The Bill James Handbook 2016

Baseball Info Solutions

www.baseballinfosolutions.com

Published by ACTA Sports

A Division of ACTA Publications

Cover Design by Tom A. Wright
Front Cover Photo by Brad Mills, USA TODAY Sports
Back Cover Photo by Mike Dinovo, USA TODAY Sports

First Edition: November 2015

Published by:
ACTA Sports, a division of ACTA Publications
4848 North Clark Street
Chicago, IL 60640
(800) 397-2282
www.actasports.com www.actapublications.com

ISBN: 978-0-87946-545-2
ISSN: 1940-8668

Printed in the United States of America by McNaughton & Gunn

Dedication

This book is dedicated to my wife Katy, my newborn son Jackson, and my aptly named dog Posey. They all have made, and continue to make, my dream to work in the sports industry possible.

A big thank you is also deserved for every stat-checker, query-writer, code-debugger, intro-author, and everyone else at BIS who contributed in any way this season.

Greg Thomas

Table of Contents

Introduction

The moment you believe you start to finally understand the game, baseball provides a rude awakening. This time last year, the San Francisco Giants were the toast of baseball. Well, next year will be another even year; their three World Series titles this decade have all been on years that ended in an even number. No one could quite believe that the Royals had made their run to the World Series, but it was clear that the Tigers were the class of the AL Central. Ditto for the Nationals in the NL East.

Continuing in the AL East, the Orioles had wrapped up their second playoff appearance and first division title in the last three years, but the Red Sox were primed for a rebound. Meanwhile, the Yankees were too old, and the Blue Jays were up to 21 years since they had last reached the postseason. The Athletics were sitting on three consecutive postseason berths and always seemed to find a way to win despite their payroll limitations. The Rangers were too thin in their rotation behind Yu Darvish and looked fated for another 90-loss season.

Most assuredly, the Pirates were a wonderful success story, but the 89-loss Cubs and the 92-loss Astros were still several years away from being competitive.

The 2015 season was incredible drama and the perfect illustration why one can never sit comfortably on their opinions and apparent knowledge of the game. It may not have been enough time for you to process everything that has changed from last year to now, but a ton of overtime hours were worked to ensure that *The Bill James Handbook* reached bookshelves by November 1, and the Handbook is the perfect source to help you set your story straight.

After the season that he had for the Cubs, Jake Arrieta needs no introduction. He led all pitchers in Win Shares with 27 this season, just edging out Zack Greinke's 26 and several clear of the rest of the field. But did you know that the team's closer Hector Rondon was tied for 12th in baseball with 16 Win Shares, more than any of Jon Lester, Jason Hammel, and Kyle Hendricks?

Much of the Astros' success has been driven by their young stars like Dallas Keuchel and Carlos Correa, but did you know that the Astros have led all teams with 2,757 shifts on balls in play over the last two seasons? Baseball Info Solutions estimates that the team has saved 47 runs with those shifts in that time. Based on an estimation of 1 extra win for every 10 extra runs, that puts the Astros' progressive defensive strategy at just short of five additional wins since 2014, or right around the value of players like Jacoby Ellsbury, Albert Pujols, and Brandon Phillips.

No one would have blamed you for calling Yu Darvish's season-ending Tommy John surgery in Spring Training the final nail in the Rangers' coffin, but then you probably would not have expected former Brewer Yovani Gallardo to increase his slider usage by four percent compared to 2014 and produce his best ERA as a full-season starter in his career.

Josh Donaldson quite suddenly became one of the best players in baseball in 2013, and so it is somewhat understandable that the Athletics believed they were trading him at his peak value to the Blue Jays. Instead, Donaldson upped his previous career high of 29 home runs from 2014 to 41 this season. Of course, the Blue Jays knew that Donaldson had a great chance to improve his power production in their home ballpark. Since 2013, O.co Coliseum in Oakland has allowed 25 percent fewer home runs to right-handed hitters than an average park, second lowest in the AL. In contrast, the Rogers Centre in Toronto has allowed right-handers to hit 14 percent more home runs than an average park, fourth best in the AL. Now, right-handers Donaldson, Troy Tulowitzki, and Edwin Encarnacion are all a part of that infield. That's not really fair to the rest of the league.

The Yankees may have entered the season with a roster full of veteran players, many of whom were past their peak seasons. However, several potential new stars emerged and helped breathe new life into the team. Greg Bird did a more than admirable job of filling in for the injured Mark Teixeira over 46 games at first base. He actually hit 11 home runs over that time. One might expect that the left-handed Bird could have benefited from the short porch in right field of Yankee Stadium; after all, left-handed hitters have hit 29 percent more home runs in that park than an average park since 2013. However, Bird actually hit 6 of his 11 home runs on the road. The Bill James Projections are optimistic that with more than 500 at-bats, Bird could club 25 home runs in 2016.

The Royals may not succeed with the formula fans are used to seeing, but that does not mean they aren't a great team. With 56 Defensive Runs Saved in 2015, the Royals just missed being the best defensive team in the AL this season (the Astros were tops in the league with a shift-driven 57 Runs Saved). The Royals have saved more runs over the last three seasons combined than anyone else in the AL, and their total of 179 Runs Saved in that time is 62 more than the AL silver medalist Orioles. The Royals were also one of the top baserunning teams in the AL; only the Blue Jays produced more Stolen Base Gain (+42) than the Royals' +36. Of course, both teams would have needed a lot of work to catch up to the Rangers' total Net Gain of +142, built on an incredible +119 Baserunning Gain, which factors in runner advancements from first to third on singles, second to home on singles, first to home on doubles, and baserunning out avoidance.

All of those statistics and many more can be found throughout this Handbook. We hope that you enjoy everything the 2015 season had to offer that we have captured in these pages, and we look forward to wondering how we ever could have been so wrong about the 2016 season this time next year.

Scott Spratt
October 15, 2015

Starting Pitcher Rankings

Joe Rosales

In sports, we often hear people use the metaphor of a bulldog to describe certain players. It is usually associated with players who exhibit a determined intensity to the way they play the game. Usually, these aren't athletes that succeed through any sort of finesse to their game. They come right at you with dogged determination to impose their will on you. Is this a reflection of how actual bulldogs really behave? Who knows? But it makes for good imagery.

One pitcher that has been referred to as a bulldog is Max Scherzer. When he signed his current mega-deal with the Washington Nationals before the start of the 2015 season, his new manager (and now old manager), Matt Williams, noted Scherzer's bulldog mentality as one of the reasons that the Nationals signed him. And, while the metaphor may be a bit overused in general, it actually seems appropriately applied to Scherzer, especially as it relates to his theoretical and entirely hypothetical quest to be the World's #1 Starting Pitcher.

Clayton Kershaw is unquestionably the best pitcher in baseball. When a player wins three Cy Young Awards in four years plus an MVP Award, you don't need a ranking system to tell you that he's the best. But, of course, we do have a ranking system, which was developed by Bill James four years ago. And when you look at the rankings that appear in the following pages, Kershaw unsurprisingly leads by a lot. That said, if you look closely at the table, you will see that on July 1st, Scherzer was only just barely behind Kershaw for the top spot. In fact, the next day, July 2nd, Scherzer actually took the lead. However, his reign only lasted five days until Kershaw took the crown back, at which point Kershaw proceeded to start pitching like Clayton Kershaw again and run away from the field.

When Scherzer took over first place, he was hitting a peak (he had just thrown a no-hitter 12 days prior) while Kershaw was hitting a valley. You could look at Scherzer's brief time in pole position as a five-day hiccup for Kershaw. However, in 2014, there were another 35 days when Kershaw relinquished the top spot in the rankings, and it was Scherzer again that was the one who took it from him. There are seven different pitchers that have occupied the #2 spot in the rankings since Kershaw first ascended to the throne on May 16, 2013, but only Scherzer has managed to actually move in front of Kershaw.

Hence the bulldog metaphor. Kershaw is a historically great pitcher, reaching sustained heights that most others aren't capable of. But that hasn't stopped Scherzer from determinedly trying to establish himself, doggedly nipping at Kershaw's heels, and every so often finding a way to break through, however briefly.

This is what is so fun about these rankings. They help us measure pitchers against each other, combining how well they have been doing recently with their career achievements. A great season will allow a pitcher to make significant moves up the rankings, but one great season isn't going to give him the top spot.

For example, Jake Arrieta had an amazing season in 2015. He jumped from 63rd at the beginning of the season up to 4th overall by the end. But he had already started to build a track record for himself in 2014 when his performance lifted him up from 154th to 62nd (the rankings continue to fluctuate every day, even over the offseason, hence Arrieta falling one spot from the end of the 2014 season to the beginning of the 2015 season...for full details on how the ranking system works, see Bill James' article on www.billjamesonline.com from September 18, 2011 called *The World's #1 Starting Pitcher*).

Other pitchers that rose significantly in the standings in 2015 include two Cleveland Indians pitchers, Carlos Carrasco and Danny Salazar. Carrasco climbed 92 spots up to 28th, while Salazar ascended 81 spots up to 50th. Combine that with Corey Kluber at #8, and that's a pretty formidable rotation. Although, it's tough for that to measure up to a Cubs rotation that has the #4 pitcher (Arrieta) and the #9 pitcher (Jon Lester) in it, or a Dodgers rotation that not only has the best pitcher in the game, but the two best pitchers in the game (Kershaw and Zack Greinke).

And Scherzer? He ended the season ranked #3, 50+ points behind Kershaw. That's a daunting deficit to be sure. But after throwing a second no-hitter of the season in his last start, we can be sure that Scherzer shouldn't be counted out for top dog status somewhere down the line.

The Starting Pitcher Rankings presented in this section capture the rankings as they stood on the first day of each month during the season, as well as the last day of the season. You can also find these rankings updated on a daily basis on www.billjamesonline.com.

Starting Pitcher Rankings

Player	April 1 Score	Rank	May 1 Score	Rank	June 1 Score	Rank	July 1 Score	Rank	Aug 1 Score	Rank	Sept 1 Score	Rank	Oct 4 Score	Rank
Kershaw,Clayton	572.8	1	568.1	1	573.3	1	585.9	1	616.6	1	626.1	1	636.3	1
Greinke,Zack	501.3	10	515.7	7	537.0	5	553.1	5	577.4	3	585.5	2	594.6	2
Scherzer,Max	524.8	4	543.7	3	563.3	2	584.6	2	582.3	2	564.8	6	583.8	3
Arrieta,Jake	417.3	63	439.0	43	452.5	37	476.3	26	504.4	17	539.8	8	577.7	4
Bumgarner,Madison	536.7	2	532.5	4	539.0	4	553.8	4	543.3	7	568.7	4	577.2	5
Price,David	519.3	5	520.6	6	528.5	8	544.1	7	555.3	4	571.5	3	577.1	6
Sale,Chris	516.5	6	507.9	10	531.3	7	563.0	3	554.7	5	564.9	5	555.6	7
Kluber,Corey	490.1	13	493.1	12	515.9	10	520.3	10	536.5	9	552.0	7	547.2	8
Lester,Jon	510.3	7	505.2	11	514.8	11	510.6	11	531.7	10	522.5	14	543.2	9
Hamels,Cole	506.3	8	513.8	8	532.8	6	532.5	9	523.1	11	527.3	12	537.3	10
Keuchel,Dallas	422.0	55	462.5	22	487.4	15	507.7	12	515.4	13	531.5	10	535.0	11
Hernandez,Felix	536.2	3	551.7	2	552.7	3	547.4	6	542.7	8	525.5	13	533.1	12
Strasburg,Stephen	484.7	14	478.6	15	460.4	30	466.9	35	464.6	41	483.5	27	519.1	13
Cueto,Johnny	504.6	9	527.1	5	522.7	9	537.6	8	545.8	6	537.5	9	518.4	14
Dickey,R.A.	475.6	16	472.0	17	467.3	24	476.9	25	490.4	24	488.7	24	510.8	15
Lackey,John	438.3	34	441.1	36	466.0	26	470.1	32	491.0	22	498.4	20	509.9	16
Zimmermann,Jordan	495.1	12	486.3	14	499.4	13	504.5	13	503.5	18	510.1	16	509.1	17
Ross,Tyson	426.1	48	432.3	49	449.2	41	465.0	37	478.4	30	493.9	22	507.6	18
Gray,Sonny	430.3	42	457.8	26	485.3	17	499.2	16	517.8	12	528.8	11	507.5	19
Shields,James	474.7	17	488.5	13	497.3	14	492.3	18	501.5	19	504.8	17	507.0	20
Quintana,Jose	451.2	27	450.4	28	464.8	27	474.7	27	490.6	23	483.1	28	505.6	21
deGrom,Jacob	386.4	94	399.9	87	445.6	43	473.4	30	494.8	21	502.8	18	505.2	22
Archer,Chris	427.9	45	462.0	23	480.2	20	501.0	14	510.4	14	519.8	15	505.0	23
Liriano,Francisco	449.7	29	469.2	19	481.3	19	499.8	15	510.0	15	499.0	19	502.6	24
Cole,Gerrit	398.1	82	427.4	54	455.5	36	467.0	34	482.5	27	483.7	26	501.8	25
Lynn,Lance	465.3	20	476.2	16	479.8	21	491.8	19	498.4	20	497.1	21	490.3	26
Teheran,Julio	448.8	31	444.0	33	442.6	46	447.8	49	457.0	47	465.4	43	488.0	27
Carrasco,Carlos	354.9	120	372.4	112	402.0	87	431.7	63	444.1	59	475.0	36	486.1	28
Chen,Wei-Yin	423.6	52	435.3	45	451.6	38	473.8	28	472.3	36	474.6	37	485.3	29
Gonzalez,Gio	463.0	22	458.1	24	461.3	29	464.8	38	475.7	33	466.2	41	484.4	30
Verlander,Justin	462.6	23	447.6	30	416.6	70	407.1	86	424.0	76	462.4	45	482.2	31
Iwakuma,Hisashi	447.3	32	439.2	40	431.4	56	423.9	70	432.6	67	458.5	50	481.0	32
Miller,Shelby	420.1	58	439.0	42	475.1	22	477.2	23	482.0	28	493.1	23	481.0	33
McHugh,Collin	407.6	72	421.5	59	433.0	55	445.4	51	447.2	56	471.3	39	480.4	34
de la Rosa,Jorge	429.5	44	416.7	70	427.6	62	453.3	45	459.5	46	471.3	40	479.9	35
Leake,Mike	427.1	46	449.2	29	433.1	54	444.9	52	475.4	34	479.1	29	478.6	36
Haren,Dan	426.3	47	439.1	41	456.3	34	464.5	39	471.3	37	462.5	44	476.1	37
Kennedy,Ian	435.8	36	426.5	56	424.2	66	444.4	53	455.4	48	477.5	32	475.6	38
Richards,Garrett	405.7	74	403.0	82	425.2	65	435.5	57	452.7	50	453.2	56	474.9	39
Volquez,Edinson	425.7	49	447.0	31	457.7	31	461.0	42	467.7	39	478.2	30	474.2	40
Ventura,Yordano	412.8	69	421.5	60	439.9	47	431.4	64	430.2	72	473.0	57	473.4	41
Samardzija,Jeff	472.8	18	471.5	18	487.1	16	481.7	21	504.7	16	475.1	35	473.3	42
Gallardo,Yovani	433.9	38	440.8	37	450.6	40	482.7	20	468.3	38	476.3	34	469.4	43
Wainwright,Adam	499.6	11	508.0	9	500.3	12	492.8	17	485.0	26	477.3	33	469.0	44
Miley,Wade	425.5	50	417.1	68	439.8	53	442.5	50	449.1	55	458.0	51	468.7	45
Hammel,Jason	417.9	62	432.2	50	468.0	23	477.0	24	474.7	35	473.2	38	468.6	46
Jimenez,Ubaldo	412.2	70	435.2	46	444.9	44	459.4	43	454.3	49	447.4	62	466.5	47
Peavy,Jake	442.4	33	430.0	52	422.3	67	444.8	80	432.5	68	437.1	75	466.4	48
Kazmir,Scott	391.3	88	427.2	55	430.8	57	450.7	48	486.3	25	487.4	25	466.2	49
Salazar,Danny	345.8	131	359.8	120	388.6	102	407.8	85	436.6	63	459.8	48	465.3	50
Weaver,Jered	476.9	15	468.1	20	483.5	18	470.1	33	462.3	44	457.5	52	465.3	51
Tanaka,Masahiro	368.9	108	390.4	94	382.7	107	397.8	96	421.5	81	444.9	65	465.0	52
Happ,J.A.	389.2	90	407.9	79	414.4	75	421.2	73	412.0	92	429.8	80	464.1	53
Tillman,Chris	457.9	24	453.0	27	447.1	42	451.3	47	478.5	29	465.5	42	463.8	54
Buehrle,Mark	431.8	40	415.3	71	437.9	50	471.2	31	478.0	31	477.8	31	462.1	55
Harvey,Matt	300.0	159	344.2	131	374.7	117	401.4	91	421.3	82	451.5	59	461.3	56
Gibson,Kyle	368.2	111	384.4	98	414.0	77	428.1	68	445.8	57	443.6	68	461.3	57
Hughes,Phil	451.8	26	457.9	25	462.0	28	473.5	29	476.7	32	461.9	46	460.4	58
Fiers,Mike	340.8	134	343.4	133	382.1	109	399.1	95	423.1	77	451.7	58	459.5	59
Burnett,A.J.	422.6	53	445.5	32	466.1	25	478.4	22	460.8	45	454.0	55	459.5	60
Odorizzi,Jake	379.7	100	409.9	76	434.4	52	432.3	62	436.9	62	447.1	63	459.1	61
Colon,Bartolo	418.3	61	434.9	47	430.5	58	440.4	56	428.6	74	451.4	60	457.7	62
Wood,Alex	391.5	87	400.5	86	418.5	69	433.1	59	440.5	61	440.5	61	457.3	63
Porcello,Rick	431.9	39	439.5	39	439.3	48	429.4	65	431.4	70	444.6	66	457.2	64
Buchholz,Clay	409.8	71	414.8	73	437.0	51	461.8	40	466.2	40	458.5	49	450.2	65
Santiago,Hector	373.5	104	394.9	89	427.8	61	442.6	55	450.4	51	447.0	64	449.8	66
Estrada,Marco	322.0	145	300.0	198	324.8	170	363.8	137	384.7	120	422.0	87	449.3	67
Hendricks,Kyle	334.2	139	349.3	129	379.2	111	394.0	98	422.4	78	419.8	88	449.2	68
Sanchez,Anibal	429.6	43	433.2	48	438.4	49	465.8	36	463.1	43	456.6	53	448.3	69
Wilson,C.J.	420.2	57	438.3	44	451.0	39	461.3	41	463.2	42	456.0	54	447.7	70
Wacha,Michael	360.9	115	381.5	100	412.5	79	429.0	67	442.2	60	461.4	47	447.1	71

Starting Pitcher Rankings

Player	April 1 Score	Rank	May 1 Score	Rank	June 1 Score	Rank	July 1 Score	Rank	Aug 1 Score	Rank	Sept 1 Score	Rank	Oct 4 Score	Rank
Koehler,Tom	396.6	84	405.1	81	415.0	73	433.4	58	449.1	54	436.8	76	442.8	72
Niese,Jon	414.0	67	417.3	67	411.8	81	430.9	65	444.9	58	443.6	67	441.4	73
Cashner,Andrew	400.9	79	417.8	65	428.4	59	423.8	71	433.1	66	439.0	74	440.8	74
Bauer,Trevor	360.0	117	388.8	95	414.8	74	418.0	78	434.9	65	442.3	69	439.9	75
Martinez,Carlos	300.0	159	334.9	139	364.6	123	399.9	94	416.3	86	426.8	83	437.5	76
Syndergaard,Noah					329.4	162	349.7	158	394.7	109	409.2	100	436.3	77
Fister,Doug	468.0	19	464.3	21	456.9	33	454.6	44	449.6	52	442.1	70	433.9	78
Feldman,Scott	418.3	60	425.0	57	428.1	60	420.6	74	421.7	80	439.2	73	432.5	79
Gonzalez,Miguel	430.4	41	440.2	38	457.5	32	451.5	46	449.5	53	439.4	71	432.4	80
Lewis,Colby	346.0	130	373.2	111	378.6	113	408.4	84	420.8	83	427.9	82	431.5	81
Shoemaker,Matt	381.1	98	384.7	97	408.1	84	412.2	82	431.1	71	439.4	72	431.1	82
Eovaldi,Nathan	370.2	107	378.6	104	388.8	101	400.7	92	415.2	87	432.4	77	428.1	83
Duffy,Danny	387.3	92	403.0	83	391.1	99	389.0	106	411.6	93	424.6	86	424.4	84
Danks,John	372.6	105	379.5	103	397.0	92	390.2	105	407.9	96	415.7	90	424.2	85
Santana,Ervin	435.4	37	415.2	72	384.2	106	354.2	152	376.1	127	378.3	129	423.3	86
Ramirez,Erasmo	300.0	159	305.5	185	333.5	158	364.5	136	390.7	111	402.1	108	422.1	87
Anderson,Chase	347.2	127	361.9	119	391.9	98	406.4	87	398.1	103	410.4	98	420.6	88
Locke,Jeff	359.7	118	368.8	114	377.5	115	392.7	100	410.7	95	412.3	97	418.7	89
Harang,Aaron	404.5	76	428.1	53	455.8	35	432.4	60	427.6	75	412.8	95	417.9	90
Lohse,Kyle	449.1	30	441.7	35	442.6	45	443.0	54	435.9	64	425.9	85	417.7	91
Pineda,Michael	331.9	140	358.6	122	389.9	100	391.4	102	407.6	97	407.8	102	417.3	92
Nelson,Jimmy	300.0	159	324.7	155	360.6	129	372.3	124	406.0	99	428.9	81	417.3	93
Latos,Mat	400.1	80	394.7	90	399.0	90	411.9	83	431.5	69	426.0	84	416.6	94
Garcia,Jaime	300.0	159	300.0	198	322.3	173	362.0	141	360.1	148	395.5	116	416.5	95
Walker,Taijuan	300.0	159	311.1	172	333.4	159	382.0	117	395.0	107	414.1	92	416.3	96
Vogelsong,Ryan	397.3	83	390.9	93	426.4	64	432.4	61	429.8	73	431.3	79	416.1	97
Hutchison,Drew	390.4	89	392.5	91	415.3	72	422.7	72	412.5	90	431.8	78	416.1	98
McCullers,Lance					320.8	177	370.1	130	387.2	115	387.6	119	416.0	99
Milone,Tommy	354.4	122	359.7	121	352.5	139	384.4	113	397.1	104	400.4	110	415.3	100
Hudson,Tim	403.2	77	408.8	77	416.4	71	417.5	79	411.5	94	403.7	105	414.6	101
de la Rosa,Rubby	300.0	159	325.4	154	360.4	131	383.9	114	395.9	106	414.4	91	413.2	102
Heston,Chris	300.0	159	336.4	138	355.5	134	382.6	115	412.7	88	408.4	101	412.8	103
Peralta,Wily	415.3	64	418.9	63	427.4	63	419.9	75	416.5	85	419.4	89	411.8	104
DeSclafani,Anthony	300.0	159	340.0	134	352.7	138	370.1	129	385.7	118	403.2	106	411.2	105
Anderson,Brett	300.0	159	313.9	169	353.7	136	391.1	104	398.1	102	407.4	103	410.7	106
Young,Chris	370.9	106	357.9	123	380.7	110	396.2	97	406.9	98	399.7	111	409.0	107
Rodon,Carlos					322.1	174	344.0	164	352.9	153	385.8	122	408.9	108
Kelly,Joe	345.7	132	364.2	117	369.4	120	376.4	120	370.2	136	402.6	107	408.7	109
Vargas,Jason	422.0	54	416.8	69	421.0	68	425.1	69	421.8	79	414.1	93	405.8	110
Hellickson,Jeremy	315.1	150	324.3	157	351.6	143	366.1	134	387.8	113	399.6	112	405.6	111
Karns,Nate	300.0	159	327.0	150	363.0	125	384.7	112	401.8	100	412.8	96	405.5	112
Kendrick,Kyle	381.1	99	376.8	106	392.6	96	404.0	88	400.0	101	399.1	113	405.4	113
Ray,Robbie	300.0	159	300.0	198	306.5	198	348.2	160	369.6	137	380.5	125	405.2	114
Rodriguez,Eduardo					314.3	186	344.3	162	361.8	146	380.1	127	403.8	115
Garza,Matt	414.5	66	417.5	66	414.3	76	412.6	81	418.5	84	413.3	94	403.7	116
Sabathia,CC	300.0	159	321.6	159	337.4	154	356.1	151	363.6	142	377.3	131	400.0	117
Smyly,Drew	378.3	102	368.7	115	372.6	118	365.1	135	357.3	150	370.5	136	398.4	118
Elias,Roenis	368.4	110	355.3	126	378.7	112	386.1	108	388.1	116	381.8	124	396.9	119
Jungmann,Taylor							336.0	169	378.9	122	400.4	109	396.8	120
Norris,Bud	437.8	35	418.9	64	412.8	78	419.1	76	412.4	91	404.6	104	396.4	121
Bettis,Chad	300.0	159	300.0	198	336.0	156	363.8	138	364.6	140	365.7	142	395.6	122
Guthrie,Jeremy	424.0	51	420.4	61	410.1	83	419.0	77	412.6	89	409.2	99	392.2	123
Morton,Charlie	383.7	95	356.0	125	348.9	146	359.0	148	373.6	130	396.3	114	391.7	124
Simon,Alfredo	309.9	155	339.2	135	364.5	124	374.0	122	375.1	128	377.0	132	391.0	125
Chavez,Jesse	306.6	157	312.1	170	362.4	128	378.2	119	385.8	117	396.2	115	389.9	126
Pelfrey,Mike	300.0	159	332.3	143	356.2	133	366.2	133	372.7	132	390.1	117	389.7	127
Heaney,Andrew	300.0	159	300.0	198	300.0	210	321.4	186	358.3	149	367.1	140	388.0	128
Gausman,Kevin	349.3	126	328.3	149	300.0	210	304.9	218	337.0	169	359.4	150	387.5	129
Cosart,Jarred	382.2	96	402.7	84	398.8	91	391.3	103	377.9	124	370.2	137	386.2	130
Corbin,Patrick	300.0	159	300.0	198	300.0	210	300.0	227	337.2	168	364.4	145	383.5	131
Anderson,Cody							323.8	181	338.8	165	345.3	164	382.9	132
Wood,Travis	392.5	85	412.7	74	400.6	89	393.1	99	385.4	119	377.6	130	382.1	133
Bolsinger,Mike	300.0	159	307.0	180	342.7	150	367.8	132	387.4	114	380.4	126	381.1	134
Iglesias,Raisel				300.7	194	317.3	183	310.8	204	325.6	189	374.2	133	380.1	135
McCarthy,Brandon	412.8	68	419.0	62	411.3	82	403.8	89	396.0	105	388.3	118	380.0	136
Collmenter,Josh	391.5	86	412.6	75	406.7	85	402.6	90	394.8	108	387.1	120	378.8	137
Martinez,Nick	331.3	141	363.1	118	386.9	105	392.4	101	389.5	112	386.9	121	378.6	138
Tomlin,Josh	300.0	159	300.0	198	300.0	210	300.0	227	300.0	238	336.6	175	378.2	139
Lincecum,Tim	379.3	101	380.2	102	405.4	86	400.4	93	393.2	110	385.4	123	377.2	140
Nola,Aaron									321.7	193	356.3	153	374.5	141
Severino,Luis									341.0	169	372.5	141
Roark,Tanner	405.6	75	383.1	99	371.0	119	368.3	131	361.3	147	353.5	159	372.3	143
Graveman,Kendall			303.1	189	314.9	185	361.9	142	372.3	134	379.9	128	371.6	144
Wisler,Matt							317.8	191	333.7	176	339.1	171	367.8	145

9

Starting Pitcher Rankings

Player	April 1 Score	Rank	May 1 Score	Rank	June 1 Score	Rank	July 1 Score	Rank	Aug 1 Score	Rank	Sept 1 Score	Rank	Oct 4 Score	Rank
Duffey,Tyler											328.3	188	367.4	146
Warren,Adam	300.0	159	317.9	163	353.6	137	373.7	123	365.9	139	358.2	151	366.5	147
Fernandez,Jose	300.0	159	300.0	198	300.0	210	300.0	227	342.6	161	353.7	158	365.7	148
Eickhoff,Jerad											323.1	195	364.8	149
Rusin,Chris	300.0	159	300.0	198	310.0	190	319.6	188	337.6	167	352.2	161	364.7	150
Nolasco,Ricky	388.8	91	377.6	105	394.7	93	388.5	107	380.7	121	373.0	134	362.9	151
Hahn,Jesse	300.0	159	324.4	156	352.2	141	385.1	111	378.9	123	371.1	135	362.9	152
Nova,Ivan	300.0	159	300.0	198	300.0	210	315.3	195	332.9	177	352.9	160	362.4	153
Alvarez,Henderson	406.0	73	405.3	80	393.1	94	385.6	109	377.9	125	370.1	138	361.9	154
Bailey,Homer	419.2	59	400.5	85	392.7	95	385.2	110	377.5	126	369.7	139	361.5	155
Perez,Martin	300.0	159	300.0	198	300.0	210	300.0	227	300.4	236	333.7	178	360.4	156
Morgan,Adam							306.4	212	327.2	187	354.9	156	360.0	157
Ross,Joe							325.3	178	341.3	162	366.8	141	359.9	158
Perez,Williams					325.2	167	352.0	156	336.5	170	333.2	180	359.6	159
Bassitt,Chris	300.0	159	300.0	198	300.0	210	307.4	211	331.9	178	365.2	144	359.3	160
Owens,Henry											331.4	181	357.4	161
Despaigne,Odrisamer	327.2	142	337.6	136	349.8	145	362.9	140	375.0	129	364.3	146	357.3	162
Stults,Eric	387.0	93	396.2	88	388.5	103	381.0	118	373.2	131	365.5	143	357.2	163
Conley,Adam									301.1	229	314.6	211	354.7	164
Phelps,David	300.0	159	325.5	153	351.7	142	361.3	145	372.6	133	362.6	147	354.4	165
May,Trevor	300.0	159	320.7	161	341.2	151	370.6	127	364.3	141	360.6	148	352.4	166
Lyles,Jordan	351.8	124	369.3	113	382.3	108	376.0	121	368.3	138	360.5	149	352.3	167
Montgomery,Mike							356.6	150	370.8	135	357.0	152	348.8	168
Gee,Dillon	382.1	97	391.8	92	388.4	104	370.9	126	363.1	143	355.4	154	347.1	169
Hernandez,Roberto	360.2	116	374.1	109	378.5	114	370.5	128	362.8	144	355.0	155	346.8	170
Rodriguez,Wandy	300.0	159	308.2	177	347.4	147	361.1	146	362.3	145	354.6	157	346.3	171
Nicolino,Justin							310.1	206	302.6	226	330.9	184	346.1	172
Lorenzen,Michael			302.9	190	332.8	161	352.5	155	352.8	154	344.5	165	345.7	173
Holland,Derek	308.9	156	307.3	179	300.0	210	300.0	227	300.0	238	330.0	186	344.2	174
Norris,Daniel	300.0	159	325.7	152	319.2	179	311.7	201	303.9	220	319.7	205	343.8	175
Paxton,James	314.0	152	328.6	147	360.6	130	353.6	153	345.8	158	338.1	172	342.2	176
Moore,Matt	300.0	159	300.0	198	300.0	210	300.0	227	301.0	230	300.0	243	340.4	177
Flande,Yohan	300.0	159	300.0	198	300.0	210	300.0	227	306.8	214	339.9	170	339.9	178
Nuno,Vidal	374.0	103	352.2	127	321.2	175	300.0	227	300.0	238	319.6	206	339.4	179
Stroman,Marcus	368.6	109	343.8	132	312.8	187	300.0	227	300.0	238	300.0	243	339.0	180
Lamb,John											320.6	201	338.5	181
Davies,Zachary													337.9	182
Gonzalez,Chi Chi					309.5	191	344.1	163	334.0	175	337.9	173	337.9	183
Masterson,Justin	363.4	113	374.8	107	363.0	126	363.1	139	353.9	151	346.1	162	337.9	184
Noesi,Hector	361.9	114	365.1	116	369.1	121	361.6	144	353.8	152	346.1	163	337.8	185
Gray,Jonathan											322.6	196	336.8	186
Johnson,Erik	300.0	159	300.0	198	300.0	210	300.0	227	300.0	238	300.0	243	336.6	187
Matzek,Tyler	354.0	123	373.5	110	367.4	122	359.9	147	352.2	155	344.4	166	336.2	188
Hale,David	300.0	159	300.0	198	306.7	197	331.6	172	329.4	181	331.1	182	335.5	189
Medlen,Kris	300.0	159	300.0	198	300.0	210	300.0	227	300.0	238	312.3	215	333.9	190
Williams,Jerome	313.1	153	328.3	148	337.4	155	329.7	174	327.4	186	341.6	167	333.4	191
Sanchez,Aaron			317.4	165	352.2	140	356.7	149	348.9	157	341.2	168	332.9	192
Boyd,Matt							305.0	216	300.0	238	320.9	199	332.5	193
Godley,Zack									315.8	199	320.8	200	330.1	194
Doubront,Felix	356.9	119	332.1	144	301.1	208	300.0	227	310.2	209	325.3	193	329.8	195
Wright,Steven	300.0	159	300.0	198	318.3	181	317.6	192	325.0	190	337.7	174	329.4	196
Matz,Steven							309.4	207	316.3	198	308.6	220	328.6	197
Rea,Colin											314.2	212	328.2	198
Colome,Alex	300.0	159	310.2	173	328.0	165	350.3	157	344.0	159	336.3	176	328.0	199
Buchanan,David	336.3	137	331.5	145	325.0	168	317.5	193	329.2	182	306.2	224	327.8	200
Weber,Ryan													327.5	201
Worley,Vance	346.8	128	356.8	124	357.1	132	349.6	159	343.1	160	335.3	177	327.1	202
Frias,Carlos	300.0	159	309.0	175	323.3	172	340.6	166	334.1	174	326.3	192	326.9	203
Pena,Ariel													326.7	204
Tropeano,Nicholas	300.0	159	309.9	174	302.1	207	300.0	227	303.0	225	300.0	243	325.6	205
Greene,Shane	324.5	144	346.7	130	362.9	127	353.6	154	341.2	163	333.4	179	325.2	206
Cain,Matt	364.2	112	334.2	140	303.2	204	300.0	227	324.8	191	324.4	194	325.1	207
Verrett,Logan											314.8	210	324.7	208
Hand,Brad	319.9	147	300.0	198	308.8	192	305.5	214	300.0	238	331.0	183	324.4	209
Brooks,Aaron	300.0	159	300.0	198	300.0	210	300.0	227	310.9	207	319.0	207	324.1	210
Chacin,Jhoulys	303.1	158	300.0	198	300.0	210	300.0	227	300.0	238	317.0	208	322.7	211
Oberholtzer,Brett	349.5	125	327.0	151	320.9	176	341.8	165	338.6	166	330.8	185	322.6	212
Velasquez,Vincent							327.2	175	336.2	171	328.4	187	320.2	213
Foltynewicz,Mike			303.2	188	333.3	160	325.9	177	326.8	188	327.7	189	319.4	214
Butler,Eddie	300.0	159	323.6	148	338.7	152	331.9	171	335.3	172	327.4	190	319.2	215
Erlin,Robbie	300.0	159	300.0	198	300.0	210	300.0	227	300.0	238	300.0	243	319.1	216
Cooney,Tim			300.1	197	300.0	210	300.0	227	335.1	173	327.4	191	319.1	217
Wolf,Randy	300.0	159	300.0	198	300.0	210	300.0	227	300.0	238	316.4	209	317.7	218
Breslow,Craig													315.1	219

Starting Pitcher Rankings

Player	April 1 Score	April 1 Rank	May 1 Score	May 1 Rank	June 1 Score	June 1 Rank	July 1 Score	July 1 Rank	Aug 1 Score	Aug 1 Rank	Sept 1 Score	Sept 1 Rank	Oct 4 Score	Oct 4 Rank
Lyons,Tyler	300.0	159	300.0	198	307.4	195	313.8	197	309.7	210	301.9	238	314.7	220
Andriese,Matt			300.6	195	300.0	210	321.6	185	321.9	192	314.2	213	313.7	221
Wada,Tsuyoshi	319.6	148	300.1	196	324.4	171	337.2	167	329.5	180	321.7	197	313.5	222
Cahill,Trevor	354.4	121	351.5	128	344.0	148	336.5	168	328.7	184	321.0	198	312.7	223
Finnegan,Brandon													312.3	224
Pomeranz,Drew	300.0	159	320.7	162	338.2	153	330.7	173	328.1	185	320.4	202	312.1	225
Urena,Jose					304.6	200	335.9	170	328.9	183	320.2	204	311.9	226
Sampson,Keyvius											297.3	401	311.7	227
Smith,Josh							305.6	213	300.0	237	300.0	243	311.5	228
Cravy,Tyler							304.9	217	303.6	222	300.0	243	311.3	229
Asher,Alec											302.5	234	310.1	230
Wilson,Tyler					306.9	196	300.0	227	300.0	238	302.5	235	309.6	231
Montas,Frankie													307.7	232
Lopez,Jorge													307.5	233
Gilmartin,Sean													307.3	234
Zych,Tony													307.0	235
Ryan,Kyle	300.0	159	300.0	198	300.0	210	315.1	196	312.1	203	304.3	227	306.4	236
Wagner,Tyler			298.1	386			300.0	227	300.0	238	300.0	243	305.1	237
Banuelos,Manny									321.2	194	313.4	214	304.5	238
Garces,Frank													303.5	239
Bergman,Christian	300.0	159	304.2	186	300.0	210	300.0	227	300.0	238	300.0	243	303.2	240
Lobstein,Kyle	300.0	159	320.9	160	333.7	157	326.2	176	318.5	195	310.7	216	302.2	241
Zito,Barry	300.0	159	300.0	198	300.0	210	300.0	227	300.0	238	300.0	243	302.2	242
Wright,Mike					304.2	201	300.9	225	300.0	238	300.0	243	301.4	243
Holmberg,David	300.0	159	300.0	198	300.0	210	300.0	227	307.1	213	309.3	217	301.1	244
Marcum,Shaun	300.0	159	300.0	198	312.8	188	324.5	179	316.8	196	309.0	219	300.8	245
All Others													300.0	246

Stolen Base Attempt Times

Bill James

Rico Noel's actual first name, according to Baseball Reference and Wiki-pedia, is "Jablonski". Seems improbable, doesn't it? I can see why he prefers to be called Rico.

Rico stole 90 bases for Lake Elsinore in 2012, and was 62-for-67 in stolen base attempts in the low minors in 2011, so probably, growing up, he was the fast-est kid in Lawton, Oklahoma named "Jablonski", I'm guessing. Also, I'm pretty sure he could outrun Ray Jablonski, who played for the Cardinals in the 1950s, which probably makes him the fastest major league player ever named "Jablon-ski".

More impressive than that, he may also be the fastest player in the major leagues, period, at least the fastest going first to second. At Baseball Info Solu-tions we use some really sharp frame-counting software to record the times of every player going first to second on a stolen base attempt; not all stolen base attempts, because when a runner is picked off first and breaks for second that obviously is different, and attempts to steal third are different because sometimes runners get a 20-foot lead off of second base. Also, we don't use the times on Hit and Run attempts. Anyway, we get very precise times for every runner on steal attempts of second base.

Jablonski Rico Noel was released by the San Diego Padres in the middle of last summer, and was signed by the Yankees, who called him to the majors to be a pinch runner in September, when the rosters go to 40 men (which, by the way is a GREAT rule. I hope the powers that be never listen to these jabberdonkies who are always complaining about the 40-man roster in September. That rule has been on the books since my grandfather was a kid, and I like it. When you're fighting for the pennant, you should be able to use every weapon you can lay your hands on.) Anyway, Noel attempted to steal seven bases, and was 5-for-7 as a base stealer. That's not a fantastic record, but Noel's average time going first to second was 3.47 seconds. That's a fantastic time.

Billy Hamilton was second at 3.48; that's not a surprise...Jarrod Dyson third, that's not a surprise. This chart presents the data for every player who had six "qualifying" stolen base attempts. The difference between the top of the chart and the bottom of the chart—the difference between the fastest base stealer in the majors and the slowest—is a half a second. Alex Gordon was the slowest; he was 2-for-7 stealing bases, which I'm pretty sure is below the break-even percentage. Jay Bruce, though, was still 9-for-14 stealing bases, and David Peralta, a native of Carabobo, Venezuela whose nickname is "Freight Train", was 9 for 13, because it's tough to stop a train from stealing second.

Of course, stealing a base successfully is a complex business; it involves not merely speed, but also the ability to get a lead without being picked off first base, the ability to break at the earliest possible instant, the judgment to know when you can run and when you can't, who you can steal against and who you can't, the ability to avoid the tag at second base, and probably numerous other skills. Joc Pederson has a really good first-to-second average time, but nonetheless was 4-for-11 stealing bases.

But the fact that stealing bases successfully has all of these other dimensions isn't a reason to ignore the speed; rather, it is a reason to measure the "pure speed" if you can measure the pure speed. You can teach a player that he can run on Jon Lester but he can't run on Wade Miley; you can teach him to read the pitcher's move, you can teach him to get a lead. You can show him pictures of Yadier Molina with the word "NO" written across the face in giant letters. Maybe you can teach him how to slide, if you get to him early enough. You can't teach a player to run like Jablonski Rico Noel.

Stolen Base Attempt Times
(2B Only)

Runner	Timed Attempts	Average
Rico Noel	7	3.47
Billy Hamilton	40	3.48
Jarrod Dyson	14	3.49
Tyler Saladino	7	3.51
Billy Burns	23	3.52
Eric Young	8	3.52
Will Venable	12	3.53
Rougned Odor	6	3.53
Kevin Pillar	19	3.54
Delino DeShields	22	3.54
Carlos Gomez	10	3.54
Rajai Davis	14	3.54
Dee Gordon	53	3.54
Sam Fuld	6	3.55
Anthony Gose	22	3.55
Peter Bourjos	9	3.56
Jacoby Ellsbury	20	3.57
Brett Gardner	16	3.57
Gregory Polanco	31	3.57
Mookie Betts	16	3.57
Kevin Kiermaier	15	3.58
Cesar Hernandez	16	3.58
Jose Altuve	31	3.58
Ian Desmond	11	3.59
Charlie Blackmon	37	3.59
Starling Marte	31	3.59
Ben Revere	26	3.59
Joc Pederson	7	3.59
George Springer	12	3.59
Michael Taylor	14	3.60
Adeiny Hechavarria	7	3.60
Chris Owings	13	3.60
Carl Crawford	9	3.60
A.J. Pollock	30	3.60
Eduardo Nunez	9	3.61
Michael Brantley	6	3.61
Austin Jackson	20	3.61
Matt Duffy	12	3.61
Mike Trout	14	3.62
Cory Spangenberg	9	3.62
Cameron Maybin	20	3.62
Jose Reyes	17	3.62
Jason Kipnis	10	3.62
Justin Upton	16	3.63
Carlos Santana	7	3.63
Leonys Martin	11	3.63
Carlos Correa	9	3.63
Xander Bogaerts	6	3.63
Kolten Wong	14	3.64
Brad Miller	12	3.64
Melvin Upton Jr.	6	3.64
Steven Souza	12	3.64
Michael Bourn	15	3.64
Ryan Braun	18	3.65
Pedro Ciriaco	6	3.65
Jason Heyward	12	3.65
Odubel Herrera	19	3.65
Adam Eaton	21	3.65
Francisco Lindor	10	3.65
Jose Ramirez	13	3.65
Mark Canha	8	3.66
Jace Peterson	14	3.66
Ichiro Suzuki	9	3.66
Alex Rios	6	3.66
J.B. Shuck	11	3.67
Jean Segura	22	3.67
Jake Marisnick	17	3.67

Runner	Timed Attempts	Average
DJ LeMahieu	15	3.67
Wil Myers	6	3.68
Danny Santana	6	3.68
Avisail Garcia	13	3.68
Elvis Andrus	18	3.68
Jimmy Rollins	8	3.68
Brandon Guyer	6	3.68
Anthony Rizzo	8	3.68
Alejandro De Aza	8	3.68
Paul Goldschmidt	14	3.69
Danny Espinosa	6	3.69
Brian Dozier	9	3.69
Denard Span	9	3.69
Jose Iglesias	14	3.69
Marcus Semien	11	3.69
Ketel Marte	6	3.69
Matt Kemp	11	3.70
Dexter Fowler	17	3.70
Ender Inciarte	18	3.70
Erick Aybar	12	3.71
Brandon Barnes	6	3.71
Juan Lagares	9	3.71
Freddy Galvis	7	3.71
Gregor Blanco	13	3.72
Kelby Tomlinson	6	3.72
Nori Aoki	11	3.72
Christian Yelich	14	3.72
Bryce Harper	6	3.72
Josh Harrison	13	3.73
Aaron Hicks	7	3.73
Brandon Phillips	11	3.74
Lorenzo Cain	14	3.74
Andrew McCutchen	12	3.75
Gerardo Parra	11	3.75
Andrew Romine	7	3.75
Eddie Rosario	13	3.75
Yoenis Cespedes	7	3.75
Manny Machado	19	3.76
Justin Ruggiano	6	3.76
Chris Coghlan	7	3.76
Logan Forsythe	6	3.78
Hanley Ramirez	8	3.78
J.T. Realmuto	6	3.78
Kris Bryant	12	3.78
Alcides Escobar	11	3.79
Angel Pagan	9	3.79
Alexei Ramirez	15	3.79
Brandon Crawford	7	3.80
Logan Morrison	8	3.80
Brandon Belt	8	3.80
Todd Frazier	10	3.82
Curtis Granderson	12	3.86
David Peralta	6	3.88
Jay Bruce	6	3.90
Alex Gordon	6	3.93

Painting the Corners

Bill James

To me, the largest revelations of the modern pitch tracking systems, which began about ten years ago, are

1) That good pitchers are able to put almost all of their pitches on the very edges of the strike zone, and

2) That pitches that stray into the heart of the plate have a real tendency to get hit hard.

After a few years of watching these strike rectangles, these things may seem to be obvious, but I tell you in all sincerity that these lessons were extremely surprising to me, and I had been watching baseball games for 45 or 50 years before those pitch zone rectangles appeared. Jim Bouton wrote about this in Ball Four, but what Bouton wrote largely suggested that pitchers could not do this. I had tended to believe that Bouton was right. But you watch a game now, and you see pitch after pitch after pitch, on the very edge of the zone. Announcers now routinely assert that a pitcher's ability to pitch on the black is the key to his success. Announcers say a lot of things that don't turn out to be true, and our data so far suggests that this one may not be true, but that's getting ahead of ourselves.

For one thing—the point made forcefully by Ted Williams 50 years ago—the *edge* of the strike zone is a very significant portion of the *area* of the strike zone. The strike zone is about 17 inches by 23 inches, more or less, and that is about 391 square inches (measured in two dimensions. I understand the three-dimensional issue, but this is complicated enough.)

Anyway, if the strike zone was 15 by 21, that would be 315 square inches. If it was 19 by 25, that would be 475 square inches. A "large" strike zone, then, is 50% larger than a "small" strike zone, although we're only adding or subtracting a couple of inches on each side. Ted Williams' point about this was that if you give the pitcher an inch or two on the edge of the zone, the zone becomes much larger, and much harder for the batter to dominate. But there is a second point here: that the fact that pitchers very often throw the ball on the edges of the strike zone doesn't necessarily mean that they're doing it on purpose. Sometimes they're throwing the ball on the edges of the zone because the edges of the zone are a significant portion of the whole of the zone. Sometimes the pitcher may be throwing the ball to the right side of the plate, but it may cross the plate on the black—but on the left side. That happens.

As Bouton said, I do not believe generally that pitchers can put the ball on a spot. Our studies of pitchers hitting the catcher's target, for example, show that they very rarely do. Pitchers only hit the catcher's mitt, without the catcher moving the mitt at least a few inches, about 10% of the time. Pitchers are good, but they're not that good. They hit the black because the black is <u>there</u>.

My understanding before the pitch rectangles appeared on TV was that pitchers generally tried to throw strikes, but sometimes threw balls because they just missed the zone. My understanding now is that most pitchers most of the time, early in the count, do not aim at the strike zone; rather, they aim the pitch an inch or two outside the zone (inside or outside or up or down...this is all "outside" in one meaning of the term.) They aim the pitch an inch or two outside the zone, understanding that this gives them two ways to profit from the pitch: 1) that the batter may chase the pitch, even though it is outside the zone and in a place that is difficult to reach, and 2) that even though they have aimed for just outside the zone, they may (almost accidentally) clip the corner of the zone, and thus get a strike. Later in the count, of course, the pitcher may be in a position where he actually has to attempt to hit the zone, and this involves risk—but at the beginning, 0-0 or certainly 0-1, the pitcher is not really trying to throw the ball IN the strike zone.

If the pitcher actually aims at the edge of the zone, of course his chance of getting a strike increases, but, since he cannot actually place the ball exactly where he wants it to go, the pitcher who is aiming for the edge sometimes will accidentally throw the ball in the heart of the zone. The pitch that accidentally hits the heart of the zone can get an immediate resolution to the plate appearance—but not (most often) a resolution that the pitcher is anxious to get. The pitcher is smarter to delay that resolution to the plate appearance to the point at which it can no longer be avoided. By aiming the early pitches outside the zone, the pitcher reduces the probability of a pitch accidentally straying into the red zone. That is my current understanding of the problem.

The general purpose of this section is to build a better understanding of this issue. When a pitcher throws a pitch, that pitch is either:

a) Clearly outside the strike zone,

b) On the edge of the zone, or

c) Clearly inside the zone.

I proposed last summer to the guys I work with at Baseball Info Solutions that we track how many of each of those each pitcher throws. But when the data showed up, it showed only about 11% of pitches as being on the edge of the zone.

Well, that's crazy talk, in my opinion. My view of the game is that 70 or 80% of pitches are on the edges of the zone, *as an ordinary fan would describe the edges of the zone*. There is really no right or wrong answer here; the "edge" of the zone has no precise definition. One person could say that that pitch was on the edge of the zone; another could say that it was clearly outside the zone; who's to say? My belief is that if you sat down with 10,000 fans and watched 10,000 pitches each, you'd have a hundred million reactions there, about 70 million or 80 million of them would be "yes, that pitch was on the edge of the zone". 70 or 80%. We may not be able to fund that undertaking, but I'm just sayin'.

So I kicked that back to the research department, and they came back with a second definition that showed about 40% of pitches on the black, which I still don't think is right, but the clock is moving and there is no way to say who is right, so we've got to go forward and learn what we can.

Our data in this study does not show that putting pitches on the black is a major identifier of pitching effectiveness. The chart includes all pitchers who threw at least 2500 pitches in 2015...about 130 innings, more or less. Clayton

Kershaw is near the bottom in terms of the percentage of his pitches that are on the black, at 38.1%. Gerrit Cole is near the bottom, and Garrett Richards, and Danny Salazar, John Lackey, Matt Harvey, Jordan Zimmerman and Max Scherzer. There is really no indication, in this data, that putting pitches on the black is a major element of pitching success.

Further, at least in this data, there does not appear to be huge variation among pitchers as to how often they put pitches on the black. The lowest "on the edge" percentage in the majors, among pitchers with 2500 pitches thrown, was 37%, and the highest was 45%—8% top to bottom; actually it is close to 9%, so let's say 9%.

Also, there is not tremendous variation in pitches thrown entirely outside the zone; that ranges from 35% (James Shields) down to 24%, by Bartolo Colon and Wei-Yin Chen. The largest variation among the three categories is in pitches in the heart of the zone. That ranges from 22% (Francisco Liriano) up to 36% (Max Scherzer and Bartolo Colon), and there are many more pitches near the top and bottom of the chart than is true in the other two categories.

What does this tell us?

Well, (a) it tells us that Max Scherzer has a lot of confidence in his stuff. He's not succeeding by nibbling the corners of the zone; he is succeeding because his stuff is so good that he can put pitches in the heart of the zone and batters still can't hit it. (b) It tells us something, perhaps, a little bit, about how different pitchers approach the risk/reward equation of aiming for the edge and accidentally getting a little too much of the plate.

And (c), it tells us that we still have a lot of work to do before we understand this. Have we properly described the "edge" of the zone as 40% of pitches, or should it be 80%? How does that change with the count? Obviously you're going to throw more pitches in the zone on 2-0 than you will on 0-2, but how many more?

And what is the results profile for each of these categories? What is the contact rate on pitches in the heart of the zone? What's the contact percentage on the edge of the zone? What is the swing-and-miss percentage? How many hard hit balls result from pitches in the heart of the zone? How often do batters swing at pitches that are clearly outside the zone?

Break that down by pitches; obviously a curve ball in the heart of the zone is different from a splitter that stays up. Break it down by pitch speeds; an 89 MPH fastball is probably going to get crushed more often than a 97 MPH fastball.

It may be that the greatness of pitchers like Clayton Kershaw, Max Scherzer and Felix Hernandez actually has nothing to do with their hitting the corners of the strike zone; rather, those pitchers may succeed because they are much better at getting swings and misses outside the strike zone, and therefore they have less pressure to come inside the strike zone. Or the opposite may be true; it may be that those pitchers succeed because they are *able* to pitch in the heart of the strike zone because of the movement on their pitches. At this point, we just really don't know, quantitatively, what is going on.

There is a long, long road ahead of us before we can be said to have gained understanding in this area. I'm not really saying that it is not true that good pitchers hit the corners of the zone more often than lesser pitchers; I am just saying that it is not apparent in this data. We'll try to start here and build upward, but ignorance is inexhaustible.

Painting the Corners

Pitcher	Pitches	Clearly Not a Strike	On the Edge	In the Heart of the Zone	On the Edge Percentage	Distribution		
Chavez, Jesse	2572	737	1168	667	45.4%	29	- 45 -	26
Locke, Jeff	2780	819	1240	721	44.6%	29	- 45 -	26
Leake, Mike	2754	745	1212	797	44.0%	27	- 44 -	29
Liriano, Francisco	2983	1028	1312	643	44.0%	34	- 44 -	22
Carrasco, Carlos	2777	809	1215	753	43.8%	29	- 44 -	27
Buehrle, Mark	2829	810	1232	787	43.5%	29	- 44 -	28
Hendricks, Kyle	2793	828	1215	750	43.5%	30	- 44 -	27
Wood, Alex	2909	803	1263	843	43.4%	28	- 43 -	29
Sabathia, CC	2703	814	1160	729	42.9%	30	- 43 -	27
Gibson, Kyle	3235	1105	1380	750	42.7%	34	- 43 -	23
Niese, Jon	2701	718	1153	830	42.7%	27	- 43 -	31
Keuchel, Dallas	3492	1193	1489	810	42.6%	34	- 43 -	23
Haren, Dan	2906	863	1235	808	42.5%	30	- 42 -	28
Pineda, Michael	2548	644	1075	829	42.2%	25	- 42 -	33
de la Rosa, Rubby	3014	846	1271	897	42.2%	28	- 42 -	30
Cueto, Johnny	3268	993	1379	896	42.2%	30	- 42 -	27
Harang, Aaron	2844	816	1201	827	42.2%	29	- 42 -	29
Kluber, Corey	3273	884	1374	1015	42.0%	27	- 42 -	31
Cashner, Andrew	3109	878	1304	927	41.9%	28	- 42 -	30
Gonzalez, Gio	2947	971	1232	744	41.8%	33	- 42 -	25
Sale, Chris	3323	920	1386	1017	41.7%	28	- 42 -	31
Kennedy, Ian	2911	896	1214	801	41.7%	31	- 42 -	28
Gallardo, Yovani	3226	1049	1343	834	41.6%	33	- 42 -	26
Chen, Wei-Yin	3010	725	1253	1032	41.6%	24	- 42 -	34
Porcello, Rick	2744	737	1132	875	41.3%	27	- 41 -	32
Pelfrey, Mike	2663	761	1100	802	41.3%	29	- 41 -	30
Miley, Wade	3194	1048	1320	826	41.3%	33	- 41 -	26
Hamels, Cole	3343	1007	1382	954	41.3%	30	- 41 -	29
Hernandez, Felix	3040	958	1257	825	41.3%	32	- 41 -	27
Lohse, Kyle	2544	840	1049	655	41.2%	33	- 41 -	26
Volquez, Edinson	3298	910	1358	1030	41.2%	28	- 41 -	31
Price, David	3388	803	1393	1192	41.1%	24	- 41 -	35
Miller, Shelby	3247	858	1335	1054	41.1%	26	- 41 -	32
Anderson, Brett	2716	768	1116	832	41.1%	28	- 41 -	31
Lester, Jon	3185	1069	1308	808	41.1%	34	- 41 -	25
DeSclafani, Anthony	2913	783	1194	936	41.0%	27	- 41 -	32
Hutchison, Drew	2511	782	1029	700	41.0%	31	- 41 -	28
Sanchez, Anibal	2532	755	1036	741	40.9%	30	- 41 -	29
Greinke, Zack	3239	1100	1326	813	40.9%	34	- 41 -	25
Martinez, Carlos	2844	837	1162	845	40.9%	29	- 41 -	30
Danks, John	2918	835	1191	892	40.8%	29	- 41 -	31
Lewis, Colby	3180	897	1296	987	40.8%	28	- 41 -	31
deGrom, Jacob	2976	844	1212	920	40.7%	28	- 41 -	31
Shields, James	3336	1162	1356	818	40.6%	35	- 41 -	25
Simon, Alfredo	3059	897	1241	921	40.6%	29	- 41 -	30
Odorizzi, Jake	2755	832	1116	807	40.5%	30	- 41 -	29
Estrada, Marco	2913	835	1179	899	40.5%	29	- 40 -	31
Colon, Bartolo	2706	641	1095	970	40.5%	24	- 40 -	36
Bumgarner, Madison	3312	983	1338	991	40.4%	30	- 40 -	30
Nelson, Jimmy	2791	807	1128	856	40.4%	29	- 40 -	31
Jimenez, Ubaldo	3060	960	1233	867	40.3%	31	- 40 -	28
Arrieta, Jake	3438	1032	1383	1023	40.2%	30	- 40 -	30
Kazmir, Scott	2941	862	1181	898	40.2%	29	- 40 -	31
Tillman, Chris	2943	843	1176	924	40.0%	29	- 40 -	31
Wacha, Michael	2937	789	1169	979	39.8%	27	- 40 -	33
Walker, Taijuan	2630	781	1048	801	39.8%	30	- 40 -	30
Samardzija, Jeff	3339	900	1321	1118	39.6%	27	- 40 -	33
Lynn, Lance	3053	1048	1206	799	39.5%	34	- 40 -	26
Archer, Chris	3449	1005	1364	1080	39.5%	29	- 40 -	31
Gray, Sonny	3078	894	1213	971	39.4%	29	- 39 -	32
Happ, J.A.	2839	859	1118	862	39.4%	30	- 39 -	30
Dickey, R.A.	3264	926	1282	1056	39.3%	28	- 39 -	32
Eovaldi, Nathan	2638	780	1034	824	39.2%	30	- 39 -	31
Lackey, John	3127	850	1222	1055	39.1%	27	- 39 -	34
Scherzer, Max	3359	852	1313	1194	39.1%	25	- 39 -	36
Zimmermann, Jordan	3103	848	1211	1044	39.0%	27	- 39 -	34
Harvey, Matt	2798	810	1086	902	38.8%	29	- 39 -	32
Cole, Gerrit	3238	964	1254	1020	38.7%	30	- 39 -	32
Ross, Tyson	3229	1107	1247	875	38.6%	34	- 39 -	27
Salazar, Danny	3048	894	1172	982	38.5%	29	- 38 -	32
Santiago, Hector	3162	925	1215	1022	38.4%	29	- 38 -	32

22

Painting the Corners

Pitcher	Pitches	Clearly Not a Strike	On the Edge	In the Heart of the Zone	On the Edge Percentage	Distribution		
Teheran, Julio	3275	1068	1256	951	38.4%	33	- 38	- 29
Heston, Chris	2792	921	1071	800	38.4%	33	- 38	- 29
Kershaw, Clayton	3392	985	1292	1115	38.1%	29	- 38	- 33
Hammel, Jason	2751	887	1045	819	38.0%	32	- 38	- 30
Richards, Garrett	3250	1033	1236	981	38.0%	32	- 38	- 30
McHugh, Collin	3241	1021	1219	1001	37.6%	32	- 38	- 31
Koehler, Tom	2976	965	1115	896	37.5%	32	- 37	- 30
Quintana, Jose	3373	1092	1255	1026	37.2%	32	- 37	- 30
Fiers, Mike	3042	956	1128	958	37.1%	31	- 37	- 31
Bauer, Trevor	2869	967	1053	849	36.7%	34	- 37	- 30
Ventura, Yordano	2651	872	968	811	36.5%	33	- 37	- 31

2015 Team Statistics

Joe Rosales

The 2015 season was fascinating for the American League West. The Houston Astros were one of the season's big surprises, finishing with a winning percentage above .500 for the first time since 2008 and making the playoffs for the first time since 2005. The Astros were playing so well, in fact, that they were actually in first place for 139 days, by far the most of anyone in the division. However, they did not finish the season in first place. That honor went to the Texas Rangers. After a miserable 7-14 April, the Rangers steadied the ship over the remainder of the first half of the season, then rode a 46-28 second-half record to a division title, taking over the lead for good on September 15th. And in the midst of it all was 2014's division winner, the Los Angeles Angels. They ended up finishing third, but they led the division as late as July 28th. They also almost snuck up behind the Astros to steal their playoff spot from them, but they came up one game short.

This is the kind of information that is available in the Team Statistics section. You will find the traditional division standings and Win-Loss records, but there is also much more. The following pages delve into each team's splits against the other teams in their league, in one-run games, in each month of the season, and more.

You will also find batting, pitching, and fielding statistics for each team. For example, the AL Batting table shows that part of the Astros' success can be attributed to the fact that they led the AL with 121 stolen bases in 2015. However, they were not the most efficient team in the AL at stealing bases. While the Astros were successful on a very good 72 percent of their stolen base attempts, the AL East champion Blue Jays literally and figuratively ran away from the rest of the league with a 79 percent success rate.

Additionally, there is a Team Pitching Staff Summary, a position-by-position breakdown of Defensive Runs Saved for each team, and splits on Batting and Fielding By Position. If you want to know which team got the most innings out of its starters, or which team's shortstops dragged them down the most, this is where you would look.

2015 American League Standings

Overall

Team	W-L	Pct	GB	D1	LD1	LLd	Team	W-L	Pct	GB	D1	LD1	LLd	Team	W-L	Pct	GB	D1	LD1	LLd
EAST							**CENTRAL**							**WEST**						
Toronto Blue Jays	93-69	.574	0.0	50	10/4	6.0	Kansas City Royals	95-67	.586	0.0	163	10/4	14.5	Texas Rangers	88-74	.543	0.0	21	10/4	4.5
New York Yankees	87-75	.537	6.0	99	8/24	7.0	Minnesota Twins	83-79	.512	12.0	9	6/7	1.0	Houston Astros	86-76	.531	2.0	135	9/14	7.0
Baltimore Orioles	81-81	.500	12.0	10	7/2	0.5	Cleveland Indians	81-80	.503	13.5	0	-	0.0	Los Angeles Angels	85-77	.525	3.0	20	7/28	2.0
Tampa Bay Rays	80-82	.494	13.0	23	6/27	2.0	Chicago White Sox	76-86	.469	19.0	0	-	0.0	Seattle Mariners	76-86	.469	12.0	2	4/12	0.0
Boston Red Sox	78-84	.481	15.0	18	4/25	2.0	Detroit Tigers	74-87	.460	20.5	22	5/16	1.0	Oakland Athletics	68-94	.420	20.0	9	4/18	1.0

Wild Card Clinch Dates: New York 10/1, Houston 10/4. Division Clinch Dates:Kansas City 9/24, Toronto 9/30, Texas 10/4.
D1 = Number of days a team had at least a share of first place of their division; LD1 = Last date the team had at least a share of first place; LLd = The largest number of games that a team led their division by.

East Division

Tm	Home	Road	East	Cent	West	NL	LHS	RHS	Day	Night	Grass	Turf	1-Rn	5+Rn	XInn	April	May	June	July	Aug	Sept	Pre	Post
	AT		**VERSUS**						**CONDITIONS**				**GAME**			**MONTHLY**						**ALL-STAR**	
Tor	53-28	40-41	42-34	20-14	19-13	12-8	20-15	73-54	36-27	57-42	37-35	56-34	15-28	37-12	8-6	11-12	12-17	18-9	12-13	21-6	19-12	45-46	48-23
NYY	45-36	42-39	39-37	15-18	17-16	11-9	27-23	60-52	30-23	57-52	77-66	10-9	25-26	21-20	4-9	13-9	13-16	15-12	17-7	14-14	15-17	48-40	39-35
Bal	47-31	34-50	38-38	21-12	17-16	11-9	22-23	59-58	27-28	54-53	70-70	11-11	25-26	21-20	6-5	10-10	13-16	18-10	11-14	11-18	18-13	44-44	37-37
TB	42-42	38-40	36-40	13-19	17-17	14-6	30-23	50-59	21-28	59-54	34-34	46-48	26-30	15-14	2-13	12-10	14-15	16-12	9-16	14-13	15-16	46-45	34-37
Bos	43-38	35-46	35-41	15-18	15-18	13-7	21-25	57-59	27-26	51-58	67-76	11-8	20-19	25-23	7-7	12-10	10-19	14-14	10-15	15-12	17-14	42-47	36-37

Central Division

Tm	Home	Road	East	Cent	West	NL	LHS	RHS	Day	Night	Grass	Turf	1-Rn	5+Rn	XInn	April	May	June	July	Aug	Sept	Pre	Post
	AT		**VERSUS**						**CONDITIONS**				**GAME**			**MONTHLY**						**ALL-STAR**	
KC	51-30	44-37	18-16	44-32	20-12	13-7	31-27	64-40	30-16	65-51	92-63	3-4	23-17	26-17	10-6	15-7	14-12	15-11	17-11	19-9	15-17	52-34	43-33
Min	46-35	37-44	19-14	40-36	16-17	8-12	28-26	55-53	31-33	52-46	81-74	2-5	21-20	22-24	6-8	10-12	20-7	11-17	12-13	14-14	16-16	49-40	34-39
Cle	39-41	42-39	18-15	32-43	19-14	12-8	24-31	57-49	26-27	55-53	76-78	5-2	15-18	27-21	5-4	7-14	17-12	11-15	13-13	16-12	17-14	42-46	39-34
CWS	40-41	36-45	14-19	32-44	21-12	9-11	18-18	58-68	24-37	52-49	75-81	1-5	29-30	19-24	13-5	8-11	15-15	10-16	16-10	12-16	15-18	41-45	35-41
Det	38-43	36-44	12-20	41-34	12-22	9-11	21-17	53-70	31-28	43-59	73-82	1-5	26-22	19-31	9-8	15-8	13-16	11-13	11-16	10-17	14-17	44-44	30-43

West Division

Tm	Home	Road	East	Cent	West	NL	LHS	RHS	Day	Night	Grass	Turf	1-Rn	5+Rn	XInn	April	May	June	July	Aug	Sept	Pre	Post
	AT		**VERSUS**						**CONDITIONS**				**GAME**			**MONTHLY**						**ALL-STAR**	
Tex	43-38	45-36	23-11	18-14	36-40	11-9	35-31	53-43	23-24	65-50	85-70	3-4	27-22	22-25	5-4	7-14	19-11	14-13	10-14	18-10	20-12	42-46	46-28
Hou	53-28	33-48	18-16	14-18	38-38	16-4	30-31	56-45	28-23	58-53	86-70	0-6	21-29	21-12	8-6	15-7	16-13	15-14	12-12	15-13	13-17	49-42	37-34
LAA	49-32	36-45	16-16	17-17	44-32	8-12	25-22	60-55	20-23	65-54	81-74	4-3	35-17	19-27	5-7	11-11	16-13	14-13	14-10	14-19	20-11	48-40	37-37
Sea	36-45	40-41	15-17	14-20	39-37	8-12	22-32	52-59	24-27	52-59	71-85	5-1	28-29	21-23	10-13	10-12	14-14	11-16	12-15	14-14	15-15	41-48	35-38
Oak	34-47	34-47	10-23	14-19	33-43	11-9	15-32	53-62	25-36	43-58	66-89	2-5	19-35	23-23	7-10	9-14	11-19	15-12	10-14	13-15	10-20	41-50	27-44

Team vs. Team Breakdown

	Tor	NYY	Bal	TB	Bos	KC	Min	Cle	CWS	Det	Tex	Hou	LAA	Sea	Oak
	EAST					**CENTRAL**					**WEST**				
Toronto Blue Jays	-	13	11	9	9	4	5	4	3	4	4	3	5	2	5
New York Yankees	6	-	9	12	11	4	5	2	5	5	2	3	4	5	3
Baltimore Orioles	8	10	-	10	11	3	0	5	3	4	1	3	2	3	6
Tampa Bay Rays	10	7	9	-	10	1	2	2	5	3	2	5	3	3	4
Boston Red Sox	10	8	8	9	-	4	2	2	3	4	2	2	2	4	5
Kansas City Royals	3	2	4	6	3	-	12	10	12	10	3	2	6	4	5
Minnesota Twins	2	1	7	4	5	7	-	12	13	8	3	3	2	4	4
Cleveland Indians	3	5	1	5	4	9	7	-	9	7	3	5	4	4	3
Chicago White Sox	4	2	3	1	4	7	6	10	-	9	3	5	4	4	5
Detroit Tigers	2	2	3	3	2	9	11	11	10	-	2	3	1	4	2
Texas Rangers	2	5	6	5	4	4	3	3	3	5	-	13	7	7	9
Houston Astros	4	4	4	2	4	4	3	2	1	4	6	-	10	12	10
Los Angeles Angels	2	2	4	3	5	1	5	2	3	6	12	9	-	12	11
Seattle Mariners	4	1	3	4	3	2	3	3	3	3	12	7	7	-	13
Oakland Athletics	1	4	1	3	1	1	3	4	2	4	10	9	8	6	-

2015 National League Standings

Overall

EAST							CENTRAL							WEST						
Team	W-L	Pct	GB	D1	LD1	LLd	Team	W-L	Pct	GB	D1	LD1	LLd	Team	W-L	Pct	GB	D1	LD1	LLd
New York Mets	90-72	.556	0.0	112	10/4	9.5	St Louis Cardinals	100-62	.617	0.0	175	10/4	9.0	Los Angeles Dodgers	92-70	.568	0.0	171	10/4	8.5
Washington Nationals	83-79	.512	7.0	63	8/2	4.5	Pittsburgh Pirates	98-64	.605	2.0	0	-	0.0	San Francisco Giants	84-78	.519	8.0	2	5/29	0.5
Miami Marlins	71-91	.438	19.0	0	-	0.0	Chicago Cubs	97-65	.599	3.0	3	4/16	0.5	Arizona Diamondbacks	79-83	.488	13.0	0	-	0.0
Atlanta Braves	67-95	.414	23.0	10	4/15	2.0	Milwaukee Brewers	68-94	.420	32.0	0	-	0.0	San Diego Padres	74-88	.457	18.0	0	-	0.0
Philadelphia Phillies	63-99	.389	27.0	0	-	0.0	Cincinnati Reds	64-98	.395	36.0	8	4/14	2.5	Colorado Rockies	68-94	.420	24.0	12	4/17	1.5

Wild Card Clinch Dates: Pittsburgh 9/23, Chicago 9/25. Division Clinch Dates:New York 9/27, St Louis 9/30, Los Angeles 10/1.
D1 = Number of days a team had at least a share of first place of their division; LD1 = Last date the team had at least a share of first place; LLd = The largest number of games that a team led their division

East Division

Tm	AT		VERSUS						CONDITIONS				GAME			MONTHLY						ALL-STAR	
	Home	Road	East	Cent	West	AL	LHS	RHS	Day	Night	Grass	Turf	1-Rn	5+Rn	XInn	April	May	June	July	Aug	Sept	Pre	Post
NYM	49-32	41-40	47-29	13-20	21-12	9-11	20-16	70-56	32-17	58-55	89-68	1-4	25-24	23-23	9-6	15-8	13-15	12-15	13-12	20-8	17-14	47-42	43-30
Was	46-35	37-44	44-32	14-19	17-16	8-12	23-16	60-63	33-22	50-57	82-78	1-1	22-22	29-20	9-2	10-13	18-9	15-12	11-13	12-17	17-15	48-39	35-40
Mia	41-40	30-51	35-41	13-19	16-18	7-13	14-19	57-72	21-29	50-62	71-85	0-6	23-21	15-24	6-3	10-12	10-19	12-15	10-15	11-18	18-12	38-51	33-40
Atl	42-39	25-56	34-42	15-18	12-21	6-14	13-23	54-72	16-28	51-67	65-92	2-3	28-18	11-27	4-9	10-12	15-13	11-16	10-16	8-20	13-18	42-47	25-48
Phi	37-44	26-55	30-46	11-23	14-18	8-12	18-20	45-79	23-29	40-70	62-98	1-1	16-27	16-31	6-9	8-15	11-18	8-19	13-12	12-16	11-19	29-62	34-37

Central Division

Tm	AT		VERSUS						CONDITIONS				GAME			MONTHLY						ALL-STAR	
	Home	Road	East	Cent	West	AL	LHS	RHS	Day	Night	Grass	Turf	1-Rn	5+Rn	XInn	April	May	June	July	Aug	Sept	Pre	Post
StL	55-26	45-36	20-12	46-30	23-11	11-9	25-18	75-44	28-21	72-41	100-62	0-0	32-23	22-16	8-8	15-6	18-11	18-8	15-12	19-9	15-16	56-33	44-29
Pit	53-28	45-36	24-9	34-42	27-6	13-7	20-16	78-48	32-15	66-49	98-64	0-0	36-17	21-12	12-9	12-10	14-14	17-9	17-9	19-8	19-14	53-35	45-29
ChC	49-32	48-33	22-12	46-30	19-13	10-10	20-14	77-51	37-30	60-35	97-65	0-0	34-21	16-15	13-5	12-8	14-14	14-13	15-12	19-9	23-9	47-40	50-25
Mil	34-47	34-47	17-16	31-45	12-21	8-12	19-20	49-74	22-31	46-63	68-94	0-0	16-16	21-21	4-5	5-17	12-17	14-14	13-12	11-15	13-19	38-52	30-42
Cin	34-47	30-51	16-17	33-43	8-25	7-13	15-27	49-71	16-36	48-62	64-98	0-0	18-29	15-27	5-12	11-11	11-16	13-14	11-14	8-21	10-22	39-47	25-51

West Division

Tm	AT		VERSUS						CONDITIONS				GAME			MONTHLY						ALL-STAR	
	Home	Road	East	Cent	West	AL	LHS	RHS	Day	Night	Grass	Turf	1-Rn	5+Rn	XInn	April	May	June	July	Aug	Sept	Pre	Post
LAD	55-26	37-44	19-13	17-17	46-30	10-10	25-19	67-51	25-16	67-54	92-70	0-0	23-26	18-15	6-9	13-8	16-12	15-15	14-10	15-12	19-13	51-39	41-31
SF	47-34	37-44	18-15	15-18	38-38	13-7	22-22	62-56	30-25	54-53	84-78	0-0	19-28	25-15	6-5	9-13	21-9	12-14	14-10	13-16	15-16	46-43	38-35
Ari	39-42	40-41	15-18	14-19	39-37	11-9	19-22	60-61	21-25	58-58	79-83	0-0	20-24	20-18	9-9	10-11	13-15	14-14	13-11	13-17	16-15	42-45	37-38
SD	39-42	35-46	17-16	15-18	35-41	7-13	19-21	55-67	17-29	57-59	74-88	0-0	22-21	21-29	7-5	11-12	14-15	12-15	13-11	14-14	10-21	41-49	33-39
Col	36-45	32-49	16-18	15-17	32-44	5-15	11-32	57-62	29-26	39-68	68-94	0-0	20-24	17-24	3-5	11-10	11-16	12-17	9-15	10-18	15-18	39-49	29-45

Team vs. Team Breakdown

	EAST					CENTRAL					WEST				
	NYM	Was	Mia	Atl	Phi	StL	Pit	ChC	Mil	Cin	LAD	SF	Ari	SD	Col
New York Mets	-	11	11	11	14	3	0	0	3	7	4	3	5	2	7
Washington Nationals	8	-	10	14	12	2	4	3	4	1	2	3	4	5	3
Miami Marlins	8	9	-	9	9	1	1	3	4	4	2	5	2	2	5
Atlanta Braves	8	5	10	-	11	4	2	1	5	3	3	3	3	2	1
Philadelphia Phillies	5	7	10	8	-	2	2	5	0	2	2	1	4	5	2
St Louis Cardinals	4	4	5	2	5	-	10	11	13	12	5	4	7	3	4
Pittsburgh Pirates	6	3	6	4	5	9	-	8	9	8	5	6	5	5	6
Chicago Cubs	7	4	3	6	2	8	11	-	14	13	3	5	4	3	4
Milwaukee Brewers	3	3	2	2	7	6	10	5	-	10	3	1	2	5	1
Cincinnati Reds	0	5	3	4	4	7	11	6	9	-	4	2	1	2	2
Los Angeles Dodgers	3	4	4	3	5	2	1	4	4	6	-	8	13	14	11
San Francisco Giants	3	4	2	4	5	2	1	2	5	5	11	-	8	11	8
Arizona Diamondbacks	2	3	5	3	2	0	1	2	5	6	6	11	-	9	13
San Diego Padres	4	2	5	5	1	4	2	3	2	4	5	8	10	-	12
Colorado Rockies	0	3	2	6	5	3	1	2	5	4	8	11	6	7	-

American League Batting

Tm	G	AB	H	2B	3B	HR	(Hm	Rd)	TB	R	RBI	TBB	IBB	SO	HBP	SH	SF	ShO	SB	CS	SB%	GDP	LOB	Avg	OBP	Slg
Tor	162	5509	1480	308	17	232	(123	109)	2518	891	852	570	12	1151	54	36	62	5	88	23	.79	140	1619	.269	.340	.457
NYY	162	5567	1397	272	19	212	(114	98)	2343	764	737	554	23	1227	63	24	54	6	63	25	.72	105	1720	.251	.323	.421
Tex	162	5511	1419	279	32	172	(92	80)	2278	751	707	503	32	1233	76	43	54	11	101	39	.72	99	1714	.257	.325	.413
Bos	162	5640	1496	294	33	161	(80	81)	2339	748	706	478	28	1148	46	30	42	9	71	27	.72	127	1742	.265	.325	.415
Hou	162	5459	1363	278	26	230	(128	102)	2383	729	691	486	22	1392	56	28	43	10	121	48	.72	102	1540	.250	.315	.437
KC	162	5575	1497	300	42	139	(62	77)	2298	724	689	383	28	973	77	34	47	11	104	34	.75	133	1714	.269	.322	.412
Bal	162	5485	1370	246	20	217	(128	89)	2307	713	686	418	23	1331	51	20	32	12	44	25	.64	127	1504	.250	.307	.421
Min	162	5467	1349	277	44	156	(85	71)	2182	696	661	439	31	1264	40	30	41	8	70	38	.65	133	1524	.247	.305	.399
Oak	162	5600	1405	277	46	146	(60	86)	2212	694	661	475	21	1119	40	14	38	8	78	29	.73	124	1679	.251	.312	.395
Det	161	5605	1515	289	49	151	(69	82)	2355	689	660	455	36	1259	41	23	35	9	83	51	.62	152	1683	.270	.328	.420
Cle	161	5439	1395	303	29	141	(61	80)	2179	669	640	533	34	1157	39	47	50	12	86	28	.75	134	1763	.256	.325	.401
LAA	162	5417	1331	243	21	176	(94	82)	2144	661	621	435	34	1150	58	37	40	11	52	34	.60	116	1573	.246	.307	.396
Sea	162	5544	1379	262	22	198	(90	108)	2279	656	624	478	31	1336	36	38	35	10	69	45	.61	123	1643	.249	.311	.411
TB	162	5485	1383	278	32	167	(82	85)	2226	644	612	436	22	1310	84	19	47	10	87	45	.66	121	1601	.252	.314	.406
CWS	162	5533	1381	260	27	136	(73	63)	2103	622	595	404	22	1231	65	30	37	12	68	42	.62	125	1612	.250	.306	.380
AL	1214	82836	21160	4166	459	2634	(1341	1293)	34146	10651	10142	7047	399	18281	826	453	657	144	1185	533	.69	1861	24631	.255	.318	.412

American League Pitching

Tm	G	CG	Rel	IP	BFP	H	R	ER	HR	SH	SF	HB	TBB	IBB	SO	WP	Bk	W	L	Pct.	ShO	Sv-Op	Hld	OAvg	OOBP	OSlg	ERA
Hou	162	5	482	1441.0	5965	1308	618	572	148	27	38	43	423	17	1280	61	2	86	76	.531	13	39-58	79	.241	.299	.382	3.57
Cle	161	11	476	1432.2	5904	1274	640	584	161	26	32	48	425	27	1407	48	5	81	80	.503	10	38-50	61	.237	.297	.386	3.67
KC	162	2	493	1452.0	6112	1372	641	601	155	28	44	52	489	10	1164	62	2	95	67	.586	8	56-76	79	.249	.314	.396	3.73
TB	162	1	530	1453.1	6069	1314	642	604	175	27	40	46	477	23	1355	81	5	80	82	.494	12	60-87	113	.240	.304	.385	3.74
Tor	162	7	469	1441.0	5984	1353	670	609	173	25	49	59	397	20	1117	62	4	93	69	.574	10	34-56	60	.248	.304	.403	3.80
LAA	162	2	518	1440.2	6096	1355	675	643	166	42	50	71	466	45	1221	61	4	85	77	.525	12	46-67	82	.248	.313	.396	3.94
Bal	162	0	453	1434.2	6085	1406	693	646	174	24	44	54	483	27	1233	46	0	81	81	.500	10	43-58	54	.257	.321	.418	4.05
NYY	162	3	497	1457.2	6191	1417	698	656	182	31	39	56	474	16	1370	78	4	87	75	.537	4	48-60	80	.253	.316	.407	4.05
Min	162	2	520	1443.0	6139	1506	700	653	163	42	43	41	413	34	1046	54	2	83	79	.512	12	45-60	76	.269	.321	.418	4.07
CWS	162	7	414	1452.2	6181	1443	701	643	162	42	43	62	474	34	1359	61	2	76	86	.469	9	37-52	61	.260	.322	.410	3.98
Sea	162	6	509	1463.0	6223	1430	726	677	181	32	37	70	491	41	1283	72	5	76	86	.469	12	45-69	100	.256	.322	.412	4.16
Oak	162	5	487	1444.2	6128	1402	729	664	172	34	53	47	474	19	1179	62	4	68	94	.420	15	28-53	41	.254	.316	.400	4.14
Tex	162	5	414	1442.2	6215	1459	733	680	171	22	51	63	508	29	1095	51	5	88	74	.543	9	45-62	94	.262	.328	.419	4.24
Bos	162	3	475	1448.1	6225	1486	753	694	178	23	37	62	478	17	1218	79	10	78	84	.481	10	40-60	63	.264	.327	.424	4.31
Det	161	7	505	1447.0	6188	1491	803	746	193	44	44	46	489	32	1100	60	8	74	87	.460	12	35-59	49	.268	.330	.444	4.64
AL	1214	66	7326	21694.1	91705	21016	10422	9659	2554	469	644	820	6961	391	18423	938	62	1231	1197	.507	158	639-927	1092	.254	.316	.407	4.01

American League Fielding

Team	G	Inn	PO	Ast	OFAst	E	(Throw	Field)	TC	DP	GDP	SB	CS	SB%	CPkof	PPkof	PB	UER	UERA	FPct
Baltimore	162	1434.2	4304	1597	48	77	(42	35)	5978	134	116	62	29	.68	4	2	10	47	0.29	.987
Cleveland	161	1432.2	4298	1528	28	79	(43	36)	5905	136	119	71	39	.65	2	1	10	56	0.35	.987
Houston	162	1441.0	4323	1617	29	85	(44	41)	6025	131	108	87	27	.76	0	4	8	46	0.29	.986
Minnesota	162	1443.0	4329	1637	44	86	(40	46)	6052	150	131	93	22	.81	0	4	3	47	0.29	.986
Detroit	161	1447.0	4341	1621	35	86	(33	53)	6048	156	137	72	43	.63	3	7	5	57	0.35	.986
Kansas City	162	1452.0	4356	1611	28	88	(40	48)	6055	138	114	75	35	.68	4	7	5	40	0.25	.985
Toronto	162	1441.0	4323	1592	21	88	(42	46)	6003	145	128	60	41	.59	4	4	25	61	0.38	.985
New York	162	1457.2	4373	1594	24	92	(42	50)	6059	135	113	71	36	.66	1	8	8	42	0.26	.985
Seattle	162	1463.0	4389	1685	23	94	(38	56)	6168	155	127	65	40	.62	3	5	10	49	0.30	.985
Los Angeles	162	1440.2	4322	1491	31	93	(39	54)	5906	108	91	93	43	.68	4	6	13	45	0.28	.984
Boston	162	1448.1	4345	1625	28	97	(39	58)	6067	148	126	75	38	.66	2	8	22	59	0.37	.984
Tampa Bay	162	1453.1	4360	1408	38	95	(39	56)	5863	118	94	88	44	.67	2	4	8	38	0.24	.984
Chicago	162	1452.2	4358	1582	37	101	(52	49)	6041	159	134	75	30	.71	1	3	22	58	0.36	.983
Texas	162	1442.2	4328	1695	31	119	(52	67)	6142	169	143	82	25	.77	5	3	11	53	0.33	.981
Oakland	162	1444.2	4334	1642	27	126	(56	70)	6102	154	130	78	40	.66	1	4	14	65	0.40	.979
American League	1214	21694.1	65083	23925	472	1406	(641	765)	90414	2145	1811	1147	532	.68	36	68	174	763	0.32	.984

National League Batting

Tm	G	AB	H	2B	3B	HR	(Hm	Rd)	TB	R	RBI	TBB	IBB	SO	HBP	SH	SF	ShO	SB	CS	SB%	GDP	LOB	Avg	OBP	Slg
Col	162	5572	1479	274	49	186	(102	84)	2409	737	702	388	47	1283	33	44	34	8	97	43	.69	114	1550	.265	.315	.432
Ari	162	5649	1494	289	48	154	(69	85)	2341	720	680	490	40	1312	33	46	57	7	132	44	.75	134	1701	.264	.324	.414
Was	162	5428	1363	265	13	177	(91	86)	2185	703	665	539	38	1344	44	55	51	12	57	23	.71	129	1645	.251	.321	.403
Pit	162	5631	1462	292	27	140	(72	68)	2228	697	661	461	46	1322	89	63	41	11	98	45	.69	115	1723	.260	.323	.396
SF	162	5565	1486	288	39	136	(53	83)	2260	696	663	457	30	1159	49	45	37	15	93	36	.72	142	1719	.267	.326	.406
ChC	162	5491	1341	272	30	171	(92	79)	2186	689	657	567	47	1518	74	32	35	10	95	37	.72	102	1643	.244	.321	.398
NYM	162	5527	1351	295	17	177	(85	92)	2211	683	654	488	42	1290	68	29	32	15	51	25	.67	130	1631	.244	.312	.400
LAD	162	5385	1346	263	26	187	(97	90)	2222	667	638	563	31	1258	60	49	30	12	59	34	.63	135	1703	.250	.326	.413
Mil	162	5480	1378	274	34	145	(76	69)	2155	655	624	412	35	1299	41	55	34	16	84	29	.74	130	1541	.251	.307	.393
SD	162	5457	1324	260	36	148	(74	74)	2100	650	623	426	22	1327	40	52	42	19	82	29	.74	108	1547	.243	.300	.385
StL	162	5484	1386	288	39	137	(60	77)	2163	647	619	506	47	1267	66	30	42	15	69	38	.64	128	1716	.253	.321	.394
Cin	162	5571	1382	257	27	167	(88	79)	2194	640	613	496	38	1255	42	47	40	13	134	38	.78	112	1730	.248	.312	.394
Phi	162	5529	1374	272	37	130	(72	58)	2110	626	586	387	20	1274	54	53	29	13	88	32	.73	119	1628	.249	.303	.382
Mia	162	5463	1420	236	40	120	(53	67)	2096	613	575	375	30	1150	39	71	40	12	112	45	.71	133	1621	.260	.310	.384
Atl	162	5420	1361	251	18	100	(48	52)	1948	573	548	471	39	1107	44	67	31	17	69	33	.68	148	1741	.251	.314	.359
NL	1215	82652	20947	4076	480	2275	(1132	1143)	32808	9996	9508	7026	552	19165	776	747	575	195	1320	531	.71	1879	24839	.253	.316	.397

National League Pitching

Tm	G	CG	Rel	IP	BFP	H	R	ER	HR	SH	SF	HB	TBB	IBB	SO	WP	Bk	W	L	Pct.	ShO	Sv-Op	Hld	OAvg	OOBP	OSlg	ERA
StL	162	1	515	1464.2	6134	1359	525	478	123	66	29	45	477	37	1329	48	5	100	62	.617	15	62-77	84	.246	.310	.366	2.94
LAD	162	6	515	1445.2	5932	1317	595	553	145	37	29	38	395	32	1396	52	10	92	70	.568	21	47-68	87	.242	.297	.372	3.44
Pit	162	0	500	1489.2	6215	1392	596	532	110	38	33	75	453	38	1338	67	4	96	64	.605	13	54-68	99	.248	.311	.361	3.21
ChC	162	6	552	1461.1	5997	1276	608	546	134	36	30	46	407	38	1431	66	3	97	65	.599	21	48-67	89	.233	.290	.372	3.36
NYM	162	1	485	1462.2	6046	1341	613	557	152	63	40	44	383	43	1337	46	2	90	72	.556	14	50-71	71	.243	.296	.377	3.43
SF	162	7	557	1444.1	6009	1344	627	597	155	31	34	50	431	28	1165	40	4	84	78	.519	18	41-56	116	.246	.305	.395	3.72
Was	162	4	468	1434.2	5975	1366	635	577	145	52	39	55	364	37	1342	39	4	83	79	.512	13	41-64	77	.250	.301	.384	3.62
Mia	162	0	486	1427.0	6050	1374	678	638	141	50	55	52	508	25	1152	53	3	71	91	.438	12	35-56	80	.255	.322	.396	4.02
Ari	162	1	550	1466.2	6257	1450	713	659	182	44	46	48	500	45	1215	51	3	79	83	.488	12	44-65	85	.258	.322	.423	4.04
SD	162	1	516	1440.1	6093	1371	731	655	191	44	38	54	516	35	1393	54	3	74	88	.457	6	41-58	63	.252	.321	.414	4.09
Mil	162	1	496	1435.0	6148	1432	737	682	176	48	42	55	517	36	1260	71	5	68	94	.420	7	40-54	73	.261	.329	.422	4.28
Cin	162	2	521	1453.1	6271	1436	754	700	177	62	45	58	544	42	1252	54	11	64	98	.395	8	35-56	63	.258	.328	.420	4.33
Atl	162	3	532	1425.1	6156	1462	760	698	170	56	46	53	550	45	1148	53	9	67	95	.414	10	44-70	82	.268	.339	.426	4.41
Phi	162	1	503	1436.1	6332	1592	809	749	191	47	42	61	483	37	1153	60	7	63	99	.389	7	35-51	53	.280	.341	.445	4.69
Col	162	4	584	1426.1	6308	1579	844	799	183	57	40	48	579	42	1112	66	6	68	94	.420	4	36-61	99	.283	.353	.461	5.04
NL	1215	38	7780	21713.1	91923	21091	10225	9420	2355	731	588	782	7112	560	19023	820	79	1198	1232	.493	181	653-942	1221	.255	.318	.402	3.90

National League Fielding

Team	G	Inn	PO	Ast	OFAst	E	(Throw	Field)	TC	DP	GDP	SB	CS	SB%	CPkof	PPkof	PB	UER	UERA	FPct
Los Angeles	162	1445.2	4337	1727	29	75	30	45	6139	133	114	85	42	.67	1	10	12	42	0.26	.988
San Francisco	162	1444.1	4333	1674	17	78	35	43	6085	145	130	82	32	.72	1	3	10	30	0.19	.987
Miami	162	1427.0	4281	1589	23	77	36	41	5947	162	145	74	25	.75	0	2	11	40	0.25	.987
Arizona	162	1466.2	4400	1697	26	86	40	46	6183	146	125	73	28	.72	2	3	11	54	0.33	.986
New York	162	1462.2	4388	1599	32	88	44	44	6075	131	114	75	26	.74	0	1	4	56	0.34	.986
Cincinnati	162	1453.1	4360	1622	27	90	37	53	6072	131	117	100	31	.76	2	3	9	54	0.33	.985
Atlanta	162	1425.1	4276	1593	26	90	36	54	5959	186	165	84	33	.72	1	10	13	62	0.39	.985
Washington	162	1434.2	4304	1533	21	90	46	44	5927	125	102	53	32	.62	1	3	7	58	0.36	.985
Colorado	162	1426.1	4279	1818	26	95	47	48	6192	171	153	92	35	.72	0	4	7	45	0.28	.985
San Diego	162	1440.1	4321	1566	30	92	46	46	5979	138	119	122	60	.67	1	5	18	76	0.47	.985
St Louis	162	1464.2	4394	1617	18	96	42	54	6107	159	134	54	29	.65	1	8	5	47	0.29	.984
Chicago	162	1461.1	4384	1670	28	111	44	67	6165	120	98	137	38	.78	7	8	10	62	0.38	.982
Pittsburgh	162	1489.2	4469	1868	39	122	53	69	6459	177	154	144	43	.77	3	3	11	64	0.39	.981
Milwaukee	162	1435.0	4305	1678	18	116	64	52	6099	164	136	104	46	.69	3	4	7	55	0.34	.981
Philadelphia	162	1436.1	4309	1585	29	117	51	66	6011	145	123	79	32	.71	2	3	12	60	0.38	.981
National League	1215	21713.1	65140	24836	389	1423	651	772	91399	2233	1929	1358	532	.72	25	70	147	805	0.33	.984

Team Pitching Staff Summary

Team	Starters IP	ERA	ERA Rank	W-L	Bullpen IP	ERA	ERA Rank	W-L	Sv-Opp	Sv Pct
Arizona Diamondbacks	887.1	4.37	23	51-56	579.1	3.56	13	28-27	44-65	68%
Atlanta Braves	939.2	4.27	20	45-66	485.2	4.69	29	22-29	44-70	63%
Baltimore Orioles	915.2	4.53	25	51-62	519.0	3.21	5	30-19	43-58	74%
Boston Red Sox	947.1	4.39	24	59-60	501.0	4.24	26	19-24	40-60	67%
Chicago Cubs	946.2	3.36	3	60-39	514.2	3.38	8	37-26	48-67	72%
Chicago White Sox	1011.0	4.12	14	52-63	441.2	3.67	15	24-23	37-52	71%
Cincinnati Reds	903.2	4.58	26	42-67	549.2	3.96	22	22-31	35-56	63%
Cleveland Indians	979.1	3.94	10	65-64	453.1	3.12	4	16-16	38-50	76%
Colorado Rockies	857.2	5.27	30	41-62	568.2	4.70	30	27-32	36-61	59%
Detroit Tigers	942.0	4.78	27	47-66	505.0	4.38	27	27-21	35-59	59%
Houston Astros	983.2	3.71	8	59-46	457.1	3.27	6	27-30	39-58	67%
Kansas City Royals	912.2	4.34	22	65-53	539.1	2.72	2	30-14	56-76	74%
Los Angeles Angels	957.2	3.98	13	55-58	483.0	3.86	18	30-19	46-67	69%
Los Angeles Dodgers	978.1	3.24	2	64-42	467.1	3.91	19	28-28	47-68	69%
Miami Marlins	911.0	4.25	18	49-64	516.0	3.66	14	22-27	35-56	63%
Milwaukee Brewers	905.0	4.79	28	45-79	530.0	3.40	9	23-15	40-54	74%
Minnesota Twins	928.0	4.14	16	58-52	515.0	3.95	21	25-27	45-60	75%
New York Mets	1002.2	3.44	4	64-51	460.0	3.48	11	26-21	50-71	70%
New York Yankees	927.0	4.25	18	62-56	530.2	3.70	16	25-19	48-60	80%
Oakland Athletics	935.2	3.91	9	47-63	509.0	4.63	28	21-31	28-53	53%
Philadelphia Phillies	892.2	5.23	29	38-76	543.2	3.81	17	25-23	35-51	69%
Pittsburgh Pirates	967.1	3.53	5	67-48	522.1	2.67	1	31-16	54-68	79%
San Diego Padres	945.1	4.13	15	48-66	495.0	4.02	23	26-22	41-58	71%
San Francisco Giants	939.1	3.95	11	65-59	505.0	3.33	7	19-19	41-56	73%
Seattle Mariners	940.0	4.17	17	55-50	523.0	4.15	25	21-36	45-69	65%
St Louis Cardinals	979.2	2.99	1	72-42	485.0	2.82	3	28-20	62-77	81%
Tampa Bay Rays	914.2	3.63	6	52-45	538.2	3.93	20	28-37	60-87	69%
Texas Rangers	940.2	4.32	21	62-54	502.0	4.12	24	26-20	45-62	73%
Toronto Blue Jays	965.1	3.96	12	72-42	475.2	3.50	12	21-27	34-56	61%
Washington Nationals	966.1	3.70	7	61-54	468.1	3.46	10	22-25	41-64	64%

Team Defense
Defensive Runs Saved by Position and Team

Team	P	C	1B	2B	3B	SS	LF	CF	RF	Shifts	Total
Arizona Diamondbacks	3	-16	18	4	-2	16	9	18	10	12	72
Houston Astros	18	6	-4	3	0	-3	-5	10	12	20	57
Kansas City Royals	12	-1	-1	0	8	1	10	25	-3	5	56
San Francisco Giants	6	11	13	-4	12	23	-7	-23	2	11	44
Miami Marlins	-1	0	-9	12	12	8	6	-11	16	2	35
Pittsburgh Pirates	-1	12	-15	2	2	0	18	-9	13	9	31
Toronto Blue Jays	3	2	-2	11	9	3	-12	16	-11	12	31
Chicago Cubs	3	9	10	10	7	5	-2	-14	-10	10	28
Tampa Bay Rays	-12	-6	-11	4	-4	-10	7	42	-5	23	28
Cleveland Indians	-3	3	-5	0	9	9	-4	2	5	7	23
Baltimore Orioles	-11	4	1	-7	10	-2	4	0	-8	29	20
Detroit Tigers	2	-14	0	20	-7	3	10	-6	-3	9	14
St Louis Cardinals	-5	4	9	3	-17	-3	-6	9	21	-1	14
Los Angeles Angels	-5	8	1	-12	1	-3	5	6	7	6	14
New York Mets	8	12	5	-10	-14	-26	16	2	14	6	13
Texas Rangers	0	-4	-2	-1	17	0	5	3	-17	12	13
Los Angeles Dodgers	-4	-1	11	-13	2	-4	7	-3	5	12	12
Boston Red Sox	5	-11	1	-1	-15	-3	-6	10	17	13	10
Oakland Athletics	6	-7	-7	-3	-3	6	3	8	1	4	8
Milwaukee Brewers	-4	11	3	2	-3	-4	-2	-10	0	11	4
Washington Nationals	10	10	-8	8	-13	-2	-11	-9	7	4	-4
Cincinnati Reds	-4	-8	7	4	3	-6	-11	3	3	5	-4
San Diego Padres	-8	10	6	0	-6	-7	8	-11	-15	19	-4
Colorado Rockies	3	-19	-9	2	17	4	-12	-7	3	8	-10
Chicago White Sox	-11	14	0	1	5	-8	1	-16	-7	5	-16
Minnesota Twins	-9	-10	4	-4	0	-10	10	6	-8	2	-19
Atlanta Braves	-6	-16	1	3	-9	27	-5	-14	-8	1	-26
New York Yankees	-1	-6	-2	-12	-8	5	5	-1	-20	12	-28
Seattle Mariners	8	13	-9	-11	0	-5	-9	-26	-11	5	-45
Philadelphia Phillies	-30	-6	-13	-15	-14	-10	-16	16	-9	-6	-103

Paul Goldschmidt   Starling Marte
Ian Kinsler   Kevin Kiermaier
Nolan Arenado   Jason Heyward
Andrelton Simmons   Buster Posey
Ender Inciarte   Dallas Keuchel

THE FIELDING BIBLE AWARDS 2015

The Fielding Bible Awards 2015

John Dewan

We are celebrating the 10-year anniversary of the The Fielding Bible Awards. The original concept came about to provide an alternative to the Gold Glove Awards. One important distinction that differentiates the Fielding Bible Award from most other baseball awards is that we only have one winner for all of Major League Baseball, instead of separate winners for each league. Our intention is to stand up and say, "This is the best fielder at this position in the major leagues last season."

Nearly every year we point out how the teams in the playoffs also just happen to be the best defensive teams in baseball. This year is no exception. Each of the eight teams remaining in the playoffs as I write this is well above average defensively. It is no coincidence. Good defense saves runs leading to additional wins.

In 2015, the voting for The Fielding Bible Awards was the most decisive one in the history of the voting. Every year there are positions where it comes down to the tiebreaker, or is decided by one to three points. In 2015, the twelve-person voting panel was unanimous on three different positions and only one position was as close as four points separating first and second place. At one of the unanimous positions Kevin Kiermaier made it easy. Playing center field for the Tampa Bay Rays, he established a new record for the most Defensive Runs Saved ever recorded (42).

Every one of the ten winners of The Fielding Bible Award this year was also either the outright MLB leader in Defensive Runs Saved for his position or was tied for the lead. Today's baseball experts trust and rely on the fact that the new defensive metrics can truly measure defense.

Four players were repeat award winners this year. The expert panel rewarded Atlanta's Andrelton Simmons with his third unanimous Fielding Bible Award in a row at shortstop. Former teammate Jason Heyward, now patrolling right field for the St. Louis Cardinals, won his third award in four years. Dallas Keuchel of the Houston Astros won his second in a row as a pitcher and Arizona's first baseman Paul Goldschmidt won his second in the last three years.

There were six first time winners: catcher Buster Posey (San Francisco), second baseman Ian Kinsler (Detroit), third baseman Nolan Arenado (Colorado), left fielder Starling Marte (Pittsburgh), center fielder Kevin Kiermaier (Tampa Bay), and multi-position player Ender Inciarte (Arizona).

Here's a short refresher course on how the awards are determined: We asked our panel of twelve experts to rank 10 players at each position on a scale from one to ten. We then use the same voting technique as the Major League Baseball MVP voting. A first place vote gets 10 points, second place 9 points, third place 8 points, etc. Total up the points for each player and the player with the most points wins the award. A perfect score is 120.

Here are the Fielding Bible Awards for the 2015 season:

First Base – Paul Goldschmidt, Arizona Diamondbacks

The Arizona Diamondbacks were the best defensive team in baseball in 2015, and Paul Goldschmidt is one of the reasons why. He saved 18 runs with his defense showing tremendous range for a first baseman, especially to his right. He was listed first on 10 of the 12 ballots receiving 118 out of a possible 120 points in the voting.

Previous Winners:

2014	Adrian Gonzalez	2009	Albert Pujols
2013	Paul Goldschmidt	2008	Albert Pujols
2012	Mark Teixeira	2007	Albert Pujols
2011	Albert Pujols	2006	Albert Pujols
2010	Daric Barton		

Second Base – Ian Kinsler, Detroit Tigers

Ian Kinsler was runner-up to Dustin Pedroia in the voting for The Fielding Bible Award in 2014. But this year, partially thanks to Pedroia's injury but mostly due to his defensive brilliance, Kinsler wins his first Fielding Bible Award. Over the last three years he is by far the leader in Defensive Runs Saved with 50 compared to DJ LeMahieu's second highest total of 29 runs saved. Kinsler saved 19 runs for the Tigers in 2015 and finished with 106 points in the voting. Dee Gordon was second in Runs Saved (13) at second base in MLB and was also second in the voting.

Previous Winners:

2014	Dustin Pedroia	2009	Aaron Hill
2013	Dustin Pedroia	2008	Brandon Phillips
2012	Darwin Barney	2007	Aaron Hill
2011	Dustin Pedroia	2006	Orlando Hudson
2010	Chase Utley		

Third Base – Nolan Arenado, Colorado Rockies

His teammates gave him the nickname "Sharknado" because of his aggressive approach charging groundballs and his ability to make whirling throws to gobble up hitters at first base. Nolan Arenado has been consistently superb defensively since arriving on the scene for the Rockies in 2013, saving 30, 16 and 18 runs in the three years he's been in the majors. He garnered 116 points in the voting. Previous Fielding Bible Award winners, Adrian Beltre and Manny Machado, finishing second and third with 102 and 101 points respectively.

Previous Winners:

2014	Josh Donaldson	2009	Ryan Zimmerman
2013	Manny Machado	2008	Adrian Beltre
2012	Adrian Beltre	2007	Pedro Feliz
2011	Adrian Beltre	2006	Adrian Beltre
2010	Evan Longoria		

Shortstop – Andrelton Simmons, Atlanta Braves

Here are the words used to describe Andrelton Simmons in *The Fielding Bible—Volume IV*: "long, freakishly athletic, and extremely smooth", "quick hands", flawless transfers", "best arm strength in the game", "makes throws from deep in the hole routine". This pretty much describes everything needed to become the ultimate defensive shortstop in baseball. It is no surprise that he is already being compared to Ozzie Smith in his short career thus far. It is now three straight years that panelists have made Simmons a unanimous choice for the shortstop Fielding Bible Award. Simmons and Giant Brandon Crawford were first and second on every ballot.

Previous Winners:

2014	Andrelton Simmons	2009	Jack Wilson
2013	Andrelton Simmons	2008	Jimmy Rollins
2012	Brendan Ryan	2007	Troy Tulowitzki
2011	Troy Tulowitzki	2006	Adam Everett
2010	Troy Tulowitzki		

Left Field – Starling Marte, Pittsburgh Pirates

Starling Marte leapt into the void left by an injury to Alex Gordon, the left field Fielding Bible Award winner of the last three years. It is not without merit. Marte is a center fielder playing left covering more ground than any other left fielder in the game. He is a constant source of highlight-reel plays, and he gunned down baserunners like no other with 14 baserunner kills, the best in the majors in 2015. He received 116 out of 120 points in the voting.

Previous Winners:

2014	Alex Gordon	2009	Carl Crawford
2013	Alex Gordon	2008	Carl Crawford
2012	Alex Gordon	2007	Eric Byrnes
2011	Brett Gardner	2006	Carl Crawford
2010	Brett Gardner		

Center Field – Kevin Kiermaier, Tampa Bay Rays

Kevin Kiermaier did what no other defensive player has ever done. He recorded 42 Defensive Runs Saved, the highest total since Baseball Info Solutions developed this metric in 2003. The thing that sets him apart from all other center fielders is his ability to range deep in center stealing doubles and triples right and left. The metric that really highlights this is: he saved an incredible 65 bases on the plays he made compared to an average center fielder. That's a lot of dead doubles and triples! The next best center fielder in bases saved was Arizona's A.J. Pollock, far behind with 38. Kiermaier was a unanimous choice by the voters. Royal Lorenzo Cain was second on every ballot.

Previous Winners:

2014	Juan Lagares	2009	Franklin Gutierrez
2013	Carlos Gomez	2008	Carlos Beltran
2012	Mike Trout	2007	Andruw Jones
2011	Austin Jackson	2006	Carlos Beltran
2010	Michael Bourn		

Right Field – Jason Heyward, St. Louis Cardinals

Jason Heyward now has six straight years of double-digit Defensive Runs Saved and three Fielding Bible Awards. He has been able to accomplish this by starting and finishing every play extremely well. He excels at picking up the ball off the bat and rarely takes the wrong angle. He is not afraid to dive, demonstrating tremendous body control when doing so. He plays deeper than most right fielders enabling him to track down deeply hit balls saving extra bases. Every Fielding Bible Award voter listed Jason Heyward first on their ballot in 2015.

Previous Winners:

2014	Jason Heyward	2009	Ichiro Suzuki
2013	Gerardo Parra	2008	Franklin Gutierrez
2012	Jason Heyward	2007	Alex Rios
2011	Justin Upton	2006	Ichiro Suzuki
2010	Ichiro Suzuki		

Catcher – Buster Posey, San Francisco Giants

After so many years of unparalleled offense as a catcher, Buster Posey has now been recognized for his defense as well with his first Fielding Bible Award. Posey has always been superb defensively. He has averaged 12 Defensive Runs Saved per year over the last six years and was tied with Kevin Plawecki for the lead among backstops with 17 in 2015. It's just that when there is a person on the planet by the name of Yadier Molina, it's hard to win an award for defensive excellence at the catcher position. But he outperformed Molina in 2015 and was recognized by the voters with 116 of 120 points for the award.

Previous Winners:

2014	Jonathan Lucroy	2009	Yadier Molina
2013	Yadier Molina	2008	Yadier Molina
2012	Yadier Molina	2007	Yadier Molina
2011	Matt Wieters	2006	Ivan Rodriguez
2010	Yadier Molina		

Pitcher – Dallas Keuchel, Houston Astros

Dallas Keuchel helped himself reach 20 wins for the Astros by saving the most runs defensively as a pitcher in the game. Those 13 Defensive Runs Saved are more than any pitcher could help himself with the bat. For example, Madison Bumgarner, the best hitting pitcher in baseball, had 10 Runs Created in a super year with the bat for a pitcher. It is also the second best DRS figure posted by a pitcher since BIS began tracking the stat. Kenny Rogers had 15 in 2008. Keuchel outpointed Zach Greinke 115-107 in the voting.

Previous Winners:

2014	Dallas Keuchel	2009	Mark Buehrle
2013	R.A. Dickey	2008	Kenny Rogers
2012	Mark Buehrle	2007	Johan Santana
2011	Mark Buehrle	2006	Greg Maddux
2010	Mark Buehrle		

Multi-Position – Ender Inciarte, Arizona Diamondbacks

Ender Inciarte is the second winner of the new Multi-Position Fielding Bible Award, which was first awarded to Lorenzo Cain in 2014. It was the closest ballot of the year as Inciarte received 94 points in the voting compared to 90 points for Cubs rookie Addison Russell. Inciarte showed extreme versatility and excellence manning every outfield position. He saved 12 runs in left, 4 runs in center and 13 runs in right field defensively for the Arizona Diamondbacks.

Previous Winners:

2014 Lorenzo Cain

Background of the Fielding Bible Awards

While *The Fielding Bible, The Fielding Bible—Volume II, The Fielding Bible—Volume III, and The Fielding Bible—Volume IV* put a lot of emphasis on the numbers, especially Defensive Runs Saved and the Range and Positioning System, we feel that visual observation and subjective judgment are still very important parts of determining the best defensive players. Also, we believe people have a right to know who is voting and all the players they are voting for. Therefore, in setting up the Fielding Bible Awards, we took the following steps:

1. *We appointed a panel of experts to vote.* We have a panel of 12 experts plus three "tie-breaker" ballots. (See below.)

2. *We rate everybody in one group.* The Gold Glove vote is divided into National League and American League. We make ours different by putting everybody together. Besides, is playing shortstop in the American League one thing and playing shortstop in the National League a different thing, or are they really very much the same thing? A few years back we had a great example of this decision. Without the Fielding Bible Award, Jack Wilson wins *nada*, because he switched leagues in mid-year. According to our panelists (and unlike the Gold Glove voters), Jack was the best fielding shortstop in baseball in 2009. Period. He deserved to be recognized for that.

3. *We use a 10-man ballot and a 10-point scale.* We use a 10-man ballot. We give 10 points for first place, 9 points for second place, etc, down to 1 point for tenth place. We feel strongly that a 10-man ballot with weighted positions leads to more accurate outcomes.

4. *We defined the list of candidates.* Only players who actually were regulars at the position are candidates. This eliminates the possibility of a vote going to somebody who wasn't really playing the position.

5. *We are publishing the balloting.* We summarize the voting at each position, clearly identifying whom everybody voted for. Publishing the actual vote totals encourages the voters to take their votes more seriously. Also, we feel the public will have more respect for the voting if they have more insight into the process.

A perfect score is 120 points. If all 12 voters place one player first on their ballot, he scores 120. Three players had perfect scores of 120 this year: Andrelton Simmons, Kevin Kiermaier, and Jason Heyward.

Here are the tie-breaker rules (which came into play in our very first year, in 2010, and in 2013). They are applied one at a time until we have a winner:

1. Most first-place votes wins.
2. Count the tie-breaker ballots, highest point tally wins.
3. Award goes to player with the more Bases Saved.

Ballots were due four days after the end of the regular season. Here is this year's panel:

Since you have this book, you probably know **Bill James**, a baseball writer and analyst published for more than thirty years. Bill is the Senior Baseball Operations Advisor for the Boston Red Sox.

The **BIS Video Scouts** at Baseball Info Solutions (BIS) study every game of the season, multiple times, charting a huge list of valuable game details.

As the MLB Network on-air host of *Clubhouse Confidential* and *MLB Now*, **Brian Kenny** brings an analytical perspective on the game of baseball to a national television audience. He also won a 2003 Sports Emmy Award as host of ESPN's *Baseball Tonight*.

Dave Cameron is the Managing Editor of FanGraphs. He resides in Winston-Salem, North Carolina, where the local minor league team once forced him to watch Michael Morse play shortstop for an entire season. He has appreciated defensive value ever since.

Doug Glanville played nine seasons in Major League Baseball and was well known for his excellent outfield defense. Currently, he is a baseball analyst at ESPN on *Baseball Tonight*, *SportsCenter*, *Wednesday Night Baseball*, and ESPN.com, as well as a regular contributor to *The New York Times*, and he is the author of the book *The Game from Where I Stand*.

The man who created Strat-O-Matic Baseball, **Hal Richman**, continues to lead his company's annual in-depth analysis of each player's season. Hal cautions SOM players that his voting on this ballot may or may not reflect the eventual fielding ratings for players in his game. Ballots were due prior to the completion of his annual research effort to evaluate player defense.

Named the best sports columnist in America in 2012 by the National Sportswriters and Sportscasters Hall of Fame, **Joe Posnanski** is the National Columnist at NBC Sports.

For over twenty-five years, BIS owner **John Dewan** has collected, analyzed, and published in-depth baseball statistics and analysis. He has authored or co-authored four volumes of *The Fielding Bible*.

Mark Simon has been a researcher for ESPN Stats & Information since 2002 and currently helps oversee the Stats & Information blog and Twitter (@espnstatsinfo). He is a regular contributor on baseball (often writing on defense) for ESPNNY.com and ESPN.com, and is the author of *Numbers Don't Lie: The Biggest Numbers in Yankees History* (published by Triumph Books in June 2016).

Peter Gammons serves as on-air and online analyst for MLB Network, MLB.com and NESN (New England Sports Network). He is the 56th recipient of the J. G. Taylor Spink Award for outstanding baseball writing given by the BBWAA (Baseball Writers Association of America).

Rob Neyer has been a working writer for 25 years, and FOXSports.com's Senior Baseball Editor for some of those years. When he's not writing, he's thinking about not writing. Rob will live in Portland, Oregon for as long as they let him.

The **Tom Tango Fan Poll** represents the results of a poll taken at the website, Tango on Baseball (www.tangotiger.net). Besides hosting the website, Tom writes research articles devoted to sabermetrics and is the co-author of *The Book: Playing the Percentages in Baseball*.

Our three tie-breakers are **Ben Jedlovec**, President of Baseball Info Solutions and co-author of *The Fielding Bible—Volume III* and *The Fielding Bible—Volume IV*, **Dan Casey**, veteran Video Scout and Senior Operations Analyst at BIS, and **Sean Forman**, the founder of Baseball-Reference.com.

The Fielding Bible Awards

Below we show the final point tally for The Fielding Bible Awards in the 2015 season. We asked a panel of experts to complete a 10-man ballot ranking players from 1 to 10 based on their defensive abilities. We show the ranks in the tables below. We then awarded points in the same way as Major League Baseball's MVP voting: 10 points for a first place vote, 9 for second, etc., down to 1 point for 10th place. We cover all nine positions, looking at only their fielding work for the 2015 season. Position players are eligible if they played at least 600 innings while catchers require a minimum of 500 innings. Either can qualify with 10 Runs Saved, as well. Pitchers require a minimum of 120 innings pitched or 5 Runs Saved.

In 2014, we introduced a Multi-Position Award for fielders who are excellent defensive players but do not call any one position their home. For a player to qualify for the Multi-Position Award, he must have played at least 600 innings across all positions and played no more than 70 percent of those innings at any one position.

First Basemen

First Basemen	Bill	BIS Video Scouts	Brian	Dave	Doug	Hal	Joe	John	Mark	Peter	Rob	Tango Fan Poll	Total Points
Paul Goldschmidt	1	1	1	1	1	1	1	1	1	2	1	2	118
Adrian Gonzalez	2	2	2	4	2	3	2	2	2	4	2	6	99
Anthony Rizzo	3	4	5	3	6	4	3	3	3	1	4	5	88
Brandon Belt	4	3	4	2	3	2	4	5	9	6	3	1	86
Yonder Alonso	7	9	3	7	4	8	5	4	4	3			56
Mark Teixeira	8	6	6	6	7	5	8	8	5	10	8	4	51
Joey Votto		7	7	5	9		6	6	8	5	7		39
Eric Hosmer	6	5				10	9		6	8	10	3	31
Albert Pujols				8	8	6	7	9		9	6	8	27
Lucas Duda		8	8		5			10	10		9		16

Others receiving points: Chris Davis 15, Freddie Freeman 8, Jose Abreu 6, Miguel Cabrera 6, Mike Napoli 5, Adam Lind 4, Joe Mauer 2, Justin Smoak 2, Mitch Moreland 1

Second Basemen

Second Basemen	Bill	BIS Video Scouts	Brian	Dave	Doug	Hal	Joe	John	Mark	Peter	Rob	Tango Fan Poll	Total Points
Ian Kinsler	1	2	1	4	1	1	1	1	1	1	1		106
Dee Gordon	2	1	2	5	2	2	3	6	2	4	3	6	94
Addison Russell		5	9	1		4	2	2	4	5	2	2	74
Danny Espinosa	8	9	3	2	3	5	7	7	3	6	4	5	70
DJ LeMahieu	10	4	4	3	10	6	4	9	6	2		8	55
Brandon Phillips		6	7	9	5	3	6	5	7		10	4	48
Ryan Goins	5			6	7		8	10	8	8	8	1	38
Kolten Wong	6	8	6			9	5	3			5		35
Logan Forsythe		10	8		6	8	9	8	5	7	6		32
Dustin Pedroia	3					7				3		3	28

Others receiving points: Carlos Sanchez 24, Eric Sogard 14, Joe Panik 11, Jose Altuve 10, Brian Dozier 5, Jason Kipnis 5, Robinson Cano 3, Omar Infante 2, Chris Owings 2, Jace Peterson 1, Anthony Rendon 1, Jonathan Schoop 1, Ben Zobrist 1

Third Basemen

Third Basemen	Bill	BIS Video Scouts	Brian	Dave	Doug	Hal	Joe	John	Mark	Peter	Rob	Tango Fan Poll	Total Points
Nolan Arenado	1	1	2	2	1	1	1	1	1	1	2	2	116
Adrian Beltre	3	4	1	1	2	4	2	2	2	2	4	3	102
Manny Machado	2	3	3	3	3	2	4	3	3	3	1	1	101
Josh Donaldson	4	2	6	4	6	3	3	4	4	5	3	4	84
Matt Duffy	5	5	4	7	5	6	7	7	5	4	5	7	65
Todd Frazier		8	5	5	4	5	8	8	9	7	7		44
Martin Prado	9	6	7	9	7	9	9	5	7	10	6	10	38
Tyler Saladino	7	10					5	6	6	6	8		29
Mike Moustakas		9	8		8	8	6			8		9	21
Evan Longoria	8	7				7				9		8	16

Others receiving points: Kyle Seager 12, Jake Lamb 10, Giovanny Urshela 6, Matt Carpenter 5, Justin Turner 3, Kris Bryant 2, Trevor Plouffe 2, Juan Uribe 2, Lonnie Chisenhall 1, Luis Valbuena 1

Shortstops

Shortstops	Bill	BIS Video Scouts	Brian	Dave	Doug	Hal	Joe	John	Mark	Peter	Rob	Tango Fan Poll	Total Points
Andrelton Simmons	1	1	1	1	1	1	1	1	1	1	1	1	120
Brandon Crawford	2	2	2	2	2	2	2	2	2	2	2	2	108
Nick Ahmed	10	5	3	3	4	6	4	3	3	3	4	7	77
Adeiny Hechavarria	5	3	4	9	3	3	6	7	4	4	3	8	73
Francisco Lindor		4	5	4	5	5	3	4	5	5	5	4	72
Troy Tulowitzki	3	7	6		7	9	7	6	8	8	6	6	48
Didi Gregorius	4	6	8	5	9	7	8	8	7	7	7	10	46
J.J. Hardy	9		7		6	10	5	5	6	10	8		33
Alcides Escobar	6			6	10	4	9					5	26
Jose Iglesias		10		7		8			9	9		3	20

Others receiving points: Xander Bogaerts 17, Carlos Correa 5, Marcus Semien 5, Alexei Ramirez 4, Alexi Amarista 3, Jordy Mercer 2, Elvis Andrus 1

Left Fielders

Left Fielders	Bill	BIS Video Scouts	Brian	Dave	Doug	Hal	Joe	John	Mark	Peter	Rob	Tango Fan Poll	Total Points
Starling Marte	3	1	1	2	1	1	1	1	1	2	1	1	116
Alex Gordon	2	3	3	3	3	2	2	4	4	1	4	2	99
Yoenis Cespedes	8	2	5	1	2	6	3	3	2	3	2	7	88
Christian Yelich	4	4	2	6	4	3	4	2	3	4	5	5	86
Eddie Rosario	10	6	8	4	6	10	5	7	6		6	4	49
Brett Gardner	1	7	6	7	7	8		9	9	10		3	43
Justin Upton	5	8	4	9	5		8	8	5	6	9		43
Sam Fuld			10			7	7	6	7	9	3	6	33
Ben Revere		5	7	5	8	9				8			24
Scott Van Slyke							6	5		7	8		18

Others receiving points: Michael Brantley 16, Randal Grichuck 11, Chris Young 8, Chris Coghlan 7, Brandon Guyer 7, Colby Rasmus 6, Brandon Barnes 3, Nori Aoki 2, Marlon Byrd 1

Center Fielders

Center Fielders	Bill	BIS Video Scouts	Brian	Dave	Doug	Hal	Joe	John	Mark	Peter	Rob	Tango Fan Poll	Total Points
Kevin Kiermaier	1	1	1	1	1	1	1	1	1	1	1	1	120
Lorenzo Cain	2	2	2	2	2	2	2	2	2	2	2	2	108
Kevin Pillar	3	3	4	4	4	6	3	5	3	4	3	5	85
A.J. Pollock	6	6	3	5	3	5	4	4	6	3	6	3	78
Billy Hamilton	4	7	5	3	7	3	10	6	5	10	10	6	56
Mookie Betts	5	5	6	10	8		5	7	7	7	8		42
Leonys Martin		9		9	5		6	3	4	8	4		40
Mike Trout		4		8		4			8			4	27
Odubel Herrera		8	9		6		8	8			9		18
Carlos Gomez			10	7	9	7		9	10	9			16

Others receiving points: Jake Marisnick 16, Juan Lagares 15, Adam Jones 14, Michael Taylor 14, Andrew McCutchen 7, Gregor Blanco 1, Michael Bourn 1, Aaron Hicks 1, Joc Pederson 1

Right Fielders

Right Fielders	Bill	BIS Video Scouts	Brian	Dave	Doug	Hal	Joe	John	Mark	Peter	Rob	Tango Fan Poll	Total Points
Jason Heyward	1	1	1	1	1	1	1	1	1	1	1	1	120
Ender Inciarte	8	6	2	2		5	2	2	2	3	2	3	84
Curtis Granderson	6	5	4		2		3	4	3	2	5		65
Bryce Harper	5	3	3		6	6	4	8	9	7	8		51
Kole Calhoun	4	2	9	5		3			4		6	9	46
Ichiro Suzuki			6	4	3		5	6	5	9	4		46
Giancarlo Stanton	10		10	9	5	9	6	3	7	4	3		44
Gregory Polanco		4		6	9	4	7	5	6	6	9		43
Carlos Gonzalez	2	10	5		4	8	8		10			6	35
Jackie Bradley Jr.	3	9			2						7	2	32

Others receiving points: Josh Reddick 27, George Springer 18, Jay Bruce 13, Rusney Castillo 13, Yasiel Puig 7, J. D. Martinez 4, Gerardo Parra 4, Jose Bautista 3, Nick Markakis 3, Andre Ethier 1, Steven Souza 1

Catchers

Catchers	Bill	BIS Video Scouts	Brian	Dave	Doug	Hal	Joe	John	Mark	Peter	Rob	Tango Fan Poll	Total Points
Buster Posey	2	1	1	1	1	3	1	1	1	1	1	2	116
Yadier Molina	1	3	4	5	3	4	3	5	2	2	2	1	97
Russell Martin	3	2	3	2	9	2	4	10	8	3		3	72
Salvador Perez	5	4	5		5	1	7		9	6	10	5	53
Jason Castro		7	2	4	4	6	6	8	4	10			48
Tyler Flowers	8		7		7		2	2			5		35
Kevin Plawecki	6	8	6				5	3	10	9	9		32
Wilson Ramos		6		2			7	5			4		31
Caleb Joseph						5	4	3		6			26
Francisco Cervelli	7	5		3						8	7		25

Others receiving points: Jonathan Lucroy 24, Mike Zunino 19, Miguel Montero 18, Yan Gomes 17, Martin Maldonado, 13, Brian McCann 10, Chris Iannetta 7, Derek Norris 5, Rene Rivera 5, Yasmani Grandal 4, Tucker Barnhart 3

Pitchers

Pitchers	Bill	BIS Video Scouts	Brian	Dave	Doug	Hal	Joe	John	Mark	Peter	Rob	Ben	Total Points
Dallas Keuchel	2	2	1	1	2	1	2	1	1	1	1	2	115
Zack Greinke	1	1	2	4	1	5	1	2	3	2	2	1	107
Jacob deGrom	7	3	3	6	3	6	7		4	9	4	3	66
Clayton Kershaw	9	5	7			3	4	4	5	5	3	5	60
Jake Arrieta	6	4			6	2	3		2	3			51
Mike Leake		7	4	5	7	4		3		4	7		47
Mark Buehrle	5	9	10	2		8	10	8	7	6		10	35
Gerrit Cole	3	6			9		8		6			9	25
Johnny Cueto			3	10	10	9	6				5		23
Julio Teheran					4	7		7		7		7	23

Others receiving points: Joe Kelly 18, Odrisamer Despaigne 14, Jaime Garcia 13, Patrick Corbin 12, Wade Miley 11, Masahiro Tanaka 10, Jose Quintana 9, Collin McHugh 6, R.A. Dickey 4, Mike Fiers 3, Sonny Gray 3, Jordan Zimmermann 3, Andrew Cashner 1, Yordano Ventura 1

Multi-Position

Pitchers	Bill	BIS Video Scouts	Brian	Dave	Doug	Hal	Joe	John	Mark	Peter	Rob	Tango Fan Poll	Total Points
Ender Inciarte		2	1	3	2	4	1	1	1	2	6	4	94
Addison Russell	9	1	2	4	3	2	2	2	2	4	8	3	90
Jackie Bradley Jr.		3	4	1	1	1	4	10	4	1		1	80
Ryan Goins		5	3	2		6		5	5	5	2	2	64
Brock Holt	1	6	8		5	8		6			1		42
Lonnie Chisenhall				10			3	3	3	10	4	9	35
Sam Fuld		9	7	6		5	8	7	6			7	33
Jung Ho Kang		4	9		4		9		7		5		28
Ben Zobrist	2	7		5					10	7	7		28
Randal Grichuck		10	5		7	3				9			21

Others receiving points: Josh Harrison 21, Gerardo Parra 19, Rusney Castillo 18, Ichiro Suzuki 15, Paulo Orlando 11, Gregor Blanco 10, Ben Revere 10, Mike Aviles 8, Aaron Hill 7, Brandon Guyer 5, Daniel Murphy 5, Danny Valencia 4, Ryan Flaherty 3, Colby Rasmus 3, Eduardo Escobar 2, Jose Ramirez 2, Rajai Davis 1, Kelly Johnson 1

Q and A of Shifting

John Dewan

Q: It looks like there was more shifting in baseball again this year. Is that true?

A: Yes. It's up significantly again this year. Here is the progress over the last six years.

MLB Shifts by Season

Year	Number of Shifts
2010	2,464
2011	2,357
2012	4,577
2013	8,180
2014	13,298
2015	17,733

As you can see, teams shifted 2,357 times in 2011. In 2015 they shifted 17,733 times. That's a rate of increase of 50% per year in that time period. The growth rate was 33% in the last year (2015 vs. 2014).

(Note: the way we count shifts is based on the number of balls being put into play while the defense is in a shift. The number of shifts includes full Ted Williams shifts and what we call Partial shifts. A full Ted Williams shift is where three or more defenders are on one side of second base. A Partial shift includes all other defensive alignments where it's clear that it's a shift defense but there are two players on each side of second base.)

Q: Was it effective?

A: Once again, yes. The chart below shows how the number of runs saved as a result of the shift has increased dramatically each year.

MLB Shift Runs Saved by Season

Year	Shift Runs Saved
2010	36
2011	42
2012	76
2013	135
2014	196
2015	266

The number of runs saved as a result of a shift defense increased from 196 in 2014 to 266 in 2015. That's a 36% increase.

Q: With all the extra shifting, were there diminishing returns?

A: Since the increase in Shift Runs Saved in 2015 (36%) is more that than the increase in the number of shifts (33%), that means teams were a little more effective shifting in 2015 than they were in 2014. Another way to get at this is to look at the number of runs saved per 100 shifts each year:

MLB Runs Saved per 100 Shifts

Year	Runs Saved per 100 Shifts
2010	1.46
2011	1.78
2012	1.66
2013	1.65
2014	1.47
2015	1.50

In general, shifting saves about 1.5 runs per 100 shifts. The rate of saving runs the last couple of years is about the same as it was in 2010. That's slightly down from the period of 2011 to 2013, but not by much.

Q: At some point there has to be some diminishing returns, doesn't there?

A: In theory that's probably true, but the fact of the matter is that shifting saves runs. There are still quite a few teams who haven't yet completely embraced the philosophy. These teams are leaving runs on the table. More on this below.

Q: Is there an upper limit?

A: I think so, at least how we measure it now. The upper limit might be 40,000 shifts in a season. With 2015 being at 17,733 shifts, there is plenty of room to continue growing. Here is the Stat of the Week article from earlier this year (March 30, 2015) on this topic:

What is the Upper Limit of Shifts?

The SABR Analytics Conference took place a couple of weeks ago in Phoenix. I strongly recommend attending this annual conference if you are interested in baseball analytics. During one of the luncheons I was talking to Rob Neyer and Brian Kenny about shifts. The usage of the shift has been increasing over the last few years, but I shared with them how Baseball Info Solutions developed software almost 10 years ago now that suggested a shift on dozens of different batters rather than just the handful that were being shifted then. It took a few years for baseball to catch on, but they did and it's making a difference.

The software, called BIS-D, currently suggests a full Ted Williams shift (three infielders to the left or right of second base) on well over 100 different batters. Rob asked if it's possible to use the software to determine an upper limit on the number of shifts. If every batter suggested by the software was shifted, how many shifts would there be? Might that be the upper limit of shifts? A great idea!

The number of shifts in baseball over the last few years have been:

All Shifts on Balls in Play by Season

2010	2011	2012	2013	2014
2,464	2,357	4,577	8,180	13,298

These include both partial shifts and full Ted Williams shifts. If we limit the totals to just the full Ted Williams Shifts, we get:

Ted Williams Shifts on Balls in Play by Season

2010	2011	2012	2013	2014
1,502	1,389	3,170	3,254	8,354

In 2014, major league teams had a full shift in place 8,354 times when a ball was put in play. How does that compare with what the BIS-D software would have recommended? If you take every player that has put at least 50 ground-balls and short line drives in play in their career (and had at least one plate appearance last year), the software recommends a shift on 113 different players. Those 113 players put 24,733 balls in play.

So, the upper limit on full Ted Williams shifts in baseball might be around 25,000, compared to the 8,354 full shifts actually deployed in 2014. Teams are only shifting about a third as often as they could be, according to the BIS-D software.

The Houston Astros, who shifted more than any team last year and saved the most runs defensively (27) with the shift, are close. BIS-D recommended 971 full shifts for them. The Astros deployed 867.

Taking this one final step, teams in aggregate are using a partial shift about half as often as they do a full shift. If that strategy is correct, the upper limit on all shifts, including partial shifts, might be closer to 40,000.

Q: Which teams shifted the most?

A: The Rays and the Astros each shifted over 1,400 times in 2015. The Rockies were a distant third with 1,011 shifts. However, those 1,011 shifts would have been nearly half the league total just four years ago.

Here is a complete chart by league comparing 2014 and 2015 team by team.

American League

Team	2014	2015	Change
Rays	824	1,462	638
Astros	1,341	1,416	75
Yankees	779	929	150
Orioles	705	899	194
Blue Jays	686	884	198
Twins	478	724	246
Athletics	489	610	121
Indians	516	575	59
Rangers	490	557	67
Royals	543	538	-5
Red Sox	498	526	28
Tigers	205	520	315
Angels	357	436	79
White Sox	534	389	-145
Mariners	412	352	-60
Total	8,857	10,817	1,960
Average	590	721	131

National League

Team	2014	2015	Change
Rockies	114	1,011	897
Pirates	660	971	311
Diamondbacks	252	587	335
Padres	241	569	328
Giants	361	552	191
Reds	212	426	214
Phillies	291	384	93
Brewers	576	382	-194
Cubs	316	381	65
Dodgers	208	316	108
Cardinals	367	313	-54
Marlins	208	300	92
Mets	221	297	76
Nationals	201	216	15
Braves	213	211	-2
Total	4,441	6,916	2,475
Average	296	461	165

Q: Were they effective?

A: Yes. The Rays and Astros saved 23 and 20 runs, respectively, when employing the shift defense. The Orioles were extremely effective shifting, saving the most runs (29) while employing the sixth-most shifts in baseball in 2015 (899 shifts).

Using the rule-of-thumb that every 10 runs is worth a win, the Rays and Astros can attribute two of their wins in 2015 to this defensive strategy. The Orioles produced about three extra wins with their shifting. That's a big deal.

Q: From the chart we can see that four teams had a lot fewer shifts in 2015 than they did in 2014? What happened with them?

A: The biggest problem for teams trying to utilize the shift is getting buy-in from the manager, coaches and players on the field. Shifting is still a radical concept for some people. It's human nature. "I've been in baseball my entire life. We've been doing it this way the whole time. Why should we change now?" Well, the reason to change now is that all the analytics are clearly showing that shifting is an effective strategy.

It's just a matter of time.

Let's look at each of the three teams that dropped off. The Mariners went from 412 shifts in 2014 to 352 in 2015. They saved 9 runs in 2014 and dropped to 5 in 2015. The White Sox dropped off even further. They bucked the league-wide trend of more shifts, and paid for it. They saved 11 runs with shifting in 2014 and also dropped to just 5 in 2015.

The Milwaukee Brewers' shift total dropped the most, but their story is a little bit different. In 2014 they only saved 4 runs with 576 shifts, only 0.69 runs per 100 shifts compared to the league average of 1.47. As a result, they cut way back on their shifting, dropping by 194 shifts from 2014 to 2015. But they were much more effective in 2015 with 11 runs saved, 2.88 runs saved per 100 shifts.

The Brewers are an anomaly. League-wide shifting is up and teams are saving more and more runs.

Q: Who are some of the more interesting hitters? Specifically, how do these guys perform when shifted compared to when they are not shifted?

A: There are quite a few players who are almost always shifted now (90% of the time and more): David Ortiz, Chris Davis, Lucas Duda, Ryan Howard, Adam LaRoche. Collectively this group hit .199 on grounders and short liners with the shift in place. The 2015 MLB average was .230 on grounders and short liners with a shift on. That's 33 points lower than the MLB average of .263 with no shift on. Let's put that in a chart:

Batting Average on Grounders and Short Liners

Name	Shift Percentage	When Shifted	No Shift
MLB Overall	18%	.230	.263

But the more interesting hitters are those that were not shifted as frequently as David Ortiz and clan. Here is a sampling of players who were not shifted all the time but were severely hampered when shifted:

Batting Average on Grounders and Short Liners

Name	Shift Percentage	When Shifted	No Shift
Prince Fielder	65%	.250	.337
Adrian Gonzalez	62%	.148	.195
Edwin Encarnacion	56%	.196	.260
Curtis Granderson	54%	.192	.392
Albert Pujols	48%	.196	.240

Edwin Encarnacion and Albert Pujols are particularly interesting in that they are right-handed hitters. Teams are becoming more and more comfortable shifting on righties, despite the fact that there is a bigger gap on the first base side of second with the first baseman needing to stay closer to the bag.

Q: Are there any hitters who have figured out how to beat the shift?

A: Overall, hitters generally don't beat the shift. When we studied this a few years back we found only one player who seemed to have a strategy that proved effective at times. Carlos Pena was one of those rare hitters these days who could bunt. He was successful bunting against the shift in selected situations (leading off an inning, for example). However, for the most part, hitters have not yet figured it out. Nevertheless, for reasons that I believe have mostly to do with sample size, some hitters hit better when shifted in 2015 than they did when not shifted. Here is a sampling:

Batting Average on Grounders and Short Liners

Name	Shift Percentage	When Shifted	No Shift
Carlos Gonzalez	66%	.265	.173
Kyle Seager	58%	.270	.226
Jay Bruce	63%	.212	.167

Q: Does the pitcher make a difference?

A: Right now, the way the pitcher makes the most difference is that there are still quite a few pitchers who can't stand shifting. It takes them out of their rhythm, they say. It is very frustrating for them to see that occasional groundball go right through the spot where a defender would be in a conventional defense.

This too will change. As time goes forward and pitchers start coming up through college and the minors where shifts are also being employed more and more, shifting will become natural to them as well.

Q: What about groundball pitchers vs. flyball pitchers?

A: Let me refer you to a really cool book that came out this year called *Big Data Baseball* by Travis Sawchik. It's the story of how the Pittsburgh Pirates brought themselves out of a 20-year playoff drought by employing analytics. One of the most important elements was this: Use the two-seam fastball more often. The two-seam fastball has a natural sinking effect compared to the four-seamer, which produces more strikeouts. Combine that with shift analytics. The theory, which has worked well for the Pirates, is that shifting will turn a higher percentage of those groundballs into outs.

Big Data Baseball is the best baseball analytics book I've read since *Moneyball*.

Q: Football has so many different names for defenses. Will baseball move in that direction?

A: At some point the baseball community might stop calling everything a "shift" and start naming different variations of them. Right now Baseball Info Solutions has named the Ted Williams Shift and the Partial Shift. In football, there is a seemingly endless array of defensive terminology involving placement of players on defense. Let me give you a few examples: 4-3 formation, 3-4 formation, cover 2, cover 3, A-gap, B-gap, wide-9, 6-technique, 7-technique, over and under alignments, 5-technique, the flex, 20-alignment, 21-alignment, 4-3 Over, 4-3 Under, etc.

I've been watching football every week for the past 40 years and the difference between a 4-3 and a 3-4 is obvious. I know snippets about a lot of the other terminology, but as a general fan, I mostly leave that to the experts. I think we might see the same progression in baseball. Insiders in baseball will have names for different defenses, but the regular fan may simply think of it as a shift or not a shift.

Shifts by Team

American League

Team	2014	2015	Change
Rays	824	1462	638
Astros	1341	1416	75
Yankees	779	929	150
Orioles	705	899	194
Blue Jays	686	884	198
Twins	478	724	246
Athletics	489	610	121
Indians	516	575	59
Rangers	490	557	67
Royals	543	538	-5
Red Sox	498	526	28
Tigers	205	520	315
Angels	357	436	79
White Sox	534	389	-145
Mariners	412	352	-60
Total	**8857**	**10817**	**1960**
Average	**590**	**721**	**130**

National League

Team	2014	2015	Change
Rockies	114	1011	897
Pirates	660	971	311
Diamondbacks	252	587	335
Padres	241	569	328
Giants	361	552	191
Reds	212	426	214
Phillies	291	384	93
Brewers	576	382	-194
Cubs	316	381	65
Dodgers	208	316	108
Cardinals	367	313	-54
Marlins	208	300	92
Mets	221	297	76
Nationals	201	216	15
Braves	213	211	-2
Total	**4441**	**6916**	**2475**
Average	**296**	**461**	**165**

Top 30 Shifted Batters

Batter	Shifted PA	Shift Percent	Shift GSL BA	No Shift GSL BA
Ortiz,David	526	95.6	.177	.000
Davis,Chris	517	92.7	.208	.143
Duda,Lucas	405	89.8	.235	.333
Howard,Ryan	386	95.3	.143	.000
Rizzo,Anthony	384	71.0	.250	.259
McCann,Brian	383	86.8	.172	.067
Fielder,Prince	354	64.8	.250	.337
Moss,Brandon	352	85.4	.292	.304
LaRoche,Adam	347	89.7	.197	.417
Gonzalez,Carlos	342	65.8	.265	.173
Santana,Carlos	325	65.4	.190	.241
Seager,Kyle	324	58.3	.270	.226
Moustakas,Mike	323	63.1	.248	.231
Gonzalez,Adrian	311	61.8	.148	.195
Alvarez,Pedro	303	81.2	.201	.200
Rasmus,Colby	292	77.5	.178	.278
Bruce,Jay	292	63.2	.212	.167
Teixeira,Mark	288	79.1	.192	.290
Moreland,Mitch	288	72.4	.240	.306
Morales,Kendrys	278	54.1	.220	.223
Encarnacion,Edwin	275	56.0	.196	.260
Beltran,Carlos	270	63.2	.286	.220
Granderson,Curtis	264	53.7	.192	.392
Belt,Brandon	263	62.5	.293	.167
Smith,Seth	261	75.7	.265	.139
Pujols,Albert	261	47.5	.196	.240
Headley,Chase	252	50.4	.229	.287
Freeman,Freddie	246	69.1	.212	.385
Lind,Adam	241	57.8	.229	.282
Martinez,Victor	238	57.3	.190	.268

Defensive Runs Saved Leaders

Joe Rosales

The Chicago Cubs have found a special defender in Addison Russell. If you look at the Infield Runs Saved Leaders on the next page, you will see that Russell's name appears on both the 2015 second base leaderboard and the 2015 shortstop leaderboard. Given that he started the season in the minors and then split his time between two positions at the major league level, the fact that he managed to accumulate enough Runs Saved to finish in the top five at both positions is very impressive.

Defensive Runs Saved (or just Runs Saved for short) is a comprehensive accounting of how a player performs defensively. Depending on the position a player plays, Runs Saved is a combined measure of his range and positioning, his ability to field bunts, to turn double plays, to prevent baserunners from advancing either on balls in play or on stolen base attempts, to get extra strike calls, to limit earned runs, and to make extraordinary defensive plays while avoiding misplays. Positive numbers mean that a player saved his team runs, while negative numbers mean a player cost his team runs, with zero being average.

In this section you will find Runs Saved leaders and trailers for every defensive position, both for the 2015 season alone and for the last three years combined.

Infield Runs Saved Leaders

First Basemen 3-Year Leaders		Second Basemen 3-Year Leaders		Third Basemen 3-Year Leaders		Shortstops 3-Year Leaders	
Goldschmidt,Paul	32	Kinsler,Ian	50	Arenado,Nolan	64	Simmons,Andrelton	94
Rizzo,Anthony	32	LeMahieu,DJ	29	Machado,Manny	55	Crawford,Brandon	30
Gonzalez,Adrian	32	Pedroia,Dustin	29	Donaldson,Josh	43	Cozart,Zack	30
Alonso,Yonder	25	Barney,Darwin	20	Uribe,Juan	33	Hardy,J.J.	22
Napoli,Mike	21	Goins,Ryan	19	Beltre,Adrian	22	Ahmed,Nick	21
Votto,Joey	17	Sogard,Eric	15	Frazier,Todd	18	Tulowitzki,Troy	18
Belt,Brandon	15	Wong,Kolten	14	Prado,Martin	17	Florimon,Pedro	16
Morneau,Justin	11	Espinosa,Danny	12	Headley,Chase	12	Barmes,Clint	12
Adams,Matt	11	Forsythe,Logan	12	Duffy,Matt	12	Kozma,Pete	11
Pujols,Albert	11	Phillips,Brandon	11	Saladino,Tyler	12	Rojas,Miguel	11

First Basemen 3-Year Trailers		Second Basemen 3-Year Trailers		Third Basemen 3-Year Trailers		Shortstops 3-Year Trailers	
Fielder,Prince	-20	Murphy,Daniel	-29	Castellanos,Nick	-39	Lowrie,Jed	-32
Howard,Ryan	-20	Uggla,Dan	-24	Gillaspie,Conor	-26	Cabrera,Asdrubal	-31
Moss,Brandon	-16	Odor,Rougned	-18	Ramirez,Aramis	-25	Reyes,Jose	-28
Alvarez,Pedro	-13	Hill,Aaron	-15	Freese,David	-25	Nunez,Eduardo	-24
Encarnacion,Edwin	-13	Dietrich,Derek	-14	Johnson,Chris	-22	Castro,Starlin	-19
Morrison,Logan	-11	Rutledge,Josh	-13	Middlebrooks,Will	-19	Tejada,Ruben	-18

First Basemen 2015 Leaders		Second Basemen 2015 Leaders		Third Basemen 2015 Leaders		Shortstops 2015 Leaders	
Goldschmidt,Paul	18	Kinsler,Ian	19	Arenado,Nolan	18	Simmons,Andrelton	25
Rizzo,Anthony	10	Gordon,Dee	13	Beltre,Adrian	18	Crawford,Brandon	20
Gonzalez,Adrian	10	Espinosa,Danny	10	Machado,Manny	14	Ahmed,Nick	19
Alonso,Yonder	9	Russell,Addison	9	Duffy,Matt	12	Lindor,Francisco	10
Belt,Brandon	8	Forsythe,Logan	8	Saladino,Tyler	12	Russell,Addison	10
Votto,Joey	6	Sanchez,Carlos	6	Donaldson,Josh	11	Hechavarria,Adeiny	9
Lind,Adam	5	Wong,Kolten	5	Prado,Martin	9	Cozart,Zack	7
Teixeira,Mark	5	Sogard,Eric	5	Lamb,Jake	7	Semien,Marcus	5
Duda,Lucas	4	Owings,Chris	5	Frazier,Todd	6	Gregorius,Didi	5
Cabrera,Miguel	4	Phillips,Brandon	4	Turner,Justin	5	Tulowitzki,Troy	5

First Basemen 2015 Trailers		Second Basemen 2015 Trailers		Third Basemen 2015 Trailers		Shortstops 2015 Trailers	
Alvarez,Pedro	-13	Giavotella,Johnny	-12	Escobar,Yunel	-11	Santana,Danny	-15
Howard,Ryan	-9	Kendrick,Howie	-12	Sandoval,Pablo	-11	Tejada,Ruben	-15
Bour,Justin	-7	Cano,Robinson	-9	Gillaspie,Conor	-10	Suarez,Eugenio	-12
Morrison,Logan	-7	Zobrist,Ben	-7	Carpenter,Matt	-10	Flores,Wilmer	-10
Carter,Chris	-6	Odor,Rougned	-7	Castellanos,Nick	-9	Cabrera,Asdrubal	-8
Cron,C.J.	-5	Murphy,Daniel	-6	Franco,Maikel	-8	Reyes,Jose	-8

Outfield Runs Saved Leaders

Left Fielders 3-Year Leaders		Center Fielders 3-Year Leaders		Right Fielders 3-Year Leaders	
Gordon,Alex	50	Lagares,Juan	54	Heyward,Jason	61
Marte,Starling	49	Cain,Lorenzo	49	Victorino,Shane	28
Cespedes,Yoenis	29	Martin,Leonys	45	Parra,Gerardo	27
Yelich,Christian	26	Kiermaier,Kevin	43	Reddick,Josh	24
Lough,David	19	Gomez,Carlos	38	Byrd,Marlon	18
Inciarte,Ender	19	Pollock,A.J.	34	Suzuki,Ichiro	18
Van Slyke,Scott	18	Dyson,Jarrod	25	Bruce,Jay	15
Heisey,Chris	12	Hamilton,Billy	23	Cain,Lorenzo	14
Blanco,Gregor	11	Marisnick,Jake	22	Kiermaier,Kevin	13
Fuld,Sam	11	Inciarte,Ender	17	Inciarte,Ender	13

Left Fielders 3-Year Trailers		Center Fielders 3-Year Trailers		Right Fielders 3-Year Trailers	
Ramirez,Hanley	-19	Fowler,Dexter	-36	Hunter,Torii	-35
Holliday,Matt	-18	Pagan,Angel	-34	Beltran,Carlos	-26
Gattis,Evan	-14	Maybin,Cameron	-19	Garcia,Avisail	-20
Gomes,Jonny	-13	Revere,Ben	-18	Kemp,Matt	-18
Coghlan,Chris	-13	Trout,Mike	-18	Arcia,Oswaldo	-16
Arcia,Oswaldo	-11	McCutchen,Andrew	-16	Cuddyer,Michael	-16

Left Fielders 2015 Leaders		Center Fielders 2015 Leaders		Right Fielders 2015 Leaders	
Marte,Starling	24	Kiermaier,Kevin	42	Heyward,Jason	22
Cespedes,Yoenis	15	Cain,Lorenzo	18	Inciarte,Ender	13
Yelich,Christian	13	Martin,Leonys	15	Granderson,Curtis	12
Rosario,Eddie	10	Pillar,Kevin	14	Polanco,Gregory	11
Conforto,Michael	9	Pollock,A.J.	14	Suzuki,Ichiro	9
Upton,Justin	8	Herrera,Odubel	10	Stanton,Giancarlo	9
Gordon,Alex	7	Betts,Mookie	9	Calhoun,Kole	6
DeJesus,David	3	Hamilton,Billy	8	Harper,Bryce	6
Young,Chris	2	Gomez,Carlos	6	Maxwell,Justin	6
Gardner,Brett	1	Bourn,Michael	6	Bruce,Jay	5

Left Fielders 2015 Trailers		Center Fielders 2015 Trailers		Right Fielders 2015 Trailers	
Ramirez,Hanley	-19	Pagan,Angel	-20	Kemp,Matt	-15
Werth,Jayson	-10	Maybin,Cameron	-16	Beltran,Carlos	-14
Asche,Cody	-8	Eaton,Adam	-14	Garcia,Avisail	-11
Ackley,Dustin	-6	Fowler,Dexter	-12	Choo,Shin-Soo	-11
Dickerson,Corey	-6	Gose,Anthony	-12	Soler,Jorge	-8
Davis,Khris	-6	Span,Denard	-10	Cruz,Nelson	-8

Pitcher/Catcher Runs Saved Leaders

Pitchers 3-Year Leaders		Catchers 3-Year Leaders	
Keuchel,Dallas	26	Molina,Yadier	46
Greinke,Zack	21	Martin,Russell	44
Kershaw,Clayton	16	Posey,Buster	41
Teheran,Julio	16	Lucroy,Jonathan	37
Leake,Mike	15	Gomes,Yan	28
Dickey,R.A.	13	Flowers,Tyler	26
Cueto,Johnny	13	Joseph,Caleb	26
Corbin,Patrick	13	Maldonado,Martin	25
Buehrle,Mark	11	Ramos,Wilson	22
Iwakuma,Hisashi	11	Conger,Hank	20

Pitchers 3-Year Trailers		Catchers 3-Year Trailers	
Lackey,John	-17	Suzuki,Kurt	-34
Burnett,A.J.	-15	Saltalamacchia,J	-31
Lester,Jon	-14	Pierzynski,A.J.	-30
Volquez,Edinson	-13	Iannetta,Chris	-29
McAllister,Zach	-12	Rosario,Wilin	-27
Nelson,Jimmy	-12	Hundley,Nick	-26

Pitchers 2015 Leaders		Catchers 2015 Leaders	
Keuchel,Dallas	13	Plawecki,Kevin	17
Greinke,Zack	9	Posey,Buster	17
Arrieta,Jake	6	Flowers,Tyler	14
Cole,Gerrit	6	Joseph,Caleb	12
Leake,Mike	6	Castro,Jason	11
Garcia,Jaime	6	Ramos,Wilson	10
Despaigne,Odrisamer	6	Maldonado,Martin	9
Kelly,Joe	6	Molina,Yadier	9
deGrom,Jacob	6	Zunino,Mike	8
Kershaw,Clayton	5	Cervelli,Francisco	8

Pitchers 2015 Trailers		Catchers 2015 Trailers	
Lester,Jon	-8	Swihart,Blake	-16
Nelson,Jimmy	-8	Pierzynski,A.J.	-13
Lackey,John	-7	Ruiz,Carlos	-12
Volquez,Edinson	-7	Hundley,Nick	-11
Sabathia,CC	-6	Suzuki,Kurt	-9
Burnett,A.J.	-6	Castillo,Welington	-9

2015 Career Register

Scott Spratt

This section contains the complete career statistics of every active major league player up to date through the end of the 2015 season. We have also included the last five years of minor league statistics for players who have appeared in fewer than three major league seasons, whether or not those players spent any time in the minors in 2015. For players who exceed that three-year cutoff but who also spent time in the minors in 2015—likely because of a rehab assignment—they will show only their 2015 minor league statistics, which will be called out by an asterisk.

Beginning this year, we have combined all minor league data for players in a season below Double-A into one row labeled Low. In addition, we have eliminated minor league statistics for players in Double-A and Triple-A where they pitched fewer than five games or hit in fewer than 10 games.

If a player led either the AL or NL in a category, that number will appear in **boldface**.

Age is seasonal age as of June 30, 2016.

For pitchers, BFP is Batters Facing Pitcher; TBB is Total Bases on Balls (or Total Walks, intentional and unintentional); Op is Save Opportunities; Hld is Holds.

For the various levels of Class-A ball, we have used "A+" to indicate High-A and "A-" to indicate Low-A. To help readers decode our minor league abbreviations, there is a legend in the back of the book.

A pronunciation guide is provided underneath the name of select players.

In addition to a variety of traditional statistics, the Register also shows Runs Created (RC) for hitters and Component ERA (ERC) for pitchers. Runs created is a comprehensive measurement of a player's offensive production distilled into a single number. It was originally developed by Bill James. Component ERA estimates what a pitcher's ERA should have been based only on his raw pitching statistics and acts as a good indicator of whether a pitcher deserved the ERA he ended the season with. The details of the current formulas for both RC and ERC are in the Baseball Glossary at the back of the Handbook.

A player's total career numbers in the postseason appear on one line above his total regular season career numbers. Since we work hard to bring you this publication by November 1, postseason data from 2015 is not included. In addition, the Japanese baseball season extends a bit beyond our deadline, so the Japanese statistics for posted players will not include a complete record of their most recent games. Those numbers will be updated in the following year's Handbook.

David Aardsma

Pitches: R Bats: R Pos: RP-33 | ARDZ-muh | Ht: 6'3" Wt: 220 Born: 12/27/1981 Age: 34

Year	Team	Lg	G	GS	CG	GF	IP	BFP	H	R	ER	HR	SH	SF	HB	TBB	IBB	SO	WP	Bk	W	L	Pct	Sh	Sv-Op	Hld	ERC	ERA
2015	OkCity*	AAA	20	0	0	18	18.2	75	12	5	5	0	0	0	0	7	0	23	1	0	0	1	.000	0	15- -	-	1.59	2.41
2004	SF	NL	11	0	0	5	10.2	61	20	8	8	1	0	1	2	10	1	5	0	0	1	0	1.000	0	0-1	1	13.38	6.75
2006	ChC	NL	45	0	0	9	53.0	225	41	25	24	9	1	3	1	28	0	49	1	0	3	0	1.000	0	0-0	5	3.88	4.08
2007	CWS	AL	25	0	0	7	32.1	151	39	24	23	4	2	1	1	17	3	36	2	0	2	1	.667	0	0-3	3	5.93	6.40
2008	Bos	AL	47	0	0	7	48.2	228	49	32	30	4	3	2	5	35	2	49	3	0	4	2	.667	0	0-1	4	5.63	5.55
2009	Sea	AL	73	0	0	53	71.1	296	49	23	20	4	2	1	0	34	3	80	2	0	3	6	.333	0	38-42	6	2.34	2.52
2010	Sea	AL	53	0	0	43	49.2	202	33	19	19	5	7	1	2	25	5	49	2	0	0	6	.000	0	31-36	0	2.74	3.44
2012	NYY	AL	1	0	0	1	1.0	5	1	1	1	1	0	0	0	1	0	1	0	0	0	0	-	0	0-0	0	14.27	9.00
2013	NYM	NL	43	0	0	7	39.2	178	39	20	19	7	2	1	4	19	6	36	1	1	2	2	.500	0	0-2	4	4.99	4.31
2015	Atl	NL	33	0	0	9	30.2	129	25	17	16	6	0	1	1	14	3	35	1	0	1	1	.500	0	0-3	6	3.93	4.70
	9 ML YEARS		331	0	0	141	337.0	1475	296	169	160	41	17	11	16	183	22	340	12	1	16	18	.471	0	69-88	29	4.19	4.27

Fernando Abad

Pitches: L Bats: L Pos: RP-62 | ah-BAHD | Ht: 6'1" Wt: 220 Born: 12/17/1985 Age: 30

Year	Team	Lg	G	GS	CG	GF	IP	BFP	H	R	ER	HR	SH	SF	HB	TBB	IBB	SO	WP	Bk	W	L	Pct	Sh	Sv-Op	Hld	ERC	ERA
2010	Hou	NL	22	0	0	6	19.0	76	14	6	6	3	0	1	0	5	0	12	0	0	0	1	.000	0	0-0	6	2.49	2.84
2011	Hou	NL	29	0	0	1	19.2	99	28	18	16	5	1	2	1	9	0	15	0	0	1	4	.200	0	0-2	7	8.06	7.32
2012	Hou	NL	37	6	0	8	46.0	208	57	27	26	6	2	1	3	19	1	38	4	0	0	6	.000	0	0-0	3	6.13	5.09
2013	Was	NL	39	0	0	17	37.2	166	42	14	14	3	0	0	1	10	0	32	0	0	0	3	.000	0	0-1	2	4.05	3.35
2014	Oak	AL	69	0	0	17	57.1	216	34	11	10	4	1	2	4	15	3	51	0	0	2	4	.333	0	0-2	9	1.64	1.57
2015	Oak	AL	62	0	0	17	47.2	205	45	23	22	11	3	3	1	19	3	45	4	0	2	2	.500	0	0-3	1	4.63	4.15
	Postseason		1	0	0	0	0.1	1	0	0	0	0	0	0	0	0	0	0	0	0	0	0	-	0	0-0	0	0.00	0.00
	6 ML YEARS		258	6	0	66	227.1	970	220	99	94	32	7	9	10	77	7	193	8	0	5	20	.200	0	0-8	28	4.06	3.72

Jose Abreu

Bats: R Throws: R Pos: 1B-115;DH-39 | uh-BRAY-you | Ht: 6'3" Wt: 255 Born: 1/29/1987 Age: 29

Year	Team	Lg	G	AB	H	2B	3B	HR	(Hm	Rd)	TB	R	RBI	RC	TBB	IBB	SO	HBP	SH	SF	SB	CS	GDP	Avg	OBP	Slg	OPS
2014	CWS	AL	145	556	176	35	2	36	(15	21)	323	80	107	113	51	15	131	11	0	4	3	1	14	.317	.383	**.581**	.964
2015	CWS	AL	154	613	178	34	3	30	(16	14)	308	88	101	105	39	11	140	15	0	1	0	0	16	.290	.347	.502	.850
	2 ML YEARS		299	1169	354	69	5	66	(31	35)	631	168	208	218	90	26	271	26	0	5	3	1	30	.303	.364	.540	.904

A.J. Achter

Pitches: R Bats: R Pos: RP-11 | AHK-ter | Ht: 6'5" Wt: 205 Born: 8/27/1988 Age: 27

Year	Team	Lg	G	GS	CG	GF	IP	BFP	H	R	ER	HR	SH	SF	HB	TBB	IBB	SO	WP	Bk	W	L	Pct	Sh	Sv-Op	Hld	ERC	ERA
2011	Beloit	A	19	19	0	0	99.2	427	97	59	50	13	7	2	4	35	0	108	6	1	5	8	.385	0	0- -	-	4.10	4.52
2012	2 Tms	Low	37	1	0	14	74.1	290	54	25	14	5	1	2	1	15	1	86	10	1	5	2	.714	0	6- -	-	1.81	1.70
2013	NwBrit	AA	25	0	0	9	36.2	157	28	10	9	3	0	2	1	19	0	36	3	1	2	0	1.000	0	3- -	-	3.18	2.21
2013	Roch	AAA	16	0	0	6	23.2	100	17	9	8	4	0	0	0	14	0	20	0	0	1	2	.333	0	1- -	-	3.75	3.04
2014	Roch	AAA	40	0	0	18	72.0	281	44	20	19	4	4	1	2	24	0	69	3	1	4	4	.500	0	6- -	-	1.73	2.38
2015	Roch	AAA	43	0	0	34	48.0	186	28	14	14	5	2	2	1	13	2	47	2	0	4	2	.667	0	14- -	-	1.59	2.63
2014	Min	AL	7	0	0	1	11.0	49	14	7	4	2	0	0	0	3	0	5	0	0	1	0	1.000	0	0-0	0	5.74	3.27
2015	Min	AL	11	0	0	4	13.1	58	12	10	10	4	0	0	0	6	1	14	0	0	0	1	.000	0	0-0	0	4.88	6.75
	2 ML YEARS		18	0	0	5	24.1	107	26	17	14	6	0	0	0	9	1	19	0	0	1	1	.500	0	0-0	0	5.27	5.18

Dustin Ackley

Bats: L Throws: R Pos: LF-67;CF-21;PH-19;2B-10;PR-7;1B-4;DH-4;RF-2 | Ht: 6'1" Wt: 205 Born: 2/26/1988 Age: 28

Year	Team	Lg	G	AB	H	2B	3B	HR	(Hm	Rd)	TB	R	RBI	RC	TBB	IBB	SO	HBP	SH	SF	SB	CS	GDP	Avg	OBP	Slg	OPS
2011	Sea	AL	90	333	91	16	7	6	(3	3)	139	39	36	53	40	1	79	0	0	3	6	0	3	.273	.348	.417	.766
2012	Sea	AL	153	607	137	22	2	12	(2	10)	199	84	50	62	59	7	124	0	1	1	13	3	13	.226	.294	.328	.622
2013	Sea	AL	113	384	97	18	2	4	(2	2)	131	40	31	45	37	1	72	1	4	1	2	3	6	.253	.319	.341	.660
2014	Sea	AL	143	502	123	27	4	14	(8	6)	200	64	65	54	32	1	90	3	3	2	8	4	10	.245	.293	.398	.692
2015	2 Tms	AL	108	238	55	11	3	10	(7	3)	102	28	30	23	18	0	45	1	3	4	2	2	3	.231	.284	.429	.712
15	Sea	AL	85	186	40	8	1	6	(4	2)	68	22	19	13	14	0	38	1	3	3	2	2	3	.215	.270	.366	.635
15	NYY	AL	23	52	15	3	2	4	(3	1)	34	6	11	10	4	0	7	0	0	1	0	0	0	.288	.333	.654	.987
	5 ML YEARS		607	2064	503	94	18	46	(22	24)	771	255	212	237	186	10	410	5	11	11	31	12	25	.244	.306	.374	.680

Cristhian Adames

Bats: B Throws: R Pos: SS-13;PH-11;2B-2;PR-1 | kris-tee-YAHN ah-dah-MAZE | Ht: 6'0" Wt: 185 Born: 7/26/1991 Age: 24

Year	Team	Lg	G	AB	H	2B	3B	HR	(Hm	Rd)	TB	R	RBI	RC	TBB	IBB	SO	HBP	SH	SF	SB	CS	GDP	Avg	OBP	Slg	OPS
2011	Ashvll	A	108	399	109	17	2	8	(-	-)	154	63	64	58	42	0	74	7	7	4	2	0	11	.273	.350	.386	.736
2012	Mdest	A+	115	418	117	21	7	2	(-	-)	158	59	54	60	47	1	82	3	11	6	4	2	8	.280	.352	.378	.730
2013	Tulsa	AA	107	389	104	19	2	3	(-	-)	136	45	36	48	34	0	78	4	17	2	13	7	11	.267	.331	.350	.681
2014	Tulsa	AA	88	330	88	9	4	2	(-	-)	111	42	38	37	29	1	58	2	13	6	7	9	9	.267	.324	.336	.661
2014	ColSpr	AAA	38	145	49	12	0	1	(-	-)	64	19	14	26	13	0	25	0	5	0	5	1	3	.338	.392	.441	.834

		BATTING																	RUNNING			AVERAGES			
Year Team	Lg	G	AB	H	2B	3B	HR	(Hm Rd)	TB	R	RBI	RC	TBB IBB	SO	HBP	SH	SF	SB CS	GDP	Avg	OBP	Slg	OPS
2015 Albq	AAA	116	463	144	20	3	11	(- -)	203	62	51	74	36 3	56	2	8	2	11 7	12	.311	.362	.438	.800
2014 Col	NL	7	15	1	0	0	0	(0 0)	1	1	0	0	0 0	5	0	0	0	0 0	1	.067	.067	.067	.133
2015 Col	NL	26	53	13	1	0	0	(0 0)	16	4	3	4	3 1	11	1	1	0	0 1	0	.245	.298	.302	.600
2 ML YEARS		33	68	14	1	1	0	(0 0)	17	5	3	4	3 1	16	1	1	0	0 1	1	.206	.250	.250	.500

Austin Adams

Pitches: R Bats: R Pos: RP-28   Ht: 5'11" Wt: 200 Born: 8/19/1986 Age: 29

		HOW MUCH HE PITCHED						WHAT HE GAVE UP										THE RESULTS						
Year Team	Lg	G	GS	CG	GF	IP	BFP	H	R	ER	HR	SH	SF	HB	TBB IBB	SO	WP	Bk	W	L	Pct	Sh	Sv-Op	Hld	ERC	ERA
2011 Akron	AA	26	26	0	0	136.0	599	147	68	57	6	5	1	5	63 0	131	11	1	11	10	.524	0	0- -	-	4.59	3.77
2013 Akron	AA	45	0	0	13	55.0	237	44	19	16	3	0	1	2	29 1	76	7	0	3	2	.600	0	4- -	-	3.23	2.62
2014 Clmbs	AAA	42	0	0	18	54.0	214	44	16	15	4	2	0	0	16 0	52	5	0	3	2	.600	0	5- -	-	2.61	2.50
2015 Clmbs	AAA	13	0	0	10	12.0	55	13	6	6	1	1	1	0	7 1	17	1	0	2	2	.500	0	4- -	-	4.98	4.50
2014 Cle	AL	6	0	0	1	7.0	30	9	7	7	1	0	0	0	1 0	4	0	0	0	0	-	0	0-0	0	5.04	9.00
2015 Cle	AL	28	0	0	9	33.1	149	37	15	14	2	2	0	0	13 0	23	1	0	2	0	1.000	0	1-1	0	4.29	3.78
2 ML YEARS		34	0	0	10	40.1	179	46	22	21	3	2	0	0	14 0	27	1	0	2	0	1.000	0	1-1	0	4.42	4.69

Matt Adams

Bats: L Throws: R Pos: 1B-46;PH-16   Ht: 6'3" Wt: 260 Born: 8/31/1988 Age: 27

		BATTING																	RUNNING			AVERAGES			
Year Team	Lg	G	AB	H	2B	3B	HR	(Hm Rd)	TB	R	RBI	RC	TBB IBB	SO	HBP	SH	SF	SB CS	GDP	Avg	OBP	Slg	OPS
2012 StL	NL	27	86	21	6	0	2	(1 1)	33	8	13	9	5 0	24	0	0	0	0 0	3	.244	.286	.384	.669
2013 StL	NL	108	296	84	14	0	17	(10 7)	149	46	51	49	23 0	80	0	0	0	0 1	9	.284	.335	.503	.839
2014 StL	NL	142	527	152	34	5	15	(8 7)	241	55	68	65	26 5	114	3	0	7	3 2	9	.288	.321	.457	.779
2015 StL	NL	60	175	42	9	0	5	(1 4)	66	14	24	16	10 1	41	0	0	1	1 0	1	.240	.280	.377	.657
Postseason		26	93	21	3	0	4	(3 1)	36	10	11	12	8 2	24	1	0	0	0 0	2	.226	.294	.387	.681
4 ML YEARS		337	1084	299	63	5	39	(20 19)	489	123	156	139	64 6	259	3	0	8	4 3	22	.276	.316	.451	.767

Nate Adcock

Pitches: R Bats: R Pos: RP-13   Ht: 6'4" Wt: 235 Born: 2/25/1988 Age: 28

		HOW MUCH HE PITCHED						WHAT HE GAVE UP										THE RESULTS						
Year Team	Lg	G	GS	CG	GF	IP	BFP	H	R	ER	HR	SH	SF	HB	TBB IBB	SO	WP	Bk	W	L	Pct	Sh	Sv-Op	Hld	ERC	ERA
2015 Lsvlle*	AAA	22	0	0	17	24.1	106	23	11	8	0	0	0	3	7 0	20	3	0	0	2	.000	0	11- -	-	3.04	2.96
2011 KC	AL	24	3	0	5	60.1	265	63	34	31	5	3	1	5	26 3	36	4	1	1	1	.500	0	1-2	1	4.47	4.62
2012 KC	AL	12	2	0	3	34.2	148	37	13	9	4	1	2	1	13 2	22	0	0	0	3	.000	0	0-0	1	4.61	2.34
2014 Tex	AL	7	0	0	2	10.0	45	11	5	5	2	0	0	2	5 0	9	1	0	0	0	-	0	0-0	0	7.03	4.50
2015 Cin	NL	13	0	0	4	18.0	83	15	12	12	3	1	1	1	12 0	13	1	0	1	2	.333	0	0-0	0	4.73	6.00
4 ML YEARS		56	5	0	14	123.0	541	126	64	57	14	5	4	7	56 5	80	6	1	2	6	.250	0	1-2	1	4.74	4.17

Ehire Adrianza

A-ee-ray A-dree-ahn-zuh

Bats: B Throws: R Pos: 2B-20;SS-20;PH-12;1B-1;3B-1   Ht: 6'1" Wt: 170 Born: 8/21/1989 Age: 26

		BATTING																	RUNNING			AVERAGES			
Year Team	Lg	G	AB	H	2B	3B	HR	(Hm Rd)	TB	R	RBI	RC	TBB IBB	SO	HBP	SH	SF	SB CS	GDP	Avg	OBP	Slg	OPS
2015 Scrmto*	AAA	44	171	54	6	1	3	(- -)	71	16	15	29	17 0	37	2	5	0	6 1	1	.316	.384	.415	.799
2013 SF	NL	9	18	4	1	0	1	(0 1)	8	3	3	1	1 0	5	0	1	0	0 0	1	.222	.263	.444	.708
2014 SF	NL	53	97	23	6	0	0	(0 0)	29	10	5	6	5 1	22	1	2	1	1 1	2	.237	.279	.299	.578
2015 SF	NL	52	113	21	7	1	0	(0 0)	30	11	11	12	15 0	20	4	2	0	3 2	2	.186	.303	.265	.569
3 ML YEARS		114	228	48	14	1	1	(0 1)	67	24	19	19	21 1	47	5	5	1	4 3	5	.211	.290	.294	.584

Jeremy Affeldt

Pitches: L Bats: L Pos: RP-52   AFF-felt   Ht: 6'4" Wt: 225 Born: 6/6/1979 Age: 37

		HOW MUCH HE PITCHED						WHAT HE GAVE UP										THE RESULTS						
Year Team	Lg	G	GS	CG	GF	IP	BFP	H	R	ER	HR	SH	SF	HB	TBB IBB	SO	WP	Bk	W	L	Pct	Sh	Sv-Op	Hld	ERC	ERA
2002 KC	AL	34	7	0	4	77.2	353	85	44	40	8	2	1	3	37 4	67	5	2	3	4	.429	0	0-1	1	4.97	4.64
2003 KC	AL	36	18	0	5	126.0	533	126	58	55	12	2	5	5	38 1	98	2	2	7	6	.538	0	4-4	3	3.82	3.93
2004 KC	AL	38	8	0	26	76.1	344	91	49	42	6	4	4	3	32 2	49	4	3	3	4	.429	0	13-17	0	5.26	4.95
2005 KC	AL	49	0	0	13	49.2	232	56	35	29	3	0	1	0	29 2	39	5	0	0	2	.000	0	0-0	12	5.08	5.26
2006 2 Tms		54	9	0	12	97.1	448	102	74	67	13	4	4	2	55 3	48	2	0	8	8	.500	0	1-3	5	5.21	6.20
2007 Col	NL	75	0	0	11	59.0	253	47	26	23	3	3	6	3	33 9	46	6	1	4	3	.571	0	0-4	9	3.19	3.51
2008 Cin	NL	74	0	0	20	78.1	335	78	36	29	9	7	0	3	25 0	80	6	0	1	1	.500	0	0-1	5	3.98	3.33
2009 SF	NL	74	0	0	8	62.1	248	42	14	12	3	0	1	3	31 3	55	5	0	2	2	.500	0	0-0	33	2.61	1.73
2010 SF	NL	53	0	0	14	50.0	228	56	25	23	4	7	1	3	24 5	44	4	0	4	3	.571	0	4-7	7	4.99	4.14
2011 SF	NL	67	0	0	12	61.2	259	47	22	18	5	4	0	4	24 5	54	4	0	3	2	.600	0	3-6	13	2.77	2.63
2012 SF	NL	67	0	0	10	63.1	267	57	23	19	1	4	0	3	23 1	57	5	0	1	2	.333	0	3-4	16	2.98	2.70
2013 SF	NL	39	0	0	11	33.2	146	27	14	14	2	4	1	4	17 5	21	2	0	1	5	.167	0	0-4	11	3.31	3.74
2014 SF	NL	62	0	0	9	55.1	225	47	14	14	1	1	1	4	14 1	41	4	1	4	2	.667	0	0-3	18	2.47	2.28
2015 SF	NL	52	0	0	7	35.1	163	43	24	23	6	0	0	2	14 2	21	1	0	2	2	.500	0	0-0	9	5.94	5.86
06 KC	AL	27	9	0	3	70.0	320	71	51	46	9	3	3	1	42 3	28	2	0	4	6	.400	0	0-2	5	5.18	5.91
06 Col	NL	27	0	0	9	27.1	128	31	23	21	4	1	1	1	13 3	20	0	0	4	2	.667	0	1-3	0	5.29	6.91
Postseason		33	0	0	4	31.1	111	14	3	3	1	0	0	2	8 2	20	2	0	2	0	1.000	0	0-0	6	1.05	0.86
14 ML YEARS		774	42	0	162	926.0	4034	904	455	408	76	42	25	42	396 41	720	55	9	43	46	.483	0	28-54	142	4.02	3.97

Jesus Aguilar

Bats: R Throws: R Pos: 1B-4;DH-3;PH-2   AGG-you-lahr   Ht: 6'3" Wt: 250 Born: 6/30/1990 Age: 26

Year	Team	Lg	G	AB	H	2B	3B	HR	(Hm	Rd)	TB	R	RBI	RC	TBB	IBB	SO	HBP	SH	SF	SB	CS	GDP	Avg	OBP	Slg	OPS
2011	2 Tms	Low	126	462	131	30	2	23	(-	-)	234	70	82	84	46	1	126	10	0	3	2	0	8	.284	.359	.506	.865
2012	Carlina	A+	107	368	102	25	2	12	(-	-)	167	63	58	64	45	2	91	9	0	5	0	1	7	.277	.365	.454	.819
2012	Akron	AA	20	72	21	6	0	3	(-	-)	36	12	13	15	13	0	24	1	0	1	0	0	3	.292	.402	.500	.902
2013	Akron	AA	130	499	137	28	0	16	(-	-)	213	66	105	78	56	1	107	5	0	7	0	1	20	.275	.349	.427	.776
2014	Clmbs	AAA	118	427	130	31	0	19	(-	-)	218	69	77	88	64	5	96	3	0	5	0	0	11	.304	.395	.511	.905
2015	Clmbs	AAA	131	510	136	29	1	19	(-	-)	224	57	93	77	47	5	116	6	0	7	0	0	21	.267	.332	.439	.771
2014	Cle	AL	19	33	4	0	0	0	(0	0)	4	2	3	0	4	0	13	0	0	1	0	0	1	.121	.211	.121	.332
2015	Cle	AL	7	19	6	1	0	0	(0	0)	7	0	2	4	0	0	7	1	0	0	0	0	0	.316	.350	.368	.718
	2 ML YEARS		26	52	10	1	0	0	(0	0)	11	2	5	4	4	0	20	1	0	1	0	0	1	.192	.259	.212	.470

Nick Ahmed

Bats: R Throws: R Pos: SS-129;PH-6;PR-3   Ht: 6'2" Wt: 195 Born: 3/15/1990 Age: 26

Year	Team	Lg	G	AB	H	2B	3B	HR	(Hm	Rd)	TB	R	RBI	RC	TBB	IBB	SO	HBP	SH	SF	SB	CS	GDP	Avg	OBP	Slg	OPS
2011	Danvle	R+	59	248	65	13	2	4	(-	-)	94	46	24	36	30	1	46	3	1	2	18	6	2	.262	.346	.379	.725
2012	Lynbrg	A+	130	506	136	36	4	6	(-	-)	198	84	49	74	49	0	102	4	10	2	40	10	10	.269	.337	.391	.728
2013	Mobile	AA	136	487	115	21	5	4	(-	-)	158	58	46	50	33	0	72	5	7	6	26	7	10	.236	.288	.324	.613
2014	Reno	AAA	104	407	127	26	4	4	(-	-)	173	57	47	67	37	2	55	3	4	1	14	6	9	.312	.373	.425	.798
2014	Ari	NL	25	70	14	2	0	1	(-	-)	19	9	4	3	3	0	10	0	2	0	0	1	2	.200	.233	.271	.504
2015	Ari	NL	134	421	95	17	6	9	(4	5)	151	49	34	38	29	1	81	1	5	3	4	5	4	.226	.275	.359	.634
	2 ML YEARS		159	491	109	19	6	10	(5	5)	170	58	38	41	32	1	91	1	7	3	4	6	6	.222	.269	.346	.616

Andrew Albers

Pitches: L Bats: R Pos: RP-1   Ht: 6'1" Wt: 200 Born: 10/6/1985 Age: 30

Year	Team	Lg	G	GS	CG	GF	IP	BFP	H	R	ER	HR	SH	SF	HB	TBB	IBB	SO	WP	Bk	W	L	Pct	Sh	Sv-Op	Hld	ERC	ERA
2011	FtMyrs	A+	22	2	0	8	52.1	203	48	11	9	2	1	0	1	7	0	46	1	0	4	1	.800	0	4--	-	2.43	1.55
2011	NwBrit	AA	13	5	0	2	43.1	176	44	15	14	0	1	0	5	7	0	34	2	0	4	1	.800	0	0--	-	3.13	2.91
2012	NwBrit	AA	19	17	0	0	98.1	395	111	41	41	7	5	2	2	12	0	73	6	3	4	3	.571	0	0--	-	3.75	3.75
2013	Roch	AAA	22	22	3	0	132.1	533	124	46	42	14	2	3	0	32	0	116	0	1	11	5	.688	1	0--	-	3.23	2.86
2015	Buffalo	AAA	20	15	1	3	83.2	377	110	57	53	7	4	4	4	26	0	53	2	1	2	11	.154	0	0--	-	5.70	5.70
2013	Min	AL	10	10	1	0	60.0	249	64	34	27	6	2	2	2	7	0	25	0	1	2	5	.286	1	0-0	0	3.45	4.05
2015	Tor	AL	1	0	0	0	2.2	11	1	1	1	1	0	0	0	2	0	1	0	0	0	0	-	0	0-0	0	3.75	3.38
	2 ML YEARS		11	10	1	0	62.2	260	65	35	28	7	2	2	2	9	0	26	0	1	2	5	.286	1	0-0	0	3.46	4.02

Matt Albers

Pitches: R Bats: L Pos: RP-30   Ht: 6'1" Wt: 225 Born: 1/20/1983 Age: 33

Year	Team	Lg	G	GS	CG	GF	IP	BFP	H	R	ER	HR	SH	SF	HB	TBB	IBB	SO	WP	Bk	W	L	Pct	Sh	Sv-Op	Hld	ERC	ERA
2015	Charllt*	AAA	7	0	0	0	9.2	39	10	6	6	2	0	0	0	1	0	5	0	0	1	0	1.000	0	0--	-	3.80	5.59
2006	Hou	NL	4	2	0	0	15.0	66	17	10	10	1	2	0	0	7	0	11	0	0	0	2	.000	0	0-0	0	4.97	6.00
2007	Hou	NL	31	18	0	2	110.2	508	127	77	72	18	6	8	7	50	6	71	7	0	4	11	.267	0	0-0	0	5.76	5.86
2008	Bal	AL	28	3	0	5	49.0	208	43	21	19	4	1	3	2	22	1	26	1	0	3	3	.500	0	0-2	6	3.62	3.49
2009	Bal	AL	56	0	0	13	67.0	309	80	43	41	3	5	2	2	36	3	49	3	0	3	6	.333	0	0-4	10	5.41	5.51
2010	Bal	AL	62	0	0	19	75.2	329	78	41	38	6	3	0	2	34	5	49	2	0	5	3	.625	0	0-2	7	4.35	4.52
2011	Bos	AL	56	0	0	10	64.2	289	62	35	34	7	4	2	5	31	1	68	2	0	4	4	.500	0	0-3	10	4.44	4.73
2012	2 Tms		63	0	0	12	60.1	241	46	21	16	9	1	2	2	22	3	44	1	0	3	1	.750	0	0-6	9	3.13	2.39
2013	Cle	AL	56	0	0	21	63.0	262	57	25	22	2	2	0	1	23	3	35	6	0	3	1	.750	0	0-0	1	2.99	3.14
2014	Hou	AL	8	0	0	1	10.0	42	10	1	1	0	0	0	1	3	0	8	0	0	0	0	-	0	0-1	3	3.46	0.90
2015	CWS	AL	30	0	0	5	37.1	149	31	6	5	3	0	3	1	9	2	28	0	0	2	0	1.000	0	0-0	6	2.52	1.21
12	Bos	AL	40	0	0	8	39.1	157	30	14	10	6	0	2	1	15	3	25	0	0	2	0	1.000	0	0-4	7	3.16	2.29
12	Ari	NL	23	0	0	4	21.0	84	16	7	6	3	1	0	1	7	0	19	1	0	1	1	.500	0	0-2	2	3.07	2.57
	10 ML YEARS		394	23	0	88	552.2	2403	551	280	258	53	24	20	23	237	24	389	22	0	27	31	.466	0	0-18	52	4.26	4.20

Hanser Alberto

HAHN-zer al-BAIR-tow

Bats: R Throws: R Pos: 2B-24;SS-8;3B-7;PR-4;DH-3;PH-3   Ht: 5'11" Wt: 215 Born: 10/17/1992 Age: 23

Year	Team	Lg	G	AB	H	2B	3B	HR	(Hm	Rd)	TB	R	RBI	RC	TBB	IBB	SO	HBP	SH	SF	SB	CS	GDP	Avg	OBP	Slg	OPS
2011	Spkane	A-	53	187	50	8	1	0	(-	-)	60	21	16	20	9	0	15	3	1	2	7	1	6	.267	.308	.321	.629
2012	2 Tms	Low	128	525	157	28	3	8	(-	-)	215	73	72	74	20	1	49	6	3	8	24	7	17	.299	.327	.410	.737
2013	Frisco	AA	100	356	76	6	4	4	(-	-)	102	37	40	26	16	1	41	5	1	6	13	5	10	.213	.253	.287	.540
2013	MrtlBh	A+	29	97	25	5	0	0	(-	-)	30	6	7	9	4	0	8	2	1	1	3	1	7	.258	.301	.309	.610
2014	MrtlBh	A+	70	262	71	15	3	5	(-	-)	107	37	43	34	10	0	25	3	6	4	10	4	8	.271	.301	.408	.709
2014	Frisco	AA	50	178	49	6	1	2	(-	-)	63	23	15	20	6	0	17	4	2	0	7	4	2	.275	.314	.354	.668
2015	RdRck	AAA	81	310	96	19	4	4	(-	-)	135	42	32	44	9	1	33	2	7	2	5	5	6	.310	.331	.435	.767
2015	Tex	AL	41	99	22	2	1	0	(0	0)	26	12	4	3	2	0	17	0	3	0	1	0	2	.222	.238	.263	.500

Al Alburquerque

Pitches: R **Bats:** R **Pos:** RP-67
AL-buh-kur-kee **Ht:** 6'0" **Wt:** 195 **Born:** 6/10/1986 **Age:** 30

Year Team	Lg	G	GS	CG	GF	IP	BFP	H	R	ER	HR	SH	SF	HB	TBB	IBB	SO	WP	Bk	W	L	Pct	Sh	Sv-Op	Hld	ERC	ERA
2011 Det	AL	41	0	0	11	43.1	182	21	9	9	0	2	1	2	29	4	67	4	0	6	1	.857	0	0-0	6	1.73	1.87
2012 Det	AL	8	0	0	0	13.1	53	6	1	1	0	0	0	0	8	0	18	0	1	0	0	-	0	0-0	1	1.50	0.68
2013 Det	AL	53	0	0	12	49.0	220	39	25	25	5	0	1	2	34	5	70	9	1	4	3	.571	0	0-0	10	4.02	4.59
2014 Det	AL	72	0	0	15	57.1	236	46	16	16	7	0	2	3	21	1	63	2	2	3	1	.750	0	1-1	17	3.23	2.51
2015 Det	AL	67	0	0	12	62.0	271	63	29	29	4	1	2	1	33	3	58	5	4	4	1	.800	0	0-1	7	4.51	4.21
Postseason		14	0	0	5	10.0	43	7	6	6	2	1	0	0	6	2	14	1	1	1	1	.500	0	0-0	3	3.51	5.40
5 ML YEARS		241	0	0	50	225.0	962	175	80	80	16	3	6	8	125	13	276	20	8	17	6	.739	0	1-2	41	3.30	3.20

Arismendy Alcantara

Bats: B **Throws:** R **Pos:** 2B-8;PH-4;3B-2
air-es-MEN-dee al-CAHN-truh **Ht:** 5'10" **Wt:** 170 **Born:** 10/29/1991 **Age:** 24

Year Team	Lg	G	AB	H	2B	3B	HR	Hm	Rd	TB	R	RBI	RC	TBB	IBB	SO	HBP	SH	SF	SB	CS	GDP	Avg	OBP	Slg	OPS
2011 Peoria	A	99	369	100	14	5	2	-	-	130	45	37	38	16	1	76	1	4	0	8	8	3	.271	.303	.352	.655
2012 Dytona	A+	85	331	100	13	7	7	-	-	148	47	51	54	19	0	61	2	2	5	25	4	5	.302	.339	.447	.786
2013 Tenn	AA	133	494	134	36	4	15	-	-	223	69	69	86	62	6	125	2	9	4	31	6	4	.271	.352	.451	.804
2014 Iowa	AAA	89	335	103	25	11	10	-	-	180	62	41	65	25	0	83	0	3	3	21	3	2	.307	.353	.537	.890
2015 Iowa	AAA	120	454	105	20	10	12	-	-	181	72	36	54	35	0	125	0	7	3	16	6	7	.231	.285	.399	.683
2014 ChC	NL	70	278	57	11	2	10	5	5	102	31	29	23	17	0	93	2	1	2	8	5	3	.205	.254	.367	.621
2015 ChC	NL	11	26	2	0	0	0	0	0	2	5	1	1	5	0	11	0	1	0	1	0	0	.077	.226	.077	.303
2 ML YEARS		81	304	59	11	2	10	5	5	104	36	30	24	22	0	104	2	2	2	9	5	3	.194	.252	.342	.594

Scott Alexander

Pitches: L **Bats:** L **Pos:** RP-4
Ht: 6'2" **Wt:** 190 **Born:** 7/10/1989 **Age:** 26

Year Team	Lg	G	GS	CG	GF	IP	BFP	H	R	ER	HR	SH	SF	HB	TBB	IBB	SO	WP	Bk	W	L	Pct	Sh	Sv-Op	Hld	ERC	ERA
2012 2 Tms	Low	11	7	0	1	35.2	159	34	22	10	2	1	3	2	16	1	31	4	0	2	4	.333	0	0--	-	3.76	2.52
2013 2 Tms	Low	17	0	0	8	42.0	162	25	8	6	0	0	1	2	14	0	37	2	0	3	1	.750	0	2--	-	1.50	1.29
2013 NWArk	AA	24	0	0	5	33.0	150	38	20	19	0	2	0	3	18	1	40	3	0	2	0	1.000	0	1--	-	5.19	5.18
2014 NWArk	AA	35	0	0	10	48.2	204	42	26	21	3	4	2	3	16	0	36	5	0	1	2	.333	0	3--	-	3.03	3.88
2014 Omha	AAA	11	0	0	3	19.0	85	23	16	13	4	1	0	0	10	0	13	4	0	1	2	.333	0	0--	-	6.99	6.16
2015 Omha	AAA	41	0	0	29	63.1	250	48	21	18	5	0	2	1	17	1	50	10	0	2	3	.400	0	14--	-	2.27	2.56
2015 KC	AL	4	0	0	3	6.0	25	5	3	3	0	0	0	1	3	0	3	1	0	0	0	-	0	0-0	-	3.67	4.50

Cody Allen

Pitches: R **Bats:** R **Pos:** RP-70
Ht: 6'1" **Wt:** 210 **Born:** 11/20/1988 **Age:** 27

Year Team	Lg	G	GS	CG	GF	IP	BFP	H	R	ER	HR	SH	SF	HB	TBB	IBB	SO	WP	Bk	W	L	Pct	Sh	Sv-Op	Hld	ERC	ERA
2012 Cle	AL	27	0	0	9	29.0	126	29	12	12	2	1	4	1	15	0	27	0	0	0	1	.000	0	0-1	1	4.39	3.72
2013 Cle	AL	77	0	0	12	70.1	301	62	22	19	7	4	4	1	26	2	88	9	0	6	1	.857	0	2-4	11	3.24	2.43
2014 Cle	AL	76	0	0	44	69.2	279	48	21	16	7	2	2	1	26	5	91	4	0	6	4	.600	0	24-28	9	2.32	2.07
2015 Cle	AL	70	0	0	58	69.1	286	56	26	23	2	1	2	2	25	2	99	9	0	2	5	.286	0	34-38	0	2.51	2.99
Postseason		1	0	0	0	0.1	2	1	1	0	0	0	0	0	0	0	1	0	0	0	0	-	0	0-0	0	14.52	0.00
4 ML YEARS		250	0	0	123	238.1	992	195	81	70	18	8	9	4	92	9	305	22	0	14	11	.560	0	60-71	21	2.88	2.64

Abraham Almonte

Bats: B **Throws:** R **Pos:** CF-56;PH-18;LF-6;RF-2;PR-2;DH-1
Ht: 5'9" **Wt:** 210 **Born:** 6/27/1989 **Age:** 27

Year Team	Lg	G	AB	H	2B	3B	HR	Hm	Rd	TB	R	RBI	RC	TBB	IBB	SO	HBP	SH	SF	SB	CS	GDP	Avg	OBP	Slg	OPS
2015 ElPaso*	AAA	61	244	68	18	2	4	-	-	102	43	35	40	33	1	46	0	5	0	11	4	5	.279	.365	.418	.783
2013 Sea	AL	25	72	19	4	0	2	1	1	29	10	9	9	6	0	21	0	2	2	1	0	2	.264	.313	.403	.715
2014 2 Tms		59	204	47	10	1	3	2	1	68	19	15	18	12	0	60	1	2	1	4	3	5	.230	.275	.333	.609
2015 2 Tms		82	232	58	12	5	5	4	1	95	36	24	28	21	0	52	0	3	2	7	1	5	.250	.310	.409	.719
14 Sea	AL	27	106	21	5	1	1	0	1	31	10	8	10	6	0	40	1	0	0	3	1	1	.198	.248	.292	.540
14 SD	NL	32	98	26	5	0	2	2	0	37	9	7	8	6	0	20	0	2	1	1	2	4	.265	.305	.378	.682
15 SD	NL	31	54	11	3	0	0	0	0	14	6	4	3	5	0	19	0	3	0	1	1	1	.204	.271	.259	.530
15 Cle	AL	51	178	47	9	5	5	4	1	81	30	20	25	16	0	33	0	0	2	6	0	4	.264	.321	.455	.776
3 ML YEARS		166	508	124	26	6	10	7	3	192	65	48	55	39	0	133	1	7	5	12	4	12	.244	.297	.378	.675

Miguel Almonte

Pitches: R **Bats:** R **Pos:** RP-9
Ht: 6'2" **Wt:** 180 **Born:** 4/4/1993 **Age:** 23

Year Team	Lg	G	GS	CG	GF	IP	BFP	H	R	ER	HR	SH	SF	HB	TBB	IBB	SO	WP	Bk	W	L	Pct	Sh	Sv-Op	Hld	ERC	ERA
2012 Royals	R	6	2	0	1	27.0	113	22	13	7	0	0	0	4	5	0	28	3	0	2	1	.667	0	0--	-	2.15	2.33
2013 Lxngtn	A	25	25	1	0	130.2	535	115	53	45	6	2	5	7	36	0	132	10	2	6	9	.400	0	0--	-	2.84	3.10
2014 Wilmg	A+	23	22	0	0	110.0	463	107	60	55	9	3	4	11	32	1	101	8	6	6	8	.429	0	0--	-	3.81	4.50
2015 NWArk	AA	17	17	0	0	67.0	293	65	31	30	4	2	1	8	27	0	55	4	0	4	4	.500	0	0--	-	4.12	4.03
2015 Omha	AAA	11	6	0	0	36.2	155	33	24	22	3	0	2	3	15	0	41	1	2	2	2	.500	0	0--	-	3.82	5.40
2015 KC	AL	9	0	0	3	8.2	41	7	6	6	4	0	0	1	7	0	10	0	0	0	2	.000	0	0-0	-	7.83	6.23

Yonder Alonso

Bats: L Throws: R Pos: 1B-102;PH-4;3B-2   YONN-dur ah-LONN-zo   Ht: 6'1" Wt: 220 Born: 4/8/1987 Age: 29

Year	Team	Lg	G	AB	H	2B	3B	HR	(Hm	Rd)	TB	R	RBI	RC	TBB	IBB	SO	HBP	SH	SF	SB	CS	GDP	Avg	OBP	Slg	OPS
2010	Cin	NL	22	29	6	2	0	0	(0	0)	8	2	3	0	0	0	10	0	0	0	0	0	1	.207	.291	.276	.483
2011	Cin	NL	47	88	29	4	0	5	(2	3)	48	9	15	16	10	0	21	0	0	0	0	0	2	.330	.398	.545	.943
2012	SD	NL	155	549	150	39	0	9	(3	6)	216	47	62	71	62	9	101	3	1	4	3	0	14	.273	.348	.393	.741
2013	SD	NL	97	334	94	11	0	6	(4	2)	123	34	45	46	32	5	47	2	0	7	6	0	9	.281	.341	.368	.710
2014	SD	NL	84	267	64	19	1	7	(3	4)	106	27	27	26	17	1	36	1	0	3	6	1	8	.240	.285	.397	.682
2015	SD	NL	103	354	100	18	1	5	(3	2)	135	50	31	40	42	3	48	3	0	3	2	5	13	.282	.361	.381	.742
6 ML YEARS			508	1621	443	93	2	32	(15	17)	636	169	183	199	163	18	263	9	1	17	17	6	47	.273	.340	.392	.732

Aaron Altherr

Bats: R Throws: R Pos: LF-23;RF-11;CF-8;PH-2   ALL-tair   Ht: 6'5" Wt: 215 Born: 1/14/1991 Age: 25

Year	Team	Lg	G	AB	H	2B	3B	HR	(Hm	Rd)	TB	R	RBI	RC	TBB	IBB	SO	HBP	SH	SF	SB	CS	GDP	Avg	OBP	Slg	OPS
2011	2 Tms	Low	112	416	101	18	2	6	(-	-)	141	61	46	48	24	0	99	7	5	6	37	4	7	.243	.291	.339	.630
2012	Lakwd	A	110	420	106	27	6	8	(-	-)	169	65	50	58	38	1	102	6	1	6	25	8	4	.252	.319	.402	.722
2013	Clrwtr	A+	123	466	128	36	6	12	(-	-)	212	57	69	76	45	0	140	3	5	8	23	5	7	.275	.337	.455	.792
2014	Rdng	AA	120	449	106	27	2	14	(-	-)	179	54	57	53	26	1	110	8	4	5	12	6	16	.236	.287	.399	.686
2015	Rdng	AA	60	229	67	19	3	6	(-	-)	110	29	29	42	28	1	40	1	1	1	8	3	7	.293	.371	.480	.851
2015	LV	AAA	51	204	60	13	2	8	(-	-)	101	36	38	38	21	2	44	2	0	2	8	1	7	.294	.362	.495	.858
2014	Phi	NL	2	5	0	0	0	0	(0	0)	0	0	0	0	0	0	2	0	0	0	0	0	0	.000	.000	.000	.000
2015	Phi	NL	39	137	33	11	4	5	(2	3)	67	25	22	23	16	0	41	5	1	2	6	2	3	.241	.338	.489	.827
2 ML YEARS			41	142	33	11	4	5	(2	3)	67	25	22	23	16	0	43	5	1	2	6	2	3	.232	.327	.472	.799

Jose Altuve

Bats: R Throws: R Pos: 2B-153;DH-1   al-TOO-vay   Ht: 5'6" Wt: 165 Born: 5/6/1990 Age: 26

Year	Team	Lg	G	AB	H	2B	3B	HR	(Hm	Rd)	TB	R	RBI	RC	TBB	IBB	SO	HBP	SH	SF	SB	CS	GDP	Avg	OBP	Slg	OPS
2011	Hou	NL	57	221	61	10	1	2	(2	0)	79	26	12	18	5	0	29	2	5	1	7	3	5	.276	.297	.357	.654
2012	Hou	NL	147	576	167	34	4	7	(4	3)	230	80	37	76	40	0	74	6	4	4	33	11	8	.290	.340	.399	.740
2013	Hou	AL	152	626	177	31	2	5	(4	1)	227	64	52	67	32	5	85	2	4	3	35	13	24	.283	.316	.363	.678
2014	Hou	AL	158	660	225	47	3	7	(4	3)	299	85	59	106	36	7	53	5	1	5	56	9	20	.341	.377	.453	.830
2015	Hou	AL	154	638	200	40	4	15	(9	6)	293	86	66	98	33	8	67	9	3	6	38	13	17	.313	.353	.459	.812
5 ML YEARS			668	2721	830	162	14	36	(23	13)	1128	341	226	365	146	20	308	24	17	24	169	49	74	.305	.343	.415	.758

Dariel Alvarez

Bats: R Throws: R Pos: RF-12;CF-1   Ht: 6'2" Wt: 180 Born: 11/7/1988 Age: 27

Year	Team	Lg	G	AB	H	2B	3B	HR	(Hm	Rd)	TB	R	RBI	RC	TBB	IBB	SO	HBP	SH	SF	SB	CS	GDP	Avg	OBP	Slg	OPS
2013	LV	AA	13	48	21	4	1	3	(-	-)	36	7	9	13	3	0	2	0	0	1	1	2	2	.438	.471	.750	1.221
2014	Bowie	AA	91	359	111	20	1	14	(-	-)	175	52	68	58	13	0	35	2	1	6	7	4	13	.309	.332	.487	.819
2014	Norfolk	AAA	44	173	52	17	2	1	(-	-)	76	23	19	25	8	0	27	0	0	2	1	1	6	.301	.328	.439	.767
2015	Norfolk	AAA	130	512	141	24	2	16	(-	-)	217	61	72	68	16	0	63	8	0	5	7	3	14	.275	.305	.424	.729
2015	Bal	AL	12	29	7	1	0	1	(1	0)	11	3	1	3	2	0	8	0	0	0	0	0	0	.241	.290	.379	.670

Dario Alvarez

Pitches: L Bats: L Pos: RP-6   Ht: 6'1" Wt: 170 Born: 1/17/1989 Age: 27

Year	Team	Lg	G	GS	CG	GF	IP	BFP	H	R	ER	HR	SH	SF	HB	TBB	IBB	SO	WP	Bk	W	L	Pct	Sh	Sv-Op	Hld	ERC	ERA
2013	Bklyn	A-	12	12	0	0	58.0	254	48	27	20	1	0	4	7	26	1	57	9	0	2	4	.333	0	0--	-	3.10	3.10
2014	2 Tms	Low	24	6	0	6	67.2	263	44	12	9	2	3	0	2	17	0	105	8	2	9	1	.900	0	1--	-	1.55	1.20
2014	Bnghtn	AA	4	0	0	2	5.2	21	4	0	0	0	0	0	1	0	0	9	1	0	1	0	1.000	0	1--	-	1.43	0.00
2015	Bnghtn	AA	32	0	0	9	31.0	134	21	14	11	2	2	0	3	16	0	43	1	0	1	1	.500	0	0--	-	2.82	3.19
2015	LsVgs	AAA	16	0	0	2	11.0	44	6	3	3	0	0	0	3	5	0	19	0	0	2	1	.667	0	0--	-	2.35	2.45
2014	NYM	NL	4	0	0	0	1.1	8	4	2	2	1	0	0	0	0	0	1	0	0	0	-	0	0-1	1	22.76	13.50
2015	NYM	NL	6	0	0	0	3.2	19	5	5	5	2	1	0	2	1	0	2	0	1	1	0	1.000	0	0-0	1	12.00	12.27
2 ML YEARS			10	0	0	0	5.0	27	9	7	7	3	1	0	2	1	0	3	0	1	1	0	1.000	0	0-1	2	14.69	12.60

Henderson Alvarez

Pitches: R Bats: R Pos: SP-4   Ht: 6'0" Wt: 205 Born: 4/18/1990 Age: 26

Year	Team	Lg	G	GS	CG	GF	IP	BFP	H	R	ER	HR	SH	SF	HB	TBB	IBB	SO	WP	Bk	W	L	Pct	Sh	Sv-Op	Hld	ERC	ERA
2011	Tor	AL	10	10	0	0	63.2	259	64	26	25	8	1	2	4	8	0	40	2	0	1	3	.250	0	0-0	0	3.49	3.53
2012	Tor	AL	31	31	1	0	187.1	807	216	110	101	29	2	4	3	54	2	79	3	1	9	14	.391	1	0-0	0	5.01	4.85
2013	Mia	NL	17	17	1	0	102.2	418	90	42	41	2	0	4	7	27	1	57	4	1	5	6	.455	1	0-0	0	2.66	3.59
2014	Mia	NL	30	30	3	0	187.0	772	198	65	55	14	7	4	8	33	3	111	4	0	12	7	.632	3	0-0	0	3.56	2.65
2015	Mia	NL	4	4	0	0	22.1	102	28	18	16	1	4	1	0	7	1	9	3	1	0	4	.000	0	0-0	0	4.57	6.45
5 ML YEARS			92	92	5	0	563.0	2358	596	261	238	54	14	15	22	129	7	296	16	3	27	34	.443	5	0-0	0	3.89	3.80

Jose Alvarez

Pitches: L Bats: L Pos: RP-64   Ht: 5'11" Wt: 180 Born: 5/6/1989 Age: 27

			HOW MUCH HE PITCHED						WHAT HE GAVE UP												THE RESULTS						
Year	Team	Lg	G	GS	CG	GF	IP	BFP	H	R	ER	HR	SH	SF	HB	TBB	IBB	SO	WP	Bk	W	L	Pct	Sh	Sv-Op	Hld	ERC	ERA
2013	Det	AL	14	6	0	0	38.2	172	42	26	25	7	2	2	2	16	1	31	0	1	1	5	.167	0	0-0	2	5.41	5.82
2014	LAA	AL	2	0	0	1	0.2	3	1	0	0	0	0	0	0	0	0	1	0	0	0	0	-	0	0-0	0	4.47	0.00
2015	LAA	AL	64	0	0	18	67.0	283	58	29	26	5	0	1	5	23	4	59	1	0	4	3	.571	0	0-1	7	3.13	3.49
	Postseason		1	0	0	0	3.0	10	0	0	0	0	0	0	0	1	0	3	0	0	0	0	-	0	0-0	0	0.13	0.00
	3 ML YEARS		80	6	0	19	106.1	458	101	55	51	12	2	3	7	39	5	91	1	1	5	8	.385	0	0-1	9	3.92	4.32

Pedro Alvarez

Bats: L Throws: R Pos: 1B-124;PH-24;DH-5   Ht: 6'3" Wt: 250 Born: 2/6/1987 Age: 29

						BATTING																	RUNNING			AVERAGES			
Year	Team	Lg	G	AB	H	2B	3B	HR	(Hm	Rd)	TB	R	RBI	RC	TBB	IBB	SO	HBP	SH	SF	SB	CS	GDP	Avg	OBP	Slg	OPS
2010	Pit	NL	95	347	89	21	1	16	(12	4)	160	42	64	50	37	1	119	0	0	2		0	0	8	.256	.326	.461	.788
2011	Pit	NL	74	235	45	9	1	4	(0	4)	68	18	19	14	24	1	80	2	1	0		1	0	11	.191	.272	.289	.561
2012	Pit	NL	149	525	128	25	1	30	(12	18)	245	64	85	77	57	6	180	1	0	3		1	0	10	.244	.317	.467	.784
2013	Pit	NL	152	558	130	22	2	36	(16	20)	264	70	100	66	48	7	186	4	0	4		2	0	16	.233	.296	.473	.770
2014	Pit	NL	122	398	92	13	1	18	(8	10)	161	46	56	42	45	6	113	2	0	0		8	3	12	.231	.312	.405	.717
2015	Pit	NL	150	437	106	18	0	27	(14	13)	205	60	77	52	48	9	131	2	0	4		2	0	6	.243	.318	.469	.787
	Postseason		6	20	6	1	0	3	(1	2)	16	4	7	5	2	1	7	0	0	1		0	0	1	.300	.348	.800	1.148
	6 ML YEARS		742	2500	590	108	6	131	(62	69)	1103	300	401	301	259	30	809	11	1	13		14	3	63	.236	.309	.441	.750

R.J. Alvarez

Pitches: R Bats: R Pos: RP-21   Ht: 6'2" Wt: 215 Born: 6/8/1991 Age: 25

			HOW MUCH HE PITCHED						WHAT HE GAVE UP												THE RESULTS						
Year	Team	Lg	G	GS	CG	GF	IP	BFP	H	R	ER	HR	SH	SF	HB	TBB	IBB	SO	WP	Bk	W	L	Pct	Sh	Sv-Op	Hld	ERC	ERA
2012	Crpds	A	23	0	0	9	27.1	122	22	16	10	2	3	1	5	11	0	38	3	0	3	2	.600	0	0--	-	3.38	3.29
2013	InldEm	A+	37	2	0	12	48.2	208	34	16	16	2	0	1	2	27	0	79	5	1	4	2	.667	0	4--	-	2.75	2.96
2014	Ark	AA	21	0	0	2	27.0	100	13	2	1	0	0	0	3	10	2	38	0	0	0	0	-	0	1--	-	1.34	0.33
2014	SnAnt	AA	17	0	0	12	16.1	69	16	5	5	0	1	0	1	3	0	23	2	0	0	1	.000	0	6--	-	2.65	2.76
2015	Nashv	AAA	31	0	0	20	35.0	156	36	19	16	2	1	2	1	17	1	41	3	0	3	3	.500	0	5--	-	4.30	4.11
2014	SD	NL	10	0	0	4	8.0	33	3	1	1	0	0	1	1	5	1	9	1	0	0	0	-	0	0-0	1	1.42	1.13
2015	Oak	AL	21	0	0	11	20.0	100	27	23	22	7	0	2	0	13	1	23	5	0	0	0	-	0	0-1	0	9.16	9.90
	2 ML YEARS		31	0	0	15	28.0	133	30	24	23	7	0	3	1	18	2	32	6	0	0	0	-	0	0-1	1	6.56	7.39

Alexi Amarista

ah-mah-REE-stah

Bats: L Throws: R Pos: SS-85;PH-22;2B-11;LF-11;CF-7;3B-2;PR-1   Ht: 5'6" Wt: 160 Born: 4/6/1989 Age: 27

						BATTING																	RUNNING			AVERAGES			
Year	Team	Lg	G	AB	H	2B	3B	HR	(Hm	Rd)	TB	R	RBI	RC	TBB	IBB	SO	HBP	SH	SF	SB	CS	GDP	Avg	OBP	Slg	OPS
2011	LAA	AL	23	52	8	3	1	0	(0	0)	13	2	5	1	2	0	8	0	1	1		0	0	1	.154	.182	.250	.432
2012	2 Tms		106	275	66	15	5	5	(0	5)	106	36	32	31	17	1	42	0	6	2		8	4	2	.240	.282	.385	.668
2013	SD	NL	146	368	87	14	4	5	(1	4)	124	35	32	40	22	1	57	2	3	1		4	2	7	.236	.282	.337	.619
2014	SD	NL	148	423	101	13	2	5	(3	2)	133	39	40	43	29	5	69	1	8	5		12	1	6	.239	.286	.314	.600
2015	SD	NL	118	324	66	10	4	3	(1	2)	93	28	30	28	24	4	55	1	3	5		5	1	6	.204	.257	.287	.544
12	LAA	AL	1	0	0	0	0	0	(0	0)	0	1	0	0	0	0	0	0	0	0		0	0	0	-	-	-	-
12	SD	NL	105	275	66	15	5	5	(0	5)	106	35	32	31	17	1	42	0	6	2		8	4	2	.240	.282	.385	.668
	5 ML YEARS		541	1442	328	55	16	18	(5	13)	469	140	139	143	94	11	231	4	21	14		29	8	22	.227	.274	.325	.599

Brett Anderson

Pitches: L Bats: L Pos: SP-31   Ht: 6'3" Wt: 240 Born: 2/1/1988 Age: 28

			HOW MUCH HE PITCHED						WHAT HE GAVE UP												THE RESULTS						
Year	Team	Lg	G	GS	CG	GF	IP	BFP	H	R	ER	HR	SH	SF	HB	TBB	IBB	SO	WP	Bk	W	L	Pct	Sh	Sv-Op	Hld	ERC	ERA
2009	Oak	AL	30	30	1	0	175.1	735	180	94	79	20	4	4	3	45	1	150	0	1	11	11	.500	1	0-0	0	3.84	4.06
2010	Oak	AL	19	19	0	0	112.1	470	112	41	35	6	3	2	7	22	2	75	4	2	7	6	.538	0	0-0	0	3.16	2.80
2011	Oak	AL	13	13	1	0	83.1	356	86	40	37	8	4	1	7	25	1	61	0	1	3	6	.333	0	0-0	0	4.20	4.00
2012	Oak	AL	6	6	0	0	35.0	137	29	11	10	1	0	0	1	7	1	25	1	0	4	2	.667	0	0-0	0	2.13	2.57
2013	Oak	AL	16	5	0	4	44.2	200	51	32	30	5	1	0	0	21	1	46	0	0	1	4	.200	0	3-3	0	5.27	6.04
2014	Col	NL	8	8	0	0	43.1	180	44	18	14	1	1	1	0	13	3	29	0	0	1	3	.250	0	0-0	0	3.20	2.91
2015	LAD	NL	31	31	1	0	180.1	750	194	82	74	18	3	2	2	46	2	116	4	2	10	9	.526	0	0-0	0	4.05	3.69
	Postseason		2	1	0	1	6.1	24	3	1	1	0	0	0	0	3	0	7	1	0	1	0	1.000	0	0-0	0	1.34	1.42
	7 ML YEARS		123	112	3	4	674.1	2828	696	318	279	59	16	10	20	179	11	502	9	6	37	41	.474	1	3-3	0	3.78	3.72

Bryan Anderson

Bats: L Throws: R Pos: C-3;PH-1   Ht: 6'1" Wt: 200 Born: 12/16/1986 Age: 29

						BATTING																	RUNNING			AVERAGES			
Year	Team	Lg	G	AB	H	2B	3B	HR	(Hm	Rd)	TB	R	RBI	RC	TBB	IBB	SO	HBP	SH	SF	SB	CS	GDP	Avg	OBP	Slg	OPS
2015	Nashv*	AAA	82	292	59	16	0	3	(-	-)	84	31	25	23	27	0	93	2	0	1		0	0	5	.202	.273	.288	.561
2010	StL	NL	15	32	9	2	0	0	(0	0)	11	1	4	5	1	0	7	1	0	1		0	0	0	.281	.314	.344	.658
2012	StL	NL	10	12	3	1	0	0	(0	0)	4	2	0	2	1	0	6	1	0	0		1	0	0	.250	.357	.333	.690
2013	CWS	AL	10	18	1	1	0	0	(0	0)	2	1	2	0	1	0	5	0	0	0		0	0	0	.056	.105	.111	.216
2014	Oak	AL	1	1	0	0	0	0	(0	0)	0	0	0	0	0	0	0	0	0	0		0	0	1	.000	.000	.000	.000
2015	Oak	AL	4	5	2	0	0	0	(0	0)	2	0	1	1	1	0	1	0	1	0		0	0	0	.400	.429	.400	.829
	5 ML YEARS		40	68	15	4	0	0	(0	0)	19	4	7	8	4	0	19	2	1	2		1	0	1	.221	.276	.279	.556

Chase Anderson

Pitches: R **Bats:** R **Pos:** SP-27   **Ht:** 6'1" **Wt:** 194 **Born:** 11/30/1987 **Age:** 28

			HOW MUCH HE PITCHED						WHAT HE GAVE UP												THE RESULTS							
Year	Team	Lg	G	GS	CG	GF	IP	BFP	H	R	ER	HR	SH	SF	HB	TBB	IBB	SO	WP	Bk	W	L	Pct	Sh	Sv-Op	Hld	ERC	ERA
2012	Mobile	AA	21	21	0	0	104.0	422	91	35	33	9	5	1	8	25	0	97	7	0	5	1	.556	0	0--	-	3.05	2.86
2013	Reno	AAA	26	13	0	2	88.0	399	107	67	56	11	3	6	1	33	0	80	2	1	4	7	.364	0	0--	-	5.42	5.73
2014	Mobile	AA	6	6	0	0	39.0	146	22	4	3	1	0	0	2	6	0	38	0	0	4	2	.667	0	0--	-	1.12	0.69
2014	Ari	NL	21	21	0	0	114.1	486	117	56	51	16	4	4	2	40	2	105	4	0	9	7	.563	0	0-0	0	4.39	4.01
2015	Ari	NL	27	27	0	0	152.2	640	158	75	73	18	3	9	7	40	2	111	3	0	6	6	.500	0	0-0	0	4.08	4.30
	2 ML YEARS		48	48	0	0	267.0	1126	275	131	124	34	7	13	9	80	4	216	7	0	15	13	.536	0	0-0	0	4.21	4.18

Cody Anderson

Pitches: R **Bats:** R **Pos:** SP-15   **Ht:** 6'4" **Wt:** 235 **Born:** 9/14/1990 **Age:** 25

			HOW MUCH HE PITCHED						WHAT HE GAVE UP												THE RESULTS							
Year	Team	Lg	G	GS	CG	GF	IP	BFP	H	R	ER	HR	SH	SF	HB	TBB	IBB	SO	WP	Bk	W	L	Pct	Sh	Sv-Op	Hld	ERC	ERA
2012	Lk Cty	A	24	23	0	1	98.1	403	92	40	35	8	1	2	1	29	0	72	5	2	4	7	.364	0	0--	-	3.29	3.20
2013	Carlina	A+	23	23	0	0	123.1	488	105	34	32	6	4	3	5	31	0	112	7	1	9	4	.692	0	0--	-	2.65	2.34
2014	Akron	AA	25	25	0	0	125.2	544	141	78	76	17	1	0	4	45	0	81	4	2	4	11	.267	0	0--	-	5.10	5.44
2015	Akron	AA	10	10	0	0	52.0	202	44	12	10	2	2	1	1	9	0	36	2	0	3	2	.600	0	0--	-	2.20	1.73
2015	Cle	AL	15	15	1	0	91.1	365	77	32	31	9	3	3	1	24	1	44	0	1	7	3	.700	0	0-0	0	2.78	3.05

Matt Andriese

Pitches: R **Bats:** R **Pos:** RP-17; SP-8   ANN-dreese   **Ht:** 6'3" **Wt:** 215 **Born:** 8/28/1989 **Age:** 26

			HOW MUCH HE PITCHED						WHAT HE GAVE UP												THE RESULTS							
Year	Team	Lg	G	GS	CG	GF	IP	BFP	H	R	ER	HR	SH	SF	HB	TBB	IBB	SO	WP	Bk	W	L	Pct	Sh	Sv-Op	Hld	ERC	ERA
2011	Eugene	A-	12	8	0	0	41.2	161	29	8	7	0	0	1	2	10	0	42	1	0	5	1	.833	0	0--	-	1.61	1.51
2012	Lk Els	A+	27	26	0	0	146.0	603	140	72	58	9	2	3	4	38	0	131	10	1	10	8	.556	0	0--	-	3.20	3.58
2013	SnAnt	AA	15	15	0	0	76.0	314	71	26	20	3	1	0	3	17	0	63	2	0	8	2	.800	0	0--	-	2.80	2.37
2013	Tucsn	AAA	12	10	0	0	58.2	245	64	32	29	2	4	4	2	12	0	42	2	0	3	5	.375	0	0--	-	3.55	4.45
2014	Drhm	AAA	28	25	0	1	162.1	667	153	73	68	18	7	2	8	48	0	129	3	1	11	8	.579	0	0--	-	3.72	3.77
2015	Drhm	AAA	13	12	0	0	65.0	265	65	24	17	2	0	3	1	10	0	69	3	1	3	3	.500	0	0--	-	2.76	2.35
2015	TB	AL	25	8	0	8	65.2	282	69	32	30	8	1	3	2	18	1	49	2	2	3	5	.375	0	2-2	0	4.08	4.11

Elvis Andrus

Bats: R **Throws:** R **Pos:** SS-160   AHN-drews   **Ht:** 6'0" **Wt:** 195 **Born:** 8/26/1988 **Age:** 27

			BATTING																		RUNNING			AVERAGES			
Year	Team	Lg	G	AB	H	2B	3B	HR	(Hm	Rd)	TB	R	RBI	RC	TBB	IBB	SO	HBP	SH	SF	SB	CS	GDP	Avg	OBP	Slg	OPS
2009	Tex	AL	145	480	128	17	8	6	(3	3)	179	72	40	65	40	0	77	6	12	3	33	6	4	.267	.329	.373	.702
2010	Tex	AL	148	588	156	15	3	0	(0	0)	177	88	35	79	64	0	96	5	17	3	32	15	6	.265	.342	.301	.643
2011	Tex	AL	150	587	164	27	3	5	(2	3)	212	96	60	76	56	0	74	5	16	1	37	12	17	.279	.347	.361	.708
2012	Tex	AL	158	629	180	31	9	3	(1	2)	238	85	62	92	57	0	96	5	17	3	21	10	15	.286	.349	.378	.727
2013	Tex	AL	156	620	168	17	4	4	(0	4)	205	91	67	72	52	1	97	4	16	6	42	8	19	.271	.328	.331	.659
2014	Tex	AL	157	619	163	35	1	2	(1	1)	206	72	41	59	46	0	96	3	9	7	27	15	21	.263	.314	.333	.647
2015	Tex	AL	160	596	154	34	2	7	(4	3)	213	69	62	68	46	1	78	2	8	9	25	9	14	.258	.309	.357	.667
	Postseason		34	140	38	4	0	0	(0	0)	42	18	5	13	12	0	20	1	4	1	9	3	6	.271	.331	.300	.631
	7 ML YEARS		1074	4119	1113	176	30	27	(11	16)	1430	573	367	511	361	2	614	30	95	29	217	75	96	.270	.331	.347	.679

Dean Anna

Bats: L **Throws:** R **Pos:** PH-1   **Ht:** 5'11" **Wt:** 180 **Born:** 11/24/1986 **Age:** 29

			BATTING																		RUNNING			AVERAGES			
Year	Team	Lg	G	AB	H	2B	3B	HR	(Hm	Rd)	TB	R	RBI	RC	TBB	IBB	SO	HBP	SH	SF	SB	CS	GDP	Avg	OBP	Slg	OPS
2011	Lk Els	A+	44	148	46	10	2	3	(-	-)	69	25	18	29	19	1	22	5	2	3	2	0	4	.311	.400	.466	.866
2011	SnAnt	AA	71	198	50	18	1	2	(-	-)	76	45	23	34	41	2	19	3	2	2	3	0	2	.253	.385	.384	.769
2012	SnAnt	AA	129	425	115	16	3	10	(-	-)	167	75	46	70	66	1	76	11	1	7	6	4	8	.271	.377	.393	.770
2013	Tucsn	AAA	132	498	165	38	5	9	(-	-)	240	90	73	100	61	0	65	11	4	8	3	7	6	.331	.410	.482	.892
2014	S-WB	AAA	36	130	25	4	3	1	(-	-)	38	13	14	11	14	0	20	4	0	4	0	1	0	.192	.283	.292	.575
2014	Indy	AAA	29	68	16	4	0	1	(-	-)	23	13	7	11	19	0	5	0	1	1	1	0	2	.235	.398	.338	.736
2015	Memp	AAA	125	445	121	22	3	3	(-	-)	158	80	44	68	77	1	61	4	5	3	5	5	10	.272	.382	.355	.737
2014	NYY	AL	12	22	3	1	0	1	(1	0)	7	3	3	1	2	0	6	0	0	1	0	0	0	.136	.200	.318	.518
2015	StL	NL	1	1	0	0	0	0	(0	0)	0	0	0	0	0	0	0	0	0	0	0	0	0	.000	.000	.000	.000
	2 ML YEARS		13	23	3	1	0	1	(1	0)	7	3	3	1	2	0	6	0	0	1	0	0	0	.130	.192	.304	.497

Nori Aoki

Bats: L **Throws:** R **Pos:** LF-86;PH-6;RF-2;DH-1   AH-oh-kee   **Ht:** 5'9" **Wt:** 180 **Born:** 1/5/1982 **Age:** 34

			BATTING																		RUNNING			AVERAGES			
Year	Team	Lg	G	AB	H	2B	3B	HR	(Hm	Rd)	TB	R	RBI	RC	TBB	IBB	SO	HBP	SH	SF	SB	CS	GDP	Avg	OBP	Slg	OPS
2012	Mil	NL	151	520	150	37	4	10	(4	6)	225	81	50	80	43	1	55	13	7	5	30	8	6	.288	.355	.433	.787
2013	Mil	NL	155	597	171	20	3	8	(5	3)	221	80	37	80	55	1	40	11	8	3	20	12	9	.286	.356	.370	.726
2014	KC	AL	132	491	140	22	6	1	(0	1)	177	63	43	69	43	0	49	6	8	1	17	8	5	.285	.349	.360	.710
2015	SF	NL	93	355	102	12	3	5	(0	3)	135	42	26	49	30	0	25	6	1	0	14	5	8	.287	.353	.380	.733
	Postseason		14	41	8	0	0	0	(0	0)	8	7	3	5	5	0	3	1	0	1	1	0	2	.195	.292	.195	.487
	4 ML YEARS		531	1963	563	91	16	24	(11	13)	758	266	156	278	171	2	169	36	24	9	81	33	28	.287	.353	.386	.740

Elvis Araujo

Pitches: L Bats: L Pos: RP-40
ah-ROW-hoe
Ht: 6'7" Wt: 270 Born: 7/15/1991 Age: 24

Year	Team	Lg	G	GS	CG	GF	IP	BFP	H	R	ER	HR	SH	SF	HB	TBB	IBB	SO	WP	Bk	W	L	Pct	Sh	Sv-Op	Hld	ERC	ERA
2011	2 Tms	Low	15	13	0	0	69.2	293	65	34	26	2	0	2	1	25	0	63	5	1	9	1	.900	0	0- -	-	3.13	3.36
2012	Lk Cty	A	28	28	1	0	135.0	601	141	89	75	7	7	5	6	61	0	111	20	2	7	10	.412	0	0- -	-	4.33	5.00
2014	Carlina	A+	25	0	0	15	29.0	126	23	16	13	1	2	5	0	13	1	29	6	0	1	1	.500	0	8- -	-	2.53	4.03
2014	Akron	AA	18	0	0	6	21.0	90	20	7	6	2	0	1	0	15	2	21	2	0	1	0	1.000	0	3- -	-	5.19	2.57
2015	Rdng	AA	7	0	0	3	9.2	44	9	8	8	1	0	0	1	6	0	11	0	0	1	2	.333	0	0- -	-	5.00	7.45
2015	Phi	NL	40	0	0	5	34.2	151	29	17	13	1	2	0	0	19	1	34	2	0	2	1	.667	0	0-0	2	3.15	3.38

Chris Archer

Pitches: R Bats: R Pos: SP-34
Ht: 6'3" Wt: 190 Born: 9/26/1988 Age: 27

Year	Team	Lg	G	GS	CG	GF	IP	BFP	H	R	ER	HR	SH	SF	HB	TBB	IBB	SO	WP	Bk	W	L	Pct	Sh	Sv-Op	Hld	ERC	ERA
2012	TB	AL	6	4	0	1	29.1	122	23	17	15	3	1	0	1	13	0	36	2	0	1	3	.250	0	0-0	0	3.24	4.60
2013	TB	AL	23	23	2	0	128.2	525	134	49	46	15	1	5	8	38	2	101	7	0	9	7	.563	2	0-0	0	3.13	3.22
2014	TB	AL	32	32	0	0	194.2	822	177	85	72	12	4	9	8	72	1	173	8	0	10	9	.526	0	0-0	0	3.36	3.33
2015	TB	AL	34	34	1	0	212.0	868	175	85	76	19	2	2	3	66	0	252	13	0	12	13	.480	1	0-0	0	2.79	3.23
	Postseason		2	0	0	0	1.2	6	1	0	0	0	1	0	0	0	0	2	0	0	0	0	-	0	0-0	0	0.75	0.00
	4 ML YEARS		95	93	3	1	564.2	2337	482	236	209	49	8	16	20	189	3	562	30	0	32	32	.500	3	0-0	0	3.08	3.33

Oswaldo Arcia

Bats: L Throws: R Pos: LF-15;RF-4;PH-1
ARR-see-ya
Ht: 6'0" Wt: 225 Born: 5/9/1991 Age: 25

Year	Team	Lg	G	AB	H	2B	3B	HR	(Hm	Rd)	TB	R	RBI	RC	TBB	IBB	SO	HBP	SH	SF	SB	CS	GDP	Avg	OBP	Slg	OPS
2015	Roch*	AAA	79	282	56	13	0	12	(-	-)	105	31	41	27	18	0	82	6	0	5	0	1	4	.199	.257	.372	.630
2013	Min	AL	97	351	88	17	2	14	(6	8)	151	34	43	37	23	0	117	4	0	1	1	2	4	.251	.304	.430	.734
2014	Min	AL	103	372	86	16	3	20	(12	8)	168	46	57	51	31	4	127	6	0	1	1	2	6	.231	.300	.452	.752
2015	Min	AL	19	58	16	0	0	2	(2	0)	22	6	8	8	4	4	15	2	0	1	0	0	2	.276	.338	.379	.718
	3 ML YEARS		219	781	190	33	5	36	(20	16)	341	86	108	96	58	8	259	12	0	2	2	4	12	.243	.305	.437	.741

Nolan Arenado

Bats: R Throws: R Pos: 3B-157;PH-1
ahr-eh-NOD-oh
Ht: 6'2" Wt: 205 Born: 4/16/1991 Age: 25

Year	Team	Lg	G	AB	H	2B	3B	HR	(Hm	Rd)	TB	R	RBI	RC	TBB	IBB	SO	HBP	SH	SF	SB	CS	GDP	Avg	OBP	Slg	OPS
2013	Col	NL	133	486	130	29	4	10	(5	5)	197	49	52	48	23	1	72	1	2	2	2	0	16	.267	.301	.405	.706
2014	Col	NL	111	432	124	34	2	18	(16	2)	216	58	61	60	25	1	58	4	1	5	2	1	13	.287	.328	.500	.828
2015	Col	NL	157	616	177	43	4	42	(20	22)	354	97	130	116	34	13	110	4	0	11	2	5	17	.287	.323	.575	.898
	3 ML YEARS		401	1534	431	106	10	70	(41	29)	767	204	243	224	82	15	240	9	3	18	6	6	46	.281	.318	.500	.818

J.P. Arencibia

Bats: R Throws: R Pos: C-23;PH-4;DH-1
air-en-SEE-bee-uh
Ht: 6'0" Wt: 205 Born: 1/5/1986 Age: 30

Year	Team	Lg	G	AB	H	2B	3B	HR	(Hm	Rd)	TB	R	RBI	RC	TBB	IBB	SO	HBP	SH	SF	SB	CS	GDP	Avg	OBP	Slg	OPS
2015	Drham*	AAA	99	384	87	17	0	22	(-	-)	170	52	65	45	15	0	125	3	0	3	0	0	7	.227	.259	.443	.702
2010	Tor	AL	11	35	5	1	0	2	(2	0)	12	3	4	4	2	0	11	0	0	0	0	0	0	.143	.189	.343	.532
2011	Tor	AL	129	443	97	20	4	23	(13	10)	194	47	78	58	36	3	133	4	0	3	1	1	6	.219	.282	.438	.720
2012	Tor	AL	102	347	81	16	0	18	(9	9)	151	45	56	47	18	1	108	3	1	3	1	0	8	.233	.275	.435	.710
2013	Tor	AL	138	474	92	18	0	21	(13	8)	173	45	55	30	18	0	148	3	0	2	0	2	8	.194	.227	.365	.592
2014	Tex	AL	63	203	36	9	0	10	(3	7)	75	20	35	19	10	0	62	7	0	2	0	0	6	.177	.239	.369	.608
2015	TB	AL	24	71	22	3	0	6	(1	5)	43	9	17	13	1	0	22	0	0	1	0	0	1	.310	.315	.606	.921
	6 ML YEARS		467	1573	333	67	4	80	(41	39)	648	169	245	171	85	4	484	17	1	11	2	3	25	.212	.258	.412	.670

Joaquin Arias

wah-KEEN AH-ree-us
Bats: R Throws: R Pos: PH-20;3B-8;SS-8;1B-2;2B-2;PR-2;DH-1
Ht: 6'1" Wt: 165 Born: 9/21/1984 Age: 31

Year	Team	Lg	G	AB	H	2B	3B	HR	(Hm	Rd)	TB	R	RBI	RC	TBB	IBB	SO	HBP	SH	SF	SB	CS	GDP	Avg	OBP	Slg	OPS
2015	Scrmto*	AAA	10	40	11	6	0	0	(-	-)	17	4	3	4	1	0	7	0	0	0	0	0	1	.275	.293	.425	.718
2006	Tex	AL	6	11	6	1	0	0	(0	0)	7	4	1	3	1	0	0	0	0	0	0	1	0	.545	.583	.636	1.220
2008	Tex	AL	32	110	32	7	3	0	(0	0)	45	15	9	15	7	0	12	2	1	0	4	1	4	.291	.345	.409	.754
2009	Tex	AL	3	8	0	0	0	0	(0	0)	0	0	0	0	0	0	3	0	1	0	0	0	0	.000	.000	.000	.000
2010	2 Tms		72	128	33	6	1	0	(0	0)	41	23	13	10	4	0	23	0	2	0	1	0	2	.258	.280	.320	.601
2012	SF	NL	112	319	86	13	5	5	(0	5)	124	30	34	32	13	4	44	5	2	5	5	1	12	.270	.304	.389	.693
2013	SF	NL	102	225	61	9	2	1	(1	0)	77	17	19	18	4	1	33	1	4	2	1	0	4	.271	.284	.342	.627
2014	SF	NL	107	193	49	9	0	0	(0	0)	58	18	15	14	8	2	23	0	1	2	1	0	1	.254	.281	.301	.581
2015	SF	NL	40	58	12	1	0	1	(0	1)	16	5	4	3	0	0	12	0	1	0	1	0	1	.207	.207	.276	.483
10	Tex	AL	50	98	27	5	1	0	(0	0)	34	18	9	8	2	0	17	0	1	0	1	0	2	.276	.290	.347	.637
10	NYM	NL	22	30	6	1	0	0	(0	0)	7	5	4	2	2	0	6	0	1	0	0	0	0	.200	.250	.233	.483
	Postseason		20	12	5	2	0	0	(0	0)	7	5	1	1	0	0	2	0	0	0	0	0	0	.417	.417	.583	1.000
	8 ML YEARS		474	1052	279	46	11	7	(1	6)	368	112	95	95	37	7	150	8	12	9	13	3	24	.265	.293	.350	.643

Shawn Armstrong

Pitches: R **Bats:** R **Pos:** RP-8   **Ht:** 6'2" **Wt:** 225 **Born:** 9/11/1990 **Age:** 25

Year	Team	Lg	G	GS	CG	GF	IP	BFP	H	R	ER	HR	SH	SF	HB	TBB	IBB	SO	WP	Bk	W	L	Pct	Sh	Sv-Op	Hld	ERC	ERA
2012	2 Tms	Low	28	0	0	13	47.1	196	32	10	10	0	2	1	6	25	1	56	3	1	1	3	.250	0	1--	-	2.65	1.90
2012	Akron	AA	17	0	0	7	20.1	81	12	2	2	0	0	0	1	12	0	22	1	0	1	0	1.000	0	3--	-	2.27	0.89
2013	Akron	AA	30	0	0	5	33.0	153	32	18	15	2	2	1	2	21	0	43	2	0	2	3	.400	0	0--	-	4.69	4.09
2014	Akron	AA	44	0	0	34	51.0	207	39	12	12	3	2	0	1	19	1	68	2	0	6	2	.750	0	15--	-	2.53	2.12
2014	Clmbs	AAA	5	0	0	1	5.0	22	4	3	3	1	0	2	0	3	0	4	2	0	0	0	-	0	0--	-	4.36	5.40
2015	Clmbs	AAA	46	0	0	27	49.2	210	37	15	13	0	2	0	2	26	2	80	4	0	1	2	.333	0	16--	-	2.57	2.36
2015	Cle	AL	8	0	0	5	8.0	30	5	2	2	1	0	0	0	2	0	11	0	0	0	0	-	0	0-0	0	1.84	2.25

Jonathan Aro

Pitches: R **Bats:** R **Pos:** RP-6   ah-ROW   **Ht:** 6'0" **Wt:** 172 **Born:** 10/10/1990 **Age:** 25

Year	Team	Lg	G	GS	CG	GF	IP	BFP	H	R	ER	HR	SH	SF	HB	TBB	IBB	SO	WP	Bk	W	L	Pct	Sh	Sv-Op	Hld	ERC	ERA
2012	RedSx	R	11	4	0	3	38.2	163	45	21	20	4	1	0	0	9	0	34	5	0	3	4	.429	0	0--	-	4.46	4.66
2013	Lowell	A-	15	1	0	9	54.2	219	44	17	13	2	4	3	2	12	2	49	1	0	5	3	.625	0	3--	-	2.09	2.14
2014	2 Tms	Low	32	1	0	25	87.0	355	64	33	21	4	7	1	3	29	0	98	3	0	3	3	.500	0	8--	-	2.21	2.17
2015	Portlnd	AA	8	0	0	3	22.1	94	15	12	7	0	1	1	1	8	0	19	0	0	3	2	.600	0	0--	-	1.68	2.82
2015	Pwtckt	AAA	26	0	0	7	51.2	207	43	18	18	2	0	2	4	10	0	53	0	0	1	0	1.000	0	2--	-	2.35	3.14
2015	Bos	AL	6	0	0	2	10.1	49	15	8	8	2	0	1	0	4	0	8	0	0	0	1	.000	0	0-0	0	7.50	6.97

Jake Arrieta

Pitches: R **Bats:** R **Pos:** SP-33   air-ee-ETT-uh   **Ht:** 6'4" **Wt:** 225 **Born:** 3/6/1986 **Age:** 30

Year	Team	Lg	G	GS	CG	GF	IP	BFP	H	R	ER	HR	SH	SF	HB	TBB	IBB	SO	WP	Bk	W	L	Pct	Sh	Sv-Op	Hld	ERC	ERA
2010	Bal	AL	18	18	0	0	100.1	449	106	57	52	9	4	2	4	48	3	52	5	0	6	6	.500	0	0-0	0	4.74	4.66
2011	Bal	AL	22	22	0	0	119.1	523	115	70	67	21	3	2	4	59	2	93	0	0	10	8	.556	0	0-0	0	4.93	5.05
2012	Bal	AL	24	18	0	0	114.2	496	122	82	79	16	3	4	5	35	3	109	4	0	3	9	.250	0	0-0	1	4.47	6.20
2013	2 Tms		14	14	0	0	75.1	324	59	41	40	9	2	3	5	41	1	60	1	0	5	4	.556	0	0-0	0	3.82	4.78
2014	ChC	NL	25	25	1	0	156.2	614	114	46	44	5	5	3	3	41	2	167	8	0	10	5	.667	1	0-0	0	1.85	2.53
2015	ChC	NL	33	33	4	0	229.0	870	150	52	45	10	4	1	6	48	2	236	6	0	22	6	.786	3	0-0	0	1.53	1.77
13	Bal	AL	5	5	0	0	23.2	111	25	19	19	2	0	3	2	17	1	23	1	0	1	2	.333	0	0-0	0	5.91	7.23
13	ChC	NL	9	9	0	0	51.2	213	34	22	21	7	2	0	3	24	0	37	0	0	4	2	.667	0	0-0	0	2.94	3.66
6 ML YEARS			136	130	5	1	795.1	3276	666	348	327	70	21	15	27	272	13	717	24	0	56	38	.596	4	0-0	1	3.02	3.70

Bronson Arroyo

Pitches: R **Bats:** R **Pos:** P   uh-ROY-oh   **Ht:** 6'3" **Wt:** 195 **Born:** 2/24/1977 **Age:** 39

Year	Team	Lg	G	GS	CG	GF	IP	BFP	H	R	ER	HR	SH	SF	HB	TBB	IBB	SO	WP	Bk	W	L	Pct	Sh	Sv-Op	Hld	ERC	ERA
2000	Pit	NL	20	12	0	1	72.2	338	88	61	51	10	5	2	4	36	6	50	3	1	2	6	.250	0	0-0	0	6.18	6.40
2001	Pit	NL	24	13	1	1	88.1	390	99	54	50	12	4	6	4	34	6	39	4	1	5	7	.417	0	0-0	2	5.09	5.09
2002	Pit	NL	9	4	0	1	27.0	123	30	14	12	1	1	1	0	15	3	22	0	0	2	1	.667	0	0-0	1	4.64	4.00
2003	Bos	AL	6	0	0	2	17.1	66	10	5	4	0	0	0	1	4	2	14	0	0	0	0	-	0	1-1	0	1.14	2.08
2004	Bos	AL	32	29	0	0	178.2	764	171	99	80	17	5	4	20	47	3	142	5	0	10	9	.526	0	0-0	0	3.65	4.03
2005	Bos	AL	35	32	0	1	205.1	878	213	116	103	22	4	4	14	54	3	100	5	1	14	10	.583	0	0-0	0	4.04	4.51
2006	Cin	NL	35	35	3	0	240.2	992	222	98	88	31	9	2	5	64	7	184	6	0	14	11	.560	1	0-0	0	3.37	3.29
2007	Cin	NL	34	34	1	0	210.2	921	232	109	99	28	10	7	13	63	6	156	4	0	9	15	.375	0	0-0	0	4.68	4.23
2008	Cin	NL	34	34	1	0	200.0	871	219	116	106	29	13	6	6	68	2	163	6	0	15	11	.577	0	0-0	0	4.83	4.77
2009	Cin	NL	33	33	3	0	220.1	923	214	101	94	31	9	5	9	65	6	127	1	0	15	13	.536	2	0-0	0	3.94	3.84
2010	Cin	NL	33	33	2	0	215.2	880	188	95	93	29	6	5	6	59	5	121	1	1	17	10	.630	0	0-0	0	3.21	3.88
2011	Cin	NL	32	32	1	0	199.0	855	227	119	112	46	6	5	6	45	5	108	0	0	9	12	.429	1	0-0	0	5.20	5.07
2012	Cin	NL	32	32	1	0	202.0	835	209	86	84	26	7	6	5	35	1	129	3	0	12	10	.545	1	0-0	0	3.68	3.74
2013	Cin	NL	32	32	2	0	202.0	823	199	88	85	32	4	7	7	34	2	124	1	2	14	12	.538	1	0-0	0	3.63	3.79
2014	Ari	NL	14	14	1	0	86.0	357	92	40	39	10	3	2	3	19	1	47	2	0	7	4	.636	0	0-0	0	4.08	4.08
	Postseason		12	4	0	3	29.1	127	24	17	15	5	0	0	2	13	0	26	0	0	1	0	1.000	0	0-0	2	3.91	4.60
15 ML YEARS			405	369	16	6	2364.2	10016	2413	1201	1100	324	86	62	103	642	58	1526	41	6	145	131	.525	6	1-1	3	4.09	4.19

Cody Asche

Bats: L **Throws:** R **Pos:** LF-63;3B-51;PH-15   ASH-ee   **Ht:** 6'1" **Wt:** 200 **Born:** 6/30/1990 **Age:** 26

Year	Team	Lg	G	AB	H	2B	3B	HR	(Hm	Rd)	TB	R	RBI	RC	TBB	IBB	SO	HBP	SH	SF	SB	CS	GDP	Avg	OBP	Slg	OPS
2015	LV*	AAA	15	61	18	3	0	1	(-	-)	24	7	3	9	6	1	9	0	0	0	0	0	2	.295	.358	.393	.752
2013	Phi	NL	50	162	38	8	1	5	(4	1)	63	18	22	18	15	3	43	1	0	1	1	0	1	.235	.302	.389	.691
2014	Phi	NL	121	397	100	25	0	10	(6	4)	155	43	46	44	33	4	102	0	3	1	0	1	7	.252	.309	.390	.699
2015	Phi	NL	129	425	104	22	3	12	(5	7)	168	41	39	47	26	3	111	4	0	1	1	2	4	.245	.294	.395	.689
3 ML YEARS			300	984	242	55	4	27	(15	12)	386	102	107	109	74	10	256	5	3	3	2	3	12	.246	.301	.392	.693

75

Alec Asher

Pitches: R Bats: R Pos: SP-7
Ht: 6'4" Wt: 280 Born: 10/4/1991 Age: 24

Year	Team	Lg	G	GS	CG	GF	IP	BFP	H	R	ER	HR	SH	SF	HB	TBB	IBB	SO	WP	Bk	W	L	Pct	Sh	Sv-Op	Hld	ERC	ERA
2012	Spkane	A-	20	0	0	13	35.0	145	29	12	12	4	1	1	1	11	0	50	1	1	2	3	.400	0	5- -	-	2.99	3.09
2013	MrtlBh	A+	26	25	0	0	133.1	562	120	60	43	10	3	3	6	40	1	139	6	2	9	7	.563	0	0- -	-	3.10	2.90
2014	Frisco	AA	28	28	0	0	154.0	631	139	74	65	18	6	6	3	32	1	122	6	0	11	11	.500	0	0- -	-	2.96	3.80
2015	Frisco	AA	8	8	0	0	43.0	183	39	20	19	3	1	0	2	18	0	43	5	0	1	4	.200	0	0- -	-	3.63	3.98
2015	RdRck	AAA	12	12	0	0	64.2	277	71	36	34	16	1	1	0	19	0	54	4	0	3	6	.333	0	0- -	-	5.27	4.73
2015	Phi	NL	7	7	0	0	29.0	138	42	30	30	8	2	1	1	10	0	16	2	2	0	6	.000	0	0-0	0	8.10	9.31

Nevin Ashley

Bats: R Throws: R Pos: C-8;PH-4
Ht: 6'1" Wt: 215 Born: 8/14/1984 Age: 31

Year	Team	Lg	G	AB	H	2B	3B	HR	(Hm	Rd)	TB	R	RBI	RC	TBB	IBB	SO	HBP	SH	SF	SB	CS	GDP	Avg	OBP	Slg	OPS
2011	Mont	AA	80	279	77	15	1	6	(-	-)	112	35	33	46	36	2	66	14	1	2	2	3	6	.276	.384	.401	.785
2011	Drham	AAA	32	101	22	1	1	2	(-	-)	31	9	15	8	5	0	29	3	2	1	0	1	3	.218	.273	.307	.580
2012	Drham	AAA	35	110	27	6	1	5	(-	-)	50	18	13	18	15	1	25	4	1	0	1	1	3	.245	.357	.455	.811
2012	Rays	R	15	45	15	3	0	1	(-	-)	21	6	5	9	7	0	6	1	0	0	2	0	0	.333	.434	.467	.901
2013	Lsvlle	AAA	80	238	56	13	1	6	(-	-)	89	28	28	32	31	2	59	3	4	2	4	1	4	.235	.328	.374	.702
2014	Indy	AAA	70	203	50	12	1	2	(-	-)	70	21	24	25	22	0	41	5	2	2	0	0	6	.246	.332	.345	.677
2015	ColSpr	AAA	94	337	103	14	4	8	(-	-)	149	52	61	57	32	0	72	7	1	4	0	2	10	.306	.374	.442	.816
2015	Mil	NL	12	20	2	1	0	0	(0	0)	3	2	1	0	0	0	8	1	0	0	0	0	0	.100	.143	.150	.293

Scott Atchison

Pitches: R Bats: R Pos: RP-23
Ht: 6'2" Wt: 200 Born: 3/29/1976 Age: 40

Year	Team	Lg	G	GS	CG	GF	IP	BFP	H	R	ER	HR	SH	SF	HB	TBB	IBB	SO	WP	Bk	W	L	Pct	Sh	Sv-Op	Hld	ERC	ERA
2004	Sea	AL	25	0	0	8	30.2	133	29	12	12	4	2	1	0	14	2	36	2	0	2	3	.400	0	0-0	4	4.08	3.52
2005	Sea	AL	6	0	0	2	6.2	27	7	5	5	1	0	0	0	1	0	9	0	0	0	0	-	0	0-0	0	3.77	6.75
2007	SF	NL	22	0	0	4	30.2	131	32	14	14	5	1	2	1	10	0	25	2	0	0	0	-	0	0-1	5	4.65	4.11
2010	Bos	AL	43	1	0	8	60.0	253	58	37	30	9	1	2	1	19	2	41	4	0	2	3	.400	0	0-0	7	3.92	4.50
2011	Bos	AL	17	0	0	4	30.1	122	31	11	11	0	1	2	2	6	0	17	2	0	1	0	1.000	0	1-1	0	3.15	3.26
2012	Bos	AL	42	0	0	7	51.1	200	42	10	9	2	1	2	0	9	3	36	2	0	2	1	.667	0	0-1	5	1.91	1.58
2013	NYM	NL	51	0	0	10	45.1	194	45	24	22	4	2	3	0	12	0	28	5	0	3	3	.500	0	0-0	10	3.33	4.37
2014	Cle	AL	70	0	0	11	72.0	280	60	24	22	4	1	1	0	14	4	49	1	0	6	0	1.000	0	2-7	14	2.16	2.75
2015	Cle	AL	23	0	0	7	19.2	87	23	15	15	6	0	2	1	4	0	12	3	0	1	1	.500	0	0-1	3	5.79	6.86
	9 ML YEARS		299	1	0	61	346.2	1427	327	155	140	35	9	15	5	89	11	253	21	0	17	11	.607	0	3-11	46	3.25	3.63

Phillippe Aumont

Pitches: R Bats: L Pos: SP-1
fih-LEEP ah-MOHNT
Ht: 6'7" Wt: 240 Born: 1/7/1989 Age: 27

Year	Team	Lg	G	GS	CG	GF	IP	BFP	H	R	ER	HR	SH	SF	HB	TBB	IBB	SO	WP	Bk	W	L	Pct	Sh	Sv-Op	Hld	ERC	ERA
2015	LV*	AAA	14	10	0	0	65.0	277	49	23	17	3	2	0	3	41	0	58	7	3	3	4	.429	0	0- -	-	3.47	2.35
2015	Buffalo*	AAA	5	4	0	0	18.0	86	12	12	12	2	0	2	0	22	0	23	4	1	0	2	.000	0	0- -	-	5.49	6.00
2012	Phi	NL	18	0	0	3	14.2	65	10	6	6	0	2	0	1	9	1	14	2	0	1	0	1.000	0	2-3	5	2.50	3.68
2013	Phi	NL	22	0	0	8	19.1	95	24	11	9	0	0	1	3	13	1	19	2	1	1	3	.250	0	0-0	1	6.34	4.19
2014	Phi	NL	5	0	0	4	5.2	35	14	12	12	3	0	1	0	5	0	6	0	0	0	1	.000	0	0-0	0	21.66	19.06
2015	Phi	NL	1	1	0	0	4.0	23	5	6	6	2	0	0	0	7	0	3	1	0	0	0	.000	0	0-0	0	16.33	13.50
	4 ML YEARS		46	1	0	15	43.2	218	53	35	33	5	2	2	4	34	2	42	5	1	1	6	.143	0	2-3	6	7.32	6.80

Alex Avila

Bats: L Throws: R Pos: C-44;1B-23;PH-4;DH-1
ah-VEE-lah
Ht: 5'11" Wt: 210 Born: 1/29/1987 Age: 29

Year	Team	Lg	G	AB	H	2B	3B	HR	(Hm	Rd)	TB	R	RBI	RC	TBB	IBB	SO	HBP	SH	SF	SB	CS	GDP	Avg	OBP	Slg	OPS
2009	Det	AL	29	61	17	4	0	5	(4	1)	36	9	14	12	10	0	18	0	0	1	0	0	0	.279	.375	.590	.965
2010	Det	AL	104	294	67	12	0	7	(4	3)	100	28	31	26	36	0	71	2	1	0	2	2	12	.228	.316	.340	.656
2011	Det	AL	141	464	137	33	4	19	(10	9)	235	63	82	86	73	9	131	3	3	8	3	1	8	.295	.389	.506	.895
2012	Det	AL	116	367	89	21	2	9	(7	2)	141	42	48	53	61	2	104	2	2	2	2	0	12	.243	.352	.384	.736
2013	Det	AL	102	330	75	14	1	11	(7	4)	124	39	47	37	44	0	112	1	1	3	0	0	10	.227	.317	.376	.693
2014	Det	AL	124	390	85	22	0	11	(3	8)	140	44	47	48	61	1	151	3	1	2	0	3	6	.218	.327	.359	.686
2015	Det	AL	67	178	34	5	0	4	(2	2)	51	21	13	20	40	0	66	0	1	0	0	1	4	.191	.339	.287	.626
	Postseason		34	110	16	2	0	3	(2	1)	27	6	7	4	11	0	43	1	1	0	0	0	1	.145	.230	.245	.475
	7 ML YEARS		683	2084	504	111	7	66	(37	29)	827	246	282	282	325	12	653	11	9	16	7	7	52	.242	.345	.397	.742

Luis Avilan

Pitches: L Bats: L Pos: RP-73
ah-VEE-lan
Ht: 6'2" Wt: 220 Born: 7/19/1989 Age: 26

Year	Team	Lg	G	GS	CG	GF	IP	BFP	H	R	ER	HR	SH	SF	HB	TBB	IBB	SO	WP	Bk	W	L	Pct	Sh	Sv-Op	Hld	ERC	ERA
2012	Atl	NL	31	0	0	2	36.0	142	27	9	8	1	3	0	1	10	1	33	3	1	1	0	1.000	0	0-0	5	2.00	2.00
2013	Atl	NL	75	0	0	7	65.0	256	40	12	11	1	1	1	4	22	2	38	3	1	5	0	1.000	0	0-2	27	1.62	1.52
2014	Atl	NL	62	0	0	14	43.1	193	47	22	22	2	3	2	3	21	7	25	5	0	4	1	.800	0	0-2	8	4.55	4.57
2015	2 Tms	NL	73	0	0	9	53.1	220	48	24	24	6	1	2	1	15	2	49	2	1	2	5	.286	0	0-3	17	3.18	4.05

	HOW MUCH HE PITCHED						WHAT HE GAVE UP												THE RESULTS							
Year Team	Lg	G	GS	CG	GF	IP	BFP	H	R	ER	HR	SH	SF	HB	TBB	IBB	SO	WP	Bk	W	L	Pct	Sh	Sv-Op	Hld	ERC	ERA
15 Atl	NL	50	0	0	7	37.2	154	35	15	15	4	0	1	0	10	2	31	1	1	2	4	.333	0	0-3	11	3.16	3.58
15 LAD	NL	23	0	0	2	15.2	66	13	9	9	2	1	1	1	5	0	18	1	0	0	1	.000	0	0-0	6	3.21	5.17
Postseason		4	0	0	1	2.2	11	3	0	0	0	0	0	0	1	1	1	0	0	0	0	-	0	0-0	2	3.55	0.00
4 ML YEARS		241	0	0	32	197.2	811	162	67	65	10	8	5	9	68	12	145	13	3	12	6	.667	0	0-7	57	2.68	2.96

Mike Aviles

uh-VEE-less

Bats: R **Throws:** R **Pos:** LF-34;3B-28;SS-23;2B-11;PH-10;CF-5;PR-4;RF-1;DH-1   **Ht:** 5'10" **Wt:** 205 **Born:** 3/13/1981 **Age:** 35

						BATTING													RUNNING			AVERAGES			
Year Team	Lg	G	AB	H	2B	3B	HR	(Hm	Rd)	TB	R	RBI	RC	TBB	IBB	SO	HBP	SH	SF	SB	CS	GDP	Avg	OBP	Slg	OPS
2008 KC	AL	102	419	136	27	4	10	(4	6)	201	68	51	62	18	4	58	2	0	2	8	3	12	.325	.354	.480	.833
2009 KC	AL	36	120	22	3	1	1	(1	0)	30	10	8	4	4	0	26	0	2	1	1	0	3	.183	.208	.250	.458
2010 KC	AL	110	424	129	16	3	8	(4	4)	175	63	32	47	20	0	49	1	0	3	14	5	13	.304	.335	.413	.748
2011 2 Tms	AL	91	286	73	17	3	7	(4	3)	117	31	39	31	13	0	44	2	4	4	14	4	8	.255	.289	.409	.698
2012 Bos	AL	136	512	128	28	0	13	(7	6)	195	57	60	57	23	0	77	2	3	6	14	6	6	.250	.282	.381	.663
2013 Cle	AL	124	361	91	15	0	9	(3	6)	133	54	46	35	15	0	41	3	7	8	8	5	11	.252	.282	.368	.650
2014 Cle	AL	113	344	85	16	1	5	(2	3)	118	38	39	27	13	0	49	1	11	5	14	5	10	.247	.273	.343	.616
2015 Cle	AL	98	290	67	10	0	5	(1	4)	92	37	17	19	20	0	38	1	5	1	3	1	18	.231	.282	.317	.599
11 KC	AL	53	185	41	11	3	5	(2	3)	73	14	31	18	9	0	27	2	3	3	10	2	5	.222	.261	.395	.656
11 Bos	AL	38	101	32	6	0	2	(2	0)	44	17	8	13	4	0	17	0	1	1	4	2	3	.317	.340	.436	.775
8 ML YEARS		810	2756	731	132	12	58	(26	32)	1061	358	292	282	126	4	382	12	32	30	76	29	81	.265	.297	.385	.682

Dylan Axelrod

Pitches: R **Bats:** R **Pos:** RP-6   **Ht:** 6'0" **Wt:** 185 **Born:** 7/30/1985 **Age:** 30

		HOW MUCH HE PITCHED						WHAT HE GAVE UP												THE RESULTS							
Year Team	Lg	G	GS	CG	GF	IP	BFP	H	R	ER	HR	SH	SF	HB	TBB	IBB	SO	WP	Bk	W	L	Pct	Sh	Sv-Op	Hld	ERC	ERA
2015 Lsvlle*	AAA	22	19	0	1	105.2	458	124	65	55	13	5	4	3	28	1	69	4	0	6	8	.429	0	0--	-	4.83	4.68
2011 CWS	AL	4	3	0	1	18.2	82	18	6	6	1	0	2	1	9	2	19	0	0	1	0	1.000	0	0-0	0	3.89	2.89
2012 CWS	AL	14	7	0	4	51.0	231	56	32	31	8	0	2	4	21	0	40	1	0	2	2	.500	0	0-0	0	5.39	5.47
2013 CWS	AL	30	20	0	8	128.1	586	170	89	81	24	2	3	4	43	2	73	5	0	4	11	.267	0	0-0	0	6.55	5.68
2014 Cin	NL	5	4	0	1	18.1	72	14	6	6	5	0	0	0	4	1	20	0	0	2	1	.667	0	0-0	0	3.06	2.95
2015 Cin	NL	6	0	0	3	12.1	59	11	13	10	5	1	0	0	8	2	12	0	0	0	1	.000	0	0-0	0	5.99	7.30
5 ML YEARS		59	34	0	17	228.2	1030	269	146	134	43	3	7	9	85	7	164	6	0	9	15	.375	0	0-0	0	5.74	5.27

John Axford

Pitches: R **Bats:** R **Pos:** RP-60   **Ht:** 6'5" **Wt:** 220 **Born:** 4/1/1983 **Age:** 33

		HOW MUCH HE PITCHED						WHAT HE GAVE UP												THE RESULTS							
Year Team	Lg	G	GS	CG	GF	IP	BFP	H	R	ER	HR	SH	SF	HB	TBB	IBB	SO	WP	Bk	W	L	Pct	Sh	Sv-Op	Hld	ERC	ERA
2009 Mil	NL	7	0	0	6	7.2	34	5	3	3	0	0	0	0	6	1	9	1	0	0	0	-	0	1-1	0	2.62	3.52
2010 Mil	NL	50	0	0	43	58.0	238	42	17	16	1	2	2	1	27	3	76	4	0	8	2	.800	0	24-27	3	2.33	2.48
2011 Mil	NL	74	0	0	63	73.2	305	59	19	16	4	1	1	0	25	1	86	8	0	2	2	.500	0	**46**-48	2	2.44	1.95
2012 Mil	NL	75	0	0	54	69.1	310	61	42	36	10	1	2	2	39	2	93	10	0	5	8	.385	0	35-44	3	4.33	4.67
2013 2 Tms	NL	75	0	0	16	65.0	289	73	32	29	10	4	1	2	26	3	65	5	0	7	7	.500	0	0-7	19	5.25	4.02
2014 2 Tms	NL	62	0	0	28	54.2	243	43	26	24	6	3	4	2	36	3	63	5	0	2	4	.333	0	10-13	2	3.96	3.95
2015 Col	NL	60	0	0	43	55.2	250	56	27	26	4	0	2	0	32	4	62	1	0	4	5	.444	0	25-31	2	4.45	4.20
13 Mil	NL	62	0	0	13	54.2	245	62	29	27	10	3	1	1	23	3	54	5	0	6	7	.462	0	0-6	19	5.53	4.45
13 StL	NL	13	0	0	3	10.1	44	11	3	2	0	1	0	1	3	0	11	0	0	1	0	1.000	0	0-1	0	3.75	1.74
14 Cle	AL	49	0	0	24	43.2	196	34	21	19	6	3	3	1	30	3	51	4	0	2	3	.400	0	10-13	2	4.11	3.92
14 Pit	NL	13	0	0	4	11.0	47	9	5	5	0	0	1	1	6	0	12	1	0	0	1	.000	0	0-0	3	3.33	4.09
Postseason		12	0	0	8	12.2	51	7	2	2	1	0	0	0	6	0	18	0	0	1	0	1.000	0	3-4	0	1.91	1.42
7 ML YEARS		403	0	0	253	384.0	1669	339	166	150	35	11	12	7	191	17	454	34	0	28	28	.500	0	141-171	29	3.70	3.52

Erick Aybar

Bats: B **Throws:** R **Pos:** SS-154;PH-2;DH-1   EYE-barr   **Ht:** 5'10" **Wt:** 180 **Born:** 1/14/1984 **Age:** 32

						BATTING													RUNNING			AVERAGES			
Year Team	Lg	G	AB	H	2B	3B	HR	(Hm	Rd)	TB	R	RBI	RC	TBB	IBB	SO	HBP	SH	SF	SB	CS	GDP	Avg	OBP	Slg	OPS
2006 LAA	AL	34	40	10	1	1	0	(0	0)	13	5	2	4	0	0	8	0	0	0	1	0	1	.250	.250	.325	.575
2007 LAA	AL	79	194	46	5	1	1	(0	1)	56	18	19	16	10	0	32	2	3	2	4	4	8	.237	.279	.289	.568
2008 LAA	AL	98	346	96	18	5	3	(2	1)	133	53	39	49	14	0	45	5	9	1	7	2	2	.277	.314	.384	.699
2009 LAA	AL	137	504	157	23	9	5	(2	3)	213	70	58	73	30	1	54	5	12	9	14	7	9	.312	.353	.423	.776
2010 LAA	AL	138	534	135	18	4	5	(3	2)	176	69	29	51	35	1	81	7	11	2	22	8	7	.253	.306	.330	.636
2011 LAA	AL	143	556	155	33	8	10	(2	8)	234	71	59	72	31	1	68	6	9	3	30	6	13	.279	.322	.421	.743
2012 LAA	AL	141	517	150	31	5	8	(4	4)	215	67	45	63	22	1	61	5	7	2	20	4	11	.290	.324	.416	.740
2013 LAA	AL	138	550	149	33	5	6	(4	2)	210	68	54	61	23	1	59	3	8	5	12	7	14	.271	.301	.382	.683
2014 LAA	AL	156	589	164	30	4	7	(2	5)	223	77	68	74	36	4	62	5	3	8	16	9	10	.278	.321	.379	.700
2015 LAA	AL	156	597	161	30	1	3	(1	2)	202	74	44	60	25	1	73	4	7	5	15	6	12	.270	.301	.338	.639
Postseason		17	61	16	3	1	0	(0	0)	21	4	4	7	1	0	5	0	4	0	4	0	2	.262	.274	.344	.618
10 ML YEARS		1220	4427	1223	222	43	48	(20	28)	1675	572	417	523	226	10	543	42	69	33	141	53	87	.276	.315	.378	.694

Burke Badenhop

Pitches: R Bats: R Pos: RP-68 BADE-en-hopp Ht: 6'5" Wt: 210 Born: 2/8/1983 Age: 33

		HOW MUCH HE PITCHED			WHAT HE GAVE UP						THE RESULTS								
Year Team	Lg	G GS CG GF	IP	BFP	H	R	ER	HR SH SF HB	TBB IBB	SO	WP Bk	W	L	Pct	Sh	Sv-Op	Hld	ERC	ERA
2008 Fla	NL	13 8 0 2	47.1	218	55	34	32	7 2 2 3	21 1	35	2 0	2	3	.400	0	0-0	0	5.74	6.08
2009 Fla	NL	35 2 0 7	72.0	303	71	32	30	5 3 2 1	24 4	57	1 0	7	4	.636	0	0-1	2	3.53	3.75
2010 Fla	NL	53 0 0 16	67.2	281	62	33	30	5 5 1 2	21 5	47	1 0	2	5	.286	0	1-3	8	3.12	3.99
2011 Fla	NL	50 0 0 15	63.2	276	65	29	29	1 1 2 4	24 4	51	4 0	2	3	.400	0	1-1	5	3.65	4.10
2012 TB	AL	66 0 0 14	62.1	262	63	24	21	6 2 4 1	12 5	42	1 0	3	2	.600	0	0-0	5	3.19	3.03
2013 Mil	NL	63 0 0 23	62.1	254	62	32	24	6 7 2 0	12 4	42	2 0	2	3	.400	0	1-4	5	3.16	3.47
2014 Bos	AL	70 0 0 11	70.2	289	70	20	18	1 4 3 2	19 5	40	2 0	0	3	.000	0	1-4	13	3.03	2.29
2015 Cin	NL	68 0 0 17	66.1	285	71	30	29	4 2 3 0	20 4	36	0 0	2	4	.333	0	0-2	7	3.69	3.93
8 ML YEARS		418 10 0 105	512.1	2168	519	234	213	35 26 19 13	153 32	350	13 0	20	27	.426	0	4-15	45	3.55	3.74

Javier Baez

Bats: R Throws: R Pos: 2B-17;3B-11;SS-8;PH-6;1B-1 BYE-ezz Ht: 6'0" Wt: 190 Born: 12/1/1992 Age: 23

		BATTING												RUNNING		AVERAGES			
Year Team	Lg	G	AB	H	2B	3B	HR	(Hm Rd)	TB	R	RBI	RC	TBB IBB	SO	HBP SH SF	SB	CS	GDP	Avg	OBP	Slg	OPS
2012 2 Tms	Low	80	293	86	13	6	16	(- -)	159	50	46	57	14 1	69	11 0 3	24	5	4	.294	.346	.543	.888
2013 Dytona	A+	76	299	82	19	4	17	(- -)	160	59	57	56	21 0	78	11 0 6	12	2	8	.274	.338	.535	.873
2013 Tenn	AA	54	218	64	15	0	20	(- -)	139	39	54	48	19 2	69	0 0 3	8	2	3	.294	.346	.638	.983
2014 Iowa	AAA	104	388	101	24	2	23	(- -)	198	64	80	65	34 3	130	5 0 7	16	8	14	.260	.323	.510	.833
2015 Iowa	AAA	70	281	91	14	2	13	(- -)	148	49	61	58	21 0	76	8 1 2	17	3	6	.324	.385	.527	.911
2014 ChC	NL	52	213	36	6	0	9	(3 6)	69	25	20	12	15 0	95	1 0 0	5	1	5	.169	.227	.324	.551
2015 ChC	NL	28	76	22	6	0	1	(1 0)	31	4	4	5	4 1	24	0 0 0	1	2	0	.289	.325	.408	.733
2 ML YEARS		80	289	58	12	0	10	(4 6)	100	29	24	17	19 1	119	1 0 0	6	3	5	.201	.252	.346	.598

Pedro Baez

Pitches: R Bats: R Pos: RP-52 BYE-ezz Ht: 6'0" Wt: 230 Born: 3/11/1988 Age: 28

		HOW MUCH HE PITCHED			WHAT HE GAVE UP						THE RESULTS								
Year Team	Lg	G GS CG GF	IP	BFP	H	R	ER	HR SH SF HB	TBB IBB	SO	WP Bk	W	L	Pct	Sh	Sv-Op	Hld	ERC	ERA
2013 Rcuca	A+	32 0 0 13	34.2	163	41	17	14	3 0 5 4	15 1	32	1 0	2	2	.500	0	2--	-	5.48	3.63
2013 Chatt	AA	16 0 0 3	23.1	102	26	13	11	3 1 1 0	8 0	23	2 1	1	1	.500	0	0--	-	4.69	4.24
2014 Chatt	AA	17 0 0 13	19.1	82	15	7	6	0 0 0 1	9 1	18	2 0	2	1	.667	0	6--	-	2.53	2.79
2014 Albq	AAA	23 0 0 15	22.2	97	27	12	12	4 0 2 2	4 0	20	2 1	0	0	-	0	6--	-	5.29	4.76
2014 LAD	NL	20 0 0 8	24.0	92	16	7	7	3 1 1 0	5 1	18	0 0	0	0	-	0	0-0	5	1.79	2.63
2015 LAD	NL	52 0 0 8	51.0	208	47	22	19	4 3 3 1	11 1	60	1 1	4	2	.667	0	0-3	11	2.87	3.35
Postseason		2 0 0 0	2.1	10	1	2	2	1 0 0 1	1 0	2	0 0	0	0	-	0	0-0	0	4.86	7.71
2 ML YEARS		72 0 0 16	75.0	300	63	29	26	7 4 4 1	16 2	78	1 1	4	2	.667	0	0-3	16	2.51	3.12

Andrew Bailey

Pitches: R Bats: R Pos: RP-10 Ht: 6'3" Wt: 235 Born: 5/31/1984 Age: 32

		HOW MUCH HE PITCHED			WHAT HE GAVE UP						THE RESULTS								
Year Team	Lg	G GS CG GF	IP	BFP	H	R	ER	HR SH SF HB	TBB IBB	SO	WP Bk	W	L	Pct	Sh	Sv-Op	Hld	ERC	ERA
2015 2 Tms*	Low	8 0 0 0	8.1	37	8	6	3	2 1 0 0	2 0	12	0 0	2	0	1.000	0	0--	-	3.80	3.24
2015 Trntn*	AA	11 0 0 6	14.1	54	6	1	1	0 0 0 0	6 0	17	1 0	1	0	1.000	0	2--	-	1.05	0.63
2015 S-WB*	AAA	9 0 0 7	12.1	50	12	3	3	1 0 0 0	3 0	13	1 0	0	0	-	0	4--	-	3.28	2.19
2009 Oak	AL	68 0 0 54	83.1	323	49	17	17	5 3 2 0	24 3	91	6 0	6	3	.667	0	26-30	2	1.44	1.84
2010 Oak	AL	47 0 0 42	49.0	189	34	8	8	3 2 3 0	13 1	42	0 0	1	3	.250	0	25-28	1	1.82	1.47
2011 Oak	AL	42 0 0 37	41.2	170	34	18	15	3 1 1 0	12 2	41	0 0	0	4	.000	0	24-26	1	2.42	3.24
2012 Bos	AL	19 0 0 13	15.1	74	21	12	12	2 0 0 0	8 2	14	0 1	1	1	.500	0	6-9	1	6.73	7.04
2013 Bos	AL	30 0 0 17	28.2	116	23	12	12	7 1 0 0	12 0	39	0 0	3	1	.750	0	8-13	8	4.13	3.77
2015 NYY	AL	10 0 0 3	8.2	41	10	8	8	2 0 2 0	5 1	6	0 0	0	1	.000	0	0-0	0	6.39	8.31
6 ML YEARS		216 0 0 166	226.2	913	171	75	72	22 7 8 0	74 9	233	6 1	11	13	.458	0	89-106	12	2.44	2.86

Homer Bailey

Pitches: R Bats: R Pos: SP-2 Ht: 6'4" Wt: 225 Born: 5/3/1986 Age: 30

		HOW MUCH HE PITCHED			WHAT HE GAVE UP						THE RESULTS								
Year Team	Lg	G GS CG GF	IP	BFP	H	R	ER	HR SH SF HB	TBB IBB	SO	WP Bk	W	L	Pct	Sh	Sv-Op	Hld	ERC	ERA
2007 Cin	NL	9 9 0 0	45.1	205	43	29	29	7 1 6 3	28 1	28	1 1	4	2	.667	0	0-0	0	4.61	5.76
2008 Cin	NL	8 8 0 0	36.1	180	59	36	32	8 5 2 0	17 1	18	4 1	0	6	.000	0	0-0	0	9.31	7.93
2009 Cin	NL	20 20 0 0	113.1	496	115	61	57	12 4 4 3	52 1	86	6 0	8	5	.615	0	0-0	0	4.56	4.53
2010 Cin	NL	19 19 1 0	109.0	465	109	55	54	11 2 1 3	40 6	100	3 1	4	3	.571	1	0-0	0	4.01	4.46
2011 Cin	NL	22 22 0 0	132.0	561	136	68	65	18 4 4 5	33 2	106	4 0	9	7	.563	0	0-0	0	4.01	4.43
2012 Cin	NL	33 33 2 0	208.0	874	206	97	85	26 5 5 8	52 3	168	3 0	13	10	.565	1	0-0	0	3.73	3.68
2013 Cin	NL	32 32 2 0	209.0	849	181	88	81	20 8 4 10	54 2	199	5 2	11	12	.478	1	0-0	0	2.99	3.49
2014 Cin	NL	23 23 1 0	145.2	604	134	60	60	16 5 4 7	45 1	124	5 1	9	5	.643	0	0-0	0	3.57	3.71
2015 Cin	NL	2 2 0 0	11.1	51	16	7	7	3 0 0 0	4 2	3	0 0	0	1	.000	0	0-0	0	7.64	5.56
Postseason		2 1 0 0	9.0	32	3	1	1	0 1 1 1	1 0	12	0 0	0	0	-	0	0-0	0	0.52	1.00
9 ML YEARS		168 168 6 0	1010.0	4285	999	501	470	117 34 30 39	325 19	832	31 6	58	51	.532	4	0-0	0	3.96	4.19

Jeff Baker

Bats: R **Throws:** R **Pos:** PH-23;1B-17;2B-1;3B-1;LF-1;DH-1   **Ht:** 6'2" **Wt:** 220 **Born:** 6/21/1981 **Age:** 35

Year	Team	Lg	G	AB	H	2B	3B	HR	(Hm	Rd)	TB	R	RBI	RC	TBB	IBB	SO	HBP	SH	SF	SB	CS	GDP	Avg	OBP	Slg	OPS
2005	Col	NL	12	38	8	4	0	1	(1	0)	15	6	4	4	5	0	12	0	0	0	0	0	1	.211	.302	.395	.697
2006	Col	NL	18	57	21	7	2	5	(4	1)	47	13	21	17	1	0	14	0	0	0	2	0	0	.368	.379	.825	1.204
2007	Col	NL	85	144	32	2	2	4	(4	0)	50	17	12	8	13	1	40	2	0	0	0	0	7	.222	.296	.347	.643
2008	Col	NL	104	299	80	22	1	12	(8	4)	140	55	48	40	26	2	85	1	1	6	4	0	5	.268	.322	.468	.791
2009	2 Tms	NL	81	226	65	15	2	4	(3	1)	96	27	24	28	18	0	53	2	0	2	1	0	8	.288	.343	.425	.768
2010	ChC	NL	79	206	56	13	2	4	(3	1)	85	29	21	21	16	0	50	1	0	1	1	0	6	.272	.326	.413	.739
2011	ChC	NL	81	201	54	12	1	3	(1	2)	77	20	23	20	10	0	46	0	0	1	0	0	8	.269	.302	.383	.685
2012	3 Tms		83	188	45	12	1	4	(1	3)	71	18	25	18	11	1	48	0	0	2	4	1	7	.239	.279	.378	.656
2013	Tex	AL	74	154	43	8	0	11	(4	7)	84	21	21	26	18	1	48	2	0	1	1	0	5	.279	.360	.545	.905
2014	Mia	NL	90	208	55	10	4	3	(3	0)	82	27	28	27	13	1	51	1	0	3	1	0	8	.264	.307	.394	.701
2015	Mia	NL	41	72	15	3	0	3	(2	1)	27	11	8	5	8	0	25	0	0	0	0	0	0	.208	.288	.375	.663
09	Col	NL	12	23	3	0	1	0	(0	0)	5	0	3	0	1	0	7	0	0	0	1	0	3	.130	.167	.217	.384
09	Col	NL	69	203	62	15	1	4	(3	1)	91	27	21	28	17	0	46	2	0	2	0	0	5	.305	.362	.448	.810
12	ChC	NL	54	134	36	10	1	4	(1	3)	60	16	20	17	8	0	28	0	0	0	4	1	4	.269	.306	.448	.753
12	Det	AL	15	35	7	2	0	0	(0	0)	9	1	4	1	2	0	10	0	0	0	0	0	3	.200	.243	.257	.500
12	Atl	NL	14	19	2	0	0	0	(0	0)	2	1	1	0	1	1	10	0	0	0	0	0	0	.105	.150	.105	.255
	Postseason		4	4	2	0	0	0	(0	0)	2	0	1	1	0	0	1	0	0	0	0	0	0	.500	.500	.500	1.000
	11 ML YEARS		748	1793	474	108	15	54	(34	20)	774	244	235	214	139	6	472	9	1	16	14	1	55	.264	.318	.432	.750

Scott Baker

Pitches: R **Bats:** R **Pos:** SP-2   **Ht:** 6'4" **Wt:** 215 **Born:** 9/19/1981 **Age:** 34

Year	Team	Lg	G	GS	CG	GF	IP	BFP	H	R	ER	HR	SH	SF	HB	TBB	IBB	SO	WP	Bk	W	L	Pct	Sh	Sv-Op	Hld	ERC	ERA
2015	OkCity*	AAA	13	13	2	0	77.0	297	64	31	29	6	3	4	2	7	0	51	3	0	7	3	.700	1	0- -	-	2.06	3.39
2005	Min	AL	10	9	0	0	53.2	217	48	21	20	5	2	2	0	14	0	32	0	0	3	3	.500	0	0-0	1	2.97	3.35
2006	Min	AL	16	16	0	0	83.1	377	114	63	59	17	2	4	3	16	1	62	0	0	5	8	.385	0	0-0	0	6.26	6.37
2007	Min	AL	24	23	2	0	143.2	606	162	70	68	15	6	2	5	29	4	102	0	0	9	9	.500	1	0-0	1	4.19	4.26
2008	Min	AL	28	28	0	0	172.1	703	161	66	66	20	2	3	6	42	2	141	6	0	11	4	.733	0	0-0	0	3.31	3.45
2009	Min	AL	33	33	1	0	200.0	828	190	99	97	28	1	6	4	48	1	162	4	0	15	9	.625	1	0-0	0	3.51	4.37
2010	Min	AL	29	29	0	0	170.1	725	186	87	85	23	1	4	6	43	0	148	7	0	12	9	.571	0	0-0	0	4.43	4.49
2011	Min	AL	23	21	1	2	134.2	548	126	50	47	15	1	2	4	32	2	123	4	0	8	6	.571	0	0-0	0	3.32	3.14
2013	ChC	NL	3	3	0	0	15.0	57	9	6	6	3	1	0	0	4	0	6	0	0	0	0	-	0	0-0	0	2.13	3.60
2014	Tex	AL	25	8	0	13	80.2	332	82	49	49	15	0	3	2	14	3	55	0	0	3	4	.429	0	0-0	0	3.90	5.47
2015	LAD	AL	2	2	0	0	11.0	45	11	7	7	4	0	0	0	3	0	8	1	0	0	1	.000	0	0-0	0	5.48	5.73
	Postseason		1	0	0	0	2.1	10	3	1	1	1	0	0	0	0	0	2	0	0	0	0	-	0	0-0	0	6.14	3.86
	10 ML YEARS		193	172	4	15	1064.2	4438	1089	518	504	145	16	26	27	245	13	839	22	0	66	53	.555	2	0-0	2	3.89	4.26

Collin Balester

Pitches: R **Bats:** R **Pos:** RP-15   **Ht:** 6'4" **Wt:** 190 **Born:** 6/6/1986 **Age:** 30

Year	Team	Lg	G	GS	CG	GF	IP	BFP	H	R	ER	HR	SH	SF	HB	TBB	IBB	SO	WP	Bk	W	L	Pct	Sh	Sv-Op	Hld	ERC	ERA
2015	Indy*	AAA	8	0	0	0	14.2	63	12	6	5	1	0	2	0	5	0	8	1	0	0	0	-	0	0- -	-	2.53	3.07
2015	Altna*	AA	13	0	0	10	20.1	79	14	4	4	1	1	1	1	6	0	14	1	1	1	0	1.000	0	4- -	-	2.03	1.77
2015	Lsvlle*	AAA	21	0	0	16	22.0	83	16	5	5	1	0	0	0	3	0	13	2	0	0	0	-	0	7- -	-	1.54	2.05
2008	Was	NL	15	15	0	0	80.0	358	92	53	49	12	2	3	6	28	1	50	4	0	3	7	.300	0	0-0	0	5.40	5.51
2009	Was	NL	7	7	0	0	30.1	135	34	24	23	10	0	0	0	14	0	20	0	0	1	4	.200	0	0-0	0	6.85	6.82
2010	Was	NL	17	0	0	8	21.0	89	15	6	6	2	2	0	2	11	1	28	4	0	1	4	.200	0	0-0	0	3.26	2.57
2011	Was	NL	23	0	0	9	35.2	159	38	21	18	7	1	1	1	14	0	34	2	1	1	4	.200	0	0-1	2	5.16	4.54
2012	Det	NL	11	0	0	5	18.0	83	14	14	13	5	0	2	3	11	1	12	4	0	2	0	1.000	0	0-0	0	5.37	6.50
2015	Cin	NL	15	0	0	5	15.2	77	17	13	13	3	0	1	1	13	0	13	1	0	1	1	.500	0	0-0	2	7.34	7.47
	6 ML YEARS		88	22	0	24	200.2	901	210	131	122	39	5	7	13	91	3	157	15	1	8	17	.320	0	0-1	4	5.48	5.47

Grant Balfour

Pitches: R **Bats:** R **Pos:** RP-6   BAL-fore   **Ht:** 6'2" **Wt:** 200 **Born:** 12/30/1977 **Age:** 38

Year	Team	Lg	G	GS	CG	GF	IP	BFP	H	R	ER	HR	SH	SF	HB	TBB	IBB	SO	WP	Bk	W	L	Pct	Sh	Sv-Op	Hld	ERC	ERA
2015	Drham*	AAA	8	0	0	2	9.2	42	9	3	3	1	0	0	0	4	0	11	1	0	0	0	-	0	0- -	-	3.69	2.79
2001	Min	AL	2	0	0	1	2.2	14	3	4	4	2	1	1	0	3	0	2	0	0	0	0	-	0	0-0	0	13.78	13.50
2003	Min	AL	17	1	0	6	26.0	115	23	12	12	4	2	1	0	14	2	30	0	0	1	0	1.000	0	0-1	1	4.14	4.15
2004	Min	AL	36	0	0	14	39.1	172	35	19	19	4	2	0	2	21	1	42	3	0	4	1	.800	0	0-1	4	4.16	4.35
2007	2 Tms		25	0	0	8	24.2	121	30	21	21	2	2	3	1	20	0	30	0	0	1	2	.333	0	0-0	1	7.15	7.66
2008	TB	AL	51	0	0	12	58.1	224	28	10	10	3	3	3	0	24	1	82	2	0	6	2	.750	0	4-5	14	1.38	1.54
2009	TB	AL	73	0	0	15	67.1	289	59	38	36	6	1	2	2	33	0	69	1	0	5	4	.556	0	4-9	18	3.79	4.81
2010	TB	AL	57	0	0	8	55.1	222	43	16	14	3	2	4	0	17	2	56	4	1	2	1	.667	0	0-1	16	2.24	2.28
2011	Oak	AL	62	0	0	15	62.0	242	44	17	17	8	4	0	0	20	1	59	0	0	5	2	.714	0	2-7	26	2.49	2.47
2012	Oak	AL	75	0	0	34	74.2	289	41	21	21	4	0	3	1	28	2	72	2	0	3	2	.600	0	24-26	15	1.55	2.53
2013	Oak	AL	65	0	0	55	62.2	262	48	20	18	7	2	0	0	27	2	72	9	0	1	3	.250	0	38-41	0	2.92	2.59
2014	TB	AL	65	0	0	34	62.0	270	49	34	34	3	1	1	1	41	3	57	4	0	2	6	.250	0	12-15	11	3.52	4.91
2015	TB	AL	6	0	0	1	4.1	21	3	3	3	1	0	1	1	4	0	0	1	0	0	0	-	0	0-0	0	6.24	6.23
07	Mil	NL	3	0	0	2	2.2	18	4	6	6	1	1	0	1	4	0	3	0	0	0	2	.000	0	0-0	0	15.83	20.25
07	TB	AL	22	0	0	6	22.0	103	26	15	15	1	1	3	0	16	0	27	0	0	1	0	1.000	0	0-0	1	6.19	6.14
	Postseason		20	0	0	8	19.2	83	16	7	7	2	1	1	0	10	4	15	1	0	1	1	.500	0	2-2	2	3.41	3.20
	12 ML YEARS		534	1	0	203	539.2	2241	406	215	209	47	15	19	8	252	14	571	26	1	30	23	.566	0	84-106	107	2.94	3.49

Jett Bandy

Bats: R Throws: R Pos: C-1;PH-1   Ht: 6'4" Wt: 235 Born: 3/26/1990 Age: 26

Year Team	Lg	G	AB	H	2B	3B	HR	(Hm	Rd)	TB	R	RBI	RC	TBB	IBB	SO	HBP	SH	SF	SB	CS	GDP	Avg	OBP	Slg	OPS
2011 2 Tms	Low	48	182	56	19	0	4	(-	-)	87	34	31	35	10	0	23	18	0	4	2	0	5	.308	.393	.478	.871
2012 InldEm	A+	94	324	80	22	1	7	(-	-)	125	42	46	42	20	1	51	15	3	3	1	1	5	.247	.318	.386	.703
2013 Ark	AA	78	245	59	17	2	4	(-	-)	92	26	28	29	14	0	39	9	1	3	0	1	5	.241	.303	.376	.678
2014 Ark	AA	93	312	78	12	0	13	(-	-)	129	38	40	47	33	2	63	15	1	2	2	4	7	.250	.348	.413	.762
2015 Salt Lk	AAA	87	309	90	21	0	11	(-	-)	144	47	60	51	16	0	63	13	1	5	0	0	8	.291	.347	.466	.813
2015 LAA	AL	2	2	1	0	0	1	(0	1)	4	1	1	1	0	0	0	0	0	0	0	0	0	.500	.500	2.000	2.500

Manny Banuelos

Pitches: L Bats: R Pos: SP-6; RP-1   ban-yoo-WAY-lohss   Ht: 5'10" Wt: 205 Born: 3/13/1991 Age: 25

Year Team	Lg	G	GS	CG	GF	IP	BFP	H	R	ER	HR	SH	SF	HB	TBB	IBB	SO	WP	Bk	W	L	Pct	Sh	Sv-Op	Hld	ERC	ERA
2011 Trntn	AA	20	20	0	0	95.1	422	94	46	38	7	2	4	6	52	0	94	9	0	4	5	.444	0	0--	-	4.70	3.59
2011 S-WB	AAA	7	7	1	0	34.1	155	36	17	16	2	2	3	1	19	0	31	2	0	2	2	.500	1	0--	-	4.77	4.19
2012 S-WB	AAA	6	6	0	0	24.0	110	29	13	12	2	0	2	1	10	0	22	1	1	0	2	.000	0	0--	-	5.36	4.50
2014 Tampa	A+	5	5	0	0	12.1	50	10	4	4	0	0	0	1	2	0	14	1	0	0	0	-	0	0--	-	1.88	2.92
2014 Trntn	AA	17	16	0	0	49.0	206	48	29	25	8	0	2	3	19	0	44	8	0	1	3	.250	0	0--	-	3.67	4.59
2015 Gwnntt	AAA	16	16	1	0	84.2	350	64	24	21	2	3	3	6	40	0	69	4	0	6	2	.750	1	0--	-	2.85	2.23
2015 Atl	NL	7	6	0	0	26.1	121	30	17	15	4	0	0	3	12	0	19	1	0	1	4	.200	0	0-0	0	6.01	5.13

Clint Barmes

Bats: R Throws: R Pos: SS-89;PH-26;PR-3;1B-1   BAR-mess   Ht: 6'1" Wt: 200 Born: 3/6/1979 Age: 37

Year Team	Lg	G	AB	H	2B	3B	HR	(Hm	Rd)	TB	R	RBI	RC	TBB	IBB	SO	HBP	SH	SF	SB	CS	GDP	Avg	OBP	Slg	OPS
2003 Col	NL	12	25	8	2	0	0	(0	0)	10	2	2	3	0	0	10	2	0	1	0	0	0	.320	.357	.400	.757
2004 Col	NL	20	71	20	3	1	2	(0	2)	31	14	10	12	3	0	10	1	2	0	0	1	2	.282	.320	.437	.757
2005 Col	NL	81	350	101	19	1	10	(7	3)	152	55	46	49	16	1	36	6	4	1	6	4	4	.289	.330	.434	.764
2006 Col	NL	131	478	105	26	4	7	(3	4)	160	57	56	47	22	6	72	9	19	7	5	4	2	.220	.264	.335	.598
2007 Col	NL	27	37	8	3	0	0	(0	0)	11	5	1	1	1	1	13	0	1	0	0	0	1	.216	.237	.297	.534
2008 Col	NL	107	393	114	25	6	11	(8	3)	184	47	44	54	17	0	69	2	4	1	13	4	9	.290	.322	.468	.790
2009 Col	NL	154	550	135	32	3	23	(13	10)	242	69	76	63	31	2	121	10	6	7	12	10	6	.245	.294	.440	.734
2010 Col	NL	133	387	91	21	0	8	(4	4)	136	43	50	43	35	10	66	5	2	3	3	2	5	.235	.305	.351	.656
2011 Hou	NL	123	446	109	27	0	12	(5	7)	172	47	39	46	38	2	88	7	2	2	3	1	9	.244	.312	.386	.698
2012 Pit	NL	144	455	104	16	1	8	(3	5)	146	34	45	38	20	3	106	8	8	2	0	2	9	.229	.272	.321	.593
2013 Pit	NL	108	304	64	15	0	5	(1	4)	94	22	23	20	14	3	70	2	9	1	0	0	5	.211	.249	.309	.558
2014 Pit	NL	48	102	25	5	0	0	(0	0)	30	15	7	7	9	2	18	4	0	1	1	1	2	.245	.328	.294	.622
2015 SD	NL	98	207	48	14	1	3	(2	1)	73	24	16	17	10	2	55	4	3	0	0	1	0	.232	.281	.353	.633
Postseason		10	25	3	0	0	0	(0	0)	3	0	0	1	0	0	3	0	1	0	0	0	0	.120	.120	.120	.240
13 ML YEARS		1186	3805	932	208	17	89	(46	43)	1441	434	415	400	216	32	734	60	60	26	43	30	54	.245	.294	.379	.673

Austin Barnes

Bats: R Throws: R Pos: C-11;PH-6;PR-3;2B-1;3B-1   Ht: 5'10" Wt: 185 Born: 12/28/1989 Age: 26

Year Team	Lg	G	AB	H	2B	3B	HR	(Hm	Rd)	TB	R	RBI	RC	TBB	IBB	SO	HBP	SH	SF	SB	CS	GDP	Avg	OBP	Slg	OPS
2011 Jmstwn	A-	57	219	63	13	0	1	(-	-)	79	33	19	32	25	0	22	4	1	1	6	1	8	.288	.369	.361	.730
2012 Grnsbr	A	123	478	152	36	3	12	(-	-)	230	76	65	96	59	0	61	9	17	3	9	2	14	.318	.401	.481	.882
2013 Jupiter	A+	98	350	91	15	1	4	(-	-)	120	42	38	51	52	0	59	10	0	5	5	2	15	.260	.367	.343	.710
2013 Jaxnvl	AA	19	62	21	2	2	1	(-	-)	30	10	7	13	12	0	10	0	0	0	0	0	3	.339	.446	.484	.930
2014 Jupiter	A+	44	180	57	11	2	1	(-	-)	75	24	14	29	19	1	25	1	0	3	3	3	7	.317	.385	.417	.802
2014 Jaxnvl	AA	78	284	84	20	2	12	(-	-)	144	56	43	63	50	0	36	6	3	5	8	0	7	.296	.406	.507	.913
2015 OkCity	AAA	81	292	92	17	2	9	(-	-)	140	40	42	58	35	1	36	3	1	4	12	2	7	.315	.389	.479	.869
2015 LAD	NL	20	29	6	2	0	0	(0	0)	8	4	1	3	6	0	6	1	1	0	1	0	2	.207	.361	.276	.637

Brandon Barnes

Bats: R Throws: R Pos: LF-75;RF-21;PH-13;CF-11;PR-3   Ht: 6'2" Wt: 210 Born: 5/15/1986 Age: 30

Year Team	Lg	G	AB	H	2B	3B	HR	(Hm	Rd)	TB	R	RBI	RC	TBB	IBB	SO	HBP	SH	SF	SB	CS	GDP	Avg	OBP	Slg	OPS
2015 Albq*	AAA	33	132	27	6	0	5	(-	-)	48	19	12	13	10	0	34	1	0	0	7	3	1	.205	.266	.364	.629
2012 Hou	NL	43	98	20	3	0	1	(0	1)	26	8	7	4	5	0	29	1	1	0	1	1	1	.204	.250	.265	.515
2013 Hou	AL	136	408	98	17	1	8	(7	1)	141	46	41	47	21	0	127	8	6	2	11	11	5	.240	.289	.346	.635
2014 Col	NL	132	292	75	17	4	8	(7	1)	124	37	27	26	15	0	100	0	6	0	5	4	11	.257	.293	.425	.718
2015 Col	NL	106	255	64	13	2	2	(1	1)	87	30	17	24	21	3	67	3	1	1	4	2	6	.251	.314	.341	.655
4 ML YEARS		417	1053	257	50	7	19	(15	4)	378	121	92	101	62	3	323	12	14	3	21	18	23	.244	.293	.359	.652

Matt Barnes

Pitches: R Bats: R Pos: RP-30; SP-2   Ht: 6'4" Wt: 210 Born: 6/17/1990 Age: 26

Year Team	Lg	G	GS	CG	GF	IP	BFP	H	R	ER	HR	SH	SF	HB	TBB	IBB	SO	WP	Bk	W	L	Pct	Sh	Sv-Op	Hld	ERC	ERA
2012 2 Tms	Low	25	25	0	0	119.2	480	97	43	38	6	2	8	9	29	0	133	6	2	7	5	.583	1	0--	-	2.49	2.86
2013 PortInd	AA	24	24	0	0	108.0	480	112	62	52	11	4	2	4	46	0	135	7	0	5	10	.333	0	0--	-	4.50	4.33
2014 Pwtckt	AAA	23	22	0	0	127.2	538	119	60	56	8	4	3	3	46	0	103	6	0	8	9	.471	0	0--	-	3.40	3.95

			HOW MUCH HE PITCHED						WHAT HE GAVE UP									THE RESULTS						
Year	Team	Lg	G	GS	CG	GF	IP	BFP	H	R	ER	HR	SH	SF	HB	TBB	IBB	SO	WP	Bk	W	L	Pct	Sh	Sv-Op	Hld	ERC	ERA
2015	Pwtckt*	AAA	17	5	0	2	37.2	170	36	17	17	3	1	3	1	22	0	41	2	1	1	1	.500	0	0- -	-	4.45	4.06
2014	Bos	AL	5	0	0	3	9.0	39	11	4	4	1	0	1	0	2	0	8	0	0	0	0	-	0	0-0	0	4.72	4.00
2015	Bos	AL	32	2	0	7	43.0	199	56	28	26	9	2	0	2	15	0	39	4	0	3	4	.429	0	0-0	3	6.66	5.44
	2 ML YEARS		37	2	0	10	52.0	238	67	32	30	10	2	1	2	17	0	47	4	0	3	4	.429	0	0-0	3	6.31	5.19

Darwin Barney

Bats: R Throws: R Pos: 2B-15;3B-1;SS-1;PR-1   Ht: 5'10" Wt: 180 Born: 11/8/1985 Age: 30

			BATTING																		RUNNING			AVERAGES			
Year	Team	Lg	G	AB	H	2B	3B	HR	(Hm	Rd)	TB	R	RBI	RC	TBB	IBB	SO	HBP	SH	SF	SB	CS	GDP	Avg	OBP	Slg	OPS
2015	OkCity*	AAA	96	347	96	15	0	4	(-	-)	123	52	31	42	22	1	44	4	4	2	7	4	7	.277	.325	.354	.680
2010	ChC	NL	30	79	19	4	0	0	(0	0)	23	12	2	6	6	0	12	0	0	0	0	0	0	.241	.294	.291	.585
2011	ChC	NL	143	529	146	23	6	2	(2	0)	187	66	43	60	22	2	67	8	7	4	9	2	14	.276	.313	.353	.666
2012	ChC	NL	156	548	139	26	4	7	(7	0)	194	73	44	60	33	1	58	3	3	1	6	1	11	.254	.299	.354	.653
2013	ChC	NL	141	501	104	25	1	7	(4	3)	152	49	41	30	36	5	64	6	4	6	4	2	22	.208	.266	.303	.569
2014	2 Tms	NL	94	237	57	11	2	3	(2	1)	81	24	23	27	17	2	34	4	2	2	1	0	1	.241	.300	.342	.642
2015	2 Tms		17	27	7	1	0	2	(0	2)	14	4	4	4	1	0	2	0	2	0	0	0	0	.259	.286	.519	.804
14	ChC	NL	72	204	47	10	2	2	(2	0)	67	18	16	19	9	2	31	1	2	1	1	0	1	.230	.265	.328	.594
14	LAD	NL	22	33	10	1	0	1	(0	1)	14	6	7	8	8	0	3	3	0	1	0	0	0	.303	.467	.424	.891
15	LAD	NL	2	4	0	0	0	0	(0	0)	0	0	0	0	0	0	0	0	0	0	0	0	0	.000	.000	.000	.000
15	Tor	AL	15	23	7	1	0	2	(0	2)	14	4	4	4	1	0	2	0	2	0	0	0	0	.304	.333	.609	.942
	6 ML YEARS		581	1921	472	90	13	21	(15	6)	651	228	157	187	115	10	237	21	18	13	20	5	48	.246	.294	.339	.633

Tucker Barnhart

Bats: B Throws: R Pos: C-73;PH-9;RF-1   Ht: 5'11" Wt: 190 Born: 1/7/1991 Age: 25

			BATTING																		RUNNING			AVERAGES			
Year	Team	Lg	G	AB	H	2B	3B	HR	(Hm	Rd)	TB	R	RBI	RC	TBB	IBB	SO	HBP	SH	SF	SB	CS	GDP	Avg	OBP	Slg	OPS
2011	Dayton	A	97	326	89	24	2	3	(-	-)	126	47	43	46	37	0	59	1	3	5	2	1	9	.273	.344	.387	.731
2012	Bkrsfld	A+	59	198	55	12	1	4	(-	-)	81	26	22	31	29	0	45	1	2	1	0	2	5	.278	.371	.409	.780
2012	Pnscla	AA	41	130	26	4	1	2	(-	-)	38	10	12	9	11	0	22	0	1	0	1	1	5	.200	.262	.292	.555
2013	Pnscla	AA	98	339	88	19	1	3	(-	-)	118	31	44	46	45	2	57	3	4	4	1	0	5	.260	.348	.348	.696
2014	Lsvlle	AAA	78	256	63	9	3	1	(-	-)	81	18	29	28	28	1	34	1	4	3	0	1	6	.246	.319	.316	.636
2014	Cin	NL	21	54	10	0	0	1	(1	0)	13	3	1	2	4	1	10	0	2	0	0	0	0	.185	.241	.241	.482
2015	Cin	NL	81	242	61	9	0	3	(2	1)	79	23	18	22	25	5	45	2	2	3	0	1	10	.252	.324	.326	.650
	2 ML YEARS		102	296	71	9	0	4	(3	1)	92	26	19	24	29	6	55	2	4	3	0	1	10	.240	.309	.311	.620

Steven Baron

Bats: R Throws: R Pos: C-4   Ht: 6'0" Wt: 205 Born: 12/7/1990 Age: 25

			BATTING																		RUNNING			AVERAGES			
Year	Team	Lg	G	AB	H	2B	3B	HR	(Hm	Rd)	TB	R	RBI	RC	TBB	IBB	SO	HBP	SH	SF	SB	CS	GDP	Avg	OBP	Slg	OPS
2011	2 Tms	Low	62	214	42	14	0	4	(-	-)	68	20	21	17	18	0	55	2	2	2	6	3	6	.196	.263	.318	.580
2012	Clinton	A	64	249	60	18	2	4	(-	-)	94	29	30	28	13	1	49	2	3	4	10	1	5	.241	.280	.378	.657
2013	Hi Dsrt	A+	86	331	69	18	5	5	(-	-)	112	31	47	28	18	0	93	0	1	3	7	0	9	.208	.247	.338	.586
2014	Hi Dsrt	A+	39	142	36	10	1	1	(-	-)	51	18	23	17	10	0	27	3	0	4	3	1	1	.254	.308	.359	.667
2014	Jacksn	AA	21	69	19	4	1	0	(-	-)	25	5	6	8	7	0	12	0	0	0	1	1	3	.275	.342	.362	.704
2015	Jacksn	AA	35	107	26	5	1	0	(-	-)	33	17	13	14	20	1	27	0	1	0	3	0	4	.243	.362	.308	.671
2015	Tacom	AAA	53	184	51	12	0	3	(-	-)	72	27	20	23	10	0	38	1	1	1	4	1	8	.277	.316	.391	.708
2015	Sea	AL	4	11	0	0	0	0	(0	0)	0	0	0	0	0	0	2	0	0	0	0	0	2	.000	.000	.000	.000

Kyle Barraclough

Pitches: R Bats: R Pos: RP-25   BAIR-ah-claw   Ht: 6'3" Wt: 225 Born: 5/23/1990 Age: 26

			HOW MUCH HE PITCHED						WHAT HE GAVE UP									THE RESULTS						
Year	Team	Lg	G	GS	CG	GF	IP	BFP	H	R	ER	HR	SH	SF	HB	TBB	IBB	SO	WP	Bk	W	L	Pct	Sh	Sv-Op	Hld	ERC	ERA
2012	2 Tms	Low	15	3	0	5	35.1	148	26	15	12	2	3	3	2	13	1	33	5	0	0	3	.000	0	2- -	-	2.39	3.06
2014	2 Tms	Low	48	0	0	18	58.1	256	49	22	16	0	2	1	1	34	0	78	8	0	2	2	.500	0	11- -	-	3.20	2.47
2015	PlmBh	A+	11	0	0	7	15.0	63	9	4	1	0	0	0	0	9	0	23	3	0	1	0	1.000	0	4- -	-	2.03	0.60
2015	Sprgfld	AA	23	0	0	16	24.2	113	19	9	9	0	0	1	2	20	0	28	5	0	2	0	1.000	0	8- -	-	3.88	3.28
2015	Mia	NL	25	0	0	5	24.1	98	12	8	7	1	0	2	0	18	2	30	1	0	2	1	.667	0	0-1	6	2.25	2.59

Aaron Barrett

Pitches: R Bats: R Pos: RP-40   Ht: 6'3" Wt: 225 Born: 1/2/1988 Age: 28

			HOW MUCH HE PITCHED						WHAT HE GAVE UP									THE RESULTS						
Year	Team	Lg	G	GS	CG	GF	IP	BFP	H	R	ER	HR	SH	SF	HB	TBB	IBB	SO	WP	Bk	W	L	Pct	Sh	Sv-Op	Hld	ERC	ERA
2011	Auburn	A-	19	0	0	15	26.2	114	16	12	12	2	0	0	0	20	0	32	5	0	1	2	.333	0	9- -	-	3.06	4.05
2012	2 Tms	Low	42	0	0	33	51.2	203	34	14	12	2	0	1	2	14	0	73	8	1	3	2	.600	0	17- -	-	1.67	2.09
2013	Hrsbrg	AA	51	0	0	42	50.1	203	40	14	12	2	2	0	0	15	0	69	3	0	1	1	.500	0	26- -	-	2.25	2.15
2014	Syrcse	AAA	10	0	0	5	10.1	37	5	0	0	0	0	0	0	1	0	8	0	0	1	0	1.000	0	2- -	-	0.65	0.00
2014	Was	NL	50	0	0	12	40.2	174	33	17	12	1	1	2	1	20	2	49	6	1	3	0	1.000	0	0-0	8	2.87	2.66
2015	Was	NL	40	0	0	8	29.1	123	28	15	15	1	0	0	3	7	0	35	1	0	3	3	.500	0	0-3	10	3.17	4.60
	Postseason		2	0	0	0	0.1	3	1	0	0	0	0	0	0	2	1	0	1	0	0	0	-	0	0-0	0	44.72	0.00
	2 ML YEARS		90	0	0	20	70.0	297	61	32	27	2	1	2	4	27	2	84	7	1	6	3	.667	0	0-3	18	2.99	3.47

Yhonathan Barrios

Pitches: R Bats: B Pos: RP-5   JON-ah-tin   Ht: 5'10" Wt: 200 Born: 12/1/1991 Age: 24

Year	Team	Lg	HOW MUCH HE PITCHED						WHAT HE GAVE UP												THE RESULTS							
			G	GS	CG	GF	IP	BFP	H	R	ER	HR	SH	SF	HB	TBB	IBB	SO	WP	Bk	W	L	Pct	Sh	Sv-Op	Hld	ERC	ERA
2013	Pirates	R	10	0	0	2	11.0	42	6	1	1	0	0	0	0	4	0	10	0	0	2	1	.667	0	1- -	-	1.31	0.82
2014	2 Tms	Low	41	0	0	29	58.1	261	63	31	25	3	2	1	4	23	0	50	5	0	2	7	.222	0	15- -	-	4.38	3.86
2015	Altna	AA	20	0	0	16	24.2	98	17	7	4	1	1	0	0	9	0	12	0	1	0	1	.000	0	10- -	-	2.00	1.46
2015	Indy	AAA	13	0	0	8	15.2	72	19	8	8	0	0	1	0	8	0	9	1	0	1	2	.333	0	1- -	-	4.98	4.60
2015	Biloxi	AA	16	0	0	8	20.0	84	22	7	7	1	0	0	1	5	0	16	1	0	3	2	.600	0	6- -	-	4.00	3.15
2015	Mil	NL	5	0	0	2	6.2	22	3	0	0	0	0	0	0	0	0	7	0	0	0	0	-	0	0-0	1	0.46	0.00

Anthony Bass

Pitches: R Bats: R Pos: RP-33   Ht: 6'2" Wt: 200 Born: 11/1/1987 Age: 28

Year	Team	Lg	HOW MUCH HE PITCHED						WHAT HE GAVE UP												THE RESULTS							
			G	GS	CG	GF	IP	BFP	H	R	ER	HR	SH	SF	HB	TBB	IBB	SO	WP	Bk	W	L	Pct	Sh	Sv-Op	Hld	ERC	ERA
2011	SD	NL	27	3	0	6	48.1	198	41	9	9	3	2	0	1	21	1	24	1	0	2	0	1.000	0	0-0	4	3.28	1.68
2012	SD	NL	24	15	1	3	97.0	411	89	59	51	10	2	2	1	39	3	80	5	1	2	8	.200	0	1-1	1	3.65	4.73
2013	SD	NL	24	0	0	8	42.0	193	51	26	25	4	1	0	0	20	4	31	5	0	0	0	-	0	0-0	0	5.41	5.36
2014	Hou	AL	21	0	0	8	27.0	119	32	20	19	6	0	1	2	7	1	7	2	0	1	1	.500	0	2-4	5	5.74	6.33
2015	Tex	AL	33	0	0	9	64.0	272	66	33	32	5	3	3	1	20	1	45	1	0	0	0	-	0	0-1	0	3.81	4.50
	5 ML YEARS		129	18	1	35	278.1	1193	279	147	136	28	8	6	5	107	10	187	14	1	5	9	.357	0	3-6	9	4.07	4.40

Chris Bassitt

Pitches: R Bats: R Pos: SP-13; RP-5   Ht: 6'5" Wt: 210 Born: 2/22/1989 Age: 27

Year	Team	Lg	HOW MUCH HE PITCHED						WHAT HE GAVE UP												THE RESULTS							
			G	GS	CG	GF	IP	BFP	H	R	ER	HR	SH	SF	HB	TBB	IBB	SO	WP	Bk	W	L	Pct	Sh	Sv-Op	Hld	ERC	ERA
2011	3 Tms	Low	23	0	0	9	34.2	141	29	8	7	1	2	0	3	8	0	41	4	0	3	1	.750	0	1- -	-	2.46	1.82
2012	WinSa	A+	38	10	0	17	91.0	403	74	45	37	6	6	0	4	54	1	75	3	0	5	4	.556	0	4- -	-	3.63	3.66
2013	WinSa	A+	18	18	0	0	101.1	443	90	50	39	9	5	2	5	42	0	101	7	0	7	2	.778	0	0- -	-	3.53	3.46
2013	Brham	AA	8	8	0	0	47.2	191	35	16	12	2	3	2	4	17	0	37	1	0	4	2	.667	0	0- -	-	2.53	2.27
2014	Brham	AA	6	6	0	0	34.2	145	26	10	6	2	2	1	2	14	0	36	0	0	3	1	.750	0	0- -	-	2.67	1.56
2015	Nashv	AAA	13	10	1	0	69.0	285	59	30	28	1	1	4	3	19	0	70	3	1	2	7	.222	0	0- -	-	2.43	3.65
2014	CWS	AL	6	5	0	1	29.2	137	34	13	13	0	1	1	3	13	1	21	0	0	1	1	.500	0	0-0	0	4.57	3.94
2015	Oak	AL	18	13	0	3	86.0	361	78	36	34	5	1	1	9	30	0	64	5	0	1	8	.111	0	0-0	0	3.55	3.56
	2 ML YEARS		24	18	0	4	115.2	498	112	49	47	5	2	2	12	43	1	85	5	0	2	9	.182	0	0-0	0	3.81	3.66

Antonio Bastardo

Pitches: L Bats: R Pos: RP-66   bah-STAHR-doh   Ht: 5'11" Wt: 205 Born: 9/21/1985 Age: 30

Year	Team	Lg	HOW MUCH HE PITCHED						WHAT HE GAVE UP												THE RESULTS							
			G	GS	CG	GF	IP	BFP	H	R	ER	HR	SH	SF	HB	TBB	IBB	SO	WP	Bk	W	L	Pct	Sh	Sv-Op	Hld	ERC	ERA
2009	Phi	NL	6	5	0	0	23.2	106	26	18	17	4	0	0	2	9	0	19	0	0	2	3	.400	0	0-0	0	5.41	6.46
2010	Phi	NL	25	0	0	2	18.2	86	19	9	9	1	0	0	2	9	0	26	0	0	2	0	1.000	0	0-1	2	4.46	4.34
2011	Phi	NL	64	0	0	15	58.0	225	28	17	17	6	2	2	0	26	0	70	4	0	6	1	.857	0	8-9	17	1.69	2.64
2012	Phi	NL	65	0	0	10	52.0	224	40	26	25	7	1	2	2	26	3	81	5	0	2	5	.286	0	1-5	26	3.42	4.33
2013	Phi	NL	48	0	0	15	42.2	179	33	12	11	2	4	1	1	21	1	47	4	0	3	2	.600	0	2-5	14	2.91	2.32
2014	Phi	NL	67	0	0	17	64.0	271	43	31	28	4	3	3	2	34	4	81	5	0	5	7	.417	0	0-2	12	2.54	3.94
2015	Pit	NL	66	0	0	18	57.1	239	39	19	19	4	2	0	3	26	2	64	8	0	4	1	.800	0	1-2	9	2.50	2.98
	Postseason		5	0	0	0	1.2	8	2	0	0	1	0	0	0	1	0	2	0	0	0	0	-	0	0-0	1	5.10	0.00
	7 ML YEARS		341	5	0	77	316.1	1330	228	132	126	28	12	8	12	151	10	388	26	0	24	19	.558	0	12-24	80	2.86	3.58

Trevor Bauer

Pitches: R Bats: R Pos: SP-30; RP-1   Ht: 6'1" Wt: 200 Born: 1/17/1991 Age: 25

Year	Team	Lg	HOW MUCH HE PITCHED						WHAT HE GAVE UP												THE RESULTS							
			G	GS	CG	GF	IP	BFP	H	R	ER	HR	SH	SF	HB	TBB	IBB	SO	WP	Bk	W	L	Pct	Sh	Sv-Op	Hld	ERC	ERA
2012	Ari	NL	4	4	0	0	16.1	77	14	13	11	2	1	1	1	13	0	17	2	0	1	2	.333	0	0-0	0	5.12	6.06
2013	Cle	AL	4	4	0	0	17.0	81	15	11	10	3	0	1	1	16	0	11	1	0	1	2	.333	0	0-0	0	6.47	5.29
2014	Cle	AL	26	26	0	0	153.0	663	151	76	71	16	1	8	11	60	4	143	6	0	5	8	.385	0	0-0	0	4.27	4.18
2015	Cle	AL	31	30	1	1	176.0	744	152	90	89	23	4	1	5	79	1	170	7	1	11	12	.478	0	0-0	0	3.86	4.55
	4 ML YEARS		65	64	1	1	362.1	1565	332	190	181	44	6	11	18	168	5	341	16	1	18	24	.429	0	0-0	0	4.21	4.50

Jose Bautista

Bats: R Throws: R Pos: RF-118; DH-33; PH-2   bah-TEE-stah   Ht: 6'0" Wt: 205 Born: 10/19/1980 Age: 35

Year	Team	Lg	BATTING																				RUNNING			AVERAGES			
			G	AB	H	2B	3B	HR	(Hm	Rd)	TB	R	RBI	RC	TBB	IBB	SO	HBP	SH	SF	SB	CS	GDP	Avg	OBP	Slg	OPS
2004	4 Tms		64	88	18	3	0	0	(0	0)	21	6	2	2	7	0	40	0	1	0	0	1	1	.205	.263	.239	.502
2005	Pit	NL	11	28	4	1	0	0	(0	0)	5	3	1	0	3	0	7	0	0	0	1	0	2	.143	.226	.179	.404
2006	Pit	NL	117	400	94	20	3	16	(11	5)	168	58	51	55	46	2	110	16	3	4	2	4	12	.235	.335	.420	.755
2007	Pit	NL	142	532	135	36	2	15	(8	7)	220	75	63	71	68	1	101	4	4	6	6	3	16	.254	.339	.414	.753
2008	2 Tms		128	370	88	17	0	15	(5	10)	150	45	54	43	40	5	91	2	8	4	1	1	12	.238	.313	.405	.718
2009	Tor	AL	113	336	79	13	3	13	(5	8)	137	54	40	42	56	1	85	4	6	2	0	0	9	.235	.349	.408	.757
2010	Tor	AL	161	569	148	35	3	54	(33	21)	351	109	124	132	100	2	116	10	0	4	9	2	10	.260	.378	.617	.995
2011	Tor	AL	149	513	155	24	2	43	(20	23)	312	105	103	132	132	24	111	6	0	9	9	5	8	.302	.447	.608	1.056
2012	Tor	AL	92	332	80	14	0	27	(11	16)	175	64	65	58	59	2	63	4	0	4	5	2	6	.241	.358	.527	.886
2013	Tor	AL	118	452	117	24	0	28	(14	14)	225	82	73	81	69	2	84	3	0	4	7	2	13	.259	.358	.498	.856
2014	Tor	AL	155	553	158	27	0	35	(18	17)	290	101	103	112	104	11	96	9	1	6	6	2	18	.286	.403	.524	.928
2015	Tor	AL	153	543	136	29	3	40	(23	17)	291	108	114	113	110	2	106	5	0	6	8	2	19	.250	.377	.536	.913

				BATTING																RUNNING			AVERAGES			
Year	Team	Lg	G	AB	H	2B	3B	HR	(Hm	Rd)	TB	R	RBI	RC	TBB	IBB	SO	HBP	SH	SF	SB	CS	GDP	Avg	OBP	Slg	OPS
04	Bal	AL	16	11	3	0	0	0	(0	0)	3	3	0	1	1	0	3	0	0	0	0	0	0	.273	.333	.273	.606
04	TB	AL	12	12	2	0	0	0	(0	0)	2	1	1	0	3	0	7	0	0	0	0	1	0	.167	.333	.167	.500
04	KC	AL	13	25	5	1	0	0	(0	0)	6	1	1	0	1	0	12	0	0	0	0	0	0	.200	.231	.240	.471
04	Pit	NL	23	40	8	2	0	0	(0	0)	10	1	0	1	2	0	18	0	1	0	0	0	1	.200	.238	.250	.488
08	Pit	NL	107	314	76	15	0	12	(3	9)	127	38	44	39	38	4	77	2	6	3	1	1	10	.242	.325	.404	.729
08	Tor	AL	21	56	12	2	0	3	(2	1)	23	7	10	4	2	1	14	0	2	1	0	0	2	.214	.237	.411	.648
	12 ML YEARS		1403	4716	1212	243	16	286	(148	138)	2345	810	793	842	794	52	1010	63	23	46	58	24	131	.257	.368	.497	.865

Mike Baxter

Bats: L **Throws:** R **Pos:** PH-23;RF-10;1B-2;LF-1;DH-1   **Ht:** 6'0" **Wt:** 205 **Born:** 12/7/1984 **Age:** 31

				BATTING																RUNNING			AVERAGES			
Year	Team	Lg	G	AB	H	2B	3B	HR	(Hm	Rd)	TB	R	RBI	RC	TBB	IBB	SO	HBP	SH	SF	SB	CS	GDP	Avg	OBP	Slg	OPS
2015	Iowa*	AAA	74	222	62	9	3	1	(-	-)	80	31	20	35	39	5	45	2	0	1	7	3	3	.279	.390	.360	.751
2010	SD	NL	9	8	1	0	0	0	(0	0)	1	0	1	0	0	0	2	0	0	1	0	0	1	.125	.111	.125	.236
2011	NYM	NL	22	34	8	2	1	1	(1	0)	15	6	4	5	5	0	9	1	0	0	0	0	1	.235	.350	.441	.791
2012	NYM	NL	89	179	47	14	2	3	(1	2)	74	26	17	30	25	4	45	5	0	2	5	3	0	.263	.365	.413	.778
2013	NYM	NL	74	132	25	6	1	0	(0	0)	33	14	4	11	17	0	28	5	0	1	5	2	1	.189	.303	.250	.553
2014	LAD	NL	4	7	0	0	0	0	(0	0)	0	0	0	0	1	0	2	0	0	0	0	0	0	.000	.125	.000	.125
2015	ChC	NL	34	57	14	1	0	0	(0	0)	15	6	2	3	7	1	14	2	0	0	0	0	3	.246	.348	.263	.612
	6 ML YEARS		232	417	95	23	4	4	(2	2)	138	52	28	49	55	5	100	13	0	4	10	5	7	.228	.333	.331	.664

Brandon Beachy

Pitches: R **Bats:** R **Pos:** SP-2   BEE-chee   **Ht:** 6'2" **Wt:** 215 **Born:** 9/3/1986 **Age:** 29

			HOW MUCH HE PITCHED						WHAT HE GAVE UP											THE RESULTS						
Year	Team	Lg	G	GS	CG	GF	IP	BFP	H	R	ER	HR	SH	SF	HB	TBB	IBB	SO	WP	Bk	W	L	Pct	Sh	Sv-Op	Hld	ERC	ERA
2015	OkCity*	AAA	10	9	0	0	47.0	197	40	22	19	4	1	3	2	21	0	36	2	0	1	1	.500	0	0- -	-	3.56	3.64
2010	Atl	NL	3	3	0	0	15.0	67	16	9	5	0	0	0	0	7	3	15	1	0	0	2	.000	0	0-0	0	3.58	3.00
2011	Atl	NL	25	25	0	0	141.2	591	125	62	58	16	6	5	5	46	9	169	11	1	7	3	.700	0	0-0	0	3.27	3.68
2012	Atl	NL	13	13	1	0	81.0	319	49	24	18	6	1	2	1	29	1	68	4	0	5	5	.500	1	0-0	0	1.80	2.00
2013	Atl	NL	5	5	0	0	30.0	120	27	17	15	5	2	1	0	4	0	23	2	0	2	1	.667	0	0-0	0	2.90	4.50
2015	LAD	NL	2	2	0	0	8.0	39	10	7	7	1	1	0	0	6	2	5	0	0	0	1	.000	0	0-0	0	6.76	7.88
	5 ML YEARS		48	48	1	0	275.2	1136	227	119	103	28	10	8	6	92	15	280	18	1	14	12	.538	1	0-0	0	2.88	3.36

Chris Beck

Pitches: R **Bats:** R **Pos:** SP-1   **Ht:** 6'3" **Wt:** 225 **Born:** 9/4/1990 **Age:** 25

			HOW MUCH HE PITCHED						WHAT HE GAVE UP											THE RESULTS						
Year	Team	Lg	G	GS	CG	GF	IP	BFP	H	R	ER	HR	SH	SF	HB	TBB	IBB	SO	WP	Bk	W	L	Pct	Sh	Sv-Op	Hld	ERC	ERA
2012	Gr Falls	R+	15	6	0	0	40.1	175	51	27	21	3	0	3	0	12	0	36	3	1	4	3	.571	0	0- -	-	5.14	4.69
2013	WinSa	A+	21	21	1	0	118.2	500	117	51	41	11	4	4	4	42	0	57	3	0	11	8	.579	1	0- -	-	3.97	3.11
2013	Brham	AA	5	5	0	0	28.0	110	26	10	9	0	1	0	2	3	0	22	0	0	2	2	.500	0	0- -	-	2.32	2.89
2014	Brham	AA	20	20	1	0	116.2	492	116	50	44	7	4	3	0	31	1	57	4	0	5	8	.385	1	0- -	-	3.40	3.39
2014	Charllt	AAA	7	7	0	0	33.1	152	36	16	15	1	1	0	2	13	0	28	1	1	1	3	.250	0	0- -	-	4.07	4.05
2015	Charllt	AAA	10	10	0	0	54.1	226	50	20	19	3	0	1	2	14	0	40	3	0	3	2	.600	0	0- -	-	2.93	3.15
2015	CWS	AL	1	1	0	0	6.0	31	10	5	4	0	1	0	0	4	0	3	0	0	0	1	.000	0	0-0	0	8.52	6.00

Gordon Beckham

Bats: R **Throws:** R **Pos:** 3B-76;PH-17;2B-11;PR-6;SS-5;DH-2   **Ht:** 6'0" **Wt:** 185 **Born:** 9/16/1986 **Age:** 29

				BATTING																RUNNING			AVERAGES			
Year	Team	Lg	G	AB	H	2B	3B	HR	(Hm	Rd)	TB	R	RBI	RC	TBB	IBB	SO	HBP	SH	SF	SB	CS	GDP	Avg	OBP	Slg	OPS
2009	CWS	AL	103	378	102	28	1	14	(4	10)	174	58	63	61	41	0	65	6	1	4	7	4	10	.270	.347	.460	.808
2010	CWS	AL	131	444	112	25	2	9	(7	2)	168	58	49	52	37	0	92	7	6	4	4	6	9	.252	.317	.378	.695
2011	CWS	AL	150	499	115	23	0	10	(7	3)	168	60	44	48	35	0	111	13	7	3	5	3	6	.230	.296	.337	.633
2012	CWS	AL	151	525	123	24	0	16	(12	4)	195	62	60	58	40	0	89	7	8	2	5	4	10	.234	.296	.371	.668
2013	CWS	AL	103	371	99	22	1	5	(3	2)	138	46	24	36	28	2	56	4	1	4	5	1	10	.267	.322	.372	.694
2014	2 Tms	AL	127	446	101	27	0	9	(4	5)	155	53	44	32	22	2	81	7	3	5	3	0	17	.226	.271	.348	.618
2015	CWS	AL	100	211	44	8	0	6	(3	3)	70	24	20	17	19	1	43	2	1	4	0	1	6	.209	.275	.332	.607
	14 CWS	AL	101	390	86	24	0	7	(3	4)	131	43	36	28	19	1	70	5	3	5	3	0	12	.221	.263	.336	.598
	14 LAA	AL	26	56	15	3	0	2	(1	1)	24	10	8	4	3	1	11	2	0	0	0	0	5	.268	.328	.429	.756
	Postseason		2	1	0	0	0	0	(0	0)	0	0	0	0	0	0	1	1	0	0	0	0	0	.000	.500	.000	.500
	7 ML YEARS		865	2874	696	157	4	69	(40	29)	1068	361	304	304	222	5	537	46	27	26	29	19	68	.242	.304	.372	.676

Tim Beckham

Bats: R **Throws:** R **Pos:** 2B-38;SS-28;PH-17;DH-12;PR-7;3B-1   **Ht:** 6'0" **Wt:** 195 **Born:** 1/27/1990 **Age:** 26

				BATTING																RUNNING			AVERAGES			
Year	Team	Lg	G	AB	H	2B	3B	HR	(Hm	Rd)	TB	R	RBI	RC	TBB	IBB	SO	HBP	SH	SF	SB	CS	GDP	Avg	OBP	Slg	OPS
2011	Mont	AA	107	418	115	25	2	7	(-	-)	165	82	57	60	39	0	91	3	5	3	15	4	7	.275	.339	.395	.734
2011	Drham	AAA	24	106	27	3	2	5	(-	-)	49	12	13	13	3	0	29	1	1	0	2	1	0	.255	.282	.462	.744
2012	Drham	AAA	72	285	73	10	1	6	(-	-)	103	40	28	37	29	2	71	2	3	4	6	0	8	.256	.325	.361	.686
2013	Drham	AAA	122	460	127	25	7	4	(-	-)	178	71	51	65	44	0	108	5	8	5	17	7	17	.276	.342	.387	.729
2014	Drham	AAA	15	62	16	2	0	0	(-	-)	18	8	4	4	2	1	14	0	1	0	0	2	1	.258	.281	.290	.572
2015	Drham	AAA	11	39	12	6	0	0	(-	-)	18	5	4	7	5	0	10	0	0	1	2	1	1	.308	.378	.462	.839
2013	TB	AL	5	7	3	0	0	0	(0	0)	3	1	1	1	0	0	0	0	0	0	0	0	0	.429	.375	.429	.804
2015	TB	AL	83	203	45	7	4	9	(3	6)	87	24	37	26	13	0	69	3	0	4	3	1	3	.222	.274	.429	.702
	2 ML YEARS		88	210	48	7	4	9	(3	6)	90	25	38	27	13	0	69	3	0	5	3	1	3	.229	.277	.429	.706

Cam Bedrosian

Pitches: R **Bats**: R **Pos**: RP-34   **Ht**: 6'0" **Wt**: 230 **Born**: 10/2/1991 **Age**: 24

Year	Team	Lg	G	GS	CG	GF	IP	BFP	H	R	ER	HR	SH	SF	HB	TBB	IBB	SO	WP	Bk	W	L	Pct	Sh	Sv-Op	Hld	ERC	ERA
2012	Crpds	A	21	21	0	0	82.2	385	91	61	58	5	2	5	8	52	0	48	15	1	3	11	.214	0	0- -	-	5.74	6.31
2013	2 Tms	Low	44	2	0	23	63.0	278	59	38	32	4	2	0	6	29	1	78	9	0	1	5	.167	0	7- -	-	4.02	4.57
2014	InldEm	A+	5	0	0	4	5.2	20	1	0	0	0	0	0	0	2	0	15	0	0	0	0	-	0	1- -	-	0.40	0.00
2014	Ark	AA	30	0	0	25	32.1	114	10	5	4	1	1	0	0	10	0	57	2	0	1	0	1.000	0	15- -	-	0.70	1.11
2014	Salt Lk	AAA	8	0	0	6	7.0	35	5	6	6	0	0	0	3	6	1	10	0	0	1	1	.500	0	2- -	-	4.62	7.71
2015	Salt Lk	AAA	24	0	0	7	35.2	149	32	11	11	0	2	0	1	14	1	42	5	0	1	1	.500	0	3- -	-	2.91	2.78
2014	LAA	AL	17	0	0	4	19.1	93	23	17	14	2	0	1	0	12	1	20	1	1	0	1	.000	0	0-1	1	5.88	6.52
2015	LAA	AL	34	0	0	10	33.1	156	40	21	20	3	1	2	2	19	2	34	2	0	1	0	1.000	0	0-0	1	6.05	5.40
	2 ML YEARS		51	0	0	14	52.2	249	63	38	34	5	1	3	2	31	3	54	3	1	1	1	.500	0	0-1	2	5.99	5.81

Dallas Beeler

Pitches: R **Bats**: R **Pos**: SP-3   **Ht**: 6'5" **Wt**: 210 **Born**: 6/12/1989 **Age**: 27

Year	Team	Lg	G	GS	CG	GF	IP	BFP	H	R	ER	HR	SH	SF	HB	TBB	IBB	SO	WP	Bk	W	L	Pct	Sh	Sv-Op	Hld	ERC	ERA
2011	Peoria	A	12	11	0	0	43.1	169	35	13	8	1	3	0	2	6	0	35	0	0	1	1	.500	0	0- -	-	1.87	1.66
2011	Tenn	AA	9	9	0	0	51.2	228	68	31	26	7	3	0	2	7	0	33	0	0	1	5	.167	0	0- -	-	5.21	4.53
2012	Tenn	AA	27	27	1	0	136.0	603	166	74	64	11	5	2	4	48	1	70	3	1	6	7	.462	0	0- -	-	5.20	4.24
2013	Tenn	AA	9	9	0	0	54.2	227	43	26	19	3	2	1	6	17	0	35	1	0	4	2	.667	0	0- -	-	2.71	3.13
2014	Iowa	AAA	20	20	1	0	124.1	499	112	48	47	8	4	1	4	32	0	83	6	1	9	6	.600	0	0- -	-	2.98	3.40
2015	Iowa	AAA	21	21	0	0	110.2	485	114	64	50	5	6	2	8	37	3	83	3	0	8	5	.615	0	0- -	-	3.79	4.07
2014	ChC	NL	2	2	0	0	11.0	46	10	5	4	0	1	0	0	7	1	6	1	0	0	2	.000	0	0-0	0	3.83	3.27
2015	ChC	NL	3	3	0	0	8.1	46	14	11	9	0	0	0	0	7	2	7	0	0	0	1	.000	0	0-0	0	8.53	9.72
	2 ML YEARS		5	5	0	0	19.1	92	24	16	13	0	1	0	0	14	3	13	1	0	0	3	.000	0	0-0	0	5.78	6.05

Joe Beimel

Pitches: L **Bats**: L **Pos**: RP-53   BYE-mull   **Ht**: 6'3" **Wt**: 205 **Born**: 4/19/1977 **Age**: 39

Year	Team	Lg	G	GS	CG	GF	IP	BFP	H	R	ER	HR	SH	SF	HB	TBB	IBB	SO	WP	Bk	W	L	Pct	Sh	Sv-Op	Hld	ERC	ERA
2015	Tacom*	AAA	6	0	0	0	6.1	29	8	3	3	0	0	1	0	2	0	8	1	0	1	0	1.000	0	0- -	-	4.37	4.26
2001	Pit	NL	42	15	0	9	115.1	511	131	72	67	12	3	1	6	49	4	58	3	0	7	11	.389	0	0-0	-	5.24	5.23
2002	Pit	NL	53	8	0	8	85.1	389	88	49	44	9	7	3	4	45	12	53	2	0	2	5	.286	0	0-1	5	4.68	4.64
2003	Pit	NL	69	0	0	11	62.1	276	69	35	35	7	3	5	4	33	6	42	0	1	1	3	.250	0	0-5	12	5.62	5.05
2004	Min	AL	3	0	0	0	1.2	15	8	8	8	1	0	0	0	2	0	2	0	0	0	0	-	0	0-0	0	44.44	43.20
2005	TB	AL	7	0	0	3	11.0	51	15	4	4	1	0	0	0	4	1	3	1	0	0	0	-	0	0-0	0	5.80	3.27
2006	LAD	NL	62	0	0	10	70.0	295	70	26	23	7	4	3	0	21	3	30	6	1	2	1	.667	0	2-2	10	3.62	2.96
2007	LAD	NL	83	0	0	10	67.1	281	63	30	29	1	5	2	1	24	6	39	3	2	4	2	.667	0	1-1	16	2.93	3.88
2008	LAD	NL	71	0	0	10	49.0	214	50	11	11	0	1	4	3	21	4	32	1	1	5	1	.833	0	0-2	12	3.70	2.02
2009	2 Tms	NL	71	0	0	26	55.1	240	57	24	22	5	4	6	1	19	5	35	4	1	1	6	.143	0	1-6	13	3.84	3.58
2010	Col	NL	71	0	0	11	45.0	188	46	18	17	5	1	1	0	15	3	21	2	1	1	2	.333	0	0-1	20	4.00	3.40
2011	Pit	NL	35	0	0	9	25.1	117	34	17	15	6	1	0	1	9	1	17	0	0	1	1	.500	0	0-2	7	7.15	5.33
2014	Sea	AL	56	0	0	8	45.0	184	39	12	11	4	3	1	1	14	4	25	3	0	3	1	.750	0	0-0	9	2.93	2.20
2015	Sea	AL	53	0	0	14	47.1	196	49	25	21	8	3	3	1	16	3	22	1	0	2	1	.667	0	1-3	6	4.70	3.99
09	Was	NL	45	0	0	19	39.2	172	38	17	15	3	2	4	1	15	4	24	2	1	1	5	.167	0	1-5	10	3.46	3.40
09	Col	NL	26	0	0	7	15.2	68	19	7	7	2	2	2	0	4	1	11	2	0	0	1	.000	0	0-1	3	4.84	4.02
	Postseason		6	0	0	1	1.1	7	1	0	0	0	0	0	0	2	0	0	0	0	0	0	-	0	0-0	0	5.91	0.00
	13 ML YEARS		676	23	0	129	680.0	2957	719	331	307	66	35	29	22	272	52	379	26	7	29	34	.460	0	5-21	110	4.43	4.06

Ronald Belisario

Pitches: R **Bats**: R **Pos**: RP-6   bell-ih-SAR-ee-oh   **Ht**: 6'3" **Wt**: 240 **Born**: 12/31/1982 **Age**: 33

Year	Team	Lg	G	GS	CG	GF	IP	BFP	H	R	ER	HR	SH	SF	HB	TBB	IBB	SO	WP	Bk	W	L	Pct	Sh	Sv-Op	Hld	ERC	ERA
2015	Drham*	AAA	27	0	0	23	30.1	122	28	11	11	2	2	0	0	9	2	18	2	0	0	2	.000	0	17- -	-	3.05	3.26
2015	Pwtckt*	AAA	5	0	0	4	6.1	27	4	2	0	0	0	0	0	2	0	5	0	0	0	1	.000	0	0- -	-	1.54	0.00
2009	LAD	NL	69	0	0	13	70.2	299	52	21	16	4	3	2	6	29	7	64	4	0	4	3	.571	0	0-7	12	2.54	2.04
2010	LAD	NL	59	0	0	13	55.1	233	52	31	31	6	3	0	3	19	4	38	4	1	3	1	.750	0	2-4	16	3.72	5.04
2012	LAD	NL	68	0	0	13	71.0	286	47	22	20	3	1	0	4	29	4	69	1	0	8	1	.889	0	1-5	23	2.14	2.54
2013	LAD	NL	77	0	0	12	68.0	300	72	34	30	3	2	2	5	28	10	49	3	0	5	7	.417	0	1-5	21	4.10	3.97
2014	CWS	AL	62	0	0	19	66.1	292	78	46	41	4	3	2	5	18	7	47	2	0	4	8	.333	0	8-12	12	4.41	5.56
2015	TB	AL	6	0	0	3	8.0	36	8	7	7	0	0	0	1	4	1	6	3	0	0	0	-	0	0-0	0	3.42	7.88
	Postseason		13	0	0	2	8.1	38	8	7	7	1	0	0	1	3	1	2	1	0	0	0	-	0	0-0	0	3.89	7.56
	6 ML YEARS		341	0	0	73	339.1	1446	309	161	145	20	12	6	23	127	33	273	17	1	24	20	.545	0	12-33	84	3.31	3.85

Matt Belisle

Pitches: R **Bats**: R **Pos**: RP-34   bell-EYE-el   **Ht**: 6'4" **Wt**: 225 **Born**: 6/6/1980 **Age**: 36

Year	Team	Lg	G	GS	CG	GF	IP	BFP	H	R	ER	HR	SH	SF	HB	TBB	IBB	SO	WP	Bk	W	L	Pct	Sh	Sv-Op	Hld	ERC	ERA
2003	Cin	NL	6	0	0	2	8.2	39	10	5	5	1	2	1	1	2	0	6	0	0	1	1	.500	0	0-1	0	4.73	5.19
2005	Cin	NL	60	5	0	17	85.2	382	101	49	42	11	4	2	6	26	6	59	3	0	4	8	.333	0	1-4	8	5.08	4.41
2006	Cin	NL	30	2	0	5	40.0	180	43	18	16	5	1	2	3	19	1	26	3	0	2	0	1.000	0	0-1	0	5.29	3.60
2007	Cin	NL	30	30	1	0	177.2	771	212	111	105	26	7	9	7	43	4	125	6	1	8	9	.471	0	0-0	0	5.05	5.32
2008	Cin	NL	6	6	0	0	29.2	142	47	27	24	4	1	2	0	6	0	14	2	0	1	4	.200	0	0-0	0	6.87	7.28
2009	Col	NL	24	0	0	6	31.0	133	35	21	19	6	0	2	1	5	1	22	1	0	3	1	.750	0	0-0	1	4.50	5.52
2010	Col	NL	76	0	0	11	92.0	365	84	34	30	7	4	2	2	16	5	91	3	1	7	5	.583	0	1-2	21	2.67	2.93
2011	Col	NL	74	0	0	10	72.0	301	77	33	26	5	4	0	4	14	3	58	0	0	10	4	.714	0	0-7	14	3.65	3.25

Year	Team	Lg	G	GS	CG	GF	IP	BFP	H	R	ER	HR	SH	SF	HB	TBB	IBB	SO	WP	Bk	W	L	Pct	Sh	Sv-Op	Hld	ERC	ERA
			HOW MUCH HE PITCHED						**WHAT HE GAVE UP**												**THE RESULTS**							
2012	Col	NL	80	0	0	14	80.0	348	91	36	33	5	4	0	3	18	6	69	1	1	3	8	.273	0	3-10	26	3.87	3.71
2013	Col	NL	72	0	0	16	73.0	301	76	37	35	6	2	1	0	15	2	62	3	0	5	7	.417	0	0-5	24	3.42	4.32
2014	Col	NL	66	1	0	13	64.2	282	74	35	35	5	4	5	1	19	2	43	3	0	4	7	.364	0	0-2	6	4.31	4.87
2015	StL	NL	34	0	0	10	33.2	149	34	10	10	1	2	1	3	15	2	25	0	0	1	1	.500	0	0-1	7	4.05	2.67
Postseason			2	0	0	0	2.0	7	0	0	0	0	0	0	0	1	0	2	0	0	0	0	-	0	0-0	1	0.27	0.00
12 ML YEARS			558	44	1	104	788.0	3393	884	416	380	82	35	27	31	198	32	600	27	3	49	55	.471	0	5-33	107	4.30	4.34

Jeff Beliveau

Pitches: L Bats: L Pos: RP-5   BELL-iv-oh   Ht: 6'1" Wt: 190 Born: 1/17/1987 Age: 29

Year	Team	Lg	G	GS	CG	GF	IP	BFP	H	R	ER	HR	SH	SF	HB	TBB	IBB	SO	WP	Bk	W	L	Pct	Sh	Sv-Op	Hld	ERC	ERA
			HOW MUCH HE PITCHED						**WHAT HE GAVE UP**												**THE RESULTS**							
2012	ChC	NL	22	0	0	4	17.2	86	21	9	9	5	1	0	1	12	1	17	1	1	1	0	1.000	0	0-0	1	7.98	4.58
2013	TB	AL	1	0	0	0	0.2	4	1	0	0	0	0	0	0	1	0	0	0	0	0	0	-	0	0-0	0	10.76	0.00
2014	TB	AL	30	0	0	6	24.0	100	19	7	7	1	1	1	2	7	1	28	1	1	0	0	-	0	1-1	6	2.40	2.63
2015	TB	AL	5	0	0	0	2.2	15	6	4	4	1	0	0	0	1	0	2	0	0	0	0	-	0	0-0	1	14.72	13.50
4 ML YEARS			58	0	0	10	45.0	205	47	20	20	7	2	1	3	21	2	47	2	2	1	0	1.000	0	1-1	8	5.11	4.00

Andrew Bellatti

Pitches: R Bats: R Pos: RP-17   bell-LAH-tee   Ht: 6'1" Wt: 190 Born: 8/5/1991 Age: 24

Year	Team	Lg	G	GS	CG	GF	IP	BFP	H	R	ER	HR	SH	SF	HB	TBB	IBB	SO	WP	Bk	W	L	Pct	Sh	Sv-Op	Hld	ERC	ERA
			HOW MUCH HE PITCHED						**WHAT HE GAVE UP**												**THE RESULTS**							
2011	HudVal	A-	15	13	0	0	72.0	295	66	26	21	1	5	2	1	23	0	63	0	0	3	5	.375	0	0--	-	2.86	2.63
2012	BG	A	40	1	0	10	91.0	376	74	33	30	9	4	1	5	30	4	99	6	0	7	3	.700	0	5--	-	2.94	2.97
2013	Charltt	A+	22	0	0	7	55.0	221	39	19	18	2	0	3	1	17	0	52	2	1	6	3	.667	0	2--	-	1.91	2.95
2013	Mont	AA	14	0	0	4	26.2	122	32	24	21	6	0	2	1	11	3	18	1	1	1	1	.500	0	1--	-	6.19	7.09
2014	Mont	AA	46	0	0	23	71.0	301	69	32	29	6	3	3	0	22	0	80	1	0	2	6	.250	0	6--	-	3.43	3.68
2015	Drham	AAA	20	4	0	3	46.1	199	50	28	27	5	2	1	1	15	0	44	1	0	2	1	.667	0	1--	-	4.40	5.24
2015	TB	AL	17	0	0	6	23.1	95	16	7	6	4	2	1	1	10	0	18	0	0	3	1	.750	0	0-0	2	3.15	2.31

Brandon Belt

Bats: L Throws: L Pos: 1B-120;LF-14;PH-6   Ht: 6'5" Wt: 220 Born: 4/20/1988 Age: 28

Year	Team	Lg	G	AB	H	2B	3B	HR	(Hm	Rd)	TB	R	RBI	RC	TBB	IBB	SO	HBP	SH	SF	SB	CS	GDP	Avg	OBP	Slg	OPS
									BATTING												**RUNNING**			**AVERAGES**			
2011	SF	NL	63	187	42	6	1	9	(2	7)	77	21	18	20	20	1	57	2	0	3	3	2	3	.225	.306	.412	.718
2012	SF	NL	145	411	113	27	6	7	(5	2)	173	47	56	63	54	5	106	3	0	4	12	2	3	.275	.360	.421	.781
2013	SF	NL	150	509	147	39	4	17	(6	11)	245	76	67	82	52	6	125	3	1	3	5	2	4	.289	.360	.481	.841
2014	SF	NL	61	214	52	8	0	12	(2	10)	96	30	27	24	18	2	64	2	0	1	3	1	4	.243	.306	.449	.755
2015	SF	NL	137	492	138	33	5	18	(5	13)	235	73	68	78	56	2	147	4	0	4	9	3	3	.280	.356	.478	.834
Postseason			32	110	27	2	2	2	(1	1)	39	13	11	16	18	1	36	0	0	1	1	2	0	.245	.349	.355	.703
5 ML YEARS			556	1813	492	113	16	63	(20	43)	826	247	236	267	200	14	499	17	1	12	32	10	17	.271	.347	.456	.803

Carlos Beltran

Bats: B Throws: R Pos: RF-123;DH-8;PH-4   BELL-trahn   Ht: 6'1" Wt: 210 Born: 4/24/1977 Age: 39

Year	Team	Lg	G	AB	H	2B	3B	HR	(Hm	Rd)	TB	R	RBI	RC	TBB	IBB	SO	HBP	SH	SF	SB	CS	GDP	Avg	OBP	Slg	OPS
									BATTING												**RUNNING**			**AVERAGES**			
1998	KC	AL	14	58	16	5	3	0	(0	0)	27	12	7	9	3	0	12	1	0	1	3	0	2	.276	.317	.466	.783
1999	KC	AL	156	663	194	27	7	22	(12	10)	301	112	108	100	46	2	123	4	0	10	27	8	17	.293	.337	.454	.791
2000	KC	AL	98	372	92	15	4	7	(4	3)	136	49	44	43	35	2	69	0	2	4	13	0	12	.247	.309	.366	.675
2001	KC	AL	155	617	189	32	12	24	(7	17)	317	106	101	118	52	2	120	5	1	5	31	1	7	.306	.362	.514	.876
2002	KC	AL	162	637	174	44	7	29	(19	10)	319	114	105	117	71	1	135	4	3	7	35	7	12	.273	.346	.501	.847
2003	KC	AL	141	521	160	14	10	26	(10	16)	272	102	100	117	72	4	81	2	0	7	41	4	8	.307	.389	.522	.911
2004	2 Tms		159	599	160	36	9	38	(15	23)	328	121	104	104	92	10	101	7	3	7	42	3	8	.267	.367	.548	.915
2005	NYM	NL	151	582	155	34	2	16	(6	10)	241	83	78	88	56	5	96	2	4	6	17	6	9	.266	.330	.414	.744
2006	NYM	NL	140	510	140	38	1	41	(16	25)	303	127	116	121	95	6	99	4	1	6	18	3	6	.275	.388	.594	.982
2007	NYM	NL	144	554	153	33	3	33	(11	22)	291	93	112	97	69	10	111	2	1	10	23	2	8	.276	.353	.525	.878
2008	NYM	NL	161	606	172	40	5	27	(14	13)	303	116	112	116	92	13	96	1	1	6	25	3	11	.284	.376	.500	.876
2009	NYM	NL	81	308	100	22	1	10	(3	7)	154	50	48	54	47	10	43	1	0	1	11	1	9	.325	.415	.500	.915
2010	NYM	NL	64	220	56	11	3	7	(3	4)	94	21	27	31	30	5	39	1	0	4	3	1	4	.255	.341	.427	.768
2011	2 Tms	NL	142	520	156	39	6	22	(14	8)	273	78	84	96	71	7	88	3	0	4	4	2	18	.300	.385	.525	.910
2012	StL	NL	151	547	147	26	1	32	(20	12)	271	83	97	87	65	15	124	2	1	4	13	6	9	.269	.346	.495	.842
2013	StL	NL	145	554	164	30	2	24	(12	12)	272	79	84	91	38	1	90	1	1	6	2	1	12	.296	.339	.491	.830
2014	NYY	AL	109	403	94	23	0	15	(11	4)	162	46	49	44	37	2	80	4	0	5	3	1	11	.233	.301	.402	.703
2015	NYY	AL	133	478	132	34	1	19	(10	9)	225	57	67	69	45	2	85	2	0	6	0	0	12	.276	.337	.471	.808
04	KC	AL	69	266	74	19	2	15	(8	7)	142	51	51	57	37	7	44	2	1	3	14	3	4	.278	.367	.534	.901
04	Hou	NL	90	333	86	17	7	23	(7	16)	186	70	53	67	55	3	57	5	2	4	28	0	4	.258	.368	.559	.926
11	NYM	NL	98	353	102	30	2	15	(9	6)	181	61	66	72	60	6	61	2	0	4	3	0	9	.289	.391	.513	.904
11	SF	NL	44	167	54	9	4	7	(5	2)	92	17	18	24	11	1	27	1	0	0	1	2	9	.323	.369	.551	.920
Postseason			51	180	60	13	1	16	(7	9)	123	45	40	53	35	2	24	2	1	1	11	0	3	.333	.445	.683	1.128
18 ML YEARS			2306	8749	2454	503	78	392	(186	206)	4289	1449	1443	1522	1016	97	1592	46	18	100	311	49	175	.280	.355	.490	.845

Adrian Beltre

Bats: R **Throws:** R **Pos:** 3B-142;DH-1 **Ht:** 5'11" **Wt:** 220 **Born:** 4/7/1979 **Age:** 37

| | | | | | | | | BATTING | | | | | | | | | | | | | RUNNING | | | AVERAGES | | | |
Year	Team	Lg	G	AB	H	2B	3B	HR	(Hm	Rd)	TB	R	RBI	RC	TBB	IBB	SO	HBP	SH	SF	SB	CS	GDP	Avg	OBP	Slg	OPS
1998	LAD	NL	77	195	42	9	0	7	(5	2)	72	18	22	20	14	0	37	3	2	0	3	1	4	.215	.278	.369	.648
1999	LAD	NL	152	538	148	27	5	15	(6	9)	230	84	67	84	61	12	105	6	4	5	18	7	4	.275	.352	.428	.780
2000	LAD	NL	138	510	148	30	2	20	(7	13)	242	71	85	85	56	2	80	2	3	4	12	5	13	.290	.360	.475	.835
2001	LAD	NL	126	475	126	22	4	13	(4	9)	195	59	60	60	28	1	82	5	2	5	13	4	9	.265	.310	.411	.720
2002	LAD	NL	159	587	151	26	5	21	(7	14)	250	70	75	74	37	4	96	4	1	6	7	5	17	.257	.303	.426	.729
2003	LAD	NL	158	559	134	30	2	23	(13	10)	237	50	80	66	37	4	103	5	1	6	2	2	13	.240	.290	.424	.714
2004	LAD	NL	156	598	200	32	0	48	(23	25)	376	104	121	120	53	9	87	2	0	4	7	2	15	.334	.388	.629	1.017
2005	Sea	AL	156	603	154	36	1	19	(7	12)	249	69	87	75	38	6	108	5	0	4	3	1	15	.255	.303	.413	.716
2006	Sea	AL	156	620	166	39	4	25	(16	9)	288	88	89	85	47	4	118	10	1	3	11	5	15	.268	.328	.465	.792
2007	Sea	AL	149	595	164	41	2	26	(11	15)	287	87	99	79	38	2	104	2	0	4	14	2	18	.276	.319	.482	.802
2008	Sea	AL	143	556	148	29	1	25	(10	15)	254	74	77	71	50	10	90	2	0	4	8	2	11	.266	.327	.457	.784
2009	Sea	AL	111	449	119	27	0	8	(4	4)	170	54	44	47	19	1	74	7	0	2	13	2	19	.265	.304	.379	.683
2010	Bos	AL	154	589	189	49	2	28	(13	15)	326	84	102	103	40	10	82	5	0	7	1	1	25	.321	.365	.553	.919
2011	Tex	AL	124	487	144	33	0	32	(23	9)	273	82	105	80	25	0	53	5	0	8	1	1	13	.296	.331	.561	.892
2012	Tex	AL	156	604	194	33	2	36	(20	16)	339	95	102	109	36	8	82	5	0	9	1	0	8	.321	.359	.561	.921
2013	Tex	AL	161	631	199	32	0	30	(15	15)	321	88	92	97	50	12	78	7	0	2	1	0	17	.315	.371	.509	.880
2014	Tex	AL	148	549	178	33	1	19	(11	8)	270	79	77	99	57	13	74	3	0	5	1	1	15	.324	.388	.492	.879
2015	Tex	AL	143	567	163	32	4	18	(13	5)	257	83	83	83	41	4	65	3	0	8	1	0	18	.287	.334	.453	.788
	Postseason		22	91	23	5	0	5	(1	4)	43	15	10	8	2	1	22	2	0	1	0	0	1	.253	.281	.473	.754
	18 ML YEARS		2567	9712	2767	560	35	413	(208	205)	4636	1339	1467	1437	727	102	1518	81	14	86	118	41	249	.285	.337	.477	.814

Joaquin Benoit

Pitches: R **Bats:** R **Pos:** RP-67 ben-WAH **Ht:** 6'4" **Wt:** 250 **Born:** 7/26/1977 **Age:** 38

| | | |HOW MUCH HE PITCHED| | | | |WHAT HE GAVE UP| | | | | | | | | | |THE RESULTS| | | | | | |
Year	Team	Lg	G	GS	CG	GF	IP	BFP	H	R	ER	HR	SH	SF	HB	TBB	IBB	SO	WP	Bk	W	L	Pct	Sh	Sv-Op	Hld	ERC	ERA
2001	Tex	AL	1	1	0	0	5.0	26	8	6	6	3	0	1	0	3	0	4	0	0	0	0	-	0	0-0	0	13.11	10.80
2002	Tex	AL	17	13	0	2	84.2	405	91	51	50	6	4	3	5	58	2	59	7	0	4	5	.444	0	1-1	0	5.52	5.31
2003	Tex	AL	25	17	0	1	105.0	462	99	67	64	23	1	4	3	51	0	87	3	1	8	5	.615	0	0-0	0	5.03	5.49
2004	Tex	AL	28	15	0	2	103.0	456	113	67	65	19	2	10	8	31	0	95	3	0	3	5	.375	0	0-0	0	5.10	5.68
2005	Tex	AL	32	9	0	6	87.0	369	69	39	36	9	2	1	2	38	0	78	1	0	4	4	.500	0	0-0	5	3.15	3.72
2006	Tex	AL	56	0	0	7	79.2	347	68	49	43	5	0	3	3	38	4	85	3	0	1	1	.500	0	0-2	7	3.30	4.86
2007	Tex	AL	70	0	0	22	82.0	337	68	28	26	6	3	2	2	28	2	87	3	0	7	4	.636	0	6-13	19	2.83	2.85
2008	Tex	AL	44	0	0	8	45.0	209	40	28	25	6	2	0	0	35	2	43	3	0	3	2	.600	0	1-4	13	5.02	5.00
2010	TB	AL	63	0	0	16	60.1	217	30	10	9	6	0	2	0	11	1	75	1	0	1	2	.333	0	1-4	25	1.14	1.34
2011	Det	AL	66	0	0	13	61.0	241	47	22	20	5	1	5	2	17	1	63	3	0	4	3	.571	0	2-7	29	2.46	2.95
2012	Det	AL	73	0	0	18	71.0	288	59	31	29	14	3	3	1	22	2	84	2	0	5	3	.625	0	2-6	30	3.48	3.68
2013	Det	AL	66	0	0	43	67.0	265	47	15	15	5	4	0	1	22	2	73	2	0	4	1	.800	0	24-26	9	2.15	2.01
2014	SD	NL	53	0	0	17	54.1	205	28	10	9	3	2	2	1	14	2	64	3	1	4	2	.667	0	11-12	16	1.20	1.49
2015	SD	NL	67	0	0	11	65.1	254	36	17	17	7	2	1	2	23	1	63	2	0	6	5	.545	0	2-6	28	1.78	2.34
	Postseason		20	0	0	5	22.1	88	17	7	7	3	0	0	1	5	0	27	2	0	1	0	1.000	0	3-5	5	2.57	2.82
	14 ML YEARS		661	55	0	166	970.1	4081	803	440	414	117	26	37	30	391	19	960	36	2	54	42	.563	0	50-81	181	3.36	3.84

Christian Bergman

Pitches: R **Bats:** R **Pos:** RP-26; SP-4 **Ht:** 6'1" **Wt:** 180 **Born:** 5/4/1988 **Age:** 28

| | | |HOW MUCH HE PITCHED| | | | |WHAT HE GAVE UP| | | | | | | | | | |THE RESULTS| | | | | | |
Year	Team	Lg	G	GS	CG	GF	IP	BFP	H	R	ER	HR	SH	SF	HB	TBB	IBB	SO	WP	Bk	W	L	Pct	Sh	Sv-Op	Hld	ERC	ERA
2011	TriCity	A-	15	15	2	0	97.1	383	83	31	28	4	0	4	11	0	68	2	0	7	5	.583	2	0- -	-	2.06	2.59
2012	Mdest	A+	27	27	0	0	162.2	668	161	73	66	16	4	3	3	37	0	121	4	0	16	5	.762	0	0- -	-	3.46	3.65
2013	Tulsa	AA	27	27	1	0	171.0	682	162	76	64	25	8	4	5	23	1	111	0	0	8	7	.533	1	0- -	-	3.21	3.37
2014	ColSpr	AAA	15	15	0	0	92.1	387	96	48	43	11	7	3	2	18	0	60	1	0	5	5	.500	0	0- -	-	3.69	4.19
2014	Col	NL	10	10	0	0	54.2	249	75	37	36	9	1	1	1	10	2	31	0	0	3	5	.375	0	0-0	0	5.74	5.93
2015	Col	NL	30	4	0	6	68.1	286	82	36	36	8	2	1	0	15	1	37	4	0	3	1	.750	0	0-0	0	4.75	4.74
	2 ML YEARS		40	14	0	6	123.0	535	157	73	72	17	3	2	1	25	3	68	4	0	6	6	.500	0	0-0	0	5.19	5.27

Doug Bernier

Bats: R **Throws:** R **Pos:** 2B-2;3B-2;PH-1 burr-NEER **Ht:** 6'1" **Wt:** 185 **Born:** 6/24/1980 **Age:** 36

| | | | | | | | | BATTING | | | | | | | | | | | | | RUNNING | | | AVERAGES | | | |
Year	Team	Lg	G	AB	H	2B	3B	HR	(Hm	Rd)	TB	R	RBI	RC	TBB	IBB	SO	HBP	SH	SF	SB	CS	GDP	Avg	OBP	Slg	OPS
2015	Roch*	AAA	95	301	76	9	0	2	(-	-)	91	39	20	34	36	0	57	3	1	1	2	2	10	.252	.337	.302	.640
2008	Col	NL	2	4	0	0	0	0	(0	0)	0	0	0	0	0	0	0	0	0	0	0	0	0	.000	.000	.000	.000
2013	Min	AL	33	53	12	3	0	0	(0	0)	15	9	5	7	8	1	15	1	2	0	2	1	1	.226	.339	.283	.622
2014	Min	AL	7	7	2	0	0	0	(0	0)	2	2	0	1	1	0	2	1	0	0	0	0	0	.286	.444	.286	.730
2015	Min	AL	4	5	1	1	0	0	(0	0)	2	1	2	1	1	0	3	0	0	0	0	0	0	.200	.333	.400	.733
	4 ML YEARS		46	69	15	4	0	0	(0	0)	19	12	7	9	10	1	21	2	2	0	2	1	1	.217	.333	.275	.609

Quintin Berry

Bats: L **Throws:** L **Pos:** PR-7;LF-2;CF-2;RF-1;PH-1 **Ht:** 6'1" **Wt:** 190 **Born:** 11/21/1984 **Age:** 31

| | | | | | | | | BATTING | | | | | | | | | | | | | RUNNING | | | AVERAGES | | | |
Year	Team	Lg	G	AB	H	2B	3B	HR	(Hm	Rd)	TB	R	RBI	RC	TBB	IBB	SO	HBP	SH	SF	SB	CS	GDP	Avg	OBP	Slg	OPS
2015	Pwtckt*	AAA	106	359	82	7	1	4	(-	-)	103	44	36	43	51	0	89	5	6	5	35	6	6	.228	.329	.287	.615
2012	Det	AL	94	291	75	10	6	2	(1	1)	103	44	29	44	25	0	80	7	6	1	21	0	4	.258	.330	.354	.684
2013	Bos	AL	13	8	5	0	0	1	(0	1)	8	5	4	5	1	0	2	0	0	0	3	0	0	.625	.667	1.000	1.667

BATTING																			RUNNING			AVERAGES			
Year Team	Lg	G	AB	H	2B	3B	HR	(Hm Rd)	TB	R	RBI	RC	TBB	IBB	SO	HBP	SH	SF	SB	CS	GDP	Avg	OBP	Slg	OPS
2014 Bal	AL	10	2	0	0 0 0	(0 0)	0	3	0	0	0 0	1	0 0 0	1 0	0	.000	.000	.000	.000
2015 ChC	NL	8	1	0	0 0 0	(0 0)	0	1	0	0	0 0	1	0 0 0	2 1	0	.000	.000	.000	.000
Postseason		14	26	5	2 0 0	(0 0)	7	3	0	3	2 0	6	0 1 0	5 0	1	.192	.250	.269	.519
4 ML YEARS		125	302	80	10 6 3	(1 2)	111	53	33	49	26 0	84	7 6 1	27 1	4	.265	.336	.368	.704

Dellin Betances

Pitches: R Bats: R Pos: RP-74 DELL-inn buh-TAN-siss **Ht:** 6'8" **Wt:** 265 **Born:** 3/23/1988 **Age:** 28

	HOW MUCH HE PITCHED						WHAT HE GAVE UP											THE RESULTS						
Year Team	Lg	G	GS	CG	GF	IP	BFP	H	R	ER	HR	SH	SF	HB	TBB	IBB	SO	WP	Bk	W	L	Pct	Sh	Sv-Op	Hld	ERC	ERA
2011 NYY	AL	2	1	0	0	2.2	16	1	2	2	0	0	1	1	6	0	2	0	0	0	0	-	0	0-0	0	7.94	6.75
2013 NYY	AL	6	0	0	3	5.0	26	9	6	6	1	0	0	0	2	0	10	0	0	0	0	-	0	0-0	0	9.81	10.80
2014 NYY	AL	70	0	0	8	90.0	341	46	15	14	4	2	3	4	24	1	135	2	1	5	0	1.000	0	1-5	29	1.24	1.40
2015 NYY	AL	74	0	0	17	84.0	332	45	17	14	6	1	1	3	40	2	131	9	0	6	4	.600	0	9-13	28	1.94	1.50
4 ML YEARS		152	1	0	28	181.2	715	101	40	36	11	3	5	8	72	3	278	11	1	11	4	.733	0	10-18	50	1.73	1.78

Rafael Betancourt

Pitches: R Bats: R Pos: RP-45 BETT-an-court **Ht:** 6'2" **Wt:** 215 **Born:** 4/29/1975 **Age:** 41

	HOW MUCH HE PITCHED						WHAT HE GAVE UP											THE RESULTS						
Year Team	Lg	G	GS	CG	GF	IP	BFP	H	R	ER	HR	SH	SF	HB	TBB	IBB	SO	WP	Bk	W	L	Pct	Sh	Sv-Op	Hld	ERC	ERA
2003 Cle	AL	33	0	0	13	38.0	154	27	11	9	5	1	1	1	13	2	36	1	0	2	2	.500	0	1-3	4	2.54	2.13
2004 Cle	AL	68	0	0	21	66.2	286	71	32	29	7	1	2	0	18	6	76	5	1	5	6	.455	0	4-11	12	3.77	3.92
2005 Cle	AL	54	0	0	12	67.2	272	57	23	21	5	1	0	0	17	2	73	0	0	4	3	.571	0	1-3	10	2.49	2.79
2006 Cle	AL	50	0	0	17	56.2	231	52	25	24	7	2	2	0	11	5	48	0	0	3	4	.429	0	3-6	7	2.84	3.81
2007 Cle	AL	68	0	0	15	79.1	289	51	13	13	4	0	2	0	9	3	80	0	0	5	1	.833	0	3-6	31	1.24	1.47
2008 Cle	AL	69	0	0	21	71.0	309	76	41	40	11	4	5	0	25	5	64	2	0	3	4	.429	0	4-8	12	4.53	5.07
2009 2 Tms		61	0	0	10	56.0	227	42	20	17	4	2	4	0	20	5	61	0	0	4	3	.571	0	2-6	20	2.30	2.73
2010 Col	NL	72	0	0	18	62.1	248	52	25	25	9	3	1	0	8	2	89	7	0	5	1	.833	0	1-5	23	2.35	3.61
2011 Col	NL	68	0	0	24	62.1	237	46	21	20	7	0	2	0	8	0	73	1	2	2	0	1.000	0	8-12	22	1.84	2.89
2012 Col	NL	60	0	0	53	57.2	236	53	19	18	6	2	2	0	12	4	57	0	1	1	4	.200	0	31-38	1	2.81	2.81
2013 Col	NL	32	0	0	29	28.2	123	26	15	13	2	3	1	0	11	2	27	1	0	2	5	.286	0	16-19	0	3.12	4.08
2015 Col	NL	45	0	0	9	39.1	175	43	29	27	4	0	2	0	12	4	40	0	0	2	4	.333	0	1-4	8	3.92	6.18
09 Cle	AL	29	0	0	7	30.2	129	25	15	12	3	1	2	0	15	4	32	0	0	1	2	.333	0	1-3	8	3.21	3.52
09 Col	NL	32	0	0	3	25.1	98	17	5	5	1	1	2	0	5	1	29	0	0	3	1	.750	0	1-3	12	1.42	1.78
Postseason		10	0	0	2	12.1	49	9	8	7	2	1	1	0	2	1	12	0	0	0	0	-	0	0-0	3	1.98	5.11
12 ML YEARS		680	0	0	241	685.2	2787	596	274	256	71	19	24	1	164	40	724	17	4	38	37	.507	0	75-121	150	2.70	3.36

Christian Bethancourt

Bats: R Throws: R Pos: C-42;PH-3;PR-3 BETH-an-court **Ht:** 6'2" **Wt:** 205 **Born:** 9/2/1991 **Age:** 24

	BATTING																			RUNNING			AVERAGES			
Year Team	Lg	G	AB	H	2B	3B	HR	(Hm Rd)	TB	R	RBI	RC	TBB	IBB	SO	HBP	SH	SF	SB	CS	GDP	Avg	OBP	Slg	OPS
2015 Gwnntt*	AAA	52	202	66	19	0	4	(- -)	97	25	31	36	12	2	31	0	1	3	5	0	4	.327	.359	.480	.840
2013 Atl	NL	1	1	0	0	0	0	(0 0)	0	0	0	0	0	0	1	0	0	0	0	0	0	.000	.000	.000	.000
2014 Atl	NL	31	113	28	3	0	0	(0 0)	31	7	9	8	3	0	26	1	0	0	1	1	3	.248	.274	.274	.548
2015 Atl	NL	48	155	31	8	0	2	(1 1)	45	16	12	4	5	1	33	0	0	0	1	1	7	.200	.225	.290	.515
3 ML YEARS		80	269	59	11	0	2	(1 1)	76	23	21	12	8	1	60	1	0	0	2	2	10	.219	.245	.283	.527

Chad Bettis

Pitches: R Bats: R Pos: SP-20 **Ht:** 6'1" **Wt:** 200 **Born:** 4/26/1989 **Age:** 27

	HOW MUCH HE PITCHED						WHAT HE GAVE UP											THE RESULTS						
Year Team	Lg	G	GS	CG	GF	IP	BFP	H	R	ER	HR	SH	SF	HB	TBB	IBB	SO	WP	Bk	W	L	Pct	Sh	Sv-Op	Hld	ERC	ERA
2015 Albq*	AAA	7	7	0	0	39.0	162	41	16	16	5	0	1	1	10	0	33	1	0	3	2	.600	0	0- -	-	4.19	3.46
2013 Col	NL	16	8	0	0	44.2	208	55	34	28	6	3	1	2	20	2	30	2	1	1	3	.250	0	0-1	1	5.95	5.64
2014 Col	NL	21	0	0	9	24.2	127	42	26	25	4	5	0	1	10	2	13	5	0	0	2	.000	0	0-1	1	8.84	9.12
2015 Col	NL	20	20	0	0	115.0	502	120	56	54	11	7	2	3	42	2	98	6	0	8	6	.571	0	0-0	0	4.20	4.23
3 ML YEARS		57	28	0	9	184.1	837	217	116	107	21	15	3	6	72	6	141	13	1	9	11	.450	0	0-2	4	5.19	5.22

Mookie Betts

Bats: R Throws: R Pos: CF-133;RF-11;PR-2;DH-1;PH-1 **Ht:** 5'9" **Wt:** 180 **Born:** 10/7/1992 **Age:** 23

	BATTING																			RUNNING			AVERAGES			
Year Team	Lg	G	AB	H	2B	3B	HR	(Hm Rd)	TB	R	RBI	RC	TBB	IBB	SO	HBP	SH	SF	SB	CS	GDP	Avg	OBP	Slg	OPS
2012 Lowell	A-	71	251	67	8	1	0	(- -)	77	34	31	33	32	0	30	3	2	4	20	4	3	.267	.352	.307	.658
2013 2 Tms	Low	127	462	145	36	4	15	(- -)	234	93	65	105	81	2	57	2	4	2	38	4	7	.314	.417	.506	.923
2014 Portlnd	AA	54	214	76	18	3	6	(- -)	118	56	34	55	35	0	20	1	0	3	22	3	6	.355	.443	.551	.994
2014 Pwtckt	AAA	45	185	62	12	2	5	(- -)	93	31	31	39	26	0	30	0	0	4	11	4	2	.335	.417	.503	.920
2014 Bos	AL	52	189	55	12	1	5	(1 4)	84	34	18	30	21	0	31	2	1	0	7	3	2	.291	.368	.444	.812
2015 Bos	AL	145	597	174	42	8	18	(9 9)	286	92	77	100	46	1	82	2	3	6	21	6	2	.291	.341	.479	.820
2 ML YEARS		197	786	229	54	9	23	(10 13)	370	126	95	130	67	1	113	4	4	6	28	9	4	.291	.348	.471	.818

Jeff Bianchi

Bats: R Throws: R Pos: 3B-2;SS-1;PR-1   bee-YANK-ee   Ht: 5'11" Wt: 185 Born: 10/5/1986 Age: 29

Year	Team	Lg	G	AB	H	2B	3B	HR	(Hm	Rd)	TB	R	RBI	RC	TBB	IBB	SO	HBP	SH	SF	SB	CS	GDP	Avg	OBP	Slg	OPS
2015	Pwtckt*	AAA	43	130	34	5	1	0	(-	-)	41	13	8	14	13	0	19	0	3	0	4	2	6	.262	.329	.315	.644
2012	Mil	NL	33	69	13	2	0	3	(1	2)	24	8	9	6	4	0	13	0	2	1	0	0	1	.188	.230	.348	.578
2013	Mil	NL	100	236	56	8	1	1	(0	1)	69	22	25	19	11	0	46	1	2	2	4	4	4	.237	.272	.292	.564
2014	Mil	NL	29	70	12	1	0	0	(0	0)	13	4	6	1	3	0	17	0	0	1	0	0	1	.171	.203	.186	.388
2015	Bos	AL	3	2	0	0	0	0	(0	0)	0	0	0	0	0	0	0	0	0	0	0	0	0	.000	.000	.000	.000
	4 ML YEARS		165	377	81	11	1	4	(1	3)	106	34	40	26	18	0	76	1	4	4	4	4	6	.215	.250	.281	.531

Chad Billingsley

Pitches: R Bats: R Pos: SP-7   Ht: 6'1" Wt: 240 Born: 7/29/1984 Age: 31

Year	Team	Lg	G	GS	CG	GF	IP	BFP	H	R	ER	HR	SH	SF	HB	TBB	IBB	SO	WP	Bk	W	L	Pct	Sh	Sv-Op	Hld	ERC	ERA
2015	LV*	AAA	7	6	0	0	29.2	136	34	21	16	5	0	0	3	10	0	23	1	1	2	2	.500	0	0- -	-	5.47	4.85
2006	LAD	NL	18	16	0	0	90.0	403	92	43	38	7	4	0	3	58	3	59	5	0	7	4	.636	0	0-0	0	5.22	3.80
2007	LAD	NL	43	20	1	6	147.0	623	131	56	54	15	9	3	3	64	3	141	5	0	12	5	.706	0	0-1	3	3.70	3.31
2008	LAD	NL	35	32	1	1	200.2	859	188	76	70	14	8	5	8	80	6	201	10	0	16	10	.615	1	0-0	1	3.62	3.14
2009	LAD	NL	33	32	0	0	196.1	823	173	94	88	17	9	11	7	86	7	179	14	0	12	11	.522	0	0-0	0	3.63	4.03
2010	LAD	NL	31	31	1	0	191.2	817	176	82	76	8	7	11	10	69	7	171	4	0	12	11	.522	1	0-0	0	3.20	3.57
2011	LAD	NL	32	32	1	0	188.0	829	189	98	88	14	13	8	7	84	4	152	5	0	11	11	.500	0	0-0	0	4.19	4.21
2012	LAD	NL	25	25	0	0	149.2	634	148	66	59	11	6	3	5	45	2	128	5	0	10	9	.526	0	0-0	0	3.55	3.55
2013	LAD	NL	2	2	0	0	12.0	49	12	4	4	1	2	0	0	5	0	6	0	0	1	0	1.000	0	0-0	0	4.29	3.00
2015	Phi	NL	7	7	0	0	37.0	165	53	26	24	5	2	1	1	8	0	15	2	0	2	3	.400	0	0-0	0	6.43	5.84
	Postseason		6	3	0	0	17.0	78	20	14	13	1	0	0	0	10	2	22	2	0	1	2	.333	0	0-0	0	5.40	6.88
	9 ML YEARS		226	197	4	7	1212.1	5202	1162	545	501	92	60	42	44	499	32	1052	50	0	83	64	.565	2	0-1	4	3.84	3.72

Gregory Bird

Bats: L Throws: R Pos: 1B-46;PH-1;PR-1   Ht: 6'3" Wt: 220 Born: 11/9/1992 Age: 23

Year	Team	Lg	G	AB	H	2B	3B	HR	(Hm	Rd)	TB	R	RBI	RC	TBB	IBB	SO	HBP	SH	SF	SB	CS	GDP	Avg	OBP	Slg	OPS
2012	2 Tms	Low	28	89	30	6	1	2	(-	-)	44	13	13	20	17	1	23	2	0	1	0	0	1	.337	.450	.494	.944
2013	CtnSC	A	130	458	132	36	3	20	(-	-)	234	84	84	105	107	4	132	6	0	2	1	1	9	.288	.428	.511	.938
2014	Tampa	A+	75	274	76	22	1	7	(-	-)	121	36	32	49	45	3	70	1	0	5	1	0	5	.277	.375	.442	.817
2014	Trntn	AA	27	95	24	8	0	7	(-	-)	53	16	11	20	18	0	27	2	0	1	0	0	0	.253	.379	.558	.937
2015	Trntn	AA	49	182	47	16	0	6	(-	-)	81	29	29	30	24	1	30	5	0	1	1	1	1	.258	.358	.445	.804
2015	S-WB	AAA	34	136	41	7	1	6	(-	-)	68	15	23	24	11	0	27	1	0	2	0	0	1	.301	.353	.500	.853
2015	NYY	AL	46	157	41	9	0	11	(5	6)	83	26	31	30	19	0	53	1	0	1	0	0	1	.261	.343	.529	.871

Charlie Blackmon

Bats: L Throws: L Pos: CF-147;LF-14;RF-7;PH-4   Ht: 6'3" Wt: 210 Born: 7/1/1986 Age: 29

Year	Team	Lg	G	AB	H	2B	3B	HR	(Hm	Rd)	TB	R	RBI	RC	TBB	IBB	SO	HBP	SH	SF	SB	CS	GDP	Avg	OBP	Slg	OPS
2011	Col	NL	27	98	25	1	0	1	(1	0)	29	9	8	10	3	1	8	0	1	0	5	1	2	.255	.277	.296	.573
2012	Col	NL	42	113	32	8	0	2	(1	1)	46	15	9	11	4	0	17	3	1	0	1	2	4	.283	.325	.407	.732
2013	Col	NL	82	246	76	17	2	6	(3	3)	115	35	22	35	7	0	49	3	2	0	7	0	1	.309	.336	.467	.803
2014	Col	NL	154	593	171	27	3	19	(13	6)	261	82	72	87	31	5	96	13	6	5	28	10	3	.288	.335	.440	.775
2015	Col	NL	157	614	176	31	9	17	(7	10)	276	93	58	95	46	2	112	13	5	4	43	13	4	.287	.347	.450	.797
	5 ML YEARS		462	1664	480	84	14	45	(25	20)	727	234	169	238	91	8	282	32	15	9	84	26	14	.288	.336	.437	.773

Carson Blair

Bats: R Throws: R Pos: C-11   Ht: 6'2" Wt: 215 Born: 10/18/1989 Age: 26

Year	Team	Lg	G	AB	H	2B	3B	HR	(Hm	Rd)	TB	R	RBI	RC	TBB	IBB	SO	HBP	SH	SF	SB	CS	GDP	Avg	OBP	Slg	OPS
2011	2 Tms	Low	36	113	22	9	0	3	(-	-)	40	13	9	11	14	0	46	0	0	1	0	0	3	.195	.281	.354	.635
2012	Salem	A+	51	165	34	11	3	3	(-	-)	60	25	24	18	21	0	48	2	0	3	2	3	3	.206	.298	.364	.662
2013	2 Tms	Low	44	132	33	10	2	4	(-	-)	59	22	14	24	27	1	41	1	0	1	2	1	4	.250	.379	.447	.826
2014	Salem	A+	67	238	62	19	2	9	(-	-)	112	40	41	46	48	1	88	2	0	3	0	0	3	.261	.385	.471	.855
2014	Portlnd	AA	17	59	17	6	1	2	(-	-)	31	11	8	12	10	0	19	1	0	1	0	0	0	.288	.394	.525	.920
2015	Mdlnd	AA	55	173	47	15	4	6	(-	-)	88	24	29	35	33	0	62	1	0	1	1	0	3	.272	.389	.509	.898
2015	Nashv	AAA	33	113	25	3	0	3	(-	-)	37	9	8	10	9	0	34	1	1	2	0	0	3	.221	.280	.327	.607
2015	Oak	AL	11	31	4	0	0	1	(0	1)	7	3	3	2	4	0	18	0	0	0	0	0	1	.129	.229	.226	.454

Andres Blanco

Bats: B Throws: R Pos: PH-42;3B-36;2B-22;SS-10;PR-3;1B-1   Ht: 5'10" Wt: 195 Born: 4/11/1984 Age: 32

Year	Team	Lg	G	AB	H	2B	3B	HR	(Hm	Rd)	TB	R	RBI	RC	TBB	IBB	SO	HBP	SH	SF	SB	CS	GDP	Avg	OBP	Slg	OPS
2004	KC	AL	19	60	19	2	2	0	(0	0)	25	9	5	12	5	0	6	1	1	0	1	2	0	.317	.379	.417	.795
2005	KC	AL	26	79	17	0	1	0	(0	0)	19	6	5	3	0	0	5	1	4	2	0	1	3	.215	.220	.241	.460
2006	KC	AL	33	87	21	4	1	0	(0	0)	27	9	9	9	5	0	14	1	3	0	0	1	2	.241	.290	.310	.601
2009	ChC	NL	53	123	31	8	0	1	(1	0)	42	15	12	9	8	3	14	1	6	0	0	2	4	.252	.303	.341	.644
2010	Tex	AL	68	166	46	10	1	0	(0	0)	58	17	13	19	11	1	24	3	3	2	0	2	0	.277	.330	.349	.679

Year	Team	Lg	G	AB	H	2B	3B	HR	(Hm	Rd)	TB	R	RBI	RC	TBB	IBB	SO	HBP	SH	SF	SB	CS	GDP	Avg	OBP	Slg	OPS
2011	Tex	AL	36	76	17	3	0	2	(2	0)	26	9	3	4	4	0	14	0	2	0	0	1	1	.224	.263	.342	.605
2014	Phi	NL	25	47	13	5	0	1	(1	0)	21	4	3	6	2	1	6	0	4	0	0	0	4	.277	.306	.447	.753
2015	Phi	NL	106	233	68	22	3	7	(4	3)	117	32	25	34	21	0	44	4	3	0	1	1	11	.292	.360	.502	.863
	8 ML YEARS		366	871	232	54	8	11	(8	3)	335	101	75	96	56	5	127	11	26	4	2	10	25	.266	.317	.385	.702

Gregor Blanco

GREH-gore BLAHN-koh

Bats: L Throws: L Pos: CF-44;LF-38;PH-29;RF-22;PR-2   Ht: 5'11" Wt: 175 Born: 12/24/1983 Age: 32

Year	Team	Lg	G	AB	H	2B	3B	HR	(Hm	Rd)	TB	R	RBI	RC	TBB	IBB	SO	HBP	SH	SF	SB	CS	GDP	Avg	OBP	Slg	OPS
2008	Atl	NL	144	430	108	14	4	1	(0	1)	133	52	38	60	74	2	99	6	6	3	13	5	3	.251	.366	.309	.676
2009	Atl	NL	24	43	8	1	0	0	(0	0)	10	5	1	2	4	0	9	0	1	0	2	0	1	.186	.255	.233	.488
2010	2 Tms		85	237	67	9	4	1	(1	0)	87	31	14	30	29	1	50	0	2	1	11	4	5	.283	.360	.367	.727
2012	SF	NL	141	393	96	14	5	5	(0	3)	135	56	34	50	51	2	104	2	5	2	26	6	0	.244	.333	.344	.676
2013	SF	NL	141	452	120	17	6	3	(0	3)	158	50	41	54	52	4	95	1	3	3	14	9	10	.265	.341	.350	.690
2014	SF	NL	146	393	102	18	6	5	(2	3)	147	51	38	53	41	1	77	3	6	1	16	5	4	.260	.333	.374	.707
2015	SF	NL	115	327	95	19	3	5	(0	5)	135	59	26	41	40	7	59	2	0	3	13	5	3	.291	.368	.413	.781
10	Atl	NL	36	58	18	1	1	0	(0	0)	21	9	3	8	8	1	15	0	0	0	1	2	2	.310	.394	.362	.756
10	KC	AL	49	179	49	8	3	1	(1	0)	66	22	11	22	21	0	35	0	2	1	10	2	3	.274	.348	.369	.717
	Postseason		33	123	23	3	2	2	(0	2)	36	20	10	14	17	0	22	1	2	0	2	0	0	.187	.291	.293	.583
	7 ML YEARS		796	2275	596	91	29	20	(5	15)	805	304	192	290	291	17	493	14	23	13	95	34	26	.262	.347	.354	.701

Kyle Blanks

Bats: R Throws: R Pos: 1B-13;LF-3;DH-1;PH-1   Ht: 6'6" Wt: 265 Born: 9/11/1986 Age: 29

Year	Team	Lg	G	AB	H	2B	3B	HR	(Hm	Rd)	TB	R	RBI	RC	TBB	IBB	SO	HBP	SH	SF	SB	CS	GDP	Avg	OBP	Slg	OPS
2015	RdRck*	AAA	18	58	17	7	0	3	(-	-)	33	8	11	13	6	0	20	4	0	1	0	0	0	.293	.391	.569	.960
2009	SD	NL	54	148	37	9	0	10	(6	4)	76	24	22	21	18	1	55	6	0	0	1	1	4	.250	.355	.514	.868
2010	SD	NL	33	102	16	6	1	3	(2	1)	33	14	15	10	15	0	46	3	0	0	1	0	1	.157	.283	.324	.607
2011	SD	NL	55	170	39	7	1	7	(2	5)	69	21	26	16	16	0	51	2	0	2	2	0	3	.229	.300	.406	.706
2012	SD	NL	4	5	1	0	0	0	(0	0)	1	0	0	0	1	0	2	0	0	0	0	0	0	.200	.333	.200	.533
2013	SD	NL	88	280	68	14	0	8	(3	5)	106	31	35	39	21	1	85	5	0	2	1	1	2	.243	.305	.379	.684
2014	2 Tms		26	55	17	1	0	2	(2	0)	24	10	7	9	8	0	16	2	0	1	0	0	3	.309	.409	.436	.845
2015	Tex	AL	18	67	21	5	0	3	(2	1)	35	10	6	11	4	0	20	0	0	0	1	0	1	.313	.352	.522	.875
14	SD	NL	5	10	2	0	0	0	(0	0)	2	1	0	0	0	0	3	0	0	0	0	0	0	.200	.200	.200	.400
14	Oak	AL	21	45	15	1	0	2	(2	0)	22	9	7	9	8	0	13	2	0	1	0	0	3	.333	.446	.489	.935
	7 ML YEARS		278	827	199	42	2	33	(17	16)	344	110	111	106	83	2	275	18	0	5	6	2	14	.241	.322	.416	.738

Joe Blanton

Pitches: R Bats: R Pos: RP-32; SP-4   Ht: 6'3" Wt: 215 Born: 12/11/1980 Age: 35

| | | | HOW MUCH HE PITCHED | | | | | | WHAT HE GAVE UP | | | | | | | | | | | THE RESULTS | | | | | | |
Year	Team	Lg	G	GS	CG	GF	IP	BFP	H	R	ER	HR	SH	SF	HB	TBB	IBB	SO	WP	Bk	W	L	Pct	Sh	Sv-Op	Hld	ERC	ERA
2015	Omha*	AAA	7	6	0	0	39.1	162	34	17	17	7	0	0	2	10	0	30	2	0	3	2	.600	0	0- -	-	3.46	3.89
2004	Oak	AL	3	0	0	1	8.0	30	6	5	5	1	0	0	0	2	0	6	0	0	0	0	-	0	0-0	0	2.52	5.63
2005	Oak	AL	33	33	2	0	201.1	835	178	86	79	23	2	7	5	67	3	116	4	2	12	12	.500	0	0-0	0	3.37	3.53
2006	Oak	AL	32	31	1	0	194.1	856	241	111	104	17	3	9	5	58	4	107	3	0	16	12	.571	1	0-0	0	5.09	4.82
2007	Oak	AL	34	34	3	0	230.0	950	240	106	101	16	5	8	4	40	4	140	3	1	14	10	.583	1	0-0	0	3.30	3.95
2008	2 Tms		33	33	0	0	197.2	855	211	110	103	22	2	4	4	66	3	111	2	0	9	12	.429	1	0-0	0	4.33	4.69
2009	Phi	NL	31	31	0	0	195.1	837	198	89	88	30	11	4	8	59	4	163	7	0	12	8	.600	0	0-0	0	4.25	4.05
2010	Phi	NL	29	28	0	0	175.2	765	206	104	94	27	5	7	3	43	6	134	2	0	9	6	.600	0	0-0	0	4.81	4.82
2011	Phi	NL	11	8	0	0	41.1	180	52	23	23	5	5	2	1	9	0	35	0	0	1	2	.333	0	0-0	0	5.13	5.01
2012	2 Tms	NL	31	30	2	1	191.0	806	207	106	100	29	8	4	3	34	5	166	5	0	10	13	.435	1	0-0	0	4.00	4.71
2013	LAA	AL	28	20	0	7	132.2	611	180	96	89	29	1	5	4	34	4	108	9	0	2	14	.125	0	0-0	0	6.48	6.04
2015	2 Tms	NL	36	4	0	13	76.0	309	69	26	24	7	1	3	1	16	5	79	2	0	7	2	.778	0	2-2	0	2.77	2.84
08	Oak	AL	20	20	0	0	127.0	550	145	74	70	12	1	2	1	35	3	62	1	0	5	12	.294	0	0-0	0	4.33	4.96
08	Phi	NL	13	13	0	0	70.2	305	66	36	33	10	1	2	3	31	0	49	1	0	4	0	1.000	0	0-0	0	4.33	4.20
12	Phi	NL	21	20	2	1	133.1	560	141	74	68	22	6	3	3	18	2	115	4	0	8	9	.471	1	0-0	0	3.77	4.59
12	LAD	NL	10	10	0	0	57.2	246	66	32	32	7	2	1	0	16	3	51	1	0	2	4	.333	0	0-0	0	4.54	4.99
15	KC	AL	15	4	0	6	41.2	172	43	19	18	6	1	2	0	7	1	40	0	0	2	2	.500	0	2-2	0	3.59	3.89
15	Pit	NL	21	0	0	7	34.1	137	26	7	6	1	0	1	1	9	4	39	2	0	5	0	1.000	0	0-0	0	1.84	1.57
	Postseason		10	6	0	1	40.1	172	36	19	18	5	1	1	3	13	2	33	2	0	2	0	1.000	0	0-0	0	3.51	4.02
	11 ML YEARS		301	252	8	23	1643.1	7034	1788	862	810	206	43	53	38	428	38	1165	37	3	92	91	.503	3	2-2	0	4.25	4.44

Michael Blazek

Pitches: R Bats: R Pos: RP-45   BLAY-zek   Ht: 6'0" Wt: 205 Born: 3/16/1989 Age: 27

| | | | HOW MUCH HE PITCHED | | | | | | WHAT HE GAVE UP | | | | | | | | | | | THE RESULTS | | | | | | |
Year	Team	Lg	G	GS	CG	GF	IP	BFP	H	R	ER	HR	SH	SF	HB	TBB	IBB	SO	WP	Bk	W	L	Pct	Sh	Sv-Op	Hld	ERC	ERA
2011	Sprgfld	AA	24	24	0	0	133.2	612	148	90	81	15	6	5	9	64	2	128	11	5	11	6	.647	0	0- -	-	5.91	5.45
2012	Sprgfld	AA	40	7	0	15	80.0	328	61	37	37	11	2	2	3	34	1	83	5	0	5	8	.385	0	0- -	-	3.31	4.16
2013	Sprgfld	AA	17	0	0	12	19.2	80	11	4	2	0	0	0	0	10	1	25	0	0	0	0	-	0	7- -	-	1.56	0.92
2013	Memp	AAA	11	0	0	11	26.0	109	17	8	8	1	0	4	0	16	0	27	2	0	1	2	.333	0	2- -	-	2.62	2.77
2014	Nashv	AAA	37	17	0	8	102.1	445	106	51	47	9	4	4	3	40	0	87	5	0	4	4	.500	0	1- -	-	4.28	4.13
2013	2 Tms	NL	18	0	0	7	17.1	84	16	12	11	3	1	1	1	13	0	14	0	0	0	1	.000	0	0-0	0	5.57	5.71

Year Team	Lg	G	GS	CG	GF	IP	BFP	H	R	ER	HR	SH	SF	HB	TBB	IBB	SO	WP	Bk	W	L	Pct	Sh	Sv-Op	Hld	ERC	ERA
2015 Mil	NL	45	0	0	17	55.2	222	40	17	15	3	1	2	1	18	1	47	3	0	5	3	.625	0	0-0	4	2.11	2.43
13 StL	NL	11	0	0	3	10.1	52	10	8	8	2	0	0	1	10	0	10	0	0	0	0	-	0	0-0	0	7.25	6.97
13 Mil	NL	7	0	0	4	7.0	32	6	4	3	1	1	1	0	3	0	4	0	0	0	1	.000	0	0-0	0	3.35	3.86
2 ML YEARS		63	0	0	24	73.0	306	56	29	26	6	2	3	2	31	1	61	3	0	5	4	.556	0	0-0	4	2.85	3.21

Jerry Blevins

Pitches: L **Bats:** L **Pos:** RP-7   **Ht:** 6'6" **Wt:** 190 **Born:** 9/6/1983 **Age:** 32

Year Team	Lg	G	GS	CG	GF	IP	BFP	H	R	ER	HR	SH	SF	HB	TBB	IBB	SO	WP	Bk	W	L	Pct	Sh	Sv-Op	Hld	ERC	ERA
2007 Oak	AL	6	0	0	1	4.2	25	8	6	5	1	0	0	0	2	0	3	0	0	0	1	.000	0	0-0	0	9.08	9.64
2008 Oak	AL	36	0	0	8	37.2	156	32	14	13	2	0	1	3	13	2	35	0	0	1	3	.250	0	0-1	5	3.00	3.11
2009 Oak	AL	20	0	0	5	22.1	90	19	12	12	2	0	1	0	6	1	23	0	0	0	0	-	0	0-0	0	2.68	4.84
2010 Oak	AL	63	0	0	9	48.2	220	54	20	20	7	3	1	1	18	1	46	0	0	2	1	.667	0	1-2	11	4.81	3.70
2011 Oak	AL	26	0	0	11	28.1	122	24	14	9	2	2	3	1	14	1	26	0	0	0	0	-	0	0-0	0	3.45	2.86
2012 Oak	AL	63	0	0	17	65.1	261	45	20	18	7	5	2	5	25	5	54	2	0	5	1	.833	0	1-1	14	2.66	2.48
2013 Oak	AL	67	0	0	14	60.0	245	47	23	21	7	3	5	4	17	2	52	2	0	5	0	1.000	0	0-4	4	2.78	3.15
2014 Was	NL	64	0	0	25	57.1	240	48	31	31	3	3	3	1	23	6	66	2	0	2	3	.400	0	0-0	9	2.78	4.87
2015 NYM	NL	7	0	0	1	5.0	15	0	0	0	0	0	0	0	0	0	4	0	0	1	0	1.000	0	0-1	5	0.00	0.00
Postseason		6	0	0	1	7.0	22	1	0	0	0	0	0	0	0	0	2	0	0	0	0	-	0	0.05	0.00		
9 ML YEARS		352	0	0	91	329.1	1374	277	140	129	31	16	16	15	118	18	309	6	0	16	9	.640	0	2-9	48	3.11	3.53

Willie Bloomquist

Bats: R **Throws:** R **Pos:** PH-9;2B-8;SS-7;3B-5;LF-5;PR-4;1B-3;RF-2   **Ht:** 5'11" **Wt:** 200 **Born:** 11/27/1977 **Age:** 38

Year Team	Lg	G	AB	H	2B	3B	HR	(Hm	Rd)	TB	R	RBI	RC	TBB	IBB	SO	HBP	SH	SF	SB	CS	GDP	Avg	OBP	Slg	OPS
2002 Sea	AL	12	33	15	4	0	0	(0	0)	19	11	7	10	5	0	2	0	0	0	3	1	0	.455	.526	.576	1.102
2003 Sea	AL	89	196	49	7	2	1	(1	0)	63	30	14	18	19	1	39	1	2	2	4	1	6	.250	.317	.321	.638
2004 Sea	AL	93	188	46	10	0	2	(0	2)	62	27	18	18	10	0	48	0	3	0	13	2	2	.245	.283	.330	.613
2005 Sea	AL	82	249	64	15	2	0	(0	0)	83	27	22	26	11	0	38	1	4	2	14	1	5	.257	.289	.333	.622
2006 Sea	AL	102	251	62	6	2	1	(0	1)	75	36	15	27	24	0	40	4	2	2	16	3	3	.247	.320	.299	.619
2007 Sea	AL	91	173	48	3	0	2	(1	1)	57	28	13	16	10	0	35	1	4	0	7	5	7	.277	.321	.329	.650
2008 Sea	AL	71	165	46	1	0	0	(0	0)	47	32	9	24	25	1	29	1	1	0	14	3	1	.279	.377	.285	.662
2009 KC	AL	125	434	115	11	8	4	(0	4)	154	52	29	45	27	1	73	1	4	2	25	6	7	.265	.308	.355	.663
2010 2 Tms		83	187	50	10	1	3	(2	1)	71	31	17	19	9	0	28	0	2	1	8	5	4	.267	.299	.380	.679
2011 Ari	NL	97	350	93	10	2	4	(2	2)	119	44	26	37	23	3	51	4	2	2	20	10	3	.266	.317	.340	.657
2012 Ari	NL	80	324	98	21	5	0	(0	0)	129	47	23	46	12	0	55	0	0	2	7	10	5	.302	.325	.398	.724
2013 Ari	NL	48	139	44	5	1	0	(0	0)	51	16	14	20	8	0	11	2	0	1	0	2	3	.317	.360	.367	.727
2014 Sea	AL	47	133	37	6	0	1	(1	0)	46	15	14	18	4	1	32	0	1	1	1	1	1	.278	.297	.346	.643
2015 Sea	AL	35	69	11	1	0	0	(0	0)	12	2	4	0	2	0	13	1	0	0	1	1	2	.159	.194	.174	.368
10 KC	AL	72	170	45	10	1	3	(2	1)	66	31	17	18	8	0	25	0	2	1	8	5	4	.265	.296	.388	.684
10 Cin	NL	11	17	5	0	0	0	(0	0)	5	0	0	1	1	0	3	0	0	0	0	0	0	.294	.333	.294	.627
Postseason		5	22	7	0	0	0	(0	0)	7	3	1	3	1	0	3	0	0	0	3	0	2	.318	.348	.318	.666
14 ML YEARS		1055	2891	778	110	23	18	(7	11)	988	398	225	324	189	7	494	16	25	15	133	51	49	.269	.316	.342	.658

Brett Bochy

Pitches: R **Bats:** R **Pos:** RP-4   **Ht:** 6'2" **Wt:** 200 **Born:** 8/27/1987 **Age:** 28

Year Team	Lg	G	GS	CG	GF	IP	BFP	H	R	ER	HR	SH	SF	HB	TBB	IBB	SO	WP	Bk	W	L	Pct	Sh	Sv-Op	Hld	ERC	ERA
2011 Augsta	A	35	0	0	13	39.0	147	22	6	6	1	1	0	8	0	53	2	0	1	0	1.000	0	10- -	-	1.17	1.38
2012 Rchmd	AA	41	0	0	24	53.1	205	29	15	15	3	2	2	3	18	4	69	1	0	7	3	.700	0	14- -	-	1.52	2.53
2013 Fresno	AAA	45	0	0	13	56.1	239	51	27	25	2	3	3	3	16	0	57	2	1	1	1	.500	0	2- -	-	2.83	3.99
2014 Fresno	AAA	35	2	0	13	54.0	233	53	25	23	8	3	2	0	27	2	47	1	0	4	4	.500	0	0- -	-	4.75	3.83
2015 Scrmto	AAA	43	0	0	12	58.0	249	52	27	19	3	4	2	3	22	0	43	5	0	6	1	.857	0	0- -	-	3.25	2.95
2014 SF	NL	3	0	0	2	3.1	14	1	2	2	1	0	0	1	2	0	3	0	0	0	0	-	0	0-0	0	3.48	5.40
2015 SF	NL	4	0	0	1	3.0	12	1	0	0	0	0	0	1	1	0	3	1	0	0	0	-	0	0-0	1	1.26	0.00
2 ML YEARS		7	0	0	3	6.1	26	2	2	2	1	0	0	2	3	0	6	1	0	0	0	-	0	0-0	1	2.30	2.84

Brennan Boesch

Bats: L **Throws:** L **Pos:** PH-27;LF-8;CF-8;RF-8;DH-1;PR-1   BOSH   **Ht:** 6'4" **Wt:** 225 **Born:** 4/12/1985 **Age:** 31

Year Team	Lg	G	AB	H	2B	3B	HR	(Hm	Rd)	TB	R	RBI	RC	TBB	IBB	SO	HBP	SH	SF	SB	CS	GDP	Avg	OBP	Slg	OPS
2015 Lsvlle*	AAA	51	187	61	9	0	4	(-	-)	82	17	30	31	19	5	41	0	1	1	0	2	2	.326	.386	.439	.825
2010 Det	AL	133	464	119	26	3	14	(7	7)	193	49	67	61	40	5	99	5	0	3	7	1	5	.256	.320	.416	.736
2011 Det	AL	115	428	121	25	1	16	(9	7)	196	75	54	56	35	2	91	5	0	4	5	3	7	.283	.341	.458	.799
2012 Det	AL	132	470	113	22	2	12	(9	3)	175	52	54	47	26	1	104	5	0	2	6	3	11	.240	.286	.372	.659
2013 NYY	AL	23	51	14	2	1	3	(2	1)	27	6	8	8	2	0	9	0	0	0	0	0	2	.275	.302	.529	.831
2014 LAA	AL	27	75	14	2	0	2	(1	1)	22	6	7	3	2	1	19	0	0	2	3	0	0	.187	.203	.293	.496
2015 Cin	NL	51	89	13	2	0	1	(1	0)	18	4	5	2	4	0	30	1	0	0	1	0	0	.146	.191	.202	.394
6 ML YEARS		481	1577	394	79	7	48	(30	18)	631	192	195	177	109	9	344	16	0	11	22	7	25	.250	.303	.400	.703

Xander Bogaerts

Bats: R **Throws:** R **Pos:** SS-156;PR-1 ZAN-derr BO-garts **Ht:** 6'1" **Wt:** 210 **Born:** 10/1/1992 **Age:** 23

Year	Team	Lg	G	AB	H	2B	3B	HR	(Hm	Rd)	TB	R	RBI	RC	TBB	IBB	SO	HBP	SH	SF	SB	CS	GDP	Avg	OBP	Slg	OPS
2013	Bos	AL	18	44	11	2	0	1	(0	1)	16	7	5	4	5	0	13	0	0	1	1	0	1	.250	.320	.364	.684
2014	Bos	AL	144	538	129	28	1	12	(7	5)	195	60	46	43	39	1	138	8	2	7	2	3	11	.240	.297	.362	.660
2015	Bos	AL	156	613	196	35	3	7	(5	2)	258	84	81	88	32	1	101	3	3	3	10	2	16	.320	.355	.421	.776
	Postseason		12	27	8	3	1	0	(0	0)	13	9	2	5	6	0	9	0	0	1	0	0	1	.296	.412	.481	.893
	3 ML YEARS		318	1195	336	65	4	20	(12	8)	469	151	132	135	76	2	252	11	5	11	13	5	28	.281	.327	.392	.720

Brian Bogusevic

Bats: L **Throws:** L **Pos:** RF-14;PH-6;LF-2 boh-guh-SEVV-ick **Ht:** 6'3" **Wt:** 215 **Born:** 2/18/1984 **Age:** 32

Year	Team	Lg	G	AB	H	2B	3B	HR	(Hm	Rd)	TB	R	RBI	RC	TBB	IBB	SO	HBP	SH	SF	SB	CS	GDP	Avg	OBP	Slg	OPS
2015	LV*	AAA	118	467	138	18	3	12	(-	-)	198	65	57	76	44	4	96	3	0	1	24	5	3	.296	.359	.424	.783
2010	Hou	NL	19	28	5	3	0	0	(0	0)	8	5	3	2	3	0	12	0	0	0	1	1	2	.179	.258	.286	.544
2011	Hou	NL	87	164	47	14	1	4	(2	2)	75	22	15	19	15	1	40	1	1	1	4	2	8	.287	.348	.457	.805
2012	Hou	NL	146	355	72	9	2	7	(4	3)	106	39	28	31	41	1	96	7	0	1	15	4	6	.203	.297	.299	.596
2013	ChC	NL	47	143	39	7	1	6	(4	2)	66	18	16	18	10	1	35	1	0	1	2	0	4	.273	.323	.462	.784
2015	Phi	NL	22	58	15	3	0	2	(2	0)	24	9	5	7	3	0	21	0	0	0	2	0	1	.259	.295	.414	.709
	5 ML YEARS		321	748	178	36	4	19	(12	7)	279	93	67	77	72	3	204	9	1	3	24	7	21	.238	.311	.373	.684

Mike Bolsinger

Pitches: R **Bats:** R **Pos:** SP-21 BOWL-sing-er **Ht:** 6'1" **Wt:** 215 **Born:** 1/29/1988 **Age:** 28

			HOW MUCH HE PITCHED						WHAT HE GAVE UP											THE RESULTS							
Year	Team	Lg	G	GS	CG	GF	IP	BFP	H	R	ER	HR	SH	SF	HB	TBB	IBB	SO	WP	Bk	W	L	Pct	Sh	Sv-Op	Hld	ERC	ERA
2011	Sbend	A	32	13	0	7	101.2	398	84	35	30	6	1	3	1	25	0	91	6	0	6	6	.500	0	0- -	-	2.45	2.66
2012	Visalia	A+	7	7	0	0	38.0	160	31	15	10	1	0	2	1	13	0	49	2	1	3	2	.600	0	0- -	-	2.43	2.37
2012	Mobile	AA	15	15	0	0	77.2	335	82	40	33	5	2	3	2	38	0	64	8	1	4	3	.571	0	0- -	-	4.77	3.82
2013	Mobile	AA	9	6	1	0	43.0	176	35	14	12	0	3	1	1	15	0	31	5	0	4	0	1.000	1	0- -	-	2.35	2.51
2013	Reno	AAA	17	17	1	0	101.0	451	116	60	53	12	7	3	4	39	1	97	5	1	7	7	.500	0	0- -	-	5.17	4.72
2014	Reno	AAA	17	16	0	0	91.2	390	92	40	40	6	3	0	3	32	1	88	1	0	8	3	.727	0	0- -	-	3.80	3.93
2015	OkCity	AAA	10	8	0	0	46.2	187	30	12	12	2	2	3	3	18	0	61	4	0	3	3	.500	0	0- -	-	2.08	2.31
2014	Ari	NL	10	9	0	0	52.1	238	66	36	32	7	3	4	0	17	1	48	0	1	1	6	.143	0	0-0	0	5.42	5.50
2015	LAD	NL	21	21	0	0	109.1	466	104	49	44	11	3	2	1	45	3	98	6	1	6	6	.500	0	0-0	0	3.87	3.62
	2 ML YEARS		31	30	0	0	161.2	704	170	85	76	18	6	6	1	62	4	146	6	2	7	12	.368	0	0-0	0	4.36	4.23

Emilio Bonifacio

boh-knee-FAH-see-oh

Bats: B **Throws:** R **Pos:** PH-20;2B-17;PR-8;DH-7;CF-3;LF-2;3B-1 **Ht:** 5'11" **Wt:** 205 **Born:** 4/23/1985 **Age:** 31

Year	Team	Lg	G	AB	H	2B	3B	HR	(Hm	Rd)	TB	R	RBI	RC	TBB	IBB	SO	HBP	SH	SF	SB	CS	GDP	Avg	OBP	Slg	OPS
2015	Iowa*	AAA	13	49	23	2	0	0	(-	-)	25	12	3	14	8	0	6	0	0	0	6	1	1	.469	.544	.510	1.054
2007	Ari	NL	11	23	5	1	0	0	(0	0)	6	2	2	4	4	0	3	0	0	0	0	1	0	.217	.333	.261	.594
2008	2 Tms	NL	49	169	41	6	5	0	(0	0)	57	29	14	16	14	0	46	0	0	3	7	4	2	.243	.296	.337	.633
2009	Fla	NL	127	461	116	11	6	1	(1	0)	142	72	27	41	34	0	95	2	8	4	21	9	5	.252	.303	.308	.611
2010	Fla	NL	73	180	47	6	3	0	(0	0)	59	30	10	24	17	0	42	0	1	3	12	0	1	.261	.320	.328	.648
2011	Fla	NL	152	565	167	26	7	5	(1	4)	222	78	36	83	59	1	129	1	11	4	40	11	4	.296	.360	.393	.753
2012	Mia	NL	64	244	63	3	4	1	(1	0)	77	30	11	30	25	1	52	1	4	0	30	3	3	.258	.330	.316	.645
2013	2 Tms	AL	136	420	102	23	3	3	(1	2)	139	54	31	39	30	0	103	2	6	3	28	8	4	.243	.295	.331	.625
2014	2 Tms	NL	110	394	102	17	4	3	(2	1)	136	47	24	46	26	2	85	0	6	0	26	8	2	.259	.305	.345	.650
2015	CWS	AL	47	78	13	2	0	0	(0	0)	15	5	4	1	2	0	27	1	1	0	1	4	1	.167	.198	.192	.390
08	Ari	NL	8	12	2	1	0	0	(0	0)	3	3	2	1	0	0	5	0	0	0	1	0	0	.167	.167	.250	.417
08	Was	NL	41	157	39	5	5	0	(0	0)	54	26	12	15	14	0	41	0	0	3	6	4	2	.248	.305	.344	.649
13	Tor	AL	94	262	57	16	1	3	(1	2)	84	33	20	19	13	0	66	2	3	2	12	6	3	.218	.258	.321	.579
13	KC	AL	42	158	45	6	2	0	(0	0)	55	21	11	20	17	0	37	0	3	1	16	2	1	.285	.352	.348	.700
14	ChC	NL	69	276	77	14	3	2	(2	0)	103	35	18	37	16	2	49	0	6	0	14	6	1	.279	.318	.373	.692
14	Atl	NL	41	118	25	3	1	1	(0	1)	33	12	6	9	10	0	36	0	0	0	12	2	1	.212	.273	.280	.553
	9 ML YEARS		769	2534	656	94	32	13	(6	7)	853	347	159	284	211	4	582	7	37	18	165	48	22	.259	.316	.337	.652

Justin Bour

Bats: L **Throws:** R **Pos:** 1B-111;PH-23;DH-1 BOOR **Ht:** 6'4" **Wt:** 250 **Born:** 5/28/1988 **Age:** 28

Year	Team	Lg	G	AB	H	2B	3B	HR	(Hm	Rd)	TB	R	RBI	RC	TBB	IBB	SO	HBP	SH	SF	SB	CS	GDP	Avg	OBP	Slg	OPS
2011	Dytona	A+	133	502	139	30	1	23	(-	-)	240	65	85	83	46	5	105	2	0	8	3	2	15	.277	.335	.478	.813
2012	Tenn	AA	138	506	143	36	0	17	(-	-)	230	64	110	87	62	10	115	3	0	6	4	1	12	.283	.360	.455	.815
2013	Tenn	AA	83	317	75	17	0	18	(-	-)	146	48	64	47	36	8	63	2	0	6	0	1	8	.237	.313	.461	.774
2014	NewOr	AAA	103	385	118	27	0	18	(-	-)	199	59	72	75	39	11	57	3	0	3	3	1	7	.306	.372	.517	.889
2015	NewOr	AAA	14	51	14	1	0	1	(-	-)	18	8	5	8	11	3	6	0	0	0	1	0	2	.275	.403	.353	.756
2014	Mia	NL	39	74	21	3	0	1	(1	0)	27	10	11	13	9	1	19	0	0	0	0	0	0	.284	.361	.365	.726
2015	Mia	NL	129	409	107	20	0	23	(10	13)	196	42	73	58	34	3	101	2	0	1	0	0	19	.262	.321	.479	.800
	2 ML YEARS		168	483	128	23	0	24	(11	13)	223	52	84	71	43	4	120	2	0	1	0	0	19	.265	.327	.462	.789

Jason Bourgeois

Bats: R **Throws:** R **Pos:** CF-35;PH-23;LF-18;RF-6;PR-1   boor-ZHWAH   **Ht:** 5'9" **Wt:** 200 **Born:** 1/4/1982 **Age:** 34

							BATTING													RUNNING			AVERAGES			
Year Team	Lg	G	AB	H	2B	3B	HR	(Hm	Rd)	TB	R	RBI	RC	TBB	IBB	SO	HBP	SH	SF	SB	CS	GDP	Avg	OBP	Slg	OPS
2015 Lsvlle*	AAA	14	55	17	2	1	0	(-	-)	21	8	7	7	3	0	5	1	1	0	1	1	1	.309	.356	.382	.738
2008 CWS	AL	6	3	1	1	0	0	(0	0)	2	0	0	0	0	0	0	0	0	0	0	0	0	.333	.333	.667	1.000
2009 Mil	NL	24	37	7	0	0	1	(1	0)	10	6	3	1	3	0	7	0	0	0	3	0	2	.189	.250	.270	.520
2010 Hou	NL	69	123	27	4	1	0	(0	0)	33	16	3	8	13	0	16	0	0	0	12	4	5	.220	.294	.268	.562
2011 Hou	NL	93	238	70	8	2	1	(0	1)	85	30	16	31	10	0	24	0	4	0	31	6	5	.294	.323	.357	.680
2012 KC	AL	30	62	16	2	1	0	(0	0)	20	10	5	5	4	0	4	0	0	0	5	4	1	.258	.303	.323	.626
2013 TB	AL	9	16	3	0	0	1	(0	1)	6	2	2	1	2	0	4	0	0	0	0	0	0	.188	.278	.375	.653
2014 Cin	NL	18	33	8	0	1	0	(0	0)	10	5	1	4	1	0	6	0	0	0	0	0	1	.242	.265	.303	.568
2015 Cin	NL	68	196	47	5	2	3	(0	3)	65	28	14	20	14	0	33	1	1	0	3	1	2	.240	.294	.332	.625
8 ML YEARS		317	708	179	20	7	6	(1	5)	231	97	44	70	47	0	94	1	5	0	54	15	16	.253	.300	.326	.627

Peter Bourjos

Bats: R **Throws:** R **Pos:** CF-93;PH-33;PR-17   BORE-juss   **Ht:** 6'1" **Wt:** 185 **Born:** 3/31/1987 **Age:** 29

							BATTING													RUNNING			AVERAGES			
Year Team	Lg	G	AB	H	2B	3B	HR	(Hm	Rd)	TB	R	RBI	RC	TBB	IBB	SO	HBP	SH	SF	SB	CS	GDP	Avg	OBP	Slg	OPS
2010 LAA	AL	51	181	37	6	4	6	(1	5)	69	19	15	13	6	0	40	2	3	1	10	3	2	.204	.237	.381	.618
2011 LAA	AL	147	502	136	26	11	12	(7	5)	220	72	43	66	32	0	124	10	7	1	22	9	7	.271	.327	.438	.765
2012 LAA	AL	101	168	37	7	0	3	(1	2)	53	27	19	18	15	0	44	3	6	3	3	1	2	.220	.291	.315	.606
2013 LAA	AL	55	175	48	3	3	3	(1	2)	66	26	12	19	10	0	43	6	4	1	6	0	8	.274	.333	.377	.710
2014 StL	NL	119	264	61	9	5	4	(2	2)	92	32	24	27	20	1	78	4	5	1	9	3	5	.231	.294	.348	.643
2015 StL	NL	117	195	39	8	3	4	(2	2)	65	32	13	14	19	4	59	6	4	1	5	8	2	.200	.290	.333	.623
Postseason		5	2	0	0	0	0	(0	0)	0	0	0	0	0	0	1	0	0	0	0	0	0	.000	.000	.000	.000
6 ML YEARS		590	1485	358	59	26	32	(14	18)	565	208	126	157	102	5	388	31	29	8	55	24	26	.241	.302	.380	.682

Michael Bourn

Bats: L **Throws:** R **Pos:** CF-106;LF-29;PH-14;RF-3;PR-3;DH-1 BORN   **Ht:** 5'10" **Wt:** 180 **Born:** 12/27/1982 **Age:** 33

							BATTING													RUNNING			AVERAGES			
Year Team	Lg	G	AB	H	2B	3B	HR	(Hm	Rd)	TB	R	RBI	RC	TBB	IBB	SO	HBP	SH	SF	SB	CS	GDP	Avg	OBP	Slg	OPS
2006 Phi	NL	17	8	1	0	0	0	(0	0)	1	2	0	0	1	0	3	0	2	0	1	2	0	.125	.222	.125	.347
2007 Phi	NL	105	119	33	3	3	1	(1	0)	45	29	6	19	13	2	21	0	1	0	18	1	1	.277	.348	.378	.727
2008 Hou	NL	138	467	107	10	4	5	(3	2)	140	57	29	43	37	0	111	2	7	1	41	10	3	.229	.288	.300	.588
2009 Hou	NL	157	606	173	27	12	3	(2	1)	233	97	35	94	63	1	140	2	5	2	61	12	1	.285	.354	.384	.738
2010 Hou	NL	141	535	142	25	6	2	(0	2)	185	84	38	74	59	5	109	3	6	2	52	12	6	.265	.341	.346	.686
2011 2 Tms	NL	158	656	193	34	10	2	(2	0)	253	94	50	92	53	3	140	4	5	4	61	14	6	.294	.349	.386	.734
2012 Atl	NL	155	624	171	26	10	9	(2	7)	244	96	57	102	70	1	155	3	2	4	42	13	2	.274	.348	.391	.739
2013 Cle	AL	130	525	138	21	6	6	(2	4)	189	75	50	65	40	0	132	2	5	3	23	12	2	.263	.316	.360	.676
2014 Cle	AL	106	444	114	17	10	3	(3	0)	160	57	28	51	35	1	114	3	3	2	10	6	5	.257	.314	.360	.674
2015 2 Tms	NL	141	425	101	15	2	0	(0	0)	120	39	30	39	46	0	107	0	8	3	17	7	5	.238	.310	.282	.592
11 Hou	NL	105	429	130	26	7	1	(1	0)	173	64	32	66	38	2	90	3	2	1	39	7	5	.303	.363	.403	.766
11 Atl	NL	53	227	63	8	3	1	(1	0)	80	30	18	26	15	1	50	1	3	3	22	7	1	.278	.321	.352	.674
15 Cle	AL	95	289	71	12	1	0	(0	0)	85	29	19	27	29	0	76	0	7	1	13	5	2	.246	.313	.294	.608
15 Atl	NL	46	136	30	3	1	0	(0	0)	35	10	11	12	17	0	31	0	1	2	4	2	3	.221	.303	.257	.561
Postseason		4	10	1	0	0	0	(0	0)	1	0	1	0	0	0	4	0	0	0	0	0	0	.100	.100	.100	.200
10 ML YEARS		1248	4409	1173	178	63	31	(15	16)	1570	630	323	579	417	13	1032	19	44	21	326	89	31	.266	.331	.356	.687

Brad Boxberger

Pitches: R **Bats:** R **Pos:** RP-69   **Ht:** 6'2" **Wt:** 225 **Born:** 5/27/1988 **Age:** 28

			HOW MUCH HE PITCHED					WHAT HE GAVE UP											THE RESULTS					
Year Team	Lg	G	GS	CG	GF	IP	BFP	H	R	ER	HR	SH	SF	HB	TBB	IBB	SO	WP	Bk	W	L	Pct	Sh	Sv-Op	Hld	ERC	ERA
2012 SD	NL	24	0	0	4	27.2	120	22	12	8	3	0	1	2	18	1	33	0	0	0	0	-	0	0-0	1	4.28	2.60
2013 SD	NL	18	0	0	6	22.0	94	19	9	7	3	3	2	0	13	0	24	0	0	0	1	.000	0	1-1	0	4.43	2.86
2014 TB	AL	63	0	0	10	64.2	247	34	17	17	9	2	2	4	20	0	104	3	2	5	2	.714	0	2-5	18	1.84	2.37
2015 TB	AL	69	0	0	53	63.0	271	54	29	26	9	2	1	2	32	5	74	5	1	4	10	.286	0	41-47	2	4.01	3.71
4 ML YEARS		174	0	0	73	177.1	732	129	67	58	24	7	6	8	83	6	235	8	3	9	13	.409	0	44-53	21	3.26	2.94

Matt Boyd

Pitches: L **Bats:** L **Pos:** SP-12; RP-1   **Ht:** 6'3" **Wt:** 215 **Born:** 2/2/1991 **Age:** 25

			HOW MUCH HE PITCHED					WHAT HE GAVE UP											THE RESULTS					
Year Team	Lg	G	GS	CG	GF	IP	BFP	H	R	ER	HR	SH	SF	HB	TBB	IBB	SO	WP	Bk	W	L	Pct	Sh	Sv-Op	Hld	ERC	ERA
2013 2 Tms	Low	8	5	0	1	24.0	88	14	7	7	2	0	0	4	4	0	23	1	0	0	3	.000	0	0- -	-	1.31	2.63
2014 Dnedin	A+	16	16	1	0	90.2	357	65	20	14	4	1	1	4	20	0	103	3	1	5	3	.625	0	0- -	-	1.81	1.39
2014 Nham	AA	10	10	0	0	42.2	197	55	33	33	5	0	2	3	13	0	44	3	0	1	4	.200	0	0- -	-	5.72	6.96
2015 Nham	AA	12	12	0	0	73.2	273	39	11	9	3	1	1	1	18	0	70	2	1	6	1	.857	0	0- -	-	1.20	1.10
2015 Buffalo	AAA	6	6	0	0	39.0	153	32	13	12	5	0	0	1	6	0	37	2	0	3	1	.750	0	0- -	-	2.49	2.77
2015 2 Tms	AL	13	12	0	0	57.1	252	71	50	48	17	1	3	1	20	0	43	4	0	1	6	.143	0	0-0	0	7.04	7.53
15 Tor	AL	2	2	0	0	6.2	36	15	11	11	5	0	1	0	1	0	7	2	0	0	2	.000	0	0-0	0	17.16	14.85
15 Det	AL	11	10	0	0	50.2	216	56	39	37	12	1	2	1	19	0	36	2	0	1	4	.200	0	0-0	0	5.88	6.57

Blaine Boyer

Pitches: R Bats: R Pos: RP-68   Ht: 6'3" Wt: 225 Born: 7/11/1981 Age: 34

		HOW MUCH HE PITCHED						WHAT HE GAVE UP											THE RESULTS						
Year	Team	Lg	G	GS	CG	GF	IP	BFP	H	R	ER	HR	SH	SF	HB	TBB	IBB	SO	WP	Bk	W	L	Pct	Sh	Sv-Op	Hld	ERC	ERA
2005	Atl	NL	43	0	0	5	37.2	158	32	13	13	1	1	1	2	17	0	33	2	0	4	2	.667	0	0-2	9	3.21	3.11
2006	Atl	NL	2	0	0	0	0.2	7	4	3	3	0	0	0	0	1	0	0	0	0	0	0	-	0	0-0	1	47.92	40.50
2007	Atl	NL	5	0	0	2	5.1	26	10	3	2	0	1	0	0	1	1	3	2	0	0	0	-	0	0-0	1	7.41	3.38
2008	Atl	NL	76	0	0	18	72.0	313	73	51	47	10	3	4	2	25	4	67	2	0	2	6	.250	0	1-5	14	4.19	5.88
2009	3 Tms	NL	48	0	0	21	54.2	241	56	36	25	1	4	1	5	20	0	29	2	0	0	2	.000	0	0-0	4	3.81	4.12
2010	Ari	NL	54	0	0	11	57.0	251	59	32	27	3	3	2	1	29	1	29	2	0	3	2	.600	0	0-4	5	4.45	4.26
2011	NYM	NL	5	0	0	3	6.2	33	13	8	8	2	1	0	1	1	0	1	0	0	0	2	.000	0	1-1	0	12.04	10.80
2014	SD	NL	32	0	0	11	40.1	160	34	16	16	2	2	1	0	8	0	29	1	0	1	1	.000	0	0-0	5	2.21	3.57
2015	Min	AL	68	0	0	12	65.0	268	62	24	18	5	3	2	0	19	4	33	5	0	3	6	.333	0	1-3	19	3.20	2.49
09	Atl	NL	3	0	0	1	1.1	11	3	6	6	0	0	0	1	3	0	2	0	0	0	1	.000	0	0-0	0	23.46	40.50
09	StL	NL	15	0	0	4	16.1	70	14	10	8	1	3	0	1	5	0	9	0	0	0	0	-	0	0-0	2	2.82	4.41
09	Ari	NL	30	0	0	16	37.0	160	39	20	11	0	1	1	3	12	0	18	2	0	0	1	.000	0	0-0	2	3.71	2.68
	9 ML YEARS		333	0	0	83	339.1	1457	343	186	159	24	18	11	11	121	10	224	16	0	12	21	.364	0	3-15	58	3.85	4.22

Brad Brach

Pitches: R Bats: R Pos: RP-62   BROCK   Ht: 6'6" Wt: 215 Born: 4/12/1986 Age: 30

		HOW MUCH HE PITCHED						WHAT HE GAVE UP											THE RESULTS						
Year	Team	Lg	G	GS	CG	GF	IP	BFP	H	R	ER	HR	SH	SF	HB	TBB	IBB	SO	WP	Bk	W	L	Pct	Sh	Sv-Op	Hld	ERC	ERA
2011	SD	NL	9	0	0	4	7.0	38	9	5	4	0	0	0	1	7	4	11	1	0	0	2	.000	0	0-0	0	6.51	5.14
2012	SD	NL	67	0	0	13	66.2	280	50	28	28	11	1	3	2	33	7	55	4	0	2	4	.333	0	0-1	15	3.47	3.78
2013	SD	NL	33	0	0	6	31.0	141	36	15	11	3	0	3	0	19	0	31	4	0	1	0	1.000	0	0-0	2	6.03	3.19
2014	Bal	AL	46	0	0	8	62.1	254	48	24	22	6	2	4	1	25	1	54	2	0	7	1	.875	0	0-0	8	2.90	3.18
2015	Bal	AL	62	0	0	12	79.1	324	57	25	24	7	3	2	0	38	3	89	1	0	5	3	.625	0	1-2	14	2.78	2.72
	Postseason		2	0	0	0	2.1	10	1	0	0	0	0	0	0	2	0	1	0	0	1	0	1.000	0	0-0	0	2.03	0.00
	5 ML YEARS		217	0	0	43	246.1	1037	200	97	89	27	6	12	4	122	15	260	12	0	15	10	.600	0	1-3	39	3.48	3.25

Silvino Bracho

Pitches: R Bats: R Pos: RP-13   BRAH-cho   Ht: 5'10" Wt: 190 Born: 7/17/1992 Age: 23

		HOW MUCH HE PITCHED						WHAT HE GAVE UP											THE RESULTS						
Year	Team	Lg	G	GS	CG	GF	IP	BFP	H	R	ER	HR	SH	SF	HB	TBB	IBB	SO	WP	Bk	W	L	Pct	Sh	Sv-Op	Hld	ERC	ERA
2013	Msoula	R+	24	0	0	23	26.1	105	23	6	5	2	0	1	0	3	0	38	1	0	0	2	.000	0	11- -	-	2.17	1.71
2014	Sbend	A	45	0	0	38	43.1	163	25	10	10	3	2	1	2	8	1	70	3	0	3	2	.600	0	26- -	-	1.35	2.08
2015	Visalia	A+	6	0	0	6	6.0	20	1	0	0	0	0	0	0	1	0	14	0	0	0	0	-	0	3- -	-	0.19	0.00
2015	Mobile	AA	37	0	0	28	44.2	177	34	10	9	3	1	2	1	9	1	59	5	0	2	1	.667	0	16- -	-	1.96	1.81
2015	Ari	NL	13	0	0	3	12.1	50	9	2	2	2	0	0	1	4	1	17	1	0	0	0	-	0	1-1	0	2.95	1.46

Archie Bradley

Pitches: R Bats: R Pos: SP-8   Ht: 6'4" Wt: 230 Born: 8/10/1992 Age: 23

		HOW MUCH HE PITCHED						WHAT HE GAVE UP											THE RESULTS						
Year	Team	Lg	G	GS	CG	GF	IP	BFP	H	R	ER	HR	SH	SF	HB	TBB	IBB	SO	WP	Bk	W	L	Pct	Sh	Sv-Op	Hld	ERC	ERA
2012	Sbend	A	27	27	0	0	136.0	583	87	64	58	6	2	2	15	84	0	152	17	2	12	6	.667	0	0- -	-	2.97	3.84
2013	Visalia	A+	5	5	0	0	28.2	115	22	5	4	1	1	0	2	10	0	43	1	0	2	0	1.000	0	0- -	-	2.57	1.26
2013	Mobile	AA	21	21	2	0	123.1	506	93	35	27	5	5	4	4	59	2	119	1	0	12	5	.706	0	0- -	-	2.82	1.97
2014	Reno	AAA	5	5	0	0	24.1	113	26	14	14	0	1	2	4	12	0	23	2	1	1	4	.200	0	0- -	-	4.66	5.18
2014	Mobile	AA	12	12	1	0	54.2	240	45	27	25	2	2	2	5	36	1	46	3	0	2	3	.400	0	0- -	-	4.01	4.12
2015	Ari	NL	8	8	0	0	35.2	161	36	23	23	3	1	1	2	22	1	23	0	0	2	3	.400	0	0-0	0	5.12	5.80

Jackie Bradley Jr.

Bats: L Throws: R Pos: RF-32;CF-27;LF-17;PH-1   Ht: 5'10" Wt: 200 Born: 4/19/1990 Age: 26

			BATTING																RUNNING			AVERAGES			
Year	Team	Lg	G	AB	H	2B	3B	HR	(Hm | Rd)	TB	R	RBI	RC	TBB	IBB	SO	HBP	SH	SF	SB	CS	GDP	Avg	OBP	Slg	OPS
2015	Pwtckt*	AAA	71	282	86	18	1	9	(- | -)	133	38	29	51	30	1	44	5	1	0	4	4	4	.305	.382	.472	.853
2013	Bos	AL	37	95	18	5	0	3	(2 | 1)	32	18	10	8	10	0	31	2	0	0	2	0	1	.189	.280	.337	.617
2014	Bos	AL	127	384	76	19	2	1	(1 | 0)	102	45	30	27	31	1	121	5	1	2	8	0	10	.198	.265	.266	.531
2015	Bos	AL	74	221	55	17	4	10	(5 | 5)	110	43	43	41	27	0	69	3	1	3	3	0	5	.249	.335	.498	.832
	3 ML YEARS		238	700	149	41	6	14	(8 | 6)	244	106	83	76	68	1	221	10	2	5	13	0	16	.213	.290	.349	.638

Michael Brantley

Bats: L Throws: L Pos: LF-101;CF-28;DH-18;PH-2   Ht: 6'2" Wt: 200 Born: 5/15/1987 Age: 29

			BATTING																RUNNING			AVERAGES			
Year	Team	Lg	G	AB	H	2B	3B	HR	(Hm | Rd)	TB	R	RBI	RC	TBB	IBB	SO	HBP	SH	SF	SB	CS	GDP	Avg	OBP	Slg	OPS
2009	Cle	AL	28	112	35	4	0	0	(0 | 0)	39	10	11	16	8	0	19	0	1	0	4	4	3	.313	.358	.348	.707
2010	Cle	AL	72	297	73	9	3	3	(2 | 1)	97	38	22	32	22	0	38	0	4	2	10	2	6	.246	.296	.327	.623
2011	Cle	AL	114	451	120	24	4	7	(4 | 3)	173	63	46	56	34	2	76	3	3	5	13	5	11	.266	.318	.384	.702
2012	Cle	AL	149	552	159	37	4	6	(3 | 3)	222	63	60	76	53	12	56	0	0	4	12	9	7	.288	.348	.402	.750
2013	Cle	AL	151	556	158	26	3	10	(9 | 1)	220	66	73	86	40	1	67	4	3	8	17	4	11	.284	.332	.396	.728
2014	Cle	AL	156	611	200	45	2	20	(11 | 9)	309	94	97	114	52	4	56	8	0	5	23	1	16	.327	.385	.506	.890
2015	Cle	AL	137	529	164	45	0	15	(9 | 6)	254	68	84	94	60	8	51	2	0	5	15	1	14	.310	.379	.480	.859
	Postseason		1	4	1	0	0	0	(0 | 0)	1	0	0	0	0	0	0	0	0	0	0	0	0	.250	.250	.250	.500
	7 ML YEARS		807	3108	909	190	16	61	(38 | 23)	1314	402	393	474	269	27	363	17	11	29	94	26	68	.292	.349	.423	.772

Rob Brantly

Bats: L Throws: R Pos: C-14;PH-2   Ht: 6'1" Wt: 195 Born: 7/14/1989 Age: 26

							BATTING													RUNNING			AVERAGES			
Year Team	Lg	G	AB	H	2B	3B	HR	(Hm	Rd)	TB	R	RBI	RC	TBB	IBB	SO	HBP	SH	SF	SB	CS	GDP	Avg	OBP	Slg	OPS
2015 Brham*	AA	30	117	38	6	1	4	(-	-)	58	13	22	19	3	0	14	1	0	0	0	1	4	.325	.347	.496	.843
2015 Charllt*	AAA	23	86	25	3	0	4	(-	-)	40	11	16	13	5	0	17	0	0	3	0	0	1	.291	.319	.465	.784
2012 Mia	NL	31	100	29	8	0	3	(1	2)	46	14	8	14	13	2	16	0	0	0	1	1	1	.290	.372	.460	.832
2013 Mia	NL	67	223	47	9	0	1	(1	0)	59	11	18	14	15	1	53	2	0	3	0	0	8	.211	.263	.265	.528
2015 CWS	AL	14	33	4	1	0	1	(1	0)	8	3	6	1	2	0	8	0	0	1	0	0	1	.121	.167	.242	.409
3 ML YEARS		112	356	80	18	0	5	(3	2)	113	28	32	29	30	3	77	2	0	4	1	1	10	.225	.286	.317	.603

Ryan Braun

Bats: R Throws: R Pos: RF-130;PH-8;DH-4   Ht: 6'2" Wt: 205 Born: 11/17/1983 Age: 32

							BATTING													RUNNING			AVERAGES			
Year Team	Lg	G	AB	H	2B	3B	HR	(Hm	Rd)	TB	R	RBI	RC	TBB	IBB	SO	HBP	SH	SF	SB	CS	GDP	Avg	OBP	Slg	OPS
2007 Mil	NL	113	451	146	26	6	34	(17	17)	286	91	97	94	29	1	112	7	0	5	15	5	13	.324	.370	.634	1.004
2008 Mil	NL	151	611	174	39	7	37	(23	14)	338	92	106	100	42	4	129	6	0	4	14	4	13	.285	.335	.553	.888
2009 Mil	NL	158	635	203	39	6	32	(15	17)	350	113	114	133	57	1	121	13	0	3	20	6	7	.320	.386	.551	.937
2010 Mil	NL	157	619	188	45	1	25	(13	12)	310	101	103	104	56	1	105	6	0	3	14	3	17	.304	.365	.501	.866
2011 Mil	NL	150	563	187	38	6	33	(16	17)	336	109	111	124	58	2	93	5	0	3	33	6	9	.332	.397	.597	.994
2012 Mil	NL	154	598	191	36	3	41	(24	17)	356	108	112	125	63	15	128	11	0	5	30	7	12	.319	.391	.595	.987
2013 Mil	NL	61	225	67	14	2	9	(5	4)	112	30	38	39	27	7	56	0	0	1	4	5	3	.298	.372	.498	.869
2014 Mil	NL	135	530	141	30	6	19	(8	11)	240	68	81	74	41	3	113	6	0	3	11	5	17	.266	.324	.453	.777
2015 Mil	NL	140	506	144	27	3	25	(8	17)	252	87	84	91	54	4	115	9	0	3	24	4	20	.285	.356	.498	.854
Postseason		15	58	22	9	0	2	(2	0)	37	7	12	13	4	0	13	1	0	1	1	0	0	.379	.422	.638	1.060
9 ML YEARS		1219	4738	1441	294	40	255	(129	126)	2580	799	846	884	427	38	972	58	0	30	165	45	116	.304	.367	.545	.911

Craig Breslow

Pitches: L Bats: L Pos: RP-43; SP-2   BREHZ-loh   Ht: 6'1" Wt: 185 Born: 8/8/1980 Age: 35

			HOW MUCH HE PITCHED					WHAT HE GAVE UP												THE RESULTS					
Year Team	Lg	G	GS	CG	GF	IP	BFP	H	R	ER	HR	SH	SF	HB	TBB	IBB	SO	WP	Bk	W	L	Pct	Sh	Sv-Op	Hld	ERC	ERA
2005 SD	NL	14	0	0	3	16.1	78	15	6	4	1	0	1	1	13	0	14	1	0	0	0	-	0	0-0	1	4.98	2.20
2006 Bos	AL	13	0	0	3	12.0	55	12	5	5	0	0	2	1	6	1	12	2	1	0	2	.000	0	0-0	3	3.78	3.75
2008 2 Tms	AL	49	0	0	13	47.0	189	34	12	10	1	2	0	0	19	2	39	4	1	0	2	.000	0	1-2	5	2.12	1.91
2009 2 Tms	AL	77	0	0	9	69.2	281	48	31	26	8	4	1	3	29	0	55	3	1	8	7	.533	0	0-2	15	2.79	3.36
2010 Oak	AL	75	0	0	23	74.2	304	53	26	25	9	2	0	0	29	4	71	0	1	4	4	.500	0	5-7	16	2.53	3.01
2011 Oak	AL	67	0	0	16	59.1	261	69	29	25	4	3	2	2	21	1	44	3	0	0	2	.000	0	0-3	8	4.74	3.79
2012 2 Tms	AL	63	0	0	16	63.1	261	52	22	19	5	3	3	2	22	2	61	2	0	3	0	1.000	0	0-1	9	2.86	2.70
2013 Bos	AL	61	0	0	13	59.2	237	49	16	12	3	0	2	2	18	0	33	2	0	5	2	.714	0	0-1	13	2.66	1.81
2014 Bos	AL	60	0	0	16	54.1	260	73	40	36	8	1	0	2	28	1	37	3	1	2	4	.333	0	1-2	7	7.14	5.96
2015 Bos	AL	45	2	0	18	65.0	280	69	33	30	12	3	5	2	23	5	46	2	0	0	4	.000	0	1-4	1	4.91	4.15
08 Cle	AL	7	0	0	3	8.1	40	10	3	3	1	0	0	0	5	0	7	0	0	0	0	-	0	0-0	1	6.09	3.24
08 Min	AL	42	0	0	10	38.2	149	24	9	7	0	2	0	0	14	2	32	4	1	0	2	.000	0	1-2	5	1.49	1.63
09 Min	AL	17	0	0	5	14.1	64	11	11	10	3	2	0	1	11	0	11	3	0	1	2	.333	0	0-0	2	5.38	6.28
09 Oak	AL	60	0	0	4	55.1	217	37	20	16	5	2	1	2	18	0	44	0	1	7	5	.583	0	0-2	13	2.21	2.60
12 Ari	NL	40	0	0	12	43.1	180	38	15	13	5	2	1	1	13	0	42	1	0	2	0	1.000	0	0-0	4	3.19	2.70
12 Bos	AL	23	0	0	4	20.0	81	14	7	6	0	1	2	1	9	2	19	1	0	1	0	1.000	0	0-1	5	2.12	2.70
Postseason		10	0	0	0	7.1	36	6	3	2	0	0	1	2	7	1	6	0	0	1	0	1.000	0	0-1	4	5.16	2.45
10 ML YEARS		524	2	0	124	521.1	2206	474	220	192	51	18	16	15	208	16	412	22	5	22	27	.449	0	8-22	73	3.64	3.31

Ryan Brett

Bats: R Throws: R Pos: 2B-3;PH-1   Ht: 5'9" Wt: 180 Born: 10/9/1991 Age: 24

							BATTING													RUNNING			AVERAGES			
Year Team	Lg	G	AB	H	2B	3B	HR	(Hm	Rd)	TB	R	RBI	RC	TBB	IBB	SO	HBP	SH	SF	SB	CS	GDP	Avg	OBP	Slg	OPS
2011 Prnctn	R	61	240	72	22	5	3	(-	-)	113	42	24	46	26	1	24	2	0	2	21	3	4	.300	.370	.471	.841
2012 BG	A	100	410	117	20	3	6	(-	-)	161	77	35	65	37	3	73	4	2	3	48	8	9	.285	.348	.393	.741
2013 2 Tms	Low	52	210	70	11	4	4	(-	-)	101	38	22	41	15	0	29	4	0	0	22	7	6	.333	.389	.481	.870
2013 Mont	AA	25	105	25	6	1	3	(-	-)	42	19	16	13	8	0	14	0	0	1	4	0	2	.238	.289	.400	.689
2014 Mont	AA	107	422	128	25	6	8	(-	-)	189	64	38	69	24	1	74	5	5	3	27	7	8	.303	.346	.448	.794
2015 Drham	AAA	84	328	81	18	1	5	(-	-)	116	48	30	34	15	0	64	6	0	5	4	3	5	.247	.288	.354	.642
2015 TB	AL	3	3	2	1	0	0	(0	0)	3	0	0	2	1	0	0	0	0	0	0	0	0	.667	.750	1.000	1.750

Jake Brigham

Pitches: R Bats: R Pos: RP-12   Ht: 6'3" Wt: 210 Born: 2/10/1988 Age: 28

			HOW MUCH HE PITCHED					WHAT HE GAVE UP												THE RESULTS					
Year Team	Lg	G	GS	CG	GF	IP	BFP	H	R	ER	HR	SH	SF	HB	TBB	IBB	SO	WP	Bk	W	L	Pct	Sh	Sv-Op	Hld	ERC	ERA
2011 Frisco	AA	35	14	0	10	114.1	503	107	67	57	13	3	2	4	55	1	114	11	0	6	6	.500	0	0--	-	4.21	4.49
2012 Frisco	AA	21	21	0	0	124.0	530	122	65	59	19	6	2	6	46	1	116	12	0	5	5	.500	0	0--	-	4.49	4.28
2013 Frisco	AA	7	0	0	4	13.2	52	5	0	0	0	1	0	1	7	1	17	0	0	0	0	-	0	2--	-	1.17	0.00
2013 RdRck	AAA	26	18	0	3	113.2	499	125	65	57	7	5	4	8	46	0	78	2	0	5	5	.500	0	0--	-	4.75	4.51
2014 Indy	AAA	18	14	0	1	92.1	395	92	51	44	12	2	2	9	28	1	70	6	0	3	5	.375	0	1--	-	4.29	4.29
2015 Missi	AA	12	12	1	0	65.0	266	55	30	22	4	4	1	4	14	0	49	3	0	6	3	.667	0	0--	-	2.25	3.05
2015 Gwnntt	AAA	8	3	0	0	26.0	111	31	14	13	1	1	0	1	7	0	20	3	0	4	1	.800	0	0--	-	4.49	4.50
2015 Atl	NL	12	0	0	4	16.2	84	28	16	16	1	0	2	1	8	1	12	2	0	0	1	.000	0	0-0	0	8.53	8.64

Reid Brignac

Bats: L Throws: R Pos: PH-13;3B-2;PR-2 BRINN-yak Ht: 6'3" Wt: 215 Born: 1/16/1986 Age: 30

Year	Team	Lg	G	AB	H	2B	3B	HR	(Hm	Rd)	TB	R	RBI	RC	TBB	IBB	SO	HBP	SH	SF	SB	CS	GDP	Avg	OBP	Slg	OPS
2015	NewOr*	AAA	93	347	93	20	1	5	(-	-)	130	38	37	49	42	1	62	2	4	3	3	1	6	.268	.348	.375	.722
2008	TB	AL	4	10	0	0	0	0	(0	0)	0	1	0	0	1	0	5	0	0	0	0	0	0	.000	.091	.000	.091
2009	TB	AL	31	90	25	8	2	1	(0	1)	40	10	6	10	3	0	20	0	0	0	2	2	1	.278	.301	.444	.746
2010	TB	AL	113	301	77	13	1	8	(3	5)	116	39	45	38	20	3	77	3	0	2	3	3	6	.256	.307	.385	.692
2011	TB	AL	92	249	48	4	0	1	(0	1)	55	18	15	8	10	1	63	1	4	0	3	1	2	.193	.227	.221	.448
2012	TB	AL	16	21	2	0	0	0	(0	0)	2	1	1	0	1	0	5	0	0	0	0	0	0	.095	.136	.095	.232
2013	2 Tms		46	92	17	4	0	1	(0	1)	24	5	6	7	4	1	30	0	2	0	0	0	6	.185	.219	.261	.480
2014	Phi	NL	37	81	18	5	1	1	(1	0)	28	4	10	8	9	1	33	0	1	0	1	1	2	.222	.300	.346	.646
2015	Mia	NL	17	13	1	0	0	0	(0	0)	1	2	0	0	3	0	5	0	1	0	0	0	0	.077	.250	.077	.327
13	Col	NL	29	48	12	3	0	1	(0	1)	18	4	6	7	3	1	13	0	2	0	0	0	3	.250	.294	.375	.669
13	NYY	AL	17	44	5	1	0	0	(0	0)	6	1	0	0	1	0	17	0	0	0	0	0	3	.114	.133	.136	.270
	Postseason		5	4	0	0	0	0	(0	0)	0	0	0	0	1	0	3	0	0	0	0	0	0	.000	.200	.000	.200
	8 ML YEARS		356	857	188	34	4	12	(4	8)	266	80	83	71	51	6	238	4	8	2	9	7	17	.219	.266	.310	.576

Socrates Brito

Bats: L Throws: L Pos: PH-9;RF-5;PR-3;LF-1;CF-1 BREE-tow Ht: 6'1" Wt: 200 Born: 9/6/1992 Age: 23

Year	Team	Lg	G	AB	H	2B	3B	HR	(Hm	Rd)	TB	R	RBI	RC	TBB	IBB	SO	HBP	SH	SF	SB	CS	GDP	Avg	OBP	Slg	OPS
2011	Dbcks	R	55	236	65	3	7	1	(-	-)	85	29	29	27	13	1	50	2	1	3	18	10	5	.275	.315	.360	.675
2012	Msoula	R+	69	279	87	15	5	4	(-	-)	124	47	39	44	21	0	73	1	0	4	15	9	4	.312	.357	.444	.802
2013	Sbend	A	129	523	138	24	9	2	(-	-)	186	61	49	62	37	1	124	2	1	3	27	9	3	.264	.313	.356	.669
2014	Visalia	A+	128	518	152	30	5	10	(-	-)	222	82	62	80	36	1	109	2	0	5	38	10	6	.293	.339	.429	.767
2015	Mobile	AA	129	490	147	16	15	9	(-	-)	220	70	57	76	29	1	84	1	0	2	20	6	7	.300	.339	.449	.788
2015	Ari	NL	18	33	10	3	1	0	(0	0)	15	5	1	5	1	0	7	0	0	0	1	0	0	.303	.324	.455	.778

Zach Britton

Pitches: L Bats: L Pos: RP-64 Ht: 6'3" Wt: 195 Born: 12/22/1987 Age: 28

| | | | HOW MUCH HE PITCHED | | | | | WHAT HE GAVE UP | | | | | | | | | THE RESULTS | | | | | | |
Year	Team	Lg	G	GS	CG	GF	IP	BFP	H	R	ER	HR	SH	SF	HB	TBB	IBB	SO	WP	Bk	W	L	Pct	Sh	Sv-Op	Hld	ERC	ERA
2011	Bal	AL	28	28	0	0	154.1	666	162	93	79	12	8	7	1	62	3	97	7	0	11	11	.500	0	0-0	0	4.24	4.61
2012	Bal	AL	12	11	0	0	60.1	270	61	37	34	6	0	1	2	32	3	53	4	0	5	3	.625	0	0-0	0	4.70	5.07
2013	Bal	AL	8	7	0	0	40.0	182	52	23	22	4	1	1	1	17	1	18	1	0	2	3	.400	0	0-0	0	6.14	4.95
2014	Bal	AL	71	0	0	49	76.1	285	46	17	14	4	3	0	1	23	0	62	0	0	3	2	.600	0	37-41	1	1.62	1.65
2015	Bal	AL	64	0	0	58	65.2	253	51	16	14	3	0	0	1	14	1	79	5	0	4	1	.800	0	36-40	0	2.02	1.92
	Postseason		6	0	0	4	4.2	24	5	2	2	0	1	0	0	5	2	5	0	0	0	0	-	0	2-2	1	5.28	3.86
	5 ML YEARS		183	46	0	107	396.2	1656	372	186	163	29	12	9	6	148	8	309	17	0	25	20	.556	0	73-81	7	3.53	3.70

Mike Broadway

Pitches: R Bats: R Pos: RP-21 Ht: 6'5" Wt: 215 Born: 3/30/1987 Age: 29

| | | | HOW MUCH HE PITCHED | | | | | WHAT HE GAVE UP | | | | | | | | | THE RESULTS | | | | | | |
Year	Team	Lg	G	GS	CG	GF	IP	BFP	H	R	ER	HR	SH	SF	HB	TBB	IBB	SO	WP	Bk	W	L	Pct	Sh	Sv-Op	Hld	ERC	ERA
2012	SnAnt	AA	33	0	0	10	39.2	184	51	32	28	4	0	1	1	13	0	45	4	0	0	2	.000	0	0--	-	5.42	6.35
2013	Hrsbrg	AA	12	0	0	4	16.2	73	18	6	5	1	2	2	0	5	1	14	2	0	1	0	1.000	0	0--	-	3.66	2.70
2013	Syrcse	AA	18	0	0	13	23.2	93	16	6	6	2	0	1	0	7	0	26	1	0	1	1	.500	0	6--	-	1.95	2.28
2014	Giants	R	5	0	0	1	6.0	25	8	1	1	0	0	0	0	1	0	6	0	0	0	0	-	0	0--	-	5.89	1.50
2015	Scrmto	AAA	40	0	0	31	48.1	175	25	6	5	0	3	1	0	8	0	64	1	0	2	0	1.000	0	13--	-	0.85	0.93
2015	SF	NL	21	0	0	5	17.1	77	20	10	10	1	1	0	1	7	1	13	0	1	0	2	.000	0	0-0	2	4.86	5.19

Aaron Brooks

Pitches: R Bats: R Pos: SP-9; RP-4 Ht: 6'4" Wt: 220 Born: 4/27/1990 Age: 26

| | | | HOW MUCH HE PITCHED | | | | | WHAT HE GAVE UP | | | | | | | | | THE RESULTS | | | | | | |
Year	Team	Lg	G	GS	CG	GF	IP	BFP	H	R	ER	HR	SH	SF	HB	TBB	IBB	SO	WP	Bk	W	L	Pct	Sh	Sv-Op	Hld	ERC	ERA
2011	Idaho	R+	15	13	0	1	79.2	330	89	42	34	7	6	1	3	8	0	73	5	0	6	2	.750	0	0--	-	3.64	3.84
2012	Kane	A	27	27	1	0	153.2	670	191	99	85	18	3	9	4	26	0	120	9	0	9	12	.429	0	0--	-	4.74	4.98
2013	Wilmg	A+	10	10	0	0	56.1	233	60	28	28	4	0	1	0	11	0	43	3	0	3	3	.500	0	0--	-	3.48	4.47
2013	NWArk	AA	16	16	1	0	103.2	427	113	54	48	13	4	6	3	11	0	67	2	0	7	7	.500	1	0--	-	3.72	4.17
2014	Omha	AAA	25	23	1	1	139.0	578	151	67	60	14	4	5	1	25	2	97	4	1	12	3	.800	0	1--	-	3.73	3.88
2015	Omha	AAA	18	17	1	0	106.2	446	118	46	44	9	3	3	1	21	2	92	1	0	6	5	.545	0	0--	-	3.81	3.71
2014	KC	AL	2	1	0	1	2.2	24	12	13	13	1	0	1	2	3	0	2	0	0	0	1	.000	0	0-0	0	44.02	43.88
2015	2 Tms	AL	13	9	0	3	55.1	250	73	41	41	9	3	2	4	14	0	38	0	0	3	4	.429	0	0-0	0	6.17	6.67
15	KC	AL	2	0	0	2	4.1	18	6	3	3	0	0	0	0	0	0	3	0	0	0	0	-	0	0-0	0	4.08	6.23
15	Oak	AL	11	9	0	1	51.0	232	67	38	38	9	3	2	4	14	0	35	0	0	3	4	.429	0	0-0	0	6.35	6.71
	2 ML YEARS		15	10	0	4	58.0	274	85	54	54	10	3	3	6	17	0	40	0	0	3	5	.375	0	0-0	0	7.53	8.38

Rex Brothers

Pitches: L Bats: L Pos: RP-17 Ht: 6'0" Wt: 210 Born: 12/18/1987 Age: 28

| | | | HOW MUCH HE PITCHED | | | | | WHAT HE GAVE UP | | | | | | | | | THE RESULTS | | | | | | |
Year	Team	Lg	G	GS	CG	GF	IP	BFP	H	R	ER	HR	SH	SF	HB	TBB	IBB	SO	WP	Bk	W	L	Pct	Sh	Sv-Op	Hld	ERC	ERA
2015	Albq*	AAA	45	0	0	22	42.1	197	27	24	21	1	2	0	2	44	0	61	5	0	5	2	.714	0	3--	-	4.04	4.46
2011	Col	NL	48	0	0	6	40.2	172	33	14	13	4	0	0	0	20	2	59	2	0	1	2	.333	0	1-3	16	3.31	2.88
2012	Col	NL	75	0	0	10	67.2	295	63	33	29	5	3	3	1	37	7	83	5	1	8	2	.800	0	0-5	18	3.99	3.86

95

Year	Team	Lg	G	GS	CG	GF	IP	BFP	H	R	ER	HR	SH	SF	HB	TBB	IBB	SO	WP	Bk	W	L	Pct	Sh	Sv-Op	Hld	ERC	ERA
																				HOW MUCH HE PITCHED / WHAT HE GAVE UP / THE RESULTS								
2013	Col	NL	72	0	0	40	67.1	281	51	16	13	5	1	0	0	36	2	76	3	3	2	1	.667	0	19-21	12	3.09	1.74
2014	Col	NL	74	0	0	15	56.1	273	65	38	35	7	1	4	2	39	0	55	5	1	4	6	.400	0	0-6	15	6.43	5.59
2015	Col	NL	17	0	0	1	10.1	46	9	2	2	0	0	1	0	8	0	5	1	0	1	0	1.000	0	0-0	0	4.12	1.74
5 ML YEARS			286	0	0	72	242.1	1067	221	103	92	21	5	8	3	140	11	278	16	5	16	11	.593	0	20-35	61	4.15	3.42

Brooks Brown

Pitches: R **Bats:** L **Pos:** RP-36   **Ht:** 6'3" **Wt:** 205 **Born:** 6/20/1985 **Age:** 31

Year	Team	Lg	G	GS	CG	GF	IP	BFP	H	R	ER	HR	SH	SF	HB	TBB	IBB	SO	WP	Bk	W	L	Pct	Sh	Sv-Op	Hld	ERC	ERA
2011	Erie	AA	17	17	0	0	93.2	412	111	68	59	10	6	3	4	27	0	65	6	0	3	9	.250	0	0--	-	4.93	5.67
2012	Toledo	AAA	29	19	0	4	112.0	502	125	67	61	11	4	5	5	58	0	81	12	0	4	4	.500	0	0--	-	5.51	4.90
2013	Indy	AAA	37	8	0	8	91.0	379	95	53	48	11	4	0	2	24	1	69	3	0	6	5	.545	0	0--	-	4.08	4.75
2014	ColSpr	AAA	37	0	0	20	47.1	209	50	29	22	4	2	3	5	17	0	46	2	0	1	1	.500	0	7--	-	4.55	4.18
2015	Albq	AAA	16	0	0	1	15.0	68	20	10	10	1	0	1	0	5	0	17	0	0	0	0	-	0	0--	-	5.52	6.00
2014	Col	NL	28	0	0	9	26.0	104	20	9	8	3	0	2	1	5	1	21	1	0	0	1	.000	0	0-0	5	2.25	2.77
2015	Col	NL	36	0	0	7	33.0	147	32	18	18	2	4	0	1	16	0	20	2	0	1	3	.250	0	0-3	10	4.00	4.91
2 ML YEARS			64	0	0	16	59.0	251	52	27	26	5	4	2	2	21	1	41	3	0	1	4	.200	0	0-3	15	3.21	3.97

Domonic Brown

Bats: L **Throws:** L **Pos:** RF-50;PH-14   **Ht:** 6'5" **Wt:** 225 **Born:** 9/3/1987 **Age:** 28

Year	Team	Lg	G	AB	H	2B	3B	HR	(Hm	Rd)	TB	R	RBI	RC	TBB	IBB	SO	HBP	SH	SF	SB	CS	GDP	Avg	OBP	Slg	OPS
2015	LV*	AAA	52	210	54	12	1	2	(-	-)	74	22	26	24	14	2	37	2	0	2	10	3	4	.257	.307	.352	.659
2010	Phi	NL	35	62	13	3	0	2	(2	0)	22	8	13	5	5	1	24	0	0	3	2	1	1	.210	.257	.355	.612
2011	Phi	NL	56	184	45	10	1	5	(4	1)	72	28	19	21	25	1	35	0	0	1	3	1	2	.245	.333	.391	.725
2012	Phi	NL	56	187	44	11	2	5	(3	2)	74	21	26	25	21	2	34	2	0	2	0	0	6	.235	.316	.396	.712
2013	Phi	NL	139	496	135	21	4	27	(14	13)	245	65	83	76	39	5	97	1	0	4	8	3	5	.272	.324	.494	.818
2014	Phi	NL	144	473	111	22	1	10	(5	5)	165	47	63	54	34	4	91	1	0	4	7	1	9	.235	.285	.349	.634
2015	Phi	NL	63	189	43	6	1	5	(4	1)	66	19	25	24	14	0	36	1	0	0	3	1	2	.228	.284	.349	.634
Postseason			3	3	0	0	0	0	(0	0)	0	1	0	0	0	0	0	0	0	0	0	0	0	.000	.000	.000	.000
6 ML YEARS			493	1591	391	73	9	54	(32	22)	644	188	229	205	138	13	317	5	0	14	23	7	25	.246	.305	.405	.710

Trevor Brown

Bats: R **Throws:** R **Pos:** C-13   **Ht:** 6'2" **Wt:** 195 **Born:** 11/15/1991 **Age:** 24

Year	Team	Lg	G	AB	H	2B	3B	HR	(Hm	Rd)	TB	R	RBI	RC	TBB	IBB	SO	HBP	SH	SF	SB	CS	GDP	Avg	OBP	Slg	OPS
2012	SlKzr	A-	33	122	27	8	0	0	(-	-)	35	10	12	11	13	0	16	1	1	2	1	1	5	.221	.297	.287	.584
2013	2 Tms	Low	111	442	106	22	1	3	(-	-)	139	53	44	41	31	0	62	5	2	5	10	9	8	.240	.294	.314	.608
2014	SnJos	A+	54	195	42	5	1	2	(-	-)	55	19	22	14	12	1	33	1	0	4	0	0	5	.215	.259	.282	.541
2014	Fresno	AAA	23	72	23	4	0	0	(-	-)	27	6	13	10	7	0	13	0	1	0	0	0	1	.319	.380	.375	.755
2015	Scrmto	AAA	83	283	74	17	0	2	(-	-)	97	35	27	33	21	0	53	4	4	2	1	0	8	.261	.319	.343	.662
2015	SF	NL	13	39	9	3	0	0	(0	0)	12	1	5	3	3	0	8	0	0	1	1	1	0	.231	.279	.308	.587

Jonathan Broxton

Pitches: R **Bats:** R **Pos:** RP-66   **Ht:** 6'4" **Wt:** 305 **Born:** 6/16/1984 **Age:** 32

Year	Team	Lg	G	GS	CG	GF	IP	BFP	H	R	ER	HR	SH	SF	HB	TBB	IBB	SO	WP	Bk	W	L	Pct	Sh	Sv-Op	Hld	ERC	ERA
2005	LAD	NL	14	0	0	5	13.2	68	13	11	9	0	0	2	1	12	2	22	2	0	1	0	1.000	0	0-1	1	4.65	5.93
2006	LAD	NL	68	0	0	20	76.1	320	61	25	22	7	3	1	1	33	6	97	7	0	4	1	.800	0	3-7	12	2.97	2.59
2007	LAD	NL	83	0	0	18	82.0	334	69	30	26	6	0	1	1	25	3	99	4	0	4	4	.500	0	2-8	32	2.71	2.85
2008	LAD	NL	70	0	0	32	69.0	285	54	29	24	2	3	3	3	27	5	88	3	0	3	5	.375	0	14-22	13	2.48	3.13
2009	LAD	NL	73	0	0	58	76.0	300	44	24	22	4	0	3	1	29	1	114	2	0	7	2	.778	0	36-42	1	1.65	2.61
2010	LAD	NL	64	0	0	46	62.1	271	64	30	28	4	3	1	2	28	5	73	1	0	5	6	.455	0	22-29	3	4.21	4.04
2011	LAD	NL	14	0	0	12	12.2	62	15	10	8	2	0	0	0	9	2	10	0	0	1	2	.333	0	7-8	0	6.47	5.68
2012	2 Tms		60	0	0	39	58.0	238	56	18	16	2	2	1	3	17	0	45	0	0	4	5	.444	0	27-33	10	3.34	2.48
2013	Cin	NL	34	0	0	30.2	133	27	17	14	4	1	2	4	12	2	25	0	0	2	2	.500	0	0-3	12	3.97	4.11
2014	2 Tms		62	0	0	18	58.2	231	41	15	15	4	2	1	1	19	0	49	0	0	4	3	.571	0	7-15	23	2.14	2.30
2015	2 Tms		66	0	0	15	60.1	257	61	32	31	7	5	1	0	22	1	63	0	0	4	5	.444	0	0-3	17	4.11	4.62
12	KC	AL	35	0	0	32	35.2	151	36	11	9	1	2	1	2	14	0	25	0	0	1	2	.333	0	23-27	3	3.93	2.27
12	Cin	NL	25	0	0	7	22.1	87	20	7	7	1	0	0	1	3	0	20	0	0	3	3	.500	0	4-6	10	2.44	2.82
14	Cin	NL	51	0	0	16	48.1	189	32	10	10	3	2	1	1	17	0	37	0	0	4	2	.667	0	7-13	21	2.06	1.86
14	Mil	NL	11	0	0	2	10.1	42	9	5	5	1	0	0	0	2	0	12	0	0	0	1	.000	0	0-2	2	2.55	4.35
15	Mil	NL	40	0	0	10	36.2	156	41	24	24	5	2	1	0	10	1	37	0	0	1	2	.333	0	0-1	11	4.50	5.89
15	StL	NL	26	0	0	5	23.2	101	20	8	7	2	3	0	0	12	0	26	0	0	3	3	.500	0	0-2	6	3.53	2.66
Postseason			16	0	0	11	17.1	79	18	8	7	1	0	0	1	7	0	19	0	0	0	3	.000	0	3-5	1	4.06	3.63
11 ML YEARS			608	0	0	271	599.2	2499	505	241	215	42	19	16	17	233	27	685	19	0	39	35	.527	0	118-171	124	3.03	3.23

Keon Broxton

Bats: R **Throws:** R **Pos:** PR-6;LF-1;CF-1;RF-1   **Ht:** 6'3" **Wt:** 195 **Born:** 5/7/1990 **Age:** 26

Year	Team	Lg	G	AB	H	2B	3B	HR	(Hm	Rd)	TB	R	RBI	RC	TBB	IBB	SO	HBP	SH	SF	SB	CS	GDP	Avg	OBP	Slg	OPS
2011	2 Tms	Low	130	484	120	14	7	7	(-	-)	169	77	45	65	69	0	172	3	5	7	33	12	3	.248	.341	.349	.690
2012	Visalia	A+	130	490	131	24	1	19	(-	-)	214	84	62	72	40	0	136	4	0	2	21	8	5	.267	.326	.437	.763
2013	Mobile	AA	101	334	77	13	3	8	(-	-)	120	40	41	37	30	0	116	2	4	2	6	1	7	.231	.296	.359	.655

								BATTING												RUNNING			AVERAGES			
Year Team	Lg	G	AB	H	2B	3B	HR	(Hm	Rd)	TB	R	RBI	RC	TBB	IBB	SO	HBP	SH	SF	SB	CS	GDP	Avg	OBP	Slg	OPS
2014 Altna	AA	127	407	112	22	9	15	(-	-)	197	67	52	77	59	6	122	3	0	2	25	6	7	.275	.369	.484	.853
2015 Altna	AA	45	179	54	12	4	3	(-	-)	83	35	26	31	19	0	51	1	1	4	11	6	1	.302	.365	.464	.828
2015 Indy	AAA	88	312	80	15	8	7	(-	-)	132	51	42	52	47	0	105	2	1	5	28	9	3	.256	.352	.423	.776
2015 Pit	NL	7	2	0	0	0	0	(0	0)	0	3	0	0	0	0	1	0	0	0	1	1	0	.000	.000	.000	.000

Jay Bruce

Bats: L Throws: L Pos: RF-150;PH-5;DH-2　　　　　　**Ht: 6'3" Wt: 225 Born: 4/3/1987 Age: 29**

								BATTING												RUNNING			AVERAGES			
Year Team	Lg	G	AB	H	2B	3B	HR	(Hm	Rd)	TB	R	RBI	RC	TBB	IBB	SO	HBP	SH	SF	SB	CS	GDP	Avg	OBP	Slg	OPS
2008 Cin	NL	108	413	105	17	1	21	(13	8)	187	63	52	49	33	1	110	4	0	2	4	6	8	.254	.314	.453	.767
2009 Cin	NL	101	345	77	15	2	22	(13	9)	162	47	58	47	38	2	75	2	1	1	3	3	5	.223	.303	.470	.773
2010 Cin	NL	148	509	143	23	5	25	(19	6)	251	80	70	71	58	5	136	1	0	5	5	4	12	.281	.353	.493	.846
2011 Cin	NL	157	585	150	27	2	32	(16	16)	277	84	97	96	71	14	158	5	1	2	8	7	8	.256	.341	.474	.814
2012 Cin	NL	155	560	141	35	5	34	(21	13)	288	89	99	85	62	11	155	4	0	7	9	3	5	.252	.327	.514	.841
2013 Cin	NL	160	626	164	43	1	30	(16	14)	299	89	109	88	63	13	185	2	0	5	7	3	9	.262	.329	.478	.807
2014 Cin	NL	137	493	107	21	1	18	(10	8)	184	71	66	54	44	5	149	2	1	5	12	3	8	.217	.281	.373	.654
2015 Cin	NL	157	580	131	35	4	26	(13	13)	252	72	87	61	58	8	145	2	0	9	9	5	10	.226	.294	.434	.729
Postseason		9	31	8	2	0	2	(0	2)	16	3	6	4	4	0	4	1	0	0	0	1	0	.258	.361	.516	.877
8 ML YEARS		1123	4111	1018	216	21	208	(121	87)	1900	595	638	551	427	59	1113	22	3	36	57	34	65	.248	.319	.462	.781

Kris Bryant

Bats: R Throws: R Pos: 3B-144;LF-8;CF-7;RF-7;PH-3;1B-1;DH-1　　　　**Ht: 6'5" Wt: 215 Born: 1/4/1992 Age: 24**

								BATTING												RUNNING			AVERAGES			
Year Team	Lg	G	AB	H	2B	3B	HR	(Hm	Rd)	TB	R	RBI	RC	TBB	IBB	SO	HBP	SH	SF	SB	CS	GDP	Avg	OBP	Slg	OPS
2013 3 Tms	Low	36	128	43	14	2	9	(-	-)	88	22	32	32	11	0	35	3	0	4	1	0	5	.336	.390	.688	1.078
2014 Tenn	AA	68	248	88	20	0	22	(-	-)	174	61	58	74	43	4	77	5	0	1	8	2	3	.355	.458	.702	1.160
2014 Iowa	AAA	70	244	72	14	1	21	(-	-)	151	57	52	62	43	4	85	9	0	1	7	2	1	.295	.418	.619	1.036
2015 ChC	NL	151	559	154	31	5	26	(21	5)	273	87	99	104	77	0	**199**	9	0	5	13	4	7	.275	.369	.488	.858

David Buchanan

Pitches: R Bats: R Pos: SP-15　　　　　　　　　　**Ht: 6'3" Wt: 200 Born: 5/11/1989 Age: 27**

		HOW MUCH HE PITCHED						WHAT HE GAVE UP											THE RESULTS						
Year Team	Lg	G	GS	CG	GF	IP	BFP	H	R	ER	HR	SH	SF	HB	TBB	IBB	SO	WP	Bk	W	L	Pct	Sh	Sv-Op	Hld	ERC	ERA
2011 2 Tms	Low	26	26	1	0	157.1	651	152	75	61	10	1	6	5	43	0	110	12	0	14	7	.667	0	0--	-	3.33	3.49
2012 Rdng	AA	12	12	1	0	72.1	305	73	36	31	7	4	5	6	23	1	40	1	0	3	5	.375	1	0--	-	4.20	3.86
2013 Rdng	AA	22	22	0	0	130.2	567	142	78	70	15	7	7	6	41	0	86	5	1	6	11	.353	0	0--	-	4.53	4.82
2013 LV	AAA	6	6	0	0	39.0	164	36	14	13	2	3	1	3	12	1	22	0	0	4	2	.667	0	0--	-	3.24	3.00
2014 LV	AAA	12	12	0	0	57.0	254	67	26	25	3	2	4	3	21	0	46	3	0	6	2	.750	0	0--	-	4.85	3.95
2015 LV	AAA	10	10	0	0	54.2	240	58	20	17	2	1	3	4	20	1	30	1	0	4	2	.667	0	0--	-	4.08	2.80
2014 Phi	NL	20	20	0	0	117.2	503	120	55	49	12	6	3	8	32	2	71	0	0	6	8	.429	0	0-0	0	3.93	3.75
2015 Phi	NL	15	15	0	0	74.2	351	109	60	58	12	4	0	3	29	1	44	2	0	2	9	.182	0	0-0	0	7.60	6.99
2 ML YEARS		35	35	0	0	192.1	854	229	115	107	24	10	3	11	61	3	115	2	0	8	17	.320	0	0-0	0	5.26	5.01

Jake Buchanan

Pitches: R Bats: R Pos: RP-5　　　　　　　　　　**Ht: 6'0" Wt: 225 Born: 9/24/1989 Age: 26**

		HOW MUCH HE PITCHED						WHAT HE GAVE UP											THE RESULTS						
Year Team	Lg	G	GS	CG	GF	IP	BFP	H	R	ER	HR	SH	SF	HB	TBB	IBB	SO	WP	Bk	W	L	Pct	Sh	Sv-Op	Hld	ERC	ERA
2011 Lancst	A+	25	25	1	0	158.2	667	157	92	69	10	7	5	6	35	3	102	7	0	5	10	.333	1	0--	-	3.16	3.91
2012 CpChr	AA	27	19	0	4	134.1	595	171	85	79	11	2	3	6	33	4	83	4	0	5	9	.357	0	0--	-	5.06	5.29
2013 CpChr	AA	18	13	0	2	82.0	311	67	22	19	4	2	1	2	9	1	44	2	0	7	2	.778	0	1--	-	1.92	2.09
2013 OkCity	AAA	12	12	0	0	76.1	316	85	33	33	6	4	1	0	13	1	55	6	0	5	5	.500	0	0--	-	3.69	3.89
2014 OkCity	AAA	16	15	1	0	88.1	369	95	44	38	7	2	2	3	16	1	46	3	0	7	5	.583	1	0--	-	3.64	3.87
2015 Fresno	AAA	30	7	0	9	81.1	360	101	47	43	5	2	3	3	22	1	46	3	0	5	5	.500	0	3--	-	4.80	4.76
2014 Hou	AL	17	2	0	9	35.1	154	41	19	18	4	3	0	1	12	1	20	2	0	1	3	.250	0	0-0	0	5.00	4.58
2015 Hou	AL	5	0	0	1	9.0	37	5	2	2	1	1	0	1	4	0	5	2	0	0	0	-	0	0-0	0	2.37	2.00
2 ML YEARS		22	2	0	10	44.1	191	46	21	20	5	4	0	2	16	1	25	4	0	1	3	.250	0	0-0	0	4.41	4.06

Clay Buchholz

Pitches: R Bats: L Pos: SP-18　　　　BUCK-holtz　　　　**Ht: 6'3" Wt: 190 Born: 8/14/1984 Age: 31**

		HOW MUCH HE PITCHED						WHAT HE GAVE UP											THE RESULTS						
Year Team	Lg	G	GS	CG	GF	IP	BFP	H	R	ER	HR	SH	SF	HB	TBB	IBB	SO	WP	Bk	W	L	Pct	Sh	Sv-Op	Hld	ERC	ERA
2007 Bos	AL	4	3	1	0	22.2	88	14	6	4	0	0	1	1	10	0	22	0	0	3	1	.750	1	0-0	0	1.90	1.59
2008 Bos	AL	16	15	1	0	76.0	357	93	63	57	11	0	3	2	41	1	72	2	1	2	9	.182	0	0-0	0	6.40	6.75
2009 Bos	AL	16	16	0	0	92.0	399	91	44	43	11	3	2	3	36	1	68	1	0	7	4	.636	0	0-0	0	4.31	4.21
2010 Bos	AL	28	28	1	0	173.2	711	142	55	45	9	5	5	5	67	1	120	7	1	17	7	.708	1	0-0	0	2.88	2.33
2011 Bos	AL	14	14	0	0	82.2	353	76	34	32	10	1	4	2	31	1	60	3	0	6	3	.667	0	0-0	0	3.72	3.48
2012 Bos	AL	29	29	2	0	189.1	802	187	104	96	25	5	9	12	64	2	129	2	2	11	8	.579	1	0-0	0	4.29	4.56
2013 Bos	AL	16	16	1	0	108.1	416	75	23	21	4	1	2	1	36	0	96	1	0	12	1	.923	1	0-0	0	2.00	1.74
2014 Bos	AL	28	28	2	0	170.1	737	182	108	101	17	3	4	10	54	2	132	8	0	8	11	.421	2	0-0	0	4.37	5.34
2015 Bos	AL	18	18	1	0	113.1	469	114	48	41	6	1	2	5	23	0	107	3	0	7	7	.500	0	0-0	0	3.23	3.26
Postseason		5	5	0	0	25.2	114	28	13	12	4	0	0	2	9	1	20	2	1	0	0	-	0	0-0	0	5.04	4.21
9 ML YEARS		169	167	9	0	1028.1	4332	974	485	440	95	18	33	40	362	8	806	27	4	73	51	.589	6	0-0	0	3.72	3.85

Mark Buehrle

Pitches: L **Bats:** L **Pos:** SP-32

BURR-lee

Ht: 6'2" **Wt:** 240 **Born:** 3/23/1979 **Age:** 37

Year	Team	Lg	G	GS	CG	GF	IP	BFP	H	R	ER	HR	SH	SF	HB	TBB	IBB	SO	WP	Bk	W	L	Pct	Sh	Sv-Op	Hld	ERC	ERA
2000	CWS	AL	28	3	0	6	51.1	225	55	27	24	5	1	0	3	19	1	37	0	0	4	1	.800	0	0-2	3	4.56	4.21
2001	CWS	AL	32	32	4	0	221.1	885	188	89	81	24	9	4	8	48	2	126	1	5	16	8	.667	2	0-0	0	2.79	3.29
2002	CWS	AL	34	34	5	0	239.0	984	236	102	95	25	9	3	3	61	7	134	6	1	19	12	.613	2	0-0	0	3.53	3.58
2003	CWS	AL	35	35	2	0	230.1	978	250	124	106	22	7	7	5	61	2	119	1	0	14	14	.500	0	0-0	0	4.10	4.14
2004	CWS	AL	35	35	4	0	245.1	1016	257	119	106	33	4	6	8	51	2	165	0	0	16	10	.615	1	0-0	0	4.00	3.89
2005	CWS	AL	33	33	3	0	236.2	971	240	99	82	20	7	4	4	40	4	149	2	2	16	8	.667	1	0-0	0	3.21	3.12
2006	CWS	AL	32	32	1	0	204.0	876	247	124	113	36	6	7	6	48	5	98	0	1	12	13	.480	1	0-0	0	5.37	4.99
2007	CWS	AL	30	30	3	0	201.0	835	208	86	81	22	7	5	5	45	5	115	1	0	10	9	.526	1	0-0	0	3.75	3.63
2008	CWS	AL	34	34	1	0	218.2	918	240	106	92	22	2	6	5	52	4	140	4	0	15	12	.556	0	0-0	0	4.12	3.79
2009	CWS	AL	33	33	1	0	213.1	874	222	97	91	27	11	7	5	45	3	105	2	1	13	10	.565	1	0-0	0	3.91	3.84
2010	CWS	AL	33	33	3	0	210.1	897	246	105	100	17	6	7	1	49	1	99	3	5	13	13	.500	1	0-0	0	4.29	4.28
2011	CWS	AL	31	31	0	0	205.1	858	221	93	82	21	6	7	2	45	3	109	1	0	13	9	.591	0	0-0	0	3.86	3.59
2012	Mia	NL	31	31	1	0	202.1	828	197	88	84	26	14	7	4	40	3	125	2	0	13	13	.500	0	0-0	0	3.41	3.74
2013	Tor	AL	33	33	1	0	203.2	876	223	100	94	24	3	6	9	51	3	139	2	0	12	10	.545	1	0-0	0	4.29	4.15
2014	Tor	AL	32	32	0	0	202.0	857	228	83	76	15	6	6	4	46	0	119	2	1	13	10	.565	0	0-0	0	4.05	3.39
2015	Tor	AL	32	32	4	0	198.2	827	214	100	84	22	10	9	7	33	4	91	0	0	15	8	.652	1	0-0	0	3.79	3.81
	Postseason		6	4	1	2	30.2	124	32	14	14	3	2	1	1	1	1	16	0	0	2	1	.667	0	1-1	0	2.95	4.11
	16 ML YEARS		518	493	33	6	3283.1	13705	3472	1542	1391	361	108	91	79	734	49	1870	27	16	214	160	.572	10	0-2	3	3.89	3.81

Madison Bumgarner

Pitches: L **Bats:** R **Pos:** SP-32

Ht: 6'5" **Wt:** 235 **Born:** 8/1/1989 **Age:** 26

Year	Team	Lg	G	GS	CG	GF	IP	BFP	H	R	ER	HR	SH	SF	HB	TBB	IBB	SO	WP	Bk	W	L	Pct	Sh	Sv-Op	Hld	ERC	ERA
2009	SF	NL	4	1	0	1	10.0	40	8	2	2	2	1	1	0	3	1	10	0	0	0	0	-	0	0-0	0	3.14	1.80
2010	SF	NL	18	18	0	0	111.0	472	119	40	37	11	0	4	5	26	2	86	1	1	7	6	.538	0	0-0	0	3.98	3.00
2011	SF	NL	33	33	0	0	204.2	844	202	82	73	12	12	4	5	46	5	191	0	1	13	13	.500	0	0-0	0	3.14	3.21
2012	SF	NL	32	32	2	0	208.1	849	183	87	78	23	7	4	7	49	6	191	3	2	16	11	.593	1	0-0	0	2.95	3.37
2013	SF	NL	31	31	0	0	201.1	803	146	68	62	15	10	4	6	62	6	199	6	0	13	9	.591	0	0-0	0	2.23	2.77
2014	SF	NL	33	33	4	0	217.1	873	194	81	72	21	9	5	6	43	3	219	4	1	18	10	.643	2	0-0	0	2.83	2.98
2015	SF	NL	32	32	4	0	218.1	869	181	73	71	21	5	4	7	39	2	234	1	0	18	9	.667	2	0-0	0	2.43	2.93
	Postseason		14	12	2	1	88.1	342	63	22	21	7	6	1	4	15	1	77	0	0	7	3	.700	2	1-1	0	1.82	2.14
	7 ML YEARS		183	180	10	1	1171.0	4750	1033	433	395	105	44	26	36	268	25	1130	15	5	85	58	.594	5	0-0	0	2.83	3.04

Daniel Burawa

Pitches: R **Bats:** R **Pos:** RP-13

burr-ow-wah

Ht: 6'2" **Wt:** 210 **Born:** 12/30/1988 **Age:** 27

Year	Team	Lg	G	GS	CG	GF	IP	BFP	H	R	ER	HR	SH	SF	HB	TBB	IBB	SO	WP	Bk	W	L	Pct	Sh	Sv-Op	Hld	ERC	ERA
2011	2 Tms	Low	39	0	0	19	84.0	349	77	36	34	6	6	2	7	24	0	66	9	0	5	4	.556	0	5--	-	3.35	3.64
2013	Trntn	AA	46	0	0	16	66.0	279	47	25	19	1	4	0	0	42	1	66	7	0	6	3	.667	0	4--	-	2.83	2.59
2014	S-WB	AAA	31	0	0	8	42.1	198	47	28	28	3	1	0	0	26	0	55	6	0	3	1	.750	0	3--	-	5.27	5.95
2014	Trntn	AA	10	0	0	4	17.0	68	13	4	3	0	0	0	2	4	0	18	1	0	0	0	-	0	1--	-	2.08	1.59
2015	S-WB	AAA	32	1	0	8	49.1	203	37	17	14	2	2	1	3	21	0	39	6	0	1	3	.250	0	1--	-	2.71	2.55
2015	2 Tms		13	0	0	4	13.0	54	11	9	9	2	0	2	1	5	0	11	0	0	0	0	-	0	0-0	1	3.92	6.23
15	NYY	AL	1	0	0	0	0.2	6	3	4	4	1	0	0	0	1	0	1	0	0	0	0	-	0	0-0	0	56.63	54.00
15	Atl	NL	12	0	0	4	12.1	48	8	5	5	1	0	2	1	4	0	10	0	0	0	0	-	0	0-0	1	2.24	3.65

Enrique Burgos

Pitches: R **Bats:** R **Pos:** RP-30

BURR-gose

Ht: 6'3" **Wt:** 250 **Born:** 11/23/1990 **Age:** 25

Year	Team	Lg	G	GS	CG	GF	IP	BFP	H	R	ER	HR	SH	SF	HB	TBB	IBB	SO	WP	Bk	W	L	Pct	Sh	Sv-Op	Hld	ERC	ERA
2011	2 Tms	Low	12	11	0	0	50.1	250	63	46	42	5	1	2	9	33	0	47	8	1	4	6	.400	0	0--	-	7.41	7.51
2012	Yakima	A-	25	0	0	16	38.1	163	28	11	10	1	2	1	2	19	0	40	3	0	2	3	.400	0	4--	-	2.65	2.35
2013	Sbend	A	49	0	0	37	46.1	216	29	23	20	1	3	1	1	49	0	50	6	0	2	2	.500	0	17--	-	3.90	3.88
2014	Visalia	A+	55	0	0	47	54.2	227	37	17	15	5	0	2	2	26	0	83	8	0	3	3	.500	0	29--	-	2.70	2.47
2015	Mobile	AA	10	0	0	7	9.1	41	4	0	0	0	0	0	0	8	0	15	1	0	0	0	-	0	6--	-	1.97	0.00
2015	Reno	AAA	15	0	0	11	15.0	78	19	10	10	3	1	0	2	12	2	23	1	0	0	1	.000	0	5--	-	8.39	6.00
2015	Ari	NL	30	0	0	8	27.0	121	27	15	14	2	0	1	0	15	0	39	6	0	2	2	.500	0	2-4	2	4.47	4.67

A.J. Burnett

Pitches: R **Bats:** R **Pos:** SP-26

Ht: 6'4" **Wt:** 225 **Born:** 1/3/1977 **Age:** 39

Year	Team	Lg	G	GS	CG	GF	IP	BFP	H	R	ER	HR	SH	SF	HB	TBB	IBB	SO	WP	Bk	W	L	Pct	Sh	Sv-Op	Hld	ERC	ERA
1999	Fla	NL	7	7	0	0	41.1	182	37	23	16	3	1	3	0	25	2	33	0	0	4	2	.667	0	0-0	0	4.00	3.48
2000	Fla	NL	13	13	0	0	82.2	364	80	46	44	8	6	3	2	44	3	57	2	0	3	7	.300	0	0-0	0	4.45	4.79
2001	Fla	NL	27	27	2	0	173.1	733	145	82	78	20	6	8	7	83	3	128	7	1	11	12	.478	1	0-0	0	3.76	4.05
2002	Fla	NL	31	29	7	0	204.1	844	153	84	75	12	9	4	9	90	5	203	14	0	12	9	.571	5	0-1	0	2.77	3.30
2003	Fla	NL	4	4	0	0	23.0	106	18	13	12	2	2	1	2	18	2	21	2	0	0	2	.000	0	0-0	0	4.36	4.70
2004	Fla	NL	20	19	1	0	120.0	490	102	50	49	9	3	4	3	38	0	113	7	0	7	6	.538	0	0-0	0	2.95	3.68
2005	Fla	NL	32	32	4	0	209.0	873	184	97	80	12	7	5	7	79	1	198	12	0	12	12	.500	2	0-0	0	3.20	3.44
2006	Tor	AL	21	21	2	0	135.2	577	138	67	60	14	4	3	8	39	3	118	6	1	10	8	.556	1	0-0	0	3.97	3.98
2007	Tor	AL	25	25	2	0	165.2	691	131	74	69	23	0	2	12	66	2	176	5	0	10	8	.556	1	0-0	0	3.47	3.75
2008	Tor	AL	35	34	1	1	221.1	957	211	109	100	19	8	5	9	86	2	231	11	2	18	10	.643	0	0-0	0	3.78	4.07
2009	NYY	AL	33	33	1	0	207.0	896	193	99	93	25	2	5	10	97	0	195	17	1	13	9	.591	0	0-0	0	4.34	4.04
2010	NYY	AL	33	33	1	0	186.2	829	204	118	109	25	7	10	19	78	2	145	16	0	10	15	.400	0	0-0	0	5.43	5.26

	HOW MUCH HE PITCHED							WHAT HE GAVE UP											THE RESULTS							
Year Team	Lg	G	GS	CG	GF	IP	BFP	H	R	ER	HR	SH	SF	HB	TBB	IBB	SO	WP	Bk	W	L	Pct	Sh	Sv-Op	Hld	ERC	ERA
2011 NYY	AL	33	32	0	0	190.1	837	190	115	109	31	4	10	9	83	2	173	25	0	11	11	.500	0	0-0	0	4.83	5.15
2012 Pit	NL	31	31	1	0	202.1	851	189	86	79	18	5	8	9	62	1	180	10	0	16	10	.615	1	0-0	0	3.44	3.51
2013 Pit	NL	30	30	1	0	191.0	801	165	79	70	11	8	3	9	67	3	209	12	0	10	11	.476	0	0-0	0	3.01	3.30
2014 Phi	NL	34	34	1	0	213.2	935	205	122	109	20	11	11	16	96	2	190	9	0	8	18	.308	0	0-0	0	4.29	4.59
2015 Pit	NL	26	26	0	0	164.0	699	174	64	58	11	2	4	11	49	2	143	6	1	9	7	.563	0	0-0	0	4.10	3.18
Postseason		8	8	0	0	41.0	189	38	29	29	4	1	0	7	27	3	31	4	0	2	3	.400	0	0-0	0	5.26	6.37
17 ML YEARS		435	430	24	1	2731.1	11665	2519	1328	1210	263	85	88	143	1100	35	2513	161	6	164	157	.511	10	0-1	0	3.83	3.99

Billy Burns

Bats: B Throws: R Pos: CF-125;PH-4   Ht: 5'9" Wt: 180 Born: 8/30/1989 Age: 26

								BATTING													RUNNING			AVERAGES			
Year Team	Lg	G	AB	H	2B	3B	HR	(Hm	Rd)	TB	R	RBI	RC	TBB	IBB	SO	HBP	SH	SF	SB	CS	GDP	Avg	OBP	Slg	OPS
2011 Auburn	A-	32	107	28	3	2	1	(-	-)	38	21	18	18	12	0	22	7	2	2	13	1	0	.262	.367	.355	.722
2012 Hgrstn	A	113	398	128	14	5	0	(-	-)	152	83	41	78	65	2	68	13	8	1	38	9	2	.322	.432	.382	.814
2013 Ptomc	A+	91	330	103	8	9	0	(-	-)	129	70	29	68	52	2	37	12	6	2	54	5	5	.312	.422	.391	.813
2013 Hrsbrg	AA	30	114	37	4	0	0	(-	-)	41	26	8	23	20	0	17	2	2	0	20	2	0	.325	.434	.360	.793
2014 Mdlnd	AA	91	364	90	20	3	1	(-	-)	119	57	23	51	44	0	65	3	6	4	51	5	6	.247	.330	.327	.657
2014 Scrmto	AAA	28	109	21	2	0	0	(-	-)	23	17	5	5	9	0	19	0	3	0	3	1	2	.193	.254	.211	.465
2015 Nashv	AAA	22	91	28	2	3	0	(-	-)	36	18	3	14	9	0	17	0	1	0	5	2	0	.308	.370	.396	.766
2014 Oak	AL	13	6	1	0	0	0	(0	0)	1	4	0	0	0	0	0	0	0	0	3	1	0	.167	.167	.167	.333
2015 Oak	AL	125	520	153	18	9	5	(3	2)	204	70	42	72	26	1	81	6	1	2	26	8	5	.294	.334	.392	.726
2 ML YEARS		138	526	154	18	9	5	(3	2)	205	74	42	72	26	1	81	6	1	2	29	9	5	.293	.332	.390	.722

Emmanuel Burriss

Bats: B Throws: R Pos: PH-4;2B-1   Ht: 6'0" Wt: 190 Born: 1/17/1985 Age: 31

								BATTING													RUNNING			AVERAGES			
Year Team	Lg	G	AB	H	2B	3B	HR	(Hm	Rd)	TB	R	RBI	RC	TBB	IBB	SO	HBP	SH	SF	SB	CS	GDP	Avg	OBP	Slg	OPS
2015 Syrcse*	AAA	95	377	105	15	6	3	(-	-)	141	45	36	51	31	3	47	6	4	2	12	6	6	.279	.341	.374	.715
2008 SF	NL	95	240	68	6	1	1	(0	1)	79	37	18	22	23	1	24	5	5	1	13	5	7	.283	.357	.329	.686
2009 SF	NL	61	202	48	6	0	0	(0	0)	54	18	13	15	14	1	34	2	1	1	11	4	3	.238	.292	.267	.560
2010 SF	NL	7	5	2	0	0	0	(0	0)	2	3	0	1	0	0	1	0	0	0	0	0	0	.400	.400	.400	.800
2011 SF	NL	59	137	28	1	0	0	(0	0)	29	14	4	6	6	0	17	3	6	0	11	3	2	.204	.253	.212	.465
2012 SF	NL	60	136	29	1	0	0	(0	0)	30	15	7	4	10	1	25	1	2	1	5	3	6	.213	.270	.221	.491
2015 Was	NL	5	3	2	0	0	0	(0	0)	2	2	0	2	2	0	0	0	0	0	0	0	0	.667	.800	.667	1.467
6 ML YEARS		287	723	177	14	1	1	(0	1)	196	89	42	50	55	3	101	11	14	3	40	15	18	.245	.307	.271	.578

Jared Burton

Pitches: R Bats: R Pos: P   Ht: 6'5" Wt: 225 Born: 6/2/1981 Age: 35

	HOW MUCH HE PITCHED							WHAT HE GAVE UP												THE RESULTS							
Year Team	Lg	G	GS	CG	GF	IP	BFP	H	R	ER	HR	SH	SF	HB	TBB	IBB	SO	WP	Bk	W	L	Pct	Sh	Sv-Op	Hld	ERC	ERA
2015 RdRck*	AAA	12	0	0	2	10.0	38	4	1	1	1	1	0	1	3	0	11	0	0	0	0	-	0	1--	-	1.30	0.90
2007 Cin	NL	47	0	0	12	43.0	176	28	15	12	2	1	1	2	22	4	36	3	1	4	2	.667	0	0-3	11	2.37	2.51
2008 Cin	NL	54	0	0	12	58.2	257	56	24	21	6	2	3	2	25	3	58	2	1	5	1	.833	0	0-2	11	3.93	3.22
2009 Cin	NL	53	0	0	13	59.1	265	61	30	29	5	3	1	4	23	6	45	2	0	1	0	1.000	0	0-0	7	4.08	4.40
2010 Cin	NL	4	0	0	2	3.1	10	0	0	0	0	0	0	0	0	0	1	0	0	0	0	-	0	0-0	1	0.00	0.00
2011 Cin	NL	6	0	0	1	4.2	23	6	2	2	1	1	0	0	3	0	3	0	0	0	0	-	0	0-0	1	7.61	3.86
2012 Min	AL	64	0	0	12	62.0	245	41	21	15	5	2	1	5	16	1	55	0	0	3	2	.600	0	5-9	18	1.98	2.18
2013 Min	AL	71	0	0	14	66.0	281	61	29	28	6	2	0	5	22	5	61	2	0	2	9	.182	0	2-7	27	3.50	3.82
2014 Min	AL	68	0	0	21	64.0	272	58	34	31	6	0	3	3	25	3	46	1	0	3	5	.375	0	3-4	14	3.59	4.36
8 ML YEARS		367	0	0	87	361.0	1529	311	155	138	31	11	9	21	136	22	305	10	2	18	19	.486	0	10-25	90	3.25	3.44

Drew Butera

Bats: R Throws: R Pos: C-49;1B-8;PH-1   bue-TARE-ah   Ht: 6'1" Wt: 200 Born: 8/9/1983 Age: 32

								BATTING													RUNNING			AVERAGES			
Year Team	Lg	G	AB	H	2B	3B	HR	(Hm	Rd)	TB	R	RBI	RC	TBB	IBB	SO	HBP	SH	SF	SB	CS	GDP	Avg	OBP	Slg	OPS
2010 Min	AL	49	142	28	6	1	2	(0	2)	42	12	13	7	4	0	25	4	3	2	0	0	5	.197	.237	.296	.533
2011 Min	AL	93	234	39	9	1	2	(1	1)	56	19	23	11	11	0	42	2	6	1	0	0	7	.167	.210	.239	.449
2012 Min	AL	42	111	22	6	0	1	(1	0)	31	7	5	6	9	0	26	2	0	0	0	0	3	.198	.270	.279	.550
2013 2 Tms		6	10	1	0	0	0	(0	0)	1	0	0	0	0	0	5	0	0	0	0	0	0	.100	.100	.100	.200
2014 LAD	NL	61	170	32	6	1	3	(0	3)	49	16	14	10	17	1	41	2	1	2	0	0	1	.188	.267	.288	.555
2015 2 Tms	AL	55	107	21	3	0	1	(0	1)	27	9	5	6	6	0	26	2	5	0	0	1	0	.196	.252	.252	.505
13 Min	AL	2	3	0	0	0	0	(0	0)	0	0	0	0	0	0	1	0	0	0	0	0	0	.000	.000	.000	.000
13 LAD	NL	4	7	1	0	0	0	(0	0)	1	0	0	0	0	0	4	0	0	0	0	0	0	.143	.143	.143	.286
15 LAA	AL	10	21	4	0	0	0	(0	0)	4	3	0	0	0	0	2	0	0	0	0	1	0	.190	.190	.190	.381
15 KC	AL	45	86	17	3	0	1	(0	1)	23	6	5	6	6	0	24	2	5	0	0	0	0	.198	.266	.267	.533
6 ML YEARS		306	774	143	30	3	9	(2	7)	206	63	60	40	47	1	165	12	15	5	0	1	16	.185	.241	.266	.507

Billy Butler

Bats: R Throws: R Pos: DH-136;PH-8;1B-7   Ht: 6'1" Wt: 240 Born: 4/18/1986 Age: 30

								BATTING													RUNNING			AVERAGES			
Year Team	Lg	G	AB	H	2B	3B	HR	(Hm	Rd)	TB	R	RBI	RC	TBB	IBB	SO	HBP	SH	SF	SB	CS	GDP	Avg	OBP	Slg	OPS
2007 KC	AL	92	329	96	23	2	8	(5	3)	147	38	52	50	27	5	55	2	0	2	0	0	8	.292	.347	.447	.794
2008 KC	AL	124	443	122	22	0	11	(4	7)	177	44	55	57	33	0	57	0	0	1	0	1	23	.275	.324	.400	.724
2009 KC	AL	159	608	183	51	1	21	(16	5)	299	78	93	99	58	3	103	2	0	4	1	0	20	.301	.362	.492	.853
2010 KC	AL	158	595	189	45	0	15	(9	6)	279	77	78	91	69	8	78	5	0	9	0	0	32	.318	.388	.469	.857

Year Team	Lg	G	AB	H	2B	3B	HR	(Hm Rd)	TB	R	RBI	RC	TBB	IBB	SO	HBP	SH	SF	SB	CS	GDP	Avg	OBP	Slg	OPS
2011 KC	AL	159	597	174	44	0	19	(9 10)	275	74	95	94	66	15	95	3	0	7	2	1	16	.291	.361	.461	.822
2012 KC	AL	161	614	192	32	1	29	(11 18)	313	72	107	102	54	9	111	7	0	4	2	1	20	.313	.373	.510	.882
2013 KC	AL	**162**	582	168	27	0	15	(6 9)	240	62	82	87	79	11	102	3	0	4	0	0	**28**	.289	.374	.412	.787
2014 KC	AL	151	549	149	32	0	9	(5 4)	208	57	66	65	41	3	96	5	0	8	0	0	21	.271	.323	.379	.702
2015 Oak	AL	151	538	135	28	1	15	(9 6)	210	63	65	64	52	4	101	7	0	4	0	0	26	.251	.323	.390	.713
Postseason		13	42	11	3	0	0	(0 0)	14	3	8	7	5	0	5	0	0	2	1	0	3	.262	.327	.333	.660
9 ML YEARS		1317	4855	1408	304	5	142	(74 68)	2148	565	693	709	479	58	798	34	0	44	5	3	194	.290	.355	.442	.797

Eddie Butler

Pitches: R **Bats:** R **Pos:** SP-16   **Ht:** 6'2" **Wt:** 180 **Born:** 3/13/1991 **Age:** 25

	HOW MUCH HE PITCHED						WHAT HE GAVE UP												THE RESULTS							
Year Team	Lg	G	GS	CG	GF	IP	BFP	H	R	ER	HR	SH	SF	HB	TBB	IBB	SO	WP	Bk	W	L	Pct	Sh	Sv-Op	Hld	ERC	ERA
2012 GdJunc	R+	13	12	0	0	67.2	272	59	18	16	1	1	1	0	13	0	55	7	0	7	1	.875	0	0- -	-	2.10	2.13
2013 2 Tms	Low	22	22	0	0	122.0	494	83	45	28	9	3	1	5	46	0	118	9	0	8	5	.615	0	0- -	-	2.31	2.07
2013 Tulsa	AA	6	6	0	0	27.2	101	13	2	2	0	0	0	1	6	0	25	1	0	1	0	1.000	0	0- -	-	0.89	0.65
2014 Tulsa	AA	18	18	0	0	108.0	450	103	46	42	10	3	3	2	32	0	63	6	0	6	9	.400	0	0- -	-	3.46	3.50
2015 Albq	AAA	11	11	0	0	63.1	278	71	43	38	6	4	4	3	25	0	37	4	1	2	6	.250	0	0- -	-	4.99	5.40
2014 Col	NL	3	3	0	0	16.0	76	23	12	12	2	2	0	0	7	1	3	0	0	1	1	.500	0	0-0	0	6.98	6.75
2015 Col	NL	16	16	1	0	79.1	370	102	57	52	13	6	1	4	42	4	44	0	0	3	10	.231	0	0-0	0	7.12	5.90
2 ML YEARS		19	19	1	0	95.1	446	125	69	64	15	8	1	4	49	5	47	0	0	4	11	.267	0	0-0	0	7.09	6.04

Joey Butler

Bats: R **Throws:** R **Pos:** DH-43;LF-30;PH-24;RF-6   **Ht:** 6'2" **Wt:** 220 **Born:** 3/12/1986 **Age:** 30

Year Team	Lg	G	AB	H	2B	3B	HR	(Hm Rd)	TB	R	RBI	RC	TBB	IBB	SO	HBP	SH	SF	SB	CS	GDP	Avg	OBP	Slg	OPS
2015 Drham*	AAA	31	120	40	9	1	6	(- -)	69	21	24	27	14	0	31	3	0	0	0	0	4	.333	.416	.575	.991
2013 Tex	AL	8	12	4	2	0	0	(0 0)	6	3	1	2	3	0	6	0	0	0	0	0	0	.333	.467	.500	.967
2014 StL	NL	6	5	0	0	0	0	(0 0)	0	0	0	0	1	0	3	0	0	0	0	0	0	.000	.167	.000	.167
2015 TB	AL	88	257	71	12	0	8	(3 5)	107	30	30	28	16	0	82	3	0	0	5	2	16	.276	.326	.416	.742
3 ML YEARS		102	274	75	14	0	8	(3 5)	113	33	31	30	20	0	91	3	0	0	5	2	16	.274	.330	.412	.742

Byron Buxton

Bats: R **Throws:** R **Pos:** CF-44;PR-2   **Ht:** 6'2" **Wt:** 190 **Born:** 12/18/1993 **Age:** 22

Year Team	Lg	G	AB	H	2B	3B	HR	(Hm Rd)	TB	R	RBI	RC	TBB	IBB	SO	HBP	SH	SF	SB	CS	GDP	Avg	OBP	Slg	OPS
2012 2 Tms	Low	48	165	41	10	4	5	(- -)	74	33	20	27	19	0	41	5	0	0	11	3	0	.248	.344	.448	.792
2013 2 Tms	Low	125	488	163	19	18	12	(- -)	254	109	77	111	76	3	105	3	3	4	55	19	5	.334	.424	.520	.944
2014 FtMyrs	A+	30	121	29	4	2	4	(- -)	49	19	16	16	10	0	33	3	0	0	6	2	0	.240	.313	.405	.718
2015 Chatt	AA	59	237	67	7	12	6	(- -)	116	44	37	45	26	0	51	1	0	4	20	2	2	.283	.351	.489	.840
2015 Roch	AAA	13	55	22	3	1	1	(- -)	30	11	8	12	4	0	12	0	0	0	2	1	0	.400	.441	.545	.986
2015 Min	AL	46	129	27	7	1	2	(0 2)	42	16	6	10	6	0	44	1	2	0	2	2	1	.209	.250	.326	.576

Marlon Byrd

Bats: R **Throws:** R **Pos:** LF-88;RF-41;CF-4;PH-4;DH-2   **Ht:** 6'0" **Wt:** 245 **Born:** 8/30/1977 **Age:** 38

Year Team	Lg	G	AB	H	2B	3B	HR	(Hm Rd)	TB	R	RBI	RC	TBB	IBB	SO	HBP	SH	SF	SB	CS	GDP	Avg	OBP	Slg	OPS
2002 Phi	NL	10	35	8	2	0	1	(1 0)	13	2	1	0	1	0	8	0	0	0	0	2	0	.229	.250	.371	.621
2003 Phi	NL	135	495	150	28	4	7	(3 4)	207	86	45	72	44	3	94	7	4	3	11	1	8	.303	.366	.418	.784
2004 Phi	NL	106	346	79	13	2	5	(3 2)	111	48	33	35	22	1	68	7	2	1	2	2	10	.228	.287	.321	.608
2005 2 Tms	NL	79	229	61	15	2	2	(0 2)	86	20	26	30	19	1	50	2	5	4	5	1	5	.266	.323	.376	.698
2006 Was	NL	78	197	44	8	1	5	(1 4)	69	28	18	18	22	1	47	6	1	2	3	3	6	.223	.317	.350	.667
2007 Tex	AL	109	414	127	17	8	10	(4 6)	190	60	70	68	29	3	88	5	0	6	5	3	9	.307	.355	.459	.814
2008 Tex	AL	122	403	120	28	4	10	(7 3)	186	70	53	63	46	3	62	9	2	2	7	2	10	.298	.380	.462	.842
2009 Tex	AL	146	547	155	43	2	20	(14 6)	262	66	89	91	32	2	98	10	0	**10**	8	4	11	.283	.329	.479	.808
2010 ChC	NL	152	580	170	39	2	12	(6 6)	249	84	66	80	31	1	98	17	0	2	5	1	12	.293	.346	.429	.775
2011 ChC	NL	119	446	123	22	2	9	(4 5)	176	51	35	43	25	2	78	8	1	2	3	2	13	.276	.324	.395	.719
2012 2 Tms	NL	48	143	30	2	0	1	(0 1)	35	10	9	8	5	1	31	2	1	2	0	3	3	.210	.243	.245	.488
2013 2 Tms	NL	147	532	155	35	5	24	(9 15)	272	75	88	85	31	2	144	8	1	7	2	4	11	.291	.336	.511	.847
2014 Phi	NL	154	591	156	28	2	25	(13 12)	263	71	85	74	35	7	185	8	0	3	3	2	6	.264	.312	.445	.757
2015 2 Tms	NL	135	506	125	25	5	23	(14 9)	229	58	73	61	29	2	145	4	0	5	2	1	10	.247	.290	.453	.743
05 Phi	NL	5	13	4	0	0	0	(0 0)	4	0	0	2	1	0	3	1	0	0	0	0	0	.308	.400	.308	.708
05 Was	NL	74	216	57	15	2	2	(0 2)	82	20	26	28	18	1	47	1	5	4	5	1	5	.264	.318	.380	.698
12 ChC	NL	13	43	3	0	0	0	(0 0)	3	1	2	0	3	1	10	1	0	0	0	1	2	.070	.149	.070	.219
12 Bos	AL	35	100	27	2	0	1	(0 1)	32	9	7	8	2	0	21	1	1	2	0	2	1	.270	.286	.320	.606
13 NYM	NL	117	425	121	26	5	21	(7 14)	220	61	71	68	25	2	124	7	1	6	2	4	6	.285	.330	.518	.848
13 Pit	NL	30	107	34	9	0	3	(2 1)	52	14	17	17	6	0	20	1	0	1	0	0	5	.318	.357	.486	.843
15 Cin	NL	96	359	85	13	3	19	(11 8)	161	46	42	37	23	1	101	3	0	3	2	1	6	.237	.286	.448	.735
15 SF	NL	39	147	40	12	2	4	(3 1)	68	12	31	24	6	1	44	1	0	2	0	0	4	.272	.301	.463	.764
Postseason		6	22	8	2	0	1	(1 0)	13	4	5	3	1	0	6	0	0	0	0	0	0	.364	.391	.591	.982
14 ML YEARS		1540	5464	1503	305	39	154	(79 75)	2348	729	691	728	371	29	1196	93	17	49	56	31	114	.275	.329	.430	.759

Cesar Cabral

Pitches: L **Bats:** L **Pos:** RP-2   kuh-BRAWL   **Ht:** 6'3" **Wt:** 250 **Born:** 2/11/1989 **Age:** 27

			HOW MUCH HE PITCHED							WHAT HE GAVE UP											THE RESULTS							
Year	Team	Lg	G	GS	CG	GF	IP	BFP	H	R	ER	HR	SH	SF	HB	TBB	IBB	SO	WP	Bk	W	L	Pct	Sh	Sv-Op	Hld	ERC	ERA
2015	Norfolk*	AAA	45	0	0	11	40.0	184	42	23	22	0	2	0	3	19	1	43	6	0	2	1	.667	0	2--	-	4.03	4.95
2013	NYY	AL	8	0	0	0	3.2	15	3	1	1	0	0	0	1	1	0	6	2	0	0	0	-	0	0-0	1	3.10	2.45
2014	NYY	AL	4	0	0	0	1.0	12	4	3	3	0	0	0	3	2	0	2	1	1	0	0	-	0	0-0	1	48.50	27.00
2015	Bal	AL	2	0	0	2	1.0	3	0	0	0	0	0	0	0	1	0	1	0	0	0	0	-	0	0-0	0	1.26	0.00
	3 ML YEARS		14	0	0	2	5.2	30	7	4	4	0	0	0	4	4	0	9	3	1	0	0	-	0	0-0	2	9.21	6.35

Asdrubal Cabrera

Bats: B **Throws:** R **Pos:** SS-136;PH-8;DH-4   azz-DRUE-bull   **Ht:** 6'0" **Wt:** 205 **Born:** 11/13/1985 **Age:** 30

							BATTING												RUNNING			AVERAGES			
Year	Team	Lg	G	AB	H	2B	3B	HR	(Hm | Rd)	TB	R	RBI	RC	TBB	IBB	SO	HBP	SH	SF	SB	CS	GDP	Avg	OBP	Slg	OPS
2007	Cle	AL	45	159	45	9	2	3	(1 | 2)	67	30	22	27	17	0	29	2	5	3	0	0	7	.283	.354	.421	.775
2008	Cle	AL	114	352	91	20	0	6	(5 | 1)	129	48	47	48	46	2	77	4	11	5	4	4	8	.259	.346	.366	.713
2009	Cle	AL	131	523	161	42	4	6	(4 | 2)	229	81	68	81	44	1	89	1	10	3	17	4	13	.308	.361	.438	.799
2010	Cle	AL	97	381	105	16	1	3	(2 | 1)	132	39	29	46	25	0	60	5	11	3	6	4	10	.276	.326	.346	.673
2011	Cle	AL	151	604	165	32	3	25	(13 | 12)	278	87	92	100	44	5	119	11	4	4	17	5	10	.273	.332	.460	.792
2012	Cle	AL	143	555	150	35	1	16	(10 | 6)	235	70	68	74	52	3	99	6	1	2	9	4	18	.270	.338	.423	.762
2013	Cle	AL	136	508	123	35	2	14	(6 | 8)	204	66	64	51	35	1	114	8	6	5	9	3	10	.242	.299	.402	.700
2014	2 Tms		146	553	133	31	4	14	(6 | 8)	214	74	61	57	49	2	108	7	1	6	10	2	15	.241	.307	.387	.694
2015	TB	AL	143	505	134	28	5	15	(7 | 8)	217	66	58	53	36	4	107	3	1	6	6	3	14	.265	.315	.430	.744
	14 Cle	AL	97	378	93	22	2	9	(5 | 4)	146	54	40	36	27	1	79	7	0	4	7	2	11	.246	.305	.386	.692
	14 Was	NL	49	175	40	9	2	5	(1 | 4)	68	20	21	21	22	1	29	0	1	2	3	0	4	.229	.312	.389	.700
	Postseason		16	65	13	1	0	2	(2 | 0)	20	7	8	6	2	0	18	0	3	1	0	0	3	.200	.221	.308	.528
	9 ML YEARS		1106	4140	1107	248	22	102	(56 | 46)	1705	561	509	537	348	18	802	47	50	37	78	29	105	.267	.329	.412	.740

Everth Cabrera

Bats: B **Throws:** R **Pos:** SS-27;2B-2;PR-1   EVV-urth   **Ht:** 5'10" **Wt:** 190 **Born:** 11/17/1986 **Age:** 29

							BATTING												RUNNING			AVERAGES			
Year	Team	Lg	G	AB	H	2B	3B	HR	(Hm | Rd)	TB	R	RBI	RC	TBB	IBB	SO	HBP	SH	SF	SB	CS	GDP	Avg	OBP	Slg	OPS
2015	Scrmto*	AAA	27	108	25	3	0	0	(- | -)	28	14	7	9	9	0	16	1	1	0	7	2	4	.231	.297	.259	.556
2009	SD	NL	103	377	96	18	8	2	(1 | 1)	136	59	31	48	46	5	88	5	8	2	25	8	3	.255	.342	.361	.703
2010	SD	NL	76	212	44	6	3	1	(0 | 1)	59	22	22	15	19	3	54	2	8	0	10	6	8	.208	.279	.278	.557
2011	SD	NL	2	8	1	0	0	0	(0 | 0)	1	1	0	1	1	0	3	0	0	0	2	0	0	.125	.222	.125	.347
2012	SD	NL	115	398	98	19	3	2	(0 | 2)	129	49	24	43	43	2	110	3	5	0	44	4	3	.246	.324	.324	.648
2013	SD	NL	95	381	108	15	5	4	(1 | 3)	145	54	31	59	41	0	69	2	10	1	37	12	1	.283	.355	.381	.736
2014	SD	NL	90	357	83	13	1	3	(0 | 3)	107	36	20	31	20	0	86	1	9	4	18	8	5	.232	.272	.300	.572
2015	Bal	AL	29	96	20	2	0	0	(0 | 0)	22	7	4	5	5	0	22	1	1	2	2	0	4	.208	.250	.229	.479
	7 ML YEARS		510	1829	450	73	20	12	(2 | 10)	599	228	132	202	175	10	432	14	41	9	138	38	24	.246	.315	.328	.643

Melky Cabrera

Bats: B **Throws:** L **Pos:** LF-150;DH-8   **Ht:** 5'10" **Wt:** 210 **Born:** 8/11/1984 **Age:** 31

							BATTING												RUNNING			AVERAGES			
Year	Team	Lg	G	AB	H	2B	3B	HR	(Hm | Rd)	TB	R	RBI	RC	TBB	IBB	SO	HBP	SH	SF	SB	CS	GDP	Avg	OBP	Slg	OPS
2005	NYY	AL	6	19	4	0	0	0	(0 | 0)	4	1	0	0	0	0	2	0	0	0	0	0	0	.211	.211	.211	.421
2006	NYY	AL	130	460	129	26	2	7	(3 | 4)	180	75	50	68	56	3	59	2	5	1	12	5	9	.280	.360	.391	.752
2007	NYY	AL	150	545	149	24	8	8	(4 | 4)	213	66	73	70	43	0	68	5	10	9	13	5	14	.273	.327	.391	.718
2008	NYY	AL	129	414	103	12	1	8	(4 | 4)	141	42	37	37	29	5	58	3	4	3	9	2	11	.249	.301	.341	.641
2009	NYY	AL	154	485	133	28	1	13	(9 | 4)	202	66	68	69	43	4	59	4	4	4	10	2	15	.274	.336	.416	.752
2010	Atl	NL	147	458	117	27	3	4	(1 | 3)	162	50	42	45	42	11	64	1	5	3	7	1	8	.255	.317	.354	.671
2011	KC	AL	155	658	201	44	5	18	(6 | 12)	309	102	87	92	35	3	94	1	7	5	20	10	13	.305	.339	.470	.809
2012	SF	NL	113	459	159	25	10	11	(2 | 9)	237	84	60	83	36	4	63	0	1	5	13	5	8	.346	.390	.516	.906
2013	Tor	AL	88	344	96	15	2	3	(0 | 3)	124	39	30	39	23	0	47	0	2	3	2	2	7	.279	.322	.360	.682
2014	Tor	AL	139	568	171	35	3	16	(7 | 9)	260	81	73	84	43	3	67	3	2	5	6	2	19	.301	.351	.458	.808
2015	CWS	AL	158	629	172	36	2	12	(6 | 6)	248	70	77	81	40	2	88	2	2	10	3	0	18	.273	.314	.394	.709
	Postseason		22	75	16	2	0	1	(0 | 1)	21	8	7	5	3	0	16	0	2	0	0	0	0	.213	.244	.280	.524
	11 ML YEARS		1369	5039	1434	272	37	100	(45 | 55)	2080	676	597	668	390	35	669	21	42	48	95	34	122	.285	.336	.413	.748

Miguel Cabrera

Bats: R **Throws:** R **Pos:** 1B-107;DH-11;PH-1   **Ht:** 6'4" **Wt:** 240 **Born:** 4/18/1983 **Age:** 33

							BATTING												RUNNING			AVERAGES			
Year	Team	Lg	G	AB	H	2B	3B	HR	(Hm | Rd)	TB	R	RBI	RC	TBB	IBB	SO	HBP	SH	SF	SB	CS	GDP	Avg	OBP	Slg	OPS
2003	Fla	NL	87	314	84	21	3	12	(7 | 5)	147	39	62	51	25	3	84	2	4	1	0	2	12	.268	.325	.468	.793
2004	Fla	NL	160	603	177	31	1	33	(14 | 19)	309	101	112	92	68	5	148	6	0	8	5	2	20	.294	.366	.512	.879
2005	Fla	NL	158	613	198	43	2	33	(11 | 22)	344	106	116	108	64	12	125	2	0	6	1	0	20	.323	.385	.561	.947
2006	Fla	NL	158	576	195	50	2	26	(15 | 11)	327	112	114	132	86	27	108	10	0	4	9	6	18	.339	.430	.568	.998
2007	Fla	NL	157	588	188	38	2	34	(19 | 15)	332	91	119	122	79	23	127	5	1	7	2	1	17	.320	.401	.565	.965
2008	Det	AL	160	616	180	36	2	37	(19 | 18)	331	85	127	109	56	6	126	3	0	9	1	0	16	.292	.349	.537	.887
2009	Det	AL	160	611	198	34	0	34	(19 | 15)	334	96	103	114	68	14	107	5	0	1	6	2	22	.324	.396	.547	.942
2010	Det	AL	150	548	180	45	1	38	(17 | 21)	341	111	126	122	89	32	95	3	0	8	3	3	17	.328	.420	.622	1.042
2011	Det	AL	161	572	197	48	0	30	(15 | 15)	335	111	105	141	108	22	89	3	0	5	2	1	24	.344	.448	.586	1.033
2012	Det	AL	161	622	205	40	0	44	(28 | 16)	377	109	139	123	66	17	98	3	0	6	4	1	28	.330	.393	.606	.999
2013	Det	AL	148	555	193	26	1	44	(17 | 27)	353	103	137	146	90	19	94	5	0	2	3	0	19	.348	.442	.636	1.078

Year	Team	Lg	G	AB	H	2B	3B	HR	(Hm	Rd)	TB	R	RBI	RC	TBB	IBB	SO	HBP	SH	SF	SB	CS	GDP	Avg	OBP	Slg	OPS
									BATTING												RUNNING			AVERAGES			
2014	Det	AL	159	611	191	52	1	25	(13	12)	320	101	109	110	60	10	117	3	0	11	1	1	21	.313	.371	.524	.895
2015	Det	AL	119	429	145	28	1	18	(7	11)	229	64	76	93	77	15	82	3	0	2	1	1	19	.338	.440	.534	.974
	Postseason		55	205	57	10	0	13	(4	9)	106	29	38	34	27	7	48	2	1	0	3	0	7	.278	.368	.517	.885
13 ML YEARS			1938	7258	2331	492	16	408	(201	207)	4079	1229	1445	1463	936	205	1400	53	5	70	38	20	253	.321	.399	.562	.961

Ramon Cabrera

Bats: B **Throws:** R **Pos:** C-8;PH-6 **Ht:** 5'8" **Wt:** 195 **Born:** 11/5/1989 **Age:** 26

									BATTING												RUNNING			AVERAGES			
Year	Team	Lg	G	AB	H	2B	3B	HR	(Hm	Rd)	TB	R	RBI	RC	TBB	IBB	SO	HBP	SH	SF	SB	CS	GDP	Avg	OBP	Slg	OPS
2011	Bradtn	A+	92	327	112	25	4	3	(-	-)	154	46	53	66	38	4	29	4	3	7	5	1	9	.343	.410	.471	.881
2012	Altna	AA	112	384	106	22	2	3	(-	-)	141	47	50	50	39	1	44	0	4	1	0	3	11	.276	.342	.367	.709
2013	Erie	AA	84	312	95	22	2	0	(-	-)	121	44	54	53	44	0	34	3	0	3	4	0	6	.304	.392	.388	.780
2013	Toledo	AAA	39	149	36	9	1	1	(-	-)	50	13	15	16	14	0	21	1	1	0	0	1	8	.242	.311	.336	.647
2014	Erie	AA	107	394	109	17	0	5	(-	-)	141	42	47	49	33	0	37	0	0	4	1	0	9	.277	.329	.358	.687
2014	Altna	AA	12	46	11	5	0	1	(-	-)	19	5	5	5	3	0	6	0	0	0	1	0	0	.239	.286	.413	.699
2015	Lsvlle	AAA	86	317	92	14	0	2	(-	-)	112	29	35	41	27	0	44	0	4	3	1	1	10	.290	.343	.353	.696
2015	Cin	NL	13	30	11	1	0	1	(1	0)	15	4	3	4	0	0	5	0	0	0	0	0	1	.367	.367	.500	.867

Trevor Cahill

Pitches: R **Bats:** R **Pos:** RP-23; SP-3 KAY-hill **Ht:** 6'4" **Wt:** 240 **Born:** 3/1/1988 **Age:** 28

					HOW MUCH HE PITCHED					WHAT HE GAVE UP											THE RESULTS					
Year	Team	Lg	G	GS	CG	GF	IP	BFP	H	R	ER	HR	SH	SF	HB	TBB	IBB	SO	WP	Bk	W	L	Pct	Sh	Sv-Op	Hld	ERC	ERA
2015	OkCity*	AAA	6	6	0	0	28.2	131	32	22	20	3	3	2	0	14	0	17	3	0	1	3	.250	0	0- -	-	5.05	6.28
2015	Iowa*	AAA	5	0	0	2	7.2	30	5	0	0	0	0	0	0	3	0	7	2	0	0	0	-	0	0- -	-	1.71	0.00
2009	Oak	AL	32	32	0	0	178.2	773	185	99	92	27	4	7	4	72	1	90	5	0	10	13	.435	0	0-0	0	4.79	4.63
2010	Oak	AL	30	30	1	0	196.2	783	155	73	65	19	3	6	6	63	1	118	2	2	18	8	.692	1	0-0	0	2.81	2.97
2011	Oak	AL	34	34	0	0	207.2	901	214	102	96	19	8	6	8	82	1	147	15	0	12	14	.462	0	0-0	0	4.34	4.16
2012	Ari	NL	32	32	2	0	200.0	839	184	93	84	16	12	6	11	74	0	156	10	2	13	12	.520	1	0-0	0	3.66	3.78
2013	Ari	NL	26	25	0	1	146.2	636	143	70	65	13	9	9	6	65	2	102	17	0	8	10	.444	0	0-0	0	4.19	3.99
2014	Ari	NL	32	17	0	8	110.2	499	123	76	69	9	6	3	4	55	2	105	5	0	3	12	.200	0	1-2	0	5.11	5.61
2015	2 Tms		26	3	0	6	43.1	187	44	27	26	4	3	1	2	16	1	36	2	0	1	3	.250	0	0-0	0	4.15	5.40
15	Atl	NL	15	3	0	6	26.1	124	36	23	22	2	2	1	1	11	1	14	1	0	0	3	.000	0	0-0	0	6.22	7.52
15	ChC	NL	11	0	0	0	17.0	63	8	4	4	2	1	0	1	5	0	22	1	0	1	0	1.000	0	0-0	2	1.52	2.12
7 ML YEARS			212	173	3	15	1083.2	4618	1048	540	497	107	45	38	41	427	8	754	56	4	65	72	.474	2	1-2	2	4.05	4.13

Lorenzo Cain

Bats: R **Throws:** R **Pos:** CF-136;RF-5;DH-3;PH-1 **Ht:** 6'2" **Wt:** 205 **Born:** 4/13/1986 **Age:** 30

									BATTING												RUNNING			AVERAGES			
Year	Team	Lg	G	AB	H	2B	3B	HR	(Hm	Rd)	TB	R	RBI	RC	TBB	IBB	SO	HBP	SH	SF	SB	CS	GDP	Avg	OBP	Slg	OPS
2010	Mil	NL	43	147	45	11	1	1	(1	0)	61	17	13	23	9	0	28	1	0	1	7	1	1	.306	.348	.415	.763
2011	KC	AL	6	22	6	1	0	0	(0	0)	7	4	1	2	1	0	4	0	0	0	0	0	0	.273	.304	.318	.623
2012	KC	AL	61	222	59	9	2	7	(4	3)	93	27	31	32	15	0	56	3	0	4	10	0	4	.266	.316	.419	.734
2013	KC	AL	115	399	100	21	3	4	(3	1)	139	54	46	46	33	2	90	4	0	6	14	6	10	.251	.310	.348	.658
2014	KC	AL	133	471	142	29	4	5	(3	2)	194	55	53	67	24	2	108	4	0	3	28	5	9	.301	.339	.412	.751
2015	KC	AL	140	551	169	34	6	16	(9	7)	263	101	72	90	37	4	98	12	0	4	28	6	16	.307	.361	.477	.838
	Postseason		15	60	20	5	0	0	(0	0)	25	13	8	12	5	0	9	1	1	1	2	0	0	.333	.388	.417	.805
6 ML YEARS			498	1812	521	105	16	33	(19	14)	757	258	216	260	119	8	384	24	0	18	87	18	40	.288	.337	.418	.754

Matt Cain

Pitches: R **Bats:** R **Pos:** SP-11; RP-2 **Ht:** 6'3" **Wt:** 230 **Born:** 10/1/1984 **Age:** 31

					HOW MUCH HE PITCHED					WHAT HE GAVE UP											THE RESULTS					
Year	Team	Lg	G	GS	CG	GF	IP	BFP	H	R	ER	HR	SH	SF	HB	TBB	IBB	SO	WP	Bk	W	L	Pct	Sh	Sv-Op	Hld	ERC	ERA
2015	Scrmto*	AAA	5	3	0	1	19.2	83	18	8	7	2	0	0	1	4	0	22	0	0	1	2	.333	0	0- -	-	2.96	3.20
2005	SF	NL	7	7	1	0	46.1	181	24	12	12	4	2	1	0	19	1	30	1	0	2	1	.667	0	0-0	0	1.61	2.33
2006	SF	NL	32	31	1	1	190.2	818	157	93	88	18	11	6	6	87	1	179	9	2	13	12	.520	1	0-0	0	3.35	4.15
2007	SF	NL	32	32	1	0	200.0	832	173	84	81	14	8	5	5	79	3	163	12	0	7	16	.304	1	0-0	0	3.23	3.65
2008	SF	NL	34	34	1	0	217.2	933	206	95	91	19	7	7	7	91	9	186	7	2	8	14	.364	1	0-0	0	3.84	3.76
2009	SF	NL	33	33	4	0	217.2	886	184	73	70	22	10	6	3	73	6	171	9	0	14	8	.636	0	0-0	0	3.06	2.89
2010	SF	NL	33	33	4	0	223.1	896	181	84	78	22	6	7	4	61	4	177	8	0	13	11	.542	2	0-0	0	2.65	3.14
2011	SF	NL	33	33	1	0	221.2	907	177	82	71	9	11	6	5	63	5	179	4	0	12	11	.522	0	0-0	0	2.31	2.88
2012	SF	NL	32	32	2	0	219.1	876	177	73	69	21	11	9	9	51	1	193	8	0	16	5	.762	2	0-0	0	2.57	2.79
2013	SF	NL	30	30	0	0	184.1	760	158	85	82	23	6	2	5	55	3	158	1	0	8	10	.444	0	0-0	0	3.15	4.00
2014	SF	NL	15	15	0	0	90.1	374	81	47	42	13	3	2	2	32	2	70	2	0	2	7	.222	0	0-0	0	3.73	4.18
2015	SF	NL	13	11	0	0	60.2	271	71	39	39	12	1	4	4	20	0	41	1	0	2	4	.333	0	0-0	0	5.79	5.79
	Postseason		8	8	0	0	51.1	210	40	13	12	6	1	0	6	14	2	33	1	0	4	2	.667	0	0-0	0	2.92	2.10
11 ML YEARS			294	291	15	1	1872.0	7734	1589	767	722	177	76	55	54	631	35	1547	62	4	97	99	.495	6	0-0	0	3.07	3.47

Kole Calhoun

Bats: L **Throws:** L **Pos:** RF-157;PH-2;1B-1 **Ht:** 5'10" **Wt:** 200 **Born:** 10/14/1987 **Age:** 28

									BATTING												RUNNING			AVERAGES			
Year	Team	Lg	G	AB	H	2B	3B	HR	(Hm	Rd)	TB	R	RBI	RC	TBB	IBB	SO	HBP	SH	SF	SB	CS	GDP	Avg	OBP	Slg	OPS
2012	LAA	AL	21	23	4	1	0	0	(0	0)	5	2	1	0	2	1	6	0	0	0	1	0	0	.174	.240	.217	.457
2013	LAA	AL	58	195	55	7	2	8	(5	3)	90	29	32	33	21	0	41	1	0	5	2	2	6	.282	.347	.462	.808

Year	Team	Lg	G	AB	H	2B	3B	HR	(Hm	Rd)	TB	R	RBI	RC	TBB	IBB	SO	HBP	SH	SF	SB	CS	GDP	Avg	OBP	Slg	OPS
2014	LAA	AL	127	493	134	31	3	17	(7	10)	222	90	58	75	38	0	104	2	2	2	5	3	5	.272	.325	.450	.776
2015	LAA	AL	159	630	161	23	2	26	(16	10)	266	78	83	85	45	1	164	5	2	4	4	1	6	.256	.308	.422	.731
Postseason			3	15	5	0	0	0	(0	0)	5	1	0	1	0	0	1	0	0	0	0	0	0	.333	.333	.333	.667
4 ML YEARS			365	1341	354	62	7	51	(28	23)	583	199	174	193	106	2	315	8	4	11	12	6	17	.264	.319	.435	.754

Orlando Calixte

Bats: R **Throws:** R **Pos:** SS-1;PH-1;PR-1   ka-LEEKS-tay   **Ht:** 5'11" **Wt:** 160 **Born:** 2/3/1992 **Age:** 24

Year	Team	Lg	G	AB	H	2B	3B	HR	(Hm	Rd)	TB	R	RBI	RC	TBB	IBB	SO	HBP	SH	SF	SB	CS	GDP	Avg	OBP	Slg	OPS
2011	Kane	A	81	289	60	5	1	3	(-	-)	76	19	31	19	20	1	70	0	4	4	11	4	2	.208	.256	.263	.519
2012	2 Tms	Low	125	484	127	30	8	14	(-	-)	215	69	62	68	36	0	109	3	5	4	10	8	10	.262	.315	.444	.759
2013	NWArk	AA	123	484	121	25	4	8	(-	-)	178	59	36	56	42	2	131	3	4	3	14	11	15	.250	.312	.368	.680
2014	NWArk	AA	96	374	89	15	1	11	(-	-)	139	43	37	41	27	0	92	0	6	5	9	5	7	.238	.286	.372	.657
2015	Omha	AAA	107	354	81	11	2	8	(-	-)	120	38	27	38	27	2	84	2	11	0	22	3	8	.229	.287	.339	.626
2015	KC	AL	2	3	0	0	0	0	(0	0)	0	1	0	0	0	0	0	0	0	0	0	0	0	.000	.000	.000	.000

Alberto Callaspo

Bats: B **Throws:** R **Pos:** 3B-65;PH-34;2B-4;DH-1   ky-AHS-po   **Ht:** 5'9" **Wt:** 225 **Born:** 4/19/1983 **Age:** 33

Year	Team	Lg	G	AB	H	2B	3B	HR	(Hm	Rd)	TB	R	RBI	RC	TBB	IBB	SO	HBP	SH	SF	SB	CS	GDP	Avg	OBP	Slg	OPS
2006	Ari	NL	23	42	10	1	1	0	(0	0)	13	2	6	5	4	0	6	0	1	0	0	1	0	.238	.298	.310	.607
2007	Ari	NL	56	144	31	8	0	0	(0	0)	39	10	7	7	9	0	14	1	1	1	1	1	8	.215	.265	.271	.535
2008	KC	AL	74	213	65	8	3	0	(0	0)	79	21	16	25	19	0	14	0	1	1	2	1	6	.305	.361	.371	.731
2009	KC	AL	155	576	173	41	8	11	(6	5)	263	79	73	90	52	4	51	1	0	5	2	1	15	.300	.356	.457	.813
2010	2 Tms	AL	146	562	149	27	2	10	(2	8)	210	61	56	54	31	3	42	1	1	6	5	3	22	.265	.302	.374	.675
2011	LAA	AL	141	475	137	23	0	6	(1	5)	178	54	46	66	58	8	48	1	0	2	8	1	11	.288	.366	.375	.740
2012	LAA	AL	138	457	115	20	0	10	(3	7)	165	55	53	60	56	1	59	0	3	4	4	3	6	.252	.331	.361	.692
2013	2 Tms	AL	136	453	117	20	0	10	(5	5)	167	52	58	60	53	2	47	1	3	6	0	2	12	.258	.333	.369	.702
2014	Oak	AL	127	404	90	15	0	4	(3	1)	117	37	39	36	40	1	50	1	0	6	0	1	18	.223	.290	.290	.580
2015	2 Tms	NL	97	230	54	7	0	1	(0	1)	64	20	15	22	28	1	34	0	1	2	0	0	6	.235	.315	.278	.594
10	KC	AL	88	349	96	19	2	8	(2	6)	143	40	43	38	19	2	29	0	0	5	3	1	14	.275	.308	.410	.718
10	LAA	AL	58	213	53	8	0	2	(0	2)	67	21	13	16	12	1	13	1	1	1	2	2	8	.249	.291	.315	.605
13	LAA	AL	86	294	74	13	0	5	(2	3)	102	32	36	37	34	2	22	0	3	5	0	2	8	.252	.324	.347	.671
13	Oak	AL	50	159	43	7	0	5	(3	2)	65	20	22	23	19	0	25	1	0	1	0	0	4	.270	.350	.409	.759
15	Atl	NL	37	107	22	2	0	1	(0	1)	27	12	8	8	14	1	10	0	0	2	0	0	4	.206	.293	.252	.545
15	LAD	NL	60	123	32	5	0	0	(0	0)	37	8	7	14	14	0	24	0	1	0	0	0	2	.260	.336	.301	.637
Postseason			7	9	2	1	0	0	(0	0)	3	0	1	1	0	0	1	0	0	0	0	0	0	.222	.222	.333	.556
10 ML YEARS			1093	3556	941	170	14	52	(20	32)	1295	391	369	425	350	20	365	6	10	34	22	14	104	.265	.329	.364	.693

Arquimedes Caminero

Pitches: R **Bats:** R **Pos:** RP-73   ahr-keh-MEE-deez   **Ht:** 6'4" **Wt:** 250 **Born:** 6/16/1987 **Age:** 29

	HOW MUCH HE PITCHED						WHAT HE GAVE UP											THE RESULTS							
Year	Team	Lg	G	GS	CG	GF	IP	BFP	H	R	ER	HR	SH	SF	HB	TBB	IBB	SO	WP	Bk	W	L	Pct	Sh	Sv-Op	Hld	ERC	ERA
2013	Mia	NL	13	0	0	6	13.0	52	10	4	4	2	0	0	1	3	0	12	1	0	0	0	-	0	0-1	1	2.85	2.77
2014	Mia	NL	6	0	0	1	6.2	31	8	8	8	2	0	0	0	4	0	8	0	0	0	0	.000	0	0-0	0	7.83	10.80
2015	Pit	NL	73	0	0	19	74.2	318	63	31	30	7	1	1	6	29	2	73	6	1	5	1	.833	0	0-1	15	3.38	3.62
3 ML YEARS			92	0	0	26	94.1	401	81	43	42	11	1	1	7	36	2	93	7	1	5	2	.714	0	0-2	16	3.58	4.01

Tony Campana

Bats: L **Throws:** L **Pos:** CF   camm-PAH-nah   **Ht:** 5'8" **Wt:** 165 **Born:** 5/30/1986 **Age:** 30

Year	Team	Lg	G	AB	H	2B	3B	HR	(Hm	Rd)	TB	R	RBI	RC	TBB	IBB	SO	HBP	SH	SF	SB	CS	GDP	Avg	OBP	Slg	OPS
2011	ChC	NL	95	143	37	3	0	1	(1	0)	43	24	6	17	8	1	30	1	3	0	24	2	1	.259	.303	.301	.603
2012	ChC	NL	89	174	46	6	0	0	(0	0)	52	26	5	20	11	0	43	0	7	0	30	3	0	.264	.308	.299	.607
2013	Ari	NL	29	46	12	0	1	0	(0	0)	14	10	0	6	8	0	14	0	0	0	8	2	0	.261	.370	.304	.675
2014	2 Tms		44	75	14	1	1	0	(0	0)	17	10	5	3	0	0	16	1	0	0	4	2	0	.187	.197	.227	.424
14	Ari	NL	26	60	9	1	1	0	(0	0)	12	4	3	2	0	0	10	1	0	0	4	1	0	.150	.164	.200	.364
14	LAA	AL	18	15	5	0	0	0	(0	0)	5	6	2	1	0	0	6	0	0	0	0	1	0	.333	.333	.333	.667
4 ML YEARS			257	438	109	10	2	1	(1	0)	126	70	16	46	27	1	103	2	10	0	66	9	1	.249	.296	.288	.583

Eric Campbell

Bats: R **Throws:** R **Pos:** 3B-48;PH-17;1B-5;LF-4;PR-1   **Ht:** 6'3" **Wt:** 205 **Born:** 4/9/1987 **Age:** 29

Year	Team	Lg	G	AB	H	2B	3B	HR	(Hm	Rd)	TB	R	RBI	RC	TBB	IBB	SO	HBP	SH	SF	SB	CS	GDP	Avg	OBP	Slg	OPS
2011	Bnghtn	AA	126	405	99	23	2	4	(-	-)	138	46	46	53	54	0	75	8	2	3	6	2	13	.244	.343	.341	.683
2012	Bnghtn	AA	115	394	114	25	2	9	(-	-)	173	53	50	72	58	0	76	6	2	5	10	5	12	.297	.391	.439	.830
2013	LsVgs	AAA	120	341	107	25	3	8	(-	-)	162	61	66	76	66	0	60	10	4	4	12	4	8	.314	.435	.475	.910
2014	LsVgs	AAA	33	141	50	15	0	3	(-	-)	74	39	24	32	20	0	20	2	0	0	3	1	8	.355	.442	.525	.967
2015	LsVgs	AAA	33	113	41	9	1	5	(-	-)	67	28	18	33	25	0	20	4	0	0	7	2	3	.363	.493	.593	1.086
2014	NYM	NL	85	190	50	9	0	3	(2	1)	68	16	16	19	17	0	55	1	0	3	3	0	5	.263	.322	.358	.680
2015	NYM	NL	71	173	34	8	0	3	(0	3)	51	28	19	13	26	1	37	4	1	2	5	3	11	.197	.312	.295	.607
2 ML YEARS			156	363	84	17	0	6	(2	4)	119	44	35	32	43	1	92	5	1	5	8	3	16	.231	.317	.328	.645

Leonel Campos

Pitches: R **Bats:** R **Pos:** RP-1 LEE-oh-nel KAM-pohs **Ht:** 6'2" **Wt:** 200 **Born:** 7/17/1987 **Age:** 28

			HOW MUCH HE PITCHED					WHAT HE GAVE UP												THE RESULTS						
Year	Team	Lg	G	GS	CG	GF	IP	BFP	H	R	ER	HR	SH	SF	HB	TBB	IBB	SO	WP	Bk	W	L	Pct	Sh	Sv-Op	Hld	ERC	ERA
2013	FtWyn	A	28	0	0	8	36.1	150	19	9	9	2	0	0	1	22	0	63	7	0	2	1	.667	0	5- -	-	2.14	2.23
2013	SnAnt	AA	26	0	0	3	30.2	122	14	5	3	0	3	1	0	16	0	43	3	0	1	0	1.000	0	2- -	-	1.33	0.88
2014	ElPaso	AAA	11	0	0	1	10.0	63	20	15	13	2	0	1	0	13	0	13	4	0	0	0	-	0	0- -	-	15.71	11.70
2014	SnAnt	AA	31	14	0	8	72.1	321	69	46	45	6	2	1	3	38	0	95	9	2	2	7	.222	0	1- -	-	4.33	5.60
2015	ElPaso	AAA	38	0	0	9	49.2	199	30	17	16	2	1	0	0	21	0	68	8	0	2	0	1.000	0	1- -	-	1.77	2.90
2014	SD	NL	6	0	0	1	7.0	33	9	5	4	0	0	0	0	4	0	9	2	0	0	0	-	0	0-0	0	5.67	5.14
2015	SD	NL	1	0	0	0	1.0	5	1	1	1	0	0	0	0	1	0	1	0	0	0	0	-	0	0-0	0	5.48	9.00
	2 ML YEARS		7	0	0	1	8.0	38	10	6	5	0	0	0	0	5	0	10	2	0	0	0	-	0	0-0	0	5.64	5.63

Mark Canha

Bats: R **Throws:** R **Pos:** 1B-75;LF-58;PH-11;RF-3;DH-2;3B-1 CAN-uh **Ht:** 6'1" **Wt:** 200 **Born:** 2/15/1989 **Age:** 27

			BATTING																		RUNNING			AVERAGES			
Year	Team	Lg	G	AB	H	2B	3B	HR	(Hm	Rd)	TB	R	RBI	RC	TBB	IBB	SO	HBP	SH	SF	SB	CS	GDP	Avg	OBP	Slg	OPS
2011	Grnsbr	A	107	384	106	22	0	25	(-	-)	203	72	85	78	59	0	85	5	0	7	7	3	10	.276	.374	.529	.902
2012	Jupiter	A+	114	406	119	24	3	6	(-	-)	167	65	68	68	54	2	75	9	1	8	1	3	6	.293	.382	.411	.793
2013	Jaxnvl	AA	128	425	116	32	2	13	(-	-)	191	63	58	76	54	0	102	15	5	5	6	1	9	.273	.371	.449	.820
2014	NewOr	AAA	127	465	141	28	3	20	(-	-)	235	83	82	92	57	0	112	8	0	7	3	1	9	.303	.384	.505	.889
2015	Oak	AL	124	441	112	22	3	16	(8	8)	188	61	70	62	33	0	96	8	0	3	7	2	9	.254	.315	.426	.742

Robinson Cano

Bats: L **Throws:** R **Pos:** 2B-149;DH-6;PH-1 kuh-NOE **Ht:** 6'0" **Wt:** 210 **Born:** 10/22/1982 **Age:** 33

			BATTING																		RUNNING			AVERAGES			
Year	Team	Lg	G	AB	H	2B	3B	HR	(Hm	Rd)	TB	R	RBI	RC	TBB	IBB	SO	HBP	SH	SF	SB	CS	GDP	Avg	OBP	Slg	OPS
2005	NYY	AL	132	522	155	34	4	14	(5	9)	239	78	62	59	16	1	68	3	7	3	1	3	16	.297	.320	.458	.778
2006	NYY	AL	122	482	165	41	1	15	(9	6)	253	62	78	74	18	3	54	2	1	5	5	2	19	.342	.365	.525	.890
2007	NYY	AL	160	617	189	41	7	19	(10	9)	301	93	97	94	39	5	85	8	1	4	4	5	19	.306	.353	.488	.841
2008	NYY	AL	159	597	162	35	3	14	(7	7)	245	70	72	64	26	3	65	5	1	5	2	4	18	.271	.305	.410	.715
2009	NYY	AL	161	637	204	48	2	25	(14	11)	331	103	85	79	30	2	63	3	0	4	5	7	22	.320	.352	.520	.871
2010	NYY	AL	160	626	200	41	3	29	(16	13)	334	103	109	118	57	14	77	8	0	5	3	2	19	.319	.381	.534	.914
2011	NYY	AL	159	623	188	46	7	28	(16	12)	332	104	118	111	38	11	96	12	0	8	8	2	18	.302	.349	.533	.882
2012	NYY	AL	161	627	196	48	1	33	(22	11)	345	105	94	110	61	10	96	7	0	2	3	2	22	.313	.379	.550	.929
2013	NYY	AL	160	605	190	41	0	27	(11	16)	312	81	107	120	65	16	85	6	0	5	7	1	18	.314	.383	.516	.899
2014	Sea	AL	157	595	187	37	2	14	(9	5)	270	77	82	106	61	20	68	6	0	3	10	3	19	.314	.382	.454	.836
2015	Sea	AL	156	624	179	34	1	21	(11	10)	278	82	79	84	43	5	107	3	0	4	2	6	26	.287	.334	.446	.779
	Postseason		51	203	45	10	3	8	(5	3)	85	22	33	23	11	3	28	2	0	1	0	2	7	.222	.267	.419	.686
	11 ML YEARS		1687	6555	2015	446	31	239	(130	109)	3240	958	983	1019	454	90	864	63	10	48	50	37	216	.307	.356	.494	.850

Carter Capps

Pitches: R **Bats:** R **Pos:** RP-30 **Ht:** 6'5" **Wt:** 220 **Born:** 8/7/1990 **Age:** 25

			HOW MUCH HE PITCHED					WHAT HE GAVE UP												THE RESULTS						
Year	Team	Lg	G	GS	CG	GF	IP	BFP	H	R	ER	HR	SH	SF	HB	TBB	IBB	SO	WP	Bk	W	L	Pct	Sh	Sv-Op	Hld	ERC	ERA
2015	NewOr*	AAA	13	0	0	10	15.0	64	10	5	3	0	2	0	1	10	1	15	1	0	0	2	.000	0	3- -	-	2.74	1.80
2012	Sea	AL	18	0	0	2	25.0	109	25	11	11	0	1	1	0	11	0	28	1	0	0	0	-	0	0-0	2	3.49	3.96
2013	Sea	AL	53	0	0	11	59.0	270	73	37	36	12	2	1	2	23	4	66	5	0	3	3	.500	0	0-2	9	6.23	5.49
2014	Mia	NL	17	0	0	5	20.1	86	19	9	9	1	0	1	2	5	0	25	2	0	0	0	-	0	0-0	1	3.13	3.98
2015	Mia	NL	30	0	0	8	31.0	118	18	5	4	2	1	1	2	7	0	58	2	0	1	0	1.000	0	0-2	11	1.50	1.16
	4 ML YEARS		118	0	0	26	135.1	583	135	62	60	15	4	4	6	46	4	177	10	0	4	3	.571	0	0-4	23	4.01	3.99

Chris Capuano

Pitches: L **Bats:** L **Pos:** RP-18; SP-4 capp-ue-AHH-noe **Ht:** 6'3" **Wt:** 220 **Born:** 8/19/1978 **Age:** 37

			HOW MUCH HE PITCHED					WHAT HE GAVE UP												THE RESULTS						
Year	Team	Lg	G	GS	CG	GF	IP	BFP	H	R	ER	HR	SH	SF	HB	TBB	IBB	SO	WP	Bk	W	L	Pct	Sh	Sv-Op	Hld	ERC	ERA
2015	S-WB*	AAA	6	6	0	0	28.1	107	20	4	4	0	0	1	0	7	0	25	3	0	2	1	.667	0	0- -	-	1.58	1.27
2003	Ari	NL	9	5	0	2	33.0	139	27	19	17	3	4	1	6	11	1	23	3	0	2	4	.333	0	0-0	1	3.45	4.64
2004	Mil	NL	17	17	0	0	88.1	385	91	55	49	18	4	1	5	37	1	80	3	1	6	8	.429	0	0-0	0	5.37	4.99
2005	Mil	NL	35	35	0	0	219.0	949	212	105	97	31	14	5	12	91	6	176	3	4	18	12	.600	0	0-0	0	4.44	3.99
2006	Mil	NL	34	34	3	0	221.1	936	229	108	99	29	9	8	9	47	4	174	7	0	11	12	.478	2	0-0	0	3.84	4.03
2007	Mil	NL	29	25	0	0	150.0	669	170	93	85	20	10	3	8	54	2	132	10	0	5	12	.294	0	0-0	0	5.11	5.10
2010	Mil	NL	24	9	0	5	66.0	278	65	29	29	9	3	2	1	21	1	54	5	0	4	4	.500	0	0-0	1	3.98	3.95
2011	NYM	NL	33	31	1	0	186.0	802	198	99	94	27	9	1	5	53	5	168	4	0	11	12	.478	1	0-0	1	4.33	4.55
2012	LAD	NL	33	33	0	0	198.1	817	188	91	82	25	16	4	2	54	4	162	6	0	12	12	.500	0	0-0	0	3.51	3.72
2013	LAD	NL	24	20	0	0	105.2	457	125	57	50	11	6	3	0	24	5	81	5	0	4	7	.364	0	0-1	0	4.36	4.26
2014	2 Tms	NL	40	12	0	4	97.1	429	101	51	47	10	3	5	4	34	3	84	8	1	3	4	.429	0	0-1	4	4.14	4.35
2015	NYY	AL	22	4	0	7	40.2	196	52	38	36	6	2	1	3	22	1	38	0	0	0	4	.000	0	0-0	1	6.93	7.97
14	Bos	AL	28	0	0	4	31.2	143	34	17	16	3	0	1	1	15	2	29	4	1	1	1	.500	0	0-1	4	4.72	4.55
14	NYY	AL	12	12	0	0	65.2	286	67	34	31	7	3	4	3	19	1	55	4	0	2	3	.400	0	0-0	0	3.86	4.25
	Postseason		1	0	0	0	3.0	11	0	0	0	0	1	0	0	3	0	3	0	0	1	0	1.000	0	0-0	0	1.03	0.00
	11 ML YEARS		300	225	4	18	1405.2	6057	1458	745	685	189	80	34	55	448	33	1172	54	6	76	91	.455	3	0-2	8	4.32	4.39

Buddy Carlyle

Pitches: R Bats: L Pos: RP-11　　　　　　　　　　Ht: 6'3" Wt: 210 Born: 12/21/1977 Age: 38

			HOW MUCH HE PITCHED					WHAT HE GAVE UP										THE RESULTS					
Year	Team	Lg	G	GS	CG	GF	IP	BFP	H	R	ER	HR	SH	SF	HB	TBB	IBB	SO	WP	Bk	W	L	Pct	Sh	Sv-Op	Hld	ERC	ERA
1999	SD	NL	7	7	0	0	37.2	162	36	28	25	7	1	2	2	17	0	29	1	0	1	3	.250	0	0-0	0	4.95	5.97
2000	SD	NL	4	0	0	2	3.0	18	6	7	7	0	0	0	0	3	0	2	0	0	0	0	-	0	0-0	0	12.01	21.00
2005	LAD	NL	10	0	0	2	14.0	62	16	13	13	4	2	0	1	4	0	13	0	0	0	0	-	0	0-1	0	6.07	8.36
2007	Atl	NL	22	20	0	1	107.0	462	117	67	62	19	11	5	2	32	8	74	3	0	8	7	.533	0	0-0	0	4.71	5.21
2008	Atl	NL	45	0	0	5	62.2	259	52	26	25	5	4	0	1	26	6	59	4	1	2	0	1.000	0	0-0	4	3.03	3.59
2009	Atl	NL	16	0	0	7	21.1	107	35	23	21	5	2	1	0	12	4	12	2	0	1	0	1.000	0	0-0	2	9.78	8.86
2011	NYY	AL	8	0	0	6	7.2	34	5	4	4	1	0	0	0	7	1	9	2	0	0	1	.000	0	0-0	1	4.16	4.70
2014	NYM	NL	27	0	0	1	31.0	119	23	6	5	2	1	0	0	5	0	28	0	0	1	1	.500	0	0-0	3	1.72	1.45
2015	NYM	NL	11	0	0	1	8.0	32	8	5	5	0	0	2	0	1	0	6	1	0	1	0	1.000	0	1-1	4	2.44	5.63
	9 ML YEARS		150	27	0	28	292.1	1255	298	179	167	43	21	10	6	107	19	232	13	1	13	13	.500	0	1-2	8	4.39	5.14

David Carpenter

Pitches: R Bats: R Pos: RP-30　　　　　　　　　　Ht: 6'2" Wt: 230 Born: 7/15/1985 Age: 30

			HOW MUCH HE PITCHED					WHAT HE GAVE UP										THE RESULTS					
Year	Team	Lg	G	GS	CG	GF	IP	BFP	H	R	ER	HR	SH	SF	HB	TBB	IBB	SO	WP	Bk	W	L	Pct	Sh	Sv-Op	Hld	ERC	ERA
2011	Hou	NL	34	0	0	12	27.2	125	28	9	9	3	4	1	4	13	7	29	2	1	1	3	.250	0	1-2	3	4.62	2.93
2012	2 Tms		33	0	0	9	32.1	163	51	31	29	5	2	0	2	16	4	31	2	0	0	2	.000	0	0-1	2	8.52	8.07
2013	Atl	NL	56	0	0	14	65.2	256	45	13	13	5	2	4	3	20	3	74	4	0	4	1	.800	0	0-0	12	2.12	1.78
2014	Atl	NL	65	0	0	14	61.0	259	61	27	24	5	1	1	3	16	0	67	1	0	6	4	.600	0	3-6	19	3.59	3.54
2015	2 Tms		30	0	0	5	24.2	107	25	12	11	4	3	1	1	9	1	15	1	0	0	1	.000	0	0-2	6	4.54	4.01
12	Hou	NL	30	0	0	8	29.2	143	43	21	20	4	2	0	1	14	3	27	2	0	0	2	.000	0	0-1	2	7.38	6.07
12	Tor	AL	3	0	0	1	2.2	20	8	10	9	1	0	0	1	2	1	4	0	0	0	0	-	0	0-0	0	22.64	30.38
15	NYY	AL	22	0	0	2	18.2	82	20	11	10	3	3	1	1	7	1	11	0	0	0	1	.000	0	0-2	2	4.97	4.82
15	Was	NL	8	0	0	3	6.0	25	5	1	1	1	0	0	0	2	0	4	1	0	0	0	-	0	0-0	4	3.28	1.50
	Postseason		3	0	0	1	2.2	12	3	4	4	2	0	0	0	1	0	3	0	0	0	1	.000	0	0-1	1	9.34	13.50
	5 ML YEARS		218	0	0	54	211.1	910	210	92	86	22	12	7	13	74	15	216	10	1	11	11	.500	0	4-11	42	4.01	3.66

David Carpenter

Pitches: R Bats: R Pos: RP-4　　　　　　　　　　Ht: 6'3" Wt: 180 Born: 9/1/1987 Age: 28

			HOW MUCH HE PITCHED					WHAT HE GAVE UP										THE RESULTS					
Year	Team	Lg	G	GS	CG	GF	IP	BFP	H	R	ER	HR	SH	SF	HB	TBB	IBB	SO	WP	Bk	W	L	Pct	Sh	Sv-Op	Hld	ERC	ERA
2015	Gwnntt*	AAA	40	0	0	10	50.2	200	34	12	10	1	2	1	1	22	2	49	0	0	3	1	.750	0	2- -	2	2.08	1.78
2012	LAA	AL	28	0	0	12	39.2	172	42	21	21	6	1	1	0	17	0	28	2	0	1	2	.333	0	0-0	2	4.97	4.76
2013	LAA	AL	1	0	0	0	0.1	5	2	4	4	1	0	0	0	2	0	1	1	0	0	0	-	0	0-0	0	124.7	108.0
2014	LAA	AL	1	0	0	0	3.0	12	1	0	0	0	0	0	2	0	0	0	0	0	0	0	-	0	0-0	0	1.26	0.00
2015	Atl	NL	4	0	0	1	3.2	17	6	3	3	2	0	0	0	0	0	5	0	0	0	0	-	0	0-0	1	9.48	7.36
	4 ML YEARS		34	0	0	13	46.2	206	51	28	28	9	1	1	2	19	0	34	3	0	1	2	.333	0	0-0	3	5.55	5.40

Matt Carpenter

Bats: L Throws: R Pos: 3B-146;2B-11;1B-3;PH-3　　　　　Ht: 6'3" Wt: 215 Born: 11/26/1985 Age: 30

			BATTING																			RUNNING			AVERAGES			
Year	Team	Lg	G	AB	H	2B	3B	HR	(Hm	Rd)	TB	R	RBI	RC	TBB	IBB	SO	HBP	SH	SF	SB	CS	GDP	Avg	OBP	Slg	OPS
2011	StL	NL	7	15	1	1	0	0	(0	0)	2	0	0	0	4	0	4	0	0	0	0	0	0	.067	.263	.133	.396
2012	StL	NL	114	296	87	22	5	6	(3	3)	137	44	46	46	34	2	63	3	0	7	1	1	10	.294	.365	.463	.828
2013	StL	NL	157	626	199	55	7	11	(6	5)	301	126	78	119	72	1	98	9	3	7	3	3	4	.318	.392	.481	.873
2014	StL	NL	158	595	162	33	2	8	(4	4)	223	99	59	93	95	2	111	8	2	9	5	3	3	.272	.375	.375	.750
2015	StL	NL	154	574	156	44	3	28	(13	15)	290	101	84	108	81	5	151	6	0	4	4	3	5	.272	.365	.505	.871
	Postseason		35	119	29	8	1	5	(3	2)	54	17	15	17	10	0	34	1	0	2	1	0	1	.244	.303	.454	.757
	5 ML YEARS		590	2106	605	155	17	53	(26	27)	953	370	267	366	286	10	427	26	5	27	13	10	22	.287	.375	.453	.828

Carlos Carrasco

Pitches: R Bats: R Pos: SP-30　　　　　　　　　　Ht: 6'4" Wt: 210 Born: 3/21/1987 Age: 29

			HOW MUCH HE PITCHED					WHAT HE GAVE UP										THE RESULTS					
Year	Team	Lg	G	GS	CG	GF	IP	BFP	H	R	ER	HR	SH	SF	HB	TBB	IBB	SO	WP	Bk	W	L	Pct	Sh	Sv-Op	Hld	ERC	ERA
2009	Cle	AL	5	5	0	0	22.1	112	40	23	22	6	0	1	0	11	1	11	0	1	0	4	.000	0	0-0	0	11.36	8.87
2010	Cle	AL	7	7	1	0	44.2	188	47	20	19	6	2	1	1	14	1	38	1	0	2	2	.500	0	0-0	0	4.42	3.83
2011	Cle	AL	21	21	1	0	124.2	536	130	68	64	15	3	7	4	40	3	85	3	0	8	9	.471	0	0-0	0	4.24	4.62
2013	Cle	AL	15	7	0	5	46.2	218	64	36	35	4	2	3	1	18	2	30	2	0	1	4	.200	0	0-0	0	6.11	6.75
2014	Cle	AL	40	14	1	12	134.0	529	103	40	38	7	2	3	1	29	1	140	4	0	8	7	.533	1	1-1	0	2.00	2.55
2015	Cle	AL	30	30	3	0	183.2	730	154	75	74	18	1	6	5	43	2	216	5	0	14	12	.538	1	0-0	0	2.72	3.63
	6 ML YEARS		118	84	6	17	556.0	2313	538	262	252	56	10	21	14	155	10	520	15	1	33	38	.465	2	1-1	0	3.53	4.08

Ezequiel Carrera

Bats: L Throws: L Pos: LF-46;RF-35;PR-9;PH-8;CF-5　　ee-ZEEK-ee-ull　　Ht: 5'10" Wt: 185 Born: 6/11/1987 Age: 29

			BATTING																			RUNNING			AVERAGES			
Year	Team	Lg	G	AB	H	2B	3B	HR	(Hm	Rd)	TB	R	RBI	RC	TBB	IBB	SO	HBP	SH	SF	SB	CS	GDP	Avg	OBP	Slg	OPS
2015	Buffalo*	AAA	30	116	32	5	0	1	(-	-)	40	18	10	15	12	0	16	1	4	0	6	2	0	.276	.349	.345	.694
2011	Cle	AL	68	202	49	8	3	0	(0	0)	63	27	14	25	16	0	35	1	7	0	10	5	4	.243	.301	.312	.613
2012	Cle	AL	48	147	40	6	3	2	(0	2)	58	20	11	17	8	1	35	1	1	1	8	1	3	.272	.312	.395	.707
2013	2 Tms		15	17	3	0	0	0	(0	0)	3	3	1	1	1	0	5	2	1	0	0	0	1	.176	.300	.176	.476
2014	Det	AL	45	69	18	4	1	0	(0	0)	24	12	2	6	3	1	14	1	0	0	7	1	2	.261	.301	.348	.649
2015	Tor	AL	91	172	47	8	0	3	(1	2)	64	27	26	26	11	0	45	2	5	2	2	1	1	.273	.321	.372	.693

Year	Team	Lg	G	AB	H	2B	3B	HR	(Hm	Rd)	TB	R	RBI	RC	TBB	IBB	SO	HBP	SH	SF	SB	CS	GDP	Avg	OBP	Slg	OPS
13	Phi	NL	13	13	1	0	0	0	(0	0)	1	2	0	0	1	0	4	2	0	0	0	0	0	.077	.250	.077	.327
13	Cle	AL	2	4	2	0	0	0	(0	0)	2	1	1	1	0	0	1	0	1	0	0	0	1	.500	.500	.500	1.000
	Postseason		3	1	0	0	0	0	(0	0)	0	0	0	0	1	0	0	0	0	0	1	0	0	.000	.500	.000	.500
	5 ML YEARS		267	607	157	26	7	5	(1	4)	212	89	54	75	39	2	134	7	14	3	27	8	11	.259	.309	.349	.659

Scott Carroll

Pitches: R **Bats:** R **Pos:** RP-18 **Ht:** 6'4" **Wt:** 215 **Born:** 9/24/1984 **Age:** 31

			HOW MUCH HE PITCHED					WHAT HE GAVE UP										THE RESULTS						
Year	Team	Lg	G	GS	CG	GF	IP	BFP	H	R	ER	HR	SH	SF	HB	TBB	IBB	SO	WP	Bk	W	L	Pct	Sh	Sv-Op	Hld	ERC	ERA
2011	Lsvlle	AAA	25	25	0	0	145.1	652	186	92	87	12	3	3	3	47	0	85	2	3	7	8	.467	0	0- -	-	5.38	5.39
2012	Lsvlle	AAA	25	0	0	7	39.2	180	51	26	26	4	1	2	1	16	1	27	1	0	2	3	.400	0	0- -	-	5.93	5.90
2012	Charltt	AAA	9	8	0	0	47.2	194	39	21	20	6	0	1	1	18	0	36	1	1	2	3	.400	0	0- -	-	3.33	3.78
2013	Brstol	R+	5	5	0	0	16.0	69	17	4	3	0	0	0	0	4	0	15	0	0	0	0	-	0	0- -	-	3.07	1.69
2013	Brham	AA	6	6	0	0	25.0	103	25	15	12	2	0	1	0	2	0	14	0	0	0	2	.000	0	0- -	-	2.82	4.32
2015	Charltt	AAA	16	16	0	0	83.0	361	85	41	32	8	4	3	2	29	1	45	3	1	7	4	.636	0	0- -	-	4.01	3.47
2014	CWS	AL	26	19	0	5	129.1	573	147	81	69	13	3	4	12	45	1	64	5	1	5	10	.333	0	0-0	-	5.07	4.80
2015	CWS	AL	18	0	0	8	36.2	162	40	19	14	2	1	2	3	13	2	27	4	0	1	1	.500	0	0-0	0	4.31	3.44
	2 ML YEARS		44	19	0	13	166.0	735	187	100	83	15	4	6	15	58	3	91	9	1	6	11	.353	0	0-0	0	4.90	4.50

Chris Carter

Bats: R **Throws:** R **Pos:** 1B-115;PH-14;DH-8 **Ht:** 6'4" **Wt:** 250 **Born:** 12/18/1986 **Age:** 29

						BATTING															RUNNING			AVERAGES			
Year	Team	Lg	G	AB	H	2B	3B	HR	(Hm	Rd)	TB	R	RBI	RC	TBB	IBB	SO	HBP	SH	SF	SB	CS	GDP	Avg	OBP	Slg	OPS
2010	Oak	AL	24	70	13	1	0	3	(1	2)	23	8	7	5	7	0	21	0	0	1	1	0	3	.186	.256	.329	.585
2011	Oak	AL	15	44	6	0	0	0	(0	0)	6	2	0	0	2	0	20	0	0	0	0	0	1	.136	.174	.136	.310
2012	Oak	AL	67	218	52	12	0	16	(5	11)	112	38	39	36	39	1	83	0	0	3	0	0	4	.239	.350	.514	.864
2013	Hou	AL	148	506	113	24	2	29	(10	19)	228	64	82	74	70	1	212	4	0	5	2	0	8	.223	.320	.451	.770
2014	Hou	AL	145	507	115	21	1	37	(21	16)	249	68	88	74	56	6	182	5	0	4	5	2	12	.227	.308	.491	.799
2015	Hou	AL	129	391	78	17	0	24	(17	7)	167	50	64	55	57	1	151	6	0	5	1	2	5	.199	.307	.427	.734
	6 ML YEARS		528	1736	377	75	3	109	(54	55)	785	230	280	244	231	9	669	15	0	18	9	4	33	.217	.312	.452	.764

Curt Casali

Bats: R **Throws:** R **Pos:** C-37;PH-2;DH-1 cuh-SAL-ee **Ht:** 6'2" **Wt:** 230 **Born:** 11/9/1988 **Age:** 27

						BATTING															RUNNING			AVERAGES			
Year	Team	Lg	G	AB	H	2B	3B	HR	(Hm	Rd)	TB	R	RBI	RC	TBB	IBB	SO	HBP	SH	SF	SB	CS	GDP	Avg	OBP	Slg	OPS
2011	2 Tms	Low	35	111	27	9	0	3	(-	-)	45	17	16	17	19	0	14	3	2	1	0	0	5	.243	.366	.405	.771
2012	2 Tms	Low	94	330	89	25	0	9	(-	-)	141	43	43	54	38	2	46	12	4	1	2	1	11	.270	.365	.427	.792
2013	Charltt	A+	46	165	44	6	1	5	(-	-)	67	15	22	24	18	0	31	1	0	0	1	0	8	.267	.342	.406	.748
2013	Mont	AA	35	120	46	11	0	5	(-	-)	72	25	31	33	21	1	18	3	0	1	0	0	2	.383	.483	.600	1.083
2014	Mont	AA	22	70	22	5	0	1	(-	-)	30	7	13	17	23	0	16	3	0	0	0	0	1	.314	.500	.429	.929
2014	Drham	AAA	46	156	37	10	0	3	(-	-)	56	11	15	20	22	0	50	2	1	2	0	0	8	.237	.335	.359	.694
2015	Drham	AAA	32	112	23	4	0	4	(-	-)	39	14	13	14	17	0	29	3	0	0	1	0	3	.205	.326	.348	.674
2014	TB	AL	30	72	12	3	0	0	(0	0)	15	10	3	3	8	0	23	2	2	0	0	0	2	.167	.268	.208	.477
2015	TB	AL	38	101	24	6	0	10	(7	3)	60	13	18	14	8	0	34	2	1	1	0	0	2	.238	.304	.594	.898
	2 ML YEARS		68	173	36	9	0	10	(7	3)	75	23	21	17	16	0	57	4	3	1	0	0	4	.208	.289	.434	.722

Andrew Cashner

Pitches: R **Bats:** R **Pos:** SP-31 **Ht:** 6'5" **Wt:** 225 **Born:** 9/11/1986 **Age:** 29

			HOW MUCH HE PITCHED						WHAT HE GAVE UP											THE RESULTS							
Year	Team	Lg	G	GS	CG	GF	IP	BFP	H	R	ER	HR	SH	SF	HB	TBB	IBB	SO	WP	Bk	W	L	Pct	Sh	Sv-Op	Hld	ERC	ERA
2010	ChC	NL	53	0	0	9	54.1	248	55	34	29	8	6	2	4	30	5	50	4	1	2	6	.250	0	0-1	16	5.22	4.80
2011	ChC	NL	7	1	0	0	10.2	39	3	2	2	1	0	0	0	4	0	8	0	0	0	1	.000	0	0-0	1	0.91	1.69
2012	SD	NL	33	5	0	5	46.1	196	42	23	22	5	3	1	1	19	1	52	2	0	3	4	.429	0	0-4	6	3.73	4.27
2013	SD	NL	31	26	1	2	175.0	707	151	69	60	12	6	3	4	47	3	128	5	0	10	9	.526	1	0-0	1	2.74	3.09
2014	SD	NL	19	19	2	0	123.1	506	110	42	35	7	3	4	1	29	3	93	2	0	5	7	.417	2	0-0	0	2.57	2.55
2015	SD	NL	31	31	0	0	184.2	804	200	111	89	19	8	6	6	66	2	165	3	0	6	16	.273	0	0-0	0	4.53	4.34
	6 ML YEARS		174	82	3	16	594.1	2500	561	277	237	52	26	16	16	195	14	496	16	1	26	42	.382	3	0-5	24	3.48	3.59

Santiago Casilla

Pitches: R **Bats:** R **Pos:** RP-67 cuh-SEE-ya **Ht:** 6'0" **Wt:** 210 **Born:** 7/25/1980 **Age:** 35

			HOW MUCH HE PITCHED						WHAT HE GAVE UP											THE RESULTS							
Year	Team	Lg	G	GS	CG	GF	IP	BFP	H	R	ER	HR	SH	SF	HB	TBB	IBB	SO	WP	Bk	W	L	Pct	Sh	Sv-Op	Hld	ERC	ERA
2004	Oak	AL	4	0	0	2	5.2	32	5	8	8	3	0	0	1	9	0	5	0	0	0	0	-	0	0-0	0	13.22	12.71
2005	Oak	AL	3	0	0	3	3.0	12	2	1	1	0	0	0	0	1	0	1	1	0	0	0	-	0	0-0	0	1.57	3.00
2006	Oak	AL	2	0	0	1	2.1	10	2	3	3	0	0	0	0	2	0	2	0	0	0	0	-	0	0-0	0	4.61	11.57
2007	Oak	AL	46	0	0	10	50.2	219	43	25	25	6	0	3	1	23	6	52	5	0	3	1	.750	0	2-5	12	3.39	4.44
2008	Oak	AL	51	0	0	9	50.1	229	60	22	22	5	3	2	3	20	2	43	6	0	2	1	.667	0	2-3	7	5.34	3.93
2009	Oak	AL	46	0	0	15	48.1	233	61	36	32	6	1	3	3	25	3	35	5	0	1	2	.333	0	0-0	5	6.32	5.96
2010	SF	NL	52	0	0	13	55.1	225	40	14	12	2	2	1	4	26	4	56	10	0	7	2	.778	0	2-3	11	2.68	1.95
2011	SF	NL	49	0	0	20	51.2	211	33	11	10	1	4	0	2	25	1	45	5	0	2	2	.500	0	6-7	6	2.11	1.74
2012	SF	NL	73	0	0	37	63.1	272	55	24	20	8	2	1	2	22	4	55	1	0	7	6	.538	0	25-31	12	3.24	2.84
2013	SF	NL	57	0	0	12	50.0	208	39	14	12	2	2	3	2	25	6	38	8	0	7	2	.778	0	2-3	22	2.88	2.16

	HOW MUCH HE PITCHED					WHAT HE GAVE UP											THE RESULTS							
Year Team Lg	G	GS	CG	GF	IP	BFP	H	R	ER	HR	SH	SF	HB	TBB	IBB	SO	WP	Bk	W	L	Pct	Sh	Sv-Op	Hld	ERC	ERA
2014 SF NL	54	0	0	31	58.1	218	35	13	11	3	2	0	3	15	2	45	3	1	3	3	.500	0	19-23	10	1.56	1.70
2015 SF NL	67	0	0	55	58.0	244	51	19	18	6	2	1	2	23	2	62	1	0	4	2	.667	0	38-44	4	3.52	2.79
Postseason	24	0	0	8	19.0	79	13	3	2	0	0	0	2	5	1	20	3	0	1	0	1.000	0	4-4	4	1.61	0.95
12 ML YEARS	504	0	0	208	497.0	2113	426	190	174	42	18	14	23	216	30	439	45	1	36	21	.632	0	96-119	85	3.40	3.15

Nick Castellanos

Bats: R Throws: R Pos: 3B-145;DH-7;PH-3   cahs-teh-YAHN-ohs   Ht: 6'4" Wt: 210 Born: 3/4/1992 Age: 24

							BATTING												RUNNING			AVERAGES			
Year Team Lg	G	AB	H	2B	3B	HR	(Hm Rd)	TB	R	RBI	RC	TBB	IBB	SO	HBP	SH	SF	SB	CS	GDP	Avg	OBP	Slg	OPS
2013 Det AL	11	18	5	0	0	0	(0 0)	5	1	0	1	0	0	1	0	0	0	0	0	0	.278	.278	.278	.556
2014 Det AL	148	533	138	31	4	11	(6 5)	210	50	66	63	36	3	140	3	0	7	2	2	7	.259	.306	.394	.700
2015 Det AL	154	549	140	33	6	15	(6 9)	230	42	73	66	39	1	152	1	0	6	0	3	21	.255	.303	.419	.721
Postseason	3	10	1	0	0	1	(0 1)	4	1	1	0	2	1	1	0	0	0	0	0	0	.100	.250	.400	.650
3 ML YEARS	313	1100	283	64	10	26	(12 14)	445	93	139	130	75	4	293	4	0	13	2	5	28	.257	.304	.405	.708

Rusney Castillo

ROOZ-knee

Bats: R Throws: R Pos: RF-48;LF-24;CF-6;PH-5;PR-4;DH-2   Ht: 5'9" Wt: 195 Born: 7/9/1987 Age: 28

							BATTING												RUNNING			AVERAGES			
Year Team Lg	G	AB	H	2B	3B	HR	(Hm Rd)	TB	R	RBI	RC	TBB	IBB	SO	HBP	SH	SF	SB	CS	GDP	Avg	OBP	Slg	OPS
2015 Pwtckt AAA	40	156	44	7	0	3	(- -)	60	17	17	22	14	0	28	0	0	2	10	2	3	.282	.337	.385	.722
2014 Bos AL	10	36	12	1	0	2	(2 0)	19	6	6	9	3	0	6	1	0	0	3	0	0	.333	.400	.528	.928
2015 Bos AL	80	273	69	10	2	5	(4 1)	98	35	29	30	13	0	54	1	1	1	4	5	11	.253	.288	.359	.647
2 ML YEARS	90	309	81	11	2	7	(6 1)	117	41	35	39	16	0	60	2	1	1	7	5	11	.262	.302	.379	.680

Welington Castillo

WELL-ing-tunn

Bats: R Throws: R Pos: C-88;PH-21;DH-2   Ht: 5'10" Wt: 210 Born: 4/24/1987 Age: 29

							BATTING												RUNNING			AVERAGES			
Year Team Lg	G	AB	H	2B	3B	HR	(Hm Rd)	TB	R	RBI	RC	TBB	IBB	SO	HBP	SH	SF	SB	CS	GDP	Avg	OBP	Slg	OPS
2010 ChC NL	7	20	6	4	0	1	(0 1)	13	3	5	3	1	0	7	0	0	0	0	0	0	.300	.333	.650	.983
2011 ChC NL	4	13	2	0	0	0	(0 0)	2	0	0	0	0	0	4	0	0	0	0	0	1	.154	.154	.154	.308
2012 ChC NL	52	170	45	11	0	5	(4 1)	71	16	22	22	17	2	51	2	0	1	0	0	4	.265	.337	.418	.754
2013 ChC NL	113	380	104	23	0	8	(1 7)	151	41	32	44	34	3	97	11	1	2	2	0	13	.274	.349	.397	.746
2014 ChC NL	110	380	90	19	0	13	(7 6)	148	28	46	44	26	0	102	7	2	2	0	0	7	.237	.296	.389	.686
2015 3 Tms	110	342	81	15	1	19	(7 12)	155	42	57	41	25	1	92	6	0	5	0	0	12	.237	.296	.453	.750
15 ChC NL	24	43	7	2	0	2	(1 1)	15	5	5	2	3	1	12	1	0	0	0	0	0	.163	.234	.349	.583
15 Sea AL	6	25	4	0	0	0	(0 0)	4	3	2	0	1	0	5	0	0	2	0	0	2	.160	.179	.160	.339
15 Ari NL	80	274	70	13	1	17	(6 11)	136	34	50	39	21	0	75	5	0	3	0	0	10	.255	.317	.496	.813
6 ML YEARS	396	1305	328	72	1	46	(19 27)	540	130	162	154	103	6	353	26	3	10	2	0	37	.251	.316	.414	.730

Angel Castro

AHN-hell

Pitches: R Bats: R Pos: RP-5   Ht: 5'11" Wt: 200 Born: 11/14/1982 Age: 33

	HOW MUCH HE PITCHED						WHAT HE GAVE UP												THE RESULTS							
Year Team Lg	G	GS	CG	GF	IP	BFP	H	R	ER	HR	SH	SF	HB	TBB	IBB	SO	WP	Bk	W	L	Pct	Sh	Sv-Op	Hld	ERC	ERA
2013 Albq AAA	25	19	0	1	116.1	501	123	50	45	7	3	4	4	37	2	91	5	0	8	5	.615	0	0- -	-	3.91	3.48
2014 Memp AAA	26	14	0	5	94.1	398	96	51	42	11	2	0	2	26	1	63	2	0	8	6	.571	0	1- -	-	3.88	4.01
2015 Nashv AAA	38	2	0	23	60.1	249	54	23	21	6	2	2	3	19	0	45	0	0	2	1	.667	0	8- -	-	3.41	3.13
2015 Oak AL	5	0	0	3	4.0	22	8	1	1	1	0	0	0	3	0	4	0	0	0	1	.000	0	0-0	0	14.13	2.25

Daniel Castro

Bats: R Throws: R Pos: 2B-12;SS-10;PH-8;3B-5   Ht: 5'11" Wt: 175 Born: 11/14/1992 Age: 23

							BATTING												RUNNING			AVERAGES			
Year Team Lg	G	AB	H	2B	3B	HR	(Hm Rd)	TB	R	RBI	RC	TBB	IBB	SO	HBP	SH	SF	SB	CS	GDP	Avg	OBP	Slg	OPS
2013 Lynbrg A+	26	88	25	1	1	0	(- -)	28	10	7	10	7	0	6	0	1	0	3	1	1	.284	.337	.318	.655
2014 Lynbrg A+	70	257	75	16	3	1	(- -)	100	33	34	32	10	0	20	1	10	1	7	4	8	.292	.320	.389	.709
2014 Missi AA	51	173	48	9	1	4	(- -)	71	23	20	21	5	0	18	1	0	1	2	1	5	.277	.300	.410	.710
2015 Missi AA	23	90	35	5	0	0	(- -)	40	17	10	16	4	0	8	0	3	1	4	2	5	.389	.411	.444	.855
2015 Gwnntt AAA	89	310	83	9	0	0	(- -)	92	19	36	31	22	0	32	1	7	5	1	1	7	.268	.314	.297	.610
2015 Atl NL	33	96	23	2	1	2	(2 0)	33	14	5	4	3	0	15	0	1	0	0	0	4	.240	.263	.344	.606

Jason Castro

Bats: L Throws: R Pos: C-103;PH-1   Ht: 6'3" Wt: 215 Born: 6/18/1987 Age: 29

							BATTING												RUNNING			AVERAGES			
Year Team Lg	G	AB	H	2B	3B	HR	(Hm Rd)	TB	R	RBI	RC	TBB	IBB	SO	HBP	SH	SF	SB	CS	GDP	Avg	OBP	Slg	OPS
2010 Hou NL	67	195	40	8	1	2	(1 1)	56	26	8	12	22	2	41	0	0	0	0	0	4	.205	.286	.287	.573
2012 Hou NL	87	257	66	15	2	6	(3 3)	103	29	29	33	31	2	61	1	2	4	0	0	8	.257	.334	.401	.735
2013 Hou AL	120	435	120	35	1	18	(13 5)	211	63	56	76	50	3	130	2	0	4	2	1	4	.276	.350	.485	.835
2014 Hou AL	126	465	103	21	2	14	(10 4)	170	43	56	45	34	1	151	9	1	3	1	0	11	.222	.286	.366	.651
2015 Hou AL	104	337	71	19	0	11	(8 3)	123	38	31	29	33	1	115	2	0	3	0	0	5	.211	.283	.365	.648
5 ML YEARS	504	1689	400	98	6	51	(35 16)	663	199	180	195	170	9	498	14	3	14	3	1	32	.237	.309	.393	.702

Miguel Castro

Pitches: R Bats: R Pos: RP-18   Ht: 6'5" Wt: 190 Born: 12/24/1994 Age: 21

Year Team	Lg	G	GS	CG	GF	IP	BFP	H	R	ER	HR	SH	SF	HB	TBB	IBB	SO	WP	Bk	W	L	Pct	Sh	Sv-Op	Hld	ERC	ERA
2014 3 Tms	Low	16	15	0	0	80.1	315	50	25	24	6	0	2	2	30	0	78	5	2	8	3	.727	0	0--	-	2.02	2.69
2015 Buffalo	AAA	13	5	0	2	19.2	99	26	15	10	4	1	1	2	12	0	21	2	0	1	3	.250	0	0--	-	8.07	4.58
2015 Albq	AAA	11	0	0	4	13.2	55	6	3	2	0	1	2	1	7	2	10	4	0	2	0	1.000	0	0--	-	1.26	1.32
2015 2 Tms		18	0	0	12	17.2	83	21	13	12	4	0	2	0	10	2	18	2	1	0	3	.000	0	4-6	1	6.61	6.11
15 Tor	AL	13	0	0	9	12.1	57	15	7	6	2	0	2	0	6	2	12	2	1	0	2	.000	0	4-6	1	5.86	4.38
15 Col	NL	5	0	0	3	5.1	26	6	6	6	2	0	0	0	4	0	6	0	0	0	1	.000	0	0-0	0	8.41	10.13

Simon Castro

Pitches: R Bats: R Pos: RP-11   SEE-moan   Ht: 6'5" Wt: 230 Born: 4/9/1988 Age: 28

Year Team	Lg	G	GS	CG	GF	IP	BFP	H	R	ER	HR	SH	SF	HB	TBB	IBB	SO	WP	Bk	W	L	Pct	Sh	Sv-Op	Hld	ERC	ERA
2011 Tucsn	AAA	6	6	0	0	25.2	130	37	30	29	5	0	1	0	18	0	21	6	1	2	2	.500	0	0--	-	8.88	10.17
2011 SnAnt	AA	16	16	0	0	89.1	375	95	48	43	9	1	2	6	16	0	73	3	1	5	6	.455	0	0--	-	3.85	4.33
2012 Brham	AA	15	15	0	0	90.0	380	89	50	37	4	2	4	3	21	0	72	1	0	6	4	.600	0	0--	-	3.09	3.70
2012 Charlt	AAA	5	5	0	0	25.0	109	32	13	12	2	0	0	2	6	0	16	1	0	1	1	.500	0	0--	-	5.40	4.32
2013 Charlt	AAA	27	12	0	4	92.2	400	98	61	60	14	1	3	3	33	0	82	2	1	3	7	.300	0	0--	-	4.77	5.83
2015 Albq	AAA	36	0	0	13	57.0	247	53	27	24	6	3	2	3	20	0	74	3	2	5	5	.500	0	0--	-	3.65	3.79
2013 CWS	AL	4	0	0	4	6.2	28	5	2	2	1	1	0	1	3	0	6	0	0	0	1	.000	0	0-0	0	3.90	2.70
2015 Col	NL	11	0	0	2	10.1	47	11	7	7	0	2	0	1	5	0	9	0	0	2	0	1.000	0	0-0	0	4.37	6.10
2 ML YEARS		15	0	0	6	17.0	75	16	9	9	1	3	0	2	8	0	15	0	0	2	1	.667	0	0-0	0	4.20	4.76

Starlin Castro

Bats: R Throws: R Pos: SS-109;2B-38;PH-14   STARR-linn   Ht: 6'0" Wt: 190 Born: 3/24/1990 Age: 26

Year Team	Lg	G	AB	H	2B	3B	HR	(Hm Rd)	TB	R	RBI	RC	TBB	IBB	SO	HBP	SH	SF	SB	CS	GDP	Avg	OBP	Slg	OPS
2010 ChC	NL	125	463	139	31	5	3	(1 2)	189	53	41	56	29	7	71	6	4	4	10	8	14	.300	.347	.408	.755
2011 ChC	NL	158	674	207	36	9	10	(4 6)	291	91	66	93	35	2	96	2	0	4	22	9	20	.307	.341	.432	.773
2012 ChC	NL	162	646	183	29	12	14	(7 7)	278	78	78	91	36	5	100	4	0	5	25	13	15	.283	.323	.430	.753
2013 ChC	NL	161	666	163	34	2	10	(9 1)	231	59	44	55	30	0	129	7	1	1	9	6	21	.245	.284	.347	.631
2014 ChC	NL	134	528	154	33	1	14	(3 11)	231	58	65	72	34	4	100	4	0	2	4	4	18	.292	.339	.438	.777
2015 ChC	NL	151	547	145	23	2	11	(3 8)	205	52	69	54	21	6	91	5	1	4	5	5	18	.265	.296	.375	.671
6 ML YEARS		891	3524	991	186	31	62	(27 35)	1425	391	363	421	186	24	587	28	6	20	75	45	106	.281	.321	.404	.725

Garin Cecchini

Bats: L Throws: R Pos: 1B-1;DH-1;PH-1;PR-1   chick-KEE-nee   Ht: 6'3" Wt: 220 Born: 4/20/1991 Age: 25

Year Team	Lg	G	AB	H	2B	3B	HR	(Hm Rd)	TB	R	RBI	RC	TBB	IBB	SO	HBP	SH	SF	SB	CS	GDP	Avg	OBP	Slg	OPS
2011 Lowell	A-	32	114	34	12	1	3	(- -)	57	21	23	24	17	0	19	2	0	0	12	1	3	.298	.398	.500	.898
2012 Grnvlle	A	118	455	139	38	4	4	(- -)	197	84	62	89	61	5	90	7	0	3	51	6	13	.305	.394	.433	.827
2013 Salem	A+	63	214	75	19	4	5	(- -)	117	44	33	55	43	0	34	5	0	0	15	7	3	.350	.469	.547	1.016
2013 Portlnd	AA	66	240	71	14	3	2	(- -)	97	36	28	46	51	2	52	2	0	2	8	2	7	.296	.420	.404	.825
2014 Pwtckt	AAA	114	407	107	21	1	7	(- -)	151	52	57	56	44	2	99	5	1	1	11	1	17	.263	.341	.371	.712
2015 Pwtckt	AAA	117	422	90	14	0	7	(- -)	125	34	28	39	40	2	100	4	1	2	9	0	15	.213	.286	.296	.583
2014 Bos	AL	11	31	8	3	0	1	(1 0)	14	6	4	5	3	0	11	2	0	0	0	0	0	.258	.361	.452	.813
2015 Bos	AL	2	4	0	0	0	0	(0 0)	0	0	0	0	0	0	3	0	0	0	0	0	0	.000	.000	.000	.000
2 ML YEARS		13	35	8	3	0	1	(1 0)	14	6	4	5	3	0	14	2	0	0	0	0	0	.229	.325	.400	.725

Brett Cecil

Pitches: L Bats: R Pos: RP-63   SEE-sill   Ht: 6'3" Wt: 220 Born: 7/2/1986 Age: 29

Year Team	Lg	G	GS	CG	GF	IP	BFP	H	R	ER	HR	SH	SF	HB	TBB	IBB	SO	WP	Bk	W	L	Pct	Sh	Sv-Op	Hld	ERC	ERA
2009 Tor	AL	18	17	0	1	93.1	422	116	59	55	17	0	2	5	38	0	69	0	0	7	4	.636	0	0-0	0	6.53	5.30
2010 Tor	AL	28	28	0	0	172.2	726	175	87	81	18	1	6	1	54	2	117	7	1	15	7	.682	0	0-0	0	3.88	4.22
2011 Tor	AL	20	20	2	0	123.2	532	122	68	65	22	3	5	6	42	1	87	1	0	4	11	.267	1	0-0	0	4.47	4.73
2012 Tor	AL	21	9	0	2	61.1	270	70	40	39	11	3	3	3	23	0	51	0	0	2	4	.333	0	0-0	1	5.68	5.72
2013 Tor	AL	60	0	0	12	60.2	250	44	20	19	4	3	2	3	23	3	70	5	1	5	1	.833	0	1-3	11	2.42	2.82
2014 Tor	AL	66	0	0	17	53.1	234	46	16	16	2	0	3	1	27	4	76	1	0	2	3	.400	0	5-7	24	3.16	2.70
2015 Tor	AL	63	0	0	24	54.1	214	39	17	15	4	1	0	2	13	3	70	4	0	5	5	.500	0	5-8	9	1.95	2.48
7 ML YEARS		276	74	2	56	619.1	2648	612	307	290	78	11	21	21	220	13	540	18	2	40	35	.533	1	11-18	45	4.13	4.21

Darrell Ceciliani

Bats: L Throws: L Pos: PH-21;LF-17;CF-7   ses-see-lee-AH-nee   Ht: 6'1" Wt: 220 Born: 6/22/1990 Age: 26

Year Team	Lg	G	AB	H	2B	3B	HR	(Hm Rd)	TB	R	RBI	RC	TBB	IBB	SO	HBP	SH	SF	SB	CS	GDP	Avg	OBP	Slg	OPS
2011 Savann	A	109	421	109	23	4	4	(- -)	152	62	40	60	52	0	96	8	7	0	25	8	4	.259	.351	.361	.712
2012 Stluci	A+	23	85	28	6	1	1	(- -)	39	19	10	16	10	0	13	1	0	1	2	0	0	.329	.402	.459	.861
2013 Bnghtn	AA	114	418	112	17	6	6	(- -)	159	61	44	56	29	2	105	6	4	4	31	7	10	.268	.322	.380	.702
2014 Bnghtn	AA	107	395	114	17	4	7	(- -)	160	59	54	55	22	1	89	6	1	6	16	7	6	.289	.331	.405	.736
2015 LsVgs	AAA	70	229	79	19	4	9	(- -)	133	50	36	52	21	2	48	1	0	3	16	4	7	.345	.398	.581	.978
2015 NYM	NL	39	68	14	2	0	1	(1 0)	19	5	3	6	4	0	25	2	0	0	5	1	0	.206	.270	.279	.550

Xavier Cedeno

Pitches: L Bats: L Pos: RP-66   seh-DAYN-yo   Ht: 6'0" Wt: 215 Born: 8/26/1986 Age: 29

				HOW MUCH HE PITCHED						WHAT HE GAVE UP													THE RESULTS							
Year	Team	Lg	G	GS	CG	GF	IP	BFP	H	R	ER	HR	SH	SF	HB	TBB	IBB	SO	WP	Bk	W	L	Pct	Sh	Sv-Op	Hld	ERC	ERA
2011	Hou	NL	3	0	0	0	1.2	11	7	5	5	2	0	0	0	0	0	0	0	0	0	0	-	0	0-0	0	43.10	27.00
2012	Hou	NL	44	0	0	12	31.0	138	30	15	13	3	2	3	1	14	1	36	3	0	0	1	.000	0	1-3	6	4.05	3.77
2013	2 Tms		16	0	0	3	12.1	60	15	12	9	0	1	0	2	8	0	9	0	0	0	0	-	0	0-0	2	6.24	6.57
2014	Was	NL	9	0	0	4	7.0	30	10	4	3	1	0	0	0	0	0	5	0	0	0	0	-	0	0-0	0	5.27	3.86
2015	2 Tms		66	0	0	10	46.0	189	40	13	12	4	0	0	2	14	2	47	6	0	4	1	.800	0	1-3	19	3.05	2.35
13	Hou	AL	5	0	0	0	6.1	37	10	11	8	0	1	0	2	7	0	3	0	0	0	0	-	0	0-0	0	11.27	11.37
13	Was	NL	11	0	0	3	6.0	23	5	1	1	0	0	0	0	1	0	6	0	0	0	0	-	0	0-0	2	1.84	1.50
15	Was	NL	5	0	0	1	3.0	15	3	2	2	1	0	0	1	2	0	4	2	0	0	0	-	0	0-2	0	8.41	6.00
15	TB	AL	61	0	0	9	43.0	174	37	11	10	3	0	0	1	12	2	43	4	0	4	1	.800	0	1-1	19	2.74	2.09
5 ML YEARS			138	0	0	29	98.0	428	102	49	42	10	3	3	5	36	3	97	9	0	4	2	.667	0	2-6	27	4.34	3.86

Juan Centeno

Bats: L Throws: R Pos: C-7;PH-3   sen-TAIN-no   Ht: 5'9" Wt: 195 Born: 11/16/1989 Age: 26

									BATTING												RUNNING			AVERAGES			
Year	Team	Lg	G	AB	H	2B	3B	HR	(Hm	Rd)	TB	R	RBI	RC	TBB	IBB	SO	HBP	SH	SF	SB	CS	GDP	Avg	OBP	Slg	OPS
2015	ColSpr*	AAA	51	176	52	6	3	0	(-	-)	64	11	24	20	5	0	19	1	1	4	2	2	9	.295	.312	.364	.675
2013	NYM	NL	4	10	3	0	0	0	(0	0)	3	0	1	1	0	0	1	0	0	0	0	0	0	.300	.300	.300	.600
2014	NYM	NL	10	30	6	0	0	0	(0	0)	6	1	2	2	3	0	5	0	0	0	0	0	2	.200	.273	.200	.473
2015	Mil	NL	10	21	1	1	0	0	(0	0)	2	0	0	0	2	0	7	0	0	0	0	0	0	.048	.130	.095	.226
3 ML YEARS			24	61	10	1	0	0	(0	0)	11	1	3	3	5	0	13	0	0	0	0	0	2	.164	.227	.180	.408

Francisco Cervelli

Bats: R Throws: R Pos: C-128;PH-5;DH-1   serr-VELL-ee   Ht: 6'1" Wt: 205 Born: 3/6/1986 Age: 30

									BATTING												RUNNING			AVERAGES			
Year	Team	Lg	G	AB	H	2B	3B	HR	(Hm	Rd)	TB	R	RBI	RC	TBB	IBB	SO	HBP	SH	SF	SB	CS	GDP	Avg	OBP	Slg	OPS
2008	NYY	AL	3	5	0	0	0	0	(0	0)	0	0	0	0	0	0	3	0	0	0	0	0	1	.000	.000	.000	.000
2009	NYY	AL	42	94	28	4	0	1	(0	1)	35	13	11	11	2	0	11	0	4	1	0	3	1	.298	.309	.372	.682
2010	NYY	AL	93	266	72	11	3	0	(0	0)	89	27	38	40	33	1	42	6	8	4	1	1	7	.271	.359	.335	.694
2011	NYY	AL	43	124	33	4	0	4	(2	2)	49	17	22	17	9	0	29	2	1	1	4	1	4	.266	.324	.395	.719
2012	NYY	AL	3	1	0	0	0	0	(0	0)	0	1	0	0	1	0	0	0	0	0	0	0	0	.000	.500	.000	.500
2013	NYY	AL	17	52	14	3	0	3	(3	0)	26	12	8	9	8	0	9	1	0	0	0	0	1	.269	.377	.500	.877
2014	NYY	AL	49	146	44	11	1	2	(1	1)	63	18	13	19	11	0	41	5	0	0	1	0	5	.301	.370	.432	.802
2015	Pit	NL	130	451	133	17	5	7	(6	1)	181	56	43	62	46	1	94	8	4	1	1	1	12	.295	.370	.401	.771
Postseason			3	3	0	0	0	0	(0	0)	0	0	0	0	0	0	2	0	0	0	0	0	0	.000	.000	.000	.000
8 ML YEARS			380	1139	324	50	9	17	(12	5)	443	144	135	158	110	2	229	22	17	7	7	6	31	.284	.357	.389	.746

Yoenis Cespedes

Bats: R Throws: R Pos: LF-134;CF-40;DH-3;PH-3   yo-EHN-ess SESS-peh-des   Ht: 5'10" Wt: 210 Born: 10/18/1985 Age: 30

									BATTING												RUNNING			AVERAGES			
Year	Team	Lg	G	AB	H	2B	3B	HR	(Hm	Rd)	TB	R	RBI	RC	TBB	IBB	SO	HBP	SH	SF	SB	CS	GDP	Avg	OBP	Slg	OPS
2012	Oak	AL	129	487	142	25	5	23	(11	12)	246	70	82	90	43	5	102	7	0	3	16	4	9	.292	.356	.505	.861
2013	Oak	AL	135	529	127	21	4	26	(14	12)	234	74	80	65	37	5	137	5	0	3	7	7	8	.240	.294	.442	.737
2014	2 Tms	AL	152	600	156	36	6	22	(13	9)	270	89	100	85	35	3	128	5	0	7	7	2	13	.260	.301	.450	.751
2015	2 Tms		159	633	184	42	6	35	(10	25)	343	101	105	103	33	5	141	5	0	5	7	5	14	.291	.328	.542	.870
14	Oak	AL	101	399	102	26	3	17	(11	6)	185	62	67	55	28	3	80	1	0	4	3	2	8	.256	.303	.464	.767
14	Bos	AL	51	201	54	10	3	5	(2	3)	85	27	33	30	7	0	48	2	0	3	4	0	5	.269	.296	.423	.719
15	Det	AL	102	403	118	28	2	18	(5	13)	204	62	61	58	19	2	87	1	0	4	3	4	9	.293	.323	.506	.829
15	NYM	NL	57	230	66	14	4	17	(5	12)	139	39	44	45	14	3	54	4	0	1	4	1	5	.287	.337	.604	.942
Postseason			10	40	14	2	1	1	(1	0)	21	4	6	8	2	0	6	1	0	0	2	0	0	.350	.395	.525	.920
4 ML YEARS			575	2249	609	124	21	106	(48	58)	1093	334	367	343	148	18	508	20	0	18	37	18	44	.271	.319	.486	.805

Jhoulys Chacin

Pitches: R Bats: R Pos: SP-4; RP-1   yoo-LEES cha-SEEN   Ht: 6'3" Wt: 215 Born: 1/7/1988 Age: 28

				HOW MUCH HE PITCHED						WHAT HE GAVE UP													THE RESULTS							
Year	Team	Lg	G	GS	CG	GF	IP	BFP	H	R	ER	HR	SH	SF	HB	TBB	IBB	SO	WP	Bk	W	L	Pct	Sh	Sv-Op	Hld	ERC	ERA
2015	Clmbs*	AAA	7	7	0	0	42.0	176	39	17	15	3	1	1	0	15	0	25	4	0	1	3	.250	0	0- -	-	3.34	3.21
2015	Reno*	AAA	13	13	0	0	86.2	361	79	37	31	8	5	3	5	30	0	63	1	1	6	3	.667	0	0- -	-	3.22	3.22
2009	Col	NL	9	1	0	3	11.0	48	6	6	6	1	1	0	0	11	0	13	2	0	0	1	.000	0	0-0	0	3.87	4.91
2010	Col	NL	28	21	0	2	137.1	583	114	64	50	10	6	5	9	61	5	138	4	0	9	11	.450	0	0-0	0	3.33	3.28
2011	Col	NL	31	31	2	0	194.0	827	168	87	78	20	5	3	4	87	1	150	7	0	11	14	.440	1	0-0	0	3.61	3.62
2012	Col	NL	14	14	0	0	69.0	314	80	35	34	10	1	1	2	32	0	45	3	0	3	5	.375	0	0-0	0	5.73	4.43
2013	Col	NL	31	31	0	0	197.1	816	188	82	76	11	3	7	3	61	3	126	5	1	14	10	.583	0	0-0	0	3.26	3.47
2014	Col	NL	11	11	0	0	63.1	272	63	38	38	8	2	3	1	28	1	42	4	0	1	7	.125	0	0-0	0	4.52	5.40
2015	Ari	NL	5	4	0	0	26.2	111	24	11	10	4	1	0	0	10	0	21	0	0	2	1	.667	0	0-0	0	3.80	3.38
7 ML YEARS			129	113	2	5	698.2	2971	643	323	292	64	19	19	19	290	10	535	25	1	40	49	.449	1	0-0	0	3.74	3.76

Andrew Chafin

Pitches: L **Bats:** R **Pos:** RP-66   **Ht:** 6'2" **Wt:** 225 **Born:** 6/17/1990 **Age:** 26

		HOW MUCH HE PITCHED						WHAT HE GAVE UP										THE RESULTS					
Year	Team	Lg	G	GS	CG	GF	IP	BFP	H	R	ER	HR	SH	SF	HB	TBB	IBB	SO	WP	Bk	W	L	Pct	Sh	Sv-Op	Hld	ERC	ERA
2012	Visalia	A+	30	22	0	3	122.1	542	112	74	67	12	4	2	2	69	0	150	10	1	6	6	.500	0	0- -	-	4.26	4.93
2013	Visalia	A+	6	6	0	0	31.0	138	32	16	16	1	0	2	0	14	1	32	4	1	3	1	.750	0	0- -	-	3.84	4.65
2013	Mobile	AA	21	21	2	0	126.1	523	118	46	40	5	5	5	3	41	0	87	13	1	10	7	.588	0	0- -	-	3.16	2.85
2014	Mobile	AA	9	9	0	0	55.0	226	49	14	12	4	3	1	1	19	0	41	3	2	4	1	.800	0	0- -	-	3.22	1.96
2014	Reno	AAA	17	16	0	0	92.2	419	111	62	55	11	4	1	2	39	3	73	3	1	5	6	.455	0	0- -	-	5.50	5.34
2014	Ari	NL	3	3	0	0	14.0	60	13	6	6	0	2	0	1	8	1	10	2	0	0	1	.000	0	0-0	0	3.92	3.86
2015	Ari	NL	66	0	0	6	75.0	306	56	23	23	3	3	2	1	30	6	58	2	0	5	1	.833	0	2-2	16	2.30	2.76
	2 ML YEARS		69	3	0	6	89.0	366	69	29	29	3	5	2	2	38	7	68	4	0	5	2	.714	0	2-2	16	2.54	2.93

Joba Chamberlain

Pitches: R **Bats:** R **Pos:** RP-36   JOBB-ah CHAME-berr-linn   **Ht:** 6'2" **Wt:** 250 **Born:** 9/23/1985 **Age:** 30

		HOW MUCH HE PITCHED						WHAT HE GAVE UP										THE RESULTS					
Year	Team	Lg	G	GS	CG	GF	IP	BFP	H	R	ER	HR	SH	SF	HB	TBB	IBB	SO	WP	Bk	W	L	Pct	Sh	Sv-Op	Hld	ERC	ERA
2015	Buffalo*	AAA	7	0	0	3	5.0	28	9	10	8	0	0	0	0	4	0	7	0	0	0	1	.000	0	2- -	-	9.71	14.40
2015	Omha*	AAA	8	0	0	2	7.0	33	11	5	5	0	0	0	0	2	0	9	2	1	1	0	1.000	0	0- -	-	6.23	6.43
2007	NYY	AL	19	0	0	3	24.0	91	12	2	1	1	1	0	1	6	0	34	1	0	2	0	1.000	0	1-1	8	1.16	0.38
2008	NYY	AL	42	12	0	5	100.1	417	87	32	29	5	2	1	2	39	3	118	4	2	4	3	.571	0	0-1	19	3.04	2.60
2009	NYY	AL	32	31	0	0	157.1	709	167	94	83	21	6	5	12	76	2	133	5	2	9	6	.600	0	0-0	0	5.32	4.75
2010	NYY	AL	73	0	0	18	71.2	305	71	37	35	6	0	1	1	22	2	77	5	1	3	4	.429	0	3-7	26	3.53	4.40
2011	NYY	AL	27	0	0	3	28.2	110	23	10	9	3	0	1	1	7	0	24	1	0	2	0	1.000	0	0-1	12	2.76	2.83
2012	NYY	AL	22	0	0	5	20.2	95	26	11	10	3	0	1	2	6	2	22	0	0	1	0	1.000	0	0-0	4	5.63	4.35
2013	NYY	AL	45	0	0	14	42.0	198	47	23	23	8	0	1	1	26	1	38	3	0	2	1	.667	0	1-1	5	6.38	4.93
2014	Det	AL	69	0	0	10	63.0	263	57	26	25	3	1	2	3	24	3	59	3	0	2	5	.286	0	2-6	29	3.29	3.57
2015	2 Tms	AL	36	0	0	15	27.2	128	38	20	15	6	1	0	1	9	0	23	2	0	0	2	.000	0	0-2	8	7.09	4.88
15	Det	AL	30	0	0	10	22.0	101	32	15	10	5	1	0	1	5	0	15	1	0	0	2	.000	0	0-2	8	7.34	4.09
15	KC	AL	6	0	0	5	5.2	27	6	5	5	1	0	0	0	4	0	8	1	0	0	0	-	0	0-0	0	6.14	7.94
	Postseason		21	0	0	1	16.0	79	23	10	9	1	1	1	2	6	0	15	2	0	1	0	1.000	0	0-2	4	6.64	5.06
	9 ML YEARS		365	43	0	73	535.1	2316	528	255	230	56	11	12	24	215	13	528	24	5	25	21	.543	0	7-19	111	4.19	3.87

Aroldis Chapman

Pitches: L **Bats:** L **Pos:** RP-65   ah-ROLL-diss   **Ht:** 6'4" **Wt:** 215 **Born:** 2/28/1988 **Age:** 28

		HOW MUCH HE PITCHED						WHAT HE GAVE UP										THE RESULTS					
Year	Team	Lg	G	GS	CG	GF	IP	BFP	H	R	ER	HR	SH	SF	HB	TBB	IBB	SO	WP	Bk	W	L	Pct	Sh	Sv-Op	Hld	ERC	ERA
2010	Cin	NL	15	0	0	3	13.1	51	9	4	3	0	0	0	0	5	0	19	2	0	2	2	.500	0	0-1	4	1.82	2.03
2011	Cin	NL	54	0	0	13	50.0	207	24	21	20	2	1	0	2	41	0	71	4	0	4	1	.800	0	1-3	13	2.69	3.60
2012	Cin	NL	68	0	0	52	71.2	276	35	13	12	4	0	1	4	23	0	122	4	0	5	5	.500	0	38-43	0	1.35	1.51
2013	Cin	NL	68	0	0	55	63.2	258	37	18	18	7	1	0	3	29	0	112	6	0	4	5	.444	0	38-43	0	2.33	2.54
2014	Cin	NL	54	0	0	44	54.0	202	21	12	12	1	1	1	2	24	0	106	4	0	3	0	1.000	0	36-38	0	1.18	2.00
2015	Cin	NL	65	0	0	54	66.1	278	43	13	12	3	0	2	5	33	1	116	7	0	4	4	.500	0	33-36	0	2.45	1.63
	Postseason		5	0	0	3	4.2	24	5	4	1	0	0	0	1	2	0	4	2	0	0	1	.000	0	0-1	4	4.11	1.93
	6 ML YEARS		324	0	0	221	319.0	1272	169	81	77	17	3	4	16	155	1	546	27	0	19	20	.487	0	146-164	23	1.89	2.17

Kevin Chapman

Pitches: L **Bats:** L **Pos:** RP-3   **Ht:** 6'3" **Wt:** 225 **Born:** 2/19/1988 **Age:** 28

		HOW MUCH HE PITCHED						WHAT HE GAVE UP										THE RESULTS					
Year	Team	Lg	G	GS	CG	GF	IP	BFP	H	R	ER	HR	SH	SF	HB	TBB	IBB	SO	WP	Bk	W	L	Pct	Sh	Sv-Op	Hld	ERC	ERA
2015	Fresno*	AAA	49	0	0	19	53.0	245	60	35	28	3	4	2	2	26	0	61	0	0	3	2	.600	0	8- -	-	4.93	4.75
2013	Hou	AL	25	0	0	20.1	87		13	6	4	1	2	0	1	13	2	15	3	0	1	1	.500	0	1-4	5	2.69	1.77
2014	Hou	AL	21	0	0	1	21.1	97	22	11	11	3	3	1	0	11	0	19	0	0	2	0	1.000	0	0-1	5	4.90	4.64
2015	Hou	AL	3	0	0	0	5.1	22	4	2	2	1	0	0	0	3	0	8	0	0	0	0	-	0	0-0	1	4.05	3.38
	3 ML YEARS		49	0	0	3	47.0	206	39	19	17	5	5	1	1	27	2	42	3	0	3	1	.750	0	1-5	10	3.82	3.26

Tyler Chatwood

Pitches: R **Bats:** R **Pos:** P   **Ht:** 6'0" **Wt:** 185 **Born:** 12/16/1989 **Age:** 26

		HOW MUCH HE PITCHED						WHAT HE GAVE UP										THE RESULTS					
Year	Team	Lg	G	GS	CG	GF	IP	BFP	H	R	ER	HR	SH	SF	HB	TBB	IBB	SO	WP	Bk	W	L	Pct	Sh	Sv-Op	Hld	ERC	ERA
2011	LAA	AL	27	25	0	0	142.0	633	166	81	75	14	6	3	6	71	4	74	3	1	6	11	.353	0	0-0	0	5.78	4.75
2012	Col	NL	19	12	0	3	64.2	294	74	43	39	9	4	2	0	33	2	41	4	0	5	6	.455	0	1-1	0	5.62	5.43
2013	Col	NL	20	20	1	0	111.1	476	118	44	39	5	2	4	4	41	5	66	10	0	8	5	.615	0	0-0	0	4.05	3.15
2014	Col	NL	4	4	0	0	24.0	101	21	13	12	4	0	2	2	8	0	20	2	0	1	0	1.000	0	0-0	0	3.91	4.50
	4 ML YEARS		70	61	1	3	342.0	1504	379	181	165	32	12	11	12	153	11	201	19	1	20	22	.476	0	1-1	0	5.03	4.34

Jesse Chavez

Pitches: R **Bats:** R **Pos:** SP-26; RP-4   CHAH-vezz   **Ht:** 6'2" **Wt:** 160 **Born:** 8/21/1983 **Age:** 32

		HOW MUCH HE PITCHED						WHAT HE GAVE UP										THE RESULTS					
Year	Team	Lg	G	GS	CG	GF	IP	BFP	H	R	ER	HR	SH	SF	HB	TBB	IBB	SO	WP	Bk	W	L	Pct	Sh	Sv-Op	Hld	ERC	ERA
2008	Pit	NL	15	0	0	6	15.0	74	20	11	11	2	3	1	0	9	2	16	2	0	0	1	.000	0	0-2	0	6.76	6.60
2009	Pit	NL	73	0	0	24	67.1	286	69	33	30	11	1	1	1	22	3	47	5	0	1	4	.200	0	0-4	15	4.39	4.01
2010	2 Tms		51	0	0	26	62.2	280	69	44	41	11	5	3	1	23	7	45	2	0	5	5	.500	0	0-1	6	4.45	5.89
2011	KC	AL	4	0	0	3	7.2	39	12	9	9	3	0	0	0	5	0	8	0	0	0	0	-	0	0-0	0	11.48	10.57
2012	2 Tms	AL	13	2	0	3	24.2	123	34	29	27	7	0	1	3	11	1	30	1	0	1	1	.500	0	0-0	1	8.32	9.85
2013	Oak	AL	35	0	0	16	57.1	248	50	27	25	3	6	2	3	20	4	55	5	0	2	4	.333	0	1-2	1	2.85	3.92

Year	Team	Lg	HOW MUCH HE PITCHED						WHAT HE GAVE UP												THE RESULTS							
			G	GS	CG	GF	IP	BFP	H	R	ER	HR	SH	SF	HB	TBB	IBB	SO	WP	Bk	W	L	Pct	Sh	Sv-Op	Hld	ERC	ERA
2014	Oak	AL	32	21	0	5	146.0	621	142	64	56	17	1	4	5	49	3	136	7	0	8	8	.500	0	0-0	0	3.89	3.45
2015	Oak	AL	30	26	0	3	157.0	672	164	78	73	18	4	6	2	48	2	136	3	0	7	15	.318	0	1-1	0	4.08	4.18
10	Atl	NL	28	0	0	16	36.2	162	40	24	24	6	3	2	1	12	3	29	0	0	3	2	.600	0	0-0	0	4.65	5.89
10	KC	AL	23	0	0	10	26.0	118	29	20	17	5	2	1	0	11	4	16	2	0	2	3	.400	0	0-1	6	5.13	5.88
12	Tor	AL	9	2	0	2	21.1	102	25	22	20	6	0	1	2	10	1	27	0	0	1	1	.500	0	0-0	6	6.90	8.44
12	Oak	AL	4	0	0	1	3.1	21	9	7	7	1	0	0	1	1	0	3	1	0	0	0	-	0	0-0	0	18.70	18.90
8 ML YEARS			253	49	0	86	537.2	2343	560	295	272	72	20	18	15	187	22	473	25	0	24	38	.387	0	2-10	22	4.35	4.55

Bruce Chen

Pitches: L Bats: L Pos: SP-2   Ht: 6'2" Wt: 215 Born: 6/19/1977 Age: 39

Year	Team	Lg	HOW MUCH HE PITCHED						WHAT HE GAVE UP												THE RESULTS							
			G	GS	CG	GF	IP	BFP	H	R	ER	HR	SH	SF	HB	TBB	IBB	SO	WP	Bk	W	L	Pct	Sh	Sv-Op	Hld	ERC	ERA
2015	Clmbs*	AAA	5	5	2	0	31.0	111	19	6	6	4	0	0	1	3	0	23	0	0	2	1	.667	0	0- -		1.50	1.74
1998	Atl	NL	4	4	0	0	20.1	91	23	9	9	3	1	0	1	9	1	17	0	0	2	0	1.000	0	0-0	0	5.55	3.98
1999	Atl	NL	16	7	0	3	51.0	214	38	32	31	11	1	1	2	27	3	45	0	0	2	2	.500	0	0-0	0	4.07	5.47
2000	2 Tms	NL	37	15	0	4	134.0	559	116	54	49	18	8	3	2	46	4	112	4	1	7	4	.636	0	0-0	0	3.35	3.29
2001	2 Tms	NL	27	27	0	0	146.0	634	146	90	79	29	4	7	1	59	4	126	5	0	7	7	.500	0	0-0	0	4.75	4.87
2002	3 Tms	NL	55	6	0	9	77.2	360	85	53	48	16	2	3	2	43	5	80	4	0	2	5	.286	0	0-0	0	5.99	5.56
2003	2 Tms		16	2	0	4	24.1	110	26	16	15	6	3	3	2	10	1	20	0	0	0	1	.000	0	0-0	1	5.81	5.55
2004	Bal	AL	8	7	1	0	47.2	196	39	19	16	7	2	1	0	16	0	32	0	0	2	1	.667	0	0-0	0	3.13	3.02
2005	Bal	AL	34	32	1	0	197.1	832	187	94	84	33	3	3	9	63	0	133	2	1	13	10	.565	0	0-0	0	4.12	3.83
2006	Bal	AL	40	12	0	16	98.2	453	137	81	76	28	3	5	0	35	3	70	1	0	0	7	.000	0	0-0	1	7.73	6.93
2007	Tex	AL	5	0	0	3	10.0	46	11	11	8	3	0	0	0	6	1	7	0	0	0	0	-	0	0-0	0	6.90	7.20
2009	KC	AL	17	9	0	4	62.1	279	74	42	40	12	2	2	4	25	3	45	4	0	1	6	.143	0	0-0	0	6.18	5.78
2010	KC	AL	33	23	1	4	140.1	608	136	68	65	17	6	7	3	57	4	98	3	0	12	7	.632	1	1-1	0	4.09	4.17
2011	KC	AL	25	25	1	0	155.0	654	152	71	65	18	3	5	7	50	2	97	2	0	12	8	.600	0	0-0	0	3.98	3.77
2012	KC	AL	34	34	0	0	191.2	827	215	114	108	33	3	5	8	47	3	140	5	0	11	14	.440	0	0-0	0	4.80	5.07
2013	KC	AL	34	15	0	3	121.0	498	107	46	44	13	2	5	3	36	4	78	0	1	9	4	.692	0	0-2	2	3.17	3.27
2014	KC	AL	13	7	0	6	48.1	223	69	40	40	7	2	3	1	16	1	36	0	0	2	4	.333	0	0-0	0	6.85	7.45
2015	Cle	AL	2	2	0	0	6.1	35	17	9	9	3	0	0	0	1	1	4	0	0	0	1	.000	0	0-0	0	18.67	12.79
00	Atl	NL	22	0	0	0	39.2	176	35	15	11	4	3	2	1	19	2	32	0	0	4	0	1.000	0	0-0	0	3.62	2.50
00	Phi	NL	15	15	0	0	94.1	383	81	39	38	14	5	1	1	27	2	80	4	0	3	4	.429	0	0-0	0	3.22	3.63
01	NYM	NL	16	16	0	0	86.1	381	90	53	48	19	2	4	1	31	4	79	2	0	4	5	.444	0	0-0	0	4.87	5.00
01	NYM	NL	11	11	0	0	59.2	253	56	37	31	10	2	3	0	28	0	47	3	0	3	2	.600	0	0-0	0	4.58	4.68
02	NYM	NL	1	0	0	0	0.2	3	1	0	0	0	0	0	0	0	0	0	0	0	0	0	-	0	0-0	0	4.47	0.00
02	Mon	NL	15	5	0	4	37.1	179	47	29	29	9	0	0	1	23	3	43	3	0	2	3	.400	0	0-0	0	7.69	6.99
02	Cin	NL	39	1	0	5	39.2	178	37	24	19	7	2	3	1	20	2	37	1	0	0	2	.000	0	0-0	4	4.55	4.31
03	Hou	NL	11	0	0	2	12.0	60	14	8	8	2	3	2	2	8	1	8	0	0	0	0	-	0	0-0	1	7.11	6.00
03	Bos	AL	5	2	0	2	12.1	50	12	8	7	4	0	1	0	2	0	12	0	0	1	0	1.000	0	0-0	0	4.40	5.11
17 ML YEARS			400	227	4	56	1532.0	6619	1578	849	786	257	45	53	45	546	40	1140	30	3	82	81	.503	1	1-3	8	4.64	4.62

Wei-Yin Chen

Pitches: L Bats: L Pos: SP-31   way-yin   Ht: 6'0" Wt: 195 Born: 7/21/1985 Age: 30

Year	Team	Lg	HOW MUCH HE PITCHED						WHAT HE GAVE UP												THE RESULTS							
			G	GS	CG	GF	IP	BFP	H	R	ER	HR	SH	SF	HB	TBB	IBB	SO	WP	Bk	W	L	Pct	Sh	Sv-Op	Hld	ERC	ERA
2012	Bal	AL	32	32	0	0	192.2	818	186	97	86	29	5	8	5	57	0	154	2	1	12	11	.522	0	0-0	0	3.88	4.02
2013	Bal	AL	23	23	0	0	137.0	572	142	62	62	17	2	6	2	39	2	104	3	0	7	7	.500	0	0-0	0	4.11	4.07
2014	Bal	AL	31	31	0	0	185.2	772	193	77	73	23	5	4	3	35	2	136	2	0	16	6	.727	0	0-0	0	3.67	3.54
2015	Bal	AL	31	31	0	0	191.1	792	192	78	71	28	5	8	5	41	0	153	3	0	11	8	.579	0	0-0	0	3.80	3.34
Postseason			3	3	0	0	15.1	69	22	9	8	2	0	0	0	2	0	10	0	0	1	1	.500	0	0-0	0	5.68	4.70
4 ML YEARS			117	117	0	0	706.2	2954	713	314	292	97	17	26	15	172	4	547	10	1	46	32	.590	0	0-0	0	3.85	3.72

Robinson Chirinos

Bats: R Throws: R Pos: C-78   chee-REE-nos   Ht: 6'1" Wt: 210 Born: 6/5/1984 Age: 32

Year	Team	Lg	BATTING																			RUNNING			AVERAGES			
			G	AB	H	2B	3B	HR	(Hm	Rd)	TB	R	RBI	RC	TBB	IBB	SO	HBP	SH	SF	SB	CS	GDP	Avg	OBP	Slg	OPS
2011	TB	AL	20	55	12	2	0	1	(1	0)	17	4	7	5	7	0	13	0	0	0	0	0	2	.218	.283	.309	.592
2013	Tex	AL	13	28	5	3	0	0	(0	0)	8	3	0	0	2	0	6	0	0	0	0	0	1	.179	.233	.286	.519
2014	Tex	AL	93	306	73	15	0	13	(6	7)	127	36	40	38	17	1	71	7	4	4	0	1	4	.239	.290	.415	.705
2015	Tex	AL	78	233	54	16	1	10	(4	6)	102	33	34	28	28	0	62	5	5	2	0	0	4	.232	.325	.438	.762
4 ML YEARS			204	622	144	36	1	24	(11	13)	254	76	81	71	52	1	152	12	9	6	0	1	9	.232	.301	.408	.709

Lonnie Chisenhall

Bats: L Throws: R Pos: RF-51;3B-50;PH-17;DH-4;PR-2   CHIZZ-en-hall   Ht: 6'2" Wt: 190 Born: 10/4/1988 Age: 27

Year	Team	Lg	BATTING																			RUNNING			AVERAGES			
			G	AB	H	2B	3B	HR	(Hm	Rd)	TB	R	RBI	RC	TBB	IBB	SO	HBP	SH	SF	SB	CS	GDP	Avg	OBP	Slg	OPS
2015	Clmbs*	AAA	40	157	44	13	0	3	(-	-)	66	18	21	22	11	1	35	1	1	1	1	0	2	.280	.329	.420	.750
2011	Cle	AL	66	212	54	13	0	7	(2	5)	88	27	22	24	8	1	49	1	1	1	1	0	3	.255	.284	.415	.699
2012	Cle	AL	43	142	38	6	1	5	(4	1)	61	16	16	18	8	0	27	1	0	0	2	1	2	.268	.314	.430	.741
2013	Cle	AL	94	289	65	17	0	11	(4	7)	115	30	36	31	16	0	56	2	1	0	1	0	8	.225	.270	.398	.668
2014	Cle	AL	142	478	134	29	1	13	(6	7)	204	62	59	69	39	3	99	8	4	3	3	1	8	.280	.343	.427	.770
2015	Cle	AL	106	333	82	19	1	7	(3	4)	124	38	44	39	23	3	69	1	2	3	4	1	0	.246	.294	.372	.667
Postseason			1	4	3	0	0	0	(0	0)	3	0	0	0	0	0	1	0	0	0	0	0	0	.750	.750	.750	1.500
5 ML YEARS			451	1454	373	84	3	43	(19	24)	592	173	177	181	94	7	300	13	8	7	11	3	21	.257	.306	.407	.713

Randy Choate

Pitches: L Bats: L Pos: RP-71
CHOTE
Ht: 6'1" Wt: 210 Born: 9/5/1975 Age: 40

Year	Team	Lg	G	GS	CG	GF	IP	BFP	H	R	ER	HR	SH	SF	HB	TBB	IBB	SO	WP	Bk	W	L	Pct	Sh	Sv-Op	Hld	ERC	ERA
2000	NYY	AL	22	0	0	6	17.0	75	14	10	9	3	0	1	1	8	0	12	1	0	0	1	.000	0	0-0	2	3.99	4.76
2001	NYY	AL	37	0	0	13	48.1	207	34	21	18	0	2	1	9	27	2	35	3	0	3	1	.750	0	0-0	3	3.03	3.35
2002	NYY	AL	18	0	0	11	22.1	101	18	18	15	1	0	0	3	15	0	17	3	0	0	0	-	0	0-0	4	4.13	6.04
2003	NYY	AL	5	0	0	2	3.2	16	7	3	3	0	0	0	0	1	0	1	0	0	0	0	-	0	0-0	0	9.72	7.36
2004	Ari	NL	74	0	0	17	50.2	232	52	26	26	1	0	4	5	28	11	49	1	1	2	4	.333	0	0-2	11	4.18	4.62
2005	Ari	NL	8	0	0	1	7.0	35	8	7	7	0	0	1	0	5	1	4	1	0	0	0	-	0	0-0	2	5.48	9.00
2006	Ari	NL	30	0	0	3	16.0	75	21	9	7	0	0	0	0	3	0	12	0	0	0	1	.000	0	0-0	5	4.87	3.94
2007	Ari	NL	2	0	0	0	3.0	-	3	0	0	0	0	0	0	0	0	0	0	0	0	0	-	0	0-0	0	-	-
2009	TB	AL	61	0	0	13	36.1	142	28	15	14	4	0	0	0	11	3	28	0	0	1	0	1.000	0	5-5	9	2.54	3.47
2010	TB	AL	85	0	0	8	44.2	187	41	23	21	3	2	2	3	17	5	40	4	0	4	3	.571	0	0-2	18	3.48	4.23
2011	Fla	NL	54	0	0	6	24.2	103	13	7	5	3	1	0	2	13	5	31	0	0	1	1	.500	0	0-0	14	2.16	1.82
2012	2 Tms	NL	80	0	0	4	38.2	168	29	18	13	1	2	2	5	18	3	38	2	0	0	0	-	0	1-1	20	2.76	3.03
2013	StL	NL	64	0	0	9	35.1	141	26	9	9	0	2	1	2	11	0	28	0	0	2	1	.667	0	0-1	15	2.00	2.29
2014	StL	NL	61	0	0	6	36.0	148	27	18	18	2	1	2	5	13	2	32	0	0	2	2	.500	0	0-0	10	2.78	4.50
2015	StL	NL	71	0	0	4	27.1	117	29	14	12	2	1	1	6	5	0	22	1	0	0	1	1.000	0	1-1	8	4.33	3.95
12	Mia	NL	44	0	0	4	25.1	104	16	11	7	0	1	1	3	9	0	27	2	0	0	0	-	0	1-1	15	1.79	2.49
12	LAD	NL	36	0	0	0	13.1	64	13	7	6	1	1	1	2	9	3	11	0	0	0	0	-	0	0-0	5	4.87	4.05
	Postseason		21	0	0	2	10.2	50	10	8	4	1	1	0	0	6	1	6	0	0	0	1	.000	0	0-0	1	3.87	3.38
	15 ML YEARS		672	0	0	102	408.0	1750	350	198	177	20	11	14	45	175	32	348	16	1	16	14	.533	0	7-12	117	3.36	3.90

Michael Choice

Bats: R Throws: R Pos: RF-1
Ht: 6'0" Wt: 230 Born: 11/10/1989 Age: 26

Year	Team	Lg	G	AB	H	2B	3B	HR	(Hm	Rd)	TB	R	RBI	RC	TBB	IBB	SO	HBP	SH	SF	SB	CS	GDP	Avg	OBP	Slg	OPS
2015	RdRck*	AAA	110	406	99	25	1	12	(-	-)	162	53	60	52	32	0	115	7	0	2	2	0	8	.244	.309	.399	.708
2015	Clmbs*	AAA	14	54	11	5	0	1	(-	-)	19	5	7	6	5	0	22	3	0	0	1	0	1	.204	.306	.352	.658
2013	Oak	AL	9	18	5	1	0	0	(0	0)	6	2	0	2	1	0	6	0	0	0	0	0	0	.278	.316	.333	.649
2014	Tex	AL	86	253	46	6	1	9	(4	5)	81	20	36	24	21	0	69	3	0	3	1	0	11	.182	.250	.320	.570
2015	Tex	AL	1	1	0	0	0	0	(0	0)	0	0	0	0	0	0	1	0	0	0	0	0	0	.000	.000	.000	.000
	3 ML YEARS		96	272	51	7	1	9	(4	5)	87	22	36	26	22	0	76	3	0	3	1	0	11	.188	.253	.320	.573

Shin-Soo Choo

Bats: L Throws: L Pos: RF-148;PH-4;DH-1
SHIN-sue CHEW
Ht: 5'11" Wt: 210 Born: 7/13/1982 Age: 33

Year	Team	Lg	G	AB	H	2B	3B	HR	(Hm	Rd)	TB	R	RBI	RC	TBB	IBB	SO	HBP	SH	SF	SB	CS	GDP	Avg	OBP	Slg	OPS
2005	Sea	AL	10	18	1	0	0	0	(0	0)	1	1	1	0	3	0	4	0	0	0	0	0	0	.056	.190	.056	.246
2006	2 Tms	AL	49	157	44	12	3	3	(2	1)	71	23	22	24	18	2	50	2	1	1	5	3	3	.280	.360	.452	.812
2007	Cle	AL	6	17	5	0	0	0	(0	0)	5	5	5	3	2	1	5	0	0	1	0	1	0	.294	.350	.294	.644
2008	Cle	AL	94	317	98	28	3	14	(10	4)	174	68	66	72	44	4	78	5	0	4	4	3	5	.309	.397	.549	.946
2009	Cle	AL	156	583	175	38	6	20	(11	9)	285	87	86	111	78	5	151	17	0	7	21	2	9	.300	.394	.489	.883
2010	Cle	AL	144	550	165	31	2	22	(8	14)	266	81	90	106	83	11	118	11	0	2	22	7	11	.300	.401	.484	.885
2011	Cle	AL	85	313	81	11	3	8	(7	1)	122	37	36	38	36	3	78	6	0	3	12	5	7	.259	.344	.390	.733
2012	Cle	AL	155	598	169	43	2	16	(8	8)	264	88	67	96	73	0	150	14	0	1	21	7	11	.283	.373	.441	.815
2013	Cin	NL	154	569	162	34	2	21	(10	11)	263	107	54	111	112	5	133	26	3	2	20	11	3	.285	.423	.462	.885
2014	Tex	AL	123	455	110	19	1	13	(5	8)	170	58	40	54	58	3	131	12	0	4	3	4	9	.242	.340	.374	.714
2015	Tex	AL	149	555	153	32	3	22	(12	10)	257	94	82	99	76	1	147	15	2	5	4	2	7	.276	.375	.463	.838
06	Sea	AL	4	11	1	1	0	0	(0	0)	2	0	0	0	0	0	4	1	0	0	0	0	0	.091	.167	.182	.348
06	Cle	AL	45	146	43	11	3	3	(2	1)	69	23	22	24	18	2	46	1	1	1	5	3	2	.295	.373	.473	.846
	Postseason		1	3	1	0	0	1	(0	1)	4	2	1	1	0	0	1	1	0	0	0	0	0	.333	.500	1.333	1.833
	11 ML YEARS		1125	4132	1163	248	25	139	(73	66)	1878	649	549	714	583	35	1045	108	6	30	112	45	65	.281	.382	.455	.837

Tony Cingrani

Pitches: L Bats: L Pos: RP-34; SP-1
sin-GRAHN-ee
Ht: 6'4" Wt: 210 Born: 7/5/1989 Age: 26

Year	Team	Lg	G	GS	CG	GF	IP	BFP	H	R	ER	HR	SH	SF	HB	TBB	IBB	SO	WP	Bk	W	L	Pct	Sh	Sv-Op	Hld	ERC	ERA
2015	Lsvlle*	AAA	9	6	0	0	24.2	105	20	6	5	2	1	1	2	11	0	32	1	1	0	1	.000	0	0- -	-	3.40	1.82
2012	Cin	NL	3	0	0	1	5.0	22	4	1	1	1	0	0	0	2	0	9	0	0	0	0	-	0	0-0	0	3.38	1.80
2013	Cin	NL	23	18	0	0	104.2	420	72	37	34	14	4	4	2	43	1	120	4	0	7	4	.636	0	0-0	1	2.78	2.92
2014	Cin	NL	13	11	0	2	63.1	280	62	33	32	12	2	2	1	35	2	61	1	2	2	8	.200	0	0-0	0	5.29	4.55
2015	Cin	NL	35	1	0	7	33.1	155	31	21	21	3	1	2	3	25	3	39	2	1	0	3	.000	0	0-2	9	5.19	5.67
	4 ML YEARS		74	30	0	10	206.1	877	169	92	88	30	7	8	6	105	6	229	7	3	9	15	.375	0	0-2	10	3.91	3.84

Pedro Ciriaco

see-ree-AH-koe
Bats: R Throws: R Pos: PH-46;3B-24;SS-9;2B-7;PR-4;1B-2;LF-1;DH-1
Ht: 6'0" Wt: 180 Born: 9/27/1985 Age: 30

Year	Team	Lg	G	AB	H	2B	3B	HR	(Hm	Rd)	TB	R	RBI	RC	TBB	IBB	SO	HBP	SH	SF	SB	CS	GDP	Avg	OBP	Slg	OPS
2015	Gwnntt*	AAA	20	77	18	1	0	1	(-	-)	22	8	7	5	1	0	15	1	1	0	1	0	1	.234	.253	.286	.539
2010	Pit	NL	8	6	3	1	1	0	(0	0)	6	3	1	3	0	0	3	0	0	0	0	0	0	.500	.500	1.000	1.500
2011	Pit	NL	23	33	10	2	1	0	(0	0)	14	4	6	5	1	0	6	0	0	0	2	1	1	.303	.324	.424	.748
2012	Bos	AL	76	259	76	15	2	2	(2	0)	101	33	19	32	8	2	47	0	5	0	16	3	4	.293	.315	.390	.705
2013	3 Tms		56	125	28	4	2	2	(2	0)	42	9	6	11	9	2	23	1	1	1	9	1	2	.224	.279	.336	.615
2014	KC	AL	25	47	10	2	0	0	(0	0)	12	7	2	3	0	0	9	1	1	0	4	0	2	.213	.229	.255	.484

Year Team	Lg	G	AB	H	2B	3B	HR	(Hm	Rd)	TB	R	RBI	RC	TBB	IBB	SO	HBP	SH	SF	SB	CS	GDP	Avg	OBP	Slg	OPS
								BATTING												RUNNING			AVERAGES			
2015 Atl	NL	84	142	37	8	1	1	(0	1)	50	14	15	10	2	0	38	2	2	3	4	2	1	.261	.275	.352	.627
13 Bos	AL	28	51	11	2	1	1	(1	0)	18	4	4	5	6	0	12	0	0	1	2	1	0	.216	.293	.353	.646
13 SD	NL	23	63	15	1	1	1	(1	0)	21	5	4	6	3	2	10	1	1	0	6	0	2	.238	.284	.333	.617
13 KC	AL	5	11	2	1	0	0	(0	0)	3	0	0	0	0	0	1	0	0	0	1	0	0	.182	.182	.273	.455
6 ML YEARS		272	612	164	32	7	5	(4	1)	225	70	51	64	20	4	126	4	9	4	35	7	8	.268	.294	.368	.661

Steve Cishek

Pitches: R Bats: R Pos: RP-59 SEE-sheck Ht: 6'6" Wt: 215 Born: 6/18/1986 Age: 30

Year Team	Lg	G	GS	CG	GF	IP	BFP	H	R	ER	HR	SH	SF	HB	TBB	IBB	SO	WP	Bk	W	L	Pct	Sh	Sv-Op	Hld	ERC	ERA
			HOW MUCH HE PITCHED						WHAT HE GAVE UP											THE RESULTS						
2015 Jaxnvl*	AA	5	0	0	3	6.0	23	5	0	0	0	0	0	0	0	0	4	0	0	0	0	-	0	2- -	-	1.37	0.00
2010 Fla	NL	3	0	0	2	4.1	15	1	0	0	0	0	0	0	1	0	3	0	0	0	0	-	0	0-0	0	0.35	0.00
2011 Fla	NL	45	0	0	21	54.2	229	45	18	16	1	3	0	3	19	7	55	5	0	2	1	.667	0	3-3	2	2.38	2.63
2012 Mia	NL	68	0	0	36	63.2	275	54	26	19	3	3	2	6	29	6	68	1	1	5	2	.714	0	15-19	13	3.28	2.69
2013 Mia	NL	69	0	0	62	69.2	281	53	19	18	3	3	3	2	22	6	74	1	0	4	6	.400	0	34-36	1	2.15	2.33
2014 Mia	NL	67	0	0	55	65.1	275	58	26	23	3	5	3	1	21	2	84	1	0	4	5	.444	0	39-43	0	2.78	3.17
2015 2 Tms	NL	59	0	0	23	55.1	243	55	26	22	4	1	2	1	27	3	48	1	0	2	6	.250	0	4-9	6	4.17	3.58
15 Mia	NL	32	0	0	15	32.0	144	37	19	16	2	1	2	0	14	3	28	0	0	2	6	.250	0	3-7	3	4.66	4.50
15 StL	NL	27	0	0	8	23.1	99	18	7	6	2	0	0	1	13	0	20	1	0	0	0	-	0	1-2	3	3.53	2.31
6 ML YEARS		311	0	0	199	313.0	1318	266	115	98	14	15	10	13	119	24	332	9	1	17	20	.459	0	95-110	22	2.84	2.82

Alex Claudio

Pitches: L Bats: L Pos: RP-18 Ht: 6'3" Wt: 185 Born: 1/31/1992 Age: 24

Year Team	Lg	G	GS	CG	GF	IP	BFP	H	R	ER	HR	SH	SF	HB	TBB	IBB	SO	WP	Bk	W	L	Pct	Sh	Sv-Op	Hld	ERC	ERA
			HOW MUCH HE PITCHED						WHAT HE GAVE UP											THE RESULTS						
2011 2 Tms	Low	16	0	0	4	28.1	115	22	8	6	1	1	1	3	10	1	31	0	1	5	0	1.000	0	1- -	-	2.70	1.91
2012 Rngrs	R	14	3	0	4	45.1	169	36	11	9	1	0	1	1	5	0	54	2	2	4	0	1.000	0	1- -	-	1.71	1.79
2013 Hkry	A	24	0	0	18	47.0	167	22	7	6	2	2	0	0	7	0	62	0	2	3	1	.750	0	11- -	-	0.83	1.15
2013 Frisco	AA	.21	0	0	3	31.2	129	28	16	10	2	2	0	1	11	1	29	1	0	1	5	.167	0	0- -	-	3.17	2.84
2014 MrtlBh	A+	17	2	0	8	49.1	190	38	9	6	2	3	0	2	9	0	56	2	2	4	0	1.000	0	4- -	-	1.96	1.09
2014 Frisco	AA	8	6	0	0	37.1	148	31	17	9	1	5	1	1	2	0	22	1	1	2	2	.500	0	0- -	-	1.61	2.17
2015 RdRck	AAA	29	0	0	6	40.0	163	43	13	13	2	1	2	1	7	0	35	2	1	3	1	.750	0	0- -	-	3.48	2.93
2014 Tex	AL	15	0	0	5	12.1	54	14	4	4	0	0	0	0	4	0	14	0	1	0	0	-	0	0-0	0	3.79	2.92
2015 Tex	AL	18	0	0	6	15.2	66	12	6	5	4	0	2	1	6	2	13	1	0	1	1	.500	0	0-1	3	3.74	2.87
2 ML YEARS		33	0	0	11	28.0	120	26	10	9	4	0	2	1	10	2	27	1	1	1	1	.500	0	0-1	3	3.79	2.89

Steve Clevenger

Bats: L Throws: R Pos: DH-18;C-9;PH-4;1B-1 CLEV-en-jer Ht: 5'10" Wt: 210 Born: 4/5/1986 Age: 30

Year Team	Lg	G	AB	H	2B	3B	HR	(Hm	Rd)	TB	R	RBI	RC	TBB	IBB	SO	HBP	SH	SF	SB	CS	GDP	Avg	OBP	Slg	OPS
								BATTING												RUNNING			AVERAGES			
2015 Norfolk*	AAA	75	262	80	11	0	4	(-	-)	103	28	32	41	32	3	37	1	0	6	0	1	13	.305	.375	.393	.769
2011 ChC	NL	2	4	1	1	0	0	(0	0)	2	1	0	0	0	0	0	1	0	0	0	0	0	.250	.400	.500	.900
2012 ChC	NL	69	199	40	12	0	1	(1	0)	55	16	16	12	16	0	39	0	0	0	0	1	10	.201	.260	.276	.537
2013 2 Tms		12	23	5	1	0	0	(0	0)	6	2	2	1	1	0	5	0	0	0	0	0	1	.217	.250	.261	.511
2014 Bal	AL	35	89	20	8	1	0	(0	0)	30	8	8	3	8	1	19	0	0	0	0	0	5	.225	.289	.337	.626
2015 Bal	AL	30	101	29	4	2	2	(2	0)	43	11	15	15	4	1	13	0	0	0	0	0	3	.287	.314	.426	.740
13 ChC	NL	8	8	1	0	0	0	(0	0)	1	1	0	0	1	0	3	0	0	0	0	0	0	.125	.222	.125	.347
13 Bal	AL	4	15	4	1	0	0	(0	0)	5	1	2	1	0	0	2	0	0	0	0	0	1	.267	.267	.333	.600
5 ML YEARS		148	416	95	26	3	3	(3	0)	136	38	41	31	29	2	76	1	0	0	0	1	19	.228	.280	.327	.607

Tyler Clippard

Pitches: R Bats: R Pos: RP-69 Ht: 6'3" Wt: 200 Born: 2/14/1985 Age: 31

Year Team	Lg	G	GS	CG	GF	IP	BFP	H	R	ER	HR	SH	SF	HB	TBB	IBB	SO	WP	Bk	W	L	Pct	Sh	Sv-Op	Hld	ERC	ERA
			HOW MUCH HE PITCHED						WHAT HE GAVE UP											THE RESULTS						
2007 NYY	AL	6	6	0	0	27.0	124	29	19	19	6	0	0	0	17	1	18	2	1	3	1	.750	0	0-0	0	6.37	6.33
2008 Was	NL	2	2	0	0	10.1	48	12	5	5	2	0	0	0	7	1	8	1	0	1	1	.500	0	0-0	0	6.90	4.35
2009 Was	NL	41	0	0	8	60.1	246	36	20	18	9	3	1	1	32	1	67	1	1	4	2	.667	0	0-1	3	2.79	2.69
2010 Was	NL	78	0	0	18	91.0	378	69	33	31	8	3	7	2	41	4	112	1	1	11	8	.579	0	1-11	23	2.91	3.07
2011 Was	NL	72	0	0	8	88.1	329	48	18	18	11	4	3	0	26	2	104	1	0	3	0	1.000	0	0-7	38	1.61	1.83
2012 Was	NL	74	0	0	42	72.2	307	55	32	30	7	3	4	2	29	2	84	5	0	2	6	.250	0	32-37	13	2.73	3.72
2013 Was	NL	72	0	0	6	71.0	275	37	19	19	7	2	1	1	24	1	73	2	0	6	3	.667	0	0-3	33	1.79	2.41
2014 Was	NL	75	0	0	6	70.1	278	47	22	17	5	2	2	1	23	1	82	0	0	7	4	.636	0	1-7	40	1.98	2.18
2015 2 Tms	NL	69	0	0	36	71.0	301	49	25	23	8	1	2	4	31	2	64	6	0	5	4	.556	0	19-25	8	2.72	2.92
15 Oak		37	0	0	30	38.2	167	25	12	12	3	0	1	2	21	1	38	1	0	1	3	.250	0	17-21	0	2.62	2.79
15 NYM	NL	32	0	0	6	32.1	134	24	13	11	5	1	1	2	10	1	26	5	0	4	1	.800	0	2-4	8	2.82	3.06
Postseason		6	0	0	1	6.0	23	2	1	1	1	1	0	0	2	0	7	0	0	0	0	-	0	0-0	3	1.13	1.50
9 ML YEARS		489	8	0	124	562.0	2286	382	193	180	65	18	20	14	230	15	612	19	3	42	29	.592	0	53-91	158	2.57	2.88

Alex Cobb

Pitches: R Bats: R Pos: P   Ht: 6'3" Wt: 200 Born: 10/7/1987 Age: 28

			HOW MUCH HE PITCHED						WHAT HE GAVE UP										THE RESULTS							
Year	Team	Lg	G	GS	CG	GF	IP	BFP	H	R	ER	HR	SH	SF	HB	TBB	IBB	SO	WP	Bk	W	L	Pct	Sh	Sv-Op	Hld	ERC	ERA
2011	TB	AL	9	9	0	0	52.2	224	49	21	20	3	0	1	1	21	1	37	2	0	3	2	.600	0	0-0	0	3.44	3.42
2012	TB	AL	23	23	2	0	136.1	569	130	67	61	11	3	6	9	40	2	106	8	1	11	9	.550	1	0-0	0	3.56	4.03
2013	TB	AL	22	22	1	0	143.1	578	120	46	44	13	1	2	3	45	4	134	5	1	11	3	.786	0	0-0	0	2.92	2.76
2014	TB	AL	27	27	0	0	166.1	681	142	56	53	11	4	4	10	47	1	149	8	0	10	9	.526	0	0-0	0	2.87	2.87
	Postseason		2	2	0	0	11.2	51	13	3	2	0	0	1	1	3	0	10	1	0	1	0	1.000	0	0-0	0	3.75	1.54
	4 ML YEARS		81	81	3	0	498.2	2052	441	190	178	38	8	13	23	153	8	426	23	2	35	23	.603	1	0-0	0	3.13	3.21

Chris Coghlan

COGG-lan

Bats: L Throws: R Pos: LF-99;PH-26;RF-21;2B-15;1B-5;3B-3   Ht: 6'0" Wt: 195 Born: 6/18/1985 Age: 31

						BATTING													RUNNING			AVERAGES			
Year	Team	Lg	G	AB	H	2B	3B	HR	(Hm | Rd)	TB	R	RBI	RC	TBB	IBB	SO	HBP	SH	SF	SB	CS	GDP	Avg	OBP	Slg	OPS
2009	Fla	NL	128	504	162	31	6	9	(5 | 4)	232	84	47	91	53	2	77	4	3	1	8	5	3	.321	.390	.460	.850
2010	Fla	NL	91	358	96	20	3	5	(5 | 0)	137	60	28	43	33	1	84	4	3	2	10	3	3	.268	.335	.383	.718
2011	Fla	NL	65	269	62	20	1	5	(4 | 1)	99	33	22	23	22	3	49	4	1	2	7	6	3	.230	.296	.368	.664
2012	Mia	NL	39	93	13	1	0	1	(1 | 0)	17	10	10	2	9	1	12	0	1	2	0	2	4	.140	.212	.183	.394
2013	Mia	NL	70	195	50	10	3	1	(0 | 1)	69	10	10	20	17	1	43	1	0	1	2	0	2	.256	.318	.354	.672
2014	ChC	NL	125	385	109	28	5	9	(5 | 4)	174	50	41	59	39	2	81	3	3	2	7	4	5	.283	.352	.452	.804
2015	ChC	NL	148	440	110	25	6	16	(6 | 10)	195	64	41	63	58	6	94	3	1	1	11	2	8	.250	.341	.443	.784
	7 ML YEARS		666	2244	602	135	24	46	(26 | 20)	923	311	199	301	231	16	440	19	12	11	45	22	28	.268	.340	.411	.751

Phil Coke

Pitches: L Bats: L Pos: RP-18   Ht: 6'1" Wt: 210 Born: 7/19/1982 Age: 33

			HOW MUCH HE PITCHED						WHAT HE GAVE UP										THE RESULTS							
Year	Team	Lg	G	GS	CG	GF	IP	BFP	H	R	ER	HR	SH	SF	HB	TBB	IBB	SO	WP	Bk	W	L	Pct	Sh	Sv-Op	Hld	ERC	ERA
2015	Stcktn*	A+	7	0	0	2	8.2	37	11	5	5	1	0	2	2	0	0	5	0	0	0	0	-	0	0- -	-	5.22	5.19
2015	Nashv*	AAA	10	0	0	1	14.2	74	24	16	16	1	0	0	1	7	0	14	5	0	0	3	.000	0	0- -	-	8.39	9.82
2008	NYY	AL	12	0	0	4	14.2	52	8	1	1	0	0	0	0	2	0	14	1	0	1	0	1.000	0	0-0	5	0.89	0.61
2009	NYY	AL	72	0	0	13	60.0	238	44	34	30	10	1	5	1	20	4	49	7	0	4	3	.571	0	2-7	21	2.84	4.50
2010	Det	AL	74	1	0	18	64.2	279	67	29	27	2	2	3	4	26	4	53	3	0	7	5	.583	0	2-4	17	4.00	3.76
2011	Det	AL	48	14	0	6	108.2	474	118	64	54	5	4	3	4	40	5	69	4	0	3	9	.250	0	1-2	6	4.13	4.47
2012	Det	AL	66	0	0	11	54.0	245	71	28	24	5	5	2	1	18	4	51	3	0	2	3	.400	0	1-3	20	5.56	4.00
2013	Det	AL	49	0	0	14	38.1	177	43	24	23	3	4	4	0	21	7	30	1	0	0	5	.000	0	1-3	4	4.81	5.40
2014	Det	AL	62	0	0	24	58.0	257	69	28	25	5	4	1	2	20	2	41	1	0	5	2	.714	0	1-2	5	4.96	3.88
2015	2 Tms		18	0	0	3	12.2	56	15	8	8	2	0	1	0	5	2	12	0	0	0	0	-	0	0-0	3	5.36	5.68
15	ChC	NL	16	0	0	2	10.0	45	14	7	7	1	0	1	0	3	2	9	0	0	0	0	-	0	0-0	3	5.78	6.30
15	Tor	AL	2	0	0	1	2.2	11	1	1	1	1	0	0	0	2	0	3	0	0	0	0	-	0	0-0	0	3.75	3.38
	Postseason		26	0	0	10	19.0	79	18	9	9	2	1	0	0	6	0	19	1	0	0	1	.000	0	3-3	2	3.52	4.26
	8 ML YEARS		401	15	0	89	411.0	1778	435	216	192	32	17	20	12	152	28	319	20	0	22	27	.449	0	8-21	83	4.16	4.20

Chris Colabello

cahl-uh-BELL-oh

Bats: R Throws: R Pos: 1B-34;LF-33;RF-13;PH-13;DH-12;PR-1   Ht: 6'4" Wt: 235 Born: 10/24/1983 Age: 32

						BATTING													RUNNING			AVERAGES			
Year	Team	Lg	G	AB	H	2B	3B	HR	(Hm	Rd)	TB	R	RBI	RC	TBB	IBB	SO	HBP	SH	SF	SB	CS	GDP	Avg	OBP	Slg	OPS
2015	Buffalo*	AAA	23	83	28	3	0	5	(-	-)	46	14	18	18	11	1	19	1	0	0	0	0	3	.337	.421	.554	.975
2013	Min	AL	55	160	31	3	0	7	(1	6)	55	14	17	13	20	0	58	1	0	0	0	1	5	.194	.287	.344	.631
2014	Min	AL	59	205	47	13	0	6	(2	4)	78	17	39	21	14	1	66	1	0	0	0	2	2	.229	.282	.380	.662
2015	Tor	AL	101	333	107	19	1	15	(7	8)	173	55	54	62	22	0	96	3	0	2	2	0	12	.321	.367	.520	.886
	3 ML YEARS		215	698	185	35	1	28	(10	18)	306	86	110	96	56	1	220	5	0	2	2	3	19	.265	.323	.438	.762

A.J. Cole

Pitches: R Bats: R Pos: RP-2; SP-1   Ht: 6'5" Wt: 200 Born: 1/5/1992 Age: 24

			HOW MUCH HE PITCHED						WHAT HE GAVE UP										THE RESULTS							
Year	Team	Lg	G	GS	CG	GF	IP	BFP	H	R	ER	HR	SH	SF	HB	TBB	IBB	SO	WP	Bk	W	L	Pct	Sh	Sv-Op	Hld	ERC	ERA
2011	Hgrstn	A	20	18	0	0	89.0	377	87	47	40	6	2	3	2	24	0	108	7	0	4	7	.364	0	0- -	-	3.27	4.04
2012	2 Tms	Low	27	27	0	0	133.2	558	138	72	55	14	4	2	7	29	0	133	5	2	6	10	.375	0	0- -	-	3.82	3.70
2013	Ptomc	A+	18	18	0	0	97.1	406	96	50	46	12	0	6	4	23	0	102	6	1	6	3	.667	0	0- -	-	3.69	4.25
2013	Hrsbrg	AA	7	7	0	0	45.1	175	31	13	11	3	0	0	0	10	1	49	1	0	4	2	.667	0	0- -	-	1.64	2.18
2014	Hrsbrg	AA	14	14	1	0	71.0	308	79	30	23	1	0	1	3	15	1	61	3	0	6	3	.667	1	0- -	-	3.44	2.92
2014	Syrcse	AAA	11	11	0	0	63.0	267	69	30	24	9	3	2	1	17	0	50	2	0	7	0	1.000	0	0- -	-	4.52	3.43
2015	Syrcse	AAA	21	19	0	0	105.2	443	91	40	37	9	1	3	4	34	1	76	2	0	5	6	.455	0	0- -	-	3.02	3.15
2015	Was	NL	3	1	0	1	9.1	44	14	11	6	1	1	1	0	1	1	9	1	0	0	0	-	0	1-1	0	5.38	5.79

Gerrit Cole

Pitches: R Bats: R Pos: SP-32   Ht: 6'4" Wt: 230 Born: 9/8/1990 Age: 25

			HOW MUCH HE PITCHED						WHAT HE GAVE UP										THE RESULTS							
Year	Team	Lg	G	GS	CG	GF	IP	BFP	H	R	ER	HR	SH	SF	HB	TBB	IBB	SO	WP	Bk	W	L	Pct	Sh	Sv-Op	Hld	ERC	ERA
2013	Pit	NL	19	19	0	0	117.1	469	109	43	42	7	5	2	3	28	0	100	4	0	10	7	.588	0	0-0	0	3.02	3.22

			HOW MUCH HE PITCHED					WHAT HE GAVE UP										THE RESULTS							
Year Team	Lg	G	GS	CG	GF	IP	BFP	H	R	ER	HR	SH	SF	HB	TBB	IBB	SO	WP	Bk	W	L	Pct	Sh	Sv-Op	Hld	ERC	ERA
2014 Pit	NL	22	22	0	0	138.0	571	127	58	56	11	10	0	9	40	1	138	9	1	11	5	.688	0	0-0	0	3.37	3.65
2015 Pit	NL	32	32	0	0	208.0	832	183	71	60	11	7	6	10	44	1	202	7	0	19	8	.704	0	0-0	0	2.66	2.60
Postseason		2	2	0	0	11.0	40	5	3	3	2	0	0	0	2	0	10	0	0	1	1	.500	0	0-0	0	1.24	2.45
3 ML YEARS		73	73	0	0	463.1	1872	419	172	158	29	22	8	22	112	2	440	20	1	40	20	.667	0	0-0	0	2.96	3.07

Dusty Coleman

Bats: R **Throws:** R **Pos:** 3B-2;PH-2;PR-1   **Ht:** 6'2" **Wt:** 205 **Born:** 4/20/1987 **Age:** 29

								BATTING												RUNNING			AVERAGES			
Year Team	Lg	G	AB	H	2B	3B	HR	(Hm	Rd)	TB	R	RBI	RC	TBB	IBB	SO	HBP	SH	SF	SB	CS	GDP	Avg	OBP	Slg	OPS
2011 Stcktn	A+	120	462	111	27	4	15	(-	-)	191	71	66	65	46	1	171	6	3	5	21	4	10	.240	.314	.413	.727
2011 Scrmto	AAA	10	36	12	3	0	0	(-	-)	15	5	4	4	1	0	14	0	0	0	0	2	0	.333	.351	.417	.768
2012 Mdlnd	AA	128	427	86	16	4	15	(-	-)	155	51	59	45	41	0	182	10	4	4	9	8	4	.201	.284	.363	.647
2013 Mdlnd	AA	130	484	126	34	10	3	(-	-)	189	65	61	68	57	1	155	6	5	2	17	10	7	.260	.344	.390	.735
2014 Mdlnd	AA	135	489	109	27	2	18	(-	-)	194	79	81	62	47	0	202	9	4	5	16	5	10	.223	.300	.397	.697
2015 NWArk	AA	26	92	32	9	0	2	(-	-)	47	12	18	22	14	0	23	7	0	1	4	4	1	.348	.465	.511	.976
2015 Omha	AAA	73	251	69	11	2	7	(-	-)	105	31	27	35	14	1	70	4	7	0	8	2	3	.275	.323	.418	.742
2015 KC	AL	4	5	0	0	0	0	(0	0)	0	0	0	0	0	0	3	0	0	0	0	0	0	.000	.000	.000	.000

Louis Coleman

Pitches: R **Bats:** R **Pos:** RP-4   **Ht:** 6'4" **Wt:** 205 **Born:** 4/4/1986 **Age:** 30

				HOW MUCH HE PITCHED					WHAT HE GAVE UP										THE RESULTS							
Year Team	Lg	G	GS	CG	GF	IP	BFP	H	R	ER	HR	SH	SF	HB	TBB	IBB	SO	WP	Bk	W	L	Pct	Sh	Sv-Op	Hld	ERC	ERA
2015 Omha*	AAA	38	0	0	27	64.0	256	48	12	12	4	5	1	1	23	3	63	3	0	8	2	.800	0	9- -	-	2.41	1.69
2011 KC	AL	48	0	0	11	59.2	244	44	20	19	9	1	1	3	26	6	64	4	0	1	4	.200	0	1-2	11	3.23	2.87
2012 KC	AL	42	0	0	18	51.0	217	41	23	21	10	3	0	1	26	3	65	1	0	0	0	-	0	0-0	2	4.07	3.71
2013 KC	AL	27	0	0	8	29.2	110	19	2	2	1	1	0	1	6	1	32	1	0	3	0	1.000	0	0-0	4	1.45	0.61
2014 KC	AL	31	0	0	10	34.0	154	39	21	21	6	0	1	1	18	1	24	3	0	1	0	1.000	0	1-1	1	6.25	5.56
2015 KC	AL	4	0	0	2	3.0	11	1	0	0	0	0	0	0	2	0	1	0	0	1	0	1.000	0	0-0	0	1.37	0.00
5 ML YEARS		152	0	0	49	177.1	736	144	66	63	26	5	2	6	78	11	186	9	0	6	4	.600	0	2-3	18	3.61	3.20

Tyler Collins

Bats: L **Throws:** L **Pos:** LF-37;DH-10;RF-7;PH-7;PR-1   **Ht:** 5'11" **Wt:** 215 **Born:** 6/6/1990 **Age:** 26

								BATTING												RUNNING			AVERAGES			
Year Team	Lg	G	AB	H	2B	3B	HR	(Hm	Rd)	TB	R	RBI	RC	TBB	IBB	SO	HBP	SH	SF	SB	CS	GDP	Avg	OBP	Slg	OPS
2011 2 Tms	Low	43	166	52	11	1	8	(-	-)	89	30	32	33	12	1	17	3	0	2	6	1	5	.313	.366	.536	.902
2012 Lkland	A+	126	473	137	35	5	7	(-	-)	203	68	66	82	58	2	64	6	0	5	20	3	6	.290	.371	.429	.800
2013 Erie	AA	129	466	112	29	6	21	(-	-)	204	67	79	68	51	1	122	8	0	5	4	5	3	.240	.323	.438	.760
2014 Toledo	AAA	121	468	123	17	2	18	(-	-)	198	63	62	70	49	2	116	4	0	5	12	4	6	.263	.335	.423	.758
2015 Toledo	AAA	53	190	47	10	0	2	(-	-)	63	21	20	24	22	1	40	3	0	3	9	2	3	.247	.330	.332	.662
2014 Det	AL	18	24	6	0	0	1	(0	1)	9	3	4	3	1	0	4	0	0	0	0	0	1	.250	.280	.375	.655
2015 Det	AL	60	192	51	11	3	4	(2	2)	80	18	25	27	13	0	43	1	1	0	2	1	2	.266	.316	.417	.732
2 ML YEARS		78	216	57	11	3	5	(2	3)	89	21	29	30	14	0	47	1	1	0	2	1	3	.264	.312	.412	.724

Josh Collmenter

Pitches: R **Bats:** R **Pos:** RP-32; SP-12   COLE-men-ter   **Ht:** 6'4" **Wt:** 235 **Born:** 2/7/1986 **Age:** 30

				HOW MUCH HE PITCHED					WHAT HE GAVE UP										THE RESULTS							
Year Team	Lg	G	GS	CG	GF	IP	BFP	H	R	ER	HR	SH	SF	HB	TBB	IBB	SO	WP	Bk	W	L	Pct	Sh	Sv-Op	Hld	ERC	ERA
2011 Ari	NL	31	24	0	3	154.1	621	137	61	58	17	9	2	5	28	2	100	1	1	10	10	.500	0	0-0	0	2.82	3.38
2012 Ari	NL	28	11	0	7	90.1	375	92	39	37	13	5	0	0	22	2	80	1	0	5	3	.625	0	0-0	0	3.85	3.69
2013 Ari	NL	49	0	0	10	92.0	384	79	34	32	8	8	0	2	33	8	85	3	0	5	5	.500	0	0-1	5	3.01	3.13
2014 Ari	NL	33	28	1	2	179.1	719	163	75	69	18	8	5	4	39	2	115	2	0	11	9	.550	1	1-1	0	3.02	3.46
2015 Ari	NL	44	12	1	19	121.0	499	129	53	51	18	2	6	1	24	2	63	1	0	4	6	.400	1	1-1	1	4.05	3.79
Postseason		1	1	0	0	7.0	26	2	1	1	1	0	0	1	2	0	6	0	0	1	0	1.000	0	0-0	0	1.18	1.29
5 ML YEARS		185	75	2	41	637.0	2598	600	262	247	74	32	13	12	146	16	443	8	1	35	33	.515	2	2-3	6	3.28	3.49

Alex Colome

Pitches: R **Bats:** R **Pos:** RP-30; SP-13   COHL-oh-may   **Ht:** 6'2" **Wt:** 210 **Born:** 12/31/1988 **Age:** 27

				HOW MUCH HE PITCHED					WHAT HE GAVE UP										THE RESULTS							
Year Team	Lg	G	GS	CG	GF	IP	BFP	H	R	ER	HR	SH	SF	HB	TBB	IBB	SO	WP	Bk	W	L	Pct	Sh	Sv-Op	Hld	ERC	ERA
2013 TB	AL	3	3	0	0	16.0	71	14	8	4	2	0	0	1	9	0	12	1	0	1	1	.500	0	0-0	0	4.41	2.25
2014 TB	AL	5	5	0	1	23.2	97	19	7	7	1	0	1	0	10	0	13	3	0	2	0	1.000	0	0-0	0	2.77	2.66
2015 TB	AL	43	13	0	5	109.2	457	112	50	48	9	2	7	4	31	4	88	8	0	8	5	.615	0	0-5	8	3.78	3.94
3 ML YEARS		51	19	0	6	149.1	625	145	65	59	12	2	8	5	50	4	113	12	0	11	6	.647	0	0-5	8	3.68	3.56

Bartolo Colon

Pitches: R **Bats:** R **Pos:** SP-31; RP-2   co-LONE   **Ht:** 5'11" **Wt:** 285 **Born:** 5/24/1973 **Age:** 43

				HOW MUCH HE PITCHED					WHAT HE GAVE UP										THE RESULTS							
Year Team	Lg	G	GS	CG	GF	IP	BFP	H	R	ER	HR	SH	SF	HB	TBB	IBB	SO	WP	Bk	W	L	Pct	Sh	Sv-Op	Hld	ERC	ERA
1997 Cle	AL	19	17	1	0	94.0	427	107	66	59	12	4	1	3	45	1	66	5	0	4	7	.364	0	0-0	0	5.53	5.65
1998 Cle	AL	31	31	6	0	204.0	883	205	91	84	15	10	2	3	79	5	158	4	0	14	9	.609	2	0-0	0	3.87	3.71
1999 Cle	AL	32	32	1	0	205.0	858	185	97	90	24	5	4	7	76	5	161	4	0	18	5	.783	1	0-0	0	3.68	3.95
2000 Cle	AL	30	30	2	0	188.0	807	163	86	81	21	2	3	4	98	4	212	4	0	15	8	.652	1	0-0	0	3.97	3.88
2001 Cle	AL	34	34	1	0	222.1	947	220	106	101	26	8	4	2	90	2	201	4	1	14	12	.538	0	0-0	0	4.24	4.09

			HOW MUCH HE PITCHED						WHAT HE GAVE UP											THE RESULTS							
Year	Team	Lg	G	GS	CG	GF	IP	BFP	H	R	ER	HR	SH	SF	HB	TBB	IBB	SO	WP	Bk	W	L	Pct	Sh	Sv-Op	Hld	ERC	ERA
2002	2 Tms		33	33	8	0	233.1	966	219	85	76	20	19	6	2	70	5	149	4	0	20	8	.714	3	0-0	0	3.29	2.93
2003	CWS	AL	34	34	9	0	242.0	984	223	107	104	30	5	8	5	71	3	173	8	3	15	13	.536	0	0-0	0	3.47	3.87
2004	LAA	AL	34	34	0	0	208.1	897	215	122	116	38	5	8	5	71	1	158	1	0	18	12	.600	0	0-0	0	4.64	5.01
2005	LAA	AL	33	33	2	0	222.2	906	215	93	86	26	9	4	3	43	0	157	2	1	21	8	.724	0	0-0	0	3.28	3.48
2006	LAA	AL	10	10	1	0	56.1	251	71	39	32	11	4	1	3	11	0	31	1	0	1	5	.167	1	0-0	0	5.61	5.11
2007	LAA	AL	19	18	0	0	99.1	453	132	74	70	15	4	3	5	29	1	76	1	0	6	8	.429	0	0-0	1	6.17	6.34
2008	Bos	AL	7	7	0	0	39.0	173	44	23	17	5	3	2	2	10	0	27	0	0	4	2	.667	0	0-0	0	4.53	3.92
2009	CWS	AL	12	12	0	0	62.1	276	69	42	29	13	4	3	2	21	3	38	1	0	3	6	.333	0	0-0	0	5.22	4.19
2011	NYY	AL	29	26	1	0	164.1	694	172	85	73	21	2	6	3	40	3	135	0	0	8	10	.444	1	0-0	0	3.95	4.00
2012	Oak	AL	24	24	0	0	152.1	636	161	62	58	17	3	4	1	23	3	91	0	0	10	9	.526	0	0-0	0	3.45	3.43
2013	Oak	AL	30	30	3	0	190.1	769	193	60	56	14	3	6	0	29	0	117	1	0	18	6	.750	3	0-0	0	3.07	2.65
2014	NYM	NL	31	31	0	0	202.1	846	218	97	92	22	8	4	5	30	3	151	2	0	15	13	.536	0	0-0	0	3.63	4.09
2015	NYM	NL	33	31	1	1	194.2	815	217	94	90	25	9	7	4	24	5	136	0	0	14	13	.519	1	0-0	0	3.84	4.16
02	Cle	AL	16	16	4	0	116.1	467	104	37	33	11	6	3	2	31	1	75	3	0	10	4	.714	2	0-0	0	3.09	2.55
02	Mon	NL	17	17	4	0	117.0	499	115	48	43	9	13	3	0	39	4	74	1	0	10	4	.714	1	0-0	0	3.48	3.31
	Postseason		10	10	1	0	58.1	241	59	24	24	5	1	1	2	22	1	45	0	0	2	4	.333	0	0-0	0	4.28	3.70
	18 ML YEARS		475	467	36	1	2980.2	12588	3029	1429	1314	355	107	76	57	856	44	2237	42	5	218	154	.586	13	0-0	1	3.92	3.97

Christian Colon

Bats: R **Throws:** R **Pos:** SS-21;2B-14;3B-8;PH-3;PR-3   co-LONE   **Ht:** 5'10" **Wt:** 190 **Born:** 5/14/1989 **Age:** 27

			BATTING																RUNNING			AVERAGES			
Year	Team	Lg	G	AB	H	2B	3B	HR	(Hm | Rd)	TB	R	RBI	RC	TBB	IBB	SO	HBP	SH	SF	SB	CS	GDP	Avg	OBP	Slg	OPS
2011	NWArk	AA	127	491	126	14	2	8	(- | -)	168	69	61	60	46	5	51	6	21	4	17	7	17	.257	.325	.342	.668
2012	NWArk	AA	73	273	79	9	2	5	(- | -)	107	33	27	42	31	0	27	2	7	2	12	6	5	.289	.364	.392	.756
2013	Omha	AAA	131	512	140	12	3	12	(- | -)	194	72	58	70	41	1	57	7	15	2	15	4	16	.273	.335	.379	.713
2014	Omha	AAA	86	344	107	18	0	8	(- | -)	149	55	47	58	30	0	29	3	6	5	15	4	9	.311	.366	.433	.800
2015	Omha	AAA	51	192	54	9	0	1	(- | -)	66	19	17	26	21	1	18	1	2	1	8	2	8	.281	.353	.344	.697
2014	KC	AL	21	45	15	5	1	0	(0 | 0)	22	8	6	9	3	0	4	0	1	0	2	0	1	.333	.375	.489	.864
2015	KC	AL	43	107	31	5	0	0	(0 | 0)	36	8	6	12	11	0	17	0	1	0	3	2	2	.290	.356	.336	.692
	Postseason		2	1	1	0	0	0	(0 | 0)	1	1	1	1	0	0	0	0	1	0	1	0	0	1.000	1.000	1.000	2.000
	2 ML YEARS		64	152	46	10	1	0	(0 | 0)	58	16	12	21	14	0	21	0	2	0	5	2	3	.303	.361	.382	.743

Michael Conforto

Bats: L **Throws:** R **Pos:** LF-50;PH-7   **Ht:** 6'1" **Wt:** 215 **Born:** 3/1/1993 **Age:** 23

			BATTING																RUNNING			AVERAGES			
Year	Team	Lg	G	AB	H	2B	3B	HR	(Hm	Rd)	TB	R	RBI	RC	TBB	IBB	SO	HBP	SH	SF	SB	CS	GDP	Avg	OBP	Slg	OPS
2014	Bklyn	A-	42	163	54	10	0	3	(-	-)	73	30	19	31	16	0	29	5	0	2	3	0	8	.331	.403	.448	.851
2015	StLuci	A+	46	184	52	12	0	7	(-	-)	85	25	28	30	17	6	26	3	0	2	0	1	8	.283	.350	.462	.811
2015	Bnghtn	AA	45	173	54	12	3	5	(-	-)	87	21	26	34	23	1	35	1	0	0	1	0	2	.312	.396	.503	.899
2015	NYM	NL	56	174	47	14	0	9	(4	5)	88	30	26	29	17	0	39	1	0	2	0	1	4	.270	.335	.506	.841

Hank Conger

Bats: B **Throws:** R **Pos:** C-69;PH-10;LF-1;PR-1   KONG-gerr   **Ht:** 6'2" **Wt:** 220 **Born:** 1/29/1988 **Age:** 28

			BATTING																RUNNING			AVERAGES			
Year	Team	Lg	G	AB	H	2B	3B	HR	(Hm	Rd)	TB	R	RBI	RC	TBB	IBB	SO	HBP	SH	SF	SB	CS	GDP	Avg	OBP	Slg	OPS
2010	LAA	AL	13	29	5	1	1	0	(0	0)	8	2	5	3	5	0	9	0	0	0	0	0	1	.172	.294	.276	.570
2011	LAA	AL	59	177	37	8	0	6	(2	4)	63	14	19	18	17	2	37	1	2	0	0	0	2	.209	.282	.356	.638
2012	LAA	AL	7	18	3	0	0	0	(0	0)	3	0	1	1	1	0	0	1	1	1	0	0	1	.167	.238	.167	.405
2013	LAA	AL	92	233	58	13	1	7	(3	4)	94	23	21	24	17	2	61	4	0	1	0	0	6	.249	.310	.403	.713
2014	LAA	AL	80	231	51	12	0	4	(3	1)	75	24	25	25	22	0	57	2	4	1	0	2	6	.221	.293	.325	.618
2015	Hou	AL	73	201	46	11	0	11	(8	3)	90	25	33	26	23	0	63	2	1	2	0	1	6	.229	.311	.448	.759
	Postseason		1	1	0	0	0	0	(0	0)	0	0	0	0	0	0	1	0	0	0	0	0	0	.000	.000	.000	.000
	6 ML YEARS		324	889	200	45	2	28	(16	12)	333	88	104	97	85	4	227	10	8	5	0	4	22	.225	.298	.375	.673

Adam Conley

Pitches: L **Bats:** L **Pos:** SP-11; RP-4   **Ht:** 6'3" **Wt:** 185 **Born:** 5/24/1990 **Age:** 26

			HOW MUCH HE PITCHED						WHAT HE GAVE UP											THE RESULTS							
Year	Team	Lg	G	GS	CG	GF	IP	BFP	H	R	ER	HR	SH	SF	HB	TBB	IBB	SO	WP	Bk	W	L	Pct	Sh	Sv-Op	Hld	ERC	ERA
2012	2 Tms	Low	26	26	0	0	127.0	534	117	59	49	4	1	6	3	43	0	135	8	1	11	5	.688	0	0- -	-	3.04	3.47
2013	Jaxnvl	AA	26	25	3	0	138.2	581	125	61	50	7	4	2	7	37	0	129	1	0	11	7	.611	1	0- -	-	2.86	3.25
2014	NewOr	AAA	12	11	0	1	60.0	266	65	41	40	3	3	1	3	26	0	48	1	0	3	5	.375	0	0- -	-	4.54	6.00
2015	NewOr	AAA	19	18	1	0	107.0	436	85	34	30	4	2	1	5	40	1	81	1	0	9	3	.750	1	0- -	-	2.68	2.52
2015	Mia	NL	15	11	0	1	67.0	281	65	28	28	7	1	4	3	21	1	59	0	0	4	1	.800	0	0-0	-	3.80	3.76

Carlos Contreras

Pitches: R **Bats:** R **Pos:** RP-22   conn-TRAIR-us   **Ht:** 5'11" **Wt:** 215 **Born:** 1/8/1991 **Age:** 25

			HOW MUCH HE PITCHED						WHAT HE GAVE UP											THE RESULTS							
Year	Team	Lg	G	GS	CG	GF	IP	BFP	H	R	ER	HR	SH	SF	HB	TBB	IBB	SO	WP	Bk	W	L	Pct	Sh	Sv-Op	Hld	ERC	ERA
2011	Billings	R+	18	0	0	2	36.0	165	35	20	20	5	1	1	5	23	1	38	5	0	2	1	.667	0	0- -	-	5.78	5.00
2012	2 Tms	Low	49	0	0	33	60.2	252	38	27	21	7	1	1	3	24	1	63	4	0	1	1	.500	0	20- -	-	2.28	3.12
2013	Bkrsfld	A+	18	18	0	0	90.0	377	70	43	38	9	3	3	4	41	1	96	7	3	5	7	.417	0	0- -	-	3.25	3.80
2013	Pnscla	AA	8	8	0	0	42.1	183	36	13	13	2	5	2	4	21	2	26	2	0	3	2	.600	0	0- -	-	3.55	2.76
2014	Pnscla	AA	9	3	0	3	20.0	89	15	7	6	0	0	0	1	9	0	27	3	0	2	1	.667	0	0- -	-	2.64	2.70

Year Team	Lg	G	GS	CG	GF	IP	BFP	H	R	ER	HR	SH	SF	HB	TBB	IBB	SO	WP	Bk	W	L	Pct	Sh	Sv-Op	Hld	ERC	ERA
		HOW MUCH HE PITCHED						**WHAT HE GAVE UP**												**THE RESULTS**							
2015 Lsvlle	AAA	31	0	0	12	39.2	178	32	13	13	3	2	2	0	30	4	55	6	0	2	2	.500	0	3--	-	3.99	2.95
2014 Cin	NL	17	0	0	8	19.1	94	19	16	14	2	0	1	0	17	0	19	3	1	0	1	.000	0	0-1	0	5.79	6.52
2015 Cin	NL	22	0	0	8	28.0	125	22	16	15	3	1	0	1	20	0	19	3	0	0	0	-	0	0-0	0	4.27	4.82
2 ML YEARS		39	0	0	16	47.1	219	41	32	29	5	1	1	1	37	0	38	6	1	0	1	.000	0	0-1	0	4.88	5.51

Ryan Cook

Pitches: R Bats: R Pos: RP-9   **Ht: 6'2" Wt: 215 Born: 6/30/1987 Age: 29**

Year Team	Lg	G	GS	CG	GF	IP	BFP	H	R	ER	HR	SH	SF	HB	TBB	IBB	SO	WP	Bk	W	L	Pct	Sh	Sv-Op	Hld	ERC	ERA
		HOW MUCH HE PITCHED						**WHAT HE GAVE UP**												**THE RESULTS**							
2015 Nashv*	AAA	30	0	0	20	33.1	143	32	16	15	3	1	1	3	14	1	26	2	0	4	1	.800	0	8--	-	4.25	4.05
2015 Pwtckt*	AAA	7	0	0	6	9.1	32	2	0	0	0	0	0	0	2	0	10	0	0	0	0	-	0	1--	-	0.30	0.00
2011 Ari	NL	12	0	0	5	7.2	41	11	6	6	0	0	0	0	8	0	7	1	1	0	1	.000	0	0-0	1	8.56	7.04
2012 Oak	AL	71	0	0	23	73.1	288	42	18	17	4	3	1	4	27	4	80	4	0	6	2	.750	0	14-21	21	1.68	2.09
2013 Oak	AL	71	0	0	13	67.1	294	62	22	19	2	0	4	4	25	1	67	7	0	6	4	.600	0	2-9	23	3.16	2.54
2014 Oak	AL	54	0	0	15	50.0	202	32	19	19	3	2	2	2	22	1	50	3	0	1	3	.250	0	1-3	7	2.23	3.42
2015 2 Tms	AL	9	0	0	1	8.2	54	20	19	18	4	0	0	0	7	0	6	1	0	0	2	.000	0	0-0	1	18.15	18.69
15 Oak	AL	4	0	0	0	4.1	23	7	5	5	0	0	0	0	3	0	3	0	0	0	2	.000	0	0-0	0	8.02	10.38
15 Bos	AL	5	0	0	1	4.1	31	13	14	13	4	0	0	0	4	0	3	1	0	0	0	-	0	0-0	1	29.66	27.00
Postseason		5	0	0	1	4.0	20	5	5	5	0	1	0	1	2	0	5	1	0	1	0	1.000	0	0-1	1	5.98	11.25
5 ML YEARS		217	0	0	57	207.0	879	167	84	79	13	5	7	10	89	6	210	16	1	13	12	.520	0	17-33	53	3.00	3.43

Tim Cooney

Pitches: L Bats: L Pos: SP-6   **Ht: 6'3" Wt: 195 Born: 12/19/1990 Age: 25**

Year Team	Lg	G	GS	CG	GF	IP	BFP	H	R	ER	HR	SH	SF	HB	TBB	IBB	SO	WP	Bk	W	L	Pct	Sh	Sv-Op	Hld	ERC	ERA
		HOW MUCH HE PITCHED						**WHAT HE GAVE UP**												**THE RESULTS**							
2012 Batvia	A-	13	11	1	1	55.2	220	56	24	21	4	0	1	2	8	0	43	4	0	3	3	.500	0	0--	-	3.22	3.40
2013 PlmBh	A+	6	6	1	0	36.0	146	38	14	11	1	1	1	1	4	0	23	0	0	3	3	.500	0	0--	-	2.95	2.75
2013 Sprgfld	AA	20	20	0	0	118.1	496	132	58	50	8	5	2	6	18	1	125	6	3	7	10	.412	0	0--	-	3.74	3.80
2014 Memp	AAA	26	25	1	0	158.0	663	158	66	61	21	6	3	6	47	0	119	7	0	14	6	.700	1	0--	-	4.11	3.47
2015 Memp	AAA	14	14	1	0	88.2	339	61	32	27	9	4	1	4	16	1	63	3	0	6	4	.600	1	0--	-	1.88	2.74
2015 StL	NL	6	6	0	0	31.1	130	28	12	11	3	3	0	1	10	2	29	1	0	1	0	1.000	0	0-0	0	3.20	3.16

Scott Copeland

Pitches: R Bats: R Pos: SP-3; RP-2   **Ht: 6'3" Wt: 215 Born: 12/15/1987 Age: 28**

Year Team	Lg	G	GS	CG	GF	IP	BFP	H	R	ER	HR	SH	SF	HB	TBB	IBB	SO	WP	Bk	W	L	Pct	Sh	Sv-Op	Hld	ERC	ERA
		HOW MUCH HE PITCHED						**WHAT HE GAVE UP**												**THE RESULTS**							
2011 2 Tms	Low	26	26	0	0	141.2	638	161	96	87	10	4	4	10	61	1	77	16	0	8	11	.421	0	0--	-	5.06	5.53
2012 2 Tms	Low	25	24	2	0	123.0	575	153	94	77	12	5	5	13	52	1	96	12	1	7	9	.438	0	0--	-	5.99	5.63
2013 Dnedin	A+	26	23	2	0	146.2	638	158	75	61	9	5	3	7	52	0	99	11	1	9	8	.529	0	0--	-	4.27	3.74
2014 Nham	AA	27	22	1	1	139.2	601	140	72	58	11	3	1	10	48	0	89	12	0	8	8	.500	0	0--	-	4.02	3.74
2015 Buffalo	AAA	21	20	0	0	125.0	518	119	44	41	8	0	2	4	37	0	66	5	0	11	6	.647	0	0--	-	3.34	2.95
2015 Tor	AL	5	3	0	2	15.1	69	24	11	11	1	1	1	0	2	0	6	0	0	1	1	.500	0	0-0	0	6.16	6.46

Patrick Corbin

Pitches: L Bats: L Pos: SP-16   **Ht: 6'3" Wt: 210 Born: 7/19/1989 Age: 26**

Year Team	Lg	G	GS	CG	GF	IP	BFP	H	R	ER	HR	SH	SF	HB	TBB	IBB	SO	WP	Bk	W	L	Pct	Sh	Sv-Op	Hld	ERC	ERA
		HOW MUCH HE PITCHED						**WHAT HE GAVE UP**												**THE RESULTS**							
2012 Ari	NL	22	17	0	3	107.0	454	117	56	54	14	2	5	4	25	2	86	1	0	6	8	.429	0	1-1	0	4.31	4.54
2013 Ari	NL	32	32	3	0	208.1	860	189	81	79	19	8	4	9	54	1	178	13	0	14	8	.636	0	0-0	0	3.14	3.41
2015 Ari	NL	16	16	0	0	85.0	357	91	34	34	9	2	1	2	17	0	78	4	0	6	5	.545	0	0-0	0	3.82	3.60
3 ML YEARS		70	65	3	3	400.1	1671	397	171	167	42	12	7	15	96	3	342	18	0	26	21	.553	0	1-1	0	3.59	3.75

Erik Cordier

Pitches: R Bats: R Pos: RP-8   cor-dee-YAY   **Ht: 6'4" Wt: 215 Born: 2/25/1986 Age: 30**

Year Team	Lg	G	GS	CG	GF	IP	BFP	H	R	ER	HR	SH	SF	HB	TBB	IBB	SO	WP	Bk	W	L	Pct	Sh	Sv-Op	Hld	ERC	ERA
		HOW MUCH HE PITCHED						**WHAT HE GAVE UP**												**THE RESULTS**							
2011 Gwnntt	AAA	19	19	0	0	86.0	392	88	55	49	9	2	3	7	51	1	61	10	0	5	8	.385	0	0--	-	5.37	5.13
2012 Gwnntt	AAA	8	4	0	0	24.2	113	27	15	12	1	0	0	1	21	0	15	4	0	1	1	.500	0	0--	-	6.55	4.38
2012 Missi	AA	5	0	0	1	4.0	26	8	9	9	0	0	1	1	5	0	6	3	0	0	2	.000	0	0--	-	14.34	20.25
2013 Indy	AAA	44	0	0	11	53.0	232	51	29	27	3	0	3	2	28	1	65	4	0	4	2	.667	0	4--	-	4.21	4.58
2014 Fresno	AAA	47	0	0	23	52.2	229	40	22	21	4	4	0	3	31	1	68	11	0	4	3	.571	0	3--	3.47	3.47	3.59
2015 Scrmto	AAA	31	0	0	16	34.2	150	20	9	4	0	2	4	0	25	0	43	5	0	2	1	.667	0	9--	-	2.27	1.04
2014 SF	NL	7	0	0	2	6.0	28	5	4	1	0	0	0	3	2	0	9	1	0	0	0	-	0	0-0	0	3.93	1.50
2015 Mia	NL	8	0	0	0	12.1	56	13	8	8	1	0	1	1	6	1	7	0	1	0	0	-	0	0-0	0	4.74	5.84
2 ML YEARS		15	0	0	2	18.1	84	18	12	9	1	0	1	4	8	1	16	1	1	0	0	-	0	0-0	0	4.47	4.42

John Cornely

Pitches: R Bats: R Pos: RP-1   Ht: 6'1" Wt: 205 Born: 5/17/1989 Age: 27

			HOW MUCH HE PITCHED						WHAT HE GAVE UP											THE RESULTS						
Year	Team	Lg	G	GS	CG	GF	IP	BFP	H	R	ER	HR	SH	SF	HB	TBB	IBB	SO	WP	Bk	W	L	Pct	Sh	Sv-Op	Hld	ERC	ERA
2011	Danvle	R+	15	0	0	4	33.0	135	19	13	8	3	0	1	0	19	0	50	3	0	3	1	.750	0	1--	-	2.45	2.18
2012	2 Tms	Low	43	0	0	29	58.2	260	47	20	20	5	0	0	0	38	0	94	5	0	1	3	.250	0	8--	-	3.75	3.07
2013	Lynbrg	A+	42	0	0	34	50.2	215	40	22	19	9	0	1	0	24	1	70	2	0	4	1	.800	0	11--	-	3.65	3.38
2014	Missi	AA	46	0	0	19	68.2	284	45	19	19	2	3	4	1	34	4	71	3	0	7	3	.700	0	7--	-	2.12	2.49
2015	Gwnntt	AAA	12	0	0	5	18.1	77	15	10	9	2	1	0	0	7	0	24	0	0	2	2	.500	0	1--	-	3.03	4.42
2015	Portlnd	AA	29	0	0	21	39.0	171	25	20	19	3	4	2	1	29	1	38	6	0	0	2	.000	0	2--	-	3.26	4.38
2015	Atl	NL	1	0	0	1	1.0	7	3	4	4	1	0	0	0	1	0	1	0	0	0	0	-	0	0-0	0	32.12	36.00

Carlos Corporan

Bats: B Throws: R Pos: C-31;PH-3;DH-1   KOHR-pohr-an   Ht: 6'2" Wt: 240 Born: 1/7/1984 Age: 32

						BATTING															RUNNING			AVERAGES			
Year	Team	Lg	G	AB	H	2B	3B	HR	(Hm	Rd)	TB	R	RBI	RC	TBB	IBB	SO	HBP	SH	SF	SB	CS	GDP	Avg	OBP	Slg	OPS
2009	Mil	NL	1	1	1	0	0	0	(0	0)	1	1	0	1	0	0	0	0	0	0	0	0	0	1.000	1.000	1.000	2.000
2011	Hou	NL	52	154	29	0	0	4	(0	0)	39	9	11	11	10	4	49	4	3	2	0	0	5	.188	.253	.253	.506
2012	Hou	NL	27	78	21	2	0	4	(3	1)	35	5	13	7	4	0	19	1	1	0	0	1	2	.269	.310	.449	.758
2013	Hou	AL	64	191	43	5	0	7	(4	3)	69	16	20	15	10	1	60	7	1	1	0	0	3	.225	.287	.361	.648
2014	Hou	AL	55	170	40	6	0	6	(5	1)	64	22	19	19	14	0	37	3	1	2	0	0	3	.235	.302	.376	.678
2015	Tex	AL	33	107	19	4	0	3	(2	1)	32	10	15	9	6	0	40	4	2	2	0	0	1	.178	.244	.299	.543
	6 ML YEARS		232	701	153	25	1	20	(14	6)	240	63	78	62	44	5	205	19	8	8	0	1	14	.218	.280	.342	.622

Carlos Correa

Bats: R Throws: R Pos: SS-99   coh-RAY-uh   Ht: 6'4" Wt: 210 Born: 9/22/1994 Age: 21

						BATTING															RUNNING			AVERAGES			
Year	Team	Lg	G	AB	H	2B	3B	HR	(Hm	Rd)	TB	R	RBI	RC	TBB	IBB	SO	HBP	SH	SF	SB	CS	GDP	Avg	OBP	Slg	OPS
2012	2 Tms	Low	50	190	49	14	2	3	(-	-)	76	28	12	24	12	1	44	1	1	0	6	1	1	.258	.305	.400	.705
2013	QuadC	A	117	450	144	33	3	9	(-	-)	210	73	86	86	58	4	83	8	1	2	10	10	6	.320	.405	.467	.872
2014	Lancst	A+	62	249	81	16	6	6	(-	-)	127	50	57	56	36	0	45	5	0	3	20	4	9	.325	.416	.510	.926
2015	CpChr	AA	29	117	45	15	2	7	(-	-)	85	25	32	37	15	1	25	1	0	0	15	0	3	.385	.459	.726	1.185
2015	Fresno	AAA	24	98	27	6	1	3	(-	-)	44	19	12	16	12	1	14	0	0	3	3	1	2	.276	.345	.449	.794
2015	Hou	AL	99	387	108	22	1	22	(12	10)	198	52	68	68	40	2	78	1	0	4	14	4	10	.279	.345	.512	.857

Kevin Correia

Pitches: R Bats: R Pos: SP-5   kore-AY-ah   Ht: 6'3" Wt: 200 Born: 8/24/1980 Age: 35

					HOW MUCH HE PITCHED							WHAT HE GAVE UP											THE RESULTS						
Year	Team	Lg	G	GS	CG	GF	IP	BFP	H	R	ER	HR	SH	SF	HB	TBB	IBB	SO	WP	Bk	W	L	Pct	Sh	Sv-Op	Hld	ERC	ERA
2015	Scrmto*	AAA	6	6	0	0	37.2	155	34	18	15	4	2	4	1	11	0	25	1	0	0	1	.000	0	0--	-	3.30	3.58
2003	SF	NL	10	7	0	1	39.1	173	41	16	16	6	1	1	4	18	1	28	2	0	3	1	.750	0	0-0	0	5.46	3.66
2004	SF	NL	12	1	0	5	19.0	92	25	20	17	3	3	3	1	10	0	14	0	0	1	0	1.000	0	0-0	0	7.12	8.05
2005	SF	NL	16	11	0	1	58.1	264	61	31	30	12	5	1	4	31	2	44	2	0	2	5	.286	0	0-0	0	5.94	4.63
2006	SF	NL	48	0	0	9	69.2	295	64	27	27	5	1	4	3	22	0	57	0	0	2	0	1.000	0	0-1	10	3.25	3.49
2007	SF	NL	59	8	0	9	101.2	437	94	39	39	9	4	3	2	40	7	80	1	1	4	7	.364	0	0-3	12	3.48	3.45
2008	SF	NL	25	19	0	2	110.0	514	141	80	74	15	3	5	4	47	3	66	5	0	3	8	.273	0	0-0	0	6.19	6.05
2009	SD	NL	33	33	1	0	198.0	830	194	92	86	17	9	3	4	64	6	142	5	1	12	11	.522	1	0-0	0	3.64	3.91
2010	SD	NL	28	26	0	0	145.0	641	152	89	87	20	6	5	5	64	6	115	3	0	10	10	.500	0	0-0	0	4.87	5.40
2011	Pit	NL	27	26	1	1	154.0	660	175	90	82	24	7	2	2	39	0	77	3	1	12	11	.522	0	0-0	0	4.74	4.79
2012	Pit	NL	32	28	0	0	171.0	728	176	89	80	20	14	7	3	46	2	89	2	0	12	11	.522	0	0-0	0	3.86	4.21
2013	Min	AL	31	31	0	0	185.1	792	218	89	86	24	6	5	2	45	1	101	2	0	9	13	.409	0	0-0	0	4.77	4.18
2014	2 Tms	NL	32	26	0	3	154.0	687	191	104	93	20	2	6	5	40	2	79	7	1	7	17	.292	0	0-0	0	5.19	5.44
2015	Phi	NL	5	5	0	0	23.1	114	37	23	17	4	2	2	0	8	0	14	0	0	0	3	.000	0	0-0	0	7.90	6.56
14	Min	AL	23	23	0	0	129.1	572	157	76	71	13	1	5	5	32	1	61	3	1	5	13	.278	0	0-0	0	4.80	4.94
14	LAD	NL	9	3	0	3	24.2	115	34	28	22	7	1	1	0	8	1	18	4	0	2	4	.333	0	0-0	0	7.30	8.03
	13 ML YEARS		358	221	2	31	1428.2	6227	1569	789	734	179	63	47	39	474	30	906	32	4	76	98	.437	1	0-4	22	4.62	4.62

Jarred Cosart

Pitches: R Bats: R Pos: SP-13; RP-1   KOH-zart   Ht: 6'3" Wt: 195 Born: 5/25/1990 Age: 26

					HOW MUCH HE PITCHED							WHAT HE GAVE UP											THE RESULTS						
Year	Team	Lg	G	GS	CG	GF	IP	BFP	H	R	ER	HR	SH	SF	HB	TBB	IBB	SO	WP	Bk	W	L	Pct	Sh	Sv-Op	Hld	ERC	ERA
2013	Hou	AL	10	10	0	0	60.0	246	46	15	13	3	0	2	0	35	0	33	3	0	1	1	.500	0	0-0	0	3.31	1.95
2014	2 Tms		30	30	0	0	180.1	766	173	80	74	9	3	8	3	73	1	115	7	0	13	11	.542	0	0-0	0	3.61	3.69
2015	Mia	NL	14	13	0	0	69.2	296	63	35	35	10	2	1	1	33	1	47	7	0	2	5	.286	0	0-0	0	4.24	4.52
14	Hou	AL	20	20	0	0	116.1	507	119	61	57	7	2	6	3	51	1	75	7	0	9	7	.563	0	0-0	0	4.18	4.41
14	Mia	NL	10	10	0	0	64.0	259	54	19	17	2	1	2	0	22	0	40	0	0	4	4	.500	0	0-0	0	2.64	2.39
	3 ML YEARS		54	53	0	0	310.0	1308	282	130	122	22	5	11	4	141	2	195	17	0	16	17	.485	0	0-0	0	3.69	3.54

Caleb Cotham

Pitches: R Bats: R Pos: RP-12   COTH-im   Ht: 6'3" Wt: 215 Born: 11/6/1987 Age: 28

					HOW MUCH HE PITCHED							WHAT HE GAVE UP											THE RESULTS						
Year	Team	Lg	G	GS	CG	GF	IP	BFP	H	R	ER	HR	SH	SF	HB	TBB	IBB	SO	WP	Bk	W	L	Pct	Sh	Sv-Op	Hld	ERC	ERA
2011	2 Tms	Low	13	1	0	0	23.0	104	23	9	5	1	0	1	0	10	0	32	1	0	0	1	.000	0	0--	-	3.63	1.96
2012	2 Tms	Low	23	19	0	0	101.1	422	103	44	41	5	0	2	3	29	2	76	2	0	5	7	.417	0	0--	-	3.53	3.64
2013	Trntn	AA	7	6	0	1	29.0	126	27	13	12	1	1	0	2	13	0	26	1	0	2	1	.667	0	0--	-	3.68	3.72
2013	S-WB	AAA	21	17	0	0	95.1	428	115	64	58	11	2	7	7	34	0	60	3	2	6	6	.500	0	0--	-	5.57	5.48

118

118

			HOW MUCH HE PITCHED				WHAT HE GAVE UP												THE RESULTS							
Year	Team	Lg	G GS CG GF	IP	BFP	H	R	ER	HR	SH	SF	HB	TBB	IBB	SO	WP	Bk	W	L	Pct	Sh	Sv-Op	Hld	ERC	ERA
2014	S-WB	AAA	5 5 0 0	18.1	86	25	14	11	1	0	0	0	7	0	17	1	1	0	2	.000	0	0--	-	5.70	5.40
2014	Trntn	AA	5 5 0 0	25.1	106	25	17	17	3	0	0	0	13	0	16	1	0	0	2	.000	0	0--	-	4.86	6.04
2014	3 Tms	Low	8 1 0 2	10.0	38	7	0	0	0	0	0	0	0	0	11	1	0	0	0	-	0	0--	-	1.19	0.00
2015	Trntn	AA	15 0 0 5	26.0	105	20	8 .	8	1	0	0	1	8	0	31	1	0	4	2	.667	0	1--	-	2.29	2.77
2015	S-WB	AAA	20 0 0 12	31.0	124	25	7	6	1	0	1	2	5	0	30	2	0	2	2	.500	0	1--	-	2.01	1.74
2015	NYY	AL	12 0 0 4	9.2	45	14	7	7	4	0	0	0	1	0	11	0	0	1	0	1.000	0	0-0	0	7.50	6.52

Neal Cotts

Pitches: L **Bats:** L **Pos:** RP-68 **Ht:** 6'2" **Wt:** 200 **Born:** 3/25/1980 **Age:** 36

			HOW MUCH HE PITCHED				WHAT HE GAVE UP												THE RESULTS							
Year	Team	Lg	G GS CG GF	IP	BFP	H	R	ER	HR	SH	SF	HB	TBB	IBB	SO	WP	Bk	W	L	Pct	Sh	Sv-Op	Hld	ERC	ERA
2003	CWS	AL	4 4 0 0	13.1	69	15	12	12	1	1	0	0	17	0	10	0	0	1	1	.500	0	0-0	-	8.43	8.10
2004	CWS	AL	56 1 0 12	65.1	281	61	45	41	13	0	1	3	30	2	58	8	0	4	4	.500	0	0-2	4	4.84	5.65
2005	CWS	AL	69 0 0 10	60.1	248	38	15	13	1	0	3	4	29	5	58	3	0	4	0	1.000	0	0-2	13	2.03	1.94
2006	CWS	AL	70 0 0 14	54.0	251	64	33	31	12	3	1	3	24	6	43	3	0	1	2	.333	0	1-4	14	6.24	5.17
2007	ChC	NL	16 0 0 4	16.2	76	15	9	9	1	1	2	3	9	0	14	0	0	0	1	.000	0	0-0	2	4.41	4.86
2008	ChC	NL	50 0 0 7	35.2	160	38	18	17	7	3	0	1	13	2	43	3	0	0	2	.000	0	0-2	9	4.87	4.29
2009	ChC	NL	19 0 0 3	11.0	55	14	9	9	3	0	0	1	9	0	9	0	0	0	2	.000	0	0-1	2	9.64	7.36
2013	Tex	AL	58 0 0 6	57.0	223	36	8	7	2	2	3	0	18	1	65	3	0	8	3	.727	0	1-4	11	1.57	1.11
2014	Tex	AL	73 0 0 18	66.2	286	66	33	32	6	2	1	3	23	3	63	4	2	2	9	.182	0	2-9	19	3.84	4.32
2015	2 Tms		68 0 0 10	63.1	269	58	26	24	12	3	2	4	22	2	58	2	0	1	0	1.000	0	0-0	5	4.21	3.41
15	Mil	NL	51 0 0 9	49.2	209	44	18	18	9	3	1	3	17	2	49	2	0	1	0	1.000	0	0-0	4	3.95	3.26
15	Min	AL	17 0 0 1	13.2	60	14	8	6	3	0	1	1	5	0	9	0	0	0	0	-	0	0-0	1	5.22	3.95
	Postseason		8 0 0 3	4.0	16	2	0	0	0	0	0	0	2	0	5	0	0	1	0	1.000	0	0-0	2	1.41	0.00
10 ML YEARS			483 5 0 84	443.1	1918	405	208	195	58	15	13	22	194	21	421	26	2	21	24	.467	0	4-24	79	4.06	3.96

Daniel Coulombe

Pitches: L **Bats:** L **Pos:** RP-14 KOO-lohm **Ht:** 5'10" **Wt:** 190 **Born:** 10/26/1989 **Age:** 26

			HOW MUCH HE PITCHED				WHAT HE GAVE UP												THE RESULTS							
Year	Team	Lg	G GS CG GF	IP	BFP	H	R	ER	HR	SH	SF	HB	TBB	IBB	SO	WP	Bk	W	L	Pct	Sh	Sv-Op	Hld	ERC	ERA
2012	2 Tms	Low	23 0 0 5	25.1	120	18	10	9	0	4	1	3	18	4	37	7	0	0	1	.000	0	1--	-	2.86	3.20
2013	Rcuca	A+	54 0 0 16	66.2	301	46	37	30	7	5	2	2	48	3	85	17	0	4	2	.667	0	1--	-	3.52	4.05
2014	Rcuca	A+	31 0 0 13	44.1	181	33	16	15	3	3	0	1	17	0	61	8	0	3	0	1.000	0	5--	-	2.54	3.05
2014	Chatt	AA	18 0 0 3	21.0	92	18	9	6	1	1	1	2	10	1	31	0	0	0	0	-	0	1--	-	3.45	2.57
2015	OkCity	AAA	38 0 0 9	41.1	178	35	16	15	1	2	1	2	24	0	41	1	0	3	1	.750	0	1--	-	3.58	3.27
2014	LAD	NL	5 0 0 0	4.1	22	5	3	2	1	0	0	0	2	0	4	2	0	0	0	-	0	0-0	0	5.49	4.15
2015	2 Tms		14 0 0 4	16.0	72	17	10	10	0	0	0	2	9	0	11	2	0	0	0	-	0	0-1	0	4.32	5.63
15	LAD	NL	5 0 0 3	8.1	40	9	7	7	0	0	0	0	6	0	7	1	0	0	0	-	0	0-0	0	4.87	7.56
15	Oak	AL	9 0 0 1	7.2	32	8	3	3	0	0	0	2	3	0	4	1	0	0	0	-	0	0-1	0	3.72	3.52
2 ML YEARS			19 0 0 4	20.1	94	22	13	12	1	0	0	2	11	0	15	4	0	0	0	-	0	0-1	0	4.60	5.31

Kaleb Cowart

Bats: B **Throws:** R **Pos:** 3B-33;PR-8 **Ht:** 6'3" **Wt:** 225 **Born:** 6/2/1992 **Age:** 24

							BATTING													RUNNING			AVERAGES			
Year	Team	Lg	G	AB	H	2B	3B	HR	(Hm Rd)	TB	R	RBI	RC	TBB	IBB	SO	HBP	SH	SF	SB	CS	GDP	Avg	OBP	Slg	OPS
2011	Orem	R+	72	283	80	12	3	7	(- -)	119	49	40	43	25	0	81	5	0	6	11	4	8	.283	.345	.420	.765
2012	2 Tms	Low	135	526	145	31	7	16	(- -)	238	90	103	89	67	0	111	4	1	7	14	7	11	.276	.358	.452	.810
2013	Ark	AA	132	498	110	20	1	6	(- -)	150	48	42	43	38	0	124	3	4	7	14	5	11	.221	.289	.301	.580
2014	Ark	AA	126	435	97	18	4	6	(- -)	141	48	54	46	43	2	99	3	2	4	26	7	12	.223	.295	.324	.619
2015	InldEm	A+	51	194	47	14	4	2	(- -)	75	32	23	27	22	0	43	3	0	2	10	2	10	.242	.326	.387	.712
2015	Salt Lk	AAA	62	220	71	13	3	6	(- -)	108	35	45	43	29	2	64	0	0	4	2	1	3	.323	.395	.491	.886
2015	LAA	AL	34	46	8	2	0	1	(1 0)	13	8	4	3	5	0	19	0	1	0	1	1	1	.174	.255	.283	.538

Collin Cowgill

Bats: R **Throws:** L **Pos:** LF-41;PR-10;PH-9;CF-4;RF-4 **Ht:** 5'9" **Wt:** 185 **Born:** 5/22/1986 **Age:** 30

							BATTING													RUNNING			AVERAGES			
Year	Team	Lg	G	AB	H	2B	3B	HR	(Hm Rd)	TB	R	RBI	RC	TBB	IBB	SO	HBP	SH	SF	SB	CS	GDP	Avg	OBP	Slg	OPS
2015	Salt Lk*	AAA	12	44	16	3	0	1	(- -)	22	5	4	8	2	0	5	1	0	0	0	0	0	.364	.404	.500	.904
2011	Ari	NL	37	92	22	3	0	1	(1 0)	28	8	9	8	8	1	28	0	0	0	4	2	0	.239	.300	.304	.604
2012	Oak	AL	38	104	28	2	0	1	(1 0)	33	10	9	14	11	0	27	0	0	1	3	4	3	.269	.336	.317	.654
2013	2 Tms		73	152	32	5	2	4	(3 1)	53	18	16	12	7	0	42	0	3	0	1	0	1	.211	.245	.349	.594
2014	LAA	AL	106	260	65	10	1	5	(2 3)	92	37	21	31	26	0	74	5	2	0	4	0	4	.250	.330	.354	.684
2015	LAA	AL	55	69	13	2	1	1	(0 1)	20	10	2	3	4	0	19	0	1	0	2	1	1	.188	.233	.290	.523
13	NYM	NL	23	61	11	2	0	2	(2 0)	19	7	8	5	2	0	15	0	0	0	0	0	0	.180	.206	.311	.518
13	LAA	AL	50	91	21	3	2	2	(1 1)	34	11	8	7	5	0	27	0	3	0	1	0	1	.231	.271	.374	.644
	Postseason		3	1	1	0	0	0	(0 0)	1	0	2	1	0	0	0	0	0	0	0	0	0	1.000	1.000	1.000	2.000
5 ML YEARS			309	677	160	22	4	12	(7 5)	226	83	57	68	56	1	190	5	6	1	14	7	9	.236	.299	.334	.633

Zack Cozart

Bats: R **Throws:** R **Pos:** SS-52;PH-1 COE-zart **Ht:** 6'0" **Wt:** 195 **Born:** 8/12/1985 **Age:** 30

Year	Team	Lg	G	AB	H	2B	3B	HR	(Hm	Rd)	TB	R	RBI	RC	TBB	IBB	SO	HBP	SH	SF	SB	CS	GDP	Avg	OBP	Slg	OPS
2011	Cin	NL	11	37	12	0	0	2	(2	0)	18	6	3	3	0	0	6	0	1	0	0	0	2	.324	.324	.486	.811
2012	Cin	NL	138	561	138	33	4	15	(6	9)	224	72	35	51	31	0	113	3	2	3	4	0	11	.246	.288	.399	.687
2013	Cin	NL	151	567	144	30	3	12	(7	5)	216	74	63	56	26	2	102	2	13	10	0	0	18	.254	.284	.381	.665
2014	Cin	NL	147	506	112	18	5	4	(1	3)	152	48	38	36	25	3	79	7	5	0	7	0	13	.221	.268	.300	.568
2015	Cin	NL	53	194	50	10	1	9	(4	5)	89	28	28	23	14	1	29	2	1	3	3	3	4	.258	.310	.459	.769
	Postseason		6	24	5	0	0	0	(0	0)	5	2	0	1	3	0	5	1	0	0	0	0	0	.208	.321	.208	.530
	5 ML YEARS		500	1865	456	91	13	42	(20	22)	699	228	167	169	96	6	329	14	22	16	14	3	48	.245	.284	.375	.659

Allen Craig

Bats: R **Throws:** R **Pos:** PH-13;RF-9;DH-9;LF-7;1B-6;PR-3 **Ht:** 6'2" **Wt:** 215 **Born:** 7/18/1984 **Age:** 31

Year	Team	Lg	G	AB	H	2B	3B	HR	(Hm	Rd)	TB	R	RBI	RC	TBB	IBB	SO	HBP	SH	SF	SB	CS	GDP	Avg	OBP	Slg	OPS
2015	Pwtckt*	AAA	93	343	94	14	0	4	(-	-)	120	29	30	49	49	0	70	4	0	3	0	0	9	.274	.368	.350	.718
2010	StL	NL	44	114	28	7	0	4	(3	1)	47	12	18	14	9	1	26	0	0	1	1	0	1	.246	.298	.412	.711
2011	StL	NL	75	200	63	15	0	11	(3	8)	111	33	40	37	15	0	40	1	1	2	5	0	7	.315	.362	.555	.917
2012	StL	NL	119	469	144	35	0	22	(11	11)	245	76	92	89	37	1	89	1	0	7	2	1	15	.307	.354	.522	.876
2013	StL	NL	134	508	160	29	2	13	(2	11)	232	71	97	98	40	2	100	10	0	5	2	0	12	.315	.373	.457	.830
2014	2 Tms		126	461	99	20	1	8	(5	3)	145	41	46	35	35	0	113	7	0	2	1	1	14	.215	.279	.315	.594
2015	Bos	AL	36	79	12	1	0	1	(1	0)	16	6	3	2	7	0	26	2	0	0	0	0	2	.152	.239	.203	.441
14	StL	NL	97	367	87	17	1	7	(5	2)	127	34	44	33	26	0	77	3	0	2	1	1	11	.237	.291	.346	.638
14	Bos	AL	29	94	12	3	0	1	(0	1)	18	7	2	2	9	0	36	4	0	0	1	0	3	.128	.234	.191	.425
	Postseason		34	100	26	5	1	5	(4	1)	48	14	14	14	14	1	27	2	1	1	0	2	2	.260	.359	.480	.839
	6 ML YEARS		534	1831	506	107	3	59	(25	34)	796	239	296	275	143	4	394	21	1	17	11	3	51	.276	.333	.435	.768

Tyler Cravy

Pitches: R **Bats:** R **Pos:** SP-7; RP-7 KRAY-vee **Ht:** 6'2" **Wt:** 210 **Born:** 7/13/1989 **Age:** 26

| | HOW MUCH HE PITCHED | | | | | | WHAT HE GAVE UP | | | | | | | | | | THE RESULTS | | | | | | |
Year	Team	Lg	G	GS	CG	GF	IP	BFP	H	R	ER	HR	SH	SF	HB	TBB	IBB	SO	WP	Bk	W	L	Pct	Sh	Sv-Op	Hld	ERC	ERA
2011	2 Tms	Low	29	11	0	3	90.1	399	97	59	50	6	3	1	5	29	0	110	24	0	6	6	.500	0	0- -	-	4.09	4.98
2012	Wisc	A	24	0	0	20	50.2	218	45	24	19	5	1	0	7	15	2	53	10	0	2	5	.286	0	3- -	-	3.46	3.38
2013	BrvdCt	A+	25	9	0	6	79.1	316	61	22	18	1	0	1	0	24	0	59	5	0	4	2	.667	0	0- -	-	2.00	2.04
2014	Hntsvl	AA	14	12	0	0	73.1	281	47	17	14	7	4	1	6	15	0	64	1	1	8	1	.889	0	0- -	-	1.86	1.72
2015	ColSpr	AAA	17	17	0	0	95.1	400	92	44	42	6	4	4	4	31	0	75	6	2	7	7	.500	0	0- -	-	3.55	3.97
2015	Mil	NL	14	7	0	1	42.2	193	47	30	27	5	2	0	2	22	1	35	0	0	0	8	.000	0	0-1	0	5.46	5.70

Brandon Crawford

Bats: L **Throws:** R **Pos:** SS-140;PH-5 **Ht:** 6'2" **Wt:** 215 **Born:** 1/21/1987 **Age:** 29

Year	Team	Lg	G	AB	H	2B	3B	HR	(Hm	Rd)	TB	R	RBI	RC	TBB	IBB	SO	HBP	SH	SF	SB	CS	GDP	Avg	OBP	Slg	OPS
2011	SF	NL	66	196	40	5	2	3	(0	3)	58	22	21	20	23	1	31	0	1	0	1	3	4	.204	.288	.296	.584
2012	SF	NL	143	435	108	26	3	4	(1	3)	152	44	45	40	33	6	95	3	2	3	1	4	4	.248	.304	.349	.653
2013	SF	NL	149	499	124	24	3	9	(2	7)	181	52	43	42	42	6	96	5	1	3	1	2	10	.248	.311	.363	.674
2014	SF	NL	153	491	121	20	10	10	(4	6)	191	54	69	72	59	10	129	2	2	10	5	3	4	.246	.324	.389	.713
2015	SF	NL	143	507	130	33	4	21	(8	13)	234	65	84	69	39	9	119	11	0	4	6	4	18	.256	.321	.462	.782
	Postseason		33	107	25	3	1	1	(0	1)	33	10	16	12	14	2	27	0	1	2	1	0	2	.234	.317	.308	.625
	5 ML YEARS		654	2128	523	108	22	47	(15	32)	816	237	262	243	196	32	470	21	6	20	14	16	40	.246	.313	.383	.696

Carl Crawford

Bats: L **Throws:** L **Pos:** LF-51;PH-21;DH-3;PR-3 **Ht:** 6'2" **Wt:** 230 **Born:** 8/5/1981 **Age:** 34

Year	Team	Lg	G	AB	H	2B	3B	HR	(Hm	Rd)	TB	R	RBI	RC	TBB	IBB	SO	HBP	SH	SF	SB	CS	GDP	Avg	OBP	Slg	OPS
2002	TB	AL	63	259	67	11	6	2	(1	1)	96	23	30	34	9	0	41	3	6	1	9	5	0	.259	.290	.371	.661
2003	TB	AL	151	630	177	19	9	5	(5	0)	228	80	54	80	26	4	102	1	1	3	55	10	5	.281	.309	.362	.671
2004	TB	AL	152	626	185	26	19	11	(6	5)	282	104	55	96	35	2	81	1	4	6	59	15	2	.296	.331	.450	.781
2005	TB	AL	156	644	194	33	15	15	(5	10)	302	101	81	102	27	1	84	5	5	6	46	8	11	.301	.331	.469	.800
2006	TB	AL	151	600	183	20	16	18	(7	11)	289	89	77	113	37	3	85	4	9	2	58	9	8	.305	.348	.482	.830
2007	TB	AL	143	584	184	37	9	11	(6	5)	272	93	80	97	32	5	112	5	1	2	50	10	11	.315	.355	.466	.820
2008	TB	AL	109	443	121	12	10	8	(3	5)	177	69	57	57	30	1	60	2	0	5	25	7	10	.273	.319	.400	.718
2009	TB	AL	156	606	185	28	8	15	(9	6)	274	96	68	99	51	1	99	8	2	5	60	16	7	.305	.364	.452	.816
2010	TB	AL	154	600	184	30	13	19	(11	8)	297	110	90	120	46	3	104	3	3	5	47	10	2	.307	.356	.495	.851
2011	Bos	AL	130	506	129	29	7	11	(4	7)	205	65	56	54	23	1	104	3	2	4	18	6	7	.255	.289	.405	.694
2012	Bos	AL	31	117	33	10	2	3	(2	1)	56	23	19	17	3	0	22	2	1	2	5	0	1	.282	.306	.479	.785
2013	LAD	NL	116	435	123	30	3	6	(5	1)	177	62	31	55	28	2	66	3	0	2	15	4	4	.283	.329	.407	.736
2014	LAD	NL	105	343	103	14	3	8	(5	3)	147	56	46	49	16	0	55	6	0	4	23	6	5	.300	.339	.429	.767
2015	LAD	NL	69	181	48	9	2	4	(1	3)	73	19	16	19	10	1	41	0	0	0	10	2	3	.265	.304	.403	.707
	Postseason		35	142	39	5	1	7	(5	2)	67	20	16	19	6	0	30	1	0	0	9	0	3	.275	.309	.472	.781
	14 ML YEARS		1686	6574	1916	307	122	136	(70	66)	2875	990	760	984	373	24	1056	46	34	47	480	108	76	.291	.332	.437	.769

Coco Crisp

Bats: B **Throws:** R **Pos:** LF-37;PH-17   **Ht:** 5'10" **Wt:** 185 **Born:** 11/1/1979 **Age:** 36

Year	Team	Lg	G	AB	H	2B	3B	HR	(Hm	Rd)	TB	R	RBI	RC	TBB	IBB	SO	HBP	SH	SF	SB	CS	GDP	Avg	OBP	Slg	OPS
2002	Cle	AL	32	127	33	9	2	1	(1	0)	49	16	9	19	11	0	19	0	3	2	4	1	0	.260	.314	.386	.700
2003	Cle	AL	99	414	110	15	6	3	(3	0)	146	55	27	48	23	1	51	0	7	3	15	9	4	.266	.302	.353	.655
2004	Cle	AL	139	491	146	24	2	15	(8	7)	219	78	71	72	36	4	69	0	9	2	20	13	8	.297	.344	.446	.790
2005	Cle	AL	145	594	178	42	4	16	(4	12)	276	86	69	92	44	1	81	0	13	5	15	6	7	.300	.345	.465	.810
2006	Bos	AL	105	413	109	22	2	8	(4	4)	159	58	36	51	31	1	67	1	7	0	22	4	5	.264	.317	.385	.702
2007	Bos	AL	145	526	141	28	7	6	(1	5)	201	85	60	68	50	1	84	1	9	5	28	6	12	.268	.330	.382	.712
2008	Bos	AL	118	361	102	18	3	7	(1	6)	147	55	41	49	35	0	59	1	8	4	20	7	6	.283	.344	.407	.751
2009	KC	AL	49	180	41	8	5	3	(0	3)	68	30	14	25	29	1	23	1	4	1	13	2	4	.228	.336	.378	.714
2010	Oak	AL	75	290	81	14	4	8	(6	2)	127	51	38	49	30	0	49	0	3	5	32	3	6	.279	.342	.438	.779
2011	Oak	AL	136	531	140	27	5	8	(4	4)	201	69	54	69	41	2	65	1	4	6	49	9	11	.264	.314	.379	.693
2012	Oak	AL	120	455	118	25	7	11	(6	5)	190	68	46	71	45	0	64	0	6	2	39	4	9	.259	.325	.418	.742
2013	Oak	AL	131	513	134	22	3	22	(9	13)	228	93	66	78	61	3	65	0	2	8	21	5	7	.261	.335	.444	.779
2014	Oak	AL	126	463	114	21	3	9	(4	5)	168	68	47	67	66	2	66	0	1	6	19	5	3	.246	.336	.363	.699
2015	Oak	AL	44	126	22	6	0	0	(0	0)	28	11	6	6	13	0	25	0	0	2	2	0	2	.175	.252	.222	.474
	Postseason		31	103	29	5	1	1	(0	1)	39	15	8	12	9	0	19	0	0	1	4	0	3	.282	.336	.379	.715
	14 ML YEARS		1464	5484	1469	281	53	117	(51	66)	2207	823	584	764	515	16	787	5	76	49	299	74	84	.268	.329	.402	.731

Kyle Crockett

Pitches: L **Bats:** L **Pos:** RP-31   **Ht:** 6'2" **Wt:** 175 **Born:** 12/15/1991 **Age:** 24

Year	Team	Lg	G	GS	CG	GF	IP	BFP	H	R	ER	HR	SH	SF	HB	TBB	IBB	SO	WP	Bk	W	L	Pct	Sh	Sv-Op	Hld	ERC	ERA
2013	2 Tms	Low	12	0	0	2	14.1	56	9	2	1	1	0	0	1	3	0	23	0	0	0	0	-	0	0- -	-	1.61	0.63
2013	Akron	AA	9	0	0	1	10.1	38	7	0	0	0	1	0	0	2	0	9	0	0	1	0	1.000	0	0- -	-	1.38	0.00
2014	Akron	AA	15	0	0	11	15.2	59	8	1	1	0	0	0	1	3	0	17	0	0	0	0	-	0	6- -	-	0.98	0.57
2014	Clmbs	AAA	6	0	0	2	8.2	33	7	4	1	0	1	0	0	0	0	6	0	0	0	0	-	0	0- -	-	1.29	1.04
2015	Clmbs	AAA	29	0	0	4	28.2	138	42	19	19	3	1	1	1	11	1	27	3	0	3	1	.750	0	0- -	-	6.86	5.97
2014	Cle	AL	43	0	0	7	30.0	122	26	6	6	2	2	0	3	8	2	28	0	1	4	1	.800	0	0-0	5	2.99	1.80
2015	Cle	AL	31	0	0	4	17.2	74	17	9	8	1	0	2	1	7	0	15	0	0	0	0	-	0	0-0	3	3.90	4.08
	2 ML YEARS		74	0	0	11	47.2	196	43	15	14	3	2	2	4	15	2	43	0	1	4	1	.800	0	0-0	8	3.31	2.64

C.J. Cron

Bats: R **Throws:** R **Pos:** 1B-58;DH-50;PH-11   CROHN   **Ht:** 6'4" **Wt:** 235 **Born:** 1/5/1990 **Age:** 26

Year	Team	Lg	G	AB	H	2B	3B	HR	(Hm	Rd)	TB	R	RBI	RC	TBB	IBB	SO	HBP	SH	SF	SB	CS	GDP	Avg	OBP	Slg	OPS
2011	Orem	R+	34	143	44	5	1	13	(-	-)	90	30	41	32	10	1	34	5	0	1	0	0	2	.308	.371	.629	1.000
2012	InldEm	A+	129	525	154	32	2	27	(-	-)	271	73	123	88	17	1	72	11	0	4	3	4	18	.293	.327	.516	.843
2013	Ark	AA	134	519	142	36	1	14	(-	-)	222	56	83	73	23	5	83	15	0	8	8	4	11	.274	.319	.428	.746
2014	Salt Lk	AAA	49	190	60	14	1	7	(-	-)	97	30	33	37	18	1	40	4	0	1	2	1	3	.316	.385	.511	.896
2015	Salt Lk	AAA	23	93	30	10	2	6	(-	-)	62	15	23	20	4	0	14	0	0	1	0	0	5	.323	.347	.667	1.014
2014	LAA	AL	79	242	62	12	1	11	(5	6)	109	28	37	35	10	0	61	1	0	0	0	0	10	.256	.289	.450	.739
2015	LAA	AL	113	378	99	17	1	16	(11	5)	166	37	51	46	17	1	82	5	0	3	3	1	9	.262	.300	.439	.739
	Postseason		3	9	1	1	0	0	(0	0)	2	0	0	0	2	0	4	0	0	0	0	0	0	.111	.273	.222	.495
	2 ML YEARS		192	620	161	29	2	27	(16	11)	275	65	88	81	27	1	143	6	0	3	3	1	19	.260	.296	.444	.739

Aaron Crow

Pitches: R **Bats:** R **Pos:** P   **Ht:** 6'3" **Wt:** 195 **Born:** 11/10/1986 **Age:** 29

Year	Team	Lg	G	GS	CG	GF	IP	BFP	H	R	ER	HR	SH	SF	HB	TBB	IBB	SO	WP	Bk	W	L	Pct	Sh	Sv-Op	Hld	ERC	ERA
2011	KC	AL	57	0	0	19	62.0	266	55	20	19	8	3	0	0	31	2	65	9	1	4	4	.500	0	0-7	8	4.00	2.76
2012	KC	AL	73	0	0	20	64.2	260	54	27	25	4	1	2	1	22	2	65	4	0	3	1	.750	0	2-8	19	2.81	3.48
2013	KC	AL	57	0	0	14	48.0	210	49	19	18	6	2	3	2	22	3	44	5	0	7	5	.583	0	1-4	19	4.73	3.38
2014	KC	AL	67	0	0	20	59.0	244	52	32	27	10	2	1	0	24	1	34	2	0	6	1	.857	0	3-6	11	3.97	4.12
	4 ML YEARS		254	0	0	73	233.2	980	210	98	89	28	8	6	3	99	8	208	20	1	20	11	.645	0	6-25	57	3.80	3.43

Nelson Cruz

Bats: R **Throws:** R **Pos:** RF-80;DH-72   **Ht:** 6'2" **Wt:** 230 **Born:** 7/1/1980 **Age:** 35

Year	Team	Lg	G	AB	H	2B	3B	HR	(Hm	Rd)	TB	R	RBI	RC	TBB	IBB	SO	HBP	SH	SF	SB	CS	GDP	Avg	OBP	Slg	OPS
2005	Mil	NL	8	5	1	1	0	0	(0	0)	2	1	0	1	2	0	0	0	0	0	0	0	0	.200	.429	.400	.829
2006	Tex	AL	41	130	29	3	0	6	(3	3)	50	15	22	18	7	0	32	0	0	1	1	0	1	.223	.261	.385	.645
2007	Tex	AL	96	307	72	15	2	9	(4	5)	118	35	34	32	21	1	87	2	1	1	2	4	5	.235	.287	.384	.671
2008	Tex	AL	31	115	38	9	1	7	(4	3)	70	19	26	30	17	2	28	1	0	0	3	1	1	.330	.421	.609	1.030
2009	Tex	AL	128	462	120	21	1	33	(18	15)	242	75	76	72	49	6	118	2	0	2	20	4	9	.260	.332	.524	.856
2010	Tex	AL	108	399	127	31	3	22	(13	9)	230	60	78	77	38	5	81	1	1	6	17	4	12	.318	.374	.576	.950
2011	Tex	AL	124	475	125	28	1	29	(19	10)	242	64	87	79	33	1	116	2	0	3	9	5	8	.263	.312	.509	.821
2012	Tex	AL	159	585	152	45	0	24	(18	6)	269	86	90	80	48	2	140	5	0	4	8	4	7	.260	.319	.460	.779
2013	Tex	AL	109	413	110	18	0	27	(13	14)	209	49	76	69	35	2	109	4	0	4	5	1	14	.266	.327	.506	.833
2014	Bal	AL	159	613	166	32	2	40	(15	25)	322	87	108	93	58	5	140	5	0	5	4	5	17	.271	.333	.525	.859
2015	Sea	AL	152	590	178	22	1	44	(17	27)	334	90	93	108	59	9	164	5	0	3	3	2	6	.302	.369	.566	.936
	Postseason		41	154	45	10	4	16	(10	6)	103	31	34	35	12	2	36	1	0	0	1	1	4	.292	.347	.669	1.016
	11 ML YEARS		1115	4094	1118	225	11	241	(124	117)	2088	581	690	659	364	36	1015	27	2	27	72	30	80	.273	.334	.510	.844

Tony Cruz

Bats: R **Throws:** R **Pos:** C-51;PH-28;3B-3;PR-2   **Ht:** 5'11" **Wt:** 215 **Born:** 8/18/1986 **Age:** 29

Year Team	Lg	G	AB	H	2B	3B	HR	(Hm	Rd)	TB	R	RBI	RC	TBB	IBB	SO	HBP	SH	SF	SB	CS	GDP	Avg	OBP	Slg	OPS
2011 StL	NL	38	65	17	5	0	0	(0	0)	22	8	6	7	6	1	13	1	0	0	0	1	1	.262	.333	.338	.672
2012 StL	NL	51	126	32	9	1	1	(0	1)	46	11	11	9	3	0	19	0	0	2	0	1	4	.254	.267	.365	.632
2013 StL	NL	51	123	25	6	1	1	(0	1)	36	13	13	9	4	1	25	2	0	0	0	0	7	.203	.240	.293	.533
2014 StL	NL	50	135	27	5	0	1	(1	0)	35	11	17	9	13	1	28	0	2	0	0	3	6	.200	.270	.259	.530
2015 StL	NL	69	142	29	7	1	2	(0	2)	44	6	11	5	6	0	32	0	2	1	0	0	6	.204	.235	.310	.545
Postseason		6	6	1	0	0	1	(0	1)	4	2	1	1	2	0	3	0	0	0	0	0	0	.167	.375	.667	1.042
5 ML YEARS		259	591	130	32	3	5	(1	4)	183	49	58	39	32	3	117	3	4	3	0	5	24	.220	.262	.310	.572

Michael Cuddyer

Bats: R **Throws:** R **Pos:** LF-69;PH-22;1B-18;RF-6;DH-5   cuh-DYE-err   **Ht:** 6'2" **Wt:** 220 **Born:** 3/27/1979 **Age:** 37

Year Team	Lg	G	AB	H	2B	3B	HR	(Hm	Rd)	TB	R	RBI	RC	TBB	IBB	SO	HBP	SH	SF	SB	CS	GDP	Avg	OBP	Slg	OPS
2001 Min	AL	8	18	4	2	0	0	(0	0)	6	1	1	2	2	0	6	0	0	0	1	0	1	.222	.300	.333	.633
2002 Min	AL	41	112	29	7	0	4	(2	2)	48	12	13	14	8	0	30	1	1	1	2	0	3	.259	.311	.429	.740
2003 Min	AL	35	102	25	1	3	4	(1	3)	44	14	8	10	12	0	19	0	0	0	1	1	6	.245	.325	.431	.756
2004 Min	AL	115	339	89	22	1	12	(8	4)	149	49	45	51	37	2	74	3	2	1	5	5	8	.263	.339	.440	.779
2005 Min	AL	126	422	111	25	3	12	(8	4)	178	55	42	43	41	5	93	3	1	3	4	4	19	.263	.330	.422	.752
2006 Min	AL	150	557	158	41	5	24	(15	9)	281	102	109	101	62	5	130	10	0	6	6	0	11	.284	.362	.504	.867
2007 Min	AL	144	547	151	28	5	16	(8	8)	237	87	81	82	64	1	107	7	0	5	5	0	19	.276	.356	.433	.790
2008 Min	AL	71	249	62	13	4	3	(1	2)	92	30	36	37	25	4	40	5	0	0	5	1	7	.249	.330	.369	.699
2009 Min	AL	153	588	162	34	7	32	(18	14)	306	93	94	89	54	3	118	6	0	2	6	1	22	.276	.342	.520	.862
2010 Min	AL	157	609	165	37	5	14	(7	7)	254	93	81	77	58	7	93	4	0	4	7	3	26	.271	.336	.417	.753
2011 Min	AL	139	529	150	29	2	20	(10	10)	243	70	70	75	48	3	95	4	0	3	11	1	18	.284	.346	.459	.805
2012 Col	NL	101	358	93	30	2	16	(9	7)	175	53	58	46	32	1	78	0	0	4	8	3	12	.260	.317	.489	.806
2013 Col	NL	130	489	162	31	3	20	(11	9)	259	74	84	87	46	5	100	2	0	3	10	3	13	**.331**	.389	.530	.919
2014 Col	NL	49	190	63	15	1	10	(6	4)	110	32	31	33	14	0	30	0	0	1	3	0	5	.332	.376	.579	.955
2015 NYM	NL	117	379	98	18	1	10	(4	6)	148	44	41	38	24	0	88	4	0	1	2	0	13	.259	.309	.391	.699
Postseason		22	74	25	2	1	2	(2	0)	35	5	8	4	4	1	18	0	0	0	0	2	1	.338	.372	.473	.845
15 ML YEARS		1536	5488	1522	333	42	197	(108	89)	2530	809	794	785	527	36	1101	49	4	34	75	22	183	.277	.344	.461	.805

Johnny Cueto

Pitches: R **Bats:** R **Pos:** SP-32   KWAY-toe   **Ht:** 5'11" **Wt:** 220 **Born:** 2/15/1986 **Age:** 30

	HOW MUCH HE PITCHED						WHAT HE GAVE UP											THE RESULTS						
Year Team	Lg	G	GS	CG	GF	IP	BFP	H	R	ER	HR	SH	SF	HB	TBB	IBB	SO	WP	Bk	W	L	Pct	Sh	Sv-Op	Hld	ERC	ERA
2008 Cin	NL	31	31	0	0	174.0	769	178	101	93	29	9	5	14	68	1	158	6	1	9	14	.391	0	0-0	0	4.95	4.81
2009 Cin	NL	30	30	0	0	171.1	740	172	90	84	24	5	3	14	61	0	132	4	0	11	11	.500	0	0-0	0	4.57	4.41
2010 Cin	NL	31	31	1	0	185.2	780	181	79	75	19	9	3	9	56	5	138	5	2	12	7	.632	1	0-0	0	3.75	3.64
2011 Cin	NL	24	24	3	0	156.0	631	123	51	40	8	10	4	10	47	0	104	5	1	9	5	.643	1	0-0	0	2.55	2.31
2012 Cin	NL	33	33	2	0	217.0	888	205	73	67	15	6	6	12	49	5	170	1	3	19	9	.679	0	0-0	0	3.13	2.78
2013 Cin	NL	11	11	0	0	60.2	242	46	20	19	7	2	1	1	18	1	51	1	0	5	2	.714	0	0-0	0	2.57	2.82
2014 Cin	NL	34	34	4	0	243.2	961	169	69	61	22	7	1	15	65	2	242	1	1	20	9	.690	2	0-0	0	2.18	2.25
2015 2 Tms		32	32	2	0	212.0	866	194	87	81	21	5	4	8	46	1	176	0	4	11	13	.458	2	0-0	0	3.06	3.44
15 Cin	NL	19	19	1	0	130.2	516	93	42	38	11	4	3	6	29	1	120	0	4	7	6	.538	1	0-0	0	2.00	2.62
15 KC	AL	13	13	1	0	81.1	350	101	45	43	10	1	1	2	17	0	56	0	0	4	7	.364	1	0-0	0	5.05	4.76
Postseason		3	3	0	0	8.2	42	13	6	5	3	1	1	0	2	0	3	0	0	0	2	.000	0	0-0	0	7.96	5.19
8 ML YEARS		226	226	12	0	1420.1	5877	1268	570	520	145	53	27	83	410	15	1171	23	12	96	70	.578	6	0-0	0	3.31	3.30

Brandon Cunniff

Pitches: R **Bats:** R **Pos:** RP-39   kin-IF   **Ht:** 6'0" **Wt:** 185 **Born:** 10/7/1988 **Age:** 27

	HOW MUCH HE PITCHED						WHAT HE GAVE UP											THE RESULTS						
Year Team	Lg	G	GS	CG	GF	IP	BFP	H	R	ER	HR	SH	SF	HB	TBB	IBB	SO	WP	Bk	W	L	Pct	Sh	Sv-Op	Hld	ERC	ERA
2013 Lynbrg	A+	20	0	0	11	31.2	133	20	8	7	2	1	2	1	21	2	39	2	1	1	0	1.000	0	0- -	-	2.89	1.99
2014 Lynbrg	A+	9	0	0	6	15.1	58	5	1	0	0	2	0	0	7	2	21	1	0	1	0	1.000	0	3- -	-	0.76	0.00
2014 Missi	AA	33	0	0	6	52.2	214	39	14	12	2	3	4	1	20	2	51	4	0	3	0	1.000	0	0- -	-	2.27	2.05
2015 Gwnntt	AAA	6	0	0	2	5.0	27	8	5	5	2	0	0	0	8	0	4	0	0	1	0	1.000	0	0- -	-	18.96	9.00
2015 Atl	NL	39	0	0	12	35.0	151	27	20	18	4	1	1	0	22	2	37	1	0	2	2	.500	0	0-2	5	3.71	4.63

Todd Cunningham

Bats: B **Throws:** R **Pos:** LF-22;PH-14;RF-4;PR-3;CF-2   **Ht:** 6'0" **Wt:** 205 **Born:** 3/20/1989 **Age:** 27

Year Team	Lg	G	AB	H	2B	3B	HR	(Hm	Rd)	TB	R	RBI	RC	TBB	IBB	SO	HBP	SH	SF	SB	CS	GDP	Avg	OBP	Slg	OPS
2011 2 Tms	Low	91	345	88	12	5	4	(-	-)	122	61	24	46	34	0	52	15	4	2	15	6	7	.255	.346	.354	.700
2012 Missi	AA	120	466	144	23	6	3	(-	-)	188	77	51	73	38	2	51	4	8	3	24	8	8	.309	.364	.403	.767
2013 Gwnntt	AAA	116	427	113	13	5	2	(-	-)	142	60	38	54	41	0	62	10	8	1	20	7	5	.265	.342	.333	.675
2014 Gwnntt	AAA	120	470	135	28	2	8	(-	-)	191	59	58	70	35	2	79	10	13	3	19	8	5	.287	.347	.406	.754
2015 Gwnntt	AAA	97	329	86	14	3	2	(-	-)	112	42	31	40	23	1	34	10	9	4	9	4	6	.261	.325	.340	.666
2013 Atl	NL	8	8	2	0	0	0	(0	0)	2	2	0	1	0	0	3	0	0	0	0	0	1	.250	.250	.250	.500
2015 Atl	NL	39	86	19	4	0	0	(0	0)	23	13	4	3	5	1	17	2	0	0	2	1	1	.221	.280	.267	.547
2 ML YEARS		47	94	21	4	0	0	(0	0)	25	15	4	4	5	1	20	2	0	0	2	1	2	.223	.277	.266	.543

Cheslor Cuthbert

Bats: R Throws: R Pos: 3B-17;PR-2;1B-1;2B-1;DH-1   CHESS-lohr   Ht: 6'1" Wt: 190 Born: 11/16/1992 Age: 23

Year	Team	Lg	G	AB	H	2B	3B	HR	(Hm	Rd)	TB	R	RBI	RC	TBB	IBB	SO	HBP	SH	SF	SB	CS	GDP	Avg	OBP	Slg	OPS
2011	Kane	A	81	300	80	13	1	8	(-	-)	119	33	51	44	36	1	65	2	0	4	2	0	4	.267	.345	.397	.742
2012	Wilmg	A+	124	475	114	18	0	7	(-	-)	153	47	59	47	37	0	80	2	0	3	6	3	8	.240	.296	.322	.618
2013	Wilmg	A+	60	225	63	21	2	2	(-	-)	94	32	31	34	27	0	37	0	0	2	1	2	8	.280	.354	.418	.772
2013	NWArk	AA	64	237	51	16	0	6	(-	-)	85	25	28	25	20	2	51	2	2	3	5	2	6	.215	.279	.359	.637
2014	NWArk	AA	96	355	98	19	1	10	(-	-)	149	35	48	54	36	2	67	1	0	3	9	3	12	.276	.342	.420	.761
2014	Omha	AAA	25	91	24	5	0	2	(-	-)	35	12	16	11	9	0	12	0	0	0	1	1	1	.264	.330	.385	.715
2015	Omha	AAA	104	397	110	22	1	11	(-	-)	167	55	51	59	37	1	60	1	1	2	5	2	14	.277	.339	.421	.759
2015	KC	AL	19	46	10	2	1	1	(1	0)	17	6	8	6	4	0	9	0	0	0	0	0	0	.217	.280	.370	.650

John Danks

Pitches: L Bats: L Pos: SP-30   Ht: 6'1" Wt: 210 Born: 4/15/1985 Age: 31

	HOW MUCH HE PITCHED						WHAT HE GAVE UP											THE RESULTS							
Year	Team	Lg	G	GS	CG	GF	IP	BFP	H	R	ER	HR	SH	SF	HB	TBB	IBB	SO	WP	Bk	W	L	Pct	Sh	Sv-Op	Hld	ERC	ERA
2007	CWS	AL	26	26	0	0	139.0	622	160	92	85	28	7	4	4	54	4	109	3	0	6	13	.316	0	0-0	0	5.73	5.50
2008	CWS	AL	33	33	0	0	195.0	804	182	74	72	15	2	2	4	57	1	159	7	0	12	9	.571	0	0-0	0	3.26	3.32
2009	CWS	AL	32	32	1	0	200.1	839	184	89	84	28	5	6	5	73	1	149	1	0	13	11	.542	0	0-0	0	3.89	3.77
2010	CWS	AL	32	32	1	0	213.0	878	189	93	88	18	5	0	4	70	2	162	2	1	15	11	.577	1	0-0	0	3.18	3.72
2011	CWS	AL	27	27	2	0	170.1	728	182	89	82	19	4	6	7	46	5	135	6	0	8	12	.400	1	0-0	0	4.16	4.33
2012	CWS	AL	9	9	0	0	53.2	238	57	35	34	7	3	2	1	23	0	30	5	0	3	4	.429	0	0-0	0	4.82	5.70
2013	CWS	AL	22	22	0	0	138.1	583	151	81	73	28	1	5	4	27	0	89	3	0	4	14	.222	0	0-0	0	4.61	4.75
2014	CWS	AL	32	32	0	0	193.2	855	205	106	102	25	4	7	9	74	1	129	7	0	11	11	.500	0	0-0	0	4.70	4.74
2015	CWS	AL	30	30	2	0	177.2	768	195	104	93	24	8	6	3	56	1	124	8	1	7	15	.318	1	0-0	0	4.62	4.71
	Postseason		1	1	0	0	6.2	30	7	3	3	1	0	0	0	3	0	7	0	0	1	0	1.000	0	0-0	0	4.81	4.05
	9 ML YEARS		243	243	6	0	1481.0	6315	1505	763	713	192	39	38	41	480	15	1086	42	2	79	100	.441	3	0-0	0	4.18	4.33

Jordan Danks

Bats: L Throws: R Pos: PH-3;LF-1   Ht: 6'5" Wt: 220 Born: 8/7/1986 Age: 29

Year	Team	Lg	G	AB	H	2B	3B	HR	(Hm	Rd)	TB	R	RBI	RC	TBB	IBB	SO	HBP	SH	SF	SB	CS	GDP	Avg	OBP	Slg	OPS
2015	LV*	AAA	120	408	105	27	0	6	(-	-)	150	38	46	49	34	1	122	3	2	1	5	3	4	.257	.318	.368	.686
2012	CWS	AL	50	67	15	1	0	1	(1	0)	19	12	4	3	6	0	16	0	0	2	3	1	1	.224	.280	.284	.564
2013	CWS	AL	79	160	37	7	0	5	(4	1)	59	15	12	12	18	0	57	1	0	0	7	2	5	.231	.313	.369	.682
2014	CWS	AL	51	117	26	2	0	2	(1	1)	34	14	10	9	14	1	46	0	0	1	5	3	1	.222	.303	.291	.594
2015	Phi	NL	4	4	0	0	0	0	(0	0)	0	0	0	0	0	0	2	0	0	0	0	0	0	.000	.000	.000	.000
	4 ML YEARS		184	348	78	10	0	8	(6	2)	112	41	26	24	38	1	121	1	0	3	15	6	7	.224	.300	.322	.622

Chase d'Arnaud

Bats: R Throws: R Pos: PH-7;SS-3;3B-1   dar-NO   Ht: 6'1" Wt: 205 Born: 1/21/1987 Age: 29

Year	Team	Lg	G	AB	H	2B	3B	HR	(Hm	Rd)	TB	R	RBI	RC	TBB	IBB	SO	HBP	SH	SF	SB	CS	GDP	Avg	OBP	Slg	OPS
2015	LV*	AAA	120	497	133	18	5	5	(-	-)	176	77	35	60	26	0	64	11	4	2	28	8	6	.268	.317	.354	.671
2011	Pit	NL	48	143	31	6	2	0	(0	0)	41	17	6	8	4	0	36	1	2	1	12	2	3	.217	.242	.287	.528
2012	Pit	NL	8	6	0	0	0	0	(0	0)	0	2	1	0	0	0	2	0	0	0	1	0	0	.000	.000	.000	.000
2014	Pit	NL	8	0	0	0	0	0	(0	0)	0	2	0	0	0	0	0	0	0	0	2	0	0	-	-	-	-
2015	Phi	NL	11	17	3	0	1	0	(0	0)	5	2	0	1	1	0	7	0	0	0	0	1	0	.176	.222	.294	.516
	4 ML YEARS		75	166	34	6	3	0	(0	0)	46	23	7	9	5	0	45	1	2	1	13	5	3	.205	.231	.277	.508

Travis d'Arnaud

Bats: R Throws: R Pos: C-64;PH-3   dar-NO   Ht: 6'2" Wt: 210 Born: 2/10/1989 Age: 27

Year	Team	Lg	G	AB	H	2B	3B	HR	(Hm	Rd)	TB	R	RBI	RC	TBB	IBB	SO	HBP	SH	SF	SB	CS	GDP	Avg	OBP	Slg	OPS
2013	NYM	NL	31	99	20	3	0	1	(1	0)	26	4	5	6	12	0	21	0	0	1	0	0	3	.202	.286	.263	.548
2014	NYM	NL	108	385	93	22	3	13	(5	8)	160	48	41	39	32	5	64	2	1	1	1	0	15	.242	.302	.416	.718
2015	NYM	NL	67	239	64	14	1	12	(6	6)	116	31	41	36	23	0	49	4	0	2	0	0	7	.268	.340	.485	.825
	3 ML YEARS		206	723	177	39	4	26	(12	14)	302	83	87	81	67	5	134	6	1	4	1	0	25	.245	.313	.418	.730

Yu Darvish

Pitches: R Bats: R Pos: P   YOO DARR-vish   Ht: 6'5" Wt: 215 Born: 8/16/1986 Age: 29

	HOW MUCH HE PITCHED						WHAT HE GAVE UP											THE RESULTS							
Year	Team	Lg	G	GS	CG	GF	IP	BFP	H	R	ER	HR	SH	SF	HB	TBB	IBB	SO	WP	Bk	W	L	Pct	Sh	Sv-Op	Hld	ERC	ERA
2012	Tex	AL	29	29	0	0	191.1	816	156	89	83	14	2	7	10	89	1	221	8	0	16	9	.640	0	0-0	0	3.31	3.90
2013	Tex	AL	32	32	0	0	209.2	841	145	68	66	26	0	5	8	80	1	277	7	1	13	9	.591	0	0-0	0	2.70	2.83
2014	Tex	AL	22	22	0	0	144.1	605	133	54	49	13	1	2	2	49	1	182	14	1	10	7	.588	1	0-0	0	3.39	3.06
	Postseason		1	1	0	0	6.2	27	5	3	2	0	1	1	1	0	0	7	0	0	0	1	.000	0	0-0	0	1.38	2.70
	3 ML YEARS		83	83	2	0	545.1	2262	434	211	198	53	3	14	20	218	3	680	29	2	39	25	.609	1	0-0	0	3.10	3.27

Kyle Davies

Pitches: R **Bats:** R **Pos:** RP-1
Ht: 6'1" **Wt:** 210 **Born:** 9/9/1983 **Age:** 32

Year Team	Lg	G	GS	CG	GF	IP	BFP	H	R	ER	HR	SH	SF	HB	TBB	IBB	SO	WP	Bk	W	L	Pct	Sh	Sv-Op	Hld	ERC	ERA
2015 S-WB*	AAA	27	26	0	0	152.2	633	155	61	56	8	2	6	4	37	0	99	4	1	11	8	.579	0	0- -	-	3.38	3.30
2005 Atl	NL	21	14	0	2	87.2	403	98	51	48	8	3	0	1	49	5	62	4	0	7	6	.538	0	0-1	2	5.25	4.93
2006 Atl	NL	14	14	1	0	63.1	312	90	60	59	14	3	2	3	33	0	51	3	0	3	7	.300	0	0-0	0	8.33	8.38
2007 2 Tms		28	28	0	0	136.0	628	155	102	92	22	5	3	5	70	4	99	8	1	7	15	.318	0	0-0	0	5.90	6.09
2008 KC	AL	21	21	0	0	113.0	487	121	57	51	10	1	3	2	43	0	71	8	1	9	7	.563	0	0-0	0	4.46	4.06
2009 KC	AL	22	22	1	0	123.0	538	122	76	72	18	3	4	4	66	1	86	10	0	8	9	.471	0	0-0	0	5.16	5.27
2010 KC	AL	32	32	1	0	183.2	817	206	114	109	20	3	5	2	80	1	126	5	1	8	12	.400	0	0-0	0	5.04	5.34
2011 KC	AL	13	13	0	0	61.1	293	84	52	46	7	3	6	5	26	2	50	4	0	1	9	.100	0	0-0	0	6.76	6.75
2015 NYY	AL	1	0	0	1	2.1	10	3	0	0	0	0	0	0	0	0	2	0	0	0	0	-	0	0-0	0	3.32	0.00
07 Atl	NL	17	17	0	0	86.0	389	92	61	55	12	3	2	2	44	3	59	1	1	4	8	.333	0	0-0	0	5.24	5.76
07 KC	AL	11	11	0	0	50.0	239	63	41	37	10	2	1	3	26	1	40	7	0	3	7	.300	0	0-0	0	7.09	6.66
8 ML YEARS		152	144	3	3	770.1	3488	879	512	477	99	21	23	22	367	13	547	42	3	43	65	.398	0	0-1	2	5.53	5.57

Zachary Davies

Pitches: R **Bats:** R **Pos:** SP-6
Ht: 6'0" **Wt:** 160 **Born:** 2/7/1993 **Age:** 23

Year Team	Lg	G	GS	CG	GF	IP	BFP	H	R	ER	HR	SH	SF	HB	TBB	IBB	SO	WP	Bk	W	L	Pct	Sh	Sv-Op	Hld	ERC	ERA
2012 Dlmrva	A	25	17	0	5	114.1	484	109	52	49	11	4	4	3	46	0	91	4	0	5	7	.417	0	1- -	-	3.96	3.86
2013 Frdrck	A+	26	26	0	0	148.2	619	145	72	61	10	9	3	3	38	0	132	5	1	7	9	.438	0	0- -	-	3.25	3.69
2014 Bowie	AA	21	20	0	0	110.0	465	106	50	41	8	3	1	4	32	1	109	3	0	10	7	.588	0	0- -	-	3.38	3.35
2015 Norfolk	AAA	19	18	1	0	101.1	419	91	33	32	4	6	1	1	33	0	81	3	0	5	6	.455	0	0- -	-	2.90	2.84
2015 ColSpr	AAA	5	5	0	0	27.0	128	38	17	15	2	1	0	1	12	0	21	1	0	1	2	.333	0	0- -	-	6.69	5.00
2015 Mil	NL	6	6	0	0	34.0	139	26	14	14	2	1	0	0	15	0	24	0	0	3	2	.600	0	0-0	0	2.74	3.71

Chris Davis

Bats: L **Throws:** R **Pos:** 1B-111;RF-30;DH-22
Ht: 6'3" **Wt:** 230 **Born:** 3/17/1986 **Age:** 30

Year Team	Lg	G	AB	H	2B	3B	HR	(Hm	Rd)	TB	R	RBI	RC	TBB	IBB	SO	HBP	SH	SF	SB	CS	GDP	Avg	OBP	Slg	OPS
2008 Tex	AL	80	295	84	23	2	17	(8	9)	162	51	55	44	20	1	88	1	0	1	1	2	5	.285	.331	.549	.880
2009 Tex	AL	113	391	93	15	1	21	(11	10)	173	48	59	50	24	2	150	2	0	2	0	0	6	.238	.284	.442	.726
2010 Tex	AL	45	120	23	9	0	1	(0	1)	35	7	4	5	15	3	40	0	0	1	3	0	3	.192	.279	.292	.571
2011 2 Tms	AL	59	199	53	12	0	5	(2	3)	80	25	19	23	11	1	63	0	0	0	1	0	4	.266	.305	.402	.707
2012 Bal	AL	139	515	139	20	0	33	(22	11)	258	75	85	85	37	6	169	7	0	3	2	3	8	.270	.326	.501	.827
2013 Bal	AL	160	584	167	42	1	53	(28	25)	370	103	138	134	72	12	199	10	0	7	4	1	4	.286	.370	.634	1.004
2014 Bal	AL	127	450	88	16	0	26	(13	13)	182	65	72	58	60	9	173	9	1	5	2	1	2	.196	.300	.404	.704
2015 Bal	AL	160	573	150	31	0	47	(29	18)	322	100	117	117	84	6	208	8	0	5	2	3	6	.262	.361	.562	.923
11 Tex	AL	28	76	19	3	0	3	(1	2)	31	9	6	7	5	0	24	0	0	0	0	0	2	.250	.296	.408	.704
11 Bal	AL	31	123	34	9	0	2	(1	1)	49	16	13	16	6	1	39	0	0	0	1	0	2	.276	.310	.398	.708
Postseason		6	24	5	0	0	0	(0	0)	5	1	2	1	1	0	9	1	0	0	0	0	0	.208	.269	.208	.478
8 ML YEARS		883	3127	797	168	4	203	(113	90)	1582	474	549	516	323	40	1090	37	1	24	15	10	38	.255	.330	.506	.835

Ike Davis

Bats: L **Throws:** L **Pos:** 1B-65;PH-8;DH-1
Ht: 6'4" **Wt:** 220 **Born:** 3/22/1987 **Age:** 29

Year Team	Lg	G	AB	H	2B	3B	HR	(Hm	Rd)	TB	R	RBI	RC	TBB	IBB	SO	HBP	SH	SF	SB	CS	GDP	Avg	OBP	Slg	OPS
2010 NYM	NL	147	523	138	33	1	19	(8	11)	230	73	71	75	72	6	138	1	0	5	3	2	13	.264	.351	.440	.791
2011 NYM	NL	36	129	39	8	1	7	(5	2)	70	20	25	22	17	3	31	1	0	2	0	0	5	.302	.383	.543	.925
2012 NYM	NL	156	519	118	26	0	32	(11	21)	240	66	90	68	61	3	141	1	0	3	0	2	10	.227	.308	.462	.771
2013 NYM	NL	103	317	65	14	0	9	(5	4)	106	37	33	36	57	5	101	1	0	2	4	0	9	.205	.326	.334	.661
2014 2 Tms	NL	143	360	84	19	0	11	(9	2)	136	43	51	45	63	3	78	0	0	4	0	4	8	.233	.344	.378	.722
2015 Oak	AL	74	214	49	17	0	3	(1	2)	75	19	20	23	23	0	44	0	0	2	0	0	5	.229	.301	.350	.652
14 NYM	NL	12	24	5	1	0	1	(1	0)	9	4	5	4	6	0	4	0	0	0	0	0	0	.208	.367	.375	.742
14 Pit	NL	131	336	79	18	0	10	(8	2)	127	39	46	41	57	3	74	0	0	4	0	4	8	.235	.343	.378	.721
6 ML YEARS		659	2062	493	117	2	81	(39	42)	857	258	290	269	293	20	533	4	0	18	7	8	50	.239	.332	.416	.748

Khris Davis

Bats: R **Throws:** R **Pos:** LF-108;PH-13
Ht: 5'10" **Wt:** 195 **Born:** 12/21/1987 **Age:** 28

Year Team	Lg	G	AB	H	2B	3B	HR	(Hm	Rd)	TB	R	RBI	RC	TBB	IBB	SO	HBP	SH	SF	SB	CS	GDP	Avg	OBP	Slg	OPS
2013 Mil	NL	56	136	38	10	0	11	(5	6)	81	27	27	25	11	0	34	5	0	1	3	0	4	.279	.353	.596	.949
2014 Mil	NL	144	501	122	37	2	22	(12	10)	229	70	69	58	32	0	122	10	0	6	4	1	13	.244	.299	.457	.756
2015 Mil	NL	121	392	97	16	2	27	(16	11)	198	54	66	57	44	1	122	1	0	3	6	2	9	.247	.323	.505	.828
3 ML YEARS		321	1029	257	63	4	60	(33	27)	508	151	162	140	87	1	278	16	0	10	13	3	26	.250	.315	.494	.809

Rajai Davis

RAHJ-ay

Bats: R Throws: R Pos: CF-46;LF-39;PH-24;RF-10;DH-8;PR-6   Ht: 5'9" Wt: 195 Born: 10/19/1980 Age: 35

Year	Team	Lg	G	AB	H	2B	3B	HR	(Hm	Rd)	TB	R	RBI	RC	TBB	IBB	SO	HBP	SH	SF	SB	CS	GDP	Avg	OBP	Slg	OPS
2006	Pit	NL	20	14	2	1	0	0	(0	0)	3	1	0	0	2	0	3	0	1	0	1	3	0	.143	.250	.214	.464
2007	2 Tms	NL	75	190	53	11	2	1	(0	1)	71	32	9	26	21	1	28	4	3	1	22	6	1	.279	.361	.374	.735
2008	2 Tms		113	214	52	5	4	3	(0	3)	74	30	19	24	8	0	40	1	2	1	29	6	1	.243	.272	.346	.618
2009	Oak	AL	125	390	119	27	5	3	(1	2)	165	65	48	63	29	0	70	7	2	4	41	12	12	.305	.360	.423	.784
2010	Oak	AL	143	525	149	28	3	5	(5	0)	198	66	52	62	26	0	78	4	1	5	50	11	10	.284	.320	.377	.697
2011	Tor	AL	95	320	76	21	6	1	(1	0)	112	44	29	32	15	0	63	1	1	1	34	11	4	.238	.273	.350	.623
2012	Tor	AL	142	447	115	24	3	8	(5	3)	169	64	43	59	29	3	102	6	1	4	46	13	8	.257	.309	.378	.687
2013	Tor	AL	108	331	86	16	2	6	(3	3)	124	49	24	36	21	0	67	5	1	2	45	6	8	.260	.312	.375	.687
2014	Det	AL	134	461	130	27	2	8	(4	4)	185	64	51	62	22	0	75	5	3	3	36	11	7	.282	.320	.401	.721
2015	Det	AL	112	341	88	16	11	8	(6	2)	150	55	30	37	22	0	76	3	1	3	18	8	5	.258	.306	.440	.746
07	Pit	NL	24	48	13	2	1	0	(0	0)	17	6	2	6	7	0	3	0	1	1	5	2	1	.271	.357	.354	.711
07	SF	NL	51	142	40	9	1	1	(0	1)	54	26	7	20	14	1	25	4	2	0	17	4	0	.282	.363	.380	.743
08	SF	NL	12	18	1	0	0	0	(0	0)	1	2	0	0	1	0	6	0	0	0	4	0	0	.056	.105	.056	.161
08	Oak	NL	101	196	51	5	4	3	(0	3)	73	28	19	24	7	0	34	1	2	1	25	6	1	.260	.288	.372	.660
	Postseason		3	6	2	0	0	0	(0	0)	2	0	0	1	0	0	0	0	0	0	0	0	0	.333	.333	.333	.667
	10 ML YEARS		1067	3233	870	176	38	43	(25	18)	1251	470	305	401	195	4	602	36	16	24	322	87	56	.269	.316	.387	.703

Wade Davis

Pitches: R Bats: R Pos: RP-69   Ht: 6'5" Wt: 220 Born: 9/7/1985 Age: 30

Year	Team	Lg	G	GS	CG	GF	IP	BFP	H	R	ER	HR	SH	SF	HB	TBB	IBB	SO	WP	Bk	W	L	Pct	Sh	Sv-Op	Hld	ERC	ERA
2009	TB	AL	6	6	1	0	36.1	150	33	19	15	2	0	0	0	13	1	36	1	0	2	2	.500	1	0-0	0	3.12	3.72
2010	TB	AL	29	29	0	0	168.0	722	165	77	76	24	3	6	5	62	2	113	4	0	12	10	.545	0	0-0	0	4.25	4.07
2011	TB	AL	29	29	1	0	184.0	795	190	96	91	23	5	7	8	63	1	105	6	0	11	10	.524	0	0-0	0	4.38	4.45
2012	TB	AL	54	0	0	15	70.1	284	48	20	19	5	0	1	0	29	2	87	2	0	3	0	1.000	0	0-1	6	2.25	2.43
2013	KC	AL	31	24	0	2	135.1	618	169	89	80	15	1	5	4	58	2	114	7	0	8	11	.421	0	0-0	0	5.88	5.32
2014	KC	AL	71	0	0	11	72.0	279	38	8	8	0	0	1	3	23	0	109	1	0	9	2	.818	0	3-6	33	1.23	1.00
2015	KC	AL	69	0	0	24	67.1	251	33	8	7	3	0	2	0	20	1	78	1	0	8	1	.889	0	17-18	18	1.16	0.94
	Postseason		15	1	0	3	21.2	85	16	4	3	1	0	0	0	6	0	28	1	0	3	0	1.000	0	0-0	3	1.99	1.25
	7 ML YEARS		289	88	2	52	733.1	3099	676	317	296	72	9	22	20	268	9	642	22	0	53	36	.596	1	20-25	57	3.59	3.63

Alejandro De Aza

day-AH-zah

Bats: L Throws: L Pos: LF-69;RF-37;PH-21;PR-4;CF-1;DH-1   Ht: 6'0" Wt: 195 Born: 4/11/1984 Age: 32

Year	Team	Lg	G	AB	H	2B	3B	HR	(Hm	Rd)	TB	R	RBI	RC	TBB	IBB	SO	HBP	SH	SF	SB	CS	GDP	Avg	OBP	Slg	OPS
2007	Fla	NL	45	144	33	8	2	0	(0	0)	45	14	8	11	6	1	37	1	5	2	2	0	2	.229	.261	.313	.574
2009	Fla	NL	22	20	5	1	0	0	(0	0)	6	6	3	4	5	0	5	0	1	1	0	0	0	.250	.385	.300	.685
2010	CWS	AL	19	30	9	3	0	0	(0	0)	12	7	2	4	1	0	4	0	1	0	2	1	0	.300	.323	.400	.723
2011	CWS	AL	54	152	50	11	3	4	(2	2)	79	29	23	34	17	1	34	1	1	0	12	5	2	.329	.400	.520	.920
2012	CWS	AL	131	524	147	29	6	9	(2	7)	215	81	50	79	47	3	109	9	4	1	26	12	1	.281	.349	.410	.760
2013	CWS	AL	153	607	160	27	4	17	(4	13)	246	84	62	82	50	1	147	6	6	6	20	8	8	.264	.323	.405	.728
2014	2 Tms	AL	142	477	120	24	8	8	(4	4)	184	56	41	58	39	2	119	6	3	3	17	10	7	.252	.314	.386	.700
2015	3 Tms		114	325	85	17	7	7	(3	4)	137	51	35	47	31	3	84	5	2	2	7	5	6	.262	.333	.422	.755
14	CWS	AL	122	395	96	19	5	5	(4	1)	140	45	31	45	33	2	100	6	2	3	15	7	6	.243	.309	.364	.663
14	Bal	AL	20	82	24	5	3	3	(0	3)	44	11	10	13	6	0	19	0	1	0	2	3	1	.293	.341	.537	.877
15	Bal	AL	30	103	22	4	1	3	(1	2)	37	16	7	10	7	2	34	2	0	0	2	2	1	.214	.277	.359	.636
15	Bos	AL	60	161	47	9	5	4	(2	2)	78	23	25	30	12	1	36	2	2	1	3	1	2	.292	.347	.484	.831
15	SF	NL	24	61	16	4	1	0	(0	0)	22	12	3	7	12	0	14	1	0	1	2	2	3	.262	.387	.361	.747
	Postseason		6	21	7	3	0	0	(0	0)	10	4	3	4	1	0	1	1	0	0	0	0	0	.333	.391	.476	.867
	8 ML YEARS		680	2279	609	120	30	45	(15	30)	924	328	224	319	196	11	539	28	23	15	86	41	26	.267	.331	.405	.736

Justin De Fratus

duh-FRAY-tiss

Pitches: R Bats: B Pos: RP-61   Ht: 6'4" Wt: 225 Born: 10/21/1987 Age: 28

Year	Team	Lg	G	GS	CG	GF	IP	BFP	H	R	ER	HR	SH	SF	HB	TBB	IBB	SO	WP	Bk	W	L	Pct	Sh	Sv-Op	Hld	ERC	ERA
2011	Phi	NL	5	0	0	2	4.0	17	1	2	1	0	1	0	1	3	1	3	1	0	1	0	1.000	0	0-0	0	1.39	2.25
2012	Phi	NL	13	0	0	2	10.2	44	7	5	4	0	0	0	0	5	1	8	1	0	0	0	-	0	0-0	5	1.75	3.38
2013	Phi	NL	58	0	0	12	46.2	208	45	21	20	3	2	2	5	25	3	42	6	0	3	3	.500	0	0-1	9	4.50	3.86
2014	Phi	NL	54	0	0	17	52.2	219	45	19	14	4	1	1	3	12	4	49	2	0	3	1	.750	0	0-2	5	2.54	2.39
2015	Phi	NL	61	0	0	16	80.0	362	92	52	49	9	4	5	5	32	2	68	7	0	0	2	.000	0	0-1	1	5.23	5.51
	5 ML YEARS		191	0	0	49	194.0	850	190	99	88	16	8	8	14	77	11	170	17	0	7	6	.538	0	0-4	20	3.98	4.08

Ivan De Jesus

hay-SOOS

Bats: R **Throws:** R **Pos:** PH-22;2B-20;LF-18;3B-13;SS-10;1B-4;PR-1   **Ht:** 5'11" **Wt:** 200 **Born:** 5/1/1987 **Age:** 29

								BATTING												RUNNING			AVERAGES			
Year Team	Lg	G	AB	H	2B	3B	HR	(Hm Rd)	TB	R	RBI	RC	TBB	IBB	SO	HBP	SH	SF	SB	CS	GDP	Avg	OBP	Slg	OPS
2015 Lsvlle*	AAA	50	185	56	9	3	0	(- -)	71	22	16	28	22	1	43	1	0	1	2	1	8	.303	.378	.384	.762
2011 LAD	NL	17	32	6	0	0	0	(0 0)	6	2	1	1	2	0	11	0	1	0	0	0	1	.188	.235	.188	.423
2012 2 Tms		31	41	9	3	0	0	(0 0)	12	5	4	4	3	0	13	0	0	1	1	1	1	.220	.267	.293	.559
2015 Cin	NL	76	201	49	10	2	4	(4 0)	75	15	28	23	19	0	55	1	0	1	0	2	3	.244	.311	.373	.684
12 LAD	NL	23	33	9	3	0	0	(0 0)	12	5	4	4	3	0	7	0	0	1	1	1	1	.273	.324	.364	.688
12 Bos	AL	8	8	0	0	0	0	(0 0)	0	0	0	0	0	0	6	0	0	0	0	0	0	.000	.000	.000	.000
3 ML YEARS		124	274	64	13	2	4	(4 0)	93	22	33	28	24	0	79	1	1	2	1	3	5	.234	.296	.339	.635

Jorge de la Rosa

Pitches: L **Bats:** L **Pos:** SP-26   **Ht:** 6'1" **Wt:** 215 **Born:** 4/5/1981 **Age:** 35

		HOW MUCH HE PITCHED						WHAT HE GAVE UP												THE RESULTS							
Year Team	Lg	G	GS	CG	GF	IP	BFP	H	R	ER	HR	SH	SF	HB	TBB	IBB	SO	WP	Bk	W	L	Pct	Sh	Sv-Op	Hld	ERC	ERA
2004 Mil	NL	5	5	0	0	22.2	113	29	20	16	1	1	3	1	14	0	5	3	0	0	3	.000	0	0-0	0	6.12	6.35
2005 Mil	NL	38	0	0	13	42.1	208	48	23	21	1	2	2	0	38	4	42	6	0	2	2	.500	0	0-2	5	6.04	4.46
2006 2 Tms		28	13	0	4	79.0	367	81	59	57	14	2	4	2	54	1	67	6	1	5	6	.455	0	0-0	1	6.05	6.49
2007 KC	AL	26	23	0	1	130.0	589	160	88	84	20	2	4	3	53	6	82	4	1	8	12	.400	0	0-0	0	5.93	5.82
2008 Col	NL	28	23	0	0	130.0	571	128	77	71	13	6	7	7	62	3	128	14	1	10	8	.556	0	0-0	0	4.50	4.92
2009 Col	NL	33	32	0	0	185.0	799	172	95	90	20	11	6	9	83	3	193	12	1	16	9	.640	0	0-0	0	4.11	4.38
2010 Col	NL	20	20	0	0	121.2	512	105	62	57	15	3	3	5	55	4	113	9	1	8	7	.533	0	0-0	0	3.86	4.22
2011 Col	NL	10	10	1	0	59.0	245	48	25	23	4	4	1	2	22	0	52	6	1	5	2	.714	0	0-0	0	2.88	3.51
2012 Col	NL	3	3	0	0	10.2	53	17	14	11	5	1	0	0	2	0	6	2	0	0	2	.000	0	0-0	0	9.22	9.28
2013 Col	NL	30	30	0	0	167.2	714	170	70	65	11	11	5	5	62	5	112	5	0	16	6	.727	0	0-0	0	3.92	3.49
2014 Col	NL	32	32	0	0	184.1	768	161	90	84	21	9	5	9	67	2	139	9	0	14	11	.560	0	0-0	0	3.55	4.10
2015 Col	NL	26	26	1	0	149.0	635	137	73	69	17	4	8	3	65	3	134	6	2	9	7	.563	0	0-0	0	3.94	4.17
06 Mil	NL	18	3	0	4	30.1	146	32	30	29	4	1	3	1	22	1	31	4	0	2	2	.500	0	0-0	1	5.90	8.60
06 KC	AL	10	10	0	0	48.2	221	49	29	28	10	1	1	1	32	0	36	2	1	3	4	.429	0	0-0	0	6.14	5.18
12 ML YEARS		279	217	2	18	1281.1	5574	1256	696	648	142	56	48	46	577	31	1073	82	8	93	75	.554	0	0-2	6	4.37	4.55

Rubby de la Rosa

ROO-bee

Pitches: R **Bats:** R **Pos:** SP-32   **Ht:** 6'1" **Wt:** 225 **Born:** 3/4/1989 **Age:** 27

		HOW MUCH HE PITCHED						WHAT HE GAVE UP												THE RESULTS							
Year Team	Lg	G	GS	CG	GF	IP	BFP	H	R	ER	HR	SH	SF	HB	TBB	IBB	SO	WP	Bk	W	L	Pct	Sh	Sv-Op	Hld	ERC	ERA
2011 LAD	NL	13	10	0	2	60.2	254	54	26	25	6	2	0	0	31	3	60	3	0	4	5	.444	0	0-1	1	3.94	3.71
2012 LAD	NL	1	0	0	0	0.2	4	0	2	2	0	0	0	0	2	0	0	0	0	0	0	-	0	0-0	0	7.00	27.00
2013 Bos	AL	11	0	0	7	11.1	53	15	7	7	2	0	0	3	2	0	6	1	0	0	0	.000	0	0-0	0	6.76	5.56
2014 Bos	AL	19	18	0	1	101.2	441	116	51	50	12	3	5	2	35	0	74	3	1	4	8	.333	0	0-0	0	4.96	4.43
2015 Ari	NL	32	32	0	0	188.2	809	193	103	98	32	8	5	4	63	3	150	2	2	14	9	.609	0	0-0	0	4.49	4.67
5 ML YEARS		76	60	0	10	363.0	1561	378	189	182	52	13	10	9	133	6	290	9	3	22	24	.478	0	0-1	1	4.61	4.51

Abel De Los Santos

ah-BELL

Pitches: R **Bats:** R **Pos:** RP-2   **Ht:** 6'2" **Wt:** 200 **Born:** 11/21/1992 **Age:** 23

		HOW MUCH HE PITCHED						WHAT HE GAVE UP												THE RESULTS							
Year Team	Lg	G	GS	CG	GF	IP	BFP	H	R	ER	HR	SH	SF	HB	TBB	IBB	SO	WP	Bk	W	L	Pct	Sh	Sv-Op	Hld	ERC	ERA
2011 Rngrs	R	14	12	0	0	61.1	241	55	29	25	5	2	2	4	8	0	61	4	0	7	1	.875	0	0--	-	2.72	3.67
2012 Spkane	A-	16	11	0	0	62.0	273	67	46	40	7	5	2	5	22	1	54	5	1	3	5	.375	0	0--	-	4.76	5.81
2013 Spkane	A-	20	0	0	7	41.1	169	33	16	16	4	2	1	2	13	0	48	4	1	4	1	.800	0	1--	-	2.84	3.48
2014 2 Tms	Low	30	0	0	33	56.0	230	36	15	12	2	2	2	5	18	3	65	3	2	5	3	.625	0	8--	-	1.76	1.93
2015 Hrsbrg	AA	39	0	0	22	57.2	239	53	24	22	6	3	3	1	12	1	55	3	1	4	4	.500	0	8--	-	2.91	3.43
2015 Was	NL	2	0	0	2	1.2	8	2	1	1	1	0	0	0	1	0	3	0	0	0	0	-	0	0-0	0	10.04	5.40

Jose De Paula

Pitches: L **Bats:** R **Pos:** RP-1   **Ht:** 6'1" **Wt:** 170 **Born:** 3/4/1988 **Age:** 28

		HOW MUCH HE PITCHED						WHAT HE GAVE UP												THE RESULTS							
Year Team	Lg	G	GS	CG	GF	IP	BFP	H	R	ER	HR	SH	SF	HB	TBB	IBB	SO	WP	Bk	W	L	Pct	Sh	Sv-Op	Hld	ERC	ERA
2011 Lk Els	A+	26	23	0	0	112.0	506	129	81	65	4	3	5	2	37	0	87	2	0	10	5	.667	0	0--	-	4.13	5.22
2013 SnAnt	AA	14	14	0	0	74.2	315	84	42	32	3	2	4	2	11	0	57	4	1	4	6	.400	0	0--	-	3.46	3.86
2014 Fresno	AAA	16	14	0	0	51.1	224	55	28	24	5	0	0	1	16	0	41	3	0	4	3	.571	0	1--	-	4.13	4.21
2015 S-WB	AAA	6	6	0	0	27.2	121	32	16	16	0	0	0	1	10	1	12	0	0	2	3	.400	0	0--	-	4.22	5.20
2015 NYY	AL	1	0	0	1	3.1	15	2	1	1	1	0	0	0	4	0	2	0	0	0	0	-	0	0-0	0	6.91	2.70

Cody Decker

Bats: R **Throws:** R **Pos:** PH-7;1B-3   **Ht:** 5'11" **Wt:** 225 **Born:** 1/17/1987 **Age:** 29

								BATTING												RUNNING			AVERAGES			
Year Team	Lg	G	AB	H	2B	3B	HR	(Hm Rd)	TB	R	RBI	RC	TBB	IBB	SO	HBP	SH	SF	SB	CS	GDP	Avg	OBP	Slg	OPS
2011 SnAnt	AA	49	177	42	10	1	13	(- -)	93	32	38	27	11	0	59	2	0	0	0	1	8	.237	.289	.525	.815
2011 Padres	R	10	32	11	2	0	2	(- -)	19	4	7	8	6	0	9	0	0	1	1	0	0	.344	.436	.594	1.030
2012 SnAnt	AA	104	346	91	19	1	25	(- -)	187	54	68	68	54	3	100	4	0	2	1	4	6	.263	.367	.540	.907
2012 Tucsn	AAA	32	107	23	7	0	4	(- -)	42	12	13	13	11	0	27	2	0	1	0	0	2	.215	.298	.393	.690
2013 Tucsn	AAA	113	324	88	24	5	17	(- -)	173	45	64	61	37	0	98	3	1	3	0	0	4	.272	.349	.534	.883

Year Team	Lg	G	AB	H	2B	3B	HR	(Hm	Rd)	TB	R	RBI	RC	TBB	IBB	SO	HBP	SH	SF	SB	CS	GDP	Avg	OBP	Slg	OPS
2013 SnAnt	AA	10	35	6	0	0	2	(-	-)	12	6	6	3	5	0	14	0	0	0	0	0	3	.171	.275	.343	.618
2014 ElPaso	AAA	134	449	117	25	4	27	(-	-)	231	68	79	78	51	0	150	4	0	6	0	3	11	.261	.337	.514	.852
2015 ElPaso	AAA	120	373	94	23	1	21	(-	-)	182	52	75	62	42	1	107	5	0	1	1	0	11	.252	.335	.488	.823
2015 SD	NL	8	11	0	0	0	0	(0	0)	0	0	0	1	0	0	5	0	0	1	0	0	1	.000	.000	.000	.000

Jaff Decker

Bats: L Throws: L Pos: PH-12;LF-4;RF-3;CF-2;PR-2   JEFF   Ht: 5'9" Wt: 190 Born: 2/23/1990 Age: 26

Year Team	Lg	G	AB	H	2B	3B	HR	(Hm	Rd)	TB	R	RBI	RC	TBB	IBB	SO	HBP	SH	SF	SB	CS	GDP	Avg	OBP	Slg	OPS
2015 Indy*	AAA	69	218	58	10	1	3	(-	-)	79	33	26	36	36	2	38	3	3	5	18	3	1	.266	.370	.362	.733
2013 SD	NL	13	26	4	0	0	1	(0	1)	7	3	2	0	3	0	4	0	1	1	0	1	0	.154	.233	.269	.503
2014 Pit	NL	5	5	0	0	0	0	(0	0)	0	0	0	0	0	0	3	0	0	0	0	0	0	.000	.000	.000	.000
2015 Pit	NL	23	28	6	1	1	0	(0	0)	9	8	1	4	7	0	9	0	1	0	0	0	0	.214	.371	.321	.693
3 ML YEARS		41	59	10	1	1	1	(0	1)	16	11	3	4	10	0	16	0	2	1	0	1	0	.169	.286	.271	.557

Samuel Deduno

Pitches: R Bats: R Pos: RP-7; SP-2   deh-DUE-noh   Ht: 6'3" Wt: 210 Born: 7/2/1983 Age: 32

Year Team	Lg	G	GS	CG	GF	IP	BFP	H	R	ER	HR	SH	SF	HB	TBB	IBB	SO	WP	Bk	W	L	Pct	Sh	Sv-Op	Hld	ERC	ERA
2010 Col	NL	4	0	0	3	2.2	12	3	1	1	1	0	0	0	1	0	3	0	0	0	0	-	0	0-0	1	6.59	3.38
2011 SD	NL	2	0	0	0	3.0	17	5	1	1	0	0	0	0	3	1	4	1	0	0	0	-	0	0-0	0	8.91	3.00
2012 Min	AL	15	15	0	0	79.0	347	69	40	39	10	1	2	5	53	0	57	5	0	6	5	.545	0	0-0	0	5.03	4.44
2013 Min	AL	18	18	0	0	108.0	461	105	48	46	7	3	3	9	41	0	67	8	2	8	8	.500	0	0-0	0	3.99	3.83
2014 2 Tms	AL	35	9	0	10	100.2	443	97	53	50	9	1	5	10	46	2	83	8	4	2	6	.250	0	0-0	2	4.40	4.47
2015 Hou	AL	9	2	0	4	21.0	96	24	16	16	3	1	1	3	9	0	17	3	0	0	1	.000	0	1-1	0	6.01	6.86
14 Min	AL	30	8	0	8	92.0	408	92	49	47	9	1	4	10	41	1	74	8	3	2	5	.286	0	0-0	1	4.68	4.60
14 Hou	AL	5	1	0	2	8.2	35	5	4	3	0	0	1	0	5	1	9	0	1	0	1	.000	0	0-0	1	1.76	3.12
6 ML YEARS		83	44	0	17	314.1	1376	303	159	153	30	6	11	27	153	3	231	25	6	16	20	.444	0	1-1	3	4.57	4.38

Jacob deGrom

Pitches: R Bats: L Pos: SP-30   duh-GRAHM   Ht: 6'4" Wt: 180 Born: 6/19/1988 Age: 28

Year Team	Lg	G	GS	CG	GF	IP	BFP	H	R	ER	HR	SH	SF	HB	TBB	IBB	SO	WP	Bk	W	L	Pct	Sh	Sv-Op	Hld	ERC	ERA
2012 2 Tms	Low	19	19	0	0	111.1	450	91	38	30	4	3	4	2	20	0	96	5	1	9	3	.750	0	0- -	-	1.95	2.43
2013 Bnghtn	AA	10	10	0	0	60.0	261	69	38	32	4	2	2	2	20	3	44	3	1	2	5	.286	0	0- -	-	4.54	4.80
2013 LsVgs	AAA	14	14	0	0	75.2	331	87	41	38	6	1	3	1	24	0	63	3	0	4	2	.667	0	0- -	-	4.50	4.52
2014 LsVgs	AAA	7	7	0	0	38.1	161	39	13	11	2	1	3	1	10	0	29	2	0	4	0	1.000	0	0- -	-	3.42	2.58
2014 NYM	NL	22	22	0	0	140.1	565	117	44	42	7	5	3	1	43	2	144	1	0	9	6	.600	0	0-0	0	2.57	2.69
2015 NYM	NL	30	30	0	0	191.0	751	149	59	54	16	10	7	2	38	2	205	6	0	14	8	.636	0	0-0	0	2.13	2.54
2 ML YEARS		52	52	0	0	331.1	1316	266	103	96	23	15	10	3	81	4	349	7	0	23	14	.622	0	0-0	0	2.32	2.61

David DeJesus

Bats: L Throws: L Pos: LF-63;PH-34;DH-22;RF-4;CF-2   da-HAY-soos   Ht: 5'11" Wt: 190 Born: 12/20/1979 Age: 36

Year Team	Lg	G	AB	H	2B	3B	HR	(Hm	Rd)	TB	R	RBI	RC	TBB	IBB	SO	HBP	SH	SF	SB	CS	GDP	Avg	OBP	Slg	OPS
2003 KC	AL	12	7	2	0	1	0	(0	0)	4	0	0	2	1	0	2	1	1	0	0	0	0	.286	.444	.571	1.016
2004 KC	AL	96	363	104	15	3	7	(2	5)	146	58	39	53	33	0	53	9	8	0	8	11	6	.287	.360	.402	.763
2005 KC	AL	122	461	135	31	6	9	(6	3)	205	69	56	77	42	1	76	9	5	6	5	5	6	.293	.359	.445	.804
2006 KC	AL	119	491	145	36	7	8	(4	4)	219	83	56	76	43	4	70	12	2	4	6	3	10	.295	.364	.446	.810
2007 KC	AL	157	605	157	29	9	7	(3	4)	225	101	58	87	64	7	83	23	7	4	10	4	10	.260	.351	.372	.722
2008 KC	AL	135	518	159	25	7	12	(6	6)	234	70	73	93	46	3	71	5	4	4	11	8	10	.307	.366	.452	.818
2009 KC	AL	144	558	157	28	9	13	(4	9)	242	74	71	83	51	0	87	8	5	5	4	9	10	.281	.347	.434	.781
2010 KC	AL	91	352	112	23	3	5	(2	3)	156	46	37	50	34	2	47	4	3	1	3	3	10	.318	.384	.443	.827
2011 Oak	AL	131	442	106	20	5	10	(4	6)	166	60	46	49	45	1	86	11	4	4	4	3	14	.240	.323	.376	.698
2012 ChC	NL	148	506	133	28	8	9	(4	5)	204	76	50	73	61	1	89	9	2	4	7	8	9	.263	.350	.403	.753
2013 3 Tms		122	391	98	29	3	8	(5	3)	157	52	38	51	39	0	79	6	2	1	5	3	6	.251	.327	.402	.729
2014 TB	AL	83	238	59	15	2	6	(3	3)	96	24	19	25	30	1	43	5	0	0	0	3	7	.248	.344	.403	.748
2015 2 Tms	AL	112	288	67	9	2	5	(2	3)	95	27	30	29	21	1	52	6	0	2	3	2	5	.233	.297	.330	.626
13 ChC	NL	84	284	71	19	3	6	(4	2)	114	39	27	40	29	0	55	5	0	0	3	0	3	.250	.330	.401	.732
13 Was	NL	3	3	0	0	0	0	(0	0)	0	0	0	0	0	0	1	0	1	0	0	0	0	.000	.000	.000	.000
13 TB	AL	35	104	27	10	0	2	(1	1)	43	13	11	11	10	0	23	1	1	1	2	3	3	.260	.328	.413	.741
15 TB	AL	82	232	60	8	2	5	(2	3)	87	24	26	26	19	1	39	4	0	2	3	2	4	.259	.323	.375	.698
15 LAA	AL	30	56	7	1	0	0	(0	0)	8	3	4	3	2	0	13	2	0	0	0	0	1	.125	.183	.143	.326
Postseason		5	13	3	1	0	0	(0	0)	4	2	1	2	1	0	6	2	0	0	0	0	1	.231	.375	.308	.683
13 ML YEARS		1472	5220	1434	288	65	99	(45	54)	2149	740	573	748	510	21	838	108	43	35	66	62	103	.275	.349	.412	.761

Steve Delabar

Pitches: R Bats: R Pos: RP-31   DELL-uh-bar   Ht: 6'5" Wt: 220 Born: 7/17/1983 Age: 32

Year Team	Lg	G	GS	CG	GF	IP	BFP	H	R	ER	HR	SH	SF	HB	TBB	IBB	SO	WP	Bk	W	L	Pct	Sh	Sv-Op	Hld	ERC	ERA
2015 Buffalo*	AAA	24	0	0	12	25.1	97	12	4	4	1	0	1	0	10	1	30	1	0	3	1	.750	0	1- -	-	1.26	1.42
2011 Sea	AL	6	0	0	4	7.0	28	5	2	2	1	0	0	1	4	1	7	0	0	1	1	.500	0	0-0	0	4.15	2.57
2012 2 Tms	AL	61	0	0	12	66.0	274	46	29	28	12	3	2	5	26	1	92	6	0	4	3	.571	0	0-2	12	3.18	3.82
2013 Tor	AL	55	0	0	14	58.2	253	50	25	21	4	3	3	2	29	5	82	4	1	5	5	.500	0	1-6	6	3.38	3.22
2014 Tor	AL	30	0	0	2	25.2	114	19	14	14	3	1	1	3	19	0	21	2	0	3	0	1.000	0	0-0	12	4.59	4.91

			HOW MUCH HE PITCHED						WHAT HE GAVE UP											THE RESULTS							
Year	Team	Lg	G	GS	CG	GF	IP	BFP	H	R	ER	HR	SH	SF	HB	TBB	IBB	SO	WP	Bk	W	L	Pct	Sh	Sv-Op	Hld	ERC	ERA
2015	Tor	AL	31	0	0	12	29.1	129	28	19	17	5	1	1	1	14	1	30	6	0	2	0	1.000	0	1-4	5	4.69	5.22
12	Sea	AL	34	0	0	11	36.2	148	23	17	17	9	2	0	5	11	1	46	3	0	2	1	.667	0	0-2	3	3.07	4.17
12	Tor	AL	27	0	0	1	29.1	126	23	12	11	3	1	2	0	15	0	46	3	0	2	2	.500	0	0-0	9	3.27	3.38
5 ML YEARS			183	0	0	42	186.2	798	148	89	82	25	8	7	12	92	8	232	18	1	15	9	.625	0	2-12	35	3.71	3.95

Randall Delgado

Pitches: R Bats: R Pos: RP-63; SP-1   Ht: 6'4" Wt: 220 Born: 2/9/1990 Age: 26

			HOW MUCH HE PITCHED						WHAT HE GAVE UP											THE RESULTS							
Year	Team	Lg	G	GS	CG	GF	IP	BFP	H	R	ER	HR	SH	SF	HB	TBB	IBB	SO	WP	Bk	W	L	Pct	Sh	Sv-Op	Hld	ERC	ERA
2011	Atl	NL	7	7	0	0	35.0	147	29	12	11	5	0	0	1	14	1	18	2	0	1	1	.500	0	0-0	0	3.48	2.83
2012	Atl	NL	18	17	0	0	92.2	401	89	48	45	8	5	3	4	42	4	75	6	1	4	9	.308	0	0-0	0	4.10	4.37
2013	Ari	NL	20	19	1	0	116.1	473	116	59	55	24	5	5	1	23	2	79	3	1	5	7	.417	1	0-0	0	4.03	4.26
2014	Ari	NL	47	4	0	6	77.2	339	71	44	42	6	2	2	3	35	2	86	5	0	4	4	.500	0	0-0	2	3.69	4.87
2015	Ari	NL	64	1	0	13	72.0	308	63	28	26	7	2	2	1	33	2	73	7	0	8	4	.667	0	1-3	12	3.59	3.25
5 ML YEARS			156	48	1	19	393.2	1668	368	191	179	50	14	12	10	147	11	332	22	2	22	25	.468	1	1-3	14	3.87	4.09

Matt den Dekker

Bats: L Throws: L Pos: LF-27;PH-21;RF-10;PR-3;CF-2   Ht: 6'1" Wt: 210 Born: 8/10/1987 Age: 28

				BATTING																RUNNING			AVERAGES			
Year	Team	Lg	G	AB	H	2B	3B	HR	(Hm	Rd)	TB	R	RBI	RC	TBB	IBB	SO	HBP	SH	SF	SB	CS	GDP	Avg	OBP	Slg	OPS
2015	Syrcse*	AAA	73	269	67	12	2	8	(-	-)	107	35	32	36	24	1	63	4	1	0	8	1	2	.249	.320	.398	.718
2013	NYM	NL	27	58	12	1	0	1	(0	1)	16	7	6	5	4	0	23	1	0	0	4	1	0	.207	.270	.276	.546
2014	NYM	NL	53	152	38	11	0	0	(0	0)	49	23	7	17	21	0	34	1	0	0	7	4	1	.250	.345	.322	.667
2015	Was	NL	55	99	25	6	1	5	(3	2)	48	12	12	12	9	0	20	0	2	0	0	1	0	.253	.315	.485	.800
3 ML YEARS			135	309	75	18	1	6	(3	3)	113	42	25	34	34	0	77	2	2	0	11	6	1	.243	.322	.366	.687

Chris Denorfia

Bats: R Throws: R Pos: LF-43;PH-38;RF-28;CF-6   deh-NOR-fee-uh   Ht: 6'0" Wt: 195 Born: 7/15/1980 Age: 35

				BATTING																RUNNING			AVERAGES			
Year	Team	Lg	G	AB	H	2B	3B	HR	(Hm	Rd)	TB	R	RBI	RC	TBB	IBB	SO	HBP	SH	SF	SB	CS	GDP	Avg	OBP	Slg	OPS
2005	Cin	NL	18	38	10	3	0	1	(1	0)	16	8	2	3	6	0	9	0	0	0	1	0	1	.263	.364	.421	.785
2006	Cin	NL	49	106	30	6	0	1	(0	1)	39	14	7	13	11	1	21	1	2	0	1	1	1	.283	.356	.368	.724
2008	Oak	AL	29	62	18	3	0	1	(0	1)	24	10	9	9	6	0	16	1	2	0	2	0	3	.290	.362	.387	.749
2009	Oak	AL	4	2	0	0	0	0	(0	0)	0	1	1	0	0	0	0	0	0	0	0	0	0	.000	.000	.000	.000
2010	SD	NL	99	284	77	15	2	9	(3	6)	123	41	36	37	27	3	51	2	1	3	8	4	5	.271	.335	.433	.769
2011	SD	NL	111	307	85	13	2	5	(1	4)	117	38	19	34	28	1	49	1	2	2	11	6	10	.277	.337	.381	.718
2012	SD	NL	130	348	102	19	6	8	(3	5)	157	56	36	49	27	0	52	2	2	3	13	5	9	.293	.345	.451	.796
2013	SD	NL	144	473	132	21	2	10	(6	4)	187	67	47	63	42	2	84	1	0	4	11	0	14	.279	.337	.395	.732
2014	2 Tms		121	330	76	12	4	3	(2	1)	105	36	21	31	25	0	70	0	2	1	9	3	6	.230	.284	.318	.602
2015	ChC	NL	103	212	57	11	1	3	(2	1)	79	18	19	22	15	1	56	1	2	1	0	1	7	.269	.319	.373	.691
14	SD	NL	89	248	60	10	3	1	(2	1)	79	25	16	27	18	0	51	0	2	0	8	1	4	.242	.293	.319	.612
14	Sea	AL	32	82	16	2	1	2	(0	2)	26	11	5	4	7	0	19	0	0	1	1	2	2	.195	.256	.317	.573
10 ML YEARS			808	2162	587	103	17	41	(16	25)	847	289	196	261	187	8	408	9	13	14	56	20	56	.272	.330	.392	.722

Daniel Descalso

dess-CAL-so

Bats: L Throws: R Pos: PH-48;SS-33;2B-15;1B-7;3B-5;PR-2;RF-1   Ht: 5'10" Wt: 190 Born: 10/19/1986 Age: 29

				BATTING																RUNNING			AVERAGES			
Year	Team	Lg	G	AB	H	2B	3B	HR	(Hm	Rd)	TB	R	RBI	RC	TBB	IBB	SO	HBP	SH	SF	SB	CS	GDP	Avg	OBP	Slg	OPS
2010	StL	NL	11	34	9	2	0	0	(0	0)	11	6	4	5	2	0	6	1	0	0	1	0	0	.265	.324	.324	.648
2011	StL	NL	148	326	86	20	3	1	(1	0)	115	35	28	40	33	9	65	3	10	3	2	2	3	.264	.334	.353	.687
2012	StL	NL	143	374	85	10	7	4	(0	4)	121	41	26	29	37	3	83	5	7	3	6	5	5	.227	.303	.324	.627
2013	StL	NL	123	328	78	25	1	5	(1	4)	120	43	43	40	22	5	56	3	3	2	6	3	7	.238	.290	.366	.656
2014	StL	NL	104	161	39	11	0	0	(0	0)	50	20	10	15	20	0	33	2	1	0	1	3	2	.242	.333	.311	.644
2015	Col	NL	101	185	38	3	2	5	(1	4)	60	22	22	14	20	6	45	0	4	0	1	2	3	.205	.283	.324	.607
Postseason			44	84	18	2	0	2	(1	1)	26	16	6	5	4	2	19	0	5	1	2	0	2	.214	.247	.310	.557
6 ML YEARS			630	1408	335	71	13	15	(3	12)	477	167	133	143	134	23	288	14	25	8	17	13	20	.238	.309	.339	.648

Anthony DeSclafani

DEE-skla-fa-nee

Pitches: R Bats: R Pos: SP-31   Ht: 6'1" Wt: 190 Born: 4/18/1990 Age: 26

			HOW MUCH HE PITCHED						WHAT HE GAVE UP											THE RESULTS							
Year	Team	Lg	G	GS	CG	GF	IP	BFP	H	R	ER	HR	SH	SF	HB	TBB	IBB	SO	WP	Bk	W	L	Pct	Sh	Sv-Op	Hld	ERC	ERA
2012	Lnsng	A	28	21	0	0	123.0	510	145	55	46	3	3	7	3	25	0	92	6	2	11	3	.786	0	0- -	-	4.03	3.37
2013	Jupiter	A+	12	12	0	0	54.0	214	48	18	10	3	0	1	1	9	0	53	3	0	4	2	.667	0	0- -	-	2.45	1.67
2013	Jaxnvl	AA	13	13	0	0	75.0	304	74	31	28	7	4	1	4	14	0	62	4	1	5	4	.556	0	0- -	-	3.43	3.36
2014	Jaxnvl	AA	8	8	0	0	43.0	175	45	20	20	4	3	0	0	10	0	38	2	0	3	4	.429	0	0- -	-	3.76	4.19
2014	NewOr	AAA	12	11	0	1	59.1	249	48	23	23	2	3	1	2	21	0	58	4	0	3	3	.500	0	0- -	-	2.66	3.49
2014	Mia	NL	13	5	0	0	33.0	146	40	23	23	4	4	3	2	5	0	26	2	0	2	2	.500	0	0-0	0	4.56	6.27
2015	Cin	NL	31	31	0	0	184.2	785	194	93	83	17	10	5	5	55	5	151	6	0	9	13	.409	0	0-0	0	4.00	4.05
2 ML YEARS			44	36	0	4	217.2	931	234	116	106	21	14	8	7	60	5	177	8	0	11	15	.423	0	0-0	0	4.08	4.38

Delino DeShields

Bats: R Throws: R Pos: CF-87;LF-35;PR-8;DH-7;2B-1   Ht: 5'9" Wt: 210 Born: 8/16/1992 Age: 23

								BATTING													RUNNING			AVERAGES			
Year	Team	Lg	G	AB	H	2B	3B	HR	(Hm	Rd)	TB	R	RBI	RC	TBB	IBB	SO	HBP	SH	SF	SB	CS	GDP	Avg	OBP	Slg	OPS
2011	Lxngtn	A	119	469	103	17	2	9	(-	-)	151	73	48	52	52	0	118	8	7	5	30	11	7	.220	.305	.322	.627
2012	2 Tms	Low	135	537	154	24	8	12	(-	-)	230	113	61	108	83	5	131	9	5	3	101	19	5	.287	.389	.428	.818
2013	Lancst	A+	111	451	143	25	14	5	(-	-)	211	100	54	91	57	1	91	11	13	2	51	18	8	.317	.405	.468	.873
2014	CpChr	AA	114	411	97	14	2	11	(-	-)	148	75	57	63	61	0	112	11	18	6	53	14	3	.236	.346	.360	.706
2015	Tex	AL	121	425	111	22	10	2	(2	0)	159	83	37	66	53	1	101	3	7	4	25	8	1	.261	.344	.374	.718

Ian Desmond

Bats: R Throws: R Pos: SS-155;PH-1   Ht: 6'3" Wt: 215 Born: 9/20/1985 Age: 30

								BATTING													RUNNING			AVERAGES			
Year	Team	Lg	G	AB	H	2B	3B	HR	(Hm	Rd)	TB	R	RBI	RC	TBB	IBB	SO	HBP	SH	SF	SB	CS	GDP	Avg	OBP	Slg	OPS
2009	Was	NL	21	82	23	7	2	4	(2	2)	46	9	12	10	5	0	14	0	1	1	1	0	2	.280	.318	.561	.879
2010	Was	NL	154	525	141	27	4	10	(8	2)	206	59	65	58	28	3	109	5	9	7	17	5	9	.269	.308	.392	.700
2011	Was	NL	154	584	148	27	5	8	(7	1)	209	65	49	65	35	2	139	4	11	5	25	10	9	.253	.298	.358	.656
2012	Was	NL	130	513	150	33	2	25	(16	9)	262	72	73	73	30	1	113	3	0	1	21	6	17	.292	.335	.511	.845
2013	Was	NL	158	600	168	38	3	20	(10	10)	272	77	80	81	43	3	145	5	2	5	21	6	16	.280	.331	.453	.784
2014	Was	NL	154	593	151	26	3	24	(12	12)	255	73	91	78	46	0	183	6	0	3	24	5	17	.255	.313	.430	.743
2015	Was	NL	156	583	136	27	2	19	(11	8)	224	69	62	59	45	0	187	3	6	4	13	5	9	.233	.290	.384	.674
	Postseason		9	37	10	1	0	0	(0	0)	11	4	0	2	1	0	9	0	0	0	1	0	0	.270	.289	.297	.587
	7 ML YEARS		927	3480	917	185	21	110	(66	44)	1474	424	432	424	232	9	890	26	29	26	122	37	79	.264	.312	.424	.736

Odrisamer Despaigne

Pitches: R Bats: R Pos: SP-18; RP-16   oh-DREE-sa-mehr des-PAHN-yay   Ht: 6'0" Wt: 205 Born: 4/4/1987 Age: 29

			HOW MUCH HE PITCHED					WHAT HE GAVE UP												THE RESULTS						
Year	Team	Lg	G	GS	CG	GF	IP	BFP	H	R	ER	HR	SH	SF	HB	TBB	IBB	SO	WP	Bk	W	L	Pct	Sh	Sv-Op	Hld	ERC	ERA
2014	ElPaso	AAA	5	5	0	0	23.2	121	36	20	20	3	2	4	1	13	0	29	1	0	1	3	.250	0	0- -	-	8.14	7.61
2014	SD	NL	16	16	0	0	96.1	404	85	44	36	6	8	1	5	32	0	65	0	0	4	7	.364	0	0-0	1	3.12	3.36
2015	SD	NL	34	18	0	5	125.2	547	142	82	81	17	8	3	9	32	3	69	7	0	5	9	.357	0	0-0	1	4.75	5.80
	2 ML YEARS		50	34	0	5	222.0	951	227	126	117	23	16	4	14	64	3	134	7	0	9	16	.360	0	0-0	1	4.01	4.74

Ross Detwiler

Pitches: L Bats: R Pos: RP-34; SP-7   DETT-why-lerr   Ht: 6'3" Wt: 215 Born: 3/6/1986 Age: 30

			HOW MUCH HE PITCHED					WHAT HE GAVE UP												THE RESULTS						
Year	Team	Lg	G	GS	CG	GF	IP	BFP	H	R	ER	HR	SH	SF	HB	TBB	IBB	SO	WP	Bk	W	L	Pct	Sh	Sv-Op	Hld	ERC	ERA
2007	Was	NL	1	0	0	1	1.0	4	0	0	0	0	0	0	0	0	0	1	0	0	0	0	-	0	0-0	0	0.00	0.00
2009	Was	NL	15	14	1	0	75.2	341	87	43	42	3	4	1	2	33	3	43	4	0	1	6	.143	0	0-0	0	4.65	5.00
2010	Was	NL	8	5	0	1	29.2	135	34	22	14	5	2	0	1	14	1	17	1	0	1	3	.250	0	0-0	0	5.83	4.25
2011	Was	NL	15	10	0	0	66.0	277	63	26	22	7	7	3	3	20	2	41	2	0	4	5	.444	0	0-0	1	3.64	3.00
2012	Was	NL	33	27	0	1	164.1	686	149	75	62	16	8	3	5	52	0	105	4	1	10	8	.556	0	0-0	1	3.30	3.40
2013	Was	NL	13	13	0	0	71.1	316	92	37	32	5	4	1	5	14	2	39	0	0	2	7	.222	0	0-0	0	4.96	4.04
2014	Was	NL	47	0	0	15	63.0	274	68	34	28	5	4	3	5	21	4	39	3	0	2	3	.400	0	1-2	3	4.36	4.00
2015	2 Tms		41	7	0	7	58.1	288	82	51	47	10	1	4	6	36	1	41	3	0	1	5	.167	0	0-2	2	8.67	7.25
15	Tex	AL	17	7	0	4	43.0	208	62	37	34	9	1	3	3	20	0	28	3	0	0	5	.000	0	0-1	1	8.35	7.12
15	Atl	NL	24	0	0	3	15.1	80	20	14	13	1	0	1	3	16	1	13	0	0	1	0	1.000	0	0-1	1	9.42	7.63
	Postseason		1	1	0	0	6.0	25	3	1	0	0	1	0	0	3	1	2	0	0	0	0	-	0	0-0	0	1.21	0.00
	8 ML YEARS		173	76	1	25	529.1	2321	575	288	247	50	30	15	27	190	13	326	17	1	21	37	.362	0	1-4	7	4.54	4.20

Elias Diaz

Bats: R Throws: R Pos: PH-2   Eh-lee-ahs   Ht: 6'0" Wt: 210 Born: 11/17/1990 Age: 25

								BATTING													RUNNING			AVERAGES			
Year	Team	Lg	G	AB	H	2B	3B	HR	(Hm	Rd)	TB	R	RBI	RC	TBB	IBB	SO	HBP	SH	SF	SB	CS	GDP	Avg	OBP	Slg	OPS
2011	WV	A	90	326	72	23	3	2	(-	-)	107	38	45	31	23	0	69	4	5	2	6	1	7	.221	.279	.328	.607
2012	WV	A	92	313	65	14	1	3	(-	-)	90	32	26	24	22	0	51	3	3	6	2	2	15	.208	.262	.288	.549
2013	Bradtn	A+	57	183	51	12	2	2	(-	-)	73	30	15	30	31	0	33	1	3	2	4	4	3	.279	.382	.399	.781
2014	Altna	AA	91	326	107	20	0	6	(-	-)	145	41	54	57	30	0	51	1	2	8	3	2	11	.328	.378	.445	.823
2014	Indy	AAA	10	33	5	1	0	0	(-	-)	6	4	0	0	3	0	6	1	0	0	0	1	0	.152	.243	.182	.425
2015	Indy	AAA	93	325	88	16	4	4	(-	-)	124	33	47	42	29	0	47	2	2	5	1	4	9	.271	.330	.382	.711
2015	Pit	NL	2	2	0	0	0	0	(0	0)	0	0	0	0	0	0	1	0	0	0	0	0	0	.000	.000	.000	.000

Jairo Diaz

Pitches: R Bats: R Pos: RP-21   HIGH-row   Ht: 6'0" Wt: 195 Born: 5/27/1991 Age: 25

			HOW MUCH HE PITCHED					WHAT HE GAVE UP												THE RESULTS						
Year	Team	Lg	G	GS	CG	GF	IP	BFP	H	R	ER	HR	SH	SF	HB	TBB	IBB	SO	WP	Bk	W	L	Pct	Sh	Sv-Op	Hld	ERC	ERA
2011	2 Tms	Low	15	14	0	0	76.0	331	83	51	43	4	2	1	6	30	1	54	8	0	4	4	.500	0	0- -	-	4.64	5.09
2012	2 Tms	Low	27	27	0	0	143.2	667	192	120	103	13	2	8	10	52	1	106	24	1	7	13	.350	0	0- -	-	6.13	6.45
2013	2 Tms	Low	45	0	0	26	56.1	259	65	43	37	6	3	2	4	25	2	49	8	1	0	5	.000	0	8- -	-	5.38	5.91
2014	InldEm	A+	29	0	0	16	32.0	140	31	18	17	2	2	0	1	10	1	37	8	0	2	3	.400	0	4- -	-	3.25	4.78
2014	Ark	AA	27	0	0	18	32.2	134	30	8	8	2	3	1	1	10	1	48	4	0	2	1	.667	0	11- -	-	3.15	2.20
2015	Albq	AAA	47	0	0	32	55.0	251	51	31	28	6	1	1	4	37	0	50	2	0	3	5	.375	0	8- -	-	5.11	4.58
2014	LAA	AL	5	0	0	2	5.2	24	4	2	2	0	1	0	1	3	0	6	0	0	0	0	-	0	0-0	0	2.29	3.18
2015	Col	NL	21	0	0	5	19.0	78	16	6	5	2	0	0	0	6	0	18	0	0	0	1	.000	0	0-1	7	2.93	2.37
	2 ML YEARS		26	0	0	7	24.2	102	20	8	7	2	1	0	1	9	0	26	0	0	0	1	.000	0	0-1	7	2.79	2.55

Jonathan Diaz

Bats: R **Throws:** R **Pos:** SS-6;LF-2   **Ht:** 5'9" **Wt:** 155 **Born:** 4/10/1985 **Age:** 31

Year Team	Lg	G	AB	H	2B	3B	HR	(Hm	Rd)	TB	R	RBI	RC	TBB	IBB	SO	HBP	SH	SF	SB	CS	GDP	Avg	OBP	Slg	OPS
2015 Buffalo*	AAA	118	359	80	12	2	2	(-	-)	102	37	23	39	51	6	64	6	12	2	7	3	10	.223	.328	.284	.612
2013 Bos	AL	5	4	0	0	0	0	(0	0)	0	2	0	0	0	0	0	0	0	0	0	0	0	.000	.000	.000	.000
2014 Tor	AL	23	38	6	1	0	0	(0	0)	7	3	4	2	3	0	14	2	2	0	1	0	1	.158	.256	.184	.440
2015 Tor	AL	7	13	2	0	0	0	(0	0)	2	1	2	1	1	0	3	1	1	0	0	0	0	.154	.267	.154	.421
3 ML YEARS		35	55	8	1	0	0	(0	0)	9	6	6	3	4	0	17	3	3	0	1	0	1	.145	.242	.164	.406

Jumbo Diaz

Pitches: R **Bats:** R **Pos:** RP-61   **Ht:** 6'4" **Wt:** 280 **Born:** 2/27/1984 **Age:** 32

Year Team	Lg	G	GS	CG	GF	IP	BFP	H	R	ER	HR	SH	SF	HB	TBB	IBB	SO	WP	Bk	W	L	Pct	Sh	Sv-Op	Hld	ERC	ERA
2011 Bowie	AA	34	0	0	30	32.0	132	21	9	5	2	4	1	1	13	0	38	3	0	0	2	.000	0	22--	-	2.14	1.41
2011 Norfolk	AAA	14	0	0	6	12.2	67	21	10	8	1	0	0	2	8	0	10	1	0	0	1	.000	0	1--	-	9.80	5.68
2012 Indy	AAA	41	0	0	16	45.0	197	43	19	18	3	2	2	4	19	4	37	3	0	1	2	.333	0	3--	-	3.86	3.60
2013 Lsvlle	AAA	44	0	0	27	54.1	217	35	11	10	5	1	1	1	21	3	60	1	0	3	4	.429	0	13--	-	2.14	1.66
2014 Lsvlle	AAA	30	0	0	28	33.1	134	25	6	4	1	1	1	2	10	1	31	1	0	2	2	.500	0	18--	-	2.16	1.08
2015 Lsvlle	AAA	13	0	0	11	16.0	65	11	2	2	0	0	0	1	4	0	12	0	1	0	1	.000	0	8--	-	1.57	1.13
2014 Cin	NL	36	0	0	12	34.2	142	29	13	13	3	0	2	0	14	4	37	1	0	0	1	.000	0	0-1	8	3.00	3.38
2015 Cin	NL	61	0	0	16	60.1	255	58	29	28	9	3	2	3	18	3	70	5	1	2	1	.667	0	1-5	7	3.92	4.18
2 ML YEARS		97	0	0	28	95.0	397	87	42	41	12	3	4	3	32	7	107	6	1	2	2	.500	0	1-6	15	3.58	3.88

Alex Dickerson

Bats: L **Throws:** L **Pos:** PH-10;LF-1   **Ht:** 6'3" **Wt:** 235 **Born:** 5/26/1990 **Age:** 26

Year Team	Lg	G	AB	H	2B	3B	HR	(Hm	Rd)	TB	R	RBI	RC	TBB	IBB	SO	HBP	SH	SF	SB	CS	GDP	Avg	OBP	Slg	OPS
2011 StCol	A-	41	150	47	16	1	3	(-	-)	74	25	19	29	16	1	28	5	0	2	0	0	5	.313	.393	.493	.886
2012 Bradtn	A+	129	488	144	31	3	13	(-	-)	220	65	90	79	39	1	93	7	2	5	12	7	7	.295	.353	.451	.803
2013 Altna	AA	126	451	130	36	3	17	(-	-)	223	61	68	75	27	4	89	8	2	3	10	7	14	.288	.337	.494	.832
2014 SnAnt	AA	34	137	44	11	2	3	(-	-)	68	20	24	24	9	1	28	1	0	0	0	1	2	.321	.367	.496	.864
2015 ElPaso	AAA	125	459	141	36	9	12	(-	-)	231	82	71	88	45	2	96	8	0	7	4	0	10	.307	.374	.503	.877
2015 SD	NL	11	8	2	0	0	0	(0	0)	2	0	0	0	0	0	3	0	0	0	0	0	1	.250	.250	.250	.500

Corey Dickerson

Bats: L **Throws:** R **Pos:** LF-54;PH-8;CF-3;DH-2   **Ht:** 6'1" **Wt:** 205 **Born:** 5/22/1989 **Age:** 27

Year Team	Lg	G	AB	H	2B	3B	HR	(Hm	Rd)	TB	R	RBI	RC	TBB	IBB	SO	HBP	SH	SF	SB	CS	GDP	Avg	OBP	Slg	OPS
2013 Col	NL	69	194	51	13	5	5	(4	1)	89	32	17	23	16	0	41	0	1	2	2	2	1	.263	.316	.459	.775
2014 Col	NL	131	436	136	27	6	24	(15	9)	247	74	76	79	37	6	101	1	0	4	8	7	6	.312	.364	.567	.931
2015 Col	NL	65	224	68	18	2	10	(5	5)	120	30	31	39	10	0	56	0	0	0	0	1	3	.304	.333	.536	.869
3 ML YEARS		265	854	255	58	13	39	(24	15)	456	136	124	141	63	6	198	1	1	6	10	10	10	.299	.345	.534	.879

R.A. Dickey

Pitches: R **Bats:** R **Pos:** SP-33   **Ht:** 6'3" **Wt:** 215 **Born:** 10/29/1974 **Age:** 41

Year Team	Lg	G	GS	CG	GF	IP	BFP	H	R	ER	HR	SH	SF	HB	TBB	IBB	SO	WP	Bk	W	L	Pct	Sh	Sv-Op	Hld	ERC	ERA
2001 Tex	AL	4	0	0	1	12.0	53	13	9	9	3	0	0	0	7	1	4	1	0	0	1	.000	0	0-0	0	6.57	6.75
2003 Tex	AL	38	13	1	6	116.2	513	135	68	66	16	4	3	5	38	5	94	5	2	9	8	.529	1	1-1	3	5.09	5.09
2004 Tex	AL	25	15	0	2	104.1	480	136	77	65	17	3	3	4	33	1	57	5	1	6	7	.462	0	1-1	0	6.08	5.61
2005 Tex	AL	9	4	0	2	29.2	134	29	23	22	4	0	1	2	17	0	15	2	0	1	2	.333	0	0-0	0	5.18	6.67
2006 Tex	AL	1	1	0	0	3.1	18	8	7	7	6	0	0	0	1	0	1	0	0	0	1	.000	0	0-0	0	32.05	18.90
2008 Sea	AL	32	14	0	9	112.1	500	124	65	65	15	4	6	2	51	4	58	11	1	5	8	.385	0	0-0	0	5.19	5.21
2009 Min	AL	35	1	0	13	64.1	293	74	34	33	8	2	2	4	30	1	42	4	0	1	1	.500	0	0-0	1	5.66	4.62
2010 NYM	NL	27	26	2	0	174.1	713	165	62	55	13	7	3	4	42	3	104	11	0	11	9	.550	1	0-0	1	3.11	2.84
2011 NYM	NL	33	32	1	0	208.2	876	202	85	76	18	16	7	9	54	2	134	9	1	8	13	.381	0	0-0	1	3.40	3.28
2012 NYM	NL	34	33	5	1	233.2	927	192	78	71	24	9	7	6	54	2	230	4	1	20	6	.769	3	0-0	1	2.70	2.73
2013 Tor	AL	34	34	3	0	224.2	943	207	113	105	35	2	6	10	71	0	177	7	1	14	13	.519	1	0-0	1	3.87	4.21
2014 Tor	AL	34	34	1	0	215.2	914	191	101	89	26	2	4	14	74	2	173	6	0	14	13	.519	0	0-0	1	3.58	3.71
2015 Tor	AL	33	33	2	0	214.1	884	195	97	93	25	3	11	11	61	1	126	9	2	11	11	.500	0	0-0	1	3.48	3.91
13 ML YEARS		339	240	15	34	1714.0	7248	1671	819	756	210	52	53	74	533	22	1215	73	9	100	93	.518	6	2-2	6	3.91	3.97

Jake Diekman

Pitches: L **Bats:** L **Pos:** RP-67   DEEK-man   **Ht:** 6'4" **Wt:** 200 **Born:** 1/21/1987 **Age:** 29

Year Team	Lg	G	GS	CG	GF	IP	BFP	H	R	ER	HR	SH	SF	HB	TBB	IBB	SO	WP	Bk	W	L	Pct	Sh	Sv-Op	Hld	ERC	ERA
2015 LV*	AAA	6	0	0	5	7.0	26	5	0	0	0	1	0	0	1	0	7	1	0	0	0	-	0	3--	-	1.37	0.00
2012 Phi	NL	32	0	0	7	27.1	131	25	17	12	1	0	1	3	20	3	35	1	0	1	1	.500	0	0-1	4	4.45	3.95
2013 Phi	NL	45	0	0	11	38.1	164	34	15	11	1	2	1	0	16	2	41	2	1	1	4	.200	0	0-1	11	2.89	2.58
2014 Phi	NL	73	0	0	19	71.0	313	66	36	30	4	2	7	3	35	5	100	7	0	5	5	.500	0	0-4	18	3.73	3.80
2015 2 Tms		67	0	0	7	58.1	260	53	28	26	5	0	0	3	31	0	69	2	0	2	1	.667	0	0-3	16	4.11	4.01
15 Phi	NL	41	0	0	6	36.2	175	40	23	21	3	0	0	2	24	0	49	1	0	2	1	.667	0	0-2	6	5.60	5.15
15 Tex	AL	26	0	0	1	21.2	85	13	5	5	2	0	0	1	7	0	20	1	0	0	0	-	0	0-1	10	1.89	2.08
4 ML YEARS		217	0	0	44	195.0	868	178	96	79	11	5	8	9	102	10	245	12	1	9	11	.450	0	0-9	49	3.78	3.65

Derek Dietrich

Bats: L Throws: R Pos: LF-46;3B-26;PH-17;1B-2;2B-2;DH-1   DEE-trick   Ht: 6'0" Wt: 205 Born: 7/18/1989 Age: 26

							BATTING											RUNNING			AVERAGES			
Year	Team	Lg	G	AB	H	2B	3B	HR	(Hm | Rd)	TB	R	RBI	RC	TBB	IBB	SO	HBP	SH	SF	SB	CS	GDP	Avg	OBP	Slg	OPS
2015	NewOr*	AAA	56	192	50	13	2	7	(- | -)	88	25	27	32	15	1	45	15	0	2	0	2	1	.260	.357	.458	.815
2013	Mia	NL	57	215	46	10	2	9	(3 | 6)	87	32	23	24	11	1	56	7	0	0	1	0	1	.214	.275	.405	.679
2014	Mia	NL	49	158	36	6	2	5	(1 | 4)	61	31	17	22	13	0	38	10	2	0	1	0	1	.228	.326	.386	.712
2015	Mia	NL	90	250	64	14	3	10	(3 | 7)	114	38	24	32	23	2	65	13	0	3	0	2	4	.256	.346	.456	.802
3 ML YEARS			196	623	146	30	7	24	(7 | 17)	262	101	64	78	47	3	159	30	2	3	2	2	6	.234	.317	.421	.738

Wilmer Difo

Bats: B Throws: R Pos: PH-10;PR-4;2B-2   DEE-fo   Ht: 6'0" Wt: 195 Born: 4/2/1992 Age: 24

							BATTING											RUNNING			AVERAGES			
Year	Team	Lg	G	AB	H	2B	3B	HR	(Hm | Rd)	TB	R	RBI	RC	TBB	IBB	SO	HBP	SH	SF	SB	CS	GDP	Avg	OBP	Slg	OPS
2011	Nats	R	25	88	24	4	3	0	(- | -)	34	10	8	12	10	0	8	0	5	1	5	3	0	.273	.343	.386	.730
2012	Nats	R	54	198	52	7	3	0	(- | -)	65	33	13	30	34	0	35	2	0	1	19	5	2	.263	.374	.328	.703
2013	4 Tms	Low	61	207	45	7	4	4	(- | -)	72	30	21	22	21	0	36	3	2	2	9	4	2	.217	.296	.348	.644
2014	Hgrstn	A	136	559	176	31	7	14	(- | -)	263	91	90	102	37	0	65	6	2	6	49	9	5	.315	.360	.470	.831
2015	Hrsbrg	AA	87	359	100	21	6	2	(- | -)	139	48	39	49	12	2	79	7	0	3	26	1	8	.279	.312	.387	.700
2015	Ptomc	A+	19	75	24	7	0	3	(- | -)	40	13	14	15	8	1	13	0	0	0	4	1	0	.320	.386	.533	.919
2015	Was	NL	15	11	2	0	0	0	(0 | 0)	2	1	0	0	0	0	2	0	0	0	0	0	0	.182	.182	.182	.364

Chris Dominguez

Bats: R Throws: R Pos: PH-9;1B-2;LF-2;RF-1   Ht: 6'4" Wt: 235 Born: 11/22/1986 Age: 29

							BATTING											RUNNING			AVERAGES			
Year	Team	Lg	G	AB	H	2B	3B	HR	(Hm | Rd)	TB	R	RBI	RC	TBB	IBB	SO	HBP	SH	SF	SB	CS	GDP	Avg	OBP	Slg	OPS
2011	SnJos	A+	63	258	75	10	1	11	(- | -)	120	40	40	41	18	0	73	1	0	2	8	2	7	.291	.337	.465	.802
2011	Rchmd	AA	78	295	72	22	2	7	(- | -)	119	35	45	31	9	0	78	4	0	5	1	5	5	.244	.272	.403	.675
2012	Rchmd	AA	49	188	42	9	0	2	(- | -)	57	17	19	14	7	0	50	1	0	1	3	0	4	.223	.254	.303	.557
2012	Fresno	AAA	43	174	43	11	0	3	(- | -)	63	15	25	15	2	0	47	2	0	0	1	2	6	.247	.264	.362	.626
2013	Fresno	AAA	132	466	137	24	5	15	(- | -)	216	60	65	71	23	3	112	6	0	2	4	5	23	.294	.334	.464	.798
2014	Fresno	AAA	131	496	136	23	3	21	(- | -)	228	66	85	71	22	0	143	4	0	6	21	10	10	.274	.307	.460	.766
2015	Lsvlle	AAA	96	296	66	19	0	9	(- | -)	112	32	36	31	16	1	92	6	1	2	5	3	15	.223	.275	.378	.653
2014	SF	NL	8	17	1	0	0	1	(0 | 1)	4	1	2	0	1	1	4	0	0	0	0	0	2	.059	.111	.235	.346
2015	Cin	NL	14	23	6	1	1	1	(0 | 1)	12	2	3	2	0	0	12	0	0	0	0	0	0	.261	.261	.522	.783
2 ML YEARS			22	40	7	1	1	2	(0 | 2)	16	3	5	2	1	1	16	0	0	0	0	0	2	.175	.195	.400	.595

Jose Dominguez

Pitches: R Bats: R Pos: RP-4   Ht: 6'0" Wt: 200 Born: 8/7/1990 Age: 25

			HOW MUCH HE PITCHED						WHAT HE GAVE UP										THE RESULTS						
Year	Team	Lg	G	GS	CG	GF	IP	BFP	H	R	ER	HR	SH	SF	HB	TBB	IBB	SO	WP	Bk	W	L	Pct	Sh	Sv-Op	Hld	ERC	ERA
2015	Drham*	AAA	30	2	0	8	27.2	135	36	20	19	5	0	2	0	20	0	25	7	0	0	2	.000	0	1--	-	8.03	6.18
2013	LAD	NL	9	0	0	2	8.1	39	11	3	2	0	0	0	1	3	0	4	1	0	0	0	-	0	0-0	1	5.47	2.16
2014	LAD	NL	5	0	0	2	6.1	30	7	8	8	2	0	0	1	3	0	8	0	0	0	0	-	0	0-0	0	7.23	11.37
2015	TB	AL	4	0	0	2	5.2	19	2	0	0	0	1	0	0	2	0	5	0	0	1	0	1.000	0	0-0	0	0.84	0.00
3 ML YEARS			18	0	0	6	20.1	88	20	11	10	2	1	0	2	8	0	17	1	0	1	0	1.000	0	0-0	1	4.39	4.43

Josh Donaldson

Bats: R Throws: R Pos: 3B-150;DH-7;PH-1   Ht: 6'0" Wt: 220 Born: 12/8/1985 Age: 30

							BATTING											RUNNING			AVERAGES			
Year	Team	Lg	G	AB	H	2B	3B	HR	(Hm | Rd)	TB	R	RBI	RC	TBB	IBB	SO	HBP	SH	SF	SB	CS	GDP	Avg	OBP	Slg	OPS
2010	Oak	AL	14	32	5	1	0	1	(0 | 1)	9	1	4	3	2	0	12	0	0	0	0	0	0	.156	.206	.281	.487
2012	Oak	AL	75	274	66	16	0	9	(3 | 6)	109	34	33	33	14	0	61	5	0	1	4	1	6	.241	.289	.398	.687
2013	Oak	AL	158	579	174	37	3	24	(13 | 11)	289	89	93	112	76	1	110	6	1	6	5	2	15	.301	.384	.499	.883
2014	Oak	AL	158	608	155	31	2	29	(11 | 18)	277	93	98	105	76	5	130	7	0	4	8	0	16	.255	.342	.456	.798
2015	Tor	AL	158	620	184	41	2	41	(24 | 17)	352	122	123	131	73	0	133	6	2	10	6	0	16	.297	.371	.568	.939
Postseason			11	43	10	1	0	0	(0 | 0)	11	2	0	2	3	0	14	0	0	0	0	0	1	.233	.283	.256	.538
5 ML YEARS			563	2113	584	126	7	104	(51 | 53)	1036	339	351	384	241	7	446	24	3	21	23	3	53	.276	.354	.490	.844

Sean Doolittle

Pitches: L Bats: L Pos: RP-12   Ht: 6'3" Wt: 210 Born: 9/26/1986 Age: 29

			HOW MUCH HE PITCHED						WHAT HE GAVE UP										THE RESULTS						
Year	Team	Lg	G	GS	CG	GF	IP	BFP	H	R	ER	HR	SH	SF	HB	TBB	IBB	SO	WP	Bk	W	L	Pct	Sh	Sv-Op	Hld	ERC	ERA
2015	Nashv*	AAA	6	0	0	1	6.0	21	3	2	2	2	0	0	0	0	0	13	0	0	0	0	-	0	0--	-	1.32	3.00
2012	Oak	AL	44	0	0	7	47.1	191	40	18	16	3	2	2	0	11	1	60	0	0	2	1	.667	0	1-2	18	2.36	3.04
2013	Oak	AL	70	0	0	11	69.0	266	53	24	24	4	3	0	2	13	1	60	2	0	5	5	.500	0	2-7	26	2.00	3.13
2014	Oak	AL	61	0	0	40	62.2	236	38	19	19	5	2	1	0	8	1	89	0	0	2	4	.333	0	22-26	5	1.23	2.73
2015	Oak	AL	12	0	0	7	13.2	57	12	6	6	1	0	1	0	5	0	15	0	0	1	0	1.000	0	4-5	1	3.10	3.95
Postseason			8	0	0	1	9.0	41	10	6	4	1	3	1	0	2	0	11	0	0	0	1	.000	0	0-3	2	3.75	4.00
4 ML YEARS			187	0	0	65	192.2	750	143	67	65	13	7	4	2	37	3	224	2	0	10	10	.500	0	29-40	50	1.84	3.04

Danny Dorn

Bats: L Throws: L Pos: PH-19;RF-3;1B-2   Ht: 6'2" Wt: 200 Born: 7/20/1984 Age: 31

Year	Team	Lg	G	AB	H	2B	3B	HR	(Hm	Rd)	TB	R	RBI	RC	TBB	IBB	SO	HBP	SH	SF	SB	CS	GDP	Avg	OBP	Slg	OPS
2011	Lsvlle	AAA	124	448	111	30	1	18	(-	-)	197	63	74	63	36	4	133	6	0	4	2	0	9	.248	.310	.440	.749
2012	Lsvlle	AAA	69	226	52	14	1	7	(-	-)	89	26	24	30	28	0	65	4	0	4	1	2	2	.230	.321	.394	.714
2012	Toledo	AAA	47	167	47	11	1	7	(-	-)	81	24	25	32	22	2	43	4	0	1	4	0	1	.281	.376	.485	.861
2013	Toledo	AAA	137	496	128	21	2	25	(-	-)	228	67	82	80	58	4	131	3	1	7	8	2	6	.258	.335	.460	.795
2014	Reno	AAA	73	247	75	13	6	12	(-	-)	136	42	47	52	32	1	57	2	1	6	1	1	8	.304	.380	.551	.930
2015	Reno	AAA	75	267	103	26	3	10	(-	-)	165	57	53	68	28	0	45	4	1	5	1	2	7	.386	.444	.618	1.062
2015	Ari	NL	23	30	5	1	0	0	(0	0)	6	0	3	1	2	0	10	0	0	0	0	0	1	.167	.219	.200	.419

Felix Doubront

Pitches: L Bats: L Pos: SP-12; RP-4   due-BRAWNDT   Ht: 6'2" Wt: 225 Born: 10/23/1987 Age: 28

Year	Team	Lg	G	GS	CG	GF	IP	BFP	H	R	ER	HR	SH	SF	HB	TBB	IBB	SO	WP	Bk	W	L	Pct	Sh	Sv-Op	Hld	ERC	ERA
2015	Buffalo*	AAA	9	9	0	0	48.0	194	36	15	13	1	0	0	0	18	0	43	2	0	1	3	.250	0	0- -		2.19	2.44
2010	Bos	AL	12	3	0	5	25.0	113	27	16	12	3	1	1	1	10	0	23	3	0	2	2	.500	0	2-3	1	4.72	4.32
2011	Bos	AL	11	0	0	1	10.1	47	12	7	7	1	0	1	0	8	0	6	0	0	0	0	-	0	1-1	0	6.97	6.10
2012	Bos	AL	29	29	0	0	161.0	709	162	95	87	24	1	6	5	71	0	167	5	0	11	10	.524	0	0-0	0	4.73	4.86
2013	Bos	AL	29	27	0	0	162.1	705	161	84	78	13	3	10	5	71	0	139	8	0	11	6	.647	0	0-0	0	4.18	4.32
2014	2 Tms		21	14	0	2	79.2	364	91	54	49	12	3	2	2	33	0	51	5	1	4	5	.444	0	0-0	0	5.33	5.54
2015	2 Tms		16	12	0	2	75.1	328	87	50	46	10	4	5	1	26	1	56	3	0	3	3	.500	0	1-1	0	5.09	5.50
14	Bos	AL	17	10	0	0	59.1	277	69	45	40	10	2	2	2	26	0	43	4	0	2	4	.333	0	0-0	0	5.66	6.07
14	ChC	NL	4	4	0	0	20.1	87	22	9	9	2	1	0	0	7	0	8	1	1	2	1	.667	0	0-0	0	4.36	3.98
15	Tor	AL	5	4	0	0	22.2	101	32	15	12	1	0	1	1	5	1	13	1	0	1	1	.500	0	0-0	0	5.56	4.76
15	Oak	AL	11	8	0	2	52.2	227	55	35	34	9	4	4	0	21	0	43	2	0	2	2	.500	0	1-1	0	4.89	5.81
	Postseason		4	0	0	1	7.0	27	3	1	1	0	0	0	1	3	1	4	0	0	1	0	1.000	0	0-0	0	1.26	1.29
	6 ML YEARS		118	85	0	10	513.2	2266	540	306	279	63	12	25	14	219	1	442	24	1	31	26	.544	0	4-5	1	4.74	4.89

Brian Dozier

Bats: R Throws: R Pos: 2B-157   DOUGH-zher   Ht: 5'11" Wt: 200 Born: 5/15/1987 Age: 29

Year	Team	Lg	G	AB	H	2B	3B	HR	(Hm	Rd)	TB	R	RBI	RC	TBB	IBB	SO	HBP	SH	SF	SB	CS	GDP	Avg	OBP	Slg	OPS
2012	Min	AL	84	316	74	11	1	6	(4	2)	105	33	33	24	16	0	58	1	4	3	9	2	10	.234	.271	.332	.603
2013	Min	AL	147	558	136	33	4	18	(8	10)	231	72	66	74	51	0	120	6	3	4	14	7	14	.244	.312	.414	.726
2014	Min	AL	156	598	145	33	1	23	(11	12)	249	112	71	87	89	1	129	9	3	8	21	7	8	.242	.345	.416	.762
2015	Min	AL	157	628	148	39	4	28	(13	15)	279	101	77	87	61	2	148	7	0	8	12	4	10	.236	.307	.444	.751
	4 ML YEARS		544	2100	503	116	10	75	(36	39)	864	318	247	272	217	3	455	23	10	23	56	20	42	.240	.314	.411	.726

Kyle Drabek

Pitches: R Bats: R Pos: RP-3   Ht: 6'2" Wt: 205 Born: 12/8/1987 Age: 28

Year	Team	Lg	G	GS	CG	GF	IP	BFP	H	R	ER	HR	SH	SF	HB	TBB	IBB	SO	WP	Bk	W	L	Pct	Sh	Sv-Op	Hld	ERC	ERA
2015	Charlt*	AAA	24	24	0	0	137.1	577	125	62	53	8	4	1	4	53	0	84	9	0	7	11	.389	0	0- -		3.39	3.47
2010	Tor	AL	3	3	0	0	17.0	69	18	9	9	2	1	2	0	5	0	12	2	0	0	3	.000	0	0-0	0	4.34	4.76
2011	Tor	AL	18	14	0	2	78.2	365	87	54	53	10	3	5	1	55	0	51	11	0	4	5	.444	0	0-0	0	6.30	6.06
2012	Tor	AL	13	13	0	0	71.1	317	67	41	37	10	0	1	1	47	0	47	7	0	4	7	.364	0	0-0	0	5.21	4.67
2013	Tor	AL	3	0	0	1	2.1	14	4	2	2	1	0	0	0	2	0	3	0	0	0	0	-	0	0-0	0	16.01	7.71
2014	Tor	AL	2	0	0	1	3.0	13	2	0	0	0	0	0	0	2	0	5	0	0	0	0	-	0	0-0	0	2.54	0.00
2015	CWS	AL	3	0	0	3	5.1	26	9	3	3	1	0	0	0	2	0	3	0	0	0	0	-	0	0-0	0	9.16	5.06
	6 ML YEARS		42	30	0	7	177.2	804	187	109	104	24	4	8	3	113	0	121	20	0	8	15	.348	0	0-0	0	5.79	5.27

Oliver Drake

Pitches: R Bats: R Pos: RP-13   Ht: 6'4" Wt: 210 Born: 1/13/1987 Age: 29

Year	Team	Lg	G	GS	CG	GF	IP	BFP	H	R	ER	HR	SH	SF	HB	TBB	IBB	SO	WP	Bk	W	L	Pct	Sh	Sv-Op	Hld	ERC	ERA
2011	Frdrck	A+	14	13	2	0	96.2	374	78	27	23	1	4	0	4	18	1	80	6	0	8	3	.727	0	0- -		1.96	2.14
2011	Bowie	AA	12	12	2	0	64.0	293	77	39	37	8	1	0	4	24	0	47	3	0	3	5	.375	0	0- -		5.55	5.20
2013	Bowie	AA	19	0	0	13	31.0	126	19	8	6	1	2	0	1	13	0	38	1	0	3	0	1.000	0	8- -		1.84	1.74
2014	Bowie	AA	50	0	0	47	52.2	210	41	19	18	2	1	0	0	17	0	71	4	0	4	3	.333	0	31- -		2.28	3.08
2015	Norfolk	AAA	42	0	0	34	44.0	169	23	4	4	1	0	1	0	16	0	66	2	0	1	2	.333	0	23- -		1.31	0.82
2015	Bal	AL	13	0	0	5	15.2	72	16	7	5	1	0	2	0	9	0	17	3	0	0	0	-	0	0-0	2	4.50	2.87

Stephen Drew

Bats: L Throws: R Pos: 2B-123;SS-15;PH-7;3B-4   Ht: 6'0" Wt: 190 Born: 3/16/1983 Age: 33

Year	Team	Lg	G	AB	H	2B	3B	HR	(Hm	Rd)	TB	R	RBI	RC	TBB	IBB	SO	HBP	SH	SF	SB	CS	GDP	Avg	OBP	Slg	OPS
2006	Ari	NL	59	209	66	13	7	5	(3	2)	108	27	23	31	14	4	50	0	2	1	2	0	1	.316	.357	.517	.874
2007	Ari	NL	150	543	129	28	4	12	(6	6)	201	60	60	71	60	5	100	3	5	8	9	0	4	.238	.313	.370	.683
2008	Ari	NL	152	611	178	44	11	21	(9	12)	307	91	67	97	41	6	109	1	3	7	3	3	5	.291	.333	.502	.836
2009	Ari	NL	135	533	139	29	12	12	(4	8)	228	71	65	76	49	7	91	1	5	5	5	2	5	.261	.320	.428	.748
2010	Ari	NL	151	565	157	33	12	15	(5	10)	259	83	61	84	62	2	108	3	2	1	10	5	8	.278	.352	.458	.810
2011	Ari	NL	86	321	81	21	5	5	(3	2)	127	44	45	41	30	0	74	1	1	1	4	4	3	.252	.317	.396	.713
2012	2 Tms		79	287	64	13	1	7	(4	3)	100	38	28	30	37	2	76	0	0	3	1	2	2	.223	.309	.348	.657
2013	Bos	AL	124	442	112	29	8	13	(6	7)	196	57	67	63	54	3	124	1	0	4	6	0	9	.253	.333	.443	.777

(Batting, continued)

Year	Team	Lg	G	AB	H	2B	3B	HR	Hm	Rd	TB	R	RBI	RC	TBB	IBB	SO	HBP	SH	SF	SB	CS	GDP	Avg	OBP	Slg	OPS
2014	2 Tms	AL	85	271	44	14	1	7	(4	3)	81	18	26	19	27	3	75	0	0	2	1	1	1	.162	.237	.299	.536
2015	NYY	AL	131	383	77	16	1	17	(9	8)	146	43	44	40	37	1	71	1	4	3	0	2	7	.201	.271	.381	.652
12	Ari	NL	40	135	26	8	1	2	(0	2)	42	17	12	12	19	1	35	0	0	1	0	1	1	.193	.290	.311	.601
12	Oak	AL	39	152	38	5	0	5	(4	1)	58	21	16	18	18	1	41	0	0	2	1	1	1	.250	.326	.382	.707
14	Bos	AL	39	131	23	6	1	4	(2	2)	43	11	11	12	14	2	39	0	0	0	1	1	1	.176	.255	.328	.583
14	NYY	AL	46	140	21	8	0	3	(2	1)	38	7	15	7	13	1	36	0	0	2	0	0	0	.150	.219	.271	.491
Postseason			28	104	22	3	2	3	(2	1)	38	10	9	8	5	0	33	0	0	1	1	0	1	.212	.245	.365	.611
10 ML YEARS			1152	4165	1047	240	62	114	(53	61)	1753	532	486	552	411	33	874	11	22	37	41	18	45	.251	.318	.421	.739

Brandon Drury

Bats: R **Throws:** R **Pos:** 3B-11;2B-6;PH-4;SS-1   DROO-ree   **Ht:** 6'1" **Wt:** 215 **Born:** 8/21/1992 **Age:** 23

Year	Team	Lg	G	AB	H	2B	3B	HR	Hm	Rd	TB	R	RBI	RC	TBB	IBB	SO	HBP	SH	SF	SB	CS	GDP	Avg	OBP	Slg	OPS
2011	Danvle	R+	63	265	92	23	0	8	(-	-)	139	40	54	50	6	1	35	4	0	3	3	0	6	.347	.367	.525	.891
2012	Rome	A	123	445	102	22	3	6	(-	-)	148	47	51	40	20	0	73	7	3	5	3	4	14	.229	.270	.333	.603
2013	Sbend	A	134	526	159	51	4	15	(-	-)	263	78	85	96	47	6	92	5	0	5	1	1	10	.302	.362	.500	.862
2014	Visalia	A+	107	430	129	35	1	19	(-	-)	223	73	81	81	41	2	76	5	0	2	4	3	16	.300	.366	.519	.885
2014	Mobile	AA	29	105	31	7	0	4	(-	-)	50	12	14	17	7	0	19	2	0	2	0	0	1	.295	.345	.476	.821
2015	Mobile	AA	67	273	76	14	1	3	(-	-)	101	22	36	30	11	0	41	2	0	5	4	6	7	.278	.306	.370	.676
2015	Reno	AAA	63	251	83	26	0	2	(-	-)	115	43	25	44	21	0	35	2	0	2	0	2	6	.331	.384	.458	.842
2015	Ari	NL	20	56	12	3	0	2	(0	2)	21	3	8	4	2	0	8	1	0	0	0	0	5	.214	.254	.375	.629

Lucas Duda

Bats: L **Throws:** R **Pos:** 1B-129;PH-8   DOO-duh   **Ht:** 6'4" **Wt:** 255 **Born:** 2/3/1986 **Age:** 30

Year	Team	Lg	G	AB	H	2B	3B	HR	Hm	Rd	TB	R	RBI	RC	TBB	IBB	SO	HBP	SH	SF	SB	CS	GDP	Avg	OBP	Slg	OPS
2010	NYM	NL	29	84	17	6	0	4	(3	1)	35	11	13	5	6	0	22	1	0	1	0	0	2	.202	.261	.417	.678
2011	NYM	NL	100	301	88	21	3	10	(2	8)	145	38	50	44	33	3	57	7	1	5	1	0	5	.292	.370	.482	.852
2012	NYM	NL	121	401	96	15	0	15	(9	6)	156	43	57	58	51	0	120	4	0	3	1	0	5	.239	.329	.389	.718
2013	NYM	NL	100	318	71	16	0	15	(9	6)	132	42	33	38	55	4	102	9	0	2	0	3	1	.223	.352	.415	.767
2014	NYM	NL	153	514	130	27	0	30	(14	16)	247	74	92	91	69	8	135	9	0	4	3	2	9	.253	.349	.481	.830
2015	NYM	NL	135	471	115	33	0	27	(19	8)	229	67	73	69	66	7	138	14	0	3	0	2	12	.244	.352	.486	.838
6 ML YEARS			638	2089	517	118	3	101	(56	45)	944	275	318	305	280	22	574	44	1	18	5	7	34	.247	.346	.452	.798

Brian Duensing

Pitches: L **Bats:** L **Pos:** RP-55   DUNN-sing   **Ht:** 6'0" **Wt:** 200 **Born:** 2/22/1983 **Age:** 33

Year	Team	Lg	G	GS	CG	GF	IP	BFP	H	R	ER	HR	SH	SF	HB	TBB	IBB	SO	WP	Bk	W	L	Pct	Sh	Sv-Op	Hld	ERC	ERA
2009	Min	AL	24	9	0	3	84.0	359	84	37	34	7	3	2	3	31	1	53	1	0	5	2	.714	0	0-0	1	4.00	3.64
2010	Min	AL	53	13	1	11	130.2	535	122	42	38	11	4	0	3	35	5	78	1	0	10	3	.769	1	0-0	5	3.18	2.62
2011	Min	AL	32	28	1	0	161.2	711	193	102	94	21	7	6	1	52	3	115	3	0	9	14	.391	1	0-0	0	5.12	5.23
2012	Min	AL	55	11	0	8	109.0	472	126	71	62	10	2	3	2	27	3	69	5	0	4	12	.250	0	0-1	7	4.31	5.12
2013	Min	AL	73	0	0	9	61.0	268	68	28	27	4	2	2	2	22	4	56	6	0	6	2	.750	0	1-4	15	4.35	3.98
2014	Min	AL	62	0	0	10	54.1	229	52	20	20	6	1	2	1	20	2	33	2	0	3	3	.500	0	0-4	7	3.84	3.31
2015	Min	AL	55	0	0	9	48.2	209	46	24	23	5	2	1	4	21	4	24	3	0	4	1	.800	0	1-2	6	4.17	4.25
Postseason			2	2	0	0	8.0	39	14	10	10	2	0	0	0	2	0	4	1	0	0	2	.000	0	0-0	0	9.43	11.25
7 ML YEARS			354	61	2	50	649.1	2783	691	324	298	64	21	16	16	208	22	428	21	0	41	37	.526	2	2-11	45	4.19	4.13

Tyler Duffey

Pitches: R **Bats:** R **Pos:** SP-10   **Ht:** 6'3" **Wt:** 220 **Born:** 12/27/1990 **Age:** 25

Year	Team	Lg	G	GS	CG	GF	IP	BFP	H	R	ER	HR	SH	SF	HB	TBB	IBB	SO	WP	Bk	W	L	Pct	Sh	Sv-Op	Hld	ERC	ERA
2012	Elizab	R+	12	0	0	5	19.0	67	10	3	3	1	0	0	0	2	0	27	1	0	2	0	1.000	0	2--	-	0.94	1.42
2013	2 Tms	Low	24	18	0	1	121.0	500	116	56	49	8	3	1	5	23	0	91	4	0	7	7	.500	0	0--	-	2.97	3.64
2014	NwBrit	AA	18	18	0	0	111.1	452	104	52	47	14	2	6	5	19	0	84	4	0	8	3	.727	0	0--	-	3.19	3.80
2015	Chatt	AA	8	8	0	0	52.2	210	46	19	15	0	1	1	0	12	0	54	1	0	2	2	.500	0	0--	-	2.26	2.56
2015	Roch	AAA	14	14	1	0	85.1	349	73	32	24	1	1	3	1	18	0	68	3	0	5	6	.455	1	0--	-	2.07	2.53
2015	Min	AL	10	10	0	0	58.0	242	56	20	20	4	3	0	0	20	0	53	1	0	5	1	.833	0	0-0	0	3.51	3.10

Danny Duffy

Pitches: L **Bats:** L **Pos:** SP-24; RP-6   **Ht:** 6'3" **Wt:** 205 **Born:** 12/21/1988 **Age:** 27

Year	Team	Lg	G	GS	CG	GF	IP	BFP	H	R	ER	HR	SH	SF	HB	TBB	IBB	SO	WP	Bk	W	L	Pct	Sh	Sv-Op	Hld	ERC	ERA
2011	KC	AL	20	20	0	0	105.1	474	119	66	66	15	2	2	5	51	1	87	4	1	4	8	.333	0	0-0	0	5.76	5.64
2012	KC	AL	6	6	0	0	27.2	121	26	13	12	2	0	0	0	18	1	28	0	1	2	2	.500	0	0-0	0	4.58	3.90
2013	KC	AL	5	5	0	0	24.1	104	19	5	5	0	0	0	0	14	0	22	2	0	2	0	1.000	0	0-0	0	3.02	1.85
2014	KC	AL	31	25	0	1	149.1	606	113	52	42	12	3	4	5	53	2	113	5	0	9	12	.429	0	0-0	0	2.62	2.53
2015	KC	AL	30	24	0	1	136.2	588	137	64	62	15	3	5	9	53	0	102	11	0	7	8	.467	0	1-1	2	4.44	4.08
Postseason			3	0	0	0	4.2	21	3	2	2	0	1	1	0	4	0	5	0	0	1	0	1.000	0	0-0	0	3.03	3.86
5 ML YEARS			92	80	0	2	443.1	1893	414	200	187	44	8	11	20	189	4	352	22	2	24	30	.444	0	1-1	3	4.01	3.80

Matt Duffy

Bats: R **Throws:** R **Pos:** PH-5;1B-2;3B-2   **Ht:** 6'3" **Wt:** 215 **Born:** 2/6/1989 **Age:** 27

Year	Team	Lg	G	AB	H	2B	3B	HR	(Hm	Rd)	TB	R	RBI	RC	TBB	IBB	SO	HBP	SH	SF	SB	CS	GDP	Avg	OBP	Slg	OPS
2011	TriCity	A-	63	235	70	20	1	2	(-	-)	98	36	37	37	15	0	41	13	1	2	2	2	9	.298	.370	.417	.787
2012	Lxngtn	A	134	492	138	32	1	16	(-	-)	220	73	70	91	48	0	106	41	0	6	6	3	11	.280	.387	.447	.834
2013	Lancst	A+	100	371	120	20	4	19	(-	-)	205	74	84	80	30	2	80	18	1	4	0	2	6	.323	.397	.553	.950
2013	CpChr	AA	24	89	22	4	0	5	(-	-)	41	11	10	12	3	0	22	3	0	0	1	1	3	.247	.295	.461	.755
2014	CpChr	AA	49	202	61	11	1	6	(-	-)	92	23	35	31	7	0	36	5	1	1	2	1	5	.302	.340	.455	.795
2014	OkCity	AAA	87	315	88	11	3	12	(-	-)	141	47	49	47	21	0	70	7	4	5	0	3	17	.279	.333	.448	.781
2015	Fresno	AAA	127	490	144	29	2	20	(-	-)	237	94	104	90	48	0	90	12	0	7	4	1	20	.294	.366	.484	.850
2015	Hou	AL	8	8	3	1	0	0	(0	0)	4	0	3	2	1	0	2	0	0	0	0	0	0	.375	.444	.500	.944

Matt Duffy

Bats: R **Throws:** R **Pos:** 3B-134;2B-9;PH-9;SS-3;1B-1;PR-1   **Ht:** 6'2" **Wt:** 170 **Born:** 1/15/1991 **Age:** 25

Year	Team	Lg	G	AB	H	2B	3B	HR	(Hm	Rd)	TB	R	RBI	RC	TBB	IBB	SO	HBP	SH	SF	SB	CS	GDP	Avg	OBP	Slg	OPS
2012	SlKzr	A-	47	182	45	4	0	1	(-	-)	52	31	16	24	26	0	22	7	0	1	10	1	7	.247	.361	.286	.647
2013	2 Tms	Low	104	393	119	20	4	9	(-	-)	174	65	57	72	52	1	57	4	4	1	25	7	9	.303	.389	.443	.832
2014	Rchmd	AA	97	367	122	24	4	3	(-	-)	163	53	62	70	42	2	66	2	0	6	20	4	8	.332	.398	.444	.842
2014	SF	NL	34	60	16	2	0	0	(0	0)	18	5	8	8	1	0	14	2	1	0	0	1	1	.267	.302	.300	.602
2015	SF	NL	149	573	169	28	6	12	(7	5)	245	77	77	84	30	0	96	5	2	2	12	0	22	.295	.334	.428	.762
	Postseason		8	6	1	0	0	0	(0	0)	1	2	0	0	0	0	2	0	1	0	0	0	0	.167	.167	.167	.333
	2 ML YEARS		183	633	185	30	6	12	(7	5)	263	82	85	92	31	0	110	7	3	2	12	1	23	.292	.331	.415	.747

Zach Duke

Pitches: L **Bats:** L **Pos:** RP-71   **Ht:** 6'2" **Wt:** 210 **Born:** 4/19/1983 **Age:** 33

Year	Team	Lg	G	GS	CG	GF	IP	BFP	H	R	ER	HR	SH	SF	HB	TBB	IBB	SO	WP	Bk	W	L	Pct	Sh	Sv-Op	Hld	ERC	ERA
2005	Pit	NL	14	14	0	0	84.2	341	79	20	17	3	3	1	2	23	2	58	1	0	8	2	.800	0	0-0	0	2.96	1.81
2006	Pit	NL	34	34	2	0	215.1	935	255	116	107	17	13	4	7	68	6	117	8	1	10	15	.400	1	0-0	0	4.82	4.47
2007	Pit	NL	20	19	0	0	107.1	482	161	74	66	14	2	4	3	25	2	41	0	1	3	8	.273	0	0-0	0	6.96	5.53
2008	Pit	NL	31	31	1	0	185.0	829	230	111	99	19	14	4	1	47	1	87	2	2	5	14	.263	1	0-0	0	4.99	4.82
2009	Pit	NL	32	32	3	0	213.0	891	231	101	96	23	18	10	3	49	0	106	2	1	11	16	.407	1	0-0	0	4.05	4.06
2010	Pit	NL	29	29	0	0	159.0	730	212	115	101	25	9	6	4	51	2	96	4	3	8	15	.348	0	0-0	0	6.22	5.72
2011	Ari	NL	21	9	0	5	76.2	338	101	42	42	6	3	3	1	19	0	32	1	0	3	4	.429	0	1-1	0	5.27	4.93
2012	Was	NL	8	0	0	3	13.2	56	11	2	2	0	0	0	0	4	0	10	0	0	1	0	1.000	0	0-0	0	2.00	1.32
2013	2 Tms	NL	26	1	0	3	31.1	142	39	23	21	3	2	2	1	10	3	18	2	0	1	2	.333	0	0-0	1	5.04	6.03
2014	Mil	NL	74	0	0	13	58.2	238	49	19	16	3	0	0	0	17	1	74	3	0	5	1	.833	0	0-4	12	2.46	2.45
2015	CWS	AL	71	0	0	14	60.2	255	47	26	23	9	2	1	3	32	4	66	0	0	3	6	.333	0	1-3	26	3.82	3.41
13	Was	NL	12	1	0	1	20.2	101	31	22	20	2	2	2	1	8	3	11	1	0	1	1	.500	0	0-0	0	6.83	8.71
13	Cin	NL	14	0	0	2	10.2	41	8	1	1	1	0	0	0	2	0	7	1	0	0	1	.000	0	0-0	1	2.01	0.84
11 ML YEARS			360	169	6	38	1205.1	5237	1415	649	590	122	66	35	31	345	21	705	23	8	58	83	.411	3	2-8	39	4.74	4.41

Ryan Dull

Pitches: R **Bats:** R **Pos:** RP-13   **Ht:** 5'10" **Wt:** 175 **Born:** 10/2/1989 **Age:** 26

Year	Team	Lg	G	GS	CG	GF	IP	BFP	H	R	ER	HR	SH	SF	HB	TBB	IBB	SO	WP	Bk	W	L	Pct	Sh	Sv-Op	Hld	ERC	ERA
2012	2 Tms	Low	21	0	0	11	31.2	133	29	11	9	2	2	0	2	9	1	47	5	0	5	1	.833	0	5--	-	3.11	2.56
2013	2 Tms	Low	35	0	0	30	48.1	182	29	10	10	1	3	2	1	6	1	66	3	0	2	4	.333	0	18--	-	1.06	1.86
2013	Mdlnd	AA	10	0	0	8	11.2	54	15	9	6	2	0	0	0	3	0	12	2	0	0	1	.000	0	1--	-	5.44	4.63
2014	Mdlnd	AA	40	0	0	24	56.1	239	52	24	18	6	3	1	3	15	4	61	5	1	5	5	.500	0	6--	-	3.21	2.88
2015	Mdlnd	AA	35	0	0	27	45.0	173	29	3	3	1	0	1	0	13	1	52	0	0	3	1	.750	0	12--	-	1.51	0.60
2015	Nashv	AAA	12	0	0	4	16.0	61	10	2	2	1	0	0	0	3	1	21	0	0	0	1	1.000	0	0--	-	1.32	1.13
2015	Oak	AL	13	0	0	3	17.0	66	12	8	8	4	0	1	0	6	1	16	0	0	1	2	.333	0	1-2	2	3.19	4.24

Mike Dunn

Pitches: L **Bats:** L **Pos:** RP-72   **Ht:** 6'0" **Wt:** 210 **Born:** 5/23/1985 **Age:** 31

Year	Team	Lg	G	GS	CG	GF	IP	BFP	H	R	ER	HR	SH	SF	HB	TBB	IBB	SO	WP	Bk	W	L	Pct	Sh	Sv-Op	Hld	ERC	ERA
2009	NYY	AL	4	0	0	3	4.0	20	3	3	3	1	0	0	0	5	0	5	1	0	0	0	-	0	0-0	0	7.17	6.75
2010	Atl	NL	25	0	0	5	19.0	88	15	4	4	1	0	0	0	17	2	27	2	0	2	0	1.000	0	0-0	1	4.19	1.89
2011	Fla	NL	72	0	0	11	63.0	267	51	28	24	9	4	2	2	31	2	68	3	0	5	6	.455	0	0-4	15	3.77	3.43
2012	Mia	NL	60	0	0	8	44.0	208	49	31	24	3	2	4	0	29	8	47	2	0	0	3	.000	0	1-6	18	5.10	4.91
2013	Mia	NL	75	0	0	15	67.2	282	53	21	20	5	1	3	0	28	4	72	2	0	3	4	.429	0	2-5	18	2.68	2.66
2014	Mia	NL	75	0	0	15	57.0	245	47	25	20	4	4	1	2	22	1	67	2	0	10	6	.625	0	1-4	22	3.03	3.16
2015	Mia	NL	72	0	0	9	54.0	235	46	27	27	6	0	1	2	29	1	65	2	0	2	5	.286	0	0-3	23	3.96	4.50
	Postseason		3	0	0	0	1.1	6	2	0	0	0	0	0	0	0	0	2	0	0	0	0	-	0	0-1	0	4.47	0.00
7 ML YEARS			383	0	0	66	308.2	1345	264	139	122	29	11	11	8	161	18	351	14	0	22	24	.478	0	4-22	97	3.67	3.56

Adam Duvall

Bats: R Throws: R Pos: LF-15;PH-9;1B-4   Ht: 6'1" Wt: 205 Born: 9/4/1988 Age: 27

Year Team	Lg	G	AB	H	2B	3B	HR	(Hm	Rd)	TB	R	RBI	RC	TBB	IBB	SO	HBP	SH	SF	SB	CS	GDP	Avg	OBP	Slg	OPS
2011 Augsta	A	116	431	123	30	4	22	(-	-)	227	69	87	89	59	4	98	14	1	5	4	4	9	.285	.385	.527	.912
2012 SnJos	A+	134	534	138	24	4	30	(-	-)	260	101	100	89	47	0	116	10	1	6	8	2	18	.258	.327	.487	.814
2013 Rchmd	AA	105	385	97	23	4	17	(-	-)	179	61	58	59	35	2	72	5	2	3	2	1	5	.252	.320	.465	.785
2014 Fresno	AAA	91	359	107	22	3	27	(-	-)	216	67	90	76	30	0	82	5	0	0	2	0	7	.298	.360	.602	.962
2015 Scrmto	AAA	100	402	113	25	2	26	(-	-)	220	60	80	72	25	2	91	4	0	6	4	1	12	.281	.325	.547	.872
2015 Lsvlle	AAA	25	95	18	4	0	4	(-	-)	34	11	7	9	6	0	23	3	0	0	1	0	2	.189	.260	.358	.618
2014 SF	NL	28	73	14	2	0	3	(2	1)	25	8	5	4	3	0	20	1	0	0	0	0	0	.192	.234	.342	.576
2015 Cin	NL	27	64	14	2	0	5	(3	2)	31	6	9	9	6	1	26	2	0	0	0	0	0	.219	.306	.484	.790
2 ML YEARS		55	137	28	4	0	8	(5	3)	56	14	14	13	9	1	46	3	0	0	0	0	0	.204	.268	.409	.677

Allan Dykstra

Bats: L Throws: R Pos: 1B-13   DIKE-stra   Ht: 6'5" Wt: 215 Born: 5/21/1987 Age: 29

Year Team	Lg	G	AB	H	2B	3B	HR	(Hm	Rd)	TB	R	RBI	RC	TBB	IBB	SO	HBP	SH	SF	SB	CS	GDP	Avg	OBP	Slg	OPS
2011 Bnghtn	AA	121	390	104	22	1	19	(-	-)	185	57	78	76	69	2	131	12	0	4	1	1	4	.267	.389	.474	.864
2012 Bnghtn	AA	62	191	50	9	0	7	(-	-)	80	35	25	39	51	2	65	4	0	2	1	0	5	.262	.423	.419	.842
2013 Bnghtn	AA	122	372	102	22	0	21	(-	-)	187	56	82	89	102	2	123	9	0	6	0	0	8	.274	.436	.503	.938
2014 LsVgs	AAA	117	343	96	23	3	16	(-	-)	173	62	74	79	84	2	97	7	0	5	0	0	5	.280	.426	.504	.930
2015 Drham	AAA	39	132	28	7	0	3	(-	-)	44	17	15	19	34	1	35	0	0	1	0	0	3	.212	.371	.333	.705
2015 TB	AL	13	31	4	0	0	1	(1	0)	7	3	4	4	6	0	12	1	0	0	0	0	2	.129	.289	.226	.515

Jarrod Dyson

juh-ROD

Bats: L Throws: R Pos: CF-37;LF-27;PR-19;RF-17;PH-5;DH-2   Ht: 5'10" Wt: 160 Born: 8/15/1984 Age: 31

Year Team	Lg	G	AB	H	2B	3B	HR	(Hm	Rd)	TB	R	RBI	RC	TBB	IBB	SO	HBP	SH	SF	SB	CS	GDP	Avg	OBP	Slg	OPS
2010 KC	AL	18	57	12	4	2	1	(1	0)	23	11	5	9	6	0	16	0	2	0	9	1	2	.211	.286	.404	.689
2011 KC	AL	26	44	9	1	0	0	(0	0)	10	8	3	7	7	0	14	0	1	1	11	1	0	.205	.308	.227	.535
2012 KC	AL	102	292	76	8	5	0	(0	0)	94	52	9	36	30	1	56	1	4	3	30	5	5	.260	.328	.322	.650
2013 KC	AL	87	213	55	9	4	2	(2	0)	78	30	17	28	21	1	45	1	3	1	34	6	4	.258	.326	.366	.692
2014 KC	AL	120	260	70	4	4	1	(1	0)	85	33	24	32	22	0	52	0	6	2	36	7	5	.269	.324	.327	.651
2015 KC	AL	90	200	50	8	6	2	(2	0)	76	31	18	25	14	0	37	4	6	1	26	3	3	.250	.311	.380	.691
Postseason		13	16	2	0	0	0	(0	0)	2	2	0	0	2	0	4	0	1	0	1	2	1	.125	.222	.125	.347
6 ML YEARS		443	1066	272	34	21	6	(6	0)	366	165	76	137	100	2	220	6	22	8	146	23	19	.255	.320	.343	.664

Sam Dyson

Pitches: R Bats: R Pos: RP-75   Ht: 6'1" Wt: 210 Born: 5/7/1988 Age: 28

Year Team	Lg	G	GS	CG	GF	IP	BFP	H	R	ER	HR	SH	SF	HB	TBB	IBB	SO	WP	Bk	W	L	Pct	Sh	Sv-Op	Hld	ERC	ERA
2012 Tor	AL	2	0	0	0	0.2	8	4	3	3	0	0	0	0	2	0	1	0	0	0	0	-	0	0-0	0	56.02	40.50
2013 Mia	NL	5	1	0	1	11.0	54	16	12	11	2	1	1	1	5	1	5	0	0	0	2	.000	0	0-0	0	7.96	9.00
2014 Mia	NL	31	0	0	12	42.0	181	41	14	10	1	2	0	3	15	4	33	1	0	3	1	.750	0	0-1	0	3.36	2.14
2015 2 Tms		75	0	0	16	75.1	309	65	26	22	4	4	1	4	21	1	71	8	0	5	4	.556	0	2-4	21	2.77	2.63
15 Mia	NL	44	0	0	10	44.0	190	41	21	18	3	3	1	3	17	1	41	6	0	3	3	.500	0	0-2	9	3.63	3.68
15 Tex	AL	31	0	0	6	31.1	119	24	5	4	1	1	0	1	4	0	30	2	0	2	1	.667	0	2-2	12	1.68	1.15
4 ML YEARS		113	1	0	29	129.0	552	126	55	46	7	7	2	8	43	6	110	9	0	8	7	.533	0	2-5	21	3.53	3.21

Ed Easley

Bats: R Throws: R Pos: C-3;PH-2   Ht: 6'0" Wt: 205 Born: 12/21/1985 Age: 30

Year Team	Lg	G	AB	H	2B	3B	HR	(Hm	Rd)	TB	R	RBI	RC	TBB	IBB	SO	HBP	SH	SF	SB	CS	GDP	Avg	OBP	Slg	OPS
2011 Mobile	AA	83	289	79	16	0	4	(-	-)	107	37	37	40	32	1	51	4	1	2	1	2	12	.273	.352	.370	.722
2012 Mobile	AA	67	204	54	7	0	2	(-	-)	67	18	23	27	31	0	30	0	0	4	1	1	7	.265	.356	.328	.684
2013 Reno	AAA	87	293	98	22	1	6	(-	-)	140	39	49	55	28	1	50	3	1	3	2	2	6	.334	.394	.478	.872
2014 Memp	AAA	80	277	82	17	1	10	(-	-)	131	43	43	47	22	0	46	7	3	3	0	4	16	.296	.359	.473	.832
2015 Memp	AAA	88	279	70	12	0	4	(-	-)	94	26	36	35	39	1	44	2	1	2	1	2	8	.251	.345	.337	.682
2015 StL	NL	4	6	0	0	0	0	(0	0)	0	0	1	0	0	0	1	0	0	1	0	0	1	.000	.000	.000	.000

Adam Eaton

Bats: L Throws: L Pos: CF-145;DH-7;PH-2   Ht: 5'8" Wt: 185 Born: 12/6/1988 Age: 27

Year Team	Lg	G	AB	H	2B	3B	HR	(Hm	Rd)	TB	R	RBI	RC	TBB	IBB	SO	HBP	SH	SF	SB	CS	GDP	Avg	OBP	Slg	OPS
2012 Ari	NL	22	85	22	3	2	2	(1	1)	35	19	5	13	14	0	15	3	1	0	2	3	0	.259	.382	.412	.794
2013 Ari	NL	66	250	63	10	4	3	(2	1)	90	40	22	27	17	0	44	6	3	1	5	2	4	.252	.314	.360	.674
2014 CWS	AL	123	486	146	26	10	1	(1	0)	195	76	35	77	43	0	83	5	2	2	15	9	4	.300	.362	.401	.763
2015 CWS	AL	153	610	175	28	9	14	(6	8)	263	98	56	96	58	2	131	14	5	2	18	8	5	.287	.361	.431	.792
4 ML YEARS		364	1431	406	67	25	20	(10	10)	583	233	118	213	132	2	273	28	11	5	40	22	13	.284	.355	.407	.762

Jon Edwards

Pitches: R **Bats:** R **Pos:** RP-22

Ht: 6'5" **Wt:** 235 **Born:** 1/8/1988 **Age:** 28

			HOW MUCH HE PITCHED					WHAT HE GAVE UP										THE RESULTS						
Year	Team	Lg	G	GS	CG	GF	IP	BFP	H	R	ER	HR	SH	SF	HB	TBB	IBB	SO	WP	Bk	W	L	Pct	Sh	Sv-Op	Hld	ERC	ERA
2012	3 Tms	Low	18	0	0	6	28.0	126	14	10	5	1	0	1	1	29	1	34	7	1	1	0	1.000	0	1--	-	3.29	1.61
2013	MrtlBh	A+	26	0	0	14	40.1	179	28	19	16	0	2	1	2	31	0	51	5	0	3	1	.750	0	4--	-	3.22	3.57
2013	Frisco	AA	9	0	0	3	15.1	68	15	10	9	3	1	1	0	8	0	16	2	0	0	1	.000	0	0--	-	5.11	5.28
2014	Frisco	AA	22	0	0	6	33.1	148	27	26	19	4	2	1	0	23	1	36	5	0	1	2	.333	0	0--	-	4.21	5.13
2014	RdRck	AAA	12	0	0	5	15.2	71	15	6	5	0	0	1	1	9	0	26	0	0	1	1	.500	0	0--	-	3.96	2.87
2015	RdRck	AAA	32	0	0	29	31.2	117	18	5	5	1	0	0	0	8	0	44	0	0	2	1	.667	0	20--	-	1.28	1.42
2015	ElPaso	AAA	5	0	0	5	5.0	19	3	0	0	0	0	0	0	3	0	7	0	0	0	0	-	0	3--	-	2.30	0.00
2014	Tex	AL	9	0	0	3	8.1	43	13	5	4	0	0	0	1	5	0	9	2	0	0	0	-	0	0-0	1	7.97	4.32
2015	2 Tms		22	0	0	7	16.2	75	12	8	8	4	0	2	0	16	0	22	2	0	0	0	-	0	0-0	2	5.92	4.32
15	Tex	AL	11	0	0	2	6.0	31	6	4	4	1	0	1	0	8	0	6	1	0	0	0	-	0	0-0	2	8.67	6.00
15	SD	NL	11	0	0	5	10.2	44	6	4	4	3	0	1	0	8	0	16	1	0	0	0	-	0	0-0	0	4.41	3.38
	2 ML YEARS		31	0	0	10	25.0	118	25	13	12	4	0	2	1	21	0	31	4	0	0	0	-	0	0-0	3	6.61	4.32

Carl Edwards Jr.

Pitches: R **Bats:** R **Pos:** RP-5

Ht: 6'3" **Wt:** 170 **Born:** 9/3/1991 **Age:** 24

			HOW MUCH HE PITCHED					WHAT HE GAVE UP										THE RESULTS						
Year	Team	Lg	G	GS	CG	GF	IP	BFP	H	R	ER	HR	SH	SF	HB	TBB	IBB	SO	WP	Bk	W	L	Pct	Sh	Sv-Op	Hld	ERC	ERA
2012	2 Tms	Low	14	13	0	0	67.0	257	32	13	11	0	2	0	3	25	0	85	3	1	5	3	.625	0	0--	-	1.21	1.48
2013	2 Tms		24	24	1	0	116.1	468	76	33	24	1	6	1	3	41	0	155	12	1	8	2	.800	0	0--	-	1.67	1.86
2014	Tenn	AA	10	10	0	0	48.0	193	30	14	13	1	2	2	1	21	0	46	3	0	1	2	.333	0	0--	-	1.88	2.44
2015	Tenn	AA	13	0	0	6	23.2	100	11	12	7	1	1	0	0	17	0	36	1	0	2	2	.500	0	4--	-	2.02	2.66
2015	Iowa	AAA	23	0	0	6	31.2	132	15	11	10	0	1	0	1	24	1	39	3	0	3	1	.750	0	2--	-	2.04	2.84
2015	ChC	NL	5	0	0	3	4.2	19	3	3	2	0	0	0	0	3	0	4	0	0	0	0	-	0	0-0	0	2.50	3.86

Jerad Eickhoff

Pitches: R **Bats:** R **Pos:** SP-8

EYE-koff

Ht: 6'4" **Wt:** 240 **Born:** 7/2/1990 **Age:** 25

			HOW MUCH HE PITCHED					WHAT HE GAVE UP										THE RESULTS						
Year	Team	Lg	G	GS	CG	GF	IP	BFP	H	R	ER	HR	SH	SF	HB	TBB	IBB	SO	WP	Bk	W	L	Pct	Sh	Sv-Op	Hld	ERC	ERA
2011	2 Tms	Low	14	0	0	9	19.0	68	9	5	5	1	0	0	4	0	0	22	1	0	1	2	.333	0	3--	-	1.00	2.37
2012	Hkry	A	26	25	0	0	126.2	545	132	75	66	22	3	5	5	38	0	90	8	2	13	7	.650	0	0--	-	4.58	4.69
2013	Frisco	AA	6	6	0	0	29.0	128	34	24	24	6	1	1	0	14	0	13	1	0	1	1	.500	0	0--	-	6.69	7.45
2013	MrtlBh	A+	21	21	0	0	116.0	476	110	52	44	9	3	4	7	26	2	80	11	0	7	3	.700	0	0--	-	3.22	3.41
2014	Frisco	AA	27	26	0	0	154.1	636	129	76	70	17	4	2	7	52	0	144	12	0	10	9	.526	0	0--	-	3.21	4.08
2015	RdRck	AAA	18	17	0	0	101.2	427	95	49	48	12	2	6	4	33	1	93	4	1	9	4	.692	0	0--	-	3.70	4.25
2015	Phi	NL	8	8	0	6	51.0	203	40	16	15	5	0	1	0	13	0	49	1	0	3	3	.500	0	0-0	0	2.40	2.65

Roenis Elias

Pitches: L **Bats:** L **Pos:** SP-20; RP-2

roh-EN-ees ehl-LEE-us

Ht: 6'1" **Wt:** 190 **Born:** 8/1/1988 **Age:** 27

			HOW MUCH HE PITCHED					WHAT HE GAVE UP										THE RESULTS						
Year	Team	Lg	G	GS	CG	GF	IP	BFP	H	R	ER	HR	SH	SF	HB	TBB	IBB	SO	WP	Bk	W	L	Pct	Sh	Sv-Op	Hld	ERC	ERA
2011	3 Tms	Low	11	8	0	0	48.1	212	53	28	23	7	0	1	3	21	0	41	4	0	5	2	.714	0	0--	-	5.51	4.28
2012	Hi Dsrt	A+	26	26	0	0	148.1	613	136	80	62	19	3	7	8	41	0	128	2	8	11	6	.647	0	0--	-	3.57	3.76
2013	Jacksn	AA	22	22	0	0	130.0	544	112	57	46	9	6	2	4	50	1	121	2	3	6	11	.353	0	0--	-	3.17	3.18
2015	Tacom	AAA	12	12	0	0	61.1	281	80	54	50	9	0	1	4	18	0	47	5	3	4	2	.667	0	0--	-	6.03	7.34
2014	Sea	AL	29	29	1	0	163.2	693	151	77	70	16	4	4	11	64	3	143	6	4	10	12	.455	1	0-0	0	3.89	3.85
2015	Sea	AL	22	20	0	0	115.1	490	106	57	53	15	1	4	9	44	1	97	1	1	5	8	.385	0	0-0	1	4.10	4.14
	2 ML YEARS		51	49	1	0	279.0	1183	257	134	123	31	5	8	20	108	4	240	7	5	15	20	.429	1	0-0	1	3.98	3.97

Brian Ellington

Pitches: R **Bats:** R **Pos:** RP-23

Ht: 6'4" **Wt:** 195 **Born:** 8/4/1990 **Age:** 25

			HOW MUCH HE PITCHED					WHAT HE GAVE UP										THE RESULTS						
Year	Team	Lg	G	GS	CG	GF	IP	BFP	H	R	ER	HR	SH	SF	HB	TBB	IBB	SO	WP	Bk	W	L	Pct	Sh	Sv-Op	Hld	ERC	ERA
2012	Jmstwn	A-	18	0	0	4	30.0	134	20	11	8	2	0	0	2	25	0	33	3	0	2	0	1.000	0	0--	-	3.90	2.40
2013	3 Tms	Low	24	3	0	4	65.0	293	56	40	30	3	3	1	12	35	0	52	1	0	4	4	.500	0	0--	-	4.12	4.15
2014	Jupiter	A+	35	0	0	15	47.1	217	51	28	25	2	1	1	3	24	0	56	2	1	2	2	.500	0	0--	-	4.70	4.75
2015	Jaxnvl	AA	25	0	0	6	43.0	169	28	13	12	0	3	2	1	13	0	47	2	0	4	1	.800	0	0--	-	1.53	2.51
2015	Mia	NL	23	0	0	9	25.0	105	17	10	8	1	0	2	2	13	2	18	1	0	2	1	.667	0	0-0	2	2.59	2.88

A.J. Ellis

Bats: R **Throws:** R **Pos:** C-62; PH-2

Ht: 6'2" **Wt:** 230 **Born:** 4/9/1981 **Age:** 35

			BATTING																		RUNNING			AVERAGES			
Year	Team	Lg	G	AB	H	2B	3B	HR	(Hm	Rd)	TB	R	RBI	RC	TBB	IBB	SO	HBP	SH	SF	SB	CS	GDP	Avg	OBP	Slg	OPS
2008	LAD	NL	4	3	0	0	0	0	(0	0)	0	1	0	0	0	0	2	0	0	0	0	0	0	.000	.000	.000	.000
2009	LAD	NL	8	10	1	0	0	0	(0	0)	1	0	1	0	0	0	1	0	0	0	0	0	0	.100	.100	.100	.200
2010	LAD	NL	44	108	30	5	0	0	(0	0)	35	6	16	16	14	1	18	1	4	1	0	0	5	.278	.363	.324	.687
2011	LAD	NL	31	85	23	1	1	2	(0	2)	32	8	11	11	14	0	16	3	1	0	0	1	2	.271	.392	.376	.769
2012	LAD	NL	133	423	114	20	1	13	(6	7)	175	44	52	61	65	11	107	7	6	4	0	0	17	.270	.373	.414	.786
2013	LAD	NL	115	390	93	17	1	10	(2	8)	142	43	52	43	45	1	78	3	4	6	0	2	11	.238	.318	.364	.682
2014	LAD	NL	93	283	54	9	0	3	(0	3)	72	21	25	22	53	5	57	4	3	4	0	0	15	.191	.323	.254	.577
2015	LAD	NL	63	181	43	9	0	7	(3	4)	73	24	21	25	32	1	38	1	3	0	0	0	4	.238	.355	.403	.758
	Postseason		14	44	17	5	1	2	(2	0)	30	7	5	11	7	1	7	1	1	0	0	0	0	.386	.481	.682	1.163
	8 ML YEARS		491	1483	358	61	3	35	(11	24)	530	147	178	178	223	19	317	19	21	15	0	3	54	.241	.345	.357	.702

Jacoby Ellsbury

Bats: L Throws: L Pos: CF-110;PH-4 Ht: 6'1" Wt: 195 Born: 9/11/1983 Age: 32

Year	Team	Lg	G	AB	H	2B	3B	HR	(Hm	Rd)	TB	R	RBI	RC	TBB	IBB	SO	HBP	SH	SF	SB	CS	GDP	Avg	OBP	Slg	OPS
2007	Bos	AL	33	116	41	7	1	3	(3	0)	59	20	18	26	8	0	15	1	0	2	9	0	2	.353	.394	.509	.902
2008	Bos	AL	145	554	155	22	7	9	(4	5)	218	98	47	71	41	2	80	7	4	3	50	11	10	.280	.336	.394	.729
2009	Bos	AL	153	624	188	27	10	8	(4	4)	259	94	60	97	49	3	74	6	6	6	70	12	13	.301	.355	.415	.770
2010	Bos	AL	18	78	15	4	0	0	(0	0)	19	10	5	4	4	0	9	1	0	0	7	1	0	.192	.241	.244	.485
2011	Bos	AL	158	660	212	46	5	32	(15	17)	364	119	105	134	52	1	98	9	3	5	39	15	8	.321	.376	.552	.928
2012	Bos	AL	74	303	82	18	0	4	(3	1)	112	43	26	37	19	0	43	0	0	1	14	3	5	.271	.313	.370	.682
2013	Bos	AL	134	577	172	31	8	9	(5	4)	246	92	53	90	47	3	92	5	1	2	52	4	12	.298	.355	.426	.781
2014	NYY	AL	149	575	156	27	5	16	(7	9)	241	71	70	84	49	5	93	3	0	7	39	5	9	.271	.328	.419	.747
2015	NYY	AL	111	452	116	15	2	7	(3	4)	156	66	33	51	35	1	86	7	1	3	21	9	6	.257	.318	.345	.663
	Postseason		38	133	40	11	2	0	(0	0)	55	26	17	25	13	2	24	0	0	1	11	2	4	.301	.361	.414	.774
	9 ML YEARS		975	3939	1137	197	38	88	(43	45)	1674	613	417	594	304	15	590	39	15	29	301	60	65	.289	.343	.425	.768

Jake Elmore

Bats: R Throws: R Pos: 1B-25;3B-9;2B-7;SS-7;LF-6;PH-4;PR-2;DH-1 Ht: 5'9" Wt: 185 Born: 6/15/1987 Age: 29

Year	Team	Lg	G	AB	H	2B	3B	HR	(Hm	Rd)	TB	R	RBI	RC	TBB	IBB	SO	HBP	SH	SF	SB	CS	GDP	Avg	OBP	Slg	OPS
2015	Drham*	AAA	57	198	49	4	0	0	(-	-)	53	20	12	24	38	0	30	3	1	0	4	4	3	.247	.377	.268	.644
2012	Ari	NL	30	68	13	4	0	0	(0	0)	17	1	7	3	5	0	6	0	0	0	0	0	1	.191	.247	.250	.497
2013	Hou	NL	52	120	29	4	0	2	(1	1)	39	16	6	13	13	0	20	0	2	1	6	1	6	.242	.313	.325	.638
2014	Cin	NL	5	11	2	0	0	0	(0	0)	2	0	0	0	1	0	4	0	0	0	0	0	0	.182	.250	.182	.432
2015	TB	AL	51	141	29	5	0	2	(2	0)	40	10	16	10	12	1	25	0	2	3	1	1	6	.206	.263	.284	.547
	4 ML YEARS		138	340	73	13	0	4	(3	1)	98	27	29	26	31	1	55	0	4	4	2	7	8	.215	.277	.288	.566

Edwin Encarnacion

Bats: R Throws: R Pos: DH-85;1B-59;PH-2 Ht: 6'1" Wt: 230 Born: 1/7/1983 Age: 33

Year	Team	Lg	G	AB	H	2B	3B	HR	(Hm	Rd)	TB	R	RBI	RC	TBB	IBB	SO	HBP	SH	SF	SB	CS	GDP	Avg	OBP	Slg	OPS
2005	Cin	NL	69	211	49	16	0	9	(3	6)	92	25	31	24	20	2	60	3	0	0	3	0	8	.232	.308	.436	.744
2006	Cin	NL	117	406	112	33	1	15	(7	8)	192	60	72	66	41	3	78	13	0	3	6	3	9	.276	.359	.473	.831
2007	Cin	NL	139	502	145	25	1	16	(10	6)	220	66	76	86	39	4	86	14	0	1	8	1	5	.289	.356	.438	.794
2008	Cin	NL	146	506	127	29	1	26	(15	11)	236	75	68	72	61	1	102	10	0	5	1	0	13	.251	.340	.466	.807
2009	2 Tms		85	293	66	11	2	13	(5	8)	120	35	39	37	37	0	67	5	0	3	2	1	5	.225	.320	.410	.729
2010	Tor	AL	96	332	81	16	0	21	(7	14)	160	47	51	41	29	1	60	2	0	4	1	0	9	.244	.305	.482	.787
2011	Tor	AL	134	481	131	36	0	17	(14	3)	218	70	55	67	43	2	77	3	0	3	8	2	17	.272	.334	.453	.787
2012	Tor	AL	151	542	152	24	0	42	(23	19)	302	93	110	124	84	12	94	11	0	7	13	3	6	.280	.384	.557	.941
2013	Tor	AL	142	530	144	29	1	36	(12	24)	283	90	104	102	82	7	62	4	0	5	7	1	20	.272	.370	.534	.904
2014	Tor	AL	128	477	128	27	2	34	(19	15)	261	75	98	86	62	6	82	2	0	1	2	0	18	.268	.354	.547	.901
2015	Tor	AL	146	528	146	31	0	39	(19	21)	294	94	111	110	77	5	98	9	0	10	3	2	14	.277	.372	.557	.929
09	Cin	NL	43	139	29	6	1	5	(3	2)	52	10	16	19	24	0	38	2	0	0	1	1	3	.209	.333	.374	.707
09	Tor	AL	42	154	37	5	1	8	(2	6)	68	25	23	18	13	0	29	3	0	3	1	0	2	.240	.306	.442	.748
	11 ML YEARS		1353	4808	1281	277	8	268	(133	135)	2378	730	815	815	575	43	866	76	0	42	54	13	124	.266	.351	.495	.846

Nathan Eovaldi

Pitches: R Bats: R Pos: SP-27 eh-VOLL-dee Ht: 6'2" Wt: 215 Born: 2/13/1990 Age: 26

Year	Team	Lg	G	GS	CG	GF	IP	BFP	H	R	ER	HR	SH	SF	HB	TBB	IBB	SO	WP	Bk	W	L	Pct	Sh	Sv-Op	Hld	ERC	ERA
2011	LAD	NL	10	6	0	1	34.2	146	28	14	14	2	2	0	2	20	0	23	0	0	1	2	.333	0	0-0	1	3.75	3.63
2012	2 Tms	NL	22	22	0	0	119.1	526	133	59	57	10	1	6	3	47	3	78	1	0	4	13	.235	0	0-0	0	4.67	4.30
2013	Mia	NL	18	18	0	0	106.1	451	100	44	40	7	6	1	1	40	3	78	3	0	4	6	.400	0	0-0	0	3.41	3.39
2014	Mia	NL	33	33	0	0	199.2	854	223	107	97	14	9	5	7	43	5	142	6	0	6	14	.300	0	0-0	0	3.89	4.37
2015	NYY	AL	27	27	0	0	154.1	673	175	72	72	10	3	3	3	49	1	121	8	0	14	3	.824	0	0-0	0	4.34	4.20
12	LAD	NL	10	10	0	0	56.1	241	63	27	26	5	0	3	0	20	2	34	1	0	1	6	.143	0	0-0	0	4.54	4.15
12	Mia	NL	12	12	0	0	63.0	285	70	32	31	5	1	3	3	27	1	44	0	0	3	7	.300	0	0-0	0	4.79	4.43
	5 ML YEARS		110	106	0	1	614.1	2650	659	296	280	43	21	15	16	199	11	442	18	0	29	38	.433	0	0-0	1	4.06	4.10

Robbie Erlin

Pitches: L Bats: R Pos: SP-3 Ht: 6'0" Wt: 195 Born: 10/8/1990 Age: 25

Year	Team	Lg	G	GS	CG	GF	IP	BFP	H	R	ER	HR	SH	SF	HB	TBB	IBB	SO	WP	Bk	W	L	Pct	Sh	Sv-Op	Hld	ERC	ERA
2015	ElPaso*	AAA	24	24	1	0	125.1	562	151	90	78	22	6	4	6	37	0	105	5	0	7	6	.538	1	0- -	-	5.55	5.60
2013	SD	NL	11	9	0	2	54.2	227	53	26	25	6	3	1	0	15	0	40	3	0	3	3	.500	0	0-0	0	3.50	4.12
2014	SD	NL	13	11	0	1	61.1	264	71	34	34	6	2	4	1	15	1	46	4	0	4	5	.444	0	0-0	0	4.39	4.99
2015	SD	NL	3	3	0	0	17.0	65	16	9	9	1	0	0	1	2	0	10	1	0	1	2	.333	0	0-0	0	2.84	4.76
	3 ML YEARS		27	23	0	3	133.0	556	140	69	68	13	5	5	2	32	1	96	8	0	8	10	.444	0	0-0	0	3.82	4.60

Alcides Escobar

Bats: R **Throws:** R **Pos:** SS-148   al-SEE-dess   **Ht:** 6'1" **Wt:** 185 **Born:** 12/16/1986 **Age:** 29

Year	Team	Lg	G	AB	H	2B	3B	HR	(Hm	Rd)	TB	R	RBI	RC	TBB	IBB	SO	HBP	SH	SF	SB	CS	GDP	Avg	OBP	Slg	OPS
2008	Mil	NL	9	4	2	0	0	0	(0	0)	2	2	0	0	0	0	1	0	0	0	0	0	0	.500	.500	.500	1.000
2009	Mil	NL	38	125	38	3	1	1	(0	1)	46	20	11	16	4	0	18	2	2	1	4	2	0	.304	.333	.368	.701
2010	Mil	NL	145	506	119	14	10	4	(3	1)	165	57	41	51	36	7	70	3	4	3	10	4	8	.235	.288	.326	.614
2011	KC	AL	158	548	139	21	8	4	(0	4)	188	69	46	46	25	1	73	4	18	3	26	9	10	.254	.290	.343	.633
2012	KC	AL	155	605	177	30	7	5	(5	0)	236	68	52	72	27	2	100	8	8	0	35	5	14	.293	.331	.390	.721
2013	KC	AL	158	607	142	20	4	4	(1	3)	182	57	52	51	19	1	84	3	9	4	22	0	12	.234	.259	.300	.559
2014	KC	AL	162	579	165	34	5	3	(2	1)	218	74	50	68	23	1	83	6	8	4	31	6	12	.285	.317	.377	.694
2015	KC	AL	148	612	157	20	5	3	(0	3)	196	76	47	60	26	1	75	8	11	5	17	5	10	.257	.293	.320	.614
	Postseason		15	65	19	5	0	1	(0	1)	27	8	5	9	1	0	11	0	4	0	1	1	1	.292	.303	.415	.718
	8 ML YEARS		973	3586	939	142	40	24	(11	13)	1233	423	299	364	160	13	504	34	60	20	145	31	66	.262	.298	.344	.642

Eduardo Escobar

Bats: B **Throws:** R **Pos:** SS-71;LF-35;2B-11;DH-7;PH-6;3B-5;RF-1;PR-1   **Ht:** 5'10" **Wt:** 185 **Born:** 1/5/1989 **Age:** 27

Year	Team	Lg	G	AB	H	2B	3B	HR	(Hm	Rd)	TB	R	RBI	RC	TBB	IBB	SO	HBP	SH	SF	SB	CS	GDP	Avg	OBP	Slg	OPS
2011	CWS	AL	9	7	2	0	0	0	(0	0)	2	0	0	1	0	0	1	0	0	0	0	0	0	.286	.286	.286	.571
2012	2 Tms	AL	50	131	28	4	1	0	(0	0)	34	18	9	12	11	0	31	1	2	1	3	0	0	.214	.278	.260	.537
2013	Min	AL	66	165	39	5	2	3	(2	1)	57	23	10	14	11	0	34	0	2	1	0	2	0	.236	.282	.345	.628
2014	Min	AL	133	433	119	35	2	6	(2	4)	176	52	37	53	24	1	93	2	4	2	1	1	6	.275	.315	.406	.721
2015	Min	AL	127	409	107	31	4	12	(2	10)	182	48	58	55	28	1	86	2	2	5	2	3	7	.262	.309	.445	.754
	12 CWS	AL	36	87	18	4	1	0	(0	0)	24	14	3	7	9	0	23	0	1	0	2	0	0	.207	.281	.276	.557
	12 Min	AL	14	44	10	0	0	0	(0	0)	10	4	6	5	2	0	8	1	1	1	1	0	0	.227	.271	.227	.498
	5 ML YEARS		385	1145	295	75	9	21	(6	15)	451	141	114	135	74	2	245	5	10	9	6	6	13	.258	.303	.394	.697

Yunel Escobar

Bats: R **Throws:** R **Pos:** 3B-134;DH-3;PH-1   you-NELL   **Ht:** 6'2" **Wt:** 215 **Born:** 11/2/1982 **Age:** 33

Year	Team	Lg	G	AB	H	2B	3B	HR	(Hm	Rd)	TB	R	RBI	RC	TBB	IBB	SO	HBP	SH	SF	SB	CS	GDP	Avg	OBP	Slg	OPS
2007	Atl	NL	94	319	104	25	0	5	(3	2)	144	54	28	52	27	1	44	5	2	2	5	3	6	.326	.385	.451	.837
2008	Atl	NL	136	514	148	24	2	10	(5	5)	206	71	60	70	59	4	62	5	7	2	2	5	24	.288	.366	.401	.766
2009	Atl	NL	141	528	158	26	2	14	(7	7)	230	89	76	90	57	3	62	10	7	2	5	4	21	.299	.377	.436	.812
2010	2 Tms		135	497	127	19	0	4	(2	2)	158	60	35	53	56	1	57	5	9	0	6	2	18	.256	.337	.318	.655
2011	Tor	AL	133	513	149	24	3	11	(8	3)	212	77	48	84	61	1	70	6	5	5	3	3	14	.290	.369	.413	.782
2012	Tor	AL	145	558	141	22	1	9	(6	3)	192	58	51	51	35	1	70	4	7	4	5	1	21	.253	.300	.344	.644
2013	TB	AL	153	508	130	27	1	9	(5	4)	186	61	56	60	57	2	73	3	6	4	4	4	19	.256	.332	.366	.698
2014	TB	AL	137	476	123	18	0	7	(2	5)	162	33	39	49	43	3	60	4	4	2	1	1	15	.258	.324	.340	.664
2015	Was		139	535	168	25	1	9	(5	4)	222	75	56	78	45	0	70	8	1	2	2	2	24	.314	.375	.415	.790
	10 Atl	NL	75	261	62	12	0	0	(0	0)	74	28	19	25	37	1	31	1	2	0	5	1	9	.238	.334	.284	.618
	10 Tor	AL	60	236	65	7	0	4	(2	2)	84	32	16	28	19	0	26	4	7	0	1	1	9	.275	.340	.356	.696
	Postseason		5	19	8	2	0	0	(0	0)	10	3	2	4	0	0	1	0	0	0	0	0	1	.421	.421	.526	.947
	9 ML YEARS		1213	4448	1248	210	10	78	(43	35)	1712	578	449	587	440	16	568	50	48	23	33	25	162	.281	.350	.385	.735

Danny Espinosa

Bats: B **Throws:** R **Pos:** 2B-81;3B-16;PH-13;SS-8;1B-5;LF-5;PR-2   **Ht:** 6'0" **Wt:** 210 **Born:** 4/25/1987 **Age:** 29

Year	Team	Lg	G	AB	H	2B	3B	HR	(Hm	Rd)	TB	R	RBI	RC	TBB	IBB	SO	HBP	SH	SF	SB	CS	GDP	Avg	OBP	Slg	OPS
2010	Was	NL	28	103	22	4	1	6	(4	2)	46	16	15	15	9	1	30	0	2	0	0	0	2	.214	.277	.447	.723
2011	Was	NL	158	573	135	29	5	21	(11	10)	237	72	66	83	57	4	166	19	5	4	17	6	6	.236	.323	.414	.737
2012	Was	NL	160	594	147	37	2	17	(7	10)	239	82	56	69	46	4	189	13	3	2	20	6	11	.247	.315	.402	.717
2013	Was	NL	44	158	25	9	0	3	(2	1)	43	11	12	8	4	0	47	3	1	1	0	1	5	.158	.193	.272	.465
2014	Was	NL	114	333	73	14	3	8	(5	3)	117	31	27	26	18	5	122	12	0	1	8	1	5	.219	.283	.351	.634
2015	Was	NL	118	367	88	21	1	13	(6	7)	150	59	37	40	33	5	106	6	3	3	5	2	6	.240	.311	.409	.719
	Postseason		7	19	1	0	0	0	(0	0)	1	0	0	0	2	0	8	0	0	0	0	0	0	.053	.143	.053	.195
	6 ML YEARS		622	2128	490	114	12	68	(35	33)	832	271	213	241	167	19	660	53	12	11	51	17	29	.230	.301	.391	.692

Marco Estrada

Pitches: R **Bats:** R **Pos:** SP-28; RP-6   **Ht:** 6'0" **Wt:** 200 **Born:** 7/5/1983 **Age:** 32

Year	Team	Lg	G	GS	CG	GF	IP	BFP	H	R	ER	HR	SH	SF	HB	TBB	IBB	SO	WP	Bk	W	L	Pct	Sh	Sv-Op	Hld	ERC	ERA
2008	Was	NL	11	0	0	3	12.2	63	17	13	11	4	0	0	2	5	1	10	0	0	0	0	-	0	0-1	3	8.13	7.82
2009	Was	NL	4	1	0	1	7.1	33	6	6	5	1	1	0	0	4	0	9	1	0	0	1	.000	0	0-0	0	3.67	6.14
2010	Mil	NL	7	1	0	0	11.1	58	14	13	12	3	1	0	1	6	0	13	2	0	0	0	-	0	0-0	0	7.17	9.53
2011	Mil	NL	43	7	0	12	92.2	381	83	45	42	11	7	1	2	29	2	88	4	2	4	8	.333	0	0-3	4	3.39	4.08
2012	Mil	NL	29	23	0	0	138.1	562	129	62	56	18	7	3	0	29	0	143	4	1	5	7	.417	0	0-0	1	3.18	3.64
2013	Mil	NL	21	21	0	0	128.0	512	109	56	55	19	3	2	2	29	0	118	3	0	7	4	.636	0	0-0	0	3.01	3.87
2014	Mil	NL	39	18	0	3	150.2	624	137	77	73	29	4	4	3	44	0	127	2	1	7	6	.538	0	0-0	0	3.85	4.36
2015	Tor	AL	34	28	0	3	181.0	725	134	67	63	24	2	3	5	55	2	131	2	0	13	8	.619	0	0-0	0	2.64	3.13
	Postseason		4	0	0	2	6.0	27	7	4	4	0	0	0	0	2	0	9	1	0	0	0	-	0	0-0	0	3.91	6.00
	8 ML YEARS		188	99	0	22	722.0	2958	629	339	317	109	25	13	15	201	5	639	18	4	36	34	.514	0	0-4	8	3.31	3.95

Andre Ethier

Bats: L **Throws:** L **Pos:** RF-80;LF-51;PH-27;CF-1;DH-1 EE-thee-er **Ht:** 6'2" **Wt:** 210 **Born:** 4/10/1982 **Age:** 34

Year	Team	Lg	G	AB	H	2B	3B	HR	(Hm	Rd)	TB	R	RBI	RC	TBB	IBB	SO	HBP	SH	SF	SB	CS	GDP	Avg	OBP	Slg	OPS
2006	LAD	NL	126	396	122	20	7	11	(9	2)	189	50	55	62	34	2	77	5	0	6	5	5	11	.308	.365	.477	.842
2007	LAD	NL	153	447	127	32	2	13	(8	5)	202	50	64	65	46	12	68	4	0	8	0	4	10	.284	.350	.452	.802
2008	LAD	NL	141	525	160	38	5	20	(10	10)	268	90	77	99	59	0	88	4	1	7	6	3	6	.305	.375	.510	.885
2009	LAD	NL	160	596	162	42	3	31	(22	9)	303	92	106	94	72	10	116	13	0	4	6	4	19	.272	.361	.508	.869
2010	LAD	NL	139	517	151	33	1	23	(14	9)	255	71	82	89	59	11	102	3	0	6	2	1	11	.292	.364	.493	.857
2011	LAD	NL	135	487	142	30	0	11	(8	3)	205	67	62	73	58	9	103	3	0	3	0	1	8	.292	.368	.421	.789
2012	LAD	NL	149	556	158	36	1	20	(14	6)	256	79	89	89	50	6	124	9	0	3	2	2	13	.284	.351	.460	.812
2013	LAD	NL	142	482	131	33	2	12	(6	6)	204	54	52	62	61	11	95	7	0	3	4	3	9	.272	.360	.423	.783
2014	LAD	NL	130	341	85	17	6	4	(4	0)	126	29	42	42	31	3	74	6	1	1	2	2	5	.249	.322	.370	.691
2015	LAD	NL	142	395	116	20	7	14	(9	5)	192	54	53	59	43	2	75	4	0	3	2	3	11	.294	.366	.486	.852
	Postseason		30	91	21	5	1	3	(1	2)	37	14	6	9	13	0	25	1	0	0	0	1	1	.231	.333	.407	.740
	10 ML YEARS		1417	4742	1354	301	34	159	(104	55)	2200	636	682	734	513	66	922	58	2	44	29	28	103	.286	.359	.464	.823

Dana Eveland

Pitches: L **Bats:** L **Pos:** RP-10 EVE-land **Ht:** 6'1" **Wt:** 235 **Born:** 10/29/1983 **Age:** 32

Year	Team	Lg	G	GS	CG	GF	IP	BFP	H	R	ER	HR	SH	SF	HB	TBB	IBB	SO	WP	Bk	W	L	Pct	Sh	Sv-Op	Hld	ERC	ERA
2015	Pwtckt*	AAA	16	0	0	7	23.1	91	17	4	4	0	1	0	4	3	0	20	1	0	2	0	1.000	0	2- -	-	1.77	1.54
2015	Norfolk*	AAA	16	3	0	3	30.1	123	25	9	8	0	1	1	3	11	0	22	0	0	2	0	1.000	0	0- -	-	2.80	2.37
2005	Mil	NL	27	0	0	9	31.2	146	40	21	21	2	0	1	1	18	3	23	1	0	1	1	.500	0	1-2	7	6.16	5.97
2006	Mil	NL	9	5	0	1	27.2	141	39	25	25	4	1	1	5	16	2	32	2	0	0	3	.000	0	0-1	0	8.30	8.13
2007	Ari	NL	5	1	0	0	5.0	28	8	8	8	0	0	1	0	5	0	3	1	0	1	0	1.000	0	0-0	0	9.25	14.40
2008	Oak	AL	29	29	1	0	168.0	737	172	82	81	10	2	5	12	77	2	118	6	1	9	9	.500	0	0-0	0	4.47	4.34
2009	Oak	AL	13	9	0	2	44.0	221	70	39	35	4	1	2	0	26	1	22	2	0	2	4	.333	0	0-0	0	8.50	7.16
2010	2 Tms		12	10	0	1	54.1	262	72	44	41	4	0	4	4	32	2	24	4	0	3	5	.375	0	0-0	0	6.90	6.79
2011	LAD	NL	5	5	0	0	29.2	118	28	10	10	1	1	0	2	6	0	16	0	0	3	2	.600	0	0-0	0	2.98	3.03
2012	Bal	AL	14	2	0	6	32.1	145	32	18	17	3	0	2	5	13	3	18	0	0	0	1	.000	0	0-0	0	4.38	4.73
2014	NYM	NL	30	0	0	10	27.1	115	24	8	8	2	0	0	4	6	1	27	0	0	1	1	.500	0	1-2	2	3.02	2.63
2015	Atl	NL	10	0	0	1	3.1	18	5	2	2	1	0	1	0	3	1	4	1	0	0	1	.000	0	0-0	1	10.42	5.40
10	Tor	AL	9	9	0	0	44.2	213	57	35	32	4	0	2	2	27	1	21	3	0	3	4	.429	0	0-0	0	6.69	6.45
10	Pit	NL	3	1	0	1	9.2	49	15	9	9	0	0	2	2	5	1	3	1	0	0	1	.000	0	0-0	0	7.85	8.38
	10 ML YEARS		154	61	1	24	423.1	1931	490	257	248	31	5	17	33	202	15	287	17	1	20	27	.426	0	2-5	10	5.40	5.27

Jeurys Familia

Pitches: R **Bats:** R **Pos:** RP-76 jeh-REES fuh-MEAL-yuh **Ht:** 6'3" **Wt:** 240 **Born:** 10/10/1989 **Age:** 26

Year	Team	Lg	G	GS	CG	GF	IP	BFP	H	R	ER	HR	SH	SF	HB	TBB	IBB	SO	WP	Bk	W	L	Pct	Sh	Sv-Op	Hld	ERC	ERA
2012	NYM	NL	8	1	0	4	12.1	52	10	8	8	0	0	0	0	9	0	10	0	0	0	0	-	0	0-0	0	3.76	5.84
2013	NYM	NL	9	0	0	3	10.2	52	12	5	5	2	2	0	0	9	1	8	3	0	0	0	-	0	1-1	0	7.20	4.22
2014	NYM	NL	76	0	0	16	77.1	322	59	26	19	3	4	2	2	32	5	73	9	0	2	5	.286	0	5-10	23	2.45	2.21
2015	NYM	NL	76	0	0	65	78.0	308	59	16	16	6	1	1	2	19	1	86	4	0	2	2	.500	0	43-48	1	2.19	1.85
	4 ML YEARS		169	1	0	88	178.1	734	140	55	48	11	7	3	4	69	7	177	16	0	4	7	.364	0	49-59	24	2.66	2.42

Buck Farmer

Pitches: R **Bats:** L **Pos:** RP-9; SP-5 **Ht:** 6'4" **Wt:** 225 **Born:** 2/20/1991 **Age:** 25

Year	Team	Lg	G	GS	CG	GF	IP	BFP	H	R	ER	HR	SH	SF	HB	TBB	IBB	SO	WP	Bk	W	L	Pct	Sh	Sv-Op	Hld	ERC	ERA
2013	Conn	A-	12	11	0	0	32.0	134	32	13	11	1	1	2	0	7	0	33	1	0	0	3	.000	0	0- -	-	2.89	3.09
2014	Wmich	A	18	18	0	0	103.2	420	91	37	30	6	2	1	3	24	0	116	7	1	10	5	.667	0	0- -	-	2.65	2.60
2015	Toledo	AAA	16	16	0	0	86.2	368	85	45	40	6	0	2	3	25	0	76	3	0	7	3	.700	0	0- -	-	3.43	4.15
2014	Det	AL	4	2	0	0	9.1	46	12	12	12	2	0	0	2	5	0	11	0	0	1	0	.000	0	0-0	0	8.29	11.57
2015	Det	AL	14	5	0	0	40.1	186	53	35	33	10	1	1	3	17	2	24	1	0	0	4	.000	0	0-0	0	7.65	7.36
	2 ML YEARS		18	7	0	1	49.2	232	65	47	45	12	1	1	5	22	2	35	1	0	0	5	.000	0	0-0	0	7.77	8.15

Danny Farquhar

Pitches: R **Bats:** R **Pos:** RP-43 FARK-kwahr **Ht:** 5'9" **Wt:** 185 **Born:** 2/17/1987 **Age:** 29

Year	Team	Lg	G	GS	CG	GF	IP	BFP	H	R	ER	HR	SH	SF	HB	TBB	IBB	SO	WP	Bk	W	L	Pct	Sh	Sv-Op	Hld	ERC	ERA
2015	Tacom*	AAA	27	1	0	11	38.0	157	40	17	13	3	0	0	0	10	0	41	1	0	1	1	.500	0	3- -	1	3.79	3.08
2011	Tor	AL	3	0	0	2	2.0	11	4	4	3	0	0	1	0	2	0	1	0	0	0	0	-	0	0-0	0	13.16	13.50
2013	Sea	AL	46	0	0	27	55.2	228	44	29	26	2	1	2	0	22	4	79	2	1	0	3	.000	0	16-20	2	2.44	4.20
2014	Sea	AL	66	0	0	22	71.0	290	58	23	21	5	1	1	4	22	1	81	6	2	3	1	.750	0	1-3	13	2.78	2.66
2015	Sea	AL	43	0	0	10	51.0	219	53	33	29	9	1	1	1	17	2	48	1	1	1	8	.111	0	1-3	8	4.60	5.12
	4 ML YEARS		158	0	0	61	179.2	748	159	89	79	16	3	5	5	63	7	209	9	4	4	12	.250	0	18-26	23	3.25	3.96

Andrew Faulkner

Pitches: L **Bats:** R **Pos:** RP-11   **Ht:** 6'3" **Wt:** 200 **Born:** 9/12/1992 **Age:** 23

Year	Team	Lg	G	GS	CG	GF	IP	BFP	H	R	ER	HR	SH	SF	HB	TBB	IBB	SO	WP	Bk	W	L	Pct	Sh	Sv-Op	Hld	ERC	ERA
2011	Rngrs	R	12	7	0	0	25.0	96	17	9	6	1	0	0	1	4	0	27	3	0	0	2	.000	0	0- -		1.50	2.16
2012	Hkry	A	29	10	0	7	94.0	424	97	56	45	2	1	1	8	44	0	74	10	0	5	5	.500	0	0- -		4.23	4.31
2013	Hkry	A	21	19	0	0	111.1	490	123	54	43	8	6	2	5	37	0	84	3	0	6	5	.545	0	0- -		4.35	3.48
2014	MrtlBh	A+	21	18	0	1	104.0	420	86	26	24	1	3	5	3	31	0	100	3	0	10	1	.909	0	1- -		2.35	2.08
2014	Frisco	AA	7	6	0	0	30.2	134	28	22	17	3	0	2	0	14	0	33	0	0	4	4	.333	0	0- -		3.71	4.99
2015	Frisco	AA	28	15	0	3	92.1	405	84	50	43	9	4	3	6	47	0	90	1	0	7	4	.636	0	1- -		4.24	4.19
2015	RdRck	AAA	6	0	0	3	8.0	26	2	0	0	0	0	0	0	1	0	13	0	0	0	0	-	0	0- -		0.27	0.00
2015	Tex	AL	11	0	0	1	9.2	40	8	3	3	2	0	0	0	3	1	10	0	0	0	0	-	0	0-0	2	3.27	2.79

Taylor Featherston

Bats: R **Throws:** R **Pos:** 3B-39;2B-33;SS-22;PR-22;PH-5;DH-1   **Ht:** 6'1" **Wt:** 185 **Born:** 10/8/1989 **Age:** 26

Year	Team	Lg	G	AB	H	2B	3B	HR	(Hm	Rd)	TB	R	RBI	RC	TBB	IBB	SO	HBP	SH	SF	SB	CS	GDP	Avg	OBP	Slg	OPS
2011	TriCity	A-	49	169	39	8	3	2	(-	-)	59	19	20	19	17	1	38	3	3	0	3	1	4	.231	.312	.349	.661
2012	Ashvll	A	105	378	113	30	4	12	(-	-)	187	75	53	77	53	0	87	8	1	4	15	4	5	.299	.393	.495	.887
2013	Mdest	A+	116	469	137	31	10	13	(-	-)	227	87	81	80	30	0	110	9	2	6	17	4	14	.292	.342	.484	.826
2014	Tulsa	AA	127	497	129	33	4	16	(-	-)	218	69	57	73	38	3	114	9	3	3	14	6	3	.260	.322	.439	.760
2015	LAA	AL	101	154	25	5	1	2	(0	2)	38	23	9	7	7	0	46	3	4	1	4	2	3	.162	.212	.247	.459

Scott Feldman

Pitches: R **Bats:** L **Pos:** SP-18   **Ht:** 6'7" **Wt:** 220 **Born:** 2/7/1983 **Age:** 33

Year	Team	Lg	G	GS	CG	GF	IP	BFP	H	R	ER	HR	SH	SF	HB	TBB	IBB	SO	WP	Bk	W	L	Pct	Sh	Sv-Op	Hld	ERC	ERA
2005	Tex	AL	8	0	0	3	9.1	37	9	1	1	0	0	0	0	2	1	4	0	0	0	1	.000	0	0-0	1	2.48	0.96
2006	Tex	AL	36	0	0	5	41.1	175	42	19	18	4	2	1	4	10	0	30	0	0	0	2	.000	0	0-1	7	3.94	3.92
2007	Tex	AL	29	0	0	10	39.0	192	44	26	25	3	0	2	3	32	5	19	2	2	1	2	.333	0	0-0	0	6.40	5.77
2008	Tex	AL	28	25	0	2	151.1	651	161	103	89	22	1	9	10	56	2	74	4	2	6	8	.429	0	0-0	0	5.03	5.29
2009	Tex	AL	34	31	0	0	189.2	791	178	87	86	18	1	3	9	65	0	113	5	2	17	8	.680	0	0-0	0	3.74	4.08
2010	Tex	AL	29	22	0	2	141.1	641	181	98	86	18	5	8	5	45	2	75	11	0	7	11	.389	0	0-0	0	5.71	5.48
2011	Tex	AL	11	2	0	5	32.0	129	25	14	14	3	0	1	2	10	0	22	2	0	2	1	.667	0	0-0	0	2.83	3.94
2012	Tex	AL	29	21	0	5	123.2	536	139	79	70	14	0	5	1	32	2	96	2	1	6	11	.353	0	0-0	0	4.27	5.09
2013	2 Tms		30	30	2	0	181.2	758	159	87	78	19	7	7	9	56	1	132	7	1	12	12	.500	1	0-0	0	3.24	3.86
2014	Hou	AL	29	29	2	0	180.1	765	185	86	75	16	2	7	11	50	5	107	6	1	8	12	.400	1	0-0	0	3.89	3.74
2015	Hou	AL	18	18	0	0	108.1	451	115	49	47	13	1	5	0	27	1	61	8	0	5	5	.500	0	0-0	0	4.01	3.90
13	ChC	NL	15	15	1	0	91.0	376	79	42	35	10	6	4	3	25	0	67	4	0	7	6	.538	0	0-0	0	3.05	3.46
13	Bal		15	15	1	0	90.2	382	80	45	43	9	1	3	6	31	1	65	3	1	5	6	.455	1	0-0	0	3.44	4.27
	Postseason		9	0	0	1	13.2	56	8	5	5	0	2	0	2	6	2	11	0	0	1	0	1.000	0	0-1	0	1.75	3.29
11	ML YEARS		281	178	4	32	1198.0	5126	1238	649	589	130	19	48	54	385	19	733	47	9	64	73	.467	2	0-1	8	4.20	4.42

Michael Feliz

Pitches: R **Bats:** R **Pos:** RP-5   **Ht:** 6'4" **Wt:** 225 **Born:** 6/28/1993 **Age:** 23

Year	Team	Lg	G	GS	CG	GF	IP	BFP	H	R	ER	HR	SH	SF	HB	TBB	IBB	SO	WP	Bk	W	L	Pct	Sh	Sv-Op	Hld	ERC	ERA
2011	Astros	R	12	10	0	0	50.0	225	53	35	24	2	3	4	1	21	0	44	1	0	0	3	.000	0	0- -		4.02	4.32
2012	2 Tms	Low	13	9	0	1	64.2	265	53	24	22	3	0	2	1	23	0	63	2	1	6	1	.857	0	0- -		2.67	3.06
2013	TriCity	A-	14	10	0	2	69.0	273	53	19	15	2	2	1	3	13	1	78	4	0	4	2	.667	0	1- -		1.83	1.96
2014	QuadC	A	25	19	0	1	102.2	441	104	53	46	6	3	1	5	37	0	111	7	0	8	6	.571	0	0- -		3.92	4.03
2015	Lancst	A+	8	5	0	0	32.2	144	30	19	16	2	2	5	2	12	0	33	2	0	1	1	.500	0	0- -		3.33	4.41
2015	CpChr	AA	15	12	0	3	78.2	301	52	19	19	5	0	0	0	20	0	70	3	1	6	3	.667	0	1- -		1.67	2.17
2015	Hou	AL	5	0	0	5	8.0	38	9	7	7	2	0	0	4	0	0	7	0	1	0	0	-	0	0-0	0	6.79	7.88

Neftali Feliz

Pitches: R **Bats:** R **Pos:** RP-48   neff-TAH-lee   **Ht:** 6'3" **Wt:** 225 **Born:** 5/2/1988 **Age:** 28

Year	Team	Lg	G	GS	CG	GF	IP	BFP	H	R	ER	HR	SH	SF	HB	TBB	IBB	SO	WP	Bk	W	L	Pct	Sh	Sv-Op	Hld	ERC	ERA
2015	RdRck*	AAA	10	0	0	2	11.0	55	15	11	9	1	1	2	1	4	1	11	1	0	0	1	.000	0	0- -		5.82	7.36
2009	Tex	AL	20	0	0	3	31.0	117	13	6	6	2	1	0	3	8	0	39	0	0	1	0	1.000	0	2-3	9	1.14	1.74
2010	Tex	AL	70	0	0	59	69.1	269	43	21	21	5	1	0	5	18	1	71	5	0	4	3	.571	0	40-43	3	1.75	2.73
2011	Tex	AL	64	0	0	56	62.1	252	42	22	19	4	3	2	0	30	1	54	2	1	2	3	.400	0	32-38	0	2.45	2.74
2012	Tex	AL	8	7	1	0	42.2	175	28	15	15	5	0	0	2	23	0	37	0	0	3	1	.750	0	0-0	0	3.11	3.16
2013	Tex	AL	6	0	0	2	4.2	21	5	0	0	0	0	1	0	2	0	4	0	0	0	0	-	0	0-0	0	4.78	0.00
2014	Tex	AL	30	0	0	22	31.2	122	20	7	7	5	1	0	0	11	0	21	1	0	2	1	.667	0	13-14	0	2.38	1.99
2015	2 Tms	AL	48	0	0	24	48.0	212	57	34	34	5	1	1	1	18	6	39	4	0	3	4	.429	0	10-17	5	5.03	6.38
15	Tex	AL	18	0	0	12	19.2	91	24	10	10	2	0	0	0	9	3	16	2	0	1	2	.333	0	6-9	0	5.26	4.58
15	Det	AL	30	0	0	12	28.1	121	33	24	24	3	1	1	1	9	3	23	2	0	2	2	.500	0	4-8	5	4.87	7.62
	Postseason		18	0	0	15	18.2	76	8	4	4	1	1	0	1	13	1	23	1	0	0	0	-	0	7-8	0	2.04	1.93
7	ML YEARS		246	7	1	166	289.2	1168	208	105	102	26	7	4	12	110	8	265	12	1	15	12	.556	0	97-115	14	2.60	3.17

Jose Fernandez

Pitches: R Bats: R Pos: SP-11   Ht: 6'2" Wt: 215 Born: 7/31/1992 Age: 23

			HOW MUCH HE PITCHED						WHAT HE GAVE UP										THE RESULTS						
Year	Team	Lg	G	GS	CG	GF	IP	BFP	H	R	ER	HR	SH	SF	HB	TBB	IBB	SO	WP	Bk	W	L	Pct	Sh	Sv-Op	Hld	ERC	ERA
2013	Mia	NL	28	28	0	0	172.2	681	111	47	42	10	3	4	5	58	5	187	3	1	12	6	.667	0	0-0	0	1.85	2.19
2014	Mia	NL	8	8	0	0	51.2	205	36	19	14	4	0	0	0	13	1	70	2	1	4	2	.667	0	0-0	0	1.80	2.44
2015	Mia	NL	11	11	0	0	64.2	265	61	21	21	4	0	4	2	14	0	79	2	0	6	1	.857	0	0-0	0	2.95	2.92
	3 ML YEARS		47	47	0	0	289.0	1151	208	87	77	18	3	8	7	85	6	336	7	2	22	9	.710	0	0-0	0	2.07	2.40

Jeff Ferrell

Pitches: R Bats: R Pos: RP-9   Ht: 6'3" Wt: 185 Born: 11/23/1990 Age: 25

			HOW MUCH HE PITCHED						WHAT HE GAVE UP										THE RESULTS						
Year	Team	Lg	G	GS	CG	GF	IP	BFP	H	R	ER	HR	SH	SF	HB	TBB	IBB	SO	WP	Bk	W	L	Pct	Sh	Sv-Op	Hld	ERC	ERA
2011	Wmich	A	6	6	0	0	28.1	119	28	13	11	3	0	1	1	12	0	24	3	0	2	1	.667	0	0--	-	4.46	3.49
2012	Wmich	A	23	16	0	4	92.0	377	76	44	40	9	3	3	3	29	0	81	6	0	7	5	.583	0	1--	-	2.94	3.91
2013	Lkland	A+	25	19	0	3	119.1	500	121	61	53	15	2	2	3	36	0	77	5	0	6	6	.500	0	0--	-	4.11	4.00
2014	Erie	AA	25	25	0	0	138.0	612	174	85	85	17	3	4	4	38	0	92	1	0	10	9	.526	0	0--	-	5.41	5.54
2015	Erie	AA	17	1	0	15	27.0	105	21	5	5	4	1	0	1	4	0	35	0	0	0	0	-	0	12--	-	2.41	1.67
2015	Toledo	AAA	11	0	0	10	11.1	46	8	6	6	3	0	0	0	5	1	10	0	0	0	1	.000	0	4--	-	3.59	4.76
2015	Det	AL	9	0	0	2	11.1	50	12	8	8	3	0	1	0	4	0	6	0	0	0	0	-	0	0-0	0	5.28	6.35

Tommy Field

Bats: R Throws: R Pos: 2B-14;SS-1;PH-1;PR-1   Ht: 5'10" Wt: 185 Born: 2/22/1987 Age: 29

						BATTING															RUNNING			AVERAGES			
Year	Team	Lg	G	AB	H	2B	3B	HR	(Hm	Rd)	TB	R	RBI	RC	TBB	IBB	SO	HBP	SH	SF	SB	CS	GDP	Avg	OBP	Slg	OPS
2015	RdRck*	AAA	103	369	91	23	3	14	(-	-)	162	51	44	61	53	1	82	7	0	6	5	1	6	.247	.347	.439	.786
2011	Col	NL	16	48	13	0	0	0	(0	0)	13	4	3	4	3	0	14	0	0	0	0	0	1	.271	.314	.271	.585
2012	Col	NL	2	2	0	0	0	0	(0	0)	0	0	0	0	1	0	1	0	0	0	0	0	0	.000	.333	.000	.333
2013	LAA	AL	15	26	4	0	0	0	(0	0)	4	4	0	0	1	0	7	0	0	0	0	0	0	.154	.185	.154	.339
2015	Tex	AL	14	41	8	1	0	2	(2	0)	15	6	5	4	2	0	16	1	1	0	1	0	0	.195	.250	.366	.616
	4 ML YEARS		47	117	25	1	0	2	(2	0)	32	14	8	8	7	0	38	1	1	0	1	0	1	.214	.264	.274	.538

Prince Fielder

Bats: L Throws: R Pos: DH-139;1B-18;PH-1   Ht: 5'11" Wt: 275 Born: 5/9/1984 Age: 32

						BATTING															RUNNING			AVERAGES			
Year	Team	Lg	G	AB	H	2B	3B	HR	(Hm	Rd)	TB	R	RBI	RC	TBB	IBB	SO	HBP	SH	SF	SB	CS	GDP	Avg	OBP	Slg	OPS
2005	Mil	NL	39	59	17	4	0	2	(2	0)	27	2	10	10	2	0	17	0	0	1	0	0	0	.288	.306	.458	.764
2006	Mil	NL	157	569	154	35	1	28	(11	17)	275	82	81	84	59	5	125	12	0	8	7	2	17	.271	.347	.483	.831
2007	Mil	NL	158	573	165	35	2	50	(27	23)	354	109	119	125	90	21	121	14	0	4	2	2	9	.288	.395	.618	1.013
2008	Mil	NL	159	588	162	30	2	34	(18	16)	298	86	102	105	84	19	134	12	0	10	3	2	12	.276	.372	.507	.879
2009	Mil	NL	162	591	177	35	3	46	(23	23)	356	103	141	134	110	21	138	9	0	9	2	3	14	.299	.412	.602	1.014
2010	Mil	NL	161	578	151	25	0	32	(18	14)	272	94	83	94	114	17	138	21	0	1	1	0	12	.261	.401	.471	.871
2011	Mil	NL	162	569	170	36	1	38	(24	14)	322	95	120	120	107	32	106	10	0	6	1	1	17	.299	.415	.566	.981
2012	Det	AL	162	581	182	33	1	30	(18	12)	307	83	108	116	85	18	84	17	0	7	1	0	19	.313	.412	.528	.940
2013	Det	AL	162	624	174	36	0	25	(13	12)	285	82	106	94	75	5	117	9	0	4	1	1	20	.279	.362	.457	.819
2014	Tex	AL	42	150	37	8	0	3	(3	0)	54	19	16	18	25	11	24	2	0	1	0	0	5	.247	.360	.360	.720
2015	Tex	AL	158	613	187	28	0	23	(11	12)	284	78	98	110	64	14	88	11	0	5	0	0	21	.305	.378	.463	.841
	Postseason		39	144	28	5	0	5	(4	1)	48	12	11	11	14	5	32	5	0	1	0	1	7	.194	.287	.333	.620
	11 ML YEARS		1522	5495	1576	305	10	311	(168	143)	2834	833	984	1010	815	163	1092	117	0	56	18	11	146	.287	.387	.516	.903

Daniel Fields

Bats: L Throws: R Pos: LF-1   Ht: 6'2" Wt: 215 Born: 1/23/1991 Age: 25

						BATTING															RUNNING			AVERAGES			
Year	Team	Lg	G	AB	H	2B	3B	HR	(Hm	Rd)	TB	R	RBI	RC	TBB	IBB	SO	HBP	SH	SF	SB	CS	GDP	Avg	OBP	Slg	OPS
2011	Lkland	A+	124	432	95	14	4	8	(-	-)	141	57	46	46	49	0	133	7	5	2	4	4	9	.220	.308	.326	.635
2012	Lkland	A+	62	244	65	11	4	1	(-	-)	87	31	26	29	19	1	55	1	0	3	14	7	5	.266	.318	.357	.675
2012	Erie	AA	29	106	28	4	0	2	(-	-)	38	13	7	16	13	0	21	2	0	1	9	1	1	.264	.352	.358	.711
2013	Erie	AA	118	457	130	27	6	10	(-	-)	199	71	58	75	45	2	130	8	1	4	24	7	8	.284	.356	.435	.791
2014	Toledo	AAA	75	274	60	10	3	6	(-	-)	94	29	26	27	15	0	76	6	2	2	8	2	2	.219	.273	.343	.616
2015	Toledo	AAA	122	447	102	25	8	7	(-	-)	164	59	41	61	66	2	146	7	3	3	17	7	13	.228	.335	.367	.701
2015	Det	AL	1	3	1	1	0	0	(0	0)	2	1	0	0	0	0	2	0	0	0	0	0	0	.333	.333	.667	1.000

Josh Fields

Pitches: R Bats: R Pos: RP-54   Ht: 6'0" Wt: 195 Born: 8/19/1985 Age: 30

			HOW MUCH HE PITCHED						WHAT HE GAVE UP										THE RESULTS						
Year	Team	Lg	G	GS	CG	GF	IP	BFP	H	R	ER	HR	SH	SF	HB	TBB	IBB	SO	WP	Bk	W	L	Pct	Sh	Sv-Op	Hld	ERC	ERA
2015	Fresno*	AAA	5	0	0	1	6.0	27	5	2	2	0	0	0	0	4	0	3	1	0	0	0	-	0	0--	-	3.35	3.00
2013	Hou	AL	41	0	0	16	38.0	160	31	21	21	8	1	0	0	18	4	40	0	0	1	3	.250	0	5-6	6	3.94	4.97
2014	Hou	AL	54	0	0	16	54.2	231	50	29	27	2	0	5	2	17	3	70	0	0	4	6	.400	0	4-8	8	2.87	4.45
2015	Hou	AL	54	0	0	19	50.2	209	39	20	20	2	2	1	1	19	3	67	1	0	4	1	.800	0	0-2	5	2.35	3.55
	3 ML YEARS		149	0	0	51	143.1	600	120	70	68	12	3	6	3	54	10	177	1	0	9	10	.474	0	9-16	19	2.95	4.27

Casey Fien

Pitches: R **Bats:** R **Pos:** RP-62
FEEN
Ht: 6'2" **Wt:** 210 **Born:** 10/21/1983 **Age:** 32

		HOW MUCH HE PITCHED						WHAT HE GAVE UP										THE RESULTS						
Year	Team	Lg	G	GS	CG	GF	IP	BFP	H	R	ER	HR	SH	SF	HB	TBB	IBB	SO	WP	Bk	W	L	Pct	Sh	Sv-Op	Hld	ERC	ERA
2009	Det	AL	9	0	0	5	11.1	53	13	11	10	2	0	2	0	6	0	9	0	0	0	1	.000	0	0-0	0	5.92	7.94
2010	Det	AL	2	0	0	2	2.2	12	4	3	3	2	1	0	0	0	0	0	0	0	0	0	-	0	0-0	0	9.96	10.13
2012	Min	AL	35	0	0	7	35.0	141	25	9	8	3	1	2	1	9	4	32	0	0	2	1	.667	0	0-0	6	1.90	2.06
2013	Min	AL	73	0	0	20	62.0	244	51	28	27	9	3	2	0	12	3	73	2	0	5	2	.714	0	0-2	17	2.59	3.92
2014	Min	AL	73	0	0	15	63.1	260	64	29	28	7	2	4	0	10	0	51	2	0	5	6	.455	0	1-5	26	3.25	3.98
2015	Min	AL	62	0	0	6	63.1	257	61	26	25	6	2	3	0	8	0	41	0	0	4	6	.400	0	0-4	18	2.77	3.55
	6 ML YEARS		254	0	0	55	237.2	967	218	106	101	29	9	13	1	45	7	206	4	0	16	16	.500	0	1-11	67	2.92	3.82

Mike Fiers

Pitches: R **Bats:** R **Pos:** SP-30; RP-1
FIRES
Ht: 6'2" **Wt:** 200 **Born:** 6/15/1985 **Age:** 31

		HOW MUCH HE PITCHED						WHAT HE GAVE UP										THE RESULTS						
Year	Team	Lg	G	GS	CG	GF	IP	BFP	H	R	ER	HR	SH	SF	HB	TBB	IBB	SO	WP	Bk	W	L	Pct	Sh	Sv-Op	Hld	ERC	ERA
2011	Mil	NL	2	0	0	2	2.0	10	2	0	0	0	0	0	0	3	0	2	0	0	0	0	-	0	0-0	0	8.25	0.00
2012	Mil	NL	23	22	0	1	127.2	539	125	56	53	12	4	4	2	36	0	135	4	0	9	10	.474	0	0-0	0	3.50	3.74
2013	Mil	NL	11	3	0	4	22.1	103	28	20	18	8	1	2	0	6	0	15	1	0	1	4	.200	0	0-0	0	6.65	7.25
2014	Mil	NL	14	10	0	1	71.2	274	46	19	17	7	2	1	0	17	1	76	1	0	6	5	.545	0	0-0	0	1.68	2.13
2015	2 Tms		31	30	1	0	180.1	761	162	83	74	24	3	8	6	64	5	180	8	0	7	10	.412	1	0-0	0	3.64	3.69
15	Mil	NL	21	21	0	0	118.0	509	117	57	51	14	3	6	5	43	5	121	6	0	5	9	.357	0	0-0	0	4.11	3.89
15	Hou	AL	10	9	1	0	62.1	252	45	26	23	10	0	2	1	21	0	59	2	0	2	1	.667	1	0-0	0	2.78	3.32
	5 ML YEARS		81	65	1	8	404.0	1687	363	178	162	51	10	15	8	126	6	408	14	0	23	29	.442	1	0-0	0	3.39	3.61

Cole Figueroa

Bats: L **Throws:** R **Pos:** 3B-2
figg-uh-ROE-ah
Ht: 5'10" **Wt:** 185 **Born:** 6/30/1987 **Age:** 29

		BATTING																		RUNNING			AVERAGES			
Year	Team	Lg	G	AB	H	2B	3B	HR	(Hm | Rd)	TB	R	RBI	RC	TBB	IBB	SO	HBP	SH	SF	SB	CS	GDP	Avg	OBP	Slg	OPS
2011	Mont	AA	114	410	116	20	6	5	(- | -)	163	71	51	67	55	0	41	8	11	4	9	5	6	.283	.375	.398	.773
2012	Mont	AA	25	86	27	6	1	3	(- | -)	44	17	12	18	17	2	9	0	0	2	1	2	1	.314	.419	.512	.931
2012	Drham	AAA	88	311	89	17	4	2	(- | -)	120	32	42	43	26	1	22	3	4	3	3	2	6	.286	.344	.386	.730
2013	Drham	AAA	129	461	132	20	4	3	(- | -)	169	65	62	69	54	0	30	4	6	8	10	2	10	.286	.361	.367	.727
2014	Drham	AAA	71	262	74	13	3	3	(- | -)	102	33	33	42	39	0	29	1	5	5	4	1	5	.282	.371	.389	.761
2015	S-WB	AAA	121	449	131	19	1	3	(- | -)	161	45	44	61	44	2	27	3	5	6	4	4	9	.292	.355	.359	.713
2014	TB	AL	23	43	10	2	1	0	(0 | 0)	14	6	6	4	4	0	4	0	0	2	0	0	0	.233	.286	.326	.611
2015	NYY	AL	2	8	2	2	0	0	(0 | 0)	4	2	0	0	0	0	0	0	0	0	0	0	0	.250	.250	.500	.750
	2 ML YEARS		25	51	12	4	1	0	(0 | 0)	18	8	6	4	4	0	4	0	0	2	0	0	0	.235	.281	.353	.634

Brandon Finnegan

Pitches: L **Bats:** L **Pos:** RP-16; SP-4
Ht: 5'11" **Wt:** 185 **Born:** 4/14/1993 **Age:** 23

		HOW MUCH HE PITCHED						WHAT HE GAVE UP										THE RESULTS						
Year	Team	Lg	G	GS	CG	GF	IP	BFP	H	R	ER	HR	SH	SF	HB	TBB	IBB	SO	WP	Bk	W	L	Pct	Sh	Sv-Op	Hld	ERC	ERA
2014	Wilmg	A+	5	5	0	0	15.0	49	5	1	1	1	0	0	0	2	0	13	1	0	0	1	.000	0	0- -	-	0.59	0.60
2014	NWArk	AA	8	0	0	3	12.0	56	15	9	3	2	0	0	1	2	0	13	1	0	0	3	.000	0	0- -	-	5.06	2.25
2015	NWArk	AA	5	3	0	1	13.0	61	10	9	4	1	0	0	0	12	0	13	0	0	0	1	.000	0	1- -	-	4.52	2.77
2015	Omha	AAA	6	4	0	0	14.0	65	17	12	11	1	0	0	0	7	0	19	0	0	0	2	.000	0	0- -	-	5.46	7.07
2015	Lsvlle	AAA	8	8	0	0	30.1	140	31	22	21	3	2	1	2	17	0	30	3	0	0	3	.000	0	0- -	-	5.01	6.23
2014	KC	AL	7	0	0	1	7.0	28	6	1	1	0	0	0	0	1	0	10	0	0	0	1	.000	0	0-0	0	1.77	1.29
2015	2 Tms		20	4	0	3	48.0	197	37	19	19	8	3	1	1	21	0	45	0	0	5	2	.714	0	0-1	0	3.55	3.56
15	KC	AL	14	0	0	3	24.1	99	16	8	8	3	1	1	1	13	0	21	0	0	3	0	1.000	0	0-1	0	3.14	2.96
15	Cin	NL	6	4	0	0	23.2	98	21	11	11	5	2	0	0	8	0	24	0	0	2	2	.500	0	0-0	0	3.96	4.18
	Postseason		7	0	0	0	6.0	31	9	7	7	0	3	0	0	5	1	4	0	0	1	1	.500	0	0-1	0	7.77	10.50
	2 ML YEARS		27	4	0	4	55.0	225	43	20	20	8	3	1	1	22	0	55	0	0	5	3	.625	0	0-1	0	3.30	3.27

Doug Fister

Pitches: R **Bats:** L **Pos:** SP-15; RP-10
Ht: 6'8" **Wt:** 210 **Born:** 2/4/1984 **Age:** 32

		HOW MUCH HE PITCHED						WHAT HE GAVE UP										THE RESULTS						
Year	Team	Lg	G	GS	CG	GF	IP	BFP	H	R	ER	HR	SH	SF	HB	TBB	IBB	SO	WP	Bk	W	L	Pct	Sh	Sv-Op	Hld	ERC	ERA
2009	Sea	AL	11	10	0	1	61.0	256	63	29	28	11	0	2	0	15	0	36	1	0	3	4	.429	0	0-0	0	4.36	4.13
2010	Sea	AL	28	28	0	0	171.0	720	187	85	78	13	2	4	6	32	2	93	8	3	6	14	.300	0	0-0	0	3.73	4.11
2011	2 Tms		32	31	3	0	216.1	875	193	76	68	11	4	9	12	37	2	146	3	1	11	13	.458	0	0-0	0	2.53	2.83
2012	Det	AL	26	26	2	0	161.2	673	166	73	62	15	3	0	7	37	1	137	1	0	10	10	.500	1	0-0	0	3.33	3.45
2013	Det	AL	33	32	1	0	208.2	881	229	91	85	14	2	5	16	44	2	159	7	0	14	9	.609	0	0-0	0	4.00	3.67
2014	Was	NL	25	25	1	0	164.0	662	153	52	44	18	6	2	7	24	0	98	5	0	16	6	.727	1	0-0	0	2.98	2.41
2015	Was	NL	25	15	0	2	103.0	449	120	56	48	14	7	5	6	24	3	63	1	0	5	7	.417	0	1-1	0	4.79	4.19
11	Sea	AL	21	21	3	0	146.0	602	139	57	54	7	3	7	9	32	2	89	3	1	3	12	.200	0	0-0	0	3.02	3.33
11	Det	AL	11	10	0	0	70.1	273	54	19	14	4	1	2	3	5	0	57	0	0	8	1	.889	0	0-0	0	1.63	1.79
	Postseason		9	8	0	0	55.1	232	54	16	16	2	2	0	3	16	0	40	1	1	4	2	.667	0	0-0	0	3.32	2.60
	7 ML YEARS		180	167	7	3	1085.2	4516	1101	462	413	96	24	25	56	213	10	732	26	4	65	63	.508	2	1-1	0	3.49	3.42

Ryan Flaherty

Bats: L Throws: R Pos: 2B-56;SS-15;1B-11;3B-8;RF-5;PR-3;PH-2;LF-1   Ht: 6'3" Wt: 220 Born: 7/27/1986 Age: 29

Year	Team	Lg	G	AB	H	2B	3B	HR	(Hm	Rd)	TB	R	RBI	RC	TBB	IBB	SO	HBP	SH	SF	SB	CS	GDP	Avg	OBP	Slg	OPS
2012	Bal	AL	77	153	33	2	1	6	(3	3)	55	15	19	15	6	0	43	3	3	1	1	0	3	.216	.258	.359	.617
2013	Bal	AL	85	246	55	11	0	10	(6	4)	96	28	27	27	19	3	62	5	1	0	2	0	2	.224	.293	.390	.683
2014	Bal	AL	102	281	62	15	1	7	(7	0)	100	33	32	34	22	2	68	5	3	1	1	0	3	.221	.288	.356	.644
2015	Bal	AL	91	267	54	8	3	9	(2	7)	95	34	31	24	26	2	81	4	2	2	0	0	8	.202	.281	.356	.637
	Postseason		11	32	9	0	0	2	(0	2)	15	5	5	4	4	0	9	0	0	0	0	0	0	.281	.361	.469	.830
	4 ML YEARS		355	947	204	36	5	32	(18	14)	346	110	109	100	73	7	254	17	9	4	4	0	16	.215	.282	.365	.648

Yohan Flande

Pitches: L Bats: L Pos: SP-10; RP-9   YO-hahn FLAHN-day   Ht: 6'2" Wt: 180 Born: 1/27/1986 Age: 30

Year	Team	Lg	G	GS	CG	GF	IP	BFP	H	R	ER	HR	SH	SF	HB	TBB	IBB	SO	WP	Bk	W	L	Pct	Sh	Sv-Op	Hld	ERC	ERA
2011	Gwnntt	AAA	33	19	0	3	137.0	596	155	70	61	9	5	9	4	38	2	104	4	1	8	8	.500	0	1--	-	4.16	4.01
2012	Gwnntt	AAA	29	27	0	0	147.2	638	153	75	69	11	6	5	5	55	1	106	12	1	6	11	.353	0	0--	-	4.14	4.21
2013	Gwnntt	AAA	31	19	1	3	131.1	575	142	70	61	9	5	3	4	46	1	92	2	1	9	7	.563	0	1--	-	4.20	4.18
2014	ColSpr	AAA	18	16	0	0	88.0	396	112	58	55	9	1	4	2	33	1	67	3	1	3	11	.214	0	0--	-	5.75	5.63
2015	NwBrit	AA	6	6	1	0	39.2	146	27	7	6	1	2	0	0	4	0	30	1	2	5	0	1.000	1	0--	-	1.26	1.36
2015	Albq	AAA	6	6	0	0	31.2	154	55	30	25	8	0	1	1	7	1	11	1	1	3	3	.500	0	0--	-	9.31	7.11
2014	Col	NL	16	10	0	2	59.0	241	55	34	34	5	5	4	2	16	2	34	0	0	0	6	.000	0	0-0	1	3.26	5.19
2015	Col	NL	19	10	0	2	68.1	296	73	36	36	14	5	1	1	25	3	43	1	1	3	3	.500	0	0-0	0	5.11	4.74
	2 ML YEARS		35	20	0	4	127.1	537	128	70	70	19	10	5	3	41	5	77	1	1	3	9	.250	0	0-0	1	4.22	4.95

Kendry Flores

Pitches: R Bats: R Pos: RP-6; SP-1   Ht: 6'2" Wt: 175 Born: 11/24/1991 Age: 24

Year	Team	Lg	G	GS	CG	GF	IP	BFP	H	R	ER	HR	SH	SF	HB	TBB	IBB	SO	WP	Bk	W	L	Pct	Sh	Sv-Op	Hld	ERC	ERA
2011	SlKzr	A-	12	11	0	0	48.0	213	59	35	27	5	1	2	2	14	0	47	2	1	4	3	.571	0	0--	-	5.19	5.06
2012	SlKzr	A-	10	8	0	0	42.1	184	44	26	21	4	1	0	1	11	0	34	3	0	1	3	.250	0	0--	-	3.58	4.46
2013	Augsta	A	22	22	1	0	141.2	551	113	47	43	11	5	2	4	17	2	137	4	0	10	6	.625	0	0--	-	1.97	2.73
2014	SnJos	A+	20	20	0	0	105.2	446	101	57	48	14	1	2	5	32	0	112	6	0	6	4	.600	0	0--	-	3.86	4.09
2015	Jaxnvl	AA	9	9	0	0	56.2	211	33	14	13	3	1	1	2	15	0	42	2	1	3	3	.500	0	0--	-	1.52	2.06
2015	NewOr	AAA	10	10	0	0	58.2	234	49	19	17	3	0	0	1	14	0	42	1	0	3	2	.600	0	0--	-	2.40	2.61
2015	Mia	NL	7	1	0	3	12.2	57	16	8	7	0	0	1	1	4	1	9	0	0	1	2	.333	0	0-0	0	4.70	4.97

Ramon Flores

Bats: L Throws: L Pos: LF-11;RF-1   Ht: 5'10" Wt: 190 Born: 3/26/1992 Age: 24

Year	Team	Lg	G	AB	H	2B	3B	HR	(Hm	Rd)	TB	R	RBI	RC	TBB	IBB	SO	HBP	SH	SF	SB	CS	GDP	Avg	OBP	Slg	OPS
2011	CtnSC	A	125	468	124	26	2	11	(-	-)	187	59	59	72	61	1	93	3	2	0	13	2	5	.265	.353	.400	.753
2012	Tampa	A+	131	517	156	29	7	6	(-	-)	217	83	39	85	54	1	85	5	2	5	24	9	4	.302	.370	.420	.790
2013	Trntn	AA	136	534	139	25	6	6	(-	-)	194	79	55	75	77	0	98	2	3	4	7	6	11	.260	.353	.363	.717
2014	S-WB	AAA	63	235	58	17	4	7	(-	-)	104	30	23	37	33	0	45	1	0	2	3	2	5	.247	.339	.443	.782
2015	S-WB	AAA	73	276	79	11	2	7	(-	-)	115	43	34	46	39	1	43	3	0	3	3	2	5	.286	.377	.417	.794
2015	Tacom	AAA	14	52	22	6	0	2	(-	-)	34	11	7	16	11	1	6	0	0	0	0	0	2	.423	.524	.654	1.178
2015	NYY	AL	12	32	7	1	0	0	(0	0)	8	3	0	1	0	0	4	0	1	0	0	0	0	.219	.219	.250	.469

Wilmer Flores

Bats: R Throws: R Pos: SS-103;2B-37;PH-4   Ht: 6'3" Wt: 205 Born: 8/6/1991 Age: 24

Year	Team	Lg	G	AB	H	2B	3B	HR	(Hm	Rd)	TB	R	RBI	RC	TBB	IBB	SO	HBP	SH	SF	SB	CS	GDP	Avg	OBP	Slg	OPS
2013	NYM	NL	27	95	20	5	0	1	(0	1)	28	8	13	7	5	0	23	0	0	1	0	0	5	.211	.248	.295	.542
2014	NYM	NL	78	259	65	13	1	6	(4	2)	98	28	29	25	12	2	31	1	1	1	1	0	6	.251	.286	.378	.664
2015	NYM	NL	137	483	127	22	0	16	(8	8)	197	55	59	58	19	2	63	4	2	2	0	1	12	.263	.295	.408	.703
	3 ML YEARS		242	837	212	40	1	23	(12	11)	323	91	101	90	36	4	117	5	3	4	1	1	19	.253	.287	.386	.673

Pedro Florimon

Bats: B Throws: R Pos: SS-17;PR-9;2B-3;PH-1   FLOOR-ih-moan   Ht: 6'2" Wt: 185 Born: 12/10/1986 Age: 29

Year	Team	Lg	G	AB	H	2B	3B	HR	(Hm	Rd)	TB	R	RBI	RC	TBB	IBB	SO	HBP	SH	SF	SB	CS	GDP	Avg	OBP	Slg	OPS
2015	Indy*	AAA	65	196	48	12	3	2	(-	-)	72	21	18	25	21	1	55	0	4	2	12	3	3	.245	.315	.367	.682
2011	Bal	AL	4	8	1	1	0	0	(0	0)	2	1	2	1	1	0	6	0	0	0	0	0	0	.125	.222	.250	.472
2012	Min	AL	43	137	30	5	2	1	(1	0)	42	16	10	8	10	0	30	0	3	0	3	1	3	.219	.272	.307	.579
2013	Min	AL	134	403	89	17	0	9	(3	6)	133	44	44	38	33	1	115	2	5	3	15	6	7	.221	.284	.330	.611
2014	Min	AL	33	76	7	1	1	0	(0	0)	10	7	1	7	8	0	22	0	2	0	6	0	2	.092	.179	.132	.310
2015	Pit	NL	24	23	2	0	1	0	(0	0)	4	5	1	7	2	0	12	0	0	0	1	0	0	.087	.160	.174	.334
	5 ML YEARS		238	647	129	24	4	10	(4	6)	191	73	58	47	54	1	185	2	11	3	25	7	12	.199	.262	.295	.557

Tyler Flowers

Bats: R **Throws:** R **Pos:** C-110;1B-2;DH-1;PH-1 **Ht:** 6'4" **Wt:** 245 **Born:** 1/24/1986 **Age:** 30

Year	Team	Lg	G	AB	H	2B	3B	HR	(Hm	Rd)	TB	R	RBI	RC	TBB	IBB	SO	HBP	SH	SF	SB	CS	GDP	Avg	OBP	Slg	OPS
2009	CWS	AL	10	16	3	1	0	0	(0	0)	4	3	0	2	3	0	8	1	0	0	0	0	1	.188	.350	.250	.600
2010	CWS	AL	8	11	1	0	0	0	(0	0)	1	2	0	1	4	0	5	0	0	0	0	0	0	.091	.333	.091	.424
2011	CWS	AL	38	110	23	5	1	5	(3	2)	45	13	16	13	14	0	38	3	0	2	0	1	2	.209	.310	.409	.719
2012	CWS	AL	52	136	29	6	0	7	(5	2)	56	19	13	13	12	0	56	4	1	0	2	1	2	.213	.296	.412	.708
2013	CWS	AL	84	256	50	11	0	10	(7	3)	91	24	24	14	14	1	94	4	0	1	0	1	9	.195	.247	.355	.603
2014	CWS	AL	127	407	98	16	1	15	(7	8)	161	42	50	43	25	0	159	8	1	1	0	1	10	.241	.297	.396	.693
2015	CWS	AL	112	331	79	12	0	9	(3	6)	118	21	39	36	21	0	104	6	2	1	0	1	8	.239	.295	.356	.652
7 ML YEARS			431	1267	283	51	2	46	(25	21)	476	124	142	122	93	1	464	26	4	5	2	5	32	.223	.289	.376	.665

Gavin Floyd

Pitches: R **Bats:** R **Pos:** RP-7 **Ht:** 6'4" **Wt:** 245 **Born:** 1/27/1983 **Age:** 33

Year	Team	Lg	G	GS	CG	GF	IP	BFP	H	R	ER	HR	SH	SF	HB	TBB	IBB	SO	WP	Bk	W	L	Pct	Sh	Sv-Op	Hld	ERC	ERA
2004	Phi	NL	6	4	0	0	28.1	126	25	11	11	1	1	0	5	16	0	24	1	1	2	0	1.000	0	0-0	0	4.33	3.49
2005	Phi	NL	7	4	0	0	26.0	127	30	31	29	5	1	1	3	16	2	17	2	0	1	2	.333	0	0-0	0	6.82	10.04
2006	Phi	NL	11	11	1	0	54.1	264	70	48	44	14	2	5	3	32	3	34	2	0	4	3	.571	1	0-0	0	8.02	7.29
2007	CWS	AL	16	10	0	4	70.0	314	85	45	41	17	3	2	6	19	0	49	1	0	1	5	.167	0	0-0	0	6.22	5.27
2008	CWS	AL	33	33	1	0	206.1	878	190	107	88	30	7	5	9	70	6	145	9	0	17	8	.680	0	0-0	0	3.80	3.84
2009	CWS	AL	30	30	1	0	193.0	797	178	93	87	21	2	3	2	59	4	163	8	0	11	11	.500	0	0-0	0	3.38	4.06
2010	CWS	AL	31	31	1	0	187.1	798	199	92	85	14	3	4	6	58	4	151	9	1	10	13	.435	0	0-0	0	4.03	4.08
2011	CWS	AL	31	30	1	1	193.2	798	180	97	94	22	4	8	11	45	2	151	12	1	12	13	.480	0	0-0	0	3.36	4.37
2012	CWS	AL	29	29	0	0	168.0	724	166	84	80	22	3	3	14	63	2	144	8	0	12	11	.522	0	0-0	0	4.50	4.29
2013	CWS	AL	5	5	0	0	24.1	110	27	15	14	4	2	2	0	12	1	25	1	0	0	4	.000	0	0-0	0	5.48	5.18
2014	Atl	NL	9	9	0	0	54.1	229	55	23	16	6	4	2	3	13	0	45	6	0	2	2	.500	0	0-0	0	3.81	2.65
2015	Cle	AL	7	0	0	2	13.1	55	11	4	4	0	0	0	1	4	0	7	1	0	0	0	-	0	0-0	0	2.40	2.70
Postseason			1	1	0	0	3.0	16	5	4	4	2	0	0	0	2	0	4	0	0	0	1	.000	0	0-0	0	14.65	12.00
12 ML YEARS			215	196	5	7	1219.0	5220	1216	650	593	156	32	35	63	407	24	955	60	3	72	72	.500	1	0-0	0	4.18	4.38

Mike Foltynewicz

Pitches: R **Bats:** R **Pos:** SP-15; RP-3 — fohl-tuh-NEH-vich — **Ht:** 6'4" **Wt:** 220 **Born:** 10/7/1991 **Age:** 24

Year	Team	Lg	G	GS	CG	GF	IP	BFP	H	R	ER	HR	SH	SF	HB	TBB	IBB	SO	WP	Bk	W	L	Pct	Sh	Sv-Op	Hld	ERC	ERA
2011	Lxngtn	A	26	26	0	0	134.0	581	149	84	74	10	3	4	7	51	0	88	8	1	5	11	.313	0	0--	-	4.78	4.97
2012	Lxngtn	A	27	27	0	0	152.0	653	145	65	53	11	4	2	5	62	0	125	6	0	14	4	.778	0	0--	-	3.79	3.14
2013	Lancst	A+	7	5	0	1	26.0	122	31	16	11	4	0	1	0	14	0	29	5	1	1	0	1.000	0	0--	-	6.11	3.81
2013	CpChr	AA	23	16	0	4	103.1	424	75	39	33	8	3	2	5	52	0	95	9	2	5	3	.625	0	3--	-	3.11	2.87
2014	OkCity	AAA	18	18	0	0	102.2	448	98	63	58	10	1	7	10	52	2	102	9	4	7	7	.500	0	0--	-	4.68	5.08
2015	Gwnntt	AAA	10	10	1	0	56.2	242	52	28	22	7	1	0	0	26	0	63	1	0	1	6	.143	0	0--	-	4.03	3.49
2014	Hou	AL	16	0	0	9	18.2	84	23	11	11	3	0	0	0	7	0	14	3	0	0	1	.000	0	0-0	1	5.80	5.30
2015	Atl	NL	18	15	0	1	86.2	399	112	63	55	17	2	6	4	29	0	77	3	1	4	6	.400	0	0-0	1	6.43	5.71
2 ML YEARS			34	15	0	10	105.1	483	135	74	66	20	2	6	4	36	0	91	6	1	4	7	.364	0	0-0	2	6.31	5.64

Logan Forsythe

Bats: R **Throws:** R **Pos:** 2B-126;1B-26;3B-9;DH-7;PH-4;PR-1 **Ht:** 6'1" **Wt:** 205 **Born:** 1/14/1987 **Age:** 29

Year	Team	Lg	G	AB	H	2B	3B	HR	(Hm	Rd)	TB	R	RBI	RC	TBB	IBB	SO	HBP	SH	SF	SB	CS	GDP	Avg	OBP	Slg	OPS
2011	SD	NL	62	150	32	9	1	0	(0	0)	43	12	12	15	12	3	33	3	2	2	3	1	3	.213	.281	.287	.568
2012	SD	NL	91	315	86	13	3	6	(5	1)	123	45	26	37	28	0	57	6	0	1	8	2	6	.273	.343	.390	.733
2013	SD	NL	75	220	47	6	1	6	(2	4)	73	22	19	16	19	2	54	2	1	1	6	1	5	.214	.281	.332	.613
2014	TB	AL	110	301	67	12	1	6	(2	4)	99	32	26	26	25	0	71	4	2	4	2	0	9	.223	.287	.329	.616
2015	TB	AL	153	540	152	33	2	17	(8	9)	240	69	68	73	55	2	111	14	0	6	9	4	12	.281	.359	.444	.804
5 ML YEARS			491	1526	384	73	8	35	(17	18)	578	180	151	167	139	7	326	29	5	14	28	8	35	.252	.323	.379	.702

Dexter Fowler

Bats: B **Throws:** R **Pos:** CF-152;PH-6 **Ht:** 6'5" **Wt:** 195 **Born:** 3/22/1986 **Age:** 30

Year	Team	Lg	G	AB	H	2B	3B	HR	(Hm	Rd)	TB	R	RBI	RC	TBB	IBB	SO	HBP	SH	SF	SB	CS	GDP	Avg	OBP	Slg	OPS
2008	Col	NL	13	26	4	0	0	0	(0	0)	4	3	0	0	0	0	5	1	0	0	0	1	0	.154	.185	.154	.339
2009	Col	NL	135	433	115	29	10	4	(2	2)	176	73	34	68	67	1	116	1	14	3	27	10	4	.266	.363	.406	.770
2010	Col	NL	132	439	114	20	14	6	(5	1)	180	73	36	68	57	0	104	2	7	0	13	8	5	.260	.347	.410	.757
2011	Col	NL	125	481	128	35	15	5	(3	2)	208	84	45	79	68	3	130	6	7	1	12	9	6	.266	.363	.432	.796
2012	Col	NL	143	454	136	18	11	13	(10	3)	215	72	53	81	68	1	128	0	6	2	12	5	5	.300	.389	.474	.863
2013	Col	NL	119	415	109	18	3	12	(7	5)	169	71	42	62	65	1	105	6	4	2	19	9	5	.263	.369	.407	.776
2014	Hou	AL	116	434	120	21	4	8	(5	3)	173	61	35	65	66	2	108	3	1	1	11	4	6	.276	.375	.399	.774
2015	ChC	NL	156	596	149	29	8	17	(11	6)	245	102	46	77	84	1	154	5	2	3	20	7	5	.250	.346	.411	.757
Postseason			4	14	3	0	0	0	(0	0)	3	1	2	1	1	0	3	0	1	2	0	0	1	.214	.235	.214	.450
8 ML YEARS			939	3278	875	170	65	65	(43	22)	1370	539	291	500	475	9	850	24	41	12	114	53	36	.267	.363	.418	.781

Jeff Francis

Pitches: L Bats: L Pos: RP-14   Ht: 6'5" Wt: 220 Born: 1/8/1981 Age: 35

			HOW MUCH HE PITCHED						WHAT HE GAVE UP											THE RESULTS							
Year	Team	Lg	G	GS	CG	GF	IP	BFP	H	R	ER	HR	SH	SF	HB	TBB	IBB	SO	WP	Bk	W	L	Pct	Sh	Sv-Op	Hld	ERC	ERA
2015	Buffalo*	AAA	19	14	0	1	92.0	373	84	28	24	3	0	0	3	13	0	79	2	0	6	3	.667	0	0- -	-	2.33	2.35
2004	Col	NL	7	7	0	0	36.2	164	42	22	21	8	2	1	1	13	1	32	2	0	3	2	.600	0	0-0	0	5.62	5.15
2005	Col	NL	33	33	0	0	183.2	828	228	119	116	26	6	10	8	70	5	128	2	0	14	12	.538	0	0-0	0	5.94	5.68
2006	Col	NL	32	32	1	0	199.0	843	187	101	92	18	7	7	13	69	15	117	0	0	13	11	.542	1	0-0	0	3.63	4.16
2007	Col	NL	34	34	1	0	215.1	922	234	103	101	25	7	4	7	63	7	165	1	1	17	9	.654	1	0-0	0	4.37	4.22
2008	Col	NL	24	24	0	0	143.2	636	164	84	80	21	6	4	3	49	4	94	0	0	4	10	.286	0	0-0	0	5.00	5.01
2010	Col	NL	20	19	0	0	104.1	441	119	61	58	11	6	4	2	23	3	67	1	0	4	6	.400	0	0-0	0	4.29	5.00
2011	KC	AL	31	31	1	0	183.0	803	224	102	98	19	7	8	5	39	5	91	5	1	6	16	.273	0	0-0	0	4.67	4.82
2012	Col	NL	24	24	0	0	113.0	502	145	71	70	15	10	3	8	22	5	76	2	0	6	7	.462	0	0-0	0	5.34	5.58
2013	Col	NL	23	12	0	4	70.1	324	89	54	49	12	4	4	1	24	2	63	5	0	3	5	.375	0	0-0	0	5.82	6.27
2014	3 Tms		12	1	0	9	20.0	82	18	13	13	3	1	1	1	3	1	15	1	0	1	2	.333	0	1-1	0	2.96	5.85
2015	Tor	AL	14	0	0	5	22.0	100	27	16	15	3	0	0	1	9	0	21	2	0	1	2	.333	0	0-0	0	5.96	6.14
14	Cin	NL	1	1	0	0	5.0	20	5	3	3	1	0	0	0	0	0	4	0	0	0	1	.000	0	0-0	0	3.05	5.40
14	Oak	AL	9	0	0	7	13.1	55	11	9	9	1	1	1	1	3	1	10	1	0	0	1	.000	0	1-1	0	2.46	6.08
14	NYY	AL	2	0	0	2	1.2	7	2	1	1	1	0	0	0	0	0	1	0	0	1	0	1.000	0	0-0	0	6.66	5.40
	Postseason		3	3	0	0	16.2	75	21	9	9	3	0	0	2	6	2	15	0	0	2	1	.667	0	0-0	0	6.57	4.86
	11 ML YEARS		254	217	3	18	1291.0	5645	1477	746	713	161	56	46	50	384	48	869	21	2	72	82	.468	2	1-1	0	4.77	4.97

Maikel Franco

Bats: R Throws: R Pos: 3B-75;1B-2;PH-2   MY-kell   Ht: 6'1" Wt: 215 Born: 8/26/1992 Age: 23

							BATTING												RUNNING			AVERAGES			
Year	Team	Lg	G	AB	H	2B	3B	HR	(Hm | Rd)	TB	R	RBI	RC	TBB	IBB	SO	HBP	SH	SF	SB	CS	GDP	Avg	OBP	Slg	OPS
2011	2 Tms	Low	71	267	66	19	1	3	(- | -)	96	25	44	32	26	2	45	2	0	1	0	0	9	.247	.318	.360	.677
2012	Lakwd	A	132	503	141	32	3	14	(- | -)	221	70	84	77	38	0	80	7	0	6	3	1	24	.280	.336	.439	.775
2013	Clrwtr	A+	65	264	79	23	1	16	(- | -)	152	42	52	52	20	1	39	2	0	3	0	0	14	.299	.349	.576	.925
2013	Rdng	AA	69	277	94	13	2	15	(- | -)	156	47	51	54	10	1	31	2	0	3	1	2	5	.339	.363	.563	.926
2014	LV	AAA	133	521	134	33	4	16	(- | -)	223	64	78	68	30	0	81	2	0	3	3	1	16	.257	.299	.428	.727
2015	LV	AAA	33	141	50	12	1	4	(- | -)	76	15	24	28	8	1	25	0	0	2	2	0	3	.355	.384	.539	.923
2014	Phi	NL	16	56	10	2	0	0	(0 | 0)	12	5	5	1	1	0	13	0	0	1	0	0	1	.179	.190	.214	.404
2015	Phi	NL	80	304	85	22	1	14	(7 | 7)	151	45	50	48	26	2	52	4	0	1	1	0	8	.280	.343	.497	.840
	2 ML YEARS		96	360	95	24	1	14	(7 | 7)	163	50	55	49	27	2	65	4	0	2	1	0	9	.264	.321	.453	.773

Jeff Francoeur

Bats: R Throws: R Pos: RF-85;PH-31;LF-20;DH-2   frann-COOR   Ht: 6'4" Wt: 220 Born: 1/8/1984 Age: 32

							BATTING												RUNNING			AVERAGES			
Year	Team	Lg	G	AB	H	2B	3B	HR	(Hm | Rd)	TB	R	RBI	RC	TBB	IBB	SO	HBP	SH	SF	SB	CS	GDP	Avg	OBP	Slg	OPS
2005	Atl	NL	70	257	77	20	1	14	(11 | 3)	141	41	45	50	11	3	58	4	0	2	3	2	4	.300	.336	.549	.884
2006	Atl	NL	162	651	169	24	6	29	(19 | 10)	292	83	103	91	23	6	132	9	0	3	1	6	15	.260	.293	.449	.742
2007	Atl	NL	162	642	188	40	0	19	(7 | 12)	285	84	105	97	42	5	129	5	0	7	5	2	14	.293	.338	.444	.782
2008	Atl	NL	155	599	143	33	3	11	(5 | 6)	215	70	71	49	39	5	111	10	0	4	0	1	18	.239	.294	.359	.653
2009	2 Tms	NL	157	593	166	32	4	15	(7 | 8)	251	72	76	59	23	5	92	6	1	9	6	4	13	.280	.309	.423	.732
2010	2 Tms		139	454	113	18	2	13	(5 | 8)	174	52	65	46	30	8	81	8	0	11	8	3	9	.249	.300	.383	.683
2011	KC	AL	153	601	171	47	4	20	(10 | 10)	286	77	87	83	37	3	123	8	0	10	22	10	17	.285	.329	.476	.805
2012	KC	AL	148	561	132	26	3	16	(7 | 9)	212	58	49	50	34	9	119	7	0	1	4	7	14	.235	.287	.378	.665
2013	2 Tms		81	245	50	10	2	3	(1 | 2)	73	20	17	11	9	2	61	2	0	0	3	0	7	.204	.238	.298	.536
2014	SD	NL	10	24	2	0	0	0	(0 | 0)	2	2	1	0	3	0	7	0	0	0	0	0	0	.083	.179	.083	.262
2015	Phi	NL	119	326	84	16	1	13	(9 | 4)	141	34	45	34	13	0	77	1	0	3	0	2	10	.258	.286	.433	.718
09	Atl	NL	82	304	76	12	2	5	(3 | 2)	107	32	35	25	12	2	46	3	1	4	5	1	10	.250	.282	.352	.634
09	NYM	NL	75	289	90	20	2	10	(4 | 6)	144	40	41	34	11	3	46	3	0	5	1	3	3	.311	.338	.498	.836
10	NYM	NL	124	401	95	16	2	11	(5 | 6)	148	43	54	39	29	8	76	7	0	10	8	2	7	.237	.293	.369	.662
10	Tex	AL	15	53	18	2	0	2	(0 | 2)	26	9	11	7	1	0	5	1	0	1	0	1	2	.340	.357	.491	.848
13	KC	AL	59	183	38	8	2	3	(1 | 2)	59	19	13	10	8	2	49	2	0	0	2	0	5	.208	.249	.322	.571
13	SF	NL	22	62	12	2	0	0	(0 | 0)	14	1	4	1	1	0	12	0	0	0	1	0	2	.194	.206	.226	.432
	Postseason		13	41	7	2	1	0	(0 | 0)	11	3	2	3	3	1	7	1	1	0	0	0	2	.171	.244	.268	.513
	11 ML YEARS		1356	4953	1295	266	26	153	(81 | 72)	2072	593	664	570	264	46	990	60	1	51	52	37	121	.261	.304	.418	.722

Kevin Frandsen

Bats: R Throws: R Pos: 1B-4;PH-3   FRAND-zen   Ht: 6'0" Wt: 190 Born: 5/24/1982 Age: 34

							BATTING												RUNNING			AVERAGES			
Year	Team	Lg	G	AB	H	2B	3B	HR	(Hm | Rd)	TB	R	RBI	RC	TBB	IBB	SO	HBP	SH	SF	SB	CS	GDP	Avg	OBP	Slg	OPS
2015	Reno*	AAA	26	81	25	2	0	0	(- | -)	27	8	7	9	6	0	8	0	1	1	0	1	1	.309	.352	.333	.686
2015	Scrmto*	AAA	86	323	88	15	1	4	(- | -)	117	38	41	42	18	1	19	13	3	2	5	2	13	.272	.334	.362	.696
2006	SF	NL	41	93	20	4	0	2	(0 | 2)	30	12	7	7	3	0	14	6	0	0	1	0	3	.215	.284	.323	.607
2007	SF	NL	109	264	71	12	1	5	(1 | 4)	100	26	31	29	21	3	24	5	3	3	4	3	17	.269	.331	.379	.710
2008	SF	NL	1	1	0	0	0	0	(0 | 0)	0	0	0	0	0	0	0	0	0	0	0	0	0	.000	.000	.000	.000
2009	SF	NL	23	50	7	2	0	0	(0 | 0)	9	3	1	0	3	0	4	1	0	0	0	0	2	.140	.204	.180	.384
2010	LAA	AL	54	160	40	11	0	0	(0 | 0)	51	24	14	16	9	0	10	1	3	0	2	0	5	.250	.294	.319	.613
2012	Phi	NL	55	195	66	10	3	2	(1 | 1)	88	24	14	30	9	2	18	5	1	0	1	0	4	.338	.383	.451	.834
2013	Phi	NL	119	252	59	10	1	5	(2 | 3)	86	27	26	21	12	0	29	11	1	2	1	0	10	.234	.296	.341	.637
2014	Was	NL	105	220	57	8	0	1	(0 | 1)	68	17	17	21	6	0	26	7	2	1	0	0	7	.259	.299	.309	.608
2015	SF	NL	7	11	2	0	0	0	(0 | 0)	2	1	0	0	1	0	3	0	1	0	0	0	2	.182	.250	.182	.432
	Postseason		1	1	0	0	0	0	(0 | 0)	0	0	0	0	0	0	0	0	0	0	0	0	0	.000	.000	.000	.000
	9 ML YEARS		514	1246	322	57	5	15	(4 | 11)	434	134	110	124	64	5	128	36	11	6	7	5	50	.258	.312	.348	.660

Nick Franklin

Bats: B Throws: R Pos: 2B-17;SS-11;1B-10;PH-8;PR-5;DH-3   Ht: 6'1" Wt: 195 Born: 3/2/1991 Age: 25

Year	Team	Lg	G	AB	H	2B	3B	HR	(Hm	Rd)	TB	R	RBI	RC	TBB	IBB	SO	HBP	SH	SF	SB	CS	GDP	Avg	OBP	Slg	OPS
2015	Drham*	AAA	57	192	51	10	1	11	(-	-)	96	26	30	34	27	0	48	0	0	2	4	3	2	.266	.353	.500	.853
2013	Sea	AL	102	369	83	20	1	12	(4	8)	141	38	45	48	42	1	113	0	0	1	6	1	2	.225	.303	.382	.686
2014	2 Tms	AL	28	81	13	2	1	1	(1	0)	20	7	6	6	6	0	32	1	0	2	2	0	2	.160	.222	.247	.469
2015	TB	AL	44	101	16	4	1	3	(2	1)	31	11	7	4	7	0	37	0	1	0	1	0	2	.158	.213	.307	.520
14	Sea	AL	17	47	6	0	1	0	(0	0)	8	3	2	1	3	0	21	1	0	1	1	0	0	.128	.192	.170	.363
14	TB	AL	11	34	7	2	0	1	(1	0)	12	4	4	5	3	0	11	0	0	1	1	0	2	.206	.263	.353	.616
3 ML YEARS			174	551	112	26	3	16	(7	9)	192	56	58	58	55	1	182	1	1	3	9	1	6	.203	.275	.348	.624

Jason Frasor

Pitches: R Bats: R Pos: RP-32   FRAY-zer   Ht: 5'9" Wt: 180 Born: 8/1/1977 Age: 38

Year	Team	Lg	G	GS	CG	GF	IP	BFP	H	R	ER	HR	SH	SF	HB	TBB	IBB	SO	WP	Bk	W	L	Pct	Sh	Sv-Op	Hld	ERC	ERA
2004	Tor	AL	63	0	0	37	68.1	299	64	31	31	4	3	3	2	36	3	54	4	2	4	6	.400	0	17-19	8	3.97	4.08
2005	Tor	AL	67	0	0	12	74.2	305	67	31	27	8	2	1	3	28	2	62	1	0	3	5	.375	0	1-3	15	3.72	3.25
2006	Tor	AL	51	0	0	12	50.0	215	47	24	24	8	0	3	2	17	1	51	3	0	3	2	.600	0	0-1	12	3.98	4.32
2007	Tor	AL	51	0	0	18	57.0	242	47	29	29	3	1	2	2	23	1	59	2	1	1	5	.167	0	3-6	4	2.88	4.58
2008	Tor	AL	49	0	0	21	47.1	208	36	23	22	4	0	2	1	32	4	42	6	0	1	2	.333	0	0-1	4	3.62	4.18
2009	Tor	AL	61	0	0	36	57.2	227	43	17	16	4	1	2	2	16	3	56	2	0	7	3	.700	0	11-14	4	2.22	2.50
2010	Tor	AL	69	0	0	18	63.2	279	61	30	26	4	1	0	4	27	6	65	5	0	3	4	.429	0	4-8	14	3.72	3.68
2011	2 Tms	AL	64	0	0	10	60.0	261	58	25	24	7	2	4	3	26	3	57	3	0	3	3	.500	0	0-2	14	4.26	3.60
2012	Tor	AL	50	0	0	9	43.2	191	42	20	20	6	1	2	2	22	1	53	5	1	1	1	.500	0	0-3	12	4.74	4.12
2013	Tex	AL	61	0	0	11	49.0	200	36	15	14	4	1	2	0	20	3	48	2	0	4	3	.571	0	0-1	10	2.50	2.57
2014	Tex	AL	61	0	0	11	47.1	196	40	17	14	3	0	5	2	18	2	46	3	0	4	1	.800	0	0-2	10	3.05	2.64
2015	2 Tms		32	0	0	10	28.0	124	27	5	4	1	1	1	0	18	3	22	2	0	1	0	1.000	0	0-1	4	4.22	1.29
11	Tor	AL	44	0	0	6	42.1	178	38	15	14	4	2	3	2	15	1	37	2	0	2	1	.667	0	0-2	10	3.46	2.98
11	CWS	AL	20	0	0	4	17.2	83	20	10	10	3	0	1	1	11	2	20	1	0	1	2	.333	0	0-0	4	6.37	5.09
14	Tex	AL	38	0	0	6	29.2	129	27	14	11	2	0	3	1	14	1	30	2	0	1	1	.500	0	0-2	10	3.68	3.34
14	KC	AL	23	0	0	5	17.2	67	13	3	3	1	0	2	1	4	1	16	1	0	3	0	1.000	0	0-0	0	2.07	1.53
15	KC	AL	26	0	0	10	23.1	104	24	5	4	1	1	1	0	15	2	18	2	0	1	0	1.000	0	0-1	2	4.72	1.54
15	Atl	NL	6	0	0	0	4.2	20	3	0	0	0	0	0	0	3	1	4	0	0	0	0	-	0	0-0	2	2.03	0.00
Postseason			7	0	0	2	5.1	23	5	1	1	0	0	0	0	2	0	3	1	0	2	0	1.000	0	0-0	0	2.88	1.69
12 ML YEARS			679	0	0	205	646.2	2747	568	267	251	56	13	27	23	283	32	615	38	4	35	35	.500	0	36-61	111	3.53	3.49

Todd Frazier

Bats: R Throws: R Pos: 3B-155;PH-2   Ht: 6'3" Wt: 220 Born: 2/12/1986 Age: 30

Year	Team	Lg	G	AB	H	2B	3B	HR	(Hm	Rd)	TB	R	RBI	RC	TBB	IBB	SO	HBP	SH	SF	SB	CS	GDP	Avg	OBP	Slg	OPS
2011	Cin	NL	41	112	26	5	0	6	(2	4)	49	17	15	13	7	0	27	2	0	0	1	0	2	.232	.289	.438	.727
2012	Cin	NL	128	422	115	26	6	19	(10	9)	210	55	67	59	36	1	103	3	0	4	3	2	9	.273	.331	.498	.829
2013	Cin	NL	150	531	124	29	3	19	(12	7)	216	63	73	67	50	1	125	14	2	3	6	5	14	.234	.314	.407	.721
2014	Cin	NL	157	597	163	22	1	29	(20	9)	274	88	80	84	52	2	139	7	0	4	20	8	9	.273	.336	.459	.795
2015	Cin	NL	157	619	158	43	1	35	(19	16)	308	82	89	73	44	3	137	7	1	7	13	8	19	.255	.309	.498	.806
Postseason			5	10	2	1	0	0	(0	0)	3	0	1	0	1	0	3	0	0	0	0	0	0	.200	.273	.300	.573
5 ML YEARS			633	2281	586	125	11	108	(63	45)	1057	305	324	296	189	7	531	33	3	18	43	23	53	.257	.321	.463	.784

Freddie Freeman

Bats: L Throws: R Pos: 1B-117;PH-3;DH-1   Ht: 6'5" Wt: 225 Born: 9/12/1989 Age: 26

Year	Team	Lg	G	AB	H	2B	3B	HR	(Hm	Rd)	TB	R	RBI	RC	TBB	IBB	SO	HBP	SH	SF	SB	CS	GDP	Avg	OBP	Slg	OPS
2010	Atl	NL	20	24	4	1	0	1	(0	1)	8	3	1	0	0	0	8	0	0	0	0	0	1	.167	.167	.333	.500
2011	Atl	NL	157	571	161	32	0	21	(9	12)	256	67	76	79	53	3	142	6	0	5	4	4	15	.282	.346	.448	.795
2012	Atl	NL	147	540	140	33	2	23	(12	11)	246	91	94	82	64	4	129	7	0	9	2	0	10	.259	.340	.456	.796
2013	Atl	NL	147	551	176	27	2	23	(16	7)	276	89	109	124	66	10	121	7	0	5	1	0	11	.319	.396	.501	.897
2014	Atl	NL	162	607	175	43	4	18	(7	11)	280	93	78	101	90	4	145	8	0	3	3	4	18	.288	.386	.461	.847
2015	Atl	NL	118	416	115	27	0	18	(5	13)	196	62	66	77	56	4	98	7	0	2	3	1	6	.276	.370	.471	.841
Postseason			5	20	8	2	0	0	(0	0)	10	4	0	2	2	0	5	0	0	0	0	0	0	.400	.455	.500	.955
6 ML YEARS			751	2709	771	163	8	104	(49	55)	1262	405	424	463	329	25	643	35	0	24	13	9	61	.285	.366	.466	.832

Sam Freeman

Pitches: L Bats: R Pos: RP-54   Ht: 5'11" Wt: 165 Born: 6/24/1987 Age: 29

Year	Team	Lg	G	GS	CG	GF	IP	BFP	H	R	ER	HR	SH	SF	HB	TBB	IBB	SO	WP	Bk	W	L	Pct	Sh	Sv-Op	Hld	ERC	ERA
2015	RdRck*	AAA	8	0	0	2	8.0	33	5	1	1	0	0	0	0	6	0	8	0	0	0	0	-	0	0- -	-	2.79	1.13
2012	StL	NL	24	0	0	7	20.0	86	17	13	12	2	1	0	1	10	0	18	0	0	0	2	.000	0	0-0	2	3.84	5.40
2013	StL	NL	13	0	0	2	12.1	50	8	3	3	0	0	0	0	5	0	8	2	0	1	0	1.000	0	0-0	1	1.67	2.19
2014	StL	NL	44	0	0	9	38.0	169	34	13	11	2	1	1	4	19	0	35	3	0	2	0	1.000	0	0-0	11	3.89	2.61
2015	Tex	AL	54	0	0	10	38.1	171	31	13	13	4	0	1	3	25	0	40	0	0	0	0	-	0	0-0	12	4.31	3.05
Postseason			1	0	0	0	0.0	2	0	0	0	0	0	0	0	2	0	0	0	0	0	0	-	0	0-0	0	-	-
4 ML YEARS			135	0	0	28	108.2	476	90	42	39	8	3	2	8	59	0	101	5	0	3	2	.600	0	0-0	26	3.74	3.23

David Freese

Bats: R **Throws:** R **Pos:** 3B-113;DH-6;PH-2 — FREEZE — **Ht:** 6'2" **Wt:** 225 **Born:** 4/28/1983 **Age:** 33

Year	Team	Lg	G	AB	H	2B	3B	HR	(Hm	Rd)	TB	R	RBI	RC	TBB	IBB	SO	HBP	SH	SF	SB	CS	GDP	Avg	OBP	Slg	OPS
2009	StL	NL	17	31	10	2	0	1	(0	1)	15	3	7	4	2	0	7	0	0	1	0	0	1	.323	.353	.484	.837
2010	StL	NL	70	240	71	12	1	4	(3	1)	97	28	36	36	21	0	59	4	4	1	1	1	7	.296	.361	.404	.765
2011	StL	NL	97	333	99	16	1	10	(6	4)	147	41	55	50	24	0	75	4	0	2	1	0	18	.297	.350	.441	.791
2012	StL	NL	144	501	147	25	1	20	(8	12)	234	70	79	79	57	2	122	7	0	2	3	3	19	.293	.372	.467	.839
2013	StL	NL	138	462	121	26	1	9	(4	5)	176	53	60	48	47	1	106	9	0	3	1	2	26	.262	.340	.381	.721
2014	LAA	AL	134	462	120	25	1	10	(6	4)	177	53	55	55	38	0	124	6	0	5	1	3	10	.260	.321	.383	.704
2015	LAA	AL	121	424	109	27	0	14	(9	5)	178	53	56	60	31	0	107	12	0	3	1	1	12	.257	.323	.420	.743
	Postseason		51	174	49	15	1	8	(4	4)	90	21	30	31	19	2	47	2	0	1	0	1	8	.282	.357	.517	.874
	7 ML YEARS		721	2453	677	133	5	68	(36	32)	1024	301	348	332	220	3	600	42	4	17	8	10	93	.276	.344	.417	.761

Carlos Frias

Pitches: R **Bats:** R **Pos:** SP-13; RP-4 — FREE-us — **Ht:** 6'4" **Wt:** 195 **Born:** 11/13/1989 **Age:** 26

Year	Team	Lg	G	GS	CG	GF	IP	BFP	H	R	ER	HR	SH	SF	HB	TBB	IBB	SO	WP	Bk	W	L	Pct	Sh	Sv-Op	Hld	ERC	ERA
2011	Rcuca	A+	12	0	0	6	16.0	76	17	13	11	3	1	2	0	17	0	11	4	0	1	1	.500	0	0--	-	8.46	6.19
2012	2 Tms	Low	18	16	0	1	83.2	372	92	57	44	5	4	3	4	29	0	72	13	0	7	5	.583	0	0--	-	4.26	4.73
2013	2 Tms	Low	20	20	0	0	114.1	486	118	48	41	7	0	5	5	34	0	97	8	2	7	6	.538	0	0--	-	3.78	3.23
2013	Chatt	AA	8	2	0	4	16.0	68	15	7	7	2	0	0	2	7	1	8	0	0	1	1	.500	0	0--	-	4.63	3.94
2014	Chatt	AA	5	5	0	0	32.0	136	34	16	12	2	1	0	2	9	0	14	1	0	2	1	.667	0	0--	-	4.00	3.38
2014	Albq	AAA	16	15	2	0	91.2	399	114	57	51	4	3	2	2	21	0	65	7	3	8	4	.667	0	0--	-	4.50	5.01
2015	OkCity	AAA	8	3	0	1	21.1	90	24	9	7	2	0	0	0	5	0	19	3	0	2	0	1.000	0	0--	-	4.13	2.95
2014	LAD	NL	15	2	0	7	32.1	137	33	22	22	4	0	0	0	7	1	29	2	0	1	1	.500	0	0-0	1	3.50	6.12
2015	LAD	NL	17	13	0	1	77.2	333	88	38	35	7	4	4	3	26	1	43	3	0	5	5	.500	0	0-0	0	4.78	4.06
	2 ML YEARS		32	15	0	8	110.0	470	121	60	57	11	4	4	3	33	2	72	5	0	6	6	.500	0	0-0	1	4.39	4.66

Christian Friedrich

Pitches: L **Bats:** R **Pos:** RP-68 — FREE-drick — **Ht:** 6'4" **Wt:** 215 **Born:** 7/8/1987 **Age:** 28

Year	Team	Lg	G	GS	CG	GF	IP	BFP	H	R	ER	HR	SH	SF	HB	TBB	IBB	SO	WP	Bk	W	L	Pct	Sh	Sv-Op	Hld	ERC	ERA
2012	Col	NL	16	16	0	0	84.2	377	102	61	58	14	6	2	2	30	0	74	8	0	5	8	.385	0	0-0	0	5.71	6.17
2014	Col	NL	16	3	0	3	24.1	110	25	21	16	3	1	2	2	10	1	27	5	0	0	4	.000	0	0-0	3	4.59	5.92
2015	Col	NL	68	0	0	13	58.1	270	75	37	34	5	4	6	1	25	2	45	3	0	0	4	.000	0	0-0	9	5.76	5.25
	3 ML YEARS		100	19	0	16	167.1	757	202	119	108	22	11	10	5	65	3	146	16	0	5	16	.238	0	0-0	12	5.56	5.81

Ernesto Frieri

Pitches: R **Bats:** R **Pos:** RP-22 — free-AIR-ee — **Ht:** 6'2" **Wt:** 205 **Born:** 7/19/1985 **Age:** 30

Year	Team	Lg	G	GS	CG	GF	IP	BFP	H	R	ER	HR	SH	SF	HB	TBB	IBB	SO	WP	Bk	W	L	Pct	Sh	Sv-Op	Hld	ERC	ERA
2015	Drham*	AAA	8	0	0	3	7.1	38	6	6	3	1	0	1	0	10	0	5	1	0	0	1	.000	0	1--	-	7.06	3.68
2015	Rays*	R	6	5	0	1	7.2	31	3	3	1	0	0	0	1	3	0	5	1	0	0	1	.000	0	0--	-	1.11	1.17
2009	SD	NL	2	0	0	2	2.0	7	0	0	0	0	0	0	0	1	0	2	0	0	0	0	-	0	0-0	0	0.27	0.00
2010	SD	NL	33	0	0	12	31.2	128	18	7	6	2	0	0	0	17	3	41	2	0	1	1	.500	0	0-0	7	1.99	1.71
2011	SD	NL	59	0	0	20	63.0	276	51	21	19	3	1	1	9	34	5	76	1	1	1	2	.333	0	0-0	4	3.60	2.71
2012	2 Tms		67	0	0	51	66.0	269	35	20	17	9	1	1	7	30	0	98	1	0	5	2	.714	0	23-26	7	2.43	2.32
2013	LAA	AL	67	0	0	51	68.2	292	55	29	29	11	2	2	3	30	1	98	1	0	2	4	.333	0	37-41	2	3.64	3.80
2014	2 Tms		48	0	0	30	41.2	184	47	34	34	11	0	0	2	14	2	48	0	0	1	4	.200	0	11-14	3	5.89	7.34
2015	TB	AL	22	0	0	6	23.1	100	20	12	12	6	0	2	1	11	0	19	1	0	0	1	.000	0	2-3	0	4.84	4.63
12	SD	NL	11	0	0	5	11.2	50	9	5	3	2	0	0	2	4	0	18	0	0	1	0	1.000	0	0-0	1	3.67	2.31
12	LAA	AL	56	0	0	46	54.1	219	26	15	14	7	1	1	5	26	0	80	1	0	4	2	.667	0	23-26	6	2.18	2.32
14	LAA	AL	34	0	0	22	31.0	133	33	22	22	8	0	0	1	9	1	38	0	0	0	3	.000	0	11-14	3	5.21	6.39
14	Pit	NL	14	0	0	8	10.2	51	14	12	12	3	0	0	1	5	1	10	0	0	1	1	.500	0	0-0	0	7.97	10.13
	7 ML YEARS		298	0	0	172	296.1	1256	226	123	117	42	4	6	22	137	11	382	6	1	11	13	.458	0	73-84	23	3.52	3.55

Eric Fryer

Bats: R **Throws:** R **Pos:** C-15;PH-1 — **Ht:** 6'2" **Wt:** 215 **Born:** 8/26/1985 **Age:** 30

Year	Team	Lg	G	AB	H	2B	3B	HR	(Hm	Rd)	TB	R	RBI	RC	TBB	IBB	SO	HBP	SH	SF	SB	CS	GDP	Avg	OBP	Slg	OPS
2015	Roch*	AAA	67	222	65	7	1	2	(-	-)	80	28	19	31	25	0	47	1	0	0	1	2	3	.293	.367	.360	.727
2011	Pit	NL	10	26	7	0	0	0	(0	0)	7	5	0	2	3	1	7	0	0	0	1	1	0	.269	.345	.269	.614
2012	Pit	NL	6	4	1	0	0	0	(0	0)	1	0	0	1	1	0	1	0	0	0	0	0	0	.250	.400	.250	.650
2013	Min	AL	6	13	5	1	0	1	(1	0)	9	2	4	5	3	0	3	0	0	0	0	0	1	.385	.500	.692	1.192
2014	Min	AL	28	75	16	4	0	1	(0	1)	23	11	5	6	5	0	15	1	0	0	1	0	0	.213	.272	.307	.578
2015	Min	AL	15	22	5	2	0	0	(0	0)	7	2	2	3	5	1	11	0	0	0	0	0	0	.227	.370	.318	.689
	5 ML YEARS		65	140	34	7	0	2	(1	1)	47	20	11	17	17	1	37	1	0	0	2	1	1	.243	.329	.336	.665

Kyuji Fujikawa

Pitches: R Bats: L Pos: RP-2   CUE-jee foo-jee-KOW-uh   Ht: 6'0" Wt: 190 Born: 7/21/1980 Age: 35

		HOW MUCH HE PITCHED						WHAT HE GAVE UP												THE RESULTS						
Year	Team	Lg	G	GS	CG	GF	IP	BFP	H	R	ER	HR	SH	SF	HB	TBB	IBB	SO	WP	Bk	W	L	Pct	Sh	Sv-Op	Hld	ERC	ERA
2015	RdRck*	AAA	10	0	0	0	9.1	41	6	4	4	1	1	0	0	9	0	8	1	0	0	0	-	0	0- -	-	4.44	3.86
2013	ChC	NL	12	0	0	5	12.0	50	11	7	7	1	0	0	2	2	0	14	2	0	1	1	.500	0	2-3	1	3.26	5.25
2014	ChC	NL	15	0	0	6	13.0	64	18	8	7	2	0	1	2	6	2	17	2	0	0	0	-	0	0-0	0	7.41	4.85
2015	Tex	AL	2	0	0	0	1.2	8	2	3	3	1	0	0	1	0	0	1	0	0	0	0	-	0	0-0	0	10.04	16.20
	3 ML YEARS		29	0	0	11	26.2	122	31	18	17	4	0	1	5	8	2	32	4	0	1	1	.500	0	2-3	1	5.59	5.74

Sam Fuld

Bats: L Throws: L Pos: LF-57;CF-43;RF-16;PH-13;PR-12;DH-3   Ht: 5'10" Wt: 175 Born: 11/20/1981 Age: 34

							BATTING												RUNNING			AVERAGES			
Year	Team	Lg	G	AB	H	2B	3B	HR	(Hm | Rd)	TB	R	RBI	RC	TBB	IBB	SO	HBP	SH	SF	SB	CS	GDP	Avg	OBP	Slg	OPS
2007	ChC	NL	14	6	0	0	0	0	(0 | 0)	0	3	0	0	3	0	3	0	0	0	0	0	0	.000	.333	.000	.333
2009	ChC	NL	65	97	29	6	1	1	(1 | 0)	40	17	2	15	17	1	10	1	0	0	2	1	1	.299	.409	.412	.821
2010	ChC	NL	19	28	4	1	0	0	(0 | 0)	5	3	3	1	3	0	5	0	0	0	0	0	2	.143	.226	.179	.404
2011	TB	AL	105	308	74	18	5	3	(2 | 1)	111	41	27	37	32	0	49	1	4	1	20	8	3	.240	.313	.360	.673
2012	TB	AL	44	98	25	3	2	0	(0 | 0)	32	14	5	13	8	0	14	1	0	0	7	2	0	.255	.318	.327	.644
2013	TB	AL	119	176	35	0	3	2	(2 | 0)	47	25	17	14	17	0	28	1	4	2	8	2	6	.199	.270	.267	.537
2014	2 Tms	AL	113	351	84	16	4	4	(0 | 4)	120	40	36	47	43	2	63	0	6	2	21	4	2	.239	.321	.342	.663
2015	Oak	AL	120	290	57	16	3	2	(1 | 1)	85	34	22	22	30	1	55	2	2	1	9	3	6	.197	.276	.293	.569
	14 Oak	AL	60	187	39	6	4	3	(0 | 3)	62	25	19	22	17	1	34	0	3	0	9	1	2	.209	.275	.332	.606
	14 Min	AL	53	164	45	10	0	1	(0 | 1)	58	15	17	25	26	1	29	0	3	2	12	3	0	.274	.370	.354	.723
	Postseason		6	9	2	0	0	0	(0 | 0)	2	2	0	1	1	0	3	0	0	0	0	0	0	.222	.300	.222	.522
	8 ML YEARS		599	1354	308	60	18	12	(6 | 6)	440	177	112	149	153	4	227	6	16	6	67	20	20	.227	.307	.325	.632

Charlie Furbush

Pitches: L Bats: L Pos: RP-33   FUR-bush   Ht: 6'5" Wt: 215 Born: 4/11/1986 Age: 30

				HOW MUCH HE PITCHED						WHAT HE GAVE UP												THE RESULTS					
Year	Team	Lg	G	GS	CG	GF	IP	BFP	H	R	ER	HR	SH	SF	HB	TBB	IBB	SO	WP	Bk	W	L	Pct	Sh	Sv-Op	Hld	ERC	ERA
2011	2 Tms	AL	28	12	0	1	85.1	372	97	59	52	16	2	4	6	30	2	67	2	1	4	10	.286	0	0-0	1	5.72	5.48
2012	Sea	AL	48	0	0	8	46.1	182	28	15	14	3	2	1	2	16	4	53	5	0	5	2	.714	0	0-0	6	1.72	2.72
2013	Sea	AL	71	0	0	5	65.0	280	48	33	27	5	2	5	3	29	2	80	3	0	2	6	.250	0	0-6	20	2.71	3.74
2014	Sea	AL	67	0	0	13	42.1	177	40	17	17	4	2	1	3	9	0	51	2	0	1	5	.167	0	1-1	20	3.26	3.61
2015	Sea	AL	33	0	0	4	21.2	82	9	6	5	2	1	0	2	5	2	17	5	0	1	1	.500	0	0-0	13	1.08	2.08
	11 Det	AL	17	2	0	1	32.1	139	36	18	13	5	2	1	3	14	1	26	0	1	1	3	.250	0	0-0	1	5.96	3.62
	11 Sea	AL	11	10	0	0	53.0	233	61	41	39	11	0	3	3	16	1	41	2	0	3	7	.300	0	0-0	0	5.57	6.62
	5 ML YEARS		247	12	0	31	260.2	1093	222	130	115	30	9	11	16	89	10	268	17	1	13	24	.351	0	1-7	60	3.31	3.97

Rocky Gale

Bats: R Throws: R Pos: C-6;PH-5   Ht: 6'1" Wt: 175 Born: 2/22/1988 Age: 28

							BATTING												RUNNING			AVERAGES			
Year	Team	Lg	G	AB	H	2B	3B	HR	(Hm | Rd)	TB	R	RBI	RC	TBB	IBB	SO	HBP	SH	SF	SB	CS	GDP	Avg	OBP	Slg	OPS
2011	2 Tms	Low	53	161	34	4	0	1	(- | -)	41	16	23	10	13	0	35	3	4	4	0	2	3	.211	.276	.255	.531
2012	Lk Els	A+	14	50	9	1	0	1	(- | -)	13	3	6	2	1	0	8	0	1	0	1	0	3	.180	.196	.260	.456
2012	Tucsn	AAA	41	123	21	6	0	0	(- | -)	27	12	11	4	6	0	22	0	2	0	0	0	6	.171	.209	.220	.429
2013	SnAnt	AA	62	207	51	5	0	1	(- | -)	59	15	22	16	10	0	19	2	3	2	0	4	8	.246	.285	.285	.570
2014	ElPaso	AAA	77	228	69	12	0	0	(- | -)	81	21	35	27	10	1	33	0	2	3	1	0	4	.303	.328	.355	.683
2015	ElPaso	AAA	102	322	99	16	4	1	(- | -)	126	34	39	45	17	2	59	5	4	3	1	1	10	.307	.349	.391	.740
2015	SD	NL	11	10	1	0	0	0	(0 | 0)	1	0	0	0	0	0	1	0	0	0	0	0	1	.100	.100	.100	.200

Yovani Gallardo

Pitches: R Bats: R Pos: SP-33   guy-YARR-doe   Ht: 6'2" Wt: 205 Born: 2/27/1986 Age: 30

				HOW MUCH HE PITCHED						WHAT HE GAVE UP												THE RESULTS					
Year	Team	Lg	G	GS	CG	GF	IP	BFP	H	R	ER	HR	SH	SF	HB	TBB	IBB	SO	WP	Bk	W	L	Pct	Sh	Sv-Op	Hld	ERC	ERA
2007	Mil	NL	20	17	0	1	110.1	466	103	48	45	8	4	3	2	37	2	101	3	0	9	5	.643	0	0-0	0	3.30	3.67
2008	Mil	NL	4	4	0	0	24.0	97	22	5	5	3	2	1	0	8	0	20	0	0	0	0	-	0	0-0	0	3.66	1.88
2009	Mil	NL	30	30	1	0	185.2	793	150	78	77	21	5	3	5	94	5	204	9	0	13	12	.520	0	0-0	0	3.57	3.73
2010	Mil	NL	31	31	2	0	185.0	803	178	89	79	12	11	4	3	75	5	200	7	1	14	7	.667	2	0-0	0	3.61	3.84
2011	Mil	NL	33	33	1	0	207.1	865	193	92	81	27	10	7	1	59	1	207	12	0	17	10	.630	1	0-0	0	3.43	3.52
2012	Mil	NL	33	33	0	0	204.0	860	185	86	83	26	11	6	0	81	3	204	5	0	16	9	.640	0	0-0	0	3.72	3.66
2013	Mil	NL	31	31	0	0	180.2	773	180	92	84	18	8	7	3	66	1	144	5	0	12	10	.545	0	0-0	0	3.98	4.18
2014	Mil	NL	32	32	0	0	192.1	817	195	86	75	21	8	3	4	54	2	146	8	0	8	11	.421	0	0-0	0	3.79	3.51
2015	Tex	AL	33	33	0	0	184.1	793	193	76	70	15	1	3	1	68	0	121	10	0	13	11	.542	0	0-0	0	4.13	3.42
	Postseason		5	4	0	0	26.0	109	22	9	6	2	1	0	0	13	3	20	4	0	1	2	.333	0	0-0	0	3.34	2.08
	9 ML YEARS		247	244	4	1	1473.2	6267	1399	652	599	151	60	37	19	542	19	1347	59	1	102	75	.576	3	0-0	0	3.71	3.66

Joey Gallo

Bats: L Throws: R Pos: LF-19;3B-15;PH-5;DH-2;CF-1;PR-1   Ht: 6'5" Wt: 230 Born: 11/19/1993 Age: 22

							BATTING												RUNNING			AVERAGES			
Year	Team	Lg	G	AB	H	2B	3B	HR	(Hm | Rd)	TB	R	RBI	RC	TBB	IBB	SO	HBP	SH	SF	SB	CS	GDP	Avg	OBP	Slg	OPS
2012	2 Tms	Low	59	206	56	12	1	22	(- | -)	136	53	52	56	48	3	78	3	0	3	6	0	0	.272	.412	.660	1.072
2013	2 Tms	Low	111	411	103	23	5	40	(- | -)	256	86	88	88	50	1	172	5	0	1	15	1	2	.251	.338	.623	.961
2014	MrtlBh	A+	58	189	61	9	3	21	(- | -)	139	53	50	61	51	3	64	2	0	4	5	3	3	.323	.463	.735	1.199

Year	Team	Lg	G	AB	H	2B	3B	HR	(Hm	Rd)	TB	R	RBI	RC	TBB	IBB	SO	HBP	SH	SF	SB	CS	GDP	Avg	OBP	Slg	OPS
2014	Frisco	AA	68	250	58	10	0	21	(-	-)	131	44	56	45	36	4	115	3	1	1	2	0	0	.232	.334	.524	.858
2015	Frisco	AA	34	121	38	10	1	9	(-	-)	77	21	31	31	24	0	49	0	0	1	1	0	0	.314	.425	.636	1.061
2015	RdRck	AAA	53	200	39	9	0	14	(-	-)	90	20	32	27	27	2	90	0	0	1	1	0	3	.195	.289	.450	.739
2015	Tex	AL	36	108	22	3	1	6	(4	2)	45	16	14	13	15	3	57	0	0	0	3	0	0	.204	.301	.417	.717

Freddy Galvis

Bats: B Throws: R Pos: SS-146;2B-4;PH-2   GAL-viss   Ht: 5'10" Wt: 190 Born: 11/14/1989 Age: 26

Year	Team	Lg	G	AB	H	2B	3B	HR	(Hm	Rd)	TB	R	RBI	RC	TBB	IBB	SO	HBP	SH	SF	SB	CS	GDP	Avg	OBP	Slg	OPS
2012	Phi	NL	58	190	43	15	1	3	(3	0)	69	14	24	14	7	0	29	0	3	0	0	0	6	.226	.254	.363	.617
2013	Phi	NL	70	205	48	5	4	6	(4	2)	79	13	19	20	13	2	45	1	3	0	1	0	5	.234	.283	.385	.668
2014	Phi	NL	43	119	21	3	1	4	(2	2)	38	14	12	9	8	0	30	0	0	1	1	0	0	.176	.227	.319	.546
2015	Phi	NL	151	559	147	14	5	7	(6	1)	192	63	50	64	30	1	103	3	7	4	10	1	11	.263	.302	.343	.645
	4 ML YEARS		322	1073	259	37	11	20	(15	5)	378	104	105	107	58	3	207	4	13	5	12	1	22	.241	.282	.352	.634

Frank Garces

Pitches: L Bats: L Pos: RP-39; SP-1   GAR-sehs   Ht: 5'11" Wt: 175 Born: 1/17/1990 Age: 26

	HOW MUCH HE PITCHED								WHAT HE GAVE UP										THE RESULTS							
Year	Team	Lg	G	GS	CG	GF	IP	BFP	H	R	ER	HR	SH	SF	HB	TBB	IBB	SO	WP	Bk	W	L	Pct	Sh	Sv-Op	Hld	ERC	ERA
2012	FtWyn	A	25	25	0	0	121.2	508	102	51	38	3	10	4	1	55	1	112	4	2	9	6	.600	0	0- -	-	2.94	2.81
2013	Lk Els	A+	26	26	0	0	120.2	556	131	86	76	15	4	5	13	57	0	126	4	3	7	9	.438	0	0- -	-	5.43	5.67
2014	SnAnt	AA	51	0	0	15	65.1	268	46	17	14	3	5	1	3	24	3	74	1	0	2	5	.286	0	8- -	-	2.15	1.93
2015	ElPaso	AAA	19	0	0	6	21.2	96	17	8	7	2	0	2	0	15	1	17	3	1	1	0	1.000	0	3- -	-	3.83	2.91
2014	SD	NL	15	0	0	0	9.0	37	8	2	2	1	0	0	1	1	0	10	0	0	0	0	-	0	0-1	3	2.82	2.00
2015	SD	NL	40	1	0	11	38.0	173	41	23	22	9	1	2	1	22	1	30	3	0	0	1	.000	0	0-0	0	6.46	5.21
	2 ML YEARS		55	1	0	12	47.0	210	49	25	24	10	1	2	2	23	1	40	3	0	0	1	.000	0	0-1	3	5.69	4.60

Adonis Garcia

Bats: R Throws: R Pos: 3B-42;LF-10;PH-8   ah-DOH-niss   Ht: 5'9" Wt: 190 Born: 4/12/1985 Age: 31

Year	Team	Lg	G	AB	H	2B	3B	HR	(Hm	Rd)	TB	R	RBI	RC	TBB	IBB	SO	HBP	SH	SF	SB	CS	GDP	Avg	OBP	Slg	OPS
2012	Tampa	A+	29	106	25	7	1	1	(-	-)	37	11	15	10	9	0	18	0	0	0	0	2	3	.236	.296	.349	.645
2012	Trntn	AA	28	118	34	12	0	4	(-	-)	58	17	14	19	5	0	18	2	0	1	2	1	1	.288	.325	.492	.817
2013	S-WB	AAA	50	199	51	9	1	3	(-	-)	71	17	10	22	11	0	21	5	1	0	4	4	8	.256	.312	.357	.668
2014	S-WB	AAA	86	342	109	20	3	9	(-	-)	162	58	45	58	17	0	51	4	0	5	11	3	12	.319	.353	.474	.827
2015	Gwnntt	AAA	87	331	94	17	1	3	(-	-)	122	43	47	40	15	2	41	1	0	3	5	1	9	.284	.314	.369	.683
2015	Atl	NL	58	191	53	12	0	10	(8	2)	95	20	26	16	5	0	35	0	0	2	0	0	0	.277	.293	.497	.790

Avisail Garcia

Bats: R Throws: R Pos: RF-130;DH-17;PH-2   ah-vee-sigh-EEL   Ht: 6'4" Wt: 240 Born: 6/12/1991 Age: 25

Year	Team	Lg	G	AB	H	2B	3B	HR	(Hm	Rd)	TB	R	RBI	RC	TBB	IBB	SO	HBP	SH	SF	SB	CS	GDP	Avg	OBP	Slg	OPS
2012	Det	AL	23	47	15	0	0	0	(0	0)	15	7	3	5	3	1	10	1	0	0	0	2	1	.319	.373	.319	.692
2013	2 Tms	AL	72	244	69	7	3	7	(3	4)	103	31	31	30	9	0	59	1	0	2	3	3	8	.283	.309	.422	.731
2014	CWS	AL	46	172	42	8	0	7	(2	5)	71	19	29	20	14	1	44	2	0	2	4	1	5	.244	.305	.413	.718
2015	CWS	AL	148	553	142	17	2	13	(8	5)	202	66	59	58	36	3	141	8	0	4	7	7	13	.257	.309	.365	.675
13	Det	AL	30	83	20	3	1	2	(1	1)	31	12	10	7	4	0	21	0	0	1	0	1	3	.241	.273	.373	.646
13	CWS	AL	42	161	49	4	2	5	(2	3)	72	19	21	23	5	0	38	1	0	1	3	2	5	.304	.327	.447	.775
	Postseason		12	23	6	1	0	0	(0	0)	7	0	4	4	2	0	5	0	0	0	1	0	0	.261	.320	.304	.624
	4 ML YEARS		289	1016	268	32	5	27	(13	14)	391	123	122	113	62	5	254	12	0	8	14	13	27	.264	.311	.385	.696

Greg Garcia

Bats: L Throws: R Pos: PH-29;SS-12;2B-10;3B-4;PR-2   Ht: 6'0" Wt: 190 Born: 8/8/1989 Age: 26

Year	Team	Lg	G	AB	H	2B	3B	HR	(Hm	Rd)	TB	R	RBI	RC	TBB	IBB	SO	HBP	SH	SF	SB	CS	GDP	Avg	OBP	Slg	OPS
2011	2 Tms	Low	105	360	102	21	6	2	(-	-)	141	56	26	58	48	1	66	12	9	2	8	6	6	.283	.384	.392	.776
2012	Sprgfld	AA	124	412	117	20	3	10	(-	-)	173	81	51	78	80	4	83	7	4	1	10	5	4	.284	.408	.420	.828
2013	Memp	AAA	116	354	96	23	4	3	(-	-)	136	50	35	58	49	1	70	11	10	0	14	2	10	.271	.377	.384	.761
2014	Memp	AAA	106	382	103	12	3	8	(-	-)	145	60	40	55	41	2	95	11	5	2	7	5	4	.270	.356	.380	.735
2015	Memp	AAA	94	330	97	19	2	0	(-	-)	120	47	36	54	48	1	55	5	4	1	16	3	11	.294	.391	.364	.754
2014	StL	NL	14	14	2	1	0	0	(0	0)	3	2	1	1	1	0	6	3	0	0	0	0	0	.143	.333	.214	.548
2015	StL	NL	49	75	18	5	0	2	(1	1)	29	7	4	7	10	1	12	1	1	0	0	0	2	.240	.337	.387	.724
	2 ML YEARS		63	89	20	6	0	2	(1	1)	32	9	5	8	11	1	18	4	1	0	0	0	2	.225	.337	.360	.696

Jaime Garcia

Pitches: L Bats: L Pos: SP-20   HY-may   Ht: 6'2" Wt: 215 Born: 7/8/1986 Age: 29

	HOW MUCH HE PITCHED								WHAT HE GAVE UP										THE RESULTS							
Year	Team	Lg	G	GS	CG	GF	IP	BFP	H	R	ER	HR	SH	SF	HB	TBB	IBB	SO	WP	Bk	W	L	Pct	Sh	Sv-Op	Hld	ERC	ERA
2008	StL	NL	10	1	0	4	16.0	69	14	10	10	4	0	0	1	8	0	8	3	0	1	1	.500	0	0-0	3	5.15	5.63
2010	StL	NL	28	28	1	0	163.1	695	151	64	49	9	3	3	3	64	4	132	4	1	13	8	.619	1	0-0	0	3.34	2.70
2011	StL	NL	32	32	2	0	194.2	826	207	100	77	15	10	5	2	50	2	156	12	1	13	7	.650	2	0-0	0	3.73	3.56
2012	StL	NL	20	20	0	0	121.2	515	136	58	53	7	8	7	0	30	1	98	12	1	7	7	.500	0	0-0	0	3.86	3.92
2013	StL	NL	9	9	0	0	55.1	234	57	26	22	6	2	0	0	15	0	43	3	0	5	2	.714	0	0-0	0	3.78	3.58

HOW MUCH HE PITCHED							WHAT HE GAVE UP												THE RESULTS							
Year	Team	Lg	G	GS	CG	GF	IP	BFP	H	R	ER	HR	SH	SF	HB	TBB	IBB	SO	WP	Bk	W	L	Pct	Sh	Sv-Op	Hld	ERC	ERA
2014	StL	NL	7	7	0	0	43.2	177	39	20	20	6	0	0	3	7	0	39	1	0	3	1	.750	0	0-0	0	3.08	4.12
2015	StL	NL	20	20	0	0	129.2	510	106	37	35	6	3	3	3	30	0	97	4	0	10	6	.625	0	0-0	0	2.31	2.43
	Postseason		6	6	0	0	27.2	120	29	13	13	3	1	0	1	11	2	24	1	0	0	2	.000	0	0-0	0	4.48	4.23
	7 ML YEARS		126	117	3	4	724.1	3026	710	315	266	53	26	18	12	204	7	573	39	3	52	32	.619	3	0-0	3	3.39	3.31

Jason Garcia

Pitches: R **Bats:** R **Pos:** RP-21 **Ht:** 6'0" **Wt:** 185 **Born:** 11/21/1992 **Age:** 23

HOW MUCH HE PITCHED							WHAT HE GAVE UP												THE RESULTS							
Year	Team	Lg	G	GS	CG	GF	IP	BFP	H	R	ER	HR	SH	SF	HB	TBB	IBB	SO	WP	Bk	W	L	Pct	Sh	Sv-Op	Hld	ERC	ERA
2011	Lowell	A-	13	13	0	0	55.2	258	52	38	24	1	1	1	6	36	0	40	4	0	3	3	.500	0	0- -	-	4.39	3.88
2012	Grnvlle	A	28	22	0	3	115.1	534	135	85	79	8	0	4	8	67	0	95	13	3	6	6	.500	0	2- -	-	5.96	6.16
2013	Grnvlle	A	9	1	0	5	36.1	158	33	20	17	3	0	1	3	16	0	36	3	1	2	2	.500	0	1- -	-	3.91	4.21
2014	2 Tms	Low	14	7	0	5	56.0	241	50	26	23	0	3	1	5	24	0	59	7	1	3	2	.600	0	3- -	-	3.24	3.70
2015	Bowie	AA	9	0	0	4	15.0	66	12	8	7	2	0	0	1	9	1	14	2	1	1	2	.333	0	0- -	-	4.11	4.20
2015	Bal	AL	21	0	0	9	29.2	132	25	19	14	3	0	1	2	17	1	22	2	0	1	0	1.000	0	0-0	0	4.02	4.25

Leury Garcia

lay-OOH-ree

Bats: B **Throws:** R **Pos:** PR-5;CF-4;SS-3;2B-2;LF-2;DH-2;PH-2 **Ht:** 5'8" **Wt:** 170 **Born:** 3/18/1991 **Age:** 25

BATTING																		RUNNING			AVERAGES			
Year	Team	Lg	G	AB	H	2B	3B	HR	(Hm | Rd)	TB	R	RBI	RC	TBB	IBB	SO	HBP	SH	SF	SB	CS	GDP	Avg	OBP	Slg	OPS
2015	Charllt*	AAA	90	349	104	19	3	3	(- | -)	138	57	31	50	20	0	66	4	9	3	30	12	3	.298	.340	.395	.736
2013	2 Tms	AL	45	101	20	1	1	0	(0 | 0)	23	10	2	4	7	0	34	0	2	1	7	2	0	.198	.248	.228	.475
2014	CWS	AL	74	145	24	3	0	1	(0 | 1)	30	13	6	0	5	1	48	0	4	1	11	1	6	.166	.192	.207	.399
2015	CWS	AL	18	14	3	0	0	0	(0 | 0)	3	0	1	2	1	0	7	0	0	0	1	0	0	.214	.267	.214	.481
13	Tex	AL	25	52	10	0	1	0	(0 | 0)	12	8	1	2	3	0	16	0	2	0	1	0	0	.192	.236	.231	.467
13	CWS	AL	20	49	10	1	0	0	(0 | 0)	11	2	1	2	4	0	18	0	0	1	6	2	0	.204	.259	.224	.484
	3 ML YEARS		137	260	47	4	1	1	(0 | 1)	56	23	9	6	13	1	89	0	6	2	19	3	6	.181	.218	.215	.434

Luis Garcia

Pitches: R **Bats:** R **Pos:** RP-72 **Ht:** 6'3" **Wt:** 230 **Born:** 1/30/1987 **Age:** 29

HOW MUCH HE PITCHED							WHAT HE GAVE UP												THE RESULTS							
Year	Team	Lg	G	GS	CG	GF	IP	BFP	H	R	ER	HR	SH	SF	HB	TBB	IBB	SO	WP	Bk	W	L	Pct	Sh	Sv-Op	Hld	ERC	ERA
2013	Phi	NL	24	0	0	6	31.1	138	27	15	13	3	0	0	1	23	0	23	3	0	1	1	.500	0	0-0	1	4.85	3.73
2014	Phi	NL	13	0	0	5	14.0	69	14	12	10	2	1	0	0	13	0	12	4	0	1	0	1.000	0	0-0	0	6.43	6.43
2015	Phi	NL	72	0	0	14	66.2	304	72	28	26	4	3	2	0	37	8	63	6	1	4	6	.400	0	2-4	16	4.59	3.51
	3 ML YEARS		109	0	0	25	112.0	511	113	55	49	9	4	2	1	73	8	98	13	1	6	7	.462	0	2-4	17	4.89	3.94

Yimi Garcia

Pitches: R **Bats:** R **Pos:** RP-58; SP-1 YIM-ee **Ht:** 6'1" **Wt:** 210 **Born:** 8/18/1990 **Age:** 25

HOW MUCH HE PITCHED							WHAT HE GAVE UP												THE RESULTS							
Year	Team	Lg	G	GS	CG	GF	IP	BFP	H	R	ER	HR	SH	SF	HB	TBB	IBB	SO	WP	Bk	W	L	Pct	Sh	Sv-Op	Hld	ERC	ERA
2011	Ogden	R+	20	1	0	10	52.1	223	46	23	18	4	3	2	4	19	2	71	2	2	4	2	.667	0	4- -	-	3.32	3.10
2012	2 Tms	Low	49	0	0	40	52.1	233	49	24	17	0	2	2	1	23	3	82	4	1	6	5	.545	0	16- -	-	2.94	2.92
2013	Chatt	AA	49	0	0	44	60.1	230	35	17	17	9	1	0	2	14	1	85	1	0	4	6	.400	0	19- -	-	1.74	2.54
2014	Albq	AAA	47	0	0	20	61.0	259	58	23	21	5	0	3	5	18	0	69	0	0	4	2	.667	0	5- -	-	3.59	3.10
2015	OkCity	AAA	9	0	0	2	10.2	45	9	5	5	1	1	0	0	5	0	12	0	0	0	0	-	0	0- -	-	3.46	4.22
2014	LAD	NL	8	0	0	5	10.0	36	6	2	2	2	0	0	0	1	0	9	0	0	0	0	-	0	0-0	1	1.59	1.80
2015	LAD	NL	59	1	0	15	56.2	225	44	23	21	8	0	2	2	10	1	68	1	0	3	5	.375	0	1-6	11	2.40	3.34
	2 ML YEARS		67	1	0	20	66.2	261	50	25	23	10	0	2	2	11	1	77	1	0	3	5	.375	0	1-6	12	2.27	3.11

Brett Gardner

Bats: L **Throws:** L **Pos:** LF-119;CF-40;PH-5;PR-2 **Ht:** 5'10" **Wt:** 185 **Born:** 8/24/1983 **Age:** 32

BATTING																		RUNNING			AVERAGES			
Year	Team	Lg	G	AB	H	2B	3B	HR	(Hm | Rd)	TB	R	RBI	RC	TBB	IBB	SO	HBP	SH	SF	SB	CS	GDP	Avg	OBP	Slg	OPS
2008	NYY	AL	42	127	29	5	2	0	(0 | 0)	38	18	16	17	8	0	30	2	3	1	13	1	0	.228	.283	.299	.582
2009	NYY	AL	108	248	67	6	6	3	(1 | 2)	94	48	23	38	26	0	40	3	6	1	26	5	3	.270	.345	.379	.724
2010	NYY	AL	150	477	132	20	7	5	(5 | 0)	181	97	47	77	79	1	101	5	5	3	47	9	6	.277	.383	.379	.762
2011	NYY	AL	159	510	132	19	8	7	(4 | 3)	188	87	36	77	60	1	93	8	8	2	49	13	5	.259	.345	.369	.713
2012	NYY	AL	16	31	10	2	0	0	(0 | 0)	12	7	3	7	5	0	7	0	1	0	2	2	0	.323	.417	.387	.804
2013	NYY	AL	145	539	147	33	10	8	(6 | 2)	224	81	52	88	52	1	127	8	7	3	24	8	8	.273	.344	.416	.759
2014	NYY	AL	148	555	142	25	8	17	(8 | 9)	234	87	58	81	56	0	134	6	13	6	21	5	3	.256	.327	.422	.749
2015	NYY	AL	151	571	148	26	3	16	(12 | 4)	228	94	66	90	68	1	135	6	8	3	20	5	8	.259	.343	.399	.742
	Postseason		33	65	14	1	0	0	(0 | 0)	15	8	7	5	4	0	17	0	2	1	5	2	0	.215	.257	.231	.488
	8 ML YEARS		919	3058	807	136	44	56	(36 | 20)	1199	519	301	475	354	4	667	38	51	19	202	48	33	.264	.346	.392	.738

Dustin Garneau

Bats: R Throws: R Pos: C-22 | GARR-noh | Ht: 6'0" Wt: 200 Born: 8/13/1987 Age: 28

Year	Team	Lg	G	AB	H	2B	3B	HR	(Hm	Rd)	TB	R	RBI	RC	TBB	IBB	SO	HBP	SH	SF	SB	CS	GDP	Avg	OBP	Slg	OPS
2011	Ashvll	A	100	341	87	29	4	17	(-	-)	175	71	67	67	58	0	70	7	1	5	7	7	3	.255	.370	.513	.883
2012	Mdest	A+	86	300	73	18	3	6	(-	-)	115	35	29	41	40	0	41	2	2	4	2	3	6	.243	.332	.383	.716
2013	Tulsa	AA	96	326	77	17	1	13	(-	-)	135	36	47	45	25	0	57	13	4	4	4	2	2	.236	.313	.414	.727
2014	Tulsa	AA	34	115	31	7	0	2	(-	-)	44	14	20	17	14	0	19	4	0	2	2	3	2	.270	.363	.383	.746
2014	ColSpr	AAA	44	148	32	9	2	5	(-	-)	60	17	22	18	14	0	21	3	1	0	2	1	4	.216	.297	.405	.702
2015	Albq	AAA	81	303	83	16	0	15	(-	-)	144	44	61	50	28	2	44	2	3	4	2	1	6	.274	.335	.475	.811
2015	Col	NL	22	70	11	3	0	2	(0	2)	20	6	8	5	6	2	14	0	0	0	0	0	2	.157	.224	.286	.509

Matt Garza

Pitches: R Bats: R Pos: SP-25; RP-1 | GARR-suh | Ht: 6'4" Wt: 215 Born: 11/26/1983 Age: 32

Year	Team	Lg	G	GS	CG	GF	IP	BFP	H	R	ER	HR	SH	SF	HB	TBB	IBB	SO	WP	Bk	W	L	Pct	Sh	Sv-Op	Hld	ERC	ERA
2006	Min	AL	10	9	0	0	50.0	232	62	33	32	6	0	3	0	23	0	38	1	0	3	6	.333	0	0-0	0	5.82	5.76
2007	Min	AL	16	15	0	1	83.0	367	96	44	34	8	1	4	4	32	4	67	4	0	5	7	.417	0	0-0	0	5.08	3.69
2008	TB	AL	30	30	3	0	184.2	772	170	83	76	19	3	9	6	59	2	128	3	2	11	9	.550	2	0-0	0	3.47	3.70
2009	TB	AL	32	32	0	0	203.0	861	177	93	89	25	2	8	11	79	0	189	3	0	8	12	.400	0	0-0	0	3.69	3.95
2010	TB	AL	33	32	3	1	204.2	855	193	94	89	28	1	6	7	63	2	150	12	2	15	10	.600	1	1-1	0	3.80	3.91
2011	ChC	NL	31	31	2	0	198.0	839	186	90	73	14	11	2	3	63	5	197	6	0	10	10	.500	0	0-0	0	3.21	3.32
2012	ChC	NL	18	18	0	0	103.2	424	90	48	45	15	5	1	4	32	0	96	1	0	5	7	.417	0	0-0	0	3.50	3.91
2013	2 Tms		24	24	1	0	155.1	652	150	73	66	20	8	3	5	42	3	136	6	0	10	6	.625	0	0-0	0	3.66	3.82
2014	Mil	NL	27	27	1	0	163.1	680	143	77	66	12	9	4	4	50	2	126	3	1	8	8	.500	1	0-0	0	2.92	3.64
2015	Mil	NL	26	25	0	1	148.2	666	176	102	93	23	7	2	2	57	3	104	7	0	6	14	.300	0	0-0	0	5.51	5.63
13	ChC	NL	11	11	0	0	71.0	293	61	26	25	8	2	1	4	20	2	62	2	0	6	1	.857	0	0-0	0	3.12	3.17
13	Tex	AL	13	13	1	0	84.1	359	89	47	41	12	6	2	1	22	1	74	4	0	4	5	.444	0	0-0	0	4.14	4.38
	Postseason		5	5	0	0	31.0	131	26	13	12	5	0	1	1	14	0	29	2	0	2	1	.667	0	0-0	0	3.95	3.48
10 ML YEARS			247	243	10	3	1494.1	6348	1443	737	663	170	47	42	46	500	21	1231	46	5	81	89	.476	4	1-1	0	3.82	3.99

Evan Gattis

Bats: R Throws: R Pos: DH-136;LF-11;PH-6 | GAT-iss | Ht: 6'4" Wt: 260 Born: 8/18/1986 Age: 29

Year	Team	Lg	G	AB	H	2B	3B	HR	(Hm	Rd)	TB	R	RBI	RC	TBB	IBB	SO	HBP	SH	SF	SB	CS	GDP	Avg	OBP	Slg	OPS
2013	Atl	NL	105	354	86	21	0	21	(13)	170	144	44	65	43	21	4	81	4	0	3	0	0	10	.243	.291	.480	.771
2014	Atl	NL	108	369	97	17	1	22	(12	10)	182	41	52	45	22	3	97	8	0	2	0	0	9	.263	.317	.493	.810
2015	Hou	AL	153	566	139	20	11	27	(15	12)	262	66	88	73	30	3	119	3	0	5	0	1	13	.246	.285	.463	.748
	Postseason		4	14	5	0	0	0	(0	0)	5	3	1	3	2	0	3	0	0	0	0	0	0	.357	.438	.357	.795
3 ML YEARS			366	1289	322	58	12	70	(35	35)	614	151	205	161	73	10	297	15	0	10	0	1	32	.250	.296	.476	.772

Kevin Gausman

Pitches: R Bats: L Pos: SP-17; RP-8 | GAHZ-man | Ht: 6'3" Wt: 190 Born: 1/6/1991 Age: 25

Year	Team	Lg	G	GS	CG	GF	IP	BFP	H	R	ER	HR	SH	SF	HB	TBB	IBB	SO	WP	Bk	W	L	Pct	Sh	Sv-Op	Hld	ERC	ERA
2013	Bal	AL	20	5	0	3	47.2	201	51	30	30	8	2	1	0	13	2	49	4	0	3	5	.375	0	0-2	2	4.41	5.66
2014	Bal	AL	20	20	1	0	113.1	476	111	48	45	7	3	7	1	38	0	88	9	0	7	7	.500	0	0-0	0	3.52	3.57
2015	Bal	AL	25	17	0	1	112.1	470	109	56	53	17	2	3	2	29	1	103	7	0	4	7	.364	0	0-0	1	3.74	4.25
	Postseason		3	0	0	1	8.0	27	4	1	1	0	0	0	0	2	0	7	0	0	0	0	-	0	0-0	0	1.05	1.13
3 ML YEARS			65	42	1	4	273.1	1147	271	134	128	32	7	11	3	80	3	240	20	0	14	19	.424	0	0-2	3	3.77	4.21

Cory Gearrin

Pitches: R Bats: R Pos: RP-7 | GARE-inn | Ht: 6'3" Wt: 215 Born: 4/14/1986 Age: 30

Year	Team	Lg	G	GS	CG	GF	IP	BFP	H	R	ER	HR	SH	SF	HB	TBB	IBB	SO	WP	Bk	W	L	Pct	Sh	Sv-Op	Hld	ERC	ERA
2015	Scrmto*	AAA	33	0	0	6	43.0	183	38	15	13	4	1	0	3	14	1	46	2	1	2	2	.500	0	0--	-	3.29	2.72
2011	Atl	NL	18	0	0	4	18.1	75	17	16	16	0	0	1	2	12	4	25	1	0	1	1	.500	0	0-1	3	3.84	7.85
2012	Atl	NL	22	0	0	7	20.0	80	17	4	4	1	0	0	2	5	0	20	2	0	0	1	.000	0	0-1	4	2.86	1.80
2013	Atl	NL	37	0	0	12	31.0	133	30	13	13	2	1	0	4	16	2	23	3	0	2	1	.667	0	1-3	1	4.73	3.77
2015	SF	NL	7	0	0	0	3.2	13	1	2	2	0	0	0	0	1	0	5	0	0	0	0	-	0	0-0	3	0.47	4.91
4 ML YEARS			84	0	0	23	73.0	311	65	35	35	3	1	1	8	34	6	73	6	0	3	3	.500	0	1-5	11	3.69	4.32

Dillon Gee

Pitches: R Bats: R Pos: SP-7; RP-1 | JEE | Ht: 6'1" Wt: 205 Born: 4/28/1986 Age: 30

Year	Team	Lg	G	GS	CG	GF	IP	BFP	H	R	ER	HR	SH	SF	HB	TBB	IBB	SO	WP	Bk	W	L	Pct	Sh	Sv-Op	Hld	ERC	ERA
2015	LsVgs*	AAA	14	14	2	0	88.1	380	105	50	45	7	6	3	2	18	0	63	2	0	8	3	.727	0	0--	-	4.32	4.58
2010	NYM	NL	5	5	0	0	33.0	136	25	10	8	2	3	0	0	15	2	17	0	0	2	2	.500	0	0-0	0	2.66	2.18
2011	NYM	NL	30	27	1	1	160.2	706	150	85	79	18	10	5	14	71	4	114	6	1	13	6	.684	0	0-0	0	4.23	4.43
2012	NYM	NL	17	17	0	0	109.2	463	108	56	50	12	2	3	6	29	0	97	0	0	6	7	.462	0	0-0	0	3.74	4.10
2013	NYM	NL	32	32	2	0	199.0	841	208	84	80	24	9	3	7	47	0	142	4	0	12	11	.522	0	0-0	0	3.97	3.62
2014	NYM	NL	22	22	0	0	137.1	570	128	61	61	18	7	3	5	43	0	94	3	1	7	8	.467	0	0-0	0	3.77	4.00
2015	NYM	NL	8	7	0	0	39.2	183	55	29	26	5	2	2	1	11	3	25	0	0	0	3	.000	0	0-0	0	5.98	5.90
6 ML YEARS			114	110	3	1	679.1	2899	674	325	304	79	33	16	33	216	9	489	13	3	40	37	.519	0	0-0	0	4.00	4.03

Steve Geltz

Pitches: R **Bats:** R **Pos:** RP-68; SP-2 **Ht:** 5'10" **Wt:** 210 **Born:** 11/1/1987 **Age:** 28

	HOW MUCH HE PITCHED							WHAT HE GAVE UP											THE RESULTS							
Year Team	Lg	G	GS	CG	GF	IP	BFP	H	R	ER	HR	SH	SF	HB	TBB	IBB	SO	WP	Bk	W	L	Pct	Sh	Sv-Op	Hld	ERC	ERA
2012 LAA	AL	2	0	0	2	2.0	11	2	1	1	0	0	1	0	3	0	1	0	0	0	0	-	0	0-0	0	7.45	4.50
2014 TB	AL	11	0	0	1	8.1	37	6	3	3	3	0	0	2	5	0	14	0	0	0	1	.000	0	0-1	0	6.25	3.24
2015 TB	AL	70	2	0	12	67.1	269	45	31	28	8	2	0	2	26	3	61	4	0	2	6	.250	0	2-5	20	2.48	3.74
3 ML YEARS		83	2	0	15	77.2	317	53	35	32	11	2	1	4	34	3	76	4	0	2	7	.222	0	2-6	20	2.96	3.71

Scooter Gennett

Bats: L **Throws:** R **Pos:** 2B-108;PH-17 jen-ETT **Ht:** 5'10" **Wt:** 185 **Born:** 5/1/1990 **Age:** 26

	BATTING																				RUNNING			AVERAGES			
Year Team	Lg	G	AB	H	2B	3B	HR	(Hm	Rd)	TB	R	RBI	RC	TBB	IBB	SO	HBP	SH	SF	SB	CS	GDP	Avg	OBP	Slg	OPS
2015 ColSpr*	AAA	17	75	23	7	1	2	(-	-)	38	12	11	12	4	0	10	0	0	0	0	1	1	.307	.342	.507	.848
2013 Mil	NL	69	213	69	11	2	6	(0	6)	102	29	21	35	10	0	42	1	5	1	2	1	0	.324	.356	.479	.834
2014 Mil	NL	137	440	127	31	3	9	(6	3)	191	55	54	59	22	5	67	0	8	4	6	3	11	.289	.320	.434	.754
2015 Mil	NL	114	375	99	18	4	6	(5	1)	143	42	29	36	12	5	68	4	0	0	1	3	11	.264	.294	.381	.675
3 ML YEARS		320	1028	295	60	9	21	(11	10)	436	126	104	130	44	10	177	5	13	5	9	7	22	.287	.318	.424	.742

Craig Gentry

Bats: R **Throws:** R **Pos:** LF-13;CF-8;RF-6;PH-3;PR-2;DH-1 JEN-tree **Ht:** 6'2" **Wt:** 190 **Born:** 11/29/1983 **Age:** 32

	BATTING																				RUNNING			AVERAGES			
Year Team	Lg	G	AB	H	2B	3B	HR	(Hm	Rd)	TB	R	RBI	RC	TBB	IBB	SO	HBP	SH	SF	SB	CS	GDP	Avg	OBP	Slg	OPS
2015 Nashv*	AAA	101	398	102	13	0	5	(-	-)	130	64	25	47	36	0	76	3	4	5	25	7	9	.256	.319	.327	.646
2009 Tex	AL	11	17	2	1	0	0	(0	0)	3	4	1	1	2	0	5	0	0	0	0	0	0	.118	.211	.176	.387
2010 Tex	AL	20	33	7	0	0	0	(0	0)	7	4	3	1	1	0	11	0	0	1	1	0	1	.212	.229	.212	.441
2011 Tex	AL	64	133	36	5	1	1	(1	0)	46	26	13	21	10	1	27	6	3	1	18	0	2	.271	.347	.346	.693
2012 Tex	AL	122	240	73	12	3	1	(0	1)	94	31	26	33	14	1	41	10	5	0	13	7	4	.304	.367	.392	.759
2013 Tex	AL	106	246	69	12	4	2	(2	0)	95	39	22	42	29	2	46	8	3	1	24	3	5	.280	.373	.386	.759
2014 Oak	AL	94	232	59	6	1	0	(0	0)	67	38	12	27	17	2	44	5	2	0	20	2	2	.254	.319	.289	.608
2015 Oak	AL	26	50	6	0	2	0	(0	0)	10	6	3	2	4	0	15	1	0	1	1	1	0	.120	.196	.200	.396
Postseason		14	17	5	0	0	0	(0	0)	5	2	1	3	1	0	4	1	1	0	2	1	0	.294	.368	.294	.663
7 ML YEARS		443	951	252	36	11	4	(3	1)	322	148	80	127	77	6	189	30	13	4	77	13	14	.265	.338	.339	.677

Gonzalez Germen

Pitches: R **Bats:** R **Pos:** RP-34; SP-1 hare-MEN **Ht:** 6'1" **Wt:** 200 **Born:** 9/23/1987 **Age:** 28

	HOW MUCH HE PITCHED							WHAT HE GAVE UP											THE RESULTS							
Year Team	Lg	G	GS	CG	GF	IP	BFP	H	R	ER	HR	SH	SF	HB	TBB	IBB	SO	WP	Bk	W	L	Pct	Sh	Sv-Op	Hld	ERC	ERA
2015 Iowa*	AAA	24	0	0	8	33.1	145	29	16	14	3	1	2	1	17	0	27	2	1	5	1	.833	0	4- -		3.80	3.78
2013 NYM	NL	29	0	0	8	34.1	149	32	15	15	1	0	0	0	16	1	33	2	0	1	2	.333	0	1-3	1	3.37	3.93
2014 NYM	NL	25	0	0	9	30.1	133	30	16	16	7	1	0	1	14	1	31	1	0	0	0	-	0	0-1	0	5.31	4.75
2015 2 Tms	NL	35	1	0	5	38.2	176	41	19	19	4	1	0	0	26	3	33	3	0	0	0	-	0	1-3	2	5.50	4.42
15 ChC	NL	6	0	0	2	6.0	29	8	5	5	0	1	0	0	5	2	8	0	0	0	0	-	0	0-0	0	6.58	7.50
15 Col	NL	29	1	0	3	32.2	147	33	14	14	4	0	0	0	21	1	25	3	0	0	0	-	0	1-3	2	5.29	3.86
3 ML YEARS		89	1	0	22	103.1	458	103	50	50	12	2	0	1	56	5	97	6	0	1	2	.333	0	2-7	3	4.72	4.35

Johnny Giavotella

Bats: R **Throws:** R **Pos:** 2B-128;PH-2;SS-1 gee-uh-vo-TELL-uh **Ht:** 5'8" **Wt:** 185 **Born:** 7/10/1987 **Age:** 28

	BATTING																				RUNNING			AVERAGES			
Year Team	Lg	G	AB	H	2B	3B	HR	(Hm	Rd)	TB	R	RBI	RC	TBB	IBB	SO	HBP	SH	SF	SB	CS	GDP	Avg	OBP	Slg	OPS
2011 KC	AL	46	178	44	9	4	2	(2	0)	67	20	21	15	6	0	32	1	0	2	5	2	4	.247	.273	.376	.649
2012 KC	AL	53	181	43	7	1	1	(1	0)	55	21	15	14	8	0	35	0	0	0	3	0	4	.238	.270	.304	.574
2013 KC	AL	14	41	9	3	0	0	(0	0)	12	4	4	5	5	0	4	2	0	0	0	0	0	.220	.333	.293	.626
2014 KC	AL	12	37	8	1	0	1	(0	1)	12	8	5	2	1	0	5	2	0	1	0	1	1	.216	.268	.324	.593
2015 LAA	AL	129	453	123	25	5	4	(3	1)	170	51	49	63	32	0	59	2	9	6	2	1	7	.272	.318	.375	.694
5 ML YEARS		254	890	227	45	10	8	(6	2)	316	104	94	99	52	0	135	7	9	9	10	4	16	.255	.299	.355	.654

Kyle Gibson

Pitches: R **Bats:** R **Pos:** SP-32 **Ht:** 6'6" **Wt:** 210 **Born:** 10/23/1987 **Age:** 28

	HOW MUCH HE PITCHED							WHAT HE GAVE UP											THE RESULTS							
Year Team	Lg	G	GS	CG	GF	IP	BFP	H	R	ER	HR	SH	SF	HB	TBB	IBB	SO	WP	Bk	W	L	Pct	Sh	Sv-Op	Hld	ERC	ERA
2013 Min	AL	10	10	0	0	51.0	238	69	38	37	7	0	2	5	20	0	29	4	0	2	4	.333	0	0-0	0	6.98	6.53
2014 Min	AL	31	31	0	0	179.1	757	178	91	89	12	4	3	2	57	0	107	11	0	13	12	.520	0	0-0	0	3.54	4.47
2015 Min	AL	32	32	1	0	194.2	821	186	88	83	18	6	6	7	65	6	145	7	0	11	11	.500	0	0-0	0	3.63	3.84
3 ML YEARS		73	73	1	0	425.0	1816	433	217	209	37	10	11	14	142	6	281	22	0	26	27	.491	0	0-0	0	3.96	4.43

Ken Giles

Pitches: R **Bats:** R **Pos:** RP-69 **Ht:** 6'2" **Wt:** 205 **Born:** 9/20/1990 **Age:** 25

	HOW MUCH HE PITCHED							WHAT HE GAVE UP											THE RESULTS							
Year Team	Lg	G	GS	CG	GF	IP	BFP	H	R	ER	HR	SH	SF	HB	TBB	IBB	SO	WP	Bk	W	L	Pct	Sh	Sv-Op	Hld	ERC	ERA
2012 2 Tms	Low	39	6	0	18	82.0	367	64	35	32	6	1	4	6	50	0	111	9	0	4	3	.571	0	8- -	-	3.66	3.51
2013 Clrwtr	A+	24	0	0	12	25.2	120	23	19	18	4	0	3	1	19	0	34	1	0	2	2	.500	0	6- -	-	5.30	6.31
2014 Rdng	AA	13	0	0	12	15.0	57	8	3	2	0	0	0	0	5	0	29	0	0	0	0	-	0	7- -	-	1.20	1.20

Year Team	Lg	G	GS	CG	GF	IP	BFP	H	R	ER	HR	SH	SF	HB	TBB	IBB	SO	WP	Bk	W	L	Pct	Sh	Sv-Op	Hld	ERC	ERA
2014 LV	AAA	11	0	0	7	13.1	57	10	4	4	0	1	1	1	8	0	9	1	0	2	0	1.000	0	5- -	-	3.09	2.70
2014 Phi	NL	44	0	0	11	45.2	166	25	7	6	1	2	1	0	11	1	64	1	0	3	1	.750	0	1-1	13	1.15	1.18
2015 Phi	NL	69	0	0	28	70.0	298	59	23	14	2	1	2	1	25	2	87	1	0	6	3	.667	0	15-20	12	2.53	1.80
2 ML YEARS		113	0	0	39	115.2	464	84	30	20	3	3	3	1	36	3	151	2	0	9	4	.692	0	16-21	25	1.88	1.56

Conor Gillaspie

Bats: L **Throws:** R **Pos:** 3B-69;PH-5;1B-2;DH-2;2B-1   guh-LESS-pee   **Ht:** 6'1" **Wt:** 195 **Born:** 7/18/1987 **Age:** 28

Year Team	Lg	G	AB	H	2B	3B	HR	(Hm	Rd)	TB	R	RBI	RC	TBB	IBB	SO	HBP	SH	SF	SB	CS	GDP	Avg	OBP	Slg	OPS
2008 SF	NL	8	5	1	0	0	0	(0	0)	1	1	0	1	2	0	0	0	0	0	0	0	0	.200	.429	.200	.629
2011 SF	NL	15	19	5	0	0	1	(1	0)	8	2	2	4	2	0	1	0	0	0	0	0	0	.263	.333	.421	.754
2012 SF	NL	6	20	3	1	0	0	(0	0)	4	2	2	0	0	0	2	0	0	0	0	0	0	.150	.150	.200	.350
2013 CWS	AL	134	408	100	14	3	13	(8	5)	159	46	40	46	37	4	79	1	0	6	0	1	7	.245	.305	.390	.695
2014 CWS	AL	130	464	131	31	5	7	(3	4)	193	50	57	68	36	4	78	3	0	3	0	4	5	.282	.336	.416	.752
2015 2 Tms	AL	75	237	54	15	2	4	(3	1)	85	14	24	20	13	2	47	1	0	2	0	1	2	.228	.269	.359	.627
15 CWS	AL	58	173	41	11	1	3	(2	1)	63	10	15	14	9	1	34	1	0	2	0	1	2	.237	.276	.364	.640
15 LAA	AL	17	64	13	4	1	1	(1	0)	22	4	9	6	4	1	13	0	0	0	0	0	0	.203	.250	.344	.594
6 ML YEARS		368	1153	294	61	10	25	(15	10)	450	115	125	139	90	10	207	5	0	11	0	6	14	.255	.309	.390	.699

Cole Gillespie

Bats: R **Throws:** R **Pos:** CF-31;RF-17;PH-12;LF-10;PR-4   gil-EH-spee   **Ht:** 6'0" **Wt:** 205 **Born:** 6/20/1984 **Age:** 32

Year Team	Lg	G	AB	H	2B	3B	HR	(Hm	Rd)	TB	R	RBI	RC	TBB	IBB	SO	HBP	SH	SF	SB	CS	GDP	Avg	OBP	Slg	OPS
2015 NewOr*	AAA	67	247	72	15	1	0	(-	-)	89	30	23	35	27	1	31	1	0	6	7	2	7	.291	.356	.360	.716
2010 Ari	NL	45	104	24	8	0	2	(2	0)	38	11	12	10	7	1	29	1	0	1	1	1	2	.231	.283	.365	.649
2011 Ari	NL	5	6	2	0	0	1	(1	0)	5	2	4	3	1	0	1	0	0	0	0	0	0	.333	.429	.833	1.262
2013 2 Tms	NL	28	59	12	2	0	0	(0	0)	14	6	4	5	7	1	13	1	1	1	0	0	2	.203	.294	.237	.531
2014 2 Tms	AL	35	74	18	2	0	1	(0	1)	23	9	5	7	6	0	13	0	1	0	2	2	3	.243	.300	.311	.611
2015 Mia	NL	67	145	42	10	2	2	(1	1)	62	17	16	21	10	0	27	0	1	1	4	1	5	.290	.333	.428	.761
13 SF	NL	3	9	0	0	0	0	(0	0)	0	0	0	0	1	1	0	0	0	0	0	0	0	.000	.100	.000	.100
13 ChC	NL	25	50	12	2	0	0	(0	0)	14	6	4	5	6	0	13	1	1	1	0	0	2	.240	.328	.280	.608
14 Sea	AL	34	71	18	2	0	1	(0	1)	23	9	5	7	6	0	13	0	1	0	2	2	3	.254	.312	.324	.636
14 Tor	AL	1	3	0	0	0	0	(0	0)	0	0	0	0	0	0	0	0	0	0	0	0	0	.000	.000	.000	.000
5 ML YEARS		180	388	98	22	2	6	(4	2)	142	45	41	46	31	2	83	2	3	3	7	4	12	.253	.309	.366	.675

Sean Gilmartin

Pitches: L **Bats:** L **Pos:** RP-49; SP-1   **Ht:** 6'2" **Wt:** 205 **Born:** 5/8/1990 **Age:** 26

Year Team	Lg	G	GS	CG	GF	IP	BFP	H	R	ER	HR	SH	SF	HB	TBB	IBB	SO	WP	Bk	W	L	Pct	Sh	Sv-Op	Hld	ERC	ERA
2011 2 Tms	Low	6	6	0	0	23.1	95	21	8	8	3	0	0	2	0	0	31	3	0	2	2	.500	0	0- -	-	2.42	3.09
2012 Missi	AA	20	20	3	0	119.1	483	111	49	47	9	3	2	4	26	0	86	2	1	5	8	.385	0	0- -	-	3.02	3.54
2012 Gwnntt	AAA	7	7	0	0	37.2	167	41	22	20	6	3	1	0	13	1	25	0	0	1	2	.333	0	0- -	-	4.63	4.78
2013 Gwnntt	AAA	17	17	0	0	91.0	412	112	61	58	12	3	6	1	33	1	65	4	0	3	8	.273	0	0- -	-	5.50	5.74
2014 NwBrit	AA	12	12	0	0	72.0	302	76	30	25	2	3	4	3	16	0	74	3	1	7	3	.700	0	0- -	-	3.39	3.13
2014 Roch	AAA	14	14	0	0	73.2	308	69	39	35	7	2	1	1	28	1	59	3	0	2	4	.333	0	0- -	-	3.71	4.28
2015 NYM	NL	50	1	0	13	57.1	235	50	17	17	2	2	1	2	18	5	54	1	0	3	2	.600	0	0-1	2	2.67	2.67

Chris Gimenez

Bats: R **Throws:** R **Pos:** C-36   JIMM-inn-ezz   **Ht:** 6'2" **Wt:** 220 **Born:** 12/27/1982 **Age:** 33

Year Team	Lg	G	AB	H	2B	3B	HR	(Hm	Rd)	TB	R	RBI	RC	TBB	IBB	SO	HBP	SH	SF	SB	CS	GDP	Avg	OBP	Slg	OPS
2015 RdRck*	AAA	69	247	60	10	0	6	(-	-)	88	28	33	30	24	0	62	3	1	2	0	0	8	.243	.315	.356	.671
2009 Cle	AL	45	111	16	2	0	3	(0	3)	27	12	7	3	17	0	36	0	1	1	1	1	3	.144	.256	.243	.499
2010 Cle	AL	28	58	11	5	0	1	(1	0)	19	6	8	5	8	0	22	0	1	0	0	0	1	.190	.288	.328	.615
2011 Sea	AL	24	59	12	1	0	1	(0	1)	16	6	6	5	10	0	13	0	0	1	0	1	1	.203	.314	.271	.585
2012 TB	AL	42	100	26	4	0	1	(0	1)	33	10	9	10	8	0	24	0	1	0	0	0	4	.260	.315	.330	.645
2013 TB	AL	4	3	1	0	0	0	(0	0)	2	0	0	0	1	0	1	0	0	0	0	0	0	.333	.500	.667	1.167
2014 2 Tms	AL	42	116	28	10	0	0	(0	0)	38	13	11	12	12	1	29	0	0	0	0	1	3	.241	.313	.328	.640
2015 Tex	AL	36	98	25	6	1	5	(3	2)	48	19	14	15	10	0	19	1	4	0	2	0	2	.255	.330	.490	.820
14 Tex	AL	34	107	28	10	0	0	(0	0)	38	13	11	12	11	1	26	0	0	0	0	1	3	.262	.331	.355	.686
14 Cle	AL	8	9	0	0	0	0	(0	0)	0	0	0	0	1	0	3	0	0	0	0	0	0	.000	.100	.000	.100
7 ML YEARS		221	545	119	29	1	11	(4	7)	183	66	55	50	66	1	144	1	7	2	3	3	15	.218	.303	.336	.639

Mychal Givens

Pitches: R **Bats:** R **Pos:** RP-22   michael   **Ht:** 6'0" **Wt:** 210 **Born:** 5/13/1990 **Age:** 26

Year Team	Lg	G	GS	CG	GF	IP	BFP	H	R	ER	HR	SH	SF	HB	TBB	IBB	SO	WP	Bk	W	L	Pct	Sh	Sv-Op	Hld	ERC	ERA
2013 Dlmrva	A	28	0	0	12	42.2	179	34	20	20	1	1	1	3	19	0	36	11	1	2	3	.400	0	3- -	-	2.92	4.22
2014 Frdrck	A+	18	0	0	6	33.1	141	21	20	12	2	1	1	2	16	0	27	4	3	1	2	.333	0	3- -	-	2.31	3.24
2014 Bowie	AA	18	0	0	8	25.1	122	19	12	11	0	2	0	6	23	0	28	9	0	0	0	-	0	0- -	-	4.68	3.91
2015 Bowie	AA	35	0	0	20	57.1	227	38	14	11	1	1	2	3	16	0	79	9	0	4	2	.667	0	15- -	-	1.64	1.73
2015 Bal	AL	22	0	0	5	30.0	117	20	7	6	1	1	1	1	6	0	38	0	0	2	0	1.000	0	0-0	4	1.49	1.80

Zack Godley

Pitches: R Bats: R Pos: SP-6; RP-3 Ht: 6'3" Wt: 245 Born: 4/21/1990 Age: 26

Year	Team	Lg	G	GS	CG	GF	IP	BFP	H	R	ER	HR	SH	SF	HB	TBB	IBB	SO	WP	Bk	W	L	Pct	Sh	Sv-Op	Hld	ERC	ERA
2013	2 Tms	Low	14	0	0	0	26.2	104	22	7	6	0	1	1	0	5	0	28	6	0	2	0	1.000	0	0- -	-	1.84	2.03
2014	2 Tms	Low	40	0	0	30	55.1	241	49	24	19	3	3	1	2	24	1	77	7	0	4	3	.571	0	15- -	-	3.29	3.09
2015	Visalia	A+	14	12	0	0	75.1	306	64	26	19	3	3	0	3	19	0	78	2	0	8	3	.727	0	0- -	-	2.50	2.27
2015	Mobile	AA	7	5	0	1	24.1	100	21	12	11	2	1	0	3	10	0	12	0	0	2	1	.667	0	0- -	-	3.92	4.07
2015	Ari	NL	9	6	0	1	36.2	150	29	13	13	4	1	1	3	17	1	34	2	0	5	1	.833	0	0-0	0	3.67	3.19

Erik Goeddel

Pitches: R Bats: R Pos: RP-35 gah-DELL Ht: 6'3" Wt: 190 Born: 12/20/1988 Age: 27

Year	Team	Lg	G	GS	CG	GF	IP	BFP	H	R	ER	HR	SH	SF	HB	TBB	IBB	SO	WP	Bk	W	L	Pct	Sh	Sv-Op	Hld	ERC	ERA
2011	2 Tms	Low	18	16	0	1	77.2	315	63	30	28	5	2	1	1	24	2	69	5	0	3	5	.375	0	0- -	-	2.53	3.24
2012	Stluci	A+	22	20	0	1	108.1	467	110	51	41	4	4	1	1	43	0	98	13	0	5	6	.455	0	0- -	-	3.75	3.41
2013	Bnghtn	AA	25	25	0	0	134.0	585	135	72	65	14	5	5	7	58	1	125	10	1	9	7	.563	0	0- -	-	4.51	4.37
2014	LsVgs	AAA	49	0	0	17	63.2	296	77	41	38	6	1	4	1	30	0	64	6	0	3	2	.600	0	0- -	-	5.53	5.37
2015	Stluci	A+	5	0	0	0	4.2	23	6	4	4	0	1	1	0	3	0	5	1	0	0	0	-	0	0- -	-	5.77	7.71
2015	Bnghtn	AA	6	0	0	1	6.0	27	7	2	2	0	0	0	0	3	0	6	0	0	0	0	-	0	0- -	-	4.72	3.00
2014	NYM	NL	6	0	0	5	6.2	26	3	2	2	0	0	0	0	4	1	6	1	0	0	0	-	0	0-0	0	1.37	2.70
2015	NYM	NL	35	0	0	9	33.1	132	24	9	9	1	0	3	2	9	2	34	2	0	1	1	.500	0	0-0	2	1.89	2.43
	2 ML YEARS		41	0	0	14	40.0	158	27	11	11	1	0	3	2	13	3	40	3	0	1	1	.500	0	0-0	2	1.79	2.48

David Goforth

Pitches: R Bats: R Pos: RP-20 Ht: 5'10" Wt: 205 Born: 10/11/1988 Age: 27

Year	Team	Lg	G	GS	CG	GF	IP	BFP	H	R	ER	HR	SH	SF	HB	TBB	IBB	SO	WP	Bk	W	L	Pct	Sh	Sv-Op	Hld	ERC	ERA
2011	Helena	R+	19	0	0	9	40.2	173	44	25	20	5	3	0	1	10	0	42	3	2	0	4	.000	0	2- -	-	4.19	4.43
2012	Wisc	A	28	28	0	0	150.2	651	154	91	78	16	3	3	9	63	0	93	11	8	10	8	.556	0	0- -	-	4.65	4.66
2013	BrvdCt	A+	14	14	0	0	78.1	328	67	33	27	4	3	2	5	28	0	58	4	0	7	5	.583	0	0- -	-	3.05	3.10
2013	Hntsvl	AA	20	4	1	9	46.2	189	32	19	17	1	2	1	1	18	0	36	5	0	4	3	.571	1	5- -	-	1.98	3.28
2014	Hntsvl	AA	54	0	0	44	64.2	282	60	28	27	2	3	0	2	29	2	44	4	0	5	4	.556	0	27- -	-	3.40	3.76
2015	ColSpr	AAA	38	0	0	19	47.0	198	36	15	14	2	4	1	0	27	4	34	10	0	0	4	.000	0	4- -	-	2.97	2.68
2015	Mil	NL	20	0	0	9	24.2	111	32	13	11	4	2	2	0	8	2	24	2	0	1	0	1.000	0	0-0	0	5.87	4.01

Ryan Goins

GO-inns

Bats: L Throws: R Pos: 2B-66;SS-58;PR-3;3B-2;LF-2;RF-2;PH-1 Ht: 5'10" Wt: 185 Born: 2/13/1988 Age: 28

Year	Team	Lg	G	AB	H	2B	3B	HR	(Hm	Rd)	TB	R	RBI	RC	TBB	IBB	SO	HBP	SH	SF	SB	CS	GDP	Avg	OBP	Slg	OPS
2013	Tor	AL	34	119	30	5	0	2	(2	0)	41	11	8	11	2	0	28	0	0	0	0	0	1	.252	.264	.345	.609
2014	Tor	AL	67	181	34	6	3	1	(1	0)	49	14	15	7	5	0	42	0	6	1	0	1	4	.188	.209	.271	.479
2015	Tor	AL	128	376	94	16	4	5	(4	1)	133	52	45	48	39	0	83	1	7	5	2	1	12	.250	.318	.354	.672
	3 ML YEARS		229	676	158	27	7	8	(7	1)	223	77	68	66	46	0	153	1	13	6	2	2	17	.234	.281	.330	.611

Paul Goldschmidt

Bats: R Throws: R Pos: 1B-157;DH-2;PH-1 Ht: 6'3" Wt: 225 Born: 9/10/1987 Age: 28

Year	Team	Lg	G	AB	H	2B	3B	HR	(Hm	Rd)	TB	R	RBI	RC	TBB	IBB	SO	HBP	SH	SF	SB	CS	GDP	Avg	OBP	Slg	OPS
2011	Ari	NL	48	156	39	9	1	8	(2	6)	74	28	26	26	20	0	53	0	0	1	4	0	4	.250	.333	.474	.808
2012	Ari	NL	145	514	147	43	1	20	(10	10)	252	82	82	86	60	4	130	4	0	9	18	3	9	.286	.359	.490	.850
2013	Ari	NL	160	602	182	36	3	36	(17	19)	332	103	125	131	99	19	145	3	0	5	15	7	25	.302	.401	.551	.952
2014	Ari	NL	109	406	122	39	1	19	(10	9)	220	75	69	83	64	10	110	2	0	3	9	3	10	.300	.396	.542	.938
2015	Ari	NL	159	567	182	38	2	33	(13	20)	323	103	110	135	118	29	151	2	0	7	21	5	16	.321	.435	.570	1.005
	Postseason		4	16	7	0	0	2	(1	1)	13	4	6	5	2	0	5	1	0	0	1	0	0	.438	.526	.813	1.339
	5 ML YEARS		621	2245	672	165	8	116	(52	64)	1201	391	412	461	361	62	589	11	0	25	67	18	64	.299	.395	.535	.930

Brandon Gomes

Pitches: R Bats: R Pos: RP-63 GOHMS Ht: 5'11" Wt: 190 Born: 7/15/1984 Age: 31

Year	Team	Lg	G	GS	CG	GF	IP	BFP	H	R	ER	HR	SH	SF	HB	TBB	IBB	SO	WP	Bk	W	L	Pct	Sh	Sv-Op	Hld	ERC	ERA
2011	TB	AL	40	0	0	17	37.0	160	34	15	12	3	1	3	1	16	0	32	1	0	2	1	.667	0	0-0	5	3.69	2.92
2012	TB	AL	15	0	0	4	17.2	83	16	12	10	2	0	1	2	12	3	15	1	0	2	2	.500	0	0-0	0	4.76	5.09
2013	TB	AL	26	0	0	9	19.1	82	18	15	14	4	1	2	0	7	3	29	1	0	3	1	.750	0	0-0	4	3.94	6.52
2014	TB	AL	29	0	0	5	34.0	138	28	14	14	5	0	1	0	11	2	24	3	0	2	2	.500	0	0-0	4	3.07	3.71
2015	TB	AL	63	0	0	13	59.0	245	55	28	28	10	3	2	3	15	2	44	4	1	2	6	.250	0	1-3	16	3.75	4.27
	Postseason		3	0	0	0	2.1	10	1	2	2	1	0	0	0	2	0	3	0	0	0	0	-	0	0-0	0	4.86	7.71
	5 ML YEARS		173	0	0	48	167.0	709	151	84	78	24	5	9	6	61	10	144	10	1	11	12	.478	0	1-3	25	3.74	4.20

Jonny Gomes

Bats: R **Throws:** R **Pos:** LF-59;PH-38;RF-8;DH-5   GOHMS   **Ht:** 6'1" **Wt:** 230 **Born:** 11/22/1980 **Age:** 35

Year	Team	Lg	G	AB	H	2B	3B	HR	(Hm	Rd)	TB	R	RBI	RC	TBB	IBB	SO	HBP	SH	SF	SB	CS	GDP	Avg	OBP	Slg	OPS
2003	TB	AL	8	15	2	1	0	0	(0	0)	3	1	0	0	0	0	6	1	0	0	0	0	0	.133	.188	.200	.388
2004	TB	AL	5	14	1	0	0	0	(0	0)	1	0	1	0	1	0	6	0	0	0	0	0	0	.071	.133	.071	.205
2005	TB	AL	101	348	98	13	6	21	(11	10)	186	61	54	62	39	1	113	14	1	5	9	5	6	.282	.372	.534	.906
2006	TB	AL	117	385	83	21	1	20	(7	13)	166	53	59	53	61	2	116	6	0	9	1	5	10	.216	.325	.431	.757
2007	TB	AL	107	348	85	20	2	17	(10	7)	160	48	49	47	35	1	126	7	0	4	12	4	1	.244	.322	.460	.782
2008	TB	AL	77	154	28	5	1	8	(2	6)	59	23	21	18	15	1	46	7	0	1	8	1	1	.182	.282	.383	.666
2009	Cin	NL	98	281	75	17	0	20	(11	9)	152	39	51	47	26	2	85	5	0	2	3	1	8	.267	.338	.541	.879
2010	Cin	NL	148	511	136	24	3	18	(11	7)	220	77	86	83	39	3	123	12	0	9	5	3	4	.266	.327	.431	.758
2011	2 Tms	NL	120	311	65	12	1	14	(8	6)	121	41	43	36	48	1	105	8	0	5	7	3	2	.209	.325	.389	.714
2012	Oak	AL	99	279	73	10	0	18	(7	11)	137	46	47	54	44	2	104	8	1	1	3	1	2	.262	.377	.491	.868
2013	Bos	AL	116	312	77	17	0	13	(5	8)	133	49	52	54	43	3	89	6	0	5	1	0	6	.247	.344	.426	.771
2014	2 Tms	AL	112	273	64	8	0	6	(4	2)	90	28	37	36	35	2	88	6	0	7	0	0	6	.234	.327	.330	.657
2015	2 Tms		95	225	48	9	0	7	(6	1)	78	29	26	23	31	1	81	3	0	3	1	1	6	.213	.313	.347	.660
11	Cin	NL	77	218	46	8	0	11	(7	4)	87	30	31	28	38	1	74	5	0	4	5	3	1	.211	.336	.399	.735
11	Was	NL	43	93	19	4	1	3	(1	2)	34	11	12	8	10	0	31	3	0	1	2	0	1	.204	.299	.366	.665
14	Bos	AL	78	209	49	7	0	6	(4	2)	74	22	32	30	26	0	70	6	0	5	0	0	5	.234	.329	.354	.683
14	Oak	AL	34	64	15	1	0	0	(0	0)	16	6	5	6	9	2	18	0	0	2	0	0	1	.234	.320	.250	.570
15	Atl	NL	83	195	43	7	0	7	(6	1)	71	27	22	22	28	1	67	3	0	2	1	1	5	.221	.325	.364	.689
15	KC	AL	12	30	5	2	0	0	(0	0)	7	2	4	1	3	0	14	0	0	1	0	0	1	.167	.235	.233	.469
	Postseason		19	49	7	2	0	1	(0	1)	12	8	5	3	5	2	15	1	0	0	0	0	2	.143	.236	.245	.481
	13 ML YEARS		1203	3456	835	157	14	162	(82	80)	1506	495	526	513	417	19	1088	83	2	51	50	24	52	.242	.333	.436	.769

Yan Gomes

Bats: R **Throws:** R **Pos:** C-91;DH-4;PH-1   YAHN GOHMS   **Ht:** 6'2" **Wt:** 215 **Born:** 7/19/1987 **Age:** 28

Year	Team	Lg	G	AB	H	2B	3B	HR	(Hm	Rd)	TB	R	RBI	RC	TBB	IBB	SO	HBP	SH	SF	SB	CS	GDP	Avg	OBP	Slg	OPS
2012	Tor	AL	43	98	20	4	0	4	(3	1)	36	9	13	11	6	0	32	3	1	3	0	0	3	.204	.264	.367	.631
2013	Cle	AL	88	293	86	18	2	11	(6	5)	141	45	38	42	18	0	67	7	0	4	2	0	12	.294	.345	.481	.826
2014	Cle	AL	135	485	135	25	3	21	(9	12)	229	61	74	65	24	3	120	3	0	6	0	0	13	.278	.313	.472	.785
2015	Cle	AL	95	363	84	22	0	12	(5	7)	142	38	45	25	13	1	104	7	0	6	0	0	11	.231	.267	.391	.659
	Postseason		1	4	2	1	0	0	(0	0)	3	0	0	0	0	0	0	0	0	0	0	0	0	.500	.500	.750	1.250
	4 ML YEARS		361	1239	325	69	5	48	(23	25)	548	153	170	143	61	4	323	20	1	19	2	0	39	.262	.303	.442	.746

Carlos Gomez

Bats: R **Throws:** R **Pos:** CF-111;DH-2;PH-2;2B-1;PR-1   **Ht:** 6'3" **Wt:** 220 **Born:** 12/4/1985 **Age:** 30

Year	Team	Lg	G	AB	H	2B	3B	HR	(Hm	Rd)	TB	R	RBI	RC	TBB	IBB	SO	HBP	SH	SF	SB	CS	GDP	Avg	OBP	Slg	OPS
2007	NYM	NL	58	125	29	3	0	2	(1	1)	38	14	12	11	8	2	27	3	0	3	12	3	0	.232	.288	.304	.592
2008	Min	AL	153	577	149	24	7	7	(3	4)	208	79	59	66	25	0	142	7	3	2	33	11	7	.258	.296	.360	.657
2009	Min	AL	137	315	72	15	5	3	(1	2)	106	51	28	33	22	0	72	4	7	1	14	7	1	.229	.287	.337	.623
2010	Mil	NL	97	291	72	11	5	3	(3	2)	104	38	24	28	17	1	72	4	6	0	18	3	10	.247	.298	.357	.655
2011	Mil	NL	94	231	52	11	3	8	(4	4)	93	37	24	25	15	0	64	2	8	2	16	2	2	.225	.276	.403	.679
2012	Mil	NL	137	415	108	19	4	19	(11	8)	192	72	51	59	20	1	98	8	6	3	37	6	6	.260	.305	.463	.768
2013	Mil	NL	147	536	152	27	10	24	(15	9)	271	80	73	81	37	2	146	10	1	6	40	7	11	.284	.338	.506	.843
2014	Mil	NL	148	574	163	34	4	23	(13	10)	274	95	73	98	47	0	141	19	1	3	34	12	11	.284	.356	.477	.833
2015	2 Tms		115	435	111	29	1	12	(6	6)	178	61	56	63	31	1	101	7	3	1	17	9	5	.255	.314	.409	.724
15	Mil	NL	74	286	75	20	1	8	(6	2)	121	42	43	45	23	0	70	5	0	0	7	6	4	.262	.328	.423	.751
15	Hou	AL	41	149	36	9	0	4	(0	4)	57	19	13	18	8	1	31	2	3	1	10	3	1	.242	.288	.383	.670
	Postseason		9	18	5	0	0	1	(0	1)	8	4	2	2	1	0	4	2	2	0	2	1	0	.278	.381	.444	.825
	9 ML YEARS		1086	3499	908	173	37	103	(57	46)	1464	527	400	464	222	7	863	64	35	21	221	60	53	.260	.314	.418	.732

Hector Gomez

Bats: R **Throws:** R **Pos:** 2B-27;PH-23;3B-12;SS-8;PR-5;LF-1   **Ht:** 6'2" **Wt:** 195 **Born:** 3/5/1988 **Age:** 28

Year	Team	Lg	G	AB	H	2B	3B	HR	(Hm	Rd)	TB	R	RBI	RC	TBB	IBB	SO	HBP	SH	SF	SB	CS	GDP	Avg	OBP	Slg	OPS
2015	ElPaso*	AAA	29	106	38	11	4	3	(-	-)	66	16	22	25	7	2	17	1	0	1	2	0	3	.358	.400	.623	1.023
2011	Col	NL	2	6	2	0	0	0	(0	0)	2	1	0	1	1	1	2	0	0	0	0	0	0	.333	.429	.333	.762
2014	Mil	NL	15	20	3	1	0	0	(0	0)	4	2	1	1	1	0	9	0	0	0	0	0	0	.150	.190	.200	.390
2015	Mil	NL	66	127	23	11	2	1	(1	0)	41	15	7	9	3	0	40	2	2	0	0	0	1	.181	.212	.323	.535
	3 ML YEARS		83	153	28	12	2	1	(1	0)	47	18	8	10	5	1	51	2	2	0	0	0	1	.183	.219	.307	.526

Jeanmar Gomez

Pitches: R **Bats:** R **Pos:** RP-65   JENN-marr   **Ht:** 6'3" **Wt:** 220 **Born:** 2/10/1988 **Age:** 28

Year	Team	Lg	G	GS	CG	GF	IP	BFP	H	R	ER	HR	SH	SF	HB	TBB	IBB	SO	WP	Bk	W	L	Pct	Sh	Sv-Op	Hld	ERC	ERA
2010	Cle	AL	11	11	0	0	57.2	265	73	36	30	7	0	3	2	22	3	34	1	0	4	5	.444	0	0-0	0	5.75	4.68
2011	Cle	AL	11	10	0	0	58.1	259	73	31	29	6	0	2	1	15	1	31	2	0	5	3	.625	0	0-0	0	4.99	4.47
2012	Cle	AL	20	17	0	1	90.2	395	95	66	60	15	2	7	4	34	5	47	2	0	5	8	.385	0	0-0	0	4.83	5.96
2013	Pit	NL	34	8	0	6	80.2	333	65	35	30	6	4	6	3	28	3	53	6	0	3	0	1.000	0	0-0	3	2.75	3.35
2014	Pit	NL	44	0	0	20	62.0	270	70	24	22	6	3	2	2	23	7	38	2	0	2	2	.500	0	1-1	2	4.70	3.19
2015	Phi	NL	65	0	0	21	74.2	319	82	28	25	4	1	4	2	17	4	50	3	0	2	3	.400	0	0-3	7	3.63	3.01
	Postseason		1	0	0	0	4.0	17	3	2	0	0	1	0	0	2	0	0	0	0	0	0	-	0	0-0	0	2.40	0.00
	6 ML YEARS		185	46	0	48	424.0	1841	458	220	196	44	10	24	14	139	23	253	16	0	21	21	.500	0	1-4	12	4.31	4.16

Marco Gonzales

Pitches: L Bats: L Pos: SP-1   Ht: 6'1" Wt: 195 Born: 2/16/1992 Age: 24

Year	Team	Lg	G	GS	CG	GF	IP	BFP	H	R	ER	HR	SH	SF	HB	TBB	IBB	SO	WP	Bk	W	L	Pct	Sh	Sv-Op	Hld	ERC	ERA
2013	2 Tms	Low	8	6	0	0	23.1	93	18	8	7	1	0	0	0	8	0	23	2	0	0	0	-	0	0- -	-	2.35	2.70
2014	PlmBh	A+	6	6	0	0	37.2	150	34	8	6	1	0	0	0	8	0	32	0	0	2	2	.500	0	0- -	-	2.44	1.43
2014	Sprgfld	AA	7	7	0	0	38.2	160	33	14	10	2	0	0	0	10	1	46	2	0	3	2	.600	0	0- -	-	2.37	2.33
2014	Memp	AAA	8	8	0	0	45.2	188	43	18	17	7	4	1	3	9	0	39	2	0	4	1	.800	0	0- -	-	3.58	3.35
2015	Memp	AAA	14	14	0	0	69.1	312	91	43	42	10	4	1	1	24	1	51	1	0	1	5	.167	0	0- -	-	6.17	5.45
2014	StL	NL	10	5	0	0	34.2	156	32	16	16	4	0	1	1	21	1	31	0	0	4	2	.667	0	0-0	1	4.59	4.15
2015	StL	NL	1	1	0	0	2.2	16	7	4	4	1	0	1	0	1	0	1	0	0	0	0	-	0	0-0	0	17.70	13.50
	Postseason		6	0	0	0	6.0	24	4	3	3	0	1	0	0	2	0	4	0	0	2	1	.667	0	0-1	1	1.57	4.50
	2 ML YEARS		11	6	0	0	37.1	172	39	20	20	5	0	2	1	22	1	32	0	0	4	2	.667	0	0-0	1	5.36	4.82

Adrian Gonzalez

Bats: L Throws: L Pos: 1B-149;PH-7;DH-3   Ht: 6'2" Wt: 220 Born: 5/8/1982 Age: 34

Year	Team	Lg	G	AB	H	2B	3B	HR	(Hm	Rd)	TB	R	RBI	RC	TBB	IBB	SO	HBP	SH	SF	SB	CS	GDP	Avg	OBP	Slg	OPS
2004	Tex	AL	16	42	10	3	0	1	(1	0)	16	7	7	7	2	0	6	0	0	0	0	0	0	.238	.273	.381	.654
2005	Tex	AL	43	150	34	7	1	6	(3	3)	61	17	17	13	10	2	37	0	0	2	0	0	3	.227	.272	.407	.678
2006	SD	NL	156	570	173	38	1	24	(10	14)	285	83	82	82	52	9	113	3	1	5	0	1	24	.304	.362	.500	.862
2007	SD	NL	161	646	182	46	3	30	(10	20)	324	101	100	108	65	9	140	3	0	6	0	0	6	.282	.347	.502	.849
2008	SD	NL	162	616	172	32	1	36	(14	22)	314	103	119	107	74	18	142	7	0	3	0	0	24	.279	.361	.510	.871
2009	SD	NL	160	552	153	27	2	40	(12	28)	304	90	99	109	119	22	109	5	1	4	1	1	23	.277	.407	.551	.958
2010	SD	NL	160	591	176	33	0	31	(11	20)	302	87	101	122	93	35	114	2	2	4	0	0	15	.298	.393	.511	.904
2011	Bos	AL	159	630	213	45	3	27	(10	17)	345	108	117	121	74	20	119	6	0	5	1	0	28	.338	.410	.548	.957
2012	2 Tms		159	629	188	47	1	18	(9	9)	291	75	108	113	42	5	110	5	0	8	2	0	10	.299	.344	.463	.806
2013	LAD	NL	157	583	171	34	0	22	(11	11)	269	69	100	89	47	6	98	1	0	10	1	0	12	.293	.342	.461	.803
2014	LAD	NL	159	591	163	41	0	27	(13	14)	285	83	116	95	56	9	112	2	0	11	1	1	13	.276	.335	.482	.817
2015	LAD	NL	156	571	157	33	0	28	(17	11)	274	76	90	84	62	10	107	6	0	3	0	1	21	.275	.350	.480	.830
12	Bos	AL	123	484	145	37	1	15	(8	7)	227	63	86	89	31	4	81	5	0	7	0	0	9	.300	.343	.469	.812
12	LAD	NL	36	145	43	10	1	3	(1	2)	64	12	22	24	11	1	29	0	0	1	2	0	1	.297	.344	.441	.785
	Postseason		18	68	20	2	0	4	(3	1)	34	10	10	7	7	1	12	0	0	0	0	0	1	.294	.360	.500	.860
	12 ML YEARS		1648	6171	1792	384	12	290	(121	169)	3070	899	1056	1050	696	145	1207	40	4	61	6	4	179	.290	.363	.497	.860

Carlos Gonzalez

Bats: L Throws: L Pos: RF-151;PH-3   Ht: 6'1" Wt: 220 Born: 10/17/1985 Age: 30

Year	Team	Lg	G	AB	H	2B	3B	HR	(Hm	Rd)	TB	R	RBI	RC	TBB	IBB	SO	HBP	SH	SF	SB	CS	GDP	Avg	OBP	Slg	OPS
2008	Oak	AL	85	302	73	22	1	4	(3	1)	109	31	26	30	13	1	81	0	1	0	4	1	7	.242	.273	.361	.634
2009	Col	NL	89	278	79	14	7	13	(7	6)	146	53	29	42	28	3	70	3	5	3	16	4	3	.284	.353	.525	.878
2010	Col	NL	145	587	197	34	9	34	(26	8)	351	111	117	116	40	8	135	2	0	7	26	8	9	.336	.376	.598	.974
2011	Col	NL	127	481	142	27	3	26	(16	10)	253	92	92	95	48	8	105	7	0	6	20	5	11	.295	.363	.526	.889
2012	Col	NL	135	518	157	31	5	22	(13	9)	264	89	85	88	56	11	115	2	0	3	20	5	11	.303	.371	.510	.881
2013	Col	NL	110	391	118	23	6	26	(12	14)	231	72	70	69	41	2	118	1	0	3	21	3	7	.302	.367	.591	.958
2014	Col	NL	70	260	62	15	1	11	(5	6)	112	35	38	32	19	2	70	1	0	1	3	0	7	.238	.292	.431	.723
2015	Col	NL	153	554	150	25	2	40	(24	16)	299	87	97	94	46	6	133	1	1	6	2	0	11	.271	.325	.540	.864
	Postseason		4	17	10	2	0	1	(1	0)	15	5	1	5	2	0	1	0	0	0	2	1	0	.588	.632	.882	1.514
	8 ML YEARS		914	3371	978	191	34	176	(106	70)	1765	570	554	568	291	41	827	17	7	29	112	26	66	.290	.347	.524	.870

Chi Chi Gonzalez

Pitches: R Bats: R Pos: SP-10; RP-4   Ht: 6'3" Wt: 210 Born: 1/15/1992 Age: 24

Year	Team	Lg	G	GS	CG	GF	IP	BFP	H	R	ER	HR	SH	SF	HB	TBB	IBB	SO	WP	Bk	W	L	Pct	Sh	Sv-Op	Hld	ERC	ERA
2013	2 Tms	Low	14	14	0	0	42.2	183	45	24	18	2	2	0	1	16	0	35	1	1	0	4	.000	0	0- -	-	4.06	3.80
2014	MrtlBh	A+	11	11	0	0	65.0	276	56	22	19	3	1	1	6	16	0	49	5	0	5	2	.714	0	0- -	-	2.66	2.63
2014	Frisco	AA	15	14	0	1	73.0	300	67	30	22	3	4	3	4	25	0	64	3	0	7	4	.636	0	0- -	-	3.21	2.71
2015	RdRck	AAA	16	16	0	0	88.1	377	95	40	35	3	1	2	4	31	0	56	1	1	8	7	.533	0	0- -	-	4.11	3.57
2015	Tex	AL	14	10	1	1	67.0	280	49	33	29	6	1	2	3	32	1	30	2	1	4	6	.400	1	0-0	0	3.00	3.90

Gio Gonzalez

Pitches: L Bats: R Pos: SP-31   Ht: 6'0" Wt: 210 Born: 9/19/1985 Age: 30

JEE-oh

Year	Team	Lg	G	GS	CG	GF	IP	BFP	H	R	ER	HR	SH	SF	HB	TBB	IBB	SO	WP	Bk	W	L	Pct	Sh	Sv-Op	Hld	ERC	ERA
2008	Oak	AL	10	7	0	3	34.0	163	32	34	29	9	2	1	3	25	1	34	1	0	1	4	.200	0	0-0	0	6.54	7.68
2009	Oak	AL	20	17	0	0	98.2	455	113	66	63	14	2	3	1	56	2	109	2	0	6	7	.462	0	0-0	0	5.96	5.75
2010	Oak	AL	33	33	1	0	200.2	851	171	75	72	15	5	2	4	92	1	171	4	1	15	9	.625	0	0-0	0	3.39	3.23
2011	Oak	AL	32	32	1	0	202.0	864	175	81	70	17	3	2	8	91	1	197	6	1	16	12	.571	0	0-0	0	3.56	3.12
2012	Was	NL	32	32	2	0	199.1	822	149	69	64	9	9	7	5	76	3	207	10	1	21	8	.724	1	0-0	0	2.37	2.89
2013	Was	NL	32	32	1	0	195.2	819	169	79	73	17	7	1	2	76	1	192	4	1	11	8	.579	1	0-0	0	3.23	3.36
2014	Was	NL	27	27	0	0	158.2	653	134	66	63	10	7	4	3	56	0	162	2	0	10	10	.500	0	0-0	0	2.91	3.57
2015	Was	NL	31	31	0	0	175.2	758	181	79	74	8	3	9	4	69	3	169	4	0	11	8	.579	0	0-0	0	3.92	3.79
	Postseason		3	3	0	0	14.0		10	7	5	0	0	1	0	12	0	11	2	0	0	0	-	0	0-0	0	3.46	3.21
	8 ML YEARS		217	211	4	3	1264.2	5385	1124	551	508	99	38	29	30	541	12	1241	33	4	91	66	.580	2	0-0	0	3.50	3.62

Marwin Gonzalez

MARR-win

Bats: B **Throws:** R **Pos:** 1B-43;SS-32;3B-21;PH-17;2B-15;LF-15;PR-6;DH-3 **Ht:** 6'1" **Wt:** 205 **Born:** 3/14/1989 **Age:** 27

									BATTING											RUNNING			AVERAGES			
Year Team	Lg	G	AB	H	2B	3B	HR	(Hm	Rd)	TB	R	RBI	RC	TBB	IBB	SO	HBP	SH	SF	SB	CS	GDP	Avg	OBP	Slg	OPS
2012 Hou	NL	80	205	48	13	0	2	(1	1)	67	21	12	12	13	0	29	0	1	0	3	3	9	.234	.280	.327	.607
2013 Hou	AL	72	204	45	8	0	4	(2	2)	65	22	14	10	9	0	37	0	8	1	6	2	5	.221	.252	.319	.571
2014 Hou	AL	103	285	79	15	1	6	(3	3)	114	33	23	26	17	0	58	4	4	0	2	4	6	.277	.327	.400	.727
2015 Hou	AL	120	344	96	18	1	12	(6	6)	152	44	34	39	16	0	74	3	7	0	4	5	9	.279	.317	.442	.759
4 ML YEARS		375	1038	268	54	2	24	(12	12)	398	120	83	87	55	0	198	7	20	1	15	14	29	.258	.300	.383	.683

Miguel Gonzalez

Pitches: R **Bats:** R **Pos:** SP-26 **Ht:** 6'1" **Wt:** 170 **Born:** 5/27/1984 **Age:** 32

			HOW MUCH HE PITCHED					WHAT HE GAVE UP											THE RESULTS						
Year Team	Lg	G	GS	CG	GF	IP	BFP	H	R	ER	HR	SH	SF	HB	TBB	IBB	SO	WP	Bk	W	L	Pct	Sh	Sv-Op	Hld	ERC	ERA
2012 Bal	AL	18	15	0	0	105.1	434	92	38	38	13	1	2	5	35	2	77	3	2	9	4	.692	0	0-0	0	3.49	3.25
2013 Bal	AL	30	28	0	1	171.1	712	157	81	72	24	3	6	3	53	3	120	4	0	11	8	.579	0	0-0	0	3.58	3.78
2014 Bal	AL	27	26	1	0	159.0	671	155	61	57	25	0	3	8	51	1	111	4	1	10	9	.526	1	0-0	0	4.25	3.23
2015 Bal	AL	26	26	0	0	144.2	622	151	81	79	24	2	2	8	51	2	109	4	0	9	12	.429	0	0-0	0	4.88	4.91
Postseason		2	2	0	0	12.2	52	9	3	2	0	1	0	2	4	1	12	1	0	0	1	.000	0	0-0	0	2.07	1.42
4 ML YEARS		101	95	1	1	580.1	2439	555	261	246	86	6	13	24	190	8	417	15	3	39	33	.542	1	0-0	0	4.06	3.82

Severino Gonzalez

Pitches: R **Bats:** R **Pos:** SP-7 **Ht:** 6'2" **Wt:** 155 **Born:** 9/28/1992 **Age:** 23

			HOW MUCH HE PITCHED					WHAT HE GAVE UP											THE RESULTS						
Year Team	Lg	G	GS	CG	GF	IP	BFP	H	R	ER	HR	SH	SF	HB	TBB	IBB	SO	WP	Bk	W	L	Pct	Sh	Sv-Op	Hld	ERC	ERA
2013 2 Tms	Low	24	13	0	1	97.0	380	76	27	21	5	2	4	3	22	1	113	2	1	6	5	.545	0	0- -	-	2.17	1.95
2014 Rdng	AA	27	27	0	0	158.2	675	169	89	81	23	2	3	9	34	0	115	3	1	9	13	.409	0	0- -	-	4.23	4.59
2015 LV	AAA	16	16	0	0	88.0	381	106	54	50	8	1	1	5	18	0	45	3	0	2	7	.222	0	0- -	-	4.66	5.11
2015 Phi	NL	7	7	0	0	30.2	143	44	27	27	5	1	4	4	7	0	28	0	1	3	3	.500	0	0-0	0	7.06	7.92

Nicholas Goody

Pitches: R **Bats:** R **Pos:** RP-7 **Ht:** 5'11" **Wt:** 195 **Born:** 7/6/1991 **Age:** 24

			HOW MUCH HE PITCHED					WHAT HE GAVE UP											THE RESULTS						
Year Team	Lg	G	GS	CG	GF	IP	BFP	H	R	ER	HR	SH	SF	HB	TBB	IBB	SO	WP	Bk	W	L	Pct	Sh	Sv-Op	Hld	ERC	ERA
2012 3 Tms	Low	23	0	0	18	32.0	123	20	4	4	0	0	0	1	9	0	52	1	0	1	2	.333	0	7- -	-	1.44	1.13
2014 Tampa	A+	12	4	0	0	15.1	62	10	4	4	1	1	0	1	5	0	27	1	0	2	0	1.000	0	0- -	-	2.01	2.35
2014 Trntn	AA	15	0	0	5	16.0	78	20	12	12	3	3	1	0	10	2	19	1	0	0	3	.000	0	0- -	-	6.83	6.75
2015 Trntn	AA	29	0	0	20	41.2	171	29	8	8	2	1	1	2	14	0	59	2	0	1	1	.500	0	4- -	-	2.07	1.73
2015 S-WB	AAA	14	0	0	8	20.2	82	14	4	3	0	2	0	0	7	0	25	3	0	1	1	.500	0	4- -	-	1.64	1.31
2015 NYY	AL	7	0	0	5	5.2	26	6	3	3	0	0	0	1	3	0	3	0	0	0	0	-	0	0-0	0	4.90	4.76

Alex Gordon

Bats: L **Throws:** R **Pos:** LF-101;DH-2;PH-1 **Ht:** 6'1" **Wt:** 220 **Born:** 2/10/1984 **Age:** 32

									BATTING											RUNNING			AVERAGES			
Year Team	Lg	G	AB	H	2B	3B	HR	(Hm	Rd)	TB	R	RBI	RC	TBB	IBB	SO	HBP	SH	SF	SB	CS	GDP	Avg	OBP	Slg	OPS
2007 KC	AL	151	543	134	36	4	15	(8	7)	223	60	60	69	41	4	137	13	1	2	14	4	12	.247	.314	.411	.725
2008 KC	AL	134	493	128	35	1	16	(9	7)	213	72	59	71	66	5	120	6	1	5	9	2	8	.260	.351	.432	.783
2009 KC	AL	49	164	38	6	0	6	(2	4)	62	28	22	16	21	0	43	2	1	1	5	0	5	.232	.324	.378	.703
2010 KC	AL	74	242	52	10	0	8	(5	3)	86	34	20	23	34	1	62	2	2	1	1	5	9	.215	.315	.355	.671
2011 KC	AL	151	611	185	45	4	23	(12	11)	307	101	87	103	67	2	139	7	0	3	17	8	9	.303	.376	.502	.879
2012 KC	AL	161	642	189	51	5	14	(8	7)	292	93	72	94	73	3	140	3	0	3	10	5	14	.294	.368	.455	.822
2013 KC	AL	156	633	168	27	6	20	(10	10)	267	90	81	90	52	7	141	9	0	6	11	3	4	.265	.327	.422	.749
2014 KC	AL	156	563	150	34	1	19	(11	8)	243	87	74	95	65	5	126	11	0	4	12	3	11	.266	.351	.432	.783
2015 KC	AL	104	354	96	18	0	13	(4	9)	153	40	48	60	49	7	92	14	0	5	2	5	2	.271	.377	.432	.809
Postseason		15	54	11	6	0	1	(0	1)	20	7	11	6	6	2	16	3	0	0	4	0	1	.204	.317	.370	.688
9 ML YEARS		1136	4245	1140	262	21	134	(67	67)	1846	605	523	621	468	34	1000	67	5	30	81	35	74	.269	.348	.435	.783

Dee Gordon

Bats: L **Throws:** R **Pos:** 2B-145;PH-1 **Ht:** 5'11" **Wt:** 170 **Born:** 4/22/1988 **Age:** 28

									BATTING											RUNNING			AVERAGES			
Year Team	Lg	G	AB	H	2B	3B	HR	(Hm	Rd)	TB	R	RBI	RC	TBB	IBB	SO	HBP	SH	SF	SB	CS	GDP	Avg	OBP	Slg	OPS
2011 LAD	NL	56	224	68	9	2	0	(0	0)	81	34	11	25	7	0	27	0	2	0	24	7	1	.304	.325	.362	.686
2012 LAD	NL	87	303	69	9	2	1	(0	1)	85	38	17	22	20	0	62	3	2	2	32	10	5	.228	.280	.281	.561
2013 LAD	NL	38	94	22	1	1	1	(0	1)	28	9	6	9	10	2	21	1	1	0	10	2	0	.234	.314	.298	.612
2014 LAD	NL	148	609	176	24	12	2	(2	0)	230	92	34	76	31	0	107	4	3	3	64	19	3	.289	.326	.378	.704
2015 Mia	NL	145	615	205	24	8	4	(2	2)	257	88	46	94	25	2	91	2	6	5	58	20	6	.333	.359	.418	.776
Postseason		6	17	3	0	0	0	(0	0)	3	0	2	0	2	0	6	0	0	0	1	1	0	.176	.263	.176	.440
5 ML YEARS		474	1845	540	67	25	8	(5	3)	681	261	114	226	93	4	308	10	14	10	188	58	15	.293	.328	.369	.698

Terrance Gore

Bats: R **Throws:** R **Pos:** PR-5;LF-4;DH-2;PH-1   **Ht:** 5'7" **Wt:** 165 **Born:** 6/8/1991 **Age:** 25

Year	Team	Lg	G	AB	H	2B	3B	HR	(Hm	Rd)	TB	R	RBI	RC	TBB	IBB	SO	HBP	SH	SF	SB	CS	GDP	Avg	OBP	Slg	OPS
2011	Royals	R	35	94	32	2	2	0	(-	-)	38	22	16	22	17	0	21	4	1	1	17	0	0	.340	.447	.404	.852
2012	Burlgtn	R+	61	227	58	4	2	0	(-	-)	66	50	13	36	36	0	52	9	4	0	36	2	2	.256	.379	.291	.669
2013	Lxngtn	A	128	455	98	6	3	0	(-	-)	110	76	24	54	62	0	120	19	5	0	68	8	3	.215	.334	.242	.576
2014	Wilmg	A+	89	252	55	8	1	0	(-	-)	65	34	15	24	20	0	66	4	9	2	36	4	4	.218	.284	.258	.542
2014	Omha	AAA	17	20	5	0	0	0	(-	-)	5	8	0	3	2	0	4	1	3	0	11	3	0	.250	.348	.250	.598
2015	NWArk	AA	85	222	63	4	1	0	(-	-)	69	42	16	35	26	0	50	3	8	0	39	2	0	.284	.367	.311	.677
2014	KC	AL	11	1	0	0	0	0	(0	0)	0	5	0	1	0	0	0	1	0	0	5	0	0	.000	.000	.000	.500
2015	KC	AL	9	3	0	0	0	0	(0	0)	0	1	0	0	0	0	1	1	0	0	3	0	0	.000	.250	.000	.250
	Postseason		6	0	0	0	0	0	(0	0)	0	2	0	0	0	0	0	0	0	0	3	0	0	-	-	-	-
	2 ML YEARS		20	4	0	0	0	0	(0	0)	0	6	0	1	0	0	1	2	0	0	8	0	0	.000	.333	.000	.333

Tom Gorzelanny

Pitches: L **Bats:** R **Pos:** RP-48   gore-zah-LAWN-ee   **Ht:** 6'2" **Wt:** 210 **Born:** 7/12/1982 **Age:** 33

Year	Team	Lg	G	GS	CG	GF	IP	BFP	H	R	ER	HR	SH	SF	HB	TBB	IBB	SO	WP	Bk	W	L	Pct	Sh	Sv-Op	Hld	ERC	ERA
2015	Toledo*	AAA	9	0	0	3	9.0	39	5	4	4	2	0	0	0	9	1	11	1	0	0	0	-	0	0--	-	4.81	4.00
2005	Pit	NL	3	1	0	0	6.0	32	10	8	8	1	1	0	0	3	0	3	0	0	0	1	.000	0	0-0	0	8.76	12.00
2006	Pit	NL	11	11	0	0	61.2	267	50	29	26	3	7	4	4	31	2	40	3	0	2	5	.286	0	0-0	0	3.23	3.79
2007	Pit	NL	32	32	1	0	201.2	874	214	90	87	18	3	9	11	68	3	135	5	1	14	10	.583	1	0-0	0	4.31	3.88
2008	Pit	NL	21	21	0	0	105.1	490	120	79	78	20	3	6	1	70	0	67	5	1	6	9	.400	0	0-0	0	6.86	6.66
2009	2 Tms	NL	22	7	0	2	47.0	204	45	30	29	6	3	3	1	17	0	47	1	0	7	3	.700	0	0-1	2	3.88	5.55
2010	ChC	NL	29	23	0	3	136.1	604	136	70	62	11	4	6	2	68	4	119	0	0	7	9	.438	0	1-1	1	4.30	4.09
2011	Was	NL	30	15	0	1	105.0	447	102	50	47	15	8	4	6	33	5	95	5	1	4	6	.400	0	0-1	4	4.03	4.03
2012	Was	NL	45	1	0	11	72.0	306	65	27	23	7	3	2	2	30	1	62	4	0	4	2	.667	0	1-1	9	3.68	2.88
2013	Mil	NL	43	10	0	4	85.1	356	77	41	37	11	1	2	2	31	1	83	2	0	3	6	.333	0	0-1	6	3.70	3.90
2014	Mil	NL	23	0	0	7	21.0	95	22	3	2	1	0	0	2	8	0	23	0	0	0	0	-	0	0-0	1	4.15	0.86
2015	Det	AL	48	0	0	14	39.1	181	45	28	26	4	2	0	2	23	2	36	1	0	2	2	.500	0	0-0	2	5.89	5.95
09	Pit	NL	9	0	0	2	8.2	36	6	5	5	0	1	0	0	4	0	7	0	0	3	1	.750	0	0-1	1	2.02	5.19
09	ChC	NL	13	7	0	0	38.1	168	39	25	24	6	2	3	1	13	0	40	1	0	4	2	.667	0	0-0	1	4.33	5.63
	Postseason		1	0	0	1	0.1	2	1	0	0	0	0	0	0	0	0	0	0	0	0	0	-	0	0-0	0	14.52	0.00
	11 ML YEARS		307	121	1	42	880.2	3856	886	455	425	97	35	36	33	382	18	710	26	3	49	53	.480	1	2-5	24	4.44	4.34

Anthony Gose

Bats: L **Throws:** L **Pos:** CF-137;PH-3;PR-2   GOASE   **Ht:** 6'1" **Wt:** 190 **Born:** 8/10/1990 **Age:** 25

Year	Team	Lg	G	AB	H	2B	3B	HR	(Hm	Rd)	TB	R	RBI	RC	TBB	IBB	SO	HBP	SH	SF	SB	CS	GDP	Avg	OBP	Slg	OPS
2012	Tor	AL	56	166	37	7	3	1	(0	1)	53	25	11	21	17	0	59	2	4	0	15	3	1	.223	.303	.319	.622
2013	Tor	AL	52	147	38	6	5	2	(2	0)	60	15	12	13	5	0	37	0	1	0	4	3	5	.259	.283	.408	.691
2014	Tor	AL	94	239	54	8	1	2	(2	0)	70	31	13	19	25	0	74	5	4	1	15	5	9	.226	.311	.293	.604
2015	Det	AL	140	485	123	24	8	5	(1	4)	178	73	26	45	45	0	145	3	2	0	23	11	11	.254	.321	.367	.688
	4 ML YEARS		342	1037	252	45	17	10	(5	5)	361	144	62	98	92	0	315	10	11	1	57	22	26	.243	.311	.348	.659

Tuffy Gosewisch

Bats: R **Throws:** R **Pos:** C-37;PH-1   GOES-uh-wish   **Ht:** 5'11" **Wt:** 200 **Born:** 8/17/1983 **Age:** 32

Year	Team	Lg	G	AB	H	2B	3B	HR	(Hm	Rd)	TB	R	RBI	RC	TBB	IBB	SO	HBP	SH	SF	SB	CS	GDP	Avg	OBP	Slg	OPS
2013	Ari	NL	14	45	8	2	0	0	(0	0)	10	1	3	0	0	0	8	0	1	1	0	0	3	.178	.174	.222	.396
2014	Ari	NL	41	129	29	8	0	1	(0	1)	40	6	7	5	3	0	24	0	0	0	0	0	6	.225	.242	.310	.553
2015	Ari	NL	38	128	27	6	0	1	(1	0)	36	9	13	8	8	0	23	1	0	1	2	1	2	.211	.261	.281	.542
	3 ML YEARS		93	302	64	16	0	2	(1	1)	86	16	23	13	11	0	55	1	1	2	2	1	11	.212	.241	.285	.525

Phil Gosselin

Bats: R **Throws:** R **Pos:** PH-21;2B-16;3B-7;LF-3;PR-1   GAHSS-eh-lin   **Ht:** 6'1" **Wt:** 200 **Born:** 10/3/1988 **Age:** 27

Year	Team	Lg	G	AB	H	2B	3B	HR	(Hm	Rd)	TB	R	RBI	RC	TBB	IBB	SO	HBP	SH	SF	SB	CS	GDP	Avg	OBP	Slg	OPS
2013	Atl	NL	4	6	2	0	0	0	(0	0)	2	2	0	1	1	1	2	0	0	0	0	0	0	.333	.429	.333	.762
2014	Atl	NL	46	128	34	4	0	1	(1	0)	41	17	3	10	5	0	27	2	1	0	2	2	1	.266	.304	.320	.624
2015	2 Tms	NL	44	106	33	9	1	3	(2	1)	53	19	15	22	9	0	16	2	0	1	2	1	2	.311	.373	.500	.873
15	Atl	NL	20	40	13	4	0	0	(0	0)	17	2	2	6	2	0	5	0	0	0	2	0	0	.325	.357	.425	.782
15	Ari	NL	24	66	20	5	1	3	(2	1)	36	17	13	16	7	0	11	2	0	1	0	1	2	.303	.382	.545	.927
	3 ML YEARS		94	240	69	13	1	4	(3	1)	96	38	18	33	15	1	45	4	1	1	4	3	3	.288	.338	.400	.738

Trevor Gott

Pitches: R **Bats:** R **Pos:** RP-48   **Ht:** 6'0" **Wt:** 190 **Born:** 8/26/1992 **Age:** 23

Year	Team	Lg	G	GS	CG	GF	IP	BFP	H	R	ER	HR	SH	SF	HB	TBB	IBB	SO	WP	Bk	W	L	Pct	Sh	Sv-Op	Hld	ERC	ERA
2013	2 Tms	Low	31	0	0	11	36.0	147	27	13	10	1	0	2	2	15	0	41	1	0	2	2	.500	0	4--	-	2.59	2.50
2014	Lk Els	A+	29	0	0	25	31.1	133	28	13	11	3	4	2	1	9	2	31	1	0	2	4	.333	0	16--	-	2.98	3.16
2014	SnAnt	AA	10	0	0	0	11.2	55	11	8	6	0	3	0	0	9	0	11	0	0	0	0	-	0	0--	-	4.30	4.63

Year	Team	Lg	G	GS	CG	GF	IP	BFP	H	R	ER	HR	SH	SF	HB	TBB	IBB	SO	WP	Bk	W	L	Pct	Sh	Sv-Op	Hld	ERC	ERA
2014	Ark	AA	13	0	0	8	17.2	68	11	3	3	1	0	1	0	7	0	18	1	0	2	1	.667	0	2- -	-	1.64	1.53
2015	Ark	AA	18	0	0	16	19.2	81	19	9	7	0	1	1	1	7	0	20	1	0	1	0	1.000	0	8- -	-	3.36	3.20
2015	Salt Lk	AAA	7	0	0	4	8.1	37	7	0	0	0	2	0	1	5	0	10	0	0	0	0	-	0	0- -	-	3.68	0.00
2015	LAA	AL	48	0	0	7	47.2	202	43	18	16	2	2	3	3	16	3	27	1	0	4	2	.667	0	0-4	14	3.03	3.02

Matt Grace

Pitches: L **Bats:** L **Pos:** RP-26   **Ht:** 6'3" **Wt:** 205 **Born:** 12/14/1988 **Age:** 27

			HOW MUCH HE PITCHED						WHAT HE GAVE UP												THE RESULTS							
Year	Team	Lg	G	GS	CG	GF	IP	BFP	H	R	ER	HR	SH	SF	HB	TBB	IBB	SO	WP	Bk	W	L	Pct	Sh	Sv-Op	Hld	ERC	ERA
2011	Hgrstn	A	26	25	0	0	132.1	591	169	92	76	8	2	6	6	38	0	85	11	0	12	7	.632	0	0- -	-	5.15	5.17
2012	Ptomc	A+	26	24	2	1	141.1	632	178	95	76	10	5	2	3	48	0	83	13	0	9	12	.429	1	0- -	-	5.25	4.84
2013	Ptomc	A+	14	0	0	2	28.1	120	26	11	10	0	3	1	3	7	0	24	2	0	3	0	1.000	0	0- -	-	2.74	3.18
2013	Hrsbrg	AA	28	0	0	4	38.0	158	42	17	16	2	1	1	1	7	1	31	3	0	6	3	.667	0	1- -	-	3.62	3.79
2014	Hrsbrg	AA	22	0	0	8	35.1	154	32	10	4	0	1	4	0	12	1	32	1	0	3	1	.750	0	3- -	-	2.49	1.02
2014	Syrcse	AAA	28	0	0	4	41.2	160	28	6	6	1	1	0	3	12	1	30	0	0	2	0	1.000	0	0- -	-	1.85	1.30
2015	Syrcse	AAA	38	0	0	10	48.2	198	43	16	13	1	7	2	0	16	0	31	0	0	0	2	.000	0	1- -	-	2.72	2.40
2015	Was	NL	26	0	0	5	17.0	84	26	11	8	0	0	2	1	8	2	14	1	0	2	1	.667	0	0-2	4	6.71	4.24

J.R. Graham

Pitches: R **Bats:** R **Pos:** RP-38; SP-1   **Ht:** 6'0" **Wt:** 210 **Born:** 1/14/1990 **Age:** 26

			HOW MUCH HE PITCHED						WHAT HE GAVE UP												THE RESULTS							
Year	Team	Lg	G	GS	CG	GF	IP	BFP	H	R	ER	HR	SH	SF	HB	TBB	IBB	SO	WP	Bk	W	L	Pct	Sh	Sv-Op	Hld	ERC	ERA
2011	Danvle	R+	13	8	0	3	57.2	227	52	15	11	0	1	0	1	13	0	52	4	1	5	2	.714	0	0- -	-	2.43	1.72
2012	Lynbrg	A+	17	17	1	0	102.2	398	88	34	30	6	4	2	2	17	0	68	2	0	9	1	.900	0	0- -	-	2.35	2.63
2012	Missi	AA	9	9	0	0	45.1	187	35	17	16	2	0	1	2	17	0	42	2	0	3	1	.750	0	0- -	-	2.57	3.18
2013	Missi	AA	8	8	0	0	35.2	150	39	16	16	0	1	1	0	10	1	28	1	0	1	3	.250	0	0- -	-	3.45	4.04
2014	Missi	AA	27	19	0	1	71.1	319	79	47	44	2	10	4	6	26	1	50	1	0	1	5	.167	0	0- -	-	4.29	5.55
2015	Min	AL	39	1	0	19	63.2	283	73	41	35	10	2	2	4	21	0	53	5	1	1	1	.500	0	0-1	0	5.31	4.95

Yasmani Grandal

Bats: B **Throws:** R **Pos:** C-107;PH-10;1B-6   yaz-MON-ee gran-DAHL   **Ht:** 6'1" **Wt:** 225 **Born:** 11/8/1988 **Age:** 27

			BATTING																			RUNNING			AVERAGES			
Year	Team	Lg	G	AB	H	2B	3B	HR	(Hm	Rd)	TB	R	RBI	RC	TBB	IBB	SO	HBP	SH	SF	SB	CS	GDP	Avg	OBP	Slg	OPS
2012	SD	NL	60	192	57	7	1	8	(3	5)	90	28	36	37	31	1	39	1	0	2	0	0	8	.297	.394	.469	.863
2013	SD	NL	28	88	19	8	1	0	(1	0)	30	13	9	12	18	2	18	1	0	1	0	0	1	.216	.352	.341	.693
2014	SD	NL	128	377	85	19	1	15	(7	8)	151	47	49	45	58	1	115	2	0	6	3	0	7	.225	.327	.401	.728
2015	LAD	NL	115	355	83	12	0	16	(8	8)	143	43	47	47	65	1	92	2	1	3	0	1	16	.234	.353	.403	.756
4 ML YEARS			331	1012	244	46	2	40	(19	21)	414	131	141	141	172	5	264	6	1	12	3	1	32	.241	.351	.409	.760

Curtis Granderson

Bats: L **Throws:** R **Pos:** RF-149;PH-13;CF-2;DH-1   **Ht:** 6'1" **Wt:** 200 **Born:** 3/16/1981 **Age:** 35

			BATTING																			RUNNING			AVERAGES			
Year	Team	Lg	G	AB	H	2B	3B	HR	(Hm	Rd)	TB	R	RBI	RC	TBB	IBB	SO	HBP	SH	SF	SB	CS	GDP	Avg	OBP	Slg	OPS
2004	Det	AL	9	25	6	1	1	0	(0	0)	9	2	0	2	3	0	8	0	0	0	0	0	1	.240	.321	.360	.681
2005	Det	AL	47	162	44	6	3	8	(5	3)	80	18	20	26	10	0	43	0	2	0	1	1	2	.272	.314	.494	.808
2006	Det	AL	159	596	155	31	9	19	(7	12)	261	90	68	89	66	0	174	4	7	6	8	5	4	.260	.335	.438	.773
2007	Det	AL	158	612	185	38	23	23	(10	13)	338	122	74	106	52	3	141	5	5	2	26	1	3	.302	.361	.552	.913
2008	Det	AL	141	553	155	26	13	22	(11	11)	273	112	66	100	71	1	111	3	1	1	12	4	7	.280	.365	.494	.858
2009	Det	AL	160	631	157	23	8	30	(10	20)	286	91	71	92	72	4	141	2	3	2	20	6	1	.249	.327	.453	.780
2010	NYY	AL	136	466	115	17	7	24	(10	14)	218	76	67	71	53	3	116	2	4	3	12	2	3	.247	.324	.468	.792
2011	NYY	AL	156	583	153	26	10	41	(21	20)	322	136	119	113	85	0	169	12	4	7	25	10	12	.262	.364	.552	.916
2012	NYY	AL	160	596	138	18	4	43	(26	17)	293	102	106	92	75	4	195	5	1	7	10	3	5	.232	.319	.492	.811
2013	NYY	AL	61	214	49	13	2	7	(2	5)	87	31	15	23	27	1	69	1	2	1	8	2	1	.229	.317	.407	.723
2014	NYM	NL	155	564	128	27	2	20	(7	13)	219	73	66	70	79	1	141	6	0	5	8	2	1	.227	.326	.388	.714
2015	NYM	NL	157	580	150	33	2	26	(12	14)	265	98	70	104	91	3	151	7	0	4	11	6	3	.259	.364	.457	.821
Postseason			36	131	30	6	3	6	(4	2)	60	16	17	22	20	1	38	1	1	1	5	1	2	.229	.333	.458	.791
12 ML YEARS			1499	5582	1435	259	84	263	(125	138)	2651	951	742	888	684	20	1459	47	29	38	141	42	43	.257	.341	.475	.816

Kendall Graveman

Pitches: R **Bats:** R **Pos:** SP-21   **Ht:** 6'2" **Wt:** 185 **Born:** 12/21/1990 **Age:** 25

			HOW MUCH HE PITCHED						WHAT HE GAVE UP												THE RESULTS							
Year	Team	Lg	G	GS	CG	GF	IP	BFP	H	R	ER	HR	SH	SF	HB	TBB	IBB	SO	WP	Bk	W	L	Pct	Sh	Sv-Op	Hld	ERC	ERA
2013	Lnsng	A	10	10	0	0	39.2	171	41	23	19	3	1	2	1	13	0	25	0	1	1	3	.250	0	0- -	-	3.89	4.31
2014	2 Tms	Low	20	20	0	0	123.0	488	100	31	25	1	4	3	4	24	0	89	2	0	10	4	.714	0	0- -	-	1.93	1.83
2014	Buffalo	AAA	6	6	0	0	38.1	145	34	8	8	1	1	0	0	5	0	22	0	0	3	2	.600	0	0- -	-	2.17	1.88
2014	Tor	AL	5	0	0	1	4.2	18	4	2	2	0	0	0	0	0	0	4	1	0	0	0	-	0	0-0	0	1.44	3.86
2015	Oak	AL	21	21	1	0	115.2	502	126	57	52	15	1	2	5	38	0	77	4	0	6	9	.400	0	0-0	0	4.72	4.05
2 ML YEARS			26	21	1	1	120.1	520	130	59	54	15	1	2	5	38	0	81	5	0	6	9	.400	0	0-0	0	4.56	4.04

Jonathan Gray

Pitches: R **Bats:** R **Pos:** SP-9 **Ht:** 6'4" **Wt:** 235 **Born:** 11/5/1991 **Age:** 24

Year Team	Lg	G	GS	CG	GF	IP	BFP	H	R	ER	HR	SH	SF	HB	TBB	IBB	SO	WP	Bk	W	L	Pct	Sh	Sv-Op	Hld	ERC	ERA
2013 2 Tms	Low	9	9	0	0	37.1	144	25	11	8	0	2	1	1	8	0	51	1	1	4	0	1.000	0	0--	-	1.41	1.93
2014 Tulsa	AA	24	24	0	0	124.1	508	107	58	54	10	6	5	4	41	0	113	5	0	10	5	.667	0	0--	-	3.10	3.91
2015 Albq	AAA	21	20	1	0	114.1	507	129	61	55	9	2	1	4	41	2	110	9	1	6	6	.500	0	0--	-	4.58	4.33
2015 Col	NL	9	9	0	0	40.2	185	52	26	25	4	2	4	2	14	2	40	3	0	0	2	.000	0	0-0	0	5.60	5.53

Sonny Gray

Pitches: R **Bats:** R **Pos:** SP-31 **Ht:** 5'11" **Wt:** 195 **Born:** 11/7/1989 **Age:** 26

Year Team	Lg	G	GS	CG	GF	IP	BFP	H	R	ER	HR	SH	SF	HB	TBB	IBB	SO	WP	Bk	W	L	Pct	Sh	Sv-Op	Hld	ERC	ERA
2013 Oak	AL	12	10	0	0	64.0	261	51	22	19	4	0	3	0	20	0	67	2	1	5	3	.625	0	0-0	0	2.42	2.67
2014 Oak	AL	33	33	2	0	219.0	899	187	84	75	15	8	5	7	74	2	183	15	0	14	10	.583	2	0-0	0	2.99	3.08
2015 Oak	AL	31	31	3	0	208.0	831	166	71	63	17	1	4	2	59	0	169	13	0	14	7	.667	2	0-0	0	2.53	2.73
Postseason		2	2	0	0	13.0	53	10	3	3	1	1	0	0	6	1	12	0	0	0	1	.000	0	0-0	0	2.87	2.08
3 ML YEARS		76	74	5	0	491.0	1991	404	177	157	36	9	12	9	153	2	419	30	1	33	20	.623	4	0-0	0	2.72	2.88

Grant Green

Bats: R **Throws:** R **Pos:** 2B-11;PR-6;1B-5;DH-2;SS-1;LF-1;PH-1 **Ht:** 6'3" **Wt:** 180 **Born:** 9/27/1987 **Age:** 28

Year Team	Lg	G	AB	H	2B	3B	HR	(Hm	Rd)	TB	R	RBI	RC	TBB	IBB	SO	HBP	SH	SF	SB	CS	GDP	Avg	OBP	Slg	OPS
2015 Salt Lk*	AAA	93	385	118	26	7	5	(-	-)	173	59	43	58	18	0	70	2	4	5	2	3	11	.306	.337	.449	.786
2013 2 Tms	AL	45	140	35	8	1	1	(1	0)	48	16	17	16	10	0	44	1	0	2	0	0	3	.250	.301	.343	.644
2014 LAA	AL	43	99	27	5	0	1	(1	0)	35	7	11	8	2	0	20	0	0	2	1	4	3	.273	.282	.354	.635
2015 LAA	AL	21	42	8	0	0	1	(0	1)	11	6	3	1	2	1	14	0	0	0	0	1	2	.190	.227	.262	.489
13 Oak	AL	5	15	0	0	0	0	(0	0)	0	0	1	0	0	0	6	0	0	1	0	0	0	.000	.000	.000	.000
13 LAA	AL	40	125	35	8	1	1	(1	0)	48	16	16	16	10	0	38	1	0	1	0	0	3	.280	.336	.384	.720
3 ML YEARS		109	281	70	13	1	3	(2	1)	94	29	31	25	14	1	78	1	0	4	1	5	8	.249	.283	.335	.618

Shane Greene

Pitches: R **Bats:** R **Pos:** SP-16; RP-2 **Ht:** 6'4" **Wt:** 210 **Born:** 11/17/1988 **Age:** 27

Year Team	Lg	G	GS	CG	GF	IP	BFP	H	R	ER	HR	SH	SF	HB	TBB	IBB	SO	WP	Bk	W	L	Pct	Sh	Sv-Op	Hld	ERC	ERA
2011 CtnSC	A	27	27	0	0	138.0	615	141	88	67	9	2	2	10	68	0	128	14	0	5	14	.263	0	0--	-	4.62	4.37
2012 Tampa	A+	24	23	0	0	112.0	505	113	80	65	5	2	4	10	63	0	101	9	1	4	7	.364	0	0--	-	4.75	5.22
2013 Tampa	A+	13	13	0	0	75.0	313	83	36	30	4	2	1	3	10	0	69	2	0	4	6	.400	0	0--	-	3.48	3.60
2013 Trntn	AA	14	13	1	1	79.1	349	92	35	28	6	2	2	7	20	0	68	1	2	8	4	.667	1	0--	-	4.57	3.18
2014 S-WB	AAA	15	13	0	0	66.1	297	79	39	34	3	1	2	0	26	1	57	3	1	5	2	.714	0	0--	-	4.70	4.61
2015 Toledo	AAA	7	7	0	0	35.0	152	37	15	15	2	0	2	3	11	0	21	1	0	1	1	.500	0	0--	-	4.10	3.86
2014 NYY	AL	15	14	0	0	78.2	345	81	38	33	8	0	1	6	29	0	51	1	0	5	4	.556	0	0-0	0	4.43	3.78
2015 Det	AL	18	16	0	1	83.2	373	103	67	64	13	2	4	6	27	4	50	1	0	4	8	.333	0	0-0	0	5.83	6.88
2 ML YEARS		33	30	0	1	162.1	718	184	105	97	21	2	5	12	56	4	131	2	0	9	12	.429	0	0-0	0	5.13	5.38

Nick Greenwood

Pitches: L **Bats:** R **Pos:** RP-1 **Ht:** 6'1" **Wt:** 180 **Born:** 9/28/1987 **Age:** 28

Year Team	Lg	G	GS	CG	GF	IP	BFP	H	R	ER	HR	SH	SF	HB	TBB	IBB	SO	WP	Bk	W	L	Pct	Sh	Sv-Op	Hld	ERC	ERA
2011 Sprgfld	AA	59	0	0	15	77.1	330	79	42	37	9	6	1	5	21	0	52	5	0	2	4	.333	0	2--	-	4.06	4.31
2012 Memp	AAA	49	4	0	12	77.2	336	87	43	38	6	2	4	5	23	2	47	5	0	4	3	.571	0	0--	-	4.45	4.40
2013 Memp	AAA	22	7	0	4	54.1	242	65	39	34	9	6	3	1	19	4	24	2	0	2	8	.200	0	0--	-	5.46	5.63
2013 Sprgfld	AA	11	7	1	1	40.2	182	50	25	18	3	2	1	2	11	1	22	2	0	3	4	.429	0	0--	-	4.79	3.98
2014 Memp	AAA	27	5	0	5	50.2	201	42	18	17	4	5	1	2	10	0	37	5	0	4	4	.500	0	0--	-	2.47	3.02
2015 Memp	AAA	32	22	0	3	129.0	568	166	88	83	16	3	5	5	25	1	60	6	1	13	6	.684	0	0--	-	5.24	5.79
2014 StL	NL	19	1	0	8	36.0	145	36	19	19	5	0	0	1	5	1	17	0	0	2	1	.667	0	0-0	1	3.44	4.75
2015 StL	NL	1	0	0	1	0.0	2	2	2	2	1	0	0	0	0	0	0	0	0	0	1	.000	0	0-1	-	-	-
2 ML YEARS		20	1	0	9	36.0	147	38	21	21	6	0	0	1	5	1	17	0	0	2	2	.500	0	0-1	1	3.92	5.25

Luke Gregerson

Pitches: R **Bats:** L **Pos:** RP-64 **Ht:** 6'3" **Wt:** 200 **Born:** 5/14/1984 **Age:** 32

Year Team	Lg	G	GS	CG	GF	IP	BFP	H	R	ER	HR	SH	SF	HB	TBB	IBB	SO	WP	Bk	W	L	Pct	Sh	Sv-Op	Hld	ERC	ERA
2009 SD	NL	72	0	0	7	75.0	318	62	29	27	3	3	1	3	31	9	93	4	0	2	4	.333	0	1-7	27	2.72	3.24
2010 SD	NL	80	0	0	9	78.1	297	47	30	28	8	1	1	1	18	2	89	0	0	4	7	.364	0	2-7	40	1.56	3.22
2011 SD	NL	61	0	0	11	55.2	241	57	23	17	2	5	1	2	19	3	34	2	0	3	3	.500	0	0-4	16	3.55	2.75
2012 SD	NL	77	0	0	15	71.2	294	57	19	19	7	5	0	3	21	3	72	3	0	2	0	1.000	0	9-13	24	2.64	2.39
2013 SD	NL	73	0	0	17	66.1	268	49	24	20	3	4	1	4	18	2	64	1	0	6	8	.429	0	4-9	25	2.07	2.71
2014 Oak	AL	72	0	0	17	72.1	284	58	20	17	6	3	1	1	15	3	59	6	0	5	5	.500	0	3-11	22	2.25	2.12
2015 Hou	AL	64	0	0	53	61.0	239	48	24	21	5	2	0	2	10	2	59	1	0	7	3	.700	0	31-36	3	2.09	3.10
Postseason		1	0	0	0	0.2	4	1	1	0	0	0	0	0	1	0	2	1	0	0	0	-	0	0-0	1	10.76	0.00
7 ML YEARS		499	0	0	129	480.1	1941	378	169	149	34	23	5	16	132	24	470	17	0	29	30	.492	0	50-87	154	2.36	2.79

Kevin Gregg

Pitches: R Bats: R Pos: RP-11   Ht: 6'6" Wt: 245 Born: 6/20/1978 Age: 38

			HOW MUCH HE PITCHED						WHAT HE GAVE UP										THE RESULTS						
Year	Team	Lg	G	GS	CG	GF	IP	BFP	H	R	ER	HR	SH	SF	HB	TBB	IBB	SO	WP	Bk	W	L	Pct	Sh	Sv-Op	Hld	ERC	ERA
2015	Tacom*	AAA	7	0	0	3	9.1	39	8	3	3	0	1	0	1	5	0	8	0	0	0	0	-	0	0- -	-	3.21	2.89
2003	LAA	AL	5	3	0	0	24.2	97	18	9	9	3	0	0	1	8	0	14	0	0	2	0	1.000	0	0-0	-	2.74	3.28
2004	LAA	AL	55	0	0	23	87.2	377	86	43	41	6	4	5	3	28	3	84	13	1	5	2	.714	0	1-2	3	3.47	4.21
2005	LAA	AL	33	2	0	9	64.1	290	70	37	36	8	1	1	3	29	2	52	5	0	1	2	.333	0	0-1	1	5.08	5.04
2006	LAA	AL	32	3	0	12	78.1	341	88	41	36	10	0	3	2	21	0	71	6	0	3	4	.429	0	0-0	-	4.51	4.14
2007	Fla	NL	74	0	0	55	84.0	355	63	34	33	7	3	0	6	40	1	87	6	0	0	5	.000	0	32-36	6	3.15	3.54
2008	Fla	NL	72	0	0	59	68.2	296	51	30	26	3	3	1	4	37	4	58	7	0	7	8	.467	0	29-38	4	2.90	3.41
2009	ChC	NL	72	0	0	51	68.2	298	60	38	36	13	0	3	3	30	2	71	7	0	5	6	.455	0	23-30	1	4.19	4.72
2010	Tor	AL	63	0	0	56	59.0	254	52	24	23	4	1	3	1	30	1	58	3	0	2	6	.250	0	37-43	3	3.66	3.51
2011	Bal	AL	63	0	0	48	59.2	275	58	35	29	7	4	1	2	40	4	53	2	0	0	3	.000	0	22-29	5	5.10	4.37
2012	Bal	AL	40	0	0	13	43.2	200	50	26	24	6	0	1	3	24	2	37	0	0	3	2	.600	0	0-0	-	6.15	4.95
2013	ChC	NL	62	0	0	52	62.0	269	53	26	24	6	4	1	1	32	2	56	1	0	2	6	.250	0	33-38	3	3.67	3.48
2014	Mia	NL	12	0	0	2	9.0	41	11	10	10	2	0	0	0	5	0	6	1	0	0	0	-	0	0-2	4	7.23	10.00
2015	Cin	NL	11	0	0	2	10.2	51	13	12	12	3	1	0	0	5	0	14	1	0	0	2	.000	0	0-1	-	6.78	10.13
	Postseason		2	0	0	0	4.0	18	4	0	0	0	0	0	0	2	0	3	1	0	0	0	-	0	0-0	-	3.63	0.00
	13 ML YEARS		594	8	0	382	720.1	3144	673	365	339	78	21	19	29	329	21	661	52	1	30	46	.395	0	177-220	24	4.07	4.24

Didi Gregorius

Bats: L Throws: R Pos: SS-155;PH-4;PR-1   dee-dee greh-GORE-ee-us   Ht: 6'2" Wt: 205 Born: 2/18/1990 Age: 26

						BATTING															RUNNING			AVERAGES			
Year	Team	Lg	G	AB	H	2B	3B	HR	(Hm	Rd)	TB	R	RBI	RC	TBB	IBB	SO	HBP	SH	SF	SB	CS	GDP	Avg	OBP	Slg	OPS
2012	Cin	NL	8	20	6	0	0	0	(0	0)	6	1	2	2	0	0	5	0	1	0	0	0	0	.300	.300	.300	.600
2013	Ari	NL	103	357	90	16	3	7	(3	4)	133	47	28	42	37	5	65	6	2	1	0	2	4	.252	.332	.373	.704
2014	Ari	NL	80	270	61	9	5	6	(3	3)	98	35	27	37	22	3	52	3	2	2	3	0	1	.226	.290	.363	.653
2015	NYY	AL	155	525	139	24	2	9	(6	3)	194	57	56	64	33	0	85	11	3	6	5	3	4	.265	.318	.370	.688
	4 ML YEARS		346	1172	296	49	10	22	(12	10)	431	140	113	145	92	8	207	20	8	9	8	5	9	.253	.316	.368	.683

Zack Greinke

Pitches: R Bats: R Pos: SP-32   GRAIN-key   Ht: 6'0" Wt: 195 Born: 10/21/1983 Age: 32

					HOW MUCH HE PITCHED							WHAT HE GAVE UP									THE RESULTS						
Year	Team	Lg	G	GS	CG	GF	IP	BFP	H	R	ER	HR	SH	SF	HB	TBB	IBB	SO	WP	Bk	W	L	Pct	Sh	Sv-Op	Hld	ERC	ERA
2004	KC	AL	24	24	0	0	145.0	599	143	64	64	26	3	2	8	26	3	100	1	1	8	11	.421	0	0-0	-	3.85	3.97
2005	KC	AL	33	33	2	0	183.0	829	233	125	118	23	4	4	13	53	0	114	4	2	5	17	.227	0	0-0	-	5.71	5.80
2006	KC	AL	3	0	0	1	6.1	28	7	3	3	1	0	0	0	3	2	5	0	0	1	0	1.000	0	0-0	-	4.93	4.26
2007	KC	AL	52	14	0	7	122.0	507	122	52	50	12	3	4	3	36	5	106	3	1	7	7	.500	0	1-1	12	3.77	3.69
2008	KC	AL	32	32	1	0	202.1	851	202	87	78	21	2	4	4	56	1	183	8	1	13	10	.565	0	0-0	-	3.68	3.47
2009	KC	AL	33	33	6	0	229.1	915	195	64	55	11	8	3	4	51	0	242	5	0	16	8	.667	3	0-0	-	2.39	2.16
2010	KC	AL	33	33	3	0	220.0	919	219	114	102	18	6	7	7	55	1	181	4	0	10	14	.417	0	0-0	-	3.48	4.17
2011	Mil	NL	28	28	0	0	171.2	715	161	82	73	19	6	1	4	45	0	201	10	0	16	6	.727	0	0-0	-	3.35	3.83
2012	2 Tms		34	34	0	0	212.1	868	200	84	82	18	7	2	2	54	0	200	8	0	15	5	.750	0	0-0	-	3.17	3.48
2013	LAD	NL	28	28	0	0	177.2	717	152	54	52	13	13	1	7	46	1	148	5	0	15	4	.789	1	0-0	-	2.78	2.63
2014	LAD	NL	32	32	0	0	202.1	821	190	69	61	19	2	4	2	43	3	207	12	0	17	8	.680	0	0-0	-	3.03	2.71
2015	LAD	NL	32	32	1	0	222.2	843	148	43	41	14	6	2	5	40	1	200	7	0	19	3	.864	0	0-0	-	1.56	1.66
12	Mil	NL	21	21	0	0	123.0	504	120	49	47	7	3	0	0	28	0	122	4	0	9	3	.750	0	0-0	-	3.02	3.44
12	LAA	AL	13	13	0	0	89.1	364	80	35	35	11	4	2	2	26	0	78	4	0	6	2	.750	0	0-0	-	3.38	3.53
	Postseason		7	7	0	0	44.2	182	39	21	18	4	1	0	2	8	0	37	1	0	2	2	.500	0	0-0	-	2.64	3.63
	12 ML YEARS		364	323	14	8	2094.2	8612	1972	841	779	195	60	34	59	508	17	1887	67	5	142	93	.604	4	1-1	12	3.22	3.35

Randal Grichuk

Bats: R Throws: R Pos: LF-49;CF-37;PH-19;RF-13;PR-2   GRICH-ick   Ht: 6'1" Wt: 195 Born: 8/13/1991 Age: 24

						BATTING															RUNNING			AVERAGES			
Year	Team	Lg	G	AB	H	2B	3B	HR	(Hm	Rd)	TB	R	RBI	RC	TBB	IBB	SO	HBP	SH	SF	SB	CS	GDP	Avg	OBP	Slg	OPS
2011	3 Tms	Low	53	199	51	12	7	3	(-	-)	86	27	25	25	8	0	46	4	0	5	0	1	2	.256	.292	.432	.724
2012	InldEm	A+	135	537	160	30	9	18	(-	-)	262	79	71	89	23	3	92	9	2	4	16	6	10	.298	.335	.488	.823
2013	Ark	AA	128	500	128	27	8	22	(-	-)	237	85	64	74	28	2	91	9	2	3	9	5	10	.256	.306	.474	.780
2014	Memp	AAA	108	436	113	23	2	25	(-	-)	215	73	71	67	28	2	108	6	0	2	8	5	13	.259	.311	.493	.805
2014	StL	NL	47	110	27	6	1	3	(2	1)	44	11	8	7	5	0	31	0	1	0	0	2	4	.245	.278	.400	.678
2015	StL	NL	103	323	89	23	7	17	(10	7)	177	49	47	47	22	2	110	4	0	1	4	2	6	.276	.329	.548	.877
	Postseason		9	35	6	0	0	2	(0	2)	12	3	3	2	1	0	13	0	0	0	0	0	0	.171	.194	.343	.537
	2 ML YEARS		150	433	116	29	8	20	(12	8)	221	60	55	54	27	2	141	4	1	1	4	4	10	.268	.316	.510	.827

A.J. Griffin

Pitches: R Bats: R Pos: P   Ht: 6'5" Wt: 230 Born: 1/28/1988 Age: 28

					HOW MUCH HE PITCHED							WHAT HE GAVE UP									THE RESULTS						
Year	Team	Lg	G	GS	CG	GF	IP	BFP	H	R	ER	HR	SH	SF	HB	TBB	IBB	SO	WP	Bk	W	L	Pct	Sh	Sv-Op	Hld	ERC	ERA
2011	2 Tms	Low	20	20	0	0	122.2	485	100	41	37	10	5	4	4	19	0	128	3	1	9	3	.750	0	0- -	-	2.21	2.71
2011	Mdlnd	AA	6	6	0	0	32.0	146	39	24	23	6	0	0	2	11	0	20	0	0	2	3	.400	0	0- -	-	6.00	6.47
2012	Mdlnd	AA	7	7	0	0	43.1	164	31	12	12	4	1	1	1	7	0	44	1	0	3	1	.750	0	0- -	-	1.85	2.49
2012	Scrmto	AAA	10	10	2	0	58.2	238	48	27	20	3	0	2	4	11	1	47	2	0	4	2	.667	0	0- -	-	2.23	3.07
2012	Oak	AL	15	15	0	0	82.1	336	74	29	28	10	0	2	1	19	0	64	0	0	7	1	.875	0	0-0	-	3.06	3.06
2013	Oak	AL	32	32	1	0	200.0	823	171	91	85	36	4	4	4	54	2	171	7	0	14	10	.583	1	0-0	-	3.33	3.83
	Postseason		1	1	0	0	5.0	21	7	2	2	1	0	0	0	0	0	3	0	0	0	0	-	0	0-0	-	5.60	3.60
	2 ML YEARS		47	47	1	0	282.1	1159	245	120	113	46	4	6	5	73	2	235	7	0	21	11	.656	1	0-0	-	3.25	3.60

Jason Grilli

Pitches: R **Bats:** R **Pos:** RP-36
GRILL-ee
Ht: 6'4" **Wt:** 230 **Born:** 11/11/1976 **Age:** 39

Year	Team	Lg	G	GS	CG	GF	IP	BFP	H	R	ER	HR	SH	SF	HB	TBB	IBB	SO	WP	Bk	W	L	Pct	Sh	Sv-Op	Hld	ERC	ERA
2000	Fla	NL	1	1	0	0	6.2	35	11	4	4	0	2	0	2	2	0	3	0	0	1	0	1.000	0	0-0	0	7.84	5.40
2001	Fla	NL	6	5	0	1	26.2	115	30	18	18	6	1	0	2	11	0	17	0	0	2	2	.500	0	0-0	0	6.44	6.08
2004	CWS	AL	8	8	1	0	45.0	203	52	38	37	11	2	1	3	20	0	26	2	0	2	3	.400	0	0-0	0	6.67	7.40
2005	Det	AL	3	2	0	0	16.0	63	14	6	6	1	1	1	0	6	0	5	0	0	1	1	.500	0	0-0	0	3.27	3.38
2006	Det	AL	51	0	0	18	62.0	270	61	31	29	6	2	4	5	25	3	31	5	0	2	3	.400	0	0-0	9	4.23	4.21
2007	Det	AL	57	0	0	13	79.2	352	81	46	42	5	1	5	5	32	1	62	5	0	5	3	.625	0	0-2	11	4.09	4.74
2008	2 Tms		60	0	0	16	75.0	323	67	27	25	2	1	3	2	38	7	69	4	0	3	3	.500	0	1-2	4	3.34	3.00
2009	2 Tms		52	0	0	11	45.2	212	50	27	27	4	2	1	1	27	2	49	2	0	2	3	.400	0	1-1	7	5.25	5.32
2011	Pit	NL	28	0	0	4	32.2	140	24	10	9	2	1	0	4	15	5	37	3	0	2	1	.667	0	1-1	9	2.79	2.48
2012	Pit	NL	64	0	0	11	58.2	244	45	20	19	7	2	1	2	22	4	90	0	0	1	6	.143	0	2-5	32	2.85	2.91
2013	Pit	NL	54	0	0	41	50.0	202	40	15	15	4	1	0	1	13	0	74	1	0	0	2	.000	0	33-35	2	2.44	2.70
2014	2 Tms		62	0	0	22	54.0	235	51	26	24	4	5	3	4	21	2	57	1	0	1	5	.167	0	12-17	12	3.73	4.00
2015	Atl	NL	36	0	0	29	33.2	140	28	13	11	2	0	1	0	10	1	45	2	0	3	4	.429	0	24-26	0	2.43	2.94
08	Det	AL	9	0	0	4	13.2	59	12	5	5	1	0	0	1	7	1	10	1	0	0	1	.000	0	0-1	0	3.85	3.29
08	Col	NL	51	0	0	12	61.1	264	55	22	20	1	1	3	1	31	6	59	3	0	3	2	.600	0	1-1	4	3.23	2.93
09	Col	NL	22	0	0	6	19.1	99	29	13	13	2	1	1	0	13	2	22	2	0	0	1	.000	0	1-1	3	8.02	6.05
09	Tex	AL	30	0	0	5	26.1	113	21	14	14	2	1	0	1	14	0	27	0	0	2	2	.500	0	0-0	4	3.44	4.78
14	Pit	NL	22	0	0	16	20.1	93	22	11	11	4	1	0	1	11	1	21	0	0	0	2	.000	0	11-15	1	5.99	4.87
14	LAA	AL	40	0	0	6	33.2	142	29	15	13	0	4	3	3	10	1	36	1	0	1	3	.250	0	1-2	11	2.53	3.48
	Postseason		11	0	0	4	8.1	33	4	0	0	0	0	0	0	4	1	7	0	0	0	0	-	0	1-1	1	1.21	0.00
13 ML YEARS			482	16	1	166	585.2	2534	554	281	266	54	21	20	31	242	25	565	25	0	25	36	.410	0	74-89	86	3.90	4.09

Justin Grimm

Pitches: R **Bats:** R **Pos:** RP-62
Ht: 6'3" **Wt:** 210 **Born:** 8/16/1988 **Age:** 27

Year	Team	Lg	G	GS	CG	GF	IP	BFP	H	R	ER	HR	SH	SF	HB	TBB	IBB	SO	WP	Bk	W	L	Pct	Sh	Sv-Op	Hld	ERC	ERA
2012	Tex	AL	5	2	0	3	14.0	65	22	14	14	1	0	2	0	3	0	13	3	0	1	1	.500	0	0-0	0	6.54	9.00
2013	2 Tms		27	17	0	3	98.0	442	120	70	65	15	4	2	2	34	1	76	4	0	7	9	.438	0	0-0	3	5.61	5.97
2014	ChC	NL	73	0	0	19	69.0	292	59	32	29	4	1	3	4	27	2	70	8	0	5	2	.714	0	0-1	11	3.14	3.78
2015	ChC	NL	62	0	0	11	49.2	204	31	18	11	4	0	3	1	26	1	67	8	0	3	5	.375	0	3-6	15	2.48	1.99
13	Tex	AL	17	17	0	0	89.0	406	116	67	63	15	2	2	1	31	1	68	4	0	7	7	.500	0	0-0	0	6.21	6.37
13	ChC	NL	10	0	0	3	9.0	36	4	3	2	0	2	0	1	3	0	8	0	0	0	2	.000	0	0-0	3	1.12	2.00
4 ML YEARS			167	19	0	36	230.2	1003	232	134	119	24	5	10	7	90	4	226	23	0	16	17	.485	0	3-7	29	4.17	4.64

Robbie Grossman

Bats: B **Throws:** L **Pos:** LF-17;PH-5;RF-4;PR-4;DH-2
Ht: 6'0" **Wt:** 205 **Born:** 9/16/1989 **Age:** 26

									BATTING											RUNNING			AVERAGES			
Year	Team	Lg	G	AB	H	2B	3B	HR	(Hm Rd)	TB	R	RBI	RC	TBB	IBB	SO	HBP	SH	SF	SB	CS	GDP	Avg	OBP	Slg	OPS
2015	Fresno*	AAA	93	347	88	16	1	5	(- -)	121	54	37	47	55	2	85	1	1	4	14	8	9	.254	.354	.349	.703
2013	Hou	AL	63	257	69	14	0	4	(3 1)	95	29	21	37	23	0	70	2	5	1	6	7	2	.268	.332	.370	.702
2014	Hou	AL	103	360	84	14	2	6	(2 4)	120	42	37	48	55	1	105	2	3	2	9	3	7	.233	.337	.333	.670
2015	Hou	AL	24	49	7	2	0	1	(1 0)	12	7	5	4	5	0	17	0	0	0	0	0	0	.143	.222	.245	.467
3 ML YEARS			190	666	160	30	2	11	(6 5)	227	78	63	89	83	1	192	4	8	3	15	10	9	.240	.327	.341	.668

Mayckol Guaipe

Pitches: R **Bats:** R **Pos:** RP-21
michael GOO-why-pay
Ht: 6'4" **Wt:** 235 **Born:** 8/11/1990 **Age:** 25

Year	Team	Lg	G	GS	CG	GF	IP	BFP	H	R	ER	HR	SH	SF	HB	TBB	IBB	SO	WP	Bk	W	L	Pct	Sh	Sv-Op	Hld	ERC	ERA
2011	Pulski	R+	14	14	0	0	64.0	286	66	37	26	2	0	2	12	20	0	49	7	1	5	6	.455	0	0--	-	4.09	3.66
2012	2 Tms	Low	13	13	0	0	70.1	299	73	37	28	5	3	4	8	17	0	40	4	0	5	0	1.000	0	0--	-	3.96	3.58
2013	Hi Dsrt	A+	35	3	0	18	59.0	261	59	39	37	5	1	2	8	29	0	57	3	0	3	4	.429	0	5--	-	4.99	5.64
2014	Jacksn	AA	40	0	0	32	56.0	226	45	20	18	4	3	2	3	9	0	56	1	0	1	3	.250	0	12--	-	2.15	2.89
2015	Tacom	AAA	38	0	0	19	47.0	194	49	17	15	3	1	1	1	10	0	36	2	0	0	4	.000	0	5--	-	3.48	2.87
2015	Sea	AL	21	0	0	2	26.2	121	34	19	16	5	1	1	3	13	1	22	1	0	0	3	.000	0	0-3	2	7.61	5.40

Deolis Guerra

Pitches: R **Bats:** R **Pos:** RP-10
day-OH-lis GAIR-uh
Ht: 6'5" **Wt:** 245 **Born:** 4/17/1989 **Age:** 27

Year	Team	Lg	G	GS	CG	GF	IP	BFP	H	R	ER	HR	SH	SF	HB	TBB	IBB	SO	WP	Bk	W	L	Pct	Sh	Sv-Op	Hld	ERC	ERA
2011	NwBrit	AA	37	10	0	5	95.0	414	102	67	59	11	4	5	4	28	0	95	11	0	8	7	.533	0	1--	-	4.31	5.59
2012	NwBrit	AA	7	0	0	2	12.2	44	5	1	1	0	0	0	1	1	0	15	2	0	2	0	1.000	0	1--	-	0.57	0.71
2012	Roch	AAA	29	0	0	7	57.1	245	59	33	31	7	2	0	2	21	1	56	5	0	2	3	.400	0	0--	-	4.45	4.87
2014	Roch	AAA	36	1	0	11	52.0	223	51	28	25	5	0	1	0	18	0	54	3	0	2	2	.500	0	0--	-	3.68	4.33
2015	Indy	AAA	25	0	0	9	36.2	137	21	6	5	1	0	2	0	8	1	37	3	0	2	1	.667	0	4--	-	1.16	1.23
2015	Pit	NL	10	0	0	4	16.2	74	26	12	12	5	0	0	1	3	0	17	2	0	2	0	1.000	0	0-0	0	8.96	6.48

Javy Guerra

Pitches: R Bats: R Pos: RP-3 | GEHR-uh | Ht: 6'1" Wt: 190 Born: 10/31/1985 Age: 30

		HOW MUCH HE PITCHED						WHAT HE GAVE UP										THE RESULTS						
Year Team	Lg	G	GS	CG	GF	IP	BFP	H	R	ER	HR	SH	SF	HB	TBB	IBB	SO	WP	Bk	W	L	Pct	Sh	Sv-Op	Hld	ERC	ERA
2011 LAD	NL	47	0	0	38	46.2	195	37	12	12	2	3	1	3	18	1	38	2	0	2	2	.500	0	21-23	-	2.73	2.31
2012 LAD	NL	45	0	0	17	45.0	196	44	13	13	1	4	2	1	23	5	37	1	0	2	3	.400	0	8-13	4	3.76	2.60
2013 LAD	NL	9	0	0	5	10.2	55	15	9	8	1	0	1	1	6	0	12	0	0	0	0	-	0	0-0	0	7.24	6.75
2014 CWS	AL	42	0	0	10	46.1	198	41	15	15	3	2	4	5	20	5	38	2	0	2	4	.333	0	1-6	7	3.60	2.91
2015 CWS	AL	3	0	0	0	1.2	7	2	0	0	0	0	0	0	1	0	0	0	0	0	0	-	0	0-0	1	5.91	0.00
5 ML YEARS		146	0	0	70	150.1	651	139	49	48	7	9	8	10	68	11	125	5	0	6	9	.400	0	30-42	12	3.63	2.87

Junior Guerra

Pitches: R Bats: R Pos: RP-3 | GAIR-uh | Ht: 6'0" Wt: 205 Born: 1/16/1985 Age: 31

		HOW MUCH HE PITCHED						WHAT HE GAVE UP										THE RESULTS						
Year Team	Lg	G	GS	CG	GF	IP	BFP	H	R	ER	HR	SH	SF	HB	TBB	IBB	SO	WP	Bk	W	L	Pct	Sh	Sv-Op	Hld	ERC	ERA
2015 Brham	AA	5	3	0	2	19.2	74	15	5	5	2	0	0	2	4	0	26	2	0	2	3	.400	0	0--	-	2.69	2.29
2015 Charllt	AAA	26	8	0	13	63.2	264	44	24	24	5	4	2	1	29	0	79	6	1	2	4	.333	0	7--	-	2.54	3.39
2015 CWS	AL	3	0	0	3	4.0	18	7	3	3	1	0	0	0	1	1	3	1	0	0	0	-	0	0-0	0	9.70	6.75

Alex Guerrero

Bats: R Throws: R Pos: PH-54;LF-29;3B-22;DH-4 | guh-RAIR-oh | Ht: 6'0" Wt: 215 Born: 11/20/1986 Age: 29

		BATTING																			RUNNING			AVERAGES			
Year Team	Lg	G	AB	H	2B	3B	HR	(Hm	Rd)	TB	R	RBI	RC	TBB	IBB	SO	HBP	SH	SF	SB	CS	GDP	Avg	OBP	Slg	OPS
2014 2 Tms	Low	12	42	15	5	1	2	(-	-)	28	9	8	11	5	0	7	1	0	2	0	0	0	.357	.420	.667	1.087
2014 Albq	AAA	65	243	80	14	5	15	(-	-)	149	38	49	52	10	0	44	4	0	1	4	0	2	.329	.364	.613	.978
2014 LAD	NL	11	13	1	0	0	0	(0	0)	1	0	0	0	0	0	6	0	0	0	0	0	0	.077	.077	.077	.154
2015 LAD	NL	106	219	51	9	1	11	(5	6)	95	25	36	25	7	0	57	2	0	2	1	0	7	.233	.261	.434	.695
2 ML YEARS		117	232	52	9	1	11	(5	6)	96	25	36	25	7	0	63	2	0	2	1	0	7	.224	.251	.414	.665

Preston Guilmet

Pitches: R Bats: R Pos: RP-5 | GILL-met | Ht: 6'2" Wt: 200 Born: 7/27/1987 Age: 28

		HOW MUCH HE PITCHED						WHAT HE GAVE UP										THE RESULTS						
Year Team	Lg	G	GS	CG	GF	IP	BFP	H	R	ER	HR	SH	SF	HB	TBB	IBB	SO	WP	Bk	W	L	Pct	Sh	Sv-Op	Hld	ERC	ERA
2015 Buffalo*	AAA	10	0	0	2	14.1	56	10	2	2	0	0	2	0	3	1	12	0	0	0	0	-	0	0--	-	1.34	1.26
2015 Drham*	AAA	13	0	0	6	15.0	65	14	4	4	1	0	0	0	6	0	16	0	0	0	0	-	0	3--	-	3.40	2.40
2015 ColSpr*	AAA	13	0	0	5	18.0	68	11	5	5	0	2	2	0	4	1	14	2	0	2	2	.500	0	1--	-	1.16	2.50
2013 Cle	AL	4	0	0	1	5.1	28	8	6	6	0	0	0	0	3	0	1	0	0	0	0	-	0	0-0	0	6.48	10.13
2014 Bal	AL	10	0	0	4	10.1	43	8	6	6	2	0	1	0	2	0	12	1	0	0	1	.000	0	0-0	1	2.47	5.23
2015 2 Tms		5	0	0	3	7.1	35	9	9	9	2	0	2	0	4	0	6	0	0	0	0	-	0	0-0	0	7.27	11.05
15 TB	AL	3	0	0	2	5.1	23	5	3	3	1	0	1	0	2	0	5	0	0	0	0	-	0	0-0	0	4.14	5.06
15 Mil	NL	2	0	0	1	2.0	12	4	6	6	1	0	1	0	2	0	1	0	0	0	0	-	0	0-0	0	17.51	27.00
3 ML YEARS		19	0	0	8	23.0	106	25	21	21	4	0	3	0	9	0	19	1	0	0	1	.000	0	0-0	1	4.80	8.22

Jason Gurka

Pitches: L Bats: L Pos: RP-9 | gurr-KAH | Ht: 6'0" Wt: 180 Born: 1/10/1988 Age: 28

		HOW MUCH HE PITCHED						WHAT HE GAVE UP										THE RESULTS						
Year Team	Lg	G	GS	CG	GF	IP	BFP	H	R	ER	HR	SH	SF	HB	TBB	IBB	SO	WP	Bk	W	L	Pct	Sh	Sv-Op	Hld	ERC	ERA
2011 2 Tms	Low	33	0	0	15	53.1	220	47	21	17	6	4	2	3	11	0	67	3	0	3	1	.750	0	1--	-	2.95	2.87
2012 Frdrck	A+	20	1	0	6	45.1	179	30	12	11	1	2	1	7	12	2	43	0	0	1	2	.333	0	1--	-	1.91	2.18
2012 Bowie	AA	12	0	0	5	20.0	94	19	8	8	3	1	1	4	12	0	22	0	0	2	3	.400	0	1--	-	5.73	3.60
2013 Bowie	AA	20	0	0	9	39.2	170	35	13	13	2	2	0	6	18	1	46	1	0	2	2	.500	0	4--	-	3.92	2.95
2014 Bowie	AA	30	3	0	5	64.0	260	50	21	17	4	3	1	2	18	0	60	2	0	3	1	.750	0	0--	-	2.35	2.39
2015 NwBrit	AA	14	0	0	0	23.1	91	17	6	6	0	1	0	1	6	0	20	2	1	3	0	1.000	0	0--	-	1.77	2.31
2015 Albq	AAA	21	1	0	6	39.2	167	42	14	14	3	1	1	3	12	1	33	1	0	2	1	.667	0	0--	-	4.25	3.18
2015 Col	NL	9	0	0	4	7.2	39	16	8	8	1	0	0	0	2	0	7	0	0	0	0	-	0	0-0	0	11.05	9.39

Jeremy Guthrie

Pitches: R Bats: R Pos: SP-24; RP-6 | | Ht: 6'1" Wt: 205 Born: 4/8/1979 Age: 37

		HOW MUCH HE PITCHED						WHAT HE GAVE UP										THE RESULTS						
Year Team	Lg	G	GS	CG	GF	IP	BFP	H	R	ER	HR	SH	SF	HB	TBB	IBB	SO	WP	Bk	W	L	Pct	Sh	Sv-Op	Hld	ERC	ERA
2004 Cle	AL	6	0	0	2	11.2	49	9	6	6	1	0	0	1	6	0	7	1	0	0	0	-	0	0-0	0	3.58	4.63
2005 Cle	AL	1	0	0	1	6.0	29	9	4	4	2	1	1	0	2	0	3	0	0	0	0	-	0	0-0	0	8.58	6.00
2006 Cle	AL	9	1	0	1	19.1	93	24	15	15	2	0	0	2	15	1	14	3	0	0	0	-	0	0-0	0	7.78	6.98
2007 Bal	AL	32	26	0	3	175.1	723	165	78	72	23	4	6	4	47	2	123	8	1	7	5	.583	0	0-1	0	3.55	3.70
2008 Bal	AL	30	30	1	0	190.2	796	176	82	77	24	2	2	7	58	2	120	3	0	10	12	.455	0	0-0	0	3.59	3.63
2009 Bal	AL	33	33	1	0	200.0	874	224	120	112	35	1	8	9	60	1	110	1	1	10	17	.370	0	0-0	0	5.08	5.04
2010 Bal	AL	32	32	0	0	209.1	872	193	93	89	25	3	9	16	50	1	119	1	1	11	14	.440	0	0-0	0	3.44	3.83
2011 Bal	AL	34	32	2	1	208.0	889	213	113	100	26	5	10	9	66	5	130	0	0	9	17	.346	0	0-0	0	4.21	4.33
2012 2 Tms		33	29	0	0	181.2	788	206	109	96	30	8	6	9	50	2	101	2	2	8	12	.400	0	0-1	0	5.03	4.76
2013 KC	AL	33	33	3	0	211.2	905	236	99	95	30	2	8	8	59	1	111	7	0	15	12	.556	2	0-0	0	4.76	4.04
2014 KC	AL	32	32	1	0	202.2	864	215	100	93	23	2	10	14	49	0	124	3	0	13	11	.542	0	0-0	0	4.18	4.13
2015 KC	AL	30	24	0	4	148.1	664	186	101	98	29	1	6	9	44	1	84	4	0	8	8	.500	0	0-0	0	6.16	5.95
12 Col	NL	19	15	0	0	90.2	422	122	72	64	21	5	3	7	31	2	45	1	1	3	9	.250	0	0-1	0	7.26	6.35
12 KC	AL	14	14	0	0	91.0	366	84	37	32	9	3	3	2	19	0	56	1	1	5	3	.625	0	0-0	0	3.06	3.16
Postseason		3	3	0	0	13.1	53	11	6	6	0	0	2	1	2	0	5	0	0	1	1	.500	0	0-0	0	1.93	4.05
12 ML YEARS		305	272	8	12	1764.2	7546	1856	920	857	250	33	66	88	506	16	1046	33	5	91	108	.457	2	0-2	0	4.42	4.37

Franklin Gutierrez

Bats: R **Throws:** R **Pos:** LF-42;PH-13;DH-6;RF-4;PR-1   **Ht:** 6'2" **Wt:** 200 **Born:** 2/21/1983 **Age:** 33

Year	Team	Lg					BATTING														RUNNING			AVERAGES			
			G	AB	H	2B	3B	HR	(Hm	Rd)	TB	R	RBI	RC	TBB	IBB	SO	HBP	SH	SF	SB	CS	GDP	Avg	OBP	Slg	OPS
2015	Tacom*	AAA	48	180	57	12	0	7	(-	-)	90	34	31	37	23	0	43	4	0	2	2	0	6	.317	.402	.500	.902
2005	Cle	AL	7	1	0	0	0	0	(0	0)	0	2	0	0	1	0	1	0	0	0	0	0	0	.000	.500	.000	.500
2006	Cle	AL	43	136	37	9	0	1	(1	0)	49	21	8	12	3	0	28	0	2	0	0	0	4	.272	.288	.360	.648
2007	Cle	AL	100	271	72	13	2	13	(10	3)	128	41	36	36	21	1	77	1	5	3	8	3	7	.266	.318	.472	.790
2008	Cle	AL	134	399	99	26	2	8	(6	2)	153	54	41	37	27	1	87	8	4	2	9	3	10	.248	.307	.383	.691
2009	Sea	AL	153	565	160	24	1	18	(7	11)	240	85	70	80	46	3	122	3	13	2	16	5	14	.283	.339	.425	.764
2010	Sea	AL	152	568	139	25	3	12	(6	6)	206	61	64	61	50	5	137	1	2	8	25	3	10	.245	.303	.363	.666
2011	Sea	AL	92	322	72	13	0	1	(0	1)	88	26	19	25	16	1	56	1	3	2	13	2	6	.224	.261	.273	.534
2012	Sea	AL	40	150	39	10	1	4	(2	2)	63	18	17	19	9	0	31	2	1	1	3	1	5	.260	.309	.420	.729
2013	Sea	AL	41	145	36	7	0	10	(6	4)	73	18	24	16	5	0	43	0	1	0	3	1	2	.248	.273	.503	.777
2015	Sea	AL	59	171	50	11	0	15	(6	9)	106	27	35	30	14	1	54	3	0	1	0	0	5	.292	.354	.620	.974
	Postseason		10	29	6	0	0	1	(0	1)	9	5	4	3	5	0	11	0	0	0	0	0	1	.207	.324	.310	.634
10 ML YEARS			821	2728	704	138	9	82	(44	38)	1106	353	314	316	192	12	635	19	31	19	77	18	63	.258	.309	.405	.715

Brandon Guyer

Bats: R **Throws:** R **Pos:** LF-60;PH-43;RF-41;CF-23;DH-5   GUY-er   **Ht:** 6'2" **Wt:** 200 **Born:** 1/28/1986 **Age:** 30

Year	Team	Lg					BATTING														RUNNING			AVERAGES			
			G	AB	H	2B	3B	HR	(Hm	Rd)	TB	R	RBI	RC	TBB	IBB	SO	HBP	SH	SF	SB	CS	GDP	Avg	OBP	Slg	OPS
2011	TB	AL	15	41	8	1	0	2	(1	1)	15	7	3	2	1	0	9	0	1	0	0	0	1	.195	.214	.366	.580
2012	TB	AL	3	7	1	0	0	1	(0	1)	4	2	1	0	0	0	1	0	0	0	0	0	0	.143	.143	.571	.714
2014	TB	AL	97	259	69	15	1	3	(1	2)	95	37	26	37	16	0	52	11	7	1	6	1	3	.266	.334	.367	.701
2015	TB	AL	128	332	88	21	2	8	(5	3)	137	51	28	51	25	0	61	24	3	1	10	4	5	.265	.359	.413	.771
4 ML YEARS			243	639	166	37	3	14	(7	7)	251	97	58	90	42	0	123	35	11	2	16	5	9	.260	.338	.393	.731

Jedd Gyorko

Bats: R **Throws:** R **Pos:** 2B-93;SS-29;PH-16;1B-1;DH-1   JERK-oh   **Ht:** 5'10" **Wt:** 205 **Born:** 9/23/1988 **Age:** 27

Year	Team	Lg					BATTING														RUNNING			AVERAGES			
			G	AB	H	2B	3B	HR	(Hm	Rd)	TB	R	RBI	RC	TBB	IBB	SO	HBP	SH	SF	SB	CS	GDP	Avg	OBP	Slg	OPS
2015	ElPaso*	AAA	16	61	17	1	0	4	(-	-)	30	8	9	10	7	0	11	1	0	0	0	1	3	.279	.362	.492	.854
2013	SD	NL	125	486	121	26	0	23	(13	10)	216	62	63	48	33	1	123	4	0	2	1	1	14	.249	.301	.444	.745
2014	SD	NL	111	400	84	17	1	10	(7	3)	133	37	51	42	36	1	100	4	0	3	3	2	8	.210	.280	.333	.612
2015	SD	NL	128	421	104	15	0	16	(9	7)	167	34	57	46	27	1	107	5	0	5	0	1	13	.247	.297	.397	.694
3 ML YEARS			364	1307	309	58	1	49	(29	20)	516	133	171	136	96	3	330	13	0	10	4	4	35	.236	.293	.395	.688

Nick Hagadone

Pitches: L **Bats:** L **Pos:** RP-36   HAGG-uh-donn   **Ht:** 6'5" **Wt:** 230 **Born:** 1/1/1986 **Age:** 30

Year	Team	Lg	HOW MUCH HE PITCHED						WHAT HE GAVE UP											THE RESULTS						
			G	GS	CG	GF	IP	BFP	H	R	ER	HR	SH	SF	HB	TBB	IBB	SO	WP	Bk	W	L	Pct	Sh	Sv-Op	Hld	ERC	ERA
2011	Cle	AL	9	0	0	3	11.0	42	4	6	5	0	0	1	1	6	0	11	2	0	1	0	1.000	0	0-0	0	1.35	4.09
2012	Cle	AL	27	0	0	10	25.1	116	26	18	18	4	0	2	0	15	0	26	2	0	1	0	1.000	0	1-2	2	5.37	6.39
2013	Cle	AL	36	0	0	6	31.1	133	24	21	19	4	2	1	0	21	1	30	3	0	1	0	1.000	0	0-1	0	4.08	5.46
2014	Cle	AL	35	0	0	4	23.1	91	18	7	7	3	1	0	0	6	2	27	0	0	1	0	1.000	0	0-0	3	2.46	2.70
2015	Cle	AL	36	0	0	6	27.1	124	30	16	13	3	1	1	0	12	1	28	2	0	0	1	.000	0	0-0	5	4.68	4.28
5 ML YEARS			143	0	0	24	118.1	506	102	68	62	14	4	5	1	60	4	122	9	0	3	2	.600	0	1-3	12	3.85	4.72

Matt Hague

Bats: R **Throws:** R **Pos:** PH-6;1B-3;3B-1;DH-1   HAIG   **Ht:** 6'3" **Wt:** 225 **Born:** 8/20/1985 **Age:** 30

Year	Team	Lg					BATTING														RUNNING			AVERAGES			
			G	AB	H	2B	3B	HR	(Hm	Rd)	TB	R	RBI	RC	TBB	IBB	SO	HBP	SH	SF	SB	CS	GDP	Avg	OBP	Slg	OPS
2015	Buffalo*	AAA	136	523	177	33	1	11	(-	-)	245	70	92	105	61	1	65	10	0	2	5	1	15	.338	.416	.468	.885
2012	Pit	NL	30	70	16	2	0	0	(0	0)	18	5	7	4	3	0	14	1	0	0	1	0	1	.229	.270	.257	.527
2014	Pit	NL	3	2	0	0	0	0	(0	0)	0	0	0	0	0	0	1	0	0	0	0	0	0	.000	.000	.000	.000
2015	Tor	AL	10	12	3	1	0	0	(0	0)	4	1	0	1	2	1	4	1	0	0	0	0	1	.250	.400	.333	.733
3 ML YEARS			43	84	19	3	0	0	(0	0)	22	6	7	5	5	1	19	2	0	0	1	0	2	.226	.286	.262	.548

Jesse Hahn

Pitches: R **Bats:** R **Pos:** SP-16   **Ht:** 6'5" **Wt:** 190 **Born:** 7/30/1989 **Age:** 26

Year	Team	Lg	HOW MUCH HE PITCHED						WHAT HE GAVE UP											THE RESULTS						
			G	GS	CG	GF	IP	BFP	H	R	ER	HR	SH	SF	HB	TBB	IBB	SO	WP	Bk	W	L	Pct	Sh	Sv-Op	Hld	ERC	ERA
2012	HudVal	A-	14	14	0	0	52.0	211	38	18	16	0	1	2	2	15	0	55	2	0	2	2	.500	0	0- -	-	1.78	2.77
2013	2 Tms	Low	20	20	0	0	69.0	286	59	21	16	1	1	1	3	18	0	67	8	0	2	1	.667	0	0- -	-	2.36	2.09
2014	SnAnt	AA	13	10	0	0	42.1	172	34	13	9	1	1	1	1	15	0	38	0	1	2	1	.667	0	0- -	-	2.49	1.91
2014	SD	NL	14	12	0	2	73.1	306	57	26	25	4	3	1	4	32	1	70	4	0	7	4	.636	0	0-0	0	2.91	3.07
2015	Oak	AL	16	16	1	0	96.2	406	88	46	36	5	1	2	8	25	1	64	7	0	6	6	.500	1	0-0	0	3.00	3.35
2 ML YEARS			30	28	1	2	170.0	712	145	72	61	9	4	3	12	57	2	134	11	0	13	10	.565	1	0-0	0	2.96	3.23

David Hale

Pitches: R Bats: R Pos: SP-12; RP-5   Ht: 6'2" Wt: 210 Born: 9/27/1987 Age: 28

		HOW MUCH HE PITCHED						WHAT HE GAVE UP										THE RESULTS							
Year Team	Lg	G	GS	CG	GF	IP	BFP	H	R	ER	HR	SH	SF	HB	TBB	IBB	SO	WP	Bk	W	L	Pct	Sh	Sv-Op	Hld	ERC	ERA
2015 Albq*	AAA	11	11	0	0	50.0	231	68	40	37	4	4	0	2	21	1	37	2	0	0	3	.000	0	0--	-	6.39	6.66
2013 Atl	NL	2	2	0	0	11.0	46	11	1	1	0	0	0	0	1	0	14	0	0	1	0	1.000	0	0-0	0	2.18	0.82
2014 Atl	NL	45	6	0	13	87.1	383	89	38	32	5	1	3	3	39	8	44	5	0	4	5	.444	0	0-0	4	4.05	3.30
2015 Col	NL	17	12	0	5	78.1	346	95	56	53	14	3	2	2	20	2	61	11	0	5	5	.500	0	0-0	0	5.33	6.09
Postseason		1	0	0	1	0.1	1	0	0	0	0	0	0	0	0	0	0	0	0	0	0	-	0	0-0	0	0.00	0.00
3 ML YEARS		64	20	0	13	176.2	775	195	95	86	19	4	5	5	60	10	119	16	0	10	10	.500	0	0-0	4	4.48	4.38

Cody Hall

Pitches: R Bats: R Pos: RP-7   Ht: 6'4" Wt: 220 Born: 1/6/1988 Age: 28

		HOW MUCH HE PITCHED						WHAT HE GAVE UP										THE RESULTS							
Year Team	Lg	G	GS	CG	GF	IP	BFP	H	R	ER	HR	SH	SF	HB	TBB	IBB	SO	WP	Bk	W	L	Pct	Sh	Sv-Op	Hld	ERC	ERA
2011 Slkzr	A-	23	0	0	20	27.1	125	21	8	8	1	2	0	4	19	1	42	5	0	3	1	.750	0	4--	-	3.87	2.63
2012 2 Tms	Low	45	0	0	35	47.2	205	48	13	10	0	2	0	5	16	2	64	1	0	4	1	.800	0	21--	-	3.52	1.89
2013 SnJos	A+	26	0	0	5	33.2	125	15	8	5	2	2	0	1	7	0	48	2	0	2	0	1.000	0	2--	-	0.96	1.34
2013 Rchmd	AA	20	0	0	15	26.1	105	17	8	7	4	1	0	2	8	0	27	1	0	2	2	.500	0	8--	-	2.46	2.39
2014 Rchmd	AA	47	0	0	28	51.2	204	42	18	18	3	3	0	0	14	1	57	1	1	1	4	.200	0	11--	-	2.38	3.14
2015 Scrmto	AAA	43	0	0	8	67.2	293	67	30	26	3	2	4	0	26	0	55	2	0	1	3	.250	0	3--	-	3.52	3.46
2015 SF	NL	7	0	0	1	8.1	41	10	6	6	1	0	0	1	4	0	7	0	0	0	0	-	0	0-0	0	5.92	6.48

Cole Hamels

Pitches: L Bats: L Pos: SP-32   Ht: 6'3" Wt: 200 Born: 12/27/1983 Age: 32

		HOW MUCH HE PITCHED						WHAT HE GAVE UP										THE RESULTS							
Year Team	Lg	G	GS	CG	GF	IP	BFP	H	R	ER	HR	SH	SF	HB	TBB	IBB	SO	WP	Bk	W	L	Pct	Sh	Sv-Op	Hld	ERC	ERA
2006 Phi	NL	23	23	0	0	132.1	558	117	66	60	19	6	8	3	48	4	145	5	0	9	8	.529	0	0-0	0	3.61	4.08
2007 Phi	NL	28	28	2	0	183.1	743	163	72	69	25	5	5	3	43	4	177	5	0	15	5	.750	0	0-0	0	3.12	3.39
2008 Phi	NL	33	33	2	0	227.1	914	193	89	78	28	6	2	1	53	7	196	0	0	14	10	.583	2	0-0	0	2.76	3.09
2009 Phi	NL	32	32	2	0	193.2	814	206	95	93	24	7	5	5	43	4	168	1	0	10	11	.476	2	0-0	0	3.98	4.32
2010 Phi	NL	33	33	1	0	208.2	856	185	74	71	26	7	0	8	61	5	211	3	0	12	11	.522	0	0-0	0	3.36	3.06
2011 Phi	NL	32	31	3	0	216.0	850	169	68	67	19	9	3	5	44	2	194	3	3	14	9	.609	0	0-0	0	2.23	2.79
2012 Phi	NL	31	31	2	0	215.1	867	190	80	73	24	6	4	3	52	3	216	3	2	17	6	.739	2	0-0	0	2.98	3.05
2013 Phi	NL	33	33	1	0	220.0	905	205	94	88	21	11	3	9	50	5	202	4	0	8	14	.364	0	0-0	0	3.15	3.60
2014 Phi	NL	30	30	0	0	204.2	829	176	60	56	14	7	7	8	59	3	198	6	1	9	9	.500	1	0-0	0	2.88	2.46
2015 2 Tms		32	32	2	0	212.1	880	190	88	86	22	6	2	10	62	3	215	9	4	13	8	.619	1	0-0	0	3.28	3.65
15 Phi	NL	20	20	1	0	128.2	537	113	53	52	12	5	1	6	39	3	137	7	2	6	7	.462	1	0-0	0	3.13	3.64
15 Tex	AL	12	12	1	0	83.2	343	77	35	34	10	1	1	4	23	0	78	2	2	7	1	.875	0	0-0	0	3.54	3.66
Postseason		13	13	1	0	81.2	326	65	29	28	9	3	2	2	21	1	77	0	0	7	4	.636	1	0-0	0	2.62	3.09
10 ML YEARS		307	306	15	0	2013.2	8216	1794	786	741	222	70	39	55	515	40	1922	39	10	121	91	.571	7	0-0	0	3.10	3.31

Billy Hamilton

Bats: B Throws: R Pos: CF-110;PH-2;PR-2   Ht: 6'0" Wt: 160 Born: 9/9/1990 Age: 25

							BATTING													RUNNING			AVERAGES			
Year Team	Lg	G	AB	H	2B	3B	HR	(Hm	Rd)	TB	R	RBI	RC	TBB	IBB	SO	HBP	SH	SF	SB	CS	GDP	Avg	OBP	Slg	OPS
2013 Cin	NL	13	19	7	2	0	0	(0	0)	9	9	1	5	2	0	4	0	1	0	13	1	0	.368	.429	.474	.902
2014 Cin	NL	152	563	141	25	8	6	(3	3)	200	72	48	64	34	0	117	1	9	4	56	23	1	.250	.292	.355	.648
2015 Cin	NL	114	412	93	8	3	4	(2	2)	119	56	28	32	28	0	75	1	9	4	57	8	5	.226	.274	.289	.563
3 ML YEARS		279	994	241	35	11	10	(5	5)	328	137	77	101	64	0	196	2	19	8	126	32	6	.242	.287	.330	.617

Josh Hamilton

Bats: L Throws: L Pos: LF-35;RF-11;PH-9;DH-1   Ht: 6'4" Wt: 240 Born: 5/21/1981 Age: 35

							BATTING													RUNNING			AVERAGES			
Year Team	Lg	G	AB	H	2B	3B	HR	(Hm	Rd)	TB	R	RBI	RC	TBB	IBB	SO	HBP	SH	SF	SB	CS	GDP	Avg	OBP	Slg	OPS
2015 RdRck*	AAA	11	37	10	3	0	0	(	)	13	1	5	3	1	1	10	0	0	0	0	0	0	.270	.289	.351	.641
2007 Cin	NL	90	298	87	17	2	19	(11	8)	165	52	47	58	33	4	65	4	0	2	3	3	6	.292	.368	.554	.922
2008 Tex	AL	156	624	190	35	5	32	(19	13)	331	98	130	119	64	9	126	7	0	9	9	1	8	.304	.371	.530	.901
2009 Tex	AL	89	336	90	19	2	10	(6	4)	143	43	54	51	24	2	79	1	0	4	8	3	5	.268	.315	.426	.741
2010 Tex	AL	133	518	186	40	3	32	(22	10)	328	95	100	121	43	5	95	5	1	4	8	1	11	.359	.411	.633	1.044
2011 Tex	AL	121	487	145	31	5	25	(14	11)	261	80	94	78	39	13	93	2	0	10	8	1	8	.298	.346	.536	.882
2012 Tex	AL	148	562	160	31	2	43	(22	21)	324	103	128	108	60	13	162	5	0	9	7	4	9	.285	.354	.577	.930
2013 LAA	AL	151	576	144	32	5	21	(9	12)	249	73	79	67	47	4	158	4	0	9	4	0	16	.250	.307	.432	.739
2014 LAA	AL	89	338	89	21	0	10	(0	10)	140	43	44	49	32	5	108	5	0	6	3	3	2	.263	.331	.414	.745
2015 Tex	AL	50	170	43	8	0	8	(7	1)	75	22	25	19	10	0	52	0	0	2	0	0	1	.253	.291	.441	.732
Postseason		37	145	30	8	0	6	(2	4)	56	18	23	17	14	7	25	0	0	3	4	1	5	.207	.272	.386	.658
9 ML YEARS		1027	3909	1134	234	24	200	(110	90)	2016	609	701	670	352	55	938	33	1	55	50	16	66	.290	.349	.516	.865

Jason Hammel

Pitches: R Bats: R Pos: SP-31   Ht: 6'6" Wt: 225 Born: 9/2/1982 Age: 33

		HOW MUCH HE PITCHED						WHAT HE GAVE UP										THE RESULTS							
Year Team	Lg	G	GS	CG	GF	IP	BFP	H	R	ER	HR	SH	SF	HB	TBB	IBB	SO	WP	Bk	W	L	Pct	Sh	Sv-Op	Hld	ERC	ERA
2006 TB	AL	9	9	0	0	44.0	208	61	38	38	7	0	3	1	21	0	32	3	2	0	6	.000	0	0-0	0	7.40	7.77
2007 TB	AL	24	14	0	2	85.0	384	100	58	58	12	2	0	2	40	1	64	3	0	3	5	.375	0	0-0	0	5.86	6.14
2008 TB	AL	40	5	0	21	78.1	346	83	45	40	11	2	2	2	35	4	44	7	0	4	4	.500	0	2-2	0	4.94	4.60
2009 Col	NL	34	30	1	0	176.2	771	203	94	85	17	10	9	9	42	6	133	4	0	10	8	.556	1	0-0	0	4.37	4.33

Year	Team	Lg	G	GS	CG	GF	IP	BFP	H	R	ER	HR	SH	SF	HB	TBB	IBB	SO	WP	Bk	W	L	Pct	Sh	Sv-Op	Hld	ERC	ERA
2010	Col	NL	30	30	0	0	177.2	770	201	97	95	18	11	6	6	47	1	141	13	2	10	9	.526	0	0-0	0	4.41	4.81
2011	Col	NL	32	27	0	2	170.1	739	175	100	90	21	11	6	6	68	3	94	8	1	7	13	.350	0	1-1	0	4.54	4.76
2012	Bal	AL	20	20	1	0	118.0	493	104	48	45	9	3	1	2	42	2	113	3	0	8	6	.571	1	0-0	0	3.14	3.43
2013	Bal	AL	26	23	0	1	139.1	611	155	81	77	22	2	8	8	48	1	96	1	0	7	8	.467	0	1-1	1	5.19	4.97
2014	2 Tms		30	29	0	1	176.1	715	154	70	68	23	3	4	8	44	2	158	6	0	10	11	.476	0	0-0	0	3.21	3.47
2015	ChC	NL	31	31	0	0	170.2	710	158	79	71	23	4	6	6	40	4	172	10	0	10	7	.588	0	0-0	0	3.32	3.74
14	ChC	NL	17	17	0	0	108.2	429	88	36	36	16	0	2	5	23	2	104	4	0	8	5	.615	0	0-0	0	2.51	2.98
14	Oak	AL	13	12	0	1	67.2	286	66	34	32	13	1	1	3	21	0	54	2	0	2	6	.250	0	0-0	0	4.42	4.26
	Postseason		4	3	0	1	15.0	63	13	8	8	1	0	0	0	9	2	16	0	0	0	1	.000	0	0-0	0	3.82	4.80
10 ML YEARS			276	218	2	27	1336.1	5747	1394	710	667	163	48	45	50	427	24	1047	58	5	69	77	.473	1	4-4	2	4.28	4.49

Brad Hand

Pitches: L **Bats:** L **Pos:** RP-26; SP-12 **Ht:** 6'3" **Wt:** 215 **Born:** 3/20/1990 **Age:** 26

Year	Team	Lg	G	GS	CG	GF	IP	BFP	H	R	ER	HR	SH	SF	HB	TBB	IBB	SO	WP	Bk	W	L	Pct	Sh	Sv-Op	Hld	ERC	ERA
2011	Fla	NL	12	12	0	0	60.0	263	53	32	28	10	4	3	1	35	1	38	0	1	1	8	.111	0	0-0	0	4.68	4.20
2012	Mia	NL	1	1	0	0	3.2	23	6	7	7	1	0	0	0	6	1	3	0	0	0	1	.000	0	0-0	0	14.74	17.18
2013	Mia	NL	7	2	0	2	20.2	82	13	7	7	2	0	0	0	8	0	15	1	0	1	1	.500	0	0-0	0	2.10	3.05
2014	Mia	NL	32	16	0	5	111.0	474	112	56	54	10	6	2	2	39	3	67	5	0	3	8	.273	0	1-1	0	3.91	4.38
2015	Mia	NL	38	12	0	7	93.1	408	107	55	55	9	5	2	3	32	1	67	2	0	4	7	.364	0	0-0	2	4.83	5.30
5 ML YEARS			90	43	0	14	288.2	1250	291	157	151	32	15	7	6	120	6	190	8	1	9	25	.265	0	1-1	2	4.33	4.71

Donovan Hand

Pitches: R **Bats:** R **Pos:** RP-1 **Ht:** 6'3" **Wt:** 235 **Born:** 4/20/1986 **Age:** 30

Year	Team	Lg	G	GS	CG	GF	IP	BFP	H	R	ER	HR	SH	SF	HB	TBB	IBB	SO	WP	Bk	W	L	Pct	Sh	Sv-Op	Hld	ERC	ERA
2011	Hntsvl	AA	9	0	0	2	11.1	48	16	3	3	0	1	0	0	1	0	12	0	0	0	0	-	0	1- -	-	4.62	2.38
2011	Nashv	AAA	38	0	0	11	53.0	234	65	24	22	6	6	1	0	20	1	32	2	0	2	6	.250	0	1- -	-	5.48	3.74
2012	Nashv	AAA	44	3	0	6	79.2	332	90	35	34	7	4	1	1	18	2	54	2	0	3	3	.500	0	0- -	-	4.16	3.84
2013	Nashv	AAA	20	0	0	5	35.2	152	34	15	13	4	1	0	0	11	1	38	2	0	3	1	.750	0	0- -	-	3.43	3.28
2014	Nashv	AAA	47	8	0	28	79.2	361	100	51	46	9	4	2	4	22	2	71	2	0	4	8	.333	0	13- -	-	5.24	5.20
2015	Lsvlle	AAA	33	11	0	2	97.0	414	113	55	53	11	3	5	4	18	1	52	1	0	1	6	.143	0	0- -	-	4.43	4.92
2013	Mil	NL	31	7	0	5	68.1	286	71	29	28	10	1	5	5	21	1	37	3	0	1	5	.167	0	0-1	2	4.70	3.69
2015	Cin	NL	1	0	0	0	3.0	13	2	0	0	0	0	1	1	1	0	3	0	0	0	0	-	0	0-0	0	2.54	0.00
2 ML YEARS			32	7	0	5	71.1	299	73	29	28	10	1	6	6	22	1	40	3	0	1	5	.167	0	0-1	2	4.60	3.53

Ryan Hanigan

Bats: R **Throws:** R **Pos:** C-53;PH-1 HANN-eh-gann **Ht:** 6'0" **Wt:** 215 **Born:** 8/16/1980 **Age:** 35

							BATTING															RUNNING			AVERAGES			
Year	Team	Lg	G	AB	H	2B	3B	HR	(Hm	Rd)	TB	R	RBI	RC	TBB	IBB	SO	HBP	SH	SF	SB	CS	GDP	Avg	OBP	Slg	OPS
2007	Cin	NL	5	10	3	1	0	0	(0	0)	4	3	2	2	1	1	2	0	0	0	0	0	0	.300	.364	.400	.764
2008	Cin	NL	31	85	23	2	0	2	(1	1)	31	9	9	12	10	1	9	3	0	0	0	0	2	.271	.367	.365	.732
2009	Cin	NL	90	251	66	6	1	3	(3	0)	83	22	11	25	37	7	31	2	2	1	0	0	9	.263	.361	.331	.692
2010	Cin	NL	70	203	61	11	0	5	(2	3)	87	25	40	41	33	4	21	4	1	2	0	0	6	.300	.405	.429	.834
2011	Cin	NL	91	266	71	6	0	6	(4	2)	95	27	31	38	35	3	32	2	1	0	0	0	3	.267	.356	.357	.714
2012	Cin	NL	112	317	87	14	0	2	(0	2)	107	25	24	40	44	13	37	3	4	3	0	0	6	.274	.365	.338	.703
2013	Cin	NL	75	222	44	8	0	2	(1	1)	58	17	21	18	29	9	27	6	2	1	0	1	7	.198	.306	.261	.567
2014	TB	AL	84	225	49	9	0	5	(4	1)	73	18	34	27	31	0	39	3	2	2	1	0	6	.218	.318	.324	.642
2015	Bos	AL	54	174	43	8	0	2	(2	0)	57	28	16	18	20	0	39	4	1	1	0	0	6	.247	.337	.328	.664
	Postseason		7	22	3	0	0	0	(0	0)	3	3	3	3	0	0	3	1	0	0	0	0	1	.136	.174	.136	.310
9 ML YEARS			612	1753	447	65	1	27	(17	10)	595	174	188	221	240	38	237	27	13	10	1	1	45	.255	.352	.339	.691

J.A. Happ

Pitches: L **Bats:** L **Pos:** SP-31; RP-1 JAY **Ht:** 6'5" **Wt:** 205 **Born:** 10/19/1982 **Age:** 33

Year	Team	Lg	G	GS	CG	GF	IP	BFP	H	R	ER	HR	SH	SF	HB	TBB	IBB	SO	WP	Bk	W	L	Pct	Sh	Sv-Op	Hld	ERC	ERA
2007	Phi	NL	1	1	0	0	4.0	21	7	5	5	3	0	0	0	2	0	5	0	0	0	1	.000	0	0-0	0	15.13	11.25
2008	Phi	NL	8	4	0	1	31.2	138	28	13	13	3	2	1	1	14	1	26	1	0	1	0	1.000	0	0-0	1	3.55	3.69
2009	Phi	NL	35	23	3	4	166.0	685	149	55	54	20	7	6	5	56	2	119	2	0	12	4	.750	2	0-0	0	3.57	2.93
2010	2 Tms		16	16	1	0	87.1	374	73	37	33	8	5	4	1	47	1	70	4	0	6	4	.600	1	0-0	0	3.69	3.40
2011	Hou	NL	28	28	0	0	156.1	698	157	103	93	21	12	8	2	83	5	134	3	2	6	15	.286	0	0-0	0	4.86	5.35
2012	2 Tms		28	24	0	3	144.2	627	147	79	77	19	9	4	2	56	1	144	7	0	10	11	.476	0	0-0	1	4.37	4.79
2013	Tor	AL	18	18	0	0	92.2	415	91	53	47	10	1	3	2	45	0	77	5	0	5	7	.417	0	0-0	0	4.36	4.56
2014	Tor	AL	30	26	0	2	158.0	673	160	79	74	22	1	5	2	51	0	133	1	0	11	11	.500	0	0-0	0	4.17	4.22
2015	2 Tms		32	31	0	0	172.0	717	173	71	69	16	2	0	2	45	4	151	6	0	11	8	.579	0	0-0	0	3.56	3.61
10	Phi	NL	3	3	0	0	15.1	70	13	4	3	1	1	1	0	12	0	9	1	0	1	0	1.000	0	0-0	0	4.40	1.76
10	Hou	NL	13	13	1	0	72.0	304	60	33	30	7	4	3	1	35	1	61	3	0	5	4	.556	1	0-0	0	3.53	3.75
12	Hou	NL	18	18	0	0	104.1	457	112	58	56	17	7	2	1	39	0	98	5	0	7	9	.438	0	0-0	0	4.36	4.83
12	Tor	AL	10	6	0	3	40.1	170	35	21	21	2	2	2	1	17	1	46	2	0	3	2	.600	0	0-0	1	3.16	4.69
15	Sea	AL	21	20	0	0	108.2	468	121	58	56	13	1	0	2	32	3	82	4	0	4	6	.400	0	0-0	0	4.49	4.64
15	Pit	NL	11	11	0	0	63.1	249	52	13	13	3	1	0	0	13	1	69	2	0	7	2	.778	0	0-0	0	2.12	1.85
	Postseason		8	1	0	0	9.1	46	12	5	5	1	0	0	0	8	0	10	0	0	0	0	-	0	0-0	1	7.96	4.82
9 ML YEARS			196	171	4	10	1012.2	4348	985	495	465	122	39	31	17	399	14	859	29	2	62	61	.504	3	0-0	2	4.09	4.13

Aaron Harang

Pitches: R **Bats:** R **Pos:** SP-29   huh-RANG   **Ht:** 6'7" **Wt:** 260 **Born:** 5/9/1978 **Age:** 38

Year Team	Lg	G	GS	CG	GF	IP	BFP	H	R	ER	HR	SH	SF	HB	TBB	IBB	SO	WP	Bk	W	L	Pct	Sh	Sv-Op	Hld	ERC	ERA
2002 Oak	AL	16	15	0	0	78.1	354	78	44	42	7	3	4	3	45	2	64	1	0	5	4	.556	0	0-0	0	4.76	4.83
2003 2 Tms		16	15	0	1	76.1	327	89	47	45	11	5	1	1	19	0	42	3	1	5	6	.455	0	0-0	0	4.84	5.31
2004 Cin	NL	28	28	1	0	161.0	711	177	90	87	26	13	6	5	53	5	125	7	0	10	9	.526	1	0-0	0	4.81	4.86
2005 Cin	NL	32	32	1	0	211.2	887	217	93	90	22	11	5	8	51	3	163	6	0	11	13	.458	0	0-0	0	3.77	3.83
2006 Cin	NL	36	35	6	0	234.1	993	242	109	98	28	21	8	8	56	8	216	6	1	16	11	.593	2	0-0	0	3.82	3.76
2007 Cin	NL	34	34	2	0	231.2	948	213	100	96	28	4	5	8	52	3	218	12	1	16	6	.727	1	0-0	0	3.22	3.73
2008 Cin	NL	30	29	1	0	184.1	793	205	104	98	35	11	7	2	50	5	153	2	0	6	17	.261	1	0-0	0	4.83	4.78
2009 Cin	NL	26	26	2	0	162.1	703	186	82	76	24	6	2	4	43	6	142	6	0	6	14	.300	1	0-0	0	4.76	4.21
2010 Cin	NL	22	20	0	1	111.2	504	139	71	66	16	4	3	4	38	0	82	9	0	6	7	.462	0	0-0	0	5.75	5.32
2011 SD	NL	28	28	0	0	170.2	719	175	73	69	20	5	2	3	58	4	124	3	0	14	7	.667	0	0-0	0	4.22	3.64
2012 LAD	NL	31	31	0	0	179.2	786	167	85	72	14	9	10	4	85	10	131	4	0	10	10	.500	0	0-0	0	3.76	3.61
2013 2 Tms		26	26	2	0	143.1	626	153	91	86	26	1	6	6	40	1	113	4	0	5	12	.294	2	0-0	0	4.62	5.40
2014 Atl	NL	33	33	0	0	204.1	876	215	88	81	15	11	6	1	71	4	161	9	0	12	12	.500	0	0-0	0	3.98	3.57
2015 Phi	NL	29	29	0	0	172.1	748	189	100	93	26	8	2	6	51	3	108	4	0	6	15	.286	0	0-0	0	4.68	4.86
03 Oak	AL	7	6	0	1	30.1	136	41	19	18	5	2	1	0	9	0	16	0	1	1	3	.250	0	0-0	0	6.32	5.34
03 Cin	NL	9	9	0	0	46.0	191	48	28	27	6	3	0	1	10	0	26	3	0	4	3	.571	0	0-0	0	3.94	5.28
13 Sea	AL	22	22	2	0	120.1	526	133	81	77	21	1	6	5	28	1	87	3	0	5	11	.313	2	0-0	0	4.58	5.76
13 NYM	NL	4	4	0	0	23.0	100	20	10	9	5	0	0	1	12	0	26	1	0	0	1	.000	0	0-0	0	4.84	3.52
14 ML YEARS		387	381	15	2	2322.0	9975	2445	1177	1099	298	112	67	63	712	54	1842	76	3	128	143	.472	8	0-0	0	4.27	4.26

Blaine Hardy

Pitches: L **Bats:** L **Pos:** RP-70   **Ht:** 6'2" **Wt:** 230 **Born:** 3/14/1987 **Age:** 29

Year Team	Lg	G	GS	CG	GF	IP	BFP	H	R	ER	HR	SH	SF	HB	TBB	IBB	SO	WP	Bk	W	L	Pct	Sh	Sv-Op	Hld	ERC	ERA
2011 Omha	AAA	23	0	0	11	29.0	146	38	25	23	7	1	0	1	19	1	23	0	0	2	3	.400	0	0--	-	8.09	7.14
2011 NWArk	AA	19	0	0	13	39.2	163	28	11	7	2	1	0	2	16	1	41	6	0	2	1	.667	0	8--	-	2.36	1.59
2012 NWArk	AA	10	0	0	6	20.2	86	17	8	6	3	0	1	2	9	0	13	4	0	1	1	.500	0	3--	-	4.04	2.61
2012 Omha	AAA	30	0	0	11	54.2	244	69	24	23	6	5	3	0	22	2	45	1	0	3	2	.600	0	1--	-	5.76	3.79
2013 Erie	AA	16	0	0	2	27.2	108	16	8	5	1	2	0	0	12	0	26	1	0	2	2	.500	0	1--	-	1.72	1.63
2013 Toledo	AAA	14	9	1	1	64.0	253	46	12	12	7	0	0	2	19	0	53	0	0	6	1	.857	1	0--	-	2.43	1.69
2014 Toledo	AAA	20	6	0	5	47.0	185	35	14	14	2	3	0	1	13	1	53	1	0	3	2	.600	0	0--	-	2.04	2.68
2014 Det	AL	38	0	0	7	39.0	167	34	12	11	1	1	2	1	20	3	31	1	0	2	1	.667	0	0-1	4	3.28	2.54
2015 Det	AL	70	0	0	11	61.1	265	61	23	21	3	4	1	1	22	2	55	5	0	5	3	.625	0	0-3	13	3.38	3.08
2 ML YEARS		108	0	0	18	100.1	432	95	35	32	3	4	6	2	42	5	86	6	0	7	4	.636	0	0-4	17	3.34	2.87

J.J. Hardy

Bats: R **Throws:** R **Pos:** SS-114   **Ht:** 6'1" **Wt:** 200 **Born:** 8/19/1982 **Age:** 33

Year Team	Lg	G	AB	H	2B	3B	HR	(Hm	Rd)	TB	R	RBI	RC	TBB	IBB	SO	HBP	SH	SF	SB	CS	GDP	Avg	OBP	Slg	OPS
2005 Mil	NL	124	372	92	22	1	9	(6	3)	143	46	50	49	44	7	48	1	8	2	0	0	10	.247	.327	.384	.711
2006 Mil	NL	35	128	31	5	0	5	(4	1)	51	13	14	13	10	0	23	0	0	1	1	1	4	.242	.295	.398	.693
2007 Mil	NL	151	592	164	30	1	26	(15	11)	274	89	80	84	40	1	73	1	4	1	2	3	13	.277	.323	.463	.786
2008 Mil	NL	146	569	161	31	4	24	(14	10)	272	78	74	78	52	3	98	1	5	2	2	1	18	.283	.343	.478	.821
2009 Mil	NL	115	414	95	16	2	11	(6	5)	148	53	47	32	43	0	85	2	1	5	0	1	14	.229	.302	.357	.659
2010 Min	AL	101	340	91	19	3	6	(1	5)	134	44	38	41	28	1	54	0	3	4	1	1	8	.268	.320	.394	.714
2011 Bal	AL	129	527	142	27	0	30	(15	15)	259	76	80	78	31	3	92	2	2	5	0	0	10	.269	.310	.491	.801
2012 Bal	AL	158	663	158	30	2	22	(15	7)	258	85	68	71	38	4	106	3	7	2	0	0	21	.238	.282	.389	.671
2013 Bal	AL	159	601	158	27	0	25	(11	14)	260	66	76	71	38	3	73	0	3	2	2	1	14	.263	.306	.433	.738
2014 Bal	AL	141	529	142	28	0	9	(5	4)	197	56	52	60	29	1	104	4	3	4	0	0	12	.268	.309	.372	.682
2015 Bal	AL	114	411	90	14	0	8	(4	4)	128	45	37	32	20	0	88	0	2	4	0	0	11	.219	.253	.311	.564
Postseason		20	76	18	5	0	1	(1	0)	26	6	7	8	6	1	12	0	0	0	0	0	1	.237	.293	.342	.635
11 ML YEARS		1373	5146	1324	249	13	175	(96	79)	2124	651	616	609	373	23	844	14	38	32	8	8	135	.257	.307	.413	.720

Dan Haren

Pitches: R **Bats:** R **Pos:** SP-32   **Ht:** 6'5" **Wt:** 215 **Born:** 9/17/1980 **Age:** 35

Year Team	Lg	G	GS	CG	GF	IP	BFP	H	R	ER	HR	SH	SF	HB	TBB	IBB	SO	WP	Bk	W	L	Pct	Sh	Sv-Op	Hld	ERC	ERA
2003 StL	NL	14	14	0	0	72.2	320	84	44	44	9	4	2	5	22	0	43	3	0	3	7	.300	0	0-0	0	5.07	5.08
2004 StL	NL	14	5	0	0	46.0	195	45	23	23	4	4	2	2	17	2	32	1	0	3	3	.500	0	0-0	0	3.91	4.50
2005 Oak	AL	34	34	3	0	217.0	897	212	101	90	26	3	5	6	53	5	163	6	0	14	12	.538	0	0-0	0	3.58	3.73
2006 Oak	AL	34	34	2	0	223.0	920	224	109	102	31	3	10		45	6	176	10	0	14	13	.519	0	0-0	0	3.72	4.12
2007 Oak	AL	34	34	1	0	222.2	935	214	91	76	24	2	8	3	55	1	192	10	0	15	9	.625	0	0-0	0	3.32	3.07
2008 Ari	NL	33	33	1	0	216.0	881	204	86	80	19	7	3	6	40	4	206	11	0	16	8	.667	1	0-0	0	2.96	3.33
2009 Ari	NL	33	33	1	0	229.1	909	192	83	80	27	8	3	4	38	2	223	13	0	14	10	.583	2	0-0	0	2.50	3.14
2010 2 Tms		35	35	2	0	235.0	994	245	110	102	31	6	10	8	54	6	216	12	2	12	12	.500	0	0-0	0	3.88	3.91
2011 LAA	AL	35	34	4	1	238.1	953	211	91	84	20	12	5	4	33	1	192	6	0	16	10	.615	3	0-0	0	2.45	3.17
2012 LAA	AL	30	30	1	0	176.2	747	190	95	85	28	7	8	3	38	3	142	5	1	12	13	.480	1	0-0	0	4.20	4.33
2013 Was	NL	31	30	0	0	169.2	717	179	92	88	28	8	4	7	31	0	151	8	1	10	14	.417	0	1-1	0	4.09	4.67
2014 LAD	NL	32	32	0	0	186.0	776	183	101	83	27	6	5	3	36	7	145	8	1	13	11	.542	0	0-0	0	3.43	4.02
2015 2 Tms		32	32	0	0	187.1	768	174	79	75	31	8	5	8	38	2	132	5	0	11	9	.550	0	0-0	0	3.50	3.60
10 Ari	NL	21	21	1	0	141.0	607	161	79	72	23	6	4	3	29	4	141	8	1	7	8	.467	0	0-0	0	4.55	4.60
10 LAA	AL	14	14	1	0	94.0	387	84	31	30	8	0	6	5	25	2	75	4	1	5	4	.556	0	0-0	0	2.94	2.87
15 Mia	NL	21	21	0	0	129.0	524	116	50	49	21	6	4	7	25	1	88	2	0	7	7	.500	0	0-0	0	3.35	3.42
15 ChC	NL	11	11	0	0	58.1	244	58	29	26	10	2	1	1	13	1	44	3	0	4	2	.667	0	0-0	0	3.83	4.01
Postseason		7	2	0	0	19.1	86	24	7	7	3	1	0	0	7	0	16	2	0	2	0	1.000	0	0-0	0	5.83	3.26
13 ML YEARS		391	380	16	4	2419.2	10022	2357	1105	1009	305	78	63	67	500	39	2013	98	5	153	131	.539	6	1-1	0	3.43	3.75

Bryce Harper

Bats: L **Throws:** R **Pos:** RF-140;CF-13;DH-1   **Ht:** 6'3" **Wt:** 215 **Born:** 10/16/1992 **Age:** 23

								BATTING													RUNNING			AVERAGES			
Year	Team	Lg	G	AB	H	2B	3B	HR	(Hm	Rd)	TB	R	RBI	RC	TBB	IBB	SO	HBP	SH	SF	SB	CS	GDP	Avg	OBP	Slg	OPS
2012	Was	NL	139	533	144	26	9	22	(10	12)	254	98	59	82	56	0	120	2	3	3	18	6	8	.270	.340	.477	.817
2013	Was	NL	118	424	116	24	3	20	(13	7)	206	71	58	73	61	4	94	5	3	4	11	4	4	.274	.368	.486	.854
2014	Was	NL	100	352	96	10	2	13	(5	8)	149	41	32	43	38	4	104	1	3	1	2	2	6	.273	.344	.423	.768
2015	Was	NL	153	521	172	38	1	42	(23	19)	338	118	99	138	124	15	131	5	0	4	6	4	15	.330	.460	.649	1.109
Postseason			9	40	8	2	1	4	(2	2)	24	6	6	4	2	0	11	0	0	0	0	0	0	.200	.238	.600	.838
4 ML YEARS			510	1830	528	98	15	97	(51	46)	947	328	248	336	279	23	449	13	9	12	37	16	33	.289	.384	.517	.902

Mitchell Harris

Pitches: R **Bats:** R **Pos:** RP-26   **Ht:** 6'4" **Wt:** 215 **Born:** 11/7/1985 **Age:** 30

			HOW MUCH HE PITCHED						WHAT HE GAVE UP										THE RESULTS							
Year	Team	Lg	G	GS	CG	GF	IP	BFP	H	R	ER	HR	SH	SF	HB	TBB	IBB	SO	WP	Bk	W	L	Pct	Sh	Sv-Op	Hld	ERC	ERA
2013	StCol	A-	20	0	0	7	33.1	135	22	4	3	0	4	0	2	15	1	29	3	2	4	1	.800	0	1--	-	2.06	0.81
2014	PlmBh	A+	8	0	0	5	12.1	51	8	6	6	1	0	0	0	6	0	9	0	0	0	2	.000	0	0--	-	2.39	4.38
2014	Sprgfld	AA	33	0	0	12	43.2	180	38	19	19	5	1	1	0	13	1	34	5	0	2	0	1.000	0	1--	-	3.02	3.92
2015	Memp	AAA	25	0	0	17	26.2	117	30	13	10	1	1	0	1	10	4	20	0	0	0	4	.000	0	4--	-	4.16	3.38
2015	StL	NL	26	0	0	7	27.0	122	30	14	11	4	1	0	0	13	0	15	2	0	2	1	.667	0	0-0	0	5.38	3.67

Will Harris

Pitches: R **Bats:** R **Pos:** RP-68   **Ht:** 6'4" **Wt:** 225 **Born:** 8/28/1984 **Age:** 31

			HOW MUCH HE PITCHED						WHAT HE GAVE UP										THE RESULTS							
Year	Team	Lg	G	GS	CG	GF	IP	BFP	H	R	ER	HR	SH	SF	HB	TBB	IBB	SO	WP	Bk	W	L	Pct	Sh	Sv-Op	Hld	ERC	ERA
2012	Col	NL	20	0	0	10	17.2	89	27	18	16	3	2	1	1	6	1	19	4	0	1	1	.500	0	0-0	3	7.39	8.15
2013	Ari	NL	61	0	0	11	52.2	217	50	17	17	3	0	4	2	15	1	53	4	0	4	1	.800	0	0-1	4	3.25	2.91
2014	Ari	NL	29	0	0	8	29.0	120	27	14	14	3	1	1	2	9	2	35	1	0	0	3	.000	0	0-1	3	3.62	4.34
2015	Hou	AL	68	0	0	18	71.0	276	42	18	15	8	2	1	1	22	1	68	2	0	5	5	.500	0	2-6	13	1.79	1.90
4 ML YEARS			178	0	0	47	170.1	702	146	67	62	17	5	7	6	52	5	175	11	0	10	10	.500	0	2-8	23	3.04	3.28

Josh Harrison

Bats: R **Throws:** R **Pos:** 3B-72;2B-37;RF-12;LF-10;PH-10;PR-1   **Ht:** 5'8" **Wt:** 195 **Born:** 7/8/1987 **Age:** 28

								BATTING													RUNNING			AVERAGES			
Year	Team	Lg	G	AB	H	2B	3B	HR	(Hm	Rd)	TB	R	RBI	RC	TBB	IBB	SO	HBP	SH	SF	SB	CS	GDP	Avg	OBP	Slg	OPS
2011	Pit	NL	65	195	53	13	2	1	(1	0)	73	21	16	19	3	0	24	0	5	1	4	1	6	.272	.281	.374	.656
2012	Pit	NL	104	249	58	9	5	3	(1	2)	86	34	16	22	10	0	37	7	7	3	7	3	3	.233	.279	.345	.624
2013	Pit	NL	60	88	22	1	2	3	(1	2)	36	10	14	11	2	0	10	3	2	0	2	0	4	.250	.290	.409	.699
2014	Pit	NL	143	520	164	38	7	13	(4	9)	255	77	52	84	22	1	81	4	2	2	18	7	6	.315	.347	.490	.837
2015	Pit	NL	114	418	120	29	1	4	(2	2)	163	57	28	48	19	1	71	7	3	2	10	8	4	.287	.327	.390	.717
Postseason			3	4	2	0	0	0	(0	0)	2	1	0	0	0	0	1	0	0	0	0	1	0	.500	.500	.500	1.000
5 ML YEARS			486	1470	417	90	17	24	(9	15)	613	199	126	184	56	2	223	21	19	8	41	19	23	.284	.318	.417	.735

Matt Harrison

Pitches: L **Bats:** L **Pos:** SP-3   **Ht:** 6'4" **Wt:** 240 **Born:** 9/16/1985 **Age:** 30

			HOW MUCH HE PITCHED						WHAT HE GAVE UP										THE RESULTS							
Year	Team	Lg	G	GS	CG	GF	IP	BFP	H	R	ER	HR	SH	SF	HB	TBB	IBB	SO	WP	Bk	W	L	Pct	Sh	Sv-Op	Hld	ERC	ERA
2015	RdRck*	AAA	5	5	0	0	28.2	128	34	21	19	0	2	3	1	12	0	18	1	0	1	3	.250	0	0--	-	4.66	5.97
2008	Tex	AL	15	15	1	0	83.2	372	100	57	51	12	1	5	2	31	2	42	2	2	9	3	.750	1	0-0	0	5.53	5.49
2009	Tex	AL	11	11	2	0	63.1	283	81	43	43	9	1	1	2	23	0	34	0	0	4	5	.444	0	0-0	0	6.17	6.11
2010	Tex	AL	37	6	0	9	78.1	356	80	45	41	10	2	8	2	39	3	46	0	0	3	2	.600	0	2-3	4	4.71	4.71
2011	Tex	AL	31	30	0	0	185.2	772	180	79	70	13	8	5	1	57	1	126	6	1	14	9	.609	0	0-0	0	3.40	3.39
2012	Tex	AL	32	32	4	0	213.1	876	210	82	78	22	1	2	1	59	0	133	2	0	18	11	.621	2	0-0	0	3.63	3.29
2013	Tex	AL	2	2	0	0	10.2	51	14	11	10	2	0	1	0	7	2	12	0	0	0	2	.000	0	0-0	0	7.54	8.44
2014	Tex	AL	4	4	0	0	17.1	84	20	8	8	1	1	0	1	12	0	10	1	0	1	1	.500	0	0-0	0	5.98	4.15
2015	Tex	AL	3	3	0	0	16.0	69	19	12	12	3	0	1	0	6	0	5	0	1	1	2	.333	0	0-0	0	5.94	6.75
Postseason			5	4	0	0	18.1	83	20	13	11	2	0	0	0	9	1	16	1	0	1	2	.333	0	0-0	0	4.88	5.40
8 ML YEARS			135	103	7	9	668.1	2863	704	337	313	72	14	23	9	234	8	408	15	4	50	35	.588	4	2-3	4	4.31	4.21

Corey Hart

Bats: R **Throws:** R **Pos:** PH-24;1B-8;RF-3;DH-1   **Ht:** 6'6" **Wt:** 240 **Born:** 3/24/1982 **Age:** 34

								BATTING													RUNNING			AVERAGES			
Year	Team	Lg	G	AB	H	2B	3B	HR	(Hm	Rd)	TB	R	RBI	RC	TBB	IBB	SO	HBP	SH	SF	SB	CS	GDP	Avg	OBP	Slg	OPS
2015	Indy*	AAA	13	42	7	1	0	2	(-	-)	14	4	7	2	1	0	15	0	0	0	0	0	0	.167	.186	.333	.519
2004	Mil	NL	1	1	0	0	0	0	(0	0)	0	0	0	0	0	0	1	0	0	0	0	0	0	.000	.000	.000	.000
2005	Mil	NL	21	57	11	2	1	2	(2	0)	21	9	7	4	6	0	11	0	0	0	2	0	6	.193	.270	.368	.638
2006	Mil	NL	87	237	67	13	2	9	(6	3)	111	32	33	30	17	1	58	0	0	2	5	8	7	.283	.328	.468	.796
2007	Mil	NL	140	505	149	33	9	24	(15	9)	272	86	81	94	36	3	99	13	5	7	23	7	6	.295	.353	.539	.892
2008	Mil	NL	157	612	164	45	6	20	(7	13)	281	76	91	81	27	2	109	5	4	9	23	7	17	.268	.300	.459	.759
2009	Mil	NL	115	419	109	24	3	12	(9	3)	175	64	48	51	43	0	92	6	1	3	11	6	9	.260	.335	.418	.753
2010	Mil	NL	145	558	158	34	4	31	(16	15)	293	91	102	83	45	2	140	6	0	5	7	6	14	.283	.340	.525	.865
2011	Mil	NL	130	492	140	25	4	26	(17	9)	251	80	63	79	51	1	114	4	3	1	7	6	12	.285	.356	.510	.866
2012	Mil	NL	149	562	152	35	4	30	(22	8)	285	91	83	87	44	5	151	11	2	3	5	0	13	.270	.334	.507	.841

Year	Team	Lg	G	AB	H	2B	3B	HR	(Hm	Rd)	TB	R	RBI	RC	TBB	IBB	SO	HBP	SH	SF	SB	CS	GDP	Avg	OBP	Slg	OPS
2014	Sea	AL	68	232	47	9	0	6	(2	4)	74	17	21	21	16	1	59	6	0	1	2	0	1	.203	.271	.319	.590
2015	Pit	NL	35	54	12	1	0	2	(1	1)	19	3	9	6	1	1	19	1	0	1	0	0	5	.222	.246	.352	.597
	Postseason		14	54	13	0	0	2	(1	1)	19	6	5	4	3	0	11	1	1	1	0	0	1	.241	.288	.352	.640
	11 ML YEARS		1048	3729	1009	221	33	162	(97	65)	1782	549	538	536	286	16	853	52	15	32	85	40	90	.271	.329	.478	.806

Matt Harvey

Pitches: R Bats: R Pos: SP-29   Ht: 6'4" Wt: 215 Born: 3/27/1989 Age: 27

			HOW MUCH HE PITCHED						WHAT HE GAVE UP										THE RESULTS						
Year	Team	Lg	G	GS	CG	GF	IP	BFP	H	R	ER	HR	SH	SF	HB	TBB	IBB	SO	WP	Bk	W	L	Pct	Sh	Sv-Op	Hld	ERC	ERA
2012	NYM	NL	10	10	0	0	59.1	245	42	19	18	5	3	3	3	26	0	70	3	0	3	5	.375	0	0-0	0	2.75	2.73
2013	NYM	NL	26	26	1	0	178.1	690	135	46	45	7	5	4	4	31	1	191	0	0	9	5	.643	1	0-0	0	1.76	2.27
2015	NYM	NL	29	29	0	0	189.1	755	156	62	57	18	7	2	5	37	2	188	4	0	13	8	.619	0	0-0	0	2.44	2.71
	3 ML YEARS		65	65	1	0	427.0	1690	333	127	120	30	15	9	12	94	3	449	9	0	25	18	.581	1	0-0	0	2.19	2.53

Chris Hatcher

Pitches: R Bats: B Pos: RP-49   Ht: 6'1" Wt: 200 Born: 1/12/1985 Age: 31

			HOW MUCH HE PITCHED						WHAT HE GAVE UP										THE RESULTS						
Year	Team	Lg	G	GS	CG	GF	IP	BFP	H	R	ER	HR	SH	SF	HB	TBB	IBB	SO	WP	Bk	W	L	Pct	Sh	Sv-Op	Hld	ERC	ERA
2015	OkCity*	AAA	5	0	0	1	4.1	20	5	4	4	0	1	0	0	2	0	3	2	0	1	0	1.000	0	0- --	-	4.31	8.31
2011	Fla	NL	11	0	0	4	10.1	48	14	8	8	2	0	3	0	4	1	8	2	0	0	0	-	0	0-0	0	6.69	6.97
2012	Mia	NL	11	0	0	7	14.2	66	17	9	7	3	0	0	1	6	0	10	1	0	0	0	-	0	0-0	0	6.19	4.30
2013	Mia	NL	7	0	0	2	8.2	44	13	13	12	1	0	0	0	4	1	7	0	0	0	1	.000	0	0-0	0	6.92	12.46
2014	Mia	NL	52	0	0	15	56.0	232	55	22	21	4	1	1	0	12	1	60	1	2	0	3	.000	0	0-2	6	3.03	3.38
2015	LAD	NL	49	0	0	12	39.0	166	35	19	16	4	2	1	3	13	2	45	3	0	3	5	.375	0	4-6	13	3.46	3.69
	5 ML YEARS		130	0	0	40	128.2	556	134	71	64	14	3	5	4	39	5	130	7	2	3	9	.250	0	4-8	19	4.01	4.48

Marcus Hatley

Pitches: R Bats: R Pos: RP-2   Ht: 6'5" Wt: 220 Born: 3/26/1988 Age: 28

			HOW MUCH HE PITCHED						WHAT HE GAVE UP										THE RESULTS						
Year	Team	Lg	G	GS	CG	GF	IP	BFP	H	R	ER	HR	SH	SF	HB	TBB	IBB	SO	WP	Bk	W	L	Pct	Sh	Sv-Op	Hld	ERC	ERA
2011	Tenn	AA	22	0	0	9	29.0	123	30	17	15	2	1	1	2	11	1	20	4	0	3	0	1.000	0	4- --	-	4.33	4.66
2011	2 Tms	Low	26	0	0	18	30.2	130	19	9	7	0	1	0	5	19	1	40	3	0	2	1	.667	0	7- --	-	2.75	2.05
2012	Tenn	AA	28	0	0	13	45.0	183	36	18	17	3	5	3	0	20	3	46	2	0	3	1	.750	0	4- --	-	2.93	3.40
2012	Iowa	AAA	12	0	0	4	15.1	69	14	14	14	0	0	0	0	10	0	18	5	0	1	0	1.000	0	0- --	-	3.78	8.22
2013	Tenn	AA	14	0	0	5	18.0	78	13	6	6	1	3	0	0	14	2	25	4	0	1	2	.333	0	2- --	-	3.54	3.00
2013	Iowa	AAA	35	0	0	10	42.2	185	40	23	20	2	0	1	1	21	0	49	5	0	3	2	.600	0	0- --	-	3.81	4.22
2014	Iowa	AAA	45	0	0	26	47.0	210	52	27	24	6	6	6	1	13	4	58	1	1	2	6	.250	0	1- --	-	4.15	4.60
2015	Memp	AAA	36	0	0	17	48.2	211	52	20	17	3	3	2	1	19	2	31	1	0	4	4	.500	0	5- --	-	4.20	3.14
2015	StL	NL	2	0	0	1	1.1	7	1	0	0	0	0	0	0	2	0	2	0	0	0	0	-	0	0-0	0	5.91	0.00

LaTroy Hawkins

Pitches: R Bats: R Pos: RP-42   Ht: 6'5" Wt: 220 Born: 12/21/1972 Age: 43

			HOW MUCH HE PITCHED						WHAT HE GAVE UP										THE RESULTS						
Year	Team	Lg	G	GS	CG	GF	IP	BFP	H	R	ER	HR	SH	SF	HB	TBB	IBB	SO	WP	Bk	W	L	Pct	Sh	Sv-Op	Hld	ERC	ERA
2015	Albq*	AAA	5	0	0	0	4.2	24	8	4	4	0	0	0	0	1	0	4	1	0	0	0	-	0	0- --	-	6.31	7.71
1995	Min	AL	6	6	1	0	27.0	131	39	29	26	3	0	3	1	12	0	9	1	1	2	3	.400	0	0-0	0	7.14	8.67
1996	Min	AL	7	6	0	1	26.1	124	42	24	24	8	1	1	0	9	0	24	1	1	1	1	.500	0	0-0	0	9.49	8.20
1997	Min	AL	20	20	0	0	103.1	478	134	71	67	19	2	2	4	47	0	58	6	3	6	12	.333	0	0-0	0	7.01	5.84
1998	Min	AL	33	33	0	0	190.1	840	227	126	111	27	4	10	5	61	1	105	10	2	7	14	.333	0	0-0	0	5.31	5.25
1999	Min	AL	33	33	1	0	174.1	803	238	136	129	29	1	5	1	60	2	103	9	0	10	14	.417	0	0-0	0	6.55	6.66
2000	Min	AL	66	0	0	38	87.2	370	85	34	33	7	4	1	1	32	1	59	6	0	2	5	.286	0	14-14	7	3.70	3.39
2001	Min	AL	62	0	0	51	51.1	248	59	34	34	3	1	4	1	39	3	36	7	0	1	5	.167	0	28-37	1	6.02	5.96
2002	Min	AL	65	0	0	15	80.1	310	63	23	19	5	2	3	0	15	1	63	5	0	6	0	1.000	0	0-3	13	1.99	2.13
2003	Min	AL	74	0	0	12	77.1	310	69	20	16	4	4	1	1	15	1	75	5	0	9	3	.750	0	2-8	28	2.48	1.86
2004	ChC	NL	77	0	0	50	82.0	333	72	27	24	10	6	2	2	14	5	69	2	0	5	4	.556	0	25-34	4	2.66	2.63
2005	2 Tms		66	0	0	21	56.1	247	58	27	24	7	3	1	0	24	3	43	1	0	2	8	.200	0	6-15	15	4.41	3.83
2006	Bal	AL	60	0	0	12	60.1	261	73	30	30	4	1	2	0	15	3	27	2	0	3	2	.600	0	0-4	16	4.37	4.48
2007	Col	NL	62	0	0	10	55.1	225	52	21	21	6	2	1	0	16	1	29	2	0	2	5	.286	0	0-5	18	3.43	3.42
2008	2 Tms		57	0	0	15	62.0	252	53	29	27	3	1	3	0	22	4	48	3	0	3	1	.750	0	1-2	13	2.75	3.92
2009	Hou	NL	65	0	0	34	63.1	259	60	16	15	7	2	2	2	16	2	45	2	0	1	4	.200	0	11-15	19	3.42	2.13
2010	Mil	NL	18	0	0	5	16.0	74	21	15	15	2	1	0	2	6	1	18	1	0	0	3	.000	0	0-2	6	6.55	8.44
2011	Mil	NL	52	0	0	10	48.1	204	50	15	13	1	1	1	0	13	1	28	2	0	3	1	.750	0	0-0	20	2.91	2.42
2012	LAA	NL	48	0	0	7	42.0	178	45	20	17	5	3	1	0	13	1	23	0	0	2	3	.400	0	1-4	6	4.27	3.64
2013	NYM	NL	72	0	0	28	70.2	288	71	27	23	6	3	5	1	10	2	55	1	0	3	2	.600	0	13-16	12	3.03	2.93
2014	Col	NL	57	0	0	48	54.1	226	52	23	20	3	0	2	0	13	2	32	3	0	4	3	.571	0	23-26	1	2.85	3.31
2015	2 Tms		42	0	0	16	38.2	162	44	16	14	4	1	0	0	7	1	34	1	0	3	1	.750	0	3-5	7	4.00	3.26
05	ChC	NL	21	0	0	12	19.0	80	18	9	7	4	1	0	0	7	0	13	0	0	1	4	.200	0	4-8	0	4.44	3.32
05	SF	NL	45	0	0	9	37.1	167	40	18	17	3	2	1	0	17	3	30	1	0	1	4	.200	0	2-7	15	4.36	4.10
08	NYY	AL	33	0	0	11	41.0	173	42	26	26	3	1	2	0	17	3	23	2	0	1	1	.500	0	0-1	1	4.09	5.71
08	Hou	NL	24	0	0	4	21.0	79	11	3	1	0	0	1	0	5	1	25	1	0	2	0	1.000	0	1-1	12	0.95	0.43
15	Col	NL	24	0	0	11	22.1	89	22	9	9	3	0	0	0	4	1	20	1	0	2	1	.667	0	2-4	3	3.39	3.63
15	Tor	AL	18	0	0	5	16.1	73	22	7	5	1	1	0	0	3	0	14	0	0	1	0	1.000	0	1-1	4	4.86	2.76
	Postseason		19	0	0	4	15.2	65	13	7	6	0	3	1	0	6	1	17	0	0	1	0	1.000	0	0-0	4	2.35	3.45
	21 ML YEARS		1042	98	2	373	1467.1	6323	1607	763	702	163	43	50	21	456	35	983	70	7	75	94	.444	0	127-190	186	4.37	4.31

Brett Hayes

Bats: R **Throws:** R **Pos:** C-14   **Ht:** 6'1" **Wt:** 210 **Born:** 2/13/1984 **Age:** 32

Year	Team	Lg	G	AB	H	2B	3B	HR	(Hm	Rd)	TB	R	RBI	RC	TBB	IBB	SO	HBP	SH	SF	SB	CS	GDP	Avg	OBP	Slg	OPS
2015	Clmbs*	AAA	51	164	31	7	0	2	(-	-)	44	11	17	8	6	0	42	1	4	1	0	1	2	.189	.221	.268	.489
2009	Fla	NL	14	11	3	1	0	1	(0	1)	7	5	2	1	0	0	4	1	0	0	0	0	1	.273	.333	.636	.970
2010	Fla	NL	26	77	16	6	1	2	(1	1)	30	6	6	7	6	1	26	0	0	0	0	0	1	.208	.265	.390	.655
2011	Fla	NL	64	130	30	9	0	5	(3	2)	54	19	16	13	11	2	39	0	3	0	0	0	2	.231	.291	.415	.706
2012	Mia	NL	39	114	23	6	0	0	(0	0)	29	7	3	2	4	3	49	0	0	0	1	0	1	.202	.229	.254	.483
2013	KC	AL	5	18	5	3	0	1	(0	1)	11	2	2	3	0	0	3	0	0	0	0	0	0	.278	.278	.611	.889
2014	KC	AL	27	52	7	1	0	1	(1	0)	11	3	2	0	1	0	12	0	0	0	0	0	1	.135	.151	.212	.362
2015	Cle	AL	14	32	5	0	0	3	(1	2)	14	4	6	3	3	0	7	0	1	0	0	0	0	.156	.229	.438	.666
7 ML YEARS			189	434	89	26	1	13	(6	7)	156	46	37	29	25	6	140	1	4	0	1	0	6	.205	.250	.359	.609

Chase Headley

Bats: B **Throws:** R **Pos:** 3B-155;PH-5;1B-1;PR-1   HEDD-lee   **Ht:** 6'2" **Wt:** 210 **Born:** 5/9/1984 **Age:** 32

Year	Team	Lg	G	AB	H	2B	3B	HR	(Hm	Rd)	TB	R	RBI	RC	TBB	IBB	SO	HBP	SH	SF	SB	CS	GDP	Avg	OBP	Slg	OPS
2007	SD	NL	8	18	4	1	0	0	(0	0)	5	1	0	1	2	0	4	1	0	0	0	0	2	.222	.333	.278	.611
2008	SD	NL	91	331	89	19	2	9	(4	5)	139	34	38	42	30	1	104	5	0	2	4	1	5	.269	.337	.420	.757
2009	SD	NL	156	543	142	31	2	12	(7	5)	213	62	64	68	62	3	133	5	0	2	10	2	19	.262	.342	.392	.734
2010	SD	NL	161	610	161	29	3	11	(3	8)	229	77	58	70	56	3	139	3	1	4	17	5	11	.264	.327	.375	.702
2011	SD	NL	113	381	110	28	1	4	(1	3)	152	43	44	61	52	8	92	2	1	3	13	2	6	.289	.374	.399	.773
2012	SD	NL	161	604	173	31	2	31	(13	18)	301	95	115	112	86	2	157	4	0	5	17	6	7	.286	.376	.498	.875
2013	SD	NL	141	520	130	35	2	13	(5	8)	208	59	50	64	67	7	142	11	0	2	8	4	9	.250	.347	.400	.747
2014	2 Tms		135	470	114	20	1	13	(7	6)	175	55	49	54	51	1	122	9	0	1	7	3	17	.243	.328	.372	.700
2015	NYY	AL	156	580	150	29	1	11	(6	5)	214	74	62	71	51	0	135	7	0	4	0	2	17	.259	.324	.369	.693
14	SD	NL	77	279	64	12	1	7	(2	5)	99	27	32	29	22	0	73	5	0	1	4	1	12	.229	.296	.355	.651
14	NYY	AL	58	191	50	8	0	6	(5	1)	76	28	17	25	29	1	49	4	0	0	3	2	5	.262	.371	.398	.768
9 ML YEARS			1122	4057	1073	223	14	104	(46	58)	1636	500	480	543	457	25	1028	47	2	23	76	25	93	.264	.344	.403	.747

Andrew Heaney

Pitches: L **Bats:** L **Pos:** SP-18   HEE-nee   **Ht:** 6'2" **Wt:** 185 **Born:** 6/5/1991 **Age:** 25

Year	Team	Lg	G	GS	CG	GF	IP	BFP	H	R	ER	HR	SH	SF	HB	TBB	IBB	SO	WP	Bk	W	L	Pct	Sh	Sv-Op	Hld	ERC	ERA
2012	2 Tms	Low	6	6	0	0	27.0	124	32	17	13	0	1	1	2	6	0	30	0	0	1	2	.333	0	0- -	-	3.76	4.33
2013	Jupiter	A+	13	12	0	1	61.2	258	45	11	6	2	2	0	6	17	0	66	3	0	5	2	.714	0	0- -	-	2.06	0.88
2013	Jaxnvl	AA	6	6	1	0	33.2	138	31	11	11	2	1	0	0	9	0	23	0	0	4	1	.800	0	0- -	-	2.89	2.94
2014	Jaxnvl	AA	9	8	0	0	53.2	218	45	16	14	2	2	1	0	13	0	52	5	0	4	2	.667	0	0- -	-	2.23	2.35
2014	NewOr	AAA	15	15	1	0	83.2	350	75	45	36	9	0	2	4	23	0	91	3	0	5	4	.556	1	0- -	-	3.23	3.87
2015	Salt Lk	AAA	14	14	0	0	78.1	354	95	49	41	2	2	5	3	25	0	74	7	0	6	2	.750	0	0- -	-	4.50	4.71
2014	Mia	NL	7	5	0	2	29.1	126	32	19	19	6	2	0	3	7	0	20	2	0	0	3	.000	0	0-0	0	5.17	5.83
2015	LAA	AL	18	18	0	0	105.2	438	99	41	41	9	1	3	6	28	1	78	4	0	6	4	.600	0	0-0	0	3.35	3.49
2 ML YEARS			25	23	0	2	135.0	564	131	60	60	15	3	3	9	35	1	98	6	0	6	7	.462	0	0-0	0	3.72	4.00

Slade Heathcott

Bats: L **Throws:** L **Pos:** RF-9;CF-8;PR-3;PH-1   **Ht:** 6'1" **Wt:** 190 **Born:** 9/28/1990 **Age:** 25

Year	Team	Lg	G	AB	H	2B	3B	HR	(Hm	Rd)	TB	R	RBI	RC	TBB	IBB	SO	HBP	SH	SF	SB	CS	GDP	Avg	OBP	Slg	OPS
2011	2 Tms	Low	53	215	60	11	4	5	(-	-)	94	38	17	31	19	0	58	4	3	1	6	7	1	.279	.347	.437	.784
2012	2 Tms	Low	65	232	70	18	2	5	(-	-)	107	41	29	43	25	0	70	5	2	1	19	4	1	.302	.380	.461	.841
2013	Trntn	AA	103	399	104	22	7	8	(-	-)	164	59	49	55	36	1	107	4	3	2	15	8	2	.261	.327	.411	.738
2015	S-WB	AAA	64	251	67	7	3	2	(-	-)	86	25	27	27	18	0	61	0	1	1	6	5	5	.267	.315	.343	.657
2015	NYY	AL	17	25	10	2	0	2	(1	1)	18	6	8	8	2	0	5	0	0	1	0	1	0	.400	.429	.720	1.149

Adeiny Hechavarria

Bats: R **Throws:** R **Pos:** SS-130   a-DAY-nee hetch-a-VA-ree-a   **Ht:** 6'2" **Wt:** 215 **Born:** 4/15/1989 **Age:** 27

Year	Team	Lg	G	AB	H	2B	3B	HR	(Hm	Rd)	TB	R	RBI	RC	TBB	IBB	SO	HBP	SH	SF	SB	CS	GDP	Avg	OBP	Slg	OPS
2012	Tor	AL	41	126	32	8	0	2	(1	1)	46	10	15	15	4	0	32	1	5	1	0	0	2	.254	.280	.365	.645
2013	Mia	NL	148	543	123	14	8	3	(1	2)	162	30	42	37	30	1	96	0	4	1	11	10	19	.227	.267	.298	.565
2014	Mia	NL	146	536	148	20	10	1	(0	1)	191	53	34	49	26	5	86	1	4	6	7	5	21	.276	.308	.356	.664
2015	Mia	NL	130	470	132	17	6	5	(3	2)	176	54	48	49	23	4	78	2	0	4	7	2	18	.281	.315	.374	.689
4 ML YEARS			465	1675	435	59	24	11	(5	6)	575	147	139	150	83	10	292	4	13	12	25	17	60	.260	.294	.343	.638

Austin Hedges

Bats: R **Throws:** R **Pos:** C-47;PH-9   **Ht:** 6'1" **Wt:** 200 **Born:** 8/18/1992 **Age:** 23

Year	Team	Lg	G	AB	H	2B	3B	HR	(Hm	Rd)	TB	R	RBI	RC	TBB	IBB	SO	HBP	SH	SF	SB	CS	GDP	Avg	OBP	Slg	OPS
2012	FtWyn	A	96	337	94	28	0	10	(-	-)	152	44	56	51	23	1	62	7	2	4	14	9	8	.279	.334	.451	.785
2013	Lk Els	A+	66	233	63	22	1	4	(-	-)	99	34	30	35	22	0	45	6	1	4	5	4	7	.270	.343	.425	.768
2013	SnAnt	AA	20	67	15	3	0	0	(-	-)	18	4	8	5	6	1	9	1	1	0	3	1	1	.224	.297	.269	.566
2014	SnAnt	AA	113	427	96	19	2	6	(-	-)	137	31	44	36	23	1	89	3	2	2	1	3	19	.225	.268	.321	.589
2015	ElPaso	AAA	21	71	23	8	0	2	(-	-)	37	12	15	14	8	0	8	0	0	0	1	0	1	.324	.392	.521	.914
2015	SD	NL	56	137	23	2	0	3	(2	1)	34	13	11	7	8	1	38	1	3	3	0	0	1	.168	.215	.248	.463

Chris Heisey

Bats: R Throws: R Pos: LF-12;RF-12;CF-10;PH-5;PR-3   HY-zee   Ht: 6'1" Wt: 215 Born: 12/14/1984 Age: 31

Year Team	Lg	G	AB	H	2B	3B	HR	(Hm	Rd)	TB	R	RBI	RC	TBB	IBB	SO	HBP	SH	SF	SB	CS	GDP	Avg	OBP	Slg	OPS
2015 OkCity*	AAA	66	216	52	8	1	15	(-	-)	107	46	41	42	39	1	57	6	0	1	3	0	6	.241	.370	.495	.866
2015 Buffalo*	AAA	17	58	9	0	0	2	(-	-)	15	5	2	4	9	0	16	0	0	0	0	0	0	.155	.269	.259	.527
2010 Cin	NL	97	201	51	10	1	8	(2	6)	87	33	21	22	16	1	57	6	1	2	1	2	3	.254	.324	.433	.757
2011 Cin	NL	120	279	71	9	1	18	(11	7)	136	44	50	40	19	3	78	5	1	4	6	1	1	.254	.309	.487	.797
2012 Cin	NL	120	347	92	16	5	7	(4	3)	139	44	31	42	18	0	81	7	3	0	6	3	8	.265	.315	.401	.715
2013 Cin	NL	87	224	53	11	1	9	(6	3)	93	29	23	26	9	0	51	5	4	2	3	0	4	.237	.279	.415	.694
2014 Cin	NL	119	275	61	15	2	8	(4	4)	104	34	22	22	15	0	64	2	5	2	9	2	3	.222	.265	.378	.643
2015 LAD	NL	33	55	10	2	0	2	(2	0)	18	8	9	10	15	2	17	0	0	1	2	0	1	.182	.347	.327	.674
Postseason		6	6	0	0	0	0	(0	0)	0	1	0	0	0	0	2	0	0	0	0	0	1	.000	.000	.000	.000
6 ML YEARS		576	1381	338	63	10	52	(29	23)	577	192	156	162	92	6	348	25	14	12	25	9	20	.245	.301	.418	.719

Jeremy Hellickson

Pitches: R Bats: R Pos: SP-27   Ht: 6'1" Wt: 190 Born: 4/8/1987 Age: 29

Year Team	Lg	G	GS	CG	GF	IP	BFP	H	R	ER	HR	SH	SF	HB	TBB	IBB	SO	WP	Bk	W	L	Pct	Sh	Sv-Op	Hld	ERC	ERA
2010 TB	AL	10	4	0	0	36.1	149	32	14	14	5	0	1	2	8	2	33	2	0	4	0	1.000	0	0-1	0	3.10	3.47
2011 TB	AL	29	29	2	0	189.0	774	146	64	62	21	1	2	4	72	8	117	8	1	13	10	.565	1	0-0	0	2.89	2.95
2012 TB	AL	31	31	0	0	177.0	741	163	68	61	25	4	3	4	59	3	124	5	0	10	11	.476	0	0-0	0	3.73	3.10
2013 TB	AL	32	31	0	1	174.0	737	185	103	100	24	2	5	4	50	0	135	7	2	12	10	.545	0	0-0	0	4.40	5.17
2014 TB	AL	13	13	0	0	63.2	281	71	35	32	8	0	1	2	21	1	54	8	0	1	5	.167	0	0-0	0	4.70	4.52
2015 Ari	NL	27	27	0	0	146.0	636	151	79	75	22	8	6	6	43	3	121	5	0	9	12	.429	0	0-0	0	4.25	4.62
Postseason		2	2	0	0	5.0	22	5	3	3	3	0	0	0	3	0	1	0	0	0	1	.000	0	0-0	0	8.99	5.40
6 ML YEARS		142	135	2	1	786.0	3318	748	363	344	105	15	18	22	253	17	584	35	3	49	48	.505	1	0-1	0	3.81	3.94

Heath Hembree

Pitches: R Bats: R Pos: RP-22   HEHM-bree   Ht: 6'4" Wt: 210 Born: 1/13/1989 Age: 27

Year Team	Lg	G	GS	CG	GF	IP	BFP	H	R	ER	HR	SH	SF	HB	TBB	IBB	SO	WP	Bk	W	L	Pct	Sh	Sv-Op	Hld	ERC	ERA
2015 Pwtckt*	AAA	29	0	0	20	31.2	128	23	10	8	1	4	1	2	10	0	32	4	0	0	5	.000	0	8--	-	2.15	2.27
2013 SF	NL	9	0	0	2	7.2	29	4	0	0	0	0	0	0	2	0	12	0	0	0	0	-	0	0-0	0	1.02	0.00
2014 Bos	AL	6	0	0	3	10.0	43	11	5	5	1	0	0	0	5	2	6	1	0	0	0	-	0	0-0	0	4.94	4.50
2015 Bos	AL	22	0	0	9	25.1	106	25	10	10	5	0	0	0	9	2	15	1	0	2	0	1.000	0	0-0	1	4.46	3.55
3 ML YEARS		37	0	0	14	43.0	178	40	15	15	6	0	0	0	16	4	33	2	0	2	0	1.000	0	0-0	1	3.79	3.14

Kyle Hendricks

Pitches: R Bats: R Pos: SP-32   Ht: 6'3" Wt: 190 Born: 12/7/1989 Age: 26

Year Team	Lg	G	GS	CG	GF	IP	BFP	H	R	ER	HR	SH	SF	HB	TBB	IBB	SO	WP	Bk	W	L	Pct	Sh	Sv-Op	Hld	ERC	ERA
2011 Spkane	A-	20	0	0	8	32.2	122	20	7	7	0	0	0	0	4	0	36	2	0	2	2	.500	0	3--	-	1.00	1.93
2012 2 Tms	Low	25	24	2	0	147.2	590	140	57	49	11	7	4	7	18	0	123	4	1	6	8	.429	0	0--	-	2.80	2.99
2013 Tenn	AA	21	21	1	0	126.1	508	107	34	26	3	3	2	5	26	0	101	1	0	10	3	.769	1	0--	-	2.23	1.85
2013 Iowa	AAA	6	6	0	0	40.0	159	35	12	11	2	0	1	1	8	0	27	1	0	3	1	.750	0	0--	-	2.49	2.48
2014 Iowa	AAA	17	17	0	0	102.2	416	98	46	41	5	8	0	2	23	4	97	1	0	10	5	.667	0	0--	-	2.90	3.59
2014 ChC	NL	13	13	0	0	80.1	321	72	24	22	4	4	1	4	15	2	47	0	0	7	2	.778	0	0-0	0	2.61	2.46
2015 ChC	NL	32	32	1	0	180.0	739	166	82	79	17	6	0	8	43	1	167	3	1	8	7	.533	1	0-0	0	3.18	3.95
2 ML YEARS		45	45	1	0	260.1	1060	238	106	101	21	10	1	12	58	3	214	3	1	15	9	.625	1	0-0	0	3.00	3.49

Liam Hendriks

Pitches: R Bats: R Pos: RP-58   Ht: 6'1" Wt: 205 Born: 2/10/1989 Age: 27

Year Team	Lg	G	GS	CG	GF	IP	BFP	H	R	ER	HR	SH	SF	HB	TBB	IBB	SO	WP	Bk	W	L	Pct	Sh	Sv-Op	Hld	ERC	ERA
2011 Min	AL	4	4	0	0	23.1	100	29	16	16	3	0	1	0	6	0	16	1	0	0	2	.000	0	0-0	0	5.26	6.17
2012 Min	AL	16	16	1	0	85.1	381	106	61	53	17	3	1	4	26	3	50	4	0	1	8	.111	0	0-0	0	6.03	5.59
2013 Min	AL	10	8	0	1	47.1	224	67	39	36	10	0	2	3	14	1	34	1	0	1	3	.250	0	0-0	0	7.16	6.85
2014 2 Tms	AL	9	6	0	0	32.2	143	38	21	19	3	0	2	3	7	0	23	1	0	1	2	.333	0	0-0	1	4.56	5.23
2015 Tor	AL	58	0	0	14	64.2	261	59	23	21	3	0	2	2	11	1	71	0	0	5	0	1.000	0	0-2	5	2.51	2.92
14 Tor	AL	3	3	0	0	13.1	57	12	9	9	3	0	0	2	4	0	8	0	0	1	0	1.000	0	0-0	0	4.58	6.08
14 KC	AL	6	3	0	0	19.1	86	26	12	10	0	0	2	1	3	0	15	1	0	0	2	.000	0	0-0	1	4.52	4.66
5 ML YEARS		97	34	1	15	253.1	1109	299	160	145	36	3	8	12	64	5	194	11	0	8	15	.348	0	0-2	6	4.99	5.15

Cesar Hernandez

Bats: B Throws: R Pos: 2B-88;PH-25;SS-12;3B-10;PR-2   Ht: 5'10" Wt: 166 Born: 5/23/1990 Age: 26

Year Team	Lg	G	AB	H	2B	3B	HR	(Hm	Rd)	TB	R	RBI	RC	TBB	IBB	SO	HBP	SH	SF	SB	CS	GDP	Avg	OBP	Slg	OPS
2013 Phi	NL	34	121	35	5	0	0	(0	0)	40	17	10	13	9	0	26	1	0	0	3	3	2	.289	.344	.331	.674
2014 Phi	NL	66	114	27	2	0	1	(1	0)	32	13	4	7	9	1	33	0	1	1	1	1	1	.237	.290	.281	.571
2015 Phi	NL	127	405	110	20	4	1	(1	0)	141	57	35	52	40	1	86	2	4	1	19	5	6	.272	.339	.348	.687
3 ML YEARS		227	640	172	27	4	2	(2	0)	213	87	49	72	58	2	145	3	5	2	20	9	9	.269	.331	.333	.664

David Hernandez

Pitches: R **Bats:** R **Pos:** RP-40 **Ht:** 6'3" **Wt:** 245 **Born:** 5/13/1985 **Age:** 31

Year	Team	Lg	G	GS	CG	GF	IP	BFP	H	R	ER	HR	SH	SF	HB	TBB	IBB	SO	WP	Bk	W	L	Pct	Sh	Sv-Op	Hld	ERC	ERA
2015 Mobile*	AA		5	1	0	1	4.0	15	0	0	0	0	1	0	0	2	0	6	1	0	0	0	-	0	0- -	-	0.25	0.00
2009 Bal	AL		20	19	0	0	101.1	462	118	62	61	27	2	3	1	46	0	68	3	0	4	10	.286	0	0-0	0	6.55	5.42
2010 Bal	AL		41	8	0	16	79.1	348	72	40	38	9	1	3	4	42	4	72	9	0	8	8	.500	0	2-6	2	4.28	4.31
2011 Ari	NL		74	0	0	28	69.1	291	49	27	26	4	3	2	2	30	1	77	7	1	5	3	.625	0	11-14	23	2.40	3.38
2012 Ari	NL		72	0	0	21	68.1	278	48	21	19	4	0	1	3	22	1	98	4	1	2	3	.400	0	4-10	25	2.10	2.50
2013 Ari	NL		62	0	0	12	62.1	263	50	33	31	10	2	0	4	24	4	66	6	0	5	6	.455	0	2-8	15	3.45	4.48
2015 Ari	NL		40	0	0	7	33.2	144	33	18	16	6	1	0	3	11	0	33	1	0	1	5	.167	0	0-0	7	4.62	4.28
Postseason			4	0	0	1	5.0	17	2	2	2	1	0	0	0	0	0	5	0	0	0	0	-	0	0-0	0	0.74	3.60
6 ML YEARS			309	27	0	84	414.1	1786	370	201	191	60	9	9	17	175	10	414	30	2	25	35	.417	0	19-38	72	3.96	4.15

Felix Hernandez

Pitches: R **Bats:** R **Pos:** SP-31 **Ht:** 6'3" **Wt:** 225 **Born:** 4/8/1986 **Age:** 30

Year	Team	Lg	G	GS	CG	GF	IP	BFP	H	R	ER	HR	SH	SF	HB	TBB	IBB	SO	WP	Bk	W	L	Pct	Sh	Sv-Op	Hld	ERC	ERA
2005 Sea	AL		12	12	0	0	84.1	328	61	26	25	5	1	2	2	23	0	77	3	0	4	4	.500	0	0-0	0	2.08	2.67
2006 Sea	AL		31	31	2	0	191.0	816	195	105	96	23	2	3	6	60	2	176	11	0	12	14	.462	1	0-0	0	4.11	4.52
2007 Sea	AL		30	30	1	0	190.1	808	209	88	83	20	6	1	3	53	4	165	7	1	14	7	.667	1	0-0	0	4.27	3.92
2008 Sea	AL		31	31	2	0	200.2	857	198	85	77	17	4	6	8	80	7	175	8	1	9	11	.450	0	0-0	0	4.05	3.45
2009 Sea	AL		34	34	2	0	238.2	977	200	81	66	15	6	11	8	71	0	217	17	1	19	5	.792	1	0-0	0	2.72	2.49
2010 Sea	AL		34	34	6	0	249.2	1001	194	80	63	17	6	3	8	70	1	232	14	1	13	12	.520	1	0-0	0	2.39	2.27
2011 Sea	AL		33	33	5	0	233.2	964	218	99	90	19	3	7	7	67	0	222	12	1	14	14	.500	0	0-0	0	3.31	3.47
2012 Sea	AL		33	33	5	0	232.0	939	209	84	79	14	2	2	12	56	0	223	13	2	13	9	.591	5	0-0	0	2.94	3.06
2013 Sea	AL		31	31	0	0	204.1	822	185	74	69	15	4	6	3	46	1	216	13	0	12	10	.545	0	0-0	0	2.83	3.04
2014 Sea	AL		34	34	0	0	236.0	912	170	68	56	16	4	5	5	46	1	248	18	0	15	6	.714	0	0-0	0	1.81	2.14
2015 Sea	AL		31	31	2	0	201.2	826	180	80	79	23	4	4	9	58	0	191	10	0	18	9	.667	2	0-0	0	3.37	3.53
11 ML YEARS			334	334	25	0	2262.1	9250	2019	870	783	184	42	50	71	630	16	2142	126	7	143	101	.586	11	0-0	0	3.05	3.11

Gorkys Hernandez

Bats: R **Throws:** R **Pos:** LF-4;PR-3;RF-2;PH-1   GORE-keez   **Ht:** 6'1" **Wt:** 190 **Born:** 9/7/1987 **Age:** 28

Year	Team	Lg	G	AB	H	2B	3B	HR	(Hm	Rd)	TB	R	RBI	RC	TBB	IBB	SO	HBP	SH	SF	SB	CS	GDP	Avg	OBP	Slg	OPS
2011 Indy	AAA		126	424	120	25	9	1	(-	-)	166	48	40	61	35	0	91	8	7	1	21	9	5	.283	.348	.392	.740
2012 Indy	AAA		67	237	61	11	2	2	(-	-)	82	43	25	32	34	0	64	2	6	2	13	7	0	.257	.353	.346	.699
2013 NewOr	AAA		90	309	85	11	4	4	(-	-)	116	45	22	40	22	1	96	4	4	1	22	9	5	.275	.330	.375	.706
2013 Omha	AAA		34	121	28	6	1	2	(-	-)	42	14	10	12	8	0	29	2	2	2	3	3	2	.231	.286	.347	.633
2014 Charllt	AAA		47	176	41	10	0	0	(-	-)	51	19	8	16	13	0	44	2	1	1	6	0	6	.233	.292	.290	.581
2015 Indy	AAA		104	340	98	16	3	6	(-	-)	138	51	42	56	41	0	78	2	5	3	17	3	5	.288	.365	.406	.771
2012 2 Tms	NL		70	156	30	2	3	3	(2	1)	47	18	13	15	13	0	42	3	1	0	7	2	2	.192	.267	.301	.569
2015 Pit	NL		8	5	0	0	0	0	(0	0)	0	0	0	0	0	0	0	0	0	0	1	0	0	.000	.000	.000	.000
12 Pit	NL		25	24	2	0	0	0	(0	0)	2	2	2	0	1	0	5	1	0	0	2	0	1	.083	.154	.083	.237
12 Mia	NL		45	132	28	2	3	3	(2	1)	45	16	11	15	12	0	37	2	1	0	5	2	1	.212	.288	.341	.629
2 ML YEARS			78	161	30	2	3	3	(2	1)	47	18	13	15	13	0	42	3	1	0	8	2	2	.186	.260	.292	.552

Kiké Hernandez

kee-KAY

Bats: R **Throws:** R **Pos:** 2B-20;CF-19;LF-17;SS-16;PH-11;PR-5;RF-2;3B-1   **Ht:** 5'11" **Wt:** 200 **Born:** 8/24/1991 **Age:** 24

Year	Team	Lg	G	AB	H	2B	3B	HR	(Hm	Rd)	TB	R	RBI	RC	TBB	IBB	SO	HBP	SH	SF	SB	CS	GDP	Avg	OBP	Slg	OPS
2011 Lxngtn	A		62	215	53	11	0	2	(-	-)	70	30	17	26	31	0	33	0	3	0	0	2	8	.247	.341	.326	.667
2012 Lancst	A+		100	378	104	25	7	5	(-	-)	158	52	49	52	22	0	43	3	5	3	4	2	9	.275	.318	.418	.736
2012 CpChr	AA		23	81	20	2	0	1	(-	-)	25	7	3	7	4	0	9	2	1	0	2	2	4	.247	.299	.309	.607
2013 CpChr	AA		116	437	103	18	2	13	(-	-)	164	53	46	51	34	2	70	5	5	2	5	3	13	.236	.297	.375	.672
2014 CpChr	AA		10	40	13	3	0	1	(-	-)	19	9	5	7	3	0	3	0	0	0	0	0	0	.325	.372	.475	.847
2014 OkCity	AAA		67	264	89	17	2	8	(-	-)	134	41	31	50	18	1	25	2	2	3	6	5	10	.337	.380	.508	.887
2014 NewOr	AAA		21	72	18	5	0	2	(-	-)	29	8	6	10	10	0	13	1	0	1	0	1	1	.250	.345	.403	.748
2015 OkCity	AAA		16	59	10	2	0	1	(-	-)	15	6	9	3	4	0	14	0	0	1	1	0	2	.169	.219	.254	.473
2014 2 Tms			42	121	30	6	3	3	(1	2)	51	13	14	18	12	0	21	1	0	0	0	0	0	.248	.321	.421	.742
2015 LAD	NL		76	202	62	12	2	7	(2	5)	99	24	22	32	11	0	46	2	1	0	0	2	3	.307	.346	.490	.836
14 Hou	AL		24	81	23	4	2	1	(1	0)	34	10	8	14	8	0	11	0	0	0	0	0	0	.284	.348	.420	.768
14 Mia	NL		18	40	7	2	1	2	(0	2)	17	3	6	4	4	0	10	1	0	0	0	0	0	.175	.267	.425	.692
2 ML YEARS			118	323	92	18	5	10	(3	7)	150	37	36	50	23	0	67	3	1	2	0	2	4	.285	.336	.464	.801

Oscar Hernandez

Bats: R **Throws:** R **Pos:** C-13;PH-5;PR-1 **Ht:** 6'1" **Wt:** 220 **Born:** 7/9/1993 **Age:** 22

Year	Team	Lg	G	AB	H	2B	3B	HR	(Hm	Rd)	TB	R	RBI	RC	TBB	IBB	SO	HBP	SH	SF	SB	CS	GDP	Avg	OBP	Slg	OPS
2012 Prnctn	R+		49	160	37	9	1	5	(-	-)	63	25	24	24	23	0	31	8	0	4	0	1	8	.231	.349	.394	.742
2013 2 Tms	Low		46	176	40	6	0	6	(-	-)	64	23	34	19	13	2	25	2	0	1	9	1	3	.227	.286	.364	.650
2014 BG	A		94	362	90	18	5	9	(-	-)	145	43	63	44	25	1	78	4	1	5	3	6	6	.249	.301	.401	.701
2015 Ari	NL		18	31	5	1	0	0	(0	0)	6	4	1	2	3	0	15	1	1	0	0	0	0	.161	.257	.194	.451

Roberto Hernandez

Pitches: R **Bats:** R **Pos:** SP-11; RP-9   **Ht:** 6'4" **Wt:** 230 **Born:** 8/30/1980 **Age:** 35

			HOW MUCH HE PITCHED						WHAT HE GAVE UP											THE RESULTS						
Year	Team	Lg	G	GS	CG	GF	IP	BFP	H	R	ER	HR	SH	SF	HB	TBB	IBB	SO	WP	Bk	W	L	Pct	Sh	Sv-Op	Hld	ERC	ERA
2006	Cle	AL	38	7	0	12	74.2	340	88	46	45	9	2	4	7	31	3	58	3	1	1	10	.091	0	0-3	10	5.69	5.42
2007	Cle	AL	32	32	2	0	215.0	879	199	78	73	16	2	4	11	61	2	137	5	1	19	8	.704	1	0-0	0	3.32	3.06
2008	Cle	AL	22	22	1	0	120.2	549	126	80	73	7	1	4	9	70	0	58	8	1	8	7	.533	1	0-0	0	5.07	5.44
2009	Cle	AL	24	24	0	0	125.1	596	151	97	88	16	4	2	8	70	0	79	5	1	5	12	.294	0	0-0	0	6.38	6.32
2010	Cle	AL	33	33	4	0	210.1	880	203	98	88	17	2	10	9	72	0	124	3	0	13	14	.481	1	0-0	0	3.77	3.77
2011	Cle	AL	32	32	0	0	188.2	833	205	125	110	22	9	7	14	60	3	109	3	1	7	15	.318	0	0-0	0	4.59	5.25
2012	Cle	AL	3	3	0	0	14.1	62	17	15	12	4	0	2	1	3	0	2	1	0	0	3	.000	0	0-0	0	6.03	7.53
2013	TB	AL	32	24	1	3	151.0	643	164	87	82	24	3	5	13	38	8	113	3	0	6	13	.316	0	1-1	0	4.74	4.89
2014	2 Tms	NL	32	29	0	1	164.2	722	156	84	75	19	10	5	9	73	7	105	5	0	8	11	.421	0	0-1	0	4.17	4.10
2015	Hou	NL	20	11	0	6	84.2	357	90	48	41	9	0	3	1	26	2	42	1	0	3	5	.375	0	0-0	0	4.20	4.36
14	Phi	NL	23	20	0	1	121.0	527	108	57	52	11	7	3	7	55	7	75	4	0	6	8	.429	0	0-1	0	3.72	3.87
14	LAD	NL	9	9	0	0	43.2	195	48	27	23	8	3	2	2	18	0	30	1	0	2	3	.400	0	0-0	0	5.50	4.74
	Postseason		3	3	0	0	15.0	66	13	12	12	2	0	0	0	11	0	12	0	0	0	1	.000	0	0-0	0	5.02	7.20
	10 ML YEARS		268	217	8	22	1349.1	5861	1399	758	687	143	33	46	82	504	25	827	37	5	70	98	.417	3	1-5	10	4.47	4.58

Dilson Herrera

Bats: R **Throws:** R **Pos:** 2B-29;PH-3   DILL-sun   **Ht:** 5'10" **Wt:** 150 **Born:** 3/3/1994 **Age:** 22

									BATTING												RUNNING			AVERAGES			
Year	Team	Lg	G	AB	H	2B	3B	HR	(Hm	Rd)	TB	R	RBI	RC	TBB	IBB	SO	HBP	SH	SF	SB	CS	GDP	Avg	OBP	Slg	OPS
2012	2 Tms	Low	60	227	65	12	5	8	(-	-)	111	48	29	39	19	0	47	0	10	0	12	4	3	.286	.341	.489	.830
2013	2 Tms	Low	116	442	118	27	3	11	(-	-)	184	75	60	64	40	1	116	8	6	7	14	6	6	.267	.334	.416	.750
2014	Stluci	A+	67	283	87	16	2	3	(-	-)	116	48	23	44	18	0	44	4	2	2	14	3	4	.307	.355	.410	.765
2014	Bnghtn	AA	61	241	82	17	3	10	(-	-)	135	50	48	54	29	0	52	2	0	6	9	4	5	.340	.406	.560	.967
2015	LsVgs	AAA	81	327	107	23	2	11	(-	-)	167	68	50	62	28	0	59	3	3	3	13	9	2	.327	.382	.511	.893
2014	NYM	NL	18	59	13	0	1	3	(0	3)	24	6	11	7	7	0	17	0	0	0	0	0	3	.220	.303	.407	.710
2015	NYM	NL	31	90	19	3	1	3	(2	1)	33	7	6	11	11	1	23	2	0	0	2	0	2	.211	.311	.367	.677
	2 ML YEARS		49	149	32	3	2	6	(2	4)	57	13	17	18	18	1	40	2	0	0	2	0	5	.215	.308	.383	.690

Elian Herrera

EH-lee-ahn

Bats: B **Throws:** R **Pos:** 3B-47;2B-36;PH-14;RF-3;LF-1;PR-1   **Ht:** 5'10" **Wt:** 205 **Born:** 2/1/1985 **Age:** 31

									BATTING												RUNNING			AVERAGES			
Year	Team	Lg	G	AB	H	2B	3B	HR	(Hm	Rd)	TB	R	RBI	RC	TBB	IBB	SO	HBP	SH	SF	SB	CS	GDP	Avg	OBP	Slg	OPS
2015	ColSpr*	AAA	56	210	75	15	2	3	(-	-)	103	33	27	42	20	0	29	0	3	0	4	1	3	.357	.413	.490	.904
2012	LAD	NL	67	187	47	10	1	1	(0	1)	62	26	17	20	23	0	50	2	2	0	4	2	5	.251	.340	.332	.671
2013	LAD	NL	4	8	2	0	0	0	(0	0)	2	0	0	0	0	0	2	0	0	0	0	0	0	.250	.250	.250	.500
2014	Mil	NL	69	135	37	7	1	0	(0	0)	46	14	5	9	3	1	36	0	1	1	4	1	2	.274	.288	.341	.629
2015	Mil	NL	83	256	62	18	0	7	(5	2)	101	29	33	26	18	1	72	0	1	2	3	1	4	.242	.290	.395	.684
	4 ML YEARS		223	586	148	35	2	8	(5	3)	211	69	55	55	44	2	160	2	4	3	11	4	11	.253	.306	.360	.666

Jonathan Herrera

Bats: B **Throws:** R **Pos:** PH-31;2B-29;3B-16;PR-6;SS-1   **Ht:** 5'9" **Wt:** 180 **Born:** 11/3/1984 **Age:** 31

									BATTING												RUNNING			AVERAGES			
Year	Team	Lg	G	AB	H	2B	3B	HR	(Hm	Rd)	TB	R	RBI	RC	TBB	IBB	SO	HBP	SH	SF	SB	CS	GDP	Avg	OBP	Slg	OPS
2008	Col	NL	28	61	14	1	1	0	(0	0)	17	5	3	6	4	0	10	0	1	0	1	1	0	.230	.277	.279	.556
2010	Col	NL	76	222	63	6	2	1	(0	1)	76	34	21	29	25	1	36	0	7	3	2	2	2	.284	.352	.342	.694
2011	Col	NL	104	281	68	5	1	3	(2	1)	84	28	14	24	28	0	40	1	10	0	4	4	7	.242	.313	.299	.612
2012	Col	NL	86	225	59	9	1	3	(3	0)	79	29	12	22	16	3	39	2	7	0	4	1	5	.262	.317	.351	.668
2013	Col	NL	81	195	57	7	2	1	(0	1)	71	16	16	22	14	3	24	0	4	2	3	2	6	.292	.336	.364	.701
2014	Bos	AL	42	90	21	1	2	0	(0	0)	26	10	9	9	7	0	24	3	3	1	1	3	3	.233	.307	.289	.596
2015	ChC	NL	73	126	29	5	1	2	(1	1)	42	14	14	11	2	1	23	0	4	0	3	0	3	.230	.242	.333	.576
	7 ML YEARS		490	1200	311	34	10	10	(6	4)	395	136	89	123	96	8	196	6	36	6	18	13	26	.259	.316	.329	.645

Kelvin Herrera

Pitches: R **Bats:** R **Pos:** RP-72   **Ht:** 5'10" **Wt:** 200 **Born:** 12/31/1989 **Age:** 26

						HOW MUCH HE PITCHED			WHAT HE GAVE UP											THE RESULTS						
Year	Team	Lg	G	GS	CG	GF	IP	BFP	H	R	ER	HR	SH	SF	HB	TBB	IBB	SO	WP	Bk	W	L	Pct	Sh	Sv-Op	Hld	ERC	ERA
2011	KC	AL	2	0	0	0	2.0	9	2	3	3	1	1	0	1	0	0	0	0	0	0	1	.000	0	0-0	1	7.30	13.50
2012	KC	AL	76	0	0	10	84.1	344	79	24	22	4	5	0	2	21	6	77	3	1	4	3	.571	0	3-4	19	2.84	2.35
2013	KC	AL	59	0	0	16	58.1	245	48	27	25	9	0	3	2	21	2	74	5	0	5	7	.417	0	2-4	20	3.35	3.86
2014	KC	AL	70	0	0	12	70.0	285	54	12	11	0	4	0	3	26	0	59	1	0	4	3	.571	0	0-1	20	2.31	1.41
2015	KC	AL	72	0	0	8	69.2	286	52	23	21	5	1	5	2	26	1	64	4	0	4	3	.571	0	0-7	21	2.53	2.71
	Postseason		11	0	0	0	15.0	61	11	3	3	0	0	0	0	7	0	16	0	0	1	0	1.000	0	0-0	3	2.31	1.80
	5 ML YEARS		279	0	0	46	284.1	1169	235	89	82	19	11	8	10	94	9	274	13	1	17	17	.500	0	5-16	81	2.76	2.60

Odubel Herrera

Bats: L **Throws:** R **Pos:** CF-136;PH-16;PR-2   oh-DOO-bull   **Ht:** 5'11" **Wt:** 200 **Born:** 12/29/1991 **Age:** 24

Year	Team	Lg	G	AB	H	2B	3B	HR	(Hm	Rd)	TB	R	RBI	RC	TBB	IBB	SO	HBP	SH	SF	SB	CS	GDP	Avg	OBP	Slg	OPS
2011	Hkry	A	119	464	142	26	3	3	(-	-)	183	72	56	68	24	0	78	8	7	2	34	11	12	.306	.349	.394	.744
2012	MrtlBh	A+	126	500	142	22	6	5	(-	-)	191	72	46	69	33	3	99	7	7	4	27	7	9	.284	.335	.382	.717
2013	Frisco	AA	101	389	100	12	7	2	(-	-)	132	37	30	39	17	0	67	1	3	2	15	5	11	.257	.289	.339	.628
2013	MrtlBh	A+	29	95	28	2	1	1	(-	-)	35	13	5	16	16	0	19	1	2	1	2	2	1	.295	.398	.368	.767
2014	MrtlBh	A+	29	111	33	3	1	0	(-	-)	38	26	11	19	23	0	21	0	1	2	9	3	1	.297	.412	.342	.754
2014	Frisco	AA	96	368	118	16	4	2	(-	-)	148	47	47	57	29	1	70	3	6	2	12	7	4	.321	.373	.402	.775
2015	Phi	NL	147	495	147	30	3	8	(4	4)	207	64	41	66	28	0	129	8	5	1	16	8	6	.297	.344	.418	.762

Chris Herrmann

Bats: L **Throws:** R **Pos:** C-38;PH-5;1B-2;RF-2;PR-1   HERR-men   **Ht:** 6'0" **Wt:** 200 **Born:** 11/24/1987 **Age:** 28

Year	Team	Lg	G	AB	H	2B	3B	HR	(Hm	Rd)	TB	R	RBI	RC	TBB	IBB	SO	HBP	SH	SF	SB	CS	GDP	Avg	OBP	Slg	OPS
2015	Roch*	AAA	23	73	19	3	0	1	(-	-)	25	9	6	11	11	0	13	2	0	2	3	0	2	.260	.364	.342	.706
2012	Min	AL	7	18	1	0	0	0	(0	0)	1	0	1	0	1	0	5	0	0	0	0	0	0	.056	.105	.056	.161
2013	Min	AL	57	157	32	7	0	4	(1	3)	51	16	18	15	18	0	49	0	3	0	0	1	3	.204	.286	.325	.611
2014	Min	AL	33	75	16	3	0	0	(0	0)	19	8	4	5	4	0	17	0	0	0	1	0	0	.213	.253	.253	.506
2015	Min	AL	45	103	15	5	1	2	(2	0)	28	13	10	8	7	0	37	2	1	0	0	0	1	.146	.214	.272	.486
4 ML YEARS			142	353	64	15	1	6	(3	3)	99	37	33	28	30	0	108	2	4	0	1	1	6	.181	.249	.280	.530

Keith Hessler

Pitches: L **Bats:** L **Pos:** RP-18   **Ht:** 6'4" **Wt:** 215 **Born:** 3/15/1989 **Age:** 27

Year	Team	Lg	G	GS	CG	GF	IP	BFP	H	R	ER	HR	SH	SF	HB	TBB	IBB	SO	WP	Bk	W	L	Pct	Sh	Sv-Op	Hld	ERC	ERA
2011	Msoula	R+	23	1	0	2	43.2	188	32	17	14	3	3	1	2	20	0	62	7	0	4	0	1.000	0	0- -	-	2.72	2.89
2012	Sbend	A	39	7	0	5	90.0	387	86	40	32	3	3	5	5	44	0	75	9	1	2	5	.286	0	1- -	-	4.00	3.20
2013	Visalia	A+	26	26	0	0	137.0	623	161	97	89	24	10	8	10	64	1	126	7	0	8	7	.533	0	0- -	-	6.36	5.85
2014	Visalia	A+	44	0	0	12	59.1	275	79	31	29	3	2	2	5	18	0	78	4	0	4	2	.667	0	1- -	-	5.54	4.40
2015	Visalia	A+	10	0	0	2	14.2	55	11	0	0	0	0	0	0	2	0	20	1	0	1	0	1.000	0	0- -	-	1.46	0.00
2015	Mobile	AA	24	0	0	7	25.1	95	17	2	2	1	2	0	0	5	3	32	1	0	3	1	.750	0	1- -	-	1.39	0.71
2015	Reno	AAA	17	0	0	2	19.0	75	14	12	12	3	1	0	0	8	0	13	1	0	1	1	.500	0	0- -	-	3.25	5.68
2015	Ari	NL	18	0	0	1	12.1	57	16	11	11	4	0	1	2	4	1	12	1	0	0	1	.000	0	0-2	1	6.95	8.03

Chris Heston

Pitches: R **Bats:** R **Pos:** SP-31   **Ht:** 6'3" **Wt:** 195 **Born:** 4/10/1988 **Age:** 28

Year	Team	Lg	G	GS	CG	GF	IP	BFP	H	R	ER	HR	SH	SF	HB	TBB	IBB	SO	WP	Bk	W	L	Pct	Sh	Sv-Op	Hld	ERC	ERA
2011	Augusta	A	24	24	1	0	151.0	614	144	64	53	10	5	4	8	40	1	131	7	0	12	4	.750	0	0- -	-	3.38	3.16
2012	Rchmd	AA	25	25	1	0	148.2	595	124	43	37	2	10	3	4	40	1	135	12	0	9	8	.529	0	0- -	-	2.30	2.24
2013	Fresno	AAA	19	19	1	0	108.2	495	129	75	70	14	6	5	9	46	2	97	8	1	7	6	.538	1	0- -	-	5.84	5.80
2014	Fresno	AAA	28	28	1	0	173.0	716	152	76	65	16	4	1	9	51	1	125	11	0	12	9	.571	4	0- -	-	3.17	3.38
2014	SF	NL	3	1	0	2	5.1	24	6	3	3	0	0	1	0	3	0	4	1	0	0	0	-	0	0-0	-	4.74	5.06
2015	SF	NL	31	31	2	0	177.2	746	169	82	78	16	2	0	13	64	3	141	5	1	12	11	.522	1	0-0	0	3.94	3.95
2 ML YEARS			34	32	2	2	183.0	770	175	85	81	16	2	1	13	67	3	145	6	1	12	11	.522	1	0-0	0	3.96	3.98

Jason Heyward

Bats: L **Throws:** L **Pos:** RF-144;CF-10;PH-8   **Ht:** 6'5" **Wt:** 245 **Born:** 8/9/1989 **Age:** 26

Year	Team	Lg	G	AB	H	2B	3B	HR	(Hm	Rd)	TB	R	RBI	RC	TBB	IBB	SO	HBP	SH	SF	SB	CS	GDP	Avg	OBP	Slg	OPS
2010	Atl	NL	142	520	144	29	5	18	(9	9)	237	83	72	96	91	2	128	10	0	2	11	6	13	.277	.393	.456	.849
2011	Atl	NL	128	396	90	18	2	14	(5	9)	154	50	42	49	51	4	93	4	0	3	9	2	7	.227	.319	.389	.708
2012	Atl	NL	158	587	158	30	6	27	(9	18)	281	93	82	87	58	1	152	2	0	3	21	8	5	.269	.335	.479	.814
2013	Atl	NL	104	382	97	22	1	14	(10	4)	163	67	38	55	48	1	73	8	1	0	2	4	7	.254	.349	.427	.776
2014	Atl	NL	149	573	155	26	3	11	(5	6)	220	74	58	84	67	3	98	6	0	3	20	4	2	.271	.351	.384	.735
2015	StL	NL	154	547	160	33	4	13	(5	8)	240	79	60	78	56	4	90	2	0	3	23	3	13	.293	.359	.439	.797
Postseason			9	39	6	1	0	1	(0	1)	10	1	4	2	1	0	16	0	0	0	0	0	1	.154	.175	.256	.431
6 ML YEARS			835	3005	804	158	21	97	(43	54)	1295	446	352	449	371	15	634	32	1	14	86	27	47	.268	.353	.431	.784

Aaron Hicks

Bats: B **Throws:** R **Pos:** CF-88;RF-16;LF-4;PH-1   **Ht:** 6'2" **Wt:** 210 **Born:** 10/2/1989 **Age:** 26

Year	Team	Lg	G	AB	H	2B	3B	HR	(Hm	Rd)	TB	R	RBI	RC	TBB	IBB	SO	HBP	SH	SF	SB	CS	GDP	Avg	OBP	Slg	OPS
2015	Roch*	AAA	38	149	50	13	4	3	(-	-)	80	26	20	31	17	0	30	0	0	2	11	6	3	.336	.399	.537	.936
2013	Min	AL	81	281	54	11	3	8	(3	5)	95	37	27	25	24	0	84	2	4	2	9	3	0	.192	.259	.338	.597
2014	Min	AL	69	186	40	8	0	1	(0	1)	51	22	18	22	36	0	56	0	2	1	4	3	2	.215	.341	.274	.615
2015	Min	AL	97	352	90	11	3	11	(6	5)	140	48	33	45	34	2	66	2	0	2	13	3	6	.256	.323	.398	.721
3 ML YEARS			247	819	184	30	6	20	(9	11)	286	107	78	92	94	2	206	4	6	5	26	9	8	.225	.306	.349	.655

John Hicks

Bats: R **Throws:** R **Pos:** C-14;DH-2;PH-2;3B-1   **Ht:** 6'2" **Wt:** 210 **Born:** 8/31/1989 **Age:** 26

Year	Team	Lg	G	AB	H	2B	3B	HR	(Hm	Rd)	TB	R	RBI	RC	TBB	IBB	SO	HBP	SH	SF	SB	CS	GDP	Avg	OBP	Slg	OPS
2011	Clinton	A	38	139	43	9	2	2	(-	-)	62	21	26	20	5	0	17	1	0	3	2	3	3	.309	.331	.446	.777
2012	Hi Dsrt	A+	121	506	158	32	2	15	(-	-)	239	87	79	85	28	2	73	3	0	1	22	8	11	.312	.351	.472	.824
2013	Jacksn	AA	80	296	70	14	1	4	(-	-)	98	40	29	32	22	0	62	6	1	2	13	4	8	.236	.301	.331	.632
2014	Jacksn	AA	53	189	56	10	2	3	(-	-)	79	29	27	29	20	0	42	0	1	1	6	3	6	.296	.362	.418	.780
2014	Tacom	AAA	28	101	28	2	1	2	(-	-)	38	13	20	13	7	0	24	2	0	2	1	0	3	.277	.330	.376	.707
2015	Tacom	AAA	83	298	73	15	1	6	(-	-)	108	39	35	32	17	0	71	0	1	4	9	2	6	.245	.282	.362	.645
2015	Sea	AL	17	32	2	1	0	0	(0	0)	3	1	1	0	1	0	18	0	1	0	1	1	0	.063	.091	.094	.185

Aaron Hill

Bats: R **Throws:** R **Pos:** 2B-47;3B-38;PH-38;DH-2   **Ht:** 5'11" **Wt:** 200 **Born:** 3/21/1982 **Age:** 34

Year	Team	Lg	G	AB	H	2B	3B	HR	(Hm	Rd)	TB	R	RBI	RC	TBB	IBB	SO	HBP	SH	SF	SB	CS	GDP	Avg	OBP	Slg	OPS
2005	Tor	AL	105	361	99	25	3	3	(3	0)	139	49	40	50	34	0	41	5	3	4	2	1	5	.274	.342	.385	.727
2006	Tor	AL	155	546	159	28	3	6	(4	2)	211	70	50	68	42	5	66	9	4	5	5	2	15	.291	.349	.386	.735
2007	Tor	AL	160	608	177	47	2	17	(8	9)	279	87	78	88	41	1	102	0	3	5	4	3	21	.291	.333	.459	.792
2008	Tor	AL	55	205	54	14	0	2	(1	1)	74	19	20	24	16	0	31	3	4	1	4	2	4	.263	.324	.361	.685
2009	Tor	AL	158	682	195	37	0	36	(21	15)	340	103	108	110	42	1	98	5	1	4	6	2	17	.286	.330	.499	.829
2010	Tor	AL	138	528	108	22	0	26	(15	11)	208	70	68	57	41	2	85	8	1	2	2	2	8	.205	.271	.394	.665
2011	2 Tms		137	520	128	27	3	8	(4	4)	185	61	61	61	35	1	72	7	2	7	21	7	10	.246	.299	.356	.655
2012	Ari	NL	156	609	184	44	6	26	(14	12)	318	93	85	101	52	7	86	4	1	2	14	5	15	.302	.360	.522	.882
2013	Ari	NL	87	327	95	21	1	11	(7	4)	151	45	41	45	29	2	48	5	0	1	1	4	6	.291	.356	.462	.818
2014	Ari	NL	133	501	122	26	3	10	(6	4)	184	52	60	48	28	0	92	5	0	7	4	3	16	.244	.287	.367	.654
2015	Ari	NL	116	313	72	18	0	6	(3	3)	108	32	39	30	31	0	54	1	0	8	7	2	9	.230	.295	.345	.640
11	Tor	AL	104	396	89	15	1	6	(3	3)	124	38	45	38	23	1	53	4	0	6	16	3	8	.225	.270	.313	.584
11	Ari	NL	33	124	39	12	2	2	(1	1)	61	23	16	23	12	0	19	3	2	1	5	4	2	.315	.386	.492	.878
	Postseason		5	18	5	0	0	1	(1	0)	8	3	1	2	5	0	3	0	0	0	0	0	1	.278	.435	.444	.879
	11 ML YEARS		1400	5200	1393	309	21	151	(86	65)	2197	681	650	682	391	19	775	52	19	46	70	33	126	.268	.323	.423	.745

Rich Hill

Pitches: L **Bats:** L **Pos:** SP-4   **Ht:** 6'5" **Wt:** 220 **Born:** 3/11/1980 **Age:** 36

			HOW MUCH HE PITCHED					WHAT HE GAVE UP										THE RESULTS						
Year	Team	Lg	G	GS	CG	GF	IP	BFP	H	R	ER	HR	SH	SF	HB	TBB	IBB	SO	WP	Bk	W	L	Pct	Sh	Sv-Op	Hld	ERC	ERA
2015	Syrcse*	AAA	25	0	0	9	21.2	101	12	9	7	1	2	1	5	21	0	32	3	0	2	2	.500	0	0- -	-	4.19	2.91
2015	Pwtckt*	AAA	5	5	0	0	32.1	128	27	11	10	3	0	0	2	9	0	29	0	0	3	2	.600	0	0- -	-	3.05	2.78
2005	ChC	NL	10	4	0	1	23.2	115	25	24	24	3	1	0	1	17	1	21	0	0	0	2	.000	0	0-0	0	5.81	9.13
2006	ChC	NL	17	16	2	1	99.1	417	83	51	46	16	8	3	2	39	1	90	3	0	6	7	.462	1	0-0	0	3.59	4.17
2007	ChC	NL	32	32	0	0	195.0	812	170	89	85	27	9	4	12	63	3	183	1	1	11	8	.579	1	0-0	0	3.56	3.92
2008	ChC	NL	5	5	0	0	19.2	89	13	9	9	2	0	1	0	18	0	15	1	0	1	1	1.000	0	0-0	0	4.38	4.12
2009	Bal	AL	14	13	0	0	57.2	275	68	53	50	7	2	2	1	40	2	46	1	1	3	3	.500	0	0-0	0	6.55	7.80
2010	Bos	AL	6	0	0	0	4.0	18	5	0	0	0	0	0	0	1	0	3	0	0	1	0	1.000	0	0-0	1	4.05	0.00
2011	Bos	AL	9	0	0	3	8.0	30	3	0	0	0	0	0	1	3	0	12	1	0	0	0	-	0	0-0	3	1.10	0.00
2012	Bos	AL	25	0	0	3	19.2	83	17	4	4	0	0	0	0	11	1	21	0	0	1	0	1.000	0	0-0	6	3.24	1.83
2013	Cle	AL	63	0	0	3	38.2	182	38	30	27	3	1	2	2	29	6	51	6	1	1	2	.333	0	0-2	13	5.07	6.28
2014	2 Tms		16	0	0	3	5.1	29	7	2	2	0	0	0	1	6	1	9	1	0	0	0	-	0	0-0	1	8.55	3.38
2015	Bos	AL	4	4	1	0	29.0	106	14	5	5	2	0	0	0	5	0	36	0	0	2	1	.667	1	0-0	0	1.13	1.55
14	LAA		2	0	0	0	0.0	4	1	1	1	0	0	0	0	3	0	0	1	0	0	0	-	0	0-0	0	-	-
14	NYY		14	0	0	2	5.1	25	6	1	1	0	0	0	1	3	1	9	0	0	0	0	-	0	0-0	1	5.10	1.69
	Postseason		1	1	0	0	3.0	18	6	3	3	1	0	0	1	2	0	3	0	0	0	1	.000	0	0-0	0	15.68	9.00
	11 ML YEARS		201	74	3	13	500.0	2156	443	267	252	60	21	13	23	232	15	487	14	3	26	23	.531	2	0-2	24	3.96	4.54

Taylor Hill

Pitches: R **Bats:** R **Pos:** RP-6   **Ht:** 6'3" **Wt:** 230 **Born:** 3/12/1989 **Age:** 27

			HOW MUCH HE PITCHED					WHAT HE GAVE UP										THE RESULTS						
Year	Team	Lg	G	GS	CG	GF	IP	BFP	H	R	ER	HR	SH	SF	HB	TBB	IBB	SO	WP	Bk	W	L	Pct	Sh	Sv-Op	Hld	ERC	ERA
2011	Auburn	A-	9	5	0	0	31.1	128	32	12	11	1	1	0	3	3	0	27	2	0	0	2	.000	0	0- -	-	2.98	3.16
2012	2 Tms	Low	27	23	1	2	139.1	615	161	91	76	14	4	2	7	34	0	71	7	1	11	7	.611	1	0- -	-	4.47	4.91
2013	Ptomc	A+	15	14	2	0	84.1	333	73	31	28	6	3	2	4	11	0	54	4	0	6	2	.750	2	0- -	-	2.39	2.99
2013	Hrsbrg	AA	11	11	0	0	69.2	284	67	25	21	7	1	4	1	16	0	41	1	0	2	7	.222	0	0- -	-	3.32	2.71
2014	Syrcse	AAA	25	24	4	1	144.0	587	136	48	45	15	2	4	9	25	0	86	3	0	11	7	.611	2	1- -	-	3.20	2.81
2015	Syrcse	AAA	22	22	0	0	118.2	541	163	80	69	9	3	4	6	29	1	70	3	0	3	10	.231	0	0- -	-	5.63	5.23
2014	Was	NL	3	1	0	2	9.0	45	16	9	9	0	1	0	2	3	1	5	0	0	0	1	.000	0	0-0	0	8.83	9.00
2015	Was	NL	6	0	0	4	12.0	51	14	5	5	2	0	0	1	4	0	9	0	0	0	0	-	0	0-0	0	5.96	3.75
	2 ML YEARS		9	1	0	6	21.0	96	30	14	14	2	1	0	3	7	1	14	0	0	0	1	.000	0	0-0	0	7.20	6.00

Dalier Hinojosa

Pitches: R **Bats:** R **Pos:** RP-19   DAH-lee-air hee-no-HO-sah   **Ht:** 6'1" **Wt:** 230 **Born:** 2/10/1986 **Age:** 30

			HOW MUCH HE PITCHED					WHAT HE GAVE UP										THE RESULTS						
Year	Team	Lg	G	GS	CG	GF	IP	BFP	H	R	ER	HR	SH	SF	HB	TBB	IBB	SO	WP	Bk	W	L	Pct	Sh	Sv-Op	Hld	ERC	ERA
2014	Pwtckt	AAA	41	0	0	12	61.2	254	39	27	26	5	3	4	1	33	2	65	6	2	3	5	.375	0	3- -	-	2.53	3.79
2015	Pwtckt	AAA	19	0	0	3	42.0	178	39	21	15	2	0	3	1	17	0	39	2	0	3	1	.750	0	0- -	-	3.46	3.21
2015	LV	AAA	10	0	0	5	13.0	57	14	8	8	1	0	1	0	5	0	13	2	0	1	0	1.000	0	0- -	-	4.26	5.54
2015	2 Tms		19	0	0	5	24.2	102	15	3	2	1	0	0	1	11	1	23	1	0	2	0	1.000	0	0-1	3	1.89	0.73
15	Bos	AL	1	0	0	1	1.2	9	0	0	0	0	0	0	1	3	0	2	0	0	0	0	-	0	0-0	0	4.82	0.00
15	Phi	NL	18	0	0	4	23.0	93	15	3	2	1	0	0	0	8	1	21	1	0	2	0	1.000	0	0-1	3	1.68	0.78

Luke Hochevar

Pitches: R **Bats:** R **Pos:** RP-49 HOE-chay-vur **Ht:** 6'5" **Wt:** 225 **Born:** 9/15/1983 **Age:** 32

Year	Team	Lg	G	GS	CG	GF	IP	BFP	H	R	ER	HR	SH	SF	HB	TBB	IBB	SO	WP	Bk	W	L	Pct	Sh	Sv-Op	Hld	ERC	ERA
2015	Omha*	AAA	9	4	0	0	10.1	52	16	9	9	2	0	0	0	8	0	10	2	0	0	1	.000	0	0- -	-	10.39	7.84
2007	KC	AL	4	1	0	1	12.2	54	11	4	3	1	1	0	3	4	0	5	1	0	0	1	.000	0	0-0	0	3.86	2.13
2008	KC	AL	22	22	0	0	129.0	566	143	84	79	12	1	2	5	47	1	72	7	0	6	12	.333	0	0-0	0	4.67	5.51
2009	KC	AL	25	25	2	0	143.0	631	167	109	104	23	2	0	8	46	0	106	9	0	7	13	.350	1	0-0	0	5.46	6.55
2010	KC	AL	18	17	1	0	103.0	450	110	61	55	9	2	2	4	37	1	76	2	1	6	6	.500	0	0-0	0	4.34	4.81
2011	KC	AL	31	31	0	0	198.0	835	192	110	103	23	2	2	7	62	4	128	7	2	11	11	.500	0	0-0	0	3.80	4.68
2012	KC	AL	32	32	2	0	185.1	800	202	127	118	27	4	3	13	61	3	144	8	0	8	16	.333	1	0-0	0	4.99	5.73
2013	KC	AL	58	0	0	22	70.1	262	41	15	15	8	2	0	1	17	1	82	2	0	5	2	.714	0	2-5	0	1.62	1.92
2015	KC	AL	49	0	0	16	50.2	214	49	23	21	7	0	1	1	16	0	49	3	0	1	1	.500	0	1-2	6	3.90	3.73
	8 ML YEARS		239	128	5	39	892.0	3812	915	533	498	110	14	10	42	290	10	662	39	3	44	62	.415	2	3-7	15	4.30	5.02

L.J. Hoes

Bats: R **Throws:** R **Pos:** RF-5;LF-3;PH-1;PR-1 HOSE **Ht:** 6'0" **Wt:** 200 **Born:** 3/5/1990 **Age:** 26

Year	Team	Lg	G	AB	H	2B	3B	HR	(Hm	Rd)	TB	R	RBI	RC	TBB	IBB	SO	HBP	SH	SF	SB	CS	GDP	Avg	OBP	Slg	OPS
2015	Fresno*	AAA	99	370	109	24	3	3	(-	-)	148	69	53	63	52	1	62	3	1	3	26	8	8	.295	.383	.400	.783
2012	Bal	AL	2	1	0	0	0	0	(0	0)	0	0	0	0	0	0	0	0	0	0	0	0	0	.000	.000	.000	.000
2013	2 Tms	AL	47	170	48	7	2	1	(0	1)	62	24	10	21	12	0	35	1	0	1	7	1	4	.282	.332	.365	.696
2014	Hou	AL	55	122	21	5	0	3	(2	1)	35	12	11	5	10	0	31	0	1	3	0	0	5	.172	.230	.287	.517
2015	Hou	AL	8	15	4	0	0	0	(0	0)	4	1	1	1	1	0	3	0	0	0	0	0	0	.267	.313	.267	.579
13	Bal	AL	1	3	0	0	0	0	(0	0)	0	0	0	0	0	0	1	0	0	0	0	0	0	.000	.000	.000	.000
13	Hou	AL	46	167	48	7	2	1	(0	1)	62	24	10	21	12	0	34	1	0	1	7	1	4	.287	.337	.371	.708
	4 ML YEARS		112	308	73	12	2	4	(2	2)	101	37	22	27	23	0	69	1	1	4	7	1	9	.237	.289	.328	.617

Bryan Holaday

Bats: R **Throws:** R **Pos:** C-18;PH-6;DH-2;1B-1;2B-1 HAHL-ih-daye **Ht:** 6'0" **Wt:** 205 **Born:** 11/19/1987 **Age:** 28

Year	Team	Lg	G	AB	H	2B	3B	HR	(Hm	Rd)	TB	R	RBI	RC	TBB	IBB	SO	HBP	SH	SF	SB	CS	GDP	Avg	OBP	Slg	OPS
2015	Toledo*	AAA	50	161	36	8	0	2	(-	-)	50	18	17	14	10	0	35	4	2	2	1	1	2	.224	.282	.311	.593
2012	Det	AL	6	12	3	1	0	0	(0	0)	4	3	0	1	0	0	2	0	1	0	0	0	0	.250	.250	.333	.583
2013	Det	AL	16	27	8	1	0	1	(1	0)	12	8	2	3	2	0	3	1	3	0	0	0	0	.296	.367	.444	.811
2014	Det	AL	62	156	36	5	1	0	(0	0)	43	14	15	11	8	0	37	1	2	4	1	1	1	.231	.266	.276	.542
2015	Det	AL	24	64	18	5	0	2	(1	1)	29	3	13	9	1	0	13	0	0	0	0	0	0	.281	.292	.453	.745
	Postseason		1	2	0	0	0	0	(0	0)	0	0	0	0	0	0	1	0	0	0	0	0	0	.000	.000	.000	.000
	4 ML YEARS		108	259	65	12	1	3	(2	1)	88	28	30	24	11	0	55	2	6	4	1	1	4	.251	.283	.340	.622

Derek Holland

Pitches: L **Bats:** B **Pos:** SP-10 **Ht:** 6'2" **Wt:** 215 **Born:** 10/9/1986 **Age:** 29

Year	Team	Lg	G	GS	CG	GF	IP	BFP	H	R	ER	HR	SH	SF	HB	TBB	IBB	SO	WP	Bk	W	L	Pct	Sh	Sv-Op	Hld	ERC	ERA
2009	Tex	AL	33	21	0	0	138.1	611	160	98	94	26	2	3	4	47	0	107	3	3	8	13	.381	1	0-1	2	5.52	6.12
2010	Tex	AL	14	10	0	2	57.1	253	55	30	26	6	0	2	4	24	0	54	0	1	3	4	.429	0	0-0	1	4.17	4.08
2011	Tex	AL	32	32	4	0	198.0	843	201	97	87	22	1	3	6	67	1	162	2	1	16	5	.762	4	0-0	0	4.15	3.95
2012	Tex	AL	29	27	0	1	175.1	730	162	100	91	32	5	4	3	52	0	145	1	0	12	7	.632	0	0-0	0	3.86	4.67
2013	Tex	AL	33	33	2	0	213.0	894	210	90	81	20	8	9	3	64	0	189	9	1	10	9	.526	2	0-0	0	3.64	3.42
2014	Tex	AL	6	5	0	0	37.0	145	34	8	6	0	2	1	0	5	1	25	1	0	2	0	1.000	0	0-0	0	2.07	1.46
2015	Tex	AL	10	10	1	0	58.2	245	59	32	32	11	3	1	5	17	2	41	1	0	3	4	.571	1	0-0	0	4.71	4.91
	Postseason		13	4	0	2	35.2	149	32	17	15	7	0	0	1	15	0	24	2	0	3	0	1.000	0	0-0	2	4.46	3.79
	7 ML YEARS		157	138	8	3	877.2	3721	881	455	417	117	21	23	25	276	4	723	17	6	55	41	.573	8	0-1	3	4.12	4.28

Greg Holland

Pitches: R **Bats:** R **Pos:** RP-48 **Ht:** 5'10" **Wt:** 205 **Born:** 11/20/1985 **Age:** 30

Year	Team	Lg	G	GS	CG	GF	IP	BFP	H	R	ER	HR	SH	SF	HB	TBB	IBB	SO	WP	Bk	W	L	Pct	Sh	Sv-Op	Hld	ERC	ERA
2010	KC	AL	15	0	0	10	18.2	87	23	15	14	3	1	0	0	8	0	23	2	0	0	1	.000	0	0-0	0	5.88	6.75
2011	KC	AL	46	0	0	15	60.0	233	37	13	12	3	1	1	1	19	3	74	7	0	5	1	.833	0	4-6	18	1.60	1.80
2012	KC	AL	67	0	0	36	67.0	289	58	22	22	2	4	3	0	34	7	91	3	1	7	4	.636	0	16-20	9	3.07	2.96
2013	KC	AL	68	0	0	61	67.0	255	40	11	9	3	1	1	0	18	1	103	2	0	2	1	.667	0	47-50	1	1.41	1.21
2014	KC	AL	65	0	0	60	62.1	240	37	13	10	3	1	1	0	20	0	90	9	0	1	3	.250	0	46-48	0	1.54	1.44
2015	KC	AL	48	0	0	40	44.2	193	39	20	19	2	3	1	0	26	1	49	7	0	3	2	.600	0	32-37	5	3.68	3.83
	Postseason		11	0	0	10	11.0	43	4	1	1	0	0	0	0	5	1	15	0	0	0	0	-	0	7-7	0	0.86	0.82
	6 ML YEARS		309	0	0	222	319.2	1297	234	94	86	16	11	7	1	125	12	430	30	1	18	12	.600	0	145-161	28	2.29	2.42

Matt Holliday

Bats: R **Throws:** R **Pos:** LF-64;PH-5;DH-4 **Ht:** 6'4" **Wt:** 250 **Born:** 1/15/1980 **Age:** 36

Year	Team	Lg	G	AB	H	2B	3B	HR	(Hm	Rd)	TB	R	RBI	RC	TBB	IBB	SO	HBP	SH	SF	SB	CS	GDP	Avg	OBP	Slg	OPS
2004	Col	NL	121	400	116	31	3	14	(10	4)	195	65	57	61	31	0	86	6	1	1	3	3	9	.290	.349	.488	.837
2005	Col	NL	125	479	147	24	7	19	(12	7)	242	68	87	88	36	1	79	7	0	4	14	3	11	.307	.361	.505	.866
2006	Col	NL	155	602	196	45	5	34	(22	12)	353	119	114	112	47	3	110	15	0	3	10	5	22	.326	.387	.586	.973
2007	Col	NL	158	636	**216**	**50**	6	36	(25	11)	386	120	137	134	63	7	126	10	0	4	11	4	23	**.340**	.405	.607	1.012
2008	Col	NL	139	539	173	38	2	25	(15	10)	290	107	88	104	74	6	104	8	0	2	28	2	9	.321	.409	.538	.947

Year Team	Lg	G	AB	H	2B	3B	HR	(Hm Rd)	TB	R	RBI	RC	TBB	IBB	SO	HBP	SH	SF	SB	CS	GDP	Avg	OBP	Slg	OPS
2009 2 Tms		156	581	182	39	3	24	(16 8)	299	94	109	112	72	8	101	10	0	7	14	7	13	.313	.394	.515	.909
2010 StL	NL	158	596	186	45	1	28	(13 15)	317	95	103	107	69	10	93	8	0	2	9	5	13	.312	.390	.532	.922
2011 StL	NL	124	446	132	36	0	22	(12 10)	234	83	75	81	60	4	93	8	0	2	2	1	21	.296	.388	.525	.912
2012 StL	NL	157	599	177	36	2	27	(13 14)	298	95	102	99	75	3	132	9	0	5	4	4	16	.295	.379	.497	.877
2013 StL	NL	141	520	156	31	1	22	(14 8)	255	103	94	99	69	5	86	9	0	4	6	1	31	.300	.389	.490	.879
2014 StL	NL	156	574	156	37	0	20	(13 7)	253	83	90	97	74	4	100	17	0	2	4	1	20	.272	.370	.441	.811
2015 StL	NL	73	229	64	16	1	4	(0 4)	94	24	35	44	39	5	49	6	0	3	2	1	9	.279	.394	.410	.804
09 Oak	AL	93	346	99	23	1	11	(7 4)	157	52	54	62	46	3	58	6	0	2	12	3	8	.286	.378	.454	.831
09 StL	NL	63	235	83	16	2	13	(9 4)	142	42	55	50	26	5	43	4	0	5	2	4	5	.353	.419	.604	1.023
Postseason		68	263	67	9	1	13	(5 8)	117	40	36	30	16	0	55	6	0	0	1	1	5	.255	.312	.445	.757
12 ML YEARS		1663	6201	1901	428	31	275	(165 110)	3216	1056	1091	1138	709	56	1159	113	1	39	107	37	197	.307	.386	.519	.904

David Holmberg

Pitches: L Bats: R Pos: SP-6 Ht: 6'3" Wt: 245 Born: 7/19/1991 Age: 24

Year Team	Lg	G	GS	CG	GF	IP	BFP	H	R	ER	HR	SH	SF	HB	TBB	IBB	SO	WP	Bk	W	L	Pct	Sh	Sv-Op	Hld	ERC	ERA
2015 Lsvlle* AAA	21	19	0	0	120.1	527	142	63	58	14	4	4	3	41	0	71	4	0	7	7	.500	0	0--	-	5.18	4.34
2013 Ari	NL	1	1	0	0	3.2	20	6	3	3	0	0	1	0	3	0	0	0	0	0	0	-	0	0-0	0	8.70	7.36
2014 Cin	NL	7	5	0	1	30.0	137	27	16	16	8	2	2	6	16	1	18	2	0	2	2	.500	0	0-0	0	6.03	4.80
2015 Cin	NL	6	6	0	0	28.1	136	36	24	24	10	4	2	2	16	0	15	1	0	1	4	.200	0	0-0	0	8.86	7.62
3 ML YEARS		14	12	0	1	62.0	293	69	43	43	18	6	5	8	35	1	33	3	0	3	6	.333	0	0-0	0	7.46	6.24

Brock Holt

Bats: L Throws: R Pos: 2B-58;3B-33;RF-21;LF-14;SS-11;1B-8;PH-6;CF-2;PR-2;DH-1 Ht: 5'10" Wt: 180 Born: 6/11/1988 Age: 28

Year Team	Lg	G	AB	H	2B	3B	HR	(Hm Rd)	TB	R	RBI	RC	TBB	IBB	SO	HBP	SH	SF	SB	CS	GDP	Avg	OBP	Slg	OPS
2012 Pit	NL	24	65	19	2	1	0	(0 0)	23	6	3	10	4	0	14	0	2	1	0	0	1	.292	.329	.354	.682
2013 Bos	AL	26	59	12	2	0	0	(0 0)	14	9	11	7	7	0	4	0	3	3	1	0	0	.203	.275	.237	.513
2014 Bos	AL	106	449	126	23	5	4	(1 3)	171	68	29	56	33	0	98	2	5	3	12	2	7	.281	.331	.381	.711
2015 Bos	AL	129	454	127	27	6	2	(1 1)	172	56	45	65	46	0	97	3	4	2	8	1	7	.280	.349	.379	.727
4 ML YEARS		285	1027	284	54	12	6	(2 4)	380	139	88	138	90	0	213	5	14	9	21	3	15	.277	.335	.370	.705

Tyler Holt

Bats: R Throws: R Pos: CF-9;LF-3;RF-2 Ht: 5'10" Wt: 200 Born: 3/10/1989 Age: 27

Year Team	Lg	G	AB	H	2B	3B	HR	(Hm Rd)	TB	R	RBI	RC	TBB	IBB	SO	HBP	SH	SF	SB	CS	GDP	Avg	OBP	Slg	OPS
2011 Knstn	A+	123	449	114	18	4	2	(- -)	146	66	26	66	78	0	106	2	5	2	34	6	5	.254	.365	.325	.691
2012 Carlina	A+	81	316	83	10	7	0	(- -)	107	48	22	41	38	0	62	4	4	0	16	8	4	.263	.349	.339	.688
2012 Akron	AA	55	216	54	5	2	0	(- -)	63	29	12	24	24	0	41	1	6	1	13	4	9	.250	.326	.292	.618
2013 Akron	AA	133	521	139	24	9	2	(- -)	187	83	42	71	55	0	90	3	7	3	28	7	16	.267	.338	.359	.697
2014 Akron	AA	39	124	37	4	1	0	(- -)	43	13	14	23	27	0	26	0	2	3	11	2	0	.298	.416	.347	.762
2014 Clmbs	AAA	59	227	70	15	0	2	(- -)	91	61	16	44	39	0	45	3	3	0	20	4	5	.308	.416	.401	.817
2015 Clmbs	AAA	101	368	111	17	4	0	(- -)	136	63	28	61	50	0	62	2	8	2	25	5	8	.302	.386	.370	.756
2014 Cle	AL	36	71	19	2	0	0	(0 0)	21	4	2	6	3	0	25	1	1	0	2	2	1	.268	.307	.296	.602
2015 2 Tms		14	31	3	0	0	0	(0 0)	3	4	0	6	3	0	11	0	0	0	1	0	0	.097	.176	.097	.273
15 Cle	AL	9	20	2	0	0	0	(0 0)	2	2	0	1	0	9	0	0	0	0	0	0	.100	.143	.100	.243
15 Cin	NL	5	11	1	0	0	0	(0 0)	1	2	0	2	2	0	2	0	0	0	1	0	0	.091	.231	.091	.322
2 ML YEARS		50	102	22	2	0	0	(0 0)	24	8	2	6	6	0	36	1	1	0	3	2	1	.216	.266	.235	.501

J.J. Hoover

Pitches: R Bats: R Pos: RP-67 Ht: 6'3" Wt: 245 Born: 8/13/1987 Age: 28

Year Team	Lg	G	GS	CG	GF	IP	BFP	H	R	ER	HR	SH	SF	HB	TBB	IBB	SO	WP	Bk	W	L	Pct	Sh	Sv-Op	Hld	ERC	ERA
2012 Cin	NL	28	0	0	6	30.2	123	17	7	7	2	2	2	2	13	1	31	0	0	1	0	1.000	0	1-2	1	1.64	2.05
2013 Cin	NL	69	0	0	23	66.0	269	47	21	21	6	3	3	2	26	6	67	1	0	5	5	.500	0	3-5	13	2.46	2.86
2014 Cin	NL	54	0	0	22	62.2	275	56	36	34	13	1	5	1	31	3	75	0	0	1	10	.091	0	0-4	1	4.52	4.88
2015 Cin	NL	67	0	0	12	64.1	264	44	24	21	7	5	2	2	31	1	52	3	0	8	2	.800	0	1-7	18	2.87	2.94
Postseason		3	0	0	0	3.1	10	0	0	0	0	0	0	0	2	0	2	0	0	0	0	-	0	0-0	0	0.45	0.00
4 ML YEARS		218	0	0	63	223.2	931	164	88	83	28	11	12	5	101	11	225	4	0	15	17	.469	0	5-18	33	3.00	3.34

Eric Hosmer

Bats: L Throws: L Pos: 1B-154;PH-3;RF-1;DH-1;PR-1 HOZZ-mer Ht: 6'4" Wt: 225 Born: 10/24/1989 Age: 26

Year Team	Lg	G	AB	H	2B	3B	HR	(Hm Rd)	TB	R	RBI	RC	TBB	IBB	SO	HBP	SH	SF	SB	CS	GDP	Avg	OBP	Slg	OPS
2011 KC	AL	128	523	153	27	3	19	(3 16)	243	66	78	71	34	7	82	1	0	5	11	5	13	.293	.334	.465	.799
2012 KC	AL	152	535	124	22	2	14	(8 6)	192	65	60	61	56	4	95	2	0	5	16	1	10	.232	.304	.359	.663
2013 KC	AL	159	623	188	34	3	17	(10 7)	279	86	79	88	51	4	100	1	1	4	11	4	15	.302	.353	.448	.801
2014 KC	AL	131	503	136	35	1	9	(5 4)	200	54	58	62	35	4	93	3	0	6	4	2	12	.270	.318	.398	.716
2015 KC	AL	158	599	178	33	5	18	(10 8)	275	98	93	94	61	6	108	3	1	3	7	3	16	.297	.363	.459	.822
Postseason		15	57	20	3	1	2	(1 1)	31	8	12	13	9	1	16	0	0	0	1	1	1	.351	.439	.544	.983
5 ML YEARS		728	2783	779	151	14	77	(36 41)	1189	369	368	376	237	25	478	10	2	23	49	15	66	.280	.336	.427	.763

T.J. House

Pitches: L **Bats:** R **Pos:** SP-4 **Ht:** 6'1" **Wt:** 205 **Born:** 9/29/1989 **Age:** 26

Year	Team	Lg	G	GS	CG	GF	IP	BFP	H	R	ER	HR	SH	SF	HB	TBB	IBB	SO	WP	Bk	W	L	Pct	Sh	Sv-Op	Hld	ERC	ERA
2011	Knstn	A+	25	24	1	0	130.0	581	133	85	75	12	6	8	6	66	0	89	8	0	6	12	.333	1	0- -	-	4.77	5.19
2012	Akron	AA	23	23	1	0	124.1	524	114	59	55	7	6	3	7	44	0	90	2	1	8	5	.615	1	0- -	-	3.38	3.98
2013	Clmbs	AAA	24	24	2	0	141.2	629	163	76	68	11	5	5	4	54	0	110	4	0	7	10	.412	0	0- -	-	4.83	4.32
2014	Clmbs	AAA	10	10	0	0	57.0	233	56	25	24	3	2	1	2	16	0	42	1	0	1	4	.200	0	0- -	-	3.45	3.79
2014	Cle	AL	19	18	0	1	102.0	429	113	41	38	10	1	1	7	22	1	80	1	0	5	3	.625	0	0-0	0	4.30	3.35
2015	Cle	AL	4	4	0	0	13.0	73	21	19	19	1	0	1	2	12	1	7	0	0	0	4	.000	0	0-0	0	10.45	13.15
	2 ML YEARS		23	22	0	1	115.0	502	134	60	57	11	1	2	9	34	2	87	1	0	5	7	.417	0	0-0	0	4.95	4.46

Adrian Houser

Pitches: R **Bats:** R **Pos:** RP-2 HOW-zer **Ht:** 6'4" **Wt:** 230 **Born:** 2/2/1993 **Age:** 23

Year	Team	Lg	G	GS	CG	GF	IP	BFP	H	R	ER	HR	SH	SF	HB	TBB	IBB	SO	WP	Bk	W	L	Pct	Sh	Sv-Op	Hld	ERC	ERA
2011	2 Tms	Low	12	11	0	0	48.0	215	49	28	23	1	3	2	0	25	0	44	12	0	2	4	.333	0	0- -	-	4.03	4.31
2012	Grnvlle	R+	11	11	0	0	58.0	245	53	28	27	1	0	1	5	23	1	54	6	0	3	4	.429	0	0- -	-	3.38	4.19
2013	TriCity	A-	14	9	0	1	50.0	216	57	25	19	1	3	2	5	10	0	39	6	0	0	4	.000	0	0- -	-	3.91	3.42
2014	QuadC	A	25	17	0	3	108.2	458	99	55	50	5	0	1	11	37	0	93	9	0	5	6	.455	0	0- -	-	3.42	4.14
2015	CpChr	AA	7	5	0	0	33.1	152	39	26	23	6	3	0	1	15	0	23	4	0	1	2	.333	0	0- -	-	6.00	6.21
2015	Biloxi	AA	7	7	0	0	37.0	152	33	16	12	4	3	0	1	6	0	32	0	0	4	1	.800	0	0- -	-	2.68	2.92
2015	Lancst	A+	12	8	0	2	49.2	219	48	30	24	3	0	2	8	20	0	55	4	0	2	2	.500	0	0- -	-	4.26	4.35
2015	Mil	NL	2	0	0	2	2.0	8	1	0	0	0	0	0	0	2	0	0	0	0	0	0	-	0	0-0	0	3.21	0.00

Ryan Howard

Bats: L **Throws:** L **Pos:** 1B-116;PH-11;DH-6 **Ht:** 6'4" **Wt:** 250 **Born:** 11/19/1979 **Age:** 36

						BATTING																	RUNNING			AVERAGES			
Year	Team	Lg	G	AB	H	2B	3B	HR	(Hm	Rd)	TB	R	RBI	RC	TBB	IBB	SO	HBP	SH	SF	SB	CS	GDP	Avg	OBP	Slg	OPS
2004	Phi	NL	19	39	11	5	0	2	(1	1)	22	5	5	7	2	0	13	1	0	0	0	0	2	.282	.333	.564	.897
2005	Phi	NL	88	312	90	17	2	22	(11	11)	177	52	63	50	33	8	100	1	0	2	0	1	6	.288	.356	.567	.924
2006	Phi	NL	159	581	182	25	1	58	(29	29)	383	104	149	138	108	37	181	9	0	6	0	0	7	.313	.425	.659	1.084
2007	Phi	NL	144	529	142	26	0	47	(23	24)	309	94	136	119	107	35	199	5	0	7	1	0	13	.268	.392	.584	.976
2008	Phi	NL	162	610	153	26	4	48	(26	22)	331	105	146	117	81	17	199	3	0	6	1	1	11	.251	.339	.543	.881
2009	Phi	NL	160	616	172	37	4	45	(18	27)	352	105	141	117	75	8	186	6	0	6	8	1	11	.279	.360	.571	.931
2010	Phi	NL	143	550	152	23	5	31	(16	15)	278	87	108	94	59	11	157	8	0	3	1	1	14	.276	.353	.505	.859
2011	Phi	NL	152	557	141	30	1	33	(17	16)	272	81	116	91	75	16	172	7	0	5	1	0	10	.253	.346	.488	.835
2012	Phi	NL	71	260	57	11	0	14	(10	4)	110	28	56	35	25	7	99	4	0	3	0	0	8	.219	.295	.423	.718
2013	Phi	NL	80	286	76	20	2	11	(9	2)	133	34	43	36	23	4	95	2	0	6	0	0	6	.266	.319	.465	.784
2014	Phi	NL	153	569	127	18	1	23	(12	11)	216	65	95	71	67	7	190	7	0	5	0	0	10	.223	.310	.380	.690
2015	Phi	NL	129	467	107	29	1	23	(13	10)	207	53	77	57	27	2	138	5	0	3	0	0	11	.229	.277	.443	.720
	Postseason		46	170	44	13	1	8	(6	2)	83	22	33	28	26	7	67	1	0	2	1	1	1	.259	.357	.488	.845
	12 ML YEARS		1460	5376	1410	267	21	357	(185	172)	2790	813	1135	932	682	152	1729	58	0	52	12	4	109	.262	.349	.519	.868

J.P. Howell

Pitches: L **Bats:** L **Pos:** RP-65 **Ht:** 6'0" **Wt:** 180 **Born:** 4/25/1983 **Age:** 33

Year	Team	Lg	G	GS	CG	GF	IP	BFP	H	R	ER	HR	SH	SF	HB	TBB	IBB	SO	WP	Bk	W	L	Pct	Sh	Sv-Op	Hld	ERC	ERA
2005	KC	AL	15	15	0	0	72.2	328	73	55	50	9	3	3	6	39	0	54	7	0	3	5	.375	0	0-0	0	5.18	6.19
2006	TB	AL	8	8	0	0	42.1	187	52	25	24	4	0	2	3	14	0	33	1	0	1	3	.250	0	0-0	0	5.51	5.10
2007	TB	AL	10	10	0	0	51.0	244	69	45	43	8	2	1	3	21	0	49	3	0	1	6	.143	0	0-0	0	6.84	7.59
2008	TB	AL	64	0	0	9	89.1	370	62	29	22	6	6	1	4	39	1	92	5	0	6	1	.857	0	3-5	14	2.51	2.22
2009	TB	AL	69	0	0	41	66.2	278	47	22	21	7	2	1	3	33	3	79	3	1	7	5	.583	0	17-25	4	2.99	2.84
2011	TB	AL	46	0	0	5	30.2	138	30	24	21	5	1	1	2	18	1	26	2	2	2	3	.400	0	1-2	10	5.43	6.16
2012	TB	AL	55	0	0	10	50.1	203	39	17	17	7	2	0	4	22	2	42	1	0	1	0	1.000	0	0-0	3	3.68	3.04
2013	LAD	NL	67	0	0	6	62.0	246	42	15	15	2	1	3	1	23	3	54	3	0	4	1	.800	0	0-0	11	1.92	2.18
2014	LAD	NL	68	0	0	8	49.0	199	31	14	13	2	4	0	1	25	1	48	3	0	3	3	.500	0	0-0	27	2.26	2.39
2015	LAD	NL	65	0	0	18	44.0	190	47	9	7	3	0	1	2	14	1	39	3	1	6	1	.857	0	1-4	9	4.07	1.43
	Postseason		23	0	0	3	19.1	85	20	7	7	2	1	2	2	7	1	23	2	0	0	3	.000	0	0-1	4	4.48	3.26
	10 ML YEARS		467	33	0	97	558.0	2383	492	255	233	58	21	13	29	248	12	516	31	4	34	28	.548	0	22-36	78	3.75	3.76

Daniel Hudson

Pitches: R **Bats:** R **Pos:** RP-63; SP-1 **Ht:** 6'3" **Wt:** 235 **Born:** 3/9/1987 **Age:** 29

Year	Team	Lg	G	GS	CG	GF	IP	BFP	H	R	ER	HR	SH	SF	HB	TBB	IBB	SO	WP	Bk	W	L	Pct	Sh	Sv-Op	Hld	ERC	ERA
2009	CWS	AL	6	2	0	0	18.2	82	16	9	7	3	0	1	1	9	0	14	1	0	1	1	.500	0	0-0	0	4.15	3.38
2010	2 Tms		14	14	0	0	95.1	372	68	26	26	8	2	2	4	27	1	84	5	0	8	2	.800	0	0-0	0	2.26	2.45
2011	Ari	NL	33	33	3	0	222.0	921	217	98	86	17	6	6	8	50	1	169	4	1	16	12	.571	0	0-0	0	3.26	3.49
2012	Ari	NL	9	9	0	0	45.1	202	62	37	37	9	2	1	0	12	0	37	2	0	3	2	.600	0	0-0	0	6.56	7.35
2014	Ari	NL	3	0	0	0	2.2	13	4	4	4	0	0	0	0	0	0	2	0	0	0	1	.000	0	0-0	0	4.08	13.50
2015	Ari	NL	64	0	0	13	67.2	290	64	34	29	7	1	3	0	25	2	71	5	0	4	3	.571	0	4-6	20	3.58	3.86
10	CWS	AL	3	3	0	0	15.2	71	17	11	11	1	1	1	0	11	0	14	2	0	1	1	.500	0	0-0	0	5.69	6.32
10	Ari	NL	11	11	0	0	79.2	301	51	15	15	7	1	1	4	16	1	70	3	0	7	1	.875	0	0-0	0	1.70	1.69
	Postseason		1	1	0	0	5.1	24	9	5	5	1	0	0	0	0	0	6	0	0	0	1	.000	0	0-0	0	7.35	8.44
	6 ML YEARS		129	59	3	14	451.2	1880	431	208	189	44	11	13	13	123	4	377	17	1	32	21	.604	0	4-6	20	3.42	3.77

Tim Hudson

Pitches: R **Bats:** R **Pos:** SP-22; RP-2   **Ht:** 6'1" **Wt:** 175 **Born:** 7/14/1975 **Age:** 40

			HOW MUCH HE PITCHED						WHAT HE GAVE UP										THE RESULTS							
Year	Team	Lg	G	GS	CG	GF	IP	BFP	H	R	ER	HR	SH	SF	HB	TBB	IBB	SO	WP	Bk	W	L	Pct	Sh	Sv-Op	Hld	ERC	ERA
1999	Oak	AL	21	21	1	0	136.1	580	121	56	49	8	1	2	4	62	2	132	6	0	11	2	.846	0	0-0	0	3.50	3.23
2000	Oak	AL	32	32	2	0	202.1	847	169	100	93	24	5	7	7	82	5	169	7	0	20	6	.769	2	0-0	0	3.43	4.14
2001	Oak	AL	35	35	3	0	235.0	980	216	100	88	20	12	8	6	71	5	181	9	1	18	9	.667	0	0-0	0	3.22	3.37
2002	Oak	AL	34	34	4	0	238.1	983	237	87	79	19	6	5	8	62	9	152	7	1	15	9	.625	2	0-0	0	3.51	2.98
2003	Oak	AL	34	34	3	0	240.0	967	197	84	72	15	11	2	10	61	9	162	6	0	16	7	.696	2	0-0	0	2.47	2.70
2004	Oak	AL	27	27	3	0	188.2	793	194	82	74	8	7	4	12	44	3	103	4	1	12	6	.667	2	0-0	0	3.44	3.53
2005	Atl	NL	29	29	2	0	192.0	817	194	79	75	20	9	1	9	65	5	115	4	0	14	9	.609	0	0-0	0	4.12	3.52
2006	Atl	NL	35	35	2	0	218.1	959	235	129	118	25	8	3	9	79	10	141	7	0	13	12	.520	1	0-0	0	4.54	4.86
2007	Atl	NL	34	34	1	0	224.1	925	221	87	83	10	11	6	8	53	8	132	5	2	16	10	.615	1	0-0	0	3.12	3.33
2008	Atl	NL	23	22	1	0	142.0	573	125	53	50	11	5	4	2	40	5	85	3	1	11	7	.611	1	0-0	0	2.90	3.17
2009	Atl	NL	7	7	0	0	42.1	180	49	17	17	4	1	0	0	13	0	30	0	0	2	1	.667	0	0-0	0	4.70	3.61
2010	Atl	NL	34	34	1	0	228.2	920	189	74	72	20	9	2	9	74	8	139	5	0	17	9	.654	1	0-0	0	2.95	2.83
2011	Atl	NL	33	33	1	0	215.0	884	189	86	77	14	6	7	15	56	6	158	10	0	16	10	.615	1	0-0	0	2.91	3.22
2012	Atl	NL	28	28	1	0	179.0	749	168	77	72	12	10	4	9	48	2	102	3	0	16	7	.696	1	0-0	0	3.18	3.62
2013	Atl	NL	21	21	0	0	131.1	534	120	60	58	10	5	1	2	36	3	95	2	0	8	7	.533	0	0-0	0	3.05	3.97
2014	SF	NL	31	31	1	0	189.1	789	199	86	75	15	5	5	7	34	3	120	2	0	9	13	.409	0	0-0	0	3.49	3.57
2015	SF	NL	24	22	0	0	123.2	525	134	62	61	13	2	3	7	37	1	64	4	0	8	9	.471	0	0-0	0	4.51	4.44
	Postseason		14	13	1	0	75.2	322	75	38	31	6	4	3	4	22	1	53	1	0	1	4	.200	0	0-0	0	3.63	3.69
	17 ML YEARS		482	479	26	0	3126.2	13005	2957	1319	1213	248	113	64	124	917	84	2080	84	6	222	133	.625	13	0-0	0	3.37	3.49

David Huff

Pitches: L **Bats:** B **Pos:** RP-2; SP-1   **Ht:** 6'1" **Wt:** 210 **Born:** 8/22/1984 **Age:** 31

			HOW MUCH HE PITCHED						WHAT HE GAVE UP										THE RESULTS							
Year	Team	Lg	G	GS	CG	GF	IP	BFP	H	R	ER	HR	SH	SF	HB	TBB	IBB	SO	WP	Bk	W	L	Pct	Sh	Sv-Op	Hld	ERC	ERA
2015	OkCity*	AAA	23	4	0	6	57.1	221	49	18	14	4	4	2	0	8	0	43	1	0	5	2	.714	0	0--	-	2.23	2.20
2009	Cle	AL	23	23	0	0	128.1	574	159	82	80	16	2	2	1	41	1	65	1	0	11	8	.579	0	0-0	0	5.33	5.61
2010	Cle	AL	15	15	1	0	79.2	369	101	61	55	14	3	3	3	34	1	37	2	0	2	11	.154	0	0-0	0	6.50	6.21
2011	Cle	AL	11	10	0	1	50.2	227	55	35	23	6	0	3	0	17	1	36	4	0	2	6	.250	0	0-0	0	4.23	4.09
2012	Cle	AL	6	4	0	0	26.2	114	30	14	10	5	0	1	1	5	0	19	0	0	3	1	.750	0	0-0	0	4.67	3.38
2013	2 Tms	AL	14	2	0	4	37.2	151	33	23	23	7	1	1	1	9	1	31	1	0	3	1	.750	0	0-0	0	3.45	5.50
2014	2 Tms	AL	46	0	0	16	59.0	258	61	25	22	5	2	0	1	23	2	39	1	0	4	1	.800	0	0-0	4	4.10	3.36
2015	LAD	NL	3	1	0	1	6.0	30	11	6	6	2	1	0	0	1	0	4	0	0	0	0	-	0	0-0	0	11.33	9.00
13	Cle	AL	3	0	0	1	3.0	15	7	5	5	0	0	0	0	1	0	5	0	0	0	0	-	0	0-0	0	12.85	15.00
13	NYY	AL	11	2	0	3	34.2	136	26	18	18	7	1	1	1	8	1	26	1	0	3	1	.750	0	0-0	0	2.82	4.67
14	SF	NL	16	0	0	3	20.0	92	27	15	14	2	0	0	1	6	0	11	0	0	1	0	1.000	0	0-0	1	5.92	6.30
14	NYY	AL	30	0	0	13	39.0	166	34	10	8	3	2	0	0	17	2	28	1	0	3	1	.750	0	0-0	3	3.25	1.85
	7 ML YEARS		118	55	1	22	388.0	1723	450	246	219	55	9	10	8	130	6	231	9	0	25	28	.472	0	0-0	4	5.07	5.08

Jared Hughes

Pitches: R **Bats:** R **Pos:** RP-76   **Ht:** 6'7" **Wt:** 245 **Born:** 7/4/1985 **Age:** 30

			HOW MUCH HE PITCHED						WHAT HE GAVE UP										THE RESULTS							
Year	Team	Lg	G	GS	CG	GF	IP	BFP	H	R	ER	HR	SH	SF	HB	TBB	IBB	SO	WP	Bk	W	L	Pct	Sh	Sv-Op	Hld	ERC	ERA
2011	Pit	NL	12	0	0	1	11.0	46	9	5	5	1	1	0	0	4	0	10	0	0	0	1	.000	0	0-0	2	2.85	4.09
2012	Pit	NL	66	0	0	20	75.2	316	65	30	24	7	1	0	5	22	4	50	5	0	2	2	.500	0	2-4	11	2.99	2.85
2013	Pit	NL	29	0	0	8	32.0	148	37	17	17	2	2	1	2	16	1	23	2	0	2	3	.400	0	0-0	3	5.27	4.78
2014	Pit	NL	63	0	0	16	64.1	256	51	21	14	4	6	2	6	19	5	36	2	0	7	5	.583	0	0-2	13	2.68	1.96
2015	Pit	NL	76	0	0	11	67.0	284	70	21	17	3	6	4	7	19	2	36	3	0	3	1	.750	0	0-3	21	3.93	2.28
	Postseason		1	0	0	0	1.0	7	3	2	2	0	0	0	0	1	0	1	0	0	0	0	-	0	0-0	0	19.55	18.00
	5 ML YEARS		246	0	0	56	250.0	1050	232	94	77	17	16	7	20	80	12	155	12	0	14	12	.538	0	2-9	50	3.42	2.77

Phil Hughes

Pitches: R **Bats:** R **Pos:** SP-25; RP-2   **Ht:** 6'5" **Wt:** 250 **Born:** 6/24/1986 **Age:** 30

			HOW MUCH HE PITCHED						WHAT HE GAVE UP										THE RESULTS							
Year	Team	Lg	G	GS	CG	GF	IP	BFP	H	R	ER	HR	SH	SF	HB	TBB	IBB	SO	WP	Bk	W	L	Pct	Sh	Sv-Op	Hld	ERC	ERA
2007	NYY	AL	13	13	0	0	72.2	306	64	39	36	8	2	1	2	29	0	58	4	0	5	3	.625	0	0-0	0	3.61	4.46
2008	NYY	AL	8	8	0	0	34.0	157	43	26	25	3	1	3	1	15	0	23	2	0	0	4	.000	0	0-0	0	5.84	6.62
2009	NYY	AL	51	7	0	6	86.0	351	68	31	29	8	0	4	5	28	1	96	4	2	8	3	.727	0	3-6	18	2.86	3.03
2010	NYY	AL	31	29	0	0	176.1	730	162	83	82	25	2	5	0	58	1	146	9	1	18	8	.692	0	0-0	0	3.65	4.19
2011	NYY	AL	17	14	1	1	74.2	334	84	48	48	9	3	3	4	27	2	47	3	0	5	5	.500	1	0-0	0	4.92	5.79
2012	NYY	AL	32	32	1	0	191.1	815	196	101	89	35	1	4	6	46	0	165	3	0	16	13	.552	0	0-0	0	4.19	4.33
2013	NYY	AL	30	29	0	0	145.2	642	170	91	84	24	3	11	5	42	4	121	6	0	4	14	.222	0	0-0	0	5.13	5.19
2014	Min	AL	32	32	1	0	209.2	855	221	88	82	16	3	7	5	16	1	186	1	0	16	10	.615	0	0-0	0	3.05	3.52
2015	Min	AL	27	25	1	1	155.1	651	184	76	76	29	1	3	2	16	0	94	1	0	11	9	.550	0	0-0	0	4.59	4.40
	Postseason		18	5	0	2	39.2	176	41	20	20	5	1	0	0	18	3	38	3	0	2	4	.333	0	0-1	2	4.49	4.54
	9 ML YEARS		241	189	4	8	1145.2	4841	1192	583	551	157	16	41	30	277	9	936	33	3	83	69	.546	1	3-6	18	4.02	4.34

Nick Hundley

Bats: R **Throws:** R **Pos:** C-102; PH-2   **Ht:** 6'1" **Wt:** 205 **Born:** 9/8/1983 **Age:** 32

			BATTING																				RUNNING			AVERAGES			
Year	Team	Lg	G	AB	H	2B	3B	HR	(Hm	Rd)	TB	R	RBI	RC	TBB	IBB	SO	HBP	SH	SF	SB	CS	GDP	Avg	OBP	Slg	OPS
2008	SD	NL	60	198	47	7	1	5	(4	1)	71	21	24	17	11	0	52	2	0	5	0	0	1	.237	.278	.359	.636
2009	SD	NL	78	256	61	15	2	8	(4	4)	104	23	30	33	28	1	76	1	1	3	5	1	2	.238	.313	.406	.719
2010	SD	NL	85	273	68	18	2	8	(7	1)	114	33	43	37	25	0	66	1	2	6	0	5	8	.249	.308	.418	.726
2011	SD	NL	82	281	81	16	5	9	(6	3)	134	34	29	40	22	3	74	4	0	1	1	1	3	.288	.347	.477	.824

				BATTING																			RUNNING			AVERAGES			
Year	Team	Lg	G	AB	H	2B	3B	HR	(Hm	Rd)	TB	R	RBI	RC	TBB	IBB	SO	HBP	SH	SF	SB	CS	GDP	Avg	OBP	Slg	OPS
2012	SD	NL	58	204	32	7	1	3	(1	2)	50	14	22	6	15	2	56	2	1	3	0	3	4	.157	.219	.245	.464
2013	SD	NL	114	373	87	19	0	13	(6	7)	145	35	44	36	26	5	98	5	1	3	1	0	7	.233	.290	.389	.679
2014	2 Tms		83	218	53	7	0	6	(4	2)	78	18	22	21	10	0	63	0	2	3	1	0	3	.243	.273	.358	.631
2015	Col	NL	103	366	110	21	5	10	(7	3)	171	45	43	44	21	0	76	1	0	1	5	6	8	.301	.339	.467	.807
14	SD	NL	33	59	16	3	0	1	(1	0)	22	1	3	5	0	0	13	0	0	0	0	0	1	.271	.271	.373	.644
14	Bal	AL	50	159	37	4	0	5	(3	2)	56	17	19	16	10	0	50	0	2	3	1	0	2	.233	.273	.352	.625
	Postseason		5	15	1	0	0	0	(0	0)	1	0	1	0	0	0	5	0	0	0	0	0	0	.067	.067	.067	.133
	8 ML YEARS		663	2169	539	110	16	62	(39	23)	867	223	257	234	158	11	561	16	7	25	13	16	36	.249	.301	.400	.701

Tommy Hunter

Pitches: R **Bats:** R **Pos:** RP-58   **Ht:** 6'3" **Wt:** 250 **Born:** 7/3/1986 **Age:** 29

			HOW MUCH HE PITCHED							WHAT HE GAVE UP											THE RESULTS						
Year	Team	Lg	G	GS	CG	GF	IP	BFP	H	R	ER	HR	SH	SF	HB	TBB	IBB	SO	WP	Bk	W	L	Pct	Sh	Sv-Op	Hld	ERC	ERA
2008	Tex	AL	3	3	0	0	11.0	63	23	20	20	4	0	0	1	3	0	9	0	0	0	2	.000	0	0-0	0	12.66	16.36
2009	Tex	AL	19	19	1	0	112.0	475	113	55	51	13	2	1	2	33	2	64	6	1	9	6	.600	0	0-0	0	3.86	4.10
2010	Tex	AL	23	22	1	0	128.0	536	126	55	53	21	3	2	3	33	0	68	1	0	13	4	.765	0	0-0	0	3.95	3.73
2011	2 Tms	AL	20	11	0	2	84.2	367	100	50	44	12	2	2	4	15	1	45	0	0	4	4	.500	0	0-1	1	4.65	4.68
2012	Bal	AL	33	20	0	5	133.2	573	161	85	81	32	3	6	4	27	2	77	0	1	7	8	.467	0	0-1	0	5.63	5.45
2013	Bal	AL	68	0	0	20	86.1	336	71	28	27	11	1	0	2	14	1	68	0	0	6	5	.545	0	4-6	21	2.53	2.81
2014	Bal	AL	60	0	0	24	60.2	241	55	22	20	4	1	2	1	12	3	45	2	0	3	2	.600	0	11-17	12	2.65	2.97
2015	2 Tms	AL	58	0	0	17	60.1	249	61	29	28	7	1	3	1	14	2	47	2	0	4	2	.667	0	1-2	7	3.65	4.18
11	Tex	AL	8	0	0	2	15.1	62	12	6	5	1	1	1	0	5	0	10	0	0	1	1	.500	0	0-1	1	2.44	2.93
11	Bal	AL	12	11	0	0	69.1	305	88	44	39	11	1	1	4	10	1	35	0	0	3	3	.500	0	0-0	1	5.19	5.06
15	Bal	AL	39	0	0	12	44.2	180	41	19	18	3	1	3	1	11	2	32	2	0	2	2	.500	0	0-1	6	2.92	3.63
15	ChC	NL	19	0	0	5	15.2	69	20	10	10	4	0	0	0	3	0	15	0	0	2	0	1.000	0	1-1	1	5.91	5.74
	Postseason		7	3	0	2	14.1	65	19	8	7	2	0	2	1	2	0	15	0	1	0	2	.000	0	0-0	0	5.35	4.40
	8 ML YEARS		284	75	2	68	676.2	2840	710	344	324	104	13	16	18	151	11	423	11	2	46	33	.582	0	16-27	41	4.11	4.31

Torii Hunter

Bats: R **Throws:** R **Pos:** RF-123;DH-14;PH-4   **Ht:** 6'2" **Wt:** 220 **Born:** 7/18/1975 **Age:** 40

				BATTING																			RUNNING			AVERAGES			
Year	Team	Lg	G	AB	H	2B	3B	HR	(Hm	Rd)	TB	R	RBI	RC	TBB	IBB	SO	HBP	SH	SF	SB	CS	GDP	Avg	OBP	Slg	OPS
1997	Min	AL	1	0	0	0	0	0	(0	0)	0	0	0	0	0	0	0	0	0	0	0	0	0	-	-	-	-
1998	Min	AL	6	17	4	1	0	0	(0	0)	5	0	2	1	2	0	6	0	0	0	0	1	1	.235	.316	.294	.610
1999	Min	AL	135	384	98	17	2	9	(2	7)	146	52	35	44	26	1	72	6	1	5	10	6	9	.255	.309	.380	.689
2000	Min	AL	99	336	94	14	7	5	(4	1)	137	44	44	39	18	2	68	2	0	2	4	3	13	.280	.318	.408	.726
2001	Min	AL	148	564	147	32	5	27	(13	14)	270	82	92	79	29	0	125	8	1	1	9	6	12	.261	.306	.479	.784
2002	Min	AL	148	561	162	37	4	29	(13	16)	294	89	94	85	35	3	118	5	0	3	23	8	17	.289	.334	.524	.859
2003	Min	AL	154	581	145	31	4	26	(12	14)	262	83	102	76	50	7	106	5	0	6	6	7	15	.250	.312	.451	.762
2004	Min	AL	138	520	141	37	0	23	(9	14)	247	79	81	69	40	4	101	7	0	2	21	7	23	.271	.330	.475	.805
2005	Min	AL	98	372	100	24	1	14	(6	8)	168	63	56	53	34	3	65	6	0	4	23	7	8	.269	.337	.452	.788
2006	Min	AL	147	557	155	21	2	31	(15	16)	273	86	98	81	45	2	108	5	0	4	12	6	19	.278	.336	.490	.826
2007	Min	AL	160	600	172	45	1	28	(11	17)	303	94	107	99	40	10	101	5	0	5	18	9	17	.287	.334	.505	.839
2008	LAA	AL	146	551	153	37	2	21	(10	11)	257	85	78	80	50	6	108	6	0	1	19	5	15	.278	.344	.466	.810
2009	LAA	AL	119	451	135	26	1	22	(15	7)	229	74	90	84	47	4	92	3	0	5	18	4	9	.299	.366	.508	.873
2010	LAA	AL	152	573	161	36	0	23	(8	15)	266	76	90	93	61	6	106	7	0	5	9	12	22	.281	.354	.464	.819
2011	LAA	AL	156	580	152	24	2	23	(15	8)	249	80	82	79	62	2	125	4	0	3	5	7	24	.262	.336	.429	.765
2012	LAA	AL	140	534	167	24	1	16	(7	9)	241	81	92	89	38	1	133	8	1	3	9	1	15	.313	.365	.451	.817
2013	Det	AL	144	606	184	37	5	17	(8	9)	282	90	84	81	26	0	113	7	3	10	3	2	11	.304	.334	.465	.800
2014	Det	AL	142	549	157	33	2	17	(8	9)	245	71	83	66	23	0	89	7	0	7	4	3	18	.286	.319	.446	.765
2015	Min	AL	139	521	125	22	0	22	(10	12)	213	67	81	65	35	1	105	6	0	5	2	5	14	.240	.293	.409	.702
	Postseason		48	186	51	12	1	4	(1	3)	77	26	20	19	17	2	32	2	2	1	3	2	7	.274	.340	.414	.754
	19 ML YEARS		2372	8857	2452	498	39	353	(166	187)	4087	1296	1391	1263	661	52	1741	97	6	71	195	99	262	.277	.331	.461	.793

Drew Hutchison

Pitches: R **Bats:** L **Pos:** SP-28; RP-2   **Ht:** 6'3" **Wt:** 195 **Born:** 8/22/1990 **Age:** 25

			HOW MUCH HE PITCHED							WHAT HE GAVE UP											THE RESULTS						
Year	Team	Lg	G	GS	CG	GF	IP	BFP	H	R	ER	HR	SH	SF	HB	TBB	IBB	SO	WP	Bk	W	L	Pct	Sh	Sv-Op	Hld	ERC	ERA
2012	Tor	AL	11	11	0	0	58.2	257	59	31	30	8	1	1	5	20	0	49	1	0	5	3	.625	0	0-0	0	4.43	4.60
2014	Tor	AL	32	32	1	0	184.2	786	173	92	92	23	4	10	1	60	1	184	4	2	11	13	.458	1	0-0	0	3.70	4.48
2015	Tor	AL	30	28	1	0	150.1	664	179	103	93	22	0	6	11	44	0	129	7	0	13	5	.722	1	0-0	0	5.44	5.57
	3 ML YEARS		73	71	2	0	393.2	1707	411	226	215	53	5	17	23	124	1	362	12	2	29	21	.580	2	0-0	0	4.45	4.92

Colt Hynes

Pitches: L **Bats:** L **Pos:** RP-5   **Ht:** 5'11" **Wt:** 200 **Born:** 6/28/1985 **Age:** 31

			HOW MUCH HE PITCHED							WHAT HE GAVE UP											THE RESULTS						
Year	Team	Lg	G	GS	CG	GF	IP	BFP	H	R	ER	HR	SH	SF	HB	TBB	IBB	SO	WP	Bk	W	L	Pct	Sh	Sv-Op	Hld	ERC	ERA
2011	SnAnt	AA	45	0	0	17	58.0	250	64	29	24	1	2	2	2	20	2	41	3	0	0	6	.000	0	1- -	-	3.98	3.72
2011	Tucsn	AAA	22	0	0	5	26.1	116	35	16	16	1	0	2	2	9	0	12	3	0	2	1	.667	0	0- -	-	5.90	5.47
2012	Tucsn	AAA	30	21	0	4	126.2	582	190	93	81	11	7	3	3	29	0	74	8	0	6	9	.400	0	0- -	-	6.41	5.76
2013	SnAnt	AA	10	0	0	0	12.1	44	10	1	1	0	1	0	0	0	0	16	1	0	1	0	1.000	0	0- -	-	1.39	0.73
2013	Tucsn	AAA	31	0	0	9	35.0	139	33	10	7	1	2	1	1	2	0	42	4	0	1	0	1.000	0	4- -	-	2.17	1.80
2014	Albq	AAA	42	0	0	11	53.0	221	56	25	24	6	1	2	1	10	0	46	2	0	1	3	.250	0	2- -	-	3.73	4.08
2014	Buffalo	AAA	7	0	0	2	8.2	31	4	1	1	1	0	0	0	1	0	7	0	0	0	1	.000	0	0- -	-	0.94	1.04
2015	Buffalo	AAA	37	0	0	10	34.1	154	35	14	13	2	2	2	5	15	2	27	2	0	0	2	.000	0	1- -	-	4.50	3.41

Year	Team	Lg	G	GS	CG	GF	IP	BFP	H	R	ER	HR	SH	SF	HB	TBB	IBB	SO	WP	Bk	W	L	Pct	Sh	Sv-Op	Hld	ERC	ERA

			HOW MUCH HE PITCHED						WHAT HE GAVE UP										THE RESULTS								
Year	Team	Lg	G	GS	CG	GF	IP	BFP	H	R	ER	HR	SH	SF	HB	TBB	IBB	SO	WP	Bk	W	L	Pct	Sh	Sv-Op	Hld	ERC	ERA
2015	Nham	AA	10	0	0	4	13.1	51	9	5	5	0	0	0	0	3	0	12	1	0	2	1	.667	0	0--	-	1.40	3.38
2013	SD	NL	22	0	0	6	17.0	84	25	17	17	3	0	0	1	9	2	13	1	0	0	0	-	0	0-0	1	8.20	9.00
2015	Tor	AL	5	0	0	1	3.0	18	8	2	2	0	0	0	0	2	1	4	0	0	0	0	-	0	0-0	0	15.27	6.00
2 ML YEARS			27	0	0	7	20.0	102	33	19	19	3	0	0	1	11	3	17	1	0	0	0	-	0	0-0	1	9.21	8.55

Chris Iannetta

Bats: R Throws: R Pos: C-85;PH-5;1B-2;DH-1   eye-ah-NETT-ah   Ht: 6'0" Wt: 230 Born: 4/8/1983 Age: 33

			BATTING																			RUNNING			AVERAGES			
Year	Team	Lg	G	AB	H	2B	3B	HR	(Hm	Rd)	TB	R	RBI	RC	TBB	IBB	SO	HBP	SH	SF	SB	CS	GDP	Avg	OBP	Slg	OPS
2006	Col	NL	21	77	20	4	0	2	(0	2)	30	12	10	9	13	2	17	1	1	1	0	1	1	.260	.370	.390	.759
2007	Col	NL	67	197	43	8	3	4	(1	3)	69	22	27	27	29	3	58	5	1	2	0	0	3	.218	.330	.350	.681
2008	Col	NL	104	333	88	22	2	18	(11	7)	168	50	65	65	56	0	92	14	2	2	0	0	6	.264	.390	.505	.895
2009	Col	NL	93	289	66	15	2	16	(8	8)	133	41	52	47	43	3	75	11	1	6	0	1	4	.228	.344	.460	.804
2010	Col	NL	61	188	37	6	1	9	(7	2)	72	20	27	21	30	2	48	4	0	1	1	0	4	.197	.318	.383	.701
2011	Col	NL	112	345	82	17	1	14	(10	4)	143	51	55	62	70	5	89	5	2	4	6	3	10	.238	.370	.414	.785
2012	LAA	AL	79	221	53	6	1	9	(3	6)	88	27	26	27	29	0	60	2	0	1	1	3	4	.240	.332	.398	.730
2013	LAA	AL	115	325	73	15	0	11	(1	10)	121	40	39	44	68	2	100	2	0	4	0	1	8	.225	.358	.372	.731
2014	LAA	AL	108	306	77	22	0	7	(6	1)	120	41	43	56	54	3	91	8	0	5	3	0	3	.252	.373	.392	.765
2015	LAA	AL	92	272	51	10	0	10	(3	7)	91	28	34	27	41	1	83	1	0	3	0	1	11	.188	.293	.335	.628
Postseason			3	10	1	0	0	1	(1	0)	4	1	1	0	1	0	2	0	0	0	0	0	0	.100	.182	.400	.582
10 ML YEARS			852	2553	590	125	10	100	(50	50)	1035	332	378	385	433	21	713	53	7	29	11	10	54	.231	.351	.405	.756

Edgar Ibarra

Pitches: L Bats: L Pos: RP-2   ee-BAR-uh   Ht: 6'0" Wt: 190 Born: 5/31/1989 Age: 27

			HOW MUCH HE PITCHED						WHAT HE GAVE UP										THE RESULTS								
Year	Team	Lg	G	GS	CG	GF	IP	BFP	H	R	ER	HR	SH	SF	HB	TBB	IBB	SO	WP	Bk	W	L	Pct	Sh	Sv-Op	Hld	ERC	ERA
2011	FtMyrs	A+	32	16	1	2	106.1	498	133	73	61	13	2	5	7	49	0	77	12	0	5	10	.333	1	0--	-	6.24	5.16
2012	FtMyrs	A+	18	0	0	6	45.0	206	49	28	18	1	2	2	6	16	0	41	6	1	1	3	.250	0	2--	-	4.23	3.60
2012	NwBrit	AA	24	0	0	10	33.2	151	40	27	23	6	1	2	1	15	0	28	2	0	2	1	.667	0	0--	-	6.21	6.15
2013	NwBrit	AA	31	0	0	4	42.1	172	32	11	9	2	0	1	2	20	3	40	3	0	2	2	.500	0	2--	-	2.76	1.91
2013	Roch	AAA	16	0	0	3	18.1	73	9	4	4	1	1	2	1	9	0	14	0	0	1	0	1.000	0	0--	-	1.75	1.96
2014	Roch	AAA	31	0	0	7	49.2	218	50	19	19	3	0	2	0	23	0	42	3	0	5	0	1.000	0	0--	-	4.06	3.44
2014	NwBrit	AA	9	0	0	6	14.1	64	17	12	11	1	1	2	1	5	0	16	1	0	2	1	.667	0	1--	-	5.03	6.91
2015	Salt Lk	AAA	49	1	0	7	61.1	283	70	45	37	5	5	7	0	33	2	66	6	0	3	3	.500	0	2--	-	5.20	5.43
2015	LAA	AL	2	0	0	1	4.0	19	4	1	1	0	0	0	0	3	0	3	1	0	0	0	-	0	0-0	0	4.54	2.25

Jose Iglesias

Bats: R Throws: R Pos: SS-119;PR-2;PH-1   ee-GLAY-see-us   Ht: 5'11" Wt: 185 Born: 1/5/1990 Age: 26

			BATTING																			RUNNING			AVERAGES			
Year	Team	Lg	G	AB	H	2B	3B	HR	(Hm	Rd)	TB	R	RBI	RC	TBB	IBB	SO	HBP	SH	SF	SB	CS	GDP	Avg	OBP	Slg	OPS
2011	Bos	AL	10	6	2	0	0	0	(0	0)	2	3	0	0	0	0	2	0	0	0	0	0	0	.333	.333	.333	.667
2012	Bos	AL	25	68	8	2	0	1	(0	1)	13	5	2	0	4	0	16	3	2	0	1	0	2	.118	.200	.191	.391
2013	2 Tms	AL	109	350	106	16	2	3	(1	2)	135	39	29	45	15	0	60	11	4	2	5	2	7	.303	.349	.386	.735
2015	Det	AL	120	416	125	17	3	2	(1	1)	154	44	23	47	25	2	44	6	4	3	11	8	10	.300	.347	.370	.717
13	Bos	AL	63	215	71	10	2	1	(0	1)	88	27	19	34	11	0	30	6	0	2	3	1	4	.330	.376	.409	.785
13	Det	AL	46	135	35	6	0	2	(1	1)	47	12	10	11	4	0	30	5	4	0	2	1	3	.259	.306	.348	.654
Postseason			11	26	6	0	0	0	(0	0)	6	2	1	0	1	0	5	1	3	0	0	1	1	.231	.286	.231	.516
4 ML YEARS			264	840	241	35	5	6	(2	4)	304	91	54	92	44	2	122	20	10	5	17	10	19	.287	.336	.362	.697

Raisel Iglesias

Pitches: R Bats: R Pos: SP-16; RP-2   rye-SELL   Ht: 6'2" Wt: 185 Born: 1/4/1990 Age: 26

			HOW MUCH HE PITCHED						WHAT HE GAVE UP										THE RESULTS								
Year	Team	Lg	G	GS	CG	GF	IP	BFP	H	R	ER	HR	SH	SF	HB	TBB	IBB	SO	WP	Bk	W	L	Pct	Sh	Sv-Op	Hld	ERC	ERA
2015	Lsvlle	AAA	6	6	0	0	29.0	121	26	12	11	4	3	0	0	8	0	21	1	0	1	3	.250	0	0--	-	3.22	3.41
2015	Cin	NL	18	16	0	1	95.1	395	81	45	44	11	4	0	7	28	0	104	2	2	3	7	.300	0	0-0	0	3.24	4.15

Ender Inciarte

Bats: L Throws: L Pos: RF-77;LF-47;CF-22;PH-11   END-er in-see-ARR-tay   Ht: 5'10" Wt: 185 Born: 10/29/1990 Age: 25

			BATTING																			RUNNING			AVERAGES			
Year	Team	Lg	G	AB	H	2B	3B	HR	(Hm	Rd)	TB	R	RBI	RC	TBB	IBB	SO	HBP	SH	SF	SB	CS	GDP	Avg	OBP	Slg	OPS
2011	Sbend	A	116	450	118	19	5	1	(-	-)	150	73	25	54	47	1	59	2	12	3	26	15	8	.262	.333	.333	.666
2012	2 Tms	Low	127	473	145	28	10	2	(-	-)	199	82	47	83	53	2	63	2	11	4	46	12	8	.307	.376	.421	.797
2013	Mobile	AA	128	473	133	17	3	5	(-	-)	171	69	25	63	27	1	47	6	8	2	43	8	8	.281	.327	.362	.688
2014	Reno	AAA	26	109	34	4	2	2	(-	-)	48	22	12	18	10	1	21	0	0	1	7	2	1	.312	.367	.440	.807
2014	Ari	NL	118	418	116	18	2	4	(1	3)	150	54	27	49	25	0	53	0	4	0	19	3	3	.278	.318	.359	.677
2015	Ari	NL	132	524	159	27	5	6	(1	5)	214	73	45	69	26	0	58	4	2	5	21	10	8	.303	.338	.408	.747
2 ML YEARS			250	942	275	45	7	10	(2	8)	364	127	72	118	51	0	111	4	6	5	40	13	11	.292	.329	.386	.716

Omar Infante

Bats: R **Throws:** R **Pos:** 2B-124;PH-1;PR-1 — in-FAHN-tay — **Ht:** 5'11" **Wt:** 195 **Born:** 12/26/1981 **Age:** 34

Year Team	Lg	G	AB	H	2B	3B	HR	(Hm Rd)	TB	R	RBI	RC	TBB	IBB	SO	HBP	SH	SF	SB	CS	GDP	Avg	OBP	Slg	OPS
2002 Det	AL	18	72	24	3	0	1	(0 1)	30	4	6	12	3	0	10	0	0	0	0	1	0	.333	.360	.417	.777
2003 Det	AL	69	221	49	6	1	0	(0 0)	57	24	8	16	18	0	37	0	3	2	6	3	1	.222	.278	.258	.536
2004 Det	AL	142	503	133	27	9	16	(7 9)	226	69	55	69	40	3	112	1	7	5	13	7	4	.264	.317	.449	.766
2005 Det	AL	121	406	90	28	2	9	(3 6)	149	36	43	38	16	0	73	2	8	2	8	0	5	.222	.254	.367	.621
2006 Det	AL	78	224	62	11	4	4	(0 4)	93	35	25	26	14	0	45	3	2	2	3	2	5	.277	.325	.415	.740
2007 Det	AL	66	166	45	6	1	2	(0 2)	59	24	17	23	9	0	29	0	2	1	4	1	4	.271	.307	.355	.662
2008 Atl	NL	96	317	93	24	3	3	(1 2)	132	45	40	45	22	2	44	2	2	5	0	1	4	.293	.338	.416	.755
2009 Atl	NL	70	203	62	9	1	2	(1 1)	79	24	27	29	19	0	28	1	2	4	2	0	5	.305	.361	.389	.750
2010 Atl	NL	134	471	151	15	3	8	(1 7)	196	65	47	70	29	1	62	0	4	2	7	6	14	.321	.359	.416	.775
2011 Fla	NL	148	579	160	24	8	7	(2 5)	221	55	49	66	34	1	67	2	17	8	4	2	12	.276	.315	.382	.696
2012 2 Tms		149	554	152	30	7	12	(5 7)	232	69	53	58	21	0	65	1	8	4	17	3	9	.274	.300	.419	.719
2013 Det	AL	118	453	144	24	3	10	(7 3)	204	54	51	64	20	1	44	0	0	3	5	2	11	.318	.345	.450	.795
2014 KC	AL	135	528	133	21	3	6	(2 4)	178	50	66	55	33	3	68	2	5	7	9	3	7	.252	.295	.337	.632
2015 KC	AL	124	440	97	23	7	2	(0 2)	140	39	44	31	9	0	69	0	2	4	2	2	8	.220	.234	.318	.552
12 Mia	NL	85	328	94	23	2	8	(2 6)	145	42	33	36	12	0	42	1	4	2	10	1	7	.287	.312	.442	.754
12 Det	AL	64	226	58	7	5	4	(3 1)	87	27	20	22	9	0	23	0	4	2	7	2	2	.257	.283	.385	.668
Postseason		45	161	41	7	0	1	(1 0)	51	16	9	16	12	2	40	1	1	2	3	1	4	.255	.307	.317	.624
14 ML YEARS		1468	5137	1395	251	52	82	(29 53)	1996	593	531	602	287	11	753	14	62	49	80	33	89	.272	.309	.389	.698

Travis Ishikawa

Bats: L **Throws:** L **Pos:** PH-29;1B-12;LF-6 — ee-shee-COW-wuh — **Ht:** 6'3" **Wt:** 220 **Born:** 9/24/1983 **Age:** 32

Year Team	Lg	G	AB	H	2B	3B	HR	(Hm Rd)	TB	R	RBI	RC	TBB	IBB	SO	HBP	SH	SF	SB	CS	GDP	Avg	OBP	Slg	OPS
2015 Scrmto*	AAA	34	133	36	8	0	4	(- -)	56	17	19	20	13	0	41	2	0	1	0	0	1	.271	.342	.421	.763
2006 SF	NL	12	24	7	3	1	0	(0 0)	12	1	4	4	1	0	6	0	0	0	0	1	0	.292	.320	.500	.820
2008 SF	NL	33	95	26	6	0	3	(1 2)	41	12	15	17	9	1	27	0	0	0	1	0	1	.274	.337	.432	.768
2009 SF	NL	120	326	85	10	2	9	(7 2)	126	49	39	44	30	3	89	4	1	2	2	2	7	.261	.329	.387	.715
2010 SF	NL	116	158	42	11	0	3	(0 3)	62	18	22	19	13	2	29	0	1	1	0	0	3	.266	.320	.392	.712
2012 Mil	NL	94	152	39	12	1	4	(2 2)	65	19	30	24	13	3	42	4	4	1	0	0	4	.257	.329	.428	.757
2013 2 Tms	AL	7	19	2	0	0	0	(0 0)	2	0	1	0	1	0	10	0	0	0	0	0	0	.105	.150	.105	.255
2014 2 Tms	AL	62	107	27	4	1	3	(2 1)	42	9	18	13	9	1	34	1	0	2	0	0	3	.252	.311	.393	.703
2015 2 Tms	NL	44	63	13	3	0	1	(0 1)	19	6	8	7	9	0	20	1	0	0	0	0	2	.206	.306	.302	.607
13 Bal	AL	6	17	2	0	0	0	(0 0)	2	0	1	0	1	0	8	0	0	0	0	0	0	.118	.167	.118	.284
13 NYY	AL	1	2	0	0	0	0	(0 0)	0	0	0	0	0	0	2	0	0	0	0	0	0	.000	.000	.000	.000
14 Pit	NL	15	34	7	1	1	1	(1 0)	13	2	3	3	3	0	11	0	0	0	0	0	1	.206	.263	.382	.646
14 SF	NL	47	73	20	3	0	2	(1 1)	29	7	15	10	6	1	23	1	0	1	0	0	1	.274	.333	.397	.731
15 SF	NL	6	5	0	0	0	0	(0 0)	0	1	0	0	1	0	3	0	0	0	0	0	0	.000	.167	.000	.167
15 Pit	NL	38	58	13	3	0	1	(0 1)	19	5	8	7	8	0	17	0	0	0	0	0	2	.224	.318	.328	.646
Postseason		26	49	12	3	0	1	(1 0)	18	4	8	8	6	0	13	1	0	0	0	0	1	.245	.339	.367	.707
8 ML YEARS		488	944	241	49	5	23	(12 11)	369	114	137	128	85	10	257	9	6	6	3	2	21	.255	.321	.391	.712

Hisashi Iwakuma

Pitches: R **Bats:** R **Pos:** SP-20 — he-SAH-shee ee-wuh-KOO-muh — **Ht:** 6'3" **Wt:** 210 **Born:** 4/12/1981 **Age:** 35

Year Team	Lg	G	GS	CG	GF	IP	BFP	H	R	ER	HR	SH	SF	HB	TBB	IBB	SO	WP	Bk	W	L	Pct	Sh	Sv-Op	Hld	ERC	ERA
2012 Sea	AL	30	16	0	6	125.1	519	117	49	44	17	1	1	3	43	3	101	5	0	9	5	.643	0	2-2	0	3.87	3.16
2013 Sea	AL	33	33	0	0	219.2	866	179	69	65	25	3	6	2	42	4	185	10	0	14	6	.700	0	0-0	0	2.43	2.66
2014 Sea	AL	28	28	0	0	179.0	709	167	70	70	20	0	1	2	21	2	154	2	0	15	9	.625	0	0-0	0	2.77	3.52
2015 Sea	AL	20	20	1	0	129.2	516	117	53	51	18	4	3	1	21	1	111	1	0	9	5	.643	1	0-0	0	2.93	3.54
4 ML YEARS		111	97	1	6	653.2	2610	580	241	230	80	8	11	8	127	10	551	18	0	47	25	.653	1	2-2	0	2.88	3.17

Maicer Izturis

Bats: B **Throws:** R **Pos:** 2B — MY-sare izz-TOUR-iss — **Ht:** 5'8" **Wt:** 155 **Born:** 9/12/1980 **Age:** 35

Year Team	Lg	G	AB	H	2B	3B	HR	(Hm Rd)	TB	R	RBI	RC	TBB	IBB	SO	HBP	SH	SF	SB	CS	GDP	Avg	OBP	Slg	OPS
2004 Mon	NL	32	107	22	5	2	1	(1 0)	34	10	4	8	10	1	20	2	2	0	4	0	1	.206	.286	.318	.603
2005 LAA	AL	77	191	47	8	4	1	(0 1)	66	18	15	25	17	2	21	0	1	1	9	3	5	.246	.306	.346	.652
2006 LAA	AL	104	352	103	21	3	5	(1 4)	145	64	44	56	38	1	35	3	5	1	14	6	7	.293	.365	.412	.777
2007 LAA	AL	102	336	97	17	2	6	(4 2)	136	47	51	65	33	2	39	0	1	4	7	1	4	.289	.349	.405	.753
2008 LAA	AL	79	290	78	14	2	3	(1 2)	105	44	37	39	26	0	27	1	2	2	11	2	9	.269	.329	.362	.691
2009 LAA	AL	114	387	116	22	3	8	(3 5)	168	74	65	66	35	2	41	5	3	7	13	5	7	.300	.359	.434	.794
2010 LAA	AL	61	212	53	13	1	3	(0 3)	77	27	27	30	21	0	27	2	1	2	7	3	1	.250	.321	.363	.684
2011 LAA	AL	122	449	124	35	0	5	(1 4)	174	51	38	53	33	3	65	8	0	4	9	6	6	.276	.334	.388	.722
2012 LAA	AL	100	289	74	11	0	2	(1 2)	91	35	20	28	25	0	38	2	3	0	17	2	10	.256	.320	.315	.634
2013 Tor	AL	107	365	86	12	0	5	(4 1)	113	33	32	26	27	0	38	1	3	3	1	5	11	.236	.288	.310	.597
2014 Tor	AL	11	35	10	1	0	0	(0 0)	11	3	1	4	2	0	4	0	1	0	1	0	0	.286	.324	.314	.639
Postseason		10	29	6	3	0	0	(0 0)	9	3	2	2	1	1	5	0	0	1	3	0	0	.207	.226	.310	.536
11 ML YEARS		909	3013	810	159	17	39	(15 24)	1120	406	334	400	267	11	355	24	22	24	93	33	61	.269	.331	.372	.703

Austin Jackson

Bats: R Throws: R Pos: CF-115;RF-22;PH-16;LF-4;PR-1　　　　　Ht: 6'1" Wt: 205 Born: 2/1/1987 Age: 29

Year	Team	Lg	G	AB	H	2B	3B	HR	(Hm	Rd)	TB	R	RBI	RC	TBB	IBB	SO	HBP	SH	SF	SB	CS	GDP	Avg	OBP	Slg	OPS
2010	Det	AL	151	618	181	34	10	4	(0	4)	247	103	41	84	47	4	170	1	8	3	27	6	5	.293	.345	.400	.745
2011	Det	AL	153	591	147	22	11	10	(5	5)	221	90	45	67	56	3	181	4	14	3	22	5	11	.249	.317	.374	.690
2012	Det	AL	137	543	163	29	10	16	(6	10)	260	103	66	90	67	0	134	2	2	3	12	9	9	.300	.377	.479	.856
2013	Det	AL	129	552	150	30	7	12	(3	9)	230	99	49	73	52	0	129	4	3	3	8	4	12	.272	.337	.417	.754
2014	2 Tms	AL	154	597	153	30	6	4	(2	2)	207	71	47	58	47	0	144	2	1	9	20	6	15	.256	.308	.347	.655
2015	2 Tms		136	491	131	25	3	9	(5	4)	189	56	48	63	29	0	126	3	3	1	17	10	5	.267	.311	.385	.696
14	Det	AL	100	374	102	25	5	4	(2	2)	149	52	33	42	35	0	85	2	1	8	9	4	9	.273	.332	.398	.730
14	Sea	AL	54	223	51	5	1	0	(0	0)	58	19	14	16	12	0	59	0	0	1	11	2	6	.229	.267	.260	.527
15	Sea	AL	107	419	114	18	3	8	(5	3)	162	46	38	52	24	0	107	1	3	1	15	9	4	.272	.312	.387	.699
15	ChC		29	72	17	7	0	1	(0	1)	27	10	10	11	5	0	19	2	0	0	2	1	1	.236	.304	.375	.679
	Postseason		35	133	31	7	1	2	(1	1)	46	18	11	15	19	0	53	1	2	0	2	1	2	.233	.333	.346	.679
	6 ML YEARS		860	3392	925	170	47	55	(21	34)	1354	522	296	435	298	7	884	19	26	22	106	40	57	.273	.333	.399	.732

Edwin Jackson

Pitches: R Bats: R Pos: RP-47　　　　　Ht: 6'3" Wt: 210 Born: 9/9/1983 Age: 32

Year	Team	Lg	G	GS	CG	GF	IP	BFP	H	R	ER	HR	SH	SF	HB	TBB	IBB	SO	WP	Bk	W	L	Pct	Sh	Sv-Op	Hld	ERC	ERA
2003	LAD	NL	4	3	0	0	22.0	91	17	6	6	2	1	1	1	11	1	19	3	0	2	1	.667	0	0-0	0	3.36	2.45
2004	LAD	NL	8	5	0	1	24.2	113	31	20	20	7	1	0	0	11	1	16	0	0	2	1	.667	0	0-0	0	7.21	7.30
2005	LAD	NL	7	6	0	0	28.2	134	31	22	20	2	0	2	1	17	0	13	2	1	2	2	.500	0	0-0	0	5.13	6.28
2006	TB	AL	23	1	0	7	36.1	174	42	27	22	2	2	2	1	25	0	27	3	1	0	0	-	0	0-0	0	5.86	5.45
2007	TB	AL	32	31	1	0	161.0	755	195	116	103	19	5	6	4	88	3	128	7	1	5	15	.250	1	0-0	0	6.11	5.76
2008	TB	AL	32	31	1	0	183.1	792	199	91	90	23	3	3	2	77	1	108	7	1	14	11	.560	1	0-1	0	4.99	4.42
2009	Det	AL	33	33	1	0	214.0	890	200	93	86	27	4	2	5	70	3	161	6	0	13	9	.591	1	0-0	0	3.72	3.62
2010	2 Tms		32	32	1	0	209.1	902	214	111	104	21	6	4	6	78	4	181	20	0	10	12	.455	1	0-0	0	4.20	4.47
2011	2 Tms		32	31	1	1	199.2	861	225	92	84	16	15	6	2	62	4	148	9	2	12	9	.571	1	0-0	0	4.34	3.79
2012	Was	NL	31	31	1	0	189.2	790	173	90	85	23	9	8	2	58	5	168	3	0	10	11	.476	1	0-0	0	3.36	4.03
2013	ChC	NL	31	31	0	0	175.1	777	197	110	97	16	8	3	5	59	7	135	14	0	8	18	.308	0	0-0	0	4.46	4.98
2014	ChC	NL	28	27	0	0	140.2	633	168	105	99	18	6	4	3	63	3	123	9	0	6	15	.286	0	0-0	0	5.75	6.33
2015	2 Tms	NL	47	0	0	18	55.2	228	44	25	19	4	1	3	1	21	1	40	5	1	4	3	.571	0	1-2	5	2.75	3.07
10	Ari	NL	21	21	1	0	134.1	587	141	80	77	13	6	2	5	60	2	104	13	0	6	10	.375	1	0-0	0	4.72	5.16
10	CWS	AL	11	11	0	0	75.0	315	73	31	27	8	0	2	1	18	2	77	7	0	4	2	.667	0	0-0	0	3.32	3.24
11	CWS	AL	19	19	1	0	121.2	522	134	55	53	8	6	4	0	39	2	97	7	1	7	7	.500	1	0-0	0	4.10	3.92
11	StL	NL	13	12	0	1	78.0	339	91	37	31	8	9	2	2	23	2	51	2	1	5	2	.714	0	0-0	0	4.73	3.58
15	ChC	NL	23	0	0	11	31.0	134	30	14	11	0	1	2	1	12	1	23	3	1	2	1	.667	0	0-1	0	3.19	3.19
15	Atl	NL	24	0	0	7	24.2	94	14	11	8	4	0	1	0	9	0	17	2	0	2	2	.500	0	1-1	5	2.16	2.92
	Postseason		9	5	0	2	28.0	124	30	17	17	6	2	0	0	15	1	23	0	0	1	2	.333	0	0-0	1	5.97	5.46
	13 ML YEARS		340	262	5	27	1640.1	7140	1736	908	835	180	61	44	33	640	33	1267	88	7	88	107	.451	3	1-3	5	4.51	4.58

Jay Jackson

Pitches: R Bats: R Pos: RP-6　　　　　Ht: 6'1" Wt: 195 Born: 10/27/1987 Age: 28

Year	Team	Lg	G	GS	CG	GF	IP	BFP	H	R	ER	HR	SH	SF	HB	TBB	IBB	SO	WP	Bk	W	L	Pct	Sh	Sv-Op	Hld	ERC	ERA
2011	Iowa	AAA	26	26	0	0	146.2	654	180	90	87	10	10	4	4	46	1	97	4	0	8	14	.364	0	0--	-	4.90	5.34
2012	Iowa	AAA	37	3	0	3	86.1	394	105	67	63	14	4	4	3	43	1	76	5	0	3	7	.300	0	0--	-	6.50	6.57
2013	Jaxnvl	AA	14	14	0	0	79.2	319	59	32	28	6	1	1	3	22	0	73	0	2	3	6	.333	0	0--	-	2.25	3.16
2013	NewOr	AAA	7	4	0	0	25.0	110	29	16	13	3	1	1	0	11	0	20	1	0	1	1	.500	0	0--	-	5.45	4.68
2014	Indy	AAA	25	12	0	4	84.2	386	91	50	46	8	5	3	4	36	3	87	6	0	5	4	.556	0	0--	-	4.56	4.89
2014	Nashv	AAA	6	6	0	0	26.2	121	29	15	15	4	1	1	0	16	0	28	0	0	0	3	.000	0	0--	-	5.86	5.06
2015	SnAnt	AA	6	0	0	3	10.2	39	7	2	2	0	1	0	0	1	0	16	0	0	1	0	1.000	0	1--	-	1.09	1.69
2015	ElPaso	AAA	48	0	0	25	63.2	256	56	21	18	2	2	1	2	17	2	70	1	0	3	3	.500	0	14--	-	2.63	2.54
2015	SD	NL	6	0	0	1	4.1	20	7	3	3	0	0	0	0	1	0	4	0	0	0	0	-	0	0-0	0	6.40	6.23

Luke Jackson

Pitches: R Bats: R Pos: RP-7　　　　　Ht: 6'2" Wt: 205 Born: 8/24/1991 Age: 24

Year	Team	Lg	G	GS	CG	GF	IP	BFP	H	R	ER	HR	SH	SF	HB	TBB	IBB	SO	WP	Bk	W	L	Pct	Sh	Sv-Op	Hld	ERC	ERA
2011	Hkry	A	19	19	0	0	75.0	358	83	57	47	9	0	5	4	48	0	78	12	1	5	6	.455	0	0--	-	5.95	5.64
2012	2 Tms	Low	26	26	1	0	129.2	569	130	72	67	6	2	5	9	65	0	146	9	1	10	7	.588	0	0--	-	4.45	4.65
2013	MrtlBh	A+	19	19	0	0	101.0	417	79	30	27	6	1	1	3	47	0	104	6	0	9	4	.692	0	0--	-	3.05	2.41
2013	Frisco	AA	6	4	0	0	27.0	103	13	2	2	0	0	1	0	12	0	30	3	0	2	0	1.000	0	0--	-	1.29	0.67
2014	Frisco	AA	15	14	0	1	83.1	335	58	28	28	5	1	3	4	24	0	83	8	1	8	2	.800	0	1--	-	2.01	3.02
2014	RdRck	AAA	11	10	0	0	40.0	201	56	49	46	9	0	3	2	28	0	43	2	0	1	3	.250	0	0--	-	9.20	10.35
2015	RdRck	AAA	39	5	0	9	66.1	294	62	37	32	3	1	4	1	35	0	79	11	0	2	3	.400	0	0--	-	3.82	4.34
2015	Tex	AL	7	0	0	4	6.1	27	5	3	3	1	0	0	0	2	0	6	1	0	0	0	-	0	0-0	0	2.81	4.26

Ryan Jackson

Bats: R Throws: R Pos: 2B-17;SS-3;3B-2;PR-1　　　　　Ht: 6'3" Wt: 180 Born: 5/10/1988 Age: 28

Year	Team	Lg	G	AB	H	2B	3B	HR	(Hm	Rd)	TB	R	RBI	RC	TBB	IBB	SO	HBP	SH	SF	SB	CS	GDP	Avg	OBP	Slg	OPS
2015	Omha*	AAA	19	59	18	3	0	1	(-	-)	24	9	2	9	7	1	13	0	2	0	0	1	1	.305	.379	.407	.786
2015	Salt Lk*	AAA	85	314	92	16	3	1	(-	-)	117	33	26	46	40	0	66	0	7	2	1	3	12	.293	.371	.373	.743

Year Team	Lg	G	AB	H	2B	3B	HR	(Hm	Rd)	TB	R	RBI	RC	TBB	IBB	SO	HBP	SH	SF	SB	CS	GDP	Avg	OBP	Slg	OPS
2012 StL	NL	13	17	2	0	0	0	(0	0)	2	2	0	0	1	0	3	0	0	0	0	0	1	.118	.167	.118	.284
2013 StL	NL	7	7	0	0	0	0	(0	0)	0	0	0	0	0	0	2	0	0	0	0	0	0	.000	.000	.000	.000
2015 LAA	AL	22	9	0	0	0	0	(0	0)	0	0	0	0	1	0	5	0	4	0	0	0	1	.000	.100	.000	.100
3 ML YEARS		42	33	2	0	0	0	(0	0)	2	2	0	0	2	0	10	0	4	0	0	0	2	.061	.114	.061	.175

Juan Jaime

Pitches: R **Bats:** R **Pos:** RP-2   HIGH-may   **Ht:** 6'2" **Wt:** 250 **Born:** 8/2/1987 **Age:** 28

Year Team	Lg	G	GS	CG	GF	IP	BFP	H	R	ER	HR	SH	SF	HB	TBB	IBB	SO	WP	Bk	W	L	Pct	Sh	Sv-Op	Hld	ERC	ERA
2012 Lynbrg	A+	42	0	0	37	51.1	219	31	19	18	4	1	2	4	33	4	73	7	0	1	3	.250	0	18--	-	2.86	3.16
2013 Missi	AA	35	0	0	2	42.0	188	30	19	19	1	4	2	5	28	1	70	7	0	2	5	.286	0	0--	-	3.31	4.07
2014 Gwnntt	AAA	43	0	0	37	41.0	185	27	18	16	1	0	0	1	36	0	63	5	0	1	0	1.000	0	18--	-	3.38	3.51
2015 Tulsa	AA	11	0	0	3	11.2	53	8	5	5	0	1	1	0	12	0	20	4	0	0	2	.000	0	0--	-	4.00	3.86
2015 OkCity	AAA	7	0	0	2	9.2	43	10	2	2	0	0	0	3	3	0	7	1	0	0	0	-	0	0--	-	4.47	1.86
2015 3 Tms	Low	11	0	0	6	10.2	43	5	2	1	0	0	1	0	5	0	20	0	1	0	0	-	0	2--	-	1.23	0.84
2014 Atl	NL	16	0	0	4	12.1	62	14	8	8	1	2	0	1	9	0	18	3	0	0	0	-	0	0-0	0	6.13	5.84
2015 Atl	NL	2	0	0	1	1.1	8	0	1	1	0	1	0	0	4	1	1	0	0	0	1	.000	0	0-0	0	5.11	6.75
2 ML YEARS		18	0	0	5	13.2	70	14	9	9	1	3	0	1	13	1	19	3	0	0	1	.000	0	0-0	0	6.12	5.93

Paul Janish

Bats: R **Throws:** R **Pos:** SS-13;2B-1;PH-1   YONN-ish   **Ht:** 6'2" **Wt:** 200 **Born:** 10/12/1982 **Age:** 33

Year Team	Lg	G	AB	H	2B	3B	HR	(Hm	Rd)	TB	R	RBI	RC	TBB	IBB	SO	HBP	SH	SF	SB	CS	GDP	Avg	OBP	Slg	OPS
2015 Norfolk*	AAA	95	302	71	7	2	0	(-	-)	82	29	21	28	31	0	41	4	5	2	2	1	6	.235	.313	.272	.584
2008 Cin	NL	38	80	15	2	0	1	(1	0)	20	5	6	5	7	0	18	2	0	0	0	0	2	.188	.270	.250	.520
2009 Cin	NL	90	256	54	21	0	1	(1	0)	78	36	16	18	26	1	40	5	5	0	2	0	8	.211	.296	.305	.601
2010 Cin	NL	82	200	52	10	0	5	(0	5)	77	23	25	31	22	2	30	2	3	1	1	3	4	.260	.338	.385	.723
2011 Cin	NL	114	336	72	14	0	1	(0	0)	88	27	23	21	18	1	46	4	3	5	3	2	7	.214	.259	.262	.521
2012 Atl	NL	55	167	31	6	1	0	(0	0)	39	18	9	13	17	0	30	2	0	0	1	0	0	.186	.269	.234	.502
2013 Atl	NL	52	41	7	2	0	0	(0	0)	9	7	2	1	3	0	11	0	0	1	0	0	3	.171	.222	.220	.442
2015 Bal	AL	14	35	10	3	0	0	(0	0)	13	4	3	3	0	0	3	0	0	1	0	0	0	.286	.278	.371	.649
Postseason		2	1	0	0	0	0	(0	0)	0	0	0	0	0	0	0	0	1	0	0	0	0	.000	.000	.000	.000
7 ML YEARS		445	1115	241	58	2	7	(2	5)	324	120	84	92	93	4	178	15	11	8	7	5	25	.216	.284	.291	.574

Travis Jankowski

Bats: L **Throws:** R **Pos:** CF-23;RF-11;PH-2;PR-1   **Ht:** 6'2" **Wt:** 190 **Born:** 6/15/1991 **Age:** 25

Year Team	Lg	G	AB	H	2B	3B	HR	(Hm	Rd)	TB	R	RBI	RC	TBB	IBB	SO	HBP	SH	SF	SB	CS	GDP	Avg	OBP	Slg	OPS
2012 2 Tms	Low	61	246	69	10	4	1	(-	-)	90	33	27	29	13	0	45	1	1	4	17	7	4	.280	.314	.366	.680
2013 Lk Els	A+	122	493	141	19	6	1	(-	-)	175	89	38	76	54	0	96	2	3	4	71	14	3	.286	.356	.355	.711
2014 3 Tms	Low	17	65	15	2	0	0	(-	-)	17	13	5	7	10	1	9	1	1	0	7	1	3	.231	.342	.262	.604
2014 SnAnt	AA	29	100	24	4	1	0	(-	-)	30	14	10	10	8	0	14	1	1	2	10	2	2	.240	.297	.300	.597
2015 SnAnt	AA	73	282	89	11	5	1	(-	-)	113	50	13	49	36	1	40	1	2	0	23	8	5	.316	.395	.401	.796
2015 ElPaso	AAA	24	97	38	6	2	0	(-	-)	48	19	12	23	13	0	10	1	1	1	9	3	0	.392	.464	.495	.959
2015 SD	NL	34	90	19	2	2	2	(0	2)	31	9	12	10	4	0	24	0	2	0	2	1	1	.211	.245	.344	.589

Kenley Jansen

Pitches: R **Bats:** B **Pos:** RP-54   KEN-lee JANN-sen   **Ht:** 6'5" **Wt:** 265 **Born:** 9/30/1987 **Age:** 28

Year Team	Lg	G	GS	CG	GF	IP	BFP	H	R	ER	HR	SH	SF	HB	TBB	IBB	SO	WP	Bk	W	L	Pct	Sh	Sv-Op	Hld	ERC	ERA
2015 Rcuca*	A+	6	5	0	0	5.1	21	6	3	3	1	0	0	0	1	0	8	0	0	0	1	.000	0	0--	-	4.90	5.06
2010 LAD	NL	25	0	0	8	27.0	109	12	2	2	0	1	0	1	15	1	41	1	0	1	0	1.000	0	4-4	4	1.40	0.67
2011 LAD	NL	51	0	0	13	53.2	218	30	17	17	3	0	1	2	26	0	96	0	2	2	1	.667	0	5-6	9	1.96	2.85
2012 LAD	NL	65	0	0	40	65.0	252	33	18	17	6	0	1	3	22	1	99	3	0	5	3	.625	0	25-32	8	1.55	2.35
2013 LAD	NL	75	0	0	45	76.2	292	48	16	16	6	0	0	3	18	1	111	2	0	4	3	.571	0	28-32	16	1.65	1.88
2014 LAD	NL	68	0	0	57	65.1	268	55	20	20	5	1	2	0	19	2	101	2	0	2	3	.400	0	44-49	0	2.60	2.76
2015 LAD	NL	54	0	0	50	52.1	200	33	14	14	6	0	2	2	8	0	80	0	0	2	1	.667	0	36-38	1	1.58	2.41
Postseason		7	0	0	7	5.1	23	6	2	2	0	0	0	0	1	0	12	0	0	0	0	-	0	3-3	0	3.17	3.38
6 ML YEARS		338	0	0	213	340.0	1339	211	87	86	26	2	6	11	108	5	528	8	2	16	11	.593	0	142-161	38	1.81	2.28

Casey Janssen

Pitches: R **Bats:** R **Pos:** RP-48   JANN-sen   **Ht:** 6'4" **Wt:** 205 **Born:** 9/17/1981 **Age:** 34

Year Team	Lg	G	GS	CG	GF	IP	BFP	H	R	ER	HR	SH	SF	HB	TBB	IBB	SO	WP	Bk	W	L	Pct	Sh	Sv-Op	Hld	ERC	ERA
2006 Tor	AL	19	17	0	1	94.0	407	103	58	53	12	2	2	7	21	3	44	3	2	6	10	.375	0	0-0	0	4.32	5.07
2007 Tor	AL	70	0	0	21	72.2	297	67	22	19	4	0	3	3	20	2	39	4	0	2	3	.400	0	6-11	24	3.06	2.35
2009 Tor	AL	21	5	0	0	40.0	192	59	29	26	5	1	2	2	14	1	24	1	0	2	4	.333	0	1-1	2	7.04	5.85
2010 Tor	AL	56	0	0	16	68.2	298	74	29	28	8	0	1	4	21	1	63	3	0	5	2	.714	0	0-0	2	4.48	3.67
2011 Tor	AL	55	0	0	11	55.2	223	47	14	14	2	1	4	2	14	1	53	2	0	6	0	1.000	0	2-4	7	2.44	2.26
2012 Tor	AL	62	0	0	47	63.2	242	44	18	18	7	1	1	3	11	1	67	2	1	1	1	.500	0	22-25	2	1.93	2.54
2013 Tor	AL	56	0	0	44	52.2	210	39	17	15	3	0	2	2	13	1	50	0	0	4	1	.800	0	34-36	1	2.02	2.56
2014 Tor	AL	50	0	0	42	45.2	192	47	22	20	6	3	1	1	7	0	28	0	0	3	3	.500	0	25-30	0	3.48	3.94
2015 Was	NL	48	0	0	12	40.0	166	38	22	22	5	3	1	1	8	3	27	1	0	2	5	.286	0	0-3	13	3.14	4.95
9 ML YEARS		437	22	0	199	533.0	2227	518	231	215	52	11	13	25	129	13	395	16	3	31	29	.517	0	90-110	50	3.44	3.63

John Jaso

Bats: L Throws: R Pos: DH-48;PH-22;LF-7;RF-1   JAY-soe   Ht: 6'2" Wt: 205 Born: 9/19/1983 Age: 32

Year	Team	Lg	G	AB	H	2B	3B	HR	(Hm	Rd)	TB	R	RBI	RC	TBB	IBB	SO	HBP	SH	SF	SB	CS	GDP	Avg	OBP	Slg	OPS
2008	TB	AL	5	10	2	0	0	0	(0	0)	2	2	0	0	0	0	2	0	0	0	0	0	1	.200	.200	.200	.400
2010	TB	AL	109	339	89	18	3	5	(1	4)	128	57	44	57	59	1	39	2	1	3	4	0	8	.263	.372	.378	.750
2011	TB	AL	89	246	55	15	1	5	(3	2)	87	26	27	20	25	0	36	1	1	0	1	2	9	.224	.298	.354	.651
2012	Sea	AL	108	294	81	19	2	10	(6	4)	134	41	50	68	56	1	51	5	1	5	5	0	6	.276	.394	.456	.850
2013	Oak	AL	70	207	56	12	0	3	(0	3)	77	31	21	36	38	0	45	2	1	1	2	1	5	.271	.387	.372	.759
2014	Oak	AL	99	307	81	18	3	9	(5	4)	132	42	40	44	28	1	60	7	0	2	2	0	5	.264	.337	.430	.767
2015	TB	AL	70	185	53	17	0	5	(3	2)	85	23	22	32	28	1	39	1	0	2	1	2	5	.286	.380	.459	.839
Postseason			5	14	3	0	0	0	(0	0)	3	0	1	1	1	0	3	0	0	0	0	0	0	.214	.267	.214	.481
7 ML YEARS			550	1588	417	99	9	37	(18	19)	645	222	204	257	234	4	272	18	4	13	15	5	39	.263	.361	.406	.767

Jon Jay

Bats: L Throws: L Pos: CF-54;PH-18;LF-17;RF-7;PR-1   Ht: 5'11" Wt: 195 Born: 3/15/1985 Age: 31

Year	Team	Lg	G	AB	H	2B	3B	HR	(Hm	Rd)	TB	R	RBI	RC	TBB	IBB	SO	HBP	SH	SF	SB	CS	GDP	Avg	OBP	Slg	OPS
2010	StL	NL	105	287	86	19	2	4	(2	2)	121	47	27	40	24	0	50	3	8	1	2	4	5	.300	.359	.422	.780
2011	StL	NL	159	455	135	24	2	10	(5	5)	193	56	37	56	28	1	81	7	9	4	6	7	11	.297	.344	.424	.768
2012	StL	NL	117	443	135	22	4	4	(3	1)	177	70	40	65	34	3	71	15	9	1	19	7	9	.305	.373	.400	.773
2013	StL	NL	157	548	151	27	2	7	(2	5)	203	75	67	74	52	7	103	14	9	5	10	5	13	.276	.351	.370	.721
2014	StL	NL	140	413	125	16	3	3	(0	3)	156	52	46	57	28	3	78	20	3	4	6	3	17	.303	.372	.378	.750
2015	StL	NL	79	210	44	5	1	1	(0	1)	54	15	10	11	19	5	36	11	3	2	0	2	7	.210	.306	.257	.563
Postseason			57	189	44	4	1	0	(0	0)	50	24	15	20	19	1	29	4	4	2	5	2	4	.233	.313	.265	.578
6 ML YEARS			757	2356	676	113	14	29	(12	17)	904	325	227	303	185	19	419	70	41	17	43	28	62	.287	.354	.384	.738

Jeremy Jeffress

Pitches: R Bats: R Pos: RP-72   JEFF-ress   Ht: 6'0" Wt: 215 Born: 9/21/1987 Age: 28

Year	Team	Lg	G	GS	CG	GF	IP	BFP	H	R	ER	HR	SH	SF	HB	TBB	IBB	SO	WP	Bk	W	L	Pct	Sh	Sv-Op	Hld	ERC	ERA
2010	Mil	NL	10	0	0	5	10.0	42	8	4	3	0	0	1	0	6	1	8	1	0	1	0	1.000	0	0-0	0	2.96	2.70
2011	KC	AL	14	0	0	6	15.1	67	12	8	8	1	2	0	0	11	0	13	1	0	1	1	.500	0	1-2	0	3.87	4.70
2012	KC	AL	13	0	0	6	13.1	73	19	14	10	0	0	0	0	13	0	13	1	0	0	0	-	0	0-0	0	7.87	6.75
2013	Tor	AL	10	0	0	3	10.1	43	8	1	1	1	0	0	0	5	0	12	0	0	1	0	1.000	0	0-0	0	3.17	0.87
2014	2 Tms		32	0	0	12	32.0	135	35	10	10	1	3	1	2	10	2	29	1	0	1	1	.500	0	0-1	6	4.06	2.81
2015	Mil	NL	72	0	0	6	68.0	285	64	22	20	5	3	0	3	22	5	67	4	2	5	0	1.000	0	0-5	23	3.36	2.65
14	Tor	AL	3	0	0	3	3.1	21	8	4	4	0	0	1	2	3	0	4	0	0	0	0	-	0	0-0	0	19.06	10.80
14	Mil	NL	29	0	0	9	28.2	114	27	6	6	1	3	0	0	7	2	25	1	0	1	1	.500	0	0-1	6	2.75	1.88
6 ML YEARS			151	0	0	40	149.0	645	146	59	52	8	8	2	5	67	8	142	8	2	9	2	.818	0	1-8	29	3.90	3.14

Chad Jenkins

Pitches: R Bats: R Pos: RP-2   Ht: 6'4" Wt: 235 Born: 12/22/1987 Age: 28

Year	Team	Lg	G	GS	CG	GF	IP	BFP	H	R	ER	HR	SH	SF	HB	TBB	IBB	SO	WP	Bk	W	L	Pct	Sh	Sv-Op	Hld	ERC	ERA
2015	Buffalo*	AAA	41	11	0	10	93.2	404	98	37	31	5	0	5	2	26	1	60	3	0	8	6	.571	0	2--	-	3.54	2.98
2012	Tor	AL	13	3	0	6	32.0	136	32	16	16	5	1	0	1	11	1	16	0	0	1	3	.250	0	0-0	0	4.36	4.50
2013	Tor	AL	10	3	0	0	33.1	132	31	13	10	3	1	0	1	6	2	15	0	0	1	0	1.000	0	0-0	0	2.92	2.70
2014	Tor	AL	21	0	0	12	31.2	136	34	10	9	2	0	0	1	6	1	18	0	0	1	1	.500	0	0-0	2	3.40	2.56
2015	Tor	AL	2	0	0	1	3.2	17	3	2	2	1	0	0	0	3	0	2	0	0	0	0	-	0	0-0	0	5.91	4.91
4 ML YEARS			46	6	0	19	100.2	421	100	41	37	11	2	0	3	26	4	51	0	0	3	4	.429	0	0-0	2	3.62	3.31

Dan Jennings

Pitches: L Bats: L Pos: RP-53   Ht: 6'3" Wt: 210 Born: 4/17/1987 Age: 29

Year	Team	Lg	G	GS	CG	GF	IP	BFP	H	R	ER	HR	SH	SF	HB	TBB	IBB	SO	WP	Bk	W	L	Pct	Sh	Sv-Op	Hld	ERC	ERA
2012	Mia	NL	22	0	0	4	19.0	86	18	5	4	2	0	0	2	11	1	8	0	0	1	0	1.000	0	0-0	2	4.85	1.89
2013	Mia	NL	47	0	0	6	40.2	171	39	17	17	1	0	2	0	16	2	38	3	0	2	4	.333	0	0-2	1	3.27	3.76
2014	Mia	NL	47	0	0	12	40.1	182	45	11	6	3	2	3	0	17	1	38	2	0	0	2	.000	0	0-2	3	4.50	1.34
2015	CWS	AL	53	0	0	17	56.1	244	55	28	25	3	4	1	0	24	6	46	4	0	2	3	.400	0	0-0	4	3.52	3.99
4 ML YEARS			169	0	0	39	156.1	683	157	61	52	9	6	6	2	68	10	130	9	0	5	9	.357	0	0-4	10	3.86	2.99

Desmond Jennings

Bats: R Throws: R Pos: LF-21;CF-10;DH-1;PH-1   Ht: 6'2" Wt: 210 Born: 10/30/1986 Age: 29

Year	Team	Lg	G	AB	H	2B	3B	HR	(Hm	Rd)	TB	R	RBI	RC	TBB	IBB	SO	HBP	SH	SF	SB	CS	GDP	Avg	OBP	Slg	OPS
2010	TB	AL	17	21	4	1	1	0	(0	0)	7	5	2	2	2	0	4	1	0	0	2	2	0	.190	.292	.333	.625
2011	TB	AL	63	247	64	9	4	10	(3	7)	111	44	25	45	31	1	59	6	3	0	20	6	1	.259	.356	.449	.805
2012	TB	AL	132	505	124	19	7	13	(9	4)	196	85	47	62	46	1	120	5	6	1	31	2	7	.246	.314	.388	.702
2013	TB	AL	139	527	133	31	6	14	(6	8)	218	82	54	74	64	0	115	3	3	5	20	8	6	.252	.334	.414	.748
2014	TB	AL	123	479	117	30	2	10	(2	8)	181	64	36	55	47	0	108	6	9	1	15	6	10	.244	.319	.378	.697
2015	TB	AL	28	97	26	2	1	1	(0	1)	33	9	7	10	8	0	17	1	0	2	5	3	2	.268	.324	.340	.664
Postseason			11	33	10	2	0	2	(2	0)	18	5	4	6	5	0	5	0	0	0	1	0	0	.303	.395	.545	.940
6 ML YEARS			502	1876	468	92	21	48	(20	28)	746	289	171	248	198	2	423	22	21	9	93	27	26	.249	.327	.398	.724

Kevin Jepsen

Pitches: R Bats: R Pos: RP-75   Ht: 6'3" Wt: 235 Born: 7/26/1984 Age: 31

Year	Team	Lg	G	GS	CG	GF	IP	BFP	H	R	ER	HR	SH	SF	HB	TBB	IBB	SO	WP	Bk	W	L	Pct	Sh	Sv-Op	Hld	ERC	ERA
2008	LAA	AL	9	0	0	0	8.1	36	8	5	4	0	0	0	0	4	0	7	1	0	0	1	.000	0	0-0	3	3.46	4.32
2009	LAA	AL	54	0	0	13	54.2	237	63	33	30	2	0	2	0	19	2	48	6	0	6	4	.600	0	1-2	17	4.27	4.94
2010	LAA	AL	68	0	0	4	59.0	253	54	26	26	2	4	2	2	29	5	61	8	0	2	4	.333	0	0-4	27	3.53	3.97
2011	LAA	AL	16	0	0	5	13.0	68	21	11	11	2	1	1	1	9	4	6	5	0	1	2	.333	0	0-1	2	9.45	7.62
2012	LAA	AL	49	0	0	11	44.2	178	39	17	15	3	3	1	2	12	1	38	1	0	3	2	.600	0	2-4	18	2.93	3.02
2013	LAA	AL	45	0	0	7	36.0	164	41	21	18	3	3	1	1	14	4	36	2	0	1	3	.250	0	0-2	8	4.50	4.50
2014	LAA	AL	74	0	0	10	65.0	260	45	19	19	4	0	1	2	23	2	75	5	0	2	0	.000	0	2-4	22	2.16	2.63
2015	2 Tms		75	0	0	23	69.2	285	52	20	18	5	1	5	0	27	1	59	5	0	3	6	.333	0	15-20	24	2.48	2.33
15	TB	AL	46	0	0	6	41.2	176	34	15	13	4	1	5	0	20	1	34	2	0	2	5	.286	0	5-9	22	3.31	2.81
15	Min	AL	29	0	0	17	28.0	109	18	5	5	1	0	0	0	7	0	25	3	0	1	1	.500	0	10-11	2	1.46	1.61
	Postseason		8	0	0	0	7.0	38	12	6	5	2	0	0	0	6	1	4	0	0	1	1	.500	0	0-0	1	12.28	6.43
	8 ML YEARS		390	0	0	73	350.1	1481	323	152	141	21	12	13	8	137	19	330	33	0	16	24	.400	0	20-37	121	3.36	3.62

Cesar Jimenez

Pitches: L Bats: L Pos: RP-19   hee-MEN-ehs   Ht: 6'0" Wt: 215 Born: 11/12/1984 Age: 31

Year	Team	Lg	G	GS	CG	GF	IP	BFP	H	R	ER	HR	SH	SF	HB	TBB	IBB	SO	WP	Bk	W	L	Pct	Sh	Sv-Op	Hld	ERC	ERA
2015	LV*	AAA	41	1	0	14	57.1	243	61	23	23	4	0	1	0	18	1	40	1	0	3	5	.375	0	4- -	-	3.90	3.61
2006	Sea	AL	4	1	0	1	7.1	38	13	12	12	4	0	0	0	4	0	3	2	0	0	0	-	0	0-0	0	14.01	14.73
2008	Sea	AL	31	0	0	8	34.1	141	32	13	13	2	2	1	1	13	0	26	2	0	0	2	.000	0	0-4	4	3.59	3.41
2011	Sea	AL	8	0	0	1	6.2	30	6	4	4	0	0	0	0	3	0	7	2	0	1	0	1.000	0	0-0	0	2.83	5.40
2013	Phi	NL	19	0	0	5	17.0	76	14	7	7	1	1	2	1	10	0	11	2	1	1	1	.500	0	0-0	3	3.66	3.71
2014	Phi	NL	16	0	0	8	16.0	65	14	3	3	1	0	1	0	7	0	8	0	0	0	0	-	0	0-0	3	3.44	1.69
2015	2 Tms	NL	19	0	0	4	23.0	91	17	8	8	2	0	0	0	8	0	25	0	0	0	0	-	0	0-0	4	2.49	3.13
15	Phi	NL	3	0	0	2	3.1	10	1	0	0	0	0	0	0	0	0	4	0	0	0	0	-	0	0-0	0	0.23	0.00
15	Mil	NL	16	0	0	2	19.2	81	16	8	8	2	0	0	0	8	0	21	0	0	0	0	-	0	0-0	4	3.13	3.66
	6 ML YEARS		97	3	0	27	104.1	441	96	47	47	10	3	4	2	45	0	80	8	1	2	3	.400	0	0-4	8	3.86	4.05

Luis Jimenez

Bats: R Throws: R Pos: PH-8;3B-7;PR-2;2B-1;DH-1   Ht: 6'1" Wt: 205 Born: 1/18/1988 Age: 28

Year	Team	Lg	G	AB	H	2B	3B	HR	(Hm	Rd)	TB	R	RBI	RC	TBB	IBB	SO	HBP	SH	SF	SB	CS	GDP	Avg	OBP	Slg	OPS
2015	Pwtckt*	AAA	14	57	8	0	1	2	(-	-)	16	4	6	1	0	0	9	0	0	0	0	0	1	.140	.140	.281	.421
2013	LAA	AL	34	104	27	6	0	0	(0	0)	33	15	5	9	2	0	28	3	0	1	0	2	2	.260	.291	.317	.608
2014	LAA	AL	18	37	6	2	0	0	(0	0)	8	3	2	2	0	0	13	2	2	0	0	0	1	.162	.205	.216	.421
2015	2 Tms		16	16	1	0	0	0	(0	0)	1	1	0	0	1	0	6	0	0	0	0	0	0	.063	.118	.063	.180
15	Mil	NL	15	15	1	0	0	0	(0	0)	1	1	0	0	1	0	6	0	0	0	0	0	0	.067	.125	.067	.192
15	Bos	AL	1	1	0	0	0	0	(0	0)	0	0	0	0	0	0	0	0	0	0	0	0	0	.000	.000	.000	.000
	3 ML YEARS		68	157	34	8	0	0	(0	0)	42	19	7	11	3	0	47	5	2	1	0	2	3	.217	.253	.268	.521

Ubaldo Jimenez

Pitches: R Bats: R Pos: SP-32   ooh-BALL-doh   Ht: 6'5" Wt: 210 Born: 1/22/1984 Age: 32

Year	Team	Lg	G	GS	CG	GF	IP	BFP	H	R	ER	HR	SH	SF	HB	TBB	IBB	SO	WP	Bk	W	L	Pct	Sh	Sv-Op	Hld	ERC	ERA
2006	Col	NL	2	1	0	0	7.2	30	5	4	3	1	0	0	0	3	0	3	0	0	0	0	-	0	0-0	0	2.48	3.52
2007	Col	NL	15	15	0	0	82.0	354	70	46	39	10	3	1	6	37	4	68	3	0	4	4	.500	0	0-0	0	3.80	4.28
2008	Col	NL	34	34	1	0	198.2	868	182	97	88	11	7	4	10	103	4	172	16	0	12	12	.500	0	0-0	0	3.92	3.99
2009	Col	NL	33	33	1	0	218.0	914	183	87	84	13	15	6	10	85	6	198	8	3	15	12	.556	0	0-0	0	3.03	3.47
2010	Col	NL	33	33	4	0	221.2	894	164	73	71	10	7	1	9	92	7	214	16	1	19	8	.704	2	0-0	0	2.57	2.88
2011	2 Tms		32	32	2	0	188.1	822	186	111	98	17	2	2	9	78	5	180	8	0	10	13	.435	1	0-0	0	4.13	4.68
2012	Cle	AL	31	31	0	0	176.2	805	190	116	106	25	2	3	8	95	3	143	16	1	9	17	.346	0	0-0	0	5.55	5.40
2013	Cle	AL	32	32	0	0	182.2	777	163	75	67	16	1	11	3	80	0	194	8	0	13	9	.591	0	0-0	0	3.61	3.30
2014	Bal	AL	25	22	0	0	125.1	553	113	68	67	14	3	4	4	77	0	116	4	0	6	9	.400	0	0-0	1	4.62	4.81
2015	Bal	AL	32	32	0	0	184.0	791	182	89	84	20	1	4	11	68	1	168	6	0	12	10	.545	0	0-0	0	4.21	4.11
11	Col	NL	21	21	2	0	123.0	532	118	68	61	10	2	2	7	51	5	118	6	0	6	9	.400	1	0-0	0	3.94	4.46
11	Cle	AL	11	11	0	0	65.1	290	68	43	37	7	0	0	2	27	0	62	2	0	4	4	.500	0	0-0	0	4.48	5.10
	Postseason		5	5	0	0	28.0	123	26	11	11	3	0	1	1	16	2	24	1	0	0	2	.000	0	0-0	0	4.47	3.54
	10 ML YEARS		269	265	8	0	1585.0	6808	1438	766	707	137	41	33	70	718	30	1456	85	5	100	94	.515	3	0-0	1	3.83	4.01

Brian Johnson

Pitches: L Bats: L Pos: SP-1   Ht: 6'4" Wt: 235 Born: 12/7/1990 Age: 25

Year	Team	Lg	G	GS	CG	GF	IP	BFP	H	R	ER	HR	SH	SF	HB	TBB	IBB	SO	WP	Bk	W	L	Pct	Sh	Sv-Op	Hld	ERC	ERA
2013	3 Tms	Low	19	19	0	0	85.0	350	60	31	24	4	2	0	4	35	0	84	8	1	2	6	.250	0	0- -	-	2.39	2.54
2014	Salem	A+	5	5	0	0	25.2	109	23	13	11	0	1	0	1	7	0	33	3	1	3	1	.750	0	0- -	-	2.30	3.86
2014	Portlnd	AA	20	20	2	0	118.0	452	78	29	23	6	4	4	0	32	0	99	5	0	10	2	.833	0	0- -	-	1.67	1.75
2015	Pwtckt	AAA	18	18	1	0	96.0	390	74	34	27	6	1	2	4	32	0	90	5	0	9	6	.600	1	0- -	-	2.55	2.53
2015	Bos	AL	1	1	0	0	4.1	19	3	4	4	0	0	1	0	4	0	3	0	0	0	1	.000	0	0-0	0	3.72	8.31

Chris Johnson

Bats: R **Throws:** R **Pos:** 1B-30;3B-27;PH-20;DH-14   **Ht:** 6'3" **Wt:** 225 **Born:** 10/1/1984 **Age:** 31

Year	Team	Lg	G	AB	H	2B	3B	HR	(Hm	Rd)	TB	R	RBI	RC	TBB	IBB	SO	HBP	SH	SF	SB	CS	GDP	Avg	OBP	Slg	OPS
2009	Hou	NL	11	22	2	0	0	0	(0	0)	2	1	1	0	1	0	6	0	0	0	0	0	0	.091	.130	.091	.221
2010	Hou	NL	94	341	105	22	2	11	(6	5)	164	40	52	55	15	2	91	2	0	4	3	0	8	.308	.337	.481	.818
2011	Hou	NL	107	378	95	21	3	7	(2	5)	143	32	42	42	16	3	97	7	0	4	2	2	2	.251	.291	.378	.670
2012	2 Tms	NL	136	488	137	28	5	15	(8	7)	220	48	76	75	31	2	132	4	1	4	5	1	18	.281	.326	.451	.777
2013	Atl	NL	142	514	165	34	0	12	(4	8)	235	54	68	77	29	5	116	2	0	2	0	0	20	.321	.358	.457	.816
2014	Atl	NL	153	582	153	27	0	10	(5	5)	210	43	58	59	23	2	159	2	2	2	6	0	23	.263	.292	.361	.653
2015	2 Tms	NL	83	243	62	11	0	3	(3	0)	82	18	18	22	10	0	74	1	0	1	2	1	5	.255	.286	.337	.624
12	Hou	NL	92	341	95	21	3	8	(8	0)	146	36	41	47	23	1	92	3	0	1	4	1	12	.279	.329	.428	.757
12	Ari	NL	44	147	42	7	2	7	(0	7)	74	12	35	28	8	1	40	1	1	3	1	0	6	.286	.321	.503	.824
15	Atl	NL	56	153	36	7	0	2	(2	0)	49	12	11	11	7	0	49	1	0	1	2	1	3	.235	.272	.320	.592
15	Cle	AL	27	90	26	4	0	1	(1	0)	33	6	7	11	3	0	25	0	0	0	0	0	2	.289	.312	.367	.678
	Postseason		4	16	7	0	0	0	(0	0)	7	1	5	4	0	0	5	0	0	0	0	0	0	.438	.438	.438	.875
	7 ML YEARS		726	2568	719	143	10	58	(28	30)	1056	236	315	330	125	14	675	18	3	17	18	4	76	.280	.316	.411	.727

Dan Johnson

Bats: L **Throws:** R **Pos:** 1B-6;PH-6;PR-1   **Ht:** 6'2" **Wt:** 210 **Born:** 8/10/1979 **Age:** 36

Year	Team	Lg	G	AB	H	2B	3B	HR	(Hm	Rd)	TB	R	RBI	RC	TBB	IBB	SO	HBP	SH	SF	SB	CS	GDP	Avg	OBP	Slg	OPS
2015	Memp*	AAA	94	350	91	19	1	15	(-	-)	157	51	62	57	45	1	64	3	0	5	0	1	3	.260	.345	.449	.793
2005	Oak	AL	109	375	103	21	0	15	(2	13)	169	54	58	56	50	1	52	1	0	8	0	1	11	.275	.355	.451	.806
2006	Oak	AL	91	286	67	13	1	9	(4	5)	109	30	37	33	40	2	45	0	0	5	0	0	6	.234	.323	.381	.704
2007	Oak	AL	117	416	98	20	1	18	(9	9)	174	53	62	58	72	4	77	3	0	4	0	0	12	.236	.349	.418	.768
2008	2 Tms	AL	11	26	5	0	0	2	(1	1)	11	3	4	3	3	0	7	0	0	0	0	0	0	.192	.276	.423	.699
2010	TB	AL	40	111	22	3	0	7	(4	3)	46	15	23	20	25	0	27	1	0	3	1	0	1	.198	.343	.414	.757
2011	TB	AL	31	84	10	1	0	2	(1	1)	17	7	4	0	6	0	18	1	0	0	0	0	3	.119	.187	.202	.389
2012	CWS	AL	14	22	8	1	0	3	(0	3)	18	8	6	9	9	1	3	0	0	0	0	0	0	.364	.548	.818	1.367
2013	Bal	AL	3	5	0	0	0	0	(0	0)	0	0	0	0	0	0	1	0	0	0	0	0	0	.000	.000	.000	.000
2014	Tor	AL	15	38	8	2	0	1	(0	1)	13	8	7	7	7	0	10	1	0	2	0	0	1	.211	.333	.342	.675
2015	StL	NL	12	19	3	0	0	0	(0	0)	3	1	2	2	2	0	4	0	0	0	0	0	0	.158	.238	.158	.396
08	Oak	AL	1	1	0	0	0	0	(0	0)	0	0	0	0	0	0	0	0	0	0	0	0	0	.000	.000	.000	.000
08	TB	AL	10	25	5	0	0	2	(1	1)	11	3	4	3	3	0	7	0	0	0	0	0	0	.200	.286	.440	.726
	Postseason		5	9	2	1	0	0	(0	0)	3	1	0	0	3	0	4	0	0	0	0	0	1	.222	.417	.333	.750
	10 ML YEARS		443	1382	324	61	2	57	(21	36)	560	179	203	188	214	8	244	7	0	22	1	1	35	.234	.335	.405	.741

Erik Johnson

Pitches: R **Bats:** R **Pos:** SP-6   **Ht:** 6'3" **Wt:** 230 **Born:** 12/30/1989 **Age:** 26

			HOW MUCH HE PITCHED						WHAT HE GAVE UP										THE RESULTS						
Year	Team	Lg	G	GS	CG	GF	IP	BFP	H	R	ER	HR	SH	SF	HB	TBB	IBB	SO	WP	Bk	W	L	Pct	Sh	Sv-Op	Hld	ERC	ERA
2015	Charltt*	AAA	23	22	0	0	132.2	535	108	40	35	5	6	4	2	41	0	136	8	0	11	8	.579	0	0- -	-	2.44	2.37
2013	CWS	AL	5	5	0	0	27.2	128	32	16	10	5	0	2	1	11	0	18	2	0	3	2	.600	0	0-0	0	5.55	3.25
2014	CWS	AL	5	5	0	0	23.2	109	27	18	17	1	0	1	2	15	1	18	3	0	1	1	.500	0	0-0	0	5.82	6.46
2015	CWS	AL	6	6	0	0	35.0	151	32	14	13	8	1	3	1	17	0	30	3	0	3	1	.750	0	0-0	0	5.01	3.34
	3 ML YEARS		16	16	0	0	86.1	388	91	48	40	14	1	6	4	43	1	66	8	0	7	4	.636	0	0-0	0	5.43	4.17

Jim Johnson

Pitches: R **Bats:** R **Pos:** RP-72   **Ht:** 6'6" **Wt:** 240 **Born:** 6/27/1983 **Age:** 33

			HOW MUCH HE PITCHED						WHAT HE GAVE UP										THE RESULTS						
Year	Team	Lg	G	GS	CG	GF	IP	BFP	H	R	ER	HR	SH	SF	HB	TBB	IBB	SO	WP	Bk	W	L	Pct	Sh	Sv-Op	Hld	ERC	ERA
2006	Bal	AL	1	1	0	0	3.0	21	9	8	8	1	0	1	1	3	0	0	0	0	0	1	.000	0	0-0	0	26.81	24.00
2007	Bal	AL	1	0	0	1	2.0	11	3	2	2	0	1	0	0	2	0	1	0	0	0	0	-	0	0-0	0	8.58	9.00
2008	Bal	AL	54	0	0	18	68.2	281	54	18	17	0	2	1	3	28	3	38	1	1	2	4	.333	0	1-1	19	2.45	2.23
2009	Bal	AL	64	0	0	29	70.0	300	73	32	32	8	2	2	3	23	3	49	2	1	4	6	.400	0	10-16	14	4.28	4.11
2010	Bal	AL	26	0	0	6	26.1	117	32	11	10	2	3	0	1	5	1	22	4	0	1	1	.500	0	1-6	11	4.26	3.42
2011	Bal	AL	69	0	0	20	91.0	366	80	30	27	5	4	2	2	21	3	58	2	1	6	5	.545	0	9-14	18	2.58	2.67
2012	Bal	AL	71	0	0	63	68.2	269	55	21	19	3	1	0	3	15	1	41	1	0	2	1	.667	0	51-54	0	2.22	2.49
2013	Bal	AL	74	0	0	63	70.1	291	72	26	23	5	2	0	7	18	4	56	2	0	3	8	.273	0	50-59	0	3.89	2.94
2014	2 Tms	AL	54	0	0	21	53.1	263	69	46	42	5	3	2	6	35	6	42	4	0	5	7	.714	0	2-3	2	7.13	7.09
2015	2 Tms	NL	72	0	0	15	66.2	291	77	36	33	5	3	3	5	20	2	50	3	0	2	6	.250	0	10-17	25	4.70	4.46
14	Oak	AL	38	0	0	18	40.1	200	60	33	32	5	2	2	3	23	3	28	4	0	4	2	.667	0	2-3	2	8.28	7.14
14	Det	AL	16	0	0	3	13.0	63	9	13	10	0	1	0	3	12	3	14	0	0	1	0	1.000	0	0-0	0	3.86	6.92
15	Atl	NL	49	0	0	13	48.0	196	45	14	12	2	3	2	1	14	2	33	2	0	2	3	.400	0	9-13	20	3.02	2.25
15	LAD	NL	23	0	0	2	18.2	95	32	22	21	3	0	1	4	6	0	17	1	0	0	3	.000	0	1-4	5	9.81	10.13
	Postseason		5	0	0	3	5.1	25	8	6	5	2	0	0	0	1	0	4	0	0	0	1	.000	0	2-3	0	8.18	8.44
	10 ML YEARS		486	1	0	236	520.0	2210	524	230	213	34	20	12	31	170	23	357	19	3	25	34	.424	0	134-170	89	3.80	3.69

Kelly Johnson

Bats: L **Throws:** R **Pos:** LF-29;2B-28;PH-26;1B-25;3B-12;RF-8;SS-1;DH-1   **Ht:** 6'1" **Wt:** 195 **Born:** 2/22/1982 **Age:** 34

Year	Team	Lg	G	AB	H	2B	3B	HR	(Hm	Rd)	TB	R	RBI	RC	TBB	IBB	SO	HBP	SH	SF	SB	CS	GDP	Avg	OBP	Slg	OPS
2005	Atl	NL	87	290	70	12	3	9	(2	7)	115	46	40	41	40	1	75	1	2	1	2	1	11	.241	.334	.397	.731
2007	Atl	NL	147	521	144	26	10	16	(5	11)	238	91	68	87	79	3	117	4	2	2	9	5	8	.276	.375	.457	.831
2008	Atl	NL	150	547	157	39	6	12	(5	7)	244	86	69	87	52	3	113	2	9	4	11	6	7	.287	.349	.446	.795
2009	Atl	NL	106	303	68	20	3	8	(4	4)	118	47	29	31	32	1	54	3	6	2	7	2	4	.224	.303	.389	.692
2010	Ari	NL	154	585	166	36	5	26	(16	10)	290	93	71	92	79	1	148	2	3	2	13	7	12	.284	.370	.496	.865

Year Team	Lg	G	AB	H	2B	3B	HR	(Hm Rd)	TB	R	RBI	RC	TBB	IBB	SO	HBP	SH	SF	SB	CS	GDP	Avg	OBP	Slg	OPS
2011 2 Tms		147	545	121	27	7	21	(10 11)	225	75	58	70	60	2	163	4	4	0	16	6	3	.222	.304	.413	.717
2012 Tor	AL	142	507	114	19	2	16	(10 6)	185	61	55	63	62	4	159	5	2	4	14	2	8	.225	.313	.365	.678
2013 TB	AL	118	366	86	12	2	16	(6 10)	150	41	52	49	35	1	99	3	0	3	7	4	4	.235	.305	.410	.715
2014 3 Tms	AL	106	265	57	14	2	7	(5 2)	96	29	27	30	29	0	71	2	0	1	2	2	3	.215	.296	.362	.659
2015 2 Tms	AL	111	310	82	11	0	14	(7 7)	135	38	47	41	23	2	81	0	0	1	2	1	8	.265	.314	.435	.750
11 Ari	NL	114	430	90	23	5	18	(10 8)	177	59	49	53	44	2	132	3	4	0	13	3	3	.209	.287	.412	.699
11 Tor	AL	33	115	31	4	2	3	(0 3)	48	16	9	17	16	0	31	1	0	0	3	3	0	.270	.364	.417	.781
14 NYY	AL	77	201	44	9	2	6	(5 1)	75	21	22	25	23	0	50	2	0	1	2	1	2	.219	.304	.373	.677
14 Bos	AL	10	25	4	1	0	0	(0 0)	5	1	1	0	0	0	10	0	0	0	0	0	1	.160	.160	.200	.360
14 Bal	AL	19	39	9	4	0	1	(0 1)	16	7	4	5	6	0	11	0	0	0	0	1	0	.231	.333	.410	.744
15 Atl	NL	62	182	50	5	0	9	(5 4)	82	20	34	27	13	1	43	0	0	1	1	1	4	.275	.321	.451	.772
15 NYM	NL	49	128	32	6	0	5	(2 3)	53	18	13	14	10	1	38	0	0	0	1	0	4	.250	.304	.414	.718
Postseason		8	7	1	0	1	0	(0 0)	3	0	0	1	1	0	2	0	0	0	0	0	0	.143	.250	.429	.679
10 ML YEARS		1268	4239	1065	216	40	145	(70 75)	1796	607	516	591	491	17	1080	26	28	20	83	36	64	.251	.331	.424	.755

Micah Johnson

Bats: L Throws: R Pos: 2B-33;PH-2;PR-2 **Ht:** 6'0" **Wt:** 210 **Born:** 12/18/1990 **Age:** 25

Year Team	Lg	G	AB	H	2B	3B	HR	(Hm Rd)	TB	R	RBI	RC	TBB	IBB	SO	HBP	SH	SF	SB	CS	GDP	Avg	OBP	Slg	OPS
2012 Gr Falls	R+	69	271	74	10	5	4	(- -)	106	49	25	44	43	1	74	1	3	0	19	6	9	.273	.375	.391	.766
2013 2 Tms	Low	126	515	162	24	15	7	(- -)	237	104	57	96	50	2	94	4	8	2	83	26	3	.315	.378	.460	.838
2014 Brham	AA	37	146	48	9	1	3	(- -)	68	18	16	28	21	0	27	1	1	1	10	7	1	.329	.414	.466	.880
2014 Charllt	AAA	65	273	75	10	5	2	(- -)	101	30	28	33	16	0	42	1	9	3	12	6	4	.275	.314	.370	.684
2015 Charllt	AAA	78	311	98	17	3	8	(- -)	145	54	36	58	32	0	63	0	4	4	28	7	4	.315	.375	.466	.841
2015 CWS	AL	36	100	23	4	0	0	(0 0)	27	10	4	8	9	0	30	2	2	0	3	2	0	.230	.306	.270	.576

Reed Johnson

Bats: R Throws: R Pos: PH-13;LF-3;RF-1 **Ht:** 5'10" **Wt:** 180 **Born:** 12/8/1976 **Age:** 39

Year Team	Lg	G	AB	H	2B	3B	HR	(Hm Rd)	TB	R	RBI	RC	TBB	IBB	SO	HBP	SH	SF	SB	CS	GDP	Avg	OBP	Slg	OPS
2003 Tor	AL	114	412	121	21	2	10	(6 4)	176	79	52	64	20	1	67	20	1	4	5	3	10	.294	.353	.427	.780
2004 Tor	AL	141	537	145	25	2	10	(8 2)	204	68	61	65	28	2	98	12	3	2	6	3	17	.270	.320	.380	.699
2005 Tor	AL	142	398	107	21	6	8	(4 4)	164	55	58	57	22	1	82	16	2	1	5	6	8	.269	.332	.412	.744
2006 Tor	AL	134	461	147	34	2	12	(4 8)	221	86	49	76	33	4	81	21	1	1	8	2	9	.319	.390	.479	.869
2007 Tor	AL	79	275	65	13	2	2	(1 1)	88	31	14	24	16	0	56	11	5	0	4	2	7	.236	.305	.320	.625
2008 ChC	NL	109	333	101	21	0	6	(3 3)	140	52	50	57	19	1	68	12	5	5	5	6	3	.303	.358	.420	.778
2009 ChC	NL	65	165	42	10	2	4	(3 1)	68	23	22	19	13	0	27	6	1	1	2	1	5	.255	.330	.412	.742
2010 LAD	NL	102	202	53	11	2	2	(1 1)	74	24	15	18	5	0	50	4	2	2	2	2	3	.262	.291	.366	.657
2011 ChC	NL	111	246	76	22	1	5	(4 1)	115	33	28	35	5	1	63	11	2	2	2	1	4	.309	.348	.467	.816
2012 2 Tms	NL	119	269	78	14	3	3	(0 3)	107	30	20	37	13	1	61	6	0	0	2	2	4	.290	.337	.398	.735
2013 Atl	NL	74	123	30	7	1	1	(1 0)	42	13	11	15	6	0	32	6	1	0	0	0	3	.244	.331	.341	.653
2014 Mia	NL	113	187	44	15	0	2	(0 2)	65	24	25	19	1	0	37	8	2	3	0	1	4	.235	.266	.348	.614
2015 Was	NL	17	22	5	1	0	0	(0 0)	6	0	3	2	0	0	6	1	0	1	0	0	1	.227	.250	.273	.523
12 ChC	NL	76	169	51	9	3	3	(0 3)	75	23	16	26	10	1	43	4	0	0	2	1	3	.302	.355	.444	.799
12 Atl	NL	43	100	27	5	0	0	(0 0)	32	7	4	11	3	0	18	2	0	0	0	1	1	.270	.305	.320	.625
Postseason		3	2	1	0	0	0	(0 0)	1	1	0	1	1	1	0	0	0	0	0	0	0	.500	.667	.500	1.167
13 ML YEARS		1320	3630	1014	215	23	65	(35 30)	1470	518	408	488	181	11	728	134	25	22	41	29	78	.279	.335	.405	.740

Steve Johnson

Pitches: R Bats: R Pos: RP-6 **Ht:** 6'1" **Wt:** 220 **Born:** 8/31/1987 **Age:** 28

Year Team	Lg	G	GS	CG	GF	IP	BFP	H	R	ER	HR	SH	SF	HB	TBB	IBB	SO	WP	Bk	W	L	Pct	Sh	Sv-Op	Hld	ERC	ERA
2015 Norfolk*	AAA	32	3	0	6	54.2	213	43	14	14	2	1	1	1	16	1	67	2	0	4	1	.800	0	1- -	-	2.31	2.30
2012 Bal	AL	12	4	0	3	38.1	151	23	9	9	4	1	0	0	18	1	46	1	0	4	0	1.000	0	0-0	0	2.31	2.11
2013 Bal	AL	9	1	0	2	15.2	73	14	13	13	2	0	0	0	13	1	20	1	0	1	1	.500	0	0-0	1	5.23	7.47
2015 Bal	AL	6	0	0	2	5.1	29	8	6	6	2	0	0	0	5	0	3	1	0	0	0	-	0	0-0	0	12.01	10.13
3 ML YEARS		27	5	0	7	59.1	253	45	28	28	8	1	0	0	36	2	69	3	0	5	1	.833	0	0-0	1	3.75	4.25

Adam Jones

Bats: R Throws: R Pos: CF-134;DH-3 **Ht:** 6'2" **Wt:** 215 **Born:** 8/1/1985 **Age:** 30

Year Team	Lg	G	AB	H	2B	3B	HR	(Hm Rd)	TB	R	RBI	RC	TBB	IBB	SO	HBP	SH	SF	SB	CS	GDP	Avg	OBP	Slg	OPS
2006 Sea	AL	32	74	16	4	0	1	(0 1)	23	6	8	4	2	0	22	0	0	0	3	1	3	.216	.237	.311	.548
2007 Sea	AL	41	65	16	2	1	2	(1 1)	26	16	4	5	4	0	21	1	1	0	2	1	0	.246	.300	.400	.700
2008 Bal	AL	132	477	129	21	7	9	(4 5)	191	61	57	56	23	0	108	7	2	5	10	3	12	.270	.311	.400	.711
2009 Bal	AL	119	473	131	22	3	19	(11 8)	216	83	70	71	36	3	93	7	2	3	10	4	13	.277	.335	.457	.792
2010 Bal	AL	149	581	165	25	5	19	(9 10)	257	76	69	72	23	1	119	13	2	2	7	7	17	.284	.325	.442	.767
2011 Bal	AL	151	567	159	26	2	25	(19 6)	264	68	83	77	29	2	113	9	1	12	12	4	16	.280	.319	.466	.785
2012 Bal	AL	162	648	186	39	3	32	(17 15)	327	103	82	101	34	0	126	13	0	2	16	7	15	.287	.334	.505	.839
2013 Bal	AL	160	653	186	35	1	33	(17 16)	322	100	108	101	25	4	136	8	0	3	14	3	15	.285	.318	.493	.811
2014 Bal	AL	159	644	181	30	2	29	(14 15)	302	88	96	92	19	1	133	12	0	7	7	1	11	.281	.311	.469	.780
2015 Bal	AL	137	546	147	25	3	27	(12 15)	259	74	82	73	24	3	102	8	0	3	3	1	21	.269	.308	.474	.782
Postseason		13	53	8	0	0	1	(1 0)	11	6	4	3	3	0	15	1	0	1	1	0	1	.151	.207	.208	.414
10 ML YEARS		1242	4728	1316	229	27	196	(107 89)	2187	675	659	652	219	14	973	78	6	37	84	32	123	.278	.319	.463	.781

Garrett Jones

Bats: L Throws: L Pos: RF-24;1B-21;PH-13;LF-4;DH-4;PR-2   Ht: 6'5" Wt: 235 Born: 6/21/1981 Age: 35

Year	Team	Lg	G	AB	H	2B	3B	HR	(Hm	Rd)	TB	R	RBI	RC	TBB	IBB	SO	HBP	SH	SF	SB	CS	GDP	Avg	OBP	Slg	OPS
2007	Min	AL	31	77	16	2	1	2	(1	1)	26	7	5	3	6	0	20	0	0	1	1	1	2	.208	.262	.338	.600
2009	Pit	NL	82	314	92	21	1	21	(13	8)	178	45	44	47	40	8	76	1	0	3	10	2	6	.293	.372	.567	.938
2010	Pit	NL	158	592	146	34	1	21	(11	10)	245	64	86	69	53	2	123	1	0	8	7	3	18	.247	.306	.414	.720
2011	Pit	NL	148	423	103	30	1	16	(8	8)	183	51	58	57	48	2	104	2	0	4	6	3	7	.243	.321	.433	.753
2012	Pit	NL	145	475	130	28	3	27	(13	14)	245	68	86	84	33	2	103	0	0	7	2	0	3	.274	.317	.516	.832
2013	Pit	NL	144	403	94	26	2	15	(6	9)	169	41	51	39	31	0	101	2	0	4	2	0	10	.233	.289	.419	.708
2014	Mia	NL	146	496	122	33	2	15	(7	8)	204	59	53	52	46	4	116	1	0	4	0	1	10	.246	.309	.411	.720
2015	NYY	AL	57	144	31	4	1	5	(2	3)	52	12	17	13	8	0	37	0	0	0	0	0	1	.215	.257	.361	.618
	Postseason		2	2	0	0	0	0	(0	0)	0	0	0	0	0	0	1	0	0	0	0	0	0	.000	.000	.000	.000
	8 ML YEARS		911	2924	734	178	12	122	(61	61)	1302	347	400	364	265	18	680	7	0	31	28	10	57	.251	.312	.445	.757

James Jones

Bats: L Throws: L Pos: CF-20;PR-7;RF-6;PH-3;LF-2;DH-1   Ht: 6'4" Wt: 200 Born: 9/24/1988 Age: 27

Year	Team	Lg	G	AB	H	2B	3B	HR	(Hm	Rd)	TB	R	RBI	RC	TBB	IBB	SO	HBP	SH	SF	SB	CS	GDP	Avg	OBP	Slg	OPS
2011	Hi Dsrt	A+	31	77	16	4	5	1	(-	-)	112	42	29	44	42	4	92	4	1	16	3	5	.247	.347	.378	.725
2012	Hi Dsrt	A+	126	493	151	28	12	14	(-	-)	245	109	76	92	54	1	124	5	3	4	26	17	6	.306	.378	.497	.875
2013	Jacksn	AA	101	363	100	14	10	6	(-	-)	152	44	45	56	40	2	72	0	2	0	28	9	7	.275	.347	.419	.766
2014	Tacom	AAA	37	156	44	6	3	2	(-	-)	62	24	15	22	13	0	31	1	3	0	7	3	4	.282	.341	.397	.739
2015	Tacom	AAA	72	265	72	12	7	1	(-	-)	101	47	24	38	38	0	43	2	3	2	25	4	5	.272	.365	.381	.746
2014	Sea	AL	108	312	78	9	5	0	(0	0)	97	46	9	26	12	0	67	0	4	0	27	1	4	.250	.278	.311	.589
2015	Sea	AL	28	29	3	1	0	0	(0	0)	4	1	0	0	2	0	13	0	0	0	1	1	0	.103	.161	.138	.299
	2 ML YEARS		136	341	81	10	5	0	(0	0)	101	47	9	26	14	0	80	0	4	0	28	2	4	.238	.268	.296	.564

Nate Jones

Pitches: R Bats: R Pos: RP-19   Ht: 6'5" Wt: 220 Born: 1/28/1986 Age: 30

			HOW MUCH HE PITCHED					WHAT HE GAVE UP										THE RESULTS						
Year	Team	Lg	G	GS	CG	GF	IP	BFP	H	R	ER	HR	SH	SF	HB	TBB	IBB	SO	WP	Bk	W	L	Pct	Sh	Sv-Op	Hld	ERC	ERA
2015	Charltt*	AAA	6	0	0	6	6.1	24	3	1	1	1	0	0	2	0	4	1	0	0	0-	-		1.54	1.42
2012	CWS	AL	65	0	0	11	71.2	301	67	19	19	4	2	4	1	32	3	65	5	0	8	0	1.000	0	0-3	7	3.67	2.39
2013	CWS	AL	70	0	0	17	78.0	315	69	40	36	5	3	6	1	26	1	89	8	1	4	5	.444	0	0-4	16	3.09	4.15
2014	CWS	AL	2	0	0	0	0.0	5	2	4	4	0	0	0	0	3	0	0	0	0				0	0-1	0		
2015	CWS	AL	19	0	0	3	19.0	72	12	7	7	5	2	0	0	6	0	27	0	0	2	2	.500	0	0-1	6	2.87	3.32
	4 ML YEARS		156	0	0	31	168.2	693	150	70	66	14	7	10	2	67	4	181	13	1	14	7	.667	0	0-9	29	3.46	3.52

Taylor Jordan

Pitches: R Bats: R Pos: RP-3; SP-1   Ht: 6'5" Wt: 210 Born: 1/17/1989 Age: 27

			HOW MUCH HE PITCHED					WHAT HE GAVE UP										THE RESULTS						
Year	Team	Lg	G	GS	CG	GF	IP	BFP	H	R	ER	HR	SH	SF	HB	TBB	IBB	SO	WP	Bk	W	L	Pct	Sh	Sv-Op	Hld	ERC	ERA
2015	Syrcse*	AAA	19	19	0	0	103.2	429	92	38	34	4	4	1	5	27	1	61	2	0	5	6	.455	0	0- -		2.70	2.95
2013	Was	NL	9	9	0	0	51.2	220	59	27	21	3	2	1	3	11	0	29	1	0	1	3	.250	0	0-0	0	4.13	3.66
2014	Was	NL	5	5	0	0	25.2	124	34	20	16	3	2	2	2	8	1	17	0	0	0	3	.000	0	0-0	0	5.70	5.61
2015	Was	NL	4	1	0	0	17.0	77	20	10	10	0	1	1	0	6	0	11	1	0	0	2	.000	0	0-0	0	4.03	5.29
	3 ML YEARS		18	15	0	0	94.1	421	113	57	47	6	5	4	5	25	1	57	2	0	1	8	.111	0	0-0	0	4.53	4.48

Caleb Joseph

Bats: R Throws: R Pos: C-94;DH-3;PH-2;1B-1   Ht: 6'3" Wt: 180 Born: 6/18/1986 Age: 30

Year	Team	Lg	G	AB	H	2B	3B	HR	(Hm	Rd)	TB	R	RBI	RC	TBB	IBB	SO	HBP	SH	SF	SB	CS	GDP	Avg	OBP	Slg	OPS
2011	Bowie	AA	108	375	96	15	1	7	(-	-)	134	42	41	49	40	1	60	6	4	5	2	9	.256	.333	.357	.691
2012	Bowie	AA	80	279	76	17	1	12	(-	-)	131	38	48	47	29	1	60	3	2	4	2	0	6	.272	.343	.470	.812
2012	Norfolk	AAA	22	68	14	4	1	0	(-	-)	20	6	7	6	8	0	10	0	0	0	0	0	2	.206	.289	.294	.584
2013	Bowie	AA	135	518	155	31	2	22	(-	-)	256	74	97	90	39	2	92	3	0	10	4	2	11	.299	.346	.494	.840
2014	Norfolk	AAA	22	92	24	7	0	2	(-	-)	37	8	11	10	3	0	22	0	0	0	0	0	0	.261	.284	.402	.686
2014	Bal	AL	82	246	51	9	0	9	(4	5)	87	22	28	22	17	0	69	3	6	3	0	1	6	.207	.264	.354	.618
2015	Bal	AL	100	320	75	16	1	11	(5	6)	126	38	49	44	27	2	72	3	3	1	0	0	7	.234	.299	.394	.693
	Postseason		3	9	2	0	0	0	(0	0)	2	0	1	1	0	0	4	0	0	1	0	0	0	.222	.200	.222	.422
	2 ML YEARS		182	566	126	25	1	20	(9	11)	213	60	77	66	44	2	141	6	9	4	0	1	13	.223	.284	.376	.660

Matt Joyce

Bats: L Throws: R Pos: LF-64;DH-17;PH-17;RF-2   Ht: 6'2" Wt: 200 Born: 8/3/1984 Age: 31

Year	Team	Lg	G	AB	H	2B	3B	HR	(Hm	Rd)	TB	R	RBI	RC	TBB	IBB	SO	HBP	SH	SF	SB	CS	GDP	Avg	OBP	Slg	OPS
2015	Salt Lk*	AAA	11	36	12	1	0	2	(-	-)	19	3	6	8	5	0	9	1	0	1	0	0	1	.333	.419	.528	.946
2008	Det	AL	92	242	61	16	3	12	(6	6)	119	40	33	36	31	0	65	2	0	2	0	2	3	.252	.339	.492	.831
2009	TB	AL	11	32	6	1	0	3	(2	1)	16	3	7	5	3	0	7	1	0	1	1	0	0	.188	.270	.500	.770
2010	TB	AL	77	216	52	15	3	10	(4	6)	103	30	40	41	40	2	55	2	0	3	2	2	2	.241	.360	.477	.837
2011	TB	AL	141	462	128	32	2	19	(11	8)	221	69	75	77	49	9	106	4	0	7	13	1	7	.277	.347	.478	.825
2012	TB	AL	124	399	96	18	3	17	(4	13)	171	55	59	59	55	4	102	6	1	1	4	3	10	.241	.341	.429	.769
2013	TB	AL	140	413	97	22	0	18	(8	10)	173	61	47	51	59	0	87	2	0	7	7	3	8	.235	.328	.419	.747

			BATTING																	RUNNING			AVERAGES			
Year	Team	Lg	G	AB	H	2B	3B	HR	(Hm | Rd)	TB	R	RBI	RC	TBB	IBB	SO	HBP	SH	SF	SB	CS	GDP	Avg	OBP	Slg	OPS
2014	TB	AL	140	418	106	23	2	9	(2 | 7)	160	51	52	52	62	4	111	4	0	9	2	5	11	.254	.349	.383	.732
2015	LAA	AL	93	247	43	12	1	5	(4 | 1)	72	17	21	15	30	1	67	4	1	2	0	3	5	.174	.272	.291	.564
	Postseason		12	32	5	1	0	1	(0 | 1)	9	1	4	3	1	0	13	0	0	0	1	0	0	.156	.182	.281	.463
	8 ML YEARS		818	2429	589	139	14	93	(41 | 52)	1035	326	334	336	329	20	600	25	2	32	29	19	46	.242	.335	.426	.761

Taylor Jungmann

Pitches: R Bats: R Pos: SP-21   YOUNG-men   **Ht: 6'6" Wt: 220 Born: 12/18/1989 Age: 26**

			HOW MUCH HE PITCHED					WHAT HE GAVE UP											THE RESULTS						
Year	Team	Lg	G	GS	CG	GF	IP	BFP	H	R	ER	HR	SH	SF	HB	TBB	IBB	SO	WP	Bk	W	L	Pct	Sh	Sv-Op	Hld	ERC	ERA
2012	BrvdCt	A+	26	26	1	0	153.0	656	159	70	60	7	3	0	11	46	0	99	10	2	11	6	.647	0	0--	-	3.83	3.53
2013	Hntsvl	AA	26	26	0	0	139.1	595	117	75	67	11	5	2	10	73	1	82	9	1	10	10	.500	0	0--	-	3.86	4.33
2014	Hntsvl	AA	9	9	0	0	52.0	220	52	21	16	4	5	0	3	15	0	46	6	0	4	4	.500	0	0--	-	3.73	2.77
2014	Nashv	AAA	19	18	0	0	101.2	435	88	48	45	7	2	1	12	46	0	101	10	1	8	6	.571	0	0--	-	3.83	3.98
2015	ColSpr	AAA	11	9	0	0	59.1	258	61	44	42	2	0	1	4	29	0	54	10	0	2	3	.400	0	0--	-	4.50	6.37
2015	Mil	NL	21	21	1	0	119.1	501	106	55	50	11	2	5	8	47	1	107	8	0	9	8	.529	0	0-0	0	3.69	3.77

Tommy Kahnle

Pitches: R Bats: R Pos: RP-36   KAIN-lee   **Ht: 6'1" Wt: 235 Born: 8/7/1989 Age: 26**

			HOW MUCH HE PITCHED					WHAT HE GAVE UP											THE RESULTS						
Year	Team	Lg	G	GS	CG	GF	IP	BFP	H	R	ER	HR	SH	SF	HB	TBB	IBB	SO	WP	Bk	W	L	Pct	Sh	Sv-Op	Hld	ERC	ERA
2011	CtnSC	A	40	0	0	12	81.0	363	69	50	38	1	1	2	1	49	0	112	11	1	3	5	.375	0	2--	-	3.36	4.22
2012	Tampa	A+	30	0	0	18	55.0	222	30	16	15	3	5	1	2	24	1	72	4	1	2	1	.667	0	6--	-	1.70	2.45
2013	Trntn	AA	46	0	0	35	60.0	257	38	20	19	4	3	3	0	45	0	74	7	0	1	3	.250	0	15--	-	3.19	2.85
2015	Albq	AAA	21	0	0	13	27.0	112	19	14	14	3	1	1	1	12	0	28	5	0	1	3	.250	0	6--	-	2.85	4.67
2014	Col	NL	54	0	0	7	68.2	285	51	39	32	7	2	3	1	31	2	63	7	0	2	1	.667	0	0-2	8	2.91	4.19
2015	Col	NL	36	0	0	8	33.1	155	31	22	18	3	1	2	0	28	1	39	3	0	0	1	.000	0	2-3	10	5.31	4.86
	2 ML YEARS		90	0	0	15	102.0	440	82	61	50	10	3	5	1	59	3	102	10	0	2	2	.500	0	2-5	18	3.65	4.41

Jung Ho Kang

Bats: R Throws: R Pos: 3B-77;SS-60;PH-16;PR-2   GAHNG   **Ht: 6'0" Wt: 215 Born: 4/5/1987 Age: 29**

			BATTING																	RUNNING			AVERAGES			
Year	Team	Lg	G	AB	H	2B	3B	HR	(Hm	Rd)	TB	R	RBI	RC	TBB	IBB	SO	HBP	SH	SF	SB	CS	GDP	Avg	OBP	Slg	OPS
2015	Pit	NL	126	421	121	24	2	15	(5	10)	194	60	58	60	28	0	99	17	0	1	5	4	10	.287	.355	.461	.816

Nate Karns

Pitches: R Bats: R Pos: SP-26; RP-1   **Ht: 6'3" Wt: 225 Born: 11/25/1987 Age: 28**

			HOW MUCH HE PITCHED					WHAT HE GAVE UP											THE RESULTS						
Year	Team	Lg	G	GS	CG	GF	IP	BFP	H	R	ER	HR	SH	SF	HB	TBB	IBB	SO	WP	Bk	W	L	Pct	Sh	Sv-Op	Hld	ERC	ERA
2013	Was	NL	3	3	0	0	12.0	61	17	11	10	5	1	0	1	6	0	11	0	0	0	1	.000	0	0-0	0	9.80	7.50
2014	TB	AL	2	2	0	0	12.0	49	7	6	6	3	0	0	2	4	0	13	0	0	1	1	.500	0	0-0	0	3.12	4.50
2015	TB	AL	27	26	0	0	147.0	621	132	62	60	19	3	4	5	56	1	145	15	0	7	5	.583	0	0-0	0	3.77	3.67
	3 ML YEARS		32	31	0	0	171.0	731	156	79	76	27	4	4	8	66	1	169	15	0	8	7	.533	0	0-0	0	4.09	4.00

Munenori Kawasaki

Bats: L Throws: R Pos: 2B-17;PR-8;3B-3;PH-1   moo-neh-NO-ree kah-wah-SAH-kee   **Ht: 5'11" Wt: 175 Born: 6/3/1981 Age: 35**

			BATTING																	RUNNING			AVERAGES			
Year	Team	Lg	G	AB	H	2B	3B	HR	(Hm	Rd)	TB	R	RBI	RC	TBB	IBB	SO	HBP	SH	SF	SB	CS	GDP	Avg	OBP	Slg	OPS
2015	Buffalo*	AAA	62	196	48	8	0	0	(-	-)	56	18	8	21	24	0	32	2	4	1	8	4	3	.245	.332	.286	.618
2012	Sea	AL	61	104	20	1	0	0	(0	0)	21	13	7	7	8	0	18	1	2	0	2	2	2	.192	.257	.202	.459
2013	Tor	AL	96	240	55	6	5	1	(1	0)	74	27	24	28	32	0	41	4	10	3	7	1	5	.229	.326	.308	.634
2014	Tor	AL	82	240	62	7	1	0	(0	0)	71	31	17	27	22	0	49	3	8	1	1	0	3	.258	.327	.296	.623
2015	Tor	AL	23	28	6	2	0	0	(0	0)	8	6	2	2	4	0	6	0	2	0	0	1	1	.214	.313	.286	.598
	4 ML YEARS		262	612	143	16	6	1	(1	0)	174	77	50	64	66	0	114	8	22	4	10	4	11	.234	.314	.284	.599

Scott Kazmir

Pitches: L Bats: L Pos: SP-31   KAZ-meer   **Ht: 6'0" Wt: 185 Born: 1/24/1984 Age: 32**

			HOW MUCH HE PITCHED					WHAT HE GAVE UP											THE RESULTS						
Year	Team	Lg	G	GS	CG	GF	IP	BFP	H	R	ER	HR	SH	SF	HB	TBB	IBB	SO	WP	Bk	W	L	Pct	Sh	Sv-Op	Hld	ERC	ERA
2004	TB	AL	8	7	0	0	33.1	152	33	22	21	4	0	0	2	21	0	41	3	0	2	3	.400	0	0-0	0	5.36	5.67
2005	TB	AL	32	32	0	0	186.0	818	172	90	78	12	6	9	10	100	0	174	7	1	10	9	.526	0	0-0	0	4.13	3.77
2006	TB	AL	24	24	1	0	144.2	610	132	59	52	15	0	5	2	52	3	163	6	0	10	8	.556	1	0-0	0	3.47	3.24
2007	TB	AL	34	34	0	0	206.2	887	196	91	80	18	6	3	7	89	1	239	10	0	13	9	.591	0	0-0	0	3.97	3.48
2008	TB	AL	27	27	0	0	152.1	641	123	61	59	23	4	5	4	70	2	166	5	0	12	8	.600	0	0-0	0	3.69	3.49
2009	2 Tms	AL	26	26	0	0	147.1	647	149	85	80	16	1	4	6	60	0	117	13	0	10	9	.526	0	0-0	0	4.36	4.89
2010	LAA	AL	28	28	0	0	150.0	682	158	103	99	25	3	6	12	79	2	93	6	0	9	15	.375	0	0-0	0	5.74	5.94
2011	LAA	AL	1	1	0	0	1.2	16	5	5	5	1	0	0	2	2	0	0	1	0	0	0	-	0	0-0	0	35.08	27.00
2013	Cle	AL	29	29	0	0	158.0	672	162	76	71	19	2	1	3	47	1	162	5	1	10	9	.526	0	0-0	0	4.02	4.04
2014	Oak	AL	32	32	2	0	190.1	777	171	81	75	16	5	1	4	50	1	164	9	1	15	9	.625	0	0-0	0	3.00	3.55
2015	2 Tms	AL	31	31	0	0	183.0	763	162	77	63	20	5	6	9	59	0	155	5	2	7	11	.389	0	0-0	0	3.41	3.10
09	TB	AL	20	20	0	0	111.0	504	121	77	73	15	1	4	5	50	0	91	10	0	8	7	.533	0	0-0	0	5.18	5.92
09	LAA	AL	6	6	0	0	36.1	143	28	8	7	1	0	0	1	10	0	26	3	0	2	2	.500	0	0-0	0	2.13	1.73

Year Team	Lg	G	GS	CG	GF	IP	BFP	H	R	ER	HR	SH	SF	HB	TBB	IBB	SO	WP	Bk	W	L	Pct	Sh	Sv-Op	Hld	ERC	ERA
15 Oak	AL	18	18	0	0	109.2	440	84	35	29	7	3	4	3	35	0	101	2	2	5	5	.500	0	0-0	0	2.45	2.38
15 Hou	AL	13	13	0	0	73.1	323	78	42	34	13	2	2	6	24	0	54	3	0	2	6	.250	0	0-0	0	5.01	4.17
Postseason		8	7	0	0	36.1	176	37	22	21	5	3	2	3	26	0	26	2	0	1	2	.333	0	0-0	0	5.92	5.20
11 ML YEARS		272	271	3	0	1553.1	6663	1463	750	683	169	32	40	61	629	13	1474	69	6	98	90	.521	1	0-0	0	3.98	3.96

Keone Kela

Pitches: R **Bats:** R **Pos:** RP-68   KEY-oh-nee KELL-uh   **Ht:** 6'1" **Wt:** 230 **Born:** 4/16/1993 **Age:** 23

Year Team	Lg	G	GS	CG	GF	IP	BFP	H	R	ER	HR	SH	SF	HB	TBB	IBB	SO	WP	Bk	W	L	Pct	Sh	Sv-Op	Hld	ERC	ERA
2012 Rngrs	R	9	0	0	1	11.1	43	4	4	2	0	0	0	1	4	0	15	0	0	0	1	.000	0	0--	-	0.91	1.59
2013 3 Tms	Low	27	0	0	9	39.0	182	43	17	15	1	1	1	6	15	0	52	7	4	5	4	.556	0	3--	-	4.49	3.46
2014 MrtlBh	A+	8	0	0	8	10.1	44	9	3	3	0	0	0	0	4	0	13	3	0	0	1	.000	0	5--	-	2.60	2.61
2014 Frisco	AA	36	0	0	23	38.2	166	22	14	8	1	0	1	2	27	0	55	4	0	2	1	.667	0	5--	-	2.53	1.86
2015 Tex	AL	68	0	0	11	60.1	243	52	18	16	4	1	0	0	18	0	68	6	1	7	5	.583	0	1-4	22	2.79	2.39

Shawn Kelley

Pitches: R **Bats:** R **Pos:** RP-53   **Ht:** 6'2" **Wt:** 220 **Born:** 4/26/1984 **Age:** 32

Year Team	Lg	G	GS	CG	GF	IP	BFP	H	R	ER	HR	SH	SF	HB	TBB	IBB	SO	WP	Bk	W	L	Pct	Sh	Sv-Op	Hld	ERC	ERA
2009 Sea	AL	41	0	0	4	46.0	191	45	23	23	9	2	2	3	9	1	41	2	1	5	4	.556	0	0-4	9	4.02	4.50
2010 Sea	AL	22	0	0	7	25.0	112	26	11	11	5	0	0	1	12	2	26	0	0	3	1	.750	0	0-0	3	5.38	3.96
2011 Sea	AL	10	0	0	2	12.2	47	7	0	0	0	0	0	0	3	1	10	0	0	0	0	-	0	0-0	1	1.01	0.00
2012 Sea	AL	47	0	0	10	44.1	190	43	20	16	5	4	3	0	15	6	45	2	1	2	4	.333	0	0-2	6	3.49	3.25
2013 NYY	AL	57	0	0	13	53.1	227	47	28	26	8	0	2	0	23	2	71	8	0	4	2	.667	0	0-1	11	3.80	4.39
2014 NYY	AL	59	0	0	15	51.2	220	45	26	26	5	3	1	1	20	4	67	3	0	3	6	.333	0	4-7	12	3.20	4.53
2015 SD	NL	53	0	0	14	51.1	205	41	18	14	4	0	4	0	15	4	63	0	0	2	2	.500	0	0-0	7	2.40	2.45
7 ML YEARS		289	0	0	73	284.1	1192	254	126	116	36	9	12	5	97	20	323	15	2	19	19	.500	0	4-14	49	3.39	3.67

Casey Kelly

Pitches: R **Bats:** R **Pos:** SP-2; RP-1   **Ht:** 6'3" **Wt:** 215 **Born:** 10/4/1989 **Age:** 26

Year Team	Lg	G	GS	CG	GF	IP	BFP	H	R	ER	HR	SH	SF	HB	TBB	IBB	SO	WP	Bk	W	L	Pct	Sh	Sv-Op	Hld	ERC	ERA
2011 SnAnt	AA	27	27	0	0	142.1	615	153	74	63	8	6	5	8	46	0	105	7	2	11	6	.647	0	0--	-	4.14	3.98
2015 SnAnt	AA	26	14	0	3	80.0	364	92	56	45	7	1	4	2	34	0	58	3	3	1	8	.111	0	1--	-	4.98	5.06
2012 SD	NL	6	6	0	0	29.0	136	39	23	20	5	3	0	2	10	1	26	0	0	2	3	.400	0	0-0	0	6.65	6.21
2015 SD	NL	3	2	0	1	11.1	56	19	13	10	1	0	0	1	3	0	7	0	0	0	2	.000	0	0-0	0	7.89	7.94
2 ML YEARS		9	8	0	1	40.1	192	58	36	30	6	3	0	3	13	1	33	0	0	2	5	.286	0	0-0	0	6.99	6.69

Don Kelly

Bats: L **Throws:** R **Pos:** 1B-1;3B-1;PR-1   **Ht:** 6'4" **Wt:** 190 **Born:** 2/15/1980 **Age:** 36

Year Team	Lg	G	AB	H	2B	3B	HR	(Hm	Rd)	TB	R	RBI	RC	TBB	IBB	SO	HBP	SH	SF	SB	CS	GDP	Avg	OBP	Slg	OPS
2015 Jupiter*	A+	12	39	7	1	1	0	(-	-)	10	5	4	3	9	0	5	0	0	1	0	1	0	.179	.327	.256	.583
2007 Pit	NL	25	27	4	0	0	0	(0	0)	4	2	0	1	3	0	3	2	0	0	0	0	1	.148	.281	.148	.429
2009 Det	AL	31	56	14	3	1	0	(0	0)	19	8	3	7	4	0	10	1	1	0	1	0	0	.250	.311	.339	.651
2010 Det	AL	119	238	58	4	0	9	(4	5)	89	30	27	26	8	0	42	2	1	2	3	0	1	.244	.272	.374	.646
2011 Det	AL	113	257	63	8	3	7	(1	6)	98	35	28	27	14	0	32	3	6	1	2	1	8	.245	.291	.381	.672
2012 Det	AL	75	113	21	2	1	1	(1	0)	28	14	7	6	14	0	22	0	0	0	2	0	2	.186	.276	.248	.523
2013 Det	AL	112	216	48	6	1	6	(4	2)	74	33	23	27	27	1	28	2	2	4	2	0	4	.222	.309	.343	.652
2014 Det	AL	95	163	40	5	1	0	(0	0)	47	24	7	14	20	1	29	1	1	0	6	1	6	.245	.332	.288	.620
2015 Mia	NL	2	1	0	0	0	0	(0	0)	0	0	0	0	0	0	0	0	0	0	0	0	0	.000	.000	.000	.000
Postseason		24	34	9	1	0	1	(0	1)	13	5	3	3	3	0	9	0	0	1	1	0	0	.265	.316	.382	.698
8 ML YEARS		572	1071	248	28	7	23	(10	13)	359	146	95	108	90	2	166	11	11	7	16	2	22	.232	.296	.335	.631

Joe Kelly

Pitches: R **Bats:** R **Pos:** SP-25   **Ht:** 6'1" **Wt:** 190 **Born:** 6/9/1988 **Age:** 28

Year Team	Lg	G	GS	CG	GF	IP	BFP	H	R	ER	HR	SH	SF	HB	TBB	IBB	SO	WP	Bk	W	L	Pct	Sh	Sv-Op	Hld	ERC	ERA
2012 StL	NL	24	16	0	4	107.0	457	112	50	42	10	4	1	3	36	2	75	4	0	5	7	.417	0	0-0	0	4.17	3.53
2013 StL	NL	37	15	0	8	124.0	532	124	42	37	10	2	2	5	44	4	79	3	0	10	5	.667	0	0-1	3	3.88	2.69
2014 2 Tms		17	17	0	0	96.1	415	88	48	45	8	2	4	7	42	0	66	3	0	6	4	.600	0	0-0	0	3.92	4.20
2015 Bos	AL	25	25	0	0	134.1	586	145	76	72	15	0	5	6	49	0	110	9	0	10	6	.625	0	0-0	0	4.69	4.82
14 StL	NL	7	7	0	0	35.0	156	41	19	17	3	1	1	3	10	0	25	0	0	2	2	.500	0	0-0	0	4.82	4.37
14 Bos	AL	10	10	0	0	61.1	259	47	29	28	5	1	3	4	32	0	41	3	0	4	2	.667	0	0-0	0	3.43	4.11
Postseason		11	4	0	1	29.1	127	26	13	12	2	1	0	1	13	1	24	1	0	0	1	.000	0	0-0	0	3.42	3.68
4 ML YEARS		103	73	0	12	461.2	1990	469	216	196	43	8	12	21	171	6	330	19	0	31	22	.585	0	0-1	2	4.19	3.82

Ryan Kelly

Pitches: R **Bats:** R **Pos:** RP-17 **Ht:** 6'2" **Wt:** 180 **Born:** 10/30/1987 **Age:** 28

			HOW MUCH HE PITCHED						WHAT HE GAVE UP										THE RESULTS						
Year	Team	Lg	G	GS	CG	GF	IP	BFP	H	R	ER	HR	SH	SF	HB	TBB	IBB	SO	WP	Bk	W	L	Pct	Sh	Sv-Op	Hld	ERC	ERA
2011	MrtlBh	A+	40	5	0	17	82.0	341	74	44	36	6	5	5	2	23	1	64	8	0	3	6	.333	0	9- -	-	2.97	3.95
2012	SnAnt	AA	39	0	0	9	47.1	196	39	20	14	2	2	1	2	15	1	47	1	0	4	1	.800	0	1- -	-	2.56	2.66
2012	Tucsn	AAA	6	0	0	1	7.2	39	15	7	6	0	0	0	0	2	0	4	2	0	0	0	-	0	0- -	-	8.59	7.04
2013	SnAnt	AA	37	0	0	4	47.1	208	49	27	27	8	1	1	2	20	1	37	1	0	1	2	.333	0	1- -	-	5.02	5.13
2013	Tucsn	AAA	14	1	0	4	20.0	85	22	8	8	1	1	0	0	9	1	18	1	0	1	1	.500	0	1- -	-	4.61	3.60
2014	Lynbrg	A+	8	0	0	8	12.0	43	4	3	3	1	0	0	0	2	0	14	1	0	1	1	.500	0	5- -	-	0.63	2.25
2014	Missi	AA	22	0	0	17	28.0	113	18	10	10	3	1	0	0	10	1	35	1	0	2	2	.500	0	5- -	-	2.03	3.21
2015	Missi	AA	17	0	0	16	18.2	75	13	2	1	0	2	1	0	6	0	18	0	0	1	1	.500	0	10- -	-	1.64	0.48
2015	Gwnntt	AAA	24	0	0	18	28.1	102	12	4	3	0	2	1	1	7	1	30	1	0	3	1	.750	0	13- -	-	0.81	0.95
2015	Atl	NL	17	0	0	8	16.2	74	21	14	13	5	1	0	0	6	0	10	0	0	0	0	-	0	0-1	0	7.13	7.02

Matt Kemp

Bats: R **Throws:** R **Pos:** RF-149;DH-3;PH-2 **Ht:** 6'4" **Wt:** 210 **Born:** 9/23/1984 **Age:** 31

					BATTING														RUNNING			AVERAGES			
Year	Team	Lg	G	AB	H	2B	3B	HR	(Hm | Rd)	TB	R	RBI	RC	TBB	IBB	SO	HBP	SH	SF	SB	CS	GDP	Avg	OBP	Slg	OPS
2006	LAD	NL	52	154	39	7	1	7	(4 | 3)	69	30	23	20	9	1	53	0	0	3	6	0	1	.253	.289	.448	.737
2007	LAD	NL	98	292	100	12	5	10	(9 | 1)	152	47	42	49	16	0	66	0	0	3	10	5	6	.342	.373	.521	.894
2008	LAD	NL	155	606	176	38	5	18	(14 | 4)	278	93	76	86	46	6	153	1	1	3	35	11	11	.290	.340	.459	.799
2009	LAD	NL	159	606	180	25	7	26	(13 | 13)	297	97	101	100	52	6	139	3	0	6	34	8	14	.297	.352	.490	.842
2010	LAD	NL	162	602	150	25	6	28	(15 | 13)	271	82	89	74	53	4	170	4	0	9	19	15	14	.249	.310	.450	.760
2011	LAD	NL	161	602	195	33	4	**39**	(19 | 20)	**353**	**115**	**126**	129	74	24	159	6	0	7	40	11	16	.324	.399	.586	.986
2012	LAD	NL	106	403	122	22	2	23	(13 | 10)	217	74	69	75	40	8	103	3	0	3	9	4	10	.303	.367	.538	.906
2013	LAD	NL	73	263	71	15	0	6	(0 | 6)	104	35	33	27	22	3	76	2	0	3	9	0	11	.270	.328	.395	.723
2014	LAD	NL	150	541	155	38	3	25	(17 | 8)	274	77	89	79	52	3	145	0	0	6	8	5	21	.287	.346	.506	.852
2015	SD	NL	154	596	158	31	3	23	(10 | 13)	264	80	100	81	39	0	147	5	0	8	12	2	17	.265	.312	.443	.755
	Postseason		20	79	20	3	0	3	(2 | 1)	32	6	7	2	5	0	28	0	0	0	0	2	3	.253	.298	.405	.703
	10 ML YEARS		1270	4665	1346	246	36	205	(117 | 88)	2279	730	748	720	403	55	1211	24	1	51	182	61	121	.289	.345	.489	.833

Howie Kendrick

Bats: R **Throws:** R **Pos:** 2B-113;PH-4 **Ht:** 5'11" **Wt:** 220 **Born:** 7/12/1983 **Age:** 32

					BATTING														RUNNING			AVERAGES			
Year	Team	Lg	G	AB	H	2B	3B	HR	(Hm | Rd)	TB	R	RBI	RC	TBB	IBB	SO	HBP	SH	SF	SB	CS	GDP	Avg	OBP	Slg	OPS
2006	LAA	AL	72	267	76	21	1	4	(2 | 2)	111	25	30	32	9	2	44	4	0	3	6	0	5	.285	.314	.416	.730
2007	LAA	AL	88	338	109	24	2	5	(3 | 2)	152	55	39	41	9	2	61	4	1	1	5	4	15	.322	.347	.450	.796
2008	LAA	AL	92	340	104	26	2	3	(1 | 2)	143	43	37	50	12	3	58	4	1	4	11	4	8	.306	.333	.421	.754
2009	LAA	AL	105	374	109	21	3	10	(5 | 5)	166	61	61	58	20	1	71	4	2	0	11	4	8	.291	.334	.444	.778
2010	LAA	AL	158	616	172	41	4	10	(4 | 6)	251	67	75	81	28	2	94	5	4	5	14	4	16	.279	.313	.407	.721
2011	LAA	AL	140	537	153	30	6	18	(5 | 13)	249	86	63	69	33	3	119	10	3	0	14	6	18	.285	.338	.464	.802
2012	LAA	AL	147	550	158	32	3	8	(4 | 4)	220	57	67	65	29	1	115	4	6	5	14	6	26	.287	.325	.400	.725
2013	LAA	AL	122	478	142	21	4	13	(9 | 4)	210	55	54	57	23	5	89	6	3	3	6	3	16	.297	.335	.439	.775
2014	LAA	AL	157	617	181	33	5	7	(0 | 7)	245	85	75	94	48	4	110	4	3	2	14	5	15	.293	.347	.397	.744
2015	LAD	NL	117	464	137	22	2	9	(6 | 3)	190	64	54	62	27	1	82	2	1	1	6	2	17	.295	.336	.409	.746
	Postseason		16	59	11	1	1	1	(1 | 0)	17	5	2	3	1	0	16	0	2	1	3	0	1	.186	.197	.288	.485
	10 ML YEARS		1198	4581	1341	271	32	87	(39 | 48)	1937	598	555	609	238	28	843	47	24	24	101	38	144	.293	.333	.423	.755

Kyle Kendrick

Pitches: R **Bats:** R **Pos:** SP-27 **Ht:** 6'3" **Wt:** 210 **Born:** 8/26/1984 **Age:** 31

			HOW MUCH HE PITCHED						WHAT HE GAVE UP										THE RESULTS						
Year	Team	Lg	G	GS	CG	GF	IP	BFP	H	R	ER	HR	SH	SF	HB	TBB	IBB	SO	WP	Bk	W	L	Pct	Sh	Sv-Op	Hld	ERC	ERA
2007	Phi	NL	20	20	0	0	121.0	499	129	53	52	16	4	7	7	25	3	49	0	0	10	4	.714	0	0-0	0	4.23	3.87
2008	Phi	NL	31	30	0	1	155.2	722	194	103	95	23	8	4	**14**	57	2	68	4	1	11	9	.550	0	0-0	0	6.05	5.49
2009	Phi	NL	9	2	0	2	26.1	112	27	11	10	1	1	2	1	9	0	15	0	1	3	1	.750	0	0-0	0	3.75	3.42
2010	Phi	NL	33	31	1	1	180.2	771	199	103	95	26	9	6	3	49	4	84	1	2	11	10	.524	0	0-0	0	4.51	4.73
2011	Phi	NL	34	15	0	5	114.2	478	110	50	41	14	6	3	7	30	5	59	1	1	8	6	.571	0	0-1	0	3.66	3.22
2012	Phi	NL	37	25	1	2	159.1	674	154	76	69	20	8	4	7	49	4	116	1	0	11	12	.478	1	0-1	2	3.84	3.90
2013	Phi	NL	30	30	2	0	182.0	800	207	104	95	18	11	7	7	47	4	110	3	1	10	13	.435	1	0-0	0	4.33	4.70
2014	Phi	NL	32	32	0	0	199.0	865	214	108	102	25	**17**	5	11	57	4	121	5	0	10	13	.435	0	0-0	0	4.39	4.61
2015	Col	NL	27	27	0	0	142.1	629	172	102	**100**	33	5	2	7	45	2	80	4	0	7	13	.350	0	0-0	0	6.21	6.32
	Postseason		1	1	0	0	3.2	18	5	5	5	2	0	0	0	2	1	2	0	0	0	1	.000	0	0-0	0	9.97	12.27
	9 ML YEARS		253	212	4	11	1281.0	5550	1406	710	659	176	69	35	64	368	28	702	19	6	81	81	.500	2	0-2	2	4.62	4.63

Ian Kennedy

Pitches: R **Bats:** R **Pos:** SP-30 **Ht:** 6'0" **Wt:** 200 **Born:** 12/19/1984 **Age:** 31

			HOW MUCH HE PITCHED						WHAT HE GAVE UP										THE RESULTS						
Year	Team	Lg	G	GS	CG	GF	IP	BFP	H	R	ER	HR	SH	SF	HB	TBB	IBB	SO	WP	Bk	W	L	Pct	Sh	Sv-Op	Hld	ERC	ERA
2007	NYY	AL	3	3	0	0	19.0	77	13	6	4	1	0	0	0	9	0	15	0	0	1	0	1.000	0	0-0	0	2.42	1.89
2008	NYY	AL	10	9	0	1	39.2	194	50	37	36	5	1	4	1	26	0	27	3	0	0	4	.000	0	0-0	0	6.93	8.17
2009	NYY	AL	1	0	0	0	1.0	6	0	0	0	0	0	0	0	2	0	1	0	0	0	0	-	0	0-0	1	7.00	0.00
2010	Ari	NL	32	32	0	0	194.0	810	163	87	82	26	11	5	10	70	2	168	**16**	0	9	10	.474	0	0-0	0	3.47	3.80
2011	Ari	NL	33	33	1	0	222.0	900	186	73	71	19	9	9	9	55	0	198	11	1	**21**	4	.840	1	0-0	0	2.71	2.88
2012	Ari	NL	33	33	1	0	208.1	899	216	101	93	28	13	5	**14**	55	4	187	5	4	15	12	.556	0	0-0	0	4.18	4.02
2013	2 Tms	NL	31	31	0	0	181.1	794	180	108	99	27	8	5	12	73	1	163	10	1	7	10	.412	0	0-0	0	4.64	4.91
2014	SD	NL	33	33	0	0	201.0	846	189	85	81	16	9	8	4	70	4	207	11	0	13	13	.500	1	0-0	0	3.47	3.63
2015	SD	NL	30	30	0	0	168.1	713	166	95	80	31	8	2	4	52	4	174	5	1	9	15	.375	0	0-0	0	4.37	4.28

		HOW MUCH HE PITCHED						WHAT HE GAVE UP												THE RESULTS						
Year	Team	Lg	G	GS	CG	GF	IP	BFP	H	R	ER	HR	SH	SF	HB	TBB	IBB	SO	WP	Bk	W	L	Pct	Sh	Sv-Op	Hld	ERC	ERA
13	Ari	NL	21	21	0	0	124.0	549	128	79	72	18	8	5	10	48	1	108	9	0	3	8	.273	0	0-0		4.82	5.23
13	SD	NL	10	10	0	0	57.1	245	52	29	27	9	0	0	2	25	0	55	1	1	4	2	.667	0	0-0		4.26	4.24
	Postseason		2	2	0	0	12.2	57	13	6	6	1	0	2	3	3	0	8	1	0	0	1	.000	0	0-0		4.25	4.26
	9 ML YEARS		206	204	2	1	1234.2	5239	1163	592	546	153	59	38	58	412	15	1140	61	7	75	68	.524	1	0-0		3.82	3.98

Logan Kensing

Pitches: R Bats: R Pos: RP-19 **Ht: 6'1" Wt: 190 Born: 7/3/1982 Age: 33**

		HOW MUCH HE PITCHED						WHAT HE GAVE UP												THE RESULTS						
Year	Team	Lg	G	GS	CG	GF	IP	BFP	H	R	ER	HR	SH	SF	HB	TBB	IBB	SO	WP	Bk	W	L	Pct	Sh	Sv-Op	Hld	ERC	ERA
2015	Tacom*	AAA	19	0	0	3	32.1	135	29	11	8	1	1	1	2	10	0	25	2	1	2	0	1.000	0	1- -	-	2.95	2.23
2004	Fla	NL	5	3	0	2	13.2	66	19	15	15	1	5	0	1	9	0	7	2	0	0	3	.000	0	0-0		10.74	9.88
2005	Fla	NL	3	0	0	0	5.2	31	11	7	7	2	0	1	0	3	0	4	0	0	0	0	-	0	0-0	1	12.96	11.12
2006	Fla	NL	37	0	0	10	37.2	161	30	19	19	6	3	0	3	19	2	45	0	0	1	3	.250	0	1-7	14	4.02	4.54
2007	Fla	NL	9	0	0	1	13.1	59	11	2	2	0	1	0	2	7	2	13	0	0	3	0	1.000	0	0-0	0	3.15	1.35
2008	Fla	NL	48	0	0	7	55.1	254	50	26	26	7	1	2	4	33	5	55	7	0	3	1	.750	0	0-3	5	4.50	4.23
2009	2 Tms	NL	32	0	0	12	35.1	172	54	35	35	8	3	1	0	17	1	19	4	1	1	2	.333	0	1-3	1	8.78	8.92
2013	Col	NL	1	0	0	1	0.2	2	0	0	0	0	0	0	0	1	0	1	0	0	0	0	-	0	0-0	0	3.22	0.00
2015	Sea	AL	19	0	0	4	15.1	64	12	10	10	2	0	1	0	7	0	13	2	0	2	1	.667	0	0-0	9	3.31	5.87
09	Fla	NL	6	0	0	2	7.1	40	14	8	8	1	1	0	0	5	0	7	2	1	0	1	.000	0	0-0	0	11.61	9.82
09	Was	NL	26	0	0	10	28.0	132	40	27	27	7	2	1	0	12	1	12	2	0	1	1	.500	0	1-3	1	8.04	8.68
	8 ML YEARS		154	3	0	36	177.0	809	187	114	114	30	8	6	10	96	10	157	15	1	10	10	.500	0	2-13	30	5.63	5.80

Max Kepler

Bats: L Throws: L Pos: RF-2;PH-2 **Ht: 6'4" Wt: 205 Born: 2/10/1993 Age: 23**

			BATTING																RUNNING			AVERAGES			
Year	Team	Lg	G	AB	H	2B	3B	HR	(Hm | Rd)	TB	R	RBI	RC	TBB	IBB	SO	HBP	SH	SF	SB	CS	GDP	Avg	OBP	Slg	OPS
2011	Elizab	R+	50	191	50	11	3	1	(- | -)	70	29	24	26	23	0	54	3	2	2	1	1	6	.262	.347	.366	.714
2012	Elizab	R+	59	232	69	16	5	10	(- | -)	125	40	49	50	27	0	33	8	0	2	7	0	5	.297	.387	.539	.925
2013	Crpds	A	61	236	56	11	3	9	(- | -)	100	35	40	33	24	1	43	2	0	1	2	0	2	.237	.312	.424	.736
2014	FtMyrs	A+	102	364	96	20	6	5	(- | -)	143	53	59	50	34	0	62	5	2	2	6	2	4	.264	.333	.393	.726
2015	Chatt	AA	112	407	131	32	13	9	(- | -)	216	76	71	93	67	4	63	2	1	5	18	4	3	.322	.416	.531	.947
2015	Min	AL	3	7	1	0	0	0	(0 | 0)	1	0	0	0	0	0	3	0	0	0	0	0	0	.143	.143	.143	.286

Clayton Kershaw

Pitches: L Bats: L Pos: SP-33 **Ht: 6'4" Wt: 225 Born: 3/19/1988 Age: 28**

			HOW MUCH HE PITCHED						WHAT HE GAVE UP												THE RESULTS						
Year	Team	Lg	G	GS	CG	GF	IP	BFP	H	R	ER	HR	SH	SF	HB	TBB	IBB	SO	WP	Bk	W	L	Pct	Sh	Sv-Op	Hld	ERC	ERA
2008	LAD	NL	22	21	0	0	107.2	470	109	51	51	11	3	3	1	52	3	100	7	0	5	5	.500	0	0-0	1	4.53	4.26
2009	LAD	NL	31	30	0	1	171.0	701	119	55	53	7	11	2	1	91	4	185	11	2	8	8	.500	0	0-0	0	2.60	2.79
2010	LAD	NL	32	32	1	0	204.1	848	160	73	66	13	8	4	7	81	9	212	5	2	13	10	.565	1	0-0	0	2.72	2.91
2011	LAD	NL	33	33	5	0	233.1	912	174	66	59	15	11	2	3	54	2	248	5	1	21	5	.808	2	0-0	0	2.00	2.28
2012	LAD	NL	33	33	2	0	227.2	901	170	70	64	16	18	4	5	63	5	229	6	2	14	9	.609	2	0-0	0	2.20	2.53
2013	LAD	NL	33	33	3	0	236.0	908	164	55	48	11	8	3	3	52	4	232	12	2	16	9	.640	2	0-0	0	1.65	1.83
2014	LAD	NL	27	27	6	0	198.1	749	139	42	39	9	6	1	2	31	0	239	7	2	21	3	.875	2	0-0	0	1.53	1.77
2015	LAD	NL	33	33	4	0	232.2	890	163	62	55	15	4	0	5	42	1	301	9	3	16	7	.696	3	0-0	0	1.67	2.13
	Postseason		11	8	0	0	51.0	213	45	32	29	6	3	1	1	18	2	58	9	0	1	5	.167	0	0-0	0	3.39	5.12
	8 ML YEARS		244	242	21	1	1611.0	6379	1198	474	435	97	69	19	27	466	26	1746	62	14	114	56	.671	12	0-0	1	2.16	2.43

Dallas Keuchel

Pitches: L Bats: L Pos: SP-33 KY-kull **Ht: 6'3" Wt: 210 Born: 1/1/1988 Age: 28**

			HOW MUCH HE PITCHED						WHAT HE GAVE UP												THE RESULTS						
Year	Team	Lg	G	GS	CG	GF	IP	BFP	H	R	ER	HR	SH	SF	HB	TBB	IBB	SO	WP	Bk	W	L	Pct	Sh	Sv-Op	Hld	ERC	ERA
2012	Hou	NL	16	16	1	0	85.1	377	93	56	50	14	9	3	1	39	1	38	2	0	3	8	.273	0	0-0	0	5.39	5.27
2013	Hou	AL	31	22	0	2	153.2	682	184	96	88	20	2	3	5	52	3	123	7	0	6	10	.375	0	0-0	0	5.33	5.15
2014	Hou	AL	29	29	5	0	200.0	808	187	71	65	11	4	5	7	48	2	146	7	0	12	9	.571	1	0-0	0	3.02	2.93
2015	Hou	AL	33	33	3	0	232.0	911	185	68	64	17	1	3	2	51	0	216	9	0	20	8	.714	2	0-0	0	2.26	2.48
	4 ML YEARS		109	100	9	2	671.0	2778	649	291	267	62	16	14	15	190	6	523	25	0	41	35	.539	3	0-0	2	3.51	3.58

Kevin Kiermaier

Bats: L Throws: R Pos: CF-148;PH-9;PR-3;RF-2 KEER-my-urr **Ht: 6'1" Wt: 215 Born: 4/22/1990 Age: 26**

			BATTING																RUNNING			AVERAGES			
Year	Team	Lg	G	AB	H	2B	3B	HR	(Hm | Rd)	TB	R	RBI	RC	TBB	IBB	SO	HBP	SH	SF	SB	CS	GDP	Avg	OBP	Slg	OPS
2013	TB	AL	1	0	0	0	0	0	(0 | 0)	0	0	0	0	0	0	0	0	0	0	0	0	0	-	-	-	-
2014	TB	AL	108	331	87	16	8	10	(4 | 6)	149	35	35	37	23	2	71	3	5	2	5	4	3	.263	.315	.450	.765
2015	TB	AL	151	505	133	25	12	10	(5 | 5)	212	62	40	66	24	0	95	2	2	2	18	5	7	.263	.298	.420	.718
	Postseason		1	0	0	0	0	0	(0 | 0)	0	0	0	0	0	0	0	0	0	0	0	0	0	-	-	-	-
	3 ML YEARS		260	836	220	41	20	20	(9 | 11)	361	97	75	103	47	2	166	5	7	4	23	9	10	.263	.305	.432	.737

Craig Kimbrel

Pitches: R **Bats:** R **Pos:** RP-61   KIM-brull   **Ht:** 5'11" **Wt:** 220 **Born:** 5/28/1988 **Age:** 28

			HOW MUCH HE PITCHED						WHAT HE GAVE UP											THE RESULTS						
Year	Team	Lg	G	GS	CG	GF	IP	BFP	H	R	ER	HR	SH	SF	HB	TBB	IBB	SO	WP	Bk	W	L	Pct	Sh	Sv-Op	Hld	ERC	ERA
2010	Atl	NL	21	0	0	7	20.2	88	9	2	1	0	0	0	0	16	1	40	4	0	4	0	1.000	0	1-1	2	1.72	0.44
2011	Atl	NL	79	0	0	64	77.0	306	48	19	18	3	1	2	1	32	1	127	4	0	4	3	.571	0	46-54	1	1.88	2.10
2012	Atl	NL	63	0	0	56	62.2	231	27	7	7	3	0	0	2	14	0	116	5	0	3	1	.750	0	42-45	0	0.93	1.01
2013	Atl	NL	68	0	0	67	67.0	258	39	10	9	4	0	0	3	20	2	98	3	0	4	3	.571	0	50-54	0	1.58	1.21
2014	Atl	NL	63	0	0	54	61.2	244	30	13	11	2	3	0	3	26	0	95	6	0	0	3	.000	0	47-51	0	1.41	1.61
2015	SD		61	0	0	53	59.1	239	40	19	17	6	0	0	1	22	1	87	4	0	4	2	.667	0	39-43	0	2.31	2.58
	Postseason		6	0	0	4	6.2	21	1	2	1	0	0	0	0	3	0	10	0	0	0	1	.000	0	1-1	1	0.54	1.35
	6 ML YEARS		355	0	0	294	348.1	1366	193	70	63	18	4	2	9	130	5	563	26	0	19	12	.613	0	225-248	2	1.58	1.63

Ian Kinsler

Bats: R **Throws:** R **Pos:** 2B-153;DH-1;PH-1   **Ht:** 6'0" **Wt:** 200 **Born:** 6/22/1982 **Age:** 34

						BATTING															RUNNING			AVERAGES			
Year	Team	Lg	G	AB	H	2B	3B	HR	(Hm	Rd)	TB	R	RBI	RC	TBB	IBB	SO	HBP	SH	SF	SB	CS	GDP	Avg	OBP	Slg	OPS
2006	Tex	AL	120	423	121	27	1	14	(10	4)	192	65	55	65	40	1	64	3	1	7	11	4	12	.286	.347	.454	.801
2007	Tex	AL	130	483	127	22	2	20	(12	8)	213	96	61	79	62	2	83	9	8	4	23	2	14	.263	.355	.441	.796
2008	Tex	AL	121	518	165	41	4	18	(4	14)	268	102	71	106	45	1	67	6	7	7	26	2	12	.319	.375	.517	.892
2009	Tex	AL	144	566	143	32	4	31	(20	11)	276	101	86	99	59	0	77	6	3	6	31	5	9	.253	.327	.488	.814
2010	Tex	AL	103	391	112	20	1	9	(4	5)	161	73	45	59	56	2	57	7	2	4	15	5	11	.286	.382	.412	.794
2011	Tex	AL	155	620	158	34	4	32	(16	16)	296	121	77	100	89	2	71	8	4	2	30	4	17	.255	.355	.477	.832
2012	Tex	AL	157	655	168	42	5	19	(14	5)	277	105	72	83	60	0	90	10	1	5	21	9	14	.256	.326	.423	.749
2013	Tex	AL	136	545	151	31	2	13	(5	8)	225	85	72	84	51	0	59	8	3	7	15	11	5	.277	.344	.413	.757
2014	Det	AL	161	684	188	40	4	17	(9	8)	287	100	92	89	29	1	79	5	3	5	15	4	20	.275	.307	.420	.727
2015	Det	AL	154	624	185	35	7	11	(6	5)	267	94	73	81	43	0	80	3	0	5	10	6	13	.296	.342	.428	.770
	Postseason		37	134	39	7	1	4	(1	3)	60	18	20	24	24	1	19	1	1	1	6	5	3	.291	.400	.448	.848
	10 ML YEARS		1381	5509	1518	324	34	184	(100	84)	2462	942	704	845	534	9	727	65	32	52	197	52	127	.276	.344	.447	.791

Brandon Kintzler

Pitches: R **Bats:** R **Pos:** RP-7   **Ht:** 5'10" **Wt:** 190 **Born:** 8/1/1984 **Age:** 31

			HOW MUCH HE PITCHED						WHAT HE GAVE UP											THE RESULTS						
Year	Team	Lg	G	GS	CG	GF	IP	BFP	H	R	ER	HR	SH	SF	HB	TBB	IBB	SO	WP	Bk	W	L	Pct	Sh	Sv-Op	Hld	ERC	ERA
2015	ColSpr*	AAA	16	0	0	1	19.0	81	23	13	11	0	1	0	0	4	0	14	6	0	1	1	.500	0	0- -	-	3.85	5.21
2010	Mil	NL	7	0	0	2	7.1	33	10	6	6	2	1	0	0	4	1	9	1	0	0	1	.000	0	0-0	0	8.67	7.36
2011	Mil	NL	9	0	0	3	14.2	61	14	9	6	3	0	2	0	3	0	15	0	1	1	1	.500	0	0-0	0	3.65	3.68
2012	Mil	NL	14	0	0	1	16.2	72	18	7	7	1	0	0	0	7	1	14	1	0	3	0	1.000	0	0-0	2	4.30	3.78
2013	Mil	NL	71	0	0	11	77.0	305	66	26	23	2	4	2	1	16	2	58	1	0	3	3	.500	0	0-4	26	2.21	2.69
2014	Mil	NL	64	0	0	13	58.1	239	62	22	21	8	4	1	0	16	3	31	1	0	3	3	.500	0	0-3	8	4.28	3.24
2015	Mil	NL	7	0	0	4	7.0	36	12	6	5	1	0	0	0	5	0	7	1	0	0	1	.000	0	0-0	0	10.76	6.43
	6 ML YEARS		172	0	0	34	181.0	746	182	76	68	17	9	5	1	51	7	134	5	1	10	9	.526	0	0-7	36	3.65	3.38

Jason Kipnis

Bats: L **Throws:** R **Pos:** 2B-124;DH-16;PH-3   KIP-niss   **Ht:** 5'11" **Wt:** 195 **Born:** 4/3/1987 **Age:** 29

						BATTING															RUNNING			AVERAGES			
Year	Team	Lg	G	AB	H	2B	3B	HR	(Hm	Rd)	TB	R	RBI	RC	TBB	IBB	SO	HBP	SH	SF	SB	CS	GDP	Avg	OBP	Slg	OPS
2011	Cle	AL	36	136	37	9	1	7	(3	4)	69	24	19	22	11	0	34	2	0	1	5	0	0	.272	.333	.507	.841
2012	Cle	AL	152	591	152	22	4	14	(5	9)	224	86	76	88	67	2	109	5	3	6	31	7	12	.257	.335	.379	.714
2013	Cle	AL	149	564	160	36	4	17	(7	10)	255	86	84	99	76	3	143	3	5	10	30	7	10	.284	.366	.452	.818
2014	Cle	AL	129	500	120	25	1	6	(3	3)	165	61	41	44	50	2	100	2	1	2	22	3	15	.240	.310	.330	.640
2015	Cle	AL	141	565	171	43	7	9	(6	3)	255	86	52	92	57	6	107	9	4	6	12	8	5	.303	.372	.451	.823
	Postseason		1	4	0	0	0	0	(0	0)	0	0	0	0	0	0	0	0	0	0	0	0	0	.000	.000	.000	.000
	5 ML YEARS		607	2356	640	135	17	53	(24	29)	968	343	272	345	261	13	493	21	13	25	100	25	42	.272	.346	.411	.757

Phil Klein

Pitches: R **Bats:** R **Pos:** RP-9; SP-2   **Ht:** 6'7" **Wt:** 260 **Born:** 4/30/1989 **Age:** 27

			HOW MUCH HE PITCHED						WHAT HE GAVE UP											THE RESULTS						
Year	Team	Lg	G	GS	CG	GF	IP	BFP	H	R	ER	HR	SH	SF	HB	TBB	IBB	SO	WP	Bk	W	L	Pct	Sh	Sv-Op	Hld	ERC	ERA
2011	2 Tms	Low	12	0	0	2	20.1	98	20	13	9	1	1	0	1	16	0	31	4	0	1	2	.333	0	0- -	-	5.17	3.98
2012	2 Tms	Low	40	0	0	24	62.1	243	39	13	12	3	2	0	4	23	0	67	3	1	6	0	1.000	0	8- -	-	2.03	1.73
2013	MrtlBh	A+	7	0	0	4	13.2	52	6	4	3	0	0	0	2	3	0	12	0	0	1	0	1.000	0	0- -	-	0.99	1.98
2013	Frisco	AA	29	2	0	2	53.2	244	45	23	15	3	2	0	2	44	1	74	7	0	5	1	.833	0	0- -	-	4.62	2.52
2014	Frisco	AA	24	0	0	14	33.1	129	15	3	3	0	5	1	1	14	0	42	4	0	3	0	1.000	0	10- -	-	1.18	0.81
2014	RdRck	AAA	9	0	0	0	18.1	67	7	0	0	0	0	0	2	6	1	28	1	0	0	0	-	0	0- -	-	0.97	0.00
2015	RdRck	AAA	18	10	0	0	63.2	263	49	25	21	2	1	1	3	27	0	58	2	0	2	1	.667	0	0- -	-	2.68	2.97
2014	Tex	AL	17	0	0	3	19.0	79	11	6	6	3	0	0	2	10	5	23	1	1	1	2	.333	0	0-0	0	2.69	2.84
2015	Tex	AL	11	2	0	3	17.1	86	23	15	13	4	0	0	0	10	0	12	1	0	1	0	1.000	0	0-0	2	7.62	6.75
	2 ML YEARS		28	2	0	6	36.1	165	34	21	19	7	0	0	2	20	5	35	2	1	2	2	.500	0	0-0	2	4.87	4.71

Corey Kluber

Pitches: R **Bats:** R **Pos:** SP-32 CLUE-burr **Ht:** 6'4" **Wt:** 215 **Born:** 4/10/1986 **Age:** 30

Year Team	Lg	G	GS	CG	GF	IP	BFP	H	R	ER	HR	SH	SF	HB	TBB	IBB	SO	WP	Bk	W	L	Pct	Sh	Sv-Op	Hld	ERC	ERA
2011 Cle	AL	3	0	0	2	4.1	25	6	4	4	0	0	0	0	3	0	5	1	0	0	0	-	0	0-0	0	8.12	8.31
2012 Cle	AL	12	12	0	0	63.0	281	76	44	36	9	1	0	4	18	0	54	2	0	2	5	.286	0	0-0	0	5.38	5.14
2013 Cle	AL	26	24	0	1	147.1	608	153	67	63	15	4	2	5	33	0	136	1	0	11	5	.688	0	0-0	0	3.83	3.85
2014 Cle	AL	34	34	3	0	235.2	951	207	72	64	14	5	2	6	51	3	269	3	0	18	9	.667	1	0-0	0	2.57	2.44
2015 Cle	AL	32	32	4	0	222.0	886	189	92	86	22	7	4	11	45	3	245	6	1	9	16	.360	0	0-0	0	2.74	3.49
5 ML YEARS		107	102	7	3	672.1	2751	631	279	253	60	17	8	28	150	6	709	13	1	40	35	.533	1	0-0	0	3.17	3.39

Corey Knebel

Pitches: R **Bats:** R **Pos:** RP-48 kuh-NAY-bull **Ht:** 6'4" **Wt:** 210 **Born:** 11/26/1991 **Age:** 24

Year Team	Lg	G	GS	CG	GF	IP	BFP	H	R	ER	HR	SH	SF	HB	TBB	IBB	SO	WP	Bk	W	L	Pct	Sh	Sv-Op	Hld	ERC	ERA
2013 Wmich	A	31	0	0	30	31.0	117	14	4	3	0	2	0	0	10	0	41	4	0	2	1	.667	0	15--	-	0.95	0.87
2014 Erie	AA	11	0	0	8	15.0	61	8	4	2	1	0	1	0	8	0	23	1	0	3	0	1.000	0	1--	-	1.94	1.20
2014 Toledo	AAA	14	0	0	3	18.1	69	6	4	4	0	2	1	2	9	0	20	1	0	1	1	.500	0	2--	-	1.17	1.96
2014 RdRck	AAA	9	0	0	1	12.0	50	9	5	5	2	0	0	1	5	0	20	0	0	1	0	1.000	0	0--	-	3.56	3.75
2015 ColSpr	AAA	16	0	0	14	15.1	65	14	8	8	1	1	0	0	7	1	22	1	0	1	2	.333	0	6--	-	3.51	4.70
2014 Det	AL	8	0	0	4	8.2	39	11	7	6	0	0	0	0	3	0	11	1	0	0	0	-	0	0-0	0	4.65	6.23
2015 Mil	NL	48	0	0	15	50.1	209	44	18	18	8	0	0	2	17	1	58	1	0	0	0	-	0	0-1	3	3.69	3.22
2 ML YEARS		56	0	0	19	59.0	248	55	25	24	8	0	0	2	20	1	69	2	0	0	0	-	0	0-1	3	3.83	3.66

Guido Knudson

Pitches: R **Bats:** R **Pos:** RP-4 GHEE-do ka-NUDE-sun **Ht:** 6'1" **Wt:** 185 **Born:** 8/5/1989 **Age:** 26

Year Team	Lg	G	GS	CG	GF	IP	BFP	H	R	ER	HR	SH	SF	HB	TBB	IBB	SO	WP	Bk	W	L	Pct	Sh	Sv-Op	Hld	ERC	ERA
2011 2 Tms	Low	18	0	0	7	26.1	111	22	14	10	0	3	3	2	7	0	23	2	0	1	2	.333	0	0--	-	2.27	3.42
2012 2 Tms	Low	16	0	0	8	30.1	130	31	18	13	3	1	0	1	6	1	27	2	0	0	1	.000	0	0--	-	3.37	3.86
2013 Wmich	A	42	0	0	10	50.1	197	41	12	10	3	3	0	3	10	2	38	1	0	1	2	.333	0	0--	-	2.35	1.79
2014 Erie	AA	28	2	0	8	61.1	266	64	31	29	4	3	1	2	26	2	66	2	0	1	6	.143	0	2--	-	4.30	4.26
2014 Lkland	A+	12	0	0	10	17.1	71	13	6	6	1	1	0	0	6	0	23	2	0	2	1	.667	0	5--	-	2.26	3.12
2015 Erie	AA	8	1	0	3	17.1	76	16	6	6	2	0	1	0	8	0	16	1	0	0	0	-	0	1--	-	3.91	3.12
2015 Toledo	AAA	32	0	0	16	42.1	174	28	12	11	1	2	3	0	21	3	44	2	0	1	2	.333	0	10--	-	2.06	2.34
2015 Det	AL	4	0	0	2	5.0	31	13	10	10	5	0	0	0	3	1	6	1	0	0	0	-	0	0-0	0	25.32	18.00

Tom Koehler

Pitches: R **Bats:** R **Pos:** SP-31; RP-1 COLE-err **Ht:** 6'3" **Wt:** 235 **Born:** 6/29/1986 **Age:** 30

Year Team	Lg	G	GS	CG	GF	IP	BFP	H	R	ER	HR	SH	SF	HB	TBB	IBB	SO	WP	Bk	W	L	Pct	Sh	Sv-Op	Hld	ERC	ERA
2012 Mia	NL	8	1	0	0	13.1	56	15	8	8	4	0	0	0	2	1	13	0	0	0	1	.000	0	0-0	0	4.99	5.40
2013 Mia	NL	29	23	0	2	143.0	601	140	72	70	14	3	2	5	54	2	92	7	0	5	10	.333	0	0-0	0	4.08	4.41
2014 Mia	NL	32	32	0	0	191.1	803	177	84	81	16	6	5	7	71	0	153	4	0	10	10	.500	0	0-0	0	3.63	3.81
2015 Mia	NL	32	31	0	0	187.1	800	180	96	85	22	6	5	6	77	3	137	2	0	11	14	.440	0	0-0	0	4.17	4.08
4 ML YEARS		101	87	0	2	535.0	2260	512	260	244	56	15	12	18	204	6	395	13	0	26	35	.426	0	0-0	0	3.97	4.10

Michael Kohn

Pitches: R **Bats:** R **Pos:** RP-6 KAHN **Ht:** 6'2" **Wt:** 200 **Born:** 6/26/1986 **Age:** 30

Year Team	Lg	G	GS	CG	GF	IP	BFP	H	R	ER	HR	SH	SF	HB	TBB	IBB	SO	WP	Bk	W	L	Pct	Sh	Sv-Op	Hld	ERC	ERA
2015 Gwnntt*	AAA	7	0	0	2	10.0	41	9	5	5	0	0	0	0	5	0	11	0	0	0	1	.000	0	0--	-	3.39	4.50
2010 LAA	AL	24	0	0	8	21.1	95	17	5	5	0	4	0	0	16	1	20	0	0	2	0	1.000	0	1-1	1	3.45	2.11
2011 LAA	AL	14	0	0	7	12.1	60	14	10	10	6	0	0	1	9	0	9	1	0	1	0	1.000	0	1-2	1	9.92	7.30
2013 LAA	AL	63	0	0	13	53.0	231	42	22	22	7	1	1	3	28	3	52	4	0	1	4	.200	0	0-2	8	3.72	3.74
2014 LAA	AL	25	0	0	4	23.2	102	11	9	8	1	0	1	2	20	1	26	3	0	2	1	.667	0	0-0	3	2.73	3.04
2015 Atl	NL	6	0	0	1	4.2	19	0	0	0	0	0	0	0	6	0	4	0	0	0	0	-	0	0-0	1	1.53	0.00
5 ML YEARS		132	0	0	33	115.0	506	84	46	45	14	5	2	6	79	5	111	8	0	5	6	.455	0	2-5	14	3.96	3.52

George Kontos

Pitches: R **Bats:** R **Pos:** RP-73 KAHN-tose **Ht:** 6'3" **Wt:** 215 **Born:** 6/12/1985 **Age:** 31

Year Team	Lg	G	GS	CG	GF	IP	BFP	H	R	ER	HR	SH	SF	HB	TBB	IBB	SO	WP	Bk	W	L	Pct	Sh	Sv-Op	Hld	ERC	ERA
2011 NYY	AL	7	0	0	4	6.0	24	4	2	2	1	0	0	0	3	0	6	0	0	0	0	-	0	0-0	0	3.20	3.00
2012 SF	NL	44	0	0	9	43.2	177	34	15	12	3	0	2	0	12	0	44	1	0	2	1	.667	0	0-1	5	2.23	2.47
2013 SF	NL	52	0	0	9	55.1	238	60	30	27	7	1	4	2	18	2	47	1	0	2	2	.500	0	0-1	5	4.59	4.39
2014 SF	NL	24	0	0	7	32.1	125	24	10	10	1	0	0	0	11	3	27	1	0	4	0	1.000	0	0-0	1	2.07	2.78
2015 SF	NL	73	0	0	12	73.1	284	57	20	19	9	1	3	0	12	3	44	3	0	4	4	.500	0	0-2	14	2.14	2.33
Postseason		8	0	0	1	5.1	22	6	4	4	1	1	0	0	1	0	2	0	0	0	0	-	0	0-0	1	4.65	6.75
5 ML YEARS		200	0	0	41	210.2	848	179	77	70	21	2	9	2	56	8	168	6	0	12	7	.632	0	0-4	25	2.77	2.99

Pete Kozma

KAHZ-muh

Bats: R **Throws:** R **Pos:** SS-31;PH-20;PR-18;2B-17;3B-13;1B-1;LF-1;DH-1   **Ht:** 6'0" **Wt:** 190 **Born:** 4/11/1988 **Age:** 28

							BATTING													RUNNING			AVERAGES			
Year	Team	Lg	G	AB	H	2B	3B	HR	(Hm | Rd)	TB	R	RBI	RC	TBB	IBB	SO	HBP	SH	SF	SB	CS	GDP	Avg	OBP	Slg	OPS
2011	StL	NL	16	17	3	1	0	0	(0 | 0)	4	2	1	2	4	0	4	0	1	0	0	0	0	.176	.333	.235	.569
2012	StL	NL	26	72	24	5	3	2	(0 | 2)	41	11	14	13	7	1	19	0	1	2	2	0	4	.333	.383	.569	.952
2013	StL	NL	143	410	89	20	0	1	(0 | 1)	112	44	35	39	34	8	91	0	1	3	3	1	6	.217	.275	.273	.548
2014	StL	NL	14	23	7	3	0	0	(0 | 0)	10	4	0	3	3	0	4	0	0	0	0	0	0	.304	.385	.435	.819
2015	StL	NL	76	99	15	0	0	0	(0 | 0)	15	15	2	4	10	2	21	1	1	0	3	1	0	.152	.236	.152	.388
	Postseason		29	82	14	3	0	1	(0 | 1)	20	11	9	13	12	3	24	2	1	0	3	1	1	.171	.292	.244	.536
	5 ML YEARS		275	621	138	29	3	3	(0 | 3)	182	76	52	61	58	11	139	1	4	5	8	2	10	.222	.288	.293	.581

Erik Kratz

Bats: R **Throws:** R **Pos:** C-7;PH-7;1B-2   **Ht:** 6'4" **Wt:** 240 **Born:** 6/15/1980 **Age:** 36

							BATTING													RUNNING			AVERAGES			
Year	Team	Lg	G	AB	H	2B	3B	HR	(Hm	Rd)	TB	R	RBI	RC	TBB	IBB	SO	HBP	SH	SF	SB	CS	GDP	Avg	OBP	Slg	OPS
2015	Omha*	AAA	15	56	12	2	0	4	(-	-)	26	7	12	7	5	0	9	0	0	1	0	0	2	.214	.274	.464	.738
2015	Tacom*	AAA	10	39	8	4	0	0	(-	-)	12	3	5	3	3	0	7	1	0	0	0	0	1	.205	.279	.308	.587
2015	LV*	AAA	26	77	24	8	1	3	(-	-)	43	14	15	19	18	0	18	0	0	2	1	0	1	.312	.433	.558	.991
2010	Pit	NL	9	34	4	0	0	0	(0	0)	4	2	1	0	2	0	9	0	0	0	0	0	0	.118	.167	.118	.284
2011	Phi	NL	2	6	2	1	0	0	(0	0)	3	0	0	1	0	0	1	0	0	0	0	0	0	.333	.333	.500	.833
2012	Phi	NL	50	141	35	9	0	9	(6	3)	71	14	26	20	11	2	34	2	0	3	0	0	2	.248	.306	.504	.809
2013	Phi	NL	68	197	42	7	0	9	(5	4)	76	21	26	15	18	4	45	1	0	2	0	0	11	.213	.280	.386	.666
2014	2 Tms	AL	47	110	24	4	0	5	(1	4)	43	12	13	7	4	1	22	0	0	1	0	0	4	.218	.243	.391	.634
2015	2 Tms	AL	16	26	5	2	0	0	(0	0)	7	3	3	1	1	0	5	0	0	1	0	0	0	.192	.214	.269	.484
14	Tor	AL	34	81	16	3	0	3	(1	2)	28	8	10	5	3	0	12	0	0	0	0	0	3	.198	.226	.346	.572
14	KC	AL	13	29	8	1	0	2	(0	2)	15	4	3	2	1	1	10	0	0	1	0	0	1	.276	.290	.517	.808
15	KC	AL	4	4	0	0	0	0	(0	0)	0	0	1	0	0	0	2	0	0	1	0	0	0	.000	.000	.000	.000
15	Phi	NL	12	22	5	2	0	0	(0	0)	7	3	2	1	1	0	3	0	0	0	0	0	0	.227	.261	.318	.579
	6 ML YEARS		192	514	112	23	0	23	(12	11)	204	52	69	44	36	7	116	3	0	7	0	0	17	.218	.270	.397	.667

Marc Krauss

Bats: L **Throws:** R **Pos:** 1B-20;DH-7;LF-1;PH-1   **Ht:** 6'2" **Wt:** 245 **Born:** 10/5/1987 **Age:** 28

							BATTING													RUNNING			AVERAGES			
Year	Team	Lg	G	AB	H	2B	3B	HR	(Hm	Rd)	TB	R	RBI	RC	TBB	IBB	SO	HBP	SH	SF	SB	CS	GDP	Avg	OBP	Slg	OPS
2015	Salt Lk*	AAA	47	159	46	8	3	4	(-	-)	72	23	29	32	35	0	38	0	0	1	0	1	4	.289	.415	.453	.868
2015	Toledo*	AAA	23	85	21	4	2	0	(-	-)	29	14	9	12	18	1	26	0	0	0	2	2	0	.247	.379	.341	.720
2013	Hou	AL	52	134	28	9	0	4	(1	3)	49	11	13	12	10	0	45	1	0	1	2	0	2	.209	.267	.366	.633
2014	Hou	AL	67	186	36	6	0	6	(2	4)	60	16	21	15	21	0	54	1	0	0	0	0	7	.194	.279	.323	.601
2015	3 Tms	AL	27	78	11	3	0	2	(0	2)	20	3	8	2	3	0	31	0	0	0	0	0	0	.141	.173	.256	.429
15	LAA	AL	11	35	5	2	0	1	(0	1)	10	2	5	2	3	0	11	0	0	0	0	0	0	.143	.211	.286	.496
15	TB	AL	4	10	1	1	0	0	(0	0)	2	0	1	0	0	0	7	0	0	0	0	0	0	.100	.100	.200	.300
15	Det	AL	12	33	5	0	0	1	(0	1)	8	1	2	0	0	0	13	0	0	0	0	0	0	.152	.152	.242	.394
	3 ML YEARS		146	398	75	18	0	12	(3	9)	129	30	42	29	34	0	130	2	0	1	2	0	9	.188	.255	.324	.579

Ian Krol

KROHL

Pitches: L **Bats:** L **Pos:** RP-33   **Ht:** 6'1" **Wt:** 210 **Born:** 5/9/1991 **Age:** 25

			HOW MUCH HE PITCHED					WHAT HE GAVE UP											THE RESULTS						
Year	Team	Lg	G	GS	CG	GF	IP	BFP	H	R	ER	HR	SH	SF	HB	TBB	IBB	SO	WP	Bk	W	L	Pct	Sh	Sv-Op	Hld	ERC	ERA
2015	Toledo*	AAA	28	0	0	5	31.1	128	21	10	8	0	1	1	0	13	0	34	3	0	1	1	.500	0	1- -	-	1.79	2.30
2013	Was	NL	32	0	0	10	27.1	117	28	12	12	5	2	1	0	8	1	22	2	0	2	1	.667	0	0-1	2	4.24	3.95
2014	Det	AL	45	0	0	5	32.2	154	42	23	18	6	0	1	2	13	4	28	1	1	0	0	-	0	1-4	10	6.35	4.96
2015	Det	AL	33	0	0	6	28.0	129	31	19	18	4	2	0	2	17	1	26	0	0	2	3	.400	0	0-1	1	6.23	5.79
	3 ML YEARS		110	0	0	21	88.0	400	101	54	48	15	4	2	4	38	6	76	3	1	4	4	.500	0	1-6	13	5.64	4.91

Kyle Kubitza

kuh-BIT-sah

Bats: L **Throws:** R **Pos:** 3B-13;PH-3;PR-3;2B-2;LF-2;DH-1   **Ht:** 6'3" **Wt:** 210 **Born:** 7/15/1990 **Age:** 25

							BATTING													RUNNING			AVERAGES			
Year	Team	Lg	G	AB	H	2B	3B	HR	(Hm	Rd)	TB	R	RBI	RC	TBB	IBB	SO	HBP	SH	SF	SB	CS	GDP	Avg	OBP	Slg	OPS
2011	Danvle	R+	44	162	52	16	3	1	(-	-)	77	36	34	33	24	0	38	1	1	2	9	3	0	.321	.407	.475	.883
2012	Rome	A	128	448	107	24	9	9	(-	-)	176	68	59	66	73	1	127	5	1	4	18	11	5	.239	.349	.393	.742
2013	Lynbrg	A+	132	435	113	28	6	12	(-	-)	189	75	57	73	80	0	132	6	3	3	8	16	5	.260	.380	.434	.814
2014	Missi	AA	132	440	130	31	11	8	(-	-)	207	76	55	90	77	8	133	7	0	5	21	6	8	.295	.405	.470	.875
2015	Salt Lk	AAA	117	457	124	43	5	7	(-	-)	198	63	50	76	60	1	125	4	0	5	7	1	4	.271	.357	.433	.791
2015	LAA	AL	19	36	7	0	0	0	(0	0)	7	6	1	1	3	0	15	0	0	0	0	0	2	.194	.256	.194	.451

Tommy La Stella

Bats: L **Throws:** R **Pos:** PH-16;2B-14;3B-12   **Ht:** 5'11" **Wt:** 190 **Born:** 1/31/1989 **Age:** 27

							BATTING													RUNNING			AVERAGES			
Year	Team	Lg	G	AB	H	2B	3B	HR	(Hm	Rd)	TB	R	RBI	RC	TBB	IBB	SO	HBP	SH	SF	SB	CS	GDP	Avg	OBP	Slg	OPS
2011	Rome	A	63	232	76	13	5	9	(-	-)	126	46	40	50	26	0	28	5	3	4	2	2	5	.328	.401	.543	.944
2012	2 Tms	Low	90	311	93	22	6	6	(-	-)	145	47	59	62	40	2	25	12	3	10	13	2	2	.299	.389	.466	.855
2013	Missi	AA	81	283	97	21	2	4	(-	-)	134	32	41	58	37	3	34	2	1	0	7	1	6	.343	.422	.473	.896
2014	Gwnntt	AAA	47	167	49	6	1	1	(-	-)	60	18	23	26	25	0	14	2	0	4	1	1	4	.293	.384	.359	.743

Year Team	Lg	G	AB	H	2B	3B	HR	(Hm	Rd)	TB	R	RBI	RC	TBB	IBB	SO	HBP	SH	SF	SB	CS	GDP	Avg	OBP	Slg	OPS
								BATTING												**RUNNING**			**AVERAGES**			
2015 Tenn	AA	10	36	9	3	0	0	(-	-)	12	9	3	4	3	0	1	1	0	0	0	0	1	.250	.325	.333	.658
2014 Atl	NL	93	319	80	16	1	1	(1	0)	101	22	31	36	36	2	40	1	3	1	2	1	8	.251	.328	.317	.644
2015 ChC	NL	33	67	18	6	0	1	(1	0)	27	4	11	10	5	0	7	1	0	1	2	0	1	.269	.324	.403	.727
2 ML YEARS		126	386	98	22	1	2	(2	0)	128	26	42	46	41	2	47	2	3	2	4	1	9	.254	.327	.332	.659

John Lackey

Pitches: R Bats: R Pos: SP-33   Ht: 6'6" Wt: 235 Born: 10/23/1978 Age: 37

Year Team	Lg	G	GS	CG	GF	IP	BFP	H	R	ER	HR	SH	SF	HB	TBB	IBB	SO	WP	Bk	W	L	Pct	Sh	Sv-Op	Hld	ERC	ERA
		HOW MUCH HE PITCHED						**WHAT HE GAVE UP**												**THE RESULTS**							
2002 LAA	AL	18	18	1	0	108.1	465	113	52	44	10	0	4	4	33	0	69	7	2	9	4	.692	0	0-0	0	4.03	3.66
2003 LAA	AL	33	33	2	0	204.0	885	223	117	105	31	2	6	10	66	4	151	11	1	10	16	.385	2	0-0	0	4.88	4.63
2004 LAA	AL	33	32	1	0	198.1	855	215	108	103	22	9	4	8	60	4	144	11	1	14	13	.519	1	0-0	0	4.39	4.67
2005 LAA	AL	33	33	1	0	209.0	892	208	85	80	13	1	2	11	71	3	199	18	0	14	5	.737	0	0-0	0	3.76	3.44
2006 LAA	AL	33	33	3	0	217.2	922	203	98	86	14	8	6	9	72	4	190	16	0	13	11	.542	2	0-0	0	3.31	3.56
2007 LAA	AL	33	33	2	0	224.0	929	219	87	75	18	1	1	12	52	2	179	9	1	19	9	.679	2	0-0	0	3.40	**3.01**
2008 LAA	AL	24	24	3	0	163.1	675	161	71	68	26	5	1	10	40	1	130	5	0	12	5	.706	0	0-0	0	4.10	3.75
2009 LAA	AL	27	27	1	0	176.1	748	177	84	75	17	9	10	9	47	1	139	6	0	11	8	.579	1	0-0	0	3.73	3.83
2010 Bos	AL	33	33	0	0	215.0	930	233	114	105	18	4	5	9	72	2	156	3	0	14	11	.560	0	0-0	0	4.37	4.40
2011 Bos	AL	28	28	0	0	160.0	743	203	119	**114**	20	2	6	**19**	56	1	108	11	0	12	12	.500	0	0-0	0	6.11	6.41
2013 Bos	AL	29	29	2	0	189.1	778	179	80	74	26	3	3	6	40	0	161	4	0	10	13	.435	0	0-0	0	3.42	3.52
2014 2 Tms		31	31	1	0	198.0	833	206	94	84	24	6	3	1	47	1	164	4	2	14	10	.583	0	0-0	0	3.81	3.82
2015 StL	NL	33	**33**	1	0	218.0	896	211	71	67	21	11	4	4	53	5	175	5	3	13	10	.565	0	0-0	0	3.34	2.77
14 Bos	AL	21	21	1	0	137.1	572	137	60	55	15	2	3	0	32	0	116	3	1	11	7	.611	0	0-0	0	3.46	3.60
14 StL	NL	10	10	0	0	60.2	261	69	34	29	9	4	0	1	15	1	48	1	1	3	3	.500	0	0-0	0	4.63	4.30
Postseason		21	18	0	0	117.0	490	110	42	40	4	3	4	3	37	5	89	7	0	7	5	.583	0	0-0	1	3.02	3.08
13 ML YEARS		388	387	18	0	2481.1	10551	2551	1180	1080	260	61	55	112	709	28	1965	110	10	165	127	.565	8	0-0	0	3.99	3.92

Tyler Ladendorf

Bats: R Throws: R Pos: LF-3;PH-3;2B-2;CF-2;3B-1;SS-1   Ht: 6'0" Wt: 190 Born: 3/7/1988 Age: 28

Year Team	Lg	G	AB	H	2B	3B	HR	(Hm	Rd)	TB	R	RBI	RC	TBB	IBB	SO	HBP	SH	SF	SB	CS	GDP	Avg	OBP	Slg	OPS
								BATTING												**RUNNING**			**AVERAGES**			
2011 Mdlnd	AA	125	432	97	17	3	6	(-	-)	138	55	35	45	47	0	87	6	7	2	6	5	10	.225	.308	.319	.627
2012 Mdlnd	AA	104	416	100	20	1	9	(-	-)	149	59	54	52	42	0	89	11	4	3	7	4	14	.240	.324	.358	.682
2013 Mdlnd	AA	83	266	70	16	1	6	(-	-)	106	34	40	38	27	2	45	5	2	2	2	0	8	.263	.340	.398	.738
2014 Scrmto	AAA	78	273	81	18	3	2	(-	-)	111	44	43	45	35	0	56	2	0	4	3	1	4	.297	.376	.407	.782
2015 Nashv	AAA	20	83	22	2	1	1	(-	-)	29	3	8	9	5	0	23	1	0	1	0	1	1	.265	.311	.349	.661
2015 Oak	AL	9	17	4	0	1	0	(0	0)	6	3	2	0	1	0	2	0	0	0	0	0	0	.235	.278	.353	.631

Aaron Laffey

Pitches: L Bats: L Pos: RP-3   LAFF-ee   Ht: 6'0" Wt: 200 Born: 4/15/1985 Age: 31

Year Team	Lg	G	GS	CG	GF	IP	BFP	H	R	ER	HR	SH	SF	HB	TBB	IBB	SO	WP	Bk	W	L	Pct	Sh	Sv-Op	Hld	ERC	ERA
		HOW MUCH HE PITCHED						**WHAT HE GAVE UP**												**THE RESULTS**							
2015 Albq*	AAA	27	12	0	1	90.0	410	103	45	39	7	7	3	1	42	4	63	5	1	5	4	.556	0	0- -	-	4.92	3.90
2007 Cle	AL	9	9	0	0	49.1	207	54	26	25	2	1	2	4	12	0	25	2	1	4	2	.667	0	0-0	0	4.02	4.56
2008 Cle	AL	16	16	0	0	93.2	409	103	52	44	10	2	0	9	31	1	43	5	1	5	7	.417	0	0-0	0	4.86	4.23
2009 Cle	AL	25	19	0	3	121.2	539	140	69	60	9	0	4	2	57	1	59	1	1	7	9	.438	0	1-1	0	5.20	4.44
2010 Cle	AL	29	5	0	1	55.2	253	62	30	28	1	0	3	2	28	1	28	1	0	2	3	.400	0	0-0	5	4.61	4.53
2011 2 Tms	AL	47	0	0	7	53.1	247	67	24	23	7	2	2	3	21	3	30	2	1	3	2	.600	0	0-1	5	5.89	3.88
2012 Tor	AL	22	16	0	1	100.2	429	100	56	51	17	2	0	5	37	1	48	2	0	4	6	.400	0	0-0	0	4.65	4.56
2013 2 Tms		5	3	0	1	12.2	64	18	10	10	1	2	2	2	10	0	9	0	0	0	0	-	0	0-0	0	9.19	7.11
2015 Col	NL	3	0	0	0	7.1	33	8	3	3	1	2	0	1	3	1	3	0	0	1	0	1.000	0	0-0	0	5.27	3.68
11 Sea	AL	36	0	0	7	42.2	197	54	20	19	7	2	1	1	16	3	24	2	1	1	1	.500	0	0-1	5	5.92	4.01
11 NYY	AL	11	0	0	0	10.2	50	13	4	4	0	0	1	2	5	0	6	0	0	2	1	.667	0	0-0	0	5.66	3.38
13 NYM	NL	4	2	0	1	10.0	50	16	8	8	1	1	1	2	5	0	9	0	0	0	0	-	0	0-0	0	9.47	7.20
13 Tor	AL	1	1	0	0	2.2	14	2	2	2	0	1	1	0	5	0	0	0	0	0	0	-	0	0-0	0	7.93	6.75
Postseason		1	0	0	0	4.2	16	1	0	0	0	0	0	0	1	0	3	0	0	0	0	-	0	0-0	0	0.30	0.00
8 ML YEARS		156	68	0	13	494.1	2181	552	270	244	48	11	13	28	199	8	245	13	4	26	29	.473	0	1-2	10	5.01	4.44

Bobby LaFromboise

Pitches: L Bats: L Pos: RP-11   lah-frahm-BOYCE   Ht: 6'4" Wt: 225 Born: 6/25/1986 Age: 30

Year Team	Lg	G	GS	CG	GF	IP	BFP	H	R	ER	HR	SH	SF	HB	TBB	IBB	SO	WP	Bk	W	L	Pct	Sh	Sv-Op	Hld	ERC	ERA
		HOW MUCH HE PITCHED						**WHAT HE GAVE UP**												**THE RESULTS**							
2015 Indy*	AAA	54	0	0	10	54.1	222	41	18	18	5	1	1	0	21	1	52	1	1	1	2	.333	0	0- -	-	2.64	2.98
2013 Sea	AL	10	0	0	4	10.2	47	12	8	7	0	1	0	0	4	1	11	0	0	0	1	.000	0	0-0	1	3.77	5.91
2014 Pit	NL	6	0	0	1	3.2	14	3	1	1	0	0	0	0	0	0	4	0	0	0	0	-	0	0-0	2	2.49	2.45
2015 Pit	NL	11	0	0	4	8.0	29	5	1	1	1	0	0	0	1	0	8	0	0	0	0	-	0	0-0	0	1.50	1.13
Postseason		1	0	0	0	0.2	1	0	0	0	0	0	0	0	0	0	0	0	0	0	0	-	0	0-0	0	0.00	0.00
3 ML YEARS		27	0	0	9	22.1	90	20	10	9	2	1	0	0	5	1	23	1	0	0	1	.000	0	0-0	3	2.74	3.63

Juan Lagares

Bats: R Throws: R Pos: CF-137;PH-12;RF-2;PR-2   luh-GAR-ess   Ht: 6'1" Wt: 215 Born: 3/17/1989 Age: 27

Year Team	Lg	G	AB	H	2B	3B	HR	(Hm	Rd)	TB	R	RBI	RC	TBB	IBB	SO	HBP	SH	SF	SB	CS	GDP	Avg	OBP	Slg	OPS
2013 NYM	NL	121	392	95	21	5	4	(1	3)	138	35	34	36	20	4	96	2	5	2	6	3	6	.242	.281	.352	.633
2014 NYM	NL	116	416	117	24	3	4	(2	2)	159	46	47	53	20	1	87	7	3	6	13	4	6	.281	.321	.382	.703
2015 NYM	NL	143	441	114	16	5	6	(2	4)	158	47	41	51	16	2	87	4	1	3	7	3	6	.259	.289	.358	.647
3 ML YEARS		380	1249	326	61	13	14	(5	9)	455	128	122	140	56	7	270	13	9	11	26	10	18	.261	.297	.364	.662

Gerald Laird

Bats: R Throws: R Pos: C-1   Ht: 6'1" Wt: 230 Born: 11/13/1979 Age: 36

Year Team	Lg	G	AB	H	2B	3B	HR	(Hm	Rd)	TB	R	RBI	RC	TBB	IBB	SO	HBP	SH	SF	SB	CS	GDP	Avg	OBP	Slg	OPS
2003 Tex	AL	19	44	12	2	1	1	(0	1)	19	9	4	5	5	0	11	1	0	0	0	0	2	.273	.360	.432	.792
2004 Tex	AL	49	147	33	6	0	1	(1	0)	42	20	16	11	12	0	35	2	4	3	0	1	5	.224	.287	.286	.572
2005 Tex	AL	13	40	9	2	0	1	(0	1)	14	7	4	4	2	0	7	0	0	0	0	0	1	.225	.262	.350	.612
2006 Tex	AL	78	243	72	20	1	7	(3	4)	115	46	22	24	12	0	54	2	1	2	3	1	7	.296	.332	.473	.805
2007 Tex	AL	120	407	91	18	3	9	(6	3)	142	48	47	45	30	1	103	2	5	4	6	2	3	.224	.278	.349	.627
2008 Tex	AL	95	344	95	24	0	6	(3	3)	137	54	41	46	23	2	63	6	4	4	2	4	5	.276	.329	.398	.727
2009 Det	AL	135	413	93	23	2	4	(1	3)	132	49	33	41	40	0	68	10	10	4	5	0	11	.225	.306	.320	.626
2010 Det	AL	89	270	56	11	0	5	(2	3)	82	22	25	22	18	0	57	3	6	2	3	1	7	.207	.263	.304	.567
2011 StL	AL	37	95	22	7	1	1	(1	0)	34	11	12	10	9	3	19	1	2	1	1	1	3	.232	.302	.358	.660
2012 Det	AL	63	174	49	8	1	2	(0	2)	65	24	11	19	14	0	21	1	1	0	0	0	4	.282	.337	.374	.710
2013 Atl	NL	47	121	34	8	0	1	(1	0)	45	12	13	18	14	0	23	3	2	1	1	1	4	.281	.367	.372	.739
2014 Atl	NL	53	152	31	8	0	0	(0	0)	39	12	10	9	14	2	33	1	0	0	0	0	6	.204	.275	.257	.532
2015 Ari	NL	1	2	0	0	0	0	(0	0)	0	0	0	0	0	0	0	0	0	0	0	0	0	.000	.000	.000	.000
Postseason		11	22	1	0	0	0	(0	0)	1	0	0	0	0	0	6	1	0	0	0	0	0	.045	.087	.045	.132
13 ML YEARS		799	2452	597	137	9	38	(18	20)	866	314	238	254	193	8	494	32	35	22	21	11	58	.243	.305	.353	.658

Junior Lake

Bats: R Throws: R Pos: LF-10;RF-10;PH-9;CF-3;DH-2;PR-1   Ht: 6'3" Wt: 215 Born: 3/27/1990 Age: 26

Year Team	Lg	G	AB	H	2B	3B	HR	(Hm	Rd)	TB	R	RBI	RC	TBB	IBB	SO	HBP	SH	SF	SB	CS	GDP	Avg	OBP	Slg	OPS
2015 Iowa*	AAA	58	197	62	10	0	7	(-	-)	93	37	31	37	30	0	53	1	1	2	9	9	6	.315	.404	.472	.876
2015 Norfolk*	AAA	15	50	15	3	0	0	(-	-)	18	2	5	8	10	0	16	0	0	1	3	2	0	.300	.410	.360	.770
2013 ChC	NL	64	236	67	16	0	6	(4	2)	101	26	16	26	13	0	68	4	1	0	4	4	2	.284	.332	.428	.760
2014 ChC	NL	108	308	65	10	3	9	(5	4)	108	30	25	18	14	0	110	1	1	2	7	3	3	.211	.246	.351	.597
2015 2 Tms		29	80	16	7	0	1	(0	1)	26	4	5	6	4	0	29	0	0	0	4	0	1	.200	.238	.325	.563
15 ChC	NL	21	58	13	4	0	1	(0	1)	20	2	5	6	4	0	20	0	0	0	4	0	1	.224	.274	.345	.619
15 Bal	AL	8	22	3	3	0	0	(0	0)	6	2	0	0	0	0	9	0	0	0	0	0	0	.136	.136	.273	.409
3 ML YEARS		201	624	148	33	3	16	(9	7)	235	60	46	50	31	0	207	5	2	2	15	7	6	.237	.278	.377	.655

Ryan LaMarre

Bats: R Throws: L Pos: CF-13;PH-4;PR-3;LF-2;RF-1   la-MARR   Ht: 6'1" Wt: 205 Born: 11/21/1988 Age: 27

Year Team	Lg	G	AB	H	2B	3B	HR	(Hm	Rd)	TB	R	RBI	RC	TBB	IBB	SO	HBP	SH	SF	SB	CS	GDP	Avg	OBP	Slg	OPS
2011 Bkrsfld	A+	117	445	124	17	3	6	(-	-)	165	78	47	66	42	1	97	8	2	6	52	14	8	.279	.347	.371	.718
2012 Pnscla	AA	133	482	127	22	3	5	(-	-)	170	68	32	68	60	0	119	10	4	2	30	10	5	.263	.356	.353	.708
2013 Pnscla	AA	126	451	111	19	4	10	(-	-)	168	55	39	58	44	1	93	11	6	3	23	13	8	.246	.326	.373	.699
2014 Lsvlle	AAA	17	50	10	2	0	1	(-	-)	15	6	6	5	8	0	17	0	1	0	1	1	0	.200	.310	.300	.610
2015 Lsvlle	AAA	91	300	77	17	1	8	(-	-)	120	33	18	38	18	0	88	5	3	3	11	4	7	.257	.307	.400	.707
2015 Cin	NL	21	25	2	0	0	0	(0	0)	2	2	0	0	0	0	9	0	1	0	0	0	1	.080	.080	.080	.160

Jake Lamb

Bats: L Throws: R Pos: 3B-95;PH-11;1B-8   Ht: 6'3" Wt: 205 Born: 10/9/1990 Age: 25

Year Team	Lg	G	AB	H	2B	3B	HR	(Hm	Rd)	TB	R	RBI	RC	TBB	IBB	SO	HBP	SH	SF	SB	CS	GDP	Avg	OBP	Slg	OPS
2012 Msoula	R+	67	280	92	22	5	9	(-	-)	151	47	57	59	24	1	51	7	0	4	8	2	8	.329	.390	.539	.930
2013 2 Tms	Low	69	248	75	22	0	13	(-	-)	136	48	52	58	50	2	75	3	0	3	0	0	10	.302	.421	.548	.969
2014 Mobile	AA	103	374	119	35	5	14	(-	-)	206	60	79	83	50	3	99	6	0	9	0	0	7	.318	.399	.551	.949
2014 Ari	NL	37	126	29	4	1	4	(2	2)	47	15	11	7	6	0	37	0	0	1	1	1	4	.230	.263	.373	.636
2015 Ari	NL	107	350	92	15	5	6	(1	5)	135	38	34	39	36	3	97	1	0	3	3	2	5	.263	.331	.386	.716
2 ML YEARS		144	476	121	19	6	10	(3	7)	182	53	45	46	42	3	134	1	0	4	4	3	9	.254	.314	.382	.696

John Lamb

Pitches: L Bats: L Pos: SP-10   Ht: 6'4" Wt: 205 Born: 7/10/1990 Age: 25

Year Team	Lg	G	GS	CG	GF	IP	BFP	H	R	ER	HR	SH	SF	HB	TBB	IBB	SO	WP	Bk	W	L	Pct	Sh	Sv-Op	Hld	ERC	ERA
2011 NWArk	AA	8	8	0	0	35.0	149	33	15	12	3	0	1	1	13	1	22	1	0	1	2	.333	0	0--	-	3.61	3.09
2012 2 Tms	Low	6	6	0	0	13.0	58	15	10	10	2	0	0	4	4	0	14	1	0	0	1	.000	0	0--	-	4.86	6.92
2013 Wilmg	A+	19	19	0	0	92.2	399	109	61	58	13	2	3	4	19	0	76	1	0	4	12	.250	0	0--	-	4.79	5.63
2014 Omha	AAA	27	26	0	0	138.1	616	137	78	61	19	7	2	9	68	0	131	8	0	8	10	.444	0	0--	-	4.92	3.97
2015 Omha	AAA	17	17	0	0	94.1	382	80	35	28	7	2	3	4	29	0	96	1	2	9	1	.900	0	0--	-	2.97	2.67
2015 Cin	NL	10	10	0	0	49.2	220	58	32	32	8	2	1	2	19	0	58	0	0	1	5	.167	0	0-0	0	5.69	5.80

Andrew Lambo

Bats: L Throws: L Pos: PH-14;RF-5;LF-3   Ht: 6'3" Wt: 215 Born: 8/11/1988 Age: 27

Year	Team	Lg	G	AB	H	2B	3B	HR	(Hm	Rd)	TB	R	RBI	RC	TBB	IBB	SO	HBP	SH	SF	SB	CS	GDP	Avg	OBP	Slg	OPS
2013	Pit	NL	18	30	7	2	0	1	(0	1)	12	4	2	1	3	0	11	0	0	0	0	1	0	.233	.303	.400	.703
2014	Pit	NL	21	39	10	4	0	0	(0	0)	14	3	1	1	0	0	8	0	0	0	0	0	2	.256	.256	.359	.615
2015	Pit	NL	20	25	1	1	0	0	(0	0)	2	1	0	0	2	0	8	0	0	0	0	0	0	.040	.111	.080	.191
	3 ML YEARS		59	94	18	7	0	1	(0	1)	28	8	3	2	5	0	27	0	0	0	0	1	2	.191	.232	.298	.530

Adam LaRoche

Bats: L Throws: L Pos: DH-74;1B-48;PH-9   luh-ROASH   Ht: 6'3" Wt: 205 Born: 11/6/1979 Age: 36

Year	Team	Lg	G	AB	H	2B	3B	HR	(Hm	Rd)	TB	R	RBI	RC	TBB	IBB	SO	HBP	SH	SF	SB	CS	GDP	Avg	OBP	Slg	OPS
2004	Atl	NL	110	324	90	27	1	13	(7	6)	158	45	45	43	27	1	78	1	2	2	0	0	10	.278	.333	.488	.821
2005	Atl	NL	141	451	117	28	0	20	(11	9)	205	53	78	63	39	7	87	4	2	6	0	2	15	.259	.320	.455	.775
2006	Atl	NL	149	492	140	38	1	32	(11	21)	276	89	90	83	55	5	128	2	1	7	0	2	9	.285	.354	.561	.915
2007	Pit	NL	152	563	153	42	0	21	(10	11)	258	71	88	84	62	5	131	3	0	4	1	1	18	.272	.345	.458	.803
2008	Pit	NL	136	492	133	32	3	25	(14	11)	246	66	85	76	54	7	122	2	0	6	1	1	9	.270	.341	.500	.841
2009	3 Tms		150	555	154	38	2	25	(15	10)	271	78	83	84	69	12	142	0	0	5	2	2	11	.277	.355	.488	.843
2010	Ari	NL	151	560	146	37	2	25	(13	12)	262	75	100	84	48	4	172	3	0	4	0	1	8	.261	.320	.468	.788
2011	Was	NL	43	151	26	4	0	3	(1	2)	39	15	15	11	25	0	37	0	0	1	1	0	2	.172	.288	.258	.546
2012	Was	NL	154	571	155	35	1	33	(17	16)	291	76	100	92	67	7	138	0	0	9	1	1	10	.271	.343	.510	.853
2013	Was	NL	152	511	121	19	3	20	(9	11)	206	70	62	68	72	10	131	3	0	4	4	1	13	.237	.332	.403	.735
2014	Was	NL	140	494	128	19	0	26	(14	12)	225	73	92	83	82	9	108	2	0	8	3	0	13	.259	.362	.455	.817
2015	CWS	AL	127	429	89	21	0	12	(4	8)	146	41	44	39	49	0	133	4	0	2	0	0	10	.207	.293	.340	.634
09	Pit		87	324	80	25	1	12	(7	5)	143	46	40	38	41	6	81	0	0	3	2	2	9	.247	.329	.441	.770
09	Bos	AL	6	19	5	2	0	1	(1	0)	10	2	3	3	0	0	2	0	0	0	0	0	1	.263	.263	.526	.789
09	Atl	NL	57	212	69	11	1	12	(7	5)	118	30	40	43	28	6	59	0	0	2	0	0	1	.325	.401	.557	.957
	Postseason		17	60	12	2	0	4	(1	3)	26	7	12	7	10	1	13	0	1	0	0	0	1	.200	.314	.433	.748
	12 ML YEARS		1605	5593	1452	340	13	255	(126	129)	2583	752	882	810	649	67	1407	24	5	58	13	11	128	.260	.336	.462	.798

Mat Latos

Pitches: R Bats: R Pos: SP-21; RP-3   LAY-tos   Ht: 6'6" Wt: 245 Born: 12/9/1987 Age: 28

Year	Team	Lg	G	GS	CG	GF	IP	BFP	H	R	ER	HR	SH	SF	HB	TBB	IBB	SO	WP	Bk	W	L	Pct	Sh	Sv-Op	Hld	ERC	ERA
2009	SD	NL	10	10	0	0	50.2	212	43	29	26	7	3	1	0	23	1	39	0	2	4	5	.444	0	0-0	0	3.72	4.62
2010	SD	NL	31	31	1	0	184.2	748	150	63	60	16	4	1	2	50	3	189	5	1	14	10	.583	1	0-0	0	2.52	2.92
2011	SD	NL	31	31	0	0	194.1	799	168	82	75	16	8	7	1	62	3	185	5	0	9	14	.391	0	0-0	0	2.93	3.47
2012	Cin	NL	33	33	2	0	209.1	858	179	87	81	25	9	3	4	64	9	185	3	1	14	4	.778	0	0-0	0	3.08	3.48
2013	Cin	NL	32	32	1	0	210.2	881	197	82	74	14	12	3	10	58	5	187	8	0	14	7	.667	0	0-0	0	3.16	3.16
2014	Cin	NL	16	16	0	0	102.1	420	92	42	37	9	8	1	2	26	2	74	1	0	5	5	.500	0	0-0	0	2.94	3.25
2015	3 Tms		24	21	0	2	116.1	494	120	67	64	13	6	5	1	32	1	100	10	1	4	10	.286	0	0-0	0	3.84	4.95
15	Mia	NL	16	16	0	0	88.1	372	85	46	44	8	4	3	1	25	0	79	9	0	4	7	.364	0	0-0	0	3.36	4.48
15	LAD	NL	6	5	0	1	24.1	106	31	19	18	3	2	2	0	6	1	18	1	1	0	3	.000	0	0-0	0	5.22	6.66
15	LAA	AL	2	0	0	1	3.2	16	4	2	2	2	0	0	0	1	0	3	0	0	0	0	-	0	0-0	0	7.04	4.91
	Postseason		2	1	0	0	8.1	39	11	7	6	2	0	0	0	2	0	5	0	0	0	1	.000	0	0-0	0	6.03	6.48
	7 ML YEARS		177	174	4	2	1068.1	4412	949	452	417	100	50	21	20	315	24	959	32	5	64	55	.538	1	0-0	0	3.06	3.51

Ryan Lavarnway

Bats: R Throws: R Pos: C-30;PH-7;1B-1   luh-VARN-way   Ht: 6'4" Wt: 240 Born: 8/7/1987 Age: 28

Year	Team	Lg	G	AB	H	2B	3B	HR	(Hm	Rd)	TB	R	RBI	RC	TBB	IBB	SO	HBP	SH	SF	SB	CS	GDP	Avg	OBP	Slg	OPS
2015	Gwnntt*	AAA	13	41	11	2	0	2	(-	-)	19	5	8	7	8	0	7	0	0	0	0	0	0	.268	.388	.463	.851
2011	Bos	AL	17	39	9	2	0	2	(0	2)	17	5	8	4	4	0	10	0	0	0	0	0	1	.231	.302	.436	.738
2012	Bos	AL	46	153	24	8	0	2	(0	2)	38	11	12	4	11	0	41	0	0	2	0	0	4	.157	.211	.248	.459
2013	Bos	AL	25	77	23	7	0	1	(1	0)	33	8	14	11	2	0	17	2	0	1	0	0	3	.299	.329	.429	.758
2014	Bos	AL	9	10	0	0	0	0	(0	0)	0	0	0	0	0	0	3	0	0	0	0	0	1	.000	.000	.000	.000
2015	2 Tms		37	94	18	6	0	2	(0	2)	30	6	6	4	12	1	28	0	0	0	0	0	5	.191	.283	.319	.602
15	Bal	AL	10	28	3	1	0	0	(0	0)	4	1	0	0	4	0	7	0	0	0	0	0	1	.107	.219	.143	.362
15	Atl	NL	27	66	15	5	0	2	(0	2)	26	5	6	4	8	1	21	0	0	0	0	0	4	.227	.311	.394	.705
	5 ML YEARS		134	373	74	23	0	7	(1	6)	118	30	40	23	29	1	99	2	0	3	0	0	14	.198	.258	.316	.574

Brett Lawrie

Bats: R Throws: R Pos: 3B-109;2B-42;DH-1;PH-1   LORI   Ht: 6'0" Wt: 210 Born: 1/18/1990 Age: 26

Year	Team	Lg	G	AB	H	2B	3B	HR	(Hm	Rd)	TB	R	RBI	RC	TBB	IBB	SO	HBP	SH	SF	SB	CS	GDP	Avg	OBP	Slg	OPS
2011	Tor	AL	43	150	44	8	4	9	(5	4)	87	26	25	33	16	1	31	3	2	0	7	1	0	.293	.373	.580	.953
2012	Tor	AL	125	494	135	26	3	11	(7	4)	200	73	48	65	33	0	86	5	2	2	13	8	9	.273	.324	.405	.729
2013	Tor	AL	107	401	102	18	0	11	(4	7)	159	41	46	45	30	1	68	7	1	3	9	5	8	.254	.315	.397	.712
2014	Tor	AL	70	259	64	9	0	12	(7	5)	109	27	38	39	16	0	49	5	0	2	0	0	10	.247	.301	.421	.722
2015	Oak	AL	149	562	146	29	3	16	(6	10)	229	64	60	65	28	1	144	5	3	4	5	2	8	.260	.299	.407	.706
	5 ML YEARS		494	1866	491	90	13	59	(29	30)	784	231	217	247	123	3	378	25	8	11	34	16	25	.263	.316	.420	.736

Tommy Layne

Pitches: L Bats: L Pos: RP-64 **Ht: 6'2" Wt: 190 Born: 11/2/1984 Age: 31**

Year Team	Lg	G	GS	CG	GF	IP	BFP	H	R	ER	HR	SH	SF	HB	TBB	IBB	SO	WP	Bk	W	L	Pct	Sh	Sv-Op	Hld	ERC	ERA
2015 Pwtckt*	AAA	7	0	0	4	7.2	32	8	3	3	0	0	0	0	2	0	9	0	0	0	0	-	0	3--	-	3.13	3.52
2012 SD	NL	26	0	0	5	16.2	68	9	6	6	0	1	0	3	2	0	25	0	0	2	0	1.000	0	2-3	7	1.20	3.24
2013 SD	NL	14	0	0	2	8.2	39	10	4	2	1	1	0	2	5	0	6	1	0	0	2	.000	0	0-0	1	7.38	2.08
2014 Bos	AL	30	0	0	3	19.0	76	14	4	2	0	0	1	1	8	1	14	2	0	2	1	.667	0	0-1	9	2.32	0.95
2015 Bos	AL	64	0	0	9	47.2	207	41	22	21	3	2	1	2	27	2	45	1	0	2	1	.667	0	1-2	9	3.80	3.97
4 ML YEARS		134	0	0	19	92.0	390	74	36	31	4	4	2	8	43	3	90	4	0	6	4	.600	0	3-6	25	3.18	3.03

Raudel Lazo

Pitches: L Bats: L Pos: RP-7 RAH-dell **Ht: 5'9" Wt: 165 Born: 4/12/1989 Age: 27**

Year Team	Lg	G	GS	CG	GF	IP	BFP	H	R	ER	HR	SH	SF	HB	TBB	IBB	SO	WP	Bk	W	L	Pct	Sh	Sv-Op	Hld	ERC	ERA
2012 Jupiter	A+	41	0	0	12	59.0	240	53	17	16	4	3	3	0	16	2	61	3	2	7	1	.875	0	3--	-	2.81	2.44
2013 Jaxnvl	AA	5	0	0	4	7.0	25	3	0	0	1	0	0	0	1	0	9	0	0	1	0	1.000	0	1--	-	0.60	0.00
2014 2 Tms	Low	8	3	0	0	8.0	31	5	5	5	2	0	1	0	2	0	6	0	0	0	0	-	0	0--	-	2.38	5.63
2015 Jaxnvl	AA	18	0	0	4	29.1	119	29	11	7	2	0	0	1	7	0	32	0	0	3	2	.600	0	0--	-	3.42	2.15
2015 Jupiter	A+	8	0	0	5	12.0	44	7	2	2	0	0	1	0	2	1	12	0	0	1	1	.500	0	1--	-	0.96	1.50
2015 Mia	NL	7	0	0	1	5.2	24	5	2	2	1	0	1	0	2	0	5	0	0	0	0	-	0	0-0	1	3.68	3.18

Mike Leake

Pitches: R Bats: R Pos: SP-30 LEEK **Ht: 5'10" Wt: 190 Born: 11/12/1987 Age: 28**

Year Team	Lg	G	GS	CG	GF	IP	BFP	H	R	ER	HR	SH	SF	HB	TBB	IBB	SO	WP	Bk	W	L	Pct	Sh	Sv-Op	Hld	ERC	ERA
2010 Cin	NL	24	22	0	0	138.1	604	158	77	65	19	7	3	3	49	2	91	2	0	8	4	.667	0	0-0	-	5.12	4.23
2011 Cin	NL	29	26	0	2	167.2	693	159	74	72	23	3	6	8	38	3	118	2	1	12	9	.571	0	0-0	-	3.53	3.86
2012 Cin	NL	30	30	2	0	179.0	757	201	97	91	26	6	7	3	41	3	116	3	0	8	9	.471	0	0-0	-	4.50	4.58
2013 Cin	NL	31	31	0	0	192.1	801	193	78	72	21	8	5	6	48	4	122	2	0	14	7	.667	0	0-0	-	3.69	3.37
2014 Cin	NL	33	33	0	0	214.1	902	217	93	88	23	7	7	13	50	3	164	4	0	11	13	.458	0	0-0	-	3.77	3.70
2015 2 Tms	NL	30	30	2	0	192.0	778	174	80	79	22	6	3	3	49	5	119	6	2	11	10	.524	1	0-0	-	3.18	3.70
15 Cin	NL	21	21	1	0	136.2	556	123	55	54	14	6	2	2	34	4	90	3	1	9	5	.643	0	0-0	-	3.01	3.56
15 SF	NL	9	9	1	0	55.1	222	51	25	25	8	0	1	1	15	1	29	3	1	2	5	.286	1	0-0	-	3.61	4.07
Postseason		1	1	0	0	4.1	20	6	5	5	2	1	0	0	2	0	1	0	0	0	1	.000	0	0-0	0	10.00	10.38
6 ML YEARS		177	172	4	2	1083.2	4535	1102	499	467	134	37	31	36	275	20	730	19	3	64	52	.552	1	0-0	0	3.89	3.88

Jack Leathersich

Pitches: L Bats: R Pos: RP-17 **Ht: 5'11" Wt: 200 Born: 7/14/1990 Age: 25**

Year Team	Lg	G	GS	CG	GF	IP	BFP	H	R	ER	HR	SH	SF	HB	TBB	IBB	SO	WP	Bk	W	L	Pct	Sh	Sv-Op	Hld	ERC	ERA
2011 Bklyn	A-	9	0	0	1	12.2	47	6	1	1	0	0	0	0	3	0	26	0	0	0	0	-	0	1--	-	0.86	0.71
2012 2 Tms	Low	38	0	0	8	72.0	306	51	29	24	3	3	2	10	32	0	113	3	0	2	6	.250	0	2--	-	2.78	3.00
2013 Bnghtn	AA	24	0	0	12	29.1	124	19	5	5	1	1	1	1	16	1	55	0	1	2	0	1.000	0	3--	-	2.35	1.53
2013 LsVgs	AAA	28	0	0	4	29.0	148	32	33	25	2	0	1	3	29	0	47	4	0	2	0	1.000	0	0--	-	7.30	7.76
2014 Bnghtn	AA	37	0	0	12	46.0	199	38	17	15	1	0	2	4	21	0	79	2	0	3	3	.500	0	1--	-	3.09	2.93
2014 LsVgs	AAA	11	0	0	3	8.1	42	8	6	5	2	0	1	1	7	0	14	0	0	0	0	-	0	0--	-	6.97	5.40
2015 LsVgs	AAA	13	0	0	7	13.1	57	10	8	8	3	0	0	1	7	0	22	1	0	0	0	-	0	0--	-	4.34	5.40
2015 NYM	NL	17	0	0	6	11.2	52	12	3	3	0	0	0	1	7	0	14	0	0	0	1	.000	0	0-0	2	4.75	2.31

Sam LeCure

Pitches: R Bats: R Pos: RP-19 leh-CURE **Ht: 6'0" Wt: 210 Born: 5/4/1984 Age: 32**

Year Team	Lg	G	GS	CG	GF	IP	BFP	H	R	ER	HR	SH	SF	HB	TBB	IBB	SO	WP	Bk	W	L	Pct	Sh	Sv-Op	Hld	ERC	ERA
2015 Lsvlle*	AAA	41	0	0	15	60.0	261	63	39	35	7	2	1	2	24	2	44	1	0	5	4	.556	0	1--	-	4.60	5.25
2010 Cin	NL	15	6	0	4	48.0	217	50	24	24	6	1	2	5	25	3	37	1	0	2	5	.286	0	0-0	0	5.36	4.50
2011 Cin	NL	43	4	0	7	77.2	307	57	33	32	10	4	0	4	21	3	73	0	0	1	1	.667	0	0-0	5	2.55	3.71
2012 Cin	NL	48	0	0	12	57.1	237	46	22	20	3	4	1	1	23	2	61	2	0	3	3	.500	0	0-1	7	2.73	3.14
2013 Cin	NL	63	0	0	15	61.0	251	50	18	18	4	1	0	1	24	0	66	0	0	2	1	.667	0	1-3	17	2.95	2.66
2014 Cin	NL	62	0	0	16	56.2	251	62	27	24	6	2	3	3	24	1	48	5	0	1	4	.200	0	0-1	17	4.99	3.81
2015 Cin	NL	19	0	0	1	20.0	83	16	9	7	2	1	1	0	7	0	15	0	0	0	2	.000	0	0-1	3	2.77	3.15
Postseason		4	0	0	1	5.0	19	3	0	0	0	0	1	0	2	1	5	0	0	1	0	1.000	0	0-0	0	1.39	0.00
6 ML YEARS		250	10	0	55	320.2	1346	281	133	125	31	13	7	14	124	9	300	8	0	10	16	.385	0	1-6	49	3.48	3.51

C.C. Lee

Pitches: R Bats: R Pos: RP-2 **Ht: 5'11" Wt: 190 Born: 10/21/1986 Age: 29**

Year Team	Lg	G	GS	CG	GF	IP	BFP	H	R	ER	HR	SH	SF	HB	TBB	IBB	SO	WP	Bk	W	L	Pct	Sh	Sv-Op	Hld	ERC	ERA
2015 Clmbs*	AAA	48	0	0	12	58.1	239	53	25	22	3	1	3	5	26	0	65	2	0	4	3	.571	0	5--	-	3.18	3.39
2013 Cle	AL	8	0	0	1	4.1	22	4	3	2	0	0	2	1	3	0	4	0	0	0	0	-	0	0-0	1	4.51	4.15
2014 Cle	AL	37	0	0	6	28.0	127	30	15	14	3	2	1	3	12	1	26	3	0	1	1	.500	0	0-1	4	4.98	4.50
2015 Cle	AL	2	0	0	0	1.2	10	4	1	1	0	0	0	0	1	0	3	0	0	0	0	-	0	0-0	0	13.02	5.40
3 ML YEARS		47	0	0	7	34.0	159	38	19	17	3	2	3	4	16	1	33	3	0	1	1	.500	0	0-1	5	5.27	4.50

Cliff Lee

Pitches: L Bats: L Pos: P   Ht: 6'3" Wt: 205 Born: 8/30/1978 Age: 37

Year Team	Lg	G	GS	CG	GF	IP	BFP	H	R	ER	HR	SH	SF	HB	TBB	IBB	SO	WP	Bk	W	L	Pct	Sh	Sv-Op	Hld	ERC	ERA
2002 Cle	AL	2	2	0	0	10.1	44	6	2	2	0	1	0	0	8	1	6	0	1	0	1	.000	0	0-0	0	2.38	1.74
2003 Cle	AL	9	9	0	0	52.1	210	41	28	21	7	1	1	2	20	1	44	3	0	3	3	.500	0	0-0	0	3.29	3.61
2004 Cle	AL	33	33	0	0	179.0	802	188	113	108	30	2	6	11	81	1	161	6	0	14	8	.636	0	0-0	0	5.31	5.43
2005 Cle	AL	32	32	1	0	202.0	838	194	91	85	22	5	7	0	52	1	143	4	0	18	5	.783	0	0-0	0	3.35	3.79
2006 Cle	AL	33	33	1	0	200.2	882	224	114	98	29	3	6	8	58	3	129	3	0	14	11	.560	0	0-0	0	4.69	4.40
2007 Cle	AL	20	16	1	1	97.1	443	112	73	68	17	3	2	7	36	1	66	5	0	5	8	.385	0	0-0	0	5.59	6.29
2008 Cle	AL	31	31	4	0	223.1	891	214	68	63	12	2	3	5	34	1	170	4	0	22	3	.880	2	0-0	0	2.75	2.54
2009 2 Tms		34	34	6	0	231.2	969	245	88	83	17	11	9	5	43	1	181	7	0	14	13	.519	2	0-0	0	3.45	3.22
2010 2 Tms	AL	28	28	7	0	212.1	843	195	84	75	16	4	6	1	18	2	185	3	1	12	9	.571	1	0-0	0	2.31	3.18
2011 Phi	NL	32	32	6	0	232.2	920	197	66	62	18	6	4	6	42	0	238	0	0	17	8	.680	6	0-0	0	2.44	2.40
2012 Phi	NL	30	30	0	0	211.0	847	207	79	74	26	3	4	0	28	0	207	4	0	6	9	.400	0	0-0	0	3.11	3.16
2013 Phi	NL	31	31	2	0	222.2	876	193	77	71	22	5	3	4	32	0	222	1	0	14	8	.636	1	0-0	0	2.50	2.87
2014 Phi	NL	13	13	1	0	81.1	352	100	40	33	7	7	3	1	12	0	72	1	0	4	5	.444	0	0-0	0	4.27	3.65
09 Cle	AL	22	22	3	0	152.0	641	165	53	53	10	6	5	3	33	1	107	6	0	7	9	.438	1	0-0	0	3.68	3.14
09 Phi	NL	12	12	3	0	79.2	328	80	35	30	7	5	4	2	10	0	74	1	0	7	4	.636	1	0-0	0	3.03	3.39
10 Sea	AL	13	13	5	0	103.2	408	92	31	27	5	0	3	0	6	0	89	2	1	8	3	.727	1	0-0	0	1.91	2.34
10 Tex	AL	15	15	2	0	108.2	435	103	53	48	11	4	3	1	12	2	96	1	0	4	6	.400	0	0-0	0	2.71	3.98
Postseason		11	11	3	0	82.0	320	66	27	23	2	1	0	1	10	0	89	2	0	7	3	.700	0	0-0	0	1.68	2.52
13 ML YEARS		328	324	29	1	2156.2	8917	2116	923	843	223	53	54	50	464	12	1824	41	2	143	91	.611	12	0-0	0	3.37	3.52

Zach Lee

Pitches: R Bats: R Pos: SP-1   Ht: 6'4" Wt: 210 Born: 9/13/1991 Age: 24

Year Team	Lg	G	GS	CG	GF	IP	BFP	H	R	ER	HR	SH	SF	HB	TBB	IBB	SO	WP	Bk	W	L	Pct	Sh	Sv-Op	Hld	ERC	ERA
2011 Gt Lks	A	24	24	0	0	109.0	468	101	51	42	9	2	9	7	32	0	91	8	0	9	6	.600	0	0--	-	3.31	3.47
2012 Rcuca	A+	12	12	0	0	55.1	234	60	31	28	9	0	1	1	10	0	52	0	0	2	3	.400	0	0--	-	4.14	4.55
2012 Chatt	AA	13	13	0	0	65.2	281	69	37	31	6	4	0	1	22	3	51	0	0	4	3	.571	0	0--	-	4.06	4.25
2013 Chatt	AA	28	25	1	0	142.2	583	132	55	51	13	6	3	4	35	1	131	5	0	10	10	.500	1	0--	-	3.15	3.22
2014 Albq	AAA	28	27	0	0	150.2	667	177	105	90	18	7	5	6	54	0	97	5	0	7	13	.350	0	0--	-	5.28	5.38
2015 OkCity	AAA	19	19	1	0	113.1	451	107	40	34	5	7	4	4	19	0	81	2	0	11	6	.647	0	0--	-	2.75	2.70
2015 LAD	NL	1	1	0	0	4.2	24	11	7	7	1	0	0	0	1	0	3	0	0	0	1	.000	0	0-0	0	14.18	13.50

DJ LeMahieu

Bats: R Throws: R Pos: 2B-149;PH-1   la-MAY-hugh   Ht: 6'4" Wt: 215 Born: 7/13/1988 Age: 27

Year Team	Lg	G	AB	H	2B	3B	HR	(Hm	Rd)	TB	R	RBI	RC	TBB	IBB	SO	HBP	SH	SF	SB	CS	GDP	Avg	OBP	Slg	OPS
2011 ChC	NL	37	60	15	2	0	0	(0	0)	17	3	4	3	1	0	12	0	1	0	0	0	2	.250	.262	.283	.546
2012 Col	NL	81	229	68	12	4	2	(1	1)	94	26	22	28	13	4	42	0	3	2	1	2	8	.297	.332	.410	.742
2013 Col	NL	109	404	113	21	3	2	(1	1)	146	39	28	42	19	2	67	1	7	3	18	7	13	.280	.311	.361	.673
2014 Col	NL	149	494	132	15	5	5	(2	3)	172	59	42	47	33	7	97	2	7	2	10	10	13	.267	.315	.348	.663
2015 Col	NL	150	564	170	21	5	6	(3	3)	219	85	61	75	50	4	107	1	3	2	23	3	20	.301	.358	.388	.746
5 ML YEARS		526	1751	498	71	17	15	(7	8)	648	212	157	195	116	17	325	4	21	9	52	22	56	.284	.329	.370	.699

Arnold Leon

Pitches: R Bats: R Pos: RP-19   lay-OHN   Ht: 6'1" Wt: 205 Born: 9/6/1988 Age: 27

Year Team	Lg	G	GS	CG	GF	IP	BFP	H	R	ER	HR	SH	SF	HB	TBB	IBB	SO	WP	Bk	W	L	Pct	Sh	Sv-Op	Hld	ERC	ERA
2011 As	R	5	5	0	0	6.1	26	6	6	6	0	0	0	0	4	0	8	0	0	0	1	.000	0	0--	-	4.33	8.53
2012 Stcktn	A+	12	0	0	4	15.1	77	26	13	9	1	0	0	1	5	0	25	3	0	0	1	.000	0	0--	-	7.94	5.28
2012 Mdlnd	AA	10	0	0	3	15.2	64	17	5	4	0	1	1	0	3	0	18	1	0	1	0	1.000	0	1--	-	3.15	2.30
2012 Scrmto	AAA	22	0	0	5	35.2	144	26	9	7	4	2	0	2	15	0	31	5	0	3	0	1.000	0	0--	-	3.08	1.77
2013 Mdlnd	AA	13	13	0	0	72.2	313	87	40	31	9	2	1	4	11	0	48	2	0	4	5	.444	0	0--	-	4.59	3.84
2013 Scrmto	AAA	12	11	0	0	71.1	300	81	36	35	4	0	2	3	13	0	49	3	0	5	3	.625	0	0--	-	3.89	4.42
2014 Scrmto	AAA	27	27	0	0	145.0	640	170	84	80	12	0	7	6	51	0	128	14	2	10	7	.588	0	0--	-	4.97	4.97
2015 Nashv	AAA	20	6	0	3	58.0	243	52	21	19	7	0	2	2	19	0	55	3	2	2	5	.286	0	1--	-	3.49	2.95
2015 Oak	AL	19	0	0	9	26.2	115	30	14	13	3	1	2	0	9	3	19	0	0	0	2	.000	0	0-0	0	4.50	4.39

Sandy Leon

Bats: B Throws: R Pos: C-37;PH-4;DH-2;3B-1   lay-OHN   Ht: 5'10" Wt: 225 Born: 3/13/1989 Age: 27

Year Team	Lg	G	AB	H	2B	3B	HR	(Hm	Rd)	TB	R	RBI	RC	TBB	IBB	SO	HBP	SH	SF	SB	CS	GDP	Avg	OBP	Slg	OPS
2015 Pwtckt*	AAA	26	99	26	4	0	1	(-	-)	33	8	13	11	10	0	23	2	0	0	0	1	1	.263	.342	.333	.676
2012 Was	NL	12	30	8	2	0	0	(0	0)	10	2	2	2	4	0	11	2	0	0	0	0	1	.267	.389	.333	.722
2013 Was	NL	2	1	0	0	0	0	(0	0)	0	0	0	0	0	0	1	0	0	0	0	0	0	.000	.000	.000	.000
2014 Was	NL	20	64	10	1	0	1	(0	1)	14	7	3	2	6	0	20	0	0	1	0	0	0	.156	.229	.219	.447
2015 Bos	AL	41	114	21	2	0	0	(0	0)	23	8	3	1	7	1	28	1	6	0	0	1	4	.184	.238	.202	.439
4 ML YEARS		75	209	39	5	0	1	(0	1)	47	17	8	5	17	1	60	3	6	0	0	1	6	.187	.258	.225	.483

Dominic Leone

Pitches: R Bats: R Pos: RP-13   LEE-own   Ht: 5'11" Wt: 210 Born: 10/26/1991 Age: 24

Year	Team	Lg	G	GS	CG	GF	IP	BFP	H	R	ER	HR	SH	SF	HB	TBB	IBB	SO	WP	Bk	W	L	Pct	Sh	Sv-Op	Hld	ERC	ERA
2012	Everett	A-	19	0	0	14	33.0	136	20	6	5	0	3	0	1	19	1	39	1	0	3	0	1.000	0	5- -	-	2.09	1.36
2013	2 Tms	Low	32	0	0	21	46.0	183	37	12	11	2	2	2	1	13	0	47	4	1	0	1	.000	0	12- -	-	2.39	2.15
2013	Jacksn	AA	16	0	0	13	18.0	71	12	6	5	2	0	0	0	5	1	17	2	2	1	2	.333	0	4- -	-	1.90	2.50
2015	Tacom	AAA	8	0	0	6	9.1	42	10	8	8	1	0	0	0	5	0	8	0	0	1	1	.500	0	1- -	-	5.09	7.71
2015	Mobile	AA	19	0	0	1	27.2	117	22	12	12	1	1	2	1	12	1	28	3	0	1	2	.333	0	0- -	-	2.72	3.90
2014	Sea	AL	57	0	0	3	66.1	272	52	18	16	4	1	3	3	25	3	70	4	0	8	2	.800	0	0-2	7	2.71	2.17
2015	2 Tms		13	0	0	6	15.0	74	19	15	14	2	0	1	1	9	2	9	2	0	0	5	.000	0	0-1	1	6.63	8.40
15	Sea	AL	10	0	0	5	11.1	54	11	9	8	1	0	0	0	9	2	7	2	0	0	4	.000	0	0-0	1	4.93	6.35
15	Ari	NL	3	0	0	1	3.2	20	8	6	6	1	0	1	1	0	0	2	0	0	0	1	.000	0	0-1	0	12.63	14.73
	2 ML YEARS		70	0	0	9	81.1	346	71	33	30	6	1	4	4	34	5	79	6	0	8	7	.533	0	0-3	8	3.36	3.32

Jon Lester

Pitches: L Bats: L Pos: SP-32   Ht: 6'4" Wt: 240 Born: 1/7/1984 Age: 32

Year	Team	Lg	G	GS	CG	GF	IP	BFP	H	R	ER	HR	SH	SF	HB	TBB	IBB	SO	WP	Bk	W	L	Pct	Sh	Sv-Op	Hld	ERC	ERA
2006	Bos	AL	15	15	0	0	81.1	367	91	43	43	7	2	8	5	43	1	60	5	0	7	2	.778	0	0-0	0	5.52	4.76
2007	Bos	AL	12	11	0	0	63.0	275	61	33	32	10	1	5	1	31	0	50	1	0	4	0	1.000	0	0-0	0	4.78	4.57
2008	Bos	AL	33	33	2	0	210.1	874	202	78	75	14	6	3	10	66	1	152	3	1	16	6	.727	2	0-0	0	3.55	3.21
2009	Bos	AL	32	32	2	0	203.1	843	186	80	77	20	2	6	10	64	0	225	6	0	15	8	.652	0	0-0	0	3.35	3.41
2010	Bos	AL	32	32	2	0	208.0	861	167	81	75	14	4	6	10	83	0	225	6	0	19	9	.679	0	0-0	0	3.00	3.25
2011	Bos	AL	31	31	0	0	191.2	799	166	77	74	20	2	2	11	75	0	182	4	0	15	9	.625	0	0-0	0	3.62	3.47
2012	Bos	AL	33	33	3	0	205.1	876	216	117	110	25	5	7	4	68	2	166	6	0	9	14	.391	0	0-0	0	4.36	4.82
2013	Bos	AL	33	33	1	0	213.1	903	209	94	89	19	1	1	7	67	0	177	5	0	15	8	.652	1	0-0	0	3.69	3.75
2014	2 Tms	AL	32	32	1	0	219.2	885	194	76	60	16	6	5	5	48	0	220	3	0	16	11	.593	1	0-0	0	2.70	2.46
2015	ChC	NL	32	32	1	0	205.0	828	183	83	76	16	5	4	7	47	0	207	8	0	11	12	.478	1	0-0	0	2.88	3.34
14	Bos	AL	21	21	0	0	143.0	580	128	52	40	9	5	2	4	32	0	149	2	0	10	7	.588	0	0-0	0	2.73	2.52
14	Oak	AL	11	11	1	0	76.2	305	66	24	20	7	1	3	1	16	0	71	1	0	6	4	.600	1	0-0	0	2.65	2.35
	Postseason		14	12	0	2	84.0	340	67	26	24	8	5	0	2	23	0	73	0	0	6	4	.600	0	0-0	0	2.58	2.57
	10 ML YEARS		285	284	12	0	1801.0	7511	1675	762	711	161	34	47	63	592	4	1664	47	1	127	79	.617	4	0-0	0	3.52	3.55

Colby Lewis

Pitches: R Bats: R Pos: SP-33   Ht: 6'4" Wt: 245 Born: 8/2/1979 Age: 36

Year	Team	Lg	G	GS	CG	GF	IP	BFP	H	R	ER	HR	SH	SF	HB	TBB	IBB	SO	WP	Bk	W	L	Pct	Sh	Sv-Op	Hld	ERC	ERA
2002	Tex	AL	15	4	0	4	34.1	168	42	26	24	4	2	0	2	26	2	28	3	1	1	3	.250	0	0-2	1	7.22	6.29
2003	Tex	AL	26	26	0	0	127.0	594	163	104	103	23	2	2	5	70	1	88	5	0	10	9	.526	0	0-0	0	7.38	7.30
2004	Tex	AL	3	3	0	0	15.1	71	13	7	7	1	0	0	1	13	0	11	0	0	1	1	.500	0	0-0	0	4.98	4.11
2006	Det	AL	2	0	0	1	3.0	18	8	1	1	1	0	0	0	1	0	5	0	0	0	0	-	0	0-0	0	17.35	3.00
2007	Oak	AL	26	1	0	8	37.2	170	44	28	27	7	1	2	3	14	3	23	1	1	2	2	.000	0	0-1	3	5.79	6.45
2010	Tex	AL	32	32	1	0	201.0	844	174	90	83	21	4	4	6	65	0	196	9	0	12	13	.480	0	0-0	0	3.15	3.72
2011	Tex	AL	32	32	2	0	200.1	839	187	103	98	35	4	5	6	56	1	169	4	0	14	10	.583	1	0-0	0	3.82	4.40
2012	Tex	AL	16	16	2	0	105.0	427	99	48	40	16	1	2	6	14	0	93	2	0	6	6	.500	0	0-0	0	3.28	3.43
2014	Tex	AL	29	29	2	0	170.1	762	211	107	98	25	3	9	8	48	5	133	3	1	10	14	.417	1	0-0	0	5.46	5.18
2015	Tex	AL	33	33	2	0	204.2	861	211	114	106	26	2	11	11	42	2	142	5	0	17	9	.654	1	0-0	0	3.86	4.66
	Postseason		8	8	0	0	50.0	204	32	15	13	7	0	0	2	22	0	44	3	0	4	1	.800	0	0-0	0	2.72	2.34
	10 ML YEARS		214	176	9	13	1098.2	4754	1152	628	587	159	19	35	48	349	14	888	32	3	71	67	.514	3	0-3	4	4.48	4.81

Adam Liberatore

Pitches: L Bats: L Pos: RP-39   LEE-ber-ah-toor   Ht: 6'3" Wt: 240 Born: 5/12/1987 Age: 29

Year	Team	Lg	G	GS	CG	GF	IP	BFP	H	R	ER	HR	SH	SF	HB	TBB	IBB	SO	WP	Bk	W	L	Pct	Sh	Sv-Op	Hld	ERC	ERA
2011	Charltt	A+	38	1	0	6	90.1	373	88	34	31	3	5	2	4	31	4	70	4	0	6	5	.545	0	1- -	-	3.48	3.09
2012	Mont	AA	33	0	0	24	52.0	223	53	18	17	4	3	1	6	20	1	27	1	0	3	4	.429	0	8- -	-	4.53	2.94
2012	Drham	AAA	16	0	0	6	21.0	89	18	3	3	0	0	1	0	8	0	21	4	0	1	1	.500	0	1- -	-	2.52	1.29
2013	Drham	AAA	43	0	0	12	60.1	255	50	27	24	1	7	3	1	25	0	69	4	0	5	3	.625	0	0- -	-	2.68	3.58
2014	Drham	AAA	54	0	0	20	65.0	247	43	14	12	1	1	0	1	15	0	86	3	0	6	1	.857	0	4- -	-	1.47	1.66
2015	OkCity	AAA	19	0	0	7	21.2	91	18	9	9	2	3	1	1	10	0	18	1	0	0	1	.000	0	3- -	-	3.56	3.74
2015	LAD	NL	39	0	0	5	29.2	122	26	14	14	3	0	1	0	9	4	29	1	0	2	2	.500	0	0-1	10	2.85	4.25

Tim Lincecum

Pitches: R Bats: L Pos: SP-15   LIN-suh-come   Ht: 5'11" Wt: 170 Born: 6/15/1984 Age: 32

Year	Team	Lg	G	GS	CG	GF	IP	BFP	H	R	ER	HR	SH	SF	HB	TBB	IBB	SO	WP	Bk	W	L	Pct	Sh	Sv-Op	Hld	ERC	ERA
2007	SF	NL	24	24	0	0	146.1	618	122	70	65	12	9	7	2	65	5	150	10	0	7	5	.583	0	0-0	0	3.21	4.00
2008	SF	NL	34	33	2	0	227.0	928	182	72	66	11	11	3	6	84	1	265	17	2	18	5	.783	1	0-0	0	2.69	2.62
2009	SF	NL	32	32	4	0	225.1	905	168	69	62	10	12	5	6	68	2	261	11	0	15	7	.682	2	0-0	0	2.14	2.48
2010	SF	NL	33	33	1	0	212.1	897	194	84	81	18	9	5	5	76	7	231	9	0	16	10	.615	1	0-0	0	3.37	3.43
2011	SF	NL	33	33	1	0	217.0	900	176	74	66	15	13	1	6	86	5	220	9	0	13	14	.481	0	0-0	0	2.92	2.74
2012	SF	NL	33	33	0	0	186.0	825	183	111	107	23	11	6	4	90	3	190	17	2	10	15	.400	0	0-0	0	4.50	5.18
2013	SF	NL	32	32	1	0	197.2	841	184	102	96	21	10	4	7	76	8	193	11	2	10	14	.417	1	0-0	0	3.76	4.37
2014	SF	NL	33	26	1	3	155.2	673	154	86	82	19	4	4	5	63	0	134	15	1	12	9	.571	0	1-1	0	4.33	4.74
2015	SF	NL	15	15	0	0	76.1	333	75	37	35	7	3	2	1	38	2	60	5	0	7	4	.636	0	0-0	0	4.35	4.13
	Postseason		13	6	0	2	56.1	217	34	16	15	3	1	3	1	14	0	65	0	0	5	2	.714	1	0-0	2	1.45	2.40
	9 ML YEARS		269	261	10	3	1643.2	6920	1438	705	660	136	78	37	42	646	33	1704	104	7	108	83	.565	7	1-1	0	3.32	3.61

Brad Lincoln

Pitches: R Bats: L Pos: P   Ht: 6'0" Wt: 225 Born: 5/25/1985 Age: 31

Year	Team	Lg	G	GS	CG	GF	IP	BFP	H	R	ER	HR	SH	SF	HB	TBB	IBB	SO	WP	Bk	W	L	Pct	Sh	Sv-Op	Hld	ERC	ERA
2015	Indy*	AAA	39	4	0	13	60.1	277	60	32	28	3	2	2	4	41	3	57	2	0	6	2	.750	0	2--	-	4.97	4.18
2010	Pit	NL	11	9	0	0	52.2	240	66	42	39	9	3	4	5	15	0	25	1	0	1	4	.200	0	0-0	0	5.99	6.66
2011	Pit	NL	12	8	0	0	47.2	211	54	27	25	4	2	2	2	16	4	29	0	0	2	3	.400	0	0-0	0	4.46	4.72
2012	2 Tms		52	5	0	10	88.0	362	80	37	36	14	4	1	1	24	2	88	1	0	5	2	.714	0	1-2	9	3.49	3.68
2013	Tor	AL	22	0	0	7	31.2	148	28	17	14	4	2	0	3	22	0	25	2	0	1	2	.333	0	0-0	0	5.04	3.98
2014	Phi	NL	2	0	0	1	2.1	13	5	3	3	1	0	0	1	0	0	2	0	0	0	0	-	0	0-0	0	14.73	11.57
12	Pit	NL	28	5	0	6	59.1	239	51	19	18	8	2	0	1	14	1	60	0	0	4	2	.667	0	1-2	5	2.97	2.73
12	Tor	AL	24	0	0	4	28.2	123	29	18	18	6	2	1	0	10	1	28	1	0	1	0	1.000	0	0-0	4	4.63	5.65
5 ML YEARS			99	22	0	18	222.1	974	233	126	117	32	11	7	12	77	6	169	4	0	9	11	.450	0	1-2	9	4.59	4.74

Adam Lind

Bats: L Throws: L Pos: 1B-138;PH-14;DH-1   Ht: 6'2" Wt: 195 Born: 7/17/1983 Age: 32

									BATTING												RUNNING			AVERAGES			
Year	Team	Lg	G	AB	H	2B	3B	HR	(Hm	Rd)	TB	R	RBI	RC	TBB	IBB	SO	HBP	SH	SF	SB	CS	GDP	Avg	OBP	Slg	OPS
2006	Tor	AL	18	60	22	8	0	2	(0	2)	36	8	8	13	5	0	12	0	0	0	0	0	0	.367	.415	.600	1.015
2007	Tor	AL	89	290	69	14	0	11	(10	1)	116	34	46	38	16	0	65	1	2	2	1	2	7	.238	.278	.400	.678
2008	Tor	AL	88	326	92	16	4	9	(2	7)	143	48	40	39	16	3	59	2	1	4	2	0	8	.282	.316	.439	.755
2009	Tor	AL	151	587	179	46	0	35	(14	21)	330	93	114	114	58	7	110	5	0	4	1	1	15	.305	.370	.562	.932
2010	Tor	AL	150	569	135	32	3	23	(15	8)	242	57	72	65	38	3	144	3	0	3	0	0	10	.237	.287	.425	.712
2011	Tor	AL	125	499	125	16	0	26	(12	14)	219	56	87	67	32	4	107	3	0	8	1	1	12	.251	.295	.439	.734
2012	Tor	AL	93	321	82	14	2	11	(6	5)	133	28	45	47	29	1	61	0	0	3	0	0	10	.255	.314	.414	.729
2013	Tor	AL	143	465	134	26	1	23	(9	14)	231	67	67	76	51	5	103	1	0	4	1	0	20	.288	.357	.497	.854
2014	Tor	AL	96	290	93	24	2	6	(5	1)	139	38	40	54	28	3	48	0	0	0	0	0	8	.321	.381	.479	.860
2015	Mil	NL	149	502	139	32	0	20	(10	10)	231	72	87	91	66	11	100	1	0	3	0	0	7	.277	.360	.460	.820
10 ML YEARS			1102	3909	1070	228	12	166	(83	83)	1820	501	606	604	339	37	809	16	3	31	6	4	97	.274	.332	.466	.797

Jacob Lindgren

Pitches: L Bats: L Pos: RP-7   Ht: 5'11" Wt: 205 Born: 3/12/1993 Age: 23

Year	Team	Lg	G	GS	CG	GF	IP	BFP	H	R	ER	HR	SH	SF	HB	TBB	IBB	SO	WP	Bk	W	L	Pct	Sh	Sv-Op	Hld	ERC	ERA
2014	Trntn	AA	8	0	0	0	11.2	49	6	6	5	0	1	0	0	9	1	18	3	0	1	1	.500	0	0--	-	2.08	3.86
2014	3 Tms	Low	11	0	0	3	13.1	55	6	2	1	0	0	0	1	4	0	30	6	0	1	0	1.000	0	1--	-	0.96	0.68
2015	S-WB	AAA	15	0	0	3	22.0	92	16	7	3	0	1	1	0	10	1	29	2	0	1	1	.500	0	3--	-	2.09	1.23
2015	NYY	AL	7	0	0	2	7.0	29	5	4	4	3	0	1	0	4	0	8	0	0	0	0	-	0	0-1	0	5.49	5.14

Francisco Lindor

Bats: B Throws: R Pos: SS-98;PH-2;DH-1   lin-DOHR   Ht: 5'11" Wt: 190 Born: 11/14/1993 Age: 22

									BATTING												RUNNING			AVERAGES			
Year	Team	Lg	G	AB	H	2B	3B	HR	(Hm	Rd)	TB	R	RBI	RC	TBB	IBB	SO	HBP	SH	SF	SB	CS	GDP	Avg	OBP	Slg	OPS
2012	Lk Cty	A	122	490	126	24	3	6	(-	-)	174	83	42	68	61	8	78	11	4	1	27	12	19	.257	.352	.355	.707
2013	Carlina	A+	83	327	100	19	6	1	(-	-)	134	51	27	55	35	0	39	2	6	3	20	5	7	.306	.373	.410	.783
2013	Akron	AA	21	76	22	3	1	1	(-	-)	30	14	7	13	14	0	7	1	0	0	5	2	1	.289	.407	.395	.801
2014	Akron	AA	88	342	95	13	4	6	(-	-)	134	51	48	51	40	0	61	1	1	3	25	9	11	.278	.352	.392	.744
2014	Clmbs	AAA	38	165	45	4	0	5	(-	-)	64	24	14	18	9	1	36	0	4	2	3	7	3	.273	.307	.388	.695
2015	Clmbs	AAA	59	229	65	11	5	2	(-	-)	92	26	22	33	25	0	38	0	5	3	9	7	1	.284	.350	.402	.752
2015	Cle	AL	99	390	122	22	4	12	(8	4)	188	50	51	64	27	0	69	1	13	7	12	2	12	.313	.353	.482	.835

Francisco Liriano

Pitches: L Bats: L Pos: SP-31   Ht: 6'2" Wt: 225 Born: 10/26/1983 Age: 32

Year	Team	Lg	G	GS	CG	GF	IP	BFP	H	R	ER	HR	SH	SF	HB	TBB	IBB	SO	WP	Bk	W	L	Pct	Sh	Sv-Op	Hld	ERC	ERA
2005	Min	AL	6	4	0	2	23.2	93	19	15	15	4	0	0	0	7	0	33	0	0	1	2	.333	0	0-0	0	3.15	5.70
2006	Min	AL	28	16	0	2	121.0	473	89	31	29	9	4	2	1	32	0	144	9	1	12	3	.800	0	1-1	1	2.12	2.16
2008	Min	AL	14	14	0	0	76.0	329	74	40	33	7	2	3	1	32	1	67	3	0	6	4	.600	0	0-0	0	3.97	3.91
2009	Min	AL	29	24	0	2	136.2	609	147	93	88	21	5	6	6	65	0	122	5	1	5	13	.278	0	0-0	0	5.46	5.80
2010	Min	AL	31	31	0	0	191.2	806	184	77	77	9	6	2	10	58	0	201	10	1	14	10	.583	0	0-0	0	3.34	3.62
2011	Min	AL	26	24	1	0	134.1	591	125	81	76	14	0	6	7	75	1	112	9	0	9	10	.474	1	0-0	0	4.58	5.09
2012	2 Tms		34	28	0	2	156.2	693	143	97	93	19	4	8	7	87	5	167	11	1	6	12	.333	0	0-0	1	4.47	5.34
2013	Pit	NL	26	26	2	0	161.0	666	134	54	54	9	3	1	0	63	0	163	7	2	16	8	.667	0	0-0	0	2.86	3.02
2014	Pit	NL	29	29	0	0	162.1	691	130	68	61	13	6	5	4	81	3	175	12	0	7	10	.412	0	0-0	0	3.28	3.38
2015	Pit	NL	31	31	0	0	186.2	773	155	75	70	15	2	1	5	70	1	205	10	1	12	7	.632	0	0-0	0	3.04	3.38
12	Min	AL	22	17	0	2	100.0	440	89	63	59	12	2	7	4	55	4	109	6	1	3	10	.231	0	0-0	1	4.27	5.31
12	CWS	AL	12	11	0	0	56.2	253	54	34	34	7	2	1	3	32	1	58	5	0	3	2	.600	0	0-0	0	4.83	5.40
Postseason			4	3	0	0	20.2	84	14	9	8	1	0	0	2	7	0	18	2	0	1	0	1.000	0	0-0	0	2.20	3.48
10 ML YEARS			254	227	3	8	1350.0	5724	1200	631	596	120	32	34	41	570	11	1389	76	7	88	79	.527	1	1-1	2	3.59	3.97

Radhames Liz

Pitches: R **Bats:** R **Pos:** RP-14 rah-DAH-mez **Ht:** 6'2" **Wt:** 200 **Born:** 10/6/1983 **Age:** 32

Year Team	Lg	G	GS	CG	GF	IP	BFP	H	R	ER	HR	SH	SF	HB	TBB	IBB	SO	WP	Bk	W	L	Pct	Sh	Sv-Op	Hld	ERC	ERA
2015 Indy*	AAA	16	10	0	1	64.1	265	44	15	10	0	1	1	5	24	1	74	4	0	4	5	.444	0	0- -	-	1.94	1.40
2007 Bal	AL	9	4	0	5	24.2	122	25	21	19	3	1	1	1	23	1	24	3	0	0	2	.000	0	0-0	0	6.49	6.93
2008 Bal	AL	17	17	0	0	84.1	393	99	67	63	16	1	3	3	51	3	57	6	0	6	6	.500	0	0-0	0	6.84	6.72
2009 Bal	AL	2	0	0	0	1.1	16	8	10	10	1	0	0	2	2	0	1	0	0	0	-	-	0	0-0	0	68.38	67.50
2015 Pit	NL	14	0	0	7	23.1	106	26	11	11	4	0	0	3	12	2	27	1	0	1	4	.200	0	0-1	0	6.32	4.24
4 ML YEARS		42	21	0	12	133.2	637	158	109	103	24	2	4	9	88	6	109	10	0	7	12	.368	0	0-1	0	7.15	6.94

Jose Lobaton

Bats: B **Throws:** R **Pos:** C-42;PH-2 LOE-bah-tone **Ht:** 6'1" **Wt:** 215 **Born:** 10/21/1984 **Age:** 31

Year Team	Lg	G	AB	H	2B	3B	HR	(Hm	Rd)	TB	R	RBI	RC	TBB	IBB	SO	HBP	SH	SF	SB	CS	GDP	Avg	OBP	Slg	OPS
2009 SD	NL	7	17	3	0	0	0	(0	0)	3	0	0	0	0	0	5	0	0	0	0	0	1	.176	.176	.176	.353
2011 TB	AL	15	34	4	1	0	0	(0	0)	5	2	0	0	4	0	8	1	0	0	0	0	2	.118	.231	.147	.378
2012 TB	AL	69	167	37	10	0	2	(1	1)	53	16	20	19	24	1	46	2	2	2	0	1	6	.222	.323	.317	.640
2013 TB	AL	100	277	69	15	2	7	(5	2)	109	38	32	32	30	0	65	0	2	2	0	1	5	.249	.320	.394	.714
2014 Was	NL	66	214	50	9	0	2	(2	0)	65	18	12	13	15	1	61	1	0	0	0	0	5	.234	.287	.304	.591
2015 Was	NL	44	136	27	4	0	3	(1	2)	40	11	20	14	15	1	40	1	1	2	0	0	5	.199	.279	.294	.573
Postseason		4	7	2	0	0	1	(1	0)	5	1	1	1	0	0	2	0	0	0	0	0	0	.286	.286	.714	1.000
6 ML YEARS		301	845	190	39	2	14	(9	5)	275	85	84	78	88	3	225	5	5	6	0	2	24	.225	.300	.325	.625

Kyle Lobstein

Pitches: L **Bats:** L **Pos:** SP-11; RP-2 LOB-steen **Ht:** 6'3" **Wt:** 200 **Born:** 8/12/1989 **Age:** 26

Year Team	Lg	G	GS	CG	GF	IP	BFP	H	R	ER	HR	SH	SF	HB	TBB	IBB	SO	WP	Bk	W	L	Pct	Sh	Sv-Op	Hld	ERC	ERA
2011 Charltt	A+	22	21	1	0	121.1	510	120	54	50	11	8	2	3	30	1	85	4	0	9	9	.500	0	0- -	-	3.42	3.71
2012 Mont	AA	27	27	0	0	144.0	624	140	73	65	12	8	7	2	69	0	129	4	0	7	7	.533	0	0- -	-	4.20	4.06
2013 Erie	AA	15	15	2	0	95.1	383	92	35	33	6	3	2	0	27	0	83	1	1	7	4	.636	0	0- -	-	3.33	3.12
2013 Toledo	AAA	13	13	0	0	72.1	311	73	32	28	2	3	6	4	25	0	65	1	0	6	3	.667	0	0- -	-	3.63	3.48
2014 Toledo	AAA	26	25	1	0	146.0	639	174	71	66	10	5	6	4	42	1	127	3	0	9	11	.450	0	0- -	-	4.62	4.07
2014 Det	AL	7	6	0	1	39.1	164	35	20	19	3	1	1	0	14	2	27	0	0	1	2	.333	0	0-0	0	3.07	4.35
2015 Det	AL	13	11	0	2	63.2	280	78	43	42	7	0	1	0	23	1	32	2	1	3	8	.273	0	0-0	0	5.38	5.94
2 ML YEARS		20	17	0	3	103.0	444	113	63	61	10	1	2	0	37	3	59	2	1	4	10	.286	0	0-0	0	4.45	5.33

Jeff Locke

Pitches: L **Bats:** L **Pos:** SP-30 LOCK **Ht:** 6'0" **Wt:** 195 **Born:** 11/20/1987 **Age:** 28

Year Team	Lg	G	GS	CG	GF	IP	BFP	H	R	ER	HR	SH	SF	HB	TBB	IBB	SO	WP	Bk	W	L	Pct	Sh	Sv-Op	Hld	ERC	ERA
2011 Pit	NL	4	4	0	0	16.2	78	21	12	12	3	1	1	1	10	0	5	0	0	0	3	.000	0	0-0	0	7.62	6.48
2012 Pit	NL	8	6	0	1	34.1	148	36	21	21	6	1	0	1	11	0	34	0	0	1	3	.250	0	0-0	0	4.68	5.50
2013 Pit	NL	30	30	0	0	166.1	711	146	69	65	11	8	10	6	84	4	125	8	2	10	7	.588	0	0-0	0	3.72	3.52
2014 Pit	NL	21	21	0	0	131.1	548	127	63	57	16	4	3	4	40	2	89	1	0	7	6	.538	0	0-0	0	3.81	3.91
2015 Pit	NL	30	30	0	0	168.1	736	179	95	84	15	7	8	7	60	4	129	5	0	8	11	.421	0	0-0	0	4.30	4.49
5 ML YEARS		93	91	0	1	517.0	2221	509	260	239	51	23	22	19	205	10	382	14	2	26	30	.464	0	0-0	0	4.11	4.16

Adam Loewen

Pitches: L **Bats:** L **Pos:** RP-20 **Ht:** 6'6" **Wt:** 235 **Born:** 4/9/1984 **Age:** 32

Year Team	Lg	G	GS	CG	GF	IP	BFP	H	R	ER	HR	SH	SF	HB	TBB	IBB	SO	WP	Bk	W	L	Pct	Sh	Sv-Op	Hld	ERC	ERA
2015 LV*	AAA	33	0	0	17	46.0	196	29	14	11	1	4	1	2	32	0	60	1	0	1	3	.250	0	10- -	-	2.83	2.15
2015 Rdng*	AA	7	0	0	0	12.1	51	10	4	2	1	1	1	1	5	1	13	2	0	1	0	1.000	0	0- -	-	3.20	1.46
2006 Bal	AL	22	19	0	1	112.1	504	111	72	67	8	1	4	8	62	0	98	3	1	6	6	.500	0	0-0	1	4.70	5.37
2007 Bal	AL	6	6	0	0	30.1	143	27	14	12	1	1	0	3	26	0	22	1	1	2	0	1.000	0	0-0	0	5.11	3.56
2008 Bal	AL	7	4	0	0	21.1	102	25	19	19	5	0	2	0	18	0	14	2	0	2	0	.000	0	0-0	1	8.37	8.02
2015 Phi	NL	20	0	0	7	19.1	93	20	15	15	3	1	1	3	17	1	22	5	0	1	0	1.000	0	0-0	0	7.51	6.98
4 ML YEARS		55	29	0	8	183.1	842	183	120	113	17	3	7	14	123	1	156	11	2	9	8	.529	0	0-0	2	5.45	5.55

Boone Logan

Pitches: L **Bats:** R **Pos:** RP-60 **Ht:** 6'5" **Wt:** 215 **Born:** 8/13/1984 **Age:** 31

Year Team	Lg	G	GS	CG	GF	IP	BFP	H	R	ER	HR	SH	SF	HB	TBB	IBB	SO	WP	Bk	W	L	Pct	Sh	Sv-Op	Hld	ERC	ERA
2006 CWS	AL	21	0	0	4	17.1	93	21	18	16	2	1	1	3	15	2	15	1	0	0	0	-	0	1-2	2	7.56	8.31
2007 CWS	AL	68	0	0	13	50.2	226	59	30	28	7	2	6	0	20	3	35	2	0	2	1	.667	0	0-2	11	5.18	4.97
2008 CWS	AL	55	0	0	12	42.1	197	57	31	28	7	2	0	1	14	3	42	1	0	2	3	.400	0	0-1	3	6.24	5.95
2009 Atl	NL	20	0	0	7	17.1	82	21	12	10	1	0	2	0	9	3	10	0	0	1	1	.500	0	0-0	1	5.29	5.19
2010 NYY	AL	51	0	0	8	40.0	169	34	13	13	6	0	1	0	20	3	38	1	0	2	0	1.000	0	0-0	13	6.12	2.93
2011 NYY	AL	64	0	0	6	41.2	185	43	20	16	4	2	1	4	13	1	46	1	0	5	3	.625	0	0-2	10	4.04	3.46
2012 NYY	AL	80	0	0	8	55.1	239	48	23	23	6	1	3	2	28	6	68	3	0	7	2	.778	0	1-4	23	3.78	3.74
2013 NYY	AL	61	0	0	9	39.0	159	33	15	14	7	3	3	0	18	4	50	3	0	5	2	.714	0	0-2	11	3.38	3.23
2014 Col	NL	35	0	0	8	25.0	116	31	20	19	6	2	2	1	11	1	32	3	0	2	3	.400	0	0-4	7	6.84	6.84
2015 Col	NL	60	0	0	12	35.1	168	40	17	17	3	1	2	5	17	1	44	3	0	0	3	.000	0	0-4	23	5.43	4.33
Postseason		13	0	0	2	7.2	30	7	2	2	1	0	0	0	0	0	9	0	0	0	0	-	0	0-0	2	2.83	2.35
10 ML YEARS		515	0	0	87	364.0	1634	387	199	184	46	14	19	18	160	29	380	18	0	26	18	.591	0	2-21	104	4.81	4.55

Kyle Lohse

Pitches: R Bats: R Pos: SP-22; RP-15 LOESH Ht: 6'2" Wt: 215 Born: 10/4/1978 Age: 37

Year	Team	Lg	G	GS	CG	GF	IP	BFP	H	R	ER	HR	SH	SF	HB	TBB	IBB	SO	WP	Bk	W	L	Pct	Sh	Sv-Op	Hld	ERC	ERA
2001	Min	AL	19	16	0	2	90.1	402	102	60	57	16	1	5	8	29	0	64	5	0	4	7	.364	0	0-0	0	5.43	5.68
2002	Min	AL	32	31	1	0	180.2	783	181	92	85	26	3	3	9	70	2	124	8	0	13	8	.619	1	0-1	0	4.55	4.23
2003	Min	AL	33	33	2	0	201.0	850	211	107	103	28	8	5	5	45	1	130	10	1	14	11	.560	1	0-0	0	4.00	4.61
2004	Min	AL	35	34	1	1	194.0	883	240	128	115	28	5	7	7	76	5	111	6	0	9	13	.409	1	0-0	0	5.89	5.34
2005	Min	AL	31	30	0	1	178.2	769	211	85	83	22	3	7	9	44	5	86	4	1	9	13	.409	1	0-0	0	4.91	4.18
2006	2 Tms		34	19	0	6	126.2	566	150	83	82	15	8	5	6	44	4	97	3	1	5	10	.333	0	0-0	0	5.21	5.83
2007	2 Tms	NL	34	32	2	0	192.2	829	207	109	99	22	14	4	12	57	3	122	3	0	9	12	.429	1	0-0	0	4.45	4.62
2008	StL	NL	33	33	0	0	200.0	839	211	88	84	18	6	4	3	49	1	119	5	0	15	6	.714	0	0-0	0	3.77	3.78
2009	StL	NL	23	22	1	0	117.2	512	125	69	62	16	3	5	3	36	2	77	3	1	6	10	.375	1	0-0	0	4.33	4.74
2010	StL	NL	18	18	0	0	92.0	431	129	75	67	9	5	4	3	35	2	54	1	0	4	8	.333	0	0-0	0	6.50	6.55
2011	StL	NL	30	30	1	0	188.1	775	178	80	71	16	8	6	3	42	1	111	1	0	14	8	.636	1	0-0	0	3.05	3.39
2012	StL	NL	33	33	0	0	211.0	864	192	74	67	19	11	7	4	38	1	143	1	0	16	3	.842	0	0-0	0	2.72	2.86
2013	Mil	NL	32	32	2	0	198.2	806	196	78	74	26	8	2	3	36	1	125	1	0	11	10	.524	1	0-0	0	3.45	3.35
2014	Mil	NL	31	31	2	0	198.1	817	183	87	78	22	9	9	8	45	0	141	1	0	13	9	.591	2	0-0	0	3.21	3.54
2015	Mil	NL	37	22	0	5	152.1	665	180	99	99	29	7	4	4	43	3	108	5	0	5	13	.278	0	2-2	2	5.42	5.85
06	Min	AL	22	8	0	5	63.2	295	80	50	50	8	1	3	6	25	2	46	1	1	2	5	.286	0	0-0	0	6.10	7.07
06	Cin	NL	12	11	0	1	63.0	271	70	33	32	7	7	2	0	19	2	51	2	0	3	5	.375	0	0-0	0	4.36	4.57
07	Cin	NL	21	21	2	0	131.2	561	143	76	67	16	8	4	6	33	1	80	3	0	6	12	.333	1	0-0	0	4.32	4.58
07	Phi	NL	13	11	0	0	61.0	268	64	33	32	6	6	0	6	24	2	42	0	0	3	0	1.000	0	0-0	0	4.71	4.72
	Postseason		13	8	0	3	46.1	199	49	26	25	8	1	0	1	13	1	39	1	0	2	5	.286	0	0-0	0	4.46	4.86
	15 ML YEARS		455	416	12	15	2522.1	10791	2696	1314	1226	312	99	77	87	689	33	1612	57	4	147	141	.510	9	2-3	2	4.25	4.37

Ryan Lollis

Bats: L Throws: L Pos: LF-3;RF-1;PH-1 LAW-liss Ht: 6'2" Wt: 185 Born: 12/16/1986 Age: 29

Year	Team	Lg	G	AB	H	2B	3B	HR	(Hm	Rd)	TB	R	RBI	RC	TBB	IBB	SO	HBP	SH	SF	SB	CS	GDP	Avg	OBP	Slg	OPS
2011	2 Tms	Low	94	347	106	24	2	2	(-	-)	140	57	42	57	43	0	56	3	0	2	10	5	4	.305	.385	.403	.788
2012	SnJos	A+	75	318	94	18	3	5	(-	-)	133	49	39	46	27	0	53	0	0	4	5	6	5	.296	.347	.418	.765
2012	Fresno	AAA	50	175	54	9	2	3	(-	-)	76	27	21	30	25	1	26	0	3	1	2	3	6	.309	.393	.434	.827
2013	Rchmd	AA	136	469	125	24	2	8	(-	-)	177	60	57	66	50	2	61	8	8	4	6	3	13	.267	.345	.377	.722
2014	Rchmd	AA	70	203	44	4	3	1	(-	-)	57	21	17	17	17	0	28	1	3	2	2	0	3	.217	.278	.281	.559
2014	SnJos	A+	26	109	30	3	0	3	(-	-)	42	15	11	14	7	0	8	0	2	0	4	0	1	.275	.319	.385	.704
2015	SnJos	A+	30	113	39	8	2	1	(-	-)	54	28	11	23	15	0	19	2	1	0	3	2	4	.345	.431	.478	.909
2015	Scrmto	AAA	72	279	92	22	2	4	(-	-)	130	42	29	50	25	2	37	2	2	4	6	4	4	.330	.384	.466	.850
2015	SF	NL	5	12	2	0	0	0	(0	0)	2	0	0	0	1	0	1	0	0	0	1	0	0	.167	.231	.167	.397

Steve Lombardozzi

Bats: B Throws: R Pos: PH-11;PR-1 lahm-bar-DOZE-ee Ht: 6'0" Wt: 200 Born: 9/20/1988 Age: 27

Year	Team	Lg	G	AB	H	2B	3B	HR	(Hm	Rd)	TB	R	RBI	RC	TBB	IBB	SO	HBP	SH	SF	SB	CS	GDP	Avg	OBP	Slg	OPS
2015	Indy*	AAA	97	355	100	15	0	0	(-	-)	115	30	37	44	32	2	40	4	2	1	14	4	7	.282	.347	.324	.671
2011	Was	NL	13	31	6	1	0	0	(0	0)	7	3	1	2	1	0	4	0	0	0	0	0	0	.194	.219	.226	.445
2012	Was	NL	126	384	105	16	3	3	(2	1)	136	40	27	46	19	1	46	6	6	1	5	3	1	.273	.317	.354	.671
2013	Was	NL	118	290	75	15	1	2	(1	1)	98	25	22	24	8	1	34	1	5	3	4	3	6	.259	.278	.338	.616
2014	Bal	AL	20	73	21	1	1	0	(0	0)	24	6	2	6	0	0	14	1	0	0	1	0	1	.288	.297	.329	.626
2015	Pit	NL	12	10	0	0	0	0	(0	0)	0	1	0	0	1	0	4	0	0	0	0	0	0	.000	.091	.000	.091
	Postseason		3	3	1	0	0	0	(0	0)	1	0	0	0	0	0	0	0	0	0	0	0	0	.333	.333	.333	.667
	5 ML YEARS		289	788	207	33	5	5	(3	2)	265	75	52	78	29	2	102	8	11	4	10	6	8	.263	.294	.336	.631

James Loney

Bats: L Throws: L Pos: 1B-101;PH-7;DH-1 Ht: 6'3" Wt: 235 Born: 5/7/1984 Age: 32

Year	Team	Lg	G	AB	H	2B	3B	HR	(Hm	Rd)	TB	R	RBI	RC	TBB	IBB	SO	HBP	SH	SF	SB	CS	GDP	Avg	OBP	Slg	OPS
2006	LAD	NL	48	102	29	6	5	4	(1	3)	57	20	18	17	8	1	10	1	0	0	1	0	8	.284	.342	.559	.901
2007	LAD	NL	96	344	114	18	4	15	(5	10)	185	41	67	71	28	5	48	1	0	2	0	1	6	.331	.381	.538	.919
2008	LAD	NL	161	595	172	35	6	13	(5	8)	258	66	90	79	45	6	85	3	1	7	7	4	25	.289	.338	.434	.772
2009	LAD	NL	158	576	162	25	2	13	(1	12)	230	73	90	84	70	10	68	0	1	4	7	3	16	.281	.357	.399	.756
2010	LAD	NL	161	588	157	41	2	10	(6	4)	232	67	88	81	52	9	95	4	0	4	10	5	14	.267	.329	.395	.723
2011	LAD	NL	158	531	153	30	1	12	(7	5)	221	56	65	71	42	7	67	1	3	5	4	0	8	.288	.339	.416	.755
2012	2 Tms		144	434	108	20	0	6	(0	6)	146	37	41	34	28	7	51	0	1	2	0	3	21	.249	.293	.336	.630
2013	TB	AL	158	549	164	33	0	13	(7	6)	236	54	75	75	44	6	77	0	1	4	3	1	16	.299	.348	.430	.778
2014	TB	AL	155	600	174	27	0	9	(4	5)	228	59	69	68	41	2	80	4	0	6	4	0	21	.290	.336	.380	.716
2015	TB	AL	104	361	101	16	0	4	(3	1)	129	25	32	40	23	5	34	1	0	3	2	4	10	.280	.322	.357	.680
12	LAD	NL	114	334	85	18	0	4	(0	4)	115	32	33	28	23	7	39	0	1	1	0	3	16	.254	.302	.344	.646
12	Bos	AL	30	100	23	2	0	2	(0	2)	31	5	8	6	5	0	12	0	0	1	0	0	5	.230	.264	.310	.574
	Postseason		22	79	28	5	0	3	(1	2)	42	6	16	16	9	1	13	1	0	0	0	0	4	.354	.427	.532	.959
	10 ML YEARS		1343	4680	1334	251	20	99	(39	60)	1922	498	635	620	381	58	615	15	7	37	38	21	145	.285	.338	.411	.749

Evan Longoria

Bats: R **Throws:** R **Pos:** 3B-148;DH-11;PH-1;PR-1   **Ht:** 6'2" **Wt:** 210 **Born:** 10/7/1985 **Age:** 30

Year	Team	Lg	G	AB	H	2B	3B	HR	(Hm	Rd)	TB	R	RBI	RC	TBB	IBB	SO	HBP	SH	SF	SB	CS	GDP	Avg	OBP	Slg	OPS
2008	TB	AL	122	448	122	31	2	27	(18	9)	238	67	85	72	46	4	122	6	0	8	7	0	8	.272	.343	.531	.874
2009	TB	AL	157	584	164	44	0	33	(16	17)	307	100	113	102	72	11	140	8	0	7	9	0	27	.281	.364	.526	.889
2010	TB	AL	151	574	169	46	5	22	(10	12)	291	96	104	99	72	12	124	5	0	10	15	5	15	.294	.372	.507	.879
2011	TB	AL	133	483	118	26	1	31	(14	17)	239	78	99	91	80	6	93	6	0	5	3	2	11	.244	.355	.495	.850
2012	TB	AL	74	273	79	14	0	17	(8	9)	144	39	55	55	33	6	61	3	0	3	2	3	14	.289	.369	.527	.896
2013	TB	AL	160	614	165	39	3	32	(15	17)	306	91	88	90	70	10	162	3	0	6	1	0	16	.269	.343	.498	.842
2014	TB	AL	**162**	624	158	26	1	22	(12	10)	252	83	91	83	57	11	133	9	1	9	5	0	15	.253	.320	.404	.724
2015	TB	AL	160	604	163	35	1	21	(10	11)	263	74	73	77	51	8	132	6	0	9	3	1	11	.270	.328	.435	.764
Postseason			30	115	22	5	0	9	(4	5)	54	16	21	13	11	0	38	0	0	0	1	0	4	.191	.262	.470	.731
8 ML YEARS			1119	4204	1138	261	13	205	(103	102)	2040	628	708	669	481	68	967	46	1	57	45	11	117	.271	.348	.485	.833

Javier Lopez

Pitches: L **Bats:** L **Pos:** RP-77   **Ht:** 6'4" **Wt:** 220 **Born:** 7/11/1977 **Age:** 38

Year	Team	Lg	G	GS	CG	GF	IP	BFP	H	R	ER	HR	SH	SF	HB	TBB	IBB	SO	WP	Bk	W	L	Pct	Sh	Sv-Op	Hld	ERC	ERA
2003	Col	NL	75	0	0	11	58.1	242	58	25	24	1	5	0	4	12	2	40	1	3	4	1	.800	0	1-2	15	3.44	3.70
2004	Col	NL	64	0	0	10	40.2	187	45	34	34	1	1	0	3	26	4	20	3	0	1	2	.333	0	0-1	12	5.28	7.52
2005	2 Tms	NL	32	0	0	6	16.1	87	26	20	20	2	1	0	1	11	3	12	0	0	1	1	.500	0	2-4	6	8.82	11.02
2006	Bos	AL	27	0	0	8	16.2	69	13	10	5	1	0	1	2	10	1	11	0	0	1	0	1.000	0	1-1	6	3.96	2.70
2007	Bos	AL	61	0	0	11	40.2	174	36	16	14	2	1	1	4	18	2	26	1	0	2	1	.667	0	0-2	13	3.59	3.10
2008	Bos	AL	70	0	0	10	59.1	247	53	18	16	4	1	1	2	27	0	38	1	0	2	0	1.000	0	0-1	10	3.73	2.43
2009	Bos	AL	14	0	0	5	11.2	64	20	13	12	1	1	1	2	9	0	5	1	0	0	2	.000	0	0-0	0	11.00	9.26
2010	2 Tms	NL	77	0	0	18	57.2	235	50	17	15	2	1	2	2	20	3	38	3	0	4	2	.667	0	0-0	11	2.85	2.34
2011	SF	NL	70	0	0	17	53.0	222	42	16	16	0	3	0	3	26	6	40	1	0	5	2	.714	0	1-3	20	2.69	2.72
2012	SF	NL	70	0	0	19	36.0	153	37	13	10	1	1	1	0	14	3	28	2	0	3	0	1.000	0	7-9	18	3.60	2.50
2013	SF	NL	69	0	0	14	39.1	161	30	10	8	1	4	1	0	12	5	37	1	0	4	2	.667	0	1-1	15	1.82	1.83
2014	SF	NL	65	0	0	14	37.2	167	31	14	13	2	3	2	2	19	6	22	1	0	1	1	.500	0	0-2	12	3.00	3.11
2015	SF	NL	77	0	0	14	39.1	147	19	8	7	1	0	0	0	16	3	26	1	0	0	1	1.000	0	0-0	20	1.26	1.60
05	Col	NL	3	0	0	1	2.0	13	7	5	5	0	0	0	0	0	0	1	0	0	0	0	-	0	0-1	0	18.39	22.50
05	Ari	NL	29	0	0	5	14.1	74	19	15	15	2	1	0	1	11	3	11	0	0	1	1	.500	0	2-3	6	7.63	9.42
10	Pit	NL	50	0	0	14	38.2	166	39	14	12	2	1	2	2	18	3	22	3	0	2	2	.500	0	0-0	6	4.24	2.79
10	SF	NL	27	0	0	4	19.0	69	11	3	3	0	0	0	0	2	0	16	0	0	2	0	1.000	0	0-0	5	0.90	1.42
Postseason			31	0	0	2	17.1	72	16	6	6	0	1	1	0	6	1	15	1	0	1	1	.500	0	0-0	9	2.72	3.12
13 ML YEARS			771	0	0	157	506.2	2155	460	214	194	23	18	10	25	220	38	343	16	3	29	14	.674	0	13-26	158	3.43	3.45

Jorge Lopez

Pitches: R **Bats:** R **Pos:** SP-2   **Ht:** 6'3" **Wt:** 190 **Born:** 2/10/1993 **Age:** 23

Year	Team	Lg	G	GS	CG	GF	IP	BFP	H	R	ER	HR	SH	SF	HB	TBB	IBB	SO	WP	Bk	W	L	Pct	Sh	Sv-Op	Hld	ERC	ERA
2015	Biloxi	AA	24	24	0	0	143.1	572	105	37	36	9	3	1	3	52	0	137	13	0	12	5	.706	0	0--	-	2.43	2.26
2015	Mil	NL	2	2	0	0	10.0	46	14	6	6	0	0	0	1	5	0	10	1	0	1	1	.500	0	0-0	0	6.87	5.40

Michael Lorenzen

Pitches: R **Bats:** R **Pos:** SP-21; RP-6   **Ht:** 6'3" **Wt:** 205 **Born:** 1/4/1992 **Age:** 24

Year	Team	Lg	G	GS	CG	GF	IP	BFP	H	R	ER	HR	SH	SF	HB	TBB	IBB	SO	WP	Bk	W	L	Pct	Sh	Sv-Op	Hld	ERC	ERA
2013	Pnscla	AA	7	0	0	0	6.0	28	6	3	3	1	1	0	0	6	0	5	0	0	0	0	-	0	0--	-	7.48	4.50
2013	3 Tms	Low	15	1	0	6	15.0	67	14	5	4	1	0	0	3	7	1	14	0	0	1	1	.500	0	4--	-	4.41	2.40
2014	Pnscla	AA	24	24	0	0	120.2	504	112	50	42	9	6	5	6	44	0	84	7	0	4	6	.400	0	0--	-	3.64	3.13
2015	Lsvlle	AAA	6	6	1	0	43.0	165	34	9	9	3	1	0	0	8	0	19	2	0	4	2	.667	1	0--	-	2.09	1.88
2015	Cin	NL	27	21	0	1	113.1	515	131	70	68	18	2	1	6	57	6	83	4	0	4	9	.308	0	0-0	1	6.09	5.40

David Lough

Bats: L **Throws:** L **Pos:** LF-49;CF-26;PR-13;PH-4;RF-2 LOW   **Ht:** 5'10" **Wt:** 175 **Born:** 1/20/1986 **Age:** 30

Year	Team	Lg	G	AB	H	2B	3B	HR	(Hm	Rd)	TB	R	RBI	RC	TBB	IBB	SO	HBP	SH	SF	SB	CS	GDP	Avg	OBP	Slg	OPS
2015	Norfolk*	AAA	14	58	15	1	1	0	(-	-)	18	7	6	5	3	0	9	0	0	1	1	1	0	.259	.290	.310	.601
2012	KC	AL	20	59	14	2	1	0	(0	0)	18	7	9	2	4	0	9	1	0	1	0	0	2	.237	.292	.305	.597
2013	KC	AL	96	315	90	17	4	5	(1	4)	130	35	33	38	10	0	52	3	4	3	5	2	1	.286	.311	.413	.724
2014	Bal	AL	112	174	43	6	3	4	(3	1)	67	31	16	19	15	0	33	1	6	1	8	5	3	.247	.309	.385	.694
2015	Bal	AL	84	134	27	1	1	4	(3	1)	42	14	12	13	5	0	36	2	3	0	2	4	0	.201	.241	.313	.555
Postseason			2	1	0	0	0	0	(0	0)	0	0	0	0	0	0	0	0	0	0	0	0	0	.000	.000	.000	.000
4 ML YEARS			312	682	174	26	9	13	(7	6)	257	89	63	75	34	0	130	7	13	5	16	11	8	.255	.295	.377	.672

Aaron Loup

Pitches: L **Bats:** L **Pos:** RP-60 LOOP   **Ht:** 5'11" **Wt:** 205 **Born:** 12/19/1987 **Age:** 28

Year	Team	Lg	G	GS	CG	GF	IP	BFP	H	R	ER	HR	SH	SF	HB	TBB	IBB	SO	WP	Bk	W	L	Pct	Sh	Sv-Op	Hld	ERC	ERA
2015	Buffalo*	AAA	5	0	0	2	6.0	30	9	3	3	0	0	0	1	4	0	5	0	1	0	0	-	0	0--	-	8.44	4.50
2012	Tor	AL	33	0	0	3	30.2	117	26	10	9	0	2	1	0	2	0	21	1	1	0	2	.000	0	0-1	6	1.59	2.64

Year	Team	Lg	G	GS	CG	GF	IP	BFP	H	R	ER	HR	SH	SF	HB	TBB	IBB	SO	WP	Bk	W	L	Pct	Sh	Sv-Op	Hld	ERC	ERA
			HOW MUCH HE PITCHED						WHAT HE GAVE UP												THE RESULTS							
2013	Tor	AL	64	0	0	12	69.1	282	66	23	19	5	2	4	7	13	4	53	2	0	4	6	.400	0	2-3	8	3.20	2.47
2014	Tor	AL	71	0	0	15	68.2	283	50	25	24	4	3	3	6	30	5	56	5	0	4	4	.500	0	4-8	13	2.75	3.15
2015	Tor	AL	60	0	0	6	42.1	186	47	24	21	6	2	0	6	7	0	46	0	0	2	5	.286	0	0-4	9	4.54	4.46
4 ML YEARS			228	0	0	36	211.0	868	189	82	73	15	9	8	19	52	9	176	8	1	10	17	.370	0	6-16	36	3.05	3.11

Mark Lowe

Pitches: R **Bats:** L **Pos:** RP-57   **Ht:** 6'3" **Wt:** 210 **Born:** 6/7/1983 **Age:** 33

Year	Team	Lg	G	GS	CG	GF	IP	BFP	H	R	ER	HR	SH	SF	HB	TBB	IBB	SO	WP	Bk	W	L	Pct	Sh	Sv-Op	Hld	ERC	ERA
			HOW MUCH HE PITCHED						WHAT HE GAVE UP												THE RESULTS							
2015	Tacom*	AAA	7	0	0	6	9.0	32	7	1	1	1	0	0	0	0	0	11	0	0	0	1	.000	0	1- -	-	1.68	1.00
2006	Sea	AL	15	0	0	3	18.2	75	12	4	4	1	1	0	2	9	1	20	1	0	1	0	1.000	0	0-0	6	2.61	1.93
2007	Sea	AL	4	0	0	1	2.2	13	2	2	2	1	0	0	0	3	0	3	0	0	0	0	-	0	0-0	2	7.69	6.75
2008	Sea	AL	57	0	0	19	63.2	303	78	44	38	6	3	3	4	34	0	55	2	0	1	5	.167	0	1-5	1	6.10	5.37
2009	Sea	AL	75	0	0	18	80.0	339	71	39	29	7	0	4	0	29	1	69	4	0	2	7	.222	0	3-13	26	3.16	3.26
2010	2 Tms	AL	14	0	0	5	13.1	61	18	9	8	2	0	1	0	6	1	12	1	0	1	3	.250	0	0-0	4	6.82	5.40
2011	Tex	AL	52	0	0	10	45.0	196	46	26	19	6	1	1	0	19	4	42	3	0	2	3	.400	0	1-3	11	4.38	3.80
2012	Tex	AL	36	0	0	12	39.1	162	35	15	15	5	0	3	0	13	0	28	4	2	2	0	.000	0	0-0	1	3.41	3.43
2013	LAA	AL	11	0	0	2	11.2	56	11	12	12	1	2	0	0	11	1	7	2	0	1	0	1.000	0	0-0	1	5.60	9.26
2014	Cle	AL	7	0	0	1	7.0	39	10	7	3	2	0	1	0	6	4	6	1	0	0	1	.000	0	0-0	0	8.50	3.86
2015	2 Tms	AL	57	0	0	13	55.0	215	46	15	12	4	0	2	1	12	1	61	2	0	1	3	.250	0	1-5	17	2.49	1.96
10	Sea	AL	11	0	0	4	10.1	45	11	5	4	1	0	1	0	5	1	7	1	0	1	3	.250	0	0-0	4	4.70	3.48
10	Tex	AL	3	0	0	1	3.0	16	7	4	4	1	0	0	0	1	0	5	0	0	0	0	-	0	0-0	0	15.67	12.00
15	Sea	AL	34	0	0	8	36.0	144	31	6	4	1	0	0	1	11	1	47	2	0	0	1	.000	0	0-2	12	2.67	1.00
15	Tor	AL	23	0	0	5	19.0	71	15	9	8	3	0	2	0	1	0	14	0	0	1	2	.333	0	1-3	5	2.07	3.79
Postseason			4	0	0	1	1.2	13	7	7	7	1	0	0	0	1	0	1	0	0	0	1	.000	0	0-0	0	35.40	37.80
10 ML YEARS			328	0	0	84	336.1	1459	329	173	142	35	7	15	7	142	13	303	20	2	9	24	.273	0	6-26	69	4.08	3.80

Jed Lowrie

Bats: B **Throws:** R **Pos:** 3B-47;SS-17;PH-6;DH-2   LAU-ree   **Ht:** 6'0" **Wt:** 180 **Born:** 4/17/1984 **Age:** 32

Year	Team	Lg	G	AB	H	2B	3B	HR	(Hm	Rd)	TB	R	RBI	RC	TBB	IBB	SO	HBP	SH	SF	SB	CS	GDP	Avg	OBP	Slg	OPS
			BATTING																		RUNNING			AVERAGES			
2008	Bos	AL	81	260	67	25	3	2	(0	2)	104	34	46	35	35	0	68	1	2	8	1	0	8	.258	.339	.400	.739
2009	Bos	AL	32	68	10	2	0	2	(1	1)	18	5	11	5	6	0	20	0	0	2	0	0	0	.147	.211	.265	.475
2010	Bos	AL	55	171	49	14	0	9	(3	6)	90	31	24	32	25	0	25	1	0	0	1	1	2	.287	.381	.526	.907
2011	Bos	AL	88	309	78	14	4	6	(3	3)	118	40	36	33	23	2	60	2	1	6	1	1	6	.252	.303	.382	.685
2012	Hou	NL	97	340	83	18	0	16	(9	7)	149	43	42	45	43	0	65	2	0	2	2	0	3	.244	.331	.438	.769
2013	Oak	AL	154	603	175	45	2	15	(7	8)	269	80	75	88	50	3	91	2	3	4	1	0	17	.290	.344	.446	.791
2014	Oak	AL	136	502	125	29	3	6	(4	2)	178	59	50	52	51	5	79	5	2	6	0	0	14	.249	.321	.355	.676
2015	Hou	AL	69	230	51	14	0	9	(5	4)	92	35	30	29	28	5	43	3	0	2	1	0	3	.222	.312	.400	.712
Postseason			18	56	9	2	0	1	(0	1)	14	6	5	4	7	0	15	1	1	1	0	0	1	.161	.262	.250	.512
8 ML YEARS			712	2483	638	161	12	65	(32	33)	1018	327	314	319	261	15	451	16	8	30	7	2	53	.257	.328	.410	.738

Jonathan Lucroy

Bats: R **Throws:** R **Pos:** C-86;PH-11;1B-7;DH-1   LOO-croy   **Ht:** 6'0" **Wt:** 195 **Born:** 6/13/1986 **Age:** 30

Year	Team	Lg	G	AB	H	2B	3B	HR	(Hm	Rd)	TB	R	RBI	RC	TBB	IBB	SO	HBP	SH	SF	SB	CS	GDP	Avg	OBP	Slg	OPS
			BATTING																		RUNNING			AVERAGES			
2010	Mil	NL	75	277	70	9	0	4	(4	0)	91	24	26	23	18	1	44	1	0	1	4	2	9	.253	.300	.329	.628
2011	Mil	NL	136	430	114	16	1	12	(8	4)	168	45	59	50	29	0	99	2	4	3	2	1	7	.265	.313	.391	.703
2012	Mil	NL	96	316	101	17	4	12	(7	5)	162	46	58	61	22	1	44	4	1	3	4	1	12	.320	.368	.513	.881
2013	Mil	NL	147	521	146	25	6	18	(9	9)	237	59	82	78	46	2	69	5	0	8	9	1	16	.280	.340	.455	.795
2014	Mil	NL	153	585	176	53	2	13	(6	7)	272	73	69	90	66	3	71	2	0	2	4	4	13	.301	.373	.465	.837
2015	Mil	NL	103	371	98	20	3	7	(3	4)	145	51	43	46	36	0	64	1	1	6	1	0	18	.264	.326	.391	.717
Postseason			10	32	8	1	0	1	(1	0)	12	3	5	4	0	0	8	0	0	0	0	0	0	.250	.250	.375	.625
6 ML YEARS			710	2500	705	140	16	66	(37	29)	1075	298	337	348	217	7	391	15	6	23	24	9	75	.282	.340	.430	.770

Lucas Luetge

Pitches: L **Bats:** L **Pos:** RP-1   LOOT-key   **Ht:** 6'4" **Wt:** 205 **Born:** 3/24/1987 **Age:** 29

Year	Team	Lg	G	GS	CG	GF	IP	BFP	H	R	ER	HR	SH	SF	HB	TBB	IBB	SO	WP	Bk	W	L	Pct	Sh	Sv-Op	Hld	ERC	ERA
			HOW MUCH HE PITCHED						WHAT HE GAVE UP												THE RESULTS							
2015	Tacom*	AAA	29	0	0	6	49.0	232	57	31	29	8	3	4	1	23	0	37	4	0	3	2	.600	0	2- -	-	5.86	5.33
2012	Sea	AL	63	0	0	16	40.2	178	37	20	18	3	1	3	1	24	6	38	5	0	2	2	.500	0	2-3	12	4.01	3.98
2013	Sea	AL	35	0	0	15	37.0	165	42	22	20	2	2	3	2	16	2	27	4	0	1	3	.250	0	0-0	1	4.81	4.86
2014	Sea	AL	12	0	0	4	9.0	38	6	5	5	3	0	0	0	5	0	7	1	0	0	0	-	0	0-0	0	4.31	5.00
2015	Sea	AL	1	0	0	1	2.1	8	0	0	0	0	0	0	0	2	0	2	0	0	0	0	-	0	0-0	0	0.81	0.00
4 ML YEARS			111	0	0	36	89.0	389	85	47	43	8	3	6	3	47	8	74	10	0	3	5	.375	0	2-3	13	4.28	4.35

Jordan Lyles

Pitches: R **Bats:** R **Pos:** SP-10   **Ht:** 6'4" **Wt:** 230 **Born:** 10/19/1990 **Age:** 25

Year	Team	Lg	G	GS	CG	GF	IP	BFP	H	R	ER	HR	SH	SF	HB	TBB	IBB	SO	WP	Bk	W	L	Pct	Sh	Sv-Op	Hld	ERC	ERA
			HOW MUCH HE PITCHED						WHAT HE GAVE UP												THE RESULTS							
2011	Hou	NL	20	15	0	2	94.0	415	107	61	56	14	7	1	5	26	1	67	0	0	2	8	.200	0	0-0	0	4.87	5.36
2012	Hou	NL	25	25	1	0	141.1	628	159	97	80	20	6	4	5	42	4	99	2	0	5	12	.294	1	0-0	0	4.67	5.09

Year Team	Lg	G	GS	CG	GF	IP	BFP	H	R	ER	HR	SH	SF	HB	TBB	IBB	SO	WP	Bk	W	L	Pct	Sh	Sv-Op	Hld	ERC	ERA
2013 Hou	AL	27	25	0	1	141.2	642	165	98	88	17	0	3	11	49	1	93	5	2	7	9	.438	0	1-1	1	5.20	5.59
2014 Col	NL	22	22	0	0	126.2	546	127	64	61	12	4	3	8	46	1	90	6	0	7	4	.636	0	0-0	0	4.17	4.33
2015 Col	NL	10	10	0	0	49.0	212	54	32	28	2	3	1	3	19	1	30	2	0	2	5	.286	0	0-0	0	4.51	5.14
5 ML YEARS		104	97	1	3	552.2	2443	612	352	313	65	20	12	32	182	8	379	15	2	23	38	.377	1	1-1	1	4.71	5.10

Lance Lynn

Pitches: R **Bats:** R **Pos:** SP-31 · **Ht:** 6'5" **Wt:** 240 **Born:** 5/12/1987 **Age:** 29

Year Team	Lg	G	GS	CG	GF	IP	BFP	H	R	ER	HR	SH	SF	HB	TBB	IBB	SO	WP	Bk	W	L	Pct	Sh	Sv-Op	Hld	ERC	ERA
2011 StL	NL	18	2	0	2	34.2	136	25	12	12	3	1	0	1	11	1	40	1	0	1	1	.500	0	1-2	3	2.37	3.12
2012 StL	NL	35	29	0	2	176.0	744	168	76	74	16	4	3	10	64	3	180	3	0	18	7	.720	0	0-0	1	3.87	3.78
2013 StL	NL	33	33	0	0	201.2	856	189	92	89	14	11	8	11	76	0	198	6	0	15	10	.600	0	0-0	0	3.67	3.97
2014 StL	NL	33	33	2	0	203.2	866	185	72	62	13	6	4	7	72	1	181	7	0	15	10	.600	1	0-0	0	3.24	2.74
2015 StL	NL	31	31	0	0	175.1	751	172	66	59	13	9	2	5	68	5	167	2	0	12	11	.522	0	0-0	0	3.83	3.03
Postseason		23	7	0	3	51.0	227	55	29	25	6	2	3	1	25	5	48	0	0	5	4	.556	0	0-0	3	4.97	4.41
5 ML YEARS		150	128	2	4	791.1	3353	739	318	296	59	31	17	34	291	10	766	19	0	61	39	.610	1	1-2	4	3.58	3.37

Tyler Lyons

Pitches: L **Bats:** B **Pos:** RP-9; SP-8 · **Ht:** 6'4" **Wt:** 200 **Born:** 2/21/1988 **Age:** 28

Year Team	Lg	G	GS	CG	GF	IP	BFP	H	R	ER	HR	SH	SF	HB	TBB	IBB	SO	WP	Bk	W	L	Pct	Sh	Sv-Op	Hld	ERC	ERA
2015 Memp*	AAA	16	16	2	0	94.2	397	104	34	33	12	1	2	2	13	0	96	0	1	9	5	.643	1	0- -	-	3.83	3.14
2013 StL	NL	12	8	0	1	53.0	223	49	29	28	5	1	0	3	16	0	43	0	0	2	4	.333	0	0-0	0	3.46	4.75
2014 StL	NL	11	4	0	1	36.2	155	33	23	18	4	1	1	2	11	2	36	0	0	0	4	.000	0	0-0	0	3.29	4.42
2015 StL	NL	17	8	0	1	60.0	255	59	29	25	12	3	2	1	15	0	60	4	0	3	1	.750	0	0-0	0	4.04	3.75
3 ML YEARS		40	20	0	3	149.2	633	141	81	71	21	5	3	6	42	2	139	4	0	5	9	.357	0	0-0	0	3.65	4.27

Dixon Machado

Bats: R **Throws:** R **Pos:** SS-24;PH-2 · **Ht:** 6'1" **Wt:** 170 **Born:** 2/22/1992 **Age:** 24

Year Team	Lg	G	AB	H	2B	3B	HR	(Hm	Rd)	TB	R	RBI	RC	TBB	IBB	SO	HBP	SH	SF	SB	CS	GDP	Avg	OBP	Slg	OPS
2011 Wmich	A	124	429	101	1	2	0	(-	-)	106	47	28	40	46	1	77	4	10	2	25	5	12	.235	.314	.247	.561
2012 Lkland	A+	119	421	82	16	1	2	(-	-)	106	59	37	35	51	0	61	1	16	1	23	5	14	.195	.283	.252	.534
2013 2 Tms	Low	44	177	41	7	2	1	(-	-)	55	22	14	15	11	1	24	0	5	0	1	0	6	.232	.277	.311	.587
2014 Lkland	A+	41	159	40	8	1	1	(-	-)	53	30	8	20	23	0	34	1	3	1	2	1	5	.252	.348	.333	.681
2014 Erie	AA	90	292	89	23	1	5	(-	-)	129	45	32	53	40	0	36	3	4	3	8	5	10	.305	.391	.442	.832
2015 Toledo	AAA	127	509	133	22	1	4	(-	-)	169	61	48	58	36	0	85	4	15	3	15	3	16	.261	.313	.332	.645
2015 Det	AL	24	68	16	3	0	0	(0	0)	19	6	5	5	7	0	14	0	3	0	1	0	3	.235	.307	.279	.586

Manny Machado

Bats: R **Throws:** R **Pos:** 3B-156;SS-7 · muh-CHAH-doe · **Ht:** 6'3" **Wt:** 185 **Born:** 7/6/1992 **Age:** 23

Year Team	Lg	G	AB	H	2B	3B	HR	(Hm	Rd)	TB	R	RBI	RC	TBB	IBB	SO	HBP	SH	SF	SB	CS	GDP	Avg	OBP	Slg	OPS
2012 Bal	AL	51	191	50	8	3	7	(7	0)	85	24	26	29	9	0	38	0	1	2	2	0	6	.262	.294	.445	.739
2013 Bal	AL	156	667	189	51	3	14	(5	9)	288	88	71	87	29	0	113	2	9	3	6	7	15	.283	.314	.432	.746
2014 Bal	AL	82	327	91	14	0	12	(9	3)	141	38	32	44	20	2	68	3	2	2	2	0	13	.278	.324	.431	.755
2015 Bal	AL	162	633	181	30	1	35	(21	14)	318	102	86	107	70	2	111	4	2	4	20	8	17	.286	.359	.502	.861
Postseason		6	19	3	1	0	1	(0	1)	7	2	1	2	1	2	6	0	2	0	0	0	1	.158	.238	.368	.607
4 ML YEARS		451	1818	511	103	7	68	(42	26)	832	252	215	267	128	4	330	9	14	10	30	15	51	.281	.330	.458	.787

Jean Machi

Pitches: R **Bats:** R **Pos:** RP-59 · GENE ma-CHEE · **Ht:** 6'0" **Wt:** 255 **Born:** 2/1/1982 **Age:** 34

Year Team	Lg	G	GS	CG	GF	IP	BFP	H	R	ER	HR	SH	SF	HB	TBB	IBB	SO	WP	Bk	W	L	Pct	Sh	Sv-Op	Hld	ERC	ERA
2012 SF	NL	8	0	0	5	6.2	28	7	5	5	2	0	0	0	1	0	4	0	0	0	0	-	0	0-0	0	4.56	6.75
2013 SF	NL	51	0	0	6	53.0	211	46	15	14	2	1	1	0	12	3	51	2	0	3	1	.750	0	0-2	11	2.30	2.38
2014 SF	NL	71	0	0	13	66.1	249	45	19	19	5	5	1	1	18	3	51	5	1	7	1	.875	0	2-5	17	1.93	2.58
2015 2 Tms		59	0	0	17	58.0	257	59	35	33	8	2	3	1	22	0	42	3	0	2	0	1.000	0	4-4	4	4.31	5.12
15 SF	NL	33	0	0	8	35.0	159	38	21	20	3	2	2	1	14	0	22	1	0	1	0	1.000	0	0-0	2	4.43	5.14
15 Bos	AL	26	0	0	9	23.0	98	21	14	13	5	0	1	0	8	0	20	2	0	1	0	1.000	0	4-4	2	4.09	5.09
Postseason		7	0	0	0	5.2	28	9	5	5	2	0	0	0	2	0	4	0	0	0	0	-	0	0-1	0	9.46	7.94
4 ML YEARS		189	0	0	44	184.0	745	157	74	71	17	8	5	2	53	6	148	10	1	12	2	.857	0	6-11	32	2.84	3.47

Ryan Madson

Pitches: R **Bats:** L **Pos:** RP-68 · **Ht:** 6'6" **Wt:** 210 **Born:** 8/28/1980 **Age:** 35

Year Team	Lg	G	GS	CG	GF	IP	BFP	H	R	ER	HR	SH	SF	HB	TBB	IBB	SO	WP	Bk	W	L	Pct	Sh	Sv-Op	Hld	ERC	ERA
2003 Phi	NL	1	0	0	0	2.0	6	0	0	0	0	0	0	0	0	0	0	0	0	0	0	-	0	0-0	0	0.00	0.00
2004 Phi	NL	52	1	0	14	77.0	312	68	23	20	6	1	1	5	19	4	55	7	0	9	3	.750	0	1-2	7	2.95	2.34
2005 Phi	NL	78	0	0	10	87.0	365	84	44	40	11	5	5	6	25	6	79	6	1	6	5	.545	0	0-7	32	3.83	4.14
2006 Phi	NL	50	17	0	8	134.1	620	176	92	85	20	9	3	10	50	4	99	12	0	11	9	.550	0	2-4	6	6.50	5.69
2007 Phi	NL	38	0	0	9	56.0	237	48	19	19	5	2	2	2	23	4	43	2	2	2	2	.500	0	1-2	7	3.28	3.05
2008 Phi	NL	76	0	0	14	82.2	340	79	29	28	6	3	1	2	23	4	67	2	1	4	2	.667	0	1-3	17	3.20	3.05

208

Year	Team	Lg	G	GS	CG	GF	IP	BFP	H	R	ER	HR	SH	SF	HB	TBB	IBB	SO	WP	Bk	W	L	Pct	Sh	Sv-Op	Hld	ERC	ERA
							HOW MUCH HE PITCHED					WHAT HE GAVE UP												THE RESULTS				
2009	Phi	NL	79	0	0	28	77.1	320	73	29	28	7	3	1	3	22	3	78	1	0	5	5	.500	0	10-16	26	3.39	3.26
2010	Phi	NL	55	0	0	21	53.0	217	42	16	15	4	2	0	4	13	3	64	2	0	6	2	.750	0	5-10	15	2.42	2.55
2011	Phi	NL	62	0	0	46	60.2	246	54	16	16	2	6	1	1	16	8	62	0	0	4	2	.667	0	32-34	3	2.45	2.37
2015	KC	AL	68	0	0	12	63.1	248	47	17	15	5	0	3	2	14	1	58	1	0	1	2	.333	0	3-5	20	2.08	2.13
	Postseason		33	0	0	11	35.0	145	33	9	9	2	2	2	1	10	2	43	2	0	2	1	.667	0	2-6	7	3.09	2.31
	10 ML YEARS		559	18	0	162	693.1	2911	671	285	266	66	31	18	34	205	37	605	33	4	48	32	.600	0	55-83	133	3.59	3.45

Kenta Maeda

Pitches: R Bats: R Pos: P mah-AY-duh **Ht: 6'0" Wt: 154 Born: 4/11/1988 Age: 28**

Year	Team	Lg	G	GS	CG	GF	IP	BFP	H	R	ER	HR	SH	SF	HB	TBB	IBB	SO	WP	Bk	W	L	Pct	Sh	Sv-Op	Hld	ERC	ERA
							HOW MUCH HE PITCHED					WHAT HE GAVE UP												THE RESULTS				
2011	HiroCrp	IND	31	31	4	0	216.0	864	178	61	59	14	-	-	6	43	0	192	4	0	10	12	.455	2	0--	-	2.29	2.46
2012	HiroCrp	IND	29	29	5	0	206.1	820	161	46	35	6	-	-	9	44	1	171	2	0	14	7	.667	2	0--	-	1.99	1.53
2013	HiroCrp	IND	26	26	3	0	175.2	690	129	46	41	13	-	-	2	40	1	158	1	0	15	7	.682	1	0--	-	1.96	2.10
2014	HiroCrp	IND	27	27	1	0	187.0	746	164	61	54	12	-	-	2	41	1	161	4	1	11	9	.550	1	0--	-	2.59	2.60
2015	HiroCrp	IND	28	28	5	0	199.1	791	162	49	48	5	-	-	6	38	0	170	3	0	15	8	.652	0	0--	-	2.00	2.17

Mikie Mahtook

MIKE-ee MAH-took

Bats: R Throws: R Pos: LF-16;CF-13;RF-12;PH-5;PR-4;DH-3 **Ht: 6'1" Wt: 200 Born: 11/30/1989 Age: 26**

Year	Team	Lg	G	AB	H	2B	3B	HR	(Hm	Rd)	TB	R	RBI	RC	TBB	IBB	SO	HBP	SH	SF	SB	CS	GDP	Avg	OBP	Slg	OPS
								BATTING													RUNNING			AVERAGES			
2012	Charltt	A+	92	341	99	15	7	5	(-	-)	143	44	37	55	29	2	71	10	0	6	19	6	7	.290	.358	.419	.777
2012	Mont	AA	39	153	38	10	1	4	(-	-)	62	17	25	19	11	0	31	3	0	2	4	3	3	.248	.308	.405	.713
2013	Mont	AA	132	511	130	30	8	7	(-	-)	197	71	68	68	43	0	102	10	0	4	25	8	18	.254	.322	.386	.708
2014	Drham	AAA	132	489	143	33	6	12	(-	-)	224	56	68	85	46	4	137	10	0	5	18	5	9	.292	.362	.458	.820
2015	Drham	AAA	98	385	96	27	3	4	(-	-)	141	35	45	46	22	0	98	9	0	2	10	1	3	.249	.304	.366	.670
2015	TB	AL	41	105	31	5	1	9	(3	6)	65	22	19	22	6	0	31	3	1	0	4	3	0	.295	.351	.619	.970

Luke Maile

MAY-lee

Bats: R Throws: R Pos: C-15;PH-2 **Ht: 6'3" Wt: 225 Born: 2/6/1991 Age: 25**

Year	Team	Lg	G	AB	H	2B	3B	HR	(Hm	Rd)	TB	R	RBI	RC	TBB	IBB	SO	HBP	SH	SF	SB	CS	GDP	Avg	OBP	Slg	OPS
								BATTING													RUNNING			AVERAGES			
2012	HudVal	A-	61	216	60	10	3	3	(-	-)	85	30	41	35	31	0	36	4	0	1	3	1	4	.278	.377	.394	.771
2013	BG	A	95	361	102	25	3	4	(-	-)	145	45	49	54	41	0	54	0	0	5	8	2	10	.283	.351	.402	.753
2014	Mont	AA	97	351	94	19	3	5	(-	-)	134	43	37	48	35	0	76	5	0	2	2	1	13	.268	.341	.382	.723
2015	Drham	AAA	89	294	61	9	1	5	(-	-)	87	38	29	28	35	0	50	4	1	3	1	1	11	.207	.298	.296	.594
2015	TB	AL	15	35	6	3	0	0	(0	0)	9	2	2	1	0	0	8	0	0	0	0	0	3	.171	.171	.257	.429

Martin Maldonado

mar-TEEN

Bats: R Throws: R Pos: C-74;PH-6;1B-1 **Ht: 6'0" Wt: 225 Born: 8/16/1986 Age: 29**

Year	Team	Lg	G	AB	H	2B	3B	HR	(Hm	Rd)	TB	R	RBI	RC	TBB	IBB	SO	HBP	SH	SF	SB	CS	GDP	Avg	OBP	Slg	OPS
								BATTING													RUNNING			AVERAGES			
2011	Mil	NL	3	1	0	0	0	0	(0	0)	0	0	0	0	0	0	1	0	0	0	0	0	0	.000	.000	.000	.000
2012	Mil	NL	78	233	62	9	0	8	(6	2)	95	22	30	28	17	0	56	2	4	0	1	1	5	.266	.321	.408	.729
2013	Mil	NL	67	183	31	7	1	4	(1	3)	52	13	22	14	13	1	53	3	3	0	0	0	2	.169	.236	.284	.520
2014	Mil	NL	52	111	26	5	0	4	(2	2)	43	14	16	14	11	1	32	3	1	0	0	0	4	.234	.320	.387	.707
2015	Mil	NL	79	229	48	7	0	4	(4	0)	67	19	22	20	23	3	65	1	1	2	0	1	6	.210	.282	.293	.575
	5 ML YEARS		279	757	167	28	1	20	(13	7)	257	68	90	76	64	5	207	9	9	2	1	2	17	.221	.288	.339	.628

Seth Maness

MAY-ness

Pitches: R Bats: R Pos: RP-76 **Ht: 6'0" Wt: 190 Born: 10/14/1988 Age: 27**

Year	Team	Lg	G	GS	CG	GF	IP	BFP	H	R	ER	HR	SH	SF	HB	TBB	IBB	SO	WP	Bk	W	L	Pct	Sh	Sv-Op	Hld	ERC	ERA
							HOW MUCH HE PITCHED					WHAT HE GAVE UP												THE RESULTS				
2013	StL	NL	66	0	0	4	62.0	249	65	17	16	4	4	0	1	13	7	35	2	0	5	2	.714	0	1-3	15	3.41	2.32
2014	StL	NL	73	0	0	17	80.1	317	77	29	26	7	5	4	2	11	3	55	2	1	6	4	.600	0	3-3	11	2.90	2.91
2015	StL	NL	76	0	0	13	63.1	270	77	35	30	7	4	1	1	13	4	46	2	0	4	2	.667	0	3-6	20	4.65	4.26
	Postseason		15	0	0	2	10.2	41	11	2	1	1	0	1	0	0	0	5	0	0	1	0	1.000	0	0-1	1	2.77	0.84
	3 ML YEARS		215	0	0	34	205.2	836	219	81	72	18	13	5	4	37	14	136	6	1	15	8	.652	0	7-12	46	3.57	3.15

Jeff Manship

Pitches: R Bats: R Pos: RP-32 **Ht: 6'2" Wt: 205 Born: 1/16/1985 Age: 31**

Year	Team	Lg	G	GS	CG	GF	IP	BFP	H	R	ER	HR	SH	SF	HB	TBB	IBB	SO	WP	Bk	W	L	Pct	Sh	Sv-Op	Hld	ERC	ERA
							HOW MUCH HE PITCHED					WHAT HE GAVE UP												THE RESULTS				
2015	Clmbs*	AAA	23	0	0	7	31.2	127	25	7	7	3	2	2	0	9	1	31	1	0	0	2	.000	0	2--	-	2.46	1.99
2009	Min	AL	11	5	0	1	31.2	146	39	21	20	4	1	3	1	15	0	21	2	0	1	1	.500	0	0-0	0	6.11	5.68
2010	Min	AL	13	1	0	1	29.0	124	34	20	17	3	1	1	0	6	0	21	0	0	2	1	.667	0	0-0	0	4.31	5.28
2011	Min	AL	5	0	0	1	3.1	19	5	3	3	0	0	2	0	4	1	2	0	0	0	0	-	0	0-0	0	8.73	8.10
2012	Min	AL	12	0	0	2	21.2	98	29	19	19	4	1	0	1	7	1	12	0	0	0	0	-	0	0-0	1	6.67	7.89
2013	Col	NL	11	4	0	3	30.2	139	37	25	24	6	0	3	0	12	1	18	0	0	0	5	.000	0	0-0	0	5.87	7.04
2014	Phi	NL	20	0	0	7	23.0	105	24	17	17	1	3	0	0	14	5	16	0	0	1	2	.333	0	0-0	0	4.30	6.65
2015	Cle	AL	32	0	0	7	39.1	144	20	4	4	1	0	4	1	10	0	33	0	0	1	0	1.000	0	0-0	3	1.14	0.92
	7 ML YEARS		104	10	0	22	178.2	775	188	109	104	19	6	13	3	68	8	123	2	0	5	9	.357	0	0-0	4	4.35	5.24

Shaun Marcum

Pitches: R **Bats:** R **Pos:** SP-6; RP-1 **Ht:** 6'0" **Wt:** 195 **Born:** 12/14/1981 **Age:** 34

Year Team	Lg	G	GS	CG	GF	IP	BFP	H	R	ER	HR	SH	SF	HB	TBB	IBB	SO	WP	Bk	W	L	Pct	Sh	Sv-Op	Hld	ERC	ERA
2015 Clmbs*	AAA	16	14	0	0	88.1	359	85	36	32	7	3	2	0	21	0	67	2	0	7	4	.636	0	0- -	-	3.16	3.26
2005 Tor	AL	5	0	0	3	8.0	32	6	0	0	0	0	0	0	4	0	4	0	0	0	0	-	0	0-0	-	2.58	0.00
2006 Tor	AL	21	14	0	3	78.1	357	87	44	44	14	1	2	4	38	3	65	1	0	3	4	.429	0	0-0	0	5.80	5.06
2007 Tor	AL	38	25	0	6	159.0	660	149	76	73	27	3	3	5	49	1	122	1	0	12	6	.667	0	1-2	1	4.00	4.13
2008 Tor	AL	25	25	0	0	151.1	630	126	60	57	21	1	3	8	50	2	123	3	0	9	7	.563	0	0-0	0	3.32	3.39
2010 Tor	AL	31	31	1	0	195.1	800	175	84	79	24	1	3	6	43	3	165	3	0	13	8	.619	0	0-0	0	3.24	3.64
2011 Mil	NL	33	33	0	0	200.2	823	175	84	79	22	6	6	0	57	3	158	6	0	13	7	.650	0	0-0	0	2.97	3.54
2012 Mil	NL	21	21	0	0	124.0	527	116	57	51	16	6	2	4	41	2	109	3	2	7	4	.636	0	0-0	0	3.71	3.70
2013 NYM	NL	14	12	0	2	78.1	334	85	48	46	7	6	4	4	21	2	60	2	0	1	10	.091	0	0-0	0	4.17	5.29
2015 Cle	AL	7	6	0	1	35.0	142	32	21	21	9	0	0	1	11	3	30	2	0	3	2	.600	0	0-0	0	4.44	5.40
Postseason		3	3	0	0	9.2	49	17	16	16	3	1	0	0	5	1	5	0	0	0	3	.000	0	0-0	0	11.38	14.90
9 ML YEARS		195	167	1	15	1030.0	4305	957	474	450	140	24	23	32	314	19	836	21	2	61	48	.560	0	1-2	1	3.66	3.93

Sugar Marimon

Pitches: R **Bats:** R **Pos:** RP-16   mah-REE-mohn   **Ht:** 6'1" **Wt:** 195 **Born:** 9/30/1988 **Age:** 27

Year Team	Lg	G	GS	CG	GF	IP	BFP	H	R	ER	HR	SH	SF	HB	TBB	IBB	SO	WP	Bk	W	L	Pct	Sh	Sv-Op	Hld	ERC	ERA
2011 Kane	A	13	13	0	0	66.0	269	55	30	27	6	5	0	2	20	0	54	5	1	3	5	.375	0	0- -	-	2.89	3.68
2012 Wilmg	A+	14	9	0	4	68.0	274	51	16	16	5	4	1	4	18	1	60	6	1	4	2	.667	0	1- -	-	2.29	2.12
2012 NWArk	AA	12	12	0	0	66.2	288	66	34	34	9	1	2	6	29	0	36	4	0	3	6	.333	0	0- -	-	4.90	4.59
2013 NWArk	AA	27	26	2	0	148.1	644	159	86	71	26	6	7	4	45	0	119	6	4	6	14	.300	0	0- -	-	4.70	4.31
2014	AAA	15	15	0	0	83.1	353	88	36	33	10	2	1	5	26	1	67	4	0	5	4	.556	0	0- -	-	4.52	3.56
2015 Gwnntt	AAA	17	14	0	0	81.2	338	75	34	30	4	0	6	3	26	0	49	3	0	5	4	.556	0	0- -	-	3.16	3.31
2015 Atl	NL	16	0	0	5	25.2	117	30	21	21	3	1	2	0	14	0	14	0	0	0	1	.000	0	0-0	0	5.86	7.36

Michael Mariot

Pitches: R **Bats:** R **Pos:** RP-2   MARE-ee-utt   **Ht:** 6'0" **Wt:** 190 **Born:** 10/20/1988 **Age:** 27

Year Team	Lg	G	GS	CG	GF	IP	BFP	H	R	ER	HR	SH	SF	HB	TBB	IBB	SO	WP	Bk	W	L	Pct	Sh	Sv-Op	Hld	ERC	ERA
2011 Wilmg	A+	28	9	0	14	100.1	426	99	47	38	7	2	2	2	21	0	80	9	0	8	4	.667	0	5- -	-	3.05	3.41
2012 NWArk	AA	31	14	0	4	113.2	470	111	48	43	12	3	2	4	30	2	81	7	0	6	3	.667	0	1- -	-	3.62	3.40
2013 Omha	AAA	47	1	0	34	60.2	261	59	31	24	4	1	4	2	25	2	66	7	0	4	5	.444	0	11- -	-	3.82	3.56
2014 Omha	AAA	14	0	0	6	20.0	87	19	11	11	2	0	0	0	7	0	25	2	0	2	1	.667	0	2- -	-	3.48	4.95
2015 Omha	AAA	42	0	0	26	62.0	255	52	23	16	3	3	1	3	16	1	72	6	0	4	2	.667	0	8- -	-	2.49	2.32
2014 KC	AL	17	0	0	8	25.0	118	31	21	18	2	0	2	0	12	1	21	5	1	1	0	1.000	0	0-0	0	5.43	6.48
2015 KC	AL	2	0	0	1	3.0	12	2	1	1	1	0	0	0	2	0	1	0	0	0	0	-	0	0-0	0	5.24	3.00
2 ML YEARS		19	0	0	9	28.0	130	33	22	19	3	0	2	0	14	1	22	5	1	1	0	1.000	0	0-0	0	5.42	6.11

Jake Marisnick

mah-RIZ-nick

Bats: R **Throws:** R **Pos:** CF-99;LF-16;RF-13;PR-13;PH-5;DH-1 **Ht:** 6'4" **Wt:** 220 **Born:** 3/30/1991 **Age:** 25

Year Team	Lg	G	AB	H	2B	3B	HR	(Hm	Rd)	TB	R	RBI	RC	TBB	IBB	SO	HBP	SH	SF	SB	CS	GDP	Avg	OBP	Slg	OPS
2013 Mia	NL	40	109	20	2	1	1	(1	0)	27	6	5	7	6	0	27	1	1	1	3	1	1	.183	.231	.248	.478
2014 2 Tms		65	221	55	8	0	3	(3	0)	72	21	19	19	8	3	67	3	2	3	8	4	2	.249	.281	.326	.607
2015 Hou	AL	133	339	80	15	4	9	(4	5)	130	46	36	40	18	0	105	5	6	4	24	9	2	.236	.281	.383	.665
14 Mia	NL	14	48	8	0	0	0	(0	0)	8	3	0	1	3	1	19	0	0	0	5	0	0	.167	.216	.167	.382
14 Hou	AL	51	173	47	8	0	3	(3	0)	64	18	19	18	5	2	48	3	2	3	6	3	2	.272	.299	.370	.669
3 ML YEARS		238	669	155	25	5	13	(8	5)	229	73	60	66	32	3	199	9	9	8	38	13	5	.232	.273	.342	.615

Nick Markakis

mar-KAY-kiss

Bats: L **Throws:** L **Pos:** RF-153;DH-3 **Ht:** 6'1" **Wt:** 190 **Born:** 11/17/1983 **Age:** 32

Year Team	Lg	G	AB	H	2B	3B	HR	(Hm	Rd)	TB	R	RBI	RC	TBB	IBB	SO	HBP	SH	SF	SB	CS	GDP	Avg	OBP	Slg	OPS
2006 Bal	AL	147	491	143	25	2	16	(9	7)	220	72	62	67	43	3	72	3	3	2	2	0	15	.291	.351	.448	.799
2007 Bal	AL	161	637	191	43	3	23	(15	8)	309	97	112	103	61	5	112	5	1	6	18	6	22	.300	.362	.485	.848
2008 Bal	AL	157	595	182	48	1	20	(11	9)	292	106	87	113	99	7	113	2	0	10	10	7	10	.306	.406	.491	.897
2009 Bal	AL	161	642	188	45	2	18	(8	10)	291	94	101	97	56	0	98	3	0	10	6	2	12	.293	.347	.453	.801
2010 Bal	AL	160	629	187	45	3	12	(8	4)	274	79	60	99	73	9	93	2	0	5	7	2	18	.297	.370	.436	.805
2011 Bal	AL	160	641	182	31	1	15	(8	7)	260	72	73	90	62	6	75	7	0	6	12	3	16	.284	.351	.406	.756
2012 Bal	AL	104	420	125	28	3	13	(9	4)	198	59	54	69	42	3	51	4	0	5	1	1	11	.298	.363	.471	.834
2013 Bal	AL	160	634	172	24	0	10	(6	4)	226	89	59	66	55	3	76	3	0	8	1	2	17	.271	.329	.356	.685
2014 Bal	AL	155	642	177	27	1	14	(8	6)	248	81	50	82	62	4	84	4	0	2	4	2	10	.276	.342	.386	.729
2015 Atl	NL	156	612	181	38	1	3	(1	2)	230	73	53	81	70	11	83	3	0	1	2	1	17	.296	.370	.376	.746
Postseason		7	31	8	1	0	1	(1	0)	12	4	3	4	1	0	3	0	0	0	1	0	0	.258	.281	.387	.668
10 ML YEARS		1521	5943	1728	354	17	144	(83	61)	2548	822	711	867	623	51	857	36	4	46	63	26	148	.291	.359	.429	.788

Matt Marksberry

Pitches: L Bats: L Pos: RP-31   Ht: 6'1" Wt: 200 Born: 8/25/1990 Age: 25

Year Team	Lg	G	GS	CG	GF	IP	BFP	H	R	ER	HR	SH	SF	HB	TBB	IBB	SO	WP	Bk	W	L	Pct	Sh	Sv-Op	Hld	ERC	ERA
2013 Danvle	R+	12	6	0	0	33.2	149	32	22	19	1	1	2	4	16	0	40	5	0	1	3	.250	0	0--	-	4.05	5.08
2014 2 Tms	Low	24	22	0	0	115.0	493	104	58	48	10	3	3	3	53	0	100	12	0	6	10	.375	0	0--	-	3.81	3.76
2015 Carlina	A+	22	0	0	9	35.2	143	22	11	11	2	1	1	2	13	1	35	1	0	3	1	.750	0	2--	-	1.88	2.78
2015 Gwnntt	AAA	11	0	0	1	10.1	41	10	3	3	0	1	0	1	1	0	8	0	0	0	0	-	0	1--	-	2.18	2.61
2015 Atl	NL	31	0	0	4	23.1	108	22	16	13	2	0	2	1	16	2	21	3	0	0	3	.000	0	0-3	5	4.71	5.01

Jason Marquis

Pitches: R Bats: L Pos: SP-9   marr-KEE   Ht: 6'1" Wt: 220 Born: 8/21/1978 Age: 37

Year Team	Lg	G	GS	CG	GF	IP	BFP	H	R	ER	HR	SH	SF	HB	TBB	IBB	SO	WP	Bk	W	L	Pct	Sh	Sv-Op	Hld	ERC	ERA
2000 Atl	NL	15	0	0	7	23.1	103	23	16	13	4	1	1	1	12	1	17	1	0	1	0	1.000	0	0-1	1	5.13	5.01
2001 Atl	NL	38	16	0	9	129.1	556	113	62	50	14	6	5	4	59	4	98	1	2	5	6	.455	0	0-2	2	3.70	3.48
2002 Atl	NL	22	22	0	0	114.1	507	127	66	64	19	4	3	3	49	3	84	4	0	8	9	.471	0	0-0	0	5.43	5.04
2003 Atl	NL	21	2	0	10	40.2	182	43	27	25	3	0	3	2	18	2	19	2	0	0	0	-	0	1-1	0	4.45	5.53
2004 StL	NL	32	32	0	0	201.1	874	215	90	83	26	5	6	10	70	1	138	6	0	15	7	.682	0	0-0	0	4.69	3.71
2005 StL	NL	33	32	3	0	207.0	868	206	110	95	29	4	3	5	69	2	100	10	3	13	14	.481	1	0-0	0	4.23	4.13
2006 StL	NL	33	33	0	0	194.1	870	221	136	130	35	12	3	16	75	2	96	2	1	14	16	.467	0	0-0	0	5.79	6.02
2007 ChC	NL	34	33	1	0	191.2	846	190	111	98	22	13	1	13	76	6	109	3	0	12	9	.571	1	0-0	0	4.28	4.60
2008 ChC	NL	29	28	0	0	167.0	738	172	87	84	15	10	7	8	70	6	91	8	1	11	9	.550	0	0-0	1	4.35	4.53
2009 Col	NL	33	33	2	0	216.0	921	218	104	97	15	10	10	4	80	6	115	6	1	15	13	.536	1	0-0	0	3.86	4.04
2010 Was	NL	13	13	0	0	58.2	276	76	47	43	9	3	0	8	24	0	31	1	1	2	9	.182	0	0-0	0	6.93	6.60
2011 2 Tms	NL	23	23	1	0	132.0	587	154	74	65	11	9	5	5	43	1	76	1	0	8	6	.571	1	0-0	0	4.72	4.43
2012 2 Tms		22	22	1	0	127.2	561	146	86	74	23	6	4	4	42	3	91	6	0	8	11	.421	1	0-0	0	5.31	5.22
2013 SD	NL	20	20	0	0	117.2	518	111	61	53	18	8	6	4	68	2	72	2	0	9	5	.643	0	0-0	0	5.04	4.05
2015 Cin	NL	9	9	0	0	47.1	216	64	37	34	10	3	4	1	14	2	37	3	0	3	4	.429	0	0-0	0	6.62	6.46
11 Was	NL	20	20	1	0	120.2	524	132	58	53	8	8	5	4	39	1	71	1	0	8	5	.615	1	0-0	0	4.19	3.95
11 Ari	NL	3	3	0	0	11.1	63	22	16	12	3	1	0	1	4	0	5	0	0	0	1	.000	0	0-0	0	11.25	9.53
12 Min	AL	7	7	0	0	34.0	160	52	33	32	9	1	2	3	14	0	12	1	0	2	4	.333	0	0-0	0	9.67	8.47
12 SD	NL	15	15	1	0	93.2	401	94	53	42	14	5	2	1	28	3	79	5	0	6	7	.462	1	0-0	0	3.97	4.04
Postseason		11	3	0	6	23.2	115	25	17	12	6	4	1	0	18	1	14	0	0	0	2	.000	0	0-0	0	6.85	4.56
15 ML YEARS		377	318	8	26	1968.1	8623	2079	1114	1008	253	94	61	88	769	41	1174	56	9	124	118	.512	5	1-4	4	4.73	4.61

Deven Marrero

Bats: R Throws: R Pos: 3B-13;SS-6;PR-6;2B-3;DH-3;PH-1   Ht: 6'1" Wt: 195 Born: 8/25/1990 Age: 25

Year Team	Lg	G	AB	H	2B	3B	HR	(Hm	Rd)	TB	R	RBI	RC	TBB	IBB	SO	HBP	SH	SF	SB	CS	GDP	Avg	OBP	Slg	OPS
2012 Lowell	A-	64	246	66	14	3	2	(-	-)	92	45	24	38	34	0	48	1	2	1	24	6	6	.268	.358	.374	.732
2013 Salem	A+	85	332	85	20	0	2	(-	-)	111	50	21	44	42	0	60	1	1	0	21	2	7	.256	.341	.334	.676
2013 Portlnd	AA	19	72	17	0	0	0	(-	-)	17	7	5	7	10	0	16	0	1	2	6	0	2	.236	.321	.236	.558
2014 Portlnd	AA	68	268	78	19	2	5	(-	-)	116	42	39	45	34	0	57	2	0	3	12	7	8	.291	.371	.433	.804
2014 Pwtckt	AAA	50	186	39	11	0	1	(-	-)	53	23	20	14	12	0	37	1	2	1	4	1	6	.210	.260	.285	.545
2015 Pwtckt	AAA	102	375	96	13	1	6	(-	-)	129	49	29	44	33	0	87	2	5	4	12	5	10	.256	.316	.344	.660
2015 Bos	AL	25	53	12	0	0	1	(0	1)	15	8	3	4	3	0	19	0	0	0	2	1	0	.226	.268	.283	.551

Evan Marshall

Pitches: R Bats: R Pos: RP-13   Ht: 6'2" Wt: 225 Born: 4/18/1990 Age: 26

Year Team	Lg	G	GS	CG	GF	IP	BFP	H	R	ER	HR	SH	SF	HB	TBB	IBB	SO	WP	Bk	W	L	Pct	Sh	Sv-Op	Hld	ERC	ERA
2011 2 Tms	Low	26	0	0	18	29.0	121	24	10	4	2	0	1	0	7	1	31	5	0	0	0	1.000	0	6--	-	2.23	1.24
2012 Mobile	AA	42	0	0	35	48.2	215	55	24	19	2	2	1	2	16	4	27	2	0	6	3	.667	0	16--	-	4.10	3.51
2013 Reno	AAA	54	0	0	27	58.0	273	75	32	28	2	2	3	5	30	2	59	8	0	3	6	.333	0	3--	-	6.14	4.34
2014 Reno	AAA	14	0	0	5	16.2	62	10	1	1	0	0	0	0	5	0	19	0	0	0	0	1.000	0	1--	-	1.37	0.54
2015 Reno	AAA	31	0	0	3	32.1	163	47	28	23	1	2	1	3	13	2	25	4	0	3	2	.600	0	0--	-	6.19	6.40
2014 Ari	NL	57	0	0	11	49.1	210	50	17	15	3	2	1	2	17	3	54	3	0	4	4	.500	0	0-1	19	3.76	2.74
2015 Ari	NL	13	0	0	4	13.1	61	20	9	9	3	0	0	0	5	1	7	1	0	0	2	.000	0	0-2	2	8.27	6.08
2 ML YEARS		70	0	0	15	62.2	271	70	26	24	6	2	1	2	22	4	61	4	0	4	6	.400	0	0-3	21	4.62	3.45

Alfredo Marte

Bats: R Throws: R Pos: LF-2;RF-1;DH-1;PR-1   marr-TAY   Ht: 5'11" Wt: 200 Born: 3/31/1989 Age: 27

Year Team	Lg	G	AB	H	2B	3B	HR	(Hm	Rd)	TB	R	RBI	RC	TBB	IBB	SO	HBP	SH	SF	SB	CS	GDP	Avg	OBP	Slg	OPS
2015 Salt Lk*	AAA	97	343	109	25	3	7	(-	-)	161	54	55	63	36	2	81	2	0	5	7	2	4	.318	.381	.469	.850
2013 Ari	NL	22	43	8	3	0	0	(0	0)	11	4	4	4	4	0	12	1	0	0	0	0	0	.186	.271	.256	.527
2014 Ari	NL	44	106	18	5	1	2	(1	1)	31	8	9	7	6	0	34	1	1	0	1	0	2	.170	.221	.292	.514
2015 LAA	AL	5	6	2	0	0	0	(0	0)	2	0	0	1	1	0	1	0	0	0	0	0	0	.333	.500	.333	.833
3 ML YEARS		71	155	28	8	1	2	(1	1)	44	12	13	12	11	0	47	3	1	0	1	0	2	.181	.249	.284	.532

Jefry Marte

Bats: R **Throws:** R **Pos:** 1B-22;3B-7;PH-7;DH-3;PR-3   marr-TAY   **Ht:** 6'1" **Wt:** 220 **Born:** 6/21/1991 **Age:** 25

Year	Team	Lg	G	AB	H	2B	3B	HR	(Hm	Rd)	TB	R	RBI	RC	TBB	IBB	SO	HBP	SH	SF	SB	CS	GDP	Avg	OBP	Slg	OPS
2011	Stluci	A+	131	483	120	22	2	7	(-	-)	167	56	55	58	41	4	86	7	0	6	14	2	11	.248	.313	.346	.659
2012	Bnghtn	AA	129	462	116	20	3	9	(-	-)	169	61	58	57	43	1	76	6	0	2	9	5	20	.251	.322	.366	.687
2013	Mdlnd	AA	66	245	68	17	1	2	(-	-)	93	33	28	36	25	1	49	4	0	4	8	1	4	.278	.349	.380	.729
2014	Mdlnd	AA	107	405	104	17	0	10	(-	-)	151	50	53	54	45	0	69	3	1	6	9	3	11	.257	.331	.373	.704
2015	Toledo	AAA	95	357	98	25	3	15	(-	-)	174	49	65	60	31	0	64	7	0	4	8	5	6	.275	.341	.487	.828
2015	Det	AL	33	80	17	4	0	4	(1	3)	33	9	11	6	8	0	22	0	2	0	0	0	2	.213	.284	.413	.697

Ketel Marte

Bats: B **Throws:** R **Pos:** SS-51;2B-4;CF-2;PR-2   kuh-TELL mar-TAY   **Ht:** 6'1" **Wt:** 165 **Born:** 10/12/1993 **Age:** 22

Year	Team	Lg	G	AB	H	2B	3B	HR	(Hm	Rd)	TB	R	RBI	RC	TBB	IBB	SO	HBP	SH	SF	SB	CS	GDP	Avg	OBP	Slg	OPS
2012	2 Tms	Low	69	265	66	4	2	0	(-	-)	74	39	24	22	14	0	38	0	7	0	15	4	5	.249	.287	.279	.566
2013	2 Tms	Low	117	464	137	15	7	1	(-	-)	169	79	37	56	19	0	50	1	11	3	20	11	9	.295	.322	.364	.687
2014	Jacksn	AA	109	443	134	27	6	2	(-	-)	179	63	46	61	19	1	65	1	4	5	23	10	6	.302	.329	.404	.733
2014	Tacom	AAA	19	80	25	5	0	2	(-	-)	36	16	9	14	8	0	13	0	0	2	6	0	1	.313	.367	.450	.817
2015	Tacom	AAA	65	261	82	12	2	3	(-	-)	107	41	29	42	20	0	32	0	3	3	20	3	4	.314	.359	.410	.769
2015	Sea	AL	57	219	62	14	3	2	(1	1)	88	25	17	33	24	0	43	0	2	2	8	4	1	.283	.351	.402	.753

Starling Marte

Bats: R **Throws:** R **Pos:** LF-141;CF-18;PR-6;PH-2   marr-TAY   **Ht:** 6'1" **Wt:** 185 **Born:** 10/9/1988 **Age:** 27

Year	Team	Lg	G	AB	H	2B	3B	HR	(Hm	Rd)	TB	R	RBI	RC	TBB	IBB	SO	HBP	SH	SF	SB	CS	GDP	Avg	OBP	Slg	OPS
2012	Pit	NL	47	167	43	3	6	5	(3	2)	73	18	17	21	8	0	50	3	2	2	12	5	5	.257	.300	.437	.737
2013	Pit	NL	135	510	143	26	10	12	(5	7)	225	83	35	74	25	2	138	24	6	1	41	15	6	.280	.343	.441	.784
2014	Pit	NL	135	495	144	29	6	13	(5	8)	224	73	56	70	33	0	131	17	0	0	30	11	5	.291	.356	.453	.808
2015	Pit	NL	153	579	166	30	2	19	(10	9)	257	84	81	81	27	3	123	19	3	5	30	10	14	.287	.337	.444	.780
	Postseason		7	28	4	1	0	1	(0	1)	8	2	1	1	1	0	6	1	0	0	1	0	1	.143	.200	.286	.486
	4 ML YEARS		470	1751	496	88	24	49	(23	26)	779	258	189	246	93	5	442	63	11	8	113	41	30	.283	.340	.445	.785

Chris Martin

Pitches: R **Bats:** R **Pos:** RP-24   **Ht:** 6'8" **Wt:** 215 **Born:** 6/2/1986 **Age:** 30

			HOW MUCH HE PITCHED						WHAT HE GAVE UP											THE RESULTS						
Year	Team	Lg	G	GS	CG	GF	IP	BFP	H	R	ER	HR	SH	SF	HB	TBB	IBB	SO	WP	Bk	W	L	Pct	Sh	Sv-Op	Hld	ERC	ERA
2011	2 Tms	Low	20	1	0	10	68.1	260	45	11	11	1	5	1	6	12	0	52	0	0	6	1	.857	0	4- -	-	1.50	1.45
2012	Portlnd	AA	23	12	0	3	76.1	328	83	42	38	4	0	2	6	18	0	65	2	0	3	6	.333	0	0- -	-	3.90	4.48
2013	Portlnd	AA	12	0	0	10	21.0	74	9	0	0	0	0	0	0	6	0	27	0	0	2	0	1.000	0	3- -	-	0.87	0.00
2013	Pwtckt	AAA	30	0	0	16	51.0	212	51	19	18	3	3	0	4	10	2	47	0	0	3	3	.500	0	2- -	-	3.28	3.18
2014	ColSpr	AAA	25	0	0	16	26.2	121	33	15	15	2	3	0	2	9	1	36	0	0	1	3	.250	0	5- -	-	5.25	4.39
2015	S-WB	AAA	20	0	0	5	28.1	122	26	12	10	1	2	0	1	10	0	25	1	0	0	1	.000	0	2- -	-	3.07	3.18
2014	Col	NL	16	0	0	1	15.2	69	22	12	12	2	0	0	0	4	0	14	1	2	0	0	-	0	0-0	3	6.30	6.89
2015	NYY	AL	24	0	0	8	20.2	99	28	13	13	2	0	0	1	6	1	18	3	0	0	2	.000	0	1-1	5	5.52	5.66
	2 ML YEARS		40	0	0	9	36.1	168	50	25	25	4	0	0	1	10	1	32	4	2	0	2	.000	0	1-1	8	5.85	6.19

Cody Martin

Pitches: R **Bats:** R **Pos:** RP-23; SP-2   **Ht:** 6'3" **Wt:** 230 **Born:** 9/4/1989 **Age:** 26

			HOW MUCH HE PITCHED						WHAT HE GAVE UP											THE RESULTS						
Year	Team	Lg	G	GS	CG	GF	IP	BFP	H	R	ER	HR	SH	SF	HB	TBB	IBB	SO	WP	Bk	W	L	Pct	Sh	Sv-Op	Hld	ERC	ERA
2011	2 Tms	Low	22	0	0	20	33.1	122	20	7	4	2	1	1	1	5	1	49	1	0	1	0	1.000	0	9- -	-	1.30	1.08
2012	Lynbrg	A+	22	19	1	0	107.1	445	93	49	35	7	3	6	7	34	2	123	1	0	12	7	.632	1	0- -	-	3.05	2.93
2013	Missi	AA	16	11	0	2	67.0	281	63	23	21	3	1	1	0	27	0	71	2	1	3	3	.500	0	0- -	-	3.43	2.82
2013	Gwnntt	AAA	13	11	1	1	69.2	292	59	30	27	6	3	2	2	31	0	66	2	0	3	4	.429	0	1- -	-	3.47	3.49
2014	Gwnntt	AAA	27	26	1	1	156.0	667	151	66	61	17	6	2	7	56	0	142	0	0	7	8	.467	0	1- -	-	3.98	3.52
2015	Gwnntt	AAA	7	6	0	1	34.1	135	24	11	8	2	3	1	1	9	0	33	1	0	1	3	.250	0	1- -	-	1.90	2.10
2015	Nashv	AAA	11	11	0	0	60.0	270	59	36	34	6	3	3	3	31	2	58	5	0	4	4	.500	0	0- -	-	4.53	5.10
2015	2 Tms		25	2	0	4	30.2	141	40	27	27	8	2	2	2	12	0	27	2	0	2	5	.286	0	0-3	7	7.54	7.92
15	Atl	NL	21	0	0	2	21.2	92	24	13	13	4	2	1	1	7	0	24	1	0	2	3	.400	0	0-3	7	5.37	5.40
15	Oak	AL	4	2	0	2	9.0	49	16	14	14	4	0	1	1	5	0	3	1	0	0	2	.000	0	0-0	0	13.36	14.00

Leonys Martin

Bats: L **Throws:** R **Pos:** CF-92;PH-6;DH-2;PR-2   lay-OH-nees mar-TEEN   **Ht:** 6'2" **Wt:** 200 **Born:** 3/6/1988 **Age:** 28

Year	Team	Lg	G	AB	H	2B	3B	HR	(Hm	Rd)	TB	R	RBI	RC	TBB	IBB	SO	HBP	SH	SF	SB	CS	GDP	Avg	OBP	Slg	OPS
2011	Tex	AL	8	8	3	1	0	0	(0	0)	4	2	0	1	0	0	1	0	0	0	0	0	0	.375	.375	.500	.875
2012	Tex	AL	24	46	8	5	2	0	(0	0)	17	6	6	4	4	0	12	0	1	1	3	0	2	.174	.235	.370	.605
2013	Tex	AL	147	457	119	21	6	8	(3	5)	176	66	49	58	28	0	104	8	13	3	36	9	6	.260	.313	.385	.698
2014	Tex	AL	155	533	146	13	7	7	(4	3)	194	68	40	64	39	3	114	2	7	2	31	12	4	.274	.325	.364	.689
2015	Tex	AL	95	288	63	12	0	5	(1	4)	90	26	25	22	16	1	69	2	3	1	14	5	5	.219	.264	.313	.576
	5 ML YEARS		429	1332	339	52	15	20	(8	12)	481	168	120	149	87	4	300	12	23	7	84	26	17	.255	.305	.361	.666

Rafael Martin

Pitches: R Bats: R Pos: RP-13   mar-TEEN   Ht: 6'3" Wt: 220 Born: 5/16/1984 Age: 32

			HOW MUCH HE PITCHED						WHAT HE GAVE UP												THE RESULTS						
Year	Team	Lg	G	GS	CG	GF	IP	BFP	H	R	ER	HR	SH	SF	HB	TBB	IBB	SO	WP	Bk	W	L	Pct	Sh	Sv-Op	Hld	ERC	ERA
2011	Ptomc	A+	6	0	0	1	8.0	33	6	2	1	0	0	0	0	2	0	10	1	0	1	0	1.000	0	0- -	-	1.71	1.13
2011	Hrsbrg	AA	32	0	0	21	35.2	144	26	8	7	1	3	0	3	9	1	44	5	0	4	1	.800	0	13- -	-	1.95	1.77
2012	Syrcse	AAA	13	0	0	2	17.2	85	16	14	14	2	1	1	3	11	0	15	3	1	0	0	-	0	0- -	-	4.94	7.13
2012	Hrsbrg	AA	15	0	0	4	17.0	83	21	15	14	4	1	0	2	12	0	14	2	0	0	0	-	0	0- -	-	7.85	7.41
2013	2 Tms	Low	21	0	0	4	31.0	123	15	5	3	1	1	1	1	14	0	39	2	0	0	0	-	0	2- -	-	1.47	0.87
2014	Hrsbrg	AA	11	0	0	3	20.0	80	15	7	6	1	1	0	1	5	0	20	0	0	2	1	.667	0	1- -	-	2.10	2.70
2014	Syrcse	AAA	25	0	0	16	33.2	126	20	4	3	0	0	0	0	7	0	42	0	0	1	1	.500	0	10- -	-	1.13	0.80
2015	Syrcse	AAA	46	0	0	31	56.0	222	41	21	20	4	3	2	1	16	2	68	2	0	5	5	.500	0	12- -	-	2.13	3.21
2015	Was	NL	13	0	0	5	12.1	56	12	9	7	4	0	1	1	5	0	25	0	0	2	0	1.000	0	0-0	0	5.66	5.11

Russell Martin

Bats: R Throws: R Pos: C-117;PH-9;DH-5;2B-2   Ht: 5'10" Wt: 205 Born: 2/15/1983 Age: 33

			BATTING																			RUNNING			AVERAGES			
Year	Team	Lg	G	AB	H	2B	3B	HR	(Hm	Rd)	TB	R	RBI	RC	TBB	IBB	SO	HBP	SH	SF	SB	CS	GDP	Avg	OBP	Slg	OPS
2006	LAD	NL	121	415	117	26	4	10	(8	2)	181	65	65	58	45	8	57	4	1	3	10	5	17	.282	.355	.436	.792
2007	LAD	NL	151	540	158	32	3	19	(8	11)	253	87	87	84	67	1	89	7	0	6	21	9	16	.293	.374	.469	.843
2008	LAD	NL	155	553	155	25	0	13	(6	7)	219	87	69	89	90	8	83	5	0	2	18	6	16	.280	.385	.396	.781
2009	LAD	NL	143	505	126	19	0	7	(3	4)	166	63	53	62	69	9	80	11	2	1	11	6	18	.250	.352	.329	.680
2010	LAD	NL	97	331	82	13	0	5	(2	3)	110	45	26	40	48	7	61	4	1	3	6	2	7	.248	.347	.332	.679
2011	NYY	AL	125	417	99	17	0	18	(8	10)	170	57	65	56	50	1	81	5	1	3	8	2	19	.237	.324	.408	.732
2012	NYY	AL	133	422	89	18	0	21	(13	8)	170	50	53	50	53	0	95	8	2	0	6	1	13	.211	.311	.403	.713
2013	Pit	NL	127	438	99	21	0	15	(6	9)	165	51	55	47	58	2	108	8	1	1	9	5	13	.226	.327	.377	.703
2014	Pit	NL	111	379	110	20	0	11	(3	8)	163	45	67	66	59	5	78	15	2	5	4	4	16	.290	.402	.430	.832
2015	Tor	AL	129	441	106	23	2	23	(13	10)	202	76	77	66	53	1	106	8	0	5	4	5	22	.240	.329	.458	.787
Postseason			40	136	29	6	0	4	(2	2)	47	17	16	12	17	0	30	6	0	2	1	0	3	.213	.323	.346	.669
10 ML YEARS			1292	4441	1141	214	9	142	(70	72)	1799	626	617	618	592	42	838	75	10	29	97	45	157	.257	.352	.405	.757

Carlos Martinez

Pitches: R Bats: R Pos: SP-29; RP-2   Ht: 6'0" Wt: 185 Born: 9/21/1991 Age: 24

			HOW MUCH HE PITCHED						WHAT HE GAVE UP												THE RESULTS						
Year	Team	Lg	G	GS	CG	GF	IP	BFP	H	R	ER	HR	SH	SF	HB	TBB	IBB	SO	WP	Bk	W	L	Pct	Sh	Sv-Op	Hld	ERC	ERA
2013	StL	NL	21	1	0	5	28.1	124	31	16	16	1	1	1	3	9	1	24	0	0	2	1	.667	0	1-1	3	4.20	5.08
2014	StL	NL	57	7	0	13	89.1	386	90	41	40	4	7	1	4	36	8	84	8	1	2	4	.333	0	1-6	17	3.79	4.03
2015	StL	NL	31	29	0	1	179.2	755	168	65	60	13	9	4	8	63	5	184	8	1	14	7	.667	0	0-0	1	3.51	3.01
Postseason			16	0	0	1	16.2	65	10	6	6	0	1	1	1	7	1	13	1	0	1	0	1.000	0	0-0	5	1.70	3.24
3 ML YEARS			109	37	0	19	297.1	1265	289	122	116	18	17	6	15	108	14	292	16	2	18	12	.600	0	2-7	21	3.66	3.51

J.D. Martinez

Bats: R Throws: R Pos: RF-148;DH-10;PH-1   Ht: 6'3" Wt: 220 Born: 8/21/1987 Age: 28

			BATTING																			RUNNING			AVERAGES			
Year	Team	Lg	G	AB	H	2B	3B	HR	(Hm	Rd)	TB	R	RBI	RC	TBB	IBB	SO	HBP	SH	SF	SB	CS	GDP	Avg	OBP	Slg	OPS
2011	Hou	NL	53	208	57	13	0	6	(3	3)	88	29	35	30	13	1	48	2	0	3	0	1	4	.274	.319	.423	.742
2012	Hou	NL	113	395	95	14	3	11	(5	6)	148	34	55	45	40	0	96	1	0	2	0	2	18	.241	.311	.375	.685
2013	Hou	AL	86	296	74	17	0	7	(4	3)	112	24	36	29	10	0	82	0	0	3	2	0	8	.250	.272	.378	.650
2014	Det	AL	123	441	139	30	3	23	(13	10)	244	57	76	75	30	5	126	3	0	6	6	3	8	.315	.358	.553	.912
2015	Det	AL	158	596	168	33	2	38	(20	18)	319	93	102	100	53	7	178	5	0	3	3	2	11	.282	.344	.535	.879
Postseason			3	12	3	1	0	2	(0	2)	10	2	5	3	0	0	4	0	0	0	0	0	0	.250	.250	.833	1.083
5 ML YEARS			533	1936	533	107	8	85	(45	40)	911	237	304	279	146	13	530	11	0	17	11	8	49	.275	.327	.471	.798

Michael Martinez

Bats: B Throws: R Pos: LF-9;PR-5;CF-2;DH-2;3B-1;RF-1;PH-1   Ht: 5'9" Wt: 175 Born: 9/16/1982 Age: 33

			BATTING																			RUNNING			AVERAGES			
Year	Team	Lg	G	AB	H	2B	3B	HR	(Hm	Rd)	TB	R	RBI	RC	TBB	IBB	SO	HBP	SH	SF	SB	CS	GDP	Avg	OBP	Slg	OPS
2015	Clmbs*	AAA	102	363	105	24	5	5	(-	-)	154	53	42	56	32	0	60	0	3	3	11	3	3	.289	.344	.424	.768
2011	Phi	NL	88	209	41	5	2	3	(1	2)	59	25	24	20	18	0	35	0	5	2	3	0	2	.196	.258	.282	.540
2012	Phi	NL	45	115	20	3	0	2	(1	1)	29	10	7	5	5	2	21	0	2	0	0	0	4	.174	.208	.252	.461
2013	Phi	NL	29	40	7	0	0	0	(0	0)	7	5	3	3	0	0	12	0	0	0	1	0	1	.175	.175	.175	.350
2014	Pit	NL	26	39	5	1	0	0	(0	0)	6	2	2	1	4	1	13	0	1	0	0	0	0	.128	.209	.154	.363
2015	Cle	AL	16	30	8	2	0	0	(0	0)	10	7	2	3	1	0	12	0	1	0	0	1	1	.267	.290	.333	.624
Postseason			2	0	0	0	0	0	(0	0)	0	1	0	0	0	0	0	0	0	0	0	0	0	-	-	-	-
5 ML YEARS			204	433	81	11	2	5	(2	3)	111	49	38	32	28	3	93	0	9	2	4	1	8	.187	.235	.256	.492

Nick Martinez

Pitches: R Bats: L Pos: SP-21; RP-3   Ht: 6'1" Wt: 200 Born: 8/5/1990 Age: 25

			HOW MUCH HE PITCHED						WHAT HE GAVE UP												THE RESULTS						
Year	Team	Lg	G	GS	CG	GF	IP	BFP	H	R	ER	HR	SH	SF	HB	TBB	IBB	SO	WP	Bk	W	L	Pct	Sh	Sv-Op	Hld	ERC	ERA
2011	2 Tms	Low	15	11	0	0	58.2	249	58	24	15	0	2	1	2	18	0	56	4	0	3	3	.500	0	0- -	-	3.09	2.30
2012	Hkry	A	31	20	0	4	117.1	503	121	66	63	8	0	5	4	37	0	109	6	0	8	6	.571	0	1- -	-	3.83	4.83
2013	MrtlBh	A+	22	21	1	0	119.1	499	106	47	38	5	1	3	7	38	0	105	7	3	10	7	.588	0	0- -	-	3.00	2.87
2013	Frisco	AA	5	4	0	1	32.0	112	11	6	4	1	2	0	0	7	0	23	2	0	2	0	1.000	0	0- -	-	0.63	1.13

Year	Team	Lg	G	GS	CG	GF	IP	BFP	H	R	ER	HR	SH	SF	HB	TBB	IBB	SO	WP	Bk	W	L	Pct	Sh	Sv-Op	Hld	ERC	ERA
2015	RdRck	AAA	6	6	0	0	31.0	125	32	12	10	1	0	1	2	7	0	18	4	0	1	1	.500	0	0- -	-	3.56	2.90
2014	Tex	AL	29	24	0	3	140.1	610	150	79	71	18	1	6	3	55	1	77	7	0	5	12	.294	0	0-0	0	4.76	4.55
2015	Tex	AL	24	21	0	1	125.0	558	135	66	55	16	1	5	13	46	2	77	4	0	7	7	.500	0	0-0	0	4.99	3.96
2 ML YEARS			53	45	0	4	265.1	1168	285	145	126	34	2	11	16	101	3	154	11	0	12	19	.387	0	0-0	2	4.87	4.27

Victor Martinez

Bats: B Throws: R Pos: DH-104;1B-10;PH-6   **Ht: 6'2" Wt: 210 Born: 12/23/1978 Age: 37**

										BATTING												RUNNING			AVERAGES			
Year	Team	Lg	G	AB	H	2B	3B	HR	(Hm	Rd)	TB	R	RBI	RC	TBB	IBB	SO	HBP	SH	SF	SB	CS	GDP	Avg	OBP	Slg	OPS
2002	Cle	AL	12	32	9	1	0	1	(1	0)	13	2	5	5	3	0	2	0	0	1	0	0	1	.281	.333	.406	.740
2003	Cle	AL	49	159	46	4	0	1	(0	1)	53	15	16	17	13	0	21	1	0	1	1	1	8	.289	.345	.333	.678
2004	Cle	AL	141	520	147	38	1	23	(8	15)	256	77	108	90	60	11	69	5	0	6	0	1	16	.283	.359	.492	.851
2005	Cle	AL	147	547	167	33	0	20	(10	10)	260	73	80	90	63	9	78	5	0	7	0	1	16	.305	.378	.475	.853
2006	Cle	AL	153	572	181	37	0	16	(4	12)	266	82	93	96	71	8	78	3	0	6	0	0	27	.316	.391	.465	.856
2007	Cle	AL	147	562	169	40	0	25	(12	13)	284	78	114	108	62	12	76	10	0	11	0	0	19	.301	.374	.505	.879
2008	Cle	AL	73	266	74	17	0	2	(2	0)	97	30	35	36	24	4	32	1	0	3	0	0	12	.278	.337	.365	.701
2009	2 Tms	AL	155	588	178	33	1	23	(7	16)	282	88	108	101	75	3	74	3	0	6	1	0	17	.303	.381	.480	.861
2010	Bos	AL	127	493	149	32	1	20	(10	10)	243	64	79	74	40	5	52	0	0	5	1	0	17	.302	.351	.493	.844
2011	Det	AL	145	540	178	40	0	12	(5	7)	254	76	103	103	46	6	51	2	0	7	1	0	20	.330	.380	.470	.850
2013	Det	AL	159	605	182	36	0	14	(7	7)	260	68	83	75	54	10	62	1	0	8	0	2	23	.301	.355	.430	.785
2014	Det	AL	151	561	188	33	0	32	(15	17)	317	87	103	115	70	28	42	4	0	6	3	2	17	.335	.409	.565	.974
2015	Det	AL	120	440	108	20	0	11	(6	5)	161	39	64	41	31	8	52	7	0	7	0	0	18	.245	.301	.366	.667
09	Cle	AL	99	377	107	21	1	15	(6	9)	175	56	67	64	51	3	51	2	0	5	0	0	11	.284	.368	.464	.832
09	Bos	AL	56	211	71	12	0	8	(1	7)	107	32	41	37	24	0	23	1	0	1	1	0	6	.336	.405	.507	.912
Postseason			39	149	47	8	1	6	(4	2)	75	22	22	25	11	3	23	3	0	0	0	0	3	.315	.374	.503	.878
13 ML YEARS			1579	5885	1776	364	3	200	(87	113)	2746	779	991	951	612	104	689	42	0	74	7	7	211	.302	.367	.467	.834

Nick Masset

Pitches: R Bats: R Pos: RP-28   MASS-et   **Ht: 6'5" Wt: 235 Born: 5/17/1982 Age: 34**

Year	Team	Lg	G	GS	CG	GF	IP	BFP	H	R	ER	HR	SH	SF	HB	TBB	IBB	SO	WP	Bk	W	L	Pct	Sh	Sv-Op	Hld	ERC	ERA
2015	NewOr*	AAA	5	0	0	2	6.0	20	3	1	1	0	0	0	0	0	0	3	0	0	0	0	-	0	2- -	-	0.57	1.50
2006	Tex	AL	8	0	0	7	8.2	36	9	4	4	0	0	2	2	2	0	4	0	0	0	0	-	0	0-0	4	4.05	4.15
2007	CWS	AL	27	1	0	4	39.1	193	52	33	31	2	1	3	2	26	5	21	4	0	2	3	.400	0	0-1	2	6.63	7.09
2008	2 Tms	AL	42	1	0	12	62.0	271	71	32	27	7	3	1	2	26	4	43	3	1	2	0	1.000	0	1-3	2	5.27	3.92
2009	Cin	NL	74	0	0	15	76.0	292	54	22	20	6	1	1	0	24	0	70	6	0	5	1	.833	0	0-2	20	2.24	2.37
2010	Cin	NL	82	0	0	22	76.2	322	64	31	29	7	3	2	1	33	3	85	8	0	4	4	.500	0	2-5	20	3.23	3.40
2011	Cin	NL	75	0	0	21	70.1	313	76	30	29	5	2	1	1	31	6	62	2	4	3	6	.333	0	1-7	14	4.37	3.71
2014	Col	NL	51	0	0	14	45.0	211	56	31	29	3	1	4	5	24	0	36	2	0	2	0	1.000	0	0-2	6	6.38	5.80
2015	2 Tms	NL	28	0	0	5	25.0	113	30	15	13	3	0	2	2	9	3	18	4	0	2	2	.500	0	0-0	6	5.36	4.68
08	CWS	AL	32	1	0	11	44.2	203	55	26	23	4	3	1	2	21	4	32	2	1	1	0	1.000	0	1-1	1	5.78	4.63
08	Cin	AL	10	0	0	1	17.1	68	16	6	4	3	0	0	0	5	0	11	1	0	1	0	1.000	0	0-2	1	3.93	2.08
15	Mia	NL	8	0	0	2	9.2	41	12	3	2	0	0	2	1	1	0	6	1	0	0	0	-	0	0-0	1	4.06	1.86
15	Atl	NL	20	0	0	3	15.1	72	18	12	11	3	0	0	1	8	3	12	3	0	2	2	.500	0	0-0	5	6.22	6.46
Postseason			2	0	0	1	2.0	10	2	1	1	0	0	0	0	2	2	1	0	0	0	0	-	0	0-0	0	3.46	4.50
8 ML YEARS			387	2	0	100	403.0	1751	412	198	182	33	11	16	15	175	21	339	29	5	20	16	.556	0	4-20	66	4.32	4.06

Justin Masterson

Pitches: R Bats: R Pos: SP-9; RP-9   **Ht: 6'6" Wt: 260 Born: 3/22/1985 Age: 31**

Year	Team	Lg	G	GS	CG	GF	IP	BFP	H	R	ER	HR	SH	SF	HB	TBB	IBB	SO	WP	Bk	W	L	Pct	Sh	Sv-Op	Hld	ERC	ERA
2008	Bos	AL	36	9	0	6	88.1	365	68	31	31	10	1	1	8	40	3	68	1	0	6	5	.545	0	0-1	3	3.51	3.16
2009	2 Tms	AL	42	16	1	4	129.1	568	128	73	65	12	10	7	8	60	3	119	5	0	4	10	.286	0	0-1	6	4.45	4.50
2010	Cle	AL	34	29	0	0	180.0	802	197	107	94	14	5	4	11	73	4	140	12	0	6	13	.316	1	0-0	2	4.68	4.70
2011	Cle	AL	34	33	1	0	216.0	908	211	89	77	11	5	5	11	65	4	158	5	0	12	10	.545	0	0-0	0	3.43	3.21
2012	Cle	AL	34	34	1	0	206.1	906	212	122	113	18	6	11	13	88	1	159	14	0	11	15	.423	0	0-0	0	4.51	4.93
2013	Cle	AL	32	29	3	2	193.0	803	156	75	74	13	5	2	17	76	0	195	8	0	14	10	.583	3	0-0	0	3.17	3.45
2014	2 Tms	AL	28	25	0	1	128.2	592	141	90	84	12	8	1	15	69	2	116	14	0	7	9	.438	0	0-0	0	5.63	5.88
2015	Bos	AL	18	9	0	4	59.1	273	68	38	37	7	0	1	10	27	0	49	7	1	4	2	.667	0	0-0	2	6.08	5.61
09	Bos	AL	31	6	0	4	72.0	312	72	38	36	7	9	6	6	25	2	67	3	0	3	3	.500	0	0-1	6	4.13	4.50
09	Cle	AL	11	10	1	0	57.1	256	56	35	29	5	1	1	2	35	1	52	2	0	1	7	.125	0	0-0	0	4.85	4.55
14	Cle	AL	19	19	0	0	98.0	452	106	66	60	6	4	1	11	56	2	93	9	0	4	6	.400	0	0-0	0	5.40	5.51
14	StL	NL	9	6	0	1	30.2	140	35	24	24	6	4	0	4	13	0	23	5	0	3	3	.500	0	0-0	0	6.34	7.04
Postseason			10	0	0	1	11.2	47	11	3	2	0	1	0	2	5	0	11	0	0	1	0	1.000	0	0-1	4	4.23	1.54
8 ML YEARS			258	184	7	17	1201.0	5217	1181	625	575	97	40	32	93	498	17	1004	66	1	64	74	.464	4	0-2	13	4.22	4.31

Marcos Mateo

Pitches: R Bats: R Pos: RP-26   **Ht: 6'1" Wt: 220 Born: 4/18/1984 Age: 32**

Year	Team	Lg	G	GS	CG	GF	IP	BFP	H	R	ER	HR	SH	SF	HB	TBB	IBB	SO	WP	Bk	W	L	Pct	Sh	Sv-Op	Hld	ERC	ERA
2015	ElPaso*	AAA	25	0	0	16	32.0	131	20	8	6	1	1	1	1	12	1	40	2	0	3	0	1.000	0	9- -	-	1.67	1.69
2010	ChC	NL	21	0	0	6	21.2	93	20	15	14	6	0	2	1	9	1	26	1	0	0	1	.000	0	0-0	1	5.07	5.82
2011	ChC	NL	23	0	0	8	23.0	98	24	11	11	2	1	0	0	10	0	25	1	0	1	2	.333	0	0-0	2	4.50	4.30
2015	SD	NL	26	0	0	6	27.0	113	22	16	12	5	1	1	3	9	1	33	1	0	1	1	.500	0	0-1	1	3.75	4.00
3 ML YEARS			70	0	0	19	71.2	304	66	42	37	13	2	3	4	28	2	84	3	0	2	4	.333	0	0-1	4	4.39	4.65

Jeff Mathis

Bats: R Throws: R Pos: C-30;PH-2   Ht: 6'0" Wt: 205 Born: 3/31/1983 Age: 33

Year	Team	Lg	G	AB	H	2B	3B	HR	(Hm	Rd)	TB	R	RBI	RC	TBB	IBB	SO	HBP	SH	SF	SB	CS	GDP	Avg	OBP	Slg	OPS
2005	LAA	AL	5	3	1	0	0	0	(0	0)	1	1	0	0	0	0	1	0	0	0	0	0	0	.333	.333	.333	.667
2006	LAA	AL	23	55	8	2	0	2	(1	1)	16	9	6	4	7	1	14	0	0	1	0	0	0	.145	.238	.291	.529
2007	LAA	AL	59	171	36	12	0	4	(3	1)	60	24	23	13	15	0	49	2	3	4	0	1	3	.211	.276	.351	.627
2008	LAA	AL	94	283	55	8	0	9	(4	5)	90	35	42	33	30	4	90	3	8	4	2	2	1	.194	.275	.318	.593
2009	LAA	AL	84	237	50	8	0	5	(3	2)	73	26	28	24	22	0	73	4	8	1	2	3	2	.211	.288	.308	.596
2010	LAA	AL	68	205	40	6	1	3	(2	1)	57	19	18	10	6	0	59	1	3	3	3	0	3	.195	.219	.278	.497
2011	LAA	AL	93	247	43	12	0	3	(1	2)	64	18	22	12	15	2	75	2	14	3	1	2	3	.174	.225	.259	.484
2012	Tor	AL	71	211	46	13	0	8	(5	3)	83	25	27	18	9	0	68	0	6	1	1	0	2	.218	.249	.393	.642
2013	Mia	NL	73	232	42	7	1	5	(3	2)	66	14	29	15	21	4	76	1	1	1	0	0	5	.181	.251	.284	.535
2014	Mia	NL	64	175	35	7	0	2	(1	1)	48	12	12	11	15	2	64	0	5	0	0	0	2	.200	.263	.274	.537
2015	Mia	NL	32	93	15	4	1	2	(1	1)	27	9	12	3	7	1	24	0	0	3	0	0	2	.161	.214	.290	.504
	Postseason		10	20	9	5	0	0	(0	0)	14	2	2	3	0	0	5	0	1	0	0	0	0	.450	.450	.700	1.150
	11 ML YEARS		666	1912	371	79	3	43	(24	19)	585	192	219	143	147	14	593	13	48	21	9	8	23	.194	.254	.306	.560

Ryan Mattheus

Pitches: R Bats: R Pos: RP-58   MATH-yooz   Ht: 6'3" Wt: 220 Born: 11/10/1983 Age: 32

Year	Team	Lg	G	GS	CG	GF	IP	BFP	H	R	ER	HR	SH	SF	HB	TBB	IBB	SO	WP	Bk	W	L	Pct	Sh	Sv-Op	Hld	ERC	ERA
2015	Salt Lk*	AAA	11	0	0	8	12.2	51	10	5	4	2	1	0	0	2	1	12	1	0	0	2	.000	0	1--	-	2.22	2.84
2011	Was	NL	35	0	0	12	32.0	136	26	11	10	1	4	1	2	15	3	12	1	1	2	2	.500	0	0-0	8	2.94	2.81
2012	Was	NL	66	0	0	11	66.1	265	57	22	21	8	2	4	3	19	5	41	3	0	5	3	.625	0	0-0	18	3.19	2.85
2013	Was	NL	37	0	0	13	51.1	166	52	26	25	1	0	3	0	15	0	22	4	1	0	2	.000	0	0-3	6	6.53	6.37
2014	Was	NL	7	0	0	4	8.2	35	7	1	1	0	0	0	1	4	0	4	0	0	0	0	-	0	0-0	3	3.22	1.04
2015	2 Tms		58	0	0	15	56.0	253	67	31	25	3	4	3	2	18	2	37	6	1	2	4	.333	0	0-1	8	4.54	4.02
15	LAA	AL	1	0	0	1	1.0	4	0	0	0	0	0	0	0	1	0	2	0	0	0	0	-	0	0-0	0	0.95	0.00
15	Cin	NL	57	0	0	14	55.0	249	67	31	25	3	4	3	2	17	2	35	6	1	2	4	.333	0	0-1	8	4.62	4.09
	Postseason		3	0	0	0	3.0	12	3	2	2	0	0	0	0	1	0	0	0	0	1	0	1.000	0	0-0	0	3.35	6.00
	5 ML YEARS		203	0	0	55	198.1	855	209	91	82	13	10	11	8	71	10	116	14	3	9	11	.450	0	0-4	40	4.08	3.72

Brian Matusz

Pitches: L Bats: L Pos: RP-58   MATT-uss   Ht: 6'5" Wt: 190 Born: 2/11/1987 Age: 29

Year	Team	Lg	G	GS	CG	GF	IP	BFP	H	R	ER	HR	SH	SF	HB	TBB	IBB	SO	WP	Bk	W	L	Pct	Sh	Sv-Op	Hld	ERC	ERA
2009	Bal	AL	8	8	0	0	44.2	196	52	24	23	6	2	2	0	14	0	38	0	0	5	2	.714	0	0-0	0	4.91	4.63
2010	Bal	AL	32	32	0	0	175.2	760	173	88	84	19	6	6	7	63	3	143	1	0	10	12	.455	0	0-0	0	3.98	4.30
2011	Bal	AL	12	12	0	0	49.2	245	81	60	59	18	1	2	0	24	1	38	0	0	1	9	.100	0	0-0	0	10.88	10.69
2012	Bal	AL	34	16	0	2	98.0	441	112	61	53	15	2	3	0	41	4	81	0	0	6	10	.375	0	0-0	4	5.25	4.87
2013	Bal	AL	65	0	0	9	51.0	208	43	21	20	3	1	2	2	16	2	50	0	0	2	1	.667	0	0-4	18	2.77	3.53
2014	Bal	AL	63	0	0	11	51.2	226	51	23	20	7	0	2	3	17	4	53	3	0	2	3	.400	0	0-3	14	3.98	3.48
2015	Bal	AL	58	0	0	16	49.0	206	38	18	16	5	2	1	3	20	3	56	2	0	1	4	.200	0	0-2	2	3.02	2.94
	Postseason		7	0	0	3	5.1	20	3	2	2	2	0	0	0	2	1	7	1	0	0	1	.000	0	0-0	2	3.15	3.38
	7 ML YEARS		272	68	0	38	519.2	2282	550	295	275	73	14	18	15	195	17	459	6	0	27	41	.397	0	0-9	38	4.64	4.76

Steven Matz

Pitches: L Bats: R Pos: SP-6   Ht: 6'2" Wt: 200 Born: 5/29/1991 Age: 25

Year	Team	Lg	G	GS	CG	GF	IP	BFP	H	R	ER	HR	SH	SF	HB	TBB	IBB	SO	WP	Bk	W	L	Pct	Sh	Sv-Op	Hld	ERC	ERA
2012	Kngspt	R+	6	6	0	0	29.0	119	16	10	5	1	0	0	1	17	0	34	0	0	2	1	.667	0	0--	-	2.14	1.55
2013	Savann	A	21	21	1	0	106.1	428	86	36	31	4	1	2	5	38	0	121	0	1	5	6	.455	1	0--	-	2.75	2.62
2014	Stluci	A+	12	12	0	0	69.0	289	66	21	17	0	3	1	5	21	0	62	2	0	4	4	.500	0	0--	-	3.11	2.22
2014	Bnghtn	AA	12	12	1	0	71.1	287	66	23	18	3	3	2	2	14	0	69	0	0	6	5	.545	0	0--	-	2.68	2.27
2015	LsVgs	AAA	15	14	0	0	90.1	359	69	25	22	6	2	1	1	31	0	94	0	0	7	4	.636	0	0--	-	2.51	2.19
2015	NYM	NL	6	6	0	0	35.2	149	34	9	9	4	1	1	1	10	0	34	0	0	4	0	1.000	0	0-0	0	3.55	2.27

Tyler Matzek

Pitches: L Bats: L Pos: SP-5   MATT-zick   Ht: 6'3" Wt: 230 Born: 10/19/1990 Age: 25

Year	Team	Lg	G	GS	CG	GF	IP	BFP	H	R	ER	HR	SH	SF	HB	TBB	IBB	SO	WP	Bk	W	L	Pct	Sh	Sv-Op	Hld	ERC	ERA
2011	2 Tms	Low	22	22	0	0	97.0	457	79	72	67	6	8	2	4	96	0	111	19	0	5	7	.417	0	0--	-	5.39	6.22
2012	Mdest	A+	28	28	0	0	142.1	649	134	85	73	7	3	1	5	95	0	153	9	0	6	8	.429	0	0--	-	4.52	4.62
2013	Tulsa	AA	26	26	0	0	142.1	627	147	67	60	13	8	5	5	76	0	95	5	2	8	9	.471	0	0--	-	4.99	3.79
2014	ColSpr	AAA	12	12	0	0	66.2	303	70	40	30	8	6	2	0	31	0	61	3	0	4	5	.556	0	0--	-	4.62	4.05
2015	Albq	AAA	10	1	0	5	11.1	57	5	12	11	1	0	0	1	17	0	15	3	0	0	1	.000	0	1--	-	5.24	8.74
2014	Col	NL	20	19	1	1	117.2	503	120	53	53	9	4	3	3	44	1	91	3	0	6	11	.353	1	0-0	0	4.06	4.05
2015	Col	NL	5	5	0	0	22.0	102	21	10	10	2	1	1	3	19	0	15	2	0	2	1	.667	0	0-0	0	6.45	4.09
	2 ML YEARS		25	24	1	1	139.2	605	141	63	63	11	5	4	6	63	1	106	5	0	8	12	.400	1	0-0	0	4.42	4.06

Joe Mauer

Bats: L **Throws:** R **Pos:** 1B-137;DH-20;PH-3   **Ht:** 6'5" **Wt:** 225 **Born:** 4/19/1983 **Age:** 33

Year	Team	Lg	G	AB	H	2B	3B	HR	(Hm	Rd)	TB	R	RBI	RC	TBB	IBB	SO	HBP	SH	SF	SB	CS	GDP	Avg	OBP	Slg	OPS
2004	Min	AL	35	107	33	8	1	6	(4	2)	61	18	17	21	11	0	14	1	0	3	1	0	1	.308	.369	.570	.939
2005	Min	AL	131	489	144	26	2	9	(4	5)	201	61	55	78	61	12	64	1	0	3	13	1	9	.294	.372	.411	.783
2006	Min	AL	140	521	181	36	4	13	(3	10)	264	86	84	103	79	21	54	1	0	7	8	3	24	.347	.429	.507	.936
2007	Min	AL	109	406	119	27	3	7	(2	5)	173	62	60	69	57	10	51	3	2	3	7	1	11	.293	.382	.426	.808
2008	Min	AL	146	536	176	31	4	9	(7	2)	242	98	85	103	84	8	50	1	1	11	1	1	21	.328	.413	.451	.864
2009	Min	AL	138	523	191	30	1	28	(16	12)	307	94	96	123	76	14	63	2	0	5	4	1	13	.365	.444	.587	1.031
2010	Min	AL	137	510	167	43	1	9	(1	8)	239	88	75	91	65	14	53	3	0	6	1	4	19	.327	.402	.469	.871
2011	Min	AL	82	296	85	15	0	3	(0	3)	109	38	30	39	32	7	38	3	0	2	0	0	9	.287	.360	.368	.729
2012	Min	AL	147	545	174	31	4	10	(4	6)	243	81	85	108	90	10	88	2	1	3	8	4	23	.319	.416	.446	.861
2013	Min	AL	113	445	144	35	0	11	(5	6)	212	62	47	74	61	7	89	0	0	2	0	1	7	.324	.404	.476	.880
2014	Min	AL	120	455	126	27	2	4	(3	1)	169	60	55	66	60	12	96	1	0	2	3	0	12	.277	.361	.371	.732
2015	Min	AL	158	592	157	34	2	10	(6	4)	225	69	66	85	67	12	112	1	1	5	2	1	22	.265	.338	.380	.718
	Postseason		9	35	10	1	0	0	(0	0)	11	1	1	2	4	0	7	0	0	0	0	0	0	.286	.359	.314	.673
	12 ML YEARS		1456	5425	1697	343	24	119	(55	64)	2445	817	755	960	743	127	772	19	5	52	48	17	171	.313	.394	.451	.845

Brandon Maurer

Pitches: R **Bats:** R **Pos:** RP-53   MAUW-er   **Ht:** 6'5" **Wt:** 220 **Born:** 7/3/1990 **Age:** 25

			HOW MUCH HE PITCHED						WHAT HE GAVE UP										THE RESULTS					
Year	Team	Lg	G	GS	CG	GF	IP	BFP	H	R	ER	HR	SH	SF	HB	TBB	IBB	SO	WP	Bk	W	L	Pct	Sh	Sv-Op	Hld	ERC	ERA
2013	Sea	AL	22	14	0	3	90.0	402	114	66	63	16	1	2	6	27	0	70	9	0	5	8	.385	0	0-0	0	6.20	6.30
2014	Sea	AL	38	7	0	4	69.2	301	74	39	36	6	2	3	0	19	2	55	3	0	1	4	.200	0	0-1	5	3.70	4.65
2015	SD	NL	53	0	0	10	51.0	206	39	19	17	3	1	2	1	15	1	39	1	0	7	4	.636	0	0-1	12	2.23	3.00
	3 ML YEARS		113	21	0	17	210.2	909	227	124	116	25	4	7	7	61	3	164	13	0	13	16	.448	0	0-2	17	4.31	4.96

Justin Maxwell

Bats: R **Throws:** R **Pos:** RF-58;PH-29;LF-19;CF-3   **Ht:** 6'5" **Wt:** 225 **Born:** 11/6/1983 **Age:** 32

Year	Team	Lg	G	AB	H	2B	3B	HR	(Hm	Rd)	TB	R	RBI	RC	TBB	IBB	SO	HBP	SH	SF	SB	CS	GDP	Avg	OBP	Slg	OPS
2007	Was	NL	15	26	7	0	0	2	(0	2)	13	5	5	4	1	0	8	0	0	0	0	0	0	.269	.296	.500	.796
2009	Was	NL	40	89	22	4	1	4	(1	3)	40	13	9	15	12	0	32	1	0	0	6	1	1	.247	.343	.449	.793
2010	Was	NL	67	104	15	6	0	3	(1	2)	30	16	12	11	25	2	43	0	0	2	5	1	3	.144	.305	.288	.594
2012	Hou	NL	124	315	72	13	3	18	(10	8)	145	46	53	52	32	0	114	3	0	2	9	4	6	.229	.304	.460	.764
2013	2 Tms	AL	75	234	59	16	3	7	(4	3)	102	35	25	28	23	0	78	4	0	1	6	2	4	.252	.328	.436	.764
2014	KC	AL	20	40	6	1	0	0	(0	0)	7	4	3	2	2	0	20	2	0	1	0	1	0	.150	.222	.175	.397
2015	SF	NL	100	249	52	8	2	7	(1	6)	85	26	26	24	20	1	76	3	1	1	2	1	4	.209	.275	.341	.616
13	Hou	AL	40	137	33	10	2	2	(0	2)	53	21	8	13	12	0	43	2	0	0	4	1	1	.241	.311	.387	.698
13	KC	AL	35	97	26	6	1	5	(4	1)	49	14	17	15	11	0	35	2	0	1	2	1	3	.268	.351	.505	.857
	7 ML YEARS		441	1057	233	48	9	41	(17	24)	422	145	133	136	115	3	371	13	1	7	28	10	18	.220	.303	.399	.702

Trevor May

Pitches: R **Bats:** R **Pos:** RP-32; SP-16   **Ht:** 6'5" **Wt:** 240 **Born:** 9/23/1989 **Age:** 26

			HOW MUCH HE PITCHED						WHAT HE GAVE UP										THE RESULTS					
Year	Team	Lg	G	GS	CG	GF	IP	BFP	H	R	ER	HR	SH	SF	HB	TBB	IBB	SO	WP	Bk	W	L	Pct	Sh	Sv-Op	Hld	ERC	ERA
2011	Clrwtr	A+	27	27	3	0	151.1	631	121	65	61	8	5	7	5	67	0	208	8	0	10	8	.556	2	0- -	-	2.99	3.63
2012	Rdng	AA	28	28	0	0	149.2	660	139	87	81	22	8	4	11	78	0	151	8	1	10	13	.435	0	0- -	-	4.82	4.87
2013	NwBrit	AA	27	27	2	0	151.2	659	149	79	76	14	2	0	8	67	0	159	8	0	9	9	.500	2	0- -	-	4.33	4.51
2014	Roch	AAA	18	18	1	0	98.1	400	75	33	31	4	0	3	0	39	0	94	2	0	8	6	.571	1	0- -	-	2.45	2.84
2014	Min	AL	10	9	0	0	45.2	213	59	41	40	7	0	1	2	22	1	44	3	0	3	6	.333	0	0-0	0	6.80	7.88
2015	Min	AL	48	16	0	9	114.2	492	127	53	51	11	3	4	4	26	2	110	4	0	8	9	.471	0	0-2	7	4.06	4.00
	2 ML YEARS		58	25	0	9	160.1	705	186	94	91	18	3	5	6	48	3	154	7	0	11	15	.423	0	0-2	7	4.80	5.11

John Mayberry

Bats: R **Throws:** R **Pos:** PH-34;LF-19;RF-11   **Ht:** 6'6" **Wt:** 235 **Born:** 12/21/1983 **Age:** 32

Year	Team	Lg	G	AB	H	2B	3B	HR	(Hm	Rd)	TB	R	RBI	RC	TBB	IBB	SO	HBP	SH	SF	SB	CS	GDP	Avg	OBP	Slg	OPS
2015	Charllt*	AAA	13	37	6	1	0	0	(-	-)	7	2	0	1	3	1	7	0	0	0	0	0	0	.162	.225	.189	.414
2009	Phi	NL	39	57	12	3	0	4	(1	3)	27	8	8	5	2	0	23	1	0	0	0	0	0	.211	.250	.474	.724
2010	Phi	NL	11	12	4	0	0	2	(0	2)	10	4	6	4	1	0	4	0	0	0	0	1	0	.333	.385	.833	1.218
2011	Phi	NL	104	267	73	17	1	15	(7	8)	137	49	49	44	26	2	55	2	0	1	8	3	6	.273	.341	.513	.854
2012	Phi	NL	149	441	108	24	0	14	(7	7)	174	53	46	47	34	2	111	2	0	2	1	0	17	.245	.301	.395	.695
2013	Phi	NL	134	353	80	23	1	11	(7	4)	138	47	39	36	27	1	90	3	0	1	5	3	6	.227	.286	.391	.677
2014	2 Tms		78	146	31	10	0	7	(3	4)	62	15	23	19	20	0	35	1	0	1	0	0	2	.212	.310	.425	.734
2015	NYM	NL	59	110	18	6	1	3	(1	2)	35	8	9	6	9	0	33	0	0	0	1	0	2	.164	.227	.318	.545
14	Phi	NL	63	122	26	7	0	6	(2	4)	51	11	21	17	15	0	30	1	0	0	0	0	1	.213	.304	.418	.722
14	Tor	AL	15	24	5	3	0	1	(1	0)	11	4	2	2	5	0	5	0	0	1	0	0	1	.208	.333	.458	.792
	Postseason		2	4	0	0	0	0	(0	0)	0	0	0	0	0	0	1	0	0	0	0	0	0	.000	.000	.000	.000
	7 ML YEARS		574	1386	326	83	3	56	(26	30)	583	172	180	161	119	5	351	9	0	5	15	7	35	.235	.299	.421	.720

Cameron Maybin

Bats: R Throws: R Pos: CF-139;PR-3;PH-2   Ht: 6'3" Wt: 215 Born: 4/4/1987 Age: 29

						BATTING												RUNNING			AVERAGES			
Year	Team	Lg	G	AB	H	2B	3B	HR	(Hm | Rd)	TB	R	RBI	RC	TBB	IBB	SO	HBP	SH	SF	SB	CS	GDP	Avg	OBP	Slg	OPS
2007 Det	AL	24	49	7	3	0	1	(0 | 1)	13	8	2	2	3	0	21	1	0	0	5	0	0	.143	.208	.265	.473
2008 Fla	NL	8	32	16	2	0	0	(0 | 0)	18	9	2	8	3	0	8	0	1	0	4	0	0	.500	.543	.563	1.105
2009 Fla	NL	54	176	44	12	2	4	(1 | 3)	72	30	13	15	17	1	51	1	4	1	1	3	2	.250	.318	.409	.727
2010 Fla	NL	82	291	68	7	3	8	(5 | 3)	105	46	28	37	24	1	92	5	1	2	9	2	4	.234	.302	.361	.663
2011 SD	NL	137	516	136	24	8	9	(2 | 7)	203	82	40	69	44	2	125	2	4	2	40	8	6	.264	.323	.393	.716
2012 SD	NL	147	507	123	20	5	8	(3 | 5)	177	67	45	52	44	1	110	4	3	3	26	7	12	.243	.306	.349	.656
2013 SD	NL	14	51	8	1	0	1	(0 | 1)	12	7	5	0	4	1	9	1	1	0	4	1	3	.157	.232	.235	.467
2014 SD	NL	95	251	59	13	4	1	(0 | 1)	83	24	15	22	19	2	56	1	0	1	4	3	8	.235	.290	.331	.621
2015 Atl	NL	141	505	135	18	2	10	(5 | 5)	187	65	59	64	45	1	102	1	1	3	23	6	16	.267	.327	.370	.697
9 ML YEARS		702	2378	596	100	24	42	(16 | 26)	870	338	209	269	203	9	574	16	15	11	116	30	51	.251	.313	.366	.678

Vin Mazzaro

Pitches: R Bats: R Pos: RP-10   muh-ZA-roh   Ht: 6'2" Wt: 220 Born: 9/27/1986 Age: 29

		HOW MUCH HE PITCHED						WHAT HE GAVE UP											THE RESULTS							
Year	Team	Lg	G	GS	CG	GF	IP	BFP	H	R	ER	HR	SH	SF	HB	TBB	IBB	SO	WP	Bk	W	L	Pct	Sh	Sv-Op	Hld	ERC	ERA
2015 NewOr*	AAA	11	1	0	4	20.0	85	22	7	7	0	1	0	1	4	1	22	3	0	3	1	.750	0	1- -	-	3.27	3.15
2015 Gwnntt*	AAA	17	0	0	5	26.2	112	22	8	7	0	0	0	1	13	0	18	0	0	1	0	1.000	0	1- -	-	2.96	2.36
2009 Oak	AL	17	17	0	0	91.1	423	120	61	54	12	1	3	4	39	3	59	5	0	4	9	.308	0	0-0	0	6.49	5.32
2010 Oak	AL	24	18	0	4	122.1	537	127	70	58	19	4	4	4	50	0	79	5	0	6	8	.429	0	0-0	0	4.86	4.27
2011 KC	AL	7	4	0	2	28.1	131	39	26	26	4	3	3	1	15	1	10	2	0	1	1	.500	0	0-0	0	7.67	8.26
2012 KC	AL	18	6	0	4	44.0	198	55	29	28	3	1	2	3	19	2	26	1	0	4	3	.571	0	0-0	0	5.80	5.73
2013 Pit	NL	57	0	0	17	73.2	304	68	23	23	3	1	3	1	21	3	46	5	1	8	2	.800	0	1-3	6	2.95	2.81
2014 Pit	NL	5	0	0	1	10.1	46	8	4	4	2	1	0	1	5	0	7	0	0	0	0	-	0	0-0	0	3.99	3.48
2015 Mia	NL	10	0	0	5	12.0	55	15	6	5	0	0	2	0	6	1	6	0	0	0	0	-	0	0-0	0	5.04	3.75
Postseason		3	0	0	0	1.2	5	0	0	0	0	0	0	0	0	0	2	0	0	0	0	-	0	0-0	0	0.00	0.00
7 ML YEARS		138	45	0	33	382.0	1694	432	219	198	43	13	15	16	155	10	233	18	1	23	23	.500	0	1-3	6	5.12	4.66

Cory Mazzoni

Pitches: R Bats: R Pos: RP-8   Ht: 6'1" Wt: 200 Born: 10/19/1989 Age: 26

		HOW MUCH HE PITCHED						WHAT HE GAVE UP											THE RESULTS							
Year	Team	Lg	G	GS	CG	GF	IP	BFP	H	R	ER	HR	SH	SF	HB	TBB	IBB	SO	WP	Bk	W	L	Pct	Sh	Sv-Op	Hld	ERC	ERA
2011 2 Tms	Low	12	1	0	0	13.0	54	12	4	2	1	0	0	2	3	0	18	1	0	2	1	.667	0	0- -	-	3.50	1.38
2012 Stluci	A+	12	12	0	0	63.2	265	64	28	23	3	4	2	1	16	0	48	4	2	5	1	.833	0	0- -	-	3.26	3.25
2012 Bnghtn	AA	14	14	2	0	80.2	347	90	45	40	9	1	4	2	20	1	56	4	2	5	5	.500	1	0- -	-	4.28	4.46
2013 Bnghtn	AA	13	12	0	0	66.0	282	70	43	32	4	4	2	2	19	0	74	2	1	5	3	.625	0	0- -	-	3.83	4.36
2014 LsVgs	AAA	9	9	0	0	52.0	220	54	29	27	6	3	1	3	12	0	49	0	0	5	1	.833	0	0- -	-	3.97	4.67
2015 ElPaso	AAA	26	0	0	9	34.0	142	25	17	15	0	1	2	0	12	1	46	1	1	1	3	.250	0	5- -	-	1.79	3.97
2015 SD	NL	8	0	0	4	8.2	53	23	22	20	2	0	1	0	5	0	8	0	0	0	0	-	0	0-0	0	17.75	20.77

Zach McAllister

Pitches: R Bats: R Pos: RP-60; SP-1   Ht: 6'6" Wt: 240 Born: 12/8/1987 Age: 28

		HOW MUCH HE PITCHED						WHAT HE GAVE UP											THE RESULTS							
Year	Team	Lg	G	GS	CG	GF	IP	BFP	H	R	ER	HR	SH	SF	HB	TBB	IBB	SO	WP	Bk	W	L	Pct	Sh	Sv-Op	Hld	ERC	ERA
2011 Cle	AL	4	4	0	0	17.2	84	26	16	12	1	0	0	0	7	1	14	0	0	0	1	.000	0	0-0	0	6.41	6.11
2012 Cle	AL	22	22	0	0	125.1	543	133	78	59	19	2	5	1	38	0	110	0	2	6	8	.429	0	0-0	0	4.37	4.24
2013 Cle	AL	24	24	0	0	134.1	579	134	65	56	13	0	3	6	49	2	101	7	1	9	9	.500	0	0-0	0	4.06	3.75
2014 Cle	AL	22	15	0	2	86.0	377	96	54	50	7	1	3	6	28	1	74	3	0	4	7	.364	0	0-0	1	4.54	5.23
2015 Cle	AL	61	1	0	9	69.0	299	70	28	23	7	1	1	3	23	4	84	3	0	4	4	.500	0	1-2	12	3.95	3.00
5 ML YEARS		133	66	0	11	432.1	1882	459	241	200	47	4	14	10	145	8	383	13	3	23	29	.442	0	1-2	13	4.26	4.16

Matt McBride

Bats: R Throws: R Pos: PH-12;1B-4;LF-3;RF-2   Ht: 6'2" Wt: 215 Born: 5/23/1985 Age: 31

						BATTING												RUNNING			AVERAGES			
Year	Team	Lg	G	AB	H	2B	3B	HR	(Hm | Rd)	TB	R	RBI	RC	TBB	IBB	SO	HBP	SH	SF	SB	CS	GDP	Avg	OBP	Slg	OPS
2015 Albq*	AAA	78	308	101	30	1	12	(- | -)	169	59	49	63	23	1	41	4	0	2	5	1	3	.328	.380	.549	.929
2012 Col	NL	31	78	16	2	0	2	(1 | 1)	24	8	11	7	1	0	17	1	0	1	0	0	4	.205	.222	.308	.530
2014 Col	NL	21	31	7	2	0	2	(1 | 1)	15	6	6	4	2	0	12	1	0	0	0	0	0	.226	.294	.484	.778
2015 Col	NL	20	42	7	0	0	0	(0 | 0)	7	5	0	0	0	0	4	1	0	0	0	0	0	.167	.186	.167	.353
3 ML YEARS		72	151	30	4	0	4	(2 | 2)	46	19	17	11	3	0	33	3	0	1	0	0	4	.199	.228	.305	.532

Brian McCann

Bats: L Throws: R Pos: C-126;PH-13;1B-10;DH-4   Ht: 6'3" Wt: 220 Born: 2/20/1984 Age: 32

						BATTING												RUNNING			AVERAGES			
Year	Team	Lg	G	AB	H	2B	3B	HR	(Hm | Rd)	TB	R	RBI	RC	TBB	IBB	SO	HBP	SH	SF	SB	CS	GDP	Avg	OBP	Slg	OPS
2005 Atl	NL	59	180	50	7	0	5	(2 | 3)	72	20	23	25	18	5	26	1	4	1	1	1	5	.278	.345	.400	.745
2006 Atl	NL	130	442	147	34	0	24	(10 | 14)	253	61	93	94	41	8	54	3	0	6	2	0	12	.333	.388	.572	.961
2007 Atl	NL	139	504	136	38	0	18	(6 | 12)	228	51	92	68	35	7	74	5	2	6	0	1	19	.270	.320	.452	.772
2008 Atl	NL	145	509	153	42	1	23	(10 | 13)	266	68	87	84	57	4	64	4	0	5	5	0	17	.301	.373	.523	.896
2009 Atl	NL	138	488	137	35	1	21	(12 | 9)	237	63	94	83	49	3	83	5	3	6	4	1	17	.281	.349	.486	.834
2010 Atl	NL	143	479	129	25	0	21	(13 | 8)	217	63	77	76	74	10	98	9	0	4	5	2	12	.269	.375	.453	.828
2011 Atl	NL	128	466	126	19	0	24	(15 | 9)	217	51	71	76	57	14	89	2	0	2	3	2	10	.270	.351	.466	.817
2012 Atl	NL	121	439	101	14	0	20	(11 | 9)	175	44	67	45	44	7	76	1	0	3	3	0	15	.230	.300	.399	.698

Year	Team	Lg	G	AB	H	2B	3B	HR	(Hm	Rd)	TB	R	RBI	RC	TBB	IBB	SO	HBP	SH	SF	SB	CS	GDP	Avg	OBP	Slg	OPS
									BATTING												**RUNNING**			**AVERAGES**			
2013	Atl	NL	102	356	91	13	0	20	(12	8)	164	43	57	51	39	3	66	5	0	2	0	1	9	.256	.336	.461	.796
2014	NYY	AL	140	495	115	15	1	23	(19	4)	201	57	75	58	32	1	77	7	0	4	0	0	16	.232	.286	.406	.692
2015	NYY	AL	135	465	108	15	1	26	(16	10)	203	68	94	77	52	3	97	11	0	7	0	0	7	.232	.320	.437	.756
	Postseason		12	43	9	1	0	3	(2	1)	19	4	9	5	5	0	16	0	0	1	0	0	0	.209	.286	.442	.728
11 ML YEARS			1380	4823	1293	257	4	225	(126	99)	2233	589	830	737	498	65	804	53	9	44	23	8	139	.268	.340	.463	.803

James McCann

Bats: R **Throws:** R **Pos:** C-112;PH-6;DH-1   **Ht:** 6'2" **Wt:** 210 **Born:** 6/13/1990 **Age:** 26

Year	Team	Lg	G	AB	H	2B	3B	HR	(Hm	Rd)	TB	R	RBI	RC	TBB	IBB	SO	HBP	SH	SF	SB	CS	GDP	Avg	OBP	Slg	OPS
2011	2 Tms	Low	14	48	7	2	0	1	(-	-)	12	1	7	3	3	0	13	2	0	1	0	0	1	.146	.222	.250	.472
2012	Lkland	A+	45	160	46	10	0	0	(-	-)	56	24	20	21	10	1	29	5	0	2	3	0	5	.288	.345	.350	.695
2012	Erie	AA	64	220	44	12	0	2	(-	-)	62	15	19	12	8	0	44	0	1	1	2	2	11	.200	.227	.282	.509
2013	Erie	AA	119	441	122	30	1	8	(-	-)	178	50	54	60	30	1	85	7	1	7	3	3	12	.277	.328	.404	.731
2014	Toledo	AAA	109	417	123	34	0	7	(-	-)	178	49	54	64	25	0	90	9	2	7	9	2	11	.295	.343	.427	.770
2014	Det	AL	9	12	3	1	0	0	(0	0)	4	2	0	1	0	0	2	0	0	0	1	0	0	.250	.250	.333	.583
2015	Det	AL	114	401	106	18	5	7	(3	2)	155	32	41	34	16	0	90	3	4	1	0	1	17	.264	.297	.387	.683
2 ML YEARS			123	413	109	19	5	7	(5	2)	159	34	41	35	16	0	92	3	4	1	1	1	17	.264	.296	.385	.681

Brandon McCarthy

Pitches: R **Bats:** R **Pos:** SP-4   **Ht:** 6'7" **Wt:** 225 **Born:** 7/7/1983 **Age:** 32

Year	Team	Lg	G	GS	CG	GF	IP	BFP	H	R	ER	HR	SH	SF	HB	TBB	IBB	SO	WP	Bk	W	L	Pct	Sh	Sv-Op	Hld	ERC	ERA
2005	CWS	AL	12	10	0	0	67.0	277	62	30	30	13	1	1	2	17	0	48	1	1	3	2	.600	0	0-0	2	3.83	4.03
2006	CWS	AL	53	2	0	13	84.2	354	77	44	44	17	3	1	0	33	9	69	5	0	4	7	.364	0	0-1	11	4.10	4.68
2007	Tex	AL	23	22	0	0	101.2	459	111	62	55	9	3	5	3	48	0	59	4	1	5	10	.333	0	0-0	0	4.89	4.87
2008	Tex	AL	5	5	0	0	22.0	93	20	11	10	3	0	2	1	8	0	10	0	0	1	1	.500	0	0-0	0	3.87	4.09
2009	Tex	AL	17	17	1	0	97.1	420	96	55	50	13	0	5	3	36	0	65	0	0	7	4	.636	1	0-0	0	4.22	4.62
2011	Oak	AL	25	25	5	0	170.2	690	168	73	63	11	4	9	0	25	1	123	3	0	9	9	.500	1	0-0	0	2.80	3.32
2012	Oak	AL	18	18	0	0	111.0	469	115	44	40	10	5	4	6	24	2	73	0	0	8	6	.571	0	0-0	0	3.67	3.24
2013	Ari	NL	22	22	2	0	135.0	577	161	71	68	13	6	1	5	21	3	76	1	1	5	11	.313	1	0-0	0	4.29	4.53
2014	2 Tms		32	32	1	0	200.0	836	222	100	90	25	3	4	3	33	4	175	4	0	10	15	.400	1	0-0	0	3.98	4.05
2015	LAD	NL	4	4	0	0	23.0	94	24	15	15	9	0	0	0	4	0	29	0	0	3	0	1.000	0	0-0	0	5.39	5.87
14	Ari	NL	18	18	0	0	109.2	466	131	65	61	15	2	3	2	20	4	93	3	0	3	10	.231	0	0-0	0	4.64	5.01
14	NYY	AL	14	14	1	0	90.1	370	91	35	29	10	1	1	1	13	0	82	1	0	7	5	.583	1	0-0	0	3.23	2.89
10 ML YEARS			211	157	9	13	1012.1	4269	1056	505	465	123	25	32	23	249	19	727	18	3	55	65	.458	4	0-1	11	3.92	4.13

Lance McCullers

Pitches: R **Bats:** L **Pos:** SP-22   **Ht:** 6'2" **Wt:** 205 **Born:** 10/2/1993 **Age:** 22

Year	Team	Lg	G	GS	CG	GF	IP	BFP	H	R	ER	HR	SH	SF	HB	TBB	IBB	SO	WP	Bk	W	L	Pct	Sh	Sv-Op	Hld	ERC	ERA
2012	2 Tms	Low	8	8	0	0	26.0	113	20	13	10	2	0	1	1	12	0	29	3	0	0	4	.000	0	0--	-	2.93	3.46
2013	QuadC	A	25	19	0	3	104.2	447	92	49	37	3	6	1	6	49	1	117	4	2	6	5	.545	0	0--	-	3.41	3.18
2014	Lancst	A+	25	18	0	6	97.0	436	95	63	59	18	0	0	7	56	0	115	11	1	3	6	.333	0	4--	-	5.67	5.47
2015	CpChr	AA	7	5	0	2	32.0	129	16	4	2	1	0	0	2	14	0	48	4	0	3	1	.750	0	1--	-	1.53	0.56
2015	Hou	AL	22	22	1	0	125.2	520	106	49	45	10	0	3	5	43	2	129	8	1	6	7	.462	0	0-0	0	3.02	3.22

Andrew McCutchen

Bats: R **Throws:** R **Pos:** CF-152;DH-3;PH-2   **Ht:** 5'10" **Wt:** 190 **Born:** 10/10/1986 **Age:** 29

Year	Team	Lg	G	AB	H	2B	3B	HR	(Hm	Rd)	TB	R	RBI	RC	TBB	IBB	SO	HBP	SH	SF	SB	CS	GDP	Avg	OBP	Slg	OPS
2009	Pit	NL	108	433	124	26	9	12	(8	4)	204	74	54	78	54	2	83	2	0	4	22	5	3	.286	.365	.471	.836
2010	Pit	NL	154	570	163	35	5	16	(8	8)	256	94	56	86	70	1	89	5	1	7	33	10	6	.286	.365	.449	.814
2011	Pit	NL	158	572	148	34	5	23	(10	13)	261	87	89	102	89	3	126	9	2	6	23	10	7	.259	.364	.456	.820
2012	Pit	NL	157	593	194	29	6	31	(15	16)	328	107	96	125	70	13	132	5	0	5	20	12	9	.327	.400	.553	.953
2013	Pit	NL	157	583	185	38	5	21	(9	12)	296	97	84	105	78	12	101	9	0	4	27	10	13	.317	.404	.508	.911
2014	Pit	NL	146	548	172	38	6	25	(10	15)	297	89	83	109	84	8	115	10	0	6	18	3	9	.314	.410	.542	.952
2015	Pit	NL	157	566	165	36	3	23	(13	10)	276	91	96	120	98	12	133	12	0	9	11	5	9	.292	.401	.488	.889
	Postseason		7	24	7	1	0	0	(0	0)	8	3	0	3	6	1	4	0	0	0	0	0	0	.292	.433	.333	.767
7 ML YEARS			1037	3865	1151	236	39	151	(73	78)	1918	639	558	725	543	51	779	52	3	41	154	55	56	.298	.388	.496	.884

T.J. McFarland

Pitches: L **Bats:** L **Pos:** RP-30   **Ht:** 6'3" **Wt:** 220 **Born:** 6/8/1989 **Age:** 27

Year	Team	Lg	G	GS	CG	GF	IP	BFP	H	R	ER	HR	SH	SF	HB	TBB	IBB	SO	WP	Bk	W	L	Pct	Sh	Sv-Op	Hld	ERC	ERA
2015	Norfolk*	AAA	16	9	0	2	52.2	210	42	20	17	0	0	2	0	14	0	31	1	0	2	3	.400	0	1--	-	1.94	2.91
2013	Bal	AL	38	1	0	8	74.2	331	83	37	35	7	2	1	0	28	5	58	2	0	4	1	.800	0	0-0	4	4.40	4.22
2014	Bal	AL	37	1	0	14	58.2	255	70	22	18	2	5	0	4	13	2	34	0	0	4	2	.667	0	0-0	5	4.23	2.76
2015	Bal	AL	30	0	0	7	40.1	188	52	26	22	4	0	0	0	18	5	26	3	0	2	2	.500	0	0-0	3	5.68	4.91
3 ML YEARS			105	2	0	29	173.2	774	205	85	75	13	7	1	4	59	12	118	5	0	10	5	.667	0	0-0	8	4.63	3.89

Jake McGee

Pitches: L **Bats:** L **Pos:** RP-39   **Ht:** 6'1" **Wt:** 195 **Born:** 8/29/1990 **Age:** 25

			HOW MUCH HE PITCHED					WHAT HE GAVE UP												THE RESULTS						
Year	Team	Lg	G	GS	CG	GF	IP	BFP	H	R	ER	HR	SH	SF	HB	TBB	IBB	SO	WP	Bk	W	L	Pct	Sh	Sv-Op	Hld	ERC	ERA
2010	TB	AL	8	0	0	3	5.0	20	2	1	1	0	0	0	0	3	0	6	0	0	0	0	-	0	0-0	0	1.32	1.80
2011	TB	AL	37	0	0	9	28.0	124	30	14	14	5	1	0	0	12	1	27	0	0	5	2	.714	0	0-0	4	5.09	4.50
2012	TB	AL	69	0	0	13	55.1	212	33	13	12	3	0	2	1	11	4	73	3	0	5	2	.714	0	0-2	19	1.26	1.95
2013	TB	AL	71	0	0	6	62.2	260	52	28	28	8	1	3	1	22	5	75	4	0	5	3	.625	0	1-5	27	3.07	4.02
2014	TB	AL	73	0	0	31	71.1	274	48	15	15	2	1	1	2	16	1	90	1	0	5	2	.714	0	19-23	14	1.55	1.89
2015	TB	AL	39	0	0	6	37.1	147	27	11	10	3	0	1	1	8	1	48	1	0	1	2	.333	0	6-10	19	1.92	2.41
	Postseason		5	0	0	1	3.1	17	3	2	2	0	1	0	1	3	1	3	0	0	0	1	.000	0	0-0	2	5.03	5.40
	6 ML YEARS		297	0	0	68	259.2	1037	192	82	80	21	3	7	5	72	12	319	9	0	21	11	.656	0	26-40	83	2.16	2.77

Casey McGehee

Bats: R **Throws:** R **Pos:** PH-50;3B-42;1B-21;DH-2   McGEE   **Ht:** 6'1" **Wt:** 220 **Born:** 10/12/1982 **Age:** 33

			BATTING																		RUNNING			AVERAGES		
Year	Team	Lg	G	AB	H	2B	3B	HR	(Hm	Rd)	TB	R	RBI	RC	TBB	IBB	SO	HBP	SH	SF	SB	CS	GDP	Avg	OBP	Slg	OPS
2015	Scrmto*	AAA	10	42	15	3	0	2	(-	-)	24	7	7	9	3	0	5	0	0	1	0	0	0	.357	.391	.571	.963
2008	ChC	NL	9	24	4	1	0	0	(0	0)	5	1	5	0	0	0	8	0	0	1	0	0	1	.167	.160	.208	.368
2009	Mil	NL	116	355	107	20	1	16	(6	10)	177	58	66	65	34	2	67	1	0	4	0	2	13	.301	.360	.499	.859
2010	Mil	NL	157	610	174	38	1	23	(13	10)	283	70	104	93	50	5	102	2	0	8	1	1	18	.285	.337	.464	.801
2011	Mil	NL	155	546	122	24	2	13	(8	5)	189	46	67	50	45	4	104	1	0	8	0	3	19	.223	.280	.346	.626
2012	2 Tms		114	318	69	16	1	9	(1	8)	114	36	41	30	29	0	70	2	0	3	1	1	10	.217	.284	.358	.643
2014	Mia	NL	160	616	177	29	1	4	(1	3)	220	56	76	78	67	3	102	1	0	7	4	2	31	.287	.355	.357	.712
2015	2 Tms	NL	109	237	47	12	0	2	(1	1)	65	14	20	8	21	0	50	0	0	0	1	1	18	.198	.264	.274	.538
12	Pit	NL	92	265	61	13	1	8	(1	7)	100	27	35	26	24	0	60	2	0	2	1	1	7	.230	.297	.377	.674
12	NYY	AL	22	53	8	3	0	1	(0	1)	14	9	6	4	5	0	10	0	0	1	0	0	3	.151	.220	.264	.484
15	SF	NL	49	127	27	5	0	2	(1	1)	38	7	11	4	11	0	28	0	0	0	1	0	15	.213	.275	.299	.575
15	Mia	NL	60	110	20	7	0	0	(0	0)	27	7	9	4	10	0	22	0	0	0	1	0	3	.182	.250	.245	.495
	Postseason		6	5	1	0	0	0	(0	0)	1	0	0	1	1	0	2	0	0	0	0	0	0	.200	.333	.200	.533
	7 ML YEARS		820	2706	700	140	6	67	(30	37)	1053	281	379	324	246	14	503	7	0	31	7	10	110	.259	.319	.389	.708

Scott McGough

Pitches: R **Bats:** R **Pos:** RP-6   mick-GUFF   **Ht:** 6'0" **Wt:** 170 **Born:** 10/31/1989 **Age:** 26

			HOW MUCH HE PITCHED						WHAT HE GAVE UP											THE RESULTS						
Year	Team	Lg	G	GS	CG	GF	IP	BFP	H	R	ER	HR	SH	SF	HB	TBB	IBB	SO	WP	Bk	W	L	Pct	Sh	Sv-Op	Hld	ERC	ERA
2011	2 Tms	Low	26	0	0	24	26.0	107	26	10	8	1	1	0	1	6	1	33	3	1	1	5	.167	0	10- -	-	3.16	2.77
2012	2 Tms	Low	50	0	0	26	64.0	283	64	30	27	3	5	1	2	30	5	56	3	4	5	6	.455	0	6- -	-	3.92	3.80
2013	Jaxnvl	AA	36	0	0	11	61.2	251	48	21	18	4	3	0	0	18	3	56	0	1	4	3	.571	0	1- -	-	2.19	2.63
2015	Jaxnvl	AA	10	0	0	3	13.1	58	14	5	4	1	1	0	0	6	0	4	1	1	0	0	-	0	0- -	-	4.43	2.70
2015	NewOr	AAA	13	0	0	5	17.0	68	9	5	4	1	0	0	0	9	0	12	2	0	0	1	.000	0	1- -	-	1.90	2.12
2015	Mia	NL	6	0	0	3	6.2	35	12	7	7	0	0	0	0	4	0	4	0	0	0	0	-	0	0-0	0	9.09	9.45

Dustin McGowan

Pitches: R **Bats:** R **Pos:** RP-13; SP-1   **Ht:** 6'3" **Wt:** 240 **Born:** 3/24/1982 **Age:** 34

			HOW MUCH HE PITCHED						WHAT HE GAVE UP											THE RESULTS						
Year	Team	Lg	G	GS	CG	GF	IP	BFP	H	R	ER	HR	SH	SF	HB	TBB	IBB	SO	WP	Bk	W	L	Pct	Sh	Sv-Op	Hld	ERC	ERA
2015	LV*	AAA	31	1	0	20	39.2	186	41	19	18	2	1	2	1	24	0	28	2	0	2	2	.500	0	15- -	-	4.65	4.08
2005	Tor	AL	13	7	0	4	45.1	205	49	34	32	7	0	4	7	17	0	34	7	0	1	3	.250	0	0-0	1	5.47	6.35
2006	Tor	AL	16	3	0	3	27.1	143	35	27	22	2	0	1	2	25	2	22	3	1	1	2	.333	0	0-1	1	7.72	7.24
2007	Tor	AL	27	27	2	0	169.2	705	146	80	77	14	0	6	2	61	3	144	13	0	12	10	.545	1	0-0	0	3.07	4.08
2008	Tor	AL	19	19	1	0	111.1	474	115	60	54	9	2	8	5	38	1	85	5	0	6	7	.462	0	0-0	0	4.13	4.37
2011	Tor	AL	5	4	0	0	21.0	96	20	15	15	4	0	1	1	13	0	20	3	0	0	2	.000	0	0-0	0	5.50	6.43
2013	Tor	AL	25	0	0	8	25.2	114	19	11	7	2	0	0	2	12	1	26	3	0	0	0	-	0	0-1	6	2.83	2.45
2014	Tor	AL	53	8	0	9	82.0	354	80	41	38	13	0	2	3	33	1	61	2	0	5	3	.625	0	1-5	10	4.50	4.17
2015	Phi	NL	14	1	0	3	23.1	118	29	21	18	7	0	0	0	20	1	21	1	0	1	2	.333	0	0-0	0	9.07	6.94
	8 ML YEARS		172	69	3	25	505.2	2209	493	289	263	58	2	22	22	219	9	413	37	1	26	29	.473	1	1-7	18	4.30	4.68

Collin McHugh

Pitches: R **Bats:** R **Pos:** SP-32   mick-HYOO   **Ht:** 6'2" **Wt:** 190 **Born:** 6/19/1987 **Age:** 29

			HOW MUCH HE PITCHED						WHAT HE GAVE UP											THE RESULTS						
Year	Team	Lg	G	GS	CG	GF	IP	BFP	H	R	ER	HR	SH	SF	HB	TBB	IBB	SO	WP	Bk	W	L	Pct	Sh	Sv-Op	Hld	ERC	ERA
2012	NYM	NL	8	4	0	1	21.1	99	27	21	18	5	2	1	2	8	2	17	0	0	0	4	.000	0	0-0	0	6.83	7.59
2013	2 Tms	NL	7	5	0	2	26.0	125	45	29	29	6	2	2	0	5	0	11	0	0	0	4	.000	0	0-0	0	8.82	10.04
2014	Hou	AL	25	25	0	0	154.2	619	117	53	47	13	6	4	6	41	1	157	6	0	11	9	.550	0	0-0	0	2.34	2.73
2015	Hou	AL	32	32	0	0	203.2	859	207	89	88	19	5	4	9	53	2	171	5	0	19	7	.731	0	0-0	0	3.75	3.89
13	NYM	NL	3	1	0	2	7.0	34	12	8	8	2	0	1	0	3	0	3	0	0	0	1	.000	0	0-0	0	10.77	10.29
13	Col	NL	4	4	0	0	19.0	91	33	21	21	4	2	1	0	2	0	8	0	0	0	3	.000	0	0-0	0	8.14	9.95
	4 ML YEARS		72	66	0	3	405.2	1702	396	192	182	43	15	11	17	107	5	356	11	0	30	24	.556	0	0-0	0	3.60	4.04

Michael McKenry

Bats: R **Throws:** R **Pos:** C-32;PH-25;DH-1 **Ht:** 5'10" **Wt:** 205 **Born:** 3/4/1985 **Age:** 31

Year Team	Lg	G	AB	H	2B	3B	HR	(Hm	Rd)	TB	R	RBI	RC	TBB	IBB	SO	HBP	SH	SF	SB	CS	GDP	Avg	OBP	Slg	OPS
2010 Col	NL	6	8	0	0	0	0	(0	0)	0	0	0	0	1	0	5	0	0	0	0	0	0	.000	.111	.000	.111
2011 Pit	NL	58	180	40	12	0	2	(1	1)	58	17	11	12	14	2	49	0	5	2	0	1	3	.222	.276	.322	.598
2012 Pit	NL	88	240	56	14	0	12	(3	9)	106	25	39	32	29	1	73	3	0	3	0	0	7	.233	.320	.442	.762
2013 Pit	NL	41	115	25	6	0	3	(2	1)	40	9	14	11	5	0	24	2	0	0	0	0	2	.217	.262	.348	.610
2014 Col	NL	57	168	53	9	0	8	(4	4)	86	23	22	28	22	1	42	1	1	0	0	3	6	.315	.398	.512	.910
2015 Col	NL	58	127	26	7	3	4	(3	1)	51	20	17	15	22	0	41	2	0	1	2	2	2	.205	.329	.402	.731
6 ML YEARS		308	838	200	48	3	29	(13	16)	341	94	103	98	93	4	234	8	6	6	2	6	20	.239	.319	.407	.725

Andrew McKirahan

Pitches: L **Bats:** R **Pos:** RP-27 mick-KEER-a-han **Ht:** 6'2" **Wt:** 195 **Born:** 2/8/1990 **Age:** 26

Year Team	Lg	G	GS	CG	GF	IP	BFP	H	R	ER	HR	SH	SF	HB	TBB	IBB	SO	WP	Bk	W	L	Pct	Sh	Sv-Op	Hld	ERC	ERA
2011 2 Tms	Low	15	0	0	6	16.2	70	12	3	3	1	0	1	0	8	0	23	1	0	0	2	.000	0	0--	-	2.58	1.62
2012 Peoria	A	9	0	0	5	10.0	40	6	2	2	0	0	0	2	4	0	11	0	0	0	0	-	0	2--	-	2.16	1.80
2013 3 Tms	Low	21	0	0	4	29.0	116	21	11	9	0	0	0	4	9	0	37	2	0	3	0	1.000	0	0--	-	2.24	2.79
2014 Dytona	A+	23	0	0	18	36.1	148	29	6	4	1	0	2	2	8	0	33	1	1	2	1	.667	0	8--	-	2.08	0.99
2014 Tenn	AA	21	0	0	8	28.2	117	28	13	11	3	2	0	0	6	0	24	3	0	0	3	.000	0	2--	-	3.27	3.45
2015 Gwnntt	AAA	6	0	0	3	5.2	25	6	2	2	2	0	0	0	3	0	8	0	1	0	0	-	0	0--	-	7.03	3.18
2015 Atl	NL	27	0	0	4	27.1	129	40	18	18	2	0	1	2	10	2	22	0	0	1	0	1.000	0	0-1	4	6.76	5.93

Nate McLouth

Bats: L **Throws:** R **Pos:** LF mc-CLOWTH **Ht:** 5'10" **Wt:** 190 **Born:** 10/28/1981 **Age:** 34

Year Team	Lg	G	AB	H	2B	3B	HR	(Hm	Rd)	TB	R	RBI	RC	TBB	IBB	SO	HBP	SH	SF	SB	CS	GDP	Avg	OBP	Slg	OPS
2005 Pit	NL	41	109	28	6	0	5	(2	3)	49	20	12	9	3	0	20	5	2	1	2	0	3	.257	.305	.450	.755
2006 Pit	NL	106	270	63	16	2	7	(3	4)	104	50	16	25	18	0	59	5	3	1	10	1	7	.233	.293	.385	.678
2007 Pit	NL	137	329	85	21	3	13	(5	8)	151	62	38	52	39	2	77	9	3	2	22	1	2	.258	.351	.459	.810
2008 Pit	NL	152	597	165	46	4	26	(15	11)	297	113	94	105	65	11	93	12	5	6	23	3	5	.276	.356	.497	.853
2009 2 Tms	NL	129	507	130	27	2	20	(9	11)	221	86	70	85	68	1	99	9	3	4	19	6	8	.256	.352	.436	.788
2010 Atl	NL	85	242	46	12	1	6	(5	1)	78	30	24	23	33	2	57	5	6	2	7	2	3	.190	.298	.322	.620
2011 Atl	NL	81	267	61	12	2	4	(4	0)	89	35	16	36	44	4	52	3	7	0	4	2	4	.228	.344	.333	.677
2012 2 Tms	NL	89	266	64	14	1	7	(4	3)	101	39	20	30	27	1	61	2	2	1	12	1	2	.241	.314	.380	.694
2013 Bal	AL	146	531	137	31	4	12	(7	5)	212	76	36	71	53	1	86	4	4	1	30	7	7	.258	.329	.399	.729
2014 Was	NL	79	139	24	6	0	1	(1	0)	33	10	7	8	16	1	35	5	1	1	4	1	0	.173	.280	.237	.517
09 Pit	NL	45	168	43	7	1	9	(5	4)	79	27	34	33	21	0	29	4	0	2	7	0	2	.256	.349	.470	.819
09 Atl	NL	84	339	87	20	1	11	(4	7)	142	59	36	52	47	1	70	5	3	2	12	6	6	.257	.354	.419	.773
12 Pit	NL	34	57	8	2	0	0	(0	0)	10	4	2	1	5	0	18	0	0	0	0	0	0	.140	.210	.175	.385
12 Bal	AL	55	209	56	12	1	7	(4	3)	91	35	18	29	22	1	43	2	2	1	12	1	2	.268	.342	.435	.777
Postseason		9	28	9	1	0	1	(0	1)	13	3	5	4	1	0	3	0	0	1	3	1	0	.321	.333	.464	.798
10 ML YEARS		1045	3257	803	191	19	101	(55	46)	1335	521	333	444	366	23	639	59	36	19	133	24	41	.247	.332	.410	.742

Yoervis Medina

Pitches: R **Bats:** R **Pos:** RP-17 yo-EHR-viss meh-DEE-nah **Ht:** 6'3" **Wt:** 245 **Born:** 7/27/1988 **Age:** 27

Year Team	Lg	G	GS	CG	GF	IP	BFP	H	R	ER	HR	SH	SF	HB	TBB	IBB	SO	WP	Bk	W	L	Pct	Sh	Sv-Op	Hld	ERC	ERA
2015 Iowa*	AAA	28	0	0	8	34.1	161	40	25	24	3	3	1	2	21	2	35	5	0	0	2	.000	0	1--	-	5.98	6.29
2013 Sea	AL	63	0	0	19	68.0	291	49	22	22	5	2	1	4	40	7	71	8	0	4	6	.400	0	1-4	19	3.15	2.91
2014 Sea	AL	66	0	0	19	57.0	247	48	18	17	3	0	4	5	28	3	60	8	0	5	3	.625	0	0-1	21	3.47	2.68
2015 2 Tms		17	0	0	5	21.0	97	23	12	11	2	0	0	0	11	0	16	1	0	1	0	1.000	0	1-2	3	4.96	4.71
15 Sea	AL	12	0	0	3	12.0	54	11	5	4	1	0	0	0	7	0	9	1	0	1	0	1.000	0	1-2	3	4.10	3.00
15 ChC	NL	5	0	0	2	9.0	43	12	7	7	1	0	0	0	4	0	7	0	0	0	0	-	0	0-0	0	6.17	7.00
3 ML YEARS		146	0	0	43	146.0	635	120	52	50	10	2	5	9	79	10	147	17	0	10	9	.526	0	2-7	43	3.52	3.08

Kris Medlen

Pitches: R **Bats:** B **Pos:** SP-8; RP-7 MEDD-linn **Ht:** 5'10" **Wt:** 190 **Born:** 10/7/1985 **Age:** 30

Year Team	Lg	G	GS	CG	GF	IP	BFP	H	R	ER	HR	SH	SF	HB	TBB	IBB	SO	WP	Bk	W	L	Pct	Sh	Sv-Op	Hld	ERC	ERA
2009 Atl	NL	37	4	0	10	67.2	294	65	34	32	5	6	2	2	30	2	72	3	1	3	5	.375	0	0-2	1	3.90	4.26
2010 Atl	NL	31	14	0	5	107.2	438	108	48	44	13	7	3	3	21	1	83	1	0	6	2	.750	0	0-0	1	3.60	3.68
2011 Atl	NL	2	0	0	0	2.1	8	1	0	0	0	0	0	0	0	0	2	0	0	0	0	-	0	0-0	0	0.40	0.00
2012 Atl	NL	50	12	2	7	138.0	520	103	26	24	6	1	0	0	23	0	120	3	0	10	1	.909	1	1-2	7	1.69	1.57
2013 Atl	NL	32	31	0	1	197.0	820	194	77	68	18	9	2	8	47	1	157	2	0	15	12	.556	0	0-0	0	3.48	3.11
2015 KC	AL	15	8	0	2	58.1	243	56	30	26	6	0	1	2	18	0	40	3	0	6	2	.750	0	0-0	0	3.71	4.01
Postseason		2	2	0	0	10.1	48	12	10	7	2	1	2	2	1	0	8	0	0	0	2	.000	0	0-0	0	4.88	6.10
6 ML YEARS		167	69	2	26	571.0	2323	527	215	194	48	23	8	15	139	4	474	12	2	40	22	.645	1	1-4	9	3.09	3.06

Jenrry Mejia

Pitches: R Bats: R Pos: RP-7   HENN-ree mah-HEE-ah   Ht: 6'0" Wt: 205 Born: 10/11/1989 Age: 26

		HOW MUCH HE PITCHED						WHAT HE GAVE UP											THE RESULTS						
Year	Team	Lg	G	GS	CG	GF	IP	BFP	H	R	ER	HR	SH	SF	HB	TBB	IBB	SO	WP	Bk	W	L	Pct	Sh	Sv-Op	Hld	ERC	ERA
2010	NYM	NL	33	3	0	8	39.0	183	46	21	20	3	0	1	3	20	2	22	7	0	0	4	.000	0	0-1	2	5.57	4.62
2012	NYM	NL	5	3	0	1	16.0	74	20	10	10	2	1	0	0	9	0	8	1	0	1	2	.333	0	0-0	0	6.55	5.63
2013	NYM	NL	5	5	0	0	27.1	112	28	9	7	2	0	4	0	4	0	27	1	0	1	2	.333	0	0-0	0	3.05	2.30
2014	NYM	NL	63	7	0	49	93.2	417	98	41	38	9	2	0	4	41	8	98	5	0	6	6	.500	0	28-31	3	4.45	3.65
2015	NYM	NL	7	0	0	1	7.1	27	4	0	0	0	1	0	0	2	1	7	0	0	1	0	1.000	0	0-0	3	1.03	0.00
5 ML YEARS			113	18	0	59	183.1	813	196	81	75	16	4	5	7	76	11	162	14	0	9	14	.391	0	28-32	7	4.47	3.68

Mark Melancon

Pitches: R Bats: R Pos: RP-78   muh-LANN-sun   Ht: 6'2" Wt: 210 Born: 3/28/1985 Age: 31

		HOW MUCH HE PITCHED						WHAT HE GAVE UP											THE RESULTS						
Year	Team	Lg	G	GS	CG	GF	IP	BFP	H	R	ER	HR	SH	SF	HB	TBB	IBB	SO	WP	Bk	W	L	Pct	Sh	Sv-Op	Hld	ERC	ERA
2009	NYY	AL	13	0	0	4	16.1	74	13	8	7	0	0	0	4	10	0	10	3	0	0	1	.000	0	0-1	0	3.94	3.86
2010	2 Tms		22	0	0	4	21.1	90	19	13	10	2	0	1	1	8	0	22	2	0	2	0	1.000	0	0-1	8	3.53	4.22
2011	Hou	NL	71	0	0	47	74.1	309	65	28	23	5	2	0	2	26	6	66	1	0	8	4	.667	0	20-25	3	2.98	2.78
2012	Bos	AL	41	0	0	17	45.0	194	45	31	31	8	1	2	3	12	1	41	2	0	0	2	.000	0	1-2	2	4.24	6.20
2013	Pit	NL	72	0	0	24	71.0	279	60	15	11	1	0	1	1	8	0	70	6	0	3	2	.600	0	16-21	26	1.78	1.39
2014	Pit	NL	72	0	0	48	71.0	277	51	15	15	2	1	1	3	11	1	71	3	0	3	5	.375	0	33-37	14	1.54	1.90
2015	Pit	NL	78	0	0	63	76.2	293	57	22	19	4	1	1	2	14	2	62	3	0	3	2	.600	0	51-53	1	1.82	2.23
10	NYY	AL	2	0	0	2	4.0	19	7	5	4	1	0	1	0	0	0	3	0	0	0	0	-	0	0-0	0	7.95	9.00
10	Hou	NL	20	0	0	2	17.1	71	12	8	6	1	0	0	1	8	0	19	2	0	2	0	1.000	0	0-1	8	2.65	3.12
Postseason			5	0	0	2	4.2	19	5	4	4	2	0	0	0	1	0	3	0	0	1	0	1.000	0	0-1	0	6.16	7.71
7 ML YEARS			369	0	0	207	375.2	1516	310	132	116	22	5	6	16	89	10	342	20	0	19	16	.543	0	121-140	54	2.41	2.78

Roman Mendez

Pitches: R Bats: R Pos: RP-15   Ht: 6'3" Wt: 235 Born: 7/25/1990 Age: 25

		HOW MUCH HE PITCHED						WHAT HE GAVE UP											THE RESULTS						
Year	Team	Lg	G	GS	CG	GF	IP	BFP	H	R	ER	HR	SH	SF	HB	TBB	IBB	SO	WP	Bk	W	L	Pct	Sh	Sv-Op	Hld	ERC	ERA
2011	Hkry	A	26	20	0	1	117.0	509	117	44	43	7	4	2	6	45	0	130	11	1	9	1	.900	0	1--	-	3.92	3.31
2012	2 Tms	Low	21	15	0	3	79.0	340	76	46	43	8	6	3	8	26	0	78	3	0	4	7	.364	0	1--	-	3.99	4.90
2012	Frisco	AA	5	0	0	1	12.1	51	8	3	2	2	0	0	1	4	1	9	0	0	2	0	1.000	0	1--	-	2.43	1.46
2013	Frisco	AA	16	0	0	8	24.2	99	12	6	5	1	3	1	2	11	2	24	2	0	2	0	1.000	0	2--	-	1.52	1.82
2014	RdRck	AAA	25	0	0	12	31.1	144	39	16	14	4	0	1	2	12	0	30	1	0	0	1	.000	0	3--	-	5.91	4.02
2015	RdRck	AAA	30	0	0	15	35.2	146	32	11	11	5	0	0	1	9	0	33	2	0	3	2	.600	0	5--	-	3.33	2.78
2014	Tex	AL	30	0	0	6	33.0	136	20	8	8	2	0	2	2	17	2	22	2	0	0	1	.000	0	0-0	10	2.31	2.18
2015	2 Tms	AL	15	0	0	7	13.2	58	14	8	8	2	0	1	1	8	1	10	0	0	0	1	.000	0	0-1	0	5.97	5.27
15	Tex	AL	12	0	0	5	11.2	49	11	7	7	1	0	0	1	7	1	9	0	0	0	1	.000	0	0-1	0	5.02	5.40
15	Bos	AL	3	0	0	2	2.0	9	3	1	1	1	0	0	0	1	0	1	0	0	0	0	-	0	0-0	0	12.15	4.50
2 ML YEARS			45	0	0	13	46.2	194	34	16	16	4	0	3	3	25	3	32	2	0	0	2	.000	0	0-1	10	3.25	3.09

Jordy Mercer

Bats: R Throws: R Pos: SS-115;PH-3   Ht: 6'3" Wt: 215 Born: 8/27/1986 Age: 29

							BATTING													RUNNING			AVERAGES			
Year	Team	Lg	G	AB	H	2B	3B	HR	(Hm	Rd)	TB	R	RBI	RC	TBB	IBB	SO	HBP	SH	SF	SB	CS	GDP	Avg	OBP	Slg	OPS
2012	Pit	NL	42	62	13	5	1	1	(1	0)	23	7	5	6	4	0	14	1	0	1	0	1	0	.210	.265	.371	.636
2013	Pit	NL	103	333	95	22	2	8	(1	7)	145	33	27	46	22	6	62	4	5	1	3	2	7	.285	.336	.435	.772
2014	Pit	NL	149	506	129	27	2	12	(3	9)	196	56	55	45	35	12	89	4	5	5	4	1	14	.255	.305	.387	.693
2015	Pit	NL	116	394	96	21	0	3	(0	3)	126	34	34	34	27	7	73	2	4	3	3	2	7	.244	.293	.320	.613
Postseason			6	12	2	0	0	0	(0	0)	2	0	0	0	1	1	4	0	0	0	0	0	0	.167	.231	.167	.397
4 ML YEARS			410	1295	333	75	5	24	(5	19)	490	130	121	131	88	25	238	11	14	10	10	6	28	.257	.308	.378	.686

Devin Mesoraco

Bats: R Throws: R Pos: PH-13;C-6;DH-4   mezz-er-OCK-oh   Ht: 6'1" Wt: 220 Born: 6/19/1988 Age: 28

							BATTING													RUNNING			AVERAGES			
Year	Team	Lg	G	AB	H	2B	3B	HR	(Hm	Rd)	TB	R	RBI	RC	TBB	IBB	SO	HBP	SH	SF	SB	CS	GDP	Avg	OBP	Slg	OPS
2011	Cin	NL	18	50	9	3	0	2	(2	0)	18	5	6	5	3	1	10	0	0	0	0	0	1	.180	.226	.360	.586
2012	Cin	NL	54	165	35	8	0	5	(4	1)	58	17	14	10	17	4	33	1	0	1	1	1	2	.212	.288	.352	.640
2013	Cin	NL	103	323	77	13	0	9	(5	4)	117	31	42	30	24	4	61	0	0	5	0	2	9	.238	.287	.362	.649
2014	Cin	NL	114	384	105	25	0	25	(14	11)	205	54	80	76	41	4	103	12	0	3	1	3	5	.273	.359	.534	.893
2015	Cin	NL	23	45	8	1	1	0	(0	0)	11	2	2	3	5	0	9	1	0	0	1	0	0	.178	.275	.244	.519
Postseason			1	1	0	0	0	0	(0	0)	0	0	0	0	0	0	0	0	0	0	0	0	0	.000	.000	.000	.000
5 ML YEARS			312	967	234	50	1	41	(25	16)	409	109	144	124	90	13	216	14	0	9	3	6	17	.242	.313	.423	.736

Alex Meyer

Pitches: R Bats: R Pos: RP-2   MY-er   Ht: 6'9" Wt: 225 Born: 1/3/1990 Age: 26

		HOW MUCH HE PITCHED						WHAT HE GAVE UP											THE RESULTS						
Year	Team	Lg	G	GS	CG	GF	IP	BFP	H	R	ER	HR	SH	SF	HB	TBB	IBB	SO	WP	Bk	W	L	Pct	Sh	Sv-Op	Hld	ERC	ERA
2012	2 Tms	Low	25	25	1	0	129.0	521	97	44	41	6	6	5	5	45	0	139	9	0	10	6	.625	1	0--	-	2.41	2.86
2013	NwBrit	AA	13	13	0	0	70.0	299	60	29	25	3	0	2	3	29	0	84	5	1	4	3	.571	0	0--	-	3.09	3.21
2014	Roch	AAA	27	27	0	0	130.1	565	116	58	51	10	7	5	8	64	0	153	5	0	7	7	.500	0	0--	-	3.90	3.52
2015	Roch	AAA	38	8	0	6	92.0	418	101	54	49	4	3	3	5	48	1	100	6	0	4	5	.444	0	0--	-	4.91	4.79
2015	Min	AL	2	0	0	0	2.2	15	4	5	5	2	1	0	0	3	0	3	0	0	0	0	-	0	0-0	0	16.82	16.88

Will Middlebrooks

Bats: R Throws: R Pos: 3B-69;PH-12;SS-8;1B-2   Ht: 6'3" Wt: 220 Born: 9/9/1988 Age: 27

Year Team	Lg	G	AB	H	2B	3B	HR	(Hm	Rd)	TB	R	RBI	RC	TBB	IBB	SO	HBP	SH	SF	SB	CS	GDP	Avg	OBP	Slg	OPS
2015 ElPaso*	AAA	38	153	39	5	1	4	(-	-)	58	13	19	16	8	1	35	0	0	3	1	2		.255	.287	.379	.666
2012 Bos	AL	75	267	77	14	0	15	(9	6)	136	34	54	46	13	0	70	3	0	3	4	1	8	.288	.325	.509	.835
2013 Bos	AL	94	348	79	18	0	17	(4	13)	148	41	49	29	20	3	98	2	1	3	3	1	13	.227	.271	.425	.696
2014 Bos	AL	63	215	41	10	0	2	(1	1)	57	14	19	15	15	1	70	4	0	0	1	1	7	.191	.256	.265	.522
2015 SD	NL	83	255	54	7	2	9	(1	8)	92	23	29	20	11	0	60	0	0	4	2	1	4	.212	.241	.361	.602
Postseason		10	25	4	2	0	0	(0	0)	6	2	1	2	3	1	10	0	0	0	0	0	0	.160	.250	.240	.490
4 ML YEARS		315	1085	251	49	2	43	(15	28)	433	112	151	110	59	4	298	9	1	10	10	4	32	.231	.274	.399	.673

Wade Miley

Pitches: L Bats: L Pos: SP-32   MY-lee   Ht: 6'0" Wt: 220 Born: 11/13/1986 Age: 29

Year Team	Lg	G	GS	CG	GF	IP	BFP	H	R	ER	HR	SH	SF	HB	TBB	IBB	SO	WP	Bk	W	L	Pct	Sh	Sv-Op	Hld	ERC	ERA
2011 Ari	NL	8	7	0	0	40.0	180	48	24	20	6	3	1	0	18	0	25	1	0	4	2	.667	0	0-0	0	5.90	4.50
2012 Ari	NL	32	29	0	0	194.2	807	193	79	72	14	8	3	2	37	0	144	6	1	16	11	.593	0	0-0	0	3.05	3.33
2013 Ari	NL	33	33	0	0	202.2	847	201	88	80	21	6	2	4	66	4	147	13	0	10	10	.500	0	0-0	0	3.88	3.55
2014 Ari	NL	33	33	0	0	201.1	866	207	103	97	23	8	9	4	75	3	183	9	0	8	12	.400	0	0-0	0	4.31	4.34
2015 Bos	AL	32	32	1	0	193.2	831	201	98	96	17	3	2	4	64	0	147	10	1	11	11	.500	0	0-0	0	4.01	4.46
5 ML YEARS		138	134	1	0	832.1	3531	850	388	365	81	28	17	14	260	7	646	39	2	49	46	.516	0	0-0	0	3.90	3.95

Andrew Miller

Pitches: L Bats: L Pos: RP-60   Ht: 6'7" Wt: 210 Born: 5/21/1985 Age: 31

Year Team	Lg	G	GS	CG	GF	IP	BFP	H	R	ER	HR	SH	SF	HB	TBB	IBB	SO	WP	Bk	W	L	Pct	Sh	Sv-Op	Hld	ERC	ERA
2006 Det	AL	8	0	0	3	10.1	51	8	9	7	0	0	0	2	10	0	6	1	0	0	1	.000	0	0-0	1	4.79	6.10
2007 Det	AL	13	13	0	0	64.0	309	73	43	40	8	3	1	7	39	0	56	4	1	5	5	.500	0	0-0	0	6.31	5.63
2008 Fla	NL	29	20	0	1	107.1	492	120	78	70	7	10	7	4	56	4	89	4	0	6	10	.375	0	0-0	0	5.04	5.87
2009 Fla	NL	20	14	0	1	80.0	366	85	52	43	7	6	4	2	43	1	59	10	0	3	5	.375	0	0-0	1	4.90	4.84
2010 Fla	NL	9	7	0	1	32.2	171	51	34	31	6	5	2	1	26	2	28	5	0	1	5	.167	0	0-0	0	10.20	8.54
2011 Bos	AL	17	12	0	1	65.0	310	77	43	40	8	6	5	3	41	0	50	2	1	6	3	.667	0	0-0	0	6.48	5.54
2012 Bos	AL	53	0	0	4	40.1	169	28	15	15	3	0	3	2	20	1	51	1	0	3	2	.600	0	0-0	13	2.76	3.35
2013 Bos	AL	37	0	0	11	30.2	135	25	12	9	3	1	0	2	17	0	48	2	0	1	2	.333	0	0-1	6	3.83	2.64
2014 2 Tms	AL	73	0	0	15	62.1	242	33	16	14	3	2	2	5	17	2	103	3	0	5	5	.500	0	1-2	22	1.36	2.02
2015 NYY	AL	60	0	0	53	61.2	246	33	16	14	5	1	2	5	20	1	100	2	0	3	2	.600	0	36-38	0	1.61	2.04
14 Bos	AL	50	0	0	12	42.1	170	25	13	11	2	2	2	4	13	2	69	2	0	3	5	.375	0	0-0	13	1.62	2.34
14 Bal	AL	23	0	0	3	20.0	72	8	3	3	1	0	0	1	4	0	34	1	0	2	0	1.000	0	1-2	9	0.86	1.35
Postseason		5	0	0	0	7.1	24	1	0	0	0	0	0	1	1	0	8	0	0	0	0	-	0	0-0	2	0.26	0.00
10 ML YEARS		319	66	0	91	554.1	2491	533	318	283	50	34	26	33	289	11	590	34	2	33	40	.452	0	37-41	45	4.41	4.59

Brad Miller

Bats: L Throws: R Pos: SS-89;CF-20;LF-15;2B-11;DH-10;PH-8;RF-6;PR-6;3B-2   Ht: 6'2" Wt: 200 Born: 10/18/1989 Age: 26

Year Team	Lg	G	AB	H	2B	3B	HR	(Hm	Rd)	TB	R	RBI	RC	TBB	IBB	SO	HBP	SH	SF	SB	CS	GDP	Avg	OBP	Slg	OPS
2013 Sea	AL	76	306	81	11	6	8	(3	5)	128	41	36	41	24	0	52	1	2	2	5	3	2	.265	.318	.418	.737
2014 Sea	AL	123	367	81	15	4	10	(4	6)	134	47	36	41	34	2	95	2	3	3	4	2	2	.221	.288	.365	.653
2015 Sea	AL	144	438	113	22	4	11	(6	5)	176	44	46	58	47	0	101	2	4	6	13	4	7	.258	.329	.402	.730
3 ML YEARS		343	1111	275	48	14	29	(13	16)	438	132	118	140	105	2	248	5	9	11	22	9	11	.248	.313	.394	.707

Justin Miller

Pitches: R Bats: R Pos: RP-34   Ht: 6'3" Wt: 215 Born: 6/13/1987 Age: 29

Year Team	Lg	G	GS	CG	GF	IP	BFP	H	R	ER	HR	SH	SF	HB	TBB	IBB	SO	WP	Bk	W	L	Pct	Sh	Sv-Op	Hld	ERC	ERA
2011 Frisco	AA	48	0	0	29	69.2	278	46	14	14	2	1	1	4	24	3	77	5	0	9	1	.900	0	13--	-	1.86	1.81
2013 Frisco	AA	16	0	0	5	16.0	75	16	12	11	1	0	1	4	7	0	21	4	0	1	0	1.000	0	2--	-	4.80	6.19
2013 RdRck	AAA	11	0	0	4	11.0	58	14	16	12	4	0	1	0	9	0	12	2	0	1	0	1.000	0	1--	-	9.32	9.82
2014 Toledo	AAA	38	0	0	22	44.2	173	30	9	9	2	1	1	4	12	0	39	2	0	2	1	.667	0	5--	-	1.98	1.81
2015 NwBrit	AA	6	0	0	2	10.2	46	7	3	1	0	0	0	2	4	1	10	0	1	1	1	.500	0	0--	-	1.97	0.84
2015 Albq	AAA	25	0	0	16	27.1	114	20	7	7	2	0	0	2	8	0	33	1	0	0	2	.000	0	7--	-	2.28	2.30
2014 Det	AL	8	0	0	4	12.1	53	14	9	7	2	1	2	0	2	0	5	0	0	1	0	1.000	0	0-0	0	4.21	5.11
2015 Col	NL	34	0	0	9	33.1	129	21	15	15	2	0	0	1	11	0	38	2	0	3	3	.500	0	1-2	7	1.75	4.05
2 ML YEARS		42	0	0	13	45.2	182	35	24	22	4	1	2	0	13	0	43	2	0	4	3	.571	0	1-2	7	2.36	4.34

Shelby Miller

Pitches: R Bats: R Pos: SP-33   Ht: 6'3" Wt: 215 Born: 10/10/1990 Age: 25

Year Team	Lg	G	GS	CG	GF	IP	BFP	H	R	ER	HR	SH	SF	HB	TBB	IBB	SO	WP	Bk	W	L	Pct	Sh	Sv-Op	Hld	ERC	ERA
2012 StL	NL	6	1	0	1	13.2	54	9	2	2	0	0	0	1	4	0	16	0	0	1	0	1.000	0	0-0	0	1.65	1.32
2013 StL	NL	31	31	1	0	173.1	722	152	65	59	20	7	3	5	57	0	169	2	0	15	9	.625	1	0-0	0	3.34	3.06
2014 StL	NL	32	31	1	0	183.0	764	160	78	76	22	7	4	2	73	4	127	4	0	10	9	.526	1	0-0	0	3.56	3.74
2015 Atl	NL	33	33	2	0	205.1	860	183	82	69	13	8	4	6	73	8	171	5	2	6	17	.261	2	0-0	0	3.12	3.02
Postseason		5	2	0	0	13.2	61	16	8	8	1	1	1	1	6	0	12	0	0	0	0	-	0	0-0	0	5.46	5.27
4 ML YEARS		102	96	4	1	575.1	2400	504	227	206	55	22	11	14	207	12	483	11	2	32	35	.478	4	0-0	1	3.29	3.22

Brad Mills

Pitches: L Bats: R Pos: SP-1   Ht: 6'0" Wt: 190 Born: 3/5/1985 Age: 31

		HOW MUCH HE PITCHED						WHAT HE GAVE UP										THE RESULTS						
Year	Team	Lg	G	GS	CG	GF	IP	BFP	H	R	ER	HR	SH	SF	HB	TBB	IBB	SO	WP	Bk	W	L	Pct	Sh	Sv-Op	Hld	ERC	ERA
2015	Nashv*	AAA	24	24	0	0	137.1	577	134	74	69	12	3	5	3	55	0	95	6	0	5	12	.294	0	0--	-	4.05	4.52
2009	Tor	AL	2	2	0	0	7.2	42	14	12	12	4	0	1	0	6	0	9	0	0	0	1	.000	0	0-0	0	15.52	14.09
2010	Tor	AL	7	3	0	0	22.1	98	20	14	14	2	0	1	1	13	1	18	1	0	1	0	1.000	0	0-0	1	4.26	5.64
2011	Tor	AL	5	4	0	0	18.1	91	23	20	20	4	0	0	2	12	1	18	1	0	1	2	.333	0	0-0	0	7.97	9.82
2012	LAA	AL	1	1	0	0	5.0	18	3	0	0	0	0	0	0	0	0	6	0	0	1	0	1.000	0	0-0	0	0.75	0.00
2014	2 Tms	AL	5	3	0	1	20.2	101	29	22	21	5	0	1	2	11	0	19	1	0	1	1	.500	0	0-0	0	8.84	9.15
2015	Oak	AL	1	1	0	0	5.0	23	7	3	3	1	0	0	1	1	0	1	0	0	0	0	-	0	0-0	0	7.46	5.40
14	Oak	AL	3	3	0	0	16.1	73	19	9	8	2	0	0	1	7	0	14	1	0	1	1	.500	0	0-0	0	5.67	4.41
14	Tor	AL	2	0	0	1	4.1	28	10	13	13	3	0	1	1	4	0	5	0	0	0	0	-	0	0-0	0	23.14	27.00
6 ML YEARS			21	14	0	1	79.0	373	96	71	70	16	0	3	6	43	2	71	3	0	4	4	.500	0	0-0	0	7.09	7.97

Tommy Milone

Pitches: L Bats: L Pos: SP-23; RP-1   mah-LONE   Ht: 6'0" Wt: 220 Born: 2/16/1987 Age: 29

		HOW MUCH HE PITCHED						WHAT HE GAVE UP										THE RESULTS						
Year	Team	Lg	G	GS	CG	GF	IP	BFP	H	R	ER	HR	SH	SF	HB	TBB	IBB	SO	WP	Bk	W	L	Pct	Sh	Sv-Op	Hld	ERC	ERA
2015	Roch*	AAA	5	5	1	0	38.2	140	25	3	3	2	0	0	0	3	0	47	1	0	4	0	1.000	1	0--	-	1.20	0.70
2011	Was	NL	5	5	0	0	26.0	110	28	11	11	2	3	2	2	4	2	15	0	0	1	0	1.000	0	0-0	0	3.55	3.81
2012	Oak	AL	31	31	1	0	190.0	791	207	90	79	24	3	3	4	36	2	137	2	0	13	10	.565	0	0-0	0	4.04	3.74
2013	Oak	AL	28	26	1	0	156.1	667	160	83	72	25	0	6	2	39	2	126	1	0	12	9	.571	0	0-0	0	3.98	4.14
2014	2 Tms	AL	22	21	0	1	118.0	519	128	63	55	16	1	2	5	37	2	75	0	0	6	4	.600	0	0-0	0	4.55	4.19
2015	Min	AL	24	23	0	1	128.2	543	128	64	56	17	6	7	1	36	1	91	3	0	9	5	.643	0	1-1	0	3.79	3.92
14	Oak	AL	16	16	0	0	96.1	405	91	42	38	12	1	2	4	26	2	61	0	0	6	3	.667	0	0-0	0	3.53	3.55
14	Min	AL	6	5	0	1	21.2	114	37	21	17	4	0	0	1	11	0	14	0	0	0	1	.000	0	0-0	0	9.76	7.06
Postseason			1	1	0	0	6.0	25	5	1	1	0	0	0	1	1	0	6	1	0	0	0	-	0	0-0	0	2.26	1.50
5 ML YEARS			110	106	2	2	619.0	2630	651	311	273	84	13	20	14	152	9	444	6	0	41	28	.594	0	1-1	0	4.05	3.97

Mike Minor

Pitches: L Bats: R Pos: P   Ht: 6'4" Wt: 220 Born: 12/26/1987 Age: 28

		HOW MUCH HE PITCHED						WHAT HE GAVE UP										THE RESULTS						
Year	Team	Lg	G	GS	CG	GF	IP	BFP	H	R	ER	HR	SH	SF	HB	TBB	IBB	SO	WP	Bk	W	L	Pct	Sh	Sv-Op	Hld	ERC	ERA
2010	Atl	NL	9	8	0	1	40.2	185	53	28	27	6	1	3	1	11	0	43	0	0	3	2	.600	0	0-0	0	5.71	5.98
2011	Atl	NL	15	15	0	0	82.2	361	93	39	38	7	3	1	1	30	5	77	2	0	5	3	.625	0	0-0	0	4.51	4.14
2012	Atl	NL	30	30	0	0	179.1	728	151	88	82	26	8	8	5	56	7	145	3	0	11	10	.524	0	0-0	0	3.28	4.12
2013	Atl	NL	32	32	1	0	204.2	820	177	79	73	22	5	6	1	46	2	181	0	0	13	9	.591	0	0-0	0	2.76	3.21
2014	Atl	NL	25	25	0	0	145.1	637	165	77	77	21	6	2	6	44	2	120	5	0	6	12	.333	0	0-0	0	4.93	4.77
Postseason			1	1	0	0	6.1	26	8	1	1	0	1	0	0	1	0	5	0	0	1	0	1.000	0	0-0	0	4.11	1.42
5 ML YEARS			111	110	1	1	652.2	2731	639	311	297	82	23	20	14	187	16	566	15	0	38	36	.514	0	0-0	0	3.76	4.10

Bryan Mitchell

Pitches: R Bats: L Pos: RP-18; SP-2   Ht: 6'3" Wt: 200 Born: 4/19/1991 Age: 25

		HOW MUCH HE PITCHED						WHAT HE GAVE UP										THE RESULTS						
Year	Team	Lg	G	GS	CG	GF	IP	BFP	H	R	ER	HR	SH	SF	HB	TBB	IBB	SO	WP	Bk	W	L	Pct	Sh	Sv-Op	Hld	ERC	ERA
2011	Stnlld	A-	14	14	0	0	61.2	275	65	34	28	5	1	2	5	31	0	59	10	0	1	3	.250	0	0--	-	5.07	4.09
2012	CtnSC	A	27	26	0	0	120.0	530	107	74	61	7	2	2	8	72	0	121	18	1	9	11	.450	0	0--	-	4.24	4.58
2013	Tampa	A+	24	23	1	0	126.2	570	144	83	72	5	4	8	6	53	0	104	23	0	4	11	.267	0	0--	-	4.66	5.12
2014	Trntn	AA	14	13	0	1	61.1	272	64	36	33	6	1	3	0	29	1	60	6	0	2	5	.286	0	0--	-	4.55	4.84
2014	S-WB	AAA	9	8	0	0	41.2	178	45	18	17	5	0	2	0	16	0	34	4	0	4	2	.667	0	0--	-	4.73	3.67
2015	S-WB	AAA	15	15	1	0	75.0	316	63	29	26	1	2	1	0	37	0	61	6	0	5	5	.500	0	0--	-	2.99	3.12
2014	NYY	AL	3	1	0	0	11.0	44	10	3	3	0	0	0	2	3	0	7	0	0	0	1	.000	0	0-0	0	3.34	2.45
2015	NYY	AL	20	2	0	8	29.2	143	37	24	21	4	0	0	2	16	1	29	6	0	0	2	.000	0	1-1	1	6.51	6.37
2 ML YEARS			23	3	0	9	40.2	187	47	27	24	4	0	0	4	19	1	36	6	0	0	3	.000	0	1-1	1	5.62	5.31

Yadier Molina

Bats: R Throws: R Pos: C-134;PH-3;DH-1   YAH-dee-air   Ht: 5'11" Wt: 220 Born: 7/13/1982 Age: 33

			BATTING																		RUNNING			AVERAGES			
Year	Team	Lg	G	AB	H	2B	3B	HR	(Hm	Rd)	TB	R	RBI	RC	TBB	IBB	SO	HBP	SH	SF	SB	CS	GDP	Avg	OBP	Slg	OPS
2004	StL	NL	51	135	36	6	0	2	(1	1)	48	12	15	15	13	3	20	0	2	1	0	1	4	.267	.329	.356	.684
2005	StL	NL	114	385	97	15	1	8	(6	2)	138	36	49	46	23	3	30	2	8	3	2	3	10	.252	.295	.358	.654
2006	StL	NL	129	417	90	26	0	6	(2	4)	134	29	49	35	26	2	41	8	8	2	1	2	15	.216	.274	.321	.595
2007	StL	NL	111	353	97	15	0	6	(4	2)	130	30	40	38	34	5	43	3	2	4	1	1	18	.275	.340	.368	.708
2008	StL	NL	124	444	135	18	0	7	(2	5)	174	37	56	57	32	4	29	1	3	5	0	2	21	.304	.349	.392	.740
2009	StL	NL	140	481	141	23	1	6	(5	1)	184	45	54	64	50	2	39	6	6	1	9	3	27	.293	.366	.383	.749
2010	StL	NL	136	465	122	19	0	6	(1	5)	159	34	62	51	42	6	51	7	2	5	8	4	19	.262	.329	.342	.671
2011	StL	NL	139	475	145	32	1	14	(5	9)	221	55	65	65	33	4	44	1	5	4	4	5	21	.305	.349	.465	.814
2012	StL	NL	138	505	159	28	0	22	(9	13)	253	65	76	91	45	4	55	5	3	5	12	3	14	.315	.373	.501	.874
2013	StL	NL	136	505	161	44	0	12	(5	7)	241	68	80	84	30	4	55	3	0	3	3	2	14	.319	.359	.477	.836
2014	StL	NL	110	404	114	21	0	7	(3	4)	156	40	38	47	28	4	55	6	1	6	1	1	14	.282	.333	.386	.719
2015	StL	NL	136	488	132	23	1	4	(3	1)	171	34	61	48	32	3	59	0	1	9	1	1	16	.270	.310	.350	.660
Postseason			86	307	89	17	0	3	(2	1)	115	25	31	32	25	5	36	1	1	1	1	1	11	.290	.344	.375	.719
12 ML YEARS			1464	5057	1429	270	5	100	(46	54)	2009	485	645	644	388	44	521	42	41	48	44	28	189	.283	.336	.397	.733

Johnny Monell

Bats: L **Throws:** R **Pos:** PH-15;C-12 MO-nell **Ht:** 6'0" **Wt:** 210 **Born:** 3/27/1986 **Age:** 30

								BATTING											RUNNING			AVERAGES			
Year	Team	Lg	G	AB	H	2B	3B	HR	(Hm Rd)	TB	R	RBI	RC	TBB	IBB	SO	HBP	SH	SF	SB	CS	GDP	Avg	OBP	Slg	OPS
2011	Rchmd	AA	119	385	96	24	1	10	(- -)	152	46	49	53	48	2	93	3	1	3	0	3	14	.249	.335	.395	.730
2012	Rchmd	AA	108	323	83	27	1	11	(- -)	145	38	50	52	41	1	84	5	0	5	2	2	10	.257	.345	.449	.794
2013	Fresno	AAA	121	415	114	27	2	20	(- -)	205	71	64	77	59	2	105	2	0	5	6	3	11	.275	.364	.494	.858
2014	Norfolk	AAA	30	91	19	4	0	1	(- -)	26	10	7	7	8	1	16	1	0	0	1	0	4	.209	.280	.286	.566
2014	Albq	AAA	38	115	30	8	1	3	(- -)	49	11	17	16	10	0	24	0	0	1	3	0	7	.261	.317	.426	.744
2015	LsVgs	AAA	71	256	83	16	0	7	(- -)	120	34	51	48	27	2	39	2	0	3	6	2	6	.324	.389	.469	.858
2013	SF	NL	8	8	1	0	0	0	(0 0)	1	2	1	0	0	0	3	1	0	0	0	0	0	.125	.222	.125	.347
2015	NYM	NL	27	48	8	2	0	0	(0 0)	10	5	4	0	4	0	13	0	0	0	0	0	5	.167	.231	.208	.439
	2 ML YEARS		35	56	9	2	0	0	(0 0)	11	7	5	0	4	0	16	1	0	0	0	0	5	.161	.230	.196	.426

Frankie Montas

Pitches: R **Bats:** R **Pos:** RP-5; SP-2 MOHN-tahs **Ht:** 6'2" **Wt:** 185 **Born:** 3/21/1993 **Age:** 23

			HOW MUCH HE PITCHED					WHAT HE GAVE UP										THE RESULTS							
Year	Team	Lg	G	GS	CG	GF	IP	BFP	H	R	ER	HR	SH	SF	HB	TBB	IBB	SO	WP	Bk	W	L	Pct	Sh	Sv-Op	Hld	ERC	ERA
2012	2 Tms	Low	13	10	0	0	44.1	182	39	23	18	0	3	0	3	13	0	45	4	0	1	5	.167	0	0- -	-	2.66	3.65
2013	2 Tms	Low	24	23	1	1	111.0	495	114	75	67	11	5	3	5	50	0	127	17	1	5	11	.313	0	0- -	-	4.47	5.43
2014	2 Tms	Low	14	14	1	0	76.0	296	51	19	13	3	1	2	2	21	0	79	3	2	5	0	1.000	0	0- -	-	1.72	1.54
2015	Brham	AA	23	23	1	0	112.0	465	89	49	37	3	4	5	1	48	0	108	4	1	5	5	.500	1	0- -	-	2.64	2.97
2015	CWS	AL	7	2	0	2	15.0	66	14	8	8	1	0	0	0	9	1	20	0	0	0	2	.000	0	0-0	0	4.16	4.80

Jesus Montero

Bats: R **Throws:** R **Pos:** 1B-27;DH-7;PH-6 **Ht:** 6'3" **Wt:** 235 **Born:** 11/28/1989 **Age:** 26

								BATTING											RUNNING			AVERAGES			
Year	Team	Lg	G	AB	H	2B	3B	HR	(Hm Rd)	TB	R	RBI	RC	TBB	IBB	SO	HBP	SH	SF	SB	CS	GDP	Avg	OBP	Slg	OPS
2015	Tacom*	AAA	98	394	140	18	6	18	(- -)	224	70	85	86	29	1	71	2	0	5	3	1	10	.355	.398	.569	.966
2011	NYY	AL	18	61	20	4	0	4	(3 1)	36	9	12	12	7	2	17	1	0	0	0	0	0	.328	.406	.590	.996
2012	Sea	AL	135	515	134	20	0	15	(6 9)	199	46	62	52	29	4	99	2	0	7	0	2	15	.260	.298	.386	.685
2013	Sea	AL	29	101	21	1	1	3	(1 2)	33	6	9	9	8	0	21	0	0	1	0	1	2	.208	.264	.327	.590
2014	Sea	AL	6	17	4	0	0	1	(1 0)	7	1	2	1	0	0	3	0	0	0	0	0	1	.235	.235	.412	.647
2015	Sea	AL	38	112	25	6	0	5	(3 2)	46	11	19	12	4	0	32	0	0	0	0	0	2	.223	.250	.411	.661
	Postseason		1	2	2	0	0	0	(0 0)	2	1	1	2	0	0	0	0	0	0	0	0	0	1.000	1.000	1.000	2.000
	5 ML YEARS		226	806	204	31	1	28	(14 14)	321	73	104	86	48	6	172	3	0	8	0	3	22	.253	.295	.398	.693

Miguel Montero

Bats: L **Throws:** R **Pos:** C-109;PH-18;DH-1 **Ht:** 5'11" **Wt:** 210 **Born:** 7/9/1983 **Age:** 32

								BATTING											RUNNING			AVERAGES			
Year	Team	Lg	G	AB	H	2B	3B	HR	(Hm Rd)	TB	R	RBI	RC	TBB	IBB	SO	HBP	SH	SF	SB	CS	GDP	Avg	OBP	Slg	OPS
2006	Ari	NL	6	16	4	1	0	0	(0 0)	5	0	3	2	1	0	3	0	0	0	0	0	0	.250	.294	.313	.607
2007	Ari	NL	84	214	48	7	0	10	(7 3)	85	30	37	19	20	2	35	3	1	6	0	0	1	.224	.292	.397	.689
2008	Ari	NL	70	184	47	16	1	5	(1 4)	80	24	18	21	19	3	49	2	1	1	0	0	1	.255	.330	.435	.765
2009	Ari	NL	128	425	125	30	0	16	(5 11)	203	61	59	65	38	5	78	3	2	2	1	2	6	.294	.355	.478	.832
2010	Ari	NL	85	297	79	20	2	9	(0 9)	130	36	43	38	29	3	71	2	0	3	0	1	10	.266	.332	.438	.770
2011	Ari	NL	140	493	139	36	1	18	(8 10)	231	65	86	84	47	10	97	8	1	4	1	1	14	.282	.351	.469	.820
2012	Ari	NL	141	486	139	25	2	15	(4 11)	213	65	88	92	73	6	130	12	0	2	0	0	15	.286	.391	.438	.829
2013	Ari	NL	116	413	95	14	0	11	(8 3)	142	44	42	42	51	4	110	5	0	6	0	0	18	.230	.318	.344	.662
2014	Ari	NL	136	489	119	23	0	13	(5 8)	181	40	72	63	56	11	97	9	0	6	0	4	12	.243	.329	.370	.699
2015	ChC	NL	113	347	86	11	0	15	(8 7)	142	36	53	52	49	5	103	4	0	3	1	1	9	.248	.345	.409	.754
	Postseason		9	27	8	2	0	0	(0 0)	10	4	2	3	3	1	6	0	0	0	0	0	0	.296	.367	.370	.737
	10 ML YEARS		1019	3364	881	183	6	112	(46 66)	1412	401	501	478	383	49	773	48	5	33	3	9	92	.262	.343	.420	.762

Rafael Montero

Pitches: R **Bats:** R **Pos:** RP-4; SP-1 **Ht:** 6'0" **Wt:** 185 **Born:** 10/17/1990 **Age:** 25

			HOW MUCH HE PITCHED					WHAT HE GAVE UP										THE RESULTS							
Year	Team	Lg	G	GS	CG	GF	IP	BFP	H	R	ER	HR	SH	SF	HB	TBB	IBB	SO	WP	Bk	W	L	Pct	Sh	Sv-Op	Hld	ERC	ERA
2011	3 Tms	Low	13	8	0	1	53.0	226	48	21	15	3	1	1	5	13	0	46	3	0	4	3	.571	0	1- -	-	2.96	2.55
2012	2 Tms	Low	20	20	1	0	122.0	479	96	37	32	6	0	4	3	19	0	110	2	2	11	5	.688	0	0- -	-	1.88	2.36
2013	Bnghtn	AA	11	11	0	0	66.2	261	51	21	18	2	1	0	0	10	0	72	0	2	7	3	.700	0	0- -	-	1.60	2.43
2013	LsVgs	AAA	16	16	0	0	88.2	363	85	35	30	4	1	2	0	25	0	78	1	1	5	4	.556	0	0- -	-	3.09	3.05
2014	LsVgs	AAA	16	16	0	0	80.0	338	69	43	32	4	1	3	1	34	0	80	2	1	6	4	.600	0	0- -	-	3.12	3.60
2015	2 Tms	Low	5	4	0	0	11.0	43	10	2	2	0	0	0	0	3	0	7	0	0	0	0	-	0	0- -	-	2.62	1.64
2014	NYM	NL	10	8	0	1	44.1	194	44	21	20	8	0	0	0	23	0	42	0	0	1	3	.250	0	0-0	0	5.16	4.06
2015	NYM	NL	5	1	0	1	10.0	46	9	6	5	0	1	0	0	5	3	13	0	0	0	1	.000	0	0-0	1	2.50	4.50
	2 ML YEARS		15	9	0	2	54.1	240	53	27	25	8	1	0	0	28	3	55	0	0	1	4	.200	0	0-0	1	4.62	4.14

Mike Montgomery

Pitches: L **Bats:** L **Pos:** SP-16 **Ht:** 6'4" **Wt:** 200 **Born:** 7/1/1989 **Age:** 26

			HOW MUCH HE PITCHED					WHAT HE GAVE UP										THE RESULTS							
Year	Team	Lg	G	GS	CG	GF	IP	BFP	H	R	ER	HR	SH	SF	HB	TBB	IBB	SO	WP	Bk	W	L	Pct	Sh	Sv-Op	Hld	ERC	ERA
2011	Omha	AAA	28	27	0	0	150.2	664	157	95	89	15	4	4	7	69	0	129	14	1	5	11	.313	0	0- -	-	4.78	5.32
2012	Omha	AAA	17	17	1	0	91.2	428	110	74	58	12	7	6	3	43	0	67	4	1	3	6	.333	0	0- -	-	5.81	5.69
2012	NWArk	AA	10	10	0	0	58.0	259	69	44	43	12	2	2	3	21	0	44	5	0	2	6	.250	0	0- -	-	6.12	6.67

HOW MUCH HE PITCHED						WHAT HE GAVE UP												THE RESULTS							
Year Team	Lg	G GS CG GF	IP	BFP	H	R	ER	HR	SH	SF	HB	TBB	IBB	SO	WP	Bk	W	L	Pct	Sh	Sv-Op	Hld	ERC	ERA
2013 Drham	AAA	20 19 1 0	108.2	474	111	65	57	9	4	2	6	48	0	77	15	0	7	8	.467	0	0- -	-	4.52	4.72
2014 Drham	AAA	25 25 0 0	126.0	539	117	68	60	9	2	6	5	48	0	98	11	1	10	5	.667	0	0- -	-	3.55	4.29
2015 Tacom	AAA	11 11 0 0	65.1	270	59	32	30	3	2	2	3	19	0	58	7	0	4	3	.571	0	0- -	-	2.98	4.13
2015 Sea	AL	16 16 2 0	90.0	395	92	49	46	11	0	0	4	37	1	64	10	0	4	6	.400	2	0-0	0	4.56	4.60

Adam Moore

Bats: R **Throws:** R **Pos:** C-1   **Ht:** 6'3" **Wt:** 220 **Born:** 5/8/1984 **Age:** 32

								BATTING											RUNNING			AVERAGES			
Year Team	Lg	G	AB	H	2B	3B	HR	(Hm | Rd)	TB	R	RBI	RC	TBB	IBB	SO	HBP	SH	SF	SB	CS	GDP	Avg	OBP	Slg	OPS
2015 Clmbs*	AAA	92	330	93	20	0	6	(- | -)	131	30	44	43	23	0	101	0	1	1	0	0	12	.282	.328	.397	.725
2009 Sea	AL	6	23	5	1	0	1	(1 | 0)	9	4	2	2	0	0	7	1	0	0	1	0	1	.217	.250	.391	.641
2010 Sea	AL	60	205	40	6	0	4	(1 | 3)	58	12	15	9	8	1	63	2	1	2	0	1	3	.195	.230	.283	.513
2011 Sea	AL	2	6	1	1	0	0	(0 | 0)	2	0	0	0	0	0	2	0	0	0	0	0	0	.167	.167	.333	.500
2012 KC	AL	4	11	2	1	0	1	(1 | 0)	6	1	2	2	1	0	3	0	0	0	0	0	0	.182	.250	.545	.795
2013 KC	AL	5	10	3	1	0	0	(0 | 0)	4	1	0	1	1	0	2	0	0	0	1	0	0	.300	.364	.400	.764
2014 SD	NL	9	10	2	1	0	0	(0 | 0)	3	1	1	2	2	1	5	0	0	0	0	0	0	.200	.333	.300	.633
2015 Cle	AL	1	4	1	0	0	0	(0 | 0)	1	0	1	0	0	0	2	0	0	0	0	0	0	.250	.250	.250	.500
7 ML YEARS		87	269	54	11	0	6	(3 | 3)	83	19	21	16	12	2	84	3	1	2	2	1	4	.201	.241	.309	.550

Matt Moore

Pitches: L **Bats:** L **Pos:** SP-12   **Ht:** 6'3" **Wt:** 210 **Born:** 6/18/1989 **Age:** 27

HOW MUCH HE PITCHED						WHAT HE GAVE UP												THE RESULTS							
Year Team	Lg	G GS CG GF	IP	BFP	H	R	ER	HR	SH	SF	HB	TBB	IBB	SO	WP	Bk	W	L	Pct	Sh	Sv-Op	Hld	ERC	ERA
2015 Drham*	AAA	7 7 0 0	40.1	166	35	18	16	6	1	0	2	12	0	58	2	0	2	3	.400	0	0- -	-	3.50	3.57
2011 TB	AL	3 1 0 0	9.1	40	9	3	3	1	0	0	0	3	0	15	2	0	1	0	1.000	0	0-0	1	3.54	2.89
2012 TB	AL	31 31 0 0	177.1	759	158	85	75	18	3	4	7	81	5	175	8	1	11	11	.500	0	0-0	0	3.83	3.81
2013 TB	AL	27 27 1 0	150.1	642	119	58	55	14	5	6	4	76	1	143	17	1	17	4	.810	1	0-0	0	3.36	3.29
2014 TB	AL	2 2 0 0	10.0	44	10	3	3	1	0	0	0	5	0	6	0	0	0	2	.000	0	0-0	0	4.48	2.70
2015 TB	AL	12 12 0 0	63.0	278	74	40	38	9	0	3	4	23	1	46	6	0	3	4	.429	0	0-0	0	5.63	5.43
Postseason		4 2 0 0	16.1	69	12	9	8	1	0	0	2	6	1	15	2	0	1	1	.500	0	0-0	0	2.60	4.41
5 ML YEARS		75 73 1 0	410.0	1763	370	189	174	43	8	13	15	188	7	385	33	2	32	21	.604	1	0-0	1	3.92	3.82

Tyler Moore

Bats: R **Throws:** R **Pos:** PH-50;1B-39;LF-20;RF-1;PR-1   **Ht:** 6'2" **Wt:** 220 **Born:** 1/30/1987 **Age:** 29

								BATTING											RUNNING			AVERAGES			
Year Team	Lg	G	AB	H	2B	3B	HR	(Hm	Rd)	TB	R	RBI	RC	TBB	IBB	SO	HBP	SH	SF	SB	CS	GDP	Avg	OBP	Slg	OPS
2012 Was	NL	75	156	41	9	0	10	(3	7)	80	20	29	26	14	0	46	1	0	0	3	0	3	.263	.327	.513	.840
2013 Was	NL	63	167	37	9	0	4	(2	2)	58	16	21	17	8	1	58	1	1	1	0	0	1	.222	.260	.347	.607
2014 Was	NL	42	91	21	2	0	4	(1	3)	35	8	14	10	7	0	29	2	0	0	0	0	2	.231	.300	.385	.685
2015 Was	NL	97	187	38	12	0	6	(3	3)	68	14	27	19	11	2	45	1	0	1	0	0	2	.203	.250	.364	.614
Postseason		1	1	1	0	0	0	(0	0)	1	0	2	1	0	0	0	0	0	0	0	0	0	1.000	1.000	1.000	2.000
4 ML YEARS		277	601	137	32	0	24	(9	15)	241	58	91	72	40	3	178	5	1	2	3	0	8	.228	.281	.401	.682

Franklin Morales

Pitches: L **Bats:** L **Pos:** RP-67   **Ht:** 6'1" **Wt:** 210 **Born:** 1/24/1986 **Age:** 30

HOW MUCH HE PITCHED						WHAT HE GAVE UP												THE RESULTS							
Year Team	Lg	G GS CG GF	IP	BFP	H	R	ER	HR	SH	SF	HB	TBB	IBB	SO	WP	Bk	W	L	Pct	Sh	Sv-Op	Hld	ERC	ERA
2007 Col	NL	8 8 0 0	39.1	163	34	15	15	2	4	2	2	14	1	26	0	0	3	2	.600	0	0-0	0	3.04	3.43
2008 Col	NL	5 5 0 0	25.1	120	28	18	18	2	2	2	1	17	2	9	1	3	1	2	.333	0	0-0	0	5.58	6.39
2009 Col	NL	40 2 0 14	40.0	179	38	22	20	4	3	0	1	23	4	41	2	0	3	2	.600	0	7-8	7	4.38	4.50
2010 Col	NL	35 0 0 15	28.2	140	28	22	20	5	1	2	3	24	2	27	3	2	0	4	.000	0	3-6	10	6.53	6.28
2011 2 Tms		50 0 0 13	46.1	193	40	21	19	6	2	1	2	19	1	42	2	1	1	2	.333	0	0-0	10	3.77	3.69
2012 Bos	AL	37 9 0 5	76.1	325	64	38	32	11	0	3	6	30	3	76	3	5	3	4	.429	0	1-1	8	3.68	3.77
2013 Bos	AL	20 1 0 3	25.1	112	24	13	13	2	0	0	3	15	2	21	3	0	2	2	.500	0	0-1	4	4.86	4.62
2014 Col	NL	38 22 0 0	142.1	646	166	90	85	24	7	7	6	65	4	100	5	4	6	9	.400	0	0-0	0	5.97	5.37
2015 KC	AL	67 0 0 12	62.1	258	58	24	22	4	2	2	4	14	0	41	6	2	4	2	.667	0	0-1	8	3.04	3.18
11 Col	NL	14 0 0 4	14.0	59	10	6	6	2	1	1	0	8	1	11	1	0	0	1	.000	0	0-0	2	3.36	3.86
11 Bos	AL	36 0 0 9	32.1	134	30	15	13	4	1	0	2	11	0	31	1	1	1	1	.500	0	0-0	8	3.96	3.62
Postseason		11 2 0 0	14.0	68	18	12	12	1	0	0	2	9	1	7	0	1	0	0	-	0	0-1	1	7.16	7.71
9 ML YEARS		300 47 0 66	486.0	2136	480	263	244	60	21	19	28	221	19	383	25	17	23	29	.442	0	11-17	38	4.57	4.52

Kendrys Morales

Bats: B **Throws:** R **Pos:** DH-141;1B-9;PH-8   KEN-dreez   **Ht:** 6'1" **Wt:** 225 **Born:** 6/20/1983 **Age:** 33

								BATTING											RUNNING			AVERAGES			
Year Team	Lg	G	AB	H	2B	3B	HR	(Hm	Rd)	TB	R	RBI	RC	TBB	IBB	SO	HBP	SH	SF	SB	CS	GDP	Avg	OBP	Slg	OPS
2006 LAA	AL	57	197	46	10	1	5	(1	4)	73	21	22	19	17	1	28	0	0	1	1	1	11	.234	.293	.371	.664
2007 LAA	AL	43	119	35	10	0	4	(2	2)	57	12	15	15	6	2	21	1	0	1	0	1	5	.294	.333	.479	.812
2008 LAA	AL	27	61	13	2	0	3	(0	3)	24	7	8	3	4	0	7	1	0	0	0	1	3	.213	.273	.393	.666
2009 LAA	AL	152	566	173	43	2	34	(21	13)	322	86	108	105	46	10	117	2	0	8	3	7	15	.306	.355	.569	.924
2010 LAA	AL	51	193	56	5	0	11	(7	4)	94	29	39	34	12	3	31	5	0	1	0	0	5	.290	.346	.487	.833
2012 LAA	AL	134	484	132	26	1	22	(10	12)	226	61	73	68	31	1	116	4	0	3	0	1	11	.273	.320	.467	.787
2013 LAA	AL	156	602	167	34	0	23	(10	13)	270	64	80	85	49	6	114	5	0	1	0	0	21	.277	.336	.449	.785
2014 2 Tms	AL	98	367	80	20	0	8	(4	4)	124	28	42	29	27	3	68	3	0	4	0	0	12	.218	.274	.338	.612
2015 KC	AL	158	569	165	41	2	22	(10	12)	276	81	106	98	58	4	103	8	0	4	0	0	24	.290	.362	.485	.847

BATTING																			RUNNING			AVERAGES			
Year Team	Lg	G	AB	H	2B	3B	HR	(Hm Rd)	TB	R	RBI	RC	TBB	IBB	SO	HBP	SH	SF	SB	CS	GDP	Avg	OBP	Slg	OPS
14 Min	AL	39	154	36	11	0	1	(0 1)	50	12	18	11	6	1	27	0	0	2	0	0	4	.234	.259	.325	.584
14 Sea	AL	59	213	44	9	0	7	(4 3)	74	16	24	18	21	2	41	3	0	2	0	0	8	.207	.285	.347	.632
Postseason		16	47	9	1	0	2	(1 1)	16	3	7	3	2	0	8	1	0	1	0	0	1	.191	.235	.340	.576
9 ML YEARS		876	3158	867	191	6	132	(67 65)	1466	389	493	456	250	30	605	29	0	22	4	12	107	.275	.331	.464	.796

Brent Morel

Bats: R Throws: R Pos: 3B-2;PH-1 more-ELL **Ht: 6'2" Wt: 230 Born: 4/21/1987 Age: 29**

BATTING																			RUNNING			AVERAGES			
Year Team	Lg	G	AB	H	2B	3B	HR	(Hm Rd)	TB	R	RBI	RC	TBB	IBB	SO	HBP	SH	SF	SB	CS	GDP	Avg	OBP	Slg	OPS
2015 Indy*	AAA	81	297	79	21	2	9	(- -)	131	36	47	44	23	1	67	3	0	3	8	2	9	.266	.322	.441	.763
2015 Nashv*	AAA	34	136	45	12	0	2	(- -)	63	19	24	23	7	0	30	2	0	1	2	1	5	.331	.370	.463	.833
2010 CWS	AL	21	65	15	3	0	3	(3 0)	27	9	7	4	4	0	17	0	0	1	2	0	2	.231	.271	.415	.687
2011 CWS	AL	126	413	101	18	1	10	(6 4)	151	44	41	36	22	0	57	3	5	1	5	4	8	.245	.287	.366	.653
2012 CWS	AL	35	113	20	2	0	0	(0 0)	22	14	5	4	7	0	39	0	5	0	4	1	3	.177	.245	.195	.420
2013 CWS	AL	12	25	5	0	0	0	(0 0)	5	3	1	3	5	0	7	0	0	0	1	1	1	.200	.333	.200	.533
2014 Pit	NL	23	39	7	2	0	0	(0 0)	9	1	4	1	2	1	9	0	0	0	0	0	1	.179	.220	.231	.450
2015 Pit	NL	3	7	2	1	0	0	(0 0)	3	1	1	0	0	0	3	0	0	0	0	0	0	.286	.286	.429	.714
Postseason		1	1	0	0	0	0	(0 0)	0	0	0	0	0	0	0	0	0	0	0	0	0	.000	.000	.000	.000
6 ML YEARS		220	662	150	26	1	13	(9 4)	217	72	59	48	40	1	132	3	10	2	12	6	15	.227	.273	.328	.601

Mitch Moreland

Bats: L Throws: L Pos: 1B-120;PH-14;DH-7 **Ht: 6'2" Wt: 230 Born: 9/6/1985 Age: 30**

BATTING																			RUNNING			AVERAGES			
Year Team	Lg	G	AB	H	2B	3B	HR	(Hm Rd)	TB	R	RBI	RC	TBB	IBB	SO	HBP	SH	SF	SB	CS	GDP	Avg	OBP	Slg	OPS
2010 Tex	AL	47	145	37	4	0	9	(3 6)	68	20	25	27	25	5	36	1	0	2	3	1	3	.255	.364	.469	.833
2011 Tex	AL	134	464	120	22	1	16	(7 9)	192	60	51	56	39	6	92	4	2	3	2	2	9	.259	.320	.414	.733
2012 Tex	AL	114	327	90	18	0	15	(10 5)	153	41	50	46	23	5	71	1	2	4	1	1	8	.275	.321	.468	.789
2013 Tex	AL	147	462	107	24	1	23	(10 13)	202	60	60	55	45	1	117	3	0	8	0	0	11	.232	.299	.437	.736
2014 Tex	AL	52	167	41	9	1	2	(1 1)	58	18	23	20	12	0	43	1	2	2	0	0	7	.246	.297	.347	.644
2015 Tex	AL	132	471	131	27	0	23	(9 14)	227	51	85	74	32	2	112	7	0	5	1	0	9	.278	.330	.482	.812
Postseason		25	76	19	4	0	3	(3 0)	32	7	10	12	6	1	18	1	1	0	0	0	3	.250	.313	.421	.734
6 ML YEARS		626	2036	526	104	3	88	(40 48)	900	250	294	278	176	19	471	17	6	24	7	4	47	.258	.319	.442	.761

Diego Moreno

Pitches: R Bats: R Pos: RP-4 **Ht: 6'1" Wt: 180 Born: 7/21/1987 Age: 28**

HOW MUCH HE PITCHED							WHAT HE GAVE UP											THE RESULTS							
Year Team	Lg	G	GS	CG	GF	IP	BFP	H	R	ER	HR	SH	SF	HB	TBB	IBB	SO	WP	Bk	W	L	Pct	Sh	Sv-Op	Hld	ERC	ERA
2011 Bradtn	A+	34	0	0	21	33.2	144	26	14	12	2	1	2	3	15	0	31	4	1	2	4	.333	0	5- -	-	3.03	3.21
2011 Altna	AA	7	0	0	4	11.0	48	10	6	6	1	0	1	2	3	0	14	1	0	0	0	-	0	0- -	-	3.64	4.91
2013 Tampa	A+	18	0	0	2	27.2	122	26	16	15	2	0	1	3	10	0	25	5	0	2	4	.333	0	0- -	-	3.73	4.88
2013 Trntn	AA	6	0	0	0	9.1	36	4	1	1	0	0	1	2	2	0	12	3	0	1	0	1.000	0	0- -	-	1.08	0.96
2014 Trntn	AA	8	0	0	8	11.1	41	5	1	1	0	0	1	0	2	0	13	0	0	1	0	1.000	0	6- -	-	0.68	0.79
2014 S-WB	AAA	30	1	0	9	46.1	214	62	25	25	2	3	2	0	15	1	42	1	0	2	3	.400	0	2- -	-	5.17	4.86
2015 S-WB	AAA	26	4	0	8	53.2	207	39	14	13	1	1	4	0	16	0	42	0	0	3	0	1.000	0	1- -	-	1.89	2.18
2015 NYY	AL	4	0	0	1	10.1	45	9	6	6	1	0	0	2	3	0	8	1	0	1	0	1.000	0	0-0	-	3.58	5.23

Adam Morgan

Pitches: L Bats: L Pos: SP-15 **Ht: 6'1" Wt: 195 Born: 2/27/1990 Age: 26**

HOW MUCH HE PITCHED							WHAT HE GAVE UP											THE RESULTS							
Year Team	Lg	G	GS	CG	GF	IP	BFP	H	R	ER	HR	SH	SF	HB	TBB	IBB	SO	WP	Bk	W	L	Pct	Sh	Sv-Op	Hld	ERC	ERA
2011 Wmspt	A-	11	11	0	0	53.2	221	42	18	12	2	1	4	2	14	0	43	3	0	3	3	.500	0	0- -	-	2.11	2.01
2012 Clrwtr	A+	21	20	1	0	123.0	490	103	46	45	7	3	4	2	28	1	140	3	1	4	10	.286	0	0- -	-	2.39	3.29
2012 Rdng	AA	6	6	0	0	35.2	143	34	14	14	2	1	0	0	11	0	29	3	0	4	1	.800	0	0- -	-	3.33	3.53
2013 LV	AAA	16	16	0	0	71.1	321	84	41	32	10	4	2	5	26	1	49	3	2	2	7	.222	0	0- -	-	5.54	4.04
2015 LV	AAA	13	13	0	0	68.1	309	81	45	36	7	4	5	1	27	0	33	1	0	0	6	.000	0	0- -	-	5.17	4.74
2015 Phi	NL	15	15	0	0	84.1	352	88	45	42	14	1	3	4	17	0	49	2	1	5	7	.417	0	0-0	0	4.21	4.48

Mike Morin

Pitches: R Bats: R Pos: RP-47 MORE-in **Ht: 6'4" Wt: 220 Born: 5/3/1991 Age: 25**

HOW MUCH HE PITCHED							WHAT HE GAVE UP											THE RESULTS							
Year Team	Lg	G	GS	CG	GF	IP	BFP	H	R	ER	HR	SH	SF	HB	TBB	IBB	SO	WP	Bk	W	L	Pct	Sh	Sv-Op	Hld	ERC	ERA
2012 Orem	R+	24	0	0	9	34.2	150	34	23	19	2	2	3	1	14	4	29	6	0	2	2	.500	0	4- -	-	3.60	4.93
2013 InldEm	A+	30	0	0	24	39.0	145	30	9	8	2	1	2	1	5	0	43	0	0	3	1	.750	0	13- -	-	1.83	1.85
2013 Ark	AA	26	0	0	15	31.0	123	26	7	7	2	2	1	2	5	0	33	3	0	0	2	.000	0	10- -	-	2.39	2.03
2014 Ark	AA	5	0	0	5	5.0	17	3	0	0	0	0	0	0	0	0	6	0	0	1	0	1.000	0	3- -	-	0.80	0.00
2015 Salt Lk	AAA	14	0	0	4	17.1	83	25	14	12	3	1	1	2	6	0	19	1	0	4	2	.667	0	1- -	-	7.64	6.23
2014 LAA	AL	60	0	0	10	59.0	246	51	22	19	3	2	4	3	19	6	54	3	0	4	4	.500	0	0-2	9	2.76	2.90
2015 LAA	AL	47	0	0	10	35.1	151	36	28	25	3	2	2	2	9	2	41	0	0	4	2	.667	0	1-1	5	3.61	6.37
Postseason		1	0	0	1	1.0	6	3	2	2	1	0	1	0	0	0	1	1	0	0	0	-	0	0-0	0	25.51	18.00
2 ML YEARS		107	0	0	20	94.1	397	87	50	44	6	4	6	5	28	8	95	3	0	8	6	.571	0	1-3	14	3.07	4.20

Justin Morneau

Bats: L Throws: R Pos: 1B-44;PH-4;DH-1 | MORE-no | Ht: 6'4" Wt: 220 Born: 5/15/1981 Age: 35

Year	Team	Lg	G	AB	H	2B	3B	HR	(Hm	Rd)	TB	R	RBI	RC	TBB	IBB	SO	HBP	SH	SF	SB	CS	GDP	Avg	OBP	Slg	OPS
2003	Min	AL	40	106	24	4	0	4	(1	3)	40	14	16	11	9	1	30	0	0	0	0	0	4	.226	.287	.377	.664
2004	Min	AL	74	280	76	17	0	19	(9	10)	150	39	58	48	28	8	54	2	0	2	0	0	4	.271	.340	.536	.875
2005	Min	AL	141	490	117	23	4	22	(9	13)	214	62	79	58	44	8	94	4	0	5	0	2	12	.239	.304	.437	.741
2006	Min	AL	157	592	190	37	1	34	(17	17)	331	97	130	118	53	9	93	5	0	11	3	3	10	.321	.375	.559	.934
2007	Min	AL	157	590	160	31	3	31	(15	16)	290	84	111	95	64	11	91	5	0	9	1	1	17	.271	.343	.492	.834
2008	Min	AL	**163**	623	187	47	4	23	(12	11)	311	97	129	**122**	76	**16**	85	3	0	10	0	1	20	.300	.374	.499	.873
2009	Min	AL	135	508	139	31	1	30	(14	16)	262	85	100	91	72	12	86	3	0	7	0	0	12	.274	.363	.516	.878
2010	Min	AL	81	296	102	25	1	18	(4	14)	183	53	56	65	50	7	62	0	0	2	0	0	6	.345	.437	.618	1.055
2011	Min	AL	69	264	60	16	0	4	(0	4)	88	19	30	28	19	1	44	3	0	2	0	0	8	.227	.285	.333	.618
2012	Min	AL	134	505	135	26	2	19	(7	12)	222	63	77	63	49	8	102	6	0	10	1	0	19	.267	.333	.440	.773
2013	2 Tms		152	572	148	36	0	17	(9	8)	235	62	77	71	50	4	110	2	0	6	0	0	13	.259	.323	.411	.734
2014	Col	NL	135	502	160	32	3	17	(11	6)	249	62	82	88	34	4	60	6	0	8	0	3	7	**.319**	.364	.496	.860
2015	Col	NL	49	168	52	10	3	3	(2	1)	77	19	15	26	13	2	25	1	0	0	0	0	2	.310	.363	.458	.821
13	Min	AL	127	495	128	32	0	17	(9	8)	211	56	74	64	37	3	98	6	0	5	0	0	10	.259	.315	.426	.741
13	Pit	NL	25	77	20	4	0	0	(0	0)	24	6	3	7	13	1	12	1	0	1	0	0	3	.260	.370	.312	.681
	Postseason		13	53	16	4	0	2	(1	1)	26	8	4	4	1	0	5	0	0	0	0	0	2	.302	.315	.491	.805
	13 ML YEARS		1487	5496	1550	335	22	241	(110	131)	2652	756	960	884	561	91	936	45	0	72	5	10	134	.282	.349	.483	.832

Akeel Morris

Pitches: R Bats: R Pos: RP-1 | ah-KEEL | Ht: 6'1" Wt: 195 Born: 11/14/1992 Age: 23

	HOW MUCH HE PITCHED							WHAT HE GAVE UP										THE RESULTS						
Year	Team	Lg	G	GS	CG	GF	IP	BFP	H	R	ER	HR	SH	SF	HB	TBB	IBB	SO	WP	Bk	W	L	Pct	Sh	Sv-Op	Hld	ERC	ERA
2011	Kngspt	R+	11	11	1	0	51.1	226	30	28	22	5	2	1	3	38	0	61	8	0	3	2	.600	0	0- -	-	3.22	3.86
2012	Kngspt	R+	11	6	0	3	38.1	179	38	37	34	7	2	1	4	22	1	50	3	0	0	6	.000	0	2- -	-	5.61	7.98
2013	Bklyn	A-	14	3	0	7	45.0	183	29	7	5	1	1	0	1	23	0	60	1	0	4	1	.800	0	1- -	-	2.24	1.00
2014	Savann	A	41	0	0	28	57.0	211	19	5	4	1	4	0	1	22	0	89	5	1	4	1	.800	0	16- -	-	0.86	0.63
2015	Stluci	A+	24	0	0	20	32.0	120	11	6	6	1	1	2	0	14	0	46	2	1	0	1	.000	0	13- -	-	0.99	1.69
2015	Bnghtn	AA	23	0	0	9	29.1	117	17	8	8	1	0	1	0	15	1	35	2	3	0	1	.000	0	0- -	-	1.90	2.45
2015	NYM	NL	1	0	0	0	0.2	8	3	5	5	1	0	0	0	3	0	0	0	0	0	0	-	0	0-0	0	75.11	67.50

Bryan Morris

Pitches: R Bats: L Pos: RP-67 | | Ht: 6'3" Wt: 225 Born: 3/28/1987 Age: 29

	HOW MUCH HE PITCHED							WHAT HE GAVE UP										THE RESULTS						
Year	Team	Lg	G	GS	CG	GF	IP	BFP	H	R	ER	HR	SH	SF	HB	TBB	IBB	SO	WP	Bk	W	L	Pct	Sh	Sv-Op	Hld	ERC	ERA
2012	Pit	NL	5	0	0	2	5.0	20	2	2	1	0	0	1	1	2	0	6	1	0	0	0	-	0	0-0	0	1.32	1.80
2013	Pit	NL	55	0	0	21	65.0	270	57	25	25	8	0	5	2	28	5	37	6	0	5	7	.417	0	0-0	7	3.78	3.46
2014	2 Tms		60	0	0	10	64.1	272	58	17	13	6	7	3	4	24	6	50	8	1	8	1	.889	0	0-7	17	3.50	1.82
2015	Mia	NL	67	0	0	18	63.0	277	67	26	22	3	4	0	3	26	0	47	2	0	5	4	.556	0	0-2	18	4.31	3.14
14	Pit	NL	21	0	0	7	23.2	103	25	11	10	4	2	2	2	12	3	14	3	1	4	0	1.000	0	0-3	4	5.75	3.80
14	Mia	NL	39	0	0	3	40.2	169	33	6	3	2	5	1	2	12	3	36	5	0	4	1	.800	0	0-4	13	2.39	0.66
	Postseason		1	0	0	1	1.0	4	1	0	0	0	0	0	0	0	0	1	0	0	0	0	-	0	0-0	1	1.95	0.00
	4 ML YEARS		187	0	0	51	197.1	839	184	70	61	17	11	9	10	80	11	140	17	1	18	12	.600	0	0-9	42	3.78	2.78

Logan Morrison

Bats: L Throws: L Pos: 1B-140;PH-11;PR-6;RF-3;LF-1 | | Ht: 6'2" Wt: 240 Born: 8/25/1987 Age: 28

Year	Team	Lg	G	AB	H	2B	3B	HR	(Hm	Rd)	TB	R	RBI	RC	TBB	IBB	SO	HBP	SH	SF	SB	CS	GDP	Avg	OBP	Slg	OPS
2010	Fla	NL	62	244	69	20	7	2	(1	1)	109	43	18	41	41	0	51	2	0	0	0	1	4	.283	.390	.447	.837
2011	Fla	NL	123	462	114	25	4	23	(12	11)	216	54	72	55	54	3	99	5	0	4	2	1	9	.247	.330	.468	.797
2012	Mia	NL	93	296	68	15	1	11	(4	7)	118	30	36	27	31	2	58	4	0	3	1	0	9	.230	.308	.399	.707
2013	Mia	NL	85	293	71	13	4	6	(1	5)	110	32	36	37	38	5	56	2	0	0	0	0	10	.242	.333	.375	.709
2014	Sea	AL	99	336	88	20	0	11	(7	4)	141	41	38	46	24	1	59	3	0	2	5	2	9	.262	.315	.420	.735
2015	Sea	AL	146	457	103	15	3	17	(7	10)	175	47	54	53	47	5	81	4	1	2	8	4	7	.225	.302	.383	.685
	6 ML YEARS		608	2088	513	108	19	70	(32	38)	869	247	254	259	235	16	404	20	1	11	16	8	48	.246	.326	.416	.742

Brandon Morrow

Pitches: R Bats: R Pos: SP-5 | | Ht: 6'3" Wt: 210 Born: 7/26/1984 Age: 31

	HOW MUCH HE PITCHED							WHAT HE GAVE UP										THE RESULTS						
Year	Team	Lg	G	GS	CG	GF	IP	BFP	H	R	ER	HR	SH	SF	HB	TBB	IBB	SO	WP	Bk	W	L	Pct	Sh	Sv-Op	Hld	ERC	ERA
2007	Sea	AL	60	0	0	18	63.1	289	56	29	29	3	4	4	1	50	5	66	4	0	3	4	.429	0	0-2	18	4.47	4.12
2008	Sea	AL	45	5	0	24	64.2	265	40	26	24	10	1	0	0	34	1	75	5	0	3	4	.429	0	10-12	3	2.84	3.34
2009	Sea	AL	26	10	0	9	69.2	313	66	38	34	10	1	2	0	44	1	63	3	0	2	4	.333	0	6-8	1	4.99	4.39
2010	Tor	AL	26	26	1	0	146.1	629	136	76	73	11	2	4	9	66	0	178	8	0	10	7	.588	1	0-0	0	3.99	4.49
2011	Tor	AL	30	30	0	0	179.1	777	162	103	94	21	4	9	12	69	1	203	12	1	11	11	.500	0	0-0	0	3.79	4.72
2012	Tor	AL	21	21	3	0	124.2	504	99	45	41	12	1	3	2	41	0	108	3	0	10	7	.588	3	0-0	0	2.73	2.96
2013	Tor	AL	10	10	0	0	54.1	242	63	39	34	12	0	0	2	18	0	42	1	0	2	3	.400	0	0-0	0	5.60	5.63
2014	Tor	AL	13	6	0	2	33.1	148	37	21	21	2	1	0	0	18	0	30	1	1	1	3	.250	0	0-0	1	5.09	5.67
2015	SD	NL	5	5	0	0	33.0	126	29	10	10	3	1	1	0	7	0	23	0	0	2	0	1.000	0	0-0	0	2.84	2.73
	9 ML YEARS		236	113	4	53	768.2	3293	687	387	360	84	15	26	25	347	9	788	37	2	44	43	.506	4	16-22	23	3.87	4.22

Michael Morse

Bats: R **Throws:** R **Pos:** 1B-58;PH-39;LF-6;DH-1   **Ht:** 6'5" **Wt:** 245 **Born:** 3/22/1982 **Age:** 34

Year	Team	Lg	G	AB	H	2B	3B	HR	(Hm	Rd)	TB	R	RBI	RC	TBB	IBB	SO	HBP	SH	SF	SB	CS	GDP	Avg	OBP	Slg	OPS
2005	Sea	AL	72	230	64	10	1	3	(3	0)	85	27	23	28	18	0	50	8	0	2	3	1	9	.278	.349	.370	.718
2006	Sea	AL	21	43	16	5	0	0	(0	0)	21	5	11	9	3	0	7	0	0	2	1	0	2	.372	.396	.488	.884
2007	Sea	AL	9	18	8	2	0	0	(0	0)	10	1	3	6	1	0	4	1	0	0	0	0	0	.444	.500	.556	1.056
2008	Sea	AL	5	9	2	1	0	0	(0	0)	3	0	0	1	1	0	4	1	0	0	0	0	0	.222	.364	.333	.697
2009	Was	NL	32	52	13	3	0	3	(3	0)	25	4	10	8	3	0	16	0	0	0	0	0	1	.250	.291	.481	.772
2010	Was	NL	98	266	77	12	2	15	(6	9)	138	36	41	42	22	1	64	4	0	1	0	1	6	.289	.352	.519	.870
2011	Was	NL	146	522	158	36	0	31	(11	20)	287	73	95	96	36	5	126	13	0	4	2	3	9	.303	.360	.550	.910
2012	Was	NL	102	406	118	17	1	18	(7	11)	191	53	62	57	16	0	97	4	0	4	0	1	14	.291	.321	.470	.791
2013	2 Tms	NL	88	312	67	13	0	13	(5	8)	119	34	27	24	21	1	87	3	0	1	0	0	12	.215	.270	.381	.651
2014	SF	NL	131	438	122	32	3	16	(6	10)	208	48	61	55	31	0	121	9	0	4	0	0	19	.279	.336	.475	.811
2015	2 Tms	NL	98	229	53	7	1	5	(1	4)	77	14	19	20	23	0	76	4	0	0	0	0	10	.231	.313	.336	.649
13	Sea	AL	76	283	64	13	0	13	(5	8)	116	31	27	24	20	1	80	3	0	1	0	0	10	.226	.283	.410	.693
13	Bal	AL	12	29	3	0	0	0	(0	0)	3	3	0	0	1	0	7	0	0	0	0	0	2	.103	.133	.103	.237
15	Mia	NL	53	160	34	4	0	4	(0	4)	50	8	12	9	12	0	55	2	0	0	0	0	6	.213	.276	.313	.588
15	Pit	NL	45	69	19	3	1	1	(1	0)	27	6	7	11	11	0	21	2	0	0	0	0	4	.275	.390	.391	.782
	Postseason		15	39	11	1	0	2	(2	0)	18	5	7	5	1	0	9	0	0	1	0	0	1	.282	.293	.462	.754
	11 ML YEARS		802	2525	698	138	8	104	(42	62)	1164	295	352	346	175	7	652	47	0	18	6	6	82	.276	.333	.461	.794

Charlie Morton

Pitches: R **Bats:** R **Pos:** SP-23   **Ht:** 6'5" **Wt:** 225 **Born:** 11/12/1983 **Age:** 32

Year	Team	Lg	G	GS	CG	GF	IP	BFP	H	R	ER	HR	SH	SF	HB	TBB	IBB	SO	WP	Bk	W	L	Pct	Sh	Sv-Op	Hld	ERC	ERA
2008	Atl	NL	16	15	0	0	74.2	345	80	56	51	9	5	4	2	41	2	48	2	0	4	8	.333	0	0-0		5.21	6.15
2009	Pit	NL	18	18	1	0	97.0	416	102	49	49	7	1	1	5	40	0	62	4	0	5	9	.357	1	0-0		4.56	4.55
2010	Pit	NL	17	17	0	0	79.2	382	112	79	67	15	6	6	7	26	3	59	5	1	2	12	.143	0	0-0		7.10	7.57
2011	Pit	NL	29	29	2	0	171.2	769	186	82	73	6	12	6	13	77	5	110	9	1	10	10	.500	1	0-0		4.52	3.83
2012	Pit	NL	9	9	0	0	50.1	223	62	30	26	5	5	2	2	11	1	25	4	0	2	6	.250	0	0-0		4.74	4.65
2013	Pit	NL	20	20	0	0	116.0	493	113	51	42	6	2		**16**	36	1	85	5	0	7	4	.636	0	0-0		3.84	3.26
2014	Pit	NL	26	26	0	0	157.1	666	143	76	65	9	7	5	**19**	57	2	126	8	0	6	12	.333	0	0-0		3.64	3.72
2015	Pit	NL	23	23	0	0	129.0	563	137	77	69	13	4	0	12	41	6	96	2	1	9	9	.500	0	0-0		4.41	4.81
	Postseason		1	1	0	0	5.2	24	3	2	2	1	1	0	0	4	0	4	0	0	0	1	.000	0	0-0		3.16	3.18
	8 ML YEARS		158	157	3	0	875.2	3857	935	500	442	70	46	26	76	329	20	611	39	3	45	70	.391	2	0-0		4.55	4.54

Jon Moscot

Pitches: R **Bats:** R **Pos:** SP-3   **Ht:** 6'4" **Wt:** 210 **Born:** 8/15/1991 **Age:** 24

Year	Team	Lg	G	GS	CG	GF	IP	BFP	H	R	ER	HR	SH	SF	HB	TBB	IBB	SO	WP	Bk	W	L	Pct	Sh	Sv-Op	Hld	ERC	ERA
2012	2 Tms	Low	12	11	0	0	27.1	115	22	12	8	2	1	1	2	11	0	27	4	0	0	2	.000	0	0--	-	3.12	2.63
2013	Bkrsfld	A+	22	22	0	0	115.2	491	109	66	59	17	5	3	6	36	2	112	8	1	2	14	.125	0	0--	-	3.88	4.59
2013	Pnscla	AA	6	6	0	0	31.0	138	34	12	11	3	2	0	3	12	1	28	3	0	2	1	.667	0	0--	-	4.92	3.19
2014	Pnscla	AA	25	25	2	0	149.1	634	145	60	52	11	8	7	8	43	2	111	5	0	7	10	.412	0	0--	-	3.47	3.13
2015	Lsvlle	AAA	9	9	0	0	54.1	225	50	20	19	5	3	3	0	19	0	34	7	0	7	1	.875	0	0--	-	3.44	3.15
2015	Cin	NL	3	3	0	0	11.2	50	11	6	6	2	0	1	0	5	0	6	1	0	1	1	.500	0	0-0		4.37	4.63

Brandon Moss

Bats: L **Throws:** R **Pos:** RF-82;1B-42;PH-19;LF-10;DH-5   **Ht:** 6'0" **Wt:** 210 **Born:** 9/16/1983 **Age:** 32

Year	Team	Lg	G	AB	H	2B	3B	HR	(Hm	Rd)	TB	R	RBI	RC	TBB	IBB	SO	HBP	SH	SF	SB	CS	GDP	Avg	OBP	Slg	OPS
2007	Bos	AL	15	25	7	2	1	0	(0	0)	11	6	1	3	4	0	6	0	0	0	0	0	0	.280	.379	.440	.819
2008	2 Tms		79	236	58	15	3	8	(4	4)	103	19	34	30	21	1	70	1	0	5	1	2	2	.246	.304	.436	.741
2009	Pit	NL	133	385	91	20	4	7	(4	3)	140	47	41	37	34	3	84	4	0	1	1	5	7	.236	.304	.364	.668
2010	Pit	NL	17	26	4	1	0	0	(0	0)	5	2	2	2	1	0	6	0	0	0	0	0	1	.154	.185	.192	.377
2011	Phi	NL	5	6	0	0	0	0	(0	0)	0	0	0	0	0	0	2	0	0	0	0	0	0	.000	.000	.000	.000
2012	Oak	AL	84	265	77	18	0	21	(9	12)	158	48	52	50	26	2	90	3	0	2	1	1	5	.291	.358	.596	.954
2013	Oak	AL	145	446	114	23	3	30	(10	20)	213	73	87	79	50	3	140	6	0	3	4	2	4	.256	.337	.522	.859
2014	Oak	AL	147	500	117	23	2	25	(12	13)	219	70	81	78	67	7	153	10	0	3	0	1	6	.234	.334	.438	.772
2015	2 Tms	NL	145	469	106	24	2	19	(4	15)	191	47	58	43	49	4	148	5	0	3	0	1	12	.226	.304	.407	.711
08	Bos	AL	34	78	23	5	1	2	(1	1)	36	7	11	11	6	0	25	0	0	2	1	1	1	.295	.337	.462	.799
08	Pit	NL	45	158	35	10	2	6	(3	3)	67	12	23	19	15	1	45	1	0	3	0	1	1	.222	.288	.424	.712
15	Cle	AL	94	337	73	17	1	15	(2	13)	137	36	50	32	32	2	106	3	0	3	0	0	9	.217	.288	.407	.695
15	StL	NL	51	132	33	7	1	4	(2	2)	54	11	8	11	17	2	42	2	0	0	0	1	3	.250	.344	.409	.753
	Postseason		11	38	6	0	0	3	(0	3)	15	4	6	4	6	1	22	1	0	0	0	0	0	.158	.289	.395	.684
	9 ML YEARS		770	2358	574	126	15	110	(43	67)	1060	312	356	322	252	20	699	29	0	17	8	11	39	.243	.322	.450	.771

Jason Motte

Pitches: R **Bats:** R **Pos:** RP-57   **Ht:** 6'0" **Wt:** 205 **Born:** 6/22/1982 **Age:** 34

Year	Team	Lg	G	GS	CG	GF	IP	BFP	H	R	ER	HR	SH	SF	HB	TBB	IBB	SO	WP	Bk	W	L	Pct	Sh	Sv-Op	Hld	ERC	ERA
2008	StL	NL	12	0	0	4	11.0	40	5	2	1	0	1	0	0	3	0	16	0	0	0	0	-	0	1-1	4	0.89	0.82
2009	StL	NL	69	0	0	14	56.2	244	57	32	30	10	0	3	2	23	1	54	2	1	4	4	.500	0	0-3	15	4.86	4.76
2010	StL	NL	56	0	0	13	52.1	208	41	13	13	5	1	3	0	18	3	54	1	0	2	3	.667	0	2-3	12	2.24	2.24
2011	StL	NL	78	0	0	27	68.0	268	49	22	17	2	1	3	5	16	2	63	1	0	5	2	.714	0	9-13	18	1.87	2.25
2012	StL	NL	67	0	0	58	72.0	279	49	23	22	9	2	1	2	17	1	86	0	0	4	5	.444	0	**42-49**	0	2.08	2.75

			HOW MUCH HE PITCHED						WHAT HE GAVE UP									THE RESULTS						
Year	Team	Lg	G	GS	CG	GF	IP	BFP	H	R	ER	HR	SH	SF	HB	TBB	IBB	SO	WP	Bk	W	L	Pct	Sh	Sv-Op	Hld	ERC	ERA
2014	StL	NL	29	0	0	10	25.0	110	29	14	13	7	0	2	0	9	0	17	1	0	1	0	1.000	0	0-0	1	6.22	4.68
2015	ChC	NL	57	0	0	18	48.1	206	48	21	21	4	3	2	2	11	5	34	2	0	8	1	.889	0	6-7	9	3.18	3.91
	Postseason		19	0	0	16	21.2	79	12	6	5	2	0	0	0	2	0	10	0	0	1	1	.500	0	8-8	0	1.07	2.08
	7 ML YEARS		368	0	0	144	333.1	1355	278	127	117	37	8	14	11	97	12	324	7	1	26	14	.650	0	60-76	59	2.94	3.16

Mike Moustakas

Bats: L **Throws:** R **Pos:** 3B-146;PH-4   moo-STOCK-us   **Ht:** 6'0" **Wt:** 215 **Born:** 9/11/1988 **Age:** 27

			BATTING																	RUNNING			AVERAGES			
Year	Team	Lg	G	AB	H	2B	3B	HR	(Hm | Rd)	TB	R	RBI	RC	TBB	IBB	SO	HBP	SH	SF	SB	CS	GDP	Avg	OBP	Slg	OPS
2011	KC	AL	89	338	89	18	1	5	(3 | 2)	124	26	30	31	22	0	51	1	2	2	2	0	5	.263	.309	.367	.675
2012	KC	AL	149	563	136	34	1	20	(10 | 10)	232	69	73	64	39	4	124	7	0	5	5	2	4	.242	.296	.412	.708
2013	KC	AL	136	472	110	26	0	12	(5 | 7)	172	42	42	35	32	1	83	5	1	4	2	4	13	.233	.287	.364	.651
2014	KC	AL	140	457	97	21	1	15	(5 | 10)	165	45	54	44	35	1	74	3	1	4	1	0	12	.212	.271	.361	.632
2015	KC	AL	147	549	156	34	1	22	(9 | 13)	258	73	82	85	43	1	76	13	4	5	1	2	14	.284	.348	.470	.817
	Postseason		15	52	12	2	0	5	(2 | 3)	29	9	7	6	2	0	9	0	1	0	0	0	1	.231	.259	.558	.817
	5 ML YEARS		661	2379	588	133	4	74	(32 | 42)	951	255	281	259	171	7	408	29	8	20	11	8	48	.247	.303	.400	.703

Steven Moya

Bats: L **Throws:** R **Pos:** RF-5;LF-2;DH-2;PH-1;PR-1   MOY-uh   **Ht:** 6'7" **Wt:** 260 **Born:** 8/9/1991 **Age:** 24

			BATTING																	RUNNING			AVERAGES			
Year	Team	Lg	G	AB	H	2B	3B	HR	(Hm | Rd)	TB	R	RBI	RC	TBB	IBB	SO	HBP	SH	SF	SB	CS	GDP	Avg	OBP	Slg	OPS
2011	Wmich	A	86	323	66	10	1	13	(- | -)	117	38	39	26	12	1	127	1	0	1	1	1	4	.204	.234	.362	.597
2012	Wmich	A	59	243	70	14	3	9	(- | -)	117	28	47	37	11	1	59	1	1	2	5	3	4	.288	.319	.481	.801
2013	Lkland	A+	93	365	93	19	5	12	(- | -)	158	52	55	48	18	0	106	4	0	1	6	0	9	.255	.296	.433	.729
2014	Erie	AA	133	515	142	33	3	35	(- | -)	286	81	105	90	23	2	161	3	0	8	16	4	7	.276	.306	.555	.861
2015	Toledo	AAA	126	500	120	30	0	20	(- | -)	210	53	74	60	27	0	162	4	1	3	5	4	12	.240	.280	.420	.703
2014	Det	AL	11	8	3	0	0	0	(0 | 0)	3	2	0	1	0	0	2	0	0	0	0	0	0	.375	.375	.375	.750
2015	Det	AL	9	22	4	0	1	0	(0 | 0)	6	1	0	1	3	0	10	0	0	0	0	0	0	.182	.280	.273	.553
	2 ML YEARS		20	30	7	0	1	0	(0 | 0)	9	3	0	2	3	0	12	0	0	0	0	0	0	.233	.303	.300	.603

Peter Moylan

Pitches: R **Bats:** R **Pos:** RP-22   **Ht:** 6'2" **Wt:** 225 **Born:** 12/2/1978 **Age:** 37

			HOW MUCH HE PITCHED						WHAT HE GAVE UP									THE RESULTS						
Year	Team	Lg	G	GS	CG	GF	IP	BFP	H	R	ER	HR	SH	SF	HB	TBB	IBB	SO	WP	Bk	W	L	Pct	Sh	Sv-Op	Hld	ERC	ERA
2015	Gwnntt*	AAA	27	0	0	15	28.2	115	22	10	10	1	2	0	3	9	0	24	2	0	2	0	1.000	0	6--	-	2.57	3.14
2006	Atl	NL	15	0	0	5	15.0	68	18	8	8	1	1	0	0	5	1	14	0	0	0	0	-	0	0-0	0	4.47	4.80
2007	Atl	NL	80	0	0	16	90.0	359	65	27	18	6	4	4	7	31	12	63	2	0	5	3	.625	0	1-2	8	2.36	1.80
2008	Atl	NL	7	0	0	2	5.2	25	5	1	1	1	0	0	1	1	0	5	0	0	0	1	.000	0	1-2	4	3.51	1.59
2009	Atl	NL	87	0	0	6	73.0	309	65	29	23	0	4	3	2	35	8	61	1	0	6	2	.750	0	0-5	25	3.06	2.84
2010	Atl	NL	85	0	0	7	63.2	271	53	24	21	5	5	2	2	37	6	52	3	0	6	2	.750	0	1-4	21	3.75	2.97
2011	Atl	NL	13	0	0	2	8.1	38	12	3	3	0	0	0	0	3	0	10	0	0	2	1	.667	0	0-0	2	5.87	3.24
2012	Atl	NL	8	0	0	3	5.0	21	3	3	1	1	1	0	0	2	0	2	1	0	1	0	1.000	0	1-1	1	2.40	1.80
2013	LAD	NL	14	0	0	7	15.1	70	23	11	11	3	0	0	0	7	1	6	0	0	1	0	1.000	0	0-0	1	8.59	6.46
2015	Atl	NL	22	0	0	2	10.1	44	12	5	4	1	0	0	0	6	0	8	0	1	1	0	1.000	0	0-1	3	3.20	3.48
	Postseason		4	0	0	1	1.0	6	1	0	0	0	0	0	0	0	0	1	0	0	0	0	-	0	0-1	0	1.26	0.00
	9 ML YEARS		331	0	0	50	286.1	1205	256	111	90	18	15	9	12	121	28	221	7	1	22	9	.710	0	4-15	65	3.38	2.83

Edward Mujica

Pitches: R **Bats:** R **Pos:** RP-49   moo-HEE-kah   **Ht:** 6'3" **Wt:** 220 **Born:** 5/10/1984 **Age:** 32

			HOW MUCH HE PITCHED						WHAT HE GAVE UP									THE RESULTS						
Year	Team	Lg	G	GS	CG	GF	IP	BFP	H	R	ER	HR	SH	SF	HB	TBB	IBB	SO	WP	Bk	W	L	Pct	Sh	Sv-Op	Hld	ERC	ERA
2006	Cle	AL	10	0	0	2	18.1	78	25	6	6	1	0	2	1	0	0	12	0	0	0	1	.000	0	0-0	0	4.50	2.95
2007	Cle	AL	10	0	0	5	13.0	60	19	12	12	3	0	1	0	2	0	7	0	0	0	0	-	0	0-0	0	6.63	8.31
2008	Cle	AL	33	0	0	13	38.2	168	46	29	29	5	0	4	1	10	3	27	1	0	3	2	.600	0	0-2	1	4.82	6.75
2009	SD	NL	67	4	0	15	93.2	393	101	47	41	14	1	3	0	19	4	76	3	1	3	5	.375	0	2-3	11	4.00	3.94
2010	SD	NL	59	0	0	24	69.2	268	59	29	28	14	1	0	0	6	0	72	1	0	2	1	.667	0	0-1	4	2.68	3.62
2011	Fla	NL	67	0	0	11	76.0	297	64	27	25	7	5	1	2	14	5	63	1	0	9	6	.600	0	0-3	17	2.46	2.96
2012	2 Tms	NL	70	0	0	16	65.1	258	56	24	22	7	1	1	1	12	3	47	1	0	0	3	.000	0	2-8	30	2.58	3.03
2013	StL	NL	65	0	0	49	64.2	255	60	20	20	9	3	1	1	5	1	46	0	1	2	1	.667	0	37-41	5	2.75	2.78
2014	Bos	AL	64	0	0	31	60.0	253	69	28	26	6	2	2	0	14	2	43	1	0	2	4	.333	0	8-9	3	4.28	3.90
2015	2 Tms	NL	49	0	0	13	47.1	194	52	28	25	10	2	1	1	7	2	30	1	3	3	5	.375	0	1-5	4	4.49	4.75
12	Mia	NL	41	0	0	14	39.0	161	36	21	19	6	0	1	1	9	2	26	0	0	0	3	.000	0	2-6	12	3.35	4.38
12	StL	NL	29	0	0	2	26.1	97	20	3	3	1	1	0	0	3	1	21	1	0	0	0	-	0	0-2	18	1.57	1.03
15	Bos	AL	11	0	0	4	13.2	56	15	7	7	3	1	0	1	3	0	8	0	2	1	1	.500	0	0-1	0	5.32	4.61
15	Oak	AL	38	0	0	9	33.2	138	37	21	18	7	1	1	0	4	2	22	1	1	2	4	.333	0	1-4	4	4.17	4.81
	Postseason		11	0	0	3	9.2	39	10	3	3	1	0	1	0	1	0	4	0	0	1	0	1.000	0	0-0	2	3.16	2.79
	10 ML YEARS		494	4	0	179	546.2	2224	551	250	234	76	15	16	7	89	20	423	9	5	24	28	.462	0	50-72	75	3.48	3.85

Max Muncy

Bats: L **Throws:** R **Pos:** 1B-23;3B-16;PH-11;PR-1   **Ht:** 6'0" **Wt:** 205 **Born:** 8/25/1990 **Age:** 25

Year	Team	Lg	G	AB	H	2B	3B	HR	(Hm	Rd)	TB	R	RBI	RC	TBB	IBB	SO	HBP	SH	SF	SB	CS	GDP	Avg	OBP	Slg	OPS
2012	Burlgtn	A	64	229	63	20	2	4	(-	-)	99	34	23	41	41	2	37	1	0	3	3	1	2	.275	.383	.432	.816
2013	Stcktn	A+	93	351	100	13	1	21	(-	-)	178	67	76	74	64	9	68	7	0	6	1	1	2	.285	.400	.507	.907
2013	Mdlnd	AA	47	172	43	12	2	4	(-	-)	71	22	24	25	24	1	34	0	0	1	0	1	3	.250	.340	.413	.753
2014	Mdlnd	AA	122	435	115	23	3	7	(-	-)	165	59	63	73	87	5	92	2	0	6	7	2	1	.264	.385	.379	.764
2015	Nashv	AAA	60	212	58	14	1	4	(-	-)	86	24	35	31	26	1	58	1	0	4	0	1	5	.274	.350	.406	.755
2015	Oak	AL	45	102	21	8	1	3	(1	2)	40	14	9	9	9	0	31	0	0	1	0	0	0	.206	.268	.392	.660

Danny Muno

Bats: B **Throws:** R **Pos:** PH-11;3B-5;2B-1;DH-1   MYOO-no   **Ht:** 5'11" **Wt:** 195 **Born:** 2/9/1989 **Age:** 27

Year	Team	Lg	G	AB	H	2B	3B	HR	(Hm	Rd)	TB	R	RBI	RC	TBB	IBB	SO	HBP	SH	SF	SB	CS	GDP	Avg	OBP	Slg	OPS
2011	Bklyn	A-	59	220	78	23	3	2	(-	-)	113	45	24	54	43	0	39	3	1	0	9	4	2	.355	.466	.514	.980
2012	Stluci	A+	81	289	81	16	2	6	(-	-)	119	36	39	53	50	0	53	3	6	4	19	3	7	.280	.387	.412	.799
2013	Bnghtn	AA	127	449	112	27	2	9	(-	-)	170	86	67	74	92	0	97	9	6	5	15	11	3	.249	.384	.379	.762
2014	LsVgs	AAA	117	359	93	13	1	14	(-	-)	150	74	62	61	60	1	82	7	5	4	9	5	10	.259	.372	.418	.790
2015	LsVgs	AAA	83	274	76	14	1	3	(-	-)	101	44	24	38	35	0	50	2	2	1	6	7	4	.277	.362	.369	.731
2015	NYM	NL	17	27	4	1	0	0	(0	0)	5	2	4	0	11	0	1	0	1	0	1	0	1	.148	.258	.185	.443

Toru Murata

Pitches: R **Bats:** L **Pos:** SP-1   TOH-roo moo-RAH-tah   **Ht:** 6'0" **Wt:** 175 **Born:** 5/20/1985 **Age:** 31

			HOW MUCH HE PITCHED						WHAT HE GAVE UP										THE RESULTS						
Year	Team	Lg	G	GS	CG	GF	IP	BFP	H	R	ER	HR	SH	SF	HB	TBB	IBB	SO	WP	Bk	W	L	Pct	Sh	Sv-Op	Hld	ERC	ERA
2011	Knstn	A+	22	5	0	4	49.2	191	37	14	13	2	0	2	1	10	1	58	2	0	3	2	.600	0	2--	-	1.80	2.36
2012	Akron	AA	24	8	0	5	65.2	268	59	22	19	1	5	0	2	19	3	59	2	0	3	1	.750	0	0--	-	2.65	2.60
2013	Akron	AA	23	23	0	0	131.0	552	143	76	61	18	2	5	8	21	0	104	4	2	6	6	.500	0	0--	-	4.15	4.19
2013	Clmbs	AAA	5	5	0	0	27.0	128	37	19	17	7	1	1	2	8	0	15	1	1	0	3	.000	0	0--	-	7.28	5.67
2014	Akron	AA	13	8	0	0	54.2	237	60	31	28	6	0	4	4	18	1	35	2	0	5	4	.556	0	0--	-	4.76	4.61
2014	Clmbs	AAA	14	12	0	1	72.0	309	79	44	43	14	3	2	5	20	0	44	1	0	5	3	.625	0	0--	-	5.18	5.38
2015	Clmbs	AAA	27	26	1	1	164.1	666	148	59	53	16	4	0	5	45	1	101	6	0	15	4	.789	0	0--	-	3.21	2.90
2015	Cle	AL	1	1	0	0	3.1	16	4	5	3	2	0	0	0	1	0	2	0	0	0	1	.000	0	0-0	0	7.80	8.10

Daniel Murphy

Bats: L **Throws:** R **Pos:** 2B-69;3B-42;1B-17;PH-8;DH-1   **Ht:** 6'1" **Wt:** 215 **Born:** 4/1/1985 **Age:** 31

Year	Team	Lg	G	AB	H	2B	3B	HR	(Hm	Rd)	TB	R	RBI	RC	TBB	IBB	SO	HBP	SH	SF	SB	CS	GDP	Avg	OBP	Slg	OPS
2008	NYM	NL	49	131	41	9	3	2	(1	1)	62	24	17	26	18	1	28	1	0	1	0	2	4	.313	.397	.473	.871
2009	NYM	NL	155	508	135	38	4	12	(7	5)	217	60	63	60	38	4	69	0	4	6	4	2	13	.266	.313	.427	.741
2011	NYM	NL	109	391	125	28	2	6	(2	4)	175	49	49	57	24	2	42	3	3	2	5	5	14	.320	.362	.448	.809
2012	NYM	NL	156	571	166	40	3	6	(1	5)	230	62	65	78	36	5	82	1	0	4	10	2	12	.291	.332	.403	.735
2013	NYM	NL	161	658	188	38	4	13	(6	7)	273	92	78	86	32	2	95	2	0	5	23	3	13	.286	.319	.415	.733
2014	NYM	NL	143	596	172	37	2	9	(4	5)	240	79	57	78	39	3	86	2	0	5	13	5	15	.289	.332	.403	.734
2015	NYM	NL	130	499	140	38	2	14	(7	7)	224	56	73	71	31	10	38	2	0	6	2	2	15	.281	.322	.449	.770
	7 ML YEARS		903	3354	967	228	20	62	(28	34)	1421	422	402	456	218	27	440	11	7	29	57	21	86	.288	.331	.424	.755

David Murphy

Bats: L **Throws:** L **Pos:** LF-53;DH-41;PH-37;RF-17   **Ht:** 6'3" **Wt:** 210 **Born:** 10/18/1981 **Age:** 34

Year	Team	Lg	G	AB	H	2B	3B	HR	(Hm	Rd)	TB	R	RBI	RC	TBB	IBB	SO	HBP	SH	SF	SB	CS	GDP	Avg	OBP	Slg	OPS
2006	Bos	AL	20	22	5	1	0	1	(0	1)	9	4	2	4	4	0	4	0	0	0	0	0	1	.227	.346	.409	.755
2007	2 Tms	AL	46	105	36	12	2	2	(1	1)	58	17	14	23	7	0	20	0	0	0	0	0	1	.343	.384	.552	.936
2008	Tex	AL	108	415	114	28	3	15	(8	7)	193	64	74	62	31	3	70	0	2	6	7	2	7	.275	.321	.465	.786
2009	Tex	AL	128	432	116	24	1	17	(8	9)	193	61	57	60	49	3	106	1	2	9	9	4	5	.269	.338	.447	.785
2010	Tex	AL	138	419	122	26	2	12	(7	5)	188	54	65	68	45	2	71	0	0	3	14	2	6	.291	.358	.449	.806
2011	Tex	AL	120	404	111	14	2	11	(8	3)	162	46	46	52	33	3	61	0	1	2	11	6	11	.275	.328	.401	.729
2012	Tex	AL	147	457	139	29	3	15	(7	8)	219	65	61	84	54	7	74	4	0	4	10	5	7	.304	.380	.479	.859
2013	Tex	AL	142	436	96	26	1	13	(9	4)	163	51	45	37	37	2	59	1	0	1	1	4	11	.220	.282	.374	.656
2014	Cle	AL	129	416	109	25	1	8	(6	2)	160	40	58	59	36	2	61	2	1	7	2	3	6	.262	.319	.385	.703
2015	2 Tms	AL	132	361	102	18	1	10	(3	7)	152	38	50	44	20	1	49	1	1	5	0	2	6	.283	.318	.421	.739
07	Bos	AL	3	2	1	0	0	0	(0	0)	1	1	0	1	0	0	1	0	0	0	0	0	0	.500	.500	1.500	2.000
07	Tex	AL	43	103	35	12	1	2	(1	1)	55	16	14	22	7	0	19	0	0	0	0	0	1	.340	.382	.534	.916
15	Cle	AL	84	206	61	12	1	5	(2	3)	90	22	27	28	16	1	29	1	1	4	0	1	4	.296	.344	.437	.781
15	LAA	AL	48	155	41	6	0	5	(1	4)	62	16	23	16	4	0	20	0	0	1	0	1	2	.265	.281	.400	.681
	Postseason		27	70	18	4	1	1	(1	0)	27	11	6	12	13	3	14	0	0	0	1	0	0	.257	.373	.386	.759
	10 ML YEARS		1110	3467	950	203	16	104	(57	47)	1497	440	472	491	316	23	575	9	7	37	54	28	61	.274	.333	.432	.765

John Ryan Murphy

Bats: R Throws: R Pos: C-65;PH-3;PR-3   Ht: 5'11" Wt: 205 Born: 5/13/1991 Age: 25

							BATTING														RUNNING			AVERAGES			
Year Team	Lg	G	AB	H	2B	3B	HR	(Hm	Rd)	TB	R	RBI	RC	TBB	IBB	SO	HBP	SH	SF	SB	CS	GDP	Avg	OBP	Slg	OPS
2013 NYY	AL	16	26	4	1	0	0	(0	0)	5	3	1	0	1	0	9	0	0	0	0	0	0	.154	.185	.192	.377
2014 NYY	AL	32	81	23	4	0	1	(1	0)	30	7	9	10	4	0	22	0	0	0	0	0	0	.284	.318	.370	.688
2015 NYY	AL	67	155	43	9	1	3	(1	2)	63	21	14	17	12	0	43	1	1	3	0	0	4	.277	.327	.406	.734
3 ML YEARS		115	262	70	14	1	4	(2	2)	98	31	24	27	17	0	74	1	1	3	0	0	4	.267	.311	.374	.685

Tom Murphy

Bats: R Throws: R Pos: C-11   Ht: 6'1" Wt: 220 Born: 4/3/1991 Age: 25

							BATTING														RUNNING			AVERAGES			
Year Team	Lg	G	AB	H	2B	3B	HR	(Hm	Rd)	TB	R	RBI	RC	TBB	IBB	SO	HBP	SH	SF	SB	CS	GDP	Avg	OBP	Slg	OPS
2012 TriCity	A-	55	212	61	13	3	6	(-	-)	98	26	38	34	14	1	52	7	1	3	1	1	3	.288	.349	.462	.811
2013 Ashvll	A	80	288	83	26	2	19	(-	-)	170	55	74	64	37	0	87	10	3	3	4	5	2	.288	.385	.590	.975
2013 Tulsa	AA	20	69	20	5	0	3	(-	-)	34	9	9	11	4	0	16	1	0	0	0	0	1	.290	.338	.493	.831
2014 Tulsa	AA	27	94	20	4	0	5	(-	-)	39	16	15	13	14	0	27	1	0	0	0	0	4	.213	.321	.415	.736
2015 NwBrit	AA	72	265	66	17	1	13	(-	-)	124	36	44	41	23	1	80	5	0	1	5	2	3	.249	.320	.468	.788
2015 Albq	AAA	33	129	35	9	2	7	(-	-)	69	19	19	20	5	1	43	1	0	1	0	1	3	.271	.301	.535	.836
2015 Col	NL	11	35	9	1	0	3	(3	0)	19	5	9	9	4	1	10	0	0	0	0	0	0	.257	.333	.543	.876

Colton Murray

Pitches: R Bats: R Pos: RP-8   Ht: 6'0" Wt: 195 Born: 4/22/1990 Age: 26

		HOW MUCH HE PITCHED						WHAT HE GAVE UP												THE RESULTS						
Year Team	Lg	G	GS	CG	GF	IP	BFP	H	R	ER	HR	SH	SF	HB	TBB	IBB	SO	WP	Bk	W	L	Pct	Sh	Sv-Op	Hld	ERC	ERA
2011 Wmspt	A-	22	0	0	7	30.0	131	28	12	10	1	2	0	1	12	0	23	2	0	1	2	.333	0	0--	-	3.29	3.00
2012 2 Tms	Low	44	0	0	24	60.1	262	60	34	25	4	1	3	5	21	1	62	7	1	1	4	.200	0	8--	-	3.89	3.73
2013 Clrwtr	A+	47	0	0	33	66.1	291	66	38	37	6	2	2	2	27	2	75	7	0	5	7	.417	0	11--	-	4.02	5.02
2014 Clrwtr	A+	11	0	0	8	17.1	75	16	4	4	0	0	1	0	8	1	17	3	0	2	2	.500	0	2--	-	3.06	2.08
2014 Rdng	AA	36	2	0	14	59.0	235	39	22	15	5	2	1	2	22	0	60	4	0	1	5	.167	0	6--	-	2.27	2.29
2015 Rdng	AA	21	0	0	10	35.2	147	31	10	10	1	0	2	0	10	0	36	0	0	6	1	.857	0	1--	-	2.44	2.52
2015 LV	AAA	31	0	0	15	42.0	171	24	16	13	2	0	2	1	21	0	41	2	0	2	2	.500	0	2--	-	1.98	2.79
2015 Phi	NL	8	0	0	6	7.2	37	11	5	5	2	0	0	0	2	0	9	1	0	0	1	.000	0	0-0	0	6.98	5.87

Wil Myers

Bats: R Throws: R Pos: CF-38;1B-22;LF-4;PH-3;RF-2;PR-1   Ht: 6'3" Wt: 205 Born: 12/10/1990 Age: 25

							BATTING														RUNNING			AVERAGES			
Year Team	Lg	G	AB	H	2B	3B	HR	(Hm	Rd)	TB	R	RBI	RC	TBB	IBB	SO	HBP	SH	SF	SB	CS	GDP	Avg	OBP	Slg	OPS
2013 TB	AL	88	335	98	23	0	13	(5	8)	160	50	53	52	33	6	91	1	0	4	5	2	10	.293	.354	.478	.831
2014 TB	AL	87	325	72	14	0	6	(2	4)	104	37	35	32	34	3	90	0	0	2	6	1	10	.222	.294	.320	.614
2015 SD	NL	60	225	57	13	1	8	(3	5)	96	40	29	35	27	0	55	1	0	0	5	2	2	.253	.336	.427	.763
Postseason		5	20	2	0	0	0	(0	0)	2	0	0	0	1	0	7	0	0	0	0	0	0	.100	.143	.100	.243
3 ML YEARS		235	885	227	50	1	27	(10	17)	360	127	117	119	94	9	236	2	0	6	16	5	22	.256	.327	.407	.734

Mike Napoli

Bats: R Throws: R Pos: 1B-111;LF-11;PH-11;DH-3;PR-1   NAPP-uh-lee   Ht: 6'1" Wt: 225 Born: 10/31/1981 Age: 34

							BATTING														RUNNING			AVERAGES			
Year Team	Lg	G	AB	H	2B	3B	HR	(Hm	Rd)	TB	R	RBI	RC	TBB	IBB	SO	HBP	SH	SF	SB	CS	GDP	Avg	OBP	Slg	OPS
2006 LAA	AL	99	268	61	13	0	16	(10	6)	122	47	42	40	51	0	90	5	0	1	2	3	2	.228	.360	.455	.815
2007 LAA	AL	75	219	54	11	1	10	(5	5)	97	40	34	35	33	2	63	5	1	5	5	2	5	.247	.351	.443	.794
2008 LAA	AL	78	227	62	9	1	20	(10	10)	133	39	49	46	35	5	70	5	1	6	7	3	3	.273	.374	.586	.960
2009 LAA	AL	114	382	104	22	1	20	(10	10)	188	60	56	53	40	1	103	7	0	3	3	3	6	.272	.350	.492	.842
2010 LAA	AL	140	453	108	24	1	26	(13	13)	212	60	68	60	42	2	137	11	0	4	4	2	15	.238	.316	.468	.784
2011 Tex	AL	113	369	118	25	0	30	(13	17)	233	72	75	90	58	2	85	3	0	2	4	1	10	.320	.414	.631	1.046
2012 Tex	AL	108	352	80	9	2	24	(11	13)	165	53	56	54	56	5	125	7	0	2	1	0	9	.227	.343	.469	.812
2013 Bos	AL	139	498	129	38	2	23	(11	12)	240	79	92	79	73	3	187	6	0	1	1	1	15	.259	.360	.482	.842
2014 Bos	AL	119	415	103	20	0	17	(6	11)	174	49	55	49	78	3	133	4	0	3	3	2	12	.248	.370	.419	.789
2015 2 Tms	AL	133	407	91	20	1	18	(13	5)	167	46	50	50	57	3	118	4	0	1	3	3	11	.224	.324	.410	.734
15 Bos	AL	98	329	68	18	1	13	(9	4)	127	37	40	36	45	2	99	3	0	1	3	1	10	.207	.307	.386	.693
15 Tex	AL	35	78	23	2	0	5	(4	1)	40	9	10	14	12	1	19	1	0	0	0	2	1	.295	.396	.513	.908
Postseason		47	138	35	6	0	7	(1	6)	62	20	26	24	19	2	46	3	0	2	1	0	2	.254	.352	.449	.801
10 ML YEARS		1118	3590	910	191	9	204	(102	102)	1731	545	577	561	523	26	1111	57	2	28	33	21	88	.253	.355	.482	.837

Chris Narveson

Pitches: L Bats: L Pos: RP-13; SP-2   NARR-vih-son   Ht: 6'3" Wt: 205 Born: 12/20/1981 Age: 34

		HOW MUCH HE PITCHED						WHAT HE GAVE UP												THE RESULTS						
Year Team	Lg	G	GS	CG	GF	IP	BFP	H	R	ER	HR	SH	SF	HB	TBB	IBB	SO	WP	Bk	W	L	Pct	Sh	Sv-Op	Hld	ERC	ERA
2015 NewOr*	AAA	10	4	0	1	26.0	123	38	16	15	4	2	0	0	10	0	29	2	0	0	3	.000	0	0--	-	7.25	5.19
2006 StL	NL	9	1	0	1	9.1	40	6	5	5	1	0	0	1	5	0	12	1	0	0	0	-	0	0-0	0	3.06	4.82
2009 Mil	NL	21	4	0	5	47.0	205	45	22	20	7	2	3	2	16	1	46	4	0	2	0	1.000	0	0-0	0	3.96	3.83
2010 Mil	NL	37	28	0	2	167.2	724	172	96	93	21	8	5	5	59	3	137	6	0	12	9	.571	0	0-1	3	4.30	4.99
2011 Mil	NL	30	28	0	0	161.2	699	160	82	80	17	6	4	1	65	1	126	4	1	11	8	.579	0	0-0	0	4.06	4.45
2012 Mil	NL	2	2	0	0	9.0	41	10	8	7	2	1	2	0	4	0	5	0	0	1	1	.500	0	0-0	0	5.69	7.00

Year Team	Lg	HOW MUCH HE PITCHED						WHAT HE GAVE UP												THE RESULTS							
		G	GS	CG	GF	IP	BFP	H	R	ER	HR	SH	SF	HB	TBB	IBB	SO	WP	Bk	W	L	Pct	Sh	Sv-Op	Hld	ERC	ERA
2013 Mil	NL	2	0	0	1	2.0	8	1	0	0	0	0	0	0	1	0	0	1	0	0	0	-	0	0-0	0	1.41	0.00
2015 Mia	NL	15	2	0	3	30.1	121	24	15	15	7	0	0	0	9	0	32	0	0	3	1	.750	0	0-0	0	3.40	4.45
Postseason		6	0	0	2	7.1	33	7	9	9	5	0	1	0	2	1	13	0	0	0	0	-	0	0-0	0	6.33	11.05
7 ML YEARS		112	65	0	12	427.0	1838	418	228	220	55	17	14	9	159	5	358	16	2	29	19	.604	0	0-1	3	4.09	4.64

Joe Nathan

Pitches: R Bats: R Pos: RP-1

Ht: 6'4" Wt: 230 Born: 11/22/1974 Age: 41

Year Team	Lg	HOW MUCH HE PITCHED						WHAT HE GAVE UP												THE RESULTS							
		G	GS	CG	GF	IP	BFP	H	R	ER	HR	SH	SF	HB	TBB	IBB	SO	WP	Bk	W	L	Pct	Sh	Sv-Op	Hld	ERC	ERA
1999 SF	NL	19	14	0	2	90.1	395	84	45	42	17	2	0	1	46	0	54	2	0	7	4	.636	0	1-1	0	4.78	4.18
2000 SF	NL	20	15	0	0	93.1	426	89	63	54	12	5	5	4	63	4	61	5	0	5	2	.714	0	0-1	0	5.23	5.21
2002 SF	NL	4	0	0	3	3.2	12	1	0	0	0	0	0	0	0	0	2	0	0	0	0	-	0	0-0	0	0.17	0.00
2003 SF	NL	78	0	0	9	79.0	316	51	26	26	7	2	4	3	33	3	83	4	1	12	4	.750	0	0-3	20	2.34	2.96
2004 Min	AL	73	0	0	63	72.1	284	48	14	13	3	2	0	2	23	3	89	5	0	1	2	.333	0	44-47	0	1.78	1.62
2005 Min	AL	69	0	0	58	70.0	276	46	22	21	5	1	2	0	22	4	94	2	0	7	4	.636	0	43-48	0	1.83	2.70
2006 Min	AL	64	0	0	61	68.1	262	38	12	12	3	3	2	1	16	4	95	3	0	7	0	1.000	0	36-38	0	1.18	1.58
2007 Min	AL	68	0	0	60	71.2	282	54	15	15	4	2	2	1	19	2	77	3	0	4	2	.667	0	37-41	0	2.08	1.88
2008 Min	AL	68	0	0	57	67.2	261	43	13	10	5	1	0	2	18	4	74	2	0	1	2	.333	0	39-45	0	1.67	1.33
2009 Min	AL	70	0	0	62	68.2	271	42	16	16	7	1	0	2	22	1	89	4	0	2	2	.500	0	47-52	0	1.89	2.10
2011 Min	AL	48	0	0	33	44.2	191	38	26	24	7	1	2	3	14	2	43	3	0	2	1	.667	0	14-17	8	3.38	4.84
2012 Tex	AL	66	0	0	62	64.1	257	55	23	20	7	1	3	2	13	1	78	5	0	3	5	.375	0	37-40	0	2.73	2.80
2013 Tex	AL	67	0	0	61	64.2	250	36	10	10	2	3	2	1	22	3	73	4	0	6	2	.750	0	43-46	0	1.39	1.39
2014 Det	AL	62	0	0	54	58.0	259	60	32	31	5	1	2	1	29	3	54	4	1	5	4	.556	0	35-42	0	4.53	4.81
2015 Det	AL	1	0	0	1	0.1	1	0	0	0	0	0	0	0	0	0	1	0	0	0	0	-	0	1-1	0	0.00	0.00
Postseason		10	0	0	5	10.0	52	14	9	9	2	0	1	0	8	3	12	1	0	0	2	.000	0	1-3	0	8.32	8.10
15 ML YEARS		777	29	0	586	917.0	3743	685	317	294	84	25	24	23	340	31	967	46	2	62	34	.646	0	377-422	28	2.62	2.89

Daniel Nava

NAH-vah

Bats: B Throws: L Pos: RF-34;1B-13;PH-13;LF-12;PR-2;DH-1

Ht: 5'11" Wt: 200 Born: 2/22/1983 Age: 33

Year Team	Lg	BATTING																		RUNNING			AVERAGES			
		G	AB	H	2B	3B	HR	(Hm	Rd)	TB	R	RBI	RC	TBB	IBB	SO	HBP	SH	SF	SB	CS	GDP	Avg	OBP	Slg	OPS
2015 Pwtckt*	AAA	10	36	9	1	0	1	(-	-)	13	4	8	5	4	0	11	2	0	0	2	0	2	.250	.357	.361	.718
2010 Bos	AL	60	161	39	14	1	1	(1	0)	58	23	26	26	19	1	46	8	0	0	1	1	5	.242	.351	.360	.711
2012 Bos	AL	88	267	65	21	0	6	(1	5)	104	38	33	33	37	1	63	9	2	2	3	0	5	.243	.352	.390	.742
2013 Bos	AL	134	458	139	29	0	12	(5	7)	204	77	66	79	51	2	93	15	4	8	0	2	10	.303	.385	.445	.831
2014 Bos	AL	113	363	98	21	0	4	(0	4)	131	41	37	49	33	1	81	10	0	4	2	5	9	.270	.346	.361	.706
2015 2 Tms	AL	60	139	27	4	0	1	(1	0)	34	13	10	15	20	0	36	5	1	1	1	0	4	.194	.315	.245	.560
15 Bos	AL	29	66	10	2	0	0	(0	0)	12	6	7	5	8	0	17	2	1	1	0	0	3	.152	.260	.182	.442
15 TB	AL	31	73	17	2	0	1	(1	0)	22	7	3	10	12	0	19	3	0	0	1	0	1	.233	.364	.301	.665
Postseason		9	25	5	1	0	0	(0	0)	6	1	2	2	3	0	9	0	0	0	0	1	1	.200	.286	.240	.526
5 ML YEARS		455	1388	368	89	1	24	(8	16)	531	192	172	202	160	5	319	47	7	13	9	5	29	.265	.358	.383	.740

Dioner Navarro

Bats: B Throws: R Pos: C-39;DH-11;PH-7

dee-AHN-err

Ht: 5'9" Wt: 205 Born: 2/9/1984 Age: 32

Year Team	Lg	BATTING																		RUNNING			AVERAGES			
		G	AB	H	2B	3B	HR	(Hm	Rd)	TB	R	RBI	RC	TBB	IBB	SO	HBP	SH	SF	SB	CS	GDP	Avg	OBP	Slg	OPS
2004 NYY	AL	5	7	3	0	0	0	(0	0)	3	2	1	1	0	0	0	0	0	0	0	0	1	.429	.429	.429	.857
2005 LAD	NL	50	176	48	9	0	3	(3	0)	66	21	14	18	20	1	21	2	1	0	0	0	3	.273	.354	.375	.729
2006 2 Tms		81	268	68	9	0	6	(4	2)	95	28	28	27	31	6	51	1	1	1	2	1	7	.254	.332	.354	.687
2007 TB	AL	119	388	88	19	2	9	(5	4)	138	46	44	35	33	3	67	1	7	5	3	1	11	.227	.286	.356	.641
2008 TB	AL	120	427	126	27	0	7	(4	3)	174	43	54	59	34	1	49	3	3	3	0	4	16	.295	.349	.407	.757
2009 TB	AL	115	376	82	15	0	8	(4	4)	121	38	32	22	18	1	51	5	8	3	5	2	14	.218	.261	.322	.583
2010 TB	AL	48	124	24	5	0	1	(1	0)	32	11	7	4	12	0	20	1	5	0	0	1	3	.194	.270	.258	.528
2011 LAD	NL	64	176	34	6	1	5	(3	2)	57	13	17	14	20	4	35	1	3	2	0	0	5	.193	.276	.324	.600
2012 Cin	NL	24	69	20	3	1	2	(0	2)	31	6	12	10	2	1	12	0	1	1	0	0	1	.290	.306	.449	.755
2013 ChC	NL	89	240	72	7	0	13	(9	4)	118	31	34	43	23	1	36	2	0	1	0	1	4	.300	.365	.492	.856
2014 Tor	AL	139	481	132	22	0	12	(9	3)	190	40	69	68	32	1	76	1	0	6	3	0	12	.274	.317	.395	.712
2015 Tor	AL	54	171	42	7	0	5	(3	2)	64	17	20	21	17	1	29	0	0	4	0	0	0	.246	.307	.374	.682
06 LAD	NL	25	75	21	2	0	2	(1	1)	29	5	8	8	11	4	18	0	0	1	1	0	1	.280	.372	.387	.759
06 TB	AL	56	193	47	7	0	4	(3	1)	66	23	20	19	20	2	33	1	1	1	1	1	6	.244	.316	.342	.658
Postseason		18	62	18	4	0	0	(0	0)	22	4	5	6	5	0	13	0	0	0	1	0	2	.290	.343	.355	.698
12 ML YEARS		908	2903	739	129	4	71	(45	26)	1089	296	332	322	242	20	447	17	29	26	13	10	75	.255	.313	.375	.688

Efren Navarro

Bats: L Throws: L Pos: 1B-29;LF-15;PH-8;RF-3;DH-2;PR-2

EFF-ren

Ht: 6'0" Wt: 210 Born: 5/14/1986 Age: 30

Year Team	Lg	BATTING																		RUNNING			AVERAGES			
		G	AB	H	2B	3B	HR	(Hm	Rd)	TB	R	RBI	RC	TBB	IBB	SO	HBP	SH	SF	SB	CS	GDP	Avg	OBP	Slg	OPS
2015 Salt Lk*	AAA	72	283	93	24	1	2	(-	-)	125	53	29	49	27	1	55	0	0	6	0	1	11	.329	.380	.442	.821
2011 LAA	AL	8	10	2	1	0	0	(0	0)	3	1	0	0	1	0	1	0	1	0	0	0	1	.200	.273	.300	.573
2013 LAA	AL	4	4	1	0	0	0	(0	0)	1	0	1	1	2	0	1	0	0	0	1	0	0	.250	.500	.250	.750
2014 LAA	AL	64	159	39	10	1	1	(1	0)	54	17	14	19	13	2	27	0	2	0	1	3	0	.245	.302	.340	.642
2015 LAA	AL	54	83	21	4	0	0	(1	0)	25	9	5	5	5	1	16	0	0	0	0	2	5	.253	.295	.301	.597
Postseason		1	1	0	0	0	0	(0	0)	0	0	0	0	0	0	1	0	0	0	0	0	0	.000	.000	.000	.000
4 ML YEARS		130	256	63	15	1	1	(1	0)	83	27	20	25	21	3	45	0	3	0	2	5	6	.246	.303	.324	.627

Rey Navarro

Bats: B Throws: R Pos: 2B-9;PH-2   Ht: 5'10" Wt: 185 Born: 12/22/1989 Age: 26

Year	Team	Lg	G	AB	H	2B	3B	HR	(Hm	Rd)	TB	R	RBI	RC	TBB	IBB	SO	HBP	SH	SF	SB	CS	GDP	Avg	OBP	Slg	OPS
2011	Wilmg	A+	72	277	79	17	7	8	(-	-)	134	34	41	45	18	1	39	4	1	1	5	4	6	.285	.337	.484	.820
2011	NWArk	AA	55	188	51	8	0	1	(-	-)	62	26	18	22	14	1	26	4	1	2	6	3	5	.271	.332	.330	.662
2012	NWArk	AA	109	400	100	14	3	3	(-	-)	129	51	39	42	30	0	41	4	9	6	9	4	9	.250	.305	.323	.627
2012	Omha	AAA	17	60	18	3	0	1	(-	-)	24	7	9	10	8	0	7	1	1	0	1	0	3	.300	.391	.400	.791
2013	NWArk	AA	119	446	126	21	4	12	(-	-)	191	61	58	60	19	1	54	2	7	7	6	6	13	.283	.310	.428	.738
2014	Pnscla	AA	67	255	70	17	2	9	(-	-)	118	40	34	40	27	0	32	0	5	4	4	7	2	.275	.339	.463	.802
2014	Lsvlle	AAA	65	230	68	17	0	3	(-	-)	94	24	24	34	19	0	26	1	0	1	1	1	1	.296	.351	.409	.759
2015	Norfolk	AAA	89	360	94	20	1	6	(-	-)	134	49	23	43	27	0	48	0	4	3	4	4	6	.261	.310	.372	.682
2015	Bal	AL	10	29	8	2	0	1	(1	0)	13	5	3	3	0	0	3	0	1	0	0	0	0	.276	.276	.448	.724

Kristopher Negron

neh-GRONE

Bats: R Throws: R Pos: SS-10;LF-10;PH-7;2B-6;CF-5;PR-4;1B-2;3B-2;RF-2   Ht: 6'0" Wt: 190 Born: 2/1/1986 Age: 30

Year	Team	Lg	G	AB	H	2B	3B	HR	(Hm	Rd)	TB	R	RBI	RC	TBB	IBB	SO	HBP	SH	SF	SB	CS	GDP	Avg	OBP	Slg	OPS
2015	Lsvlle*	AAA	59	204	44	5	1	4	(-	-)	63	13	15	18	15	1	47	4	5	2	3	1	6	.216	.280	.309	.589
2012	Cin	NL	4	4	1	0	0	0	(-	-)	1	2	0	1	1	0	2	0	0	0	0	0	0	.250	.400	.250	.650
2014	Cin	NL	49	144	39	10	1	6	(3	3)	69	19	17	23	12	0	40	1	1	0	5	0	2	.271	.331	.479	.810
2015	Cin	NL	43	93	13	2	0	0	(0	0)	15	5	2	2	9	0	23	3	2	0	2	0	2	.140	.238	.161	.399
	3 ML YEARS		96	241	53	12	1	6	(3	3)	85	26	19	26	22	0	65	4	3	0	7	0	4	.220	.296	.353	.649

Jimmy Nelson

Pitches: R Bats: R Pos: SP-30   Ht: 6'6" Wt: 245 Born: 6/5/1989 Age: 27

Year	Team	Lg	G	GS	CG	GF	IP	BFP	H	R	ER	HR	SH	SF	HB	TBB	IBB	SO	WP	Bk	W	L	Pct	Sh	Sv-Op	Hld	ERC	ERA
2013	Mil	NL	4	1	0	0	10.0	37	2	1	1	0	0	1	0	5	0	8	1	0	0	0	-	0	0-0	0	0.64	0.90
2014	Mil	NL	14	12	0	1	69.1	311	82	42	38	6	1	2	8	19	0	57	4	0	2	9	.182	0	0-0	0	4.96	4.93
2015	Mil	NL	30	30	0	0	177.1	752	163	89	81	18	4	7	13	65	4	148	11	1	11	13	.458	0	0-0	0	3.79	4.11
	3 ML YEARS		48	43	0	1	256.2	1100	247	132	120	24	5	10	21	89	4	213	16	1	13	22	.371	0	0-0	0	3.92	4.21

Hector Neris

NAIR-ess

Pitches: R Bats: R Pos: RP-32   Ht: 6'2" Wt: 215 Born: 6/14/1989 Age: 27

Year	Team	Lg	G	GS	CG	GF	IP	BFP	H	R	ER	HR	SH	SF	HB	TBB	IBB	SO	WP	Bk	W	L	Pct	Sh	Sv-Op	Hld	ERC	ERA
2011	2 Tms	Low	34	0	0	10	59.0	247	51	24	18	7	1	1	2	17	0	72	3	1	3	2	.600	0	0--	-	3.10	2.75
2012	Clrwtr	A+	50	0	0	22	78.2	322	64	34	31	7	2	1	4	25	3	94	5	4	2	1	.667	0	6--	-	2.85	3.55
2013	Rdng	AA	46	8	0	16	97.0	415	89	51	49	14	1	4	2	39	0	93	4	4	6	4	.600	0	0--	-	3.99	4.55
2014	LV	AAA	37	1	0	11	58.0	245	50	29	27	5	1	0	6	19	1	58	3	2	4	3	.571	0	2--	-	3.31	4.19
2014	Rdng	AA	11	0	0	3	19.1	76	12	4	4	3	2	0	0	10	0	12	0	0	2	0	1.000	0	0--	-	2.99	1.86
2015	LV	AAA	27	0	0	10	37.1	173	38	16	15	1	3	0	0	24	1	35	2	0	1	3	.250	0	1--	-	4.43	3.62
2014	Phi	NL	1	0	0	1	1.0	3	0	0	0	0	0	0	0	0	0	1	0	0	1	0	1.000	0	0-0	-	0.00	0.00
2015	Phi	NL	32	0	0	8	40.1	170	38	19	17	8	1	0	4	10	0	41	3	0	2	2	.500	0	0-0	2	4.21	3.79
	2 ML YEARS		33	0	0	9	41.1	173	38	19	17	8	1	0	4	10	0	42	3	0	3	2	.600	0	0-0	2	4.01	3.70

Angel Nesbitt

AHN-hell

Pitches: R Bats: R Pos: RP-24   Ht: 6'1" Wt: 240 Born: 12/4/1990 Age: 25

Year	Team	Lg	G	GS	CG	GF	IP	BFP	H	R	ER	HR	SH	SF	HB	TBB	IBB	SO	WP	Bk	W	L	Pct	Sh	Sv-Op	Hld	ERC	ERA
2012	Conn	A-	20	0	0	10	36.1	167	49	23	19	1	4	2	4	11	0	23	6	0	4	3	.571	0	0--	-	5.66	4.71
2013	Wmich	A	52	0	0	22	67.0	282	60	33	24	5	1	4	1	21	1	54	4	0	3	4	.429	0	3--	-	2.99	3.22
2014	Lkland	A+	24	0	0	19	34.1	131	23	3	3	1	0	0	0	8	1	36	1	0	2	0	1.000	0	14--	-	1.38	0.79
2014	Erie	AA	24	0	0	15	32.1	130	20	8	8	3	1	0	1	15	1	36	2	0	1	0	1.000	0	6--	-	2.42	2.23
2015	Toledo	AAA	27	0	0	6	40.1	190	54	30	28	3	3	1	0	21	0	30	2	0	1	5	.167	0	0--	-	6.43	6.25
2015	Det	AL	24	0	0	6	21.2	98	22	14	13	2	2	1	4	8	2	14	3	0	1	1	.500	0	0-2	2	4.49	5.40

Pat Neshek

NEE-sheck

Pitches: R Bats: B Pos: RP-66   Ht: 6'3" Wt: 210 Born: 9/4/1980 Age: 35

Year	Team	Lg	G	GS	CG	GF	IP	BFP	H	R	ER	HR	SH	SF	HB	TBB	IBB	SO	WP	Bk	W	L	Pct	Sh	Sv-Op	Hld	ERC	ERA
2006	Min	AL	32	0	0	3	37.0	138	23	9	9	6	0	5	0	53	0	0	4	2	.667	0	0-2	10	1.68	2.19		
2007	Min	AL	74	0	0	20	70.1	278	44	25	23	7	4	5	2	27	5	74	2	0	7	2	.778	0	0-3	15	2.12	2.94
2008	Min	AL	15	0	0	3	13.1	56	12	7	7	2	1	1	0	4	1	15	0	0	0	1	.000	0	0-2	6	3.29	4.73
2010	Min	AL	11	0	0	3	9.0	43	7	5	5	1	0	0	1	8	0	9	0	0	0	1	.000	0	0-1	1	5.13	5.00
2011	SD	NL	25	0	0	13	24.2	112	19	12	11	4	1	0	1	22	1	20	1	0	1	1	.500	0	0-0	4	5.37	4.01
2012	Oak	AL	24	0	0	5	19.2	77	10	3	3	3	0	2	1	6	1	16	1	0	2	1	.667	0	0-2	4	1.66	1.37
2013	Oak	AL	45	0	0	17	40.1	177	40	17	15	6	0	3	0	15	2	29	1	0	2	1	.667	0	0-0	1	4.06	3.35
2014	StL	NL	71	0	0	17	67.1	255	44	14	14	4	2	2	2	9	2	68	1	0	7	2	.778	0	6-10	25	1.38	1.87
2015	Hou	AL	66	0	0	8	54.2	223	49	25	22	8	4	1	2	12	1	51	1	0	3	6	.333	0	1-4	28	3.23	3.62
	Postseason		11	0	0	3	9.1	33	4	3	3	2	0	0	0	0	0	8	0	0	2	0	.000	0	0-1	3	0.82	2.89
	9 ML YEARS		363	0	0	89	336.1	1359	248	117	109	41	12	15	9	109	13	335	7	0	26	17	.605	0	7-24	90	2.58	2.92

Juan Nicasio

Pitches: R Bats: R Pos: RP-52; SP-1 ni-KAH-see-oh **Ht:** 6'4" **Wt:** 250 **Born:** 8/31/1986 **Age:** 29

Year	Team	Lg	G	GS	CG	GF	IP	BFP	H	R	ER	HR	SH	SF	HB	TBB	IBB	SO	WP	Bk	W	L	Pct	Sh	Sv-Op	Hld	ERC	ERA
2011	Col	NL	13	13	0	0	71.2	299	73	35	33	8	1	0	1	18	3	58	1	0	4	4	.500	0	0-0	0	3.69	4.14
2012	Col	NL	11	11	0	0	58.0	257	72	37	34	7	3	1	1	22	1	54	4	0	2	3	.400	0	0-0	0	5.74	5.28
2013	Col	NL	31	31	0	0	157.2	703	168	97	90	17	6	1	5	64	7	119	6	2	9	9	.500	0	0-0	0	4.52	5.14
2014	Col	NL	33	14	0	7	93.2	409	107	59	56	19	5	2	1	31	1	63	3	1	6	6	.500	0	0-0	0	5.43	5.38
2015	LAD	NL	53	1	0	12	58.1	260	59	25	25	1	3	0	1	32	6	65	2	0	1	3	.250	0	1-3	14	4.00	3.86
	5 ML YEARS		141	70	0	19	439.1	1928	479	253	238	52	18	4	9	167	18	359	16	3	22	25	.468	0	1-3	15	4.66	4.88

Justin Nicolino

Pitches: L Bats: L Pos: SP-12 **Ht:** 6'3" **Wt:** 190 **Born:** 11/22/1991 **Age:** 24

Year	Team	Lg	G	GS	CG	GF	IP	BFP	H	R	ER	HR	SH	SF	HB	TBB	IBB	SO	WP	Bk	W	L	Pct	Sh	Sv-Op	Hld	ERC	ERA
2011	2 Tms	Low	15	12	1	1	61.0	231	39	12	9	0	1	0	1	13	0	73	1	3	6	2	.750	0	0- -	-	1.30	1.33
2012	Lnsng	A	28	22	0	0	124.1	495	112	41	34	6	3	2	5	21	1	119	4	1	10	4	.714	0	0- -	-	2.54	2.46
2013	Jupiter	A+	18	18	1	0	96.2	385	89	27	24	4	2	3	2	18	0	64	1	1	5	2	.714	0	0- -	-	2.61	2.23
2013	Jaxnvl	AA	9	9	1	0	45.1	205	63	29	25	2	4	2	2	12	0	31	1	0	3	2	.600	0	0- -	-	5.64	4.96
2014	Jaxnvl	AA	28	28	2	0	170.1	686	163	68	55	10	7	4	5	20	1	81	2	0	14	4	.778	2	0- -	-	2.62	2.91
2015	NewOr	AAA	20	20	0	0	115.0	487	134	51	45	11	5	2	4	29	2	63	0	0	7	7	.500	0	0- -	-	4.64	3.52
2015	Mia	NL	12	12	0	0	74.0	301	72	33	33	8	5	3	3	20	2	23	2	0	5	4	.556	0	0-0	0	3.73	4.01

Jon Niese

Pitches: L Bats: L Pos: SP-29; RP-4 NIECE **Ht:** 6'3" **Wt:** 220 **Born:** 10/27/1986 **Age:** 29

Year	Team	Lg	G	GS	CG	GF	IP	BFP	H	R	ER	HR	SH	SF	HB	TBB	IBB	SO	WP	Bk	W	L	Pct	Sh	Sv-Op	Hld	ERC	ERA
2008	NYM	NL	3	3	0	0	14.0	69	20	11	11	2	1	0	0	8	0	11	0	0	1	1	.500	0	0-0	0	7.71	7.07
2009	NYM	NL	5	5	0	0	25.2	110	27	12	12	1	2	1	0	9	0	18	1	0	1	1	.500	0	0-0	0	3.76	4.21
2010	NYM	NL	30	30	2	0	173.2	770	192	97	81	20	9	4	9	62	3	148	5	0	9	10	.474	1	0-0	0	4.77	4.20
2011	NYM	NL	27	26	0	0	157.1	694	178	88	77	14	**16**	2	5	44	4	138	3	0	11	11	.500	0	0-0	0	4.27	4.40
2012	NYM	NL	30	30	0	0	190.1	788	174	77	72	22	8	4	4	49	2	155	6	0	13	9	.591	0	0-0	0	3.21	3.40
2013	NYM	NL	24	24	1	0	143.0	621	158	68	59	10	6	0	4	48	1	105	5	0	8	8	.500	1	0-0	0	4.32	3.71
2014	NYM	NL	30	30	0	0	187.2	786	193	80	71	17	10	5	7	45	0	138	3	0	9	11	.450	0	0-0	0	3.72	3.40
2015	NYM	NL	33	29	0	1	176.2	770	192	93	81	20	**16**	4	9	55	2	113	2	0	9	10	.474	0	0-0	0	4.49	4.13
	8 ML YEARS		182	177	3	1	1068.1	4608	1134	526	464	106	68	20	38	320	12	826	25	0	61	61	.500	2	0-0	0	4.13	3.91

Kirk Nieuwenhuis

Bats: L Throws: R Pos: LF-34;PH-29;CF-16;RF-7;PR-5 NEW-enn-hice **Ht:** 6'3" **Wt:** 225 **Born:** 8/7/1987 **Age:** 28

Year	Team	Lg	G	AB	H	2B	3B	HR	(Hm	Rd)	TB	R	RBI	RC	TBB	IBB	SO	HBP	SH	SF	SB	CS	GDP	Avg	OBP	Slg	OPS
2015	LsVgs*	AAA	27	105	34	6	3	8	(-	-)	70	21	29	26	10	0	21	1	1	2	2	0	2	.324	.381	.667	1.048
2012	NYM	NL	91	282	71	12	1	7	(5	2)	106	40	28	28	25	0	98	2	3	2	4	4	2	.252	.315	.376	.691
2013	NYM	NL	47	95	18	4	1	3	(2	1)	32	10	14	8	12	1	32	0	0	1	2	0	1	.189	.278	.337	.615
2014	NYM	NL	61	112	29	14	1	3	(1	2)	54	16	16	16	16	3	39	0	0	2	4	0	1	.259	.346	.482	.828
2015	2 Tms		74	128	25	11	0	4	(3	1)	48	21	14	14	10	0	49	3	0	0	2	2	2	.195	.270	.375	.645
15	NYM	NL	64	106	22	9	0	4	(3	1)	43	17	13	10	8	0	40	3	0	0	2	1	2	.208	.282	.406	.688
15	LAA	AL	10	22	3	2	0	0	(0	0)	5	4	1	0	2	0	9	0	0	0	0	1	0	.136	.208	.227	.436
	4 ML YEARS		273	617	143	40	3	17	(11	6)	240	87	72	62	63	4	218	5	3	5	12	6	6	.232	.306	.389	.695

Wil Nieves

Bats: R Throws: R Pos: C-4;1B-2;PH-1 nee-YEV-es **Ht:** 5'11" **Wt:** 190 **Born:** 9/25/1977 **Age:** 38

Year	Team	Lg	G	AB	H	2B	3B	HR	(Hm	Rd)	TB	R	RBI	RC	TBB	IBB	SO	HBP	SH	SF	SB	CS	GDP	Avg	OBP	Slg	OPS
2015	Gwnntt*	AAA	22	63	15	3	0	0	(-	-)	18	5	8	6	8	0	14	0	0	0	0	0	8	.238	.324	.286	.610
2002	SD	NL	28	72	13	3	1	0	(0	0)	18	2	3	4	4	4	15	0	0	0	1	0	1	.181	.224	.250	.474
2005	NYY	AL	3	4	0	0	0	0	(0	0)	0	0	0	0	0	0	1	0	0	0	0	0	0	.000	.000	.000	.000
2006	NYY	AL	6	6	0	0	0	0	(0	0)	0	0	0	0	0	0	1	0	0	0	0	0	0	.000	.000	.000	.000
2007	NYY	AL	26	61	10	4	0	0	(0	0)	14	6	8	4	2	0	9	0	3	0	0	0	3	.164	.190	.230	.420
2008	Was	NL	68	176	46	9	1	1	(1	0)	60	15	20	20	13	1	29	0	5	2	0	1	7	.261	.309	.341	.650
2009	Was	NL	72	224	58	6	0	1	(0	1)	67	20	26	21	17	1	45	3	0	5	1	0	7	.259	.313	.299	.612
2010	Was	NL	59	158	32	8	0	3	(1	2)	49	10	16	9	8	2	29	1	4	1	0	0	6	.203	.244	.310	.554
2011	Mil	NL	20	50	7	2	0	0	(0	0)	9	2	0	0	3	1	12	0	1	0	0	0	1	.140	.189	.180	.369
2012	2 Tms	NL	32	83	25	3	0	2	(0	2)	34	7	8	9	4	2	17	0	1	1	0	1	3	.301	.330	.410	.739
2013	Ari	NL	71	195	58	11	0	1	(1	0)	72	16	22	21	8	0	32	0	0	3	0	0	7	.297	.320	.369	.690
2014	Phi	NL	36	122	31	8	0	1	(1	0)	42	9	7	6	1	0	34	2	2	1	1	0	2	.254	.270	.344	.614
2015	SD	NL	6	13	1	0	0	1	(1	0)	4	1	4	2	1	0	4	0	0	0	0	0	0	.077	.143	.308	.451
12	Col	NL	16	47	14	2	0	1	(0	1)	19	3	5	6	3	1	9	0	0	1	0	0	3	.298	.333	.404	.738
12	Ari	NL	16	36	11	1	0	1	(0	1)	15	4	3	3	1	1	8	0	1	0	0	1	0	.306	.324	.417	.741
	12 ML YEARS		427	1164	281	54	2	10	(5	5)	369	88	114	96	61	11	228	6	16	13	3	2	39	.241	.280	.317	.597

Rico Noel

Bats: R **Throws:** R **Pos:** PR-12;DH-3;RF-2;PH-2   **Ht:** 5'8" **Wt:** 170 **Born:** 1/11/1989 **Age:** 27

Year	Team	Lg	G	AB	H	2B	3B	HR	(Hm	Rd)	TB	R	RBI	RC	TBB	IBB	SO	HBP	SH	SF	SB	CS	GDP	Avg	OBP	Slg	OPS
2011	2 Tms	Low	126	475	116	22	5	3	(-	-)	157	89	46	68	50	0	94	18	10	1	62	5	6	.244	.338	.331	.669
2012	Lk Els	A+	134	514	139	14	2	0	(-	-)	157	79	30	71	62	2	151	8	8	1	90	23	5	.270	.357	.305	.663
2013	SnAnt	AA	131	496	132	23	5	0	(-	-)	165	74	41	68	52	0	119	13	10	5	59	19	3	.266	.348	.333	.681
2014	ElPaso	AAA	109	333	86	11	1	2	(-	-)	105	49	27	44	41	2	81	3	6	2	32	6	4	.258	.343	.315	.658
2015	ElPaso	AAA	33	66	16	1	1	0	(-	-)	19	11	6	9	9	0	17	1	2	2	10	1	0	.242	.333	.288	.621
2015	S-WB	AAA	22	17	1	0	0	0	(-	-)	1	5	0	0	4	0	7	1	1	0	9	3	2	.059	.273	.059	.332
2015	Trntn	AA	12	33	4	0	0	0	(-	-)	4	3	1	1	5	1	10	1	1	0	4	1	1	.121	.256	.121	.378
2015	NYY	AL	15	2	1	0	0	0	(0	0)	1	5	0	0	0	0	0	0	0	0	5	2	0	.500	.500	.500	1.000

Hector Noesi

Pitches: R **Bats:** R **Pos:** SP-5; RP-5   noh-EH-see   **Ht:** 6'3" **Wt:** 205 **Born:** 1/26/1987 **Age:** 29

Year	Team	Lg	G	GS	CG	GF	IP	BFP	H	R	ER	HR	SH	SF	HB	TBB	IBB	SO	WP	Bk	W	L	Pct	Sh	Sv-Op	Hld	ERC	ERA
2015	Charllt*	AAA	11	10	0	0	65.0	250	46	25	24	7	3	2	0	16	0	56	1	0	4	4	.500	0	0- -	-	2.10	3.32
2011	NYY	AL	30	2	0	14	56.1	247	63	29	28	6	1	2	2	22	4	45	4	0	2	2	.500	0	0-0	4	4.85	4.47
2012	Sea	AL	22	18	0	4	106.2	453	107	71	69	21	3	7	2	39	1	68	1	2	2	12	.143	0	0-0	0	4.77	5.82
2013	Sea	AL	12	1	0	4	27.1	134	42	21	20	3	1	1	1	12	4	21	2	0	0	1	.000	0	0-0	0	7.45	6.59
2014	3 Tms	AL	33	27	1	3	172.1	733	180	98	91	28	4	7	2	56	1	123	9	1	8	12	.400	0	0-0	0	4.55	4.75
2015	CWS	AL	10	5	0	4	32.2	154	41	26	25	7	0	0	1	17	1	22	3	1	0	4	.000	0	0-0	0	7.08	6.89
14	Sea	AL	2	0	0	2	1.0	6	2	3	3	1	0	1	0	0	0	2	1	0	0	1	.000	0	0-0	0	13.47	27.00
14	Tex	AL	3	0	0	1	5.1	28	11	7	7	0	0	0	0	2	0	4	0	0	0	0	-	0	0-0	0	9.94	11.81
14	CWS	AL	28	27	1	0	166.0	699	167	88	81	27	4	6	2	54	1	117	8	1	8	11	.421	0	0-0	0	4.34	4.39
	5 ML YEARS		107	53	1	29	395.1	1721	433	245	233	65	9	17	8	146	11	279	19	4	12	31	.279	0	0-0	4	5.05	5.30

Aaron Nola

Pitches: R **Bats:** R **Pos:** SP-13   NO-luh   **Ht:** 6'1" **Wt:** 195 **Born:** 6/4/1993 **Age:** 23

Year	Team	Lg	G	GS	CG	GF	IP	BFP	H	R	ER	HR	SH	SF	HB	TBB	IBB	SO	WP	Bk	W	L	Pct	Sh	Sv-Op	Hld	ERC	ERA
2014	Clrwtr	A+	7	6	0	1	31.1	121	24	12	11	4	2	1	0	5	0	30	1	0	2	3	.400	0	0- -	-	2.15	3.16
2014	Rdng	AA	5	5	0	0	24.0	98	25	7	7	4	1	0	0	5	0	15	0	0	2	0	1.000	0	0- -	-	4.09	2.63
2015	Rdng	AA	12	12	0	0	76.2	288	59	17	16	4	3	2	3	9	0	59	0	0	7	3	.700	0	0- -	-	1.82	1.88
2015	LV	AAA	6	6	0	0	32.2	141	38	14	13	3	0	0	0	9	0	33	0	0	1	1	.750	0	0- -	-	4.47	3.58
2015	Phi	NL	13	13	0	0	77.2	318	74	31	31	11	1	1	2	19	1	68	0	0	6	2	.750	0	0-0	0	3.62	3.59

Ricky Nolasco

Pitches: R **Bats:** R **Pos:** SP-8; RP-1   **Ht:** 6'2" **Wt:** 235 **Born:** 12/13/1982 **Age:** 33

Year	Team	Lg	G	GS	CG	GF	IP	BFP	H	R	ER	HR	SH	SF	HB	TBB	IBB	SO	WP	Bk	W	L	Pct	Sh	Sv-Op	Hld	ERC	ERA
2006	Fla	NL	35	22	0	0	140.0	613	157	86	75	20	8	6	10	41	5	99	7	0	11	11	.500	0	0-0	2	4.89	4.82
2007	Fla	NL	5	4	0	0	21.1	99	26	16	13	3	3	5	1	9	2	11	1	0	1	2	.333	0	0-0	0	5.71	5.48
2008	Fla	NL	34	32	1	0	212.1	868	192	88	83	28	6	9	6	42	6	186	1	3	15	8	.652	1	0-0	0	3.03	3.52
2009	Fla	NL	31	31	2	0	185.0	785	188	111	104	23	8	5	2	44	7	195	2	0	13	9	.591	0	0-0	0	3.62	5.06
2010	Fla	NL	26	26	1	0	157.2	665	169	82	79	24	5	6	2	33	1	147	5	0	14	9	.609	0	0-0	0	4.11	4.51
2011	Fla	NL	33	33	2	0	206.0	891	244	117	107	20	11	5	3	44	8	148	6	0	10	12	.455	1	0-0	0	4.34	4.67
2012	Mia	NL	31	31	3	0	191.0	832	214	100	95	18	19	6	8	47	9	125	8	1	12	13	.480	2	0-0	0	4.14	4.48
2013	2 Tms	NL	34	33	0	0	199.1	834	195	90	82	17	10	3	10	46	1	165	5	0	13	11	.542	0	0-0	0	3.38	3.70
2014	Min	AL	27	27	1	0	159.0	695	203	96	95	22	4	5	5	38	1	115	5	0	6	12	.333	0	0-0	0	5.53	5.38
2015	Min	AL	9	8	0	1	37.1	173	50	31	28	3	0	2	1	14	2	35	1	1	5	2	.714	0	0-0	0	5.82	6.75
13	Mia	NL	18	18	0	0	112.1	468	112	50	48	11	7	3	4	25	1	90	4	0	5	8	.385	0	0-0	0	3.49	3.85
13	LAD	NL	16	15	0	0	87.0	366	83	40	34	6	3	0	6	21	0	75	1	0	8	3	.727	0	0-0	0	3.25	3.52
	Postseason		1	1	0	0	4.0	16	3	3	3	1	1	0	0	1	0	4	0	0	0	1	.000	0	0-0	0	3.01	6.75
	10 ML YEARS		265	247	10	1	1509.0	6455	1638	817	761	178	74	51	48	358	42	1226	41	5	100	89	.529	4	0-0	2	4.10	4.54

Sean Nolin

Pitches: L **Bats:** L **Pos:** SP-6   **Ht:** 6'4" **Wt:** 230 **Born:** 12/26/1989 **Age:** 26

Year	Team	Lg	G	GS	CG	GF	IP	BFP	H	R	ER	HR	SH	SF	HB	TBB	IBB	SO	WP	Bk	W	L	Pct	Sh	Sv-Op	Hld	ERC	ERA
2015	Nashv*	AAA	14	12	0	0	47.1	201	40	15	14	5	2	2	4	19	0	38	0	0	2	2	.500	0	0- -	-	3.60	2.66
2013	Tor	AL	1	1	0	0	1.1	11	7	6	6	1	0	0	1	1	0	1	0	0	0	1	.000	0	0-0	0	52.56	40.50
2014	Tor	AL	1	0	0	1	1.0	4	1	1	1	0	0	0	0	0	0	0	0	0	0	0	-	0	0-0	0	7.45	9.00
2015	Oak	AL	6	6	0	0	29.0	134	35	19	17	4	1	5	0	12	0	15	3	1	1	2	.333	0	0-0	0	5.49	5.28
	3 ML YEARS		8	7	0	0	31.1	149	43	26	24	6	1	5	0	13	0	15	3	1	1	3	.250	0	0-0	0	6.99	6.89

Nick Noonan

Bats: L **Throws:** R **Pos:** SS-5;PH-5;1B-3;PR-2   **Ht:** 6'1" **Wt:** 175 **Born:** 5/4/1989 **Age:** 27

Year	Team	Lg	G	AB	H	2B	3B	HR	(Hm	Rd)	TB	R	RBI	RC	TBB	IBB	SO	HBP	SH	SF	SB	CS	GDP	Avg	OBP	Slg	OPS
2011	Rchmd	AA	71	260	55	11	0	3	(-	-)	75	28	25	24	33	5	60	2	2	2	2	2	6	.212	.303	.288	.591
2011	Fresno	AAA	13	37	11	0	0	1	(-	-)	14	6	4	5	4	0	2	0	0	0	1	0	1	.297	.366	.378	.744
2011	SnJos	A+	28	122	30	6	1	1	(-	-)	41	14	16	13	12	0	18	0	0	1	1	2	3	.246	.311	.336	.647
2012	Fresno	AAA	129	490	145	26	3	9	(-	-)	204	65	62	74	40	2	84	1	5	5	7	3	10	.296	.347	.416	.763
2013	Fresno	AAA	48	165	42	13	1	0	(-	-)	57	20	20	19	17	0	44	1	2	3	1	2	2	.255	.323	.345	.668

Year	Team	Lg	G	AB	H	2B	3B	HR	(Hm	Rd)	TB	R	RBI	RC	TBB	IBB	SO	HBP	SH	SF	SB	CS	GDP	Avg	OBP	Slg	OPS
2014	Fresno	AAA	104	379	90	16	0	3	(-	-)	115	38	24	32	20	0	98	4	2	1	6	5	8	.237	.282	.303	.586
2015	S-WB	AAA	67	244	64	13	0	1	(-	-)	80	28	26	26	17	0	68	1	3	4	1	1	5	.262	.308	.328	.636
2015	Scrmto	AAA	19	64	17	1	0	2	(-	-)	24	6	10	8	5	0	15	0	0	1	1	0	1	.266	.314	.375	.689
2013	SF	NL	62	105	23	2	0	0	(0	0)	25	12	5	5	6	3	24	0	0	0	0	0	1	.219	.261	.238	.499
2015	SF	NL	14	22	2	1	0	1	(1	0)	6	2	3	0	2	0	8	0	0	0	0	0	1	.091	.167	.273	.439
	2 ML YEARS		76	127	25	3	0	1	(1	0)	31	14	8	5	8	3	32	0	0	0	0	0	2	.197	.244	.244	.489

Bud Norris

Pitches: R **Bats:** R **Pos:** RP-27; SP-11   **Ht:** 6'0" **Wt:** 195 **Born:** 3/2/1985 **Age:** 31

Year	Team	Lg	G	GS	CG	GF	IP	BFP	H	R	ER	HR	SH	SF	HB	TBB	IBB	SO	WP	Bk	W	L	Pct	Sh	Sv-Op	Hld	ERC	ERA
2009	Hou	NL	11	10	0	0	55.2	249	59	29	28	9	1	3	3	25	1	54	3	0	6	3	.667	0	0-0	0	5.26	4.53
2010	Hou	NL	27	27	0	0	153.2	683	151	94	84	18	6	4	6	77	3	158	5	2	9	10	.474	0	0-0	0	4.61	4.92
2011	Hou	NL	31	31	0	0	186.0	795	177	93	78	24	9	4	5	70	7	176	3	2	6	11	.353	0	0-0	0	3.96	3.77
2012	Hou	NL	29	29	0	0	168.1	733	165	90	87	23	7	2	8	66	2	165	8	0	7	13	.350	0	0-0	0	4.34	4.65
2013	2 Tms	AL	32	30	0	2	176.2	773	196	89	82	17	6	3	5	67	0	147	4	0	10	12	.455	0	0-0	0	4.75	4.18
2014	Bal	AL	28	28	0	0	165.1	687	149	68	67	20	1	4	14	52	2	139	3	0	15	8	.652	0	0-0	0	3.72	3.65
2015	2 Tms	AL	38	11	0	7	83.0	377	100	68	62	15	3	2	4	31	0	71	2	0	3	11	.214	0	0-2	2	5.96	6.72
	13	Hou	AL	21	21	0	0	126.0	541	135	62	55	11	4	3	4	43	0	90	3	0	6	9	.400	0	0-0	0	4.34	3.93
	13	Bal	AL	11	9	0	2	50.2	232	61	27	27	6	2	0	1	24	0	57	1	0	4	3	.571	0	0-0	0	5.81	4.80
	15	Bal	AL	18	11	0	2	66.1	305	84	57	52	14	3	2	3	25	0	50	0	0	2	9	.182	0	0-1	0	6.60	7.06
	15	SD	NL	20	0	0	5	16.2	72	16	11	10	1	0	0	1	6	0	21	2	0	1	2	.333	0	0-1	2	3.62	5.40
	Postseason		2	2	0	0	10.2	46	11	4	4	1	0	0	0	2	0	9	1	0	1	0	1.000	0	0-0	0	3.22	3.38
	7 ML YEARS		196	166	0	9	988.2	4297	997	531	488	126	33	22	45	388	15	910	28	4	56	68	.452	0	0-2	2	4.46	4.44

Daniel Norris

Pitches: L **Bats:** L **Pos:** SP-13   **Ht:** 6'2" **Wt:** 195 **Born:** 4/25/1993 **Age:** 23

Year	Team	Lg	G	GS	CG	GF	IP	BFP	H	R	ER	HR	SH	SF	HB	TBB	IBB	SO	WP	Bk	W	L	Pct	Sh	Sv-Op	Hld	ERC	ERA
2012	2 Tms	Low	13	12	0	0	42.2	207	58	44	40	4	1	5	2	18	0	43	4	0	2	4	.333	0	0- -	-	6.26	8.44
2013	2 Tms	Low	24	23	0	0	90.2	400	85	46	40	6	1	2	4	46	0	100	11	0	2	7	.222	0	0- -	-	4.05	3.97
2014	Dnedin	A+	13	13	0	0	66.0	262	50	11	9	0	4	1	0	18	0	76	6	0	6	0	1.000	0	0- -	-	1.77	1.23
2014	Nham	AA	8	8	0	0	35.2	155	32	18	18	5	0	0	2	17	0	49	3	1	3	1	.750	0	0- -	-	4.31	4.54
2014	Buffalo	AAA	5	4	0	0	22.2	85	14	8	8	2	0	0	0	8	0	38	0	0	3	1	.750	0	0- -	-	2.01	3.18
2015	Buffalo	AAA	16	16	0	0	90.2	405	96	50	43	5	4	3	1	41	0	78	6	0	3	10	.231	0	0- -	-	4.28	4.27
2014	Tor	AL	5	1	0	2	6.2	30	5	4	4	1	0	1	0	5	0	4	0	0	0	0	-	0	0-0	1	4.31	5.40
2015	2 Tms	AL	13	13	0	0	60.0	251	53	31	25	9	1	4	2	19	0	45	3	0	3	2	.600	0	0-0	0	3.55	3.75
	15	Tor	AL	5	5	0	0	23.1	103	23	11	10	3	1	2	2	12	0	18	2	0	1	1	.500	0	0-0	0	5.10	3.86
	15	Det	AL	8	8	0	0	36.2	148	30	20	15	6	0	2	0	7	0	27	1	0	2	1	.667	0	0-0	0	2.64	3.68
	2 ML YEARS		18	14	0	2	66.2	281	58	35	29	10	1	5	2	24	0	49	3	0	3	2	.600	0	0-0	1	3.63	3.92

Derek Norris

Bats: R **Throws:** R **Pos:** C-128;1B-17;PH-14;DH-1   **Ht:** 6'0" **Wt:** 210 **Born:** 2/14/1989 **Age:** 27

Year	Team	Lg	G	AB	H	2B	3B	HR	(Hm	Rd)	TB	R	RBI	RC	TBB	IBB	SO	HBP	SH	SF	SB	CS	GDP	Avg	OBP	Slg	OPS
2012	Oak	AL	60	209	42	8	1	7	(3	4)	73	19	34	27	21	1	66	1	0	1	5	1	6	.201	.276	.349	.625
2013	Oak	AL	98	264	65	6	3	9	(6	3)	108	41	30	40	37	1	71	4	1	2	5	0	5	.246	.345	.409	.754
2014	Oak	AL	127	385	104	19	1	10	(7	3)	155	46	55	66	54	2	86	1	1	1	2	2	12	.270	.361	.403	.763
2015	SD	NL	147	515	129	33	2	14	(9	5)	208	65	62	66	35	1	131	6	0	1	4	1	5	.250	.305	.404	.709
	Postseason		7	18	2	0	0	0	(0	0)	2	1	1	1	0	0	9	0	0	0	0	1	0	.111	.111	.111	.222
	4 ML YEARS		432	1373	340	76	4	40	(25	15)	544	171	181	199	147	5	354	12	2	5	16	4	28	.248	.325	.396	.721

Ivan Nova

Pitches: R **Bats:** R **Pos:** SP-17   ee-VAHN   **Ht:** 6'4" **Wt:** 235 **Born:** 1/12/1987 **Age:** 29

Year	Team	Lg	G	GS	CG	GF	IP	BFP	H	R	ER	HR	SH	SF	HB	TBB	IBB	SO	WP	Bk	W	L	Pct	Sh	Sv-Op	Hld	ERC	ERA
2010	NYY	AL	10	7	0	3	42.0	185	44	22	21	4	1	1	1	17	2	26	2	0	1	2	.333	0	0-1	0	4.31	4.50
2011	NYY	AL	28	27	0	1	165.1	704	163	74	68	13	2	6	6	57	3	98	11	0	16	4	.800	0	0-0	0	3.76	3.70
2012	NYY	AL	28	28	0	0	170.1	748	194	100	95	28	3	6	10	56	3	153	6	2	12	8	.600	0	0-0	0	5.32	5.02
2013	NYY	AL	23	20	3	2	139.1	586	135	49	48	9	2	3	14	44	3	116	3	0	9	6	.600	2	0-0	0	3.77	3.10
2014	NYY	AL	4	4	0	0	20.2	96	32	19	19	6	0	2	2	6	0	12	1	0	2	2	.500	0	0-0	0	9.40	8.27
2015	NYY	AL	17	17	0	0	94.0	413	99	54	53	13	3	2	7	33	0	63	5	0	6	11	.353	0	0-0	0	4.75	5.07
	Postseason		2	1	0	0	8.1	34	7	4	4	2	0	0	0	4	0	8	0	0	1	1	.500	0	0-0	0	4.66	4.32
	6 ML YEARS		110	103	3	6	631.2	2732	667	318	304	73	11	20	40	213	11	468	28	2	46	33	.582	2	0-1	0	4.52	4.33

Eduardo Nunez

Bats: R **Throws:** R **Pos:** SS-27;3B-16;DH-14;PH-9;PR-9;LF-3;2B-1   **Ht:** 6'0" **Wt:** 195 **Born:** 6/15/1987 **Age:** 29

Year	Team	Lg	G	AB	H	2B	3B	HR	(Hm	Rd)	TB	R	RBI	RC	TBB	IBB	SO	HBP	SH	SF	SB	CS	GDP	Avg	OBP	Slg	OPS
2010	NYY	AL	30	50	14	1	0	1	(0	1)	18	12	7	8	3	0	2	0	0	0	5	0	4	.280	.321	.360	.681
2011	NYY	AL	112	309	82	18	2	5	(2	3)	119	38	30	42	22	2	37	0	6	1	22	6	6	.265	.313	.385	.698
2012	NYY	AL	38	89	26	4	1	1	(1	0)	35	14	11	15	6	0	12	1	0	4	11	2	1	.292	.330	.393	.723
2013	NYY	AL	90	304	79	17	4	3	(2	1)	113	38	28	31	20	1	51	3	4	5	10	3	3	.260	.307	.372	.679

Year	Team	Lg	G	AB	H	2B	3B	HR	(Hm	Rd)	TB	R	RBI	RC	TBB	IBB	SO	HBP	SH	SF	SB	CS	GDP	Avg	OBP	Slg	OPS
2014	Min	AL	72	204	51	7	4	4	(4	0)	78	26	24	21	5	0	31	1	3	0	9	3	7	.250	.271	.382	.654
2015	Min	AL	72	188	53	14	1	4	(3	1)	81	23	20	25	12	0	29	1	2	1	8	4	1	.282	.327	.431	.758
	Postseason		6	11	3	1	1	1	(0	1)	9	4	1	1	0	0	0	0	0	0	2	0	0	.273	.273	.818	1.091
	6 ML YEARS		414	1144	305	61	12	18	(12	6)	444	151	120	142	68	3	162	6	15	11	65	18	22	.267	.308	.388	.696

Vidal Nuno

Pitches: L **Bats:** L **Pos:** RP-25; SP-10   vee-DOLL NOON-yo   **Ht:** 5'11" **Wt:** 210 **Born:** 7/26/1987 **Age:** 28

			HOW MUCH HE PITCHED						WHAT HE GAVE UP												THE RESULTS						
Year	Team	Lg	G	GS	CG	GF	IP	BFP	H	R	ER	HR	SH	SF	HB	TBB	IBB	SO	WP	Bk	W	L	Pct	Sh	Sv-Op	Hld	ERC	ERA
2015	Reno*	AAA	8	8	0	0	50.2	210	51	22	19	7	3	0	1	8	0	41	1	0	3	3	.500	0	0- -	-	3.45	3.38
2013	NYY	AL	5	3	0	2	20.0	82	16	5	5	2	0	0	1	6	0	9	0	0	1	2	.333	0	0-0	0	2.81	2.25
2014	2 Tms		31	28	0	1	161.2	679	157	89	82	25	3	7	6	46	1	129	5	0	2	12	.143	0	0-0	0	3.98	4.56
2015	2 Tms		35	10	0	8	89.0	376	90	38	37	15	1	7	5	22	2	81	3	2	1	5	.167	0	0-0	4	4.20	3.74
14	NYY	AL	17	14	0	1	78.0	339	86	52	47	15	0	6	2	26	1	60	4	0	2	5	.286	0	0-0	0	5.18	5.42
14	Ari	NL	14	14	0	0	83.2	340	71	37	35	10	3	1	4	20	0	69	1	0	0	7	.000	0	0-0	0	2.96	3.76
15	Ari	NL	3	0	0	1	14.1	58	10	3	3	1	0	0	0	5	1	19	0	1	0	1	.000	0	0-0	0	2.01	1.88
15	Sea	AL	32	10	0	7	74.2	318	80	35	34	14	1	7	5	17	1	62	3	1	1	4	.200	0	0-0	4	4.67	4.10
	3 ML YEARS		71	41	0	11	270.2	1137	263	132	124	42	4	14	12	74	3	219	8	2	4	19	.174	0	0-0	4	3.96	4.12

Scott Oberg

Pitches: R **Bats:** R **Pos:** RP-64   **Ht:** 6'2" **Wt:** 205 **Born:** 3/13/1990 **Age:** 26

			HOW MUCH HE PITCHED						WHAT HE GAVE UP												THE RESULTS						
Year	Team	Lg	G	GS	CG	GF	IP	BFP	H	R	ER	HR	SH	SF	HB	TBB	IBB	SO	WP	Bk	W	L	Pct	Sh	Sv-Op	Hld	ERC	ERA
2012	GdJunc	R+	25	0	0	22	27.0	111	20	9	7	2	3	0	0	6	0	29	0	0	0	2	.000	0	13- -	-	1.83	2.33
2013	Mdest	A+	56	0	0	49	53.1	221	34	14	11	4	3	0	0	27	1	61	3	0	1	6	.143	0	33- -	-	2.34	1.86
2014	Tulsa	AA	27	0	0	24	27.1	109	22	8	8	1	0	1	1	6	0	21	1	0	0	1	.000	0	15- -	-	2.15	2.63
2015	Albq	AAA	7	0	0	4	8.0	39	14	1	1	0	0	0	0	2	0	11	0	0	1	0	1.000	0	2- -	-	7.17	1.13
2015	Col	NL	64	0	0	11	58.1	259	58	35	33	10	3	1	6	31	2	44	6	1	3	4	.429	0	1-3	15	5.60	5.09

Brett Oberholtzer

Pitches: L **Bats:** L **Pos:** SP-8   OH-ber-holt-zer   **Ht:** 6'1" **Wt:** 225 **Born:** 7/1/1989 **Age:** 26

			HOW MUCH HE PITCHED						WHAT HE GAVE UP												THE RESULTS						
Year	Team	Lg	G	GS	CG	GF	IP	BFP	H	R	ER	HR	SH	SF	HB	TBB	IBB	SO	WP	Bk	W	L	Pct	Sh	Sv-Op	Hld	ERC	ERA
2015	Fresno*	AAA	12	12	0	0	70.0	291	71	35	30	9	2	1	0	12	0	52	3	0	7	4	.636	0	0- -	-	3.40	3.86
2013	Hou	AL	13	10	2	1	71.2	293	66	26	22	7	0	1	1	13	0	45	0	0	4	5	.444	1	0-0	0	2.82	2.76
2014	Hou	AL	24	24	0	0	143.2	623	170	73	70	12	5	10	3	28	0	94	2	3	5	13	.278	0	0-0	0	4.22	4.39
2015	Hou	AL	8	8	0	0	38.1	171	44	21	19	4	1	2	1	17	0	27	2	0	2	2	.500	0	0-0	0	5.31	4.46
	3 ML YEARS		45	42	2	1	253.2	1087	280	120	111	23	6	13	5	58	0	166	4	3	11	20	.355	1	0-0	0	3.97	3.94

Peter O'Brien

Bats: R **Throws:** R **Pos:** PH-6;LF-3   **Ht:** 6'4" **Wt:** 235 **Born:** 7/15/1990 **Age:** 25

			BATTING																			RUNNING			AVERAGES			
Year	Team	Lg	G	AB	H	2B	3B	HR	(Hm	Rd)	TB	R	RBI	RC	TBB	IBB	SO	HBP	SH	SF	SB	CS	GDP	Avg	OBP	Slg	OPS
2012	2 Tms	Low	52	212	45	10	0	10	(-	-)	85	29	34	21	10	1	62	3	0	2	0	1	10	.212	.256	.401	.656
2013	2 Tms	Low	119	447	130	39	4	22	(-	-)	243	78	96	85	41	2	134	6	0	12	0	1	13	.291	.350	.544	.893
2014	Tampa	A+	30	112	36	9	1	10	(-	-)	77	19	19	25	4	1	29	2	0	1	0	0	1	.321	.353	.688	1.040
2014	Trntn	AA	72	274	67	14	1	23	(-	-)	152	47	51	45	16	0	77	4	0	0	0	0	8	.245	.296	.555	.851
2015	Reno	AAA	131	490	139	35	9	26	(-	-)	270	77	107	89	31	0	124	7	1	5	1	3	11	.284	.332	.551	.883
2015	Ari	NL	8	10	4	1	0	1	(1	0)	8	1	3	3	2	0	5	0	0	0	0	0	0	.400	.500	.800	1.300

Darren O'Day

Pitches: R **Bats:** R **Pos:** RP-68   **Ht:** 6'4" **Wt:** 220 **Born:** 10/22/1982 **Age:** 33

			HOW MUCH HE PITCHED						WHAT HE GAVE UP												THE RESULTS						
Year	Team	Lg	G	GS	CG	GF	IP	BFP	H	R	ER	HR	SH	SF	HB	TBB	IBB	SO	WP	Bk	W	L	Pct	Sh	Sv-Op	Hld	ERC	ERA
2008	LAA	AL	30	0	0	17	43.1	194	49	24	22	2	2	1	4	14	6	29	1	0	0	1	.000	0	0-0	1	4.20	4.57
2009	2 Tms		68	0	0	15	58.2	233	41	14	12	3	1	3	5	18	1	56	1	0	2	1	.667	0	2-2	20	2.20	1.84
2010	Tex	AL	72	0	0	14	62.0	240	43	15	14	5	1	3	5	12	2	45	0	0	6	2	.750	0	0-2	22	1.93	2.03
2011	Tex	AL	16	0	0	7	16.2	74	17	10	10	7	1	1	2	5	0	18	0	0	0	1	.000	0	0-0	3	6.45	5.40
2012	Bal	AL	69	0	0	10	67.0	263	49	17	17	6	3	1	6	14	2	69	0	0	7	1	.875	0	0-2	15	2.06	2.28
2013	Bal	AL	68	0	0	18	62.0	247	47	16	15	7	1	1	5	15	1	59	1	0	5	3	.625	0	2-6	20	2.60	2.18
2014	Bal	AL	68	0	0	18	68.2	271	42	14	13	6	1	2	8	19	4	73	0	0	5	2	.714	0	4-8	25	1.92	1.70
2015	Bal	AL	68	0	0	19	65.1	257	47	13	11	5	0	1	5	14	1	82	0	0	6	2	.750	0	6-11	18	2.09	1.52
09	NYM	NL	4	0	0	1	3.0	17	5	2	0	0	0	1	1	1	0	2	0	0	0	0	-	0	0-0	0	7.72	0.00
09	Tex	AL	64	0	0	14	55.2	216	36	12	12	3	1	2	4	17	1	54	1	0	2	1	.667	0	2-2	20	1.95	1.94
	Postseason		20	0	0	1	14.1	57	11	8	8	4	1	0	1	3	0	15	0	0	0	3	.000	0	0-0	5	3.46	5.02
	8 ML YEARS		459	0	0	118	443.2	1779	335	123	114	41	10	13	37	111	17	431	3	0	31	13	.705	0	14-31	124	2.46	2.31

Rougned Odor

Bats: L Throws: R Pos: 2B-119;PH-5;PR-1   ROOG-ned oh-DORE   Ht: 5'11" Wt: 190 Born: 2/3/1994 Age: 22

										BATTING												RUNNING			AVERAGES			
Year	Team	Lg	G	AB	H	2B	3B	HR	(Hm	Rd)	TB	R	RBI	RC	TBB	IBB	SO	HBP	SH	SF	SB	CS	GDP	Avg	OBP	Slg	OPS
2011	Spkane	A-	58	233	61	9	3	2	(-	-)	82	33	29	28	13	0	37	9	1	2	10	4	5	.262	.323	.352	.675
2012	Hkry	A	109	432	112	23	4	10	(-	-)	173	60	47	56	25	0	65	10	2	2	19	10	4	.259	.313	.400	.714
2013	MrtlBh	A+	100	377	115	33	4	5	(-	-)	171	65	59	66	26	1	67	15	2	5	27	8	7	.305	.369	.454	.822
2013	Frisco	AA	30	134	41	8	2	6	(-	-)	71	20	19	25	9	1	24	1	0	0	5	2	3	.306	.354	.530	.884
2014	Frisco	AA	32	129	36	2	1	6	(-	-)	58	21	17	18	7	0	22	0	1	1	6	3	4	.279	.314	.450	.763
2015	RdRck	AAA	30	108	38	12	2	5	(-	-)	69	26	19	28	12	1	10	2	2	0	3	1	2	.352	.426	.639	1.065
2014	Tex	AL	114	386	100	14	7	9	(4	5)	155	39	48	46	17	1	71	5	6	3	4	7	7	.259	.297	.402	.698
2015	Tex	AL	120	426	111	21	9	16	(7	9)	198	54	61	62	23	2	79	14	2	5	6	7	3	.261	.316	.465	.781
	2 ML YEARS		234	812	211	35	16	25	(11	14)	353	93	109	108	40	3	150	19	8	8	10	14	10	.260	.307	.435	.742

Jake Odorizzi

Pitches: R Bats: R Pos: SP-28   oh-duh-RIZZ-ee   Ht: 6'2" Wt: 190 Born: 3/27/1990 Age: 26

			HOW MUCH HE PITCHED					WHAT HE GAVE UP										THE RESULTS							
Year	Team	Lg	G	GS	CG	GF	IP	BFP	H	R	ER	HR	SH	SF	HB	TBB	IBB	SO	WP	Bk	W	L	Pct	Sh	Sv-Op	Hld	ERC	ERA
2012	KC	AL	2	2	0	0	7.1	34	8	4	4	1	0	0	0	4	0	4	0	0	0	1	.000	0	0-0	0	5.34	4.91
2013	TB	AL	7	4	0	2	29.2	122	28	13	13	3	0	1	2	8	0	22	1	0	0	1	.000	0	1-1	0	3.62	3.94
2014	TB	AL	31	31	0	0	168.0	719	156	79	77	20	3	8	5	59	0	174	3	0	11	13	.458	0	0-0	0	3.68	4.13
2015	TB	AL	28	28	0	0	169.1	700	149	65	63	18	4	3	3	46	0	150	5	1	9	9	.500	0	0-0	0	3.02	3.35
	4 ML YEARS		68	65	0	2	374.1	1575	341	161	157	42	7	12	10	117	0	350	9	1	20	24	.455	0	1-1	0	3.40	3.77

Eric O'Flaherty

Pitches: L Bats: L Pos: RP-41   Ht: 6'2" Wt: 220 Born: 2/5/1985 Age: 31

			HOW MUCH HE PITCHED					WHAT HE GAVE UP										THE RESULTS							
Year	Team	Lg	G	GS	CG	GF	IP	BFP	H	R	ER	HR	SH	SF	HB	TBB	IBB	SO	WP	Bk	W	L	Pct	Sh	Sv-Op	Hld	ERC	ERA
2006	Sea	AL	15	0	0	5	11.0	57	18	9	5	2	1	0	0	6	3	6	2	0	0	0	-	0	0-0	1	8.63	4.09
2007	Sea	AL	56	0	0	9	52.1	221	45	26	26	1	0	2	5	20	1	36	4	1	7	1	.875	0	0-1	4	3.04	4.47
2008	Sea	AL	7	0	0	1	6.2	42	16	15	15	2	0	1	2	4	2	4	0	0	0	1	.000	0	0-0	2	17.12	20.25
2009	Atl	NL	78	0	0	8	56.1	236	52	23	19	2	1	1	6	18	4	39	2	0	2	1	.667	0	0-2	15	3.26	3.04
2010	Atl	NL	56	0	0	7	44.0	181	37	14	12	2	1	0	1	18	2	36	3	0	3	2	.600	0	0-1	9	2.97	2.45
2011	Atl	NL	78	0	0	5	73.2	301	59	9	8	2	7	2	3	21	8	67	1	0	2	4	.333	0	0-4	32	2.13	0.98
2012	Atl	NL	64	0	0	7	57.1	230	47	14	11	3	3	1	2	19	2	46	1	0	3	0	1.000	0	0-3	28	2.71	1.73
2013	Atl	NL	19	0	0	2	18.0	70	12	5	5	2	0	1	0	5	1	11	0	0	3	0	1.000	0	0-1	12	1.93	2.50
2014	Oak	AL	21	0	0	6	20.0	80	15	5	5	3	1	0	2	4	0	15	3	0	1	0	1.000	0	1-2	3	2.68	2.25
2015	2 Tms		41	0	0	8	30.0	159	47	30	27	2	2	0	2	18	2	21	1	0	1	2	.333	0	0-1	4	7.97	8.10
15	Oak	AL	25	0	0	5	21.1	108	29	17	14	1	2	0	0	13	1	15	0	0	1	2	.333	0	0-1	3	6.26	5.91
15	NYM	NL	16	0	0	3	8.2	51	18	13	13	1	0	0	2	5	1	6	1	0	0	0	-	0	0-0	1	12.63	13.50
	Postseason		1	0	0	0	1.0	4	2	0	0	0	0	0	0	0	0	0	0	0	0	0	-	0	0-0	0	9.49	0.00
	10 ML YEARS		435	0	0	58	369.1	1577	348	150	133	21	16	8	23	133	25	281	17	1	22	11	.667	0	1-15	110	3.44	3.24

Alexi Ogando

Pitches: R Bats: R Pos: RP-64   oh-GONE-doh   Ht: 6'4" Wt: 195 Born: 10/5/1983 Age: 32

			HOW MUCH HE PITCHED					WHAT HE GAVE UP										THE RESULTS							
Year	Team	Lg	G	GS	CG	GF	IP	BFP	H	R	ER	HR	SH	SF	HB	TBB	IBB	SO	WP	Bk	W	L	Pct	Sh	Sv-Op	Hld	ERC	ERA
2010	Tex	AL	44	0	0	12	41.2	171	31	6	6	2	3	2	1	16	2	39	3	0	4	1	.800	0	0-2	7	2.34	1.30
2011	Tex	AL	31	29	1	2	169.0	693	149	73	66	16	2	3	7	43	0	126	5	0	13	8	.619	1	0-0	0	3.01	3.51
2012	Tex	AL	58	1	0	11	66.0	263	49	26	24	9	0	3	2	17	1	66	5	0	2	0	1.000	0	3-6	12	2.50	3.27
2013	Tex	AL	23	18	0	0	104.1	428	87	38	36	11	2	3	5	41	1	72	6	1	7	4	.636	0	0-0	0	3.44	3.11
2014	Tex	AL	27	0	0	10	25.0	122	33	19	19	1	1	0	1	15	1	22	4	0	2	3	.400	0	1-2	7	6.34	6.84
2015	Bos	AL	64	0	0	16	65.1	277	59	29	29	12	0	2	3	28	2	53	1	2	3	1	.750	0	0-4	12	4.43	3.99
	Postseason		18	0	0	2	19.0	81	16	6	5	3	0	0	0	10	2	23	1	0	2	0	1.000	0	0-3	4	3.95	2.37
	6 ML YEARS		247	48	1	51	471.1	1954	408	191	180	51	8	13	19	160	7	378	24	3	31	17	.646	1	4-14	38	3.32	3.44

Nefi Ogando

Pitches: R Bats: R Pos: RP-4   Ht: 6'2" Wt: 220 Born: 6/3/1989 Age: 27

			HOW MUCH HE PITCHED					WHAT HE GAVE UP										THE RESULTS							
Year	Team	Lg	G	GS	CG	GF	IP	BFP	H	R	ER	HR	SH	SF	HB	TBB	IBB	SO	WP	Bk	W	L	Pct	Sh	Sv-Op	Hld	ERC	ERA
2011	Lowell	A-	15	2	0	1	57.1	261	53	26	18	2	2	3	2	31	0	38	5	0	1	5	.167	0	0- -	-	3.71	2.83
2012	Grnvlle	A	38	0	0	12	75.1	331	72	34	31	3	1	1	5	34	1	54	7	1	4	4	.500	0	2- -	-	3.81	3.70
2013	Salem	A+	33	0	0	15	55.0	240	49	34	25	5	1	4	2	27	0	44	8	0	2	3	.400	0	3- -	-	3.86	4.09
2014	Rdng	AA	48	0	0	27	56.0	262	64	41	39	6	4	4	6	28	0	57	3	1	5	1	.833	0	7- -	-	5.76	6.27
2015	Rdng	AA	24	0	0	11	34.2	144	25	11	11	2	0	1	1	19	1	33	4	0	2	3	.400	0	2- -	-	2.97	2.86
2015	LV	AAA	21	0	0	6	28.1	127	27	11	9	1	0	0	4	12	1	22	1	0	2	2	.500	0	1- -	-	3.85	2.86
2015	Phi	NL	4	0	0	1	4.0	21	7	5	4	0	0	0	2	2	0	2	0	0	0	0	-	0	0-0	0	8.06	9.00

Ross Ohlendorf

Pitches: R Bats: R Pos: RP-21   OH-lenn-dorf   Ht: 6'4" Wt: 240 Born: 8/8/1982 Age: 33

			HOW MUCH HE PITCHED					WHAT HE GAVE UP										THE RESULTS							
Year	Team	Lg	G	GS	CG	GF	IP	BFP	H	R	ER	HR	SH	SF	HB	TBB	IBB	SO	WP	Bk	W	L	Pct	Sh	Sv-Op	Hld	ERC	ERA
2015	RdRck*	AAA	26	0	0	9	35.0	153	38	18	17	2	2	1	1	13	1	41	6	0	4	5	.444	0	0- -	-	4.21	4.37
2007	NYY	AL	6	0	0	3	6.1	26	5	2	2	1	0	0	0	2	0	9	0	0	0	0	-	0	0-0	1	2.94	2.84
2008	2 Tms		30	5	0	3	62.2	300	86	49	45	10	1	1	1	31	3	49	10	1	1	4	.200	0	0-0	4	7.16	6.46
2009	Pit	NL	29	29	0	0	176.2	725	165	80	77	25	11	8	7	53	1	109	2	1	11	10	.524	0	0-0	0	3.84	3.92

Year	Team	Lg	G	GS	CG	GF	IP	BFP	H	R	ER	HR	SH	SF	HB	TBB	IBB	SO	WP	Bk	W	L	Pct	Sh	Sv-Op	Hld	ERC	ERA
			HOW MUCH HE PITCHED						**WHAT HE GAVE UP**												**THE RESULTS**							
2010	Pit	NL	21	21	0	0	108.1	475	106	54	49	12	9	8	6	44	2	79	5	0	1	11	.083	0	0-0	0	4.20	4.07
2011	Pit	NL	9	9	0	0	38.2	194	60	38	35	9	5	3	6	15	2	27	2	0	1	3	.250	0	0-0	0	9.12	8.15
2012	SD	NL	13	9	0	2	48.2	233	62	44	42	7	4	0	5	24	0	39	2	1	4	4	.500	0	0-0	0	6.37	7.77
2013	Was	NL	16	7	0	1	60.1	247	56	22	22	8	3	0	1	14	1	45	1	0	4	1	.800	0	0-1	1	3.30	3.28
2015	Tex	AL	21	0	0	6	19.1	85	21	8	8	4	0	1	0	7	2	19	0	0	3	1	.750	0	1-2	1	4.96	3.72
08	NYY	AL	25	0	0	3	40.0	187	50	31	29	7	0	0	1	19	3	36	6	0	1	1	.500	0	0-0	4	6.39	6.53
08	Pit	NL	5	5	0	0	22.2	113	36	18	16	3	1	1	0	12	0	13	4	1	0	3	.000	0	0-0	0	8.59	6.35
	Postseason		1	0	0	1	1.0	9	4	3	3	1	0	0	1	1	0	0	0	0	0	0	-	0	0-0	0	47.63	27.00
	8 ML YEARS		145	80	0	15	521.0	2285	561	297	280	76	33	21	22	190	11	376	22	3	25	34	.424	0	1-3	13	4.84	4.84

Hector Olivera

Bats: R **Throws:** R **Pos:** 3B-21;PH-3 oh-li-VAIR-ah **Ht:** 6'2" **Wt:** 220 **Born:** 4/5/1985 **Age:** 31

Year	Team	Lg	G	AB	H	2B	3B	HR	(Hm	Rd)	TB	R	RBI	RC	TBB	IBB	SO	HBP	SH	SF	SB	CS	GDP	Avg	OBP	Slg	OPS
											BATTING										**RUNNING**			**AVERAGES**			
2015	3 Tms	Low	12	33	6	1	0	0	(-	-)	7	5	0	2	4	0	3	0	0	0	0	0	3	.182	.270	.212	.482
2015	Gwnntt	AAA	10	39	9	3	0	0	(-	-)	12	5	3	3	2	0	4	1	0	0	0	0	1	.231	.286	.308	.593
2015	Atl	NL	24	79	20	4	1	2	(0	2)	32	4	11	11	5	0	12	2	0	1	0	0	2	.253	.310	.405	.715

Edgar Olmos

Pitches: L **Bats:** L **Pos:** RP-4; SP-2 OAL-moase **Ht:** 6'4" **Wt:** 220 **Born:** 4/12/1990 **Age:** 26

Year	Team	Lg	G	GS	CG	GF	IP	BFP	H	R	ER	HR	SH	SF	HB	TBB	IBB	SO	WP	Bk	W	L	Pct	Sh	Sv-Op	Hld	ERC	ERA
			HOW MUCH HE PITCHED						**WHAT HE GAVE UP**												**THE RESULTS**							
2011	Jupiter	A+	28	28	0	0	127.2	627	167	110	94	13	3	8	10	81	2	101	16	2	4	17	.190	0	0--	-	7.22	6.63
2012	Jupiter	A+	24	13	0	0	89.1	394	83	50	43	5	0	4	7	48	0	78	10	0	1	5	.167	0	0--	-	4.23	4.33
2012	Jaxnvl	AA	9	1	0	3	16.2	72	8	1	1	0	1	0	0	16	0	13	2	0	0	1	.000	0	0--	-	2.66	0.54
2013	Jaxnvl	AA	38	0	0	8	50.1	222	47	20	14	1	1	0	1	27	0	41	6	0	4	2	.667	0	1--	-	3.71	2.50
2014	Jaxnvl	AA	18	0	0	10	26.1	113	22	16	13	5	2	2	1	13	0	16	1	0	1	0	1.000	0	2--	-	4.30	4.44
2014	NewOr	AAA	33	0	0	15	51.1	211	49	24	22	4	1	0	2	17	1	44	2	0	2	3	.400	0	1--	-	3.65	3.86
2015	Tacom	AAA	20	2	0	7	33.0	146	32	14	13	0	1	2	6	13	1	34	3	0	1	1	.500	0	1--	-	3.81	3.55
2013	Mia	NL	5	0	0	2	5.0	24	7	9	4	2	1	0	0	3	1	2	0	0	0	1	.000	0	0-0	0	9.81	7.20
2015	Sea	AL	6	2	0	1	14.0	67	16	8	7	1	0	1	1	8	1	4	1	0	1	0	1.000	0	0-0	0	5.39	4.50
	2 ML YEARS		11	2	0	3	19.0	91	23	17	11	3	1	1	1	11	2	6	1	0	1	1	.500	0	0-0	0	6.48	5.21

Tyler Olson

Pitches: L **Bats:** R **Pos:** RP-11 **Ht:** 6'3" **Wt:** 195 **Born:** 10/2/1989 **Age:** 26

Year	Team	Lg	G	GS	CG	GF	IP	BFP	H	R	ER	HR	SH	SF	HB	TBB	IBB	SO	WP	Bk	W	L	Pct	Sh	Sv-Op	Hld	ERC	ERA
			HOW MUCH HE PITCHED						**WHAT HE GAVE UP**												**THE RESULTS**							
2013	Everett	A-	18	8	1	3	54.0	243	61	33	26	1	1	3	3	20	0	48	6	0	1	4	.333	1	1--	-	4.25	4.33
2014	Hi Dsrt	A+	5	5	0	0	23.0	100	21	8	8	0	0	4	0	10	0	27	2	0	2	1	.667	0	0--	-	3.15	3.13
2014	Jacksn	AA	22	22	1	0	125.1	528	126	55	49	8	7	4	7	25	0	100	2	0	10	7	.588	0	0--	-	3.27	3.52
2015	Tacom	AAA	25	6	0	3	54.1	243	61	40	27	7	1	2	2	17	0	53	0	2	3	5	.375	0	1--	-	4.67	4.47
2015	Sea	AL	11	0	0	4	13.1	65	18	8	8	2	2	0	1	10	7	8	0	1	1	1	.500	0	0-0	1	7.64	5.40

Mike Olt

Bats: R **Throws:** R **Pos:** 3B-26;1B-5;PH-3 AULT **Ht:** 6'2" **Wt:** 210 **Born:** 8/27/1988 **Age:** 27

Year	Team	Lg	G	AB	H	2B	3B	HR	(Hm	Rd)	TB	R	RBI	RC	TBB	IBB	SO	HBP	SH	SF	SB	CS	GDP	Avg	OBP	Slg	OPS
											BATTING										**RUNNING**			**AVERAGES**			
2015	Iowa*	AAA	59	211	56	14	0	9	(-	-)	97	30	25	32	20	0	71	2	0	1	0	1	4	.265	.330	.460	.793
2012	Tex	AL	16	33	5	1	0	0	(0	0)	6	2	5	2	5	0	13	0	0	2	1	1	1	.152	.250	.182	.432
2014	ChC	NL	89	225	36	8	0	12	(4	8)	80	23	33	19	25	0	100	3	0	5	0	1	3	.160	.248	.356	.604
2015	2 Tms		30	94	18	0	0	4	(2	2)	30	7	5	4	7	0	35	1	0	0	0	1	2	.191	.255	.319	.574
15	ChC	NL	6	15	2	0	0	1	(2	1)	5	1	1	0	0	0	6	1	0	0	0	0	0	.133	.188	.333	.521
15	CWS	AL	24	79	16	0	0	3	(2	1)	25	6	4	4	7	0	29	0	0	0	0	1	2	.203	.267	.316	.584
	3 ML YEARS		135	352	59	9	0	16	(6	10)	116	32	43	25	37	0	148	4	0	7	1	3	6	.168	.250	.330	.580

Shawn O'Malley

Bats: B **Throws:** R **Pos:** CF-14;PH-8;LF-4;3B-3;RF-3;PR-3;DH-1 **Ht:** 5'11" **Wt:** 175 **Born:** 12/28/1987 **Age:** 28

Year	Team	Lg	G	AB	H	2B	3B	HR	(Hm	Rd)	TB	R	RBI	RC	TBB	IBB	SO	HBP	SH	SF	SB	CS	GDP	Avg	OBP	Slg	OPS
											BATTING										**RUNNING**			**AVERAGES**			
2011	Mont	AA	79	308	85	8	5	1	(-	-)	106	55	23	43	42	2	58	4	7	1	24	13	2	.276	.369	.344	.713
2012	Drham	AAA	67	216	53	4	2	2	(-	-)	67	32	18	24	17	0	49	3	7	4	11	1	1	.245	.304	.310	.614
2012	Mont	AA	35	121	28	3	3	0	(-	-)	37	22	5	14	17	0	24	2	3	1	7	3	1	.231	.333	.306	.639
2013	Mont	AA	91	321	84	12	6	3	(-	-)	117	53	32	46	32	0	60	6	11	3	24	3	3	.262	.337	.364	.702
2014	Ark	AA	11	32	6	0	1	0	(-	-)	8	3	5	3	6	0	8	0	1	1	1	0	0	.188	.308	.250	.558
2014	Salt Lk	AAA	89	318	105	19	9	3	(-	-)	151	60	38	65	39	0	44	7	9	3	13	4	4	.330	.411	.475	.886
2015	Tacom	AAA	89	310	92	11	5	5	(-	-)	128	50	39	47	19	1	47	5	8	2	20	7	2	.297	.345	.413	.758
2014	LAA	AL	11	16	3	0	0	0	(0	0)	3	3	1	1	0	0	8	0	0	0	2	0	0	.188	.188	.188	.375
2015	Sea	AL	24	42	11	1	0	1	(0	1)	15	10	7	11	12	0	14	0	2	1	3	0	0	.262	.418	.357	.775
	2 ML YEARS		35	58	14	1	0	1	(0	1)	18	13	8	12	12	0	22	0	2	1	5	0	0	.241	.366	.310	.677

Paulo Orlando

Bats: R **Throws:** R **Pos:** RF-45;LF-37;PR-7;CF-5;PH-3;DH-2 **Ht:** 6'2" **Wt:** 210 **Born:** 11/1/1985 **Age:** 30

												BATTING									RUNNING			AVERAGES			
Year	Team	Lg	G	AB	H	2B	3B	HR	(Hm	Rd)	TB	R	RBI	RC	TBB	IBB	SO	HBP	SH	SF	SB	CS	GDP	Avg	OBP	Slg	OPS
2011	Omha	AAA	58	187	44	10	2	1	(-	-)	61	24	27	17	11	0	30	1	6	0	6	3	6	.235	.281	.326	.608
2011	NWArk	AA	45	167	51	5	10	4	(-	-)	88	30	24	32	13	0	35	3	2	2	8	4	3	.305	.362	.527	.889
2012	NWArk	AA	116	420	117	18	2	6	(-	-)	157	54	40	56	30	2	57	4	3	5	21	6	11	.279	.329	.374	.703
2013	Omha	AAA	92	293	81	9	3	5	(-	-)	111	41	46	38	22	0	56	1	7	3	8	3	3	.276	.326	.379	.705
2014	Omha	AAA	136	501	151	21	9	6	(-	-)	208	61	63	80	39	1	86	5	5	4	34	9	9	.301	.355	.415	.770
2015	Omha	AAA	41	170	47	11	0	3	(-	-)	67	20	17	23	8	1	32	1	1	2	9	0	1	.276	.309	.394	.704
2015	KC	AL	86	241	60	14	6	7	(4	3)	107	31	27	30	5	0	53	2	2	1	3	3	0	.249	.269	.444	.713

Ryan O'Rourke

Pitches: L **Bats:** R **Pos:** RP-28 **Ht:** 6'3" **Wt:** 230 **Born:** 4/30/1988 **Age:** 28

				HOW MUCH HE PITCHED						WHAT HE GAVE UP									THE RESULTS						
Year	Team	Lg	G	GS	CG	GF	IP	BFP	H	R	ER	HR	SH	SF	HB	TBB	IBB	SO	WP	Bk	W	L	Pct	Sh	Sv-Op	Hld	ERC	ERA
2011	Beloit	A	34	17	0	5	110.1	472	116	45	39	7	7	4	2	32	1	107	5	2	5	5	.500	0	1- -	-	3.72	3.18
2012	2 Tms	Low	38	2	0	12	74.1	324	83	51	46	8	2	3	1	20	2	72	9	0	2	6	.250	0	2- -	-	4.22	5.57
2013	FtMyrs	A+	17	0	0	7	28.1	110	19	7	7	3	1	1	0	8	0	21	2	0	5	1	.833	0	3- -	-	2.02	2.22
2013	NwBrit	AA	17	0	0	5	17.1	72	15	10	9	0	1	1	0	7	2	19	3	0	0	2	.000	0	2- -	-	2.54	4.67
2014	NwBrit	AA	50	0	0	17	40.2	174	36	24	19	5	1	2	0	16	1	52	1	0	2	4	.333	0	4- -	-	3.46	4.20
2015	Roch	AAA	20	0	0	8	13.2	61	13	9	9	1	0	2	0	7	0	22	1	0	0	0	-	0	0- -	-	3.95	5.93
2015	Min	AL	28	0	0	7	22.0	97	16	15	15	3	1	1	0	15	2	24	2	0	0	0	-	0	0-0	0	3.69	6.14

David Ortiz

Bats: L **Throws:** L **Pos:** DH-134;1B-9;PH-3 **Ht:** 6'3" **Wt:** 230 **Born:** 11/18/1975 **Age:** 40

												BATTING									RUNNING			AVERAGES			
Year	Team	Lg	G	AB	H	2B	3B	HR	(Hm	Rd)	TB	R	RBI	RC	TBB	IBB	SO	HBP	SH	SF	SB	CS	GDP	Avg	OBP	Slg	OPS
1997	Min	AL	15	49	16	3	0	1	(0	1)	22	10	6	7	2	0	19	0	0	0	0	0	1	.327	.353	.449	.802
1998	Min	AL	86	278	77	20	0	9	(2	7)	124	47	46	46	39	3	72	5	0	4	1	0	8	.277	.371	.446	.817
1999	Min	AL	10	20	0	0	0	0	(0	0)	0	1	0	0	5	0	12	0	0	0	0	0	2	.000	.200	.000	.200
2000	Min	AL	130	415	117	36	1	10	(7	3)	185	59	63	66	57	2	81	0	0	6	1	0	13	.282	.364	.446	.810
2001	Min	AL	89	303	71	17	1	18	(6	12)	144	46	48	46	40	8	68	1	1	2	1	0	6	.234	.324	.475	.799
2002	Min	AL	125	412	112	32	1	20	(5	15)	206	52	75	62	43	0	87	3	0	8	1	2	5	.272	.339	.500	.839
2003	Bos	AL	128	448	129	39	2	31	(17	14)	265	79	101	80	58	8	83	1	0	2	0	0	9	.288	.369	.592	.961
2004	Bos	AL	150	582	175	47	3	41	(17	24)	351	94	139	127	75	8	133	4	0	8	0	0	12	.301	.380	.603	.983
2005	Bos	AL	159	601	180	40	1	47	(20	27)	363	119	148	137	102	9	124	1	0	9	1	0	13	.300	.397	.604	1.001
2006	Bos	AL	151	558	160	29	2	54	(22	32)	355	115	137	129	119	23	117	4	0	5	1	0	12	.287	.413	.636	1.049
2007	Bos	AL	149	549	182	52	1	35	(16	19)	341	116	117	138	111	12	103	4	0	3	3	1	16	.332	.445	.621	1.066
2008	Bos	AL	109	416	110	30	1	23	(12	11)	211	74	89	82	70	12	74	1	1	3	1	0	11	.264	.369	.507	.877
2009	Bos	AL	150	541	129	35	1	28	(18	10)	250	77	99	79	74	5	134	5	0	7	0	2	9	.238	.332	.462	.794
2010	Bos	AL	145	518	140	36	1	32	(15	17)	274	86	102	94	82	14	145	2	0	4	0	1	12	.270	.370	.529	.899
2011	Bos	AL	146	525	162	40	1	29	(13	16)	291	84	96	97	78	12	83	1	0	1	1	1	24	.309	.398	.554	.953
2012	Bos	AL	90	324	103	26	0	23	(13	10)	198	65	60	75	56	13	51	0	0	3	0	1	6	.318	.415	.611	1.026
2013	Bos	AL	137	518	160	38	2	30	(12	18)	292	84	103	102	76	27	88	1	0	5	4	0	21	.309	.395	.564	.959
2014	Bos	AL	142	518	136	27	0	35	(11	24)	268	59	104	91	75	22	95	3	0	6	0	0	18	.263	.355	.517	.873
2015	Bos	AL	146	528	144	37	0	37	(15	22)	292	73	108	87	77	16	95	0	0	9	0	1	16	.273	.360	.553	.913
	Postseason		82	295	87	21	2	17	(12	5)	163	51	60	69	57	11	71	2	0	3	0	1	4	.295	.409	.553	.962
	19 ML YEARS		2257	8103	2303	584	18	503	(221	282)	4432	1340	1641	1545	1239	194	1664	36	2	85	15	9	214	.284	.378	.547	.925

Josh Osich

Pitches: L **Bats:** L **Pos:** RP-35 OH-sitch **Ht:** 6'2" **Wt:** 230 **Born:** 9/3/1988 **Age:** 27

				HOW MUCH HE PITCHED						WHAT HE GAVE UP									THE RESULTS						
Year	Team	Lg	G	GS	CG	GF	IP	BFP	H	R	ER	HR	SH	SF	HB	TBB	IBB	SO	WP	Bk	W	L	Pct	Sh	Sv-Op	Hld	ERC	ERA
2011	Ms	Jap	28	-	10	-	232.0	885	156	42	37	5	-	-	6	36	-	276	10	1	18	6	.750	6	0- -	-	1.37	1.44
2012	SnJos	A+	27	2	0	6	32.1	138	34	14	13	1	1	1	0	11	0	34	3	0	0	2	.000	0	1- -	-	3.67	3.62
2013	SnJos	A+	34	0	0	20	40.1	162	32	13	11	1	1	0	0	10	1	48	4	1	3	1	.750	0	12- -	-	1.94	2.45
2013	Rchmd	AA	22	0	0	9	29.2	122	26	16	16	2	2	0	0	12	0	28	4	0	2	3	.400	0	3- -	-	3.28	4.85
2014	Rchmd	AA	28	0	0	3	33.1	143	28	18	14	4	2	0	1	20	0	27	4	0	1	0	1.000	0	0- -	-	4.33	3.78
2015	Rchmd	AA	31	0	0	28	34.0	137	23	6	6	1	2	0	1	10	1	34	4	0	1	0	1.000	0	19- -	-	1.66	1.59
2015	Scrmto	AAA	6	0	0	5	7.0	27	3	1	0	0	0	0	2	0	11	1	0	1	0	1.000	0	1- -	-	0.80	0.00
2015	SF	NL	35	0	0	6	28.2	120	24	12	7	4	1	1	0	8	0	27	2	0	2	0	1.000	0	0-2	11	2.88	2.20

Sean O'Sullivan

Pitches: R **Bats:** R **Pos:** SP-13 **Ht:** 6'1" **Wt:** 255 **Born:** 9/1/1987 **Age:** 28

				HOW MUCH HE PITCHED						WHAT HE GAVE UP									THE RESULTS						
Year	Team	Lg	G	GS	CG	GF	IP	BFP	H	R	ER	HR	SH	SF	HB	TBB	IBB	SO	WP	Bk	W	L	Pct	Sh	Sv-Op	Hld	ERC	ERA
2015	LV*	AAA	9	9	0	0	56.1	233	48	23	20	3	2	0	1	19	0	41	2	1	5	2	.714	0	0- -	-	2.80	3.20
2009	LAA	AL	12	10	0	1	51.2	227	60	34	34	12	2	4	1	16	1	29	1	0	4	2	.667	0	0-0	-	5.66	5.92
2010	2 Tms	AL	19	14	0	3	83.2	368	90	53	51	15	0	3	1	31	2	43	4	2	4	6	.400	0	0-0	-	4.93	5.49
2011	KC	AL	12	10	0	1	58.1	273	78	52	47	10	3	4	2	26	1	19	3	0	2	6	.250	0	0-1	-	7.03	7.25
2013	SD	NL	7	3	0	2	25.0	118	31	12	11	0	1	2	1	14	1	12	0	0	0	2	.000	0	0-0	-	5.40	3.96
2014	Phi	NL	3	2	0	0	12.2	52	15	9	9	3	1	0	0	2	0	7	0	0	0	1	.000	0	0-0	-	5.29	6.39
2015	Phi	NL	13	13	0	0	71.0	328	94	49	48	16	4	5	6	20	5	35	3	0	1	6	.143	0	0-0	-	6.67	6.08
	10	LAA	AL	5	1	0	2	13.0	49	7	3	3	1	0	0	0	4	2	6	0	0	1	0	1.000	0	0-0	-	1.33	2.08
	10	KC	AL	14	13	0	1	70.2	319	83	50	48	14	0	3	1	27	0	37	4	2	3	6	.333	0	0-0	-	5.76	6.11
	6 ML YEARS		66	52	0	8	302.1	1366	368	209	200	56	11	18	11	109	10	145	11	2	11	23	.324	0	0-1	-	5.92	5.95

Roberto Osuna

Pitches: R **Bats:** R **Pos:** RP-68   **Ht:** 6'2" **Wt:** 230 **Born:** 2/7/1995 **Age:** 21

		HOW MUCH HE PITCHED					WHAT HE GAVE UP										THE RESULTS						
Year	Team	Lg	G	GS	CG	GF	IP	BFP	H	R	ER	HR	SH	SF	HB	TBB	IBB	SO	WP	Bk	W	L	Pct	Sh	Sv-Op	Hld	ERC	ERA
2012	2 Tms	Low	12	9	0	0	43.2	180	32	14	11	2	1	2	3	15	0	49	3	1	2	0	1.000	0	0--	-	2.34	2.27
2013	Lnsng	A	10	10	0	0	42.1	176	39	28	26	6	2	0	2	11	0	51	8	0	3	5	.375	0	0--	-	3.55	5.53
2014	2 Tms	Low	8	8	0	0	23.0	104	28	16	16	3	1	0	3	9	0	32	0	0	0	2	.000	0	0--	-	6.26	6.26
2015	Tor	AL	68	0	0	39	69.2	271	48	21	20	7	1	2	1	16	2	75	5	0	1	6	.143	0	20-23	7	1.89	2.58

Shohei Otani

Pitches: R **Bats:** L **Pos:** P   sho-HAY   **Ht:** 6'3" **Wt:** 189 **Born:** 7/5/1994 **Age:** 21

		HOW MUCH HE PITCHED					WHAT HE GAVE UP										THE RESULTS						
Year	Team	Lg	G	GS	CG	GF	IP	BFP	H	R	ER	HR	SH	SF	HB	TBB	IBB	SO	WP	Bk	W	L	Pct	Sh	Sv-Op	Hld	ERC	ERA
2013	Nippon	IND	13	11	0	-	61.2	274	57	30	29	4	-	-	8	33	0	46	2	0	3	0	1.000	0	0--	-	4.47	4.23
2014	Nippon	IND	24	24	3	0	155.1	639	125	50	45	7	-	-	4	57	0	179	6	1	11	4	.733	2	0--	-	2.66	2.61
2015	Nippon	IND	22	22	5	0	160.2	621	100	40	40	7	-	-	3	46	0	196	9	0	15	5	.750	3	0--	-	1.57	2.24

Dan Otero

Pitches: R **Bats:** R **Pos:** RP-41   oh-TEHR-oh   **Ht:** 6'3" **Wt:** 215 **Born:** 2/19/1985 **Age:** 31

		HOW MUCH HE PITCHED					WHAT HE GAVE UP										THE RESULTS						
Year	Team	Lg	G	GS	CG	GF	IP	BFP	H	R	ER	HR	SH	SF	HB	TBB	IBB	SO	WP	Bk	W	L	Pct	Sh	Sv-Op	Hld	ERC	ERA
2015	Nashv*	AAA	15	2	0	4	27.2	108	23	7	6	1	1	0	0	4	1	19	0	0	2	0	1.000	0	0--	-	1.86	1.95
2012	SF	NL	12	0	0	4	12.1	57	19	11	8	0	0	0	2	2	1	8	1	0	0	0	-	0	0-0	6	5.18	5.84
2013	Oak	AL	33	0	0	8	39.0	159	42	7	6	0	1	0	0	6	1	27	0	0	2	0	1.000	0	0-1	8	2.90	1.38
2014	Oak	AL	72	0	0	14	86.2	349	80	24	22	4	4	3	2	15	7	45	1	0	8	2	.800	0	1-4	12	2.47	2.28
2015	Oak	AL	41	0	0	6	46.2	204	64	35	35	7	1	3	2	6	2	28	1	0	2	4	.333	0	0-1	2	5.70	6.75
	Postseason		5	0	0	0	7.0	28	7	2	2	0	1	0	0	1	0	3	0	0	1	0	1.000	0	0-0	1	2.52	2.57
	4 ML YEARS		158	0	0	32	184.2	769	205	77	71	11	6	6	6	29	11	108	3	0	12	6	.667	0	1-6	22	3.54	3.46

Adam Ottavino

Pitches: R **Bats:** B **Pos:** RP-10   ott-tah-VEE-no   **Ht:** 6'5" **Wt:** 220 **Born:** 11/22/1985 **Age:** 30

		HOW MUCH HE PITCHED					WHAT HE GAVE UP										THE RESULTS						
Year	Team	Lg	G	GS	CG	GF	IP	BFP	H	R	ER	HR	SH	SF	HB	TBB	IBB	SO	WP	Bk	W	L	Pct	Sh	Sv-Op	Hld	ERC	ERA
2010	StL	NL	5	3	0	0	22.1	110	37	21	21	5	1	0	0	9	1	12	1	0	0	2	.000	0	0-0	0	9.22	8.46
2012	Col	NL	53	0	0	6	79.0	339	76	42	40	9	3	1	1	34	7	81	8	0	5	1	.833	0	0-2	6	4.01	4.56
2013	Col	NL	51	0	0	6	78.1	335	73	27	23	5	6	4	2	31	5	78	9	1	1	3	.250	0	0-0	8	3.42	2.64
2014	Col	NL	75	0	0	16	65.0	272	67	26	26	6	2	3	4	16	1	70	4	0	1	4	.200	0	1-6	21	3.87	3.60
2015	Col	NL	10	0	0	5	10.1	35	3	0	0	0	0	0	1	2	0	13	0	0	1	0	1.000	0	3-3	3	0.56	0.00
	5 ML YEARS		194	3	0	32	255.0	1091	256	116	110	25	12	8	8	92	14	254	22	1	8	10	.444	0	4-11	38	3.99	3.88

Henry Owens

Pitches: L **Bats:** L **Pos:** SP-11   **Ht:** 6'6" **Wt:** 220 **Born:** 7/21/1992 **Age:** 23

		HOW MUCH HE PITCHED					WHAT HE GAVE UP										THE RESULTS						
Year	Team	Lg	G	GS	CG	GF	IP	BFP	H	R	ER	HR	SH	SF	HB	TBB	IBB	SO	WP	Bk	W	L	Pct	Sh	Sv-Op	Hld	ERC	ERA
2012	Grnvlle	A	23	22	0	0	101.2	450	100	58	55	10	4	2	6	47	0	130	5	0	12	5	.706	0	0--	-	4.43	4.87
2013	Salem	A+	20	20	0	0	104.2	431	66	39	34	6	3	1	7	53	0	123	8	0	8	5	.615	0	0--	-	2.51	2.92
2013	Portlnd	AA	6	6	0	0	30.1	125	18	8	6	3	0	0	2	15	0	46	3	0	3	1	.750	0	0--	-	2.51	1.78
2014	Portlnd	AA	20	20	3	0	121.0	493	89	36	35	6	0	1	3	47	0	126	6	0	14	4	.778	2	0--	-	2.42	2.60
2014	Pwtckt	AAA	6	6	0	0	38.0	156	32	17	17	4	1	1	3	12	0	44	0	0	3	1	.750	0	0--	-	3.29	4.03
2015	Pwtckt	AAA	21	21	0	0	122.1	499	84	47	43	7	0	5	3	56	0	103	4	1	3	8	.273	0	0--	-	2.48	3.16
2015	Bos	AL	11	11	0	0	63.0	272	62	35	32	7	0	2	3	24	0	50	4	1	4	4	.500	0	0-0	0	4.18	4.57

Chris Owings

Bats: R **Throws:** R **Pos:** 2B-115;SS-35;PH-10;PR-1   **Ht:** 5'10" **Wt:** 190 **Born:** 8/12/1991 **Age:** 24

			BATTING																	RUNNING			AVERAGES			
Year	Team	Lg	G	AB	H	2B	3B	HR	(Hm	Rd)	TB	R	RBI	RC	TBB	IBB	SO	HBP	SH	SF	SB	CS	GDP	Avg	OBP	Slg	OPS
2013	Ari	NL	20	55	16	5	0	0	(0	0)	21	5	5	7	6	1	10	0	0	0	2	0	0	.291	.361	.382	.742
2014	Ari	NL	91	310	81	15	6	6	(1	5)	126	34	26	38	16	0	67	2	2	2	8	1	4	.261	.300	.406	.706
2015	Ari	NL	147	515	117	27	5	4	(3	1)	166	59	43	41	26	3	144	1	7	3	16	4	9	.227	.264	.322	.587
	3 ML YEARS		258	880	214	47	11	10	(4	6)	313	98	74	86	48	4	221	3	9	5	26	5	13	.243	.283	.356	.639

Marcell Ozuna

Bats: R **Throws:** R **Pos:** CF-111;RF-15;PH-2   oh-ZUNE-uh   **Ht:** 6'1" **Wt:** 225 **Born:** 11/12/1990 **Age:** 25

			BATTING																	RUNNING			AVERAGES			
Year	Team	Lg	G	AB	H	2B	3B	HR	(Hm	Rd)	TB	R	RBI	RC	TBB	IBB	SO	HBP	SH	SF	SB	CS	GDP	Avg	OBP	Slg	OPS
2015	NewOr*	AAA	33	120	38	12	1	5	(-	-)	67	21	11	25	11	1	23	1	0	0	1	0	6	.317	.379	.558	.937
2013	Mia	NL	70	275	73	17	4	3	(0	3)	107	31	32	35	13	0	57	2	1	0	5	1	6	.265	.303	.389	.693
2014	Mia	NL	153	565	152	26	5	23	(12	11)	257	72	85	74	41	1	164	1	0	5	3	1	12	.269	.317	.455	.772
2015	Mia	NL	123	459	119	27	0	10	(2	8)	176	47	44	48	30	1	110	3	0	2	2	3	10	.259	.308	.383	.691
	3 ML YEARS		346	1299	344	70	9	36	(14	22)	540	150	161	157	84	2	331	6	1	7	10	5	28	.265	.311	.416	.727

Jordan Pacheco

Bats: R Throws: R Pos: C-18;PH-12;1B-2;3B-1 puh-CHECK-oh Ht: 6'1" Wt: 200 Born: 1/30/1986 Age: 30

Year	Team	Lg	G	AB	H	2B	3B	HR	(Hm	Rd)	TB	R	RBI	RC	TBB	IBB	SO	HBP	SH	SF	SB	CS	GDP	Avg	OBP	Slg	OPS
2015	Reno*	AAA	58	161	33	11	1	2	(-	-)	52	26	15	17	19	1	26	3	0	2	0	0	5	.205	.297	.323	.620
2011	Col	NL	21	84	24	1	0	2	(2	0)	31	5	14	12	3	0	9	1	0	0	0	0	2	.286	.318	.369	.687
2012	Col	NL	132	475	147	32	3	5	(4	1)	200	51	54	64	22	2	61	3	1	4	7	2	13	.309	.341	.421	.762
2013	Col	NL	95	247	59	15	0	1	(1	0)	77	23	22	21	10	0	38	3	1	1	0	0	4	.239	.276	.312	.588
2014	2 Tms	NL	69	153	39	10	1	0	(0	0)	51	10	16	17	9	0	27	1	1	1	0	0	6	.255	.299	.333	.632
2015	Ari	NL	29	66	16	0	0	2	(2	0)	22	8	8	6	9	0	14	1	0	2	1	0	6	.242	.333	.333	.667
14	Col	NL	22	72	17	6	1	0	(0	0)	25	4	8	8	6	0	15	1	0	1	0	0	3	.236	.300	.347	.647
14	Ari	NL	47	81	22	4	0	0	(0	0)	26	6	8	9	3	0	12	0	1	0	0	0	3	.272	.298	.321	.619
	5 ML YEARS		346	1025	285	58	4	10	(9	1)	381	97	114	120	53	2	149	9	3	8	8	2	31	.278	.317	.372	.689

Angel Pagan

Bats: B Throws: R Pos: CF-124;PH-9;DH-1;PR-1 AIN-jell pah-GAHN Ht: 6'2" Wt: 200 Born: 7/2/1981 Age: 34

Year	Team	Lg	G	AB	H	2B	3B	HR	(Hm	Rd)	TB	R	RBI	RC	TBB	IBB	SO	HBP	SH	SF	SB	CS	GDP	Avg	OBP	Slg	OPS
2006	ChC	NL	77	170	42	6	2	5	(4	1)	67	28	18	21	15	0	28	0	1	1	4	2	3	.247	.306	.394	.701
2007	ChC	NL	71	148	39	10	2	4	(3	1)	65	21	21	23	10	0	32	0	1	2	4	1	0	.264	.306	.439	.745
2008	NYM	NL	31	91	25	7	1	0	(0	0)	34	12	13	15	11	0	18	0	1	2	4	0	0	.275	.346	.374	.720
2009	NYM	NL	88	343	105	22	11	6	(5	1)	167	54	32	53	25	2	56	0	5	3	14	7	3	.306	.350	.487	.837
2010	NYM	NL	151	579	168	31	7	11	(6	5)	246	80	69	90	44	5	97	1	6	3	37	9	9	.290	.340	.425	.765
2011	NYM	NL	123	478	125	24	4	7	(4	3)	178	68	56	64	44	4	62	1	4	5	32	7	4	.262	.322	.372	.694
2012	SF	NL	154	605	174	38	15	8	(1	7)	266	95	56	91	48	5	97	0	2	4	29	7	6	.288	.338	.440	.778
2013	SF	NL	71	280	79	16	3	5	(3	2)	116	44	30	41	23	0	36	0	2	9	4	1	.282	.334	.414	.749
2014	SF	NL	96	383	115	21	3	3	(1	2)	149	56	27	50	25	1	53	1	1	3	16	6	5	.300	.342	.389	.731
2015	SF	NL	133	512	134	21	3	3	(1	2)	170	55	37	48	32	0	93	1	0	6	12	4	12	.262	.303	.332	.635
	Postseason		16	69	13	3	1	2	(1	1)	24	10	6	3	4	0	12	0	0	1	1	1	0	.188	.230	.348	.578
	10 ML YEARS		995	3589	1006	196	50	52	(28	24)	1458	513	359	496	277	17	572	4	21	31	161	47	43	.280	.330	.406	.736

Joe Panik

Bats: L Throws: R Pos: 2B-99;PH-4 PAN-ick Ht: 6'1" Wt: 190 Born: 10/30/1990 Age: 25

Year	Team	Lg	G	AB	H	2B	3B	HR	(Hm	Rd)	TB	R	RBI	RC	TBB	IBB	SO	HBP	SH	SF	SB	CS	GDP	Avg	OBP	Slg	OPS
2011	SlKzr	A-	69	270	92	10	3	6	(-	-)	126	49	54	52	28	0	25	2	0	4	13	5	8	.341	.401	.467	.868
2012	SnJos	A+	130	535	159	27	4	7	(-	-)	215	93	76	85	58	1	54	5	2	5	10	4	13	.297	.368	.402	.770
2013	Rchmd	AA	137	522	134	27	4	4	(-	-)	181	64	57	66	58	1	68	5	8	6	10	5	16	.257	.333	.347	.680
2014	Fresno	AAA	74	293	94	14	4	5	(-	-)	131	50	45	51	27	2	33	3	1	2	3	2	9	.321	.382	.447	.829
2014	SF	NL	73	269	82	10	2	1	(0	1)	99	31	18	33	16	0	33	0	1	1	0	0	4	.305	.343	.368	.711
2015	SF	NL	100	382	119	27	2	8	(4 | 4)	174	59	37	60	38	0	42	1	5	3	4	3	2	7	.312	.378	.455	.833
	Postseason		17	73	17	2	2	1	(1	0)	26	7	8	7	4	0	6	0	1	0	0	0	1	.233	.273	.356	.629
	2 ML YEARS		173	651	201	37	4	9	(4	5)	273	90	55	93	54	0	75	5	4	5	3	2	11	.309	.364	.419	.783

Jonathan Papelbon

Pitches: R Bats: R Pos: RP-59 PAHP-ill-bonn Ht: 6'4" Wt: 225 Born: 11/23/1980 Age: 35

			HOW MUCH HE PITCHED						WHAT HE GAVE UP										THE RESULTS						
Year	Team	Lg	G	GS	CG	GF	IP	BFP	H	R	ER	HR	SH	SF	HB	TBB	IBB	SO	WP	Bk	W	L	Pct	Sh	Sv-Op	Hld	ERC	ERA
2005	Bos	AL	17	3	0	4	34.0	148	33	11	10	4	1	0	3	17	2	34	1	0	3	1	.750	0	0-1	4	4.82	2.65
2006	Bos	AL	59	0	0	49	68.1	257	40	8	7	3	1	2	1	13	2	75	2	0	4	2	.667	0	35-41	1	1.22	0.92
2007	Bos	AL	59	0	0	53	58.1	224	30	12	12	5	0	0	4	15	0	84	0	0	1	3	.250	0	37-40	2	1.43	1.85
2008	Bos	AL	67	0	0	62	69.1	273	58	24	18	4	4	1	0	8	0	77	2	0	5	4	.556	0	41-46	0	1.92	2.34
2009	Bos	AL	66	0	0	59	68.0	285	54	15	14	5	1	2	4	24	1	76	0	0	1	1	.500	0	38-41	0	2.78	1.85
2010	Bos	AL	65	0	0	53	67.0	287	57	34	29	7	5	0	2	28	4	76	4	0	5	7	.417	0	37-45	0	3.32	3.90
2011	Bos	AL	63	0	0	54	64.1	255	50	22	21	3	0	1	3	10	1	87	1	0	4	1	.800	0	31-34	0	1.86	2.94
2012	Phi	NL	70	0	0	64	70.0	284	56	22	19	8	3	0	4	18	1	92	0	0	5	6	.455	0	38-42	0	2.75	2.44
2013	Phi	NL	61	0	0	54	61.2	254	59	23	20	6	0	3	1	11	1	57	2	0	5	1	.833	0	29-36	0	2.98	2.92
2014	Phi	NL	66	0	0	52	66.1	259	45	15	15	2	3	0	5	15	1	63	1	0	2	3	.400	0	39-43	0	1.68	2.04
2015	2 Tms	NL	59	0	0	51	63.1	260	53	22	15	7	2	2	7	12	2	56	0	1	4	3	.571	0	24-26	0	2.82	2.13
15	Phi	NL	37	0	0	34	39.2	161	31	9	7	3	1	0	4	8	1	40	0	0	2	1	.667	0	17-17	0	2.36	1.59
15	Was	NL	22	0	0	17	23.2	99	22	13	8	4	1	2	3	4	1	16	0	1	2	2	.500	0	7-9	0	3.64	3.04
	Postseason		18	0	0	12	27.0	100	14	3	3	0	0	1	0	8	3	23	0	0	2	1	.667	0	7-9	0	1.01	1.00
	11 ML YEARS		652	3	0	555	690.2	2786	535	208	180	54	20	11	34	171	15	777	13	1	39	32	.549	0	349-395	7	2.33	2.35

Jimmy Paredes

pah-REY-dez

Bats: B Throws: R Pos: DH-81;PH-11;3B-8;2B-6;RF-2;LF-1;PR-1 Ht: 6'3" Wt: 200 Born: 11/25/1988 Age: 27

Year	Team	Lg	G	AB	H	2B	3B	HR	(Hm	Rd)	TB	R	RBI	RC	TBB	IBB	SO	HBP	SH	SF	SB	CS	GDP	Avg	OBP	Slg	OPS
2011	Hou	NL	46	168	48	8	2	2	(0	2)	66	16	18	23	9	0	47	0	1	1	5	4	3	.286	.320	.393	.713
2012	Hou	NL	24	74	14	1	0	0	(0	0)	17	7	3	3	6	0	21	0	0	2	2	1	0	.189	.244	.230	.474
2013	Hou	AL	48	125	24	4	0	1	(1	0)	31	8	10	8	6	0	44	1	1	2	4	1	0	.192	.231	.248	.479
2014	2 Tms	AL	27	63	18	4	0	2	(2	0)	28	12	8	6	2	0	16	0	0	0	4	0	1	.286	.308	.444	.752
2015	Bal	AL	104	363	100	17	2	10	(6	4)	151	46	42	47	19	0	111	0	0	2	4	4	8	.275	.310	.416	.726

Year Team	Lg	G	AB	H	2B	3B	HR	(Hm	Rd)	TB	R	RBI	RC	TBB	IBB	SO	HBP	SH	SF	SB	CS	GDP	Avg	OBP	Slg	OPS
14 KC	AL	9	10	2	0	0	0	(0	0)	2	3	0	0	0	0	3	0	0	0	2	0	0	.200	.200	.200	.400
14 Bal	AL	18	53	16	4	0	2	(2	0)	26	9	8	6	2	0	13	0	0	0	2	0	1	.302	.327	.491	.818
Postseason		1	0	0	0	0	0	(0	0)	0	0	0	0	1	0	0	0	0	0	0	0	0	-	1.000	-	-
5 ML YEARS		249	793	204	34	5	15	(9	6)	293	89	81	87	42	0	239	1	2	7	19	13	13	.257	.293	.369	.662

Byung-ho Park

Bats: R **Throws:** R **Pos:** 1B   **Ht:** 6'1" **Wt:** 194 **Born:** 7/10/1986 **Age:** 29

Year Team	Lg	G	AB	H	2B	3B	HR	(Hm	Rd)	TB	R	RBI	RC	TBB	IBB	SO	HBP	SH	SF	SB	CS	GDP	Avg	OBP	Slg	OPS
2011 2 Tms	Low	66	201	51	11	2	13	(-	-)	105	31	31	37	26	0	76	2	0	1	2	0	5	.254	.343	.522	.866
2012 Nexen	IND	133	469	136	34	0	31	(-	-)	263	76	105	105	73	3	111	11	0	7	20	9	6	.290	.393	.561	.954
2013 Nexen	IND	128	450	143	17	0	37	(-	-)	271	91	117	119	92	4	96	8	0	6	10	2	9	.318	.437	.602	1.039
2014 Nexen	IND	128	459	139	16	2	52	(-	-)	315	126	124	132	96	3	142	12	0	4	8	3	13	.303	.433	.686	1.119
2015 Nexen	IND	140	528	181	35	1	53	(-	-)	377	129	146	153	78	6	161	12	0	4	10	3	10	.343	.436	.714	1.150

Jarrett Parker

Bats: L **Throws:** L **Pos:** RF-9;PH-8;LF-5;CF-4   **Ht:** 6'4" **Wt:** 210 **Born:** 1/1/1989 **Age:** 27

Year Team	Lg	G	AB	H	2B	3B	HR	(Hm	Rd)	TB	R	RBI	RC	TBB	IBB	SO	HBP	SH	SF	SB	CS	GDP	Avg	OBP	Slg	OPS
2011 SnJos	A+	127	486	123	25	3	13	(-	-)	193	81	61	77	74	1	144	8	2	1	20	5	9	.253	.360	.397	.757
2012 SnJos	A+	122	409	101	21	7	15	(-	-)	181	71	67	73	70	3	175	8	2	2	28	6	2	.247	.360	.443	.809
2013 Rchmd	AA	131	444	109	18	5	18	(-	-)	191	72	57	70	60	0	161	15	5	0	13	11	7	.245	.355	.430	.785
2014 Rchmd	AA	100	363	100	20	6	12	(-	-)	168	52	58	65	45	2	103	10	0	1	11	4	8	.275	.370	.463	.833
2014 Fresno	AAA	24	79	22	5	0	3	(-	-)	36	13	10	12	9	0	23	1	0	0	1	2	1	.278	.360	.456	.815
2015 Scrmto	AAA	124	434	123	25	3	23	(-	-)	223	74	74	86	62	3	164	4	0	4	19	7	3	.283	.375	.514	.889
2015 SF	NL	21	49	17	2	0	6	(1	5)	37	11	14	12	5	0	21	0	0	0	1	1	1	.347	.407	.755	1.163

Jarrod Parker

Pitches: R **Bats:** R **Pos:** P   **Ht:** 6'1" **Wt:** 195 **Born:** 11/24/1988 **Age:** 27

Year Team	Lg	G	GS	CG	GF	IP	BFP	H	R	ER	HR	SH	SF	HB	TBB	IBB	SO	WP	Bk	W	L	Pct	Sh	Sv-Op	Hld	ERC	ERA
2011 Ari	NL	1	1	0	0	5.2	22	4	0	0	0	2	0	0	1	0	1	0	0	0	0	-	0	0-0	0	1.36	0.00
2012 Oak	AL	29	29	0	0	181.1	751	166	71	70	17	7	8	3	63	3	140	10	0	13	8	.619	0	0-0	0	3.24	3.47
2013 Oak	AL	32	32	1	0	197.0	818	178	92	87	25	8	4	7	63	2	134	7	0	12	8	.600	0	0-0	0	3.57	3.97
Postseason		4	3	0	0	18.0	77	21	11	10	1	2	0	1	4	0	12	2	0	1	2	.333	0	0-0	0	4.29	5.00
3 ML YEARS		62	62	1	0	384.0	1591	348	163	157	36	17	12	10	127	5	275	17	0	25	16	.610	0	0-0	0	3.37	3.68

Kyle Parker

Bats: R **Throws:** R **Pos:** LF-28;PH-13;RF-5;1B-2   **Ht:** 6'0" **Wt:** 205 **Born:** 9/30/1989 **Age:** 26

Year Team	Lg	G	AB	H	2B	3B	HR	(Hm	Rd)	TB	R	RBI	RC	TBB	IBB	SO	HBP	SH	SF	SB	CS	GDP	Avg	OBP	Slg	OPS
2011 Ashvll	A	117	445	127	23	1	21	(-	-)	215	75	95	82	48	1	133	14	1	8	2	0	20	.285	.367	.483	.850
2012 Mdest	A+	102	390	120	18	6	23	(-	-)	219	86	73	90	66	1	88	6	0	1	1	2	14	.308	.415	.562	.976
2013 Tulsa	AA	123	480	138	23	3	23	(-	-)	236	70	74	81	40	1	99	4	0	4	6	6	14	.288	.345	.492	.836
2014 ColSpr	AAA	128	502	145	31	3	15	(-	-)	227	73	72	77	33	1	102	4	0	3	4	3	14	.289	.336	.452	.788
2015 Albq	AAA	93	357	100	19	4	9	(-	-)	154	53	58	51	24	1	102	2	2	3	6	4	15	.280	.326	.431	.758
2014 Col	NL	18	26	5	1	0	0	(0	0)	6	1	1	1	0	0	14	0	0	0	0	0	0	.192	.192	.231	.423
2015 Col	NL	46	106	19	3	1	3	(3	0)	33	10	11	4	6	0	37	0	0	0	1	0	2	.179	.223	.311	.535
2 ML YEARS		64	132	24	4	1	3	(3	0)	39	11	12	5	6	0	51	0	0	0	1	0	2	.182	.217	.295	.513

Chris Parmelee

Bats: L **Throws:** L **Pos:** 1B-25;RF-8;PH-2   PAR-muh-lee   **Ht:** 6'1" **Wt:** 220 **Born:** 2/24/1988 **Age:** 28

Year Team	Lg	G	AB	H	2B	3B	HR	(Hm	Rd)	TB	R	RBI	RC	TBB	IBB	SO	HBP	SH	SF	SB	CS	GDP	Avg	OBP	Slg	OPS
2015 Norfolk*	AAA	63	239	75	13	0	6	(-	-)	106	33	32	43	29	2	52	1	0	3	3	1	4	.314	.386	.444	.830
2011 Min	AL	21	76	27	6	0	4	(2	2)	45	8	14	19	12	0	13	0	0	0	0	0	3	.355	.443	.592	1.035
2012 Min	AL	64	192	44	10	2	5	(1	4)	73	18	19	18	13	1	52	4	0	1	0	0	4	.229	.290	.380	.671
2013 Min	AL	101	294	67	13	0	8	(2	6)	104	21	24	27	33	0	81	3	0	3	1	1	6	.228	.309	.354	.663
2014 Min	AL	87	250	64	11	0	7	(3	4)	96	27	28	19	17	0	64	2	0	1	0	3	7	.256	.307	.384	.691
2015 Bal	AL	32	97	21	7	1	4	(3	1)	42	11	9	9	4	0	26	1	0	0	0	1	1	.216	.255	.433	.688
5 ML YEARS		305	909	223	47	3	28	(11	17)	360	85	94	92	79	1	236	10	0	5	1	5	21	.245	.311	.396	.707

Bobby Parnell

Pitches: R **Bats:** R **Pos:** RP-30   **Ht:** 6'3" **Wt:** 205 **Born:** 9/8/1984 **Age:** 31

Year Team	Lg	G	GS	CG	GF	IP	BFP	H	R	ER	HR	SH	SF	HB	TBB	IBB	SO	WP	Bk	W	L	Pct	Sh	Sv-Op	Hld	ERC	ERA
2015 StLuci*	A+	7	2	0	2	6.2	37	11	8	8	0	1	0	0	7	0	5	2	0	2	0	.000	0	0- -	-	10.08	10.80
2015 Bnghtn*	AA	8	0	0	2	7.1	39	11	10	10	1	0	1	1	7	0	6	1	0	2	0	.000	0	0- -	-	10.93	12.27
2008 NYM	NL	6	0	0	3	5.0	23	3	3	3	0	0	0	0	2	0	3	1	0	0	0	0-0	0	0-0	0	1.59	5.40
2009 NYM	NL	68	8	0	14	88.1	413	101	56	52	8	3	1	4	46	2	74	6	1	4	8	.333	0	1-5	16	5.37	5.30
2010 NYM	NL	41	0	0	10	35.0	149	41	13	11	1	2	0	0	8	2	33	0	0	0	1	.000	0	0-2	9	3.80	2.83
2011 NYM	NL	60	0	0	23	59.1	268	60	29	24	4	6	0	2	27	4	64	8	1	4	6	.400	0	6-12	11	4.01	3.64
2012 NYM	NL	74	0	0	23	68.2	288	65	24	19	4	4	0	2	20	2	61	1	0	5	4	.556	0	7-12	18	3.08	2.49

	HOW MUCH HE PITCHED					WHAT HE GAVE UP				THE RESULTS		
Year Team	Lg	G GS CG GF	IP	BFP	H R ER HR SH SF HB	TBB IBB	SO WP Bk	W L Pct Sh Sv-Op Hld	ERC ERA
2013 NYM	NL	49 0 0 41	50.0	198	38 17 12 1 2 3 1	12 3	44 1 0	5 5 .500 0 22-26 0	1.78 2.16
2014 NYM	NL	1 0 0 0	1.0	6	2 1 1 0 0 0 0	1 0	1 0 0	0 0 - 0 0-1 0	12.01 9.00
2015 NYM	NL	30 0 0 8	24.0	112	30 20 17 0 1 1 0	17 1	13 4 0	2 4 .333 0 1-3 5	6.12 6.38
8 ML YEARS		329 8 0 122	331.1	1453	340 163 139 18 18 7 8	133 14	293 21 2	20 28 .417 0 37-61 59	3.89 3.78

Gerardo Parra
heh-RAHR-doh PAR-uh

Bats: L **Throws:** L **Pos:** RF-63;LF-53;CF-41;PH-21;PR-1   **Ht:** 5'11" **Wt:** 210 **Born:** 5/6/1987 **Age:** 29

		BATTING																	RUNNING			AVERAGES			
Year Team	Lg	G	AB	H	2B	3B	HR	(Hm Rd)	TB	R	RBI	RC	TBB	IBB	SO	HBP	SH	SF	SB	CS	GDP	Avg	OBP	Slg	OPS
2009 Ari	NL	120	455	132	21	8	5	(4 1)	184	59	60	58	25	1	89	1	4	6	5	7	18	.290	.324	.404	.729
2010 Ari	NL	133	364	95	19	6	3	(1 2)	135	31	30	38	23	10	76	2	3	1	1	0	8	.261	.308	.371	.679
2011 Ari	NL	141	445	130	20	8	8	(3 5)	190	55	46	71	43	16	82	3	0	2	15	1	8	.292	.357	.427	.784
2012 Ari	NL	133	385	105	21	2	7	(5 2)	151	58	36	50	33	4	77	4	6	2	15	9	4	.273	.335	.392	.727
2013 Ari	NL	156	601	161	43	4	10	(6 4)	242	79	48	69	48	3	100	3	7	4	10	10	12	.268	.323	.403	.726
2014 2 Tms	NL	150	529	138	22	4	9	(3 6)	195	64	40	46	32	5	100	5	6	2	9	7	10	.261	.308	.369	.677
2015 2 Tms	NL	155	547	159	36	5	14	(8 6)	247	83	51	71	28	3	92	5	4	5	14	4	8	.291	.328	.452	.780
14 Ari	NL	104	406	105	18	3	6	(2 4)	147	51	30	37	24	3	72	4	4	2	5	5	6	.259	.305	.362	.667
14 Mil	NL	46	123	33	4	1	3	(1 2)	48	13	10	9	8	2	28	1	2	0	4	2	4	.268	.318	.390	.708
15 Mil	NL	100	323	106	24	5	9	(4 5)	167	53	31	47	20	2	57	3	1	4	9	3	7	.328	.369	.517	.886
15 Bal	AL	55	224	53	12	0	5	(4 1)	80	30	20	24	8	1	35	2	3	1	5	1	1	.237	.268	.357	.625
Postseason		5	18	1	1	0	0	(0 0)	2	1	0	0	1	0	7	0	0	0	0	0	0	.056	.105	.111	.216
7 ML YEARS		988	3326	920	182	37	56	(30 26)	1344	429	311	403	232	42	616	23	30	22	69	38	68	.277	.326	.404	.730

Manny Parra
PAR-uh

Pitches: L **Bats:** L **Pos:** RP-40   **Ht:** 6'3" **Wt:** 215 **Born:** 10/30/1982 **Age:** 33

		HOW MUCH HE PITCHED				WHAT HE GAVE UP				THE RESULTS		
Year Team	Lg	G GS CG GF	IP	BFP	H R ER HR SH SF HB	TBB IBB	SO WP Bk	W L Pct Sh Sv-Op Hld	ERC ERA
2007 Mil	NL	9 2 0 3	26.1	116	25 13 11 1 1 3 2	12 0	26 1 0	0 1 .000 0 0-0 0	3.83 3.76
2008 Mil	NL	32 29 0 0	166.0	741	181 91 81 18 10 2 2	75 1	147 17 2	10 8 .556 0 0-0 0	4.89 4.39
2009 Mil	NL	27 27 0 0	140.0	671	179 108 99 19 5 3 1	77 5	116 4 1	11 11 .500 0 0-0 0	6.51 6.36
2010 Mil	NL	42 16 0 9	122.0	560	135 76 68 18 6 7 3	63 3	129 14 1	3 10 .231 0 0-0 0	5.53 5.02
2012 Mil	NL	62 0 0 8	58.2	273	62 39 33 3 0 1 3	35 2	61 6 0	2 3 .400 0 0-2 9	4.88 5.06
2013 Cin	NL	57 0 0 8	46.0	188	40 18 17 5 3 1 1	15 0	56 4 0	2 3 .400 0 0-1 16	3.28 3.33
2014 Cin	NL	53 0 0 8	36.2	164	39 20 19 4 4 0 1	18 1	34 2 0	0 3 .000 0 1-2 16	4.94 4.66
2015 Cin	NL	40 0 0 5	32.1	130	32 15 14 2 1 2 0	6 1	23 1 0	1 2 .333 0 0-1 6	2.97 3.90
Postseason		3 0 0 0	3.0	12	3 0 0 0 0 0 0	1 0	4 0 0	0 0 - 0 0-0 0	3.35 0.00
8 ML YEARS		322 74 0 41	628.0	2843	693 380 342 70 30 19 13	301 13	592 49 4	29 41 .414 0 1-6 48	5.09 4.90

Andy Parrino
puh-REE-no

Bats: B **Throws:** R **Pos:** SS-10;3B-6;PH-2;PR-2   **Ht:** 6'0" **Wt:** 190 **Born:** 10/31/1985 **Age:** 30

		BATTING																	RUNNING			AVERAGES			
Year Team	Lg	G	AB	H	2B	3B	HR	(Hm Rd)	TB	R	RBI	RC	TBB	IBB	SO	HBP	SH	SF	SB	CS	GDP	Avg	OBP	Slg	OPS
2015 Nashv*	AAA	80	287	78	9	3	5	(- -)	108	32	24	38	30	0	81	2	1	1	0	2	7	.272	.344	.376	.720
2011 SD	NL	24	44	8	1	0	0	(0 0)	9	3	4	4	9	1	17	1	0	1	1	0	1	.182	.327	.205	.532
2012 SD	NL	55	116	24	5	0	1	(1 0)	32	9	6	9	17	7	35	2	2	1	1	0	2	.207	.316	.276	.592
2013 Oak	AL	14	34	4	2	0	0	(0 0)	6	2	1	0	2	0	12	0	1	0	0	0	1	.118	.167	.176	.343
2014 Oak	AL	21	46	7	3	0	1	(1 0)	13	4	3	0	3	0	14	1	0	1	0	0	0	.152	.216	.283	.498
2015 Oak	AL	17	6	0	0	0	0	(0 0)	0	1	0	0	2	0	5	0	0	0	0	0	0	.000	.250	.000	.250
5 ML YEARS		131	246	43	11	0	2	(2 0)	60	19	14	13	33	8	83	4	2	3	2	0	5	.175	.280	.244	.524

Spencer Patton

Pitches: R **Bats:** R **Pos:** RP-27   **Ht:** 6'1" **Wt:** 200 **Born:** 2/20/1988 **Age:** 28

		HOW MUCH HE PITCHED				WHAT HE GAVE UP				THE RESULTS		
Year Team	Lg	G GS CG GF	IP	BFP	H R ER HR SH SF HB	TBB IBB	SO WP Bk	W L Pct Sh Sv-Op Hld	ERC ERA
2011 Idaho	R+	19 2 0 6	39.2	179	42 20 15 0 0 1 2	15 0	56 9 0	3 1 .750 0 2- - -	3.66 3.40
2012 Idaho	R+	16 8 0 0	57.0	259	67 43 40 4 4 2 5	21 0	84 6 0	0 7 .000 0 0- - -	5.06 6.32
2013 Wilmg	A+	25 2 0 9	64.1	257	49 19 14 5 1 2 3	20 0	76 5 0	5 2 .714 0 2- - -	2.57 1.96
2013 NWArk	AA	12 0 0 1	18.0	69	9 4 3 1 2 0 3	6 1	27 0 0	0 0 - 0 0- - -	1.66 1.50
2014 Omha	AAA	34 0 0 27	46.1	188	26 21 21 9 2 1 2	22 2	60 2 1	4 3 .571 0 14- - -	2.71 4.08
2014 RdRck	AAA	15 0 0 13	16.0	67	16 6 6 1 1 1 0	3 1	25 3 0	1 1 .500 0 4- - -	2.86 3.38
2015 RdRck	AAA	26 0 0 17	27.0	114	21 6 5 1 0 0 2	9 0	36 2 0	2 0 1.000 0 11- - -	2.44 1.67
2014 Tex	AL	9 0 0 2	9.1	35	6 1 1 0 0 0 0	2 0	8 0 0	1 0 1.000 0 0-0 2	1.29 0.96
2015 Tex	AL	27 0 0 6	24.0	109	24 24 24 5 1 0 4	12 0	28 1 0	1 1 .500 0 0-0 3	6.04 9.00
2 ML YEARS		36 0 0 8	33.1	144	30 25 25 5 1 0 4	14 0	36 1 0	2 1 .667 0 0-0 5	4.46 6.75

Ben Paulsen

Bats: L **Throws:** R **Pos:** 1B-91;PH-21;LF-19;PR-2;RF-1   **Ht:** 6'4" **Wt:** 210 **Born:** 10/27/1987 **Age:** 28

		BATTING																	RUNNING			AVERAGES			
Year Team	Lg	G	AB	H	2B	3B	HR	(Hm Rd)	TB	R	RBI	RC	TBB	IBB	SO	HBP	SH	SF	SB	CS	GDP	Avg	OBP	Slg	OPS
2011 Tulsa	AA	136	547	132	29	4	19	(- -)	226	69	78	68	40	6	132	4	2	4	2	3	8	.241	.296	.413	.709
2012 Tulsa	AA	120	436	110	18	3	13	(- -)	173	58	53	54	37	3	113	2	0	3	1	4	9	.252	.312	.397	.709
2013 ColSpr	AAA	123	459	134	32	10	18	(- -)	240	64	79	82	37	2	128	2	0	4	2	2	7	.292	.345	.523	.867
2014 ColSpr	AAA	117	435	128	32	6	20	(- -)	232	76	76	87	58	4	119	2	0	2	4	5	10	.294	.378	.533	.912

Year Team	Lg	G	AB	H	2B	3B	HR	(Hm	Rd)	TB	R	RBI	RC	TBB	IBB	SO	HBP	SH	SF	SB	CS	GDP	Avg	OBP	Slg	OPS
							BATTING													**RUNNING**			**AVERAGES**			
2015 Albq	AAA	36	125	32	8	2	3	(-	-)	53	19	15	19	15	0	34	1	0	0	1	0	3	.256	.340	.424	.764
2014 Col	NL	31	63	20	4	0	4	(1	3)	36	8	10	11	2	1	19	1	0	0	0	0	1	.317	.348	.571	.920
2015 Col	NL	116	325	90	19	4	11	(6	5)	150	42	49	42	23	0	92	2	1	3	1	2	5	.277	.326	.462	.787
2 ML YEARS		147	388	110	23	4	15	(7	8)	186	50	59	53	25	1	111	3	1	3	1	2	6	.284	.329	.479	.809

James Paxton

Pitches: L Bats: L Pos: SP-13   Ht: 6'4" Wt: 235 Born: 11/6/1988 Age: 27

		HOW MUCH HE PITCHED						WHAT HE GAVE UP												THE RESULTS							
Year Team	Lg	G	GS	CG	GF	IP	BFP	H	R	ER	HR	SH	SF	HB	TBB	IBB	SO	WP	Bk	W	L	Pct	Sh	Sv-Op	Hld	ERC	ERA
2013 Sea	AL	4	4	0	0	24.0	94	15	5	4	2	0	0	0	7	2	21	0	0	3	0	1.000	0	0-0	0	1.61	1.50
2014 Sea	AL	13	13	0	0	74.0	303	60	29	25	3	3	1	1	29	2	59	7	0	6	4	.600	0	0-0	0	2.69	3.04
2015 Sea	AL	13	13	0	0	67.0	297	67	34	29	8	0	3	0	29	1	56	5	0	3	4	.429	0	0-0	0	4.22	3.90
3 ML YEARS		30	30	0	0	165.0	694	142	68	58	13	3	4	1	65	5	136	12	0	12	8	.600	0	0-0	0	3.11	3.16

James Pazos

Pitches: L Bats: R Pos: RP-11   pah-ZOHSS   Ht: 6'3" Wt: 230 Born: 5/5/1991 Age: 25

		HOW MUCH HE PITCHED						WHAT HE GAVE UP												THE RESULTS							
Year Team	Lg	G	GS	CG	GF	IP	BFP	H	R	ER	HR	SH	SF	HB	TBB	IBB	SO	WP	Bk	W	L	Pct	Sh	Sv-Op	Hld	ERC	ERA
2012 StnIld	A-	28	0	0	9	40.1	168	29	9	8	0	0	1	0	19	0	39	3	0	2	2	.500	0	3--	-	2.18	1.79
2013 Tampa	Low	25	0	0	13	34.1	142	28	15	15	3	1	2	3	9	0	33	2	0	3	1	.750	0	1--	-	2.79	3.93
2014 Tampa	A+	18	1	0	16	25.0	106	23	13	11	0	0	1	2	6	0	33	1	0	0	2	.000	0	4--	-	2.62	3.96
2014 Trntn	AA	28	0	0	15	42.0	168	28	7	7	0	0	1	1	19	0	42	4	0	0	1	.000	0	6--	-	2.04	1.50
2015 Trntn	AA	6	0	0	4	9.2	32	4	2	2	1	0	1	0	0	0	12	1	0	0	0	-	0	1--	-	0.60	1.90
2015 S-WB	AAA	21	0	0	6	33.0	138	25	6	4	0	0	1	2	15	0	37	2	0	3	1	.750	0	2--	-	2.55	1.09
2015 NYY	AL	11	0	0	1	5.0	21	3	0	0	0	1	0	0	3	0	3	1	0	0	0	-	0	0-0	0	2.03	0.00

Brad Peacock

Pitches: R Bats: R Pos: SP-1   Ht: 6'1" Wt: 210 Born: 2/2/1988 Age: 28

		HOW MUCH HE PITCHED						WHAT HE GAVE UP												THE RESULTS							
Year Team	Lg	G	GS	CG	GF	IP	BFP	H	R	ER	HR	SH	SF	HB	TBB	IBB	SO	WP	Bk	W	L	Pct	Sh	Sv-Op	Hld	ERC	ERA
2011 Was	NL	3	2	0	0	12.0	48	7	1	1	0	0	0	0	6	0	4	1	0	2	0	1.000	0	0-1	0	1.71	0.75
2013 Hou	AL	18	14	0	1	83.1	365	78	51	48	15	1	1	3	37	0	77	4	0	5	6	.455	0	0-0	2	4.54	5.18
2014 Hou	AL	28	24	0	3	131.2	589	136	80	69	20	0	6	4	70	4	119	6	0	4	9	.308	0	0-0	1	5.29	4.72
2015 Hou	AL	1	1	0	0	5.0	22	5	3	3	0	0	1	1	2	0	3	0	0	0	1	.000	0	0-0	0	4.20	5.40
4 ML YEARS		50	41	0	4	232.0	1024	226	135	121	35	1	8	8	115	4	203	11	0	11	16	.407	0	0-1	3	4.79	4.69

Steve Pearce

Bats: R Throws: R Pos: LF-41;1B-28;2B-18;PH-10;RF-8;DH-1   Ht: 5'11" Wt: 200 Born: 4/13/1983 Age: 33

								BATTING												RUNNING			AVERAGES			
Year Team	Lg	G	AB	H	2B	3B	HR	(Hm Rd)	TB	R	RBI	RC	TBB	IBB	SO	HBP	SH	SF	SB	CS	GDP	Avg	OBP	Slg	OPS	
2007 Pit	NL	23	68	20	5	1	0	(0 0)	27	13	6	9	5	0	12	0	0	0	2	1	2	.294	.342	.397	.740
2008 Pit	NL	37	109	27	7	0	4	(0 4)	46	6	15	13	5	0	22	3	0	2	2	0	1	.248	.294	.422	.716
2009 Pit	NL	60	165	34	13	1	4	(3 1)	61	19	16	17	21	0	43	0	0	0	1	0	0	.206	.296	.370	.665
2010 Pit	NL	15	29	8	2	1	0	(0 0)	12	4	5	5	7	0	6	0	0	2	0	0	0	.276	.395	.414	.809
2011 Pit	NL	50	94	19	2	0	1	(1 0)	24	8	10	5	7	0	21	1	1	2	0	0	6	.202	.260	.255	.515
2012 3 Tms		61	159	38	8	1	4	(2 2)	60	16	26	24	20	1	41	3	2	4	1	2	4	.239	.328	.377	.705
2013 Bal	AL	44	119	31	7	0	4	(3 1)	50	14	13	20	15	2	25	4	0	0	1	0	0	.261	.362	.420	.782
2014 Bal	AL	102	338	99	26	0	21	(12 9)	188	51	49	66	40	1	76	4	0	1	5	0	4	.293	.373	.556	.930
2015 Bal	AL	92	294	64	13	1	15	(7 8)	124	42	40	33	23	1	69	7	0	1	1	1	11	.218	.289	.422	.711
12 Bal	AL	28	71	18	4	0	3	(2 1)	31	8	14	12	8	0	17	0	2	2	0	1	1	.254	.321	.437	.758
12 Hou	AL	21	63	16	4	1	0	(0 0)	22	2	8	9	7	1	16	3	0	2	1	1	3	.254	.347	.349	.696
12 NYY	AL	12	25	4	0	0	1	(0 1)	7	6	4	3	5	0	8	0	0	0	0	0	0	.160	.300	.280	.580
Postseason		7	27	4	1	0	0	(0 0)	5	4	1	2	2	0	3	1	0	0	0	0	0	.148	.233	.185	.419
9 ML YEARS		484	1375	340	83	5	53	(28 25)	592	173	180	192	143	5	315	22	3	12	13	4	30	.247	.325	.431	.756

Jake Peavy

Pitches: R Bats: R Pos: SP-19   Ht: 6'1" Wt: 195 Born: 5/31/1981 Age: 35

		HOW MUCH HE PITCHED						WHAT HE GAVE UP												THE RESULTS							
Year Team	Lg	G	GS	CG	GF	IP	BFP	H	R	ER	HR	SH	SF	HB	TBB	IBB	SO	WP	Bk	W	L	Pct	Sh	Sv-Op	Hld	ERC	ERA
2015 Scrmto*	AAA	6	6	0	0	32.1	144	39	22	22	5	0	2	2	9	0	28	1	0	0	3	.000	0	0--	-	5.43	6.12
2002 SD	NL	17	17	0	0	97.2	430	106	54	49	11	5	2	3	33	4	90	4	1	6	7	.462	0	0-0	0	4.41	4.52
2003 SD	NL	32	32	0	0	194.2	827	173	94	89	33	7	5	6	82	3	156	2	0	12	11	.522	0	0-0	0	4.13	4.11
2004 SD	NL	27	27	0	0	166.1	694	146	49	42	13	5	6	11	53	4	173	1	1	15	6	.714	0	0-0	0	3.18	2.27
2005 SD	NL	30	30	3	0	203.0	812	162	70	65	18	4	5	7	50	3	216	3	1	13	7	.650	3	0-0	0	2.49	2.88
2006 SD	NL	32	32	2	0	202.1	846	187	93	92	23	5	1	6	62	11	215	4	0	11	14	.440	0	0-0	0	3.42	4.09
2007 SD	NL	34	34	0	0	223.1	898	169	67	63	13	5	7	6	68	5	240	4	0	19	6	.760	0	0-0	0	2.27	2.54
2008 SD	NL	27	27	1	0	173.2	709	146	57	55	17	7	1	5	59	1	166	6	0	10	11	.476	0	0-0	0	3.12	2.85
2009 2 Tms		16	16	1	0	101.2	410	80	41	39	8	3	2	1	34	0	110	2	2	9	6	.600	0	0-0	0	2.63	3.45
2010 CWS	AL	17	17	1	0	107.0	450	98	55	55	13	1	5	5	34	2	93	2	1	7	6	.538	1	0-0	0	3.59	4.63
2011 CWS	AL	19	18	1	0	111.2	470	117	61	61	10	1	5	3	24	4	95	4	0	7	7	.500	1	0-0	0	3.59	4.92
2012 CWS	AL	32	32	4	0	219.0	882	191	88	82	27	1	6	10	49	1	194	3	2	11	12	.478	1	0-0	0	3.07	3.37
2013 2 Tms	AL	23	23	2	0	144.2	590	130	70	67	20	2	3	2	36	0	121	0	2	12	5	.706	0	0-0	0	3.25	4.17
2014 2 Tms		32	32	0	0	202.2	852	196	91	84	23	8	11	9	63	2	158	5	2	7	13	.350	0	0-0	0	3.83	3.73
2015 SF	NL	19	19	0	0	110.2	448	99	45	44	12	5	1	2	25	1	78	2	1	8	6	.571	0	0-0	0	2.97	3.58
09 SD	NL	13	13	1	0	81.2	335	69	38	36	7	2	2	1	28	0	92	2	1	6	5	.500	0	0-0	0	3.00	3.97

			HOW MUCH HE PITCHED			WHAT HE GAVE UP										THE RESULTS						
Year	Team	Lg	G	GS	CG	GF	IP	BFP	H	R	ER	HR	SH	SF	HB	TBB	IBB	SO	WP	Bk	W	L	Pct	Sh	Sv-Op	Hld	ERC	ERA
09	CWS	AL	3	3	0	0	20.0	75	11	3	3	1	1	0	0	6	0	18	0	1	3	0	1.000	0	0-0	0	1.38	1.35
13	CWS	AL	13	13	1	0	80.0	324	74	41	38	14	1	2	1	17	0	76	0	1	8	4	.667	0	0-0	0	3.49	4.28
13	Bos	AL	10	10	1	0	64.2	266	56	29	29	6	1	1	1	19	0	45	0	1	4	1	.800	0	0-0	0	2.96	4.04
14	Bos	AL	20	20	0	0	124.0	538	131	67	65	20	4	5	3	46	1	100	2	1	1	9	.100	0	0-0	0	4.83	4.72
14	SF	NL	12	12	0	0	78.2	314	65	24	19	3	4	6	6	17	1	58	3	1	6	4	.600	0	0-0	0	2.40	2.17
	Postseason		9	9	0	0	38.1	178	53	34	34	4	3	1	0	17	4	21	1	0	1	5	.167	0	0-0	0	6.48	7.98
	14 ML YEARS		357	356	15	0	2258.1	9318	2000	935	887	241	59	60	76	672	41	2105	42	13	147	117	.557	6	0-0	0	3.22	3.53

Joc Pederson

Bats: L **Throws:** L **Pos:** CF-147;PH-9;PR-1   JOCK   **Ht:** 6'1" **Wt:** 215 **Born:** 4/21/1992 **Age:** 24

							BATTING													RUNNING			AVERAGES			
Year	Team	Lg	G	AB	H	2B	3B	HR	(Hm | Rd)	TB	R	RBI	RC	TBB	IBB	SO	HBP	SH	SF	SB	CS	GDP	Avg	OBP	Slg	OPS
2011	2 Tms	Low	84	316	102	20	2	11	(- | -)	159	58	65	69	43	3	63	5	1	5	26	5	5	.323	.407	.503	.910
2012	Rcuca	A+	110	434	136	26	4	18	(- | -)	224	96	70	89	51	1	81	10	2	2	26	14	4	.313	.396	.516	.913
2013	Chatt	AA	123	439	122	24	3	22	(- | -)	218	81	58	89	70	5	114	5	2	3	31	8	4	.278	.381	.497	.878
2014	Albq	AAA	121	445	135	17	4	33	(- | -)	259	106	78	113	100	3	149	5	1	2	30	13	7	.303	.435	.582	1.017
2014	LAD	NL	18	28	4	0	0	0	(0 | 0)	4	1	0	1	9	0	11	0	1	0	0	1	0	.143	.351	.143	.494
2015	LAD	NL	151	480	101	19	1	26	(13 | 13)	200	67	54	62	92	6	170	9	2	2	4	7	5	.210	.346	.417	.763
	2 ML YEARS		169	508	105	19	1	26	(13 | 13)	204	68	54	63	101	6	181	9	3	2	4	7	6	.207	.347	.402	.748

Dustin Pedroia

Bats: R **Throws:** R **Pos:** 2B-92;DH-1   peh-DROY-uh   **Ht:** 5'8" **Wt:** 175 **Born:** 8/17/1983 **Age:** 32

							BATTING													RUNNING			AVERAGES			
Year	Team	Lg	G	AB	H	2B	3B	HR	(Hm | Rd)	TB	R	RBI	RC	TBB	IBB	SO	HBP	SH	SF	SB	CS	GDP	Avg	OBP	Slg	OPS
2006	Bos	AL	31	89	17	4	0	2	(1 | 1)	27	5	7	3	7	0	7	1	1	0	0	1	1	.191	.258	.303	.561
2007	Bos	AL	139	520	165	39	1	8	(5 | 3)	230	86	50	79	47	1	42	7	5	2	7	1	8	.317	.380	.442	.823
2008	Bos	AL	157	653	213	54	2	17	(7 | 10)	322	118	83	107	50	1	52	7	7	9	20	1	17	.326	.376	.493	.869
2009	Bos	AL	154	626	185	48	1	15	(10 | 8)	280	115	72	104	74	3	45	5	3	6	20	8	19	.296	.371	.447	.819
2010	Bos	AL	75	302	87	24	1	12	(4 | 8)	149	53	41	52	37	1	38	4	2	6	9	1	7	.288	.367	.493	.860
2011	Bos	AL	159	635	195	37	3	21	(13 | 8)	301	102	91	114	86	6	85	1	2	7	26	8	12	.307	.387	.474	.861
2012	Bos	AL	141	563	163	39	3	15	(9 | 6)	253	81	65	84	48	3	60	5	1	6	20	6	9	.290	.347	.449	.797
2013	Bos	AL	160	641	193	42	2	9	(7 | 2)	266	91	84	99	73	4	75	3	0	7	17	5	24	.301	.372	.415	.787
2014	Bos	AL	135	551	153	39	0	7	(2 | 5)	207	72	53	65	51	1	75	1	0	6	6	6	14	.278	.337	.376	.712
2015	Bos	AL	93	381	111	19	1	12	(4 | 8)	168	46	42	55	38	1	51	2	1	3	2	2	6	.291	.356	.441	.797
	Postseason		44	178	44	13	0	5	(2 | 3)	72	30	25	22	19	0	25	2	1	2	3	1	4	.247	.323	.404	.728
	10 ML YEARS		1244	4961	1482	339	14	118	(62 | 56)	2203	769	588	762	511	21	530	36	22	52	127	39	117	.299	.365	.444	.809

Carlos Peguero

Bats: L **Throws:** L **Pos:** LF-25;PH-10;RF-9;CF-1   peh-GEHR-oh   **Ht:** 6'5" **Wt:** 260 **Born:** 2/22/1987 **Age:** 29

							BATTING													RUNNING			AVERAGES			
Year	Team	Lg	G	AB	H	2B	3B	HR	(Hm | Rd)	TB	R	RBI	RC	TBB	IBB	SO	HBP	SH	SF	SB	CS	GDP	Avg	OBP	Slg	OPS
2015	Pwtckt*	AAA	26	97	23	4	0	7	(- | -)	48	9	21	15	9	0	33	1	0	1	0	0	1	.237	.306	.495	.800
2011	Sea	AL	46	143	28	3	2	6	(4 | 2)	53	14	19	12	8	2	54	3	0	1	0	1	0	.196	.252	.371	.622
2012	Sea	AL	17	56	10	2	1	2	(1 | 1)	20	2	7	5	1	0	28	0	0	0	0	0	0	.179	.193	.357	.550
2013	Sea	AL	2	6	2	0	0	1	(1 | 0)	5	1	1	1	1	1	2	0	0	0	1	0	0	.333	.429	.833	1.262
2014	KC	AL	4	9	2	1	0	0	(0 | 0)	3	1	1	1	1	0	5	0	0	0	0	0	0	.222	.300	.333	.633
2015	2 Tms	AL	34	75	14	4	0	4	(0 | 4)	30	11	9	10	13	0	37	1	0	1	2	0	1	.187	.311	.400	.711
15	Tex	AL	30	70	13	4	0	4	(0 | 4)	29	10	9	10	12	0	36	1	0	1	2	0	1	.186	.310	.414	.724
15	Bos	AL	4	5	1	0	0	0	(0 | 0)	1	1	0	0	1	0	1	0	0	0	0	0	0	.200	.333	.200	.533
	5 ML YEARS		103	289	56	10	3	13	(6 | 7)	111	29	37	29	24	3	126	4	0	2	3	1	1	.194	.263	.384	.647

Mike Pelfrey

Pitches: R **Bats:** R **Pos:** SP-30   PELL-free   **Ht:** 6'7" **Wt:** 240 **Born:** 1/14/1984 **Age:** 32

			HOW MUCH HE PITCHED						WHAT HE GAVE UP												THE RESULTS						
Year	Team	Lg	G	GS	CG	GF	IP	BFP	H	R	ER	HR	SH	SF	HB	TBB	IBB	SO	WP	Bk	W	L	Pct	Sh	Sv-Op	Hld	ERC	ERA
2006	NYM	NL	4	4	0	0	21.1	99	25	14	13	1	1	1	3	12	0	13	2	0	2	1	.667	0	0-0	0	6.05	5.48
2007	NYM	NL	15	13	0	0	72.2	342	85	47	45	6	3	6	3	39	1	45	3	0	3	8	.273	0	0-0	0	5.99	5.57
2008	NYM	NL	32	32	2	0	200.2	851	209	86	83	12	11	5	13	64	1	110	2	0	13	11	.542	0	0-0	0	4.04	3.72
2009	NYM	NL	31	31	0	0	184.1	824	213	112	103	18	8	5	7	66	8	107	1	6	10	12	.455	0	0-0	0	4.83	5.03
2010	NYM	NL	34	33	0	1	204.0	870	213	88	83	12	17	4	6	68	5	113	1	1	15	9	.625	0	1-1	0	3.89	3.66
2011	NYM	NL	34	33	2	0	193.2	860	220	111	102	21	10	8	7	65	7	105	2	2	7	13	.350	0	0-0	0	4.70	4.74
2012	NYM	NL	3	3	0	0	19.2	85	24	5	5	0	1	0	0	4	0	13	1	0	0	0	-	0	0-0	0	3.82	2.29
2013	Min	AL	29	29	0	0	152.2	680	184	92	88	13	1	7	6	53	0	101	1	0	5	13	.278	0	0-0	0	5.13	5.19
2014	Min	AL	5	5	0	0	23.2	119	29	23	21	5	2	2	2	18	0	10	1	0	0	3	.000	0	0-0	0	8.18	7.99
2015	Min	AL	30	30	0	0	164.2	714	198	86	78	11	3	3	12	45	1	86	5	0	6	11	.353	0	0-0	0	4.89	4.26
	10 ML YEARS		217	213	4	1	1237.1	5444	1400	664	621	99	60	38	65	434	23	703	19	9	61	81	.430	0	1-1	0	4.70	4.52

Ariel Pena

Pitches: R **Bats:** R **Pos:** SP-5; RP-1   arr-ee-EL   **Ht:** 6'3" **Wt:** 250 **Born:** 5/20/1989 **Age:** 27

			HOW MUCH HE PITCHED						WHAT HE GAVE UP												THE RESULTS						
Year	Team	Lg	G	GS	CG	GF	IP	BFP	H	R	ER	HR	SH	SF	HB	TBB	IBB	SO	WP	Bk	W	L	Pct	Sh	Sv-Op	Hld	ERC	ERA
2011	InldEm	A+	27	27	1	0	151.2	680	154	88	75	10	5	3	7	81	0	180	15	0	10	6	.625	0	0- -	-	4.63	4.45
2012	Ark	AA	19	19	0	0	114.1	475	94	43	38	14	2	4	6	42	0	111	7	0	6	6	.500	0	0- -	-	3.15	2.99
2012	Hntsvl	AA	7	7	0	0	32.1	153	40	26	26	5	4	2	5	23	0	29	3	0	0	2	.000	0	0- -	-	8.42	7.24

Year	Team	Lg	G	GS	CG	GF	IP	BFP	H	R	ER	HR	SH	SF	HB	TBB	IBB	SO	WP	Bk	W	L	Pct	Sh	Sv-Op	Hld	ERC	ERA
2013	Hntsvl	AA	27	27	0	0	142.1	604	115	63	59	17	4	5	2	79	1	131	10	0	8	9	.471	0	0- -	-	3.85	3.73
2014	Nashv	AAA	25	24	0	0	128.1	548	96	69	65	12	4	2	5	75	0	140	12	0	9	8	.529	0	0- -	-	3.52	4.56
2015	ColSpr	AAA	43	7	0	5	82.2	349	77	41	38	7	2	3	3	32	1	83	6	0	2	2	.500	0	0- -	-	3.71	4.14
2015	Mil	NL	6	5	0	0	27.1	120	24	14	13	2	2	1	2	14	2	27	2	0	2	1	.667	0	0-0	0	3.78	4.28

Brayan Pena

Bats: B **Throws:** R **Pos:** C-86;PH-19;1B-5;DH-1   BRIAN   **Ht:** 5'9" **Wt:** 240 **Born:** 1/7/1982 **Age:** 34

										BATTING														RUNNING			AVERAGES			
Year	Team	Lg	G	AB	H	2B	3B	HR	(Hm	Rd)	TB	R	RBI	RC	TBB	IBB	SO	HBP	SH	SF	SB	CS	GDP	Avg	OBP	Slg	OPS
2005	Atl	NL	18	39	7	2	0	0	(0	0)	9	2	4	0	1	1	7	0	0	0	0	0	1	.179	.200	.231	.431
2006	Atl	NL	23	41	11	2	0	1	(0	1)	16	9	5	4	2	0	5	0	0	0	0	0	2	.268	.302	.390	.693
2007	Atl	NL	16	33	7	0	0	1	(1	0)	10	2	3	0	0	0	3	0	0	0	0	1	2	.212	.212	.303	.515
2008	Atl	NL	14	14	4	1	0	0	(0	0)	5	3	0	0	1	0	2	0	0	0	0	0	0	.286	.333	.357	.690
2009	KC	AL	64	165	45	10	0	6	(3	3)	73	17	18	18	12	2	18	0	4	2	0	0	5	.273	.318	.442	.761
2010	KC	AL	60	158	40	10	0	1	(0	1)	53	11	19	16	12	0	27	1	1	2	2	0	8	.253	.306	.335	.642
2011	KC	AL	72	222	55	11	0	3	(0	3)	75	17	24	23	12	0	24	2	0	4	0	0	6	.248	.288	.338	.625
2012	KC	AL	68	212	50	10	1	2	(1	1)	68	16	25	19	9	0	24	0	1	4	0	1	7	.236	.262	.321	.583
2013	Det	AL	71	229	68	11	0	4	(1	3)	91	19	22	19	6	0	26	2	2	4	0	2	7	.297	.315	.397	.713
2014	Cin	NL	115	348	88	18	1	5	(3	2)	123	23	26	31	20	2	42	0	1	3	2	3	8	.253	.291	.353	.645
2015	Cin	NL	108	333	91	17	0	0	(0	0)	108	17	18	34	29	1	34	2	2	1	2	0	10	.273	.334	.324	.659
	Postseason		1	3	1	0	0	0	(0	0)	1	0	1	0	0	0	0	0	0	0	0	0	1	.333	.333	.333	.667
	11 ML YEARS		629	1794	466	92	2	23	(9	14)	631	136	164	164	104	6	212	7	11	20	6	7	56	.260	.300	.352	.651

Francisco Pena

Bats: R **Throws:** R **Pos:** C-8;PH-1   **Ht:** 6'2" **Wt:** 230 **Born:** 10/12/1989 **Age:** 26

										BATTING														RUNNING			AVERAGES			
Year	Team	Lg	G	AB	H	2B	3B	HR	(Hm	Rd)	TB	R	RBI	RC	TBB	IBB	SO	HBP	SH	SF	SB	CS	GDP	Avg	OBP	Slg	OPS
2011	Stluci	A+	95	319	71	13	0	5	(-	-)	99	28	37	27	20	0	50	3	0	0	3	1	8	.223	.275	.310	.585
2012	Stluci	A+	41	142	36	10	1	4	(-	-)	60	19	22	19	11	0	29	0	1	1	0	0	1	.254	.305	.423	.728
2012	Bnghtn	AA	40	126	25	7	0	3	(-	-)	41	14	17	13	16	1	25	2	1	0	1	0	2	.198	.299	.325	.624
2013	Bnghtn	AA	21	69	17	6	0	0	(-	-)	23	4	4	7	7	1	4	1	1	1	0	1	6	.246	.321	.333	.654
2013	LsVgs	AAA	68	218	56	15	1	9	(-	-)	100	22	39	30	10	1	40	3	1	4	1	0	5	.257	.294	.459	.752
2014	Omha	AAA	96	342	82	13	0	27	(-	-)	176	53	61	50	16	1	65	5	2	5	0	3	12	.240	.280	.515	.795
2015	Omha	AAA	95	342	86	20	1	13	(-	-)	147	42	48	46	23	1	56	4	3	2	4	1	6	.251	.305	.430	.734
2014	KC	AL	1	0	0	0	0	0	(0	0)	0	0	0	0	0	0	0	0	0	0	0	0	0	-	-	-	-
2015	KC	AL	8	7	1	0	0	0	(0	0)	1	0	0	0	0	0	3	0	0	0	0	0	1	.143	.143	.143	.286
	2 ML YEARS		9	7	1	0	0	0	(0	0)	1	0	0	0	0	0	3	0	0	0	0	0	1	.143	.143	.143	.286

Hunter Pence

Bats: R **Throws:** R **Pos:** RF-51;DH-1;PH-1   **Ht:** 6'4" **Wt:** 220 **Born:** 4/13/1983 **Age:** 33

										BATTING														RUNNING			AVERAGES			
Year	Team	Lg	G	AB	H	2B	3B	HR	(Hm	Rd)	TB	R	RBI	RC	TBB	IBB	SO	HBP	SH	SF	SB	CS	GDP	Avg	OBP	Slg	OPS
2007	Hou	NL	108	456	147	30	9	17	(7	10)	246	57	69	77	26	0	95	1	0	1	11	5	10	.322	.360	.539	.899
2008	Hou	NL	157	595	160	34	4	25	(14	11)	277	78	83	82	40	2	124	4	0	3	11	10	14	.269	.318	.466	.783
2009	Hou	NL	159	585	165	26	5	25	(14	11)	276	76	72	80	58	1	109	1	0	3	14	11	25	.282	.346	.472	.818
2010	Hou	NL	156	614	173	29	3	25	(14	11)	283	93	91	89	41	2	105	0	0	3	18	9	11	.282	.325	.461	.786
2011	2 Tms	NL	154	606	190	38	5	22	(5	17)	304	84	97	102	56	3	124	1	0	5	8	2	15	.314	.370	.502	.871
2012	2 Tms	NL	160	617	156	26	4	24	(9	15)	262	87	104	81	56	2	145	7	1	7	5	2	15	.253	.319	.425	.743
2013	SF	NL	162	629	178	35	5	27	(10	17)	304	91	99	91	52	3	115	3	0	3	22	3	17	.283	.339	.483	.822
2014	SF	NL	162	650	180	29	10	20	(5	15)	289	106	74	96	52	3	130	3	0	3	13	6	13	.277	.332	.445	.777
2015	SF	NL	52	207	57	13	1	9	(3	6)	99	30	40	28	16	0	48	0	0	0	4	1	8	.275	.327	.478	.806
11	Hou	NL	100	399	123	26	3	11	(4	7)	188	49	62	63	30	1	86	1	0	2	7	1	7	.308	.356	.471	.828
11	Phi	NL	54	207	67	12	2	11	(1	10)	116	35	35	39	26	2	38	0	0	3	1	1	8	.324	.394	.560	.954
12	Phi	NL	101	398	108	15	2	17	(7	10)	178	59	59	50	37	1	85	3	0	2	4	2	14	.271	.336	.447	.784
12	SF	NL	59	219	48	11	2	7	(2	5)	84	28	45	31	19	1	60	4	1	5	1	0	1	.219	.287	.384	.671
	Postseason		38	147	39	8	0	2	(0	2)	53	22	16	14	12	1	28	0	0	1	4	3	3	.265	.319	.361	.679
	9 ML YEARS		1270	4959	1406	260	46	194	(81	113)	2340	702	729	726	397	16	995	20	1	28	106	49	128	.284	.337	.472	.809

Cliff Pennington

Bats: B **Throws:** R **Pos:** 2B-33;SS-29;PH-29;3B-18;LF-8;PR-7;DH-1   **Ht:** 5'10" **Wt:** 195 **Born:** 6/15/1984 **Age:** 32

										BATTING														RUNNING			AVERAGES			
Year	Team	Lg	G	AB	H	2B	3B	HR	(Hm	Rd)	TB	R	RBI	RC	TBB	IBB	SO	HBP	SH	SF	SB	CS	GDP	Avg	OBP	Slg	OPS
2008	Oak	AL	36	99	24	5	0	0	(0	0)	29	14	9	12	13	0	18	2	2	1	4	1	1	.242	.339	.293	.632
2009	Oak	AL	60	208	58	11	3	4	(3	1)	87	27	21	29	19	0	46	1	1	0	7	5	5	.279	.342	.418	.760
2010	Oak	AL	156	508	127	26	8	6	(2	4)	187	64	46	66	50	0	96	3	12	3	29	5	7	.250	.319	.368	.687
2011	Oak	AL	148	515	136	26	2	8	(3	5)	190	57	58	73	42	1	104	1	8	4	14	9	5	.264	.319	.369	.687
2012	Oak	AL	125	418	90	18	2	6	(0	6)	130	50	28	37	35	0	90	2	5	2	15	6	1	.215	.278	.311	.589
2013	Ari	NL	96	269	65	13	1	1	(1	0)	83	25	18	23	26	5	54	1	2	1	2	0	7	.242	.310	.309	.618
2014	Ari	NL	68	177	46	5	3	2	(1	1)	62	21	10	19	20	0	36	3	1	0	6	1	1	.260	.340	.350	.690
2015	2 Tms		105	210	44	6	0	3	(1	2)	59	24	21	18	27	2	49	1	7	4	3	0	6	.210	.298	.281	.578
15	Ari	NL	72	135	32	3	0	1	(1	0)	38	15	10	10	16	2	29	0	4	2	3	0	4	.237	.314	.281	.595
15	Tor	AL	33	75	12	3	0	2	(0	2)	21	9	11	8	11	0	20	1	3	2	0	0	2	.160	.270	.280	.550
	Postseason		5	14	4	0	0	0	(0	0)	4	1	1	2	3	0	4	0	0	0	0	0	0	.286	.412	.286	.697
	8 ML YEARS		794	2404	589	110	19	30	(11	19)	827	282	211	277	232	8	493	14	38	15	80	27	33	.245	.313	.344	.657

David Peralta

Bats: L **Throws:** L **Pos:** LF-124;PH-21;RF-9;CF-1　　pah-RALL-tah　　**Ht:** 6'1" **Wt:** 215 **Born:** 8/14/1987 **Age:** 28

Year	Team	Lg	G	AB	H	2B	3B	HR	(Hm	Rd)	TB	R	RBI	RC	TBB	IBB	SO	HBP	SH	SF	SB	CS	GDP	Avg	OBP	Slg	OPS
2011	RioGrnd	IND	85	339	133	30	5	17	(-	-)	224	76	81	89	19	0	44	7	2	6	7	2	-	.392	.429	.661	1.089
2012	Wichita	IND	98	377	125	30	5	3	(-	-)	174	65	70	72	36	1	36	5	0	5	25	8	-	.332	.392	.462	.854
2013	2 Tms	Low	93	390	136	29	4	16	(-	-)	221	71	80	80	17	2	50	2	0	4	5	1	8	.349	.375	.567	.942
2014	Mobile	AA	53	202	60	17	1	6	(-	-)	97	33	46	35	18	2	21	2	0	1	2	0	5	.297	.359	.480	.839
2014	Ari	NL	88	329	94	12	9	8	(5	3)	148	40	36	38	16	0	60	1	1	1	6	3	9	.286	.320	.450	.770
2015	Ari	NL	149	462	144	26	10	17	(8	9)	241	61	78	83	44	2	107	4	0	7	9	4	7	.312	.371	.522	.893
	2 ML YEARS		237	791	238	38	19	25	(13	12)	389	101	114	121	60	2	167	5	1	8	15	7	16	.301	.351	.492	.842

Jhonny Peralta

Bats: R **Throws:** R **Pos:** SS-148;PH-6;DH-2　　pah-RALL-tah　　**Ht:** 6'2" **Wt:** 215 **Born:** 5/28/1982 **Age:** 34

Year	Team	Lg	G	AB	H	2B	3B	HR	(Hm	Rd)	TB	R	RBI	RC	TBB	IBB	SO	HBP	SH	SF	SB	CS	GDP	Avg	OBP	Slg	OPS
2003	Cle	AL	77	242	55	10	1	4	(3	1)	79	24	21	24	20	0	65	4	2	2	1	3	5	.227	.295	.326	.621
2004	Cle	AL	8	25	6	1	0	0	(0	0)	7	2	2	2	3	0	6	0	0	0	0	1	0	.240	.321	.280	.601
2005	Cle	AL	141	504	147	35	4	24	(14	10)	262	82	78	87	58	3	128	3	1	4	0	2	12	.292	.366	.520	.885
2006	Cle	AL	149	569	146	28	3	13	(7	6)	219	84	68	66	56	0	152	1	3	3	0	1	19	.257	.323	.385	.708
2007	Cle	AL	152	574	155	27	1	21	(16	5)	247	87	72	85	61	2	146	4	1	7	4	4	12	.270	.341	.430	.771
2008	Cle	AL	154	605	167	42	4	23	(11	12)	286	104	89	84	48	2	126	4	2	5	3	1	26	.276	.331	.473	.804
2009	Cle	AL	151	582	148	35	1	11	(2	9)	218	57	83	63	51	0	134	4	2	6	0	2	20	.254	.316	.375	.690
2010	2 Tms	AL	148	551	137	30	2	15	(4	11)	216	60	81	71	53	2	103	1	0	10	1	0	11	.249	.311	.392	.703
2011	Det	AL	146	525	157	25	3	21	(13	8)	251	68	86	77	40	2	95	2	0	9	0	2	17	.299	.345	.478	.824
2012	Det	AL	150	531	127	32	3	13	(6	7)	204	58	63	53	49	3	105	2	1	2	1	2	20	.239	.305	.384	.689
2013	Det	AL	107	409	124	30	0	11	(7	4)	187	50	55	62	35	2	98	1	1	2	3	3	9	.303	.358	.457	.815
2014	StL	NL	157	560	147	38	0	21	(8	13)	248	61	75	74	58	2	112	6	0	4	3	2	19	.263	.336	.443	.779
2015	StL	NL	155	579	159	26	1	17	(9	8)	238	64	71	65	50	6	111	5	0	6	1	4	23	.275	.334	.411	.745
10	Cle	AL	91	334	82	23	2	7	(3	4)	130	37	43	41	32	1	69	1	0	6	1	0	7	.246	.308	.389	.698
10	Det	AL	57	217	55	7	0	8	(1	7)	86	23	38	30	21	1	34	0	0	4	0	0	4	.253	.314	.396	.710
	Postseason		54	197	52	14	0	8	(5	3)	90	17	25	24	14	0	39	1	1	1	2	0	9	.264	.315	.457	.771
	13 ML YEARS		1695	6256	1675	359	23	194	(100	94)	2662	801	844	813	582	24	1381	37	13	60	17	27	193	.268	.331	.426	.756

Joel Peralta

Pitches: R **Bats:** R **Pos:** RP-33　　joe-ELL pah-RALL-tah　　**Ht:** 5'10" **Wt:** 210 **Born:** 3/23/1976 **Age:** 40

Year	Team	Lg	G	GS	CG	GF	IP	BFP	H	R	ER	HR	SH	SF	HB	TBB	IBB	SO	WP	Bk	W	L	Pct	Sh	Sv-Op	Hld	ERC	ERA
2005	LAA	AL	28	0	0	10	34.2	145	28	15	15	6	2	1	0	14	2	30	2	0	1	0	1.000	0	0-0	0	3.40	3.89
2006	KC	AL	64	0	0	21	73.2	304	74	37	36	10	1	3	2	17	2	57	5	0	1	3	.250	0	1-3	17	3.80	4.40
2007	KC	AL	62	0	0	18	87.2	366	93	39	37	9	2	4	2	19	5	66	2	0	1	3	.250	0	1-5	7	3.75	3.80
2008	KC	AL	40	0	0	12	52.2	224	56	37	35	15	1	3	2	14	0	38	1	0	1	2	.333	0	0-1	1	5.38	5.98
2009	Col	NL	27	0	0	6	24.2	113	27	17	17	3	0	1	3	12	2	22	0	0	3	0	.000	0	0-1	6	5.51	6.20
2010	Was	NL	39	0	0	10	49.0	189	30	12	11	5	2	1	1	9	4	49	0	0	1	0	1.000	0	0-2	9	1.43	2.02
2011	TB	AL	71	0	0	18	67.2	256	44	23	22	7	2	2	0	18	3	61	3	0	3	4	.429	0	6-8	19	1.84	2.93
2012	TB	AL	77	0	0	9	67.0	264	49	28	27	9	0	1	1	17	2	84	5	0	2	6	.250	0	2-5	37	2.36	3.63
2013	TB	AL	80	0	0	12	71.1	291	47	31	27	7	2	0	0	34	1	74	1	0	3	8	.273	0	1-4	41	2.53	3.41
2014	TB	AL	69	0	0	12	63.1	265	60	31	31	9	2	1	1	15	1	74	2	0	3	4	.429	0	1-7	18	3.41	4.41
2015	LAD	NL	33	0	0	7	29.0	121	28	14	14	6	0	0	4	8	1	24	1	0	3	1	.750	0	3-3	3	4.04	4.34
	Postseason		6	0	0	2	5.2	23	4	0	0	0	0	0	0	3	0	4	1	0	0	0	-	0	0-1	1	2.41	0.00
	11 ML YEARS		590	0	0	135	620.2	2538	536	284	272	86	14	17	12	177	23	579	22	0	19	34	.358	0	15-39	158	3.18	3.94

Wily Peralta

Pitches: R **Bats:** R **Pos:** SP-20　　pah-RALL-tah　　**Ht:** 6'1" **Wt:** 245 **Born:** 5/8/1989 **Age:** 27

Year	Team	Lg	G	GS	CG	GF	IP	BFP	H	R	ER	HR	SH	SF	HB	TBB	IBB	SO	WP	Bk	W	L	Pct	Sh	Sv-Op	Hld	ERC	ERA
2012	Mil	NL	6	5	0	1	29.0	113	24	8	8	0	3	0	0	11	0	23	1	0	2	1	.667	0	0-0	0	2.61	2.48
2013	Mil	NL	32	32	2	0	183.1	802	187	107	89	19	11	3	7	73	3	129	12	0	11	15	.423	1	0-0	0	4.32	4.37
2014	Mil	NL	32	32	0	0	198.2	838	198	88	78	23	9	3	7	61	0	154	7	0	17	11	.607	0	0-0	0	3.98	3.53
2015	Mil	NL	20	20	0	0	108.2	478	130	60	57	14	4	3	4	37	2	60	5	1	5	10	.333	0	0-0	0	5.40	4.72
	4 ML YEARS		90	89	2	1	519.2	2231	539	263	232	56	27	9	18	182	5	366	25	1	35	37	.486	1	0-0	0	4.30	4.02

Jose Peraza

Bats: R **Throws:** R **Pos:** 2B-6;CF-1;PR-1　　per-AH-zuh　　**Ht:** 6'0" **Wt:** 180 **Born:** 4/30/1994 **Age:** 22

Year	Team	Lg	G	AB	H	2B	3B	HR	(Hm	Rd)	TB	R	RBI	RC	TBB	IBB	SO	HBP	SH	SF	SB	CS	GDP	Avg	OBP	Slg	OPS
2012	2 Tms	Low	53	206	61	7	3	1	(-	-)	77	38	28	30	13	0	24	4	5	0	25	5	2	.296	.350	.374	.724
2013	Rome	A	114	448	129	18	8	1	(-	-)	166	72	47	67	34	1	64	6	9	7	64	15	8	.288	.341	.371	.712
2014	Lynbrg	A+	66	284	97	13	8	1	(-	-)	129	44	27	51	10	1	32	3	3	4	35	7	5	.342	.365	.454	.820
2014	Missi	AA	44	185	62	7	3	1	(-	-)	78	35	17	30	7	0	15	1	2	0	25	8	5	.335	.363	.422	.784
2015	Gwnntt	AAA	96	391	115	10	7	3	(-	-)	148	52	37	51	15	3	35	2	12	7	26	7	7	.294	.318	.379	.697
2015	OkCity	AAA	22	90	26	3	1	1	(-	-)	34	11	5	11	2	0	10	0	2	0	7	0	1	.289	.304	.378	.682
2015	LAD	NL	7	22	4	1	1	0	(0	0)	7	3	1	2	2	1	2	0	1	0	3	0	0	.182	.250	.318	.568

Carlos Perez

Bats: R Throws: R Pos: C-80;PH-4;1B-2;DH-1;PR-1　　　　Ht: 6'0" Wt: 210 Born: 10/27/1990 Age: 25

Year Team	Lg	G	AB	H	2B	3B	HR	(Hm	Rd)	TB	R	RBI	RC	TBB	IBB	SO	HBP	SH	SF	SB	CS	GDP	Avg	OBP	Slg	OPS
2011 Lnsng	A	95	383	98	17	6	3	(-	-)	136	58	41	47	37	1	74	2	1	6	6	2	8	.256	.320	.355	.675
2012 2 Tms	Low	97	361	103	28	6	5	(-	-)	158	59	50	59	41	1	55	4	5	5	3	3	12	.285	.360	.438	.798
2013 CpChr	AA	16	53	15	4	0	1	(-	-)	22	6	5	8	4	0	11	2	1	0	0	0	1	.283	.356	.415	.771
2013 OkCity	AAA	75	264	71	14	0	2	(-	-)	91	29	32	32	25	0	39	0	3	4	1	1	5	.269	.328	.345	.672
2014 OkCity	AAA	88	301	78	16	2	6	(-	-)	116	33	34	40	29	0	54	1	6	3	3	0	10	.259	.323	.385	.709
2015 Salt Lk	AAA	17	72	26	8	0	2	(-	-)	40	11	12	16	7	0	7	0	0	0	1	0	2	.361	.418	.556	.973
2015 LAA	AL	86	260	65	13	0	4	(4	0)	90	20	21	26	19	0	49	0	2	2	2	0	7	.250	.299	.346	.645

Eury Perez

Bats: R Throws: R Pos: LF-29;PH-12;RF-6;CF-3;DH-1;PR-1　　YERR-ee　　　　Ht: 6'0" Wt: 190 Born: 5/30/1990 Age: 26

Year Team	Lg	G	AB	H	2B	3B	HR	(Hm	Rd)	TB	R	RBI	RC	TBB	IBB	SO	HBP	SH	SF	SB	CS	GDP	Avg	OBP	Slg	OPS
2015 Gwnntt*	AAA	64	236	70	8	2	2	(-	-)	88	35	21	37	22	0	39	6	6	1	28	8	2	.297	.370	.373	.743
2012 Was	NL	13	5	1	0	0	0	(0	0)	1	3	0	0	0	0	0	0	0	0	3	0	0	.200	.200	.200	.400
2013 Was	NL	9	8	1	0	0	0	(0	0)	1	1	0	0	0	0	3	0	0	0	1	0	0	.125	.125	.125	.250
2014 NYY	AL	4	10	2	0	0	0	(0	0)	2	2	0	1	0	0	3	0	0	0	1	0	0	.200	.200	.200	.400
2015 Atl	NL	47	119	32	4	0	0	(0	0)	36	10	5	10	7	1	23	4	3	0	3	1	3	.269	.331	.303	.633
4 ML YEARS		73	142	36	4	0	0	(0	0)	40	16	5	11	7	1	29	4	3	0	8	1	3	.254	.307	.282	.589

Hernan Perez

AIR-nahn

Bats: R Throws: R Pos: 3B-80;PH-22;2B-19;1B-7;SS-6;PR-5;DH-1　　　　Ht: 6'1" Wt: 185 Born: 3/26/1991 Age: 25

Year Team	Lg	G	AB	H	2B	3B	HR	(Hm	Rd)	TB	R	RBI	RC	TBB	IBB	SO	HBP	SH	SF	SB	CS	GDP	Avg	OBP	Slg	OPS
2012 Det	AL	2	2	1	0	0	0	(0	0)	1	1	0	0	0	0	0	0	0	0	0	0	0	.500	.500	.500	1.000
2013 Det	AL	34	66	13	0	1	0	(0	0)	15	13	5	4	2	0	15	0	2	1	1	0	2	.197	.217	.227	.445
2014 Det	AL	8	5	1	0	0	0	(0	0)	1	1	0	0	1	0	1	0	0	0	0	0	0	.200	.333	.200	.533
2015 2 Tms		112	263	64	15	2	1	(0	1)	86	14	21	23	5	1	59	0	3	1	5	1	6	.243	.257	.327	.584
15 Det	AL	22	33	2	0	0	0	(0	0)	2	1	0	0	1	0	11	0	0	0	1	0	2	.061	.088	.061	.149
15 Mil	NL	90	230	62	15	2	1	(0	1)	84	13	21	23	4	1	48	0	3	1	4	1	4	.270	.281	.365	.646
Postseason		4	2	0	0	0	0	(0	0)	0	1	0	0	0	0	0	0	0	0	0	0	1	.000	.000	.000	.000
4 ML YEARS		156	336	79	15	3	1	(0	1)	103	29	26	27	8	1	75	0	5	2	6	1	8	.235	.251	.307	.558

Juan Perez

Bats: R Throws: R Pos: PH-9;LF-8;CF-5;2B-1;PR-1　　　　Ht: 5'11" Wt: 185 Born: 11/13/1986 Age: 29

Year Team	Lg	G	AB	H	2B	3B	HR	(Hm	Rd)	TB	R	RBI	RC	TBB	IBB	SO	HBP	SH	SF	SB	CS	GDP	Avg	OBP	Slg	OPS
2015 Scrmto*	AAA	83	321	85	24	3	7	(-	-)	136	41	37	44	17	2	62	2	4	0	17	2	11	.265	.306	.424	.730
2013 SF	NL	34	89	23	5	0	1	(1	0)	31	8	8	10	6	0	21	0	1	1	2	0	3	.258	.302	.348	.650
2014 SF	NL	61	100	17	7	0	1	(0	1)	27	13	3	2	5	0	25	2	2	0	0	1	3	.170	.224	.270	.494
2015 SF	NL	22	39	11	3	0	0	(0	0)	14	5	2	2	1	0	6	0	0	0	1	0	1	.282	.300	.359	.659
Postseason		14	25	5	1	0	0	(0	0)	6	3	3	3	2	2	6	0	3	1	0	0	0	.200	.250	.240	.490
3 ML YEARS		117	228	51	15	0	2	(1	1)	72	26	13	14	12	0	52	2	3	1	3	1	7	.224	.267	.316	.583

Martin Perez

Pitches: L Bats: L Pos: SP-14　　mar-TEEN　　　　Ht: 6'0" Wt: 195 Born: 4/4/1991 Age: 25

		HOW MUCH HE PITCHED						WHAT HE GAVE UP										THE RESULTS						
Year Team	Lg	G	GS	CG	GF	IP	BFP	H	R	ER	HR	SH	SF	HB	TBB	IBB	SO	WP	Bk	W	L	Pct	Sh	Sv-Op	Hld	ERC	ERA
2012 Tex	AL	12	6	0	2	38.0	177	47	26	23	3	1	1	2	15	1	25	5	2	1	4	.200	0	0-0	0	5.33	5.45
2013 Tex	AL	20	20	1	0	124.1	529	129	55	50	15	2	3	3	37	0	84	9	2	10	6	.625	0	0-0	0	4.14	3.62
2014 Tex	AL	8	8	2	0	51.1	207	50	25	25	3	1	0	1	19	1	35	1	0	4	3	.571	2	0-0	0	3.82	4.38
2015 Tex	AL	14	14	0	0	78.2	339	88	45	39	3	0	3	2	24	1	48	1	0	3	6	.333	0	0-0	0	4.04	4.46
4 ML YEARS		54	48	3	2	292.1	1252	314	151	137	24	4	7	8	95	3	192	16	4	18	19	.486	2	0-0	0	4.21	4.22

Oliver Perez

Pitches: L Bats: L Pos: RP-70　　　　Ht: 6'3" Wt: 220 Born: 8/15/1981 Age: 34

		HOW MUCH HE PITCHED						WHAT HE GAVE UP										THE RESULTS						
Year Team	Lg	G	GS	CG	GF	IP	BFP	H	R	ER	HR	SH	SF	HB	TBB	IBB	SO	WP	Bk	W	L	Pct	Sh	Sv-Op	Hld	ERC	ERA
2002 SD	NL	16	15	0	0	90.0	387	71	37	35	13	5	3	5	48	1	94	3	0	4	5	.444	0	0-0	0	3.93	3.50
2003 2 Tms	NL	24	24	0	0	126.2	579	129	80	77	22	5	2	4	77	3	141	7	1	4	10	.286	0	0-0	0	5.66	5.47
2004 Pit	NL	30	30	2	0	196.0	805	145	71	65	22	9	5	9	81	2	239	2	1	12	10	.545	1	0-0	0	2.99	2.98
2005 Pit	NL	20	20	0	0	103.0	471	102	68	67	23	5	4	6	70	1	97	3	0	7	5	.583	0	0-0	0	6.44	5.85
2006 2 Tms	NL	22	22	1	0	112.2	529	129	90	82	20	5	10	6	68	0	102	5	1	3	13	.188	1	0-0	0	6.62	6.55
2007 NYM	NL	29	29	0	0	177.0	765	153	90	70	22	4	7	7	79	1	174	6	0	15	10	.600	0	0-0	0	3.76	3.56
2008 NYM	NL	34	34	0	0	194.0	847	167	100	91	24	9	7	11	105	4	180	9	1	10	7	.588	0	0-0	0	4.21	4.22
2009 NYM	NL	14	14	0	0	66.0	324	69	51	50	12	5	4	4	58	2	62	2	0	3	4	.429	0	0-0	0	7.16	6.82
2010 NYM	NL	17	7	0	4	46.1	234	54	37	35	9	1	3	4	42	3	37	4	0	0	5	.000	0	0-0	0	8.27	6.80
2012 Sea	AL	33	0	0	6	29.2	123	27	7	7	1	1	1	0	10	2	24	2	0	1	3	.250	0	0-2	5	2.82	2.12
2013 Sea	AL	61	0	0	22	53.0	229	50	23	22	6	6	1	0	26	3	74	1	0	3	3	.500	0	2-3	8	4.23	3.74
2014 Ari	NL	68	0	0	11	58.2	256	50	25	19	5	4	0	7	24	2	76	3	3	3	4	.429	0	0-1	15	3.53	2.91
2015 2 Tms		70	0	0	15	41.0	183	39	24	19	4	1	0	4	15	2	51	3	0	2	4	.333	0	0-3	10	3.81	4.17
03 SD	NL	19	19	0	0	103.2	473	103	65	62	20	4	2	3	65	2	117	6	1	4	7	.364	0	0-0	0	5.74	5.38

			HOW MUCH HE PITCHED						WHAT HE GAVE UP													THE RESULTS							
Year	Team	Lg	G	GS	CG	GF	IP	BFP	H	R	ER	HR	SH	SF	HB	TBB	IBB	SO	WP	Bk	W	L	Pct	Sh	Sv-Op	Hld	ERC	ERA
03	Pit	NL	5	5	0	0	23.0	106	26	15	15	2	1	0	1	12	1	24	1	0	0	3	.000	0	0-0	0	5.29	5.87
06	Pit	NL	15	15	0	0	76.0	364	88	64	56	13	5	8	3	51	0	61	4	1	2	10	.167	0	0-0	0	6.85	6.63
06	NYM	NL	7	7	1	0	36.2	165	41	26	26	7	0	2	3	17	0	41	1	0	1	3	.250	1	0-0	0	6.16	6.38
15	Ari	NL	48	0	0	11	29.0	128	25	12	10	2	1	0	4	11	1	37	2	0	2	1	.667	0	0-3	7	3.38	3.10
15	Hou	AL	22	0	0	4	12.0	55	14	12	9	2	0	0	0	4	1	14	1	0	0	3	.000	0	0-0	3	4.89	6.75
	Postseason		2	2	0	0	11.2	50	13	6	6	3	2	0	1	3	1	7	0	0	1	0	1.000	0	0-0	0	5.61	4.63
	13 ML YEARS		438	195	3	58	1294.0	5732	1185	703	639	183	55	46	68	703	26	1351	50	7	67	83	.447	2	2-9	38	4.63	4.44

Roberto Perez

Bats: R **Throws:** R **Pos:** C-69;DH-1   **Ht:** 5'11" **Wt:** 225 **Born:** 12/23/1988 **Age:** 27

			BATTING																			RUNNING			AVERAGES			
Year	Team	Lg	G	AB	H	2B	3B	HR	(Hm	Rd)	TB	R	RBI	RC	TBB	IBB	SO	HBP	SH	SF	SB	CS	GDP	Avg	OBP	Slg	OPS
2011	Knstn	A+	94	284	64	16	1	2	(-	-)	88	30	30	38	62	2	79	1	3	1	1	0	7	.225	.365	.310	.675
2012	Akron	AA	95	283	60	16	2	1	(-	-)	83	31	31	33	49	0	67	6	7	4	0	1	11	.212	.336	.293	.630
2013	Akron	AA	32	93	23	5	0	2	(-	-)	34	10	10	19	32	0	25	3	0	0	1	1	4	.247	.453	.366	.819
2013	Clmbs	AAA	67	187	33	12	0	0	(-	-)	45	16	24	12	22	0	59	3	6	4	0	1	6	.176	.269	.241	.509
2014	Clmbs	AAA	53	174	53	11	1	8	(-	-)	90	29	43	37	29	1	51	1	4	1	1	0	5	.305	.405	.517	.922
2014	Cle	AL	29	85	23	5	0	1	(1	0)	31	10	4	8	5	0	26	0	5	0	0	0	2	.271	.311	.365	.676
2015	Cle	AL	70	184	42	9	1	7	(4	3)	74	30	21	24	33	1	64	2	5	2	0	0	9	.228	.348	.402	.751
	2 ML YEARS		99	269	65	14	1	8	(5	3)	105	40	25	32	38	1	90	2	10	2	0	0	11	.242	.338	.390	.728

Salvador Perez

Bats: R **Throws:** R **Pos:** C-139;DH-2;1B-1;PH-1   **Ht:** 6'3" **Wt:** 240 **Born:** 5/10/1990 **Age:** 26

			BATTING																			RUNNING			AVERAGES			
Year	Team	Lg	G	AB	H	2B	3B	HR	(Hm	Rd)	TB	R	RBI	RC	TBB	IBB	SO	HBP	SH	SF	SB	CS	GDP	Avg	OBP	Slg	OPS
2011	KC	AL	39	148	49	8	2	3	(1	2)	70	20	21	26	7	0	20	1	0	2	0	0	5	.331	.361	.473	.834
2012	KC	AL	76	289	87	16	0	11	(3	8)	136	38	39	36	12	3	27	1	0	3	0	0	14	.301	.328	.471	.798
2013	KC	AL	138	496	145	25	3	13	(6	7)	215	48	79	77	21	2	63	4	0	5	0	0	13	.292	.323	.433	.757
2014	KC	AL	150	578	150	28	2	17	(8	9)	233	57	70	55	22	2	85	3	0	3	1	0	22	.260	.289	.403	.692
2015	KC	AL	142	531	138	25	0	21	(9	12)	226	52	70	60	13	4	82	4	0	5	1	0	23	.260	.280	.426	.706
	Postseason		15	58	12	1	0	1	(1	0)	16	4	6	3	1	0	10	1	0	0	0	0	2	.207	.233	.276	.509
	5 ML YEARS		545	2042	569	102	7	65	(27	38)	880	215	279	254	75	11	277	13	0	18	2	0	77	.279	.306	.431	.737

Williams Perez

Pitches: R **Bats:** R **Pos:** SP-20; RP-3   **Ht:** 6'1" **Wt:** 230 **Born:** 5/21/1991 **Age:** 25

			HOW MUCH HE PITCHED						WHAT HE GAVE UP													THE RESULTS							
Year	Team	Lg	G	GS	CG	GF	IP	BFP	H	R	ER	HR	SH	SF	HB	TBB	IBB	SO	WP	Bk	W	L	Pct	Sh	Sv-Op	Hld	ERC	ERA
2011	2 Tms	Low	13	6	0	1	39.1	179	40	18	12	2	0	1	6	17	0	38	1	0	4	0	1.000	0	0- -	-	4.47	2.75
2012	Danvle	R+	13	9	0	1	56.1	234	54	31	26	5	0	1	4	9	0	54	1	0	4	3	.571	0	1- -	-	3.09	4.15
2013	2 Tms	Low	23	22	1	0	125.0	524	123	55	49	9	4	4	5	36	0	106	6	0	11	6	.647	0	0- -	-	3.55	3.53
2014	Missi	AA	26	25	0	0	133.0	555	119	49	43	4	7	4	11	39	0	94	9	2	7	6	.538	0	0- -	-	2.96	2.91
2015	Gwnntt	AAA	8	8	0	0	38.2	154	32	8	5	1	1	1	1	10	0	36	0	0	3	1	.750	0	0- -	-	2.32	1.16
2015	Atl	NL	23	20	1	1	116.2	514	130	66	62	13	3	5	9	51	2	73	4	1	7	6	.538	0	1-1	0	5.41	4.78

Glen Perkins

Pitches: L **Bats:** L **Pos:** RP-60   **Ht:** 6'0" **Wt:** 215 **Born:** 3/2/1983 **Age:** 33

			HOW MUCH HE PITCHED						WHAT HE GAVE UP													THE RESULTS							
Year	Team	Lg	G	GS	CG	GF	IP	BFP	H	R	ER	HR	SH	SF	HB	TBB	IBB	SO	WP	Bk	W	L	Pct	Sh	Sv-Op	Hld	ERC	ERA
2006	Min	AL	4	0	0	0	5.2	20	3	1	1	0	0	0	0	0	0	6	0	0	0	0	-	0	0-0	1	0.60	1.59
2007	Min	AL	19	0	0	3	28.2	115	23	10	10	2	1	1	2	12	0	20	2	0	0	0	-	0	0-0	3	3.32	3.14
2008	Min	AL	26	26	0	0	151.0	661	183	81	74	25	7	4	3	39	0	74	2	1	12	4	.750	0	0-0	0	5.30	4.41
2009	Min	AL	18	17	0	0	96.1	423	120	64	63	13	1	3	1	23	0	45	2	1	6	7	.462	0	0-0	0	5.14	5.89
2010	Min	AL	13	1	0	5	21.2	98	29	16	14	3	1	2	4	5	1	14	0	0	1	1	.500	0	0-0	0	6.56	5.82
2011	Min	AL	65	0	0	17	61.2	253	55	19	17	2	5	1	1	21	5	65	3	0	4	4	.500	0	2-5	17	2.81	2.48
2012	Min	AL	70	0	0	43	70.1	281	57	25	20	8	3	2	1	16	3	78	3	0	3	1	.750	0	16-20	11	2.63	2.56
2013	Min	AL	61	0	0	53	62.2	240	43	16	16	5	2	1	3	15	0	77	0	0	2	0	1.000	0	36-40	0	2.01	2.30
2014	Min	AL	63	0	0	56	61.2	260	62	29	25	7	2	5	2	11	2	66	3	0	4	3	.571	0	34-41	0	3.33	3.65
2015	Min	AL	60	0	0	45	57.0	238	58	21	21	9	1	0	0	10	2	54	4	0	3	5	.375	0	32-35	3	3.56	3.32
	Postseason		1	0	0	0	0.1	3	2	0	0	0	0	0	0	0	0	0	0	0	0	0	-	0	0-0	0	39.65	0.00
	10 ML YEARS		399	44	0	224	616.2	2589	633	282	261	74	23	19	19	152	13	499	19	2	35	25	.583	0	120-141	35	3.86	3.81

Vinnie Pestano

Pitches: R **Bats:** R **Pos:** RP-19   peh-STAH-no   **Ht:** 6'0" **Wt:** 210 **Born:** 2/20/1985 **Age:** 31

			HOW MUCH HE PITCHED						WHAT HE GAVE UP													THE RESULTS							
Year	Team	Lg	G	GS	CG	GF	IP	BFP	H	R	ER	HR	SH	SF	HB	TBB	IBB	SO	WP	Bk	W	L	Pct	Sh	Sv-Op	Hld	ERC	ERA
2015	Salt Lk*	AAA	35	0	0	24	34.1	131	18	8	8	1	1	1	4	8	1	42	4	0	1	3	.250	0	10- -	-	1.29	2.10
2010	Cle	AL	5	0	0	5	5.0	23	4	2	2	0	0	0	0	5	0	8	0	0	0	0	-	0	1-1	0	4.56	3.60
2011	Cle	AL	68	0	0	20	62.0	250	41	16	16	5	0	0	3	24	3	84	0	0	1	2	.333	0	2-6	23	2.26	2.32
2012	Cle	AL	70	0	0	13	70.0	286	53	20	20	7	0	2	4	24	1	76	1	0	3	5	.500	0	2-5	36	2.77	2.57
2013	Cle	AL	37	0	0	21	35.1	159	37	18	16	6	0	2	1	21	1	37	2	0	1	2	.333	0	6-9	6	5.84	4.08
2014	2 Tms	AL	25	0	0	5	18.2	78	18	8	6	3	0	1	0	5	0	26	2	0	0	1	.000	0	3-3	3	3.74	2.89
2015	LAA	AL	19	0	0	3	11.2	60	15	9	7	3	0	2	1	8	2	13	1	0	1	0	1.000	0	0-2	0	8.08	5.40

	HOW MUCH HE PITCHED			WHAT HE GAVE UP				THE RESULTS		
Year Team Lg	G GS CG GF	IP BFP	H R ER HR SH SF HB	TBB IBB	SO WP Bk	W L	Pct Sh	Sv-Op Hld	ERC ERA
14 Cle AL	13 0 0 2	9.0 40	13 7 5 2 0 0 0	1 0	13 1 0	0 1	.000 0	0-0 0	6.43 5.00
14 LAA AL	12 0 0 3	9.2 38	5 1 1 1 0 1 0	4 0	13 1 0	0 0	- 0	0-0 1	1.70 0.93
Postseason	2 0 0 1	1.0 4	1 0 0 0 0 0 0	0 0	1 0 0	0 0	- 0	0-0 0	1.95 0.00
6 ML YEARS	224 0 0 67	202.2 856	168 73 67 24 0 7 9	87 7	244 6 0	6 8	.429 0	11-23 66	3.50 2.98

Jace Peterson

Bats: L Throws: R Pos: 2B-144;PH-11;PR-2   JAYCE   Ht: 6'0" Wt: 200 Born: 5/9/1990 Age: 26

				BATTING														RUNNING			AVERAGES			
Year Team	Lg	G	AB	H	2B	3B	HR	(Hm Rd)	TB	R	RBI	RC	TBB IBB	SO	HBP	SH	SF	SB	CS	GDP	Avg	OBP	Slg	OPS
2011 Eugene	A-	73	276	67	9	5	2	(- -)	92	48	27	42	50 1	53	2	2	3	39	10	4	.243	.360	.333	.693
2012 FtWyn	A	117	444	127	23	9	2	(- -)	174	78	48	76	62 0	63	5	8	2	51	13	4	.286	.378	.392	.770
2013 Lk Els	A+	113	423	128	17	13	7	(- -)	192	78	66	82	54 0	58	5	7	7	42	10	6	.303	.382	.454	.836
2014 SnAnt	AA	18	74	23	3	0	1	(- -)	29	10	7	11	9 0	9	0	0	0	4	3	1	.311	.386	.392	.777
2014 ElPaso	AAA	68	248	76	21	6	2	(- -)	115	44	39	49	42 0	50	1	6	2	12	6	3	.306	.406	.464	.870
2014 SD	NL	27	53	6	0	0	0	(0 0)	6	3	0	0	2 1	18	1	2	0	2	0	1	.113	.161	.113	.274
2015 Atl	NL	152	528	126	23	5	6	(1 5)	177	55	52	56	56 4	120	3	7	3	12	10	5	.239	.314	.335	.649
2 ML YEARS		179	581	132	23	5	6	(1 5)	183	58	52	56	58 5	138	4	9	3	14	10	6	.227	.300	.315	.615

Shane Peterson

Bats: L Throws: L Pos: PH-39;LF-33;CF-20;RF-9;1B-2;DH-1;PR-1   Ht: 6'0" Wt: 210 Born: 2/11/1988 Age: 28

				BATTING														RUNNING			AVERAGES			
Year Team	Lg	G	AB	H	2B	3B	HR	(Hm Rd)	TB	R	RBI	RC	TBB IBB	SO	HBP	SH	SF	SB	CS	GDP	Avg	OBP	Slg	OPS
2011 Mdlnd	AA	59	227	59	16	1	3	(- -)	86	33	27	35	30 1	38	5	0	1	11	1	6	.260	.357	.379	.736
2011 Scrmto	AAA	46	167	49	7	3	6	(- -)	80	31	32	31	23 0	37	0	0	1	2	1	6	.293	.377	.479	.856
2012 Mdlnd	AA	48	157	43	11	3	2	(- -)	66	27	23	34	44 3	47	3	1	0	9	3	1	.274	.441	.420	.862
2012 Scrmto	AAA	39	131	51	7	1	7	(- -)	81	36	23	36	23 1	31	1	2	0	4	3	0	.389	.484	.618	1.102
2013 Scrmto	AAA	126	463	116	25	1	12	(- -)	179	70	79	73	77 1	127	4	3	6	17	2	10	.251	.358	.387	.745
2014 Scrmto	AAA	137	543	167	40	5	11	(- -)	250	101	90	100	66 4	139	2	8	6	11	4	14	.308	.381	.460	.841
2015 ColSpr	AAA	47	172	55	10	2	7	(- -)	90	26	27	34	17 0	41	2	1	0	1	1	5	.320	.387	.523	.911
2013 Oak	AL	2	7	1	0	0	0	(0 0)	1	1	1	0	1 0	3	0	0	0	0	0	0	.143	.250	.143	.393
2015 Mil	NL	93	201	52	7	3	2	(0 2)	71	22	16	20	20 1	55	0	3	1	0	1	3	.259	.324	.353	.678
2 ML YEARS		95	208	53	7	3	2	(0 2)	72	23	17	20	21 1	58	0	3	1	0	1	3	.255	.322	.346	.668

Gregorio Petit

Bats: R Throws: R Pos: 2B-13;PH-4;3B-3;PR-1   peh-TEET   Ht: 5'10" Wt: 195 Born: 12/10/1984 Age: 31

				BATTING														RUNNING			AVERAGES			
Year Team	Lg	G	AB	H	2B	3B	HR	(Hm Rd)	TB	R	RBI	RC	TBB IBB	SO	HBP	SH	SF	SB	CS	GDP	Avg	OBP	Slg	OPS
2015 S-WB*	AAA	46	174	40	10	0	2	(- -)	56	19	15	14	8 1	22	0	1	0	0	0	7	.230	.264	.322	.586
2008 Oak	AL	14	23	8	2	0	0	(0 0)	10	4	0	2	2 0	9	0	0	0	0	0	0	.348	.400	.435	.835
2009 Oak	AL	11	31	7	1	0	0	(0 0)	8	2	1	1	0 0	6	0	0	0	0	0	0	.226	.226	.258	.484
2014 Hou	AL	37	97	27	8	0	2	(1 1)	41	14	9	10	1 0	25	2	0	0	0	1	1	.278	.300	.423	.723
2015 NYY	AL	20	42	7	3	0	0	(0 0)	10	7	5	2	3 1	16	0	1	1	0	0	0	.167	.217	.238	.455
4 ML YEARS		82	193	49	14	0	2	(1 1)	69	27	15	15	6 1	56	2	1	1	0	1	3	.254	.282	.358	.640

Yusmeiro Petit

Pitches: R Bats: R Pos: RP-41; SP-1   yooz-MAIR-oh peh-TEET   Ht: 6'1" Wt: 250 Born: 11/22/1984 Age: 31

	HOW MUCH HE PITCHED			WHAT HE GAVE UP				THE RESULTS		
Year Team Lg	G GS CG GF	IP BFP	H R ER HR SH SF HB	TBB IBB	SO WP Bk	W L	Pct Sh	Sv-Op Hld	ERC ERA
2006 Fla NL	15 1 0 5	26.1 129	46 28 28 7 1 0 0	9 1	20 0 0	1 1	.500 0	0-0 0	10.07 9.57
2007 Ari NL	14 10 0 2	57.0 243	58 30 29 12 1 1 0	18 1	40 0 1	3 4	.429 0	0-0 0	4.56 4.58
2008 Ari NL	19 8 0 6	56.1 229	45 29 27 12 4 2 1	14 2	42 3 1	3 5	.375 0	0-0 0	3.08 4.31
2009 Ari NL	23 17 0 2	89.2 407	102 62 58 19 3 0 1	34 1	74 3 0	3 10	.231 0	0-0 0	5.44 5.82
2012 SF NL	1 1 0 0	4.2 22	7 2 2 0 1 0 0	4 0	1 1 0	0 0	- 0	0-0 0	9.14 3.86
2013 SF NL	8 7 1 0	48.0 196	46 19 19 4 2 0 0	11 1	47 0 0	4 1	.800 0	0-0 0	3.08 3.56
2014 SF NL	39 12 1 14	117.0 461	97 51 48 12 0 3 1	22 5	133 0 0	5 5	.500 0	0-0 0	2.40 3.69
2015 SF NL	42 1 0 15	76.0 316	75 32 31 11 1 6 1	15 2	59 3 0	1 1	.500 0	1-1 0	3.48 3.67
Postseason	4 0 0 0	12.2 47	7 2 2 0 0 0 0	4 1	13 1 0	3 0	1.000 0	0-0 0	1.18 1.42
8 ML YEARS	161 57 2 44	475.0 2003	476 253 242 77 13 13 3	127 13	416 10 2	20 27	.426 1	1-1 0	3.94 4.59

Jake Petricka

Pitches: R Bats: R Pos: RP-62   puh-TRICH-kuh   Ht: 6'5" Wt: 205 Born: 6/5/1988 Age: 28

	HOW MUCH HE PITCHED			WHAT HE GAVE UP				THE RESULTS		
Year Team Lg	G GS CG GF	IP BFP	H R ER HR SH SF HB	TBB IBB	SO WP Bk	W L	Pct Sh	Sv-Op Hld	ERC ERA
2013 CWS AL	16 0 0 3	19.1 85	20 7 7 0 1 1 1	10 1	10 4 0	1 1	.500 0	0-1 0	4.18 3.26
2014 CWS AL	67 0 0 33	73.0 307	67 24 24 3 3 4 2	33 4	55 2 0	1 6	.143 0	14-18 10	3.52 2.96
2015 CWS AL	62 0 0 18	52.0 220	56 21 21 2 3 1 1	18 4	33 2 0	4 3	.571 0	2-3 12	3.91 3.63
3 ML YEARS	145 0 0 54	144.1 612	143 52 52 5 7 6 4	61 9	98 8 0	6 10	.375 0	16-22 22	3.75 3.24

Jonathan Pettibone

Pitches: R Bats: L Pos: P Ht: 6'6" Wt: 225 Born: 7/19/1990 Age: 25

		HOW MUCH HE PITCHED						WHAT HE GAVE UP											THE RESULTS						
Year Team	Lg	G	GS	CG	GF	IP	BFP	H	R	ER	HR	SH	SF	HB	TBB	IBB	SO	WP	Bk	W	L	Pct	Sh	Sv-Op	Hld	ERC	ERA
2011 Clrwtr	A+	27	27	0	0	161.0	654	149	62	53	5	7	7	6	34	1	115	7	2	10	11	.476	0	0--	-	2.68	2.96
2012 Rdng	AA	19	19	1	0	117.1	488	115	52	43	9	7	2	5	27	0	81	4	0	9	7	.563	0	0--	-	3.33	3.30
2012 LV	AAA	7	7	1	0	42.1	176	31	12	12	0	2	0	0	22	0	32	2	0	4	1	.800	1	0--	-	2.45	2.55
2014 LV	AAA	5	5	0	0	26.1	106	22	11	10	0	1	1	0	6	0	13	2	0	2	0	1.000	0	0--	-	1.96	3.42
2013 Phi	NL	18	18	0	0	100.1	437	109	50	45	9	8	2	5	38	3	66	1	0	5	4	.556	0	0-0	0	4.62	4.04
2014 Phi	NL	2	2	0	0	9.0	47	17	10	9	2	1	0	0	3	1	6	0	0	0	1	.000	0	0-0	0	10.08	9.00
2 ML YEARS		20	20	0	0	109.1	484	126	60	54	11	9	2	5	41	4	72	1	0	5	5	.500	0	0-0	0	5.03	4.45

Tommy Pham

Bats: R Throws: R Pos: CF-33;LF-18;PH-12;RF-3;PR-1   FAM   Ht: 6'1" Wt: 175 Born: 3/8/1988 Age: 28

		BATTING																RUNNING			AVERAGES			
Year Team	Lg	G	AB	H	2B	3B	HR	(Hm | Rd)	TB	R	RBI	RC	TBB	IBB	SO	HBP	SH	SF	SB	CS	GDP	Avg	OBP	Slg	OPS
2011 Sprgfld	AA	40	142	42	11	3	5	(- | -)	74	31	16	27	18	0	39	1	2	2	3	3	6	.296	.374	.521	.895
2012 Sprgfld	AA	12	39	6	2	0	1	(- | -)	11	3	3	2	4	0	19	0	0	0	0	0	1	.154	.233	.282	.515
2013 Sprgfld	AA	45	163	49	6	6	6	(- | -)	85	27	28	33	20	0	42	4	0	1	6	3	4	.301	.388	.521	.910
2013 Memp	AAA	30	106	28	6	1	1	(- | -)	39	6	13	12	7	0	25	0	0	0	2	1	4	.264	.304	.368	.678
2014 Memp	AAA	104	346	112	16	6	10	(- | -)	170	63	44	70	38	1	81	4	0	2	20	2	8	.324	.395	.491	.886
2015 Memp	AAA	48	171	56	10	1	6	(- | -)	86	29	39	36	22	0	36	0	0	3	9	0	5	.327	.398	.503	.901
2014 StL	NL	6	2	0	0	0	0	(0 | 0)	0	0	0	0	0	0	2	0	0	0	0	0	0	.000	.000	.000	.000
2015 StL	NL	52	153	41	7	5	5	(1 | 4)	73	28	18	26	19	1	41	0	0	1	2	0	1	.268	.347	.477	.824
2 ML YEARS		58	155	41	7	5	5	(1 | 4)	73	28	18	26	19	1	43	0	0	1	2	0	1	.265	.343	.471	.814

Josh Phegley

Bats: R Throws: R Pos: C-68;PH-8;PR-1   FEG-lee   Ht: 5'10" Wt: 225 Born: 2/12/1988 Age: 28

		BATTING																RUNNING			AVERAGES			
Year Team	Lg	G	AB	H	2B	3B	HR	(Hm | Rd)	TB	R	RBI	RC	TBB	IBB	SO	HBP	SH	SF	SB	CS	GDP	Avg	OBP	Slg	OPS
2013 CWS	AL	65	204	42	7	0	4	(2 | 2)	61	14	22	12	5	0	41	0	2	2	2	0	6	.206	.223	.299	.522
2014 CWS	AL	11	37	8	2	0	3	(3 | 0)	19	4	7	2	0	0	11	0	0	0	0	0	0	.216	.211	.514	.724
2015 Oak	AL	73	225	56	16	1	9	(6 | 3)	101	27	34	32	14	0	51	3	0	1	0	0	5	.249	.300	.449	.749
3 ML YEARS		149	466	106	25	1	16	(11 | 5)	181	45	63	46	19	0	103	3	2	4	2	0	11	.227	.260	.388	.649

David Phelps

Pitches: R Bats: R Pos: SP-19; RP-4   Ht: 6'2" Wt: 200 Born: 10/9/1986 Age: 29

		HOW MUCH HE PITCHED						WHAT HE GAVE UP											THE RESULTS						
Year Team	Lg	G	GS	CG	GF	IP	BFP	H	R	ER	HR	SH	SF	HB	TBB	IBB	SO	WP	Bk	W	L	Pct	Sh	Sv-Op	Hld	ERC	ERA
2012 NYY	AL	33	11	0	5	99.2	414	81	38	37	14	4	3	6	38	2	96	2	2	4	4	.500	0	0-0	2	3.48	3.34
2013 NYY	AL	22	12	0	3	86.2	376	88	50	48	8	1	2	5	35	1	79	2	0	6	5	.545	0	0-1	1	4.38	4.98
2014 NYY	AL	32	17	1	5	113.0	497	115	62	55	13	4	3	7	46	2	92	2	1	5	5	.500	0	1-1	5	4.52	4.38
2015 Mia	NL	23	19	0	1	112.0	482	119	59	56	11	2	5	4	33	0	77	2	0	4	8	.333	0	0-0	0	4.13	4.50
Postseason		3	0	0	1	3.1	19	7	4	3	0	0	0	0	1	0	2	0	0	0	2	.000	0	0-0	0	8.97	8.10
4 ML YEARS		110	59	1	14	411.1	1769	403	209	196	46	11	13	22	152	5	344	8	3	19	22	.463	0	1-2	8	4.13	4.29

Brandon Phillips

Bats: R Throws: R Pos: 2B-141;PH-7;SS-1   Ht: 6'0" Wt: 210 Born: 6/28/1981 Age: 35

		BATTING																RUNNING			AVERAGES			
Year Team	Lg	G	AB	H	2B	3B	HR	(Hm | Rd)	TB	R	RBI	RC	TBB	IBB	SO	HBP	SH	SF	SB	CS	GDP	Avg	OBP	Slg	OPS
2002 Cle	AL	11	31	8	3	1	0	(0 | 0)	13	5	4	5	3	0	6	1	1	0	0	0	0	.258	.343	.419	.762
2003 Cle	AL	112	370	77	18	1	6	(3 | 3)	115	36	33	22	14	0	77	3	5	1	4	5	12	.208	.242	.311	.553
2004 Cle	AL	6	22	4	2	0	0	(0 | 0)	6	1	1	0	2	0	5	0	0	0	0	2	1	.182	.250	.273	.523
2005 Cle	AL	6	9	0	0	0	0	(0 | 0)	0	1	0	0	0	0	4	0	0	0	0	0	0	.000	.000	.000	.000
2006 Cin	NL	149	536	148	28	1	17	(9 | 8)	229	65	75	74	35	3	88	6	4	6	25	2	19	.276	.324	.427	.751
2007 Cin	NL	158	650	187	26	6	30	(17 | 13)	315	107	94	88	33	4	109	12	2	5	32	8	26	.288	.331	.485	.816
2008 Cin	NL	141	559	146	24	7	21	(13 | 8)	247	80	78	74	39	6	93	5	0	6	23	10	13	.261	.312	.442	.754
2009 Cin	NL	153	584	161	30	5	20	(10 | 10)	261	78	98	80	44	3	75	6	2	8	25	9	21	.276	.329	.447	.776
2010 Cin	NL	155	626	172	33	5	18	(10 | 8)	269	100	59	77	46	1	83	8	6	1	16	12	14	.275	.332	.430	.762
2011 Cin	NL	150	610	183	38	1	18	(14 | 4)	279	94	82	92	44	3	85	9	5	6	14	9	15	.300	.353	.457	.810
2012 Cin	NL	147	580	163	30	1	18	(15 | 3)	249	86	77	78	28	2	79	8	3	4	15	2	19	.281	.321	.429	.750
2013 Cin	NL	151	606	158	24	2	18	(7 | 11)	240	80	103	82	39	6	98	8	4	9	5	3	19	.261	.310	.396	.706
2014 Cin	NL	121	462	123	25	0	8	(3 | 5)	172	44	51	53	23	1	74	6	2	2	3	2	13	.266	.306	.372	.678
2015 Cin	NL	148	588	173	19	2	12	(9 | 3)	232	69	70	78	27	1	68	4	1	3	23	3	13	.294	.328	.395	.723
Postseason		9	40	13	4	0	2	(0 | 2)	23	3	8	10	0	0	5	0	0	1	1	0	0	.325	.317	.575	.892
14 ML YEARS		1608	6233	1703	300	33	186	(110 | 76)	2627	846	825	803	377	30	944	76	35	55	184	68	185	.273	.320	.421	.741

A.J. Pierzynski

Bats: L Throws: R Pos: C-107;PH-6;DH-1   perr-ZINN-ski   Ht: 6'3" Wt: 235 Born: 12/30/1976 Age: 39

		BATTING																RUNNING			AVERAGES			
Year Team	Lg	G	AB	H	2B	3B	HR	(Hm | Rd)	TB	R	RBI	RC	TBB	IBB	SO	HBP	SH	SF	SB	CS	GDP	Avg	OBP	Slg	OPS
1998 Min	AL	7	10	3	0	0	0	(0 | 0)	3	1	1	2	1	0	2	1	0	1	0	0	6	.300	.385	.300	.685
1999 Min	AL	9	22	6	2	0	0	(0 | 0)	8	3	3	3	1	0	4	1	0	0	0	0	0	.273	.333	.364	.697
2000 Min	AL	33	88	27	5	1	2	(1 | 1)	40	12	11	14	5	0	14	2	0	1	1	0	1	.307	.354	.455	.809
2001 Min	AL	114	381	110	33	2	7	(3 | 4)	168	51	55	50	16	4	57	4	1	3	1	7	7	.289	.322	.441	.763
2002 Min	AL	130	440	132	31	6	6	(2 | 4)	193	54	49	60	13	1	61	11	2	3	1	2	14	.300	.334	.439	.773

			BATTING																			RUNNING			AVERAGES			
Year	Team	Lg	G	AB	H	2B	3B	HR	(Hm	Rd)	TB	R	RBI	RC	TBB	IBB	SO	HBP	SH	SF	SB	CS	GDP	Avg	OBP	Slg	OPS
2003	Min	AL	137	487	152	35	3	11	(6	5)	226	63	74	80	24	12	55	15	2	5	3	1	13	.312	.360	.464	.824
2004	SF	NL	131	471	128	28	2	11	(3	8)	193	45	77	58	19	4	27	15	2	3	0	1	27	.272	.319	.410	.729
2005	CWS	AL	128	460	118	21	0	18	(12	6)	193	61	56	55	23	5	68	12	1	1	0	2	13	.257	.308	.420	.728
2006	CWS	AL	140	509	150	24	0	16	(9	7)	222	65	64	68	22	6	72	8	3	1	1	0	10	.295	.333	.436	.769
2007	CWS	AL	136	472	124	24	0	14	(8	6)	190	54	50	49	25	5	66	8	1	3	1	1	21	.263	.309	.403	.712
2008	CWS	AL	134	534	150	31	1	13	(7	6)	222	66	60	64	19	5	71	8	3	6	1	0	14	.281	.312	.416	.728
2009	CWS	AL	138	504	151	22	1	13	(8	5)	214	57	49	59	24	6	52	1	3	3	1	1	18	.300	.331	.425	.755
2010	CWS	AL	128	474	128	29	0	9	(7	2)	184	43	56	51	15	2	39	6	6	2	3	4	17	.270	.300	.388	.688
2011	CWS	AL	129	464	133	29	1	8	(5	3)	188	38	48	53	23	6	33	5	2	6	0	0	19	.287	.323	.405	.728
2012	CWS	AL	135	479	133	18	4	27	(18	9)	240	68	77	79	28	5	78	8	1	4	0	0	8	.278	.326	.501	.827
2013	Tex	AL	134	503	137	24	1	17	(10	7)	214	48	70	61	11	2	76	9	0	6	1	1	14	.272	.297	.425	.722
2014	2 Tms		102	338	85	12	1	5	(1	4)	114	25	37	31	14	2	54	5	1	4	0	1	13	.251	.288	.337	.625
2015	Atl	NL	113	407	122	24	1	9	(5	4)	175	38	49	51	19	2	37	7	0	3	0	2	19	.300	.339	.430	.769
14	Bos	AL	72	256	65	10	1	4	(1	3)	89	19	31	23	9	2	40	4	1	4	0	0	11	.254	.286	.348	.633
14	StL	NL	30	82	20	2	0	1	(0	1)	25	6	6	8	5	0	14	1	0	0	0	1	2	.244	.295	.305	.600
	Postseason		32	106	31	5	1	5	(3	2)	53	16	18	20	11	1	14	2	1	1	2	3	2	.292	.367	.500	.867
	18 ML YEARS		1978	7043	1989	392	24	186	(105	81)	2987	792	886	888	302	67	866	126	28	55	14	23	228	.282	.321	.424	.745

Kevin Pillar

Bats: R **Throws:** R **Pos:** CF-142;LF-14;RF-3;PH-1;PR-1 pih-LAHR **Ht:** 6'0" **Wt:** 205 **Born:** 1/4/1989 **Age:** 27

			BATTING																			RUNNING			AVERAGES			
Year	Team	Lg	G	AB	H	2B	3B	HR	(Hm	Rd)	TB	R	RBI	RC	TBB	IBB	SO	HBP	SH	SF	SB	CS	GDP	Avg	OBP	Slg	OPS
2013	Tor	AL	36	102	21	4	0	3	(1	2)	34	11	13	9	4	0	29	2	2	0	0	1	0	.206	.250	.333	.583
2014	Tor	AL	53	116	31	9	0	2	(2	0)	46	19	7	8	4	0	28	1	0	1	1	2	3	.267	.295	.397	.692
2015	Tor	AL	159	586	163	31	2	12	(6	6)	234	76	56	73	28	1	85	5	4	5	25	4	9	.278	.314	.399	.713
	3 ML YEARS		248	804	215	44	2	17	(9	8)	314	106	76	90	36	1	142	8	6	6	26	7	12	.267	.303	.391	.694

Stolmy Pimentel

Pitches: R **Bats:** R **Pos:** RP-8 STOLE-mee PIM-en-tell **Ht:** 6'3" **Wt:** 230 **Born:** 2/1/1990 **Age:** 26

			HOW MUCH HE PITCHED						WHAT HE GAVE UP											THE RESULTS						
Year	Team	Lg	G	GS	CG	GF	IP	BFP	H	R	ER	HR	SH	SF	HB	TBB	IBB	SO	WP	Bk	W	L	Pct	Sh	Sv-Op	Hld	ERC	ERA
2015	RdRck*	AAA	17	12	0	2	71.2	330	86	44	43	9	1	5	5	33	0	60	6	1	5	3	.625	0	0- -	-	6.01	5.40
2013	Pit	NL	5	0	0	1	9.1	38	6	4	2	0	0	1	0	2	0	9	2	0	0	0	-	0	0-0	1	1.19	1.93
2014	Pit	NL	20	0	0	11	32.2	148	34	19	19	5	0	1	2	16	2	38	2	0	2	1	.667	0	0-0	5	5.17	5.23
2015	Tex	AL	8	0	0	5	11.1	46	11	5	5	1	1	1	0	3	0	7	1	0	0	1	.000	0	0-0	0	3.41	3.97
	3 ML YEARS		33	0	0	17	53.1	232	51	28	26	6	1	3	2	21	2	54	5	0	2	2	.500	0	0-0	1	3.93	4.39

Branden Pinder

Pitches: R **Bats:** R **Pos:** RP-25 **Ht:** 6'3" **Wt:** 225 **Born:** 1/26/1989 **Age:** 27

			HOW MUCH HE PITCHED						WHAT HE GAVE UP											THE RESULTS						
Year	Team	Lg	G	GS	CG	GF	IP	BFP	H	R	ER	HR	SH	SF	HB	TBB	IBB	SO	WP	Bk	W	L	Pct	Sh	Sv-Op	Hld	ERC	ERA
2011	Stnlld	A-	24	0	0	22	31.0	116	16	4	4	1	3	0	3	5	0	38	1	0	2	2	.500	0	14- -	-	1.12	1.16
2012	Tampa	A+	41	0	0	28	67.2	307	70	27	21	1	5	1	5	29	7	67	8	0	2	6	.250	0	9- -	-	3.75	2.79
2013	Trntn	AA	19	0	0	13	24.1	117	28	19	17	2	2	2	2	16	1	22	1	1	1	1	.500	0	5- -	-	6.08	6.29
2013	Tampa	A+	21	5	0	6	49.0	192	39	20	19	4	0	4	4	11	0	50	4	0	1	2	.333	0	1- -	-	2.63	3.49
2014	Trntn	AA	12	0	0	9	16.0	57	7	1	1	0	1	0	0	2	0	18	1	0	2	0	1.000	0	4- -	-	0.60	0.56
2014	S-WB	AAA	13	0	0	6	16.2	69	17	7	7	2	0	1	0	5	0	12	1	0	1	0	1.000	0	1- -	-	4.03	3.78
2015	S-WB	AAA	23	0	0	12	35.1	147	31	15	11	3	0	2	0	10	0	36	4	1	1	3	.250	0	1- -	-	2.82	2.80
2015	NYY	AL	25	0	0	10	27.2	122	28	9	9	4	0	1	0	14	1	25	0	1	0	2	.000	0	0-0	0	4.85	2.93

Michael Pineda

Pitches: R **Bats:** R **Pos:** SP-27 pah-NAY-dah **Ht:** 6'7" **Wt:** 260 **Born:** 1/18/1989 **Age:** 27

			HOW MUCH HE PITCHED						WHAT HE GAVE UP											THE RESULTS						
Year	Team	Lg	G	GS	CG	GF	IP	BFP	H	R	ER	HR	SH	SF	HB	TBB	IBB	SO	WP	Bk	W	L	Pct	Sh	Sv-Op	Hld	ERC	ERA
2011	Sea	AL	28	28	0	0	171.0	696	133	76	71	18	4	3	5	55	1	173	9	0	9	10	.474	0	0-0	0	2.73	3.74
2014	NYY	AL	13	13	0	0	76.1	290	56	18	16	5	2	1	0	7	0	59	3	1	5	5	.500	0	0-0	0	1.51	1.89
2015	NYY	AL	27	27	1	0	160.2	668	176	83	78	21	4	6	3	21	0	156	4	0	12	10	.545	0	0-0	0	3.82	4.37
	3 ML YEARS		68	68	1	0	408.0	1654	365	177	165	44	10	10	8	83	1	388	16	1	26	25	.510	0	0-0	0	2.88	3.64

Yohan Pino

Pitches: R **Bats:** R **Pos:** RP-6; SP-1 PEEN-oh **Ht:** 6'2" **Wt:** 190 **Born:** 12/26/1983 **Age:** 32

			HOW MUCH HE PITCHED						WHAT HE GAVE UP											THE RESULTS						
Year	Team	Lg	G	GS	CG	GF	IP	BFP	H	R	ER	HR	SH	SF	HB	TBB	IBB	SO	WP	Bk	W	L	Pct	Sh	Sv-Op	Hld	ERC	ERA
2011	Nham	AA	36	10	1	8	95.2	385	90	47	44	15	1	0	3	14	0	104	3	0	4	8	.333	0	0- -	-	3.28	4.14
2012	Nham	AA	25	22	2	1	134.0	552	122	58	53	17	1	3	7	29	1	111	4	0	10	8	.556	0	0- -	-	3.23	3.56
2013	Lsvlle	AAA	31	16	1	11	121.1	502	114	52	44	7	2	8	1	30	2	107	2	1	5	7	.417	1	6- -	-	2.88	3.26
2014	Roch	AAA	16	9	2	2	73.0	290	47	21	20	9	1	1	3	24	0	72	3	1	10	2	.833	2	0- -	-	2.26	2.47
2015	Omha	AAA	16	14	1	0	78.2	332	83	41	41	12	0	0	1	20	0	69	1	0	6	3	.667	0	0- -	-	4.23	4.69
2014	Min	AL	11	11	0	0	60.1	258	66	34	34	8	2	4	1	14	0	50	2	0	2	5	.286	0	0-0	0	4.20	5.07
2015	KC	AL	7	1	0	3	19.1	82	23	11	7	2	0	0	0	3	0	13	0	0	0	2	.000	0	0-0	0	4.20	3.26
	2 ML YEARS		18	12	0	3	79.2	340	89	45	41	10	2	4	1	17	0	63	2	0	2	7	.222	0	0-0	0	4.20	4.63

Jose Pirela

Bats: R **Throws:** R **Pos:** 2B-27;PH-7;PR-6;LF-2;DH-2;RF-1 **Ht:** 5'11" **Wt:** 215 **Born:** 11/21/1989 **Age:** 26

Year Team	Lg	G	AB	H	2B	3B	HR	(Hm	Rd)	TB	R	RBI	RC	TBB	IBB	SO	HBP	SH	SF	SB	CS	GDP	Avg	OBP	Slg	OPS
2011 Trntn	AA	128	468	112	21	4	8	(-	-)	165	50	45	50	25	1	88	13	8	7	9	7	7	.239	.292	.353	.645
2012 Trntn	AA	82	317	93	19	3	8	(-	-)	142	55	33	53	26	1	48	6	7	2	9	3	4	.293	.356	.448	.804
2013 Trntn	AA	124	459	125	27	5	10	(-	-)	192	73	62	76	56	0	61	9	1	5	18	3	11	.272	.359	.418	.777
2014 S-WB	AAA	130	535	163	21	11	10	(-	-)	236	87	60	84	37	2	74	3	2	4	15	7	7	.305	.345	.441	.792
2015 S-WB	AAA	60	231	75	14	1	3	(-	-)	100	40	23	41	24	0	22	2	0	2	5	2	7	.325	.390	.433	.823
2014 NYY	AL	7	24	8	1	2	0	(0	0)	13	6	3	4	1	0	4	0	0	0	0	0	1	.333	.360	.542	.902
2015 NYY	AL	37	74	17	3	0	1	(1	0)	23	7	5	3	2	0	16	0	1	1	1	0	4	.230	.247	.311	.558
2 ML YEARS		44	98	25	4	2	1	(1	0)	36	13	8	7	3	0	20	0	1	1	1	0	5	.255	.275	.367	.642

Stephen Piscotty

Bats: R **Throws:** R **Pos:** LF-55;RF-15;1B-11;PH-2;CF-1 **Ht:** 6'3" **Wt:** 210 **Born:** 1/14/1991 **Age:** 25

Year Team	Lg	G	AB	H	2B	3B	HR	(Hm	Rd)	TB	R	RBI	RC	TBB	IBB	SO	HBP	SH	SF	SB	CS	GDP	Avg	OBP	Slg	OPS
2012 QuadC	A	55	210	62	18	1	4	(-	-)	94	29	27	37	18	1	25	9	0	0	3	0	9	.295	.376	.448	.823
2013 PlmBh	A+	63	243	71	14	2	9	(-	-)	116	30	35	39	18	2	27	3	0	0	4	5	4	.292	.348	.477	.826
2013 Sprgfld	AA	49	184	55	9	0	6	(-	-)	82	17	24	31	19	1	19	1	1	2	7	3	12	.299	.344	.446	.810
2014 Memp	AAA	136	500	144	32	0	9	(-	-)	203	70	69	76	43	2	61	10	1	2	11	5	18	.288	.355	.406	.761
2015 Memp	AAA	87	320	87	28	2	11	(-	-)	152	54	41	56	46	0	62	3	0	3	5	6	13	.272	.366	.475	.841
2015 StL	NL	63	233	71	15	4	7	(4	3)	115	29	39	41	20	2	56	1	0	2	2	1	7	.305	.359	.494	.853

Kevin Plawecki

Bats: R **Throws:** R **Pos:** C-70;PH-3   plah-WEH-kee **Ht:** 6'2" **Wt:** 225 **Born:** 2/26/1991 **Age:** 25

Year Team	Lg	G	AB	H	2B	3B	HR	(Hm	Rd)	TB	R	RBI	RC	TBB	IBB	SO	HBP	SH	SF	SB	CS	GDP	Avg	OBP	Slg	OPS
2012 Bklyn	A	61	216	54	8	0	7	(-	-)	83	26	27	31	25	0	24	8	0	3	0	0	7	.250	.345	.384	.729
2013 2 Tms	Low	125	449	137	38	1	8	(-	-)	201	60	80	82	42	2	53	24	1	5	1	0	15	.305	.390	.448	.838
2014 Bnghtn	AA	58	224	73	18	0	6	(-	-)	109	33	43	41	16	0	27	5	0	4	0	0	12	.326	.378	.487	.864
2014 LsVgs	AAA	43	152	43	6	0	5	(-	-)	64	25	21	23	14	1	21	1	2	1	0	0	4	.283	.345	.421	.766
2015 LsVgs	AAA	22	85	19	5	1	1	(-	-)	29	7	9	7	3	0	12	2	0	0	0	0	3	.224	.267	.341	.608
2015 NYM	NL	73	233	51	9	0	3	(1	2)	69	18	21	22	17	4	60	4	1	3	0	0	4	.219	.280	.296	.576

Trevor Plouffe

Bats: R **Throws:** R **Pos:** 3B-140;1B-17   PLOOF **Ht:** 6'2" **Wt:** 215 **Born:** 6/15/1986 **Age:** 30

Year Team	Lg	G	AB	H	2B	3B	HR	(Hm	Rd)	TB	R	RBI	RC	TBB	IBB	SO	HBP	SH	SF	SB	CS	GDP	Avg	OBP	Slg	OPS
2010 Min	AL	22	41	6	1	0	2	(1	1)	13	7	6	2	0	0	14	0	2	1	0	0	0	.146	.143	.317	.460
2011 Min	AL	81	286	68	18	1	8	(3	5)	112	47	31	31	25	0	71	4	2	3	3	3	6	.238	.305	.392	.697
2012 Min	AL	119	422	99	19	1	24	(15	9)	192	56	55	48	37	0	92	4	0	2	1	3	9	.235	.301	.455	.756
2013 Min	AL	129	477	121	22	1	14	(8	6)	187	44	52	49	34	1	112	6	1	4	2	1	11	.254	.309	.392	.701
2014 Min	AL	136	520	134	40	2	14	(8	6)	220	69	80	74	53	2	109	4	0	5	2	1	12	.258	.328	.423	.751
2015 Min	AL	152	573	140	35	4	22	(13	9)	249	74	86	79	50	0	124	4	1	4	2	1	28	.244	.307	.435	.742
6 ML YEARS		639	2319	568	135	9	84	(48	36)	973	297	310	283	199	3	522	22	6	19	10	9	66	.245	.308	.420	.728

Gregory Polanco

Bats: L **Throws:** L **Pos:** RF-144;PH-10;LF-8;CF-2   puh-LAHN-ko **Ht:** 6'5" **Wt:** 230 **Born:** 9/14/1991 **Age:** 24

Year Team	Lg	G	AB	H	2B	3B	HR	(Hm	Rd)	TB	R	RBI	RC	TBB	IBB	SO	HBP	SH	SF	SB	CS	GDP	Avg	OBP	Slg	OPS
2011 2 Tms	Low	51	179	41	4	4	3	(-	-)	62	34	35	26	24	0	35	3	2	5	18	0	1	.229	.322	.346	.669
2012 WV	A	116	437	142	26	6	16	(-	-)	228	84	85	89	44	1	64	2	1	1	40	15	8	.325	.388	.522	.910
2013 Bradtn	A+	57	218	68	17	0	6	(-	-)	103	29	30	41	16	0	37	3	2	2	24	4	4	.312	.364	.472	.836
2013 Altna	AA	68	243	64	13	2	6	(-	-)	99	36	41	38	36	1	36	1	1	5	13	7	3	.263	.354	.407	.762
2014 Indy	AAA	69	274	90	17	5	7	(-	-)	138	51	51	54	28	2	49	1	0	2	16	6	3	.328	.390	.504	.894
2014 Pit	NL	89	277	65	9	0	7	(5	2)	95	50	33	32	30	1	59	0	2	2	14	5	1	.235	.307	.343	.650
2015 Pit	NL	153	593	152	35	6	9	(6	3)	226	83	52	73	55	6	121	1	1	2	27	10	5	.256	.320	.381	.701
2 ML YEARS		242	870	217	44	6	16	(11	5)	321	133	85	105	85	7	180	1	3	4	41	15	6	.249	.316	.369	.685

Jorge Polanco

Bats: B **Throws:** R **Pos:** SS-4;PH-1   puh-LAHN-ko **Ht:** 5'11" **Wt:** 200 **Born:** 7/5/1993 **Age:** 22

Year Team	Lg	G	AB	H	2B	3B	HR	(Hm	Rd)	TB	R	RBI	RC	TBB	IBB	SO	HBP	SH	SF	SB	CS	GDP	Avg	OBP	Slg	OPS
2011 Twins	R	51	172	43	8	3	1	(-	-)	60	21	16	20	15	0	24	3	2	1	6	4	4	.250	.319	.349	.668
2012 Elizab	R+	51	173	55	15	2	5	(-	-)	89	35	27	35	20	0	26	3	3	5	6	3	2	.318	.388	.514	.903
2013 Crpds	A	115	465	143	32	10	5	(-	-)	210	76	78	78	42	2	59	3	3	10	4	4	4	.308	.362	.452	.813
2014 FtMyrs	A+	94	378	110	17	6	6	(-	-)	157	61	45	60	46	1	60	1	1	6	10	8	8	.291	.364	.415	.780
2014 NwBrit	AA	37	146	41	6	0	1	(-	-)	50	13	16	16	9	0	28	0	2	0	7	3	0	.281	.323	.342	.665
2015 Chatt	AA	95	394	114	17	3	6	(-	-)	155	55	47	55	35	0	63	0	0	2	18	10	7	.289	.346	.393	.739
2015 Roch	AAA	22	88	25	6	0	0	(-	-)	31	7	6	10	4	0	10	0	0	2	1	0	3	.284	.309	.352	.661
2014 Min	AL	5	6	2	1	1	0	(0	0)	5	2	3	4	2	0	2	0	0	0	0	0	0	.333	.500	.833	1.333
2015 Min	AL	4	10	3	0	0	0	(0	0)	3	1	1	3	2	0	1	0	0	0	1	0	0	.300	.417	.300	.717
2 ML YEARS		9	16	5	1	1	0	(0	0)	8	3	4	7	4	0	3	0	0	0	1	0	0	.313	.450	.500	.950

A.J. Pollock

Bats: R Throws: R Pos: CF-151;PH-7;PR-1   Ht: 6'1" Wt: 195 Born: 12/5/1987 Age: 28

Year	Team	Lg	G	AB	H	2B	3B	HR	(Hm	Rd)	TB	R	RBI	RC	TBB	IBB	SO	HBP	SH	SF	SB	CS	GDP	Avg	OBP	Slg	OPS
2012	Ari	NL	31	81	20	4	1	2	(2	0)	32	8	8	9	9	1	11	0	1	2	1	2	2	.247	.315	.395	.710
2013	Ari	NL	137	443	119	28	5	8	(3	5)	181	64	38	58	33	1	82	2	3	1	12	3	5	.269	.322	.409	.730
2014	Ari	NL	75	265	80	19	6	7	(7	0)	132	41	24	43	19	0	46	2	1	0	14	3	4	.302	.353	.498	.851
2015	Ari	NL	157	609	192	39	6	20	(9	11)	303	111	76	106	53	0	89	2	0	9	39	7	19	.315	.367	.498	.865
4 ML YEARS			400	1398	411	90	18	37	(21	16)	648	224	146	216	114	2	228	6	5	12	66	15	30	.294	.347	.464	.811

Drew Pomeranz

Pitches: L Bats: R Pos: RP-44; SP-9   POMM-er-anze   Ht: 6'5" Wt: 240 Born: 11/22/1988 Age: 27

Year	Team	Lg	G	GS	CG	GF	IP	BFP	H	R	ER	SH	SF	HB	TBB	IBB	SO	WP	Bk	W	L	Pct	Sh	Sv-Op	Hld	ERC	ERA
2011	Col	NL	4	4	0	0	18.1	77	19	11	11	0	1	1	5	0	13	1	0	2	1	.667	0	0-0	0	3.36	5.40
2012	Col	NL	22	22	0	0	96.2	434	97	57	53	14	8	4	46	2	83	8	1	2	9	.182	0	0-0	0	4.78	4.93
2013	Col	NL	8	4	0	0	21.2	105	25	15	15	4	1	1	19	1	19	0	0	0	4	.000	0	0-0	0	8.04	6.23
2014	Oak	AL	20	10	0	4	69.0	278	51	22	18	7	1	0	26	0	64	0	0	5	4	.556	0	0-0	0	2.70	2.35
2015	Oak	AL	53	9	0	9	86.0	357	71	44	35	8	4	5	31	2	82	2	0	5	6	.455	0	3-6	12	3.05	3.66
5 ML YEARS			107	49	0	13	291.2	1251	263	149	132	33	15	10	127	4	261	11	1	14	24	.368	0	3-6	12	3.87	4.07

Dalton Pompey

Bats: B Throws: R Pos: CF-21;PR-7;LF-6;DH-3   pom-PAY   Ht: 6'2" Wt: 195 Born: 12/11/1992 Age: 23

Year	Team	Lg	G	AB	H	2B	3B	HR	(Hm	Rd)	TB	R	RBI	RC	TBB	IBB	SO	HBP	SH	SF	SB	CS	GDP	Avg	OBP	Slg	OPS
2011	2 Tms	Low	60	226	54	10	2	5	(-	-)	83	49	17	36	38	0	58	4	2	0	23	1	2	.239	.358	.367	.725
2012	3 Tms	Low	20	70	20	4	3	0	(-	-)	30	14	8	11	10	0	14	0	2	0	5	1	0	.286	.375	.429	.804
2013	Lnsng	A	115	437	114	22	9	6	(-	-)	172	68	40	70	63	1	106	5	3	3	38	10	4	.261	.358	.394	.752
2014	Dnedin	A+	70	276	88	12	6	6	(-	-)	130	49	34	57	35	0	56	2	2	2	29	2	3	.319	.397	.471	.868
2014	Nham	AA	31	112	33	5	3	3	(-	-)	53	20	12	20	14	0	18	1	0	0	8	5	2	.295	.378	.473	.851
2014	Buffalo	AAA	12	53	19	5	0	0	(-	-)	24	15	5	10	3	0	10	0	0	0	6	0	0	.358	.393	.453	.846
2015	Buffalo	AAA	65	253	72	7	4	1	(-	-)	90	44	18	38	36	2	41	1	2	3	16	7	5	.285	.372	.356	.728
2015	Nham	AA	31	133	47	2	3	6	(-	-)	73	26	22	29	11	0	23	2	1	1	7	3	0	.353	.408	.549	.957
2014	Tor	AL	17	39	9	1	2	1	(1	0)	17	5	4	3	4	0	12	0	0	0	1	0	0	.231	.302	.436	.738
2015	Tor	AL	34	94	21	8	0	2	(1	1)	35	17	6	9	7	0	23	2	0	0	5	1	1	.223	.291	.372	.664
2 ML YEARS			51	133	30	9	2	3	(2	1)	52	22	10	12	11	0	35	2	0	0	6	1	1	.226	.295	.391	.685

Rick Porcello

Pitches: R Bats: R Pos: SP-28   pore-SELL-oh   Ht: 6'5" Wt: 200 Born: 12/27/1988 Age: 27

Year	Team	Lg	G	GS	CG	GF	IP	BFP	H	R	ER	SH	SF	HB	TBB	IBB	SO	WP	Bk	W	L	Pct	Sh	Sv-Op	Hld	ERC	ERA
2009	Det	AL	31	31	0	0	170.2	720	176	81	75	23	4	2	52	0	89	6	1	14	9	.609	0	0-0	0	4.24	3.96
2010	Det	AL	27	27	0	0	162.2	700	188	96	89	18	1	2	38	2	84	11	3	10	12	.455	0	0-0	0	4.56	4.92
2011	Det	AL	31	31	0	0	182.0	784	210	103	96	18	5	5	46	1	104	12	0	14	9	.609	0	0-0	0	4.57	4.75
2012	Det	AL	31	31	0	0	176.1	783	226	101	90	16	2	3	44	3	107	6	0	10	12	.455	0	0-0	0	5.16	4.59
2013	Det	AL	32	29	1	1	177.0	736	185	87	85	18	4	3	42	4	142	6	1	13	8	.619	0	0-0	0	3.79	4.32
2014	Det	AL	32	31	3	1	204.2	840	211	89	78	18	3	4	41	4	129	0	0	15	13	.536	3	0-0	0	3.50	3.43
2015	Bos	AL	28	28	0	0	172.0	737	196	103	94	25	2	5	38	0	149	12	1	9	15	.375	0	0-0	0	4.76	4.92
Postseason			8	2	0	4	16.1	71	18	10	8	0	0	1	2	2	13	1	0	0	2	.000	0	0-0	0	3.06	4.41
7 ML YEARS			212	208	4	2	1245.1	5300	1392	660	607	136	21	24	41	301	14	804	53	6	85	78	.521	3	0-0	0	4.34	4.39

Buster Posey

Bats: R Throws: R Pos: C-106;1B-42;PH-6;DH-3   Ht: 6'1" Wt: 215 Born: 3/27/1987 Age: 29

Year	Team	Lg	G	AB	H	2B	3B	HR	(Hm	Rd)	TB	R	RBI	RC	TBB	IBB	SO	HBP	SH	SF	SB	CS	GDP	Avg	OBP	Slg	OPS
2009	SF	NL	7	17	2	0	0	0	(0	0)	2	1	0	0	0	0	4	0	0	0	0	0	0	.118	.118	.118	.235
2010	SF	NL	108	406	124	23	2	18	(6	12)	205	58	67	70	30	5	55	4	0	3	0	2	12	.305	.357	.505	.862
2011	SF	NL	45	162	46	5	0	4	(1	3)	63	17	21	26	18	3	30	4	0	1	3	0	4	.284	.368	.389	.756
2012	SF	NL	148	530	178	39	1	24	(7	17)	291	78	103	111	69	7	96	2	0	9	1	1	19	.336	.408	.549	.957
2013	SF	NL	148	520	153	34	1	15	(8	7)	234	61	72	77	60	8	70	8	0	7	2	1	15	.294	.371	.450	.821
2014	SF	NL	147	547	170	28	2	22	(11	11)	268	72	89	94	47	5	69	3	0	8	0	1	16	.311	.364	.490	.854
2015	SF	NL	150	557	177	28	0	19	(6	13)	262	74	95	96	56	10	52	3	0	7	2	0	17	.318	.379	.470	.849
Postseason			48	188	46	3	0	4	(1	3)	61	16	21	18	20	4	40	1	0	1	1	1	4	.245	.319	.324	.644
7 ML YEARS			753	2739	850	157	6	102	(39	63)	1325	361	447	474	280	38	376	24	0	35	8	5	83	.310	.375	.484	.859

Martin Prado

Bats: R Throws: R Pos: 3B-124;2B-11;PH-1   mar-TEEN PRAH-doe   Ht: 6'1" Wt: 190 Born: 10/27/1983 Age: 32

Year	Team	Lg	G	AB	H	2B	3B	HR	(Hm	Rd)	TB	R	RBI	RC	TBB	IBB	SO	HBP	SH	SF	SB	CS	GDP	Avg	OBP	Slg	OPS
2006	Atl	NL	24	42	11	1	1	1	(1	0)	17	3	9	9	5	0	7	0	2	0	0	0	2	.262	.340	.405	.745
2007	Atl	NL	28	59	17	3	0	0	(0	0)	20	5	2	6	3	0	6	0	0	0	0	0	0	.288	.323	.339	.662
2008	Atl	NL	78	228	73	18	4	2	(1	1)	105	36	33	39	21	0	29	1	2	2	3	1	3	.320	.377	.461	.838
2009	Atl	NL	128	450	138	38	0	11	(4	7)	209	64	49	57	36	1	59	2	11	4	1	3	17	.307	.358	.464	.822
2010	Atl	NL	140	599	184	40	3	15	(4	11)	275	100	66	86	40	2	86	3	3	6	5	3	13	.307	.350	.459	.809
2011	Atl	NL	129	551	143	26	2	13	(9	4)	212	66	57	57	34	1	52	1	1	3	4	8	16	.260	.302	.385	.687
2012	Atl	NL	156	617	186	42	6	10	(6	4)	270	81	70	96	58	2	69	2	4	9	17	4	19	.301	.359	.438	.796

Year Team	Lg	G	AB	H	2B	3B	HR	(Hm	Rd)	TB	R	RBI	RC	TBB	IBB	SO	HBP	SH	SF	SB	CS	GDP	Avg	OBP	Slg	OPS
2013 Ari	NL	155	609	172	36	2	14	(7	7)	254	70	82	72	47	2	53	2	0	6	3	5	29	.282	.333	.417	.750
2014 2 Tms		143	536	151	26	4	12	(7	5)	221	62	58	66	26	0	80	7	0	4	3	1	20	.282	.321	.412	.733
2015 Mia	NL	129	500	144	22	4	9	(5	4)	197	52	63	70	37	4	68	5	1	8	1	0	9	.288	.338	.394	.732
14 Ari	NL	106	403	109	17	4	5	(3	2)	149	44	42	43	23	0	57	6	0	4	2	1	17	.270	.317	.370	.686
14 NYY	AL	37	133	42	9	0	7	(4	3)	72	18	16	23	3	0	23	1	0	0	1	0	3	.316	.336	.541	.877
Postseason		1	5	1	0	0	0	(0	0)	1	0	0	0	0	0	1	0	0	0	0	0	0	.200	.200	.200	.400
10 ML YEARS		1110	4191	1219	252	24	87	(44	43)	1780	539	489	558	307	12	509	23	24	42	37	25	128	.291	.339	.425	.764

Alex Presley

Bats: L **Throws:** L **Pos:** LF-4;PR-2;CF-1;RF-1 　　　　　**Ht:** 5'10" **Wt:** 195 **Born:** 7/25/1985 **Age:** 30

Year Team	Lg	G	AB	H	2B	3B	HR	(Hm	Rd)	TB	R	RBI	RC	TBB	IBB	SO	HBP	SH	SF	SB	CS	GDP	Avg	OBP	Slg	OPS
2015 Fresno*	AAA	89	332	97	14	1	3	(-	-)	122	48	49	46	27	2	41	1	5	2	15	4	6	.292	.345	.367	.713
2010 Pit	NL	19	23	6	1	0	0	(0	0)	7	2	0	1	1	0	8	0	1	0	1	1	0	.261	.292	.304	.596
2011 Pit	NL	52	215	64	12	6	4	(1	3)	100	27	20	35	13	1	40	1	1	1	9	3	1	.298	.339	.465	.804
2012 Pit	NL	104	346	82	14	7	10	(2	8)	140	46	25	31	18	0	72	2	4	0	9	7	5	.237	.279	.405	.683
2013 2 Tms		57	185	51	5	2	3	(2	1)	69	17	15	17	9	0	39	1	0	0	1	4	3	.276	.313	.373	.686
2014 Hou	AL	89	254	62	6	1	6	(4	2)	88	22	19	29	13	0	44	1	1	2	5	1	3	.244	.281	.346	.628
2015 Hou	AL	8	12	3	0	0	0	(0	0)	3	1	1	2	1	0	5	0	0	0	0	0	0	.250	.308	.250	.558
13 Pit	NL	29	72	19	1	1	2	(2	0)	28	8	4	5	1	0	18	0	0	0	1	1	1	.264	.274	.389	.663
13 Min	AL	28	113	32	4	1	1	(0	1)	41	9	11	12	8	0	21	1	0	0	1	3	2	.283	.336	.363	.699
6 ML YEARS		329	1035	268	38	16	23	(9	14)	407	115	80	115	55	1	208	5	7	3	25	16	12	.259	.299	.393	.692

Ryan Pressly

Pitches: R **Bats:** R **Pos:** RP-27 　　　　　**Ht:** 6'3" **Wt:** 210 **Born:** 12/15/1988 **Age:** 27

		HOW MUCH HE PITCHED						WHAT HE GAVE UP											THE RESULTS						
Year Team	Lg	G	GS	CG	GF	IP	BFP	H	R	ER	HR	SH	SF	HB	TBB	IBB	SO	WP	Bk	W	L	Pct	Sh	Sv-Op	Hld	ERC	ERA
2015 Roch*	AAA	7	0	0	4	10.0	41	6	7	5	1	0	1	0	6	0	15	3	0	0	2	.000	0	0- --	-	2.73	4.50
2013 Min	AL	49	0	0	18	76.2	315	71	37	33	5	2	3	0	27	1	49	7	0	3	3	.500	0	0-0	1	3.31	3.87
2014 Min	AL	25	0	0	5	28.1	122	30	10	9	2	3	1	1	8	2	14	1	0	2	0	1.000	0	0-1	2	3.98	2.86
2015 Min	AL	27	0	0	6	27.2	119	27	9	9	0	1	1	0	12	1	22	2	0	3	2	.600	0	0-0	4	3.31	2.93
3 ML YEARS		101	0	0	29	132.2	556	128	56	51	8	5	7	1	47	4	85	10	0	8	5	.615	0	0-1	7	3.46	3.46

David Price

Pitches: L **Bats:** L **Pos:** SP-32 　　　　　**Ht:** 6'6" **Wt:** 210 **Born:** 8/26/1985 **Age:** 30

		HOW MUCH HE PITCHED						WHAT HE GAVE UP											THE RESULTS						
Year Team	Lg	G	GS	CG	GF	IP	BFP	H	R	ER	HR	SH	SF	HB	TBB	IBB	SO	WP	Bk	W	L	Pct	Sh	Sv-Op	Hld	ERC	ERA
2008 TB	AL	5	1	0	0	14.0	57	9	4	3	1	0	1	1	4	0	12	0	0	0	0	-	0	0-0	1	1.86	1.93
2009 TB	AL	23	23	0	0	128.1	557	119	72	63	17	3	2	4	54	0	102	2	0	10	7	.588	0	0-0	0	4.05	4.42
2010 TB	AL	32	31	2	0	208.2	861	170	71	63	15	4	3	5	79	1	188	5	3	19	6	.760	1	0-0	0	2.91	2.72
2011 TB	AL	34	**34**	0	0	224.1	918	192	93	87	22	4	7	9	63	5	218	2	0	12	13	.480	0	0-0	0	2.97	3.49
2012 TB	AL	31	31	2	0	211.0	836	173	63	60	16	2	3	5	59	2	205	8	1	**20**	5	**.800**	1	0-0	0	2.67	**2.56**
2013 TB	AL	27	27	**4**	0	186.2	740	178	78	69	16	1	2	3	27	0	151	0	0	10	8	.556	0	0-0	0	2.89	3.33
2014 2 Tms		34	**34**	3	0	248.1	**1009**	230	100	90	25	4	3	5	38	1	**271**	2	0	15	12	.556	0	0-0	0	2.79	3.26
2015 2 Tms		32	32	3	0	220.1	888	190	70	60	17	4	8	3	47	2	225	4	0	18	5	.783	1	0-0	0	2.54	**2.45**
14 TB	AL	23	23	2	0	170.2	689	156	68	59	20	3	3	5	23	1	189	2	0	11	8	.579	0	0-0	0	2.79	3.11
14 Det	AL	11	11	1	0	77.2	320	74	32	31	5	1	0	0	15	0	82	0	0	4	4	.500	0	0-0	0	2.77	3.59
15 Det	AL	21	21	3	0	146.0	592	133	50	41	13	4	5	3	29	2	138	3	0	9	4	.692	1	0-0	0	2.83	2.53
15 Tor	AL	11	11	0	0	74.1	296	57	20	19	4	0	3	0	18	0	87	1	0	9	1	.900	0	0-0	0	2.00	2.30
Postseason		10	5	0	5	40.0	168	40	22	20	7	0	1	1	9	0	36	1	0	1	5	.167	0	1-1	0	3.95	4.50
8 ML YEARS		218	213	14	0	1441.2	5866	1261	551	495	129	22	29	35	371	11	1372	29	4	104	56	.650	3	0-0	0	2.89	3.09

Jason Pridie

Bats: L **Throws:** R **Pos:** PH-4;RF-2;LF-1;CF-1 　　　PRY-dee　　　**Ht:** 6'1" **Wt:** 205 **Born:** 10/9/1983 **Age:** 32

Year Team	Lg	G	AB	H	2B	3B	HR	(Hm	Rd)	TB	R	RBI	RC	TBB	IBB	SO	HBP	SH	SF	SB	CS	GDP	Avg	OBP	Slg	OPS
2015 Nashv*	AAA	127	478	148	24	7	20	(-	-)	246	84	89	97	55	5	102	2	0	5	20	3	5	.310	.380	.515	.894
2008 Min	AL	10	4	0	0	0	0	(0	0)	0	3	0	0	1	0	1	0	1	0	0	0	0	.000	.200	.000	.200
2009 Min	AL	1	0	0	0	0	0	(0	0)	0	0	0	0	0	0	0	0	0	0	0	0	0	-	-	-	-
2011 NYM	NL	101	208	48	11	3	4	(3	1)	77	28	20	22	24	2	64	0	3	1	7	1	2	.231	.309	.370	.679
2012 Phi	NL	9	10	3	1	0	1	(1	0)	7	1	3	2	0	0	0	0	0	0	0	0	0	.300	.300	.700	1.000
2013 Bal	AL	4	10	2	0	0	0	(0	0)	2	0	1	1	0	0	2	0	0	0	0	0	0	.200	.200	.200	.400
2014 Col	NL	2	4	0	0	0	0	(0	0)	0	1	0	0	0	0	2	0	0	0	0	0	0	.000	.000	.000	.000
2015 Oak	AL	6	9	0	0	0	0	(0	0)	0	0	0	0	1	0	4	0	0	0	0	0	0	.000	.100	.000	.100
7 ML YEARS		133	245	53	12	3	5	(4	1)	86	33	24	25	26	2	73	0	4	1	7	1	2	.216	.290	.351	.641

Yasiel Puig

Bats: R **Throws:** R **Pos:** RF-78;PH-5 　　　yah-SEE-el PWEEG　　　**Ht:** 6'2" **Wt:** 255 **Born:** 12/7/1990 **Age:** 25

Year Team	Lg	G	AB	H	2B	3B	HR	(Hm	Rd)	TB	R	RBI	RC	TBB	IBB	SO	HBP	SH	SF	SB	CS	GDP	Avg	OBP	Slg	OPS
2013 LAD	NL	104	382	122	21	2	19	(9	10)	204	66	42	62	36	6	97	11	0	3	11	8	6	.319	.391	.534	.925
2014 LAD	NL	148	558	165	37	9	16	(8	8)	268	92	69	95	67	3	124	12	2	1	11	7	7	.296	.382	.480	.863
2015 LAD	NL	79	282	72	12	3	11	(6	5)	123	30	38	35	26	1	66	2	0	1	3	3	1	.255	.322	.436	.758
Postseason		14	51	16	1	2	0	(0	0)	21	10	5	6	2	0	22	0	0	0	0	1	2	.314	.364	.412	.775
3 ML YEARS		331	1222	359	70	14	46	(23	23)	595	188	149	192	129	10	287	25	2	5	25	18	14	.294	.371	.487	.858

Albert Pujols

Bats: R **Throws:** R **Pos:** 1B-95;DH-62;3B-1   POO-holes   **Ht:** 6'3" **Wt:** 230 **Born:** 1/16/1980 **Age:** 36

Year	Team	Lg	G	AB	H	2B	3B	HR	(Hm	Rd)	TB	R	RBI	RC	TBB	IBB	SO	HBP	SH	SF	SB	CS	GDP	Avg	OBP	Slg	OPS
2001	Stl	NL	161	590	194	47	4	37	(18	19)	360	112	130	132	69	6	93	9	1	7	1	3	21	.329	.403	.610	1.013
2002	Stl	NL	157	590	185	40	2	34	(14	20)	331	118	127	121	72	13	69	9	0	4	2	4	20	.314	.394	.561	.955
2003	Stl	NL	157	591	212	51	1	43	(21	22)	394	137	124	160	79	12	65	10	0	5	5	1	13	.359	.439	.667	1.106
2004	Stl	NL	154	592	196	51	2	46	(18	28)	389	133	123	143	84	12	52	7	0	9	5	5	21	.331	.415	.657	1.072
2005	Stl	NL	161	591	195	38	2	41	(23	18)	360	129	117	139	97	27	65	9	0	3	16	2	19	.330	.430	.609	1.039
2006	Stl	NL	143	535	177	33	1	49	(24	25)	359	119	137	146	92	28	50	4	0	3	7	2	20	.331	.431	.671	1.102
2007	Stl	NL	158	565	185	38	1	32	(12	20)	321	99	103	118	99	22	58	7	0	8	2	6	27	.327	.429	.568	.997
2008	Stl	NL	148	524	187	44	0	37	(19	18)	342	100	116	130	104	34	54	5	0	8	7	3	16	.357	.462	.653	1.114
2009	Stl	NL	160	568	186	45	1	47	(22	25)	374	124	135	145	115	44	64	9	0	8	16	4	23	.327	.443	.658	1.101
2010	Stl	NL	159	587	183	39	1	42	(17	25)	350	115	118	131	103	38	76	4	0	6	14	4	23	.312	.414	.596	1.011
2011	Stl	NL	147	579	173	29	0	37	(16	21)	313	105	99	100	61	15	58	4	0	7	9	1	29	.299	.366	.541	.906
2012	LAA	AL	154	607	173	50	0	30	(14	16)	313	85	105	100	52	16	76	5	0	6	8	1	19	.285	.343	.516	.859
2013	LAA	AL	99	391	101	19	0	17	(8	9)	171	49	64	54	40	8	55	5	0	7	1	1	18	.258	.330	.437	.767
2014	LAA	AL	159	633	172	37	1	28	(13	15)	295	89	105	86	48	11	71	5	0	9	5	1	28	.272	.324	.466	.790
2015	LAA	AL	157	602	147	22	0	40	(20	20)	289	85	95	82	50	10	72	6	0	3	5	3	15	.244	.307	.480	.787
Postseason			77	279	90	18	1	19	(7	12)	167	55	54	68	49	20	40	5	0	1	1	2	6	.323	.431	.599	1.030
15 ML YEARS			2274	8545	2666	583	16	560	(259	301)	4961	1599	1698	1787	1165	296	978	98	1	93	103	41	312	.312	.397	.581	.977

Zach Putnam

Pitches: R **Bats:** R **Pos:** RP-49   **Ht:** 6'2" **Wt:** 225 **Born:** 7/3/1987 **Age:** 28

			HOW MUCH HE PITCHED					WHAT HE GAVE UP												THE RESULTS						
Year	Team	Lg	G	GS	CG	GF	IP	BFP	H	R	ER	HR	SH	SF	HB	TBB	IBB	SO	WP	Bk	W	L	Pct	Sh	Sv-Op	Hld	ERC	ERA
2011	Cle	AL	8	0	0	3	7.1	34	10	5	5	1	0	0	2	0	0	9	1	0	1	1	.500	0	0-1	0	5.82	6.14
2012	Col	NL	2	0	0	0	2.0	9	3	0	0	0	1	0	0	1	0	0	0	0	0	0	-	0	0-0	0	7.26	0.00
2013	ChC	NL	5	0	0	1	3.1	19	9	7	7	1	0	1	0	0	0	4	0	0	0	0	-	0	0-0	0	15.42	18.90
2014	CWS	AL	49	0	0	13	54.2	213	39	14	12	2	1	1	1	20	1	46	5	0	5	3	.625	0	6-7	16	2.21	1.98
2015	CWS	AL	49	0	0	16	48.2	212	42	24	22	7	4	4	4	24	5	64	5	0	3	3	.500	0	0-3	6	4.14	4.07
5 ML YEARS			113	0	0	33	116.0	487	103	50	46	11	6	6	7	45	6	123	11	0	9	7	.563	0	6-11	22	3.58	3.57

Kevin Quackenbush

Pitches: R **Bats:** R **Pos:** RP-57   **Ht:** 6'4" **Wt:** 220 **Born:** 11/28/1988 **Age:** 27

			HOW MUCH HE PITCHED					WHAT HE GAVE UP												THE RESULTS						
Year	Team	Lg	G	GS	CG	GF	IP	BFP	H	R	ER	HR	SH	SF	HB	TBB	IBB	SO	WP	Bk	W	L	Pct	Sh	Sv-Op	Hld	ERC	ERA
2011	2 Tms	Low	35	0	0	32	42.0	158	25	3	3	1	0	0	0	12	0	71	1	0	2	1	.667	0	18- -	-	1.30	0.64
2012	Lk Els	A+	52	0	0	46	57.2	229	42	9	6	1	2	0	0	22	0	70	3	0	3	2	.600	0	27- -	-	2.13	0.94
2013	SnAnt	AA	29	0	0	23	31.0	121	16	4	1	1	1	1	3	10	1	46	0	1	2	0	1.000	0	13- -	-	1.41	0.29
2013	Tucsn	AAA	28	0	0	11	34.0	151	33	14	11	0	1	0	2	19	1	38	0	0	8	2	.800	0	4- -	-	3.99	2.91
2014	ElPaso	AAA	13	0	0	9	14.1	55	9	2	2	1	0	0	0	4	0	12	0	0	0	0	-	0	6- -	-	1.37	1.26
2015	ElPaso	AAA	9	0	0	4	11.2	39	6	1	1	0	1	1	0	2	0	14	0	0	1	0	1.000	0	2- -	-	0.93	0.77
2014	SD	NL	56	0	0	18	54.1	222	42	15	15	2	1	3	2	18	4	56	1	1	3	3	.500	0	6-7	10	2.25	2.48
2015	SD	NL	57	0	0	19	58.1	243	52	28	26	6	1	4	1	20	3	58	0	1	3	2	.600	0	0-1	2	3.28	4.01
2 ML YEARS			113	0	0	37	112.2	465	94	43	41	8	2	7	3	38	7	114	1	2	6	5	.545	0	6-8	12	2.77	3.28

Chad Qualls

Pitches: R **Bats:** R **Pos:** RP-60   **Ht:** 6'4" **Wt:** 235 **Born:** 8/17/1978 **Age:** 37

			HOW MUCH HE PITCHED					WHAT HE GAVE UP												THE RESULTS						
Year	Team	Lg	G	GS	CG	GF	IP	BFP	H	R	ER	HR	SH	SF	HB	TBB	IBB	SO	WP	Bk	W	L	Pct	Sh	Sv-Op	Hld	ERC	ERA
2004	Hou	NL	25	0	0	4	33.0	141	34	13	13	3	0	1	4	8	1	24	0	0	4	0	1.000	0	1-2	9	4.02	3.55
2005	Hou	NL	77	0	0	19	79.2	329	73	33	29	7	4	3	6	23	2	60	1	0	6	4	.600	0	0-0	22	3.42	3.28
2006	Hou	NL	81	0	0	13	88.2	356	76	38	37	10	4	4	6	28	6	56	0	0	7	3	.700	0	0-6	23	3.36	3.76
2007	Hou	NL	79	0	0	16	82.2	345	84	29	28	10	6	2	3	25	5	78	2	0	6	5	.545	0	5-10	21	4.07	3.05
2008	Ari	NL	77	0	0	21	73.2	300	61	29	23	4	4	3	3	18	2	71	6	0	4	8	.333	0	9-17	22	2.40	2.81
2009	Ari	NL	51	0	0	44	52.0	217	53	23	21	5	1	0	2	7	2	45	2	0	2	2	.500	0	24-29	3	3.17	3.63
2010	2 Tms		70	0	0	29	59.0	281	85	56	48	7	4	4	2	21	4	49	4	0	3	4	.429	0	12-19	11	6.63	7.32
2011	SD	NL	77	0	0	20	74.1	306	73	30	29	7	7	1	0	20	5	43	4	0	6	8	.429	0	0-5	22	3.38	3.51
2012	3 Tms		60	0	0	15	52.1	231	63	34	31	7	2	2	0	14	4	27	3	0	2	1	.667	0	0-5	14	4.78	5.33
2013	Mia	NL	66	0	0	12	62.0	252	57	18	18	4	4	0	2	19	7	49	1	0	5	2	.714	0	0-2	15	3.09	2.61
2014	Hou	AL	58	0	0	41	51.1	213	54	22	19	5	2	0	2	5	2	43	1	1	1	5	.167	0	19-25	2	3.22	3.33
2015	Hou	AL	60	0	0	17	49.1	202	46	24	24	6	1	4	2	9	1	46	3	0	3	5	.375	0	4-6	10	3.13	4.38
10	Ari	NL	43	0	0	28	38.0	190	61	41	35	5	4	2	1	15	4	34	3	0	1	4	.200	0	12-16	3	7.80	8.29
10	TB	AL	27	0	0	1	21.0	91	24	15	13	2	0	2	1	6	0	15	1	0	2	0	1.000	0	0-3	8	4.64	5.57
12	Phi	NL	35	0	0	8	31.1	140	39	18	16	7	1	0	0	9	3	19	2	0	1	1	.500	0	0-5	12	5.74	4.60
12	NYY	AL	8	0	0	4	7.1	33	10	5	5	0	0	1	0	3	1	2	1	0	1	0	1.000	0	0-0	0	5.38	6.14
12	Pit	NL	17	0	0	5	13.2	58	14	11	10	0	1	1	0	2	0	6	0	0	0	0	-	0	0-0	2	2.48	6.59
Postseason			17	0	0	0	22.2	94	24	13	13	3	1	0	0	7	3	17	0	0	1	1	.500	0	0-2	2	4.20	5.16
12 ML YEARS			781	0	0	251	758.0	3173	759	349	320	75	39	24	32	197	41	591	27	0	49	47	.510	0	74-126	171	3.64	3.80

Jose Quintana

Pitches: L Bats: R Pos: SP-32   KIN-tahn-ah   Ht: 6'1" Wt: 220 Born: 1/24/1989 Age: 27

			HOW MUCH HE PITCHED						WHAT HE GAVE UP													THE RESULTS							
Year Team	Lg	G	GS	CG	GF	IP	BFP	H	R	ER	HR	SH	SF	HB	TBB	IBB	SO	WP	Bk	W	L	Pct	Sh	Sv-Op	Hld	ERC	ERA
2012 CWS	AL	25	22	0	2	136.1	568	142	62	57	14	5	1	3	42	4	81	10	2	6	6	.500	0	0-0	0	4.13	3.76
2013 CWS	AL	33	33	0	0	200.0	832	188	83	78	23	3	6	5	56	2	164	2	1	9	7	.563	0	0-0	0	3.47	3.51
2014 CWS	AL	32	32	0	0	200.1	830	197	87	74	10	4	6	2	52	3	178	7	0	9	11	.450	0	0-0	0	3.15	3.32
2015 CWS	AL	32	32	1	0	206.1	862	218	81	77	16	4	4	8	44	4	177	5	0	9	10	.474	1	0-0	0	3.67	3.36
4 ML YEARS		122	119	1	2	743.0	3092	745	313	286	63	16	17	18	194	13	600	24	3	33	34	.493	1	0-0	0	3.55	3.46

Ryan Raburn

Bats: R Throws: R Pos: DH-35;PH-29;LF-18;RF-17   RAY-burn   Ht: 6'0" Wt: 185 Born: 4/17/1981 Age: 35

								BATTING												RUNNING			AVERAGES			
Year Team	Lg	G	AB	H	2B	3B	HR	(Hm	Rd)	TB	R	RBI	RC	TBB	IBB	SO	HBP	SH	SF	SB	CS	GDP	Avg	OBP	Slg	OPS
2004 Det	AL	12	29	4	1	0	0	(0	0)	5	4	1	1	2	0	15	0	0	0	1	0	0	.138	.194	.172	.366
2007 Det	AL	49	138	42	12	2	4	(2	2)	70	28	27	21	8	1	33	0	1	1	3	0	7	.304	.340	.507	.847
2008 Det	AL	92	182	43	10	1	4	(2	2)	67	26	20	20	16	1	49	0	1	0	3	1	2	.236	.298	.368	.666
2009 Det	AL	113	261	76	11	2	16	(9	7)	139	44	45	42	26	2	60	2	1	1	5	4	6	.291	.359	.533	.891
2010 Det	AL	113	371	104	25	1	15	(5	10)	176	54	62	54	27	0	92	8	1	3	2	2	8	.280	.340	.474	.814
2011 Det	AL	121	387	99	22	2	14	(7	7)	167	53	49	48	21	2	114	3	4	3	1	1	4	.256	.297	.432	.729
2012 Det	AL	66	205	35	14	0	1	(0	1)	52	14	12	8	13	0	53	2	1	1	1	1	7	.171	.226	.254	.480
2013 Cle	AL	87	243	66	18	0	16	(8	8)	132	40	55	47	29	0	67	4	0	1	0	0	4	.272	.357	.543	.901
2014 Cle	AL	74	195	39	7	0	4	(0	4)	58	18	22	11	13	1	51	1	0	3	0	0	8	.200	.250	.297	.547
2015 Cle	AL	82	173	52	16	1	8	(2	6)	94	22	29	30	23	3	44	4	0	1	0	0	5	.301	.393	.543	.936
Postseason		10	31	9	2	0	2	(1	1)	17	4	5	4	5	0	9	0	0	0	0	0	3	.290	.389	.548	.937
10 ML YEARS		809	2184	560	136	9	82	(35	47)	960	303	322	282	178	10	578	24	9	14	16	9	51	.256	.318	.440	.757

Alexei Ramirez

Bats: R Throws: R Pos: SS-152;PH-2;DH-1   ah-lexx-AY   Ht: 6'2" Wt: 180 Born: 9/22/1981 Age: 34

								BATTING												RUNNING			AVERAGES			
Year Team	Lg	G	AB	H	2B	3B	HR	(Hm	Rd)	TB	R	RBI	RC	TBB	IBB	SO	HBP	SH	SF	SB	CS	GDP	Avg	OBP	Slg	OPS
2008 CWS	AL	136	480	139	22	2	21	(13	8)	228	65	77	78	18	3	61	3	4	4	13	9	14	.290	.317	.475	.792
2009 CWS	AL	148	542	150	14	1	15	(9	6)	211	71	68	74	49	3	66	1	6	8	14	5	15	.277	.333	.389	.723
2010 CWS	AL	156	585	165	29	2	18	(11	7)	252	83	70	72	27	2	82	2	7	5	13	8	12	.282	.313	.431	.744
2011 CWS	AL	158	614	165	31	2	15	(7	8)	245	81	70	74	51	1	84	6	8	5	7	5	19	.269	.328	.399	.727
2012 CWS	AL	158	593	157	24	4	9	(6	3)	216	59	73	70	16	2	77	4	4	4	20	7	15	.265	.287	.364	.651
2013 CWS	AL	158	637	181	39	2	6	(5	1)	242	68	48	67	26	2	68	3	4	4	30	9	17	.284	.313	.380	.693
2014 CWS	AL	158	622	170	35	2	15	(8	7)	254	82	74	79	24	0	81	6	1	4	21	4	21	.273	.305	.408	.713
2015 CWS	AL	154	583	145	33	0	10	(7	3)	208	54	62	50	31	2	68	1	1	6	17	7	18	.249	.285	.357	.642
Postseason		4	12	3	0	0	0	(0	0)	3	1	2	1	1	0	1	0	0	2	0	0	0	.250	.267	.250	.517
8 ML YEARS		1226	4656	1272	227	15	109	(66	43)	1856	563	542	564	242	15	587	26	35	40	135	54	131	.273	.310	.399	.709

Aramis Ramirez

Bats: R Throws: R Pos: 3B-122;PH-11;1B-5;DH-2   ah-RAH-miss   Ht: 6'1" Wt: 205 Born: 6/25/1978 Age: 38

								BATTING												RUNNING			AVERAGES			
Year Team	Lg	G	AB	H	2B	3B	HR	(Hm	Rd)	TB	R	RBI	RC	TBB	IBB	SO	HBP	SH	SF	SB	CS	GDP	Avg	OBP	Slg	OPS
1998 Pit	NL	72	251	59	9	1	6	(3	3)	88	23	24	26	18	0	72	4	1	1	0	1	3	.235	.296	.351	.646
1999 Pit	NL	18	56	10	2	1	0	(0	0)	14	2	7	4	6	0	9	0	1	1	0	0	0	.179	.254	.250	.504
2000 Pit	NL	73	254	65	15	2	6	(4	2)	102	19	35	28	10	0	36	5	1	4	0	0	9	.256	.293	.402	.695
2001 Pit	NL	158	603	181	40	0	34	(16	18)	323	83	112	108	40	4	100	8	0	4	5	4	9	.300	.350	.536	.886
2002 Pit	NL	142	522	122	26	0	18	(7	11)	202	51	71	49	29	3	95	8	0	11	2	0	17	.234	.279	.387	.666
2003 2 Tms	NL	159	607	165	32	2	27	(10	17)	282	75	106	88	42	3	99	10	0	11	2	2	21	.272	.324	.465	.788
2004 ChC	NL	145	547	174	32	1	36	(22	14)	316	99	103	100	49	6	62	3	0	7	0	2	25	.318	.373	.578	.951
2005 ChC	NL	123	463	140	30	0	31	(11	20)	263	72	92	79	35	4	60	6	0	2	0	1	15	.302	.358	.568	.926
2006 ChC	NL	157	594	173	38	4	38	(14	24)	333	93	119	109	50	4	63	9	0	7	2	1	15	.291	.352	.561	.912
2007 ChC	NL	132	506	157	35	4	26	(17	9)	278	72	101	95	43	8	66	4	0	5	0	0	13	.310	.366	.549	.915
2008 ChC	NL	149	554	160	44	1	27	(17	10)	287	97	111	108	74	7	94	11	0	6	2	2	13	.289	.380	.518	.898
2009 ChC	NL	82	306	97	14	1	15	(7	8)	158	46	65	66	28	3	43	8	0	0	2	1	8	.317	.389	.516	.905
2010 ChC	NL	124	465	112	21	1	25	(14	11)	210	61	83	64	34	3	90	3	0	5	0	0	10	.241	.294	.452	.745
2011 ChC	NL	149	565	173	35	1	26	(14	12)	288	80	93	96	43	5	69	10	0	8	1	1	12	.306	.361	.510	.871
2012 Mil	NL	149	570	171	50	3	27	(15	12)	308	92	105	97	44	3	82	12	0	4	9	2	14	.300	.360	.540	.901
2013 Mil	NL	92	304	86	18	0	12	(6	6)	140	43	49	44	36	0	55	8	0	3	0	1	8	.283	.370	.461	.831
2014 Mil	NL	133	494	141	23	1	15	(7	8)	211	47	66	66	21	2	75	13	0	3	0	3	18	.285	.330	.427	.757
2015 2 Tms	NL	137	475	117	31	1	17	(5	12)	201	43	75	51	31	3	68	5	0	5	1	0	23	.246	.297	.423	.720
03 Pit	NL	96	375	105	25	1	12	(6	6)	168	44	67	49	25	3	68	7	0	8	1	1	17	.280	.330	.448	.778
03 ChC	NL	63	232	60	7	1	15	(4	11)	114	31	39	39	17	0	31	3	0	3	1	1	4	.259	.314	.491	.805
15 Mil	NL	81	279	69	18	0	11	(4	7)	120	25	42	28	16	3	42	4	0	3	1	0	12	.247	.295	.430	.725
15 Pit	NL	56	196	48	13	1	6	(1	5)	81	18	33	23	15	0	26	1	0	2	0	0	11	.245	.299	.413	.712
Postseason		18	67	13	2	1	4	(1	3)	29	7	10	8	9	0	15	1	0	0	0	0	5	.194	.299	.433	.732
18 ML YEARS		2194	8136	2303	495	24	386	(188	198)	4004	1098	1417	1278	633	58	1238	127	3	87	29	18	233	.283	.341	.492	.833

Erasmo Ramirez

Pitches: R Bats: R Pos: SP-27; RP-7   eh-RASS-moh   Ht: 5'11" Wt: 200 Born: 5/2/1990 Age: 26

		HOW MUCH HE PITCHED						WHAT HE GAVE UP												THE RESULTS							
Year	Team	Lg	G	GS	CG	GF	IP	BFP	H	R	ER	HR	SH	SF	HB	TBB	IBB	SO	WP	Bk	W	L	Pct	Sh	Sv-Op	Hld	ERC	ERA
2012	Sea	AL	16	8	0	2	59.0	238	47	26	22	6	1	5	3	12	1	48	0	0	1	3	.250	0	0-0	0	2.42	3.36
2013	Sea	AL	14	13	0	0	72.1	321	79	44	40	12	0	3	3	26	0	57	0	0	5	3	.625	0	0-0	0	5.04	4.98
2014	Sea	AL	17	14	0	0	75.1	338	82	44	44	13	1	1	6	34	2	60	3	0	1	6	.143	0	0-0	0	5.68	5.26
2015	TB	AL	34	27	0	5	163.1	666	145	73	68	16	1	1	9	40	0	126	3	0	11	6	.647	0	0-0	0	3.11	3.75
	4 ML YEARS		81	62	0	7	370.0	1563	353	187	174	47	3	10	21	112	3	291	6	0	18	18	.500	0	0-0	0	3.84	4.23

Hanley Ramirez

Bats: R Throws: R Pos: LF-92;DH-11;PH-2;3B-1   Ht: 6'2" Wt: 225 Born: 12/23/1983 Age: 32

			BATTING																	RUNNING			AVERAGES			
Year	Team	Lg	G	AB	H	2B	3B	HR	(Hm	Rd)	TB	R	RBI	RC	TBB	IBB	SO	HBP	SH	SF	SB	CS	GDP	Avg	OBP	Slg	OPS
2005	Bos	AL	2	2	0	0	0	0	(0	0)	0	0	0	0	0	0	2	0	0	0	0	0	0	.000	.000	.000	.000
2006	Fla	NL	158	633	185	46	11	17	(9	8)	304	119	59	101	56	0	128	4	5	2	51	15	7	.292	.353	.480	.833
2007	Fla	NL	154	639	212	48	6	29	(15	14)	359	125	81	115	52	3	95	7	4	4	51	14	10	.332	.386	.562	.948
2008	Fla	NL	153	589	177	34	4	33	(17	16)	318	**125**	67	116	92	9	122	8	0	4	35	12	5	.301	.400	.540	.940
2009	Fla	NL	151	576	197	42	1	24	(17	7)	313	101	106	122	61	14	101	9	1	5	27	8	9	**.342**	.410	.543	.954
2010	Fla	NL	142	543	163	28	2	21	(12	9)	258	92	76	90	64	12	93	7	0	5	32	10	14	.300	.378	.475	.853
2011	Fla	NL	92	338	82	16	0	10	(5	5)	128	55	45	46	44	3	66	2	1	0	20	10	6	.243	.333	.379	.712
2012	2 Tms	NL	157	604	155	29	4	24	(11	13)	264	79	92	81	54	4	132	6	0	3	21	7	17	.257	.322	.437	.759
2013	LAD	NL	86	304	105	25	2	20	(8	12)	194	62	57	69	27	3	52	3	0	2	10	2	5	.345	.402	.638	1.040
2014	LAD	NL	128	449	127	35	0	13	(8	5)	201	64	71	69	56	2	84	6	0	1	14	5	10	.283	.369	.448	.817
2015	Bos	AL	105	401	100	12	1	19	(8	11)	171	59	53	47	21	2	71	4	0	4	6	3	11	.249	.291	.426	.717
12	Mia	NL	93	353	87	18	2	14	(7	7)	151	49	48	42	37	1	72	3	0	2	14	4	11	.246	.322	.428	.749
12	LAD	NL	64	251	68	11	2	10	(4	6)	113	30	44	39	17	3	60	3	0	1	7	3	6	.271	.324	.450	.774
	Postseason		13	45	16	5	1	1	(0	1)	26	7	9	9	6	3	7	2	0	0	2	0	2	.356	.453	.578	1.031
	11 ML YEARS		1328	5078	1503	315	31	210	(110	100)	2510	881	707	856	527	52	946	56	11	30	267	86	94	.296	.367	.494	.861

J.C. Ramirez

Pitches: R Bats: R Pos: RP-20   Ht: 6'4" Wt: 250 Born: 8/16/1988 Age: 27

			HOW MUCH HE PITCHED						WHAT HE GAVE UP												THE RESULTS							
Year	Team	Lg	G	GS	CG	GF	IP	BFP	H	R	ER	HR	SH	SF	HB	TBB	IBB	SO	WP	Bk	W	L	Pct	Sh	Sv-Op	Hld	ERC	ERA
2011	Rdng	AA	26	26	3	0	144.0	627	144	84	72	15	4	5	4	55	0	89	5	4	11	13	.458	1	0- -	-	4.10	4.50
2012	Rdng	AA	16	16	0	0	27.1	115	20	14	11	3	0	0	1	14	0	18	1	0	0	2	.000	0	3- -	-	3.25	3.62
2012	LV	AAA	29	0	0	11	40.0	164	36	19	19	3	0	1	2	17	1	34	5	0	3	2	.600	0	1- -	-	3.79	4.28
2013	LV	AAA	30	0	0	9	42.0	191	42	24	22	2	1	1	0	23	1	36	4	0	4	2	.667	0	3- -	-	4.12	4.71
2014	Akron	AA	10	0	0	7	13.0	53	5	3	3	1	0	0	0	8	0	14	2	0	1	0	1.000	0	1- -	-	1.59	2.08
2014	Clmbs	AAA	25	0	0	15	31.1	132	33	16	12	5	1	1	1	11	0	15	2	0	1	3	.250	0	2- -	-	4.90	3.45
2015	Reno	AAA	23	0	0	6	25.0	106	22	8	8	0	1	1	0	10	0	18	0	0	0	1	.000	0	1- -	-	2.72	2.88
2015	Tacom	AAA	14	0	0	10	18.0	76	17	6	5	2	2	0	1	7	1	18	2	0	1	1	.500	0	0- -	-	4.01	2.50
2013	Phi	NL	18	0	0	2	24.0	116	30	22	20	6	1	4	0	15	1	16	0	0	0	1	.000	0	0-0	3	7.59	7.50
2015	2 Tms	NL	20	0	0	6	23.2	106	25	14	14	3	0	0	1	11	3	16	1	0	1	2	.333	0	0-3	2	4.79	5.32
15	Ari	NL	12	0	0	4	15.1	63	15	7	7	1	0	0	0	4	2	11	1	0	1	1	.500	0	0-2	2	3.04	4.11
15	Sea	AL	8	0	0	2	8.1	43	10	7	7	2	0	0	1	7	1	5	0	0	0	1	.000	0	0-1	0	8.47	7.56
	2 ML YEARS		38	0	0	8	47.2	222	55	36	34	9	1	4	1	26	4	32	1	0	1	3	.250	0	0-3	5	6.16	6.42

Jose Ramirez

Pitches: R Bats: R Pos: RP-8   Ht: 6'3" Wt: 190 Born: 1/21/1990 Age: 26

			HOW MUCH HE PITCHED						WHAT HE GAVE UP												THE RESULTS							
Year	Team	Lg	G	GS	CG	GF	IP	BFP	H	R	ER	HR	SH	SF	HB	TBB	IBB	SO	WP	Bk	W	L	Pct	Sh	Sv-Op	Hld	ERC	ERA
2011	2 Tms	Low	21	21	0	0	103.1	467	119	76	65	12	4	6	5	43	0	99	6	1	5	12	.294	0	0- -	-	5.33	5.66
2012	Tampa	A+	21	18	0	1	98.2	424	92	43	35	7	3	1	5	30	1	94	4	0	7	6	.538	0	2- -	-	3.24	3.19
2013	Trntn	AA	9	8	0	1	42.1	165	28	15	13	7	0	1	3	15	0	50	7	0	1	3	.250	0	1- -	-	2.90	2.76
2013	S-WB	AAA	8	8	0	0	31.1	137	29	20	17	3	0	0	4	21	0	28	2	0	1	3	.250	0	0- -	-	5.52	4.88
2014	S-WB	AAA	9	0	0	2	12.1	60	13	4	2	0	0	1	0	10	1	16	1	0	3	0	1.000	0	1- -	-	5.31	1.46
2015	S-WB	AAA	32	0	0	21	49.2	210	40	18	16	1	0	1	2	23	1	56	3	0	3	0	1.000	0	10- -	-	2.84	2.90
2015	Tacom	AAA	9	0	0	6	13.0	61	16	14	13	5	1	1	0	7	0	10	1	0	1	1	.500	0	0- -	-	8.32	9.00
2014	NYY	AL	8	0	0	5	10.0	49	11	6	6	2	0	0	2	7	0	10	0	0	0	2	.000	0	0-0	0	7.60	5.40
2015	2 Tms	AL	8	0	0	2	7.2	52	15	14	11	0	0	0	3	10	1	5	3	0	1	0	1.000	0	0-0	0	14.28	12.91
15	NYY	AL	3	0	0	1	3.0	20	6	5	5	0	0	0	1	4	0	2	3	0	0	0	-	0	0-0	0	15.12	15.00
15	Sea	AL	5	0	0	1	4.2	32	9	9	6	0	0	0	2	6	1	3	0	0	1	0	1.000	0	0-0	0	13.76	11.57
	2 ML YEARS		16	0	0	7	17.2	101	26	20	17	2	0	0	5	17	1	15	3	0	1	2	.333	0	0-0	0	10.50	8.66

Jose Ramirez

Bats: B Throws: R Pos: SS-46;2B-33;3B-13;PH-3;PR-3;LF-2;DH-1   Ht: 5'9" Wt: 180 Born: 9/17/1992 Age: 23

			BATTING																	RUNNING			AVERAGES			
Year	Team	Lg	G	AB	H	2B	3B	HR	(Hm	Rd)	TB	R	RBI	RC	TBB	IBB	SO	HBP	SH	SF	SB	CS	GDP	Avg	OBP	Slg	OPS
2015	Clmbs*	AAA	44	174	51	13	2	1	(-	-)	71	29	12	27	17	2	9	0	3	1	15	4	3	.293	.354	.408	.762
2013	Cle	AL	15	12	4	0	0	0	(0	0)	4	6	0	2	2	0	2	0	0	0	0	1	0	.333	.429	.500	.929
2014	Cle	AL	68	237	62	10	2	2	(1	1)	82	27	17	25	13	0	35	1	**13**	2	10	1	3	.262	.300	.346	.646
2015	Cle	AL	97	315	69	14	3	6	(1	5)	107	50	27	28	32	0	39	1	5	2	10	4	5	.219	.291	.340	.631
	3 ML YEARS		180	564	135	24	6	8	(2	6)	195	82	44	55	47	0	76	2	18	4	20	6	8	.239	.298	.346	.644

Neil Ramirez

Pitches: R **Bats:** R **Pos:** RP-19

Ht: 6'4" **Wt:** 190 **Born:** 5/25/1989 **Age:** 27

Year	Team	Lg	G	GS	CG	GF	IP	BFP	H	R	ER	HR	SH	SF	HB	TBB	IBB	SO	WP	Bk	W	L	Pct	Sh	Sv-Op	Hld	ERC	ERA
2011	RdRck	AAA	18	18	0	0	74.1	318	63	34	30	6	1	1	6	35	0	86	7	0	4	3	.571	0	0- -	-	3.72	3.63
2011	Frisco	AA	6	6	0	0	19.0	77	13	4	4	1	0	1	1	8	0	24	1	1	1	0	1.000	0	0- -	-	2.42	1.89
2012	RdRck	AAA	15	15	0	0	74.0	331	78	65	63	12	4	2	6	31	0	63	6	0	6	8	.429	0	0- -	-	5.24	7.66
2012	Frisco	AA	13	12	0	0	49.1	208	47	26	23	6	0	5	5	16	0	45	5	1	2	5	.286	0	0- -	-	4.15	4.20
2013	Frisco	AA	21	21	0	0	103.0	416	77	46	44	8	4	3	5	42	0	127	10	2	9	3	.750	0	0- -	-	2.87	3.84
2014	Iowa	AAA	6	0	0	1	7.0	33	7	6	6	2	0	0	0	5	0	11	0	0	0	0	.-	0	0- -	-	6.69	7.71
2015	Tenn	AAA	6	0	0	0	5.1	22	3	2	2	0	0	0	0	3	0	8	0	0	1	1	.500	0	0- -	-	1.76	3.38
2014	ChC	NL	50	0	0	10	43.2	177	29	11	7	2	0	0	2	17	0	53	3	1	3	3	.500	0	3-5	16	2.12	1.44
2015	ChC	NL	19	0	0	4	14.0	60	12	5	5	1	0	2	0	6	0	15	2	0	1	0	1.000	0	0-0	2	3.14	3.21
	2 ML YEARS		69	0	0	14	57.2	237	41	16	12	3	0	2	2	23	0	68	5	1	4	3	.571	0	3-5	18	2.36	1.87

Noe Ramirez

Pitches: R **Bats:** R **Pos:** RP-17

no-AY

Ht: 6'3" **Wt:** 205 **Born:** 12/22/1989 **Age:** 26

Year	Team	Lg	G	GS	CG	GF	IP	BFP	H	R	ER	HR	SH	SF	HB	TBB	IBB	SO	WP	Bk	W	L	Pct	Sh	Sv-Op	Hld	ERC	ERA
2012	Grnville	A	16	16	0	0	84.2	350	89	43	39	12	2	5	3	19	0	82	2	1	2	7	.222	0	0- -	-	4.19	4.15
2013	Salem	A+	21	0	0	5	47.0	182	41	13	11	0	2	1	4	9	0	44	3	0	2	1	.667	0	1- -	-	2.46	2.11
2013	Portlnd	AA	15	0	0	9	28.2	113	22	9	9	4	1	1	2	8	0	31	0	0	1	1	.500	0	5- -	-	2.99	2.83
2014	Portlnd	AA	42	0	0	31	67.1	268	56	17	16	0	4	1	3	16	1	56	6	1	2	1	.667	0	18- -	-	2.16	2.14
2015	Pwtckt	AAA	30	1	0	20	42.2	176	33	13	11	1	2	3	1	18	0	38	1	0	4	1	.800	0	3- -	-	2.55	2.32
2015	Bos	AL	17	0	0	3	13.0	61	13	12	6	3	0	0	2	7	0	13	1	0	0	1	.000	0	0-0	4	6.15	4.15

A.J. Ramos

Pitches: R **Bats:** R **Pos:** RP-71

Ht: 5'10" **Wt:** 205 **Born:** 9/20/1986 **Age:** 29

Year	Team	Lg	G	GS	CG	GF	IP	BFP	H	R	ER	HR	SH	SF	HB	TBB	IBB	SO	WP	Bk	W	L	Pct	Sh	Sv-Op	Hld	ERC	ERA
2012	Mia	NL	11	0	0	4	9.1	40	8	4	4	2	0	0	1	4	0	13	0	0	0	0	.-	0	0-1	1	4.65	3.86
2013	Mia	NL	68	0	0	18	80.0	338	58	32	28	4	1	3	2	43	3	86	1	0	3	4	.429	0	0-4	11	2.80	3.15
2014	Mia	NL	68	0	0	12	64.0	270	36	16	15	1	3	1	3	43	7	73	7	0	7	0	1.000	0	0-3	20	2.19	2.11
2015	Mia	NL	71	0	0	51	70.1	277	45	18	18	6	1	2	3	26	0	87	2	0	2	4	.333	0	32-38	4	2.21	2.30
	4 ML YEARS		218	0	0	85	223.2	925	147	70	65	13	5	6	9	116	10	259	10	0	12	8	.600	0	32-46	36	2.52	2.62

Cesar Ramos

Pitches: L **Bats:** L **Pos:** RP-65

Ht: 6'2" **Wt:** 200 **Born:** 6/22/1984 **Age:** 32

Year	Team	Lg	G	GS	CG	GF	IP	BFP	H	R	ER	HR	SH	SF	HB	TBB	IBB	SO	WP	Bk	W	L	Pct	Sh	Sv-Op	Hld	ERC	ERA
2009	SD	NL	5	2	0	0	14.2	62	19	5	5	0	0	0	0	4	0	10	0	0	0	1	.000	0	0-0	0	4.78	3.07
2010	SD	NL	14	0	0	4	8.1	47	18	11	11	1	0	0	0	4	0	9	1	1	0	1	.000	0	0-0	2	11.97	11.88
2011	TB	AL	59	0	0	9	43.2	192	36	22	19	4	1	2	3	25	8	31	1	0	0	1	.000	0	0-2	3	3.64	3.92
2012	TB	AL	17	1	0	9	30.0	120	19	7	7	2	0	0	2	10	0	29	0	0	1	0	1.000	0	0-0	1	1.98	2.10
2013	TB	AL	48	0	0	25	67.1	288	66	31	31	6	2	4	2	22	6	53	3	0	2	2	.500	0	1-1	5	3.55	4.14
2014	TB	AL	43	7	0	14	82.2	360	73	39	34	8	3	3	1	39	7	66	4	0	2	6	.250	0	0-0	2	3.53	3.70
2015	LAA	AL	65	0	0	21	52.1	221	55	17	16	2	3	3	3	15	0	43	5	0	2	1	.667	0	0-2	5	3.78	2.75
	7 ML YEARS		251	10	0	82	299.0	1290	286	132	123	23	9	12	11	119	21	241	14	1	7	12	.368	0	1-5	13	3.68	3.70

Wilson Ramos

Bats: R **Throws:** R **Pos:** C-125;PH-3;DH-1

Ht: 6'0" **Wt:** 230 **Born:** 8/10/1987 **Age:** 28

Year	Team	Lg	G	AB	H	2B	3B	HR	(Hm	Rd)	TB	R	RBI	RC	TBB	IBB	SO	HBP	SH	SF	SB	CS	GDP	Avg	OBP	Slg	OPS
2010	2 Tms		22	79	22	7	0	1	(1	0)	32	5	5	10	2	0	12	1	0	0	0	0	2	.278	.305	.405	.710
2011	Was	NL	113	389	104	22	1	15	(8	7)	173	48	52	43	38	8	76	2	4	2	0	2	19	.267	.334	.445	.779
2012	Was	NL	25	83	22	2	0	3	(1	2)	33	11	10	12	12	2	19	0	0	1	0	0	1	.265	.354	.398	.752
2013	Was	NL	78	287	78	9	0	16	(6	10)	135	29	59	40	15	1	42	0	0	1	0	1	12	.272	.307	.470	.777
2014	Was	NL	88	341	91	12	0	11	(3	8)	136	32	47	35	17	2	57	0	0	3	0	0	17	.267	.299	.399	.698
2015	Was	NL	128	475	109	16	0	15	(10	5)	170	41	68	39	21	2	101	0	0	8	0	0	16	.229	.258	.358	.616
10	Min	AL	7	27	8	3	0	0	(0	0)	11	2	1	3	0	0	3	1	0	0	0	0	1	.296	.321	.407	.729
10	Was	NL	15	52	14	4	0	1	(1	0)	21	3	4	7	2	0	9	0	0	0	0	0	0	.269	.296	.404	.700
	Postseason		4	17	2	0	0	0	(0	0)	2	1	0	0	1	0	6	0	1	0	0	0	1	.118	.167	.118	.284
	6 ML YEARS		454	1654	426	68	1	61	(29	32)	679	166	241	179	105	15	307	3	4	15	0	3	67	.258	.301	.411	.711

Anthony Ranaudo

Pitches: R **Bats:** R **Pos:** SP-2; RP-2

ran-AW-doh

Ht: 6'7" **Wt:** 230 **Born:** 9/9/1989 **Age:** 26

Year	Team	Lg	G	GS	CG	GF	IP	BFP	H	R	ER	HR	SH	SF	HB	TBB	IBB	SO	WP	Bk	W	L	Pct	Sh	Sv-Op	Hld	ERC	ERA
2011	2 Tms	Low	26	26	0	0	127.0	536	115	63	56	10	2	4	13	46	0	117	7	0	9	6	.600	0	0- -	-	3.72	3.97
2012	Portlnd	AA	9	9	0	0	37.2	180	41	29	28	4	1	4	3	27	0	27	4	0	1	3	.250	0	0- -	-	6.26	6.69
2013	Portlnd	AA	19	19	0	0	109.2	442	80	39	36	9	2	4	3	40	0	106	1	1	8	4	.667	0	0- -	-	2.53	2.95
2013	Pwtckt	AAA	6	5	0	1	30.1	126	32	11	10	1	1	0	0	7	0	21	0	0	3	1	.750	0	0- -	-	3.31	2.97
2014	Pwtckt	AAA	24	24	1	0	138.0	568	112	45	40	9	1	6	4	54	0	111	2	0	14	4	.778	1	0- -	-	2.94	2.61

Year	Team	Lg	G	GS	CG	GF	IP	BFP	H	R	ER	HR	SH	SF	HB	TBB	IBB	SO	WP	Bk	W	L	Pct	Sh	Sv-Op	Hld	ERC	ERA
2015	RdRck	AAA	21	21	0	0	118.0	513	123	65	60	14	3	4	4	46	0	90	2	0	7	6	.538	0	0--	-	4.57	4.58
2014	Bos	AL	7	7	0	0	39.1	170	39	21	21	10	0	4	0	16	0	15	2	0	4	3	.571	0	0-0	0	5.14	4.81
2015	Tex	AL	4	2	0	0	15.1	73	18	13	13	2	2	1	1	8	0	11	0	0	0	1	.000	0	0-0	0	5.96	7.63
	2 ML YEARS		11	9	0	0	54.2	243	57	34	34	12	2	5	1	24	0	26	2	0	4	4	.500	0	0-0	0	5.38	5.60

Colby Rasmus

Bats: L **Throws:** L **Pos:** LF-72;CF-43;RF-43;PH-12   **Ht:** 6'2" **Wt:** 195 **Born:** 8/11/1986 **Age:** 29

Year	Team	Lg	G	AB	H	2B	3B	HR	(Hm	Rd)	TB	R	RBI	RC	TBB	IBB	SO	HBP	SH	SF	SB	CS	GDP	Avg	OBP	Slg	OPS
2009	StL	NL	147	474	119	22	2	16	(7	9)	193	72	52	60	36	3	95	3	5	2	3	1	5	.251	.307	.407	.714
2010	StL	NL	144	464	128	28	3	23	(11	12)	231	85	66	76	63	9	148	1	2	4	12	8	5	.276	.361	.498	.859
2011	2 Tms		129	471	106	24	6	14	(4	10)	184	75	53	50	50	2	116	0	2	3	5	2	10	.225	.298	.391	.688
2012	Tor	AL	151	565	126	21	5	23	(8	15)	226	75	75	74	47	5	149	7	2	4	4	3	7	.223	.289	.400	.689
2013	Tor	AL	118	417	115	26	1	22	(14	8)	209	57	66	76	37	0	135	3	0	1	0	1	4	.276	.338	.501	.840
2014	Tor	AL	104	346	78	21	1	18	(7	11)	155	45	40	38	29	2	124	1	0	0	4	0	1	.225	.287	.448	.735
2015	Hou	AL	137	432	103	23	2	25	(12	13)	205	67	61	67	47	0	154	2	1	3	2	1	6	.238	.314	.475	.789
11	StL	NL	94	338	83	14	6	11	(4	7)	142	61	40	43	45	2	77	0	1	2	5	2	8	.246	.332	.420	.753
11	Tor	AL	35	133	23	10	0	3	(0	3)	42	14	13	7	5	0	39	0	1	1	0	0	2	.173	.201	.316	.517
	Postseason		3	9	4	3	0	0	(0	0)	7	1	1	1	2	0	1	0	0	0	0	0	1	.444	.545	.778	1.323
	7 ML YEARS		930	3169	775	165	20	141	(63	78)	1403	476	413	441	309	21	921	17	12	17	30	16	38	.245	.313	.443	.756

Cory Rasmus

Pitches: R **Bats:** R **Pos:** RP-15; SP-1   **Ht:** 6'0" **Wt:** 200 **Born:** 11/6/1987 **Age:** 28

Year	Team	Lg	G	GS	CG	GF	IP	BFP	H	R	ER	HR	SH	SF	HB	TBB	IBB	SO	WP	Bk	W	L	Pct	Sh	Sv-Op	Hld	ERC	ERA
2015	Salt Lk*	AAA	10	3	0	2	15.1	59	9	5	4	0	1	1	0	2	0	25	0	0	0	1	.000	0	1--	-	0.92	2.35
2013	2 Tms		19	0	0	6	21.2	103	24	15	13	6	0	1	0	13	2	20	0	1	1	1	.500	0	0-1	2	6.55	5.40
2014	LAA	AL	30	6	0	7	56.0	225	42	17	16	5	0	2	0	17	1	57	0	0	3	2	.600	0	0-0	0	2.31	2.57
2015	LAA	AL	16	1	0	5	20.2	88	15	12	12	3	1	0	1	11	2	27	0	0	0	0	-	0	0-1	1	3.41	5.23
13	Atl	NL	3	0	0	2	6.2	31	8	6	6	4	0	0	0	3	0	6	0	0	0	0	-	0	0-0	0	9.21	8.10
13	LAA	AL	16	0	0	4	15.0	72	16	9	7	2	0	1	0	10	2	14	0	1	1	1	.500	0	0-1	2	5.34	4.20
	Postseason		1	0	0	1	2.2	9	0	0	0	0	0	0	0	1	0	2	0	0	0	0	-	0	0-0	0	0.16	0.00
	3 ML YEARS		65	7	0	18	98.1	416	81	44	41	14	1	3	1	41	5	104	0	1	4	3	.571	0	0-2	3	3.37	3.75

Rob Rasmussen

Pitches: L **Bats:** R **Pos:** RP-20   **Ht:** 5'10" **Wt:** 170 **Born:** 4/2/1989 **Age:** 27

Year	Team	Lg	G	GS	CG	GF	IP	BFP	H	R	ER	HR	SH	SF	HB	TBB	IBB	SO	WP	Bk	W	L	Pct	Sh	Sv-Op	Hld	ERC	ERA
2011	Jupiter	A+	28	27	1	0	148.1	645	140	75	60	10	7	7	9	71	7	118	9	0	12	10	.545	1	0--	-	4.03	3.64
2012	Jupiter	A+	16	16	0	0	87.2	376	83	52	38	6	4	2	1	36	0	75	11	0	4	7	.364	0	0--	-	3.64	3.90
2012	CpChr	AA	11	10	0	0	54.1	232	58	30	29	6	1	2	1	18	0	44	2	0	4	4	.500	0	0--	-	4.39	4.80
2013	Chatt	AA	16	14	0	1	81.1	327	60	26	23	5	0	1	3	28	0	76	6	0	3	4	.429	0	0--	-	2.41	2.55
2013	Albq	AAA	12	10	0	0	54.1	257	64	42	39	10	3	3	3	32	0	37	2	0	0	7	.000	0	0--	-	6.81	6.46
2014	Buffalo	AAA	35	0	0	8	43.0	177	32	15	13	0	1	0	1	17	0	44	6	0	1	1	.500	0	1--	-	2.15	2.72
2015	Buffalo	AAA	33	1	0	6	41.0	170	26	11	11	1	1	1	0	20	0	39	4	0	4	1	.800	0	1--	-	1.98	2.41
2014	Tor	AL	10	0	0	4	11.1	50	8	4	4	1	0	0	2	7	0	13	2	0	0	0	-	0	0-0	2	3.87	3.18
2015	2 Tms	AL	20	0	0	6	15.1	79	26	18	17	2	0	0	0	8	0	17	4	0	2	1	.667	0	0-0	2	9.14	9.98
15	Tor	AL	1	0	0	1	1.0	4	1	0	0	0	0	0	0	0	0	1	0	0	0	0	-	0	0-0	0	1.95	0.00
15	Sea	AL	19	0	0	5	14.1	75	25	18	17	2	0	0	0	8	0	16	4	0	2	1	.667	0	0-0	2	9.74	10.67
	2 ML YEARS		30	0	0	10	26.2	129	34	22	21	3	0	0	2	15	0	30	6	0	2	1	.667	0	0-0	4	6.76	7.09

Josh Ravin

Pitches: R **Bats:** R **Pos:** RP-9   **Ht:** 6'4" **Wt:** 230 **Born:** 1/21/1988 **Age:** 28

Year	Team	Lg	G	GS	CG	GF	IP	BFP	H	R	ER	HR	SH	SF	HB	TBB	IBB	SO	WP	Bk	W	L	Pct	Sh	Sv-Op	Hld	ERC	ERA
2011	Carlina	A+	6	6	0	0	28.0	131	30	25	22	2	1	2	1	23	1	21	3	0	2	0	.000	0	0--	-	6.23	7.07
2011	Bkrsfld	A+	19	19	0	0	95.2	432	79	66	49	13	0	3	15	59	0	93	11	1	2	8	.200	0	0--	-	4.82	4.61
2012	Pnscla	AA	20	0	0	3	24.0	113	23	16	13	3	1	1	1	20	0	22	5	0	1	3	.250	0	0--	-	5.98	4.88
2013	Pnscla	AA	38	0	0	10	40.1	187	44	26	25	4	3	0	3	27	1	39	10	0	1	3	.250	0	0--	-	6.08	5.58
2013	Lsvlle	AAA	10	0	0	2	10.2	53	12	9	8	1	0	1	0	11	0	9	1	0	0	0	-	0	0--	-	7.50	6.75
2014	Chatt	AA	12	0	0	9	14.2	63	12	7	5	1	0	1	0	7	0	17	0	0	1	1	.500	0	4--	-	3.10	3.07
2014	Albq	AAA	11	0	0	6	10.2	50	12	6	5	1	0	1	0	7	0	8	0	0	1	0	1.000	0	2--	-	5.78	4.22
2015	OkCity	AAA	22	0	0	10	28.0	124	23	12	12	2	1	2	1	16	0	38	4	0	3	1	.750	0	3--	-	3.60	3.86
2015	LAD	NL	9	0	0	4	9.1	47	13	7	7	3	0	0	1	4	0	12	1	0	2	1	.667	0	0-0	0	8.54	6.75

Robbie Ray

Pitches: L **Bats:** L **Pos:** SP-23   **Ht:** 6'2" **Wt:** 195 **Born:** 10/1/1991 **Age:** 24

Year	Team	Lg	G	GS	CG	GF	IP	BFP	H	R	ER	HR	SH	SF	HB	TBB	IBB	SO	WP	Bk	W	L	Pct	Sh	Sv-Op	Hld	ERC	ERA
2011	Hgrstn	A	20	20	0	0	89.0	375	71	36	31	3	3	1	12	38	0	95	8	0	2	3	.400	0	0--	-	3.18	3.13
2012	Ptomc	A+	22	21	0	1	105.2	485	122	85	77	14	3	4	11	49	0	86	13	1	4	12	.250	0	0--	-	5.96	6.56
2013	Ptomc	A+	16	16	3	0	84.0	341	60	30	29	9	3	1	4	41	0	100	7	0	6	3	.667	0	0--	-	3.21	3.11
2013	Hrsbrg	AA	11	11	1	0	58.0	255	56	28	24	4	1	0	6	21	0	60	1	0	5	2	.714	1	0--	-	3.86	3.72
2014	Toledo	AAA	20	19	0	0	100.1	435	106	51	47	6	3	3	3	44	0	75	6	1	7	6	.538	0	0--	-	4.47	4.22

Year	Team	Lg		HOW MUCH HE PITCHED							WHAT HE GAVE UP											THE RESULTS							
			G	GS	CG	GF	IP	BFP	H	R	ER	HR	SH	SF	HB	TBB	IBB	SO	WP	Bk	W	L	Pct	Sh	Sv-Op	Hld	ERC	ERA
2015	Reno	AAA	9	9	0	0	41.2	187	44	21	17	1	3	0	0	27	1	57	1	0	2	3	.400	0	0--	-	4.86	3.67
2014	Det	AL	9	6	0	1	28.2	136	43	26	26	5	1	1	0	11	0	19	2	1	1	4	.200	0	0-0	1	7.72	8.16
2015	Ari	NL	23	23	0	0	127.2	545	121	56	50	9	7	6	8	49	3	119	2	0	5	12	.294	0	0-0	0	3.75	3.52
	2 ML YEARS		32	29	0	1	156.1	681	164	82	76	14	8	7	8	60	3	138	4	1	6	16	.273	0	0-0	1	4.42	4.38

Colin Rea

Pitches: R Bats: R Pos: SP-6   ray   Ht: 6'5" Wt: 220 Born: 7/1/1990 Age: 25

Year	Team	Lg		HOW MUCH HE PITCHED							WHAT HE GAVE UP											THE RESULTS							
			G	GS	CG	GF	IP	BFP	H	R	ER	HR	SH	SF	HB	TBB	IBB	SO	WP	Bk	W	L	Pct	Sh	Sv-Op	Hld	ERC	ERA
2011	Eugene	A-	15	15	0	0	53.0	228	47	18	13	2	0	2	6	21	0	43	6	2	3	4	.429	0	0--	-	3.44	2.21
2012	FtWyn	A	31	19	0	4	103.0	460	106	61	47	9	6	3	8	47	0	80	8	0	5	10	.333	0	0--	-	4.68	4.11
2013	2 Tms	Low	31	12	0	5	86.0	389	77	45	39	4	3	6	5	61	3	83	10	2	2	6	.250	0	0--	-	4.48	4.08
2014	Lk Els	A+	28	28	0	0	139.0	597	151	65	60	11	2	0	7	37	0	118	4	2	11	9	.550	0	0--	-	4.10	3.88
2015	SnAnt	AA	12	12	0	0	75.0	283	50	15	9	1	1	0	1	11	0	60	1	0	3	2	.600	0	0--	-	1.28	1.08
2015	ElPaso	AAA	6	6	0	0	26.2	120	29	14	12	2	0	0	2	12	1	20	0	0	2	2	.500	0	0--	-	4.83	4.05
2015	SD	NL	6	6	0	0	31.2	133	29	16	15	2	1	2	1	11	0	26	0	0	2	2	.500	0	0-0	0	3.29	4.26

J.T. Realmuto

Bats: R Throws: R Pos: C-118;PH-7;PR-3   ray-al-MOO-toh   Ht: 6'1" Wt: 205 Born: 3/18/1991 Age: 25

Year	Team	Lg		BATTING										RUNNING			AVERAGES			
			G	AB	H	2B	3B	HR	(Hm | Rd)	TB	R	RBI	RC	TBB	IBB	SO	HBP	SH	SF	SB	CS	GDP	Avg	OBP	Slg	OPS

Year	Team	Lg	G	AB	H	2B	3B	HR	(Hm	Rd)	TB	R	RBI	RC	TBB	IBB	SO	HBP	SH	SF	SB	CS	GDP	Avg	OBP	Slg	OPS
2011	Grnsbr	A	96	348	100	16	3	12	(-	-)	158	46	49	56	26	0	78	6	1	0	13	6	9	.287	.347	.454	.801
2012	Jupiter	A+	123	446	114	16	0	8	(-	-)	154	63	46	53	37	1	64	7	3	6	13	5	17	.256	.319	.345	.664
2013	Jaxnvl	AA	106	368	88	21	3	5	(-	-)	130	41	39	45	36	0	68	5	0	7	9	1	7	.239	.310	.353	.663
2014	Jaxnvl	AA	97	375	111	24	6	8	(-	-)	171	66	62	66	41	2	59	3	0	4	18	5	11	.296	.366	.456	.822
2014	Mia	NL	11	29	7	1	1	0	(0	0)	10	4	9	4	1	0	8	0	0	0	0	0	2	.241	.267	.345	.611
2015	Mia	NL	126	441	114	21	7	10	(6	4)	179	49	47	44	19	2	70	2	1	4	8	4	11	.259	.290	.406	.696
	2 ML YEARS		137	470	121	22	8	10	(6	4)	189	53	56	48	20	2	78	2	1	4	8	4	13	.257	.288	.402	.690

Chris Rearick

Pitches: L Bats: L Pos: RP-5   Ht: 6'3" Wt: 200 Born: 12/5/1987 Age: 28

Year	Team	Lg	G	GS	CG	GF	IP	BFP	H	R	ER	HR	SH	SF	HB	TBB	IBB	SO	WP	Bk	W	L	Pct	Sh	Sv-Op	Hld	ERC	ERA
2011	BG	A	50	0	0	43	81.1	315	49	18	15	3	6	3	7	16	0	89	6	1	7	2	.778	0	20--	-	1.42	1.66
2012	Charltt	A+	35	0	0	35	45.1	190	35	12	9	0	1	3	2	15	4	59	3	0	2	3	.400	0	20--	-	1.96	1.79
2012	Mont	AA	15	0	0	5	24.2	107	22	14	12	4	1	2	2	8	1	26	2	0	2	1	.667	0	2--	-	3.74	4.38
2013	SnAnt	AA	35	0	0	10	38.0	154	31	11	8	1	3	0	1	10	1	42	1	0	3	0	1.000	0	0--	-	2.20	1.89
2014	SnAnt	AA	7	0	0	0	7.1	30	8	3	3	2	0	0	0	0	0	9	1	0	1	0	1.000	0	0--	-	3.96	3.68
2014	ElPaso	AAA	33	0	0	8	36.1	147	31	13	11	2	0	0	0	9	1	38	2	0	2	0	1.000	0	0--	-	2.41	2.72
2015	ElPaso	AAA	37	0	0	12	43.0	203	48	28	25	5	3	3	3	30	1	28	2	1	0	3	.000	0	0--	-	6.43	5.23
2015	SnAnt	AA	5	0	0	4	6.0	24	5	0	0	0	0	0	0	1	0	9	1	0	0	0	-	0	2--	-	1.74	0.00
2015	SD	NL	5	0	0	1	3.0	16	6	4	4	2	1	0	0	2	0	4	0	0	0	0	-	0	0-0	1	18.50	12.00

Anthony Recker

Bats: R Throws: R Pos: C-28;PH-4;PR-2;1B-1;3B-1   Ht: 6'2" Wt: 240 Born: 8/29/1983 Age: 32

Year	Team	Lg	G	AB	H	2B	3B	HR	(Hm	Rd)	TB	R	RBI	RC	TBB	IBB	SO	HBP	SH	SF	SB	CS	GDP	Avg	OBP	Slg	OPS
2015	LsVgs*	AAA	27	94	23	3	1	8	(-	-)	52	17	21	18	12	0	26	2	0	0	0	0	3	.245	.343	.553	.896
2011	Oak	AL	5	17	3	1	0	0	(0	0)	4	3	0	0	4	0	7	0	0	0	0	0	0	.176	.333	.235	.569
2012	2 Tms	AL	22	49	7	2	0	1	(0	1)	12	4	4	0	6	0	15	2	1	0	0	0	1	.143	.263	.245	.508
2013	NYM	NL	50	135	29	7	0	6	(4	2)	54	17	19	13	13	1	49	0	1	2	0	1	1	.215	.280	.400	.680
2014	NYM	NL	58	174	35	9	0	7	(3	4)	65	18	27	17	10	0	64	1	2	2	1	1	2	.201	.246	.374	.620
2015	NYM	NL	32	80	10	1	0	2	(0	2)	17	6	5	3	11	2	35	1	0	0	1	0	1	.125	.239	.213	.452
12	Oak	AL	13	31	4	1	0	0	(0	0)	5	3	0	0	4	0	13	1	1	0	0	0	1	.129	.250	.161	.411
12	ChC	NL	9	18	3	1	0	1	(0	1)	7	1	4	0	2	0	2	1	0	0	0	0	1	.167	.286	.389	.675
	5 ML YEARS		167	455	84	20	0	16	(7	9)	152	48	55	33	44	3	170	4	4	4	2	2	5	.185	.260	.334	.594

Josh Reddick

Bats: L Throws: R Pos: RF-143;PH-13;DH-2;CF-1   Ht: 6'2" Wt: 180 Born: 2/19/1987 Age: 29

Year	Team	Lg	G	AB	H	2B	3B	HR	(Hm	Rd)	TB	R	RBI	RC	TBB	IBB	SO	HBP	SH	SF	SB	CS	GDP	Avg	OBP	Slg	OPS
2009	Bos	AL	27	59	10	4	0	2	(0	2)	20	5	4	4	2	0	17	1	0	0	0	0	0	.169	.210	.339	.549
2010	Bos	AL	29	62	12	3	1	1	(1	0)	20	5	5	1	1	0	15	0	0	0	0	1	1	.194	.206	.323	.529
2011	Bos	AL	87	254	71	18	3	7	(2	5)	116	41	28	33	19	1	50	1	0	4	1	2	1	.280	.327	.457	.784
2012	Oak	AL	156	611	148	29	5	32	(18	14)	283	85	85	73	55	8	151	2	1	4	11	1	15	.242	.305	.463	.768
2013	Oak	AL	114	385	87	19	2	12	(2	10)	146	54	56	53	46	1	86	2	1	7	9	2	4	.226	.307	.379	.686
2014	Oak	AL	109	363	96	16	7	12	(5	7)	162	53	54	54	28	0	63	1	0	3	1	1	3	.264	.316	.446	.763
2015	Oak	AL	149	526	143	25	4	20	(7	13)	236	66	77	83	49	1	65	0	1	2	10	2	7	.272	.333	.449	.781
	Postseason		11	38	8	1	0	2	(0	2)	15	5	2	2	5	1	15	0	0	0	0	0	1	.211	.302	.395	.697
	7 ML YEARS		671	2260	567	114	22	86	(35	51)	983	310	309	301	200	11	447	7	3	20	33	8	31	.251	.311	.435	.746

Todd Redmond

Pitches: R Bats: R Pos: RP-6; SP-1

Ht: 6'3" Wt: 240 Born: 5/17/1985 Age: 31

			HOW MUCH HE PITCHED						WHAT HE GAVE UP										THE RESULTS						
Year	Team	Lg	G	GS	CG	GF	IP	BFP	H	R	ER	HR	SH	SF	HB	TBB	IBB	SO	WP	Bk	W	L	Pct	Sh	Sv-Op	Hld	ERC	ERA
2015	Buffalo*	AAA	23	10	0	2	78.2	339	86	36	35	5	2	1	2	25	4	57	2	0	3	7	.300	0	1- -	-	4.06	4.00
2012	Cin	NL	1	1	0	0	3.1	22	7	4	4	1	0	0	0	5	0	2	0	0	0	1	.000	0	0-0	0	18.68	10.80
2013	Tor	AL	17	14	0	2	77.0	324	70	38	37	13	1	1	6	23	2	76	1	0	4	3	.571	0	0-0	0	3.91	4.32
2014	Tor	AL	42	0	0	14	75.0	314	73	33	27	5	2	5	2	27	6	60	2	0	1	4	.200	0	1-1	0	3.60	3.24
2015	Tor	AL	7	1	0	1	16.0	72	17	13	13	3	0	0	1	7	0	13	1	0	0	0	-	0	0-0	1	5.46	7.31
	4 ML YEARS		67	16	0	17	171.1	732	167	88	81	22	3	6	9	62	8	151	4	0	5	8	.385	0	1-1	1	4.15	4.25

Addison Reed

Pitches: R Bats: L Pos: RP-55

Ht: 6'4" Wt: 230 Born: 12/27/1988 Age: 27

			HOW MUCH HE PITCHED						WHAT HE GAVE UP										THE RESULTS						
Year	Team	Lg	G	GS	CG	GF	IP	BFP	H	R	ER	HR	SH	SF	HB	TBB	IBB	SO	WP	Bk	W	L	Pct	Sh	Sv-Op	Hld	ERC	ERA
2015	Reno*	AAA	11	0	0	9	10.1	45	8	2	2	1	0	0	0	5	1	11	1	0	1	1	.500	0	5- -	-	2.87	1.74
2011	CWS	AL	6	0	0	2	7.1	33	10	3	3	1	0	0	0	1	0	12	0	0	0	0	-	0	0-0	0	5.24	3.68
2012	CWS	AL	62	0	0	44	55.0	238	57	30	29	6	0	4	2	18	3	54	0	1	3	2	.600	0	29-33	4	4.09	4.75
2013	CWS	AL	68	0	0	59	71.1	295	56	31	30	6	3	6	2	23	2	72	2	0	5	4	.556	0	40-48	0	2.56	3.79
2014	Ari	NL	62	0	0	55	59.1	252	57	31	28	11	1	1	1	15	2	69	3	0	1	7	.125	0	32-38	0	3.76	4.25
2015	2 Tms	NL	55	0	0	14	56.0	241	58	21	21	3	1	0	0	19	6	51	2	0	3	3	.500	0	4-8	14	3.52	3.38
15	Ari	NL	38	0	0	11	40.2	181	47	19	19	2	1	0	0	14	5	34	2	0	2	2	.500	0	3-5	8	4.10	4.20
15	NYM	NL	17	0	0	3	15.1	60	11	2	2	1	0	0	0	5	1	17	0	0	1	1	.500	0	1-3	6	2.10	1.17
	5 ML YEARS		253	0	0	174	249.0	1059	238	116	111	27	5	11	5	76	13	258	7	1	12	16	.429	0	105-127	18	3.47	4.01

Chris Reed

Pitches: L Bats: L Pos: RP-2

Ht: 6'3" Wt: 225 Born: 5/20/1990 Age: 26

			HOW MUCH HE PITCHED						WHAT HE GAVE UP										THE RESULTS						
Year	Team	Lg	G	GS	CG	GF	IP	BFP	H	R	ER	HR	SH	SF	HB	TBB	IBB	SO	WP	Bk	W	L	Pct	Sh	Sv-Op	Hld	ERC	ERA
2012	Rcuca	A+	7	6	0	1	35.0	140	25	12	12	1	1	1	1	14	0	38	0	0	1	4	.200	0	0- -	-	2.29	3.09
2012	Chatt	AA	12	11	0	0	35.1	155	31	19	19	2	3	0	4	20	0	29	3	0	0	4	.000	0	0- -	-	4.23	4.84
2013	Chatt	AA	29	25	1	0	137.2	587	128	64	59	9	5	0	6	63	1	106	7	1	4	11	.267	1	0- -	-	3.89	3.86
2014	Chatt	AA	23	23	0	0	137.0	578	114	70	49	10	9	2	7	55	2	116	12	0	4	8	.333	0	0- -	-	3.15	3.22
2014	Albq	AAA	5	5	0	0	21.1	113	37	28	26	5	2	0	2	11	0	18	2	0	0	3	.000	0	0- -	-	10.79	10.97
2015	Tulsa	AA	16	0	0	4	23.2	109	22	21	19	2	2	1	0	18	1	16	3	0	2	2	.500	0	1- -	-	4.88	7.23
2015	OkCity	AAA	8	0	0	3	11.0	43	11	4	4	0	0	1	0	4	0	5	1	0	0	0	-	0	0- -	-	3.59	3.27
2015	NewOr	AAA	14	0	0	5	20.2	92	18	9	9	3	2	0	1	13	1	23	3	1	1	0	1.000	0	0- -	-	4.70	3.92
2015	Mia	NL	2	0	0	1	4.0	18	6	2	2	0	1	0	0	1	0	1	0	0	0	0	-	0	0-0	0	5.79	4.50

Michael Reed

Bats: R Throws: R Pos: RF-3;PH-3;PR-1

Ht: 6'0" Wt: 190 Born: 11/18/1992 Age: 23

			BATTING																RUNNING			AVERAGES			
Year	Team	Lg	G	AB	H	2B	3B	HR	(Hm | Rd)	TB	R	RBI	RC	TBB	IBB	SO	HBP	SH	SF	SB	CS	GDP	Avg	OBP	Slg	OPS
2011	Brewrs	R	14	56	13	4	2	0	(- | -)	21	11	5	6	5	1	17	0	1	0	1	0	0	.232	.319	.375	.670
2012	2 Tms	Low	59	211	53	5	1	1	(- | -)	63	34	25	27	32	0	66	1	4	1	14	1	1	.251	.351	.299	.650
2013	Wisc	A	118	455	130	23	13	1	(- | -)	182	68	40	77	71	3	108	4	7	2	26	10	15	.286	.385	.400	.785
2014	BrvdCt	A+	110	365	93	20	5	5	(- | -)	138	50	47	65	78	0	79	9	2	3	33	13	8	.255	.396	.378	.774
2015	Biloxi	AA	93	313	87	20	5	5	(- | -)	132	43	49	57	53	1	80	3	0	8	25	7	6	.278	.379	.422	.801
2015	ColSpr	AAA	38	126	31	13	2	0	(- | -)	48	19	21	18	20	0	31	1	0	1	1	0	3	.246	.351	.381	.732
2015	Mil	NL	7	6	2	1	0	0	(0 | 0)	3	2	0	1	0	0	3	0	0	0	0	0	0	.333	.333	.500	.833

Rob Refsnyder

Bats: R Throws: R Pos: 2B-15;PH-2;PR-1

REF-snide-er

Ht: 6'1" Wt: 205 Born: 3/26/1991 Age: 25

			BATTING																RUNNING			AVERAGES			
Year	Team	Lg	G	AB	H	2B	3B	HR	(Hm | Rd)	TB	R	RBI	RC	TBB	IBB	SO	HBP	SH	SF	SB	CS	GDP	Avg	OBP	Slg	OPS
2012	CtnSC	A	46	162	39	8	0	4	(- | -)	59	22	22	21	16	0	25	3	0	1	11	1	7	.241	.319	.364	.683
2013	2 Tms	Low	130	467	137	32	3	6	(- | -)	193	75	57	90	84	0	82	13	2	3	23	6	13	.293	.413	.413	.826
2014	Trntn	AA	60	228	78	19	5	6	(- | -)	125	35	30	45	14	0	38	2	0	5	5	5	8	.342	.385	.548	.933
2014	S-WB	AAA	77	287	85	19	1	8	(- | -)	130	47	33	51	41	0	67	2	1	2	4	4	8	.296	.386	.453	.839
2015	S-WB	AAA	117	450	122	28	2	9	(- | -)	181	66	56	72	56	1	73	9	1	6	12	2	12	.271	.359	.402	.761
2015	NYY	AL	16	43	13	3	0	2	(1 | 1)	22	3	5	6	3	1	7	0	0	0	2	0	3	.302	.348	.512	.859

Nolan Reimold

RYE-mold

Bats: R Throws: R Pos: LF-37;RF-13;PH-10;CF-9;DH-4;PR-3

Ht: 6'4" Wt: 205 Born: 10/12/1983 Age: 32

			BATTING																RUNNING			AVERAGES			
Year	Team	Lg	G	AB	H	2B	3B	HR	(Hm | Rd)	TB	R	RBI	RC	TBB	IBB	SO	HBP	SH	SF	SB	CS	GDP	Avg	OBP	Slg	OPS
2015	Norfolk*	AAA	54	197	54	13	0	2	(- | -)	73	25	15	29	26	0	42	2	0	1	5	1	4	.274	.363	.371	.733
2009	Bal	AL	104	358	100	18	2	15	(8 | 7)	167	49	45	57	47	1	77	3	0	3	8	2	8	.279	.365	.466	.831
2010	Bal	AL	39	116	24	5	0	3	(0 | 3)	38	9	14	6	12	0	26	1	0	2	0	0	6	.207	.282	.328	.610
2011	Bal	AL	87	267	66	10	3	13	(8 | 5)	121	40	45	48	28	1	57	6	0	4	7	2	4	.247	.328	.453	.781
2012	Bal	AL	16	67	21	6	0	5	(0 | 5)	42	10	10	15	2	0	14	0	0	0	1	0	3	.313	.333	.627	.960
2013	Bal	AL	40	128	25	3	0	5	(3 | 2)	43	17	12	7	10	2	41	0	0	2	0	1	4	.195	.250	.336	.586
2014	2 Tms		29	69	16	5	0	3	(1 | 2)	30	5	13	9	6	0	32	0	0	3	1	0	0	.232	.282	.435	.717

							BATTING													RUNNING			AVERAGES			
Year	Team	Lg	G	AB	H	2B	3B	HR	(Hm | Rd)	TB	R	RBI	RC	TBB	IBB	SO	HBP	SH	SF	SB	CS	GDP	Avg	OBP	Slg	OPS
2015	Bal	AL	61	170	42	5	1	6	(5 | 1)	67	24	20	27	23	2	47	2	0	0	0	0	2	.247	.344	.394	.738
14	Tor	AL	22	52	11	4	0	2	(0 | 2)	21	3	9	6	6	0	22	0	0	2	1	0	0	.212	.283	.404	.687
14	Ari	NL	7	17	5	1	0	1	(1 | 0)	9	2	4	3	0	0	10	0	0	1	0	0	0	.294	.278	.529	.807
	7 ML YEARS		376	1175	294	52	6	50	(25 | 25)	508	154	159	169	128	6	294	12	0	14	17	5	27	.250	.327	.432	.759

Anthony Rendon

Bats: R **Throws:** R **Pos:** 2B-59;3B-28;PH-2   ren-DOAN   **Ht:** 6'1" **Wt:** 210 **Born:** 6/6/1990 **Age:** 26

							BATTING													RUNNING			AVERAGES			
Year	Team	Lg	G	AB	H	2B	3B	HR	(Hm | Rd)	TB	R	RBI	RC	TBB	IBB	SO	HBP	SH	SF	SB	CS	GDP	Avg	OBP	Slg	OPS
2013	Was	NL	98	351	93	23	1	7	(3 | 4)	139	40	35	43	31	3	69	5	2	5	1	1	7	.265	.329	.396	.725
2014	Was	NL	153	613	176	39	6	21	(10 | 11)	290	111	83	97	58	2	104	5	2	5	17	3	11	.287	.351	.473	.824
2015	Was	NL	80	311	82	16	0	5	(3 | 2)	113	43	25	39	36	0	70	4	0	4	1	2	8	.264	.344	.363	.707
	Postseason		4	19	7	0	0	0	(0 | 0)	7	0	1	3	1	0	2	0	0	0	1	0	0	.368	.400	.368	.768
	3 ML YEARS		331	1275	351	78	7	33	(16 | 17)	542	194	143	179	125	5	243	14	4	14	19	6	26	.275	.343	.425	.768

Ben Revere

Bats: L **Throws:** R **Pos:** LF-112;CF-43;RF-12;PH-8;PR-1   **Ht:** 5'9" **Wt:** 170 **Born:** 5/3/1988 **Age:** 28

							BATTING													RUNNING			AVERAGES			
Year	Team	Lg	G	AB	H	2B	3B	HR	(Hm | Rd)	TB	R	RBI	RC	TBB	IBB	SO	HBP	SH	SF	SB	CS	GDP	Avg	OBP	Slg	OPS
2010	Min	AL	13	28	5	0	0	0	(0 | 0)	5	1	2	0	2	0	5	0	0	0	1	1	1	.179	.233	.179	.412
2011	Min	AL	117	450	120	9	5	0	(0 | 0)	139	56	30	51	26	1	41	2	3	6	34	9	7	.267	.310	.309	.619
2012	Min	AL	124	511	150	13	6	0	(0 | 0)	175	70	32	62	29	1	54	3	6	4	40	9	8	.294	.333	.342	.675
2013	Phi	NL	88	315	96	9	3	0	(0 | 0)	111	37	17	39	16	1	36	0	5	0	22	8	10	.305	.338	.352	.691
2014	Phi	NL	151	601	184	13	7	2	(1 | 1)	217	71	28	71	13	1	49	4	7	1	49	8	11	.306	.325	.361	.686
2015	2 Tms		152	592	181	22	7	2	(1 | 1)	223	84	45	78	32	0	64	2	5	3	31	7	5	.306	.342	.377	.719
15	Phi	NL	96	366	109	13	6	1	(1 | 0)	137	49	26	45	19	0	36	1	2	0	24	5	4	.298	.334	.374	.709
15	Tor	AL	56	226	72	9	1	1	(0 | 1)	86	35	19	33	13	0	28	1	3	3	7	2	1	.319	.354	.381	.734
	6 ML YEARS		645	2497	736	66	28	4	(2 | 2)	870	319	154	301	118	3	249	11	26	8	176	42	42	.295	.328	.348	.677

Jo-Jo Reyes

Pitches: L **Bats:** L **Pos:** RP-1   **Ht:** 6'2" **Wt:** 230 **Born:** 11/20/1984 **Age:** 31

			HOW MUCH HE PITCHED						WHAT HE GAVE UP										THE RESULTS							
Year	Team	Lg	G	GS	CG	GF	IP	BFP	H	R	ER	HR	SH	SF	HB	TBB	IBB	SO	WP	Bk	W	L	Pct	Sh	Sv-Op	Hld	ERC	ERA
2015	Salt Lk*	AAA	15	11	0	2	68.0	302	83	41	36	8	5	6	2	23	0	45	4	0	4	5	.444	0	1- -	-	5.42	4.76
2007	Atl	NL	11	10	0	0	50.2	230	55	39	35	9	5	2	1	30	2	27	1	0	2	2	.500	0	0-0	0	6.06	6.22
2008	Atl	NL	23	22	0	0	113.0	512	134	77	73	18	9	3	3	52	4	78	2	0	3	11	.214	0	0-0	0	5.97	5.81
2009	Atl	NL	6	5	0	0	27.0	119	27	25	21	4	1	1	1	13	3	21	0	0	0	2	.000	0	0-0	0	4.73	7.00
2010	Atl	NL	1	0	0	0	3.1	23	10	9	9	2	0	0	0	3	0	2	0	0	0	0	-	0	0-0	0	26.51	24.30
2011	2 Tms	AL	29	25	1	1	140.2	641	176	99	87	21	3	3	7	48	0	87	7	0	7	11	.389	0	0-0	0	5.87	5.57
2015	LAA	AL	1	0	0	0	0.1	1	0	0	0	0	0	0	0	0	0	0	0	0	1	0	1.000	0	0-0	0	0.00	0.00
11	Tor	AL	20	20	1	0	110.0	504	140	78	66	14	3	3	6	35	0	64	6	0	5	8	.385	0	0-0	0	5.71	5.40
11	Bal	AL	9	5	0	1	30.2	137	36	21	21	7	0	0	1	13	0	23	1	0	2	3	.400	0	0-0	0	6.42	6.16
	6 ML YEARS		71	62	1	1	335.0	1526	402	249	225	54	18	9	12	146	9	215	10	0	13	26	.333	0	0-0	0	5.99	6.04

Jose Reyes

Bats: B **Throws:** R **Pos:** SS-116   **Ht:** 6'0" **Wt:** 195 **Born:** 6/11/1983 **Age:** 33

							BATTING													RUNNING			AVERAGES			
Year	Team	Lg	G	AB	H	2B	3B	HR	(Hm | Rd)	TB	R	RBI	RC	TBB	IBB	SO	HBP	SH	SF	SB	CS	GDP	Avg	OBP	Slg	OPS
2003	NYM	NL	69	274	84	12	4	5	(1 | 4)	119	47	32	46	13	0	36	0	2	3	13	3	1	.307	.334	.434	.769
2004	NYM	NL	53	220	56	16	2	2	(1 | 1)	82	33	14	25	5	0	31	0	4	0	19	2	1	.255	.271	.373	.644
2005	NYM	NL	161	696	190	24	17	7	(2 | 5)	269	99	58	84	27	0	78	2	4	4	60	15	7	.273	.300	.386	.687
2006	NYM	NL	153	647	194	30	17	19	(9 | 10)	315	122	81	121	53	6	81	1	2	0	64	17	6	.300	.354	.487	.841
2007	NYM	NL	160	681	191	36	12	12	(5 | 7)	287	119	57	99	77	13	78	1	5	1	78	21	6	.280	.354	.421	.775
2008	NYM	NL	159	688	204	37	19	16	(9 | 7)	327	113	68	117	66	4	82	1	5	3	56	15	9	.297	.358	.475	.833
2009	NYM	NL	36	147	41	7	2	2	(1 | 1)	58	18	15	20	18	1	19	0	0	1	11	2	2	.279	.355	.395	.750
2010	NYM	NL	133	563	159	29	10	11	(8 | 3)	241	83	54	76	31	4	63	2	4	3	30	10	8	.282	.321	.428	.749
2011	NYM	NL	126	537	181	31	16	7	(4 | 3)	265	101	44	90	43	9	41	0	2	4	39	7	5	.337	.384	.493	.877
2012	Mia	NL	160	642	184	37	12	11	(4 | 7)	278	86	57	92	63	9	56	0	5	6	40	11	10	.287	.347	.433	.780
2013	Tor	AL	93	382	113	20	0	10	(7 | 3)	163	58	37	61	34	2	47	1	0	2	15	6	6	.296	.353	.427	.780
2014	Tor	AL	143	610	175	33	4	9	(5 | 4)	243	94	51	77	38	1	73	1	2	4	30	2	4	.287	.328	.398	.726
2015	2 Tms		116	481	132	25	2	7	(5 | 2)	182	57	53	63	26	0	62	0	9	3	24	6	5	.274	.310	.378	.688
15	Tor	AL	69	288	82	17	0	4	(3 | 1)	111	36	34	42	17	0	38	0	4	2	16	2	3	.285	.322	.385	.708
15	Col	NL	47	193	50	8	2	3	(2 | 1)	71	21	19	21	9	0	24	0	5	1	8	4	3	.259	.291	.368	.659
	Postseason		10	44	11	1	1	1	(1 | 0)	17	7	5	6	3	1	5	0	0	0	3	1	0	.250	.298	.386	.684
	13 ML YEARS		1562	6568	1904	337	117	118	(63 | 55)	2829	1030	621	971	494	53	747	9	44	34	479	117	71	.290	.339	.431	.770

Mark Reynolds

Bats: R **Throws:** R **Pos:** 1B-100;PH-27;3B-22;LF-5;DH-3;2B-1;RF-1;PR-1   **Ht:** 6'2" **Wt:** 220 **Born:** 8/3/1983 **Age:** 32

							BATTING													RUNNING			AVERAGES			
Year	Team	Lg	G	AB	H	2B	3B	HR	(Hm | Rd)	TB	R	RBI	RC	TBB	IBB	SO	HBP	SH	SF	SB	CS	GDP	Avg	OBP	Slg	OPS
2007	Ari	NL	111	366	102	20	4	17	(7 | 10)	181	62	62	62	37	4	129	5	1	5	0	0	5	.279	.349	.495	.843
2008	Ari	NL	152	539	129	28	4	28	(13 | 15)	247	87	97	82	64	0	204	3	1	6	11	2	10	.239	.320	.458	.779
2009	Ari	NL	155	578	150	30	1	44	(19 | 25)	314	98	102	94	76	3	223	5	0	3	24	9	4	.260	.349	.543	.892
2010	Ari	NL	145	499	99	17	2	32	(21 | 11)	216	79	85	77	83	7	211	9	0	5	7	4	8	.198	.320	.433	.753
2011	Bal	AL	155	534	118	27	1	37	(17 | 20)	258	84	86	77	75	2	196	7	0	4	6	4	11	.221	.323	.483	.806

				BATTING																		RUNNING			AVERAGES			
Year	Team	Lg	G	AB	H	2B	3B	HR	(Hm	Rd)	TB	R	RBI	RC	TBB	IBB	SO	HBP	SH	SF	SB	CS	GDP	Avg	OBP	Slg	OPS
2012	Bal	AL	135	457	101	26	0	23	(11	12)	196	65	69	68	73	2	159	6	0	2	1	3	19	.221	.335	.429	.763
2013	2 Tms	AL	135	445	98	14	0	21	(9	12)	175	55	67	55	51	1	154	5	0	3	3	1	9	.220	.306	.393	.699
2014	Mil	NL	130	378	74	9	0	22	(9	13)	149	47	45	41	47	3	122	3	1	4	5	1	8	.196	.287	.394	.681
2015	StL	NL	140	382	88	21	2	13	(4	9)	152	35	48	38	44	2	121	4	0	2	2	3	10	.230	.315	.398	.713
13	Cle	AL	99	335	72	8	0	15	(8	7)	125	40	48	39	43	1	123	3	0	3	3	0	7	.215	.307	.373	.680
13	NYY	AL	36	110	26	6	0	6	(1	5)	50	15	19	16	8	0	31	2	0	0	0	1	2	.236	.300	.455	.755
	Postseason		13	48	7	0	0	2	(1	1)	13	3	3	2	3	0	19	3	0	0	1	0	1	.146	.241	.271	.512
	9 ML YEARS		1258	4178	959	192	13	237	(110	127)	1888	612	661	594	550	24	1519	47	3	34	59	28	88	.230	.324	.452	.775

Matt Reynolds

Pitches: L Bats: L Pos: RP-18 **Ht: 6'5" Wt: 240 Born: 10/2/1984 Age: 31**

			HOW MUCH HE PITCHED						WHAT HE GAVE UP										THE RESULTS							
Year	Team	Lg	G	GS	CG	GF	IP	BFP	H	R	ER	HR	SH	SF	HB	TBB	IBB	SO	WP	Bk	W	L	Pct	Sh	Sv-Op	Hld	ERC	ERA
2015	Reno*	AAA	45	0	0	13	50.0	218	54	31	31	5	1	5	4	18	1	43	4	0	3	6	.333	0	0- -		4.73	5.58
2010	Col	NL	21	0	0	2	18.0	70	10	4	4	2	1	1	2	5	0	17	1	0	1	0	1.000	0	0-0	2	1.87	2.00
2011	Col	NL	73	0	0	9	50.2	211	48	24	23	10	1	4	0	18	5	50	5	2	1	2	.333	0	0-2	18	4.18	4.09
2012	Col	NL	71	0	0	16	57.1	249	65	31	28	11	6	3	0	17	4	51	5	1	3	1	.750	0	0-0	9	4.96	4.40
2013	Ari	NL	30	0	0	9	27.1	111	25	7	6	2	0	1	1	5	1	23	0	0	0	2	.000	0	2-3	5	2.71	1.98
2015	Ari	NL	18	0	0	3	13.2	62	14	7	7	6	0	0	1	7	2	18	0	0	0	0	-	0	0-1	3	7.30	4.61
	5 ML YEARS		213	0	0	39	167.0	703	162	73	68	31	8	9	4	52	12	159	11	3	5	5	.500	0	2-6	30	4.14	3.66

Clayton Richard

Pitches: L Bats: L Pos: RP-20; SP-3 **Ht: 6'5" Wt: 245 Born: 9/12/1983 Age: 32**

			HOW MUCH HE PITCHED						WHAT HE GAVE UP										THE RESULTS							
Year	Team	Lg	G	GS	CG	GF	IP	BFP	H	R	ER	HR	SH	SF	HB	TBB	IBB	SO	WP	Bk	W	L	Pct	Sh	Sv-Op	Hld	ERC	ERA
2015	Indy*	AAA	9	9	0	0	56.0	237	53	20	13	3	2	1	4	13	1	25	1	0	4	2	.667	0	0- -		3.02	2.09
2008	CWS	AL	13	8	0	3	47.2	215	61	37	32	5	0	1	0	13	2	29	1	1	2	5	.286	0	0-0	0	5.06	6.04
2009	2 Tms		38	26	1	3	153.0	663	154	81	75	17	8	5	3	71	0	114	7	3	9	5	.643	0	0-0	0	4.60	4.41
2010	SD	NL	33	33	1	0	201.2	861	206	89	84	16	6	2	4	78	6	153	4	2	14	9	.609	1	0-0	0	4.09	3.75
2011	SD	NL	18	18	0	0	99.2	427	104	52	43	8	4	1	2	38	2	53	3	1	5	9	.357	0	0-0	0	4.22	3.88
2012	SD	NL	33	33	1	0	218.2	910	228	110	97	31	3	6	6	42	4	107	4	2	14	14	.500	1	0-0	0	3.87	3.99
2013	SD	NL	12	11	0	1	52.2	239	65	44	41	13	6	1	0	21	1	24	0	0	2	5	.286	0	0-0	0	6.55	7.01
2015	ChC	NL	23	3	0	0	42.1	181	47	18	18	3	0	0	1	7	1	22	4	0	4	2	.667	0	0-0	2	3.56	3.83
09	CWS	AL	26	14	1	3	89.0	387	94	50	46	10	3	4	3	37	0	66	5	2	4	3	.571	0	0-0	0	4.76	4.65
09	CWS	AL	12	12	0	0	64.0	276	60	31	29	7	5	1	0	34	0	48	2	1	5	2	.714	0	0-0	0	4.38	4.08
	Postseason		2	0	0	0	6.1	25	5	1	1	0	0	0	0	3	0	6	0	0	0	0	-	0	0-0	0	2.74	1.42
	7 ML YEARS		170	132	3	7	815.2	3496	865	431	390	93	27	16	16	270	16	502	23	9	50	49	.505	2	0-0	2	4.32	4.30

Garrett Richards

Pitches: R Bats: R Pos: SP-32 **Ht: 6'3" Wt: 210 Born: 5/27/1988 Age: 28**

			HOW MUCH HE PITCHED						WHAT HE GAVE UP										THE RESULTS							
Year	Team	Lg	G	GS	CG	GF	IP	BFP	H	R	ER	HR	SH	SF	HB	TBB	IBB	SO	WP	Bk	W	L	Pct	Sh	Sv-Op	Hld	ERC	ERA
2011	LAA	AL	7	3	0	2	14.0	62	16	11	9	4	0	0	0	7	0	9	2	0	0	2	.000	0	0-0	0	6.97	5.79
2012	LAA	AL	30	9	0	4	71.0	318	77	46	37	7	2	4	3	34	1	47	2	0	4	3	.571	0	1-3	5	5.04	4.69
2013	LAA	AL	47	17	1	6	145.0	620	151	73	67	12	9	3	1	44	4	101	11	0	7	8	.467	0	1-2	5	3.78	4.16
2014	LAA	AL	26	26	1	0	168.2	678	124	51	49	5	0	3	7	51	1	164	22	1	13	4	.765	1	0-0	0	2.06	2.61
2015	LAA	AL	32	32	1	0	207.1	865	181	94	84	20	6	10	5	76	2	176	17	0	15	12	.556	1	0-0	0	3.32	3.65
	5 ML YEARS		142	87	3	12	606.0	2543	549	275	246	48	17	20	16	212	8	497	54	1	39	29	.574	2	2-5	10	3.31	3.65

C.J. Riefenhauser

Pitches: L Bats: L Pos: RP-17   REEF-en-how-zer   **Ht: 6'0" Wt: 195 Born: 1/30/1990 Age: 26**

			HOW MUCH HE PITCHED						WHAT HE GAVE UP										THE RESULTS							
Year	Team	Lg	G	GS	CG	GF	IP	BFP	H	R	ER	HR	SH	SF	HB	TBB	IBB	SO	WP	Bk	W	L	Pct	Sh	Sv-Op	Hld	ERC	ERA
2011	2 Tms	Low	26	25	1	0	138.1	554	112	53	43	10	8	5	3	36	0	123	4	1	7	8	.467	1	0- -		2.48	2.80
2012	Charltt	A+	23	14	0	4	96.1	415	98	55	51	11	2	4	6	32	1	103	2	1	7	8	.467	0	1- -		4.25	4.76
2012	Mont	AA	9	1	0	0	18.1	80	15	7	7	4	0	2	3	8	0	15	0	0	1	1	.500	0	0- -		4.65	3.44
2013	Mont	AA	34	0	0	20	53.0	197	28	10	3	3	2	0	1	11	0	48	0	0	4	0	1.000	0	11- -		1.17	0.51
2013	Drham	AAA	17	0	0	4	20.2	82	14	9	7	2	0	0	0	8	0	22	1	0	2	1	.667	0	0- -		2.36	3.05
2014	Drham	AAA	39	0	0	12	57.2	240	41	13	9	3	2	1	3	24	0	53	4	0	3	3	.500	0	1- -		2.46	1.40
2015	Drham	AAA	29	0	0	4	34.2	139	25	12	11	3	1	3	3	7	1	34	1	0	4	2	.667	0	1- -		1.75	2.86
2014	TB	AL	7	0	0	1	5.1	24	6	5	5	0	0	0	0	3	1	2	0	0	0	0	-	0	0-0	0	4.39	8.44
2015	TB	AL	17	0	0	4	14.2	62	15	10	9	3	1	1	0	7	0	7	0	0	1	0	1.000	0	0-0	0	5.54	5.52
	2 ML YEARS		24	0	0	5	20.0	86	21	15	14	3	1	1	0	10	1	9	0	0	1	0	1.000	0	0-0	0	5.25	6.30

Andre Rienzo

Pitches: R Bats: R Pos: RP-14   ree-ENN-zo   **Ht: 6'3" Wt: 190 Born: 7/5/1988 Age: 27**

			HOW MUCH HE PITCHED						WHAT HE GAVE UP										THE RESULTS							
Year	Team	Lg	G	GS	CG	GF	IP	BFP	H	R	ER	HR	SH	SF	HB	TBB	IBB	SO	WP	Bk	W	L	Pct	Sh	Sv-Op	Hld	ERC	ERA
2015	NewOr*	AAA	15	14	0	0	77.2	321	66	36	26	5	1	1	3	32	0	56	12	1	2	6	.250	0	0- -		3.29	3.01
2013	CWS	AL	10	10	0	0	56.0	250	55	34	30	11	2	1	2	28	0	38	4	0	2	3	.400	0	0-0	0	5.18	4.82
2014	CWS	AL	18	11	0	3	64.2	312	82	54	49	12	2	2	5	33	0	51	6	1	4	5	.444	0	0-0	0	7.05	6.82
2015	Mia	NL	14	0	0	5	19.2	89	17	14	13	2	1	0	1	13	1	15	3	0	0	1	.000	0	0-0	0	4.41	5.95
	3 ML YEARS		42	21	0	8	140.1	651	154	102	92	25	5	3	8	74	1	104	13	1	6	9	.400	0	0-0	0	5.91	5.90

Alex Rios

Bats: R **Throws:** R **Pos:** RF-105 **Ht:** 6'5" **Wt:** 210 **Born:** 2/18/1981 **Age:** 35

Year Team	Lg	G	AB	H	2B	3B	HR	(Hm	Rd)	TB	R	RBI	RC	TBB	IBB	SO	HBP	SH	SF	SB	CS	GDP	Avg	OBP	Slg	OPS
2004 Tor	AL	111	426	122	24	7	1	(0	1)	163	55	28	49	31	0	84	2	1	0	15	3	14	.286	.338	.383	.720
2005 Tor	AL	146	481	126	23	6	10	(5	5)	191	71	59	56	28	1	101	5	0	5	14	9	14	.262	.306	.397	.703
2006 Tor	AL	128	450	136	33	6	17	(12	5)	232	68	82	83	35	1	89	3	0	10	15	6	10	.302	.349	.516	.865
2007 Tor	AL	161	643	191	43	7	24	(13	11)	320	114	85	105	55	3	103	6	0	7	17	4	9	.297	.354	.498	.852
2008 Tor	AL	155	635	185	47	8	15	(9	6)	293	91	79	92	44	2	112	2	0	5	32	8	20	.291	.337	.461	.798
2009 2 Tms	AL	149	582	144	31	2	17	(15	2)	230	63	71	64	37	1	107	6	1	7	24	5	21	.247	.296	.395	.691
2010 CWS	AL	147	567	161	29	3	21	(10	11)	259	89	88	84	38	4	93	7	0	5	34	14	21	.284	.334	.457	.791
2011 CWS	AL	145	537	122	22	2	13	(7	6)	187	64	44	35	27	4	68	2	0	4	11	6	20	.227	.265	.348	.613
2012 CWS	AL	157	605	184	37	8	25	(16	9)	312	93	91	103	26	3	92	4	0	5	23	6	18	.304	.334	.516	.850
2013 2 Tms	AL	156	616	171	33	4	18	(7	11)	266	83	81	78	41	2	108	2	0	2	42	7	17	.278	.324	.432	.756
2014 Tex	AL	131	492	138	30	8	4	(1	3)	196	54	54	53	23	3	93	1	0	5	17	9	19	.280	.311	.398	.709
2015 KC	AL	105	385	98	22	2	4	(1	3)	136	40	32	29	15	0	67	5	0	6	9	0	10	.255	.287	.353	.640
09 Tor	AL	108	436	115	25	2	14	(12	2)	186	52	62	60	31	1	78	6	0	6	19	3	14	.264	.317	.427	.744
09 CWS	AL	41	146	29	6	0	3	(3	0)	44	11	9	4	6	0	29	0	1	1	5	2	7	.199	.229	.301	.530
13 CWS	AL	109	430	119	22	2	12	(6	6)	181	57	55	51	32	2	78	1	0	1	26	6	12	.277	.328	.421	.749
13 Tex	AL	47	186	52	11	2	6	(1	5)	85	26	26	27	9	0	30	1	0	1	16	1	5	.280	.315	.457	.772
12 ML YEARS		1691	6419	1778	374	63	169	(96	73)	2785	885	794	831	400	24	1117	45	2	61	253	77	193	.277	.321	.434	.755

Rene Rivera

Bats: R **Throws:** R **Pos:** C-107;1B-7;PH-2;DH-1   ruh-NAY   **Ht:** 5'10" **Wt:** 215 **Born:** 7/31/1983 **Age:** 32

Year Team	Lg	G	AB	H	2B	3B	HR	(Hm	Rd)	TB	R	RBI	RC	TBB	IBB	SO	HBP	SH	SF	SB	CS	GDP	Avg	OBP	Slg	OPS
2004 Sea	AL	2	3	0	0	0	0	(0	0)	0	0	0	0	0	0	1	0	0	0	0	0	0	.000	.000	.000	.000
2005 Sea	AL	16	48	19	3	0	1	(0	1)	25	3	6	8	1	0	11	0	1	0	0	0	0	.396	.408	.521	.929
2006 Sea	AL	35	99	15	4	0	2	(1	1)	25	8	4	4	3	0	29	1	3	0	1	0	2	.152	.184	.253	.437
2011 Min	AL	45	104	15	3	0	1	(0	1)	21	9	5	3	8	0	32	1	0	1	0	0	2	.144	.211	.202	.412
2013 SD	NL	23	67	17	3	1	0	(0	0)	22	4	7	6	2	1	16	0	0	2	0	0	1	.254	.268	.328	.596
2014 SD	NL	103	294	74	18	1	11	(1	10)	127	27	44	41	27	3	76	3	3	2	0	0	6	.252	.319	.432	.751
2015 TB	AL	110	298	53	14	0	5	(4	1)	82	16	26	16	11	0	86	3	5	2	0	0	4	.178	.213	.275	.489
7 ML YEARS		334	913	193	45	2	20	(6	14)	302	67	92	78	52	4	251	8	12	7	1	0	15	.211	.258	.331	.589

Yadiel Rivera

Bats: R **Throws:** R **Pos:** 2B-4;SS-2;3B-1   YA-dee-el   **Ht:** 6'3" **Wt:** 180 **Born:** 5/2/1992 **Age:** 24

Year Team	Lg	G	AB	H	2B	3B	HR	(Hm	Rd)	TB	R	RBI	RC	TBB	IBB	SO	HBP	SH	SF	SB	CS	GDP	Avg	OBP	Slg	OPS
2011 2 Tms	Low	106	433	102	16	8	9	(-	-)	161	53	43	43	18	0	125	3	6	0	7	3	7	.236	.271	.372	.643
2012 Wisc	A	127	465	115	26	5	12	(-	-)	187	60	49	56	26	0	119	4	6	5	7	3	12	.247	.290	.402	.692
2013 BrvdCt	A+	129	478	115	16	2	5	(-	-)	150	51	37	47	32	0	80	9	4	1	13	8	8	.241	.300	.314	.614
2014 BrvdCt	A+	66	231	59	8	2	3	(-	-)	80	35	17	26	16	0	50	4	1	2	5	3	6	.255	.312	.346	.659
2014 Hntsvl	AA	58	183	48	9	6	2	(-	-)	75	31	13	23	10	1	36	1	2	0	5	2	4	.262	.304	.410	.714
2015 Biloxi	AA	52	184	51	9	3	1	(-	-)	69	23	16	24	17	0	30	2	5	0	8	7	4	.277	.345	.375	.720
2015 ColSpr	AAA	81	289	68	8	4	1	(-	-)	87	32	28	22	10	0	53	2	3	2	4	3	12	.235	.264	.301	.565
2015 Mil	NL	7	14	1	0	0	0	(0	0)	1	0	0	0	0	0	4	0	1	0	0	0	0	.071	.071	.071	.143

Felipe Rivero

Pitches: L **Bats:** L **Pos:** RP-49 **Ht:** 6'2" **Wt:** 200 **Born:** 7/5/1991 **Age:** 24

Year Team	Lg	G	GS	CG	GF	IP	BFP	H	R	ER	HR	SH	SF	HB	TBB	IBB	SO	WP	Bk	W	L	Pct	Sh	Sv-Op	Hld	ERC	ERA
2011 Prnctn	R+	14	12	0	1	60.1	262	64	36	31	7	0	6	13	0	57	0	1	3	3	.500	0	0--	-	4.13	4.62
2012 BG	A	27	21	0	0	113.1	476	115	56	43	5	3	6	6	29	1	98	7	2	8	8	.500	0	0--	-	3.44	3.41
2013 Charltt	A+	25	23	2	2	127.0	542	122	63	48	7	5	3	7	52	1	91	8	0	9	7	.563	2	0--	-	3.84	3.40
2014 Hrsbrg	AA	10	10	0	0	43.2	197	45	30	20	4	3	1	2	18	0	38	2	0	2	7	.222	0	0--	-	4.28	4.12
2015 Syrcse	AAA	8	0	0	2	6.2	32	8	5	5	0	0	0	0	5	0	5	0	0	0	2	.000	0	0--	-	5.88	6.75
2015 Was	NL	49	0	0	17	48.1	189	35	15	15	2	0	1	1	11	2	43	2	1	2	1	.667	0	2-3	6	1.74	2.79

Anthony Rizzo

Bats: L **Throws:** L **Pos:** 1B-160 **Ht:** 6'3" **Wt:** 240 **Born:** 8/8/1989 **Age:** 26

Year Team	Lg	G	AB	H	2B	3B	HR	(Hm	Rd)	TB	R	RBI	RC	TBB	IBB	SO	HBP	SH	SF	SB	CS	GDP	Avg	OBP	Slg	OPS
2011 SD	NL	49	128	18	8	1	1	(1	0)	31	9	9	7	21	1	46	4	0	0	2	1	2	.141	.281	.242	.523
2012 ChC	NL	87	337	96	15	0	15	(7	8)	156	44	48	57	27	1	62	3	0	1	3	2	7	.285	.342	.463	.805
2013 ChC	NL	160	606	141	40	2	23	(13	10)	254	71	80	74	76	7	127	6	0	2	6	5	12	.233	.323	.419	.742
2014 ChC	NL	140	524	150	28	1	32	(14	**18**)	276	89	78	99	73	7	116	15	0	4	5	4	8	.286	.386	.527	.913
2015 ChC	NL	**160**	586	163	38	3	31	(11	20)	300	94	101	115	78	9	105	**30**	0	7	17	6	9	.278	.387	.512	.899
5 ML YEARS		596	2181	568	129	7	102	(46	56)	1017	307	316	352	275	25	456	58	0	14	33	18	38	.260	.356	.466	.823

Donn Roach

Pitches: R **Bats:** R **Pos:** SP-1 **Ht:** 6'0" **Wt:** 195 **Born:** 12/14/1989 **Age:** 26

		HOW MUCH HE PITCHED				WHAT HE GAVE UP												THE RESULTS						
Year Team	Lg	G	GS	CG	GF	IP	BFP	H	R	ER	HR	SH	SF	HB	TBB	IBB	SO	WP	Bk	W	L	Pct	Sh	Sv-Op	Hld	ERC	ERA
2011 Crpds	A	45	0	0	7	70.1	305	73	33	27	1	4	4	3	20	1	68	11	0	5	5	.500	0	2--	-	3.32	3.45
2012 2 Tms	Low	14	13	0	0	88.1	355	77	26	19	2	2	0	5	14	0	73	4	0	10	1	.909	0	0--	-	2.24	1.94
2013 SnAnt	AA	28	28	0	0	142.2	600	138	73	56	7	5	2	5	40	0	77	11	0	8	12	.400	0	0--	-	3.22	3.53
2014 ElPaso	AAA	19	13	0	1	77.1	366	98	56	45	2	5	2	7	40	0	44	4	1	4	6	.400	0	0--	-	5.93	5.24
2015 Iowa	AAA	15	15	1	0	89.0	357	83	26	23	6	4	1	3	16	2	33	3	0	7	2	.778	0	0--	-	2.82	2.33
2015 Lsvlle	AAA	7	7	0	0	42.0	189	57	32	28	2	2	3	1	7	0	18	1	0	2	4	.333	0	0--	-	4.82	6.00
2014 SD	NL	16	1	0	5	30.1	140	36	17	16	2	3	1	4	15	1	17	4	0	1	0	1.000	0	0-0	-	5.87	4.75
2015 ChC	NL	1	1	0	0	3.1	18	8	4	4	0	0	0	0	1	0	1	0	0	0	1	.000	0	0-0	0	12.26	10.80
2 ML YEARS		17	2	0	5	33.2	158	44	21	20	2	3	1	4	16	1	18	4	0	1	1	.500	0	0-0	0	6.44	5.35

Tanner Roark

Pitches: R **Bats:** R **Pos:** RP-28; SP-12 ROW-ark **Ht:** 6'2" **Wt:** 235 **Born:** 10/5/1986 **Age:** 29

		HOW MUCH HE PITCHED				WHAT HE GAVE UP												THE RESULTS						
Year Team	Lg	G	GS	CG	GF	IP	BFP	H	R	ER	HR	SH	SF	HB	TBB	IBB	SO	WP	Bk	W	L	Pct	Sh	Sv-Op	Hld	ERC	ERA
2013 Was	NL	14	5	0	1	53.2	204	38	11	9	1	3	2	0	11	0	40	0	0	7	1	.875	0	0-0	1	1.54	1.51
2014 Was	NL	31	31	1	0	198.2	798	178	64	63	16	5	2	6	39	1	138	0	0	15	10	.600	1	0-0	0	2.76	2.85
2015 Was	NL	40	12	0	8	111.0	467	119	55	54	17	4	4	5	26	3	70	0	0	4	7	.364	0	1-2	4	4.39	4.38
Postseason		2	0	0	1	2.2	12	3	1	1	1	0	0	0	0	0	3	0	0	0	1	.000	0	0-0	0	4.33	3.38
3 ML YEARS		85	48	1	9	363.1	1469	335	130	126	34	12	8	11	76	4	248	0	0	26	18	.591	1	1-2	5	3.02	3.12

Ken Roberts

Pitches: L **Bats:** L **Pos:** RP-15 **Ht:** 6'1" **Wt:** 200 **Born:** 3/9/1988 **Age:** 28

		HOW MUCH HE PITCHED				WHAT HE GAVE UP												THE RESULTS						
Year Team	Lg	G	GS	CG	GF	IP	BFP	H	R	ER	HR	SH	SF	HB	TBB	IBB	SO	WP	Bk	W	L	Pct	Sh	Sv-Op	Hld	ERC	ERA
2011 TriCity	A-	27	0	0	18	38.2	148	26	10	8	2	1	0	2	7	1	39	2	0	4	2	.667	0	10--	-	1.59	1.86
2012 Ashvll	A	50	0	0	22	68.0	265	53	16	14	4	1	1	3	9	0	56	7	0	4	1	.800	0	0--	-	1.90	1.85
2013 Mdest	A+	41	0	0	17	55.1	228	52	15	8	0	2	0	2	9	0	44	3	0	0	0	-	0	4--	-	2.33	1.30
2013 Tulsa	AA	12	0	0	4	16.1	79	21	15	13	4	1	1	1	13	0	6	2	0	1	1	.500	0	0--	-	9.47	7.16
2014 Tulsa	AA	47	0	0	17	78.1	298	52	22	20	3	5	2	2	20	2	54	2	0	9	2	.818	0	2--	-	1.64	2.30
2015 Albq	AAA	23	0	0	5	31.2	141	50	24	18	3	2	0	0	4	0	28	2	0	1	3	.250	0	0--	-	6.56	5.12
2015 2 Tms	NL	15	0	0	4	13.2	65	22	11	11	0	1	2	1	3	0	6	0	0	1	1	.500	0	0-1	0	6.50	7.24
15 Col	NL	9	0	0	3	9.1	43	13	6	6	0	0	1	1	2	0	5	0	0	0	1	.000	0	0-0	0	5.25	5.79
15 Phi	NL	6	0	0	1	4.1	22	9	5	5	0	1	1	0	1	0	1	0	0	1	0	1.000	0	0-1	0	9.46	10.38

Daniel Robertson

Bats: R **Throws:** R **Pos:** LF-27;PH-9;CF-7;PR-4;RF-1 **Ht:** 5'8" **Wt:** 205 **Born:** 9/30/1985 **Age:** 30

		BATTING																		RUNNING			AVERAGES			
Year Team	Lg	G	AB	H	2B	3B	HR	(Hm	Rd)	TB	R	RBI	RC	TBB	IBB	SO	HBP	SH	SF	SB	CS	GDP	Avg	OBP	Slg	OPS
2011 SnAnt	AA	124	438	124	23	5	5	(-	-)	172	97	44	70	55	2	51	7	5	3	20	6	8	.283	.370	.393	.762
2012 Tucsn	AAA	129	490	148	28	4	2	(-	-)	190	71	38	75	48	0	58	6	8	1	18	8	13	.302	.371	.388	.758
2013 Tucsn	AAA	136	484	138	24	9	2	(-	-)	186	91	53	78	60	1	63	10	5	6	23	6	10	.285	.371	.384	.756
2015 Salt Lk	AAA	60	245	65	16	0	1	(-	-)	84	27	20	29	24	0	32	2	1	3	6	6	4	.265	.332	.343	.675
2014 Tex	AL	70	177	48	9	1	0	(0	0)	59	23	21	23	17	0	28	0	2	1	6	4	3	.271	.333	.333	.667
2015 LAA	AL	37	75	21	2	0	0	(0	0)	23	10	7	8	2	1	7	0	3	0	0	0	1	.280	.299	.307	.605
2 ML YEARS		107	252	69	11	1	0	(0	0)	82	33	28	31	19	1	35	0	5	1	6	4	4	.274	.324	.325	.649

David Robertson

Pitches: R **Bats:** R **Pos:** RP-60 **Ht:** 5'11" **Wt:** 195 **Born:** 4/9/1985 **Age:** 31

		HOW MUCH HE PITCHED				WHAT HE GAVE UP												THE RESULTS						
Year Team	Lg	G	GS	CG	GF	IP	BFP	H	R	ER	HR	SH	SF	HB	TBB	IBB	SO	WP	Bk	W	L	Pct	Sh	Sv-Op	Hld	ERC	ERA
2008 NYY	AL	25	0	0	8	30.1	131	29	18	18	3	0	3	0	15	2	36	6	0	4	0	1.000	0	0-0	0	4.12	5.34
2009 NYY	AL	45	0	0	20	43.2	191	36	19	16	4	0	0	1	23	1	63	6	0	2	1	.667	0	1-1	5	3.51	3.30
2010 NYY	AL	64	0	0	10	61.1	273	59	26	26	5	5	3	3	33	6	71	7	2	4	5	.444	0	1-3	14	4.29	3.82
2011 NYY	AL	70	0	0	8	66.2	272	40	9	8	1	1	0	1	35	6	100	6	1	4	0	1.000	0	1-4	34	1.85	1.08
2012 NYY	AL	65	0	0	17	60.2	248	52	19	18	5	0	1	1	19	0	81	1	1	2	7	.222	0	2-5	30	2.95	2.67
2013 NYY	AL	70	0	0	9	66.1	262	51	15	15	5	3	0	2	18	1	77	1	0	5	1	.833	0	3-5	33	2.37	2.04
2014 NYY	AL	63	0	0	55	64.1	259	45	23	22	7	1	0	1	23	2	96	0	0	4	5	.444	0	39-44	0	2.41	3.08
2015 CWS	AL	60	0	0	53	63.1	250	46	27	24	7	0	0	1	13	2	86	4	0	6	5	.545	0	34-41	0	2.00	3.41
Postseason		19	0	0	7	17.0	73	15	7	7	2	1	0	1	5	3	17	1	0	3	0	1.000	0	0-0	2	2.99	3.71
8 ML YEARS		462	0	0	180	456.2	1886	358	156	147	37	10	7	10	179	20	610	31	4	31	24	.564	0	81-103	116	2.78	2.90

Clint Robinson

Bats: L **Throws:** L **Pos:** 1B-44;PH-44;LF-27;RF-11;DH-3 **Ht:** 6'5" **Wt:** 245 **Born:** 2/16/1985 **Age:** 31

		BATTING																		RUNNING			AVERAGES			
Year Team	Lg	G	AB	H	2B	3B	HR	(Hm	Rd)	TB	R	RBI	RC	TBB	IBB	SO	HBP	SH	SF	SB	CS	GDP	Avg	OBP	Slg	OPS
2012 KC	AL	4	4	0	0	0	0	(0	0)	0	0	0	0	0	0	2	0	0	0	0	0	0	.000	.000	.000	.000
2014 LAD	NL	9	9	3	0	0	0	(0	0)	3	3	2	2	1	0	1	0	0	0	0	0	0	.333	.400	.333	.733
2015 Was	NL	126	309	84	15	1	10	(5	5)	131	44	34	47	37	4	52	5	0	1	0	0	6	.272	.358	.424	.782
3 ML YEARS		139	322	87	15	1	10	(5	5)	134	47	36	49	38	4	55	5	0	1	0	0	6	.270	.355	.416	.771

Shane Robinson

Bats: R **Throws:** R **Pos:** LF-55;CF-15;RF-12;PR-12;PH-7;DH-3   **Ht:** 5'9" **Wt:** 165 **Born:** 10/30/1984 **Age:** 31

								BATTING												RUNNING			AVERAGES			
Year Team	Lg	G	AB	H	2B	3B	HR	(Hm Rd)	TB	R	RBI	RC	TBB	IBB	SO	HBP	SH	SF	SB	CS	GDP	Avg	OBP	Slg	OPS
2009 StL	NL	11	25	6	1	0	0	(0 0)	7	1	1	1	0	0	2	0	0	1	1	0	1	.240	.231	.280	.511
2011 StL	NL	9	7	0	0	0	0	(0 0)	0	0	0	0	1	0	2	0	0	0	0	0	1	.000	.125	.000	.125
2012 StL	NL	102	166	42	8	0	3	(1 2)	59	20	16	15	14	2	32	0	0	1	1	0	5	.253	.309	.355	.665
2013 StL	NL	99	144	36	2	1	2	(1 1)	46	22	16	18	23	0	17	0	0	4	5	1	2	.250	.345	.319	.664
2014 StL	NL	47	60	9	1	1	0	(0 0)	12	3	4	0	6	0	10	0	0	0	0	1	3	.150	.227	.200	.427
2015 Min	AL	83	180	45	7	3	0	(0 0)	58	28	16	21	12	0	29	1	3	1	6	1	4	.250	.299	.322	.621
Postseason		18	24	5	1	0	1	(0 1)	9	4	4	0	1	0	4	0	0	0	0	0	1	.208	.240	.375	.615
6 ML YEARS		351	582	138	19	5	5	(2 3)	182	74	53	55	56	2	92	1	3	7	13	3	16	.237	.302	.313	.615

Hansel Robles

Pitches: R **Bats:** R **Pos:** RP-57   ROH-blace   **Ht:** 5'11" **Wt:** 185 **Born:** 8/13/1990 **Age:** 25

		HOW MUCH HE PITCHED						WHAT HE GAVE UP											THE RESULTS						
Year Team	Lg	G	GS	CG	GF	IP	BFP	H	R	ER	HR	SH	SF	HB	TBB	IBB	SO	WP	Bk	W	L	Pct	Sh	Sv-Op	Hld	ERC	ERA
2011 Kngspt	R+	15	0	0	4	37.0	160	28	13	11	2	1	0	10	16	1	42	1	1	3	1	.750	0	1- -	-	3.56	2.68
2012 Bklyn	A-	12	12	0	0	72.2	272	47	14	9	0	1	1	4	10	0	66	2	1	6	1	.857	0	0- -	-	1.26	1.11
2013 2 Tms	Low	18	17	0	0	95.1	409	95	44	40	8	5	4	8	31	0	71	4	1	5	5	.500	0	0- -	-	4.00	3.78
2014 Bnghtn	AA	30	18	1	3	110.2	477	107	57	53	10	3	5	7	43	4	106	4	1	7	6	.538	1	0- -	-	4.04	4.31
2015 LsVgs	AAA	5	0	0	0	7.2	30	6	0	0	0	0	0	0	1	0	10	0	0	1	0	1.000	0	0- -	-	1.49	0.00
2015 NYM	NL	57	0	0	7	54.0	217	37	27	22	8	1	2	2	18	1	61	2	1	4	3	.571	0	0-4	12	2.57	3.67

Fernando Rodney

Pitches: R **Bats:** R **Pos:** RP-68   **Ht:** 5'11" **Wt:** 220 **Born:** 3/18/1977 **Age:** 39

		HOW MUCH HE PITCHED						WHAT HE GAVE UP											THE RESULTS						
Year Team	Lg	G	GS	CG	GF	IP	BFP	H	R	ER	HR	SH	SF	HB	TBB	IBB	SO	WP	Bk	W	L	Pct	Sh	Sv-Op	Hld	ERC	ERA
2002 Det	AL	20	0	0	10	18.0	89	25	15	12	2	2	1	0	12	2	10	0	1	1	3	.250	0	0-4	0	6.77	6.00
2003 Det	AL	27	0	0	11	29.2	143	35	20	20	2	3	3	1	17	1	33	0	0	1	3	.250	0	3-6	3	5.46	6.07
2005 Det	AL	39	0	0	26	44.0	185	39	14	14	5	2	0	2	17	3	42	2	0	2	3	.400	0	9-15	3	3.59	2.86
2006 Det	AL	63	0	0	30	71.2	304	51	36	28	6	2	0	8	34	4	65	3	0	7	4	.636	0	7-11	18	3.01	3.52
2007 Det	AL	48	0	0	12	50.2	223	46	27	24	5	4	2	3	21	0	54	4	0	2	6	.250	0	1-3	12	3.74	4.26
2008 Det	AL	38	0	0	25	40.1	188	34	22	22	3	1	2	3	30	5	49	3	0	0	6	.000	0	13-19	5	4.29	4.91
2009 Det	AL	73	0	0	65	75.2	330	70	38	37	8	4	2	2	41	4	61	5	0	2	5	.286	0	37-38	0	4.31	4.40
2010 LAA	AL	72	0	0	30	68.0	308	70	33	32	4	1	0	5	35	1	53	4	0	4	3	.571	0	14-21	21	4.63	4.24
2011 LAA	AL	39	0	0	15	32.0	150	26	18	16	1	3	0	3	28	0	26	2	0	3	5	.375	0	3-7	10	4.66	4.50
2012 TB	AL	76	0	0	65	74.2	282	43	9	5	2	4	2	3	15	1	76	4	0	2	2	.500	0	48-50	0	1.22	0.60
2013 TB	AL	68	0	0	55	66.2	290	53	27	25	3	1	1	1	36	3	82	4	1	5	4	.556	0	37-45	0	3.02	3.38
2014 Sea	AL	69	0	0	64	66.1	286	61	24	21	3	4	1	3	28	3	76	4	0	1	6	.143	0	**48-51**	0	3.42	2.85
2015 2 Tms		68	0	0	32	62.2	277	59	36	33	9	1	1	8	29	3	58	6	0	7	5	.583	0	16-23	9	4.76	4.74
15 Sea	AL	54	0	0	28	50.2	227	51	32	32	8	1	1	5	25	3	43	5	0	5	5	.500	0	16-22	7	5.25	5.68
15 ChC	NL	14	0	0	4	12.0	50	8	4	1	1	0	0	3	4	0	15	1	0	2	0	1.000	0	0-1	2	2.88	0.75
Postseason		10	0	0	2	10.0	45	7	6	4	0	3	0	1	8	1	13	1	0	1	0	1.000	0	0-2	3	3.38	3.60
13 ML YEARS		700	0	0	440	700.1	3055	612	319	289	53	32	15	42	341	30	685	41	2	37	55	.402	0	236-293	81	3.67	3.71

Carlos Rodon

Pitches: L **Bats:** L **Pos:** SP-23; RP-3   roh-DON   **Ht:** 6'3" **Wt:** 235 **Born:** 12/10/1992 **Age:** 23

		HOW MUCH HE PITCHED						WHAT HE GAVE UP											THE RESULTS						
Year Team	Lg	G	GS	CG	GF	IP	BFP	H	R	ER	HR	SH	SF	HB	TBB	IBB	SO	WP	Bk	W	L	Pct	Sh	Sv-Op	Hld	ERC	ERA
2014 2 Tms	Low	6	3	0	0	12.1	55	11	5	4	0	0	0	0	5	0	20	1	0	0	0	-	0	0- -	0	2.64	2.92
2015 CWS	AL	26	23	1	1	139.1	607	130	63	58	11	6	5	8	71	0	139	7	0	9	6	.600	0	0-0	0	4.25	3.75

Alex Rodriguez

Bats: R **Throws:** R **Pos:** DH-136;PH-12;3B-4;1B-2   **Ht:** 6'3" **Wt:** 225 **Born:** 7/27/1975 **Age:** 40

								BATTING												RUNNING			AVERAGES			
Year Team	Lg	G	AB	H	2B	3B	HR	(Hm Rd)	TB	R	RBI	RC	TBB	IBB	SO	HBP	SH	SF	SB	CS	GDP	Avg	OBP	Slg	OPS
1994 Sea	AL	17	54	11	0	0	0	(0 0)	11	4	2	3	3	0	20	0	1	1	3	0	0	.204	.241	.204	.445
1995 Sea	AL	48	142	33	6	2	5	(1 4)	58	15	19	15	6	0	42	0	1	0	4	2	0	.232	.264	.408	.672
1996 Sea	AL	146	601	215	**54**	1	36	(18 18)	379	**141**	123	144	59	1	104	4	6	7	15	4	15	**.358**	.414	.631	1.045
1997 Sea	AL	141	587	176	40	3	23	(16 7)	291	100	84	100	41	1	99	5	4	1	29	6	14	.300	.350	.496	.846
1998 Sea	AL	161	**686**	213	35	5	42	(18 24)	384	123	124	135	45	0	121	10	3	4	46	13	12	.310	.360	.560	.919
1999 Sea	AL	129	502	143	25	0	42	(20 22)	294	110	111	102	56	2	109	5	1	8	21	7	12	.285	.357	.586	.943
2000 Sea	AL	148	554	175	34	2	41	(13 28)	336	134	132	138	100	5	121	7	0	11	15	4	10	.316	.420	.606	1.026
2001 Tex	AL	162	632	201	34	1	52	(26 26)	393	133	135	148	75	6	131	16	0	9	18	3	17	.318	.399	.622	1.021
2002 Tex	AL	162	624	187	27	2	57	(34 23)	389	125	**142**	152	87	12	122	10	0	4	9	4	14	.300	.392	.623	1.015
2003 Tex	AL	161	607	181	30	6	47	(26 21)	364	**124**	118	131	87	10	126	15	0	6	17	3	16	.298	.396	**.600**	.995
2004 NYY	AL	155	601	172	24	2	36	(17 19)	308	112	106	112	80	6	131	10	0	7	28	4	18	.286	.375	.512	.888
2005 NYY	AL	162	605	194	29	1	48	(26 22)	369	**124**	130	137	91	8	139	16	0	3	21	6	8	.321	.421	**.610**	1.031
2006 NYY	AL	154	572	166	26	1	35	(20 15)	299	113	121	112	90	8	139	8	0	4	15	4	22	.290	.392	.523	.914
2007 NYY	AL	158	583	183	31	0	**54**	(26 28)	376	**143**	156	159	95	11	120	21	0	9	24	4	15	.314	.422	.645	1.067
2008 NYY	AL	138	510	154	33	0	35	(21 14)	292	104	103	97	65	9	117	14	0	6	18	3	16	.302	.392	.573	.965
2009 NYY	AL	124	444	127	17	1	30	(18 12)	236	78	100	89	80	7	97	8	0	3	14	2	13	.286	.402	.532	.933
2010 NYY	AL	137	522	141	29	2	30	(15 15)	264	74	125	93	59	1	98	3	0	11	4	3	7	.270	.341	.506	.847
2011 NYY	AL	99	373	103	21	0	16	(9 7)	172	67	62	61	47	1	80	5	0	3	4	1	13	.276	.362	.461	.823
2012 NYY	AL	122	463	126	17	1	18	(8 10)	199	74	57	66	51	3	116	10	0	5	13	1	13	.272	.353	.430	.783

Year Team	Lg	G	AB	H	2B	3B	HR	(Hm	Rd)	TB	R	RBI	RC	TBB	IBB	SO	HBP	SH	SF	SB	CS	GDP	Avg	OBP	Slg	OPS
								BATTING												**RUNNING**			**AVERAGES**			
2013 NYY	AL	44	156	38	7	0	7	(2	5)	66	21	19	19	23	1	43	2	0	0	4	2	5	.244	.348	.423	.771
2015 NYY	AL	151	523	131	22	1	33	(18	15)	254	83	86	83	84	5	145	6	0	7	4	0	17	.250	.356	.486	.842
Postseason		75	274	72	16	0	13	(5	8)	127	43	41	43	39	4	75	9	1	3	8	3	6	.263	.369	.464	.833
21 ML YEARS		2719	10341	3070	541	31	687	(352	335)	5734	2002	2055	2096	1324	97	2220	175	16	108	326	76	257	.297	.382	.554	.937

Eduardo Rodriguez

Pitches: L Bats: L Pos: SP-21　　　　Ht: 6'2" Wt: 210 Born: 4/7/1993 Age: 23

Year Team	Lg	G	GS	CG	GF	IP	BFP	H	R	ER	HR	SH	SF	HB	TBB	IBB	SO	WP	Bk	W	L	Pct	Sh	Sv-Op	Hld	ERC	ERA
		HOW MUCH HE PITCHED						**WHAT HE GAVE UP**												**THE RESULTS**							
2011 2 Tms	Low	12	11	0	1	48.2	197	34	20	12	1	0	1	2	18	0	50	2	1	1	1	.500	0	1--	-	2.06	2.22
2012 Dlmrva	A	22	22	1	0	107.0	454	103	56	44	4	3	6	5	30	0	73	2	2	5	7	.417	0	0--	-	3.13	3.70
2013 Frdrck	A+	14	14	0	0	85.1	351	78	36	27	4	4	0	2	25	0	66	2	0	6	4	.600	0	0--	-	2.97	2.85
2013 Bowie	AA	11	11	1	0	59.2	252	53	28	28	5	0	2	2	24	1	59	1	1	4	3	.571	0	0--	-	3.48	4.22
2014 Bowie	AA	16	16	1	0	82.2	362	90	50	44	5	1	3	0	29	1	69	4	5	3	7	.300	0	0--	-	4.04	4.79
2014 Portlnd	AA	6	6	0	0	37.1	147	30	4	4	1	1	1	2	8	0	39	2	0	3	1	.750	0	0--	-	2.17	0.96
2015 Pwtckt	AAA	8	8	1	0	48.1	190	46	22	16	2	1	2	0	7	0	44	1	0	4	3	.571	0	0--	-	2.57	2.98
2015 Bos	AL	21	21	0	0	121.2	522	120	55	52	13	5	4	4	37	1	98	4	1	10	6	.625	0	0-0	0	3.73	3.85

Fernando Rodriguez

Pitches: R Bats: R Pos: RP-56　　　　Ht: 6'3" Wt: 235 Born: 6/18/1984 Age: 32

Year Team	Lg	G	GS	CG	GF	IP	BFP	H	R	ER	HR	SH	SF	HB	TBB	IBB	SO	WP	Bk	W	L	Pct	Sh	Sv-Op	Hld	ERC	ERA
		HOW MUCH HE PITCHED						**WHAT HE GAVE UP**												**THE RESULTS**							
2015 Nashv*	AAA	10	1	0	3	16.0	71	8	5	5	2	1	0	0	6	0	18	0	0	0	0	-	0	0--	-	1.61	2.81
2009 LAA	AL	1	0	0	0	0.2	6	1	3	2	1	0	0	0	2	0	1	1	0	0	0	-	0	0-0	0	31.03	27.00
2011 Hou	NL	47	0	0	11	52.1	231	51	24	23	6	5	0	3	30	5	57	2	0	2	3	.400	0	0-0	6	4.90	3.96
2012 Hou	NL	71	0	0	9	70.1	309	68	45	42	10	2	2	1	34	7	78	10	0	2	10	.167	0	0-4	13	4.39	5.37
2014 Oak	AL	7	0	0	3	9.0	33	4	1	1	0	0	0	0	2	0	4	0	0	1	0	1.000	0	0-0	1	0.76	1.00
2015 Oak	AL	56	0	0	12	58.2	242	43	27	25	4	1	1	1	24	1	65	4	0	4	2	.667	0	0-2	6	2.51	3.84
5 ML YEARS		182	0	0	35	191.0	821	167	100	93	21	8	3	5	92	13	205	17	0	9	15	.375	0	0-6	26	3.76	4.38

Francisco Rodriguez

Pitches: R Bats: R Pos: RP-60　　　　Ht: 6'0" Wt: 195 Born: 1/7/1982 Age: 34

Year Team	Lg	G	GS	CG	GF	IP	BFP	H	R	ER	HR	SH	SF	HB	TBB	IBB	SO	WP	Bk	W	L	Pct	Sh	Sv-Op	Hld	ERC	ERA
		HOW MUCH HE PITCHED						**WHAT HE GAVE UP**												**THE RESULTS**							
2002 LAA	AL	5	0	0	4	5.2	21	3	0	0	0	0	0	1	2	1	13	0	0	0	0	-	0	0-0	0	1.52	0.00
2003 LAA	AL	59	0	0	23	86.0	334	50	30	29	12	2	4	2	35	5	95	7	0	8	3	.727	0	2-6	7	2.25	3.03
2004 LAA	AL	69	0	0	29	84.0	335	51	21	17	2	2	1	1	33	1	123	5	0	4	1	.800	0	12-19	27	1.64	1.82
2005 LAA	AL	66	0	0	58	67.1	270	45	20	20	7	1	1	0	32	3	91	8	0	2	5	.286	0	**45-50**	0	2.52	2.67
2006 LAA	AL	69	0	0	58	73.0	296	52	16	14	6	3	0	1	28	5	98	10	0	2	3	.400	0	**47-51**	0	2.35	1.73
2007 LAA	AL	64	0	0	56	67.1	285	50	22	21	3	1	4	4	34	0	90	7	1	5	2	.714	0	40-46	0	2.74	2.81
2008 LAA	AL	76	0	0	69	68.1	288	54	21	17	4	1	1	2	34	4	77	6	0	2	3	.400	0	**62-69**	0	3.06	2.24
2009 NYM	NL	70	0	0	66	68.0	295	51	34	28	7	4	1	1	38	6	73	1	0	3	6	.333	0	35-42	0	3.18	3.71
2010 NYM	NL	53	0	0	46	57.1	236	45	14	14	3	1	1	2	21	4	67	3	1	4	2	.667	0	25-30	0	2.53	2.20
2011 2 Tms	NL	73	0	0	36	71.2	307	67	22	21	4	2	1	2	26	4	79	4	0	6	2	.750	0	23-29	17	3.25	2.64
2012 Mil	NL	78	0	0	13	72.0	305	65	37	35	8	1	3	0	31	1	72	6	0	2	7	.222	0	3-10	32	3.73	4.38
2013 2 Tms	NL	48	0	0	23	46.2	193	42	14	14	7	3	0	1	14	4	54	2	0	3	2	.600	0	10-10	5	3.44	2.70
2014 Mil	NL	69	0	0	66	68.0	268	49	23	23	14	2	0	1	18	1	73	0	0	5	5	.500	0	44-49	0	2.77	3.04
2015 Mil	NL	60	0	0	55	57.0	216	38	15	14	6	1	2	0	11	1	62	3	0	1	3	.250	0	38-40	0	1.69	2.21
11 NYM	NL	42	0	0	34	42.2	187	44	15	15	3	2	1	2	16	4	46	2	0	2	2	.500	0	23-26	0	3.94	3.16
11 Mil	NL	31	0	0	2	29.0	120	23	7	6	1	0	0	0	10	0	33	2	0	4	0	1.000	0	0-3	17	2.32	1.86
13 Mil	NL	25	0	0	18	24.2	97	17	3	3	2	2	0	0	9	3	26	0	0	1	1	.500	0	10-10	1	2.10	1.09
13 Bal	AL	23	0	0	5	22.0	96	25	11	11	5	1	0	1	5	1	28	2	0	2	1	.667	0	0-0	4	5.11	4.50
Postseason		26	0	0	8	36.2	158	32	15	12	5	1	3	1	18	2	49	5	0	5	4	.556	0	3-5	6	3.99	2.95
14 ML YEARS		859	0	0	602	892.1	3658	662	289	267	83	24	19	15	357	40	1067	62	2	47	44	.516	0	386-451	88	2.66	2.69

Paco Rodriguez

Pitches: L Bats: L Pos: RP-18　　　　Ht: 6'3" Wt: 220 Born: 4/16/1991 Age: 25

Year Team	Lg	G	GS	CG	GF	IP	BFP	H	R	ER	HR	SH	SF	HB	TBB	IBB	SO	WP	Bk	W	L	Pct	Sh	Sv-Op	Hld	ERC	ERA
		HOW MUCH HE PITCHED						**WHAT HE GAVE UP**												**THE RESULTS**							
2012 LAD	NL	11	0	0	2	6.2	26	3	1	1	0	0	0	0	4	1	6	0	0	0	1	.000	0	0-0	1	1.37	1.35
2013 LAD	NL	76	0	0	11	54.1	208	30	15	14	5	3	1	2	19	4	63	3	0	3	4	.429	0	2-5	20	1.68	2.32
2014 LAD	NL	19	0	0	1	14.0	53	12	6	6	1	1	0	0	4	0	14	0	0	1	0	1.000	0	0-1	4	2.95	3.86
2015 LAD	NL	18	0	0	4	10.1	42	10	3	3	0	0	0	0	3	0	8	0	0	0	0	-	0	0-0	4	2.90	2.61
Postseason		2	0	0	0	0.2	8	4	2	2	1	0	0	0	2	1	1	0	0	0	0	-	0	0-0	0	75.08	27.00
4 ML YEARS		124	0	0	18	85.1	329	55	25	24	6	4	2	2	30	5	91	3	0	4	5	.444	0	2-6	28	1.98	2.53

Sean Rodriguez

Bats: R Throws: R Pos: 1B-102;PR-17;LF-16;PH-15;RF-14;3B-8;2B-7;SS-3　　　　Ht: 6'0" Wt: 200 Born: 4/26/1985 Age: 31

Year Team	Lg	G	AB	H	2B	3B	HR	(Hm	Rd)	TB	R	RBI	RC	TBB	IBB	SO	HBP	SH	SF	SB	CS	GDP	Avg	OBP	Slg	OPS
								BATTING												**RUNNING**			**AVERAGES**			
2008 LAA	AL	59	167	34	8	1	3	(2	1)	53	18	10	12	14	0	55	3	2	1	3	1	3	.204	.276	.317	.593
2009 LAA	AL	12	25	5	0	0	2	(0	2)	11	4	4	2	3	0	7	0	0	1	0	0	2	.200	.276	.440	.716
2010 TB	AL	118	343	86	19	2	9	(5	4)	136	53	40	38	21	1	97	8	5	1	13	3	10	.251	.308	.397	.705
2011 TB	AL	131	373	83	20	3	8	(4	4)	133	45	36	41	38	2	87	18	5	2	11	7	8	.223	.323	.357	.679
2012 TB	AL	112	301	64	14	1	6	(3	3)	98	36	32	32	27	1	75	3	8	3	5	0	7	.213	.281	.326	.607

Year	Team	Lg	BATTING																			RUNNING			AVERAGES			
			G	AB	H	2B	3B	HR	(Hm	Rd)	TB	R	RBI	RC	TBB	IBB	SO	HBP	SH	SF	SB	CS	GDP	Avg	OBP	Slg	OPS
2013	TB	AL	96	195	48	10	1	5	(3	2)	75	21	23	21	17	0	59	5	3	2	1	3	3	.246	.320	.385	.704
2014	TB	AL	96	237	50	13	3	12	(7	5)	105	30	41	29	10	0	66	6	3	3	2	1	3	.211	.258	.443	.701
2015	Pit	NL	139	224	55	12	1	4	(2	2)	81	25	17	17	5	0	63	6	5	0	2	2	9	.246	.281	.362	.642
	Postseason		12	28	5	1	0	1	(0	1)	9	6	2	1	2	0	5	0	0	0	0	0	0	.179	.233	.321	.555
	8 ML YEARS		763	1865	425	96	12	49	(26	23)	692	232	203	192	135	4	509	49	31	13	37	17	45	.228	.295	.371	.666

Wandy Rodriguez

Pitches: L Bats: B Pos: SP-15; RP-2 — WAHN-dee — Ht: 5'10" Wt: 195 Born: 1/18/1979 Age: 37

Year	Team	Lg	HOW MUCH HE PITCHED						WHAT HE GAVE UP												THE RESULTS							
			G	GS	CG	GF	IP	BFP	H	R	ER	HR	SH	SF	HB	TBB	IBB	SO	WP	Bk	W	L	Pct	Sh	Sv-Op	Hld	ERC	ERA
2015	Omha*	AAA	5	0	0	1	8.0	32	5	1	1	0	0	1	0	4	0	7	0	0	0	0	0--		0	-	1.92	1.13
2005	Hou	NL	25	22	0	0	128.2	560	135	82	79	19	3	3	8	53	2	80	3	3	10	10	.500	0	0-0	0	5.08	5.53
2006	Hou	NL	30	24	0	1	135.2	611	154	96	85	17	7	4	6	63	7	98	6	0	9	10	.474	0	0-0	0	5.45	5.64
2007	Hou	NL	31	31	1	0	182.2	782	179	102	93	22	6	4	5	62	2	158	3	0	9	13	.409	1	0-0	0	3.94	4.58
2008	Hou	NL	25	25	0	0	137.1	587	136	65	54	14	2	5	5	44	3	131	2	3	9	7	.563	0	0-0	0	3.82	3.54
2009	Hou	NL	33	33	1	0	205.2	849	192	77	69	21	8	4	5	63	5	193	2	1	14	12	.538	1	0-0	0	3.47	3.02
2010	Hou	NL	32	32	0	0	195.0	822	183	95	78	16	6	5	9	68	3	178	8	0	11	12	.478	0	0-0	0	3.60	3.60
2011	Hou	NL	30	30	0	0	191.0	808	182	81	74	25	7	3	5	69	7	166	5	0	11	11	.500	0	0-0	0	3.95	3.49
2012	2 Tms	NL	34	**33**	0	1	205.2	875	205	99	86	21	6	5	3	56	4	139	5	0	12	13	.480	0	0-0	0	3.55	3.76
2013	Pit	NL	12	12	0	0	62.2	260	58	26	25	10	1	1	4	12	1	46	1	1	6	4	.600	0	0-0	0	3.43	3.59
2014	Pit	NL	6	6	0	0	26.2	125	37	25	20	10	2	1	0	8	1	20	0	1	0	2	.000	0	0-0	0	7.91	6.75
2015	Tex	AL	17	15	0	1	86.1	392	99	48	47	10	1	5	3	36	2	72	3	0	6	4	.600	0	0-0	0	5.16	4.90
	12 Hou	NL	21	21	0	0	130.2	558	134	66	55	13	5	3	2	32	2	89	5	0	7	9	.438	0	0-0	0	3.57	3.79
	12 Pit	NL	13	12	0	1	75.0	317	71	33	31	8	1	2	1	24	2	50	0	0	5	4	.556	0	0-0	0	3.50	3.72
	Postseason		3	0	0	1	4.2	22	5	2	2	2	1	0	0	5	1	4	0	0	0	1	.000	0	0-0	0	10.58	3.86
	11 ML YEARS		275	263	2	3	1557.1	6671	1560	796	710	185	49	40	53	534	37	1281	38	9	97	98	.497	2	0-0	0	4.09	4.10

Chaz Roe

Pitches: R Bats: R Pos: RP-36 — ROW — Ht: 6'5" Wt: 190 Born: 10/9/1986 Age: 29

Year	Team	Lg	HOW MUCH HE PITCHED						WHAT HE GAVE UP												THE RESULTS							
			G	GS	CG	GF	IP	BFP	H	R	ER	HR	SH	SF	HB	TBB	IBB	SO	WP	Bk	W	L	Pct	Sh	Sv-Op	Hld	ERC	ERA
2015	Norfolk*	AAA	17	0	0	10	24.2	100	17	6	6	0	1	0	3	9	1	22	0	0	3	1	.750	0	2--	0	2.10	2.19
2013	Ari	NL	21	0	0	4	22.1	95	18	10	10	3	2	1	0	13	3	24	1	0	1	0	1.000	0	0-2	1	3.78	4.03
2014	NYY	AL	3	0	0	2	2.0	13	3	3	2	0	0	1	0	3	0	4	1	0	0	0	-	0	0-0	0	9.89	9.00
2015	Bal	AL	36	0	0	6	41.1	177	44	19	19	4	1	1	1	17	2	38	0	0	4	2	.667	0	0-1	4	4.62	4.14
	3 ML YEARS		60	0	0	12	65.2	285	65	32	31	7	3	3	1	33	5	66	2	0	5	2	.714	0	0-3	5	4.48	4.25

Esmil Rogers

Pitches: R Bats: R Pos: RP-18 — ESS-mill — Ht: 6'3" Wt: 200 Born: 8/14/1985 Age: 30

Year	Team	Lg	HOW MUCH HE PITCHED						WHAT HE GAVE UP												THE RESULTS							
			G	GS	CG	GF	IP	BFP	H	R	ER	HR	SH	SF	HB	TBB	IBB	SO	WP	Bk	W	L	Pct	Sh	Sv-Op	Hld	ERC	ERA
2015	S-WB*	AAA	7	7	0	0	34.2	147	37	16	13	0	1	1	1	12	0	28	2	2	1	1	.500	0	0--	-	3.73	3.38
2009	Col	NL	1	1	0	0	4.0	16	3	2	2	0	1	0	0	2	0	3	0	0	0	0	-	0	0-0	0	2.58	4.50
2010	Col	NL	28	8	0	5	72.0	333	94	59	49	5	4	3	5	26	2	66	5	2	2	3	.400	0	0-1	1	5.70	6.13
2011	Col	NL	18	13	0	1	83.0	404	110	65	65	14	4	4	6	47	5	63	5	1	6	6	.500	0	0-0	0	7.49	7.05
2012	2 Tms	NL	67	0	0	19	78.2	348	83	42	41	7	2	2	5	30	4	83	10	0	3	3	.500	0	0-2	8	4.37	4.69
2013	Tor	AL	44	20	0	5	137.2	598	152	76	73	21	0	4	6	44	2	96	7	2	5	9	.357	0	0-1	4	4.92	4.77
2014	2 Tms	AL	34	1	0	13	45.2	202	50	30	29	8	2	0	2	17	0	44	1	1	2	0	1.000	0	0-1	1	5.23	5.72
2015	NYY	AL	18	0	0	3	33.0	153	41	29	23	5	0	3	2	14	0	31	6	0	1	1	.500	0	0-0	1	6.24	6.27
	12 Col	AL	23	0	0	6	25.2	131	36	23	23	2	0	0	2	18	2	29	5	0	0	2	.000	0	0-2	2	7.71	8.06
	12 Cle	AL	44	0	0	13	53.0	217	47	19	18	5	2	2	3	12	2	54	5	0	3	1	.750	0	0-0	6	2.93	3.06
	14 Tor	AL	16	0	0	9	20.2	96	28	17	16	5	0	0	1	7	0	21	1	0	0	0	-	0	0-0	1	7.27	6.97
	14 NYY	AL	18	1	0	4	25.0	106	22	13	13	3	2	0	1	10	0	23	0	1	2	0	1.000	0	0-1	3	3.71	4.68
	7 ML YEARS		210	43	0	46	454.0	2054	533	303	282	60	11	16	26	180	13	386	34	6	19	22	.463	0	0-5	18	5.50	5.59

Jason Rogers

Bats: R Throws: R Pos: PH-58;1B-24;3B-3;LF-3;DH-1 — Ht: 6'1" Wt: 255 Born: 3/13/1988 Age: 28

Year	Team	Lg	BATTING																			RUNNING			AVERAGES			
			G	AB	H	2B	3B	HR	(Hm	Rd)	TB	R	RBI	RC	TBB	IBB	SO	HBP	SH	SF	SB	CS	GDP	Avg	OBP	Slg	OPS
2011	2 Tms	Low	71	267	74	16	2	7	(-	-)	115	32	40	40	24	2	53	2	2	4	6	2	2	.277	.337	.431	.767
2012	2 Tms	Low	133	472	142	35	1	11	(-	-)	212	72	66	92	79	3	88	5	0	2	12	1	13	.301	.405	.449	.854
2013	Hntsvl	AA	133	481	130	25	2	22	(-	-)	225	69	87	82	59	1	86	1	0	8	7	2	11	.270	.346	.468	.814
2014	Hntsvl	AA	77	287	81	18	2	7	(-	-)	124	42	43	46	31	1	56	3	0	3	5	1	10	.282	.355	.432	.787
2014	Nashv	AAA	57	206	65	11	4	11	(-	-)	117	36	39	44	22	0	38	1	0	3	0	0	10	.316	.379	.568	.947
2015	ColSpr	AAA	33	122	42	8	0	8	(-	-)	74	25	24	32	24	1	23	0	0	1	0	0	2	.344	.449	.607	1.056
2014	Mil	NL	8	9	1	1	0	0	(0	0)	2	0	0	0	1	0	1	0	0	0	0	0	0	.111	.200	.222	.422
2015	Mil	NL	86	152	45	6	2	4	(2	2)	67	22	16	22	15	0	34	2	0	0	0	0	0	.296	.367	.441	.808
	2 ML YEARS		94	161	46	7	2	4	(2	2)	69	22	16	22	16	0	35	2	0	0	0	0	2	.286	.358	.429	.786

Miguel Rojas

Bats: R Throws: R Pos: SS-32;PH-14;2B-9;3B-9;PR-4   Ht: 6'0" Wt: 150 Born: 2/24/1989 Age: 27

Year	Team	Lg	G	AB	H	2B	3B	HR	(Hm	Rd)	TB	R	RBI	RC	TBB	IBB	SO	HBP	SH	SF	SB	CS	GDP	Avg	OBP	Slg	OPS
2011	Carlina	AA	68	239	62	6	0	0	(-	-)	68	26	24	21	16	0	39	0	7	3	11	7	5	.259	.302	.285	.587
2012	Pnscla	AA	58	143	30	1	0	0	(-	-)	31	14	10	9	16	0	17	1	0	0	2	3	7	.210	.294	.217	.511
2012	Lsvlle	AAA	44	129	24	3	0	1	(-	-)	30	9	7	6	7	1	16	0	7	1	0	0	3	.186	.226	.233	.459
2013	Chatt	AA	130	420	98	12	2	5	(-	-)	129	45	32	43	40	0	49	3	13	2	10	4	13	.233	.303	.307	.610
2014	Albq	AAA	51	159	48	9	0	4	(-	-)	69	27	13	25	10	3	21	3	0	1	7	3	4	.302	.353	.434	.787
2015	NewOr	AAA	65	249	75	15	4	3	(-	-)	107	32	23	36	13	1	26	4	7	2	2	5	7	.301	.343	.430	.773
2014	LAD	NL	85	149	27	3	0	1	(0	1)	33	16	9	6	10	1	28	2	1	0	0	0	5	.181	.242	.221	.464
2015	Mia	NL	60	142	40	7	1	1	(1	0)	52	13	17	15	11	1	16	0	2	2	0	1	4	.282	.329	.366	.695
	Postseason		1	1	0	0	0	0	(0	0)	0	0	0	0	0	0	0	0	0	0	0	0	0	.000	.000	.000	.000
	2 ML YEARS		145	291	67	10	1	2	(1	1)	85	29	26	21	21	2	44	2	3	2	0	1	9	.230	.285	.292	.577

David Rollins

Pitches: L Bats: L Pos: RP-20   Ht: 6'1" Wt: 210 Born: 12/21/1989 Age: 26

Year	Team	Lg	G	GS	CG	GF	IP	BFP	H	R	ER	HR	SH	SF	HB	TBB	IBB	SO	WP	Bk	W	L	Pct	Sh	Sv-Op	Hld	ERC	ERA
2011	2 Tms	Low	7	7	0	0	35.2	137	28	7	7	2	0	0	0	3	0	29	2	1	4	0	1.000	0	0--	-	1.62	1.77
2012	2 Tms	Low	24	24	0	0	108.2	448	91	43	36	7	4	1	4	45	0	100	5	0	7	4	.636	0	0--	-	3.22	2.98
2013	Lancst	A+	23	14	0	7	97.1	405	81	50	43	9	1	3	4	32	0	96	3	1	8	5	.615	0	3--	-	2.98	3.98
2013	CpChr	AA	6	6	0	0	33.0	142	38	18	16	4	1	1	1	10	0	32	1	1	3	0	.000	0	0--	-	4.93	4.36
2014	CpChr	AA	27	12	0	9	78.0	331	74	38	33	7	0	3	2	22	1	77	0	2	3	4	.429	0	1--	-	3.29	3.81
2015	Tacom	AAA	7	0	0	0	9.1	34	7	0	0	0	0	0	0	1	0	8	1	0	0	0	-	0	0--	-	1.43	0.00
2015	Sea	AL	20	0	0	7	25.0	118	37	21	21	3	1	0	2	8	1	21	0	0	0	2	.000	0	0-0	1	7.14	7.56

Jimmy Rollins

Bats: B Throws: R Pos: SS-134;PH-13;PR-3   Ht: 5'7" Wt: 175 Born: 11/27/1978 Age: 37

Year	Team	Lg	G	AB	H	2B	3B	HR	(Hm	Rd)	TB	R	RBI	RC	TBB	IBB	SO	HBP	SH	SF	SB	CS	GDP	Avg	OBP	Slg	OPS
2000	Phi	NL	14	53	17	1	1	0	(0	0)	20	5	5	8	2	0	7	0	0	0	3	0	0	.321	.345	.377	.723
2001	Phi	NL	158	656	180	29	12	14	(8	6)	275	97	54	96	48	2	108	2	9	5	46	8	5	.274	.323	.419	.743
2002	Phi	NL	154	637	156	33	10	11	(3	8)	242	82	60	72	54	3	103	4	6	4	31	13	14	.245	.306	.380	.686
2003	Phi	NL	156	628	165	42	6	8	(5	3)	243	85	62	76	54	4	113	0	5	2	20	12	9	.263	.320	.387	.707
2004	Phi	NL	154	657	190	43	12	14	(8	6)	299	119	73	108	57	3	73	3	6	2	30	9	4	.289	.348	.455	.803
2005	Phi	NL	158	677	196	38	11	12	(5	7)	292	115	54	100	47	8	71	4	2	2	41	6	9	.290	.338	.431	.770
2006	Phi	NL	158	689	191	45	9	25	(15	10)	329	127	83	114	57	2	80	5	0	7	36	4	12	.277	.334	.478	.811
2007	Phi	NL	162	716	212	38	20	30	(18	12)	380	139	94	124	49	5	85	7	0	6	41	6	11	.296	.344	.531	.875
2008	Phi	NL	137	556	154	38	9	11	(5	6)	243	76	59	95	58	7	55	5	3	3	47	3	11	.277	.349	.437	.786
2009	Phi	NL	155	672	168	43	5	21	(10	11)	284	100	77	88	44	1	70	2	2	5	31	8	7	.250	.296	.423	.719
2010	Phi	NL	88	350	85	16	3	8	(4	4)	131	48	41	54	40	2	32	1	0	3	17	1	4	.243	.320	.374	.694
2011	Phi	NL	142	567	152	22	2	16	(7	9)	226	87	63	82	58	5	59	3	0	3	30	8	9	.268	.338	.399	.736
2012	Phi	NL	156	632	158	33	5	23	(11	12)	270	102	68	88	62	2	96	0	2	3	30	5	9	.250	.316	.427	.743
2013	Phi	NL	160	600	151	36	2	6	(4	2)	209	65	39	70	59	6	93	1	3	3	22	6	12	.252	.318	.348	.667
2014	Phi	NL	138	538	131	22	4	17	(7	10)	212	78	55	69	64	2	100	1	3	3	28	6	6	.243	.323	.394	.717
2015	LAD	NL	144	517	116	24	3	13	(7	6)	185	71	41	58	44	0	86	1	3	3	12	8	12	.224	.285	.358	.643
	Postseason		46	188	47	12	1	3	(1	2)	70	27	15	16	16	0	34	2	1	1	11	4	5	.250	.314	.372	.686
	16 ML YEARS		2234	9145	2422	503	114	229	(116	113)	3840	1396	928	1282	797	52	1231	38	42	52	465	103	134	.265	.325	.420	.745

Jamie Romak

Bats: R Throws: R Pos: PH-9;LF-2;1B-1;PR-1   RO-mack   Ht: 6'2" Wt: 220 Born: 9/30/1985 Age: 30

Year	Team	Lg	G	AB	H	2B	3B	HR	(Hm	Rd)	TB	R	RBI	RC	TBB	IBB	SO	HBP	SH	SF	SB	CS	GDP	Avg	OBP	Slg	OPS
2011	NWArk	AA	124	439	110	21	1	23	(-	-)	202	66	71	73	55	2	88	8	1	2	6	1	13	.251	.343	.460	.803
2012	Omha	AAA	11	34	5	2	0	0	(-	-)	7	5	2	1	2	0	8	1	0	0	0	0	0	.147	.216	.206	.422
2012	Memp	AAA	31	112	31	8	1	0	(-	-)	41	9	12	14	8	0	24	1	1	2	0	0	10	.277	.325	.366	.691
2012	Sprgfld	AA	64	243	66	11	2	10	(-	-)	111	46	42	42	31	1	53	4	0	3	6	2	6	.272	.359	.457	.816
2013	Memp	AAA	134	458	111	32	1	22	(-	-)	211	69	74	71	49	1	115	6	2	3	6	1	12	.242	.322	.461	.782
2014	Albq	AAA	108	418	117	30	3	24	(-	-)	225	65	85	76	34	0	107	4	0	6	4	1	9	.280	.335	.538	.874
2015	Reno	AAA	129	486	138	42	3	27	(-	-)	267	87	100	98	60	0	143	4	0	7	6	1	11	.284	.363	.549	.912
2014	LAD	NL	15	21	1	1	0	0	(0	0)	2	2	3	0	2	0	8	0	0	0	0	0	1	.048	.130	.095	.226
2015	Ari	NL	12	15	5	2	0	0	(0	0)	7	2	1	2	1	0	6	0	0	0	0	0	0	.333	.375	.467	.842
	2 ML YEARS		27	36	6	3	0	0	(0	0)	9	4	4	2	3	0	14	0	0	0	0	0	1	.167	.231	.250	.481

Enny Romero

Pitches: L Bats: L Pos: RP-23   ENN-nee   Ht: 6'3" Wt: 215 Born: 1/24/1991 Age: 25

Year	Team	Lg	G	GS	CG	GF	IP	BFP	H	R	ER	HR	SH	SF	HB	TBB	IBB	SO	WP	Bk	W	L	Pct	Sh	Sv-Op	Hld	ERC	ERA
2011	BG	A	26	26	0	0	114.0	503	104	67	54	9	3	3	4	68	0	140	14	3	5	5	.500	0	0--	-	4.37	4.26
2012	Charltt	A+	25	23	1	0	126.0	539	89	67	55	5	3	10	7	76	0	107	12	0	5	7	.417	1	0--	-	3.04	3.93
2013	Mont	AA	27	27	0	0	140.1	594	110	51	43	9	5	3	2	73	1	110	4	3	11	7	.611	0	0--	-	3.16	2.76
2014	Drham	AAA	25	25	0	0	126.0	553	128	69	63	13	2	6	2	52	0	117	6	1	5	11	.313	0	0--	-	4.26	4.50
2015	Drham	AAA	17	3	0	2	46.1	201	48	26	25	5	1	2	1	17	0	45	4	1	1	1	.500	0	1--	-	4.28	4.86
2013	TB	AL	1	1	0	0	4.2	18	1	0	0	0	0	0	0	4	0	0	0	0	0	0	-	0	0-0	0	1.35	0.00
2015	TB	AL	23	0	0	7	30.0	140	39	18	17	1	1	1	0	13	0	31	2	0	0	2	.000	0	0-2	3	5.38	5.10
	2 ML YEARS		24	1	0	7	34.2	158	40	18	17	1	1	1	0	17	0	31	2	0	0	2	.000	0	0-2	3	4.74	4.41

Stefen Romero

Bats: R **Throws:** R **Pos:** LF-6;RF-5;PR-2;CF-1;PH-1   STEFF-ehn   **Ht:** 6'2" **Wt:** 220 **Born:** 10/17/1988 **Age:** 27

Year	Team	Lg	G	AB	H	2B	3B	HR	(Hm	Rd)	TB	R	RBI	RC	TBB	2	SO	HBP	SH	SF	SB	CS	GDP	Avg	OBP	Slg	OPS
2011	Clinton	A	116	429	120	22	4	16	(-	-)	198	62	65	69	32	2	69	11	1	5	16	9	7	.280	.342	.462	.803
2012	Hi Dsrt	A+	60	258	92	19	3	11	(-	-)	150	47	51	56	13	3	35	3	0	2	6	2	7	.357	.391	.581	.973
2012	Jacksn	AA	56	216	75	15	4	12	(-	-)	134	38	50	50	14	0	37	5	0	5	6	3	6	.347	.392	.620	1.012
2013	Tacom	AAA	93	375	104	23	4	11	(-	-)	168	51	74	57	28	0	87	4	0	4	8	4	4	.277	.331	.448	.779
2014	Tacom	AAA	36	151	54	7	2	12	(-	-)	101	26	36	35	8	0	28	1	0	3	1	3	6	.358	.387	.669	1.055
2015	Tacom	AAA	116	476	139	37	4	17	(-	-)	235	77	79	81	29	0	85	4	0	7	10	1	10	.292	.333	.494	.827
2014	Sea	AL	72	177	34	6	2	3	(1	2)	53	19	11	7	4	0	48	6	2	1	0	4	5	.192	.234	.299	.533
2015	Sea	AL	13	21	4	1	0	1	(0	1)	8	6	3	3	3	0	6	0	0	0	0	0	0	.190	.292	.381	.673
	2 ML YEARS		85	198	38	7	2	4	(1	3)	61	25	14	10	7	0	54	6	2	1	0	4	5	.192	.241	.308	.549

Andrew Romine

ROW-mine

Bats: B **Throws:** R **Pos:** 3B-59;SS-27;PR-19;1B-17;2B-13;PH-4;LF-2;DH-1   **Ht:** 6'1" **Wt:** 200 **Born:** 12/24/1985 **Age:** 30

Year	Team	Lg	G	AB	H	2B	3B	HR	(Hm	Rd)	TB	R	RBI	RC	TBB	IBB	SO	HBP	SH	SF	SB	CS	GDP	Avg	OBP	Slg	OPS
2010	LAA	AL	5	11	1	0	0	0	(0	0)	1	0	0	0	0	0	4	0	1	0	0	0	0	.091	.091	.091	.182
2011	LAA	AL	10	16	2	0	0	0	(0	0)	2	2	0	0	1	0	6	0	1	0	1	0	0	.125	.176	.125	.301
2012	LAA	AL	12	17	7	0	0	0	(0	0)	7	2	1	5	3	0	3	0	1	0	1	0	0	.412	.500	.412	.912
2013	LAA	AL	47	108	28	3	0	0	(0	0)	31	9	10	12	7	0	24	1	6	1	1	0	2	.259	.308	.287	.595
2014	Det	AL	94	251	57	6	0	2	(1	1)	69	30	12	17	18	0	60	0	4	0	12	2	5	.227	.279	.275	.554
2015	Det	AL	109	184	47	5	0	2	(0	2)	58	25	15	13	11	1	46	3	4	1	10	5	4	.255	.307	.315	.622
	Postseason		3	11	2	0	0	0	(0	0)	2	0	0	0	0	0	4	0	0	0	0	0	0	.182	.182	.182	.364
	6 ML YEARS		277	587	142	14	0	4	(1	3)	168	68	38	47	40	1	143	4	17	2	25	7	11	.242	.294	.286	.580

Austin Romine

ROW-mine

Bats: R **Throws:** R **Pos:** 1B-1   **Ht:** 6'0" **Wt:** 215 **Born:** 11/22/1988 **Age:** 27

Year	Team	Lg	G	AB	H	2B	3B	HR	(Hm	Rd)	TB	R	RBI	RC	TBB	IBB	SO	HBP	SH	SF	SB	CS	GDP	Avg	OBP	Slg	OPS
2015	S-WB*	AAA	92	338	88	19	0	7	(-	-)	128	38	49	41	22	1	53	4	0	2	0	1	12	.260	.311	.379	.690
2011	NYY	AL	9	19	3	0	0	0	(0	0)	3	2	0	1	1	0	5	0	0	0	0	0	0	.158	.200	.158	.358
2013	NYY	AL	60	135	28	9	0	1	(0	1)	40	15	10	8	8	0	37	1	3	1	1	0	7	.207	.255	.296	.551
2014	NYY	AL	7	13	3	1	0	0	(0	0)	4	2	1	2	0	0	4	0	0	0	0	0	0	.231	.231	.308	.538
2015	NYY	AL	1	2	0	0	0	0	(0	0)	0	0	0	0	0	0	0	0	0	0	0	0	0	.000	.000	.000	.000
	4 ML YEARS		77	169	34	10	0	1	(0	1)	47	19	11	10	9	0	46	1	3	1	1	0	7	.201	.244	.278	.523

Sergio Romo

Pitches: R **Bats:** R **Pos:** RP-70   **Ht:** 5'11" **Wt:** 185 **Born:** 3/4/1983 **Age:** 33

			HOW MUCH HE PITCHED						WHAT HE GAVE UP									THE RESULTS								
Year	Team	Lg	G	GS	CG	GF	IP	BFP	H	R	ER	HR	SH	SF	HB	TBB	IBB	SO	WP	Bk	W	L	Pct	Sh	Sv-Op	Hld	ERC	ERA
2008	SF	NL	29	0	0	8	34.0	130	16	13	8	3	2	1	3	8	1	33	0	0	3	1	.750	0	0-0	5	1.27	2.12
2009	SF	NL	45	0	0	9	34.0	143	30	15	15	1	2	0	1	11	0	41	2	0	5	2	.714	0	2-2	10	2.76	3.97
2010	SF	NL	68	0	0	13	62.0	247	46	16	15	6	2	2	4	14	2	70	0	0	5	3	.625	0	0-4	21	2.26	2.18
2011	SF	NL	65	0	0	16	48.0	175	29	8	8	2	2	0	0	5	1	70	0	0	3	1	.750	0	1-2	23	1.08	1.50
2012	SF	NL	69	0	0	27	55.1	215	37	11	11	5	2	0	3	10	1	63	2	0	4	2	.667	0	14-15	23	1.72	1.79
2013	SF	NL	65	0	0	52	60.1	250	53	20	17	5	1	1	1	12	3	58	1	0	5	8	.385	0	38-43	0	2.47	2.54
2014	SF	NL	64	0	0	35	58.0	230	43	24	24	9	2	0	4	12	2	59	2	0	6	4	.600	0	23-28	11	2.54	3.72
2015	SF	NL	70	0	0	14	57.1	230	51	20	19	3	2	0	1	10	2	71	4	0	0	5	.000	0	2-4	34	2.37	2.98
	Postseason		25	0	0	13	21.1	81	16	5	5	2	0	0	0	2	0	20	1	0	3	1	.750	0	4-6	4	1.68	2.11
	8 ML YEARS		475	0	0	174	409.0	1620	305	127	117	34	15	4	17	82	12	465	11	0	31	26	.544	0	80-98	127	2.03	2.57

Bruce Rondon

Pitches: R **Bats:** R **Pos:** RP-35   ron-DOAN   **Ht:** 6'3" **Wt:** 275 **Born:** 12/9/1990 **Age:** 25

			HOW MUCH HE PITCHED						WHAT HE GAVE UP									THE RESULTS								
Year	Team	Lg	G	GS	CG	GF	IP	BFP	H	R	ER	HR	SH	SF	HB	TBB	IBB	SO	WP	Bk	W	L	Pct	Sh	Sv-Op	Hld	ERC	ERA
2011	Wmich	A	41	0	0	33	40.0	179	22	11	9	0	4	2	5	34	1	61	11	1	2	2	.500	0	19- -	-	2.96	2.03
2012	Lkland	A+	22	0	0	21	23.1	92	12	5	5	1	1	1	1	10	1	34	1	0	1	0	1.000	0	15- -	-	1.55	1.93
2012	Erie	AA	21	0	0	19	21.2	90	15	4	2	1	0	0	4	9	0	23	2	1	0	1	.000	0	12- -	-	2.86	0.83
2012	Toledo	AAA	9	0	0	8	8.0	37	5	3	2	1	0	0	0	7	1	9	0	0	1	0	1.000	0	2- -	-	3.60	2.25
2013	Toledo	AAA	30	0	0	26	29.2	118	14	6	5	1	1	1	2	13	0	40	2	0	1	1	.500	0	14- -	-	1.48	1.52
2015	Toledo	AAA	13	0	0	3	12.2	61	16	11	10	1	1	1	0	6	0	14	0	0	2	2	.500	0	1- -	-	5.51	7.11
2013	Det	AL	30	0	0	12	28.2	122	28	11	11	2	1	2	0	11	0	30	7	1	1	2	.333	0	1-3	5	3.69	3.45
2015	Det	AL	35	0	0	15	31.0	145	31	22	20	3	3	2	2	19	1	36	2	0	1	0	1.000	0	5-9	3	4.97	5.81
	2 ML YEARS		65	0	0	27	59.2	267	59	33	31	5	4	4	2	30	1	66	9	1	2	2	.500	0	6-12	8	4.35	4.68

Hector Rondon

Pitches: R **Bats:** R **Pos:** RP-72   rahn-DOHN   **Ht:** 6'3" **Wt:** 180 **Born:** 2/26/1988 **Age:** 28

			HOW MUCH HE PITCHED						WHAT HE GAVE UP									THE RESULTS								
Year	Team	Lg	G	GS	CG	GF	IP	BFP	H	R	ER	HR	SH	SF	HB	TBB	IBB	SO	WP	Bk	W	L	Pct	Sh	Sv-Op	Hld	ERC	ERA
2013	ChC	NL	45	0	0	14	54.2	242	52	29	29	6	4	3	3	25	5	44	4	0	2	1	.667	0	0-1	5	4.10	4.77
2014	ChC	NL	64	0	0	44	63.1	255	52	21	17	2	0	1	0	15	0	63	0	0	4	4	.500	0	29-33	1	2.10	2.42
2015	ChC	NL	72	0	0	47	70.0	281	55	19	13	4	3	1	3	15	2	69	5	1	6	4	.600	0	30-34	8	2.12	1.67
	3 ML YEARS		181	0	0	105	188.0	778	159	69	59	12	7	5	6	55	7	176	9	1	12	9	.571	0	59-68	11	2.65	2.82

Jorge Rondon

Pitches: R Bats: R Pos: RP-10   rahn-DOHN   Ht: 6'1" Wt: 215 Born: 2/16/1988 Age: 28

			HOW MUCH HE PITCHED						WHAT HE GAVE UP													THE RESULTS							
Year	Team	Lg	G	GS	CG	GF	IP	BFP	H	R	ER	HR	SH	SF	HB	TBB	IBB	SO	WP	Bk	W	L	Pct	Sh	Sv-Op	Hld	ERC	ERA
2011	PlmBh	A+	21	0	0	17	26.2	118	29	13	12	1	6	3	0	13	2	27	5	0	1	5	.167	0	6--	-	4.36	4.05
2011	Sprgfld	AA	37	0	0	24	37.1	188	43	45	38	4	3	1	5	33	2	30	8	0	1	8	.111	0	7--	-	7.54	9.16
2012	Sprgfld	AA	33	0	0	13	34.0	145	29	14	13	1	0	3	4	16	0	30	5	4	2	1	.667	0	4--	-	3.56	3.44
2012	Memp	AAA	13	0	0	6	15.0	64	12	6	6	1	0	0	0	8	0	20	0	1	1	0	1.000	0	1--	-	3.25	3.60
2013	Memp	AAA	51	0	0	11	67.2	308	72	31	23	6	0	6	2	37	3	42	7	1	3	5	.375	0	1--	-	4.96	3.06
2014	Memp	AAA	51	0	0	22	62.1	264	59	23	21	3	2	3	3	20	1	51	5	1	5	4	.556	0	10--	-	3.28	3.03
2015	Albq	AAA	5	0	0	1	6.2	24	2	1	1	0	0	0	1	2	0	4	1	0	0	0	-	0	0--	-	0.83	1.35
2015	Norfolk	AAA	30	0	0	8	54.0	209	38	14	14	0	3	1	0	17	0	46	0	1	3	1	.750	0	1--	-	1.72	2.33
2014	StL	NL	1	0	0	0	1.0	4	0	0	0	0	0	0	0	1	0	0	0	0	0	0	-	0	0-0	0	0.95	0.00
2015	2 tms		10	0	0	3	14.1	81	28	26	21	3	0	0	0	9	0	9	1	0	0	1	.000	0	0-0	0	13.19	13.19
15	Col	NL	2	0	0	1	1.0	15	8	11	10	0	0	0	0	3	0	1	0	0	0	0	-	0	0-0	0	69.50	90.00
15	Bal	AL	8	0	0	2	13.1	66	20	15	11	3	0	0	0	6	0	8	1	0	0	1	.000	0	0-0	0	8.22	7.43
2 ML YEARS			11	0	0	3	15.1	85	28	26	21	3	0	0	0	10	0	9	1	0	0	1	.000	0	0-0	0	11.04	12.33

Adam Rosales

Bats: R Throws: R Pos: 1B-19;2B-19;3B-14;PR-8;PH-4;LF-1;DH-1   Ht: 6'1" Wt: 200 Born: 5/20/1983 Age: 33

			BATTING																		RUNNING			AVERAGES			
Year	Team	Lg	G	AB	H	2B	3B	HR	(Hm	Rd)	TB	R	RBI	RC	TBB	IBB	SO	HBP	SH	SF	SB	CS	GDP	Avg	OBP	Slg	OPS
2008	Cin	NL	18	29	6	1	0	0	(0	0)	7	0	2	2	1	0	4	0	0	0	1	0	0	.207	.233	.241	.475
2009	Cin	NL	87	230	49	10	1	4	(2	2)	73	23	19	22	26	0	46	5	2	3	1	2	2	.213	.303	.317	.620
2010	Oak	AL	80	255	69	8	2	7	(1	6)	102	31	31	31	19	0	65	1	2	2	2	2	1	.271	.321	.400	.721
2011	Oak	AL	24	61	6	0	0	2	(0	2)	12	5	8	0	4	0	13	1	0	2	0	0	4	.098	.162	.197	.358
2012	Oak	AL	42	99	22	5	0	2	(1	1)	33	12	8	6	11	1	24	0	0	1	0	0	4	.222	.297	.333	.631
2013	2 Tms	AL	68	147	28	5	0	5	(2	3)	48	15	12	6	10	1	34	4	4	1	0	0	4	.190	.259	.327	.586
2014	Tex	AL	56	164	43	7	0	4	(2	2)	62	20	19	23	13	0	42	3	0	0	4	2	5	.262	.328	.378	.706
2015	Tex	AL	55	114	26	4	0	3	(1	2)	39	14	7	9	10	0	30	1	0	0	4	4	4	.228	.296	.342	.638
13	Oak	AL	51	136	26	5	0	4	(2	2)	43	11	8	5	10	1	31	4	4	0	0	0	4	.191	.267	.316	.583
13	Tex	AL	17	11	2	0	0	1	(0	1)	5	4	4	1	0	0	3	0	0	1	0	0	0	.182	.167	.455	.621
8 ML YEARS			430	1099	249	40	3	27	(9	18)	376	120	106	99	94	2	258	15	8	9	12	10	24	.227	.294	.342	.636

Eddie Rosario

Bats: L Throws: R Pos: LF-86;RF-34;PH-5;CF-4   Ht: 6'1" Wt: 180 Born: 9/28/1991 Age: 24

			BATTING																		RUNNING			AVERAGES			
Year	Team	Lg	G	AB	H	2B	3B	HR	(Hm	Rd)	TB	R	RBI	RC	TBB	IBB	SO	HBP	SH	SF	SB	CS	GDP	Avg	OBP	Slg	OPS
2011	Elizab	R	67	270	91	9	9	21	(-	-)	181	71	60	68	27	2	60	0	1	0	17	6	5	.337	.397	.670	1.068
2012	2 Tms	Low	100	411	123	35	4	13	(-	-)	205	62	74	69	32	1	71	1	0	5	11	11	10	.299	.347	.499	.846
2013	FtMyrs	A+	52	207	68	13	5	6	(-	-)	109	40	35	39	17	1	29	2	0	5	3	6	5	.329	.377	.527	.903
2013	NwBrit	AA	70	289	82	19	3	4	(-	-)	119	40	38	40	21	1	67	0	1	2	7	4	3	.284	.330	.412	.742
2014	NwBrit	AA	79	316	75	20	3	8	(-	-)	125	40	36	35	17	0	68	1	0	2	8	4	5	.237	.277	.396	.672
2015	Roch	AAA	23	95	23	2	1	3	(-	-)	36	11	12	10	5	0	17	0	0	0	1	1	2	.242	.280	.379	.659
2015	Min	AL	122	453	121	18	15	13	(10	3)	208	60	50	58	15	3	118	0	3	3	11	6	5	.267	.289	.459	.748

Wilin Rosario

Bats: R Throws: R Pos: 1B-53;PH-28;DH-6;C-2   wih-LEAN roh-SORRY-oh   Ht: 5'11" Wt: 220 Born: 2/23/1989 Age: 27

			BATTING																		RUNNING			AVERAGES			
Year	Team	Lg	G	AB	H	2B	3B	HR	(Hm	Rd)	TB	R	RBI	RC	TBB	IBB	SO	HBP	SH	SF	SB	CS	GDP	Avg	OBP	Slg	OPS
2015	Albq*	AAA	38	148	44	12	1	7	(-	-)	79	18	23	25	5	0	31	2	0	0	1	1	7	.297	.329	.534	.863
2011	Col	NL	16	54	11	3	1	3	(1	2)	25	6	8	4	2	0	20	0	0	1	0	0	1	.204	.228	.463	.691
2012	Col	NL	117	396	107	19	0	28	(18	10)	210	67	71	56	25	2	99	1	0	4	4	5	10	.270	.312	.530	.843
2013	Col	NL	121	449	131	22	1	21	(10	11)	218	63	79	62	15	0	109	1	0	1	4	1	7	.292	.315	.486	.801
2014	Col	NL	106	382	102	25	0	13	(7	6)	166	46	54	40	23	5	70	0	0	5	1	0	17	.267	.305	.435	.739
2015	Col	NL	87	231	62	14	1	6	(4	2)	96	22	29	21	8	2	56	1	1	1	2	1	8	.268	.295	.416	.710
5 ML YEARS			447	1512	413	83	3	71	(40	31)	715	204	241	183	73	9	354	3	1	12	11	7	43	.273	.306	.473	.779

Trevor Rosenthal

Pitches: R Bats: R Pos: RP-68   Ht: 6'2" Wt: 220 Born: 5/29/1990 Age: 26

			HOW MUCH HE PITCHED						WHAT HE GAVE UP													THE RESULTS							
Year	Team	Lg	G	GS	CG	GF	IP	BFP	H	R	ER	HR	SH	SF	HB	TBB	IBB	SO	WP	Bk	W	L	Pct	Sh	Sv-Op	Hld	ERC	ERA
2012	StL	NL	19	0	0	7	22.2	89	14	7	7	2	1	0	1	7	0	25	1	0	0	2	.000	0	0-0	3	1.89	2.78
2013	StL	NL	74	0	0	15	75.1	311	63	25	22	4	3	0	6	20	0	108	3	0	2	4	.333	0	3-8	29	2.68	2.63
2014	StL	NL	72	0	0	59	70.1	308	57	25	25	2	2	4	4	42	5	87	1	1	2	6	.250	0	45-51	2	3.36	3.20
2015	StL	NL	68	0	0	57	68.2	287	62	16	16	3	1	0	1	25	3	83	7	0	2	4	.333	0	48-51	0	3.04	2.10
Postseason			21	0	0	13	24.0	91	13	2	2	0	0	0	0	8	2	38	1	1	1	0	1.000	0	7-9	2	1.16	0.75
4 ML YEARS			233	0	0	138	237.0	995	196	73	70	11	7	4	12	94	8	303	12	1	6	16	.273	0	96-110	34	2.91	2.66

Seth Rosin

Pitches: R **Bats:** R **Pos:** RP-1 ro-ZEEN **Ht:** 6'6" **Wt:** 265 **Born:** 11/2/1988 **Age:** 27

			HOW MUCH HE PITCHED							WHAT HE GAVE UP											THE RESULTS							
Year	Team	Lg	G	GS	CG	GF	IP	BFP	H	R	ER	HR	SH	SF	HB	TBB	IBB	SO	WP	Bk	W	L	Pct	Sh	Sv-Op	Hld	ERC	ERA
2011	Augsta	A	39	10	0	10	89.0	365	81	44	33	3	5	0	2	30	0	93	2	0	2	3	.400	0	2- -	-	3.06	3.34
2012	2 Tms	Low	37	8	0	16	68.1	282	56	34	31	6	3	2	1	22	1	75	2	1	2	2	.500	0	10- -	-	2.74	4.08
2013	Rdng	AA	26	23	1	1	126.2	531	120	69	61	13	4	6	3	35	1	96	3	1	9	6	.600	0	0- -	-	3.38	4.33
2014	LV	AAA	17	1	0	6	23.0	105	31	17	16	3	1	2	0	9	2	20	2	0	1	3	.250	0	2- -	-	6.28	6.26
2014	Rdng	AA	26	0	0	12	35.1	144	33	9	9	3	0	3	0	10	0	24	1	1	2	2	.500	0	1- -	-	3.23	2.29
2015	LV	AAA	47	0	0	18	68.1	300	76	27	25	4	2	4	0	21	2	49	4	0	4	3	.571	0	3- -	-	3.92	3.29
2014	Tex	AL	3	0	0	2	4.0	19	6	3	3	0	0	0	0	1	0	3	0	0	1	0	1.000	0	0-0	-	5.46	6.75
2015	Phi	NL	1	0	0	1	2.0	14	7	5	5	1	0	1	1	1	0	0	1	0	0	0	.-	0	0-0	0	32.37	22.50
	2 ML YEARS		4	0	0	3	6.0	33	13	8	8	1	0	1	1	2	0	3	1	0	1	0	1.000	0	0-0	0	13.00	12.00

Cody Ross

Bats: R **Throws:** L **Pos:** RF-5;LF-4;PH-3;DH-1 **Ht:** 5'11" **Wt:** 195 **Born:** 12/23/1980 **Age:** 35

						BATTING															RUNNING			AVERAGES			
Year	Team	Lg	G	AB	H	2B	3B	HR	(Hm	Rd)	TB	R	RBI	RC	TBB	IBB	SO	HBP	SH	SF	SB	CS	GDP	Avg	OBP	Slg	OPS
2003	Det	AL	6	19	4	1	0	1	(1	0)	8	1	5	4	1	0	3	1	1	0	0	0	0	.211	.286	.421	.707
2005	LAD	NL	14	25	4	1	0	0	(0	0)	5	1	1	0	1	0	10	0	0	0	0	0	1	.160	.192	.200	.392
2006	3 Tms	NL	101	269	61	12	2	13	(6	7)	116	34	46	36	22	0	65	4	1	2	1	1	8	.227	.293	.431	.724
2007	Fla	NL	66	173	58	19	0	12	(8	4)	113	35	39	42	20	3	38	3	0	1	2	0	2	.335	.411	.653	1.064
2008	Fla	NL	145	461	120	29	5	22	(7	15)	225	59	73	68	33	2	116	7	0	5	6	1	5	.260	.316	.488	.804
2009	Fla	NL	151	559	151	37	1	24	(13	11)	262	73	90	75	34	1	122	9	0	2	5	2	18	.270	.321	.469	.790
2010	2 Tms	NL	153	525	141	28	3	14	(5	9)	217	71	65	68	37	4	121	5	0	2	9	2	9	.269	.322	.413	.735
2011	SF	NL	121	405	97	25	0	14	(6	8)	164	54	52	53	49	4	96	4	0	3	5	2	10	.240	.325	.405	.730
2012	Bos	AL	130	476	127	34	1	22	(13	9)	229	70	81	76	42	3	129	3	1	6	2	3	11	.267	.326	.481	.807
2013	Ari	NL	94	317	88	17	1	8	(4	4)	131	33	38	37	25	1	50	3	1	5	3	2	10	.278	.331	.413	.745
2014	Ari	NL	83	202	51	8	0	2	(1	1)	65	15	15	16	15	0	44	1	0	1	0	0	3	.252	.306	.322	.628
2015	Oak	AL	9	22	2	0	0	0	(0	0)	2	3	3	0	3	0	6	0	0	0	0	0	0	.091	.200	.091	.291
06	LAD	NL	8	14	7	1	1	2	(0	2)	16	4	9	6	0	0	2	0	0	0	1	0	0	.500	.500	1.143	1.643
06	Cin	NL	2	5	1	0	0	0	(0	0)	1	0	0	1	0	0	2	0	0	0	0	0	0	.200	.200	.200	.400
06	Fla	NL	91	250	53	11	1	11	(6	5)	99	30	37	29	22	0	61	4	1	2	0	1	8	.212	.284	.396	.680
10	Fla	NL	120	452	120	24	3	11	(5	6)	183	60	58	58	30	4	100	4	0	1	9	1	7	.265	.316	.405	.721
10	SF	NL	33	73	21	4	0	3	(0	3)	34	11	7	10	7	0	21	1	0	1	0	1	2	.288	.354	.466	.819
	Postseason		15	51	15	5	0	5	(0	5)	35	11	10	12	7	0	11	1	0	0	0	0	1	.294	.390	.686	1.076
	12 ML YEARS		1073	3453	904	211	13	132	(64	68)	1537	449	508	475	282	18	800	40	4	27	33	13	77	.262	.322	.445	.768

David Ross

Bats: R **Throws:** R **Pos:** C-59;PH-14;PR-1 **Ht:** 6'2" **Wt:** 230 **Born:** 3/19/1977 **Age:** 39

						BATTING															RUNNING			AVERAGES			
Year	Team	Lg	G	AB	H	2B	3B	HR	(Hm	Rd)	TB	R	RBI	RC	TBB	IBB	SO	HBP	SH	SF	SB	CS	GDP	Avg	OBP	Slg	OPS
2002	LAD	NL	8	10	2	1	0	1	(0	1)	6	2	2	2	2	0	4	1	0	0	0	0	0	.200	.385	.600	.985
2003	LAD	NL	40	124	32	7	0	10	(5	5)	69	19	18	18	13	0	42	2	0	1	0	0	4	.258	.336	.556	.892
2004	LAD	NL	70	165	28	3	1	5	(2	3)	48	13	15	11	15	1	62	5	0	5	0	0	3	.170	.253	.291	.544
2005	2 Tms	NL	51	125	30	8	1	3	(2	1)	49	11	15	13	6	0	28	2	2	3	0	0	3	.240	.279	.392	.671
2006	Cin	NL	90	247	63	15	1	21	(13	8)	143	37	52	43	37	7	75	3	4	5	0	0	4	.255	.353	.579	.932
2007	Cin	NL	112	311	63	10	0	17	(12	5)	124	32	39	27	30	4	92	0	5	2	0	0	9	.203	.271	.399	.670
2008	2 Tms		60	142	32	9	0	3	(1	2)	50	18	13	19	32	4	39	1	6	1	0	1	3	.225	.369	.352	.721
2009	Atl	NL	54	128	35	9	0	7	(2	5)	65	18	20	20	21	0	39	1	1	0	0	0	1	.273	.380	.508	.888
2010	Atl	NL	59	121	35	13	2	2	(2	0)	58	15	28	22	20	0	28	1	2	1	0	1	5	.289	.392	.479	.871
2011	Atl	NL	52	152	40	7	0	6	(2	4)	65	14	23	22	16	0	51	0	3	0	0	1	4	.263	.333	.428	.761
2012	Atl	NL	62	176	45	7	0	9	(4	5)	79	18	23	21	18	0	60	0	0	2	1	0	5	.256	.321	.449	.770
2013	Bos	AL	36	102	22	5	0	4	(3	1)	39	11	10	7	11	0	42	1	2	0	1	0	3	.216	.298	.382	.681
2014	Bos	AL	50	152	28	7	0	7	(4	3)	56	16	15	13	16	1	58	0	2	1	0	1	1	.184	.260	.368	.629
2015	ChC	NL	72	159	28	9	0	1	(1	0)	40	6	9	8	20	7	61	0	2	1	1	0	1	.176	.267	.252	.518
05	Pit	NL	40	108	24	8	0	3	(2	1)	41	9	15	9	6	0	24	1	1	3	0	0	3	.222	.263	.380	.642
05	SD	NL	11	17	6	0	1	0	(0	0)	8	2	0	4	0	0	4	1	1	0	0	0	0	.353	.389	.471	.859
08	Cin	NL	52	134	31	9	0	3	(1	2)	49	17	13	19	32	4	36	1	5	1	0	1	3	.231	.381	.366	.747
08	Bos	AL	8	8	1	0	0	0	(0	0)	1	1	0	0	0	0	3	0	1	0	0	0	0	.125	.125	.125	.250
	Postseason		14	32	9	3	0	1	(1	0)	15	3	4	4	2	0	11	0	1	0	0	0	0	.281	.324	.469	.792
	14 ML YEARS		816	2114	483	110	5	96	(53	43)	891	230	282	246	257	24	681	17	28	22	3	4	46	.228	.314	.421	.736

Joe Ross

Pitches: R **Bats:** R **Pos:** SP-13; RP-3 **Ht:** 6'4" **Wt:** 205 **Born:** 5/21/1993 **Age:** 23

			HOW MUCH HE PITCHED							WHAT HE GAVE UP											THE RESULTS							
Year	Team	Lg	G	GS	CG	GF	IP	BFP	H	R	ER	HR	SH	SF	HB	TBB	IBB	SO	WP	Bk	W	L	Pct	Sh	Sv-Op	Hld	ERC	ERA
2012	3 Tms	Low	15	15	0	0	54.2	233	51	28	26	3	1	4	1	22	0	56	3	0	0	4	.000	0	0- -	-	3.48	4.28
2013	FtWyn	A	23	23	0	0	122.1	524	124	55	51	7	8	6	5	40	1	79	4	0	5	8	.385	0	0- -	-	3.72	3.75
2014	Lk Els	A+	19	19	0	0	101.2	436	101	52	45	6	4	3	7	28	2	87	3	0	8	6	.571	0	0- -	-	3.47	3.98
2015	Hrsbrg	AA	9	9	0	0	51.1	206	46	18	16	3	3	0	3	12	0	54	1	0	2	2	.500	0	0- -	-	2.92	2.81
2015	Syrcse	AAA	5	5	0	0	24.2	93	15	6	6	2	0	0	0	7	0	15	2	0	3	1	.750	0	0- -	-	1.65	2.19
2015	Was	NL	16	13	0	1	76.2	314	64	33	31	7	3	1	2	21	0	69	1	0	5	5	.500	0	0-0	0	2.74	3.64

Robbie Ross

Pitches: L **Bats:** L **Pos:** RP-54   **Ht:** 5'11" **Wt:** 215 **Born:** 6/24/1989 **Age:** 27

			HOW MUCH HE PITCHED						WHAT HE GAVE UP										THE RESULTS							
Year	Team	Lg	G	GS	CG	GF	IP	BFP	H	R	ER	HR	SH	SF	HB	TBB	IBB	SO	WP	Bk	W	L	Pct	Sh	Sv-Op	Hld	ERC	ERA
2012	Tex	AL	58	0	0	9	65.0	265	55	21	16	3	1	2	2	23	3	47	1	1	6	0	1.000	0	0-0	9	2.83	2.22
2013	Tex	AL	65	0	0	16	62.1	267	63	21	21	4	0	0	5	19	2	58	2	0	4	2	.667	0	0-1	15	3.79	3.03
2014	Tex	AL	27	12	0	4	78.1	365	103	65	54	9	2	2	7	30	2	51	6	0	3	6	.333	0	0-0	2	6.34	6.20
2015	Bos	AL	54	0	0	18	60.2	259	59	28	26	7	2	2	3	20	2	53	1	0	0	2	.000	0	6-8	12	3.89	3.86
	4 ML YEARS		204	12	0	47	266.1	1156	280	135	117	23	5	6	17	92	9	209	10	1	13	10	.565	0	6-9	38	4.27	3.95

Tyson Ross

Pitches: R **Bats:** R **Pos:** SP-33   **Ht:** 6'5" **Wt:** 230 **Born:** 4/22/1987 **Age:** 29

			HOW MUCH HE PITCHED						WHAT HE GAVE UP										THE RESULTS							
Year	Team	Lg	G	GS	CG	GF	IP	BFP	H	R	ER	HR	SH	SF	HB	TBB	IBB	SO	WP	Bk	W	L	Pct	Sh	Sv-Op	Hld	ERC	ERA
2010	Oak	AL	26	2	0	9	39.1	169	39	24	24	4	1	4	0	20	0	32	5	0	1	4	.200	0	1-2	2	4.60	5.49
2011	Oak	AL	9	6	0	1	36.0	145	33	12	11	1	1	0	0	13	1	24	2	0	3	3	.500	0	0-0	0	3.09	2.75
2012	Oak	AL	18	13	0	3	73.1	342	96	56	53	7	3	3	5	37	3	46	2	1	2	11	.154	0	0-0	0	6.68	6.50
2013	SD	NL	35	16	0	4	125.0	504	100	51	44	8	3	5	7	44	4	119	7	0	3	8	.273	0	0-0	0	2.84	3.17
2014	SD	NL	31	31	2	0	195.2	811	165	75	61	13	10	4	9	72	2	195	12	0	13	14	.481	1	0-0	0	3.07	2.81
2015	SD	NL	33	**33**	1	0	196.0	823	172	78	71	9	3	3	8	**84**	3	212	**14**	0	10	12	.455	0	0-0	0	3.33	3.26
	6 ML YEARS		152	101	3	21	665.1	2794	605	296	264	42	21	19	29	270	13	628	42	1	32	52	.381	1	1-2	2	3.55	3.57

Zac Rosscup

Pitches: L **Bats:** R **Pos:** RP-33   ROSS-cup   **Ht:** 6'2" **Wt:** 220 **Born:** 6/9/1988 **Age:** 28

			HOW MUCH HE PITCHED						WHAT HE GAVE UP										THE RESULTS							
Year	Team	Lg	G	GS	CG	GF	IP	BFP	H	R	ER	HR	SH	SF	HB	TBB	IBB	SO	WP	Bk	W	L	Pct	Sh	Sv-Op	Hld	ERC	ERA
2015	Iowa*	AAA	11	0	0	0	11.1	48	8	7	6	1	0	0	1	4	0	20	2	0	0	0	-	0	0--	-	2.49	4.76
2013	ChC	NL	10	0	0	3	6.2	30	3	1	1	1	0	0	0	7	1	7	0	0	0	0	-	0	0-0	0	3.56	1.35
2014	ChC	NL	18	0	0	5	13.1	66	14	14	14	2	0	0	0	12	1	21	0	0	1	0	1.000	0	0-0	1	6.54	9.45
2015	ChC	NL	33	0	0	6	26.2	118	26	13	13	5	2	0	0	13	0	29	1	0	2	1	.667	0	0-2	6	4.85	4.39
	3 ML YEARS		61	0	0	14	46.2	214	43	28	28	8	2	0	0	32	2	57	1	0	3	1	.750	0	0-2	7	5.14	5.40

Ryan Rua

Bats: R **Throws:** R **Pos:** LF-22;1B-4;RF-4;PH-1   ROO-ah   **Ht:** 6'2" **Wt:** 205 **Born:** 3/11/1990 **Age:** 26

			BATTING																	RUNNING			AVERAGES			
Year	Team	Lg	G	AB	H	2B	3B	HR	(Hm	Rd)	TB	R	RBI	RC	TBB	IBB	SO	HBP	SH	SF	SB	CS	GDP	Avg	OBP	Slg	OPS
2011	2 Tms	Low	52	188	57	12	5	4	(-	-)	91	43	37	36	21	0	40	2	1	2	10	0	5	.303	.376	.484	.860
2012	Spkane	A-	74	280	82	16	1	7	(-	-)	121	40	43	47	29	0	64	6	2	3	4	1	8	.293	.368	.432	.800
2013	Hkry	A	104	367	92	24	1	29	(-	-)	205	70	82	76	49	2	91	12	0	2	13	2	4	.251	.356	.559	.914
2013	Frisco	AA	23	86	20	2	1	3	(-	-)	33	19	9	10	7	0	24	2	0	2	1	0	2	.233	.305	.384	.689
2014	Frisco	AA	71	257	77	13	1	10	(-	-)	122	34	38	46	30	2	55	1	0	0	5	3	5	.300	.375	.475	.850
2014	RdRck	AAA	58	214	67	13	2	8	(-	-)	108	31	36	41	21	0	42	4	0	2	1	2	3	.313	.382	.505	.886
2015	RdRck	AAA	40	142	28	5	0	6	(-	-)	51	18	22	17	18	0	45	4	0	1	3	0	5	.197	.303	.359	.662
2014	Tex	AL	28	105	31	7	0	2	(1	1)	44	11	14	13	2	0	18	2	0	0	1	0	6	.295	.321	.419	.740
2015	Tex	AL	28	83	16	5	0	4	(2	2)	33	10	7	5	3	0	32	0	0	0	0	0	2	.193	.221	.398	.619
	2 ML YEARS		56	188	47	12	0	6	(3	3)	77	21	21	18	5	0	50	2	0	0	1	0	8	.250	.277	.410	.686

Drew Rucinski

Pitches: R **Bats:** R **Pos:** RP-3; SP-1   ruh-SIN-ski   **Ht:** 6'2" **Wt:** 190 **Born:** 12/30/1988 **Age:** 27

			HOW MUCH HE PITCHED						WHAT HE GAVE UP										THE RESULTS							
Year	Team	Lg	G	GS	CG	GF	IP	BFP	H	R	ER	HR	SH	SF	HB	TBB	IBB	SO	WP	Bk	W	L	Pct	Sh	Sv-Op	Hld	ERC	ERA
2011	3 Tms	Low	22	0	0	5	37.0	161	36	13	12	3	5	2	6	10	0	47	2	0	4	0	1.000	0	0--	-	3.88	2.92
2013	InldEm	A+	5	5	0	0	29.0	115	29	11	6	0	0	1	1	4	0	21	0	0	2	2	.500	0	0--	-	2.67	1.86
2014	Ark	AA	26	26	2	0	148.2	610	142	61	52	7	4	6	6	41	0	140	10	0	10	6	.625	1	0--	-	3.23	3.15
2015	Salt Lk	AAA	22	22	0	0	112.1	509	141	73	71	21	4	2	5	44	0	87	2	0	5	7	.417	0	0--	-	6.50	5.69
2014	LAA	AL	3	0	0	2	7.1	34	9	4	4	0	0	0	1	2	0	8	0	0	0	0	-	0	0-0	0	4.52	4.91
2015	LAA	AL	4	1	0	2	7.0	35	10	6	6	1	0	0	1	6	0	4	2	0	0	2	.000	0	0-0	0	10.39	7.71
	2 ML YEARS		7	1	0	4	14.1	69	19	10	10	1	0	0	2	8	0	12	2	0	0	2	.000	0	0-0	0	7.16	6.28

Darin Ruf

Bats: R **Throws:** R **Pos:** 1B-66;PH-29;LF-22   ROUGH   **Ht:** 6'3" **Wt:** 250 **Born:** 7/28/1986 **Age:** 29

			BATTING																	RUNNING			AVERAGES			
Year	Team	Lg	G	AB	H	2B	3B	HR	(Hm	Rd)	TB	R	RBI	RC	TBB	IBB	SO	HBP	SH	SF	SB	CS	GDP	Avg	OBP	Slg	OPS
2012	Phi	NL	12	33	11	2	1	3	(1	2)	24	4	10	5	2	1	12	0	0	2	0	0	1	.333	.351	.727	1.079
2013	Phi	NL	73	251	62	11	0	14	(11	3)	115	36	30	33	33	1	91	7	0	2	0	0	4	.247	.348	.458	.806
2014	Phi	NL	52	102	24	8	0	3	(3	0)	41	13	8	9	8	0	32	4	1	2	0	0	2	.235	.305	.402	.712
2015	Phi	NL	106	268	63	12	0	12	(6	6)	111	30	39	34	21	0	69	5	0	3	1	0	7	.235	.300	.414	.714
	4 ML YEARS		243	654	160	33	1	32	(21	11)	291	83	87	81	64	2	204	16	1	9	1	0	14	.245	.323	.445	.768

Justin Ruggiano

roo-jee-AH-no

Bats: R **Throws:** R **Pos:** LF-22;PH-19;CF-15;RF-13;PR-4;DH-2   **Ht:** 6'1" **Wt:** 210 **Born:** 4/12/1982 **Age:** 34

Year Team	Lg	G	AB	H	2B	3B	HR	(Hm	Rd)	TB	R	RBI	RC	TBB	IBB	SO	HBP	SH	SF	SB	CS	GDP	Avg	OBP	Slg	OPS
2015 Tacom*	AAA	49	179	53	9	0	10	(-	-)	92	27	29	35	23	1	51	3	0	0	6	4	7	.296	.385	.514	.899
2007 TB	AL	7	14	3	0	0	0	(0	0)	3	2	3	1	1	0	5	0	0	0	0	0	0	.214	.267	.214	.481
2008 TB	AL	45	76	15	4	0	2	(2	0)	25	9	7	4	4	0	27	1	0	0	2	0	2	.197	.247	.329	.576
2011 TB	AL	46	105	26	4	0	4	(3	1)	42	11	13	16	4	0	26	0	1	1	1	1	2	.248	.273	.400	.673
2012 Mia	NL	91	288	90	23	1	13	(4	9)	154	38	36	46	29	0	84	0	1	1	14	8	6	.313	.374	.535	.909
2013 Mia	NL	128	424	94	18	1	18	(3	15)	168	49	50	42	41	1	114	5	1	0	15	8	9	.222	.298	.396	.694
2014 ChC	NL	81	224	63	13	1	6	(2	4)	96	29	28	32	18	0	70	3	1	4	2	4	2	.281	.337	.429	.766
2015 2 Tms		57	125	31	8	1	6	(1	5)	59	20	15	20	14	0	41	2	0	0	5	2	1	.248	.333	.472	.805
15 Sea	AL	36	70	15	4	0	2	(1	1)	25	8	3	9	11	0	27	0	0	0	3	2	0	.214	.321	.357	.678
15 LAD	NL	21	55	16	4	1	4	(0	4)	34	12	12	11	3	0	14	2	0	0	2	0	1	.291	.350	.618	.968
7 ML YEARS		455	1256	322	70	4	49	(15	34)	547	158	152	161	111	1	367	11	4	6	39	23	22	.256	.321	.436	.756

Carlos Ruiz

Bats: R **Throws:** R **Pos:** C-83;PH-4   **Ht:** 5'10" **Wt:** 205 **Born:** 1/22/1979 **Age:** 37

Year Team	Lg	G	AB	H	2B	3B	HR	(Hm	Rd)	TB	R	RBI	RC	TBB	IBB	SO	HBP	SH	SF	SB	CS	GDP	Avg	OBP	Slg	OPS
2006 Phi	NL	27	69	18	1	1	3	(2	1)	30	5	10	10	5	2	8	1	2	1	0	0	3	.261	.316	.435	.751
2007 Phi	NL	115	374	97	29	2	6	(4	2)	148	42	54	49	42	10	49	5	5	3	6	1	17	.259	.340	.396	.735
2008 Phi	NL	117	320	70	14	0	4	(2	2)	96	47	31	28	44	6	38	4	4	1	1	2	14	.219	.320	.300	.620
2009 Phi	NL	107	322	82	26	1	9	(5	4)	137	32	43	49	47	8	39	4	4	2	3	2	8	.255	.355	.425	.780
2010 Phi	NL	121	371	112	28	1	8	(3	5)	166	43	53	62	55	13	54	6	0	1	1	0	8	.302	.400	.447	.847
2011 Phi	NL	132	410	116	23	0	6	(1	5)	157	49	40	59	48	10	48	10	3	1	1	0	7	.283	.371	.383	.754
2012 Phi	NL	114	372	121	32	0	16	(8	8)	201	56	68	75	29	6	50	16	0	4	4	0	6	.325	.394	.540	.935
2013 Phi	NL	92	310	83	16	0	5	(4	1)	114	30	37	34	18	3	39	7	4	2	1	0	11	.268	.320	.368	.688
2014 Phi	NL	110	381	96	25	1	6	(2	4)	141	43	31	50	46	1	60	12	1	5	4	2	11	.252	.347	.370	.717
2015 Phi	NL	86	284	60	13	1	2	(1	1)	81	23	22	19	28	2	43	4	3	1	1	1	13	.211	.290	.285	.575
Postseason		46	142	36	8	1	4	(3	1)	58	19	15	24	24	3	16	5	1	0	3	0	2	.254	.380	.408	.789
10 ML YEARS		1021	3213	855	207	7	65	(32	33)	1271	370	389	435	362	61	428	69	26	21	21	9	98	.266	.351	.396	.746

Nick Rumbelow

Pitches: R **Bats:** R **Pos:** RP-17   **Ht:** 6'0" **Wt:** 190 **Born:** 9/6/1991 **Age:** 24

		HOW MUCH HE PITCHED						WHAT HE GAVE UP									THE RESULTS						
Year Team	Lg	G	GS	CG	GF	IP	BFP	H	R	ER	HR	SH	SF	HB	TBB	IBB	SO	WP	Bk	W	L	Pct	Sh	Sv-Op	Hld	ERC	ERA
2013 Stnlld	A-	19	0	0	14	23.0	89	12	13	6	1	0	2	1	5	0	20	2	0	2	2	.500	0	7--	-	1.14	2.35
2014 2 Tms	Low	27	0	0	19	35.1	142	24	7	7	0	1	3	1	12	0	47	10	0	5	1	.833	0	6--	-	1.70	1.78
2014 Trntn	AA	7	0	0	6	7.1	28	4	4	3	0	0	0	0	1	0	15	1	0	0	0	-	0	1--	-	0.83	3.68
2014 S-WB	AAA	10	0	0	3	15.2	68	17	7	7	2	0	1	0	5	0	19	1	0	0	1	.000	0	1--	-	4.40	4.02
2015 S-WB	AAA	37	0	0	22	52.2	220	47	28	25	4	2	1	0	13	0	57	6	0	2	3	.400	0	8--	-	2.68	4.27
2015 NYY	AL	17	0	0	6	15.2	68	16	8	7	2	0	0	0	5	1	15	2	1	1	1	.500	0	0-0	0	3.87	4.02

Cameron Rupp

Bats: R **Throws:** R **Pos:** C-80;PH-1   **Ht:** 6'2" **Wt:** 260 **Born:** 9/28/1988 **Age:** 27

Year Team	Lg	G	AB	H	2B	3B	HR	(Hm	Rd)	TB	R	RBI	RC	TBB	IBB	SO	HBP	SH	SF	SB	CS	GDP	Avg	OBP	Slg	OPS
2013 Phi	NL	4	13	4	1	0	0	(0	0)	5	1	2	2	1	0	4	0	0	0	0	0	0	.308	.357	.385	.742
2014 Phi	NL	18	60	11	4	0	0	(0	0)	15	4	6	3	4	0	20	0	0	0	0	0	5	.183	.234	.250	.484
2015 Phi	NL	81	270	63	9	1	9	(4	5)	101	24	28	29	24	5	71	3	0	2	0	1	8	.233	.301	.374	.675
3 ML YEARS		103	343	78	14	1	9	(4	5)	121	29	36	34	29	5	95	3	0	2	0	1	13	.227	.292	.353	.645

Chris Rusin

RUSS-inn

Pitches: L **Bats:** L **Pos:** SP-22; RP-2   **Ht:** 6'2" **Wt:** 195 **Born:** 10/22/1986 **Age:** 29

		HOW MUCH HE PITCHED						WHAT HE GAVE UP									THE RESULTS						
Year Team	Lg	G	GS	CG	GF	IP	BFP	H	R	ER	HR	SH	SF	HB	TBB	IBB	SO	WP	Bk	W	L	Pct	Sh	Sv-Op	Hld	ERC	ERA
2015 Albq*	AAA	7	6	0	0	34.1	161	47	28	24	6	0	0	0	11	1	18	2	1	3	2	.600	0	0--	-	6.31	6.29
2012 ChC	NL	7	7	0	0	29.2	135	38	22	21	4	0	3	0	11	0	21	0	0	2	3	.400	0	0-0	0	6.46	6.37
2013 ChC	NL	13	13	0	0	66.1	282	66	30	29	8	1	1	3	24	3	36	1	0	2	6	.250	0	0-0	0	4.21	3.93
2014 ChC	NL	4	0	0	2	12.2	58	16	10	10	1	1	0	0	5	1	8	1	0	0	0	-	0	0-0	0	5.24	7.11
2015 Col	NL	24	22	2	0	131.2	594	170	88	78	19	2	0	3	41	5	86	2	2	6	10	.375	1	0-0	0	5.80	5.33
4 ML YEARS		48	42	2	2	240.1	1069	290	150	138	32	4	1	9	81	9	151	4	2	10	19	.345	1	0-0	0	5.40	5.17

Addison Russell

Bats: R **Throws:** R **Pos:** 2B-86;SS-61;PH-1   **Ht:** 6'0" **Wt:** 200 **Born:** 1/23/1994 **Age:** 22

Year Team	Lg	G	AB	H	2B	3B	HR	(Hm	Rd)	TB	R	RBI	RC	TBB	IBB	SO	HBP	SH	SF	SB	CS	GDP	Avg	OBP	Slg	OPS
2012 3 Tms	Low	55	217	80	10	9	7	(-	-)	129	46	45	54	23	0	48	2	1	1	16	2	3	.369	.432	.594	1.027
2013 Stcktn	A+	107	429	118	29	10	17	(-	-)	218	85	60	87	61	0	116	11	0	3	21	3	8	.275	.377	.508	.885
2014 Mdlnd	AA	13	48	16	3	1	1	(-	-)	24	7	8	10	8	0	8	1	0	0	3	2	3	.333	.439	.500	.939
2014 Tenn	AA	50	193	57	11	4	12	(-	-)	104	32	36	33	9	0	36	2	0	0	2	2	7	.295	.333	.539	.872
2015 Iowa	AAA	11	44	14	4	0	1	(-	-)	21	7	9	7	1	0	7	0	0	1	1	0	0	.318	.326	.477	.803
2015 ChC	NL	142	475	115	29	1	13	(8	5)	185	60	54	53	42	2	149	3	1	2	4	3	4	.242	.307	.389	.696

James Russell

Pitches: L **Bats:** L **Pos:** RP-49   **Ht:** 6'4" **Wt:** 205 **Born:** 1/8/1986 **Age:** 30

			HOW MUCH HE PITCHED						WHAT HE GAVE UP										THE RESULTS							
Year	Team	Lg	G	GS	CG	GF	IP	BFP	H	R	ER	HR	SH	SF	HB	TBB	IBB	SO	WP	Bk	W	L	Pct	Sh	Sv-Op	Hld	ERC	ERA
2015	Iowa*	AAA	9	0	0	6	11.0	43	8	5	3	0	0	0	0	4	0	13	0	0	2	0	1.000	0	3- -	-	1.99	2.45
2010	ChC	NL	57	0	0	11	49.0	219	55	37	27	11	3	4	4	11	0	42	2	0	1	1	.500	0	0-2	6	5.12	4.96
2011	ChC	NL	64	5	0	10	67.2	292	76	37	31	12	4	6	2	14	4	43	1	0	1	6	.143	0	0-2	6	4.51	4.12
2012	ChC	NL	77	0	0	19	69.1	292	67	28	25	5	2	3	1	23	7	55	1	1	7	1	.875	0	2-5	13	3.35	3.25
2013	ChC	NL	74	0	0	7	52.2	214	46	21	21	7	1	1	1	18	6	37	1	0	1	6	.143	0	0-8	19	3.37	3.59
2014	2 Tms	NL	66	1	0	15	57.2	238	45	20	19	3	7	1	1	20	3	42	1	0	0	2	.000	0	1-3	6	2.37	2.97
2015	ChC	NL	49	0	0	8	34.0	148	42	24	20	3	1	1	0	9	2	20	0	0	0	2	.000	0	1-3	8	4.75	5.29
14	ChC	NL	44	0	0	7	33.1	142	24	14	13	3	5	1	1	16	2	26	1	0	0	2	.000	0	1-3	5	2.76	3.51
14	Atl	NL	22	1	0	8	24.1	96	21	6	6	0	2	0	0	4	1	16	0	0	0	0	-	0	0-0	1	1.86	2.22
6 ML YEARS			387	6	0	70	330.1	1403	331	167	143	41	18	16	9	95	22	239	6	1	10	18	.357	0	4-23	58	3.80	3.90

Josh Rutledge

Bats: R **Throws:** R **Pos:** 2B-30;3B-5;PR-5;DH-3;PH-3   **Ht:** 6'1" **Wt:** 190 **Born:** 4/21/1989 **Age:** 27

						BATTING															RUNNING			AVERAGES			
Year	Team	Lg	G	AB	H	2B	3B	HR	(Hm	Rd)	TB	R	RBI	RC	TBB	IBB	SO	HBP	SH	SF	SB	CS	GDP	Avg	OBP	Slg	OPS
2015	Salt Lk*	AAA	78	310	85	19	3	5	(-	-)	125	45	32	42	19	0	67	5	0	3	2	1	6	.274	.323	.403	.727
2012	Col	NL	73	277	76	20	5	8	(5	3)	130	37	37	37	9	0	54	4	0	1	7	0	8	.274	.306	.469	.775
2013	Col	NL	88	285	67	6	1	7	(5	2)	96	45	19	28	22	1	62	2	4	1	12	0	2	.235	.294	.337	.630
2014	Col	NL	105	309	83	16	7	4	(1	3)	125	44	33	42	20	0	83	6	5	2	2	3	6	.269	.323	.405	.728
2015	Bos	AL	39	74	21	1	0	1	(1	0)	25	11	10	11	5	1	26	2	1	3	0	0	0	.284	.333	.338	.671
4 ML YEARS			305	945	247	43	13	20	(12	8)	376	137	99	118	56	2	225	14	10	7	21	3	16	.261	.310	.398	.708

Brendan Ryan

Bats: R **Throws:** R **Pos:** 2B-26;3B-14;SS-6;PH-5;1B-3;PR-3;RF-2   **Ht:** 6'2" **Wt:** 195 **Born:** 3/26/1982 **Age:** 34

						BATTING															RUNNING			AVERAGES			
Year	Team	Lg	G	AB	H	2B	3B	HR	(Hm	Rd)	TB	R	RBI	RC	TBB	IBB	SO	HBP	SH	SF	SB	CS	GDP	Avg	OBP	Slg	OPS
2007	StL	NL	67	180	52	9	0	4	(2	2)	73	30	12	21	15	0	19	1	3	0	7	0	3	.289	.347	.406	.752
2008	StL	NL	80	197	48	9	0	0	(0	0)	57	30	10	12	16	0	31	2	3	0	7	2	4	.244	.307	.289	.596
2009	StL	NL	129	390	114	19	7	3	(1	2)	156	55	37	48	24	3	56	6	6	3	14	7	9	.292	.340	.400	.740
2010	StL	NL	139	439	98	19	3	2	(0	2)	129	50	36	37	33	5	60	2	9	3	11	4	6	.223	.279	.294	.573
2011	Sea	AL	123	436	108	19	3	3	(0	3)	142	51	39	46	34	0	87	10	9	5	13	3	7	.248	.313	.326	.639
2012	Sea	AL	141	407	79	19	3	3	(2	1)	113	42	31	35	44	0	98	5	8	6	11	5	4	.194	.277	.278	.555
2013	2 Tms	AL	104	319	63	12	0	4	(1	3)	87	30	22	17	23	1	73	2	4	1	4	2	11	.197	.255	.273	.528
2014	NYY	AL	49	114	19	4	0	0	(0	0)	23	5	8	2	4	0	30	3	1	2	0	2	2	.167	.211	.202	.413
2015	NYY	AL	47	96	22	6	2	0	(0	0)	32	10	8	9	5	0	29	1	1	0	0	0	1	.229	.275	.333	.608
13	Sea	AL	87	260	50	10	0	3	(1	2)	69	23	21	14	21	1	60	1	4	1	4	2	11	.192	.254	.265	.520
13	NYY	AL	17	59	13	2	0	1	(0	1)	18	7	1	3	2	0	13	1	0	0	0	0	0	.220	.258	.305	.563
Postseason			3	12	1	1	0	0	(0	0)	2	0	0	0	0	0	2	0	0	0	0	0	0	.083	.083	.167	.250
9 ML YEARS			879	2578	603	116	18	19	(6	13)	812	303	203	227	198	9	483	32	44	20	67	25	47	.234	.295	.315	.610

Kyle Ryan

Pitches: L **Bats:** L **Pos:** RP-10; SP-6   **Ht:** 6'5" **Wt:** 210 **Born:** 9/25/1991 **Age:** 24

			HOW MUCH HE PITCHED						WHAT HE GAVE UP											THE RESULTS							
Year	Team	Lg	G	GS	CG	GF	IP	BFP	H	R	ER	HR	SH	SF	HB	TBB	IBB	SO	WP	Bk	W	L	Pct	Sh	Sv-Op	Hld	ERC	ERA
2011	Wmich	A	24	24	0	0	137.0	562	145	56	48	3	4	7	9	30	1	99	5	1	6	10	.375	0	0- -	-	3.54	3.15
2012	Wmich	A	28	28	1	0	158.2	669	176	85	66	11	7	9	6	29	0	105	6	1	7	8	.467	0	0- -	-	3.79	3.74
2013	Lkland	A+	24	24	0	0	142.0	584	132	58	50	12	3	3	8	37	0	90	1	1	12	7	.632	0	0- -	-	3.32	3.17
2014	Erie	AA	21	21	1	0	126.2	531	140	67	64	15	2	5	1	32	1	78	4	1	7	10	.412	1	0- -	-	4.32	4.55
2014	Toledo	AAA	5	5	0	0	33.0	120	21	8	6	0	1	0	0	5	0	20	0	2	3	0	1.000	0	0- -	-	1.16	1.64
2015	Toledo	AAA	17	17	0	0	103.0	440	117	55	48	3	4	1	1	33	1	63	2	0	4	9	.308	0	0- -	-	4.13	4.19
2014	Det	AL	6	1	0	1	10.1	41	10	3	3	0	0	0	0	2	0	4	0	1	2	0	1.000	0	0-0	0	2.57	2.61
2015	Det	AL	16	6	0	3	56.1	237	60	29	28	9	2	1	1	20	0	30	1	0	2	4	.333	0	0-0	0	4.94	4.47
2 ML YEARS			22	7	0	4	66.2	278	70	32	31	9	2	1	1	22	0	34	1	1	4	4	.500	0	0-0	0	4.55	4.19

Hyun-Jin Ryu

Pitches: L **Bats:** R **Pos:** P   he-YUN-jin ree-YOO   **Ht:** 6'2" **Wt:** 255 **Born:** 3/25/1987 **Age:** 29

			HOW MUCH HE PITCHED						WHAT HE GAVE UP											THE RESULTS							
Year	Team	Lg	G	GS	CG	GF	IP	BFP	H	R	ER	HR	SH	SF	HB	TBB	IBB	SO	WP	Bk	W	L	Pct	Sh	Sv-Op	Hld	ERC	ERA
2013	LAD	NL	30	30	2	0	192.0	783	182	67	64	15	7	3	1	49	4	154	5	0	14	8	.636	1	0-0	0	3.13	3.00
2014	LAD	NL	26	26	0	0	152.0	631	152	60	57	8	6	2	3	29	2	139	2	0	14	7	.667	0	0-0	0	3.00	3.38
Postseason			3	3	0	0	16.0	63	14	5	5	1	0	0	0	3	0	9	0	0	1	0	1.000	0	0-0	0	2.44	2.81
2 ML YEARS			56	56	2	0	344.0	1414	334	127	121	23	13	5	4	78	6	293	7	0	28	15	.651	1	0-0	0	3.07	3.17

Marc Rzepczynski

Pitches: L **Bats:** L **Pos:** RP-72   zepp-CHINN-ski   **Ht:** 6'2" **Wt:** 220 **Born:** 8/29/1985 **Age:** 30

			HOW MUCH HE PITCHED						WHAT HE GAVE UP											THE RESULTS							
Year	Team	Lg	G	GS	CG	GF	IP	BFP	H	R	ER	HR	SH	SF	HB	TBB	IBB	SO	WP	Bk	W	L	Pct	Sh	Sv-Op	Hld	ERC	ERA
2009	Tor	AL	11	11	0	0	61.1	261	51	27	25	7	2	1	2	30	0	60	4	1	2	4	.333	0	0-0	0	3.65	3.67
2010	Tor	AL	14	12	0	0	63.2	287	72	37	35	8	1	2	5	30	1	57	4	1	4	4	.500	0	0-0	2	5.71	4.95
2011	2 Tms		71	0	0	7	62.0	256	50	27	23	3	2	0	4	26	1	61	6	0	2	6	.250	0	0-4	18	3.04	3.34
2012	StL	NL	70	0	0	14	46.2	196	46	22	22	7	0	0	0	17	2	33	3	0	1	3	.250	0	0-5	18	4.21	4.24
2013	2 Tms		38	0	0	10	30.2	129	27	13	11	2	1	1	4	10	3	29	0	0	0	0	-	0	0-0	6	3.28	3.23

Year	Team	Lg	G	GS	CG	GF	IP	BFP	H	R	ER	HR	SH	SF	HB	TBB	IBB	SO	WP	Bk	W	L	Pct	Sh	Sv-Op	Hld	ERC	ERA
2014	Cle	AL	73	0	0	8	46.0	196	42	19	14	1	1	2	3	19	3	46	2	0	0	3	.000	0	1-2	13	3.27	2.74
2015	2 Tms		72	0	0	7	35.0	158	40	29	22	3	2	2	3	14	4	41	2	0	2	4	.333	0	0-4	16	4.94	5.66
11	Tor	AL	43	0	0	6	39.1	158	28	16	13	2	1	0	3	15	0	33	5	0	2	3	.400	0	0-3	10	2.52	2.97
11	StL	NL	28	0	0	1	22.2	98	22	11	10	1	1	0	1	11	1	28	1	0	0	3	.000	0	0-1	8	4.01	3.97
13	StL	NL	11	0	0	4	10.1	50	16	9	9	1	0	1	1	4	1	9	0	0	0	0	-	0	0-0	0	7.69	7.84
13	Cle	AL	27	0	0	6	20.1	79	11	4	2	1	1	0	3	6	2	20	0	0	0	0	-	0	0-0	6	1.57	0.89
15	Cle	AL	45	0	0	6	20.1	94	23	15	10	1	1	0	1	10	3	24	1	0	2	3	.400	0	0-2	12	4.66	4.43
15	SD	NL	27	0	0	1	14.2	64	17	14	12	2	1	2	2	4	1	17	1	0	0	1	.000	0	0-2	4	5.32	7.36
Postseason			18	0	0	1	10.2	44	10	5	5	0	0	0	1	2	0	13	1	0	1	0	1.000	0	0-1	7	2.64	4.22
7 ML YEARS			349	23	0	46	345.1	1483	328	174	152	31	9	8	20	146	14	327	21	2	11	24	.314	0	1-15	73	4.02	3.96

CC Sabathia

Pitches: L **Bats:** L **Pos:** SP-29   **Ht:** 6'7" **Wt:** 285 **Born:** 7/21/1980 **Age:** 35

Year	Team	Lg	G	GS	CG	GF	IP	BFP	H	R	ER	HR	SH	SF	HB	TBB	IBB	SO	WP	Bk	W	L	Pct	Sh	Sv-Op	Hld	ERC	ERA
2001	Cle	AL	33	33	0	0	180.1	763	149	93	88	19	3	5	7	95	1	171	7	3	17	5	.773	0	0-0	0	3.86	4.39
2002	Cle	AL	33	33	2	0	210.0	891	198	109	102	17	5	10	1	88	2	149	6	3	13	11	.542	0	0-0	0	3.74	4.37
2003	Cle	AL	30	30	2	0	197.2	832	190	85	79	19	10	4	6	66	3	141	4	2	13	9	.591	1	0-0	0	3.70	3.60
2004	Cle	AL	30	30	1	0	188.0	787	176	90	86	20	3	6	7	72	3	139	1	1	11	10	.524	1	0-0	0	3.91	4.12
2005	Cle	AL	31	31	1	0	196.2	823	185	92	88	19	6	3	7	62	1	161	7	0	15	10	.600	0	0-0	0	3.55	4.03
2006	Cle	AL	28	28	6	0	192.2	802	182	83	69	17	8	5	7	44	3	172	3	0	12	11	.522	2	0-0	0	3.13	3.22
2007	Cle	AL	34	34	4	0	241.0	975	238	94	86	20	6	6	8	37	1	209	1	0	19	7	.731	1	0-0	0	3.12	3.21
2008	2 Tms		35	35	10	0	253.0	1023	223	85	76	19	9	6	7	59	1	251	2	2	17	10	.630	5	0-0	0	2.78	2.70
2009	NYY	AL	34	34	2	0	230.0	938	197	96	86	18	4	9	9	67	7	197	5	0	19	8	.704	0	0-0	0	2.89	3.37
2010	NYY	AL	34	34	2	0	237.2	970	209	92	84	20	5	8	7	74	6	197	8	1	21	7	.750	0	0-0	0	3.11	3.18
2011	NYY	AL	33	33	3	0	237.1	985	230	87	79	17	8	7	7	61	4	230	2	1	19	8	.704	1	0-0	0	3.27	3.00
2012	NYY	AL	28	28	2	0	200.0	833	184	89	75	22	4	3	8	44	2	197	4	1	15	6	.714	0	0-0	0	3.10	3.38
2013	NYY	AL	32	32	2	0	211.0	908	224	122	112	28	8	8	4	65	5	175	7	1	14	13	.519	0	0-0	0	4.32	4.78
2014	NYY	AL	8	8	0	0	46.0	209	58	31	27	10	1	1	4	10	0	48	2	0	3	4	.429	0	0-0	0	5.98	5.28
2015	NYY	AL	29	29	1	0	167.1	726	188	92	88	28	5	6	6	50	3	137	5	1	6	10	.375	0	0-0	0	5.01	4.73
08	Cle	AL	18	18	3	0	122.1	507	117	54	52	13	3	3	3	34	1	123	1	2	6	8	.429	2	0-0	0	3.52	3.83
08	Mil	NL	17	17	7	0	130.2	516	106	31	24	6	6	3	4	25	0	128	1	0	11	2	.846	3	0-0	0	2.13	1.65
Postseason			19	18	1	0	107.1	478	116	57	54	14	5	0	5	51	8	101	4	1	9	5	.643	0	0-0	0	5.19	4.53
15 ML YEARS			452	452	38	0	2988.2	12465	2831	1340	1225	293	85	87	95	894	42	2574	64	16	214	129	.624	12	0-0	0	3.51	3.69

Casey Sadler

Pitches: R **Bats:** R **Pos:** SP-1   **Ht:** 6'4" **Wt:** 225 **Born:** 7/13/1990 **Age:** 25

Year	Team	Lg	G	GS	CG	GF	IP	BFP	H	R	ER	HR	SH	SF	HB	TBB	IBB	SO	WP	Bk	W	L	Pct	Sh	Sv-Op	Hld	ERC	ERA
2011	WV	A	35	0	0	19	66.2	268	51	20	18	5	3	1	7	17	0	57	6	0	5	5	.500	0	4--	-	2.56	2.43
2012	Bradtn	A+	32	17	0	6	130.1	544	125	63	54	7	4	4	11	35	0	93	4	1	4	6	.400	0	2--	-	3.40	3.73
2013	Altna	AA	23	23	1	0	130.1	535	116	54	48	11	3	2	9	42	1	67	2	0	11	7	.611	0	0--	-	3.42	3.31
2014	Indy	AAA	21	21	1	0	124.2	506	124	49	42	11	3	4	4	24	1	77	2	1	11	4	.733	0	0--	-	3.35	3.03
2015	Indy	AAA	13	13	2	0	81.0	334	72	41	38	9	3	2	0	25	0	48	2	0	6	5	.545	0	0--	-	3.20	4.22
2014	Pit	NL	6	0	0	2	10.1	49	12	9	9	0	0	2	1	5	0	7	1	0	0	1	.000	0	0-0	0	4.80	7.84
2015	Pit	NL	1	1	0	0	5.0	19	4	2	2	1	0	0	0	1	0	5	0	0	1	0	1.000	0	0-0	0	2.98	3.60
2 ML YEARS			7	1	0	2	15.1	68	16	11	11	1	0	2	1	6	0	12	1	0	1	1	.500	0	0-0	0	4.25	6.46

Tyler Saladino

Bats: R **Throws:** R **Pos:** 3B-60;SS-11;PH-2;PR-2;1B-1   **Ht:** 6'0" **Wt:** 200 **Born:** 7/20/1989 **Age:** 26

Year	Team	Lg	G	AB	H	2B	3B	HR	(Hm	Rd)	TB	R	RBI	RC	TBB	IBB	SO	HBP	SH	SF	SB	CS	GDP	Avg	OBP	Slg	OPS
2011	WinSa	A+	102	397	107	26	9	16	(-	-)	199	75	55	55	51	1	90	9	4	3	7	7	9	.270	.363	.501	.864
2012	Brham	AA	112	418	99	15	4	4	(-	-)	134	71	39	61	75	0	91	8	2	6	38	8	5	.237	.359	.321	.680
2012	Charlt	AAA	15	49	11	2	0	0	(-	-)	13	9	6	4	4	0	16	1	1	0	1	0	1	.224	.296	.265	.562
2013	Brham	AA	118	424	97	17	2	5	(-	-)	133	49	55	49	51	0	86	6	6	6	28	8	15	.229	.316	.314	.630
2014	Charlt	AAA	82	294	91	16	4	9	(-	-)	142	41	43	53	27	0	50	1	1	2	7	1	4	.310	.367	.483	.850
2015	Charlt	AAA	52	196	50	7	2	4	(-	-)	73	28	29	31	22	0	33	4	2	7	25	2	6	.255	.332	.372	.704
2015	CWS	AL	68	236	53	6	4	4	(4	0)	79	33	20	19	12	0	51	2	3	1	8	2	9	.225	.267	.335	.602

Fernando Salas

Pitches: R **Bats:** R **Pos:** RP-72   SAH-lahss   **Ht:** 6'2" **Wt:** 200 **Born:** 5/30/1985 **Age:** 31

Year	Team	Lg	G	GS	CG	GF	IP	BFP	H	R	ER	HR	SH	SF	HB	TBB	IBB	SO	WP	Bk	W	L	Pct	Sh	Sv-Op	Hld	ERC	ERA
2010	StL	NL	27	0	0	11	30.2	133	28	13	12	4	1	1	0	15	2	29	2	0	0	0	-	0	0-1	1	4.03	3.52
2011	StL	NL	68	0	0	46	75.0	295	50	20	19	7	3	0	2	21	3	75	2	0	5	6	.455	0	24-30	6	1.94	2.28
2012	StL	NL	65	0	0	23	58.2	256	56	28	28	5	5	0	1	27	5	60	4	0	1	4	.200	0	0-3	7	3.85	4.30
2013	StL	NL	27	0	0	14	28.0	118	27	15	14	3	1	4	1	6	1	22	2	0	0	3	.000	0	0-2	2	3.22	4.50
2014	LAA	AL	57	0	0	11	58.2	239	50	22	22	5	4	1	1	14	4	61	1	1	5	0	1.000	0	0-1	8	2.54	3.38
2015	LAA	AL	72	0	0	13	63.2	269	61	34	30	8	5	4	3	12	5	74	3	0	5	2	.714	0	0-2	17	3.17	4.24
Postseason			18	0	0	3	20.1	83	16	10	8	2	0	0	0	4	1	18	1	1	0	1	.000	0	0-0	4	2.05	3.54
6 ML YEARS			316	0	0	118	314.2	1310	272	132	125	32	19	10	8	95	20	321	14	1	16	15	.516	0	24-39	41	2.95	3.58

Danny Salazar

Pitches: R Bats: L Pos: SP-30   SAL-uh-zarr   Ht: 6'0" Wt: 195 Born: 1/11/1990 Age: 26

			HOW MUCH HE PITCHED						WHAT HE GAVE UP										THE RESULTS						
Year	Team	Lg	G	GS	CG	GF	IP	BFP	H	R	ER	HR	SH	SF	HB	TBB	IBB	SO	WP	Bk	W	L	Pct	Sh	Sv-Op	Hld	ERC	ERA
2013	Cle	AL	10	10	0	0	52.0	211	44	18	18	7	1	0	0	15	0	65	3	0	2	3	.400	0	0-0	0	3.05	3.12
2014	Cle	AL	20	20	1	0	110.0	474	117	57	52	13	1	5	3	35	4	120	3	0	6	8	.429	1	0-0	0	4.30	4.25
2015	Cle	AL	30	30	0	0	185.0	757	156	79	71	23	3	4	7	53	1	195	3	2	14	10	.583	0	0-0	0	3.10	3.45
	Postseason		1	1	0	0	4.0	18	4	3	3	1	0	0	0	2	1	4	0	0	0	1	.000	0	0-0	0	5.04	6.75
	3 ML YEARS		60	60	1	0	347.0	1442	317	154	141	43	5	9	10	103	5	380	9	2	22	21	.512	1	0-0	0	3.46	3.66

Chris Sale

Pitches: L Bats: L Pos: SP-31   SAIL   Ht: 6'6" Wt: 180 Born: 3/30/1989 Age: 27

			HOW MUCH HE PITCHED						WHAT HE GAVE UP										THE RESULTS						
Year	Team	Lg	G	GS	CG	GF	IP	BFP	H	R	ER	HR	SH	SF	HB	TBB	IBB	SO	WP	Bk	W	L	Pct	Sh	Sv-Op	Hld	ERC	ERA
2010	CWS	AL	21	0	0	8	23.1	92	15	5	5	2	1	0	0	10	0	32	1	0	2	1	.667	0	4-4	2	2.30	1.93
2011	CWS	AL	58	0	0	17	71.0	288	52	22	22	6	3	0	2	27	3	79	2	0	2	2	.500	0	8-10	16	2.55	2.79
2012	CWS	AL	30	29	1	0	192.0	772	167	66	65	19	1	3	6	51	5	192	6	0	17	8	.680	0	0-1	0	3.00	3.05
2013	CWS	AL	30	30	4	0	214.1	866	184	81	73	23	4	14	4	46	2	226	8	1	11	14	.440	1	0-0	0	2.92	3.07
2014	CWS	AL	26	26	2	0	174.0	685	129	48	42	13	2	3	11	39	2	208	3	0	12	4	.750	0	0-0	0	2.18	2.17
2015	CWS	AL	31	31	1	0	208.2	854	185	88	79	23	2	3	13	42	0	274	7	0	13	11	.542	0	0-0	0	3.00	3.41
	6 ML YEARS		196	116	8	25	883.1	3557	732	310	286	86	11	13	46	215	12	1011	27	1	57	40	.588	1	12-15	18	2.76	2.91

Jarrod Saltalamacchia

Bats: B Throws: R Pos: C-47;PH-29;1B-4;DH-2   salt-ah-luh-MOCK-ee-ah   Ht: 6'4" Wt: 235 Born: 5/2/1985 Age: 31

			BATTING																	RUNNING			AVERAGES			
Year	Team	Lg	G	AB	H	2B	3B	HR	(Hm	Rd)	TB	R	RBI	RC	TBB	IBB	SO	HBP	SH	SF	SB	CS	GDP	Avg	OBP	Slg	OPS
2007	2 Tms		93	308	82	13	1	11	(6	5)	130	39	33	32	19	1	75	1	0	1	0	0	8	.266	.310	.422	.732
2008	Tex	AL	61	198	50	13	0	3	(2	1)	72	27	26	29	31	1	74	0	0	1	0	2	1	.253	.352	.364	.716
2009	Tex	AL	84	283	66	12	0	9	(6	3)	105	34	34	30	22	1	97	1	3	1	0	2	3	.233	.290	.371	.661
2010	2 Tms	AL	12	24	4	3	0	0	(0	0)	7	2	2	3	6	0	5	0	0	0	0	0	0	.167	.333	.292	.625
2011	Bos	AL	103	358	84	23	3	16	(6	10)	161	52	56	43	24	1	119	3	0	1	1	0	7	.235	.288	.450	.737
2012	Bos	AL	121	405	90	17	1	25	(12	13)	184	55	59	49	38	0	139	1	0	4	0	1	5	.222	.288	.454	.742
2013	Bos	AL	121	425	116	40	0	14	(9	5)	198	68	65	60	43	3	139	0	0	2	4	1	7	.273	.338	.466	.804
2014	Mia	NL	114	373	82	20	0	11	(5	6)	135	43	44	34	55	4	143	2	0	5	0	1	11	.220	.320	.362	.681
2015	2 Tms	NL	79	200	45	15	0	9	(7	2)	87	26	24	21	23	0	69	2	1	1	0	0	5	.225	.310	.435	.745
07	Atl	NL	47	141	40	6	0	4	(4	0)	58	11	12	13	10	1	28	1	0	1	0	0	4	.284	.333	.411	.745
07	Tex	AL	46	167	42	7	1	7	(2	5)	72	28	21	19	9	0	47	0	0	0	0	0	4	.251	.290	.431	.721
10	Tex	AL	2	5	1	0	0	0	(0	0)	1	0	1	1	0	0	1	0	0	0	0	0	0	.200	.200	.200	.400
10	Bos	AL	10	19	3	3	0	0	(0	0)	6	2	1	2	6	0	4	0	0	0	0	0	0	.158	.360	.316	.676
15	Mia	NL	9	29	2	1	0	1	(1	0)	6	3	1	0	4	0	12	0	0	0	0	0	2	.069	.182	.207	.389
15	Ari	NL	70	171	43	14	0	8	(6	2)	81	23	23	21	19	0	57	2	1	1	0	0	3	.251	.332	.474	.805
	Postseason		10	32	6	1	0	0	(0	0)	7	1	5	2	3	0	19	0	0	0	0	0	0	.188	.257	.219	.476
	9 ML YEARS		788	2574	619	156	5	98	(53	45)	1079	346	343	301	261	11	860	10	4	16	5	7	47	.240	.311	.419	.730

Jeff Samardzija

Pitches: R Bats: R Pos: SP-32   suh-MAHR-jah   Ht: 6'5" Wt: 225 Born: 1/23/1985 Age: 31

			HOW MUCH HE PITCHED						WHAT HE GAVE UP										THE RESULTS						
Year	Team	Lg	G	GS	CG	GF	IP	BFP	H	R	ER	HR	SH	SF	HB	TBB	IBB	SO	WP	Bk	W	L	Pct	Sh	Sv-Op	Hld	ERC	ERA
2008	ChC	NL	26	0	0	6	27.2	124	24	12	7	0	1	1	1	15	2	25	2	0	1	0	1.000	0	1-4	3	3.08	2.28
2009	ChC	NL	20	2	0	7	34.2	161	46	29	29	7	4	1	1	15	1	21	2	0	1	3	.250	0	0-0	0	7.13	7.53
2010	ChC	NL	7	3	0	0	19.1	100	21	22	18	4	0	0	2	20	1	9	1	0	2	2	.500	0	0-0	0	8.45	8.38
2011	ChC	NL	75	0	0	18	88.0	380	64	35	29	5	3	2	5	50	3	87	8	0	8	4	.667	0	0-2	13	3.05	2.97
2012	ChC	NL	28	28	1	0	174.2	723	157	79	74	20	5	4	4	56	2	180	10	0	9	13	.409	0	0-0	0	3.41	3.81
2013	ChC	NL	33	33	2	0	213.2	914	210	109	103	25	4	2	8	78	3	214	11	0	8	13	.381	1	0-0	0	4.11	4.34
2014	2 Tms		33	33	2	0	219.2	879	191	86	73	20	3	7	10	43	3	202	10	0	7	13	.350	2	0-0	0	2.74	2.99
2015	CWS	AL	32	32	2	0	214.0	910	228	122	118	29	4	9	12	49	0	163	5	0	11	13	.458	2	0-0	0	4.24	4.96
14	ChC	NL	17	17	0	0	108.0	449	99	44	34	7	3	4	6	31	3	103	6	0	2	7	.222	0	0-0	0	3.14	2.83
14	Oak	AL	16	16	2	0	111.2	430	92	42	39	13	0	3	4	12	0	99	4	0	5	6	.455	0	0-0	0	2.34	3.14
	Postseason		1	0	0	0	1.0	4	2	1	1	0	0	0	0	0	0	0	0	0	0	0	-	0	0-0	0	9.49	9.00
	8 ML YEARS		254	131	7	31	991.2	4191	941	494	451	110	24	26	43	326	15	901	49	0	47	61	.435	3	1-6	16	3.75	4.09

Keyvius Sampson

Pitches: R Bats: R Pos: SP-12; RP-1   KEY-vuss   Ht: 6'2" Wt: 225 Born: 1/6/1991 Age: 25

			HOW MUCH HE PITCHED						WHAT HE GAVE UP										THE RESULTS						
Year	Team	Lg	G	GS	CG	GF	IP	BFP	H	R	ER	HR	SH	SF	HB	TBB	IBB	SO	WP	Bk	W	L	Pct	Sh	Sv-Op	Hld	ERC	ERA
2011	FtWyn	A	24	24	0	0	118.0	481	81	42	38	8	1	2	6	49	0	143	7	2	12	3	.800	0	0- -	-	2.48	2.90
2012	SnAnt	AA	26	25	0	0	122.1	532	108	70	68	11	4	3	4	57	1	122	8	2	8	11	.421	0	0- -	-	3.67	5.00
2013	Tucsn	AAA	9	9	0	0	38.0	182	44	32	30	5	6	2	1	29	0	25	2	1	2	3	.400	0	0- -	-	6.97	7.11
2013	SnAnt	AA	19	18	0	0	103.1	411	74	31	26	9	3	1	3	33	2	110	6	0	10	4	.714	0	0- -	-	2.32	2.26
2014	ElPaso	AAA	38	14	0	5	91.2	425	91	73	68	19	3	3	3	68	0	94	8	0	2	5	.286	0	0- -	-	6.47	6.68
2015	Pnscla	AA	8	8	0	0	43.2	189	35	11	9	2	1	0	2	22	0	41	3	0	1	2	.333	0	0- -	-	3.33	1.85
2015	Lsvlle	AAA	8	7	0	1	39.0	178	40	22	22	1	2	2	2	22	0	33	2	0	1	2	.333	0	0- -	-	4.46	5.08
2015	Cin	NL	13	12	0	0	52.1	251	67	43	38	7	2	6	2	26	0	42	4	0	2	6	.250	0	0-0	0	6.23	6.54

Aaron Sanchez

Pitches: R Bats: R Pos: RP-30; SP-11   Ht: 6'4" Wt: 200 Born: 7/1/1992 Age: 23

Year Team	Lg	G	GS	CG	GF	IP	BFP	H	R	ER	HR	SH	SF	HB	TBB	IBB	SO	WP	Bk	W	L	Pct	Sh	Sv-Op	Hld	ERC	ERA
2011 2 Tms	Low	14	9	0	3	54.1	241	53	33	32	4	4	1	2	26	0	56	3	0	3	3	.500	0	1--	-	4.15	5.30
2012 Lnsng	A	25	18	0	3	90.1	377	64	33	25	3	3	3	7	51	0	97	6	2	8	5	.615	0	0--	-	3.03	2.49
2013 Dnedin	A+	22	20	0	1	86.1	360	63	40	32	4	0	3	5	40	0	75	4	1	4	5	.444	0	0--	-	2.73	3.34
2014 Nham	AA	14	14	0	0	66.0	285	52	34	28	2	2	2	7	40	1	57	2	1	3	4	.429	0	0--	-	3.64	3.82
2014 Buffalo	AAA	8	6	0	0	34.1	150	36	20	16	4	2	2	1	17	1	27	2	1	0	3	.000	0	0--	-	5.06	4.19
2014 Tor	AL	24	0	0	6	33.0	121	14	5	4	1	2	0	1	9	0	27	1	0	2	2	.500	0	3-3	7	0.96	1.09
2015 Tor	AL	41	11	0	10	92.1	380	74	35	33	9	2	1	3	44	2	66	8	0	7	6	.538	0	0-1	10	3.47	3.22
2 ML YEARS		65	11	0	10	125.1	501	88	40	37	10	4	1	4	53	2	88	9	0	9	8	.529	0	3-4	17	2.63	2.66

Anibal Sanchez

Pitches: R Bats: R Pos: SP-25   ah-NEE-bahl   Ht: 6'0" Wt: 205 Born: 2/27/1984 Age: 32

Year Team	Lg	G	GS	CG	GF	IP	BFP	H	R	ER	HR	SH	SF	HB	TBB	IBB	SO	WP	Bk	W	L	Pct	Sh	Sv-Op	Hld	ERC	ERA
2006 Fla	NL	18	17	2	0	114.1	469	90	39	36	9	3	1	4	46	1	72	4	1	10	3	.769	1	0-0	0	2.96	2.83
2007 Fla	NL	6	6	0	0	30.0	151	43	17	16	3	2	2	2	19	1	14	3	0	2	1	.667	0	0-0	0	7.90	4.80
2008 Fla	NL	10	10	0	0	51.2	241	54	35	32	7	4	2	6	27	2	50	1	0	2	5	.286	0	0-0	0	5.40	5.57
2009 Fla	NL	16	16	0	0	86.0	383	84	39	37	10	2	2	1	46	5	71	0	1	4	8	.333	0	0-0	0	4.51	3.87
2010 Fla	NL	32	32	1	0	195.0	841	192	89	77	10	13	3	7	70	5	157	7	0	13	12	.520	1	0-0	0	3.56	3.55
2011 Fla	NL	32	32	3	0	196.1	830	187	85	80	20	12	1	5	64	8	202	4	5	8	9	.471	2	0-0	0	3.57	3.67
2012 2 Tms		31	31	1	0	195.2	820	200	95	84	20	5	7	5	48	3	167	7	1	9	13	.409	1	0-0	0	3.70	3.86
2013 Det	AL	29	29	1	0	182.0	746	156	56	52	9	4	4	2	54	1	202	7	0	14	8	.636	1	0-0	0	2.63	2.57
2014 Det	AL	22	21	0	0	126.0	514	108	55	48	4	3	4	3	30	1	102	5	0	8	5	.615	0	0-0	0	2.35	3.43
2015 Det	AL	25	25	1	0	157.0	660	152	89	87	29	5	2	1	49	1	138	5	3	10	10	.500	1	0-0	0	4.14	4.99
12 Mia	NL	19	19	0	0	121.0	504	119	59	53	12	4	5	2	33	2	110	4	1	5	7	.417	0	0-0	0	3.55	3.94
12 Det	AL	12	12	1	0	74.2	316	81	36	31	8	1	2	3	15	1	57	3	0	4	6	.400	1	0-0	0	3.95	3.74
Postseason		7	6	0	0	38.2	161	31	14	12	5	0	1	0	14	1	43	4	0	2	4	.333	0	0-0	1	2.96	2.79
10 ML YEARS		221	219	9	0	1334.0	5655	1266	599	549	121	53	28	36	453	28	1175	43	11	80	74	.519	7	0-0	0	3.56	3.70

Carlos Sanchez

Bats: B Throws: R Pos: 2B-117;PH-5;DH-1   Ht: 5'11" Wt: 195 Born: 6/29/1992 Age: 24

Year Team	Lg	G	AB	H	2B	3B	HR	(Hm	Rd)	TB	R	RBI	RC	TBB	IBB	SO	HBP	SH	SF	SB	CS	GDP	Avg	OBP	Slg	OPS
2011 2 Tms	Low	68	280	80	11	1	1	(-	-)	96	48	30	34	20	0	51	10	7	1	8	10	5	.286	.354	.343	.697
2012 WinSa	A+	92	365	115	14	6	1	(-	-)	144	58	42	57	31	0	64	7	7	6	19	10	8	.315	.394	.395	.769
2012 Brham	AA	30	119	44	9	1	0	(-	-)	55	17	13	23	10	0	22	2	1	1	7	5	2	.370	.424	.462	.886
2012 Charllt	AAA	11	39	10	2	0	0	(-	-)	12	4	1	2	0	0	6	0	0	0	0	0	1	.256	.256	.308	.564
2013 Charllt	AAA	112	432	104	20	2	0	(-	-)	128	50	28	40	29	1	76	4	11	3	16	7	9	.241	.293	.296	.589
2014 Charllt	AAA	110	437	128	19	6	7	(-	-)	180	60	57	67	36	0	84	5	10	6	16	4	15	.293	.349	.412	.761
2015 Charllt	AAA	29	131	45	10	0	2	(-	-)	61	17	17	22	4	0	28	1	1	0	5	2	1	.344	.368	.466	.833
2014 CWS	AL	28	100	25	5	0	0	(0	0)	30	6	5	5	3	0	25	0	0	1	1	1	1	.250	.269	.300	.569
2015 CWS	AL	120	389	87	23	1	5	(2	3)	127	40	31	30	19	0	81	5	6	1	2	2	9	.224	.268	.326	.595
2 ML YEARS		148	489	112	28	1	5	(2	3)	157	46	36	35	22	0	106	5	6	2	3	3	10	.229	.268	.321	.589

Gary Sanchez

Bats: R Throws: R Pos: PH-2   Ht: 6'2" Wt: 230 Born: 12/2/1992 Age: 23

Year Team	Lg	G	AB	H	2B	3B	HR	(Hm	Rd)	TB	R	RBI	RC	TBB	IBB	SO	HBP	SH	SF	SB	CS	GDP	Avg	OBP	Slg	OPS
2011 CtnSC	A	82	301	77	16	1	17	(-	-)	146	49	52	50	36	0	93	2	0	4	2	1	9	.256	.335	.485	.820
2012 2 Tms		116	435	126	29	1	18	(-	-)	211	65	85	73	32	0	106	5	0	2	15	4	13	.290	.344	.485	.829
2013 Tampa	A+	94	362	92	21	0	13	(-	-)	152	38	61	50	28	1	71	5	0	4	3	1	8	.254	.313	.420	.733
2013 Trntn	AA	23	92	23	6	0	2	(-	-)	35	12	10	14	13	0	16	4	0	1	0	0	3	.250	.364	.380	.744
2014 Trntn	AA	110	429	116	19	0	13	(-	-)	174	48	65	61	43	0	91	2	0	3	1	1	15	.270	.338	.406	.743
2015 Trntn	AA	58	233	61	14	0	12	(-	-)	111	33	36	37	18	1	50	2	0	1	6	0	2	.262	.319	.476	.795
2015 S-WB	AAA	35	132	39	9	0	6	(-	-)	66	17	26	22	11	0	28	1	0	2	1	2	7	.295	.349	.500	.849
2015 NYY	AL	2	2	0	0	0	0	(0	0)	0	0	0	0	0	0	1	0	0	0	0	0	0	.000	.000	.000	.000

Hector Sanchez

Bats: B Throws: R Pos: C-16;PH-12   Ht: 6'0" Wt: 235 Born: 11/17/1989 Age: 26

Year Team	Lg	G	AB	H	2B	3B	HR	(Hm	Rd)	TB	R	RBI	RC	TBB	IBB	SO	HBP	SH	SF	SB	CS	GDP	Avg	OBP	Slg	OPS
2015 Scrmto*	AAA	37	139	38	6	0	4	(-	-)	56	18	14	18	9	0	25	1	1	2	0	0	4	.273	.318	.403	.721
2011 SF	NL	13	31	8	2	0	0	(0	0)	10	0	1	2	3	0	6	0	0	0	0	0	1	.258	.324	.323	.646
2012 SF	NL	74	218	61	15	0	3	(1	2)	85	22	34	22	5	0	52	1	0	3	0	0	8	.280	.295	.390	.685
2013 SF	NL	63	129	32	4	0	3	(0	3)	45	8	19	14	7	0	29	3	0	1	0	0	1	.248	.300	.349	.649
2014 SF	NL	66	163	32	8	0	3	(1	2)	49	8	28	12	8	1	55	2	0	4	0	1	2	.196	.237	.301	.538
2015 SF	NL	28	56	10	4	0	1	(0	1)	17	5	5	3	2	0	14	0	1	0	0	0	1	.179	.207	.304	.510
Postseason		4	11	1	0	0	0	(0	0)	1	1	0	1	2	0	7	0	0	0	0	0	0	.091	.231	.091	.322
5 ML YEARS		244	597	143	33	0	10	(2	8)	206	43	87	53	25	1	156	6	1	8	0	1	13	.240	.274	.345	.619

Tony Sanchez

Bats: R Throws: R Pos: C-2;PH-1   Ht: 5'11" Wt: 220 Born: 5/20/1988 Age: 28

Year	Team	Lg	G	AB	H	2B	3B	HR	(Hm	Rd)	TB	R	RBI	RC	TBB	IBB	SO	HBP	SH	SF	SB	CS	GDP	Avg	OBP	Slg	OPS
2015	Indy*	AAA	94	313	74	20	2	3	(-	-)	107	38	47	41	45	2	65	8	0	5	4	3	9	.236	.342	.342	.684
2013	Pit	NL	22	60	14	4	0	2	(1	1)	24	9	5	4	3	0	14	2	0	1	0	0	2	.233	.288	.400	.688
2014	Pit	NL	26	75	20	1	0	2	(0	2)	27	3	13	9	3	0	28	1	0	1	0	0	0	.267	.300	.360	.660
2015	Pit	NL	3	8	3	0	0	0	(0	0)	3	2	0	1	1	0	3	0	0	0	0	0	0	.375	.444	.375	.819
3 ML YEARS			51	143	37	5	0	4	(1	3)	54	14	18	14	7	0	45	3	0	2	0	0	2	.259	.303	.378	.681

Pablo Sandoval

Bats: B Throws: R Pos: 3B-123;PH-4   Ht: 5'11" Wt: 255 Born: 8/11/1986 Age: 29

Year	Team	Lg	G	AB	H	2B	3B	HR	(Hm	Rd)	TB	R	RBI	RC	TBB	IBB	SO	HBP	SH	SF	SB	CS	GDP	Avg	OBP	Slg	OPS
2008	SF	NL	41	145	50	10	1	3	(1	2)	71	24	24	24	4	1	14	1	0	4	0	0	6	.345	.357	.490	.847
2009	SF	NL	153	572	189	44	5	25	(13	12)	318	79	90	113	52	13	83	4	0	5	5	5	10	.330	.387	.556	.943
2010	SF	NL	152	563	151	34	3	13	(9	4)	230	61	63	55	47	12	81	1	0	5	3	2	26	.268	.323	.409	.732
2011	SF	NL	117	426	134	26	3	23	(7	16)	235	55	70	72	32	9	63	0	1	7	2	4	12	.315	.357	.552	.909
2012	SF	NL	108	396	112	25	2	12	(7	5)	177	59	63	60	38	4	59	1	0	7	1	1	13	.283	.342	.447	.789
2013	SF	NL	141	525	146	27	2	14	(6	8)	219	52	79	78	47	5	79	6	0	6	0	0	19	.278	.341	.417	.758
2014	SF	NL	157	588	164	26	3	16	(9	7)	244	68	73	78	39	6	85	4	0	7	0	0	16	.279	.324	.415	.739
2015	Bos	AL	126	470	115	25	1	10	(4	6)	172	43	47	46	25	1	73	7	1	2	0	0	14	.245	.292	.366	.658
Postseason			39	154	53	13	0	6	(3	3)	84	21	20	27	10	3	22	2	0	1	0	0	7	.344	.389	.545	.935
8 ML YEARS			995	3685	1061	217	20	116	(56	60)	1666	441	509	526	284	51	537	24	2	43	11	12	116	.288	.339	.452	.791

Jerry Sands

Bats: R Throws: R Pos: RF-32;PH-12;1B-11;LF-7;PR-2;DH-1   Ht: 6'4" Wt: 225 Born: 9/28/1987 Age: 28

Year	Team	Lg	G	AB	H	2B	3B	HR	(Hm	Rd)	TB	R	RBI	RC	TBB	IBB	SO	HBP	SH	SF	SB	CS	GDP	Avg	OBP	Slg	OPS
2015	Clmbs*	AAA	66	223	64	12	1	14	(-	-)	120	41	46	50	45	0	40	4	0	4	1	2	7	.287	.409	.538	.948
2011	LAD	NL	61	198	50	15	0	4	(2	2)	77	20	26	25	25	0	51	1	2	1	3	3	5	.253	.338	.389	.727
2012	LAD	NL	9	23	4	2	0	0	(0	0)	6	2	1	1	1	0	9	0	0	0	0	0	0	.174	.208	.261	.469
2014	TB	AL	12	21	4	0	0	1	(1	0)	7	1	4	1	0	0	6	1	0	0	0	0	2	.190	.227	.333	.561
2015	Cle	AL	50	123	29	5	1	4	(2	2)	48	11	19	15	9	0	36	0	0	1	0	0	0	.236	.286	.390	.676
4 ML YEARS			132	365	87	22	1	9	(5	4)	138	34	50	42	35	0	102	2	2	2	3	3	7	.238	.307	.378	.685

Miguel Sano

Bats: R Throws: R Pos: DH-69;3B-9;1B-2;PH-2   sah-NO   Ht: 6'4" Wt: 260 Born: 5/11/1993 Age: 23

Year	Team	Lg	G	AB	H	2B	3B	HR	(Hm	Rd)	TB	R	RBI	RC	TBB	IBB	SO	HBP	SH	SF	SB	CS	GDP	Avg	OBP	Slg	OPS
2011	Elizab	R	66	267	78	18	7	20	(-	-)	170	58	59	58	23	0	77	2	0	1	5	4	4	.292	.352	.637	.988
2012	Beloit	A	129	457	118	28	4	28	(-	-)	238	75	100	93	80	4	144	8	0	8	8	3	10	.258	.373	.521	.893
2013	FtMyrs	A+	56	206	68	15	2	16	(-	-)	135	51	48	55	29	2	61	6	0	2	9	2	2	.330	.424	.655	1.079
2013	NwBrit	AA	67	233	55	15	3	19	(-	-)	133	35	55	47	36	2	81	4	0	3	2	1	6	.236	.344	.571	.915
2015	Chatt	AA	66	241	66	18	1	15	(-	-)	131	55	48	51	38	2	68	3	0	4	5	1	5	.274	.374	.544	.918
2015	Min	AL	80	279	75	17	1	18	(10	8)	148	46	52	62	53	1	119	1	0	2	1	1	4	.269	.385	.530	.916

Carlos Santana

Bats: B Throws: R Pos: 1B-132;DH-21;PH-1   Ht: 5'11" Wt: 210 Born: 4/8/1986 Age: 30

Year	Team	Lg	G	AB	H	2B	3B	HR	(Hm	Rd)	TB	R	RBI	RC	TBB	IBB	SO	HBP	SH	SF	SB	CS	GDP	Avg	OBP	Slg	OPS
2010	Cle	AL	46	150	39	13	0	6	(2	4)	70	23	22	25	37	2	29	1	0	4	3	0	3	.260	.401	.467	.868
2011	Cle	AL	155	552	132	35	2	27	(14	13)	252	84	79	81	97	7	133	2	0	7	5	3	15	.239	.351	.457	.808
2012	Cle	AL	143	507	128	27	2	18	(7	11)	213	72	76	77	91	4	101	3	0	8	3	5	21	.252	.365	.420	.785
2013	Cle	AL	154	541	145	39	1	20	(12	8)	246	75	74	93	93	6	110	4	0	4	3	1	7	.268	.377	.455	.832
2014	Cle	AL	152	541	125	25	0	27	(13	14)	231	68	85	88	113	5	124	3	0	3	5	2	13	.231	.365	.427	.792
2015	Cle	AL	154	550	127	29	2	19	(6	13)	217	72	85	80	108	8	122	3	0	5	11	3	20	.231	.357	.395	.752
Postseason			1	4	2	1	0	0	(0	0)	3	0	0	0	0	0	1	0	0	0	0	0	0	.500	.500	.750	1.250
6 ML YEARS			804	2841	696	168	7	117	(54	63)	1229	394	421	444	539	32	619	16	0	31	30	14	79	.245	.365	.433	.798

Danny Santana

Bats: B Throws: R Pos: SS-66;PH-12;PR-8;CF-5;DH-5;RF-1   Ht: 5'11" Wt: 185 Born: 11/7/1990 Age: 25

Year	Team	Lg	G	AB	H	2B	3B	HR	(Hm	Rd)	TB	R	RBI	RC	TBB	IBB	SO	HBP	SH	SF	SB	CS	GDP	Avg	OBP	Slg	OPS
2011	Beloit	A	104	365	90	15	5	7	(-	-)	136	55	41	41	25	0	98	4	10	5	24	15	6	.247	.298	.373	.671
2012	FtMyrs	A+	121	507	145	21	9	8	(-	-)	208	70	60	69	29	2	77	5	3	3	17	11	4	.286	.329	.410	.739
2013	NwBrit	AA	131	539	160	22	10	2	(-	-)	208	66	45	72	24	1	94	8	11	5	30	13	8	.297	.333	.386	.719
2014	Roch	AAA	24	97	26	7	2	0	(-	-)	37	15	7	12	6	0	28	0	2	0	4	1	1	.268	.311	.381	.692
2015	Roch	AAA	35	152	49	10	4	3	(-	-)	76	24	15	26	7	0	25	0	1	2	6	3	3	.322	.348	.500	.848
2014	Min	AL	101	405	129	27	7	7	(3	4)	191	70	40	72	19	0	98	3	2	1	20	4	3	.319	.353	.472	.824
2015	Min	AL	91	261	56	10	5	0	(0	0)	76	30	21	16	6	1	68	3	7	0	8	4	7	.215	.241	.291	.532
2 ML YEARS			192	666	185	37	12	7	(3	4)	267	100	61	88	25	1	166	6	9	1	28	8	10	.278	.309	.401	.710

Domingo Santana

Bats: R **Throws:** R **Pos:** RF-25;CF-24;LF-14;PH-5   **Ht:** 6'5" **Wt:** 225 **Born:** 4/7/1993 **Age:** 23

								BATTING												RUNNING			AVERAGES			
Year Team	Lg	G	AB	H	2B	3B	HR	(Hm Rd)	TB	R	RBI	RC	TBB	IBB	SO	HBP	SH	SF	SB	CS	GDP	Avg	OBP	Slg	OPS
2011 2 Tms	Low	113	418	120	33	4	12	(- -)	197	58	53	72	32	3	135	17	0	0	5	1	5	.287	.362	.471	.833
2012 Lancst	A+	119	457	138	26	6	23	(- -)	245	87	97	95	55	0	148	9	0	4	7	1	10	.302	.385	.536	.921
2013 CpChr	AA	112	416	105	23	2	25	(- -)	207	72	64	73	46	1	139	13	0	1	12	5	7	.252	.345	.498	.842
2014 OkCity	AAA	120	443	131	27	2	16	(- -)	210	63	81	83	64	1	149	2	0	4	6	4	3	.296	.384	.474	.858
2015 Fresno	AAA	75	275	88	18	3	16	(- -)	160	62	59	65	48	1	91	3	0	0	1	4	2	.320	.426	.582	1.008
2015 ColSpr	AAA	20	79	30	5	1	2	(- -)	43	13	18	17	6	0	17	0	0	0	1	1	3	.380	.424	.544	.968
2014 Hou	AL	6	17	0	0	0	0	(0 0)	0	0	1	0	1	0	14	0	0	0	0	0	0	.000	.000	.000	.056
2015 2 Tms		52	160	38	7	0	8	(3 5)	69	20	26	28	20	0	63	5	0	2	4	1	2	.238	.337	.431	.768
15 Hou	AL	14	39	10	2	0	2	(0 2)	18	6	8	8	2	0	17	1	0	0	2	1	1	.256	.310	.462	.771
15 Mil	NL	38	121	28	5	0	6	(3 3)	51	14	18	20	18	0	46	4	0	2	2	0	1	.231	.345	.421	.766
2 ML YEARS		58	177	38	7	0	8	(3 5)	69	21	26	28	21	0	77	5	0	2	4	1	2	.215	.312	.390	.702

Ervin Santana

Pitches: R **Bats:** R **Pos:** SP-17   **Ht:** 6'2" **Wt:** 175 **Born:** 12/12/1982 **Age:** 33

		HOW MUCH HE PITCHED						WHAT HE GAVE UP												THE RESULTS						
Year Team	Lg	G	GS	CG	GF	IP	BFP	H	R	ER	HR	SH	SF	HB	TBB	IBB	SO	WP	Bk	W	L	Pct	Sh	Sv-Op	Hld	ERC	ERA
2005 LAA	AL	23	23	1	0	133.2	583	139	73	69	17	1	4	8	47	2	99	4	0	12	8	.600	1	0-0	0	4.51	4.65
2006 LAA	AL	33	33	0	0	204.0	846	181	106	97	21	4	10	11	70	2	141	10	2	16	8	.667	0	0-0	0	3.51	4.28
2007 LAA	AL	28	26	0	1	150.0	675	174	103	96	26	3	2	8	58	3	126	7	0	7	14	.333	0	0-0	0	5.69	5.76
2008 LAA	AL	32	32	2	0	219.0	897	198	89	85	23	3	5	8	47	2	214	5	1	16	7	.696	1	0-0	0	3.00	3.49
2009 LAA	AL	24	23	2	0	139.2	614	159	83	78	24	2	1	10	47	4	107	4	0	8	8	.500	2	0-0	1	5.47	5.03
2010 LAA	AL	33	33	4	0	222.2	954	221	104	97	27	8	8	12	73	2	169	11	1	17	10	.630	1	0-0	0	4.10	3.92
2011 LAA	AL	33	33	4	0	228.2	949	207	95	86	26	4	7	8	72	4	178	10	1	11	12	.478	1	0-0	0	3.45	3.38
2012 LAA	AL	30	30	1	0	178.0	764	165	109	102	39	2	2	9	61	2	133	4	0	9	13	.409	1	0-0	0	4.38	5.16
2013 KC	AL	32	32	0	0	211.0	859	190	85	76	26	2	3	6	51	3	161	6	0	9	10	.474	0	0-0	0	3.19	3.24
2014 Atl	NL	31	31	0	0	196.0	817	193	90	86	16	12	12	4	63	4	179	9	0	14	10	.583	0	0-0	0	3.68	3.95
2015 Min	AL	17	17	0	0	108.0	457	104	50	48	12	4	2	4	36	2	82	3	0	7	5	.583	0	0-0	0	3.82	4.00
Postseason		8	2	0	3	22.2	101	21	17	14	4	1	1	3	9	1	14	0	0	2	2	.500	0	0-0	0	4.55	5.56
11 ML YEARS		316	313	14	1	1990.2	8415	1931	987	920	257	45	56	88	625	30	1589	73	5	126	105	.545	7	0-0	1	3.94	4.16

Hector Santiago

Pitches: L **Bats:** R **Pos:** SP-32; RP-1   **Ht:** 6'0" **Wt:** 215 **Born:** 12/16/1987 **Age:** 28

		HOW MUCH HE PITCHED						WHAT HE GAVE UP												THE RESULTS						
Year Team	Lg	G	GS	CG	GF	IP	BFP	H	R	ER	HR	SH	SF	HB	TBB	IBB	SO	WP	Bk	W	L	Pct	Sh	Sv-Op	Hld	ERC	ERA
2011 CWS	AL	2	0	0	1	5.1	18	1	0	0	0	0	0	0	1	1	2	1	0	0	0	-	0	0-0	0	0.16	0.00
2012 CWS	AL	42	4	0	19	70.1	306	54	26	26	10	2	1	7	40	1	79	5	2	4	1	.800	0	4-6	4	4.11	3.33
2013 CWS	AL	34	23	0	4	149.0	656	137	69	59	17	3	3	15	72	2	137	2	0	4	9	.308	0	0-0	0	4.43	3.56
2014 LAA	AL	30	24	0	2	127.1	544	120	63	53	15	1	3	3	53	3	108	5	1	6	9	.400	0	0-0	1	4.02	3.75
2015 LAA	AL	33	32	0	0	180.2	776	156	80	72	29	4	4	10	71	5	162	1	3	9	9	.500	0	0-0	0	3.82	3.59
Postseason		1	0	0	0	1.1	7	1	2	2	1	0	0	0	2	0	0	0	0	0	0	-	0	0-0	0	12.98	13.50
5 ML YEARS		141	83	0	26	532.2	2300	468	238	210	71	10	11	35	237	12	488	14	6	23	28	.451	0	4-6	5	4.02	3.55

Sergio Santos

Pitches: R **Bats:** R **Pos:** RP-14   **Ht:** 6'4" **Wt:** 215 **Born:** 7/4/1983 **Age:** 32

		HOW MUCH HE PITCHED						WHAT HE GAVE UP												THE RESULTS						
Year Team	Lg	G	GS	CG	GF	IP	BFP	H	R	ER	HR	SH	SF	HB	TBB	IBB	SO	WP	Bk	W	L	Pct	Sh	Sv-Op	Hld	ERC	ERA
2015 OkCity*	AAA	6	0	0	0	4.2	21	5	2	2	0	0	0	0	3	0	8	0	0	0	0	-	0	0--	0	4.78	3.86
2010 CWS	AL	56	0	0	13	51.2	235	53	18	17	2	2	1	3	26	3	56	8	0	2	2	.500	0	1-3	14	4.22	2.96
2011 CWS	AL	63	0	0	50	63.1	260	41	25	25	6	1	1	3	29	5	92	5	0	4	5	.444	0	30-36	2	2.46	3.55
2012 Tor	AL	6	0	0	4	5.0	24	6	5	5	1	0	1	0	4	0	4	1	0	0	1	.000	0	2-4	0	7.98	9.00
2013 Tor	AL	29	0	0	6	25.2	90	11	5	5	1	0	2	0	4	2	28	1	0	1	1	.500	0	1-3	8	0.69	1.75
2014 Tor	AL	26	0	0	14	21.0	106	28	22	20	5	0	2	0	18	2	29	4	0	0	3	.000	0	5-8	0	9.19	8.57
2015 2 Tms		14	0	0	8	16.1	73	16	9	9	3	0	1	0	7	1	18	4	0	0	0	-	0	0-0	0	4.40	4.96
15 LAD	NL	12	0	0	6	13.1	61	13	7	7	2	0	1	0	7	1	15	4	0	0	0	-	0	0-0	0	4.48	4.73
15 NYY	AL	2	0	0	2	3.0	12	3	2	2	1	0	0	0	0	0	3	0	0	0	0	-	0	0-0	0	3.79	6.00
6 ML YEARS		194	0	0	95	183.0	788	155	84	81	18	3	8	6	88	13	227	23	0	7	12	.368	0	39-54	24	3.52	3.98

Luis Sardinas

Bats: B **Throws:** R **Pos:** 2B-16;SS-14;PH-6;3B-3   sar-DEEN-yas   **Ht:** 6'1" **Wt:** 150 **Born:** 5/16/1993 **Age:** 23

								BATTING												RUNNING			AVERAGES			
Year Team	Lg	G	AB	H	2B	3B	HR	(Hm Rd)	TB	R	RBI	RC	TBB	IBB	SO	HBP	SH	SF	SB	CS	GDP	Avg	OBP	Slg	OPS
2011 Rngrs	R	14	52	16	2	1	0	(- -)	20	11	7	8	4	0	10	2	0	2	2	1	0	.308	.367	.385	.751
2012 Hkry	A	96	374	109	14	2	2	(- -)	133	65	30	52	29	0	52	4	2	3	32	9	5	.291	.346	.356	.702
2013 MrtlBh	A+	97	383	114	15	3	1	(- -)	138	69	31	55	32	1	54	7	5	5	27	8	5	.298	.358	.360	.719
2013 Frisco	AA	29	135	35	4	0	1	(- -)	42	12	15	12	4	0	21	1	1	0	5	2	4	.259	.286	.311	.597
2014 Frisco	AA	21	87	22	5	1	0	(- -)	29	12	9	7	3	0	12	0	0	0	1	1	1	.253	.278	.333	.611
2014 RdRck	AAA	60	262	76	15	2	1	(- -)	98	39	28	31	8	0	39	0	2	1	9	4	6	.290	.310	.374	.684
2015 ColSpr	AAA	103	390	110	17	5	1	(- -)	140	51	33	47	20	0	54	1	5	0	16	4	17	.282	.319	.359	.678
2014 Tex	AL	43	115	30	6	0	0	(0 0)	36	12	8	9	5	0	21	2	3	0	5	1	5	.261	.303	.313	.616
2015 Mil	NL	36	97	19	0	1	0	(0 0)	21	8	4	5	6	1	25	0	1	1	0	0	3	.196	.240	.216	.457
2 ML YEARS		79	212	49	6	1	0	(0 0)	57	20	12	14	11	1	46	2	4	1	5	1	8	.231	.274	.269	.543

Michael Saunders

Bats: L **Throws:** R **Pos:** RF-6;LF-3   **Ht:** 6'4" **Wt:** 225 **Born:** 11/19/1986 **Age:** 29

									BATTING											RUNNING			AVERAGES			
Year	Team	Lg	G	AB	H	2B	3B	HR	(Hm | Rd)	TB	R	RBI	RC	TBB	IBB	SO	HBP	SH	SF	SB	CS	GDP	Avg	OBP	Slg	OPS
2009	Sea	AL	46	122	27	1	3	0	(0 | 0)	34	13	4	8	6	0	40	0	1	0	4	1	1	.221	.258	.279	.537
2010	Sea	AL	100	289	61	11	2	10	(5 | 5)	106	29	33	31	35	0	84	0	2	1	6	3	1	.211	.295	.367	.662
2011	Sea	AL	58	161	24	5	0	2	(1 | 1)	35	16	8	2	12	1	56	0	5	1	6	2	1	.149	.207	.217	.424
2012	Sea	AL	139	507	125	31	3	19	(8 | 11)	219	71	57	67	43	0	132	1	1	1	21	4	6	.247	.306	.432	.738
2013	Sea	AL	132	406	96	23	3	12	(5 | 7)	161	59	46	49	54	4	118	1	1	6	13	5	6	.236	.323	.397	.720
2014	Sea	AL	78	231	63	11	3	8	(4 | 4)	104	38	34	37	26	1	59	0	2	4	4	5	2	.273	.341	.450	.791
2015	Tor	AL	9	31	6	0	0	0	(0 | 0)	6	2	3	3	5	0	10	0	0	0	0	0	1	.194	.306	.194	.499
7 ML YEARS			562	1747	402	82	14	51	(23 | 28)	665	228	185	197	181	6	499	2	12	13	54	20	18	.230	.301	.381	.682

Rob Scahill

Pitches: R **Bats:** L **Pos:** RP-28   SKAY-hill   **Ht:** 6'2" **Wt:** 210 **Born:** 2/15/1987 **Age:** 29

				HOW MUCH HE PITCHED					WHAT HE GAVE UP										THE RESULTS						
Year	Team	Lg	G	GS	CG	GF	IP	BFP	H	R	ER	HR	SH	SF	HB	TBB	IBB	SO	WP	Bk	W	L	Pct	Sh	Sv-Op	Hld	ERC	ERA
2015 Indy*	AAA		6	0	0	2	6.2	31	7	3	3	0	0	0	0	3	0	6	0	0	0	0	-	0	0--	-	3.58	4.05
2012	Col	NL	6	0	0	3	8.2	33	7	1	1	0	0	0	0	3	0	4	0	0	0	0	-	0	0-0	0	2.43	1.04
2013	Col	NL	23	0	0	6	33.1	149	40	19	19	5	3	0	4	9	1	20	1	0	1	0	1.000	0	0-0	1	5.55	5.13
2014	Col	NL	12	0	0	3	15.0	72	17	8	8	3	0	2	1	9	2	11	0	0	1	0	1.000	0	0-1	0	6.37	4.80
2015	Pit	NL	28	0	0	13	30.2	142	33	15	9	3	1	1	1	16	5	24	1	0	2	4	.333	0	0-0	1	4.70	2.64
4 ML YEARS			69	0	0	25	87.2	396	97	43	37	11	4	3	6	37	8	59	2	0	4	4	.500	0	0-1	2	5.06	3.80

Jordan Schafer

Bats: L **Throws:** L **Pos:** CF-26;LF-1;PH-1;PR-1   **Ht:** 6'1" **Wt:** 205 **Born:** 9/4/1986 **Age:** 29

									BATTING											RUNNING			AVERAGES			
Year	Team	Lg	G	AB	H	2B	3B	HR	(Hm	Rd)	TB	R	RBI	RC	TBB	IBB	SO	HBP	SH	SF	SB	CS	GDP	Avg	OBP	Slg	OPS
2009	Atl	NL	50	167	34	8	0	2	(0	2)	48	18	8	11	27	3	63	0	0	1	2	1	2	.204	.313	.287	.600
2011	2 Tms	NL	82	302	73	10	3	2	(0	2)	95	46	13	34	28	0	70	2	4	1	22	4	4	.242	.309	.315	.624
2012	Hou	NL	106	313	66	10	4	2	(4	0)	92	40	23	32	36	3	106	3	6	1	27	9	3	.211	.297	.294	.591
2013	Atl	NL	94	231	57	8	3	3	(0	3)	80	32	21	31	29	2	73	0	5	0	22	6	1	.247	.331	.346	.677
2014	2 Tms	NL	104	210	50	9	1	1	(0	1)	64	26	15	20	22	1	48	0	8	0	30	7	1	.238	.310	.305	.615
2015	Min	AL	27	69	15	3	0	0	(0	0)	18	9	5	5	3	0	23	0	2	0	0	3	0	.217	.250	.261	.511
11	Atl	NL	52	196	47	6	3	1	(0	1)	62	32	7	22	18	0	42	1	4	0	15	4	3	.240	.307	.316	.623
11	Hou	NL	30	106	26	4	0	1	(0	1)	33	14	6	12	10	0	28	1	0	1	7	0	1	.245	.314	.311	.625
14	Atl	NL	63	80	13	4	0	0	(0	0)	17	9	2	3	10	1	20	0	3	0	15	2	1	.163	.256	.213	.468
14	Min	AL	41	130	37	5	1	1	(0	1)	47	17	13	17	12	0	28	0	5	0	15	5	0	.285	.345	.362	.707
Postseason		1	1	0	0	0	0	(0	0)	0	0	0	0	0	0	1	0	0	0	0	0	0	.000	.000	.000	.000
6 ML YEARS			463	1292	295	48	9	12	(4	8)	397	171	85	133	145	9	383	5	25	3	103	30	11	.228	.308	.307	.615

Logan Schafer

Bats: L **Throws:** L **Pos:** CF-49;PH-21;PR-3;LF-1   **Ht:** 6'1" **Wt:** 190 **Born:** 9/8/1986 **Age:** 29

									BATTING											RUNNING			AVERAGES			
Year	Team	Lg	G	AB	H	2B	3B	HR	(Hm	Rd)	TB	R	RBI	RC	TBB	IBB	SO	HBP	SH	SF	SB	CS	GDP	Avg	OBP	Slg	OPS
2015 ColSpr*	AAA		72	260	67	15	2	1	(-	-)	89	29	17	27	14	0	35	0	5	3	3	1	5	.258	.292	.342	.635
2011	Mil	NL	8	3	1	0	0	0	(0	0)	1	1	0	0	1	0	1	0	1	0	0	0	0	.333	.500	.333	.833
2012	Mil	NL	16	23	7	1	2	0	(0	0)	12	3	5	4	1	0	3	0	0	1	0	1	0	.304	.320	.522	.842
2013	Mil	NL	134	298	63	15	3	4	(2	2)	96	29	33	31	25	1	60	3	11	0	7	1	5	.211	.279	.322	.601
2014	Mil	NL	65	116	21	9	1	0	(0	0)	32	13	8	11	15	3	27	1	3	1	2	1	0	.181	.278	.276	.554
2015	Mil	NL	69	122	27	6	1	1	(1	0)	38	17	6	8	12	0	29	2	6	1	1	0	3	.221	.299	.311	.611
5 ML YEARS			292	562	119	31	7	5	(3	2)	179	63	52	54	54	4	120	6	21	3	10	3	8	.212	.286	.319	.605

Scott Schebler

Bats: L **Throws:** R **Pos:** PH-12;LF-7;RF-6   SHEB-ler   **Ht:** 6'0" **Wt:** 225 **Born:** 10/6/1990 **Age:** 25

									BATTING											RUNNING			AVERAGES			
Year	Team	Lg	G	AB	H	2B	3B	HR	(Hm	Rd)	TB	R	RBI	RC	TBB	IBB	SO	HBP	SH	SF	SB	CS	GDP	Avg	OBP	Slg	OPS
2011	Ogden	R+	70	295	84	17	8	13	(-	-)	156	44	58	50	13	2	97	5	0	2	1	1	4	.285	.324	.529	.853
2012	Gt Lks	A	137	515	134	32	8	6	(-	-)	200	67	67	64	30	3	99	10	2	3	17	11	8	.260	.312	.388	.700
2013	Rcuca	A+	125	477	141	29	13	27	(-	-)	277	95	91	99	35	0	140	15	4	3	16	5	5	.296	.360	.581	.941
2014	Chatt	AA	135	489	137	23	14	28	(-	-)	272	82	73	100	45	4	110	22	1	3	10	4	8	.280	.365	.556	.921
2015	OkCity	AAA	121	432	104	16	9	13	(-	-)	177	57	50	62	40	8	93	12	0	1	15	2	6	.241	.322	.410	.731
2015	LAD	NL	19	36	9	0	0	3	(1	2)	18	6	4	4	3	1	13	1	0	0	2	1	0	.250	.325	.500	.825

Tanner Scheppers

Pitches: R **Bats:** R **Pos:** RP-42   **Ht:** 6'4" **Wt:** 200 **Born:** 1/17/1987 **Age:** 29

				HOW MUCH HE PITCHED					WHAT HE GAVE UP										THE RESULTS						
Year	Team	Lg	G	GS	CG	GF	IP	BFP	H	R	ER	HR	SH	SF	HB	TBB	IBB	SO	WP	Bk	W	L	Pct	Sh	Sv-Op	Hld	ERC	ERA
2015 Frisco*	AA		6	0	0	0	5.2	24	4	2	1	0	0	0	0	3	0	8	1	0	0	0	-	0	0--	-	2.29	1.59
2015 RdRck*	AAA		13	0	0	6	14.0	59	11	5	3	0	1	3	1	8	2	11	4	0	0	2	.000	0	2--	-	2.97	1.93
2012	Tex	AL	39	0	0	13	32.1	152	47	18	16	6	3	1	2	9	3	30	4	0	1	1	.500	0	1-1	4	7.05	4.45
2013	Tex	AL	76	0	0	11	76.2	302	58	21	16	6	0	0	7	24	4	59	4	0	6	2	.750	0	1-3	27	2.71	1.88
2014	Tex	AL	8	4	0	0	23.0	111	31	24	23	6	0	1	3	10	0	17	2	0	0	1	.000	0	0-0	1	8.21	9.00
2015	Tex	AL	42	0	0	7	38.1	176	37	25	24	6	0	3	2	23	3	32	1	0	4	1	.800	0	0-3	12	5.09	5.63
4 ML YEARS			165	4	0	31	170.1	741	173	88	79	24	3	5	14	66	10	138	11	0	11	5	.688	0	2-7	44	4.69	4.17

Max Scherzer

Pitches: R **Bats:** R **Pos:** SP-33　　　　SHERR-zer　　　　**Ht:** 6'3" **Wt:** 215 **Born:** 7/27/1984 **Age:** 31

Year	Team	Lg	G	GS	CG	GF	IP	BFP	H	R	ER	HR	SH	SF	HB	TBB	IBB	SO	WP	Bk	W	L	Pct	Sh	Sv-Op	Hld	ERC	ERA
2008	Ari	NL	16	7	0	2	56.0	237	48	24	19	5	4	2	5	21	1	66	2	0	0	4	.000	0	0-0	0	3.45	3.05
2009	Ari	NL	30	30	0	0	170.1	741	166	94	78	20	5	6	10	63	1	174	5	1	9	11	.450	0	0-0	0	4.12	4.12
2010	Det	AL	31	31	0	0	195.2	800	174	84	76	20	5	5	7	70	1	184	8	0	12	11	.522	0	0-0	0	3.56	3.50
2011	Det	AL	33	33	0	0	195.0	833	207	101	96	29	3	7	7	56	1	174	12	0	15	9	.625	0	0-0	0	4.48	4.43
2012	Det	AL	32	32	0	0	187.2	787	179	82	78	23	5	1	5	60	2	231	2	1	16	7	.696	0	0-0	0	3.77	3.74
2013	Det	AL	32	32	0	0	214.1	836	152	73	69	18	2	8	4	56	0	240	6	1	21	3	.875	0	0-0	0	2.07	2.90
2014	Det	AL	33	33	1	0	220.1	904	196	80	77	18	4	8	6	63	1	252	10	1	18	5	.783	1	0-0	0	3.04	3.15
2015	Was	NL	33	33	4	0	228.2	899	176	74	71	27	11	2	5	34	2	276	10	1	14	12	.538	3	0-0	0	2.11	2.79
	Postseason		12	10	0	0	62.2	258	46	27	26	5	1	0	4	25	1	80	3	0	4	3	.571	0	0-0	1	2.75	3.73
8 ML YEARS			240	231	5	2	1468.0	6037	1298	612	564	160	39	39	49	423	9	1597	55	5	105	62	.629	4	0-0	0	3.21	3.46

Brian Schlitter

Pitches: R **Bats:** R **Pos:** RP-10　　　　**Ht:** 6'5" **Wt:** 235 **Born:** 12/21/1985 **Age:** 30

Year	Team	Lg	G	GS	CG	GF	IP	BFP	H	R	ER	HR	SH	SF	HB	TBB	IBB	SO	WP	Bk	W	L	Pct	Sh	Sv-Op	Hld	ERC	ERA
2015	Iowa*	AAA	45	0	0	41	44.2	194	41	11	8	1	1	1	1	26	1	35	1	0	2	3	.400	0	23- -	-	3.88	1.61
2010	ChC	NL	7	0	0	3	8.0	48	18	11	11	2	0	1	1	5	1	7	0	0	0	1	.000	0	0-0	0	15.07	12.38
2014	ChC	NL	61	0	0	5	56.1	242	58	29	26	2	5	1	2	19	4	31	0	0	2	3	.400	0	0-4	12	3.57	4.15
2015	ChC	NL	10	0	0	3	7.1	35	12	6	6	2	0	0	0	2	0	4	0	0	1	2	.333	0	0-2	0	8.97	7.36
3 ML YEARS			78	0	0	11	71.2	325	88	46	43	6	5	1	3	26	5	42	0	0	3	6	.333	0	0-6	12	5.15	5.40

Jonathan Schoop

Bats: R **Throws:** R **Pos:** 2B-84;PH-2　　　　SCOPE　　　　**Ht:** 6'1" **Wt:** 225 **Born:** 10/16/1991 **Age:** 24

Year	Team	Lg	G	AB	H	2B	3B	HR	(Hm	Rd)	TB	R	RBI	RC	TBB	IBB	SO	HBP	SH	SF	SB	CS	GDP	Avg	OBP	Slg	OPS
2013	Bal	AL	5	14	4	0	0	1	(0	1)	7	5	1	1	1	0	2	0	0	0	0	0	2	.286	.333	.500	.833
2014	Bal	AL	137	455	95	18	0	16	(5	11)	161	48	45	32	13	0	122	8	5	0	2	0	12	.209	.244	.354	.598
2015	Bal	AL	86	305	85	17	0	15	(9	6)	147	34	39	40	9	0	79	4	1	2	2	0	9	.279	.306	.482	.788
	Postseason		7	21	4	1	0	0	(0	0)	5	3	2	2	3	0	4	0	0	0	2	0	0	.190	.292	.238	.530
3 ML YEARS			228	774	184	35	0	32	(15	17)	315	87	85	73	23	0	203	12	6	2	4	0	23	.238	.270	.407	.677

Andrew Schugel

Pitches: R **Bats:** R **Pos:** RP-5　　　　SHOO-gul　　　　**Ht:** 6'0" **Wt:** 205 **Born:** 6/27/1989 **Age:** 27

Year	Team	Lg	G	GS	CG	GF	IP	BFP	H	R	ER	HR	SH	SF	HB	TBB	IBB	SO	WP	Bk	W	L	Pct	Sh	Sv-Op	Hld	ERC	ERA
2011	2 Tms	Low	29	16	0	5	110.0	468	95	45	37	3	1	3	8	45	0	95	13	0	5	5	.500	0	1- -	-	3.14	3.03
2012	Ark	AA	27	27	0	0	140.1	575	117	54	45	9	6	4	6	55	1	109	5	0	6	8	.429	0	0- -	-	3.14	2.89
2013	Salt Lk	AAA	19	19	0	0	89.1	415	121	74	70	12	0	4	4	33	0	76	7	0	4	6	.400	0	0- -	-	6.54	7.05
2014	Mobile	AA	26	26	0	0	147.2	613	142	60	57	3	4	6	6	50	2	117	5	0	6	4	.600	0	0- -	-	3.30	3.47
2015	Reno	AAA	9	9	1	0	38.0	193	65	45	43	4	1	4	2	17	0	27	6	0	2	7	.222	0	0- -	-	9.03	10.18
2015	Mobile	AA	12	12	0	0	77.1	308	74	21	19	5	2	0	2	15	0	52	7	0	7	2	.778	0	0- -	-	3.03	2.21
2015	Ari	NL	5	0	0	2	9.0	51	17	13	5	2	0	0	0	5	2	5	0	0	0	0	-	0	0-0	0	10.46	5.00

Bo Schultz

Pitches: R **Bats:** R **Pos:** RP-31　　　　**Ht:** 6'3" **Wt:** 220 **Born:** 9/25/1985 **Age:** 30

Year	Team	Lg	G	GS	CG	GF	IP	BFP	H	R	ER	HR	SH	SF	HB	TBB	IBB	SO	WP	Bk	W	L	Pct	Sh	Sv-Op	Hld	ERC	ERA
2011	Stcktn	A+	7	0	0	2	6.2	37	11	14	11	0	1	1	1	5	0	4	1	0	0	0	-	0	0- -	-	9.15	14.85
2012	Visalia	A+	29	0	0	28	34.0	152	41	21	17	3	2	1	0	10	3	36	2	0	4	2	.667	0	11- -	-	4.51	4.50
2012	Mobile	AA	17	0	0	7	21.1	92	20	8	5	0	2	0	1	7	1	13	1	0	2	3	.400	0	0- -	-	2.81	2.11
2013	Reno	AAA	17	0	0	7	19.2	93	29	12	12	4	1	0	1	7	1	23	4	0	0	2	.000	0	0- -	-	7.83	5.49
2013	Mobile	AA	20	16	0	3	85.0	346	62	29	27	3	5	2	7	29	0	52	10	0	5	4	.556	0	1- -	-	2.34	2.86
2014	Reno	AAA	28	23	1	0	135.1	619	174	109	93	17	5	4	4	46	2	82	4	1	10	8	.556	0	0- -	-	5.76	6.18
2015	Buffalo	AAA	16	0	0	13	21.1	83	15	4	4	1	1	1	0	7	1	18	1	0	2	1	.667	0	7- -	-	1.96	1.69
2014	Ari	NL	4	0	0	3	8.0	36	13	7	7	1	0	1	0	1	1	5	0	0	0	1	.000	0	0-0	0	6.86	7.88
2015	Tor	AL	31	0	0	10	43.0	173	32	19	17	7	0	2	1	14	0	31	2	0	0	1	.000	0	1-3	4	2.92	3.56
2 ML YEARS			35	0	0	13	51.0	209	45	26	24	8	0	3	1	15	1	36	2	0	0	2	.000	0	1-3	4	3.47	4.24

Skip Schumaker

SHOO-mock-er

Bats: L **Throws:** R **Pos:** PH-81;LF-40;2B-12;RF-4;CF-2;DH-2　　　　**Ht:** 5'10" **Wt:** 190 **Born:** 2/3/1980 **Age:** 36

Year	Team	Lg	G	AB	H	2B	3B	HR	(Hm	Rd)	TB	R	RBI	RC	TBB	IBB	SO	HBP	SH	SF	SB	CS	GDP	Avg	OBP	Slg	OPS
2005	StL	NL	27	24	6	1	0	0	(0	0)	7	9	1	2	2	0	2	0	0	0	1	0	0	.250	.308	.292	.599
2006	StL	NL	28	54	10	1	0	1	(0	1)	14	3	2	2	5	1	6	0	1	0	2	1	1	.185	.254	.259	.513
2007	StL	NL	88	177	59	12	2	2	(1	1)	81	19	19	30	8	0	20	0	1	2	1	1	5	.333	.358	.458	.816
2008	StL	NL	153	540	163	22	5	8	(4	4)	219	87	46	74	47	2	60	2	4	1	8	2	19	.302	.359	.406	.765
2009	StL	NL	153	532	161	34	1	4	(2	2)	209	85	35	74	52	2	69	0	1	1	2	2	4	.303	.364	.393	.757
2010	StL	NL	137	476	126	18	1	5	(1	4)	161	66	42	61	43	2	64	4	2	4	5	3	7	.265	.328	.338	.667
2011	StL	NL	117	367	104	19	0	2	(1	1)	129	34	38	43	27	3	50	2	1	3	0	2	10	.283	.333	.351	.685
2012	StL	NL	107	272	75	14	4	1	(1	0)	100	37	28	34	27	2	50	0	3	2	1	1	6	.276	.339	.368	.707
2013	LAD	NL	125	319	84	16	0	2	(1	1)	106	31	30	34	28	0	54	5	3	0	2	2	11	.263	.332	.332	.665

						BATTING															RUNNING			AVERAGES			
Year Team	Lg	G	AB	H	2B	3B	HR	(Hm Rd)	TB	R	RBI	RC	TBB	IBB	SO	HBP	SH	SF	SB	CS	GDP	Avg	OBP	Slg	OPS			
2014 Cin	NL	83	247	58	12	0	2	(1 1)	76	22	22	22	18	0	50	1	3	2	2	1	3	.235	.287	.308	.595			
2015 Cin	NL	131	244	59	20	0	1	(1 0)	82	23	21	24	23	2	51	0	1	0	2	2	7	.242	.306	.336	.642			
Postseason		30	55	13	3	0	0	(0 0)	16	3	8	6	3	2	10	1	0	1	0	0	3	.236	.283	.291	.574			
11 ML YEARS		1149	3252	905	169	13	28	(13 15)	1184	416	284	400	280	14	476	14	19	16	26	17	73	.278	.337	.364	.701			

Kyle Schwarber

Bats: L **Throws:** R **Pos:** LF-41;C-21;PH-9;DH-6;RF-4   SHWAR-burr   **Ht:** 6'0" **Wt:** 235 **Born:** 3/5/1993 **Age:** 23

						BATTING															RUNNING			AVERAGES			
Year Team	Lg	G	AB	H	2B	3B	HR	(Hm Rd)	TB	R	RBI	RC	TBB	IBB	SO	HBP	SH	SF	SB	CS	GDP	Avg	OBP	Slg	OPS			
2014 3 Tms	Low	72	262	90	18	2	18	(- -)	166	55	53	67	39	2	57	4	0	6	5	2	6	.344	.428	.634	1.061			
2015 Tenn	AA	58	197	63	10	1	13	(- -)	114	39	39	50	42	1	49	1	1	2	1	0	5	.320	.438	.579	1.017			
2015 Iowa	AAA	17	60	20	7	1	3	(- -)	38	7	10	14	7	0	23	0	0	0	0	0	0	.333	.403	.633	1.036			
2015 ChC	NL	69	232	57	6	1	16	(7 9)	113	52	43	39	36	1	77	4	0	1	3	3	4	.246	.355	.487	.842			

Evan Scribner

Pitches: R **Bats:** R **Pos:** RP-54   SKRIBB-nurr   **Ht:** 6'3" **Wt:** 190 **Born:** 7/19/1985 **Age:** 30

		HOW MUCH HE PITCHED						WHAT HE GAVE UP										THE RESULTS							
Year Team	Lg	G	GS	CG	GF	IP	BFP	H	R	ER	HR	SH	SF	HB	TBB	IBB	SO	WP	Bk	W	L	Pct	Sh	Sv-Op	Hld	ERC	ERA
2011 SD	NL	10	0	0	5	14.0	64	18	11	11	1	0	0	0	4	0	10	0	0	0	0	-	0	0-0	0	4.92	7.07
2012 Oak	AL	30	0	0	5	35.1	148	30	11	10	2	0	0	0	12	0	30	1	0	2	0	1.000	0	1-1	1	2.70	2.55
2013 Oak	AL	18	0	0	12	26.2	114	26	13	13	3	0	0	0	7	0	19	2	0	0	0	-	0	0-0	0	3.38	4.39
2014 Oak	AL	13	0	0	6	11.2	47	11	6	6	4	0	0	1	0	0	11	0	0	1	0	1.000	0	0-0	0	3.89	4.63
2015 Oak	AL	54	0	0	14	60.0	238	58	31	29	14	0	1	2	4	0	64	2	0	2	2	.500	0	0-4	8	3.57	4.35
Postseason		1	0	0	1	2.0	6	0	0	0	0	0	0	0	0	0	3	0	0	0	0	-	0	0-0	0	0.00	0.00
5 ML YEARS		125	0	0	50	147.2	611	143	72	69	24	0	1	3	27	0	134	5	0	5	2	.714	0	1-5	9	3.50	4.21

Xavier Scruggs

Bats: R **Throws:** R **Pos:** 1B-11;PH-6   ZAY-vyer   **Ht:** 6'1" **Wt:** 220 **Born:** 9/23/1987 **Age:** 28

						BATTING															RUNNING			AVERAGES			
Year Team	Lg	G	AB	H	2B	3B	HR	(Hm Rd)	TB	R	RBI	RC	TBB	IBB	SO	HBP	SH	SF	SB	CS	GDP	Avg	OBP	Slg	OPS			
2011 PlmBh	A+	117	411	107	27	3	21	(- -)	203	57	63	72	40	1	125	13	1	6	4	1	11	.260	.340	.494	.834			
2012 Sprgfld	AA	130	452	106	26	1	22	(- -)	200	64	91	70	58	0	150	9	0	3	8	4	15	.235	.331	.442	.774			
2013 Sprgfld	AA	133	448	111	18	1	29	(- -)	218	67	81	86	82	2	177	12	1	3	11	7	5	.248	.376	.487	.863			
2014 Memp	AAA	135	472	135	29	3	21	(- -)	233	82	87	86	53	0	114	11	0	2	3	5	19	.286	.370	.494	.864			
2015 Memp	AAA	109	383	91	22	1	14	(- -)	157	54	57	57	54	1	103	8	0	4	4	3	9	.238	.341	.410	.751			
2014 StL	NL	9	15	3	1	0	0	(0 0)	4	0	2	2	2	0	7	1	0	0	0	0	0	.200	.333	.267	.600			
2015 StL	NL	17	42	11	2	0	0	(0 0)	13	5	7	5	0	0	10	1	0	0	1	0	2	.262	.279	.310	.589			
2 ML YEARS		26	57	14	3	0	0	(0 0)	17	5	9	7	2	0	17	2	0	0	1	0	2	.246	.295	.298	.593			

Corey Seager

Bats: L **Throws:** R **Pos:** SS-21;3B-6;PH-2   SEE-gurr   **Ht:** 6'4" **Wt:** 215 **Born:** 4/27/1994 **Age:** 22

						BATTING															RUNNING			AVERAGES			
Year Team	Lg	G	AB	H	2B	3B	HR	(Hm Rd)	TB	R	RBI	RC	TBB	IBB	SO	HBP	SH	SF	SB	CS	GDP	Avg	OBP	Slg	OPS			
2012 Ogden	R+	46	175	54	9	2	8	(- -)	91	34	33	36	21	1	33	2	1	3	8	2	4	.309	.383	.520	.903			
2013 2 Tms	Low	101	372	100	20	4	16	(- -)	176	55	72	64	46	4	89	3	1	4	10	4	10	.269	.351	.473	.824			
2014 Chatt	AA	38	148	51	16	3	2	(- -)	79	28	27	29	10	0	39	0	1	2	1	1	6	.345	.381	.534	.915			
2014 Rcuca	A+	80	327	115	34	2	18	(- -)	207	61	70	81	30	2	76	5	0	3	5	1	6	.352	.411	.633	1.044			
2015 Tulsa	AA	20	80	30	7	1	5	(- -)	54	17	15	20	5	1	11	0	0	1	1	1	2	.375	.407	.675	1.082			
2015 OkCity	AAA	105	421	117	30	2	13	(- -)	190	64	61	66	32	2	65	5	0	6	3	0	9	.278	.332	.451	.783			
2015 LAD	NL	27	98	33	8	1	4	(3 1)	55	17	17	19	14	1	19	1	0	0	2	0	2	.337	.425	.561	.986			

Kyle Seager

Bats: L **Throws:** R **Pos:** 3B-160;SS-1;PH-1   SEE-gurr   **Ht:** 6'0" **Wt:** 210 **Born:** 11/3/1987 **Age:** 28

						BATTING															RUNNING			AVERAGES			
Year Team	Lg	G	AB	H	2B	3B	HR	(Hm Rd)	TB	R	RBI	RC	TBB	IBB	SO	HBP	SH	SF	SB	CS	GDP	Avg	OBP	Slg	OPS			
2011 Sea	AL	53	182	47	13	0	3	(0 3)	69	22	13	16	13	0	36	2	2	2	3	1	4	.258	.312	.379	.691			
2012 Sea	AL	155	594	154	35	1	20	(5 15)	251	62	86	88	46	1	110	5	2	4	13	5	9	.259	.316	.423	.738			
2013 Sea	AL	160	615	160	32	2	22	(8 14)	262	79	69	90	68	1	122	7	0	5	9	3	8	.260	.338	.426	.764			
2014 Sea	AL	159	590	158	27	4	25	(16 9)	268	71	96	96	52	3	118	8	1	3	7	5	12	.268	.334	.454	.788			
2015 Sea	AL	161	623	166	37	0	26	(7 19)	281	85	74	75	54	6	98	5	0	4	6	6	17	.266	.328	.451	.779			
5 ML YEARS		688	2604	685	144	7	96	(36 60)	1131	319	338	365	233	11	484	27	5	18	38	20	50	.263	.328	.434	.762			

Jean Segura

Bats: R **Throws:** R **Pos:** SS-140;PH-3   GENE seg-ER-uh   **Ht:** 5'10" **Wt:** 205 **Born:** 3/17/1990 **Age:** 26

						BATTING															RUNNING			AVERAGES			
Year Team	Lg	G	AB	H	2B	3B	HR	(Hm Rd)	TB	R	RBI	RC	TBB	IBB	SO	HBP	SH	SF	SB	CS	GDP	Avg	OBP	Slg	OPS			
2012 2 Tms		45	151	39	4	3	0	(0 0)	49	19	14	16	13	3	23	0	1	1	7	1	1	.258	.315	.325	.640			
2013 Mil	NL	146	588	173	20	10	12	(7 5)	249	74	49	72	25	1	84	6	2	2	44	13	17	.294	.329	.423	.752			
2014 Mil	NL	146	513	120	14	6	5	(3 2)	167	61	31	45	28	7	70	4	10	2	20	9	13	.246	.289	.326	.614			
2015 Mil	NL	142	560	144	16	5	6	(4 2)	188	57	50	57	13	2	93	6	3	2	25	6	14	.257	.281	.336	.616			
12 LAA	AL	1	3	0	0	0	0	(0 0)	0	0	0	0	0	0	2	0	0	0	0	0	0	.000	.000	.000	.000			
12 Mil	NL	44	148	39	4	3	0	(0 0)	49	19	14	16	13	3	21	0	1	1	7	1	1	.264	.321	.331	.652			
4 ML YEARS		479	1812	482	54	24	23	(14 9)	653	211	144	190	79	11	270	16	16	7	96	29	45	.266	.301	.360	.662			

Marcus Semien

Bats: R Throws: R Pos: SS-152;PH-8   SIM-ee-inn   Ht: 6'1" Wt: 195 Born: 9/17/1990 Age: 25

								BATTING												RUNNING			AVERAGES			
Year	Team	Lg	G	AB	H	2B	3B	HR	(Hm | Rd)	TB	R	RBI	RC	TBB	IBB	SO	HBP	SH	SF	SB	CS	GDP	Avg	OBP	Slg	OPS
2013	CWS	AL	21	69	18	4	0	2	(2 | 0)	28	7	7	7	1	0	22	0	0	1	2	2	1	.261	.268	.406	.673
2014	CWS	AL	64	231	54	10	2	6	(4 | 2)	86	30	28	31	21	0	70	1	2	0	3	0	6	.234	.300	.372	.673
2015	Oak	AL	155	556	143	23	7	15	(5 | 10)	225	65	45	57	42	1	132	1	1	1	11	5	16	.257	.310	.405	.715
	3 ML YEARS		240	856	215	37	9	23	(11 | 12)	339	102	80	95	64	1	224	2	3	2	16	7	23	.251	.304	.396	.700

Luis Severino

Pitches: R Bats: R Pos: SP-11   Ht: 6'0" Wt: 195 Born: 2/20/1994 Age: 22

			HOW MUCH HE PITCHED					WHAT HE GAVE UP										THE RESULTS							
Year	Team	Lg	G	GS	CG	GF	IP	BFP	H	R	ER	HR	SH	SF	HB	TBB	IBB	SO	WP	Bk	W	L	Pct	Sh	Sv-Op	Hld	ERC	ERA
2013	2 Tms	Low	10	8	0	0	44.0	179	37	14	12	1	0	2	2	10	0	53	3	0	4	2	.667	0	0--	-	2.27	2.45
2014	2 Tms	Low	18	18	0	0	88.0	357	73	28	24	2	4	0	3	21	1	98	4	0	4	3	.571	0	0--	-	2.20	2.45
2014	Trntn	AA	6	6	0	0	25.0	100	20	8	7	1	0	0	0	6	0	29	0	1	2	2	.500	0	0--	-	2.07	2.52
2015	Trntn	AA	8	8	0	0	38.0	157	32	17	14	2	2	1	2	10	0	48	1	1	2	2	.500	0	0--	-	2.58	3.32
2015	S-WB	AAA	11	11	0	0	61.1	239	40	18	13	0	1	1	3	17	0	50	3	0	7	0	1.000	0	0--	-	1.54	1.91
2015	NYY	AL	11	11	0	0	62.1	255	53	21	20	9	0	0	2	22	0	56	2	1	5	3	.625	0	0-0	0	3.57	2.89

Pedro Severino

Bats: R Throws: R Pos: C-2;PH-1   Ht: 6'2" Wt: 200 Born: 7/20/1993 Age: 22

								BATTING												RUNNING			AVERAGES			
Year	Team	Lg	G	AB	H	2B	3B	HR	(Hm | Rd)	TB	R	RBI	RC	TBB	IBB	SO	HBP	SH	SF	SB	CS	GDP	Avg	OBP	Slg	OPS
2011	Nats	R	32	115	21	4	1	2	(- | -)	33	16	9	8	10	0	27	2	2	0	0	0	4	.183	.260	.287	.547
2012	Nats	R	38	109	24	3	1	0	(- | -)	29	9	8	9	9	0	4	4	2	1	0	0	3	.220	.301	.266	.567
2013	Hgrstn	A	84	282	68	19	2	1	(- | -)	94	28	45	26	13	0	54	1	3	3	1	0	7	.241	.274	.333	.608
2014	Ptomc	A+	94	291	72	15	1	9	(- | -)	116	41	36	37	21	0	57	5	6	3	2	0	5	.247	.306	.399	.705
2015	Hrsbrg	AA	91	329	81	13	0	5	(- | -)	109	33	34	32	19	1	51	1	6	2	1	2	12	.246	.288	.331	.619
2015	Was	NL	2	4	1	1	0	0	(0 | 0)	2	1	0	0	0	0	1	0	0	0	0	0	0	.250	.250	.500	.750

Richie Shaffer

Bats: R Throws: R Pos: 1B-10;PH-9;3B-8;DH-8;RF-2;LF-1   SHAY-fer   Ht: 6'3" Wt: 220 Born: 3/15/1991 Age: 25

								BATTING												RUNNING			AVERAGES			
Year	Team	Lg	G	AB	H	2B	3B	HR	(Hm | Rd)	TB	R	RBI	RC	TBB	IBB	SO	HBP	SH	SF	SB	CS	GDP	Avg	OBP	Slg	OPS
2012	HudVal	A-	33	117	36	5	2	4	(- | -)	57	25	26	23	16	1	31	4	0	1	0	0	1	.308	.406	.487	.893
2013	Charltt	A+	122	469	119	33	1	11	(- | -)	187	55	73	62	35	2	106	6	0	9	6	0	4	.254	.308	.399	.707
2014	Mont	AA	119	427	95	28	4	19	(- | -)	188	58	64	64	56	1	119	5	1	2	4	0	10	.222	.318	.440	.759
2015	Mont	AA	39	149	39	10	0	7	(- | -)	70	22	27	27	23	0	49	1	1	1	3	0	3	.262	.362	.470	.832
2015	Drham	AAA	69	244	66	17	1	19	(- | -)	142	42	45	50	31	3	74	3	0	4	1	1	3	.270	.355	.582	.937
2015	TB	AL	31	74	14	3	0	4	(2 | 2)	29	11	6	4	10	0	32	3	0	1	0	1	2	.189	.307	.392	.699

Bryan Shaw

Pitches: R Bats: B Pos: RP-74   Ht: 6'1" Wt: 210 Born: 11/8/1987 Age: 28

			HOW MUCH HE PITCHED					WHAT HE GAVE UP										THE RESULTS							
Year	Team	Lg	G	GS	CG	GF	IP	BFP	H	R	ER	HR	SH	SF	HB	TBB	IBB	SO	WP	Bk	W	L	Pct	Sh	Sv-Op	Hld	ERC	ERA
2011	Ari	NL	33	0	0	8	28.1	122	30	9	8	2	0	0	4	8	1	24	1	0	1	0	1.000	0	0-0	9	4.31	2.54
2012	Ari	NL	64	0	0	19	59.1	252	60	29	23	4	4	2	2	24	3	41	4	1	1	6	.143	0	2-4	10	4.08	3.49
2013	Cle	AL	70	0	0	11	75.0	316	60	31	27	4	4	2	4	28	2	73	5	0	7	3	.700	0	1-5	12	2.71	3.24
2014	Cle	AL	80	0	0	16	76.1	313	61	26	22	6	5	2	2	22	4	64	4	1	5	5	.500	0	2-9	24	2.45	2.59
2015	Cle	AL	74	0	0	19	64.0	265	59	24	21	8	1	0	1	19	1	54	3	0	3	3	.500	0	2-6	23	3.47	2.95
	Postseason		5	0	0	1	5.2	18	1	0	0	0	0	1	0	1	0	5	0	0	0	0	-	0	0-0	1	0.22	0.00
	5 ML YEARS		321	0	0	73	303.0	1268	270	119	101	24	14	6	13	101	11	256	17	2	17	17	.500	0	7-24	78	3.20	3.00

Travis Shaw

Bats: L Throws: R Pos: 1B-55;3B-8;PH-2;PR-2;LF-1   Ht: 6'4" Wt: 225 Born: 4/16/1990 Age: 26

								BATTING												RUNNING			AVERAGES			
Year	Team	Lg	G	AB	H	2B	3B	HR	(Hm	Rd)	TB	R	RBI	RC	TBB	IBB	SO	HBP	SH	SF	SB	CS	GDP	Avg	OBP	Slg	OPS
2011	2 Tms	Low	59	211	56	14	0	8	(-	-)	94	34	37	37	35	0	47	2	0	2	3	0	4	.265	.372	.445	.817
2012	Salem	A+	99	354	108	31	3	16	(-	-)	193	69	73	81	59	3	81	7	0	3	11	2	8	.305	.411	.545	.957
2012	Portlnd	AA	31	110	25	13	0	3	(-	-)	47	13	12	18	21	0	34	1	0	1	1	1	1	.227	.353	.427	.781
2013	Portlnd	AA	127	444	98	21	4	16	(-	-)	175	57	50	66	78	2	117	5	0	2	7	3	3	.221	.342	.394	.736
2014	Portlnd	AA	47	177	54	8	1	11	(-	-)	97	35	37	39	29	1	23	1	1	0	5	3	8	.305	.406	.548	.954
2014	Pwtckt	AAA	81	313	82	21	1	10	(-	-)	135	43	41	45	28	2	76	1	0	4	2	0	8	.262	.321	.431	.752
2015	Pwtckt	AAA	77	289	72	12	2	5	(-	-)	103	29	30	34	26	1	54	4	1	2	0	1	7	.249	.318	.356	.674
2015	Bos	AL	65	226	62	10	0	13	(8	5)	111	31	36	35	18	1	57	2	0	2	0	1	1	.274	.331	.491	.822

James Shields

Pitches: R Bats: R Pos: SP-33   Ht: 6'3" Wt: 215 Born: 12/20/1981 Age: 34

			HOW MUCH HE PITCHED					WHAT HE GAVE UP										THE RESULTS							
Year	Team	Lg	G	GS	CG	GF	IP	BFP	H	R	ER	HR	SH	SF	HB	TBB	IBB	SO	WP	Bk	W	L	Pct	Sh	Sv-Op	Hld	ERC	ERA
2006	TB	AL	21	21	1	0	124.2	540	141	69	67	18	4	3	5	38	5	104	9	0	6	8	.429	0	0-0	0	4.92	4.84
2007	TB	AL	31	31	1	0	215.0	874	202	98	92	28	4	5	10	36	0	184	9	0	12	8	.600	0	0-0	0	3.24	3.85
2008	TB	AL	33	33	3	0	215.0	877	208	94	85	24	6	0	12	40	0	160	6	0	14	8	.636	2	0-0	0	3.41	3.56
2009	TB	AL	33	33	0	0	219.2	930	239	113	101	29	6	3	1	52	1	167	3	1	11	12	.478	0	0-0	0	4.16	4.14

				HOW MUCH HE PITCHED							WHAT HE GAVE UP												THE RESULTS							
Year	Team	Lg	G	GS	CG	GF	IP	BFP	H	R	ER	HR	SH	SF	HB	TBB	IBB	SO	WP	Bk	W	L	Pct	Sh	Sv-Op	Hld	ERC	ERA
2010	TB	AL	34	33	0	0	203.1	899	246	128	117	34	5	2	5	51	2	187	13	2	13	15	.464	0	0-0	0	5.21	5.18
2011	TB	AL	33	33	11	0	249.1	975	195	83	78	26	5	3	5	65	1	225	4	0	16	12	.571	4	0-0	0	2.58	2.82
2012	TB	AL	33	33	3	0	227.2	944	208	103	89	25	3	2	11	58	2	223	7	1	15	10	.600	2	0-0	0	3.28	3.52
2013	KC	AL	34	34	2	0	228.2	946	215	82	80	20	6	7	8	68	0	196	11	2	13	9	.591	0	0-0	0	3.45	3.15
2014	KC	AL	34	34	1	0	227.0	939	224	95	81	23	3	7	11	44	0	180	12	2	14	8	.636	1	0-0	0	3.41	3.21
2015	SD	NL	33	33	0	0	202.1	860	189	93	88	33	6	1	9	81	5	216	7	1	13	7	.650	0	0-0	0	4.34	3.91
Postseason			11	11	0	0	59.1	269	76	37	36	8	1	1	6	15	0	45	6	0	3	6	.333	0	0-0	0	5.80	5.46
10 ML YEARS			319	318	22	0	2112.2	8784	2067	958	878	260	48	33	77	533	16	1842	81	9	127	97	.567	9	0-0	0	3.69	3.74

Matt Shoemaker

Pitches: R Bats: R Pos: SP-24; RP-1 · SHOO-may-kerr · Ht: 6'2" Wt: 225 Born: 9/27/1986 Age: 29

				HOW MUCH HE PITCHED							WHAT HE GAVE UP												THE RESULTS							
Year	Team	Lg	G	GS	CG	GF	IP	BFP	H	R	ER	HR	SH	SF	HB	TBB	IBB	SO	WP	Bk	W	L	Pct	Sh	Sv-Op	Hld	ERC	ERA
2013	LAA	AL	1	1	0	0	5.0	19	2	0	0	0	0	0	0	2	0	5	1	0	0	0	—	0	0-0	0	0.95	0.00
2014	LAA	AL	27	20	0	5	136.0	543	122	49	46	14	3	5	4	24	0	124	5	0	16	4	.800	0	0-0	0	2.84	3.04
2015	LAA	AL	25	24	0	1	135.1	569	135	70	67	24	4	4	4	35	2	116	3	0	7	10	.412	0	0-0	0	4.12	4.46
Postseason			1	1	0	0	6.0	23	5	1	1	0	1	0	0	0	0	6	0	0	0	0	—	0	0-0	0	1.37	1.50
3 ML YEARS			53	45	0	6	276.1	1131	259	119	113	38	7	9	8	61	2	245	9	0	23	14	.622	0	0-0	0	3.40	3.68

Chasen Shreve

Pitches: L Bats: L Pos: RP-59 · CHASE-en SHREEVE · Ht: 6'3" Wt: 185 Born: 7/12/1990 Age: 25

				HOW MUCH HE PITCHED							WHAT HE GAVE UP												THE RESULTS							
Year	Team	Lg	G	GS	CG	GF	IP	BFP	H	R	ER	HR	SH	SF	HB	TBB	IBB	SO	WP	Bk	W	L	Pct	Sh	Sv-Op	Hld	ERC	ERA
2011	Rome	A	34	0	0	12	70.0	308	77	33	30	3	6	1	2	26	4	68	15	0	5	6	.455	0	4--	-	4.12	3.86
2012	Lynbrg	A+	32	0	0	13	46.0	190	44	16	11	2	4	1	0	17	1	41	3	0	4	4	.500	0	1--	-	3.40	2.15
2012	Missi	AA	11	0	0	3	18.1	86	17	8	8	1	0	0	0	16	1	16	0	0	2	1	.667	0	0--	-	5.06	3.93
2013	Missi	AA	36	0	0	15	42.2	192	43	25	21	1	8	4	0	22	4	28	1	0	3	1	.750	0	0--	-	3.76	4.43
2013	Lynbrg	A+	14	0	0	5	19.2	84	15	7	6	1	0	0	0	8	0	15	2	0	0	1	.000	0	2--	-	2.41	2.75
2014	Missi	AA	36	0	0	21	54.1	207	42	16	15	2	0	0	1	9	1	76	1	0	3	2	.600	0	7--	-	1.81	2.48
2014	Gwnntt	AAA	10	0	0	5	9.2	38	9	4	4	2	1	1	0	3	0	11	0	0	2	1	.667	0	2--	-	4.33	3.72
2014	Atl	NL	15	0	0	4	12.1	50	10	1	1	0	1	0	0	3	0	15	1	0	0	0	—	0	0-0	2	1.88	0.73
2015	NYY	AL	59	0	0	13	58.1	251	49	21	20	10	2	0	1	33	2	64	4	0	6	2	.750	0	0-1	10	4.39	3.09
2 ML YEARS			74	0	0	17	70.2	301	59	22	21	10	3	0	1	36	2	79	5	0	6	2	.750	0	0-1	12	3.91	2.67

J.B. Shuck

Bats: L Throws: L Pos: PH-37;RF-27;CF-11;LF-10;PR-2 · Ht: 5'11" Wt: 195 Born: 6/18/1987 Age: 29

							BATTING														RUNNING			AVERAGES			
Year	Team	Lg	G	AB	H	2B	3B	HR	(Hm	Rd)	TB	R	RBI	RC	TBB	IBB	SO	HBP	SH	SF	SB	CS	GDP	Avg	OBP	Slg	OPS
2011	Hou	NL	37	81	22	2	1	0	(0	0)	26	9	3	9	11	1	7	0	0	0	2	0	3	.272	.359	.321	.680
2013	LAA	AL	129	437	128	20	3	2	(1	1)	160	60	39	54	27	0	54	1	6	7	8	4	10	.293	.331	.366	.697
2014	2 Tms	AL	38	110	16	1	0	2	(1	1)	23	12	9	3	3	1	12	0	1	0	2	0	1	.145	.168	.209	.377
2015	CWS	AL	79	143	38	8	2	0	(0	0)	50	15	15	20	16	0	16	1	3	2	7	5	2	.266	.340	.350	.689
14	LAA	AL	22	84	14	1	0	2	(1	1)	21	10	9	3	3	1	11	0	1	0	2	0	0	.167	.195	.250	.445
14	Cle	AL	16	26	2	0	0	0	(0	0)	2	2	0	0	0	0	1	0	0	0	0	0	1	.077	.077	.077	.154
4 ML YEARS			283	771	204	31	6	4	(2	2)	259	96	66	86	57	2	89	2	10	9	19	9	16	.265	.313	.336	.649

Kevin Siegrist

Pitches: L Bats: L Pos: RP-81 · SEE-grist · Ht: 6'5" Wt: 215 Born: 7/20/1989 Age: 26

				HOW MUCH HE PITCHED							WHAT HE GAVE UP												THE RESULTS							
Year	Team	Lg	G	GS	CG	GF	IP	BFP	H	R	ER	HR	SH	SF	HB	TBB	IBB	SO	WP	Bk	W	L	Pct	Sh	Sv-Op	Hld	ERC	ERA
2013	StL	NL	45	0	0	15	39.2	152	17	2	2	1	0	0	1	18	1	50	0	0	3	1	.750	0	0-0	11	1.27	0.45
2014	StL	NL	37	0	0	5	30.1	140	32	23	23	5	1	1	2	16	0	37	1	0	1	4	.200	0	0-2	16	5.59	6.82
2015	StL	NL	81	0	0	13	74.2	312	53	20	18	4	3	4	3	34	2	90	0	0	7	1	.875	0	6-10	28	2.52	2.17
Postseason			9	0	0	1	6.0	25	6	3	2	1	0	1	0	0	0	3	2	0	0	0	—	0	0-0	1	2.73	3.00
3 ML YEARS			163	0	0	33	144.2	604	102	45	43	10	4	5	6	68	3	177	1	0	11	6	.647	0	6-12	55	2.67	2.68

Andrelton Simmons

Bats: R Throws: R Pos: SS-147;PH-1 · ANN-drel-ton · Ht: 6'2" Wt: 195 Born: 9/4/1989 Age: 26

							BATTING														RUNNING			AVERAGES			
Year	Team	Lg	G	AB	H	2B	3B	HR	(Hm	Rd)	TB	R	RBI	RC	TBB	IBB	SO	HBP	SH	SF	SB	CS	GDP	Avg	OBP	Slg	OPS
2012	Atl	NL	49	166	48	8	2	3	(3	0)	69	17	19	23	12	1	21	1	0	3	1	0	5	.289	.335	.416	.751
2013	Atl	NL	157	606	150	27	6	17	(5	12)	240	76	59	60	40	1	55	3	5	4	6	5	16	.248	.296	.396	.692
2014	Atl	NL	146	540	132	18	4	7	(3	4)	179	44	46	41	32	4	60	0	2	2	4	5	25	.244	.286	.331	.617
2015	Atl	NL	147	535	142	23	2	4	(2	2)	181	60	44	48	39	6	48	6	1	2	5	3	19	.265	.321	.338	.660
Postseason			5	16	4	1	0	0	(0	0)	5	0	2	1	2	0	3	0	1	0	0	0	1	.250	.333	.313	.646
4 ML YEARS			499	1847	472	76	14	31	(13	18)	669	197	168	172	123	12	184	10	8	11	16	13	65	.256	.304	.362	.666

Alfredo Simon

Pitches: R Bats: R Pos: SP-31 — si-MOHN — Ht: 6'6" Wt: 265 Born: 5/8/1981 Age: 35

		HOW MUCH HE PITCHED						WHAT HE GAVE UP												THE RESULTS							
Year Team	Lg	G	GS	CG	GF	IP	BFP	H	R	ER	HR	SH	SF	HB	TBB	IBB	SO	WP	Bk	W	L	Pct	Sh	Sv-Op	Hld	ERC	ERA
2008 Bal	AL	4	1	0	0	13.0	59	16	10	9	4	0	1	2	2	0	8	2	0	0	0	-	0	0-0	0	6.45	6.23
2009 Bal	AL	2	2	0	0	6.1	28	8	7	7	5	0	0	0	2	0	3	0	0	0	1	.000	0	0-0	0	10.74	9.95
2010 Bal	AL	49	0	0	35	49.1	222	54	30	27	10	1	2	2	22	2	37	1	0	4	2	.667	0	17-21	1	5.66	4.93
2011 Bal	AL	23	16	0	1	115.2	499	128	69	63	15	1	4	4	40	6	83	2	2	4	9	.308	0	0-0	0	4.83	4.90
2012 Cin	NL	36	0	0	13	61.0	269	65	22	18	2	2	3	6	22	1	52	9	0	3	2	.600	0	1-1	1	4.16	2.66
2013 Cin	NL	63	0	0	20	87.2	359	68	31	28	8	5	2	8	26	2	63	4	0	6	4	.600	0	1-3	6	2.75	2.87
2014 Cin	NL	32	32	0	0	196.1	818	180	80	75	22	7	4	12	56	7	127	3	0	15	10	.600	0	0-0	0	3.49	3.44
2015 Det	AL	31	31	2	0	187.0	820	201	112	105	24	9	6	8	68	1	117	14	0	13	12	.520	1	0-0	0	4.73	5.05
Postseason		2	0	0	1	2.1	11	3	0	0	0	1	0	0	1	0	1	0	0	0	0	-	0	0-0	0	4.93	0.00
8 ML YEARS		240	82	2	69	716.1	3074	721	361	332	90	25	22	42	238	19	490	35	2	45	40	.529	1	19-25	8	4.23	4.17

Jon Singleton

Bats: L Throws: L Pos: 1B-14;DH-4;PH-4 — Ht: 6'2" Wt: 225 Born: 9/18/1991 Age: 24

		BATTING																		RUNNING			AVERAGES			
Year Team	Lg	G	AB	H	2B	3B	HR	(Hm	Rd)	TB	R	RBI	RC	TBB	IBB	SO	HBP	SH	SF	SB	CS	GDP	Avg	OBP	Slg	OPS
2011 2 Tms	Low	128	449	134	23	1	13	(-	-)	198	68	63	81	70	3	123	4	0	7	3	3	14	.298	.392	.441	.833
2012 CpChr	AA	131	461	131	27	4	21	(-	-)	229	94	79	95	88	5	131	1	0	5	7	2	6	.284	.396	.497	.893
2013 CpChr	AA	11	38	10	2	1	2	(-	-)	20	5	8	8	9	0	16	0	0	1	0	0	0	.263	.396	.526	.922
2013 OkCity	AAA	73	245	54	13	0	6	(-	-)	85	31	31	33	46	1	89	0	0	3	1	0	4	.220	.340	.347	.687
2014 OkCity	AAA	54	195	52	10	1	14	(-	-)	106	37	43	43	42	6	52	1	0	1	1	1	4	.267	.397	.544	.941
2015 Fresno	AAA	102	378	96	25	2	22	(-	-)	191	72	83	72	64	2	99	1	0	5	2	1	6	.254	.359	.505	.865
2014 Hou	AL	95	310	52	13	0	13	(7	6)	104	42	44	28	50	1	134	1	0	1	2	3	4	.168	.285	.335	.620
2015 Hou	AL	19	47	9	2	0	1	(1	0)	14	6	6	5	10	0	17	0	0	1	1	0	0	.191	.328	.298	.625
2 ML YEARS		114	357	61	15	0	14	(8	6)	118	48	50	33	60	1	151	1	0	2	3	3	4	.171	.290	.331	.621

Tony Sipp

Pitches: L Bats: L Pos: RP-60 — Ht: 6'0" Wt: 190 Born: 7/12/1983 Age: 32

		HOW MUCH HE PITCHED						WHAT HE GAVE UP												THE RESULTS							
Year Team	Lg	G	GS	CG	GF	IP	BFP	H	R	ER	HR	SH	SF	HB	TBB	IBB	SO	WP	Bk	W	L	Pct	Sh	Sv-Op	Hld	ERC	ERA
2009 Cle	AL	46	0	0	8	40.0	168	27	16	13	5	3	1	0	25	2	48	3	0	2	0	1.000	0	0-0	9	3.29	2.93
2010 Cle	AL	70	0	0	16	63.0	266	48	30	29	12	3	2	2	39	3	69	4	0	2	2	.500	0	1-3	15	4.42	4.14
2011 Cle	AL	69	0	0	17	62.1	251	45	22	21	10	1	2	0	24	3	57	2	1	6	3	.667	0	0-1	24	2.87	3.03
2012 Cle	AL	63	0	0	7	55.0	233	47	29	27	9	2	1	1	23	1	51	3	0	1	2	.333	0	1-2	12	3.80	4.42
2013 Ari	NL	56	0	0	11	37.2	175	35	22	20	6	3	1	3	22	2	42	3	1	3	2	.600	0	0-2	3	4.90	4.78
2014 Hou	AL	56	0	0	13	50.2	198	28	19	19	5	2	0	0	17	2	63	3	0	4	3	.571	0	4-6	11	1.57	3.38
2015 Hou	AL	60	0	0	12	54.1	216	41	13	12	5	2	1	1	15	1	62	4	0	3	4	.429	0	0-3	13	2.34	1.99
7 ML YEARS		420	0	0	84	363.0	1507	271	151	141	52	16	8	7	165	14	392	22	2	21	16	.568	0	6-17	87	3.22	3.50

Grady Sizemore

Bats: L Throws: L Pos: RF-42;LF-32;PH-26;DH-10 — Ht: 6'2" Wt: 205 Born: 8/2/1982 Age: 33

		BATTING																		RUNNING			AVERAGES			
Year Team	Lg	G	AB	H	2B	3B	HR	(Hm	Rd)	TB	R	RBI	RC	TBB	IBB	SO	HBP	SH	SF	SB	CS	GDP	Avg	OBP	Slg	OPS
2004 Cle	AL	43	138	34	6	2	4	(2	2)	56	15	24	21	14	0	34	5	0	2	2	0	0	.246	.333	.406	.739
2005 Cle	AL	158	640	185	37	11	22	(10	12)	310	111	81	101	52	1	132	7	5		22	10	17	.289	.348	.484	.832
2006 Cle	AL	162	655	190	53	11	28	(14	14)	349	134	76	121	78	8	153	13	1	4	22	6	2	.290	.375	.533	.907
2007 Cle	AL	162	628	174	34	5	24	(11	13)	290	118	78	123	101	9	155	17	0	2	33	10	3	.277	.390	.462	.852
2008 Cle	AL	157	634	170	39	5	33	(21	12)	318	101	90	121	98	14	130	11	0	2	38	5	5	.268	.374	.502	.876
2009 Cle	AL	106	436	108	20	6	18	(5	13)	194	73	64	68	60	1	92	4	2	1	13	8	4	.248	.343	.445	.788
2010 Cle	AL	33	128	27	6	2	0	(0	0)	37	15	13	11	9	0	35	2	0	1	4	2	1	.211	.271	.289	.560
2011 Cle	AL	71	268	60	21	1	10	(6	4)	113	34	32	28	18	1	85	6	0	3	0	2	4	.224	.285	.422	.706
2014 2 Tms		112	347	81	19	4	5	(1	4)	123	35	27	39	33	0	76	0	0	1	6	1	10	.233	.299	.354	.654
2015 2 Tms		97	273	69	17	0	6	(4	2)	104	24	33	30	20	0	60	2	0	1	3	3	3	.253	.307	.381	.688
14 Bos	AL	52	185	40	10	2	2	(2	2)	60	14	15	18	19	0	41	0	0	1	5	0	6	.216	.288	.324	.612
14 Phi	NL	60	162	41	9	2	3	(1	2)	63	21	12	21	14	0	35	0	0	0	1	1	4	.253	.313	.389	.701
15 Phi	NL	39	98	24	5	0	0	(0	0)	29	4	6	8	6	0	23	0	0	0	0	0	2	.245	.288	.296	.584
15 TB	AL	58	175	45	12	0	6	(4	2)	75	20	27	22	14	0	37	2	0	1	3	3	1	.257	.318	.429	.746
Postseason		11	43	12	2	1	2	(0	2)	22	9	3	5	8	3	9	1	0	1	2	1	2	.279	.396	.512	.908
10 ML YEARS		1101	4147	1098	252	47	150	(74	76)	1894	660	518	663	483	34	952	67	8	19	143	47	49	.265	.349	.457	.806

Tyler Skaggs

Pitches: L Bats: L Pos: P — Ht: 6'4" Wt: 215 Born: 7/13/1991 Age: 24

		HOW MUCH HE PITCHED						WHAT HE GAVE UP												THE RESULTS							
Year Team	Lg	G	GS	CG	GF	IP	BFP	H	R	ER	HR	SH	SF	HB	TBB	IBB	SO	WP	Bk	W	L	Pct	Sh	Sv-Op	Hld	ERC	ERA
2012 Ari	NL	6	6	0	0	29.1	133	30	20	19	6	1	0	2	13	0	21	1	0	1	3	.250	0	0-0	0	5.31	5.83
2013 Ari	NL	7	7	0	0	38.2	170	38	23	22	7	2	2	2	15	2	36	2	0	2	3	.400	0	0-0	0	4.56	5.12
2014 LAA	AL	18	18	0	0	113.0	464	107	59	54	9	2	5	4	30	1	86	7	0	5	5	.500	0	0-0	0	3.31	4.30
3 ML YEARS		31	31	0	0	181.0	767	175	102	95	22	3	7	8	58	3	143	10	0	8	11	.421	0	0-0	0	3.88	4.72

Carson Smith

Pitches: R Bats: R Pos: RP-70   Ht: 6'6" Wt: 215 Born: 10/19/1989 Age: 26

			HOW MUCH HE PITCHED						WHAT HE GAVE UP												THE RESULTS						
Year Team	Lg	G	GS	CG	GF	IP	BFP	H	R	ER	HR	SH	SF	HB	TBB	IBB	SO	WP	Bk	W	L	Pct	Sh	Sv-Op	Hld	ERC	ERA
2012 Hi Dsrt	A+	49	0	0	32	62.0	271	54	22	20	2	5	2	5	28	2	77	9	1	5	1	.833	0	15- -	-	3.29	2.90
2013 Jacksn	AA	44	0	0	37	50.0	203	33	12	10	1	1	0	5	17	3	71	7	0	1	3	.250	0	15- -	-	1.88	1.80
2014 Tacom	AAA	39	0	0	30	43.0	182	44	19	14	1	1	1	1	13	0	45	2	0	1	3	.250	0	10- -	-	3.40	2.93
2014 Sea	AL	9	0	0	1	8.1	29	2	0	0	0	0	0	0	3	0	10	0	0	1	0	1.000	0	0-0	3	0.55	0.00
2015 Sea	AL	70	0	0	24	70.0	284	49	19	18	2	3	0	7	22	4	92	6	0	2	5	.286	0	13-18	22	2.04	2.31
2 ML YEARS		79	0	0	25	78.1	313	51	19	18	2	3	0	7	25	4	102	6	0	3	5	.375	0	13-18	25	1.80	2.07

Chad Smith

Pitches: R Bats: R Pos: RP-2   Ht: 6'3" Wt: 215 Born: 10/2/1989 Age: 26

			HOW MUCH HE PITCHED						WHAT HE GAVE UP												THE RESULTS						
Year Team	Lg	G	GS	CG	GF	IP	BFP	H	R	ER	HR	SH	SF	HB	TBB	IBB	SO	WP	Bk	W	L	Pct	Sh	Sv-Op	Hld	ERC	ERA
2012 3 Tms	Low	14	8	0	3	45.2	185	40	15	14	2	0	1	1	14	0	48	4	0	1	2	.333	0	2- -	-	2.84	2.76
2013 Wmich	AA	43	2	0	8	72.0	286	58	19	17	3	2	2	0	22	2	73	3	0	5	4	.556	0	1- -	-	2.35	2.13
2014 Erie	AA	12	0	0	2	20.0	78	15	3	3	0	0	0	0	6	0	18	2	0	1	0	1.000	0	1- -	-	1.88	1.35
2014 Toledo	AAA	22	0	0	6	27.0	119	38	15	15	2	2	2	0	5	0	22	1	1	4	3	.571	0	0- -	-	5.48	5.00
2015 Nashv	AAA	8	0	0	6	11.2	52	13	3	3	0	0	0	0	5	0	7	2	0	1	1	.500	0	2- -	-	4.07	2.31
2015 Salt Lk	AAA	6	0	0	0	8.1	45	18	9	9	1	0	0	1	2	0	6	0	0	0	0	-	0	0- -	-	11.65	9.72
2014 Det	AL	10	0	0	5	11.2	50	15	7	7	1	0	0	0	3	0	9	0	0	0	0	-	0	0-0	0	5.24	5.40
2015 Oak	AL	2	0	0	0	1.1	13	5	5	5	0	0	0	1	3	0	2	1	0	0	0	-	0	0-0	0	36.01	33.75
2 ML YEARS		12	0	0	5	13.0	63	20	12	12	1	0	0	1	6	0	11	1	0	0	0	-	0	0-0	0	7.96	8.31

Joe Smith

Pitches: R Bats: R Pos: RP-70   Ht: 6'2" Wt: 205 Born: 3/22/1984 Age: 32

			HOW MUCH HE PITCHED						WHAT HE GAVE UP												THE RESULTS						
Year Team	Lg	G	GS	CG	GF	IP	BFP	H	R	ER	HR	SH	SF	HB	TBB	IBB	SO	WP	Bk	W	L	Pct	Sh	Sv-Op	Hld	ERC	ERA
2007 NYM	NL	54	0	0	14	44.1	205	48	18	17	3	2	0	7	21	4	45	2	0	3	2	.600	0	0-0	10	5.04	3.45
2008 NYM	NL	82	0	0	12	63.1	271	51	28	25	4	4	0	4	31	4	52	1	0	6	3	.667	0	0-3	18	3.23	3.55
2009 Cle	AL	37	0	0	5	34.0	142	30	16	13	4	1	1	0	13	0	30	2	0	0	0	-	0	0-1	10	3.49	3.44
2010 Cle	AL	53	0	0	7	40.0	170	30	18	17	4	1	0	1	24	2	32	0	1	2	2	.500	0	0-1	17	3.53	3.83
2011 Cle	AL	71	0	0	13	67.0	267	52	16	15	1	2	2	2	21	1	45	2	0	3	3	.500	0	0-3	16	2.19	2.01
2012 Cle	AL	72	0	0	12	67.0	278	53	27	22	4	1	1	2	25	4	53	1	1	7	4	.636	0	0-3	21	2.60	2.96
2013 Cle	AL	70	0	0	20	63.0	259	54	17	16	5	3	0	3	23	2	54	3	0	6	2	.750	0	3-8	25	3.23	2.29
2014 LAA	AL	76	0	0	26	74.2	285	45	16	15	4	3	0	6	15	3	68	4	0	7	2	.778	0	15-19	18	1.47	1.81
2015 LAA	AL	70	0	0	13	65.1	271	64	26	26	4	2	1	2	19	4	57	1	0	5	5	.500	0	5-9	32	3.36	3.58
Postseason		3	0	0	1	2.2	10	1	0	0	0	0	0	0	0	0	3	0	0	0	0	-	0	0-0	0	0.28	0.00
9 ML YEARS		585	0	0	122	518.2	2148	427	182	166	33	19	5	27	192	24	436	16	2	39	23	.629	0	23-47	167	2.92	2.88

Josh Smith

Pitches: R Bats: R Pos: SP-7; RP-2   Ht: 6'2" Wt: 220 Born: 8/7/1987 Age: 28

			HOW MUCH HE PITCHED						WHAT HE GAVE UP												THE RESULTS						
Year Team	Lg	G	GS	CG	GF	IP	BFP	H	R	ER	HR	SH	SF	HB	TBB	IBB	SO	WP	Bk	W	L	Pct	Sh	Sv-Op	Hld	ERC	ERA
2011 Dayton	A	26	26	0	0	142.1	579	122	57	47	10	1	3	8	33	0	166	5	0	14	7	.667	0	0- -	-	2.71	2.97
2012 Bkrsfld	A+	27	27	1	0	147.0	626	143	71	62	15	2	5	9	46	0	140	8	0	9	8	.529	0	0- -	-	3.84	3.80
2013 Pnscla	AA	28	28	0	0	160.0	674	148	65	58	16	9	5	7	50	2	139	5	0	11	9	.550	0	0- -	-	3.46	3.26
2014 Lsvlle	AAA	28	24	1	1	159.0	719	174	90	83	8	5	8	7	66	1	123	2	1	10	7	.588	0	0- -	-	4.38	4.70
2015 Lsvlle	AAA	15	12	0	1	86.1	365	84	37	36	2	1	4	6	24	1	69	1	0	3	5	.375	0	0- -	-	3.18	3.75
2015 Pnscla	AA	9	9	0	0	56.0	226	51	23	19	5	1	4	2	9	0	53	0	0	5	4	.556	0	0- -	-	2.76	3.05
2015 Cin	NL	9	7	0	0	32.2	161	42	27	25	5	0	2	5	21	3	30	0	0	0	4	.000	0	0-0	0	7.82	6.89

Seth Smith

Bats: L Throws: L Pos: LF-65;RF-55;PH-21;DH-20;PR-2   Ht: 6'3" Wt: 210 Born: 9/30/1982 Age: 33

							BATTING															RUNNING			AVERAGES			
Year Team	Lg	G	AB	H	2B	3B	HR	(Hm	Rd)	TB	R	RBI	RC	TBB	IBB	SO	HBP	SH	SF	SB	CS	GDP	Avg	OBP	Slg	OPS
2007 Col	NL	7	8	5	0	1	0	(0	0)	7	4	0	3	0	0	1	0	0	0	0	0	0	.625	.625	.875	1.500
2008 Col	NL	67	108	28	7	0	4	(2	2)	47	13	15	18	15	0	23	0	0	0	1	0	0	.259	.350	.435	.785
2009 Col	NL	133	335	98	20	4	15	(8	7)	171	61	55	63	46	3	67	2	1	3	4	1	5	.293	.378	.510	.889
2010 Col	NL	133	358	88	19	5	17	(12	5)	168	55	52	51	35	1	67	2	0	3	2	1	5	.246	.314	.469	.783
2011 Col	NL	147	476	135	32	9	15	(9	6)	230	67	59	73	46	7	93	4	0	7	10	2	9	.284	.347	.483	.830
2012 Oak	AL	125	383	92	23	2	14	(6	8)	161	55	52	52	50	7	98	5	0	3	2	2	4	.240	.333	.420	.754
2013 Oak	AL	117	368	93	27	0	8	(3	5)	144	49	40	46	39	4	94	3	0	0	0	0	10	.253	.329	.391	.721
2014 SD	NL	136	443	118	31	5	12	(8	4)	195	55	48	68	69	3	87	4	0	4	1	1	9	.266	.367	.440	.807
2015 Sea	AL	136	395	98	31	5	12	(7	5)	175	54	42	54	47	4	99	4	1	5	0	0	15	.248	.330	.443	.773
Postseason		18	42	11	2	0	2	(1	1)	19	6	7	7	5	2	13	1	0	0	0	0	0	.262	.354	.452	.807
9 ML YEARS		1001	2874	755	190	31	97	(55	42)	1298	413	363	428	347	29	629	24	2	25	20	7	57	.263	.344	.452	.796

Will Smith

Pitches: L **Bats:** R **Pos:** RP-76 **Ht:** 6'5" **Wt:** 260 **Born:** 7/10/1989 **Age:** 26

		HOW MUCH HE PITCHED						WHAT HE GAVE UP												THE RESULTS							
Year Team	Lg	G	GS	CG	GF	IP	BFP	H	R	ER	HR	SH	SF	HB	TBB	IBB	SO	WP	Bk	W	L	Pct	Sh	Sv-Op	Hld	ERC	ERA
2012 KC	AL	16	16	0	0	89.2	396	111	54	53	12	2	5	1	33	1	59	4	0	6	9	.400	0	0-0		5.75	5.32
2013 KC	AL	19	1	0	4	33.1	131	24	16	12	6	0	4	1	7	1	43	0	0	2	1	.667	0	0-3	6	2.47	3.24
2014 Mil	NL	78	0	0	6	65.2	286	62	31	27	6	1	1	3	31	6	86	7	0	1	3	.250	0	1-6	30	4.02	3.70
2015 Mil	NL	76	0	0	11	63.1	264	52	23	19	5	1	2	1	24	1	91	5	0	7	2	.778	0	0-4	20	2.91	2.70
4 ML YEARS		189	17	0	21	252.0	1077	249	124	111	29	4	12	6	95	8	279	16	0	16	15	.516	0	1-13	56	4.09	3.96

Justin Smoak

Bats: B **Throws:** L **Pos:** 1B-110;PH-27;DH-4;PR-1 SMOKE **Ht:** 6'4" **Wt:** 230 **Born:** 12/5/1986 **Age:** 29

		BATTING																	RUNNING			AVERAGES			
Year Team	Lg	G	AB	H	2B	3B	HR	(Hm Rd)	TB	R	RBI	RC	TBB	IBB	SO	HBP	SH	SF	SB	CS	GDP	Avg	OBP	Slg	OPS
2010 2 Tms	AL	100	348	76	14	0	13	(4 9)	129	40	48	42	46	4	91	0	0	3	1	0	9	.218	.307	.371	.678
2011 Sea	AL	123	427	100	24	0	15	(10 5)	169	38	55	55	55	4	105	3	0	4	0	0	10	.234	.323	.396	.719
2012 Sea	AL	132	483	105	14	0	19	(4 15)	176	49	51	50	49	2	111	1	0	2	1	0	12	.217	.290	.364	.654
2013 Sea	AL	131	454	108	19	0	20	(9 11)	187	53	50	60	64	1	119	2	0	1	0	0	11	.238	.334	.412	.746
2014 Sea	AL	80	248	50	13	0	7	(4 3)	84	28	30	23	24	0	66	2	0	2	0	1	8	.202	.275	.339	.614
2015 Tor	AL	132	296	67	16	1	18	(8 10)	139	44	59	49	29	0	86	2	0	1	0	0	10	.226	.299	.470	.768
10 Tex	AL	70	235	49	10	0	8	(4 4)	83	29	34	30	38	4	57	0	0	2	1	0	6	.209	.316	.353	.670
10 Sea	AL	30	113	27	4	0	5	(0 5)	46	11	14	12	8	0	34	0	0	1	0	0	3	.239	.287	.407	.694
6 ML YEARS		698	2256	506	100	1	92	(39 53)	884	252	293	279	267	11	578	10	0	13	2	1	60	.224	.308	.392	.699

Jake Smolinski

Bats: R **Throws:** R **Pos:** LF-52;RF-16;PH-13;PR-3;DH-2 smoh-LYNN-skee **Ht:** 5'11" **Wt:** 205 **Born:** 2/9/1989 **Age:** 27

		BATTING																	RUNNING			AVERAGES			
Year Team	Lg	G	AB	H	2B	3B	HR	(Hm Rd)	TB	R	RBI	RC	TBB	IBB	SO	HBP	SH	SF	SB	CS	GDP	Avg	OBP	Slg	OPS
2011 Jaxnvl	AA	116	396	97	26	0	7	(- -)	144	42	36	54	59	5	57	1	3	3	6	5	8	.245	.342	.364	.706
2012 Jaxnvl	AA	112	408	105	24	3	7	(- -)	156	71	42	69	78	1	74	10	2	2	9	4	8	.257	.388	.382	.770
2013 Jaxnvl	AA	24	56	11	1	0	0	(- -)	12	8	4	6	13	1	10	1	0	0	1	0	0	.196	.357	.214	.571
2013 NewOr	AAA	95	314	81	14	2	9	(- -)	126	36	31	47	37	3	61	5	0	1	8	1	8	.258	.345	.401	.746
2014 Frisco	AA	72	266	71	15	3	10	(- -)	122	43	35	45	32	0	54	4	0	5	6	2	4	.267	.349	.459	.807
2015 RdRck	AAA	12	45	19	5	0	4	(- -)	36	9	14	14	4	0	7	1	0	0	0	1	0	.422	.480	.800	1.280
2015 Nashv	AAA	25	86	30	9	0	5	(- -)	54	16	17	20	8	0	9	1	0	2	2	1	1	.349	.402	.628	1.030
2014 Tex	AL	24	86	30	5	0	3	(1 2)	44	12	12	15	3	0	24	3	0	0	0	0	0	.349	.391	.512	.903
2015 2 Tms	AL	76	166	32	7	2	6	(2 4)	61	24	26	17	19	0	39	3	0	4	1	1	3	.193	.281	.367	.649
15 Tex	AL	35	60	8	1	0	1	(0 1)	12	12	6	4	11	0	20	1	0	2	1	0	1	.133	.270	.200	.470
15 Oak	AL	41	106	24	6	2	5	(2 3)	49	12	20	13	8	0	19	2	0	2	0	1	2	.226	.288	.462	.750
2 ML YEARS		100	252	62	12	2	9	(3 6)	105	36	38	32	22	0	63	6	0	4	1	1	4	.246	.317	.417	.734

Drew Smyly

Pitches: L **Bats:** L **Pos:** SP-12 SMY-lee **Ht:** 6'3" **Wt:** 190 **Born:** 6/13/1989 **Age:** 27

		HOW MUCH HE PITCHED						WHAT HE GAVE UP												THE RESULTS							
Year Team	Lg	G	GS	CG	GF	IP	BFP	H	R	ER	HR	SH	SF	HB	TBB	IBB	SO	WP	Bk	W	L	Pct	Sh	Sv-Op	Hld	ERC	ERA
2012 Det	AL	23	18	0	0	99.1	416	93	49	44	12	2	3	2	33	1	94	3	0	4	3	.571	0	0-0	1	3.68	3.99
2013 Det	AL	63	0	0	9	76.0	303	62	20	20	4	0	1	1	17	1	81	5	0	6	0	1.000	0	2-6	21	2.21	2.37
2014 2 Tms	AL	28	25	1	0	153.0	618	136	57	55	18	1	3	1	42	2	133	8	0	9	10	.474	1	0-0	1	3.17	3.24
2015 TB	AL	12	12	0	0	66.2	275	58	24	23	11	1	1	1	20	0	77	2	0	5	2	.714	0	0-0	0	3.45	3.11
14 Det	AL	21	18	0	0	105.1	445	111	48	46	14	0	3	1	31	1	89	4	0	6	9	.400	0	0-0	1	4.26	3.93
14 TB	AL	7	7	1	0	47.2	173	25	9	9	4	1	0	0	11	1	44	4	0	3	1	.750	1	0-0	0	1.28	1.70
Postseason		10	0	0	1	7.0	30	3	3	2	0	0	0	0	6	1	7	0	0	1	0	1.000	0	0-0	2	1.81	2.57
4 ML YEARS		126	55	1	9	395.0	1612	349	150	142	45	4	8	5	112	4	385	18	0	24	15	.615	1	2-6	23	3.15	3.24

Travis Snider

Bats: L **Throws:** L **Pos:** LF-42;RF-22;PH-20;DH-5 **Ht:** 6'0" **Wt:** 235 **Born:** 2/2/1988 **Age:** 28

		BATTING																	RUNNING			AVERAGES			
Year Team	Lg	G	AB	H	2B	3B	HR	(Hm Rd)	TB	R	RBI	RC	TBB	IBB	SO	HBP	SH	SF	SB	CS	GDP	Avg	OBP	Slg	OPS
2015 Indy*	AAA	10	35	11	1	0	1	(- 1)	15	5	4	6	4	0	3	0	0	1	0	0	1	.314	.375	.429	.804
2008 Tor	AL	24	73	22	6	0	2	(1 1)	34	9	13	13	5	0	23	0	0	2	0	0	0	.301	.338	.466	.803
2009 Tor	AL	77	241	58	14	1	9	(5 4)	101	34	29	30	29	1	78	3	2	1	1	1	5	.241	.328	.419	.748
2010 Tor	AL	82	298	76	20	0	14	(9 5)	138	36	32	40	21	2	79	0	0	6	6	3	3	.255	.304	.463	.767
2011 Tor	AL	49	187	42	14	0	3	(2 1)	65	23	30	21	11	1	56	1	1	2	9	3	5	.225	.269	.348	.616
2012 2 Tms		60	164	41	7	1	4	(3 1)	62	23	17	21	17	0	48	1	0	3	2	0	2	.250	.319	.378	.697
2013 Pit	NL	111	261	56	12	2	5	(4 1)	87	28	25	23	24	3	75	0	0	3	2	3	1	.215	.281	.333	.614
2014 Pit	NL	140	322	85	15	1	13	(4 9)	141	37	38	42	34	2	67	2	1	0	1	1	10	.264	.338	.438	.776
2015 2 Tms	NL	87	237	55	12	2	4	(3 1)	83	24	24	28	26	2	66	2	0	0	1	0	3	.232	.313	.350	.663
12 Tor	AL	10	36	9	2	0	3	(2 1)	20	6	8	7	3	0	14	0	0	1	0	0	0	.250	.300	.556	.856
12 Pit	NL	50	128	32	5	1	1	(1 0)	42	17	9	14	14	0	34	1	0	2	2	0	2	.250	.324	.328	.652
15 Bal	AL	69	211	50	9	2	3	(2 1)	72	23	20	25	23	1	56	2	0	0	1	0	3	.237	.318	.341	.659
15 Pit	NL	18	26	5	3	0	1	(1 0)	11	1	8	3	3	1	10	0	0	0	0	0	0	.192	.269	.423	.699
Postseason		2	3	0	0	0	0	(0 0)	0	0	0	0	0	0	3	0	0	0	0	0	0	.000	.000	.000	.000
8 ML YEARS		630	1783	435	100	7	54	(31 23)	711	214	212	218	167	11	492	9	4	8	22	11	29	.244	.311	.399	.709

Miguel Socolovich

Pitches: R Bats: R Pos: RP-28　　　　　　　　　　　　　　Ht: 6'1" Wt: 195 Born: 7/24/1986 Age: 29

Year Team	Lg	G	GS	CG	GF	IP	BFP	H	R	ER	HR	SH	SF	HB	TBB	IBB	SO	WP	Bk	W	L	Pct	Sh	Sv-Op	Hld	ERC	ERA
2011 Charlt	AAA	29	2	0	7	48.0	214	46	24	21	2	2	0	0	25	1	63	5	0	3	2	.600	0	1--	-	3.78	3.94
2011 Brham	AA	5	0	0	3	7.0	22	0	0	0	0	0	0	0	2	0	7	0	0	0	0	-	0	1--	-	0.10	0.00
2012 Norfolk	AAA	28	0	0	12	52.0	203	33	13	11	4	0	2	3	14	0	52	1	0	4	0	1.000	0	2--	-	1.83	1.90
2014 LsVgs	AAA	51	0	0	9	59.1	260	68	26	24	5	0	3	0	19	1	68	4	0	2	2	.500	0	3--	-	4.43	3.64
2015 Memp	AAA	21	0	0	4	32.2	126	18	9	9	1	2	2	1	12	0	36	1	0	2	2	.500	0	0--	-	1.52	2.48
2012 2 Tms		12	0	0	2	16.1	72	15	11	11	3	0	0	0	9	0	12	0	1	0	0	-	0	0-1	1	4.79	6.06
2015 StL	NL	28	0	0	11	29.2	125	25	7	6	1	2	0	0	10	1	27	1	0	4	1	.800	0	0-0	1	2.45	1.82
12 Bal	AL	6	0	0	1	10.1	47	11	8	8	2	0	0	0	6	0	6	0	1	0	0	-	0	0-1	0	5.91	6.97
12 ChC	NL	6	0	0	1	6.0	25	4	3	3	1	0	0	0	3	0	6	0	0	0	0	-	0	0-0	1	3.05	4.50
2 ML YEARS		40	0	0	13	46.0	197	40	18	17	4	2	0	0	19	1	39	1	1	4	1	.800	0	0-1	2	3.22	3.33

Eric Sogard

Bats: L Throws: R Pos: 2B-96;SS-17;PH-9;PR-6;DH-2;3B-1　　SO-guard　　　　　　　Ht: 5'10" Wt: 190 Born: 5/22/1986 Age: 30

Year Team	Lg	G	AB	H	2B	3B	HR	(Hm	Rd)	TB	R	RBI	RC	TBB	IBB	SO	HBP	SH	SF	SB	CS	GDP	Avg	OBP	Slg	OPS
2010 Oak	AL	4	7	3	0	0	0	(0	0)	3	0	0	1	2	0	1	0	0	0	0	1	0	.429	.556	.429	.984
2011 Oak	AL	27	70	14	3	0	0	(0	2)	23	7	4	3	4	0	13	0	0	0	0	0	2	.200	.243	.329	.572
2012 Oak	AL	37	102	17	3	1	2	(0	2)	28	8	7	7	5	0	17	0	1	0	2	0	1	.167	.206	.275	.480
2013 Oak	AL	130	368	98	24	3	2	(0	2)	134	45	35	43	27	2	51	5	6	4	10	5	4	.266	.322	.364	.686
2014 Oak	AL	117	291	65	10	0	1	(1	0)	78	38	22	27	31	0	37	1	4	2	11	4	6	.223	.298	.268	.567
2015 Oak	AL	120	372	92	12	3	1	(1	0)	113	40	37	36	23	1	50	2	3	1	6	1	9	.247	.294	.304	.598
Postseason		5	13	1	0	0	0	(0	0)	1	0	0	0	1	0	3	0	1	0	0	0	0	.077	.143	.077	.220
6 ML YEARS		435	1210	289	52	7	8	(2	6)	379	138	105	117	92	3	169	8	14	7	29	11	22	.239	.295	.313	.609

Donovan Solano

Bats: R Throws: R Pos: PH-30;3B-10;SS-10;2B-7;PR-4　　sol-ON-oh　　　　　　　Ht: 5'9" Wt: 205 Born: 12/17/1987 Age: 28

Year Team	Lg	G	AB	H	2B	3B	HR	(Hm	Rd)	TB	R	RBI	RC	TBB	IBB	SO	HBP	SH	SF	SB	CS	GDP	Avg	OBP	Slg	OPS
2015 NewOr*	AAA	36	140	38	3	0	0	(-	-)	41	10	6	11	4	0	24	0	1	2	0	1	3	.271	.288	.293	.581
2012 Mia	NL	93	285	84	11	3	2	(0	2)	107	29	28	35	21	1	58	2	3	5	7	0	5	.295	.342	.375	.717
2013 Mia	NL	102	361	90	13	1	3	(0	3)	114	33	34	38	23	3	57	7	2	2	3	1	11	.249	.305	.316	.621
2014 Mia	NL	111	310	78	11	1	3	(1	2)	100	26	28	35	19	0	61	3	7	1	1	2	5	.252	.300	.323	.623
2015 Mia	NL	55	90	17	3	1	0	(0	0)	22	6	7	3	1	0	18	2	1	0	0	0	4	.189	.215	.244	.459
4 ML YEARS		361	1046	269	38	6	8	(1	7)	343	94	97	111	64	4	194	14	13	8	11	3	25	.257	.307	.328	.634

Jhonatan Solano

Bats: R Throws: R Pos: C-6;PH-1　　　　JOHN-uh-tun sol-ON-oh　　　　　　Ht: 5'9" Wt: 212 Born: 8/12/1985 Age: 30

Year Team	Lg	G	AB	H	2B	3B	HR	(Hm	Rd)	TB	R	RBI	RC	TBB	IBB	SO	HBP	SH	SF	SB	CS	GDP	Avg	OBP	Slg	OPS
2015 NewOr*	AAA	55	193	44	7	0	3	(-	-)	60	13	22	16	10	1	27	2	1	2	0	0	7	.228	.271	.311	.581
2012 Was	NL	12	35	11	3	0	2	(1	1)	20	6	6	6	2	1	5	0	0	0	1	0	0	.314	.351	.571	.923
2013 Was	NL	24	48	7	2	0	0	(0	0)	9	2	2	0	2	0	7	0	0	0	0	1	4	.146	.180	.188	.368
2015 Mia	NL	7	20	1	1	0	0	(0	0)	2	1	2	0	1	0	1	0	0	0	0	0	0	.050	.095	.100	.195
3 ML YEARS		43	103	19	6	0	2	(1	1)	31	9	10	6	5	1	13	0	0	0	1	1	4	.184	.222	.301	.523

Yangervis Solarte

YAWN-gurr-veess soh-LAHR-tay

Bats: B Throws: R Pos: 3B-92;1B-28;PH-23;2B-19;DH-1　　　　　　Ht: 5'11" Wt: 195 Born: 7/7/1987 Age: 28

Year Team	Lg	G	AB	H	2B	3B	HR	(Hm	Rd)	TB	R	RBI	RC	TBB	IBB	SO	HBP	SH	SF	SB	CS	GDP	Avg	OBP	Slg	OPS
2011 NwBrit	AA	121	459	151	36	3	7	(-	-)	214	64	49	78	24	2	38	5	7	2	5	4	18	.329	.367	.466	.834
2012 RdRck	AAA	130	518	150	28	0	11	(-	-)	211	69	54	76	41	1	44	3	0	6	3	1	29	.290	.342	.407	.749
2013 RdRck	AAA	133	526	145	31	0	12	(-	-)	212	66	75	72	39	3	69	2	2	8	3	0	22	.276	.323	.403	.727
2014 2 Tms		131	469	122	19	1	10	(5	5)	173	56	48	59	53	1	58	4	3	6	0	1	13	.260	.336	.369	.705
2015 SD	NL	152	526	142	33	4	14	(5	9)	225	63	63	74	34	0	56	6	2	3	1	0	15	.270	.320	.428	.748
14 NYY	AL	75	252	64	14	0	6	(3	3)	96	26	31	33	30	0	34	3	1	3	0	0	8	.254	.337	.381	.718
14 SD	NL	56	217	58	5	1	4	(2	2)	77	30	17	26	23	1	24	1	2	3	0	1	5	.267	.336	.355	.691
2 ML YEARS		283	995	264	52	5	24	(10	14)	398	119	111	133	87	1	114	10	5	9	1	1	28	.265	.328	.400	.728

Jorge Soler

Bats: R Throws: R Pos: RF-95;PH-7;DH-1　　　　HOR-hay so-LAIR　　　　　Ht: 6'4" Wt: 215 Born: 2/25/1992 Age: 24

Year Team	Lg	G	AB	H	2B	3B	HR	(Hm	Rd)	TB	R	RBI	RC	TBB	IBB	SO	HBP	SH	SF	SB	CS	GDP	Avg	OBP	Slg	OPS
2012 2 Tms	Low	34	134	40	7	0	5	(-	-)	62	28	25	24	12	2	19	3	0	0	12	1	3	.299	.369	.463	.832
2013 Dytona	A+	55	210	59	13	1	8	(-	-)	98	38	35	35	21	1	38	1	0	4	5	1	3	.281	.343	.467	.810
2014 Tenn	AA	22	65	27	9	1	6	(-	-)	56	13	22	24	12	0	15	0	0	2	0	0	1	.415	.494	.862	1.355
2014 Iowa	AAA	32	110	31	11	1	8	(-	-)	68	22	29	24	17	2	26	0	0	0	0	1	4	.282	.378	.618	.996
2014 ChC	NL	24	89	26	8	1	5	(1	4)	51	11	20	15	6	0	24	0	0	2	1	0	3	.292	.330	.573	.903
2015 ChC	NL	101	366	96	18	1	10	(7	3)	146	39	47	43	32	5	121	3	0	3	3	1	9	.262	.324	.399	.723
2 ML YEARS		125	455	122	26	2	15	(8	7)	197	50	67	58	38	5	145	3	0	5	4	1	12	.268	.325	.433	.758

Sammy Solis

Pitches: L **Bats:** R **Pos:** RP-18   SOH-lees   **Ht:** 6'5" **Wt:** 230 **Born:** 8/10/1988 **Age:** 27

			HOW MUCH HE PITCHED			WHAT HE GAVE UP						THE RESULTS								
Year Team	Lg	G GS CG GF	IP	BFP	H	R	ER	HR SH SF HB	TBB IBB	SO	WP Bk	W	L	Pct	Sh	Sv-Op	Hld	ERC	ERA
2011 2 Tms	Low	17 17 0 0	96.2	403	100	38	35	8 1 2 4	23 0	93	6 1	8	3	.727	0	0--	-	3.73	3.26
2013 2 Tms	Low	14 13 0 0	59.2	243	59	23	22	3 1 2 0	19 0	43	3 0	2	1	.667	0	0--	-	3.50	3.32
2015 Hrsbrg	AA	11 1 0 4	13.1	64	19	10	10	0 1 1 2	5 0	11	3 0	0	3	.000	0	2--	-	6.33	6.75
2015 Syrcse	AAA	9 0 0 3	13.1	53	8	3	3	0 1 1 1	5 0	11	1 0	0	0	-	0	2--	-	1.64	2.03
2015 Was	NL	18 0 0 6	21.1	94	25	11	8	2 1 2 1	4 2	17	0 0	1	1	.500	0	0-0	1	4.08	3.38

Joakim Soria

Pitches: R **Bats:** R **Pos:** RP-72   wah-KEEM SORE-ee-uh   **Ht:** 6'3" **Wt:** 200 **Born:** 5/18/1984 **Age:** 32

			HOW MUCH HE PITCHED			WHAT HE GAVE UP						THE RESULTS								
Year Team	Lg	G GS CG GF	IP	BFP	H	R	ER	HR SH SF HB	TBB IBB	SO	WP Bk	W	L	Pct	Sh	Sv-Op	Hld	ERC	ERA
2007 KC	AL	62 0 0 38	69.0	270	46	20	19	3 1 3 1	19 3	75	2 0	2	3	.400	0	17-21	9	1.63	2.48
2008 KC	AL	63 0 0 57	67.1	260	39	13	12	5 2 2 6	19 1	66	1 1	2	3	.400	0	42-45	0	1.72	1.60
2009 KC	AL	47 0 0 41	53.0	222	44	14	13	5 1 2 2	16 1	69	3 0	3	2	.600	0	30-33	0	2.80	2.21
2010 KC	AL	66 0 0 56	65.2	270	53	13	13	4 3 4 2	16 1	71	3 1	1	2	.333	0	43-46	0	2.27	1.78
2011 KC	AL	60 0 0 47	60.1	256	60	29	27	7 3 2 2	17 0	60	1 0	5	5	.500	0	28-35	0	3.80	4.03
2013 Tex	AL	26 0 0 9	23.2	101	18	10	10	2 1 0 1	14 2	28	2 0	1	0	1.000	0	0-0	6	3.45	3.80
2014 2 Tms	AL	48 0 0 37	44.1	182	38	19	16	2 1 2 2	6 2	48	1 0	2	4	.333	0	18-20	1	2.04	3.25
2015 2 Tms		72 0 0 40	67.2	272	55	20	19	8 1 1 2	19 1	64	5 0	3	1	.750	0	24-30	11	2.87	2.53
14 Tex	AL	35 0 0 32	33.1	133	25	12	10	0 1 1 1	4 1	42	0 0	1	3	.250	0	17-19	0	1.38	2.70
14 Det	AL	13 0 0 5	11.0	49	13	7	6	2 0 1 1	2 1	6	1 0	1	1	.500	0	1-1	1	4.92	4.91
15 Det	AL	43 0 0 35	41.0	165	32	13	13	8 1 0 2	11 1	36	0 0	3	1	.750	0	23-26	0	3.15	2.85
15 Pit	NL	29 0 0 5	26.2	107	23	7	6	0 0 1 0	8 0	28	5 0	0	0	-	0	1-4	11	2.39	2.03
Postseason		2 0 0 1	1.0	9	4	5	5	0 0 0 0	2 1	0	0 0	0	1	.000	0	0-1	0	29.61	45.00
8 ML YEARS		444 0 0 325	451.0	1833	353	138	129	36 13 16 18	126 11	481	18 2	19	20	.487	0	202-230	27	2.45	2.57

Rafael Soriano

Pitches: R **Bats:** R **Pos:** RP-6   **Ht:** 6'4" **Wt:** 230 **Born:** 12/19/1979 **Age:** 36

			HOW MUCH HE PITCHED			WHAT HE GAVE UP						THE RESULTS								
Year Team	Lg	G GS CG GF	IP	BFP	H	R	ER	HR SH SF HB	TBB IBB	SO	WP Bk	W	L	Pct	Sh	Sv-Op	Hld	ERC	ERA
2015 Tenn*	AA	5 0 0 1	5.0	19	3	1	0	0 0 0 0	3 0	4	0 0	0	0	-	0	0--	-	2.30	0.00
2015 Iowa*	AAA	5 0 0 0	5.0	17	2	1	1	1 0 0 0	0 0	6	0 0	0	0	-	0	0--	-	0.74	1.80
2002 Sea	AL	10 8 0 1	47.1	202	45	25	24	8 1 0 0	16 1	32	2 0	0	3	.000	0	1-1	0	3.93	4.56
2003 Sea	AL	40 0 0 12	53.0	201	30	9	9	2 0 1 3	12 1	68	0 0	3	0	1.000	0	1-2	5	1.32	1.53
2004 Sea	AL	6 0 0 0	3.1	23	9	6	5	0 0 0 0	3 0	3	0 0	0	3	.000	0	0-1	0	15.97	13.50
2005 Sea	AL	7 0 0 4	7.1	30	6	2	2	0 0 1 0	1 0	9	0 0	0	0	-	0	0-0	1	2.00	2.45
2006 Sea	AL	53 0 0 14	60.0	241	44	15	15	6 1 1 2	21 0	65	2 0	1	2	.333	0	2-6	18	2.64	2.25
2007 Atl	NL	71 0 0 28	72.0	276	47	26	24	12 0 0 2	15 2	70	0 0	3	3	.500	0	9-12	19	2.05	3.00
2008 Atl	NL	14 0 0 5	14.0	57	7	5	4	1 0 0 0	9 2	16	1 0	0	1	.000	0	3-4	0	2.27	2.57
2009 Atl	NL	77 0 0 52	75.2	307	53	25	25	6 4 2 1	27 4	102	0 0	1	6	.143	0	27-31	6	2.18	2.97
2010 TB	AL	64 0 0 56	62.1	237	36	14	12	4 0 1 1	14 2	57	0 0	3	2	.600	0	**45-48**	0	1.33	1.73
2011 NYY	AL	42 0 0 8	39.1	164	33	18	18	4 1 0 1	18 2	36	0 0	2	3	.400	0	2-5	23	3.51	4.12
2012 NYY	AL	69 0 0 54	67.2	279	55	17	17	6 0 1 1	24 4	69	3 0	2	1	.667	0	42-46	4	2.79	2.26
2013 Was	NL	68 0 0 58	66.2	277	65	24	23	7 1 0 0	17 2	51	3 0	3	3	.500	0	43-49	0	3.36	3.11
2014 Was	NL	64 0 0 48	62.0	252	51	23	22	4 0 2 2	19 0	59	2 0	4	1	.800	0	32-39	0	2.70	3.19
2015 ChC	NL	6 0 0 3	5.2	25	8	4	4	2 0 0 0	1 0	4	0 0	0	0	1.000	0	0-1	0	7.66	6.35
Postseason		11 0 0 4	14.1	48	8	4	4	3 2 0 0	0 0	8	0 0	0	1	.000	0	1-1	1	1.28	2.51
14 ML YEARS		591 8 0 343	636.1	2571	489	213	204	62 8 9 15	197 20	641	13 0	24	28	.462	0	207-245	76	2.55	2.89

Geovany Soto

Bats: R **Throws:** R **Pos:** C-73;PH-4;DH-3   **Ht:** 6'1" **Wt:** 235 **Born:** 1/20/1983 **Age:** 33

				BATTING														RUNNING			AVERAGES			
Year Team	Lg	G	AB	H	2B	3B	HR	(Hm Rd)	TB	R	RBI	RC	TBB IBB	SO	HBP SH SF	SB CS GDP				Avg	OBP	Slg	OPS
2005 ChC	NL	1	1	0	0	0	0	(0 0)	0	0	0	0	0 0	0	0 0 0	0 0 0				.000	.000	.000	.000
2006 ChC	NL	11	25	5	1	0	0	(0 0)	6	1	2	0	0 0	5	1 0 0	0 0 0				.200	.231	.240	.471
2007 ChC	NL	18	54	21	6	0	3	(2 1)	36	12	8	13	5 0	14	0 0 1	0 0 1				.389	.433	.667	1.100
2008 ChC	NL	141	494	141	35	2	23	(11 12)	249	66	86	81	62 6	121	2 0 5	0 1 11				.285	.364	.504	.868
2009 ChC	NL	102	331	72	19	1	11	(6 5)	126	27	47	34	50 3	77	3 0 5	1 0 19				.218	.321	.381	.702
2010 ChC	NL	105	322	90	19	0	17	(12 5)	160	47	53	59	62 4	83	0 0 3	0 1 5				.280	.393	.497	.890
2011 ChC	NL	125	421	96	26	0	17	(7 10)	173	46	54	43	45 3	124	6 0 2	0 0 12				.228	.310	.411	.721
2012 2 Tms		99	324	64	12	1	11	(3 8)	111	45	39	30	30 1	76	3 2 2	1 0 12				.198	.270	.343	.613
2013 Tex	AL	54	163	40	9	0	9	(7 2)	76	20	22	23	20 0	60	0 1 0	1 2 6				.245	.328	.466	.794
2014 2 Tms	AL	24	80	20	6	0	1	(1 0)	29	8	11	6	6 0	19	0 1 0	0 0 6				.250	.302	.363	.665
2015 CWS	AL	78	187	41	8	0	9	(6 3)	76	20	21	19	21 0	63	1 1 0	0 1 2				.219	.301	.406	.708
12 ChC	NL	52	176	35	6	1	6	(2 4)	61	26	14	15	19 1	35	2 0 0	0 0 6				.199	.284	.347	.631
12 Tex	AL	47	148	29	6	0	5	(1 4)	50	19	25	15	11 0	41	1 2 2	1 0 6				.196	.253	.338	.591
14 Tex	AL	10	38	9	2	0	1	(1 0)	14	5	3	1	0 0	11	0 0 0	0 0 3				.237	.237	.368	.605
14 Oak	AL	14	42	11	4	0	0	(0 0)	15	3	8	5	6 0	8	0 1 0	0 0 3				.262	.354	.357	.711
Postseason		7	20	3	1	0	1	(0 1)	7	1	2	1	3 0	6	0 0 0	0 0 0				.150	.261	.350	.611
11 ML YEARS		758	2402	590	141	4	101	(55 46)	1042	292	343	308	301 17	642	16 5 18	3 5 70				.246	.331	.434	.765

Giovanni Soto

Pitches: L **Bats:** L **Pos:** RP-6   **Ht:** 6'2" **Wt:** 190 **Born:** 5/18/1991 **Age:** 25

		HOW MUCH HE PITCHED							WHAT HE GAVE UP												THE RESULTS								
Year	Team	Lg	G	GS	CG	GF	IP	BFP	H	R	ER	HR	SH	SF	HB	TBB	IBB	SO	WP	Bk	W	L	Pct	Sh	Sv-Op	Hld	ERC	ERA
2011	2 Tms	Low	18	12	0	1	69.0	290	60	30	24	5	2	0	7	22	0	71	1	1	4	4	.500	0	0- -	-	3.26	3.13
2012	Akron	AA	22	22	2	0	121.1	513	111	62	53	10	4	2	8	49	0	100	6	0	6	9	.400	0	0- -	-	3.82	3.93
2013	Clmbs	AAA	9	1	0	2	8.2	41	8	5	5	0	1	1	0	9	0	8	0	0	0	1	.000	0	0- -	-	5.46	5.19
2014	Akron	AA	37	0	0	10	53.0	212	45	24	19	2	0	3	1	12	1	49	4	0	0	2	.000	0	1- -	-	2.31	3.23
2015	Clmbs	AAA	46	1	0	6	53.2	219	35	22	16	1	2	0	1	29	1	51	4	0	2	1	.667	0	2- -	-	2.32	2.68
2015	Cle	AL	6	0	0	1	3.1	13	3	0	0	0	0	0	0	0	0	0	0	0	0	0	-	0	0-0	0	1.57	0.00

Steven Souza

Bats: R **Throws:** R **Pos:** RF-103;PH-7;DH-3   SOO-zuh   **Ht:** 6'4" **Wt:** 225 **Born:** 4/24/1989 **Age:** 27

					BATTING															RUNNING			AVERAGES			
Year	Team	Lg	G	AB	H	2B	3B	HR	(Hm	Rd)	TB	R	RBI	RC	TBB	IBB	SO	HBP	SH	SF	SB	CS	GDP	Avg	OBP	Slg	OPS
2011	Ptomc	A+	122	390	89	17	2	11	(-	-)	143	58	56	60	75	3	131	8	0	5	25	9	5	.228	.360	.367	.726
2012	2 Tms	Low	97	353	105	22	3	23	(-	-)	202	64	85	73	35	3	74	6	1	5	14	8	6	.297	.366	.572	.938
2013	Hrsbrg	AA	77	273	82	23	1	15	(-	-)	152	54	44	62	41	1	76	5	0	4	20	6	9	.300	.396	.557	.953
2014	Syrcse	AAA	96	346	120	25	2	18	(-	-)	203	62	75	88	52	3	75	3	0	6	26	7	1	.347	.430	.587	1.017
2014	Was	NL	21	23	3	0	0	2	(1	1)	9	2	2	1	3	0	7	0	0	0	0	0	1	.130	.231	.391	.622
2015	TB	AL	110	373	84	15	1	16	(6	10)	149	59	40	40	46	0	144	5	1	1	12	6	7	.225	.318	.399	.717
	2 ML YEARS		131	396	87	15	1	18	(7	11)	158	61	42	41	49	0	151	5	1	1	12	6	8	.220	.313	.399	.712

Denard Span

Bats: L **Throws:** L **Pos:** CF-61   **Ht:** 6'0" **Wt:** 210 **Born:** 2/27/1984 **Age:** 32

					BATTING															RUNNING			AVERAGES			
Year	Team	Lg	G	AB	H	2B	3B	HR	(Hm	Rd)	TB	R	RBI	RC	TBB	IBB	SO	HBP	SH	SF	SB	CS	GDP	Avg	OBP	Slg	OPS
2008	Min	AL	93	347	102	16	7	6	(2	4)	150	70	47	68	50	3	60	4	8	2	18	7	3	.294	.387	.432	.819
2009	Min	AL	145	578	180	16	10	8	(5	3)	240	97	68	100	70	3	89	10	12	6	23	10	7	.311	.392	.415	.807
2010	Min	AL	153	629	166	24	10	3	(0	3)	219	85	58	85	60	0	74	4	10	4	26	12	4	.264	.331	.348	.679
2011	Min	AL	70	284	75	11	5	2	(1	1)	102	37	16	32	27	0	36	0	0	0	6	1	3	.264	.328	.359	.687
2012	Min	AL	128	516	146	38	4	4	(2	2)	204	71	41	69	47	0	62	0	4	1	17	6	10	.283	.342	.395	.738
2013	Was	NL	153	610	170	28	11	4	(2	2)	232	75	47	74	42	0	77	2	7	1	20	6	11	.279	.327	.380	.707
2014	Was	NL	147	610	184	39	8	5	(1	4)	254	94	37	94	50	1	65	2	3	3	31	7	6	.302	.355	.416	.771
2015	Was	NL	61	246	74	17	0	5	(0	5)	106	38	22	45	25	0	26	1	1	2	11	0	5	.301	.365	.431	.796
	Postseason		10	47	12	1	0	0	(0	0)	13	1	1	2	1	0	5	0	0	0	1	0	2	.255	.271	.277	.547
	8 ML YEARS		950	3820	1097	189	55	37	(13	24)	1507	567	336	567	371	7	489	23	45	17	152	41	57	.287	.352	.395	.747

Cory Spangenberg

SPAN-jen-burg

Bats: L **Throws:** R **Pos:** 2B-70;PH-21;3B-19;RF-2;LF-1;CF-1;DH-1   **Ht:** 6'0" **Wt:** 195 **Born:** 3/16/1991 **Age:** 25

					BATTING															RUNNING			AVERAGES			
Year	Team	Lg	G	AB	H	2B	3B	HR	(Hm	Rd)	TB	R	RBI	RC	TBB	IBB	SO	HBP	SH	SF	SB	CS	GDP	Avg	OBP	Slg	OPS
2011	2 Tms	Low	72	275	87	17	1	3	(-	-)	115	55	44	54	45	1	57	5	3	2	25	6	1	.316	.419	.418	.837
2012	Lk Els	A+	98	384	104	12	8	1	(-	-)	135	53	40	48	26	1	72	6	6	4	27	9	4	.271	.324	.352	.675
2013	Lk Els	A+	54	226	67	13	6	4	(-	-)	104	33	31	40	23	1	51	1	3	0	17	3	1	.296	.364	.460	.824
2013	SnAnt	AA	76	287	83	10	3	2	(-	-)	105	35	20	36	17	0	61	2	11	2	19	11	2	.289	.331	.366	.697
2014	SnAnt	AA	66	281	93	17	8	2	(-	-)	132	38	22	46	15	1	63	0	8	0	14	9	2	.331	.365	.470	.835
2014	SD	NL	20	62	18	2	1	2	(1	1)	28	7	9	9	2	0	14	0	1	0	4	2	1	.290	.313	.452	.764
2015	SD	NL	108	303	82	17	5	4	(3	1)	121	38	21	40	28	1	75	2	8	3	9	4	4	.271	.333	.399	.733
	2 ML YEARS		128	365	100	19	6	6	(4	2)	149	45	30	49	30	1	89	2	9	3	13	6	5	.274	.330	.408	.738

George Springer

Bats: R **Throws:** R **Pos:** RF-93;CF-10;PR-1   **Ht:** 6'3" **Wt:** 215 **Born:** 9/19/1989 **Age:** 26

					BATTING															RUNNING			AVERAGES			
Year	Team	Lg	G	AB	H	2B	3B	HR	(Hm	Rd)	TB	R	RBI	RC	TBB	IBB	SO	HBP	SH	SF	SB	CS	GDP	Avg	OBP	Slg	OPS
2012	Lancst	A+	106	433	137	18	10	22	(-	-)	241	101	82	98	56	4	131	6	0	5	28	6	6	.316	.398	.557	.955
2012	CpChr	AA	22	73	16	3	0	2	(-	-)	25	8	5	7	6	0	25	1	1	0	4	2	1	.219	.288	.342	.630
2013	CpChr	AA	73	273	81	20	0	19	(-	-)	158	56	55	64	42	1	96	5	2	1	23	5	1	.297	.399	.579	.978
2013	OkCity	AAA	62	219	68	7	4	18	(-	-)	137	50	53	60	41	0	65	4	0	2	22	3	2	.311	.425	.626	1.050
2014	OkCity	AAA	13	51	18	4	1	3	(-	-)	33	17	9	15	9	0	15	1	0	0	4	0	0	.353	.459	.647	1.106
2014	Hou	AL	78	295	68	8	1	20	(5	15)	138	45	51	45	39	4	114	9	0	2	5	2	4	.231	.336	.468	.804
2015	Hou	AL	102	388	107	19	2	16	(9	7)	178	59	41	60	50	0	109	8	2	3	16	4	4	.276	.367	.459	.826
	2 ML YEARS		180	683	175	27	3	36	(14	22)	316	104	92	105	89	4	223	17	2	5	21	6	8	.256	.354	.463	.817

Craig Stammen

Pitches: R **Bats:** R **Pos:** RP-5   STAMM-enn   **Ht:** 6'4" **Wt:** 230 **Born:** 3/9/1984 **Age:** 32

				HOW MUCH HE PITCHED					WHAT HE GAVE UP												THE RESULTS								
Year	Team	Lg	G	GS	CG	GF	IP	BFP	H	R	ER	HR	SH	SF	HB	TBB	IBB	SO	WP	Bk	W	L	Pct	Sh	Sv-Op	Hld	ERC	ERA
2009	Was	NL	19	19	1	0	105.2	448	112	67	60	14	4	3	3	24	1	48	7	0	4	7	.364	0	0-0	0	4.03	5.11
2010	Was	NL	35	19	3	0	128.0	562	151	78	73	13	5	6	1	41	4	85	3	0	4	4	.500	0	0-0	1	4.79	5.13
2011	Was	NL	7	0	0	2	10.1	38	3	1	1	0	0	0	0	4	0	12	1	0	1	1	.500	0	0-0	1	0.67	0.87
2012	Was	NL	59	0	0	15	88.1	370	70	27	23	7	5	1	2	36	4	87	3	0	6	1	.857	0	1-2	10	2.84	2.34
2013	Was	NL	55	0	0	14	81.2	339	78	30	25	4	8	4	2	27	3	79	2	1	7	6	.538	0	0-1	7	3.32	2.76

			HOW MUCH HE PITCHED						WHAT HE GAVE UP													THE RESULTS							
Year Team	Lg	G	GS	CG	GF	IP	BFP	H	R	ER	HR	SH	SF	HB	TBB	IBB	SO	WP	Bk	W	L	Pct	Sh	Sv-Op	Hld	ERC	ERA
2014 Was	NL	49	0	0	15	72.2	304	78	34	31	5	3	1	3	14	2	56	1	1	4	5	.444	0	0-0	7	3.61	3.84
2015 Was	NL	5	0	0	0	4.0	17	2	0	0	0	0	1	0	3	1	3	0	0	0	0	-	0	0-0	2	1.66	0.00
Postseason		6	0	0	0	7.0	34	8	4	4	1	1	1	3	2	0	5	0	0	0	0	-	0	0-0	1	6.41	5.14
7 ML YEARS		229	38	1	49	490.2	2078	494	237	213	43	25	16	11	149	15	370	17	2	26	24	.520	0	1-3	28	3.70	3.91

Cody Stanley

Bats: L **Throws:** R **Pos:** PH-7;C-2   **Ht:** 5'10" **Wt:** 190 **Born:** 12/21/1988 **Age:** 27

							BATTING														RUNNING			AVERAGES			
Year Team	Lg	G	AB	H	2B	3B	HR	(Hm	Rd)	TB	R	RBI	RC	TBB	IBB	SO	HBP	SH	SF		SB	CS	GDP	Avg	OBP	Slg	OPS
2011 QuadC	A	101	379	100	24	2	11	(-	-)	161	54	66	52	27	3	92	4	0	3		4	2	8	.264	.317	.425	.742
2012 2 Tms	Low	48	167	47	10	1	3	(-	-)	68	12	35	21	6	0	36	1	0	6		1	0	2	.281	.300	.407	.707
2013 PlmBh	A+	23	84	19	1	2	1	(-	-)	27	7	11	6	2	0	17	2	0	2		0	1	0	.226	.256	.321	.577
2013 Sprgfld	AA	75	272	68	10	0	5	(-	-)	93	31	34	29	16	1	54	2	2	2		4	0	6	.250	.295	.342	.636
2014 Sprgfld	AA	103	385	109	16	2	12	(-	-)	165	47	43	61	35	1	68	3	1	9		13	2	7	.283	.340	.429	.769
2015 Memp	AAA	93	271	65	11	0	7	(-	-)	97	36	45	31	24	1	50	3	0	6		2	1	6	.240	.303	.358	.661
2015 StL	NL	9	10	4	1	0	0	(0	0)	5	2	3	3	0	0	3	0	0	0		0	0	0	.400	.400	.500	.900

Giancarlo Stanton

Bats: R **Throws:** R **Pos:** RF-71;DH-3   john-CAHR-loh   **Ht:** 6'6" **Wt:** 240 **Born:** 11/8/1989 **Age:** 26

							BATTING														RUNNING			AVERAGES			
Year Team	Lg	G	AB	H	2B	3B	HR	(Hm	Rd)	TB	R	RBI	RC	TBB	IBB	SO	HBP	SH	SF		SB	CS	GDP	Avg	OBP	Slg	OPS
2010 Fla	NL	100	359	93	21	1	22	(7	15)	182	45	59	56	34	6	123	2	0	1		5	2	7	.259	.326	.507	.833
2011 Fla	NL	150	516	135	30	5	34	(16	18)	277	79	87	81	70	6	166	9	0	6		5	5	11	.262	.356	.537	.893
2012 Mia	NL	123	449	130	30	1	37	(16	21)	273	75	86	79	46	9	143	5	0	1		6	2	5	.290	.361	**.608**	.969
2013 Mia	NL	116	425	106	26	0	24	(15	9)	204	62	62	66	74	5	140	4	0	1		1	0	10	.249	.365	.480	.845
2014 Mia	NL	145	539	155	31	1	37	(24	13)	299	89	105	109	94	24	170	3	0	2		13	1	16	.288	.395	**.555**	.950
2015 Mia	NL	74	279	74	12	1	27	(13	14)	169	47	67	54	34	6	95	2	0	3		4	2	5	.265	.346	.606	.952
6 ML YEARS		708	2567	693	150	9	181	(91	90)	1404	397	466	445	352	56	837	25	0	14		34	12	54	.270	.362	.547	.909

Max Stassi

Bats: R **Throws:** R **Pos:** C-10;DH-1;PH-1   STASS-ee   **Ht:** 5'10" **Wt:** 200 **Born:** 3/15/1991 **Age:** 25

							BATTING														RUNNING			AVERAGES			
Year Team	Lg	G	AB	H	2B	3B	HR	(Hm	Rd)	TB	R	RBI	RC	TBB	IBB	SO	HBP	SH	SF		SB	CS	GDP	Avg	OBP	Slg	OPS
2015 Fresno*	AAA	84	294	62	8	2	13	(-	-)	113	37	43	32	26	1	93	3	2	3		1	1	4	.211	.279	.384	.663
2013 Hou	AL	3	7	2	0	0	0	(0	0)	2	0	1	0	0	0	2	1	0	0		0	0	1	.286	.375	.286	.661
2014 Hou	AL	7	20	7	2	0	0	(0	0)	9	2	4	4	0	0	6	0	0	0		0	0	0	.350	.350	.450	.800
2015 Hou	AL	11	15	6	0	0	1	(1	0)	9	4	2	3	1	0	5	0	1	0		0	0	1	.400	.438	.600	1.038
3 ML YEARS		21	42	15	2	0	1	(1	0)	20	6	7	7	1	0	13	1	1	0		0	0	2	.357	.386	.476	.863

Tim Stauffer

Pitches: R **Bats:** R **Pos:** RP-18   STOFF-er   **Ht:** 6'1" **Wt:** 220 **Born:** 6/2/1982 **Age:** 34

			HOW MUCH HE PITCHED						WHAT HE GAVE UP													THE RESULTS							
Year Team	Lg	G	GS	CG	GF	IP	BFP	H	R	ER	HR	SH	SF	HB	TBB	IBB	SO	WP	Bk	W	L	Pct	Sh	Sv-Op	Hld	ERC	ERA
2015 LsVgs*	AAA	8	8	1	0	54.1	218	46	17	15	4	2	0	3	10	0	35	3	0	4	1	.800	0	0- -	-	2.51	2.48
2005 SD	NL	15	14	0	0	81.0	355	92	50	48	10	2	0	2	29	0	49	0	0	3	6	.333	0	0-0	0	5.00	5.33
2006 SD	NL	1	1	0	0	6.0	21	3	2	1	0	0	0	0	1	0	2	0	0	1	0	1.000	0	0-0	0	0.84	1.50
2007 SD	NL	2	2	0	0	7.2	45	15	18	18	5	0	0	1	6	0	6	0	0	0	1	.000	0	0-0	0	18.32	21.13
2009 SD	NL	14	14	0	0	73.0	316	71	31	29	8	2	1	5	34	1	53	1	0	4	7	.364	0	0-0	0	4.60	3.58
2010 SD	NL	32	7	0	12	82.2	326	65	18	17	3	3	0	2	24	5	61	0	0	6	5	.545	0	0-0	6	2.23	1.85
2011 SD	NL	31	31	0	0	185.2	777	180	81	77	20	14	3	8	53	5	128	4	1	9	12	.429	0	0-0	0	3.67	3.73
2012 SD	NL	1	1	0	0	5.0	24	7	4	3	1	0	0	0	3	0	5	0	0	0	0	-	0	0-0	0	8.40	5.40
2013 SD	NL	43	0	0	8	69.2	284	59	29	29	7	3	2	4	20	1	64	0	0	3	1	.750	0	0-1	7	3.06	3.75
2014 SD	NL	44	3	0	22	64.1	273	67	25	25	4	2	1	2	23	4	67	1	1	6	2	.750	0	0-1	1	3.98	3.50
2015 2 Tms		18	0	0	7	20.2	100	32	18	16	6	0	1	1	9	2	14	2	0	1	0	1.000	0	0-1	1	9.48	6.97
15 Min	AL	13	0	0	5	15.0	73	24	13	11	4	0	1	0	7	2	6	2	0	1	0	1.000	0	0-0	1	9.47	6.60
15 NYM	NL	5	0	0	2	5.2	27	8	5	5	2	0	0	1	2	0	8	0	0	0	0	-	0	0-1	0	9.47	7.94
10 ML YEARS		201	73	0	49	595.2	2521	591	276	263	64	26	8	25	202	18	449	8	2	33	34	.493	0	0-2	8	4.02	3.97

Chris Stewart

Bats: R **Throws:** R **Pos:** C-52;PH-10   **Ht:** 6'4" **Wt:** 210 **Born:** 2/19/1982 **Age:** 34

							BATTING														RUNNING			AVERAGES			
Year Team	Lg	G	AB	H	2B	3B	HR	(Hm	Rd)	TB	R	RBI	RC	TBB	IBB	SO	HBP	SH	SF		SB	CS	GDP	Avg	OBP	Slg	OPS
2006 CWS	AL	6	8	0	0	0	0	(0	0)	0	0	0	0	0	0	2	0	0	0		0	0	0	.000	.000	.000	.000
2007 Tex	AL	17	37	9	2	0	0	(0	0)	11	4	3	3	3	0	6	0	3	0		0	0	0	.243	.300	.297	.597
2008 NYY	AL	1	3	0	0	0	0	(0	0)	0	0	0	0	0	0	1	0	0	0		0	0	0	.000	.000	.000	.000
2010 SD	NL	2	0	0	0	0	0	(0	0)	0	0	0	0	0	0	0	0	0	0		0	0	0	.-	.-	.-	.-
2011 SF	NL	67	162	33	8	0	3	(1	2)	50	20	10	10	16	4	18	2	3	0		0	0	2	.204	.283	.309	.592
2012 NYY	AL	55	141	34	8	0	1	(0	0)	45	15	13	10	10	0	21	1	3	2		2	0	1	.241	.292	.319	.611
2013 NYY	AL	109	294	62	6	0	4	(3	1)	80	28	25	24	30	0	49	6	4	8		4	0	8	.211	.293	.272	.566
2014 Pit	NL	49	136	40	5	0	0	(0	0)	45	9	10	15	12	2	27	3	2	1		0	1	2	.294	.362	.331	.693
2015 Pit	NL	58	159	46	8	0	0	(0	0)	54	9	15	17	6	0	29	2	3	2		0	0	3	.289	.320	.340	.659
Postseason		1	0	0	0	0	0	(0	0)	0	0	0	0	0	0	0	0	0	0		0	0	0	.-	.-	.-	.-
9 ML YEARS		364	940	224	37	0	8	(5	3)	285	85	76	79	77	6	153	14	20	9		6	1	18	.238	.303	.303	.606

Matt Stites

Pitches: R Bats: L Pos: RP-11   Ht: 5'11" Wt: 195 Born: 5/28/1990 Age: 26

Year	Team	Lg	G	GS	CG	GF	IP	BFP	H	R	ER	HR	SH	SF	HB	TBB	IBB	SO	WP	Bk	W	L	Pct	Sh	Sv-Op	Hld	ERC	ERA
2011	2 Tms	Low	26	0	0	11	34.2	127	14	7	7	1	0	0	1	8	0	39	3	2	4	0	1.000	0	5--	-	0.82	1.82
2012	FtWyn	A	42	0	0	37	48.2	175	25	7	4	4	1	1	1	3	0	60	2	1	2	0	1.000	0	13--	-	0.92	0.74
2013	SnAnt	AA	46	0	0	22	52.0	202	37	16	12	6	1	1	1	8	1	51	1	0	2	2	.500	0	14--	-	1.82	2.08
2014	Mobile	AA	12	0	0	6	12.0	46	10	5	5	0	2	0	0	3	0	8	0	0	0	1	.000	0	3--	-	2.16	3.75
2014	Reno	AAA	17	0	0	17	16.0	64	13	6	4	1	0	1	0	6	0	15	0	0	0	0	-	0	12--	-	2.83	2.25
2015	Reno	AAA	23	0	0	9	25.2	119	31	16	11	2	0	2	0	14	0	14	2	0	1	1	.500	0	3--	-	5.72	3.86
2014	Ari	NL	37	0	0	11	33.0	148	33	23	21	6	3	1	1	16	1	26	2	0	0	0	-	0	0-0	2	5.01	5.73
2015	Ari	NL	11	0	0	6	8.2	44	14	14	12	1	0	1	0	5	0	6	0	0	0	0	-	0	0-0	0	8.80	12.46
	2 ML YEARS		48	0	0	17	41.2	192	47	37	33	7	3	2	1	21	1	32	2	0	0	0	-	0	0-0	2	5.76	7.13

Drew Storen

Pitches: R Bats: B Pos: RP-58   STORE-inn   Ht: 6'1" Wt: 195 Born: 8/11/1987 Age: 28

Year	Team	Lg	G	GS	CG	GF	IP	BFP	H	R	ER	HR	SH	SF	HB	TBB	IBB	SO	WP	Bk	W	L	Pct	Sh	Sv-Op	Hld	ERC	ERA
2010	Was	NL	54	0	0	22	55.1	232	48	24	22	3	6	2	3	22	3	52	3	0	4	4	.500	0	5-7	10	3.19	3.58
2011	Was	NL	73	0	0	52	75.1	303	57	24	23	8	1	1	2	20	4	74	2	0	6	3	.667	0	43-48	3	2.35	2.75
2012	Was	NL	37	0	0	17	30.1	116	22	8	8	0	2	1	1	8	0	24	1	0	3	1	.750	0	4-5	10	1.79	2.37
2013	Was	NL	68	0	0	20	61.2	267	65	34	31	7	3	1	1	19	2	58	2	0	4	2	.667	0	3-8	24	4.08	4.52
2014	Was	NL	65	0	0	18	56.1	224	44	8	7	2	3	2	3	11	3	46	4	0	2	1	.667	0	11-14	20	1.93	1.12
2015	Was	NL	58	0	0	35	55.0	228	45	23	21	4	1	1	5	16	2	67	2	0	2	2	.500	0	29-34	5	2.79	3.44
	Postseason		6	0	0	5	5.1	25	7	5	5	0	0	1	0	3	0	7	0	0	1	1	.500	0	1-3	5	5.85	8.44
	6 ML YEARS		355	0	0	164	334.0	1370	281	121	112	24	14	9	15	96	14	321	14	0	21	13	.618	0	95-116	72	2.73	3.02

Dan Straily

Pitches: R Bats: R Pos: SP-3; RP-1   STRAY-lee   Ht: 6'2" Wt: 215 Born: 12/1/1988 Age: 27

Year	Team	Lg	G	GS	CG	GF	IP	BFP	H	R	ER	HR	SH	SF	HB	TBB	IBB	SO	WP	Bk	W	L	Pct	Sh	Sv-Op	Hld	ERC	ERA
2015	Fresno*	AAA	22	22	1	0	122.2	542	147	69	65	13	0	5	4	25	0	124	7	2	10	9	.526	0	0--	-	4.50	4.77
2012	Oak	AL	7	7	0	0	39.1	172	36	19	17	11	1	1	2	16	1	32	0	0	2	1	.667	0	0-0	0	4.94	3.89
2013	Oak	AL	27	27	0	0	152.1	640	132	74	67	16	4	5	7	57	0	124	7	0	10	8	.556	0	0-0	0	3.46	3.96
2014	2 Tms		14	8	0	0	52.0	231	53	41	39	10	0	1	2	24	1	47	2	0	1	3	.250	0	0-0	0	5.22	6.75
2015	Hou	AL	4	3	0	0	16.2	76	16	11	10	2	0	0	1	8	0	14	1	0	0	1	.000	0	0-0	0	4.38	5.40
14	Oak	AL	7	7	0	0	38.1	159	33	21	21	9	0	1	1	15	1	34	2	0	1	2	.333	0	0-0	0	4.31	4.93
14	ChC	NL	7	1	0	0	13.2	72	20	20	18	1	0	0	1	9	0	13	0	0	0	1	.000	0	0-0	0	7.78	11.85
	Postseason		1	1	0	0	6.0	22	4	3	3	1	0	0	1	0	0	8	0	0	0	0	-	0	0-0	0	1.99	4.50
	4 ML YEARS		52	45	0	0	260.1	1119	237	145	133	39	5	7	12	105	2	217	10	0	13	13	.500	0	0-0	0	4.08	4.60

Stephen Strasburg

Pitches: R Bats: R Pos: SP-23   STRAHS-berg   Ht: 6'4" Wt: 230 Born: 7/20/1988 Age: 27

Year	Team	Lg	G	GS	CG	GF	IP	BFP	H	R	ER	HR	SH	SF	HB	TBB	IBB	SO	WP	Bk	W	L	Pct	Sh	Sv-Op	Hld	ERC	ERA
2010	Was	NL	12	12	0	0	68.0	274	56	25	22	5	2	2	0	17	0	92	2	0	5	3	.625	0	0-0	0	2.41	2.91
2011	Was	NL	5	5	0	0	24.0	88	15	5	4	0	1	1	0	2	0	24	0	0	1	1	.500	0	0-0	0	0.97	1.50
2012	Was	NL	28	28	0	0	159.1	653	136	62	56	15	6	4	4	48	1	197	5	0	15	6	.714	0	0-0	0	2.97	3.16
2013	Was	NL	30	30	1	0	183.0	731	136	71	61	16	5	1	12	56	1	191	7	3	8	9	.471	1	0-0	0	2.58	3.00
2014	Was	NL	34	34	0	0	215.0	868	198	86	75	23	9	4	5	43	4	242	7	0	14	11	.560	0	0-0	0	3.02	3.14
2015	Was	NL	23	23	0	0	127.1	523	115	56	49	14	5	1	3	26	0	155	4	0	11	7	.611	0	0-0	0	2.92	3.46
	Postseason		1	1	0	0	5.0	25	8	2	1	0	1	0	1	1	0	2	0	0	0	1	.000	0	0-0	0	6.68	1.80
	6 ML YEARS		132	132	1	0	776.2	3137	656	305	267	73	28	13	24	192	6	901	25	3	54	37	.593	1	0-0	0	2.75	3.09

Ryan Strausborger

Bats: R Throws: R Pos: LF-18;PR-12;DH-4;RF-1;PH-1   STROSS-burger   Ht: 6'0" Wt: 185 Born: 3/4/1988 Age: 28

Year	Team	Lg	G	AB	H	2B	3B	HR	(Hm	Rd)	TB	R	RBI	RC	TBB	IBB	SO	HBP	SH	SF	SB	CS	GDP	Avg	OBP	Slg	OPS
2011	MrtlBh	A+	126	488	132	29	9	8	(-	-)	203	71	57	76	45	1	91	15	6	5	31	12	5	.270	.347	.416	.763
2012	Frisco	AA	116	433	107	15	11	6	(-	-)	162	62	46	57	33	3	101	7	3	6	26	0	6	.247	.309	.374	.683
2013	Frisco	AA	133	461	100	20	5	10	(-	-)	160	50	51	50	38	5	102	7	11	1	28	9	4	.217	.286	.347	.633
2014	RdRck	AAA	88	325	84	17	4	5	(-	-)	124	50	22	46	29	1	55	2	2	2	21	0	6	.258	.321	.382	.703
2015	RdRck	AAA	86	345	96	21	2	10	(-	-)	151	54	34	54	24	0	66	3	7	2	27	5	4	.278	.329	.438	.767
2015	Tex	AL	31	45	9	0	0	1	(1	0)	12	9	3	2	3	0	11	0	1	2	2	1	1	.200	.240	.267	.507

Huston Street

Pitches: R Bats: R Pos: RP-62   Ht: 6'0" Wt: 195 Born: 8/2/1983 Age: 32

Year	Team	Lg	G	GS	CG	GF	IP	BFP	H	R	ER	HR	SH	SF	HB	TBB	IBB	SO	WP	Bk	W	L	Pct	Sh	Sv-Op	Hld	ERC	ERA
2005	Oak	AL	67	0	0	47	78.1	306	53	17	15	3	3	2	2	26	4	72	1	0	5	1	.833	0	23-27	1	1.87	1.72
2006	Oak	AL	69	0	0	55	70.2	290	64	28	26	4	3	3	2	13	3	67	4	0	4	4	.500	0	37-48	1	2.49	3.31
2007	Oak	AL	48	0	0	35	50.0	199	35	20	16	5	2	1	0	12	3	63	0	0	5	2	.714	0	16-21	5	1.84	2.88
2008	Oak	AL	63	0	0	37	70.0	291	58	29	29	6	3	3	1	27	6	69	2	0	7	5	.583	0	18-25	5	2.98	3.73
2009	Col	NL	64	0	0	52	61.2	240	43	22	21	7	3	2	0	13	4	70	0	0	4	1	.800	0	35-37	2	1.83	3.06
2010	Col	NL	44	0	0	39	47.1	187	39	21	19	5	0	1	2	11	4	45	2	1	4	4	.500	0	20-25	0	2.66	3.61
2011	Col	NL	62	0	0	47	58.1	239	62	28	25	10	3	1	1	9	1	55	0	0	1	4	.200	0	29-33	4	4.03	3.86

HOW MUCH HE PITCHED							WHAT HE GAVE UP												THE RESULTS							
Year Team	Lg	G	GS	CG	GF	IP	BFP	H	R	ER	HR	SH	SF	HB	TBB	IBB	SO	WP	Bk	W	L	Pct	Sh	Sv-Op	Hld	ERC	ERA
2012 SD	NL	40	0	0	36	39.0	144	17	8	8	2	1	1	0	11	1	47	1	0	2	1	.667	0	23-24	0	0.99	1.85
2013 SD	NL	58	0	0	52	56.2	222	44	17	17	12	0	1	0	14	1	46	4	0	2	5	.286	0	33-35	0	3.00	2.70
2014 2 Tms		61	0	0	51	59.1	229	42	9	9	4	1	0	0	14	3	57	0	0	2	2	.500	0	41-44	0	1.77	1.37
2015 LAA	AL	62	0	0	51	62.1	255	52	22	22	7	2	3	0	20	5	57	6	0	3	3	.500	0	40-45	0	2.85	3.18
14 SD	NL	33	0	0	28	33.0	121	18	4	4	3	0	0	0	7	0	34	0	0	1	0	1.000	0	24-25	0	1.33	1.09
14 LAA	AL	28	0	0	23	26.1	108	24	5	5	1	1	0	0	7	3	23	0	0	1	2	.333	0	17-19	0	2.53	1.71
Postseason		10	0	0	7	12.0	54	14	9	9	2	1	1	0	6	1	8	0	0	0	3	.000	0	3-4	0	5.92	6.75
11 ML YEARS		638	0	0	502	653.2	2598	509	221	207	65	21	18	8	170	35	648	20	1	39	32	.549	0	315-364	18	2.38	2.85

Hunter Strickland

Pitches: R Bats: R Pos: RP-55   Ht: 6'4" Wt: 220 Born: 9/24/1988 Age: 27

HOW MUCH HE PITCHED							WHAT HE GAVE UP												THE RESULTS							
Year Team	Lg	G	GS	CG	GF	IP	BFP	H	R	ER	HR	SH	SF	HB	TBB	IBB	SO	WP	Bk	W	L	Pct	Sh	Sv-Op	Hld	ERC	ERA
2012 Bradtn	A+	10	9	0	1	45.1	188	47	16	15	5	0	1	6	8	0	25	1	0	2	2	.500	0	0--	-	4.11	2.98
2012 Altna	AA	23	9	0	9	41.1	184	49	23	21	5	1	3	3	14	0	32	1	0	2	2	.500	0	1--	-	5.41	4.57
2013 SnJos	A+	20	0	0	18	21.0	76	10	2	2	1	1	0	1	5	1	23	0	0	1	0	1.000	0	9--	-	1.11	0.86
2014 Rchmd	AA	38	0	0	27	35.2	135	25	10	8	3	1	2	0	4	0	48	1	0	1	1	.500	0	11--	-	1.52	2.02
2015 Scrmto	AAA	15	0	0	10	21.2	80	14	5	4	0	1	0	1	3	0	25	1	0	1	1	.500	0	5--	-	1.25	1.66
2014 SF	NL	9	0	0	5	7.0	25	5	0	0	0	0	0	0	0	0	9	0	0	1	0	1.000	0	1-1	1	1.08	0.00
2015 SF	NL	55	0	0	11	51.1	191	34	14	14	4	0	0	2	10	1	50	1	0	3	3	.500	0	0-2	20	1.72	2.45
Postseason		8	0	0	3	8.1	34	9	7	7	6	0	0	0	2	0	8	1	0	1	0	1.000	0	1-2	1	8.47	7.56
2 ML YEARS		64	0	0	16	58.1	216	39	14	14	4	0	0	2	10	1	59	1	0	4	3	.571	0	1-3	21	1.63	2.16

Marcus Stroman

Pitches: R Bats: R Pos: SP-4   Ht: 5'8" Wt: 180 Born: 5/1/1991 Age: 25

HOW MUCH HE PITCHED							WHAT HE GAVE UP												THE RESULTS							
Year Team	Lg	G	GS	CG	GF	IP	BFP	H	R	ER	HR	SH	SF	HB	TBB	IBB	SO	WP	Bk	W	L	Pct	Sh	Sv-Op	Hld	ERC	ERA
2012 Vancvr	A-	7	0	0	2	11.1	45	8	5	4	0	0	0	0	3	0	15	0	0	1	0	1.000	0	0--	-	1.55	3.18
2012 Nham	AA	8	0	0	0	8.0	38	8	3	3	1	1	0	0	6	0	8	1	0	2	0	1.000	0	0--	-	5.55	3.38
2013 Nham	AA	20	20	0	0	111.2	459	99	48	41	13	3	2	3	27	0	129	4	0	9	5	.643	0	0--	-	3.04	3.30
2014 Buffalo	AAA	7	7	1	0	35.2	146	32	14	12	1	1	0	2	9	0	45	0	0	2	4	.333	0	0--	-	2.74	3.03
2014 Tor	AL	26	20	1	1	130.2	534	125	56	53	7	0	2	3	28	1	111	9	1	11	6	.647	1	1-1	0	2.93	3.65
2015 Tor	AL	4	4	0	0	27.0	103	20	5	5	2	0	0	1	6	0	18	2	1	4	0	1.000	0	0-0	0	2.16	1.67
2 ML YEARS		30	24	1	1	157.2	637	145	61	58	9	0	2	4	34	1	129	11	2	15	6	.714	1	1-1	0	2.80	3.31

Pedro Strop

Pitches: R Bats: R Pos: RP-76   STROPE   Ht: 6'1" Wt: 220 Born: 6/13/1985 Age: 31

HOW MUCH HE PITCHED							WHAT HE GAVE UP												THE RESULTS							
Year Team	Lg	G	GS	CG	GF	IP	BFP	H	R	ER	HR	SH	SF	HB	TBB	IBB	SO	WP	Bk	W	L	Pct	Sh	Sv-Op	Hld	ERC	ERA
2009 Tex	AL	7	0	0	3	7.0	30	6	6	6	0	0	0	0	4	0	9	0	0	0	0	-	0	0-0	0	3.27	7.71
2010 Tex	AL	15	0	0	5	10.2	60	17	12	12	2	1	0	1	11	0	11	5	1	0	0	-	0	0-0	1	11.92	10.13
2011 2 Tms	AL	23	0	0	6	22.0	90	15	5	5	0	2	1	1	10	0	21	2	2	2	1	.667	0	0-2	4	2.15	2.05
2012 Bal	AL	70	0	0	17	66.1	283	52	18	18	2	1	1	4	37	2	58	5	0	5	2	.714	0	3-10	24	3.22	2.44
2013 2 Tms		66	0	0	22	57.1	254	45	30	29	5	7	0	6	26	2	66	8	1	2	5	.286	0	1-4	17	3.21	4.55
2014 ChC	NL	65	0	0	13	61.0	244	40	19	15	2	0	1	4	25	3	71	6	1	2	4	.333	0	2-6	21	2.12	2.21
2015 ChC	NL	76	0	0	12	68.0	270	39	24	22	5	1	3	4	29	6	81	6	0	2	6	.250	0	3-5	28	1.94	2.91
11 Tex	AL	11	0	0	4	9.2	44	7	4	4	0	1	1	1	7	0	9	2	2	0	1	.000	0	0-1	0	3.34	3.72
11 Bal	AL	12	0	0	2	12.1	46	8	1	1	0	1	0	0	3	0	12	0	0	2	0	1.000	0	0-1	4	1.39	0.73
13 Bal	AL	29	0	0	15	22.1	111	23	19	18	4	4	0	2	15	2	24	5	1	0	3	.000	0	0-3	3	5.81	7.25
13 ChC	NL	37	0	0	7	35.0	143	22	11	11	1	3	0	4	11	0	42	3	0	2	2	.500	0	1-1	14	1.80	2.83
Postseason		2	0	0	0	2.1	9	1	0	0	0	0	0	0	1	0	2	0	0	1	0	1.000	0	0-0	0	1.08	0.00
7 ML YEARS		322	0	0	78	292.1	1231	214	114	107	16	12	6	20	142	13	317	32	5	13	18	.419	0	9-27	95	2.84	3.29

Drew Stubbs

Bats: R Throws: R Pos: CF-42;LF-21;PH-17;PR-8;RF-4   Ht: 6'4" Wt: 205 Born: 10/4/1984 Age: 31

BATTING																				RUNNING			AVERAGES			
Year Team	Lg	G	AB	H	2B	3B	HR	(Hm	Rd)	TB	R	RBI	RC	TBB	IBB	SO	HBP	SH	SF	SB	CS	GDP	Avg	OBP	Slg	OPS
2015 Albq*	AAA	38	137	36	4	3	2	(-	-)	52	22	20	22	24	0	39	2	0	2	6	3	3	.263	.376	.380	.755
2009 Cin	NL	42	180	48	5	1	8	(7	1)	79	27	17	22	15	0	49	0	1	0	10	4	1	.267	.323	.439	.762
2010 Cin	NL	150	514	131	19	6	22	(13	9)	228	91	77	74	55	2	168	5	3	6	30	6	6	.255	.329	.444	.773
2011 Cin	NL	158	604	147	22	3	15	(9	6)	220	92	44	66	63	1	205	7	6	1	40	10	2	.243	.321	.364	.686
2012 Cin	NL	136	493	105	13	2	14	(6	8)	164	75	40	45	42	0	166	2	6	1	30	7	2	.213	.277	.333	.610
2013 Cle	AL	146	430	100	21	2	10	(4	6)	155	59	45	50	44	1	141	2	2	3	17	2	3	.233	.305	.360	.665
2014 Col	NL	132	388	112	22	4	15	(12	3)	187	67	43	58	30	1	136	1	2	3	20	3	4	.289	.339	.482	.821
2015 2 Tms		78	123	24	4	2	5	(4	1)	47	20	10	13	14	1	60	1	2	0	5	1	1	.195	.283	.382	.665
15 Col	NL	51	102	22	3	2	5	(4	1)	44	14	10	12	9	1	50	1	2	0	2	1	1	.216	.286	.431	.717
15 Tex	AL	27	21	2	1	0	0	(0	0)	3	6	0	1	5	0	10	0	0	0	3	0	0	.095	.269	.143	.412
Postseason		8	28	5	1	1	0	(0	0)	8	4	1	1	2	0	7	0	0	0	0	0	0	.179	.233	.286	.519
7 ML YEARS		842	2732	667	106	20	89	(55	34)	1080	431	276	328	263	6	925	18	22	14	152	33	19	.244	.313	.395	.708

Eric Stults

Pitches: L **Bats:** L **Pos:** SP-8; RP-1 **Ht:** 6'2" **Wt:** 220 **Born:** 12/9/1979 **Age:** 36

			HOW MUCH HE PITCHED							WHAT HE GAVE UP											THE RESULTS							
Year	Team	Lg	G	GS	CG	GF	IP	BFP	H	R	ER	HR	SH	SF	HB	TBB	IBB	SO	WP	Bk	W	L	Pct	Sh	Sv-Op	Hld	ERC	ERA
2015	Tulsa*	AA	10	8	1	2	53.1	224	47	25	20	2	2	2	2	15	1	35	1	0	4	4	.500	0	1--	-	2.64	3.38
2015	OkCity*	AAA	6	6	0	0	36.2	147	34	15	13	3	2	2	0	6	0	26	0	0	2	1	.667	0	0--	-	2.69	3.19
2006	LAD	NL	6	2	0	2	17.2	73	17	12	11	4	2	0	0	7	0	5	0	0	1	0	1.000	0	0-0	0	4.91	5.60
2007	LAD	NL	12	5	0	0	38.2	179	50	26	25	5	1	1	1	17	2	30	2	0	1	4	.200	0	0-0	1	6.25	5.82
2008	LAD	NL	7	7	1	0	38.2	167	38	18	15	6	2	0	1	13	2	30	0	0	2	3	.400	1	0-0	0	4.07	3.49
2009	LAD	NL	10	10	1	0	50.0	223	51	27	27	3	3	0	4	26	2	33	2	0	4	3	.571	1	0-0	0	4.67	4.86
2011	Col	NL	6	0	0	2	12.0	53	11	8	8	4	0	0	1	4	1	7	0	0	0	0	-	0	0-0	0	4.94	6.00
2012	2 Tms		20	15	0	2	99.0	413	92	38	32	7	9	5	2	27	0	55	1	1	8	3	.727	0	0-0	0	3.06	2.91
2013	SD	NL	33	33	2	0	203.2	857	219	97	89	18	10	6	2	40	2	131	2	1	11	13	.458	0	0-0	0	3.63	3.93
2014	SD	NL	32	32	0	0	176.0	763	197	93	84	26	13	6	4	45	3	111	3	0	8	17	.320	0	0-0	0	4.54	4.30
2015	Atl	NL	9	8	0	1	47.2	196	48	31	31	10	3	1	0	13	1	31	1	0	1	5	.167	0	0-0	0	4.42	5.85
	12 CWS	AL	2	1	0	1	6.2	30	6	2	2	0	0	0	1	4	0	4	0	0	0	-	0	0-0	0	4.14	2.70
	12 SD	NL	18	14	0	1	92.1	383	86	36	30	7	9	5	1	23	0	51	1	1	8	3	.727	0	0-0	0	2.98	2.92
	9 ML YEARS		135	112	4	7	683.1	2924	723	350	322	83	43	19	15	192	13	433	11	2	36	48	.429	2	0-0	1	4.13	4.24

Eugenio Suarez

Bats: R **Throws:** R **Pos:** SS-96;PH-2;3B-1 ay-yoo-HAY-nee-oh SWA-rez **Ht:** 5'11" **Wt:** 180 **Born:** 7/18/1991 **Age:** 24

						BATTING												RUNNING			AVERAGES			
Year	Team	Lg	G	AB	H	2B	3B	HR	(Hm | Rd)	TB	R	RBI	RC	TBB	IBB	SO	HBP	SH	SF	SB	CS	GDP	Avg	OBP	Slg	OPS
2011	2 Tms	Low	70	248	66	18	5	7	(- | -)	115	48	33	40	21	0	47	6	4	0	11	5	5	.266	.338	.464	.802
2012	Wmich	A	135	511	147	34	5	6	(- | -)	209	82	67	87	65	2	116	15	5	7	21	9	6	.288	.380	.409	.789
2013	Lkland	A+	25	103	32	6	2	1	(- | -)	45	17	12	19	14	0	25	4	0	1	2	3	3	.311	.410	.437	.847
2013	Erie	AA	111	442	112	24	4	9	(- | -)	171	53	45	57	46	0	98	6	2	0	9	11	8	.253	.332	.387	.719
2014	Erie	AA	42	155	44	14	1	6	(- | -)	78	26	29	27	15	0	38	0	0	0	7	2	4	.284	.347	.503	.850
2014	Toledo	AAA	12	43	13	4	0	2	(- | -)	23	6	7	10	6	0	9	2	0	1	2	0	2	.302	.404	.535	.939
2015	Lsvlle	AAA	57	203	52	9	2	8	(- | -)	89	30	25	32	26	1	40	3	5	1	3	4	5	.256	.348	.438	.786
2014	Det	AL	85	244	59	9	1	4	(2 | 2)	82	33	23	30	22	1	67	5	5	1	3	2	3	.242	.316	.336	.652
2015	Cin	NL	97	372	104	19	2	13	(4 | 9)	166	42	48	49	17	0	94	3	4	2	4	1	7	.280	.315	.446	.761
	Postseason		1	1	0	0	0	0	(0 | 0)	0	0	0	0	0	0	0	0	0	0	0	0	0	.000	.000	.000	.000
	2 ML YEARS		182	616	163	28	3	17	(6 | 11)	248	75	71	79	39	1	161	8	9	3	7	3	10	.265	.315	.403	.718

Jesus Sucre

Bats: R **Throws:** R **Pos:** C-50 SUE-cray **Ht:** 6'0" **Wt:** 225 **Born:** 4/30/1988 **Age:** 28

						BATTING												RUNNING			AVERAGES			
Year	Team	Lg	G	AB	H	2B	3B	HR	(Hm | Rd)	TB	R	RBI	RC	TBB	IBB	SO	HBP	SH	SF	SB	CS	GDP	Avg	OBP	Slg	OPS
2013	Sea	AL	8	26	5	0	0	0	(0 | 0)	5	1	3	1	2	0	1	0	0	1	0	0	2	.192	.241	.192	.434
2014	Sea	AL	21	61	13	2	0	0	(0 | 0)	15	4	5	6	0	0	17	0	3	0	0	0	0	.213	.213	.246	.459
2015	Sea	AL	52	127	20	6	0	1	(1 | 0)	29	9	7	1	6	0	21	0	9	0	0	0	6	.157	.195	.228	.424
	3 ML YEARS		81	214	38	8	0	1	(1 | 0)	49	14	15	8	8	0	39	0	12	1	0	0	8	.178	.206	.229	.435

Eric Surkamp

Pitches: L **Bats:** L **Pos:** RP-1 SIR-camp **Ht:** 6'5" **Wt:** 220 **Born:** 7/16/1987 **Age:** 28

						HOW MUCH HE PITCHED					WHAT HE GAVE UP									THE RESULTS							
Year	Team	Lg	G	GS	CG	GF	IP	BFP	H	R	ER	HR	SH	SF	HB	TBB	IBB	SO	WP	Bk	W	L	Pct	Sh	Sv-Op	Hld	ERC	ERA
2015	Charllt*	AAA	11	1	0	4	25.2	102	19	8	8	3	0	0	0	9	1	30	0	0	3	0	1.000	0	1--	-	2.62	2.81
2015	OkCity*	AAA	16	15	1	0	88.1	381	97	39	35	8	4	3	4	23	0	70	2	0	9	3	.750	0	0--	-	4.18	3.57
2011	SF	NL	6	6	0	0	26.2	126	32	18	17	1	2	2	2	17	1	13	0	0	2	2	.500	0	0-0	0	6.03	5.74
2013	SF	NL	1	1	0	0	2.2	18	9	7	7	2	0	0	2	0	0	0	0	0	0	1	.000	0	0-0	0	32.56	23.63
2014	CWS	AL	35	0	0	2	24.1	107	22	14	13	3	3	0	1	13	3	20	0	0	2	0	1.000	0	0-0	7	4.81	4.81
2015	LAD	NL	1	0	0	0	3.1	16	4	4	4	2	0	0	2	1	0	4	0	0	0	0	-	0	0-0	0	12.47	10.80
	4 ML YEARS		43	7	0	2	57.0	267	67	43	41	8	5	2	7	31	4	37	0	0	4	3	.571	0	0-0	7	6.48	6.47

Andrew Susac

Bats: R **Throws:** R **Pos:** C-40;PH-13 SOO-sack **Ht:** 6'1" **Wt:** 215 **Born:** 3/22/1990 **Age:** 26

						BATTING												RUNNING			AVERAGES			
Year	Team	Lg	G	AB	H	2B	3B	HR	(Hm | Rd)	TB	R	RBI	RC	TBB	IBB	SO	HBP	SH	SF	SB	CS	GDP	Avg	OBP	Slg	OPS
2012	SnJos	A+	102	361	88	16	3	9	(- | -)	137	58	52	52	55	0	100	6	2	2	1	1	8	.244	.351	.380	.731
2013	Rchmd	AA	84	262	67	17	0	12	(- | -)	120	32	46	46	42	0	68	3	1	2	1	0	7	.256	.362	.458	.820
2014	Fresno	AAA	63	213	57	9	0	10	(- | -)	96	34	32	38	34	1	50	5	0	1	0	0	4	.268	.379	.451	.830
2014	SF	NL	35	88	24	8	0	3	(1 | 2)	41	13	19	16	7	0	28	0	0	0	0	0	0	.273	.326	.466	.792
2015	SF	NL	52	133	29	7	2	3	(2 | 1)	49	14	14	13	14	0	43	1	0	0	0	0	2	.218	.297	.368	.666
	Postseason		4	4	1	0	0	0	(0 | 0)	1	0	0	1	0	0	1	0	0	0	0	0	0	.250	.250	.250	.500
	2 ML YEARS		87	221	53	15	2	6	(3 | 3)	90	27	33	29	21	0	71	1	0	0	0	0	2	.240	.309	.407	.716

Ichiro Suzuki

EE-chee-row soo-ZOO-kee

Bats: L **Throws:** R **Pos:** RF-73;PH-45;LF-30;CF-7;DH-2   **Ht:** 5'11" **Wt:** 170 **Born:** 10/22/1973 **Age:** 42

Year	Team	Lg	G	AB	H	2B	3B	HR	(Hm	Rd)	TB	R	RBI	RC	TBB	IBB	SO	HBP	SH	SF	SB	CS	GDP	Avg	OBP	Slg	OPS
2001	Sea	AL	157	692	242	34	8	8	(5	3)	316	127	69	124	30	10	53	8	4	4	56	14	3	.350	.381	.457	.838
2002	Sea	AL	157	647	208	27	8	8	(4	4)	275	111	51	110	68	27	62	5	3	5	31	15	8	.321	.388	.425	.813
2003	Sea	AL	159	679	212	29	8	13	(8	5)	296	111	62	107	36	7	69	6	3	1	34	8	3	.312	.352	.436	.788
2004	Sea	AL	161	704	262	24	5	8	(4	4)	320	101	60	125	49	19	63	4	2	3	36	11	6	.372	.414	.455	.869
2005	Sea	AL	162	679	206	21	12	15	(8	7)	296	111	68	109	48	23	66	4	2	6	33	8	5	.303	.350	.436	.786
2006	Sea	AL	161	695	224	20	9	9	(6	3)	289	110	49	107	49	16	71	5	1	2	45	2	2	.322	.370	.416	.786
2007	Sea	AL	161	678	238	22	7	6	(3	3)	292	111	68	128	49	13	77	3	4	2	37	8	7	.351	.396	.431	.827
2008	Sea	AL	162	686	213	20	7	6	(3	3)	265	103	42	100	51	12	65	5	3	4	43	4	8	.310	.361	.386	.747
2009	Sea	AL	146	639	225	31	4	11	(6	5)	297	88	46	111	32	15	71	4	2	1	26	9	1	.352	.386	.465	.851
2010	Sea	AL	162	680	214	30	3	6	(1	5)	268	74	43	96	45	13	86	3	3	1	42	9	3	.315	.359	.394	.754
2011	Sea	AL	161	677	184	22	3	5	(4	1)	227	80	47	80	39	13	69	0	1	4	40	7	11	.272	.310	.335	.645
2012	2 Tms	AL	162	629	178	28	6	9	(6	3)	245	77	55	63	22	5	61	2	5	5	29	7	12	.283	.307	.390	.696
2013	NYY	AL	150	520	136	15	3	7	(5	2)	178	57	35	56	26	4	63	1	6	2	20	4	6	.262	.297	.342	.639
2014	NYY	AL	143	359	102	13	2	1	(1	0)	122	42	22	39	21	1	68	1	2	1	15	3	3	.284	.324	.340	.664
2015	Mia	NL	153	398	91	5	6	1	(1	0)	111	45	21	30	31	1	51	0	5	4	11	5	8	.229	.282	.279	.561
12	Sea	AL	95	402	105	15	5	4	(1	3)	142	49	28	33	17	4	40	0	0	4	15	2	10	.261	.288	.353	.642
12	NYY	AL	67	227	73	13	1	5	(5	0)	103	28	27	30	5	1	21	2	5	1	14	5	2	.322	.340	.454	.794
Postseason			19	78	27	4	0	1	(1	0)	34	10	8	11	7	2	9	0	1	0	4	3	0	.346	.400	.436	.836
15 ML YEARS			2357	9362	2935	341	91	113	(65	48)	3797	1348	738	1385	596	179	995	51	46	46	498	114	86	.314	.356	.406	.762

Kurt Suzuki

Bats: R **Throws:** R **Pos:** C-130;PH-3   **Ht:** 5'11" **Wt:** 205 **Born:** 10/4/1983 **Age:** 32

Year	Team	Lg	G	AB	H	2B	3B	HR	(Hm	Rd)	TB	R	RBI	RC	TBB	IBB	SO	HBP	SH	SF	SB	CS	GDP	Avg	OBP	Slg	OPS
2007	Oak	AL	68	213	53	13	0	7	(4	3)	87	27	39	33	24	0	39	3	3	5	0	0	4	.249	.327	.408	.735
2008	Oak	AL	148	530	148	25	1	7	(5	2)	196	54	42	66	44	2	69	11	2	1	2	3	20	.279	.346	.370	.716
2009	Oak	AL	147	570	156	37	1	15	(8	7)	240	74	88	77	28	0	59	8	1	7	8	2	14	.274	.313	.421	.734
2010	Oak	AL	131	435	120	18	2	13	(8	5)	181	55	71	54	33	3	49	12	0	4	3	2	22	.242	.303	.366	.669
2011	Oak	AL	134	460	109	26	0	14	(8	6)	177	54	44	42	38	1	64	7	3	7	2	2	14	.237	.301	.385	.686
2012	2 Tms		118	408	96	20	0	6	(3	3)	134	36	43	39	20	3	73	5	4	5	2	0	5	.235	.276	.328	.605
2013	2 Tms		94	285	66	13	1	5	(2	3)	96	25	32	34	22	6	35	3	2	4	2	0	2	.232	.290	.337	.627
2014	Min	AL	131	452	130	34	0	3	(1	2)	173	37	61	65	34	0	46	9	1	7	0	1	9	.288	.345	.383	.727
2015	Min	AL	131	433	104	17	0	5	(3	2)	136	36	50	46	29	4	59	7	6	4	0	0	14	.240	.296	.314	.610
12	Oak	AL	75	262	57	15	0	1	(1	0)	75	19	18	16	9	0	53	3	2	2	1	0	3	.218	.250	.286	.536
12	Was	NL	43	146	39	5	0	5	(2	3)	59	17	25	23	11	3	20	2	2	3	1	0	2	.267	.321	.404	.725
13	Was	NL	79	252	56	11	1	3	(0	3)	78	19	25	26	20	6	32	3	2	4	2	0	2	.222	.283	.310	.593
13	Oak	AL	15	33	10	2	0	2	(2	0)	18	6	7	8	2	0	3	0	0	0	0	0	0	.303	.343	.545	.888
Postseason			5	17	4	0	0	0	(0	0)	4	0	2	2	2	0	4	0	0	0	0	0	0	.235	.316	.235	.551
9 ML YEARS			1102	3846	982	203	5	75	(42	33)	1420	398	470	456	272	19	493	65	22	44	19	10	104	.255	.312	.369	.681

Anthony Swarzak

SWORE-zack

Pitches: R **Bats:** R **Pos:** RP-10   **Ht:** 6'4" **Wt:** 215 **Born:** 9/10/1985 **Age:** 30

Year	Team	Lg	G	GS	CG	GF	IP	BFP	H	R	ER	HR	SH	SF	HB	TBB	IBB	SO	WP	Bk	W	L	Pct	Sh	Sv-Op	Hld	ERC	ERA
2015	Clmbs*	AAA	6	0	0	3	5.0	22	6	2	2	0	0	0	0	1	0	5	1	1	0	1	.000	0	0- -	-	3.60	3.60
2009	Min	AL	12	12	0	0	59.0	268	76	43	41	12	1	1	2	20	0	34	0	0	3	7	.300	0	0-0	0	6.50	6.25
2011	Min	AL	27	11	0	2	102.0	441	111	53	49	9	2	3	6	26	1	55	3	1	4	7	.364	0	0-0	0	4.11	4.32
2012	Min	AL	44	5	0	9	96.2	413	106	57	54	15	3	6	0	31	8	62	3	0	3	6	.333	0	0-1	1	4.63	5.03
2013	Min	AL	48	0	0	8	96.0	387	89	33	31	7	2	5	1	22	1	69	1	0	3	2	.600	0	0-2	3	2.94	2.91
2014	Min	AL	50	4	0	11	86.0	378	100	48	44	5	1	2	0	28	5	47	0	2	3	2	.600	0	0-1	3	4.29	4.60
2015	Cle	AL	10	0	0	3	13.1	61	18	9	5	1	0	0	0	4	1	13	0	0	0	0	-	0	0-0	0	5.34	3.38
6 ML YEARS			191	32	0	33	453.0	1948	500	243	224	49	9	17	9	131	16	280	7	3	16	24	.400	0	0-4	7	4.32	4.45

Darnell Sweeney

Bats: B **Throws:** R **Pos:** PH-14;LF-12;2B-9;CF-2;3B-1;RF-1;PR-1   **Ht:** 6'1" **Wt:** 195 **Born:** 2/1/1991 **Age:** 25

Year	Team	Lg	G	AB	H	2B	3B	HR	(Hm	Rd)	TB	R	RBI	RC	TBB	IBB	SO	HBP	SH	SF	SB	CS	GDP	Avg	OBP	Slg	OPS
2012	2 Tms	Low	67	265	78	9	6	5	(-	-)	114	46	33	48	33	1	49	3	3	4	27	6	3	.294	.374	.430	.804
2013	Rcuca	A+	134	552	152	34	16	11	(-	-)	251	79	77	87	43	1	151	5	6	7	48	20	5	.275	.329	.455	.784
2014	Chatt	AA	132	490	141	34	5	14	(-	-)	227	88	57	89	77	1	117	5	10	4	15	16	4	.288	.387	.463	.850
2015	OkCity	AAA	116	472	128	30	4	9	(-	-)	193	69	49	68	42	4	116	3	1	4	32	13	10	.271	.332	.409	.741
2015	Phi	NL	37	85	15	4	1	3	(1	2)	30	9	11	8	13	0	27	0	0	0	0	2	1	.176	.286	.353	.639

Blake Swihart

SWY-hart

Bats: B **Throws:** R **Pos:** C-83;PH-4   **Ht:** 6'1" **Wt:** 205 **Born:** 4/3/1992 **Age:** 24

Year	Team	Lg	G	AB	H	2B	3B	HR	(Hm	Rd)	TB	R	RBI	RC	TBB	IBB	SO	HBP	SH	SF	SB	CS	GDP	Avg	OBP	Slg	OPS
2012	Grnvlle	A	92	344	90	17	4	7	(-	-)	136	44	53	44	26	0	68	0	0	8	6	2	5	.262	.307	.395	.702
2013	Salem	A+	103	376	112	29	7	2	(-	-)	161	45	42	60	41	2	63	1	1	3	7	8	9	.298	.366	.428	.794

Year Team	Lg	G	AB	H	2B	3B	HR	(Hm	Rd)	TB	R	RBI	RC	TBB	IBB	SO	HBP	SH	SF	SB	CS	GDP	Avg	OBP	Slg	OPS
2014 Portlnd	AA	92	347	104	23	3	12	(-	-)	169	47	55	61	29	1	65	1	0	3	7	1	8	.300	.353	.487	.840
2014 Pwtckt	AAA	18	69	18	3	1	1	(-	-)	26	6	9	7	2	0	15	0	0	0	1	0	1	.261	.282	.377	.659
2015 Pwtckt	AAA	20	74	23	3	0	0	(-	-)	26	7	11	9	6	0	14	0	0	0	1	1	2	.311	.363	.351	.714
2015 Bos	AL	84	288	79	17	1	5	(2	3)	113	47	31	34	18	0	77	1	2	0	4	2	8	.274	.319	.392	.712

Nick Swisher

Bats: B **Throws:** L **Pos:** DH-28;LF-25;PH-13;1B-12;RF-3   **Ht:** 6'0" **Wt:** 195 **Born:** 11/25/1980 **Age:** 35

Year Team	Lg	G	AB	H	2B	3B	HR	(Hm	Rd)	TB	R	RBI	RC	TBB	IBB	SO	HBP	SH	SF	SB	CS	GDP	Avg	OBP	Slg	OPS
2004 Oak	AL	20	60	15	4	0	2	(1	1)	25	11	8	8	8	0	11	2	0	1	0	0	2	.250	.352	.417	.769
2005 Oak	AL	131	462	109	32	1	21	(11	10)	206	66	74	62	55	3	110	4	0	1	0	1	9	.236	.322	.446	.768
2006 Oak	AL	157	556	141	24	2	35	(17	18)	274	106	95	95	97	7	152	11	2	6	1	2	13	.254	.372	.493	.864
2007 Oak	AL	150	539	141	36	1	22	(8	14)	245	84	78	89	100	12	131	10	1	9	3	2	13	.262	.381	.455	.836
2008 CWS	AL	153	497	109	21	1	24	(19	5)	204	86	69	69	82	6	135	4	1	4	3	3	14	.219	.332	.410	.743
2009 NYY	AL	150	498	124	35	1	29	(8	21)	248	84	82	84	97	2	126	3	3	6	0	0	13	.249	.371	.498	.869
2010 NYY	AL	150	566	163	33	3	29	(15	14)	289	91	89	100	58	0	139	6	3	2	1	2	13	.288	.359	.511	.870
2011 NYY	AL	150	526	137	30	0	23	(12	11)	236	81	85	90	95	6	125	5	1	8	2	2	18	.260	.374	.449	.822
2012 NYY	AL	148	537	146	36	0	24	(11	13)	254	75	93	98	77	2	141	4	1	5	2	3	9	.272	.364	.473	.837
2013 Cle	AL	145	549	135	27	2	22	(11	11)	232	74	63	77	77	3	138	4	0	4	0	1	11	.246	.341	.423	.763
2014 Cle	AL	97	360	75	20	0	8	(6	2)	119	33	42	34	36	0	111	0	1	4	0	0	7	.208	.278	.331	.608
2015 2 Tms		76	219	43	9	0	6	(2	4)	70	14	25	21	35	1	54	3	0	3	0	0	9	.196	.312	.320	.631
15 Cle	AL	30	101	20	4	0	2	(1	1)	30	6	8	5	8	1	24	1	0	1	0	0	2	.198	.261	.297	.558
15 Atl	AL	46	118	23	5	0	4	(1	3)	40	8	17	16	27	0	30	2	0	2	0	0	7	.195	.349	.339	.688
Postseason		47	158	26	9	0	4	(3	1)	47	16	8	10	24	0	48	1	1	1	0	0	4	.165	.277	.297	.575
12 ML YEARS		1527	5369	1338	307	11	245	(121	124)	2402	805	803	825	817	42	1373	56	13	53	13	15	131	.249	.351	.447	.799

Noah Syndergaard

Pitches: R **Bats:** L **Pos:** SP-24   sin-DER-gard   **Ht:** 6'6" **Wt:** 240 **Born:** 8/29/1992 **Age:** 23

		HOW MUCH HE PITCHED						WHAT HE GAVE UP										THE RESULTS							
Year Team	Lg	G	GS	CG	GF	IP	BFP	H	R	ER	HR	SH	SF	HB	TBB	IBB	SO	WP	Bk	W	L	Pct	Sh	Sv-Op	Hld	ERC	ERA
2011 3 Tms	Low	13	11	0	1	59.0	238	46	14	12	1	1	1	0	18	0	68	2	0	5	2	.714	0	0- -	-	2.06	1.83
2012 Lnsng	A	27	19	0	2	103.2	420	81	41	30	3	0	4	3	31	0	122	1	0	8	5	.615	0	1- -	-	2.22	2.60
2013 Stluci	A+	12	12	0	0	63.2	258	61	25	22	3	1	1	1	16	0	64	4	1	3	3	.500	0	0- -	-	3.07	3.11
2013 Bnghtn	AA	11	11	0	0	54.0	214	46	23	18	8	0	0	0	12	0	69	2	0	6	1	.857	0	0- -	-	2.95	3.00
2014 LsVgs	AAA	26	26	0	0	133.0	583	154	77	68	11	4	4	6	43	1	145	6	0	9	7	.563	0	0- -	-	4.76	4.60
2015 LsVgs	AAA	5	5	1	0	29.2	113	20	7	6	2	1	0	0	8	0	34	1	0	3	0	1.000	1	0- -	-	1.82	1.82
2015 NYM	NL	24	24	0	0	150.0	603	126	60	54	19	5	3	3	31	2	166	6	0	9	7	.563	0	0-0	0	2.70	3.24

Matt Szczur

Bats: R **Throws:** R **Pos:** LF-26;PH-24;CF-6;RF-4;PR-4   SEE-zur   **Ht:** 6'0" **Wt:** 200 **Born:** 7/20/1989 **Age:** 26

Year Team	Lg	G	AB	H	2B	3B	HR	(Hm	Rd)	TB	R	RBI	RC	TBB	IBB	SO	HBP	SH	SF	SB	CS	GDP	Avg	OBP	Slg	OPS
2011 2 Tms	Low	109	447	131	22	3	10	(-	-)	189	75	46	66	26	0	48	3	2	2	24	5	6	.293	.335	.423	.758
2012 Dytona	A+	78	295	87	19	4	2	(-	-)	120	68	34	55	47	1	50	4	2	4	38	12	2	.295	.394	.407	.801
2012 Tenn	AA	35	143	30	7	4	2	(-	-)	51	24	6	15	14	0	29	1	0	0	4	2	0	.210	.285	.357	.641
2013 Tenn	AA	128	512	144	27	4	3	(-	-)	188	78	44	70	50	0	75	6	3	3	22	12	11	.281	.350	.367	.717
2014 Iowa	AAA	116	414	108	16	1	1	(-	-)	129	52	24	46	30	1	78	3	9	1	30	7	9	.261	.315	.312	.626
2015 Iowa	AAA	70	267	78	12	2	8	(-	-)	118	40	31	45	22	0	51	6	4	1	20	5	4	.292	.355	.442	.796
2014 ChC	NL	33	62	14	2	0	2	(1	1)	22	6	5	7	4	0	11	0	0	0	0	0	1	.226	.273	.355	.628
2015 ChC	NL	47	72	16	5	0	1	(1	0)	24	5	8	6	6	0	15	0	1	1	2	0	1	.222	.278	.333	.612
2 ML YEARS		80	134	30	7	0	3	(2	1)	46	11	13	13	10	0	26	0	1	1	2	0	2	.224	.276	.343	.619

Jose Tabata

Bats: R **Throws:** R **Pos:** PH-18;RF-5;LF-3;DH-1;PR-1   TAH-bah-tah   **Ht:** 5'11" **Wt:** 210 **Born:** 8/12/1988 **Age:** 27

Year Team	Lg	G	AB	H	2B	3B	HR	(Hm	Rd)	TB	R	RBI	RC	TBB	IBB	SO	HBP	SH	SF	SB	CS	GDP	Avg	OBP	Slg	OPS
2015 Indy*	AAA	44	148	43	6	1	0	(-	-)	51	19	5	19	16	1	16	1	0	0	2	2	9	.291	.364	.345	.708
2015 OkCity*	AAA	28	89	20	4	0	2	(-	-)	30	6	8	9	8	0	13	0	1	1	1	0	1	.225	.286	.337	.623
2010 Pit	NL	102	405	121	21	4	4	(3	1)	162	61	35	59	28	0	57	2	5	1	19	7	7	.299	.346	.400	.746
2011 Pit	NL	91	334	89	18	1	4	(3	1)	121	53	21	41	40	1	61	4	1	3	16	7	8	.266	.349	.362	.711
2012 Pit	NL	103	333	81	20	3	3	(1	2)	116	43	16	31	29	0	58	6	6	0	8	12	7	.243	.315	.348	.664
2013 Pit	NL	106	308	87	17	5	6	(4	2)	132	35	33	45	23	0	45	5	5	0	3	1	6	.282	.342	.429	.771
2014 Pit	NL	80	174	49	5	2	0	(0	0)	58	14	17	17	7	0	26	2	1	2	1	2	12	.282	.314	.333	.647
2015 Pit	NL	27	38	11	0	0	0	(0	0)	11	2	4	4	2	0	7	1	0	0	0	1	3	.289	.341	.289	.631
Postseason		5	6	0	0	0	0	(0	0)	0	0	0	0	0	0	2	0	0	0	0	0	0	.000	.000	.000	.000
6 ML YEARS		509	1592	438	81	15	17	(11	6)	600	208	126	197	129	1	254	20	18	6	47	30	43	.275	.336	.377	.713

Masahiro Tanaka

Pitches: R **Bats:** R **Pos:** SP-24   mah-sah-HEE-roh tuh-NAH-kah   **Ht:** 6'2" **Wt:** 210 **Born:** 11/1/1988 **Age:** 27

		HOW MUCH HE PITCHED						WHAT HE GAVE UP										THE RESULTS							
Year Team	Lg	G	GS	CG	GF	IP	BFP	H	R	ER	HR	SH	SF	HB	TBB	IBB	SO	WP	Bk	W	L	Pct	Sh	Sv-Op	Hld	ERC	ERA
2011 Tohoku	IND	27	27	14	0	226.1	866	171	35	32	8	-	-	5	27	0	241	7	0	19	5	.792	6	0- -	-	1.60	1.27
2012 Tohoku	IND	22	22	8	0	173.0	696	160	45	36	4	-	-	9	19	0	169	4	0	10	4	.714	3	0- -	-	2.15	1.87

Year	Team	Lg	G	GS	CG	GF	IP	BFP	H	R	ER	HR	SH	SF	HB	TBB	IBB	SO	WP	Bk	W	L	Pct	Sh	Sv-Op	Hld	ERC	ERA
								HOW MUCH HE PITCHED						WHAT HE GAVE UP										THE RESULTS				
2013	Tohoku	IND	28	27	8	1	212.0	822	168	35	30	6	-	-	3	32	0	183	9	0	24	0	1.000	2	1- -	-	1.77	1.27
2014	NYY	AL	20	20	3	0	136.1	542	123	47	42	15	2	3	4	21	0	141	4	0	13	5	.722	1	0-0	0	2.83	2.77
2015	NYY	AL	24	24	1	0	154.0	609	126	66	60	25	1	8	1	27	0	139	4	0	12	7	.632	0	0-0	0	2.65	3.51
	2 ML YEARS		44	44	4	0	290.1	1151	249	113	102	40	3	11	5	48	0	280	8	0	25	12	.676	1	0-0	0	2.74	3.16

Travis Tartamella

Bats: R **Throws:** R **Pos:** C-3   **Ht:** 6'0" **Wt:** 205 **Born:** 12/17/1987 **Age:** 28

Year	Team	Lg	G	AB	H	2B	3B	HR	(Hm	Rd)	TB	R	RBI	RC	TBB	IBB	SO	HBP	SH	SF	SB	CS	GDP	Avg	OBP	Slg	OPS
							BATTING														RUNNING			AVERAGES			
2011	PlmBh	A+	20	64	13	3	0	1	(-	-)	19	6	8	5	7	0	22	0	1	1	0	0	2	.203	.278	.297	.575
2011	Sprgfld	AA	15	46	7	1	1	0	(-	-)	10	4	5	1	3	0	13	0	2	0	0	0	0	.152	.204	.217	.421
2012	Sprgfld	AA	37	132	21	6	0	1	(-	-)	30	8	7	3	4	0	37	2	1	0	0	0	6	.159	.196	.227	.423
2013	Memp	AAA	53	176	43	4	0	3	(-	-)	56	11	18	17	14	1	54	1	1	1	0	1	2	.244	.302	.318	.620
2014	Sprgfld	AA	65	217	37	6	0	1	(-	-)	46	11	20	8	15	0	55	2	0	1	0	0	4	.171	.230	.212	.442
2015	Memp	AAA	40	118	24	5	0	0	(-	-)	29	9	9	6	6	1	38	0	4	3	0	0	1	.203	.236	.246	.482
2015	StL	NL	3	2	1	0	0	0	(0	0)	1	0	0	0	0	0	0	0	0	0	0	0	0	.500	.500	.500	1.000

Chris Taylor

Bats: R **Throws:** R **Pos:** SS-28;PR-7;2B-4;DH-2;3B-1   **Ht:** 6'1" **Wt:** 195 **Born:** 8/29/1990 **Age:** 25

Year	Team	Lg	G	AB	H	2B	3B	HR	(Hm	Rd)	TB	R	RBI	RC	TBB	IBB	SO	HBP	SH	SF	SB	CS	GDP	Avg	OBP	Slg	OPS
							BATTING														RUNNING			AVERAGES			
2012	2 Tms	Low	49	183	59	12	1	2	(-	-)	79	31	22	36	23	0	22	8	2	2	17	6	2	.322	.417	.432	.848
2013	Hi Dsrt	A+	67	269	90	16	7	1	(-	-)	141	62	44	64	44	0	62	2	0	4	20	2	4	.335	.426	.524	.950
2013	Jacksn	AA	67	256	75	12	4	1	(-	-)	98	46	16	44	40	1	55	2	1	1	18	3	4	.293	.391	.383	.774
2014	Tacom	AAA	75	302	99	22	7	5	(-	-)	150	63	37	61	35	1	74	3	1	5	14	6	7	.328	.397	.497	.894
2015	Tacom	AAA	86	343	103	26	6	4	(-	-)	147	56	32	61	50	0	61	2	0	1	16	8	4	.300	.391	.429	.820
2014	Sea	AL	47	136	39	8	0	0	(0	0)	47	16	9	18	11	0	39	2	1	1	5	2	3	.287	.347	.346	.692
2015	Sea	AL	37	94	16	3	1	0	(0	0)	21	9	1	1	6	0	31	0	2	0	3	2	0	.170	.220	.223	.443
	2 ML YEARS		84	230	55	11	1	0	(0	0)	68	25	10	19	17	0	70	2	3	1	8	4	3	.239	.296	.296	.592

Michael Taylor

Bats: R **Throws:** R **Pos:** CF-96;LF-38;PH-6;PR-4;RF-3   **Ht:** 6'3" **Wt:** 210 **Born:** 3/26/1991 **Age:** 25

Year	Team	Lg	G	AB	H	2B	3B	HR	(Hm	Rd)	TB	R	RBI	RC	TBB	IBB	SO	HBP	SH	SF	SB	CS	GDP	Avg	OBP	Slg	OPS
							BATTING														RUNNING			AVERAGES			
2011	Hgrstn	A	126	442	112	26	7	13	(-	-)	191	64	68	61	32	0	120	6	4	4	23	12	7	.253	.310	.432	.742
2012	Ptomc	A+	109	384	93	33	2	3	(-	-)	139	51	37	47	40	0	113	3	3	1	19	9	6	.242	.318	.362	.680
2013	Ptomc	A+	133	509	134	41	6	10	(-	-)	217	79	87	85	55	1	131	8	2	7	51	7	10	.263	.340	.426	.767
2014	Hrsbrg	AA	98	384	120	17	2	22	(-	-)	207	74	61	84	50	2	130	4	2	1	34	8	3	.313	.396	.539	.935
2014	Syrcse	AAA	12	44	10	3	1	1	(-	-)	18	7	3	6	7	0	14	0	1	0	3	1	0	.227	.333	.409	.742
2014	Was	NL	17	39	8	3	0	1	(0	1)	14	5	5	3	3	0	17	1	0	0	0	2	1	.205	.279	.359	.638
2015	Was	NL	138	472	108	15	2	14	(6	8)	169	49	63	60	35	9	158	1	1	2	16	3	5	.229	.282	.358	.640
	2 ML YEARS		155	511	116	18	2	15	(6	9)	183	54	68	63	38	9	175	2	1	2	16	5	6	.227	.282	.358	.640

Junichi Tazawa

Pitches: R **Bats:** R **Pos:** RP-61   joo-NEE-chee tuh-ZAH-wah   **Ht:** 5'11" **Wt:** 200 **Born:** 6/6/1986 **Age:** 30

Year	Team	Lg	G	GS	CG	GF	IP	BFP	H	R	ER	HR	SH	SF	HB	TBB	IBB	SO	WP	Bk	W	L	Pct	Sh	Sv-Op	Hld	ERC	ERA
								HOW MUCH HE PITCHED						WHAT HE GAVE UP										THE RESULTS				
2009	Bos	AL	6	4	0	1	25.1	130	43	23	21	4	0	3	3	9	0	13	0	0	2	3	.400	0	0-0	0	9.14	7.46
2011	Bos	AL	3	0	0	2	3.0	13	3	2	2	1	0	0	0	1	0	4	0	0	0	0	-	0	0-0	0	5.31	6.00
2012	Bos	AL	37	0	0	13	44.0	172	37	7	7	1	1	1	2	5	0	45	0	0	1	1	.500	0	1-1	5	1.94	1.43
2013	Bos	AL	71	0	0	10	68.1	284	70	25	24	9	2	5	1	12	1	72	3	1	5	4	.556	0	0-8	25	3.55	3.16
2014	Bos	AL	71	0	0	12	63.0	261	58	23	20	5	1	1	0	17	1	64	5	0	4	3	.571	0	0-5	16	2.97	2.86
2015	Bos	AL	61	0	0	13	58.2	247	65	28	27	5	0	1	1	13	1	56	9	1	2	7	.222	0	3-10	16	3.96	4.14
	Postseason		13	0	0	0	7.1	26	6	1	1	0	0	0	0	1	0	6	1	0	1	0	1.000	0	0-0	6	1.84	1.23
	6 ML YEARS		249	4	0	51	262.1	1107	276	108	101	25	4	11	7	57	3	254	17	2	14	18	.438	0	4-24	62	3.69	3.47

Everett Teaford

Pitches: L **Bats:** L **Pos:** RP-4   **Ht:** 6'0" **Wt:** 160 **Born:** 5/15/1984 **Age:** 32

Year	Team	Lg	G	GS	CG	GF	IP	BFP	H	R	ER	HR	SH	SF	HB	TBB	IBB	SO	WP	Bk	W	L	Pct	Sh	Sv-Op	Hld	ERC	ERA
								HOW MUCH HE PITCHED						WHAT HE GAVE UP										THE RESULTS				
2015	Drhm*	AAA	26	19	0	1	102.2	457	122	70	61	12	2	1	5	33	0	72	3	0	5	9	.357	0	0- -	-	5.18	5.35
2011	KC	AL	26	3	0	7	44.0	175	36	17	16	8	1	3	1	14	0	28	2	0	2	1	.667	0	1-1	1	3.50	3.27
2012	KC	AL	18	5	0	3	61.1	263	68	34	34	11	0	1	2	21	0	35	2	1	1	4	.200	0	0-0	0	5.31	4.99
2013	KC	AL	1	0	0	0	0.2	3	1	0	0	0	0	0	0	0	0	0	0	0	0	0	-	0	0-0	0	4.47	0.00
2015	TB	AL	4	0	0	2	5.2	24	5	1	1	0	0	0	1	3	1	4	0	0	0	0	-	0	0-0	0	3.77	1.59
	4 ML YEARS		49	8	0	12	111.2	465	110	52	51	19	1	4	4	38	1	67	4	1	3	5	.375	0	1-1	1	4.50	4.11

Taylor Teagarden

Bats: R Throws: R Pos: C-6;PH-4   Ht: 6'0" Wt: 210 Born: 12/21/1983 Age: 32

Year	Team	Lg	G	AB	H	2B	3B	HR	(Hm	Rd)	TB	R	RBI	RC	TBB	IBB	SO	HBP	SH	SF	SB	CS	GDP	Avg	OBP	Slg	OPS
2015	Iowa*	AAA	63	197	60	12	1	5	(-	-)	89	26	31	34	23	1	70	2	0	2	0	0	3	.305	.379	.452	.831
2008	Tex	AL	16	47	15	5	0	6	(3	3)	38	10	17	15	5	0	19	1	0	0	0	0	0	.319	.396	.809	1.205
2009	Tex	AL	60	198	43	13	0	6	(2	4)	74	26	24	16	14	0	76	1	3	2	0	0	6	.217	.270	.374	.644
2010	Tex	AL	28	71	11	1	0	4	(1	3)	24	10	6	5	8	0	34	2	4	0	0	0	0	.155	.259	.338	.597
2011	Tex	AL	14	34	8	2	0	0	(0	0)	10	3	2	2	2	0	13	0	0	0	0	0	0	.235	.278	.294	.572
2012	Bal	AL	22	57	9	3	0	2	(2	0)	18	4	9	6	5	0	23	0	2	0	0	0	1	.158	.226	.316	.542
2013	Bal	AL	23	60	10	2	0	2	(0	2)	18	3	5	2	1	0	18	0	1	0	0	1	0	.167	.180	.300	.480
2014	NYM	NL	9	28	4	0	0	1	(1	0)	7	1	5	2	2	0	7	0	0	0	0	0	1	.143	.200	.250	.450
2015	ChC	NL	8	15	3	0	0	0	(0	0)	3	0	2	1	0	0	4	0	0	0	0	0	1	.200	.200	.200	.400
	8 ML YEARS		180	510	103	26	0	21	(9	12)	192	57	70	49	37	0	194	4	10	2	0	1	9	.202	.260	.376	.637

Julio Teheran

Pitches: R Bats: R Pos: SP-33   tay-RONN   Ht: 6'2" Wt: 200 Born: 1/27/1991 Age: 25

	HOW MUCH HE PITCHED							WHAT HE GAVE UP											THE RESULTS							
Year	Team	Lg	G	GS	CG	GF	IP	BFP	H	R	ER	HR	SH	SF	HB	TBB	IBB	SO	WP	Bk	W	L	Pct	Sh	Sv-Op	Hld	ERC	ERA
2011	Atl	NL	5	3	0	0	19.2	87	21	11	11	4	2	1	0	8	0	10	1	0	1	1	.500	0	0-0	0	5.19	5.03
2012	Atl	NL	2	1	0	0	6.1	24	5	4	4	0	0	0	0	1	0	5	0	0	0	0	-	0	0-0	0	1.64	5.68
2013	Atl	NL	30	30	0	0	185.2	774	173	69	66	22	8	5	13	45	4	170	2	0	14	8	.636	0	0-0	0	3.45	3.20
2014	Atl	NL	33	33	4	0	221.0	884	188	82	71	22	13	4	4	51	4	186	1	1	14	13	.519	2	0-0	0	2.71	2.89
2015	Atl	NL	33	33	0	0	200.2	843	189	99	90	27	10	3	9	73	3	171	2	0	11	8	.579	0	0-0	0	4.07	4.04
	Postseason		1	1	0	0	2.2	17	8	6	6	1	0	1	0	1	0	5	1	0	0	1	.000	0	0-0	0	20.77	20.25
	5 ML YEARS		103	100	4	0	633.1	2612	576	265	242	75	33	13	26	178	11	542	6	1	40	30	.571	2	0-0	0	3.41	3.44

Mark Teixeira

Bats: B Throws: R Pos: 1B-108;DH-3;PH-2   tuh-SHARE-uh   Ht: 6'3" Wt: 225 Born: 4/11/1980 Age: 36

Year	Team	Lg	G	AB	H	2B	3B	HR	(Hm	Rd)	TB	R	RBI	RC	TBB	IBB	SO	HBP	SH	SF	SB	CS	GDP	Avg	OBP	Slg	OPS
2003	Tex	AL	146	529	137	29	5	26	(19	7)	254	66	84	78	44	5	120	14	0	2	1	2	14	.259	.331	.480	.811
2004	Tex	AL	145	545	153	34	2	38	(18	20)	305	101	112	120	68	12	117	10	0	2	4	1	6	.281	.370	.560	.929
2005	Tex	AL	162	644	194	41	3	43	(30	13)	370	112	144	148	72	5	124	11	0	3	4	0	18	.301	.379	.575	.954
2006	Tex	AL	162	628	177	45	1	33	(12	21)	323	99	110	114	89	12	128	4	0	6	2	0	17	.282	.371	.514	.886
2007	2 Tms		132	494	151	33	2	30	(14	16)	278	86	105	116	72	13	112	7	0	2	0	0	7	.306	.400	.563	.963
2008	2 Tms		157	574	177	41	0	33	(19	14)	317	102	121	119	97	13	93	7	0	7	2	0	17	.308	.410	.552	.962
2009	NYY	AL	156	609	178	43	3	39	(24	15)	344	103	122	112	81	9	114	12	0	5	2	0	13	.292	.383	.565	.948
2010	NYY	AL	158	601	154	36	0	33	(19	14)	289	113	108	110	93	6	122	13	0	5	0	1	15	.256	.365	.481	.846
2011	NYY	AL	156	589	146	26	1	39	(22	17)	291	90	111	106	76	3	110	11	0	8	4	1	12	.248	.341	.494	.835
2012	NYY	AL	123	451	113	27	1	24	(12	12)	214	66	84	69	54	1	83	7	0	12	2	1	11	.251	.332	.475	.807
2013	NYY	AL	15	53	8	1	0	3	(2	1)	18	5	12	6	8	2	19	1	0	1	0	0	1	.151	.270	.340	.609
2014	NYY	AL	123	440	95	14	0	22	(10	12)	175	56	62	51	58	3	109	6	0	4	1	1	13	.216	.313	.398	.711
2015	NYY	AL	111	392	100	22	0	31	(14	17)	215	57	79	71	59	6	85	6	0	5	2	0	7	.255	.357	.548	.906
07	Tex	AL	78	286	85	24	1	13	(5	8)	150	48	49	58	45	10	66	3	0	1	0	0	5	.297	.397	.524	.921
07	Atl	NL	54	208	66	9	1	17	(9	8)	128	38	56	58	27	3	46	4	0	1	0	0	2	.317	.404	.615	1.020
08	Atl	NL	103	381	108	27	0	20	(11	9)	195	63	78	69	65	9	70	3	0	2	0	0	13	.283	.390	.512	.902
08	LAA	AL	54	193	69	14	0	13	(8	5)	122	39	43	50	32	4	23	4	0	5	2	0	4	.358	.449	.632	1.081
	Postseason		40	153	34	6	0	3	(2	1)	49	21	14	15	24	2	34	4	0	2	1	0	3	.222	.339	.320	.659
	13 ML YEARS		1746	6549	1783	392	18	394	(215	179)	3393	1056	1254	1220	871	90	1336	109	0	62	24	7	151	.272	.364	.518	.882

Ruben Tejada

Bats: R Throws: R Pos: SS-81;3B-19;2B-13;PH-7;PR-1   Ht: 5'11" Wt: 200 Born: 10/27/1989 Age: 26

Year	Team	Lg	G	AB	H	2B	3B	HR	(Hm	Rd)	TB	R	RBI	RC	TBB	IBB	SO	HBP	SH	SF	SB	CS	GDP	Avg	OBP	Slg	OPS
2010	NYM	NL	78	216	46	12	0	1	(0	1)	61	28	15	16	22	3	38	8	6	3	2	2	2	.213	.305	.282	.588
2011	NYM	NL	96	328	93	15	1	0	(0	0)	110	31	36	41	35	3	50	6	4	3	5	1	6	.284	.360	.335	.696
2012	NYM	NL	114	464	134	26	0	1	(0	1)	163	53	25	49	27	0	73	5	3	2	4	4	9	.289	.333	.351	.685
2013	NYM	NL	57	208	42	12	0	0	(0	0)	54	20	10	15	15	0	24	1	3	0	2	1	3	.202	.259	.260	.519
2014	NYM	NL	119	355	84	11	0	5	(1	4)	110	30	34	42	50	11	73	8	4	2	1	2	8	.237	.342	.310	.652
2015	NYM	NL	116	360	94	23	0	3	(2	1)	126	36	28	42	38	5	70	5	2	2	2	1	6	.261	.338	.350	.688
	6 ML YEARS		580	1931	493	99	1	10	(3	7)	624	198	148	205	187	22	328	33	22	12	16	11	34	.255	.330	.323	.653

Tomas Telis

Bats: B Throws: R Pos: PH-12;C-11;DH-1   TOE-maas tay-LEASE   Ht: 5'8" Wt: 215 Born: 6/18/1991 Age: 25

Year	Team	Lg	G	AB	H	2B	3B	HR	(Hm	Rd)	TB	R	RBI	RC	TBB	IBB	SO	HBP	SH	SF	SB	CS	GDP	Avg	OBP	Slg	OPS
2011	Hkry	A	115	461	137	28	0	11	(-	-)	198	67	69	66	18	0	35	6	5	4	12	6	17	.297	.329	.430	.759
2012	MrtlBh	A+	117	450	111	24	1	4	(-	-)	149	45	43	44	17	2	53	7	3	7	9	2	18	.247	.283	.331	.614
2013	Frisco	AA	91	348	92	19	0	4	(-	-)	123	32	43	37	10	1	46	4	3	4	8	2	13	.264	.290	.353	.643
2014	Frisco	AA	70	267	81	16	2	2	(-	-)	107	31	33	39	17	1	29	1	3	7	7	1	14	.303	.339	.401	.740
2014	RdRck	AAA	36	139	48	7	2	3	(-	-)	68	18	17	24	6	1	12	1	1	1	1	1	4	.345	.377	.489	.866
2015	RdRck	AAA	70	282	82	15	1	5	(-	-)	114	43	25	37	14	2	31	1	3	0	1	2	15	.291	.327	.404	.731
2015	NewOr	AAA	13	48	16	0	0	0	(-	-)	16	3	4	7	5	1	6	0	1	1	2	0	5	.333	.389	.333	.722
2014	Tex	AL	18	68	17	2	0	0	(0	0)	19	7	8	7	1	0	10	1	1	0	0	0	2	.250	.271	.279	.551

Year Team	Lg	G	AB	H	2B	3B	HR	(Hm Rd)	TB	R	RBI	RC	TBB	IBB	SO	HBP	SH	SF	SB	CS	GDP	Avg	OBP	Slg	OPS
2015 2 Tms		23	38	6	0	0	0	(0 0)	6	2	2	1	1	1	4	2	0	0	0	0	2	.158	.220	.158	.377
15 Tex	AL	6	11	2	0	0	0	(0 0)	2	1	2	1	0	0	1	1	0	0	0	0	0	.182	.250	.182	.432
15 Mia	NL	17	27	4	0	0	0	(0 0)	4	1	0	0	1	1	3	1	0	0	0	0	0	.148	.207	.148	.355
2 ML YEARS		41	106	23	2	0	0	(0 0)	25	9	10	8	2	1	14	3	1	0	0	0	4	.217	.252	.236	.488

Ryan Tepera

Pitches: R Bats: R Pos: RP-32
tuh-PAIR-uh
Ht: 6'1" Wt: 180 Born: 11/3/1987 Age: 28

Year Team	Lg	G	GS	CG	GF	IP	BFP	H	R	ER	HR	SH	SF	HB	TBB	IBB	SO	WP	Bk	W	L	Pct	Sh	Sv-Op	Hld	ERC	ERA
2011 Dnedin A+		27	23	0	2	146.1	612	156	75	72	13	3	1	5	38	1	93	11	0	11	6	.647	0	0- -	-	4.03	4.43
2012 Dnedin A+		5	5	1	0	21.0	101	27	19	18	3	0	0	2	12	0	14	1	1	1	3	.250	0	0- -	-	7.33	7.71
2012 Nham AA		16	15	0	0	74.1	345	82	44	40	4	3	5	7	37	0	57	6	0	7	3	.700	0	0- -	-	5.01	4.84
2013 Nham AA		33	20	0	8	116.0	517	109	65	58	11	4	5	12	56	0	105	6	0	10	8	.556	0	1- -	-	4.40	4.50
2014 Buffalo AAA		51	0	0	23	64.0	278	66	29	26	4	2	1	1	24	4	67	5	0	7	3	.700	0	2- -	-	3.82	3.66
2015 Buffalo AAA		21	0	0	6	34.0	130	16	5	4	1	0	0	0	13	1	37	3	0	3	1	.750	0	3- -	-	1.20	1.06
2015 Tor AL		32	0	0	12	33.0	128	23	14	12	8	0	0	3	6	0	22	2	0	0	2	.000	0	1-1	0	2.87	3.27

Nick Tepesch

Pitches: R Bats: R Pos: P
TEP-ish
Ht: 6'4" Wt: 225 Born: 10/12/1988 Age: 27

Year Team	Lg	G	GS	CG	GF	IP	BFP	H	R	ER	HR	SH	SF	HB	TBB	IBB	SO	WP	Bk	W	L	Pct	Sh	Sv-Op	Hld	ERC	ERA
2011 Hkry A		29	23	2	1	138.1	583	147	70	62	14	6	4	13	33	0	118	1	0	7	5	.583	0	0- -	-	4.27	4.03
2012 MrtlBh A+		12	12	1	0	71.2	299	68	27	23	3	3	2	7	18	0	59	3	0	5	3	.625	1	0- -	-	3.24	2.89
2012 Frisco AA		16	14	0	0	90.1	382	97	47	43	10	3	3	3	26	0	68	3	2	6	3	.667	0	0- -	-	4.34	4.28
2014 RdRck AAA		7	7	1	0	45.2	178	36	8	8	1	1	1	2	9	0	41	2	0	6	1	.857	1	0- -	-	1.98	1.58
2013 Tex AL		19	17	0	1	93.0	407	100	53	50	12	1	4	7	27	3	76	0	0	4	6	.400	0	0-0	-	4.49	4.84
2014 Tex AL		23	22	0	1	126.0	537	128	66	61	15	3	4	7	44	2	56	1	0	5	11	.313	0	0-0	-	4.37	4.36
2 ML YEARS		42	39	0	2	219.0	944	228	119	111	27	4	8	14	71	5	132	1	0	9	17	.346	0	0-0	0	4.42	4.56

Joey Terdoslavich

Bats: B Throws: R Pos: PH-16;1B-12;LF-2
ter-DOSS-low-vitch
Ht: 6'2" Wt: 200 Born: 9/9/1988 Age: 27

Year Team	Lg	G	AB	H	2B	3B	HR	(Hm Rd)	TB	R	RBI	RC	TBB	IBB	SO	HBP	SH	SF	SB	CS	GDP	Avg	OBP	Slg	OPS
2015 Gwnntt* AAA		42	146	41	11	1	4	(- -)	66	23	24	28	29	1	33	0	0	4	1	1	5	.281	.391	.452	.843
2013 Atl	NL	55	79	17	4	0	0	(0 0)	21	11	4	6	12	1	24	0	0	1	1	0	2	.215	.315	.266	.581
2014 Atl	NL	9	10	3	2	0	0	(0 0)	5	1	2	1	0	0	3	1	0	0	0	0	1	.300	.364	.500	.864
2015 Atl	NL	28	56	12	4	1	1	(1 0)	21	5	4	3	3	1	14	0	0	0	0	0	0	.214	.254	.375	.629
3 ML YEARS		92	145	32	10	1	1	(1 0)	47	17	10	10	15	2	41	1	0	1	1	0	3	.221	.296	.324	.620

Joe Thatcher

Pitches: L Bats: L Pos: RP-43
Ht: 6'2" Wt: 230 Born: 10/4/1981 Age: 34

Year Team	Lg	G	GS	CG	GF	IP	BFP	H	R	ER	HR	SH	SF	HB	TBB	IBB	SO	WP	Bk	W	L	Pct	Sh	Sv-Op	Hld	ERC	ERA
2015 Fresno* AAA		9	0	0	3	8.2	34	4	1	1	0	0	0	1	4	0	10	1	0	0	0	-	0	0- -	-	1.50	1.04
2007 SD	NL	22	0	0	5	21.0	85	13	6	3	1	0	0	1	6	2	16	0	0	2	2	.500	0	0-0	5	1.49	1.29
2008 SD	NL	25	0	0	7	25.2	128	42	25	24	4	2	3	0	13	2	17	0	0	0	4	.000	0	0-3	5	8.91	8.42
2009 SD	NL	52	0	0	7	45.0	188	37	14	14	2	1	2	4	18	7	55	2	1	1	0	1.000	0	0-1	9	2.87	2.80
2010 SD	NL	65	0	0	12	35.0	137	23	5	5	1	3	2	1	7	2	45	0	0	1	0	1.000	0	0-0	11	1.37	1.29
2011 SD	NL	18	0	0	5	10.0	44	8	5	5	1	0	0	0	7	1	9	0	0	0	0	-	0	0-0	2	3.96	4.50
2012 SD	NL	55	0	0	13	31.2	141	30	13	12	2	2	2	3	14	3	39	0	1	1	4	.200	0	1-1	14	3.82	3.41
2013 2 Tms		72	0	0	16	39.1	164	40	14	14	4	1	2	1	10	0	36	3	0	3	2	.600	0	0-4	15	3.75	3.20
2014 2 Tms		53	0	0	9	30.1	135	36	16	13	3	1	2	4	4	1	27	1	0	2	1	.667	0	0-1	6	4.42	3.86
2015 Hou	AL	43	0	0	3	22.2	100	23	8	8	1	2	2	0	12	0	26	0	0	1	3	.250	0	0-0	6	4.28	3.18
13 SD	NL	50	0	0	13	30.0	121	28	7	7	3	0	1	1	4	0	29	2	0	3	1	.750	0	0-2	11	2.83	2.10
13 Ari	NL	22	0	0	3	9.1	43	12	7	7	1	1	1	0	6	0	7	1	0	0	1	.000	0	0-2	4	7.19	6.75
14 Ari	NL	37	0	0	7	24.0	100	23	10	7	3	1	1	2	3	1	25	1	0	1	0	1.000	0	0-1	4	3.14	2.63
14 LAA	AL	16	0	0	2	6.1	35	13	6	6	0	0	1	2	1	0	2	0	0	1	1	.500	0	0-0	2	9.96	8.53
9 ML YEARS		405	0	0	77	260.2	1122	252	106	98	19	12	15	14	91	18	270	6	2	11	16	.407	0	1-10	70	3.58	3.38

Dale Thayer

Pitches: R Bats: R Pos: RP-38
Ht: 6'0" Wt: 210 Born: 12/17/1980 Age: 35

Year Team	Lg	G	GS	CG	GF	IP	BFP	H	R	ER	HR	SH	SF	HB	TBB	IBB	SO	WP	Bk	W	L	Pct	Sh	Sv-Op	Hld	ERC	ERA
2015 ElPaso* AAA		7	0	0	4	9.2	37	5	1	1	1	0	0	0	3	0	10	0	0	2	0	1.000	0	0- -	-	1.47	0.93
2009 TB	AL	11	0	0	3	13.2	59	18	9	7	3	0	0	0	1	0	8	1	0	0	0	-	0	1-1	0	5.38	4.61
2010 TB	AL	1	0	0	0	2.0	13	6	6	6	1	0	0	2	0	0	2	0	0	0	0	-	0	0-0	0	24.30	27.00
2011 NYM	NL	11	0	0	7	10.1	42	12	4	4	0	1	2	0	0	0	5	0	0	0	3	.000	0	0-0	1	2.78	3.48
2012 SD	NL	64	0	0	21	57.2	235	53	24	22	4	4	4	1	12	4	47	2	0	2	2	.500	0	7-10	22	2.68	3.43
2013 SD	NL	69	0	0	13	65.0	270	59	25	24	8	3	1	2	22	2	64	2	0	3	5	.375	0	1-4	18	3.60	3.32
2014 SD	NL	70	0	0	25	65.1	265	53	19	17	9	1	0	2	16	3	62	1	0	4	5	.444	0	0-1	13	2.75	2.34
2015 SD	NL	38	0	0	5	37.2	158	37	17	17	5	1	1	0	15	4	25	2	0	2	2	.500	0	0-1	6	4.13	4.06
7 ML YEARS		264	0	0	74	251.2	1042	239	104	97	30	10	8	5	66	13	213	8	0	11	17	.393	0	9-17	59	3.41	3.47

Caleb Thielbar

Pitches: L Bats: R Pos: RP-6 THEEL-bar Ht: 6'0" Wt: 205 Born: 1/31/1987 Age: 29

Year Team	Lg	G	GS	CG	GF	IP	BFP	H	R	ER	HR	SH	SF	HB	TBB	IBB	SO	WP	Bk	W	L	Pct	Sh	Sv-Op	Hld	ERC	ERA
2015 Roch*	AAA	29	0	0	9	32.0	142	30	10	10	1	3	1	1	18	3	19	0	0	5	3	.625	0	0- -	-	3.80	2.81
2015 ElPaso*	AAA	9	0	0	3	12.1	52	9	1	1	1	0	0	1	5	0	7	0	0	0	0	-	0	0- -	-	2.78	0.73
2013 Min	AL	49	0	0	16	46.0	171	24	11	9	4	0	1	0	14	4	39	1	0	3	2	.600	0	0-0	1	1.38	1.76
2014 Min	AL	54	0	0	7	47.2	206	51	19	18	3	1	6	1	16	1	35	0	0	2	1	.667	0	0-1	7	4.01	3.40
2015 Min	AL	6	0	0	1	5.0	20	5	3	3	0	1	0	0	0	0	5	1	0	0	0	-	0	0-0	1	1.95	5.40
3 ML YEARS		109	0	0	24	98.2	397	80	33	30	7	2	7	1	30	5	79	2	0	5	3	.625	0	0-1	9	2.53	2.74

Josh Thole

Bats: L Throws: R Pos: C-18 TOE-lee Ht: 6'1" Wt: 205 Born: 10/28/1986 Age: 29

Year Team	Lg	G	AB	H	2B	3B	HR	(Hm	Rd)	TB	R	RBI	RC	TBB	IBB	SO	HBP	SH	SF	SB	CS	GDP	Avg	OBP	Slg	OPS
2015 Buffalo*	AAA	45	149	34	5	0	0	(-	-)	39	12	17	14	20	0	20	0	1	0	0	0	2	.228	.320	.262	.581
2009 NYM	NL	17	53	17	2	1	0	(0	0)	21	2	9	9	4	0	5	0	0	2	1	0	1	.321	.356	.396	.752
2010 NYM	NL	73	202	56	7	1	3	(2	1)	74	17	17	28	24	1	25	1	0	1	0	1	8	.277	.357	.366	.723
2011 NYM	NL	114	340	91	17	0	3	(1	2)	117	22	40	39	38	6	47	4	1	3	0	2	8	.268	.345	.344	.690
2012 NYM	NL	104	321	75	15	0	1	(0	1)	93	24	21	24	27	6	50	1	4	1	0	0	12	.234	.294	.290	.584
2013 Tor	AL	45	120	21	3	1	1	(0	1)	29	11	8	7	12	0	25	1	2	0	0	0	3	.175	.256	.242	.497
2014 Tor	AL	57	133	33	4	0	0	(0	0)	37	11	7	11	14	0	25	0	3	0	0	3	4	.248	.320	.278	.598
2015 Tor	AL	18	49	10	2	0	0	(0	0)	12	5	2	2	3	0	9	0	0	0	0	0	2	.204	.250	.245	.495
7 ML YEARS		428	1218	303	50	3	8	(3	5)	383	92	104	120	122	13	186	7	10	6	2	5	38	.249	.319	.314	.634

Ian Thomas

Pitches: L Bats: R Pos: RP-13; SP-1 Ht: 6'4" Wt: 215 Born: 4/20/1987 Age: 29

Year Team	Lg	G	GS	CG	GF	IP	BFP	H	R	ER	HR	SH	SF	HB	TBB	IBB	SO	WP	Bk	W	L	Pct	Sh	Sv-Op	Hld	ERC	ERA
2012 Rome	A	26	0	0	12	45.2	193	45	19	16	4	1	0	0	15	0	58	1	1	5	0	1.000	0	6- -	-	3.63	3.15
2013 Missi	AA	39	13	0	8	104.1	419	72	34	32	7	4	2	1	37	2	123	1	1	7	8	.467	0	1- -	-	2.11	2.76
2014 Gwnntt	AAA	6	1	0	2	13.2	56	12	6	6	1	0	2	0	5	0	16	2	0	0	1	.000	0	1- -	-	3.17	3.95
2015 Gwnntt	AAA	7	0	0	1	12.2	43	5	0	0	0	0	1	0	1	0	16	0	0	0	0	-	0	0- -	-	0.46	0.00
2015 OkCity	AAA	14	6	0	1	42.1	195	55	29	27	5	2	2	0	15	0	38	3	0	4	1	.800	0	0- -	-	5.70	5.74
2014 Atl	NL	16	0	0	4	10.2	48	10	5	5	0	1	0	0	6	1	13	1	0	1	2	.333	0	0-0	3	3.37	4.22
2015 2 Tms	NL	14	1	0	4	23.1	98	20	11	10	2	1	0	0	11	0	23	1	0	1	1	.500	0	0-0	0	3.51	3.86
15 Atl	NL	5	0	0	1	5.1	25	4	3	2	1	1	0	0	5	0	5	1	0	0	0	-	0	0-0	0	5.34	3.38
15 LAD	NL	9	1	0	3	18.0	73	16	8	8	1	0	0	0	6	0	18	0	0	1	1	.500	0	0-0	0	3.01	4.00
2 ML YEARS		30	1	0	8	34.0	146	30	16	15	2	2	1	0	17	1	36	2	0	2	3	.400	0	0-0	3	3.48	3.97

Aaron Thompson

Pitches: L Bats: L Pos: RP-41 Ht: 6'3" Wt: 205 Born: 2/28/1987 Age: 29

Year Team	Lg	G	GS	CG	GF	IP	BFP	H	R	ER	HR	SH	SF	HB	TBB	IBB	SO	WP	Bk	W	L	Pct	Sh	Sv-Op	Hld	ERC	ERA
2015 Roch*	AAA	21	0	0	11	17.0	71	16	7	7	0	0	0	0	4	0	11	0	0	1	1	.500	0	1- -	-	2.44	3.71
2011 Pit	NL	4	1	0	0	7.2	41	13	6	6	2	1	0	0	6	0	1	0	0	0	0	-	0	0-0	0	11.83	7.04
2014 Min	AL	7	0	0	2	7.1	31	8	2	2	0	0	1	0	2	1	6	0	0	0	0	-	0	0-0	1	3.20	2.45
2015 Min	AL	41	0	0	5	32.1	137	32	19	18	2	2	3	0	11	2	17	1	0	1	3	.250	0	0-1	9	3.43	5.01
3 ML YEARS		52	1	0	7	47.1	209	53	27	26	4	3	4	0	19	3	24	1	0	1	3	.250	0	0-1	10	4.54	4.94

Trayce Thompson

Bats: R Throws: R Pos: RF-18;LF-12;CF-10;PH-5;PR-4;DH-1 Ht: 6'3" Wt: 210 Born: 3/15/1991 Age: 25

Year Team	Lg	G	AB	H	2B	3B	HR	(Hm	Rd)	TB	R	RBI	RC	TBB	IBB	SO	HBP	SH	SF	SB	CS	GDP	Avg	OBP	Slg	OPS
2011 Knapol	A	136	519	125	36	2	24	(-	-)	237	95	87	81	60	1	172	10	4	4	8	4	10	.241	.329	.457	.785
2012 WinSa	A+	116	449	114	28	5	22	(-	-)	218	77	90	76	45	1	144	6	2	8	18	3	2	.254	.325	.486	.810
2012 Brham	AA	14	50	14	1	1	3	(-	-)	26	10	6	10	8	0	16	0	0	0	2	0	1	.280	.379	.520	.899
2013 Brham	AA	135	507	116	24	5	15	(-	-)	195	78	73	70	60	0	139	13	2	8	25	8	5	.229	.321	.385	.706
2014 Brham	AA	133	518	123	34	6	16	(-	-)	217	86	59	76	65	0	151	4	3	5	20	5	5	.237	.324	.419	.743
2015 Charllt	AAA	104	388	101	23	4	13	(-	-)	171	53	39	53	23	0	79	2	2	2	11	5	8	.260	.304	.441	.744
2015 CWS	AL	44	122	36	8	3	5	(3	2)	65	17	16	20	13	0	26	0	0	0	1	0	3	.295	.363	.533	.896

Tyler Thornburg

Pitches: R Bats: R Pos: RP-24 Ht: 5'11" Wt: 190 Born: 9/29/1988 Age: 27

Year Team	Lg	G	GS	CG	GF	IP	BFP	H	R	ER	HR	SH	SF	HB	TBB	IBB	SO	WP	Bk	W	L	Pct	Sh	Sv-Op	Hld	ERC	ERA
2015 ColSpr*	AAA	17	17	0	0	88.2	396	106	55	52	16	4	1	1	36	0	57	3	0	2	7	.222	0	0- -	-	5.97	5.28
2012 Mil	NL	8	3	0	3	22.0	95	24	11	11	8	1	0	1	7	0	20	1	0	0	0	-	0	0-0	0	6.44	4.50
2013 Mil	NL	18	7	0	4	66.2	270	53	17	15	1	4	1	3	26	2	48	2	1	3	1	.750	0	0-0	0	2.59	2.03
2014 Mil	NL	27	0	0	9	29.2	131	24	14	14	1	1	0	0	21	0	28	4	0	3	1	.750	0	0-0	5	3.71	4.25
2015 Mil	NL	24	0	0	9	34.1	151	31	22	14	7	0	2	3	12	1	34	3	1	0	2	.000	0	0-0	1	4.20	3.67
4 ML YEARS		77	10	0	20	152.2	647	132	64	54	17	6	4	7	66	3	130	10	2	6	4	.600	0	0-0	6	3.70	3.18

Matt Thornton

Pitches: L **Bats:** L **Pos:** RP-60   **Ht:** 6'6" **Wt:** 235 **Born:** 9/15/1976 **Age:** 39

		HOW MUCH HE PITCHED						WHAT HE GAVE UP										THE RESULTS						
Year	Team	Lg	G	GS	CG	GF	IP	BFP	H	R	ER	HR	SH	SF	HB	TBB	IBB	SO	WP	Bk	W	L	Pct	Sh	Sv-Op	Hld	ERC	ERA
2004	Sea	AL	19	1	0	8	32.2	148	30	15	15	2	2	1	0	25	1	30	2	0	1	2	.333	0	0-0	0	4.75	4.13
2005	Sea	AL	55	0	0	15	57.0	262	54	33	33	13	1	1	0	42	2	57	7	0	0	4	.000	0	0-1	5	6.06	5.21
2006	CWS	AL	63	0	0	20	54.0	227	46	20	20	5	1	3	1	21	4	49	1	0	5	3	.625	0	2-5	18	3.12	3.33
2007	CWS	AL	68	0	0	13	56.1	249	59	31	30	4	0	2	2	26	6	55	3	0	4	4	.500	0	2-7	17	4.35	4.79
2008	CWS	AL	74	0	0	12	67.1	268	48	20	20	5	1	1	2	19	2	77	3	0	5	3	.625	0	1-6	20	2.07	2.67
2009	CWS	AL	70	0	0	17	72.1	291	58	22	22	5	2	1	1	20	2	87	4	0	6	3	.667	0	4-9	24	2.40	2.74
2010	CWS	AL	61	0	0	13	60.2	239	41	18	18	3	0	2	2	20	5	81	1	0	5	4	.556	0	8-10	21	1.89	2.67
2011	CWS	AL	62	0	0	20	59.2	262	60	34	22	3	3	3	0	21	5	63	2	0	2	5	.286	0	3-7	20	3.32	3.32
2012	CWS	AL	74	0	0	18	65.0	266	63	27	25	4	1	0	3	17	4	53	2	0	4	10	.286	0	3-7	26	3.29	3.46
2013	2 Tms	AL	60	0	0	6	43.1	187	47	20	18	4	4	1	2	15	1	30	2	0	0	4	.000	0	0-1	19	4.50	3.74
2014	2 Tms		64	0	0	8	36.0	152	33	9	7	0	2	2	5	8	2	28	0	0	1	3	.250	0	0-4	18	2.69	1.75
2015	Was	NL	60	0	0	12	41.1	171	33	12	10	2	2	1	1	11	3	23	1	0	2	1	.667	0	0-1	18	2.12	2.18
13	CWS	AL	40	0	0	3	28.0	116	25	14	12	4	2	0	2	10	1	21	1	0	0	3	.000	0	0-1	18	3.94	3.86
13	Bos	AL	20	0	0	3	15.1	71	22	6	6	0	2	1	0	5	0	9	1	0	0	1	.000	0	0-0	1	5.55	3.52
14	NYY	AL	46	0	0	6	24.2	107	23	9	7	0	2	2	4	6	2	20	0	0	0	3	.000	0	0-4	12	2.83	2.55
14	Was	NL	18	0	0	2	11.1	45	10	0	0	0	0	0	1	2	0	8	0	0	1	0	1.000	0	0-0	6	2.39	0.00
	Postseason		6	0	0	1	5.2	26	5	1	1	0	1	0	0	4	2	3	0	0	0	1	.000	0	0-0	1	3.13	1.59
12 ML YEARS			730	1	0	162	645.2	2722	572	261	240	50	19	18	19	245	37	633	28	0	35	46	.432	0	23-58	206	3.24	3.35

Chris Tillman

Pitches: R **Bats:** R **Pos:** SP-31   **Ht:** 6'5" **Wt:** 200 **Born:** 4/15/1988 **Age:** 28

		HOW MUCH HE PITCHED						WHAT HE GAVE UP										THE RESULTS						
Year	Team	Lg	G	GS	CG	GF	IP	BFP	H	R	ER	HR	SH	SF	HB	TBB	IBB	SO	WP	Bk	W	L	Pct	Sh	Sv-Op	Hld	ERC	ERA
2009	Bal	AL	12	12	0	0	65.0	285	77	40	39	15	0	0	2	24	1	39	4	0	2	5	.286	0	0-0	0	6.28	5.40
2010	Bal	AL	11	11	0	0	53.2	236	51	37	35	9	1	3	1	31	1	31	2	0	2	5	.286	0	0-0	0	5.12	5.87
2011	Bal	AL	13	13	0	0	62.0	287	77	41	38	5	1	1	4	25	0	46	1	1	3	5	.375	0	0-0	0	5.58	5.52
2012	Bal	AL	15	15	0	0	86.0	347	66	38	28	12	1	2	1	24	0	66	5	0	9	3	.750	0	0-0	0	2.65	2.93
2013	Bal	AL	33	33	1	0	206.1	845	184	87	85	33	4	6	3	68	2	179	6	1	16	7	.696	0	0-0	0	3.72	3.71
2014	Bal	AL	34	34	1	0	207.1	871	189	83	77	21	1	5	4	66	1	150	8	0	13	6	.684	1	0-0	0	3.33	3.34
2015	Bal	AL	31	31	0	0	173.0	741	176	96	96	20	3	8	5	64	1	120	4	0	11	11	.500	0	0-0	0	4.32	4.99
	Postseason		2	2	0	0	9.1	42	11	7	7	3	0	0	0	3	0	9	0	0	1	0	1.000	0	0-0	0	6.29	6.75
7 ML YEARS			149	149	2	0	853.1	3612	820	423	398	115	11	25	20	302	6	631	30	2	56	42	.571	1	0-0	0	4.02	4.20

Shawn Tolleson

Pitches: R **Bats:** R **Pos:** RP-73   TAHL-eh-son   **Ht:** 6'2" **Wt:** 220 **Born:** 1/19/1988 **Age:** 28

		HOW MUCH HE PITCHED						WHAT HE GAVE UP										THE RESULTS						
Year	Team	Lg	G	GS	CG	GF	IP	BFP	H	R	ER	HR	SH	SF	HB	TBB	IBB	SO	WP	Bk	W	L	Pct	Sh	Sv-Op	Hld	ERC	ERA
2012	LAD	NL	40	0	0	12	37.2	160	30	19	18	4	2	1	1	20	1	39	0	0	3	1	.750	0	0-0	2	3.59	4.30
2013	LAD	NL	1	0	0	0	0.0	2	0	0	0	0	0	0	0	2	0	0	0	0	0	0		0	0-0	0		-
2014	Tex	AL	64	0	0	10	71.2	296	56	23	22	10	2	3	1	28	5	69	4	0	3	1	.750	0	0-0	7	3.06	2.76
2015	Tex	AL	73	0	0	53	72.1	298	66	25	24	9	2	1	2	17	5	76	0	0	6	4	.600	0	35-37	6	3.11	2.99
4 ML YEARS			178	0	0	75	181.2	756	152	67	64	23	6	5	4	67	11	184	4	0	12	6	.667	0	35-37	15	3.23	3.17

Steve Tolleson

Bats: R **Throws:** R **Pos:** 2B-11;SS-4;LF-3;PH-2;RF-1;PR-1   **Ht:** 5'11" **Wt:** 185 **Born:** 11/1/1983 **Age:** 32

			BATTING																	RUNNING			AVERAGES			
Year	Team	Lg	G	AB	H	2B	3B	HR	(Hm | Rd)	TB	R	RBI	RC	TBB	IBB	SO	HBP	SH	SF	SB	CS	GDP	Avg	OBP	Slg	OPS
2010	Oak	AL	25	49	14	3	0	1	(1 | 0)	20	5	4	7	4	0	9	0	0	0	0	0	0	.286	.340	.408	.748
2012	Bal	AL	29	71	13	3	0	2	(2 | 0)	22	4	6	7	4	0	17	0	1	0	1	0	2	.183	.227	.310	.537
2014	Tor	AL	109	170	43	7	2	3	(2 | 1)	63	21	16	16	12	0	49	2	4	1	3	1	3	.253	.308	.371	.679
2015	Tor	AL	19	41	11	5	1	0	(0 | 0)	18	9	3	4	4	0	9	0	0	0	2	0	1	.268	.333	.439	.772
4 ML YEARS			182	331	81	18	3	6	(5 | 1)	123	39	29	34	24	0	84	2	5	1	6	1	6	.245	.299	.372	.670

Yasmany Tomas

yahz-MAH-nee toe-MAHS

Bats: R **Throws:** R **Pos:** RF-57;3B-31;PH-22;LF-6;1B-4;DH-3   **Ht:** 6'2" **Wt:** 255 **Born:** 11/14/1990 **Age:** 25

			BATTING																	RUNNING			AVERAGES			
Year	Team	Lg	G	AB	H	2B	3B	HR	(Hm | Rd)	TB	R	RBI	RC	TBB	IBB	SO	HBP	SH	SF	SB	CS	GDP	Avg	OBP	Slg	OPS
2015	Ari	NL	118	406	111	19	3	9	(4 | 5)	163	40	48	32	17	0	110	2	0	1	5	2	16	.273	.305	.401	.707

Josh Tomlin

Pitches: R **Bats:** R **Pos:** SP-10   **Ht:** 6'1" **Wt:** 190 **Born:** 10/19/1984 **Age:** 31

		HOW MUCH HE PITCHED						WHAT HE GAVE UP										THE RESULTS						
Year	Team	Lg	G	GS	CG	GF	IP	BFP	H	R	ER	HR	SH	SF	HB	TBB	IBB	SO	WP	Bk	W	L	Pct	Sh	Sv-Op	Hld	ERC	ERA
2010	Cle	AL	12	12	1	0	73.0	301	72	38	37	10	3	3	3	19	3	43	1	0	6	4	.600	0	0-0	0	3.89	4.56
2011	Cle	AL	26	26	0	0	165.1	662	157	80	78	24	1	3	3	21	2	89	3	0	12	7	.632	0	0-0	0	3.11	4.25
2012	Cle	AL	21	16	0	0	103.1	452	126	74	73	18	2	3	3	25	3	56	4	0	5	8	.385	0	0-0	0	5.34	6.36
2013	Cle	AL	1	0	0	0	2.0	9	2	0	0	0	0	0	0	0	0	0	0	0	0	0		0	0-0	0	1.68	0.00
2014	Cle	AL	25	16	1	6	104.0	446	120	66	55	18	1	3	1	14	3	94	6	0	6	9	.400	1	0-0	4	4.28	4.76
2015	Cle	AL	10	10	2	0	65.2	251	47	22	22	13	0	0	2	8	0	57	1	0	7	2	.778	0	0-0	0	2.24	3.02
6 ML YEARS			95	80	4	6	513.1	2121	524	280	265	83	7	12	12	87	11	339	15	0	36	30	.545	1	0-0	0	3.75	4.65

Kelby Tomlinson

Bats: R **Throws:** R **Pos:** 2B-50;PH-4;SS-1   **Ht:** 6'3" **Wt:** 180 **Born:** 6/16/1990 **Age:** 26

Year	Team	Lg	G	AB	H	2B	3B	HR	(Hm	Rd)	TB	R	RBI	RC	TBB	IBB	SO	HBP	SH	SF	SB	CS	GDP	Avg	OBP	Slg	OPS
2011	2 Tms	Low	39	149	53	10	5	2	(-	-)	79	34	27	33	15	0	24	1	0	1	11	2	2	.356	.416	.530	.946
2012	Augsta	A	123	450	101	9	4	1	(-	-)	121	57	36	45	53	0	105	5	6	6	36	11	5	.224	.309	.269	.578
2013	2 Tms	Low	39	162	45	8	1	1	(-	-)	58	22	18	20	15	0	39	1	0	1	6	2	6	.278	.341	.358	.699
2013	Rchmd	AA	33	96	19	5	0	0	(-	-)	24	13	4	8	16	0	27	0	4	0	3	1	1	.198	.313	.250	.563
2014	Rchmd	AA	126	433	116	9	6	1	(-	-)	140	63	32	57	44	1	82	5	8	4	49	12	7	.268	.340	.323	.663
2015	Rchmd	AA	64	253	82	18	3	1	(-	-)	109	43	28	45	25	0	37	3	5	3	16	6	3	.324	.387	.431	.818
2015	Scrmto	AAA	33	136	43	1	1	2	(-	-)	52	21	15	19	7	0	22	2	2	2	5	3	2	.316	.354	.382	.736
2015	SF	NL	54	178	54	6	3	2	(2	0)	72	23	20	22	14	0	40	1	0	0	5	4	3	.303	.358	.404	.762

Michael Tonkin

Pitches: R **Bats:** R **Pos:** RP-26   TAHN-kin   **Ht:** 6'7" **Wt:** 220 **Born:** 11/19/1989 **Age:** 26

Year	Team	Lg	G	GS	CG	GF	IP	BFP	H	R	ER	HR	SH	SF	HB	TBB	IBB	SO	WP	Bk	W	L	Pct	Sh	Sv-Op	Hld	ERC	ERA
2015	Roch*	AAA	33	0	0	23	41.0	151	25	5	5	2	0	0	1	5	0	46	4	0	2	1	.667	0	14- -	-	1.22	1.10
2013	Min	AL	9	0	0	6	11.1	47	9	6	1	0	0	0	0	3	0	10	1	0	0	0	-	0	0-0	0	1.82	0.79
2014	Min	AL	25	0	0	8	19.0	87	23	13	10	2	2	1	2	6	0	16	1	0	0	0	-	0	0-0	4	5.36	4.74
2015	Min	AL	26	0	0	10	23.1	99	21	9	9	4	0	1	1	9	2	19	1	0	0	0	-	0	0-0	5	3.99	3.47
	3 ML YEARS		60	0	0	24	53.2	233	53	28	20	6	2	2	3	18	2	45	3	0	0	0	-	0	0-0	9	3.94	3.35

Alex Torres

Pitches: L **Bats:** L **Pos:** RP-39   **Ht:** 5'10" **Wt:** 185 **Born:** 12/8/1987 **Age:** 28

Year	Team	Lg	G	GS	CG	GF	IP	BFP	H	R	ER	HR	SH	SF	HB	TBB	IBB	SO	WP	Bk	W	L	Pct	Sh	Sv-Op	Hld	ERC	ERA
2015	LsVgs*	AAA	10	0	0	1	7.2	34	6	1	1	0	0	2	0	4	0	9	1	0	0	0	-	0	0- -	-	2.53	1.17
2011	TB	AL	4	0	0	2	8.0	39	8	4	3	0	0	0	1	7	2	9	0	0	1	1	.500	0	0-0	0	5.11	3.38
2013	TB	AL	39	0	0	5	58.0	226	32	12	11	1	1	1	3	20	1	62	1	0	4	2	.667	0	0-1	5	1.43	1.71
2014	SD	NL	70	0	0	12	54.0	241	46	25	20	2	2	2	3	33	1	51	6	0	2	1	.667	0	0-1	7	3.74	3.33
2015	NYM	NL	39	0	0	11	34.1	154	26	16	12	6	1	0	1	26	1	35	3	0	0	0	-	0	1-2	7	4.70	3.15
	Postseason		3	0	0	0	4.0	15	2	0	0	0	0	0	0	1	0	5	0	0	0	0	-	0	0-0	0	0.94	0.00
	4 ML YEARS		152	0	0	30	154.1	660	112	57	46	9	4	3	8	86	5	157	10	0	7	4	.636	0	1-4	19	3.02	2.68

Carlos Torres

Pitches: R **Bats:** R **Pos:** RP-59   **Ht:** 6'1" **Wt:** 180 **Born:** 10/22/1982 **Age:** 33

Year	Team	Lg	G	GS	CG	GF	IP	BFP	H	R	ER	HR	SH	SF	HB	TBB	IBB	SO	WP	Bk	W	L	Pct	Sh	Sv-Op	Hld	ERC	ERA
2009	CWS	AL	8	5	0	2	28.1	130	30	20	19	5	3	3	2	17	2	22	0	0	1	2	.333	0	0-0	0	6.05	6.04
2010	CWS	AL	5	1	0	1	13.2	71	23	13	13	2	0	1	0	9	1	13	0	0	0	1	.000	0	0-0	0	9.84	8.56
2012	Col	NL	31	0	0	9	53.0	231	49	31	31	2	6	4	4	26	1	42	6	0	5	3	.625	0	0-0	1	3.85	5.26
2013	NYM	NL	33	9	0	4	86.1	352	79	34	33	15	4	1	4	17	1	75	4	1	4	6	.400	0	0-0	3	3.47	3.44
2014	NYM	NL	73	1	0	20	97.0	405	89	35	33	11	2	1	2	38	4	96	6	0	8	6	.571	0	2-5	12	3.77	3.06
2015	NYM	NL	59	0	0	19	57.2	243	61	32	30	5	1	3	0	18	6	48	5	0	5	6	.455	0	0-1	11	3.86	4.68
	6 ML YEARS		209	16	0	57	336.0	1432	331	165	159	40	16	13	12	125	15	296	21	1	23	24	.489	0	2-6	27	4.13	4.26

Ronald Torreyes

Bats: R **Throws:** R **Pos:** 2B-4;3B-3;PH-2;PR-2   tore-RAY-ess   **Ht:** 5'10" **Wt:** 150 **Born:** 9/2/1992 **Age:** 23

Year	Team	Lg	G	AB	H	2B	3B	HR	(Hm	Rd)	TB	R	RBI	RC	TBB	IBB	SO	HBP	SH	SF	SB	CS	GDP	Avg	OBP	Slg	OPS
2011	Dayton	A	67	278	99	9	5	3	(-	-)	127	53	41	50	14	1	19	6	7	1	12	7	7	.356	.398	.457	.855
2012	Dytona	A+	115	421	111	23	5	6	(-	-)	162	62	47	57	32	1	29	10	5	6	13	4	2	.264	.326	.385	.711
2013	Tenn	AA	65	224	59	14	4	2	(-	-)	87	32	25	33	22	0	15	6	9	4	4	0	8	.263	.340	.388	.728
2013	CpChr	AA	38	151	42	6	2	0	(-	-)	52	19	12	16	6	0	14	1	4	0	1	1	3	.278	.310	.344	.654
2014	OkCity	AAA	126	460	137	20	5	2	(-	-)	173	65	46	62	25	0	26	10	21	3	12	9	10	.298	.345	.376	.721
2015	Fresno	AAA	19	70	14	1	0	0	(-	-)	15	7	5	1	1	0	9	0	1	0	0	1	3	.200	.211	.214	.426
2015	Nham	AA	16	50	7	2	0	0	(-	-)	9	4	9	1	4	0	2	0	0	0	2	0	4	.140	.204	.180	.384
2015	Tulsa	AA	62	249	73	13	2	4	(-	-)	102	39	19	36	20	0	23	2	1	2	3	3	3	.293	.348	.410	.758
2015	OkCity	AAA	13	49	15	2	1	0	(-	-)	19	10	3	6	2	0	4	1	0	1	0	0	2	.306	.340	.388	.727
2015	LAD	NL	8	6	2	1	0	0	(0	0)	3	1	1	2	1	0	1	0	1	0	0	0	0	.333	.429	.500	.929

Matt Tracy

Pitches: L **Bats:** L **Pos:** RP-1   **Ht:** 6'3" **Wt:** 212 **Born:** 11/26/1988 **Age:** 27

Year	Team	Lg	G	GS	CG	GF	IP	BFP	H	R	ER	HR	SH	SF	HB	TBB	IBB	SO	WP	Bk	W	L	Pct	Sh	Sv-Op	Hld	ERC	ERA
2011	StnIld	A-	17	6	0	5	47.1	196	41	20	16	1	0	0	3	16	0	48	2	1	1	2	.333	0	0- -	-	2.87	3.04
2012	Tampa	A+	18	18	2	0	99.0	409	88	47	36	3	9	2	5	39	0	64	5	0	5	7	.417	0	0- -	-	3.26	3.27
2013	Trntn	AA	14	13	0	0	63.2	286	67	42	39	6	0	2	7	37	0	60	0	0	4	5	.444	0	0- -	-	5.70	5.51
2014	Trntn	AA	16	15	0	0	88.1	381	97	35	32	3	1	2	4	34	0	50	4	1	8	2	.800	0	0- -	-	4.38	3.26
2014	S-WB	AAA	12	11	0	1	62.2	276	74	38	31	8	3	0	4	21	0	39	0	0	1	6	.143	0	1- -	-	5.43	4.45
2015	S-WB	AAA	13	6	0	3	39.1	178	45	28	25	3	1	3	4	19	0	26	2	1	0	3	.000	0	0- -	-	5.60	5.72
2015	Trntn	AA	16	5	0	5	51.0	206	45	17	13	2	2	1	0	16	0	40	1	0	1	3	.250	0	0- -	-	2.79	2.29
2015	NYY	AL	1	0	0	1	2.0	11	2	3	0	0	0	0	0	2	0	1	0	0	0	0	-	0	0-0	0	4.93	0.00

Devon Travis

Bats: R **Throws:** R **Pos:** 2B-62;PH-1;PR-1   DEV-in   **Ht:** 5'9" **Wt:** 195 **Born:** 2/21/1991 **Age:** 25

										BATTING												RUNNING			AVERAGES			
Year	Team	Lg	G	AB	H	2B	3B	HR	(Hm	Rd)	TB	R	RBI	RC	TBB	IBB	SO	HBP	SH	SF		SB	CS	GDP	Avg	OBP	Slg	OPS
2012	2 Tms	A-	25	93	26	2	2	3	(-	-)	41	17	11	15	8	0	10	3	2	1		3	1	3	.280	.352	.441	.793
2013	2 Tms	Low	132	504	177	28	4	16	(-	-)	261	93	76	112	53	2	64	10	2	7		22	4	8	.351	.418	.518	.936
2014	Erie	AA	100	396	118	20	7	10	(-	-)	182	68	52	68	37	1	60	2	2	4		16	5	16	.298	.358	.460	.817
2015	Tor	AL	62	217	66	18	0	8	(4	4)	108	38	35	40	18	0	43	2	0	1		3	1	4	.304	.361	.498	.859

Blake Treinen

Pitches: R **Bats:** R **Pos:** RP-60   TRY-nen   **Ht:** 6'5" **Wt:** 230 **Born:** 6/30/1988 **Age:** 28

				HOW MUCH HE PITCHED					WHAT HE GAVE UP										THE RESULTS							
Year	Team	Lg	G	GS	CG	GF	IP	BFP	H	R	ER	HR	SH	SF	HB	TBB	IBB	SO	WP	Bk	W	L	Pct	Sh	Sv-Op	Hld	ERC	ERA
2011	2 Tms	Low	21	0	0	14	30.0	123	23	13	11	1	3	0	1	8	0	36	2	0	1	1	.500	0	2- -	-	2.03	3.30
2012	Stcktn	A+	24	15	1	1	103.0	448	116	60	50	11	0	3	4	23	0	92	5	0	7	7	.500	0	0- -	-	4.22	4.37
2013	Hrsbrg	AA	21	20	0	0	118.2	506	125	54	48	9	0	4	4	33	2	86	8	1	6	7	.462	0	0- -	-	3.84	3.64
2014	Syrcse	AAA	16	16	0	0	80.2	339	78	34	30	4	4	3	4	20	0	64	2	0	8	2	.800	0	0- -	-	3.14	3.35
2015	Syrcse	AAA	5	0	0	3	12.0	43	6	0	0	0	0	0	0	1	0	14	3	0	0	0	-	0	0- -	-	0.66	0.00
2014	Was	NL	15	7	0	6	50.2	214	57	17	14	1	0	0	2	13	1	30	1	0	2	3	.400	0	0-0	0	3.86	2.49
2015	Was	NL	60	0	0	17	67.2	280	62	32	29	4	1	1	2	32	6	65	4	0	2	5	.286	0	0-3	10	3.76	3.86
	2 ML YEARS		75	7	0	23	118.1	494	119	49	43	5	1	1	4	45	7	95	5	0	4	8	.333	0	0-3	10	3.80	3.27

Nicholas Tropeano

Pitches: R **Bats:** R **Pos:** SP-7; RP-1   TROH-pee-ah-no   **Ht:** 6'4" **Wt:** 205 **Born:** 8/27/1990 **Age:** 25

				HOW MUCH HE PITCHED					WHAT HE GAVE UP										THE RESULTS							
Year	Team	Lg	G	GS	CG	GF	IP	BFP	H	R	ER	HR	SH	SF	HB	TBB	IBB	SO	WP	Bk	W	L	Pct	Sh	Sv-Op	Hld	ERC	ERA
2011	TriCity	A-	12	12	0	0	53.1	222	42	18	14	1	1	1	1	21	0	63	6	1	3	2	.600	0	0- -	-	2.44	2.36
2012	2 Tms	Low	27	26	0	0	158.0	656	149	66	53	11	6	3	5	47	0	166	12	0	12	7	.632	0	0- -	-	3.32	3.02
2013	CpChr	AA	28	20	1	6	133.2	562	140	65	61	15	5	5	3	39	0	130	5	0	7	10	.412	0	5- -	-	4.16	4.11
2014	OkCity	AAA	23	20	0	1	124.2	486	90	44	42	11	1	2	4	33	1	120	5	0	9	5	.643	0	0- -	-	2.22	3.03
2015	Salt Lk	AAA	16	16	1	0	88.0	393	97	51	47	9	3	3	3	36	0	96	3	0	3	6	.333	0	0- -	-	4.83	4.81
2014	Hou	AL	4	4	0	0	21.2	91	19	12	11	0	1	1	1	9	1	13	1	0	1	3	.250	0	0-0	0	2.92	4.57
2015	LAA	AL	8	7	0	0	37.2	161	40	18	16	2	2	1	0	10	0	38	0	0	3	2	.600	0	0-0	0	3.53	3.82
	2 ML YEARS		12	11	0	0	59.1	252	59	30	27	2	3	2	1	19	1	51	1	0	4	5	.444	0	0-0	0	3.31	4.10

Mike Trout

Bats: R **Throws:** R **Pos:** CF-156;DH-4   **Ht:** 6'2" **Wt:** 230 **Born:** 8/7/1991 **Age:** 24

										BATTING												RUNNING			AVERAGES			
Year	Team	Lg	G	AB	H	2B	3B	HR	(Hm	Rd)	TB	R	RBI	RC	TBB	IBB	SO	HBP	SH	SF		SB	CS	GDP	Avg	OBP	Slg	OPS
2011	LAA	AL	40	123	27	6	0	5	(1	4)	48	20	16	14	9	0	30	2	0	1		4	0	2	.220	.281	.390	.672
2012	LAA	AL	139	559	182	27	8	30	(16	14)	315	**129**	83	**127**	67	4	139	6	0	7		**49**	5	7	.326	.399	.564	.963
2013	LAA	AL	157	589	190	39	9	27	(13	14)	328	**109**	97	141	**110**	10	136	9	0	8		33	7	8	.323	.432	.557	.988
2014	LAA	AL	157	602	173	39	9	36	(19	17)	**338**	115	111	131	83	6	**184**	10	0	10		16	2	6	.287	.377	.561	.939
2015	LAA	AL	159	575	172	32	6	41	(20	21)	339	104	90	**131**	92	14	158	10	0	5		11	7	11	.299	.402	**.590**	**.991**
	Postseason		3	12	1	0	0	1	(0	1)	4	1	1	0	3	0	2	0	0	0		0	1	0	.083	.267	.333	.600
	5 ML YEARS		652	2448	744	143	32	139	(69	70)	1368	477	397	544	361	34	647	37	0	31		113	21	34	.304	.397	.559	.956

Mark Trumbo

Bats: R **Throws:** R **Pos:** RF-76;DH-30;1B-23;LF-13;PH-10   **Ht:** 6'4" **Wt:** 225 **Born:** 1/16/1986 **Age:** 30

										BATTING												RUNNING			AVERAGES			
Year	Team	Lg	G	AB	H	2B	3B	HR	(Hm	Rd)	TB	R	RBI	RC	TBB	IBB	SO	HBP	SH	SF		SB	CS	GDP	Avg	OBP	Slg	OPS
2010	LAA	AL	8	15	1	0	0	0	(0	0)	1	2	2	0	1	0	8	0	0	0		0	0	0	.067	.125	.067	.192
2011	LAA	AL	149	539	137	31	1	29	(14	15)	257	65	87	69	25	6	120	5	0	4		9	4	17	.254	.291	.477	.768
2012	LAA	AL	144	544	146	19	3	32	(12	20)	267	66	95	80	36	3	153	4	0	2		4	5	12	.268	.317	.491	.808
2013	LAA	AL	159	620	145	30	2	34	(19	15)	281	85	100	74	54	6	184	0	0	4		5	2	18	.234	.294	.453	.747
2014	Ari	NL	88	328	77	15	1	14	(7	7)	136	37	61	44	28	3	89	1	0	5		2	3	8	.235	.293	.415	.707
2015	2 Tms		142	508	133	23	3	22	(12	10)	228	62	64	58	36	1	132	0	0	1		0	0	12	.262	.310	.449	.759
15	Ari	NL	46	174	45	10	3	9	(4	5)	88	23	23	21	10	0	39	0	0	0		0	0	4	.259	.299	.506	.805
15	Sea	AL	96	334	88	13	0	13	(8	5)	140	39	41	37	26	1	93	0	0	1		0	0	8	.263	.316	.419	.735
	6 ML YEARS		690	2554	639	118	10	131	(64	67)	1170	317	409	325	180	19	686	10	0	16		20	14	67	.250	.300	.458	.758

Chin-hui Tsao

Pitches: R **Bats:** R **Pos:** RP-5   chin-wee sow   **Ht:** 6'1" **Wt:** 210 **Born:** 6/2/1981 **Age:** 35

				HOW MUCH HE PITCHED					WHAT HE GAVE UP										THE RESULTS							
Year	Team	Lg	G	GS	CG	GF	IP	BFP	H	R	ER	HR	SH	SF	HB	TBB	IBB	SO	WP	Bk	W	L	Pct	Sh	Sv-Op	Hld	ERC	ERA
2015	OkCity*	AAA	30	0	0	19	39.0	155	31	16	12	3	0	1	0	11	4	42	1	0	2	1	.667	0	7- -	-	2.41	2.77
2003	Col	NL	9	8	0	1	43.1	196	48	30	29	11	3	0	4	20	1	29	0	0	3	3	.500	0	0-0	0	6.56	6.02
2004	Col	NL	10	0	0	5	9.1	37	7	4	4	2	1	0	0	1	0	11	0	0	0	0	-	0	1-2	1	2.21	3.86
2005	Col	NL	10	0	0	9	11.0	56	16	8	8	3	1	1	1	5	1	4	1	0	1	0	1.000	0	3-4	0	8.44	6.55
2007	LAD	NL	21	0	0	6	24.2	97	18	12	12	3	0	0	1	8	0	16	0	0	1	0	1.000	0	0-1	3	2.74	4.38
2015	LAD	NL	5	0	0	0	7.0	37	15	9	8	3	0	0	0	3	1	7	0	0	1	1	.500	0	0-0	0	15.20	10.29
	5 ML YEARS		55	8	0	21	95.1	423	104	63	61	22	5	1	6	37	3	67	1	0	5	5	.500	0	4-7	4	5.75	5.76

Preston Tucker

Bats: L **Throws:** L **Pos:** LF-79;PH-15;RF-14;DH-3;PR-2   **Ht:** 6'0" **Wt:** 217 **Born:** 7/6/1990 **Age:** 25

							BATTING													RUNNING			AVERAGES			
Year	Team	Lg	G	AB	H	2B	3B	HR	(Hm | Rd)	TB	R	RBI	RC	TBB	IBB	SO	HBP	SH	SF	SB	CS	GDP	Avg	OBP	Slg	OPS
2012	TriCity	A-	42	165	53	7	0	8	(- | -)	84	32	38	32	18	0	16	2	0	2	1	2	4	.321	.390	.509	.899
2013	Lancst	A+	75	298	97	18	1	15	(- | -)	162	61	74	62	29	1	45	2	0	4	3	0	4	.326	.384	.544	.928
2013	CpChr	AA	60	237	62	14	1	10	(- | -)	108	36	29	38	27	1	46	4	0	0	0	1	6	.262	.347	.456	.803
2014	CpChr	AA	65	261	72	17	0	17	(- | -)	140	41	43	48	26	5	46	3	0	0	3	3	5	.276	.348	.536	.885
2014	OkCity	AAA	73	275	79	18	0	7	(- | -)	118	38	51	44	31	3	74	0	0	3	2	0	4	.287	.356	.429	.785
2015	Fresno	AAA	33	129	38	4	0	11	(- | -)	75	20	35	26	12	1	25	1	0	1	1	0	6	.295	.357	.581	.938
2015	Hou	AL	98	300	73	19	0	13	(5 | 8)	131	35	33	34	20	0	68	3	0	0	0	2	3	.243	.297	.437	.734

Samuel Tuivailala

Pitches: R **Bats:** R **Pos:** RP-14   TOO-ee-vah-la-la   **Ht:** 6'3" **Wt:** 195 **Born:** 10/19/1992 **Age:** 23

			HOW MUCH HE PITCHED					WHAT HE GAVE UP									THE RESULTS							
Year	Team	Lg	G	GS	CG	GF	IP	BFP	H	R	ER	HR	SH	SF	HB	TBB	IBB	SO	WP	Bk	W	L	Pct	Sh	Sv-Op	Hld	ERC	ERA
2012	Jhscty	R+	11	0	0	1	13.0	64	12	6	6	1	0	0	0	13	0	23	1	0	0	0	-	0	0--	-	5.69	4.15
2013	Peoria	A	28	0	0	7	35.1	159	31	22	21	0	1	1	4	20	1	50	4	0	0	3	.000	0	1--	-	3.63	5.35
2014	PlmBch	A+	29	0	0	13	37.2	162	29	16	15	1	0	2	2	18	0	64	4	0	0	1	.000	0	3--	-	2.77	3.58
2014	Sprgfld	AA	17	0	0	3	21.0	88	18	8	6	0	1	0	1	9	1	30	2	0	2	1	.667	0	1--	-	2.87	2.57
2015	Memp	AAA	43	0	0	37	45.0	188	28	9	8	2	0	0	3	26	2	43	6	0	3	1	.750	0	17--	-	2.55	1.60
2014	StL	NL	2	0	0	0	1.0	10	5	4	4	2	0	0	0	2	0	1	0	0	0	0	-	0	0-0	0	72.46	36.00
2015	StL	NL	14	0	0	5	14.2	65	13	5	5	2	0	0	0	8	1	20	3	0	0	1	.000	0	0-0	2	4.06	3.07
	2 ML YEARS		16	0	0	5	15.2	75	18	9	9	4	0	0	0	10	1	21	3	0	0	1	.000	0	0-0	2	6.93	5.17

Troy Tulowitzki

Bats: R **Throws:** R **Pos:** SS-121;PH-7;DH-1   too-luh-WIT-skee   **Ht:** 6'3" **Wt:** 215 **Born:** 10/10/1984 **Age:** 31

									BATTING												RUNNING			AVERAGES			
Year	Team	Lg	G	AB	H	2B	3B	HR	(Hm	Rd)	TB	R	RBI	RC	TBB	IBB	SO	HBP	SH	SF	SB	CS	GDP	Avg	OBP	Slg	OPS
2006	Col	NL	25	96	23	2	0	1	(0	1)	28	15	6	10	10	3	25	1	1	0	3	0	1	.240	.318	.292	.609
2007	Col	NL	155	609	177	33	5	24	(15	9)	292	104	99	95	57	3	130	9	5	2	7	6	14	.291	.359	.479	.838
2008	Col	NL	101	377	99	24	2	8	(4	4)	151	48	46	42	38	5	56	2	2	2	1	6	16	.263	.332	.401	.732
2009	Col	NL	151	543	161	25	9	32	(17	15)	300	101	92	96	73	4	112	3	0	9	20	11	20	.297	.377	.552	.930
2010	Col	NL	122	470	148	32	3	27	(15	12)	267	89	95	88	48	4	78	5	1	5	11	2	17	.315	.381	.568	.949
2011	Col	NL	143	537	162	36	2	30	(17	13)	292	81	105	101	59	12	79	4	1	5	9	3	16	.302	.372	.544	.916
2012	Col	NL	47	181	52	8	2	8	(3	5)	88	33	27	27	19	1	19	2	0	1	2	2	7	.287	.360	.486	.846
2013	Col	NL	126	446	139	27	0	25	(14	11)	241	72	82	80	57	5	85	4	0	5	1	0	9	.312	.391	.540	.931
2014	Col	NL	91	315	107	18	1	21	(14	7)	190	71	52	70	54	4	57	5	0	5	1	1	4	.340	.432	.603	1.035
2015	2 Tms		128	486	136	27	0	17	(11	6)	214	77	70	69	38	5	114	6	0	4	1	0	17	.280	.337	.440	.777
15	Col	NL	87	323	97	19	0	12	(7	5)	152	46	53	53	24	4	72	1	0	3	0	0	13	.300	.348	.471	.818
15	Tor		41	163	39	8	0	5	(4	1)	62	31	17	16	14	1	42	5	0	1	1	0	4	.239	.317	.380	.697
	Postseason		15	57	12	5	0	1	(0	1)	20	3	6	3	4	0	17	1	0	1	0	1	3	.211	.270	.351	.621
	10 ML YEARS		1089	4060	1204	232	24	193	(110	83)	2063	691	674	678	449	46	755	41	10	38	56	31	121	.297	.369	.508	.877

Jacob Turner

Pitches: R **Bats:** R **Pos:** P   **Ht:** 6'5" **Wt:** 215 **Born:** 5/21/1991 **Age:** 25

			HOW MUCH HE PITCHED					WHAT HE GAVE UP									THE RESULTS							
Year	Team	Lg	G	GS	CG	GF	IP	BFP	H	R	ER	HR	SH	SF	HB	TBB	IBB	SO	WP	Bk	W	L	Pct	Sh	Sv-Op	Hld	ERC	ERA
2011	Det	AL	3	3	0	0	12.2	60	17	13	12	3	0	1	1	4	0	8	0	0	0	1	.000	0	0-0	0	7.03	8.53
2012	2 Tms		10	10	0	0	55.0	231	50	32	27	9	1	2	0	16	3	36	5	0	2	5	.286	0	0-0	0	3.42	4.42
2013	Mia	NL	20	20	1	0	118.0	514	116	55	49	11	8	5	4	54	5	77	11	0	3	8	.273	0	0-0	0	4.25	3.74
2014	2 Tms	NL	28	18	0	4	113.0	501	148	81	77	12	6	4	1	33	2	71	6	1	6	11	.353	0	0-0	1	5.59	6.13
12	Det	AL	3	3	0	0	12.1	61	17	11	11	4	0	1	0	7	1	7	1	0	1	1	.500	0	0-0	0	8.66	8.03
12	Mia	NL	7	7	0	0	42.2	170	33	21	16	5	1	1	0	9	2	29	4	0	1	4	.200	0	0-0	0	2.20	3.38
14	Mia	NL	20	12	0	4	78.1	352	106	54	52	8	2	3	1	23	1	54	3	1	4	7	.364	0	0-0	0	5.84	5.97
14	ChC	NL	8	6	0	0	34.2	149	42	27	25	4	4	1	0	10	1	17	3	0	2	4	.333	0	0-0	1	5.03	6.49
	4 ML YEARS		61	51	1	4	298.2	1306	331	181	165	35	15	12	6	107	10	192	22	1	11	25	.306	0	0-0	1	4.69	4.97

Justin Turner

Bats: R **Throws:** R **Pos:** 3B-100;PH-19;1B-10;2B-5;SS-1   **Ht:** 5'11" **Wt:** 205 **Born:** 11/23/1984 **Age:** 31

									BATTING												RUNNING			AVERAGES			
Year	Team	Lg	G	AB	H	2B	3B	HR	(Hm	Rd)	TB	R	RBI	RC	TBB	IBB	SO	HBP	SH	SF	SB	CS	GDP	Avg	OBP	Slg	OPS
2009	Bal	AL	12	18	3	0	0	0	(0	0)	3	2	3	1	4	0	3	0	0	0	0	0	1	.167	.318	.167	.485
2010	2 Tms		9	17	1	1	0	0	(0	0)	2	1	0	0	1	0	3	0	0	0	0	0	0	.059	.111	.118	.229
2011	NYM	NL	117	435	113	30	0	4	(3	1)	155	49	51	59	39	2	59	10	2	1	7	2	9	.260	.334	.356	.690
2012	NYM	NL	94	171	46	13	1	2	(2	0)	67	20	19	19	9	0	24	4	0	1	1	1	9	.269	.319	.392	.711
2013	NYM	NL	86	200	56	13	1	2	(0	2)	77	12	16	17	11	1	34	1	1	1	0	1	6	.280	.319	.385	.704
2014	LAD	NL	109	288	98	21	1	7	(5	2)	142	46	43	55	28	1	58	4	0	2	6	1	6	.340	.404	.493	.897
2015	LAD	NL	126	385	113	26	1	16	(8	8)	189	55	60	65	36	1	71	13	1	4	5	2	10	.294	.370	.491	.861
10	Bal	AL	5	9	0	0	0	0	(0	0)	0	0	0	0	0	0	3	0	0	0	0	0	0	.000	.000	.000	.000
10	NYM	NL	4	8	1	1	0	0	(0	0)	2	1	0	0	1	0	0	0	0	0	0	0	0	.125	.222	.250	.472
	Postseason		2	2	0	0	0	0	(0	0)	0	0	0	0	0	0	1	0	0	0	0	0	0	.000	.000	.000	.000
	7 ML YEARS		553	1514	430	104	4	31	(18	13)	635	185	192	216	128	5	252	32	4	9	19	7	41	.284	.351	.419	.770

Trea Turner

Bats: R **Throws:** R **Pos:** 2B-12;PR-7;SS-6;PH-6   TRAY   **Ht:** 6'1" **Wt:** 175 **Born:** 6/30/1993 **Age:** 23

Year Team	Lg	G	AB	H	2B	3B	HR	(Hm	Rd)	TB	R	RBI	RC	TBB	IBB	SO	HBP	SH	SF	SB	CS	GDP	Avg	OBP	Slg	OPS
2014 2 Tms	Low	69	279	90	16	2	5	(-	-)	125	45	24	55	35	1	67	5	1	1	23	4	4	.323	.406	.448	.854
2015 SnAnt	AA	58	227	73	13	3	5	(-	-)	107	31	35	42	24	0	48	0	2	1	11	4	5	.322	.385	.471	.856
2015 Hrsbrg	AA	10	39	14	4	1	0	(-	-)	20	6	4	7	1	0	8	0	0				2	.359	.366	.513	.879
2015 Syrcse	AAA	48	188	59	7	3	3	(-	-)	81	31	15	31	13	0	41	0	1	3	14	2	2	.314	.353	.431	.784
2015 Was	NL	27	40	9	1	0	1	(0	1)	13	5	1	2	4	0	12	0	0	0	2	2	0	.225	.295	.325	.620

Koji Uehara

Pitches: R **Bats:** R **Pos:** RP-43   KOH-jee ooh-ih-HAR-uh   **Ht:** 6'2" **Wt:** 195 **Born:** 4/3/1975 **Age:** 41

		HOW MUCH HE PITCHED						WHAT HE GAVE UP												THE RESULTS							
Year Team	Lg	G	GS	CG	GF	IP	BFP	H	R	ER	HR	SH	SF	HB	TBB	IBB	SO	WP	Bk	W	L	Pct	Sh	Sv-Op	Hld	ERC	ERA
2009 Bal	AL	12	12	0	0	66.2	279	71	33	30	7	1	3	0	12	1	48	0	0	2	4	.333	0	0-0	0	3.56	4.05
2010 Bal	AL	43	0	0	22	44.0	174	37	15	14	5	1	0	0	5	0	55	1	0	1	2	.333	0	13-15	6	2.22	2.86
2011 2 Tms	AL	65	0	0	22	65.0	243	38	17	17	11	1	1	0	9	1	85	0	0	2	3	.400	0	0-1	22	1.48	1.83
2012 Tex	AL	37	0	0	13	36.0	130	20	7	7	4	1	1	0	3	0	43	1	0	0	0	-	0	1-1	7	1.12	1.75
2013 Bos	AL	73	0	0	40	74.1	265	33	10	9	5	1	1	1	9	2	101	1	0	4	1	.800	0	21-24	13	0.79	1.09
2014 Bos	AL	64	0	0	50	64.1	249	51	18	18	10	3	1	1	8	0	80	1	0	6	5	.545	0	26-31	1	2.35	2.52
2015 Bos	AL	43	0	0	38	40.1	160	28	14	10	3	1	1	0	9	1	47	4	0	2	4	.333	0	25-27	0	1.67	2.23
11 Bal	AL	43	0	0	19	47.0	174	25	9	9	6	1	1	0	8	1	62	0	0	1	1	.500	0	0-1	13	1.27	1.72
11 Tex	AL	22	0	0	3	18.0	69	13	8	8	5	0	0	0	1	0	23	0	0	1	2	.333	0	0-0	9	2.21	4.00
Postseason		17	0	0	13	16.0	60	12	6	6	4	0	0	0	2	0	20	0	0	1	1	.500	0	7-7	0	2.63	3.38
7 ML YEARS		337	12	0	185	390.2	1500	278	114	105	45	9	8	2	55	5	459	8	0	17	19	.472	0	86-99	49	1.75	2.42

Dan Uggla

Bats: R **Throws:** R **Pos:** PH-37;2B-31;1B-1;DH-1   UGG-luh   **Ht:** 5'11" **Wt:** 210 **Born:** 3/11/1980 **Age:** 36

Year Team	Lg	G	AB	H	2B	3B	HR	(Hm	Rd)	TB	R	RBI	RC	TBB	IBB	SO	HBP	SH	SF	SB	CS	GDP	Avg	OBP	Slg	OPS
2006 Fla	NL	154	611	172	26	7	27	(10	17)	293	105	90	97	48	1	123	9	7	8	6	6	5	.282	.339	.480	.818
2007 Fla	NL	159	632	155	49	3	31	(18	13)	303	113	88	81	68	0	167	13	4	11	2	1	10	.245	.326	.479	.805
2008 Fla	NL	146	531	138	37	1	32	(15	17)	273	97	92	93	77	6	171	8	0	3	5	5	10	.260	.360	.514	.874
2009 Fla	NL	158	564	137	27	1	31	(21	10)	259	84	90	81	92	4	150	7	1	4	2	1	10	.243	.354	.459	.813
2010 Fla	NL	159	589	169	31	0	33	(14	19)	299	100	105	101	78	2	149	2	0	5	4	1	10	.287	.369	.508	.877
2011 Atl	NL	161	600	140	22	1	36	(18	18)	272	88	82	78	62	2	156	7	0	3	1	3	9	.233	.311	.453	.764
2012 Atl	NL	154	523	115	29	0	19	(7	12)	201	86	78	83	94	5	168	10	0	3	4	3	8	.220	.348	.384	.732
2013 Atl	NL	136	448	80	10	3	22	(8	14)	162	60	55	48	77	2	171	9	0	3	2	0	7	.179	.309	.362	.671
2014 2 Tms	NL	52	141	21	3	0	2	(0	2)	30	14	10	6	11	0	46	4	0	1	0	0	3	.149	.229	.213	.442
2015 Was	NL	67	120	22	4	2	2	(0	2)	36	12	16	13	19	0	40	1	0	1	0	1	1	.183	.298	.300	.598
14 Atl	NL	48	130	21	3	0	2	(0	2)	30	13	10	6	10	0	40	4	0	1	0	0	3	.162	.241	.231	.472
14 SF	NL	4	11	0	0	0	0	(0	0)	0	1	0	0	1	0	6	0	0	0	0	0	0	.000	.083	.000	.083
Postseason		1	4	0	0	0	0	(0	0)	0	1	0	0	1	0	0	0	0	0	0	0	0	.000	.200	.000	.200
10 ML YEARS		1346	4759	1149	238	18	235	(111	124)	2128	759	706	681	626	22	1341	70	12	42	26	21	75	.241	.336	.447	.783

Justin Upton

Bats: R **Throws:** R **Pos:** LF-146;PH-4;DH-1   **Ht:** 6'2" **Wt:** 205 **Born:** 8/25/1987 **Age:** 28

Year Team	Lg	G	AB	H	2B	3B	HR	(Hm	Rd)	TB	R	RBI	RC	TBB	IBB	SO	HBP	SH	SF	SB	CS	GDP	Avg	OBP	Slg	OPS
2007 Ari	NL	43	140	31	8	3	2	(2	0)	51	17	11	13	11	4	37	1	0	0	2	0	3	.221	.283	.364	.647
2008 Ari	NL	108	356	89	19	6	15	(12	3)	165	52	42	47	54	6	121	4	0	3	1	4	3	.250	.353	.463	.816
2009 Ari	NL	138	526	158	30	7	26	(14	12)	280	84	86	94	55	3	137	2	1	4	20	5	10	.300	.366	.532	.899
2010 Ari	NL	133	495	135	27	3	17	(8	9)	219	73	69	73	64	5	152	4	1	7	18	8	20	.273	.356	.442	.799
2011 Ari	NL	159	592	171	39	5	31	(20	11)	313	105	88	103	59	9	126	19	0	1	21	9	8	.289	.369	.529	.898
2012 Ari	NL	150	554	155	24	4	17	(11	6)	238	107	67	82	63	5	121	5	0	6	18	8	7	.280	.355	.430	.785
2013 Atl	NL	149	558	147	27	2	27	(13	14)	259	94	70	84	75	4	161	5	1	4	8	1	12	.263	.354	.464	.818
2014 Atl	NL	154	566	153	34	2	29	(18	11)	278	77	102	84	60	1	171	6	0	8	8	4	10	.270	.342	.491	.833
2015 SD	NL	150	542	136	26	3	26	(15	11)	246	85	81	85	68	5	159	4	0	5	19	5	10	.251	.336	.454	.790
Postseason		15	48	11	2	1	2	(0	2)	21	7	4	7	10	0	13	2	0	0	1	0	0	.229	.383	.438	.821
9 ML YEARS		1184	4329	1175	234	35	190	(113	77)	2049	694	616	665	509	42	1185	50	3	41	115	44	83	.271	.352	.473	.825

Melvin Upton Jr.

Bats: R **Throws:** R **Pos:** CF-63;PH-34;PR-2   **Ht:** 6'3" **Wt:** 185 **Born:** 8/21/1984 **Age:** 31

Year Team	Lg	G	AB	H	2B	3B	HR	(Hm	Rd)	TB	R	RBI	RC	TBB	IBB	SO	HBP	SH	SF	SB	CS	GDP	Avg	OBP	Slg	OPS
2015 ElPaso*	AAA	13	50	14	2	0	1	(-	-)	19	10	6	7	4	0	12	0	0	0	4	0	1	.280	.333	.380	.713
2004 TB	AL	45	159	41	8	2	4	(2	2)	65	19	12	22	15	0	46	1	1	1	4	1	1	.258	.324	.409	.733
2006 TB	AL	50	175	43	5	0	1	(0	1)	51	20	10	17	13	0	40	1	0	0	11	3	1	.246	.302	.291	.593
2007 TB	AL	129	474	142	25	1	24	(13	11)	241	86	82	93	65	4	154	4	1	4	22	8	14	.300	.386	.508	.894
2008 TB	AL	145	531	145	37	2	9	(4	5)	213	85	67	87	97	4	134	2	3	7	44	16	13	.273	.383	.401	.784
2009 TB	AL	144	560	135	33	4	11	(7	4)	209	79	55	68	57	0	152	3	3	3	42	14	7	.241	.313	.373	.686
2010 TB	AL	154	536	127	38	4	18	(7	11)	227	89	62	74	67	1	164	2	1	4	42	9	13	.237	.322	.424	.745
2011 TB	AL	153	560	136	27	4	23	(9	14)	240	82	81	79	71	4	161	4	2	3	36	12	16	.243	.331	.429	.759
2012 TB	AL	146	573	141	29	3	28	(17	11)	260	79	78	71	45	0	169	1	4	8	31	6	13	.246	.298	.454	.752
2013 Atl	NL	126	391	72	14	0	9	(7	2)	113	30	26	21	44	2	151	3	1	6	12	5	7	.184	.268	.289	.557

							BATTING														RUNNING			AVERAGES			
Year Team	Lg	G	AB	H	2B	3B	HR	(Hm Rd)	TB	R	RBI	RC	TBB	IBB	SO	HBP	SH	SF	SB	CS	GDP	Avg	OBP	Slg	OPS
2014 Atl	NL	141	519	108	19	5	12	(6 6)	173	67	35	47	57	5	173	1	3	2	20	7	6	.208	.287	.333	.620
2015 SD	NL	87	205	53	12	4	5	(2 3)	88	23	17	33	21	2	62	0	2	0	9	3	1	.259	.327	.429	.757
Postseason		28	104	27	6	1	7	(2 5)	56	20	18	17	9	1	32	0	0	1	9	2	4	.260	.316	.538	.854
11 ML YEARS		1320	4683	1143	247	29	144	(75 69)	1880	659	525	612	552	22	1406	22	21	38	273	84	92	.244	.324	.401	.726

Jose Urena

Pitches: R **Bats:** R **Pos:** RP-11; SP-9   oo-RAY-nuh   **Ht:** 6'3" **Wt:** 175 **Born:** 9/12/1991 **Age:** 24

		HOW MUCH HE PITCHED						WHAT HE GAVE UP											THE RESULTS							
Year Team	Lg	G	GS	CG	GF	IP	BFP	H	R	ER	HR	SH	SF	HB	TBB	IBB	SO	WP	Bk	W	L	Pct	Sh	Sv-Op	Hld	ERC	ERA
2011 Jmstwn	A-	15	15	0	0	72.2	315	74	38	35	4	1	2	3	29	0	48	1	2	4	7	.364	0	0--	-	4.04	4.33
2012 Grnsbr	A	27	22	1	4	138.1	572	143	67	52	13	3	2	1	29	0	101	7	2	9	6	.600	0	2--	-	3.54	3.38
2013 Jupiter	A+	27	26	0	0	149.2	618	148	69	62	8	3	5	6	29	0	107	3	0	10	7	.588	0	0--	-	3.08	3.73
2014 Jaxnvl	AA	26	25	0	0	162.0	652	155	65	60	14	7	6	2	29	1	121	4	0	13	8	.619	0	0--	-	2.99	3.33
2015 NewOr	AAA	11	11	1	0	67.2	276	65	23	20	4	2	1	3	19	0	41	3	0	6	1	.857	1	0--	-	3.41	2.66
2015 Mia	NL	20	9	0	4	61.2	274	73	37	36	5	3	5	3	25	2	28	2	1	1	5	.167	0	0-1	0	5.27	5.25

Juan Uribe

Bats: R **Throws:** R **Pos:** 3B-92;PH-25;2B-8;DH-1   oo-REE-bay   **Ht:** 6'0" **Wt:** 245 **Born:** 3/22/1979 **Age:** 37

							BATTING														RUNNING			AVERAGES			
Year Team	Lg	G	AB	H	2B	3B	HR	(Hm Rd)	TB	R	RBI	RC	TBB	IBB	SO	HBP	SH	SF	SB	CS	GDP	Avg	OBP	Slg	OPS
2001 Col	NL	72	273	82	15	11	8	(3 5)	143	32	53	44	8	1	55	2	0	0	3	0	6	.300	.325	.524	.849
2002 Col	NL	155	566	136	25	7	6	(4 2)	193	69	49	53	34	1	120	5	7	6	9	2	17	.240	.286	.341	.627
2003 Col	NL	87	316	80	19	3	10	(6 4)	135	45	33	45	17	0	60	3	6	1	7	2	3	.253	.297	.427	.724
2004 CWS	AL	134	502	142	31	6	23	(16 7)	254	82	74	81	32	1	96	3	11	5	9	11	10	.283	.327	.506	.833
2005 CWS	AL	146	481	121	23	3	16	(10 6)	198	58	71	59	34	0	77	4	11	10	4	6	7	.252	.301	.412	.712
2006 CWS	AL	132	463	109	28	2	21	(13 8)	204	53	71	52	13	1	82	3	9	7	1	1	10	.235	.257	.441	.698
2007 CWS	AL	150	513	120	18	2	20	(15 5)	202	55	68	52	34	2	112	4	7	1	1	9	6	.234	.284	.394	.678
2008 CWS	AL	110	324	80	22	1	7	(5 2)	125	38	40	43	22	0	64	1	5	1	1	3	5	.247	.296	.386	.682
2009 SF	NL	122	398	115	26	4	16	(9 7)	197	50	55	55	25	2	82	1	3	5	3	1	7	.289	.329	.495	.824
2010 SF	NL	148	521	129	24	2	24	(13 11)	229	64	85	66	45	6	92	4	0	5	1	2	20	.248	.310	.440	.749
2011 LAD	NL	77	270	55	12	0	4	(3 1)	79	21	28	13	17	2	60	6	0	2	2	0	12	.204	.264	.293	.557
2012 LAD	NL	66	162	31	9	0	2	(1 1)	46	15	17	13	13	0	37	2	1	1	0	1	6	.191	.258	.284	.542
2013 LAD	NL	132	388	108	22	2	12	(6 6)	170	47	50	51	30	3	81	2	3	3	5	0	12	.278	.331	.438	.769
2014 LAD	NL	103	386	120	23	0	9	(5 4)	170	36	54	48	15	2	77	1	0	2	0	1	15	.311	.337	.440	.777
2015 3 Tms	NL	119	360	91	17	0	14	(6 8)	150	40	43	41	34	3	80	2	0	1	2	0	12	.253	.320	.417	.737
15 LAD	NL	29	81	20	2	0	1	(0 1)	25	6	6	6	5	0	9	0	0	1	1	0	5	.247	.287	.309	.596
15 Atl	NL	46	151	43	6	0	7	(3 4)	70	17	17	20	15	2	37	1	0	0	1	0	5	.285	.353	.464	.817
15 NYM	NL	44	128	28	9	0	6	(3 3)	55	17	20	15	14	1	34	1	0	0	0	0	2	.219	.301	.430	.730
Postseason		44	157	32	6	0	5	(4 1)	53	15	24	15	7	0	44	1	3	1	2	0	5	.204	.241	.338	.579
15 ML YEARS		1753	5923	1519	314	43	192	(115 77)	2495	705	791	718	373	24	1175	43	63	54	48	39	148	.256	.303	.421	.724

Henry Urrutia

Bats: L **Throws:** R **Pos:** LF-8;DH-1;PH-1   oo-ROOT-ee-ah   **Ht:** 6'5" **Wt:** 200 **Born:** 2/13/1987 **Age:** 29

							BATTING														RUNNING			AVERAGES			
Year Team	Lg	G	AB	H	2B	3B	HR	(Hm Rd)	TB	R	RBI	RC	TBB	IBB	SO	HBP	SH	SF	SB	CS	GDP	Avg	OBP	Slg	OPS
2013 Bowie	AA	52	200	73	16	0	7	(- -)	110	33	37	45	24	2	36	0	0	0	1	1	4	.365	.433	.550	.983
2013 Norfolk	AAA	29	114	36	5	1	2	(- -)	49	16	13	17	8	0	15	0	0	1	0	0	2	.316	.358	.430	.788
2014 Norfolk	AAA	51	204	55	12	1	0	(- -)	69	14	17	19	5	0	50	0	0	2	2	1	8	.270	.284	.338	.623
2014 Orioles	R	14	49	9	1	0	0	(- -)	10	4	2	1	3	0	11	0	0	0	0	0	1	.184	.231	.204	.435
2015 Norfolk	AAA	115	460	134	22	1	10	(- -)	188	58	53	66	40	1	81	0	0	5	1	3	12	.291	.345	.409	.753
2013 Bal	AL	24	58	16	0	1	0	(0 0)	18	5	2	4	0	0	11	0	0	0	0	0	2	.276	.276	.310	.586
2015 Bal	AL	10	34	9	1	0	1	(1 0)	13	3	6	6	2	0	3	0	0	0	0	0	1	.265	.306	.382	.688
2 ML YEARS		34	92	25	1	1	1	(1 0)	31	8	8	10	2	0	14	0	0	0	0	0	3	.272	.287	.337	.624

Giovanny Urshela

Bats: R **Throws:** R **Pos:** 3B-80;PH-1   URR-sha-lah   **Ht:** 6'0" **Wt:** 215 **Born:** 10/11/1991 **Age:** 24

							BATTING														RUNNING			AVERAGES			
Year Team	Lg	G	AB	H	2B	3B	HR	(Hm Rd)	TB	R	RBI	RC	TBB	IBB	SO	HBP	SH	SF	SB	CS	GDP	Avg	OBP	Slg	OPS
2011 Lk Cty	A	126	505	120	24	2	9	(- -)	175	57	46	46	14	1	69	4	2	4	3	0	12	.238	.262	.347	.608
2012 Carlina	A+	114	439	122	30	1	14	(- -)	196	50	59	62	16	0	60	7	5	8	1	1	17	.278	.309	.446	.755
2013 Akron	AA	116	445	120	23	2	8	(- -)	171	42	43	50	14	0	48	1	4	2	1	1	17	.270	.292	.384	.676
2014 Akron	AA	24	90	27	9	0	5	(- -)	51	15	19	17	6	1	16	1	0	1	1	1	2	.300	.347	.567	.914
2014 Clmbs	AAA	105	396	109	27	6	13	(- -)	187	63	65	62	30	1	52	3	1	1	0	2	11	.275	.330	.472	.802
2015 Clmbs	AAA	22	81	22	5	1	3	(- -)	38	12	9	11	3	0	12	0	0	0	0	0	4	.272	.298	.469	.767
2015 Cle	AL	81	267	60	8	1	6	(3 3)	88	25	21	19	18	0	58	2	1	0	0	1	9	.225	.279	.330	.608

Chase Utley

Bats: L **Throws:** R **Pos:** 2B-88;PH-11;1B-6;3B-3;DH-3   UTT-lee   **Ht:** 6'1" **Wt:** 190 **Born:** 12/17/1978 **Age:** 37

							BATTING														RUNNING			AVERAGES			
Year Team	Lg	G	AB	H	2B	3B	HR	(Hm Rd)	TB	R	RBI	RC	TBB	IBB	SO	HBP	SH	SF	SB	CS	GDP	Avg	OBP	Slg	OPS
2003 Phi	NL	43	134	32	10	1	2	(1 1)	50	13	21	19	11	0	22	6	0	1	2	0	3	.239	.322	.373	.696
2004 Phi	NL	94	267	71	11	2	13	(8 5)	125	36	57	37	15	1	40	2	1	2	4	1	6	.266	.308	.468	.776
2005 Phi	NL	147	543	158	39	6	28	(12 16)	293	93	105	102	69	5	109	9	0	7	16	3	10	.291	.376	.540	.915
2006 Phi	NL	160	658	203	40	4	32	(16 16)	347	131	102	122	63	1	132	14	0	4	15	4	9	.309	.379	.527	.906
2007 Phi	NL	132	530	176	48	5	22	(14 8)	300	104	103	111	50	1	89	25	1	7	9	1	7	.332	.410	.566	.976

Year	Team	Lg	G	AB	H	2B	3B	HR	(Hm	Rd)	TB	R	RBI	RC	TBB	IBB	SO	HBP	SH	SF	SB	CS	GDP	Avg	OBP	Slg	OPS
2008	Phi	NL	159	607	177	41	4	33	(20	13)	325	113	104	113	64	14	104	27	1	8	14	2	9	.292	.380	.535	.915
2009	Phi	NL	156	571	161	28	4	31	(16	15)	290	112	93	115	88	3	110	24	0	4	23	0	5	.282	.397	.508	.905
2010	Phi	NL	115	425	117	20	2	16	(10	6)	189	75	65	83	63	3	63	18	0	5	13	2	4	.275	.387	.445	.832
2011	Phi	NL	103	398	103	21	6	11	(8	3)	169	54	44	57	39	4	47	14	1	2	14	0	3	.259	.344	.425	.769
2012	Phi	NL	83	301	77	15	2	11	(8	3)	129	48	45	49	43	7	43	12	0	6	11	1	4	.256	.365	.429	.793
2013	Phi	NL	131	476	135	25	6	18	(8	10)	226	73	69	78	45	4	79	5	0	5	8	3	12	.284	.348	.475	.823
2014	Phi	NL	155	589	159	36	6	11	(6	5)	240	74	78	86	53	12	85	13	0	9	10	1	8	.270	.339	.407	.746
2015	2 Tms	NL	107	373	79	21	2	8	(3	5)	128	37	39	30	32	4	64	10	0	8	4	0	7	.212	.286	.343	.629
15	Phi	NL	73	249	54	12	1	5	(1	4)	83	23	30	19	22	4	35	4	0	7	3	0	6	.217	.284	.333	.617
15	LAD	NL	34	124	25	9	1	3	(2	1)	45	14	9	11	10	0	29	6	0	1	1	0	1	.202	.291	.363	.654
	Postseason		46	164	43	7	1	10	(5	5)	82	38	25	34	34	3	38	5	0	1	10	2	3	.262	.402	.500	.902
	13 ML YEARS		1585	5872	1648	355	50	236	(130	106)	2811	963	925	1002	635	59	987	179	4	68	143	18	87	.281	.365	.479	.843

Luis Valbuena

Bats: L **Throws**: R **Pos**: 3B-99;1B-31;PH-6;DH-2;2B-1   val-BWAY-nah   **Ht**: 5'10" **Wt**: 200 **Born**: 11/30/1985 **Age**: 30

Year	Team	Lg	G	AB	H	2B	3B	HR	(Hm	Rd)	TB	R	RBI	RC	TBB	IBB	SO	HBP	SH	SF	SB	CS	GDP	Avg	OBP	Slg	OPS
2008	Sea	AL	18	49	12	5	0	0	(0	0)	17	6	1	5	4	0	11	1	0	0	0	0	0	.245	.315	.347	.662
2009	Cle	AL	103	368	92	25	3	10	(2	8)	153	52	31	35	26	0	83	0	2	2	2	3	8	.250	.298	.416	.714
2010	Cle	AL	91	275	53	12	0	2	(1	1)	71	22	24	21	28	1	61	3	2	2	1	2	5	.193	.273	.258	.531
2011	Cle	AL	17	43	9	0	0	1	(0	1)	12	4	1	2	1	0	9	0	0	0	1	0	0	.209	.227	.279	.506
2012	ChC	NL	90	265	58	20	0	4	(2	2)	90	26	28	27	36	1	55	0	0	2	0	2	6	.219	.310	.340	.650
2013	ChC	NL	108	331	72	15	1	12	(4	8)	125	34	37	43	53	4	63	4	1	2	1	4	4	.218	.331	.378	.708
2014	ChC	NL	149	478	119	33	4	16	(7	9)	208	68	51	65	65	4	113	2	1	1	1	2	8	.249	.341	.435	.776
2015	Hou	AL	132	434	97	18	0	25	(15	10)	190	62	56	51	50	1	106	6	0	3	1	0	13	.224	.310	.438	.748
	8 ML YEARS		708	2243	512	128	8	70	(31	39)	866	274	229	249	263	11	501	16	6	12	7	13	44	.228	.312	.386	.698

Jordany Valdespin

Bats: L **Throws**: R **Pos**: RF-1;PH-1   jor-DAN-ee VAL-dah-spin   **Ht**: 6'0" **Wt**: 190 **Born**: 12/23/1987 **Age**: 28

Year	Team	Lg	G	AB	H	2B	3B	HR	(Hm	Rd)	TB	R	RBI	RC	TBB	IBB	SO	HBP	SH	SF	SB	CS	GDP	Avg	OBP	Slg	OPS
2015	NewOr*	AAA	76	256	75	12	3	2	(-	-)	99	34	20	36	18	1	31	5	4	3	7	3	6	.293	.348	.387	.734
2012	NYM	NL	94	191	46	9	1	8	(5	3)	81	28	26	20	10	0	44	2	3	0	10	3	2	.241	.286	.424	.710
2013	NYM	NL	66	133	25	3	1	4	(2	2)	42	16	16	10	8	0	28	3	0	0	4	3	1	.188	.250	.316	.566
2014	Mia	NL	52	98	21	2	1	3	(1	2)	34	8	10	11	9	0	16	0	6	0	1	0	1	.214	.280	.347	.627
2015	Mia	NL	2	4	0	0	0	0	(0	0)	0	0	0	0	0	0	1	0	0	0	0	0	0	.000	.000	.000	.000
	4 ML YEARS		214	426	92	14	3	15	(8	7)	157	52	52	41	27	0	89	5	9	0	15	6	4	.216	.271	.369	.639

Jose Valdez

Pitches: R **Bats**: R **Pos**: RP-7   **Ht**: 6'1" **Wt**: 200 **Born**: 3/1/1990 **Age**: 26

			HOW MUCH HE PITCHED						WHAT HE GAVE UP											THE RESULTS						
Year	Team	Lg	G	GS	CG	GF	IP	BFP	H	R	ER	HR	SH	SF	HB	TBB	IBB	SO	WP	Bk	W	L	Pct	Sh	Sv-Op	Hld	ERC	ERA
2012	Tigers	R	23	0	0	23	22.0	90	15	3	2	0	0	0	0	10	0	28	5	1	0	1	.000	0	15- -	-	1.98	0.82
2013	2 Tms	Low	50	0	0	46	49.1	207	32	16	15	1	0	0	1	34	1	67	6	2	2	2	.500	0	33- -	-	2.82	2.74
2014	Erie	AA	47	0	0	41	57.0	246	56	27	26	6	0	1	1	26	1	66	3	1	2	3	.400	0	18- -	-	4.33	4.11
2015	Toledo	AAA	43	0	0	24	57.0	247	49	23	21	3	3	1	0	38	2	43	5	1	4	5	.444	0	5- -	-	4.01	3.32
2015	Det	AL	7	0	0	3	9.0	39	10	4	4	2	0	0	0	4	0	4	2	0	0	1	.000	0	0-1	0	6.01	4.00

Danny Valencia

vuh-LENN-see-yah

Bats: R **Throws**: R **Pos**: 3B-55;LF-32;PH-13;1B-5;RF-5;2B-3;DH-3;PR-3   **Ht**: 6'2" **Wt**: 220 **Born**: 9/19/1984 **Age**: 31

Year	Team	Lg	G	AB	H	2B	3B	HR	(Hm	Rd)	TB	R	RBI	RC	TBB	IBB	SO	HBP	SH	SF	SB	CS	GDP	Avg	OBP	Slg	OPS
2010	Min	AL	85	299	93	18	1	7	(4	3)	134	30	40	50	20	0	46	0	0	3	2	0	11	.311	.351	.448	.799
2011	Min	AL	154	564	139	28	2	15	(9	6)	216	63	72	57	40	2	102	0	0	4	2	6	15	.246	.294	.383	.677
2012	2 Tms	AL	44	154	29	6	1	3	(3	0)	46	14	21	7	3	0	38	0	0	4	0	1	6	.188	.199	.299	.497
2013	Bal	AL	52	161	49	14	1	8	(4	4)	89	20	23	25	8	0	33	0	0	1	0	2	5	.304	.335	.553	.888
2014	2 Tms	AL	86	264	68	16	1	4	(3	1)	98	20	30	25	14	0	62	2	0	4	1	1	8	.258	.296	.371	.667
2015	2 Tms	AL	105	345	100	23	1	18	(7	11)	179	59	66	57	29	3	80	1	1	2	2	2	13	.290	.345	.519	.864
12	Min	AL	34	126	25	6	1	2	(2	0)	39	13	17	7	3	0	32	0	0	3	0	1	5	.198	.212	.310	.522
12	Bos	AL	10	28	4	0	0	1	(1	0)	7	1	4	0	0	0	6	0	0	1	0	0	1	.143	.138	.250	.388
14	KC	AL	36	110	31	5	0	2	(0	2)	42	8	11	8	7	0	27	1	0	0	0	0	4	.282	.328	.382	.710
14	Tor	AL	50	154	37	11	1	2	(1	1)	56	12	19	17	7	0	35	1	0	3	1	1	4	.240	.273	.364	.636
15	Tor	AL	58	162	48	13	0	7	(4	3)	82	26	29	26	9	0	40	0	1	1	2	1	4	.296	.331	.506	.838
15	Oak	AL	47	183	52	10	1	11	(3	8)	97	33	37	31	20	3	40	1	0	1	0	1	9	.284	.356	.530	.886
	Postseason		3	9	2	1	0	0	(0	0)	3	1	2	1	1	0	3	0	0	1	0	0	0	.222	.273	.333	.606
	6 ML YEARS		526	1787	478	105	7	55	(28	27)	762	206	252	221	114	5	361	3	1	18	7	12	58	.267	.310	.426	.736

Scott Van Slyke

Bats: R Throws: R Pos: LF-55;PH-25;RF-22;1B-21;CF-3;DH-1   Ht: 6'4" Wt: 220 Born: 7/24/1986 Age: 29

							BATTING													RUNNING			AVERAGES			
Year	Team	Lg	G	AB	H	2B	3B	HR	(Hm | Rd)	TB	R	RBI	RC	TBB	IBB	SO	HBP	SH	SF	SB	CS	GDP	Avg	OBP	Slg	OPS
2012	LAD	NL	27	54	9	2	0	2	(1 | 1)	17	4	7	4	2	0	14	0	1	0	1	0	2	.167	.196	.315	.511
2013	LAD	NL	53	129	31	8	0	7	(4 | 3)	60	13	19	15	20	0	37	1	0	2	1	1	7	.240	.342	.465	.807
2014	LAD	NL	98	212	63	13	1	11	(2 | 9)	111	32	29	34	28	0	71	4	0	2	4	2	3	.297	.386	.524	.910
2015	LAD	NL	96	222	53	14	0	6	(4 | 2)	85	19	30	26	23	2	62	4	1	3	3	1	5	.239	.317	.383	.700
	Postseason		3	1	0	0	0	0	(0 | 0)	0	0	0	0	0	0	0	0	0	0	0	0	0	.000	.000	.000	.000
	4 ML YEARS		274	617	156	37	1	26	(11 | 15)	273	68	85	79	73	2	184	9	2	7	9	4	17	.253	.337	.442	.780

Jason Vargas

Pitches: L Bats: L Pos: SP-9   Ht: 6'0" Wt: 215 Born: 2/2/1983 Age: 33

			HOW MUCH HE PITCHED						WHAT HE GAVE UP											THE RESULTS							
Year	Team	Lg	G	GS	CG	GF	IP	BFP	H	R	ER	HR	SH	SF	HB	TBB	IBB	SO	WP	Bk	W	L	Pct	Sh	Sv-Op	Hld	ERC	ERA
2005	Fla	NL	17	13	1	0	73.2	325	71	34	33	4	4	1	4	31	4	59	0	0	5	5	.500	0	0-0	0	3.68	4.03
2006	Fla	NL	12	5	0	3	43.0	213	50	39	35	9	4	4	4	30	3	25	2	0	1	2	.333	0	0-0	0	7.30	7.33
2007	NYM	NL	2	2	0	0	10.1	51	17	14	14	4	0	0	0	2	1	4	1	1	0	1	.000	0	0-0	0	8.95	12.19
2009	Sea	AL	23	14	0	4	91.2	385	98	53	50	16	3	6	3	24	1	54	1	0	3	6	.333	0	0-0	0	4.64	4.91
2010	Sea	AL	31	31	0	0	192.2	811	187	86	81	18	4	7	1	54	3	116	1	4	9	12	.429	1	0-0	0	3.37	3.78
2011	Sea	AL	32	32	4	0	201.0	857	205	105	95	22	3	4	4	59	4	131	3	1	10	13	.435	3	0-0	0	3.86	4.25
2012	Sea	AL	33	33	2	0	217.1	887	201	94	93	35	3	6	3	55	1	141	5	0	14	11	.560	2	0-0	0	3.57	3.85
2013	LAA	AL	24	24	3	0	150.0	644	162	68	67	17	3	3	5	46	2	109	0	1	9	8	.529	2	0-0	0	4.40	4.02
2014	KC	AL	30	30	1	0	187.0	790	197	82	77	19	3	1	6	41	4	128	1	1	11	10	.524	1	0-0	0	3.76	3.71
2015	KC	AL	9	9	0	0	43.0	183	46	20	19	5	0	0	1	12	0	27	0	0	5	2	.714	0	0-0	0	4.22	3.98
	Postseason		3	3	0	0	15.1	61	11	6	6	3	0	0	0	6	0	11	1	0	1	0	1.000	0	0-0	0	3.20	3.52
	10 ML YEARS		213	193	11	7	1209.2	5146	1234	595	564	149	27	32	31	354	23	794	14	8	67	70	.489	6	0-0	0	3.99	4.20

Kennys Vargas

Bats: B Throws: R Pos: DH-29;1B-18;PH-11   KEN-ee   Ht: 6'5" Wt: 280 Born: 8/1/1990 Age: 25

							BATTING													RUNNING			AVERAGES			
Year	Team	Lg	G	AB	H	2B	3B	HR	(Hm	Rd)	TB	R	RBI	RC	TBB	IBB	SO	HBP	SH	SF	SB	CS	GDP	Avg	OBP	Slg	OPS
2011	Elizab	R+	44	174	56	11	0	6	(-	-)	85	27	33	32	15	0	50	1	0	1	0	0	1	.322	.377	.489	.865
2012	Beloit	A	41	154	49	10	1	11	(-	-)	94	22	36	39	28	3	41	1	0	3	0	0	4	.318	.419	.610	1.030
2013	FtMyrs	A+	125	457	122	33	1	19	(-	-)	214	68	93	77	50	3	105	7	0	6	0	0	20	.267	.344	.468	.813
2014	NwBrit	AA	97	356	100	17	0	17	(-	-)	168	50	63	62	43	3	68	3	0	3	0	2	10	.281	.360	.472	.832
2015	Roch	AAA	38	122	34	6	0	6	(-	-)	58	20	22	25	26	1	39	2	0	1	0	0	2	.279	.411	.475	.886
2015	Chatt	AA	35	122	35	3	2	7	(-	-)	63	20	24	27	26	2	32	2	0	1	0	0	4	.287	.417	.516	.934
2014	Min	AL	53	215	59	10	1	9	(8	1)	98	26	38	27	12	2	63	3	0	4	0	0	5	.274	.316	.456	.772
2015	Min	AL	58	175	42	4	0	5	(5	0)	61	18	17	13	9	0	54	0	0	0	0	0	7	.240	.277	.349	.626
	2 ML YEARS		111	390	101	14	1	14	(13	1)	159	44	55	40	21	2	117	3	0	4	0	0	12	.259	.299	.408	.707

Anthony Varvaro

Pitches: R Bats: R Pos: RP-9   var-VAR-oh   Ht: 6'0" Wt: 190 Born: 10/31/1984 Age: 31

			HOW MUCH HE PITCHED						WHAT HE GAVE UP											THE RESULTS							
Year	Team	Lg	G	GS	CG	GF	IP	BFP	H	R	ER	HR	SH	SF	HB	TBB	IBB	SO	WP	Bk	W	L	Pct	Sh	Sv-Op	Hld	ERC	ERA
2010	Sea	AL	4	0	0	2	4.0	24	6	5	5	2	0	0	0	6	0	5	1	0	0	1	.000	0	0-0	0	16.26	11.25
2011	Atl	NL	18	0	0	9	24.0	96	15	7	7	3	2	1	0	11	4	23	1	0	0	2	.000	0	0-1	1	2.28	2.63
2012	Atl	NL	12	0	0	5	16.2	76	16	11	10	2	1	0	2	9	1	21	3	0	1	1	.500	0	0-0	0	4.88	5.40
2013	Atl	NL	62	0	0	30	73.1	306	68	25	23	3	2	0	1	25	3	43	7	0	3	1	.750	0	1-3	6	3.07	2.82
2014	Atl	NL	61	0	0	17	54.2	218	46	18	16	5	0	3	0	13	1	50	5	0	3	3	.500	0	0-1	13	2.57	2.63
2015	Bos	AL	9	0	0	2	11.0	51	14	5	5	0	0	0	0	6	1	8	1	0	1	1	.000	0	0-0	0	5.36	4.09
	6 ML YEARS		166	0	0	65	183.2	771	165	71	66	15	5	4	3	70	10	150	18	0	7	9	.438	0	1-5	20	3.32	3.23

Christian Vazquez

Bats: R Throws: R Pos: C   VAZ-kehz   Ht: 5'9" Wt: 195 Born: 8/21/1990 Age: 25

							BATTING													RUNNING			AVERAGES			
Year	Team	Lg	G	AB	H	2B	3B	HR	(Hm	Rd)	TB	R	RBI	RC	TBB	IBB	SO	HBP	SH	SF	SB	CS	GDP	Avg	OBP	Slg	OPS
2011	Grnvlle	A	105	392	111	27	3	18	(-	-)	198	71	84	72	43	2	84	5	0	4	1	1	10	.283	.358	.505	.863
2012	Salem	A+	81	293	78	17	0	7	(-	-)	116	43	41	44	40	0	70	4	3	2	2	2	7	.266	.360	.396	.756
2012	Portlnd	AA	20	73	15	4	0	0	(-	-)	19	11	5	5	8	0	9	0	0	1	0	0	1	.205	.280	.260	.541
2013	Portlnd	AA	96	342	99	19	1	5	(-	-)	135	48	48	55	47	0	44	3	3	4	7	5	9	.289	.376	.395	.771
2014	Pwtckt	AAA	66	244	68	17	0	3	(-	-)	94	35	20	32	21	2	52	1	2	2	0	1	14	.279	.336	.385	.721
2014	Bos	AL	55	175	42	9	0	1	(1	0)	54	15	20	19	19	1	33	0	3	4	0	0	4	.240	.308	.309	.617

Donnie Veal

Pitches: L Bats: L Pos: RP-5   VEEL   Ht: 6'4" Wt: 235 Born: 9/18/1984 Age: 31

			HOW MUCH HE PITCHED						WHAT HE GAVE UP											THE RESULTS							
Year	Team	Lg	G	GS	CG	GF	IP	BFP	H	R	ER	HR	SH	SF	HB	TBB	IBB	SO	WP	Bk	W	L	Pct	Sh	Sv-Op	Hld	ERC	ERA
2015	Gwnntt*	AAA	17	0	0	5	16.0	59	9	3	0	0	0	1	0	2	0	13	1	0	2	0	1.000	0	0--	-	0.88	0.00
2009	Pit	NL	19	0	0	10	16.1	87	18	13	13	2	0	1	2	20	0	16	2	0	1	0	1.000	0	0-0	1	8.89	7.16
2012	CWS	AL	24	0	0	5	13.0	49	5	2	2	0	0	0	4	0	19	0	0	0	0		0	1-1	4	0.75	1.38
2013	CWS	AL	50	0	0	9	29.1	126	26	16	15	3	0	0	0	16	1	29	4	0	2	3	.400	0	0-1	13	4.02	4.60
2014	CWS	AL	7	0	0	3	6.0	32	6	5	5	0	0	1	1	7	1	6	1	0	0	0		0	0-0	2	6.41	7.50
2015	Atl	NL	5	0	0	2	4.1	24	8	7	7	3	1	0	1	2	0	3	2	0	0	0		0	0-1	0	16.52	14.54
	5 ML YEARS		105	0	0	25	69.0	318	63	43	42	8	1	2	4	49	2	73	9	0	3	3	.500	0	1-3	20	5.08	5.48

Vincent Velasquez

Pitches: R **Bats:** B **Pos:** RP-12; SP-7 **Ht:** 6'3" **Wt:** 205 **Born:** 6/7/1992 **Age:** 24

			HOW MUCH HE PITCHED						WHAT HE GAVE UP										THE RESULTS						
Year	Team	Lg	G	GS	CG	GF	IP	BFP	H	R	ER	HR	SH	SF	HB	TBB	IBB	SO	WP	Bk	W	L	Pct	Sh	Sv-Op	Hld	ERC	ERA
2012	TriCity	A-	9	9	0	0	45.2	190	37	19	17	2	0	4	3	17	0	51	4	2	4	1	.800	0	0- -	-	2.83	3.35
2013	2 Tms	Low	28	19	0	4	124.2	518	104	53	49	9	2	5	8	41	0	142	6	1	9	6	.600	0	3- -	-	2.97	3.54
2014	2 Tms	Low	18	13	0	2	63.2	264	50	26	25	6	1	0	6	25	1	91	2	0	7	5	.583	0	0- -	-	3.23	3.53
2015	CpChr	AA	9	5	0	1	33.0	130	20	9	7	2	0	1	1	13	0	45	1	0	4	0	1.000	0	0- -	-	1.94	1.91
2015	Hou	AL	19	7	0	5	55.2	231	50	28	27	5	0	0	2	21	0	58	3	0	1	1	.500	0	0-0	0	3.58	4.37

Will Venable

Bats: L **Throws:** L **Pos:** CF-63;LF-39;PH-33;RF-21;PR-5   VENN-uh-bull **Ht:** 6'3" **Wt:** 205 **Born:** 10/29/1982 **Age:** 33

			BATTING																RUNNING			AVERAGES			
Year	Team	Lg	G	AB	H	2B	3B	HR	(Hm | Rd)	TB	R	RBI	RC	TBB	IBB	SO	HBP	SH	SF	SB	CS	GDP	Avg	OBP	Slg	OPS
2008	SD	NL	28	110	29	4	2	2	(0 | 2)	43	16	10	15	13	1	21	0	0	1	1	1	1	.264	.339	.391	.730
2009	SD	NL	95	293	75	14	2	12	(5 | 7)	129	38	38	34	25	2	89	4	2	0	6	1	6	.256	.323	.440	.763
2010	SD	NL	131	392	96	11	7	13	(6 | 7)	160	60	51	57	45	8	128	3	0	5	29	7	3	.245	.324	.408	.732
2011	SD	NL	121	370	91	14	7	9	(6 | 3)	146	49	44	52	31	4	92	5	1	4	26	3	2	.246	.310	.395	.704
2012	SD	NL	148	417	110	26	8	9	(2 | 7)	179	62	45	66	41	2	94	5	5	2	24	6	6	.264	.335	.429	.765
2013	SD	NL	151	481	129	22	8	22	(15 | 7)	233	64	53	56	29	4	118	2	2	1	22	6	6	.268	.312	.484	.796
2014	SD	NL	146	406	91	13	2	8	(5 | 3)	132	47	33	41	33	2	107	4	3	2	11	6	6	.224	.288	.325	.613
2015	2 Tms		135	349	85	13	3	6	(1 | 5)	122	40	33	46	37	3	94	2	2	0	16	1	8	.244	.320	.350	.669
15	SD	NL	98	283	73	10	3	6	(1 | 5)	107	34	30	39	25	1	73	0	0	0	11	1	8	.258	.318	.378	.696
15	Tex	AL	37	66	12	3	0	0	(0 | 0)	15	6	3	7	12	2	21	2	2	0	5	0	0	.182	.325	.227	.552
8 ML YEARS			955	2818	706	117	39	81	(40 | 41)	1144	376	307	367	254	26	743	25	15	15	135	31	34	.251	.317	.406	.722

Pat Venditte

Pitches: B **Bats:** B **Pos:** RP-26   ven-DET-ee **Ht:** 6'1" **Wt:** 180 **Born:** 6/30/1985 **Age:** 31

			HOW MUCH HE PITCHED						WHAT HE GAVE UP										THE RESULTS						
Year	Team	Lg	G	GS	CG	GF	IP	BFP	H	R	ER	HR	SH	SF	HB	TBB	IBB	SO	WP	Bk	W	L	Pct	Sh	Sv-Op	Hld	ERC	ERA
2011	Trntn	AA	51	0	0	21	90.0	373	80	37	34	7	3	8	3	31	0	88	5	1	3	7	.300	0	0- -	-	3.28	3.40
2012	S-WB	AAA	7	0	0	6	13.0	56	11	4	4	1	1	1	1	6	1	12	0	0	1	1	.500	0	0- -	-	3.47	2.77
2013	Trntn	AA	8	0	0	1	11.1	49	13	5	5	1	0	0	0	3	1	13	1	1	1	2	.333	0	0- -	-	4.13	3.97
2013	3 Tms	Low	13	6	0	0	17.1	71	14	8	6	0	1	1	1	5	0	17	2	0	0	2	.000	0	0- -	-	2.22	3.12
2014	Trntn	AA	15	0	0	6	22.0	83	11	3	2	2	0	0	0	5	0	30	0	0	1	0	1.000	0	1- -	-	1.18	0.82
2014	S-WB	AAA	26	2	0	7	56.1	239	54	21	21	4	3	2	1	17	0	53	3	2	2	5	.286	0	0- -	-	3.30	3.36
2015	Nashv	AAA	23	1	0	2	40.2	166	27	8	7	2	3	1	2	15	0	40	1	2	1	0	1.000	0	0- -	-	2.05	1.55
2015	Oak	AL	26	0	0	7	28.2	119	22	14	14	3	1	1	0	12	0	23	0	0	2	2	.500	0	0- -	2	2.90	4.40

Yordano Ventura

Pitches: R **Bats:** R **Pos:** SP-28   your-DON-oh ven-TOUR-uh **Ht:** 6'0" **Wt:** 180 **Born:** 6/3/1991 **Age:** 25

			HOW MUCH HE PITCHED						WHAT HE GAVE UP										THE RESULTS						
Year	Team	Lg	G	GS	CG	GF	IP	BFP	H	R	ER	HR	SH	SF	HB	TBB	IBB	SO	WP	Bk	W	L	Pct	Sh	Sv-Op	Hld	ERC	ERA
2013	KC	AL	3	3	0	0	15.1	64	13	6	6	3	0	0	0	6	0	11	1	0	1	0	1.000	0	0-0	0	3.83	3.52
2014	KC	AL	31	30	0	0	183.0	782	168	70	65	14	3	4	5	69	1	159	11	1	14	10	.583	0	0-0	0	3.44	3.20
2015	KC	AL	28	28	0	0	163.1	693	154	75	74	14	1	4	9	58	1	156	10	0	13	8	.619	0	0-0	0	3.71	4.08
Postseason			5	4	0	0	25.1	104	23	9	9	3	0	1	0	9	0	14	1	0	1	0	1.000	0	0-1	0	3.60	3.20
3 ML YEARS			62	61	0	0	361.2	1539	335	151	145	31	4	8	14	133	2	326	22	1	27	19	.587	0	0-0	0	3.58	3.61

Drew VerHagen

Pitches: R **Bats:** R **Pos:** RP-20   verr-HAY-gen **Ht:** 6'6" **Wt:** 230 **Born:** 10/22/1990 **Age:** 25

			HOW MUCH HE PITCHED						WHAT HE GAVE UP										THE RESULTS						
Year	Team	Lg	G	GS	CG	GF	IP	BFP	H	R	ER	HR	SH	SF	HB	TBB	IBB	SO	WP	Bk	W	L	Pct	Sh	Sv-Op	Hld	ERC	ERA
2012	2 Tms	Low	10	6	0	0	31.0	132	25	15	12	0	0	2	3	14	0	19	8	0	0	3	.000	0	0- -	-	2.90	3.48
2013	Lkland	A+	12	11	0	1	67.1	276	49	27	21	1	3	4	5	27	1	35	4	0	5	3	.625	0	0- -	-	2.36	2.81
2013	Erie	AA	12	12	1	0	60.0	248	53	24	20	3	5	1	4	17	0	40	5	0	2	5	.286	1	0- -	-	2.94	3.00
2014	Toledo	AAA	19	19	0	0	110.1	465	117	47	45	5	5	2	8	25	1	63	5	0	6	7	.462	0	0- -	-	3.67	3.67
2015	Toledo	AAA	15	0	0	5	27.2	117	26	13	11	0	3	4	1	11	0	21	2	0	1	3	.250	0	1- -	-	3.22	3.58
2015	Erie	AA	5	0	0	3	6.2	25	6	2	2	1	0	0	0	2	0	5	2	0	2	0	1.000	0	2- -	-	3.87	2.70
2014	Det	AL	1	1	0	0	5.0	20	5	3	3	0	0	0	0	3	0	4	0	0	0	1	.000	0	0-0	0	4.67	5.40
2015	Det	AL	20	0	0	2	26.1	106	18	6	6	1	1	0	1	14	2	13	1	0	2	0	1.000	0	0-1	3	2.61	2.05
2 ML YEARS			21	1	0	2	31.1	126	23	9	9	1	1	0	1	17	2	17	1	0	2	1	.667	0	0-1	3	2.91	2.59

Justin Verlander

Pitches: R **Bats:** R **Pos:** SP-20 **Ht:** 6'5" **Wt:** 225 **Born:** 2/20/1983 **Age:** 33

			HOW MUCH HE PITCHED						WHAT HE GAVE UP										THE RESULTS						
Year	Team	Lg	G	GS	CG	GF	IP	BFP	H	R	ER	HR	SH	SF	HB	TBB	IBB	SO	WP	Bk	W	L	Pct	Sh	Sv-Op	Hld	ERC	ERA
2005	Det	AL	2	2	0	0	11.1	54	15	9	9	1	0	0	1	5	0	7	1	0	0	2	.000	0	0-0	0	6.41	7.15
2006	Det	AL	30	30	1	0	186.0	776	187	78	75	21	2	4	6	60	1	124	5	1	17	9	.654	1	0-0	0	4.12	3.63
2007	Det	AL	32	32	1	0	201.2	866	181	88	82	20	3	1	19	67	3	183	17	2	18	6	.750	1	0-0	0	3.53	3.66
2008	Det	AL	33	33	1	0	201.0	880	195	119	108	18	4	6	14	87	8	163	6	3	11	17	.393	0	0-0	0	4.17	4.84
2009	Det	AL	35	35	3	0	240.0	982	219	99	92	20	6	4	6	63	5	269	8	4	19	9	.679	1	0-0	0	3.06	3.45
2010	Det	AL	33	33	4	0	224.1	925	190	89	84	14	6	8	6	71	0	219	11	2	18	9	.667	0	0-0	0	2.79	3.37
2011	Det	AL	34	34	4	0	251.0	969	174	73	67	24	2	3	3	57	0	250	7	2	24	5	.828	2	0-0	0	1.92	2.40
2012	Det	AL	33	33	6	0	238.1	956	192	81	70	19	4	3	5	60	2	239	2	1	17	8	.680	1	0-0	0	2.45	2.64
2013	Det	AL	34	34	0	0	218.1	925	212	94	84	19	2	6	4	75	1	217	3	1	13	12	.520	0	0-0	0	3.68	3.46

Year	Team	Lg	G	GS	CG	GF	IP	BFP	H	R	ER	HR	SH	SF	HB	TBB	IBB	SO	WP	Bk	W	L	Pct	Sh	Sv-Op	Hld	ERC	ERA
			HOW MUCH HE PITCHED						**WHAT HE GAVE UP**												**THE RESULTS**							
2014	Det	AL	32	32	0	0	206.0	893	223	114	104	18	6	5	5	65	1	159	5	1	15	12	.556	0	0-0	0	4.19	4.54
2015	Det	AL	20	20	1	0	133.1	535	113	56	50	13	1	6	3	32	1	113	2	0	5	8	.385	1	0-0	0	2.75	3.38
	Postseason		16	16	1	0	98.1	401	77	40	37	13	1	1	1	30	0	112	6	1	7	5	.583	1	0-0	0	2.77	3.39
11 ML YEARS			318	318	21	0	2111.1	8761	1901	900	825	187	36	46	72	642	22	1943	67	17	157	97	.618	7	0-0	0	3.22	3.52

Logan Verrett

Pitches: R **Bats:** R **Pos:** RP-14; SP-4 — vuh-RETT — **Ht:** 6'2" **Wt:** 190 **Born:** 6/19/1990 **Age:** 26

Year	Team	Lg	G	GS	CG	GF	IP	BFP	H	R	ER	HR	SH	SF	HB	TBB	IBB	SO	WP	Bk	W	L	Pct	Sh	Sv-Op	Hld	ERC	ERA
			HOW MUCH HE PITCHED						**WHAT HE GAVE UP**												**THE RESULTS**							
2012	2 Tms	Low	17	17	2	0	103.1	415	87	43	31	11	0	3	3	13	0	93	5	0	5	2	.714	1	0- -	-	2.32	2.70
2013	Bnghtn	AA	24	24	0	0	146.0	586	136	72	69	21	3	3	3	31	0	132	4	1	12	6	.667	0	0- -	-	3.41	4.25
2014	LsVgs	AAA	28	28	1	0	162.0	699	188	94	78	17	3	9	7	34	0	119	9	1	11	5	.688	0	0- -	-	4.44	4.33
2015	LsVgs	AAA	18	11	0	0	64.2	273	69	35	33	6	2	3	1	19	0	53	4	0	5	3	.625	0	0- -	-	4.11	4.59
2015	2 Tms		18	4	0	4	47.2	190	34	20	19	6	2	3	2	15	4	39	1	0	1	2	.333	0	1-2	0	2.48	3.59
15	Tex	AL	4	0	0	1	9.0	42	11	7	6	1	0	2	0	4	1	3	1	0	0	1	.000	0	0-0	0	5.30	6.00
15	NYM	NL	14	4	0	3	38.2	148	23	13	13	5	2	1	2	11	3	36	0	0	1	1	.500	0	1-2	0	1.90	3.03

Shane Victorino

Bats: R **Throws:** R **Pos:** RF-34;LF-29;PH-13;CF-3;PR-1 — **Ht:** 5'9" **Wt:** 190 **Born:** 11/30/1980 **Age:** 35

Year	Team	Lg	G	AB	H	2B	3B	HR	(Hm	Rd)	TB	R	RBI	RC	TBB	IBB	SO	HBP	SH	SF	SB	CS	GDP	Avg	OBP	Slg	OPS
			BATTING																		**RUNNING**			**AVERAGES**			
2003	SD	NL	36	73	11	2	0	0	(0	0)	13	8	4	1	7	0	17	1	1	1	7	2	5	.151	.232	.178	.410
2005	Phi	NL	21	17	5	0	0	2	(1	1)	11	5	8	4	0	0	3	0	0	2	0	0	0	.294	.263	.647	.910
2006	Phi	NL	153	415	119	19	8	6	(3	3)	172	70	46	58	24	0	54	14	8	1	4	3	5	.287	.346	.414	.760
2007	Phi	NL	131	456	128	23	3	12	(6	6)	193	78	46	65	37	1	62	10	5	2	37	4	10	.281	.347	.423	.770
2008	Phi	NL	146	570	167	30	8	14	(6	8)	255	102	58	86	45	2	69	7	5	0	36	11	8	.293	.352	.447	.799
2009	Phi	NL	156	620	181	39	13	10	(4	6)	276	102	62	99	60	1	71	6	4	4	25	8	5	.292	.358	.445	.803
2010	Phi	NL	147	587	152	26	10	18	(13	5)	252	84	69	89	53	5	79	7	0	1	34	6	7	.259	.327	.429	.756
2011	Phi	NL	132	519	145	27	16	17	(6	11)	255	95	61	86	55	1	63	6	6	0	19	3	4	.279	.355	.491	.847
2012	2 Tms		154	595	152	29	7	11	(4	7)	228	72	55	76	53	1	80	0	6	9	39	6	5	.255	.321	.383	.704
2013	Bos	AL	122	477	140	26	2	15	(7	8)	215	82	61	77	25	0	75	18	10	2	21	3	5	.294	.351	.451	.801
2014	Bos	AL	30	123	33	6	1	2	(1	1)	47	14	12	13	6	0	21	1	1	2	2	0	3	.268	.303	.382	.685
2015	2 Tms		71	178	41	4	2	1	(0	1)	52	19	7	19	16	1	32	5	3	2	7	0	4	.230	.308	.292	.601
12	Phi	NL	101	387	101	17	5	9	(3	6)	155	46	40	50	35	1	49	2	5	2	24	4	4	.261	.324	.401	.724
12	LAD	NL	53	208	51	12	2	2	(1	1)	73	26	15	26	18	0	31	4	4	1	15	2	1	.245	.316	.351	.667
15	Bos	AL	33	94	23	2	0	1	(0	1)	28	10	4	10	9	0	14	2	1	0	5	0	3	.245	.324	.298	.622
15	LAA	AL	38	84	18	2	2	0	(0	0)	24	9	3	9	7	1	18	3	2	2	2	0	1	.214	.292	.286	.577
	Postseason		60	226	58	11	2	7	(4	3)	94	31	42	42	17	4	29	11	4	1	10	1	3	.257	.337	.416	.753
12 ML YEARS			1299	4630	1274	231	70	108	(51	57)	1969	731	489	673	381	12	626	81	52	20	231	46	61	.275	.340	.425	.765

Carlos Villanueva

Pitches: R **Bats:** R **Pos:** RP-35 — vee-ah-new-AY-vah — **Ht:** 6'2" **Wt:** 215 **Born:** 11/28/1983 **Age:** 32

Year	Team	Lg	G	GS	CG	GF	IP	BFP	H	R	ER	HR	SH	SF	HB	TBB	IBB	SO	WP	Bk	W	L	Pct	Sh	Sv-Op	Hld	ERC	ERA
			HOW MUCH HE PITCHED						**WHAT HE GAVE UP**												**THE RESULTS**							
2006	Mil	NL	10	6	0	2	53.2	215	43	22	22	8	1	0	4	11	1	39	0	0	2	2	.500	0	0-0	0	2.85	3.69
2007	Mil	NL	59	6	0	8	114.1	489	101	52	50	16	4	1	3	53	3	99	3	0	8	5	.615	0	1-3	16	4.03	3.94
2008	Mil	NL	47	9	0	9	108.1	464	112	53	49	18	9	1	3	30	1	93	4	0	4	7	.364	0	1-1	11	4.29	4.07
2009	Mil	NL	64	6	0	23	96.0	422	102	58	57	13	4	0	2	35	8	83	4	0	4	10	.286	0	3-8	9	4.44	5.34
2010	Mil	NL	50	6	0	5	52.2	231	48	27	27	7	0	3	4	22	1	67	5	0	2	0	1.000	0	1-4	14	4.08	4.61
2011	Tor	AL	33	13	0	3	107.0	454	103	49	48	11	1	6	4	32	3	68	4	0	6	4	.600	0	0-1	0	3.57	4.04
2012	Tor	AL	38	16	0	9	125.1	521	113	59	58	23	2	4	3	46	4	122	6	1	7	7	.500	0	0-0	2	4.08	4.16
2013	ChC	NL	47	15	0	5	128.2	524	117	58	58	14	7	3	3	40	4	103	0	0	7	8	.467	0	0-1	0	3.43	4.06
2014	ChC	NL	42	5	0	15	77.2	343	89	42	40	6	3	2	3	19	4	72	3	0	5	7	.417	0	2-2	3	4.10	4.64
2015	StL	NL	35	0	0	20	61.0	250	50	21	20	6	1	2	2	21	2	55	1	0	4	3	.571	0	2-2	0	2.98	2.95
	Postseason		2	0	0	0	3.2	11	0	0	0	0	0	0	0	0	0	3	0	0	0	0	-	0	0-0	1	0.00	0.00
10 ML YEARS			425	76	0	99	924.2	3913	878	441	429	122	32	22	31	309	31	801	30	1	49	53	.480	0	10-22	57	3.84	4.18

Jonathan Villar

vee-YARR

Bats: B **Throws:** R **Pos:** SS-22;3B-12;PH-10;PR-9;LF-5;DH-4;2B-3;CF-2 — **Ht:** 6'1" **Wt:** 215 **Born:** 5/2/1991 **Age:** 25

Year	Team	Lg	G	AB	H	2B	3B	HR	(Hm	Rd)	TB	R	RBI	RC	TBB	IBB	SO	HBP	SH	SF	SB	CS	GDP	Avg	OBP	Slg	OPS
			BATTING																		**RUNNING**			**AVERAGES**			
2015	Fresno*	AAA	70	280	76	13	5	5	(-	-)	114	59	32	43	27	0	76	3	3	0	35	9	5	.271	.342	.407	.749
2013	Hou	AL	58	210	51	9	2	1	(0	1)	67	26	8	22	24	1	71	0	7	0	18	8	5	.243	.321	.319	.640
2014	Hou	AL	87	263	55	13	2	7	(4	3)	93	31	27	24	19	1	80	2	4	1	17	4	4	.209	.267	.354	.620
2015	Hou	AL	53	116	33	7	1	2	(0	2)	48	18	11	15	10	0	29	0	1	1	7	2	3	.284	.339	.414	.752
3 ML YEARS			198	589	139	29	5	10	(3	7)	208	75	46	61	53	2	180	2	12	2	42	14	12	.236	.300	.353	.653

Pedro Villarreal

Pitches: R Bats: R Pos: RP-29   VEE-uh-ree-al   Ht: 6'1" Wt: 235 Born: 12/9/1987 Age: 28

			HOW MUCH HE PITCHED						WHAT HE GAVE UP												THE RESULTS							
Year	Team	Lg	G	GS	CG	GF	IP	BFP	H	R	ER	HR	SH	SF	HB	TBB	IBB	SO	WP	Bk	W	L	Pct	Sh	Sv-Op	Hld	ERC	ERA
2015	Lsvlle*	AAA	19	0	0	8	26.0	107	26	11	11	0	1	2	0	4	1	21	0	0	1	0	1.000	0	1- -	-	2.42	3.81
2012	Cin	NL	1	0	0	1	1.0	3	0	0	0	0	0	0	0	0	0	1	0	0	0	0	-	0	0-0	0	0.00	0.00
2013	Cin	NL	2	1	0	0	5.2	32	13	8	8	4	0	0	0	3	0	4	0	0	0	1	.000	0	0-0	0	20.07	12.71
2014	Cin	NL	12	0	0	1	14.2	62	11	7	7	1	0	1	1	7	1	12	1	0	0	2	.000	0	0-0	0	2.95	4.30
2015	Cin	NL	29	0	0	10	50.0	214	57	24	19	6	2	3	3	12	2	29	0	1	1	3	.250	0	0-0	0	4.62	3.42
	4 ML YEARS		44	1	0	12	71.1	311	81	39	34	11	2	4	4	22	3	46	1	1	1	6	.143	0	0-0	0	5.09	4.29

Nick Vincent

Pitches: R Bats: R Pos: RP-26   Ht: 6'0" Wt: 180 Born: 7/12/1986 Age: 29

			HOW MUCH HE PITCHED						WHAT HE GAVE UP												THE RESULTS							
Year	Team	Lg	G	GS	CG	GF	IP	BFP	H	R	ER	HR	SH	SF	HB	TBB	IBB	SO	WP	Bk	W	L	Pct	Sh	Sv-Op	Hld	ERC	ERA
2015	ElPaso*	AAA	40	0	0	5	50.1	209	48	21	17	5	2	3	0	15	0	68	0	0	5	3	.625	0	1- -	-	3.44	3.04
2012	SD	NL	27	0	0	3	26.1	105	19	5	5	2	1	0	1	7	0	28	1	0	2	0	1.000	0	0-1	5	2.13	1.71
2013	SD	NL	45	0	0	7	46.1	180	33	11	11	1	4	0	2	11	3	49	0	0	6	3	.667	0	1-1	10	1.67	2.14
2014	SD	NL	63	0	0	7	55.0	215	44	22	22	5	3	0	2	11	1	62	1	0	1	2	.333	0	0-2	20	2.39	3.60
2015	SD	NL	26	0	0	8	23.0	100	25	8	6	0	0	1	0	10	1	22	0	0	0	1	.000	0	0-2	0	3.95	2.35
	4 ML YEARS		161	0	0	25	150.2	600	121	46	44	8	8	1	5	39	5	161	2	0	9	6	.600	0	1-6	35	2.34	2.63

Arodys Vizcaino

Pitches: R Bats: R Pos: RP-36   ah-ROH-dis vees-kai-EE-no   Ht: 6'0" Wt: 190 Born: 11/13/1990 Age: 25

			HOW MUCH HE PITCHED						WHAT HE GAVE UP												THE RESULTS							
Year	Team	Lg	G	GS	CG	GF	IP	BFP	H	R	ER	HR	SH	SF	HB	TBB	IBB	SO	WP	Bk	W	L	Pct	Sh	Sv-Op	Hld	ERC	ERA
2011	Atl	NL	17	0	0	2	17.1	77	16	9	9	1	0	0	1	9	1	17	5	0	1	1	.500	0	0-2	5	3.89	4.67
2014	ChC	NL	5	0	0	1	5.0	22	5	3	3	1	0	0	0	3	0	4	0	0	0	0	-	0	0-0	0	5.79	5.40
2015	Atl	NL	36	0	0	25	33.2	139	27	7	6	1	2	0	0	13	2	37	7	0	3	1	.750	0	9-10	3	2.42	1.60
	3 ML YEARS		58	0	0	32	56.0	238	48	19	18	3	2	0	1	25	3	58	12	0	4	2	.667	0	9-12	8	3.13	2.89

Ryan Vogelsong

Pitches: R Bats: R Pos: SP-22; RP-11   VOH-gull-song   Ht: 6'4" Wt: 215 Born: 7/22/1977 Age: 38

			HOW MUCH HE PITCHED						WHAT HE GAVE UP												THE RESULTS							
Year	Team	Lg	G	GS	CG	GF	IP	BFP	H	R	ER	HR	SH	SF	HB	TBB	IBB	SO	WP	Bk	W	L	Pct	Sh	Sv-Op	Hld	ERC	ERA
2000	SF	NL	4	0	0	3	6.0	24	4	0	0	0	0	0	0	2	0	6	0	0	0	0	-	0	0-0	0	1.57	0.00
2001	2 Tms	NL	15	2	0	8	34.2	164	39	31	26	6	0	1	2	20	1	24	2	0	0	5	.000	0	0-0	1	6.20	6.75
2003	Pit	NL	6	5	0	0	22.0	108	30	19	16	1	3	1	2	9	3	15	1	0	2	2	.500	0	0-0	0	5.72	6.55
2004	Pit	NL	31	26	0	4	133.0	610	148	99	96	22	8	6	10	67	7	92	3	0	6	13	.316	0	0-0	0	5.89	6.50
2005	Pit	NL	44	0	0	19	81.1	369	82	43	40	5	1	4	8	40	1	52	7	0	2	2	.500	0	0-1	1	4.51	4.43
2006	Pit	NL	20	0	0	7	38.0	178	44	27	27	2	5	4	7	16	2	27	4	1	0	0	-	0	0-0	0	5.31	6.39
2011	SF	NL	30	28	1	1	179.2	752	164	62	54	15	10	3	5	61	6	139	1	1	13	7	.650	1	0-0	0	3.32	2.71
2012	SF	NL	31	31	0	0	189.2	788	171	76	71	17	7	4	8	62	7	158	3	0	14	9	.609	0	0-0	0	3.33	3.37
2013	SF	NL	19	19	0	0	103.2	467	124	73	66	15	4	4	6	38	2	67	3	0	4	6	.400	0	0-0	0	5.64	5.73
2014	SF	NL	32	32	1	0	184.2	780	178	86	82	18	10	3	9	58	2	151	2	0	8	13	.381	0	0-0	0	3.71	4.00
2015	SF	NL	33	22	0	6	135.0	598	140	76	70	17	3	6	3	58	2	108	1	0	9	11	.450	0	0-1	0	4.62	4.67
01	SF	NL	13	0	0	8	28.2	130	29	21	18	5	0	1	2	14	0	17	2	0	0	3	.000	0	0-0	1	5.26	5.65
01	Pit	NL	2	2	0	0	6.0	34	10	10	8	1	0	0	0	6	1	7	0	0	0	2	.000	0	0-0	0	11.03	12.00
	Postseason		8	7	0	1	37.0	155	32	12	12	1	0	0	1	16	0	29	0	0	3	0	1.000	0	0-0	0	3.11	2.92
	11 ML YEARS		265	165	2	48	1107.2	4838	1124	590	548	118	51	36	60	431	33	839	27	2	58	68	.460	1	0-2	2	4.32	4.45

Stephen Vogt

Bats: L Throws: R Pos: C-100;1B-25;PH-21;DH-8   VOTE   Ht: 6'0" Wt: 215 Born: 11/1/1984 Age: 31

			BATTING																		RUNNING			AVERAGES			
Year	Team	Lg	G	AB	H	2B	3B	HR	(Hm	Rd)	TB	R	RBI	RC	TBB	IBB	SO	HBP	SH	SF	SB	CS	GDP	Avg	OBP	Slg	OPS
2012	TB	AL	18	25	0	0	0	0	(0	0)	0	0	0	0	2	0	2	0	0	0	0	0	0	.000	.074	.000	.074
2013	Oak	AL	47	135	34	6	1	4	(3	1)	54	18	16	15	9	1	28	0	2	2	0	1	2	.252	.295	.400	.695
2014	Oak	AL	84	269	75	10	2	9	(4	5)	116	26	35	38	16	2	39	1	0	1	0	0	2	.279	.321	.431	.752
2015	Oak	AL	136	445	116	21	3	18	(5	13)	197	58	71	75	56	6	97	2	0	8	0	2	9	.261	.341	.443	.783
	Postseason		6	19	3	0	1	0	(0	0)	5	2	1	1	2	0	8	0	0	0	0	0	0	.158	.238	.263	.501
	4 ML YEARS		285	874	225	37	6	31	(12	19)	367	102	122	128	83	9	166	3	2	11	1	3	13	.257	.320	.420	.740

Edinson Volquez

Pitches: R Bats: R Pos: SP-33; RP-1   VOLE-kezz   Ht: 6'0" Wt: 220 Born: 7/3/1983 Age: 32

			HOW MUCH HE PITCHED						WHAT HE GAVE UP												THE RESULTS							
Year	Team	Lg	G	GS	CG	GF	IP	BFP	H	R	ER	HR	SH	SF	HB	TBB	IBB	SO	WP	Bk	W	L	Pct	Sh	Sv-Op	Hld	ERC	ERA
2005	Tex	AL	6	3	0	0	12.2	75	25	22	20	3	0	1	2	10	0	11	0	0	0	4	.000	0	0-0	0	14.15	14.21
2006	Tex	AL	8	8	0	0	33.1	164	52	28	27	7	0	1	1	17	0	15	0	0	1	6	.143	0	0-0	0	9.27	7.29
2007	Tex	AL	6	6	0	0	34.0	149	34	18	17	4	0	2	2	15	0	29	0	0	2	1	.667	0	0-0	0	4.63	4.50
2008	Cin	NL	33	32	0	1	196.0	838	167	82	70	14	6	5	14	93	5	206	10	1	17	6	.739	0	0-0	0	3.61	3.21
2009	Cin	NL	9	9	0	0	49.2	218	34	25	24	6	2	1	5	32	0	47	2	1	4	2	.667	0	0-0	0	3.77	4.35
2010	Cin	NL	12	12	0	0	62.2	275	59	30	30	6	3	1	4	35	0	67	5	0	4	3	.571	0	0-0	0	4.60	4.31
2011	Cin	NL	20	20	0	0	108.2	489	106	72	69	19	5	6	4	65	3	104	5	2	5	7	.417	0	0-0	0	5.42	5.71
2012	SD	NL	32	32	1	0	182.2	802	160	88	84	14	5	4	9	105	6	174	9	1	11	11	.500	1	0-0	0	4.04	4.14
2013	2 Tms	NL	33	32	0	0	170.1	777	193	114	108	19	9	4	3	77	2	142	16	0	9	12	.429	0	0-0	0	5.11	5.71
2014	Pit	NL	32	31	1	0	192.2	809	166	75	65	17	13	6	14	71	6	140	15	0	13	7	.650	0	0-0	0	3.37	3.04

Year Team	Lg	G	GS	CG	GF	IP	BFP	H	R	ER	HR	SH	SF	HB	TBB	IBB	SO	WP	Bk	W	L	Pct	Sh	Sv-Op	Hld	ERC	ERA
2015 KC	AL	34	33	1	0	200.1	850	190	89	79	16	5	7	8	72	1	155	3	0	13	9	.591	0	0-0	0	3.66	3.55
13 SD	NL	27	27	0	0	142.1	659	168	100	95	14	7	3	3	69	2	116	11	0	9	10	.474	0	0-0	0	5.45	6.01
13 LAD	NL	6	5	0	0	28.0	118	25	14	13	5	2	1	0	8	0	26	5	0	0	2	.000	0	0-0	0	3.45	4.18
Postseason		2	2	0	0	6.2	34	9	9	9	1	0	1	0	5	0	3	0	0	0	2	.000	0	0-0	0	7.94	12.15
11 ML YEARS		225	218	3	1	1243.0	5446	1186	643	593	125	48	38	65	592	23	1090	65	5	79	68	.537	1	0-0	0	4.30	4.29

Chris Volstad

Pitches: R **Bats:** R **Pos:** RP-1   VOHL-stadd   **Ht:** 6'8" **Wt:** 230 **Born:** 9/23/1986 **Age:** 29

Year Team	Lg	G	GS	CG	GF	IP	BFP	H	R	ER	HR	SH	SF	HB	TBB	IBB	SO	WP	Bk	W	L	Pct	Sh	Sv-Op	Hld	ERC	ERA
2015 Indy*	AAA	27	25	0	0	155.2	655	159	61	55	3	4	7	9	43	3	97	6	0	11	7	.611	0	0--	-	3.40	3.18
2008 Fla	NL	15	14	0	0	84.1	365	76	30	27	3	6	1	5	36	4	52	0	0	6	4	.600	0	0-0	0	3.30	2.88
2009 Fla	NL	29	29	1	0	159.0	682	169	100	92	29	8	3	3	59	3	107	8	0	9	13	.409	1	0-0	0	5.05	5.21
2010 Fla	NL	30	30	2	0	175.0	758	187	94	89	17	8	7	8	60	5	102	8	1	12	9	.571	1	0-0	0	4.38	4.58
2011 Fla	NL	29	29	0	0	165.2	719	187	96	90	23	12	10	1	49	6	117	2	1	5	13	.278	0	0-0	0	4.63	4.89
2012 ChC	NL	21	21	0	0	111.1	507	137	81	78	16	5	8	3	43	4	61	2	1	3	12	.200	0	0-0	0	5.73	6.31
2013 Col	NL	6	0	0	1	8.1	47	19	10	10	1	0	0	2	1	0	3	0	0	0	0	-	0	0-0	1	12.25	10.80
2015 Pit	NL	1	0	0	0	2.0	7	2	0	0	0	0	0	0	0	0	0	0	0	0	0	-	0	0-0	0	2.31	0.00
7 ML YEARS		131	123	3	1	705.2	3085	777	411	386	89	39	29	22	248	22	442	20	3	35	51	.407	2	0-0	1	4.74	4.92

Joey Votto

Bats: L **Throws:** R **Pos:** 1B-156;PH-2   VAH-toe   **Ht:** 6'2" **Wt:** 220 **Born:** 9/10/1983 **Age:** 32

Year Team	Lg	G	AB	H	2B	3B	HR	(Hm	Rd)	TB	R	RBI	RC	TBB	IBB	SO	HBP	SH	SF	SB	CS	GDP	Avg	OBP	Slg	OPS
2007 Cin	NL	24	84	27	7	0	4	(4	0)	46	11	17	17	5	1	15	0	0	0	1	0	0	.321	.360	.548	.907
2008 Cin	NL	151	526	156	32	3	24	(14	10)	266	69	84	91	59	9	102	2	0	2	7	5	7	.297	.368	.506	.874
2009 Cin	NL	131	469	151	38	1	25	(14	11)	266	82	84	99	70	10	106	4	0	1	4	1	8	.322	.414	.567	.981
2010 Cin	NL	150	547	177	36	2	37	(18	19)	328	106	113	132	91	8	125	7	0	3	16	5	11	.324	.424	.600	1.024
2011 Cin	NL	161	599	185	40	3	29	(13	16)	318	101	103	131	110	15	129	4	0	6	8	6	20	.309	.416	.531	.947
2012 Cin	NL	111	374	126	44	0	14	(10	4)	212	59	56	97	94	18	85	5	0	2	5	3	8	.337	.474	.567	1.041
2013 Cin	NL	162	581	177	30	3	24	(11	13)	285	101	73	121	135	19	138	4	0	6	6	3	15	.305	.435	.491	.926
2014 Cin	NL	62	220	56	16	0	6	(6	0)	90	32	23	36	47	2	49	3	0	2	1	1	5	.255	.390	.409	.799
2015 Cin	NL	158	545	171	33	2	29	(14	15)	295	95	80	135	143	15	135	5	0	2	11	3	11	.314	.459	.541	1.000
Postseason		9	32	8	0	0	0	(0	0)	8	3	1	3	4	0	9	0	0	1	0	0	1	.250	.324	.250	.574
9 ML YEARS		1110	3945	1226	276	14	192	(104	88)	2106	656	633	859	754	97	884	34	0	24	59	27	85	.311	.423	.534	.957

Michael Wacha

Pitches: R **Bats:** R **Pos:** SP-30   WOCK-uh   **Ht:** 6'6" **Wt:** 210 **Born:** 7/1/1991 **Age:** 24

Year Team	Lg	G	GS	CG	GF	IP	BFP	H	R	ER	HR	SH	SF	HB	TBB	IBB	SO	WP	Bk	W	L	Pct	Sh	Sv-Op	Hld	ERC	ERA
2013 StL	NL	15	9	0	2	64.2	260	52	20	20	5	1	3	0	19	0	65	3	0	4	1	.800	0	0-1	0	2.52	2.78
2014 StL	NL	19	19	0	0	107.0	447	95	41	38	6	1	2	5	33	0	94	2	0	5	6	.455	0	0-0	0	3.00	3.20
2015 StL	NL	30	30	0	0	181.1	762	162	74	68	19	8	3	6	58	4	153	4	1	17	7	.708	0	0-0	0	3.28	3.38
Postseason		6	5	0	1	31.0	123	18	12	12	4	0	0	1	13	3	33	0	0	4	2	.667	0	0-0	0	2.16	3.48
3 ML YEARS		64	58	0	2	353.0	1469	309	135	126	30	10	8	11	110	4	312	9	1	26	14	.650	0	0-1	0	3.05	3.21

Tsuyoshi Wada

Pitches: L **Bats:** L **Pos:** SP-7; RP-1   sue-YO-she WAH-duh   **Ht:** 5'11" **Wt:** 180 **Born:** 2/21/1981 **Age:** 35

Year Team	Lg	G	GS	CG	GF	IP	BFP	H	R	ER	HR	SH	SF	HB	TBB	IBB	SO	WP	Bk	W	L	Pct	Sh	Sv-Op	Hld	ERC	ERA
2011	Jap	26	26	4	0	184.2	726	145	33	31	7	-	-	4	40	0	168	5	0	16	5	.762	2	0--	-	2.02	1.51
2013 Norfolk	AAA	19	19	0	0	102.2	442	112	50	46	9	3	2	4	35	0	80	1	0	5	6	.455	0	0--	-	4.50	4.03
2014 Iowa	AAA	19	18	0	0	113.2	464	104	36	35	13	2	1	2	28	2	120	3	0	10	6	.625	0	0--	-	3.18	2.77
2015 Iowa	AAA	16	16	0	0	86.2	372	93	44	38	4	1	6	0	26	1	62	4	0	4	5	.444	0	0--	-	3.68	3.95
2014 ChC	NL	13	13	0	0	69.1	289	67	28	25	7	2	1	3	19	1	57	0	0	4	4	.500	0	0-0	0	3.59	3.25
2015 ChC	NL	8	7	0	0	32.1	136	30	14	13	5	1	1	1	11	1	31	1	0	1	1	.500	0	0-0	0	3.90	3.62
2 ML YEARS		21	20	0	0	101.2	425	97	42	38	12	3	2	4	30	2	88	1	0	5	5	.500	0	0-0	0	3.69	3.36

Tyler Wagner

Pitches: R **Bats:** R **Pos:** SP-3   **Ht:** 6'3" **Wt:** 195 **Born:** 1/24/1991 **Age:** 25

Year Team	Lg	G	GS	CG	GF	IP	BFP	H	R	ER	HR	SH	SF	HB	TBB	IBB	SO	WP	Bk	W	L	Pct	Sh	Sv-Op	Hld	ERC	ERA
2012 Helena	R+	14	13	0	0	48.2	233	63	51	42	6	0	1	3	22	0	47	4	0	1	4	.200	0	0--	-	6.36	7.77
2013 Wisc	A	27	25	1	2	148.2	613	129	59	53	10	3	4	3	56	0	116	12	0	10	8	.556	1	0--	-	3.18	3.21
2014 BrvdCt	A+	25	25	1	0	150.0	595	118	41	31	10	4	6	1	48	0	118	6	1	13	6	.684	0	0--	-	2.53	1.86
2015 Biloxi	AA	25	25	2	0	152.1	609	130	45	38	7	4	4	3	45	0	120	4	1	11	5	.688	1	0--	-	2.71	2.25
2015 Mil	NL	3	3	0	0	13.2	67	22	11	11	1	2	1	0	7	0	5	1	0	0	2	.000	0	0-0	0	8.26	7.24

Adam Wainwright

Pitches: R Bats: R Pos: SP-4; RP-3   Ht: 6'7" Wt: 235 Born: 8/30/1981 Age: 34

Year	Team	Lg	G	GS	CG	GF	IP	BFP	H	R	ER	HR	SH	SF	HB	TBB	IBB	SO	WP	Bk	W	L	Pct	Sh	Sv-Op	Hld	ERC	ERA
2005	StL	NL	2	0	0	1	2.0	9	2	3	3	1	0	0	0	1	0	0	0	0	0	0	-	0	0-0	0	7.30	13.50
2006	StL	NL	61	0	0	10	75.0	309	64	26	26	6	4	1	4	22	2	72	3	0	2	1	.667	0	3-5	17	2.92	3.12
2007	StL	NL	32	32	1	0	202.0	882	212	93	83	13	9	5	9	70	4	136	6	0	14	12	.538	0	0-0	0	4.01	3.70
2008	StL	NL	20	20	1	0	132.0	544	122	51	47	12	6	4	3	34	1	91	3	0	11	3	.786	0	0-0	0	3.14	3.20
2009	StL	NL	34	34	1	0	233.0	970	216	75	68	17	10	5	3	66	1	212	7	0	19	8	.704	0	0-0	0	3.08	2.63
2010	StL	NL	33	33	5	0	230.1	910	186	68	62	15	13	6	4	56	2	213	2	0	20	11	.645	2	0-0	0	2.36	2.42
2012	StL	NL	32	32	3	0	198.2	831	196	96	87	15	9	6	6	52	3	184	5	2	14	13	.519	2	0-0	0	3.41	3.94
2013	StL	NL	34	34	5	0	241.2	956	223	83	79	15	13	2	6	35	2	219	5	0	19	9	.679	2	0-0	0	2.60	2.94
2014	StL	NL	32	32	5	0	227.0	898	184	64	60	10	8	3	7	50	5	179	4	1	20	9	.690	3	0-0	0	2.20	2.38
2015	StL	NL	7	4	0	2	28.0	111	25	7	5	0	2	0	0	4	0	20	0	0	2	1	.667	0	0-0	0	1.97	1.61
	Postseason		21	12	1	9	83.2	343	79	32	29	8	2	2	2	15	0	90	3	0	4	4	.500	0	4-5	0	2.97	3.12
	10 ML YEARS		287	221	21	13	1569.2	6420	1430	566	520	104	74	32	42	390	20	1326	35	3	121	67	.644	9	3-5	17	2.90	2.98

Jordan Walden

Pitches: R Bats: R Pos: RP-12   Ht: 6'5" Wt: 250 Born: 11/16/1987 Age: 28

Year	Team	Lg	G	GS	CG	GF	IP	BFP	H	R	ER	HR	SH	SF	HB	TBB	IBB	SO	WP	Bk	W	L	Pct	Sh	Sv-Op	Hld	ERC	ERA
2010	LAA	AL	16	0	0	5	15.1	65	13	4	4	1	0	0	0	7	0	23	1	1	0	1	.000	0	1-1	6	3.21	2.35
2011	LAA	AL	62	0	0	42	60.1	253	49	22	20	3	4	2	1	26	3	67	6	0	5	5	.500	0	32-42	2	2.82	2.98
2012	LAA	AL	45	0	0	20	39.0	172	35	15	15	3	0	1	0	18	1	48	7	0	3	2	.600	0	1-2	8	3.42	3.46
2013	Atl	NL	50	0	0	9	47.0	193	39	19	18	4	1	0	1	14	4	54	6	0	4	3	.571	0	1-3	14	2.63	3.45
2014	Atl	NL	58	0	0	8	50.0	205	33	17	16	2	0	1	0	27	1	62	9	0	0	2	.000	0	3-5	20	2.41	2.88
2015	StL	NL	12	0	0	2	10.1	42	7	1	1	0	0	1	0	4	1	12	2	0	1	0	1.000	0	1-1	8	1.63	0.87
	Postseason		2	0	0	0	2.2	13	3	4	4	0	0	0	1	1	0	3	0	0	0	0	-	0	0-0	0	5.24	13.50
	6 ML YEARS		243	0	0	86	222.0	930	176	78	74	13	5	5	2	96	10	266	31	1	12	14	.462	0	39-54	58	2.76	3.00

Kyle Waldrop

Bats: L Throws: L Pos: PH-1   Ht: 6'2" Wt: 215 Born: 11/26/1991 Age: 24

Year	Team	Lg	G	AB	H	2B	3B	HR	(Hm	Rd)	TB	R	RBI	RC	TBB	IBB	SO	HBP	SH	SF	SB	CS	GDP	Avg	OBP	Slg	OPS
2011	Billings	R+	68	278	76	22	9	5	(-	-)	131	38	29	39	10	0	65	3	1	1	4	4	5	.273	.305	.471	.776
2012	Dayton	A	117	416	118	21	6	8	(-	-)	175	59	50	63	38	5	77	4	7	4	10	6	14	.284	.346	.421	.767
2013	Bkrsfld	A+	129	504	130	32	4	21	(-	-)	233	66	54	72	32	0	121	2	0	2	20	8	5	.258	.304	.462	.766
2014	Bkrsfld	A+	65	256	92	20	1	6	(-	-)	132	54	32	55	22	0	56	3	2	5	11	2	6	.359	.409	.516	.925
2014	Pnscla	AA	66	232	73	17	3	8	(-	-)	120	27	35	41	17	1	44	0	1	2	3	4	8	.315	.359	.517	.876
2015	Pnscla	AA	67	242	67	13	3	6	(-	-)	104	21	31	32	12	1	61	2	0	3	2	2	2	.277	.313	.430	.742
2015	Lsvlle	AAA	55	205	38	6	0	1	(-	-)	47	8	13	7	7	1	54	0	0	1	0	1	4	.185	.211	.229	.441
2015	Cin	NL	1	1	0	0	0	0	(0	0)	0	0	0	0	0	0	1	0	0	0	0	0	0	.000	.000	.000	.000

Christian Walker

Bats: R Throws: R Pos: PH-3;1B-2;DH-2   Ht: 6'0" Wt: 220 Born: 3/28/1991 Age: 25

Year	Team	Lg	G	AB	H	2B	3B	HR	(Hm	Rd)	TB	R	RBI	RC	TBB	IBB	SO	HBP	SH	SF	SB	CS	GDP	Avg	OBP	Slg	OPS
2012	Abrdn	A-	22	81	23	5	0	2	(-	-)	34	12	9	13	10	0	14	2	0	0	2	1	1	.284	.376	.420	.796
2013	2 Tms	Low	86	331	103	22	0	11	(-	-)	158	44	55	58	28	0	57	6	0	5	2	3	9	.311	.370	.477	.848
2013	Bowie	AA	17	62	15	5	0	0	(-	-)	20	7	1	6	6	0	10	1	0	0	0	0	1	.242	.319	.323	.641
2014	Bowie	AA	95	366	110	15	2	20	(-	-)	189	58	77	70	38	0	83	3	0	4	2	1	6	.301	.367	.516	.884
2014	Norfolk	AAA	44	166	43	10	0	6	(-	-)	71	15	19	25	18	1	49	2	0	2	0	0	4	.259	.335	.428	.763
2015	Norfolk	AAA	138	534	137	33	1	18	(-	-)	226	68	74	75	49	2	136	6	0	3	1	3	20	.257	.324	.423	.748
2014	Bal	AL	6	18	3	1	0	1	(1	0)	7	1	1	0	1	0	9	0	0	0	0	0	0	.167	.211	.389	.599
2015	Bal	AL	7	9	1	0	0	0	(0	0)	1	0	0	1	3	0	4	0	0	0	0	0	0	.111	.333	.111	.444
	2 ML YEARS		13	27	4	1	0	1	(1	0)	8	1	1	1	4	0	13	0	0	0	0	0	0	.148	.258	.296	.554

Neil Walker

Bats: B Throws: R Pos: 2B-146;PH-15   Ht: 6'3" Wt: 210 Born: 9/10/1985 Age: 30

Year	Team	Lg	G	AB	H	2B	3B	HR	(Hm	Rd)	TB	R	RBI	RC	TBB	IBB	SO	HBP	SH	SF	SB	CS	GDP	Avg	OBP	Slg	OPS
2009	Pit	NL	17	36	7	1	0	0	(0	0)	8	5	0	2	4	0	11	0	0	0	1	0	1	.194	.275	.222	.497
2010	Pit	NL	110	426	126	29	3	12	(5	7)	197	57	66	66	34	1	83	3	2	4	2	3	4	.296	.349	.462	.811
2011	Pit	NL	159	596	163	36	4	12	(5	7)	243	76	83	77	54	5	112	4	0	9	9	6	15	.273	.334	.408	.742
2012	Pit	NL	129	472	132	27	0	14	(7	7)	201	62	69	72	47	1	104	2	1	8	7	5	11	.280	.342	.426	.768
2013	Pit	NL	133	478	120	24	4	16	(8	8)	200	62	53	62	50	4	85	15	5	3	1	2	14	.251	.339	.418	.757
2014	Pit	NL	137	512	139	25	3	23	(10	13)	239	74	76	72	45	2	88	11	1	2	2	2	12	.271	.342	.467	.809
2015	Pit	NL	151	543	146	32	3	16	(8	8)	232	69	71	73	44	5	110	8	0	8	4	1	9	.269	.328	.427	.756
	Postseason		7	28	2	1	0	0	(0	0)	3	1	1	1	2	0	7	0	0	0	0	0	0	.071	.133	.107	.240
	7 ML YEARS		836	3063	833	174	17	93	(42	51)	1320	405	418	424	278	18	593	43	9	33	26	19	66	.272	.338	.431	.769

Taijuan Walker

Pitches: R Bats: R Pos: SP-29　　　　TIE-wahn　　　　Ht: 6'4" Wt: 235 Born: 8/13/1992 Age: 23

Year	Team	Lg	G	GS	CG	GF	IP	BFP	H	R	ER	HR	SH	SF	HB	TBB	IBB	SO	WP	Bk	W	L	Pct	Sh	Sv-Op	Hld	ERC	ERA
2013	Sea	AL	3	3	0	0	15.0	60	11	7	6	0	0	2	0	4	0	12	0	0	1	0	1.000	0	0-0	0	1.63	3.60
2014	Sea	AL	8	5	1	2	38.0	160	31	12	11	2	0	0	3	18	1	34	2	1	2	3	.400	0	0-0	0	3.34	2.61
2015	Sea	AL	29	29	1	0	169.2	706	163	92	86	25	4	5	9	40	1	157	4	1	11	8	.579	0	0-0	0	3.74	4.56
3 ML YEARS			40	37	2	2	222.2	926	205	111	103	27	4	7	12	62	2	203	6	2	14	11	.560	0	0-0	0	3.52	4.16

Brett Wallace

Bats: L Throws: R Pos: PH-50;1B-17;3B-5;DH-2　　　　Ht: 6'2" Wt: 235 Born: 8/26/1986 Age: 29

										BATTING											RUNNING			AVERAGES			
Year	Team	Lg	G	AB	H	2B	3B	HR	(Hm	Rd)	TB	R	RBI	RC	TBB	IBB	SO	HBP	SH	SF	SB	CS	GDP	Avg	OBP	Slg	OPS
2015	ElPaso*	AAA	61	239	73	13	0	8	(-	-)	110	34	37	43	24	1	56	6	0	2	1	0	9	.305	.380	.460	.840
2010	Hou	NL	51	144	32	6	1	2	(1	1)	46	14	13	10	8	3	50	7	0	0	0	0	3	.222	.296	.319	.615
2011	Hou	NL	115	336	87	22	0	5	(2	3)	124	37	29	31	36	4	91	3	1	2	1	1	12	.259	.334	.369	.703
2012	Hou	NL	66	229	58	10	1	9	(1	8)	97	24	24	27	18	1	73	6	0	1	0	0	2	.253	.323	.424	.746
2013	Hou	AL	79	262	58	14	1	13	(6	7)	113	35	36	34	18	0	104	5	0	0	1	1	5	.221	.284	.431	.716
2015	SD	NL	64	96	29	6	0	5	(4	1)	50	14	16	18	10	1	31	1	0	0	0	0	1	.302	.374	.521	.895
5 ML YEARS			375	1067	264	58	3	34	(15	19)	430	124	118	120	90	9	349	22	1	3	2	2	23	.247	.318	.403	.721

Zach Walters

Bats: B Throws: R Pos: PH-5;LF-3;2B-2;3B-2;SS-2;PR-2;RF-1　　　　Ht: 6'2" Wt: 210 Born: 9/5/1989 Age: 26

										BATTING											RUNNING			AVERAGES			
Year	Team	Lg	G	AB	H	2B	3B	HR	(Hm	Rd)	TB	R	RBI	RC	TBB	IBB	SO	HBP	SH	SF	SB	CS	GDP	Avg	OBP	Slg	OPS
2015	Clmbs*	AAA	91	341	85	21	3	10	(-	-)	142	39	48	46	30	3	79	2	1	5	3	0	8	.249	.310	.416	.726
2013	Was	NL	8	8	3	0	1	0	(0	0)	5	2	1	2	1	0	0	0	0	0	0	0	1	.375	.444	.625	1.069
2014	2 Tms		62	127	23	3	0	10	(4	6)	56	16	17	10	9	0	48	1	0	0	0	0	0	.181	.241	.441	.682
2015	Cle	AL	12	30	4	0	0	0	(0	0)	4	0	3	0	0	0	15	0	0	0	0	0	0	.133	.133	.133	.267
14	Was	NL	32	39	8	1	0	3	(0	3)	18	7	5	4	4	0	16	0	0	0	0	0	0	.205	.279	.462	.741
14	Cle	AL	30	88	15	2	0	7	(4	3)	38	9	12	6	5	0	32	1	0	0	0	0	0	.170	.223	.432	.655
3 ML YEARS			82	165	30	3	1	10	(4	6)	65	18	21	12	10	0	63	1	0	0	0	0	1	.182	.233	.394	.627

Adam Warren

Pitches: R Bats: R Pos: RP-26; SP-17　　　　Ht: 6'1" Wt: 225 Born: 8/25/1987 Age: 28

Year	Team	Lg	G	GS	CG	GF	IP	BFP	H	R	ER	HR	SH	SF	HB	TBB	IBB	SO	WP	Bk	W	L	Pct	Sh	Sv-Op	Hld	ERC	ERA
2012	NYY	AL	1	1	0	0	2.1	17	8	6	6	2	0	0	0	2	0	1	0	0	0	0	-	0	0-0	0	33.34	23.14
2013	NYY	AL	34	2	0	17	77.0	331	80	29	29	10	0	0	2	30	2	64	3	0	3	2	.600	0	1-1	1	4.60	3.39
2014	NYY	AL	69	0	0	11	78.2	324	63	27	26	4	5	4	3	24	1	76	4	0	3	6	.333	0	3-6	23	2.45	2.97
2015	NYY	AL	43	17	0	5	131.1	534	114	51	48	10	2	2	7	39	1	104	7	0	7	7	.500	0	1-1	3	3.07	3.29
4 ML YEARS			147	20	0	33	289.1	1206	265	113	109	26	7	6	12	95	4	245	14	0	13	15	.464	0	5-8	27	3.44	3.39

Tony Watson

Pitches: L Bats: L Pos: RP-77　　　　Ht: 6'4" Wt: 225 Born: 5/30/1985 Age: 31

Year	Team	Lg	G	GS	CG	GF	IP	BFP	H	R	ER	HR	SH	SF	HB	TBB	IBB	SO	WP	Bk	W	L	Pct	Sh	Sv-Op	Hld	ERC	ERA
2011	Pit	NL	43	0	0	6	41.0	174	34	18	18	6	2	1	1	20	4	37	0	0	2	2	.500	0	0-1	19	3.75	3.95
2012	Pit	NL	68	0	0	10	53.1	215	37	21	20	5	2	2	1	23	1	53	1	0	5	2	.714	0	0-2	16	2.62	3.38
2013	Pit	NL	67	0	0	14	71.2	280	51	19	19	5	3	1	6	12	1	54	2	0	3	1	.750	0	2-4	22	1.88	2.39
2014	Pit	NL	78	0	0	3	77.1	305	64	16	14	5	5	3	6	15	0	81	0	0	10	2	.833	0	2-9	34	2.54	1.63
2015	Pit	NL	77	0	0	4	75.1	293	55	17	16	3	1	3	4	17	1	62	1	0	4	1	.800	0	1-3	41	1.92	1.91
Postseason			4	0	0	0	4.0	17	4	1	1	1	0	0	0	1	0	1	0	0	0	0	-	0	0-0	1	4.38	2.25
5 ML YEARS			333	0	0	37	318.2	1267	241	91	87	24	13	10	18	87	7	287	4	0	24	8	.750	0	5-19	123	2.39	2.46

Jered Weaver

Pitches: R Bats: R Pos: SP-26　　　　Ht: 6'7" Wt: 210 Born: 10/4/1982 Age: 33

Year	Team	Lg	G	GS	CG	GF	IP	BFP	H	R	ER	HR	SH	SF	HB	TBB	IBB	SO	WP	Bk	W	L	Pct	Sh	Sv-Op	Hld	ERC	ERA
2006	LAA	AL	19	19	0	0	123.0	490	94	36	35	15	2	2	3	33	1	105	2	0	11	2	.846	0	0-0	0	2.57	2.56
2007	LAA	AL	28	28	0	0	161.0	695	178	77	70	17	5	5	2	45	3	115	4	0	13	7	.650	0	0-0	0	4.24	3.91
2008	LAA	AL	30	30	0	0	176.2	745	173	88	85	20	1	4	6	54	4	152	3	0	11	10	.524	0	0-0	0	3.80	4.33
2009	LAA	AL	33	33	4	0	211.0	882	196	91	88	26	6	8	4	66	3	174	3	0	16	8	.667	2	0-0	0	3.56	3.75
2010	LAA	AL	34	34	4	0	224.1	905	187	83	75	23	2	5	0	54	0	233	7	1	13	12	.520	0	0-0	0	2.59	3.01
2011	LAA	AL	33	33	4	0	235.2	926	182	65	63	20	5	5	3	56	0	198	8	0	18	8	.692	2	0-0	0	2.27	2.41
2012	LAA	AL	30	30	3	0	188.2	739	147	63	59	20	0	4	4	45	0	142	2	0	20	5	.800	2	0-0	0	2.48	2.81
2013	LAA	AL	24	24	0	0	154.1	634	139	58	56	17	1	3	7	37	0	117	2	0	11	8	.579	0	0-0	0	3.17	3.27
2014	LAA	AL	34	34	1	0	213.1	888	193	87	85	27	5	4	6	65	1	169	3	0	18	9	.667	0	0-0	0	3.46	3.59
2015	LAA	AL	26	26	1	0	159.0	669	163	84	82	24	5	2	12	33	3	90	2	0	7	12	.368	1	0-0	0	4.09	4.64
Postseason			7	4	0	2	27.2	107	15	8	8	5	0	1	0	12	0	28	0	0	2	1	.667	0	0-0	1	2.37	2.60
10 ML YEARS			291	291	13	0	1847.0	7573	1652	732	698	209	32	42	47	488	15	1495	36	1	138	81	.630	7	0-0	0	3.16	3.40

Daniel Webb

Pitches: R Bats: R Pos: RP-27

Ht: 6'3" Wt: 215 Born: 8/18/1989 Age: 26

Year Team	Lg	G	GS	CG	GF	IP	BFP	H	R	ER	HR	SH	SF	HB	TBB	IBB	SO	WP	Bk	W	L	Pct	Sh	Sv-Op	Hld	ERC	ERA
2015 Charllt*	AAA	18	0	0	9	28.1	125	25	12	12	3	0	1	2	15	0	24	4	0	2	1	.667	0	2--	-	4.22	3.81
2013 CWS	AL	9	0	0	4	11.1	46	9	4	4	0	0	1	0	4	0	10	1	0	0	0	-	0	0-0	1	2.20	3.18
2014 CWS	AL	57	0	0	26	67.2	296	59	31	30	6	1	3	2	42	5	58	13	0	6	5	.545	0	0-2	4	4.18	3.99
2015 CWS	AL	27	0	0	6	30.0	150	41	26	21	3	0	1	1	22	1	22	2	0	1	0	1.000	0	0-1	0	7.82	6.30
3 ML YEARS		93	0	0	36	109.0	492	109	61	55	9	1	5	3	68	6	90	16	0	7	5	.583	0	0-3	5	4.88	4.54

Ryan Webb

Pitches: R Bats: R Pos: RP-40

Ht: 6'6" Wt: 245 Born: 2/5/1986 Age: 30

Year Team	Lg	G	GS	CG	GF	IP	BFP	H	R	ER	HR	SH	SF	HB	TBB	IBB	SO	WP	Bk	W	L	Pct	Sh	Sv-Op	Hld	ERC	ERA
2015 Clmbs*	AAA	5	0	0	2	8.0	28	4	1	1	0	0	0	0	1	0	5	1	1	1	1	.500	0	0--	-	0.76	1.13
2009 SD	NL	28	0	0	9	25.2	117	27	14	11	3	2	1	1	11	1	19	4	0	2	1	.667	0	0-0	6	4.54	3.86
2010 SD	NL	54	0	0	15	59.0	253	64	21	19	1	1	1	1	19	5	44	2	1	3	1	.750	0	0-2	9	3.61	2.90
2011 Fla	NL	53	0	0	10	50.2	214	48	20	18	2	3	1	2	20	5	31	1	1	2	4	.333	0	0-4	8	3.39	3.20
2012 Mia	NL	65	0	0	21	60.1	270	72	30	27	2	0	2	4	20	8	44	0	0	4	3	.571	0	0-0	10	4.44	4.03
2013 Mia	NL	66	0	0	19	80.1	332	70	30	26	5	11	5	2	27	5	54	4	0	2	6	.250	0	0-3	4	2.91	2.91
2014 Bal	AL	51	0	0	13	49.1	207	50	21	21	2	1	0	1	12	2	37	1	1	3	3	.500	0	0-0	11	3.15	3.83
2015 Cle	AL	40	0	0	11	50.2	204	46	21	18	4	1	1	2	12	2	31	1	0	1	0	1.000	0	0-0	2	2.99	3.20
7 ML YEARS		357	0	0	98	376.0	1597	377	157	140	19	19	11	13	121	28	260	13	3	17	18	.486	0	0-9	48	3.48	3.35

Ryan Weber

Pitches: R Bats: R Pos: SP-5

Ht: 6'0" Wt: 180 Born: 8/12/1990 Age: 25

Year Team	Lg	G	GS	CG	GF	IP	BFP	H	R	ER	HR	SH	SF	HB	TBB	IBB	SO	WP	Bk	W	L	Pct	Sh	Sv-Op	Hld	ERC	ERA
2011 2 Tms	Low	15	6	0	6	49.2	200	42	17	15	2	0	0	4	11	0	35	1	2	2	0	1.000	0	2--	-	2.55	2.72
2012 2 Tms	Low	35	16	0	9	117.1	514	136	72	64	5	5	5	7	23	2	94	1	0	7	9	.438	0	2--	-	3.89	4.91
2013 2 Tms	Low	24	16	1	1	96.2	403	95	54	44	7	4	1	11	15	2	83	1	0	6	6	.500	0	0--	-	3.26	4.10
2014 Missi	AA	32	13	0	2	101.1	436	129	59	51	7	7	5	1	16	0	62	1	2	5	6	.455	0	0--	-	4.52	4.53
2015 Missi	AA	11	3	0	1	26.1	101	23	8	8	1	0	1	0	1	0	24	0	0	2	0	1.000	0	1--	-	1.77	2.73
2015 Gwnntt	AAA	27	6	0	4	73.1	281	60	18	18	7	3	1	3	9	0	35	2	0	6	3	.667	0	3--	-	2.30	2.21
2015 Atl	NL	5	5	0	0	28.1	109	25	15	15	3	0	0	2	6	0	19	0	0	0	3	.000	0	0-0	0	3.26	4.76

Allen Webster

Pitches: R Bats: R Pos: SP-5; RP-4

Ht: 6'2" Wt: 190 Born: 2/10/1990 Age: 26

Year Team	Lg	G	GS	CG	GF	IP	BFP	H	R	ER	HR	SH	SF	HB	TBB	IBB	SO	WP	Bk	W	L	Pct	Sh	Sv-Op	Hld	ERC	ERA
2015 Reno*	AAA	15	15	0	0	77.0	368	117	70	70	8	2	3	3	26	0	62	3	1	4	6	.400	0	0--	-	7.16	8.18
2013 Bos	AL	8	7	0	1	30.1	145	37	30	29	7	0	5	2	18	0	23	1	0	1	2	.333	0	0-0	0	7.56	8.60
2014 Bos	AL	11	11	0	0	59.0	259	58	35	33	3	0	4	7	28	0	36	2	0	5	3	.625	0	0-0	0	4.46	5.03
2015 Ari	NL	9	5	0	1	31.0	142	32	28	20	10	1	1	2	20	1	17	1	0	1	1	.500	0	0-0	0	7.38	5.81
3 ML YEARS		28	23	0	2	120.1	546	127	93	82	20	1	10	11	66	1	76	4	0	7	6	.538	0	0-0	0	5.96	6.13

Jemile Weeks

Bats: B Throws: R Pos: 2B-3

jah-MYLE

Ht: 5'9" Wt: 170 Born: 1/26/1987 Age: 29

Year Team	Lg	G	AB	H	2B	3B	HR	(Hm	Rd)	TB	R	RBI	RC	TBB	IBB	SO	HBP	SH	SF	SB	CS	GDP	Avg	OBP	Slg	OPS
2015 Pwtckt*	AAA	70	235	48	11	2	1	(-	-)	66	25	6	22	29	1	53	2	0	0	7	0	6	.204	.297	.281	.578
2011 Oak	AL	97	406	123	26	8	2	(1	1)	171	50	36	64	21	1	62	4	2	4	22	11	3	.303	.340	.421	.761
2012 Oak	AL	118	444	98	15	8	2	(1	1)	135	54	20	42	50	0	70	5	9	3	16	5	5	.221	.305	.304	.609
2013 Oak	AL	8	9	1	0	0	0	(0	0)	1	3	0	0	0	0	5	0	0	0	0	0	0	.111	.111	.111	.222
2014 2 Tms	AL	17	37	11	3	1	0	(0	0)	16	8	3	6	4	0	2	1	2	1	2	0	1	.297	.372	.432	.805
2015 Bos	AL	3	9	3	0	0	0	(0	0)	3	1	1	1	0	0	2	0	0	0	0	0	0	.333	.333	.333	.667
14 Bal	AL	3	11	3	0	1	0	(0	0)	5	2	0	1	0	0	0	0	2	0	0	0	1	.273	.273	.455	.727
14 Bos	AL	14	26	8	3	0	0	(0	0)	11	6	3	5	4	0	2	1	0	1	2	0	0	.308	.406	.423	.829
5 ML YEARS		243	905	236	44	17	4	(2	2)	326	116	60	113	75	1	141	10	13	8	40	16	9	.261	.322	.360	.682

Rickie Weeks

Bats: R Throws: R Pos: LF-19;PH-19;DH-11

Ht: 5'10" Wt: 220 Born: 9/13/1982 Age: 33

Year Team	Lg	G	AB	H	2B	3B	HR	(Hm	Rd)	TB	R	RBI	RC	TBB	IBB	SO	HBP	SH	SF	SB	CS	GDP	Avg	OBP	Slg	OPS
2003 Mil	NL	7	12	2	1	0	0	(0	0)	3	1	0	0	1	0	6	1	0	0	0	0	0	.167	.286	.250	.536
2005 Mil	NL	96	360	86	13	2	13	(8	5)	142	56	42	49	40	2	96	11	2	1	15	2	11	.239	.333	.394	.727
2006 Mil	NL	95	359	100	15	3	8	(6	2)	145	73	34	53	30	1	92	19	2	3	19	5	6	.279	.363	.404	.766
2007 Mil	NL	118	409	96	21	6	16	(5	11)	177	87	36	65	78	5	116	14	3	2	25	2	3	.235	.374	.433	.807
2008 Mil	NL	129	475	111	22	7	14	(3	11)	189	89	46	67	66	0	115	14	1	4	19	5	5	.234	.342	.398	.740
2009 Mil	NL	37	147	40	5	2	9	(7	2)	76	28	24	27	12	0	39	3	0	0	2	2	1	.272	.340	.517	.857
2010 Mil	NL	160	651	175	32	4	29	(16	13)	302	112	83	110	76	0	184	25	0	2	11	4	5	.269	.366	.464	.830
2011 Mil	NL	118	453	122	26	2	20	(10	10)	212	77	49	68	50	3	107	8	1	3	9	2	6	.269	.350	.468	.818
2012 Mil	NL	157	588	135	29	4	21	(10	11)	235	85	63	77	74	2	169	13	0	2	16	3	9	.230	.328	.400	.728
2013 Mil	NL	104	350	73	20	1	10	(6	4)	125	40	24	28	40	0	105	9	0	0	7	3	13	.209	.306	.357	.663

Year	Team	Lg	G	AB	H	2B	3B	HR	(Hm	Rd)	TB	R	RBI	RC	TBB	IBB	SO	HBP	SH	SF	SB	CS	GDP	Avg	OBP	Slg	OPS
2014	Mil	NL	121	252	69	19	1	8	(4	4)	114	36	29	38	25	0	73	8	0	1	3	4	7	.274	.357	.452	.809
2015	Sea	AL	37	84	14	1	0	2	(0	2)	21	7	9	7	9	0	25	2	0	0	0	0	3	.167	.263	.250	.513
	Postseason		14	45	6	1	1	2	(2	0)	15	5	4	2	2	0	8	2	0	0	0	0	3	.133	.204	.333	.537
	12 ML YEARS		1179	4140	1023	204	32	150	(75	75)	1741	691	439	589	501	13	1127	127	9	18	126	32	69	.247	.345	.421	.765

Jayson Werth

Bats: R **Throws:** R **Pos:** LF-76;RF-14;PH-3;DH-1 **Ht:** 6'5" **Wt:** 240 **Born:** 5/20/1979 **Age:** 37

Year	Team	Lg	G	AB	H	2B	3B	HR	(Hm	Rd)	TB	R	RBI	RC	TBB	IBB	SO	HBP	SH	SF	SB	CS	GDP	Avg	OBP	Slg	OPS
2002	Tor	AL	15	46	12	2	1	0	(0	0)	16	4	6	5	6	0	11	0	0	1	1	0	4	.261	.340	.348	.687
2003	Tor	AL	26	48	10	4	0	2	(0	2)	20	7	10	6	3	0	22	0	0	0	1	0	0	.208	.255	.417	.672
2004	LAD	NL	89	290	76	11	3	16	(11	5)	141	56	47	47	30	0	85	4	1	1	4	1	1	.262	.338	.486	.825
2005	LAD	NL	102	337	79	22	2	7	(1	6)	126	46	43	44	48	2	114	6	1	3	11	2	10	.234	.338	.374	.711
2007	Phi	NL	94	255	76	11	3	8	(1	7)	117	43	49	57	44	1	73	2	2	1	7	1	0	.298	.404	.459	.863
2008	Phi	NL	134	418	114	16	3	24	(11	13)	208	73	67	74	57	1	119	4	0	3	20	1	2	.273	.363	.498	.861
2009	Phi	NL	159	571	153	26	1	36	(21	15)	289	98	99	107	91	8	156	8	0	6	20	3	11	.268	.373	.506	.879
2010	Phi	NL	156	554	164	46	2	27	(18	9)	295	106	85	91	82	6	147	7	0	9	13	3	11	.296	.388	.532	.921
2011	Was	NL	150	561	130	26	1	20	(10	10)	218	69	58	74	74	5	160	10	0	4	19	3	10	.232	.330	.389	.718
2012	Was	NL	81	300	90	21	3	5	(4	1)	132	42	31	48	42	2	57	1	0	1	8	2	3	.300	.387	.440	.827
2013	Was	NL	129	462	147	24	0	25	(13	12)	246	84	82	94	60	3	101	5	0	5	10	1	9	.318	.398	.532	.931
2014	Was	NL	147	534	156	37	1	16	(5	11)	243	85	82	104	83	3	113	9	0	3	9	1	9	.292	.394	.455	.849
2015	Was	NL	88	331	73	16	1	12	(6	6)	127	51	42	38	38	0	84	3	0	6	0	1	8	.221	.302	.384	.685
	Postseason		53	191	47	10	2	14	(10	4)	103	33	27	30	33	4	63	1	0	1	5	0	3	.246	.358	.539	.898
	13 ML YEARS		1370	4707	1280	262	21	198	(101	97)	2178	764	701	789	658	31	1242	59	4	43	123	19	78	.272	.365	.463	.828

Matt West

Pitches: R **Bats:** R **Pos:** RP-2 **Ht:** 6'1" **Wt:** 200 **Born:** 11/21/1988 **Age:** 27

| | | | HOW MUCH HE PITCHED | | | | | | WHAT HE GAVE UP | | | | | | | | | | THE RESULTS | | | | | | | |
Year	Team	Lg	G	GS	CG	GF	IP	BFP	H	R	ER	HR	SH	SF	HB	TBB	IBB	SO	WP	Bk	W	L	Pct	Sh	Sv-Op	Hld	ERC	ERA
2011	2 Tms	Low	24	0	0	22	27.0	104	24	9	9	3	1	0	3	1	0	35	2	0	1	2	.333	0	9--	-	2.70	3.00
2012	MrtlBh	A+	17	0	0	6	20.1	94	18	16	15	1	1	0	2	16	0	14	2	1	0	3	.000	0	0--	-	4.97	6.64
2014	Frisco	AA	8	0	0	4	13.1	48	7	1	1	1	0	0	1	2	0	10	3	0	2	0	1.000	0	3--	-	1.26	0.68
2014	RdRck	AAA	33	1	0	7	43.1	199	53	25	20	4	0	1	5	16	1	54	4	0	3	3	.500	0	1--	-	5.63	4.15
2015	Nham	AA	7	0	0	1	12.1	49	9	1	0	0	0	0	1	4	0	17	1	0	0	0	-	0	1--	-	2.12	0.00
2015	Tulsa	AA	12	0	0	2	16.0	61	8	4	1	0	1	0	1	4	0	17	2	0	1	1	.500	0	0--	-	1.06	0.56
2015	OkCity	AAA	14	0	0	3	23.0	109	31	24	20	3	0	1	0	9	0	17	2	0	1	1	.500	0	0--	-	6.19	7.83
2014	Tex	AL	3	0	0	1	4.0	18	6	3	3	0	0	0	0	1	0	3	0	0	0	0	-	0	0-0	0	5.79	6.75
2015	LAD	NL	2	0	0	2	3.0	11	2	0	0	0	0	0	0	1	0	2	0	0	0	0	-	0	0-0	0	1.73	0.00
	2 ML YEARS		5	0	0	3	7.0	29	8	3	3	0	0	0	0	2	0	5	0	0	0	0	-	0	0-0	0	3.90	3.86

Zack Wheeler

Pitches: R **Bats:** L **Pos:** P **Ht:** 6'4" **Wt:** 195 **Born:** 5/30/1990 **Age:** 26

| | | | HOW MUCH HE PITCHED | | | | | | WHAT HE GAVE UP | | | | | | | | | | THE RESULTS | | | | | | | |
Year	Team	Lg	G	GS	CG	GF	IP	BFP	H	R	ER	HR	SH	SF	HB	TBB	IBB	SO	WP	Bk	W	L	Pct	Sh	Sv-Op	Hld	ERC	ERA
2011	2 Tms	Low	22	22	0	0	115.0	495	100	50	45	7	2	4	8	52	1	129	9	0	9	7	.563	0	0--	-	3.45	3.52
2012	Bnghtn	AA	19	19	1	0	116.0	474	92	46	42	2	2	8	11	43	0	117	6	1	10	6	.625	1	0--	-	2.74	3.26
2012	Buffalo	AAA	6	6	1	0	33.0	134	23	13	12	2	3	2	1	16	0	31	2	0	2	2	.500	1	0--	-	2.70	3.27
2013	LsVgs	AAA	13	13	0	0	68.2	291	61	35	30	9	1	2	2	27	0	73	1	0	4	2	.667	0	0--	-	3.75	3.93
2013	NYM	NL	17	17	0	0	100.0	431	90	42	38	10	3	7	4	46	2	84	6	0	7	5	.583	0	0-0	0	3.88	3.42
2014	NYM	NL	32	32	1	0	185.1	794	167	84	73	14	5	3	11	79	3	187	9	0	11	11	.500	1	0-0	0	3.68	3.54
	2 ML YEARS		49	49	1	0	285.1	1225	257	126	111	24	8	10	15	125	5	271	15	0	18	16	.529	1	0-0	0	3.75	3.50

Chase Whitley

Pitches: R **Bats:** R **Pos:** SP-4 **Ht:** 6'3" **Wt:** 215 **Born:** 6/14/1989 **Age:** 27

| | | | HOW MUCH HE PITCHED | | | | | | WHAT HE GAVE UP | | | | | | | | | | THE RESULTS | | | | | | | |
Year	Team	Lg	G	GS	CG	GF	IP	BFP	H	R	ER	HR	SH	SF	HB	TBB	IBB	SO	WP	Bk	W	L	Pct	Sh	Sv-Op	Hld	ERC	ERA
2011	Tampa	A+	23	0	0	14	48.1	190	41	13	9	2	1	0	3	10	0	40	4	0	0	1	.000	0	6--	-	2.51	1.68
2011	Trntn	AA	19	1	0	6	42.2	188	46	21	16	6	2	3	0	19	0	37	1	1	3	4	.429	0	1--	-	5.03	3.38
2012	S-WB	AAA	41	2	0	9	80.1	318	61	30	29	7	1	4	2	25	1	66	5	1	9	5	.643	0	1--	-	2.53	3.25
2013	S-WB	AAA	29	5	0	6	67.2	277	61	24	23	3	1	4	4	21	0	62	7	0	3	2	.600	0	3--	-	3.13	3.06
2014	S-WB	AAA	10	6	0	0	31.1	122	22	7	7	1	1	1	0	8	0	37	0	0	3	2	.600	0	0--	-	1.54	2.01
2014	NYY	AL	24	12	0	3	75.2	330	94	44	44	10	1	2	4	18	0	60	2	0	4	3	.571	0	0-0	0	5.37	5.23
2015	NYY	AL	4	4	0	0	19.1	84	20	9	9	3	0	0	2	5	0	16	2	0	1	2	.333	0	0-0	0	4.47	4.19
	2 ML YEARS		28	16	0	3	95.0	414	114	53	53	13	1	2	6	23	0	76	4	0	5	5	.500	0	0-0	0	5.18	5.02

Joe Wieland

Pitches: R **Bats:** R **Pos:** SP-2   WEE-land **Ht:** 6'3" **Wt:** 210 **Born:** 1/21/1990 **Age:** 26

| | | | HOW MUCH HE PITCHED | | | | | | WHAT HE GAVE UP | | | | | | | | | | THE RESULTS | | | | | | | |
Year	Team	Lg	G	GS	CG	GF	IP	BFP	H	R	ER	HR	SH	SF	HB	TBB	IBB	SO	WP	Bk	W	L	Pct	Sh	Sv-Op	Hld	ERC	ERA
2015	OkCity*	AAA	22	21	0	1	113.2	488	135	64	58	7	4	5	3	25	0	92	2	1	10	5	.667	1	0--	-	4.29	4.59
2012	SD	NL	5	5	0	0	27.2	119	26	16	14	5	1	2	1	9	2	24	1	0	0	4	.000	0	0-0	0	3.94	4.55
2014	SD	NL	4	2	0	0	11.1	54	16	9	9	3	0	1	0	5	0	8	0	1	1	0	1.000	0	0-0	0	8.09	7.15
2015	LAD	NL	2	2	0	0	8.2	40	10	8	8	2	0	1	0	5	1	4	0	0	0	1	.000	0	0-0	0	6.56	8.31
	3 ML YEARS		11	9	0	0	47.2	213	52	33	31	10	1	4	1	19	3	36	1	1	1	5	.167	0	0-0	0	5.31	5.85

Matt Wieters

Bats: B **Throws:** R **Pos:** C-55;DH-12;PH-7;1B-3 WEE-ters **Ht:** 6'5" **Wt:** 230 **Born:** 5/21/1986 **Age:** 30

Year	Team	Lg	G	AB	H	2B	3B	HR	(Hm	Rd)	TB	R	RBI	RC	TBB	IBB	SO	HBP	SH	SF	SB	CS	GDP	Avg	OBP	Slg	OPS
2009	Bal	AL	96	354	102	15	1	9	(5	4)	146	35	43	43	28	2	86	1	0	2	0	0	11	.288	.340	.412	.753
2010	Bal	AL	130	446	111	22	1	11	(3	8)	168	37	55	47	47	7	94	2	0	7	0	1	13	.249	.319	.377	.695
2011	Bal	AL	139	500	131	28	0	22	(13	9)	225	72	68	76	48	3	84	2	0	1	1	0	16	.262	.328	.450	.778
2012	Bal	AL	144	526	131	27	1	23	(11	12)	229	67	83	73	60	4	112	4	0	3	3	0	17	.249	.329	.435	.764
2013	Bal	AL	148	523	123	29	0	22	(13	9)	218	59	79	65	43	5	104	0	1	12	2	0	7	.235	.287	.417	.704
2014	Bal	AL	26	104	32	5	0	5	(2	3)	52	13	18	17	6	0	19	0	0	2	0	1	1	.308	.339	.500	.839
2015	Bal	AL	75	258	69	14	1	8	(3	5)	109	24	25	33	21	0	67	0	0	3	0	0	4	.267	.319	.422	.742
	Postseason		6	24	3	1	0	0	(0	0)	4	2	0	0	2	0	4	0	0	0	0	0	0	.125	.192	.167	.359
	7 ML YEARS		758	2711	699	140	4	100	(50	50)	1147	307	371	354	253	21	566	9	1	30	6	2	69	.258	.320	.423	.743

Tom Wilhelmsen

Pitches: R **Bats:** R **Pos:** RP-53 will-HELM-senn **Ht:** 6'6" **Wt:** 220 **Born:** 12/16/1983 **Age:** 32

			HOW MUCH HE PITCHED						WHAT HE GAVE UP										THE RESULTS						
Year	Team	Lg	G	GS	CG	GF	IP	BFP	H	R	ER	HR	SH	SF	HB	TBB	IBB	SO	WP	Bk	W	L	Pct	Sh	Sv-Op	Hld	ERC	ERA
2011	Sea	AL	25	0	0	10	32.2	136	25	13	12	2	0	2	2	13	0	30	6	1	2	0	1.000	0	0-0	3	2.78	3.31
2012	Sea	AL	73	0	0	48	79.1	326	59	24	22	5	1	2	2	29	3	87	3	0	4	3	.571	0	29-34	7	2.38	2.50
2013	Sea	AL	59	0	0	40	59.0	251	45	28	27	2	3	3	1	33	5	45	6	0	0	3	.000	0	24-29	2	2.87	4.12
2014	Sea	AL	57	2	0	18	79.1	317	47	22	20	6	1	3	2	36	6	72	4	0	3	2	.600	0	1-3	8	2.03	2.27
2015	Sea	AL	53	0	0	20	62.0	267	56	24	22	3	4	3	2	29	3	60	2	0	2	2	.500	0	13-15	7	3.49	3.19
	5 ML YEARS		267	2	0	136	312.1	1297	232	111	103	18	9	13	9	140	17	294	21	1	11	10	.524	0	67-81	27	2.63	2.97

Adam Wilk

Pitches: L **Bats:** L **Pos:** RP-1 **Ht:** 6'2" **Wt:** 181 **Born:** 12/9/1987 **Age:** 28

			HOW MUCH HE PITCHED						WHAT HE GAVE UP										THE RESULTS						
Year	Team	Lg	G	GS	CG	GF	IP	BFP	H	R	ER	HR	SH	SF	HB	TBB	IBB	SO	WP	Bk	W	L	Pct	Sh	Sv-Op	Hld	ERC	ERA
2015	Salt Lk*	AAA	27	25	1	0	145.0	652	189	106	90	16	5	1	2	40	0	105	6	1	7	11	.389	0	0--	-	5.46	5.59
2011	Det	AL	5	0	0	1	13.1	57	14	10	8	3	0	0	0	3	0	10	0	0	0	-	-	0	0-0	0	4.40	5.40
2012	Det	AL	3	3	0	0	11.0	55	21	11	10	4	0	1	0	3	0	7	0	0	0	3	.000	0	0-0	0	11.90	8.18
2015	LAA	AL	1	0	0	1	2.0	10	2	1	1	1	0	0	1	1	0	2	0	0	0	-	-	0	0-0	0	9.87	4.50
	3 ML YEARS		9	3	0	2	26.1	122	37	22	19	8	0	1	1	7	0	19	0	0	0	3	.000	0	0-0	0	7.68	6.49

Jackson Williams

Bats: R **Throws:** R **Pos:** C-7;PH-2 **Ht:** 5'11" **Wt:** 200 **Born:** 5/14/1986 **Age:** 30

Year	Team	Lg	G	AB	H	2B	3B	HR	(Hm	Rd)	TB	R	RBI	RC	TBB	IBB	SO	HBP	SH	SF	SB	CS	GDP	Avg	OBP	Slg	OPS
2011	Fresno	AAA	56	125	23	3	0	1	(-	-)	29	13	12	8	17	1	36	2	1	2	0	2	3	.184	.288	.232	.520
2011	Rchmd	AA	18	53	11	2	0	3	(-	-)	22	8	9	6	5	0	9	1	0	0	0	0	0	.208	.288	.415	.703
2012	Fresno	AAA	86	295	73	15	1	11	(-	-)	123	34	40	35	13	2	62	2	1	3	0	0	12	.247	.281	.417	.698
2013	Fresno	AAA	85	261	60	14	2	5	(-	-)	93	30	30	28	21	0	48	2	2	3	0	0	3	.230	.289	.356	.646
2014	ColSpr	AAA	72	242	62	15	0	4	(-	-)	89	26	34	34	37	1	57	1	3	3	3	3	6	.256	.353	.368	.721
2015	Rchmd	AAA	83	276	63	9	1	1	(-	-)	77	26	18	26	29	1	50	5	1	1	1	2	5	.228	.312	.279	.591
2014	Col	NL	7	14	3	0	0	1	(1	0)	6	1	3	3	2	0	4	0	0	0	0	0	1	.214	.313	.429	.741
2015	SF	NL	7	10	2	1	0	0	(0	0)	3	1	1	2	4	0	1	0	0	0	1	0	0	.200	.429	.300	.729
	2 ML YEARS		14	24	5	1	0	1	(1	0)	9	2	4	5	6	0	5	0	0	0	1	0	1	.208	.367	.375	.742

Jerome Williams

Pitches: R **Bats:** R **Pos:** SP-21; RP-12 **Ht:** 6'3" **Wt:** 260 **Born:** 12/4/1981 **Age:** 34

			HOW MUCH HE PITCHED						WHAT HE GAVE UP										THE RESULTS						
Year	Team	Lg	G	GS	CG	GF	IP	BFP	H	R	ER	HR	SH	SF	HB	TBB	IBB	SO	WP	Bk	W	L	Pct	Sh	Sv-Op	Hld	ERC	ERA
2003	SF	NL	21	21	2	0	131.0	545	116	54	48	10	6	3	7	49	3	88	2	1	7	5	.583	1	0-0	0	3.42	3.30
2004	SF	NL	22	22	0	0	129.1	559	123	69	61	14	4	9	17	44	1	80	2	1	10	7	.588	0	0-0	0	4.14	4.24
2005	2 Tms	NL	22	20	0	0	122.2	532	119	62	58	14	11	8	10	49	1	70	2	0	6	10	.375	0	0-0	1	4.34	4.26
2006	ChC	NL	5	2	0	1	12.1	61	15	12	10	2	0	3	1	11	1	5	0	0	0	2	.000	0	0-0	0	8.42	7.30
2007	Was	NL	6	6	0	0	30.0	140	34	26	24	6	1	1	0	18	0	15	2	1	0	5	.000	0	0-0	0	6.43	7.20
2011	LAA	AL	10	6	0	1	44.0	184	45	20	18	6	0	1	1	15	0	28	0	0	4	0	1.000	0	0-0	0	4.45	3.68
2012	LAA	AL	32	15	1	7	137.2	572	139	73	70	17	0	4	5	35	1	98	1	0	6	8	.429	1	1-1	0	3.91	4.58
2013	LAA	AL	37	25	0	8	169.1	728	181	93	86	23	1	3	4	55	2	107	5	0	9	10	.474	0	0-0	0	4.53	4.57
2014	3 Tms	AL	37	11	0	14	115.0	497	125	64	61	12	3	2	6	36	2	82	2	0	6	7	.462	0	0-3	2	4.47	4.77
2015	Phi	NL	33	21	0	3	121.0	553	161	83	78	22	2	4	5	34	3	74	4	0	4	12	.250	0	1-2	4	6.27	5.80
05	SF	NL	4	3	0	0	16.2	73	21	12	12	2	1	0	1	4	1	11	0	0	0	2	.000	0	0-0	0	5.32	6.48
05	ChC	NL	18	17	0	0	106.0	459	98	50	46	12	10	8	9	45	0	59	2	0	6	8	.429	0	0-0	1	4.19	3.91
14	Hou	AL	26	0	0	14	47.2	219	59	33	32	7	3	1	3	16	1	38	2	0	1	4	.200	0	0-3	2	5.70	6.04
14	Tex	AL	2	2	0	0	10.0	48	18	11	11	0	0	0	0	3	0	6	0	0	1	1	.500	0	0-0	0	8.02	9.90
14	Phi	NL	9	9	0	0	57.1	230	48	20	18	5	0	1	3	17	1	38	0	0	4	2	.667	0	0-0	0	2.99	2.83
	Postseason		1	1	0	0	2.0	13	5	3	3	0	1	0	0	1	0	1	0	0	0	0	-	0	0-0	0	12.20	13.50
	10 ML YEARS		225	149	3	34	1012.1	4371	1058	556	514	126	28	38	56	346	14	647	20	3	52	66	.441	2	2-6	7	4.51	4.57

Mason Williams

Bats: L Throws: R Pos: CF-8   Ht: 6'1" Wt: 185 Born: 8/21/1991 Age: 24

Year	Team	Lg	G	AB	H	2B	3B	HR	(Hm	Rd)	TB	R	RBI	RC	TBB	IBB	SO	HBP	SH	SF	SB	CS	GDP	Avg	OBP	Slg	OPS
2011	StnIsld	A-	68	269	94	11	6	3	(-	-)	126	42	31	50	20	0	41	2	4	3	28	12	1	.349	.395	.468	.863
2012	2 Tms	Low	91	359	107	22	4	11	(-	-)	170	68	35	59	24	1	47	4	7	3	20	13	3	.298	.346	.474	.820
2013	Tampa	A+	100	406	106	21	3	3	(-	-)	142	56	24	49	39	0	61	2	11	3	15	9	7	.261	.327	.350	.676
2013	Trntn	AA	17	72	11	3	1	1	(-	-)	19	7	4	2	1	0	18	0	3	0	0	0	2	.153	.164	.264	.428
2014	Trntn	AA	128	507	113	18	4	5	(-	-)	154	67	40	48	47	1	68	1	7	1	21	8	21	.223	.290	.304	.593
2015	Trntn	AA	34	120	38	7	0	0	(-	-)	45	14	11	20	19	1	17	0	4	1	11	6	0	.317	.407	.375	.782
2015	S-WB	AAA	20	81	26	7	1	0	(-	-)	35	12	11	13	8	1	6	0	2	0	2	1	3	.321	.382	.432	.814
2015	NYY	AL	8	21	6	3	0	1	(0	1)	12	3	3	4	1	0	3	0	0	0	0	0	0	.286	.318	.571	.890

Mac Williamson

Bats: R Throws: R Pos: LF-6;RF-3;DH-2;PH-1   Ht: 6'5" Wt: 240 Born: 7/15/1990 Age: 25

Year	Team	Lg	G	AB	H	2B	3B	HR	(Hm	Rd)	TB	R	RBI	RC	TBB	IBB	SO	HBP	SH	SF	SB	CS	GDP	Avg	OBP	Slg	OPS
2012	2 Tms	A	33	131	42	8	0	9	(-	-)	77	26	32	27	8	0	24	4	0	1	0	0	7	.321	.375	.588	.963
2013	SnJos	A+	136	520	152	31	2	25	(-	-)	262	94	89	102	51	3	132	21	0	5	10	1	13	.292	.375	.504	.879
2014	SnJos	A+	23	85	27	7	0	3	(-	-)	43	16	11	19	13	0	14	2	0	0	6	1	3	.318	.420	.506	.926
2015	Rchmd	AA	69	259	76	16	2	5	(-	-)	111	41	42	42	25	4	53	5	0	1	3	1	8	.293	.366	.429	.794
2015	Scrmto	AAA	54	189	47	12	0	8	(-	-)	83	35	31	33	26	1	55	11	0	1	1	0	3	.249	.370	.439	.809
2015	SF	NL	10	32	7	0	1	0	(0	0)	9	2	1	1	0	0	8	1	0	1	0	0	1	.219	.235	.281	.517

Alex Wilson

Pitches: R Bats: R Pos: RP-58; SP-1   Ht: 6'0" Wt: 215 Born: 11/3/1986 Age: 29

Year	Team	Lg	G	GS	CG	GF	IP	BFP	H	R	ER	HR	SH	SF	HB	TBB	IBB	SO	WP	Bk	W	L	Pct	Sh	Sv-Op	Hld	ERC	ERA
2013	Bos	AL	26	0	0	9	27.2	127	34	16	15	0	0	1	1	14	1	22	1	0	1	1	.500	0	0-0	1	5.19	4.88
2014	Bos	AL	18	0	0	3	28.1	109	20	8	6	3	0	1	2	5	0	19	1	0	1	0	1.000	0	0-1	0	2.08	1.91
2015	Det	AL	59	1	0	16	70.0	273	61	19	17	5	2	2	2	11	1	38	2	0	3	3	.500	0	2-4	7	2.47	2.19
	3 ML YEARS		103	1	0	28	126.0	509	115	43	38	8	2	4	5	30	2	79	4	0	5	4	.556	0	2-5	8	2.94	2.71

Bobby Wilson

Bats: R Throws: R Pos: C-55;PH-2;DH-1   Ht: 6'0" Wt: 220 Born: 4/8/1983 Age: 33

Year	Team	Lg	G	AB	H	2B	3B	HR	(Hm	Rd)	TB	R	RBI	RC	TBB	IBB	SO	HBP	SH	SF	SB	CS	GDP	Avg	OBP	Slg	OPS
2015	Drham*	AAA	17	49	9	1	0	0	(-	-)	10	3	0	2	6	1	11	0	0	0	0	0	1	.184	.273	.204	.477
2008	LAA	AL	7	6	1	0	0	0	(0	0)	1	0	1	0	1	0	3	0	0	0	0	0	0	.167	.286	.167	.452
2009	LAA	AL	12	5	1	1	0	0	(0	0)	2	0	0	0	0	0	1	0	1	0	0	0	1	.200	.200	.400	.600
2010	LAA	AL	40	96	22	6	0	4	(3	1)	40	12	15	12	8	0	23	0	2	0	0	0	3	.229	.288	.417	.705
2011	LAA	AL	57	111	21	8	0	1	(0	1)	32	5	8	7	10	1	16	0	4	2	0	2	2	.189	.252	.288	.540
2012	LAA	AL	75	171	36	5	0	3	(2	1)	50	19	13	13	15	0	33	1	13	1	0	0	7	.211	.277	.292	.569
2014	Ari	NL	2	4	1	0	0	0	(0	0)	1	0	0	0	0	0	0	0	0	0	0	0	0	.250	.250	.250	.500
2015	2 Tms	AL	56	132	25	5	0	1	(1	0)	33	8	14	12	11	0	39	1	2	1	0	1	1	.189	.255	.250	.505
15	TB	AL	25	55	8	0	0	0	(0	0)	8	3	4	2	4	0	20	0	0	0	0	0	1	.145	.203	.145	.349
15	Tex	AL	31	77	17	5	0	1	(1	0)	25	5	10	10	7	0	19	1	2	1	0	1	0	.221	.291	.325	.615
	7 ML YEARS		249	525	107	25	0	9	(6	3)	159	44	51	44	45	1	115	2	22	4	0	3	14	.204	.267	.303	.570

C.J. Wilson

Pitches: L Bats: L Pos: SP-21   Ht: 6'1" Wt: 210 Born: 11/18/1980 Age: 35

Year	Team	Lg	G	GS	CG	GF	IP	BFP	H	R	ER	HR	SH	SF	HB	TBB	IBB	SO	WP	Bk	W	L	Pct	Sh	Sv-Op	Hld	ERC	ERA
2005	Tex	AL	24	6	0	5	48.0	220	63	39	37	5	1	2	2	18	1	30	4	1	1	7	.125	0	1-1	4	6.03	6.94
2006	Tex	AL	44	0	0	12	44.1	191	39	23	20	7	1	0	5	18	1	43	0	0	2	4	.333	0	1-2	7	4.25	4.06
2007	Tex	AL	66	0	0	22	68.1	285	50	25	23	4	2	4	6	33	1	63	5	0	2	1	.667	0	12-14	15	3.01	3.03
2008	Tex	AL	50	0	0	41	46.1	214	49	35	31	8	1	1	2	27	2	41	3	0	2	2	.500	0	24-28	1	5.77	6.02
2009	Tex	AL	74	0	0	30	73.2	323	66	29	23	3	3	0	6	32	3	84	3	0	5	6	.455	0	14-18	19	3.40	2.81
2010	Tex	AL	33	33	3	0	204.0	850	161	83	76	10	1	3	10	93	0	170	7	1	15	8	.652	0	0-0	0	3.03	3.35
2011	Tex	AL	34	34	3	0	223.1	915	191	89	73	16	3	5	10	74	0	206	6	0	16	7	.696	1	0-0	0	3.07	2.94
2012	LAA	AL	34	34	0	0	202.1	865	181	102	86	19	4	6	6	91	2	173	4	1	13	10	.565	0	0-0	0	3.75	3.83
2013	LAA	AL	33	33	0	0	212.1	913	200	93	80	15	4	2	8	85	3	188	14	2	17	7	.708	0	0-0	0	3.66	3.39
2014	LAA	AL	31	31	1	0	175.2	761	169	95	88	17	3	7	11	85	5	151	9	0	13	10	.565	1	0-0	0	4.46	4.51
2015	LAA	AL	21	21	0	0	132.0	553	118	59	57	13	2	4	10	46	2	110	11	1	8	8	.500	0	0-0	0	3.60	3.89
	Postseason		11	10	0	0	53.0	237	49	35	31	10	3	1	4	30	6	44	3	0	1	6	.143	0	0-0	0	5.08	5.26
	11 ML YEARS		444	192	7	110	1430.1	6090	1287	672	594	117	25	34	76	602	20	1259	66	6	94	70	.573	2	52-63	46	3.69	3.74

Josh Wilson

Bats: R Throws: R Pos: 2B-11;3B-10;SS-2;PR-2;DH-1   Ht: 6'0" Wt: 175 Born: 3/26/1981 Age: 35

Year	Team	Lg	G	AB	H	2B	3B	HR	(Hm	Rd)	TB	R	RBI	RC	TBB	IBB	SO	HBP	SH	SF	SB	CS	GDP	Avg	OBP	Slg	OPS
2015	Toledo*	AAA	79	262	66	14	1	3	(-	-)	91	30	30	31	22	0	70	4	2	3	10	2	5	.252	.316	.347	.663
2005	Fla	NL	11	10	1	1	0	0	(0	0)	2	2	0	0	0	0	4	1	0	0	0	0	0	.100	.182	.200	.382
2007	2 Tms		105	282	67	15	3	2	(0	2)	94	28	24	24	17	0	57	5	3	3	6	2	5	.238	.290	.333	.623
2009	3 Tms		72	192	42	11	1	3	(1	2)	64	19	13	14	12	1	44	4	3	0	1	2	4	.219	.279	.333	.612
2010	Sea	AL	108	361	82	14	2	2	(1	1)	106	22	25	31	14	0	74	12	0	1	5	0	6	.227	.278	.294	.572

321

									BATTING														RUNNING			AVERAGES			
Year	Team	Lg	G	AB	H	2B	3B	HR	(Hm	Rd)	TB	R	RBI	RC	TBB	IBB	SO	HBP	SH	SF	SB	CS	GDP	Avg	OBP	Slg	OPS
2011	2 Tms	NL	60	85	19	5	0	2	(0	2)	30	13	5	7	4	0	22	0	3	0	1	0	0	.224	.258	.353	.611
2013	Ari	NL	30	60	12	1	1	1	(1	0)	18	9	4	2	5	0	17	0	0	0	0	0	6	.200	.262	.300	.562
2014	Tex	AL	24	67	16	4	0	0	(0	0)	20	7	8	6	2	0	14	1	2	0	1	0	3	.239	.271	.299	.570
2015	Det	AL	21	38	12	3	0	0	(0	0)	15	4	5	5	0	0	15	2	1	0	0	0	1	.316	.350	.395	.745
07	Was	NL	15	19	1	0	0	0	(0	0)	1	3	0	0	5	0	6	1	0	0	0	0		.053	.280	.053	.333
07	TB	AL	90	263	66	15	3	2	(0	2)	93	25	24	24	12	0	51	4	3	3	6	2	5	.251	.291	.354	.644
09	Ari	NL	11	26	6	1	0	0	(0	0)	7	1	2	4	3	0	3	1	0	0	0	0	2	.231	.333	.269	.603
09	SD	NL	16	38	4	2	0	0	(0	0)	6	2	1	1	3	1	9	1	1	0	0	0		.105	.190	.158	.348
09	Sea	AL	45	128	32	8	1	3	(1	2)	51	16	10	9	6	0	32	2	2	0	1	2		.250	.294	.398	.693
11	Ari	NL	6	10	2	1	0	0	(0	0)	3	3	1	1	0	0	1	0	0	0	0	0	0	.200	.200	.300	.500
11	Mil	NL	54	75	17	4	0	2	(0	2)	27	10	4	6	4	0	21	0	3	0	1	0		.227	.266	.360	.626
	8 ML YEARS		431	1095	251	54	7	10	(3	7)	349	104	84	89	54	1	247	25	12	4	14	4	25	.229	.280	.319	.599

Justin Wilson

Pitches: L Bats: L Pos: RP-74　　　　**Ht: 6'2" Wt: 205 Born: 8/18/1987 Age: 28**

			HOW MUCH HE PITCHED					WHAT HE GAVE UP											THE RESULTS							
Year	Team	Lg	G	GS	CG	GF	IP	BFP	H	R	ER	HR	SH	SF	HB	TBB	IBB	SO	WP	Bk	W	L	Pct	Sh	Sv-Op	Hld	ERC	ERA
2012	Pit	NL	8	0	0	3	4.2	26	10	1	1	0	1	0	0	3	0	7	1	0	0		-	0	0-0	0	11.83	1.93
2013	Pit	NL	58	0	0	8	73.2	295	50	17	17	4	3	1	3	28	1	59	5	0	6	1	.857	0	0-3	14	2.20	2.08
2014	Pit	NL	70	0	0	15	60.0	256	49	30	28	4	0	0	3	30	5	61	4	0	3	4	.429	0	0-3	16	3.29	4.20
2015	NYY	AL	74	0	0	3	61.0	244	49	21	21	3	2	0	2	20	0	66	4	0	5	0	1.000	0	0-2	29	2.63	3.10
	Postseason		3	0	0	0	3.0	14	3	1	1	0	0	0	0	2	0	4	1	0		-	0	0-0	0	4.23	3.00
	4 ML YEARS		210	0	0	29	199.1	821	158	69	67	11	6	1	8	81	6	193	14	0	14	5	.737	0	0-8	59	2.83	3.03

Tyler Wilson

Pitches: R Bats: R Pos: SP-5; RP-4　　　　**Ht: 6'2" Wt: 185 Born: 9/25/1989 Age: 26**

			HOW MUCH HE PITCHED					WHAT HE GAVE UP											THE RESULTS							
Year	Team	Lg	G	GS	CG	GF	IP	BFP	H	R	ER	HR	SH	SF	HB	TBB	IBB	SO	WP	Bk	W	L	Pct	Sh	Sv-Op	Hld	ERC	ERA
2011	2 Tms	Low	8	8	0	0	33.0	123	19	7	7	4	0	0	1	5	0	27	1	0	0	0	-	0	0--	-	1.43	1.91
2012	2 Tms	Low	25	25	0	0	143.0	575	125	68	61	16	0	2	7	30	0	143	5	2	10	10	.500	0	0--	-	2.98	3.84
2013	Frdrck	A+	11	11	0	0	62.1	264	57	34	31	4	1	1	1	25	0	48	1	0	1	1	.500	0	0--	-	3.43	4.48
2013	Bowie	AA	16	16	1	0	89.1	374	85	40	38	13	1	4	2	22	0	70	5	0	7	5	.583	0	0--	-	3.55	3.83
2014	Bowie	AA	16	16	0	0	96.2	408	101	47	40	10	2	4	1	22	0	91	8	0	10	5	.667	0	0--	-	3.69	3.72
2014	Norfolk	AAA	12	12	0	0	70.0	285	61	30	28	8	6	2	1	21	0	66	7	1	4	3	.571	0	0--	-	3.18	3.60
2015	Norfolk	AAA	17	17	0	0	94.1	385	94	35	34	8	2	1	4	18	0	63	0	0	5	5	.500	0	0--	-	3.37	3.24
2015	Bal	AL	9	5	0	2	36.0	149	39	14	14	1	0	2	1	11	1	13	0	0	2	2	.500	0	0-0	0	3.90	3.50

Daniel Winkler

Pitches: R Bats: R Pos: RP-2　　　　**Ht: 6'3" Wt: 200 Born: 2/2/1990 Age: 26**

			HOW MUCH HE PITCHED					WHAT HE GAVE UP											THE RESULTS							
Year	Team	Lg	G	GS	CG	GF	IP	BFP	H	R	ER	HR	SH	SF	HB	TBB	IBB	SO	WP	Bk	W	L	Pct	Sh	Sv-Op	Hld	ERC	ERA
2011	Casper	R+	12	12	0	0	57.1	251	64	31	25	6	0	0	3	19	0	65	6	3	4	3	.571	0	0--	-	4.55	3.92
2012	Ashvll	A	25	25	0	0	145.1	644	152	80	72	16	2	7	22	47	0	136	4	1	11	10	.524	0	0--	-	4.70	4.46
2013	Mdest	A+	22	22	0	0	130.1	510	84	48	43	15	1	6	9	37	0	152	4	1	12	5	.706	0	0--	-	2.19	2.97
2013	Tulsa	AA	5	5	0	0	26.2	108	23	11	9	3	0	1	1	10	0	23	2	0	1	2	.333	0	0--	-	3.60	3.04
2014	Tulsa	AA	12	12	1	0	70.0	262	33	11	11	5	1	0	6	17	0	71	1	0	5	2	.714	1	0--	-	1.28	1.41
2015	Atl	NL	2	0	0	0	1.2	8	2	2	2	2	0	0	0	1	0	2	0	0	0	0	-	0	0-0	0	14.99	10.80

Matt Wisler

Pitches: R Bats: R Pos: SP-19; RP-1　　WISS-lurr　　**Ht: 6'3" Wt: 195 Born: 9/12/1992 Age: 23**

			HOW MUCH HE PITCHED					WHAT HE GAVE UP											THE RESULTS							
Year	Team	Lg	G	GS	CG	GF	IP	BFP	H	R	ER	HR	SH	SF	HB	TBB	IBB	SO	WP	Bk	W	L	Pct	Sh	Sv-Op	Hld	ERC	ERA
2012	FtWyn	A	24	23	1	0	114.0	461	95	39	32	1	5	5	5	28	0	113	5	2	5	4	.556	1	0--	-	2.22	2.53
2013	Lk Els	A+	6	6	0	0	31.0	119	22	7	7	1	0	0	1	6	0	28	0	1	2	1	.667	0	0--	-	1.64	2.03
2013	SnAnt	AA	20	20	0	0	105.0	417	85	36	35	7	1	5	2	27	0	103	3	0	8	5	.615	0	0--	-	2.45	3.00
2014	SnAnt	AA	6	6	0	0	30.0	120	26	7	7	2	3	0	0	6	0	35	2	0	1	0	1.000	0	0--	-	2.42	2.10
2014	ElPaso	AAA	22	22	0	0	116.2	514	131	68	65	19	1	3	5	36	0	101	6	1	9	5	.643	0	0--	-	5.01	5.01
2015	Gwnntt	AAA	12	12	0	0	65.0	273	68	34	31	5	3	0	1	13	0	49	1	1	3	4	.429	0	0--	-	3.43	4.29
2015	Atl	NL	20	19	0	0	109.0	478	119	59	57	16	4	5	4	40	4	72	2	3	8	8	.500	0	0-0	0	4.91	4.71

Asher Wojciechowski

Pitches: R Bats: R Pos: SP-3; RP-2　　wo-jah-HOW-ski　　**Ht: 6'4" Wt: 235 Born: 12/21/1988 Age: 27**

			HOW MUCH HE PITCHED					WHAT HE GAVE UP											THE RESULTS							
Year	Team	Lg	G	GS	CG	GF	IP	BFP	H	R	ER	HR	SH	SF	HB	TBB	IBB	SO	WP	Bk	W	L	Pct	Sh	Sv-Op	Hld	ERC	ERA
2011	Dnedin	A+	25	22	0	0	130.1	571	156	79	68	15	0	1	4	31	1	96	3	1	11	9	.550	0	0--	-	4.75	4.70
2012	Dnedin	A	18	18	0	0	93.1	381	91	40	37	3	3	2	5	22	0	76	3	0	7	3	.700	0	0--	-	3.15	3.57
2012	CpChr	AA	8	8	0	0	43.2	178	30	14	11	0	1	1	5	14	0	34	0	2	2	2	.500	0	0--	-	1.94	2.27
2013	CpChr	AA	6	3	0	3	26.0	98	17	6	6	1	0	1	0	7	1	27	0	0	2	1	.667	0	1--	-	1.58	2.08
2013	OkCity	AAA	22	21	2	0	134.0	554	116	56	53	10	1	2	1	44	1	104	4	0	9	7	.563	1	0--	-	2.93	3.56
2014	OkCity	AAA	15	14	0	1	76.0	330	89	46	40	10	1	0	4	21	1	59	4	0	4	4	.500	0	0--	-	5.06	4.74
2015	Fresno	AAA	20	20	1	0	115.1	511	129	68	63	13	6	5	6	41	0	87	11	0	8	4	.667	0	0--	-	4.87	4.92
2015	Hou	AL	5	3	0	2	16.1	79	23	13	13	2	0	2	0	7	0	16	1	0	0	1	.000	0	0-0	0	6.66	7.16

Randy Wolf

Pitches: L **Bats:** L **Pos:** SP-7; RP-1   **Ht:** 6'0" **Wt:** 205 **Born:** 8/22/1976 **Age:** 39

			HOW MUCH HE PITCHED						WHAT HE GAVE UP												THE RESULTS							
Year Team	Lg	G	GS	CG	GF	IP	BFP	H	R	ER	HR	SH	SF	HB	TBB	IBB	SO	WP	Bk	W	L	Pct	Sh	Sv-Op	Hld	ERC	ERA
2015 Buffalo*	AAA	23	23	1	0	139.2	571	139	44	40	4	6	7	4	40	0	106	4	0	9	2	.818	0	0- -	-	3.36	2.58
1999 Phi	NL	22	21	0	0	121.2	552	126	78	75	20	5	1	5	67	0	116	4	0	6	9	.400	0	0-0	0	5.54	5.55
2000 Phi	NL	32	32	1	0	206.1	889	210	107	100	25	10	8	8	83	2	160	1	0	11	9	.550	0	0-0	0	4.54	4.36
2001 Phi	NL	28	25	4	1	163.0	684	150	74	67	15	11	7	10	51	4	152	1	0	10	11	.476	2	0-0	0	3.46	3.70
2002 Phi	NL	31	31	3	0	210.2	855	172	77	75	23	7	6	7	63	5	172	4	0	11	9	.550	2	0-0	0	2.88	3.20
2003 Phi	NL	33	33	2	0	200.0	850	176	101	94	27	8	4	6	78	4	177	6	0	16	10	.615	2	0-0	0	3.67	4.23
2004 Phi	NL	23	23	1	0	136.2	585	145	73	65	20	6	3	5	36	4	89	2	0	5	8	.385	1	0-0	0	4.29	4.28
2005 Phi	NL	13	13	0	0	80.0	346	87	40	39	14	4	1	6	26	2	61	1	0	6	4	.600	0	0-0	0	5.17	4.39
2006 Phi	NL	12	12	0	0	56.2	261	63	37	35	13	2	3	2	33	2	44	2	0	4	0	1.000	0	0-0	0	6.63	5.56
2007 LAD	NL	18	18	0	0	102.2	458	110	55	54	10	5	5	6	39	2	94	4	0	9	6	.600	0	0-0	0	4.52	4.73
2008 2 Tms	NL	33	33	1	0	190.1	823	191	100	91	21	10	4	12	71	4	162	3	0	12	12	.500	1	0-0	0	4.30	4.30
2009 LAD	NL	34	34	0	0	214.1	862	178	81	77	24	12	2	6	58	1	160	4	0	11	7	.611	0	0-0	0	2.89	3.23
2010 Mil	NL	34	34	1	0	215.2	936	213	107	100	29	9	6	9	87	6	142	2	0	13	12	.520	1	0-0	0	4.39	4.17
2011 Mil	NL	33	33	0	0	212.1	903	214	95	87	23	13	6	13	66	1	134	4	1	13	10	.565	0	0-0	0	4.10	3.69
2012 2 Tms		30	26	0	1	157.2	699	196	103	99	23	10	4	7	52	1	104	2	2	5	10	.333	0	0-0	0	5.85	5.65
2014 Mia	NL	6	4	0	1	25.2	113	33	17	15	4	1	0	0	6	0	19	1	0	1	3	.250	0	1-1	0	5.49	5.26
2015 Det	AL	8	7	0	0	34.2	161	46	28	24	5	0	1	1	15	1	28	3	0	0	5	.000	0	0-0	1	6.64	6.23
08 SD	NL	21	21	0	0	119.2	522	123	69	63	14	6	2	8	47	0	105	2	0	6	10	.375	0	0-0	0	4.63	4.74
08 Hou	NL	12	12	1	0	70.2	301	68	31	28	7	4	2	4	24	4	57	1	0	6	2	.750	1	0-0	0	3.77	3.57
12 Mil	NL	25	24	0	0	142.1	633	179	94	90	21	8	4	6	45	1	96	2	2	3	10	.231	0	0-0	0	5.86	5.69
12 Bal	AL	5	2	0	1	15.1	66	17	9	9	2	2	0	1	7	0	8	0	0	2	0	1.000	0	0-0	0	5.74	5.28
Postseason		4	4	0	0	19.0	92	24	14	14	5	1	0	1	11	2	12	0	0	1	1	.500	0	0-0	0	7.71	6.63
16 ML YEARS		390	379	13	3	2328.1	9977	2310	1173	1097	296	113	61	103	831	39	1814	44	3	133	125	.516	9	1-1	1	4.22	4.24

Kolten Wong

Bats: L **Throws:** R **Pos:** 2B-147;PH-7   COLT-enn   **Ht:** 5'9" **Wt:** 185 **Born:** 10/10/1990 **Age:** 25

				BATTING															RUNNING			AVERAGES			
Year Team	Lg	G	AB	H	2B	3B	HR	(Hm	Rd)	TB	R	RBI	RC	TBB	IBB	SO	HBP	SH	SF	SB	CS	GDP	Avg	OBP	Slg	OPS
2013 StL	NL	32	59	9	1	0	0	(0	0)	10	6	0	0	3	0	12	0	0	0	3	0	2	.153	.194	.169	.363
2014 StL	NL	113	402	100	14	3	12	(10	2)	156	52	42	41	21	3	71	4	5	1	20	4	12	.249	.292	.388	.680
2015 StL	NL	150	557	146	28	1	11	(6	5)	215	71	61	67	36	2	95	15	0	5	15	8	10	.262	.321	.386	.707
Postseason		15	35	8	3	1	3	(2	1)	22	4	6	5	1	1	6	0	0	0	2	0	2	.229	.250	.629	.879
3 ML YEARS		295	1018	255	43	7	23	(15	8)	381	129	103	108	60	5	178	19	5	6	38	12	24	.250	.303	.374	.677

Alex Wood

Pitches: L **Bats:** R **Pos:** SP-32   **Ht:** 6'4" **Wt:** 215 **Born:** 1/12/1991 **Age:** 25

				HOW MUCH HE PITCHED						WHAT HE GAVE UP										THE RESULTS						
Year Team	Lg	G	GS	CG	GF	IP	BFP	H	R	ER	HR	SH	SF	HB	TBB	IBB	SO	WP	Bk	W	L	Pct	Sh	Sv-Op	Hld	ERC	ERA
2013 Atl	NL	31	11	0	9	77.2	327	76	29	27	3	6	4	1	27	1	77	4	2	3	3	.500	0	0-0	1	3.40	3.13
2014 Atl	NL	35	24	1	2	171.2	694	151	58	53	16	7	3	6	45	1	170	5	0	11	11	.500	0	0-0	2	3.04	2.78
2015 2 Tms	NL	32	32	0	0	189.2	801	198	86	81	15	15	3	4	59	4	139	6	1	12	12	.500	0	0-0	0	3.94	3.84
15 Atl	NL	20	20	0	0	119.1	509	132	50	47	8	11	1	2	36	2	90	5	0	7	6	.538	0	0-0	0	4.15	3.54
15 LAD	NL	12	12	0	0	70.1	292	66	36	34	7	4	2	2	23	2	49	1	1	5	6	.455	0	0-0	0	3.58	4.35
Postseason		2	0	0	0	3.1	14	3	4	0	1	0	0	0	0	0	3	1	0	0	0	-	0	0-0	0	2.79	0.00
3 ML YEARS		98	67	1	11	439.0	1822	425	173	161	34	28	10	11	131	6	386	15	3	26	26	.500	0	0-0	3	3.48	3.30

Travis Wood

Pitches: L **Bats:** R **Pos:** RP-45; SP-9   **Ht:** 5'11" **Wt:** 175 **Born:** 2/6/1987 **Age:** 29

				HOW MUCH HE PITCHED						WHAT HE GAVE UP										THE RESULTS						
Year Team	Lg	G	GS	CG	GF	IP	BFP	H	R	ER	HR	SH	SF	HB	TBB	IBB	SO	WP	Bk	W	L	Pct	Sh	Sv-Op	Hld	ERC	ERA
2010 Cin	NL	17	17	0	0	102.2	419	85	45	40	9	3	3	4	26	1	86	0	1	5	4	.556	0	0-0	0	2.64	3.51
2011 Cin	NL	22	18	0	2	106.0	463	118	57	57	10	9	7	4	40	5	76	2	0	6	6	.500	0	0-0	0	4.73	4.84
2012 ChC	NL	26	26	0	0	156.0	649	133	80	74	25	9	4	8	54	3	119	2	1	6	13	.316	0	0-0	0	3.65	4.27
2013 ChC	NL	32	32	0	0	200.0	821	163	73	69	18	7	4	8	66	2	144	6	0	9	12	.429	0	0-0	0	2.90	3.11
2014 ChC	NL	31	31	0	0	173.2	781	190	110	97	20	8	4	7	76	1	146	2	0	8	13	.381	0	0-0	0	5.00	5.03
2015 ChC	NL	54	9	0	12	100.2	419	86	48	43	11	1	2	1	39	5	118	2	0	5	4	.556	0	4-4	3	3.27	3.84
Postseason		1	0	0	0	3.1	12	1	0	0	0	0	0	0	1	1	3	0	0	0	0	-	0	0-0	0	0.38	0.00
6 ML YEARS		182	133	0	14	839.0	3552	775	413	380	93	37	24	32	301	17	689	14	2	39	52	.429	0	4-4	3	3.69	4.08

Rob Wooten

Pitches: R **Bats:** R **Pos:** RP-4   WOOT-enn   **Ht:** 6'1" **Wt:** 200 **Born:** 7/21/1985 **Age:** 30

				HOW MUCH HE PITCHED						WHAT HE GAVE UP										THE RESULTS						
Year Team	Lg	G	GS	CG	GF	IP	BFP	H	R	ER	HR	SH	SF	HB	TBB	IBB	SO	WP	Bk	W	L	Pct	Sh	Sv-Op	Hld	ERC	ERA
2015 ColSpr*	AAA	44	1	0	10	52.0	228	56	29	27	9	2	4	2	14	2	50	0	1	5	2	.714	0	1- -	-	4.49	4.67
2013 Mil	NL	27	0	0	6	27.2	115	27	12	12	1	1	0	1	8	2	18	0	0	3	1	.750	0	0-1	3	3.16	3.90
2014 Mil	NL	40	0	0	15	34.1	147	42	18	18	1	0	1	1	8	0	29	0	0	1	4	.200	0	0-0	11	4.39	4.72
2015 Mil	NL	4	0	0	0	6.0	30	5	8	8	1	1	0	1	6	0	6	1	0	0	0	-	0	0-0	0	6.61	12.00
3 ML YEARS		71	0	0	21	68.0	292	74	38	38	3	2	1	3	22	2	53	1	0	4	5	.444	0	0-1	19	4.06	5.03

Brandon Workman

Pitches: R Bats: R Pos: P
Ht: 6'5" Wt: 225 Born: 8/13/1988 Age: 27

		HOW MUCH HE PITCHED						WHAT HE GAVE UP										THE RESULTS						
Year	Team	Lg	G	GS	CG	GF	IP	BFP	H	R	ER	HR	SH	SF	HB	TBB	IBB	SO	WP	Bk	W	L	Pct	Sh	Sv-Op	Hld	ERC	ERA
2011	Grnvlle	A	26	26	0	0	131.0	540	128	67	54	10	5	4	5	33	0	115	6	1	6	7	.462	0	0- -	-	3.42	3.71
2012	Salem	A+	20	20	0	0	113.2	454	104	47	43	10	4	3	1	20	0	107	6	1	7	7	.500	0	0- -	-	2.76	3.40
2012	Portlnd	AA	5	5	0	0	25.0	101	23	12	11	2	1	2	0	5	0	23	0	0	3	1	.750	0	0- -	-	2.77	3.96
2013	Portlnd	AA	11	10	0	0	65.2	259	51	29	25	6	2	2	1	17	0	74	3	0	5	1	.833	0	0- -	-	2.42	3.43
2013	Pwtckt	AAA	6	6	0	0	35.1	152	39	13	11	6	2	0	2	13	0	34	1	0	3	1	.750	0	0- -	-	5.47	2.80
2014	Pwtckt	AAA	11	11	0	0	61.1	253	61	28	28	10	1	3	0	17	1	55	1	0	7	1	.875	0	0- -	-	4.03	4.11
2013	Bos	AL	20	3	0	5	41.2	180	44	23	23	5	2	1	0	15	1	47	1	0	6	3	.667	0	0-1	1	4.34	4.97
2014	Bos	AL	19	15	0	2	87.0	378	88	57	50	11	3	3	1	36	0	70	2	0	1	10	.091	0	0-0	1	4.43	5.17
	Postseason		7	0	0	0	8.2	35	7	1	0	0	1	0	0	3	1	4	0	0	0	1	.000	0	0-0	0	2.09	0.00
	2 ML YEARS		39	18	0	7	128.2	558	132	80	73	16	5	4	1	51	1	117	3	0	7	13	.350	0	0-1	2	4.40	5.11

Vance Worley

Pitches: R Bats: R Pos: RP-15; SP-8
Ht: 6'2" Wt: 250 Born: 9/25/1987 Age: 28

		HOW MUCH HE PITCHED						WHAT HE GAVE UP										THE RESULTS						
Year	Team	Lg	G	GS	CG	GF	IP	BFP	H	R	ER	HR	SH	SF	HB	TBB	IBB	SO	WP	Bk	W	L	Pct	Sh	Sv-Op	Hld	ERC	ERA
2015	Indy*	AAA	5	5	0	0	34.0	134	30	10	9	4	0	0	2	5	0	21	0	0	3	1	.750	0	0- -	-	2.89	2.38
2010	Phi	NL	5	2	0	2	13.0	51	8	2	2	1	2	0	4	4	0	12	1	0	1	1	.500	0	0-0	0	1.66	1.38
2011	Phi	NL	25	21	1	0	131.2	553	116	47	44	10	9	5	3	46	2	119	2	1	11	3	.786	0	0-0	2	3.12	3.01
2012	Phi	NL	23	23	0	0	133.0	590	154	69	62	12	11	3	6	47	4	107	1	0	6	9	.400	0	0-0	0	4.87	4.20
2013	Min	AL	10	10	0	0	48.2	234	82	43	39	9	0	1	3	15	1	25	1	0	1	5	.167	0	0-0	0	9.17	7.21
2014	Pit	NL	18	17	1	0	110.2	458	112	43	35	9	6	4	3	22	1	79	4	0	8	4	.667	1	0-0	0	3.35	2.85
2015	Pit	NL	23	8	0	6	71.2	310	81	36	32	6	3	2	2	21	3	49	3	0	4	6	.400	0	0-1	0	4.34	4.02
	Postseason		2	0	0	0	1.1	8	3	1	1	0	0	0	0	1	0	0	0	0	0	0	-	0	0-0	1	12.64	6.75
	6 ML YEARS		104	81	2	8	508.2	2196	553	240	214	47	31	15	17	155	11	391	12	1	31	28	.525	1	0-1	2	4.25	3.79

David Wright

Bats: R Throws: R Pos: 3B-38
Ht: 6'0" Wt: 205 Born: 12/20/1982 Age: 33

			BATTING																		RUNNING			AVERAGES			
Year	Team	Lg	G	AB	H	2B	3B	HR	(Hm	Rd)	TB	R	RBI	RC	TBB	IBB	SO	HBP	SH	SF	SB	CS	GDP	Avg	OBP	Slg	OPS
2004	NYM	NL	69	263	77	17	1	14	(8	6)	138	41	40	42	14	0	40	3	0	3	6	0	7	.293	.332	.525	.857
2005	NYM	NL	160	575	176	42	1	27	(12	15)	301	99	102	105	72	2	113	7	0	3	17	7	16	.306	.388	.523	.912
2006	NYM	NL	154	582	181	40	5	26	(13	13)	309	96	116	119	66	13	113	5	0	8	20	5	15	.311	.381	.531	.912
2007	NYM	NL	160	604	196	42	1	30	(16	14)	330	113	107	127	94	6	115	6	0	7	34	5	14	.325	.416	.546	.963
2008	NYM	NL	160	626	189	42	2	33	(21	12)	334	115	124	116	94	5	118	4	0	11	15	5	15	.302	.390	.534	.924
2009	NYM	NL	144	535	164	39	3	10	(5	5)	239	88	72	86	74	8	140	3	0	6	27	9	16	.307	.390	.447	.837
2010	NYM	NL	157	587	166	36	3	29	(12	17)	295	87	103	97	69	9	161	2	0	12	19	11	12	.283	.354	.503	.856
2011	NYM	NL	102	389	99	23	1	14	(5	9)	166	60	61	58	52	4	97	3	0	3	13	2	5	.254	.345	.427	.771
2012	NYM	NL	156	581	178	41	2	21	(12	9)	286	91	93	105	81	16	112	3	0	5	15	10	15	.306	.391	.492	.883
2013	NYM	NL	112	430	132	23	6	18	(6	12)	221	63	58	78	55	5	79	5	0	2	17	3	11	.307	.390	.514	.904
2014	NYM	NL	134	535	144	30	1	8	(6	2)	200	54	63	60	42	5	113	4	0	5	8	5	22	.269	.324	.374	.698
2015	NYM	NL	38	152	44	7	0	5	(1	4)	66	24	17	25	22	0	36	0	0	0	2	1	4	.289	.379	.434	.814
	Postseason		10	37	8	3	0	1	(0	1)	14	3	6	5	5	1	8	0	0	0	0	0	0	.216	.310	.378	.688
	12 ML YEARS		1546	5859	1746	382	26	235	(117	118)	2885	931	956	1018	735	73	1237	45	0	65	193	63	152	.298	.377	.492	.869

Mike Wright

Pitches: R Bats: R Pos: SP-9; RP-3
Ht: 6'6" Wt: 215 Born: 1/3/1990 Age: 26

		HOW MUCH HE PITCHED						WHAT HE GAVE UP										THE RESULTS						
Year	Team	Lg	G	GS	CG	GF	IP	BFP	H	R	ER	HR	SH	SF	HB	TBB	IBB	SO	WP	Bk	W	L	Pct	Sh	Sv-Op	Hld	ERC	ERA
2011	3 Tms	Low	8	8	0	0	45.2	195	50	31	29	6	2	1	3	10	0	42	6	0	3	2	.600	0	0- -	-	4.39	5.72
2012	Frdrck	A+	8	8	0	0	46.1	186	47	16	15	3	2	1	1	5	0	35	0	0	5	2	.714	0	0- -	-	2.94	2.91
2012	Bowie	AA	12	12	0	0	62.1	267	71	38	34	7	1	0	3	17	0	45	6	0	5	3	.625	0	0- -	-	4.74	4.91
2013	Bowie	AA	26	26	0	0	143.2	625	152	65	52	9	3	4	10	39	1	136	9	1	11	3	.786	0	0- -	-	3.84	3.26
2014	Norfolk	AAA	26	26	0	0	142.2	622	159	87	73	10	6	5	5	41	2	103	5	0	5	11	.313	0	0- -	-	4.15	4.61
2015	Norfolk	AAA	15	14	0	0	81.0	315	59	21	20	4	0	2	3	25	0	63	4	0	9	1	.900	0	0- -	-	2.24	2.22
2015	Bal	AL	12	9	0	0	44.2	204	52	30	30	9	0	2	5	18	3	26	2	0	3	5	.375	0	0-0	0	6.20	6.04

Steven Wright

Pitches: R Bats: R Pos: SP-9; RP-7
Ht: 6'1" Wt: 215 Born: 8/30/1984 Age: 31

		HOW MUCH HE PITCHED						WHAT HE GAVE UP										THE RESULTS						
Year	Team	Lg	G	GS	CG	GF	IP	BFP	H	R	ER	HR	SH	SF	HB	TBB	IBB	SO	WP	Bk	W	L	Pct	Sh	Sv-Op	Hld	ERC	ERA
2015	Pwtckt*	AAA	8	8	1	0	52.0	221	55	31	22	2	1	2	2	15	0	42	5	0	2	5	.286	0	0- -	-	3.72	3.81
2013	Bos	AL	4	1	0	2	13.1	59	12	8	8	0	0	0	1	9	0	10	2	0	2	0	1.000	0	0-0	0	4.22	5.40
2014	Bos	AL	6	1	0	3	21.0	86	21	8	6	2	0	0	0	4	0	22	1	0	0	1	.000	0	0-0	0	3.25	2.57
2015	Bos	AL	16	9	0	3	72.2	310	67	38	33	12	1	1	1	27	0	52	2	0	5	4	.556	0	0-0	0	3.99	4.09
	3 ML YEARS		26	11	0	8	107.0	455	100	54	47	14	1	1	2	40	0	84	5	0	7	5	.583	0	0-0	0	3.89	3.95

Wesley Wright

Pitches: L **Bats:** R **Pos:** RP-11 **Ht:** 5'11" **Wt:** 185 **Born:** 1/28/1985 **Age:** 31

Year	Team	Lg	G	GS	CG	GF	IP	BFP	H	R	ER	HR	SH	SF	HB	TBB	IBB	SO	WP	Bk	W	L	Pct	Sh	Sv-Op	Hld	ERC	ERA
2015	Norfolk*	AAA	10	0	0	1	11.2	56	15	11	10	1	0	2	1	7	2	5	3	0	0	2	.000	0	0--	-	6.59	7.71
2015	Salt Lk*	AAA	12	0	0	2	12.2	48	9	2	2	0	0	0	0	5	0	13	0	0	0	1	.000	0	0--	-	2.10	1.42
2008	Hou	NL	71	0	0	15	55.2	250	45	34	31	8	1	1	4	34	4	57	2	1	4	3	.571	0	1-1	13	4.21	5.01
2009	Hou	NL	49	0	0	5	44.2	204	53	27	27	9	0	2	0	25	3	47	2	0	3	4	.429	0	0-2	6	6.64	5.44
2010	Hou	NL	14	4	0	3	33.0	148	37	27	21	6	2	1	3	13	0	29	0	0	1	2	.333	0	0-0	5	5.78	5.73
2011	Hou	NL	21	0	0	5	12.0	44	6	2	2	1	0	0	0	5	0	11	1	0	0	0	-	0	0-1	3	1.68	1.50
2012	Hou	NL	77	0	0	13	52.1	223	45	20	19	4	1	0	6	17	0	54	1	0	2	2	.500	0	1-2	19	3.26	3.27
2013	2 Tms	AL	71	0	0	17	53.2	232	54	24	22	7	1	2	3	19	2	55	2	0	0	4	.000	0	0-4	9	4.31	3.69
2014	ChC	NL	58	0	0	15	48.1	209	48	19	17	2	2	3	2	19	2	37	2	0	0	3	.000	0	0-2	9	3.69	3.17
2015	2 Tms	AL	11	0	0	4	7.1	31	6	4	3	1	0	2	0	3	1	5	0	0	0	0	-	0	0-0	0	3.10	3.68
13	Hou	AL	55	0	0	13	41.1	184	45	20	18	5	1	2	3	16	2	40	2	0	0	4	.000	0	0-4	8	4.89	3.92
13	TB	AL	16	0	0	4	12.1	48	9	4	4	2	0	0	0	3	0	15	0	0	0	0	-	0	0-0	1	2.47	2.92
15	Bal	AL	2	0	0	2	1.2	7	2	1	1	0	0	1	0	0	0	0	0	0	0	0	-	0	0-0	0	2.89	5.40
15	LAA	AL	9	0	0	2	5.2	24	4	3	2	1	0	1	0	3	1	5	0	0	0	0	-	0	0-0	0	3.16	3.18
	Postseason		2	0	0	1	0.2	4	1	0	0	0	0	0	0	1	1	1	0	0	0	0	-	0	0-0	0	6.98	0.00
8 ML YEARS			372	4	0	77	307.0	1341	294	157	142	38	7	11	18	135	12	295	10	1	10	18	.357	0	2-12	59	4.33	4.16

Kirby Yates

Pitches: R **Bats:** L **Pos:** RP-20 **Ht:** 5'10" **Wt:** 210 **Born:** 3/25/1987 **Age:** 29

Year	Team	Lg	G	GS	CG	GF	IP	BFP	H	R	ER	HR	SH	SF	HB	TBB	IBB	SO	WP	Bk	W	L	Pct	Sh	Sv-Op	Hld	ERC	ERA
2011	2 Tms	Low	20	4	0	11	40.0	166	20	9	8	0	1	0	6	24	0	48	1	2	2	1	.667	0	2--	-	2.09	1.80
2012	Mont	AA	50	0	0	39	68.0	285	48	21	20	4	4	1	1	39	2	94	8	0	4	2	.667	0	16--	-	2.90	2.65
2013	Drham	AAA	51	0	0	38	61.2	249	38	14	13	2	2	2	5	23	2	93	6	0	3	2	.600	0	20--	-	1.83	1.90
2014	Drham	AAA	21	0	0	21	25.0	97	10	1	1	0	1	0	1	9	0	35	0	1	1	0	1.000	0	16--	-	0.93	0.36
2015	Drham	AAA	23	0	0	10	25.1	117	27	16	15	5	1	0	2	12	0	34	3	0	1	2	.333	0	6--	-	5.69	5.33
2014	TB	AL	37	0	0	12	36.0	156	33	16	15	4	0	1	3	15	3	42	2	0	0	2	.000	0	1-2	0	3.94	3.75
2015	TB	AL	20	0	0	10	20.1	92	23	18	18	10	0	0	1	7	0	21	0	0	1	0	1.000	0	0-0	0	7.58	7.97
2 ML YEARS			57	0	0	22	56.1	248	56	34	33	14	0	1	4	22	3	63	2	0	1	2	.333	0	1-2	0	5.23	5.27

Christian Yelich

Bats: L **Throws:** R **Pos:** LF-103;CF-36;PH-3 YELL-itch **Ht:** 6'2" **Wt:** 195 **Born:** 12/5/1991 **Age:** 24

Year	Team	Lg	G	AB	H	2B	3B	HR	(Hm	Rd)	TB	R	RBI	RC	TBB	IBB	SO	HBP	SH	SF	SB	CS	GDP	Avg	OBP	Slg	OPS
2013	Mia	NL	62	240	69	12	1	4	(0	4)	95	34	16	35	31	1	66	1	0	1	10	0	4	.288	.370	.396	.766
2014	Mia	NL	144	582	165	30	6	9	(2	7)	234	94	54	87	70	3	137	3	3	2	21	7	9	.284	.362	.402	.764
2015	Mia	NL	126	476	143	30	2	7	(1	6)	198	63	44	64	47	2	101	2	0	0	16	5	13	.300	.366	.416	.782
3 ML YEARS			332	1298	377	72	9	20	(3	17)	527	191	114	186	148	6	304	6	3	3	47	12	26	.290	.365	.406	.771

Rafael Ynoa

Bats: B **Throws:** R **Pos:** PH-41;LF-19;3B-10;SS-8;2B-5 ee-NO-uh **Ht:** 6'0" **Wt:** 190 **Born:** 8/7/1987 **Age:** 28

Year	Team	Lg	G	AB	H	2B	3B	HR	(Hm	Rd)	TB	R	RBI	RC	TBB	IBB	SO	HBP	SH	SF	SB	CS	GDP	Avg	OBP	Slg	OPS
2011	Rcuca	A+	126	466	128	21	3	5	(-	-)	170	61	54	59	42	0	69	2	9	7	13	11	14	.275	.333	.365	.697
2012	Chatt	AA	113	421	117	23	4	0	(-	-)	148	58	37	61	58	0	70	1	9	4	23	9	11	.278	.364	.352	.715
2013	Chatt	AA	128	484	129	30	1	6	(-	-)	179	56	33	63	51	2	69	1	7	0	16	11	7	.267	.338	.370	.708
2014	ColSpr	AAA	115	427	127	31	3	5	(-	-)	179	66	32	64	38	2	78	2	4	2	7	7	10	.297	.356	.419	.775
2015	Albq	AAA	56	224	64	12	4	1	(-	-)	87	29	11	30	16	1	36	0	3	0	5	1	2	.286	.333	.388	.722
2014	Col	NL	19	67	23	6	1	0	(0	0)	31	5	13	13	4	0	9	0	0	0	0	0	1	.343	.380	.463	.843
2015	Col	NL	72	127	33	8	1	0	(0	0)	43	14	9	13	3	0	28	0	1	0	1	0	2	.260	.277	.339	.616
2 ML YEARS			91	194	56	14	2	0	(0	0)	74	19	22	26	7	0	37	0	1	0	1	0	3	.289	.313	.381	.695

Chris Young

Pitches: R **Bats:** R **Pos:** SP-18; RP-16 **Ht:** 6'10" **Wt:** 255 **Born:** 5/25/1979 **Age:** 37

Year	Team	Lg	G	GS	CG	GF	IP	BFP	H	R	ER	HR	SH	SF	HB	TBB	IBB	SO	WP	Bk	W	L	Pct	Sh	Sv-Op	Hld	ERC	ERA
2004	Tex	AL	7	7	0	0	36.1	158	36	21	19	7	1	2	0	10	0	27	1	0	3	2	.600	0	0-0	0	4.26	4.71
2005	Tex	AL	31	31	0	0	164.2	700	162	84	78	19	2	4	7	45	2	137	3	0	12	7	.632	0	0-0	0	3.71	4.26
2006	SD	NL	31	31	0	0	179.1	735	134	72	69	28	8	3	6	69	4	164	6	1	11	5	.688	0	0-0	0	3.12	3.46
2007	SD	NL	30	30	0	0	173.0	705	118	66	60	10	3	6	7	72	0	167	7	4	9	8	.529	0	0-0	0	2.35	3.12
2008	SD	NL	18	18	1	0	102.1	434	84	46	45	13	4	1	1	48	4	93	3	1	7	6	.538	0	0-0	0	3.50	3.96
2009	SD	NL	14	14	0	0	76.0	336	70	47	44	12	4	5	2	40	3	50	1	0	4	6	.400	0	0-0	0	4.55	5.21
2010	SD	NL	4	4	0	0	20.0	82	10	2	2	1	1	0	0	11	0	15	1	0	2	0	1.000	0	0-0	0	1.72	0.90
2011	NYM	NL	4	4	0	0	24.0	95	12	5	5	3	1	0	1	11	0	22	0	0	1	0	1.000	0	0-0	0	2.04	1.88
2012	NYM	NL	20	20	0	0	115.0	493	119	58	53	16	9	4	2	36	5	80	3	0	4	9	.308	0	0-0	0	4.19	4.15
2014	Sea	AL	30	29	0	0	165.0	688	143	70	67	26	4	9	3	60	3	108	5	1	12	9	.571	0	0-0	0	3.63	3.65
2015	KC	AL	34	18	0	3	123.1	500	91	44	42	16	4	2	0	43	0	83	5	0	11	6	.647	0	0-1	2	2.66	3.06
	Postseason		1	1	0	0	6.2	25	4	0	0	0	0	0	0	2	1	9	0	0	1	0	1.000	0	0-0	0	1.22	0.00
11 ML YEARS			223	206	1	3	1179.0	4926	979	515	484	151	41	34	31	445	21	946	35	7	76	58	.567	0	0-1	2	3.31	3.69

Chris Young

Bats: R **Throws:** R **Pos:** RF-76;LF-55;CF-15;PR-14;PH-13;DH-2   **Ht:** 6'2" **Wt:** 200 **Born:** 9/5/1983 **Age:** 32

Year	Team	Lg	G	AB	H	2B	3B	HR	(Hm	Rd)	TB	R	RBI	RC	TBB	IBB	SO	HBP	SH	SF	SB	CS	GDP	Avg	OBP	Slg	OPS
2006	Ari	NL	30	70	17	4	0	2	(1	1)	27	10	10	11	6	0	12	1	0	1	2	1	0	.243	.308	.386	.693
2007	Ari	NL	148	569	135	29	3	32	(14	18)	266	85	68	68	43	1	141	6	1	5	27	6	5	.237	.295	.467	.763
2008	Ari	NL	160	625	155	42	7	22	(9	13)	277	85	85	84	62	2	165	1	6	5	14	5	10	.248	.315	.443	.758
2009	Ari	NL	134	433	92	28	4	15	(7	8)	173	54	42	47	59	2	133	4	3	2	11	4	3	.212	.311	.400	.711
2010	Ari	NL	156	584	150	33	0	27	(20	7)	264	94	91	86	74	0	145	2	1	3	28	7	10	.257	.341	.452	.793
2011	Ari	NL	156	567	134	38	3	20	(14	6)	238	89	71	84	80	4	139	4	1	7	22	9	3	.236	.331	.420	.751
2012	Ari	NL	101	325	75	24	0	14	(5	9)	141	36	41	46	36	0	79	2	0	0	8	3	4	.231	.311	.434	.745
2013	Oak	AL	107	335	67	18	3	12	(4	8)	127	46	40	32	36	3	93	2	0	2	10	3	7	.200	.280	.379	.659
2014	2 Tms		111	325	72	20	0	11	(8	3)	125	40	38	37	32	2	70	5	1	3	8	3	3	.222	.299	.385	.683
2015	NYY	AL	140	318	80	20	1	14	(6	8)	144	53	42	46	30	2	73	3	3	2	3	1	6	.252	.320	.453	.773
14	NYM	NL	88	254	52	12	0	8	(6	2)	88	31	28	25	25	2	54	4	1	3	7	3	3	.205	.283	.346	.630
14	NYY	AL	23	71	20	8	0	3	(2	1)	37	9	10	12	7	0	16	1	0	0	1	0	0	.282	.354	.521	.876
	Postseason		12	43	14	2	0	5	(3	2)	31	9	9	12	9	0	18	1	0	0	3	2	0	.326	.453	.721	1.174
10 ML YEARS			1243	4151	977	256	21	169	(88	81)	1782	592	528	541	458	16	1050	30	16	30	133	42	51	.235	.314	.429	.743

Delmon Young

Bats: R **Throws:** R **Pos:** RF-40;PH-11;DH-4;LF-2   **Ht:** 6'3" **Wt:** 240 **Born:** 9/14/1985 **Age:** 30

Year	Team	Lg	G	AB	H	2B	3B	HR	(Hm	Rd)	TB	R	RBI	RC	TBB	IBB	SO	HBP	SH	SF	SB	CS	GDP	Avg	OBP	Slg	OPS
2006	TB	AL	30	126	40	9	1	3	(1	2)	60	16	10	15	1	0	24	3	0	1	2	2	0	.317	.336	.476	.812
2007	TB	AL	162	645	186	38	4	13	(9	4)	263	65	93	90	26	2	127	3	0	7	10	3	23	.288	.316	.408	.723
2008	Min	AL	152	575	167	28	4	10	(7	3)	233	80	69	74	35	7	105	7	1	5	14	5	19	.290	.336	.405	.741
2009	Min	AL	108	395	112	16	2	12	(7	5)	168	50	60	46	12	1	92	4	0	5	2	5	17	.284	.308	.425	.733
2010	Min	AL	153	570	170	46	1	21	(6	15)	281	77	112	94	28	5	81	6	0	9	5	4	16	.298	.333	.493	.826
2011	2 Tms	AL	124	473	127	21	1	12	(8	4)	186	54	64	57	23	2	85	2	0	5	1	0	19	.268	.302	.393	.695
2012	Det	AL	151	574	153	27	1	18	(9	9)	236	54	74	62	20	1	112	7	0	7	0	2	20	.267	.296	.411	.707
2013	2 Tms		103	334	87	16	0	11	(3	8)	136	30	38	36	20	0	78	4	0	3	0	0	8	.260	.307	.407	.715
2014	Bal	AL	83	242	73	11	1	7	(4	3)	107	27	30	34	10	0	51	3	0	0	2	0	6	.302	.337	.442	.779
2015	Bal	AL	52	174	47	6	0	2	(2	0)	59	20	16	16	4	0	29	1	0	1	0	0	8	.270	.289	.339	.628
11	Min	AL	84	305	81	16	0	4	(1	3)	109	26	32	32	18	2	55	0	0	2	1	0	12	.266	.305	.357	.662
11	Det	AL	40	168	46	5	1	8	(7	1)	77	28	32	25	5	0	30	2	0	3	0	0	7	.274	.298	.458	.756
13	Phi	NL	80	272	71	13	0	8	(3	5)	108	22	31	30	14	0	69	3	0	2	0	0	7	.261	.302	.397	.699
13	TB	AL	23	62	16	3	0	3	(0	3)	28	8	7	6	6	0	9	1	0	1	0	0	1	.258	.329	.452	.780
	Postseason		37	126	33	4	1	9	(5	4)	66	14	22	13	8	2	28	2	0	1	1	1	4	.262	.314	.524	.838
10 ML YEARS			1118	4108	1162	218	11	109	(56	53)	1729	473	566	524	179	18	784	40	1	43	36	21	136	.283	.316	.421	.737

Eric Young

Bats: B **Throws:** R **Pos:** LF-18;CF-16;PH-16;PR-15;RF-2   **Ht:** 5'10" **Wt:** 195 **Born:** 5/25/1985 **Age:** 31

Year	Team	Lg	G	AB	H	2B	3B	HR	(Hm	Rd)	TB	R	RBI	RC	TBB	IBB	SO	HBP	SH	SF	SB	CS	GDP	Avg	OBP	Slg	OPS
2015	Gwnntt*	AAA	67	234	58	6	3	1	(-	-)	73	36	27	32	33	1	43	4	8	1	24	3	7	.248	.349	.312	.661
2009	Col	NL	30	57	14	1	0	1	(1	0)	18	7	1	2	4	0	12	0	0	0	4	4	1	.246	.295	.316	.611
2010	Col	NL	51	172	42	5	1	0	(0	0)	49	26	8	16	17	0	32	0	0	0	17	6	2	.244	.312	.285	.597
2011	Col	NL	77	198	49	4	3	0	(0	0)	59	34	10	27	26	0	38	3	1	1	27	4	1	.247	.342	.298	.640
2012	Col	NL	98	174	55	7	2	4	(2	2)	78	36	15	29	13	0	31	4	5	0	14	2	1	.316	.377	.448	.825
2013	2 Tms	NL	148	539	134	27	7	2	(1	1)	181	70	32	58	46	1	100	2	10	1	46	11	6	.249	.310	.336	.645
2014	NYM	NL	100	280	64	10	5	1	(0	1)	87	48	17	30	24	1	60	5	5	2	30	6	2	.229	.299	.311	.610
2015	2 Tms	NL	53	85	13	4	2	0	(0	0)	21	16	5	6	6	1	18	1	2	0	6	2	1	.153	.217	.247	.464
13	Col	NL	57	165	40	9	3	1	(0	1)	58	22	6	14	11	0	33	0	4	0	8	4	1	.242	.290	.352	.641
13	NYM	NL	91	374	94	18	4	1	(1	0)	123	48	26	44	35	1	67	2	6	1	38	7	5	.251	.318	.329	.647
15	Atl	NL	35	77	13	4	2	0	(0	0)	21	7	5	6	6	1	17	0	2	0	3	0	1	.169	.229	.273	.502
15	NYM	NL	18	8	0	0	0	0	(0	0)	0	9	0	0	0	0	1	1	0	0	3	2	0	.000	.111	.000	.111
	Postseason		2	1	0	0	0	0	(0	0)	0	0	0	0	0	0	0	0	0	0	0	0	0	.000	.000	.000	.000
7 ML YEARS			557	1505	371	58	20	8	(4	4)	493	237	88	168	136	3	291	15	23	4	144	35	14	.247	.314	.328	.642

Brad Ziegler

Pitches: R **Bats:** R **Pos:** RP-66   ZIGG-lerr   **Ht:** 6'4" **Wt:** 220 **Born:** 10/10/1979 **Age:** 36

Year	Team	Lg	G	GS	CG	GF	IP	BFP	H	R	ER	HR	SH	SF	HB	TBB	IBB	SO	WP	Bk	W	L	Pct	Sh	Sv-Op	Hld	ERC	ERA
2008	Oak	AL	47	0	0	21	59.2	229	47	8	7	2	4	3	1	22	3	30	0	0	3	0	1.000	0	11-13	9	2.60	1.06
2009	Oak	AL	69	0	0	23	73.1	313	82	27	25	2	1	3	1	28	4	54	0	0	2	4	.333	0	7-10	14	4.25	3.07
2010	Oak	AL	64	0	0	12	60.2	257	54	24	22	4	1	1	3	28	9	41	0	1	3	7	.300	0	0-4	18	3.48	3.26
2011	2 Tms		66	0	0	16	58.1	239	53	21	14	0	1	2	1	19	3	44	1	0	3	2	.600	0	1-2	10	2.68	2.16
2012	Ari	NL	77	0	0	15	68.2	263	54	21	19	2	2	2	1	21	2	42	1	0	6	1	.857	0	0-2	17	2.33	2.49
2013	Ari	NL	78	0	0	33	73.0	297	61	20	18	3	2	2	3	22	6	44	0	0	8	1	.889	0	13-15	11	2.51	2.22
2014	Ari	NL	68	0	0	11	67.0	281	60	29	26	5	2	4	3	24	6	54	0	0	5	3	.625	0	1-9	29	3.22	3.49
2015	Ari	NL	66	0	0	46	68.0	263	48	17	14	3	1	0	1	17	3	36	2	0	0	3	.000	0	30-32	4	1.74	1.85
11	Oak	AL	43	0	0	12	37.2	160	38	14	10	0	1	1	1	13	3	29	1	0	3	2	.600	0	1-2	6	3.21	2.39
11	Ari	NL	23	0	0	4	20.2	79	15	7	4	0	0	1	0	6	0	15	0	0	0	0	-	0	0-0	4	1.77	1.74
	Postseason		2	0	0	0	0.1	7	4	4	4	0	0	0	0	2	1	0	0	1	0	0	-	0	0-0	0	115.8	108.0
8 ML YEARS			535	0	0	177	528.2	2142	459	167	145	21	14	17	14	181	36	345	4	1	30	21	.588	0	63-87	112	2.83	2.47

Ryan Zimmerman

Bats: R Throws: R Pos: 1B-93;PH-3;LF-1   Ht: 6'3" Wt: 220 Born: 9/28/1984 Age: 31

Year Team	Lg	G	AB	H	2B	3B	HR	(Hm	Rd)	TB	R	RBI	RC	TBB	IBB	SO	HBP	SH	SF	SB	CS	GDP	Avg	OBP	Slg	OPS
2005 Was	NL	20	58	23	10	0	0	(0	0)	33	6	6	9	3	0	12	0	0	1	0	0	1	.397	.419	.569	.988
2006 Was	NL	157	614	176	47	3	20	(10	10)	289	84	110	101	61	7	120	2	1	4	11	8	15	.287	.351	.471	.822
2007 Was	NL	162	653	174	43	5	24	(11	13)	299	99	91	83	61	3	125	3	0	5	4	1	26	.266	.330	.458	.788
2008 Was	NL	106	428	121	24	1	14	(7	7)	189	51	51	48	31	1	71	3	0	4	1	1	12	.283	.333	.442	.774
2009 Was	NL	157	610	178	37	3	33	(17	16)	320	110	106	96	72	9	119	2	0	9	2	0	22	.292	.364	.525	.888
2010 Was	NL	142	525	161	32	0	25	(9	16)	268	85	85	97	69	6	98	4	0	5	4	1	16	.307	.388	.510	.899
2011 Was	NL	101	395	114	21	2	12	(7	5)	175	52	49	58	41	4	73	1	0	3	3	1	14	.289	.355	.443	.798
2012 Was	NL	145	578	163	36	1	25	(16	9)	276	93	95	84	57	8	116	2	0	4	5	2	20	.282	.346	.478	.824
2013 Was	NL	147	568	156	26	2	26	(7	19)	264	84	79	83	60	2	133	2	0	3	6	0	16	.275	.344	.465	.809
2014 Was	NL	61	214	60	19	1	5	(1	4)	96	26	38	32	22	0	37	0	0	4	0	0	6	.280	.342	.449	.790
2015 Was	NL	95	346	86	25	1	16	(9	7)	161	43	73	49	33	0	79	1	0	10	1	0	13	.249	.308	.465	.773
Postseason		9	25	9	1	0	2	(1	1)	16	3	4	5	0	0	6	0	0	1	0	0	0	.360	.346	.640	.986
11 ML YEARS		1293	4989	1412	320	19	200	(94	106)	2370	733	783	740	510	40	983	20	1	52	37	14	161	.283	.349	.475	.824

Jordan Zimmermann

Pitches: R Bats: R Pos: SP-33   Ht: 6'2" Wt: 225 Born: 5/23/1986 Age: 30

Year Team	Lg	G	GS	CG	GF	IP	BFP	H	R	ER	HR	SH	SF	HB	TBB	IBB	SO	WP	Bk	W	L	Pct	Sh	Sv-Op	Hld	ERC	ERA
2009 Was	NL	16	16	0	0	91.1	391	95	51	47	10	5	3	4	29	0	92	0	0	3	5	.375	0	0-0	0	4.25	4.63
2010 Was	NL	7	7	0	0	31.0	135	31	20	17	8	1	1	2	10	1	27	0	0	1	2	.333	0	0-0	0	5.02	4.94
2011 Was	NL	26	26	1	0	161.1	662	154	62	57	12	8	2	7	31	2	124	3	1	8	11	.421	0	0-0	0	3.02	3.18
2012 Was	NL	32	32	0	0	195.2	805	186	69	64	18	8	4	8	43	2	153	3	0	12	8	.600	0	0-0	0	3.22	2.94
2013 Was	NL	32	32	4	0	213.1	865	192	81	77	19	9	4	7	40	0	161	3	0	19	9	.679	2	0-0	0	2.79	3.25
2014 Was	NL	32	32	3	0	199.2	800	185	67	59	13	5	3	6	29	0	182	4	0	14	5	.737	2	0-0	0	2.64	2.66
2015 Was	NL	33	33	0	0	201.2	831	204	89	82	24	8	2	8	39	3	164	2	1	13	10	.565	0	0-0	0	3.63	3.66
Postseason		3	2	0	0	12.2	47	10	6	6	1	1	0	0	1	0	11	0	0	0	1	.000	0	0-0	0	1.80	4.26
7 ML YEARS		178	178	8	0	1094.0	4489	1047	439	403	104	44	19	42	221	8	903	15	2	70	50	.583	4	0-0	0	3.20	3.32

Barry Zito

Pitches: L Bats: L Pos: SP-2; RP-1   Ht: 6'2" Wt: 205 Born: 5/13/1978 Age: 38

Year Team	Lg	G	GS	CG	GF	IP	BFP	H	R	ER	HR	SH	SF	HB	TBB	IBB	SO	WP	Bk	W	L	Pct	Sh	Sv-Op	Hld	ERC	ERA
2015 Nashv*	AAA	24	22	1	0	138.0	590	121	66	53	10	2	5	5	60	0	91	3	0	8	7	.533	0	0--	-	3.47	3.46
2000 Oak	AL	14	14	1	0	92.2	376	64	30	28	6	1	0	2	45	2	78	2	0	7	4	.636	1	0-0	0	2.63	2.72
2001 Oak	AL	35	35	3	0	214.1	902	184	92	83	18	5	4	13	80	0	205	6	1	17	8	.680	2	0-0	0	3.33	3.49
2002 Oak	AL	35	35	1	0	229.1	939	182	79	70	24	9	7	9	78	2	182	2	1	23	5	.821	0	0-0	0	2.92	2.75
2003 Oak	AL	35	35	4	0	231.2	957	186	98	85	19	7	7	6	88	3	146	9	0	14	12	.538	1	0-0	0	2.91	3.30
2004 Oak	AL	34	34	0	0	213.0	926	216	116	106	28	7	9	9	81	2	163	4	1	11	11	.500	0	0-0	0	4.45	4.48
2005 Oak	AL	35	35	0	0	228.1	953	185	106	98	26	8	7	13	89	0	171	4	0	14	13	.519	0	0-0	0	3.32	3.86
2006 Oak	AL	34	34	0	0	221.0	945	211	99	94	27	7	6	13	99	5	151	4	0	16	10	.615	0	0-0	0	4.47	3.83
2007 SF	NL	34	33	0	0	196.2	850	182	105	99	24	12	4	4	83	4	131	5	0	11	13	.458	0	0-0	0	3.91	4.53
2008 SF	NL	32	32	0	0	180.0	818	186	115	103	16	8	14	4	102	10	120	3	0	10	17	.370	0	0-0	0	4.81	5.15
2009 SF	NL	33	33	1	0	192.0	813	179	89	86	21	11	1	8	81	8	154	2	2	10	13	.435	0	0-0	0	4.00	4.03
2010 SF	NL	34	33	1	1	199.1	848	184	97	92	20	13	7	7	84	7	150	7	0	9	14	.391	0	0-0	0	3.85	4.15
2011 SF	NL	13	9	0	3	53.2	225	51	35	35	10	0	2	0	24	1	32	1	0	3	4	.429	0	0-0	0	4.71	5.87
2012 SF	NL	32	32	1	0	184.1	799	186	91	85	20	12	4	5	70	6	114	1	0	15	8	.652	1	0-0	0	4.15	4.15
2013 SF	NL	30	25	0	0	133.1	608	173	94	85	19	5	1	4	54	2	86	5	1	5	11	.313	0	0-0	0	6.39	5.74
2015 Oak	AL	3	2	0	1	7.0	37	12	8	8	4	0	0	0	6	0	2	0	0	0	0	-	0	0-0	0	16.04	10.29
Postseason		10	10	0	0	60.1	252	50	19	19	7	1	0	3	23	1	46	1	0	6	3	.667	0	0-0	0	3.35	2.83
15 ML YEARS		433	421	12	9	2576.2	11001	2381	1254	1157	282	105	73	97	1064	52	1885	50	8	165	143	.536	5	0-0	0	3.90	4.04

Ben Zobrist

Bats: B Throws: R Pos: 2B-69;LF-45;DH-6;RF-5;3B-4;PH-4   ZOH-brist   Ht: 6'3" Wt: 210 Born: 5/26/1981 Age: 35

Year Team	Lg	G	AB	H	2B	3B	HR	(Hm	Rd)	TB	R	RBI	RC	TBB	IBB	SO	HBP	SH	SF	SB	CS	GDP	Avg	OBP	Slg	OPS
2006 TB	AL	52	183	41	6	2	2	(2	0)	57	10	18	13	10	1	26	0	2	3	2	3	2	.224	.260	.311	.572
2007 TB	AL	31	97	15	2	0	1	(0	1)	20	8	9	7	3	0	21	1	2	2	2	0	1	.155	.184	.206	.391
2008 TB	AL	62	198	50	10	2	12	(4	8)	100	32	30	31	25	1	37	2	0	2	3	0	4	.253	.339	.505	.844
2009 TB	AL	152	501	149	28	7	27	(18	9)	272	91	91	109	91	4	104	2	1	4	17	6	7	.297	.405	.543	.948
2010 TB	AL	151	541	129	28	2	10	(3	7)	191	77	75	84	92	1	107	3	7	12	24	3	10	.238	.346	.353	.699
2011 TB	AL	156	588	158	46	6	20	(9	11)	276	99	91	100	77	1	128	2	2	5	19	6	9	.269	.353	.469	.822
2012 TB	AL	157	560	151	39	7	20	(8	12)	264	88	74	72	97	7	103	3	2	6	14	9	13	.270	.377	.471	.848
2013 TB	AL	157	612	168	36	3	12	(7	5)	246	77	71	85	72	4	91	7	1	6	11	3	18	.275	.354	.402	.756
2014 TB	AL	146	570	155	34	3	10	(4	6)	225	83	52	75	75	4	84	1	2	6	10	5	8	.272	.354	.395	.749
2015 2 Tms	AL	126	467	129	36	3	13	(5	8)	210	76	56	72	62	3	56	1	0	5	3	4	8	.276	.359	.450	.809
15 Oak	AL	67	235	63	20	2	6	(2	4)	105	39	33	38	33	2	26	0	0	3	1	1	5	.268	.354	.447	.801
15 KC	AL	59	232	66	16	1	7	(3	4)	105	37	23	34	29	1	30	1	0	2	2	3	3	.284	.364	.453	.816
Postseason		21	66	14	2	0	2	(1	1)	22	7	3	2	6	0	14	1	0	0	0	0	1	.212	.288	.333	.621
10 ML YEARS		1190	4317	1145	265	35	127	(60	67)	1861	641	567	671	604	26	757	22	19	51	105	39	80	.265	.355	.431	.786

Mike Zunino

Bats: R **Throws:** R **Pos:** C-112;PH-1   zoo-NEE-no   **Ht:** 6'2" **Wt:** 220 **Born:** 3/25/1991 **Age:** 25

								BATTING												RUNNING			AVERAGES			
Year Team	Lg	G	AB	H	2B	3B	HR	(Hm Rd)	TB	R	RBI	RC	TBB	IBB	SO	HBP	SH	SF	SB	CS	GDP	Avg	OBP	Slg	OPS
2015 Tacom*	AAA	10	41	13	2	0	3	(- -)	24	7	8	8	0	0	8	2	0	0	0	0	2	.317	.349	.585	.934
2013 Sea	AL	52	173	37	5	0	5	(3 2)	57	22	14	13	16	0	49	3	0	1	1	0	5	.214	.290	.329	.620
2014 Sea	AL	131	438	87	20	2	22	(10 12)	177	51	60	39	17	1	158	17	0	4	0	3	13	.199	.254	.404	.658
2015 Sea	AL	112	350	61	11	0	11	(6 5)	105	28	28	14	21	0	132	5	8	2	0	1	6	.174	.230	.300	.530
3 ML YEARS		295	961	185	36	2	38	(19 19)	339	101	102	66	54	1	339	25	8	7	1	4	24	.193	.252	.353	.605

Tony Zych

Pitches: R **Bats:** R **Pos:** RP-12; SP-1   zick   **Ht:** 6'3" **Wt:** 190 **Born:** 8/7/1990 **Age:** 25

			HOW MUCH HE PITCHED					WHAT HE GAVE UP												THE RESULTS						
Year Team	Lg	G	GS	CG	GF	IP	BFP	H	R	ER	HR	SH	SF	HB	TBB	IBB	SO	WP	Bk	W	L	Pct	Sh	Sv-Op	Hld	ERC	ERA
2012 Dytona	A+	27	0	0	24	36.2	145	32	16	13	0	1	1	2	7	1	36	2	0	3	3	.500	0	6- -	-	2.23	3.19
2012 Tenn	AA	20	0	0	5	24.2	112	26	12	12	1	0	0	3	12	0	28	1	0	2	1	.667	0	0- -	-	4.77	4.38
2013 Tenn	AA	47	0	0	16	56.0	243	51	30	19	2	4	2	1	21	1	40	2	0	5	5	.500	0	3- -	-	2.99	3.05
2014 Tenn	AA	45	0	0	16	58.1	254	75	36	33	3	2	3	3	18	0	35	3	0	4	5	.444	0	2- -	-	5.44	5.09
2015 Jacksn	AA	15	0	0	14	16.2	62	11	4	4	0	0	0	3	0	0	18	0	1	0	0	-	0	5- -	-	1.28	2.16
2015 Tacom	AAA	25	0	0	14	31.2	135	34	12	12	2	1	0	2	9	0	37	4	0	1	2	.333	0	4- -	-	4.08	3.41
2015 Sea	AL	13	1	0	4	18.1	76	17	6	5	1	0	0	2	3	0	24	1	0	0	0	-	0	0-0	1	2.88	2.45

2015 Fielding Statistics

Scott Spratt

The Total Runs Saved column on the right side of the ensuing tables tells you how many runs Baseball Info Solutions estimates each fielder saved or cost his team defensively in 2015. For example, Paul Goldschmidt saved the Diamondbacks 18 runs. Ian Kinsler saved the Tigers 19 runs. Nolan Arenado and Adrian Beltre saved the Rockies and Rangers 18 runs apiece. Those totals show you how important good defensive play can be. Those run totals are enough to contribute nearly two wins to their clubs based on the prevailing estimate of 10 runs per extra win, and that's before those players even held a bat.

If you head over to the center field regulars table, you'll notice that Kevin Kiermaier saved the Rays 42 runs. That is not a misprint. Kiermaier was so exceptional in center field that he contributed more than four wins on defense. BIS has Defense Runs Saved data back to 2003, and Kiermaier set the record for the most runs a player has saved his team in a season. That record was previously held by Andrelton Simmons, who saved the Braves 41 runs at shortstop in 2013.

As you might expect from a record-setting performance, Kiermaier set the pace for center fielders in all aspects of defense. He saved the Rays 29 runs with his range and positioning. Lorenzo Cain of the Royals was closest behind him at 21. Kiermaier saved six runs thanks to his Good Fielding Plays and avoidance of Defensive Misplays. That was tied for the most among center fielders with home run thief Mike Trout, whose three home run robberies were the most in baseball this season (Kiermaier had two). Finally, Kiermaier saved seven runs with his arm, which nearly doubled up the closest center fielder to him (Mookie Betts with four Outfield Arm Runs Saved).

There are plenty more defensive nuggets in this section both for regulars and backups at the eight non-pitcher positions. The tables include the total of Bases Saved (BSv)—previously referred to as PM—and Runs Saved split by component and in total for each player at every position that he played. For non-catchers, Plus/Minus Runs Saved (+/-) has been renamed to Range and Positioning Runs Saved (R/P). For catchers, there is a new component called Strike Zone Runs Saved (SZ) that measures their ability to draw extra strike calls due to catcher framing. Also for catchers, the Other Runs Saved component is the combined total of Bunt Runs Saved and Adjusted Earned Runs Saved.

The tables also include traditional statistics such as putouts, assists, errors, and fielding percentage. To qualify as a regular, a player must have played at least 750 innings at the position or 600 if he is a catcher. For the regulars, each position is ordered from most Runs Saved to fewest. A more detailed description of Runs Saved can be found in the glossary.

Fielding data for pitchers can be found in the "Pitchers Hitting, Fielding, and Holding Runners" section.

First Basemen - Regulars

Player	Tm	G	GS	Inn	PO	A	E	DP	Pct.	Bases Saved	Runs Saved R/P	GFP/ DME	Bunts/ GDP	Total
Goldschmidt,Paul	Ari	157	155	1381.2	1378	123	5	129	.997	+17	12	4	2	18
Rizzo,Anthony	ChC	160	160	1430.1	1330	126	9	102	.994	+8	6	2	2	10
Gonzalez,Adrian	LAD	149	145	1254.1	1267	116	6	100	.996	+6	4	5	1	10
Alonso,Yonder	SD	102	92	826.1	817	54	3	71	.997	+6	5	4	0	9
Belt,Brandon	SF	120	117	1050.0	1060	71	3	91	.997	+11	8	-3	3	8
Votto,Joey	Cin	156	156	1377.1	1212	139	9	122	.993	+5	4	0	2	6
Lind,Adam	Mil	138	134	1163.2	1098	82	4	124	.997	+4	3	2	0	5
Teixeira,Mark	NYY	108	105	913.2	897	48	3	76	.997	+3	2	4	-1	5
Pujols,Albert	LAA	95	95	804.0	718	55	5	57	.994	+7	5	0	-1	4
Duda,Lucas	NYM	129	127	1127.2	1039	77	3	87	.997	+5	4	1	-1	4
Cabrera,Miguel	Det	107	107	932.1	903	76	4	96	.996	+4	3	2	-1	4
Davis,Chris	Bal	111	108	947.0	882	53	3	77	.997	+3	2	1	1	4
Napoli,Mike	TOT	111	101	899.0	851	71	7	77	.992	+6	5	-1	-1	3
Freeman,Freddie	Atl	117	110	958.0	893	63	4	103	.996	+1	1	0	2	3
Moreland,Mitch	Tex	120	110	982.1	975	64	4	109	.996	+4	2	1	-1	2
Abreu,Jose	CWS	115	115	1017.0	952	60	11	100	.989	0	0	0	1	1
Hosmer,Eric	KC	154	152	1354.2	1261	101	4	121	.997	-3	-2	3	0	1
Mauer,Joe	Min	137	135	1188.0	1151	86	5	113	.996	0	0	1	-1	0
Zimmerman,Ryan	Was	93	92	792.1	726	49	4	63	.995	-3	-2	0	1	-1
Loney,James	TB	101	92	815.1	729	42	6	58	.992	-1	-1	0	-1	-2
Santana,Carlos	Cle	132	132	1157.0	1061	77	3	110	.997	-3	-2	-1	-2	-5
Carter,Chris	Hou	115	105	913.1	911	67	8	85	.992	-3	-2	-4	0	-6
Bour,Justin	Mia	111	101	899.2	836	47	6	106	.993	-7	-5	-1	-1	-7
Morrison,Logan	Sea	140	115	1104.2	1055	71	4	106	.996	-8	-6	2	-3	-7
Howard,Ryan	Phi	116	112	957.1	871	66	6	75	.994	-9	-6	-2	-1	-9
Alvarez,Pedro	Pit	124	119	906.1	966	68	23	98	.978	-9	-6	-7	0	-13

Second Basemen - Regulars

Player	Tm	G	GS	Inn	PO	A	E	DP	Pct.	Range	Bases Saved	Runs Saved R/P	GFP/ DME	GDP	Total
Kinsler,Ian	Det	153	151	1324.0	289	425	13	109	.982	4.85	+23	17	-2	4	19
Gordon,Dee	Mia	145	144	1270.0	293	434	6	111	.992	5.15	+16	12	-1	2	13
Forsythe,Logan	TB	126	123	1073.1	164	299	7	43	.985	3.88	+10	8	1	-1	8
Sanchez,Carlos	CWS	117	112	996.1	229	268	5	83	.990	4.49	+3	3	-1	4	6
Wong,Kolten	StL	147	140	1278.2	312	410	17	107	.977	5.08	+6	4	-1	2	5
Sogard,Eric	Oak	96	87	775.2	168	268	5	56	.989	5.06	+5	4	1	0	5
Owings,Chris	Ari	115	101	918.2	154	289	4	65	.991	4.34	+1	1	3	1	5
Phillips,Brandon	Cin	141	141	1228.0	261	394	6	79	.991	4.80	+9	6	0	-2	4
Infante,Omar	KC	124	121	1060.1	193	319	10	67	.981	4.35	+9	6	0	-3	3
Gennett,Scooter	Mil	108	93	819.0	176	273	7	71	.985	4.93	+7	5	0	-2	3
Altuve,Jose	Hou	153	153	1330.2	247	417	5	81	.993	4.49	+2	2	0	1	3
LeMahieu,DJ	Col	149	146	1284.0	300	452	9	120	.988	5.27	0	0	1	2	3
Panik,Joe	SF	99	95	843.1	191	268	2	64	.996	4.90	-1	-1	2	1	2
Kipnis,Jason	Cle	124	124	1082.2	203	311	7	69	.987	4.27	+4	3	-1	-1	1
Utley,Chase	TOT	88	87	751.1	154	230	8	53	.980	4.60	-1	0	0	-1	-1
Peterson,Jace	Atl	144	137	1218.0	287	395	9	109	.987	5.04	-1	-1	0	0	-1
Walker,Neil	Pit	146	135	1224.2	236	418	7	103	.989	4.81	-8	-6	3	1	-2
Pedroia,Dustin	Bos	92	92	799.2	165	271	6	61	.986	4.91	0	0	-1	-2	-3
Drew,Stephen	NYY	123	94	892.1	158	267	7	59	.984	4.29	-5	-3	0	0	-3
Dozier,Brian	Min	157	157	1383.0	304	456	8	111	.990	4.95	-4	-3	0	-2	-5
Odor,Rougned	Tex	119	113	1007.1	207	350	17	97	.970	4.98	-6	-5	-2	0	-7
Cano,Robinson	Sea	149	149	1316.1	287	403	6	104	.991	4.72	-11	-8	-1	0	-9
Kendrick,Howie	LAD	113	112	989.0	193	296	5	52	.990	4.45	-13	-10	0	-2	-12
Giavotella,Johnny	LAA	128	124	1094.2	216	307	12	64	.978	4.30	-13	-10	-1	-1	-12

Third Basemen - Regulars

Player	Tm	G	GS	Inn	PO	A	E	DP	Pct.	Range	Bases Saved	Runs Saved R/P	GFP/ DME	Bunts/ GDP	Total
Arenado,Nolan	Col	157	156	1362.0	105	385	17	42	.966	3.24	+20	15	3	0	18
Beltre,Adrian	Tex	142	142	1237.2	105	267	17	28	.956	2.71	+18	14	0	4	18
Machado,Manny	Bal	156	156	1367.2	132	337	19	38	.961	3.09	+18	14	0	0	14
Duffy,Matt	SF	134	129	1150.1	78	250	12	20	.965	2.57	+16	12	0	0	12
Donaldson,Josh	Tor	150	150	1317.0	137	287	18	32	.959	2.90	+14	11	0	0	11
Prado,Martin	Mia	124	118	1034.0	72	218	7	28	.976	2.52	+9	6	2	1	9
Lamb,Jake	Ari	95	87	782.2	47	203	7	14	.973	2.87	+10	7	0	0	7
Frazier,Todd	Cin	155	155	1371.1	102	274	19	21	.952	2.47	+8	6	1	-1	6

Player	Tm	G	GS	Inn	PO	A	E	DP	Pct.	Range	Bases Saved	Runs Saved R/P	GFP/ DME	Bunts/ GDP	Total
Turner,Justin	LAD	100	88	774.0	39	175	9	18	.960	2.49	+6	5	-1	1	5
Moustakas,Mike	KC	146	140	1254.0	112	257	12	21	.969	2.65	+7	5	1	-2	4
Bryant,Kris	ChC	144	136	1209.1	81	249	17	21	.951	2.46	+5	4	-1	0	3
Seager,Kyle	Sea	160	159	1421.0	94	352	16	37	.965	2.82	-1	-1	1	1	1
Plouffe,Trevor	Min	140	138	1217.0	101	276	11	32	.972	2.79	+3	3	0	-4	-1
Valbuena,Luis	Hou	99	93	835.0	54	168	6	20	.974	2.39	-2	-2	1	0	-1
Longoria,Evan	TB	148	147	1293.1	109	259	9	29	.976	2.56	-3	-2	1	0	-1
Freese,David	LAA	113	112	913.2	54	179	8	13	.967	2.30	-5	-4	0	2	-2
Lawrie,Brett	Oak	109	106	930.2	69	197	18	15	.937	2.57	-1	-1	-2	0	-3
Headley,Chase	NYY	155	148	1320.0	99	302	23	25	.946	2.73	-3	-3	-1	-2	-6
Ramirez,Aramis	TOT	122	120	965.1	62	202	10	20	.964	2.46	-10	-7	-1	0	-8
Castellanos,Nick	Det	145	142	1175.2	92	249	12	27	.966	2.61	-11	-9	-1	1	-9
Carpenter,Matt	StL	146	141	1244.0	77	234	14	25	.957	2.25	-13	-10	0	0	-10
Escobar,Yunel	Was	134	134	1126.2	56	171	7	14	.970	1.81	-11	-8	-2	-1	-11
Sandoval,Pablo	Bos	123	122	1034.2	78	200	15	19	.949	2.42	-14	-11	1	-1	-11

Shortstops - Regulars

Player	Tm	G	GS	Inn	PO	A	E	DP	Pct.	Range	Bases Saved	Runs Saved R/P	GFP/ DME	GDP	Total
Simmons,Andrelton	Atl	147	145	1279.1	235	444	8	126	.988	4.78	+20	15	5	5	25
Crawford,Brandon	SF	140	136	1200.1	191	427	13	89	.979	4.63	+22	16	2	2	20
Ahmed,Nick	Ari	129	116	1042.1	190	368	13	84	.977	4.82	+19	15	1	3	19
Lindor,Francisco	Cle	98	97	865.1	132	247	10	60	.974	3.94	+13	10	0	0	10
Hechavarria,Adeiny	Mia	130	129	1120.1	173	373	9	93	.984	4.39	+14	11	-2	0	9
Semien,Marcus	Oak	152	147	1304.2	214	407	35	99	.947	4.28	+4	4	1	0	5
Tulowitzki,Troy	TOT	121	120	1025.1	153	361	8	85	.985	4.51	+4	4	0	1	5
Gregorius,Didi	NYY	155	147	1330.0	177	430	13	77	.979	4.11	+4	3	1	1	5
Hardy,J.J.	Bal	114	112	994.2	141	301	3	57	.993	4.00	+4	3	1	0	4
Desmond,Ian	Was	155	155	1359.0	226	417	27	94	.960	4.26	+1	0	0	1	1
Correa,Carlos	Hou	99	99	870.2	112	265	13	41	.967	3.90	+1	1	1	-2	0
Mercer,Jordy	Pit	115	108	986.1	148	351	7	78	.986	4.55	-1	-1	1	0	0
Andrus,Elvis	Tex	160	159	1404.2	248	516	22	114	.972	4.90	+2	1	0	-2	-1
Escobar,Alcides	KC	148	148	1306.2	217	418	13	80	.980	4.37	+1	1	0	-2	-1
Bogaerts,Xander	Bos	156	154	1360.1	236	429	11	95	.984	4.40	+2	1	1	-3	-1
Segura,Jean	Mil	140	139	1232.1	177	426	19	98	.969	4.40	+5	4	-6	-1	-3
Aybar,Erick	LAA	154	154	1335.2	244	359	17	71	.973	4.06	-1	-1	-1	-1	-3
Iglesias,Jose	Det	119	115	1019.1	162	315	11	81	.977	4.21	-9	-7	2	2	-3
Castro,Starlin	ChC	109	104	943.0	143	323	18	58	.963	4.45	-1	-1	-1	-2	-4
Miller,Brad	Sea	89	83	750.1	109	269	14	56	.964	4.53	-2	-1	-3	0	-4
Galvis,Freddy	Phi	146	144	1263.2	206	398	17	87	.973	4.30	-10	-7	1	0	-6
Ramirez,Alexei	CWS	152	151	1349.2	206	462	16	105	.977	4.45	-10	-8	-1	3	-6
Peralta,Jhonny	StL	148	147	1287.2	157	420	8	88	.986	4.03	-5	-4	-1	-2	-7
Rollins,Jimmy	LAD	134	128	1134.1	166	350	9	65	.983	4.09	-9	-7	2	-2	-7
Cabrera,Asdrubal	TB	136	131	1141.0	150	284	9	51	.980	3.42	-10	-8	2	-2	-8
Reyes,Jose	TOT	116	116	996.0	147	338	16	70	.968	4.38	-16	-12	1	3	-8
Flores,Wilmer	NYM	103	96	835.2	119	267	14	62	.965	4.16	-10	-7	-2	-1	-10
Suarez,Eugenio	Cin	96	95	841.1	147	265	19	59	.956	4.41	-14	-10	-3	1	-12

Left Fielders - Regulars

Player	Tm	G	GS	Inn	PO	A	E	DP	Pct.	Range	Bases Saved	Runs Saved R/P	GFP/ DME	Throws	Total
Marte,Starling	Pit	141	133	1186.1	180	15	1	0	.995	1.48	+22	11	5	8	24
Cespedes,Yoenis	TOT	134	113	1022.1	247	10	5	1	.981	2.26	+17	9	0	6	15
Yelich,Christian	Mia	103	86	786.2	182	5	2	0	.989	2.14	+24	11	0	2	13
Upton,Justin	SD	146	145	1260.1	235	9	3	0	.988	1.74	+21	10	2	-4	8
Gordon,Alex	KC	101	100	864.2	193	4	0	1	1.000	2.05	+8	4	0	3	7
Gardner,Brett	NYY	119	104	942.2	178	6	0	1	1.000	1.76	+3	2	1	-2	1
Byrd,Marlon	TOT	88	86	754.2	153	2	0	0	1.000	1.85	+1	1	1	-1	1
Revere,Ben	TOT	112	93	848.0	187	3	0	0	1.000	2.02	+3	2	0	-2	0
Coghlan,Chris	ChC	99	87	750.2	128	8	0	0	1.000	1.63	-3	-1	1	0	0
Brantley,Michael	Cle	101	94	828.2	172	7	2	1	.989	1.94	-9	-3	1	1	-1
Peralta,David	Ari	124	109	982.0	211	3	2	0	.991	1.96	+15	7	-3	-6	-2
Cabrera,Melky	CWS	150	150	1324.2	220	8	5	0	.979	1.55	-15	-7	2	3	-2
Davis,Khris	Mil	108	107	871.1	171	1	5	0	.972	1.78	+3	1	-1	-6	-6

Center Fielders - Regulars

Player	Tm	G	GS	Inn	PO	A	E	DP	Pct.	Range	Bases Saved	R/P	GFP/ DME	Throws	Total
Kiermaier,Kevin	TB	148	129	1174.2	410	15	5	3	.988	3.26	+65	29	6	7	42
Cain,Lorenzo	KC	136	136	1173.1	389	6	10	2	.975	3.03	+37	21	-2	-1	18
Pollock,A.J.	Ari	151	143	1303.2	347	5	3	0	.992	2.43	+38	16	2	-4	14
Pillar,Kevin	Tor	142	139	1236.0	404	7	2	0	.995	2.99	+24	13	0	1	14
Herrera,Odubel	Phi	136	121	1065.0	341	5	5	1	.986	2.92	+32	15	-2	-3	10
Betts,Mookie	Bos	133	130	1157.0	335	10	4	2	.989	2.68	+8	5	0	4	9
Hamilton,Billy	Cin	110	109	975.2	273	8	0	1	1.000	2.59	+7	5	2	1	8
Gomez,Carlos	TOT	111	109	959.2	269	5	7	3	.975	2.57	+21	7	-2	1	6
Bourn,Michael	TOT	106	97	858.1	236	4	1	2	.996	2.52	+9	5	1	0	6
Marisnick,Jake	Hou	99	84	757.1	202	8	3	3	.986	2.50	+1	3	0	2	5
Trout,Mike	LAA	156	155	1362.2	428	7	0	1	1.000	2.87	-3	-1	6	0	5
Burns,Billy	Oak	125	118	1066.0	280	2	3	2	.989	2.38	+13	7	0	-3	4
Jones,Adam	Bal	134	134	1168.2	317	13	3	4	.991	2.54	-14	-4	1	7	4
Lagares,Juan	NYM	137	106	999.0	278	3	2	2	.993	2.53	+4	4	0	-2	2
Hicks,Aaron	Min	88	87	761.2	223	8	1	2	.996	2.73	-3	-2	2	2	2
Ellsbury,Jacoby	NYY	110	106	948.0	232	5	0	2	1.000	2.25	-1	1	1	-1	1
Jackson,Austin	TOT	115	103	939.0	279	2	3	1	.989	2.69	+1	1	-2	0	-1
Taylor,Michael	Was	96	89	802.1	228	3	3	1	.987	2.59	-7	-3	1	0	-2
Pederson,Joc	LAD	147	137	1223.0	269	5	4	1	.986	2.02	-6	-3	1	-1	-3
Ozuna,Marcell	Mia	111	104	924.2	238	5	1	0	.996	2.37	-11	-7	1	3	-3
Blackmon,Charlie	Col	147	138	1209.2	308	8	3	2	.991	2.35	+4	-1	-3	-4	-8
McCutchen,Andrew	Pit	152	151	1374.2	301	7	2	2	.994	2.02	-15	-10	0	2	-8
Gose,Anthony	Det	137	125	1120.0	352	4	4	1	.989	2.86	-20	-7	-2	-3	-12
Fowler,Dexter	ChC	152	149	1324.1	337	5	4	2	.988	2.32	-20	-7	-1	-4	-12
Eaton,Adam	CWS	145	144	1280.0	343	8	5	2	.986	2.47	-24	-13	-3	2	-14
Maybin,Cameron	Atl	139	126	1129.2	331	7	3	2	.991	2.69	-19	-10	-2	-4	-16
Pagan,Angel	SF	124	122	1061.1	258	2	4	2	.985	2.20	-26	-15	-2	-3	-20

Right Fielders - Regulars

Player	Tm	G	GS	Inn	PO	A	E	DP	Pct.	Range	Bases Saved	R/P	GFP/ DME	Throws	Total
Heyward,Jason	StL	144	136	1217.1	278	9	3	2	.990	2.12	+39	20	1	1	22
Granderson,Curtis	NYM	149	141	1275.2	279	9	5	1	.983	2.03	+23	11	1	0	12
Polanco,Gregory	Pit	144	133	1220.1	247	13	8	5	.970	1.92	+19	10	-4	5	11
Harper,Bryce	Was	140	139	1203.2	269	8	7	2	.975	2.07	+12	5	0	1	6
Calhoun,Kole	LAA	157	157	1383.2	342	11	4	1	.989	2.30	-1	-2	5	3	6
Gonzalez,Carlos	Col	151	142	1230.1	253	8	7	1	.974	1.91	+17	8	0	-3	5
Bruce,Jay	Cin	150	149	1319.2	300	11	3	0	.990	2.12	+2	2	3	0	5
Springer,George	Hou	93	93	811.2	162	6	3	3	.982	1.86	+2	2	2	1	5
Martinez,J.D.	Det	148	147	1306.1	265	15	2	3	.993	1.93	-17	-5	4	5	4
Reddick,Josh	Oak	143	134	1182.1	257	6	5	1	.981	2.00	+5	3	-2	0	1
Braun,Ryan	Mil	130	128	1121.0	205	5	2	1	.991	1.69	+6	2	-1	-2	-1
Bautista,Jose	Tor	118	118	1038.2	224	4	3	1	.987	1.98	-7	-4	1	0	-3
Souza,Steven	TB	103	101	884.0	172	8	2	3	.989	1.83	-7	-4	-2	2	-4
Markakis,Nick	Atl	153	153	1330.1	295	4	1	0	.997	2.02	+7	4	-3	-7	-6
Rios,Alex	KC	105	105	914.2	215	4	3	0	.986	2.15	-4	-1	-2	-3	-6
Hunter,Torii	Min	123	121	1035.2	231	6	5	1	.979	2.06	-14	-6	0	-2	-8
Soler,Jorge	ChC	95	93	825.2	144	4	1	1	.993	1.61	-13	-8	0	0	-8
Choo,Shin-Soo	Tex	148	144	1262.0	315	5	5	2	.985	2.28	-9	-6	0	-5	-11
Garcia,Avisail	CWS	130	129	1124.0	235	17	3	4	.988	2.02	-32	-15	2	2	-11
Beltran,Carlos	NYY	123	120	968.1	166	5	3	3	.983	1.59	-19	-11	-1	-2	-14
Kemp,Matt	SD	149	149	1282.0	269	10	8	2	.972	1.96	-17	-9	-4	-2	-15

Catchers - Regulars

Player	Tm	G	GS	Inn	PO	A	E	DP	PB	Pct.	SBA	CS	PCS	CS%	CERA	GFP/ DME	SB	SZ	Other	Total
Posey,Buster	SF	106	103	901.2	771	67	2	4	4	.998	56	17	5	.30	3.57	6	0	8	3	17
Plawecki,Kevin	NYM	70	66	602.2	558	36	1	1	2	.998	43	11	0	.26	2.79	1	1	10	5	17
Flowers,Tyler	CWS	110	100	878.1	877	63	5	10	15	.995	62	9	9	.15	3.68	0	-4	16	2	14
Joseph,Caleb	Bal	94	93	826.1	749	45	3	3	6	.996	52	15	3	.29	3.65	2	0	3	7	12
Castro,Jason	Hou	103	102	883.1	777	62	1	5	7	.999	62	20	4	.32	3.49	0	3	7	1	11
Ramos,Wilson	Was	125	123	1078.1	1026	77	6	3	3	.995	47	17	7	.36	3.43	3	2	1	4	10
Maldonado,Martin	Mil	74	66	602.2	561	34	9	7	3	.985	46	17	1	.37	4.03	0	4	3	2	9
Molina,Yadier	StL	134	131	1149.2	1064	56	7	9	4	.994	56	19	7	.34	2.79	1	1	2	5	9
Cervelli,Francisco	Pit	128	124	1099.2	992	82	7	6	10	.994	124	23	6	.19	3.50	-1	0	11	-2	8
Zunino,Mike	Sea	112	101	919.2	809	44	5	6	6	.994	54	12	10	.22	4.03	0	-1	9	0	8

| | | | | | | | | | | | | | | | | Runs Saved | | | | |
Player	Tm	G	GS	Inn	PO	A	E	DP	PB	Pct.	SBA	CS	PCS	CS%	CERA	GFP/DME	SB	SZ	Other	Total
Iannetta,Chris	LAA	85	80	718.2	624	44	3	3	6	.996	56	12	3	.21	3.88	-1	-1	7	2	7
Montero,Miguel	ChC	109	90	825.0	820	55	12	3	3	.986	86	15	3	.17	3.36	1	-1	9	-2	7
Norris,Derek	SD	128	116	1040.2	970	79	7	7	13	.993	122	38	6	.31	4.14	2	2	2	0	6
Rupp,Cameron	Phi	80	79	701.1	524	54	4	7	7	.993	51	18	2	.35	4.52	1	2	1	2	6
Grandal,Yasmani	LAD	107	100	884.1	811	60	3	5	8	.997	75	19	4	.25	3.35	1	-2	9	-2	6
Martin,Russell	Tor	117	113	994.0	799	70	4	6	19	.995	65	25	7	.38	3.86	-5	4	6	-1	4
Lucroy,Jonathan	Mil	86	86	745.0	627	53	8	8	3	.988	94	24	3	.26	4.16	0	0	4	-1	3
Realmuto,J.T.	Mia	118	116	1025.1	835	47	6	6	11	.993	58	15	1	.26	3.71	-1	0	-5	7	1
Perez,Salvador	KC	139	137	1192.1	974	90	4	10	4	.996	90	24	5	.27	3.62	4	2	-4	-1	1
Chirinos,Robinson	Tex	78	73	645.0	474	31	6	2	4	.988	38	9	3	.24	4.45	3	0	-3	0	0
Perez,Carlos	LAA	80	75	665.0	545	71	5	1	7	.992	59	18	7	.31	4.01	1	2	-1	-2	0
Gomes,Yan	Cle	91	90	800.0	746	58	3	8	6	.996	57	18	1	.32	3.56	3	0	-3	-1	-1
Vogt,Stephen	Oak	100	89	803.0	658	41	3	4	9	.996	58	15	5	.26	3.79	-1	-1	-8	7	-3
McCann,Brian	NYY	126	119	1042.1	980	69	7	5	1	.993	76	26	2	.34	3.97	-3	2	-4	1	-4
Pena,Brayan	Cin	86	84	754.1	683	31	1	4	5	.999	68	10	3	.15	4.01	0	-5	-3	3	-5
Rivera,Rene	TB	107	87	784.2	752	60	11	5	6	.987	63	23	0	.37	3.90	0	2	0	-8	-6
McCann,James	Det	112	103	943.1	723	54	0	5	3	1.000	65	24	4	.37	4.65	1	0	-6	-1	-6
Suzuki,Kurt	Min	130	123	1096.0	825	35	3	8	3	.997	88	8	6	.09	3.96	2	-6	-9	4	-9
Castillo,Welington	TOT	88	83	736.2	606	35	7	4	7	.989	42	9	2	.21	4.35	3	-2	-4	-6	-9
Hundley,Nick	Col	102	100	866.1	643	51	5	5	5	.993	69	19	7	.28	5.63	2	2	-8	-7	-11
Ruiz,Carlos	Phi	83	81	716.0	626	41	11	8	5	.984	52	6	5	.12	4.84	-1	-3	-6	-2	-12
Pierzynski,A.J.	Atl	107	104	909.2	729	44	2	7	5	.997	82	15	6	.18	4.53	-5	-3	-5	0	-13
Swihart,Blake	Bos	83	78	688.0	570	39	3	4	16	.995	54	13	3	.24	4.57	-7	0	-7	-2	-16

All Other Fielders

Player	Tm	Pos	G	GS	Inn	PO	A	E	DP	Pct.	Rng	BSv	RS
Ackley, D	TOT	1B	4	3	27	28	2	0	0	1.000	-	-1	-1
	TOT	2B	10	10	72	13	14	1	3	.964	3.38	-2	-4
	TOT	LF	67	38	377	69	1	0	0	1.000	1.67	-4	-6
	TOT	CF	21	16	139	33	1	0	1	1.000	2.20	-1	-1
	TOT	RF	2	0	2	0	0	0	0	-	.00	-2	-1
Adames, C	Col	2B	2	2	17	4	7	0	1	1.000	5.82	0	0
	Col	SS	13	11	93	15	30	2	8	.957	4.35	+2	3
Adams, M	StL	1B	46	42	352	321	32	3	30	.992	-	+7	5
Adrianza, E	SF	1B	1	1	9	5	0	0	0	1.000	-	-1	0
	SF	2B	20	13	130	27	42	2	11	.972	4.79	-3	-3
	SF	3B	1	1	7	1	2	0	0	1.000	3.86	+1	0
	SF	SS	20	16	152	24	54	1	13	.987	4.63	+6	3
Aguilar, J	Cle	1B	4	4	36	26	3	0	1	1.000	-	-1	-2
Alberto, H	Tex	2B	24	21	190	40	73	2	14	.983	5.35	+10	8
	Tex	3B	7	2	26	2	3	0	0	1.000	1.75	0	0
	Tex	SS	8	3	34	4	13	0	3	1.000	4.50	+1	1
Alcantara, A	ChC	2B	6	6	57	14	18	1	2	.970	5.05	-1	0
	ChC	3B	2	1	10	1	1	0	0	1.000	1.80	0	0
Almonte, A	TOT	LF	6	3	33	2	0	0	0	1.000	.55	0	0
	TOT	CF	56	54	481	131	4	0	1	1.000	2.49	-4	2
	TOT	RF	2	2	17	2	0	0	0	1.000	1.08	0	0
Alonso, Y	SD	3B	2	2	14	0	2	0	0	1.000	1.29	0	0
Altherr, A	Phi	LF	23	20	176	40	0	0	0	1.000	2.05	+1	1
	Phi	CF	8	5	59	20	2	0	0	1.000	3.34	+2	3
	Phi	RF	11	10	88	20	1	0	1	1.000	2.14	+1	1
Alvarez, D	Bal	CF	2	0	2	0	0	0	0	-	.00	-1	0
	Bal	RF	12	10	79	16	1	0	1	1.000	1.94	-2	-1
Amarista, A	SD	2B	11	5	51	9	18	0	1	1.000	4.80	+2	1
	SD	3B	2	0	9	1	1	0	0	1.000	2.00	0	0
	SD	SS	85	79	671	121	221	12	52	.966	4.58	0	1
	SD	LF	11	3	42	5	0	0	0	1.000	1.07	-1	0
	SD	CF	7	0	14	3	0	0	0	1.000	1.93	-3	-2
Aoki, N	SF	LF	86	82	714	135	4	0	0	1.000	1.75	-2	-1
	SF	RF	2	2	15	1	0	0	0	1.000	.59	0	0
Arcia, O	Min	LF	15	14	107	28	0	1	0	.966	2.36	-1	-1
	Min	RF	4	4	39	9	0	0	0	1.000	2.08	-2	-1
Arias, J	SF	1B	2	1	11	13	0	0	3	1.000	-	0	0
	SF	2B	2	1	10	3	3	0	0	1.000	5.40	+1	1
	SF	3B	8	2	27	2	5	0	1	1.000	2.30	-1	-1
	SF	SS	8	6	48	4	26	4	2	.882	5.63	0	2
Asche, C	Phi	3B	51	51	435	26	97	8	13	.939	2.55	-6	-3
	Phi	LF	63	61	523	107	3	2	1	.982	1.89	-12	-8
Avila, A	Det	1B	23	13	134	120	9	1	12	.992	-	-2	0
Aviles, M	Cle	2B	11	9	78	11	39	1	8	.980	5.77	0	-2
	Cle	3B	28	22	194	17	35	5	3	.912	2.41	-2	-2
	Cle	SS	23	20	172	19	52	3	10	.959	3.72	+3	1
	Cle	LF	34	25	228	49	1	1	0	.980	1.98	+1	1
	Cle	CF	5	3	28	5	0	0	0	1.000	1.61	-3	-2
	Cle	RF	1	0	1	0	0	0	0	-	.00	0	0
Baez, J	ChC	1B	1	0	1	0	0	0	0	-	-	-1	0
	ChC	2B	17	5	60	13	16	1	7	.967	4.37	0	0
	ChC	3B	11	6	64	5	19	1	1	.960	3.38	+5	4
	ChC	SS	8	5	45	7	14	0	3	1.000	4.20	-3	-1
Baker, J	Mia	1B	17	14	115	115	2	2	7	.983	-	-1	-2
	Mia	2B	1	1	3	1	2	0	0	1.000	9.00	-1	-1
	Mia	3B	1	0	1	0	0	0	0	-	.00	0	0
	Mia	LF	1	0	2	0	0	0	0	-	.00	0	0
Barmes, C	SD	1B	1	0	2	4	0	0	0	1.000	-	0	0
	SD	SS	89	51	509	87	167	8	28	.969	4.49	-3	-3
Barnes, A	LAD	2B	1	1	6	1	0	0	0	1.000	1.50	0	0
	LAD	3B	1	0	3	0	0	0	0	-	.00	0	0
Barnes, B	Col	LF	75	45	450	87	3	2	2	.978	1.80	+4	-3
	Col	CF	11	9	60	20	1	0	0	1.000	3.15	-2	1
	Col	RF	21	13	128	27	0	0	0	1.000	1.90	-3	-3
Barney, D	TOT	2B	15	6	67	10	23	1	3	.971	4.43	-2	-1
	TOT	3B	1	0	2	0	0	0	0	-	.00	0	0
	TOT	SS	1	1	7	0	3	0	0	1.000	3.86	0	0
Barnhart, T	Cin	RF	1	0	1	0	0	0	0	-	.00	-1	0
Baxter, M	ChC	1B	2	1	11	16	1	0	1	1.000	-	0	0
	ChC	LF	1	0	1	0	0	0	0	-	.00	0	0
	ChC	RF	10	8	78	15	0	1	0	.938	1.72	+2	1
Beckham, G	CWS	2B	11	7	68	22	25	0	10	1.000	6.22	0	1
	CWS	3B	76	39	429	24	96	3	7	.976	2.52	+5	6
	CWS	SS	5	4	35	9	13	1	6	.957	5.66	-1	-1
Beckham, T	TB	2B	38	21	207	31	59	5	13	.947	3.91	-4	-2
	TB	3B	1	1	9	2	2	0	0	1.000	4.00	0	-1
	TB	SS	28	22	208	23	52	2	10	.974	3.25	-3	-2
Belt, B	SF	LF	14	13	96	16	0	2	0	.889	1.49	-5	-2
Bernier, D	Min	2B	2	0	3	0	3	0	1	1.000	9.00	+1	0
	Min	3B	2	1	10	0	1	0	0	1.000	.90	0	0
Berry, Q	ChC	2B	2	0	3	0	0	0	0	-	.00	0	0
	ChC	CF	2	0	4	0	0	0	0	-	.00	0	0
	ChC	RF	1	0	2	0	0	0	0	-	.00	0	0
Betts, M	Bos	RF	11	11	97	23	0	1	0	.958	2.13	0	1
Bianchi, J	Bos	3B	2	0	6	0	2	0	0	1.000	3.00	0	0
	Bos	SS	1	0	1	1	1	0	1	1.000	18.00	0	0
Bird, G	NYY	1B	46	42	380	376	24	1	33	.998	-	-1	-3
Blackmon, C	Col	LF	14	4	63	10	1	0	0	1.000	1.57	+3	1
	Col	RF	7	4	31	9	0	0	0	1.000	2.61	0	0
Blanco, A	Phi	1B	1	1	8	11	1	0	0	1.000	-	+1	0
	Phi	2B	22	14	142	29	53	2	14	.976	5.19	-3	-1
	Phi	3B	36	26	250	19	49	3	3	.958	2.45	-5	-5
	Phi	SS	10	7	65	8	23	1	4	.969	4.29	-2	0
Blanco, G	SF	LF	38	25	249	63	1	0	1	1.000	2.31	+3	1
	SF	CF	44	34	319	84	0	1	0	.988	2.37	-10	-6
	SF	RF	22	19	164	36	0	2	0	.947	1.97	+1	-1
Blanks, K	Tex	1B	13	13	114	105	6	0	10	1.000	-	-3	-2
	Tex	LF	3	3	25	5	0	0	0	1.000	1.80	+2	1
Bloomquist, W	Sea	1B	3	3	24	24	1	0	4	1.000	-	0	0
	Sea	2B	8	2	31	6	6	0	2	1.000	3.48	+1	1
	Sea	3B	5	2	24	1	5	0	0	1.000	2.25	+1	1
	Sea	SS	7	5	39	6	14	0	1	1.000	4.62	-3	-2
	Sea	LF	5	3	26	2	0	0	0	1.000	.69	0	0
	Sea	RF	2	1	11	2	1	0	0	1.000	2.45	0	1
Boesch, B	Cin	LF	8	5	47	12	0	0	0	1.000	2.31	0	0
	Cin	CF	8	7	60	17	0	0	0	1.000	2.55	0	-2
	Cin	RF	8	3	38	7	0	0	0	1.000	1.67	-2	-1
Bogusevic, B	Phi	LF	2	1	12	3	0	0	0	1.000	2.19	+1	0
	Phi	RF	14	13	116	27	2	3	1	.906	2.24	0	0
Bonifacio, E	CWS	2B	17	11	104	27	37	3	11	.955	5.52	+2	1
	CWS	3B	1	0	1	0	0	0	0	-	.00	0	0
	CWS	LF	2	1	11	1	0	0	0	1.000	.82	0	0
	CWS	CF	3	0	4	2	0	0	0	1.000	4.50	0	0
Bourgeois, J	Cin	LF	18	6	72	11	1	0	0	1.000	1.51	-5	-1
	Cin	CF	35	31	264	70	1	2	0	.973	2.42	-10	-4
	Cin	RF	6	3	34	4	0	0	0	1.000	1.06	-4	-2
Bourjos, P	StL	CF	93	41	477	125	1	1	1	.992	2.38	-5	-4
Bourn, M	TOT	LF	29	16	166	35	3	0	1	1.000	2.06	-2	1
	TOT	RF	3	2	19	2	0	0	0	1.000	.95	-1	-1
Bradley Jr., J	Bos	LF	17	13	122	35	2	0	1	1.000	2.72	+4	3
	Bos	CF	27	25	224	61	0	0	0	1.000	2.45	+4	3
	Bos	RF	32	28	262	63	2	1	1	.985	2.23	-2	2
Brantley, M	Cle	LF	28	24	206	40	1	0	0	1.000	1.79	-2	-1
Brett, R	TB	2B	3	1	8	3	3	1	1	.857	6.75	0	0
Brignac, R	Mia	3B	2	1	10	1	0	0	0	1.000	.90	0	0
Brito, S	Ari	LF	1	0	5	0	1	0	0	1.000	1.80	0	1
	Ari	CF	1	0	4	0	0	0	0	-	.00	0	0
	Ari	RF	5	5	43	15	1	0	1	1.000	3.35	+5	3
Brown, D	Phi	RF	50	47	403	99	4	1	1	.990	2.30	-3	-1
Broxton, K	Pit	LF	1	0	0	0	0	0	0	-	.00	0	0
	Pit	CF	1	0	1	0	0	0	0	-	.00	0	0
	Pit	RF	1	0	1	0	0	0	0	-	.00	0	0
Bryant, K	ChC	1B	1	1	6	2	1	0	0	1.000	-	0	0
	ChC	LF	8	4	39	5	0	0	0	1.000	1.15	+1	1
	ChC	CF	7	1	18	2	1	0	0	1.000	1.50	-2	0
	ChC	RF	7	5	41	13	0	0	0	1.000	2.85	0	0
Burriss, E	Was	2B	1	0	1	0	1	0	0	1.000	9.00	0	0
Butera, D	TOT	1B	8	1	24	18	4	0	0	1.000	-	0	0
Butler, B	Oak	1B	7	5	57	49	7	0	4	1.000	-	0	-2
Butler, J	TB	LF	30	22	198	48	1	1	0	.980	2.23	+2	2
	TB	RF	6	2	18	7	0	0	0	1.000	3.44	0	0
Buxton, B	Min	CF	44	35	327	115	2	0	0	1.000	3.22	+7	4
Byrd, M	TOT	CF	4	3	30	9	0	0	0	1.000	2.70	-1	-1
	TOT	RF	41	37	340	79	2	0	0	1.000	2.15	-1	1

All Other Fielders

Player	Tm	Pos	G	GS	Inn	PO	A	E	DP	Pct.	Rng	BSv	RS
Cabrera, E	Bal	2B	2	2	16	4	5	0	0	1.000	5.06	+1	1
	Bal	SS	27	26	224	22	62	3	9	.966	3.37	-5	-4
Cain, L	KC	RF	5	1	19	2	0	0	0	1.000	.95	0	0
Calhoun, K	LAA	1B	1	0	1	1	0	0	0	1.000	-	0	0
Calixte, O	KC	SS	1	0	4	2	0	0	0	1.000	4.50	0	0
Callaspo, A	TOT	2B	4	4	29	11	12	0	4	1.000	7.06	-1	-1
	TOT	3B	65	50	466	26	92	5	8	.959	2.28	0	-4
Campbell, E	NYM	1B	5	3	28	30	3	0	4	1.000	-	0	0
	NYM	3B	48	39	365	28	65	8	5	.921	2.30	-3	-3
	NYM	LF	4	3	39	8	1	0	0	1.000	2.06	+2	1
Canha, M	Oak	1B	75	57	538	491	47	4	58	.993	-	-3	-3
	Oak	3B	1	0	2	0	2	0	0	1.000	9.00	0	0
	Oak	LF	58	48	414	107	0	2	0	.982	2.33	+6	-1
	Oak	RF	3	1	9	0	0	0	0	-	.00	0	0
Carpenter, M	StL	1B	3	1	10	13	1	0	2	1.000	-	0	1
	StL	2B	11	9	59	12	19	0	4	1.000	4.76	-2	-1
Carrera, E	Tor	LF	46	19	230	46	1	2	0	.959	1.84	-5	-6
	Tor	CF	5	4	32	8	0	0	0	1.000	2.25	-3	-2
	Tor	RF	35	21	195	43	0	0	0	1.000	1.98	-3	-2
Castillo, R	Bos	LF	24	24	217	42	4	0	0	1.000	1.91	+4	9
	Bos	CF	6	4	41	15	0	1	0	.938	3.27	-3	-2
	Bos	RF	48	39	356	95	2	4	0	.960	2.45	+13	8
Castro, D	Atl	2B	12	12	99	23	39	0	13	1.000	5.64	+1	3
	Atl	3B	5	1	19	3	3	1	3	.857	2.84	-1	0
	Atl	SS	10	8	77	12	23	0	10	1.000	4.09	0	1
Castro, S	ChC	2B	38	29	258	47	85	6	20	.957	4.60	+2	2
Cecchini, G	Bos	1B	1	0	4	4	1	0	1	1.000	-	0	0
Ceciliani, D	NYM	LF	17	8	85	19	2	0	1	1.000	2.21	+3	4
	NYM	CF	7	5	44	17	0	0	0	1.000	3.48	+4	2
Cespedes, Y	TOT	CF	40	39	312	81	3	2	0	.977	2.42	-8	-4
Chisenhall, L	Cle	3B	50	45	406	30	101	5	12	.963	2.91	+7	7
	Cle	RF	51	40	354	87	5	1	2	.989	2.34	+15	11
Choice, M	Tex	RF	1	0	3	0	0	1	0	.000	.00	-1	-1
Ciriaco, P	Atl	1B	2	2	16	14	1	0	4	1.000	-	0	-1
	Atl	2B	7	5	46	13	15	0	7	1.000	5.48	+1	2
	Atl	3B	24	8	102	11	16	1	1	.964	2.39	+1	2
	Atl	SS	9	9	69	12	21	0	5	1.000	4.30	+1	1
	Atl	LF	1	0	2	1	0	0	0	1.000	4.50	0	0
Clevenger, S	Bal	1B	1	0	2	4	0	0	0	1.000	-	0	0
Coghlan, C	ChC	1B	5	0	13	19	0	0	3	1.000	-	0	0
	ChC	2B	15	11	79	14	20	1	1	.971	3.89	0	-1
	ChC	3B	3	1	10	1	0	0	0	1.000	.90	0	0
	ChC	RF	21	20	148	36	1	0	0	1.000	2.25	-1	0
Colabello, C	Tor	1B	34	29	240	248	11	1	24	.996	-	-5	-4
	Tor	LF	33	33	257	47	0	2	0	.959	1.65	-13	-9
	Tor	RF	13	13	108	23	0	1	0	.958	1.92	-8	-5
Coleman, D	KC	3B	2	1	9	1	2	0	0	1.000	3.00	0	0
Collins, T	Det	LF	37	35	311	61	3	3	1	.955	1.85	-3	-3
	Det	RF	7	5	48	12	0	1	0	.923	2.27	-3	-2
Colon, C	KC	2B	14	8	90	19	25	0	9	1.000	4.40	-1	-1
	KC	3B	8	6	50	10	13	2	2	.920	4.14	+2	1
	KC	SS	21	14	141	20	47	3	9	.957	4.27	+3	2
Conforto, M	NYM	LF	50	48	390	85	6	0	0	1.000	2.10	+7	9
Conger, H	Hou	LF	1	0	2	0	0	0	0	-	.00	0	0
Cowart, K	LAA	3B	33	13	150	10	40	2	4	.962	3.00	-1	0
Cowgill, C	LAA	LF	41	12	156	36	1	0	0	1.000	2.13	+5	5
	LAA	CF	4	1	13	5	0	0	0	1.000	3.46	0	0
	LAA	RF	4	4	31	11	1	0	0	1.000	3.48	+1	1
Cozart, Z	Cin	SS	52	52	450	79	132	3	30	.986	4.22	+11	7
Craig, A	Bos	1B	6	3	33	29	3	0	3	1.000	-	0	0
	Bos	LF	7	4	49	11	0	0	0	1.000	2.03	-1	0
	Bos	RF	9	5	54	15	0	0	0	1.000	2.48	-4	-1
Crawford, C	LAD	LF	51	42	347	38	0	0	0	1.000	.99	-4	-4
Crisp, C	Oak	LF	37	27	253	51	1	0	0	1.000	1.85	+4	1
Cron, C	LAA	1B	58	54	461	385	31	6	33	.986	-	-4	-5
Cruz, N	Sea	RF	80	80	704	151	6	4	1	.975	2.01	-5	-8
Cruz, T	StL	3B	3	0	6	0	2	0	0	1.000	3.00	-1	-1
Cuddyer, M	NYM	1B	18	15	141	116	11	0	11	1.000	-	-1	-1
	NYM	LF	69	66	556	96	3	3	0	.971	1.60	-8	-3
	NYM	RF	6	6	51	7	1	0	0	1.000	1.41	0	0
Cunningham, T	Atl	LF	22	16	152	31	0	0	0	1.000	1.84	+4	2
	Atl	CF	2	2	17	13	1	0	1	1.000	7.41	+7	4

Player	Tm	Pos	G	GS	Inn	PO	A	E	DP	Pct.	Rng	BSv	RS
	Atl	RF	4	1	15	3	0	0	0	1.000	1.80	0	0
Cuthbert, C	KC	1B	1	0	1	0	0	0	0	1.000	-	0	0
	KC	2B	1	0	2	1	0	0	0	1.000	4.50	0	0
	KC	3B	17	12	115	7	31	1	3	.974	2.97	+4	3
Danks, J	Phi	RF	1	0	0	0	0	0	0	-	.00	0	0
d'Arnaud,C	Phi	3B	1	1	9	2	7	0	2	1.000	9.00	+2	1
	Phi	SS	3	2	21	3	7	0	1	1.000	4.22	-1	-1
Davis, C	Bal	RF	30	29	253	39	2	0	0	1.000	1.46	-6	-3
Davis, I	Oak	1B	65	61	525	492	41	4	53	.993	-	+1	-1
Davis, R	Det	LF	39	25	245	53	1	1	0	.982	1.99	+4	1
	Det	CF	46	36	327	93	1	0	0	1.000	2.59	+6	6
	Det	RF	10	6	64	15	0	1	0	.938	2.11	-5	-4
De Aza, A	TOT	LF	69	51	483	104	3	2	0	.982	2.00	-7	-5
	TOT	CF	1	1	8	1	0	0	0	1.000	1.13	0	0
	TOT	RF	37	29	247	48	1	0	0	1.000	1.78	-1	1
De Jesus, I	Cin	1B	4	1	16	9	2	0	1	1.000	-	+1	1
	Cin	2B	20	13	133	25	50	0	9	1.000	5.06	-2	-2
	Cin	3B	13	6	70	6	15	0	0	1.000	2.70	-2	-2
	Cin	SS	10	8	80	15	24	3	6	.929	4.37	0	0
	Cin	LF	18	14	124	30	0	2	0	.938	2.18	-7	-6
Decker, C	SD	1B	3	1	10	5	2	0	1	1.000	-	+1	0
Decker, J	Pit	LF	4	3	29	3	0	1	0	.750	.93	-1	0
	Pit	CF	2	0	3	0	0	0	0	-	.00	-1	-1
	Pit	RF	3	1	20	5	1	1	0	.857	2.70	0	1
DeJesus, D	TOT	LF	63	53	464	97	3	1	0	.990	1.94	+3	3
	TOT	CF	2	1	9	2	0	0	0	1.000	2.00	0	0
	TOT	RF	4	1	13	2	0	0	0	1.000	1.35	0	0
den Dekker, M	Was	LF	27	15	156	25	0	1	0	.962	1.44	0	0
	Was	CF	2	0	9	1	0	0	0	1.000	1.00	0	0
	Was	RF	10	5	51	7	0	0	0	1.000	1.24	+1	2
Denorfia, C	ChC	LF	43	21	217	48	5	0	0	1.000	2.20	-4	-1
	ChC	CF	6	4	33	5	0	0	0	1.000	1.35	-2	-1
	ChC	RF	28	20	181	35	0	0	0	1.000	1.74	-1	-1
Descalso, D	Col	1B	7	2	25	29	1	0	1	1.000	-	0	0
	Col	2B	15	11	99	24	24	3	8	.941	4.35	-1	-1
	Col	3B	5	4	34	3	12	0	1	1.000	3.93	-3	-1
	Col	SS	33	22	217	36	80	5	16	.959	4.80	0	0
	Col	LF	1	0	0	0	0	0	0	-	.00	0	0
DeShields, D	Tex	2B	1	0	3	0	3	0	0	1.000	9.00	0	0
	Tex	LF	35	25	240	50	3	1	2	.981	1.98	+1	1
	Tex	CF	87	85	686	202	3	5	0	.976	2.69	-11	-10
Diaz, J	Tor	SS	6	4	34	5	9	0	1	1.000	3.71	0	0
	Tor	LF	2	0	6	4	0	0	0	1.000	6.00	0	0
Dickerson, A	SD	LF	1	0	3	1	0	0	0	1.000	3.00	0	0
Dickerson, C	Col	LF	54	53	414	82	1	0	0	1.000	1.80	-4	-6
	Col	CF	3	2	19	6	0	0	0	1.000	2.84	-3	-1
Dietrich, D	Mia	1B	2	2	25	1	1	0	0	1.000	-	0	0
	Mia	2B	2	1	8	2	0	0	0	1.000	2.25	0	0
	Mia	3B	26	24	195	6	35	4	4	.911	1.90	-3	-1
	Mia	LF	46	45	355	76	0	2	0	.974	1.93	-5	-8
Difo, W	Was	2B	2	1	10	3	0	0	0	1.000	3.00	0	0
Dominguez, C	Cin	1B	2	1	10	8	0	0	0	1.000	-	0	0
	Cin	LF	2	2	16	3	0	0	0	1.000	1.69	0	0
	Cin	RF	1	1	9	2	0	0	0	1.000	2.00	0	0
Dorn, D	Ari	1B	2	1	10	7	0	0	0	1.000	-	0	0
	Ari	RF	3	2	23	3	0	0	0	1.000	1.17	0	0
Drew, S	NYY	3B	4	1	13	1	2	0	0	1.000	2.08	0	0
	NYY	SS	15	10	89	12	34	2	10	.958	4.67	0	0
Drury, B	Ari	2B	4	3	38	11	9	1	3	.952	4.74	-2	-1
	Ari	3B	11	8	80	2	14	0	1	1.000	1.81	+1	1
	Ari	SS	1	1	6	1	2	0	0	1.000	4.50	0	0
Duffy, M	Hou	1B	2	0	2	2	0	0	0	1.000	-	0	0
	Hou	3B	2	0	8	1	6	0	0	1.000	7.88	0	0
Duffy, M	SF	1B	1	1	3	0	0	0	0	-	-	0	0
	SF	2B	9	7	65	13	17	1	5	.968	4.13	-2	-2
	SF	SS	3	1	15	0	4	1	1	.800	2.35	-1	-1
Duvall, A	Cin	1B	4	2	17	17	0	0	2	1.000	-	0	0
	Cin	LF	15	15	120	24	0	0	0	1.000	1.80	0	0
Dykstra, A	TB	1B	13	11	87	92	1	2	9	.979	-	-2	-3
Dyson, J	KC	LF	27	17	176	39	4	0	2	1.000	2.20	+4	3
	KC	CF	37	23	252	70	4	2	0	.974	2.65	+6	6
	KC	RF	17	15	133	36	0	0	0	1.000	2.44	+3	2

All Other Fielders

Player	Tm	Pos	G	GS	Inn	PO	A	E	DP	Pct.	Rng	BSv	RS
Elmore, J	TB	1B	25	22	190	178	7	3	13	.984	-	-1	-2
	TB	2B	7	5	45	7	9	0	1	1.000	3.20	+1	0
	TB	3B	9	6	59	6	7	2	3	.867	1.98	-2	-2
	TB	SS	7	4	46	6	13	0	3	1.000	3.74	+2	2
	TB	LF	6	3	28	5	0	0	0	1.000	1.61	+1	0
Encarnacion, E	Tor	1B	59	59	481	466	32	3	33	.994	-	-3	0
Escobar, E	Min	2B	11	4	48	8	14	0	2	1.000	4.13	+1	1
	Min	3B	5	5	41	3	6	1	1	.900	1.98	0	1
	Min	SS	71	71	627	92	191	4	44	.986	4.06	+2	2
	Min	LF	35	27	236	60	4	1	1	.985	2.44	-5	0
	Min	RF	1	0	0	0	0	0	0	-	.00	0	0
Espinosa, D	Was	1B	5	5	44	34	3	0	4	1.000	-	0	0
	Was	2B	81	74	647	136	240	1	47	.997	5.23	+10	10
	Was	3B	16	9	109	10	18	2	0	.933	2.30	-2	-2
	Was	SS	8	5	50	5	17	0	1	1.000	3.96	-3	-3
	Was	LF	5	2	23	5	0	0	0	1.000	1.93	0	0
Ethier, A	LAD	LF	51	38	333	54	3	2	1	.966	1.54	-4	0
	LAD	CF	1	0	1	0	0	0	0	-	.00	0	0
	LAD	RF	80	68	586	123	3	2	1	.984	1.94	+7	2
Featherston, T	LAA	2B	33	25	220	48	55	2	12	.981	4.21	+3	3
	LAA	3B	39	10	138	9	32	0	3	1.000	2.68	+4	5
	LAA	SS	22	7	94	21	34	4	4	.932	5.27	+2	1
Field, T	Tex	2B	14	12	104	23	41	3	4	.955	5.54	+1	-2
	Tex	SS	1	0	4	1	1	0	0	1.000	4.50	0	0
Fielder, P	Tex	1B	18	18	148	134	9	4	15	.973	-	-6	-5
Fields, D	Det	LF	1	0	7	2	0	1	0	.667	2.57	0	-1
Figueroa, C	NYY	3B	2	2	18	0	3	1	0	.750	1.50	0	0
Flaherty, R	Bal	1B	11	8	76	92	2	0	8	1.000	-	-1	-1
	Bal	2B	56	52	448	88	132	1	35	.995	4.42	-3	0
	Bal	3B	8	6	55	3	19	1	3	.957	3.60	-1	-1
	Bal	SS	15	9	79	17	17	0	6	1.000	3.87	-4	-1
	Bal	LF	1	1	8	1	0	0	0	1.000	1.13	-2	-1
	Bal	RF	5	5	38	6	0	0	0	1.000	1.42	-1	0
Flores, R	NYY	LF	11	8	77	17	2	0	0	1.000	2.22	-2	2
	NYY	RF	1	0	4	1	0	0	0	1.000	2.25	0	0
Flores, W	NYM	2B	37	30	292	61	92	0	22	1.000	4.71	-2	-1
Florimon, P	Pit	2B	3	0	4	2	1	0	1	1.000	6.75	0	0
	Pit	SS	17	4	64	10	20	2	2	.938	4.20	0	1
Flowers, T	CWS	1B	2	0	5	3	1	0	0	1.000	-	0	0
Forsythe, L	TB	1B	26	15	138	120	6	2	10	.984	-	-4	-2
	TB	3B	9	4	46	6	13	0	0	1.000	3.72	0	0
Franco, M	Phi	1B	2	2	16	13	1	0	1	1.000	-	0	0
	Phi	3B	75	75	664	49	119	10	11	.944	2.28	-11	-8
Francoeur, J	Phi	LF	20	10	106	19	0	2	0	.905	1.62	-10	-6
	Phi	RF	85	59	553	131	5	5	1	.965	2.21	-5	-5
Frandsen, K	SF	1B	4	3	26	24	2	0	0	1.000	-	+2	1
Franklin, N	TB	1B	10	5	55	46	4	2	7	.962	-	0	0
	TB	2B	17	12	120	16	36	1	7	.981	3.90	-2	-2
	TB	SS	11	5	59	7	13	2	2	.909	3.05	-2	-2
Fuld, S	Oak	LF	57	31	308	74	7	2	3	.976	2.37	+5	8
	Oak	CF	43	35	307	99	3	2	0	.981	2.99	+9	3
	Oak	RF	16	9	91	18	1	0	0	1.000	1.87	-1	-2
Gallo, J	Tex	3B	15	13	120	8	21	5	2	.853	2.17	0	0
	Tex	LF	19	14	121	20	1	0	0	1.000	1.57	+1	2
	Tex	CF	1	1	5	1	0	0	0	1.000	1.80	0	0
Galvis, F	Phi	2B	4	3	29	9	11	0	3	1.000	6.28	-1	-1
Garcia, A	Atl	3B	42	41	345	23	63	10	6	.896	2.24	-1	-3
	Atl	LF	10	7	56	9	1	0	0	1.000	1.61	+1	1
Garcia, G	StL	2B	10	6	59	15	15	3	6	.909	4.58	-2	-1
	StL	3B	4	1	8	2	1	0	0	1.000	3.38	0	0
	StL	SS	12	7	65	10	23	1	6	.971	4.57	+2	2
Garcia, L	CWS	2B	2	0	4	0	2	0	0	1.000	4.50	0	0
	CWS	SS	3	0	5	0	0	1	0	.000	.00	0	0
	CWS	LF	2	0	4	0	0	0	0	-	.00	0	0
	CWS	CF	4	1	18	4	0	0	0	1.000	2.00	0	0
Gardner, B	NYY	CF	40	36	322	87	1	2	0	.978	2.46	-1	0
Gattis, E	Hou	LF	11	11	71	5	0	1	0	.833	.63	-6	-4
Gentry, C	Oak	LF	13	4	49	9	0	0	0	1.000	1.65	0	0
	Oak	CF	8	7	52	20	1	0	0	.955	3.63	+4	1
	Oak	RF	6	5	38	6	1	1	1	.875	1.66	-2	-1
Giavotella, J	LAA	SS	1	0	1	0	0	0	0	-	.00	0	0
Gillaspie, C	TOT	1B	2	0	5	4	1	0	0	1.000	-	0	0
	TOT	2B	1	0	1	0	0	0	0	-	.00	0	0
	TOT	3B	69	67	524	34	98	14	5	.904	2.27	-18	-10
Gillespie, C	Mia	LF	10	2	27	9	0	3	0	.750	3.00	0	0
	Mia	CF	31	17	169	44	0	1	0	.978	2.34	+1	0
	Mia	RF	17	15	119	27	0	0	0	1.000	2.05	-2	-2
Goins, R	Tor	2B	66	62	537	117	165	3	42	.989	4.73	+1	4
	Tor	3B	2	0	4	0	1	0	0	1.000	2.25	0	0
	Tor	SS	58	48	445	86	143	4	32	.983	4.63	+8	8
	Tor	LF	2	2	17	2	0	1	0	.667	1.06	-1	-1
	Tor	RF	2	0	3	0	0	0	0	-	.00	0	0
Gomes, J	TOT	LF	59	48	411	62	4	0	0	1.000	1.45	-10	-5
	TOT	RF	8	6	42	5	0	0	0	1.000	1.07	-2	-2
Gomez, C	TOT	2B	1	0	1	0	0	0	0	-	.00	0	0
Gomez, H	Mil	2B	27	18	163	31	54	1	16	.988	4.69	-1	2
	Mil	3B	12	4	47	5	8	1	0	.929	2.49	-1	-1
	Mil	SS	8	6	57	10	17	2	5	.931	4.26	-1	-1
Gonzalez, M	Hou	1B	43	20	213	203	14	1	14	.995	-	+1	1
	Hou	2B	15	9	103	17	38	1	7	.982	4.81	-1	0
	Hou	3B	21	16	134	7	22	2	1	.935	1.94	-1	0
	Hou	SS	32	29	251	34	81	3	15	.975	4.12	-2	0
	Hou	LF	15	12	97	21	1	0	0	.957	2.03	+2	2
Gore, T	KC	LF	4	0	10	0	0	0	0	-	.00	-1	-1
Gosselin, P	TOT	2B	16	15	116	21	33	2	7	.964	4.19	-4	-3
	TOT	3B	7	6	45	2	11	1	1	.929	2.60	+2	0
	TOT	LF	3	1	18	3	0	0	0	1.000	1.50	+1	-1
Grandal, Y	LAD	1B	6	2	27	26	1	0	6	1.000	-	0	-1
Granderson, C	NYM	CF	2	2	16	8	0	0	0	1.000	4.50	0	-1
Green, G	LAA	1B	5	2	25	22	0	0	1	1.000	-	0	0
	LAA	2B	11	10	76	14	19	1	4	.971	3.91	-3	-2
	LAA	SS	1	1	6	1	1	0	0	1.000	1.50	-1	0
	LAA	LF	1	0	1	1	0	0	0	1.000	9.00	0	0
Grichuk, R	StL	LF	49	37	344	60	1	2	0	.968	1.59	+14	4
	StL	CF	37	34	282	71	1	0	1	1.000	2.30	+7	5
	StL	RF	13	10	93	20	0	1	0	.952	1.93	0	-2
Grossman, R	Hou	LF	17	14	120	17	0	0	0	1.000	1.28	-3	-1
	Hou	RF	4	0	7	1	0	0	0	1.000	1.29	0	0
Guerrero, A	LAD	3B	22	18	150	10	34	1	3	.978	2.65	0	-1
	LAD	LF	29	27	206	29	1	2	0	.938	1.31	-4	-3
Gurka, J	Col	RF	1	0	1	0	0	0	0	-	.00	0	0
Gutierrez, F	Sea	LF	42	36	301	66	3	1	1	.986	2.06	+3	3
	Sea	RF	4	0	8	1	0	0	0	1.000	1.13	0	0
Guyer, B	TB	LF	60	39	358	93	2	0	1	1.000	2.39	+3	1
	TB	CF	23	17	140	35	0	1	0	.972	2.25	+3	1
	TB	RF	41	20	226	44	0	0	0	1.000	1.75	+1	-1
Gyorko, J	SD	1B	1	0	1	2	0	0	0	1.000	-	0	0
	SD	2B	93	76	714	117	230	2	46	.994	4.38	-2	-2
	SD	SS	29	28	221	37	58	1	15	.990	3.87	-6	-4
Hague, M	Tor	1B	3	2	17	17	1	0	0	1.000	-	-2	-1
	Tor	3B	3	0	1	0	0	0	0	1.000	3.00	0	0
Hamilton, J	Tex	LF	35	33	281	50	2	0	0	1.000	1.66	+1	1
	Tex	RF	11	7	64	20	0	0	0	1.000	2.83	-2	-1
Harper, B	Was	CF	13	12	100	28	1	0	0	1.000	2.60	+3	3
Harrison, J	Pit	2B	37	34	227	45	69	2	21	.983	4.53	+2	2
	Pit	3B	72	57	526	41	136	9	20	.952	3.03	-2	0
	Pit	LF	10	7	60	13	1	1	0	.933	2.10	-3	-1
	Pit	RF	12	8	82	13	0	2	0	.867	1.43	+2	0
Hart, C	Pit	1B	8	7	48	39	1	3	2	.930	-	-1	-2
	Pit	RF	3	2	22	10	0	0	0	1.000	4.09	+2	1
Headley, C	NYY	1B	1	0	1	0	0	0	0	-	-	-1	-1
Heathcott, S	NYY	CF	8	4	44	16	0	0	0	1.000	3.27	+3	1
	NYY	RF	9	2	27	4	0	0	0	1.000	1.33	-2	-1
Heisey, C	LAD	LF	12	3	38	8	0	0	0	1.000	1.89	+1	1
	LAD	CF	10	7	63	6	1	0	0	1.000	1.00	-2	0
	LAD	RF	12	7	62	13	0	0	0	1.000	1.88	+1	0
Hernandez, C	Phi	2B	88	75	678	132	234	6	47	.984	4.86	-8	-5
	Phi	3B	10	9	77	8	20	2	1	.933	3.27	+2	1
	Phi	SS	12	9	86	12	26	1	4	.974	3.96	-1	-3
Hernandez, G	Pit	LF	4	0	7	1	0	0	0	1.000	1.29	0	0
	Pit	RF	2	1	10	0	0	0	0	-	.00	0	0
Hernandez, K	LAD	2B	20	15	133	36	47	0	11	1.000	5.60	-2	-4
	LAD	3B	1	1	8	0	0	0	0	-	.00	-1	-1

All Other Fielders

Player	Tm	Pos	G	GS	Inn	PO	A	E	DP	Pct.	Rng	BSv	RS
	LAD	SS	16	11	106	11	34	2	2	.957	3.81	+3	2
	LAD	LF	17	5	66	12	2	1	0	.933	1.92	-5	1
	LAD	CF	19	18	149	32	0	0	0	1.000	1.94	-1	0
	LAD	RF	2	1	10	1	0	0	0	1.000	.90	0	0
Herrera, D	NYM	2B	29	27	243	53	85	2	19	.986	5.10	-2	-2
Herrera, E	Mil	2B	36	30	254	52	99	3	14	.981	5.34	-3	-2
	Mil	3B	47	32	317	26	72	6	8	.942	2.78	-1	1
	Mil	LF	1	0	3	3	0	0	0	1.000	10.13	0	0
	Mil	RF	3	0	6	1	0	0	0	1.000	1.50	0	0
Herrera, J	ChC	2B	29	16	174	39	46	2	11	.977	4.40	-2	-2
	ChC	3B	16	9	88	6	18	1	0	.960	2.45	+2	0
	ChC	SS	1	0	2	0	0	0	0	-	.00	0	0
Herrmann, C	Min	1B	2	0	4	3	1	0	2	1.000	-	0	0
	Min	RF	2	0	2	0	0	0	0	-	.00	0	0
Heyward, J	StL	CF	10	8	51	12	1	0	1	1.000	2.29	+3	2
Hicks, A	Min	LF	4	4	33	9	0	0	0	1.000	2.45	-2	0
	Min	RF	16	4	54	12	1	0	0	1.000	2.15	-1	-1
Hicks, J	Sea	3B	1	0	2	1	0	0	0	1.000	4.50	0	0
Hill, A	Ari	2B	47	38	342	57	118	2	21	.989	4.60	+3	1
	Ari	3B	38	33	292	23	57	4	8	.952	2.47	-5	-4
Hoes, L	Hou	LF	3	1	11	0	0	0	0	-	.00	0	0
	Hou	RF	5	3	26	6	0	0	0	1.000	2.08	+3	2
Holaday, B	Det	1B	1	0	1	1	0	0	1	1.000	-	-1	-1
	Det	2B	1	0	1	0	0	0	0	-	.00	0	0
Holliday, M	StL	LF	64	64	495	85	0	0	0	1.000	1.54	+2	-4
Holt, B	Bos	1B	8	5	49	46	3	0	6	1.000	-	0	0
	Bos	2B	58	49	431	67	137	4	32	.981	4.26	+5	2
	Bos	3B	33	24	227	16	47	3	2	.955	2.50	-4	-4
	Bos	SS	11	7	70	11	28	2	7	.951	5.01	-2	-1
	Bos	LF	14	8	71	18	1	0	0	1.000	2.42	+2	2
	Bos	CF	2	2	18	5	0	0	0	1.000	2.50	+1	0
	Bos	RF	21	20	165	44	0	0	0	1.000	2.40	+8	2
Holt, T	TOT	LF	3	1	15	3	0	0	0	1.000	1.80	+1	1
	TOT	CF	9	6	56	22	0	0	0	1.000	3.54	0	-1
	TOT	RF	2	1	10	1	0	0	0	1.000	.90	0	0
Hosmer, E	KC	RF	1	0	3	0	0	0	0	-	.00	-1	-1
Iannetta, C	LAA	1B	2	0	5	5	0	0	0	1.000	-	0	0
Inciarte, E	Ari	LF	47	42	372	97	4	2	1	.981	2.44	+17	12
	Ari	CF	22	18	152	44	2	1	0	.979	2.72	+2	4
	Ari	RF	77	56	539	113	4	3	1	.975	1.95	+15	13
Ishikawa, T	TOT	1B	12	5	62	68	7	1	9	.987	-	+1	-1
	TOT	LF	6	5	29	2	0	0	0	1.000	.62	-1	-1
Jackson, A	TOT	LF	4	2	20	2	0	0	0	1.000	.90	-1	0
	TOT	RF	22	6	90	21	1	1	1	.957	2.21	-1	0
Jackson, R	LAA	2B	17	3	47	5	12	1	1	.944	3.26	-1	-1
	LAA	3B	2	1	12	1	2	0	0	1.000	2.31	0	0
	LAA	SS	3	0	4	0	1	0	0	1.000	2.25	-1	-1
Janish, P	Bal	2B	1	0	8	2	5	0	2	1.000	7.88	+1	0
	Bal	SS	13	9	84	16	31	0	7	1.000	5.06	-1	0
Jankowski, T	SD	CF	23	21	163	35	0	1	0	.972	1.93	+4	-1
	SD	RF	11	6	71	14	1	0	0	1.000	1.91	0	0
Jaso, J	TB	LF	7	7	47	2	1	0	0	1.000	.57	0	-1
	TB	RF	1	0	2	0	0	0	0	-	.00	0	0
Jay, J	StL	LF	17	3	58	12	0	0	0	1.000	1.87	+2	1
	StL	CF	54	49	407	116	1	0	2	1.000	2.59	-1	1
	StL	RF	7	1	32	9	1	0	0	1.000	2.84	+1	1
Jennings, D	TB	LF	21	19	164	35	3	0	0	1.000	2.09	0	2
	TB	CF	10	7	61	15	0	0	0	1.000	2.21	+1	0
Jimenez, L	TOT	2B	1	0	4	0	1	0	0	1.000	4.50	0	0
	TOT	3B	7	2	25	2	4	1	1	.857	2.16	0	0
Johnson, C	TOT	1B	30	24	213	182	14	1	28	.995	-	-1	-1
	TOT	3B	27	24	195	9	33	3	4	.933	1.94	-4	-2
Johnson, D	StL	1B	6	4	37	34	4	0	0	1.000	-	-1	0
Johnson, K	TOT	1B	25	17	163	134	20	3	25	.981	-	-4	-2
	TOT	2B	28	22	204	33	61	2	9	.979	4.15	-1	-1
	TOT	3B	12	7	61	4	10	3	0	.824	2.05	-4	-2
	TOT	SS	1	1	9	2	2	1	1	.800	4.00	-1	-1
	TOT	LF	29	25	192	46	2	2	0	.960	2.25	+2	0
	TOT	RF	8	4	36	4	0	0	0	1.000	.99	-3	-1
Johnson, M	CWS	2B	33	32	280	58	76	3	14	.978	4.31	-6	-7
Johnson, R	Was	LF	3	1	14	2	0	0	0	1.000	1.26	-2	-1
	Was	RF	1	1	8	3	0	0	0	1.000	3.38	0	0
Jones, G	NYY	1B	21	10	101	103	12	0	10	1.000	-	-2	-1
	NYY	LF	4	1	16	4	0	0	0	1.000	2.20	+1	0
	NYY	RF	24	17	148	30	0	0	0	1.000	1.82	-2	-2
Jones, J	Sea	LF	2	0	4	1	0	0	0	1.000	2.25	0	0
	Sea	CF	20	6	82	18	0	0	0	1.000	1.97	-9	-5
	Sea	RF	6	0	12	2	0	0	0	1.000	1.50	0	0
Joseph, C	Bal	1B	1	0	2	2	0	0	1	1.000	-	0	0
Joyce, M	LAA	LF	64	58	468	95	2	1	0	.990	1.87	-3	-3
	LAA	RF	2	0	2	0	0	0	0	-	.00	0	0
Kang, J	Pit	3B	77	54	535	30	139	5	11	.971	2.84	+6	4
	Pit	SS	60	49	426	74	146	9	40	.961	4.65	0	0
Kawasaki, M	Tor	2B	17	8	78	9	29	0	6	1.000	4.38	+1	2
	Tor	SS	3	2	18	1	4	0	0	1.000	2.50	0	0
Kelly, D	Mia	1B	1	0	1	0	0	0	0	-	-	0	0
	Mia	3B	1	1	2	0	2	0	0	1.000	7.71	0	0
Kepler, M	Min	RF	2	1	10	3	0	0	0	1.000	2.70	0	0
Kiermaier, K	TB	RF	2	2	14	2	0	0	0	1.000	1.29	0	0
Kozma, P	StL	1B	1	0	1	0	0	0	0	-	-	0	0
	StL	2B	17	7	65	15	24	1	5	.975	5.37	+1	0
	StL	3B	13	3	63	6	19	1	0	.962	3.55	-1	-1
	StL	SS	31	8	112	18	42	2	6	.968	4.82	+3	2
	StL	LF	1	0	7	1	0	0	0	1.000	1.29	-2	-1
Kratz, E	TOT	1B	2	2	14	15	0	0	2	1.000	-	-1	0
Krauss, M	TOT	1B	20	16	143	110	11	1	13	.992	-	-3	-1
	TOT	LF	1	0	1	1	0	0	0	1.000	9.00	0	0
Kubitza, K	LAA	2B	2	0	2	0	0	0	0	-	.00	0	0
	LAA	3B	13	9	85	4	14	2	1	.900	1.91	+1	0
	LAA	LF	2	1	7	0	0	0	0	-	.00	-3	-1
La Stella, T	ChC	2B	14	11	88	12	33	0	4	1.000	4.60	+3	2
	ChC	3B	12	6	52	3	3	1	0	.857	1.04	-2	-1
Ladendorf, T	Oak	2B	2	2	18	2	5	0	1	1.000	3.50	0	0
	Oak	3B	1	0	2	1	0	0	0	1.000	4.50	0	0
	Oak	SS	1	0	2	1	0	0	0	1.000	4.50	0	0
	Oak	LF	1	3	9	4	0	0	0	1.000	4.00	-1	0
	Oak	CF	2	1	9	2	0	0	0	1.000	2.00	0	0
Lagares, J	NYM	RF	2	0	5	4	0	0	0	1.000	7.71	0	0
Lake, J	TOT	LF	10	7	70	8	1	1	0	.900	1.15	-3	-2
	TOT	CF	3	1	6	0	0	0	0	1.000	.00	-1	-1
	TOT	RF	10	8	73	16	1	1	0	.944	2.10	-5	-2
LaMarre, R	Cin	LF	2	0	3	0	0	0	0	-	.00	0	0
	Cin	CF	13	5	57	16	1	1	0	.944	2.68	+1	0
	Cin	RF	2	0	2	0	0	0	0	-	.00	0	0
Lamb, J	Ari	1B	8	2	29	27	2	0	2	1.000	-	0	0
Lambo, A	Pit	LF	3	1	11	2	0	0	0	1.000	1.69	+1	1
	Pit	RF	5	2	20	1	1	0	0	1.000	.89	-2	-1
LaRoche, A	CWS	1B	48	44	393	351	27	1	43	.997	-	-2	-1
Lavarnway, R	TOT	1B	1	1	9								
Lawrie, B	Oak	2B	42	40	361	92	114	6	28	.972	5.14	-2	-3
Leon, S	Bos	3B	1	0	1	0	0	0	0	-	.00	0	0
Lollis, R	SF	LF	3	2	18	2	0	0	0	1.000	.98	+2	1
	SF	RF	1	1	8	2	0	0	0	1.000	2.25	0	0
Lough, D	Bal	LF	49	21	238	49	2	0	0	1.000	1.93	+11	7
	Bal	CF	26	13	136	28	0	0	0	1.000	1.85	0	0
	Bal	RF	2	0	3	1	0	0	0	1.000	3.00	0	0
Lowrie, J	Hou	3B	47	45	381	25	60	3	1	.966	2.01	+1	0
	Hou	SS	17	16	153	21	53	0	6	1.000	4.35	-4	-4
Lucroy, J	Mil	1B	7	5	43	46	1	0	6	1.000	-	-1	-1
Machado, D	Det	SS	24	20	180	37	56	2	14	.979	4.66	+1	0
Machado, M	Bal	3B	7	6	53	4	15	2	3	.905	3.23	0	-1
Mahtook, M	TB	LF	16	5	69	21	0	0	0	1.000	2.74	-1	-1
	TB	CF	13	9	78	22	0	0	0	1.000	2.55	-1	-1
	TB	RF	12	10	79	20	1	1	1	.955	2.39	0	1
Maldonado, M	Mil	1B	1	3	2	0	0	0	0	1.000	-	0	0
Marisnick, J	Hou	LF	16	9	81	27	0	0	0	1.000	3.01	+5	4
	Hou	RF	13	8	85	16	0	0	0	1.000	1.69	+4	4
Marrero, D	Bos	2B	3	1	20	1	5	0	2	1.000	2.70	0	0
	Bos	3B	13	10	99	3	18	1	4	.955	1.91	-3	0
	Bos	SS	6	1	17	3	6	0	2	1.000	4.76	-1	-1
Marte, A	LAA	LF	2	1	10	2	0	0	0	1.000	1.80	+1	1
	LAA	RF	1	0	3	0	0	0	0	-	.00	0	0
Marte, J	Det	1B	22	15	122	106	11	3	9	.975	-	-2	-1
	Det	3B	7	4	53	2	15	1	3	.944	2.91	0	-1

All Other Fielders

Player	Tm	Pos	G	GS	Inn	PO	A	E	DP	Pct.	Rng	BSv	RS
Marte, K	Sea	2B	4	3	32	1	10	0	2	1.000	3.13	+2	1
	Sea	SS	51	49	440	64	150	9	31	.960	4.37	+4	2
	Sea	CF	2	2	14	3	0	0	0	1.000	1.93	-2	-1
Marte, S	Pit	CF	18	10	103	25	1	1	1	.963	2.27	-1	0
Martin, L	Tex	CF	92	71	673	218	13	1	0	.996	3.09	+10	15
Martin, R	Tor	2B	2	0	3	0	1	0	0	1.000	3.00	+1	1
Martinez, M	Cle	3B	1	0	1	0	0	0	0	1.000	9.00	0	0
	Cle	LF	9	5	53	16	0	0	0	1.000	2.72	-1	0
	Cle	CF	2	2	17	5	0	0	0	1.000	2.65	-1	0
	Cle	RF	1	0	1	0	0	0	0	-	.00	0	0
Martinez, V	Det	1B	10	10	86	81	5	1	13	.989	-	-2	-1
Maxwell, J	SF	LF	19	12	114	23	0	0	0	1.000	1.81	+1	0
	SF	CF	3	1	11	2	0	1	0	.667	1.64	+1	0
	SF	RF	58	47	429	105	3	1	1	.991	2.27	+9	6
Mayberry, J	NYM	LF	19	13	113	32	1	0	1	1.000	2.63	+4	1
	NYM	RF	11	10	80	25	0	0	0	1.000	2.81	+2	0
McBride, M	Col	1B	4	4	33	33	2	0	3	1.000	-	0	0
	Col	LF	3	3	20	4	0	0	0	1.000	1.80	0	0
	Col	RF	2	1	10	0	0	0	0	-	.00	0	0
McCann, B	NYY	1B	10	0	16	12	0	0	0	1.000	-	0	0
McGehee, C	TOT	1B	21	12	109	109	5	1	12	.991	-	0	0
	TOT	3B	42	38	330	21	65	6	6	.935	2.35	+3	1
Middlebrooks, W	SD	1B	2	1	8	10	0	0	0	1.000	-	0	0
	SD	3B	69	60	531	53	93	7	13	.954	2.47	-5	-6
	SD	SS	8	4	39	5	11	0	3	1.000	3.69	0	-1
Miller, B	Sea	2B	11	5	55	13	22	1	5	.972	5.73	+1	-1
	Sea	3B	2	1	9	0	1	1	0	.500	1.00	-1	-1
	Sea	LF	15	9	85	13	1	0	0	1.000	1.48	-3	-2
	Sea	CF	20	20	146	35	0	1	0	.972	2.16	-16	-10
	Sea	RF	6	1	22	5	0	0	0	1.000	2.05	-3	-2
Montero, J	Sea	1B	27	25	189	181	5	1	18	.995	-	-3	-2
Moore, T	Was	1B	39	23	232	216	10	0	22	1.000	-	-4	-4
	Was	LF	20	13	123	18	0	0	0	1.000	1.32	-3	-2
	Was	RF	1	0	1	0	0	0	0	-	.00	0	0
Morales, K	KC	1B	9	9	75	62	3	0	3	1.000	-	-3	-2
Morel, B	Pit	3B	2	2	14	1	3	0	1	1.000	2.57	0	0
Morneau, J	Col	1B	44	42	361	357	32	1	54	.997	-	-2	-2
Morrison, L	Sea	LF	1	1	8	0	0	0	0	-	.00	-2	-1
	Sea	RF	3	1	13	5	0	0	0	1.000	3.46	+2	1
Morse, M	TOT	1B	58	50	420	429	18	0	41	1.000	-	-3	-1
	TOT	LF	6	6	35	6	1	0	0	1.000	1.80	+1	1
Moss, B	TOT	1B	42	33	302	250	25	0	22	1.000	-	0	0
	TOT	LF	10	9	64	12	0	0	0	1.000	1.68	+3	0
	TOT	RF	82	79	689	151	6	4	1	.975	2.05	0	-2
Moya, S	Det	LF	2	2	16	8	1	0	0	1.000	5.06	+2	2
	Det	RF	5	3	29	4	1	0	1	1.000	1.55	-3	-1
Muncy, M	Oak	1B	23	17	145	137	10	2	9	.987	-	-1	0
	Oak	3B	16	10	90	5	17	4	0	.846	2.20	-1	-1
Muno, D	NYM	2B	1	1	8	0	3	0	0	1.000	3.38	+1	0
	NYM	3B	5	3	30	1	5	3	1	.667	1.80	-1	-1
Murphy, D	NYM	1B	17	14	133	117	14	1	12	.992	-	-4	-6
	NYM	2B	69	65	572	118	166	6	32	.979	4.47	-5	-6
	NYM	3B	42	41	352	16	71	6	5	.935	2.22	-3	-1
Murphy, D	TOT	LF	53	46	375	74	0	0	0	1.000	1.77	-4	-6
	TOT	RF	17	10	101	18	0	0	0	1.000	1.60	0	2
Myers, W	SD	1B	22	19	165	158	10	0	17	1.000	-	0	0
	SD	LF	4	3	28	5	0	0	0	1.000	1.63	+3	1
	SD	CF	38	33	299	67	1	0	0	1.000	2.05	-11	-7
	SD	RF	2	1	2	0	0	0	0	-	.00	0	0
Napoli, M	TOT	LF	11	11	50	2	1	2	0	.600	.54	-3	-2
Nava, D	TOT	1B	13	8	81	75	3	1	7	.987	-	+1	0
	TOT	LF	12	2	39	12	0	0	0	1.000	2.77	+3	2
	TOT	RF	34	26	225	48	3	0	1	1.000	2.04	0	2
Navarro, E	LAA	1B	29	8	107	113	5	0	7	1.000	-	+4	4
	LAA	LF	15	11	86	20	1	0	0	1.000	2.20	+2	2
	LAA	RF	3	0	6	2	0	0	0	1.000	3.00	0	0
Navarro, R	Bal	2B	9	7	68	16	19	1	6	.972	4.63	-3	-2
Negron, K	Cin	2B	1	1	8	12	16	2	0	1.000	-	0	0
	Cin	2B	6	4	38	3	13	0	4	1.000	3.76	+3	3
	Cin	3B	2	1	11	0	0	1	0	.000	.00	-2	-1
	Cin	SS	10	7	81	11	31	1	7	.977	4.67	0	-1
	Cin	LF	10	2	35	10	0	0	0	1.000	2.60	0	0
	Cin	CF	5	3	25	7	0	0	0	1.000	2.49	+1	2
	Cin	RF	2	1	9	3	0	1	0	.750	3.00	0	0
Nieuwenhuis, K	TOT	LF	34	14	151	41	0	0	0	1.000	2.44	+3	2
	TOT	CF	16	11	103	28	2	0	1	1.000	2.61	+6	3
	TOT	RF	7	2	24	8	0	0	0	1.000	3.00	+1	1
Nieves, W	SD	1B	2	0	2	3	0	0	1	1.000	-	0	0
Noel, R	NYY	RF	2	0	2	1	0	0	0	1.000	4.50	0	0
Noonan, N	SF	1B	3	2	19	24	1	0	2	1.000	-	0	0
	SF	SS	5	3	27	4	6	1	1	.909	3.33	-1	-1
Norris, D	SD	1B	17	15	108	108	1	2	8	.982	-	-2	-3
Nunez, E	Min	2B	1	1	9	3	0	0	0	1.000	3.00	0	0
	Min	3B	16	9	98	7	15	2	0	.917	2.02	+1	1
	Min	SS	27	23	209	32	71	0	10	1.000	4.43	+5	3
	Min	LF	3	2	14	4	1	1	0	.833	3.21	0	1
O'Brien, P	Ari	LF	3	1	16	1	0	0	0	1.000	.56	-1	-1
Olivera, H	Atl	3B	21	21	168	15	23	4	2	.905	2.04	-2	-1
Olt, M	TOT	1B	5	3	32	21	2	2	1	.920	-	0	0
	TOT	3B	26	23	191	19	26	4	1	.918	2.12	-4	-4
O'Malley, S	Sea	3B	3	0	6	1	1	0	0	1.000	3.00	-1	-1
	Sea	LF	4	1	11	1	0	0	0	1.000	.82	0	0
	Sea	CF	14	10	90	22	0	0	0	1.000	2.20	-1	0
	Sea	RF	3	1	13	1	0	0	0	1.000	.69	0	0
Orlando, P	KC	LF	37	27	252	53	3	2	1	.966	2.00	+2	3
	KC	CF	5	3	27	11	1	0	0	1.000	4.00	0	1
	KC	RF	45	33	325	65	1	2	0	.971	1.83	+12	4
Ortiz, D	Bos	1B	9	9	60	51	5	1	2	.982	-	0	-1
Owings, C	Ari	SS	35	29	261	37	62	1	10	.990	3.41	-3	-4
Ozuna, M	Mia	RF	15	15	123	35	0	0	0	1.000	2.57	+2	0
Pacheco, J	Ari	1B	2	0	7	5	0	0	0	1.000	-	0	0
	Ari	3B	1	0	1	0	0	0	0	-	.00	0	0
Paredes, J	Bal	2B	6	6	52	11	17	0	2	1.000	4.88	-1	-1
	Bal	3B	8	0	12	1	3	3	0	.571	3.00	-3	-3
	Bal	LF	1	0	1	1	0	0	0	1.000	9.00	0	0
	Bal	RF	2	1	8	1	0	0	0	1.000	1.13	-2	-1
Parker, J	SF	LF	5	3	33	6	0	0	0	1.000	1.64	-4	-2
	SF	CF	4	2	25	8	0	0	0	1.000	2.88	+1	1
	SF	RF	9	7	57	5	0	0	0	1.000	.79	-1	-2
Parker, K	Col	1B	2	2	12	10	2	0	0	1.000	-	+1	0
	Col	LF	28	23	189	30	0	1	0	.968	1.43	-3	-2
	Col	RF	5	2	20	5	0	0	0	1.000	2.25	0	0
Parmelee, C	Bal	1B	25	19	173	176	12	0	17	1.000	-	+2	0
	Bal	RF	8	7	55	16	1	1	1	.944	2.78	-1	0
Parra, G	TOT	LF	43	43	396	83	1	0	0	1.000	1.91	+1	-2
	TOT	CF	41	31	289	72	5	2	0	.975	2.40	-5	-1
	TOT	RF	63	52	479	99	3	0	0	1.000	1.92	-15	-7
Parrino, A	Oak	3B	6	0	10	0	1	0	1	1.000	.90	0	0
	Oak	SS	10	1	19	2	4	0	1	1.000	2.84	0	0
Paulsen, B	Col	1B	91	66	617	660	48	3	63	.996	-	-2	0
	Col	LF	19	13	103	19	0	0	0	1.000	1.67	+4	3
	Col	RF	1	0	1	0	0	0	0	-	.00	0	0
Pearce, S	Bal	1B	28	25	212	184	18	1	15	.995	-	-3	-2
	Bal	2B	18	13	122	25	35	0	7	1.000	4.44	-2	-2
	Bal	LF	41	34	306	64	3	1	0	.985	1.97	-9	-3
	Bal	RF	8	6	56	8	1	1	0	.900	1.45	0	0
Peguero, C	TOT	LF	25	15	148	32	0	0	0	1.000	1.94	+1	0
	TOT	CF	1	0	2	1	0	0	0	1.000	4.50	+1	0
	TOT	RF	9	3	34	8	1	0	0	1.000	2.38	-1	1
Pena, B	Cin	1B	5	0	13	22	1	0	1	1.000	-	-1	0
Pence, H	SF	RF	51	50	441	122	4	3	2	.977	2.57	+1	0
Pennington, C	TOT	2B	33	25	237	38	81	3	14	.975	4.53	+2	1
	TOT	3B	18	2	42	2	11	1	0	.929	2.76	-1	1
	TOT	SS	29	16	166	18	61	5	14	.940	4.29	+1	1
	TOT	LF	8	5	45	11	1	0	0	1.000	2.40	+1	3
Peralta, D	Ari	1B	1	1	7	2	0	0	0	1.000	2.57	0	0
	Ari	RF	9	5	53	14	0	0	0	1.000	2.38	+1	0
Peraza, J	LAD	2B	6	6	47	5	20	2	5	.926	4.79	-2	-2
	LAD	CF	1	0	5	2	0	0	0	1.000	3.60	0	0
Perez, C	LAA	1B	2	0	4	4	1	0	0	1.000	-	-1	-1
Perez, E	Atl	LF	29	24	226	50	2	0	0	1.000	2.07	+4	2
	Atl	CF	3	3	25	3	0	1	0	.750	1.08	-3	-3
	Atl	RF	6	3	28	8	1	0	0	1.000	2.89	-1	1
Perez, H	TOT	1B	7	1	19	15	2	0	1	1.000	-	0	0

All Other Fielders

Player	Tm	Pos	G	GS	Inn	PO	A	E	DP	Pct.	Rng	BSv	RS
	TOT	2B	19	13	108	26	33	1	5	.983	4.90	-4	-3
	TOT	3B	80	49	452	34	94	4	9	.970	2.55	+5	4
	TOT	SS	6	3	29	2	2	0	0	1.000	1.24	0	0
Perez, J	SF	2B	1	0	2	0	0	0	0	-	.00	0	0
	SF	LF	8	5	42	9	0	0	0	1.000	1.91	-1	-1
	SF	CF	5	3	28	4	1	0	0	1.000	1.61	+2	3
Perez, S	KC	1B	1	0	3	2	0	0	1	1.000	-	0	0
Peterson, S	Mil	1B	2	1	15	16	1	1	1	.944	-	0	0
	Mil	LF	33	17	175	44	3	1	0	.979	2.42	+7	6
	Mil	CF	20	20	160	44	1	2	1	.957	2.54	0	-2
	Mil	RF	9	6	58	6	0	0	0	1.000	.93	0	0
Petit, G	NYY	2B	13	11	93	24	27	1	10	.981	4.94	-1	-1
	NYY	3B	3	2	18	1	4	1	0	.833	2.50	+1	0
Pham, T	StL	LF	5	8	75	10	0	0	0	1.000	1.21	-4	-2
	StL	CF	33	29	243	52	2	0	1	1.000	2.00	+7	5
	StL	RF	3	1	11	1	0	0	0	1.000	.82	0	0
Phillips, B	Cin	SS	1	0	1	0	0	0	0	-	.00	0	0
Pillar, K	Tor	LF	14	13	120	32	3	0	1	1.000	2.63	+4	8
	Tor	RF	3	3	26	4	0	0	0	1.000	1.38	0	0
Pirela, J	NYY	2B	27	19	157	36	44	4	12	.952	4.60	-2	-3
	NYY	LF	2	1	10	1	1	0	0	1.000	1.80	-1	0
	NYY	RF	1	1	8	1	0	0	0	1.000	1.13	0	0
Piscotty, S	StL	1B	11	9	57	62	1	0	6	1.000	-	-2	-1
	StL	LF	55	40	385	54	1	2	1	.965	1.28	-4	-4
	StL	CF	1	1	5	1	0	0	0	1.000	1.80	0	0
	StL	RF	15	11	90	18	0	0	0	1.000	1.79	+2	0
Plouffe, T	Min	1B	17	13	118	122	11	1	7	.993	-	+4	4
Polanco, G	Pit	LF	8	3	52	13	0	0	0	1.000	2.25	+1	1
	Pit	CF	2	1	8	0	0	0	0	-	.00	-1	0
Polanco, J	Min	SS	4	3	28	3	12	2	2	.882	4.82	+1	0
Pompey, D	Tor	LF	6	6	49	12	1	1	0	.929	2.37	0	1
	Tor	CF	21	18	167	46	2	1	0	.980	2.59	+6	5
Posey, B	SF	1B	42	37	324	334	19	0	35	1.000	-	+3	4
Prado, M	Mia	2B	11	9	71	13	20	0	4	1.000	4.18	+2	1
Presley, A	Hou	LF	4	2	16	4	0	0	0	1.000	2.25	0	0
	Hou	CF	1	1	10	3	0	0	0	1.000	2.70	0	0
	Hou	RF	1	1	8	1	0	0	0	1.000	1.13	-2	-1
Pridie, J	Oak	LF	1	0	1	0	0	0	0	-	.00	0	0
	Oak	CF	1	1	9	1	0	0	0	1.000	1.00	0	0
	Oak	RF	2	0	9	0	0	0	0	-	.00	-1	0
Puig, Y	LAD	RF	78	71	638	132	6	1	0	.993	1.95	+1	2
Pujols, A	LAA	3B	1	0	1	0	0	0	0	-	.00	0	0
Raburn, R	Cle	LF	18	12	96	22	1	1	0	.958	2.16	-5	-2
	Cle	RF	17	12	98	21	0	0	0	1.000	1.93	-5	-3
Ramirez, A	TOT	1B	5	4	30	27	1	2	5	.933	-	-1	0
Ramirez, H	Bos	3B	1	0	4	0	0	0	0	-	.00	0	0
	Bos	LF	92	92	748	120	3	4	1	.969	1.48	-19	-19
Ramirez, J	Cle	2B	33	27	260	34	94	2	17	.985	4.43	0	1
	Cle	3B	13	12	104	8	23	1	3	.969	2.68	+7	5
	Cle	SS	46	43	384	46	99	8	20	.948	3.40	-3	-2
	Cle	LF	2	2	14	3	0	0	0	1.000	1.93	+1	1
Rasmus, C	Hou	LF	72	47	445	80	2	2	0	.976	1.66	-3	-1
	Hou	CF	43	31	256	71	2	1	1	.986	2.57	-3	0
	Hou	RF	43	37	328	84	5	2	2	.978	2.44	-8	3
Recker, A	NYM	1B	1	1	9	9	0	0	1	1.000	-	0	0
	NYM	3B	1	0	1	0	0	0	0	-	.00	0	0
Reddick, J	Oak	CF	1	0	2	1	0	0	0	1.000	4.50	0	0
Reed, M	Mil	RF	3	1	11	4	0	0	0	1.000	3.27	+1	1
Refsnyder, R	NYY	2B	15	12	106	10	41	0	7	1.000	4.33	0	-1
Reimold, N	Bal	LF	37	30	261	50	3	1	0	.981	1.83	+1	-2
	Bal	CF	9	8	59	14	0	0	0	1.000	2.14	-6	-3
	Bal	RF	13	3	46	12	1	1	0	.929	2.54	-3	-1
Rendon, A	Was	2B	59	59	494	107	137	4	35	.984	4.45	-3	-1
	Was	3B	28	19	199	10	36	0	4	1.000	2.08	0	-1
Revere, B	TOT	CF	43	35	301	88	2	0	2	1.000	2.69	+5	1
	TOT	RF	12	12	92	20	0	0	0	1.000	1.95	0	-2
Reynolds, M	StL	1B	100	72	708	680	44	6	72	.992	-	+4	3
	StL	2B	1	0	3	1	0	0	0	1.000	6.00	0	0
	StL	3B	22	17	143	7	19	3	3	.897	1.63	-8	-5
	StL	LF	5	4	36	10	0	0	0	1.000	2.50	+1	0
	StL	RF	1	1	6	0	0	0	0	-	.00	0	0
Rivera, R	TB	1B	7	2	26	17	1	0	0	1.000	-	0	0
Rivera, Y	Mil	2B	4	2	19	5	10	1	5	.938	7.11	+1	1
	Mil	3B	1	0	4	2	0	0	0	1.000	4.50	0	0
	Mil	SS	2	2	16	5	8	0	3	1.000	7.31	+2	2
Robertson, D	LAA	LF	27	11	135	40	2	0	0	1.000	2.80	+4	4
	LAA	CF	7	4	39	11	1	0	0	1.000	2.77	+3	1
	LAA	RF	1	0	3	0	0	0	0	-	.00	0	0
Robinson, C	Was	1B	44	42	365	331	25	3	21	.992	-	0	-3
	Was	LF	27	26	209	39	0	2	0	.951	1.68	-4	-5
	Was	RF	11	6	61	8	0	0	0	1.000	1.19	0	0
Robinson, S	Min	LF	55	32	305	68	3	1	1	.986	2.10	0	0
	Min	CF	15	14	117	37	1	0	0	1.000	2.92	+4	2
	Min	RF	12	2	36	6	1	0	0	1.000	1.75	-1	1
Rodriguez, A	NYY	2B	1	1	10	17	0	1	2	.944	-	0	-1
	NYY	3B	4	2	18	1	4	0	0	1.000	1.02	0	0
Rodriguez, S	Pit	1B	102	12	327	366	15	1	37	.997	-	+2	2
	Pit	2B	7	3	34	3	16	0	4	1.000	4.98	+3	2
	Pit	3B	8	3	35	3	12	0	2	1.000	3.89	0	0
	Pit	SS	3	1	13	4	3	2	2	.778	4.85	-1	-1
	Pit	LF	16	7	84	11	0	0	0	1.000	1.17	0	-1
	Pit	RF	14	8	74	18	0	0	0	1.000	2.19	+3	2
Rogers, J	Mil	1B	24	22	203	209	10	1	12	.995	-	-2	0
	Mil	3B	1	1	11	1	1	3	0	.400	1.64	-2	-2
	Mil	LF	3	2	14	0	0	0	0	-	.00	0	0
Rojas, M	Mia	2B	9	4	36	9	7	0	1	1.000	4.00	0	0
	Mia	3B	9	6	57	3	14	1	0	.944	2.68	+2	2
	Mia	SS	32	26	241	33	75	1	19	.991	4.04	+1	0
Romak, J	Ari	1B	1	0	3	3	0	1	0	.750	-	-1	-1
	Ari	LF	2	1	13	0	0	0	0	-	.00	0	0
Romero, S	Sea	LF	6	0	21	5	0	0	0	1.000	2.11	+3	0
	Sea	CF	1	1	4	0	0	0	0	-	.00	-2	-1
	Sea	RF	5	4	33	8	0	0	0	1.000	2.18	0	0
Romine, A	Det	1B	17	6	78	73	6	1	7	.988	-	-1	-1
	Det	2B	13	6	64	19	25	0	11	1.000	6.22	0	1
	Det	3B	59	9	147	14	35	2	1	.961	3.00	+3	4
	Det	SS	27	22	212	48	71	4	19	.967	5.05	+7	7
	Det	LF	2	0	3	2	0	0	0	1.000	6.00	+1	0
Romine, A	NYY	1B	1	1	6	8	1	0	1	1.000	-	0	0
Rosales, A	Tex	1B	19	10	89	87	6	0	11	1.000	-	+3	2
	Tex	2B	19	16	138	25	49	2	14	.974	4.81	-2	0
	Tex	3B	14	5	59	4	12	1	0	.941	2.44	0	-1
	Tex	LF	1	1	8	4	0	0	0	1.000	4.50	0	0
Rosario, E	Min	LF	86	83	743	157	12	5	3	.971	2.05	+1	10
	Min	CF	4	3	28	15	0	0	0	1.000	4.80	0	0
	Min	RF	34	30	265	48	4	2	1	.963	1.77	-2	1
Rosario, W	Col	1B	53	46	378	389	22	6	38	.986	-	-7	-7
Ross, C	Oak	LF	4	2	15	6	0	1	0	.857	3.60	-1	0
	Oak	RF	5	4	37	6	0	0	0	1.000	1.46	0	0
Rua, R	Tex	1B	4	0	8	7	0	0	0	1.000	-	0	0
	Tex	LF	22	21	159	32	0	0	0	1.000	1.81	0	1
	Tex	RF	4	3	25	3	0	0	0	1.000	1.08	-1	-1
Ruf, D	Phi	1B	66	43	422	416	27	3	47	.993	-	-3	-4
	Phi	LF	22	19	153	31	0	0	0	1.000	1.82	0	1
Ruggiano, J	TOT	LF	22	16	147	25	0	0	0	1.000	1.53	0	-1
	TOT	CF	15	8	88	20	0	0	0	1.000	2.04	-9	-6
	TOT	RF	4	2	35	8	0	0	0	.929	2.28	0	0
Russell, A	ChC	2B	86	84	746	151	226	9	47	.977	4.55	+14	9
	ChC	SS	61	53	471	67	139	4	29	.981	3.93	+13	10
Rutledge, J	Bos	2B	30	18	175	33	53	3	14	.966	4.41	0	0
	Bos	3B	5	1	22	1	6	1	0	.875	2.86	-2	-1
Ryan, B	NYY	1B	1	1	1	1	0	0	0	1.000	-	0	0
	NYY	2B	26	17	147	16	44	4	4	.938	3.68	-1	-1
	NYY	3B	14	7	71	9	14	0	3	1.000	2.92	-2	-2
	NYY	SS	6	5	39	9	17	1	3	.963	6.00	0	1
	NYY	RF	2	1	2	1	0	0	0	1.000	4.50	0	0
Saladino, T	CWS	1B	1	0	1	3	0	0	0	1.000	-	0	0
	CWS	3B	60	53	478	39	122	5	6	.970	3.03	+13	12
	CWS	SS	11	7	63	11	13	0	2	1.000	3.43	0	-1
Saltalamacchia, J	TOT	1B	1	1	15	14	0	0	1	1.000	-	0	0
Sands, J	Cle	1B	11	6	71	78	4	0	2	1.000	-	+3	0
	Cle	LF	7	6	51	14	0	0	0	1.000	2.47	+1	0
	Cle	RF	32	20	178	32	1	0	0	1.000	1.67	-3	-3
Sano, M	Min	1B	2	0	5	2	0	0	0	1.000	-	0	0

Player	Tm	Pos	G	GS	Inn	PO	A	E	DP	Pct.	Rng	BSv	RS
	Min	3B	9	9	77	8	15	0	0	1.000	2.69	-1	-1
Santana, D	Min	SS	66	65	578	92	191	16	47	.946	4.40	-12	-15
	Min	CF	5	3	27	8	0	0	0	1.000	2.63	+1	1
	Min	RF	1	0	1	0	0	0	0	-	.00	0	0
Santana, D	TOT	LF	14	2	50	5	0	0	0	1.000	.89	-1	0
	TOT	CF	24	21	162	37	0	1	0	.974	2.06	+1	-3
	TOT	RF	25	21	186	36	1	2	0	.949	1.79	-1	-1
Sardinas, L	Mil	2B	16	7	85	23	32	0	12	1.000	5.80	+1	1
	Mil	3B	3	3	24	1	4	1	1	.833	1.88	+1	1
	Mil	SS	14	14	121	24	45	1	10	.986	5.15	-5	-2
Saunders, M	Tor	LF	3	3	26	7	0	0	0	1.000	2.42	+2	1
	Tor	RF	6	6	49	5	3	0	0	1.000	1.46	-4	-1
Schafer, J	Min	LF	1	0	5	0	0	0	0	-	.00	0	0
	Min	CF	26	20	182	55	1	1	0	.982	2.77	-6	-3
Schafer, L	Mil	LF	1	0	1	0	0	0	0	-	.00	0	0
	Mil	CF	49	25	267	70	1	2	0	.973	2.39	-5	-6
Schebler, S	LAD	LF	7	3	39	10	0	0	0	1.000	2.31	+4	2
	LAD	RF	6	2	29	8	0	0	0	1.000	2.48	+1	0
Schoop, J	Bal	2B	84	82	721	145	235	7	50	.982	4.74	-8	-3
Schumaker, S	Cin	2B	12	4	54	2	19	0	4	1.000	3.52	-1	-1
	Cin	LF	40	32	283	61	3	4	1	.941	2.04	-2	-4
	Cin	CF	2	1	12	2	0	0	0	1.000	1.50	0	0
	Cin	RF	4	2	17	2	0	0	0	1.000	1.06	-1	0
Schwarber, K	ChC	LF	41	36	296	42	1	1	0	.977	1.31	-5	-3
	ChC	RF	4	2	14	3	0	0	0	1.000	1.93	0	0
Scruggs, X	StL	1B	11	10	83	73	8	1	8	.988	-	+2	0
Seager, C	LAD	3B	6	4	40	1	11	0	1	1.000	2.72	+1	1
	LAD	SS	21	21	192	23	70	5	12	.949	4.36	0	1
Seager, K	Sea	SS	1	0	2	0	1	0	0	1.000	4.50	0	0
Shaffer, R	TB	1B	10	8	75	64	6	0	4	1.000	-	0	-1
	TB	3B	8	4	46	6	6	1	3	.923	2.35	+1	0
	TB	LF	1	1	7	0	0	0	0	-	.00	-1	0
	TB	RF	2	0	5	2	0	0	0	1.000	3.60	0	0
Shaw, T	Bos	1B	55	50	456	419	36	3	50	.993	-	0	-1
	Bos	3B	8	5	55	5	14	0	0	1.000	3.13	+1	1
	Bos	LF	1	0	3	0	0	0	0	-	.00	-1	-1
Shuck, J	CWS	LF	10	2	35	10	0	0	0	1.000	2.57	-3	1
	CWS	CF	11	10	83	26	1	0	0	1.000	2.93	-6	-2
	CWS	RF	27	17	179	39	3	0	0	1.000	2.11	+1	3
Singleton, J	Hou	1B	14	10	96	107	5	1	9	.991	-	+1	-1
Sizemore, G	TOT	LF	32	23	201	47	2	1	0	.980	2.20	-7	-2
	TOT	RF	42	33	269	67	1	2	0	.971	2.28	-6	-6
Smith, S	Sea	LF	65	51	436	76	5	1	1	.988	1.67	-2	0
	Sea	RF	55	40	362	87	1	0	0	1.000	2.19	+6	1
Smoak, J	Tor	1B	110	71	687	666	44	4	74	.994	-	+2	4
Smolinski, J	TOT	LF	52	39	332	65	1	0	0	1.000	1.79	0	-1
	TOT	RF	16	11	104	24	4	0	1	1.000	2.42	-5	-1
Snider, T	TOT	LF	42	40	314	66	3	0	0	1.000	1.98	+1	2
	TOT	RF	22	20	166	47	2	1	1	.980	2.65	+6	4
Sogard, E	Oak	3B	1	1	8	0	2	0	0	1.000	2.25	0	0
	Oak	SS	17	14	119	22	37	1	9	.983	4.46	+2	1
Solano, D	Mia	2B	7	3	39	8	14	2	1	.917	5.08	-1	-1
	Mia	3B	10	4	58	1	15	0	0	1.000	2.48	+3	2
	Mia	SS	10	7	66	4	18	1	4	.957	3.00	-1	-1
Solarte, Y	SD	1B	28	25	219	180	16	4	21	.980	-	+2	1
	SD	2B	19	14	121	23	34	1	4	.983	4.25	+1	1
	SD	3B	92	85	741	44	130	6	11	.967	2.11	-4	-3
Span, D	Was	CF	61	61	523	149	3	1	3	.993	2.62	-21	-10
Spangenberg, C	SD	2B	70	67	555	87	173	4	39	.985	4.21	-2	0
	SD	3B	19	14	131	2	25	0	0	1.000	1.85	+4	4
	SD	LF	1	0	2	0	0	0	0	-	.00	0	0
	SD	CF	1	0	4	0	0	0	0	-	.00	0	0
	SD	RF	2	0	5	0	0	0	0	-	.00	-2	-1
Springer, G	Hou	CF	10	8	74	27	0	0	0	1.000	3.30	+1	1
Stanton, G	Mia	RF	71	71	626	149	6	3	3	.981	2.23	+15	9
Strausborger, R	Tex	LF	18	13	121	20	1	1	1	.955	1.56	-6	-3
	Tex	RF	1	1	7	1	0	0	0	1.000	1.29	+1	0
Stubbs, D	TOT	LF	21	10	99	11	0	0	0	1.000	1.00	+1	1
	TOT	CF	42	16	188	47	2	0	0	1.000	2.35	+1	0
	TOT	RF	4	0	5	2	0	0	0	1.000	3.60	+1	0
Suarez, E	Cin	3B	1	0	1	0	0	0	0	-	.00	0	0
Suzuki, I	Mia	LF	30	23	222	52	2	0	0	1.000	2.19	-1	0
	Mia	CF	7	5	50	13	0	0	0	1.000	2.32	-4	-3
	Mia	RF	73	60	551	152	3	0	0	1.000	2.53	+19	9
Sweeney, D	Phi	2B	9	8	67	14	13	2	4	.931	3.65	-3	-2
	Phi	3B	1	0	2	0	0	0	0	-	.00	0	0
	Phi	LF	12	11	88	13	0	1	0	.929	1.33	-9	-4
	Phi	CF	2	2	17	6	0	0	0	1.000	3.18	+1	1
	Phi	RF	1	0	5	2	1	0	0	1.000	5.40	0	1
Swisher, N	TOT	1B	12	10	85	85	4	0	12	1.000	-	0	-1
	TOT	LF	25	24	189	48	1	0	0	1.000	2.33	-4	-5
	TOT	RF	3	2	19	0	0	2	0	.000	-	-2	-1
Szczur, M	ChC	LF	26	8	95	16	0	0	0	1.000	1.52	-1	-1
	ChC	CF	6	4	41	6	0	0	0	1.000	1.33	-4	-2
	ChC	RF	4	0	9	2	0	0	0	1.000	2.00	0	0
Tabata, J	Pit	LF	7	5	50	3	1	0	0	1.000	.69	-2	-1
	Pit	RF	5	4	30	6	0	0	0	1.000	1.78	-2	-1
Taylor, C	Sea	2B	4	2	20	5	1	1	1	.857	2.70	-2	-2
	Sea	3B	1	0	1	0	0	0	0	-	.00	0	0
	Sea	SS	28	25	231	33	71	3	11	.972	4.05	+1	-1
Taylor, M	Was	LF	38	32	287	72	3	0	0	1.000	2.35	+7	7
	Was	RF	3	0	11	2	0	0	0	1.000	1.64	0	0
Tejada, R	NYM	2B	13	11	98	14	32	0	8	1.000	4.22	-1	0
	NYM	3B	19	18	156	14	36	2	4	.962	2.88	-1	-3
	NYM	SS	81	65	618	78	189	5	36	.982	3.89	-19	-15
Terdoslavich, J	Atl	1B	12	11	96	87	10	0	12	1.000	-	+2	2
	Atl	LF	2	0	1	0	0	0	0	-	.00	0	0
Thompson, T	CWS	LF	12	9	78	18	0	0	0	1.000	2.08	+3	2
	CWS	CF	10	7	68	14	0	0	0	1.000	1.86	0	0
	CWS	RF	18	16	150	36	0	1	0	.973	2.16	+3	1
Tolleson, S	Tor	2B	11	8	74	12	23	0	3	1.000	4.26	+3	4
	Tor	SS	4	2	22	0	6	0	0	1.000	2.45	-2	-1
	Tor	LF	3	2	14	1	0	1	0	.500	2.64	-3	-1
	Tor	RF	1	0	4	0	0	0	0	-	.00	0	0
Tomas, Y	Ari	1B	4	2	14	12	1	0	2	1.000	-	0	0
	Ari	3B	31	31	272	22	45	6	5	.918	2.22	-10	-6
	Ari	LF	6	5	31	8	0	1	0	.889	2.32	-2	-2
	Ari	RF	57	54	464	105	3	2	0	.982	2.10	-3	-6
Tomlinson, K	SF	2B	50	46	394	82	130	4	30	.981	4.84	-4	-2
	SF	SS	1	0	2	0	0	0	0	-	.00	0	0
Torreyes, R	LAD	2B	4	0	12	2	4	0	1	1.000	4.50	+1	0
	LAD	3B	3	0	5	0	0	0	0	-	.00	0	0
Travis, D	Tor	2B	62	60	510	112	171	6	39	.979	4.99	+1	1
Trumbo, M	TOT	1B	23	20	152	155	8	1	13	.994	-	0	1
	TOT	LF	13	12	90	17	0	2	0	.895	1.69	+1	-1
	TOT	RF	76	70	580	107	4	2	0	.982	1.72	-6	-3
Tucker, P	Hou	LF	79	62	554	100	2	1	0	.990	1.66	-9	-5
	Hou	RF	14	12	101	21	0	0	0	1.000	1.87	+1	0
Turner, J	LAD	1B	10	6	60	53	5	1	6	.983	-	+1	0
	LAD	2B	5	3	27	1	10	0	2	1.000	3.62	0	0
	LAD	SS	1	1	6	2	2	1	1	.800	6.00	-1	0
Turner, T	Was	2B	12	6	59	19	22	1	5	.976	6.29	+3	2
	Was	SS	6	2	26	3	4	1	2	.875	2.45	0	0
Uggla, D	Was	1B	1	0	1	0	0	0	0	-	-	0	0
	Was	2B	31	22	231	39	62	2	9	.981	3.93	0	-3
Upton Jr., M	SD	CF	63	47	441	116	6	1	0	.992	2.49	-3	2
Uribe, J	TOT	2B	8	7	58	8	14	0	4	1.000	3.89	+2	1
	TOT	3B	92	81	733	34	169	9	18	.958	2.49	+3	1
Urrutia, H	Bal	LF	8	8	73	14	1	0	0	1.000	1.85	-2	0
Urshela, G	Cle	3B	80	76	682	41	145	6	17	.969	2.45	+2	0
Utley, C	TOT	1B	6	3	29	31	4	0	2	1.000	-	0	0
	TOT	3B	3	3	25	1	8	0	0	1.000	3.24	+2	1
Valbuena, L	Hou	1B	31	27	217	205	13	1	12	.995	-	0	2
	Hou	2B	1	0	1	0	2	0	0	1.000	18.00	0	0
Valdespin, J	Mia	RF	1	1	9	1	0	0	0	1.000	1.00	0	0
Valencia, D	TOT	1B	5	1	16	12	2	0	0	1.000	-	0	0
	TOT	2B	3	0	11	2	3	0	1	1.000	4.22	0	0
	TOT	3B	55	54	485	37	109	3	10	.980	2.71	0	-3
	TOT	LF	32	27	220	44	0	1	0	.978	1.80	-3	-3
	TOT	RF	3	1	20	4	0	0	0	1.000	2.12	0	0
Van Slyke, S	LAD	1B	21	8	95	95	6	1	10	.990	-	+2	2
	LAD	LF	55	31	304	59	7	1	1	.985	1.96	+11	11
	LAD	CF	3	0	5	2	0	0	0	1.000	3.60	0	0
	LAD	RF	22	13	117	20	1	1	0	.955	1.61	0	0

Player	Tm	Pos	G	GS	Inn	PO	A	E	DP	Pct.	Rng	BSv	RS
Vargas, K	Min	1B	18	14	128	131	10	0	14	1.000	-	0	0
Venable, W	TOT	LF	39	19	221	41	1	0	0	1.000	1.71	+3	1
	TOT	CF	63	58	504	123	2	1	0	.992	2.23	-12	-5
	TOT	RF	21	4	69	7	1	0	0	1.000	1.05	-1	-1
Victorino, S	TOT	LF	29	23	202	40	5	2	1	.957	2.00	-10	-2
	TOT	CF	3	0	5	2	0	0	0	1.000	3.60	0	0
	TOT	RF	34	27	243	62	1	0	1	1.000	2.33	+8	4
Villar, J	Hou	2B	3	0	6	0	1	0	0	1.000	1.42	+1	0
	Hou	3B	12	8	82	10	15	4	3	.862	2.73	0	0
	Hou	SS	22	18	166	21	62	5	15	.943	4.49	-2	1
	Hou	LF	5	2	22	4	0	0	0	1.000	1.66	-1	0
	Hou	CF	2	0	4	2	0	0	0	1.000	4.50	0	0
Vogt, S	Oak	1B	25	20	180	182	14	2	18	.990	-	-3	-1
Walker, C	Bal	1B	2	0	4	7	0	0	1	1.000	-	0	0
Wallace, B	SD	1B	17	9	99	87	4	0	8	1.000	-	-2	-1
	SD	3B	5	1	14	0	4	1	0	.800	2.57	-1	-1
Walters, Z	Cle	2B	2	1	12	1	3	0	1	1.000	3.00	0	0
	Cle	3B	2	2	11	1	1	2	0	.500	1.64	-1	0
	Cle	SS	2	1	11	1	2	0	0	1.000	2.45	0	0
	Cle	LF	3	1	14	2	0	0	0	1.000	1.32	0	0
	Cle	RF	1	0	7	1	0	0	0	1.000	1.29	0	0
Weeks, J	Bos	2B	3	2	22	6	7	0	2	1.000	5.32	+1	0
Weeks, R	Sea	LF	19	10	89	12	0	1	0	.923	1.21	-3	-2
Werth, J	Was	LF	76	73	621	104	3	2	0	.982	1.55	-7	-10
	Was	RF	14	11	99	9	0	0	0	1.000	.82	-1	-1
Wieters, M	Bal	1B	3	2	18	22	1	0	2	1.000	-	0	0
Williams, M	NYY	CF	8	7	53	13	0	0	0	1.000	2.21	-1	-1
Williamson, M	SF	LF	6	6	46	11	0	0	0	1.000	2.15	+2	1
	SF	RF	3	1	15	5	0	0	0	1.000	2.93	-2	-1
Wilson, J	Det	2B	11	3	41	6	12	0	3	1.000	3.92	+1	0
	Det	3B	10	3	41	3	5	2	1	.800	1.76	-1	-1
	Det	SS	2	2	16	1	6	0	1	1.000	3.94	-1	-1
Wright, D	NYM	3B	38	38	338	23	55	4	2	.951	2.08	-9	-8
Yelich, C	Mia	CF	36	36	283	74	1	0	1	1.000	2.39	-8	-5
Ynoa, R	Col	2B	5	3	26	1	10	0	2	1.000	3.81	0	0
	Col	3B	10	2	30	1	5	1	0	.857	1.80	0	0
	Col	SS	8	1	26	3	14	0	3	1.000	5.88	+2	1
	Col	LF	19	13	113	22	2	1	0	.960	1.92	-5	-4
Young, C	NYY	LF	55	46	393	80	3	0	0	1.000	1.90	+4	2
	NYY	CF	15	9	91	24	0	1	0	.960	2.38	-2	-2
	NYY	RF	76	22	298	62	1	0	0	1.000	1.90	-1	-3
Young, D	Bal	LF	2	2	15	6	1	0	0	1.000	4.20	+1	2
	Bal	RF	40	37	319	56	7	2	0	.969	1.78	-8	1
Young, E	TOT	LF	18	3	50	11	0	0	0	1.000	1.97	-2	-1
	TOT	CF	16	14	110	35	0	0	0	1.000	2.87	+2	0
	TOT	RF	2	1	11	4	0	0	0	1.000	3.27	+1	1
Zimmerman, R	Was	LF	1	0	1	0	0	0	0	-	.00	0	0
Zobrist, B	TOT	2B	69	66	590	117	185	3	53	.990	4.61	-8	-7
	TOT	3B	4	3	24	2	4	0	0	1.000	2.25	0	0
	TOT	LF	45	42	347	64	1	4	0	.942	1.69	-3	-5
	TOT	RF	5	4	34	11	0	0	0	1.000	2.91	0	0

All Other Catchers

Player	Tm	G	GS	Inn	PO	A	E	DP	PB	Pct.	SBA	CS	PCS	CS%	CERA	GFP/DME	SB	SZ	Other	Total
Anderson,Bryan	Oak	3	2	17.0	10	2	1	0	0	.923	2	0	0	.00	3.71	0	0	0	0	0
Arencibia,J.P.	TB	23	18	153.0	148	12	1	0	1	.994	18	4	3	.22	3.76	0	0	-2	-1	-3
Ashley,Nevin	Mil	8	5	41.1	41	3	0	0	0	1.000	3	1	0	.33	6.10	0	0	0	0	0
Avila,Alex	Det	44	43	365.2	291	18	0	3	2	1.000	31	10	1	.32	4.55	-3	0	-5	1	-7
Bandy,Jett	LAA	1	0	1.0	1	1	0	0	0	1.000	0	0	0	-	0.00	0	0	0	0	0
Barnes,Austin	LAD	11	7	69.1	57	5	0	0	1	1.000	8	1	0	.13	5.19	1	-1	0	0	0
Barnhart,Tucker	Cin	73	67	598.0	492	42	2	0	4	.996	51	14	1	.27	4.94	-1	1	0	-3	-3
Baron,Steven	Sea	4	4	29.0	34	1	0	0	0	1.000	2	0	0	.00	2.79	0	0	0	0	0
Bethancourt,Christian	Atl	42	41	357.0	305	22	4	4	8	.988	19	8	1	.42	4.56	1	2	-4	0	-1
Blair,Carson	Oak	11	9	83.2	57	1	4	0	0	.935	5	0	2	.00	8.07	-2	-1	-3	0	-6
Brantly,Rob	CWS	14	9	87.0	82	3	0	1	2	1.000	3	2	1	.67	3.83	-1	0	-1	0	-2
Brown,Trevor	SF	13	12	108.0	77	7	1	0	0	.988	9	2	0	.22	4.25	0	-1	-2	0	-3
Butera,Drew	TOT	49	30	282.2	211	17	4	1	1	.983	22	7	2	.32	4.36	-1	2	-1	-1	-1
Cabrera,Ramon	Cin	8	6	50.0	41	5	0	0	0	1.000	5	3	0	.60	3.42	0	1	0	0	1
Casali,Curt	TB	37	32	275.1	241	15	1	4	0	.996	25	6	1	.24	3.99	-1	-1	1	0	-1
Centeno,Juan	Mil	7	5	46.0	44	3	1	0	1	.979	3	0	0	.00	7.83	0	-1	0	0	-1
Clevenger,Steve	Bal	9	6	56.0	43	3	0	0	1	1.000	5	1	0	.20	5.63	1	0	0	-1	0
Conger,Hank	Hou	69	56	514.2	472	22	4	5	1	.992	43	1	0	.02	3.55	1	-6	0	-1	-6
Corporan,Carlos	Tex	31	30	277.2	219	11	3	2	3	.987	25	5	2	.20	4.47	-1	0	0	-1	-2
Cruz,Tony	StL	51	30	287.0	251	16	0	1	1	1.000	19	2	1	.11	3.48	0	-1	-2	-1	-4
d'Arnaud,Travis	NYM	64	64	569.1	556	25	3	6	1	.995	39	10	4	.26	3.95	1	-1	4	-4	0
Easley,Ed	StL	3	1	14.0	14	0	0	0	0	1.000	0	0	0	-	3.21	0	0	0	0	0
Ellis,A.J.	LAD	62	55	492.0	515	49	0	3	3	1.000	30	8	10	.27	3.40	1	1	-7	-2	-7
Fryer,Eric	Min	15	7	69.0	52	0	1	1	0	.981	2	0	0	.00	5.48	0	0	0	0	0
Gale,Rocky	SD	6	1	17.0	18	0	0	0	0	1.000	0	0	0	-	4.24	0	0	0	0	0
Garneau,Dustin	Col	22	19	180.1	146	10	2	0	1	.987	10	5	0	.50	3.99	0	1	-5	0	-4
Gimenez,Chris	Tex	36	32	279.0	230	13	3	3	2	.988	19	1	1	.05	3.35	-1	-2	-2	1	-4
Gosewisch,Tuffy	Ari	37	34	311.1	256	24	1	0	2	.996	29	10	1	.34	3.90	2	1	-3	0	0
Hanigan,Ryan	Bos	53	51	454.1	411	25	3	4	4	.993	33	9	3	.27	4.58	-2	0	3	1	2
Hayes,Brett	Cle	14	9	85.1	74	4	1	0	0	.987	8	1	1	.13	4.96	-1	-1	-1	0	-3
Hedges,Austin	SD	47	41	350.2	366	26	4	1	2	.990	48	15	1	.31	3.85	2	1	3	0	6
Hernandez,Oscar	Ari	13	7	77.1	74	11	0	2	2	1.000	2	1	0	.50	3.03	-1	0	0	0	-1
Herrmann,Chris	Min	38	32	278.0	205	15	3	3	0	.987	19	8	0	.42	4.18	-1	3	-3	0	-1
Hicks,John	Sea	14	10	88.2	72	10	1	1	0	.988	10	5	0	.50	3.96	0	1	0	0	1
Holaday,Bryan	Det	18	15	138.0	112	5	0	1	0	1.000	13	3	1	.23	4.83	0	0	-1	0	-1
Kratz,Erik	TOT	7	3	31.0	26	2	0	1	0	1.000	0	0	1	.00	4.06	0	0	0	0	0
Laird,Gerald	Ari	1	1	4.1	3	0	0	0	0	1.000	0	0	0	-	6.23	0	0	0	0	0
Lavarnway,Ryan	TOT	30	25	225.2	189	8	2	1	1	.990	13	4	1	.31	3.99	-1	-1	-3	0	-3
Leon,Sandy	Bos	37	33	306.0	258	28	1	4	2	.997	20	10	0	.50	3.47	0	3	-1	1	3
Lobaton,Jose	Was	42	38	347.1	299	20	2	3	4	.994	30	7	1	.23	4.28	0	-1	3	-2	0
Maile,Luke	TB	15	9	88.2	76	5	0	1	1	1.000	1	1	0	1.00	3.25	0	1	0	0	1
Mathis,Jeff	Mia	30	29	246.0	210	13	1	1	0	.996	13	2	3	.15	4.76	1	-1	2	-1	1
McKenry,Michael	Col	32	31	272.1	226	8	5	0	1	.979	32	2	1	.06	3.73	0	-3	2	0	-1
Mesoraco,Devin	Cin	6	5	51.0	52	2	0	0	0	1.000	3	0	0	.00	3.35	0	-1	0	0	-1
Monell,Johnny	NYM	12	9	85.0	60	0	0	0	0	1.000	4	0	0	.00	3.07	1	0	0	0	1
Moore,Adam	Cle	1	1	9.0	4	0	0	0	0	1.000	0	0	0	-	2.00	0	0	0	0	0
Murphy,John Ryan	NYY	65	43	415.1	389	24	3	1	7	.993	27	6	2	.22	4.25	-1	-2	2	-1	-2
Murphy,Tom	Col	11	10	90.1	82	5	1	0	0	.989	7	0	1	.00	5.88	0	-1	-2	0	-3
Navarro,Dioner	Tor	39	34	320.0	242	20	4	3	2	.985	22	8	1	.36	3.15	-1	2	-3	1	-1
Nieves,Wil	SD	4	4	32.0	42	2	1	0	3	.978	5	0	0	.00	5.06	-1	-1	0	0	-2
Pacheco,Jordan	Ari	18	13	130.1	95	3	1	1	2	.990	11	2	0	.18	4.90	-1	-1	0	0	-2
Pena,Francisco	KC	8	1	21.0	12	0	0	0	0	1.000	0	0	0	-	3.86	0	0	0	0	0
Perez,Roberto	Cle	69	61	538.1	568	42	4	2	4	.993	44	16	2	.39	3.69	0	3	3	1	7
Phegley,Josh	Oak	68	62	541.0	454	53	2	3	5	.996	45	17	1	.38	4.13	-1	4	-1	0	2
Recker,Anthony	NYM	28	23	205.2	171	6	1	0	1	.994	10	0	1	.00	4.16	-1	-2	-2	-1	-6
Rosario,Wilin	Col	2	2	17.0	19	1	0	0	0	1.000	0	0	0	-	2.65	0	0	0	0	0
Ross,David	ChC	59	46	402.1	397	36	1	3	4	.998	64	15	2	.23	2.66	-2	5	0	2	5
Saltalamacchia,J	TOT	47	44	389.0	326	24	3	1	0	.992	26	4	1	.15	4.10	0	-2	-3	0	-5
Sanchez,Hector	SF	16	11	101.0	69	6	0	1	2	1.000	6	0	1	.00	3.39	-1	0	-1	0	-2
Sanchez,Tony	Pit	2	2	17.1	16	3	0	0	0	1.000	2	0	1	.00	2.08	0	0	0	0	0
Schwarber,Kyle	ChC	21	15	136.0	110	7	4	1	2	.967	15	1	2	.07	4.70	0	-2	-1	0	-3
Severino,Pedro	Was	2	1	9.0	7	1	0	0	0	1.000	0	0	0	-	1.00	0	0	0	0	0
Solano,Jhonatan	Mia	6	6	52.2	39	2	0	1	0	1.000	13	1	0	.08	4.27	0	-1	0	0	-1
Soto,Geovany	CWS	73	53	487.1	398	24	5	1	5	.988	29	8	1	.28	4.56	0	1	3	-2	2
Stanley,Cody	StL	2	0	6.0	7	0	0	0	0	1.000	0	0	0	-	3.00	-1	0	0	0	-1
Stassi,Max	Hou	10	4	43.0	39	1	0	1	0	1.000	4	1	1	.25	5.44	1	0	0	0	1
Stewart,Chris	Pit	52	36	372.2	328	37	9	2	1	.976	51	10	3	.20	2.46	0	-1	3	2	4
Sucre,Jesus	Sea	50	43	379.1	349	28	3	5	3	.992	23	10	3	.43	4.46	1	3	1	-1	4
Susac,Andrew	SF	40	33	302.2	222	18	4	3	3	.984	34	5	1	.15	4.04	-1	-4	1	1	-1
Tartamella,Travis	StL	3	0	8.0	9	0	0	0	0	1.000	0	0	0	-	4.50	0	0	0	0	0
Teagarden,Taylor	ChC	6	3	34.0	30	3	0	0	0	1.000	2	0	0	.00	1.59	0	0	0	0	0
Telis,Tomas	TOT	11	5	50.1	42	2	1	0	0	.978	3	0	1	.00	8.05	1	0	-2	0	-1
Thole,Josh	Tor	18	15	127.0	87	3	1	0	4	.989	6	0	0	.00	5.10	-1	-1	1	0	-1
Wieters,Matt	Bal	55	55	485.1	423	23	5	3	2	.989	25	7	1	.28	4.38	-1	0	-4	-2	-7
Williams,Jackson	SF	7	3	31.0	21	4	0	0	1	1.000	2	1	0	.50	4.65	0	0	0	0	0
Wilson,Bobby	TOT	55	41	373.1	323	23	2	1	2	.994	36	8	2	.22	3.54	1	0	4	1	6

Runs Saved Multi-Year Summary

Ben Jedlovec

Defensive Runs Saved and other defensive metrics of the current age are still relatively new. We've reported batting averages, strikeouts, assists, and errors for well over a century, but we have had sufficient data to calculate more sophisticated defensive metrics for barely over a decade. As such, we baseball fans are relatively inexperienced with putting them into context, which is exactly what this section aims to accomplish.

Defensive Runs Saved estimates the number of runs a player saves or costs his team relative to the average player at his position. As you can see in the Runs Saved leaderboards, the best players at a position might be 15 or 20 runs above average, while the worst might be 15 runs below average.

As this section will detail, there are players who are consistently great (Jason Heyward), consistently awful (Hanley Ramirez), and everything in between. There are improving fielders (Jason Castro), fielders whose playing time has shifted downward on the defensive spectrum (Torii Hunter), and fielders declining with age and injury (Evan Longoria). All of these are helpful placing the numbers, and the players they represent, into context.

A player must have over 2,500 innings played over the past six seasons or 700 innings in the most recent season at his primary position in order to qualify for this list. A secondary position is listed if the player has played at a second position over 1,000 innings over six seasons (or 200 innings in the most recent season).

Defensive Runs Saved By Season

Player	YOB	Pos 1	Pos 2	10	11	12	13	14	15
Abreu,Jose	1987	1B						-10	1
Ackley,Dustin	1988	2B			9	11	-4	8	-13
Ahmed,Nick	1990	SS						2	19
Alonso,Yonder	1987	1B		2	-6	2	6	9	9
Altuve,Jose	1990	2B			2	-18	-3	-7	3
Alvarez,Pedro	1987	3B	1B	-11	-9	-5	3	-5	-13
Andrus,Elvis	1988	SS		-8	6	8	11	-14	-1
Aoki,Nori	1982	RF	LF			3	10	-7	-1
Arenado,Nolan	1991	3B					30	16	18
Arencibia,J.P.	1986	C		0	-16	-4	8	-7	-3
Avila,Alex	1987	C		-3	0	5	-2	3	-7
Aybar,Erick	1984	SS		5	-1	3	-7	-3	-3
Barmes,Clint	1979	SS		11	16	13	12	3	-3
Barney,Darwin	1985	2B		6	3	29	11	10	-1
Bautista,Jose	1980	RF		-1	0	6	6	-2	-3
Beckham,Gordon	1986	2B		-4	5	-6	-3	0	6
Belt,Brandon	1988	1B			3	4	4	3	6
Beltran,Carlos	1977	RF		-4	-4	5	-7	-5	-14
Beltre,Adrian	1979	3B		20	11	13	-5	9	18
Betts,Mookie	1992	CF						4	10
Blackmon,Charlie	1986	CF			-2	5	-6	2	-7
Bogaerts,Xander	1992	SS					-1	-16	-1
Bour,Justin	1988	1B						0	-7
Bourjos,Peter	1987	CF		14	10	9	-1	7	-4
Bourn,Michael	1982	CF		28	-5	23	2	-5	6
Brantley,Michael	1987	LF	CF	-13	8	0	4	-1	-2
Braun,Ryan	1983	LF	RF	6	2	6	3	-8	-1
Bruce,Jay	1987	RF		16	0	-1	16	-7	5
Burns,Billy	1989	CF						0	4
Byrd,Marlon	1977	RF	CF	4	0	2	8	9	1
Cabrera,Asdrubal	1985	SS		-4	0	-5	-16	-17	-8
Cabrera,Everth	1986	SS		3	-2	-4	-3	3	-3
Cabrera,Melky	1984	LF		-2	-5	1	-4	-5	-2
Cabrera,Miguel	1983	1B	3B	-3	-2	-4	-18	-2	4
Cain,Lorenzo	1986	CF		8	0	5	23	22	18
Calhoun,Kole	1987	RF				1	-7	1	6
Callaspo,Alberto	1983	3B		4	5	7	-14	-2	-5
Cano,Robinson	1982	2B		18	2	15	6	0	9
Carpenter,Matt	1985	3B			-1	-5	0	-2	-10
Carter,Chris	1986	1B		-4	0	-5	-9	0	-6
Castellanos,Nick	1992	3B					-1	-30	-9
Castillo,Welington	1987	C		-1	0	-4	3	-8	-9
Castro,Jason	1987	C		0		-8	-5	2	11
Castro,Starlin	1990	SS		-3	-8	3	-8	-7	-2
Cervelli,Francisco	1986	C		1	2	0	1	1	8
Cespedes,Yoenis	1985	LF				-6	-1	10	11
Chisenhall,Lonnie	1988	3B			5	-4	1	-16	18
Choo,Shin-Soo	1982	RF		7	2	-10	-18	-12	-11
Coghlan,Chris	1985	LF		4	-11	-3	-5	-12	-1
Cozart,Zack	1985	SS			4	12	4	19	7
Crawford,Brandon	1987	SS			1	12	2	8	20
Crawford,Carl	1981	LF		8	-1	1	0	1	-4
Crisp,Coco	1979	CF		6	-1	0	3	-18	1
Cruz,Nelson	1980	RF		1	-4	-12	-3	4	-8
Cuddyer,Michael	1979	RF		-16	-12	-7	-15	-4	-4
Davis,Chris	1986	1B		3	-5	-4	-7	8	1
Davis,Ike	1987	1B		13	1	-3	1	-4	-1
Davis,Khris	1987	LF					-2	4	-6
Davis,Rajai	1980	LF		-7	-8	3	4	-10	1
Desmond,Ian	1985	SS		-6	-4	-6	-3	1	1
Donaldson,Josh	1985	3B		-2		3	12	20	11
Dozier,Brian	1987	2B				1	9	0	-5
Drew,Stephen	1983	SS	2B	0	3	-7	-2	4	-3
Duda,Lucas	1986	1B		-1	-9	-15	-12	5	4
Duffy,Matt	1991	3B						-1	9
Eaton,Adam	1988	CF				1	-2	11	-14
Ellis,A.J.	1981	C		-6	-4	-6	-4	-6	-7
Ellsbury,Jacoby	1983	CF		2	9	2	13	-3	1
Encarnacion,Edwin	1983	1B		-4	-7	-4	-7	-6	0
Escobar,Alcides	1986	SS		9	10	-2	4	-4	-1
Escobar,Yunel	1982	SS	3B	9	8	14	4	-23	-11
Espinosa,Danny	1987	2B		4	6	7	3	0	5
Ethier,Andre	1982	RF		-14	1	0	0	-7	2
Fielder,Prince	1984	1B		-17	-10	-4	-13	-2	-5
Flores,Wilmer	1991	SS				-3	-4	-11	
Flowers,Tyler	1986	C		0	8	9	1	11	14
Forsythe,Logan	1987	2B			7	-10	-2	3	6
Fowler,Dexter	1986	CF		0	-5	-12	-4	-20	-12
Francoeur,Jeff	1984	RF		16	2	-11	0	0	-11
Frazier,Todd	1986	3B			3	-1	5	8	6
Freeman,Freddie	1989	1B		0	-2	3	7	-7	3
Freese,David	1983	3B		-5	0	2	-14	-9	-2
Galvis,Freddy	1989	SS			9	-4	-4	-7	
Garcia,Avisail	1991	RF			-1	-4	-8	-11	
Gardner,Brett	1983	LF		33	23	1	5	4	1
Gennett,Scooter	1990	2B				2	-5	3	
Giavotella,Johnny	1987	2B			-1	-4	-1	0	-12
Gillaspie,Conor	1987	3B			-1	-3	-5	-12	-10
Goldschmidt,Paul	1987	1B			-3	1	13	1	18
Gomes,Jonny	1980	LF		-19	-2	-3	0	-7	-7
Gomes,Yan	1987	C				1	21	8	-1
Gomez,Carlos	1985	CF		5	16	2	32	0	6
Gonzalez,Adrian	1982	1B		-4	12	14	11	11	10
Gonzalez,Carlos	1985	LF	RF	1	8	-13	11	-5	5
Gordon,Alex	1984	LF		-3	19	24	17	26	7
Gordon,Dee	1988	2B			-3	-14	-3	-5	13
Gose,Anthony	1990	CF				3	0	2	-12
Grandal,Yasmani	1988	C				15	4	-5	5
Granderson,Curtis	1981	CF	RF	10	-2	-7	3	-5	11
Gregorius,Didi	1990	SS				1	-1	2	5
Gyorko,Jedd	1988	2B					-4	-9	-6
Hamilton,Billy	1990	CF					1	14	8
Hamilton,Josh	1981	LF		12	3	-8	-6	-1	0
Hanigan,Ryan	1980	C		12	11	23	2	4	2
Hardy,J.J.	1982	SS		-5	8	18	8	10	4
Harper,Bryce	1992	RF				14	4	0	9
Hart,Corey	1982	RF		2	-3	-6		-1	-1
Headley,Chase	1984	3B		16	0	-3	5	13	-7
Hechavarria,Adeiny	1989	SS				-1	-3	-3	9
Heyward,Jason	1989	RF		11	10	17	14	26	24
Hicks,Aaron	1989	CF					2	-3	1
Hill,Aaron	1982	2B		-2	0	-2	-9	-10	-3
Holliday,Matt	1980	LF		5	-2	-6	-13	-1	-4
Hosmer,Eric	1989	1B			-10	6	3	3	0
Howard,Ryan	1979	1B		-13	-13	-6	-1	-10	-9
Hundley,Nick	1983	C		-10	-3	-4	-12	-3	-11
Hunter,Torii	1975	RF		-7	7	12	-10	-17	-8
Iannetta,Chris	1983	C		-9	-1	-6	-22	-14	7
Iglesias,Jose	1990	SS			0	7	-1		-3
Infante,Omar	1981	2B		6	5	7	-5	1	3
Jackson,Austin	1987	CF		12	26	6	4	-1	-1
Jay,Jon	1985	CF		-5	9	1	-10	6	3
Jennings,Desmond	1986	CF		0	2	10	-6	4	2
Johnson,Chris	1984	3B		-15	-11	-10	-7	-13	-2
Johnson,Kelly	1982	2B		0	1	5	3	2	-7
Jones,Adam	1985	CF		-6	-1	-13	-1	3	4
Jones,Garrett	1981	1B		-8	-8	-9	-3	-7	-3
Joseph,Caleb	1986	C						14	12
Joyce,Matt	1984	RF		5	0	4	-3	1	-3
Kemp,Matt	1984	CF	RF	-33	-7	-10	-5	-22	-15
Kendrick,Howie	1983	2B		-5	6	2	-3	7	-12
Kiermaier,Kevin	1990	CF					0	14	42
Kinsler,Ian	1982	2B		8	17	1	11	20	19
Kipnis,Jason	1987	2B			-4	3	-1	-11	1
Lagares,Juan	1989	CF					28	26	2
Lamb,Jake	1990	3B						0	7
LaRoche,Adam	1979	1B		7	5	8	1	0	-1
Lawrie,Brett	1990	3B			11	20	3	1	-6
LeMahieu,DJ	1988	2B			1	8	11	17	3
Lind,Adam	1983	1B		-4	-5	1	-7	-3	5
Loney,James	1984	1B		4	11	6	4	-1	-2
Longoria,Evan	1985	3B		17	20	1	12	-5	-1

Player	YOB	Position 1	Position 2	DRS By Season 10	11	12	13	14	15
Lowrie,Jed	1984	SS		-3	-1	-3	-21	-10	-3
Lucroy,Jonathan	1986	C		22	19	16	11	24	2
Machado,Manny	1992	3B				7	35	6	13
Marisnick,Jake	1991	CF					7	15	13
Markakis,Nick	1983	RF		-9	5	-7	-7	0	-6
Marte,Starling	1988	LF				5	20	5	24
Martin,Leonys	1988	CF			-1	0	14	16	15
Martin,Russell	1983	C		15	18	4	21	19	5
Martinez,J.D.	1987	RF			2	-2	-9	0	4
Mathis,Jeff	1983	C		7	11	7	10	8	1
Mauer,Joe	1983	C	1B	3	4	-6	8	4	0
Maybin,Cameron	1987	CF		6	14	7	-5	2	-16
McCann,Brian	1984	C		3	9	13	6	6	-4
McCann,James	1990	C						-1	-6
McCutchen,Andrew	1986	CF		-5	2	-6	5	-13	-8
McGehee,Casey	1982	3B		-12	4	-1		-2	1
Mercer,Jordy	1986	SS				3	-2	9	0
Miller,Brad	1989	SS					-3	-5	-20
Molina,Yadier	1982	C		26	5	29	30	7	9
Montero,Miguel	1983	C		10	19	9	-2	10	7
Moreland,Mitch	1985	1B		1	-5	0	1	1	2
Morneau,Justin	1981	1B		7	-3	0	5	8	-2
Morrison,Logan	1987	1B		-4	-22	-2	-4	2	-7
Moustakas,Mike	1988	3B			1	14	-3	-2	4
Murphy,Daniel	1985	2B			6	-10	-15	-11	-5
Murphy,David	1981	LF		0	3	5	5	-13	-4
Napoli,Mike	1981	1B		-9	-7	-12	10	8	1
Navarro,Dioner	1984	C		4	0	1	1	-15	-1
Norris,Derek	1989	C				6	-1	-3	3
Odor,Rougned	1994	2B						-11	-7
Owings,Chris	1991	2B					0	6	1
Ozuna,Marcell	1990	CF					4	9	-3
Pagan,Angel	1981	CF		19	-9	-5	-9	-5	-20
Panik,Joe	1990	2B						-1	2
Parra,Gerardo	1987	RF	LF	13	14	9	37	0	-10
Pederson,Joc	1992	CF						0	-3
Pedroia,Dustin	1983	2B		3	18	11	15	17	-3
Pena,Brayan	1982	C		3	4	-2	-1	3	-5
Pence,Hunter	1983	RF		4	2	-6	-8	-1	0
Pennington,Cliff	1984	SS		13	-12	12	13	4	5
Peralta,David	1987	LF						3	-2
Peralta,Jhonny	1982	SS		3	2	-1	0	17	-7
Perez,Salvador	1990	C			-2	7	11	7	1
Peterson,Jace	1990	2B						0	-1
Phillips,Brandon	1981	2B		11	7	11	1	6	4
Pierzynski,A.J.	1976	C		-1	-3	-10	-4	-13	-13
Pillar,Kevin	1989	CF					4	3	22
Plouffe,Trevor	1986	3B		-2	-19	-8	0	6	3
Polanco,Gregory	1991	RF						-2	12
Pollock,A.J.	1987	CF				1	12	8	14
Posey,Buster	1987	C		6	5	15	16	10	21
Prado,Martin	1983	3B		8	10	18	2	9	10
Pujols,Albert	1980	1B		6	9	9	1	6	4
Ramirez,Alexei	1981	SS		20	10	14	1	-4	-6
Ramirez,Aramis	1978	3B		-15	-17	4	-12	-5	-8
Ramirez,Hanley	1983	SS	LF	-17	-11	-18	3	-9	-19
Ramos,Wilson	1987	C		3	11	-2	10	2	10
Rasmus,Colby	1986	CF		-5	-4	7	12	-6	2
Realmuto,J.T.	1991	C						0	1
Reddick,Josh	1987	RF		1	10	15	13	10	1
Revere,Ben	1988	CF	LF	0	-4	10	-3	-16	-1
Reyes,Jose	1983	SS		-5	-14	-16	-4	-16	-8
Reynolds,Mark	1983	1B	3B	-5	-21	-9	-11	6	-2
Rios,Alex	1981	RF		-1	-9	7	-4	-4	-6
Rivera,Rene	1983	C			5		9	15	-6
Rizzo,Anthony	1989	1B			2	4	16	6	10
Rodriguez,Alex	1975	3B		6	14	-2	-3		-1
Rollins,Jimmy	1978	SS		3	-6	-8	-15	4	-7
Rosario,Wilin	1989	C			-2	-18	-13	-15	-7
Ruiz,Carlos	1979	C		3	-8	4	0	1	-12
Rupp,Cameron	1988	C					0	-1	6
Ryan,Brendan	1982	SS		24	20	27	6	2	-3
Saltalamacchia,J	1985	C		-1	4	5	-5	-21	-5

Player	YOB	Position 1	Position 2	DRS By Season 10	11	12	13	14	15
Sanchez,Carlos	1992	2B						-2	6
Sandoval,Pablo	1986	3B		-1	14	-4	-5	4	-11
Santana,Carlos	1986	1B	C	-2	-17	-14	-19	-10	-5
Schoop,Jonathan	1991	2B					-1	11	-3
Schumaker,Skip	1980	2B		-13	1	0	-19	-8	-5
Seager,Kyle	1987	3B			0	-4	-8	10	1
Segura,Jean	1990	SS				0	3	2	-3
Semien,Marcus	1990	SS					5	-4	5
Simmons,Andrelton	1989	SS				19	41	28	25
Smith,Seth	1982	LF		-3	-8	2	0	3	1
Smoak,Justin	1986	1B		-2	-1	0	-8	-4	4
Sogard,Eric	1986	2B		0	4	3	4	3	6
Solarte,Yangervis	1987	3B						-7	-1
Soler,Jorge	1992	RF						1	-8
Soto,Geovany	1983	C		3	8	0	4	1	2
Souza,Steven	1989	RF						0	-4
Span,Denard	1984	CF		-4	9	19	3	-2	-10
Springer,George	1989	RF						-2	6
Stanton,Giancarlo	1989	RF		10	3	9	-6	6	9
Stubbs,Drew	1984	CF		-4	-4	1	-7	0	2
Suarez,Eugenio	1991	SS						-4	-12
Suzuki,Ichiro	1973	RF		-1	-3	5	10	1	6
Suzuki,Kurt	1983	C		8	-10	-11	-8	-17	-9
Swisher,Nick	1980	RF		-1	-4	7	7	-5	-7
Taylor,Michael	1991	CF						-1	5
Teixeira,Mark	1980	1B		6	3	17	0	2	5
Tejada,Ruben	1989	SS		-2	1	0	-6	3	-18
Thole,Josh	1986	C		2	-6	10	-4	-2	-1
Trout,Mike	1991	CF			0	19	-11	-12	5
Trumbo,Mark	1986	1B		2	8	-3	1	-8	-3
Tulowitzki,Troy	1984	SS		16	12	-6	6	7	5
Turner,Justin	1984	3B		-3	-14	-3	0	6	5
Uggla,Dan	1980	2B		-8	-15	4	-19	-2	-3
Upton,Justin	1987	RF	LF	0	3	1	-8	-3	8
Upton Jr.,Melvin	1984	CF		-16	-5	-5	0	-8	2
Uribe,Juan	1979	3B		-4	4	4	15	17	2
Utley,Chase	1978	2B		17	7	9	-4	3	0
Valbuena,Luis	1985	3B		3	-1	4	6	-11	1
Valencia,Danny	1984	3B		3	-13	-1	0	-2	-6
Venable,Will	1982	RF		12	5	-3	1	10	-5
Victorino,Shane	1980	CF		1	3	7	23	1	2
Vogt,Stephen	1984	C				0	0	0	-4
Votto,Joey	1983	1B		4	7	9	6	5	6
Walker,Neil	1985	2B		-7	-3	-4	9	-2	-2
Weeks,Rickie	1982	2B		-14	-15	-30	-15	-17	-2
Werth,Jayson	1979	RF		-2	-3	-11	0	-4	-11
Wieters,Matt	1986	C		15	22	13	-10	-4	-7
Wong,Kolten	1990	2B					0	9	5
Wright,David	1982	3B		-13	-5	16	5	13	-8
Yelich,Christian	1991	LF					1	11	8
Young,Chris	1983	CF		16	17	6	-7	1	-3
Young,Delmon	1985	LF		-11	-5	-3	-9	-4	3
Zimmerman,Ryan	1984	3B	1B	11	-5	-1	-1	-4	-1
Zobrist,Ben	1981	2B		13	19	5	9	6	-12
Zunino,Mike	1991	C					0	8	8

Baserunning

Scott Spratt

With so much attention paid to hitting, pitching, and fielding, it can be easy to forget that there is a fourth facet of baseball. And while baserunning may not quite have the same impact on team wins and losses as the former three, sometimes it neatly explains why teams you did not expect to be so good are so good and why teams you did not expect to be so bad are so bad.

This season provided several great examples. On the positive side of things, the Texas Rangers lost 95 games in 2014 and then lost perhaps their best player in Yu Darvish before the start of this season. However, the Rangers made an incredible worst-to-first transformation, and while the team can point to significant offensive improvements as a catalyst for much of that turnaround, their baserunning improvements were perhaps even more dramatic. In 2014, the Rangers produced +24 Net Gain, a solid total good for 14th-best in baseball. This season, the Rangers jumped to +142 Net Gain, the best in baseball by 32 points. And while the Rangers had some stolen base threats in their lineup—notably, Elvis Andrus and Delino DeShields produced 25 steals apiece and Leonys Martin chipped in 14— who led the team's push to +23 Stolen Base Gain, it was their other work on the basepaths that elevated the team to the top of the leaderboard. Their incredible total of +110 Baserunning Gain was fueled by the team's aggressive approach to taking extra bases on singles and doubles. In particular, Rangers players went from first to third on singles 115 times this season, 18 more than any other team.

On the opposite end of the spectrum, the Tigers and Nationals were clear preseason favorites in the AL Central and NL East. Meanwhile, both teams can point to declining baserunning as a contributor to their disappointing seasons. With -21 Net Gain in 2014, the Tigers were already a below-average baserunning team.

However, that total dropped precipitously to -107 in 2015, the worst in baseball by 36 points. The Nationals were closer to the middle of the pack this season with +18 Net Gain, but compared to last year's baseball-leading total of +113, it was a huge drop-off. The biggest culprits for those declining totals were James McCann (-28), Nick Castellanos (-25), Jose Iglesias (-23), Miguel Cabrera (-22), and Victor Martinez (-22) for the Tigers and Yunel Escobar (-21) and Anthony Rendon (-11) for the Nationals.

2015 Baserunning

Player	1st to 3rd Moved	1st to 3rd Chances	2nd to Home Moved	2nd to Home Chances	1st to Home Moved	1st to Home Chances	Bases Taken	Out Adv	Doubled Off	BR Outs	GDP	GDP Opps	BR Gain	SB Gain	Net Gain
Abreu,Jose	9	41	9	16	5	11	18	2	1	4	16	127	-3	0	-3
Ackley,Dustin	3	10	0	6	0	5	9	3	1	4	3	40	-9	-2	-11
Adams,Matt	1	11	1	3	0	1	3	0	1	1	1	37	-1	+1	0
Ahmed,Nick	8	17	6	9	2	2	18	0	0	0	4	66	+24	-6	+18
Almonte,Abraham	3	6	9	11	1	1	5	1	0	1	5	40	+4	+5	+9
Alonso,Yonder	7	25	10	14	5	11	13	3	2	5	13	63	-9	-8	-17
Altherr,Aaron	4	8	3	4	1	1	4	0	0	0	3	33	+7	+2	+9
Altuve,Jose	8	24	11	24	4	9	25	8	1	11	17	94	-21	+12	-9
Alvarez,Pedro	5	24	1	6	1	4	13	0	1	1	6	91	+7	+2	+9
Amarista,Alexi	4	16	2	4	1	2	13	1	0	1	6	71	+9	+3	+12
Andrus,Elvis	20	32	7	9	8	10	16	5	0	5	14	131	+14	+7	+21
Aoki,Nori	5	20	5	12	1	9	10	3	4	7	8	41	-23	+4	-19
Arenado,Nolan	10	23	12	20	2	4	10	3	0	3	17	126	-1	-8	-9
Asche,Cody	6	24	3	12	3	4	5	4	0	4	4	79	-8	-3	-11
Avila,Alex	1	15	2	10	0	4	4	0	2	2	4	36	-12	-2	-14
Aviles,Mike	4	23	6	10	2	4	9	1	1	2	18	63	-12	+1	-11
Aybar,Erick	15	34	15	23	5	5	39	9	1	11	12	98	+11	+3	+14
Barnes,Clint	1	9	4	8	1	1	6	2	0	2	0	30	0	-2	-2
Barnes,Brandon	7	11	5	8	1	1	6	0	2	2	6	59	+3	0	+3
Barnhart,Tucker	2	12	3	7	1	3	3	0	0	0	10	55	-5	-2	-7
Bautista,Jose	13	28	11	16	7	15	20	2	1	3	19	135	+10	+4	+14
Beckham,Gordon	4	17	6	7	0	1	9	2	1	3	6	43	-2	-2	-4
Beckham,Tim	1	11	2	8	0	2	10	1	2	3	3	37	-5	+1	-4
Belt,Brandon	9	32	8	12	2	8	13	3	0	3	3	107	+9	+3	+12
Beltran,Carlos	6	27	4	7	2	4	5	1	1	2	12	103	-6	0	-6
Beltre,Adrian	18	36	14	20	10	14	23	2	0	2	18	128	+23	+1	+24
Betts,Mookie	11	34	11	20	5	6	22	1	1	2	2	103	+24	+9	+33
Bird,Gregory	1	6	1	5	0	1	2	1	0	1	1	35	-2	0	-2
Blackmon,Charlie	20	42	13	24	4	7	23	8	1	9	4	70	+4	+17	+21
Blanco,Andres	5	17	3	3	1	4	9	1	2	3	11	51	-6	-1	-7
Blanco,Gregor	10	32	9	15	7	8	10	2	1	3	3	60	+7	+3	+10
Bogaerts,Xander	17	26	12	17	11	14	23	7	1	8	16	115	+8	+6	+14
Bour,Justin	2	18	4	16	0	7	6	4	0	4	19	104	-27	0	-27
Bourgeois,Jason	1	7	6	9	1	5	14	1	1	2	2	25	+6	+1	+7
Bourjos,Peter	5	12	4	6	3	4	6	0	0	1	2	39	+7	-11	-4
Bourn,Michael	8	23	4	10	4	6	12	1	1	2	5	92	+9	+3	+12
Bradley Jr.,Jackie	4	11	5	10	0	2	7	2	0	2	5	43	-1	+3	+2
Brantley,Michael	7	27	7	16	3	11	13	4	0	4	14	133	-7	+13	+6
Braun,Ryan	14	33	14	21	7	12	16	3	2	5	20	115	-2	+16	+14
Brown,Domonic	0	6	2	7	1	3	7	3	0	3	2	38	-5	+1	-4
Bruce,Jay	4	24	3	16	1	3	16	2	0	2	10	104	-1	-1	-2
Bryant,Kris	18	44	13	22	2	4	14	4	0	4	7	147	+13	+5	+18
Burns,Billy	13	34	9	21	3	5	20	2	2	4	5	78	+9	+10	+19
Butler,Billy	2	27	3	17	2	14	14	4	2	6	26	114	-38	0	-38
Butler,Joey	3	14	2	5	0	8	7	0	0	0	16	56	-10	+1	-9
Byrd,Marlon	5	25	5	7	2	7	13	2	3	5	10	100	-6	0	-6
Cabrera,Asdrubal	4	28	14	22	4	6	16	4	1	5	14	108	-5	0	-5
Cabrera,Melky	12	31	10	24	5	7	16	4	5	9	18	131	-17	+3	-14
Cabrera,Miguel	10	37	9	18	0	6	13	5	2	7	19	127	-21	-1	-22
Cain,Lorenzo	15	34	21	21	6	6	14	2	1	3	16	146	+19	+16	+35
Calhoun,Kole	11	32	6	11	3	11	27	5	3	8	6	108	+5	+2	+7
Callaspo,Alberto	3	15	2	5	1	3	4	2	0	2	6	51	-6	0	-6
Campbell,Eric	2	13	7	12	1	2	7	0	1	1	11	35	-6	-1	-7
Canha,Mark	9	18	6	13	2	6	13	0	0	0	9	101	+14	+3	+17
Cano,Robinson	9	36	11	18	2	10	23	2	2	4	26	129	-8	-10	-18
Carpenter,Matt	12	35	11	20	7	14	18	4	3	7	5	95	+1	-2	-1
Carrera,Ezequiel	4	11	5	6	2	2	7	1	1	2	1	36	+6	0	+6
Carter,Chris	5	20	3	10	1	3	14	2	0	2	5	78	+6	-3	+3
Castellanos,Nick	3	24	7	13	1	6	7	1	2	3	21	122	-19	-6	-25
Castillo,Rusney	3	19	3	9	4	7	9	4	0	4	11	55	-13	-6	-19
Castillo,Welington	2	11	6	10	1	5	5	2	0	2	12	79	-8	0	-8
Castro,Jason	2	13	5	10	1	3	5	0	0	0	5	54	+1	0	+1
Castro,Starlin	11	30	10	13	1	7	11	2	2	4	18	119	-6	-5	-11

2015 Baserunning

Player	1st to 3rd Moved	Chances	2nd to Home Moved	Chances	1st to Home Moved	Chances	Bases Taken	Out Adv	Doubled Off	BR Outs	GDP	GDP Opps	BR Gain	SB Gain	Net Gain
Cervelli,Francisco	4	30	9	14	7	11	21	2	1	3	12	88	+5	-1	+4
Cespedes,Yoenis	7	22	11	14	8	11	20	2	0	2	14	133	+18	-3	+15
Chirinos,Robinson	2	15	3	5	0	3	4	1	0	1	4	38	-4	0	-4
Chisenhall,Lonnie	4	9	6	9	2	5	13	1	0	1	0	72	+18	+2	+20
Choo,Shin-Soo	15	45	13	20	5	7	26	4	1	5	7	110	+18	0	+18
Ciriaco,Pedro	0	2	4	5	2	2	3	1	0	1	1	25	+2	0	+2
Coghlan,Chris	8	22	14	17	5	6	12	3	1	4	8	86	+7	+7	+14
Colabello,Chris	2	14	7	17	2	4	14	0	2	2	12	74	-3	+2	-1
Collins,Tyler	4	8	4	5	2	3	2	0	0	0	2	36	+6	0	+6
Conforto,Michael	3	9	7	10	0	1	7	0	0	0	4	36	+7	-2	+5
Conger,Hank	1	9	4	8	0	2	4	2	0	2	6	41	-8	-2	-10
Correa,Carlos	5	15	7	7	0	1	15	1	1	2	10	90	+10	+6	+16
Cozart,Zack	3	7	5	6	1	3	7	1	0	1	4	33	+5	-3	+2
Crawford,Brandon	7	27	10	14	5	7	19	2	0	2	18	109	+7	-2	+5
Crawford,Carl	1	12	5	6	1	1	6	2	1	3	3	35	-4	+6	+2
Cron,C.J.	4	16	4	6	3	5	9	1	1	2	9	73	+1	+1	+2
Cruz,Nelson	5	38	8	12	0	7	13	4	2	6	6	100	-12	-1	-13
Cuddyer,Michael	3	17	10	18	4	6	13	1	4	5	13	76	-10	+2	-8
d'Arnaud,Travis	2	14	6	8	2	3	4	0	0	0	7	54	+1	0	+1
Davis,Chris	6	45	12	26	5	10	16	3	1	4	6	121	-1	-4	-5
Davis,Ike	2	13	3	9	0	5	3	0	0	0	5	41	-5	0	-5
Davis,Khris	3	22	3	7	5	11	8	2	1	3	9	77	-8	+2	-6
Davis,Rajai	4	18	8	10	1	1	5	1	0	1	5	53	+2	+2	+4
De Aza,Alejandro	8	18	9	13	3	6	13	1	1	2	6	57	+10	-3	+7
De Jesus,Ivan	4	15	2	4	1	1	7	0	0	0	3	31	+6	-4	+2
DeJesus,David	5	13	4	7	1	6	9	1	0	1	5	45	+4	-1	+3
Denorfia,Chris	4	14	6	7	1	4	1	2	1	3	7	40	-11	-2	-13
Descalso,Daniel	4	14	3	6	0	3	6	0	0	0	3	44	+5	-3	+2
DeShields,Delino	13	30	17	22	4	5	24	3	1	4	1	72	+26	+9	+35
Desmond,Ian	13	22	8	16	5	7	19	2	0	2	9	126	+22	+3	+25
Dickerson,Corey	3	11	2	6	2	2	5	3	0	3	3	34	-5	-2	-7
Dietrich,Derek	2	22	6	11	3	3	8	1	0	1	4	44	+1	-4	-3
Donaldson,Josh	7	30	12	20	5	11	35	1	2	3	16	139	+20	+6	+26
Dozier,Brian	7	33	9	22	5	5	17	2	1	3	10	102	+2	+4	+6
Drew,Stephen	6	20	4	10	0	5	10	1	1	2	7	76	0	-4	-4
Duda,Lucas	2	25	10	16	3	5	9	1	0	1	12	118	+1	-4	-3
Duffy,Matt	10	37	18	24	8	9	17	2	2	4	22	134	+2	+12	+14
Dyson,Jarrod	6	9	7	8	3	3	8	0	0	0	3	32	+14	+20	+34
Eaton,Adam	19	46	14	20	8	10	32	5	3	8	5	86	+20	+2	+22
Ellis,A.J.	0	9	1	5	0	1	3	3	0	3	4	43	-12	0	-12
Ellsbury,Jacoby	6	30	10	15	1	3	26	1	0	1	6	63	+19	+3	+22
Encarnacion,Edwin	5	26	13	20	4	7	9	3	1	4	14	119	-8	-1	-9
Escobar,Alcides	12	32	17	22	10	14	20	2	0	2	10	73	+19	+7	+26
Escobar,Eduardo	3	23	6	14	2	7	12	3	0	3	7	76	-5	-4	-9
Escobar,Yunel	8	38	6	12	1	9	21	3	2	6	24	117	-19	-2	-21
Espinosa,Danny	6	19	13	20	3	4	9	1	0	1	6	75	+9	+1	+10
Ethier,Andre	9	30	9	12	2	7	9	3	0	3	11	99	-1	-4	-5
Featherston,Taylor	7	13	2	3	2	3	11	1	1	3	3	32	+6	0	+6
Fielder,Prince	6	44	5	19	4	13	18	2	0	2	21	156	-11	0	-11
Flaherty,Ryan	6	14	5	8	0	1	6	2	0	2	8	60	-1	0	-1
Flores,Wilmer	4	14	6	10	1	2	13	2	2	4	12	94	-3	-2	-5
Flowers,Tyler	1	21	5	10	0	0	2	0	0	0	8	62	-7	-2	-9
Forsythe,Logan	5	21	13	22	4	5	19	3	1	4	12	121	+5	+1	+6
Fowler,Dexter	16	33	9	19	6	8	25	8	2	10	5	88	+2	+6	+8
Franco,Maikel	7	20	5	11	3	6	7	1	1	2	8	65	-2	+1	-1
Francoeur,Jeff	4	11	3	8	0	4	8	4	1	5	10	66	-14	-4	-18
Frazier,Todd	8	32	5	10	3	3	20	6	4	10	19	170	-14	-3	-17
Freeman,Freddie	11	26	8	15	2	7	14	1	0	1	6	108	+16	+1	+17
Freese,David	4	23	4	10	2	3	8	4	0	5	12	70	-18	-1	-19
Fuld,Sam	7	18	4	10	3	4	10	2	2	4	6	51	-3	+3	0
Galvis,Freddy	10	31	14	16	1	2	13	3	0	3	11	116	+9	+8	+17
Garcia,Adonis	2	11	2	3	0	4	1	1	0	1	9	45	-10	0	-10
Garcia,Avisail	8	31	8	16	5	14	23	7	1	8	13	117	-8	-7	-15
Gardner,Brett	17	34	10	12	6	10	25	4	2	6	8	113	+19	+10	+29

2015 Baserunning

Player	1st to 3rd Moved	1st to 3rd Chances	2nd to Home Moved	2nd to Home Chances	1st to Home Moved	1st to Home Chances	Bases Taken	Out Adv	Doubled Off	BR Outs	GDP	GDP Opps	BR Gain	SB Gain	Net Gain
Gattis,Evan	5	21	7	14	1	7	13	5	0	5	13	103	-11	-2	-13
Gennett,Scooter	8	15	10	10	3	3	12	1	0	2	11	60	+9	-5	+4
Giavotella,Johnny	10	19	5	11	8	10	12	4	4	9	7	86	-9	0	-9
Gillaspie,Conor	2	13	3	5	0	1	4	2	0	2	2	52	-1	-2	-3
Gillespie,Cole	3	7	3	5	0	0	3	0	0	0	5	28	+1	+2	+3
Goins,Ryan	16	34	10	15	2	6	26	2	0	2	12	86	+22	0	+22
Goldschmidt,Paul	19	52	12	22	8	15	28	2	0	2	16	136	+21	+11	+32
Gomes,Jonny	1	17	7	11	1	3	6	0	1	1	6	43	-3	-1	-4
Gomes,Yan	6	18	6	9	2	4	2	1	2	3	11	90	-8	0	-8
Gomez,Carlos	9	21	8	8	3	3	9	1	2	3	5	78	+9	-1	+8
Gonzalez,Adrian	7	41	7	18	1	7	12	1	2	3	21	138	-16	-2	-18
Gonzalez,Carlos	5	25	8	13	8	12	18	1	0	1	11	107	+14	+2	+16
Gonzalez,Marwin	5	15	4	5	2	7	12	3	0	3	9	62	-1	-6	-7
Gordon,Alex	13	31	2	7	1	2	7	2	2	4	2	59	-1	-8	-9
Gordon,Dee	11	31	14	23	8	15	19	4	2	6	6	65	+2	+18	+20
Gose,Anthony	11	26	17	22	0	0	21	4	2	6	11	85	+6	+1	+7
Grandal,Yasmani	5	22	6	9	1	7	7	4	1	5	16	87	-19	-2	-21
Granderson,Curtis	14	46	10	19	11	14	19	5	2	7	3	86	+5	-1	+4
Gregorius,Didi	8	34	9	14	6	9	16	4	1	5	4	94	+5	-1	+4
Grichuk,Randal	4	16	10	14	1	1	14	1	1	2	6	65	+9	0	+9
Guerrero,Alex	2	5	2	5	0	1	5	4	0	4	7	46	-11	+1	-10
Gutierrez,Franklin	2	12	3	5	0	1	7	0	1	1	5	45	+1	0	+1
Guyer,Brandon	6	19	7	10	3	5	14	3	4	7	5	58	-5	+2	-3
Gyorko,Jedd	2	16	6	11	1	4	14	1	3	4	13	82	-8	-2	-10
Hamilton,Billy	7	18	12	12	1	1	18	0	0	0	5	71	+26	+41	+67
Hamilton,Josh	5	12	1	4	2	3	2	1	0	1	1	35	+2	0	+2
Hanigan,Ryan	2	16	5	9	3	4	7	1	0	1	6	39	0	0	0
Hardy,J.J.	0	9	9	17	3	9	11	1	0	1	11	92	+1	0	+1
Harper,Bryce	12	25	12	21	12	17	25	6	2	8	15	157	+8	-2	+6
Harrison,Josh	13	26	12	15	5	8	13	2	2	4	4	53	+10	-6	+4
Headley,Chase	7	37	14	23	3	7	25	0	3	3	17	119	+6	-4	+2
Hechavarria,Adeiny	6	16	14	22	4	5	9	1	0	1	18	98	0	+3	+3
Hernandez,Cesar	7	32	12	16	5	9	17	2	3	5	6	72	+2	+9	+11
Hernandez,Kiké	2	11	6	7	0	2	5	1	0	1	3	34	+1	-4	-3
Herrera,Elian	4	10	8	10	0	2	10	1	0	1	4	48	+9	+1	+10
Herrera,Odubel	4	19	13	18	4	9	15	2	0	2	6	81	+10	0	+10
Heyward,Jason	14	36	19	26	6	6	20	6	2	8	13	145	+6	+17	+23
Hicks,Aaron	3	20	10	16	2	5	5	2	2	4	6	53	-11	+7	-4
Hill,Aaron	1	13	8	12	3	5	8	1	0	1	9	70	+1	+3	+4
Holliday,Matt	3	15	5	10	2	8	4	3	0	3	9	63	-13	0	-13
Holt,Brock	11	29	4	11	7	10	27	1	0	1	7	92	+27	+6	+33
Hosmer,Eric	12	33	16	23	10	17	29	3	0	3	16	131	+22	+1	+23
Howard,Ryan	1	16	6	13	0	2	5	0	1	1	11	90	-7	0	-7
Hundley,Nick	7	20	5	9	0	1	6	2	1	3	8	73	-5	-7	-12
Hunter,Torii	5	27	16	19	2	5	12	1	0	1	14	105	+6	-8	-2
Iannetta,Chris	0	12	5	12	2	5	9	1	0	1	11	67	-5	-2	-7
Iglesias,Jose	7	28	6	13	4	7	4	5	0	5	10	72	-18	-5	-23
Inciarte,Ender	11	31	7	14	2	4	32	2	2	4	8	84	+19	+1	+20
Infante,Omar	4	18	6	9	4	5	11	2	2	4	8	85	0	-2	-2
Jackson,Austin	9	21	5	11	4	7	13	1	1	2	5	75	+10	-3	+7
Jaso,John	1	10	3	5	1	4	10	2	4	6	5	21	-15	-3	-18
Jay,Jon	6	19	9	10	3	5	9	3	1	4	7	44	-2	-4	-6
Johnson,Chris	5	16	3	4	2	4	4	1	1	2	5	47	-2	0	-2
Johnson,Kelly	4	15	6	11	4	6	4	0	0	1	8	71	0	0	0
Jones,Adam	5	21	9	13	3	6	12	3	2	5	21	140	-11	+1	-10
Joseph,Caleb	2	16	3	8	2	4	8	1	0	1	7	58	-1	0	-1
Joyce,Matt	2	10	1	3	1	2	9	2	0	2	5	63	+2	-6	-4
Kang,Jung Ho	12	28	12	18	1	1	16	2	1	3	10	77	+9	-3	+6
Kemp,Matt	3	19	9	15	3	7	13	4	0	4	17	136	-7	+8	+1
Kendrick,Howie	15	31	8	14	8	11	14	1	0	1	17	97	+11	+2	+13
Kiermaier,Kevin	12	24	8	16	3	5	19	1	0	1	7	82	+20	+8	+28
Kinsler,Ian	13	39	12	17	10	15	14	3	2	5	13	113	+2	-2	0
Kipnis,Jason	8	30	21	30	7	14	28	3	2	5	5	94	+18	-4	+14
Lagares,Juan	12	25	3	7	3	7	11	4	0	4	6	73	+2	+1	+3

353

2015 Baserunning

Player	1st to 3rd Moved	1st to 3rd Chances	2nd to Home Moved	2nd to Home Chances	1st to Home Moved	1st to Home Chances	Bases Taken	Out Adv	Doubled Off	BR Outs	GDP	GDP Opps	BR Gain	SB Gain	Net Gain
Lamb,Jake	4	22	4	6	3	7	9	0	0	0	5	62	+7	-1	+6
LaRoche,Adam	4	26	7	14	0	4	13	3	0	3	10	92	-4	0	-4
Lawrie,Brett	4	24	12	19	4	11	18	2	2	4	8	124	+5	+1	+6
LeMahieu,DJ	8	30	16	22	5	8	18	0	1	1	20	110	+7	+17	+24
Lind,Adam	8	28	8	19	3	7	15	4	2	6	7	88	-7	0	-7
Lindor,Francisco	8	19	6	10	4	7	19	5	1	6	12	94	0	+8	+8
Loney,James	2	27	4	14	1	3	9	5	1	6	10	75	-23	-6	-29
Longoria,Evan	9	38	17	21	4	8	21	5	1	6	11	136	+7	+1	+8
Lowrie,Jed	5	14	2	3	3	5	14	0	0	0	3	40	+16	+1	+17
Lucroy,Jonathan	6	25	6	13	3	8	7	3	1	4	18	73	-21	+1	-20
Machado,Manny	17	37	12	25	4	13	17	3	1	4	17	93	-4	+4	0
Maldonado,Martin	2	6	3	8	1	1	4	0	0	0	6	44	+1	-2	-1
Marisnick,Jake	10	18	3	6	1	1	12	0	0	0	2	58	+19	+6	+25
Markakis,Nick	12	47	16	30	4	11	20	2	3	5	17	86	-11	0	-11
Marte,Ketel	2	5	3	4	1	3	7	1	3	4	1	28	-4	0	-4
Marte,Starling	11	34	13	21	5	11	16	8	0	8	14	112	-12	+10	-2
Martin,Leonys	5	8	5	6	1	2	4	0	1	1	5	50	+4	+4	+8
Martin,Russell	5	29	10	16	3	8	15	2	1	4	22	112	-12	-6	-18
Martinez,J.D.	6	36	12	22	2	9	15	2	2	4	11	130	-4	-1	-5
Martinez,Victor	1	20	2	11	0	6	7	1	1	3	18	106	-22	0	-22
Mauer,Joe	6	20	5	13	3	7	24	2	2	4	22	133	-2	0	-2
Maxwell,Justin	3	12	7	10	0	1	4	1	0	1	4	46	+1	0	+1
Maybin,Cameron	7	17	17	21	5	8	15	3	2	5	16	102	0	+11	+11
McCann,Brian	5	28	4	10	1	9	12	2	0	2	7	101	0	0	0
McCann,James	0	17	3	13	1	5	7	3	1	4	17	79	-26	-2	-28
McCutchen,Andrew	5	44	15	23	4	15	11	1	0	1	9	136	+1	+1	+2
McGehee,Casey	6	16	0	3	0	0	3	3	1	4	18	55	-22	-1	-23
McKenry,Michael	2	10	3	6	0	1	1	0	0	0	2	32	0	-2	-2
Mercer,Jordy	6	14	7	13	4	5	9	2	0	3	7	94	+4	-1	+3
Middlebrooks,Will	2	11	5	9	0	0	2	1	0	1	4	50	-2	0	-2
Miller,Brad	4	18	8	15	1	1	14	3	2	5	7	76	-4	+5	+1
Molina,Yadier	3	25	5	9	0	4	13	2	1	3	16	106	-9	+1	-8
Montero,Miguel	4	21	6	15	2	3	10	1	1	2	9	69	-4	-1	-5
Moore,Tyler	1	7	1	7	1	2	2	0	0	0	2	30	-1	0	-1
Morales,Kendrys	10	35	10	14	2	15	18	4	0	4	24	119	-12	0	-12
Moreland,Mitch	3	18	11	13	1	5	8	0	1	2	9	108	+2	+1	+3
Morneau,Justin	3	10	2	5	1	1	5	0	0	0	2	26	+5	0	+5
Morrison,Logan	8	21	5	13	0	5	16	3	1	4	7	94	+2	0	+2
Morse,Michael	0	13	1	6	0	3	6	0	0	0	10	50	-7	0	-7
Moss,Brandon	7	27	3	10	1	4	12	1	0	1	12	117	+3	-2	+1
Moustakas,Mike	5	39	13	17	3	7	11	7	0	7	14	123	-17	-3	-20
Murphy,Daniel	3	21	6	12	3	8	8	0	0	0	15	111	-2	-2	-4
Murphy,David	3	12	6	9	4	7	9	2	0	2	6	71	+4	-4	0
Murphy,John Ryan	0	9	2	3	2	4	9	0	0	0	4	35	+6	0	+6
Myers,Wil	5	12	8	13	4	7	11	2	0	2	2	28	+7	+1	+8
Napoli,Mike	5	18	4	11	1	5	12	3	0	3	11	92	-4	-3	-7
Nava,Daniel	4	14	3	3	1	2	4	0	0	1	4	34	+1	+1	+2
Navarro,Dioner	1	10	0	4	0	3	4	1	0	1	0	29	-2	0	-2
Norris,Derek	9	33	12	23	4	7	8	3	3	6	5	95	-8	+2	-6
Nunez,Eduardo	4	9	5	6	1	2	10	1	2	3	1	25	+4	0	+4
Odor,Rougned	6	15	5	7	0	3	24	2	2	4	3	82	+17	-8	+9
Orlando,Paulo	2	8	5	9	1	2	9	1	1	2	0	46	+6	-3	+3
Ortiz,David	2	25	7	22	0	2	15	4	1	5	16	114	-18	-2	-20
Owings,Chris	9	21	11	20	5	7	26	0	3	3	9	112	+22	+8	+30
Ozuna,Marcell	9	27	8	11	0	0	6	0	0	0	10	85	+6	-4	+2
Pagan,Angel	6	22	17	22	7	9	10	4	4	8	12	100	-11	+4	-7
Panik,Joe	7	28	10	21	0	6	15	0	0	0	7	94	+10	-1	+9
Paredes,Jimmy	4	22	6	10	3	5	12	1	2	3	8	88	+1	-4	-3
Parra,Gerardo	7	30	13	22	4	6	10	4	0	5	8	106	-4	+6	+2
Paulsen,Ben	2	10	9	11	3	3	4	0	4	4	5	61	-5	-3	-8
Pearce,Steve	5	10	3	4	2	4	6	1	0	1	11	63	0	-1	-1
Pederson,Joc	4	20	7	12	4	5	11	3	3	6	5	88	-5	-10	-15
Pedroia,Dustin	6	31	8	17	4	8	10	4	3	7	6	67	-16	-2	-18
Pena,Brayan	1	18	3	11	1	5	11	1	1	2	10	63	-9	+2	-7

2015 Baserunning

Player	1st to 3rd		2nd to Home		1st to Home		Bases Taken	Out Adv	Doubled Off	BR Outs	GDP	GDP Opps	BR Gain	SB Gain	Net Gain
	Moved	Chances	Moved	Chances	Moved	Chances									
Pence,Hunter	4	8	2	7	3	3	6	1	0	2	8	40	-4	+2	-2
Pennington,Cliff	4	15	3	5	0	3	9	2	0	2	6	50	0	+3	+3
Peralta,David	10	31	7	10	4	7	20	2	2	4	7	83	+10	+1	+11
Peralta,Jhonny	4	38	8	17	5	15	11	3	2	5	23	143	-26	-7	-33
Perez,Carlos	5	11	1	7	1	4	9	0	1	1	7	51	+1	+2	+3
Perez,Hernan	4	9	2	3	1	1	4	1	0	2	6	50	-2	+3	+1
Perez,Roberto	3	11	3	10	0	2	12	0	0	0	9	44	+3	0	+3
Perez,Salvador	2	22	6	14	1	14	10	2	0	2	23	95	-23	+1	-22
Peterson,Jace	9	31	14	18	3	6	15	2	1	3	5	80	+11	-8	+3
Peterson,Shane	4	16	2	6	1	4	11	1	0	1	3	35	+5	-2	+3
Pham,Tommy	2	4	5	6	1	2	8	0	0	0	1	29	+12	+2	+14
Phegley,Josh	3	16	3	14	2	4	6	2	1	3	5	43	-11	0	-11
Phillips,Brandon	10	32	10	13	5	8	21	3	2	5	13	92	+4	+17	+21
Pierzynski,A.J.	3	28	5	15	2	6	9	1	1	2	19	90	-18	-4	-22
Pillar,Kevin	10	34	9	15	3	8	15	1	1	2	9	136	+11	+17	+28
Piscotty,Stephen	1	10	1	5	3	3	5	0	2	2	7	50	-6	0	-6
Plawecki,Kevin	2	11	5	8	0	1	4	0	1	1	4	48	0	0	0
Plouffe,Trevor	10	34	12	21	2	8	15	2	1	3	28	126	-13	0	-13
Polanco,Gregory	17	28	15	21	3	6	27	5	2	7	5	86	+19	+7	+26
Pollock,A.J.	12	34	17	27	5	5	20	2	2	4	19	129	+5	+25	+30
Posey,Buster	1	30	16	25	2	11	22	1	1	2	17	124	0	+2	+2
Prado,Martin	11	31	8	17	2	7	14	3	0	3	9	87	+2	+1	+3
Puig,Yasiel	4	15	4	7	5	5	2	1	1	2	1	64	+3	-3	0
Pujols,Albert	9	34	14	22	2	2	15	4	1	5	15	123	-3	-1	-4
Raburn,Ryan	3	6	0	1	2	3	11	1	0	1	5	39	+7	0	+7
Ramirez,Alexei	3	20	12	21	3	10	9	3	2	5	18	127	-18	+3	-15
Ramirez,Aramis	3	25	6	16	1	4	7	4	0	4	23	104	-27	+1	-26
Ramirez,Hanley	7	27	7	11	4	6	7	4	1	5	11	81	-11	0	-11
Ramirez,Jose	5	17	9	17	5	6	18	5	0	5	5	70	+5	+2	+7
Ramos,Wilson	2	11	4	10	1	3	11	1	0	1	16	85	-4	0	-4
Rasmus,Colby	8	15	12	13	6	11	12	1	0	1	6	92	+20	0	+20
Realmuto,J.T.	11	31	4	10	3	3	15	4	1	5	11	101	0	0	0
Reddick,Josh	11	33	5	9	6	8	14	2	3	5	7	109	+4	+6	+10
Reimold,Nolan	4	11	0	0	0	2	1	2	1	3	2	28	-8	0	-8
Rendon,Anthony	4	22	7	10	2	7	10	3	1	4	8	62	-8	-3	-11
Revere,Ben	12	31	15	22	8	13	29	1	2	3	5	79	+27	+17	+44
Reyes,Jose	7	23	12	18	2	8	14	7	0	7	6	76	-7	+12	+5
Reynolds,Mark	2	15	7	12	0	2	6	2	2	4	10	70	-14	-4	-18
Rios,Alex	5	19	7	9	1	4	5	3	4	7	10	79	-19	+9	-10
Rivera,Rene	0	14	1	7	0	3	7	1	1	2	4	49	-7	0	-7
Rizzo,Anthony	8	31	10	22	6	15	19	5	1	6	9	146	-1	+5	+4
Robinson,Clint	4	25	8	15	0	2	8	2	0	2	6	52	-5	0	-5
Robinson,Shane	5	13	2	9	3	4	8	1	1	2	4	32	-1	+4	+3
Rodriguez,Alex	5	20	7	16	3	9	21	2	1	3	17	151	+4	+4	+8
Rodriguez,Sean	2	12	6	9	0	0	7	2	1	3	9	57	-7	-2	-9
Rogers,Jason	2	9	6	10	1	3	3	0	1	1	2	27	-1	0	-1
Rojas,Miguel	2	5	3	5	0	1	11	2	0	2	4	25	+3	-2	+1
Rollins,Jimmy	4	20	15	23	1	3	8	3	1	4	12	92	-9	-4	-13
Romine,Andrew	5	19	6	11	1	1	9	1	0	1	4	41	+5	0	+5
Rosario,Eddie	9	20	8	8	2	3	16	1	2	3	5	83	+16	-1	+15
Rosario,Wilin	4	14	3	6	1	2	5	3	1	4	8	40	-12	0	-12
Ross,David	1	6	0	2	0	1	1	0	1	1	1	43	-1	+1	0
Ruf,Darin	3	14	0	2	0	2	3	2	0	2	7	53	-9	+1	-8
Ruiz,Carlos	2	17	2	4	1	2	12	1	1	2	13	56	-6	-1	-7
Rupp,Cameron	2	14	5	9	1	2	4	1	0	1	8	52	-5	-2	-7
Russell,Addison	7	21	9	15	1	4	10	2	0	2	8	72	+2	-2	0
Saladino,Tyler	4	12	2	2	4	6	4	0	0	0	9	48	+2	+4	+6
Saltalamacchia,Jarrod	2	10	1	9	1	2	12	1	1	2	5	50	+1	0	+1
Sanchez,Carlos	3	15	11	17	0	3	7	3	1	4	9	75	-9	-2	-11
Sandoval,Pablo	0	17	3	11	0	6	14	3	0	3	14	93	-12	0	-12
Sano,Miguel	2	19	4	15	0	5	5	5	0	5	4	65	-19	-1	-20
Santana,Carlos	8	37	7	14	9	15	14	1	2	3	20	137	-5	+5	0
Santana,Danny	5	11	5	9	3	4	12	0	0	0	7	61	+13	0	+13
Santana,Domingo	5	11	0	1	3	3	3	0	2	2	2	43	+2	+2	+4

2015 Baserunning

Player	1st to 3rd		2nd to Home		1st to Home		Bases Taken	Out Adv	Doubled Off	BR Outs	GDP	GDP Opps	BR Gain	SB Gain	Net Gain
	Moved	Chances	Moved	Chances	Moved	Chances									
Schoop,Jonathan	2	10	3	8	0	4	9	2	2	4	9	59	-11	+2	-9
Schumaker,Skip	3	11	6	10	3	4	8	1	0	1	7	57	+4	-2	+2
Schwarber,Kyle	3	9	10	11	4	4	7	0	1	1	4	68	+12	-3	+9
Seager,Kyle	14	32	9	18	0	4	26	4	1	5	17	124	+6	-6	0
Segura,Jean	9	23	14	20	5	6	15	2	0	2	14	92	+9	+13	+22
Semien,Marcus	8	29	10	15	5	5	15	2	0	2	16	110	+6	+1	+7
Shaw,Travis	2	9	4	6	0	2	10	0	0	0	1	31	+10	-2	+8
Shuck,J.B.	1	10	5	8	1	1	7	2	1	3	2	34	-2	-3	-5
Simmons,Andrelton	9	23	11	16	2	5	14	2	2	4	19	117	-4	-1	-5
Sizemore,Grady	4	15	5	7	1	4	5	0	0	0	3	50	+6	-3	+3
Smith,Seth	7	24	8	16	2	2	8	2	0	2	15	91	-5	0	-5
Smoak,Justin	0	16	2	8	0	5	7	1	1	2	10	64	-13	0	-13
Smolinski,Jake	3	7	7	8	2	2	2	0	0	0	3	29	+6	-1	+5
Snider,Travis	4	12	2	5	1	2	2	2	1	3	3	59	-5	+1	-4
Sogard,Eric	5	20	7	10	3	6	11	0	1	1	9	73	+6	+4	+10
Solarte,Yangervis	10	30	10	16	1	5	14	2	2	4	15	95	-5	+1	-4
Soler,Jorge	8	22	9	12	4	8	6	1	0	1	9	69	+4	+1	+5
Soto,Geovany	0	8	2	2	0	4	6	2	0	2	2	37	-2	-2	-4
Souza,Steven	9	24	11	14	4	4	21	3	1	4	7	88	+17	0	+17
Span,Denard	6	21	9	14	3	5	12	1	0	1	5	43	+9	+11	+20
Spangenberg,Cory	7	16	4	6	6	6	11	2	0	2	4	52	+11	+1	+12
Springer,George	8	20	6	11	3	5	11	2	2	4	4	68	+2	+8	+10
Stanton,Giancarlo	4	19	6	10	2	3	6	1	0	1	5	66	+3	0	+3
Stewart,Chris	1	9	5	7	0	0	1	0	1	1	3	29	-3	0	-3
Suarez,Eugenio	3	18	5	7	2	4	5	2	0	3	7	68	-7	+2	-5
Suzuki,Ichiro	8	30	5	9	4	6	10	2	0	2	8	71	+2	+1	+3
Suzuki,Kurt	8	24	6	18	3	8	12	1	0	1	14	89	-2	0	-2
Swihart,Blake	6	19	6	14	3	6	11	1	0	1	8	57	+3	0	+3
Swisher,Nick	1	11	1	2	0	4	2	0	0	0	9	52	-7	0	-7
Taylor,Michael	6	18	3	10	4	6	10	4	1	5	5	75	-5	+10	+5
Teixeira,Mark	7	23	0	10	1	7	7	3	0	3	7	99	-8	+2	-6
Tejada,Ruben	3	14	9	14	1	6	6	1	0	1	6	69	0	0	0
Thompson,Trayce	3	6	2	2	4	4	3	1	0	1	3	18	+2	+1	+3
Tomas,Yasmany	4	22	4	6	0	2	14	3	0	4	16	74	-11	+1	-10
Tomlinson,Kelby	4	12	1	1	4	5	3	0	0	0	3	33	+5	-3	+2
Travis,Devon	5	8	8	9	1	9	6	1	1	2	4	43	+1	+1	+2
Trout,Mike	10	21	19	22	3	4	20	1	3	4	11	142	+20	-3	+17
Trumbo,Mark	6	23	4	12	2	7	8	4	1	5	12	102	-15	0	-15
Tucker,Preston	3	13	5	7	0	2	8	2	1	3	3	49	-1	-4	-5
Tulowitzki,Troy	10	38	8	14	2	7	16	3	2	5	17	120	-8	+1	-7
Turner,Justin	7	28	7	14	3	5	11	1	2	3	10	82	-3	+1	-2
Upton Jr.,Melvin	4	6	1	2	1	1	6	0	2	2	1	37	+4	+3	+7
Upton,Justin	12	29	9	15	5	10	18	1	3	4	10	114	+10	+9	+19
Uribe,Juan	4	17	6	6	1	4	3	0	0	0	12	85	-1	+2	+1
Urshela,Giovanny	1	16	2	5	0	5	8	0	0	0	9	39	-2	-5	-7
Utley,Chase	7	16	3	5	5	7	13	3	0	3	7	68	+7	+4	+11
Valbuena,Luis	5	22	7	10	4	7	8	2	0	3	13	90	-6	+1	-5
Valencia,Danny	4	23	3	7	0	6	5	2	1	4	13	67	-21	-2	-23
Van Slyke,Scott	2	8	6	9	0	1	6	0	0	0	5	65	+7	+1	+8
Venable,Will	10	22	8	10	4	6	11	2	1	3	8	51	+5	+14	+19
Victorino,Shane	2	11	3	4	1	2	5	0	0	0	4	34	+3	+7	+10
Villar,Jonathan	4	6	5	7	1	2	5	3	2	5	3	23	-8	+3	-5
Vogt,Stephen	8	24	5	13	3	9	18	2	1	3	9	101	+6	-4	+2
Votto,Joey	9	49	9	16	3	19	20	1	1	3	11	127	-2	+5	+3
Walker,Neil	5	34	11	15	4	7	10	2	4	6	9	99	-11	+2	-9
Werth,Jayson	2	16	6	13	4	5	15	3	0	3	8	71	+2	-2	0
Wieters,Matt	3	11	1	3	0	2	3	2	0	2	4	40	-6	0	-6
Wong,Kolten	15	27	7	15	3	7	18	0	1	1	10	102	+18	-1	+17
Wright,David	2	10	2	4	2	6	5	0	1	1	4	31	-2	0	-2
Yelich,Christian	10	30	14	20	6	7	13	3	1	4	13	103	+3	+6	+9
Young,Chris	2	13	9	16	4	8	9	1	1	2	6	56	-1	+1	0
Young,Delmon	3	7	1	2	1	4	9	0	0	0	8	44	+5	0	+5
Zimmerman,Ryan	2	17	6	11	4	7	6	2	0	2	13	88	-8	+1	-7
Zobrist,Ben	10	25	13	19	5	11	11	4	1	5	8	94	0	-5	-5

2015 Baserunning

Player	1st to 3rd Moved	Chances	2nd to Home Moved	Chances	1st to Home Moved	Chances	Bases Taken	Out Adv	Doubled Off	BR Outs	GDP	GDP Opps	BR Gain	SB Gain	Net Gain
Zunino,Mike	2	9	3	5	0	2	6	2	2	4	6	76	-6	-2	-8

2015 Team Baserunning

Team	1st to 3rd Moved	Chances	2nd to Home Moved	Chances	1st to Home Moved	Chances	Bases Taken	Out Adv	Doubled Off	BR Outs	GDP	GDP Opps	BR Gain	SB Gain	Net Gain
Texas Rangers	115	321	114	170	40	83	187	23	9	33	99	1123	+119	+23	+142
Arizona D-Backs	96	326	92	169	37	67	212	21	12	34	134	1099	+66	+44	+110
Cincinnati Reds	61	290	77	137	27	70	175	19	13	34	112	1092	+20	+58	+78
Toronto Blue Jays	82	308	115	189	37	104	197	23	13	38	139	1210	+32	+42	+74
Houston Astros	82	246	85	139	30	71	166	31	7	41	102	1024	+35	+25	+60
New York Yankees	76	311	81	160	31	81	181	22	10	32	105	1152	+43	+13	+56
Cleveland Indians	76	284	91	166	42	93	179	25	11	36	132	1171	+24	+30	+54
Chicago Cubs	96	281	107	174	35	71	143	32	12	44	102	1149	+26	+21	+47
Kansas City Royals	96	314	123	176	45	96	155	32	11	43	133	1075	+5	+36	+41
San Diego Padres	77	271	99	166	39	71	150	28	15	43	107	1022	+5	+24	+29
Colorado Rockies	97	294	108	174	34	59	135	26	12	38	114	1032	+17	+11	+28
San Francisco Giants	86	322	119	196	45	87	160	24	13	38	142	1116	-3	+21	+18
Washington Nationals	75	290	88	174	42	78	171	30	7	38	128	1143	+7	+11	+18
Boston Red Sox	89	319	88	180	47	88	186	37	7	44	127	1097	+1	+17	+18
Pittsburgh Pirates	90	321	117	186	37	77	157	31	13	45	115	1123	+5	+8	+13
Los Angeles Angels	88	266	89	152	39	65	199	37	15	56	116	1065	+23	-16	+7
Milwaukee Brewers	86	287	106	174	41	75	138	25	14	42	130	1027	-20	+26	+6
Miami Marlins	85	308	98	182	35	65	135	28	5	33	133	1071	-16	+22	+6
Philadelphia Phillies	73	277	90	157	30	71	151	30	12	42	119	1065	-18	+24	+6
Oakland Athletics	83	297	84	180	38	91	158	25	15	40	124	1153	-18	+20	+2
New York Mets	72	283	98	170	39	73	139	19	13	32	130	1102	-1	+1	0
Tampa Bay Rays	69	302	98	171	31	68	189	32	18	51	121	1093	-15	-3	-18
Minnesota Twins	72	276	98	189	29	68	169	27	11	38	133	1060	-13	-6	-19
St Louis Cardinals	81	306	98	164	35	78	155	27	18	46	128	1173	-21	-7	-28
Atlanta Braves	79	303	112	183	31	73	132	18	14	34	148	1115	-32	+3	-29
Baltimore Orioles	79	283	90	165	27	71	129	28	11	39	127	1110	-36	-6	-42
Seattle Mariners	77	269	75	148	14	60	167	28	19	47	123	1071	-35	-21	-56
Chicago White Sox	74	309	100	172	35	76	160	37	15	53	125	1091	-50	-16	-66
Los Angeles Dodgers	76	295	91	159	28	66	114	29	13	42	135	1164	-62	-9	-71
Detroit Tigers	73	321	100	183	29	75	130	28	14	43	152	1158	-88	-19	-107
MLB Totals	2461	8880	2931	5105	1049	2271	4819	822	372	1219	3735	33146			

Career Baserunning

Players with 1000 Career Games
(Data goes back to 2002)

Player	1st to 3rd		2nd to Home		1st to Home		Bases Taken	Out Adv	Doubled Off	BR Outs	GDP	GDP Opps	BR Gain	SB Gain	Net Gain
	Moved	Chances	Moved	Chances	Moved	Chances									
Andrus,Elvis	131	252	104	139	46	65	181	20	18	38	96	791	+126	+67	+193
Aybar,Erick	104	219	121	162	32	53	173	37	19	58	87	869	+53	+35	+88
Barmes,Clint	55	163	73	108	28	43	104	10	9	19	54	673	+72	-17	+55
Bautista,Jose	99	275	96	153	50	96	141	26	19	45	131	1096	-4	+10	+6
Beltran,Carlos	143	426	153	245	62	115	214	21	15	37	137	1567	+127	+157	+284
Beltre,Adrian	133	427	145	244	60	126	217	39	3	42	219	1736	+24	+24	+48
Bloomquist,Willie	66	186	69	107	28	49	94	15	7	22	49	551	+43	+31	+74
Bourn,Michael	79	249	112	177	50	67	164	15	11	26	31	632	+130	+148	+278
Braun,Ryan	83	261	108	157	49	76	150	25	12	37	116	1092	+49	+75	+124
Bruce,Jay	52	187	71	125	26	49	108	18	6	24	65	890	+45	-11	+34
Butler,Billy	32	278	53	152	19	102	131	31	8	39	194	1035	-212	-1	-213
Byrd,Marlon	71	307	120	186	48	100	172	27	11	39	114	1117	+20	-6	+14
Cabrera,Asdrubal	79	226	98	147	34	70	150	38	8	50	105	917	-2	+20	+18
Cabrera,Melky	95	284	96	163	44	88	168	31	14	47	122	1037	+4	+27	+31
Cabrera,Miguel	125	540	167	296	47	134	222	39	14	55	253	1702	-113	-2	-115
Callaspo,Alberto	58	226	76	119	14	35	93	29	8	38	104	749	-70	-6	-76
Cano,Robinson	103	351	159	251	40	87	201	35	21	56	216	1500	-46	-24	-70
Choo,Shin-Soo	81	280	106	165	39	76	170	22	17	39	65	784	+56	+22	+78
Crawford,Carl	75	302	175	243	59	109	255	36	21	60	76	1282	+125	+264	+389
Crisp,Coco	92	279	148	213	57	95	187	19	11	31	84	949	+124	+151	+275
Cruz,Nelson	34	193	61	106	10	49	104	21	12	33	80	787	-50	+12	-38
Cuddyer,Michael	131	328	119	197	52	90	168	44	16	62	182	1213	-53	+30	-23
Davis,Rajai	59	139	68	101	33	41	131	10	6	16	56	585	+110	+148	+258
DeJesus,David	138	358	116	186	43	83	195	27	14	41	103	893	+83	-58	+25
Drew,Stephen	58	219	74	138	21	67	120	31	10	42	45	791	-8	+5	-3
Encarnacion,Edwin	73	252	85	135	34	84	114	23	9	32	124	1069	-17	+28	+11
Escobar,Yunel	96	320	104	149	31	74	126	28	18	47	162	911	-90	-17	-107
Ethier,Andre	67	338	125	181	35	74	110	20	9	30	103	1120	0	-27	-27
Fielder,Prince	49	395	64	166	34	112	163	29	10	39	147	1246	-116	-4	-120
Francoeur,Jeff	82	234	89	147	30	83	127	31	15	48	122	1052	-40	-22	-62
Gomes,Jonny	52	182	82	126	22	44	105	14	12	27	52	790	+50	+2	+52
Gomez,Carlos	54	148	97	125	25	36	88	29	18	47	53	666	-13	+101	+88
Gonzalez,Adrian	62	367	89	214	42	130	152	33	16	50	179	1434	-155	-2	-157
Gordon,Alex	75	262	114	168	34	65	138	14	9	23	74	832	+77	+11	+88
Granderson,Curtis	97	323	114	199	65	104	170	17	17	34	43	1056	+128	+57	+185
Hamilton,Josh	83	248	83	133	40	62	106	11	14	26	66	878	+64	+18	+82
Hardy,J.J.	66	248	81	147	27	81	120	17	9	27	135	1038	-28	-8	-36
Hart,Corey	45	149	79	116	25	47	106	19	4	24	90	742	+21	+5	+26
Headley,Chase	56	240	80	147	22	56	130	21	9	32	93	863	-15	+26	+11
Hill,Aaron	74	275	100	158	35	69	144	18	7	26	126	1126	+39	+4	+43
Holliday,Matt	140	414	177	262	63	116	190	41	14	55	197	1505	+5	+33	+38
Howard,Ryan	34	288	77	173	31	115	119	26	10	36	109	1228	-86	+4	-82
Hunter,Torii	168	381	162	248	53	103	231	53	19	73	227	1595	-11	+6	-5
Infante,Omar	86	255	103	167	35	66	119	23	18	42	89	1006	+4	+14	+18
Johnson,Kelly	60	225	71	138	37	65	134	12	8	21	64	842	+68	+11	+79
Johnson,Reed	59	221	85	131	38	70	123	20	6	27	78	648	+16	-17	-1
Jones,Adam	72	228	86	123	49	75	132	16	10	27	123	1017	+45	+20	+65
Kemp,Matt	93	251	115	168	38	64	130	35	22	58	121	1079	-31	+60	+29
Kendrick,Howie	106	254	99	163	46	78	141	26	16	44	144	927	-17	+25	+8
Kinsler,Ian	128	295	156	220	52	91	206	20	19	39	127	1013	+119	+93	+212
LaRoche,Adam	56	306	81	165	22	83	141	27	10	38	128	1240	-59	-9	-68
Lind,Adam	55	182	57	120	24	70	79	19	6	27	97	823	-51	-2	-53
Loney,James	67	262	76	143	27	63	138	25	10	37	148	976	-58	-4	-62
Longoria,Evan	58	234	92	145	26	67	124	14	11	25	117	942	0	+23	+23
Markakis,Nick	97	418	140	227	42	108	168	23	7	31	148	1174	-8	+11	+3
Martin,Russell	72	287	105	167	38	69	131	25	14	40	157	997	-63	+7	-56
Martinez,Victor	56	385	98	204	23	123	163	31	8	40	211	1409	-162	-7	-169
Mauer,Joe	116	360	133	199	50	112	205	14	11	27	171	1271	+81	+14	+95
McCann,Brian	44	259	38	127	14	88	85	27	8	36	139	1154	-155	+7	-148
McCutchen,Andrew	73	265	108	145	35	65	105	13	10	23	56	744	+55	+44	+99
Molina,Yadier	54	292	63	148	18	59	115	26	8	35	189	1091	-152	-12	-164

358

Career Baserunning

Players with 1000 Career Games
(Data goes back to 2002)

Player	1st to 3rd Moved	Chances	2nd to Home Moved	Chances	1st to Home Moved	Chances	Bases Taken	Out Adv	Doubled Off	BR Outs	GDP	GDP Opps	BR Gain	SB Gain	Net Gain
Montero,Miguel	35	200	57	108	24	63	85	23	10	33	92	704	-85	-15	-100
Morneau,Justin	54	282	89	169	26	88	145	35	5	40	134	1283	-51	-15	-66
Murphy,David	42	159	74	133	29	55	109	16	7	23	61	714	+31	-2	+29
Napoli,Mike	67	231	76	123	22	61	90	19	7	27	88	846	-10	-9	-19
Ortiz,David	58	405	96	242	26	128	182	47	15	63	184	1847	-175	-6	-181
Pedroia,Dustin	79	290	117	182	45	119	158	35	15	52	117	1033	-41	+49	+8
Pence,Hunter	91	285	93	145	58	76	162	17	10	28	128	1027	+70	+8	+78
Peralta,Jhonny	64	346	109	213	35	104	161	37	16	53	193	1426	-139	-37	-176
Phillips,Brandon	123	303	120	176	45	72	214	43	17	62	220	1245	+5	+48	+53
Pierzynski,A.J.	65	338	89	203	22	77	155	47	7	56	220	1245	-192	-20	-212
Prado,Martin	92	246	91	141	29	70	144	26	11	37	128	813	-8	-13	-21
Pujols,Albert	169	500	199	279	56	136	243	65	17	84	291	2081	-80	+26	-54
Ramirez,Alexei	71	224	109	161	41	66	135	18	14	32	131	1006	+21	+27	+48
Ramirez,Aramis	72	362	94	216	29	118	149	42	11	53	212	1536	-189	-2	-191
Ramirez,Hanley	92	277	137	206	44	76	160	44	13	58	94	975	+1	+95	+96
Reyes,Jose	122	340	173	256	46	76	251	58	19	77	71	936	+69	+245	+314
Reynolds,Mark	47	191	63	111	19	65	107	16	9	25	88	877	-5	+3	-2
Rios,Alex	86	283	151	223	39	83	186	21	18	39	193	1421	+19	+99	+118
Rodriguez,Alex	119	372	154	239	50	126	203	35	16	51	177	1672	+25	+101	+126
Rollins,Jimmy	153	456	214	312	50	106	291	36	11	47	129	1280	+161	+226	+387
Ross,Cody	52	172	65	105	10	42	96	17	5	23	77	752	+10	+7	+17
Ruiz,Carlos	42	151	67	105	12	40	80	14	12	28	98	667	-55	+3	-52
Schumaker,Skip	53	226	73	126	21	45	124	16	5	22	73	573	+15	-8	+7
Sizemore,Grady	71	240	112	155	30	52	154	11	14	25	49	772	+122	+49	+171
Smith,Seth	48	165	62	97	33	46	84	17	6	25	57	571	+13	+6	+19
Suzuki,Ichiro	160	605	210	336	68	136	311	33	17	51	83	1384	+166	+242	+408
Suzuki,Kurt	56	207	72	139	24	52	92	12	1	14	104	830	+1	-1	0
Swisher,Nick	103	334	84	156	40	98	148	25	16	41	131	1287	-2	-17	-19
Teixeira,Mark	84	377	118	205	43	122	174	42	8	50	151	1673	-27	+10	-17
Tulowitzki,Troy	93	278	103	160	24	61	144	30	14	45	121	953	-16	-6	-22
Uggla,Dan	95	289	95	141	56	99	134	30	10	40	75	978	+54	-16	+38
Upton Jr.,Melvin	98	230	97	149	27	54	165	23	12	36	92	954	+85	+105	+190
Upton,Justin	90	247	101	147	49	83	117	15	15	30	83	965	+65	+27	+92
Uribe,Juan	85	251	93	149	19	53	131	13	12	27	142	1185	+16	-33	-17
Utley,Chase	153	329	144	196	57	93	186	25	16	41	87	1357	+188	+107	+295
Victorino,Shane	98	266	106	154	42	77	164	9	16	28	61	856	+127	+139	+266
Votto,Joey	88	306	90	150	29	92	135	35	15	51	85	928	-43	+5	-38
Weeks,Rickie	84	240	116	162	38	70	147	32	23	55	69	713	+5	+62	+67
Werth,Jayson	93	300	103	159	35	70	147	22	4	27	78	1018	+87	+85	+172
Wright,David	107	342	121	186	53	119	180	32	16	51	152	1393	+8	+67	+75
Young,Chris	45	176	86	126	41	62	107	19	11	30	51	842	+53	+49	+102
Young,Delmon	51	211	83	135	25	59	130	24	9	35	136	888	-46	-6	-52
Zimmerman,Ryan	77	264	108	167	46	93	145	20	6	26	161	1198	+21	+9	+30
Zobrist,Ben	91	247	88	150	40	83	163	18	10	28	80	924	+91	+27	+118

2002-2015 MLB Averages

1st to 3rd	2nd to Home	1st to Home
28%	59%	45%

Relief Pitching

Joe Rosales

The New York Yankees had a noteworthy bullpen in 2015 because of the two out-standing relievers that they had at the back end, Andrew Miller and Dellin Betances. Miller can more appropriately be called the closer because he got most of the save opportunities. However, the Yankees represent a rare instance in which a non-closer was actually used in more high leverage situations (where both relievers were on the team all season). Betances made more appearances than Miller (74 to 60), had more long outings than Miller (12 to 8), pitched more often on consecutive days (18 to 10), and pitched in higher Leverage Index situations on average (1.9 to 1.8). So, while Miller was nominally the closer, Betances appears to have been the more trusted reliever.

This section documents the performance of the most used relievers of each major league team. To qualify, a reliever must have had at least 10 relief appearances in 2015. In addition to his performance, which is detailed in a variety of metrics, we classify each reliever with a specific role. Most modern bullpens are made up of one closer (CL), one or two set-up men (SU), left-handed pitchers who are used against left-handed hitters (LT), a long man (LM), and some number of utility relievers (UR).

The data contained in this section includes:

Usage: Games in Relief (Rel G), the number of times the pitcher entered the game before the seventh inning (Early Entry), pitching on consecutive days (Cons Days), long outings (LO), and Leverage Index (Lev Ind). We use the Leverage Index calculated by Tom Tango and published on FanGraphs.com. An average Leverage Index is 1.0. If a pitcher pitches frequently in late innings with the game on the line, his leverage index will be high. If he generally pitches in the 6th inning of 7-2 ballgames, his leverage index will be very low.

Inherited Runners: The total (#), the number that scored (Scrd), and the percentage that scored (Pct).

Saves: The conversions and opportunities for three different classifications of Saves: "Easy", "Regular", and "Tough". The definitions of each of these save types can be found in the Baseball Glossary at the end of the book.

Relief Results: Clean Outings (Clean), Blown Save Wins (BS Wins), Saves and Save Opportunities (Sv-Opp), Holds, Save/Hold Percentage (Sv/Hld Pct), Opponent OPS (Opp OPS), and reliever ERA (Rel ERA). The definitions of many of these categories can be found in the Baseball Glossary at the end of the book.

Arizona Diamondbacks

Pitcher	Pos	T	Rel G	Early Entry	Cons Days	Long	Lev Ind	#	Scrd	Pct	Easy	Reg	Tough	Clean	BS Win	BS	Holds	Sv/Hld Pct	Opp OPS	Rel ERA
Ziegler, Brad	CL	R	66	1	18	7	1.6	20	4	.20	17 - 17	10 - 11	3 - 4	54	0	2	4	.94	.524	1.85
Hudson, Daniel	SU	R	63	5	7	11	1.3	16	5	.31	4 - 4	0 - 2	0 - 0	43	1	2	20	.92	.703	4.06
Reed, Addison	SU	R	38	3	4	8	1.4	13	5	.38	0 - 0	3 - 5	0 - 0	25	0	2	8	.85	.773	4.20
Perez, Oliver	LT	L	48	7	12	2	0.8	37	9	.24	0 - 0	0 - 1	0 - 2	36	1	3	7	.70	.627	3.10
Reynolds, Matt	LT	L	18	4	5	2	0.9	14	7	.50	0 - 0	0 - 0	0 - 1	10	0	1	3	.75	.947	4.61
Hessler, Keith	LT	L	18	7	4	1	0.7	11	6	.55	0 - 0	0 - 0	0 - 2	11	0	2	1	.33	.974	8.03
Chafin, Andrew	LM	L	66	29	11	12	1.2	44	15	.34	0 - 0	2 - 2	0 - 0	47	0	0	16	1.00	.587	2.76
Delgado, Randall	LM	R	63	24	16	13	1.2	41	12	.29	0 - 1	1 - 2	0 - 0	41	0	2	12	.87	.651	2.84
Collmenter, Josh	LM	R	32	11	5	14	0.4	15	4	.27	0 - 0	1 - 1	0 - 0	23	0	0	1	1.00	.648	1.89
Hernandez, David	UR	R	40	5	5	1	0.8	13	2	.15	0 - 0	0 - 0	0 - 0	26	0	0	7	1.00	.778	4.28
Burgos, Enrique	UR	R	30	5	7	4	1.1	8	4	.50	1 - 2	1 - 2	0 - 0	18	0	2	2	.67	.709	4.67
Bracho, Silvino	UR	R	13	6	1	2	0.6	7	2	.29	1 - 1	0 - 0	0 - 0	10	0	0	0	1.00	.680	1.46
Marshall, Evan	UR	R	13	0	3	2	1.4	4	1	.25	0 - 0	0 - 1	0 - 1	6	0	2	2	.50	.999	6.08
Ramirez, J.C.	UR	R	12	6	4	4	1.2	16	6	.38	0 - 0	0 - 1	0 - 1	4	0	2	2	.50	.641	4.11
Stites, Matt	UR	R	11	2	1	1	0.1	2	0	.00	0 - 0	0 - 0	0 - 0	6	0	0	0		.958	12.46

Atlanta Braves

Pitcher	Pos	T	Rel G	Early Entry	Cons Days	Long	Lev Ind	#	Scrd	Pct	Easy	Reg	Tough	Clean	BS Win	BS	Holds	Sv/Hld Pct	Opp OPS	Rel ERA
Grilli, Jason	CL	R	36	0	7	6	1.9	0	0	.00	16 - 17	8 - 9	0 - 0	25	0	2	0	.92	.620	2.94
Johnson, Jim	SU	R	49	0	16	2	1.7	11	3	.27	4 - 4	5 - 7	0 - 2	38	0	4	20	.88	.635	2.25
Martin, Cody	SU	R	21	8	5	1	1.2	11	2	.18	0 - 0	0 - 3	0 - 0	12	1	3	7	.70	.862	5.40
Avilan, Luis	LT	L	50	9	14	1	1.5	35	6	.17	0 - 1	0 - 2	0 - 0	38	0	3	11	.79	.670	3.58
Marksberry, Matt	LT	L	31	4	10	2	0.9	14	4	.29	0 - 1	0 - 1	0 - 1	19	0	3	5	.63	.777	5.01
McKirahan, Andrew	LT	L	27	9	4	5	0.8	25	5	.20	0 - 1	0 - 0	0 - 0	14	1	1	4	.80	.843	5.93
Detwiler, Ross	LT	L	24	8	6	5	0.6	20	7	.35	0 - 0	0 - 0	0 - 1	12	0	1	1	.50	.954	7.63
Eveland, Dana	LT	L	10	1	4	0	1.6	9	3	.33	0 - 0	0 - 0	0 - 0	5	0	0	1	1.00	1.302	5.40
Marimon, Sugar	LM	R	16	10	1	6	0.3	16	5	.31	0 - 0	0 - 0	0 - 0	4	0	0	0		.919	7.36
Cunniff, Brandon	UR	R	39	9	11	3	1.0	27	4	.15	0 - 0	0 - 0	0 - 2	27	0	2	5	.71	.673	4.63
Vizcaino, Arodys	UR	R	36	1	12	4	1.6	9	1	.11	4 - 4	5 - 6	0 - 0	31	0	1	3	.92	.615	1.60
Aardsma, David	UR	R	33	8	10	6	0.8	20	4	.20	0 - 0	0 - 1	0 - 2	21	0	3	6	.67	.759	4.70
Jackson, Edwin	UR	R	24	2	6	3	0.8	11	2	.18	0 - 0	0 - 0	1 - 1	15	0	0	5	1.00	.602	2.92
Moylan, Peter	UR	R	22	2	8	0	1.1	23	5	.22	0 - 0	0 - 0	0 - 1	14	1	1	3	.75	.636	3.48
Masset, Nick	UR	R	20	2	5	1	1.2	9	0	.00	0 - 0	0 - 0	0 - 0	14	0	0	5	1.00	.883	6.46
Kelly, Ryan	UR	R	17	4	5	1	0.3	12	7	.58	0 - 1	0 - 0	0 - 0	7	0	1	0	.00	.952	7.02
Brigham, Jake	UR	R	12	2	2	4	0.4	6	5	.83	0 - 0	0 - 0	0 - 0	6	0	0	0		.988	8.64
Burawa, Daniel	UR	R	12	4	3	3	0.3	13	4	.31	0 - 0	0 - 0	0 - 0	7	0	0	1	1.00	.564	3.65
Cahill, Trevor	UR	R	12	4	2	3	0.4	5	5	1.00	0 - 0	0 - 0	0 - 0	7	0	0	0		.857	7.07

Baltimore Orioles

Pitcher	Pos	T	Rel G	Early Entry	Cons Days	Long	Lev Ind	#	Scrd	Pct	Easy	Reg	Tough	Clean	BS Win	BS	Holds	Sv/Hld Pct	Opp OPS	Rel ERA
Britton, Zach	CL	L	64	0	18	3	1.5	12	0	.00	20 - 21	13 - 16	3 - 3	53	0	4	0	.90	.547	1.92
O'Day, Darren	SU	R	68	1	17	6	1.5	23	6	.26	1 - 2	5 - 7	0 - 2	57	1	5	18	.83	.540	1.52
Matusz, Brian	LT	L	58	12	15	8	0.9	46	17	.37	0 - 0	0 - 1	0 - 1	37	0	2	2	.50	.638	2.94
Hunter, Tommy	LM	R	39	8	3	5	1.0	28	11	.39	0 - 1	0 - 0	0 - 0	22	0	1	6	.86	.650	3.63
Roe, Chaz	LM	R	36	16	4	8	0.8	22	0	.00	0 - 0	0 - 1	0 - 0	22	0	1	4	.80	.798	4.14
McFarland, T.J.	LM	L	30	14	3	10	0.8	15	1	.07	0 - 0	0 - 0	0 - 0	18	0	0	3	1.00	.814	4.91
Givens, Mychal	LM	R	22	11	3	6	0.9	13	2	.15	0 - 0	0 - 0	0 - 0	16	0	0	4	1.00	.538	1.80
Brach, Brad	UR	R	62	18	8	21	1.1	29	17	.59	0 - 0	1 - 1	0 - 1	38	0	1	14	.94	.627	2.72
Garcia, Jason	UR	R	21	9	3	7	0.2	10	3	.30	0 - 0	0 - 0	0 - 0	11	0	0	0		.717	4.25
Drake, Oliver	UR	R	13	2	0	5	0.8	1	0	.00	0 - 0	0 - 0	0 - 0	8	0	0	2	1.00	.708	2.87

Boston Red Sox

Pitcher	Pos	T	Usage					Inherited Runners			Saves			Relief Results						
			Rel G	Early Entry	Cons Days	Long	Lev Ind	#	Scrd	Pct	Easy	Reg	Tough	Clean	BS Win	BS	Holds	Sv/Hld Pct	Opp OPS	Rel ERA
Uehara, Koji	CL	R	43	0	9	1	1.7	5	0	.00	16 - 16	9 - 11	0 - 0	36	0	2	0	.93	.562	2.23
Tazawa, Junichi	SU	R	61	1	15	5	1.4	21	8	.38	3 - 4	0 - 5	0 - 1	41	1	7	16	.73	.751	4.14
Layne, Tommy	LT	L	64	11	20	6	0.9	45	9	.20	1 - 1	0 - 0	0 - 1	44	0	1	9	.91	.684	3.97
Ross, Robbie	LT	L	54	18	10	12	0.8	41	15	.37	4 - 4	2 - 3	0 - 1	31	0	2	12	.90	.729	3.86
Breslow, Craig	LT	L	43	9	4	16	0.7	27	12	.44	0 - 0	0 - 1	1 - 3	20	0	3	1	.40	.846	4.53
Ogando, Alexi	UR	R	64	12	8	10	1.0	31	9	.29	0 - 0	0 - 2	0 - 2	42	0	4	12	.75	.776	3.99
Barnes, Matt	UR	R	30	9	3	9	0.8	14	4	.29	0 - 0	0 - 0	0 - 0	19	0	0	3	1.00	.873	4.13
Machi, Jean	UR	R	26	3	8	1	1.3	20	4	.20	3 - 3	1 - 1	0 - 0	15	0	0	2	1.00	.768	5.09
Hembree, Heath	UR	R	22	7	3	4	0.4	2	1	.50	0 - 0	0 - 0	0 - 0	16	0	0	1	1.00	.795	3.55
Ramirez, Noe	UR	R	17	2	4	3	1.1	15	3	.20	0 - 0	0 - 0	0 - 0	11	0	0	4	1.00	.803	4.15
Mujica, Edward	UR	R	11	5	1	2	0.8	7	0	.00	0 - 0	0 - 1	0 - 0	7	0	1	0	.00	.836	4.61

Chicago Cubs

Pitcher	Pos	T	Usage					Inherited Runners			Saves			Relief Results						
			Rel G	Early Entry	Cons Days	Long	Lev Ind	#	Scrd	Pct	Easy	Reg	Tough	Clean	BS Win	BS	Holds	Sv/Hld Pct	Opp OPS	Rel ERA
Rondon, Hector	CL	R	72	0	23	6	2.0	14	3	.21	16 - 18	14 - 16	0 - 0	60	0	4	8	.90	.568	1.67
Strop, Pedro	SU	R	76	2	24	2	1.6	26	12	.46	1 - 1	1 - 3	1 - 1	57	0	2	28	.94	.538	2.91
Grimm, Justin	SU	R	62	27	16	4	1.2	41	11	.27	0 - 1	3 - 5	0 - 0	43	0	3	15	.86	.572	1.99
Russell, James	LT	L	49	7	12	1	0.7	26	5	.19	1 - 2	0 - 0	0 - 1	35	0	2	8	.82	.836	5.29
Rosscup, Zac	LT	L	33	4	4	4	1.2	23	8	.35	0 - 0	0 - 1	0 - 1	21	0	2	6	.75	.860	4.39
Coke, Phil	LT	L	16	4	5	0	0.8	15	4	.27	0 - 0	0 - 0	0 - 0	11	0	0	3	1.00	.914	6.30
Wood, Travis	LM	L	45	19	7	15	0.8	21	7	.33	3 - 3	1 - 1	0 - 0	31	0	0	3	1.00	.577	2.95
Jackson, Edwin	LM	R	23	9	2	8	0.5	11	4	.36	0 - 0	0 - 1	0 - 0	13	0	1	0	.00	.637	3.19
Richard, Clayton	LM	L	20	10	4	5	0.8	15	5	.33	0 - 0	0 - 0	0 - 0	11	0	0	2	1.00	.765	4.44
Motte, Jason	UR	R	57	9	18	2	1.4	21	5	.24	4 - 4	2 - 3	0 - 0	40	0	1	9	.94	.689	3.91
Hunter, Tommy	UR	R	19	3	4	0	0.5	5	1	.20	1 - 1	0 - 0	0 - 0	12	0	0	1	1.00	.864	5.74
Ramirez, Neil	UR	R	19	0	2	1	0.3	3	0	.00	0 - 0	0 - 0	0 - 0	16	0	0	2	1.00	.685	3.21
Rodney, Fernando	UR	R	14	0	3	0	1.1	2	2	1.00	0 - 0	0 - 0	0 - 1	11	0	1	2	.67	.579	0.75
Cahill, Trevor	UR	R	11	6	1	3	1.0	10	2	.20	0 - 0	0 - 0	0 - 0	6	0	0	2	1.00	.494	2.12
Schlitter, Brian	UR	R	10	4	1	2	1.5	9	4	.44	0 - 0	0 - 1	0 - 1	5	0	2	0	.00	1.006	7.36

Chicago White Sox

Pitcher	Pos	T	Usage					Inherited Runners			Saves			Relief Results						
			Rel G	Early Entry	Cons Days	Long	Lev Ind	#	Scrd	Pct	Easy	Reg	Tough	Clean	BS Win	BS	Holds	Sv/Hld Pct	Opp OPS	Rel ERA
Robertson, David	CL	R	60	0	15	8	1.9	6	3	.50	22 - 23	11 - 16	1 - 2	44	2	7	0	.83	.573	3.41
Duke, Zach	SU	L	71	1	25	5	1.4	37	7	.19	0 - 0	0 - 2	1 - 1	50	0	2	26	.93	.724	3.41
Jones, Nate	SU	R	19	1	2	1	1.3	8	0	.00	0 - 0	0 - 1	0 - 0	14	0	1	6	.86	.695	3.32
Jennings, Dan	LT	L	53	7	14	11	0.7	38	14	.37	0 - 0	0 - 0	0 - 0	34	0	0	4	1.00	.664	3.99
Carroll, Scott	LM	R	18	10	2	10	0.4	17	7	.41	0 - 0	0 - 0	0 - 0	6	0	0	0		.774	3.44
Petricka, Jake	UR	R	62	5	19	5	1.3	31	5	.16	0 - 0	2 - 3	0 - 0	43	0	1	12	.93	.716	3.63
Putnam, Zach	UR	R	49	8	5	8	1.0	21	4	.19	0 - 0	0 - 3	0 - 0	31	1	3	6	.67	.734	4.07
Albers, Matt	UR	R	30	9	6	7	0.9	25	10	.40	0 - 0	0 - 0	0 - 0	20	0	0	6	1.00	.599	1.21
Webb, Daniel	UR	R	27	10	5	9	0.6	21	11	.52	0 - 0	0 - 1	0 - 0	14	0	1	0	.00	.887	6.30

Cincinnati Reds

Pitcher	Pos	T	Rel G	Early Entry	Cons Days	Long	Lev Ind	#	Scrd	Pct	Easy	Reg	Tough	Clean	BS Win	BS	Holds	Sv/Hld Pct	Opp OPS	Rel ERA
Chapman, Aroldis	CL	L	65	0	20	9	1.8	11	6	.55	20 - 21	12 - 14	1 - 1	53	1	3	0	.92	.527	1.63
Hoover, J.J.	SU	R	67	7	12	8	1.4	12	3	.25	1 - 3	0 - 3	0 - 1	52	2	6	18	.76	.663	2.94
Cingrani, Tony	SU	L	34	10	5	6	1.3	25	9	.36	0 - 0	0 - 2	0 - 0	20	0	2	9	.82	.756	4.70
Parra, Manny	LT	L	40	9	6	2	1.0	23	5	.22	0 - 0	0 - 0	0 - 1	27	0	1	6	.86	.675	3.90
Mattheus, Ryan	LM	R	57	17	17	4	0.8	19	6	.32	0 - 0	0 - 0	0 - 1	36	0	1	8	.89	.755	4.09
Villarreal, Pedro	LM	R	29	14	3	14	0.7	18	5	.28	0 - 0	0 - 0	0 - 0	17	0	0	0		.778	3.42
Badenhop, Burke	UR	R	68	15	15	9	0.8	31	14	.45	0 - 0	0 - 2	0 - 0	43	0	2	7	.78	.706	3.93
Diaz, Jumbo	UR	R	61	8	17	8	1.0	16	4	.25	0 - 3	1 - 1	0 - 1	43	0	4	7	.67	.755	4.18
Contreras, Carlos	UR	R	22	6	0	6	0.6	2	0	.00	0 - 0	0 - 0	0 - 0	14	0	0	0		.725	4.82
LeCure, Sam	UR	R	19	8	2	3	0.6	10	2	.20	0 - 0	0 - 0	0 - 1	11	0	1	3	.75	.672	3.15
Balester, Collin	UR	R	15	8	2	3	0.5	1	0	.00	0 - 0	0 - 0	0 - 0	7	0	0	2	1.00	.797	7.47
Adcock, Nate	UR	R	13	7	1	8	0.6	0	0	.00	0 - 0	0 - 0	0 - 0	7	0	0	0		.797	6.00
Gregg, Kevin	UR	R	11	2	1	3	1.1	2	0	.00	0 - 1	0 - 0	0 - 0	4	0	1	2	.67	.849	10.13

Cleveland Indians

Pitcher	Pos	T	Rel G	Early Entry	Cons Days	Long	Lev Ind	#	Scrd	Pct	Easy	Reg	Tough	Clean	BS Win	BS	Holds	Sv/Hld Pct	Opp OPS	Rel ERA
Allen, Cody	CL	R	70	1	18	6	1.7	26	4	.15	21 - 23	6 - 6	7 - 9	52	1	4	0	.89	.596	2.99
Shaw, Bryan	SU	R	74	5	17	5	1.3	48	17	.35	1 - 1	0 - 1	1 - 4	51	1	4	23	.86	.693	2.95
Rzepczynski, Marc	SU	L	45	11	11	0	1.0	34	7	.21	0 - 0	0 - 0	0 - 2	33	0	2	12	.86	.719	4.43
Hagadone, Nick	LT	L	36	11	11	0	0.7	21	5	.24	0 - 0	0 - 0	0 - 0	23	0	0	5	1.00	.741	4.28
Crockett, Kyle	LT	L	31	10	6	0	0.5	28	4	.14	0 - 0	0 - 0	0 - 0	22	0	0	3	1.00	.697	4.08
Manship, Jeff	LM	R	32	14	3	5	0.5	33	9	.27	0 - 0	0 - 0	0 - 0	21	0	0	3	1.00	.440	0.92
Adams, Austin	LM	R	28	12	1	9	0.3	21	5	.24	1 - 1	0 - 0	0 - 0	16	0	0	0	1.00	.766	3.78
McAllister, Zach	UR	R	60	14	8	11	1.0	29	11	.38	1 - 1	0 - 1	0 - 0	39	0	1	12	.93	.646	2.49
Webb, Ryan	UR	R	40	14	5	3	0.4	24	9	.38	0 - 0	0 - 0	0 - 0	23	0	0	0		.679	3.20
Atchison, Scott	UR	R	23	4	3	2	0.5	13	5	.38	0 - 1	0 - 0	0 - 0	12	0	1	3	.75	.897	6.86
Swarzak, Anthony	UR	R	10	5	2	1	0.2	4	3	.75	0 - 0	0 - 0	0 - 0	6	0	0	0		.799	3.38

Colorado Rockies

Pitcher	Pos	T	Rel G	Early Entry	Cons Days	Long	Lev Ind	#	Scrd	Pct	Easy	Reg	Tough	Clean	BS Win	BS	Holds	Sv/Hld Pct	Opp OPS	Rel ERA
Axford, John	CL	R	60	0	14	6	1.9	5	3	.60	14 - 15	11 - 16	0 - 0	44	2	6	2	.82	.704	4.20
Logan, Boone	SU	L	60	1	16	0	1.3	35	15	.43	0 - 1	0 - 1	0 - 2	41	0	4	23	.85	.756	4.33
Brown, Brooks	SU	R	36	13	10	4	1.1	17	5	.29	0 - 0	0 - 1	0 - 2	20	0	3	10	.77	.716	4.91
Kahnle, Tommy	SU	R	36	5	10	6	1.1	14	2	.14	1 - 1	1 - 2	0 - 0	24	0	1	10	.92	.778	4.86
Diaz, Jairo	SU	R	21	1	5	1	1.1	3	1	.33	0 - 1	0 - 0	0 - 0	18	0	1	7	.88	.615	2.37
Friedrich, Christian	LT	L	68	22	14	9	0.8	40	14	.35	0 - 0	0 - 0	0 - 0	40	0	0	9	1.00	.820	5.25
Brothers, Rex	LT	L	17	4	5	1	0.9	11	4	.36	0 - 0	0 - 0	0 - 0	14	0	0	0		.748	1.74
Germen, Gonzalez	LM	R	28	12	7	8	0.9	4	1	.25	0 - 1	1 - 2	0 - 0	19	0	2	2	.60	.824	4.25
Bergman, Christian	LM	R	26	18	3	19	0.7	15	3	.20	0 - 0	0 - 0	0 - 0	12	0	0	0		.795	4.10
Oberg, Scott	UR	R	64	19	15	9	1.1	39	8	.21	1 - 2	0 - 0	0 - 1	42	0	2	15	.89	.839	5.09
Betancourt, Rafael	UR	R	45	4	10	4	1.2	17	2	.12	1 - 2	0 - 1	0 - 1	29	0	3	8	.75	.749	6.18
Miller, Justin	UR	R	34	6	10	3	0.9	14	2	.14	0 - 1	1 - 1	0 - 0	25	0	1	7	.89	.553	4.05
Hawkins, LaTroy	UR	R	24	5	6	0	1.1	7	2	.29	1 - 3	1 - 1	0 - 0	18	1	2	3	.71	.692	3.63
Castro, Simon	UR	R	11	5	0	1	0.5	3	0	.00	0 - 0	0 - 0	0 - 0	7	0	0	0		.737	6.10
Ottavino, Adam	UR	R	10	0	4	0	1.2	0	0	.00	3 - 3	0 - 0	0 - 0	10	0	0	3	1.00	.265	0.00

Detroit Tigers

Pitcher	Pos	T	Usage					Inherited Runners			Saves			Relief Results						
			Rel G	Early Entry	Cons Days	Long	Lev Ind	#	Scrd	Pct	Easy	Reg	Tough	Clean	BS Win	BS	Holds	Sv/Hld Pct	Opp OPS	Rel ERA
Soria, Joakim	CL	R	43	0	13	4	1.9	13	4	.31	11 - 12	11 - 12	1 - 2	34	0	3	0	.88	.665	2.85
Chamberlain, Joba	SU	R	30	0	11	2	1.2	16	4	.25	0 - 1	0 - 1	0 - 0	19	0	2	8	.80	.986	4.09
Hardy, Blaine	LT	L	70	14	24	7	0.9	46	13	.28	0 - 0	0 - 2	0 - 1	44	1	3	13	.81	.704	3.08
Gorzelanny, Tom	LT	L	48	11	12	5	0.7	36	14	.39	0 - 0	0 - 0	0 - 0	26	0	0	2	1.00	.878	5.95
Krol, Ian	LT	L	33	7	9	5	1.2	18	3	.17	0 - 0	0 - 1	0 - 0	23	1	1	1	.50	.847	5.79
Ryan, Kyle	LT	L	10	7	0	6	0.6	11	2	.18	0 - 0	0 - 0	0 - 0	3	0	0	0		.742	3.51
VerHagen, Drew	LM	R	20	8	6	8	1.2	12	4	.33	0 - 0	0 - 1	0 - 0	14	0	1	3	.75	.559	2.05
Alburquerque, Al	UR	R	67	15	21	11	0.8	43	15	.35	0 - 0	0 - 0	0 - 1	45	0	1	7	.88	.731	4.21
Wilson, Alex	UR	R	58	12	14	12	1.0	43	17	.40	0 - 0	1 - 3	1 - 1	39	0	2	7	.82	.625	2.28
Rondon, Bruce	UR	R	35	1	9	2	1.7	8	0	.00	2 - 2	3 - 7	0 - 1	23	0	4	3	.67	.770	5.81
Feliz, Neftali	UR	R	30	4	4	5	1.2	13	6	.46	4 - 5	0 - 2	0 - 1	18	0	4	2	.60	.854	7.62
Nesbitt, Angel	UR	R	24	5	7	2	1.0	22	8	.36	0 - 0	0 - 0	0 - 2	14	0	2	2	.50	.740	5.40

Houston Astros

Pitcher	Pos	T	Usage					Inherited Runners			Saves			Relief Results						
			Rel G	Early Entry	Cons Days	Long	Lev Ind	#	Scrd	Pct	Easy	Reg	Tough	Clean	BS Win	BS	Holds	Sv/Hld Pct	Opp OPS	Rel ERA
Gregerson, Luke	CL	R	64	0	20	2	1.8	7	1	.14	21 - 24	10 - 11	0 - 1	51	2	5	0	.86	.573	3.10
Neshek, Pat	SU	R	66	0	14	1	1.3	27	4	.15	0 - 0	1 - 3	0 - 1	49	0	3	28	.91	.709	3.62
Sipp, Tony	LT	L	60	11	10	4	1.2	34	8	.24	0 - 0	0 - 2	0 - 1	45	0	3	13	.81	.606	1.99
Thatcher, Joe	LT	L	43	12	7	1	0.9	31	9	.29	0 - 0	0 - 0	0 - 0	30	0	0	6	1.00	.726	3.18
Perez, Oliver	LT	L	22	0	8	1	1.0	12	3	.25	0 - 0	0 - 0	0 - 0	12	0	0	3	1.00	.798	6.75
Harris, Will	UR	R	68	12	12	7	1.3	34	8	.24	0 - 0	1 - 3	1 - 3	49	1	4	13	.79	.525	1.90
Qualls, Chad	UR	R	60	6	13	1	1.1	20	6	.30	3 - 3	0 - 1	1 - 2	41	0	2	10	.88	.681	4.38
Fields, Josh	UR	R	54	13	9	6	0.9	25	6	.24	0 - 0	0 - 2	0 - 0	40	0	2	5	.71	.602	3.55
Velasquez, Vincent	UR	R	12	5	0	4	0.5	10	3	.30	0 - 0	0 - 0	0 - 0	6	0	0	0		.714	5.09

Kansas City Royals

Pitcher	Pos	T	Usage					Inherited Runners			Saves			Relief Results						
			Rel G	Early Entry	Cons Days	Long	Lev Ind	#	Scrd	Pct	Easy	Reg	Tough	Clean	BS Win	BS	Holds	Sv/Hld Pct	Opp OPS	Rel ERA
Holland, Greg	CL	R	48	0	13	4	2.1	8	4	.50	23 - 25	9 - 12	0 - 0	34	2	5	0	.86	.692	3.83
Herrera, Kelvin	SU	R	72	2	17	6	1.5	20	8	.40	0 - 0	0 - 5	0 - 2	50	2	7	21	.75	.578	2.71
Davis, Wade	SU	R	69	0	14	3	1.5	12	1	.08	11 - 11	6 - 7	0 - 0	62	1	1	18	.97	.451	0.94
Madson, Ryan	SU	R	68	17	15	1	1.3	26	7	.27	1 - 1	2 - 2	0 - 2	52	0	2	20	.92	.573	2.13
Morales, Franklin	LT	L	67	20	17	3	0.7	27	5	.18	0 - 0	0 - 0	0 - 0	48	0	1	8	.89	.687	3.18
Frasor, Jason	LM	R	26	8	1	7	0.9	16	5	.31	0 - 0	0 - 0	0 - 1	19	0	1	2	.67	.769	1.54
Finnegan, Brandon	LM	L	14	8	0	6	0.5	7	2	.29	0 - 0	0 - 0	0 - 1	8	1	1	0	.00	.643	2.96
Hochevar, Luke	UR	R	50	9	8	8	0.9	18	6	.33	0 - 0	1 - 2	0 - 0	32	0	1	6	.88	.737	3.73
Young, Chris	UR	R	16	5	1	6	0.7	3	0	.00	0 - 0	0 - 1	0 - 0	11	0	1	2	.67	.524	2.59
Blanton, Joe	UR	R	11	5	2	7	0.4	4	2	.50	1 - 1	1 - 1	0 - 0	7	0	0	0	1.00	.692	2.74

Los Angeles Angels

Pitcher	Pos	T	Usage					Inherited Runners			Saves			Relief Results						
			Rel G	Early Entry	Cons Days	Long	Lev Ind	#	Scrd	Pct	Easy	Reg	Tough	Clean	BS Win	BS	Holds	Sv/Hld Pct	Opp OPS	Rel ERA
Street, Huston	CL	R	62	0	24	5	2.1	14	3	.21	24 - 26	13 - 16	3 - 3	47	1	5	0	.89	.641	3.18
Smith, Joe	SU	R	70	0	27	2	1.8	12	4	.33	0 - 2	5 - 7	0 - 0	53	0	4	32	.90	.684	3.58
Gott, Trevor	SU	R	48	9	12	3	1.3	22	9	.41	0 - 0	0 - 2	0 - 2	32	1	4	14	.78	.625	3.02
Ramos, Cesar	LT	L	65	17	19	5	0.5	66	14	.21	0 - 0	0 - 0	0 - 2	46	0	2	5	.71	.685	2.75
Alvarez, Jose	LT	L	64	16	18	11	0.7	35	12	.34	0 - 1	0 - 0	0 - 0	41	0	1	7	.88	.642	3.49
Bedrosian, Cam	LM	R	34	14	6	8	0.5	23	8	.35	0 - 0	0 - 0	0 - 0	21	0	0	1	1.00	.833	5.40
Salas, Fernando	UR	R	72	17	15	6	0.9	48	10	.21	0 - 0	0 - 2	0 - 0	44	1	2	17	.89	.716	4.24
Morin, Mike	UR	R	47	11	17	2	0.7	25	8	.32	0 - 0	1 - 1	0 - 0	31	0	0	5	1.00	.720	6.37
Pestano, Vinnie	UR	R	19	3	4	1	0.7	16	9	.56	0 - 0	0 - 0	0 - 2	10	0	2	0	.00	.951	5.40
Rasmus, Cory	UR	R	15	6	1	5	0.4	6	1	.17	0 - 1	0 - 0	0 - 0	10	0	1	1	.50	.669	5.09

Los Angeles Dodgers

Pitcher	Pos	T	Usage					Inherited Runners			Saves			Relief Results						
			Rel G	Early Entry	Cons Days	Long	Lev Ind	#	Scrd	Pct	Easy	Reg	Tough	Clean	BS Win	BS	Holds	Sv/Hld Pct	Opp OPS	Rel ERA
Jansen, Kenley	CL	R	54	0	15	2	1.5	11	6	.55	25 - 25	10 - 12	1 - 1	38	1	2	1	.95	.513	2.41
Nicasio, Juan	SU	R	52	12	10	13	1.1	18	6	.33	0 - 0	0 - 1	1 - 2	32	0	2	14	.88	.740	3.83
Hatcher, Chris	SU	R	49	3	11	2	1.2	24	11	.46	4 - 4	0 - 0	0 - 2	29	0	2	13	.89	.685	3.69
Johnson, Jim	SU	R	23	3	6	3	1.5	10	3	.30	0 - 1	1 - 3	0 - 0	12	0	3	5	.67	.966	10.13
Howell, J.P.	LT	R	65	9	19	1	1.1	39	9	.23	0 - 0	0 - 0	1 - 4	51	0	3	9	.77	.673	1.43
Liberatore, Adam	LT	L	39	5	7	0	1.0	23	10	.43	0 - 0	0 - 0	0 - 1	26	0	1	10	.91	.671	4.25
Avilan, Luis	LT	L	23	2	5	0	1.3	21	3	.14	0 - 0	0 - 0	0 - 0	16	0	0	6	1.00	.654	5.17
Rodriguez, Paco	LT	L	18	5	4	0	0.9	22	5	.23	0 - 0	0 - 0	0 - 0	12	0	0	4	1.00	.625	2.61
Garcia, Yimi	UR	R	58	9	13	3	1.1	22	5	.23	1 - 3	0 - 2	0 - 1	42	1	5	11	.71	.570	3.13
Baez, Pedro	UR	R	52	14	13	5	1.2	40	15	.38	0 - 0	0 - 2	0 - 1	33	1	3	11	.79	.693	3.35
Peralta, Joel	UR	R	33	8	7	2	0.8	12	5	.42	3 - 3	0 - 0	0 - 0	23	0	0	3	1.00	.740	4.34
Santos, Sergio	UR	R	12	2	2	1	0.4	6	1	.17	0 - 0	0 - 0	0 - 0	8	0	0	0		.762	4.73

Miami Marlins

Pitcher	Pos	T	Usage					Inherited Runners			Saves			Relief Results						
			Rel G	Early Entry	Cons Days	Long	Lev Ind	#	Scrd	Pct	Easy	Reg	Tough	Clean	BS Win	BS	Holds	Sv/Hld Pct	Opp OPS	Rel ERA
Ramos, A.J.	CL	R	71	3	17	6	1.7	25	8	.32	18 - 19	12 - 17	2 - 2	57	1	6	4	.86	.562	2.30
Dunn, Mike	SU	L	72	2	18	6	1.3	49	8	.16	0 - 0	0 - 2	0 - 1	53	0	3	23	.88	.712	4.50
Morris, Bryan	SU	R	67	6	16	9	1.1	25	4	.16	0 - 1	0 - 0	0 - 1	48	0	2	18	.90	.721	3.14
Capps, Carter	SU	R	30	1	4	5	1.1	16	6	.38	0 - 0	0 - 1	0 - 1	23	0	2	11	.85	.474	1.16
Hand, Brad	LT	L	26	11	2	8	0.3	14	1	.07	0 - 0	0 - 0	0 - 0	17	0	0	2	1.00	.680	4.71
Narveson, Chris	LT	L	13	7	0	6	0.5	8	0	.00	0 - 0	0 - 0	0 - 0	7	0	0	0		.668	3.38
Dyson, Sam	UR	R	44	11	9	5	1.0	23	12	.52	0 - 0	0 - 0	0 - 2	25	0	2	9	.82	.658	3.68
Cishek, Steve	UR	R	32	2	5	4	1.6	12	8	.67	0 - 0	3 - 7	0 - 0	19	0	4	3	.60	.782	4.50
Barraclough, Kyle	UR	R	25	9	6	4	1.3	14	2	.14	0 - 0	0 - 1	0 - 0	17	0	1	6	.86	.563	2.59
Ellington, Brian	UR	R	23	4	6	7	0.6	6	1	.17	0 - 0	0 - 0	0 - 0	16	0	0	2	1.00	.612	2.88
Rienzo, Andre	UR	R	14	6	0	4	0.3	13	5	.38	0 - 0	0 - 0	0 - 0	7	0	0	0		.744	5.95
Urena, Jose	UR	R	11	5	0	3	0.7	6	1	.17	0 - 0	0 - 1	0 - 0	5	0	1	0	.00	.847	6.46
Mazzaro, Vin	UR	R	10	2	1	2	0.3	5	2	.40	0 - 0	0 - 0	0 - 0	4	0	0	0		.850	3.75

Milwaukee Brewers

Pitcher	Pos	T	Usage					Inherited Runners			Saves			Relief Results						
			Rel G	Early Entry	Cons Days	Long	Lev Ind	#	Scrd	Pct	Easy	Reg	Tough	Clean	BS Win	BS	Holds	Sv/Hld Pct	Opp OPS	Rel ERA
Rodriguez, Francisco	CL	R	60	0	18	1	1.4	7	0	.00	26 - 26	12 - 14	0 - 0	50	1	2	0	.95	.547	2.21
Smith, Will	SU	L	76	4	26	3	1.2	44	14	.32	0 - 0	0 - 1	0 - 3	55	0	4	20	.83	.649	2.70
Jeffress, Jeremy	SU	R	72	8	19	4	1.4	31	12	.39	0 - 0	0 - 3	0 - 2	54	1	5	23	.82	.666	2.65
Broxton, Jonathan	SU	R	40	0	6	2	1.1	6	3	.50	0 - 1	0 - 0	0 - 0	26	1	1	11	.92	.800	5.89
Cotts, Neal	LM	L	51	20	13	7	0.3	26	8	.31	0 - 0	0 - 0	0 - 0	37	0	0	4	1.00	.725	3.26
Thornburg, Tyler	LM	R	24	11	1	14	0.6	12	1	.08	0 - 0	0 - 0	0 - 0	13	0	0	1	1.00	.723	3.67
Jimenez, Cesar	LM	L	16	7	2	5	0.5	2	1	.50	0 - 0	0 - 0	0 - 0	12	0	0	4	1.00	.625	3.66
Lohse, Kyle	LM	R	15	10	0	10	0.6	4	1	.25	1 - 1	1 - 1	0 - 0	7	0	0	2	1.00	.795	3.81
Knebel, Corey	UR	R	48	14	4	7	0.5	12	3	.25	0 - 0	0 - 1	0 - 0	32	0	1	3	.75	.744	3.22
Blazek, Michael	UR	R	45	14	8	11	0.6	13	4	.31	0 - 0	0 - 0	0 - 0	32	0	0	4	1.00	.557	2.43
Goforth, David	UR	R	20	7	3	4	0.3	14	3	.21	0 - 0	0 - 0	0 - 0	12	0	0	0		.862	4.01

Minnesota Twins

Pitcher	Pos	T	Usage					Inherited Runners			Saves			Relief Results						
			Rel G	Early Entry	Cons Days	Long	Lev Ind	#	Scrd	Pct	Easy	Reg	Tough	Clean	BS Win	BS	Holds	Sv/Hld Pct	Opp OPS	Rel ERA
Perkins, Glen	CL	L	60	0	14	2	1.7	13	4	.31	21 - 21	8 - 10	3 - 4	44	0	3	3	.92	.701	3.32
Jepsen, Kevin	CL	R	29	0	9	2	1.5	1	0	.00	7 - 7	3 - 4	0 - 0	26	0	1	2	.92	.445	1.61
Boyer, Blaine	SU	R	68	18	20	4	1.2	38	18	.47	0 - 0	1 - 3	0 - 0	43	0	2	19	.91	.691	2.49
Fien, Casey	SU	R	62	7	17	4	1.2	22	4	.18	0 - 0	0 - 2	0 - 2	46	0	4	18	.82	.648	3.55
Duensing, Brian	LT	L	55	19	16	3	0.8	45	10	.22	0 - 0	1 - 2	0 - 0	39	0	1	6	.88	.741	4.25
Thompson, Aaron	LT	L	41	7	13	3	1.1	34	10	.29	0 - 0	0 - 1	0 - 0	23	0	1	9	.90	.682	5.01
ORourke, Ryan	LT	L	28	10	6	4	0.5	21	4	.19	0 - 0	0 - 0	0 - 0	19	0	0	0		.660	6.14
Cotts, Neal	LT	L	17	7	3	1	0.8	12	3	.25	0 - 0	0 - 0	0 - 0	10	0	0	1	1.00	.824	3.95
Graham, J.R.	LM	R	38	14	0	18	0.4	20	11	.55	0 - 0	0 - 0	0 - 1	18	0	1	0	.00	.801	5.13
May, Trevor	UR	R	32	0	8	2	1.3	9	3	.33	0 - 0	0 - 1	0 - 1	26	0	2	7	.78	.697	2.87
Pressly, Ryan	UR	R	27	10	9	3	0.8	13	2	.15	0 - 0	0 - 0	0 - 0	18	0	0	4	1.00	.645	2.93
Tonkin, Michael	UR	R	26	5	3	4	0.5	22	8	.36	0 - 0	0 - 0	0 - 0	17	0	0	5	1.00	.793	3.47
Stauffer, Tim	UR	R	13	8	2	4	0.6	13	6	.46	0 - 0	0 - 0	0 - 0	4	0	0	1	1.00	1.132	6.60
Achter, A.J.	UR	R	11	4	1	3	0.4	9	4	.44	0 - 0	0 - 0	0 - 0	7	0	0	0		.791	6.75

New York Mets

Pitcher	Pos	T	Usage					Inherited Runners			Saves			Relief Results						
			Rel G	Early Entry	Cons Days	Long	Lev Ind	#	Scrd	Pct	Easy	Reg	Tough	Clean	BS Win	BS	Holds	Sv/Hld Pct	Opp OPS	Rel ERA
Familia, Jeurys	CL	R	76	0	26	7	1.7	21	4	.19	26 - 27	14 - 17	3 - 4	62	0	5	1	.90	.569	1.85
Clippard, Tyler	SU	R	32	0	9	2	1.2	5	1	.20	1 - 2	1 - 2	0 - 0	23	1	2	8	.83	.637	3.06
Reed, Addison	SU	R	17	0	5	0	1.3	7	5	.71	1 - 1	0 - 0	0 - 2	14	0	2	6	.78	.539	1.17
Gilmartin, Sean	LT	L	49	9	10	12	0.8	20	6	.30	0 - 0	0 - 0	0 - 1	35	0	1	2	.67	.625	2.58
Torres, Alex	LT	L	39	8	7	7	0.9	25	5	.20	0 - 0	0 - 0	1 - 2	27	0	1	7	.89	.719	3.15
Leathersich, Jack	LT	L	17	6	4	2	0.4	11	4	.36	0 - 0	0 - 0	0 - 0	12	0	0	2	1.00	.726	2.31
OFlaherty, Eric	LT	L	16	3	3	0	0.4	11	4	.36	0 - 0	0 - 0	0 - 0	6	0	0	1	1.00	1.081	13.50
Torres, Carlos	UR	R	59	7	16	9	1.0	30	12	.40	0 - 0	0 - 1	0 - 0	39	0	1	11	.92	.743	4.68
Robles, Hansel	UR	R	57	8	15	5	1.2	29	12	.41	0 - 0	0 - 3	0 - 1	34	0	4	12	.75	.659	3.67
Goeddel, Erik	UR	R	35	13	7	5	0.6	23	8	.35	0 - 0	0 - 0	0 - 0	26	0	0	2	1.00	.553	2.43
Parnell, Bobby	UR	R	30	3	6	1	1.2	15	6	.40	0 - 2	0 - 0	1 - 1	19	0	2	5	.75	.789	6.38
Carlyle, Buddy	UR	R	11	1	2	0	1.2	11	3	.27	1 - 1	0 - 0	0 - 0	7	0	0	4	1.00	.661	5.63
Verrett, Logan	UR	R	10	4	1	3	0.7	2	1	.50	0 - 1	1 - 1	0 - 0	8	0	1	0	.50	.420	2.20

New York Yankees

Pitcher	Pos	T	Rel G	Early Entry	Cons Days	Long	Lev Ind	#	Scrd	Pct	Easy	Reg	Tough	Clean	BS Win	BS	Holds	Sv/Hld Pct	Opp OPS	Rel ERA
			Usage					**Inherited Runners**			**Saves**			**Relief Results**						
Miller, Andrew	CL	L	60	0	10	8	1.8	12	1	.08	20 - 21	15 - 16	1 - 1	48	1	2	0	.95	.475	2.04
Wilson, Justin	SU	L	74	19	20	5	1.4	44	7	.16	0 - 0	0 - 1	0 - 1	56	2	2	29	.94	.602	3.10
Betances, Dellin	SU	R	74	0	18	12	1.9	41	11	.27	4 - 4	2 - 4	3 - 5	56	1	4	28	.90	.510	1.50
Shreve, Chasen	LT	L	59	18	9	10	0.9	43	15	.35	0 - 0	0 - 1	0 - 0	37	0	1	10	.91	.738	3.09
Capuano, Chris	LT	L	18	6	1	8	0.4	8	3	.38	0 - 0	0 - 0	0 - 0	8	0	0	1	1.00	.861	7.24
Pazos, James	LT	L	11	4	2	0	0.4	5	1	.20	0 - 0	0 - 0	0 - 0	10	0	0	0		.476	0.00
Warren, Adam	LM	R	26	11	5	10	0.8	17	4	.24	0 - 0	1 - 1	1 - 0	17	0	0	3	1.00	.605	2.29
Mitchell, Bryan	LM	R	18	4	0	7	0.7	8	3	.38	0 - 0	1 - 1	0 - 0	8	0	0	1	1.00	.756	6.00
Rogers, Esmil	LM	R	18	10	1	10	0.7	15	7	.47	0 - 0	0 - 0	0 - 0	6	0	0	1	1.00	.835	6.27
Pinder, Branden	UR	R	25	5	4	6	0.3	10	5	.50	0 - 0	0 - 0	0 - 0	15	0	0	0		.830	2.93
Martin, Chris	UR	R	24	9	4	2	0.7	15	7	.47	1 - 1	0 - 0	0 - 0	13	0	0	5	1.00	.777	5.66
Carpenter, David	UR	R	22	7	3	2	0.7	9	4	.44	0 - 0	0 - 2	0 - 0	13	0	2	2	.50	.869	4.82
Rumbelow, Nick	UR	R	17	4	0	1	0.5	13	3	.23	0 - 0	0 - 0	0 - 0	10	0	0	0		.722	4.02
Cotham, Caleb	UR	R	12	3	1	2	0.7	9	3	.33	0 - 0	0 - 0	0 - 0	6	0	0	0		.992	6.52
Bailey, Andrew	UR	R	10	2	0	1	0.6	6	2	.33	0 - 0	0 - 0	0 - 0	5	0	0	0		.866	8.31

Oakland Athletics

Pitcher	Pos	T	Rel G	Early Entry	Cons Days	Long	Lev Ind	#	Scrd	Pct	Easy	Reg	Tough	Clean	BS Win	BS	Holds	Sv/Hld Pct	Opp OPS	Rel ERA
			Usage					**Inherited Runners**			**Saves**			**Relief Results**						
Clippard, Tyler	CL	R	37	0	6	8	1.7	11	3	.27	9 - 9	7 - 8	1 - 4	29	0	4	0	.81	.567	2.79
Pomeranz, Drew	SU	L	44	8	11	7	1.4	28	11	.39	1 - 1	2 - 4	0 - 1	31	0	3	12	.83	.587	2.61
Abad, Fernando	LT	L	62	9	13	5	0.7	46	13	.28	0 - 0	0 - 1	0 - 2	42	0	3	1	.25	.813	4.15
OFlaherty, Eric	LT	L	25	6	4	2	0.8	11	3	.27	0 - 0	0 - 0	0 - 1	14	0	1	3	.75	.826	5.91
Doolittle, Sean	LT	L	12	2	1	4	1.6	1	1	1.00	1 - 1	3 - 4	0 - 0	7	0	1	1	.83	.651	3.95
Venditte, Pat	LM	B	26	11	6	7	0.8	18	7	.39	0 - 0	0 - 0	0 - 0	16	0	0	2	1.00	.679	4.40
Leon, Arnold	LM	R	19	9	2	8	0.6	13	7	.54	0 - 0	0 - 0	0 - 0	6	0	0	0		.779	4.39
Rodriguez, Fernando	UR	R	56	13	12	10	1.0	30	4	.13	0 - 0	0 - 1	0 - 1	39	0	2	6	.75	.589	3.84
Scribner, Evan	UR	R	54	9	14	11	0.8	21	10	.48	0 - 0	0 - 2	0 - 2	32	1	4	8	.67	.758	4.35
Otero, Dan	UR	R	41	16	11	8	0.6	24	8	.33	0 - 0	0 - 0	0 - 1	21	0	1	2	.67	.886	6.75
Mujica, Edward	UR	R	38	8	8	0	1.2	25	7	.28	0 - 1	0 - 1	1 - 2	25	0	3	4	.63	.769	4.81
Alvarez, R.J.	UR	R	21	4	7	4	0.2	12	7	.58	0 - 0	0 - 0	0 - 1	8	0	1	0	.00	1.035	9.90
Dull, Ryan	UR	R	13	1	2	2	1.5	3	1	.33	0 - 0	1 - 1	0 - 1	9	0	1	2	.75	.713	4.24

Philadelphia Phillies

Pitcher	Pos	T	Rel G	Early Entry	Cons Days	Long	Lev Ind	#	Scrd	Pct	Easy	Reg	Tough	Clean	BS Win	BS	Holds	Sv/Hld Pct	Opp OPS	Rel ERA
			Usage					**Inherited Runners**			**Saves**			**Relief Results**						
Giles, Ken	CL	R	69	0	21	10	1.5	16	3	.19	9 - 9	4 - 9	2 - 2	53	0	5	12	.84	.569	1.80
Papelbon, Jonathan	CL	R	37	0	10	1	1.3	4	1	.25	14 - 14	2 - 2	1 - 1	28	0	0	0	1.00	.597	1.59
Araujo, Elvis	LT	L	40	14	12	5	0.6	19	3	.16	0 - 0	0 - 0	0 - 0	24	0	0	2	1.00	.619	3.38
De Fratus, Justin	LM	R	61	30	13	22	0.4	26	13	.50	0 - 0	0 - 0	0 - 1	33	0	1	1	.50	.822	5.51
Diekman, Jake	LM	L	41	16	12	3	0.7	22	9	.41	0 - 0	0 - 1	0 - 1	23	0	2	6	.75	.773	5.15
Loewen, Adam	LM	L	20	7	5	5	0.4	10	1	.10	0 - 0	0 - 0	0 - 0	11	0	0	0		.900	6.98
Garcia, Luis	UR	R	72	3	18	7	1.4	22	8	.36	1 - 1	1 - 2	0 - 1	50	0	2	16	.90	.748	3.51
Gomez, Jeanmar	UR	R	65	16	17	11	0.9	22	10	.45	0 - 0	0 - 2	0 - 1	43	0	3	7	.70	.697	3.01
Neris, Hector	UR	R	32	12	5	9	0.7	13	5	.38	0 - 0	0 - 0	0 - 0	21	0	0	2	1.00	.772	3.79
Hinojosa, Dalier	UR	R	18	3	4	4	0.7	2	1	.50	0 - 0	0 - 1	0 - 0	14	1	1	3	.75	.483	0.78
McGowan, Dustin	UR	R	13	4	2	7	0.5	5	2	.40	0 - 0	0 - 0	0 - 0	5	0	0	0		.992	6.30
Williams, Jerome	UR	R	12	2	3	2	1.2	3	0	.00	0 - 0	1 - 2	0 - 0	7	0	1	4	.83	.744	3.52

Pittsburgh Pirates

Pitcher	Pos	T	Rel G	Early Entry	Cons Days	Long	Lev Ind	#	Scrd	Pct	Easy	Reg	Tough	Clean	BS Win	BS	Holds	Sv/Hld Pct	Opp OPS	Rel ERA
Melancon, Mark	CL	R	78	0	23	1	1.9	13	3	.23	32 - 34	19 - 19	0 - 0	63	0	2	1	.96	.541	2.23
Watson, Tony	SU	L	77	0	23	4	1.7	24	6	.25	0 - 1	0 - 1	1 - 1	63	0	2	41	.95	.525	1.91
Hughes, Jared	SU	R	76	19	22	6	1.2	56	9	.16	0 - 1	0 - 1	0 - 1	56	0	3	21	.88	.720	2.28
Soria, Joakim	SU	R	29	1	10	3	1.4	7	3	.43	0 - 0	1 - 3	0 - 1	22	0	3	11	.80	.571	2.03
Bastardo, Antonio	LT	L	66	9	18	9	0.8	27	3	.11	1 - 1	0 - 0	0 - 1	50	0	1	9	.91	.571	2.98
LaFromboise, Bobby	LT	L	11	3	2	1	0.4	11	3	.27	0 - 0	0 - 0	0 - 0	10	0	0	0		.564	1.13
Blanton, Joe	LM	R	21	8	4	8	0.8	3	1	.33	0 - 0	0 - 0	0 - 0	16	0	0	0		.556	1.57
Worley, Vance	LM	R	15	5	2	9	0.7	0	0	.00	0 - 0	0 - 1	0 - 0	7	1	1	0	.00	.639	2.83
Caminero, Arquimedes	UR	R	73	13	15	9	0.9	31	7	.23	0 - 1	0 - 0	0 - 0	50	0	1	15	.94	.661	3.62
Scahill, Rob	UR	R	28	6	2	7	1.1	8	1	.13	0 - 0	0 - 0	0 - 0	17	0	0	1	1.00	.761	2.64
Liz, Radhames	UR	R	14	6	1	6	1.3	0	0	.00	0 - 0	0 - 1	0 - 0	6	0	1	0	.00	.837	4.24
Guerra, Deolis	UR	R	10	4	2	5	0.9	3	2	.67	0 - 0	0 - 0	0 - 0	5	0	0	0		1.077	6.48

San Diego Padres

Pitcher	Pos	T	Rel G	Early Entry	Cons Days	Long	Lev Ind	#	Scrd	Pct	Easy	Reg	Tough	Clean	BS Win	BS	Holds	Sv/Hld Pct	Opp OPS	Rel ERA
Kimbrel, Craig	CL	R	61	0	17	5	1.8	5	1	.20	22 - 23	15 - 18	2 - 2	45	2	4	0	.91	.569	2.58
Benoit, Joaquin	SU	R	67	0	19	2	1.4	0	0	.00	2 - 2	0 - 4	0 - 0	52	1	4	28	.88	.547	2.34
Garces, Frank	LT	L	39	7	7	7	0.3	25	6	.24	0 - 0	0 - 0	0 - 0	25	0	0	0		.860	5.00
Rzepczynski, Marc	LT	L	27	7	9	0	1.0	30	10	.33	0 - 0	0 - 0	0 - 2	15	0	2	4	.67	.820	7.36
Mateo, Marcos	LM	R	26	12	6	7	0.5	14	3	.21	0 - 0	0 - 1	0 - 0	14	0	1	1	.50	.738	4.00
Despaigne, Odrisamer	LM	R	16	10	1	7	0.3	8	3	.38	0 - 0	0 - 0	0 - 0	9	0	0	0		.968	7.30
Quackenbush, Kevin	UR	R	57	4	9	11	0.4	16	4	.25	0 - 0	0 - 0	0 - 1	38	0	1	2	.67	.670	4.01
Kelley, Shawn	UR	R	53	7	6	6	0.8	31	11	.35	0 - 0	0 - 0	0 - 0	37	0	0	7	1.00	.596	2.45
Maurer, Brandon	UR	R	53	2	14	3	1.3	16	6	.38	0 - 0	0 - 0	0 - 1	38	1	1	12	.92	.568	3.00
Thayer, Dale	UR	R	38	10	8	5	1.0	12	4	.33	0 - 0	0 - 1	0 - 0	29	0	1	6	.86	.764	4.06
Vincent, Nick	UR	R	29	9	8	5	0.6	15	7	.47	0 - 0	0 - 1	0 - 1	15	0	2	0	.00	.698	2.35
Norris, Bud	UR	R	20	8	3	2	0.8	14	5	.36	0 - 0	0 - 0	0 - 1	12	1	1	2	.67	.750	5.40
Edwards, Jon	UR	R	11	2	1	1	0.2	4	2	.50	0 - 0	0 - 0	0 - 0	8	0	0	0		.775	3.38

San Francisco Giants

Pitcher	Pos	T	Rel G	Early Entry	Cons Days	Long	Lev Ind	#	Scrd	Pct	Easy	Reg	Tough	Clean	BS Win	BS	Holds	Sv/Hld Pct	Opp OPS	Rel ERA
Casilla, Santiago	CL	R	67	0	20	3	1.9	25	9	.36	26 - 29	11 - 12	1 - 3	49	1	6	0	.86	.680	2.79
Romo, Sergio	SU	R	70	1	23	0	1.5	38	7	.18	1 - 1	1 - 2	0 - 1	52	0	2	34	.95	.622	2.98
Strickland, Hunter	SU	R	55	3	16	1	1.2	31	4	.13	0 - 0	0 - 1	0 - 1	41	0	2	20	.91	.543	2.45
Osich, Josh	SU	L	35	4	12	3	1.0	21	4	.19	0 - 0	0 - 1	0 - 1	24	0	2	11	.85	.633	2.20
Lopez, Javier	LT	L	77	10	27	1	1.0	59	8	.14	0 - 0	0 - 0	0 - 0	64	0	0	20	1.00	.459	1.60
Affeldt, Jeremy	LT	L	52	11	9	1	0.8	30	6	.20	0 - 0	0 - 0	0 - 0	35	0	0	9	1.00	.818	5.86
Petit, Yusmeiro	LM	R	41	20	2	17	0.5	34	10	.29	0 - 0	1 - 1	0 - 0	24	0	0	0	1.00	.740	3.47
Kontos, George	UR	R	73	32	20	6	1.0	54	13	.24	0 - 1	0 - 1	0 - 0	52	0	2	14	.88	.595	2.33
Machi, Jean	UR	R	33	3	3	5	0.5	11	2	.18	0 - 0	0 - 0	0 - 0	23	0	0	2	1.00	.773	5.14
Broadway, Mike	UR	R	21	3	5	0	0.5	5	2	.40	0 - 0	0 - 0	0 - 0	13	0	0	2	1.00	.839	5.19
Vogelsong, Ryan	UR	R	11	4	0	7	0.7	4	0	.00	0 - 0	0 - 1	0 - 0	6	0	1	0	.00	.933	5.68

Seattle Mariners

Pitcher	Pos	T	Usage					Inherited Runners			Saves			Relief Results						
			Rel G	Early Entry	Cons Days	Long	Lev Ind	#	Scrd	Pct	Easy	Reg	Tough	Clean	BS Win	BS	Holds	Sv/Hld Pct	Opp OPS	Rel ERA
Rodney, Fernando	CL	R	54	0	13	3	2.0	5	2	.40	11 - 14	5 - 8	0 - 0	32	1	6	7	.79	.820	5.68
Wilhelmsen, Tom	CL	R	53	11	12	15	1.5	29	18	.62	7 - 7	5 - 7	1 - 1	31	0	2	7	.91	.696	3.19
Smith, Carson	SU	R	70	3	17	6	2.1	33	8	.24	8 - 9	5 - 7	0 - 2	51	0	5	22	.88	.539	2.31
Lowe, Mark	SU	R	34	6	8	5	1.0	10	1	.10	0 - 0	0 - 1	0 - 1	29	0	2	12	.86	.602	1.00
Furbush, Charlie	SU	L	33	5	10	0	1.4	16	0	.00	0 - 0	0 - 0	0 - 0	29	0	0	13	1.00	.414	2.08
Kensing, Logan	SU	R	19	5	6	2	1.2	13	4	.31	0 - 0	0 - 0	0 - 0	11	0	0	9	1.00	.672	5.87
Beimel, Joe	LT	L	53	9	14	3	0.7	30	15	.50	0 - 0	1 - 2	0 - 1	31	0	2	6	.78	.799	3.99
Nuno, Vidal	LT	L	22	4	4	5	0.5	14	4	.29	0 - 0	0 - 0	0 - 0	14	0	0	4	1.00	.647	1.93
Rasmussen, Rob	LT	L	19	6	7	3	0.8	18	5	.28	0 - 0	0 - 0	0 - 0	10	0	0	2	1.00	.977	10.67
Olson, Tyler	LT	L	11	4	3	5	1.2	7	2	.29	0 - 0	0 - 0	0 - 0	5	0	0	1	1.00	1.056	5.40
Guaipe, Mayckol	LM	R	21	15	4	9	1.1	18	6	.33	0 - 0	0 - 2	0 - 1	8	0	3	2	.40	.951	5.40
Rollins, David	LM	L	20	9	1	10	0.6	14	6	.43	0 - 0	0 - 0	0 - 0	8	0	0	1	1.00	.925	7.56
Farquhar, Danny	UR	R	43	9	9	11	0.9	23	7	.30	0 - 1	1 - 1	0 - 1	24	0	2	8	.82	.818	5.12
Medina, Yoervis	UR	R	12	3	2	2	1.1	5	1	.20	0 - 0	1 - 2	0 - 0	8	0	1	3	.80	.759	3.00
Zych, Tony	UR	R	12	4	1	3	0.7	10	2	.20	0 - 0	0 - 0	0 - 0	5	0	0	1	1.00	.642	2.87
Leone, Dominic	UR	R	10	2	1	5	1.6	6	0	.00	0 - 0	0 - 0	0 - 0	4	0	0	1	1.00	.770	6.35

St Louis Cardinals

Pitcher	Pos	T	Usage					Inherited Runners			Saves			Relief Results						
			Rel G	Early Entry	Cons Days	Long	Lev Ind	#	Scrd	Pct	Easy	Reg	Tough	Clean	BS Win	BS	Holds	Sv/Hld Pct	Opp OPS	Rel ERA
Rosenthal, Trevor	CL	R	68	0	22	6	2.1	14	3	.21	30 - 32	14 - 15	4 - 4	54	0	3	0	.94	.619	2.10
Siegrist, Kevin	SU	L	81	3	22	7	1.4	24	5	.21	3 - 4	3 - 6	0 - 0	65	1	4	28	.89	.605	2.17
Maness, Seth	SU	R	76	16	26	6	1.3	59	14	.24	1 - 1	1 - 2	1 - 3	54	0	3	20	.88	.788	4.26
Broxton, Jonathan	SU	R	26	1	7	1	1.2	6	3	.50	0 - 0	0 - 1	0 - 1	18	0	2	6	.75	.710	2.66
Walden, Jordan	SU	R	12	0	5	0	2.0	4	0	.00	0 - 0	1 - 1	0 - 0	11	0	0	8	1.00	.505	0.87
Choate, Randy	LT	L	71	7	30	1	0.9	57	8	.14	0 - 0	1 - 1	0 - 0	56	0	0	8	1.00	.720	3.95
Villanueva, Carlos	LM	R	35	13	1	13	0.8	6	1	.17	0 - 0	2 - 2	0 - 0	21	0	0	0	1.00	.677	2.95
Belisle, Matt	UR	R	34	5	7	7	1.1	11	4	.36	0 - 0	0 - 0	0 - 1	25	0	1	7	.88	.690	2.67
Socolovich, Miguel	UR	R	28	2	5	6	0.6	7	1	.14	0 - 0	0 - 0	0 - 0	20	0	0	1	1.00	.568	1.82
Cishek, Steve	UR	R	27	4	5	0	0.8	5	3	.60	1 - 1	0 - 1	0 - 0	21	0	1	3	.80	.629	2.31
Harris, Mitchell	UR	R	26	4	7	7	0.8	4	0	.00	0 - 0	0 - 0	0 - 0	19	0	0	0		.754	3.67
Tuivailala, Samuel	UR	R	14	0	4	3	1.0	3	2	.67	0 - 0	0 - 0	0 - 0	10	0	0	2	1.00	.744	3.07

Tampa Bay Rays

Pitcher	Pos	T	Usage					Inherited Runners			Saves			Relief Results						
			Rel G	Early Entry	Cons Days	Long	Lev Ind	#	Scrd	Pct	Easy	Reg	Tough	Clean	BS Win	BS	Holds	Sv/Hld Pct	Opp OPS	Rel ERA
Boxberger, Brad	CL	R	69	0	26	7	2.0	13	3	.23	31 - 32	10 - 13	0 - 2	49	2	6	2	.88	.703	3.71
Geltz, Steve	SU	R	68	18	18	8	1.3	26	3	.12	1 - 1	1 - 3	0 - 1	49	0	3	20	.88	.609	3.84
Gomes, Brandon	SU	R	64	27	10	10	1.4	40	8	.20	1 - 1	0 - 2	0 - 0	42	0	2	16	.89	.739	4.27
Cedeno, Xavier	SU	L	61	20	22	3	1.0	30	4	.13	1 - 1	0 - 0	0 - 0	50	0	0	19	1.00	.592	2.09
Jepsen, Kevin	SU	R	46	0	15	2	2.0	14	6	.43	1 - 2	4 - 6	0 - 1	32	0	4	22	.87	.635	2.81
McGee, Jake	SU	L	39	0	10	4	1.7	3	0	.00	3 - 3	3 - 7	0 - 0	33	0	4	19	.86	.544	2.41
Colome, Alex	SU	R	30	7	5	7	1.4	16	9	.56	0 - 2	0 - 1	0 - 2	19	1	5	8	.62	.584	2.66
Romero, Enny	LT	L	23	6	3	7	0.5	11	7	.64	0 - 0	0 - 0	0 - 2	12	0	2	3	.60	.798	5.10
Riefenhauser, C.J.	LT	L	17	4	5	1	0.4	10	2	.20	0 - 0	0 - 0	0 - 0	12	0	0	0		.870	5.52
Andriese, Matt	LM	R	17	6	1	9	0.6	5	3	.60	0 - 0	2 - 2	0 - 0	8	0	0	0	1.00	.746	4.75
Frieri, Ernesto	UR	R	22	1	4	2	0.5	6	1	.17	0 - 1	2 - 2	0 - 0	11	0	1	0	.67	.797	4.63
Yates, Kirby	UR	R	20	4	3	5	0.3	11	5	.45	0 - 0	0 - 0	0 - 0	7	0	0	0		1.004	7.97
Bellatti, Andrew	UR	R	17	5	5	4	1.0	9	2	.22	0 - 0	0 - 0	0 - 0	12	0	0	2	1.00	.685	2.31

Texas Rangers

Pitcher	Pos	T	Rel G	Early Entry	Cons Days	Long	Lev Ind	#	Scrd	Pct	Easy	Reg	Tough	Clean	BS Win	BS	Holds	Sv/Hld Pct	Opp OPS	Rel ERA
					Usage				Inherited Runners			Saves				Relief Results					
Tolleson, Shawn	CL	R	73	0	28	6	1.8	9	2	.22	24 - 25	11 - 12	0 - 0	57	0	2	6	.95	.675	2.99
Kela, Keone	SU	R	68	6	12	2	1.3	27	5	.19	1 - 1	0 - 2	0 - 1	51	1	3	22	.88	.615	2.39
Scheppers, Tanner	SU	R	42	6	11	3	1.2	23	6	.26	0 - 1	0 - 2	0 - 0	25	1	3	12	.80	.778	5.63
Dyson, Sam	SU	R	31	1	10	1	1.3	11	1	.09	0 - 0	1 - 1	1 - 1	26	0	0	12	1.00	.520	1.15
Diekman, Jake	SU	L	26	0	7	2	1.2	13	2	.15	0 - 1	0 - 0	0 - 0	23	0	1	10	.91	.520	2.08
Ohlendorf, Ross	SU	R	21	8	2	3	1.1	7	2	.29	1 - 2	0 - 0	0 - 0	14	0	1	7	.89	.797	3.72
Freeman, Sam	LT	L	54	12	17	6	0.9	47	11	.23	0 - 0	0 - 0	0 - 0	40	0	0	12	1.00	.683	3.05
Claudio, Alex	LT	L	18	5	4	2	1.0	15	8	.53	0 - 0	0 - 0	0 - 1	12	0	1	3	.75	.762	2.87
Faulkner, Andrew	LT	L	11	5	2	1	0.5	10	1	.10	0 - 0	0 - 0	0 - 0	8	0	0	2	1.00	.680	2.79
Detwiler, Ross	LT	L	10	2	3	2	0.7	7	2	.29	0 - 0	0 - 1	0 - 0	5	0	1	1	.50	1.040	7.71
Bass, Anthony	LM	R	33	18	7	16	0.4	24	10	.42	0 - 1	0 - 0	0 - 0	15	0	1	0	.00	.756	4.50
Patton, Spencer	UR	R	27	9	8	6	0.5	18	3	.17	0 - 0	0 - 0	0 - 0	17	0	0	3	1.00	.870	9.00
Feliz, Neftali	UR	R	18	0	4	3	2.2	7	4	.57	3 - 3	3 - 4	0 - 2	12	0	3	0	.67	.777	4.58
Mendez, Roman	UR	R	12	3	3	1	0.7	10	5	.50	0 - 0	0 - 0	0 - 1	6	0	1	0	.00	.802	5.40
Edwards, Jon	UR	R	11	4	0	0	0.8	8	2	.25	0 - 0	0 - 0	0 - 0	9	0	0	2	1.00	.906	6.00

Toronto Blue Jays

Pitcher	Pos	T	Rel G	Early Entry	Cons Days	Long	Lev Ind	#	Scrd	Pct	Easy	Reg	Tough	Clean	BS Win	BS	Holds	Sv/Hld Pct	Opp OPS	Rel ERA
					Usage				Inherited Runners			Saves				Relief Results					
Osuna, Roberto	CL	R	68	7	13	12	1.6	33	9	.27	12 - 12	7 - 10	1 - 1	46	0	3	7	.90	.591	2.58
Sanchez, Aaron	SU	R	30	0	8	2	1.2	9	5	.56	0 - 0	0 - 0	0 - 1	22	0	1	10	.91	.467	2.39
Lowe, Mark	SU	R	23	1	5	0	1.1	9	3	.33	1 - 1	0 - 1	0 - 1	16	0	2	5	.75	.632	3.79
Cecil, Brett	LT	L	63	5	13	4	1.2	24	7	.29	3 - 3	2 - 3	0 - 2	49	0	3	9	.82	.562	2.48
Loup, Aaron	LT	L	60	16	17	1	0.9	34	11	.32	0 - 1	0 - 1	0 - 2	38	0	4	9	.69	.776	4.46
Francis, Jeff	LM	L	14	9	1	6	0.3	6	4	.67	0 - 0	0 - 0	0 - 0	5	0	0	0		.814	6.14
Hendriks, Liam	UR	R	58	16	10	12	0.7	30	9	.30	0 - 0	0 - 1	0 - 1	43	0	2	5	.71	.605	2.92
Tepera, Ryan	UR	R	32	6	6	6	0.5	19	5	.26	1 - 1	0 - 0	0 - 0	20	0	0	0	1.00	.670	3.27
Schultz, Bo	UR	R	31	11	4	10	0.7	12	2	.17	1 - 1	0 - 1	0 - 1	21	0	2	4	.71	.637	3.56
Delabar, Steve	UR	R	31	5	2	7	0.8	14	5	.36	0 - 0	1 - 2	0 - 2	20	0	3	5	.67	.800	5.22
Hawkins, LaTroy	UR	R	18	4	0	1	0.9	2	0	.00	1 - 1	0 - 0	0 - 0	13	0	0	4	1.00	.782	2.76
Castro, Miguel	UR	R	13	1	3	1	1.6	10	4	.40	3 - 3	1 - 2	0 - 1	7	0	2	1	.71	.858	4.38

Washington Nationals

Pitcher	Pos	T	Rel G	Early Entry	Cons Days	Long	Lev Ind	#	Scrd	Pct	Easy	Reg	Tough	Clean	BS Win	BS	Holds	Sv/Hld Pct	Opp OPS	Rel ERA
					Usage				Inherited Runners			Saves				Relief Results					
Storen, Drew	CL	R	58	0	13	0	1.7	5	4	.80	16 - 18	13 - 16	0 - 0	44	0	5	5	.87	.603	3.44
Thornton, Matt	SU	L	60	7	9	0	1.2	33	6	.18	0 - 0	0 - 0	0 - 1	49	0	1	18	.95	.580	2.18
Janssen, Casey	SU	R	48	1	11	2	1.2	9	1	.11	0 - 2	0 - 1	0 - 0	36	0	3	13	.81	.720	4.95
Barrett, Aaron	SU	R	40	5	11	0	1.3	27	8	.30	0 - 0	0 - 1	0 - 2	26	0	3	10	.77	.636	4.60
Rivero, Felipe	LT	L	49	7	10	4	0.7	20	6	.30	1 - 1	1 - 1	0 - 1	36	0	1	6	.89	.544	2.79
Grace, Matt	LT	L	26	4	3	1	1.0	16	6	.38	0 - 0	0 - 0	0 - 2	17	0	2	4	.67	.855	4.24
Solis, Sammy	LT	L	18	6	1	5	0.4	9	6	.67	0 - 0	0 - 0	0 - 0	11	0	0	1	1.00	.718	3.38
Roark, Tanner	LM	R	28	11	2	12	0.7	17	9	.53	1 - 1	0 - 0	0 - 1	14	0	1	4	.83	.739	3.74
Treinen, Blake	UR	R	60	14	13	12	1.0	24	7	.29	0 - 1	0 - 1	0 - 0	37	0	3	10	.77	.692	3.86
Papelbon, Jonathan	UR	R	22	0	6	2	1.5	1	0	.00	5 - 5	2 - 4	0 - 0	13	1	2	0	.78	.712	3.04
Martin, Rafael	UR	R	13	1	2	4	0.4	8	0	.00	0 - 0	0 - 0	0 - 0	9	0	0	0		.852	5.11
Fister, Doug	UR	R	10	7	0	7	0.9	5	1	.20	0 - 0	1 - 1	0 - 0	6	0	0	0	1.00	.710	2.12

Pitchers Hitting, Fielding, & Holding Runners, and Hitters Pitching

Joe Rosales

We are used to talking about Madinson Bumgarner's great pitching performances, especially given what he did during the 2014 postseason to lead the Giants to their third World Series in five years. But now we are going to have to start talking about his great hitting performances as well. In 2015, Bumgarner led all pitchers in baseball by hitting five home runs. That is the most a pitcher has hit in a single season since Carlos Zambrano hit six home runs in 2006. That also helped lead the way for the whole Giants pitching staff, which hit a total of nine home runs on the season. The next highest total for any team was two. Besides Bumgarner's five, Tim Hudson hit one, Ryan Vogelsong hit one, Jake Peavy hit one, and Mike Leake hit one (as a member of the Giants...he also hit one as a member of the Reds).

In the following tables, you will find hitting statistics for pitchers, both for the 2015 season and for their careers. You will also find pitcher statistics related to fielding and holding runners on base. The column to the far right of the tables, RS, represents a pitcher's overall Defensive Runs Saved, which combines their ability to field their position (Range and Positioning Runs Saved), their ability to field Bunts (Bunt Runs Saved), their ability to control the running game (Stolen Base Runs Saved), and the good defensive plays and defensive misplays that they make that do not get captured by the other components (Good Fielding Play/Defensive Misplay Runs Saved). If there is one overarching metric to look at to get a feel for how good a pitcher is defensively, that is the one. However, there are also more specific statistics, like Pitcher Pickoffs (PPO). For example, Julio Teheran had the most PPO in baseball in 2015 with five, which is the third straight season that

Teheran has led or been tied for the lead in that category. Pretty impressive for a right-handed pitcher.

And finally, the table at the end of this section includes data on hitters pitching. Ike Davis, who was a two-way player in college, may have thought he was giving up pitching for good when he was drafted to play in the majors. But that track record actually made him the perfect choice to take the mound on two occasions in 2015 to help see the Oakland Athletics through to the end of the game in a couple blowout losses. He only gave up one hit and one walk in the two innings that he pitched, and also managed to get a strikeout. Every active position player who has pitched in the big leagues is listed in this table, both with their career pitching statistics as well as any numbers that they accrued in 2015.

Pitchers Hitting, Fielding and Holding Runners

Pitcher	T	2015 Hitting						Career Hitting										2015 Fielding and Holding Runners											
		Avg	AB	H	HR	RBI	SH	Avg	AB	H	2B	3B	HR	RBI	BB	SO	SH	Inn	PO	A	E	DP	Pct	SBA	CS	PCS	PPO	CS%	RS
Aardsma,David, Atl	R	.000	1	0	0	0	0	.000	4	0	0	0	0	0	0	2	1	30.2	0	1	1	0	.500	5	1	0	0	.20	-1
Abad,Fernando, Oak	L	-	0	0	0	0	0	.125	8	1	0	0	0	0	0	4	0	47.2	2	4	0	0	1.000	3	3	0	0	1.00	0
Achter,A.J., Min	R	-	0	0	0	0	0	-	0	0	0	0	0	0	0	0	0	13.1	1	0	1	0	.500	4	0	0	0	.00	-1
Adams,Austin, Cle	R	.000	1	0	0	0	0	.000	1	0	0	0	0	0	0	0	0	33.1	0	4	0	0	1.000	1	0	0	0	.00	0
Adcock,Nate, Cin	R	-	0	0	0	0	0	.000	1	0	0	0	0	0	0	1	0	18.0	2	3	1	0	.833	6	1	0	0	.17	-1
Affeldt,Jeremy, SF	L	.000	2	0	0	0	0	.176	17	3	0	0	0	2	2	6	0	35.1	3	6	0	0	1.000	4	0	0	0	.00	1
Albers,Andrew, Tor	L	-	0	0	0	0	0	-	0	0	0	0	0	0	0	0	0	2.2	0	0	0	0	-	0	0	0	0	-	0
Albers,Matt, CWS	R	-	0	0	0	0	0	.059	34	2	0	0	0	0	0	21	3	37.1	3	8	1	1	.917	4	0	0	0	.00	-1
Alburquerque,Al, Det	R	-	0	0	0	0	0	-	0	0	0	0	0	0	0	0	0	62.0	5	9	0	2	1.000	9	1	0	0	.11	0
Alexander,Scott, KC	L	-	0	0	0	0	0	-	0	0	0	0	0	0	0	0	0	6.0	1	1	0	0	1.000	0	0	0	0	-	0
Allen,Cody, Cle	R	-	0	0	0	0	0	-	0	0	0	0	0	0	0	0	0	69.1	2	4	0	0	1.000	5	1	0	0	.20	1
Almonte,Miguel, KC	R	-	0	0	0	0	0	-	0	0	0	0	0	0	0	0	0	8.2	1	1	0	0	1.000	1	0	0	0	.00	0
Alvarez,Dario, NYM	L	-	0	0	0	0	0	-	0	0	0	0	0	0	0	0	0	3.2	0	0	0	0	-	0	0	0	0	-	0
Alvarez,Henderson, Mia	R	.333	6	2	0	1	0	.234	94	22	4	0	1	9	1	34	12	22.1	3	4	1	0	.875	2	0	0	0	.00	-1
Alvarez,Jose, LAA	L	-	0	0	0	0	0	.000	1	0	0	0	0	0	1	0	0	67.0	6	8	0	1	1.000	0	0	0	0	-	2
Alvarez,R.J., Oak	R	-	0	0	0	0	0	-	0	0	0	0	0	0	0	0	0	20.0	2	1	0	0	1.000	0	0	0	0	-	-1
Anderson,Brett, LAD	L	.085	47	4	0	3	9	.092	65	6	3	0	0	4	5	41	10	180.1	4	47	0	1	1.000	20	10	6	0	.50	-2
Anderson,Chase, Ari	R	.104	48	5	0	3	8	.073	82	6	0	0	0	3	1	37	14	152.2	8	14	2	2	.917	8	3	0	0	.38	-1
Anderson,Cody, Cle	R	.000	3	0	0	0	0	.000	3	0	0	0	0	0	0	3	0	91.1	8	15	0	1	1.000	3	2	0	0	.67	2
Andriese,Matt, TB	R	.000	1	0	0	0	0	.000	1	0	0	0	0	0	0	0	0	65.2	4	5	0	1	1.000	4	2	0	0	.50	0
Araujo,Elvis, Phi	L	.000	1	0	0	0	0	.000	1	0	0	0	0	0	0	1	0	34.2	1	6	0	2	1.000	3	0	0	0	.00	0
Archer,Chris, TB	R	.000	5	0	0	0	0	.000	13	0	0	0	0	0	0	7	0	212.0	5	22	2	3	.931	15	8	0	0	.53	1
Armstrong,Shawn, Cle	R	-	0	0	0	0	0	-	0	0	0	0	0	0	0	0	0	5.0	0	0	0	0	-	0	0	0	0	-	0
Aro,Jonathan, Bos	R	-	0	0	0	0	0	-	0	0	0	0	0	0	0	0	0	10.1	1	0	0	0	1.000	0	0	0	0	-	0
Arrieta,Jake, ChC	R	.152	79	12	2	2	3	.154	143	22	3	2	2	8	5	75	14	229.0	33	49	4	5	.953	33	6	0	1	.18	6
Asher,Alec, Phi	R	.333	6	2	0	0	0	.333	6	2	1	0	0	0	0	3	0	29.0	3	3	0	1	1.000	2	1	0	0	.50	-1
Atchison,Scott, Cle	R	-	0	0	0	0	0	.000	2	0	0	0	0	0	0	1	0	19.2	1	2	0	0	1.000	0	0	0	0	-	0
Aumont,Phillippe, Phi	R	-	0	0	0	0	0	.000	1	0	0	0	0	0	1	1	0	4.0	0	0	0	0	-	0	0	0	0	-	0
Avilan,Luis, Atl-LAD	L	.000	1	0	0	0	0	.250	4	1	0	0	0	0	0	0	2	53.1	6	13	1	2	.950	5	1	1	0	.20	2
Axelrod,Dylan, Cin	R	.000	2	0	0	0	1	.125	8	1	0	0	0	0	0	6	1	12.1	0	1	0	0	1.000	1	0	0	0	.00	1
Axford,John, Col	R	-	0	0	0	0	0	.000	1	0	0	0	0	0	0	0	0	55.2	6	8	1	1	.933	10	2	1	0	.20	-2
Badenhop,Burke, Cin	R	.000	1	0	0	0	0	.091	33	3	1	0	0	2	1	19	5	66.1	3	9	0	1	1.000	7	2	0	0	.29	2
Baez,Pedro, LAD	R	-	0	0	0	0	0	-	0	0	0	0	0	0	0	0	0	51.0	1	4	1	0	.833	2	1	1	0	.50	-3
Bailey,Andrew, NYY	R	-	0	0	0	0	0	-	0	0	0	0	0	0	0	0	0	8.2	2	2	0	0	1.000	1	0	0	0	.00	1
Bailey,Homer, Cin	R	.000	4	0	0	0	0	.158	304	48	6	0	0	17	9	119	41	11.1	1	2	0	0	1.000	1	0	0	0	.00	0
Baker,Scott, LAD	R	.000	3	0	0	0	1	.094	32	3	1	0	0	0	0	13	0	11.0	1	1	0	0	1.000	1	0	0	0	.00	0
Balester,Collin, Cin	R	.000	1	0	0	0	0	.143	28	4	0	0	0	1	2	10	11	15.2	1	0	0	0	1.000	0	0	0	0	-	0
Balfour,Grant, TB	R	-	0	0	0	0	0	.000	2	0	0	0	0	0	0	2	0	4.1	0	0	0	0	-	0	0	0	0	-	0
Banuelos,Manny, Atl	L	.000	3	0	0	0	4	.000	3	0	0	0	0	0	0	1	4	26.1	0	2	1	0	.667	7	2	2	0	.29	-1
Barnes,Matt, Bos	R	-	0	0	0	0	0	-	0	0	0	0	0	0	0	0	0	43.0	4	3	0	0	1.000	8	1	0	0	.13	-2
Barraclough,Kyle, Mia	R	-	0	0	0	0	0	-	0	0	0	0	0	0	0	0	0	24.1	1	2	1	0	.750	5	2	0	0	.40	-1
Barrett,Aaron, Was	R	-	0	0	0	0	0	-	0	0	0	0	0	0	0	0	0	29.1	2	3	2	1	.714	5	1	0	0	.20	-1
Barrios,Yhonathan, Mil	R	-	0	0	0	0	0	-	0	0	0	0	0	0	0	0	0	6.2	0	1	0	0	1.000	0	0	0	0	-	0
Bass,Anthony, Tex	R	-	0	0	0	0	0	.105	38	4	0	1	0	6	0	17	1	64.0	6	8	1	2	.933	3	1	0	0	.33	-1
Bassitt,Chris, Oak	R	.000	2	0	0	0	0	.000	2	0	0	0	0	0	0	1	0	86.0	5	9	1	1	.933	11	4	0	0	.36	-2
Bastardo,Antonio, Pit	L	.000	2	0	0	0	1	.000	8	0	0	0	0	0	1	5	1	57.1	0	4	1	0	.800	8	0	0	0	.00	-1
Bauer,Trevor, Cle	R	.167	6	1	0	0	0	.077	13	1	0	0	0	0	1	5	1	176.0	12	13	1	3	.962	17	6	1	0	.35	-1
Beachy,Brandon, LAD	R	.000	2	0	0	0	0	.118	85	10	1	0	0	5	5	47	11	8.0	1	0	0	0	1.000	1	0	0	0	.00	0
Beck,Chris, CWS	R	-	0	0	0	0	0	-	0	0	0	0	0	0	0	0	0	6.0	0	2	0	0	1.000	1	0	0	0	.00	0
Bedrosian,Cam, LAA	R	-	0	0	0	0	0	-	0	0	0	0	0	0	0	0	0	33.1	2	4	0	0	1.000	5	2	0	0	.40	-1
Beeler,Dallas, ChC	R	.333	3	1	0	0	0	.286	7	2	1	0	0	0	0	3	0	8.1	1	2	0	0	1.000	0	0	0	0	-	0
Beimel,Joe, Sea	L	-	0	0	0	0	0	.222	45	10	1	0	0	1	2	19	6	47.1	1	14	0	2	1.000	4	4	4	2	1.00	3
Belisario,Ronald, TB	R	.000	1	0	0	0	0	.000	6	0	0	0	0	0	0	3	0	8.0	0	0	0	0	-	0	0	0	0	-	0
Belisle,Matt, StL	R	-	0	0	0	0	0	.082	85	7	3	0	0	3	3	47	18	33.2	1	7	0	0	1.000	2	1	0	0	.50	0
Beliveau,Jeff, TB	L	-	0	0	0	0	0	-	0	0	0	0	0	0	0	0	0	2.2	0	0	0	0	-	1	0	0	0	.00	0
Bellatti,Andrew, TB	R	-	0	0	0	0	0	-	0	0	0	0	0	0	0	0	0	23.1	0	2	1	0	.667	3	1	0	0	.33	-1
Benoit,Joaquin, SD	R	-	0	0	0	0	0	.000	9	0	0	0	0	0	0	4	0	65.1	3	8	0	0	1.000	8	3	0	0	.38	2
Bergman,Christian, Col	R	.167	12	2	0	0	2	.097	31	3	0	0	0	0	1	10	3	68.1	5	10	0	2	1.000	4	2	0	0	.50	2
Betances,Dellin, NYY	R	-	0	0	0	0	0	-	0	0	0	0	0	0	0	0	0	84.0	5	8	0	0	1.000	21	4	0	0	.19	-1
Betancourt,Rafael, Col	R	-	0	0	0	0	0	.000	0	0	0	0	0	0	0	0	0	39.1	2	1	0	0	1.000	5	0	0	0	.00	-1
Bettis,Chad, Col	R	.069	29	2	0	1	0	.047	43	2	0	0	1	4	18	3		115.0	12	11	0	1	1.000	4	1	0	0	.25	1
Billingsley,Chad, Phi	R	.077	13	1	1	1	1	.138	355	49	8	0	3	21	19	170	36	37.0	2	6	1	1	.889	1	1	0	0	1.00	-2
Blanton,Joe, KC-Pit	R	.000	4	0	0	0	0	.106	216	23	0	0	0	6	8	92	31	76.0	7	8	1	0	.938	7	2	0	1	.29	2
Blazek,Michael, Mil	R	.250	4	1	0	0	1	.250	4	1	1	0	0	1	0	2	0	55.2	5	9	1	0	.933	6	4	0	0	.67	3
Blevins,Jerry, NYM	L	-	0	0	0	0	0	.000	1	0	0	0	0	0	0	1	0	5.0	0	1	0	0	1.000	2	0	0	0	.00	0
Bochy,Brett, SF	R	-	0	0	0	0	0	-	0	0	0	0	0	0	0	0	0	3.0	0	0	0	0	-	0	0	0	0	-	0
Bolsinger,Mike, LAD	R	.026	38	1	0	0	2	.053	57	3	1	0	0	1	0	30	3	109.1	8	7	3	1	.833	15	6	0	0	.40	-4
Boxberger,Brad, TB	R	-	0	0	0	0	0	.000	3	0	0	0	0	0	0	1	1	63.0	1	6	2	0	.778	9	3	0	0	.33	-2
Boyd,Matt, Tor-Det	L	-	0	0	0	0	0	-	0	0	0	0	0	0	0	0	0	57.1	1	7	1	0	.889	6	5	2	0	.83	0

Pitchers Hitting, Fielding and Holding Runners

Pitcher	T	2015 Hitting						Career Hitting										2015 Fielding and Holding Runners											
		Avg	AB	H	HR	RBI	SH	Avg	AB	H	2B	3B	HR	RBI	BB	SO	SH	Inn	PO	A	E	DP	Pct	SBA	CS	PCS	PPO	CS%	RS
Boyer,Blaine, Min	R	-	0	0	0	0	0	.000	8	0	0	0	0	0	0	6	1	65.0	7	13	2	1	.909	12	4	2	0	.33	-1
Brach,Brad, Bal	R	-	0	0	0	0	0	.000	1	0	0	0	0	0	0	0	1	79.1	3	6	1	1	.900	8	2	0	0	.25	-2
Bracho,Silvino, Ari	R	-	0	0	0	0	0	-	0	0	0	0	0	0	0	0	0	12.1	1	0	0	0	1.000	1	1	0	0	1.00	0
Bradley,Archie, Ari	R	.143	14	2	0	0	0	.143	14	2	0	0	0	0	0	7	0	35.2	4	2	0	0	1.000	5	1	0	0	.20	-1
Breslow,Craig, Bos	L	-	0	0	0	0	0	.000	4	0	0	0	0	0	0	2	0	65.0	3	5	1	1	.889	3	2	0	0	.67	-1
Brigham,Jake, Atl	R	.000	1	0	0	0	1	.000	1	0	0	0	0	0	0	1	1	16.2	0	0	0	0	-	4	0	0	0	.00	-1
Britton,Zach, Bal	L	-	0	0	0	0	0	.625	8	5	1	0	1	2	0	1	0	65.2	5	21	0	1	1.000	3	3	2	0	1.00	1
Broadway,Mike, SF	R	-	0	0	0	0	0	-	0	0	0	0	0	0	0	0	0	17.1	1	2	0	0	1.000	3	3	0	0	1.00	1
Brooks,Aaron, KC-Oak	R	.000	2	0	0	0	0	.000	2	0	0	0	0	0	0	0	0	55.1	5	2	0	1	1.000	3	1	1	0	.33	-1
Brothers,Rex, Col	L	-	0	0	0	0	0	.000	4	0	0	0	0	0	0	4	1	10.1	0	2	0	1	1.000	0	0	0	0	-	1
Brown,Brooks, Col	R	-	0	0	0	0	0	.000	1	0	0	0	0	0	0	0	1	33.0	1	4	0	0	1.000	6	0	0	0	.00	0
Broxton,Jonathan, Mil-StL	R	-	0	0	0	0	0	.000	5	0	0	0	0	0	2	2	1	60.1	5	13	1	0	.947	3	1	0	0	.33	0
Buchanan,David, Phi	R	.200	20	4	0	1	1	.140	50	7	2	0	0	3	6	18	6	74.2	2	5	1	2	.875	2	1	0	0	.50	-4
Buchanan,Jake, Hou	R	-	0	0	0	0	0	.000	1	0	0	0	0	0	0	0	0	9.0	0	1	0	0	1.000	1	0	0	0	.00	0
Buchholz,Clay, Bos	R	.000	6	0	0	0	0	.182	11	2	0	0	0	0	0	3	1	113.1	9	6	2	0	.882	6	4	0	0	.67	-3
Buehrle,Mark, Tor	L	.143	7	1	0	0	1	.072	125	9	2	0	1	3	2	58	13	198.2	11	29	3	4	.930	2	2	2	1	1.00	5
Bumgarner,Madison, SF	L	.247	77	19	5	9	1	.183	367	67	10	0	11	40	18	141	36	218.1	5	19	1	1	.960	9	4	2	0	.44	0
Burawa,Daniel, NYY-Atl	R	-	0	0	0	0	0	-	0	0	0	0	0	0	0	0	0	13.0	0	1	0	0	1.000	1	0	0	0	.00	0
Burgos,Enrique, Ari	R	-	0	0	0	0	0	-	0	0	0	0	0	0	0	0	0	27.0	0	2	0	0	1.000	3	2	0	0	.67	0
Burnett,A.J., Pit	R	.119	42	5	1	5	9	.114	493	56	8	3	4	19	20	241	59	164.0	11	20	3	1	.912	42	9	2	2	.21	-6
Butler,Eddie, Col	R	.043	23	1	0	0	1	.034	29	1	0	0	0	0	0	16	1	79.1	10	15	4	2	.862	10	4	1	1	.40	1
Cabral,Cesar, Bal	L	-	0	0	0	0	0	-	0	0	0	0	0	0	0	0	0	1.0	0	0	0	0	-	0	0	0	0	-	0
Cahill,Trevor, Atl-ChC	R	.143	7	1	0	0	0	.102	157	16	2	1	0	9	3	54	15	43.1	5	10	0	1	1.000	7	2	0	0	.29	0
Cain,Matt, SF	R	.000	16	0	0	1	3	.121	552	67	10	1	6	27	21	271	70	60.2	2	4	0	0	1.000	8	1	0	0	.13	0
Caminero,Arquimedes, Pit	R	-	0	0	0	0	0	-	0	0	0	0	0	0	0	0	0	74.2	2	9	0	0	1.000	9	0	0	0	.00	-1
Campos,Leonel, SD	R	-	0	0	0	0	0	-	0	0	0	0	0	0	0	0	0	1.0	0	0	0	0	-	0	0	0	0	-	0
Capps,Carter, Mia	R	.500	2	1	0	0	0	.500	2	1	0	0	0	0	0	0	0	31.0	1	5	0	1	1.000	5	0	0	1	.00	-1
Capuano,Chris, NYY	L	.000	1	0	0	0	0	.124	371	46	10	0	1	20	9	176	38	40.2	0	10	0	0	1.000	2	1	1	0	.50	1
Carlyle,Buddy, NYM	R	-	0	0	0	0	0	.175	57	10	0	0	0	4	3	17	7	8.0	2	0	0	0	1.000	0	0	0	0	-	0
Carpenter,David, NYY-Was	R	-	0	0	0	0	0	.200	5	1	0	0	0	0	0	1	1	24.2	2	2	1	0	.800	2	1	0	0	.50	0
Carpenter,David, Atl	R	-	0	0	0	0	0	-	0	0	0	0	0	0	0	0	0	3.2	1	0	0	0	1.000	0	0	0	0	-	0
Carrasco,Carlos, Cle	R	1.000	1	1	0	0	2	.125	8	1	0	0	0	0	0	5	4	183.2	8	14	0	1	1.000	22	9	1	0	.41	0
Carroll,Scott, CWS	R	-	0	0	0	0	0	.000	0	0	0	0	0	0	0	0	0	36.2	2	4	1	0	.857	5	1	0	0	.20	1
Cashner,Andrew, SD	R	.083	60	5	0	1	0	.158	158	25	2	1	1	6	4	68	14	184.2	9	34	1	3	.977	25	11	1	2	.44	1
Casilla,Santiago, SF	R	-	0	0	0	0	0	.250	4	1	0	0	0	1	1	1	0	58.0	2	8	0	1	1.000	7	2	0	0	.29	2
Castro,Angel, Oak	R	-	0	0	0	0	0	-	0	0	0	0	0	0	0	0	0	4.0	0	0	0	0	-	0	0	0	0	-	-1
Castro,Miguel, Tor-Col	R	-	0	0	0	0	0	-	0	0	0	0	0	0	0	0	0	17.2	0	2	0	0	1.000	2	1	0	0	.50	1
Castro,Simon, Col	R	-	0	0	0	0	0	-	0	0	0	0	0	0	0	0	0	10.1	0	1	0	0	1.000	0	0	0	0	-	1
Cecil,Brett, Tor	L	-	0	0	0	0	0	.000	6	0	0	0	0	0	0	6	0	54.1	3	5	1	0	.889	4	1	1	1	.25	-2
Cedeno,Xavier, Was-TB	L	-	0	0	0	0	0	.000	1	0	0	0	0	0	0	0	0	46.0	2	8	1	1	.909	4	2	0	0	.50	0
Chacin,Jhoulys, Ari	R	.125	8	1	0	0	1	.180	211	38	5	0	1	15	7	47	14	26.2	2	4	0	0	1.000	2	2	0	0	1.00	0
Chafin,Andrew, Ari	L	.000	3	0	0	0	0	.200	5	1	0	0	0	1	0	2	0	75.0	4	10	1	1	.933	1	0	0	0	.00	1
Chamberlain,Joba, Det-KC	R	-	0	0	0	0	0	.000	6	0	0	0	0	0	1	2	2	27.2	3	3	0	0	1.000	1	0	0	1	.00	0
Chapman,Aroldis, Cin	L	.000	1	0	0	0	0	.000	2	0	0	0	0	0	0	0	1	66.1	1	2	0	0	1.000	9	1	0	1	.11	-3
Chapman,Kevin, Hou	L	-	0	0	0	0	0	-	0	0	0	0	0	0	0	0	0	5.1	0	1	0	0	1.000	1	1	1	0	1.00	0
Chavez,Jesse, Oak	R	.333	3	1	0	0	2	.091	11	1	0	0	0	0	0	10	3	157.0	10	10	2	0	.909	11	5	0	0	.45	1
Chen,Bruce, Cle	L	-	0	0	0	0	0	.152	125	19	1	0	0	3	3	58	19	6.1	0	0	0	0	-	0	0	0	0	-	0
Chen,Wei-Yin, Bal	L	-	0	0	0	0	0	.000	6	0	0	0	0	0	0	3	0	191.1	12	22	2	4	.944	7	2	1	0	.29	0
Choate,Randy, StL	L	-	0	0	0	0	0	.000	5	0	0	0	0	0	1	3	0	27.1	5	9	0	1	1.000	1	1	1	0	.50	0
Cingrani,Tony, Cin	L	.000	2	0	0	1	0	.192	52	10	1	0	0	2	0	16	8	33.1	0	6	0	1	1.000	2	0	0	1	.00	1
Cishek,Steve, Mia-StL	R	-	0	0	0	0	0	.000	1	0	0	0	0	0	0	0	0	55.1	4	7	2	0	.846	7	2	0	0	.29	0
Claudio,Alex, Tex	L	-	0	0	0	0	0	-	0	0	0	0	0	0	0	0	0	15.2	2	4	0	0	1.000	0	0	0	0	-	1
Clippard,Tyler, Oak-NYM	R	.000	1	0	0	0	0	.200	15	3	0	0	0	0	0	6	3	71.0	3	6	0	0	1.000	7	1	0	0	.14	1
Coke,Phil, ChC-Tor	L	-	0	0	0	0	0	.000	3	0	0	0	0	0	0	3	0	12.2	2	4	1	0	.857	0	0	0	0	-	1
Cole,A.J., Was	R	.000	2	0	0	0	0	.000	2	0	0	0	0	0	0	0	0	9.1	0	3	1	0	.750	0	0	0	0	-	0
Cole,Gerrit, Pit	R	.150	60	9	0	2	9	.171	140	24	0	0	1	9	5	59	14	208.0	10	37	0	1	1.000	35	10	0	0	.29	6
Coleman,Louis, KC	R	-	0	0	0	0	0	.000	1	0	0	0	0	0	0	1	0	3.0	1	0	1	0	1.000	0	0	0	0	-	0
Collmenter,Josh, Ari	R	.185	27	5	0	1	2	.128	148	19	2	0	0	6	9	50	13	121.0	17	14	0	0	1.000	7	4	2	0	.57	2
Colome,Alex, TB	R	-	0	0	0	0	0	.000	2	0	0	0	0	0	0	1	0	109.2	5	12	0	0	1.000	9	5	0	1	.56	-1
Colon,Bartolo, NYM	R	.138	58	8	0	4	4	.093	216	20	2	0	0	9	0	113	17	194.2	9	32	3	6	.932	9	3	1	1	.33	3
Conley,Adam, Mia	L	.222	18	4	0	1	4	.222	18	4	0	0	0	1	0	8	4	67.0	0	9	0	0	1.000	4	1	1	0	.25	1
Contreras,Carlos, Cin	R	-	0	0	0	0	0	.000	1	0	0	0	0	0	0	1	0	28.0	3	1	0	0	1.000	2	1	0	0	.50	0
Cook,Ryan, Oak-Bos	R	-	0	0	0	0	0	-	0	0	0	0	0	0	0	0	0	8.2	0	0	1	0	.000	3	0	0	0	.00	-1
Cooney,Tim, StL	L	.300	10	3	0	0	1	.300	10	3	0	0	0	0	0	0	1	31.1	1	5	0	0	1.000	3	3	1	0	1.00	0
Copeland,Scott, Tor	R	.000	1	0	0	0	0	.000	1	0	0	0	0	0	0	0	0	15.1	1	4	0	1	1.000	1	1	0	0	1.00	0
Corbin,Patrick, Ari	L	.120	25	3	0	3	1	.119	126	15	4	1	0	10	6	51	12	85.0	2	18	1	2	.952	1	0	0	0	.00	5
Cordier,Erik, Mia	R	-	0	0	0	0	1	-	0	0	0	0	0	0	0	0	1	12.1	0	1	0	0	1.000	1	0	0	0	.00	0
Cornely,John, Atl	R	-	0	0	0	0	0	-	0	0	0	0	0	0	0	0	0	1.0	0	0	0	0	-	0	0	0	0	-	0
Correia,Kevin, Phi	R	.167	6	1	0	0	1	.120	300	36	6	0	0	13	11	125	45	23.1	1	1	0	0	1.000	0	0	0	0	-	-1
Cosart,Jarred, Mia	R	.059	17	1	0	1	1	.132	38	5	0	0	0	1	0	15	4	69.2	1	19	0	0	1.000	2	1	0	0	.50	3

Pitchers Hitting, Fielding and Holding Runners

Pitcher	T	2015 Hitting						Career Hitting										2015 Fielding and Holding Runners											
		Avg	AB	H	HR	RBI	SH	Avg	AB	H	2B	3B	HR	RBI	BB	SO	SH	Inn	PO	A	E	DP	Pct	SBA	CS	PCS	PPO	CS%	RS
Cotham,Caleb, NYY	R	-	0	0	0	0	0	-	0	0	0	0	0	0	0	0	0	9.2	0	0	0	0	-	2	1	0	0	.50	-1
Cotts,Neal, Mil-Min	L	-	0	0	0	0	0	.500	2	1	1	0	0	0	0	1	0	63.1	2	5	0	0	1.000	8	0	0	0	.00	-3
Coulombe,Daniel, LAD-Oak	L	.000	1	0	0	0	0	.000	1	0	0	0	0	0	0	1	0	16.0	1	0	0	0	1.000	0	0	0	0	-	0
Cravy,Tyler, Mil	R	.000	8	0	0	0	2	.000	8	0	0	0	0	0	0	3	2	42.2	2	3	0	0	1.000	2	2	0	0	1.00	0
Crockett,Kyle, Cle	L	-	0	0	0	0	0	-	0	0	0	0	0	0	0	0	0	17.2	0	2	0	0	1.000	0	0	0	0	-	-1
Cueto,Johnny, Cin-KC	R	.162	37	6	0	0	5	.107	384	41	1	0	0	10	11	124	69	212.0	21	22	0	2	1.000	5	2	0	1	.40	5
Cunniff,Brandon, Atl	R	-	0	0	0	0	0	-	0	0	0	0	0	0	0	0	0	35.0	1	3	1	0	.800	1	0	0	0	.00	-1
Danks,John, CWS	L	-	0	0	0	0	0	.083	24	2	0	0	0	1	8	3	177.2	6	20	3	1	.897	10	3	1	1	.30	-2
Davies,Kyle, NYY	R	-	0	0	0	0	0	.130	69	9	1	0	2	9	4	25	16	2.1	0	1	0	0	1.000	0	0	0	0	-	0
Davies,Zachary, Mil	R	.077	13	1	0	0	1	.077	13	1	0	0	0	0	0	3	1	34.0	1	8	0	1	1.000	1	1	0	1	1.00	3
Davis,Wade, KC	R	-	0	0	0	0	0	.250	8	2	0	0	0	0	4	3	67.1	9	8	1	1	.944	5	1	0	0	.20	1
De Fratus,Justin, Phi	R	.333	3	1	0	0	0	.250	4	1	0	0	0	0	0	2	0	80.0	10	3	2	1	.867	11	5	2	0	.45	0
de la Rosa,Jorge, Col	L	.063	48	3	0	3	2	.121	340	41	4	0	0	21	4	146	28	149.0	5	22	0	0	1.000	13	3	1	0	.23	2
de la Rosa,Rubby, Ari	R	.094	64	6	0	2	4	.113	80	9	0	0	0	2	1	26	5	188.2	26	17	0	3	1.000	12	4	0	1	.33	-3
De Los Santos,Abel, Was	R	-	0	0	0	0	0	-	0	0	0	0	0	0	0	0	0	1.2	0	0	0	0	-	0	0	0	0	-	0
De Paula,Jose, NYY	L	-	0	0	0	0	0	-	0	0	0	0	0	0	0	0	0	3.1	0	0	0	0	-	0	0	0	0	-	0
Deduno,Samuel, Hou	R	-	0	0	0	0	0	.167	6	1	1	0	0	0	0	5	1	21.0	2	1	0	0	1.000	4	1	0	0	.25	0
deGrom,Jacob, NYM	R	.186	59	11	0	4	4	.200	105	21	3	0	0	6	4	29	10	191.0	17	32	0	3	1.000	10	6	0	0	.60	6
Delabar,Steve, Tor	R	-	0	0	0	0	0	-	0	0	0	0	0	0	0	0	0	29.1	2	2	0	0	1.000	2	2	0	0	1.00	0
Delgado,Randall, Ari	R	.000	1	0	0	0	1	.182	77	14	0	0	2	1	33	11	72.0	5	7	0	0	1.000	5	1	0	0	.20	2
DeSclafani,Anthony, Cin	R	.155	58	9	0	3	2	.147	68	10	1	0	0	5	4	36	2	184.2	14	21	2	0	.946	19	3	1	0	.16	-3
Despaigne,Odrisamer, SD	R	.067	30	2	0	0	3	.037	54	2	1	0	0	2	2	21	6	125.2	5	30	0	0	1.000	5	3	0	0	.60	6
Detwiler,Ross, Tex-Atl	L	.000	1	0	0	0	0	.061	115	7	0	0	0	3	3	59	9	58.1	4	15	0	1	1.000	9	5	4	0	.56	3
Diaz,Jairo, Col	R	-	0	0	0	0	0	-	0	0	0	0	0	0	0	0	0	19.0	1	1	0	0	1.000	1	0	0	0	.00	-1
Diaz,Jumbo, Cin	R	-	0	0	0	0	0	-	0	0	0	0	0	0	0	0	0	60.1	6	1	0	1	1.000	5	1	0	0	.20	-2
Dickey,R.A., Tor	R	.000	3	0	0	0	1	.176	205	36	3	0	0	11	4	36	27	214.1	11	25	0	1	1.000	10	4	2	1	.40	1
Diekman,Jake, Phi-Tex	L	-	0	0	0	0	0	-	0	0	0	0	0	0	0	0	0	58.1	1	10	1	1	.917	4	1	1	0	.25	1
Dominguez,Jose, TB	R	-	0	0	0	0	0	.000	2	0	0	0	0	0	0	2	0	5.2	0	2	0	0	1.000	0	0	0	0	-	0
Doolittle,Sean, Oak	L	-	0	0	0	0	0	.000	1	0	0	0	0	0	0	0	0	13.2	0	1	0	0	1.000	1	0	0	0	.00	0
Doubront,Felix, Tor-Oak	L	-	0	0	0	0	0	.091	11	1	0	0	0	1	6	2	75.1	4	15	0	1	1.000	14	5	3	0	.36	2
Drabek,Kyle, CWS	R	-	0	0	0	0	0	.000	2	0	0	0	0	0	0	1	0	5.1	0	0	0	0	-	0	0	0	0	-	-1
Drake,Oliver, Bal	R	-	0	0	0	0	0	-	0	0	0	0	0	0	0	0	0	15.2	1	0	0	0	1.000	0	0	0	0	-	0
Duensing,Brian, Min	L	.000	1	0	0	0	0	.000	7	0	0	0	0	0	4	0	48.2	1	13	1	1	.933	6	0	0	0	.00	1
Duffey,Tyler, Min	R	-	0	0	0	0	0	-	0	0	0	0	0	0	0	0	0	58.0	7	4	1	0	.917	0	0	0	0	-	-3
Duffy,Danny, KC	L	-	0	0	0	0	0	.000	9	0	0	0	0	0	0	5	1	136.2	2	18	3	2	.870	7	2	2	0	.29	0
Duke,Zach, CWS	L	-	0	0	0	0	0	.180	317	57	7	0	2	23	12	117	43	60.2	7	5	1	2	.923	4	1	1	0	.25	-1
Dull,Ryan, Oak	R	-	0	0	0	0	0	-	0	0	0	0	0	0	0	0	0	17.0	0	0	0	0	-	0	0	0	0	-	0
Dunn,Mike, Mia	L	1.000	1	1	0	0	0	.200	5	1	0	0	0	0	0	1	0	54.0	1	4	0	0	1.000	5	2	1	0	.40	-1
Dyson,Sam, Mia-Tex	R	-	0	0	0	0	0	.000	2	0	0	0	0	0	0	0	0	75.1	4	11	3	1	.833	9	1	0	0	.11	-3
Edwards,Jon, Tex-SD	R	-	0	0	0	0	0	-	0	0	0	0	0	0	0	0	0	16.2	1	2	0	0	1.000	6	2	0	0	.33	0
Edwards Jr.,Carl, ChC	R	.000	1	0	0	0	0	.000	1	0	0	0	0	0	0	1	0	4.2	1	1	0	0	1.000	0	0	0	0	-	0
Eickhoff,Jerad, Phi	R	.143	14	2	0	2	2	.143	14	2	0	0	0	2	0	7	2	51.0	6	5	0	0	1.000	3	2	1	0	.67	1
Elias,Roenis, Sea	L	-	0	0	0	0	0	.000	4	0	0	0	0	0	0	1	0	115.1	0	13	1	0	.929	9	4	0	0	.44	1
Ellington,Brian, Mia	R	-	0	0	0	0	0	-	0	0	0	0	0	0	0	0	0	25.0	0	5	0	0	1.000	5	1	0	0	.20	1
Eovaldi,Nathan, NYY	R	.000	5	0	0	0	0	.081	135	11	0	0	0	1	4	84	13	154.1	10	20	0	2	1.000	4	1	0	4	.25	-2
Erlin,Robbie, SD	L	.000	5	0	0	0	1	.077	39	3	0	0	0	2	2	12	3	17.0	0	2	1	0	.667	1	0	0	0	.00	-1
Estrada,Marco, Tor	R	.333	6	2	0	0	0	.152	125	19	4	0	0	7	7	57	20	181.0	10	8	1	0	.947	12	5	0	0	.42	0
Eveland,Dana, Atl	L	-	0	0	0	0	0	.045	22	1	0	0	0	0	2	13	5	3.1	1	0	0	0	1.000	0	0	0	0	-	0
Familia,Jeurys, NYM	R	-	0	0	0	0	0	.500	4	2	0	0	0	1	0	1	0	78.0	5	11	0	1	1.000	3	1	0	0	.33	1
Farmer,Buck, Det	R	.250	4	1	0	0	0	.250	4	1	0	0	0	0	3	0	40.1	2	5	1	0	.875	3	2	0	0	.67	-4
Farquhar,Danny, Sea	R	-	0	0	0	0	0	-	0	0	0	0	0	0	0	0	0	51.0	3	11	0	0	1.000	2	0	0	0	.00	2
Faulkner,Andrew, Tex	L	-	0	0	0	0	0	-	0	0	0	0	0	0	0	0	0	9.2	1	1	0	0	1.000	0	0	0	0	-	0
Feldman,Scott, Hou	R	.500	2	1	0	0	0	.169	59	10	3	0	1	9	0	23	5	108.1	10	20	2	2	.938	13	2	0	0	.15	-1
Feliz,Michael, Hou	R	-	0	0	0	0	0	-	0	0	0	0	0	0	0	0	0	8.0	0	0	0	0	-	0	0	0	0	-	0
Feliz,Neftali, Tex-Det	R	-	0	0	0	0	0	.000	2	0	0	0	0	0	0	1	0	48.0	4	3	0	2	1.000	5	3	0	0	.60	-2
Fernandez,Jose, Mia	R	.167	18	3	1	2	4	.190	84	16	2	1	2	8	0	30	13	64.2	3	1	0	0	1.000	0	0	0	0	-	-2
Ferrell,Jeff, Det	R	-	0	0	0	0	0	-	0	0	0	0	0	0	0	0	0	11.1	1	1	0	0	1.000	0	0	0	0	-	0
Fields,Josh, Hou	R	-	0	0	0	0	0	-	0	0	0	0	0	0	0	0	0	50.2	1	4	0	0	1.000	5	2	0	0	.40	-1
Fien,Casey, Min	R	-	0	0	0	0	0	-	0	0	0	0	0	0	0	0	0	63.1	5	5	0	0	1.000	6	1	1	0	.17	0
Fiers,Mike, Mil-Hou	R	.100	30	3	0	0	4	.082	85	7	0	0	0	2	0	44	18	180.1	10	21	4	0	.886	17	5	1	2	.29	5
Finnegan,Brandon, KC-Cin	L	.000	4	0	0	0	2	.000	4	0	0	0	0	0	0	2	2	58.0	6	11	0	0	1.000	4	1	0	0	.25	2
Fister,Doug, Was	R	.226	31	7	0	0	6	.153	98	15	3	0	0	2	3	41	18	103.0	8	18	3	2	.897	4	3	0	1	.75	3
Flande,Yohan, Col	L	.143	21	3	0	1	1	.121	33	4	0	0	0	2	1	16	5	68.1	4	12	1	0	.941	3	1	0	0	.33	1
Flores,Kendry, Mia	R	.000	1	0	0	0	0	.000	1	0	0	0	0	0	0	1	0	12.2	0	2	0	0	1.000	1	1	1	0	1.00	0
Floyd,Gavin, Cle	R	-	0	0	0	0	0	.068	74	5	0	0	0	2	4	43	4	13.1	1	0	0	0	1.000	1	0	0	0	.00	1
Foltynewicz,Mike, Atl	R	.071	28	2	0	3	0	.071	28	2	1	0	0	3	0	19	1	86.2	2	5	1	0	.875	9	3	0	0	.33	-4
Francis,Jeff, Tor	L	-	0	0	0	0	0	.116	303	35	7	0	16	25	102	53	22.0	1	3	0	0	1.000	1	0	0	0	.00	0
Frasor,Jason, KC-Atl	R	-	0	0	0	0	0	-	0	0	0	0	0	0	0	0	0	28.0	4	4	0	2	1.000	2	0	0	0	.00	0
Freeman,Sam, Tex	L	-	0	0	0	0	0	-	0	0	0	0	0	0	0	0	0	38.1	1	5	0	0	1.000	4	1	0	0	.25	2
Frias,Carlos, LAD	R	.048	21	1	0	0	1	.036	28	1	0	0	0	1	16	1	77.2	16	10	0	0	1.000	6	3	0	1	.50	-1

Pitchers Hitting, Fielding and Holding Runners

Pitcher	T	2015 Hitting						Career Hitting										2015 Fielding and Holding Runners											
		Avg	AB	H	HR	RBI	SH	Avg	AB	H	2B	3B	HR	RBI	BB	SO	SH	Inn	PO	A	E	DP	Pct	SBA	CS	PCS	PPO	CS%	RS
Friedrich,Christian, Col	L	.000	3	0	0	0	0	.091	33	3	0	0	0	0	3	17	1	58.1	3	4	0	0	1.000	1	0	0	0	.00	-1
Frieri,Ernesto, TB	R	-	0	0	0	0	0	.000	1	0	0	0	0	0	0	1	0	23.1	0	0	0	0	-	4	0	0	0	.00	-1
Fujikawa,Kyuji, Tex	R	-	0	0	0	0	0	-	0	0	0	0	0	0	0	0	0	1.2	0	0	0	0	-	0	0	0	0	-	0
Furbush,Charlie, Sea	L	-	0	0	0	0	0	-	0	0	0	0	0	0	0	0	0	21.2	2	3	1	0	.833	3	1	1	0	.33	-1
Gallardo,Yovani, Tex	R	.500	4	2	0	0	0	.198	420	83	21	0	12	42	12	148	35	184.1	17	21	1	2	.974	17	7	1	2	.41	1
Garces,Frank, SD	L	-	0	0	0	0	0	-	0	0	0	0	0	0	0	0	0	38.0	1	2	0	0	1.000	3	1	1	0	.33	0
Garcia,Jaime, StL	L	.098	41	4	0	1	1	.143	231	33	2	1	2	12	9	74	17	129.2	2	30	2	1	.941	5	2	1	1	.40	6
Garcia,Jason, Bal	R	-	0	0	0	0	0	-	0	0	0	0	0	0	1	0	0	29.2	3	1	1	0	.800	4	1	0	0	.25	-1
Garcia,Luis, Phi	R	-	0	0	0	0	0	.000	2	0	0	0	0	0	0	1	0	66.2	4	20	0	1	1.000	7	1	1	1	.14	2
Garcia,Yimi, LAD	R	-	0	0	0	0	0	-	0	0	0	0	0	0	0	0	0	56.2	4	5	0	1	1.000	4	1	0	0	.25	0
Garza,Matt, Mil	R	.077	39	3	0	0	7	.085	211	18	3	0	0	3	4	125	27	148.2	9	16	1	0	.962	11	5	0	0	.45	-1
Gausman,Kevin, Bal	R	-	0	0	0	0	0	.000	4	0	0	0	0	0	0	3	0	112.1	5	13	1	0	.947	5	2	0	0	.40	0
Gearrin,Cory, SF	R	-	0	0	0	0	0	-	0	0	0	0	0	0	0	0	0	3.2	0	2	0	0	1.000	0	0	0	0	-	1
Gee,Dillon, NYM	R	.100	10	1	0	0	2	.109	193	21	3	1	0	11	9	89	26	39.2	5	10	1	2	.938	4	1	0	0	.25	0
Geltz,Steve, TB	R	-	0	0	0	0	0	-	0	0	0	0	0	0	0	0	0	67.1	0	6	0	1	1.000	8	2	0	0	.25	-2
Germen,Gonzalez, ChC-Col	R	.000	1	0	0	0	0	.000	3	0	0	0	0	0	0	3	0	38.2	1	4	0	0	1.000	2	0	0	0	.00	0
Gibson,Kyle, Min	R	.200	5	1	0	0	0	.222	9	2	0	0	0	0	0	4	0	194.2	16	27	1	3	.977	11	1	0	2	.09	1
Giles,Ken, Phi	R	-	0	0	0	0	0	-	0	0	0	0	0	0	0	0	0	70.0	1	4	1	0	.833	2	0	0	0	.00	-4
Gilmartin,Sean, NYM	L	.333	6	2	0	0	0	.333	6	2	0	0	0	0	0	3	0	57.1	2	5	0	1	1.000	4	2	0	0	.50	0
Givens,Mychal, Bal	R	-	0	0	0	0	0	-	0	0	0	0	0	0	0	0	0	30.0	3	6	0	1	1.000	0	0	0	0	-	2
Godley,Zack, Ari	R	.111	9	1	0	0	1	.111	9	1	0	0	0	0	0	6	1	36.2	2	3	0	1	1.000	1	0	0	0	.00	-2
Goeddel,Erik, NYM	R	.000	1	0	0	0	0	.000	1	0	0	0	0	0	0	0	0	33.1	1	1	0	0	1.000	4	0	0	0	.00	-2
Goforth,David, Mil	R	.000	3	0	0	0	1	.000	3	0	0	0	0	0	0	1	0	24.2	1	5	0	0	1.000	5	2	1	0	.40	-1
Gomes,Brandon, TB	R	-	0	0	0	0	0	.000	1	0	0	0	0	0	1	1	0	59.0	0	6	0	0	1.000	4	1	1	1	.25	-1
Gomez,Jeanmar, Phi	R	.000	1	0	0	0	0	.158	19	3	0	0	0	0	0	11	1	74.2	4	12	0	1	1.000	5	2	0	0	.40	-1
Gonzales,Marco, StL	L	-	0	0	0	0	0	.300	10	3	2	0	0	0	0	2	2	2.2	0	0	0	0	-	0	0	0	0	-	0
Gonzalez,Chi Chi, Tex	R	-	0	0	0	0	0	-	0	0	0	0	0	0	0	0	0	67.0	4	13	0	0	1.000	1	0	0	0	.00	2
Gonzalez,Gio, Was	L	.093	43	4	0	2	10	.088	216	19	4	0	3	9	3	89	35	175.2	9	32	0	1	1.000	15	7	2	0	.47	2
Gonzalez,Miguel, Bal	R	.000	1	0	0	0	0	.000	9	0	0	0	0	0	0	3	1	144.2	10	14	0	3	1.000	4	1	0	0	.25	-1
Gonzalez,Severino, Phi	R	.100	10	1	0	1	1	.100	10	1	0	0	0	1	1	4	1	30.2	3	2	0	0	1.000	4	1	0	0	.25	-1
Goody,Nicholas, NYY	R	-	0	0	0	0	0	-	0	0	0	0	0	0	0	0	0	5.2	1	1	0	0	1.000	0	0	0	0	-	0
Gorzelanny,Tom, Det	L	-	0	0	0	0	0	.092	217	20	0	0	0	13	9	102	24	39.1	2	4	0	0	1.000	5	1	0	0	.20	1
Gott,Trevor, LAA	R	-	0	0	0	0	0	-	0	0	0	0	0	0	0	0	0	47.2	4	8	0	0	1.000	3	2	0	0	.67	1
Grace,Matt, Was	L	-	0	0	0	0	0	-	0	0	0	0	0	0	0	0	0	17.0	0	4	0	0	1.000	1	0	0	0	.00	-1
Graham,J.R., Min	R	-	0	0	0	0	0	-	0	0	0	0	0	0	0	0	0	63.2	6	11	0	0	1.000	7	1	0	0	.14	-1
Graveman,Kendall, Oak	R	-	0	0	0	0	0	-	0	0	0	0	0	0	0	0	0	115.2	11	11	2	1	.917	12	5	1	1	.42	2
Gray,Jonathan, Col	R	.000	11	0	0	0	0	.000	11	0	0	0	0	0	2	6	0	40.2	3	4	0	0	1.000	7	2	1	1	.29	-3
Gray,Sonny, Oak	R	.167	6	1	0	0	0	.125	8	1	0	0	0	0	0	5	2	208.0	37	23	0	1	1.000	9	2	0	0	.22	2
Greene,Shane, Det	R	.000	5	0	0	0	0	.000	5	0	0	0	0	0	0	5	0	83.2	4	10	2	2	.875	7	4	0	0	.57	-2
Greenwood,Nick, StL	L	-	0	0	0	0	0	.000	5	0	0	0	0	0	0	1	0	0.0	0	0	0	0	-	0	0	0	0	-	0
Gregerson,Luke, Hou	R	-	0	0	0	0	0	.000	2	0	0	0	0	0	0	1	1	61.0	3	17	0	3	1.000	3	0	0	0	.00	0
Gregg,Kevin, Cin	R	-	0	0	0	0	0	.000	6	0	0	0	0	0	0	5	0	10.2	1	0	1	0	.500	1	0	0	0	.00	0
Greinke,Zack, LAD	R	.224	67	15	2	3	8	.220	291	64	16	0	6	14	16	58	31	222.2	19	41	2	2	.968	13	6	0	2	.46	9
Grilli,Jason, Atl	R	-	0	0	0	0	0	.200	15	3	0	1	3	0	3	3	0	33.2	1	3	1	0	.800	0	0	0	0	-	1
Grimm,Justin, ChC	R	.000	1	0	0	0	0	.000	4	0	0	0	0	0	0	3	0	49.2	2	0	1	0	.667	7	0	0	0	.00	-2
Guaipe,Mayckol, Sea	R	-	0	0	0	0	0	-	0	0	0	0	0	0	0	0	0	26.2	1	1	0	0	1.000	3	2	0	0	.67	-1
Guerra,Deolis, Pit	R	.000	1	0	0	0	0	.000	1	0	0	0	0	0	0	0	0	16.2	4	2	0	0	1.000	1	0	0	0	.00	0
Guerra,Javy, CWS	R	-	0	0	0	0	0	-	0	0	0	0	0	0	1	0	0	1.2	0	0	0	0	-	0	0	0	0	-	0
Guerra,Junior, CWS	R	-	0	0	0	0	0	-	0	0	0	0	0	0	0	0	0	4.0	1	2	0	1	1.000	1	0	0	0	.00	0
Guilmet,Preston, TB-Mil	R	-	0	0	0	0	0	-	0	0	0	0	0	0	0	0	0	7.1	0	1	0	0	1.000	1	0	0	0	.00	0
Gurka,Jason, Col	L	-	0	0	0	0	0	-	0	0	0	0	0	0	0	0	0	7.2	0	1	0	0	1.000	0	0	0	0	-	0
Guthrie,Jeremy, KC	R	.250	4	1	0	0	1	.100	60	6	2	0	0	1	1	27	1	148.1	13	27	1	0	.976	11	6	2	3	.55	4
Hagadone,Nick, Cle	L	-	0	0	0	0	0	-	0	0	0	0	0	0	0	0	0	27.1	1	3	0	0	1.000	1	1	1	0	1.00	1
Hahn,Jesse, Oak	R	.000	3	0	0	0	0	.080	25	2	0	0	0	1	0	14	2	96.2	10	13	1	1	.958	6	4	0	1	.67	0
Hale,David, Col	R	.087	23	2	0	0	4	.068	44	3	0	0	0	1	0	20	5	78.1	5	7	0	1	1.000	8	0	0	0	.00	-3
Hall,Cody, SF	R	-	0	0	0	0	0	-	0	0	0	0	0	0	0	0	0	8.1	0	0	0	0	-	0	0	0	0	-	0
Hamels,Cole, Phi-Tex	L	.167	42	7	0	0	4	.174	610	106	15	2	1	28	17	257	62	212.1	10	25	2	1	.946	27	3	2	0	.11	-3
Hammel,Jason, ChC	R	.169	65	11	0	4	3	.134	268	36	5	0	1	14	6	106	34	170.2	8	23	2	1	.939	18	3	0	1	.17	-2
Hand,Brad, Mia	L	.118	17	2	0	2	6	.076	66	5	0	0	0	4	0	21	13	93.1	2	18	0	1	1.000	7	2	0	0	.29	2
Hand,Donovan, Cin	R	.000	1	0	0	0	0	.083	12	1	0	0	0	0	0	3	2	3.0	0	0	0	0	-	1	0	0	0	.00	0
Happ,J.A., Sea-Pit	L	.087	23	2	0	0	3	.089	179	16	2	0	1	6	9	79	27	172.0	4	21	2	0	.926	15	7	3	0	.47	-1
Harang,Aaron, Phi	R	.167	48	8	0	0	9	.097	670	65	8	0	1	21	5	294	69	172.1	6	15	2	0	.913	8	4	0	0	.50	-4
Hardy,Blaine, Det	L	.000	1	0	0	0	0	.000	1	0	0	0	0	0	0	0	0	61.1	2	7	0	0	1.000	1	0	0	0	.00	-1
Haren,Dan, Mia-ChC	R	.122	49	6	0	5	10	.200	414	83	26	0	2	39	17	121	41	187.1	9	9	0	1	1.000	8	2	0	0	.25	-3
Harris,Mitchell, StL	R	.000	1	0	0	0	0	.000	1	0	0	0	0	0	0	1	0	27.0	1	3	0	0	1.000	2	0	0	1	.00	0
Harris,Will, Hou	R	.000	1	0	0	0	0	.000	1	0	0	0	0	0	0	1	0	71.0	3	11	0	1	1.000	0	0	0	0	-	0
Harrison,Matt, Tex	L	.000	2	0	0	0	1	.000	18	0	0	0	0	0	1	12	3	16.0	1	1	0	0	1.000	0	0	0	0	-	-1
Harvey,Matt, NYM	R	.108	65	7	1	7	1	.128	141	18	6	0	1	12	1	65	9	189.1	6	19	2	1	.926	14	3	0	0	.21	-1
Hatcher,Chris, LAD	R	.000	1	0	0	0	0	.000	9	0	0	0	0	0	2	6	0	39.0	3	1	0	0	1.000	3	0	0	0	.00	-2
Hatley,Marcus, StL	R	-	0	0	0	0	0	-	0	0	0	0	0	0	0	0	0	1.1	0	0	0	0	-	0	0	0	0	-	0

Pitchers Hitting, Fielding and Holding Runners

Pitcher	T	2015 Hitting Avg	AB	H	HR	RBI	SH	Career Hitting Avg	AB	H	2B	3B	HR	RBI	BB	SO	SH	2015 Fielding and Holding Runners Inn	PO	A	E	DP	Pct	SBA	CS	PCS	PPO	CS%	RS
Hawkins,LaTroy, Col-Tor	R	.000	1	0	0	0	0	.000	8	0	0	0	0	0	0	7	1	38.2	2	8	0	1	1.000	4	2	0	0	.50	3
Heaney,Andrew, LAA	L	-	0	0	0	0	1	.077	13	1	0	0	0	0	0	5	2	105.2	3	8	0	1	1.000	3	0	0	0	.00	0
Hellickson,Jeremy, Ari	R	.220	41	9	0	7	3	.213	47	10	0	0	0	7	2	17	4	146.0	11	19	2	0	.938	9	1	0	0	.11	1
Hembree,Heath, Bos	R	-	0	0	0	0	0	-	0	0	0	0	0	0	0	0	0	25.1	0	1	0	0	1.000	4	2	0	0	.50	0
Hendricks,Kyle, ChC	R	.050	60	3	0	1	3	.071	84	6	1	0	0	2	4	35	6	180.0	17	29	0	2	1.000	18	5	2	2	.28	3
Hendriks,Liam, Tor	R	-	0	0	0	0	0	.000	2	0	0	0	0	0	1	1	0	64.2	4	4	0	0	1.000	8	2	0	1	.25	-2
Hernandez,David, Ari	R	-	0	0	0	0	0	.250	4	1	0	0	0	0	0	1	0	33.2	3	2	1	0	.833	2	0	0	1	.00	-1
Hernandez,Felix, Sea	R	.000	3	0	0	0	0	.108	37	4	1	0	1	7	2	17	5	201.2	13	26	2	2	.951	18	5	1	0	.28	2
Hernandez,Roberto, Hou	R	.000	2	0	0	0	0	.058	69	4	0	0	0	2	1	37	11	84.2	6	12	0	1	1.000	13	3	0	0	.23	-1
Herrera,Kelvin, KC	R	-	0	0	0	0	0	-	0	0	0	0	0	0	0	0	0	69.2	5	6	0	0	1.000	9	2	0	0	.22	-2
Hessler,Keith, Ari	L	1.000	1	1	0	0	0	1.000	1	1	0	0	0	0	0	0	0	12.1	1	2	0	0	1.000	0	0	0	0	-	1
Heston,Chris, SF	R	.196	51	10	0	3	7	.192	52	10	2	0	0	3	0	19	7	177.2	12	24	4	3	.900	11	6	1	0	.55	4
Hill,Rich, Bos	L	-	0	0	0	0	0	.123	114	14	3	0	0	6	2	51	6	29.0	1	2	1	0	.750	1	0	0	0	.00	0
Hill,Taylor, Was	R	-	0	0	0	0	0	.333	3	1	0	0	0	0	0	0	0	12.0	1	1	0	0	1.000	2	0	0	0	.00	0
Hinojosa,Dalier, Bos-Phi	R	-	0	0	0	0	0	-	0	0	0	0	0	0	0	0	0	24.2	1	0	0	0	1.000	1	0	0	0	.00	-2
Hochevar,Luke, KC	R	-	0	0	0	0	0	.063	16	1	0	0	0	0	0	10	1	50.2	4	7	0	2	1.000	4	1	0	0	.25	1
Holland,Derek, Tex	L	-	0	0	0	0	0	.000	12	0	0	0	0	0	2	6	2	58.2	1	8	1	1	.900	3	2	1	1	.67	1
Holland,Greg, KC	R	-	0	0	0	0	0	-	0	0	0	0	0	0	0	0	0	44.2	1	9	0	1	1.000	2	2	0	0	1.00	2
Holmberg,David, Cin	L	.125	8	1	0	0	1	.071	14	1	0	0	0	2	8	3	28.1	1	2	0	1.000	2	0	0	0	.00	-1			
Hoover,J.J., Cin	R	-	0	0	0	0	0	-	0	0	0	0	0	0	1	0	0	64.1	3	8	1	0	.917	2	1	0	0	.50	-1
House,T.J., Cle	L	-	0	0	0	0	0	.000	2	0	0	0	0	0	0	2	0	13.0	0	1	0	0	1.000	4	0	0	0	.00	-1
Houser,Adrian, Mil	R	-	0	0	0	0	0	-	0	0	0	0	0	0	0	0	0	2.0	1	2	0	1	1.000	0	0	0	0	-	1
Howell,J.P., LAD	L	-	0	0	0	0	0	.182	11	2	0	0	1	0	5	0	44.0	7	11	0	2	1.000	8	1	1	0	.13	0		
Hudson,Daniel, Ari	R	.000	1	0	0	0	0	.226	106	24	5	0	1	21	5	35	14	67.2	5	7	1	0	.923	10	3	1	0	.30	1
Hudson,Tim, SF	R	.184	38	7	1	1	3	.160	613	98	19	1	4	42	26	190	67	123.2	7	15	0	4	1.000	7	4	0	1	.57	-1
Huff,David, LAD	L	.000	1	0	0	0	0	.125	8	1	0	0	0	0	0	4	2	6.0	0	3	0	0	1.000	0	0	0	0	-	0
Hughes,Jared, Pit	R	-	0	0	0	0	1	.000	5	0	0	0	0	0	0	4	1	67.0	4	15	1	0	.950	14	5	2	0	.36	-2
Hughes,Phil, Min	R	.000	3	0	0	0	0	.000	15	0	0	0	0	0	0	6	3	155.1	5	17	0	1	1.000	9	2	0	0	.22	0
Hunter,Tommy, Bal-ChC	R	-	0	0	0	0	0	.000	3	0	0	0	0	0	0	2	0	60.1	9	7	0	1	1.000	12	2	0	0	.17	1
Hutchison,Drew, Tor	R	-	0	0	0	0	0	.333	6	2	0	0	0	0	0	2	0	150.1	6	15	0	3	1.000	22	8	2	0	.36	0
Hynes,Colt, Tor	L	-	0	0	0	0	0	-	0	0	0	0	0	0	0	0	0	3.0	0	0	0	0	-	0	0	0	0	-	0
Ibarra,Edgar, LAA	L	-	0	0	0	0	0	-	0	0	0	0	0	0	0	0	0	4.0	0	0	0	0	-	0	0	0	0	-	0
Iglesias,Raisel, Cin	R	.067	30	2	0	1	1	.067	30	2	0	1	0	1	0	13	1	95.1	12	14	2	1	.929	4	1	1	0	.25	2
Iwakuma,Hisashi, Sea	R	.000	2	0	0	0	1	.000	9	0	0	0	0	0	1	7	2	129.2	6	21	0	1	1.000	3	2	0	0	.67	4
Jackson,Edwin, ChC-Atl	R	.000	1	0	0	0	0	.169	248	42	3	0	2	11	11	100	22	55.2	2	6	1	0	.889	5	1	0	0	.20	0
Jackson,Jay, SD	R	-	0	0	0	0	0	-	0	0	0	0	0	0	0	0	0	4.1	0	0	0	0	-	0	0	0	0	-	0
Jackson,Luke, Tex	R	-	0	0	0	0	0	-	0	0	0	0	0	0	0	0	0	6.1	0	0	0	0	-	0	0	0	0	-	0
Jaime,Juan, Atl	R	-	0	0	0	0	0	-	0	0	0	0	0	0	0	0	0	1.1	0	1	0	0	1.000	1	0	0	0	.00	0
Jansen,Kenley, LAD	R	-	0	0	0	0	0	.333	3	1	0	0	0	1	1	1	0	52.1	0	2	1	0	.667	5	0	0	0	.00	-2
Janssen,Casey, Was	R	-	0	0	0	0	0	.000	3	0	0	0	0	0	2	1	0	40.0	4	6	0	0	1.000	1	1	0	0	1.00	1
Jeffress,Jeremy, Mil	R	-	0	0	0	0	0	-	0	0	0	0	0	0	0	0	0	68.0	4	8	2	0	.857	2	0	1	0	-	-2
Jenkins,Chad, Tor	R	-	0	0	0	0	0	.000	2	0	0	0	0	0	0	2	0	3.2	0	0	0	0	-	0	0	0	0	-	0
Jennings,Dan, CWS	L	-	0	0	0	0	0	.000	1	0	0	0	0	0	0	0	0	56.1	5	9	2	1	.875	1	0	0	0	.00	-1
Jepsen,Kevin, TB-Min	R	-	0	0	0	0	0	-	0	0	0	0	0	0	0	0	0	69.2	5	8	2	1	.867	6	2	0	0	.33	1
Jimenez,Cesar, Phi-Mil	L	-	0	0	0	0	0	.000	1	0	0	0	0	0	0	1	0	23.0	1	3	0	0	1.000	3	0	0	0	.00	0
Jimenez,Ubaldo, Bal	R	.250	8	2	0	2	0	.117	282	33	0	0	0	11	17	98	33	184.0	7	15	1	1	.957	25	3	0	0	.12	-4
Johnson,Brian, Bos	L	-	0	0	0	0	0	-	0	0	0	0	0	0	0	0	0	4.1	0	0	0	0	-	2	0	0	0	.00	0
Johnson,Erik, CWS	R	-	0	0	0	0	0	.000	3	0	0	0	0	0	0	0	0	35.0	2	2	0	0	1.000	4	3	1	0	.75	1
Johnson,Jim, Atl-LAD	R	-	0	0	0	0	0	.000	1	0	0	0	0	0	0	1	0	66.2	4	6	1	0	.909	7	0	0	0	.00	-3
Johnson,Steve, Bal	R	-	0	0	0	0	0	-	0	0	0	0	0	0	0	0	0	5.1	0	0	0	0	-	0	0	0	0	-	0
Jones,Nate, CWS	R	-	0	0	0	0	0	-	0	0	0	0	0	0	0	0	0	19.0	1	3	0	0	1.000	1	1	1	0	1.00	0
Jordan,Taylor, Was	R	.333	6	2	0	0	0	.179	28	5	0	0	0	0	9	4	17.0	1	4	0	1.000	0	0	0	0	-	1			
Jungmann,Taylor, Mil	R	.270	37	10	0	0	6	.270	37	10	2	0	0	1	12	6	119.1	11	16	1	0	.964	24	6	2	1	.25	0
Kahnle,Tommy, Col	R	-	0	0	0	0	0	.000	3	0	0	0	0	0	0	1	0	33.1	3	1	0	0	1.000	1	0	0	0	.00	-1
Karns,Nate, TB	R	.250	4	1	1	1	1	.143	7	1	0	0	1	1	0	4	3	147.0	5	13	1	0	.947	22	5	0	0	.23	-2
Kazmir,Scott, Oak-Hou	L	.250	4	1	0	1	0	.115	26	3	0	0	2	0	10	1	183.0	4	17	7	1	.750	9	0	0	1	.00	-3		
Kela,Keone, Tex	R	-	0	0	0	0	0	-	0	0	0	0	0	0	0	0	0	60.1	2	6	0	1.000	10	1	0	0	.10	-2			
Kelley,Shawn, SD	R	-	0	0	0	0	0	-	0	0	0	0	0	0	0	0	0	51.1	3	0	1	0	.750	4	3	0	0	.75	-1
Kelly,Casey, SD	R	.000	2	0	0	0	1	.167	12	2	0	0	0	0	0	4	3	11.1	0	2	0	0	1.000	0	0	0	0	-	0
Kelly,Joe, Bos	R	.200	5	1	0	1	0	.172	87	15	4	0	0	5	0	25	8	134.1	20	23	4	1	.915	10	3	0	2	.30	6
Kelly,Ryan, Atl	R	-	0	0	0	0	0	-	0	0	0	0	0	0	0	0	0	16.2	1	2	0	0	1.000	1	0	0	0	.00	0
Kendrick,Kyle, Col	R	.186	43	8	1	2	3	.139	373	52	9	1	1	9	18	157	44	142.1	10	18	2	2	.933	13	6	0	1	.46	1
Kennedy,Ian, SD	R	.095	42	4	0	0	6	.128	313	40	11	1	1	18	32	152	42	168.1	8	12	0	2	1.000	15	5	0	0	.33	-1
Kensing,Logan, Sea	R	-	0	0	0	0	0	.000	8	0	0	0	0	0	0	2	1	15.1	0	2	0	0	1.000	0	0	0	0	-	0
Kershaw,Clayton, LAD	L	.127	71	9	0	2	5	.153	472	72	6	1	1	24	20	148	80	232.2	8	45	1	1	.981	16	9	6	4	.56	5
Keuchel,Dallas, Hou	L	.200	5	1	0	0	1	.100	30	3	0	0	0	1	2	18	6	232.0	18	53	1	1	.986	5	0	0	0	.00	13
Kimbrel,Craig, SD	R	.000	1	0	0	0	0	.000	1	0	0	0	0	0	0	1	0	59.1	4	3	1	1	.875	9	1	0	0	.11	-2
Kintzler,Brandon, Mil	R	.000	1	0	0	0	0	.000	2	0	0	0	0	0	0	1	0	7.0	1	3	0	0	1.000	0	0	0	0	-	0
Klein,Phil, Tex	R	-	0	0	0	0	0	-	0	0	0	0	0	0	0	0	0	17.1	0	1	0	0	1.000	4	0	0	0	.00	-2
Kluber,Corey, Cle	R	.000	6	0	0	0	0	.077	13	1	0	0	0	0	1	6	1	222.0	16	25	0	2	1.000	23	7	0	0	.30	1

Pitchers Hitting, Fielding and Holding Runners

Pitcher	T	2015 Hitting						Career Hitting										2015 Fielding and Holding Runners											
		Avg	AB	H	HR	RBI	SH	Avg	AB	H	2B	3B	HR	RBI	BB	SO	SH	Inn	PO	A	E	DP	Pct	SBA	CS	PCS	PPO	CS%	RS
Knebel,Corey, Mil	R	-	0	0	0	0	0	-	0	0	0	0	0	0	0	0	0	50.1	3	8	0	0	1.000	4	1	0	0	.25	2
Knudson,Guido, Det	R	-	0	0	0	0	0	-	0	0	0	0	0	0	0	0	0	5.0	0	0	0	0	-	0	0	0	0	-	0
Koehler,Tom, Mia	R	.120	50	6	0	1	12	.086	140	12	1	0	0	1	3	73	22	187.1	14	20	5	2	.872	12	4	1	1	.33	-2
Kohn,Michael, Atl	R	-	0	0	0	0	0	-	0	0	0	0	0	0	0	0	0	4.2	0	0	0	0	-	0	0	0	0	-	0
Kontos,George, SF	R	.000	2	0	0	0	1	.000	5	0	0	0	0	0	0	3	3	73.1	4	7	0	1	1.000	9	2	0	0	.22	0
Krol,Ian, Det	L	-	0	0	0	0	0	-	0	0	0	0	0	0	0	0	0	28.0	0	4	1	1	.800	0	0	0	0	-	0
Lackey,John, StL	R	.113	62	7	0	3	4	.108	120	13	4	0	0	5	4	43	11	218.0	20	15	2	3	.946	12	3	0	0	.25	-7
Laffey,Aaron, Col	L	.500	2	1	0	0	0	.222	9	2	0	0	0	0	0	2	0	7.1	0	1	0	0	1.000	1	1	0	0	1.00	0
LaFromboise,Bobby, Pit	L	-	0	0	0	0	0	-	0	0	0	0	0	0	0	0	0	8.0	0	0	0	0	-	1	0	0	0	.00	0
Lamb,John, Cin	L	.063	16	1	0	1	0	.063	16	1	1	0	0	1	0	8	0	49.2	0	3	0	0	1.000	4	1	0	0	.25	-1
Latos,Mat, Mia-LAD-LAA	R	.292	24	7	0	1	10	.132	319	42	6	0	3	14	6	145	43	116.1	12	14	1	1	.963	21	5	0	0	.24	-1
Layne,Tommy, Bos	L	-	0	0	0	0	0	-	0	0	0	0	0	0	0	0	0	47.2	5	7	0	0	1.000	6	2	2	0	.33	1
Lazo,Raudel, Mia	L	-	0	0	0	0	0	-	0	0	0	0	0	0	0	0	0	5.2	0	0	0	0	-	0	0	0	0	-	0
Leake,Mike, Cin-SF	R	.116	69	8	2	8	4	.212	364	77	16	1	6	23	9	147	36	192.0	19	32	1	2	.981	6	3	0	0	.50	6
Leathersich,Jack, NYM	L	-	0	0	0	0	0	-	0	0	0	0	0	0	0	0	0	11.2	0	2	0	0	1.000	5	1	0	0	.20	-1
LeCure,Sam, Cin	R	.000	1	0	0	0	0	.091	22	2	2	0	0	1	8	2	2	20.0	2	2	0	0	1.000	3	1	1	0	.33	0
Lee,C.C., Cle	R	-	0	0	0	0	0	-	0	0	0	0	0	0	0	0	0	1.2	0	0	0	0	-	0	0	0	0	-	0
Lee,Zach, LAD	R	.000	2	0	0	0	0	.000	2	0	0	0	0	0	0	0	0	4.2	0	0	0	0	-	0	0	0	0	-	0
Leon,Arnold, Oak	R	-	0	0	0	0	0	-	0	0	0	0	0	0	0	0	0	26.2	4	1	0	0	1.000	2	0	0	0	.00	-2
Leone,Dominic, Sea-Ari	R	-	0	0	0	0	0	-	0	0	0	0	0	0	0	0	0	15.0	1	1	0	0	1.000	0	0	0	0	-	0
Lester,Jon, ChC	L	.065	62	4	0	0	6	.041	98	4	0	0	0	1	4	52	11	205.0	10	17	3	1	.900	55	11	2	0	.20	-8
Lewis,Colby, Tex	R	.000	2	0	0	0	0	.259	27	7	1	0	0	5	0	11	1	204.2	8	10	1	0	.947	15	3	0	0	.20	-4
Liberatore,Adam, LAD	L	.000	2	0	0	0	0	.000	2	0	0	0	0	0	0	2	0	29.2	1	4	0	0	1.000	3	0	0	0	.00	0
Lincecum,Tim, SF	R	.143	21	3	0	0	2	.112	474	53	4	2	0	19	34	244	70	76.1	3	7	0	0	1.000	14	1	0	0	.07	-2
Lindgren,Jacob, NYY	L	-	0	0	0	0	0	-	0	0	0	0	0	0	0	0	0	7.0	0	1	1	0	.500	0	0	0	0	-	0
Liriano,Francisco, Pit	L	.169	65	11	1	7	2	.121	174	21	2	0	1	10	8	69	14	186.2	5	24	1	1	.967	13	2	1	0	.15	3
Liz,Radhames, Pit	R	.000	1	0	0	0	0	.000	7	0	0	0	0	0	0	3	0	23.1	2	2	0	0	1.000	2	1	0	0	.50	0
Lobstein,Kyle, Det	L	-	0	0	0	0	0	-	0	0	0	0	0	0	0	0	0	63.2	3	10	0	0	1.000	5	2	1	1	.40	-1
Locke,Jeff, Pit	L	.067	45	3	0	2	7	.092	153	14	1	0	0	2	6	78	15	168.1	7	25	0	1	1.000	21	7	4	0	.33	-4
Loewen,Adam, Phi	L	.333	3	1	0	0	0	.189	37	7	1	0	1	4	3	13	0	19.1	1	4	1	0	.833	4	2	1	0	.50	0
Logan,Boone, Col	L	-	0	0	0	0	0	-	0	0	0	0	0	0	0	0	0	35.1	0	6	0	0	1.000	0	0	0	0	-	1
Lohse,Kyle, Mil	R	.231	39	9	0	1	3	.153	509	78	9	0	0	31	9	163	75	152.1	8	26	1	0	.971	12	6	0	0	.50	3
Lopez,Javier, SF	L	-	0	0	0	0	1	.091	11	1	0	0	0	1	0	5	2	39.1	4	12	0	2	1.000	0	0	0	0	-	2
Lopez,Jorge, Mil	R	.000	2	0	0	0	1	.000	2	0	0	0	0	0	0	2	1	10.0	0	1	0	0	1.000	2	1	0	0	.50	0
Lorenzen,Michael, Cin	R	.250	36	9	0	4	4	.250	36	9	0	1	0	4	0	13	4	113.1	13	11	0	3	1.000	13	5	1	0	.38	0
Loup,Aaron, Tor	L	-	0	0	0	0	0	.000	1	0	0	0	0	0	0	0	0	42.1	0	4	0	0	1.000	1	0	0	0	.00	0
Lowe,Mark, Sea-Tor	R	-	0	0	0	0	0	.000	1	0	0	0	0	0	0	1	0	55.0	2	3	0	0	1.000	4	3	0	0	.75	1
Luetge,Lucas, Sea	L	-	0	0	0	0	0	-	0	0	0	0	0	0	0	0	0	2.1	0	2	0	0	1.000	1	1	1	0	1.00	0
Lyles,Jordan, Col	R	.000	19	0	0	0	0	.132	136	18	4	0	2	7	6	64	11	49.0	2	8	1	0	.909	8	2	1	0	.25	-1
Lynn,Lance, StL	R	.160	50	8	0	1	5	.087	218	19	3	0	5	11	12	127	30	175.1	12	14	2	1	.929	5	1	1	3	.20	-3
Lyons,Tyler, StL	L	.188	16	3	0	1	2	.143	35	5	0	0	1	1	4	13	3	60.0	1	9	3	0	.769	4	0	0	0	.00	0
Machi,Jean, SF-Bos	R	.000	3	0	0	0	0	.000	5	0	0	0	0	0	0	3	1	58.0	4	10	0	0	1.000	4	1	1	0	.25	1
Madson,Ryan, KC	R	-	0	0	0	0	0	.125	48	6	1	0	0	2	2	20	7	63.1	6	13	0	4	1.000	2	1	0	0	.50	3
Maness,Seth, StL	R	.000	3	0	0	0	0	.231	13	3	0	0	0	0	5	0	0	63.1	5	11	0	1	1.000	1	0	0	0	.00	0
Manship,Jeff, Cle	R	-	0	0	0	0	0	.000	10	0	0	0	0	0	0	3	0	39.1	2	4	0	0	1.000	0	0	0	0	-	1
Marcum,Shaun, Cle	R	-	0	0	0	0	0	.132	129	17	5	0	1	8	9	44	20	35.0	3	2	0	0	1.000	2	2	0	0	1.00	1
Marimon,Sugar, Atl	R	.333	6	2	0	0	0	.333	6	2	0	0	0	0	1	3	0	25.2	0	1	0	0	1.000	3	1	0	0	.33	0
Mariot,Michael, KC	R	-	0	0	0	0	0	-	0	0	0	0	0	0	0	0	0	3.0	0	0	0	0	-	0	0	0	0	-	0
Marksberry,Matt, Atl	L	-	0	0	0	0	0	-	0	0	0	0	0	0	0	0	0	23.1	1	2	1	0	.750	3	1	1	0	.33	-1
Marquis,Jason, Cin	R	.188	16	3	0	1	1	.196	663	130	35	2	5	57	13	167	42	47.1	4	5	0	0	1.000	9	3	0	0	.33	-1
Marshall,Evan, Ari	R	-	0	0	0	0	0	-	0	0	0	0	0	0	0	0	0	13.1	1	1	0	0	1.000	0	0	0	0	-	0
Martin,Chris, NYY	R	-	0	0	0	0	0	-	0	0	0	0	0	0	0	0	0	20.2	3	2	0	0	1.000	2	0	0	0	.00	-1
Martin,Cody, Atl-Oak	R	-	0	0	0	0	1	-	0	0	0	0	0	0	0	0	1	30.2	2	2	0	0	1.000	1	0	0	0	.00	0
Martin,Rafael, Was	R	-	0	0	0	0	0	-	0	0	0	0	0	0	0	0	0	12.1	0	0	0	0	-	1	0	0	0	.00	0
Martinez,Carlos, StL	R	.143	56	8	0	0	5	.157	70	11	2	0	0	2	1	28	6	179.2	18	26	2	3	.957	7	5	0	2	.71	-1
Martinez,Nick, Tex	R	.000	4	0	0	0	0	.000	7	0	0	0	0	0	0	3	0	125.0	6	13	4	2	.826	9	2	1	0	.22	1
Masset,Nick, Mia-Atl	R	-	0	0	0	0	0	.000	5	0	0	0	0	0	0	5	1	25.0	1	0	0	0	1.000	3	1	0	0	.33	0
Masterson,Justin, Bos	R	.667	3	2	0	1	0	.212	33	7	0	0	0	2	0	13	3	59.1	6	8	1	1	.933	7	5	0	0	.71	1
Mateo,Marcos, SD	R	-	0	0	0	0	0	.000	3	0	0	0	0	0	0	1	1	27.0	1	2	0	0	1.000	2	0	0	0	.00	-1
Matthews,Ryan, LAA-Cin	R	-	0	0	0	0	0	.000	1	0	0	0	0	0	0	1	0	56.0	3	8	4	0	.733	10	0	0	0	.00	-6
Matusz,Brian, Bal	L	-	0	0	0	0	0	.125	8	1	0	0	0	0	0	6	0	49.0	0	4	0	0	1.000	1	1	1	0	1.00	-1
Matz,Steven, NYM	L	.286	14	4	0	5	0	.286	14	4	1	0	0	5	0	1	0	35.2	0	6	0	1	1.000	3	0	0	0	.00	1
Matzek,Tyler, Col	L	.375	8	3	0	0	1	.217	46	10	2	0	0	2	2	14	4	22.0	1	4	0	1	1.000	7	1	0	0	.14	0
Maurer,Brandon, SD	R	-	0	0	0	0	0	.000	1	0	0	0	0	0	0	0	1	51.0	0	3	1	0	.750	6	2	0	0	.33	-2
May,Trevor, Min	R	.000	3	0	0	0	0	.000	3	0	0	0	0	0	0	3	0	114.2	5	11	2	0	.889	12	2	1	0	.17	-5
Mazzaro,Vin, Mia	R	-	0	0	0	0	0	.176	17	3	0	0	0	1	0	10	5	12.0	0	1	0	0	1.000	1	0	0	0	.00	-1
Mazzoni,Cory, SD	R	-	0	0	0	0	0	-	0	0	0	0	0	0	0	0	0	8.2	0	0	0	0	-	1	0	0	0	.00	-1
McAllister,Zach, Cle	R	-	0	0	0	0	0	.167	6	1	0	0	0	0	0	2	0	69.0	2	3	2	0	.714	7	3	0	0	.43	-5
McCarthy,Brandon, LAD	R	.000	6	0	0	1	2	.062	81	5	0	0	4	4	4	35	8	23.0	1	3	0	1	1.000	2	1	0	0	.50	1
McCullers,Lance, Hou	R	.000	2	0	0	0	0	.000	2	0	0	0	0	0	0	1	0	125.2	11	11	1	0	.957	4	1	0	0	.25	1

Pitchers Hitting, Fielding and Holding Runners

Pitcher	T	2015 Hitting						Career Hitting										2015 Fielding and Holding Runners											
		Avg	AB	H	HR	RBI	SH	Avg	AB	H	2B	3B	HR	RBI	BB	SO	SH	Inn	PO	A	E	DP	Pct	SBA	CS	PCS	PPO	CS%	RS
McFarland,T.J., Bal	L	-	0	0	0	0	0	-	0	0	0	0	0	0	0	0	1	40.1	0	6	0	0	1.000	0	0	0	0	-	-1
McGee,Jake, TB	L	-	0	0	0	0	0	-	0	0	0	0	0	0	0	0	0	37.1	0	2	0	0	1.000	0	0	0	0	-	0
McGough,Scott, Mia	R	-	0	0	0	0	0	-	0	0	0	0	0	0	0	0	0	6.2	0	1	0	0	1.000	1	0	0	0	.00	0
McGowan,Dustin, Phi	R	.000	3	0	0	0	0	.118	17	2	0	0	0	0	0	10	1	23.1	1	5	0	1	1.000	2	1	0	0	.50	0
McHugh,Collin, Hou	R	.125	8	1	0	0	0	.100	20	2	0	0	0	0	0	8	1	203.2	13	31	1	1	.978	14	4	0	1	.29	3
McKirahan,Andrew, Atl	L	.000	1	0	0	0	0	.000	1	0	0	0	0	0	0	1	0	27.1	0	3	0	1	1.000	2	0	0	0	.00	0
Medina,Yoervis, Sea-ChC	R	-	0	0	0	0	0	-	0	0	0	0	0	0	0	0	0	21.0	3	2	1	0	.833	3	1	0	0	.33	0
Medlen,Kris, KC	R	-	0	0	0	0	1	.141	128	18	4	0	1	8	11	59	12	58.1	4	7	0	0	1.000	4	1	0	2	.25	0
Mejia,Jenrry, NYM	R	-	0	0	0	0	0	.029	34	1	0	0	0	1	0	16	3	7.1	2	0	0	0	1.000	1	0	0	0	.00	0
Melancon,Mark, Pit	R	-	0	0	0	0	0	-	0	0	0	0	0	0	1	0	0	76.2	7	16	1	1	.958	2	2	0	0	1.00	4
Mendez,Roman, Tex-Bos	R	-	0	0	0	0	0	-	0	0	0	0	0	0	0	0	0	13.2	1	2	0	0	1.000	3	1	0	0	.33	0
Meyer,Alex, Min	R	-	0	0	0	0	0	-	0	0	0	0	0	0	0	0	0	2.2	1	1	0	0	1.000	2	0	0	0	.00	0
Miley,Wade, Bos	L	.000	2	0	0	0	0	.147	197	29	5	0	1	12	8	52	26	193.2	7	30	1	1	.974	4	3	2	3	.75	5
Miller,Andrew, NYY	L	-	0	0	0	0	0	.056	72	4	0	0	0	3	0	36	4	61.2	2	2	1	0	.800	2	1	0	0	.50	0
Miller,Justin, Col	R	.000	2	0	0	0	1	.000	2	0	0	0	0	0	0	2	1	33.1	1	2	0	0	1.000	3	0	0	0	.00	1
Miller,Shelby, Atl	R	.054	56	3	0	0	11	.113	160	18	9	0	1	6	7	83	32	205.1	9	22	5	3	.861	24	6	1	0	.25	-2
Mills,Brad, Oak	L	-	0	0	0	0	0	.000	4	0	0	0	0	0	0	0	0	5.0	0	0	0	0	-	0	0	0	0	-	0
Milone,Tommy, Min	L	.000	2	0	0	0	0	.160	25	4	0	0	1	6	0	5	4	128.2	9	16	0	0	1.000	11	3	2	0	.27	-1
Mitchell,Bryan, NYY	R	.000	1	0	0	0	0	.000	1	0	0	0	0	0	0	1	0	29.2	1	3	0	0	1.000	2	0	0	0	.00	0
Montas,Frankie, CWS	R	-	0	0	0	0	0	-	0	0	0	0	0	0	0	0	0	15.0	0	1	0	0	1.000	1	1	0	0	1.00	0
Montero,Rafael, NYM	R	.000	2	0	0	0	0	.000	13	0	0	0	0	0	0	6	2	10.0	2	1	0	0	1.000	0	0	0	0	-	0
Montgomery,Mike, Sea	L	.000	3	0	0	0	0	.000	3	0	0	0	0	0	0	2	0	90.0	5	10	0	2	1.000	2	1	1	0	.50	1
Moore,Matt, TB	L	.000	1	0	0	0	1	.000	7	0	0	0	0	1	0	2	2	63.0	3	8	1	0	.917	4	2	0	0	.50	-1
Morales,Franklin, KC	L	-	0	0	0	0	0	.177	62	11	0	0	0	2	4	27	8	62.1	4	12	1	2	.941	0	0	0	1	-	4
Moreno,Diego, NYY	R	-	0	0	0	0	0	-	0	0	0	0	0	0	0	0	0	10.1	0	1	0	0	1.000	1	0	0	0	.00	0
Morgan,Adam, Phi	L	.077	26	2	0	1	1	.077	26	2	1	0	0	1	0	12	1	84.1	6	7	0	1	1.000	5	1	0	1	.20	1
Morin,Mike, LAA	R	-	0	0	0	0	0	-	0	0	0	0	0	0	0	0	0	35.1	2	3	1	0	.833	4	1	0	0	.25	-1
Morris,Akeel, NYM	R	-	0	0	0	0	0	-	0	0	0	0	0	0	0	0	0	0.2	0	0	0	0	-	0	0	0	0	-	0
Morris,Bryan, Mia	R	-	0	0	0	0	0	.167	6	1	0	0	0	0	0	3	0	63.0	2	13	1	2	.938	3	0	0	0	.00	0
Morrow,Brandon, SD	R	.000	9	0	0	0	0	.000	23	0	0	0	0	0	1	14	0	33.0	3	2	0	1	1.000	3	2	0	1	.67	0
Morton,Charlie, Pit	R	.028	36	1	0	1	6	.072	249	18	4	0	0	6	3	129	36	129.0	9	16	2	1	.926	13	0	0	0	.00	-3
Moscot,Jon, Cin	R	.250	4	1	0	0	0	.250	4	1	0	0	0	0	0	2	0	11.2	2	1	0	0	1.000	2	0	0	0	.00	0
Motte,Jason, ChC	R	-	0	0	0	0	0	.000	4	0	0	0	0	0	0	4	0	48.1	1	5	0	0	1.000	2	1	0	0	.50	0
Moylan,Peter, Atl	R	-	0	0	0	0	0	.000	7	0	0	0	0	0	1	6	0	10.1	0	2	0	0	1.000	1	0	0	0	.00	-1
Mujica,Edward, Bos-Oak	R	-	0	0	0	0	0	.182	11	2	0	0	0	0	0	4	2	47.1	1	10	2	2	.846	8	1	0	0	.13	1
Murata,Toru, Cle	R	-	0	0	0	0	0	-	0	0	0	0	0	0	0	0	0	3.1	0	1	0	0	1.000	0	0	0	0	-	0
Murray,Colton, Phi	R	-	0	0	0	0	0	-	0	0	0	0	0	0	0	0	0	7.2	0	1	0	0	1.000	1	0	0	0	.00	0
Narveson,Chris, Mia	L	.000	6	0	0	1	1	.216	116	25	3	0	0	13	5	46	16	30.1	0	5	2	0	.714	2	1	0	0	.50	0
Nathan,Joe, Det	R	-	0	0	0	0	0	.159	63	10	3	0	2	4	3	17	10	0.1	0	0	0	0	-	0	0	0	0	-	0
Nelson,Jimmy, Mil	R	.109	55	6	0	2	3	.115	78	9	2	0	0	2	1	43	4	177.1	8	21	1	3	.967	30	6	0	0	.20	-8
Neris,Hector, Phi	R	.000	1	0	0	0	0	.000	1	0	0	0	0	0	0	1	0	40.1	1	3	2	0	.667	2	1	0	0	.50	-1
Nesbitt,Angel, Det	R	-	0	0	0	0	0	-	0	0	0	0	0	0	0	0	0	21.2	2	2	0	0	1.000	1	1	0	0	1.00	-1
Neshek,Pat, Hou	R	-	0	0	0	0	0	-	0	0	0	0	0	0	0	0	0	54.2	1	6	1	0	.875	1	1	0	0	1.00	-1
Nicasio,Juan, LAD	R	.000	1	0	0	0	0	.119	101	12	2	0	0	8	6	62	14	58.1	5	7	1	0	.923	9	0	0	2	.00	-4
Nicolino,Justin, Mia	L	.040	25	1	0	0	2	.040	25	1	0	0	0	0	0	8	2	74.0	2	15	0	1	1.000	2	1	1	0	.50	1
Niese,Jon, NYM	L	.173	52	9	0	4	3	.155	317	49	6	1	0	18	33	150	29	176.2	7	39	1	4	.979	11	5	4	0	.45	-1
Noesi,Hector, CWS	R	-	0	0	0	0	0	.250	8	2	0	0	0	0	0	3	0	32.2	0	4	0	1	1.000	1	0	0	0	.00	0
Nola,Aaron, Phi	R	.087	23	2	0	1	2	.087	23	2	0	0	1	1	1	16	2	77.2	5	10	0	0	1.000	8	3	0	0	.38	-2
Nolasco,Ricky, Min	R	.000	3	0	0	0	0	.136	374	51	12	0	1	26	21	176	62	37.1	2	1	1	0	.750	3	2	0	0	.67	-1
Nolin,Sean, Oak	L	-	0	0	0	0	0	-	0	0	0	0	0	0	0	0	0	29.0	0	1	0	0	1.000	1	0	0	0	.00	0
Norris,Bud, Bal-SD	R	.000	4	0	0	0	0	.147	177	26	5	0	0	11	4	59	31	83.0	6	6	2	0	.857	8	3	0	2	.38	-1
Norris,Daniel, Tor-Det	L	.500	2	1	1	2	0	.500	2	1	0	0	1	2	1	1	0	60.0	3	8	0	1	1.000	7	2	0	0	.29	2
Nova,Ivan, NYY	R	-	0	0	0	0	0	.071	14	1	0	0	0	0	0	13	3	94.0	4	8	2	2	.857	13	3	1	0	.23	-3
Nuno,Vidal, Ari-Sea	L	.143	7	1	0	1	0	.080	25	2	0	0	0	1	0	8	0	89.0	0	13	1	1	.929	3	0	0	1	.00	0
Oberg,Scott, Col	R	-	0	0	0	0	0	-	0	0	0	0	0	0	0	0	0	58.1	6	6	0	1	1.000	4	2	0	0	.50	1
Oberholtzer,Brett, Hou	L	-	0	0	0	0	2	-	0	0	0	0	0	0	1	0	2	38.1	3	7	0	0	1.000	6	2	1	0	.33	1
O'Day,Darren, Bal	R	-	0	0	0	0	0	.000	1	0	0	0	0	0	0	1	0	65.1	2	4	0	1	1.000	5	2	0	0	.40	0
Odorizzi,Jake, TB	R	.000	4	0	0	0	0	.000	8	0	0	0	0	1	1	5	0	169.1	4	10	0	2	1.000	13	3	0	0	.23	-1
O'Flaherty,Eric, Oak-NYM	L	-	0	0	0	0	0	.000	2	0	0	0	0	0	0	2	0	30.0	2	5	0	0	1.000	2	0	0	0	.00	0
Ogando,Alexi, Bos	R	-	0	0	0	0	0	.500	6	3	0	0	0	0	0	3	0	65.1	8	6	2	0	.875	6	3	0	1	.50	0
Ogando,Nefi, Phi	R	-	0	0	0	0	0	-	0	0	0	0	0	0	0	0	0	4.1	0	0	0	0	-	0	0	0	0	-	0
Ohlendorf,Ross, Tex	R	-	0	0	0	0	0	.073	137	10	0	0	1	5	4	67	11	19.1	0	2	0	0	1.000	3	0	0	0	.00	0
Olmos,Edgar, Sea	L	-	0	0	0	0	0	-	0	0	0	0	0	0	0	0	0	14.0	0	1	0	0	1.000	2	0	0	0	.00	0
Olson,Tyler, Sea	L	-	0	0	0	0	0	-	0	0	0	0	0	0	0	0	0	13.1	1	1	0	0	1.000	0	0	0	0	-	0
O'Rourke,Ryan, Min	L	-	0	0	0	0	0	-	0	0	0	0	0	0	0	0	0	22.0	2	0	0	0	1.000	1	0	0	0	.00	0
Osich,Josh, SF	L	.000	1	0	0	0	2	.000	1	0	0	0	0	0	0	1	2	28.2	1	2	1	0	.750	0	0	0	0	-	-2
O'Sullivan,Sean, Phi	R	.100	20	2	0	0	2	.121	33	4	2	0	0	0	1	17	2	71.0	6	6	0	0	1.000	7	2	1	0	.29	-1
Osuna,Roberto, Tor	R	-	0	0	0	0	0	-	0	0	0	0	0	0	0	0	0	69.2	4	4	0	0	1.000	4	2	0	0	.50	0
Otero,Dan, Oak	R	-	0	0	0	0	0	.000	1	0	0	0	0	0	0	1	0	46.2	1	6	0	0	1.000	3	2	1	0	.67	0
Ottavino,Adam, Col	R	-	0	0	0	0	0	.083	24	2	0	0	0	1	1	17	3	10.1	0	2	0	0	1.000	3	1	0	0	.33	0

Pitchers Hitting, Fielding and Holding Runners

Pitcher	T	2015 Hitting						Career Hitting											2015 Fielding and Holding Runners											
		Avg	AB	H	HR	RBI	SH	Avg	AB	H	2B	3B	HR	RBI	BB	SO	SH	Inn	PO	A	E	DP	Pct	SBA	CS	PCS	PPO	CS%	RS
Owens,Henry, Bos	L	.000	2	0	0	0	0	.000	2	0	0	0	0	0	0	2	0	63.0	1	6	0	1	1.000	6	1	1	0	.17	-1
Papelbon,Jonathan, Phi-Was	R	-	0	0	0	0	0	-	0	0	0	0	0	0	0	0	0	63.1	7	6	2	1	.867	4	0	0	0	.00	-1
Parnell,Bobby, NYM	R	-	0	0	0	0	0	.111	9	1	0	0	0	0	0	3	0	24.0	3	3	2	2	.750	2	1	0	0	.50	0
Parra,Manny, Cin	L	-	0	0	0	0	0	.188	144	27	11	1	0	13	6	58	10	32.1	5	2	0	0	1.000	2	0	0	0	.00	0
Patton,Spencer, Tex	R	-	0	0	0	0	0	-	0	0	0	0	0	0	0	0	0	24.0	2	3	0	1	1.000	1	1	0	0	1.00	0
Paxton,James, Sea	L	.000	2	0	0	0	0	.000	4	0	0	0	0	0	1	4	1	67.0	0	6	0	1	1.000	4	0	0	0	.00	-2
Pazos,James, NYY	L	-	0	0	0	0	0	-	0	0	0	0	0	0	0	0	0	5.0	0	1	0	1	1.000	0	0	0	0	-	0
Peacock,Brad, Hou	R	-	0	0	0	0	0	.000	9	0	0	0	0	0	0	7	1	5.0	0	1	0	0	1.000	0	0	0	0	-	0
Peavy,Jake, SF	R	.194	36	7	1	3	4	.167	492	82	17	1	3	30	20	153	50	110.2	8	10	1	0	.947	10	1	0	1	.10	-1
Pelfrey,Mike, Min	R	.667	3	2	0	0	0	.104	268	28	5	0	0	13	13	72	24	164.2	8	20	0	2	1.000	10	2	0	1	.20	-3
Pena,Ariel, Mil	R	.000	7	0	0	0	0	.000	7	0	0	0	0	0	0	6	0	27.1	1	1	0	1	1.000	4	1	0	0	.25	0
Peralta,Joel, LAD	R	.000	1	0	0	0	0	.200	5	1	1	0	0	2	0	3	0	29.0	1	0	0	0	1.000	2	0	0	0	.00	-1
Peralta,Wily, Mil	R	.033	30	1	0	1	4	.081	148	12	3	0	0	4	6	64	21	108.2	11	18	2	1	.935	9	4	0	0	.44	-2
Perez,Martin, Tex	L	.000	2	0	0	0	0	.000	8	0	0	0	0	0	0	7	1	78.2	5	6	1	0	.917	2	0	0	0	.00	-2
Perez,Oliver, Ari-Hou	L	-	0	0	0	0	0	.158	341	54	1	0	0	15	14	116	39	41.0	3	6	0	1	1.000	2	0	0	0	.00	0
Perez,Williams, Atl	R	.071	28	2	0	0	4	.071	28	2	0	0	0	0	2	13	4	116.2	7	15	0	2	1.000	3	0	0	1	.00	1
Perkins,Glen, Min	L	-	0	0	0	0	0	.000	4	0	0	0	0	0	0	4	3	57.0	2	7	0	0	1.000	1	0	0	0	.00	-1
Pestano,Vinnie, LAA	R	-	0	0	0	0	0	-	0	0	0	0	0	0	0	0	0	11.2	0	0	1	0	.000	1	0	0	0	.00	0
Petit,Yusmeiro, SF	R	.000	9	0	0	0	1	.045	112	5	0	0	0	3	3	47	6	76.0	5	9	0	0	1.000	4	0	0	0	.00	-3
Petricka,Jake, CWS	R	-	0	0	0	0	0	-	0	0	0	0	0	0	0	0	0	52.0	1	6	0	1	1.000	2	0	0	0	.00	-1
Phelps,David, Mia	R	.118	34	4	0	0	5	.100	40	4	0	0	0	0	0	19	6	112.0	4	19	1	2	.958	7	2	0	0	.29	1
Pimentel,Stolmy, Tex	R	-	0	0	0	0	0	.000	6	0	0	0	0	0	0	3	0	11.1	0	3	0	1	1.000	3	1	0	0	.33	0
Pinder,Branden, NYY	R	1.000	1	1	0	1	0	1.000	1	1	1	0	0	1	0	0	0	27.2	2	3	0	1	1.000	2	0	0	0	.00	1
Pineda,Michael, NYY	R	.000	2	0	0	0	0	.143	7	1	0	0	0	0	0	3	0	160.2	9	19	2	0	.933	13	9	0	0	.69	0
Pino,Yohan, KC	R	-	0	0	0	0	0	-	0	0	0	0	0	0	0	0	0	19.1	0	1	2	0	.333	2	1	0	0	.50	-2
Pomeranz,Drew, Oak	L	-	0	0	0	0	0	.206	34	7	2	0	1	1	1	19	7	86.0	2	13	1	2	.938	11	2	2	1	.18	2
Porcello,Rick, Bos	R	.000	2	0	0	0	0	.174	23	4	0	0	0	2	0	10	3	172.0	10	19	3	3	.906	23	5	0	1	.22	-2
Pressly,Ryan, Min	R	-	0	0	0	0	0	-	0	0	0	0	0	0	0	0	0	27.2	0	1	0	1	1.000	3	2	0	0	.67	0
Price,David, Det-Tor	L	.000	9	0	0	0	0	.054	37	2	0	0	0	2	16	0	220.1	14	23	2	1	.949	2	2	1	0	1.00	2		
Putnam,Zach, CWS	R	-	0	0	0	0	0	-	0	0	0	0	0	0	0	0	0	48.2	2	8	0	0	1.000	7	1	0	0	.14	-2
Quackenbush,Kevin, SD	R	-	0	0	0	0	0	-	0	0	0	0	0	0	0	0	0	58.1	1	2	0	0	1.000	9	3	0	0	.33	-2
Qualls,Chad, Hou	R	-	0	0	0	0	0	.000	6	0	0	0	0	0	0	5	0	49.1	2	7	0	1	1.000	10	2	0	0	.20	-1
Quintana,Jose, CWS	L	.000	8	0	0	0	1	.000	22	0	0	0	0	0	1	13	3	206.1	2	27	0	1	1.000	17	6	3	1	.35	3
Ramirez,Erasmo, TB	R	.000	2	0	0	0	0	.000	8	0	0	0	0	0	4	1	163.1	7	19	1	2	.963	5	2	0	2	.40	2	
Ramirez,J.C., Ari-Sea	R	-	0	0	0	0	0	.000	1	0	0	0	0	0	0	0	0	23.2	1	1	0	0	1.000	8	1	0	0	.13	-1
Ramirez,Jose, NYY-Sea	R	-	0	0	0	0	0	-	0	0	0	0	0	0	0	0	0	7.2	0	0	0	0	-	0	0	0	0	-	0
Ramirez,Neil, ChC	R	-	0	0	0	0	0	-	0	0	0	0	0	0	0	0	0	14.0	0	0	0	0	-	1	0	0	0	.00	0
Ramirez,Noe, Bos	R	-	0	0	0	0	0	-	0	0	0	0	0	0	0	0	0	13.0	2	0	0	0	1.000	3	1	0	0	.33	0
Ramos,A.J., Mia	R	-	0	0	0	0	0	-	0	0	0	0	0	0	0	0	0	70.1	4	8	0	1	1.000	2	0	0	0	.00	0
Ramos,Cesar, LAA	L	-	0	0	0	0	0	.000	6	0	0	0	0	0	4	0	52.1	0	5	0	0	1.000	4	0	0	0	.00	-1	
Ranaudo,Anthony, Tex	R	.000	2	0	0	0	0	.000	7	0	0	0	0	0	0	5	0	15.1	1	1	0	0	1.000	2	0	0	0	.00	0
Rasmus,Cory, LAA	R	.000	1	0	0	0	0	.000	1	0	0	0	0	0	0	0	0	20.2	1	0	0	0	1.000	3	1	0	0	.33	0
Rasmussen,Rob, Tor-Sea	L	-	0	0	0	0	0	-	0	0	0	0	0	0	0	0	0	15.1	0	1	0	0	1.000	2	1	0	0	.50	0
Ravin,Josh, LAD	R	-	0	0	0	0	0	-	0	0	0	0	0	0	0	0	0	9.1	1	0	0	0	1.000	2	0	0	0	.00	0
Ray,Robbie, Ari	L	.097	31	3	0	0	5	.121	33	4	1	0	0	0	0	14	5	127.2	9	15	0	1	1.000	12	1	1	1	.08	-1
Rea,Colin, SD	R	.222	9	2	0	0	2	.222	9	2	1	0	0	1	4	2	31.2	1	5	1	1	.857	4	1	0	0	.25	1	
Rearick,Chris, SD	L	-	0	0	0	0	0	-	0	0	0	0	0	0	0	0	0	3.0	0	0	0	0	-	0	0	0	0	-	0
Redmond,Todd, Tor	R	-	0	0	0	0	0	.000	5	0	0	0	0	0	1	2	1	16.0	0	0	0	0	-	1	1	0	0	1.00	0
Reed,Addison, Ari-NYM	R	.000	2	0	0	0	0	.000	2	0	0	0	0	0	0	0	0	56.0	3	3	0	2	1.000	3	1	0	0	.33	-1
Reed,Chris, Mia	L	-	0	0	0	0	0	-	0	0	0	0	0	0	0	0	0	4.0	0	3	0	0	1.000	0	0	0	0	-	0
Reyes,Jo-Jo, LAA	L	-	0	0	0	0	0	.143	63	9	2	0	0	2	4	24	7	0.1	0	0	0	0	-	0	0	0	0	-	0
Reynolds,Matt, Ari	L	-	0	0	0	0	0	.000	5	0	0	0	0	0	1	3	1	13.2	0	2	0	0	1.000	1	0	0	0	.00	0
Richard,Clayton, ChC	L	.143	14	2	0	3	0	.120	209	25	8	0	1	20	4	94	23	42.1	5	13	0	1	1.000	1	0	0	0	.00	2
Richards,Garrett, LAA	R	-	0	0	0	0	0	.000	13	0	0	0	0	0	0	5	0	207.1	17	29	3	2	.939	11	5	1	1	.45	-4
Riefenhauser,C.J., TB	L	-	0	0	0	0	0	-	0	0	0	0	0	0	0	0	0	14.2	0	1	0	0	1.000	2	1	0	0	.50	-2
Rienzo,Andre, Mia	R	.000	2	0	0	0	0	.000	2	0	0	0	0	0	0	0	0	19.2	2	0	0	0	1.000	1	0	0	0	.00	0
Rivero,Felipe, Was	L	-	0	0	0	0	0	-	0	0	0	0	0	0	0	0	0	48.1	2	8	0	0	1.000	5	1	0	0	.20	1
Roach,Donn, ChC	R	1.000	1	1	0	1	0	.400	5	2	1	0	0	1	0	1	0	3.1	0	0	0	0	-	0	0	0	0	-	0
Roark,Tanner, Was	R	.185	27	5	0	0	2	.162	99	16	3	0	0	1	1	35	14	111.0	9	15	0	3	1.000	6	4	0	1	.67	1
Roberts,Ken, Col-Phi	L	-	0	0	0	0	0	-	0	0	0	0	0	0	0	0	0	13.2	1	2	0	0	1.000	4	1	0	0	.25	0
Robertson,David, CWS	R	-	0	0	0	0	0	-	0	0	0	0	0	0	0	0	0	63.1	4	1	0	0	1.000	4	1	0	1	.25	-1
Robles,Hansel, NYM	R	-	0	0	0	0	0	-	0	0	0	0	0	0	0	0	0	54.0	1	4	0	0	1.000	3	1	0	0	.33	0
Rodney,Fernando, Sea-ChC	R	-	0	0	0	0	0	.000	1	0	0	0	0	0	0	0	0	62.2	3	7	0	0	1.000	5	2	0	0	.40	1
Rodon,Carlos, CWS	L	.000	1	0	0	0	2	.000	1	0	0	0	0	0	0	1	2	139.1	3	19	2	2	1.000	13	3	1	0	.23	1
Rodriguez,Eduardo, Bos	L	.000	2	0	0	0	0	.000	2	0	0	0	0	0	0	2	1	121.2	5	17	2	0	.917	4	2	1	0	.50	0
Rodriguez,Fernando, Oak	R	-	0	0	0	0	0	.000	4	0	0	0	0	0	0	3	0	58.2	2	4	1	0	.857	5	3	0	0	.60	2
Rodriguez,Francisco, Mil	R	-	0	0	0	0	0	.500	2	1	0	0	0	0	0	1	0	57.0	5	2	0	0	1.000	4	2	0	0	.50	0
Rodriguez,Paco, LAD	L	-	0	0	0	0	0	.000	1	0	0	0	0	0	0	1	0	10.1	1	0	0	0	1.000	1	1	0	0	1.00	0
Rodriguez,Wandy, Tex	L	.500	2	1	0	0	0	.134	447	60	10	0	0	21	10	130	53	86.1	3	7	1	0	.909	4	0	0	0	.00	2
Roe,Chaz, Bal	R	-	0	0	0	0	0	.000	1	0	0	0	0	0	0	1	0	41.1	1	3	1	0	.800	4	3	0	0	.75	0

Pitchers Hitting, Fielding and Holding Runners

Pitcher	T	2015 Hitting						Career Hitting										2015 Fielding and Holding Runners											RS
		Avg	AB	H	HR	RBI	SH	Avg	AB	H	2B	3B	HR	RBI	BB	SO	SH	Inn	PO	A	E	DP	Pct	SBA	CS	PCS	PPO	CS%	
Rogers,Esmil, NYY	R	-	0	0	0	0	0	.208	53	11	3	0	0	1	0	21	10	33.0	3	3	1	1	.857	2	0	0	0	.00	0
Rollins,David, Sea	L	-	0	0	0	0	0	-	0	0	0	0	0	0	0	0	0	25.0	1	3	0	1	1.000	2	0	0	0	.00	1
Romero,Enny, TB	L	-	0	0	0	0	0	-	0	0	0	0	0	0	0	0	0	30.0	1	2	1	0	.750	2	0	0	0	.00	-2
Romo,Sergio, SF	R	.000	2	0	0	0	0	.000	6	0	0	0	0	0	0	4	0	57.1	4	8	0	0	1.000	8	3	1	1	.38	2
Rondon,Bruce, Det	R	-	0	0	0	0	0	-	0	0	0	0	0	0	0	0	0	31.0	3	5	0	0	1.000	5	1	0	0	.20	0
Rondon,Hector, ChC	R	-	0	0	0	0	0	-	0	0	0	0	0	0	0	0	0	70.0	8	10	0	0	1.000	9	1	1	2	.11	0
Rondon,Jorge, Col-Bal	R	-	0	0	0	0	0	-	0	0	0	0	0	0	0	0	0	14.1	1	1	0	0	1.000	0	0	0	0	-	-1
Rosenthal,Trevor, StL	R	.000	1	0	0	0	0	.000	3	0	0	0	0	0	0	3	0	68.2	1	3	0	0	1.000	3	1	0	0	.33	-2
Rosin,Seth, Phi	R	-	0	0	0	0	0	-	0	0	0	0	0	0	0	0	0	2.0	0	1	0	0	1.000	0	0	0	0	-	0
Ross,Joe, Was	R	.111	27	3	0	0	2	.111	27	3	0	0	0	0	0	11	2	76.2	6	13	1	1	.950	2	1	0	0	.50	1
Ross,Robbie, Bos	L	-	0	0	0	0	0	.000	3	0	0	0	0	0	1	1	0	60.2	5	10	0	0	1.000	0	0	0	0	-	0
Ross,Tyson, SD	R	.250	56	14	1	6	8	.203	148	30	2	1	1	9	5	61	13	196.0	12	31	4	3	.915	50	13	3	0	.26	-4
Rosscup,Zac, ChC	L	-	0	0	0	0	0	-	0	0	0	0	0	0	0	0	0	26.2	1	5	0	0	1.000	1	0	0	0	.00	0
Rucinski,Drew, LAA	R	-	0	0	0	0	0	-	0	0	0	0	0	0	0	0	0	7.0	0	1	0	0	1.000	4	1	0	0	.25	0
Rumbelow,Nick, NYY	R	-	0	0	0	0	0	-	0	0	0	0	0	0	0	0	0	15.2	0	0	0	0	-	1	0	0	0	.00	0
Rusin,Chris, Col	L	.217	46	10	1	4	4	.175	80	14	0	1	1	6	0	16	6	131.2	8	27	1	5	.972	9	4	4	1	.44	3
Russell,James, ChC	L	.000	1	0	0	0	0	.063	16	1	0	0	0	0	0	6	0	34.0	4	6	0	0	1.000	8	3	2	0	.38	0
Ryan,Kyle, Det	L	-	0	0	0	0	0	-	0	0	0	0	0	0	0	0	0	56.1	8	0	1	1	1.000	4	2	1	0	.50	1
Rzepczynski,Marc, Cle-SD	L	-	0	0	0	0	0	.000	1	0	0	0	0	0	0	1	0	35.0	4	4	3	1	.727	6	1	0	0	.17	-3
Sabathia,CC, NYY	L	.000	3	0	0	0	0	.219	114	25	3	0	3	15	1	32	3	167.1	3	7	1	0	.909	5	2	1	0	.40	-6
Sadler,Casey, Pit	R	.000	1	0	0	0	1	.000	1	0	0	0	0	0	0	0	1	5.0	1	2	0	0	1.000	1	1	1	0	1.00	0
Salas,Fernando, LAA	R	-	0	0	0	0	0	.000	4	0	0	0	0	0	0	2	0	63.2	2	10	0	1	1.000	3	0	0	0	.00	1
Salazar,Danny, Cle	R	.000	4	0	0	0	0	.000	9	0	0	0	0	0	0	9	0	185.0	11	17	3	1	.903	9	6	1	0	.67	-2
Sale,Chris, CWS	L	.111	9	1	0	0	0	.071	14	1	0	0	0	0	0	8	1	208.2	7	16	1	1	.958	9	4	3	0	.44	0
Samardzija,Jeff, CWS	R	.500	2	1	0	0	0	.130	162	21	5	0	2	10	6	65	21	214.0	7	14	0	2	1.000	16	4	0	0	.25	-4
Sampson,Keyvius, Cin	R	.000	16	0	0	0	1	.000	16	0	0	0	0	0	0	11	1	52.1	4	4	0	0	1.000	5	2	0	0	.40	1
Sanchez,Aaron, Tor	R	-	0	0	0	0	0	-	0	0	0	0	0	0	0	0	0	92.1	5	12	2	0	.895	11	7	0	0	.64	1
Sanchez,Anibal, Det	R	.000	4	0	0	0	0	.090	245	22	1	1	0	7	16	116	31	157.0	21	15	0	1	1.000	19	4	0	1	.21	2
Santana,Ervin, Min	R	-	0	0	0	0	0	.125	88	11	2	0	0	3	2	43	9	108.0	10	14	1	2	.960	8	1	0	1	.13	2
Santiago,Hector, LAA	L	.200	5	1	0	0	0	.154	13	2	0	0	0	0	5	3	3	180.2	4	20	0	3	1.000	25	8	3	1	.32	1
Santos,Sergio, LAD-NYY	R	-	0	0	0	0	0	.000	1	0	0	0	0	0	0	0	0	16.1	3	0	0	0	1.000	0	0	0	0	-	0
Scahill,Rob, Pit	R	-	0	0	0	0	0	.000	2	0	0	0	0	0	1	0	1	30.2	1	4	1	0	.833	4	1	0	0	.25	-1
Scheppers,Tanner, Tex	R	-	0	0	0	0	0	-	0	0	0	0	0	0	0	0	0	38.1	4	3	0	0	1.000	2	0	0	0	.00	0
Scherzer,Max, Was	R	.217	69	15	0	0	6	.189	148	28	3	0	4	6	6	46	16	228.2	7	22	0	0	1.000	8	2	0	0	.25	0
Schlitter,Brian, ChC	R	-	0	0	0	0	0	1.000	1	1	0	0	0	0	0	0	0	7.1	0	0	0	0	-	0	0	0	0	-	0
Schugel,Andrew, Ari	R	-	0	0	0	0	0	-	0	0	0	0	0	0	0	0	0	9.0	0	3	1	1	.750	2	1	0	0	.50	0
Schultz,Bo, Tor	R	-	0	0	0	0	0	.000	1	0	0	0	0	0	0	0	0	43.0	2	2	1	0	.800	6	0	0	0	.00	-1
Scribner,Evan, Oak	R	-	0	0	0	0	0	-	0	0	0	0	0	0	0	0	0	60.0	5	5	0	1	1.000	9	3	1	0	.33	1
Severino,Luis, NYY	R	.000	2	0	0	0	0	.000	2	0	0	0	0	0	0	0	0	62.1	5	11	1	1	.941	6	3	0	1	.50	4
Shaw,Bryan, Cle	R	-	0	0	0	0	0	-	0	0	0	0	0	0	0	0	0	64.0	7	5	0	0	1.000	6	1	0	0	.17	0
Shields,James, SD	R	.132	68	9	0	2	5	.165	115	19	3	0	0	6	3	41	6	202.1	10	30	3	2	.930	23	8	2	2	.35	0
Shoemaker,Matt, LAA	R	.000	1	0	0	0	0	.000	2	0	0	0	0	0	1	1	1	135.1	12	9	2	1	.913	15	5	0	2	.33	-4
Shreve,Chasen, NYY	L	-	0	0	0	0	0	-	0	0	0	0	0	0	0	0	0	58.1	3	4	0	0	1.000	3	2	0	0	.67	0
Siegrist,Kevin, StL	L	-	0	0	0	0	0	.000	1	0	0	0	0	0	0	1	0	74.2	1	10	3	1	.786	9	4	3	1	.44	0
Simon,Alfredo, Det	R	.000	5	0	0	0	0	.107	75	8	3	0	0	2	1	29	7	187.0	14	25	0	2	1.000	24	7	1	1	.29	1
Sipp,Tony, Hou	L	-	0	0	0	0	0	-	0	0	0	0	0	0	0	0	0	54.1	2	7	0	0	1.000	5	3	2	0	.60	0
Smith,Carson, Sea	R	-	0	0	0	0	0	-	0	0	0	0	0	0	0	0	0	70.0	11	6	1	0	.944	9	2	0	0	.22	-2
Smith,Chad, Oak	R	-	0	0	0	0	0	-	0	0	0	0	0	0	0	0	0	1.1	0	0	0	0	-	0	0	0	0	-	0
Smith,Joe, LAA	R	-	0	0	0	0	0	.000	2	0	0	0	0	0	2	0	0	65.1	3	14	2	3	.895	4	2	1	1	.50	0
Smith,Josh, Cin	R	.222	9	2	0	0	0	.222	9	2	0	1	0	0	0	4	1	32.2	1	1	1	0	.667	8	2	0	0	.25	-2
Smith,Will, Mil	L	-	0	0	0	0	0	-	0	0	0	0	0	0	0	0	0	63.1	0	4	0	0	1.000	7	2	1	0	.29	-2
Smyly,Drew, TB	L	-	0	0	0	0	0	.000	2	0	0	0	0	0	0	1	0	66.2	1	10	1	0	.917	13	4	4	0	.31	1
Socolovich,Miguel, StL	R	.000	1	0	0	0	0	.000	1	0	0	0	0	0	0	0	0	29.2	1	5	1	0	.857	5	0	0	0	.00	-1
Solis,Sammy, Was	L	.500	2	1	0	0	0	.500	2	1	0	0	0	0	0	0	0	21.1	3	4	0	0	1.000	3	0	0	0	.00	0
Soria,Joakim, Det-Pit	R	-	0	0	0	0	0	-	0	0	0	0	0	0	0	0	0	67.2	2	9	0	1	1.000	3	0	0	0	.00	1
Soriano,Rafael, ChC	R	-	0	0	0	0	0	.000	4	0	0	0	0	0	0	1	0	5.2	0	1	0	0	1.000	2	1	0	0	.50	0
Soto,Giovanni, Cle	L	-	0	0	0	0	0	-	0	0	0	0	0	0	0	0	0	3.1	0	0	0	0	-	0	0	0	0	-	0
Stammen,Craig, Was	R	-	0	0	0	0	0	.202	89	18	7	0	0	10	4	35	10	4.0	0	0	0	0	-	2	0	0	0	.00	0
Stauffer,Tim, Min-NYM	R	-	0	0	0	0	0	.150	140	21	3	0	0	12	4	63	17	20.2	0	5	0	1	1.000	0	0	0	0	-	1
Stites,Matt, Ari	R	-	0	0	0	0	0	-	0	0	0	0	0	0	0	0	0	8.2	0	2	0	0	1.000	2	0	0	0	.00	0
Storen,Drew, Was	R	-	0	0	0	0	0	.500	2	1	0	0	0	0	0	1	0	55.0	3	7	0	0	1.000	1	1	0	0	1.00	0
Straily,Dan, Hou	R	-	0	0	0	0	0	.000	3	0	0	0	0	0	2	3	0	16.2	1	1	0	0	1.000	2	0	0	0	.00	0
Strasburg,Stephen, Was	R	.132	38	5	0	0	6	.145	220	32	7	0	1	13	14	89	31	127.1	3	9	2	0	.857	6	2	1	0	.33	-2
Street,Huston, LAA	R	-	0	0	0	0	0	.000	2	0	0	0	0	0	0	1	0	62.1	3	9	0	1	1.000	5	1	0	0	.20	2
Strickland,Hunter, SF	R	.000	1	0	0	0	0	.000	1	0	0	0	0	0	0	1	0	51.1	2	7	0	0	1.000	5	3	2	0	.60	1
Stroman,Marcus, Tor	R	-	0	0	0	0	0	-	0	0	0	0	0	0	0	0	0	27.0	5	5	0	0	1.000	2	1	0	0	.50	0
Strop,Pedro, ChC	R	-	0	0	0	0	0	-	0	0	0	0	0	0	0	0	0	68.0	2	6	0	0	1.000	4	1	0	1	.25	0
Stults,Eric, Atl	L	.077	13	1	0	0	3	.166	199	33	7	0	1	12	6	76	23	47.2	3	3	0	0	1.000	3	2	1	0	.67	1
Surkamp,Eric, LAD	L	-	0	0	0	0	1	.111	9	1	0	0	0	1	1	5	1	3.1	0	0	0	0	-	0	0	0	0	-	0
Swarzak,Anthony, Cle	R	-	0	0	0	0	0	.000	5	0	0	0	0	0	0	4	0	13.1	0	2	0	0	1.000	1	0	0	0	.00	0

Pitchers Hitting, Fielding and Holding Runners

Pitcher	T	2015 Hitting						Career Hitting										2015 Fielding and Holding Runners											
		Avg	AB	H	HR	RBI	SH	Avg	AB	H	2B	3B	HR	RBI	BB	SO	SH	Inn	PO	A	E	DP	Pct	SBA	CS	PCS	PPO	CS%	RS
Syndergaard,Noah, NYM	R	.209	43	9	1	4	6	.209	43	9	1	0	1	4	1	26	6	150.0	8	11	2	0	.905	16	1	0	0	.06	-5
Tanaka,Masahiro, NYY	R	.000	7	0	0	0	0	.063	16	1	0	0	0	0	1	7	0	154.0	11	19	0	2	1.000	3	2	0	3	.67	5
Tazawa,Junichi, Bos	R	-	0	0	0	0	0	-	0	0	0	0	0	0	0	0	0	58.2	1	4	0	2	1.000	8	1	0	0	.13	-2
Teaford,Everett, TB	L	-	0	0	0	0	0	-	0	0	0	0	0	0	0	0	0	5.2	0	1	0	0	1.000	0	0	0	0	-	0
Teheran,Julio, Atl	R	.096	52	5	0	2	14	.138	181	25	4	0	0	10	6	47	28	200.2	16	30	1	5	.979	12	6	0	5	.50	5
Tepera,Ryan, Tor	R	-	0	0	0	0	0	-	0	0	0	0	0	0	0	0	0	33.0	0	4	0	1	1.000	0	0	0	0	-	0
Thatcher,Joe, Hou	L	-	0	0	0	0	0	.000	1	0	0	0	0	0	0	1	0	22.2	0	3	0	0	1.000	2	0	0	0	.00	0
Thayer,Dale, SD	R	-	0	0	0	0	0	.000	3	0	0	0	0	0	0	1	0	37.2	0	2	0	0	1.000	2	0	0	0	.00	0
Thielbar,Caleb, Min	L	-	0	0	0	0	0	-	0	0	0	0	0	0	0	0	0	5.0	1	1	0	0	1.000	0	0	0	0	-	0
Thomas,Ian, Atl-LAD	L	.000	3	0	0	0	0	.000	3	0	0	0	0	0	1	1	0	23.1	2	1	1	0	.750	2	0	0	0	.00	-1
Thompson,Aaron, Min	L	-	0	0	0	0	0	-	0	0	0	0	0	0	1	0	0	32.1	4	7	0	0	1.000	2	0	0	0	.00	1
Thornburg,Tyler, Mil	R	.000	3	0	0	0	0	.040	25	1	1	0	0	0	0	11	2	34.1	3	1	0	0	1.000	3	0	0	0	.00	0
Thornton,Matt, Was	L	-	0	0	0	0	0	.000	1	0	0	0	0	0	0	1	0	41.1	2	8	0	1	1.000	2	0	0	0	.00	1
Tillman,Chris, Bal	R	.000	2	0	0	0	0	.000	12	0	0	0	0	0	0	5	3	173.0	7	18	1	0	.962	5	1	0	0	.20	-1
Tolleson,Shawn, Tex	R	-	0	0	0	0	0	-	0	0	0	0	0	0	0	0	0	72.1	2	10	0	0	1.000	1	0	0	0	.00	0
Tomlin,Josh, Cle	R	-	0	0	0	0	0	.571	7	4	0	0	0	1	0	3	0	65.2	7	5	0	0	1.000	1	1	0	1	1.00	1
Tonkin,Michael, Min	R	-	0	0	0	0	0	-	0	0	0	0	0	0	0	0	0	23.1	2	4	0	0	1.000	5	1	0	0	.20	1
Torres,Alex, NYM	L	.000	1	0	0	0	0	.000	2	0	0	0	0	0	0	1	0	34.1	4	3	0	0	1.000	3	0	0	0	.00	0
Torres,Carlos, NYM	R	1.000	1	1	0	0	0	.118	34	4	0	0	0	2	2	19	6	57.2	5	17	0	1	1.000	3	1	0	0	.33	3
Tracy,Matt, NYY	L	-	0	0	0	0	0	-	0	0	0	0	0	0	0	0	0	2.0	0	1	0	0	-	1	0	0	0	.00	0
Treinen,Blake, Was	R	.000	2	0	0	0	2	.071	14	1	0	0	0	0	1	9	4	67.2	4	12	3	2	.842	6	2	0	0	.33	0
Tropeano,Nicholas, LAA	R	-	0	0	0	0	0	.000	1	0	0	0	0	0	1	0	0	37.2	2	2	1	0	.800	3	1	0	0	.33	0
Tsao,Chin-hui, LAD	R	1.000	1	1	0	0	0	.214	14	3	2	0	0	0	0	1	2	7.0	0	0	0	0	-	1	1	0	0	1.00	0
Tuivailala,Samuel, StL	R	-	0	0	0	0	0	-	0	0	0	0	0	0	0	0	0	14.2	2	2	0	0	1.000	2	0	0	0	.00	0
Uehara,Koji, Bos	R	-	0	0	0	0	0	.000	2	0	0	0	0	0	1	1	0	40.1	2	2	0	0	1.000	0	0	0	0	-	0
Urena,Jose, Mia	R	.077	13	1	0	0	0	.077	13	1	0	0	0	0	0	9	0	61.2	0	12	0	1	1.000	0	0	0	0	-	2
Valdez,Cesar, Det	R	-	0	0	0	0	0	-	0	0	0	0	0	0	0	0	0	9.0	0	0	0	0	-	0	0	0	0	-	0
Vargas,Jason, KC	L	-	0	0	0	0	0	.262	61	16	3	0	0	4	3	16	2	43.0	1	6	0	1	1.000	2	1	1	0	.50	1
Varvaro,Anthony, Bos	R	-	0	0	0	0	0	.000	1	0	0	0	0	0	0	1	0	11.0	2	1	0	0	1.000	2	1	0	0	.50	0
Veal,Donnie, Atl	L	-	0	0	0	0	0	-	0	0	0	0	0	0	0	0	1	4.1	0	1	0	0	1.000	0	0	0	0	-	0
Velasquez,Vincent, Hou	R	-	0	0	0	0	0	-	0	0	0	0	0	0	0	0	0	55.2	4	3	3	1	1.000	9	3	0	0	.33	1
Venditte,Pat, Oak	B	.000	1	0	0	0	0	.000	1	0	0	0	0	0	0	1	0	28.2	1	3	0	0	1.000	0	0	0	0	-	0
Ventura,Yordano, KC	R	.000	6	0	0	0	0	.100	10	1	0	0	0	0	0	8	1	163.1	15	16	2	1	.939	6	4	1	1	.67	4
VerHagen,Drew, Det	R	-	0	0	0	0	0	-	0	0	0	0	0	0	0	0	0	26.1	2	4	0	0	1.000	2	0	0	0	.00	0
Verlander,Justin, Det	R	-	0	0	0	0	0	.063	32	2	0	0	0	0	0	15	10	133.1	8	6	3	1	.824	7	4	0	2	.57	-1
Verrett,Logan, Tex-NYM	R	.000	7	0	0	0	0	.000	7	0	0	0	0	0	0	2	1	47.2	7	3	0	2	1.000	2	0	0	0	.00	-1
Villanueva,Carlos, StL	R	.000	8	0	0	0	3	.095	116	11	0	0	0	4	3	57	18	61.0	3	4	0	0	1.000	7	3	0	0	.43	0
Villarreal,Pedro, Cin	R	.167	6	1	0	2	0	.222	9	2	1	0	0	2	0	4	0	50.0	6	1	0	0	1.000	4	2	0	0	.50	-1
Vincent,Nick, SD	R	-	0	0	0	0	0	.000	2	0	0	0	0	0	0	2	0	23.0	0	1	1	1	.500	3	1	0	0	.33	-2
Vizcaino,Arodys, Atl	R	-	0	0	0	0	0	-	0	0	0	0	0	0	0	0	0	33.2	2	2	0	0	1.000	0	0	0	0	.00	0
Vogelsong,Ryan, SF	R	.139	36	5	1	2	8	.144	292	42	9	0	1	11	15	120	39	135.0	7	13	0	1	1.000	10	0	0	0	.00	-1
Volquez,Edinson, KC	R	.000	6	0	0	0	0	.083	277	23	2	0	1	8	7	142	43	200.1	7	13	2	0	.909	22	4	0	0	.18	-7
Volstad,Chris, Pit	R	-	0	0	0	0	0	.139	201	28	6	0	0	7	2	94	28	2.0	0	0	0	0	-	0	0	0	0	-	0
Wacha,Michael, StL	R	.154	52	8	0	4	6	.118	102	12	1	0	0	9	4	48	10	181.1	18	29	3	0	.940	8	3	1	0	.38	2
Wada,Tsuyoshi, ChC	L	.000	8	0	0	0	0	.036	28	1	0	0	0	0	2	15	3	32.1	1	2	0	0	1.000	0	0	0	0	.00	-1
Wagner,Tyler, Mil	R	.000	3	0	0	0	0	.000	3	0	0	0	0	0	0	2	0	13.2	1	2	0	0	1.000	1	0	0	0	.00	-1
Wainwright,Adam, StL	R	.000	10	0	0	0	0	.198	520	103	25	1	6	39	19	166	41	28.0	4	3	0	0	1.000	1	0	0	0	.00	0
Walden,Jordan, StL	R	-	0	0	0	0	0	-	0	0	0	0	0	0	0	0	0	10.1	0	0	0	0	-	3	0	0	0	.00	-1
Walker,Taijuan, Sea	R	.111	9	1	0	1	1	.111	9	1	1	0	0	1	0	5	1	169.2	12	19	4	1	.886	8	4	2	2	.50	0
Warren,Adam, NYY	R	.000	3	0	0	0	0	.000	3	0	0	0	0	0	0	1	0	131.1	6	14	1	1	.952	10	4	1	0	.40	1
Watson,Tony, Pit	L	-	0	0	0	0	0	.167	6	1	0	0	0	0	0	5	2	75.1	5	12	0	1	1.000	3	0	0	0	.00	2
Weaver,Jered, LAA	R	.000	2	0	0	0	0	.111	36	4	0	0	0	1	2	15	0	159.0	13	16	3	0	.906	32	10	3	1	.31	-2
Webb,Daniel, CWS	R	-	0	0	0	0	0	-	0	0	0	0	0	0	0	0	0	30.0	1	4	1	0	.833	4	1	0	0	.25	-1
Webb,Ryan, Cle	R	-	0	0	0	0	0	.200	5	1	0	0	0	0	4	0	0	50.2	1	15	0	1	1.000	4	0	0	0	.00	0
Weber,Ryan, Atl	R	.000	10	0	0	0	0	.000	10	0	0	0	0	0	0	8	0	28.1	5	4	1	1	.900	3	3	0	1	1.00	1
Webster,Allen, Ari	R	.000	11	0	0	0	0	.000	11	0	0	0	0	0	0	6	0	31.0	2	4	1	0	.857	5	1	0	0	.20	-1
West,Matt, LAD	R	-	0	0	0	0	0	-	0	0	0	0	0	0	0	0	0	3.0	1	1	0	0	1.000	0	0	0	0	-	0
Whitley,Chase, NYY	R	-	0	0	0	0	0	.200	5	1	0	0	0	0	0	0	0	19.1	3	3	1	0	.857	3	1	0	0	.33	0
Wieland,Joe, LAD	R	.000	1	0	0	0	1	.167	12	2	1	0	0	2	0	5	1	8.2	1	1	0	0	1.000	1	0	0	0	.00	0
Wilhelmsen,Tom, Sea	R	-	0	0	0	0	0	-	0	0	0	0	0	0	0	0	0	62.0	6	9	0	2	1.000	3	1	0	0	.33	1
Wilk,Adam, LAA	L	-	0	0	0	0	0	.000	1	0	0	0	0	0	0	1	0	2.0	0	0	0	0	-	0	0	0	0	-	0
Williams,Jerome, Phi	R	.065	31	2	0	1	4	.109	165	18	4	0	0	5	2	73	27	121.0	5	9	0	0	1.000	9	1	0	1	.11	-5
Wilson,Alex, Det	R	-	0	0	0	0	0	-	0	0	0	0	0	0	0	0	0	70.0	9	9	1	0	.947	7	4	0	1	.57	1
Wilson,C.J., LAA	L	.333	6	2	0	0	0	.138	29	4	0	1	0	3	3	10	4	132.0	4	20	2	1	.923	9	4	2	0	.44	2
Wilson,Justin, NYY	L	.000	1	0	0	0	0	.000	6	0	0	0	0	0	0	6	1	61.0	1	4	1	1	.833	7	1	0	0	.14	0
Wilson,Tyler, Bal	R	.000	2	0	0	0	1	.000	2	0	0	0	0	0	0	1	1	36.0	2	4	0	0	1.000	3	2	0	0	.67	0
Winkler,Daniel, Atl	R	-	0	0	0	0	0	-	0	0	0	0	0	0	0	0	0	1.2	1	0	0	0	1.000	0	0	0	0	-	0
Wisler,Matt, Atl	R	.138	29	4	0	1	5	.138	29	4	0	0	0	1	2	6	5	109.0	9	14	0	1	1.000	3	1	0	0	.33	2
Wojciechowski,Asher, Hou	R	-	0	0	0	0	0	-	0	0	0	0	0	0	0	0	0	16.1	0	1	1	0	.500	1	0	0	0	.00	-1
Wolf,Randy, Det	L	-	0	0	0	0	0	.184	694	128	33	0	5	58	32	231	79	34.2	0	0	0	0	1.000	1	1	0	1	1.00	2

Pitchers Hitting, Fielding and Holding Runners

Pitcher	T	2015 Hitting						Career Hitting										2015 Fielding and Holding Runners											
		Avg	AB	H	HR	RBI	SH	Avg	AB	H	2B	3B	HR	RBI	BB	SO	SH	Inn	PO	A	E	DP	Pct	SBA	CS	PCS	PPO	CS%	RS
Wood,Alex, Atl-LAD	L	.164	55	9	0	4	8	.103	117	12	2	0	0	6	6	77	14	189.2	4	27	2	3	.939	9	3	1	4	.33	-1
Wood,Travis, ChC	L	.100	30	3	0	2	0	.182	269	49	8	1	9	30	6	103	20	100.2	3	8	0	1	1.000	3	3	0	1	1.00	3
Wooten,Rob, Mil	R	.000	1	0	0	0	0	.000	2	0	0	0	0	0	0	1	0	6.0	1	2	0	0	1.000	0	0	0	0	-	0
Worley,Vance, Pit	R	.176	17	3	0	0	1	.133	135	18	4	0	0	7	2	53	15	71.2	1	14	0	2	1.000	6	2	0	0	.33	2
Wright,Mike, Bal	R	.500	2	1	0	0	1	.500	2	1	0	0	0	0	0	1	1	44.2	2	3	0	0	1.000	2	1	0	0	.50	-1
Wright,Steven, Bos	R	.000	1	0	0	0	1	.000	1	0	0	0	0	0	0	0	1	72.2	4	12	1	1	.941	5	2	0	1	.40	3
Wright,Wesley, Bal-LAA	L	-	0	0	0	0	0	.063	16	1	0	0	0	0	0	8	1	7.1	2	1	0	0	1.000	1	0	0	0	.00	0
Yates,Kirby, TB	R	-	0	0	0	0	0	-	0	0	0	0	0	0	0	0	0	20.1	0	2	1	0	.667	4	1	0	0	.25	0
Young,Chris, KC	R	.500	4	2	0	3	0	.150	206	31	6	1	1	17	10	82	27	123.1	4	10	1	0	.933	25	7	1	0	.28	-1
Ziegler,Brad, Ari	R	-	0	0	0	0	0	.143	7	1	0	0	0	0	0	3	0	68.0	4	10	2	0	.875	1	1	0	0	1.00	2
Zimmermann,Jordan, Was	R	.159	63	10	0	3	6	.169	320	54	6	0	1	15	10	97	43	201.2	16	29	2	1	.957	14	7	5	1	.50	2
Zito,Barry, Oak	L	-	0	0	0	0	0	.102	344	35	0	0	0	11	18	99	56	7.0	1	2	0	1	1.000	0	0	0	0	-	0
Zych,Tony, Sea	R	-	0	0	0	0	0	-	0	0	0	0	0	0	0	0	0	18.1	0	3	0	0	1.000	4	2	0	0	.50	-2

Hitters Pitching

Player	2015 Pitching G	W	L	Sv	IP	H	R	ER	BB	SO	ERA	Career Pitching G	W	L	Sv	IP	H	R	ER	BB	SO	ERA
Amarista,Alexi, SD	1	-	-	-	0.1	-	-	-	-	-	0.00	1	0	0	0	0.1	0	0	0	0	0	0.00
Anna,Dean, StL	-	-	-	-	-	-	-	-	-	-		1	0	0	0	1.0	3	2	2	0	0	18.00
Arencibia,J.P., TB	-	-	-	-	-	-	-	-	-	-		1	0	0	0	1.0	1	0	0	0	0	0.00
Bogusevic,Brian, Phi	-	-	-	-	-	-	-	-	-	-		1	0	0	0	1.0	3	2	2	0	0	18.00
Butera,Drew, LAA-KC	-	-	-	-	-	-	-	-	-	-		3	0	0	0	2.2	2	2	2	1	3	6.75
Cuddyer,Michael, NYM	-	-	-	-	-	-	-	-	-	-		1	0	0	0	1.0	2	0	0	1	0	0.00
Davis,Chris, Bal	-	-	-	-	-	-	-	-	-	-		1	1	0	0	2.0	2	0	0	1	2	0.00
Davis,Ike, Oak	2	-	-	-	2.0	1	-	-	1	1	0.00	2	0	0	0	2.0	1	0	0	1	1	0.00
Decker,Jaff, Pit	1	-	-	-	1.0	2	-	-	-	-	0.00	1	0	0	0	1.0	2	0	0	0	0	0.00
Denorfia,Chris, ChC	1	-	-	-	0.1	-	-	-	-	-	0.00	1	0	0	0	0.1	0	0	0	0	0	0.00
Descalso,Daniel, Col	-	-	-	-	-	-	-	-	-	-		1	0	0	0	0.1	0	0	0	0	0	0.00
Elmore,Jake, TB	1	-	-	-	1.0	3	1	1	-	-	9.00	2	0	0	0	2.0	3	1	1	0	0	4.50
Francoeur,Jeff, Phi	1	-	-	-	2.0	1	2	2	3	1	9.00	1	0	0	0	2.0	1	2	2	3	1	9.00
Franklin,Nick, TB	1	-	-	-	1.0	3	2	2	-	-	18.00	1	0	0	0	1.0	3	2	2	0	0	18.00
Fuld,Sam, Oak	-	-	-	-	-	-	-	-	-	-		1	0	0	0	0.1	0	0	0	0	0	0.00
Garcia,Leury, CWS	1	-	-	-	1.0	1	-	-	-	1	0.00	2	0	1	0	2.0	2	2	2	2	1	9.00
Gentry,Craig, Oak	-	-	-	-	-	-	-	-	-	-		1	0	0	0	1.0	3	2	2	1	0	18.00
Gimenez,Chris, Tex	-	-	-	-	-	-	-	-	-	-		1	0	0	0	1.0	0	0	0	0	1	0.00
Gomes,Jonny, Atl-KC	1	-	-	-	1.0	3	2	2	-	1	18.00	1	0	0	0	1.0	3	2	2	0	1	18.00
Harrison,Josh, Pit	-	-	-	-	-	-	-	-	-	-		1	0	0	0	0.1	0	0	0	0	0	0.00
Janish,Paul, Bal	-	-	-	-	-	-	-	-	-	-		2	0	0	0	2.0	9	11	11	2	3	49.50
Jones,Garrett, NYY	1	-	-	-	0.2	-	-	-	1	-	0.00	1	0	0	0	0.2	0	0	0	1	0	0.00
Kelly,Don, Mia	-	-	-	-	-	-	-	-	-	-		1	0	0	0	0.1	0	0	0	0	0	0.00
LaRoche,Adam, CWS	1	-	-	-	1.0	-	-	-	-	1	0.00	1	0	0	0	1.0	0	0	0	0	1	0.00
Maldonado,Martin, Mil	-	-	-	-	-	-	-	-	-	-		1	0	0	0	1.0	1	0	0	0	0	0.00
Mathis,Jeff, Mia	-	-	-	-	-	-	-	-	-	-		2	0	0	0	2.0	4	2	2	1	0	9.00
Moore,Tyler, Was	1	-	-	-	0.2	-	-	-	-	-	0.00	1	0	0	0	0.2	0	0	0	0	0	0.00
Moreland,Mitch, Tex	-	-	-	-	-	-	-	-	-	-		1	0	0	0	1.0	0	0	0	0	0	0.00
Murphy,David, Cle-LAA	1	-	-	-	0.1	2	5	-	1	-	0.00	2	0	0	0	1.1	3	5	0	1	1	0.00
Raburn,Ryan, Cle	1	-	-	-	0.2	1	2	-	1	-	0.00	2	0	0	0	1.2	1	2	0	1	1	0.00
Ramirez,Alexei, CWS	1	-	-	-	1.0	1	-	-	-	-	0.00	1	0	0	0	1.0	1	0	0	0	0	0.00
Recker,Anthony, NYM	-	-	-	-	-	-	-	-	-	-		1	0	0	0	1.0	1	2	2	1	0	18.00
Robinson,Clint, Was	1	-	-	-	1.0	1	-	-	-	1	0.00	1	0	0	0	1.0	1	0	0	0	1	0.00
Robinson,Shane, Min	1	-	-	-	1.0	-	-	-	1	1	0.00	1	0	0	0	1.0	0	0	0	1	1	0.00
Romine,Andrew, Det	-	-	-	-	-	-	-	-	-	-		1	0	0	0	1.0	4	3	3	0	1	27.00
Rosales,Adam, Tex	2	-	-	-	2.0	2	3	2	1	1	9.00	2	0	0	0	2.0	2	3	2	1	1	9.00
Ross,Cody, Oak	-	-	-	-	-	-	-	-	-	-		1	0	0	0	1.0	1	0	0	0	0	0.00
Ross,David, ChC	2	-	-	-	2.0	-	-	-	-	-	0.00	2	0	0	0	2.0	0	0	0	0	0	0.00
Ryan,Brendan, NYY	1	-	-	-	2.0	2	-	-	-	-	0.00	1	0	0	0	2.0	2	0	0	0	0	0.00
Schumaker,Skip, Cin	-	-	-	-	-	-	-	-	-	-		4	0	0	0	4.0	4	2	2	5	3	4.50
Snider,Travis, Bal-Pit	-	-	-	-	-	-	-	-	-	-		1	0	0	0	1.0	1	2	2	2	1	18.00
Sucre,Jesus, Sea	2	-	-	-	2.0	6	3	3	-	-	13.50	2	0	0	0	2.0	6	3	3	0	0	13.50
Suzuki,Ichiro, Mia	1	-	-	-	1.0	2	1	1	-	-	9.00	1	0	0	0	1.0	2	1	1	0	0	9.00
Swisher,Nick, Cle-Atl	-	-	-	-	-	-	-	-	-	-		1	0	0	0	1.0	1	0	0	1	1	0.00
Tolleson,Steve, Tor	-	-	-	-	-	-	-	-	-	-		2	0	0	0	1.0	1	0	0	0	1	0.00
Wilson,Josh, Det	1	-	-	-	1.0	2	1	1	-	-	9.00	4	0	1	0	4.0	6	4	4	3	0	9.00

386

Hitter Analysis

Ben Jedlovec

The Hitter Analysis section provides a set of detailed information on hitters who had at least 100 plate appearances in 2015. It is information that has not always been widely available because of the logistical challenges in their data collection. The data in this section covers:

PA - Plate Appearances
Pit - Pitches Seen
T - Pitches Taken
Sw - Pitches Swung At
St - Pitches Taken for a Strike
B - Pitches Taken for a Ball
S/M - Swings and Misses
F - Foul Balls Hit
InP - Pitches Hit In Play
P/PA - Pitches Per Plate Appearance
GB - Groundballs Hit
LD - Line Drives Hit
FB - Flyballs Hit

Additionally, we have a pair of categories that combine several of those fields in order to group players into two sets of groupings:

1. Very Patient, Patient, Neutral, Aggressive, or Very Aggressive
2. Groundball Hitters, Medium Hitters, or Flyball (Air) Hitters

Of note from this section:

- Spending a week in Triple-A didn't stop Kris Bryant from pacing the league in Swings and Misses. In 650 plate appearances, Bryant whiffed 448 times, or 303 more than Mookie Betts in four fewer plate appearances.
- Two partial-season players had exactly one foul ball per plate appearance, but no regulars managed to pull off that feat. Pablo Sandoval came extremely close, however, with 498 foul balls in 505 plate appearances.
- Ben Revere and Andrelton Simmons make their swings count, putting the ball in play (as opposed to whiffing or fouling off the pitch) on a little over half their swings. Joey Gallo fills the other end of the spectrum, putting the ball in play on less than one-fourth of his swings.

Hitter Analysis

Hitter	PA	PS	T	Sw	St	B	S/M	F	In P	P/PA	Group	GB	LD	FB	Hits
Jose Abreu	668	2526	1298	1228	401	897	294	460	474	3.78	Aggressive	224	98	152	Ground
Dustin Ackley*	264	1073	631	442	216	415	66	176	200	4.06	Very Patient	86	31	79	Air
Matt Adams*	186	693	329	364	96	233	83	146	135	3.73	Aggressive	55	27	52	Air
Ehire Adrianza#	134	507	268	239	71	197	39	105	95	3.78	Aggressive	48	13	29	Ground
Nick Ahmed	459	1645	858	787	298	560	167	272	348	3.58	Very Aggressive	151	56	124	Medium
Hanser Alberto	104	345	148	197	53	95	32	80	85	3.32	Very Aggressive	40	13	26	Ground
Abraham Almonte#	258	981	518	463	152	366	107	171	185	3.80	Neutral	83	35	52	Ground
Yonder Alonso*	402	1464	800	664	204	596	101	254	309	3.64	Very Aggressive	152	71	86	Ground
Aaron Altherr	161	638	375	263	119	256	64	100	99	3.96	Patient	39	22	37	Air
Jose Altuve	689	2227	1077	1150	332	745	123	447	580	3.23	Very Aggressive	268	104	202	Medium
Pedro Alvarez*	491	1916	1031	885	284	747	266	309	310	3.90	Neutral	163	63	83	Ground
Alexi Amarista*	357	1386	732	654	265	467	92	285	277	3.88	Neutral	131	56	84	Ground
Elvis Andrus	661	2445	1388	1057	483	905	151	371	535	3.70	Aggressive	241	108	163	Ground
Nori Aoki*	392	1452	796	656	274	522	59	266	331	3.70	Aggressive	198	63	65	Ground
Nolan Arenado	665	2322	1089	1233	296	793	251	465	517	3.49	Very Aggressive	178	112	227	Air
Cody Asche*	456	1722	887	835	286	601	194	326	315	3.78	Aggressive	117	72	121	Air
Alex Avila*	219	980	585	395	149	436	136	146	113	4.47	Very Patient	45	31	35	Medium
Mike Aviles	317	1196	658	538	232	426	74	206	258	3.77	Aggressive	124	41	87	Ground
Erick Aybar#	638	2155	1021	1134	320	701	143	455	536	3.38	Very Aggressive	265	106	133	Ground
Clint Barmes	224	851	385	466	132	253	103	208	155	3.80	Neutral	42	35	70	Air
Brandon Barnes	281	1052	501	551	155	346	164	197	190	3.74	Aggressive	79	49	58	Medium
Tucker Barnhart#	274	958	483	475	147	336	74	199	202	3.50	Very Aggressive	93	49	55	Ground
Jose Bautista	666	2741	1662	1079	500	1162	208	426	445	4.12	Very Patient	166	62	217	Air
Gordon Beckham	237	940	490	450	161	329	79	198	173	3.97	Patient	78	33	61	Medium
Tim Beckham	223	899	451	448	150	301	142	168	138	4.03	Very Patient	68	26	42	Ground
Brandon Belt*	556	2320	1164	1156	257	907	302	505	349	4.17	Very Patient	116	100	132	Air
Carlos Beltran#	531	2069	1129	940	370	759	157	384	399	3.90	Neutral	142	86	171	Air
Adrian Beltre	619	2288	1187	1101	404	783	177	414	510	3.70	Aggressive	212	116	182	Air
Christian Bethancourt	160	527	206	321	58	148	86	113	122	3.29	Very Aggressive	62	22	38	Ground
Mookie Betts	654	2634	1574	1060	634	940	145	392	523	4.03	Patient	198	101	220	Air
Gregory Bird*	178	746	406	340	123	283	89	146	105	4.19	Very Patient	28	23	54	Air
Charlie Blackmon*	682	2727	1559	1168	562	997	184	473	511	4.00	Patient	190	123	183	Air
Andres Blanco#	261	1008	522	486	174	348	103	191	192	3.86	Neutral	86	38	64	Medium
Gregor Blanco*	372	1419	788	631	236	552	105	255	271	3.81	Neutral	118	63	79	Ground
Xander Bogaerts	654	2530	1288	1242	485	803	240	484	518	3.87	Neutral	270	110	132	Ground
Justin Bour*	446	1707	932	775	282	650	204	262	309	3.83	Neutral	149	53	107	Ground
Jason Bourgeois	212	841	455	386	161	294	57	165	164	3.97	Patient	84	33	44	Ground
Peter Bourjos	225	822	420	402	140	280	111	150	141	3.65	Aggressive	66	22	47	Ground
Michael Bourn*	482	1902	1101	801	335	766	197	275	329	3.95	Patient	147	77	87	Ground
Jackie Bradley Jr.*	255	1067	600	467	193	407	134	177	156	4.18	Very Patient	74	24	56	Medium
Michael Brantley*	596	2149	1240	909	403	837	71	355	483	3.61	Very Aggressive	220	108	152	Ground
Ryan Braun	568	2141	1065	1076	307	758	231	450	394	3.77	Aggressive	195	76	122	Ground
Domonic Brown*	204	773	384	389	124	260	80	156	153	3.79	Aggressive	69	24	60	Air
Jay Bruce*	649	2543	1317	1226	329	988	291	491	444	3.92	Patient	164	83	196	Air
Kris Bryant	650	2651	1354	1297	315	1039	448	484	365	4.08	Patient	125	75	165	Air
Billy Burns#	555	1943	806	1137	216	590	170	525	442	3.50	Very Aggressive	217	93	121	Ground
Drew Butera	120	402	197	205	73	124	48	71	86	3.35	Very Aggressive	26	15	39	Air
Billy Butler	601	2248	1244	1004	437	807	182	381	441	3.74	Aggressive	224	78	139	Ground
Joey Butler	276	1057	506	551	137	369	180	196	175	3.83	Neutral	102	37	36	Ground
Byron Buxton	138	513	274	239	107	167	73	79	87	3.72	Aggressive	34	11	34	Air
Marlon Byrd	544	1979	788	1191	184	604	349	476	366	3.64	Very Aggressive	157	76	133	Air
Asdrubal Cabrera#	551	2067	951	1116	253	698	234	477	405	3.75	Aggressive	142	82	173	Air
Everth Cabrera#	105	407	210	197	69	141	45	75	77	3.88	Neutral	48	14	10	Ground
Melky Cabrera#	683	2572	1362	1210	486	876	152	505	553	3.77	Aggressive	254	131	164	Ground
Miguel Cabrera	511	1985	1092	893	280	812	195	349	349	3.88	Neutral	147	88	114	Medium
Lorenzo Cain	604	2294	1164	1135	338	826	207	471	457	3.81	Aggressive	208	106	143	Ground
Kole Calhoun*	686	2557	1303	1254	359	944	335	447	472	3.73	Aggressive	196	107	166	Air
Alberto Callaspo#	261	1057	658	399	226	432	41	159	199	4.05	Very Patient	75	50	72	Air
Eric Campbell	206	820	486	334	154	332	66	129	139	3.98	Patient	63	36	39	Ground
Mark Canha	485	1892	1003	889	363	640	192	349	348	3.90	Neutral	146	62	140	Air
Robinson Cano*	674	2445	1227	1218	360	867	222	475	521	3.63	Very Aggressive	263	126	132	Ground
Matt Carpenter*	665	2807	1714	1093	640	1074	225	441	427	4.22	Very Patient	126	121	177	Air
Ezequiel Carrera*	192	728	394	334	140	254	88	112	134	3.79	Aggressive	73	20	27	Ground
Chris Carter	460	1963	1062	901	295	767	324	331	245	4.27	Very Patient	73	45	127	Air
Curt Casali	113	441	237	204	65	172	66	69	69	3.90	Neutral	29	8	31	Air
Nick Castellanos	595	2317	1166	1151	346	820	335	413	403	3.89	Neutral	146	94	163	Air
Rusney Castillo	289	1040	501	539	168	333	124	194	221	3.60	Very Aggressive	139	29	51	Ground
Welington Castillo	378	1436	807	629	304	503	148	226	255	3.80	Neutral	107	47	101	Air
Daniel Castro	100	391	178	213	68	110	31	100	82	3.91	Patient	50	11	20	Ground
Jason Castro*	375	1476	778	698	231	547	219	254	225	3.94	Patient	84	55	86	Air
Starlin Castro	578	2136	1096	1040	381	715	193	386	461	3.70	Aggressive	249	78	133	Ground
Francisco Cervelli	510	2003	1174	829	384	790	152	315	362	3.93	Patient	186	75	96	Ground

Hitter Analysis

Hitter	PA	PS	T	Sw	St	B	S/M	F	In P	P/PA	Group	GB	LD	FB	Hits
Yoenis Cespedes	676	2722	1391	1331	470	921	302	532	497	4.03	Patient	207	101	188	Air
Robinson Chirinos	273	1104	628	476	207	421	101	197	178	4.04	Very Patient	61	33	78	Air
Lonnie Chisenhall*	362	1315	617	698	206	411	126	303	269	3.63	Very Aggressive	108	52	106	Air
Shin-Soo Choo*	653	2606	1514	1092	468	1046	278	399	415	3.99	Patient	209	85	117	Ground
Pedro Ciriaco	151	521	204	317	81	123	79	129	109	3.45	Very Aggressive	43	23	35	Medium
Steve Clevenger*	105	361	173	188	59	114	25	75	88	3.44	Very Aggressive	43	17	28	Ground
Chris Coghlan*	503	2016	1134	882	335	799	166	368	348	4.01	Patient	157	69	117	Medium
Chris Colabello	360	1372	683	689	196	487	203	247	239	3.81	Neutral	114	60	64	Ground
Tyler Collins*	207	752	355	397	94	261	84	163	150	3.63	Very Aggressive	59	33	56	Air
Christian Colon	119	474	271	203	104	167	31	81	91	3.98	Patient	40	24	26	Air
Michael Conforto*	194	743	423	320	128	295	67	116	137	3.83	Neutral	53	31	53	Air
Hank Conger#	229	930	510	420	163	347	114	165	141	4.06	Very Patient	48	30	61	Air
Carlos Corporan#	121	470	222	248	70	152	70	107	71	3.88	Neutral	24	16	29	Air
Carlos Correa	432	1797	992	805	323	669	159	333	313	4.16	Very Patient	152	70	91	Ground
Zack Cozart	214	749	391	358	134	257	51	138	169	3.50	Very Aggressive	64	32	70	Air
Brandon Crawford*	561	2169	1045	1124	275	770	301	431	392	3.87	Neutral	185	73	130	Ground
Carl Crawford*	193	708	341	367	112	229	82	143	140	3.67	Aggressive	60	34	46	Medium
Coco Crisp#	139	533	311	222	111	200	47	74	101	3.83	Neutral	44	18	39	Air
C.J. Cron	404	1534	756	778	262	494	160	318	299	3.80	Neutral	133	55	111	Air
Nelson Cruz	655	2632	1367	1265	376	991	370	468	427	4.02	Patient	195	87	145	Medium
Tony Cruz	151	585	279	306	99	180	67	126	113	3.87	Neutral	59	16	36	Ground
Michael Cuddyer	408	1525	741	784	246	495	182	310	292	3.74	Aggressive	142	64	86	Ground
Travis d'Arnaud	268	988	528	460	165	363	102	166	192	3.69	Aggressive	71	41	80	Air
Chris Davis*	670	2786	1468	1318	346	1122	444	504	370	4.16	Very Patient	117	91	160	Air
Ike Davis*	239	933	527	406	183	344	72	162	172	3.90	Neutral	90	34	48	Ground
Khris Davis	440	1777	919	858	263	656	277	308	273	4.04	Very Patient	116	47	110	Air
Rajai Davis	370	1382	696	686	237	459	128	289	269	3.74	Aggressive	116	59	88	Medium
Alejandro De Aza*	365	1463	761	702	247	514	155	302	245	4.01	Neutral	90	54	87	Air
Ivan De Jesus	222	959	549	410	186	363	88	175	147	4.32	Very Patient	73	35	39	Ground
David DeJesus*	317	1195	655	540	224	431	71	231	238	3.77	Aggressive	104	56	78	Medium
Matt den Dekker*	110	395	214	181	67	147	42	58	81	3.59	Very Aggressive	35	14	29	Medium
Chris Denorfia	231	925	486	439	179	307	115	165	159	4.00	Patient	79	38	38	Ground
Daniel Descalso*	209	771	396	375	125	271	81	150	144	3.69	Aggressive	62	27	51	Medium
Delino DeShields	492	1923	1175	748	440	735	165	248	335	3.91	Neutral	145	58	103	Ground
Ian Desmond	641	2365	1184	1181	365	819	327	448	406	3.69	Aggressive	212	62	123	Ground
Corey Dickerson*	234	898	388	510	115	273	123	219	168	3.84	Neutral	64	50	54	Air
Derek Dietrich*	289	1103	594	509	175	419	110	211	188	3.82	Neutral	69	37	81	Air
Josh Donaldson	711	2817	1528	1289	409	1119	313	477	499	3.96	Patient	222	86	188	Air
Brian Dozier	704	2833	1553	1280	491	1062	271	521	488	4.02	Patient	161	109	213	Air
Stephen Drew*	428	1661	973	688	325	648	105	264	319	3.88	Neutral	118	49	146	Air
Lucas Duda*	554	2266	1318	948	407	911	231	381	336	4.09	Very Patient	92	74	170	Air
Matt Duffy	612	2271	1228	1043	411	817	179	383	481	3.71	Aggressive	252	100	127	Ground
Jarrod Dyson*	225	838	449	389	147	302	60	159	170	3.72	Aggressive	83	36	35	Ground
Adam Eaton*	689	2785	1557	1228	556	1001	212	530	486	4.04	Very Patient	238	103	128	Ground
A.J. Ellis	217	930	602	328	215	387	50	132	146	4.29	Very Patient	62	30	50	Medium
Jacoby Ellsbury*	501	1881	973	908	311	662	145	390	370	3.75	Aggressive	167	89	113	Ground
Jake Elmore	158	597	339	258	134	205	34	103	121	3.78	Aggressive	49	30	38	Medium
Edwin Encarnacion	624	2517	1431	1086	410	1021	240	406	440	4.03	Very Patient	159	85	196	Air
Alcides Escobar	662	2311	1110	1201	387	723	202	446	553	3.49	Very Aggressive	257	120	161	Ground
Eduardo Escobar#	446	1762	909	853	307	602	170	353	330	3.95	Patient	137	63	126	Air
Yunel Escobar	591	1991	996	995	273	723	159	368	468	3.37	Very Aggressive	254	104	108	Ground
Danny Espinosa#	412	1515	690	825	170	520	225	333	267	3.68	Aggressive	112	46	92	Medium
Andre Ethier*	445	1709	890	819	255	635	159	337	323	3.84	Neutral	124	85	114	Air
Taylor Featherston	169	636	322	314	115	207	77	124	113	3.76	Aggressive	50	19	36	Medium
Prince Fielder*	693	2483	1293	1190	339	954	231	429	530	3.58	Very Aggressive	245	97	188	Medium
Ryan Flaherty*	301	1149	627	522	195	432	125	207	190	3.82	Neutral	92	26	67	Ground
Wilmer Flores	510	1969	1009	960	356	653	133	403	424	3.86	Neutral	176	89	156	Air
Tyler Flowers	361	1411	704	707	223	481	208	269	230	3.91	Neutral	107	39	82	Medium
Logan Forsythe	615	2540	1516	1024	562	954	178	411	435	4.13	Very Patient	172	86	176	Air
Dexter Fowler#	690	2819	1647	1172	476	1171	241	484	447	4.09	Very Patient	190	89	160	Air
Maikel Franco	335	1198	626	572	182	444	135	184	253	3.58	Very Aggressive	119	46	88	Medium
Jeff Francoeur	343	1183	517	666	162	355	164	250	252	3.45	Very Aggressive	100	60	92	Air
Nick Franklin#	109	432	208	224	47	161	75	84	65	3.96	Patient	20	14	28	Air
Todd Frazier	678	2565	1209	1356	302	907	324	542	490	3.78	Aggressive	161	93	232	Air
Freddie Freeman*	481	1871	950	921	190	760	216	385	320	3.89	Neutral	117	89	114	Air
David Freese	470	1842	1007	835	330	677	189	326	320	3.92	Patient	174	56	90	Ground
Sam Fuld*	325	1325	837	488	324	513	73	177	238	4.08	Very Patient	138	42	52	Ground
Joey Gallo*	123	504	262	242	57	205	117	74	51	4.10	Very Patient	18	14	19	Air
Freddy Galvis#	603	2288	1116	1172	392	724	214	491	467	3.79	Neutral	182	99	164	Air
Adonis Garcia	198	708	325	383	104	221	80	145	158	3.58	Very Aggressive	78	34	46	Ground
Avisail Garcia	601	2142	883	1259	204	679	379	464	416	3.56	Very Aggressive	203	102	111	Ground
Brett Gardner*	656	2732	1709	1023	618	1091	208	368	447	4.16	Very Patient	194	89	145	Medium
Evan Gattis	604	2102	1041	1061	312	729	246	363	452	3.48	Very Aggressive	206	77	169	Medium
Scooter Gennett*	391	1368	598	770	190	408	129	334	307	3.50	Very Aggressive	147	65	90	Ground
Johnny Giavotella	502	1756	955	801	343	612	112	280	409	3.50	Very Aggressive	182	94	121	Ground

Hitter Analysis

Hitter	PA	PS	T	Sw	St	B	S/M	F	In P	P/PA	Group	GB	LD	FB	Hits
Conor Gillaspie*	253	866	425	441	118	307	101	148	192	3.42	Very Aggressive	85	40	66	Medium
Cole Gillespie	157	598	334	264	113	221	43	101	120	3.81	Neutral	63	19	35	Ground
Chris Gimenez	113	435	259	176	97	162	32	61	83	3.85	Neutral	33	14	32	Air
Ryan Goins*	428	1614	913	701	330	583	125	271	305	3.77	Aggressive	159	53	82	Ground
Paul Goldschmidt	695	2917	1806	1111	527	1279	256	431	423	4.20	Very Patient	176	99	148	Air
Jonny Gomes	262	1064	697	367	268	429	105	115	147	4.06	Very Patient	56	26	65	Air
Yan Gomes	389	1471	706	765	226	480	165	335	265	3.78	Aggressive	89	70	106	Air
Carlos Gomez	477	1744	768	976	177	591	239	399	338	3.66	Aggressive	139	63	124	Air
Hector Gomez	134	488	209	279	75	134	76	114	89	3.64	Very Aggressive	31	23	31	Air
Adrian Gonzalez*	643	2485	1249	1236	301	948	251	517	467	3.86	Neutral	174	121	171	Air
Carlos Gonzalez*	608	2235	1035	1200	216	819	353	419	428	3.68	Aggressive	200	70	155	Medium
Marwin Gonzalez#	370	1310	637	673	211	426	156	240	277	3.54	Very Aggressive	117	60	87	Medium
Alex Gordon*	422	1683	982	701	279	703	157	277	267	3.99	Patient	100	66	100	Air
Dee Gordon*	653	2248	1081	1167	388	693	152	480	535	3.44	Very Aggressive	297	107	93	Ground
Anthony Gose*	535	2131	1064	1067	291	773	272	453	342	3.98	Patient	174	67	81	Ground
Tuffy Gosewisch	138	524	279	245	101	178	39	100	106	3.80	Neutral	52	23	30	Ground
Phil Gosselin	118	475	274	201	99	175	38	72	91	4.03	Patient	50	17	23	Ground
Yasmani Grandal#	426	1763	1074	689	336	738	150	272	267	4.14	Very Patient	120	45	98	Medium
Curtis Granderson*	682	2981	1863	1118	636	1227	220	465	433	4.37	Very Patient	133	117	182	Air
Didi Gregorius*	578	2093	1009	1084	303	706	231	404	449	3.62	Very Aggressive	198	94	151	Medium
Randal Grichuk	350	1391	675	716	186	489	222	280	214	3.97	Patient	81	44	89	Air
Alex Guerrero	230	802	327	475	92	235	118	193	164	3.49	Very Aggressive	68	32	64	Air
Franklin Gutierrez	189	843	489	354	167	322	102	134	118	4.46	Very Patient	48	28	42	Air
Brandon Guyer	385	1426	669	757	177	492	161	321	275	3.70	Aggressive	119	57	93	Medium
Jedd Gyorko	458	1813	930	883	286	644	211	353	319	3.96	Patient	135	67	117	Air
Billy Hamilton#	454	1677	892	785	294	598	134	301	350	3.69	Aggressive	133	61	118	Air
Josh Hamilton*	182	674	318	356	76	242	124	112	120	3.70	Aggressive	55	27	38	Ground
Ryan Hanigan	201	847	488	359	183	305	55	166	137	4.21	Very Patient	71	33	32	Ground
J.J. Hardy	437	1789	1077	712	432	645	117	266	329	4.09	Very Patient	161	57	108	Ground
Bryce Harper*	654	2682	1496	1186	316	1180	299	493	394	4.10	Very Patient	151	87	154	Air
Josh Harrison	449	1567	717	850	238	479	164	334	352	3.49	Very Aggressive	144	86	116	Medium
Chase Headley#	642	2561	1463	1098	487	976	225	424	449	3.99	Patient	193	119	136	Medium
Adeiny Hechavarria	499	1676	796	880	256	540	154	330	396	3.36	Very Aggressive	196	78	110	Ground
Austin Hedges	152	566	257	279	90	167	75	99	105	3.53	Very Aggressive	46	19	37	Medium
Cesar Hernandez#	452	1628	865	763	268	597	160	279	324	3.60	Very Aggressive	164	72	66	Ground
Kiké Hernandez	218	826	433	393	150	283	100	134	159	3.79	Aggressive	73	37	48	Ground
Dilson Herrera	103	419	246	172	73	173	34	71	67	4.06	Very Patient	22	14	31	Air
Elian Herrera#	277	1110	528	582	153	375	137	258	187	4.01	Patient	69	46	70	Air
Jonathan Herrera#	132	509	255	254	96	159	42	105	107	3.86	Neutral	45	15	37	Medium
Odubel Herrera*	537	2155	1076	1079	354	722	264	443	372	4.01	Patient	169	84	105	Ground
Chris Herrmann*	113	435	205	230	67	138	70	93	67	3.85	Neutral	31	11	23	Medium
Jason Heyward*	610	2348	1385	963	434	951	154	347	460	3.85	Neutral	263	89	108	Ground
Aaron Hicks#	390	1510	832	678	237	595	134	256	288	3.87	Neutral	117	64	99	Air
Aaron Hill	353	1291	727	564	242	485	90	207	267	3.66	Aggressive	112	53	102	Air
Matt Holliday	277	1062	546	516	117	429	112	221	183	3.83	Neutral	88	42	53	Air
Brock Holt*	509	2085	1238	847	496	742	122	362	363	4.10	Very Patient	188	85	84	Ground
Eric Hosmer*	667	2557	1394	1163	410	984	230	438	495	3.83	Neutral	254	114	119	Ground
Ryan Howard*	503	1897	861	1036	192	669	319	384	332	3.77	Aggressive	118	92	122	Air
Nick Hundley	389	1448	713	735	208	505	157	287	291	3.72	Aggressive	124	65	99	Medium
Torii Hunter	567	2087	972	1115	277	695	243	451	421	3.68	Aggressive	202	72	143	Ground
Chris Iannetta	317	1313	750	563	203	547	170	201	192	4.14	Very Patient	75	25	92	Air
Jose Iglesias	454	1690	913	777	374	539	76	322	379	3.72	Aggressive	205	77	85	Ground
Ender Inciarte*	561	1936	993	943	376	617	106	364	473	3.45	Very Aggressive	239	99	118	Ground
Omar Infante	455	1557	814	743	322	492	147	219	377	3.42	Very Aggressive	153	78	140	Air
Austin Jackson	527	2201	1226	975	442	784	206	400	369	4.18	Very Patient	185	88	89	Ground
John Jaso*	216	870	481	389	130	351	82	159	148	4.03	Patient	78	32	38	Ground
Jon Jay*	245	889	461	428	140	321	61	188	179	3.63	Very Aggressive	106	38	32	Ground
Desmond Jennings	108	418	233	185	75	158	30	73	82	3.87	Neutral	47	15	20	Ground
Chris Johnson	255	1018	512	506	154	358	156	180	170	3.99	Patient	81	36	53	Ground
Kelly Johnson*	335	1296	694	602	223	471	144	227	230	3.87	Neutral	101	54	75	Medium
Micah Johnson*	114	472	243	229	82	161	46	110	72	4.14	Very Patient	38	14	13	Ground
Adam Jones	581	1996	791	1205	182	609	272	486	447	3.44	Very Aggressive	203	79	161	Medium
Garrett Jones*	152	583	296	287	100	196	67	113	107	3.84	Neutral	49	20	38	Medium
Caleb Joseph	355	1364	710	654	229	481	146	255	252	3.84	Neutral	83	58	107	Air
Matt Joyce*	284	1074	573	501	166	407	130	188	183	3.78	Aggressive	74	32	76	Air
Jung Ho Kang	467	1881	1087	794	386	701	189	282	323	4.03	Patient	161	73	89	Ground
Matt Kemp	648	2534	1243	1291	364	879	331	503	457	3.91	Patient	198	98	161	Medium
Howie Kendrick	495	1864	910	954	296	614	181	389	384	3.77	Aggressive	225	94	64	Ground
Kevin Kiermaier*	535	1954	950	1004	296	654	199	391	414	3.65	Aggressive	194	93	119	Ground
Ian Kinsler	675	2526	1336	1190	438	898	140	501	549	3.74	Aggressive	184	138	221	Air
Jason Kipnis*	641	2540	1442	1098	509	933	181	449	468	3.96	Patient	208	124	130	Ground
Pete Kozma	111	414	234	180	77	157	29	72	79	3.73	Aggressive	22	12	41	Air
Juan Lagares	465	1811	891	920	330	561	175	387	358	3.89	Neutral	193	50	109	Ground
Jake Lamb*	390	1548	897	651	304	593	160	235	256	3.97	Patient	115	50	83	Medium
Adam LaRoche*	484	1907	1082	825	343	739	210	317	298	3.94	Patient	127	52	117	Air

Hitter Analysis

Hitter	PA	PS	T	Sw	St	B	S/M	F	In P	P/PA	Group	GB	LD	FB	Hits
Ryan Lavarnway	106	416	232	184	73	159	49	69	66	3.92	Patient	24	12	30	Air
Brett Lawrie	602	2297	1177	1120	401	776	283	412	425	3.82	Neutral	206	78	138	Ground
DJ LeMahieu	620	2451	1387	1064	486	901	167	435	462	3.95	Patient	249	119	89	Ground
Sandy Leon#	128	502	281	221	103	178	36	93	92	3.92	Patient	38	16	31	Medium
Adam Lind*	572	2254	1253	1001	410	843	201	395	405	3.94	Patient	187	76	142	Medium
Francisco Lindor#	438	1578	771	807	219	552	145	321	341	3.60	Very Aggressive	163	66	92	Ground
Jose Lobaton#	155	633	341	292	85	256	82	111	99	4.08	Very Patient	46	19	33	Medium
James Loney*	388	1306	678	628	201	477	78	220	330	3.37	Very Aggressive	141	80	109	Medium
Evan Longoria	670	2536	1350	1186	416	934	267	439	480	3.79	Aggressive	187	99	194	Air
David Lough*	144	501	252	249	93	159	57	91	101	3.48	Very Aggressive	43	19	36	Air
Jed Lowrie#	263	1086	603	483	163	440	78	216	189	4.13	Very Patient	66	40	83	Air
Jonathan Lucroy	415	1671	947	724	346	601	106	304	314	4.03	Patient	140	81	92	Ground
Manny Machado	713	2789	1582	1207	475	1107	202	477	528	3.91	Patient	226	92	199	Air
Mikie Mahtook	115	460	234	226	67	167	64	87	75	4.00	Patient	24	17	32	Air
Martin Maldonado	256	994	596	398	208	388	98	133	167	3.88	Neutral	76	33	53	Ground
Jake Marisnick	372	1449	695	754	211	484	205	305	244	3.90	Neutral	96	45	88	Air
Nick Markakis*	686	2711	1584	1127	569	1015	118	479	530	3.95	Patient	277	110	143	Ground
Ketel Marte#	247	952	535	417	175	360	78	159	180	3.85	Neutral	90	37	45	Ground
Starling Marte	633	2281	979	1302	275	704	320	518	464	3.60	Very Aggressive	242	106	102	Ground
Leonys Martin*	310	1112	583	529	213	370	136	170	223	3.59	Very Aggressive	108	32	69	Ground
Russell Martin	507	2112	1247	865	403	844	189	336	340	4.17	Very Patient	170	55	111	Ground
J.D. Martinez	657	2605	1235	1370	314	921	402	547	421	3.96	Patient	144	94	183	Air
Victor Martinez#	485	1909	1003	906	311	692	121	390	395	3.94	Patient	159	83	153	Air
Jeff Mathis	103	393	199	194	50	149	58	64	72	3.82	Neutral	29	14	28	Air
Joe Mauer*	666	2715	1611	1104	594	1017	177	441	486	4.08	Very Patient	268	116	97	Ground
Justin Maxwell	274	1030	516	514	137	379	159	180	175	3.76	Aggressive	79	36	59	Medium
John Mayberry	119	471	250	221	83	167	63	81	77	3.96	Patient	31	19	27	Air
Cameron Maybin	555	2174	1227	947	429	798	185	355	407	3.92	Patient	234	89	81	Ground
Brian McCann*	535	2094	1212	882	433	779	143	364	375	3.91	Patient	134	62	175	Air
James McCann	425	1501	714	787	245	469	188	283	316	3.53	Very Aggressive	153	71	83	Ground
Andrew McCutchen	685	2780	1575	1205	394	1181	302	461	442	4.06	Very Patient	169	104	169	Air
Casey McGehee	258	998	542	456	175	367	97	172	187	3.87	Neutral	106	35	46	Ground
Michael McKenry	152	625	376	249	122	254	68	94	87	4.11	Very Patient	33	15	39	Air
Jordy Mercer	430	1603	899	704	348	551	118	258	328	3.73	Aggressive	158	67	99	Ground
Will Middlebrooks	270	1034	554	480	196	358	128	153	199	3.83	Neutral	74	41	84	Air
Brad Miller*	497	1788	917	871	275	642	207	317	347	3.60	Very Aggressive	165	69	107	Ground
Yadier Molina	530	1812	832	980	214	618	156	385	439	3.42	Very Aggressive	209	89	140	Ground
Jesus Montero	116	384	153	231	52	101	66	85	80	3.31	Very Aggressive	36	16	28	Medium
Miguel Montero*	403	1639	843	796	208	635	235	314	247	4.07	Very Patient	100	63	84	Air
Tyler Moore	200	773	386	387	124	262	93	151	143	3.87	Neutral	57	25	61	Air
Kendrys Morales#	639	2442	1273	1169	328	945	259	440	470	3.82	Neutral	211	96	163	Medium
Mitch Moreland*	515	2033	1078	955	337	741	234	357	364	3.95	Patient	166	72	126	Medium
Justin Morneau*	182	637	305	332	81	224	62	127	143	3.50	Very Aggressive	68	27	47	Ground
Logan Morrison*	511	1940	1011	929	275	736	169	381	379	3.80	Neutral	167	61	146	Air
Michael Morse	256	1031	525	506	139	386	150	203	153	4.03	Patient	87	39	27	Ground
Brandon Moss*	526	2056	1043	1013	277	766	291	398	324	3.91	Patient	105	66	152	Air
Mike Moustakas*	614	2435	1284	1151	387	897	179	490	482	3.97	Patient	189	89	196	Air
Max Muncy*	112	489	287	202	96	191	44	81	72	4.37	Very Patient	23	9	39	Air
Daniel Murphy*	538	1891	975	916	281	694	77	372	467	3.51	Very Aggressive	200	99	168	Air
David Murphy*	391	1480	796	684	313	483	96	267	318	3.79	Aggressive	161	53	103	Ground
John Ryan Murphy	172	663	342	321	111	231	61	144	116	3.85	Neutral	54	27	34	Ground
Wil Myers	253	1076	625	451	191	434	108	173	170	4.25	Very Patient	79	28	59	Medium
Mike Napoli	469	2038	1179	859	382	797	205	364	290	4.35	Very Patient	123	45	122	Air
Daniel Nava#	166	667	393	274	143	250	49	120	105	4.02	Patient	47	19	38	Medium
Dioner Navarro#	192	746	426	320	150	276	63	111	146	3.89	Neutral	54	32	60	Air
Kristopher Negron	107	370	190	180	64	126	45	63	72	3.46	Very Aggressive	35	12	21	Ground
Kirk Nieuwenhuis*	141	587	320	267	102	218	83	105	79	4.16	Very Patient	34	16	28	Medium
Derek Norris	557	2225	1226	999	432	794	208	406	385	3.99	Patient	160	67	158	Air
Eduardo Nunez	204	723	365	358	56	291	56	141	161	3.54	Very Aggressive	88	25	42	Ground
Rougned Odor*	470	1755	911	844	292	619	144	346	354	3.73	Aggressive	157	50	136	Air
Mike Olt	102	442	253	189	79	174	70	60	59	4.33	Very Patient	31	8	20	Ground
Paulo Orlando	251	896	412	484	140	272	108	185	191	3.57	Very Aggressive	80	41	63	Medium
David Ortiz*	614	2488	1377	1111	340	1037	247	422	442	4.05	Very Patient	162	99	181	Air
Chris Owings	552	1975	916	1059	318	598	263	415	381	3.58	Very Aggressive	144	95	124	Air
Marcell Ozuna	494	1832	960	872	310	650	222	299	351	3.71	Aggressive	169	74	108	Ground
Angel Pagan#	551	2106	1232	874	458	774	98	351	425	3.82	Neutral	181	99	145	Medium
Joe Panik*	432	1592	911	681	302	609	73	261	347	3.69	Aggressive	148	79	116	Ground
Jimmy Paredes#	384	1408	587	821	142	445	288	279	254	3.67	Aggressive	123	59	70	Ground
Kyle Parker	112	400	181	219	53	128	89	61	69	3.57	Very Aggressive	32	15	22	Ground
Chris Parmelee*	102	417	214	203	71	143	36	96	71	4.09	Very Patient	15	14	41	Air
Gerardo Parra*	589	2085	942	1143	280	662	196	483	464	3.54	Very Aggressive	211	106	132	Medium
Ben Paulsen*	354	1283	555	728	139	416	218	273	237	3.62	Very Aggressive	106	52	77	Medium
Steve Pearce	325	1217	641	576	202	439	125	225	226	3.74	Aggressive	76	45	105	Air
Joc Pederson*	585	2464	1419	1045	393	1026	358	373	314	4.21	Very Patient	130	49	132	Air
Dustin Pedroia	425	1638	930	708	335	595	87	287	334	3.85	Neutral	168	59	106	Ground

Hitter Analysis

Hitter	PA	PS	T	Sw	St	B	S/M	F	In P	P/PA	Group	GB	LD	FB	Hits
Brayan Pena#	367	1343	759	584	241	518	55	227	302	3.66	Aggressive	151	66	79	Ground
Hunter Pence	223	848	462	386	147	315	110	117	159	3.80	Neutral	86	27	46	Ground
Cliff Pennington#	249	1021	576	445	162	414	93	180	172	4.10	Very Patient	69	38	50	Medium
David Peralta*	517	1923	1008	915	300	708	207	346	362	3.72	Aggressive	188	77	96	Ground
Jhonny Peralta	640	2444	1225	1219	291	934	266	479	474	3.82	Neutral	209	117	148	Medium
Carlos Perez	283	1076	584	492	200	384	80	197	215	3.80	Neutral	89	42	81	Air
Eury Perez	133	494	251	243	89	162	49	95	99	3.71	Aggressive	55	19	15	Ground
Hernan Perez	272	896	378	518	130	248	130	180	208	3.29	Very Aggressive	88	45	70	Medium
Roberto Perez	226	969	608	361	211	397	94	140	127	4.29	Very Patient	65	24	33	Ground
Salvador Perez	553	1840	849	991	287	562	171	366	454	3.33	Very Aggressive	190	94	170	Air
Jace Peterson*	597	2370	1339	1031	457	882	219	394	418	3.97	Patient	185	88	127	Ground
Shane Peterson*	226	899	486	413	143	343	98	164	150	3.98	Patient	77	39	31	Ground
Tommy Pham	173	677	398	279	140	258	68	98	113	3.91	Patient	58	24	31	Ground
Josh Phegley	243	870	413	457	128	285	105	177	175	3.58	Very Aggressive	64	36	75	Air
Brandon Phillips	623	2168	992	1176	295	697	212	440	524	3.48	Very Aggressive	234	130	158	Ground
A.J. Pierzynski*	436	1455	657	798	157	500	106	319	373	3.34	Very Aggressive	174	92	107	Ground
Kevin Pillar	628	2262	1103	1159	409	694	203	446	510	3.60	Very Aggressive	204	108	181	Air
Stephen Piscotty	256	985	493	492	141	352	110	203	179	3.85	Neutral	81	38	60	Medium
Kevin Plawecki	258	956	528	428	193	335	93	158	177	3.71	Aggressive	81	35	59	Medium
Trevor Plouffe	632	2403	1323	1080	461	862	219	407	454	3.80	Neutral	185	82	183	Air
Gregory Polanco*	652	2528	1395	1133	441	954	215	443	475	3.88	Neutral	212	92	163	Medium
A.J. Pollock	673	2361	1267	1094	436	831	172	393	529	3.51	Very Aggressive	264	109	152	Ground
Dalton Pompey#	103	376	179	197	44	135	53	73	71	3.65	Aggressive	28	11	26	Air
Buster Posey	623	2194	1159	1035	321	838	127	396	512	3.52	Very Aggressive	225	114	173	Medium
Martin Prado	551	2157	1305	852	535	770	96	315	441	3.91	Patient	206	102	132	Ground
Yasiel Puig	311	1212	570	642	124	446	171	254	217	3.90	Neutral	96	37	84	Air
Albert Pujols	661	2514	1372	1142	449	923	168	441	533	3.80	Neutral	223	85	225	Air
Ryan Raburn	201	853	489	364	142	347	85	149	130	4.24	Very Patient	57	28	45	Medium
Alexei Ramirez	622	2185	1125	1060	380	745	158	380	522	3.51	Very Aggressive	257	111	151	Ground
Aramis Ramirez	516	1815	855	960	238	617	160	388	412	3.52	Very Aggressive	157	77	178	Air
Hanley Ramirez	430	1588	797	791	239	558	149	308	334	3.69	Aggressive	167	68	99	Ground
Jose Ramirez#	355	1416	833	583	310	523	62	238	283	3.99	Patient	129	44	98	Medium
Wilson Ramos	504	1782	827	955	227	600	220	353	382	3.54	Very Aggressive	212	75	95	Ground
Colby Rasmus*	485	2011	1079	932	308	771	288	362	362	4.15	Very Patient	78	55	142	Air
J.T. Realmuto	467	1723	864	859	293	571	125	358	376	3.69	Aggressive	168	80	127	Medium
Josh Reddick*	582	2296	1299	997	423	876	149	380	464	3.95	Patient	178	97	188	Air
Nolan Reimold	195	800	478	322	159	319	79	120	123	4.10	Very Patient	60	20	43	Ground
Anthony Rendon	355	1556	973	583	354	619	90	248	245	4.38	Very Patient	110	52	81	Medium
Ben Revere*	634	2252	1296	956	521	775	99	321	536	3.55	Very Aggressive	286	138	99	Ground
Jose Reyes#	519	1804	896	908	298	598	140	337	431	3.48	Very Aggressive	183	83	149	Medium
Mark Reynolds	432	1790	962	828	277	685	255	310	263	4.14	Very Patient	109	50	104	Air
Alex Rios	411	1533	809	724	275	534	124	276	324	3.73	Aggressive	129	72	123	Air
Rene Rivera	319	1175	513	662	157	356	198	245	219	3.68	Aggressive	81	37	96	Air
Anthony Rizzo*	701	2751	1488	1263	421	1067	225	550	488	3.92	Patient	168	106	212	Air
Clint Robinson*	352	1394	773	621	221	552	107	256	258	3.96	Patient	105	64	89	Air
Shane Robinson	197	730	376	354	134	242	52	147	155	3.71	Aggressive	79	24	49	Ground
Alex Rodriguez	620	2503	1405	1098	387	1018	339	374	385	4.04	Very Patient	166	70	149	Air
Sean Rodriguez	240	847	384	463	116	268	133	164	166	3.53	Very Aggressive	75	32	50	Air
Jason Rogers	169	686	405	281	140	265	63	100	118	4.06	Very Patient	64	19	35	Ground
Miguel Rojas	157	561	280	281	94	186	46	105	130	3.57	Very Aggressive	69	30	26	Ground
Jimmy Rollins#	563	2128	1170	958	348	822	163	362	433	3.78	Aggressive	161	80	179	Air
Andrew Romine#	203	756	371	385	100	271	79	163	143	3.72	Aggressive	80	27	30	Ground
Adam Rosales	125	508	299	209	101	198	53	72	84	4.06	Very Patient	41	13	30	Medium
Eddie Rosario*	474	1692	695	997	210	485	253	403	341	3.57	Very Aggressive	131	68	136	Air
Wilin Rosario	242	859	397	462	122	275	118	167	177	3.55	Very Aggressive	96	35	45	Ground
David Ross	182	716	365	351	98	267	122	128	101	3.93	Neutral	31	18	48	Air
Darin Ruf	297	1144	593	551	193	400	141	208	202	3.85	Neutral	90	41	71	Medium
Justin Ruggiano	141	550	291	259	81	210	89	86	84	3.90	Neutral	34	16	34	Air
Carlos Ruiz	320	1236	726	510	268	458	60	205	245	3.86	Neutral	107	54	81	Medium
Cameron Rupp	299	1138	586	552	171	415	141	210	201	3.81	Neutral	86	37	76	Air
Addison Russell	523	2154	1121	1033	347	774	307	397	329	4.12	Very Patient	133	59	132	Air
Brendan Ryan	103	382	196	186	81	115	54	64	68	3.71	Aggressive	34	9	24	Ground
Tyler Saladino	254	932	509	423	178	331	73	161	189	3.67	Aggressive	98	42	43	Ground
Jarrod Saltalamacchia#	227	920	501	419	143	358	134	152	133	4.05	Very Patient	41	28	63	Air
Carlos Sanchez#	420	1615	819	796	287	532	159	322	315	3.85	Neutral	166	70	71	Ground
Pablo Sandoval#	505	1848	761	1087	200	561	189	498	400	3.66	Aggressive	195	75	129	Ground
Jerry Sands	133	536	297	238	93	204	68	82	88	4.02	Patient	40	17	31	Medium
Miguel Sano	335	1455	870	585	258	612	232	191	162	4.34	Very Patient	54	40	68	Air
Carlos Santana#	666	2863	1814	1049	540	1274	192	424	433	4.30	Very Patient	192	79	160	Air
Danny Santana#	277	940	402	538	147	255	136	202	200	3.39	Very Aggressive	98	36	47	Ground
Domingo Santana	187	781	436	345	127	309	114	132	99	4.18	Very Patient	51	19	29	Ground
Luis Sardinas#	105	396	196	200	76	120	39	87	74	3.77	Aggressive	45	10	18	Ground
Logan Schafer*	143	533	280	253	87	193	47	106	100	3.73	Aggressive	47	16	31	Ground
Jonathan Schoop	321	1122	439	683	100	339	200	254	229	3.50	Very Aggressive	98	44	86	Air
Skip Schumaker*	268	1055	547	508	195	352	95	219	194	3.94	Patient	100	52	42	Ground

Hitter Analysis

Hitter	PA	PS	T	Sw	St	B	S/M	F	In P	P/PA	Group	GB	LD	FB	Hits
Kyle Schwarber*	273	1163	641	522	187	454	169	197	156	4.26	Very Patient	63	27	66	Air
Corey Seager*	113	456	224	232	50	174	51	102	79	4.04	Very Patient	42	16	21	Ground
Kyle Seager*	686	2537	1385	1152	447	938	195	428	529	3.70	Aggressive	185	126	214	Air
Jean Segura	584	2057	953	1104	336	617	180	452	472	3.52	Very Aggressive	275	78	113	Ground
Marcus Semien	601	2370	1333	1037	464	869	220	391	426	3.94	Patient	162	98	165	Air
Travis Shaw*	248	1022	547	475	189	358	96	208	171	4.12	Very Patient	64	34	73	Air
J.B. Shuck*	165	622	359	263	127	232	34	97	132	3.77	Aggressive	73	23	32	Ground
Andrelton Simmons	583	1906	1032	874	332	700	96	288	490	3.27	Very Aggressive	271	103	108	Ground
Grady Sizemore*	296	1063	539	524	169	370	106	204	214	3.59	Very Aggressive	92	49	73	Medium
Seth Smith*	452	1905	1143	762	385	758	198	262	302	4.21	Very Patient	127	59	114	Air
Justin Smoak#	328	1262	725	537	228	497	145	181	211	3.85	Neutral	90	50	71	Medium
Jake Smolinski	192	756	413	343	133	280	67	145	131	3.94	Patient	59	20	52	Air
Travis Snider*	265	1082	569	513	163	406	129	213	171	4.08	Very Patient	81	36	54	Ground
Eric Sogard*	401	1459	858	601	352	506	64	211	326	3.64	Very Aggressive	141	70	107	Medium
Yangervis Solarte#	571	2022	1042	980	326	716	122	383	475	3.54	Very Aggressive	206	91	175	Air
Jorge Soler	404	1621	848	773	241	607	256	269	248	4.01	Patient	105	69	74	Medium
Geovany Soto	210	875	541	334	187	354	96	113	125	4.17	Very Patient	46	28	49	Air
Steven Souza	426	1717	919	798	281	638	250	317	231	4.03	Very Patient	102	45	78	Medium
Denard Span*	275	1006	585	421	196	389	41	157	223	3.66	Aggressive	112	53	57	Ground
Cory Spangenberg*	345	1290	677	613	195	482	135	238	239	3.74	Aggressive	109	54	53	Ground
George Springer	451	1790	974	816	244	730	255	277	284	3.97	Patient	128	69	85	Air
Giancarlo Stanton	318	1221	680	541	197	483	192	162	187	3.84	Neutral	65	38	84	Air
Chris Stewart	172	618	350	268	148	202	44	89	135	3.59	Very Aggressive	70	29	31	Ground
Drew Stubbs	140	596	354	242	135	219	92	85	65	4.26	Very Patient	23	8	31	Air
Eugenio Suarez	398	1581	861	720	320	541	172	264	284	3.97	Patient	114	58	107	Air
Jesus Sucre	142	525	302	223	103	199	29	79	115	3.70	Aggressive	50	17	38	Medium
Andrew Susac	148	583	323	260	99	224	78	92	90	3.94	Patient	42	17	31	Medium
Ichiro Suzuki*	438	1636	926	710	330	596	65	289	356	3.74	Aggressive	204	64	81	Ground
Kurt Suzuki	479	1749	951	798	323	628	100	314	384	3.65	Aggressive	162	73	142	Air
Blake Swihart#	309	1210	640	570	220	420	124	233	213	3.92	Patient	96	56	58	Ground
Nick Swisher#	260	1052	610	442	181	429	109	165	168	4.05	Very Patient	85	31	52	Ground
Chris Taylor	102	375	199	176	66	133	53	58	65	3.68	Aggressive	20	15	27	Air
Michael Taylor	511	1889	903	986	260	643	311	358	317	3.70	Aggressive	139	67	96	Ground
Mark Teixeira#	462	1815	1038	777	291	747	165	300	312	3.93	Patient	121	59	132	Air
Ruben Tejada	407	1549	769	780	204	565	159	327	294	3.81	Neutral	116	79	94	Medium
Trayce Thompson	135	555	318	237	96	222	59	82	96	4.11	Very Patient	37	28	31	Air
Yasmany Tomas	426	1472	635	837	185	450	224	316	297	3.46	Very Aggressive	163	65	69	Ground
Kelby Tomlinson	193	746	392	354	122	270	76	140	138	3.87	Neutral	77	38	23	Ground
Devon Travis	239	946	515	431	192	323	74	181	176	3.96	Patient	88	38	50	Ground
Mike Trout	682	2980	1864	1116	616	1248	233	461	422	4.37	Very Patient	157	103	162	Air
Mark Trumbo	545	2075	1007	1068	276	731	316	375	377	3.81	Neutral	157	68	152	Air
Preston Tucker*	323	1278	638	640	181	457	157	251	232	3.96	Patient	108	41	83	Medium
Troy Tulowitzki	534	2111	1163	948	389	774	203	369	376	3.95	Patient	154	83	139	Air
Justin Turner	439	1719	923	796	273	650	132	345	319	3.92	Patient	115	88	115	Air
Dan Uggla	141	563	324	239	96	228	66	92	81	3.99	Patient	33	14	33	Air
Justin Upton	620	2514	1400	1114	393	1007	340	385	388	4.05	Very Patient	150	67	171	Air
Melvin Upton Jr.	228	877	443	434	113	330	136	153	145	3.85	Neutral	58	34	48	Air
Juan Uribe	397	1529	741	788	161	580	176	331	281	3.85	Neutral	126	53	102	Medium
Giovanny Urshela	288	1077	459	618	130	329	123	285	210	3.74	Aggressive	87	51	71	Medium
Chase Utley*	423	1621	958	663	335	623	92	254	317	3.83	Neutral	137	63	114	Air
Luis Valbuena*	493	2056	1093	963	315	778	228	404	331	4.17	Very Patient	113	67	150	Air
Danny Valencia	378	1386	745	641	250	495	163	210	268	3.67	Aggressive	140	46	81	Ground
Scott Van Slyke	253	950	506	444	149	357	122	158	164	3.75	Aggressive	63	31	69	Air
Kennys Vargas#	184	723	385	338	120	265	103	114	121	3.93	Patient	62	31	28	Ground
Will Venable*	390	1540	848	692	282	566	162	273	257	3.95	Patient	151	45	54	Ground
Shane Victorino	204	774	461	313	189	272	55	107	151	3.79	Neutral	55	35	57	Air
Jonathan Villar#	128	501	264	237	82	182	56	92	89	3.91	Patient	50	17	20	Ground
Stephen Vogt*	511	2102	1236	866	425	811	154	356	356	4.11	Very Patient	134	78	144	Air
Joey Votto*	695	3020	1911	1109	535	1376	249	448	412	4.35	Very Patient	172	102	134	Medium
Neil Walker#	603	2336	1176	1160	347	829	217	502	441	3.87	Neutral	184	94	162	Air
Brett Wallace*	107	428	221	207	60	161	79	63	65	4.00	Patient	26	19	20	Medium
Jayson Werth	378	1571	976	595	383	593	137	205	253	4.16	Very Patient	87	55	111	Air
Matt Wieters#	282	1171	623	548	189	434	134	220	194	4.15	Very Patient	83	49	62	Medium
Bobby Wilson	147	570	299	271	103	196	67	108	96	3.88	Neutral	47	19	28	Ground
Kolten Wong*	613	2282	1133	1149	322	811	210	472	467	3.72	Aggressive	207	104	152	Medium
David Wright	174	686	383	303	113	270	63	124	116	3.94	Patient	42	29	45	Air
Christian Yelich*	525	2125	1206	919	365	841	191	353	375	4.05	Very Patient	233	84	56	Ground
Rafael Ynoa#	131	519	243	276	90	153	45	131	100	3.96	Patient	49	19	31	Ground
Chris Young	356	1418	769	649	238	531	136	263	250	3.98	Patient	88	43	116	Air
Delmon Young	180	605	242	363	50	192	88	129	146	3.36	Very Aggressive	63	35	48	Medium
Ryan Zimmerman	390	1546	909	637	335	574	132	228	277	3.96	Patient	134	46	97	Ground
Ben Zobrist#	535	2157	1364	793	484	880	94	283	416	4.03	Very Patient	203	77	134	Ground
Mike Zunino	386	1582	788	794	234	554	260	306	228	4.10	Very Patient	71	38	109	Air

For some players Swings and Misses, Fouls, and Balls in Play do not add up to overall Swings. This is because of the rare occasions when a swing results in a Catcher Interference.
Switch Hitter
* Bats Left

Pitcher Analysis

Ben Jedlovec

The Career Register section tells you the results of a pitcher's performance; meanwhile, this section provides a little more detail into how they arrived at those results. This data includes their number of batters faced and pitches thrown; strikes and balls thrown; groundballs, line drives, and flyballs allowed; percentage of strikes and swinging strike rate; and how often they worked themselves into certain counts.

A few notes you may find interesting:
- Pitching coaches will often recite the maxim, "The most important pitch is strike one." If so, Max Scherzer might be the best pitcher in baseball. He got ahead 0-1 on 537 of 899 batters faced this season, 30 more than any other pitcher in baseball (interestingly, Jose Quintana was second). As a rate, that 67 percent is also tops among starting pitchers.
- Zach Britton allowed 125 groundballs against just 15 flyballs on the entire season. Basically, the outfielders can take a nap during Orioles' ninth innings.
- Swinging strikes comprised an insane 37 percent of Carter Capps' strikes this year. (Aroldis Chapman is next best at a mere 31 percent.) Some general advice to hitters facing Capps: don't swing.
- The unheralded Evan Scribner went to a full count on 25 of the 238 batters he faced in 2015; however, only 4 batters managed to work a walk off him this year (and only two of those came in full counts). In fact, his 16-to-1 strikeout to walk ratio is the best we've seen (minimum 20 innings pitched) since Dennis Eckersley's 1990 season.

Pitcher Analysis
Pitchers with 50+ Batters Faced in 2015

Pitcher	BF	Pitches	K	BB	GB	LD	FB	Str%	S/Str	Counts 1-0	0-1	Full	2 Strike	3 Ball
David Aardsma	129	492	35	14	23	16	39	65%	24%	47	69	14	67	25
Fernando Abad	205	833	45	19	53	19	64	63%	18%	98	84	28	112	46
A.J. Achter	58	228	14	6	8	9	20	63%	21%	19	31	10	28	14
Austin Adams	149	528	23	13	52	19	40	66%	19%	44	81	19	67	23
Nate Adcock	83	338	13	12	28	11	17	54%	14%	43	32	13	35	25
Jeremy Affeldt	163	562	21	14	73	24	29	61%	10%	69	73	14	64	24
Matt Albers	149	566	28	9	65	15	31	64%	11%	62	73	12	75	24
Al Alburquerque	271	1077	58	33	85	42	49	62%	18%	116	135	34	145	60
Cody Allen	286	1139	99	25	52	41	65	64%	22%	116	150	33	171	52
Henderson Alvarez	102	334	9	7	47	19	16	62%	8%	42	46	10	32	16
Jose Alvarez	283	1015	59	23	99	37	58	66%	17%	88	162	20	139	39
R.J. Alvarez	100	394	23	13	16	13	34	59%	21%	43	48	18	51	28
Brett Anderson	750	2716	116	46	380	87	106	64%	13%	313	352	68	338	116
Chase Anderson	640	2462	111	40	198	111	162	64%	13%	244	313	94	324	119
Cody Anderson	365	1294	44	24	134	60	98	66%	13%	143	159	42	164	62
Matt Andriese	282	1088	49	18	102	35	73	64%	14%	116	139	34	135	54
Elvis Araujo	151	617	34	19	46	19	29	63%	19%	67	72	25	85	34
Chris Archer	868	3449	252	66	249	108	183	65%	20%	314	458	112	496	155
Jake Arrieta	870	3438	236	48	318	119	129	65%	18%	347	427	134	494	169
Alec Asher	138	501	16	10	39	20	49	61%	13%	56	59	17	49	28
Scott Atchison	87	338	12	4	29	16	24	67%	11%	29	47	11	47	13
Luis Avilan	220	822	49	15	72	31	47	65%	22%	81	104	27	116	42
Dylan Axelrod	59	236	12	8	12	5	21	58%	14%	31	24	9	28	17
John Axford	250	1070	62	32	87	26	42	59%	18%	122	102	44	136	70
Burke Badenhop	285	1048	36	20	106	44	77	62%	11%	116	140	29	115	54
Pedro Baez	208	831	60	11	50	25	58	67%	23%	70	115	21	119	31
Homer Bailey	51	171	3	4	22	7	13	61%	11%	19	23	4	17	10
Collin Balester	77	280	13	13	14	8	28	58%	18%	33	32	10	30	22
Manny Banuelos	121	470	19	12	35	21	31	61%	14%	46	62	22	63	30
Matt Barnes	199	790	39	15	54	30	55	65%	16%	83	92	26	106	36
Kyle Barraclough	98	464	30	18	16	13	21	59%	26%	51	46	21	69	28
Aaron Barrett	123	478	35	7	33	18	25	67%	21%	39	76	12	67	20
Anthony Bass	272	1049	45	20	98	47	57	62%	14%	99	137	38	128	56
Chris Bassitt	361	1420	64	30	113	54	87	62%	14%	164	161	48	182	73
Antonio Bastardo	239	1057	64	26	44	26	72	63%	24%	90	133	48	159	59
Trevor Bauer	744	2869	170	79	189	97	196	61%	16%	304	363	107	365	165
Cam Bedrosian	156	632	34	19	42	23	33	60%	12%	68	70	25	85	37
Joe Beimel	196	699	22	16	64	24	63	63%	12%	62	103	17	79	33
Matt Belisle	149	594	25	15	54	20	29	65%	14%	48	85	24	80	33
Andrew Bellatti	95	346	18	10	22	13	28	62%	21%	37	47	12	46	18
Joaquin Benoit	254	1038	63	23	75	28	59	63%	27%	118	116	41	147	58
Christian Bergman	286	1120	37	15	93	56	83	67%	11%	92	158	42	158	52
Dellin Betances	332	1370	131	40	74	32	49	62%	25%	134	174	57	219	80
Rafael Betancourt	175	699	40	12	27	32	62	67%	18%	63	95	21	97	30
Chad Bettis	502	1882	98	42	173	78	100	61%	17%	209	233	64	232	102
Chad Billingsley	165	576	15	8	62	32	43	64%	11%	59	80	19	62	29
Joe Blanton	309	1152	79	16	102	42	66	65%	20%	116	148	36	157	48
Michael Blazek	222	863	47	18	73	29	52	61%	18%	84	119	37	110	52
Mike Bolsinger	466	1779	98	45	164	55	90	63%	15%	210	211	58	231	92
Brad Boxberger	271	1140	74	32	58	34	68	65%	19%	120	133	33	159	55
Matt Boyd	252	1003	43	20	59	30	96	62%	14%	104	118	34	137	48
Blaine Boyer	268	934	33	19	101	51	60	66%	12%	99	128	21	111	39
Brad Brach	324	1307	89	38	84	37	69	62%	23%	135	154	51	181	80
Silvino Bracho	50	215	17	4	5	7	16	66%	24%	24	24	9	34	11
Archie Bradley	161	644	23	22	65	16	31	58%	11%	73	71	24	79	44
Craig Breslow	280	1029	46	23	72	36	97	63%	16%	126	114	33	128	55
Jake Brigham	84	308	12	8	26	24	13	63%	13%	33	37	12	38	21
Zach Britton	253	904	79	14	125	18	15	69%	24%	93	126	18	134	31
Mike Broadway	77	290	13	7	20	13	22	67%	22%	28	41	6	41	10
Aaron Brooks	250	885	38	14	82	42	65	64%	12%	93	121	32	110	43
Brooks Brown	147	574	20	16	53	23	29	58%	20%	67	61	24	66	38
Jonathan Broxton	257	997	63	22	86	32	45	66%	18%	103	119	32	138	43
David Buchanan	351	1230	44	29	127	65	76	64%	12%	134	158	30	136	57
Clay Buchholz	469	1716	107	23	160	70	101	67%	16%	165	250	50	239	68
Mark Buehrle	827	2829	91	33	311	145	221	66%	8%	316	399	71	330	111
Madison Bumgarner	869	3312	234	39	241	131	206	67%	19%	312	457	112	473	135
Daniel Burawa	54	218	11	5	20	7	10	61%	15%	20	25	10	29	16
Enrique Burgos	121	514	39	15	23	18	26	61%	26%	55	55	18	72	31

398

Pitcher Analysis
Pitchers with 50+ Batters Faced in 2015

Pitcher	BF	Pitches	K	BB	GB	LD	FB	Str%	S/Str	Counts 1-0	0-1	Full	2 Strike	3 Ball
A.J. Burnett	699	2500	143	49	261	110	118	64%	15%	272	331	71	329	121
Eddie Butler	370	1356	44	42	136	60	76	60%	12%	161	164	43	146	83
Trevor Cahill	187	679	36	16	82	25	23	61%	17%	77	82	20	85	36
Matt Cain	271	993	41	20	72	48	81	64%	14%	111	125	26	118	45
Arquimedes Caminero	318	1116	73	29	99	49	60	66%	20%	119	151	24	145	48
Carter Capps	118	445	58	7	20	10	19	69%	37%	41	68	11	75	17
Chris Capuano	196	745	38	22	56	31	43	63%	19%	70	102	27	98	42
David Carpenter	107	390	15	9	30	17	31	63%	19%	45	45	7	46	15
Carlos Carrasco	730	2777	216	43	234	87	136	68%	21%	240	407	68	400	100
Scott Carroll	162	601	27	13	70	19	29	64%	15%	58	85	21	76	33
Andrew Cashner	804	3109	165	66	261	125	165	65%	13%	309	406	112	407	163
Santiago Casilla	244	907	62	23	72	37	46	63%	17%	105	112	36	121	49
Miguel Castro	83	293	18	10	18	13	23	60%	19%	35	35	10	40	17
Brett Cecil	214	823	70	13	65	24	37	65%	24%	85	100	29	127	42
Xavier Cedeno	189	742	47	14	66	26	32	65%	23%	85	85	25	115	37
Jhoulys Chacin	111	426	21	10	37	15	26	61%	16%	50	48	17	51	23
Andrew Chafin	306	1176	58	30	121	39	47	61%	14%	141	129	40	146	69
Joba Chamberlain	128	537	23	9	39	25	29	61%	16%	53	64	32	73	36
Aroldis Chapman	278	1169	116	33	46	27	51	63%	31%	123	134	44	184	62
Jesse Chavez	672	2572	136	48	207	110	163	62%	15%	265	325	100	342	142
Wei-Yin Chen	792	3010	153	41	234	116	228	68%	14%	249	454	81	415	115
Randy Choate	117	406	22	5	50	13	18	64%	20%	41	60	10	50	16
Tony Cingrani	155	666	39	25	32	23	29	59%	21%	75	71	24	88	40
Steve Cishek	243	950	48	27	76	36	53	61%	16%	87	130	35	121	54
Alex Claudio	66	251	13	6	23	7	15	65%	17%	23	37	7	36	12
Tyler Clippard	301	1239	64	31	42	36	120	64%	19%	133	140	47	177	65
Phil Coke	56	238	12	5	23	7	9	65%	18%	23	28	7	31	12
Gerrit Cole	832	3238	202	44	272	127	168	65%	16%	317	430	112	433	147
Josh Collmenter	499	1925	63	24	139	103	161	64%	12%	207	241	62	228	85
Alex Colome	457	1702	88	31	132	81	116	63%	17%	174	237	43	216	74
Bartolo Colon	815	2706	136	24	268	132	234	70%	10%	272	418	52	360	79
Adam Conley	281	1102	59	21	80	37	80	66%	16%	117	131	37	153	52
Carlos Contreras	125	513	19	20	32	12	38	56%	20%	64	50	20	57	37
Ryan Cook	54	211	6	7	21	7	13	61%	11%	27	22	7	26	11
Tim Cooney	130	481	29	10	33	20	34	62%	15%	55	55	17	57	29
Scott Copeland	69	252	6	2	27	22	11	65%	10%	26	36	5	31	9
Patrick Corbin	357	1254	78	17	119	60	75	67%	17%	138	169	26	167	41
Erik Cordier	56	217	7	6	18	7	16	63%	12%	27	21	6	27	11
Kevin Correia	114	421	14	8	36	29	21	62%	11%	40	60	16	47	22
Jarred Cosart	296	1170	47	33	117	37	57	59%	14%	136	135	47	136	72
Neal Cotts	269	1072	58	22	67	37	76	62%	17%	120	121	30	147	53
Daniel Coulombe	72	265	11	9	29	11	12	61%	12%	32	28	8	33	16
Tyler Cravy	193	761	35	22	53	30	49	60%	13%	74	94	26	95	46
Kyle Crockett	74	281	15	7	27	12	11	66%	11%	25	43	8	37	10
Johnny Cueto	866	3268	176	46	265	136	222	66%	16%	316	427	123	430	146
Brandon Cunniff	151	610	37	22	38	19	30	57%	23%	58	73	29	80	45
John Danks	768	2918	124	56	217	120	231	65%	14%	289	389	86	384	126
Zachary Davies	139	539	24	15	57	21	21	62%	17%	55	68	15	68	28
Wade Davis	251	1050	78	20	58	31	62	64%	19%	99	127	47	160	60
Justin De Fratus	362	1445	68	32	110	51	89	61%	17%	163	160	57	178	84
Jorge de la Rosa	635	2459	134	65	219	87	115	62%	20%	263	303	82	314	132
Rubby de la Rosa	809	3014	150	63	284	105	190	64%	18%	344	361	87	392	144
Samuel Deduno	96	368	17	9	31	17	18	63%	15%	36	49	12	47	20
Jacob deGrom	751	2976	205	38	216	102	169	68%	19%	243	419	94	437	122
Steve Delabar	129	543	30	14	35	13	35	64%	21%	45	72	18	77	29
Randall Delgado	308	1281	73	33	81	34	79	61%	22%	116	163	59	175	81
Anthony DeSclafani	785	2913	151	55	251	118	187	65%	15%	291	409	74	378	121
Odrisamer Despaigne	547	2088	69	32	214	95	115	63%	9%	228	254	75	262	113
Ross Detwiler	288	1169	41	36	89	45	67	59%	13%	136	130	47	144	70
Jairo Diaz	78	277	18	6	30	9	14	65%	17%	33	32	12	36	17
Jumbo Diaz	255	1024	70	18	69	34	55	63%	23%	102	120	42	142	54
R.A. Dickey	884	3264	126	61	286	142	254	66%	14%	362	429	95	413	157
Jake Diekman	260	1097	69	31	88	24	44	62%	19%	107	136	38	156	58
Sean Doolittle	57	254	15	5	13	6	18	68%	15%	20	29	12	38	13
Felix Doubront	328	1268	56	26	112	45	81	61%	16%	164	140	45	153	73
Oliver Drake	72	298	17	9	22	7	17	63%	22%	32	34	11	44	15
Brian Duensing	209	779	24	21	81	30	47	61%	13%	84	96	25	91	37
Tyler Duffey	242	908	53	20	82	32	51	64%	16%	88	133	22	116	44
Danny Duffy	588	2360	102	53	162	103	152	64%	14%	253	283	74	326	112

Pitcher Analysis
Pitchers with 50+ Batters Faced in 2015

Pitcher	BF	Pitches	K	BB	GB	LD	FB	Str%	S/Str	1-0	0-1	Full	2 Strike	3 Ball
Zach Duke	255	1053	66	32	88	26	37	61%	18%	115	117	51	138	69
Ryan Dull	66	254	16	6	18	6	20	62%	18%	33	27	7	34	12
Mike Dunn	235	986	65	29	53	30	54	62%	20%	97	115	40	141	57
Sam Dyson	309	1106	71	21	143	35	30	65%	20%	123	143	33	150	50
Jon Edwards	75	315	22	16	7	5	25	57%	23%	35	34	8	41	24
Jerad Eickhoff	203	739	49	13	53	31	56	66%	16%	71	104	19	99	32
Roenis Elias	490	1842	97	44	148	65	122	63%	16%	196	240	69	240	100
Brian Ellington	105	445	18	13	28	12	32	61%	14%	48	52	12	56	22
Nathan Eovaldi	673	2638	121	49	259	108	129	65%	14%	272	337	81	347	118
Robbie Erlin	65	220	10	2	24	13	14	68%	13%	23	38	6	27	7
Marco Estrada	725	2913	131	55	170	82	276	64%	16%	307	339	101	389	140
Jeurys Familia	308	1173	86	19	116	40	43	67%	24%	119	159	37	174	53
Buck Farmer	186	697	24	17	62	20	55	62%	13%	75	94	26	80	37
Danny Farquhar	219	824	48	17	57	32	59	63%	17%	90	101	29	103	43
Scott Feldman	451	1771	61	27	174	84	98	63%	12%	178	227	59	219	90
Neftali Feliz	212	838	39	18	57	39	56	64%	16%	91	97	22	108	38
Jose Fernandez	265	992	79	14	67	48	52	68%	20%	103	137	29	152	39
Jeff Ferrell	50	184	6	4	16	8	16	63%	16%	21	25	7	19	11
Josh Fields	209	860	67	19	41	22	57	65%	21%	83	113	36	126	47
Casey Fien	257	985	41	8	75	42	88	67%	14%	84	145	27	134	37
Mike Fiers	761	3042	180	64	189	102	212	64%	16%	302	383	97	406	148
Brandon Finnegan	197	751	45	21	69	21	37	62%	16%	82	91	28	98	46
Doug Fister	449	1654	63	24	153	73	117	66%	8%	171	226	44	212	74
Yohan Flande	296	1068	43	25	131	34	55	62%	13%	121	139	37	117	66
Kendry Flores	57	201	9	4	15	12	16	66%	18%	22	28	2	31	8
Gavin Floyd	55	218	7	4	20	10	13	62%	13%	23	26	11	28	12
Mike Foltynewicz	399	1481	77	29	95	66	124	65%	15%	147	207	37	198	57
Jeff Francis	100	400	21	9	29	21	19	62%	15%	43	45	16	54	25
Jason Frasor	124	543	22	18	38	19	26	60%	14%	43	73	22	75	33
Sam Freeman	171	693	40	25	50	22	31	59%	18%	86	70	26	83	47
Carlos Frias	333	1181	43	26	141	56	59	64%	15%	131	155	44	145	63
Christian Friedrich	270	975	45	25	92	45	57	62%	18%	122	113	28	111	47
Ernesto Frieri	100	378	19	11	20	9	39	66%	14%	36	54	14	52	17
Charlie Furbush	82	301	17	5	27	9	20	64%	17%	30	41	10	44	13
Yovani Gallardo	793	3226	121	68	294	131	171	60%	11%	328	393	131	389	185
Frank Garces	173	677	30	22	45	25	47	61%	17%	75	73	28	86	42
Jaime Garcia	510	1857	97	30	230	62	84	66%	14%	211	236	50	243	74
Jason Garcia	132	493	22	17	40	19	32	59%	15%	61	60	19	61	31
Luis Garcia	304	1153	63	37	126	44	30	60%	21%	146	124	40	139	66
Yimi Garcia	225	842	68	10	41	25	78	69%	22%	82	117	18	127	28
Matt Garza	666	2393	104	57	218	107	159	65%	13%	257	303	68	292	119
Kevin Gausman	470	1876	103	29	149	57	127	64%	18%	212	210	65	262	91
Dillon Gee	183	616	25	11	73	28	42	70%	14%	60	93	15	78	25
Steve Geltz	269	1105	61	26	59	27	90	63%	16%	107	143	37	145	61
Gonzalez Germen	176	710	33	26	52	24	39	58%	23%	75	83	31	90	50
Kyle Gibson	821	3235	145	65	315	117	158	62%	16%	322	404	116	406	174
Ken Giles	298	1185	87	25	82	40	61	65%	23%	119	142	50	180	66
Sean Gilmartin	235	867	54	18	70	28	59	65%	19%	91	118	25	123	39
Mychal Givens	117	466	38	6	28	21	22	67%	19%	42	67	11	70	13
Zack Godley	150	574	34	17	43	21	30	62%	20%	61	71	15	68	31
Erik Goeddel	132	499	34	9	35	17	33	61%	22%	64	53	13	66	23
David Goforth	111	398	24	8	36	19	21	65%	20%	42	56	7	47	17
Brandon Gomes	245	946	44	15	63	28	87	65%	18%	91	128	34	128	45
Jeanmar Gomez	319	1173	50	17	120	54	72	63%	14%	121	151	40	137	54
Chi Chi Gonzalez	280	1048	30	32	103	43	66	61%	11%	115	136	33	113	57
Gio Gonzalez	758	2947	169	69	273	99	135	63%	16%	306	388	107	404	152
Miguel Gonzalez	622	2439	109	51	180	107	160	64%	14%	235	324	77	317	117
Severino Gonzalez	143	553	28	7	37	27	39	66%	17%	54	78	17	79	22
Tom Gorzelanny	181	674	36	23	46	24	47	58%	21%	73	88	29	81	48
Trevor Gott	202	728	27	16	87	25	40	62%	10%	89	86	21	90	33
Matt Grace	84	308	14	8	36	14	11	61%	10%	40	35	8	35	17
J.R. Graham	283	1071	53	21	99	41	62	64%	17%	119	131	32	145	51
Kendall Graveman	502	1898	77	38	189	81	108	62%	13%	204	237	64	234	97
Jonathan Gray	185	682	40	14	54	30	41	63%	17%	76	91	18	77	33
Sonny Gray	831	3078	169	59	314	99	183	64%	16%	337	402	84	407	135
Shane Greene	373	1336	50	27	123	65	93	66%	11%	142	179	31	169	52
Luke Gregerson	239	867	59	10	99	27	38	69%	23%	78	132	18	130	29
Kevin Gregg	51	213	14	5	11	8	12	64%	15%	16	27	10	29	13
Zack Greinke	843	3239	200	40	281	112	193	64%	20%	307	436	105	439	136

Pitcher Analysis
Pitchers with 50+ Batters Faced in 2015

Pitcher	BF	Pitches	K	BB	GB	LD	FB	Str%	S/Str	1-0	0-1	Full	2 Strike	3 Ball
Jason Grilli	140	591	45	10	23	22	40	68%	23%	54	73	19	91	30
Justin Grimm	204	870	67	26	49	27	33	59%	23%	82	108	42	123	57
Mayckol Guaipe	121	459	22	13	39	17	24	65%	17%	41	66	15	65	20
Deolis Guerra	74	307	17	3	19	14	18	64%	17%	36	30	11	43	14
Jeremy Guthrie	664	2475	84	44	177	133	205	64%	11%	244	337	83	297	117
Nick Hagadone	124	458	28	12	29	22	30	62%	18%	54	56	14	59	23
Jesse Hahn	406	1531	64	25	161	75	70	63%	13%	158	205	48	196	70
David Hale	346	1300	61	20	121	52	85	63%	19%	136	165	43	157	63
Cole Hamels	880	3343	215	62	278	122	183	66%	21%	344	439	112	475	166
Jason Hammel	710	2751	172	40	184	118	179	65%	18%	277	357	94	392	127
Brad Hand	408	1553	67	32	138	70	91	60%	14%	196	165	52	177	83
J.A. Happ	717	2839	151	45	212	124	174	64%	14%	288	346	101	377	136
Aaron Harang	748	2844	108	51	204	114	247	63%	12%	283	375	100	351	144
Blaine Hardy	265	968	55	22	71	44	67	65%	17%	85	140	26	123	41
Dan Haren	768	2906	132	38	176	116	283	64%	10%	279	379	100	365	130
Mitchell Harris	122	436	15	13	41	13	37	65%	13%	37	64	19	54	26
Will Harris	276	1127	68	22	93	35	54	62%	14%	111	138	44	156	57
Matt Harrison	69	271	5	6	23	12	22	58%	6%	29	33	12	29	18
Matt Harvey	755	2798	188	37	233	91	183	68%	18%	241	412	89	401	119
Chris Hatcher	166	652	45	13	44	18	40	65%	20%	65	79	21	89	30
LaTroy Hawkins	162	557	34	7	67	21	32	69%	13%	64	70	9	70	17
Andrew Heaney	438	1646	78	28	124	72	128	64%	14%	168	227	50	200	71
Jeremy Hellickson	636	2478	121	43	193	96	166	63%	17%	236	329	74	330	118
Heath Hembree	106	392	15	9	22	20	39	65%	15%	39	54	8	48	14
Kyle Hendricks	739	2793	167	43	261	111	137	65%	13%	272	380	91	370	128
Liam Hendriks	261	1034	71	11	82	40	55	69%	17%	81	148	29	160	34
David Hernandez	144	587	33	11	37	18	39	64%	17%	65	65	16	78	26
Felix Hernandez	826	3040	191	58	313	94	150	65%	17%	300	412	92	411	138
Roberto Hernandez	357	1317	42	26	148	55	82	63%	11%	131	180	33	155	64
Kelvin Herrera	286	1089	64	26	85	43	62	65%	21%	112	142	23	142	45
Keith Hessler	57	211	12	4	16	7	18	64%	15%	21	33	6	27	8
Chris Heston	746	2792	141	64	277	110	136	61%	15%	320	338	93	329	162
Rich Hill	106	434	36	5	30	10	22	69%	17%	41	61	9	67	13
Taylor Hill	51	198	9	4	19	10	8	59%	16%	27	19	7	28	8
Dalier Hinojosa	102	429	23	11	31	9	27	63%	16%	46	48	16	61	23
Luke Hochevar	214	871	49	16	55	25	68	66%	16%	79	114	35	117	46
Derek Holland	245	909	41	17	75	41	63	61%	12%	90	130	32	106	48
Greg Holland	193	717	49	26	56	25	33	64%	23%	71	103	21	100	37
David Holmberg	136	536	15	16	39	17	41	58%	9%	64	59	21	56	34
J.J. Hoover	264	1119	52	31	69	35	68	60%	18%	125	109	53	149	68
T.J. House	73	277	7	12	31	16	5	56%	9%	27	41	7	32	17
J.P. Howell	190	756	39	14	79	20	32	60%	18%	79	86	31	90	44
Daniel Hudson	290	1160	71	25	83	42	67	62%	22%	125	125	49	156	66
Tim Hudson	525	1854	64	37	231	87	94	65%	14%	194	266	46	225	78
Jared Hughes	284	966	36	19	137	38	40	66%	15%	112	120	23	121	36
Phil Hughes	651	2255	94	16	188	129	215	69%	8%	185	360	52	299	68
Tommy Hunter	249	881	47	14	83	38	64	68%	16%	85	126	26	116	39
Drew Hutchison	664	2511	129	44	188	114	173	65%	15%	235	344	83	325	126
Raisel Iglesias	395	1566	104	28	117	52	79	66%	19%	147	214	45	227	71
Hisashi Iwakuma	516	1868	111	21	191	70	118	68%	17%	165	294	40	260	58
Edwin Jackson	228	876	40	21	67	36	60	61%	18%	103	102	29	107	48
Kenley Jansen	200	795	80	8	38	12	58	72%	24%	61	125	21	134	25
Casey Janssen	166	604	27	8	37	31	58	65%	11%	52	92	15	79	27
Jeremy Jeffress	285	1066	67	22	110	45	34	62%	19%	126	132	25	143	50
Dan Jennings	244	939	46	24	110	27	32	61%	15%	104	112	31	117	50
Kevin Jepsen	285	1164	59	27	90	39	68	62%	17%	122	143	47	150	70
Cesar Jimenez	91	371	25	8	31	9	18	62%	18%	33	47	18	46	24
Ubaldo Jimenez	791	3060	168	68	262	118	154	62%	14%	311	393	121	391	173
Erik Johnson	151	637	30	17	24	24	53	61%	15%	67	76	23	80	38
Jim Johnson	291	1054	50	20	128	36	44	65%	13%	113	143	38	134	50
Nate Jones	72	281	27	6	17	5	15	65%	25%	30	37	6	42	11
Taylor Jordan	77	255	11	6	26	16	16	67%	14%	25	40	3	30	7
Taylor Jungmann	501	2045	107	47	155	69	111	62%	14%	214	246	79	279	120
Tommy Kahnle	155	654	39	28	46	20	18	59%	23%	76	69	35	86	52
Nate Karns	621	2440	145	56	171	88	149	63%	15%	263	294	85	336	128
Scott Kazmir	763	2941	155	59	225	104	196	65%	16%	296	376	105	402	138
Keone Kela	243	1031	68	18	79	32	45	65%	22%	103	128	35	159	51
Shawn Kelley	205	809	63	15	53	24	47	65%	23%	57	126	28	121	38
Casey Kelly	56	201	7	3	19	14	11	63%	10%	22	29	7	28	8

Pitcher Analysis
Pitchers with 50+ Batters Faced in 2015

Pitcher	BF	Pitches	K	BB	GB	LD	FB	Str%	S/Str	Counts				
										1-0	0-1	Full	2 Strike	3 Ball
Joe Kelly	587	2378	110	49	191	105	123	62%	13%	225	306	105	309	148
Ryan Kelly	74	259	10	6	26	7	24	64%	14%	32	35	8	32	12
Kyle Kendrick	629	2222	80	45	189	107	191	63%	11%	227	293	80	257	119
Ian Kennedy	713	2911	174	52	179	106	180	64%	17%	274	376	107	412	151
Logan Kensing	64	255	13	7	17	8	18	64%	16%	22	34	9	35	13
Clayton Kershaw	890	3392	301	42	262	114	148	68%	24%	288	489	80	516	118
Dallas Keuchel	911	3492	216	51	393	119	125	63%	17%	353	455	140	460	185
Craig Kimbrel	239	1008	87	22	59	25	44	63%	25%	93	127	36	149	49
Phil Klein	86	348	12	10	27	14	23	64%	11%	43	38	11	54	18
Corey Kluber	886	3273	245	45	242	124	205	68%	19%	320	443	83	478	119
Corey Knebel	209	831	58	17	65	26	41	66%	16%	88	101	20	122	36
Tom Koehler	800	2976	137	77	260	104	201	61%	12%	333	364	96	361	169
George Kontos	284	1053	44	12	96	50	79	66%	16%	119	136	25	135	37
Ian Krol	129	537	26	17	37	19	26	63%	14%	55	63	22	77	33
John Lackey	896	3127	175	53	297	133	215	68%	14%	259	484	79	426	107
John Lamb	220	912	58	19	52	30	56	63%	18%	91	114	32	125	47
Mat Latos	494	1804	100	32	154	85	112	66%	16%	191	242	52	226	76
Tommy Layne	207	798	45	27	70	28	30	58%	15%	95	94	32	96	53
Mike Leake	778	2754	119	49	309	129	159	66%	10%	303	371	80	345	122
Jack Leathersich	52	227	14	7	13	6	10	61%	20%	30	20	12	33	16
Sam LeCure	83	303	15	7	35	9	16	63%	16%	33	43	8	39	14
Arnold Leon	115	426	19	9	39	17	29	61%	15%	54	47	21	52	29
Dominic Leone	74	287	9	9	25	12	18	59%	18%	28	38	8	37	18
Jon Lester	828	3185	207	47	269	120	161	64%	17%	323	413	112	426	150
Colby Lewis	861	3180	142	42	222	145	291	65%	13%	320	434	98	410	148
Adam Liberatore	122	483	29	9	34	18	30	62%	18%	43	70	15	59	26
Tim Lincecum	333	1323	60	38	101	47	80	61%	18%	167	132	49	179	73
Francisco Liriano	773	2983	205	70	249	109	128	62%	24%	329	351	103	393	159
Radhames Liz	106	388	27	12	22	22	19	60%	19%	49	44	16	51	27
Kyle Lobstein	280	1009	32	23	116	44	62	61%	12%	122	127	28	109	51
Jeff Locke	736	2780	129	60	268	127	131	63%	15%	279	377	89	359	144
Adam Loewen	93	393	22	17	17	18	15	57%	21%	47	40	20	51	30
Boone Logan	168	658	44	17	42	19	37	63%	25%	65	84	26	95	38
Kyle Lohse	665	2544	108	43	192	116	190	64%	15%	240	355	73	340	116
Javier Lopez	147	545	26	16	70	15	19	61%	15%	59	69	24	66	36
Michael Lorenzen	515	1997	83	57	148	103	114	60%	15%	223	244	57	245	110
Aaron Loup	186	723	46	7	69	27	29	66%	15%	61	106	27	105	32
Mark Lowe	215	814	61	12	56	38	45	68%	21%	72	121	25	122	32
Jordan Lyles	212	767	30	19	77	40	38	60%	14%	88	98	23	80	41
Lance Lynn	751	3053	167	68	219	107	169	61%	15%	327	351	110	368	184
Tyler Lyons	255	959	60	15	68	43	62	67%	15%	101	130	24	143	35
Jean Machi	257	867	42	22	90	37	58	62%	15%	115	103	19	91	42
Ryan Madson	248	898	58	14	94	23	54	66%	21%	84	126	27	122	35
Seth Maness	270	968	46	13	114	39	51	67%	14%	89	141	20	122	32
Jeff Manship	144	550	33	10	50	22	28	64%	17%	55	71	17	71	27
Shaun Marcum	142	563	30	11	33	22	45	62%	18%	59	71	19	68	30
Sugar Marimon	117	418	14	14	32	17	38	61%	13%	55	56	12	44	24
Matt Marksberry	108	408	21	16	27	14	29	60%	16%	48	51	17	50	25
Jason Marquis	216	783	37	14	74	36	50	62%	16%	101	90	23	89	40
Evan Marshall	61	223	7	5	26	12	11	61%	21%	24	32	5	27	10
Chris Martin	99	391	18	6	39	20	15	63%	9%	35	54	17	50	20
Cody Martin	141	498	27	12	33	27	38	63%	12%	61	61	18	61	28
Rafael Martin	56	247	25	5	8	7	10	65%	28%	15	37	10	40	12
Carlos Martinez	755	2844	184	63	263	97	123	65%	17%	277	391	90	393	145
Nick Martinez	558	2119	77	46	178	101	142	62%	12%	220	283	73	264	106
Nick Masset	113	397	18	9	38	21	25	60%	14%	50	52	10	41	22
Justin Masterson	273	1010	49	27	96	34	55	60%	12%	119	119	36	115	60
Marcos Mateo	113	477	33	9	23	10	33	62%	16%	50	54	18	66	26
Ryan Mattheus	253	940	37	18	99	46	43	63%	14%	98	115	27	125	40
Brian Matusz	206	833	56	20	44	25	56	63%	21%	80	109	28	120	38
Steven Matz	149	576	34	10	46	21	34	66%	13%	57	68	20	86	26
Tyler Matzek	102	399	15	19	25	14	24	51%	14%	55	36	17	41	35
Brandon Maurer	206	790	39	15	71	33	45	62%	20%	81	102	28	103	40
Trevor May	492	1864	110	26	135	74	137	66%	16%	180	261	56	262	79
Vin Mazzaro	55	200	6	6	15	11	17	59%	14%	29	22	2	20	9
Cory Mazzoni	53	201	8	5	20	14	6	65%	9%	12	34	5	26	8
Zach McAllister	299	1222	84	23	81	39	67	65%	16%	128	151	40	172	58
Brandon McCarthy	94	367	29	4	23	13	24	69%	17%	32	54	9	55	14
Lance McCullers	520	2109	129	43	158	74	108	62%	16%	223	246	73	301	107

402

Pitcher Analysis
Pitchers with 50+ Batters Faced in 2015

Pitcher	BF	Pitches	K	BB	GB	LD	FB	Str%	S/Str	Counts 1-0	0-1	Full	2 Strike	3 Ball
T.J. McFarland	188	687	26	18	92	27	24	65%	12%	74	93	21	82	36
Jake McGee	147	620	48	8	35	14	41	68%	20%	56	83	18	90	27
Dustin McGowan	118	473	21	20	30	20	27	58%	20%	52	54	24	62	35
Collin McHugh	859	3241	171	53	279	123	213	65%	17%	326	448	100	417	148
Andrew McKirahan	129	462	22	10	46	26	20	67%	14%	54	58	10	58	20
Yoervis Medina	97	389	16	11	27	16	27	58%	15%	51	42	12	43	25
Kris Medlen	243	927	40	18	90	31	60	63%	14%	102	112	29	119	46
Mark Melancon	293	1088	62	14	122	42	48	68%	18%	110	144	38	149	46
Roman Mendez	58	234	10	8	8	10	21	58%	14%	31	23	6	29	14
Wade Miley	831	3194	147	64	296	126	185	61%	14%	322	411	118	400	183
Andrew Miller	246	966	100	20	58	22	40	67%	27%	84	141	33	159	49
Justin Miller	129	527	38	11	30	19	31	67%	20%	49	69	16	82	23
Shelby Miller	860	3247	171	73	283	108	202	66%	15%	336	429	106	443	158
Tommy Milone	543	2067	91	36	168	93	143	63%	13%	196	285	84	255	115
Bryan Mitchell	143	596	29	16	48	27	21	60%	15%	61	73	27	79	39
Frankie Montas	66	286	20	9	14	6	17	61%	22%	31	31	15	42	19
Mike Montgomery	395	1453	64	37	147	57	83	63%	15%	145	189	48	185	70
Matt Moore	278	1056	46	23	80	45	79	64%	15%	110	140	32	140	47
Franklin Morales	258	949	41	14	96	43	55	62%	12%	121	112	29	113	49
Adam Morgan	352	1246	49	17	85	56	137	65%	16%	118	179	34	156	54
Mike Morin	151	554	41	9	37	17	41	67%	24%	55	78	9	80	21
Bryan Morris	277	1006	47	26	118	35	42	65%	19%	100	139	33	123	50
Brandon Morrow	126	484	23	7	45	20	30	65%	17%	59	56	12	64	19
Charlie Morton	563	1995	96	41	232	86	87	65%	13%	209	271	54	258	90
Jon Moscot	50	185	6	5	16	6	17	63%	8%	19	23	8	25	10
Jason Motte	206	801	34	11	47	35	73	67%	11%	67	115	22	103	32
Edward Mujica	194	702	30	7	69	26	57	69%	17%	58	111	15	90	26
Chris Narveson	121	452	32	9	31	16	32	64%	18%	56	55	14	61	21
Jimmy Nelson	752	2791	148	65	263	104	153	64%	16%	294	375	76	357	124
Hector Neris	170	681	41	10	44	17	53	62%	23%	80	79	22	84	36
Angel Nesbitt	98	384	14	8	33	14	21	63%	15%	46	40	14	50	22
Pat Neshek	223	849	51	12	49	34	70	71%	15%	69	136	18	134	25
Juan Nicasio	260	1083	65	32	68	39	50	63%	18%	98	134	37	153	62
Justin Nicolino	301	1047	23	20	110	45	93	66%	8%	106	154	17	113	35
Jon Niese	770	2701	113	55	309	118	140	64%	10%	293	376	89	329	130
Hector Noesi	154	609	22	17	45	21	48	63%	18%	65	75	21	79	33
Aaron Nola	318	1117	68	19	107	45	73	65%	14%	115	158	28	145	48
Ricky Nolasco	173	665	35	14	50	34	39	62%	16%	84	74	22	87	36
Sean Nolin	134	499	15	12	44	17	43	60%	11%	55	63	19	52	28
Bud Norris	377	1463	71	31	116	61	90	63%	16%	159	195	52	193	74
Daniel Norris	251	1035	45	19	73	31	79	60%	16%	118	117	53	129	70
Ivan Nova	413	1529	63	33	150	59	97	63%	13%	184	184	43	175	69
Vidal Nuno	376	1452	81	22	111	44	108	67%	16%	131	203	40	204	51
Scott Oberg	259	1005	44	31	94	32	48	59%	15%	114	113	40	120	67
Brett Oberholtzer	171	655	27	17	61	22	42	64%	12%	67	83	20	81	32
Darren O'Day	257	1062	82	14	54	31	69	67%	23%	88	145	41	165	50
Jake Odorizzi	700	2755	150	46	183	108	199	65%	16%	278	338	97	372	129
Eric O'Flaherty	159	557	21	18	67	26	22	62%	17%	56	81	19	65	30
Alexi Ogando	277	1122	53	28	80	39	71	62%	19%	109	137	42	152	61
Ross Ohlendorf	85	387	19	7	21	14	24	61%	18%	39	40	19	51	26
Edgar Olmos	67	239	4	8	27	10	17	55%	5%	33	26	8	23	17
Tyler Olson	65	219	8	10	19	9	15	60%	12%	21	35	5	22	15
Ryan O'Rourke	97	395	24	15	23	8	26	61%	22%	43	47	17	60	25
Josh Osich	120	459	27	8	41	8	35	65%	27%	51	58	15	62	20
Sean O'Sullivan	328	1180	35	20	107	49	102	63%	10%	125	164	32	131	55
Roberto Osuna	271	1091	75	16	61	35	82	65%	23%	102	143	37	153	54
Dan Otero	204	727	28	6	81	39	47	68%	11%	56	116	15	93	20
Henry Owens	272	1058	50	24	66	31	93	62%	20%	123	116	35	133	53
Jonathan Papelbon	260	901	56	12	88	27	62	71%	19%	87	132	21	137	30
Bobby Parnell	112	408	13	17	44	19	17	57%	14%	48	49	18	40	28
Manny Parra	130	497	23	6	45	23	30	64%	17%	67	51	15	62	27
Spencer Patton	109	477	28	12	22	15	25	62%	19%	52	53	22	75	30
James Paxton	297	1111	56	29	101	36	72	60%	12%	139	131	40	129	62
Jake Peavy	448	1741	78	25	127	57	151	66%	13%	165	229	63	226	85
Mike Pelfrey	714	2663	86	45	286	127	148	63%	10%	299	330	89	321	130
Ariel Pena	120	499	27	14	28	15	32	59%	21%	59	57	19	62	32
Joel Peralta	121	482	24	8	30	18	41	67%	13%	49	61	15	62	21
Wily Peralta	478	1754	60	37	189	73	104	60%	12%	207	205	60	197	100
Martin Perez	339	1215	48	24	157	47	58	65%	13%	118	173	30	150	50

Pitcher Analysis
Pitchers with 50+ Batters Faced in 2015

Pitcher	BF	Pitches	K	BB	GB	LD	FB	Str%	S/Str	Counts 1-0	0-1	Full	2 Strike	3 Ball
Oliver Perez	183	732	51	15	39	26	44	67%	19%	62	106	26	112	40
Williams Perez	514	1870	73	51	191	76	108	62%	11%	223	233	66	212	113
Glen Perkins	238	834	54	10	58	37	77	70%	16%	86	118	19	118	29
Vinnie Pestano	60	246	13	8	9	7	22	61%	22%	30	27	11	32	18
Yusmeiro Petit	316	1113	59	15	78	51	110	67%	15%	119	140	33	162	43
Jake Petricka	220	790	33	18	107	29	28	64%	15%	77	117	23	97	41
David Phelps	482	1858	77	33	151	83	127	64%	8%	169	252	74	255	94
Branden Pinder	122	482	25	14	26	25	30	61%	20%	51	57	21	65	29
Michael Pineda	668	2548	156	21	231	105	143	68%	18%	245	363	72	362	87
Yohan Pino	82	279	13	3	23	14	27	70%	9%	26	43	5	34	6
Drew Pomeranz	357	1442	82	31	100	51	86	63%	18%	148	176	55	199	76
Rick Porcello	737	2744	149	38	243	116	173	65%	14%	290	365	84	347	117
Ryan Pressly	119	424	22	12	39	17	27	67%	14%	49	61	6	52	16
David Price	888	3388	225	47	243	139	219	69%	18%	294	486	99	493	127
Zach Putnam	212	844	64	24	50	24	40	62%	28%	87	103	30	122	51
Kevin Quackenbush	243	1044	58	20	71	34	58	64%	15%	98	134	43	148	59
Chad Qualls	202	733	46	9	85	22	35	67%	18%	70	100	16	102	25
Jose Quintana	862	3373	177	44	296	146	187	65%	15%	268	507	126	450	151
Erasmo Ramirez	666	2409	126	40	232	99	154	66%	17%	230	338	74	321	108
J.C. Ramirez	106	413	16	11	34	13	30	61%	16%	43	47	17	47	31
Jose Ramirez	52	215	5	10	14	5	15	54%	15%	20	25	9	27	17
Neil Ramirez	60	251	15	6	15	7	17	60%	20%	29	28	10	35	14
Noe Ramirez	61	249	13	7	16	7	16	63%	20%	21	39	4	33	13
A.J. Ramos	277	1087	87	26	69	26	64	63%	26%	112	139	40	160	59
Cesar Ramos	221	789	43	15	74	38	45	62%	15%	79	105	26	92	39
Anthony Ranaudo	73	293	11	8	15	12	24	62%	10%	31	31	12	42	19
Cory Rasmus	88	377	27	11	18	5	25	60%	24%	40	43	19	55	25
Rob Rasmussen	79	331	17	8	18	16	19	64%	16%	35	38	14	47	17
Robbie Ray	545	2257	119	49	154	79	123	63%	15%	212	270	96	302	139
Colin Rea	133	525	26	11	43	22	28	61%	10%	65	56	21	68	32
Todd Redmond	72	279	13	7	11	10	29	63%	17%	27	37	7	35	13
Addison Reed	241	954	51	19	72	30	65	64%	14%	104	108	28	124	45
Matt Reynolds	62	233	18	7	16	3	17	65%	26%	23	31	9	35	11
Clayton Richard	181	615	22	7	89	39	22	67%	10%	70	86	13	74	19
Garrett Richards	865	3250	176	76	327	102	167	64%	18%	345	427	110	439	161
C.J. Riefenhauser	62	253	7	7	19	5	23	64%	15%	18	36	10	34	11
Andre Rienzo	89	357	15	13	28	11	20	58%	13%	45	37	13	44	21
Felipe Rivero	189	761	43	11	60	28	44	68%	17%	71	104	18	105	28
Tanner Roark	467	1800	70	26	172	78	110	64%	12%	185	231	57	234	87
Ken Roberts	65	235	6	3	27	11	15	64%	11%	26	29	8	30	12
David Robertson	250	981	86	13	53	45	51	68%	21%	78	149	27	161	33
Hansel Robles	217	891	61	18	44	24	66	65%	20%	87	113	26	132	39
Fernando Rodney	277	1100	58	29	90	32	56	61%	17%	109	139	30	146	54
Carlos Rodon	607	2441	139	71	176	88	112	61%	17%	283	266	104	315	150
Eduardo Rodriguez	522	2009	98	37	161	88	125	64%	13%	224	245	66	257	94
Fernando Rodriguez	242	985	65	24	58	26	64	64%	21%	98	119	41	143	58
Francisco Rodriguez	216	828	62	11	65	33	42	68%	21%	79	120	22	121	30
Wandy Rodriguez	392	1594	72	36	114	70	94	62%	10%	137	208	62	206	92
Chaz Roe	177	702	38	17	61	23	33	63%	15%	69	93	23	97	34
Esmil Rogers	153	578	31	14	45	27	34	64%	17%	73	69	16	74	26
David Rollins	118	452	21	8	34	23	26	65%	18%	48	55	19	67	23
Enny Romero	140	598	31	13	44	20	30	63%	18%	68	63	26	86	38
Sergio Romo	230	881	71	10	65	34	46	68%	26%	70	140	22	144	32
Bruce Rondon	145	578	36	19	35	21	29	62%	20%	66	65	22	81	33
Hector Rondon	281	1079	69	15	100	39	52	66%	17%	104	146	31	153	41
Jorge Rondon	81	292	9	9	25	19	18	63%	14%	36	33	12	34	18
Trevor Rosenthal	287	1205	83	25	81	34	62	65%	19%	123	143	40	167	59
Joe Ross	314	1153	69	21	106	35	72	65%	19%	128	153	27	160	49
Robbie Ross	259	1006	53	20	89	44	46	64%	16%	99	131	30	138	52
Tyson Ross	823	3229	212	84	315	95	102	61%	21%	349	400	127	442	185
Zac Rosscup	118	520	29	13	26	18	29	61%	21%	50	54	29	72	36
Nick Rumbelow	68	280	15	5	21	9	18	59%	16%	33	29	11	37	16
Chris Rusin	594	2149	86	41	236	94	123	64%	14%	196	323	65	259	105
James Russell	148	557	20	9	46	31	38	64%	12%	57	68	21	65	30
Kyle Ryan	237	891	30	20	87	40	55	63%	12%	94	114	33	113	49
Marc Rzepczynski	158	575	41	14	66	20	12	61%	24%	60	72	19	74	34
CC Sabathia	726	2703	137	50	239	113	169	65%	14%	273	381	87	358	121
Fernando Salas	269	1035	74	12	60	37	74	68%	20%	91	148	24	153	36
Danny Salazar	757	3048	195	53	218	93	186	65%	19%	310	376	114	432	154

404

Pitcher Analysis
Pitchers with 50+ Batters Faced in 2015

Pitcher	BF	Pitches	K	BB	GB	LD	FB	Str%	S/Str	1-0	0-1	Full	2 Strike	3 Ball
Chris Sale	854	3323	274	42	222	115	184	68%	22%	277	485	104	507	137
Jeff Samardzija	910	3339	163	49	263	143	268	67%	15%	340	444	93	439	124
Keyvius Sampson	251	1044	42	26	70	40	69	60%	15%	113	116	42	131	63
Aaron Sanchez	380	1449	61	44	163	48	58	59%	12%	176	162	53	174	89
Anibal Sanchez	660	2532	138	49	185	97	181	63%	15%	231	346	90	320	126
Ervin Santana	457	1678	82	36	135	71	124	62%	16%	176	214	53	203	86
Hector Santiago	776	3162	162	71	158	87	283	63%	14%	330	363	118	416	166
Sergio Santos	73	252	18	7	20	14	14	63%	26%	22	41	5	34	12
Rob Scahill	142	535	24	16	61	19	19	62%	16%	54	70	17	62	31
Tanner Scheppers	176	688	32	23	48	23	48	61%	14%	79	81	21	87	36
Max Scherzer	899	3359	276	34	203	105	256	71%	23%	259	537	84	537	103
Andrew Schugel	51	191	5	5	25	7	9	64%	13%	17	31	7	27	10
Bo Schultz	173	635	31	14	62	22	43	64%	17%	66	81	18	88	29
Evan Scribner	238	921	64	4	65	38	62	72%	19%	72	148	25	148	28
Luis Severino	255	1025	56	22	89	34	52	64%	16%	95	134	34	137	50
Bryan Shaw	265	1044	54	19	87	45	58	65%	17%	102	136	49	153	64
James Shields	860	3336	216	81	244	113	187	61%	21%	341	425	128	429	196
Matt Shoemaker	569	2089	116	35	159	75	172	63%	15%	224	267	68	261	106
Chasen Shreve	251	1110	64	33	69	20	61	58%	20%	116	116	62	144	82
Kevin Siegrist	312	1282	90	34	56	37	87	62%	18%	116	171	46	180	81
Alfredo Simon	820	3059	117	68	267	133	212	62%	14%	363	365	103	354	164
Tony Sipp	216	853	62	15	52	23	59	66%	22%	77	116	26	122	36
Carson Smith	284	1068	92	22	103	27	29	64%	20%	116	145	26	160	47
Joe Smith	271	996	57	19	99	44	47	67%	12%	101	142	25	135	41
Josh Smith	161	662	30	21	40	29	36	61%	15%	67	79	20	90	37
Will Smith	264	1067	91	24	66	22	56	65%	24%	106	140	32	168	50
Drew Smyly	275	1136	77	20	64	33	77	66%	18%	109	143	35	165	50
Miguel Socolovich	125	492	27	10	41	15	30	64%	18%	41	70	19	76	28
Sammy Solis	94	365	17	4	32	15	24	65%	15%	44	41	8	48	13
Joakim Soria	272	1155	64	19	77	41	64	67%	15%	106	150	38	178	49
Tim Stauffer	100	385	14	9	40	14	21	61%	10%	41	47	16	49	23
Drew Storen	228	858	67	16	53	33	52	65%	20%	87	121	23	123	37
Dan Straily	76	291	14	8	22	11	20	63%	16%	39	28	9	33	16
Stephen Strasburg	523	2043	155	26	139	77	113	67%	17%	180	283	56	310	73
Huston Street	255	1027	57	20	60	35	79	62%	22%	113	122	30	132	48
Hunter Strickland	191	736	50	10	51	26	51	70%	22%	67	105	23	115	27
Marcus Stroman	103	373	18	6	50	14	14	67%	11%	35	55	11	52	16
Pedro Strop	270	1058	81	29	78	30	44	62%	27%	114	133	32	141	61
Eric Stults	196	754	31	13	56	31	62	65%	11%	66	107	25	100	30
Anthony Swarzak	61	198	13	4	19	14	11	70%	15%	16	34	6	28	10
Noah Syndergaard	603	2380	166	31	184	79	133	65%	20%	216	331	63	331	100
Masahiro Tanaka	609	2290	139	27	206	84	148	67%	17%	228	314	76	311	96
Junichi Tazawa	247	954	56	13	71	34	71	64%	19%	89	128	34	135	45
Julio Teheran	843	3275	171	73	228	138	208	63%	18%	363	397	119	435	174
Ryan Tepera	128	465	22	6	44	16	37	66%	15%	45	69	10	62	14
Joe Thatcher	100	411	26	12	27	13	20	62%	19%	42	47	18	55	27
Dale Thayer	158	617	25	15	44	24	48	62%	14%	69	75	20	79	31
Ian Thomas	98	407	23	11	29	15	18	63%	18%	37	53	16	59	24
Aaron Thompson	137	504	17	11	38	26	40	64%	17%	57	67	16	67	22
Tyler Thornburg	151	645	34	12	36	24	42	64%	15%	57	81	24	91	33
Matt Thornton	171	593	23	11	58	30	45	63%	14%	71	75	14	68	23
Chris Tillman	741	2943	120	64	236	115	192	63%	12%	310	355	101	363	152
Shawn Tolleson	298	1169	76	17	84	41	73	64%	17%	101	168	34	157	55
Josh Tomlin	251	949	57	8	69	30	85	68%	14%	84	134	29	134	34
Michael Tonkin	99	362	19	9	40	8	22	64%	11%	35	55	7	42	14
Alex Torres	154	640	35	26	44	16	31	57%	17%	77	65	24	78	46
Carlos Torres	243	921	48	18	85	40	51	65%	16%	94	116	28	127	44
Blake Treinen	280	1030	65	32	111	39	27	64%	18%	114	132	26	137	54
Nicholas Tropeano	161	651	38	10	42	23	44	64%	19%	58	84	26	91	37
Samuel Tuivailala	65	265	20	8	18	7	12	63%	19%	26	33	9	35	15
Koji Uehara	160	633	47	9	27	17	56	68%	29%	43	107	21	95	29
Jose Urena	274	997	28	25	103	43	68	61%	14%	115	126	27	111	49
Jason Vargas	183	687	27	12	58	27	57	62%	13%	65	94	27	85	35
Anthony Varvaro	51	199	8	6	17	10	9	60%	13%	19	27	6	25	11
Vincent Velasquez	231	976	58	21	47	33	70	64%	17%	89	117	38	127	53
Pat Venditte	119	489	23	12	27	13	42	63%	14%	45	61	23	63	30
Yordano Ventura	693	2651	156	58	244	96	127	62%	17%	280	338	89	341	140
Drew VerHagen	106	408	13	14	56	12	7	59%	11%	45	52	12	51	22
Justin Verlander	535	2150	113	32	132	76	174	65%	16%	192	291	85	291	110

Pitcher Analysis
Pitchers with 50+ Batters Faced in 2015

Pitcher	BF	Pitches	K	BB	GB	LD	FB	Str%	S/Str	Counts 1-0	0-1	Full	2 Strike	3 Ball
Logan Verrett	190	697	39	15	58	21	51	66%	18%	59	110	11	96	22
Carlos Villanueva	250	927	55	21	72	32	66	64%	20%	95	133	23	118	38
Pedro Villarreal	214	789	29	12	71	39	58	67%	13%	73	107	25	101	35
Nick Vincent	100	416	22	10	22	19	27	67%	16%	37	58	13	63	18
Arodys Vizcaino	139	556	37	13	30	24	32	64%	19%	59	66	19	80	28
Ryan Vogelsong	598	2311	108	58	188	81	152	62%	11%	237	293	86	288	129
Edinson Volquez	850	3298	155	72	279	128	200	64%	16%	352	420	103	438	164
Michael Wacha	762	2937	153	58	242	117	169	66%	16%	279	390	84	391	123
Tsuyoshi Wada	136	534	31	11	41	20	30	65%	11%	48	68	19	74	30
Tyler Wagner	67	247	5	7	27	9	17	60%	9%	26	31	8	24	17
Adam Wainwright	111	383	20	4	43	22	19	67%	13%	51	43	13	52	16
Taijuan Walker	706	2630	157	40	190	110	192	66%	16%	260	360	86	364	109
Adam Warren	534	2159	104	39	171	86	121	62%	14%	216	279	77	275	105
Tony Watson	293	1116	62	17	98	43	65	67%	18%	99	155	28	148	42
Jered Weaver	669	2448	90	33	179	99	242	64%	14%	263	343	80	310	111
Daniel Webb	150	536	22	22	53	23	29	59%	19%	65	62	18	59	37
Ryan Webb	204	671	31	12	93	33	31	67%	14%	69	103	15	85	26
Ryan Weber	109	407	19	6	52	14	15	62%	9%	49	47	17	53	20
Allen Webster	142	517	17	20	47	15	39	58%	18%	60	66	19	55	36
Chase Whitley	84	323	16	5	29	8	22	65%	17%	31	39	8	48	13
Tom Wilhelmsen	267	1067	60	29	72	35	64	61%	18%	125	118	49	143	63
Jerome Williams	553	1978	74	34	202	98	129	65%	14%	213	263	65	247	94
Alex Wilson	273	1014	38	11	111	33	76	68%	11%	105	138	27	128	33
C.J. Wilson	553	2117	110	46	165	84	134	61%	15%	225	275	81	264	122
Justin Wilson	244	1048	66	20	67	42	44	66%	19%	98	130	32	153	45
Tyler Wilson	149	520	13	11	64	22	37	63%	9%	63	66	16	60	25
Matt Wisler	478	1772	72	40	119	82	153	64%	13%	193	231	46	218	81
Asher Wojciechowski	79	311	16	7	11	17	27	61%	11%	37	33	11	41	18
Randy Wolf	161	624	28	15	52	31	34	62%	12%	74	65	19	72	32
Alex Wood	801	2909	139	59	286	133	159	64%	13%	300	391	97	365	154
Travis Wood	419	1718	118	39	89	59	110	63%	17%	160	225	63	227	95
Vance Worley	310	1143	49	21	108	49	77	64%	10%	130	142	41	145	63
Mike Wright	204	785	26	18	58	30	66	60%	13%	91	93	28	90	44
Steven Wright	310	1178	52	27	98	31	98	64%	15%	138	139	37	152	59
Kirby Yates	92	408	21	7	17	13	33	64%	16%	32	54	17	55	19
Chris Young	500	1986	83	43	92	60	209	62%	16%	213	244	68	257	110
Brad Ziegler	263	954	36	17	150	28	28	64%	14%	108	120	26	118	38
Jordan Zimmermann	831	3103	164	39	255	132	220	68%	13%	271	445	87	439	118
Tony Zych	76	274	24	3	23	6	17	68%	22%	19	46	10	37	13

Pitchers' Repertoires

Ben Jedlovec

This section includes a breakdown of how often every pitcher who appeared in a major league game in 2015 threw each type of pitch in his repertoire. This includes everything from Aroldis Chapman's fastball, which averaged 99.5 miles per hour this year, to Chris Denorfia's 55 mph "heater". Speaking of position players pitching, Alexei Ramirez's average fastball velocity of 88.8 mph topped 80 regular pitchers this season. Can you throw your changeup as often as your fastball and still be effective? Francisco Rodriguez thinks so, throwing his change on 43 percent of pitches to the tune of a 2.21 ERA and 38 saves.

If it was thrown in a game this season, it's in this section.

Player	Fastball Velocity	Fastball	Cutter	Curve	Slider	Change	Splitter	Other
Aardsma,David	91.5	68%	-	-	26%	-	6%	
Abad,Fernando	91.0	55%	20%	12%	-	13%	-	
Achter,A.J.	89.9	60%	-	-	20%	20%	-	
Adams,Austin	96.9	72%	-	-	20%	8%	-	
Adcock,Nate	93.8	76%	-	-	23%	1%	-	
Affeldt,Jeremy	90.5	66%	-	24%	-	-	10%	
Albers,Andrew	85.6	37%	-	26%	34%	3%	-	
Albers,Matt	89.7	71%	-	-	17%	12%	-	
Alburquerque,Al	93.1	44%	-	-	56%	-	-	
Alexander,Scott	92.8	76%	-	-	24%	-	-	
Allen,Cody	94.9	62%	-	37%	-	<1%	-	
Almonte,Miguel	96.5	57%	-	17%	-	26%	-	
Alvarez,Dario	91.2	64%	1%	-	34%	-	-	
Alvarez,Henderson	90.7	62%	-	2%	18%	19%	-	
Alvarez,Jose	90.9	52%	-	8%	23%	17%	-	
Alvarez,R.J.	94.0	65%	-	-	23%	12%	-	
Amarista,Alexi	80.0	100%	-	-	-	-	-	
Anderson,Brett	90.7	52%	-	12%	26%	10%	-	
Anderson,Chase	91.5	62%	<1%	14%	-	24%	-	
Anderson,Cody	92.2	58%	-	5%	15%	23%	-	
Andriese,Matt	91.3	58%	20%	13%	-	9%	-	
Araujo,Elvis	93.0	63%	-	-	34%	3%	-	
Archer,Chris	95.2	54%	-	-	39%	7%	-	
Armstrong,Shawn	93.5	75%	24%	<1%	-	-	-	
Aro,Jonathan	92.5	70%	-	-	12%	17%	-	
Arrieta,Jake	94.6	51%	29%	15%	-	5%	-	
Asher,Alec	91.4	61%	-	3%	25%	12%	-	
Atchison,Scott	90.1	34%	56%	10%	-	-	-	
Aumont,Phillippe	92.5	69%	-	29%	-	-	2%	
Avilan,Luis	93.5	63%	<1%	7%	-	30%	-	
Axelrod,Dylan	87.4	55%	-	9%	20%	16%	-	
Axford,John	96.1	68%	-	18%	14%	-	-	
Badenhop,Burke	88.6	59%	-	-	16%	26%	-	
Baez,Pedro	97.1	74%	-	-	16%	10%	-	
Bailey,Andrew	93.1	45%	40%	14%	-	-	-	
Bailey,Homer	91.1	54%	-	1%	26%	-	19%	
Baker,Scott	89.3	63%	-	-	32%	4%	-	
Balester,Collin	92.0	72%	-	21%	-	8%	-	
Balfour,Grant	89.4	57%	-	3%	31%	8%	-	
Banuelos,Manny	89.0	57%	-	12%	10%	22%	-	
Barnes,Matt	94.8	62%	-	23%	1%	15%	-	
Barraclough,Kyle	95.6	61%	-	-	38%	<1%	-	
Barrett,Aaron	94.1	60%	-	-	39%	<1%	-	
Barrios,Yhonathan	96.4	59%	-	-	4%	37%	-	
Bass,Anthony	92.6	60%	-	-	29%	12%	-	
Bassitt,Chris	93.1	56%	-	14%	22%	7%	-	
Bastardo,Antonio	92.8	75%	-	-	20%	5%	-	
Bauer,Trevor	92.8	56%	-	12%	21%	9%	-	Screwball 3%
Beachy,Brandon	89.1	63%	-	12%	17%	9%	-	
Beck,Chris	91.8	54%	-	3%	13%	30%	-	
Bedrosian,Cam	94.4	74%	-	-	25%	1%	-	
Beeler,Dallas	89.1	41%	41%	15%	-	-	3%	
Beimel,Joe	87.0	73%	-	4%	13%	10%	-	
Belisario,Ronald	91.6	88%	-	-	9%	-	3%	
Belisle,Matt	90.6	58%	-	9%	31%	2%	-	
Beliveau,Jeff	87.2	66%	22%	6%	-	6%	-	
Bellatti,Andrew	92.8	58%	-	-	22%	21%	-	

Player	Fastball Velocity	Fastball	Cutter	Curve	Slider	Change	Splitter	Other
Benoit,Joaquin	94.2	46%	-	-	20%	35%	-	
Bergman,Christian	89.6	48%	-	8%	20%	23%	-	
Betances,Dellin	97.0	49%	-	-	51%	-	-	
Betancourt,Rafael	90.7	71%	-	17%	-	12%	-	
Bettis,Chad	92.0	60%	9%	15%	-	16%	-	
Billingsley,Chad	90.7	59%	19%	12%	-	10%	-	
Blanton,Joe	90.8	49%	-	4%	32%	15%	-	
Blazek,Michael	92.9	46%	-	28%	26%	<1%	-	
Blevins,Jerry	89.8	56%	-	40%	-	4%	-	
Bochy,Brett	88.8	65%	21%	-	9%	5%	-	
Bolsinger,Mike	87.0	45%	-	35%	19%	<1%	-	
Boxberger,Brad	92.7	62%	-	4%	<1%	34%	-	
Boyd,Matt	91.1	57%	-	8%	17%	18%	-	
Boyer,Blaine	92.7	64%	-	9%	26%	<1%	-	
Brach,Brad	94.0	61%	-	-	12%	27%	-	
Bracho,Silvino	92.9	76%	-	-	20%	4%	-	
Bradley,Archie	92.2	73%	-	24%	-	3%	-	
Breslow,Craig	89.9	53%	18%	5%	-	25%	-	
Brigham,Jake	91.5	63%	-	4%	29%	4%	-	
Britton,Zach	95.9	90%	-	-	10%	-	-	
Broadway,Mike	95.1	64%	-	-	36%	<1%	-	
Brooks,Aaron	91.5	60%	-	5%	15%	21%	-	
Brothers,Rex	93.4	55%	-	-	43%	1%	-	
Brown,Brooks	93.3	56%	-	-	13%	31%	-	
Broxton,Jonathan	94.1	62%	-	2%	31%	5%	-	
Buchanan,David	89.6	45%	21%	14%	-	20%	-	
Buchanan,Jake	89.0	47%	-	15%	27%	11%	-	
Buchholz,Clay	92.0	44%	24%	15%	-	17%	-	
Buehrle,Mark	83.4	51%	16%	9%	-	25%	-	
Bumgarner,Madison	92.1	50%	-	17%	31%	2%	-	
Burawa,Daniel	94.5	71%	-	-	29%	-	-	
Burgos,Enrique	95.7	50%	-	-	50%	-	-	
Burnett,A.J.	90.9	64%	-	29%	-	7%	-	
Butler,Eddie	93.4	65%	-	6%	14%	15%	-	
Cabral,Cesar	90.0	67%	-	-	27%	7%	-	
Cahill,Trevor	91.5	55%	-	13%	17%	16%	-	
Cain,Matt	90.7	53%	-	11%	22%	14%	-	
Caminero,Arquimedes	97.9	66%	23%	-	-	-		11%
Campos,Leonel	95.1	64%	-	-	36%	-	-	
Capps,Carter	98.1	64%	-	-	36%	-	-	
Capuano,Chris	88.7	44%	-	5%	27%	24%	-	
Carlyle,Buddy	90.0	84%	12%	-	-	4%	-	
Carpenter,David	95.0	70%	-	-	29%	<1%	-	
Carpenter,David	88.8	58%	-	-	42%	-	-	
Carrasco,Carlos	94.5	56%	-	8%	22%	14%	-	
Carroll,Scott	89.9	61%	<1%	7%	14%	19%	-	
Cashner,Andrew	94.8	67%	-	3%	20%	10%	-	
Casilla,Santiago	93.3	59%	-	23%	15%	3%	-	
Castro,Angel	94.1	76%	-	-	18%	6%	-	
Castro,Miguel	96.4	61%	-	-	22%	17%	-	
Castro,Simon	91.4	55%	-	-	45%	<1%	-	
Cecil,Brett	92.3	38%	16%	40%	-	6%	-	
Cedeno,Xavier	89.6	8%	39%	17%	36%	-	-	
Chacin,Jhoulys	88.6	49%	15%	5%	23%	8%	-	
Chafin,Andrew	92.5	71%	-	-	28%	1%	-	
Chamberlain,Joba	93.9	47%	-	16%	35%	2%	-	
Chapman,Aroldis	99.5	76%	-	-	17%	8%	-	
Chapman,Kevin	91.8	58%	-	-	34%	9%	-	

Player	Fastball Velocity	Pitch Repertoire						
		Fastball	Cutter	Curve	Slider	Change	Splitter	Other
Chavez,Jesse	91.2	35%	36%	5%	6%	18%	-	
Chen,Bruce	83.9	44%	-	10%	33%	13%	-	
Chen,Wei-Yin	91.4	64%	-	8%	17%	10%	-	
Choate,Randy	83.7	62%	-	-	38%	-	-	
Cingrani,Tony	91.8	86%	-	-	12%	2%	-	
Cishek,Steve	90.8	57%	-	-	41%	1%	-	
Claudio,Alex	84.1	35%	26%	-	20%	19%	-	
Clippard,Tyler	91.5	46%	7%	1%	-	38%	8%	
Coke,Phil	93.0	62%	19%	-	14%	6%	-	
Cole,A.J.	90.5	68%	-	5%	8%	19%	-	
Cole,Gerrit	95.6	67%	-	8%	21%	4%	-	
Coleman,Louis	89.2	62%	-	-	38%	-	-	
Collmenter,Josh	84.8	67%	-	5%	-	28%	-	
Colome,Alex	94.1	55%	-	10%	23%	13%	-	
Colon,Bartolo	88.3	84%	<1%	-	9%	6%	-	
Conley,Adam	91.3	65%	-	-	15%	20%	-	
Contreras,Carlos	92.0	71%	-	17%	-	12%	-	
Cook,Ryan	93.8	68%	-	-	22%	10%	-	
Cooney,Tim	89.6	49%	-	20%	9%	23%	-	
Copeland,Scott	90.3	66%	-	6%	18%	10%	-	
Corbin,Patrick	92.4	65%	-	-	29%	6%	-	
Cordier,Erik	97.9	68%	-	-	32%	-	-	
Cornely,John	89.3	59%	-	-	41%	-	-	
Correia,Kevin	88.0	41%	27%	14%	-	17%	-	
Cosart,Jarred	94.2	76%	-	18%	-	6%	-	
Cotham,Caleb	92.6	42%	-	4%	54%	-	-	
Cotts,Neal	89.9	55%	34%	-	11%	-	-	
Coulombe,Daniel	89.6	43%	9%	19%	9%	20%	-	
Cravy,Tyler	90.8	54%	-	10%	15%	21%	-	
Crockett,Kyle	89.5	73%	-	-	23%	4%	-	
Cueto,Johnny	92.5	51%	21%	4%	8%	16%	-	
Cunniff,Brandon	93.2	64%	-	-	35%	2%	-	
Danks,John	89.4	44%	15%	12%	-	29%	-	
Davies,Kyle	90.0	68%	18%	8%	-	5%	-	
Davies,Zachary	88.8	63%	4%	8%	-	25%	-	
Davis,Ike	86.1	81%	-	-	19%	-	-	
Davis,Wade	95.9	52%	29%	19%	-	<1%	-	
De Fratus,Justin	91.5	58%	-	<1%	32%	10%	-	
de la Rosa,Jorge	91.4	32%	24%	6%	<1%	37%	-	
de la Rosa,Rubby	94.3	59%	-	<1%	21%	19%	-	
De Los Santos,Abel	94.2	58%	-	23%	13%	6%	-	
De Paula,Jose	90.5	48%	-	30%	-	21%	-	
Decker,Jaff	80.5	100%	-	-	-	-	-	
Deduno,Samuel	87.6	56%	-	37%	<1%	7%	-	
deGrom,Jacob	95.0	62%	-	10%	16%	13%	-	
Delabar,Steve	93.4	59%	-	-	11%	-	30%	
Delgado,Randall	92.9	54%	-	1%	24%	21%	-	
Denorfia,Chris	55.0	100%	-	-	-	-	-	
DeSclafani,Anthony	92.5	62%	-	7%	24%	7%	-	
Despaigne,Odrisamer	91.0	65%	8%	17%	<1%	10%	-	
Detwiler,Ross	91.8	77%	-	13%	-	10%	-	
Diaz,Jairo	97.2	60%	-	-	40%	-	-	
Diaz,Jumbo	97.3	73%	-	-	20%	-	7%	
Dickey,R.A.	81.5	11%	-	-	-	2%	-	Knuckleball 87%
Diekman,Jake	96.5	72%	-	-	24%	4%	-	
Dominguez,Jose	92.8	77%	-	-	21%	1%	-	
Doolittle,Sean	92.4	91%	-	-	4%	6%	-	
Doubront,Felix	90.8	56%	18%	13%	-	13%	-	

410

Player	Fastball Velocity	Fastball	Cutter	Curve	Slider	Change	Splitter	Other
Drabek,Kyle	90.7	31%	43%	14%	-	11%	-	
Drake,Oliver	90.6	42%	-	-	2%	-	56%	
Duensing,Brian	91.5	53%	-	8%	23%	16%	-	
Duffey,Tyler	90.2	58%	-	40%	-	2%	-	
Duffy,Danny	93.8	65%	-	<1%	23%	11%	-	
Duke,Zach	89.4	54%	16%	5%	16%	9%	-	
Dull,Ryan	90.9	54%	-	-	36%	9%	-	
Dunn,Mike	94.7	63%	-	<1%	37%	-	-	
Dyson,Sam	95.8	74%	-	-	11%	15%	-	
Edwards Jr.,Carl	93.5	64%	-	33%	-	3%	-	
Edwards,Jon	94.1	56%	-	6%	37%	-	-	
Eickhoff,Jerad	91.0	58%	-	19%	16%	7%	-	
Elias,Roenis	91.7	52%	-	22%	-	26%	-	
Ellington,Brian	96.9	77%	-	20%	-	2%	-	
Elmore,Jake	79.8	71%	-	12%	-	18%	-	
Eovaldi,Nathan	96.7	48%	-	9%	23%	20%	-	
Erlin,Robbie	90.1	63%	-	15%	-	22%	-	
Estrada,Marco	89.3	52%	8%	11%	-	28%	-	
Eveland,Dana	89.6	46%	-	-	50%	4%	-	
Familia,Jeurys	97.1	70%	-	-	22%	-	8%	
Farmer,Buck	92.5	61%	-	-	19%	21%	-	
Farquhar,Danny	92.9	30%	41%	16%	-	13%	-	
Faulkner,Andrew	93.4	67%	-	-	23%	-	10%	
Feldman,Scott	90.3	29%	43%	25%	-	-	3%	
Feliz,Michael	93.5	69%	-	-	26%	5%	-	
Feliz,Neftali	94.6	62%	-	-	27%	11%	-	
Fernandez,Jose	95.8	56%	-	4%	28%	13%	-	
Ferrell,Jeff	93.1	63%	-	11%	-	26%	-	
Fields,Josh	94.3	68%	-	15%	12%	5%	-	
Fien,Casey	92.6	55%	38%	-	7%	-	-	
Fiers,Mike	89.4	57%	9%	16%	2%	16%	-	
Finnegan,Brandon	92.7	72%	-	-	21%	7%	-	
Fister,Doug	86.2	70%	-	7%	11%	13%	-	
Flande,Yohan	90.8	54%	-	-	10%	36%	-	
Flores,Kendry	90.8	46%	20%	17%	7%	10%	-	
Floyd,Gavin	92.0	47%	33%	15%	-	4%	-	
Foltynewicz,Mike	95.0	71%	-	11%	15%	4%	-	
Francis,Jeff	86.0	42%	7%	21%	17%	14%	-	
Francoeur,Jeff	85.3	85%	-	-	13%	2%	-	
Franklin,Nick	81.4	100%	-	-	-	-	-	
Frasor,Jason	92.0	62%	-	-	20%	-	18%	
Freeman,Sam	93.8	56%	-	-	12%	32%	-	
Frias,Carlos	94.6	57%	29%	5%	-	9%	-	
Friedrich,Christian	91.1	49%	-	12%	39%	<1%	-	
Frieri,Ernesto	91.4	54%	-	-	32%	14%	-	
Fujikawa,Kyuji	89.6	58%	-	15%	-	-	27%	
Furbush,Charlie	91.3	54%	-	2%	43%	<1%	-	
Gallardo,Yovani	90.4	54%	-	12%	29%	5%	-	
Garces,Frank	90.8	56%	-	31%	-	13%	-	
Garcia,Jaime	90.2	60%	19%	6%	-	15%	-	
Garcia,Jason	93.3	65%	-	-	28%	8%	-	
Garcia,Leury	86.0	87%	-	-	13%	-	-	
Garcia,Luis	95.5	59%	-	-	41%	-	-	
Garcia,Yimi	93.4	68%	1%	-	29%	2%	-	
Garza,Matt	92.7	67%	-	14%	16%	3%	-	
Gausman,Kevin	95.3	70%	-	-	11%	4%	16%	
Gearrin,Cory	92.6	55%	-	-	43%	2%	-	
Gee,Dillon	89.4	54%	-	9%	19%	19%	-	

Player	Fastball Velocity	Pitch Repertoire						
		Fastball	Cutter	Curve	Slider	Change	Splitter	Other
Geltz,Steve	92.2	64%	-	-	21%	14%	-	
Germen,Gonzalez	94.1	57%	-	-	8%	35%	-	
Gibson,Kyle	91.8	58%	-	4%	19%	20%	-	
Giles,Ken	96.5	62%	-	-	38%	-	-	
Gilmartin,Sean	88.8	40%	-	7%	31%	21%	-	
Givens,Mychal	94.3	62%	-	-	30%	7%	-	
Godley,Zack	91.4	41%	40%	12%	-	8%	-	
Goeddel,Erik	93.0	56%	<1%	22%	-	-	22%	
Goforth,David	94.1	56%	-	<1%	43%	<1%	-	
Gomes,Brandon	91.0	40%	-	5%	32%	-	23%	
Gomes,Jonny	69.0	100%	-	-	-	-	-	
Gomez,Jeanmar	91.5	65%	2%	-	19%	14%	-	
Gonzales,Marco	89.4	64%	-	8%	-	29%	-	
Gonzalez,Chi Chi	91.4	66%	-	4%	21%	9%	-	
Gonzalez,Gio	92.0	66%	-	18%	-	16%	-	
Gonzalez,Miguel	91.1	58%	-	10%	15%	-	16%	
Gonzalez,Severino	88.9	67%	<1%	3%	14%	15%	-	
Goody,Nicholas	90.9	55%	-	-	44%	<1%	-	
Gorzelanny,Tom	90.8	58%	<1%	-	31%	10%	-	
Gott,Trevor	96.2	84%	-	14%	-	2%	-	
Grace,Matt	91.1	73%	-	-	21%	5%	-	
Graham,J.R.	94.7	67%	-	-	29%	4%	-	
Graveman,Kendall	90.7	55%	25%	-	8%	-	11%	
Gray,Jonathan	94.4	64%	-	-	19%	17%	-	
Gray,Sonny	92.9	60%	4%	14%	16%	6%	-	
Greene,Shane	91.7	49%	30%	<1%	10%	9%	-	
Greenwood,Nick	87.0	38%	-	-	13%	50%	-	
Gregerson,Luke	89.4	57%	-	-	41%	2%	-	
Gregg,Kevin	91.0	62%	11%	-	12%	-	14%	
Greinke,Zack	91.8	51%	-	9%	19%	21%	-	
Grilli,Jason	94.0	68%	-	-	32%	<1%	-	
Grimm,Justin	95.2	56%	-	37%	7%	-	-	
Guaipe,Mayckol	93.1	58%	-	<1%	38%	3%	-	
Guerra,Deolis	90.8	46%	-	15%	-	39%	-	
Guerra,Javy	92.1	75%	-	6%	17%	3%	-	
Guerra,Junior	94.1	48%	-	-	21%	-	31%	
Guilmet,Preston	87.6	57%	-	-	6%	-	37%	
Gurka,Jason	91.6	52%	-	29%	5%	14%	-	
Guthrie,Jeremy	91.7	52%	-	17%	14%	17%	-	
Hagadone,Nick	94.0	74%	17%	-	9%	-	-	
Hahn,Jesse	92.0	68%	-	17%	5%	10%	-	
Hale,David	90.4	63%	-	-	19%	18%	-	
Hall,Cody	92.8	59%	-	-	13%	-	29%	
Hamels,Cole	92.6	49%	15%	12%	-	24%	-	
Hammel,Jason	92.3	53%	-	7%	36%	4%	-	
Hand,Brad	92.1	69%	-	12%	8%	10%	-	
Hand,Donovan	87.3	44%	-	37%	2%	18%	-	
Happ,J.A.	91.9	67%	-	10%	14%	9%	-	
Harang,Aaron	89.5	60%	6%	4%	18%	11%	-	
Hardy,Blaine	88.3	41%	-	24%	18%	16%	-	
Haren,Dan	86.1	38%	41%	14%	-	-	7%	
Harris,Mitchell	94.7	54%	36%	4%	-	-	6%	
Harris,Will	91.8	80%	-	20%	-	<1%	-	
Harrison,Matt	86.5	67%	-	6%	9%	17%	-	
Harvey,Matt	95.9	61%	-	13%	14%	12%	-	
Hatcher,Chris	96.0	64%	4%	-	13%	18%	-	
Hatley,Marcus	89.3	29%	-	-	71%	-	-	
Hawkins,LaTroy	93.1	75%	-	<1%	16%	8%	-	

Player	Fastball Velocity	Pitch Repertoire						
		Fastball	Cutter	Curve	Slider	Change	Splitter	Other
Heaney,Andrew	91.4	63%	-	-	19%	18%	-	
Hellickson,Jeremy	90.1	57%	<1%	20%	-	22%	-	
Hembree,Heath	94.3	70%	-	2%	21%	7%	-	
Hendricks,Kyle	88.3	68%	5%	7%	-	20%	-	
Hendriks,Liam	94.9	66%	-	5%	26%	3%	-	
Hernandez,David	94.3	62%	-	36%	-	2%	-	
Hernandez,Felix	91.8	44%	-	22%	6%	28%	-	
Hernandez,Roberto	88.9	56%	-	-	15%	29%	-	
Herrera,Kelvin	98.1	76%	-	2%	4%	18%	-	
Hessler,Keith	92.9	73%	-	-	27%	-	-	
Heston,Chris	89.0	61%	-	14%	13%	12%	-	
Hill,Rich	90.2	50%	-	41%	1%	7%	-	
Hill,Taylor	90.9	65%	-	<1%	27%	8%	-	
Hinojosa,Dalier	93.1	64%	-	-	24%	13%	-	
Hochevar,Luke	94.5	41%	40%	19%	-	-	-	
Holland,Derek	92.9	59%	-	13%	18%	10%	-	
Holland,Greg	93.6	48%	-	5%	45%	-		2%
Holmberg,David	87.9	60%	-	9%	7%	24%	-	
Hoover,J.J.	93.4	69%	-	16%	12%	4%	-	
House,T.J.	88.5	58%	-	4%	19%	19%	-	
Houser,Adrian	94.5	83%	-	11%	-	6%	-	
Howell,J.P.	87.1	59%	-	35%	-	7%	-	
Hudson,Daniel	96.1	58%	-	-	15%	27%	-	
Hudson,Tim	88.1	55%	-	11%	24%	-		10%
Huff,David	91.9	66%	9%	2%	-	23%	-	
Hughes,Jared	93.1	82%	-	-	18%	<1%	-	
Hughes,Phil	90.7	59%	20%	16%	-	5%	-	
Hunter,Tommy	96.2	62%	13%	26%	-	-	-	
Hutchison,Drew	92.4	65%	-	-	23%	12%	-	
Hynes,Colt	88.9	56%	-	-	30%	14%	-	
Ibarra,Edgar	90.5	59%	-	-	15%	26%	-	
Iglesias,Raisel	91.7	58%	-	-	29%	13%	-	
Iwakuma,Hisashi	88.4	49%	<1%	7%	17%	-		25%
Jackson,Edwin	93.9	55%	1%	5%	35%	4%	-	
Jackson,Jay	94.6	68%	-	-	32%	-	-	
Jackson,Luke	96.1	67%	-	26%	-	6%	-	
Jaime,Juan	94.5	84%	-	-	-	16%	-	
Jansen,Kenley	92.5	90%	-	-	10%	-	-	
Janssen,Casey	88.5	43%	31%	15%	8%	3%	-	
Jeffress,Jeremy	95.4	78%	-	21%	-	2%	-	
Jenkins,Chad	89.2	76%	-	-	20%	4%	-	
Jennings,Dan	92.4	59%	-	-	41%	-	-	
Jepsen,Kevin	94.4	67%	-	23%	-	10%	-	
Jimenez,Cesar	89.0	65%	-	-	11%	24%	-	
Jimenez,Ubaldo	90.6	61%	-	5%	14%	3%	16%	
Johnson,Brian	87.5	41%	-	41%	16%	1%	-	
Johnson,Erik	91.4	73%	-	3%	16%	9%	-	
Johnson,Jim	94.3	74%	-	19%	-	7%	-	
Johnson,Steve	87.8	83%	-	6%	4%	7%	-	
Jones,Garrett	76.3	71%	-	12%	-	18%	-	
Jones,Nate	97.6	54%	-	<1%	44%	2%	-	
Jordan,Taylor	91.4	67%	-	-	22%	12%	-	
Jungmann,Taylor	92.0	68%	-	25%	-	7%	-	
Kahnle,Tommy	95.9	56%	-	-	3%	41%	-	
Karns,Nate	91.6	58%	-	29%	-	12%	-	
Kazmir,Scott	91.3	58%	12%	4%	8%	18%	-	
Kela,Keone	95.6	58%	-	32%	-	10%	-	
Kelley,Shawn	91.9	45%	-	-	55%	-	-	

Player	Fastball Velocity	Pitch Repertoire						
		Fastball	Cutter	Curve	Slider	Change	Splitter	Other
Kelly,Casey	90.8	62%	-	16%	12%	10%	-	
Kelly,Joe	95.4	66%	-	9%	14%	11%	-	
Kelly,Ryan	92.3	42%	47%	11%	-	-	-	
Kendrick,Kyle	89.0	46%	26%	8%	-	20%	-	
Kennedy,Ian	91.3	62%	8%	15%	-	15%	-	
Kensing,Logan	92.3	50%	-	-	46%	4%	-	
Kershaw,Clayton	93.6	54%	-	18%	28%	<1%	-	
Keuchel,Dallas	89.6	56%	10%	-	20%	14%	-	
Kimbrel,Craig	97.3	70%	-	30%	-	<1%	-	
Kintzler,Brandon	90.8	68%	-	-	17%	15%	-	
Klein,Phil	90.7	57%	-	-	34%	9%	-	
Kluber,Corey	92.8	52%	28%	16%	-	5%	-	
Knebel,Corey	94.9	68%	-	31%	-	<1%	-	
Knudson,Guido	93.4	62%	-	-	36%	3%	-	
Koehler,Tom	92.1	58%	-	23%	14%	5%	-	
Kohn,Michael	93.6	83%	-	-	18%	-	-	
Kontos,George	91.2	39%	33%	2%	24%	3%	-	
Krol,Ian	93.6	62%	23%	9%	-	7%	-	
Lackey,John	91.6	68%	-	8%	23%	2%	-	
Laffey,Aaron	86.2	34%	36%	5%	22%	4%	-	
LaFromboise,Bobby	88.2	45%	-	-	43%	12%	-	
Lamb,John	91.1	55%	20%	9%	-	16%	-	
LaRoche,Adam	82.3	67%	-	25%	-	8%	-	
Latos,Mat	91.5	62%	-	8%	15%	4%	11%	
Layne,Tommy	89.8	64%	21%	-	10%	5%	-	
Lazo,Raudel	90.0	50%	-	-	39%	11%	-	
Leake,Mike	90.9	44%	26%	13%	10%	7%	-	
Leathersich,Jack	91.2	85%	-	11%	-	4%	-	
LeCure,Sam	87.3	56%	-	19%	4%	21%	-	
Lee,C.C.	92.6	77%	-	-	23%	-	-	
Lee,Zach	89.6	41%	-	13%	26%	20%	-	
Leon,Arnold	91.7	59%	-	14%	17%	10%	-	
Leone,Dominic	93.3	58%	17%	-	23%	2%	-	
Lester,Jon	92.0	53%	27%	15%	-	5%	-	
Lewis,Colby	88.0	50%	-	8%	35%	7%	-	
Liberatore,Adam	93.8	78%	-	-	14%	8%	-	
Lincecum,Tim	87.2	48%	-	13%	15%	24%	-	
Lindgren,Jacob	89.4	62%	-	-	38%	-	-	
Liriano,Francisco	92.5	47%	-	-	33%	20%	-	
Liz,Radhames	94.7	69%	-	-	21%	11%	-	
Lobstein,Kyle	86.4	59%	19%	7%	-	15%	-	
Locke,Jeff	91.3	61%	-	16%	-	23%	-	
Loewen,Adam	91.6	61%	-	-	30%	8%	-	
Logan,Boone	92.6	48%	-	-	52%	-	-	
Lohse,Kyle	89.4	45%	-	7%	27%	21%	-	
Lopez,Javier	84.5	74%	19%	-	4%	3%	-	
Lopez,Jorge	93.5	72%	-	15%	-	13%	-	
Lorenzen,Michael	94.0	65%	<1%	11%	16%	7%	-	
Loup,Aaron	93.2	65%	-	-	14%	20%	-	
Lowe,Mark	95.5	50%	-	-	50%	-	-	
Luetge,Lucas	90.5	61%	-	18%	18%	3%	-	
Lyles,Jordan	92.1	62%	2%	8%	15%	13%	-	
Lynn,Lance	91.7	85%	-	5%	8%	2%	-	
Lyons,Tyler	90.1	52%	-	3%	32%	13%	-	
Machi,Jean	92.7	54%	-	-	10%	-	36%	
Madson,Ryan	94.2	51%	20%	-	-	30%	-	
Maness,Seth	89.5	66%	-	-	16%	18%	-	
Manship,Jeff	91.9	56%	-	3%	41%	<1%	-	

414

Player	Fastball Velocity	Fastball	Cutter	Curve	Slider	Change	Splitter	Other
Marcum,Shaun	85.2	42%	33%	8%	-	17%	-	
Marimon,Sugar	91.4	62%	-	20%	-	18%	-	
Mariot,Michael	92.6	70%	-	-	23%	7%	-	
Marksberry,Matt	92.5	66%	-	33%	-	1%	-	
Marquis,Jason	87.8	59%	-	-	21%	3%	18%	
Marshall,Evan	94.3	63%	-	19%	-	18%	-	
Martin,Chris	94.2	61%	24%	-	15%	-	-	
Martin,Cody	89.3	66%	-	14%	19%	<1%	-	
Martin,Rafael	89.2	70%	-	-	24%	6%	-	
Martinez,Carlos	95.3	57%	-	2%	24%	17%	-	
Martinez,Nick	89.8	61%	-	6%	22%	11%	-	
Masset,Nick	92.0	66%	9%	19%	-	-	6%	
Masterson,Justin	87.4	69%	-	-	31%	-	-	
Mateo,Marcos	94.2	47%	-	-	53%	<1%	-	
Mattheus,Ryan	92.9	77%	2%	-	14%	-	7%	
Matusz,Brian	90.7	56%	-	4%	26%	14%	-	
Matz,Steven	94.3	68%	-	20%	2%	10%	-	
Matzek,Tyler	91.6	34%	-	7%	40%	19%	-	
Maurer,Brandon	95.1	40%	43%	-	-	17%	-	
May,Trevor	92.9	60%	-	16%	5%	19%	-	
Mazzaro,Vin	92.4	62%	-	-	31%	7%	-	
Mazzoni,Cory	94.4	62%	-	-	31%	-	6%	
McAllister,Zach	95.3	74%	-	12%	12%	-	2%	
McCarthy,Brandon	93.4	63%	16%	22%	-	-	-	
McCullers,Lance	94.5	54%	-	36%	-	10%	-	
McFarland,T.J.	91.6	69%	-	-	19%	11%	-	
McGee,Jake	94.5	93%	-	7%	-	-	-	
McGough,Scott	93.5	66%	-	-	26%	8%	-	
McGowan,Dustin	93.6	67%	-	-	25%	9%	-	
McHugh,Collin	90.4	34%	-	24%	39%	4%	-	
McKirahan,Andrew	93.1	75%	-	-	25%	-	-	
Medina,Yoervis	92.8	64%	-	-	34%	2%	-	
Medlen,Kris	91.0	60%	-	21%	-	18%	-	
Mejia,Jenrry	-	-	62%	4%	28%	6%	-	
Melancon,Mark	91.5	8%	65%	27%	-	<1%	-	
Mendez,Roman	93.3	58%	-	-	24%	3%	15%	
Meyer,Alex	95.6	75%	-	25%	-	-	-	
Miley,Wade	90.8	57%	2%	8%	14%	19%	-	
Miller,Andrew	94.3	46%	-	-	54%	-	-	
Miller,Justin	94.2	59%	-	-	40%	<1%	-	
Miller,Shelby	94.0	67%	22%	10%	-	2%	-	
Mills,Brad	85.0	58%	1%	17%	-	24%	-	
Milone,Tommy	87.8	52%	10%	13%	-	25%	-	
Mitchell,Bryan	96.1	50%	20%	27%	-	3%	-	
Montas,Frankie	96.6	60%	-	-	39%	<1%	-	
Montero,Rafael	91.7	76%	-	-	16%	8%	-	
Montgomery,Mike	90.9	53%	14%	13%	-	20%	-	
Moore,Matt	92.0	59%	6%	23%	-	12%	-	
Moore,Tyler	84.0	80%	-	-	20%	-	-	
Morales,Franklin	92.8	61%	-	9%	30%	<1%	-	
Moreno,Diego	94.8	45%	-	-	24%	30%	-	
Morgan,Adam	89.0	57%	-	3%	22%	18%	-	
Morin,Mike	92.3	41%	-	-	20%	38%	-	
Morris,Akeel	92.6	68%	-	-	4%	28%	-	
Morris,Bryan	95.0	51%	36%	-	13%	-	-	
Morrow,Brandon	93.4	53%	9%	10%	16%	13%	-	
Morton,Charlie	92.0	68%	-	24%	-	9%	-	
Moscot,Jon	91.4	61%	-	11%	18%	9%	-	

Player	Fastball Velocity	Pitch Repertoire						
		Fastball	Cutter	Curve	Slider	Change	Splitter Other
Motte,Jason	95.0	84%	14%	-	2%	-	-
Moylan,Peter	90.3	73%	-	-	25%	1%	-
Mujica,Edward	90.4	50%	-	-	20%	-	31%
Murata,Toru	86.7	61%	-	9%	14%	-	16%
Murphy,David	78.3	95%	-	5%	-	-	-
Murray,Colton	93.6	58%	-	36%	7%	-	-
Narveson,Chris	89.1	44%	-	12%	21%	24%	-
Nathan,Joe	92.0	25%	-	-	75%	-	-
Nelson,Jimmy	93.5	60%	-	21%	17%	1%	-
Neris,Hector	93.2	58%	-	-	14%	-	28%
Nesbitt,Angel	94.3	52%	26%	-	7%	15%	-
Neshek,Pat	90.0	53%	-	-	39%	8%	-
Nicasio,Juan	95.1	74%	-	-	24%	2%	-
Nicolino,Justin	88.7	56%	18%	8%	-	18%	-
Niese,Jon	89.1	47%	22%	15%	3%	13%	-
Noesi,Hector	93.2	54%	-	3%	23%	20%	-
Nola,Aaron	90.5	64%	-	24%	-	12%	-
Nolasco,Ricky	90.3	53%	-	16%	26%	-	6%
Nolin,Sean	86.9	54%	5%	12%	11%	18%	-
Norris,Bud	93.8	63%	2%	-	30%	6%	-
Norris,Daniel	91.9	59%	-	10%	17%	15%	-
Nova,Ivan	93.0	65%	-	30%	-	5%	-
Nuno,Vidal	89.2	34%	5%	9%	34%	18%	-
O'Day,Darren	86.7	55%	-	-	44%	<1%	-
O'Flaherty,Eric	90.0	71%	-	-	28%	1%	-
O'Rourke,Ryan	90.6	46%	-	2%	44%	8%	-
O'Sullivan,Sean	89.6	58%	-	3%	22%	17%	-
Oberg,Scott	95.0	64%	-	12%	18%	6%	-
Oberholtzer,Brett	88.6	58%	14%	7%	-	20%	-
Odorizzi,Jake	91.3	51%	16%	3%	-	30%	-
Ogando,Alexi	94.5	64%	-	-	28%	8%	-
Ogando,Nefi	95.5	57%	-	-	42%	1%	-
Ohlendorf,Ross	93.8	60%	-	-	35%	6%	-
Olmos,Edgar	92.4	63%	-	14%	-	22%	-
Olson,Tyler	88.6	48%	-	42%	-	9%	-
Osich,Josh	95.7	47%	37%	-	-	16%	-
Osuna,Roberto	95.6	72%	-	-	14%	14%	-
Otero,Dan	89.7	76%	5%	2%	8%	10%	-
Ottavino,Adam	95.7	49%	12%	-	39%	-	-
Owens,Henry	89.2	60%	-	12%	5%	24%	-
Papelbon,Jonathan	91.4	68%	-	-	17%	-	15%
Parnell,Bobby	93.0	75%	-	25%	-	-	-
Parra,Manny	92.6	60%	-	-	34%	-	6%
Patton,Spencer	92.0	69%	-	-	26%	5%	-
Paxton,James	94.2	71%	4%	14%	-	11%	-
Pazos,James	93.8	83%	-	-	17%	-	-
Peacock,Brad	89.9	54%	-	12%	18%	16%	-
Peavy,Jake	90.2	48%	31%	9%	4%	8%	-
Pelfrey,Mike	93.3	73%	-	3%	9%	-	14%
Pena,Ariel	91.6	61%	-	-	34%	5%	-
Peralta,Joel	89.4	51%	-	19%	-	-	30%
Peralta,Wily	94.3	66%	-	-	28%	5%	-
Perez,Martin	91.8	57%	-	9%	12%	22%	-
Perez,Oliver	91.9	57%	-	-	43%	-	-
Perez,Williams	90.6	72%	-	12%	-	17%	-
Perkins,Glen	93.7	70%	-	-	30%	-	-
Pestano,Vinnie	89.8	80%	-	-	20%	-	-
Petit,Yusmeiro	88.5	50%	-	22%	17%	12%	-

Player	Fastball Velocity	Pitch Repertoire						
		Fastball	Cutter	Curve	Slider	Change	Splitter	Other
Petricka,Jake	94.1	74%	-	-	11%	15%	-	
Phelps,David	90.2	60%	18%	14%	-	8%	-	
Pimentel,Stolmy	92.0	68%	-	-	25%	-	7%	
Pinder,Branden	94.6	55%	-	12%	32%	-	-	
Pineda,Michael	92.8	54%	-	-	34%	11%	-	
Pino,Yohan	88.8	60%	-	4%	32%	4%	-	
Pomeranz,Drew	91.5	68%	-	31%	-	2%	-	
Porcello,Rick	91.0	66%	-	14%	10%	10%	-	
Pressly,Ryan	94.2	46%	-	24%	29%	<1%	-	
Price,David	94.2	53%	16%	8%	-	23%	-	
Putnam,Zach	90.5	15%	22%	-	-	-	63%	
Quackenbush,Kevin	90.7	74%	-	24%	-	-	2%	
Qualls,Chad	91.4	57%	-	-	42%	-	<1%	
Quintana,Jose	91.6	52%	7%	31%	-	10%	-	
Raburn,Ryan	81.9	100%	-	-	-	-	-	
Ramirez,Alexei	88.8	61%	-	-	36%	4%	-	
Ramirez,Erasmo	90.9	56%	-	5%	17%	23%	-	
Ramirez,J.C.	95.4	68%	-	-	26%	-	6%	
Ramirez,Jose	95.8	59%	-	-	19%	22%	-	
Ramirez,Neil	93.0	64%	-	10%	26%	<1%	-	
Ramirez,Noe	89.8	54%	-	-	21%	24%	-	
Ramos,A.J.	92.6	46%	3%	<1%	28%	23%	-	
Ramos,Cesar	89.8	47%	-	12%	36%	5%	-	
Ranaudo,Anthony	91.1	62%	-	19%	10%	8%	-	
Rasmus,Cory	91.8	43%	-	13%	13%	31%	-	
Rasmussen,Rob	93.2	56%	-	8%	32%	4%	-	
Ravin,Josh	97.1	80%	-	-	19%	<1%	-	
Ray,Robbie	93.3	72%	-	<1%	19%	9%	-	
Rea,Colin	91.2	59%	18%	19%	-	-	4%	
Rearick,Chris	89.8	57%	-	-	41%	2%	-	
Redmond,Todd	90.0	73%	-	-	24%	3%	-	
Reed,Addison	92.6	67%	-	-	32%	<1%	-	
Reed,Chris	91.1	71%	-	-	16%	14%	-	
Reyes,Jo-Jo	89.0	100%	-	-	-	-	-	
Reynolds,Matt	87.8	50%	-	-	33%	4%	13%	
Richard,Clayton	91.0	81%	4%	-	9%	6%	-	
Richards,Garrett	95.5	61%	-	6%	33%	<1%	-	
Riefenhauser,C.J.	88.9	37%	-	-	52%	11%	-	
Rienzo,Andre	90.4	46%	40%	12%	-	2%	-	
Rivero,Felipe	95.4	76%	-	-	19%	5%	-	
Roach,Donn	88.0	57%	-	25%	-	-	18%	
Roark,Tanner	92.8	67%	-	11%	15%	7%	-	
Roberts,Ken	88.5	64%	-	24%	-	-	12%	
Robertson,David	92.2	67%	-	31%	-	2%	-	
Robinson,Clint	80.5	67%	-	33%	-	-	-	
Robinson,Shane	80.7	93%	-	7%	-	-	-	
Robles,Hansel	95.7	72%	-	-	27%	<1%	-	
Rodney,Fernando	94.7	61%	-	-	<1%	38%	-	
Rodon,Carlos	93.4	60%	-	-	31%	9%	-	
Rodriguez,Eduardo	94.0	69%	-	-	12%	19%	-	
Rodriguez,Fernando	93.7	63%	18%	16%	-	3%	-	
Rodriguez,Francisco	89.6	45%	-	12%	-	43%	-	
Rodriguez,Paco	87.1	33%	30%	-	34%	4%	-	
Rodriguez,Wandy	88.4	61%	-	34%	-	5%	-	
Roe,Chaz	92.7	66%	-	-	33%	<1%	-	
Rogers,Esmil	93.3	57%	3%	19%	19%	<1%	<1%	
Rollins,David	92.4	60%	-	-	16%	24%	-	
Romero,Enny	96.1	68%	21%	-	11%	<1%	-	

Player	Fastball Velocity	Pitch Repertoire						
		Fastball	Cutter	Curve	Slider	Change	Splitter	Other
Romo,Sergio	87.5	37%	-	-	59%	4%	-	
Rondon,Bruce	97.7	60%	-	-	34%	6%	-	
Rondon,Hector	96.4	59%	3%	-	36%	3%	-	
Rondon,Jorge	95.2	63%	-	-	30%	7%	-	
Rosales,Adam	79.9	89%	-	-	-	11%	-	
Rosenthal,Trevor	97.6	74%	6%	3%	-	17%	-	
Rosin,Seth	92.8	56%	-	-	40%	4%	-	
Ross,David	71.3	100%	-	-	-	-	-	
Ross,Joe	93.4	57%	-	-	36%	7%	-	
Ross,Robbie	92.5	63%	-	20%	17%	-	-	
Ross,Tyson	92.8	52%	6%	-	42%	<1%	-	
Rosscup,Zac	92.9	60%	-	-	40%	-	-	
Rucinski,Drew	90.9	64%	-	-	14%	8%	14%	
Rumbelow,Nick	93.4	57%	-	12%	-	30%	-	
Rusin,Chris	89.5	45%	25%	3%	8%	19%	-	
Russell,James	90.0	58%	3%	11%	16%	13%	-	
Ryan,Brendan	79.4	86%	-	11%	-	4%	-	
Ryan,Kyle	88.1	57%	26%	-	7%	10%	-	
Rzepczynski,Marc	91.8	59%	-	-	39%	2%	-	
Sabathia,CC	90.1	56%	3%	-	22%	18%	-	
Sadler,Casey	90.7	70%	-	-	18%	12%	-	
Salas,Fernando	90.6	59%	-	-	26%	15%	-	
Salazar,Danny	94.8	69%	-	4%	6%	21%	-	
Sale,Chris	94.5	53%	-	-	20%	28%	-	
Samardzija,Jeff	94.2	40%	23%	-	25%	-	13%	
Sampson,Keyvius	92.1	62%	-	14%	13%	11%	-	
Sanchez,Aaron	94.9	79%	-	13%	3%	5%	-	
Sanchez,Anibal	91.9	51%	6%	8%	16%	18%	-	
Santana,Ervin	92.5	53%	-	-	34%	13%	-	
Santiago,Hector	90.3	61%	11%	5%	7%	17%	-	
Santos,Sergio	92.6	54%	-	-	38%	8%	-	
Scahill,Rob	93.6	60%	-	12%	26%	2%	-	
Scheppers,Tanner	94.8	66%	-	1%	29%	4%	-	
Scherzer,Max	94.2	59%	<1%	8%	19%	13%	-	
Schlitter,Brian	94.5	89%	-	-	11%	-	-	
Schugel,Andrew	91.7	58%	-	11%	-	31%	-	
Schultz,Bo	95.8	60%	26%	-	13%	<1%	-	
Scribner,Evan	91.1	49%	-	27%	24%	<1%	-	
Severino,Luis	95.3	52%	-	-	34%	14%	-	
Shaw,Bryan	-	-	79%	-	21%	-	<1%	
Shields,James	91.0	42%	19%	19%	-	21%	-	
Shoemaker,Matt	90.2	56%	-	8%	14%	-	22%	
Shreve,Chasen	91.4	51%	-	-	16%	-	32%	
Siegrist,Kevin	94.0	75%	-	-	7%	18%	-	
Simon,Alfredo	92.7	46%	11%	8%	-	-	35%	
Sipp,Tony	90.9	50%	-	-	26%	24%	-	
Smith,Carson	92.9	49%	-	-	45%	6%	-	
Smith,Chad	92.6	63%	-	-	38%	-	-	
Smith,Joe	88.3	70%	-	-	30%	<1%	-	
Smith,Josh	89.9	50%	-	15%	25%	11%	-	
Smith,Will	93.2	51%	-	9%	40%	-	-	
Smyly,Drew	90.3	55%	18%	24%	-	3%	-	
Socolovich,Miguel	90.3	40%	-	-	30%	30%	-	
Solis,Sammy	93.9	73%	-	16%	-	11%	-	
Soria,Joakim	92.2	71%	-	9%	11%	8%	-	
Soriano,Rafael	90.7	57%	-	19%	24%	-	-	
Soto,Giovanni	90.2	34%	34%	20%	9%	2%	-	
Stammen,Craig	91.6	39%	-	13%	48%	-	-	

Player	Fastball Velocity	Fastball	Cutter	Curve	Slider	Change	Splitter	Other
Stauffer,Tim	88.9	63%	15%	7%	-	16%	-	
Stites,Matt	93.9	63%	-	-	20%	17%	-	
Storen,Drew	94.0	54%	-	-	36%	11%	-	
Straily,Dan	89.3	47%	-	<1%	31%	21%	-	
Strasburg,Stephen	95.4	63%	-	22%	<1%	14%	-	
Street,Huston	88.5	41%	-	-	38%	22%	-	
Strickland,Hunter	96.9	71%	-	-	24%	5%	-	
Stroman,Marcus	92.0	49%	12%	11%	16%	12%	-	
Strop,Pedro	95.1	50%	-	-	49%	-	<1%	
Stults,Eric	87.3	51%	-	4%	26%	19%	-	
Sucre,Jesus	88.3	96%	-	4%	-	-	-	
Surkamp,Eric	87.8	55%	12%	27%	-	6%	-	
Suzuki,Ichiro	86.8	56%	-	33%	-	11%	-	
Swarzak,Anthony	92.2	72%	-	-	28%	-	-	
Syndergaard,Noah	97.1	62%	-	22%	2%	14%	<1%	
Tanaka,Masahiro	91.8	33%	11%	7%	21%	-	28%	
Tazawa,Junichi	93.6	62%	-	9%	9%	-	21%	
Teaford,Everett	89.4	38%	26%	23%	-	13%	-	
Teheran,Julio	91.2	62%	-	8%	23%	8%	-	
Tepera,Ryan	95.0	36%	40%	-	15%	9%	-	
Thatcher,Joe	84.5	84%	-	-	16%	-	-	
Thayer,Dale	91.9	74%	-	-	19%	6%	-	
Thielbar,Caleb	90.5	65%	-	4%	27%	4%	-	
Thomas,Ian	90.0	54%	-	11%	8%	27%	-	
Thompson,Aaron	89.8	44%	-	<1%	48%	7%	-	
Thornburg,Tyler	92.2	54%	-	17%	-	29%	-	
Thornton,Matt	93.6	72%	-	-	18%	10%	-	
Tillman,Chris	91.5	65%	8%	14%	-	13%	-	
Tolleson,Shawn	92.9	67%	<1%	-	13%	19%	-	
Tomlin,Josh	88.4	53%	27%	13%	-	7%	-	
Tonkin,Michael	94.3	73%	-	-	25%	2%	-	
Torres,Alex	91.8	60%	-	3%	9%	29%	-	
Torres,Carlos	92.5	30%	50%	19%	-	<1%	-	
Tracy,Matt	89.9	62%	-	8%	26%	5%	-	
Treinen,Blake	96.3	70%	-	-	30%	<1%	-	
Tropeano,Nicholas	91.2	55%	-	22%	-	21%	2%	
Tsao,Chin-hui	93.6	47%	-	2%	45%	7%	-	
Tuivailala,Samuel	96.4	61%	-	8%	31%	-	-	
Uehara,Koji	87.1	39%	<1%	-	-	-	60%	
Urena,Jose	93.8	62%	-	3%	18%	17%	-	
Valdez,Jose	96.0	63%	-	-	31%	6%	-	
Vargas,Jason	87.7	56%	-	15%	-	29%	-	
Varvaro,Anthony	91.1	58%	-	23%	-	19%	-	
Veal,Donnie	92.6	77%	-	13%	-	10%	-	
Velasquez,Vincent	94.6	69%	-	19%	5%	7%	-	
Venditte,Pat	84.6	44%	-	-	55%	1%	-	
Ventura,Yordano	96.3	58%	4%	24%	-	15%	-	
VerHagen,Drew	93.9	67%	-	27%	-	-	6%	
Verlander,Justin	92.8	59%	-	16%	17%	9%	-	
Verrett,Logan	90.4	56%	-	5%	24%	15%	-	
Villanueva,Carlos	88.3	42%	-	7%	37%	13%	-	
Villarreal,Pedro	92.4	54%	21%	-	21%	4%	-	
Vincent,Nick	89.6	39%	55%	<1%	-	6%	-	
Vizcaino,Arodys	97.7	68%	-	32%	-	<1%	-	
Vogelsong,Ryan	91.1	52%	19%	21%	-	9%	-	
Volquez,Edinson	93.7	51%	-	24%	-	25%	-	
Volstad,Chris	91.3	80%	-	20%	-	-	-	
Wacha,Michael	94.2	57%	13%	13%	-	17%	-	

Player	Fastball Velocity	Pitch Repertoire						
		Fastball	Cutter	Curve	Slider	Change	Splitter	Other
Wada, Tsuyoshi	88.4	62%	3%	7%	14%	14%	-	
Wagner, Tyler	89.7	44%	27%	-	11%	18%	-	
Wainwright, Adam	89.6	41%	31%	27%	-	2%	-	
Walden, Jordan	94.2	55%	-	-	27%	18%	-	
Walker, Taijuan	94.3	65%	9%	8%	-	18%	-	
Warren, Adam	92.5	45%	-	11%	29%	15%	-	
Watson, Tony	93.9	76%	-	-	5%	19%	-	
Weaver, Jered	83.3	47%	-	22%	12%	19%	-	
Webb, Daniel	94.5	67%	-	-	23%	11%	-	
Webb, Ryan	92.0	62%	-	-	22%	15%	-	
Weber, Ryan	89.6	61%	-	22%	-	17%	-	
Webster, Allen	91.5	63%	-	1%	15%	21%	-	
West, Matt	93.6	72%	-	19%	-	9%	-	
Whitley, Chase	89.1	42%	-	10%	25%	23%	-	
Wieland, Joe	90.7	63%	-	26%	-	12%	-	
Wilhelmsen, Tom	95.0	56%	24%	11%	-	10%	-	
Wilk, Adam	88.8	48%	3%	10%	-	40%	-	
Williams, Jerome	90.1	49%	27%	7%	-	17%	-	
Wilson, Alex	92.4	55%	36%	-	7%	2%	-	
Wilson, C.J.	90.3	52%	10%	10%	12%	15%	-	
Wilson, Josh	84.3	94%	-	6%	-	-	-	
Wilson, Justin	95.1	80%	14%	6%	-	-	-	
Wilson, Tyler	90.0	70%	-	1%	20%	9%	-	
Winkler, Daniel	89.4	48%	27%	-	18%	6%	-	
Wisler, Matt	93.3	62%	-	5%	23%	9%	-	
Wojciechowski, Asher	91.0	58%	10%	-	19%	13%	-	
Wolf, Randy	88.3	49%	-	15%	25%	11%	-	
Wood, Alex	89.1	62%	-	22%	-	16%	-	
Wood, Travis	90.2	60%	24%	4%	6%	6%	-	
Wooten, Rob	87.9	42%	37%	-	15%	-	5%	
Worley, Vance	88.9	67%	30%	3%	-	<1%	-	
Wright, Mike	93.2	69%	-	2%	18%	11%	-	
Wright, Steven	83.5	10%	-	-	-	-	-	Knuckleball 90%
Wright, Wesley	88.1	56%	-	29%	4%	11%	-	
Yates, Kirby	92.4	56%	-	17%	18%	9%	-	
Young, Chris	86.6	58%	-	<1%	39%	2%	-	
Ziegler, Brad	83.9	67%	-	-	11%	22%	-	
Zimmermann, Jordan	93.0	62%	-	15%	22%	<1%	-	
Zito, Barry	83.7	58%	-	20%	-	22%	-	
Zych, Tony	96.1	53%	-	-	45%	2%	-	

420

Average Fastball Velocity

Ben Jedlovec

Scanning this section, you will find one general principle to be true: pitchers tend to lose velocity over time. There are three times as many pitchers throwing at least one mph slower than they were in 2010 as there are pitchers who have gained at least one mph. Pitchers' arms wear down with age, or they may pitch through discomfort to keep their job. Jered Weaver lost the most velocity in 2015, dropping 3 mph from last year alone and 7 mph from his peak. Unfortunately, this most recent velocity dropoff came with a dramatic decline in performance. Weaver did miss over a month of the season with an injury, but his velocity sank even further upon his return.

Sometimes, pitchers develop better command or instincts over time and don't need to throw as hard as they used to. Bartolo Colon is the perfect example. While he hasn't matched his Cy Young-caliber prime, he has prolonged his career by at least five seasons foregoing velocity in favor of sharp command of his fastball.

There are exceptions to the rule, of course. A pitcher gets healthy, improves his conditioning, or moves to the bullpen and picks up some velocity. Zach McAllister gained the most velocity in 2015, transitioning from a less impressive starting pitcher to a much more dominant reliever thanks in part to a velocity jump of more than 2 mph.

This section contains the average fastball velocity by year, as tracked by Baseball Info Solutions, for each pitcher who has thrown at least 50 innings in at least three of the last four seasons.

Average Fastball Velocity by Age

Player	Age	08	09	10	11	12	13	14	15
Teheran, Julio	25				93	92	92	90	91
Lyles, Jordan	25				89	91	92	91	92
McGee, Jake	25			94	95	96	96	96	95
Alvarez, Henderson	26				93	93	93	94	91
Eovaldi, Nathan	26				94	94	96	96	97
Delgado, Randall	26				92	92	92	93	93
Herrera, Kelvin	26				96	99	98	98	98
Bumgarner, Madison	26		89	91	92	91	91	92	92
Moore, Matt	27				96	94	92	91	92
Sale, Chris	27			96	95	92	93	94	94
Reed, Addison	27				95	95	93	92	93
Porcello, Rick	27		91	91	90	92	91	90	91
Pomeranz, Drew	27				90	91	91	91	91
Strasburg, Stephen	27			97	96	96	95	95	95
Kimbrel, Craig	28			95	96	97	97	97	97
Richards, Garrett	28				95	95	96	96	95
Tillman, Chris	28		92	90	89	91	91	90	91
Kershaw, Clayton	28	94	94	93	93	93	93	93	94
Cahill, Trevor	28		90	90	89	89	89	90	92
Chapman, Aroldis	28			100	98	98	98	100	99
Gomez, Jeanmar	28			91	90	90	91	91	91
Chacin, Jhoulys	28		91	91	91	90	90	88	88
Britton, Zach	28				92	92	92	95	96
Brothers, Rex	28				95	95	93	93	93
Santiago, Hector	28				94	93	91	90	90
Latos, Mat	28		94	94	93	93	93	91	91
McAllister, Zach	28				91	92	91	93	95
Locke, Jeff	28				90	91	90	90	91
Leake, Mike	28			89	89	89	90	90	91
Shaw, Bryan	28				93	93	93	93	92
Doubront, Felix	28			91	93	92	90	89	90
Jansen, Kenley	28			94	93	92	92	94	93
Worley, Vance	28			91	90	89	88	87	
Storen, Drew	28			94	95	95	94	93	94
Cook, Ryan	29				95	95	95	94	94
Lynn, Lance	29				93	93	92	92	92
Ross, Tyson	29			93	92	92	94	93	93
Hellickson, Jeremy	29			91	91	91	90	90	90
Milone, Tommy	29				87	87	87	86	88
Matusz, Brian	29		92	90	88	91	91	91	91
Wood, Travis	29			89	89	88	88	87	89
Nova, Ivan	29			93	93	93	92	93	
Miley, Wade	29				90	91	91	91	91
Niese, Jon	29	89	89	88	90	89	89	88	89
Holland, Derek	29		93	92	94	93	94	92	93
Cashner, Andrew	29			96	95	98	95	94	95
Nicasio, Juan	29				94	94	93	92	93
Garcia, Jaime	29	89		89	89	88	87	89	89
Hunter, Tommy	29	91	89	90	90	91	95	96	95
Cecil, Brett	29		91	90	88	89	91	92	92
Hughes, Phil	30	91	93	92	91	92	92	91	92
Cishek, Steve	30			93	93	92	92	92	91
Tazawa, Junichi	30		90		92	94	94	94	94
Zimmermann, Jordan	30		93	92	93	94	94	94	93
Bailey, Homer	30	91	94	93	92	92	94	94	91
Gee, Dillon	30			89	89	90	89	89	89
Brach, Brad	30				93	92	92	93	94
Kluber, Corey	30				92	91	92	92	91
Hernandez, Felix	30	95	94	94	93	92	92	92	92
Arrieta, Jake	30			93	92	93	94	92	93
Detwiler, Ross	30		91	90	92	93	92	93	92
Gallardo, Yovani	30	90	92	93	93	92	91	91	90
Cueto, Johnny	30	93	93	93	93	92	91	92	91
Collmenter, Josh	30				87	87	88	86	85
Webb, Ryan	30		95	95	94	94	92	92	92
Morales, Franklin	30	91	93	94	95	94	93	91	93
Russell, James	30			89	88	89	89	89	90
Holland, Greg	30			96	95	96	96	96	94
Medlen, Kris	30		90	90	91	90	89		91
Bastardo, Antonio	30		92	94	93	92	92	92	93
Gonzalez, Gio	30	90	92	92	92	93	93	92	92
Swarzak, Anthony	30		90		91	92	92	92	92
Davis, Wade	30		92	92	91	94	91	95	95
Price, David	30	94	93	95	95	94	92	92	93
Hughes, Jared	30				93	92	92	92	93
Fiers, Mike	31			88	87	88	89	89	
Strop, Pedro	31		95	95	94	97	96	95	95
Salas, Fernando	31			91	91	92	90	91	91
Watson, Tony	31				91	94	94	94	94
Dunn, Mike	31		93	95	94	94	94	95	95
Danks, John	31	90	89	90	90	89	88	87	89
Robertson, David	31	91	92	92	93	92	92	92	92
Melancon, Mark	31		93	93	93	93	92	92	91
Masterson, Justin	31	89	92	91	93	92	92	89	87
Norris, Bud	31		94	94	93	92	92	93	94
Clippard, Tyler	31	89	90	92	93	92	91	92	90
Samardzija, Jeff	31	95	94	94	94	95	94	94	94
Kennedy, Ian	31	89	92	89	90	89	90	91	91
Tomlin, Josh	31			88	87	88	89	88	87
Cain, Matt	31	92	93	92	91	91	91	92	91
Kendrick, Kyle	31	90	91	89	89	89	89	89	88
Buchholz, Clay	31	93	94	94	92	91	90	90	91
Scherzer, Max	31	94	94	93	93	94	93	93	94
Ramos, Cesar	32		91	92	92	92	91	90	90
Broxton, Jonathan	32	96	98	95	94	95	93	93	94
Lincecum, Tim	32	94	92	91	92	90	90	90	87
Gregerson, Luke	32		91	91	90	89	88	88	89
Mujica, Edward	32	92	93	92	92	92	92	91	90
LeCure, Sam	32			89	90	90	89	87	87
Kelley, Shawn	32		93	93	91	92	92	92	92
Smith, Joe	32	89	90	91	90	89	90	89	88
Stammen, Craig	32		89	90	91	92	92	92	92
Sanchez, Anibal	32	90	91	91	92	92	93	92	92
Fister, Doug	32		88	88	90	89	89	88	86
Jimenez, Ubaldo	32	95	96	96	93	92	92	91	91
Lester, Jon	32	91	92	92	91	92	92	90	91
Hamels, Cole	32	90	90	91	91	90	91	91	92
Wilhelmsen, Tom	32			95	96	96	94	93	
Villanueva, Carlos	32	89	89	90	89	89	88	88	88
Garza, Matt	32	93	93	93	94	94	93	93	93
Morton, Charlie	32	91	91	93	91	90	93	91	92
Liriano, Francisco	32	91	92	94	92	93	93	93	92
Greinke, Zack	32	93	94	93	93	92	90	92	92
Ogando, Alexi	32			96	95	97	93	94	95
Hochevar, Luke	32	90	92	93	92	92	94		92
Jackson, Edwin	32	94	95	94	94	93	93	93	94
Blevins, Jerry	32	91	90	89	88	87	88	90	90
Chavez, Jesse	32	94	94	95	93	92	91	90	91
Street, Huston	32	90	92	91	90	89	89	89	89
Sipp, Tony	32		92	92	91	91	90	92	91
McCarthy, Brandon	32	89	89		90	90	90	93	93
Estrada, Marco	32	90	90	91	91	90	89	89	89
Volquez, Edinson	32	94	94	94	94	94	92	93	94
Deduno, Samuel	32		90	89	91	90	89	88	
Johnson, Jim	33	94	94	94	95	94	94	94	94
Axford, John	33		94	95	96	96	95	95	96
Romo, Sergio	33	89	90	89	89	88	87	88	87
Perkins, Glen	33	91	90	92	94	95	95	93	94
Duensing, Brian	33		91	91	91	92	92	91	91
Verlander, Justin	33	94	96	95	95	94	93	92	93
Badenhop, Burke	33	89	88	89	89	89	89	89	89
Feldman, Scott	33	90	91	90	91	91	89	88	89
Vargas, Jason	33		88	87	86	87	88	87	88
Nolasco, Ricky	33	91	91	91	91	90	90	90	90
Santana, Ervin	33	94	92	92	93	92	92	92	92
ODay, Darren'	33	87	85	86	84	85	86	87	87
Happ, J.A.	33	87	88	90	90	90	91	93	92
Weaver, Jered	33	90	89	90	89	88	86	86	83
Hammel, Jason	33	92	92	93	93	94	93	92	92
Rodriguez, Francisco	34	92	93	91	90	92	91	91	90
Shields, James	34	89	89	90	90	91	90	90	89
Williams, Jerome	34			90	91	92	90	89	

		Average FB Velocity							
Player	Age	08	09	10	11	12	13	14	15
Peavy, Jake	35	91	91	90	90	90	90	89	89
Simon, Alfredo	35	93	92	95	94	94	93	93	92
de la Rosa, Jorge	35	93	93	93	93	90	91	91	90
Thayer, Dale	35		93	93	93	94	93	92	92
Blanton, Joe	35	89	90	89	88	90	89		91
Papelbon, Jonathan	35	95	95	95	95	94	92	91	91
Wilson, C.J.	35	93	93	90	90	91	91	90	90
Haren, Dan	35	91	89	89	87	87	87	86	85
Hernandez, Roberto	35	93	93	93	93	91	92	90	89
Correia, Kevin	35	89	91	90	90	90	89	89	87
Breslow, Craig	35	89	90	89	90	89	89	88	89
Casilla, Santiago	35	94	95	97	94	94	93	94	93
Sabathia, CC	35	94	94	93	94	92	91	89	90
Belisle, Matt	36	91	92	92	92	91	91	91	91
Soriano, Rafael	36	93	93	92	92	92	91	91	91
Stults, Eric	36	89	89		91	87	87	88	87
Ziegler, Brad	36	85	85	84	85	86	86	85	84
Lewis, Colby	36			90	89	88		89	88
Young, Chris	37	87	86	85	85	85		85	87
Guthrie, Jeremy	37	93	92	93	93	93	92	92	92
Buehrle, Mark	37	85	85	85	85	85	83	83	82
Rodriguez, Wandy	37	89	90	90	89	89	89	88	88
Lohse, Kyle	37	91	90	90	89	90	90	89	89
Capuano, Chris	37			87	88	88	89	89	89
Qualls, Chad	37	93	93	92	93	93	94	93	91
Harang, Aaron	38	90	90	90	90	90	90	89	89
Balfour, Grant	38	95	93	93	93	93	93	92	89
Benoit, Joaquin	38	92		94	94	94	94	95	94
Vogelsong, Ryan	38				91	90	88	90	90
Rodney, Fernando	39	95	96	96	96	96	96	95	95
Burnett, A.J.	39	94	94	93	93	92	93	92	91
Grilli, Jason	39	92	92		92	94	93	93	94
Peralta, Joel	40	91	92	91	91	90	90	90	89
Hudson, Tim	40	90	89	91	90	89	90	89	88
Nathan, Joe	41	94	94			92	94	92	92
Dickey, R.A.	41	85	85	84	84	83	82	82	81
Colon, Bartolo	43	92	89		92	90	90	89	88

Pinch Hitting

Joe Rosales

Once a controversial mid-first round draft pick back in 2008, Brett Wallace has played for four different organizations and has struggled to establish himself as a big-leaguer. However, one positive thing that we can now definitely say about him is that he was the most productive pinch hitter of the 2015 season. Of all the players who had at least 20 at-bats as a pinch hitter in 2015, only two had an on-base plus slugging (OPS) of 1.000 or better. One of those players was Gerardo Parra, who had exactly 20 pinch hit at-bats which led to 10 hits, 2 doubles, 1 triple, and 3 RBI. Yet that pales in comparison to Wallace's line as a pinch hitter. With 43 pinch hit at-bats, Wallace had 15 hits, 3 doubles, 4 home runs, and 12 RBI. That was good for a .349/.440/.698 line (AVG/OBP/SLG), and those home run and RBI totals were the most of anyone in baseball.

Alex Guerrero of the Los Angeles Dodgers is another player who exhibited a lot of power as a pinch hitter in 2015. He hit 3 home runs and 3 doubles in his 51 pinch hit at-bats. In fact, the Dodgers had multiple pinch hitters perform well, as Andre Ethier batted .333/.385/.500 in his 24 pinch hit at-bats. That level of productivity is actually consistent with what Ethier has accomplished in the past as a pinch hitter, with a career line of .288/.404/.432.

The following pages contain a record of the pinch hit performances of all active major league baseball players. For a player's seasonal totals to be included, he needed at least 10 plate appearances or 10 total bases as a pinch hitter in 2015. For his career totals to be included, he needs at least 100 career plate appearances as a pinch hitter.

Pinch Hitting
Pinch Hitters with 10+ PAs or 10+ Total Bases in 2015

Batter	B	AB	H	2B	3B	HR	RBI	TBB	IBB	SO	GDP	Avg	OBP	Slg	OPS
Dustin Ackley	L	15	5	2	0	0	1	3	0	1	0	.333	.421	.467	.888
Cristhian Adames	B	11	4	0	0	0	0	0	0	3	0	.364	.364	.364	.727
Matt Adams	L	16	6	0	0	1	3	0	0	3	0	.375	.375	.563	.938
Ehire Adrianza	B	11	3	2	0	0	1	0	0	3	0	.273	.333	.455	.788
Abraham Almonte	B	16	5	3	0	0	1	1	0	5	1	.313	.353	.500	.853
Pedro Alvarez	L	21	7	0	0	0	5	3	0	6	0	.333	.417	.333	.750
Alexi Amarista	L	22	5	0	0	0	1	0	0	4	0	.227	.227	.227	.455
Joaquin Arias	R	20	3	1	0	0	1	0	0	7	0	.150	.150	.200	.350
Cody Asche	L	12	3	0	0	2	3	1	1	5	0	.250	.308	.750	1.058
Mike Aviles	R	9	0	0	0	0	0	0	0	0	1	.000	.000	.000	.000
Jeff Baker	R	19	2	0	0	0	1	4	0	9	0	.105	.261	.105	.366
Clint Barmes	R	22	4	1	0	0	2	2	0	6	0	.182	.250	.227	.477
Brandon Barnes	R	13	2	0	0	0	2	0	0	5	0	.154	.154	.154	.308
Mike Baxter	L	21	4	0	0	0	0	2	0	7	2	.190	.261	.190	.451
Gordon Beckham	R	15	3	0	0	0	1	1	0	6	0	.200	.235	.200	.435
Tim Beckham	R	16	4	0	1	2	4	0	0	5	0	.250	.250	.750	1.000
Andres Blanco	B	36	10	5	0	2	6	5	0	10	3	.278	.366	.583	.949
Gregor Blanco	L	25	8	1	1	0	4	1	0	6	0	.320	.333	.440	.773
Brennan Boesch	L	24	4	0	0	0	2	2	0	8	0	.167	.259	.167	.426
Emilio Bonifacio	B	18	4	0	0	0	0	1	0	6	1	.222	.300	.222	.522
Justin Bour	L	20	6	1	0	1	2	3	0	5	0	.300	.391	.500	.891
Jason Bourgeois	R	22	6	0	0	1	3	1	0	1	0	.273	.304	.409	.713
Peter Bourjos	R	25	2	0	0	1	2	1	0	10	1	.080	.172	.200	.372
Michael Bourn	L	13	1	0	0	0	0	1	0	3	0	.077	.143	.077	.220
Reid Brignac	L	9	0	0	0	0	0	3	0	5	0	.000	.250	.000	.250
Domonic Brown	L	14	1	0	0	0	0	0	0	8	0	.071	.071	.071	.143
Joey Butler	R	23	2	0	0	0	1	1	0	11	4	.087	.125	.087	.212
Alberto Callaspo	B	31	7	0	0	1	5	3	1	4	3	.226	.294	.323	.617
Eric Campbell	R	13	4	1	0	0	4	3	0	3	2	.308	.438	.385	.822
Mark Canha	R	11	0	0	0	0	1	0	0	6	0	.000	.000	.000	.000
Chris Carter	R	12	2	1	0	0	0	2	0	8	0	.167	.286	.250	.536
Welington Castillo	R	20	4	0	0	1	3	1	0	6	0	.200	.238	.350	.588
Starlin Castro	R	13	4	0	0	0	0	0	0	1	0	.308	.357	.308	.665
Darrell Ceciliani	L	17	3	1	0	0	1	1	0	9	0	.176	.263	.235	.498
Lonnie Chisenhall	L	15	3	1	0	0	2	1	0	6	0	.200	.250	.267	.517
Pedro Ciriaco	R	43	11	3	1	0	5	0	0	12	1	.256	.267	.372	.639
Chris Coghlan	L	26	6	0	1	1	2	0	0	8	3	.231	.231	.423	.654
Chris Colabello	R	12	3	0	0	0	1	1	0	4	1	.250	.308	.250	.558
Hank Conger	B	10	3	0	0	0	0	0	0	2	0	.300	.300	.300	.600
Allen Craig	R	11	2	1	0	0	1	1	0	3	0	.182	.308	.273	.580
Carl Crawford	L	19	4	1	0	1	5	1	0	5	1	.211	.250	.421	.671
Coco Crisp	B	15	6	1	0	0	4	2	0	6	0	.400	.471	.467	.937
C.J. Cron	R	10	2	1	0	1	4	0	0	4	0	.200	.200	.600	.800
Tony Cruz	R	26	3	0	0	0	1	1	0	7	0	.115	.148	.115	.264
Michael Cuddyer	R	19	6	0	0	0	3	1	0	3	0	.316	.364	.316	.679
Todd Cunningham	B	11	1	0	0	0	0	2	0	1	1	.091	.231	.091	.322
Khris Davis	R	11	4	0	0	2	3	2	0	5	1	.364	.462	.909	1.371
Rajai Davis	R	20	3	1	0	0	2	2	0	8	1	.150	.250	.200	.450
Alejandro De Aza	L	17	5	1	0	0	2	2	0	4	0	.294	.381	.353	.734
Ivan De Jesus	R	20	3	0	0	0	1	2	0	7	1	.150	.227	.200	.427
Jaff Decker	L	10	3	1	0	0	0	2	0	3	0	.300	.417	.400	.817
David DeJesus	L	29	5	1	1	0	7	1	0	6	1	.172	.194	.276	.469
Matt den Dekker	L	18	4	1	0	1	2	2	0	4	0	.222	.300	.444	.744
Chris Denorfia	R	34	11	4	1	1	2	3	0	7	2	.324	.378	.588	.967
Daniel Descalso	L	44	8	0	0	1	3	3	0	12	0	.182	.234	.250	.484
Derek Dietrich	L	14	3	1	0	0	0	1	0	3	1	.214	.353	.286	.639
Wilmer Difo	B	10	1	0	0	0	0	0	0	2	0	.100	.100	.100	.200
Danny Dorn	L	16	3	1	0	0	3	2	0	7	0	.188	.278	.250	.528
Danny Espinosa	B	11	2	0	0	1	1	2	0	5	0	.182	.308	.455	.762
Andre Ethier	L	24	8	2	1	0	4	1	0	5	1	.333	.385	.500	.885
Jeff Francoeur	R	30	11	3	0	1	11	0	0	10	2	.367	.355	.567	.922
Sam Fuld	L	12	1	0	0	0	0	1	0	2	0	.083	.154	.083	.237
Greg Garcia	L	26	9	2	0	1	1	2	0	6	1	.346	.414	.538	.952
Scooter Gennett	L	16	5	2	0	0	3	0	0	3	0	.313	.313	.438	.750
Cole Gillespie	R	9	1	0	0	0	0	2	0	4	1	.111	.273	.111	.384
Jonny Gomes	R	35	8	1	0	1	3	3	0	12	1	.229	.289	.343	.632
Hector Gomez	R	21	2	0	0	0	0	0	0	6	1	.095	.095	.095	.190
Marwin Gonzalez	B	17	2	1	0	0	0	0	0	4	0	.118	.118	.176	.294

Pinch Hitting

Pinch Hitters with 10+ PAs or 10+ Total Bases in 2015

Batter	B	AB	H	2B	3B	HR	RBI	TBB	IBB	SO	GDP	Avg	OBP	Slg	OPS
Phil Gosselin	R	20	6	2	0	0	1	1	0	8	0	.300	.333	.400	.733
Yasmani Grandal	B	7	1	0	0	0	0	3	0	3	1	.143	.400	.143	.543
Curtis Granderson	L	6	1	0	0	0	2	7	1	2	0	.167	.615	.167	.782
Randal Grichuk	R	16	3	1	0	1	2	1	0	4	1	.188	.278	.438	.715
Alex Guerrero	R	51	13	3	0	3	11	1	0	13	0	.255	.283	.490	.773
Franklin Gutierrez	R	11	2	0	0	1	6	1	0	4	0	.182	.308	.455	.762
Brandon Guyer	R	38	10	1	0	2	9	1	0	11	2	.263	.349	.447	.796
Jedd Gyorko	R	13	4	1	0	1	2	3	1	6	0	.308	.438	.615	1.053
Josh Harrison	R	9	1	0	0	0	1	1	0	2	0	.111	.200	.111	.311
Corey Hart	R	22	7	0	0	1	7	1	1	7	3	.318	.333	.455	.788
Cesar Hernandez	B	21	5	0	0	1	4	3	0	3	0	.238	.333	.381	.714
Kiké Hernandez	R	10	3	2	0	0	3	0	0	6	0	.300	.273	.500	.773
Elian Herrera	B	12	2	0	0	0	1	2	0	5	0	.167	.286	.167	.452
Jonathan Herrera	B	30	6	1	0	1	2	0	0	9	1	.200	.200	.333	.533
Odubel Herrera	L	13	5	1	0	0	1	2	0	4	0	.385	.500	.462	.962
Aaron Hill	R	30	9	3	0	0	7	6	0	3	0	.300	.395	.400	.795
Ryan Howard	L	11	2	1	0	0	1	0	0	4	0	.182	.182	.273	.455
Ender Inciarte	L	9	1	0	0	0	0	2	0	1	0	.111	.273	.111	.384
Travis Ishikawa	L	21	5	1	0	0	3	6	0	4	0	.238	.407	.286	.693
Austin Jackson	R	13	2	0	0	0	0	3	0	4	1	.154	.313	.154	.466
John Jaso	L	18	6	2	0	0	4	4	1	4	0	.333	.455	.444	.899
Jon Jay	L	14	4	0	0	0	1	2	0	4	2	.286	.375	.286	.661
Chris Johnson	R	20	3	1	0	0	1	0	0	7	0	.150	.150	.200	.350
Kelly Johnson	L	22	6	0	0	1	2	2	0	6	1	.273	.333	.409	.742
Reed Johnson	R	11	2	1	0	0	2	0	0	4	0	.182	.231	.273	.503
Garrett Jones	L	12	2	0	0	1	3	1	0	4	0	.167	.231	.417	.647
Matt Joyce	L	13	1	1	0	0	0	2	0	6	1	.077	.200	.154	.354
Jung Ho Kang	R	14	3	1	0	0	3	2	0	6	0	.214	.313	.286	.598
Pete Kozma	R	19	4	0	0	0	0	0	0	2	0	.211	.211	.211	.421
Tommy La Stella	L	14	6	2	0	0	2	1	0	1	0	.429	.467	.571	1.038
Juan Lagares	R	12	4	1	0	1	3	0	0	5	0	.333	.333	.667	1.000
Jake Lamb	L	9	1	1	0	0	3	2	0	2	0	.111	.273	.222	.495
Andrew Lambo	L	12	0	0	0	0	0	2	0	4	0	.000	.143	.000	.143
Adam Lind	L	10	4	2	0	0	4	4	2	3	0	.400	.571	.600	1.171
Steve Lombardozzi	B	10	0	0	0	0	0	1	0	4	0	.000	.091	.000	.091
Jonathan Lucroy	R	10	2	0	0	0	1	1	0	5	1	.200	.273	.200	.473
Justin Maxwell	R	24	7	0	0	0	2	5	0	10	0	.292	.414	.292	.705
John Mayberry	R	29	2	0	0	0	1	5	0	10	1	.069	.206	.069	.275
Matt McBride	R	12	2	0	0	0	0	0	0	1	0	.167	.167	.167	.333
Brian McCann	L	10	2	0	0	0	0	2	0	4	0	.200	.385	.200	.585
Casey McGehee	R	46	10	3	0	0	7	4	0	15	1	.217	.280	.283	.563
Michael McKenry	R	18	2	0	0	0	1	7	0	9	0	.111	.360	.111	.471
Devin Mesoraco	R	10	2	1	0	0	1	3	0	2	0	.200	.385	.300	.685
Will Middlebrooks	R	11	0	0	0	0	0	1	0	5	0	.000	.083	.000	.083
Johnny Monell	L	15	1	1	0	0	2	0	0	5	2	.067	.067	.133	.200
Miguel Montero	L	11	1	0	0	0	0	6	1	6	0	.091	.444	.091	.535
Tyler Moore	R	46	5	2	0	1	3	3	1	13	0	.109	.180	.217	.397
Mitch Moreland	L	12	5	1	0	0	3	1	0	3	1	.417	.500	.500	1.000
Logan Morrison	L	10	1	0	0	1	3	1	0	3	0	.100	.182	.400	.582
Michael Morse	R	32	10	1	1	1	6	7	0	9	1	.313	.436	.500	.936
Brandon Moss	L	15	3	1	0	0	1	3	0	6	0	.200	.368	.267	.635
Max Muncy	L	9	2	0	0	0	0	1	0	2	0	.222	.300	.222	.522
Danny Muno	B	9	3	1	0	0	0	1	0	5	0	.333	.400	.444	.844
David Murphy	L	35	11	1	0	3	9	0	0	4	0	.314	.306	.600	.906
Mike Napoli	R	10	2	0	0	0	0	1	0	3	0	.200	.273	.200	.473
Daniel Nava	B	13	2	0	0	0	1	0	0	3	0	.154	.154	.154	.308
Kirk Nieuwenhuis	L	25	3	1	0	1	1	2	0	14	0	.120	.185	.280	.465
Derek Norris	R	13	1	0	0	0	0	1	0	6	0	.077	.143	.077	.220
Chris Owings	R	10	4	2	0	0	2	0	0	3	0	.400	.400	.600	1.000
Jordan Pacheco	R	12	3	0	0	0	0	0	0	6	0	.250	.250	.250	.500
Jimmy Paredes	B	9	1	0	0	0	0	1	0	5	0	.111	.200	.111	.311
Kyle Parker	R	13	2	0	0	0	2	0	0	4	1	.154	.154	.154	.308
Gerardo Parra	L	20	10	2	1	0	3	1	0	3	0	.500	.524	.700	1.224
Ben Paulsen	L	20	8	1	0	0	5	1	0	7	1	.400	.429	.450	.879
Steve Pearce	R	9	0	0	0	0	0	1	0	2	1	.000	.100	.000	.100
Carlos Peguero	L	8	0	0	0	0	0	2	0	5	0	.000	.200	.000	.200
Brayan Pena	B	19	5	1	0	0	1	0	0	2	0	.263	.263	.316	.579
Cliff Pennington	B	24	7	0	0	1	3	5	0	2	1	.292	.414	.417	.830
David Peralta	L	19	6	0	0	0	2	1	0	8	0	.316	.333	.316	.649

Pinch Hitting
Pinch Hitters with 10+ PAs or 10+ Total Bases in 2015

Batter	B	AB	H	2B	3B	HR	RBI	TBB	IBB	SO	GDP	Avg	OBP	Slg	OPS
Eury Perez	R	8	1	0	0	0	0	1	0	1	1	.125	.300	.125	.425
Hernan Perez	R	21	6	1	0	0	1	1	0	6	1	.286	.318	.333	.652
Jace Peterson	L	9	2	0	0	0	0	2	0	1	0	.222	.364	.222	.586
Shane Peterson	L	34	10	3	0	1	6	3	0	17	0	.294	.342	.471	.813
Tommy Pham	R	11	1	0	0	0	0	1	0	4	0	.091	.167	.091	.258
Ryan Raburn	R	22	6	3	1	0	8	5	2	3	0	.273	.448	.500	.948
Aramis Ramirez	R	10	3	1	0	0	4	1	0	3	0	.300	.364	.400	.764
Colby Rasmus	L	8	1	0	0	1	1	4	0	4	0	.125	.417	.500	.917
Josh Reddick	L	12	4	1	0	0	2	1	0	1	0	.333	.385	.417	.801
Nolan Reimold	R	9	2	0	0	0	0	1	0	4	0	.222	.300	.222	.522
Mark Reynolds	R	24	6	2	0	0	3	3	0	5	0	.250	.333	.333	.667
Clint Robinson	L	34	6	2	0	1	4	4	0	9	0	.176	.317	.324	.641
Alex Rodriguez	R	9	4	0	0	1	3	3	1	2	0	.444	.583	.778	1.361
Sean Rodriguez	R	14	1	0	0	0	0	0	0	4	1	.071	.071	.071	.143
Jason Rogers	R	49	13	2	0	2	8	9	0	9	1	.265	.379	.429	.808
Miguel Rojas	R	12	2	1	0	0	4	0	0	5	1	.167	.154	.250	.404
Jimmy Rollins	B	13	1	0	0	0	0	0	0	4	0	.077	.077	.077	.154
Wilin Rosario	R	27	7	2	0	1	4	1	1	8	1	.259	.286	.444	.730
David Ross	R	12	2	0	0	0	1	2	0	6	0	.167	.286	.167	.452
Darin Ruf	R	29	4	0	0	1	2	0	0	11	0	.138	.138	.241	.379
Justin Ruggiano	R	16	7	2	0	1	5	1	0	5	0	.438	.471	.750	1.221
Jarrod Saltalamacchia	B	26	8	2	0	0	1	2	0	9	0	.308	.379	.385	.764
Hector Sanchez	B	12	4	1	0	0	0	0	0	4	0	.333	.333	.417	.750
Jerry Sands	R	11	4	0	0	1	5	1	0	2	0	.364	.417	.636	1.053
Danny Santana	B	11	1	0	0	0	0	1	0	1	0	.091	.167	.091	.258
Logan Schafer	L	17	2	2	0	0	1	2	0	5	1	.118	.211	.235	.446
Scott Schebler	L	10	2	0	0	0	0	1	0	1	0	.200	.333	.200	.533
Skip Schumaker	L	78	19	6	0	0	7	3	1	25	1	.244	.272	.321	.592
J.B. Shuck	L	30	8	2	1	0	6	3	0	7	1	.267	.343	.400	.743
Grady Sizemore	L	22	6	2	0	0	4	3	0	4	0	.273	.385	.364	.748
Seth Smith	L	18	5	2	0	1	2	2	0	3	1	.278	.350	.556	.906
Justin Smoak	B	25	6	2	0	0	3	2	0	6	0	.240	.296	.320	.616
Jake Smolinski	R	11	2	1	0	0	1	1	0	4	0	.182	.250	.273	.523
Travis Snider	L	18	2	1	0	0	3	2	0	8	0	.111	.200	.167	.367
Donovan Solano	R	28	4	0	1	0	2	0	0	7	1	.143	.200	.214	.414
Yangervis Solarte	B	22	4	1	0	0	2	1	0	2	2	.182	.217	.227	.445
Cory Spangenberg	L	18	4	2	0	0	1	0	0	5	0	.222	.222	.333	.556
Chris Stewart	R	8	4	1	0	0	2	0	0	1	0	.500	.444	.625	1.069
Drew Stubbs	R	16	8	2	1	1	3	1	0	3	0	.500	.529	.938	1.467
Andrew Susac	R	11	0	0	0	0	0	2	0	9	0	.000	.154	.000	.154
Ichiro Suzuki	L	42	9	0	1	0	2	3	0	6	0	.214	.267	.262	.529
Darnell Sweeney	B	11	2	1	0	1	3	3	0	5	0	.182	.357	.545	.903
Nick Swisher	B	9	2	1	0	0	2	3	0	4	0	.222	.462	.333	.795
Matt Szczur	R	23	4	2	0	0	1	1	0	4	0	.174	.208	.261	.469
Jose Tabata	R	16	4	0	0	0	2	1	0	4	0	.250	.333	.250	.583
Tomas Telis	B	10	1	0	0	0	0	1	1	1	0	.100	.250	.100	.350
Joey Terdoslavich	B	16	2	1	0	1	1	0	0	6	1	.125	.125	.375	.500
Yasmany Tomas	R	22	2	0	0	0	1	0	0	8	1	.091	.091	.091	.182
Mark Trumbo	R	10	4	0	0	1	1	0	0	3	0	.400	.400	.700	1.100
Preston Tucker	L	13	3	0	0	2	4	1	0	5	0	.231	.286	.692	.978
Justin Turner	R	17	3	0	0	2	5	1	0	5	0	.176	.222	.529	.752
Dan Uggla	R	27	4	1	0	0	2	8	0	12	0	.148	.333	.185	.519
Melvin Upton Jr.	R	26	8	2	1	0	2	8	1	4	0	.308	.471	.462	.932
Juan Uribe	R	21	4	0	0	1	2	4	1	9	0	.190	.320	.333	.653
Chase Utley	L	10	2	1	0	0	2	1	0	3	0	.200	.273	.300	.573
Danny Valencia	R	12	2	0	0	1	1	1	0	2	1	.167	.231	.417	.647
Scott Van Slyke	R	18	5	0	0	0	2	5	1	2	1	.278	.458	.278	.736
Kennys Vargas	B	11	1	0	0	0	2	0	0	5	0	.091	.091	.091	.182
Will Venable	L	29	6	0	0	1	2	4	0	10	0	.207	.303	.310	.613
Shane Victorino	R	9	2	0	0	0	0	3	0	1	1	.222	.417	.222	.639
Stephen Vogt	L	15	3	0	1	0	1	5	1	6	0	.200	.381	.333	.714
Neil Walker	B	13	4	1	0	0	2	0	0	3	0	.308	.267	.385	.651
Brett Wallace	L	43	15	3	0	4	12	7	1	15	0	.349	.440	.698	1.138
Rickie Weeks	R	18	4	1	0	1	7	0	0	6	1	.222	.263	.444	.708
Rafael Ynoa	B	40	13	6	0	0	4	1	0	13	0	.325	.341	.475	.816
Chris Young	R	12	3	1	0	0	1	0	0	2	0	.250	.250	.333	.583
Delmon Young	R	9	3	1	0	0	2	1	0	2	2	.333	.455	.444	.899
Eric Young	B	16	2	0	0	0	0	0	0	3	0	.125	.125	.125	.250

Career Pinch Hitting
Active Pinch Hitters with 100+ PAs in their careers

Batter	B	AB	H	2B	3B	HR	RBI	TBB	IBB	SO	GDP	Avg	OBP	Slg	OPS
Joaquin Arias	R	107	22	6	0	0	11	4	0	18	1	.206	.237	.262	.499
Jeff Baker	R	241	50	9	2	6	30	24	4	91	9	.207	.281	.336	.617
Mike Baxter	L	91	25	10	0	0	12	13	3	21	4	.275	.373	.385	.757
Gregor Blanco	L	102	33	7	2	0	18	8	0	27	0	.324	.363	.431	.794
Willie Bloomquist	R	108	24	1	1	1	12	6	1	20	4	.222	.265	.278	.543
Alberto Callaspo	B	126	28	2	0	3	19	16	1	20	6	.222	.308	.310	.617
Chris Denorfia	R	169	41	11	1	4	20	17	0	36	7	.243	.307	.391	.697
Daniel Descalso	L	158	29	8	0	1	14	11	0	41	1	.184	.246	.253	.499
Andre Ethier	L	118	34	6	1	3	29	21	2	33	7	.288	.404	.432	.836
Kevin Frandsen	R	151	39	4	1	2	19	7	1	21	2	.258	.309	.338	.646
Jonny Gomes	R	195	36	7	0	10	34	33	4	78	3	.185	.315	.374	.689
Josh Harrison	R	95	14	1	1	3	12	3	0	17	2	.147	.180	.274	.454
Corey Hart	R	97	31	6	1	4	23	7	2	25	7	.320	.364	.526	.890
Chris Heisey	R	142	40	8	2	11	37	12	1	39	4	.282	.338	.599	.936
Jonathan Herrera	B	94	22	3	0	1	6	12	0	18	2	.234	.324	.298	.622
Travis Ishikawa	L	165	45	9	1	2	23	17	1	41	2	.273	.344	.376	.720
John Jaso	L	93	23	5	0	3	15	21	1	21	2	.247	.383	.398	.780
Jon Jay	L	86	24	3	0	2	10	9	1	22	4	.279	.357	.384	.741
Kelly Johnson	L	109	23	3	1	2	12	22	2	30	2	.211	.344	.312	.655
Reed Johnson	R	290	79	15	0	6	42	11	1	68	9	.272	.328	.386	.714
Garrett Jones	L	100	18	4	0	1	14	10	2	27	3	.180	.257	.250	.507
Matt Joyce	L	103	19	7	1	1	16	18	2	35	2	.184	.303	.301	.604
John Mayberry	R	141	36	6	0	7	22	14	1	39	4	.255	.323	.447	.769
Brian McCann	L	89	19	5	0	3	12	10	4	25	1	.213	.307	.371	.678
Casey McGehee	R	96	25	6	0	3	21	10	2	26	4	.260	.336	.417	.753
Miguel Montero	L	90	17	2	0	3	15	19	2	33	2	.189	.351	.311	.662
Tyler Moore	R	107	13	5	0	3	12	6	1	45	1	.121	.183	.252	.435
Michael Morse	R	94	28	5	2	2	21	13	0	31	2	.298	.380	.457	.837
Brandon Moss	L	111	23	6	1	2	14	12	0	38	2	.207	.305	.333	.638
Daniel Murphy	L	90	24	2	2	3	18	8	2	19	3	.267	.320	.433	.753
David Murphy	L	100	28	4	0	4	21	13	2	18	0	.280	.353	.440	.793
David Ortiz	L	93	17	4	1	5	19	22	3	24	2	.183	.336	.409	.745
Gerardo Parra	L	104	23	5	1	1	9	5	1	23	2	.221	.261	.317	.579
Brayan Pena	B	127	32	6	0	2	15	9	0	24	4	.252	.295	.346	.641
A.J. Pierzynski	L	129	34	5	0	5	21	13	5	21	7	.264	.336	.419	.754
Ryan Raburn	R	114	21	7	1	4	23	17	3	32	2	.184	.309	.368	.677
Shane Robinson	R	107	24	4	1	0	7	16	0	19	2	.224	.323	.280	.603
Sean Rodriguez	R	91	12	1	0	1	7	11	0	37	1	.132	.248	.176	.423
Cody Ross	R	99	29	7	0	5	16	14	0	28	0	.293	.388	.515	.903
Skip Schumaker	L	251	59	15	0	1	21	13	2	56	5	.235	.277	.307	.584
Seth Smith	L	201	62	15	5	8	44	32	2	51	4	.308	.401	.552	.953
Travis Snider	L	140	30	7	0	5	20	12	1	42	2	.214	.281	.371	.652
Jose Tabata	R	88	20	4	1	0	11	7	0	20	2	.227	.303	.295	.598
Justin Turner	R	144	37	9	0	2	29	10	0	29	7	.257	.304	.361	.665
Juan Uribe	R	89	25	7	0	3	14	11	1	29	2	.281	.363	.461	.823
Jordany Valdespin	L	90	15	1	0	7	17	14	0	27	0	.167	.292	.411	.704
Will Venable	L	139	27	3	2	2	13	16	1	43	0	.194	.276	.288	.563
Shane Victorino	R	95	25	1	1	3	23	10	0	18	3	.263	.333	.389	.723
Rickie Weeks	R	101	23	2	1	3	14	15	0	38	4	.228	.345	.356	.701
Eric Young	B	146	31	3	1	1	4	18	0	36	2	.212	.307	.267	.574

Manufactured Runs, Productive Outs, & Unproductive Outs

Ben Jedlovec

The Texas Rangers were the best run manufacturing team of 2015, helping them to the third-best offense in baseball and an American League West crown. This is nothing new, exactly; the Rangers finished first in this department in 2013 thanks to the league's top two run manufacturers in Elvis Andrus and Ian Kinsler, though with Kinsler in Detroit, the Rangers slipped to third in 2014. In 2015, they found their Kinsler replacement in Delino DeShields, but the entire lineup from top to bottom got in on the act. Second-spot hitter Shin-Soo Choo led the league with 39 productive outs with third-spot hitter Prince Fielder close behind with 32 productive outs of his own. Cleanup hitter Adrian Beltre participated in 25 manufactured runs himself, second-most on the team. Andrus actually spent most of the year sixth and seventh in the lineup.

Also of note are the slugging Toronto Blue Jays. Despite their well-deserved reputation as a power-hitting bunch, the league's best offense wasn't above manufacturing a run when the time came, completing the season with 165 manufactured runs.

However, the single-best run manufacturing individual was Dee Gordon for the second year in a row. In addition to his league-leading 58 stolen bases, he furthered the Marlins' run-producing efforts at the plate with six sacrifice hits and five sacrifice flies (which is notable for a heavy groundball hitter like Gordon).

Players with the most Manufactured Runs, Productive Outs, & Unproductive Outs

Manufactured Runs	
Gordon, Dee, Mia	35
Eaton, Adam, CWS	32
Hamilton, Billy, Cin	31
Revere, Ben, Phi-Tor	31
Gose, Anthony, Det	29
Blackmon, Charlie, Col	29
Polanco, Gregory, Pit	29
Deshields, Delino, Tex	28
Aybar, Erick, LAA	28
Fowler, Dexter, ChC	27
Burns, Billy, Oak	27
Escobar, Alcides, KC	26
Beltre, Adrian, Tex	25
Braun, Ryan, Mil	25
Ellsbury, Jacoby, NYY	25
Andrus, Elvis, Tex	24
Maybin, Cameron, Atl	24
Betts, Mookie, Bos	24
Pollock, A.J., Ari	24
Dozier, Brian, Min	23
Pillar, Kevin, Tor	23
Hosmer, Eric, KC	23
Altuve, Jose, Hou	22
Marte, Starling, Pit	22
Owings, Chris, Ari	22
Hechavarria, Adeiny, Mia	22
Bogaerts, Xander, Bos	22
Simmons, Andrelton, Atl	21
Cain, Lorenzo, KC	21
Goldschmidt, Paul, Ari	21
Heyward, Jason, StL	21
Choo, Shin-Soo, Tex	20
De Aza, Alejandro, Bal-Bos-SF	20
Segura, Jean, Mil	20
Machado, Manny, Bal	20
Trout, Mike, LAA	20
Ramirez, Jose, Cle	20
Bryant, Kris, ChC	19
Gardner, Brett, NYY	19
McCutchen, Andrew, Pit	19
Peterson, Jace, Atl	19
Cano, Robinson, Sea	19
Granderson, Curtis, NYM	19
Inciarte, Ender, Ari	19
Upton, Justin, SD	18
Fielder, Prince, Tex	18
Garcia, Avisail, CWS	18
Crawford, Brandon, SF	18
Duffy, Matt, SF	18
Kang, Jung Ho, Pit	17
Ahmed, Nick, Ari	17
Rosario, Eddie, Min	17
LeMahieu, DJ, Col	17
Holt, Brock, Bos	17
Souza, Steven, TB	17
Markakis, Nick, Atl	17
Galvis, Freddy, Phi	17
Carpenter, Matt, StL	17
Donaldson, Josh, Tor	17
Escobar, Yunel, Was	17

Productive Outs	
Choo, Shin-Soo, Tex	39
Heyward, Jason, StL	36
Ramirez, Alexei, CWS	36
Andrus, Elvis, Tex	35
Cabrera, Melky, CWS	35
Molina, Yadier, StL	34
Morales, Kendrys, KC	32
Santana, Carlos, Cle	32
Fielder, Prince, Tex	32
Pujols, Albert, LAA	32
Gardner, Brett, NYY	32
Goldschmidt, Paul, Ari	31
Holt, Brock, Bos	31
McCutchen, Andrew, Pit	31
Duffy, Matt, SF	31
Prado, Martin, Mia	31
Desmond, Ian, Was	31
Kinsler, Ian, Det	31
Escobar, Alcides, KC	30
Cabrera, Asdrubal, TB	30
Gonzalez, Carlos, Col	30
Rizzo, Anthony, ChC	30
Pillar, Kevin, Tor	30
Lindor, Francisco, Cle	29
Beltre, Adrian, Tex	29
Aybar, Erick, LAA	29
Parra, Gerardo, Mil-Bal	29
Morrison, Logan, Sea	29
Donaldson, Josh, Tor	29
Reyes, Jose, Tor-Col	29
Moustakas, Mike, KC	29
Gordon, Dee, Mia	28
Revere, Ben, Phi-Tor	28
Zimmerman, Ryan, Was	28
LeMahieu, DJ, Col	28
Kipnis, Jason, Cle	28
Simmons, Andrelton, Atl	28
Eaton, Adam, CWS	28
Yelich, Christian, Mia	28
Bruce, Jay, Cin	27
Odor, Rougned, Tex	27
Castro, Starlin, ChC	27
Ortiz, David, Bos	27
Ramos, Wilson, Was	27
Utley, Chase, Phi-LAD	27
Hosmer, Eric, KC	27
Reddick, Josh, Oak	27
Walker, Neil, Pit	27
Segura, Jean, Mil	26
Escobar, Yunel, Was	26
Alvarez, Pedro, Pit	26
Bogaerts, Xander, Bos	26
Goins, Ryan, Tor	26
Marte, Starling, Pit	26
Pollock, A.J., Ari	26

Unproductive Outs	
Frazier, Todd, Cin	123
Santana, Carlos, Cle	93
Rodriguez, Alex, NYY	91
Peralta, Jhonny, StL	91
Cain, Lorenzo, KC	88
Bryant, Kris, ChC	88
Seager, Kyle, Sea	87
Martinez, J.D., Det	87
Pollock, A.J., Ari	86
Longoria, Evan, TB	86
Cespedes, Yoenis, Det-NYM	85
McCutchen, Andrew, Pit	82
Lawrie, Brett, Oak	82
Moss, Brandon, Cle-StL	82
Castro, Starlin, ChC	82
Bautista, Jose, Tor	81
Trout, Mike, LAA	81
Castellanos, Nick, Det	80
Owings, Chris, Ari	80
Semien, Marcus, Oak	80
Dozier, Brian, Min	79
Headley, Chase, NYY	79
Kinsler, Ian, Det	79
Norris, Derek, SD	78
Garcia, Avisail, CWS	78
Pillar, Kevin, Tor	78
Trumbo, Mark, Ari-Sea	77
Forsythe, Logan, TB	77
Andrus, Elvis, Tex	77
Fielder, Prince, Tex	77
Duda, Lucas, NYM	77
Rizzo, Anthony, ChC	77
Hosmer, Eric, KC	77
Ramirez, Alexei, CWS	76
Upton, Justin, SD	76
Kemp, Matt, SD	75
Jones, Adam, Bal	75
Arenado, Nolan, Col	75
Davis, Chris, Bal	75
Tulowitzki, Troy, Col-Tor	75
Bogaerts, Xander, Bos	75
Byrd, Marlon, Cin-SF	74
Desmond, Ian, Was	74
Posey, Buster, SF	73
Pujols, Albert, LAA	73
Heyward, Jason, StL	73
Donaldson, Josh, Tor	73
Reddick, Josh, Oak	73
Cabrera, Melky, CWS	73
Brantley, Michael, Cle	73

Manufactured Runs, Productive Outs, & Unproductive Outs Produced by Team

Team	Manufactured Runs	Productive Outs	Unproductive Outs
Arizona Diamondbacks	164	276	695
Atlanta Braves	144	285	644
Baltimore Orioles	99	213	674
Boston Red Sox	170	271	669
Chicago White Sox	135	251	672
Chicago Cubs	137	230	733
Cincinnati Reds	132	254	686
Cleveland Indians	131	260	735
Colorado Rockies	149	247	657
Detroit Tigers	132	210	726
Houston Astros	142	212	682
Kansas City Royals	170	255	663
Los Angeles Dodgers	103	226	693
Los Angeles Angels	154	235	636
Miami Marlins	164	310	617
Milwaukee Brewers	135	256	650
Minnesota Twins	154	214	652
New York Yankees	123	217	722
New York Mets	121	224	675
Oakland Athletics	139	239	715
Philadelphia Phillies	129	256	674
Pittsburgh Pirates	164	283	651
San Diego Padres	146	231	650
San Francisco Giants	143	260	690
Seattle Mariners	119	245	674
St Louis Cardinals	135	274	693
Tampa Bay Rays	128	211	707
Texas Rangers	195	284	627
Toronto Blue Jays	165	274	636
Washington Nationals	134	277	657

Manufactured Runs, Productive Outs, & Unproductive Outs Allowed by Team

Team	Manufactured Runs	Productive Outs	Unproductive Outs
Arizona Diamondbacks	122	253	682
Atlanta Braves	137	278	710
Baltimore Orioles	144	235	720
Boston Red Sox	166	253	715
Chicago White Sox	157	227	724
Chicago Cubs	110	217	638
Cincinnati Reds	134	279	718
Cleveland Indians	120	194	616
Colorado Rockies	174	285	671
Detroit Tigers	135	224	687
Houston Astros	132	242	643
Kansas City Royals	121	228	693
Los Angeles Dodgers	143	235	611
Los Angeles Angels	144	249	675
Miami Marlins	155	284	637
Milwaukee Brewers	165	262	695
Minnesota Twins	143	251	717
New York Yankees	146	250	648
New York Mets	130	256	650
Oakland Athletics	168	271	668
Philadelphia Phillies	163	282	701
Pittsburgh Pirates	184	273	694
San Diego Padres	166	269	657
San Francisco Giants	114	253	608
Seattle Mariners	145	214	667
St Louis Cardinals	101	257	749
Tampa Bay Rays	123	210	645
Texas Rangers	140	258	723
Toronto Blue Jays	132	238	637
Washington Nationals	142	253	656

Managers Record

Bill James

A couple of years ago, you may remember, it was widely rumored that Kansas City Royals' manager Ned Yost was a moron. I forget what the complaints about him were, because frankly I am too old to take seriously the notion that various major league managers are bumbling incompetents who should pay more attention to the cutting-edge insights of people who call in to the radio. Anyway, Ned Yost has more or less put an end to his local criticism, by the simple method of putting together a deathly efficient three-man bullpen.

In order to understand managers, you have to build an information base about what makes one manager different from another. I had this insight sometime in the 1980s, when Ralph Houk was managing the Red Sox. I looked up Ralph Houk in the Baseball Register, and it told me that he had hit .286 for Neosho in the Arkansas-Missouri League in 1939. I was struck by how spectacularly irrelevant this was to his managerial assignment. If you looked up an outfielder in the same book, it would tell you how many bases he stole, how many homers he hit, how many games he played...relevant information about his playing skills. If you looked up his manager, it told you that he hit .286 for Neosho in 1939. It was hard to imagine a less germane piece of information about his managing.

So then, what SHOULD a manager's record tell you? It should tell you how he manages his team—what he does well, what he does poorly, what he does a lot of, what he doesn't like to do, whether he has been successful, whether he hasn't. The manager's record should tell you the same kind of stuff a player's record tells you about the player.

Years ago, then, I started to think through the process of creating a record for a manager. These pages that follow, the managers' records, are the result of that process, as well as being the result of a lot of hard work by the guys at Baseball Info Solutions. But getting back to Ned Yost, it occurred to me, in thinking about his story, that there was something that could be measured there, but which we have not measured up to now. How well does the manager develop his bullpen? Ned Yost has turned around his career by developing a killer bullpen.

These managers' records are not evaluations. We're not here to tell you who is a good manager and who is not a good manager. We are here to try to help you see how one manager is different from another manager, as best we can. This amounts to a prohibition against making judgments about managers—a prohibition on us—but it is not a prohibition against making a factual record which includes elements of performance excellence. That Ned Yost has built a strong bullpen in Kansas City is a fact; no reasonable person could argue that he has not. This may then be treated as a fact, and, as a fact, it could be included in his managerial record.

OK, well...how do we create a factual record of a manager's ability to develop a strong bullpen?

We start by evaluating every relief pitcher season in baseball history on a 0-to-100 scale. I'll tell you a little bit about how I did this, but not too much because it would take 20 pages to explain every detail, and anyway people would just get hung up on the details. I created a 0-to-100 scale by putting together ten zero-to-ten scales. One scale, for example, is ERA: one point if the pitcher's ERA is below 10.00, two points if it is below 9.00, three points if it is below 8.00, four points if it is below 7.00, etc. One scale is for games pitched: one point if the pitcher pitched 34 games, two points if 41 games, three points if 48 games, four points if 55 games, etc. One scale is for WHIP, one scale is for strikeout/walk ratio, one scale is for batters faced, one scale is for saves, one scale is for sort-of-WHIP, but with different weights given to walks, hits, and home runs allowed. It's just simple stuff, but it reliably puts the best relief pitchers at the top of the scale. In 1974, when Mike Marshall became the first relief pitcher to win the Cy Young Award, the system says that the best relief pitcher in baseball was Mike Marshall. In 1981, when Rollie Fingers became the first modern relief pitcher to win the MVP Award, the system says that the best relief pitcher in baseball was Rollie Fingers; even in 1950, when Jim Konstanty won the National League MVP Award, the system says that Jim Konstanty was vastly better than any other major league reliever, which is not that helpful because most teams in 1950 didn't have any meaningful relievers. In 1979, when Bruce Sutter won the National League Cy Young Award, the system says that Bruce Sutter was the best reliever in the National League, and in 1984, when Willie Hernandez won the American League Cy Young and MVP Awards, the system says that Willie Hernandez was the best reliever in the American League.

The system is just stating the obvious; that is all that it is intended to do. But it is stating the obvious in such a form that we may then take that statement and incorporate it in the next stage of our research. The first stage of our research is asking "How good was this relief pitcher's season?" The second stage of our research is asking "How good was this team's bullpen?", and the third stage is asking "How good was this manager's record at building strong bullpens?" We'll move on to the second stage of the research in just a moment, but we'll hang up on the first question for just a moment.

According to our system, the greatest relief season of all time was by Eric Gagne in 2003. Gagne struck out 137 batters in 82 innings, saved 55 games, posted a 1.20 ERA and won the National League Cy Young Award, so it's not like this is an out-of-left-field selection, but my point is that you may agree with this or you may not; I don't really care. Maybe you think that the greatest relief season ever was by Dennis Eckersley in 1990 or Dick Radatz in 1964 or Craig Kimbrel in 2012; different people have different opinions. We can't make everybody happy, but what we can do is to create standards which give us reasonable answers, and apply those standards in a systematic way.

If the system is wrong in comparing Dennis Eckersley in 1990 to Dick Radatz in 1964, by the time we get to the third stage of the research it has become a third-decimal error. And I would argue that the system is 99% right in these first-level answers. What I mean by that is this: that if you pick two seasons at random and ask "Which of these seasons is better?", the system would agree with the average fan or the average baseball savant 99% of the time, because it's just not really that difficult to make these distinctions. Did Jake McGee have a better year in 2013, when he had a 4.02 ERA, a 75-22 strikeout/walk ratio and 1 Save, or in 2014, when he had a 1.89 ERA, a 90-16 strikeout/walk ratio and 19 Saves? It's not that hard. Very rarely is it that hard.

So anyway, we take the stage one results, which place each pitcher on a zero-to-one-hundred scale, and we move on to the stage two study, which involves comparing not pitchers but bullpens. In 2014 the Houston Astros had five relief pitchers who pitched 30 or more games for them:

Name	W	L	ERA	G	GF	SV	IP	H	R	ER	SO	BB	WHIP
Chad Qualls	1	5	3.33	58	41	19	51.1	54	22	19	43	5	1.149
Tony Sipp*	4	3	3.38	56	13	4	50.2	28	19	19	63	17	0.888
Josh Fields	4	6	4.45	54	16	4	54.2	50	29	27	70	17	1.226
Jose Veras	4	0	3.03	34	7	1	32.2	25	13	11	37	16	1.255
Darin Downs*	2	1	5.45	45	7	0	34.2	28	22	21	27	19	1.356

That's a very poor bullpen. There is nobody with 20 saves, there is nobody with an ERA below 2.00 or even below 3.00, and their peripheral numbers are not terrific. In 2014 we evaluate Qualls, then the Astros' closer, at 54 on a 0-to-100 scale, Tony Sipp at 53, Josh Fields at 48, Jose Veras as 45, and Darrin Downs at 39. We don't count "value" below 30, which is more or less a replacement level, so we state the "value" of the Astros bullpen at 90 points—24 for Qualls (54 minus 30), 23 points for Sipp, 18 points for Josh Fields, 15 points for Veras, and 9 points for Downs. 90 total.

In 2015 the Astros had seven relievers who pitched 30 or more games for them:

Name	W	L	ERA	G	GF	SV	IP	H	R	ER	SO	BB	WHIP
Luke Gregerson	7	3	3.10	64	53	31	61.0	48	24	21	59	10	0.951
Will Harris	5	5	1.90	68	18	2	71.0	42	18	15	68	22	0.901
Josh Fields	4	1	3.55	54	19	0	50.2	39	20	20	67	19	1.145
Tony Sipp*	3	4	1.99	60	12	0	54.1	41	13	12	62	15	1.031
Pat Neshek	3	6	3.62	66	8	1	54.2	49	25	22	51	12	1.116
Chad Qualls	3	5	4.38	60	17	4	49.1	46	24	24	46	9	1.115
Joe Thatcher*	1	3	3.18	43	3	0	22.2	23	8	8	26	12	1.544

Obviously, that's a much better bullpen—seven relievers against five, and more relievers reaching higher standards. Whereas the 2014 Astros bullpen scores at 90 points, the 2015 bullpen scores at 148.

In this way we can evaluate every team's bullpen every year. The best bullpen of all time, if you're curious, was the 2010 San Diego Padres' unit—Heath Bell, Luke Gregerson, Edward Mujica, Mike Adams, Joe Thatcher, Tim Stauffer, Ryan Webb and Ernesto Frieri. Bell, Adams, Thatcher, Stauffer and Frieri had ERAs under 2.00. Mujica, Gregerson and Frieri went on to become closers for other teams.

Again, you can agree with that or not, that's up to you, but no reasonable person would doubt that that was a very outstanding bullpen. After we have a "score" or "bullpen value total" for each team, then we can compare each team to the league average. The 1975 Cincinnati Reds had a four-man bullpen with all four men having ERAs in the twos. That wouldn't be a remarkable bullpen now, when seven-man and eight-man bullpens are common, but in 1975, that was the fourth-best bullpen that any team had ever had. The '75 Reds, the Big Red Machine, had so many potent weapons that the bullpen tends to be overlooked, but it was a great bullpen by the standards of the time.

That was Sparky Anderson. Sparky is interesting. Early in his career Sparky was known as "Captain Hook" because he went to the bullpen so early, and he tended to have the deepest and best bullpens in baseball. By the end of his career he had reached the other end of the spectrum; his bullpens were among the thinnest and weakest in baseball. It wasn't so much that Sparky changed as that the parade just passed him by. But I am getting a little bit ahead of myself there.

First, we create a "score" for each pitcher; second, we add up the team totals to create a score for each team; third, we compare the team score to the league average for that season, and fourth, we attribute that to the manager of the team, thus making a "manager's record" for constructing strong bullpens.

Of course, the manager is not alone in constructing the bullpen. The manager is given assets to work with by the front office; if the assets are not good, the results may not be so good. But getting back to Ned Yost, I think that no reasonable person would question that Yost deserves a good deal of the credit for the Kansas City bullpen. From 2008 to 2012 Luke Hochevar was a struggling starter. In 2013 Yost moved him to the bullpen, where he was brilliant. In 2014 Hochevar was hurt, but Yost replaced him with Kelvin Herrera, who was just as good, and at the same time moved Wade Davis, another struggling starter, into the bullpen. To say that Davis has been a "good" reliever would be ridiculous understatement; he's been a beast. When Greg Holland, Yost's closer, had to have Tommy John surgery in 2015, Yost moved Davis into the closer slot, and replaced Davis with Ryan Madson, who had been out of baseball for several years, and Madson was tremendous. Knowing who to put into which role is critical to successful managing.

One other quick point, before I deliver the results of this study. Craig Kimbrel, still a young man, has already had a somewhat historic career. Kimbrel has had four seasons as the #1 reliever in his league. Only two other pitchers in history have ever had four seasons as their league's #1 reliever: Dennis Eckersley, who also had four, and Mariano Rivera, who had six. On the other hand, Hall of Fame relievers Hoyt Wilhelm and Rollie Fingers actually had only two seasons each as the #1 relievers in their league. Fingers was competing with Goose Gossage and Sparky Lyle and Dan Quisenberry and others, but still...I thought I would mention it.

Anyway, these are the best and worst managers of all time at the art of constructing and maintaining a strong bullpen, based on this study.

1. (Best) Joe Torre (+508 points) Torre actually did not have good bullpens in New York in his first three years as a manager, 1977 to 1979; his bullpens in those years were below average. He had his first good bullpen in 1980 (Jeff Reardon, Neal Allen, Tom Hausman and Dyar Miller). Torre had very good bullpens in St. Louis from 1991 to 1993, and had tremendous bullpens with the Dodgers in 2008 and 2009. And, of course, with the Yankees he had Mariano, but in the modern era one great reliever does not make a great bullpen; you need SEVERAL guys out there in order to be rated at the top of the league.

I credit Torre with 19 strong bullpens in 27 years as a manager; actually he managed parts of 29 seasons, but we don't hold him responsible for the fragments of seasons in St. Louis in 1990 and 1995. The +508 points is calculated by comparing Torre's bullpens each season to the league average in that season. In Los Angeles in 2009, for example, Torre's eight-man bullpen has a score of 205 against a league average of 139, or +66.

2. Tony LaRussa (+379). LaRussa saw that Dennis Eckersley, a fast-fading starting pitcher, could be effective as a closer, and convinced him to buy in to the assignment. He was also for many years the foremost effective proponent of the theory that one can never have too many left-handed relievers.

3. Ron Gardenhire (+326). LaRussa managed 32 seasons, more or less. Gardenhire has managed 13 so far, but had good bullpens in 9 out of 13 seasons, including eight straight, and had great bullpens in four seasons. His best bullpen was 2006—Joe Nathan, Juan Rincon, Dennys Reyes, Jesse Crain, Matt Guerrier and Pat Neshek. Reyes pitched 66 times with a 0.89 ERA.

4. Bobby Cox (+322). Cox' best bullpen was his 2002 bullpen led by John Smoltz and Chris Hammond, backed by Mike Remlinger, Kerry Lightenberg, Darren Holmes, Kevin Gryboski and Tim Spooneybarger.

5. Jimy Williams (+283). Williams managed only 11 years—three full years in Atlanta, five years in Boston and three in Houston—but had strong bullpens in 9 of the 11 seasons. His best bullpen was in Houston in 2003—Billy Wagner, Octavio Dotel, Brad Lidge, and Ricky Stone.

6. Walter Alston (+283).

7. Buddy Black (+262).

8. Al Lopez (+246).

9. Eddie Stanky (+225). This one is a complete surprise, as Stanky (a) only managed for six seasons, and (b) was never known as a forward-thinking man. (I saw Stanky coaching a college team about 1983, years after his major league career. One of his players wandered off first base and was picked off, and Stanky, from the third base coach's box, screamed at the kid and berated him for his stupidity. It was stuff like that ended his major league career.) Anyway, despite these other issues, Stanky had among the best bullpens in the National League in 1952 and 1953, and had the best bullpens in major league history up to that point with the White Sox in 1967 and 1968. And that's why we do research—to occasionally learn things that we previously had not understood.

10. Dusty Baker (+221). Dusty Baker was the Ned Yost of his time. The guys who were too smart for their own damned good were always convinced that he was a disgrace to the managerial fraternity, in large part because they took for granted what he did well, and focused on the things that he did not do well.

Now, the <u>worst</u> managers at running a bullpen, which is perhaps a more interesting list than the other.

The worst manager ever at developing a bullpen was Jim Leyland. Leyland's struggles with his bullpens in Detroit are well documented and well known, but until doing this study, I didn't realize that this is actually a thread that runs through all of his career. Leyland had relatively poor bullpens in Pittsburgh in 1986, 1987, 1989, 1992, 1993, 1994 and 1995. The other years they were not poor, but they were not good, either. His two best relievers in Pittsburgh were Stan Belinda and Bill Landrum.

In Florida he had an OK bullpen his first season (1997) and a very poor bullpen in 1998. His bullpen in Colorado was very poor. His best bullpens in Detroit were barely above average, and his worst were historically bad. For his career, his teams were -452 compared to the league average.

Obviously, Leyland did many things well, and was a highly respected manager. But in this one area, he just was not successful. The rest of the list:

2. John McNamara (-296). McNamara, the ultimate itinerant manager, had 13 bad bullpens in 16 years of managing.

3. Phil Garner (-233).

4. Eric Wedge (-212).

5. Tony Muser (-182). Muser managed only four seasons, but had four dreadful bullpens.

6. Jerry Narron (-176). Five weak bullpens in five tries.

7. Tommy Lasorda (-175).

8. George Bamberger (-170). Bamberger was a famously successful pitching coach, but all of his successes were with starting pitchers. He never had a good bullpen; zero good bullpens in six years.

9. Bo Porter (-161). Porter has managed only two seasons, but his bullpens were so spectacularly awful that he makes the list. I recounted for you earlier his 2014 bullpen in Houston.

10. Birdie Tebbetts (-157). Eight poor bullpens in ten years of managing.

Most of the managers who were very good at running the bullpen had long careers, while many of the managers who show up on the not-so-good list had very short careers. But this leads to another question: Are there managers who have had very good careers, but who were not particularly successful at managing the bullpen?

Well, obviously there are at least two; Lasorda is in the Hall of Fame, and Leyland certainly has a chance to be thought of on that level. But there have been other very good and great managers whose records with the bullpen were not impressive, including:

1. Casey Stengel. Stengel just missed the list of bullpen failures. This may be unfair; Casey's handling of his 1950s bullpens was perhaps more unusual than unsuccessful. People remember Stengel relievers Joe Page, 1949 (who Stengel inherited with the team) and Ryne Duren, 1958-1959 (who was more colorful than actually successful), but the fact is that many of Casey's teams really had no bullpen, other than starting pitchers in exile. Casey used his best starting pitchers in relief when he needed to do that, and he shuffled pitchers back and forth between the bullpen and starting assignments. Both of these things were common practices in the 1930s, but largely extinct by the end of Casey's career.

2. Don Zimmer (-100 in his career).

3. Bill Virdon (-93. 8 poor bullpens in 13 years.)

4. Lou Piniella (-75 in 23 seasons as a manager).

5. Davey Johnson (+11) and **Earl Weaver** (+15). Weaver and Johnson weren't BAD at handling bullpens; it just wasn't their strength. They were great with starting pitchers. Sometimes you have to choose what you're going to work with.

OK, what I was assigned to write here was an introduction to the Manager's Records. The charts below document:

a) How many different lineups the manager used. Buddy Black in 2014 used 157 different lineups in 162 games. Charlie Manuel with the 2009 Phillies used only 68 lineups.

b) PL%. This is the percentage of players in the starting lineups who had the platoon advantage at the start of the game.

c) PH. Joe Maddon almost every year uses more Pinch Hitters than any other manager in his league, plus Maddon has had such a terrific career as a manager that I have almost entirely gotten over the habit of referring to him as John Maddon.

The rest of the stuff that these charts document is listed briefly at the end of the section. Lloyd McClendon loves the intentional walk, and regularly leads his league in the number of intentional walks that blow up in his face.

I can't say that we have achieved our goal here. I measure how well I am doing, sometimes, by how many people try to imitate me. I haven't noticed a lot of other people creating what I think of as descriptive records for managers, and I don't think there is any general understanding in the culture that this information even exists. But we'll keep plugging away at it, and we'll see what we can figure out.

Manny Acta

Year	Team	Lg	G	LUp	PL%	PH	PR	DS	Quick	Slow	LO	RCD	LS	Rel	SBA	SacA	RM	PO	#	Good	NG	Bomb	W	L	Pct
2007	Nationals	NL	162	101	.65	295	32	78	53	28	5	183	1	588	92	86	70	28	44	28	16	8	73	89	.451
2008	Nationals	NL	161	133	.62	293	31	39	38	46	6	119	4	517	124	95	63	24	44	27	17	8	59	102	.366
2009	Nationals	NL	87	66	.62	145	11	20	14	25	1	91	1	282	54	43	62	5	26	13	13	6	26	61	.299
2010	Indians	AL	162	142	.63	79	20	39	44	49	18	81	6	470	124	41	142	20	36	17	19	10	69	93	.426
2011	Indians	AL	162	134	.71	76	44	43	47	49	20	107	0	483	131	40	144	29	34	20	14	10	80	82	.494
2012	Indians	AL	156	116	.76	68	20	72	38	54	14	94	1	464	149	21	135	23	27	12	15	9	65	91	.417
	162-Game Average			126	.67	174	29	53	43	46	12	123	2	510	123	59	112	23	38	21	17	9	68	94	.420

Sandy Alomar, Jr.

Year	Team	Lg	G	LUp	PL%	PH	PR	DS	Quick	Slow	LO	RCD	LS	Rel	SBA	SacA	RM	PO	#	Good	NG	Bomb	W	L	Pct
2012	Indians	AL	6	6	.61	12	2	1	1	1	0	9	0	30	5	3	3	0	0	0	0	0	3	3	.500
	162-Game Average			162	.61	324	54	27	27	27	0	243	0	810	135	81	81	0	0	0	0	0	81	81	.500

Brad Ausmus

Year	Team	Lg	G	LUp	PL%	PH	PR	DS	Quick	Slow	LO	RCD	LS	Rel	SBA	SacA	RM	PO	#	Good	NG	Bomb	W	L	Pct
2014	Tigers	AL	162	103	.51	79	43	44	28	55	43	99	1	473	147	32	144	13	34	17	17	5	90	72	.556
2015	Tigers	AL	161	122	.47	83	38	50	33	59	30	131	4	505	134	37	161	7	32	18	14	7	74	87	.460
	162-Game Average			113	.49	81	41	47	31	57	37	115	3	491	141	35	153	10	33	18	16	6	82	80	.506

Dusty Baker

Year	Team	Lg	G	LUp	PL%	PH	PR	DS	Quick	Slow	LO	RCD	LS	Rel	SBA	SacA	RM	PO	#	Good	NG	Bomb	W	L	Pct
1994	Giants	NL	115	76	.53	177	16	9	29	25	2	86	12	288	154	88	78		40	24	16	8	55	60	.478
1995	Giants	NL	144	97	.41	230	36	13	32	50	8	90	8	381	184	101	77		51	32	19	14	67	77	.465
1996	Giants	NL	162	129	.51	250	17	15	24	58	15	94	8	425	166	103	96		60	37	23	15	68	94	.420
1997	Giants	NL	162	114	.71	212	17	22	46	25	17	132	4	481	170	85	93		57	36	21	12	90	72	.556
1998	Giants	NL	163	130	.62	224	20	12	43	38	8	113	5	433	153	111	41		68	42	26	9	89	74	.546
1999	Giants	NL	162	119	.62	233	16	16	30	51	27	111		450	165	113	40		41	25	16	10	86	76	.531
2000	Giants	NL	162	82	.56	233	26	22	38	50	25	91	3	384	118	86	37		26	17	9	2	97	65	.599
2001	Giants	NL	162	122	.48	261	22	19	40	48	10	114	4	439	99	95	45		49	33	16	6	90	72	.556
2002	Giants	NL	162	118	.43	223	32	38	29	56	53	106	8	417	95	89	42	41	44	28	16	10	95	66	.590
2003	Cubs	NL	162	114	.49	272	25	43	24	58	65	111	3	420	104	93	31	24	36	23	13	4	88	74	.543
2004	Cubs	NL	162	113	.44	254	16	19	37	41	42	129	8	460	94	108	71	62	33	22	11	7	89	73	.549
2005	Cubs	NL	162	121	.59	240	21	29	40	46	36	103	2	457	104	88	107	70	48	27	21	7	79	83	.488
2006	Cubs	NL	162	133	.56	271	9	26	45	39	22	165	2	542	170	108	139	46	44	28	16	11	66	96	.407
2008	Reds	NL	162	119	.58	285	28	27	26	63	39	124	2	507	132	100	101	37	40	28	12	4	74	88	.457
2009	Reds	NL	162	130	.45	252	15	35	30	62	35	115	1	478	136	120	118	23	36	29	7	4	78	84	.481
2010	Reds	NL	162	120	.46	258	19	49	36	41	22	140	0	502	136	91	157	13	32	22	10	9	91	71	.562
2011	Reds	NL	162	142	.42	240	29	42	34	51	20	115	0	501	147	102	226	33	47	26	21	5	79	83	.488
2012	Reds	NL	162	121	.43	201	19	39	33	39	30	78	4	425	114	108	148	19	33	22	11	3	97	65	.599
2013	Reds	NL	162	95	.54	236	20	27	39	40	14	90	3	461	102	110	157	21	28	23	5	3	90	72	.556
	162-Game Average			118	.52	245	22	27	35	47	26	113	4	454	137	102	118	48	44	28	16	8	84	78	.519

Jeff Banister

Year	Team	Lg	G	LUp	PL%	PH	PR	DS	Quick	Slow	LO	RCD	LS	Rel	SBA	SacA	RM	PO	#	Good	NG	Bomb	W	L	Pct
2015	Rangers	AL	162	127	.57	94	51	46	40	47	11	122	0	498	140	66	158	5	29	19	10	5	88	74	.543
	162-Game Average			127	.57	94	51	46	40	47	11	122	0	498	140	66	158	5	29	19	10	5	88	74	.543

Bud Black

Year	Team	Lg	G	LUp	PL%	PH	PR	DS	Quick	Slow	LO	RCD	LS	Rel	SBA	SacA	RM	PO	#	Good	NG	Bomb	W	L	Pct
2007	Padres	NL	163	115	.62	279	18	13	63	28	13	122	0	485	79	85	73	56	48	28	20	11	89	74	.546
2008	Padres	NL	162	113	.63	286	25	20	55	36	17	109	0	491	53	75	78	31	61	30	31	17	63	99	.389
2009	Padres	NL	162	137	.64	264	8	34	50	37	8	118	5	527	111	99	84	55	58	42	16	6	75	87	.463
2010	Padres	NL	162	135	.61	285	16	45	55	33	10	132	7	499	174	99	135	31	51	35	16	8	90	72	.556
2011	Padres	NL	162	140	.58	288	20	43	40	36	10	110	2	490	214	69	184	41	56	31	25	13	71	91	.438
2012	Padres	NL	162	132	.74	280	26	35	45	49	11	126	5	529	201	89	162	21	48	34	14	7	76	86	.469
2013	Padres	NL	162	145	.66	271	24	37	35	46	4	102	1	488	152	78	122	12	31	20	11	8	76	86	.469
2014	Padres	NL	162	157	.74	313	23	29	49	33	13	104	1	481	125	74	116	15	32	24	8	4	77	85	.475
2015	Padres	NL	65	50	.54	113	6	6	8	25	3	40	0	199	54	24	46	2	15	11	4	0	32	33	.492
	162-Game Average			134	.65	283	20	31	48	38	11	115	2	498	138	82	119	31	48	30	17	9	77	85	.475

Bruce Bochy

Year	Team	Lg	G	LUp	PL%	PH	PR	DS	Quick	Slow	LO	RCD	LS	Rel	SBA	SacA	RM	PO	#	Good	NG	Bomb	W	L	Pct
1995	Padres	NL	144	96	.59	262	30	23	44	41	17	38	3	337	170	68		38	37	19	18	11	70	74	.486
1996	Padres	NL	162	114	.52	289	29	15	51	33	10	67	12	411	164	73		65	47	29	18	12	91	71	.562
1997	Padres	NL	162	111	.60	291	26	9	45	45	3	81	11	426	200	84		58	37	20	17	11	76	86	.469
1998	Padres	NL	162	108	.65	280	62	44	44	45	9	82	12	369	116	84		27	45	31	14	10	98	64	.605
1999	Padres	NL	162	137	.60	298	51	21	44	36	4	68	5	403	241	60		29	48	29	19	13	74	88	.457
2000	Padres	NL	162	134	.52	285	44	14	41	47	14	105	5	443	184	52		27	50	21	29	11	76	86	.469
2001	Padres	NL	162	116	.60	255	54	27	32	47	6	85	10	422	173	43		23	54	31	23	13	79	83	.488
2002	Padres	NL	162	123	.66	259	44	56	39	40	17	106	4	459	115	63	74	14	61	38	23	14	66	96	.407
2003	Padres	NL	162	134	.58	339	20	29	34	43	16	100	3	473	115	63	41	6	52	33	19	12	64	98	.395
2004	Padres	NL	162	96	.54	261	28	47	47	32	15	76	3	437	77	75	96	14	39	24	15	10	87	75	.537
2005	Padres	NL	162	128	.58	285	31	49	46	36	23	87	1	456	143	89	111	16	45	33	12	8	82	80	.506
2006	Padres	NL	162	111	.60	264	64	48	43	42	24	111	2	475	154	77	110	21	63	43	20	10	88	74	.543
2007	Giants	NL	162	128	.72	264	50	45	26	50	36	132	2	496	152	86	119	10	41	29	12	3	71	91	.438
2008	Giants	NL	162	134	.68	276	32	39	24	59	42	97	6	478	154	77	155	5	59	40	19	8	72	90	.444
2009	Giants	NL	162	134	.65	231	21	52	42	40	32	84	8	457	106	93	118	5	49	32	17	10	88	74	.543
2010	Giants	NL	162	126	.55	224	45	70	29	37	40	118	12	477	87	102	144	12	58	41	17	8	92	70	.568
2011	Giants	NL	162	138	.62	245	49	42	38	38	44	108	3	480	136	79	175	11	46	36	10	6	86	76	.531
2012	Giants	NL	162	112	.75	220	32	55	22	50	31	136	9	526	157	87	176	15	42	30	12	5	94	68	.580
2013	Giants	NL	162	109	.70	263	19	45	33	52	23	143	4	524	93	78	164	7	64	46	18	6	76	86	.469
2014	Giants	NL	162	131	.66	236	29	64	45	41	19	102	1	475	83	53	147	12	35	25	10	9	88	74	.543
2015	Giants	NL	162	124	.63	230	12	21	45	32	11	137	2	557	129	54	173	8	28	20	8	3	84	78	.519
162-Game Average				122	.62	266	37	39	39	42	21	99	6	459	141	74	129	20	48	31	17	9	81	81	.500

Tim Bogar

Year	Team	Lg	G	LUp	PL%	PH	PR	DS	Quick	Slow	LO	RCD	LS	Rel	SBA	SacA	RM	PO	#	Good	NG	Bomb	W	L	Pct
2014	Rangers	AL	22	21	.56	1	5	0	10	3	3	11	0	76	29	6	23	1	9	5	4	3	14	8	.636
162-Game Average				155	.56	7	37	0	74	22	22	81	0	560	214	44	169	7	66	37	29	22	103	59	.636

Kevin Cash

Year	Team	Lg	G	LUp	PL%	PH	PR	DS	Quick	Slow	LO	RCD	LS	Rel	SBA	SacA	RM	PO	#	Good	NG	Bomb	W	L	Pct
2015	Rays	AL	162	137	.62	219	23	38	72	33	10	134	3	530	132	27	173	2	23	17	6	3	80	82	.494
162-Game Average				137	.62	219	23	38	72	33	10	134	3	530	132	27	173	2	23	17	6	3	80	82	.494

Terry Collins

Year	Team	Lg	G	LUp	PL%	PH	PR	DS	Quick	Slow	LO	RCD	LS	Rel	SBA	SacA	RM	PO	#	Good	NG	Bomb	W	L	Pct
1994	Astros	NL	115	74	.54	185	20	13	6	6	0	37	4	268	168	90		37	28	17	11	5	66	49	.574
1995	Astros	NL	144	106	.49	302	38	11	15	7	8	100	8	394	236	97		44	39	27	12	8	76	68	.528
1996	Astros	NL	162	111	.41	257	30	38	13	12	9	70	10	371	243	94		35	42	30	12	6	82	80	.506
1997	Angels	AL	162	117	.70	86	34	22	10	16	15	67	8	400	198	55		60	25	13	12	4	84	78	.519
1998	Angels	AL	162	119	.57	100	64	33	15	11	28	86	11	415	138	69		38	16	6	10	4	85	77	.525
1999	Angels	AL	133	113	.56	93	26	16	10	16	10	68	2	315	93	39		7	10	1	9	3	51	82	.383
2011	Mets	NL	162	121	.68	312	18	28	32	44	23	126	5	514	165	88	151	9	48	35	13	9	77	85	.475
2012	Mets	NL	162	141	.69	329	16	38	39	36	19	113	0	505	117	75	149	8	29	18	11	3	74	88	.457
2013	Mets	NL	162	132	.61	266	12	33	33	42	15	131	4	535	149	67	128	3	38	30	8	3	74	88	.457
2014	Mets	NL	162	135	.55	247	17	26	28	46	23	111	6	489	135	73	119	2	38	23	15	4	79	83	.488
2015	Mets	NL	162	138	.52	255	21	40	47	36	6	119	8	485	76	49	117	1	43	33	10	6	90	72	.556
162-Game Average				125	.58	233	28	29	24	26	15	99	6	450	165	76	133	23	34	22	12	5	80	82	.494

Craig Counsell

Year	Team	Lg	G	LUp	PL%	PH	PR	DS	Quick	Slow	LO	RCD	LS	Rel	SBA	SacA	RM	PO	#	Good	NG	Bomb	W	L	Pct
2015	Brewers	NL	137	106	.54	247	14	30	30	47	3	85	1	424	99	56	106	2	30	26	4	3	61	76	.445
162-Game Average				125	.54	292	17	35	35	56	4	101	1	501	117	66	125	2	35	31	5	4	72	90	.444

Tony DeFrancesco

Year	Team	Lg	G	LUp	PL%	PH	PR	DS	Quick	Slow	LO	RCD	LS	Rel	SBA	SacA	RM	PO	#	Good	NG	Bomb	W	L	Pct
2012	Astros	NL	41	41	.64	82	10	12	21	7	2	24	5	150	34	16	45	14	15	9	6	4	16	25	.390
162-Game Average				162	.64	324	40	47	83	28	8	95	20	593	134	63	178	55	59	36	24	16	63	99	.389

John Farrell

Year	Team	Lg	G	LINEUPS LUp	PL%	SUBSTITUTION PH	PR	DS	PITCHER USAGE Quick	Slow	LO	RCD	LS	Rel	TACTICS SBA	Sac	RM	PO	INTENTIONAL BB #	Good	NG	Bomb	RESULTS W	L	Pct
2011	Blue Jays	AL	162	131	.43	64	48	22	40	41	26	62	3	474	183	40	181	22	28	17	11	5	81	81	.500
2012	Blue Jays	AL	162	131	.50	94	30	16	49	44	7	84	3	495	164	46	211	15	20	11	9	7	73	89	.451
2013	Red Sox	AL	162	126	.68	93	41	20	28	46	34	71	4	450	142	32	147	5	10	5	5	3	97	65	.599
2014	Red Sox	AL	162	145	.55	101	24	17	29	53	28	107	1	493	88	26	124	4	19	11	8	2	71	91	.438
2015	Red Sox	AL	114	96	.56	55	18	20	26	28	6	62	1	326	63	27	105	2	12	6	6	1	50	64	.439
162-Game Average				134	.54	87	34	20	37	45	21	82	3	476	136	36	163	10	19	11	8	4	79	83	.488

Terry Francona

Year	Team	Lg	G	LINEUPS LUp	PL%	SUBSTITUTION PH	PR	DS	PITCHER USAGE Quick	Slow	LO	RCD	LS	Rel	TACTICS SBA	SacA	RM	PO	INTENTIONAL BB #	Good	NG	Bomb	RESULTS W	L	Pct
1997	Phillies	NL	162	98	.66	288	19	28	28	54	22	102	9	409	148	91		30	42	23	19	9	68	94	.420
1998	Phillies	NL	162	84	.53	256	20	19	34	57	20	88	7	385	142	85		16	27	10	17	8	75	87	.463
1999	Phillies	NL	162	85	.51	239	13	31	29	41	16	111	7	441	160	81		27	24	14	10	6	77	85	.475
2000	Phillies	NL	162	108	.53	278	17	14	38	43	25	102	5	414	132	89		16	32	22	10	7	65	97	.401
2004	Red Sox	AL	162	141	.65	116	65	58	41	48	32	105	8	437	98	18	91	28	28	22	6	4	98	64	.605
2005	Red Sox	AL	162	104	.67	110	46	37	25	55	30	99	3	442	57	21	79	11	28	18	10	5	95	67	.586
2006	Red Sox	AL	162	116	.59	93	54	49	36	44	13	94	9	454	74	33	98	16	25	11	14	7	86	76	.531
2007	Red Sox	AL	162	109	.60	84	34	23	41	35	32	89	4	451	120	45	90	14	20	14	6	4	96	66	.593
2008	Red Sox	AL	162	131	.59	62	40	40	50	30	20	90	11	466	155	40	87	8	17	10	7	4	95	67	.586
2009	Red Sox	AL	162	113	.58	85	47	28	36	50	30	68	6	463	165	29	68	9	24	15	9	6	95	67	.586
2010	Red Sox	AL	162	143	.62	125	48	34	32	63	49	84	3	443	85	36	125	26	30	17	13	4	89	73	.549
2011	Red Sox	AL	162	123	.67	89	44	11	52	46	27	89	4	444	144	29	163	34	11	6	5	2	90	72	.556
2013	Indians	AL	162	121	.75	78	45	24	47	34	18	122	2	540	153	41	158	5	26	15	11	6	92	70	.568
2014	Indians	AL	162	133	.78	123	16	24	37	37	18	150	7	573	131	58	128	3	51	29	22	13	85	77	.525
2015	Indians	AL	161	127	.75	138	21	13	40	36	23	85	8	476	114	63	87	4	27	20	7	5	81	80	.503
162-Game Average				116	.63	144	35	29	38	45	25	99	6	456	125	51	107	16	27	16	11	6	86	76	.531

Ron Gardenhire

Year	Team	Lg	G	LINEUPS LUp	PL%	SUBSTITUTION PH	PR	DS	PITCHER USAGE Quick	Slow	LO	RCD	LS	Rel	TACTICS SBA	SacA	RM	PO	INTENTIONAL BB #	Good	NG	Bomb	RESULTS W	L	Pct
2002	Twins	AL	161	111	.69	141	36	42	54	25	10	84	1	435	141	48	44	11	24	16	8	4	94	67	.584
2003	Twins	AL	162	126	.63	144	50	26	49	33	13	85	2	399	138	59	37	14	35	16	19	6	90	72	.556
2004	Twins	AL	162	131	.59	129	45	29	56	21	20	106	4	435	162	66	121	18	27	15	12	7	92	70	.568
2005	Twins	AL	162	135	.58	104	45	26	50	21	5	87	1	396	146	59	138	16	38	28	10	3	83	79	.512
2006	Twins	AL	162	97	.62	93	36	21	60	31	3	82	5	421	143	48	130	11	25	14	11	4	96	66	.593
2007	Twins	AL	162	139	.63	104	42	25	45	30	8	99	4	438	142	45	148	11	33	14	19	9	79	83	.488
2008	Twins	AL	163	103	.64	109	26	12	47	29	5	115	3	485	144	73	143	17	38	25	13	8	88	75	.540
2009	Twins	AL	163	129	.63	83	54	34	43	25	12	115	3	480	117	62	100	21	20	9	11	6	87	76	.534
2010	Twins	AL	162	112	.62	86	55	30	57	28	5	106	1	465	96	47	140	14	19	12	7	4	94	68	.580
2011	Twins	AL	162	150	.58	93	48	21	34	44	17	82	1	457	131	44	170	5	37	21	16	9	63	99	.389
2012	Twins	AL	162	121	.62	64	45	24	42	31	4	82	1	499	172	49	207	10	43	27	16	6	66	96	.407
2013	Twins	AL	162	139	.66	103	42	28	41	43	6	78	1	511	85	37	137	14	31	13	18	7	66	96	.407
2014	Twins	AL	162	132	.64	97	44	23	40	40	2	82	2	491	135	31	149	5	24	11	13	6	70	92	.432
162-Game Average				125	.62	104	44	26	48	31	8	92	2	455	135	51	128	13	30	17	13	6	82	80	.506

John Gibbons

Year	Team	Lg	G	LINEUPS LUp	PL%	SUBSTITUTION PH	PR	DS	PITCHER USAGE Quick	Slow	LO	RCD	LS	Rel	TACTICS SBA	SacA	RM	PO	INTENTIONAL BB #	Good	NG	Bomb	RESULTS W	L	Pct
2004	Blue Jays	AL	50	36	.68	42	3	2	16	8	7	22	1	130	34	2	47	21	11	5	6	3	20	30	.400
2005	Blue Jays	AL	162	124	.66	148	11	37	55	18	9	77	12	432	107	28	128	45	29	13	16	9	80	82	.494
2006	Blue Jays	AL	162	120	.53	112	32	40	59	33	17	94	16	482	98	20	127	40	56	32	24	12	87	75	.537
2007	Blue Jays	AL	162	131	.46	139	48	33	45	37	31	75	9	420	79	35	99	37	34	17	17	6	83	79	.512
2008	Blue Jays	AL	74	60	.48	53	15	18	12	20	12	43	0	205	70	23	39	10	26	16	10	6	35	39	.473
2013	Blue Jays	AL	162	136	.63	124	31	24	55	44	14	69	2	487	153	41	160	4	33	17	16	6	74	88	.457
2014	Blue Jays	AL	162	128	.72	202	41	49	45	37	20	73	8	449	99	49	161	6	23	17	6	2	83	79	.512
2015	Blue Jays	AL	162	129	.48	97	41	47	46	37	13	85	6	469	111	45	152	2	20	10	10	3	93	69	.574
162-Game Average				128	.58	136	33	37	49	35	18	80	8	454	111	36	135	24	34	19	16	7	82	80	.506

Kirk Gibson

Year	Team	Lg	G	LINEUPS LUp	PL%	SUBSTITUTION PH	PR	DS	PITCHER USAGE Quick	Slow	LO	RCD	LS	Rel	TACTICS SBA	SacA	RM	PO	INTENTIONAL BB #	Good	NG	Bomb	RESULTS W	L	Pct
2010	Diamondbacks	NL	83	57	.64	154	7	11	25	21	8	43	1	247	69	28	62	19	19	13	6	2	34	49	.410
2011	Diamondbacks	NL	162	118	.57	253	9	13	33	51	15	116	2	463	188	74	143	12	16	10	6	3	94	68	.580
2012	Diamondbacks	NL	162	140	.56	231	11	9	35	50	16	104	4	461	144	77	120	8	18	11	7	1	81	81	.500

Year	Team	Lg	G	LUp	PL%	PH	PR	DS	Quick	Slow	LO	RCD	LS	Rel	SBA	SacA	RM	PO	#	Good	NG	Bomb	W	L	Pct
2013	Diamondbacks	NL	162	138	.59	285	22	15	31	44	9	121	0	527	103	67	108	3	42	31	11	5	81	81	.500
2014	Diamondbacks	NL	159	135	.55	247	19	18	43	41	5	92	1	479	117	67	140	13	42	28	14	10	63	96	.396
	162-Game Average			131	.57	260	15	15	37	46	12	106	2	484	138	70	128	12	30	21	10	5	79	83	.488

Joe Girardi

Year	Team	Lg	G	LUp	PL%	PH	PR	DS	Quick	Slow	LO	RCD	LS	Rel	SBA	SacA	RM	PO	#	Good	NG	Bomb	W	L	Pct
2006	Marlins	NL	162	117	.50	250	44	66	46	40	28	76	3	438	168	97	108	42	58	37	21	7	78	84	.481
2008	Yankees	AL	162	114	.63	97	37	42	60	37	12	88	10	475	157	38	173	36	37	22	15	8	89	73	.549
2009	Yankees	AL	162	106	.73	97	61	42	36	45	27	88	13	461	139	44	83	33	28	14	14	9	103	59	.636
2010	Yankees	AL	162	114	.72	117	44	31	43	39	33	76	3	430	133	47	152	20	37	26	11	6	95	67	.586
2011	Yankees	AL	162	94	.69	72	41	53	51	36	21	88	2	465	193	50	151	26	43	30	13	4	97	65	.599
2012	Yankees	AL	162	107	.70	149	33	48	37	53	21	115	7	485	120	47	145	10	32	17	15	6	95	67	.586
2013	Yankees	AL	162	141	.59	119	15	29	42	50	23	82	4	428	146	49	131	4	34	20	14	6	85	77	.525
2014	Yankees	AL	162	142	.74	117	27	33	51	28	10	95	7	475	138	44	132	8	23	10	13	9	84	78	.519
2015	Yankees	AL	162	126	.79	118	50	57	48	34	9	80	10	497	88	32	92	6	16	8	8	4	87	75	.537
	162-Game Average			118	.68	124	39	45	46	40	20	88	7	462	142	50	130	21	34	20	14	7	90	72	.556

Fredi Gonzalez

Year	Team	Lg	G	LUp	PL%	PH	PR	DS	Quick	Slow	LO	RCD	LS	Rel	SBA	SacA	RM	PO	#	Good	NG	Bomb	W	L	Pct
2007	Marlins	NL	162	96	.50	284	29	34	33	56	20	138	5	560	139	91	79	22	60	36	24	16	71	91	.438
2008	Marlins	NL	161	106	.51	255	38	49	38	39	8	120	3	511	104	61	75	17	66	42	24	14	84	77	.522
2009	Marlins	NL	162	97	.58	281	28	49	48	26	12	116	0	530	110	86	88	20	60	38	22	15	87	75	.537
2010	Marlins	NL	70	31	.41	104	12	16	14	13	11	35	1	193	56	33	64	10	18	11	7	5	34	36	.486
2011	Braves	NL	162	119	.60	260	27	29	53	36	21	144	0	510	121	95	139	19	73	49	24	13	89	73	.549
2012	Braves	NL	162	108	.61	268	18	27	50	34	9	115	4	460	133	67	116	20	40	28	12	11	94	68	.580
2013	Braves	NL	162	115	.50	214	40	51	50	42	8	124	2	466	95	79	94	11	35	26	9	4	96	66	.593
2014	Braves	NL	162	103	.45	206	34	34	27	41	20	122	3	472	128	70	106	23	36	24	12	8	79	83	.488
2015	Braves	NL	162	140	.61	255	21	31	35	55	7	136	0	532	102	80	135	4	45	35	10	5	67	95	.414
	162-Game Average			109	.54	252	29	38	41	41	14	125	2	502	117	79	106	17	51	34	17	11	83	79	.512

Ozzie Guillen

Year	Team	Lg	G	LUp	PL%	PH	PR	DS	Quick	Slow	LO	RCD	LS	Rel	SBA	SacA	RM	PO	#	Good	NG	Bomb	W	L	Pct
2004	White Sox	AL	162	134	.58	132	35	15	28	65	48	86	8	399	129	84	97	17	36	15	21	8	83	79	.512
2005	White Sox	AL	162	112	.51	100	32	21	31	56	35	114	5	412	204	68	148	15	42	27	15	6	99	63	.611
2006	White Sox	AL	162	87	.60	135	42	38	28	68	35	83	7	398	141	61	85	27	59	39	20	9	90	72	.556
2007	White Sox	AL	162	124	.56	100	26	23	26	53	33	131	2	463	123	54	92	13	50	24	26	15	72	90	.444
2008	White Sox	AL	163	100	.52	75	49	37	42	48	14	100	3	463	101	44	98	8	42	29	13	6	89	74	.546
2009	White Sox	AL	162	124	.52	105	48	19	50	37	16	70	4	415	162	45	114	15	41	23	18	10	79	83	.488
2010	White Sox	AL	162	115	.51	85	46	36	41	51	24	61	8	407	234	60	220	25	41	26	15	10	88	74	.543
2011	White Sox	AL	160	111	.52	73	47	28	34	45	28	63	8	404	133	65	172	40	49	35	14	7	78	82	.488
2012	Marlins	NL	162	116	.60	234	23	29	24	39	27	126	2	483	190	89	137	23	61	38	23	13	69	93	.426
	162-Game Average			114	.55	116	39	27	34	51	29	93	5	427	158	63	129	20	47	28	18	9	83	79	.512

Chip Hale

Year	Team	Lg	G	LUp	PL%	PH	PR	DS	Quick	Slow	LO	RCD	LS	Rel	SBA	SacA	RM	PO	#	Good	NG	Bomb	W	L	Pct
2015	Diamondbacks	NL	162	130	.48	270	14	35	49	35	5	103	8	550	176	67	146	5	45	35	10	6	79	83	.488
	162-Game Average			130	.48	270	14	35	49	35	5	103	8	550	176	67	146	5	45	35	10	6	79	83	.488

A.J. Hinch

Year	Team	Lg	G	LUp	PL%	PH	PR	DS	Quick	Slow	LO	RCD	LS	Rel	SBA	SacA	RM	PO	#	Good	NG	Bomb	W	L	Pct
2009	Diamondbacks	NL	133	115	.63	222	10	13	24	50	24	61	5	392	113	64	41	5	24	12	12	6	58	75	.436
2010	Diamondbacks	NL	79	56	.53	120	7	4	12	40	21	39	1	207	58	19	51	7	19	9	10	9	31	48	.392
2015	Astros	AL	162	151	.63	122	40	37	33	41	19	97	0	482	169	31	128	6	17	11	6	2	86	76	.531
	162-Game Average			139	.61	201	25	23	30	57	28	85	3	468	147	49	95	8	26	14	12	6	76	86	.469

447

Clint Hurdle

Year	Team	Lg	G	LINEUPS		SUBSTITUTION			PITCHER USAGE						TACTICS				INTENTIONAL BB				RESULTS		
				LUp	PL%	PH	PR	DS	Quick	Slow	LO	RCD	LS	Rel	SBA	SacA	RM	PO	#	Good	NG	Bomb	W	L	Pct
2002	Rockies	NL	140	100	.52	274	28	41	33	45	17	104	3	437	139	46	50	13	38	22	16	11	67	73	.479
2003	Rockies	NL	162	108	.47	317	17	32	35	40	5	87	4	500	100	82	26	16	51	31	20	13	74	88	.457
2004	Rockies	NL	162	131	.57	289	18	35	36	63	20	74	1	473	77	128	67	12	84	54	30	12	68	94	.420
2005	Rockies	NL	162	135	.60	273	21	40	42	60	17	89	2	459	97	114	119	22	54	28	26	15	67	95	.414
2006	Rockies	NL	162	111	.49	259	17	22	34	52	17	107	2	499	135	156	114	28	81	45	36	23	76	86	.469
2007	Rockies	NL	163	96	.51	283	32	29	45	37	13	112	1	529	131	112	109	26	61	30	31	14	90	73	.552
2008	Rockies	NL	162	131	.49	253	20	31	40	43	16	85	2	485	178	111	116	43	49	31	18	6	74	88	.457
2009	Rockies	NL	46	42	.60	73	8	10	11	14	3	31	0	135	45	26	34	3	11	8	3	1	18	28	.391
2011	Pirates	NL	162	134	.60	278	26	63	58	27	1	134	3	549	160	101	173	20	65	39	26	13	72	90	.444
2012	Pirates	NL	162	133	.55	270	26	60	50	33	3	74	2	483	125	82	120	17	30	18	12	3	79	83	.488
2013	Pirates	NL	162	127	.51	289	24	61	61	25	7	76	3	465	136	83	172	20	26	22	4	2	94	68	.580
2014	Pirates	NL	162	123	.50	322	28	38	47	40	7	91	0	452	151	85	187	24	43	26	17	7	88	74	.543
2015	Pirates	NL	162	108	.50	269	48	76	39	40	9	124	1	500	143	81	173	9	38	31	7	3	98	64	.605
162-Game Average				122	.53	284	26	44	44	43	11	98	2	491	133	99	120	21	52	32	20	10	79	83	.488

Dan Jennings

Year	Team	Lg	G	LINEUPS		SUBSTITUTION			PITCHER USAGE						TACTICS				INTENTIONAL BB				RESULTS		
				LUp	PL%	PH	PR	DS	Quick	Slow	LO	RCD	LS	Rel	SBA	SacA	RM	PO	#	Good	NG	Bomb	W	L	Pct
2015	Marlins	NL	124	98	.53	186	14	23	32	30	4	67	3	379	120	63	97	2	22	12	10	5	55	69	.444
162-Game Average				128	.53	243	18	30	42	39	5	88	4	495	157	82	127	3	29	16	13	7	72	90	.444

Davey Johnson

Year	Team	Lg	G	LINEUPS		SUBSTITUTION			PITCHER USAGE						TACTICS				INTENTIONAL BB				RESULTS		
				LUp	PL%	PH	PR	DS	Quick	Slow	LO	RCD	LS	Rel	SBA	SacA	RM	PO	#	Good	NG	Bomb	W	L	Pct
1994	Reds	NL	115	79	.54	195	22	12	32	28	2	56	12	261	170	86	0	41	23	15	8	1	66	48	.579
1995	Reds	NL	144	105	.55	257	18	31	56	18	1	60	16	329	258	88	0	10	32	16	16	10	85	59	.590
1996	Orioles	AL	163	99	.68	85	33	38	48	48	13	67	9	378	117	62	0	6	35	13	22	11	88	74	.543
1997	Orioles	AL	162	109	.56	104	36	43	65	23	5	84	11	400	89	75	0	10	31	16	15	9	98	64	.605
1999	Dodgers	NL	162	109	.53	236	22	9	36	40	8	67	4	399	235	126	0	19	26	17	9	7	77	85	.475
2000	Dodgers	NL	162	89	.59	252	26	11	20	15	10		6	371	137	80	51	11	14	8	6	2	86	76	.531
2011	Nationals	NL	83	59	.45	143	20	23	40	13	1	51	1	271	58	51	85	6	19	10	9	6	40	43	.482
2012	Nationals	NL	162	93	.60	252	30	42	57	30	10	105	1	482	140	67	158	2	32	21	11	7	98	64	.605
2013	Nationals	NL	162	108	.54	233	23	33	46	39	27	99	0	440	116	91	148	1	17	8	9	3	86	76	.531
162-Game Average				99	.35	226	29	18	47	36	18	66	15	354	173	88	176	18	33	18	15	8	92	70	.568

Tom Lawless

Year	Team	Lg	G	LINEUPS		SUBSTITUTION			PITCHER USAGE						TACTICS				INTENTIONAL BB				RESULTS		
				LUp	PL%	PH	PR	DS	Quick	Slow	LO	RCD	LS	Rel	SBA	SacA	RM	PO	#	Good	NG	Bomb	W	L	Pct
2014	Astros	AL	24	23	.64	18	6	9	8	3	5	7	1	67	39	9	35	3	6	2	4	1	11	13	.458
162-Game Average				155	.64	122	41	61	54	20	34	47	7	452	263	61	236	20	41	14	27	7	74	88	.457

Jim Leyland

Year	Team	Lg	G	LINEUPS		SUBSTITUTION			PITCHER USAGE						TACTICS				INTENTIONAL BB				RESULTS		
				LUp	PL%	PH	PR	DS	Quick	Slow	LO	RCD	LS	Rel	SBA	SacA	RM	PO	#	Good	NG	Bomb	W	L	Pct
1994	Pirates	NL	114	94	.56	170	16	13	12	9	1	48	4	285	78	48		38	52	29	23	15	53	61	.465
1995	Pirates	NL	144	124	.56	282	8	4	13	12	11	71	4	391	139	69		51	50	30	20	10	58	86	.403
1996	Pirates	NL	162	117	.53	299	18	14	27	8	11	60	11	422	175	101		46	50	23	27	13	73	89	.451
1997	Marlins	NL	162	105	.59	258	36	31	21	12	18	65	2	404	173	91		38	41	25	16	9	92	70	.568
1998	Marlins	NL	162	96	.59	277	13	15	18	24	31	73	8	420	172	91		31	61	36	25	11	54	108	.333
1999	Rockies	NL	162	124	.56	294	11	12	11	29	21	72	5	421	113	88		11	46	24	22	14	72	90	.444
2006	Tigers	AL	162	120	.53	81	34	38	52	32	16	52	3	390	100	57	128	9	35	23	12	9	95	67	.586
2007	Tigers	AL	162	108	.53	77	31	49	46	43	14	70	5	443	133	35	123	20	41	24	17	13	88	74	.543
2008	Tigers	AL	163	131	.51	66	25	50	29	47	20	72	7	440	94	40	114	10	63	37	26	13	74	88	.457
2009	Tigers	AL	162	126	.55	125	52	50	47	47	38	86	3	439	105	60	132	19	42	26	16	6	86	77	.528
2010	Tigers	AL	162	129	.58	130	11	47	36	54	45	70	6	416	99	54	174	31	29	14	15	9	81	81	.500
2011	Tigers	AL	162	127	.63	86	42	87	43	39	39	84	1	421	69	62	172	7	34	17	17	10	95	67	.586
2012	Tigers	AL	162	121	.58	76	33	62	38	41	37	103	0	420	82	46	151	14	35	21	14	7	88	74	.543
2013	Tigers	AL	162	109	.61	105	40	34	25	48	50	77	6	428	55	42	180	6	29	16	13	8	93	69	.574
162-Game Average				120	.57	171	27	37	31	33	26	74	5	422	117	65	147	24	45	25	19	11	81	81	.500

Torey Lovullo

Year	Team	Lg	G	LINEUPS		SUBSTITUTION			PITCHER USAGE						TACTICS				INTENTIONAL BB				RESULTS		
				LUp	PL%	PH	PR	DS	Quick	Slow	LO	RCD	LS	Rel	SBA	SacA	RM	PO	#	Good	NG	Bomb	W	L	Pct
2015	Red Sox	AL	48	40	.58	17	17	4	9	16	10	28	0	149	35	10	32	0	5	3	2	1	28	20	.583
162-Game Average				135	.58	57	57	14	30	54	34	95	0	503	118	34	108	0	17	10	7	3	95	68	.583

Pete Mackanin

Year	Team	Lg	G	LUp	PL%	PH	PR	DS	Quick	Slow	LO	RCD	LS	Rel	SBA	SacA	RM	PO	#	Good	NG	Bomb	W	L	Pct
2005	Pirates	NL	26	24	.52	54	1	5	11	4	1	22	0	94	19	19	20	2	5	2	3	1	12	14	.462
2007	Reds	NL	80	57	.59	130	10	26	20	22	9	58	3	266	62	44	36	12	18	10	8	3	41	39	.513
2015	Phillies	NL	88	82	.76	143	2	16	25	26	5	58	4	278	70	48	93	9	12	7	5	2	37	51	.420
	162-Game Average			136	.66	273	11	39	47	43	13	115	6	533	126	93	124	19	29	16	13	5	75	87	.463

Joe Maddon

Year	Team	Lg	G	LUp	PL%	PH	PR	DS	Quick	Slow	LO	RCD	LS	Rel	SBA	SacA	RM	PO	#	Good	NG	Bomb	W	L	Pct
1996	Angels	AL	22	19	.64	21	5	0	7	6	6	10	3	48	11	20		6	4	3	1	1	8	14	.364
1998	Angels	AL	8	4	.57	2	4	0	1	5	3	5	3	12	2	7		0	1	0	1	0	6	2	.750
1999	Angels	AL	29	19	.58	29	4	1	6	0	4	20	0	85	23	12		7	3	1	2	1	19	10	.655
2006	Devil Rays	AL	162	145	.54	81	26	51	41	39	16	79	10	444	186	51	132	48	39	19	20	13	61	101	.377
2007	Devil Rays	AL	162	122	.53	80	19	16	31	56	19	113	1	483	179	40	118	50	31	18	13	4	66	96	.407
2008	Rays	AL	162	115	.69	133	16	39	48	37	14	112	7	448	192	31	113	26	29	15	14	8	97	65	.599
2009	Rays	AL	162	123	.66	140	21	18	28	51	23	139	3	510	255	29	99	15	22	10	12	7	84	78	.519
2010	Rays	AL	162	129	.67	174	31	18	41	34	26	135	2	491	217	42	166	12	34	28	6	3	96	66	.593
2011	Rays	AL	162	130	.67	137	16	31	34	36	47	112	6	438	217	42	187	4	38	23	15	6	91	71	.562
2012	Rays	AL	162	151	.62	156	37	52	43	38	33	123	3	472	178	40	181	7	35	25	10	6	90	72	.556
2013	Rays	AL	163	147	.64	193	27	56	52	38	16	111	6	485	111	26	117	6	38	21	17	11	92	71	.564
2014	Rays	AL	162	130	.58	123	23	15	44	35	26	110	3	494	90	54	143	2	27	20	7	3	77	85	.475
2015	Cubs	NL	162	119	.60	288	22	32	41	31	14	129	2	552	132	48	180	3	38	22	16	10	97	65	.599
	162-Game Average			130	.62	155	24	32	40	39	24	116	5	478	173	43	144	18	33	20	13	7	85	77	.525

Charlie Manuel

Year	Team	Lg	G	LUp	PL%	PH	PR	DS	Quick	Slow	LO	RCD	LS	Rel	SBA	SacA	RM	PO	#	Good	NG	Bomb	W	L	Pct
2000	Indians	AL	162	102	.64	73	40	26	21	12	20	104	7	462	147	59		30	45	28	17	9	90	72	.556
2001	Indians	AL	162	114	.61	105	30	49	28	17	10	120	3	484	120	67		43	44	30	14	11	91	71	.562
2002	Indians	AL	86	67	.61	57	10	19	14	17	25	47	0	222	57	21	34	3	21	12	9	4	39	47	.453
2005	Phillies	NL	162	80	.64	265	36	19	42	28	13	119	6	442	143	86	76	11	51	35	16	9	88	74	.543
2006	Phillies	NL	162	81	.65	301	42	49	28	43	22	126	2	500	117	79	74	16	63	35	28	12	85	77	.525
2007	Phillies	NL	162	87	.64	264	56	75	40	40	19	128	6	498	157	84	90	30	62	41	21	16	89	73	.549
2008	Phillies	NL	162	77	.65	291	62	60	33	42	24	124	1	468	161	88	92	34	64	46	18	11	92	70	.568
2009	Phillies	NL	162	68	.67	283	20	16	32	55	32	107	3	459	147	74	65	3	31	19	12	3	93	69	.574
2010	Phillies	NL	162	94	.64	276	17	19	37	50	39	114	1	451	129	64	120	3	42	27	15	6	97	65	.599
2011	Phillies	NL	162	105	.69	264	26	22	49	39	48	74	1	394	120	80	141	5	41	31	10	5	102	60	.630
2012	Phillies	NL	162	131	.68	281	22	48	35	56	30	93	5	440	139	91	125	6	33	21	12	5	81	81	.500
2013	Phillies	NL	120	90	.61	196	29	29	20	38	16	73	1	331	88	53	90	1	23	13	10	7	53	67	.442
	162-Game Average			97	.65	236	35	38	34	39	26	109	3	457	135	75	98	16	46	30	16	9	89	73	.549

Mike Matheny

Year	Team	Lg	G	LUp	PL%	PH	PR	DS	Quick	Slow	LO	RCD	LS	Rel	SBA	SacA	RM	PO	#	Good	NG	Bomb	W	L	Pct
2012	Cardinals	NL	162	122	.62	286	37	33	53	37	8	118	5	506	128	95	144	16	28	13	15	7	88	74	.543
2013	Cardinals	NL	162	89	.56	237	30	41	42	49	25	114	4	483	67	73	125	6	26	20	6	6	97	65	.599
2014	Cardinals	NL	162	119	.56	258	21	35	53	32	17	119	5	485	89	81	155	10	35	20	15	7	90	72	.556
2015	Cardinals	NL	162	135	.52	274	46	41	51	29	11	142	8	515	107	60	168	15	37	29	8	3	100	62	.617
	162-Game Average			116	.57	264	34	38	50	37	15	123	6	497	98	77	148	12	32	21	11	6	94	68	.580

Don Mattingly

Year	Team	Lg	G	LUp	PL%	PH	PR	DS	Quick	Slow	LO	RCD	LS	Rel	SBA	SacA	RM	PO	#	Good	NG	Bomb	W	L	Pct
2011	Dodgers	NL	161	140	.57	233	29	44	45	40	30	86	1	461	166	93	181	13	48	27	21	12	82	79	.509
2012	Dodgers	NL	162	127	.59	247	22	43	51	39	20	118	2	506	148	105	153	8	62	38	24	15	86	76	.531
2013	Dodgers	NL	162	145	.55	210	18	47	40	30	18	118	3	504	106	99	131	10	44	28	16	7	92	70	.568
2014	Dodgers	NL	162	124	.51	237	17	62	49	31	15	107	5	496	188	67	168	2	35	20	15	8	94	68	.580
2015	Dodgers	NL	161	136	.70	276	20	45	50	30	13	119	1	508	93	67	136	2	32	18	14	5	91	70	.565
	162-Game Average			135	.58	241	21	48	47	34	19	110	2	496	141	86	154	7	44	26	18	9	89	73	.549

Lloyd McClendon

Year	Team	Lg	G	LUp	PL%	PH	PR	DS	Quick	Slow	LO	RCD	LS	Rel	SBA	SacA	RM	PO	#	Good	NG	Bomb	W	L	Pct
2001	Pirates	NL	162	131	.51	255	17	32	45	38	2	85	5	410	166	83		52	74	44	30	19	62	100	.383
2002	Pirates	NL	161	121	.45	261	38	65	62	30	3	98	2	458	135	93	73	67	93	61	32	22	72	89	.447
2003	Pirates	NL	162	114	.57	315	27	59	46	35	27	114	10	457	123	99	55	73	58	34	24	13	75	87	.463

				LINEUPS		SUBSTITUTION			PITCHER USAGE						TACTICS				INTENTIONAL BB				RESULTS		
Year	Team	Lg	G	LUp	PL%	PH	PR	DS	Quick	Slow	LO	RCD	LS	Rel	SBA	SacA	RM	PO	#	Good	NG	Bomb	W	L	Pct
2004	Pirates	NL	161	114	.50	278	13	58	**50**	40	26	133	1	464	103	100	91	61	64	37	27	**16**	72	89	.447
2005	Pirates	NL	136	123	.53	218	8	19	37	34	15	86	5	357	84	62	83	37	60	32	28	16	55	81	.404
2014	Mariners	AL	162	141	.69	93	48	33	**61**	11		87	3	497	138	48	187	30	36	21	15	9	87	75	.537
2015	Mariners	AL	162	140	.63	133	52	50	53	31	10	114	5	509	114	49	148	**30**	41	23	**18**	**10**	76	86	.469
162-Game Average				129	.56	227	30	46	52	34	14	105	5	462	126	78	109	51	62	37	25	15	73	89	.451

Bob Melvin

				LINEUPS		SUBSTITUTION			PITCHER USAGE						TACTICS				INTENTIONAL BB				RESULTS		
Year	Team	Lg	G	LUp	PL%	PH	PR	DS	Quick	Slow	LO	RCD	LS	Rel	SBA	SacA	RM	PO	#	Good	NG	Bomb	W	L	Pct
2003	Mariners	AL	162	111	.62	81	62	33	27	46	43	56	6	366	145	44	37	5	24	14	10	4	93	69	.574
2004	Mariners	AL	162	151	.59	109	**66**	26	26	63	43	82	5	414	152	56	123	24	32	18	14	8	63	99	.389
2005	Diamondbacks	NL	162	120	.68	**310**	26	38	26	56	36	123	**11**	458	93	93	101	30	43	27	16	9	77	85	.475
2006	Diamondbacks	NL	162	114	.72	278	11	35	37	42	15	86	0	461	106	83	61	30	44	28	16	8	76	86	.469
2007	Diamondbacks	NL	162	146	.57	243	11	61	35	42	31	96	2	469	133	74	70	25	38	30	8	4	**90**	72	.556
2008	Diamondbacks	NL	162	134	.57	263	27	30	41	39	16	102	0	444	81	87	79	28	41	27	14	9	82	80	.506
2009	Diamondbacks	NL	29	29	.62	47	6	8	7	4	3	17	0	91	29	17	13	3	3	1	2	2	12	17	.414
2011	Athletics	AL	99	87	.71	33	13	17	24	23	18	59	2	283	103	34	87	23	9	5	4	3	47	52	.475
2012	Athletics	AL	162	132	.71	111	17	18	**63**	29	5	93	2	462	154	41	116	30	34	21	13	6	94	68	.580
2013	Athletics	AL	162	133	.77	166	14	35	48	28	7	84	7	447	102	32	74	8	23	18	5	3	96	66	.593
2014	Athletics	AL	162	137	.77	187	38	44	45	30	11	101	2	441	103	28	91	16	28	20	8	5	88	74	.543
2015	Athletics	AL	162	137	.65	161	24	35	53	36	10	100	**10**	487	107	17	130	20	19	8	11	8	68	**94**	.420
162-Game Average				133	.67	184	29	35	40	41	22	93	4	447	121	56	91	22	31	20	11	6	82	80	.506

Brad Mills

				LINEUPS		SUBSTITUTION			PITCHER USAGE						TACTICS				INTENTIONAL BB				RESULTS		
Year	Team	Lg	G	LUp	PL%	PH	PR	DS	Quick	Slow	LO	RCD	LS	Rel	SBA	SacA	RM	PO	#	Good	NG	Bomb	W	L	Pct
2010	Astros	NL	162	128	.50	280	17	51	29	52	**41**	121	1	507	136	90	122	8	39	30	9	5	76	86	.469
2011	Astros	NL	162	121	.49	284	31	31	25	**65**	38	125	2	503	151	95	135	11	59	38	21	9	56	**106**	.346
2012	Astros	NL	121	103	.60	181	22	22	20	49	12	102	0	391	117	54	115	11	25	12	13	6	39	82	.322
162-Game Average				128	.53	271	25	38	27	60	33	127	1	510	147	87	135	11	45	29	16	7	62	100	.383

Paul Molitor

				LINEUPS		SUBSTITUTION			PITCHER USAGE						TACTICS				INTENTIONAL BB				RESULTS		
Year	Team	Lg	G	LUp	PL%	PH	PR	DS	Quick	Slow	LO	RCD	LS	Rel	SBA	SacA	RM	PO	#	Good	NG	Bomb	W	L	Pct
2015	Twins	AL	162	124	.59	75	34	27	51	27	7	123	4	520	108	44	132	5	34	20	14	8	83	79	.512
162-Game Average				124	.59	75	34	27	51	27	7	123	4	520	108	44	132	5	34	20	14	8	83	79	.512

Pat Murphy

				LINEUPS		SUBSTITUTION			PITCHER USAGE						TACTICS				INTENTIONAL BB				RESULTS		
Year	Team	Lg	G	LUp	PL%	PH	PR	DS	Quick	Slow	LO	RCD	LS	Rel	SBA	SacA	RM	PO	#	Good	NG	Bomb	W	L	Pct
2015	Padres	NL	96	84	.56	195	12	10	19	39	11	69	2	314	56	46	60	6	19	10	9	4	42	54	.438
162-Game Average				142	.56	329	20	17	32	66	19	116	3	530	95	78	101	10	32	17	15	7	71	91	.438

Bo Porter

				LINEUPS		SUBSTITUTION			PITCHER USAGE						TACTICS				INTENTIONAL BB				RESULTS		
Year	Team	Lg	G	LUp	PL%	PH	PR	DS	Quick	Slow	LO	RCD	LS	Rel	SBA	SacA	RM	PO	#	Good	NG	Bomb	W	L	Pct
2013	Astros	AL	162	138	.60	107	40	26	48	43	14	84	6	448	171	51	155	22	32	19	13	8	51	**111**	.315
2014	Astros	AL	138	120	.66	69	21	15	28	42	16	74	2	371	120	22	127	18	26	13	13	6	59	79	.428
162-Game Average				139	.63	95	33	22	41	46	16	85	4	442	157	39	152	22	31	17	14	8	59	103	.364

Bryan Price

				LINEUPS		SUBSTITUTION			PITCHER USAGE						TACTICS				INTENTIONAL BB				RESULTS		
Year	Team	Lg	G	LUp	PL%	PH	PR	DS	Quick	Slow	LO	RCD	LS	Rel	SBA	SacA	RM	PO	#	Good	NG	Bomb	W	L	Pct
2014	Reds	NL	162	130	.54	220	21	33	35	37	26	82	3	428	174	87	135	9	33	21	12	5	76	86	.469
2015	Reds	NL	162	118	.57	263	16	26	42	48	**15**	102	2	521	172	63	144	**28**	42	29	13	7	64	**98**	.395
162-Game Average				124	.55	242	19	30	39	43	21	92	3	475	173	75	140	19	38	25	13	6	70	92	.432

Mike Redmond

				LINEUPS		SUBSTITUTION			PITCHER USAGE						TACTICS				INTENTIONAL BB				RESULTS		
Year	Team	Lg	G	LUp	PL%	PH	PR	DS	Quick	Slow	LO	RCD	LS	Rel	SBA	SacA	RM	PO	#	Good	NG	Bomb	W	L	Pct
2013	Marlins	NL	162	132	.52	240	8	9	47	30	4	88	1	471	107	81	124	2	58	42	16	7	62	**100**	.383

Year	Team	Lg	G	LUp	PL%	PH	PR	DS	Quick	Slow	LO	RCD	LS	Rel	SBA	SacA	RM	PO	#	Good	NG	Bomb	W	L	Pct
2014	Marlins	NL	162	102	.50	279	9	14	51	37	8	107	4	487	79	81	100	8	35	23	12	7	77	85	.475
2015	Marlins	NL	38	22	.39	65	6	2	11	5	0	18	0	107	37	23	21	0	3	2	1	1	16	22	.421
	162-Game Average			115	.50	261	10	11	49	32	5	95	2	477	100	83	110	4	43	30	13	7	69	93	.426

Rick Renteria

Year	Team	Lg	G	LUp	PL%	PH	PR	DS	Quick	Slow	LO	RCD	LS	Rel	SBA	SacA	RM	PO	#	Good	NG	Bomb	W	L	Pct
2014	Cubs	NL	162	137	.63	275	9	20	50	42	12	103	1	537	105	77	106	5	37	23	14	8	73	89	.451
	162-Game Average			137	.63	275	9	20	50	42	12	103	1	537	105	77	106	5	37	23	14	8	73	89	.451

Dave Roberts

Year	Team	Lg	G	LUp	PL%	PH	PR	DS	Quick	Slow	LO	RCD	LS	Rel	SBA	SacA	RM	PO	#	Good	NG	Bomb	W	L	Pct
2015	Padres	NL	1	1	.63	3	0	0	0	1	0	2	0	3	1	1	0	0	1	1	0	0	0	1	.000
	162-Game Average			162	.63	486	0	0	0	162	0	324	0	486	162	162	0	0	162	162	0	0	0	162	.000

Ron Roenicke

Year	Team	Lg	G	LUp	PL%	PH	PR	DS	Quick	Slow	LO	RCD	LS	Rel	SBA	SacA	RM	PO	#	Good	NG	Bomb	W	L	Pct
2011	Brewers	NL	162	105	.45	260	31	36	36	43	31	92	1	434	125	104	141	14	16	9	7	4	96	66	.593
2012	Brewers	NL	162	110	.45	322	20	25	36	50	23	**149**	1	512	197	91	152	8	20	12	8	2	83	79	.512
2013	Brewers	NL	162	125	.47	275	15	34	39	47	7	96	2	501	**192**	86	157	6	29	22	7	6	74	88	.457
2014	Brewers	NL	162	115	.44	253	19	37	33	48	12	114	1	478	145	**92**	127	11	20	16	4	4	82	80	.506
2015	Brewers	NL	25	24	.39	48	4	5	3	9	2	15	0	72	14	18	17	2	6	5	1	1	7	18	.280
	162-Game Average			115	.45	279	21	33	35	47	18	112	1	481	162	94	143	10	22	15	6	4	82	80	.506

Jimmy Rollins

Year	Team	Lg	G	LUp	PL%	PH	PR	DS	Quick	Slow	LO	RCD	LS	Rel	SBA	SacA	RM	PO	#	Good	NG	Bomb	W	L	Pct
2015	Dodgers	NL	1	1	.25	2	2	3	1	0	0	0	0	7	0	0	0	0	0	0	0	0	1	0	1.000
	162-Game Average			162	.25	324	324	486	162	0	0	0	0	1134	0	0	0	0	0	0	0	0	162	0	1.000

Ryne Sandberg

Year	Team	Lg	G	LUp	PL%	PH	PR	DS	Quick	Slow	LO	RCD	LS	Rel	SBA	SacA	RM	PO	#	Good	NG	Bomb	W	L	Pct
2013	Phillies	NL	42	34	.66	66	4	6	6	12	7	18	0	135	14	15	26	0	10	6	4	4	20	22	.476
2014	Phillies	NL	162	105	.70	259	20	31	37	**62**	**30**	111	0	461	135	72	140	1	**43**	**31**	12	6	73	89	.451
2015	Phillies	NL	74	58	.72	114	7	14	16	22	5	63	2	225	50	36	70	2	25	23	2	0	26	48	.351
	162-Game Average			115	.70	256	18	30	34	56	24	112	1	478	116	72	138	2	45	35	10	6	69	93	.426

Mike Scioscia

Year	Team	Lg	G	LUp	PL%	PH	PR	DS	Quick	Slow	LO	RCD	LS	Rel	SBA	SacA	RM	PO	#	Good	NG	Bomb	W	L	Pct
2000	Angels	AL	162	75	.62	110	41	4	56	42	6	95	9	441	145	63		40	44	28	16	7	82	80	.506
2001	Angels	AL	162	130	.62	118	30	8	29	41	5	81	9	384	168	66		50	47	22	25	12	75	87	.463
2002	Angels	AL	162	102	.64	**162**	57	26	36	33	34	88	8	400	168	62	52	30	24	15	9	5	99	63	.611
2003	Angels	AL	162	130	.64	134	54	40	50	48	11	60	4	375	**190**	64	79	25	38	26	12	3	77	85	.475
2004	Angels	AL	162	126	.57	94	32	44	37	40	22	61	11	343	**189**	70	**229**	22	27	18	9	3	92	70	.568
2005	Angels	AL	162	124	.65	92	37	37	47	37	24	88	9	379	**218**	58	**160**	43	24	15	9	4	95	67	.586
2006	Angels	AL	162	114	.63	103	45	38	38	49	21	99	9	380	**205**	37	**166**	22	27	18	9	6	89	73	.549
2007	Angels	AL	162	127	.66	103	26	19	39	40	14	84	4	396	**194**	41	**166**	44	22	12	10	5	94	68	.580
2008	Angels	AL	162	125	.63	74	30	36	37	48	**21**	87	1	383	177	39	151	31	32	22	10	6	**100**	62	.617
2009	Angels	AL	162	123	.69	80	26	37	47	47	33	91	1	434	211	55	**137**	**40**	35	22	13	6	97	65	.599
2010	Angels	AL	162	133	.59	96	31	23	41	52	48	76	0	410	156	58	**223**	28	33	17	16	8	80	82	.494
2011	Angels	AL	162	129	.64	88	14	24	31	37	**55**	57	1	386	187	**69**	**212**	46	34	25	9	5	86	76	.531
2012	Angels	AL	162	121	.55	73	23	47	37	47	31	96	8	444	167	**61**	**236**	33	20	11	9	7	89	73	.549
2013	Angels	AL	162	118	.56	88	26	39	31	44	29	130	8	496	116	48	**205**	41	36	19	17	11	78	84	.481
2014	Angels	AL	162	125	.58	123	46	**59**	49	39	22	141	0	543	120	35	**189**	14	41	**31**	10	5	**98**	64	.605
2015	Angels	AL	162	125	.53	117	**62**	**73**	38	38	12	**145**	4	518	86	41	168	15	**45**	**34**	11	9	85	77	.525
	162-Game Average			120	.61	103	37	35	40	43	24	93	5	420	169	54	170	33	33	21	12	6	89	74	.546

Buck Showalter

Year	Team	Lg	G	LUp	PL%	PH	PR	DS	Quick	Slow	LO	RCD	LS	Rel	SBA	SacA	RM	PO	#	Good	NG	Bomb	W	L	Pct
1994	Yankees	AL	113	79	.59	95	31	3	24	30	0	38	7	241	95	34		22	24	13	11	4	70	43	.619
1995	Yankees	AL	145	107	.68	124	30	20	29	42	37	57	6	302	80	27		29	21	14	7	1	79	65	.549
1998	Diamondbacks	NL	162	124	.62	252	17	15	34	40	7	43	6	368	111	68		13	32	16	16	9	65	97	.401
1999	Diamondbacks	NL	162	97	.63	220	20	17	37	48	25	74	3	382	176	75		15	48	29	19	8	100	62	.617
2000	Diamondbacks	NL	162	99	.60	250	32	11	46	26	18	74	12	390	141	89		10	53	28	25	16	85	77	.525
2003	Rangers	AL	162	133	.61	88	51	41	35	33	12	93	7	494	90	35	80	12	45	24	21	14	71	91	.438
2004	Rangers	AL	162	120	.64	86	15	24	53	30	12	82	10	468	105	30	88	5	29	19	10	3	89	73	.549
2005	Rangers	AL	162	98	.59	57	22	11	42	39	17	79	8	454	82	11	103	5	31	10	21	16	79	83	.488
2006	Rangers	AL	162	95	.57	39	34	22	41	27	10	85	4	489	77	30	72	8	18	11	7	5	80	82	.494
2010	Orioles	AL	57	42	.74	20	11	13	23	9	10	24	1	144	38	13	31	1	10	9	1	1	34	23	.596
2011	Orioles	AL	162	117	.53	60	39	27	43	40	14	61	2	478	106	32	133	6	42	31	11	5	69	93	.426
2012	Orioles	AL	162	120	.62	78	28	31	37	42	10	88	0	492	87	46	145	6	36	25	11	5	93	69	.574
2013	Orioles	AL	162	100	.65	90	23	21	31	39	19	84	4	473	108	37	104	4	32	11	21	13	85	77	.525
2014	Orioles	AL	162	120	.49	77	29	51	37	34	17	89	2	479	64	50	101	10	25	16	9	4	96	66	.593
2015	Orioles	AL	162	145	.60	89	21	35	35	41	6	76	8	453	69	26	95	10	27	12	15	8	81	81	.500
	162-Game Average			115	.61	117	29	25	39	37	15	75	6	438	103	43	102	11	34	19	15	8	84	78	.519

Dale Sveum

Year	Team	Lg	G	LUp	PL%	PH	PR	DS	Quick	Slow	LO	RCD	LS	Rel	SBA	SacA	RM	PO	#	Good	NG	Bomb	W	L	Pct
2008	Brewers	NL	12	3	.48	32	2	1	7	2	1	12	0	46	5	13	6	1	2	1	1	0	7	5	.583
2012	Cubs	NL	162	101	.60	277	23	44	46	48	8	117	1	493	139	61	153	13	36	24	12	8	61	101	.377
2013	Cubs	NL	162	107	.60	277	12	17	42	47	19	112	1	489	95	58	122	8	43	29	14	8	66	96	.407
	162-Game Average			102	.60	283	18	30	46	47	14	116	1	496	115	64	135	11	39	26	13	8	65	97	.401

Jim Tracy

Year	Team	Lg	G	LUp	PL%	PH	PR	DS	Quick	Slow	LO	RCD	LS	Rel	SBA	SacA	RM	PO	#	Good	NG	Bomb	W	L	Pct
2001	Dodgers	NL	162	111	.50	264	34	20	46	42	8	84	4	409	131	81		10	37	19	18	9	86	76	.531
2002	Dodgers	NL	162	102	.52	317	39	37	49	36	21	118	9	423	133	81	46	18	45	31	14	5	92	70	.568
2003	Dodgers	NL	162	103	.64	269	22	64	52	29	22	148	11	438	116	97	32	10	35	23	12	8	85	77	.525
2004	Dodgers	NL	162	94	.70	295	25	19	49	34	16	128	16	459	143	81	93	7	47	32	15	8	93	69	.574
2005	Dodgers	NL	162	129	.64	303	31	37	44	40	20	126	2	459	93	76	97	17	34	21	13	6	71	91	.438
2006	Pirates	NL	162	121	.43	264	22	22	37	43	12	156	3	505	91	80	75	12	62	39	23	15	67	95	.414
2007	Pirates	NL	162	124	.49	240	12	26	33	40	13	113	0	495	98	80	90	12	55	30	25	11	68	94	.420
2009	Rockies	NL	116	87	.63	186	25	28	28	27	27	83	3	349	116	73	82	9	40	28	12	7	74	42	.638
2010	Rockies	NL	162	135	.65	257	30	41	38	40	34	128	0	513	141	64	135	11	54	34	20	10	83	79	.512
2011	Rockies	NL	162	134	.62	252	21	30	35	47	21	129	1	517	160	94	231	18	47	27	20	11	73	89	.451
2012	Rockies	NL	162	140	.55	264	33	33	74	33	6	111	2	575	140	88	165	18	61	36	25	12	64	98	.395
	162-Game Average			119	.58	272	27	33	45	38	19	124	5	480	127	84	108	13	48	30	18	10	80	82	.494

Alan Trammell

Year	Team	Lg	G	LUp	PL%	PH	PR	DS	Quick	Slow	LO	RCD	LS	Rel	SBA	SacA	RM	PO	#	Good	NG	Bomb	W	L	Pct
2003	Tigers	AL	162	129	.72	138	29	14	48	39	15	73	14	451	161	92	66	28	35	22	13	7	43	119	.265
2004	Tigers	AL	162	131	.65	105	29	19	47	36	26	79	6	432	136	62	99	9	33	16	17	10	72	90	.444
2005	Tigers	AL	162	119	.49	75	26	16	35	39	13	87	2	425	94	56	129	11	33	21	12	7	71	91	.438
2014	Diamondbacks	NL	3	3	.63	6	2	0	1	0	0	1	0	9	2	1	3	0	1	1	0	0	1	2	.333
	162-Game Average			127	.62	107	28	16	43	38	18	80	7	436	130	70	98	16	34	20	14	8	62	100	.383

Bobby Valentine

Year	Team	Lg	G	LUp	PL%	PH	PR	DS	Quick	Slow	LO	RCD	LS	Rel	SBA	SacA	RM	PO	#	Good	NG	Bomb	W	L	Pct
1996	Mets	NL	31	28	.67	88	7	3	7	4	1	11	1	75	20	27	0	2	14	8	6	2	12	19	.387
1997	Mets	NL	162	131	.65	313	39	23	52	30	8	70	11	376	171	102	0	27	43	28	15	6	88	74	.543
1998	Mets	NL	162	124	.64	305	42	34	45	36	23	80	7	399	108	157	0	50	59	42	17	10	88	74	.543
1999	Mets	NL	163	76	.57	323	43	26	56	24	14	108	8	439	53	35	18	9	53	35	18	9	97	66	.595
2000	Mets	NL	162	118	.34	299	38	32	37	37	18	90	7	411	112	118	0	42	42	27	15	7	94	68	.580
2001	Mets	NL	162	143	.43	298	33	34	38	40	7	83	6	397	114	88	0	0	60	30	30	16	82	80	.506
2002	Mets	NL	161	122	.62	323	48	32	15	42	29	87	2	451	129	98	81	41	75	49	26	13	75	86	.466
2012	Red Sox	AL	162	143	.61	107	30	25	34	52	21	91	6	489	128	44	148	18	33	22	11	5	69	93	.426
	162-Game Average			125	.61	243	45	14	38	46	31	79	14	369	158	90	115	25	45	27	18	10	82	80	.506

Robin Ventura

Year	Team	Lg	G	LINEUPS		SUBSTITUTION			PITCHER USAGE						TACTICS				INTENTIONAL BB				RESULTS		
				LUp	PL%	PH	PR	DS	Quick	Slow	LO	RCD	LS	Rel	SBA	SacA	RM	PO	#	Good	NG	Bomb	W	L	Pct
2012	White Sox	AL	162	75	.48	72	**64**	23	39	44	34	104	4	466	152	42	174	13	29	17	12	7	85	77	.525
2013	White Sox	AL	162	116	.47	76	47	33	24	**52**	38	**133**	0	470	147	24	132	15	24	12	12	4	63	99	.389
2014	White Sox	AL	162	115	.55	85	49	44	26	**59**	29	96	5	453	121	26	150	28	42	25	17	5	73	89	.451
2015	White Sox	AL	162	114	.57	118	29	35	16	**66**	**43**	94	3	414	110	39	146	18	34	21	13	8	76	86	.469
	162-Game Average			105	.52	88	47	34	26	55	36	107	3	451	133	33	151	19	32	19	14	6	74	88	.457

Ron Washington

Year	Team	Lg	G	LINEUPS		SUBSTITUTION			PITCHER USAGE						TACTICS				INTENTIONAL BB				RESULTS		
				LUp	PL%	PH	PR	DS	Quick	Slow	LO	RCD	LS	Rel	SBA	SacA	RM	PO	#	Good	NG	Bomb	W	L	Pct
2007	Rangers	AL	162	139	.60	89	30	**53**	47	46	4	78	9	467	113	**76**	67	13	38	19	19	11	75	87	.463
2008	Rangers	AL	162	129	.64	118	16	14	31	**53**	11	85	3	458	106	53	74	20	44	19	25	**20**	79	83	.488
2009	Rangers	AL	162	123	.55	48	11	11	39	47	28	80	9	436	185	44	80	5	14	9	5	3	87	75	.537
2010	Rangers	AL	162	112	.52	86	39	31	46	42	35	110	4	481	171	**68**	160	10	24	15	9	0	90	72	.556
2011	Rangers	AL	162	106	.48	66	18	23	43	39	40	76	2	417	188	52	182	3	21	12	9	6	96	66	.593
2012	Rangers	AL	162	79	.47	94	25	37	30	48	33	91	0	428	135	46	155	22	15	10	5	5	93	69	.574
2013	Rangers	AL	163	113	.60	142	23	19	48	41	28	105	3	475	**195**	**24**	169	11	35	**24**	11	6	91	72	.558
2014	Rangers	AL	140	109	.54	96	16	16	35	51	11	65	0	400	135	43	155	6	34	25	9	4	53	87	.379
	162-Game Average			116	.55	94	23	26	41	47	24	88	4	453	156	55	132	11	29	17	12	7	84	78	.519

Eric Wedge

Year	Team	Lg	G	LINEUPS		SUBSTITUTION			PITCHER USAGE						TACTICS				INTENTIONAL BB				RESULTS		
				LUp	PL%	PH	PR	DS	Quick	Slow	LO	RCD	LS	Rel	SBA	SacA	RM	PO	#	Good	NG	Bomb	W	L	Pct
2003	Indians	AL	162	**145**	.67	117	43	27	47	34	18	89	5	428	147	67	54	12	37	22	15	8	68	94	.420
2004	Indians	AL	162	114	.72	91	34	20	44	38	22	121	0	**479**	149	57	129	28	47	26	**21**	**18**	80	82	.494
2005	Indians	AL	162	111	.66	88	18	16	45	45	15	90	3	409	98	53	79	9	20	11	9	7	93	69	.574
2006	Indians	AL	162	111	.59	98	13	13	31	52	27	48	1	377	78	40	83	15	35	21	14	11	78	84	.481
2007	Indians	AL	162	117	.60	116	41	25	34	38	20	79	2	395	113	40	108	16	42	24	18	9	**96**	66	.593
2008	Indians	AL	162	**136**	.54	112	31	18	40	35	17	78	4	399	106	56	98	5	28	6	22	11	81	81	.500
2009	Indians	AL	162	**148**	.59	63	28	11	32	41	21	67	3	445	115	52	74	8	31	14	17	9	65	97	.401
2011	Mariners	AL	162	**152**	.68	52	30	22	39	45	30	50	1	351	165	43	161	7	27	20	7	6	67	95	.414
2012	Mariners	AL	162	141	.69	87	36	21	44	35	14	89	5	451	139	45	116	8	39	20	**19**	7	75	87	.463
2013	Mariners	AL	162	143	.70	78	36	33	50	36	8	82	2	448	72	43	97	3	**48**	19	**29**	12	71	91	.438
	162-Game Average			132	.65	90	31	21	41	40	19	79	3	418	118	50	100	11	35	18	17	10	77	85	.475

Walt Weiss

Year	Team	Lg	G	LINEUPS		SUBSTITUTION			PITCHER USAGE						TACTICS				INTENTIONAL BB				RESULTS		
				LUp	PL%	PH	PR	DS	Quick	Slow	LO	RCD	LS	Rel	SBA	SacA	RM	PO	#	Good	NG	Bomb	W	L	Pct
2013	Rockies	NL	162	136	.56	260	18	32	50	42	0	96	2	503	144	80	149	15	52	28	**24**	7	74	88	.457
2014	Rockies	NL	162	134	.51	270	12	26	40	49	2	119	0	**547**	133	69	140	11	32	16	16	7	66	**96**	.407
2015	Rockies	NL	162	122	.56	262	9	36	45	47	2	125	1	**584**	140	58	138	13	42	26	16	6	68	94	.420
	162-Game Average			131	.54	264	13	31	45	46	1	113	1	545	139	69	142	13	42	23	19	7	69	93	.426

Matt Williams

Year	Team	Lg	G	LINEUPS		SUBSTITUTION			PITCHER USAGE						TACTICS				INTENTIONAL BB				RESULTS		
				LUp	PL%	PH	PR	DS	Quick	Slow	LO	RCD	LS	Rel	SBA	SacA	RM	PO	#	Good	NG	Bomb	W	L	Pct
2014	Nationals	NL	162	100	.56	248	17	33	**62**	33	11	67	1	458	124	87	91	3	26	15	11	6	**96**	66	.593
2015	Nationals	NL	162	121	.48	225	22	17	45	44	**15**	86	2	468	80	77	79	1	37	17	**20**	**10**	83	79	.512
	162-Game Average			111	.52	237	20	25	54	39	13	77	2	463	102	82	85	2	32	16	16	8	90	73	.552

Ned Yost

Year	Team	Lg	G	LINEUPS		SUBSTITUTION			PITCHER USAGE						TACTICS				INTENTIONAL BB				RESULTS		
				LUp	PL%	PH	PR	DS	Quick	Slow	LO	RCD	LS	Rel	SBA	SacA	RM	PO	#	Good	NG	Bomb	W	L	Pct
2003	Brewers	NL	162	97	.44	304	22	39	23	**59**	18	90	6	460	138	85	40	23	43	28	15	9	68	94	.420
2004	Brewers	NL	161	131	.60	283	25	20	39	41	27	63	2	423	**178**	79	108	8	27	16	11	8	67	94	.416
2005	Brewers	NL	162	99	.46	259	18	35	26	41	**42**	71	2	395	113	89	97	50	52	23	**29**	10	81	81	.500
2006	Brewers	NL	162	106	.48	238	12	14	33	44	18	77	4	427	108	80	82	16	34	14	20	12	75	87	.463
2007	Brewers	NL	162	109	.60	259	11	41	37	42	18	117	**7**	492	128	74	94	19	37	28	9	9	83	79	.512
2008	Brewers	NL	150	74	.48	217	5	16	37	39	23	69	5	399	141	61	105	31	30	17	13	7	83	67	.553
2010	Royals	AL	127	80	.57	56	25	6	22	39	20	65	0	332	127	40	128	18	25	16	9	5	55	72	.433
2011	Royals	AL	162	87	.58	36	28	16	42	42	21	56	7	420	211	65	203	19	42	27	15	5	71	91	.438
2012	Royals	AL	162	118	.57	60	34	15	48	37	10	108	1	**500**	170	37	149	25	**44**	**29**	15	**11**	72	90	.444
2013	Royals	AL	162	127	.60	79	**48**	39	43	44	21	72	2	427	185	48	168	25	21	12	9	6	86	76	.531
2014	Royals	AL	162	101	.52	51	**63**	46	37	51	26	93	1	451	**189**	45	159	3	14	7	7	3	89	73	.549
2015	Royals	AL	162	83	.57	40	40	26	51	42	13	90	3	493	138	45	126	5	10	7	3	1	**95**	67	.586
	162-Game Average			104	.54	161	28	27	37	45	22	83	3	446	156	64	125	21	32	19	13	7	79	83	.488

Categories of this record are Games Managed (G), Number of Different Lineups Used (LUp), the percentage of players who had the platoon advantage at the start of the game (PL%), Pinch Hitters Used (PH), Pinch Runners Used (PR), Defensive Substitutes Used (DS), Quick Hooks (Quick), Slow Hooks (Slow), Long Outings by Starting Pitchers (LO), Relievers Used on Consecutive Days (RCD), Long Saves (LS), Relievers Used (Rel), Stolen Base Attempts (SBA), Sacrifice Bunt Attempts (SacA), Runners Moving with the Pitch (RM), Pitchouts ordered (PO), Intentional Walks issued (#), Intentional Walks resulting in a Good Outcome (Good), Intentional Walks resulting Not in a Good Outcome (NG), Intentional Walks Blowing Up on the Manager (Bomb), Wins (W), Losses (L), and Winning Percentage (Pct).

2015 American League Managers

Manager	G	LUp	PL%	PH	PR	DS	Quick	Slow	LO	RCD	LS	Rel	SBA	SacA	RM	PO	# Good	NG	Bomb	W	L	Pct
		LINEUPS		SUBSTITUTION			PITCHER USAGE						TACTICS				INTENTIONAL BB			RESULTS		
Buck Showalter, Bal	162	145	.60	89	21	35	35	41	6	76	8	453	69	26	95	10	27	12	15	8	81	81	.500
Terry Francona, Cle	161	127	.75	138	21	13	40	36	23	85	8	476	114	63	87	4	27	20	7	5	81	80	.503
Robin Ventura, CWS	162	114	.57	118	29	35	16	66	43	94	3	414	110	39	146	18	34	21	13	8	76	86	.469
Brad Ausmus, Det	161	122	.47	83	38	50	33	59	30	131	4	505	134	37	161	7	32	18	14	7	74	87	.460
A.J. Hinch, Hou	162	151	.63	122	40	37	33	41	19	97	0	482	169	31	128	6	17	11	6	2	86	76	.531
Ned Yost, KC	162	83	.57	40	40	26	51	42	13	90	3	493	138	45	126	5	10	7	3	1	95	67	.586
Mike Scioscia, LAA	162	125	.53	117	62	73	38	38	12	145	4	518	86	41	168	15	45	34	11	9	85	77	.525
Paul Molitor, Min	162	124	.59	75	34	27	51	27	7	123	4	520	108	44	132	5	34	20	14	8	83	79	.512
Joe Girardi, NYY	162	126	.79	118	50	57	48	34	9	80	10	497	88	32	92	6	16	8	8	4	87	75	.537
Bob Melvin, Oak	162	137	.65	161	24	35	53	36	10	100	10	487	107	17	130	20	19	8	11	8	68	94	.420
Lloyd McClendon, Sea	162	140	.63	133	52	50	53	31	10	114	5	509	114	49	148	30	41	23	18	10	76	86	.469
Kevin Cash, TB	162	137	.62	219	23	38	72	33	10	134	3	530	132	27	173	2	23	17	6	3	80	82	.494
Jeff Banister, Tex	162	127	.57	94	51	46	40	47	11	122	0	498	140	66	158	5	29	19	10	5	88	74	.543
John Gibbons, Tor	162	129	.48	97	41	47	46	37	13	85	6	469	111	45	152	2	20	10	10	3	93	69	.574
162-Game Average		128	.60	112	37	40	43	41	15	104	5	488	114	40	136	9	26	16	10	5	82	80	.506

Manager	G	LUp	PL%	PH	PR	DS	Quick	Slow	LO	RCD	LS	Rel	SBA	SacA	RM	PO	# Good	NG	Bomb	W	L	Pct
		LINEUPS		SUBSTITUTION			PITCHER USAGE						TACTICS				INTENTIONAL BB			RESULTS		
John Farrell, Bos	114	96	.56	55	18	20	26	28	6	62	1	326	63	27	105	2	12	6	6	1	50	64	.439
Torey Lovullo, Bos	48	40	.58	17	17	4	9	16	10	28	0	149	35	10	32	0	5	3	2	1	28	20	.583

2015 National League Managers

Manager	G	LUp	PL%	PH	PR	DS	Quick	Slow	LO	RCD	LS	Rel	SBA	SacA	RM	PO	# Good	NG	Bomb	W	L	Pct
		LINEUPS		SUBSTITUTION			PITCHER USAGE						TACTICS				INTENTIONAL BB			RESULTS		
Chip Hale, Ari	162	130	.48	270	14	35	49	35	5	103	8	550	176	67	146	5	45	35	10	6	79	83	.488
Fredi Gonzalez, Atl	162	140	.61	255	21	31	35	55	7	136	0	532	102	80	135	4	45	35	10	5	67	95	.414
Joe Maddon, ChC	162	119	.60	288	22	32	41	31	14	129	2	552	132	48	180	3	38	22	16	10	97	65	.599
Bryan Price, Cin	162	118	.57	263	16	26	42	48	15	102	2	521	172	63	144	28	42	29	13	7	64	98	.395
Walt Weiss, Col	162	122	.56	262	9	36	45	47	2	125	1	584	140	58	138	13	42	26	16	6	68	94	.420
Don Mattingly, LAD	161	136	.70	276	20	45	50	30	13	119	1	508	93	67	136	2	32	18	14	5	91	70	.565
Terry Collins, NYM	162	138	.52	255	21	40	47	36	6	119	8	485	76	49	117	1	43	33	10	6	90	72	.556
Clint Hurdle, Pit	162	108	.50	269	48	76	39	40	9	124	1	500	143	81	173	9	38	31	7	3	98	64	.605
Bruce Bochy, SF	162	124	.63	230	12	21	45	32	11	137	2	557	129	54	173	8	28	20	8	3	84	78	.519
Mike Matheny, StL	162	135	.52	274	46	41	51	29	11	142	8	515	107	60	168	15	37	29	8	3	100	62	.617
Matt Williams, Was	162	121	.48	225	22	17	45	44	15	86	2	468	80	77	79	1	37	17	20	10	83	79	.512
162-Game Average		129	.58	266	20	33	41	44	10	116	3	518	123	68	140	8	38	26	11	5	79	83	.488

Manager	G	LUp	PL%	PH	PR	DS	Quick	Slow	LO	RCD	LS	Rel	SBA	SacA	RM	PO	# Good	NG	Bomb	W	L	Pct
		LINEUPS		SUBSTITUTION			PITCHER USAGE						TACTICS				INTENTIONAL BB			RESULTS		
Jimmy Rollins, LAD	1	1	.25	2	2	3	1	0	0	0	0	7	0	0	0	0	0	0	0	0	1	0	1.000
Mike Redmond, Mia	38	22	.39	65	6	2	11	5	0	18	0	107	37	23	21	0	3	2	1	1	16	22	.421
Dan Jennings, Mia	124	98	.53	186	14	23	32	30	4	67	3	379	120	63	97	2	22	12	10	5	55	69	.444
Ron Roenicke, Mil	25	24	.39	48	4	5	3	9	2	15	0	72	14	18	17	2	6	5	1	1	7	18	.280
Craig Counsell, Mil	137	106	.54	247	14	30	30	47	3	85	1	424	99	56	106	2	30	26	4	3	61	76	.445
Pete Mackanin, Phi	88	82	.76	143	2	16	25	26	5	58	4	278	70	48	93	9	12	7	5	2	37	51	.420
Ryne Sandberg, Phi	74	58	.72	114	7	14	16	22	5	63	2	225	50	36	70	2	25	23	2	0	26	48	.351
Bud Black, SD	65	50	.54	113	6	6	8	25	3	40	0	199	54	24	46	2	15	11	4	0	32	33	.492
Pat Murphy, SD	96	84	.56	195	12	10	19	39	11	69	2	314	56	46	60	6	19	10	9	4	42	54	.438
Dave Roberts, SD	1	1	.63	3	0	0	0	1	0	2	0	3	1	1	0	0	1	1	0	0	0	1	.000

Ballparks and Park Indices

Ben Jedlovec

A park index tells you whether a given park is favorable to hitters or pitchers compared to other MLB parks. For example, Coors Field, one mile above sea level, had a park factor of 144 in 2015, meaning the Rockies and their opponents scored 44 percent more runs at Coors than in Rockies road games. Not surprisingly, this was the highest park index in MLB.

A park with an index of exactly 100 is neutral and therefore should have no effect on a particular stat. An index above 100 means the ballpark favors that statistic. An index below 100 means the ballpark is unfavorable towards that statistic. For example, AT&T Park, home of the Giants, posted an 85 park index for runs, lowest in MLB this season and 15 percent below the league average offensive environment.

One-year park indices tend to fluctuate a little more than we are comfortable with from year to year. For example, while Coors Field was the most offense-friendly park in the National League, Cleveland's Progressive Field surprisingly held that claim in the American League at 126. That is fairly out of character for the Indians' home park. As a result, we also publish three-year park factors for those who prefer a less volatile reference point. While Coors Field holds steady at 140 over the 2013-15 time period, Progressive Field drops to 103, sixth in the AL.

We also calculate park indices for other statistics, from home runs to triples to strikeouts and even foul outs. For instance, O.co Coliseum's expansive foul territory has led to a 159 foul out park index over the past three seasons, the highest in MLB. We can also break down offensive components between left-handed and right-handed batters. Fenway Park is much kinder to right-handed power hitters (100 park index over three-years) than to lefties (70), while Oriole Park at Camden Yards plays the opposite (137 for LHB vs. 108 for RHB).

One final note: due to small dimension changes in both PETCO Park and Citi Field, we treat each as if they are completely new parks in 2015. The net impact of the renovations was that both parks moved outfield fences in to some degree, though sometimes changes to the seating configurations can also impact wind currents inside the ballpark. The change seems to have worked wonders at PETCO, where the park moved from an 88 home run park index to a 110 in 2015. However, the results are mixed in New York, where Citi Field's changes seemed to boost the lefty home run index while dropping the right-handed index a similar amount. We will see if both trends hold in 2016.

Arizona Diamondbacks - Chase Field
LF: 330　　CF: 407　　RF:335

| | 2015 Season | | | | | | | 2013-2015 | | | | | | |
| | Home Games | | | Away Games | | | | Home Games | | | Away Games | | | |
	D'Backs	Opp	Total	D'Backs	Opp	Total	Index	D'Backs	Opp	Total	D'Backs	Opp	Total	Index
G	81	81	162	81	81	162		241	241	482	245	245	490	
Avg	.270	.264	.267	.259	.252	.256	104	.264	.259	.261	.251	.261	.256	102
AB	2757	2887	5644	2892	2730	5622	100	8142	8511	16653	8735	8331	17066	99
R	366	372	738	354	341	695	106	1047	1083	2130	973	1067	2040	106
H	745	761	1506	749	689	1438	105	2146	2205	4351	2195	2172	4367	101
2B	156	176	332	133	142	275	120	451	465	916	399	448	847	111
3B	33	17	50	15	13	28	178	83	52	135	43	38	81	171
HR	69	86	155	85	96	181	85	198	252	450	204	260	464	99
BB	250	251	501	240	249	489	102	726	671	1397	681	783	1464	98
SO	655	628	1283	657	587	1244	103	1741	1867	3608	1878	1844	3722	99
Foul Outs	52	64	116	54	47	101	114	163	176	339	162	135	297	117
E	47	57	104	39	50	89	117	135	142	277	127	134	261	108
E-Infield	20	29	49	17	26	43	114	53	66	119	53	65	118	103
LHB-Avg	.283	.267	.274	.271	.248	.258	106	.259	.266	.263	.248	.260	.254	104
LHB-HR	15	41	56	20	36	56	101	65	106	171	64	96	160	109
RHB-Avg	.265	.261	.263	.254	.256	.255	103	.267	.254	.260	.254	.261	.257	101
RHB-HR	54	45	99	65	60	125	78	133	146	279	140	164	304	94

Atlanta Braves - Turner Field
LF: 335　　CF: 401　　RF:330

| | 2015 Season | | | | | | | 2013-2015 | | | | | | |
| | Home Games | | | Away Games | | | | Home Games | | | Away Games | | | |
	Braves	Opp	Total	Braves	Opp	Total	Index	Braves	Opp	Total	Braves	Opp	Total	Index
G	81	81	162	81	81	162		243	243	486	243	243	486	
Avg	.248	.250	.249	.254	.287	.270	92	.250	.243	.246	.244	.266	.255	97
AB	2633	2776	5409	2787	2673	5460	99	7935	8317	16252	8394	8039	16433	99
R	286	359	645	287	401	688	94	930	886	1816	904	1019	1923	94
H	654	695	1349	707	767	1474	92	1985	2017	4002	2046	2140	4186	96
2B	126	138	264	125	147	272	98	356	370	726	382	418	800	92
3B	11	11	22	7	22	29	77	33	31	64	28	48	76	85
HR	48	65	113	52	105	157	73	200	190	390	204	228	432	91
BB	249	289	538	222	261	483	112	767	707	1474	718	724	1442	103
SO	547	619	1166	560	529	1089	108	1915	2015	3930	1945	1666	3611	110
Foul Outs	41	60	101	53	54	107	95	154	162	316	166	165	331	97
E	43	58	101	47	32	79	128	130	153	283	130	119	249	114
E-Infield	21	28	49	23	15	38	129	62	69	131	55	53	108	121
LHB-Avg	.251	.268	.259	.275	.303	.288	90	.260	.256	.258	.265	.272	.269	96
LHB-HR	19	31	50	30	49	79	62	76	76	152	78	98	176	86
RHB-Avg	.246	.236	.241	.233	.275	.255	94	.244	.232	.238	.229	.262	.245	97
RHB-HR	29	34	63	22	56	78	83	124	114	238	126	130	256	95

Baltimore Orioles - Oriole Park at Camden Yards
LF: 333　　CF: 410　　RF:318

| | 2015 Season | | | | | | | 2013-2015 | | | | | | |
| | Home Games | | | Away Games | | | | Home Games | | | Away Games | | | |
	Orioles	Opp	Total	Orioles	Opp	Total	Index	Orioles	Opp	Total	Orioles	Opp	Total	Index
G	78	78	156	84	84	168		240	240	480	246	246	492	
Avg	.269	.257	.262	.232	.257	.244	107	.263	.250	.257	.248	.256	.252	102
AB	2643	2752	5395	2842	2727	5569	104	8103	8369	16472	8598	8160	16758	101
R	400	349	749	313	344	657	123	1123	999	2122	1040	996	2036	107
H	710	706	1416	660	700	1360	112	2135	2096	4231	2129	2090	4219	103
2B	120	148	268	126	169	295	94	381	413	794	427	455	882	92
3B	7	11	18	13	12	25	74	20	26	46	30	39	69	68
HR	128	94	222	89	80	169	136	350	279	629	290	248	538	119
BB	212	207	419	206	276	482	90	617	686	1303	618	742	1360	97
SO	596	610	1206	735	623	1358	92	1743	1797	3540	1998	1779	3777	95
Foul Outs	47	52	99	63	63	126	81	176	180	356	202	208	410	88
E	36	43	79	41	34	75	113	105	131	236	113	123	236	103
E-Infield	12	20	32	15	15	30	115	38	53	91	48	53	101	92
LHB-Avg	.265	.244	.254	.227	.247	.237	107	.256	.252	.254	.241	.253	.247	103
LHB-HR	55	55	110	38	29	67	138	152	135	287	105	105	210	137
RHB-Avg	.271	.266	.269	.236	.265	.250	108	.269	.249	.259	.252	.259	.256	101
RHB-HR	73	59	132	51	51	102	134	198	144	342	185	143	328	108

Boston Red Sox - Fenway Park
LF: 310   CF: 420   RF:302

	2015 Season							2013-2015						
	Home Games			Away Games				Home Games			Away Games			
	Red Sox	Opp	Total	Red Sox	Opp	Total	Index	Red Sox	Opp	Total	Red Sox	Opp	Total	Index
G	81	81	162	81	81	162		243	243	486	243	243	486	
Avg	.290	.263	.277	.241	.265	.253	109	.277	.257	.267	.248	.257	.252	106
AB	2785	2868	5653	2855	2755	5610	101	8239	8541	16780	8603	8209	16812	100
R	433	383	816	315	370	685	119	1176	1077	2253	1059	1047	2106	107
H	809	755	1564	687	731	1418	110	2286	2197	4483	2131	2113	4244	106
2B	176	157	333	118	142	260	127	552	490	1042	387	406	793	132
3B	15	18	33	18	14	32	102	41	47	88	41	43	84	105
HR	80	87	167	81	91	172	96	212	224	436	250	264	514	85
BB	239	219	458	239	259	498	91	812	722	1534	782	762	1544	100
SO	541	631	1172	607	587	1194	97	1799	1940	3739	1994	1785	3779	99
Foul Outs	42	54	96	65	54	119	80	129	164	293	183	203	386	76
E	56	66	122	41	42	83	147	160	166	326	109	128	237	138
E-Infield	27	29	56	19	20	39	144	70	65	135	42	52	94	144
LHB-Avg	.288	.268	.278	.245	.240	.243	115	.283	.254	.269	.253	.247	.250	107
LHB-HR	36	30	66	44	38	82	78	94	84	178	131	123	254	70
RHB-Avg	.292	.260	.276	.237	.282	.260	106	.273	.260	.266	.243	.266	.254	105
RHB-HR	44	57	101	37	53	90	113	118	140	258	119	141	260	100

Chicago Cubs - Wrigley Field
LF: 355   CF: 400   RF:353

	2015 Season							2013-2015						
	Home Games			Away Games				Home Games			Away Games			
	Cubs	Opp	Total	Cubs	Opp	Total	Index	Cubs	Opp	Total	Cubs	Opp	Total	Index
G	81	81	162	81	81	162		243	243	486	243	243	486	
Avg	.237	.231	.234	.251	.235	.243	96	.243	.242	.242	.238	.245	.241	101
AB	2613	2792	5405	2878	2684	5562	97	8012	8447	16459	8485	8034	16519	100
R	326	306	632	363	302	665	95	969	1002	1971	936	1002	1938	102
H	618	646	1264	723	630	1353	93	1947	2041	3988	2016	1965	3981	100
2B	111	136	247	161	150	311	82	408	447	855	431	436	867	99
3B	15	20	35	15	17	32	113	40	47	87	39	47	86	102
HR	92	79	171	79	55	134	131	263	215	478	237	194	431	111
BB	293	201	494	274	206	480	106	740	728	1468	708	723	1431	103
SO	716	739	1455	802	692	1494	100	2061	2067	4128	2164	1859	4023	103
Foul Outs	42	35	77	51	45	96	83	142	123	265	179	172	351	76
E	50	38	88	61	53	114	77	152	125	277	162	143	305	91
E-Infield	27	16	43	31	19	50	86	71	47	118	70	60	130	91
LHB-Avg	.221	.234	.227	.263	.230	.248	92	.246	.248	.247	.239	.229	.234	105
LHB-HR	41	33	74	53	17	70	108	117	74	191	134	65	199	97
RHB-Avg	.249	.230	.238	.242	.238	.240	99	.241	.238	.239	.237	.255	.246	97
RHB-HR	51	46	97	26	38	64	156	146	141	287	103	129	232	124

Chicago White Sox - U.S. Cellular Field
LF: 330   CF: 400   RF:335

	2015 Season							2013-2015						
	Home Games			Away Games				Home Games			Away Games			
	White Sox	Opp	Total	White Sox	Opp	Total	Index	White Sox	Opp	Total	White Sox	Opp	Total	Index
G	81	81	162	81	81	162		243	243	486	243	243	486	
Avg	.247	.247	.247	.253	.273	.263	94	.250	.252	.251	.251	.269	.260	96
AB	2734	2849	5583	2799	2709	5508	101	8155	8527	16682	8484	8139	16623	100
R	290	338	628	332	363	695	90	927	1088	2015	953	1094	2047	98
H	674	704	1378	707	739	1446	95	2035	2147	4182	2131	2188	4319	97
2B	118	130	248	142	142	284	86	352	384	736	424	416	840	87
3B	13	17	30	14	22	36	82	36	39	75	42	53	95	79
HR	73	84	157	63	78	141	110	228	259	487	211	225	436	111
BB	218	267	485	186	207	393	122	674	804	1478	558	736	1294	114
SO	621	719	1340	610	640	1250	106	1880	2028	3908	1920	1732	3652	107
Foul Outs	65	48	113	47	52	99	113	193	183	376	166	157	323	116
E	52	49	101	49	49	98	103	166	146	312	163	131	294	106
E-Infield	22	21	43	20	18	38	113	76	63	139	69	53	122	114
LHB-Avg	.233	.233	.233	.268	.272	.269	87	.240	.245	.243	.253	.275	.264	92
LHB-HR	21	31	52	23	24	47	104	77	108	185	78	90	168	109
RHB-Avg	.256	.254	.255	.242	.273	.259	99	.255	.256	.256	.250	.265	.257	99
RHB-HR	52	53	105	40	54	94	113	151	151	302	133	135	268	113

Cincinnati Reds - Great American Ballpark
LF: 328   CF: 404   RF:325

	2015 Season							2013-2015						
	Home Games			Away Games				Home Games			Away Games			
	Reds	Opp	Total	Reds	Opp	Total	Index	Reds	Opp	Total	Reds	Opp	Total	Index
G	81	81	162	81	81	162		242	242	484	244	244	488	
Avg	.255	.260	.257	.241	.256	.249	104	.248	.240	.244	.242	.249	.245	99
AB	2775	2895	5670	2796	2667	5463	104	8077	8441	16518	8388	8001	16389	102
R	344	391	735	296	363	659	112	988	971	1959	945	984	1929	102
H	707	753	1460	675	683	1358	108	2004	2022	4026	2030	1990	4020	101
2B	136	157	293	121	160	281	100	390	417	807	395	412	807	99
3B	10	6	16	17	19	36	43	30	26	56	37	42	79	70
HR	88	95	183	79	82	161	110	247	285	532	206	225	431	122
BB	264	281	545	232	263	495	106	771	761	1532	725	725	1450	105
SO	619	698	1317	636	554	1190	107	1857	2144	4001	1895	1694	3589	111
Foul Outs	56	59	115	58	38	96	115	160	174	334	169	144	313	106
E	36	43	79	54	48	102	77	109	151	260	129	154	283	93
E-Infield	11	15	26	32	21	53	49	38	54	92	60	71	131	71
LHB-Avg	.270	.270	.270	.241	.261	.251	108	.254	.246	.250	.252	.258	.255	98
LHB-HR	33	45	78	29	37	66	115	100	130	230	84	94	178	131
RHB-Avg	.245	.252	.248	.242	.253	.247	101	.244	.235	.239	.235	.241	.238	101
RHB-HR	55	50	105	50	45	95	106	147	155	302	122	131	253	117

Cleveland Indians - Progressive Field
LF: 325   CF: 405   RF:325

	2015 Season							2013-2015						
	Home Games			Away Games				Home Games			Away Games			
	Indians	Opp	Total	Indians	Opp	Total	Index	Indians	Opp	Total	Indians	Opp	Total	Index
G	80	80	160	81	81	162		242	242	484	243	243	486	
Avg	.274	.251	.262	.239	.223	.231	113	.261	.246	.254	.248	.244	.246	103
AB	2695	2758	5453	2744	2615	5359	103	8059	8430	16489	8420	8008	16428	101
R	367	359	726	302	281	583	126	1048	1001	2049	1035	954	1989	103
H	739	691	1430	656	583	1239	117	2106	2074	4180	2091	1957	4048	104
2B	177	150	327	126	104	230	140	459	437	896	418	374	792	113
3B	13	13	26	16	18	34	75	28	34	62	47	50	97	64
HR	61	88	149	80	73	153	96	220	238	458	234	205	439	104
BB	280	222	502	253	203	456	108	799	712	1511	800	731	1531	98
SO	576	707	1283	581	700	1281	98	1780	2188	3968	1849	2048	3897	101
Foul Outs	51	30	81	62	64	126	63	138	115	253	176	169	345	73
E	39	42	81	40	38	78	105	150	123	273	143	136	279	98
E-Infield	16	17	33	12	15	27	124	63	46	109	54	60	114	96
LHB-Avg	.280	.254	.269	.250	.210	.233	115	.267	.243	.256	.250	.240	.246	104
LHB-HR	35	40	75	48	36	84	90	139	114	253	134	102	236	105
RHB-Avg	.265	.247	.255	.222	.235	.229	111	.252	.249	.250	.246	.248	.247	101
RHB-HR	26	48	74	32	37	69	103	81	124	205	100	103	203	103

Colorado Rockies - Coors Field
LF: 347   CF: 415   RF:350

	2015 Season							2013-2015						
	Home Games			Away Games				Home Games			Away Games			
	Rockies	Opp	Total	Rockies	Opp	Total	Index	Rockies	Opp	Total	Rockies	Opp	Total	Index
G	81	81	162	81	81	162		243	243	486	243	243	486	
Avg	.302	.302	.302	.228	.262	.245	123	.306	.288	.297	.234	.267	.251	118
AB	2819	2912	5731	2753	2671	5424	106	8523	8722	17245	8260	7987	16247	106
R	449	483	932	288	361	649	144	1383	1314	2697	815	1108	1923	140
H	851	878	1729	628	701	1329	130	2605	2516	5121	1936	2136	4072	126
2B	151	201	352	123	162	285	117	478	551	1029	386	480	866	112
3B	35	25	60	14	16	30	189	98	60	158	28	56	84	177
HR	102	100	202	84	83	167	114	309	261	570	222	231	453	119
BB	210	287	497	178	292	470	100	648	794	1442	564	833	1397	97
SO	572	560	1132	711	552	1263	85	1636	1620	3256	2132	1630	3762	82
Foul Outs	34	36	70	62	50	112	59	119	118	237	165	149	314	71
E	48	52	100	47	41	88	114	140	173	313	151	114	265	118
E-Infield	15	25	40	20	20	40	100	47	72	119	53	47	100	119
LHB-Avg	.308	.295	.301	.229	.260	.243	124	.301	.278	.290	.237	.262	.249	116
LHB-HR	46	36	82	42	25	67	120	131	85	216	101	79	180	115
RHB-Avg	.298	.306	.302	.227	.264	.246	123	.309	.295	.302	.233	.271	.252	120
RHB-HR	56	64	120	42	58	100	111	178	176	354	121	152	273	121

Detroit Tigers - Comerica Park
LF: 345 CF: 420 RF:330

| | 2015 Season | | | | | | | 2013-2015 | | | | | | |
| | Home Games | | | Away Games | | | | Home Games | | | Away Games | | | |
	Tigers	Opp	Total	Tigers	Opp	Total	Index	Tigers	Opp	Total	Tigers	Opp	Total	Index
G	81	81	162	80	80	160		243	243	486	242	242	484	
Avg	.273	.257	.265	.267	.279	.273	97	.285	.257	.271	.269	.261	.265	102
AB	2770	2836	5606	2835	2729	5564	100	8211	8457	16668	8759	8266	17025	98
R	337	375	712	352	428	780	90	1126	1074	2200	1116	1058	2174	101
H	757	729	1486	758	762	1520	97	2341	2175	4516	2356	2160	4516	100
2B	147	136	283	142	144	286	98	430	426	856	476	429	905	97
3B	30	33	63	19	27	46	136	63	76	139	35	54	89	160
HR	69	84	153	82	109	191	80	233	215	448	249	233	482	95
BB	228	244	472	227	245	472	99	733	706	1439	696	707	1403	105
SO	581	578	1159	678	522	1200	96	1550	1852	3402	1926	1920	3846	90
Foul Outs	58	76	134	57	53	110	121	175	195	370	169	151	320	118
E	42	54	96	44	33	77	123	128	142	270	135	131	266	101
E-Infield	15	19	34	24	13	37	91	50	53	103	56	57	113	91
LHB-Avg	.236	.260	.252	.234	.281	.262	96	.261	.252	.255	.250	.260	.256	100
LHB-HR	11	36	47	15	46	61	77	58	102	160	67	108	175	95
RHB-Avg	.285	.255	.272	.280	.278	.279	97	.295	.262	.281	.277	.263	.271	104
RHB-HR	58	48	106	67	63	130	81	175	113	288	182	125	307	95

Houston Astros - Minute Maid Park
LF: 315 CF: 435 RF:326

| | 2015 Season | | | | | | | 2013-2015 | | | | | | |
| | Home Games | | | Away Games | | | | Home Games | | | Away Games | | | |
	Astros	Opp	Total	Astros	Opp	Total	Index	Astros	Opp	Total	Astros	Opp	Total	Index
G	81	81	162	81	81	162		243	243	486	243	243	486	
Avg	.253	.233	.243	.247	.248	.248	98	.243	.255	.249	.244	.262	.253	99
AB	2605	2770	5375	2854	2664	5518	97	7980	8538	16518	8383	8035	16418	101
R	367	281	648	362	337	699	93	983	1100	2083	985	1089	2074	100
H	658	646	1304	705	662	1367	95	1940	2173	4113	2047	2102	4149	99
2B	134	126	260	144	126	270	99	369	429	798	415	411	826	96
3B	14	24	38	12	13	25	156	36	64	100	25	44	69	144
HR	128	70	198	102	78	180	113	299	249	548	242	229	471	116
BB	252	191	443	234	232	466	98	714	756	1470	693	767	1460	100
SO	689	696	1385	703	584	1287	110	2193	1872	4065	2176	1629	3805	106
Foul Outs	45	50	95	73	50	123	79	137	152	289	192	179	371	77
E	37	45	82	48	55	103	80	148	144	292	168	139	307	95
E-Infield	15	15	30	16	19	35	86	62	53	115	67	55	122	94
LHB-Avg	.230	.217	.223	.235	.251	.243	92	.224	.253	.240	.234	.261	.248	97
LHB-HR	52	25	77	43	24	67	119	128	102	230	96	92	188	122
RHB-Avg	.266	.246	.256	.255	.247	.251	102	.255	.256	.256	.251	.262	.256	100
RHB-HR	76	45	121	59	54	113	109	171	147	318	146	137	283	112

Kansas City Royals - Kauffman Stadium
LF: 330 CF: 410 RF:330

| | 2015 Season | | | | | | | 2013-2015 | | | | | | |
| | Home Games | | | Away Games | | | | Home Games | | | Away Games | | | |
	Royals	Opp	Total	Royals	Opp	Total	Index	Royals	Opp	Total	Royals	Opp	Total	Index
G	81	81	162	81	81	162		243	243	486	243	243	486	
Avg	.279	.248	.263	.259	.251	.255	103	.265	.256	.260	.263	.243	.253	103
AB	2673	2765	5438	2902	2734	5636	96	8018	8442	16460	8651	8058	16709	99
R	376	313	689	348	328	676	102	1000	980	1980	1023	886	1909	104
H	746	685	1431	751	687	1438	100	2122	2165	4287	2274	1959	4233	101
2B	157	152	309	143	110	253	127	412	425	837	428	329	757	112
3B	25	23	48	17	16	33	151	58	56	114	47	38	85	136
HR	62	68	130	77	87	164	82	160	197	357	186	241	427	85
BB	196	215	411	187	274	461	92	597	658	1255	588	740	1328	96
SO	437	566	1003	536	594	1130	92	1365	1757	3122	1641	1779	3420	93
Foul Outs	48	62	110	64	55	119	96	183	189	372	190	174	364	104
E	35	44	79	53	63	116	68	129	132	261	148	167	315	83
E-Infield	15	16	31	16	26	42	74	45	56	101	57	59	116	87
LHB-Avg	.291	.242	.264	.272	.251	.261	101	.262	.260	.261	.268	.249	.258	101
LHB-HR	35	35	70	42	36	78	94	89	92	181	99	112	211	88
RHB-Avg	.272	.252	.263	.250	.252	.251	105	.267	.253	.260	.259	.238	.249	104
RHB-HR	27	33	60	35	51	86	72	71	105	176	87	129	216	82

462

Los Angeles Angels - Angel Stadium of Anaheim
LF: 330   CF: 400   RF:330

| | 2015 Season | | | | | | | 2013-2015 | | | | | | |
| | Home Games | | | Away Games | | | | Home Games | | | Away Games | | | |
	Angels	Opp	Total	Angels	Opp	Total	Index	Angels	Opp	Total	Angels	Opp	Total	Index
G	81	81	162	81	81	162		243	243	486	243	243	486	
Avg	.250	.233	.241	.242	.263	.253	95	.258	.242	.249	.255	.256	.256	98
AB	2641	2758	5399	2776	2709	5485	98	8155	8525	16680	8502	8121	16623	100
R	320	298	618	341	377	718	86	1034	979	2013	1133	1063	2196	92
H	659	642	1301	672	713	1385	94	2101	2059	4160	2170	2078	4248	98
2B	116	123	239	127	150	277	88	376	400	776	441	387	828	93
3B	11	6	17	10	13	23	75	41	22	63	50	32	82	77
HR	94	70	164	82	96	178	94	244	205	449	251	254	505	89
BB	219	237	456	216	229	445	104	718	739	1457	732	764	1496	97
SO	569	668	1237	581	553	1134	111	1776	2020	3796	1861	1743	3604	105
Foul Outs	55	66	121	47	52	99	124	167	186	353	144	183	327	108
E	48	44	92	45	44	89	103	146	148	294	142	167	309	95
E-Infield	27	20	47	20	21	41	115	63	66	129	56	67	123	105
LHB-Avg	.238	.239	.239	.234	.266	.252	95	.248	.243	.245	.249	.254	.252	97
LHB-HR	24	25	49	18	38	56	91	67	83	150	67	113	180	85
RHB-Avg	.255	.228	.242	.246	.261	.253	96	.263	.240	.252	.259	.257	.258	98
RHB-HR	70	45	115	64	58	122	94	177	122	299	184	141	325	90

Los Angeles Dodgers - Dodger Stadium
LF: 330   CF: 395   RF:330

| | 2015 Season | | | | | | | 2013-2015 | | | | | | |
| | Home Games | | | Away Games | | | | Home Games | | | Away Games | | | |
	Dodgers	Opp	Total	Dodgers	Opp	Total	Index	Dodgers	Opp	Total	Dodgers	Opp	Total	Index
G	81	81	162	81	81	162		243	243	486	243	243	486	
Avg	.251	.230	.240	.249	.255	.252	95	.254	.235	.244	.265	.250	.258	95
AB	2617	2778	5395	2768	2655	5423	99	7942	8384	16326	8494	8002	16496	99
R	340	264	604	327	331	658	92	952	859	1811	1082	935	2017	90
H	656	640	1296	690	677	1367	95	2018	1973	3991	2251	2003	4254	94
2B	140	113	253	123	116	239	106	422	373	795	424	361	785	102
3B	13	5	18	13	15	28	65	32	13	45	49	49	98	46
HR	97	69	166	90	76	166	101	233	215	448	226	199	425	107
BB	252	171	423	311	224	535	79	695	588	1283	863	696	1559	83
SO	608	730	1338	650	666	1316	102	1763	2110	3873	1887	1951	3838	102
Foul Outs	50	46	96	67	40	107	90	139	142	281	180	137	317	90
E	30	40	70	45	27	72	97	146	138	284	145	137	282	101
E-Infield	15	13	28	18	11	29	97	69	43	112	60	53	113	99
LHB-Avg	.237	.230	.234	.244	.274	.256	91	.253	.243	.248	.262	.257	.260	96
LHB-HR	58	23	81	50	29	79	106	110	78	188	86	82	168	115
RHB-Avg	.265	.231	.245	.255	.244	.249	98	.255	.231	.242	.268	.246	.257	94
RHB-HR	39	46	85	40	47	87	96	123	137	260	140	117	257	101

Miami Marlins - Marlins Park
LF: 340   CF: 416   RF:335

| | 2015 Season | | | | | | | 2013-2015 | | | | | | |
| | Home Games | | | Away Games | | | | Home Games | | | Away Games | | | |
	Marlins	Opp	Total	Marlins	Opp	Total	Index	Marlins	Opp	Total	Marlins	Opp	Total	Index
G	81	81	162	81	81	162		243	243	486	243	243	486	
Avg	.260	.250	.255	.260	.260	.260	98	.251	.253	.252	.245	.261	.253	100
AB	2668	2786	5454	2795	2599	5394	101	8000	8447	16447	8450	8026	16476	100
R	306	323	629	307	355	662	95	931	950	1881	840	1048	1888	100
H	693	697	1390	727	677	1404	99	2007	2135	4142	2069	2096	4165	99
2B	110	139	249	126	139	265	93	354	427	781	355	404	759	103
3B	22	16	38	18	13	31	121	68	65	133	39	52	91	146
HR	53	58	111	67	83	150	73	148	151	299	189	225	414	72
BB	197	261	458	178	247	425	107	693	720	1413	615	772	1387	102
SO	538	617	1155	612	535	1147	100	1745	1821	3566	2056	1698	3754	95
Foul Outs	46	53	99	53	54	107	92	143	145	288	164	148	312	92
E	34	45	79	43	43	86	92	121	140	261	141	125	266	98
E-Infield	9	16	25	21	14	35	71	46	48	94	58	50	108	87
LHB-Avg	.282	.266	.274	.266	.259	.262	104	.260	.253	.256	.246	.267	.257	100
LHB-HR	18	29	47	28	36	64	75	42	70	112	71	101	172	64
RHB-Avg	.244	.239	.241	.256	.262	.259	93	.245	.253	.249	.244	.256	.250	100
RHB-HR	35	29	64	39	47	86	72	106	81	187	118	124	242	78

Milwaukee Brewers - Miller Park
LF: 344   CF: 400   RF:345

	2015 Season							2013-2015						
	Home Games			Away Games				Home Games			Away Games			
	Brewers	Opp	Total	Brewers	Opp	Total	Index	Brewers	Opp	Total	Brewers	Opp	Total	Index
G	81	81	162	81	81	162		243	243	486	243	243	486	
Avg	.249	.260	.255	.254	.262	.258	99	.254	.257	.255	.249	.254	.251	102
AB	2694	2851	5545	2786	2633	5419	102	8014	8477	16491	8402	8038	16440	100
R	341	389	730	314	348	662	110	997	1085	2082	948	996	1944	107
H	671	741	1412	707	691	1398	101	2033	2178	4211	2092	2041	4133	102
2B	145	145	290	129	142	271	105	401	373	774	408	378	786	98
3B	21	15	36	13	18	31	113	55	29	84	50	43	93	90
HR	76	113	189	69	63	132	140	235	308	543	217	210	427	127
BB	227	239	466	185	278	463	98	675	683	1358	567	731	1298	104
SO	633	669	1302	666	591	1257	101	1740	1918	3658	1939	1713	3652	100
Foul Outs	39	47	86	59	44	103	82	138	161	299	181	169	350	85
E	58	47	105	58	45	103	102	149	150	299	180	156	336	89
E-Infield	17	20	37	18	16	34	109	54	61	115	68	59	127	91
LHB-Avg	.281	.282	.281	.261	.255	.257	109	.267	.265	.266	.259	.244	.250	107
LHB-HR	22	58	80	20	28	48	157	51	154	205	46	103	149	133
RHB-Avg	.233	.241	.237	.251	.268	.258	92	.249	.250	.249	.245	.262	.252	99
RHB-HR	54	55	109	49	35	84	130	184	154	338	171	107	278	123

Minnesota Twins - Target Field
LF: 339   CF: 411   RF:328

	2015 Season							2013-2015						
	Home Games			Away Games				Home Games			Away Games			
	Twins	Opp	Total	Twins	Opp	Total	Index	Twins	Opp	Total	Twins	Opp	Total	Index
G	81	81	162	81	81	162		243	243	486	243	243	486	
Avg	.263	.262	.262	.231	.277	.253	104	.257	.275	.267	.238	.278	.258	103
AB	2696	2848	5544	2771	2752	5523	100	8173	8711	16884	8425	8233	16658	101
R	373	323	696	323	377	700	99	1044	1147	2191	981	1118	2099	104
H	710	745	1455	639	761	1400	104	2102	2399	4501	2005	2286	4291	105
2B	134	149	283	143	146	289	98	434	492	926	444	432	876	104
3B	22	9	31	22	16	38	81	46	46	92	40	47	87	104
HR	85	79	164	71	84	155	105	220	225	445	215	253	468	94
BB	220	196	416	219	217	436	95	759	604	1363	757	675	1432	94
SO	577	530	1107	687	516	1203	92	1860	1549	3409	2163	1513	3676	91
Foul Outs	51	58	109	59	57	116	94	160	187	347	164	186	350	98
E	48	57	105	38	44	82	128	151	147	298	113	149	262	114
E-Infield	22	25	47	13	16	29	162	60	64	124	39	63	102	122
LHB-Avg	.265	.254	.259	.220	.281	.253	102	.260	.270	.265	.239	.279	.258	103
LHB-HR	26	24	50	14	35	49	100	90	84	174	86	109	195	90
RHB-Avg	.262	.268	.265	.237	.273	.254	104	.254	.280	.268	.237	.277	.257	104
RHB-HR	59	55	114	57	49	106	108	130	141	271	129	144	273	96

New York Mets - Citi Field
LF: 335   CF: 408   RF:330

	2015 Season							2012-2014						
	Home Games			Away Games				Home Games			Away Games			
	Mets	Opp	Total	Mets	Opp	Total	Index	Mets	Opp	Total	Mets	Opp	Total	Index
G	81	81	162	81	81	162		243	243	486	243	243	486	
Avg	.233	.236	.235	.255	.250	.253	93	.228	.245	.237	.254	.259	.256	92
AB	2660	2807	5467	2867	2708	5575	98	7967	8461	16428	8514	8145	16659	99
R	313	290	603	370	323	693	87	841	970	1811	1057	1041	2098	86
H	621	663	1284	730	678	1408	91	1819	2069	3888	2162	2111	4273	91
2B	144	112	256	151	123	274	95	366	392	758	458	403	861	89
3B	7	12	19	10	11	21	92	33	30	63	39	56	95	67
HR	85	79	164	92	73	165	101	185	249	434	209	205	414	106
BB	248	187	435	240	196	436	102	756	730	1486	775	725	1500	100
SO	620	698	1318	670	639	1309	103	1928	1967	3895	1970	1785	3755	105
Foul Outs	65	58	123	74	56	130	96	149	189	338	163	178	341	101
E	34	37	71	54	50	104	68	126	136	262	172	134	306	86
E-Infield	12	18	30	22	25	47	64	53	53	106	72	65	137	77
LHB-Avg	.242	.251	.247	.255	.259	.257	96	.227	.242	.234	.253	.268	.260	90
LHB-HR	49	42	91	38	34	72	124	87	106	193	104	94	198	101
RHB-Avg	.228	.224	.226	.255	.244	.250	90	.230	.246	.239	.255	.253	.254	94
RHB-HR	36	37	73	54	39	93	82	98	143	241	105	111	216	111

New York Yankees - Yankee Stadium
LF: 318   CF: 408   RF:314

| | 2015 Season | | | | | | | 2013-2015 | | | | | | |
| | Home Games | | | Away Games | | | | Home Games | | | Away Games | | | |
	Yankees	Opp	Total	Yankees	Opp	Total	Index	Yankees	Opp	Total	Yankees	Opp	Total	Index
G	81	81	162	81	81	162		243	243	486	243	243	486	
Avg	.255	.240	.248	.247	.267	.257	96	.251	.252	.252	.241	.257	.249	101
AB	2749	2862	5611	2818	2728	5546	101	8041	8555	16596	8472	8166	16638	100
R	381	358	739	383	340	723	102	1022	1035	2057	1025	998	2023	102
H	701	688	1389	696	729	1425	97	2022	2159	4181	2045	2102	4147	101
2B	133	117	250	139	143	282	88	360	395	755	406	426	832	91
3B	5	12	17	14	13	27	62	23	29	52	46	39	85	61
HR	114	105	219	98	77	175	124	277	294	571	226	223	449	127
BB	274	240	514	280	234	514	99	751	649	1400	721	660	1381	102
SO	618	697	1315	609	673	1282	101	1753	2081	3834	1821	1892	3713	104
Foul Outs	55	46	101	50	52	102	98	172	164	336	174	148	322	105
E	44	45	89	48	39	87	102	132	126	258	121	139	260	99
E-Infield	21	19	40	24	24	48	83	56	51	107	55	61	116	92
LHB-Avg	.252	.260	.255	.250	.264	.255	100	.261	.253	.257	.241	.255	.247	104
LHB-HR	77	44	121	66	17	83	146	189	110	299	148	84	232	129
RHB-Avg	.261	.226	.238	.239	.269	.259	92	.237	.252	.246	.242	.259	.252	98
RHB-HR	37	61	98	32	60	92	104	88	184	272	78	139	217	126

Oakland Athletics - O.co Coliseum
LF: 330   CF: 400   RF:330

| | 2015 Season | | | | | | | 2013-2015 | | | | | | |
| | Home Games | | | Away Games | | | | Home Games | | | Away Games | | | |
	Athletics	Opp	Total	Athletics	Opp	Total	Index	Athletics	Opp	Total	Athletics	Opp	Total	Index
G	81	81	162	81	81	162		243	243	486	243	243	486	
Avg	.257	.241	.249	.245	.267	.256	97	.253	.237	.245	.246	.249	.248	99
AB	2752	2778	5530	2848	2742	5590	99	8157	8414	16571	8509	8086	16595	100
R	351	340	691	343	389	732	94	1080	924	2004	1110	1002	2112	95
H	708	670	1378	697	732	1429	96	2066	1993	4059	2096	2017	4113	99
2B	147	120	267	130	146	276	98	424	366	790	407	339	746	106
3B	29	3	32	17	10	27	120	63	18	81	41	25	66	123
HR	60	79	139	86	93	179	78	217	218	435	261	264	525	83
BB	228	223	451	247	251	498	92	830	639	1469	804	669	1473	100
SO	496	577	1073	623	602	1225	89	1571	1805	3376	1830	1801	3631	93
Foul Outs	90	96	186	61	58	119	158	287	286	573	196	164	360	159
E	67	55	122	59	49	108	113	165	148	313	169	149	318	98
E-Infield	28	19	47	24	29	53	89	67	50	117	64	64	128	91
LHB-Avg	.252	.237	.245	.242	.260	.250	98	.247	.237	.242	.252	.257	.254	95
LHB-HR	19	38	57	37	40	77	77	92	92	184	134	112	246	75
RHB-Avg	.261	.244	.253	.247	.273	.260	97	.259	.237	.247	.240	.244	.242	102
RHB-HR	41	41	82	49	53	102	79	125	126	251	127	152	279	90

Philadelphia Phillies - Citizens Bank Park
LF: 329   CF: 401   RF:329

| | 2015 Season | | | | | | | 2013-2015 | | | | | | |
| | Home Games | | | Away Games | | | | Home Games | | | Away Games | | | |
	Phillies	Opp	Total	Phillies	Opp	Total	Index	Phillies	Opp	Total	Phillies	Opp	Total	Index
G	81	81	162	81	81	162		243	243	486	243	243	486	
Avg	.247	.273	.261	.249	.287	.268	97	.245	.257	.251	.247	.275	.261	96
AB	2691	2930	5621	2838	2761	5599	100	8151	8674	16825	8437	8101	16538	102
R	338	393	731	288	416	704	104	985	1089	2074	870	1156	2026	102
H	666	800	1466	708	792	1500	98	1999	2226	4225	2086	2227	4313	98
2B	124	154	278	148	146	294	94	373	448	821	405	444	849	95
3B	19	9	28	18	24	42	66	54	36	90	42	65	107	83
HR	72	99	171	58	92	150	114	220	269	489	175	208	383	125
BB	200	248	448	187	240	427	105	660	742	1402	587	773	1360	101
SO	613	626	1239	661	527	1188	104	1910	1947	3857	1875	1660	3535	107
Foul Outs	60	67	127	56	39	95	133	175	202	377	169	142	311	119
E	64	69	133	53	45	98	136	170	171	341	127	148	275	124
E-Infield	33	35	68	16	17	33	206	83	75	158	45	67	112	141
LHB-Avg	.252	.284	.265	.252	.301	.272	98	.251	.260	.255	.253	.272	.260	98
LHB-HR	40	34	74	30	45	75	98	120	83	203	101	87	188	110
RHB-Avg	.241	.266	.256	.246	.277	.264	97	.237	.255	.248	.239	.277	.261	95
RHB-HR	32	65	97	28	47	75	129	100	186	286	74	121	195	140

Pittsburgh Pirates - PNC Park
LF: 325   CF: 399   RF:320

	2015 Season							2013-2015						
	Home Games			Away Games				Home Games			Away Games			
	Pirates	Opp	Total	Pirates	Opp	Total	Index	Pirates	Opp	Total	Pirates	Opp	Total	Index
G	81	81	162	81	81	162		243	243	486	243	243	486	
Avg	.259	.241	.250	.261	.255	.258	97	.260	.238	.249	.250	.250	.250	100
AB	2738	2867	5605	2893	2748	5641	99	8157	8432	16589	8496	8080	16576	100
R	343	281	624	354	315	669	93	1002	847	1849	1011	957	1968	94
H	708	691	1399	754	701	1455	96	2122	2009	4131	2122	2023	4145	100
2B	128	128	256	164	129	293	88	407	343	750	433	372	805	93
3B	14	9	23	13	15	28	83	46	24	70	46	45	91	77
HR	72	58	130	68	52	120	109	203	151	354	254	188	442	80
BB	233	224	457	228	229	457	101	718	706	1424	732	761	1493	95
SO	620	691	1311	702	647	1349	98	1765	1945	3710	2131	1882	4013	92
Foul Outs	33	46	79	42	53	95	84	131	132	263	151	139	290	91
E	57	54	111	65	44	109	102	166	145	311	171	139	310	100
E-Infield	28	26	54	29	20	49	110	65	66	131	68	62	130	101
LHB-Avg	.222	.236	.230	.254	.257	.255	90	.239	.235	.237	.230	.254	.242	98
LHB-HR	30	17	47	25	19	44	110	102	47	149	98	66	164	92
RHB-Avg	.275	.244	.260	.264	.254	.259	100	.271	.240	.256	.260	.248	.255	100
RHB-HR	42	41	83	43	33	76	109	101	104	205	156	122	278	73

San Diego Padres - PETCO Park
LF: 336   CF: 396   RF:322

	2015 Season							2013-2014						
	Home Games			Away Games				Home Games			Away Games			
	Padres	Opp	Total	Padres	Opp	Total	Index	Padres	Opp	Total	Padres	Opp	Total	Index
G	81	81	162	81	81	162		162	162	324	162	162	324	
Avg	.247	.243	.245	.239	.262	.250	98	.234	.228	.231	.237	.270	.253	91
AB	2651	2760	5411	2806	2680	5486	99	5268	5560	10828	5543	5342	10885	99
R	321	345	666	329	386	715	93	558	543	1101	595	734	1329	83
H	654	670	1324	670	701	1371	97	1235	1266	2501	1313	1441	2754	91
2B	128	130	258	132	138	270	97	221	233	454	249	295	544	84
3B	17	21	38	19	29	48	80	35	24	59	21	35	56	106
HR	74	92	166	74	79	153	110	120	127	247	135	146	281	88
BB	211	258	469	215	258	473	101	489	485	974	446	502	948	103
SO	655	748	1403	672	645	1317	108	1268	1327	2595	1335	1128	2463	106
Foul Outs	52	54	106	55	43	98	110	83	90	173	97	91	188	93
E	48	50	98	44	59	103	95	86	94	180	98	95	193	93
E-Infield	16	20	36	21	23	44	82	35	33	68	29	36	65	105
LHB-Avg	.258	.252	.254	.259	.260	.259	98	.236	.232	.234	.239	.261	.250	94
LHB-HR	15	55	70	21	43	64	110	56	62	118	49	59	108	107
RHB-Avg	.241	.234	.238	.228	.263	.243	98	.233	.224	.228	.235	.276	.256	89
RHB-HR	59	37	96	53	36	89	110	64	65	129	86	87	173	76

San Francisco Giants - AT&T Park
LF: 339   CF: 399   RF:309

	2015 Season							2013-2015						
	Home Games			Away Games				Home Games			Away Games			
	Giants	Opp	Total	Giants	Opp	Total	Index	Giants	Opp	Total	Giants	Opp	Total	Index
G	81	81	162	81	81	162		244	244	488	242	242	484	
Avg	.265	.233	.249	.269	.236	.249	94	.260	.236	.248	.261	.257	.259	96
AB	2680	2762	5442	2885	2701	5586	97	8100	8339	16439	8540	8027	16567	98
R	330	276	606	366	351	717	85	942	899	1841	1048	1033	2081	88
H	711	643	1354	775	701	1476	92	2110	1969	4079	2229	2060	4289	94
2B	132	112	244	156	134	290	86	389	390	779	436	399	835	94
3B	29	27	56	10	24	34	169	78	76	154	38	48	86	180
HR	53	56	109	83	99	182	61	150	177	327	225	256	481	69
BB	232	209	441	225	222	447	101	698	672	1370	655	669	1324	104
SO	557	611	1168	602	554	1156	104	1668	1926	3594	1814	1706	3520	103
Foul Outs	30	53	83	45	49	94	91	126	155	281	167	158	325	87
E	45	39	84	33	45	78	108	148	116	264	137	129	266	98
E-Infield	17	16	33	12	19	31	106	63	49	112	47	54	101	110
LHB-Avg	.275	.239	.258	.265	.267	.266	97	.271	.240	.256	.257	.256	.257	100
LHB-HR	22	24	46	46	49	95	50	56	69	125	107	103	210	59
RHB-Avg	.257	.228	.241	.272	.255	.263	92	.251	.233	.242	.264	.257	.261	93
RHB-HR	31	32	63	37	50	87	74	94	108	202	118	153	271	76

Seattle Mariners - Safeco Field
LF: 331   CF: 401   RF:326

| | 2015 Season | | | | | | | 2013-2015 | | | | | | |
| | Home Games | | | Away Games | | | | Home Games | | | Away Games | | | |
	Mariners	Opp	Total	Mariners	Opp	Total	Index	Mariners	Opp	Total	Mariners	Opp	Total	Index
G	81	81	162	81	81	162		243	243	486	243	243	486	
Avg	.249	.238	.244	.248	.274	.261	93	.242	.237	.240	.244	.260	.252	95
AB	2711	2807	5518	2833	2783	5616	98	8060	8425	16485	8492	8212	16704	99
R	310	336	646	346	390	736	88	901	968	1869	1013	1066	2079	90
H	676	668	1344	703	762	1465	92	1951	2000	3951	2074	2137	4211	94
2B	123	125	248	139	160	299	84	358	396	754	400	431	831	92
3B	10	10	20	12	13	25	81	27	27	54	44	44	88	62
HR	90	90	180	108	91	199	92	251	239	490	271	253	524	95
BB	242	231	473	236	260	496	97	688	678	1366	715	754	1469	94
SO	690	674	1364	646	609	1255	111	1951	2061	4012	1970	1836	3806	107
Foul Outs	53	65	118	50	52	102	118	192	189	381	146	151	297	130
E	46	52	98	48	44	92	107	123	141	264	141	127	268	99
E-Infield	26	27	53	20	16	36	147	54	68	122	66	50	116	105
LHB-Avg	.257	.249	.254	.257	.277	.265	96	.254	.243	.249	.258	.258	.258	97
LHB-HR	43	35	78	52	28	80	96	156	98	254	159	101	260	98
RHB-Avg	.240	.231	.235	.239	.272	.257	91	.224	.233	.229	.225	.262	.246	93
RHB-HR	47	55	102	56	63	119	90	95	141	236	112	152	264	91

St Louis Cardinals - Busch Stadium
LF: 336   CF: 400   RF:335

| | 2015 Season | | | | | | | 2013-2015 | | | | | | |
| | Home Games | | | Away Games | | | | Home Games | | | Away Games | | | |
	Cardinals	Opp	Total	Cardinals	Opp	Total	Index	Cardinals	Opp	Total	Cardinals	Opp	Total	Index
G	81	81	162	81	81	162		243	243	486	243	243	486	
Avg	.262	.248	.255	.244	.244	.244	105	.265	.239	.252	.251	.252	.252	100
AB	2672	2850	5522	2812	2667	5479	101	8001	8418	16419	8466	8046	16512	99
R	315	250	565	332	275	607	93	1025	830	1855	1024	894	1918	97
H	701	708	1409	685	651	1336	105	2122	2016	4138	2129	2030	4159	99
2B	147	118	265	141	122	263	100	452	372	824	433	384	817	101
3B	18	15	33	21	11	32	102	40	42	82	40	39	79	104
HR	60	60	120	77	63	140	85	175	165	340	192	193	385	89
BB	258	214	472	248	263	511	92	738	665	1403	720	733	1453	97
SO	578	662	1240	689	667	1356	91	1564	1954	3518	1946	1850	3796	93
Foul Outs	48	73	121	47	38	85	141	163	194	357	161	126	287	125
E	48	40	88	48	53	101	87	122	115	237	137	137	274	86
E-Infield	23	15	38	22	27	49	78	62	39	101	63	58	121	83
LHB-Avg	.272	.250	.261	.249	.250	.250	105	.279	.244	.262	.261	.255	.258	101
LHB-HR	27	24	51	37	27	64	85	79	60	139	84	82	166	87
RHB-Avg	.255	.248	.251	.239	.239	.239	105	.254	.237	.245	.244	.250	.247	99
RHB-HR	33	36	69	40	36	76	86	96	105	201	108	111	219	90

Tampa Bay Rays - Tropicana Field Surface: FieldTurf
LF: 315   CF: 404   RF:322

| | 2015 Season | | | | | | | 2013-2015 | | | | | | |
| | Home Games | | | Away Games | | | | Home Games | | | Away Games | | | |
	Rays	Opp	Total	Rays	Opp	Total	Index	Rays	Opp	Total	Rays	Opp	Total	Index
G	84	84	168	78	78	156		246	246	492	241	241	482	
Avg	.245	.238	.241	.259	.242	.251	96	.250	.231	.240	.254	.245	.250	96
AB	2730	2887	5617	2755	2590	5345	98	8122	8509	16631	8417	7968	16385	99
R	315	332	647	329	310	639	94	975	936	1911	981	977	1958	96
H	669	687	1356	714	627	1341	94	2028	1967	3995	2137	1954	4091	96
2B	135	106	241	143	126	269	85	393	341	734	444	381	825	88
3B	13	9	22	19	10	29	72	36	36	72	43	31	74	96
HR	82	92	174	85	83	168	99	214	233	447	235	240	475	93
BB	214	234	448	222	243	465	92	804	697	1501	748	744	1492	99
SO	694	743	1437	616	612	1228	111	1816	2168	3984	1789	1934	3723	105
Foul Outs	67	79	146	64	64	128	109	195	223	418	167	198	365	113
E	44	34	78	51	44	95	76	96	106	202	146	131	277	71
E-Infield	21	11	32	21	17	38	78	41	36	77	53	47	100	75
LHB-Avg	.251	.237	.242	.265	.231	.246	98	.259	.226	.241	.258	.244	.251	96
LHB-HR	27	44	71	20	23	43	153	86	111	197	80	93	173	109
RHB-Avg	.242	.239	.241	.256	.252	.254	95	.243	.236	.240	.251	.246	.249	96
RHB-HR	55	48	103	65	60	125	80	128	122	250	155	147	302	83

Texas Rangers - Globe Life Park in Arlington
LF: 332   CF: 400   RF:325

	2015 Season							2013-2015						
	Home Games			Away Games				Home Games			Away Games			
	Rangers	Opp	Total	Rangers	Opp	Total	Index	Rangers	Opp	Total	Rangers	Opp	Total	Index
G	81	81	162	81	81	162		244	244	488	243	243	486	
Avg	.274	.266	.270	.241	.258	.249	108	.265	.261	.263	.253	.260	.257	102
AB	2746	2857	5603	2765	2710	5475	102	8120	8520	16640	8436	8128	16564	100
R	404	387	791	347	346	693	114	1076	1120	2196	1042	1022	2064	106
H	753	759	1512	666	700	1366	111	2149	2224	4373	2135	2115	4250	102
2B	148	145	293	131	135	266	108	379	422	801	422	448	870	92
3B	18	17	35	14	23	37	92	45	46	91	38	42	80	113
HR	92	85	177	80	86	166	104	228	241	469	231	247	478	98
BB	272	265	537	231	243	474	111	731	766	1497	651	745	1396	107
SO	570	554	1124	663	541	1204	91	1624	1778	3402	1838	1736	3574	95
Foul Outs	44	54	98	67	47	114	84	135	162	297	181	194	375	79
E	58	55	113	61	64	125	90	161	177	338	150	175	325	104
E-Infield	22	27	49	30	28	58	84	66	75	141	62	71	133	106
LHB-Avg	.264	.277	.270	.259	.254	.257	105	.254	.267	.261	.248	.259	.253	103
LHB-HR	52	36	88	57	33	90	97	106	119	225	110	109	219	101
RHB-Avg	.285	.258	.270	.221	.261	.243	111	.274	.256	.264	.257	.261	.259	102
RHB-HR	40	49	89	23	53	76	113	122	122	244	121	138	259	95

Toronto Blue Jays - Rogers Centre Surface: FieldTurf
LF: 328   CF: 400   RF:328

	2015 Season							2013-2015						
	Home Games			Away Games				Home Games			Away Games			
	Blue Jays	Opp	Total	Blue Jays	Opp	Total	Index	Blue Jays	Opp	Total	Blue Jays	Opp	Total	Index
G	81	81	162	81	81	162		243	243	486	243	243	486	
Avg	.278	.228	.253	.260	.268	.264	96	.267	.244	.256	.253	.263	.258	99
AB	2661	2733	5394	2848	2719	5567	97	8131	8475	16606	8464	8115	16579	100
R	450	292	742	441	378	819	91	1217	1019	2236	1109	1093	2202	102
H	739	623	1362	741	730	1471	93	2172	2072	4244	2141	2132	4273	99
2B	171	127	298	137	140	277	111	475	489	964	388	413	801	120
3B	6	17	23	11	13	24	99	36	36	72	29	51	80	90
HR	123	80	203	109	93	202	104	316	287	603	278	232	510	118
BB	296	187	483	274	210	484	103	809	678	1487	773	709	1482	100
SO	524	575	1099	627	542	1169	97	1676	1896	3572	1749	1628	3377	106
Foul Outs	78	69	147	71	68	139	109	246	200	446	222	199	421	106
E	41	38	79	47	60	107	74	143	154	297	143	150	293	101
E-Infield	13	14	27	24	19	43	63	49	56	105	65	53	118	89
LHB-Avg	.256	.232	.241	.256	.264	.261	93	.261	.250	.255	.261	.260	.261	98
LHB-HR	14	41	55	18	43	61	88	94	128	222	77	115	192	114
RHB-Avg	.286	.224	.259	.262	.272	.266	97	.272	.240	.256	.247	.264	.255	100
RHB-HR	109	39	148	91	50	141	112	222	159	381	201	117	318	121

Washington Nationals - Nationals Park
LF: 336   CF: 402   RF:335

	2015 Season							2013-2015						
	Home Games			Away Games				Home Games			Away Games			
	Nationals	Opp	Total	Nationals	Opp	Total	Index	Nationals	Opp	Total	Nationals	Opp	Total	Index
G	81	81	162	81	81	162		243	243	486	243	243	486	
Avg	.257	.243	.249	.246	.258	.252	99	.266	.246	.256	.238	.250	.244	105
AB	2653	2795	5448	2775	2669	5444	100	8049	8428	16477	8357	8067	16424	100
R	360	309	669	343	326	669	100	1071	884	1955	974	932	1906	103
H	681	678	1359	682	688	1370	99	2139	2071	4210	1992	2013	4005	105
2B	140	118	258	125	121	246	105	407	387	794	382	356	738	107
3B	3	11	14	10	18	28	50	23	21	44	44	50	94	47
HR	91	72	163	86	73	159	102	224	182	406	266	215	481	84
BB	280	181	461	259	183	442	104	770	569	1339	750	552	1302	103
SO	629	686	1315	715	656	1371	96	1809	1979	3788	2031	1887	3918	96
Foul Outs	54	68	122	48	60	108	113	158	190	348	150	159	309	112
E	50	52	102	40	48	88	116	152	160	312	145	134	279	112
E-Infield	20	26	46	17	17	34	135	60	66	126	47	50	97	130
LHB-Avg	.270	.245	.255	.295	.277	.284	90	.272	.246	.258	.240	.264	.253	102
LHB-HR	36	32	68	39	34	73	88	91	72	163	96	107	203	80
RHB-Avg	.251	.240	.246	.226	.242	.233	106	.262	.246	.254	.237	.238	.238	107
RHB-HR	55	40	95	47	39	86	114	133	110	243	170	108	278	88

2015 American League Ballpark Index Rankings

Home Park	TOTALS												LHB		RHB	
	Avg	AB	R	H	2B	3B	HR	BB	SO	FO	E	E-Inf	Avg	HR	Avg	HR
Indians (Progressive Field)	113	103	126	117	140	75	96	108	98	63	105	124	115	90	111	103
Orioles (Oriole Park at Camden Yards)	107	104	123	112	94	74	136	90	92	81	113	115	107	138	108	134
Red Sox (Fenway Park)	109	101	119	110	127	102	96	91	97	80	147	144	115	78	106	113
Rangers (Globe Life Park in Arlington)	108	102	114	111	108	92	104	111	91	84	90	84	105	97	111	113
Yankees (Yankee Stadium)	96	101	102	97	88	62	124	99	101	98	102	83	100	146	92	104
Royals (Kauffman Stadium)	103	96	102	100	127	151	82	92	92	96	68	74	101	94	105	72
Twins (Target Field)	104	100	99	104	98	81	105	95	92	94	128	162	102	100	104	108
Athletics (O.co Coliseum)	97	99	94	96	98	120	78	92	89	158	113	89	98	77	97	79
Rays (Tropicana Field)	96	98	94	94	85	72	99	92	111	109	76	78	98	153	95	80
Astros (Minute Maid Park)	98	97	93	95	99	156	113	98	110	79	80	86	92	119	102	109
Blue Jays (Rogers Centre)	96	97	91	93	111	99	104	103	97	109	74	63	93	88	97	112
White Sox (U.S. Cellular Field)	94	101	90	95	86	82	110	122	106	113	103	113	87	104	99	113
Tigers (Comerica Park)	97	100	90	97	98	136	80	99	96	121	123	91	96	77	97	81
Mariners (Safeco Field)	93	98	88	92	84	81	92	97	111	118	107	147	96	96	91	90
Angels (Angel Stadium of Anaheim)	95	98	86	94	88	75	94	104	111	124	103	115	95	91	96	94

2015 National League Ballpark Index Rankings

Home Park	TOTALS												LHB		RHB	
	Avg	AB	R	H	2B	3B	HR	BB	SO	FO	E	E-Inf	Avg	HR	Avg	HR
Rockies (Coors Field)	123	106	144	130	117	189	114	100	85	59	114	100	124	120	123	111
Reds (Great American Ballpark)	104	104	112	108	100	43	110	106	107	115	77	49	108	115	101	106
Brewers (Miller Park)	99	102	110	101	105	113	140	98	101	82	102	109	109	157	92	130
Diamondbacks (Chase Field)	104	100	106	105	120	178	85	102	103	114	117	114	106	101	103	78
Phillies (Citizens Bank Park)	97	100	104	98	94	66	114	105	104	133	136	206	98	98	97	129
Nationals (Nationals Park)	99	100	100	99	105	50	102	104	96	113	116	135	90	88	106	114
Cubs (Wrigley Field)	96	97	95	93	82	113	131	106	100	83	77	86	92	108	99	156
Marlins (Marlins Park)	98	101	95	99	93	121	73	107	100	92	92	71	104	75	93	72
Braves (Turner Field)	92	99	94	92	98	77	73	112	108	95	128	129	90	62	94	83
Pirates (PNC Park)	97	99	93	96	88	83	109	101	98	84	102	110	90	110	100	109
Padres (PETCO Park)	98	99	93	97	97	80	110	101	108	110	95	82	98	110	98	110
Cardinals (Busch Stadium)	105	101	93	105	100	102	85	92	91	141	87	78	105	85	105	86
Dodgers (Dodger Stadium)	95	99	92	95	106	65	101	79	102	90	97	97	91	106	98	96
Mets (Citi Field)	93	98	87	91	95	92	101	102	103	96	68	64	96	124	90	82
Giants (AT&T Park)	94	97	85	92	86	169	61	101	104	91	108	106	97	50	92	74

2015 AL Home Runs

Home Park	Index
Orioles	136
Yankees	124
Astros	113
White Sox	110
Twins	105
Rangers	104
Blue Jays	104
Rays	99
Red Sox	96
Indians	96
Angels	94
Mariners	92
Royals	82
Tigers	80
Athletics	78

2015 AL LHB Home Runs

Home Park	Index
Rays	153
Yankees	146
Orioles	138
Astros	119
White Sox	104
Twins	100
Rangers	97
Mariners	96
Royals	94
Angels	91
Indians	90
Blue Jays	88
Red Sox	78
Athletics	77
Tigers	77

2015 AL RHB Home Runs

Home Park	Index
Orioles	134
White Sox	113
Red Sox	113
Rangers	113
Blue Jays	112
Astros	109
Twins	108
Yankees	104
Indians	103
Angels	94
Mariners	90
Tigers	81
Rays	80
Athletics	79
Royals	72

2015 NL Home Runs

Home Park	Index
Brewers	140
Cubs	131
Rockies	114
Phillies	114
Padres	110
Reds	110
Pirates	109
Nationals	102
Mets	101
Dodgers	101
Diamondbacks	85
Cardinals	85
Marlins	73
Braves	73
Giants	61

2015 NL LHB Home Runs

Home Park	Index
Brewers	157
Mets	124
Rockies	120
Reds	115
Pirates	110
Padres	110
Cubs	108
Dodgers	106
Diamondbacks	101
Phillies	98
Nationals	88
Cardinals	85
Marlins	75
Braves	62
Giants	50

2015 NL RHB Home Runs

Home Park	Index
Cubs	156
Brewers	130
Phillies	129
Nationals	114
Rockies	111
Padres	110
Pirates	109
Reds	106
Dodgers	96
Cardinals	86
Braves	83
Mets	82
Diamondbacks	78
Giants	74
Marlins	72

2015 AL Avg	
Home Park	Index
Indians	113
Red Sox	109
Rangers	108
Orioles	107
Twins	104
Royals	103
Astros	98
Athletics	97
Tigers	97
Yankees	96
Rays	96
Blue Jays	96
Angels	95
White Sox	94
Mariners	93

2015 AL LHB Avg	
Home Park	Index
Indians	115
Red Sox	115
Orioles	107
Rangers	105
Twins	102
Royals	101
Yankees	100
Rays	98
Athletics	98
Tigers	96
Mariners	96
Angels	95
Blue Jays	93
Astros	92
White Sox	87

2015 AL RHB Avg	
Home Park	Index
Rangers	111
Indians	111
Orioles	108
Red Sox	106
Royals	105
Twins	104
Astros	102
White Sox	99
Tigers	97
Blue Jays	97
Athletics	97
Angels	96
Rays	95
Yankees	92
Mariners	91

2015 NL Avg	
Home Park	Index
Rockies	123
Cardinals	105
Diamondbacks	104
Reds	104
Nationals	99
Brewers	99
Marlins	98
Padres	98
Phillies	97
Pirates	97
Cubs	96
Dodgers	95
Giants	94
Mets	93
Braves	92

2015 NL LHB Avg	
Home Park	Index
Rockies	124
Brewers	109
Reds	108
Diamondbacks	106
Cardinals	105
Marlins	104
Padres	98
Phillies	98
Giants	97
Mets	96
Cubs	92
Dodgers	91
Braves	90
Pirates	90
Nationals	90

2015 NL RHB Avg	
Home Park	Index
Rockies	123
Nationals	106
Cardinals	105
Diamondbacks	103
Reds	101
Pirates	100
Cubs	99
Dodgers	98
Padres	98
Phillies	97
Braves	94
Marlins	93
Giants	92
Brewers	92
Mets	90

2015 AL Doubles	
Home Park	Index
Indians	140
Red Sox	127
Royals	127
Blue Jays	111
Rangers	108
Astros	99
Tigers	98
Athletics	98
Twins	98
Orioles	94
Angels	88
Yankees	88
White Sox	86
Rays	85
Mariners	84

2015 AL Triples	
Home Park	Index
Astros	156
Royals	151
Tigers	136
Athletics	120
Red Sox	102
Blue Jays	99
Rangers	92
White Sox	82
Mariners	81
Twins	81
Indians	75
Angels	75
Orioles	74
Rays	72
Yankees	62

2015 AL Errors	
Home Park	Index
Red Sox	147
Twins	128
Tigers	123
Orioles	113
Athletics	113
Mariners	107
Indians	105
Angels	103
White Sox	103
Yankees	102
Rangers	90
Astros	80
Rays	76
Blue Jays	74
Royals	68

2015 NL Doubles	
Home Park	Index
Diamondbacks	120
Rockies	117
Dodgers	106
Nationals	105
Brewers	105
Reds	100
Cardinals	100
Braves	98
Padres	97
Mets	95
Phillies	94
Marlins	93
Pirates	88
Giants	86
Cubs	82

2015 NL Triples	
Home Park	Index
Rockies	189
Diamondbacks	178
Giants	169
Marlins	121
Brewers	113
Cubs	113
Cardinals	102
Mets	92
Pirates	83
Padres	80
Braves	77
Phillies	66
Dodgers	65
Nationals	50
Reds	43

2015 NL Errors	
Home Park	Index
Phillies	136
Braves	128
Diamondbacks	117
Nationals	116
Rockies	114
Giants	108
Brewers	102
Pirates	102
Dodgers	97
Padres	95
Marlins	92
Cardinals	87
Reds	77
Cubs	77
Mets	68

2013-2015 American League Ballpark Index Rankings

Home Park	TOTALS												LHB		RHB	
	Avg	AB	R	H	2B	3B	HR	BB	SO	FO	E	E-Inf	Avg	HR	Avg	HR
Red Sox (Fenway Park)	106	100	107	106	132	105	85	100	99	76	138	144	107	70	105	100
Orioles (Oriole Park at Camden Yards)	102	101	107	103	92	68	119	97	95	88	103	92	103	137	101	108
Rangers (Globe Life Park in Arlington)	102	100	106	102	92	113	98	107	95	79	104	106	103	101	102	95
Twins (Target Field)	103	101	104	105	104	104	94	94	91	98	114	122	103	90	104	96
Royals (Kauffman Stadium)	103	99	104	101	112	136	85	96	93	104	83	87	101	88	104	82
Indians (Progressive Field)	103	101	103	104	113	64	104	98	101	73	98	96	104	105	101	103
Yankees (Yankee Stadium)	101	100	102	101	91	61	127	102	104	105	99	92	104	129	98	126
Blue Jays (Rogers Centre)	99	100	102	99	120	90	118	100	106	106	101	89	98	114	100	121
Tigers (Comerica Park)	102	98	101	100	97	160	95	105	90	118	101	91	100	95	104	95
Astros (Minute Maid Park)	99	101	100	99	96	144	116	100	106	77	95	94	97	122	100	112
White Sox (U.S. Cellular Field)	96	100	98	97	87	79	111	114	107	116	106	114	92	109	99	113
Rays (Tropicana Field)	96	99	96	96	88	96	93	99	105	113	71	75	96	109	96	83
Athletics (O.co Coliseum)	99	100	95	99	106	123	80	100	93	159	98	91	95	75	102	90
Angels (Angel Stadium of Anaheim)	98	100	92	98	93	77	89	97	105	108	95	105	97	85	98	90
Mariners (Safeco Field)	95	99	90	94	92	62	95	94	107	130	99	105	97	98	93	91

2013-2015 National League Ballpark Index Rankings

Home Park	TOTALS												LHB		RHB	
	Avg	AB	R	H	2B	3B	HR	BB	SO	FO	E	E-Inf	Avg	HR	Avg	HR
Rockies (Coors Field)	118	106	140	126	112	177	119	97	82	71	118	119	116	115	120	121
Brewers (Miller Park)	102	100	107	102	98	90	127	104	100	85	89	91	107	133	99	123
Diamondbacks (Chase Field)	102	99	106	101	111	171	99	98	99	117	108	103	104	109	101	94
Nationals (Nationals Park)	105	100	103	105	107	47	84	103	96	112	112	130	102	80	107	88
Reds (Great American Ballpark)	99	102	102	101	99	70	122	105	111	106	93	71	98	131	101	117
Phillies (Citizens Bank Park)	96	102	102	98	95	83	125	101	107	119	124	141	98	110	95	140
Cubs (Wrigley Field)	101	100	102	100	99	102	111	103	103	76	91	91	105	97	97	124
Marlins (Marlins Park)	100	100	100	99	103	146	72	102	95	92	98	87	100	64	100	78
Cardinals (Busch Stadium)	100	99	97	99	101	104	89	97	93	125	86	83	101	87	99	90
Braves (Turner Field)	97	99	94	96	92	85	91	103	110	97	114	121	96	86	97	95
Pirates (PNC Park)	100	100	94	100	93	77	80	95	92	91	100	101	98	92	100	73
Padres (PETCO Park)[1]	98	99	93	97	87	80	110	101	108	110	95	82	98	110	98	110
Dodgers (Dodger Stadium)	95	99	90	94	102	46	107	83	102	90	101	99	96	115	94	101
Giants (AT&T Park)	96	98	88	94	94	180	69	104	103	87	98	110	100	59	93	76
Mets (Citi Field)[1]	93	98	87	91	95	92	101	102	103	96	68	64	96	124	90	82

2013-2015 AL Home Runs

Home Park	Index
Yankees	127
Orioles	119
Blue Jays	118
Astros	116
White Sox	111
Indians	104
Rangers	98
Tigers	95
Mariners	95
Twins	94
Rays	93
Angels	89
Red Sox	85
Royals	85
Athletics	83

2013-2015 AL LHB Home Runs

Home Park	Index
Orioles	137
Yankees	129
Astros	122
Blue Jays	114
Rays	109
White Sox	109
Indians	105
Rangers	101
Mariners	98
Tigers	95
Twins	90
Royals	88
Angels	85
Athletics	75
Red Sox	70

2013-2015 AL RHB Home Runs

Home Park	Index
Yankees	126
Blue Jays	121
White Sox	113
Astros	112
Orioles	108
Indians	103
Red Sox	100
Twins	96
Tigers	95
Rangers	95
Mariners	91
Angels	90
Athletics	90
Rays	83
Royals	82

2013-2015 NL Home Runs

Home Park	Index
Brewers	127
Phillies	125
Reds	122
Rockies	119
Cubs	111
Padres[1]	110
Dodgers	107
Mets[1]	101
Diamondbacks	99
Braves	91
Cardinals	89
Nationals	84
Pirates	80
Marlins	72
Giants	69

2013-2015 NL LHB Home Runs

Home Park	Index
Brewers	133
Reds	131
Mets[1]	124
Rockies	115
Dodgers	115
Padres[1]	110
Phillies	110
Diamondbacks	109
Cubs	97
Pirates	92
Cardinals	87
Braves	86
Nationals	80
Marlins	64
Giants	59

2013-2015 NL RHB Home Runs

Home Park	Index
Phillies	140
Cubs	124
Brewers	123
Rockies	121
Reds	117
Padres[1]	110
Dodgers	101
Braves	95
Diamondbacks	94
Cardinals	90
Nationals	88
Mets[1]	82
Marlins	78
Giants	76
Pirates	73

1. 2015 Only

2013-2015 AL Avg	
Home Park	Index
Red Sox	106
Twins	103
Indians	103
Royals	103
Rangers	102
Tigers	102
Orioles	102
Yankees	101
Blue Jays	99
Athletics	99
Astros	99
Angels	98
White Sox	96
Rays	96
Mariners	95

2013-2015 AL LHB Avg	
Home Park	Index
Red Sox	107
Indians	104
Yankees	104
Orioles	103
Rangers	103
Twins	103
Royals	101
Tigers	100
Blue Jays	98
Angels	97
Astros	97
Mariners	97
Rays	96
Athletics	95
White Sox	92

2013-2015 AL RHB Avg	
Home Park	Index
Red Sox	105
Royals	104
Twins	104
Tigers	104
Athletics	102
Rangers	102
Orioles	101
Indians	101
Blue Jays	100
Astros	100
White Sox	99
Angels	98
Yankees	98
Rays	96
Mariners	93

2013-2015 NL Avg	
Home Park	Index
Rockies	118
Nationals	105
Diamondbacks	102
Brewers	102
Cubs	101
Cardinals	100
Marlins	100
Pirates	100
Reds	99
Padres[1]	98
Braves	97
Phillies	96
Giants	96
Dodgers	95
Mets[1]	93

2013-2015 NL LHB Avg	
Home Park	Index
Rockies	116
Brewers	107
Cubs	105
Diamondbacks	104
Nationals	102
Cardinals	101
Giants	100
Marlins	100
Padres[1]	98
Reds	98
Pirates	98
Phillies	98
Mets[1]	96
Braves	96
Dodgers	96

2013-2015 NL RHB Avg	
Home Park	Index
Rockies	120
Nationals	107
Diamondbacks	101
Reds	101
Pirates	100
Marlins	100
Cardinals	99
Brewers	99
Padres[1]	98
Cubs	97
Braves	97
Phillies	95
Dodgers	94
Giants	93
Mets[1]	90

2013-2015 AL Doubles	
Home Park	Index
Red Sox	132
Blue Jays	120
Indians	113
Royals	112
Athletics	106
Twins	104
Tigers	97
Astros	96
Angels	93
Mariners	92
Rangers	92
Orioles	92
Yankees	91
Rays	88
White Sox	87

2013-2015 AL Triples	
Home Park	Index
Tigers	160
Astros	144
Royals	136
Athletics	123
Rangers	113
Red Sox	105
Twins	104
Rays	96
Blue Jays	90
White Sox	79
Angels	77
Orioles	68
Indians	64
Mariners	62
Yankees	61

2013-2015 AL Errors	
Home Park	Index
Red Sox	138
Twins	114
White Sox	106
Rangers	104
Orioles	103
Blue Jays	101
Tigers	101
Yankees	99
Mariners	99
Athletics	98
Indians	98
Angels	95
Astros	95
Royals	83
Rays	71

2013-2015 NL Doubles	
Home Park	Index
Rockies	112
Diamondbacks	111
Nationals	107
Marlins	103
Dodgers	102
Cardinals	101
Reds	99
Cubs	99
Brewers	98
Padres[1]	97
Mets[1]	95
Phillies	95
Giants	94
Pirates	93
Braves	92

2013-2015 NL Triples	
Home Park	Index
Giants	180
Rockies	177
Diamondbacks	171
Marlins	146
Cardinals	104
Cubs	102
Mets[1]	92
Brewers	90
Braves	85
Phillies	83
Padres[1]	80
Pirates	77
Reds	70
Nationals	47
Dodgers	46

2013-2015 NL Errors	
Home Park	Index
Phillies	124
Rockies	118
Braves	114
Nationals	112
Diamondbacks	108
Dodgers	101
Pirates	100
Giants	98
Marlins	98
Padres[1]	95
Reds	93
Cubs	91
Brewers	89
Cardinals	86
Mets[1]	68

1. 2015 Only

2015 Lefty/Righty Statistics

Ben Jedlovec

Many highly touted prospects debuted in 2015, including Kris Bryant, Carlos Correa, Noah Syndergaard, and the Twins' duo of Miguel Sano and Byron Buxton, just to name a few. But for many, the most anticipated debut of 2015 was not on any prospect lists: 29-year-old switch-pitcher Pat Venditte.

We had plenty of time to see this coming. Venditte was successful enough at Creighton University to garner All-American honors and earn a 20th-round draft pick from the Yankees. The Yankees brought him along slowly through the minors even though he was certainly effective if not dominant at each level. The A's picked him up this offseason and on June 5, Venditte made his major league debut.

(For you trivia buffs, Venditte is not the first switch-pitcher in MLB history. Baseball had a handful of switch-pitchers in the 19th century, and most recently righty Greg Harris faced two batters with his left arm in 1995.)

In addition to throwing less-observant fans for a loop when he switches hands from batter to batter, Venditte adds a new wrinkle when facing switch-hitters. The "Venditte Rule" states that the pitcher must declare which arm he is going to throw with before the batter steps in, and he must stick with it throughout the at-bat.

If you've ever tried to program baseball data collection software or a baseball simulator, you've probably made some assumptions in how to handle switch-hitters. A few times each year, these assumptions are violated when a switch-hitter steps in from the abnormal side against a knuckleballer or when he's protecting an injury. This year, our scoring software and stat-checkers had fits trying to keep up with the havoc wreaked by the A's rookie reliever.

This section details platoon splits for all hitters with at least 20 plate appearances and pitchers with at least 20 batters faced in 2015, including Pat Venditte. As you can see, Venditte was far more effective against left-handed batters (.106 batting average against to go with 18 strikeouts and just 4 walks) than righties (.293, with 5 and 8, respectively).

Batters vs. Left-Handed and Right-Handed Pitchers

Batter	vs	Avg	AB	H	2B	3B	HR	RBI	BB	SO	OBP	Slg
Abreu,Jose	L	.232	142	33	8	0	3	12	12	31	.306	.352
Bats Right	R	.308	471	145	26	3	27	89	27	109	.360	.548
Ackley,Dustin	L	.136	22	3	1	0	0	0	3	6	.240	.182
Bats Left	R	.241	216	52	10	3	10	30	15	39	.288	.454
Adames,Cristhian	L	.286	21	6	0	1	0	3	2	5	.348	.381
Bats Both	R	.219	32	7	1	0	0	0	1	6	.265	.250
Adams,Matt	L	.200	25	5	1	0	0	1	2	10	.259	.240
Bats Left	R	.247	150	37	8	0	5	23	8	31	.283	.400
Adrianza,Ehire	L	.176	34	6	2	0	0	4	4	3	.282	.235
Bats Both	R	.190	79	15	5	1	0	7	11	17	.312	.278
Ahmed,Nick	L	.296	108	32	4	3	2	10	10	15	.358	.444
Bats Right	R	.201	313	63	13	3	7	24	19	66	.246	.329
Alberto,Hanser	L	.152	33	5	0	0	0	2	0	11	.152	.152
Bats Right	R	.258	66	17	2	1	0	2	2	6	.279	.318
Alcantara,Arismendy	L	.000	4	0	0	0	0	0	1	2	.200	.000
Bats Both	R	.091	22	2	0	0	0	1	4	9	.231	.091
Almonte,Abraham	L	.250	60	15	1	0	0	4	3	14	.281	.267
Bats Both	R	.250	172	43	11	5	5	20	18	38	.319	.459
Alonso,Yonder	L	.267	75	20	1	0	1	11	8	16	.349	.320
Bats Left	R	.287	279	80	17	1	4	20	34	32	.364	.398
Altherr,Aaron	L	.180	50	9	5	2	0	6	6	12	.276	.360
Bats Right	R	.276	87	24	6	2	5	16	10	29	.373	.563
Altuve,Jose	L	.372	188	70	13	2	5	14	18	25	.431	.543
Bats Right	R	.289	450	130	27	2	10	52	15	42	.319	.424
Alvarez,Dariel	L	.261	23	6	1	0	1	1	1	6	.292	.435
Bats Right	R	.167	6	1	0	0	0	0	1	2	.286	.167
Alvarez,Pedro	L	.258	62	16	1	0	3	9	3	20	.292	.419
Bats Left	R	.240	375	90	17	0	24	68	45	111	.322	.477
Amarista,Alexi	L	.211	38	8	2	0	0	4	2	7	.244	.263
Bats Left	R	.203	286	58	8	4	3	26	22	48	.259	.290
Andrus,Elvis	L	.286	210	60	14	0	5	24	16	25	.333	.424
Bats Right	R	.244	386	94	20	2	2	38	30	53	.296	.321
Aoki,Nori	L	.333	99	33	2	1	0	9	8	8	.400	.374
Bats Left	R	.270	256	69	10	2	5	17	22	17	.335	.383
Arcia,Oswaldo	L	.304	23	7	0	0	0	2	0	5	.320	.304
Bats Left	R	.257	35	9	0	0	2	6	4	10	.350	.429
Arenado,Nolan	L	.267	135	36	9	0	5	26	15	22	.333	.444
Bats Right	R	.293	481	141	34	4	37	104	19	88	.320	.611
Arencibia,J.P.	L	.259	27	7	0	0	2	4	1	11	.276	.481
Bats Right	R	.341	44	15	3	0	4	13	0	11	.341	.682
Arias,Joaquin	L	.250	36	9	1	0	0	3	0	7	.250	.278
Bats Right	R	.136	22	3	0	0	1	1	0	5	.136	.273
Asche,Cody	L	.231	78	18	3	0	1	6	5	23	.277	.308
Bats Left	R	.248	347	86	19	3	11	33	21	88	.298	.415
Ashley,Nevin	L	.000	5	0	0	0	0	0	0	3	.000	.000
Bats Right	R	.133	15	2	1	0	0	1	0	5	.188	.200
Avila,Alex	L	.133	30	4	1	0	0	0	5	13	.257	.167
Bats Left	R	.203	148	30	4	0	4	13	35	53	.355	.311
Aviles,Mike	L	.242	153	37	4	0	4	11	13	21	.304	.346
Bats Right	R	.219	137	30	6	0	1	6	7	17	.257	.285
Aybar,Erick	L	.270	174	47	8	0	0	9	3	20	.281	.316
Bats Both	R	.270	423	114	22	1	3	35	22	53	.309	.348
Baez,Javier	L	.421	19	8	4	0	0	0	1	5	.450	.632
Bats Right	R	.246	57	14	2	0	1	4	3	19	.283	.333
Baker,Jeff	L	.208	53	11	3	0	3	6	6	19	.288	.434
Bats Right	R	.211	19	4	0	0	0	2	2	6	.286	.211
Barmes,Clint	L	.242	99	24	7	0	2	11	6	30	.299	.374
Bats Right	R	.222	108	24	7	1	1	5	4	25	.263	.333
Barnes,Austin	L	.167	12	2	1	0	0	1	3	1	.375	.250
Bats Right	R	.235	17	4	1	0	0	0	3	5	.350	.294
Barnes,Brandon	L	.224	67	15	1	0	0	5	7	25	.307	.239
Bats Right	R	.261	188	49	12	2	2	12	14	42	.317	.378
Barney,Darwin	L	.333	9	3	1	0	1	2	0	0	.333	.778
Bats Right	R	.222	18	4	0	0	1	2	1	2	.263	.389
Barnhart,Tucker	L	.178	45	8	0	0	0	5	5	8	.255	.178
Bats Both	R	.269	197	53	9	0	3	13	20	37	.339	.360
Bautista,Jose	L	.231	104	24	6	1	5	20	26	19	.382	.452
Bats Right	R	.255	439	112	23	2	35	94	84	87	.376	.556
Baxter,Mike	L	1.000	3	3	0	0	0	1	1	0	1.000	1.000
Bats Left	R	.204	54	11	1	0	0	1	6	14	.295	.222
Beckham,Gordon	L	.218	87	19	1	0	3	9	8	14	.293	.333
Bats Right	R	.202	124	25	7	0	3	11	11	29	.263	.331
Beckham,Tim	L	.236	106	25	3	3	5	17	5	33	.263	.462
Bats Right	R	.206	97	20	4	1	4	20	8	36	.284	.392
Belt,Brandon	L	.264	129	34	10	0	5	18	14	41	.345	.457
Bats Left	R	.287	363	104	23	5	13	50	42	106	.360	.485

Batter	vs	Avg	AB	H	2B	3B	HR	RBI	BB	SO	OBP	Slg
Beltran,Carlos	L	.255	141	36	10	1	5	18	10	25	.305	.447
Bats Both	R	.285	337	96	24	0	14	49	35	60	.350	.481
Beltre,Adrian	L	.311	190	59	11	2	10	33	23	23	.381	.547
Bats Right	R	.276	377	104	21	2	8	50	18	42	.309	.406
Bethancourt,Christian	L	.170	47	8	2	0	0	2	3	11	.220	.213
Bats Right	R	.213	108	23	6	0	2	10	2	22	.227	.324
Betts,Mookie	L	.311	148	46	7	2	5	20	11	15	.356	.486
Bats Right	R	.285	449	128	35	6	13	57	35	67	.336	.477
Bird,Gregory	L	.238	42	10	1	0	2	7	7	15	.347	.405
Bats Left	R	.270	115	31	8	0	9	24	12	38	.341	.574
Blackmon,Charlie	L	.264	163	43	5	3	3	14	12	29	.322	.387
Bats Left	R	.295	451	133	26	6	14	44	34	83	.356	.472
Blair,Carson	L	.091	11	1	0	0	1	1	2	6	.231	.364
Bats Right	R	.150	20	3	0	0	0	2	2	12	.227	.150
Blanco,Andres	L	.349	86	30	10	0	3	8	6	13	.404	.570
Bats Both	R	.259	147	38	12	3	4	17	15	31	.335	.463
Blanco,Gregor	L	.282	71	20	3	1	1	5	5	16	.346	.394
Bats Left	R	.293	256	75	16	2	4	21	35	43	.374	.418
Blanks,Kyle	L	.333	27	9	3	0	3	4	0	7	.333	.778
Bats Right	R	.300	40	12	2	0	0	2	4	13	.364	.350
Bloomquist,Willie	L	.184	38	7	1	0	0	2	2	5	.244	.211
Bats Right	R	.129	31	4	0	0	0	2	0	8	.129	.129
Boesch,Brennan	L	.143	7	1	0	0	0	1	1	5	.250	.143
Bats Left	R	.146	82	12	2	0	1	4	3	25	.186	.207
Bogaerts,Xander	L	.365	156	57	8	1	2	12	16	23	.424	.468
Bats Right	R	.304	457	139	27	2	5	69	16	78	.330	.405
Bogusevic,Brian	L	.091	11	1	0	0	0	0	0	6	.091	.091
Bats Left	R	.298	47	14	3	0	2	5	3	15	.340	.489
Bonifacio,Emilio	L	.176	34	6	2	0	0	1	0	16	.176	.235
Bats Both	R	.159	44	7	0	0	0	3	2	11	.213	.159
Bour,Justin	L	.221	68	15	4	0	0	9	6	22	.293	.279
Bats Left	R	.270	341	92	16	0	23	64	28	79	.326	.519
Bourgeois,Jason	L	.167	54	9	1	1	1	8	4	11	.224	.278
Bats Right	R	.268	142	38	4	1	2	6	10	22	.320	.352
Bourjos,Peter	L	.203	64	13	1	0	3	4	6	23	.292	.359
Bats Right	R	.198	131	26	7	3	1	9	13	36	.289	.321
Bourn,Michael	L	.231	91	21	4	0	0	6	14	27	.324	.275
Bats Left	R	.240	334	80	11	2	0	24	32	80	.306	.284
Bradley Jr.,Jackie	L	.306	72	22	4	3	2	12	8	21	.390	.528
Bats Left	R	.221	149	33	13	1	8	32	19	48	.308	.483
Brantley,Michael	L	.294	214	63	16	0	5	35	18	30	.346	.439
Bats Left	R	.321	315	101	29	0	10	49	42	21	.401	.508
Brantly,Rob	L	.000	9	0	0	0	0	0	0	1	.000	.000
Bats Left	R	.167	24	4	1	0	1	6	2	7	.222	.333
Braun,Ryan	L	.317	120	38	8	1	6	14	18	26	.407	.550
Bats Right	R	.275	386	106	19	2	19	70	36	89	.340	.482
Brito,Socrates	L	.000	4	0	0	0	0	0	1	1	.200	.000
Bats Left	R	.345	29	10	3	1	0	1	0	6	.345	.517
Brown,Domonic	L	.238	42	10	2	1	0	5	3	7	.289	.333
Bats Left	R	.224	147	33	4	0	5	20	11	29	.283	.354
Brown,Trevor	L	.083	12	1	0	0	0	1	0	4	.077	.083
Bats Right	R	.296	27	8	3	0	0	4	3	4	.367	.407
Bruce,Jay	L	.229	166	38	9	2	4	23	14	41	.286	.380
Bats Left	R	.225	414	93	26	2	22	64	44	104	.297	.457
Bryant,Kris	L	.246	126	31	6	1	6	25	19	53	.345	.452
Bats Right	R	.284	433	123	25	4	20	74	58	146	.376	.499
Burns,Billy	L	.315	165	52	8	1	2	8	8	26	.356	.412
Bats Both	R	.285	355	101	10	8	3	34	18	55	.324	.383
Butera,Drew	L	.250	28	7	1	0	0	0	1	9	.300	.286
Bats Right	R	.177	79	14	2	0	1	5	5	17	.235	.241
Butler,Billy	L	.200	140	28	9	0	4	10	29	23	.337	.350
Bats Right	R	.269	398	107	19	1	11	55	23	78	.317	.405
Butler,Joey	L	.259	108	28	4	0	4	13	5	32	.292	.407
Bats Right	R	.289	149	43	8	0	4	17	11	50	.350	.423
Buxton,Byron	L	.116	43	5	2	0	0	1	2	18	.156	.163
Bats Right	R	.256	86	22	5	1	2	5	4	26	.297	.407
Byrd,Marlon	L	.271	129	35	11	0	6	22	10	28	.324	.496
Bats Right	R	.239	377	90	14	5	17	51	19	117	.279	.438
Cabrera,Asdrubal	L	.281	153	43	11	1	3	19	4	25	.300	.425
Bats Both	R	.259	352	91	17	4	12	39	32	82	.321	.432
Cabrera,Everth	L	.148	27	4	0	0	0	2	2	8	.194	.148
Bats Both	R	.232	69	16	2	0	0	2	3	14	.274	.261
Cabrera,Melky	L	.240	171	41	10	0	2	18	7	27	.267	.333
Bats Both	R	.286	458	131	26	2	10	59	33	61	.331	.417
Cabrera,Miguel	L	.313	80	25	4	0	5	18	21	13	.466	.550
Bats Right	R	.344	349	120	24	1	13	58	56	69	.434	.530

Batters vs. Left-Handed and Right-Handed Pitchers

Batter	vs	Avg	AB	H	2B	3B	HR	RBI	BB	SO	OBP	Slg
Cabrera,Ramon	L	.375	8	3	0	0	0	0	0	1	.375	.375
Bats Both	R	.364	22	8	1	0	1	3	0	4	.364	.545
Cain,Lorenzo	L	.335	185	62	20	1	7	26	13	28	.391	.568
Bats Right	R	.292	366	107	14	5	9	46	24	70	.346	.432
Calhoun,Kole	L	.220	200	44	6	0	8	29	17	58	.293	.370
Bats Left	R	.272	430	117	17	2	18	54	28	106	.316	.447
Callaspo,Alberto	L	.150	40	6	1	0	0	2	3	9	.209	.175
Bats Both	R	.253	190	48	6	0	1	13	25	25	.336	.300
Campbell,Eric	L	.143	35	5	2	0	1	3	7	7	.302	.286
Bats Right	R	.210	138	29	6	0	2	16	19	30	.315	.297
Canha,Mark	L	.221	149	33	2	1	3	16	10	30	.278	.309
Bats Right	R	.271	292	79	20	2	13	54	23	66	.334	.486
Cano,Robinson	L	.270	226	61	4	0	9	31	12	43	.308	.407
Bats Left	R	.296	398	118	30	1	12	48	31	64	.348	.467
Carpenter,Matt	L	.228	184	42	11	1	8	29	23	54	.322	.429
Bats Left	R	.292	390	114	33	2	20	55	58	97	.385	.541
Carrera,Ezequiel	L	.310	29	9	1	0	1	8	1	10	.333	.448
Bats Left	R	.266	143	38	7	0	2	18	10	35	.318	.357
Carter,Chris	L	.201	159	32	7	0	9	22	26	55	.321	.415
Bats Right	R	.198	232	46	10	0	15	42	31	96	.297	.435
Casali,Curt	L	.241	29	7	0	0	3	8	1	8	.313	.552
Bats Right	R	.236	72	17	6	0	7	10	7	26	.300	.611
Castellanos,Nick	L	.351	114	40	6	2	5	20	10	30	.400	.570
Bats Right	R	.230	435	100	27	4	10	53	29	122	.277	.379
Castillo,Rusney	L	.318	88	28	5	1	2	9	4	15	.351	.466
Bats Right	R	.222	185	41	5	1	3	20	9	39	.258	.308
Castillo,Welington	L	.239	92	22	3	0	6	15	10	32	.311	.467
Bats Right	R	.236	250	59	12	1	13	42	15	60	.291	.448
Castro,Daniel	L	.268	41	11	2	0	2	4	1	4	.286	.463
Bats Right	R	.218	55	12	0	1	0	1	2	11	.246	.255
Castro,Jason	L	.192	104	20	5	0	1	2	7	38	.243	.269
Bats Left	R	.219	233	51	14	0	10	29	26	77	.299	.408
Castro,Starlin	L	.281	121	34	7	0	0	10	4	20	.304	.339
Bats Right	R	.261	426	111	16	2	11	59	17	71	.294	.385
Ceciliani,Darrell	L	.286	7	2	0	0	0	0	0	2	.286	.286
Bats Left	R	.197	61	12	2	0	1	3	4	23	.269	.279
Centeno,Juan	L	.500	2	1	1	0	0	0	0	0	.500	1.000
Bats Left	R	.000	19	0	0	0	0	0	2	7	.095	.000
Cervelli,Francisco	L	.310	100	31	2	4	2	7	13	22	.386	.470
Bats Right	R	.291	351	102	15	1	5	36	33	72	.365	.382
Cespedes,Yoenis	L	.223	139	31	4	1	8	25	15	42	.297	.439
Bats Right	R	.310	494	153	38	5	27	80	18	99	.338	.571
Chirinos,Robinson	L	.265	83	22	5	1	4	11	9	22	.351	.494
Bats Right	R	.213	150	32	11	0	6	23	19	40	.310	.407
Chisenhall,Lonnie	L	.241	58	14	2	0	1	9	5	9	.297	.328
Bats Left	R	.247	275	68	17	1	6	35	18	60	.294	.382
Choo,Shin-Soo	L	.237	211	50	9	1	6	28	24	54	.333	.374
Bats Left	R	.299	344	103	23	2	16	54	52	93	.400	.517
Ciriaco,Pedro	L	.209	43	9	2	0	0	1	2	14	.261	.256
Bats Right	R	.283	99	28	6	1	1	14	0	24	.282	.394
Clevenger,Steve	L	.375	8	3	0	0	0	0	0	0	.375	.375
Bats Left	R	.280	93	26	4	2	2	15	4	13	.309	.430
Coghlan,Chris	L	.116	43	5	1	0	0	0	4	11	.208	.140
Bats Left	R	.264	397	105	24	6	16	41	54	83	.355	.476
Colabello,Chris	L	.308	91	28	3	0	7	16	8	26	.364	.571
Bats Right	R	.326	242	79	16	1	8	38	14	70	.368	.500
Collins,Tyler	L	.286	14	4	1	0	0	2	0	2	.286	.357
Bats Left	R	.264	178	47	10	3	4	23	13	41	.318	.421
Colon,Christian	L	.333	36	12	1	0	0	1	3	5	.385	.361
Bats Right	R	.268	71	19	4	0	0	5	8	12	.342	.324
Conforto,Michael	L	.214	14	3	0	0	0	1	1	3	.267	.214
Bats Left	R	.275	160	44	14	0	9	25	16	36	.341	.531
Conger,Hank	L	.175	97	17	5	0	4	11	11	33	.268	.351
Bats Both	R	.279	104	29	6	0	7	22	12	30	.353	.538
Corporan,Carlos	L	.222	36	8	2	0	1	4	1	10	.243	.361
Bats Both	R	.155	71	11	2	0	2	11	5	30	.244	.268
Correa,Carlos	L	.274	124	34	8	0	9	26	14	21	.343	.556
Bats Right	R	.281	263	74	14	1	13	42	26	57	.346	.490
Cowart,Kaleb	L	.150	20	3	0	0	0	1	1	6	.190	.150
Bats Both	R	.192	26	5	2	0	1	3	4	13	.300	.385
Cowgill,Collin	L	.225	40	9	0	1	1	2	1	8	.244	.350
Bats Right	R	.138	29	4	2	0	0	0	3	11	.219	.207
Cozart,Zack	L	.326	46	15	2	0	3	8	4	3	.365	.565
Bats Right	R	.236	148	35	8	1	6	20	10	26	.292	.426
Craig,Allen	L	.222	27	6	1	0	1	2	3	8	.300	.370
Bats Right	R	.115	52	6	0	0	0	1	4	18	.207	.115

Batter	vs	Avg	AB	H	2B	3B	HR	RBI	BB	SO	OBP	Slg
Crawford,Brandon	L	.259	143	37	10	1	4	25	5	40	.289	.427
Bats Left	R	.255	364	93	23	3	17	59	34	79	.333	.475
Crawford,Carl	L	.296	27	8	1	0	0	2	2	6	.345	.333
Bats Left	R	.260	154	40	8	2	4	14	8	35	.296	.416
Crisp,Coco	L	.200	40	8	3	0	0	1	3	6	.256	.275
Bats Both	R	.163	86	14	3	0	0	5	10	19	.250	.198
Cron,C.J.	L	.260	127	33	5	1	3	11	5	21	.286	.386
Bats Right	R	.263	251	66	12	0	13	40	12	61	.307	.466
Cruz,Nelson	L	.357	168	60	9	1	14	27	23	41	.435	.673
Bats Right	R	.280	422	118	13	0	30	66	36	123	.343	.524
Cruz,Tony	L	.231	26	6	1	0	0	2	3	7	.310	.269
Bats Right	R	.198	116	23	6	1	2	9	3	25	.217	.319
Cuddyer,Michael	L	.273	99	27	4	0	1	5	11	21	.357	.343
Bats Right	R	.254	280	71	14	1	9	36	13	67	.291	.407
Cunningham,Todd	L	.200	10	2	1	0	0	2	0	4	.273	.300
Bats Both	R	.224	76	17	3	0	0	2	5	13	.280	.263
Cuthbert,Cheslor	L	.250	20	5	2	0	0	4	1	4	.286	.350
Bats Right	R	.192	26	5	0	1	1	4	3	5	.276	.385
d'Arnaud,Travis	L	.333	45	15	4	0	4	10	7	6	.423	.689
Bats Right	R	.253	194	49	10	1	8	31	16	43	.319	.438
Davis,Chris	L	.268	190	51	8	0	10	31	16	58	.330	.468
Bats Left	R	.258	383	99	23	0	37	86	68	150	.375	.608
Davis,Ike	L	.211	19	4	3	0	0	0	0	3	.211	.368
Bats Left	R	.231	195	45	14	0	3	20	23	41	.309	.349
Davis,Khris	L	.212	104	22	5	0	6	15	13	34	.297	.433
Bats Right	R	.260	288	75	11	2	21	51	31	88	.332	.531
Davis,Rajai	L	.245	139	34	5	5	5	14	10	39	.298	.460
Bats Right	R	.267	202	54	11	6	3	16	12	37	.312	.426
De Aza,Alejandro	L	.159	44	7	0	2	0	2	3	18	.220	.250
Bats Left	R	.278	281	78	17	5	7	33	28	66	.351	.448
De Jesus,Ivan	L	.263	57	15	3	0	2	8	4	16	.306	.421
Bats Right	R	.236	144	34	7	2	2	20	15	39	.313	.354
Decker,Jaff	L	.000	6	0	0	0	0	0	1	3	.143	.000
Bats Left	R	.273	22	6	1	1	0	1	6	6	.429	.409
DeJesus,David	L	.091	11	1	0	0	0	1	0	0	.083	.091
Bats Left	R	.238	277	66	9	2	5	29	21	52	.305	.339
den Dekker,Matt	L	.154	13	2	2	0	0	1	1	0	.214	.308
Bats Left	R	.267	86	23	4	1	5	11	8	20	.330	.512
Denorfia,Chris	L	.211	76	16	5	1	0	6	9	25	.294	.303
Bats Right	R	.301	136	41	6	0	3	12	6	31	.333	.412
Descalso,Daniel	L	.167	24	4	1	0	0	4	3	5	.259	.208
Bats Left	R	.211	161	34	2	2	5	18	17	40	.287	.342
DeShields,Delino	L	.282	149	42	11	2	1	16	18	41	.363	.403
Bats Right	R	.250	276	69	11	8	1	21	35	60	.334	.359
Desmond,Ian	L	.248	117	29	7	0	5	16	13	31	.321	.436
Bats Right	R	.230	466	107	20	2	14	46	32	156	.282	.371
Dickerson,Corey	L	.268	56	15	5	0	0	6	3	19	.305	.357
Bats Left	R	.315	168	53	13	2	10	25	7	37	.343	.595
Dietrich,Derek	L	.178	45	8	0	0	1	3	2	20	.275	.244
Bats Left	R	.273	205	56	14	3	9	21	21	45	.361	.502
Dominguez,Chris	L	.111	9	1	0	0	1	1	0	6	.111	.444
Bats Right	R	.357	14	5	1	1	0	2	0	6	.357	.571
Donaldson,Josh	L	.299	117	35	12	0	9	25	18	23	.391	.632
Bats Right	R	.296	503	149	29	2	32	98	55	110	.366	.553
Dorn,Danny	L	.000	2	0	0	0	0	0	0	1	.000	.000
Bats Left	R	.179	28	5	1	0	0	3	2	9	.233	.214
Dozier,Brian	L	.232	181	42	13	2	7	21	23	37	.320	.442
Bats Right	R	.237	447	106	26	2	21	56	38	111	.301	.445
Drew,Stephen	L	.235	85	20	5	0	3	8	7	20	.290	.400
Bats Left	R	.191	298	57	11	1	14	36	30	51	.266	.376
Drury,Brandon	L	.304	23	7	1	0	2	5	0	3	.304	.609
Bats Right	R	.152	33	5	2	0	0	3	2	5	.222	.212
Duda,Lucas	L	.285	123	35	11	0	7	21	7	42	.333	.545
Bats Left	R	.230	348	80	22	0	20	52	59	96	.358	.466
Duffy,Matt	L	.252	147	37	3	1	3	17	8	19	.295	.347
Bats Right	R	.310	426	132	25	5	9	60	22	77	.348	.455
Duvall,Adam	L	.176	17	3	1	0	0	1	1	6	.263	.235
Bats Right	R	.234	47	11	1	0	5	8	5	20	.321	.574
Dykstra,Allan	L	.000	2	0	0	0	0	0	1	0	.333	.000
Bats Left	R	.138	29	4	0	0	1	4	5	12	.286	.241
Dyson,Jarrod	L	.222	36	8	2	0	0	4	3	8	.300	.278
Bats Left	R	.256	164	42	6	6	2	14	11	29	.313	.402
Eaton,Adam	L	.268	168	45	5	2	0	11	8	33	.326	.321
Bats Left	R	.294	442	130	23	7	14	45	50	98	.374	.473
Ellis,A.J.	L	.260	77	20	5	0	5	10	17	13	.394	.519
Bats Right	R	.221	104	23	4	0	2	11	15	25	.325	.317

Batters vs. Left-Handed and Right-Handed Pitchers

Batter	vs	Avg	AB	H	2B	3B	HR	RBI	BB	SO	OBP	Slg
Ellsbury,Jacoby	L	.253	154	39	5	0	2	11	12	35	.327	.325
Bats Left	R	.258	298	77	10	2	5	22	23	51	.313	.356
Elmore,Jake	L	.304	46	14	3	0	1	9	7	4	.389	.435
Bats Right	R	.158	95	15	2	0	1	7	5	21	.196	.211
Encarnacion,Edwin	L	.260	100	26	4	0	6	16	15	25	.356	.480
Bats Right	R	.280	428	120	27	0	33	95	62	73	.375	.575
Escobar,Alcides	L	.269	175	47	7	1	1	13	13	23	.316	.337
Bats Right	R	.252	437	110	13	4	2	34	13	52	.284	.314
Escobar,Eduardo	L	.277	130	36	7	0	7	21	5	30	.297	.492
Bats Both	R	.254	279	71	24	4	5	37	23	56	.314	.423
Escobar,Yunel	L	.314	121	38	3	0	2	5	11	18	.371	.388
Bats Right	R	.314	414	130	22	1	7	51	34	52	.376	.423
Espinosa,Danny	L	.261	88	23	4	0	3	5	10	24	.343	.409
Bats Both	R	.233	279	65	17	1	10	32	23	82	.300	.409
Ethier,Andre	L	.200	45	9	2	0	0	6	2	14	.229	.244
Bats Left	R	.306	350	107	18	7	14	47	41	61	.383	.517
Featherston,Taylor	L	.217	46	10	3	0	0	3	5	18	.302	.283
Bats Right	R	.139	108	15	2	1	2	6	2	28	.170	.231
Field,Tommy	L	.167	6	1	0	0	0	1	2	2	.375	.167
Bats Right	R	.200	35	7	1	0	2	4	0	14	.222	.400
Fielder,Prince	L	.252	254	64	11	0	9	36	22	51	.323	.402
Bats Left	R	.343	359	123	17	0	14	62	42	37	.416	.507
Flaherty,Ryan	L	.179	56	10	3	2	0	5	1	18	.242	.304
Bats Left	R	.209	211	44	5	1	9	26	25	63	.291	.370
Flores,Ramon	L	.250	4	1	0	0	0	0	0	1	.250	.250
Bats Left	R	.214	28	6	1	0	0	0	0	3	.214	.250
Flores,Wilmer	L	.310	100	31	8	0	7	16	6	15	.355	.600
Bats Right	R	.251	383	96	14	0	9	43	13	48	.279	.358
Florimon,Pedro	L	.143	7	1	0	1	0	1	0	4	.143	.429
Bats Both	R	.063	16	1	0	0	0	0	2	8	.167	.063
Flowers,Tyler	L	.270	63	17	4	0	1	12	8	18	.370	.381
Bats Right	R	.231	268	62	8	0	8	27	13	86	.276	.351
Forsythe,Logan	L	.299	167	50	16	2	10	33	19	31	.373	.599
Bats Right	R	.273	373	102	17	0	7	35	36	80	.353	.375
Fowler,Dexter	L	.326	135	44	7	0	4	12	16	31	.399	.467
Bats Both	R	.228	461	105	22	8	13	34	68	123	.331	.395
Franco,Maikel	L	.232	69	16	1	0	5	14	11	17	.361	.464
Bats Right	R	.294	235	69	21	1	9	36	15	35	.337	.506
Francoeur,Jeff	L	.248	133	33	7	0	3	20	6	35	.277	.368
Bats Right	R	.264	193	51	9	1	10	25	7	42	.292	.477
Franklin,Nick	L	.207	29	6	3	0	0	0	3	10	.281	.310
Bats Both	R	.139	72	10	1	1	3	7	4	27	.184	.306
Frazier,Todd	L	.261	153	40	11	0	14	26	9	37	.301	.608
Bats Right	R	.253	466	118	32	1	21	63	35	100	.311	.461
Freeman,Freddie	L	.219	114	25	8	0	1	13	20	39	.341	.316
Bats Left	R	.298	302	90	19	0	17	53	36	59	.382	.530
Freese,David	L	.213	108	23	6	0	5	10	14	24	.312	.407
Bats Right	R	.272	316	86	21	0	9	46	17	83	.328	.424
Fryer,Eric	L	.000	5	0	0	0	0	0	1	1	.167	.000
Bats Right	R	.294	17	5	2	0	0	2	4	10	.429	.412
Fuld,Sam	L	.106	47	5	1	0	1	4	5	12	.222	.191
Bats Left	R	.214	243	52	15	3	1	18	25	43	.286	.313
Gallo,Joey	L	.135	37	5	0	0	2	4	2	23	.179	.297
Bats Left	R	.239	71	17	3	1	4	10	13	34	.357	.479
Galvis,Freddy	L	.280	157	44	4	0	0	9	4	25	.296	.306
Bats Both	R	.256	402	103	10	5	7	41	26	78	.304	.358
Garcia,Adonis	L	.328	58	19	3	0	5	10	2	9	.344	.638
Bats Right	R	.256	133	34	9	0	5	16	3	26	.270	.436
Garcia,Avisail	L	.293	123	36	5	0	3	13	13	30	.353	.407
Bats Right	R	.247	430	106	12	2	10	46	23	111	.297	.353
Garcia,Greg	L	.400	5	2	1	0	0	0	2	2	.571	.600
Bats Left	R	.229	70	16	4	0	2	4	8	10	.316	.371
Gardner,Brett	L	.276	170	47	12	0	3	22	20	41	.361	.400
Bats Left	R	.252	401	101	14	3	13	44	48	94	.335	.399
Garneau,Dustin	L	.211	19	4	1	0	0	1	0	2	.211	.263
Bats Right	R	.137	51	7	2	0	2	7	6	12	.228	.294
Gattis,Evan	L	.237	198	47	8	4	7	28	10	28	.274	.424
Bats Right	R	.250	368	92	12	7	20	60	20	91	.291	.484
Gennett,Scooter	L	.114	35	4	0	1	0	1	0	10	.139	.171
Bats Left	R	.279	340	95	18	3	6	28	12	58	.310	.403
Gentry,Craig	L	.143	28	4	0	1	0	1	1	9	.194	.214
Bats Right	R	.091	22	2	0	1	0	2	3	6	.200	.182
Giavotella,Johnny	L	.250	112	28	8	0	1	12	13	16	.325	.348
Bats Right	R	.279	341	95	17	5	3	37	19	43	.316	.384
Gillaspie,Conor	L	.267	15	4	1	0	0	3	0	5	.250	.333
Bats Left	R	.225	222	50	14	2	4	21	13	42	.270	.360
Gillespie,Cole	L	.368	38	14	3	0	0	5	3	7	.405	.447
Bats Right	R	.262	107	28	7	2	2	11	7	20	.307	.421
Gimenez,Chris	L	.269	26	7	2	1	2	7	8	7	.441	.654
Bats Right	R	.250	72	18	4	0	3	7	2	12	.280	.431
Goins,Ryan	L	.212	85	18	2	2	1	12	7	23	.269	.318
Bats Left	R	.261	291	76	14	2	4	33	32	60	.332	.364
Goldschmidt,Paul	L	.364	121	44	5	1	8	24	21	34	.462	.620
Bats Right	R	.309	446	138	33	1	25	86	97	117	.428	.556
Gomes,Jonny	L	.227	97	22	3	0	5	18	23	35	.371	.412
Bats Right	R	.203	128	26	6	0	2	8	8	46	.261	.297
Gomes,Yan	L	.208	101	21	6	0	1	7	6	36	.248	.297
Bats Right	R	.240	262	63	16	0	11	38	7	68	.275	.427
Gomez,Carlos	L	.215	93	20	3	0	3	13	11	19	.302	.344
Bats Right	R	.266	342	91	26	1	9	43	20	82	.318	.427
Gomez,Hector	L	.186	43	8	3	2	1	2	0	12	.205	.419
Bats Right	R	.179	84	15	8	0	0	5	3	28	.216	.274
Gonzalez,Adrian	L	.294	163	48	11	0	4	25	11	27	.346	.436
Bats Left	R	.267	408	109	22	0	24	65	51	80	.352	.498
Gonzalez,Carlos	L	.195	159	31	3	0	5	19	6	44	.222	.308
Bats Left	R	.301	395	119	22	2	35	78	40	89	.364	.633
Gonzalez,Marwin	L	.295	139	41	8	1	6	14	10	23	.347	.496
Bats Both	R	.268	205	55	10	0	6	20	6	51	.296	.405
Gordon,Alex	L	.280	125	35	5	0	5	17	14	32	.377	.440
Bats Left	R	.266	229	61	13	0	8	31	35	60	.377	.428
Gordon,Dee	L	.350	160	56	6	2	2	15	5	24	.373	.450
Bats Left	R	.327	455	149	18	6	2	31	20	67	.353	.407
Gose,Anthony	L	.192	73	14	4	1	0	2	7	28	.272	.274
Bats Left	R	.265	412	109	20	7	5	24	38	117	.330	.383
Gosewisch,Tuffy	L	.160	25	4	1	0	0	1	3	5	.241	.200
Bats Right	R	.223	103	23	5	0	1	12	5	18	.266	.301
Gosselin,Phil	L	.286	28	8	4	0	0	3	6	4	.429	.429
Bats Right	R	.321	78	25	5	1	3	12	3	12	.349	.526
Grandal,Yasmani	L	.308	52	16	1	0	1	4	9	15	.410	.385
Bats Both	R	.221	303	67	11	0	15	43	56	77	.343	.406
Granderson,Curtis	L	.183	126	23	7	0	2	14	15	48	.273	.286
Bats Left	R	.280	454	127	26	2	24	56	76	103	.388	.504
Green,Grant	L	.083	12	1	0	0	0	0	2	4	.214	.083
Bats Right	R	.233	30	7	0	0	1	3	0	10	.233	.333
Gregorius,Didi	L	.247	146	36	5	1	1	24	10	26	.311	.315
Bats Left	R	.272	379	103	19	1	8	32	23	59	.321	.391
Grichuk,Randal	L	.265	113	30	7	2	6	14	4	34	.297	.522
Bats Right	R	.281	210	59	16	5	11	33	18	76	.345	.562
Grossman,Robbie	L	.136	22	3	0	0	0	2	2	9	.208	.136
Bats Both	R	.148	27	4	2	0	1	3	3	8	.233	.333
Guerrero,Alex	L	.238	80	19	3	0	3	11	2	20	.262	.388
Bats Right	R	.230	139	32	6	1	8	25	5	37	.260	.460
Gutierrez,Franklin	L	.317	104	33	7	0	8	19	7	28	.357	.615
Bats Right	R	.254	67	17	4	0	7	16	7	26	.351	.627
Guyer,Brandon	L	.271	188	51	12	1	7	20	17	39	.387	.457
Bats Right	R	.257	144	37	9	1	1	8	8	22	.318	.354
Gyorko,Jedd	L	.282	110	31	6	0	4	13	11	25	.358	.445
Bats Right	R	.235	311	73	9	0	12	44	16	82	.275	.379
Hamilton,Billy	L	.241	116	28	2	2	3	6	5	28	.270	.371
Bats Both	R	.220	296	65	6	1	1	22	23	47	.276	.257
Hamilton,Josh	L	.236	55	13	3	0	3	12	3	17	.271	.455
Bats Left	R	.261	115	30	5	0	5	13	7	35	.301	.435
Hanigan,Ryan	L	.364	44	16	4	0	0	2	5	8	.440	.455
Bats Right	R	.208	130	27	4	0	2	14	15	31	.302	.285
Hardy,J.J.	L	.210	119	25	2	0	1	9	5	27	.242	.252
Bats Right	R	.223	292	65	12	0	7	28	15	61	.257	.336
Harper,Bryce	L	.318	154	49	15	0	7	25	32	34	.434	.552
Bats Left	R	.335	367	123	23	1	35	74	92	97	.471	.689
Harrison,Josh	L	.302	106	32	5	1	1	6	8	17	.364	.396
Bats Right	R	.282	312	88	24	0	3	22	11	54	.314	.388
Hart,Corey	L	.107	28	3	1	0	1	3	1	14	.167	.250
Bats Right	R	.346	26	9	0	0	1	6	0	5	.333	.462
Hayes,Brett	L	.214	14	3	0	0	2	5	2	1	.313	.643
Bats Right	R	.111	18	2	0	0	1	1	1	6	.158	.278
Headley,Chase	L	.283	184	52	12	1	3	24	14	35	.335	.408
Bats Both	R	.247	396	98	17	0	8	38	37	100	.319	.351
Heathcott,Slade	L	.000	3	0	0	0	0	0	0	0	.000	.000
Bats Left	R	.455	22	10	2	0	2	8	2	5	.480	.818
Hechavarria,Adeiny	L	.352	88	31	5	1	2	13	9	15	.412	.500
Bats Right	R	.264	382	101	12	5	3	35	14	63	.291	.346
Hedges,Austin	L	.136	44	6	2	0	1	4	2	11	.170	.250
Bats Right	R	.183	93	17	0	0	2	7	6	27	.235	.247

Batters vs. Left-Handed and Right-Handed Pitchers

Batter	vs	Avg	AB	H	2B	3B	HR	RBI	BB	SO	OBP	Slg
Heisey,Chris	L	.146	41	6	2	0	1	6	10	13	.302	.268
Bats Right	R	.286	14	4	0	0	1	3	5	4	.474	.500
Hernandez,Cesar	L	.314	121	38	7	1	0	11	12	27	.381	.388
Bats Both	R	.254	284	72	13	3	1	24	28	59	.322	.331
Hernandez,Kiké	L	.423	78	33	9	2	4	16	7	17	.471	.744
Bats Right	R	.234	124	29	3	0	3	6	4	29	.262	.331
Hernandez,Oscar	L	.000	2	0	0	0	0	0	0	1	.000	.000
Bats Right	R	.172	29	5	1	0	0	1	3	14	.273	.207
Herrera,Dilson	L	.250	20	5	2	0	0	0	4	7	.375	.350
Bats Right	R	.200	70	14	1	1	3	6	7	16	.291	.371
Herrera,Elian	L	.207	82	17	6	0	3	10	3	21	.235	.390
Bats Both	R	.259	174	45	12	0	4	23	15	51	.314	.397
Herrera,Jonathan	L	.286	35	10	4	1	0	4	0	8	.286	.457
Bats Both	R	.209	91	19	1	0	2	10	2	15	.226	.286
Herrera,Odubel	L	.293	123	36	6	1	1	6	6	36	.338	.382
Bats Left	R	.298	372	111	24	2	7	35	22	93	.346	.430
Herrmann,Chris	L	.050	20	1	0	0	0	1	3	6	.174	.050
Bats Left	R	.169	83	14	5	1	2	9	4	31	.225	.325
Heyward,Jason	L	.272	162	44	7	1	2	20	18	40	.344	.364
Bats Left	R	.301	385	116	26	3	11	40	38	50	.364	.470
Hicks,Aaron	L	.307	101	31	1	0	6	11	11	27	.375	.495
Bats Both	R	.235	251	59	10	3	5	22	23	39	.302	.359
Hicks,John	L	.100	10	1	0	0	0	1	0	7	.100	.100
Bats Right	R	.045	22	1	1	0	0	0	1	11	.087	.091
Hill,Aaron	L	.236	110	26	3	0	2	7	7	25	.277	.318
Bats Right	R	.227	203	46	15	0	4	32	24	29	.303	.360
Holaday,Bryan	L	.316	19	6	2	0	1	1	0	4	.316	.579
Bats Right	R	.267	45	12	3	0	1	12	1	9	.283	.400
Holliday,Matt	L	.246	61	15	3	0	2	11	15	15	.403	.393
Bats Right	R	.292	168	49	13	1	2	24	24	34	.390	.417
Holt,Brock	L	.312	109	34	9	1	0	18	15	34	.394	.413
Bats Left	R	.270	345	93	18	5	2	27	31	63	.333	.368
Holt,Tyler	L	.111	9	1	0	0	0	0	1	1	.200	.111
Bats Right	R	.091	22	2	0	0	0	0	2	10	.167	.091
Hosmer,Eric	L	.279	244	68	11	3	4	30	19	45	.332	.398
Bats Left	R	.310	355	110	22	2	14	63	42	63	.384	.501
Howard,Ryan	L	.130	100	13	2	0	3	10	5	40	.178	.240
Bats Left	R	.256	367	94	27	1	20	67	22	98	.304	.499
Hundley,Nick	L	.292	89	26	3	2	1	8	4	24	.323	.404
Bats Right	R	.303	277	84	18	3	9	35	17	52	.345	.487
Hunter,Torii	L	.244	160	39	6	0	8	29	9	39	.291	.431
Bats Right	R	.238	361	86	16	0	14	52	26	66	.294	.399
Iannetta,Chris	L	.230	74	17	1	0	4	13	16	19	.359	.405
Bats Right	R	.172	198	34	9	0	6	21	25	64	.267	.308
Iglesias,Jose	L	.354	99	35	6	1	1	11	13	12	.425	.465
Bats Right	R	.284	317	90	11	2	1	12	12	32	.320	.341
Inciarte,Ender	L	.229	140	32	3	2	0	12	4	17	.255	.279
Bats Left	R	.331	384	127	24	3	6	33	22	41	.368	.456
Infante,Omar	L	.228	127	29	12	0	0	10	2	19	.238	.323
Bats Right	R	.217	313	68	11	7	2	34	7	50	.232	.316
Ishikawa,Travis	L	.200	5	1	0	0	0	0	1	3	.333	.200
Bats Left	R	.207	58	12	3	0	1	8	8	17	.303	.310
Jackson,Austin	L	.281	167	47	4	2	6	25	11	42	.333	.437
Bats Right	R	.259	324	84	21	1	3	23	18	84	.299	.358
Janish,Paul	L	.167	18	3	1	0	0	2	0	2	.158	.222
Bats Right	R	.412	17	7	2	0	0	1	0	1	.412	.529
Jankowski,Travis	L	.250	20	5	0	0	1	5	0	7	.250	.400
Bats Left	R	.200	70	14	2	2	1	7	4	17	.243	.329
Jaso,John	L	.308	13	4	1	0	0	2	6	4	.526	.385
Bats Left	R	.285	172	49	16	0	5	20	22	35	.365	.465
Jay,Jon	L	.158	38	6	0	0	0	3	4	6	.256	.158
Bats Left	R	.221	172	38	5	1	1	7	15	30	.317	.279
Jennings,Desmond	L	.320	25	8	1	0	0	2	1	5	.357	.360
Bats Right	R	.250	72	18	1	1	1	5	7	12	.313	.333
Johnson,Chris	L	.326	92	30	3	0	1	9	3	23	.354	.391
Bats Right	R	.212	151	32	8	0	2	9	7	51	.245	.305
Johnson,Kelly	L	.273	33	9	0	0	1	4	2	11	.314	.364
Bats Left	R	.264	277	73	11	0	13	43	21	70	.314	.444
Johnson,Micah	L	.174	23	4	0	0	0	0	2	8	.240	.174
Bats Left	R	.247	77	19	4	0	0	4	7	22	.326	.299
Johnson,Reed	L	.200	5	1	1	0	0	2	0	2	.167	.400
Bats Right	R	.235	17	4	0	0	0	1	0	4	.278	.235
Jones,Adam	L	.261	134	35	8	0	6	20	7	38	.299	.455
Bats Right	R	.272	412	112	17	3	21	62	17	64	.311	.481
Jones,Garrett	L	.130	23	3	1	0	1	4	2	5	.200	.304
Bats Left	R	.231	121	28	3	1	4	13	6	32	.268	.372

Batter	vs	Avg	AB	H	2B	3B	HR	RBI	BB	SO	OBP	Slg
Jones,James	L	.000	5	0	0	0	0	0	0	2	.000	.000
Bats Left	R	.125	24	3	1	0	0	0	2	11	.192	.167
Joseph,Caleb	L	.250	108	27	4	1	4	14	6	26	.296	.417
Bats Right	R	.226	212	48	12	0	7	35	21	46	.301	.382
Joyce,Matt	L	.048	21	1	1	0	0	1	2	12	.167	.095
Bats Left	R	.186	226	42	11	1	5	20	28	55	.282	.310
Kang,Jung Ho	L	.238	84	20	3	0	3	10	9	24	.340	.381
Bats Right	R	.300	337	101	21	2	12	48	19	75	.359	.481
Kawasaki,Munenori	L	.571	7	4	1	0	0	2	0	0	.571	.714
Bats Left	R	.095	21	2	1	0	0	0	4	6	.240	.143
Kemp,Matt	L	.280	125	35	8	0	6	28	11	26	.336	.488
Bats Right	R	.261	471	123	23	3	17	72	28	121	.305	.431
Kendrick,Howie	L	.291	110	32	5	0	2	18	7	20	.331	.391
Bats Right	R	.297	354	105	17	2	7	36	20	62	.338	.415
Kiermaier,Kevin	L	.246	142	35	5	2	2	11	6	35	.273	.352
Bats Left	R	.270	363	98	20	10	8	29	18	60	.308	.446
Kinsler,Ian	L	.305	131	40	9	2	2	9	9	9	.348	.450
Bats Right	R	.294	493	145	26	5	9	64	34	71	.341	.422
Kipnis,Jason	L	.250	212	53	14	2	3	17	12	50	.302	.377
Bats Left	R	.334	353	118	29	5	6	35	45	57	.412	.496
Kozma,Pete	L	.143	28	4	0	0	0	1	2	6	.200	.143
Bats Right	R	.155	71	11	0	0	0	1	8	15	.250	.155
Kratz,Erik	L	.267	15	4	1	0	0	0	0	3	.267	.333
Bats Right	R	.091	11	1	1	0	0	3	1	2	.154	.182
Krauss,Marc	L	.000	5	0	0	0	0	0	0	3	.000	.000
Bats Left	R	.151	73	11	3	0	2	8	3	28	.184	.274
Kubitza,Kyle	L	.250	4	1	0	0	0	0	0	1	.250	.250
Bats Left	R	.188	32	6	0	0	0	1	3	14	.257	.188
La Stella,Tommy	L	.000	4	0	0	0	0	0	0	1	.000	.000
Bats Left	R	.286	63	18	6	0	1	11	5	6	.343	.429
Lagares,Juan	L	.273	121	33	7	2	3	15	9	28	.333	.438
Bats Right	R	.253	320	81	9	3	3	26	7	59	.271	.328
Lake,Junior	L	.290	31	9	6	0	0	3	1	9	.313	.484
Bats Right	R	.143	49	7	1	0	1	2	3	20	.192	.224
LaMarre,Ryan	L	.000	3	0	0	0	0	0	0	1	.000	.000
Bats Right	R	.091	22	2	0	0	0	0	0	8	.091	.091
Lamb,Jake	L	.200	45	9	0	0	1	3	5	19	.275	.267
Bats Left	R	.272	305	83	15	5	5	31	31	78	.339	.403
Lambo,Andrew	L	.000	2	0	0	0	0	0	0	2	.000	.000
Bats Left	R	.043	23	1	1	0	0	0	2	6	.120	.087
LaRoche,Adam	L	.157	89	14	3	0	0	7	3	37	.191	.191
Bats Left	R	.221	340	75	18	0	12	37	46	96	.318	.379
Lavarnway,Ryan	L	.242	33	8	2	0	1	3	7	11	.375	.394
Bats Right	R	.164	61	10	4	0	1	3	5	17	.227	.279
Lawrie,Brett	L	.293	157	46	7	1	7	22	10	32	.341	.484
Bats Right	R	.247	405	100	22	2	9	38	18	112	.282	.378
LeMahieu,DJ	L	.316	136	43	2	1	1	13	17	26	.390	.368
Bats Right	R	.297	428	127	19	4	5	48	33	81	.348	.395
Leon,Sandy	L	.059	34	2	0	0	0	1	0	12	.059	.059
Bats Both	R	.238	80	19	2	0	0	2	7	16	.307	.263
Lind,Adam	L	.221	104	23	8	0	0	10	8	25	.277	.298
Bats Left	R	.291	398	116	24	0	20	77	58	75	.380	.503
Lindor,Francisco	L	.321	140	45	9	2	5	18	11	25	.368	.521
Bats Both	R	.308	250	77	13	2	7	33	16	44	.344	.460
Lobaton,Jose	L	.118	17	2	0	0	0	1	4	5	.286	.118
Bats Both	R	.210	119	25	4	0	3	19	11	35	.278	.319
Loney,James	L	.226	84	19	4	0	1	5	4	12	.258	.310
Bats Left	R	.296	277	82	12	0	3	27	19	22	.341	.372
Longoria,Evan	L	.342	155	53	9	1	8	28	16	30	.392	.568
Bats Right	R	.245	449	110	26	0	13	45	35	102	.306	.390
Lough,David	L	.214	14	3	0	0	0	1	2	4	.353	.214
Bats Left	R	.200	120	24	1	1	4	11	3	32	.226	.325
Lowrie,Jed	L	.267	60	16	4	0	4	9	10	10	.375	.533
Bats Both	R	.206	170	35	10	0	5	21	18	33	.288	.353
Lucroy,Jonathan	L	.255	94	24	5	0	1	13	7	18	.298	.340
Bats Right	R	.267	277	74	15	3	6	30	29	46	.335	.408
Machado,Dixon	L	.250	16	4	1	0	0	1	2	4	.333	.313
Bats Right	R	.231	52	12	2	0	0	4	5	10	.298	.269
Machado,Manny	L	.258	159	41	6	0	7	14	19	31	.335	.428
Bats Right	R	.295	474	140	24	1	28	72	51	80	.367	.527
Mahtook,Mikie	L	.294	68	20	2	1	7	15	5	20	.368	.662
Bats Right	R	.297	37	11	3	0	2	4	1	11	.316	.541
Maile,Luke	L	.238	21	5	2	0	0	1	0	3	.238	.333
Bats Right	R	.071	14	1	1	0	0	1	0	5	.071	.143
Maldonado,Martin	L	.245	53	13	3	0	3	6	8	19	.339	.472
Bats Right	R	.199	176	35	4	0	1	16	15	46	.264	.239

Batters vs. Left-Handed and Right-Handed Pitchers

Batter	vs	Avg	AB	H	2B	3B	HR	RBI	BB	SO	OBP	Slg
Marisnick,Jake	L	.204	142	29	6	2	7	20	7	45	.247	.423
Bats Right	R	.259	197	51	9	2	2	16	11	60	.307	.355
Markakis,Nick	L	.273	194	53	9	1	0	12	7	28	.305	.330
Bats Left	R	.306	418	128	29	0	3	41	63	55	.398	.397
Marrero,Deven	L	.150	20	3	0	0	0	0	0	8	.150	.150
Bats Right	R	.273	33	9	0	0	1	3	3	11	.333	.364
Marte,Jefry	L	.270	37	10	3	0	3	8	3	7	.325	.595
Bats Right	R	.163	43	7	1	0	1	3	5	15	.250	.256
Marte,Ketel	L	.257	101	26	9	1	1	9	10	20	.324	.396
Bats Both	R	.305	118	36	5	2	1	8	14	23	.373	.407
Marte,Starling	L	.246	126	31	4	0	6	18	4	27	.296	.421
Bats Right	R	.298	453	135	26	2	13	63	23	96	.347	.450
Martin,Leonys	L	.229	105	24	2	0	2	12	4	33	.261	.305
Bats Left	R	.213	183	39	10	0	3	13	12	36	.265	.317
Martin,Russell	L	.278	90	25	7	0	5	14	20	16	.414	.522
Bats Right	R	.231	351	81	16	2	18	63	33	90	.306	.442
Martinez,J.D.	L	.265	117	31	2	0	10	25	21	43	.377	.538
Bats Right	R	.286	479	137	31	2	28	77	32	135	.335	.534
Martinez,Michael	L	.222	9	2	1	0	0	0	1	3	.300	.333
Bats Both	R	.286	21	6	1	0	0	2	0	9	.286	.333
Martinez,Victor	L	.348	89	31	8	0	1	15	7	8	.398	.472
Bats Both	R	.219	351	77	12	0	10	49	24	44	.276	.339
Mathis,Jeff	L	.231	13	3	0	0	1	3	0	4	.214	.462
Bats Right	R	.150	80	12	4	1	1	9	7	20	.213	.263
Mauer,Joe	L	.267	191	51	8	2	4	26	17	34	.327	.393
Bats Left	R	.264	401	106	26	0	6	40	50	78	.344	.374
Maxwell,Justin	L	.221	86	19	3	1	1	3	9	29	.295	.314
Bats Right	R	.202	163	33	5	1	6	23	11	47	.264	.356
Mayberry,John	L	.175	57	10	4	1	2	4	5	15	.242	.386
Bats Right	R	.151	53	8	2	0	1	5	4	18	.211	.245
Maybin,Cameron	L	.237	118	28	5	1	3	10	18	31	.338	.373
Bats Right	R	.276	387	107	13	1	7	49	27	71	.323	.370
McBride,Matt	L	.200	10	2	0	0	0	0	0	2	.200	.200
Bats Right	R	.156	32	5	0	0	0	0	0	2	.182	.156
McCann,Brian	L	.241	116	28	3	0	6	26	12	26	.331	.422
Bats Left	R	.229	349	80	12	1	20	68	40	71	.316	.441
McCann,James	L	.320	97	31	7	2	4	14	6	23	.359	.557
Bats Right	R	.247	304	75	11	3	3	27	10	67	.277	.332
McCutchen,Andrew	L	.328	122	40	7	0	5	21	15	25	.410	.508
Bats Right	R	.282	444	125	29	3	18	75	83	108	.399	.482
McGehee,Casey	L	.234	47	11	2	0	0	1	10	6	.368	.277
Bats Right	R	.189	190	36	10	0	2	19	11	44	.234	.274
McKenry,Michael	L	.263	19	5	2	0	1	5	9	5	.500	.526
Bats Right	R	.194	108	21	5	3	3	12	13	36	.290	.380
Mercer,Jordy	L	.284	81	23	8	0	0	4	9	14	.356	.383
Bats Right	R	.233	313	73	13	0	3	30	18	59	.277	.304
Mesoraco,Devin	L	.077	13	1	0	1	0	1	3	4	.250	.231
Bats Right	R	.219	32	7	1	0	0	1	2	5	.286	.250
Middlebrooks,Will	L	.206	68	14	3	1	3	11	4	11	.243	.412
Bats Right	R	.214	187	40	4	1	6	18	7	49	.240	.342
Miller,Brad	L	.234	111	26	2	0	0	9	5	26	.261	.252
Bats Left	R	.266	327	87	20	4	11	37	42	75	.350	.453
Molina,Yadier	L	.232	125	29	4	0	0	14	16	16	.313	.264
Bats Right	R	.284	363	103	19	2	4	47	16	43	.309	.380
Monell,Johnny	L	.000	2	0	0	0	0	0	1	0	.333	.000
Bats Left	R	.174	46	8	2	0	0	4	3	13	.224	.217
Montero,Jesus	L	.205	73	15	3	0	2	7	4	21	.247	.329
Bats Right	R	.256	39	10	3	0	3	12	0	11	.256	.564
Montero,Miguel	L	.234	47	11	1	0	3	11	6	12	.339	.447
Bats Left	R	.250	300	75	10	0	12	42	43	91	.346	.403
Moore,Tyler	L	.204	54	11	3	0	3	14	7	12	.306	.426
Bats Right	R	.203	133	27	9	0	3	13	4	33	.225	.338
Morales,Kendrys	L	.298	238	71	13	1	4	41	22	38	.359	.412
Bats Both	R	.284	331	94	28	1	18	65	36	65	.363	.538
Moreland,Mitch	L	.245	155	38	7	0	5	21	11	40	.293	.387
Bats Left	R	.294	316	93	20	0	18	64	21	72	.348	.528
Morneau,Justin	L	.342	38	13	5	0	0	3	2	5	.375	.474
Bats Left	R	.300	130	39	5	3	3	12	11	20	.359	.454
Morrison,Logan	L	.190	142	27	8	0	0	9	10	30	.253	.246
Bats Left	R	.241	315	76	7	3	17	45	37	51	.323	.444
Morse,Michael	L	.235	68	16	2	1	1	7	8	22	.333	.338
Bats Right	R	.230	161	37	5	0	4	12	15	54	.303	.335
Moss,Brandon	L	.242	149	36	9	1	4	18	17	42	.325	.396
Bats Left	R	.219	320	70	15	1	15	40	32	106	.294	.413
Moustakas,Mike	L	.282	206	58	12	0	10	35	12	23	.338	.485
Bats Left	R	.286	343	98	22	1	12	47	31	53	.353	.461

Batter	vs	Avg	AB	H	2B	3B	HR	RBI	BB	SO	OBP	Slg
Moya,Steven	L	.000	3	0	0	0	0	0	0	2	.000	.000
Bats Left	R	.211	19	4	0	1	0	0	3	8	.318	.316
Muncy,Max	L	.000	1	0	0	0	0	0	1	1	.500	.000
Bats Left	R	.208	101	21	8	1	3	9	8	30	.264	.396
Muno,Danny	L	.000	4	0	0	0	0	0	0	2	.000	.000
Bats Both	R	.174	23	4	1	0	0	0	4	9	.296	.217
Murphy,Daniel	L	.254	126	32	7	1	1	11	4	13	.284	.349
Bats Left	R	.290	373	108	31	1	13	62	27	25	.334	.483
Murphy,David	L	.304	23	7	1	1	0	5	1	5	.360	.435
Bats Left	R	.281	338	95	17	0	10	45	19	44	.315	.420
Murphy,John Ryan	L	.266	79	21	6	0	3	9	5	21	.314	.456
Bats Right	R	.289	76	22	3	1	0	5	7	22	.341	.355
Murphy,Tom	L	.167	18	3	0	0	0	1	2	5	.250	.167
Bats Right	R	.353	17	6	1	0	3	8	2	5	.421	.941
Myers,Wil	L	.261	46	12	3	1	0	8	12	13	.424	.370
Bats Right	R	.251	179	45	10	0	8	21	15	42	.309	.441
Napoli,Mike	L	.278	151	42	5	1	12	26	27	47	.391	.563
Bats Right	R	.191	256	49	15	0	6	24	30	71	.283	.320
Nava,Daniel	L	.242	33	8	1	0	0	1	3	8	.324	.273
Bats Both	R	.179	106	19	3	0	1	9	17	28	.313	.236
Navarro,Dioner	L	.278	36	10	0	0	3	5	5	3	.366	.528
Bats Both	R	.237	135	32	7	0	2	15	12	26	.291	.333
Navarro,Efren	L	.182	11	2	0	0	0	0	0	3	.182	.182
Bats Left	R	.264	72	19	4	0	0	5	5	13	.312	.319
Navarro,Rey	L	.375	8	3	0	0	1	2	0	0	.375	.750
Bats Both	R	.238	21	5	2	0	0	1	0	3	.238	.333
Negron,Kristopher	L	.091	33	3	1	0	0	1	3	7	.189	.121
Bats Right	R	.167	60	10	1	0	0	1	6	16	.265	.183
Nieuwenhuis,Kirk	L	.000	9	0	0	0	0	1	1	6	.182	.000
Bats Left	R	.210	119	25	11	0	4	13	9	43	.277	.403
Noonan,Nick	L	.000	4	0	0	0	0	0	0	2	.000	.000
Bats Left	R	.111	18	2	1	0	1	3	2	6	.200	.333
Norris,Derek	L	.295	122	36	11	0	3	10	11	34	.351	.459
Bats Right	R	.237	393	93	22	2	11	52	24	97	.291	.387
Nunez,Eduardo	L	.210	62	13	3	0	3	10	2	11	.246	.403
Bats Right	R	.317	126	40	11	1	1	10	10	18	.365	.444
Odor,Rougned	L	.266	154	41	9	3	5	25	6	31	.320	.461
Bats Left	R	.257	272	70	12	6	11	36	17	48	.314	.467
Olivera,Hector	L	.067	15	1	0	0	0	2	2	5	.176	.067
Bats Right	R	.297	64	19	4	1	2	9	3	7	.343	.484
Olt,Mike	L	.185	27	5	0	0	2	2	0	8	.185	.407
Bats Right	R	.194	67	13	0	0	2	3	7	27	.280	.284
O'Malley,Shawn	L	.263	19	5	1	0	0	3	6	3	.423	.316
Bats Both	R	.261	23	6	0	0	1	4	6	11	.414	.391
Orlando,Paulo	L	.265	98	26	5	2	2	9	3	13	.287	.418
Bats Right	R	.238	143	34	9	4	5	18	2	40	.257	.462
Ortiz,David	L	.231	169	39	9	0	8	30	12	39	.277	.426
Bats Left	R	.292	359	105	28	0	29	78	65	56	.395	.613
Owings,Chris	L	.171	117	20	6	1	1	4	8	40	.230	.265
Bats Right	R	.244	398	97	21	4	3	39	18	104	.274	.339
Ozuna,Marcell	L	.341	85	29	7	0	2	8	7	18	.394	.494
Bats Right	R	.241	374	90	20	0	8	36	23	92	.288	.358
Pacheco,Jordan	L	.267	15	4	0	0	0	1	3	5	.368	.267
Bats Right	R	.235	51	12	0	0	2	7	6	9	.322	.353
Pagan,Angel	L	.318	148	47	6	0	0	13	10	30	.356	.358
Bats Both	R	.239	364	87	15	3	3	24	22	63	.281	.321
Panik,Joe	L	.291	86	25	4	1	1	10	11	8	.374	.395
Bats Left	R	.318	296	94	23	1	7	27	27	34	.379	.473
Paredes,Jimmy	L	.263	57	15	5	0	0	5	3	13	.300	.351
Bats Both	R	.278	306	85	12	2	10	37	16	98	.312	.428
Parker,Jarrett	L	.462	13	6	0	0	2	3	2	3	.533	.923
Bats Left	R	.306	36	11	2	0	4	11	3	18	.359	.694
Parker,Kyle	L	.194	36	7	2	1	1	4	3	11	.256	.389
Bats Right	R	.171	70	12	1	0	2	7	3	26	.205	.271
Parmelee,Chris	L	.125	16	2	1	0	0	0	0	6	.176	.188
Bats Left	R	.235	81	19	6	1	4	9	4	20	.271	.481
Parra,Gerardo	L	.238	105	25	2	1	3	13	6	19	.296	.362
Bats Left	R	.303	442	134	34	4	11	38	22	73	.336	.473
Paulsen,Ben	L	.235	34	8	1	0	0	7	3	12	.289	.265
Bats Left	R	.282	291	82	18	4	11	42	20	80	.330	.485
Pearce,Steve	L	.196	112	22	4	1	4	17	9	23	.266	.357
Bats Right	R	.231	182	42	9	0	11	23	14	46	.303	.462
Pederson,Joc	L	.216	116	25	3	0	6	14	13	48	.295	.397
Bats Left	R	.209	364	76	16	1	20	40	79	122	.361	.423
Pedroia,Dustin	L	.275	91	25	6	0	4	8	13	17	.362	.473
Bats Right	R	.297	290	86	13	1	8	34	25	34	.354	.431

Batters vs. Left-Handed and Right-Handed Pitchers

Batter	vs	Avg	AB	H	2B	3B	HR	RBI	BB	SO	OBP	Slg
Peguero,Carlos	L	.286	7	2	0	0	0	1	2	2	.500	.286
Bats Left	R	.176	68	12	4	0	4	8	11	35	.288	.412
Pena,Brayan	L	.217	92	20	3	0	0	5	11	12	.301	.250
Bats Both	R	.295	241	71	14	0	0	13	18	22	.347	.353
Pence,Hunter	L	.200	40	8	3	0	1	12	1	8	.220	.350
Bats Right	R	.293	167	49	10	1	8	28	15	40	.352	.509
Pennington,Cliff	L	.140	43	6	1	0	0	4	8	9	.264	.163
Bats Both	R	.228	167	38	5	0	3	17	19	40	.307	.311
Peralta,David	L	.250	80	20	3	2	1	14	6	23	.311	.375
Bats Left	R	.325	382	124	23	8	16	64	38	84	.384	.552
Peralta,Jhonny	L	.238	164	39	4	1	9	16	12	41	.298	.439
Bats Right	R	.289	415	120	22	0	8	55	38	70	.348	.400
Peraza,Jose	L	.267	15	4	1	1	0	1	1	0	.313	.467
Bats Right	R	.000	7	0	0	0	0	0	1	2	.125	.000
Perez,Carlos	L	.186	70	13	2	0	0	3	6	11	.247	.214
Bats Right	R	.274	190	52	11	0	4	18	13	38	.319	.395
Perez,Eury	L	.278	18	5	0	0	0	0	3	2	.409	.278
Bats Right	R	.267	101	27	4	0	0	5	4	21	.315	.307
Perez,Hernan	L	.240	100	24	8	2	1	10	1	23	.245	.390
Bats Right	R	.245	163	40	7	0	0	11	4	36	.263	.288
Perez,Juan	L	.292	24	7	2	0	0	0	1	5	.320	.375
Bats Right	R	.267	15	4	1	0	0	2	0	1	.267	.333
Perez,Roberto	L	.265	49	13	5	0	1	4	12	16	.413	.429
Bats Right	R	.215	135	29	4	1	6	17	21	48	.323	.393
Perez,Salvador	L	.215	172	37	9	0	4	17	0	26	.223	.337
Bats Right	R	.281	359	101	16	0	17	53	13	56	.307	.468
Peterson,Jace	L	.190	105	20	4	1	1	11	6	33	.234	.276
Bats Left	R	.251	423	106	19	4	5	41	50	87	.332	.350
Peterson,Shane	L	.237	38	9	1	1	0	2	5	12	.326	.316
Bats Left	R	.264	163	43	6	2	2	14	15	43	.324	.362
Petit,Gregorio	L	.115	26	3	2	0	0	5	3	11	.200	.192
Bats Right	R	.250	16	4	1	0	0	0	0	5	.250	.313
Pham,Tommy	L	.278	36	10	0	0	1	2	9	12	.422	.361
Bats Right	R	.265	117	31	7	5	4	16	10	29	.320	.513
Phegley,Josh	L	.276	116	32	7	0	5	17	8	23	.323	.466
Bats Right	R	.220	109	24	9	1	4	17	6	28	.277	.431
Phillips,Brandon	L	.303	145	44	4	0	2	15	7	11	.338	.372
Bats Right	R	.291	443	129	15	2	10	55	20	57	.325	.402
Pierzynski,A.J.	L	.265	83	22	5	0	0	7	5	10	.330	.325
Bats Left	R	.309	324	100	19	1	9	42	14	27	.342	.457
Pillar,Kevin	L	.278	144	40	6	0	2	12	8	25	.323	.361
Bats Right	R	.278	442	123	25	2	10	44	20	60	.311	.412
Pirela,Jose	L	.302	43	13	2	0	1	3	2	8	.333	.419
Bats Right	R	.129	31	4	1	0	0	2	0	8	.125	.161
Piscotty,Stephen	L	.322	59	19	5	0	2	8	6	15	.379	.508
Bats Right	R	.299	174	52	10	4	5	31	14	41	.353	.489
Plawecki,Kevin	L	.122	41	5	0	0	2	4	1	7	.143	.268
Bats Right	R	.240	192	46	9	0	1	17	16	53	.307	.302
Plouffe,Trevor	L	.250	156	39	7	2	6	26	22	27	.344	.436
Bats Right	R	.242	417	101	28	2	16	60	28	97	.293	.434
Polanco,Gregory	L	.190	126	24	5	0	2	16	9	36	.250	.278
Bats Left	R	.274	467	128	30	6	7	36	46	85	.338	.409
Pollock,A.J.	L	.326	135	44	8	1	5	18	10	18	.370	.511
Bats Right	R	.312	474	148	31	5	15	58	43	71	.366	.494
Pompey,Dalton	L	.350	20	7	2	0	0	1	2	3	.409	.450
Bats Both	R	.189	74	14	6	0	2	5	5	20	.259	.351
Posey,Buster	L	.314	137	43	10	0	5	18	9	9	.358	.496
Bats Right	R	.319	420	134	18	0	14	77	47	43	.385	.462
Prado,Martin	L	.325	114	37	8	1	2	13	13	6	.391	.465
Bats Right	R	.277	386	107	14	1	7	50	24	62	.322	.373
Puig,Yasiel	L	.279	68	19	3	0	5	10	11	15	.380	.544
Bats Right	R	.248	214	53	9	3	6	28	15	51	.302	.402
Pujols,Albert	L	.219	155	34	6	0	11	21	14	18	.282	.471
Bats Right	R	.253	447	113	16	0	29	74	36	54	.316	.483
Raburn,Ryan	L	.325	151	49	16	0	8	25	20	34	.415	.589
Bats Right	R	.136	22	3	0	1	0	4	3	10	.240	.227
Ramirez,Alexei	L	.283	127	36	7	0	2	17	8	13	.321	.386
Bats Right	R	.239	456	109	26	0	8	45	23	55	.275	.349
Ramirez,Aramis	L	.216	111	24	5	1	5	17	11	14	.285	.414
Bats Right	R	.255	364	93	26	0	12	58	20	54	.300	.426
Ramirez,Hanley	L	.230	113	26	3	1	6	20	8	26	.276	.434
Bats Right	R	.257	288	74	9	0	13	33	13	45	.296	.424
Ramirez,Jose	L	.202	94	19	3	0	2	6	10	9	.276	.298
Bats Both	R	.226	221	50	11	3	4	21	22	30	.298	.357
Ramos,Wilson	L	.233	116	27	2	0	4	19	6	24	.266	.353
Bats Right	R	.228	359	82	14	0	11	49	15	77	.255	.359
Rasmus,Colby	L	.252	119	30	5	0	7	16	20	42	.364	.471
Bats Left	R	.233	313	73	18	2	18	45	27	112	.294	.476
Realmuto,J.T.	L	.281	89	25	7	2	2	13	5	17	.319	.472
Bats Right	R	.253	352	89	14	5	8	34	14	53	.282	.389
Recker,Anthony	L	.174	23	4	0	0	2	3	5	10	.321	.435
Bats Right	R	.105	57	6	1	0	0	2	6	25	.203	.123
Reddick,Josh	L	.222	135	30	5	1	4	16	13	20	.291	.363
Bats Left	R	.289	391	113	20	3	16	61	36	45	.347	.478
Refsnyder,Rob	L	.267	30	8	2	0	0	1	3	2	.333	.333
Bats Right	R	.385	13	5	1	0	2	4	0	5	.385	.923
Reimold,Nolan	L	.278	79	22	3	1	2	8	12	25	.374	.418
Bats Right	R	.220	91	20	2	0	4	12	11	22	.317	.374
Rendon,Anthony	L	.311	61	19	4	0	0	5	6	8	.373	.377
Bats Right	R	.252	250	63	12	0	5	20	30	62	.337	.360
Revere,Ben	L	.271	155	42	5	1	0	14	10	25	.321	.316
Bats Left	R	.318	437	139	17	6	2	31	22	39	.349	.398
Reyes,Jose	L	.273	139	38	7	0	3	17	9	14	.311	.388
Bats Both	R	.275	342	94	18	2	4	36	17	48	.309	.374
Reynolds,Mark	L	.224	107	24	4	2	5	12	14	36	.314	.439
Bats Right	R	.233	275	64	17	0	8	36	30	85	.315	.382
Rios,Alex	L	.229	109	25	8	0	0	6	4	19	.267	.303
Bats Right	R	.264	276	73	14	2	4	26	11	48	.295	.373
Rivera,Rene	L	.181	94	17	6	0	0	7	3	30	.212	.245
Bats Right	R	.176	204	36	8	0	5	19	8	56	.214	.289
Rizzo,Anthony	L	.294	163	48	11	0	6	25	22	33	.409	.472
Bats Left	R	.272	423	115	27	3	25	76	56	72	.378	.527
Robertson,Daniel	L	.225	40	9	1	0	0	3	1	4	.244	.250
Bats Right	R	.343	35	12	1	0	0	4	1	3	.361	.371
Robinson,Clint	L	.424	33	14	2	0	0	2	5	8	.500	.485
Bats Left	R	.254	276	70	13	1	10	32	32	44	.341	.417
Robinson,Shane	L	.257	74	19	2	0	0	8	6	13	.309	.284
Bats Right	R	.245	106	26	5	3	0	8	6	16	.292	.349
Rodriguez,Alex	L	.263	156	41	10	1	10	27	31	48	.394	.532
Bats Right	R	.245	367	90	12	0	23	59	53	97	.340	.466
Rodriguez,Sean	L	.236	89	21	6	0	2	5	3	27	.284	.371
Bats Right	R	.252	135	34	6	1	2	12	2	36	.279	.356
Rogers,Jason	L	.271	70	19	3	0	2	6	9	19	.354	.400
Bats Right	R	.317	82	26	3	2	2	10	6	15	.378	.476
Rojas,Miguel	L	.125	24	3	1	0	0	1	1	4	.160	.167
Bats Right	R	.314	118	37	6	1	1	16	10	12	.362	.407
Rollins,Jimmy	L	.297	111	33	8	0	2	13	7	16	.339	.423
Bats Both	R	.204	406	83	16	3	11	28	37	70	.270	.340
Romero,Stefen	L	.200	15	3	1	0	1	2	2	3	.294	.467
Bats Right	R	.167	6	1	0	0	0	1	1	3	.286	.167
Romine,Andrew	L	.257	35	9	0	0	1	3	1	13	.297	.343
Bats Both	R	.255	149	38	5	0	1	12	10	33	.309	.309
Rosales,Adam	L	.217	69	15	1	0	2	4	7	23	.289	.319
Bats Right	R	.244	45	11	3	0	1	3	3	7	.306	.378
Rosario,Eddie	L	.289	114	33	2	5	4	18	4	29	.311	.500
Bats Left	R	.260	339	88	16	10	9	32	11	89	.281	.445
Rosario,Wilin	L	.282	85	24	6	0	2	7	7	16	.333	.424
Bats Right	R	.260	146	38	8	1	4	22	1	40	.270	.411
Ross,Cody	L	.125	16	2	0	0	0	1	0	5	.125	.125
Bats Right	R	.000	6	0	0	0	0	2	3	1	.333	.000
Ross,David	L	.156	45	7	2	0	0	3	5	15	.240	.200
Bats Right	R	.184	114	21	7	0	1	6	15	46	.277	.272
Rua,Ryan	L	.196	51	10	3	0	3	6	2	17	.226	.431
Bats Right	R	.188	32	6	2	0	1	1	1	15	.212	.344
Ruf,Darin	L	.371	97	36	4	0	8	22	12	18	.447	.660
Bats Right	R	.158	171	27	8	0	4	17	9	51	.208	.275
Ruggiano,Justin	L	.301	83	25	6	1	5	11	8	22	.370	.578
Bats Right	R	.143	42	6	2	0	1	4	6	19	.265	.262
Ruiz,Carlos	L	.327	55	18	7	0	1	8	3	7	.377	.509
Bats Right	R	.183	229	42	6	1	1	14	25	36	.270	.231
Rupp,Cameron	L	.303	66	20	5	1	3	9	7	12	.370	.545
Bats Right	R	.211	204	43	4	0	6	19	17	59	.279	.319
Russell,Addison	L	.156	109	17	9	0	2	9	10	35	.233	.294
Bats Right	R	.268	366	98	20	1	11	45	32	114	.328	.418
Rutledge,Josh	L	.318	22	7	1	0	0	2	2	9	.385	.364
Bats Right	R	.269	52	14	0	0	1	8	3	17	.310	.327
Ryan,Brendan	L	.283	53	15	5	2	0	6	2	13	.321	.453
Bats Right	R	.163	43	7	1	0	0	2	3	16	.217	.186
Saladino,Tyler	L	.207	58	12	2	2	1	8	6	10	.288	.362
Bats Right	R	.230	178	41	4	2	3	12	6	41	.259	.326
Saltalamacchia,Jarrod	L	.293	41	12	4	0	3	4	5	9	.370	.610
Bats Both	R	.208	159	33	11	0	6	20	18	60	.294	.390

Batters vs. Left-Handed and Right-Handed Pitchers

Batter	vs	Avg	AB	H	2B	3B	HR	RBI	BB	SO	OBP	Slg
Sanchez,Carlos	L	.218	87	19	8	0	1	9	5	17	.261	.345
Bats Both	R	.225	302	68	15	1	4	22	14	64	.270	.321
Sanchez,Hector	L	.176	17	3	1	0	0	0	1	0	.222	.235
Bats Both	R	.179	39	7	3	0	1	5	1	14	.200	.333
Sandoval,Pablo	L	.197	147	29	5	0	0	11	5	29	.234	.231
Bats Both	R	.266	323	86	20	1	10	36	20	44	.317	.427
Sands,Jerry	L	.297	64	19	5	1	2	11	4	18	.338	.500
Bats Right	R	.169	59	10	0	0	2	8	5	18	.231	.271
Sano,Miguel	L	.284	81	23	5	1	4	13	10	34	.363	.519
Bats Both	R	.263	198	52	12	0	14	39	43	85	.393	.535
Santana,Carlos	L	.268	190	51	8	0	4	24	35	36	.382	.374
Bats Both	R	.211	360	76	21	2	15	61	73	86	.345	.406
Santana,Danny	L	.253	75	19	4	1	0	4	1	21	.291	.333
Bats Both	R	.199	186	37	6	4	0	17	5	47	.220	.274
Santana,Domingo	L	.288	52	15	3	0	4	9	7	16	.373	.577
Bats Right	R	.213	108	23	4	0	4	17	13	47	.320	.361
Sardinas,Luis	L	.136	22	3	0	1	0	1	0	8	.136	.227
Bats Both	R	.213	75	16	0	0	0	3	6	17	.268	.213
Saunders,Michael	L	.667	3	2	0	0	0	1	1	0	.750	.667
Bats Left	R	.143	28	4	0	0	0	2	4	10	.250	.143
Schafer,Jordan	L	.313	16	5	1	0	0	1	0	2	.313	.375
Bats Left	R	.189	53	10	2	0	0	4	3	21	.232	.226
Schafer,Logan	L	.160	25	4	1	0	0	1	2	3	.214	.200
Bats Left	R	.237	97	23	5	1	1	5	10	26	.321	.340
Schebler,Scott	L	.000	4	0	0	0	0	0	1	2	.200	.000
Bats Left	R	.281	32	9	0	0	3	4	2	11	.343	.563
Schoop,Jonathan	L	.232	99	23	2	0	2	6	4	30	.260	.313
Bats Right	R	.301	206	62	15	0	13	33	5	49	.329	.563
Schumaker,Skip	L	.273	22	6	3	0	0	1	5	6	.407	.409
Bats Left	R	.239	222	53	17	0	1	20	18	45	.295	.329
Schwarber,Kyle	L	.143	56	8	1	0	2	11	5	27	.213	.268
Bats Left	R	.278	176	49	5	1	14	32	31	50	.396	.557
Scruggs,Xavier	L	.143	7	1	1	0	0	1	0	3	.143	.286
Bats Right	R	.286	35	10	1	0	0	6	0	7	.306	.314
Seager,Corey	L	.325	40	13	1	0	2	9	7	8	.426	.500
Bats Left	R	.345	58	20	7	1	2	8	7	11	.424	.603
Seager,Kyle	L	.297	229	68	10	0	13	35	8	44	.324	.511
Bats Left	R	.249	394	98	27	0	13	39	46	54	.330	.416
Segura,Jean	L	.283	145	41	7	2	1	8	2	16	.300	.379
Bats Right	R	.248	415	103	9	3	5	42	11	77	.274	.320
Semien,Marcus	L	.329	152	50	4	4	5	18	11	25	.372	.507
Bats Right	R	.230	404	93	19	3	10	27	31	107	.287	.366
Shaffer,Richie	L	.137	51	7	2	0	1	3	8	24	.286	.235
Bats Right	R	.304	23	7	1	0	3	3	2	8	.360	.739
Shaw,Travis	L	.329	82	27	6	0	6	16	3	19	.353	.622
Bats Left	R	.243	144	35	4	0	7	20	15	38	.319	.417
Shuck,J.B.	L	.217	23	5	2	0	0	1	5	5	.357	.304
Bats Left	R	.275	120	33	6	2	0	14	11	11	.336	.358
Simmons,Andrelton	L	.224	107	24	2	0	1	6	10	12	.294	.271
Bats Right	R	.276	428	118	21	2	3	38	29	36	.328	.355
Singleton,Jon	L	.333	9	3	1	0	0	1	1	4	.400	.444
Bats Left	R	.158	38	6	1	0	1	5	9	13	.313	.263
Sizemore,Grady	L	.333	18	6	1	0	1	2	2	2	.429	.556
Bats Left	R	.247	255	63	16	0	5	31	18	58	.298	.369
Smith,Seth	L	.200	50	10	4	0	1	4	1	19	.231	.340
Bats Left	R	.255	345	88	27	5	11	38	46	80	.343	.458
Smoak,Justin	L	.256	39	10	0	0	4	10	1	8	.275	.564
Bats Both	R	.222	257	57	16	1	14	49	28	78	.302	.455
Smolinski,Jake	L	.262	84	22	2	2	4	17	14	16	.356	.476
Bats Right	R	.122	82	10	5	0	2	9	5	23	.198	.256
Snider,Travis	L	.233	43	10	4	1	0	2	0	7	.233	.372
Bats Left	R	.232	194	45	8	1	4	26	26	59	.329	.345
Sogard,Eric	L	.210	62	13	1	0	1	8	4	18	.269	.274
Bats Left	R	.255	310	79	11	3	0	29	19	32	.299	.310
Solano,Donovan	L	.077	26	2	1	1	0	3	0	4	.077	.192
Bats Right	R	.234	64	15	2	0	0	4	1	14	.269	.266
Solano,Jhonatan	L	.000	2	0	0	0	0	0	0	0	.000	.000
Bats Right	R	.056	18	1	1	0	0	2	1	1	.105	.111
Solarte,Yangervis	L	.242	120	29	7	0	3	13	8	12	.292	.375
Bats Both	R	.278	406	113	26	4	11	50	26	44	.328	.443
Soler,Jorge	L	.240	75	18	3	0	2	13	15	29	.370	.360
Bats Right	R	.268	291	78	15	1	8	34	17	92	.311	.409
Soto,Geovany	L	.246	57	14	4	0	3	7	1	17	.306	.474
Bats Right	R	.208	130	27	4	0	6	14	16	46	.299	.377
Souza,Steven	L	.212	99	21	6	0	4	13	18	36	.336	.394
Bats Right	R	.230	274	63	9	1	12	27	28	108	.310	.401
Span,Denard	L	.197	61	12	1	0	1	6	6	9	.279	.262
Bats Left	R	.335	185	62	16	0	4	16	19	17	.393	.486
Spangenberg,Cory	L	.273	55	15	2	0	0	3	9	14	.394	.309
Bats Left	R	.270	248	67	15	5	4	18	19	61	.319	.419
Springer,George	L	.296	135	40	8	0	8	14	20	32	.403	.533
Bats Right	R	.265	253	67	11	2	8	27	30	77	.348	.419
Stanton,Giancarlo	L	.288	59	17	2	1	9	17	7	21	.358	.814
Bats Right	R	.259	220	57	10	0	18	50	27	74	.343	.550
Stewart,Chris	L	.300	30	9	1	0	0	4	2	4	.333	.333
Bats Right	R	.287	129	37	7	0	0	11	4	25	.316	.341
Strausborger,Ryan	L	.160	25	4	0	0	1	2	2	7	.214	.280
Bats Right	R	.250	20	5	0	0	0	1	1	4	.273	.250
Stubbs,Drew	L	.179	56	10	2	1	1	2	5	29	.258	.304
Bats Right	R	.209	67	14	2	1	4	8	9	31	.303	.448
Suarez,Eugenio	L	.289	83	24	4	0	4	13	6	23	.337	.482
Bats Right	R	.277	289	80	15	2	9	35	11	71	.308	.436
Sucre,Jesus	L	.289	38	11	4	0	0	4	5	3	.372	.395
Bats Right	R	.101	89	9	2	0	1	3	1	18	.111	.157
Susac,Andrew	L	.298	47	14	4	0	1	6	6	14	.377	.447
Bats Right	R	.174	86	15	3	2	2	8	8	29	.253	.326
Suzuki,Ichiro	L	.278	90	25	0	4	1	11	6	10	.323	.400
Bats Left	R	.214	308	66	5	2	0	10	25	41	.270	.244
Suzuki,Kurt	L	.257	136	35	8	0	1	17	12	18	.320	.338
Bats Right	R	.232	297	69	9	0	4	33	17	41	.284	.303
Sweeney,Darnell	L	.222	27	6	1	0	1	2	4	6	.323	.370
Bats Both	R	.155	58	9	3	1	2	9	9	21	.269	.345
Swihart,Blake	L	.225	80	18	3	0	1	6	8	19	.303	.300
Bats Both	R	.293	208	61	14	1	4	25	10	58	.326	.428
Swisher,Nick	L	.225	80	18	6	0	3	14	8	9	.304	.413
Bats Both	R	.180	139	25	3	0	3	11	27	45	.315	.266
Szczur,Matt	L	.243	37	9	4	0	1	4	3	5	.293	.432
Bats Left	R	.200	35	7	1	0	0	4	3	10	.263	.229
Tabata,Jose	L	.333	15	5	0	0	0	2	1	4	.375	.333
Bats Right	R	.261	23	6	0	0	0	2	1	3	.320	.261
Taylor,Chris	L	.241	29	7	1	1	0	1	2	7	.290	.345
Bats Right	R	.138	65	9	2	0	0		4	24	.188	.169
Taylor,Michael	L	.240	104	25	2	0	4	14	8	36	.292	.375
Bats Right	R	.226	368	83	13	2	10	49	27	122	.280	.353
Teixeira,Mark	L	.223	121	27	5	0	6	18	27	19	.373	.413
Bats Both	R	.269	271	73	17	0	25	61	32	66	.349	.609
Tejada,Ruben	L	.264	87	23	5	0	2	7	10	18	.340	.391
Bats Both	R	.260	273	71	18	0	1	21	28	52	.338	.337
Telis,Tomas	L	.333	6	2	0	0	0	2	0	1	.429	.333
Bats Both	R	.125	32	4	0	0	0	0	1	3	.176	.125
Terdoslavich,Joey	L	.111	9	1	0	1	0	1	0	1	.111	.333
Bats Both	R	.234	47	11	4	0	1	3	3	13	.280	.383
Thole,Josh	L	.250	12	3	1	0	0	1	0	2	.250	.333
Bats Left	R	.189	37	7	1	0	0	1	3	7	.250	.216
Thompson,Trayce	L	.327	55	18	5	3	2	6	3	9	.362	.636
Bats Right	R	.269	67	18	3	0	3	10	10	17	.364	.448
Tolleson,Steve	L	.318	22	7	3	1	0	3	3	3	.400	.545
Bats Right	R	.211	19	4	2	0	0		1	6	.250	.316
Tomas,Yasmany	L	.279	111	31	6	2	4	16	7	25	.319	.477
Bats Right	R	.271	295	80	13	1	5	32	10	85	.300	.373
Tomlinson,Kelby	L	.371	62	23	2	1	2	9	1	12	.381	.532
Bats Right	R	.267	116	31	4	2	0	11	13	28	.346	.336
Travis,Devon	L	.328	58	19	4	0	4	7	4	7	.371	.603
Bats Right	R	.294	160	47	14	0	4	28	14	36	.356	.456
Trout,Mike	L	.313	144	45	9	1	10	19	30	37	.434	.597
Bats Right	R	.295	431	127	23	5	31	71	62	121	.391	.587
Trumbo,Mark	L	.289	173	50	6	1	11	25	11	40	.330	.526
Bats Right	R	.248	335	83	17	2	11	39	25	92	.300	.409
Tucker,Preston	L	.200	65	13	2	0	0	1	3	16	.235	.231
Bats Left	R	.255	235	60	17	0	13	32	17	52	.314	.494
Tulowitzki,Troy	L	.350	100	35	7	0	4	15	7	25	.400	.540
Bats Right	R	.262	386	101	20	0	13	55	31	89	.321	.415
Turner,Justin	L	.248	109	27	3	0	5	16	15	25	.339	.413
Bats Right	R	.312	276	86	23	1	11	44	21	46	.383	.522
Turner,Trea	L	.375	8	3	0	0	0	0	1	1	.444	.375
Bats Right	R	.188	32	6	1	0	1	1	3	11	.257	.313
Uggla,Dan	L	.237	38	9	2	1	0	6	5	14	.326	.342
Bats Right	R	.159	82	13	2	1	2	10	14	26	.286	.280
Upton,Justin	L	.191	110	21	3	0	6	13	9	30	.258	.300
Bats Right	R	.266	432	115	23	3	23	71	58	120	.355	.493
Upton Jr.,Melvin	L	.254	71	18	6	0	2	6	13	22	.369	.423
Bats Right	R	.261	134	35	6	4	3	11	8	40	.303	.433

Batters vs. Left-Handed and Right-Handed Pitchers

Batter	vs	Avg	AB	H	2B	3B	HR	RBI	BB	SO	OBP	Slg
Uribe,Juan	L	.272	92	25	4	0	7	15	11	22	.350	.543
Bats Right	R	.246	268	66	13	0	7	28	23	58	.310	.373
Urrutia,Henry	L	.000	3	0	0	0	0	0	0	0	.000	.000
Bats Left	R	.290	31	9	1	0	1	6	2	3	.333	.419
Urshela,Giovanny	L	.275	69	19	3	0	1	4	4	12	.315	.362
Bats Right	R	.207	198	41	5	1	5	17	14	46	.266	.318
Utley,Chase	L	.186	97	18	4	1	1	7	9	21	.278	.278
Bats Left	R	.221	276	61	17	1	7	32	23	43	.289	.366
Valbuena,Luis	L	.158	114	18	3	0	5	11	15	30	.265	.316
Bats Left	R	.247	320	79	15	0	20	45	35	76	.327	.481
Valencia,Danny	L	.298	131	39	6	0	5	27	17	24	.376	.458
Bats Right	R	.285	214	61	17	1	13	39	12	56	.325	.556
Van Slyke,Scott	L	.258	93	24	4	0	3	11	17	21	.386	.398
Bats Right	R	.225	129	29	10	0	3	19	6	41	.261	.372
Vargas,Kennys	L	.364	55	20	0	0	2	8	3	16	.397	.473
Bats Both	R	.183	120	22	4	0	3	9	6	38	.222	.292
Venable,Will	L	.159	44	7	1	0	0	4	2	14	.196	.182
Bats Left	R	.256	305	78	12	3	6	29	35	80	.336	.374
Victorino,Shane	L	.243	107	26	3	2	1	4	11	19	.333	.336
Bats Right	R	.211	71	15	1	0	0	3	5	13	.269	.225
Villar,Jonathan	L	.279	61	17	5	1	1	7	4	14	.318	.443
Bats Both	R	.291	55	16	2	0	1	4	6	15	.361	.382
Vogt,Stephen	L	.239	109	26	5	1	1	19	10	24	.301	.330
Bats Left	R	.268	336	90	16	2	17	52	46	73	.353	.479
Votto,Joey	L	.331	166	55	12	1	7	28	41	39	.467	.542
Bats Left	R	.306	379	116	21	1	22	52	102	96	.456	.541
Walker,Neil	L	.237	93	22	5	0	0	9	7	13	.284	.290
Bats Both	R	.276	450	124	27	3	16	62	37	97	.337	.456
Wallace,Brett	L	.296	27	8	3	0	0	4	2	11	.345	.407
Bats Left	R	.304	69	21	3	0	5	12	8	20	.385	.565
Walters,Zach	L	.182	11	2	0	0	0	3	0	4	.182	.182
Bats Both	R	.105	19	2	0	0	0	0	0	11	.105	.105
Weeks,Rickie	L	.234	47	11	1	0	2	9	4	9	.308	.383
Bats Right	R	.081	37	3	0	0	0	0	5	16	.209	.081
Werth,Jayson	L	.218	78	17	7	0	5	16	6	22	.271	.500
Bats Right	R	.221	253	56	9	1	7	26	32	62	.311	.348
Wieters,Matt	L	.265	68	18	2	0	3	7	4	22	.301	.426
Bats Both	R	.268	190	51	12	1	5	18	17	45	.325	.421
Williams,Mason	L	.000	1	0	0	0	0	0	0	0	.000	.000
Bats Left	R	.300	20	6	3	0	1	3	1	3	.333	.600
Williamson,Mac	L	.133	15	2	0	0	0	0	0	2	.188	.133
Bats Right	R	.294	17	5	0	1	0	1	0	6	.278	.412
Wilson,Bobby	L	.105	38	4	0	0	0	2	4	14	.190	.105
Bats Right	R	.223	94	21	5	0	1	12	7	25	.282	.309
Wilson,Josh	L	.357	14	5	1	0	0	3	0	6	.357	.429
Bats Right	R	.292	24	7	2	0	0	2	0	9	.346	.375
Wong,Kolten	L	.229	166	38	5	0	1	24	6	35	.275	.277
Bats Left	R	.276	391	108	23	4	10	37	30	60	.340	.432
Wright,David	L	.351	37	13	3	0	2	4	5	6	.429	.595
Bats Right	R	.270	115	31	4	0	3	13	17	30	.364	.383
Yelich,Christian	L	.288	132	38	4	1	1	16	12	33	.347	.356
Bats Left	R	.305	344	105	26	1	6	28	35	68	.373	.439
Ynoa,Rafael	L	.260	50	13	5	0	0	5	1	12	.275	.360
Bats Both	R	.260	77	20	3	1	0	4	2	16	.278	.325
Young,Chris	L	.327	153	50	15	1	7	24	18	28	.397	.575
Bats Right	R	.182	165	30	5	0	7	18	12	45	.246	.339
Young,Delmon	L	.310	58	18	1	0	0	5	0	7	.317	.328
Bats Right	R	.250	116	29	5	0	2	11	4	22	.275	.345
Young,Eric	L	.100	10	1	1	0	0	1	0	1	.182	.200
Bats Both	R	.160	75	12	3	2	0	4	6	17	.222	.253
Zimmerman,Ryan	L	.330	91	30	9	1	7	28	8	20	.376	.681
Bats Right	R	.220	255	56	16	0	9	45	25	59	.284	.388
Zobrist,Ben	L	.329	149	49	17	1	3	16	20	18	.409	.517
Bats Both	R	.252	318	80	19	2	10	40	42	38	.335	.418
Zunino,Mike	L	.206	102	21	4	0	1	7	6	36	.248	.275
Bats Right	R	.161	248	40	7	0	10	21	15	96	.223	.310
AL	L	.258	-	-	-	-	-	-	-	-	.322	.410
	R	.254	-	-	-	-	-	-	-	-	.316	.413
NL	L	.250	-	-	-	-	-	-	-	-	.315	.385
	R	.254	-	-	-	-	-	-	-	-	.316	.401
MLB	L	.255	-	-	-	-	-	-	-	-	.319	.399
	R	.254	-	-	-	-	-	-	-	-	.316	.407

Pitchers vs. Left-Handed and Right-Handed Batters

Pitcher	vs	Avg	AB	H	2B	3B	HR	RBI	BB	SO	OBP	Slg
Aardsma,David	L	.353	34	12	2	0	3	7	6	7	.463	.676
Throws Right	R	.167	78	13	5	0	3	13	8	28	.241	.346
Abad,Fernando	L	.277	101	28	4	1	7	20	5	26	.315	.545
Throws Left	R	.218	78	17	2	1	4	10	14	19	.330	.423
Achter,A.J.	L	.267	15	4	0	0	1	3	4	6	.421	.467
Throws Right	R	.216	37	8	1	0	3	9	2	8	.256	.486
Adams,Austin	L	.267	60	16	2	2	1	11	7	10	.343	.417
Throws Right	R	.284	74	21	8	0	1	7	6	13	.338	.432
Adcock,Nate	L	.259	27	7	1	0	1	3	6	0	.382	.407
Throws Right	R	.195	41	8	4	1	2	9	6	13	.313	.488
Affeldt,Jeremy	L	.284	67	19	3	0	2	12	5	12	.342	.418
Throws Left	R	.300	80	24	3	0	4	10	9	9	.378	.488
Albers,Matt	L	.275	51	14	2	0	1	6	7	7	.356	.373
Throws Right	R	.200	85	17	2	0	2	7	2	21	.222	.294
Alburquerque,Al	L	.256	90	23	3	1	4	18	14	22	.356	.444
Throws Right	R	.278	144	40	7	0	0	10	19	36	.361	.326
Alexander,Scott	L	.333	6	2	0	0	0	1	0	1	.429	.333
Throws Left	R	.200	15	3	0	0	0	2	3	2	.333	.200
Allen,Cody	L	.176	125	22	6	0	1	11	13	50	.264	.248
Throws Right	R	.260	131	34	10	0	1	16	12	49	.317	.359
Almonte,Miguel	L	.231	13	3	0	0	0	0	5	2	.444	.231
Throws Right	R	.200	20	4	0	0	4	6	2	8	.304	.800
Alvarez,Henderson	L	.360	50	18	3	0	1	10	6	6	.429	.480
Throws Right	R	.250	40	10	3	0	0	4	1	3	.262	.325
Alvarez,Jose	L	.217	106	23	3	0	1	13	8	27	.297	.274
Throws Left	R	.236	148	35	8	1	4	22	15	32	.309	.385
Alvarez,R.J.	L	.450	40	18	4	0	4	15	2	6	.465	.850
Throws Right	R	.200	45	9	2	0	3	11	11	17	.351	.444
Anderson,Brett	L	.284	204	58	9	2	1	18	14	37	.335	.363
Throws Left	R	.276	493	136	17	1	17	55	32	79	.319	.418
Anderson,Chase	L	.262	267	70	18	1	7	29	25	58	.330	.416
Throws Right	R	.280	314	88	15	2	11	36	15	53	.315	.446
Anderson,Cody	L	.238	147	35	7	2	5	15	12	18	.300	.415
Throws Right	R	.225	187	42	7	0	4	14	12	26	.267	.326
Andriese,Matt	L	.281	121	34	3	1	5	16	10	22	.338	.446
Throws Right	R	.255	137	35	6	1	3	16	8	27	.297	.380
Araujo,Elvis	L	.243	74	18	2	1	1	7	7	17	.309	.338
Throws Left	R	.200	55	11	2	0	0	6	12	17	.343	.236
Archer,Chris	L	.222	424	94	20	0	9	40	29	132	.272	.333
Throws Right	R	.218	371	81	11	0	10	34	37	120	.293	.329
Armstrong,Shawn	L	.143	14	2	1	0	0	1	1	6	.200	.214
Throws Right	R	.214	14	3	1	0	1	1	1	5	.267	.500
Aro,Jonathan	L	.316	19	6	2	0	0	2	4	3	.435	.421
Throws Right	R	.360	25	9	4	0	2	5	0	5	.346	.760
Arrieta,Jake	L	.159	377	60	15	1	3	22	27	123	.221	.228
Throws Right	R	.207	434	90	17	3	7	26	21	113	.248	.309
Asher,Alec	L	.379	66	25	7	0	4	16	4	9	.408	.667
Throws Right	R	.293	58	17	3	1	4	13	6	7	.369	.586
Atchison,Scott	L	.179	28	5	0	0	1	3	1	6	.226	.286
Throws Right	R	.346	52	18	5	0	5	15	3	6	.375	.731
Aumont,Phillippe	L	.333	9	3	1	0	1	2	4	1	.538	.778
Throws Right	R	.286	7	2	1	0	1	4	3	2	.500	.857
Avilan,Luis	L	.271	96	26	4	0	2	13	3	24	.290	.375
Throws Left	R	.210	105	22	3	1	4	14	12	25	.294	.371
Axelrod,Dylan	L	.217	23	5	0	0	3	6	4	3	.333	.609
Throws Right	R	.222	27	6	1	0	2	6	4	9	.323	.481
Axford,John	L	.258	97	25	3	0	1	5	14	29	.351	.320
Throws Right	R	.261	119	31	5	0	3	20	18	33	.353	.378
Badenhop,Burke	L	.265	117	31	8	2	2	14	12	12	.331	.419
Throws Right	R	.280	143	40	5	0	2	26	8	24	.314	.357
Baez,Pedro	L	.255	51	13	4	1	1	4	4	16	.304	.431
Throws Right	R	.245	139	34	12	0	3	26	7	44	.282	.396
Bailey,Andrew	L	.250	12	3	0	0	0	1	2	3	.333	.250
Throws Right	R	.318	22	7	1	0	2	7	3	3	.385	.636
Bailey,Homer	L	.500	20	10	2	0	2	5	1	2	.524	.900
Throws Right	R	.222	27	6	2	0	1	2	3	1	.300	.407
Baker,Scott	L	.308	13	4	1	0	1	2	1	1	.357	.615
Throws Right	R	.241	29	7	3	0	3	5	2	7	.290	.655
Balester,Collin	L	.174	23	4	1	0	0	2	8	5	.387	.217
Throws Right	R	.333	39	13	3	1	3	10	5	8	.413	.692
Balfour,Grant	L	.400	5	2	1	0	0	1	3	0	.600	.600
Throws Right	R	.100	10	1	0	0	1	4	1	0	.182	.400
Banuelos,Manny	L	.286	28	8	1	0	1	2	5	5	.412	.429
Throws Left	R	.282	78	22	5	0	3	14	7	14	.356	.462
Barnes,Matt	L	.284	81	23	7	0	2	10	8	15	.356	.444
Throws Right	R	.333	99	33	3	0	7	19	7	24	.383	.576

Pitcher	vs	Avg	AB	H	2B	3B	HR	RBI	BB	SO	OBP	Slg
Barraclough,Kyle	L	.161	31	5	1	0	1	4	10	10	.366	.290
Throws Right	R	.149	47	7	4	0	0	6	8	20	.263	.234
Barrett,Aaron	L	.200	35	7	1	1	0	4	2	5	.263	.286
Throws Right	R	.269	78	21	3	0	1	11	5	30	.329	.346
Barrios,Yhonathan	L	.100	10	1	0	0	0	0	0	4	.100	.100
Throws Right	R	.167	12	2	1	0	0	0	0	3	.167	.250
Bass,Anthony	L	.284	102	29	5	2	2	16	13	15	.364	.431
Throws Right	R	.259	143	37	12	2	3	19	7	30	.291	.434
Bassitt,Chris	L	.217	184	40	9	2	3	17	22	36	.313	.337
Throws Right	R	.279	136	38	9	0	2	15	8	28	.342	.390
Bastardo,Antonio	L	.138	65	9	0	1	1	3	6	19	.233	.215
Throws Left	R	.210	143	30	6	0	3	14	20	45	.311	.315
Bauer,Trevor	L	.225	325	73	12	1	12	39	47	80	.326	.378
Throws Right	R	.239	330	79	17	3	11	43	32	90	.311	.409
Beachy,Brandon	L	.200	15	3	1	0	1	4	1	3	.250	.467
Throws Right	R	.412	17	7	3	0	0	3	5	2	.545	.588
Beck,Chris	L	.438	16	7	3	0	0	3	3	2	.526	.625
Throws Right	R	.300	10	3	0	1	0	2	1	1	.364	.500
Bedrosian,Cam	L	.391	46	18	2	0	2	5	7	9	.481	.565
Throws Right	R	.256	86	22	5	1	1	14	12	25	.347	.372
Beeler,Dallas	L	.474	19	9	2	0	0	4	4	2	.565	.579
Throws Right	R	.250	20	5	2	0	0	5	3	5	.348	.350
Beimel,Joe	L	.280	75	21	3	0	4	16	7	13	.345	.480
Throws Left	R	.286	98	28	3	0	4	19	9	9	.339	.439
Belisario,Ronald	L	.316	19	6	2	0	0	2	2	3	.381	.421
Throws Right	R	.154	13	2	1	0	0	3	2	3	.267	.231
Belisle,Matt	L	.256	43	11	1	1	1	6	7	10	.389	.395
Throws Right	R	.271	85	23	3	0	0	7	8	15	.333	.306
Bellatti,Andrew	L	.167	36	6	2	0	1	1	5	9	.268	.306
Throws Right	R	.222	45	10	0	1	3	8	5	9	.308	.467
Benoit,Joaquin	L	.172	122	21	3	2	6	12	10	36	.235	.377
Throws Right	R	.144	104	15	5	0	1	4	13	27	.250	.221
Bergman,Christian	L	.215	107	23	5	2	1	9	6	22	.254	.327
Throws Right	R	.366	161	59	13	1	7	27	9	15	.400	.590
Betances,Dellin	L	.135	133	18	4	0	2	5	17	57	.243	.211
Throws Right	R	.175	154	27	3	0	4	15	23	74	.285	.273
Betancourt,Rafael	L	.204	49	10	3	0	1	5	7	18	.298	.327
Throws Right	R	.295	112	33	8	2	3	21	5	22	.322	.482
Bettis,Chad	L	.252	230	58	20	1	4	27	29	44	.337	.400
Throws Right	R	.284	218	62	17	2	7	27	13	54	.329	.477
Billingsley,Chad	L	.394	71	28	5	0	4	14	4	8	.427	.634
Throws Right	R	.305	82	25	3	0	1	8	4	7	.341	.378
Blanton,Joe	L	.281	135	38	10	1	4	17	11	30	.331	.459
Throws Right	R	.203	153	31	8	1	3	10	5	49	.231	.327
Blazek,Michael	L	.184	87	16	4	0	2	9	7	21	.253	.299
Throws Right	R	.212	113	24	5	0	1	11	11	26	.278	.283
Bolsinger,Mike	L	.287	178	51	9	1	4	13	26	36	.377	.416
Throws Right	R	.224	237	53	10	0	7	30	19	62	.282	.354
Boxberger,Brad	L	.225	129	29	4	0	4	14	16	32	.308	.349
Throws Right	R	.238	105	25	3	0	5	17	16	42	.350	.410
Boyd,Matt	L	.358	67	24	4	1	6	15	5	9	.405	.716
Throws Left	R	.294	160	47	5	3	11	29	15	34	.350	.569
Boyer,Blaine	L	.169	83	14	3	0	0	6	7	11	.231	.205
Throws Right	R	.298	161	48	10	2	5	27	12	22	.345	.478
Brach,Brad	L	.184	147	27	8	0	1	10	19	37	.275	.259
Throws Right	R	.224	134	30	7	0	6	23	19	52	.318	.410
Bracho,Silvino	L	.294	17	5	2	0	1	2	3	9	.400	.588
Throws Right	R	.143	28	4	1	0	1	2	1	8	.200	.286
Bradley,Archie	L	.178	73	13	2	0	1	5	17	18	.341	.247
Throws Right	R	.371	62	23	4	1	2	14	5	5	.420	.565
Breslow,Craig	L	.295	88	26	3	1	3	13	6	14	.351	.455
Throws Left	R	.270	159	43	10	0	9	25	17	32	.333	.503
Brigham,Jake	L	.517	29	15	5	0	0	11	7	4	.595	.690
Throws Right	R	.295	44	13	4	0	1	10	1	8	.319	.455
Britton,Zach	L	.145	69	10	0	0	0	1	3	29	.181	.145
Throws Left	R	.243	169	41	6	1	3	12	11	50	.293	.343
Broadway,Mike	L	.364	33	12	2	2	0	5	2	5	.400	.545
Throws Right	R	.229	35	8	1	1	1	3	5	8	.341	.400
Brooks,Aaron	L	.292	106	31	4	1	5	16	7	24	.336	.491
Throws Right	R	.347	121	42	10	1	4	19	7	14	.397	.545
Brothers,Rex	L	.227	22	5	1	1	0	3	3	3	.308	.364
Throws Left	R	.267	15	4	0	1	0	3	5	2	.450	.400
Brown,Brooks	L	.265	49	13	4	1	1	8	8	6	.368	.449
Throws Right	R	.247	77	19	3	0	1	9	8	14	.326	.325
Broxton,Jonathan	L	.326	92	30	4	1	2	17	8	22	.376	.457
Throws Right	R	.226	137	31	4	4	5	17	14	41	.298	.423

Pitchers vs. Left-Handed and Right-Handed Batters

Pitcher	vs	Avg	AB	H	2B	3B	HR	RBI	BB	SO	OBP	Slg
Buchanan,David	L	.353	150	53	11	2	8	26	19	17	.429	.613
Throws Right	R	.339	165	56	14	1	4	27	10	27	.384	.509
Buchanan,Jake	L	.100	10	1	0	0	1	1	1	1	.182	.400
Throws Right	R	.190	21	4	4	0	0	1	3	4	.320	.381
Buchholz,Clay	L	.239	234	56	11	0	4	18	8	61	.272	.338
Throws Right	R	.284	204	58	15	0	2	22	15	46	.338	.387
Buehrle,Mark	L	.290	207	60	11	1	8	23	8	21	.319	.469
Throws Left	R	.275	561	154	35	5	14	67	25	70	.308	.430
Bumgarner,Madison	L	.206	141	29	6	0	2	11	6	49	.248	.291
Throws Left	R	.226	673	152	24	5	19	59	33	185	.266	.361
Burawa,Daniel	L	.211	19	4	0	0	1	7	2	2	.261	.368
Throws Right	R	.259	27	7	1	0	1	5	3	9	.355	.407
Burgos,Enrique	L	.293	41	12	1	0	1	5	10	14	.431	.390
Throws Right	R	.234	64	15	4	0	1	12	5	25	.286	.344
Burnett,A.J.	L	.254	272	69	9	2	4	20	32	55	.353	.346
Throws Right	R	.291	361	105	15	3	7	36	17	88	.321	.407
Butler,Eddie	L	.353	156	55	17	0	8	29	29	19	.457	.615
Throws Right	R	.292	161	47	13	1	5	27	13	25	.352	.478
Cahill,Trevor	L	.242	66	16	1	1	2	13	5	15	.306	.379
Throws Right	R	.283	99	28	5	0	2	17	11	21	.357	.394
Cain,Matt	L	.313	115	36	5	4	6	21	10	14	.377	.583
Throws Right	R	.276	127	35	12	0	6	15	10	27	.329	.512
Caminero,Arquimedes	L	.217	106	23	6	0	3	14	15	26	.323	.358
Throws Right	R	.229	175	40	7	1	4	19	14	47	.301	.349
Capps,Carter	L	.160	50	8	1	0	1	3	3	31	.204	.240
Throws Right	R	.175	57	10	1	0	1	6	4	27	.254	.246
Capuano,Chris	L	.338	65	22	8	0	0	11	8	16	.427	.462
Throws Left	R	.291	103	30	5	0	6	25	14	22	.378	.515
Carlyle,Buddy	L	.143	7	1	0	0	0	0	0	2	.143	.143
Throws Right	R	.318	22	7	3	0	0	4	1	4	.320	.455
Carpenter,David	L	.269	26	7	1	1	0	2	2	6	.321	.385
Throws Right	R	.269	67	18	4	0	4	11	7	9	.342	.507
Carrasco,Carlos	L	.216	305	66	15	1	10	31	23	95	.269	.370
Throws Right	R	.238	370	88	16	4	8	39	20	121	.284	.368
Carroll,Scott	L	.254	67	17	6	1	0	11	6	11	.307	.373
Throws Right	R	.303	76	23	5	1	2	12	7	16	.384	.474
Cashner,Andrew	L	.293	321	94	22	4	14	50	46	71	.379	.517
Throws Right	R	.267	397	106	18	2	5	45	20	94	.309	.360
Casilla,Santiago	L	.262	103	27	2	3	5	17	14	33	.356	.485
Throws Right	R	.212	113	24	2	0	1	9	9	29	.274	.257
Castro,Angel	L	.300	10	3	0	0	1	2	1	3	.364	.600
Throws Right	R	.625	8	5	0	0	0	0	2	1	.700	.625
Castro,Miguel	L	.294	34	10	2	0	2	7	6	8	.390	.529
Throws Right	R	.297	37	11	3	1	2	10	4	10	.357	.595
Castro,Simon	L	.333	15	5	1	0	0	1	2	3	.412	.400
Throws Right	R	.250	24	6	2	0	0	2	3	6	.357	.333
Cecil,Brett	L	.195	77	15	0	2	1	9	4	33	.253	.286
Throws Left	R	.198	121	24	6	0	3	9	9	37	.254	.322
Cedeno,Xavier	L	.196	97	19	2	0	1	6	4	23	.243	.247
Throws Left	R	.276	76	21	1	0	3	6	10	24	.360	.408
Chacin,Jhoulys	L	.319	47	15	1	1	3	7	7	6	.407	.574
Throws Right	R	.170	53	9	3	0	1	2	3	15	.214	.283
Chafin,Andrew	L	.182	110	20	6	0	1	13	11	24	.260	.264
Throws Left	R	.225	160	36	10	0	2	19	19	34	.306	.325
Chamberlain,Joba	L	.362	58	21	2	1	5	16	2	10	.383	.690
Throws Right	R	.288	59	17	6	1	1	8	7	13	.373	.475
Chapman,Aroldis	L	.143	63	9	2	0	0	1	11	38	.276	.175
Throws Left	R	.194	175	34	2	0	3	15	22	78	.297	.257
Chapman,Kevin	L	.154	13	2	1	0	0	1	1	7	.214	.231
Throws Left	R	.333	6	2	0	0	1	3	2	1	.500	.833
Chavez,Jesse	L	.291	337	98	22	1	14	50	23	66	.338	.487
Throws Right	R	.240	275	66	9	0	4	25	25	70	.299	.316
Chen,Bruce	L	.333	12	4	1	0	1	3	0	2	.333	.667
Throws Left	R	.591	22	13	2	0	2	4	1	2	.609	.955
Chen,Wei-Yin	L	.223	175	39	7	1	3	8	6	32	.250	.326
Throws Left	R	.274	558	153	43	3	25	63	35	121	.318	.496
Choate,Randy	L	.265	83	22	2	0	2	10	3	18	.333	.361
Throws Left	R	.333	21	7	2	0	0	3	2	4	.391	.429
Cingrani,Tony	L	.267	45	12	4	1	2	14	6	14	.382	.533
Throws Left	R	.241	79	19	7	0	1	15	19	25	.384	.367
Cishek,Steve	L	.247	81	20	5	1	1	12	17	18	.384	.370
Throws Right	R	.267	131	35	6	0	3	17	10	30	.315	.382
Claudio,Alex	L	.226	31	7	1	0	2	6	2	7	.265	.452
Throws Left	R	.192	26	5	0	1	2	6	4	6	.313	.500
Clippard,Tyler	L	.137	139	19	5	0	3	6	17	33	.231	.237
Throws Right	R	.242	124	30	6	0	5	20	14	31	.333	.411

Pitcher	vs	Avg	AB	H	2B	3B	HR	RBI	BB	SO	OBP	Slg
Coke,Phil	L	.286	28	8	2	0	1	4	2	10	.333	.464
Throws Left	R	.318	22	7	3	0	1	5	3	2	.385	.591
Cole,A.J.	L	.370	27	10	2	0	1	7	1	7	.379	.556
Throws Right	R	.286	14	4	0	0	0	2	0	2	.286	.286
Cole,Gerrit	L	.227	374	85	14	1	5	30	26	101	.287	.310
Throws Right	R	.251	391	98	17	4	6	33	18	101	.287	.361
Collmenter,Josh	L	.273	231	63	14	2	7	18	7	25	.296	.442
Throws Right	R	.281	235	66	19	1	11	33	17	38	.323	.511
Colome,Alex	L	.278	212	59	10	1	4	31	23	42	.345	.392
Throws Right	R	.264	201	53	4	0	5	26	8	46	.300	.358
Colon,Bartolo	L	.290	404	117	20	1	11	38	12	68	.309	.426
Throws Right	R	.272	367	100	21	1	14	50	12	68	.298	.450
Conley,Adam	L	.286	35	10	0	0	1	3	7	9	.395	.371
Throws Left	R	.253	217	55	14	1	6	21	14	50	.304	.410
Contreras,Carlos	L	.167	42	7	2	0	2	5	12	10	.364	.357
Throws Right	R	.246	61	15	6	0	1	9	8	9	.333	.393
Cook,Ryan	L	.556	18	10	1	0	2	8	4	1	.636	.944
Throws Right	R	.345	29	10	1	0	2	8	3	5	.406	.586
Cooney,Tim	L	.318	22	7	1	0	0	4	2	6	.400	.364
Throws Left	R	.223	94	21	6	1	3	6	8	23	.284	.404
Copeland,Scott	L	.400	35	14	2	1	1	7	2	4	.432	.600
Throws Right	R	.333	30	10	3	0	0	4	0	2	.323	.433
Corbin,Patrick	L	.211	71	15	5	0	1	4	4	21	.250	.324
Throws Left	R	.288	264	76	18	2	8	27	13	57	.326	.462
Cordier,Erik	L	.353	17	6	1	0	1	3	2	2	.421	.588
Throws Right	R	.226	31	7	1	0	0	3	4	5	.324	.258
Correia,Kevin	L	.352	54	19	6	0	3	17	8	5	.422	.630
Throws Right	R	.375	48	18	4	0	1	5	0	9	.375	.521
Cosart,Jarred	L	.228	123	28	9	3	3	11	17	26	.319	.423
Throws Right	R	.257	136	35	2	1	7	22	16	21	.340	.441
Cotham,Caleb	L	.368	19	7	2	0	2	6	1	6	.400	.789
Throws Right	R	.292	24	7	0	0	2	4	0	5	.292	.542
Cotts,Neal	L	.186	97	18	2	0	4	12	6	26	.243	.330
Throws Left	R	.286	140	40	6	0	8	16	16	32	.367	.500
Coulombe,Daniel	L	.200	30	6	1	0	0	3	5	4	.314	.233
Throws Left	R	.333	33	11	6	0	0	4	4	7	.405	.515
Cravy,Tyler	L	.263	80	21	5	0	3	9	17	16	.392	.438
Throws Right	R	.299	87	26	5	4	2	18	5	19	.351	.517
Crockett,Kyle	L	.256	43	11	2	0	0	4	4	9	.313	.302
Throws Left	R	.286	21	6	1	0	1	5	3	6	.385	.476
Cueto,Johnny	L	.215	376	81	21	1	7	31	25	96	.266	.332
Throws Right	R	.265	427	113	23	4	14	50	21	80	.308	.436
Cunniff,Brandon	L	.341	41	14	1	0	1	7	7	10	.438	.439
Throws Right	R	.151	86	13	2	1	3	14	15	27	.275	.302
Danks,John	L	.240	167	40	9	1	8	26	9	29	.285	.449
Throws Left	R	.294	528	155	38	4	16	72	47	95	.349	.472
Davies,Zachary	L	.120	50	6	0	0	1	1	9	13	.254	.180
Throws Right	R	.274	73	20	7	0	1	11	6	11	.329	.411
Davis,Wade	L	.146	130	19	3	1	2	6	13	43	.222	.231
Throws Right	R	.141	99	14	6	1	1	3	7	35	.196	.253
De Fratus,Justin	L	.221	122	27	9	0	3	14	17	24	.317	.369
Throws Right	R	.335	194	65	14	2	6	46	15	44	.389	.521
de la Rosa,Jorge	L	.240	129	31	6	1	3	19	11	40	.298	.372
Throws Left	R	.249	425	106	29	2	14	52	54	94	.333	.426
de la Rosa,Rubby	L	.315	365	115	32	0	20	63	38	60	.382	.567
Throws Right	R	.214	364	78	10	1	12	32	25	90	.265	.346
Deduno,Samuel	L	.279	43	12	2	2	2	7	4	12	.360	.558
Throws Right	R	.308	39	12	4	0	1	8	5	5	.400	.487
deGrom,Jacob	L	.245	363	89	13	0	12	32	18	104	.283	.380
Throws Right	R	.181	331	60	11	0	4	23	20	101	.225	.251
Delabar,Steve	L	.212	52	11	2	0	4	10	8	18	.317	.481
Throws Right	R	.288	59	17	7	0	1	9	6	12	.358	.458
Delgado,Randall	L	.248	101	25	5	0	1	8	18	28	.361	.327
Throws Right	R	.226	168	38	8	0	6	24	15	45	.290	.381
DeSclafani,Anthony	L	.268	366	98	26	1	12	45	40	81	.341	.443
Throws Right	R	.279	344	96	17	2	5	34	15	70	.313	.384
Despaigne,Odrisamer	L	.278	223	62	14	4	5	32	17	26	.343	.444
Throws Right	R	.294	272	80	12	1	12	41	15	43	.337	.478
Detwiler,Ross	L	.234	77	18	3	0	1	14	9	17	.348	.312
Throws Left	R	.390	164	64	14	2	9	36	27	24	.472	.665
Diaz,Jairo	L	.222	27	6	0	0	1	4	2	6	.276	.333
Throws Right	R	.222	45	10	2	0	1	2	4	12	.286	.333
Diaz,Jumbo	L	.248	105	26	8	0	4	12	12	21	.336	.438
Throws Right	R	.258	124	32	4	2	5	19	6	49	.293	.444
Dickey,R.A.	L	.228	378	86	18	3	11	38	32	48	.288	.378
Throws Right	R	.260	420	109	19	5	14	51	29	78	.317	.429

Pitchers vs. Left-Handed and Right-Handed Batters

Pitcher	vs	Avg	AB	H	2B	3B	HR	RBI	BB	SO	OBP	Slg
Diekman,Jake	L	.266	94	25	3	0	2	12	13	24	.367	.362
Throws Left	R	.212	132	28	9	0	3	19	18	45	.311	.348
Doolittle,Sean	L	.273	11	3	1	0	1	3	3	3	.429	.636
Throws Left	R	.225	40	9	2	0	0	3	2	12	.256	.275
Doubront,Felix	L	.225	71	16	1	0	1	7	5	21	.276	.282
Throws Left	R	.321	221	71	18	0	9	41	21	35	.375	.525
Drabek,Kyle	L	.571	7	4	1	0	0	1	1	1	.625	.714
Throws Right	R	.294	17	5	0	0	1	4	1	2	.333	.471
Drake,Oliver	L	.167	24	4	1	0	1	4	4	6	.276	.333
Throws Right	R	.324	37	12	2	0	0	1	5	11	.395	.378
Duensing,Brian	L	.288	66	19	5	0	0	9	10	11	.413	.364
Throws Left	R	.235	115	27	4	1	5	16	11	13	.299	.417
Duffey,Tyler	L	.257	109	28	4	1	1	6	11	33	.325	.339
Throws Right	R	.255	110	28	8	1	3	12	9	20	.311	.427
Duffy,Danny	L	.239	109	26	5	1	0	6	7	25	.291	.303
Throws Left	R	.271	409	111	13	4	15	53	46	77	.353	.433
Duke,Zach	L	.181	83	15	1	0	3	11	15	29	.303	.301
Throws Left	R	.241	133	32	7	2	6	14	17	37	.340	.459
Dull,Ryan	L	.167	24	4	0	0	3	6	6	7	.333	.542
Throws Right	R	.229	35	8	2	0	1	2	0	9	.222	.371
Dunn,Mike	L	.227	88	20	3	1	1	11	12	28	.330	.318
Throws Left	R	.226	115	26	7	1	5	18	17	37	.326	.435
Dyson,Sam	L	.229	109	25	2	0	1	9	8	26	.282	.275
Throws Right	R	.235	170	40	7	0	3	18	13	45	.303	.329
Edwards,Jon	L	.258	31	8	2	0	2	3	5	14	.351	.516
Throws Right	R	.154	26	4	0	0	2	7	11	8	.395	.385
Eickhoff,Jerad	L	.268	82	22	3	2	4	11	8	15	.330	.500
Throws Right	R	.168	107	18	4	1	1	5	5	34	.205	.252
Elias,Roenis	L	.227	97	22	5	0	1	8	8	34	.299	.309
Throws Left	R	.251	335	84	15	2	14	40	36	63	.332	.433
Ellington,Brian	L	.222	27	6	3	0	1	4	6	9	.343	.444
Throws Right	R	.180	61	11	4	0	0	4	7	9	.286	.246
Eovaldi,Nathan	L	.314	293	92	15	0	4	35	27	55	.375	.406
Throws Right	R	.258	322	83	10	1	6	27	22	66	.305	.351
Erlin,Robbie	L	.364	11	4	1	1	0	1	0	3	.364	.636
Throws Left	R	.235	51	12	1	0	1	4	2	7	.278	.314
Estrada,Marco	L	.203	374	76	11	4	15	36	29	70	.264	.374
Throws Right	R	.204	285	58	13	1	9	30	26	61	.275	.351
Familia,Jeurys	L	.214	126	27	5	0	3	10	13	34	.291	.325
Throws Right	R	.201	159	32	4	1	3	9	6	52	.235	.296
Farmer,Buck	L	.389	72	28	6	0	3	13	11	9	.470	.597
Throws Right	R	.272	92	25	4	2	7	19	6	15	.333	.587
Farquhar,Danny	L	.220	91	20	7	0	3	14	8	26	.280	.396
Throws Right	R	.306	108	33	9	1	6	17	9	22	.364	.574
Faulkner,Andrew	L	.111	18	2	1	0	0	0	1	5	.158	.167
Throws Left	R	.316	19	6	0	0	2	4	2	5	.381	.632
Feldman,Scott	L	.258	221	57	8	2	4	20	14	33	.297	.367
Throws Right	R	.294	197	58	9	1	9	25	13	28	.336	.487
Feliz,Michael	L	.250	16	4	1	0	1	3	2	3	.368	.500
Throws Right	R	.294	17	5	1	0	1	4	2	4	.368	.529
Feliz,Neftali	L	.289	97	28	3	0	3	21	10	15	.355	.412
Throws Right	R	.309	94	29	5	4	2	19	8	24	.365	.511
Fernandez,Jose	L	.333	114	38	4	2	3	10	7	30	.377	.482
Throws Right	R	.176	131	23	4	0	1	9	7	49	.217	.229
Ferrell,Jeff	L	.222	18	4	1	0	1	3	1	1	.263	.444
Throws Right	R	.296	27	8	1	0	2	5	3	5	.355	.556
Fields,Josh	L	.234	77	18	4	3	1	17	7	23	.302	.403
Throws Right	R	.193	109	21	4	0	1	3	12	44	.273	.257
Fien,Casey	L	.282	103	29	5	2	2	11	2	12	.290	.427
Throws Right	R	.227	141	32	4	0	4	13	6	29	.257	.340
Fiers,Mike	L	.227	317	72	12	3	10	35	26	78	.285	.379
Throws Right	R	.248	363	90	17	4	14	42	38	102	.324	.433
Finnegan,Brandon	L	.200	45	9	2	0	3	9	7	13	.321	.444
Throws Left	R	.222	126	28	5	1	5	11	14	32	.298	.397
Fister,Doug	L	.265	211	56	7	1	8	23	13	28	.316	.422
Throws Right	R	.327	196	64	11	2	6	27	11	35	.365	.495
Flande,Yohan	L	.262	65	17	4	1	2	9	8	9	.351	.446
Throws Left	R	.281	199	56	12	2	12	28	17	34	.336	.543
Flores,Kendry	L	.333	30	10	3	0	0	3	3	5	.382	.433
Throws Right	R	.286	21	6	0	0	0	2	1	4	.348	.286
Floyd,Gavin	L	.111	18	2	0	0	0	1	4	5	.273	.111
Throws Right	R	.281	32	9	2	0	0	3	0	2	.303	.344
Foltynewicz,Mike	L	.328	177	58	14	2	9	28	13	33	.368	.582
Throws Right	R	.298	181	54	9	0	8	30	16	44	.363	.481
Francis,Jeff	L	.359	39	14	1	0	2	9	4	7	.432	.538
Throws Left	R	.255	51	13	3	0	1	6	5	14	.321	.373

Pitcher	vs	Avg	AB	H	2B	3B	HR	RBI	BB	SO	OBP	Slg
Frasor,Jason	L	.327	52	17	6	0	1	3	6	5	.397	.500
Throws Right	R	.192	52	10	1	0	0	6	12	17	.338	.212
Freeman,Sam	L	.281	64	18	1	0	4	12	15	23	.427	.484
Throws Left	R	.167	78	13	4	0	0	6	10	17	.270	.218
Frias,Carlos	L	.357	129	46	9	0	2	11	14	14	.429	.473
Throws Right	R	.251	167	42	2	0	5	23	12	29	.297	.353
Friedrich,Christian	L	.268	112	30	2	0	2	15	9	23	.320	.339
Throws Left	R	.369	122	45	9	1	3	26	16	22	.433	.533
Frieri,Ernesto	L	.220	41	9	2	0	3	4	4	8	.283	.488
Throws Right	R	.244	45	11	1	0	3	8	7	11	.352	.467
Furbush,Charlie	L	.105	38	4	0	0	0	0	2	11	.150	.105
Throws Left	R	.139	36	5	1	0	2	3	3	6	.244	.333
Gallardo,Yovani	L	.271	358	97	18	5	9	37	37	58	.340	.425
Throws Right	R	.265	362	96	15	3	6	28	31	63	.322	.373
Garces,Frank	L	.246	69	17	1	0	4	13	13	18	.366	.435
Throws Left	R	.312	77	24	4	0	5	15	9	12	.382	.558
Garcia,Jaime	L	.250	104	26	2	0	2	8	6	23	.304	.327
Throws Left	R	.218	367	80	15	0	4	25	24	74	.266	.292
Garcia,Jason	L	.257	35	9	5	0	0	4	12	5	.449	.400
Throws Right	R	.208	77	16	4	0	3	13	5	17	.265	.377
Garcia,Luis	L	.337	104	35	6	0	2	16	17	22	.426	.452
Throws Right	R	.234	158	37	7	2	2	16	20	41	.318	.342
Garcia,Yimi	L	.172	64	11	1	0	4	9	3	19	.209	.375
Throws Right	R	.224	147	33	4	0	4	14	7	49	.266	.333
Garza,Matt	L	.303	287	87	20	1	11	40	29	45	.367	.495
Throws Right	R	.286	311	89	17	0	12	48	28	59	.347	.457
Gausman,Kevin	L	.227	225	51	15	0	5	18	18	62	.283	.360
Throws Right	R	.278	209	58	14	1	12	29	11	41	.317	.526
Gee,Dillon	L	.395	86	34	7	2	3	14	5	8	.430	.628
Throws Right	R	.259	81	21	4	0	2	12	6	17	.307	.383
Geltz,Steve	L	.196	102	20	3	0	2	13	19	34	.328	.284
Throws Right	R	.184	136	25	4	0	6	14	7	27	.229	.346
Germen,Gonzalez	L	.254	63	16	3	1	2	4	12	12	.373	.429
Throws Right	R	.291	86	25	5	2	2	13	14	21	.390	.465
Gibson,Kyle	L	.248	383	95	25	0	8	42	40	72	.326	.376
Throws Right	R	.257	354	91	16	0	10	34	25	73	.306	.387
Giles,Ken	L	.222	117	26	3	0	1	8	12	29	.300	.274
Throws Right	R	.217	152	33	6	1	1	11	13	58	.275	.289
Gilmartin,Sean	L	.260	96	25	5	0	1	8	7	25	.317	.344
Throws Left	R	.216	116	25	6	1	1	9	11	29	.287	.310
Givens,Mychal	L	.205	39	8	3	0	0	4	3	10	.273	.282
Throws Right	R	.174	69	12	5	1	1	3	3	28	.208	.319
Godley,Zack	L	.182	55	10	1	0	0	3	10	11	.328	.200
Throws Right	R	.260	73	19	4	0	4	8	7	23	.329	.479
Goeddel,Erik	L	.189	37	7	3	0	0	1	3	9	.250	.270
Throws Right	R	.210	81	17	4	0	1	11	6	25	.272	.296
Goforth,David	L	.359	39	14	1	0	1	6	4	6	.409	.462
Throws Right	R	.300	60	18	4	0	3	8	4	18	.338	.517
Gomes,Brandon	L	.192	99	19	7	0	3	8	10	18	.273	.354
Throws Right	R	.293	123	36	5	0	7	22	5	26	.326	.504
Gomez,Jeanmar	L	.256	117	30	10	0	2	15	7	18	.307	.393
Throws Right	R	.292	178	52	6	1	2	20	10	32	.325	.371
Gonzalez,Chi Chi	L	.246	114	28	5	0	1	10	14	13	.333	.316
Throws Right	R	.164	128	21	6	1	5	17	18	17	.273	.344
Gonzalez,Gio	L	.258	159	41	10	0	1	13	10	28	.302	.340
Throws Left	R	.272	514	140	21	8	7	59	59	141	.346	.385
Gonzalez,Miguel	L	.278	273	76	16	1	13	36	23	54	.343	.487
Throws Right	R	.262	286	75	10	2	11	36	28	55	.334	.427
Gonzalez,Severino	L	.426	61	26	2	1	3	11	5	9	.493	.639
Throws Right	R	.273	66	18	4	0	2	13	2	19	.282	.424
Goody,Nicholas	L	.333	12	4	2	0	0	3	0	0	.333	.500
Throws Right	R	.200	10	2	1	0	0	0	3	3	.429	.300
Gorzelanny,Tom	L	.222	72	16	3	0	2	12	10	20	.317	.347
Throws Left	R	.354	82	29	9	3	2	20	13	16	.454	.610
Gott,Trevor	L	.275	80	22	1	1	1	14	12	15	.366	.350
Throws Right	R	.214	98	21	2	1	1	10	4	12	.262	.286
Grace,Matt	L	.289	38	11	1	0	0	6	2	9	.333	.316
Throws Left	R	.429	35	15	5	0	0	9	6	5	.500	.571
Graham,J.R.	L	.277	112	31	5	1	4	22	9	22	.336	.446
Throws Right	R	.296	142	42	5	1	6	26	12	31	.359	.472
Graveman,Kendall	L	.275	222	61	9	0	4	20	24	36	.355	.369
Throws Right	R	.278	234	65	13	0	11	29	14	41	.320	.474
Gray,Jonathan	L	.295	78	23	5	1	0	7	9	21	.371	.385
Throws Right	R	.341	85	29	8	0	4	18	5	19	.372	.576
Gray,Sonny	L	.208	389	81	13	0	8	26	34	93	.275	.303
Throws Right	R	.226	376	85	10	1	9	37	25	76	.272	.330

Pitchers vs. Left-Handed and Right-Handed Batters

Pitcher	vs	Avg	AB	H	2B	3B	HR	RBI	BB	SO	OBP	Slg
Greene,Shane	L	.363	179	65	16	6	5	33	15	23	.414	.603
Throws Right	R	.245	155	38	3	2	8	26	12	27	.312	.445
Gregerson,Luke	L	.235	119	28	6	1	1	12	7	26	.278	.328
Throws Right	R	.189	106	20	1	0	4	12	3	33	.225	.311
Gregg,Kevin	L	.174	23	4	0	0	1	2	2	11	.240	.304
Throws Right	R	.409	22	9	0	0	2	9	3	3	.480	.682
Greinke,Zack	L	.194	356	69	12	0	6	19	27	83	.257	.278
Throws Right	R	.182	434	79	10	3	8	22	13	117	.208	.274
Grilli,Jason	L	.222	54	12	5	0	0	2	5	23	.283	.315
Throws Right	R	.213	75	16	6	0	2	10	5	22	.263	.373
Grimm,Justin	L	.140	57	8	2	0	1	6	9	25	.269	.228
Throws Right	R	.197	117	23	5	0	3	13	17	42	.292	.316
Guaipe,Mayckol	L	.452	42	19	4	0	3	8	8	8	.540	.762
Throws Right	R	.246	61	15	0	1	2	10	5	14	.329	.377
Guerra,Deolis	L	.250	24	6	1	0	0	2	1	5	.308	.292
Throws Right	R	.435	46	20	5	0	5	12	2	12	.458	.870
Guilmet,Preston	L	.231	13	3	0	0	1	5	3	4	.333	.462
Throws Right	R	.375	16	6	1	0	1	4	1	2	.412	.625
Gurka,Jason	L	.500	16	8	5	0	1	6	0	2	.500	1.000
Throws Left	R	.381	21	8	1	0	0	4	2	5	.435	.429
Guthrie,Jeremy	L	.325	329	107	18	2	20	64	27	47	.383	.574
Throws Right	R	.292	271	79	12	1	9	27	17	37	.338	.443
Hagadone,Nick	L	.264	53	14	1	1	1	9	4	16	.310	.377
Throws Left	R	.281	57	16	2	0	2	2	8	12	.369	.421
Hahn,Jesse	L	.286	192	55	11	0	3	24	12	33	.344	.391
Throws Right	R	.185	178	33	6	0	2	10	13	31	.249	.253
Hale,David	L	.297	148	44	10	2	7	19	10	31	.346	.534
Throws Right	R	.298	171	51	15	0	7	32	10	30	.337	.509
Hall,Cody	L	.227	22	5	1	0	0	3	2	5	.292	.273
Throws Right	R	.357	14	5	0	0	1	2	2	2	.471	.571
Hamels,Cole	L	.237	173	41	10	0	2	9	18	43	.316	.329
Throws Left	R	.238	627	149	25	2	20	70	44	172	.295	.380
Hammel,Jason	L	.235	293	69	19	3	7	25	25	78	.303	.392
Throws Right	R	.247	361	89	18	4	16	44	15	94	.277	.452
Hand,Brad	L	.206	102	21	6	0	0	12	6	29	.248	.265
Throws Left	R	.326	264	86	16	1	9	36	26	38	.391	.496
Happ,J.A.	L	.267	176	47	14	0	2	11	8	51	.299	.381
Throws Left	R	.256	492	126	24	1	14	54	37	100	.311	.394
Harang,Aaron	L	.283	304	86	17	4	10	38	35	33	.363	.464
Throws Right	R	.273	377	103	14	7	16	56	16	75	.306	.475
Hardy,Blaine	L	.241	112	27	4	1	1	17	11	23	.310	.321
Throws Left	R	.276	123	34	13	2	1	15	11	32	.331	.439
Haren,Dan	L	.277	332	92	24	1	20	39	21	64	.324	.536
Throws Right	R	.218	377	82	20	1	11	31	17	68	.259	.363
Harris,Mitchell	L	.237	38	9	0	0	0	1	7	9	.356	.237
Throws Right	R	.300	70	21	1	0	4	8	6	6	.355	.486
Harris,Will	L	.129	116	15	1	1	4	9	9	30	.197	.259
Throws Right	R	.201	134	27	3	0	4	12	13	38	.272	.313
Harrison,Matt	L	.357	14	5	0	0	1	2	2	1	.438	.571
Throws Left	R	.292	48	14	2	1	2	7	4	4	.340	.500
Harvey,Matt	L	.226	345	78	9	1	15	30	26	96	.288	.388
Throws Right	R	.218	358	78	17	2	3	25	11	92	.242	.302
Hatcher,Chris	L	.180	50	9	0	0	3	3	10	15	.328	.360
Throws Right	R	.268	97	26	8	0	1	19	3	30	.301	.381
Hawkins,LaTroy	L	.276	76	21	4	1	3	11	5	20	.321	.474
Throws Right	R	.295	78	23	0	1	1	6	2	14	.313	.359
Heaney,Andrew	L	.228	114	26	4	1	1	5	4	29	.261	.307
Throws Left	R	.255	286	73	18	0	8	27	24	49	.321	.402
Hellickson,Jeremy	L	.273	242	66	14	3	8	32	22	47	.336	.455
Throws Right	R	.257	331	85	26	1	14	40	21	74	.306	.468
Hembree,Heath	L	.256	43	11	2	1	3	4	3	6	.304	.558
Throws Right	R	.259	54	14	2	0	2	6	6	9	.333	.407
Hendricks,Kyle	L	.267	303	81	19	2	13	33	23	71	.325	.472
Throws Right	R	.225	378	85	17	1	4	44	20	96	.273	.307
Hendriks,Liam	L	.283	106	30	7	1	2	9	5	30	.321	.425
Throws Right	R	.207	140	29	4	0	1	11	6	41	.242	.257
Hernandez,David	L	.260	50	13	4	0	1	5	6	12	.339	.400
Throws Right	R	.253	79	20	3	0	5	11	5	21	.322	.481
Hernandez,Felix	L	.234	380	89	17	4	12	46	35	81	.304	.395
Throws Right	R	.246	370	91	10	1	11	27	23	110	.297	.368
Hernandez,Roberto	L	.268	157	42	8	3	2	14	17	10	.337	.395
Throws Right	R	.282	170	48	13	1	7	25	9	32	.319	.494
Herrera,Kelvin	L	.151	119	18	2	0	2	11	17	30	.252	.218
Throws Right	R	.256	133	34	6	0	3	18	9	34	.308	.368
Hessler,Keith	L	.160	25	4	0	0	2	6	2	6	.222	.400
Throws Left	R	.429	28	12	3	1	2	10	2	6	.467	.821
Heston,Chris	L	.270	318	86	19	3	12	40	38	55	.356	.462
Throws Right	R	.238	349	83	17	3	4	33	26	86	.307	.338
Hill,Rich	L	.158	19	3	0	0	0	1	1	6	.200	.158
Throws Left	R	.138	80	11	1	0	2	4	4	30	.198	.225
Hill,Taylor	L	.417	24	10	1	0	1	3	1	6	.440	.583
Throws Right	R	.182	22	4	1	1	1	4	3	3	.308	.455
Hinojosa,Dalier	L	.119	42	5	1	0	0	0	8	10	.275	.143
Throws Right	R	.208	48	10	1	0	1	3	3	13	.255	.292
Hochevar,Luke	L	.263	80	21	6	1	2	11	6	24	.310	.438
Throws Right	R	.241	116	28	4	1	5	15	10	25	.307	.422
Holland,Derek	L	.293	41	12	2	0	1	6	2	12	.326	.415
Throws Left	R	.264	178	47	10	2	10	23	15	29	.337	.511
Holland,Greg	L	.250	76	19	2	2	2	11	15	25	.370	.408
Throws Right	R	.230	87	20	6	0	0	12	11	24	.316	.299
Holmberg,David	L	.148	27	4	0	0	1	2	7	5	.314	.259
Throws Left	R	.376	85	32	3	0	9	20	9	10	.443	.729
Hoover,J.J.	L	.217	115	25	6	1	5	11	12	20	.300	.417
Throws Right	R	.174	109	19	3	3	2	10	19	32	.295	.312
House,T.J.	L	.143	7	1	0	0	0	1	0	1	.125	.143
Throws Left	R	.392	51	20	3	0	1	15	12	6	.523	.510
Howell,J.P.	L	.224	85	19	0	0	0	7	7	22	.295	.224
Throws Left	R	.318	88	28	3	0	3	8	7	17	.368	.455
Hudson,Daniel	L	.186	113	21	7	1	3	10	15	34	.279	.345
Throws Right	R	.291	148	43	6	0	4	20	10	37	.331	.412
Hudson,Tim	L	.322	205	66	10	1	4	16	25	15	.397	.439
Throws Right	R	.251	271	68	6	1	9	35	12	49	.294	.380
Huff,David	L	.333	9	3	0	0	1	2	0	0	.333	.667
Throws Left	R	.444	18	8	0	0	1	4	1	4	.500	.611
Hughes,Jared	L	.286	91	26	5	0	0	11	6	11	.343	.341
Throws Right	R	.280	157	44	5	2	3	12	13	25	.347	.395
Hughes,Phil	L	.282	333	94	15	1	14	37	9	45	.301	.459
Throws Right	R	.304	296	90	25	1	15	35	7	49	.321	.547
Hunter,Tommy	L	.276	105	29	5	1	4	16	4	22	.297	.457
Throws Right	R	.256	125	32	4	0	3	18	10	25	.314	.360
Hutchison,Drew	L	.266	312	83	17	0	11	48	25	65	.324	.426
Throws Right	R	.330	291	96	23	0	11	42	19	64	.384	.522
Iglesias,Raisel	L	.286	168	48	8	0	4	24	14	31	.348	.405
Throws Right	R	.176	188	33	13	1	7	17	14	73	.251	.367
Iwakuma,Hisashi	L	.261	245	64	12	1	8	21	9	52	.286	.416
Throws Right	R	.219	242	53	11	0	10	26	12	59	.257	.388
Jackson,Edwin	L	.171	76	13	5	0	1	7	12	16	.289	.276
Throws Right	R	.246	126	31	6	0	3	19	9	24	.292	.365
Jackson,Jay	L	.500	2	1	1	0	0	0	1	0	.667	1.000
Throws Right	R	.353	17	6	1	0	0	2	0	4	.353	.412
Jackson,Luke	L	.143	7	1	0	0	0	0	0	3	.143	.143
Throws Right	R	.222	18	4	1	0	1	3	2	3	.300	.444
Jansen,Kenley	L	.200	95	19	3	0	3	9	3	34	.240	.326
Throws Right	R	.151	93	14	2	0	3	11	5	46	.190	.269
Janssen,Casey	L	.176	51	9	3	0	1	8	6	10	.263	.294
Throws Right	R	.284	102	29	6	2	4	11	2	17	.302	.500
Jeffress,Jeremy	L	.272	92	25	4	1	2	11	10	22	.350	.402
Throws Right	R	.236	165	39	5	0	3	16	12	45	.296	.321
Jennings,Dan	L	.274	95	26	3	0	0	14	8	20	.330	.305
Throws Left	R	.242	120	29	5	0	3	19	16	26	.328	.358
Jepsen,Kevin	L	.235	136	32	1	0	4	10	18	31	.323	.331
Throws Right	R	.172	116	20	1	1	1	12	9	28	.225	.224
Jimenez,Cesar	L	.200	30	6	0	0	0	1	3	8	.273	.200
Throws Left	R	.208	53	11	2	0	2	8	5	17	.276	.358
Jimenez,Ubaldo	L	.227	362	82	19	1	13	50	35	92	.310	.392
Throws Right	R	.290	345	100	10	4	7	30	33	76	.353	.403
Johnson,Erik	L	.262	65	17	2	0	4	5	11	10	.372	.477
Throws Right	R	.234	64	15	4	0	4	8	6	20	.292	.484
Johnson,Jim	L	.295	112	33	2	0	1	9	7	26	.336	.339
Throws Right	R	.297	148	44	5	1	4	22	13	24	.367	.426
Johnson,Steve	L	.300	10	3	2	0	1	3	2	2	.417	.800
Throws Right	R	.357	14	5	1	0	1	5	3	1	.471	.643
Jones,Nate	L	.125	24	3	0	0	2	4	2	13	.192	.375
Throws Right	R	.225	40	9	1	0	3	3	4	14	.295	.475
Jordan,Taylor	L	.289	38	11	4	0	0	5	4	3	.357	.395
Throws Right	R	.290	31	9	1	0	0	4	2	8	.324	.323
Jungmann,Taylor	L	.259	212	55	12	2	3	18	26	49	.342	.377
Throws Right	R	.225	227	51	8	2	8	32	21	58	.305	.383
Kahnle,Tommy	L	.320	50	16	4	0	0	6	11	11	.429	.400
Throws Right	R	.203	74	15	5	0	3	10	17	28	.352	.392
Karns,Nate	L	.248	282	70	12	1	5	20	38	85	.338	.351
Throws Right	R	.229	271	62	9	1	14	34	18	60	.283	.424

Pitchers vs. Left-Handed and Right-Handed Batters

Pitcher	vs	Avg	AB	H	2B	3B	HR	RBI	BB	SO	OBP	Slg
Kazmir,Scott	L	.272	173	47	12	0	7	23	8	25	.312	.462
Throws Left	R	.225	511	115	16	3	13	43	51	130	.301	.344
Kela,Keone	L	.289	90	26	1	0	2	7	12	21	.373	.367
Throws Right	R	.194	134	26	8	0	2	11	6	47	.229	.299
Kelley,Shawn	L	.224	85	19	2	2	3	9	5	31	.267	.400
Throws Right	R	.218	101	22	1	0	1	13	10	32	.278	.257
Kelly,Casey	L	.286	21	6	0	0	0	3	2	2	.348	.286
Throws Right	R	.419	31	13	4	0	1	10	1	5	.455	.645
Kelly,Joe	L	.254	272	69	15	4	5	28	22	59	.309	.393
Throws Right	R	.298	255	76	10	1	10	38	27	51	.374	.463
Kelly,Ryan	L	.261	23	6	0	0	3	8	5	4	.393	.652
Throws Right	R	.341	44	15	3	0	2	10	1	6	.356	.545
Kendrick,Kyle	L	.314	261	82	18	5	15	40	29	41	.386	.594
Throws Right	R	.291	309	90	17	3	18	50	16	39	.335	.540
Kennedy,Ian	L	.256	320	82	17	7	18	43	27	93	.322	.522
Throws Right	R	.259	324	84	22	4	13	44	25	81	.316	.472
Kensing,Logan	L	.143	14	2	1	0	1	3	4	3	.333	.429
Throws Right	R	.238	42	10	2	0	1	7	3	10	.283	.357
Kershaw,Clayton	L	.203	192	39	6	1	5	15	5	77	.231	.323
Throws Left	R	.192	647	124	20	1	10	37	37	224	.239	.272
Keuchel,Dallas	L	.177	181	32	4	1	3	17	6	50	.201	.260
Throws Left	R	.227	673	153	24	1	14	49	45	166	.277	.328
Kimbrel,Craig	L	.194	108	21	5	1	3	9	14	40	.287	.343
Throws Right	R	.176	108	19	1	0	3	8	8	47	.239	.269
Kintzler,Brandon	L	.385	13	5	1	0	0	4	5	2	.556	.462
Throws Right	R	.389	18	7	1	0	1	4	0	5	.389	.611
Klein,Phil	L	.395	38	15	4	0	2	5	7	7	.489	.658
Throws Right	R	.211	38	8	0	0	2	6	3	5	.268	.368
Kluber,Corey	L	.261	429	112	31	2	11	42	30	122	.321	.420
Throws Right	R	.197	390	77	14	0	11	32	15	123	.231	.318
Knebel,Corey	L	.222	81	18	5	1	4	8	9	26	.308	.457
Throws Right	R	.239	109	26	9	0	4	13	8	32	.297	.431
Knudson,Guido	L	.778	9	7	2	0	3	6	1	0	.800	2.000
Throws Right	R	.316	19	6	0	1	2	6	2	6	.381	.737
Koehler,Tom	L	.258	365	94	11	1	16	51	41	74	.335	.425
Throws Right	R	.252	341	86	25	2	6	39	36	63	.327	.390
Kontos,George	L	.227	97	22	1	1	5	14	6	16	.272	.412
Throws Right	R	.205	171	35	7	0	4	14	6	28	.228	.316
Krol,Ian	L	.326	43	14	0	1	1	6	7	12	.442	.442
Throws Left	R	.262	65	17	4	0	3	9	10	14	.360	.462
Lackey,John	L	.271	369	100	13	1	12	30	36	56	.340	.409
Throws Right	R	.244	455	111	19	1	9	37	17	119	.271	.349
Laffey,Aaron	L	.300	10	3	1	0	1	3	2	1	.462	.700
Throws Left	R	.294	17	5	0	0	0	0	1	2	.333	.294
LaFromboise,Bobby	L	.158	19	3	1	0	1	4	0	8	.158	.368
Throws Left	R	.222	9	2	1	0	0	0	1	0	.300	.333
Lamb,John	L	.341	41	14	6	0	3	11	6	13	.449	.707
Throws Left	R	.284	155	44	8	0	5	19	13	45	.337	.432
Latos,Mat	L	.286	213	61	15	0	8	30	15	42	.333	.469
Throws Right	R	.249	237	59	17	1	5	29	17	58	.296	.392
Layne,Tommy	L	.148	88	13	2	0	0	10	11	27	.248	.170
Throws Left	R	.322	87	28	8	0	3	14	16	18	.433	.517
Lazo,Raudel	L	.429	7	3	1	0	1	1	1	1	.500	1.000
Throws Left	R	.143	14	2	0	1	0	1	1	4	.188	.286
Leake,Mike	L	.262	401	105	18	2	14	46	24	61	.305	.421
Throws Right	R	.218	316	69	18	1	8	30	25	58	.277	.358
Leathersich,Jack	L	.280	25	7	2	0	0	4	4	9	.379	.360
Throws Left	R	.263	19	5	1	0	0	0	3	5	.391	.316
LeCure,Sam	L	.138	29	4	2	0	0	1	1	8	.167	.207
Throws Right	R	.267	45	12	3	1	2	8	6	7	.346	.511
Lee,Zach	L	.563	16	9	3	0	1	6	1	0	.588	.938
Throws Right	R	.286	7	2	0	0	0	0	0	3	.286	.286
Leon,Arnold	L	.342	38	13	2	0	2	10	6	6	.432	.553
Throws Right	R	.262	65	17	4	0	1	9	3	13	.286	.369
Leone,Dominic	L	.200	30	6	3	0	0	3	7	6	.368	.300
Throws Right	R	.394	33	13	3	0	2	10	2	3	.417	.667
Lester,Jon	L	.247	178	44	7	2	4	18	8	53	.282	.376
Throws Left	R	.237	586	139	35	4	12	60	39	154	.290	.372
Lewis,Colby	L	.271	428	116	26	4	13	63	22	63	.314	.442
Throws Right	R	.260	365	95	18	0	13	40	20	79	.301	.416
Liberatore,Adam	L	.242	62	15	4	1	1	8	4	16	.284	.387
Throws Left	R	.220	50	11	2	0	2	6	5	13	.291	.380
Lincecum,Tim	L	.209	139	29	6	1	2	10	18	29	.296	.309
Throws Right	R	.307	150	46	9	0	5	25	20	31	.392	.467
Lindgren,Jacob	L	.000	7	0	0	0	0	1	1	2	.111	.000
Throws Left	R	.294	17	5	1	0	3	5	3	6	.400	.882
Liriano,Francisco	L	.207	150	31	3	1	3	15	15	42	.292	.300
Throws Left	R	.228	545	124	22	2	12	51	55	163	.300	.341
Liz,Radhames	L	.282	39	11	1	0	2	5	5	8	.378	.462
Throws Right	R	.288	52	15	2	0	2	5	7	19	.393	.442
Lobstein,Kyle	L	.244	78	19	4	1	0	7	8	14	.314	.321
Throws Left	R	.331	178	59	11	2	7	32	15	18	.381	.534
Locke,Jeff	L	.294	153	45	6	0	5	23	13	19	.360	.431
Throws Left	R	.267	501	134	26	2	10	63	47	110	.330	.387
Loewen,Adam	L	.294	34	10	1	1	1	5	6	11	.429	.471
Throws Left	R	.270	37	10	1	0	2	6	11	11	.440	.459
Logan,Boone	L	.225	71	16	2	0	0	10	9	30	.349	.254
Throws Left	R	.333	72	24	4	0	3	17	8	14	.395	.514
Lohse,Kyle	L	.285	281	80	19	2	13	45	26	54	.347	.505
Throws Right	R	.307	326	100	15	0	16	48	17	54	.343	.500
Lopez,Javier	L	.112	89	10	3	0	0	6	7	20	.177	.146
Throws Left	R	.214	42	9	2	1	1	4	9	6	.353	.381
Lopez,Jorge	L	.400	15	6	0	1	0	2	1	5	.438	.533
Throws Right	R	.320	25	8	1	0	0	3	4	5	.433	.360
Lorenzen,Michael	L	.332	193	64	16	2	9	30	31	37	.432	.575
Throws Right	R	.262	256	67	19	1	9	31	26	46	.335	.449
Loup,Aaron	L	.275	69	19	4	1	0	4	1	19	.342	.362
Throws Left	R	.275	102	28	4	1	6	20	6	27	.315	.510
Lowe,Mark	L	.276	87	24	4	0	2	11	7	25	.333	.391
Throws Right	R	.196	112	22	5	0	2	6	5	36	.229	.295
Lyles,Jordan	L	.305	95	29	8	0	0	13	16	18	.407	.389
Throws Right	R	.275	91	25	4	0	2	12	3	12	.313	.385
Lynn,Lance	L	.272	302	82	17	3	10	37	41	59	.362	.447
Throws Right	R	.247	365	90	16	1	3	23	27	108	.302	.321
Lyons,Tyler	L	.232	56	13	2	0	3	6	6	16	.317	.429
Throws Left	R	.258	178	46	7	1	9	20	9	44	.291	.461
Machi,Jean	L	.160	100	16	1	1	3	6	12	18	.250	.280
Throws Right	R	.333	129	43	15	1	5	30	10	24	.378	.581
Madson,Ryan	L	.205	112	23	5	0	2	5	6	27	.244	.304
Throws Right	R	.205	117	24	6	0	3	15	8	31	.264	.333
Maness,Seth	L	.361	83	30	6	0	0	6	7	11	.411	.434
Throws Right	R	.280	168	47	8	0	7	34	6	35	.307	.452
Manship,Jeff	L	.235	51	12	3	0	1	4	3	9	.291	.353
Throws Right	R	.103	78	8	3	0	0	8	7	24	.169	.141
Marcum,Shaun	L	.319	69	22	4	1	5	13	8	15	.397	.623
Throws Right	R	.164	61	10	2	0	4	6	3	15	.203	.393
Marimon,Sugar	L	.317	41	13	5	3	0	8	8	3	.420	.585
Throws Right	R	.288	59	17	2	1	3	13	6	11	.348	.508
Marksberry,Matt	L	.170	53	9	3	1	0	6	7	14	.267	.264
Throws Left	R	.361	36	13	4	0	2	8	9	7	.479	.639
Marquis,Jason	L	.310	100	31	6	0	2	13	6	19	.336	.430
Throws Right	R	.351	94	33	6	0	8	24	8	18	.408	.670
Marshall,Evan	L	.385	26	10	2	0	2	3	1	2	.407	.692
Throws Right	R	.333	30	10	2	0	1	5	4	5	.412	.500
Martin,Chris	L	.233	30	7	2	0	0	2	2	6	.281	.300
Throws Right	R	.339	62	21	3	0	2	15	4	12	.388	.484
Martin,Cody	L	.262	42	11	2	1	3	10	4	10	.319	.571
Throws Right	R	.358	81	29	4	1	5	14	8	17	.424	.617
Martin,Rafael	L	.357	14	5	0	0	2	5	4	4	.474	.786
Throws Right	R	.200	35	7	2	0	2	4	1	21	.243	.429
Martinez,Carlos	L	.262	321	84	17	3	9	35	38	79	.339	.417
Throws Right	R	.240	350	84	14	1	4	23	25	105	.303	.320
Martinez,Nick	L	.236	229	54	12	1	5	23	24	34	.314	.362
Throws Right	R	.307	264	81	15	5	11	37	22	43	.378	.527
Masset,Nick	L	.256	39	10	0	0	2	5	4	10	.333	.410
Throws Right	R	.328	61	20	6	0	1	8	5	8	.382	.475
Masterson,Justin	L	.310	126	39	12	2	3	18	16	22	.409	.508
Throws Right	R	.266	109	29	7	1	4	16	11	27	.355	.459
Mateo,Marcos	L	.250	40	10	0	1	3	6	7	11	.380	.525
Throws Right	R	.203	59	12	2	1	2	8	2	22	.242	.373
Mattheus,Ryan	L	.340	103	35	9	0	3	14	4	15	.355	.515
Throws Right	R	.260	123	32	5	0	0	11	14	22	.345	.301
Matusz,Brian	L	.186	102	19	3	0	4	19	4	38	.231	.333
Throws Left	R	.244	78	19	5	0	1	9	16	18	.375	.346
Matz,Steven	L	.250	32	8	0	0	0	0	7	8	.400	.250
Throws Left	R	.250	104	26	1	0	4	9	3	26	.269	.375
Matzek,Tyler	L	.214	14	3	0	1	0	2	0	1	.353	.357
Throws Left	R	.281	64	18	2	0	2	8	19	14	.440	.406
Maurer,Brandon	L	.158	95	15	3	0	1	6	5	27	.206	.221
Throws Right	R	.261	92	24	5	0	2	17	10	12	.330	.380
May,Trevor	L	.288	236	68	9	5	4	23	18	53	.340	.419
Throws Right	R	.269	219	59	15	1	7	28	8	57	.300	.443

Pitchers vs. Left-Handed and Right-Handed Batters

Pitcher	vs	Avg	AB	H	2B	3B	HR	RBI	BB	SO	OBP	Slg
Mazzaro,Vin	L	.313	16	5	2	1	0	2	4	0	.429	.563
Throws Right	R	.323	31	10	3	0	0	5	2	6	.353	.419
Mazzoni,Cory	L	.542	24	13	3	0	2	13	1	3	.538	.917
Throws Right	R	.435	23	10	5	0	0	7	4	5	.519	.652
McAllister,Zach	L	.252	127	32	4	1	1	9	10	37	.309	.323
Throws Right	R	.264	144	38	4	1	6	23	13	47	.333	.431
McCarthy,Brandon	L	.234	47	11	3	0	2	3	2	16	.265	.426
Throws Right	R	.302	43	13	0	0	7	12	2	13	.333	.791
McCullers,Lance	L	.209	239	50	13	2	3	20	19	74	.272	.318
Throws Right	R	.243	230	56	13	2	7	22	24	55	.320	.409
McFarland,T.J.	L	.232	82	19	4	0	1	9	4	16	.267	.317
Throws Left	R	.375	88	33	5	1	3	12	14	10	.461	.557
McGee,Jake	L	.200	45	9	2	0	2	6	2	13	.229	.378
Throws Left	R	.196	92	18	3	0	1	5	6	35	.253	.261
McGough,Scott	L	.667	9	6	1	0	0	4	1	1	.700	.778
Throws Right	R	.273	22	6	2	0	0	4	3	3	.360	.364
McGowan,Dustin	L	.289	45	13	0	0	6	13	9	6	.407	.689
Throws Right	R	.302	53	16	2	0	1	6	11	15	.422	.396
McHugh,Collin	L	.235	371	87	17	2	8	38	26	82	.292	.356
Throws Right	R	.288	417	120	22	0	11	44	27	89	.336	.420
McKirahan,Andrew	L	.300	60	18	1	0	1	14	4	13	.348	.367
Throws Left	R	.393	56	22	4	0	1	9	6	9	.460	.518
Medina,Yoervis	L	.311	45	14	2	0	2	9	5	6	.380	.489
Throws Right	R	.220	41	9	5	1	0	3	6	10	.319	.390
Medlen,Kris	L	.239	113	27	8	2	2	13	16	20	.336	.398
Throws Right	R	.266	109	29	1	0	4	14	2	20	.286	.385
Mejia,Jenrry	L	.200	10	2	1	0	0	0	1	2	.273	.300
Throws Right	R	.143	14	2	1	0	0	0	1	5	.200	.214
Melancon,Mark	L	.138	123	17	2	0	1	4	8	34	.201	.179
Throws Right	R	.263	152	40	7	1	3	16	6	28	.291	.382
Mendez,Roman	L	.261	23	6	1	0	1	5	7	4	.433	.435
Throws Right	R	.308	26	8	3	0	1	6	1	6	.357	.538
Miley,Wade	L	.241	170	41	13	1	3	17	10	33	.291	.382
Throws Left	R	.272	588	160	38	5	14	74	54	114	.334	.425
Miller,Andrew	L	.233	43	10	1	0	1	5	3	21	.277	.326
Throws Left	R	.131	175	23	3	0	4	10	17	79	.227	.217
Miller,Justin	L	.184	38	7	3	0	0	1	5	12	.279	.263
Throws Right	R	.175	80	14	4	1	2	10	6	26	.233	.325
Miller,Shelby	L	.262	382	100	19	4	10	37	35	72	.321	.411
Throws Right	R	.214	387	83	22	1	3	33	38	99	.294	.300
Mills,Brad	L	.400	5	2	0	0	0	0	0	0	.500	.400
Throws Left	R	.313	16	5	1	0	1	3	1	1	.353	.563
Milone,Tommy	L	.218	119	26	2	1	3	14	10	28	.275	.328
Throws Left	R	.273	374	102	24	1	14	37	26	63	.318	.455
Mitchell,Bryan	L	.264	53	14	1	0	2	7	7	17	.361	.396
Throws Right	R	.319	72	23	4	0	2	13	9	12	.402	.458
Montas,Frankie	L	.286	21	6	1	0	1	4	6	4	.444	.476
Throws Right	R	.222	36	8	2	0	0	4	3	16	.282	.278
Montero,Rafael	L	.429	7	3	1	1	0	0	3	1	.600	.857
Throws Right	R	.182	33	6	2	0	0	5	2	12	.229	.242
Montgomery,Mike	L	.303	89	27	8	0	2	13	10	19	.380	.461
Throws Left	R	.246	264	65	12	1	9	26	27	45	.323	.402
Moore,Matt	L	.265	83	22	5	0	4	16	6	10	.315	.470
Throws Left	R	.315	165	52	10	1	5	22	17	36	.387	.479
Morales,Franklin	L	.192	99	19	5	2	1	7	5	20	.245	.313
Throws Left	R	.285	137	39	11	1	3	15	9	21	.333	.445
Moreno,Diego	L	.318	22	7	2	0	1	5	3	3	.400	.545
Throws Right	R	.111	18	2	1	0	0	1	0	5	.200	.167
Morgan,Adam	L	.225	71	16	2	0	2	8	6	9	.278	.338
Throws Left	R	.281	256	72	20	0	12	31	11	40	.320	.500
Morin,Mike	L	.269	52	14	2	0	1	8	3	15	.322	.365
Throws Right	R	.262	84	22	6	1	2	15	6	26	.311	.429
Morris,Bryan	L	.297	101	30	7	2	1	12	8	16	.360	.436
Throws Right	R	.259	143	37	3	0	2	15	18	31	.346	.322
Morrow,Brandon	L	.222	63	14	2	1	1	3	5	15	.279	.333
Throws Right	R	.278	54	15	2	1	2	7	2	8	.298	.463
Morton,Charlie	L	.301	259	78	21	4	8	40	27	52	.389	.506
Throws Right	R	.239	247	59	12	0	5	20	14	44	.285	.348
Moscot,Jon	L	.238	21	5	0	0	1	2	4	2	.360	.381
Throws Right	R	.261	23	6	1	0	1	4	1	4	.280	.435
Motte,Jason	L	.294	68	20	2	1	3	8	5	11	.342	.485
Throws Right	R	.233	120	28	7	1	1	13	6	23	.277	.333
Moylan,Peter	L	.750	4	3	0	0	1	3	0	0	.750	1.500
Throws Right	R	.225	40	9	1	0	0	4	0	8	.225	.250
Mujica,Edward	L	.306	72	22	3	0	4	11	1	13	.324	.514
Throws Right	R	.270	111	30	2	0	6	18	6	17	.305	.450

Pitcher	vs	Avg	AB	H	2B	3B	HR	RBI	BB	SO	OBP	Slg
Murray,Colton	L	.231	13	3	2	0	0	1	1	3	.286	.385
Throws Right	R	.364	22	8	0	0	2	4	1	6	.391	.636
Narveson,Chris	L	.081	37	3	0	0	1	2	3	13	.150	.162
Throws Left	R	.280	75	21	4	0	6	13	6	19	.333	.573
Nelson,Jimmy	L	.302	291	88	21	1	11	41	33	61	.381	.495
Throws Right	R	.202	372	75	11	1	7	33	32	87	.275	.293
Neris,Hector	L	.267	60	16	6	0	1	6	8	15	.353	.417
Throws Right	R	.232	95	22	4	0	7	17	2	26	.277	.495
Nesbitt,Angel	L	.368	38	14	2	0	1	11	3	7	.455	.500
Throws Right	R	.178	45	8	2	0	1	4	5	7	.269	.289
Neshek,Pat	L	.276	76	21	4	1	2	12	6	21	.333	.434
Throws Right	R	.219	128	28	7	0	6	15	6	30	.259	.414
Nicasio,Juan	L	.348	69	24	6	2	0	6	17	16	.477	.493
Throws Right	R	.226	155	35	8	3	1	17	15	49	.298	.335
Nicolino,Justin	L	.283	60	17	1	1	1	5	4	8	.338	.383
Throws Left	R	.262	210	55	13	3	7	25	16	15	.316	.452
Niese,Jon	L	.305	151	46	7	1	4	18	7	27	.346	.444
Throws Left	R	.273	535	146	26	2	16	68	48	86	.338	.419
Noesi,Hector	L	.239	67	16	3	0	4	8	8	15	.329	.463
Throws Right	R	.362	69	25	6	1	3	12	9	7	.436	.609
Nola,Aaron	L	.310	116	36	7	0	4	13	9	15	.360	.474
Throws Right	R	.212	179	38	1	2	7	18	10	53	.260	.358
Nolasco,Ricky	L	.239	71	17	6	1	2	13	9	15	.321	.437
Throws Right	R	.388	85	33	8	0	1	13	5	20	.424	.518
Nolin,Sean	L	.333	39	13	1	0	2	7	5	5	.391	.513
Throws Left	R	.286	77	22	3	0	2	9	7	10	.333	.403
Norris,Bud	L	.295	190	56	19	0	9	32	18	46	.362	.537
Throws Right	R	.299	147	44	10	3	6	31	13	25	.360	.531
Norris,Daniel	L	.259	58	15	3	1	4	9	6	11	.328	.552
Throws Left	R	.228	167	38	9	2	5	18	13	34	.285	.395
Nova,Ivan	L	.312	189	59	12	2	8	28	18	19	.375	.524
Throws Right	R	.223	179	40	13	0	5	20	15	44	.302	.380
Nuno,Vidal	L	.215	79	17	4	0	1	7	3	26	.258	.304
Throws Left	R	.279	262	73	16	1	14	34	19	55	.329	.508
Oberg,Scott	L	.275	80	22	3	0	3	7	9	18	.356	.425
Throws Right	R	.261	138	36	11	0	7	30	22	26	.380	.493
Oberholtzer,Brett	L	.357	42	15	5	1	1	7	1	2	.364	.595
Throws Left	R	.269	108	29	4	0	3	13	16	25	.365	.389
O'Day,Darren	L	.210	81	17	4	0	2	9	8	23	.293	.333
Throws Right	R	.192	156	30	1	0	3	10	6	59	.236	.256
Odorizzi,Jake	L	.230	366	84	23	6	5	32	18	98	.264	.366
Throws Right	R	.234	278	65	13	2	13	27	28	52	.310	.435
O'Flaherty,Eric	L	.278	72	20	3	0	0	6	8	18	.358	.319
Throws Left	R	.415	65	27	10	0	2	16	10	3	.500	.662
Ogando,Alexi	L	.206	97	20	7	0	2	6	8	20	.271	.340
Throws Right	R	.265	147	39	2	3	10	26	20	33	.359	.524
Ogando,Nefi	L	.273	11	3	0	1	0	2	0	2	.273	.455
Throws Right	R	.500	8	4	0	0	0	2	2	0	.600	.500
Ohlendorf,Ross	L	.241	29	7	0	1	1	2	4	8	.333	.414
Throws Right	R	.292	48	14	1	0	3	8	3	11	.327	.500
Olmos,Edgar	L	.200	10	2	2	0	0	1	1	0	.333	.400
Throws Left	R	.298	47	14	2	0	1	9	7	4	.382	.404
Olson,Tyler	L	.350	20	7	3	1	0	4	3	6	.458	.600
Throws Left	R	.344	32	11	2	0	2	4	7	2	.462	.594
O'Rourke,Ryan	L	.171	41	7	1	0	1	5	7	19	.292	.268
Throws Left	R	.231	39	9	1	0	2	6	8	5	.354	.410
Osich,Josh	L	.222	63	14	2	0	2	9	5	17	.279	.349
Throws Left	R	.213	47	10	2	0	2	5	3	10	.255	.383
O'Sullivan,Sean	L	.366	123	45	11	0	12	26	13	12	.424	.748
Throws Right	R	.290	169	49	12	1	4	20	7	23	.332	.444
Osuna,Roberto	L	.206	136	28	8	2	4	13	9	35	.255	.382
Throws Right	R	.174	115	20	5	1	3	12	7	40	.224	.313
Otero,Dan	L	.328	64	21	4	0	3	16	3	11	.353	.531
Throws Right	R	.336	128	43	11	1	4	23	3	17	.356	.531
Ottavino,Adam	L	.133	15	2	0	0	0	0	1	5	.188	.133
Throws Right	R	.059	17	1	0	0	0	0	1	8	.158	.059
Owens,Henry	L	.293	41	12	1	0	2	5	6	9	.396	.463
Throws Left	R	.248	202	50	13	0	5	24	18	41	.313	.386
Papelbon,Jonathan	L	.274	117	32	3	0	6	15	8	27	.333	.453
Throws Right	R	.176	119	21	6	1	1	4	4	29	.227	.269
Parnell,Bobby	L	.333	30	10	3	0	0	5	9	3	.487	.433
Throws Right	R	.317	63	20	1	0	0	11	8	10	.389	.333
Parra,Manny	L	.271	59	16	5	1	1	10	3	13	.302	.441
Throws Left	R	.258	62	16	1	0	1	5	3	10	.288	.323
Patton,Spencer	L	.281	32	9	4	0	1	5	7	7	.425	.500
Throws Right	R	.250	60	15	3	0	4	19	5	21	.338	.500

Pitchers vs. Left-Handed and Right-Handed Batters

Pitcher	vs	Avg	AB	H	2B	3B	HR	RBI	BB	SO	OBP	Slg
Paxton,James	L	.404	57	23	3	0	2	11	10	14	.493	.561
Throws Left	R	.212	208	44	7	0	6	20	19	42	.274	.332
Pazos,James	L	.273	11	3	0	0	0	0	1	1	.333	.273
Throws Left	R	.000	6	0	0	0	0	0	2	2	.250	.000
Peacock,Brad	L	.444	9	4	2	0	0	1	1	2	.500	.667
Throws Right	R	.111	9	1	1	0	0	1	1	1	.200	.222
Peavy,Jake	L	.207	208	43	8	3	8	21	15	42	.260	.389
Throws Right	R	.271	207	56	11	3	4	22	10	36	.309	.411
Pelfrey,Mike	L	.312	298	93	19	0	6	42	40	41	.398	.436
Throws Right	R	.297	353	105	17	1	5	36	5	45	.322	.394
Pena,Ariel	L	.256	39	10	4	1	2	5	11	8	.431	.564
Throws Right	R	.226	62	14	6	0	0	7	3	19	.269	.323
Peralta,Joel	L	.229	48	11	1	0	1	4	5	10	.302	.313
Throws Right	R	.262	65	17	3	0	5	11	3	14	.294	.538
Peralta,Wily	L	.309	223	69	17	3	9	27	15	27	.355	.534
Throws Right	R	.295	207	61	13	0	5	28	22	33	.366	.430
Perez,Martin	L	.210	62	13	0	0	1	6	5	19	.279	.258
Throws Left	R	.304	247	75	14	5	2	35	19	29	.352	.425
Perez,Oliver	L	.185	92	17	4	1	1	9	5	33	.235	.283
Throws Left	R	.310	71	22	2	0	3	14	10	18	.417	.465
Perez,Williams	L	.303	234	71	14	1	9	31	25	34	.377	.487
Throws Right	R	.278	212	59	6	2	4	25	26	39	.366	.382
Perkins,Glen	L	.379	58	22	3	0	0	2	4	12	.419	.431
Throws Left	R	.213	169	36	6	0	9	22	6	42	.240	.408
Pestano,Vinnie	L	.375	16	6	2	0	0	0	2	2	.474	.500
Throws Right	R	.273	33	9	1	0	3	14	6	11	.366	.576
Petit,Yusmeiro	L	.276	123	34	4	3	6	20	10	21	.324	.504
Throws Right	R	.241	170	41	11	2	5	20	5	38	.263	.418
Petricka,Jake	L	.358	53	19	4	0	0	6	6	7	.417	.434
Throws Right	R	.257	144	37	7	0	2	8	12	26	.318	.347
Phelps,David	L	.277	195	54	9	0	6	23	17	36	.342	.415
Throws Right	R	.267	243	65	10	3	5	31	16	41	.310	.395
Pimentel,Stolmy	L	.429	14	6	0	0	1	1	0	0	.429	.643
Throws Right	R	.185	27	5	0	0	0	2	3	7	.258	.185
Pinder,Branden	L	.341	44	15	3	3	1	5	5	8	.408	.614
Throws Right	R	.206	63	13	3	0	3	7	9	17	.301	.397
Pineda,Michael	L	.272	302	82	18	3	9	35	14	72	.301	.440
Throws Right	R	.283	332	94	19	2	12	40	7	84	.301	.461
Pino,Yohan	L	.238	42	10	3	0	0	2	1	9	.256	.310
Throws Right	R	.351	37	13	1	0	2	5	2	4	.385	.541
Pomeranz,Drew	L	.152	99	15	1	0	2	13	7	33	.216	.222
Throws Left	R	.260	215	56	13	1	6	32	24	49	.335	.414
Porcello,Rick	L	.289	374	108	20	2	16	52	22	82	.334	.481
Throws Right	R	.286	308	88	15	0	9	35	16	67	.329	.422
Pressly,Ryan	L	.263	38	10	4	0	0	3	3	9	.310	.368
Throws Right	R	.254	67	17	2	0	0	4	9	13	.342	.284
Price,David	L	.262	214	56	10	1	4	11	7	47	.284	.374
Throws Left	R	.219	612	134	30	3	13	52	40	178	.267	.342
Putnam,Zach	L	.229	83	19	3	1	4	13	12	29	.337	.434
Throws Right	R	.247	93	23	2	0	3	12	12	35	.336	.366
Quackenbush,Kevin	L	.295	95	28	6	0	2	10	13	25	.378	.421
Throws Right	R	.197	122	24	4	0	4	15	7	33	.237	.328
Qualls,Chad	L	.230	61	14	3	0	1	10	4	10	.286	.328
Throws Right	R	.256	125	32	5	1	5	16	5	36	.282	.432
Quintana,Jose	L	.233	180	42	10	1	5	18	9	42	.280	.383
Throws Left	R	.283	622	176	37	6	11	54	35	135	.325	.415
Ramirez,Erasmo	L	.193	322	62	12	1	8	29	26	70	.254	.311
Throws Right	R	.284	292	83	16	0	8	34	14	56	.334	.421
Ramirez,J.C.	L	.205	39	8	1	0	0	5	7	4	.340	.231
Throws Right	R	.309	55	17	4	0	3	12	4	12	.356	.545
Ramirez,Jose	L	.400	15	6	3	0	0	6	6	3	.609	.600
Throws Right	R	.375	24	9	2	2	0	8	4	2	.483	.625
Ramirez,Neil	L	.238	21	5	1	0	0	1	3	6	.320	.286
Throws Right	R	.226	31	7	2	1	1	3	3	9	.286	.452
Ramirez,Noe	L	.200	10	2	0	0	0	3	2	3	.333	.200
Throws Right	R	.262	42	11	1	0	3	10	5	10	.367	.500
Ramos,A.J.	L	.202	109	22	6	0	2	13	13	39	.290	.312
Throws Right	R	.169	136	23	3	0	4	10	13	48	.250	.279
Ramos,Cesar	L	.274	95	26	4	0	0	11	8	21	.346	.316
Throws Left	R	.284	102	29	4	0	2	12	7	22	.324	.382
Ranaudo,Anthony	L	.265	34	9	1	0	2	13	2	10	.297	.471
Throws Right	R	.333	27	9	2	1	0	3	6	1	.471	.481
Rasmus,Cory	L	.214	42	9	2	0	2	8	7	16	.327	.405
Throws Right	R	.182	33	6	3	0	1	3	4	11	.289	.364
Rasmussen,Rob	L	.364	33	12	2	0	2	8	3	7	.417	.606
Throws Left	R	.368	38	14	3	0	0	9	5	10	.442	.447

Pitcher	vs	Avg	AB	H	2B	3B	HR	RBI	BB	SO	OBP	Slg
Ravin,Josh	L	.318	22	7	0	0	2	5	3	6	.400	.591
Throws Right	R	.300	20	6	0	0	1	5	1	6	.364	.450
Ray,Robbie	L	.262	130	34	8	3	2	15	8	32	.307	.415
Throws Left	R	.252	345	87	22	3	7	33	41	87	.339	.394
Rea,Colin	L	.225	71	16	7	0	1	10	8	18	.296	.366
Throws Right	R	.277	47	13	2	1	1	5	3	8	.333	.426
Redmond,Todd	L	.160	25	4	1	0	0	0	4	5	.300	.200
Throws Right	R	.333	39	13	3	1	3	10	3	8	.381	.692
Reed,Addison	L	.253	95	24	4	2	1	10	11	22	.330	.368
Throws Right	R	.270	126	34	8	2	2	20	8	29	.313	.413
Reynolds,Matt	L	.241	29	7	0	0	3	10	4	13	.353	.552
Throws Left	R	.280	25	7	0	0	3	4	3	5	.357	.640
Richard,Clayton	L	.234	64	15	2	0	0	7	2	10	.269	.266
Throws Left	R	.294	109	32	7	3	3	12	5	12	.325	.495
Richards,Garrett	L	.226	416	94	19	0	8	39	42	107	.299	.329
Throws Right	R	.247	352	87	16	0	12	42	34	69	.312	.395
Riefenhauser,C.J.	L	.370	27	10	2	0	3	8	4	5	.452	.778
Throws Left	R	.192	26	5	1	0	0	1	3	2	.267	.231
Rienzo,Andre	L	.217	23	5	0	0	0	3	7	3	.400	.217
Throws Right	R	.235	51	12	4	1	2	13	6	12	.328	.471
Rivero,Felipe	L	.198	86	17	4	0	0	8	5	23	.242	.244
Throws Left	R	.200	90	18	7	0	2	5	6	20	.255	.344
Roark,Tanner	L	.299	201	60	15	0	9	29	16	28	.359	.507
Throws Right	R	.261	226	59	9	1	8	30	10	42	.293	.416
Roberts,Ken	L	.462	26	12	3	0	0	2	2	1	.517	.577
Throws Left	R	.313	32	10	3	0	0	7	1	5	.314	.406
Robertson,David	L	.175	97	17	1	0	1	10	9	36	.245	.216
Throws Right	R	.210	138	29	4	3	6	19	4	50	.238	.413
Robles,Hansel	L	.167	78	13	3	1	3	13	3	30	.214	.346
Throws Right	R	.205	117	24	9	1	5	17	15	31	.295	.427
Rodney,Fernando	L	.252	103	26	9	0	4	10	18	35	.389	.456
Throws Right	R	.244	135	33	5	1	5	22	11	23	.313	.407
Rodon,Carlos	L	.194	139	27	3	1	0	12	17	41	.294	.230
Throws Left	R	.272	378	103	21	3	11	45	54	98	.367	.431
Rodriguez,Eduardo	L	.272	114	31	4	1	7	17	5	25	.311	.509
Throws Left	R	.249	357	89	16	1	6	34	32	73	.312	.350
Rodriguez,Fernando	L	.174	86	15	2	0	0	2	11	29	.268	.198
Throws Right	R	.217	129	28	7	1	4	17	13	36	.292	.380
Rodriguez,Francisco	L	.206	102	21	4	0	2	7	4	29	.234	.304
Throws Right	R	.172	99	17	2	1	4	6	7	33	.224	.333
Rodriguez,Paco	L	.292	24	7	1	0	0	6	2	6	.333	.333
Throws Left	R	.214	14	3	1	0	0	1	1	2	.267	.286
Rodriguez,Wandy	L	.294	85	25	6	1	3	14	6	15	.344	.494
Throws Left	R	.282	262	74	16	0	7	34	30	57	.356	.424
Roe,Chaz	L	.333	66	22	4	1	2	11	7	13	.397	.515
Throws Right	R	.242	91	22	8	0	2	11	10	25	.320	.396
Rogers,Esmil	L	.349	43	15	2	0	2	9	9	8	.462	.535
Throws Right	R	.286	91	26	4	0	3	17	5	23	.327	.429
Rollins,David	L	.333	33	11	1	1	2	6	3	6	.405	.606
Throws Left	R	.351	74	26	5	1	1	15	5	15	.400	.486
Romero,Enny	L	.391	46	18	3	2	0	9	4	9	.431	.543
Throws Left	R	.266	79	21	4	0	1	7	9	22	.341	.354
Romo,Sergio	L	.371	70	26	8	0	0	9	8	7	.443	.486
Throws Right	R	.170	147	25	6	1	3	12	2	64	.181	.286
Rondon,Bruce	L	.288	52	15	3	0	2	9	10	15	.403	.462
Throws Right	R	.239	67	16	5	0	1	9	9	21	.338	.358
Rondon,Hector	L	.231	121	28	8	0	2	8	8	28	.293	.347
Throws Right	R	.196	138	27	4	0	2	12	7	41	.234	.268
Rondon,Jorge	L	.357	28	10	2	0	1	7	5	4	.455	.536
Throws Right	R	.409	44	18	3	2	2	14	4	5	.458	.705
Rosenthal,Trevor	L	.194	108	21	1	1	0	4	17	41	.304	.222
Throws Right	R	.270	152	41	3	2	3	14	8	42	.311	.375
Ross,Joe	L	.279	136	38	10	1	4	14	15	27	.353	.456
Throws Right	R	.172	151	26	1	1	3	14	6	42	.209	.252
Ross,Robbie	L	.224	85	19	6	0	2	18	7	22	.284	.365
Throws Left	R	.272	147	40	7	1	5	19	13	31	.340	.435
Ross,Tyson	L	.256	352	90	17	3	5	30	49	100	.358	.364
Throws Right	R	.220	373	82	11	3	4	37	35	112	.286	.298
Rosscup,Zac	L	.158	38	6	0	1	1	4	7	12	.289	.289
Throws Left	R	.308	65	20	9	1	4	15	6	17	.366	.662
Rucinski,Drew	L	.500	12	6	1	0	1	5	6	1	.667	.833
Throws Right	R	.250	16	4	1	0	0	2	0	3	.294	.313
Rumbelow,Nick	L	.250	28	7	1	1	2	6	2	6	.300	.571
Throws Right	R	.257	35	9	1	0	0	1	3	9	.316	.286
Rusin,Chris	L	.305	128	39	8	3	5	26	5	21	.336	.531
Throws Left	R	.312	420	131	30	3	14	57	36	65	.369	.498

Pitchers vs. Left-Handed and Right-Handed Batters

Pitcher	vs	Avg	AB	H	2B	3B	HR	RBI	BB	SO	OBP	Slg
Russell,James	L	.273	66	18	4	1	0	5	5	11	.324	.364
Throws Left	R	.338	71	24	10	0	3	15	4	9	.368	.606
Ryan,Kyle	L	.333	57	19	2	1	1	9	3	6	.361	.456
Throws Left	R	.263	156	41	5	0	8	16	17	24	.339	.449
Rzepczynski,Marc	L	.255	94	24	2	0	2	14	8	30	.321	.340
Throws Left	R	.372	43	16	1	1	1	10	6	11	.460	.512
Sabathia,CC	L	.189	127	24	1	1	3	13	5	40	.235	.283
Throws Left	R	.308	532	164	21	3	25	69	45	97	.362	.500
Salas,Fernando	L	.271	107	29	6	0	4	16	3	32	.289	.439
Throws Right	R	.232	138	32	10	2	4	19	9	42	.287	.420
Salazar,Danny	L	.232	327	76	15	4	15	39	21	95	.283	.440
Throws Right	R	.220	363	80	13	3	8	28	32	100	.289	.339
Sale,Chris	L	.250	128	32	4	0	0	10	9	49	.329	.281
Throws Left	R	.230	666	153	28	3	23	72	33	225	.272	.384
Samardzija,Jeff	L	.278	425	118	21	8	21	65	29	80	.326	.513
Throws Right	R	.268	411	110	19	1	8	45	20	83	.312	.377
Sampson,Keyvius	L	.340	97	33	7	1	2	14	15	21	.425	.495
Throws Right	R	.274	124	34	9	0	5	23	11	21	.331	.468
Sanchez,Aaron	L	.282	170	48	8	0	9	21	29	22	.390	.488
Throws Right	R	.163	160	26	5	0	0	10	15	39	.242	.194
Sanchez,Anibal	L	.217	318	69	15	2	12	37	32	79	.291	.390
Throws Right	R	.291	285	83	17	1	17	45	17	59	.329	.537
Santana,Ervin	L	.260	208	54	18	2	7	31	23	34	.338	.466
Throws Right	R	.246	203	50	7	0	5	14	13	48	.297	.355
Santiago,Hector	L	.220	168	37	9	1	3	11	15	35	.294	.339
Throws Left	R	.229	519	119	28	2	26	63	56	127	.311	.441
Santos,Sergio	L	.417	24	10	2	1	2	4	1	3	.423	.833
Throws Right	R	.146	41	6	2	0	1	5	6	15	.255	.268
Scahill,Rob	L	.286	56	16	5	0	0	2	7	8	.359	.375
Throws Right	R	.254	67	17	3	0	3	12	9	16	.351	.433
Scheppers,Tanner	L	.234	64	15	3	0	3	10	12	13	.346	.422
Throws Right	R	.262	84	22	5	0	3	13	11	19	.357	.429
Scherzer,Max	L	.230	440	101	25	2	13	35	25	126	.273	.384
Throws Right	R	.184	407	75	15	1	14	33	9	150	.209	.329
Schlitter,Brian	L	.500	6	3	0	0	1	3	1	0	.571	1.000
Throws Right	R	.333	27	9	2	0	1	6	1	4	.357	.519
Schugel,Andrew	L	.429	21	9	1	0	2	8	4	2	.520	.762
Throws Right	R	.320	25	8	3	0	0	4	1	3	.346	.440
Schultz,Bo	L	.145	62	9	1	0	2	5	11	17	.270	.258
Throws Right	R	.242	95	23	3	0	5	14	3	14	.270	.432
Scribner,Evan	L	.227	97	22	4	0	6	11	2	29	.250	.454
Throws Right	R	.269	134	36	7	1	8	24	2	35	.283	.515
Severino,Luis	L	.244	123	30	7	0	3	8	14	24	.331	.374
Throws Right	R	.213	108	23	6	0	6	13	8	32	.267	.435
Shaw,Bryan	L	.226	93	21	2	1	3	14	11	18	.308	.366
Throws Right	R	.252	151	38	7	1	5	19	8	36	.294	.411
Shields,James	L	.279	383	107	16	4	23	42	51	88	.368	.522
Throws Right	R	.216	380	82	27	2	10	37	30	128	.284	.376
Shoemaker,Matt	L	.248	270	67	14	0	11	36	22	55	.305	.422
Throws Right	R	.270	252	68	14	0	13	26	13	61	.311	.480
Shreve,Chasen	L	.259	81	21	2	1	2	12	11	27	.355	.383
Throws Left	R	.209	134	28	2	1	8	20	22	37	.321	.418
Siegrist,Kevin	L	.278	79	22	4	0	2	6	18	20	.406	.405
Throws Left	R	.164	189	31	11	2	2	13	16	70	.236	.275
Simon,Alfredo	L	.289	422	122	29	8	16	48	42	57	.353	.509
Throws Right	R	.257	307	79	18	2	8	44	26	60	.327	.407
Sipp,Tony	L	.224	98	22	5	0	1	9	8	25	.287	.306
Throws Left	R	.192	99	19	6	0	4	10	7	37	.245	.374
Smith,Carson	L	.227	110	25	5	0	0	10	10	31	.315	.273
Throws Right	R	.169	142	24	6	0	2	12	12	61	.248	.254
Smith,Joe	L	.288	118	34	7	1	2	11	15	24	.370	.415
Throws Right	R	.233	129	30	4	1	2	17	4	33	.261	.326
Smith,Josh	L	.361	61	22	5	0	4	12	13	14	.481	.639
Throws Right	R	.278	72	20	5	0	1	13	8	16	.369	.389
Smith,Will	L	.257	101	26	8	0	4	21	12	43	.330	.455
Throws Left	R	.193	135	26	7	1	1	9	12	48	.264	.281
Smyly,Drew	L	.157	51	8	6	0	0	1	5	24	.232	.275
Throws Left	R	.249	201	50	7	0	11	22	15	53	.303	.448
Socolovich,Miguel	L	.156	45	7	0	0	0	3	6	11	.255	.156
Throws Right	R	.265	68	18	4	0	1	5	4	16	.306	.368
Solis,Sammy	L	.355	31	11	0	0	0	5	0	3	.364	.355
Throws Left	R	.255	55	14	3	0	2	10	4	14	.300	.418
Soria,Joakim	L	.266	124	33	5	0	5	10	5	22	.295	.427
Throws Right	R	.177	124	22	2	0	3	13	14	42	.270	.266
Soriano,Rafael	L	.545	11	6	3	0	1	4	1	2	.583	1.091
Throws Right	R	.154	13	2	0	0	1	3	0	2	.154	.385

Pitcher	vs	Avg	AB	H	2B	3B	HR	RBI	BB	SO	OBP	Slg
Stauffer,Tim	L	.448	29	13	2	0	2	7	7	4	.556	.724
Throws Right	R	.317	60	19	5	2	4	12	2	10	.344	.667
Stites,Matt	L	.375	16	6	1	0	1	4	3	2	.474	.625
Throws Right	R	.364	22	8	0	1	0	4	2	4	.400	.455
Storen,Drew	L	.284	109	31	4	0	1	9	11	28	.358	.349
Throws Right	R	.146	96	14	3	0	3	14	5	39	.212	.271
Straily,Dan	L	.243	37	9	2	1	1	5	7	5	.364	.432
Throws Right	R	.233	30	7	0	1	1	4	1	9	.281	.400
Strasburg,Stephen	L	.202	247	50	9	1	5	19	19	82	.264	.308
Throws Right	R	.270	241	65	9	3	9	30	7	73	.293	.444
Street,Huston	L	.252	115	29	3	0	6	13	13	28	.323	.435
Throws Right	R	.200	115	23	2	2	1	9	7	29	.244	.278
Strickland,Hunter	L	.185	65	12	3	0	1	3	4	11	.232	.277
Throws Right	R	.193	114	22	3	1	3	9	6	39	.246	.316
Stroman,Marcus	L	.194	67	13	1	0	1	3	5	13	.260	.254
Throws Right	R	.241	29	7	1	0	1	2	1	5	.267	.379
Strop,Pedro	L	.186	86	16	5	0	2	3	16	26	.327	.314
Throws Right	R	.156	147	23	4	0	3	26	13	55	.230	.245
Stults,Eric	L	.255	47	12	1	2	1	7	2	4	.286	.426
Throws Left	R	.273	132	36	6	2	9	20	11	27	.326	.553
Swarzak,Anthony	L	.250	20	5	2	0	0	0	1	6	.286	.350
Throws Right	R	.351	37	13	2	0	1	9	3	7	.400	.486
Syndergaard,Noah	L	.237	278	66	7	5	10	33	18	67	.284	.406
Throws Right	R	.212	283	60	10	1	9	24	13	99	.251	.350
Tanaka,Masahiro	L	.223	269	60	13	3	13	31	14	71	.258	.439
Throws Right	R	.219	302	66	20	0	12	30	13	68	.250	.404
Tazawa,Junichi	L	.299	97	29	6	1	3	19	5	22	.333	.474
Throws Right	R	.267	135	36	4	4	2	14	8	34	.310	.400
Teaford,Everett	L	.333	12	4	2	0	0	2	1	1	.429	.500
Throws Left	R	.125	8	1	1	0	0	0	2	3	.300	.250
Teheran,Julio	L	.300	367	110	20	1	18	50	47	64	.387	.507
Throws Right	R	.207	381	79	12	2	9	35	26	107	.263	.320
Tepera,Ryan	L	.137	51	7	0	0	3	4	6	9	.254	.314
Throws Right	R	.235	68	16	3	0	5	9	0	13	.246	.500
Thatcher,Joe	L	.245	53	13	1	0	1	8	10	19	.365	.321
Throws Left	R	.323	31	10	2	1	0	4	2	7	.343	.452
Thayer,Dale	L	.227	66	15	5	0	3	12	12	9	.346	.439
Throws Right	R	.293	75	22	4	0	2	8	3	16	.316	.427
Thielbar,Caleb	L	.200	10	2	1	0	0	0	0	4	.200	.300
Throws Left	R	.333	9	3	0	0	0	1	0	1	.333	.333
Thomas,Ian	L	.121	33	4	2	0	0	3	5	10	.237	.182
Throws Left	R	.308	52	16	3	0	2	7	6	13	.379	.481
Thompson,Aaron	L	.189	53	10	4	0	0	9	6	11	.262	.264
Throws Left	R	.324	68	22	2	0	2	10	5	6	.365	.441
Thornburg,Tyler	L	.232	56	13	2	0	3	10	7	16	.313	.429
Throws Right	R	.231	78	18	2	0	4	12	5	18	.299	.410
Thornton,Matt	L	.198	86	17	5	1	0	6	1	11	.205	.279
Throws Left	R	.229	70	16	3	0	2	7	10	12	.333	.357
Tillman,Chris	L	.262	332	87	20	2	3	25	37	64	.337	.361
Throws Right	R	.271	328	89	22	1	17	56	27	56	.328	.500
Tolleson,Shawn	L	.243	152	37	8	0	6	12	8	39	.290	.414
Throws Right	R	.234	124	29	4	1	3	12	9	37	.284	.355
Tomlin,Josh	L	.156	122	19	3	0	4	6	2	26	.169	.279
Throws Right	R	.235	119	28	7	2	9	15	6	31	.283	.555
Tonkin,Michael	L	.361	36	13	0	0	3	11	3	8	.400	.611
Throws Right	R	.154	52	8	1	0	1	6	6	11	.254	.231
Torres,Alex	L	.268	56	15	1	0	2	8	12	14	.406	.393
Throws Left	R	.157	70	11	2	0	4	8	14	21	.298	.357
Torres,Carlos	L	.263	80	21	4	1	2	11	9	18	.337	.413
Throws Right	R	.284	141	40	8	1	3	22	9	30	.320	.418
Treinen,Blake	L	.336	110	37	8	1	3	16	17	21	.425	.509
Throws Right	R	.187	134	25	1	0	1	10	15	44	.276	.216
Tropeano,Nicholas	L	.267	75	20	6	0	1	4	7	22	.325	.387
Throws Right	R	.274	73	20	5	0	1	9	3	16	.303	.384
Tsao,Chin-hui	L	.571	14	8	2	0	2	4	1	2	.600	1.143
Throws Right	R	.350	20	7	2	0	1	3	2	5	.409	.600
Tuivailala,Samuel	L	.217	23	5	1	0	1	3	3	9	.308	.391
Throws Right	R	.235	34	8	2	1	1	3	5	11	.333	.441
Uehara,Koji	L	.153	72	11	4	0	2	6	6	24	.215	.292
Throws Right	R	.221	77	17	4	2	1	5	3	23	.250	.364
Urena,Jose	L	.288	104	30	7	1	4	16	15	8	.380	.490
Throws Right	R	.321	134	43	9	0	1	21	10	20	.367	.410
Valdez,Jose	L	.308	13	4	0	1	0	2	3	2	.438	.462
Throws Right	R	.273	22	6	1	0	2	3	1	2	.304	.591
Vargas,Jason	L	.286	49	14	6	0	1	8	4	6	.340	.469
Throws Left	R	.264	121	32	4	0	4	9	8	21	.315	.397

Pitcher	vs	Avg	AB	H	2B	3B	HR	RBI	BB	SO	OBP	Slg
Varvaro,Anthony	L	.263	19	5	0	1	0	2	1	3	.300	.368
Throws Right	R	.346	26	9	3	0	0	5	5	5	.452	.462
Veal,Donnie	L	.500	8	4	2	0	1	4	2	0	.636	1.125
Throws Left	R	.333	12	4	0	0	2	3	0	3	.333	.833
Velasquez,Vincent	L	.214	112	24	6	0	3	11	13	28	.296	.348
Throws Right	R	.271	96	26	7	3	2	17	8	30	.340	.469
Venditte,Pat	L	.106	47	5	3	0	1	7	4	18	.173	.234
Throws Both	R	.293	58	17	7	0	2	10	8	5	.379	.517
Ventura,Yordano	L	.255	325	83	16	4	9	44	31	89	.321	.412
Throws Right	R	.240	296	71	11	2	5	23	27	67	.317	.341
VerHagen,Drew	L	.226	31	7	0	0	1	2	7	6	.368	.323
Throws Right	R	.186	59	11	1	0	0	5	7	7	.284	.203
Verlander,Justin	L	.216	120	26	8	2	8	26	17	55	.265	.355
Throws Right	R	.244	234	57	12	0	5	27	14	56	.291	.359
Verrett,Logan	L	.200	80	16	0	0	5	8	9	17	.293	.388
Throws Right	R	.205	88	18	4	1	1	15	6	22	.250	.307
Villanueva,Carlos	L	.183	93	17	8	1	3	9	11	19	.274	.387
Throws Right	R	.252	131	33	6	1	3	11	10	36	.308	.382
Villarreal,Pedro	L	.321	78	25	3	1	2	11	6	9	.364	.462
Throws Right	R	.276	116	32	5	0	4	13	6	20	.323	.422
Vincent,Nick	L	.278	36	10	2	0	0	1	9	8	.422	.333
Throws Right	R	.283	53	15	4	0	0	10	1	14	.291	.358
Vizcaino,Arodys	L	.196	56	11	3	1	0	3	8	16	.297	.286
Throws Right	R	.235	68	16	5	0	1	3	5	21	.288	.353
Vogelsong,Ryan	L	.283	237	67	14	4	14	46	27	51	.353	.553
Throws Right	R	.251	291	73	15	3	3	19	31	57	.325	.354
Volquez,Edinson	L	.240	388	93	22	2	10	36	39	80	.310	.384
Throws Right	R	.262	370	97	14	2	6	40	33	75	.330	.359
Wacha,Michael	L	.215	303	65	16	1	6	27	27	66	.284	.333
Throws Right	R	.253	384	97	15	2	13	44	31	87	.313	.404
Wada,Tsuyoshi	L	.308	26	8	4	0	1	2	3	5	.379	.577
Throws Left	R	.229	96	22	3	2	4	11	8	26	.292	.427
Wagner,Tyler	L	.333	24	8	1	1	0	3	5	1	.433	.458
Throws Right	R	.424	33	14	4	1	1	7	2	4	.457	.697
Wainwright,Adam	L	.256	43	11	5	0	0	3	2	7	.289	.372
Throws Right	R	.226	62	14	4	0	0	3	2	13	.250	.290
Walden,Jordan	L	.125	16	2	0	0	0	0	4	7	.300	.125
Throws Right	R	.238	21	5	2	0	0	1	0	5	.227	.333
Walker,Taijuan	L	.256	352	90	19	0	12	38	23	89	.303	.412
Throws Right	R	.247	296	73	12	0	13	40	17	68	.300	.419
Warren,Adam	L	.225	200	45	10	1	2	16	17	36	.288	.315
Throws Right	R	.243	284	69	10	1	8	30	22	68	.310	.370
Watson,Tony	L	.186	70	13	2	0	0	0	6	18	.278	.214
Throws Left	R	.212	198	42	5	0	3	23	11	44	.254	.283
Weaver,Jered	L	.264	318	84	19	3	12	36	19	48	.321	.456
Throws Right	R	.264	299	79	20	0	12	42	14	42	.305	.452
Webb,Daniel	L	.362	47	17	2	1	1	11	8	6	.455	.511
Throws Right	R	.304	79	24	4	0	2	17	14	16	.411	.430
Webb,Ryan	L	.224	85	19	5	1	1	4	8	14	.290	.341
Throws Right	R	.262	103	27	7	0	3	20	4	17	.300	.417
Weber,Ryan	L	.255	55	14	4	1	3	7	4	8	.328	.527
Throws Right	R	.239	46	11	0	0	0	1	2	11	.271	.239
Webster,Allen	L	.340	47	16	1	1	6	9	9	4	.439	.787
Throws Right	R	.225	71	16	2	1	4	11	11	13	.345	.451
Whitley,Chase	L	.400	30	12	2	0	3	6	2	5	.438	.767
Throws Right	R	.170	47	8	3	0	0	1	3	11	.250	.234
Wieland,Joe	L	.400	10	4	2	0	2	5	1	0	.417	1.200
Throws Right	R	.250	24	6	1	1	0	2	4	4	.357	.375
Wilhelmsen,Tom	L	.323	96	31	8	1	1	13	15	27	.416	.458
Throws Right	R	.189	132	25	4	2	2	22	14	33	.268	.295
Williams,Jerome	L	.312	215	67	14	0	3	23	19	25	.375	.419
Throws Right	R	.321	293	94	13	0	19	48	15	49	.354	.560
Wilson,Alex	L	.222	117	26	4	0	2	12	6	21	.258	.308
Throws Right	R	.252	139	35	2	2	3	19	5	17	.286	.360
Wilson,C.J.	L	.248	117	29	8	0	4	12	8	26	.310	.419
Throws Left	R	.238	374	89	13	1	9	42	38	84	.318	.350
Wilson,Justin	L	.236	72	17	4	0	0	7	10	19	.337	.292
Throws Left	R	.216	148	32	4	1	3	13	10	47	.270	.318
Wilson,Tyler	L	.282	71	20	7	0	0	8	7	4	.342	.380
Throws Right	R	.297	64	19	7	0	1	6	4	9	.343	.453
Wisler,Matt	L	.327	202	66	17	1	10	26	30	21	.416	.569
Throws Right	R	.238	223	53	16	0	6	27	10	51	.274	.390
Wojciechowski,Asher	L	.372	43	16	6	2	1	4	7	7	.451	.674
Throws Right	R	.259	27	7	2	0	1	8	0	9	.250	.444
Wolf,Randy	L	.148	27	4	0	0	0	1	3	5	.233	.148
Throws Left	R	.359	117	42	10	2	5	25	12	23	.420	.607

Pitcher	vs	Avg	AB	H	2B	3B	HR	RBI	BB	SO	OBP	Slg
Wood,Alex	L	.223	175	39	6	0	1	14	5	38	.243	.274
Throws Left	R	.292	545	159	23	5	14	59	54	101	.359	.429
Wood,Travis	L	.231	130	30	4	1	1	18	12	40	.297	.300
Throws Left	R	.228	246	56	9	1	10	23	27	78	.304	.394
Wooten,Rob	L	.167	12	2	1	0	1	3	2	5	.286	.500
Throws Right	R	.300	10	3	1	1	0	0	4	1	.533	.600
Worley,Vance	L	.307	101	31	5	0	2	12	14	18	.385	.416
Throws Right	R	.276	181	50	15	0	4	22	7	31	.311	.425
Wright,Mike	L	.322	90	29	7	0	4	11	8	11	.386	.533
Throws Right	R	.258	89	23	7	0	5	15	10	15	.350	.506
Wright,Steven	L	.234	137	32	5	0	4	13	15	29	.314	.358
Throws Right	R	.245	143	35	8	0	8	20	12	23	.301	.469
Wright,Wesley	L	.214	14	3	0	0	1	3	1	2	.267	.429
Throws Left	R	.250	12	3	1	0	0	2	2	3	.313	.333
Yates,Kirby	L	.333	33	11	2	0	5	10	4	10	.405	.848
Throws Right	R	.235	51	12	1	0	5	10	3	11	.291	.549
Young,Chris	L	.242	231	56	11	2	8	20	27	41	.320	.411
Throws Right	R	.159	220	35	11	1	8	20	16	42	.215	.327
Ziegler,Brad	L	.217	120	26	7	0	3	9	9	18	.271	.350
Throws Right	R	.179	123	22	2	0	0	5	8	18	.235	.195
Zimmermann,Jordan	L	.284	395	112	18	2	13	46	28	88	.338	.438
Throws Right	R	.243	379	92	7	0	11	38	11	76	.269	.348
Zito,Barry	L	.400	5	2	0	0	2	3	0	1	.400	1.600
Throws Left	R	.385	26	10	2	0	2	5	6	1	.500	.692
Zych,Tony	L	.200	20	4	0	0	1	2	1	9	.238	.350
Throws Right	R	.255	51	13	2	1	0	2	2	15	.309	.333
AL	L	.251	-	-	-	-	-	-	-	-	.316	.399
	R	.256	-	-	-	-	-	-	-	-	.315	.412
NL	L	.261	-	-	-	-	-	-	-	-	.333	.416
	R	.251	-	-	-	-	-	-	-	-	.307	.393
MLB	L	.256	-	-	-	-	-	-	-	-	.324	.408
	R	.253	-	-	-	-	-	-	-	-	.311	.402

2015 Leader Boards

Scott Spratt

For data hounds, you can't beat the pages of objective data in the Handbook. Beyond just the Register pages—which document every hit, home run, sacrifice fly, and everything else each active player has done in baseball over the last 10 or more years—there are tons of advanced statistics that rely on objectively measured components to make their judgments. For example, Defensive Runs Saved is a complex calculation made up of eight different components that cover everything from an outfielder's arm to a catcher's framing ability. But at its core, Defensive Runs Saved is based on specific, objective data. Did the fielder convert the play into an out? How frequently have fielders converted similar batted balls as determined by objectively measured and double-checked hit locations and hang times into outs?

This section is no exception. The many different hitter and pitcher leaderboards provide a glimpse of the top and bottom of both the AL and NL in a variety of categories. Some of those categories are simple and objective, like the Total Bases leaderboard for hitters and the Pitches Per Batter leaderboard for pitchers. Some of those categories are sophisticated and objective, like the Best OPS vs. Sliders leaderboard.

As cherished as every last measurement is, fans know that it is narratives that made them fall in love with the game in the first place. Baseball is the American Pastime because it provides such wonderful stories that can be shared between father and son or argued over by best friends. That's what's so great about the Leaderboards. They provide plenty of narrative fodder.

Seven different pitchers threw no-hitters this season: Chris Heston on June 9 versus the Mets, Max Scherzer on June 20 versus the Pirates, Cole Hamels on July 25 versus the Cubs, Hisashi Iwakuma on August 12 versus the Orioles, Mike Fiers on August 21 versus the Dodgers, Jake Arrieta on August 30 versus the Dodgers, and Max Scherzer again on October 3 versus the Mets. But which no-hitter was the best one? Flip over to the Bill James Leaderboards and you'll find the top games in baseball in 2015 as ranked by Game Score—a measurement of a pitcher's excellence in a start that factors in outs recorded, strikeouts, hits allowed, walks allowed, and runs allowed.

Game Score would tell you that a pair of Scherzer's starts were the best starts in baseball this season, with the October 3 no-hitter narrowly edging a June 14 one-hitter for the best of the best. That means that Game Score believes that Scherzer's June 14 one-hitter was better than his June 20 no-hitter six days later. Meanwhile, Game Score will also tell you that teammates Carlos Carrasco and Corey Kluber pitched a pair of one-hitters, the former on September 25 versus the Royals and the latter over eight innings on May 13 versus the Cardinals, that were just as good as or better than all six of those other no-hitters. Game Score will also tell you that 35-year-old Rich Hill, after pitching exclusively as a reliever in the majors from 2010 until mid-September this season, produced the fifth-best start in the AL when he struck out 10 Orioles and walked just one in his third start on September 25. What will free agency have in store for him after such an unusual season?

One favorite argument to have is who is the best athlete in baseball? Again, the Bill James Leaderboards provide plenty of fodder. The Power / Speed Number leaderboard combine home runs and stolen bases into a single ranking. Manny Machado has been primed for stardom since he reached the major leagues as a just-turned 20-year-old in 2012. It was tremendously exciting to see him put everything together this season with 35 home runs and 20 stolen bases. However, that performance made Machado only the runner-up in Power / Speed Number. Would you have guessed that Diamondbacks center fielder A.J. Pollock had his own 20-20 season, including exactly 20 home runs and an impressive 39 stolen bases? Pollock actually bested Machado and everyone else in baseball in Power / Speed Number and may be the most underrated player in the game.

As you flip through these pages to find your own favorite narratives, here are some definitions to help clarify parts of the leaderboards that may not be familiar to you:

BPS stands for "Batting Average plus Slugging Percentage." BPS makes more sense than OPS for some leaderboards that involve pitches.

OutZ is "Pitches Outside the Strike Zone."

Holds Adjusted Save Percentage is calculated by dividing holds plus saves by holds plus save opportunities.

2015 American League Batting Leaders

Batting Average
(minimum 502 PA)

Cabrera,Miguel, Det	.338
Bogaerts,Xander, Bos	.320
Altuve,Jose, Hou	.313
Brantley,Michael, Cle	.310
Cain,Lorenzo, KC	.307
Fielder,Prince, Tex	.305
Kipnis,Jason, Cle	.303
Cruz,Nelson, Sea	.302
Trout,Mike, LAA	.299
Hosmer,Eric, KC	.297

On Base Percentage
(minimum 502 PA)

Cabrera,Miguel, Det	.440
Trout,Mike, LAA	.402
Brantley,Michael, Cle	.379
Fielder,Prince, Tex	.378
Bautista,Jose, Tor	.377
Choo,Shin-Soo, Tex	.375
Kipnis,Jason, Cle	.372
Encarnacion,Edwin, Tor	.372
Donaldson,Josh, Tor	.371
Cruz,Nelson, Sea	.369

Slugging Average
(minimum 502 PA)

Trout,Mike, LAA	.590
Donaldson,Josh, Tor	.568
Cruz,Nelson, Sea	.566
Davis,Chris, Bal	.562
Encarnacion,Edwin, Tor	.557
Ortiz,David, Bos	.553
Bautista,Jose, Tor	.536
Martinez,J.D., Det	.535
Cabrera,Miguel, Det	.534
Abreu,Jose, CWS	.502

Home Runs

Davis,Chris, Bal	47
Cruz,Nelson, Sea	44
Donaldson,Josh, Tor	41
Trout,Mike, LAA	41
Bautista,Jose, Tor	40
Pujols,Albert, LAA	40
Encarnacion,Edwin, Tor	39
Martinez,J.D., Det	38
Ortiz,David, Bos	37
Machado,Manny, Bal	35

Games

Machado,Manny, Bal	162
Seager,Kyle, Sea	161
Andrus,Elvis, Tex	160
Davis,Chris, Bal	160
Longoria,Evan, TB	160
Calhoun,Kole, LAA	159
Pillar,Kevin, Tor	159
Trout,Mike, LAA	159
7 tied with	158

Plate Appearances

Machado,Manny, Bal	713
Donaldson,Josh, Tor	711
Dozier,Brian, Min	704
Fielder,Prince, Tex	693
Altuve,Jose, Hou	689
Eaton,Adam, CWS	689
Calhoun,Kole, LAA	686
Seager,Kyle, Sea	686
Cabrera,Melky, CWS	683
Trout,Mike, LAA	682

At Bats

Altuve,Jose, Hou	638
Machado,Manny, Bal	633
Calhoun,Kole, LAA	630
Cabrera,Melky, CWS	629
Dozier,Brian, Min	628
Cano,Robinson, Sea	624
Kinsler,Ian, Det	624
Seager,Kyle, Sea	623
Donaldson,Josh, Tor	620
3 tied with	613

Hits

Altuve,Jose, Hou	200
Bogaerts,Xander, Bos	196
Fielder,Prince, Tex	187
Kinsler,Ian, Det	185
Donaldson,Josh, Tor	184
Machado,Manny, Bal	181
Cano,Robinson, Sea	179
Abreu,Jose, CWS	178
Cruz,Nelson, Sea	178
Hosmer,Eric, KC	178

Singles

Bogaerts,Xander, Bos	151
Altuve,Jose, Hou	141
Fielder,Prince, Tex	136
Kinsler,Ian, Det	132
Escobar,Alcides, KC	129
Aybar,Erick, LAA	127
Eaton,Adam, CWS	124
Cano,Robinson, Sea	123
Cabrera,Melky, CWS	122
Hosmer,Eric, KC	122

Doubles

Brantley,Michael, Cle	45
Kipnis,Jason, Cle	43
Betts,Mookie, Bos	42
Donaldson,Josh, Tor	41
Morales,Kendrys, KC	41
Altuve,Jose, Hou	40
Dozier,Brian, Min	39
Ortiz,David, Bos	37
Seager,Kyle, Sea	37
2 tied with	36

Triples

Rosario,Eddie, Min	15
Kiermaier,Kevin, TB	12
Davis,Rajai, Det	11
Gattis,Evan, Hou	11
DeShields,Delino, Tex	10
Burns,Billy, Oak	9
Eaton,Adam, CWS	9
Odor,Rougned, Tex	9
Betts,Mookie, Bos	8
Gose,Anthony, Det	8

Total Bases

Donaldson,Josh, Tor	352
Trout,Mike, LAA	339
Cruz,Nelson, Sea	334
Davis,Chris, Bal	322
Martinez,J.D., Det	319
Machado,Manny, Bal	318
Abreu,Jose, CWS	308
Encarnacion,Edwin, Tor	294
Altuve,Jose, Hou	293
Ortiz,David, Bos	292

Runs Scored

Donaldson,Josh, Tor	122
Bautista,Jose, Tor	108
Trout,Mike, LAA	104
Machado,Manny, Bal	102
Cain,Lorenzo, KC	101
Dozier,Brian, Min	101
Davis,Chris, Bal	100
Eaton,Adam, CWS	98
Hosmer,Eric, KC	98
4 tied with	94

RBI

Donaldson,Josh, Tor	123
Davis,Chris, Bal	117
Bautista,Jose, Tor	114
Encarnacion,Edwin, Tor	111
Ortiz,David, Bos	108
Morales,Kendrys, KC	106
Martinez,J.D., Det	102
Abreu,Jose, CWS	101
Fielder,Prince, Tex	98
Pujols,Albert, LAA	95

Walks

Bautista,Jose, Tor	110
Santana,Carlos, Cle	108
Trout,Mike, LAA	92
Davis,Chris, Bal	84
Rodriguez,Alex, NYY	84
Cabrera,Miguel, Det	77
Encarnacion,Edwin, Tor	77
Ortiz,David, Bos	77
Choo,Shin-Soo, Tex	76
Donaldson,Josh, Tor	73

Strikeouts

Davis,Chris, Bal	208
Martinez,J.D., Det	178
Calhoun,Kole, LAA	164
Cruz,Nelson, Sea	164
Trout,Mike, LAA	158
Rasmus,Colby, Hou	154
Castellanos,Nick, Det	152
Carter,Chris, Hou	151
Dozier,Brian, Min	148
Choo,Shin-Soo, Tex	147

2015 American League Batting Leaders

Intentional Walks		BA Bases Loaded		Sacrifice Hits		Sacrifice Flies	
		(minimum 10 PA)					
Ortiz,David, Bos	16	Giavotella,Johnny, LAA	.700	Lindor,Francisco, Cle	13	Cabrera,Melky, CWS	10
Cabrera,Miguel, Det	15	Reddick,Josh, Oak	.667	Escobar,Alcides, KC	11	Donaldson,Josh, Tor	10
Fielder,Prince, Tex	14	Cron,C.J., LAA	.545	Giavotella,Johnny, LAA	9	Encarnacion,Edwin, Tor	10
Trout,Mike, LAA	14	Martinez,J.D., Det	.545	Sucre,Jesus, Sea	9	Andrus,Elvis, Tex	9
Mauer,Joe, Min	12	Headley,Chase, NYY	.533	Andrus,Elvis, Tex	8	Longoria,Evan, TB	9
Abreu,Jose, CWS	11	Mauer,Joe, Min	.533	Gardner,Brett, NYY	8	Ortiz,David, Bos	9
Pujols,Albert, LAA	10	Castellanos,Nick, Det	.500	Zunino,Mike, Sea	8	Bautista,Jose, Tor	8
Cruz,Nelson, Sea	9	Donaldson,Josh, Tor	.500	6 tied with	7	Beltre,Adrian, Tex	8
5 tied with	8	Martinez,Victor, Det	.500			Dozier,Brian, Min	8
		Plouffe,Trevor, Min	.471			Vogt,Stephen, Oak	8

BA Close & Late		Batting Average w/ RISP		SLG vs. LHP		SLG vs. RHP	
(minimum 50 PA)		(minimum 100 PA)		(minimum 125 PA)		(minimum 377 PA)	
Gomes,Yan, Cle	.458	Cabrera,Miguel, Det	.365	Cruz,Nelson, Sea	.673	Ortiz,David, Bos	.613
Bradley Jr.,Jackie, Bos	.372	Donaldson,Josh, Tor	.353	Donaldson,Josh, Tor	.632	Davis,Chris, Bal	.608
Trumbo,Mark, Sea	.370	Trout,Mike, LAA	.352	Forsythe,Logan, TB	.599	Trout,Mike, LAA	.587
Giavotella,Johnny, LAA	.365	Mauer,Joe, Min	.352	Trout,Mike, LAA	.597	Encarnacion,Edwin, Tor	.575
Hosmer,Eric, KC	.363	Lindor,Francisco, Cle	.350	Raburn,Ryan, Cle	.589	Bautista,Jose, Tor	.556
Odor,Rougned, Tex	.359	Castellanos,Nick, Det	.342	Young,Chris, NYY	.575	Donaldson,Josh, Tor	.553
Bogaerts,Xander, Bos	.359	Abreu,Jose, CWS	.341	Castellanos,Nick, Det	.570	Abreu,Jose, CWS	.548
Colabello,Chris, Tor	.345	Morales,Kendrys, KC	.335	Longoria,Evan, TB	.568	Morales,Kendrys, KC	.538
Andrus,Elvis, Tex	.345	Betts,Mookie, Bos	.333	Cain,Lorenzo, KC	.568	Martinez,J.D., Det	.534
Vogt,Stephen, Oak	.338	Bogaerts,Xander, Bos	.331	Napoli,Mike, Bos-Tex	.563	Cabrera,Miguel, Det	.530

Leadoff Hitters OBP		Cleanup Hitters SLG		BA vs. LHP		BA vs. RHP	
(minimum 150 PA)		(minimum 150 PA)		(minimum 125 PA)		(minimum 377 PA)	
Jaso,John, TB	.404	Ortiz,David, Bos	.670	Altuve,Jose, Hou	.372	Cabrera,Miguel, Det	.344
Kipnis,Jason, Cle	.385	Davis,Chris, Bal	.582	Bogaerts,Xander, Bos	.365	Fielder,Prince, Tex	.343
Guyer,Brandon, TB	.379	Teixeira,Mark, NYY	.579	Cruz,Nelson, Sea	.357	Kipnis,Jason, Cle	.334
Springer,George, Hou	.379	Valencia,Danny, Tor-Oak	.571	Castellanos,Nick, Det	.351	Hosmer,Eric, KC	.310
Altuve,Jose, Hou	.365	Cruz,Nelson, Sea	.559	Longoria,Evan, TB	.342	Abreu,Jose, CWS	.308
Machado,Manny, Bal	.364	Martinez,J.D., Det	.556	Cain,Lorenzo, KC	.335	Bogaerts,Xander, Bos	.304
Eaton,Adam, CWS	.360	Encarnacion,Edwin, Tor	.554	Semien,Marcus, Oak	.329	Choo,Shin-Soo, Tex	.299
Gardner,Brett, NYY	.360	Sano,Miguel, Min	.546	Zobrist,Ben, Oak-KC	.329	Cano,Robinson, Sea	.296
Marte,Ketel, Sea	.350	Cano,Robinson, Sea	.531	Young,Chris, NYY	.327	Donaldson,Josh, Tor	.296
Betts,Mookie, Bos	.338	Gattis,Evan, Hou	.500	Raburn,Ryan, Cle	.325	Machado,Manny, Bal	.295

Home BA		Away BA		OBP vs. LHP		OBP vs. RHP	
(minimum 251 PA)		(minimum 251 PA)		(minimum 125 PA)		(minimum 377 PA)	
Cabrera,Miguel, Det	.357	Eaton,Adam, CWS	.317	Cruz,Nelson, Sea	.435	Cabrera,Miguel, Det	.434
Bogaerts,Xander, Bos	.347	Trout,Mike, LAA	.316	Trout,Mike, LAA	.434	Fielder,Prince, Tex	.416
Kipnis,Jason, Cle	.347	Gregorius,Didi, NYY	.306	Altuve,Jose, Hou	.431	Kipnis,Jason, Cle	.412
Altuve,Jose, Hou	.342	Brantley,Michael, Cle	.304	Bogaerts,Xander, Bos	.424	Choo,Shin-Soo, Tex	.400
Cain,Lorenzo, KC	.337	Fielder,Prince, Tex	.301	Raburn,Ryan, Cle	.415	Ortiz,David, Bos	.395
Beltre,Adrian, Tex	.332	Cruz,Nelson, Sea	.299	Zobrist,Ben, Oak-KC	.409	Trout,Mike, LAA	.391
Donaldson,Josh, Tor	.330	Kinsler,Ian, Det	.296	Springer,George, Hou	.403	Hosmer,Eric, KC	.384
Burns,Billy, Oak	.326	Seager,Kyle, Sea	.295	Castellanos,Nick, Det	.400	Bautista,Jose, Tor	.376
Betts,Mookie, Bos	.322	Bogaerts,Xander, Bos	.291	Young,Chris, NYY	.397	Encarnacion,Edwin, Tor	.375
Choo,Shin-Soo, Tex	.317	Forsythe,Logan, TB	.290	Rodriguez,Alex, NYY	.394	Davis,Chris, Bal	.375

2015 American League Batting Leaders

Stolen Bases

Altuve,Jose, Hou	38
Cain,Lorenzo, KC	28
Burns,Billy, Oak	26
Dyson,Jarrod, KC	26
Andrus,Elvis, Tex	25
DeShields,Delino, Tex	25
Pillar,Kevin, Tor	25
Marisnick,Jake, Hou	24
Gose,Anthony, Det	23
2 tied with	21

Caught Stealing

Altuve,Jose, Hou	13
Gose,Anthony, Det	11
Andrus,Elvis, Tex	9
Ellsbury,Jacoby, NYY	9
Jackson,Austin, Sea	9
Marisnick,Jake, Hou	9
7 tied with	8

Highest SB Success Pct
(minimum 20 SBA)

Dyson,Jarrod, KC	89.7
Pillar,Kevin, Tor	86.2
Cain,Lorenzo, KC	82.4
Gardner,Brett, NYY	80.0
Springer,George, Hou	80.0
Kiermaier,Kevin, TB	78.3
Betts,Mookie, Bos	77.8
Escobar,Alcides, KC	77.3
Burns,Billy, Oak	76.5
DeShields,Delino, Tex	75.8

Lowest SB Success Pct
(minimum 20 SBA)

Kipnis,Jason, Cle	60.0
Jackson,Austin, Sea	62.5
Gose,Anthony, Det	67.6
Davis,Rajai, Det	69.2
Eaton,Adam, CWS	69.2
Ellsbury,Jacoby, NYY	70.0
Ramirez,Alexei, CWS	70.8
Aybar,Erick, LAA	71.4
Machado,Manny, Bal	71.4
Marisnick,Jake, Hou	72.7

Steals of Third

Cain,Lorenzo, KC	12
Dyson,Jarrod, KC	10
Altuve,Jose, Hou	7
Andrus,Elvis, Tex	6
Davis,Rajai, Det	6
Guyer,Brandon, TB	6
Marisnick,Jake, Hou	5
Pillar,Kevin, Tor	5
7 tied with	4

Grounded Into DP

Plouffe,Trevor, Min	28
Butler,Billy, Oak	26
Cano,Robinson, Sea	26
Morales,Kendrys, KC	24
Perez,Salvador, KC	23
Martin,Russell, Tor	22
Mauer,Joe, Min	22
Castellanos,Nick, Det	21
Fielder,Prince, Tex	21
Jones,Adam, Bal	21

Grounded Into DP Pct
(minimum 50 GIDP Ops)

Chisenhall,Lonnie, Cle	0.00
DeShields,Delino, Tex	1.39
Betts,Mookie, Bos	1.94
Gordon,Alex, KC	3.39
Marisnick,Jake, Hou	3.45
Bourn,Michael, Cle	3.64
Odor,Rougned, Tex	3.66
Gillaspie,Conor, CWS-LAA	3.85
Gregorius,Didi, NYY	4.26
Davis,Chris, Bal	4.96

Hit By Pitch

Guyer,Brandon, TB	24
Abreu,Jose, CWS	15
Choo,Shin-Soo, Tex	15
Eaton,Adam, CWS	14
Forsythe,Logan, TB	14
Gordon,Alex, KC	14
Odor,Rougned, Tex	14
Moustakas,Mike, KC	13
Cain,Lorenzo, KC	12
Freese,David, LAA	12

Pitches Seen

Trout,Mike, LAA	2980
Santana,Carlos, Cle	2863
Dozier,Brian, Min	2833
Donaldson,Josh, Tor	2817
Machado,Manny, Bal	2789
Davis,Chris, Bal	2786
Eaton,Adam, CWS	2785
Bautista,Jose, Tor	2741
Gardner,Brett, NYY	2732
Mauer,Joe, Min	2715

At Bats Per Home Run
(minimum 502 PA)

Davis,Chris, Bal	12.2
Cruz,Nelson, Sea	13.4
Encarnacion,Edwin, Tor	13.5
Bautista,Jose, Tor	13.6
Trout,Mike, LAA	14.0
Ortiz,David, Bos	14.3
Pujols,Albert, LAA	15.1
Donaldson,Josh, Tor	15.1
Martinez,J.D., Det	15.7
Rodriguez,Alex, NYY	15.8

Highest GB/FB Ratio
(minimum 502 PA)

Mauer,Joe, Min	2.76
Holt,Brock, Bos	2.24
Gose,Anthony, Det	2.15
Hosmer,Eric, KC	2.13
Bogaerts,Xander, Bos	2.05
Aybar,Erick, LAA	1.99
Cano,Robinson, Sea	1.99
Eaton,Adam, CWS	1.86
Garcia,Avisail, CWS	1.83
Burns,Billy, Oak	1.79

Lowest GB/FB Ratio
(minimum 502 PA)

Davis,Chris, Bal	0.73
Dozier,Brian, Min	0.76
Bautista,Jose, Tor	0.76
McCann,Brian, NYY	0.77
Martinez,J.D., Det	0.79
Encarnacion,Edwin, Tor	0.81
Cabrera,Asdrubal, TB	0.82
Beltran,Carlos, NYY	0.83
Kinsler,Ian, Det	0.83
Seager,Kyle, Sea	0.86

Pitches Per Plate App
(minimum 502 PA)

Trout,Mike, LAA	4.37
Santana,Carlos, Cle	4.30
Martin,Russell, Tor	4.17
Gardner,Brett, NYY	4.16
Davis,Chris, Bal	4.16
Forsythe,Logan, TB	4.13
Bautista,Jose, Tor	4.12
Vogt,Stephen, Oak	4.11
Holt,Brock, Bos	4.10
Mauer,Joe, Min	4.08

Pct Pitches Taken
(minimum 1500 Pitches)

Santana,Carlos, Cle	63.4
Zobrist,Ben, Oak-KC	63.2
Gardner,Brett, NYY	62.6
Trout,Mike, LAA	62.6
DeShields,Delino, Tex	61.1
Bautista,Jose, Tor	60.6
Hardy,J.J., Bal	60.2
Smith,Seth, Sea	60.0
Betts,Mookie, Bos	59.8
Forsythe,Logan, TB	59.7

Best BPS on OutZ
(minimum 502 PA)

Bogaerts,Xander, Bos	.622
Encarnacion,Edwin, Tor	.615
Cain,Lorenzo, KC	.610
Ortiz,David, Bos	.599
Forsythe,Logan, TB	.580
Abreu,Jose, CWS	.580
Betts,Mookie, Bos	.569
McCann,Brian, NYY	.567
Escobar,Alcides, KC	.564
Kipnis,Jason, Cle	.563

Worst BPS on OutZ
(minimum 502 PA)

Calhoun,Kole, LAA	.293
Moreland,Mitch, Tex	.302
Morrison,Logan, Sea	.316
Headley,Chase, NYY	.320
Gose,Anthony, Det	.327
Choo,Shin-Soo, Tex	.327
Plouffe,Trevor, Min	.335
Hunter,Torii, Min	.361
Garcia,Avisail, CWS	.375
Mauer,Joe, Min	.381

2015 American League Batting Leaders

Best OPS vs Fastballs
(minimum 251 PA)

Donaldson,Josh, Tor	1.066
Trout,Mike, LAA	1.066
Davis,Chris, Bal	1.016
Cabrera,Miguel, Det	.985
Morales,Kendrys, KC	.984
Cruz,Nelson, Sea	.962
Choo,Shin-Soo, Tex	.961
Teixeira,Mark, NYY	.955
Cain,Lorenzo, KC	.940
Bautista,Jose, Tor	.937

Best OPS vs Curveballs
(minimum 50 PA)

Cain,Lorenzo, KC	.927
Bautista,Jose, Tor	.906
Miller,Brad, Sea	.889
Calhoun,Kole, LAA	.878
Pillar,Kevin, Tor	.870
Gattis,Evan, Hou	.853
Martinez,J.D., Det	.853
Moustakas,Mike, KC	.852
Vogt,Stephen, Oak	.849
Fielder,Prince, Tex	.779

Best OPS vs Changeups
(minimum 50 PA)

Donaldson,Josh, Tor	1.366
Cruz,Nelson, Sea	1.074
Odor,Rougned, Tex	1.054
Smoak,Justin, Tor	1.040
Encarnacion,Edwin, Tor	1.035
Reddick,Josh, Oak	1.016
Kinsler,Ian, Det	.991
Hicks,Aaron, Min	.983
Fielder,Prince, Tex	.977
Cabrera,Asdrubal, TB	.962

Best OPS vs Sliders
(minimum 32 PA)

Zobrist,Ben, Oak-KC	1.182
Betts,Mookie, Bos	1.081
Pujols,Albert, LAA	1.078
Sanchez,Carlos, CWS	1.077
Encarnacion,Edwin, Tor	1.041
Souza,Steven, TB	1.026
Eaton,Adam, CWS	1.008
Correa,Carlos, Hou	1.000
Valbuena,Luis, Hou	.975
Escobar,Eduardo, Min	.973

OPS
(minimum 502 PA)

Trout,Mike, LAA	.991
Cabrera,Miguel, Det	.974
Donaldson,Josh, Tor	.939
Cruz,Nelson, Sea	.936
Encarnacion,Edwin, Tor	.929
Davis,Chris, Bal	.923
Ortiz,David, Bos	.913
Bautista,Jose, Tor	.913
Martinez,J.D., Det	.879
Machado,Manny, Bal	.861

OPS First Half
(minimum 260 PA)

Cabrera,Miguel, Det	1.034
Trout,Mike, LAA	1.019
Fielder,Prince, Tex	.924
Cruz,Nelson, Sea	.919
Martinez,J.D., Det	.913
Rodriguez,Alex, NYY	.898
Kipnis,Jason, Cle	.889
Machado,Manny, Bal	.886
Donaldson,Josh, Tor	.884
Teixeira,Mark, NYY	.876

OPS Second Half
(minimum 201 PA)

Encarnacion,Edwin, Tor	1.132
Ortiz,David, Bos	1.102
Davis,Chris, Bal	1.078
Choo,Shin-Soo, Tex	1.016
Donaldson,Josh, Tor	1.011
Brantley,Michael, Cle	.963
Bautista,Jose, Tor	.958
Cruz,Nelson, Sea	.957
Trout,Mike, LAA	.956
Lindor,Francisco, Cle	.930

OPS by Catchers
(minimum 251 PA)

Vogt,Stephen, Oak	.853
Martin,Russell, Tor	.793
Chirinos,Robinson, Tex	.762
McCann,Brian, NYY	.762
Perez,Salvador, KC	.715
Swihart,Blake, Bos	.714
Joseph,Caleb, Bal	.702
McCann,James, Det	.676
Gomes,Yan, Cle	.676
Perez,Carlos, LAA	.657

OPS by First Basemen
(minimum 251 PA)

Cabrera,Miguel, Det	.994
Davis,Chris, Bal	.965
Teixeira,Mark, NYY	.912
Canha,Mark, Oak	.873
Abreu,Jose, CWS	.834
Hosmer,Eric, KC	.829
Encarnacion,Edwin, Tor	.816
Moreland,Mitch, Tex	.811
Pujols,Albert, LAA	.801
Smoak,Justin, Tor	.782

OPS by Second Basemen
(minimum 251 PA)

Kipnis,Jason, Cle	.847
Altuve,Jose, Hou	.815
Pedroia,Dustin, Bos	.799
Schoop,Jonathan, Bal	.793
Cano,Robinson, Sea	.793
Odor,Rougned, Tex	.781
Kinsler,Ian, Det	.775
Forsythe,Logan, TB	.771
Zobrist,Ben, Oak-KC	.771
Dozier,Brian, Min	.751

OPS by Third Basemen
(minimum 251 PA)

Donaldson,Josh, Tor	.926
Machado,Manny, Bal	.865
Moustakas,Mike, KC	.821
Beltre,Adrian, Tex	.793
Seager,Kyle, Sea	.780
Freese,David, LAA	.750
Longoria,Evan, TB	.750
Plouffe,Trevor, Min	.744
Valbuena,Luis, Hou	.742
Lawrie,Brett, Oak	.737

OPS by Shortstops
(minimum 251 PA)

Escobar,Eduardo, Min	.864
Correa,Carlos, Hou	.857
Lindor,Francisco, Cle	.836
Cabrera,Asdrubal, TB	.776
Bogaerts,Xander, Bos	.776
Iglesias,Jose, Det	.715
Reyes,Jose, Tor	.708
Semien,Marcus, Oak	.706
Miller,Brad, Sea	.696
Gregorius,Didi, NYY	.689

OPS by Left Fielders
(minimum 251 PA)

Brantley,Michael, Cle	.839
Gordon,Alex, KC	.818
Cespedes,Yoenis, Det	.813
Rosario,Eddie, Min	.813
Gardner,Brett, NYY	.719
Cabrera,Melky, CWS	.708
Ramirez,Hanley, Bos	.690

OPS by Center Fielders
(minimum 251 PA)

Trout,Mike, LAA	.994
Cain,Lorenzo, KC	.841
Betts,Mookie, Bos	.817
Jones,Adam, Bal	.787
Eaton,Adam, CWS	.786
DeShields,Delino, Tex	.730
Burns,Billy, Oak	.729
Pillar,Kevin, Tor	.721
Hicks,Aaron, Min	.718
Kiermaier,Kevin, TB	.713

OPS by Right Fielders
(minimum 251 PA)

Cruz,Nelson, Sea	1.072
Bautista,Jose, Tor	.907
Martinez,J.D., Det	.899
Choo,Shin-Soo, Tex	.847
Springer,George, Hou	.836
Beltran,Carlos, NYY	.833
Reddick,Josh, Oak	.785
Calhoun,Kole, LAA	.728
Souza,Steven, TB	.726
Hunter,Torii, Min	.705

OPS by Designated Hitters
(minimum 125 PA)

Encarnacion,Edwin, Tor	.993
Bautista,Jose, Tor	.936
Sano,Miguel, Min	.908
Abreu,Jose, CWS	.894
Ortiz,David, Bos	.885
Morales,Kendrys, KC	.860
Butler,Joey, TB	.856
Rodriguez,Alex, NYY	.846
Fielder,Prince, Tex	.823
Jaso,John, TB	.805

2015 American League Batting Leaders

OPS Batting Left vs. LHP
(minimum 125 PA)

Rasmus,Colby, Hou	.835
Seager,Kyle, Sea	.835
Moustakas,Mike, KC	.823
Gordon,Alex, KC	.817
Holt,Brock, Bos	.807
Davis,Chris, Bal	.799
Moss,Brandon, Cle	.789
Brantley,Michael, Cle	.785
Odor,Rougned, Tex	.781
Gardner,Brett, NYY	.761

OPS Batting Left vs. RHP
(minimum 377 PA)

Ortiz,David, Bos	1.008
Davis,Chris, Bal	.984
Fielder,Prince, Tex	.923
Choo,Shin-Soo, Tex	.917
Kipnis,Jason, Cle	.908
Morales,Kendrys, KC	.901
Hosmer,Eric, KC	.885
Eaton,Adam, CWS	.847
Vogt,Stephen, Oak	.832
Beltran,Carlos, NYY	.831

OPS Batting Right vs. LHP
(minimum 125 PA)

Cruz,Nelson, Sea	1.107
Trout,Mike, LAA	1.032
Donaldson,Josh, Tor	1.024
Raburn,Ryan, Cle	1.004
Altuve,Jose, Hou	.973
Forsythe,Logan, TB	.972
Young,Chris, NYY	.972
Castellanos,Nick, Det	.970
Longoria,Evan, TB	.960
Cain,Lorenzo, KC	.959

OPS Batting Right vs. RHP
(minimum 377 PA)

Trout,Mike, LAA	.978
Cabrera,Miguel, Det	.964
Encarnacion,Edwin, Tor	.950
Bautista,Jose, Tor	.932
Donaldson,Josh, Tor	.919
Abreu,Jose, CWS	.908
Machado,Manny, Bal	.894
Martinez,J.D., Det	.870
Cruz,Nelson, Sea	.866
Betts,Mookie, Bos	.813

OPS vs. LHP
(minimum 125 PA)

Cruz,Nelson, Sea	1.107
Trout,Mike, LAA	1.032
Donaldson,Josh, Tor	1.024
Raburn,Ryan, Cle	1.004
Altuve,Jose, Hou	.973
Forsythe,Logan, TB	.972
Young,Chris, NYY	.972
Castellanos,Nick, Det	.970
Longoria,Evan, TB	.960
Cain,Lorenzo, KC	.959

OPS vs. RHP
(minimum 377 PA)

Ortiz,David, Bos	1.008
Davis,Chris, Bal	.984
Trout,Mike, LAA	.978
Cabrera,Miguel, Det	.964
Encarnacion,Edwin, Tor	.950
Bautista,Jose, Tor	.932
Fielder,Prince, Tex	.923
Donaldson,Josh, Tor	.919
Choo,Shin-Soo, Tex	.917
2 tied with	.908

RC Per 27 Outs vs. LHP
(minimum 125 PA)

Cruz,Nelson, Sea	9.7
Trout,Mike, LAA	8.7
Beltre,Adrian, Tex	8.0
Altuve,Jose, Hou	8.0
Young,Chris, NYY	7.9
Donaldson,Josh, Tor	7.7
Cain,Lorenzo, KC	7.7
Castellanos,Nick, Det	7.6
Longoria,Evan, TB	7.5
Martinez,J.D., Det	7.3

RC Per 27 Outs vs. RHP
(minimum 377 PA)

Fielder,Prince, Tex	8.5
Trout,Mike, LAA	8.0
Davis,Chris, Bal	7.7
Cabrera,Miguel, Det	7.7
Encarnacion,Edwin, Tor	7.6
Donaldson,Josh, Tor	7.5
Kipnis,Jason, Cle	7.5
Abreu,Jose, CWS	7.2
Bautista,Jose, Tor	7.1
Ortiz,David, Bos	7.0

Highest RBI %
(minimum 502 PA)

Donaldson,Josh, Tor	43.85
Trout,Mike, LAA	43.60
Davis,Chris, Bal	43.00
Encarnacion,Edwin, Tor	42.63
Abreu,Jose, CWS	41.62
Bautista,Jose, Tor	41.59
Cabrera,Miguel, Det	40.71
Betts,Mookie, Bos	39.73
McCann,Brian, NYY	39.65
Cruz,Nelson, Sea	39.51

Lowest RBI %
(minimum 502 PA)

Gose,Anthony, Det	16.76
Semien,Marcus, Oak	20.81
Escobar,Alcides, KC	24.52
Kiermaier,Kevin, TB	25.46
Aybar,Erick, LAA	25.57
Pillar,Kevin, Tor	26.06
Cabrera,Asdrubal, TB	26.68
Andrus,Elvis, Tex	27.07
Garcia,Avisail, CWS	27.44
Sandoval,Pablo, Bos	27.52

Highest Strikeout per PA
(minimum 502 PA)

Davis,Chris, Bal	.310
Gose,Anthony, Det	.271
Martinez,J.D., Det	.271
Castellanos,Nick, Det	.255
Cruz,Nelson, Sea	.250
Calhoun,Kole, LAA	.239
Lawrie,Brett, Oak	.239
Garcia,Avisail, CWS	.235
Rodriguez,Alex, NYY	.234
Trout,Mike, LAA	.232

Lowest Strikeout per PA
(minimum 502 PA)

Brantley,Michael, Cle	.086
Altuve,Jose, Hou	.097
Beltre,Adrian, Tex	.105
Zobrist,Ben, Oak-KC	.105
Pujols,Albert, LAA	.109
Ramirez,Alexei, CWS	.109
Reddick,Josh, Oak	.112
Escobar,Alcides, KC	.113
Aybar,Erick, LAA	.114
2 tied with	.118

Home Runs At Home

Davis,Chris, Bal	29
Donaldson,Josh, Tor	24
Bautista,Jose, Tor	23
Machado,Manny, Bal	21
Martinez,J.D., Det	20
Pujols,Albert, LAA	20
Trout,Mike, LAA	20
Encarnacion,Edwin, Tor	18
Rodriguez,Alex, NYY	18
3 tied with	17

Home Runs Away

Cruz,Nelson, Sea	27
Ortiz,David, Bos	22
Encarnacion,Edwin, Tor	21
Trout,Mike, LAA	21
Pujols,Albert, LAA	20
Seager,Kyle, Sea	19
Davis,Chris, Bal	18
Martinez,J.D., Det	18
3 tied with	17

2015 American League Batting Leaders

Under Age 26: AB Per HR
(minimum 502 PA)

Trout,Mike, LAA	14.0
Machado,Manny, Bal	18.1
Perez,Salvador, KC	25.3
Betts,Mookie, Bos	33.2
Hosmer,Eric, KC	33.3
Lawrie,Brett, Oak	35.1
Castellanos,Nick, Det	36.6
Semien,Marcus, Oak	37.1
Altuve,Jose, Hou	42.5
Garcia,Avisail, CWS	42.5

Under Age 26: OPS
(minimum 502 PA)

Trout,Mike, LAA	.991
Machado,Manny, Bal	.861
Hosmer,Eric, KC	.822
Betts,Mookie, Bos	.820
Altuve,Jose, Hou	.812
Bogaerts,Xander, Bos	.776
Castellanos,Nick, Det	.721
Kiermaier,Kevin, TB	.718
Semien,Marcus, Oak	.715
2 tied with	.706

Under Age 26: RC/27 Outs
(minimum 502 PA)

Trout,Mike, LAA	8.2
Betts,Mookie, Bos	6.1
Machado,Manny, Bal	5.9
Hosmer,Eric, KC	5.7
Altuve,Jose, Hou	5.5
Bogaerts,Xander, Bos	5.3
Kiermaier,Kevin, TB	4.6
Gregorius,Didi, NYY	4.3
Castellanos,Nick, Det	4.0
Lawrie,Brett, Oak	4.0

Swing and Miss %
(minimum 1500 Pitches Seen)

Carter,Chris, Hou	36.5
Davis,Chris, Bal	34.4
Zunino,Mike, Sea	33.8
Souza,Steven, TB	32.1
Springer,George, Hou	31.8
Rasmus,Colby, Hou	31.4
Rodriguez,Alex, NYY	31.2
Garcia,Avisail, CWS	30.4
Martinez,J.D., Det	29.8
Cruz,Nelson, Sea	29.7

Highest First Swing %
(minimum 502 PA)

Burns,Billy, Oak	47.0
Garcia,Avisail, CWS	44.6
Jones,Adam, Bal	42.5
Martinez,J.D., Det	40.0
Calhoun,Kole, LAA	39.5
Altuve,Jose, Hou	39.3
Cabrera,Asdrubal, TB	37.7
Davis,Chris, Bal	37.2
Sandoval,Pablo, Bos	35.5
Castellanos,Nick, Det	34.5

Lowest First Swing %
(minimum 502 PA)

Trout,Mike, LAA	10.2
Mauer,Joe, Min	11.0
Holt,Brock, Bos	12.2
Gardner,Brett, NYY	13.1
Kipnis,Jason, Cle	14.1
Forsythe,Logan, TB	14.2
Betts,Mookie, Bos	14.4
Santana,Carlos, Cle	14.7
Vogt,Stephen, Oak	14.9
McCann,Brian, NYY	15.3

Home RC Per 27 Outs
(minimum 251 PA)

Cabrera,Miguel, Det	8.6
Davis,Chris, Bal	8.5
Donaldson,Josh, Tor	8.4
Bautista,Jose, Tor	8.1
Kipnis,Jason, Cle	8.0
Encarnacion,Edwin, Tor	7.4
Altuve,Jose, Hou	7.3
McCann,Brian, NYY	7.3
Betts,Mookie, Bos	7.2
Cain,Lorenzo, KC	7.2

Road RC Per 27 Outs
(minimum 251 PA)

Trout,Mike, LAA	9.2
Fielder,Prince, Tex	7.1
Encarnacion,Edwin, Tor	7.1
Cruz,Nelson, Sea	6.8
Donaldson,Josh, Tor	6.7
Abreu,Jose, CWS	6.7
Eaton,Adam, CWS	6.5
Brantley,Michael, Cle	6.4
Martinez,J.D., Det	6.2
Machado,Manny, Bal	5.9

Lead Changing RBI

Donaldson,Josh, Tor	42
Cruz,Nelson, Sea	37
Rodriguez,Alex, NYY	37
Davis,Chris, Bal	35
Hosmer,Eric, KC	35
Gattis,Evan, Hou	33
Moreland,Mitch, Tex	33
Ortiz,David, Bos	33
Trout,Mike, LAA	33
2 tied with	32

2015 National League Batting Leaders

Batting Average (minimum 502 PA)		On Base Percentage (minimum 502 PA)		Slugging Average (minimum 502 PA)		Home Runs	
Gordon,Dee, Mia	.333	Harper,Bryce, Was	.460	Harper,Bryce, Was	.649	Arenado,Nolan, Col	42
Harper,Bryce, Was	.330	Votto,Joey, Cin	.459	Arenado,Nolan, Col	.575	Harper,Bryce, Was	42
Goldschmidt,Paul, Ari	.321	Goldschmidt,Paul, Ari	.435	Goldschmidt,Paul, Ari	.570	Gonzalez,Carlos, Col	40
Posey,Buster, SF	.318	McCutchen,Andrew, Pit	.401	Votto,Joey, Cin	.541	Frazier,Todd, Cin	35
Pollock,A.J., Ari	.315	Rizzo,Anthony, ChC	.387	Gonzalez,Carlos, Col	.540	Goldschmidt,Paul, Ari	33
Escobar,Yunel, Was	.314	Posey,Buster, SF	.379	Peralta,David, Ari	.522	Rizzo,Anthony, ChC	31
Votto,Joey, Cin	.314	Escobar,Yunel, Was	.375	Rizzo,Anthony, ChC	.512	Votto,Joey, Cin	29
Peralta,David, Ari	.312	Peralta,David, Ari	.371	Carpenter,Matt, StL	.505	Carpenter,Matt, StL	28
Inciarte,Ender, Ari	.303	Markakis,Nick, Atl	.370	Braun,Ryan, Mil	.498	Gonzalez,Adrian, LAD	28
LeMahieu,DJ, Col	.301	Cervelli,Francisco, Pit	.370	Frazier,Todd, Cin	.498	4 tied with	27

Games		Plate Appearances		At Bats		Hits	
Rizzo,Anthony, ChC	160	Rizzo,Anthony, ChC	701	Frazier,Todd, Cin	619	Gordon,Dee, Mia	205
Goldschmidt,Paul, Ari	159	Goldschmidt,Paul, Ari	695	Arenado,Nolan, Col	616	Pollock,A.J., Ari	192
Votto,Joey, Cin	158	Votto,Joey, Cin	695	Gordon,Dee, Mia	615	Goldschmidt,Paul, Ari	182
Arenado,Nolan, Col	157	Fowler,Dexter, ChC	690	Blackmon,Charlie, Col	614	Markakis,Nick, Atl	181
Blackmon,Charlie, Col	157	Markakis,Nick, Atl	686	Markakis,Nick, Atl	612	Arenado,Nolan, Col	177
Bruce,Jay, Cin	157	McCutchen,Andrew, Pit	685	Pollock,A.J., Ari	609	Posey,Buster, SF	177
Frazier,Todd, Cin	157	Blackmon,Charlie, Col	682	Fowler,Dexter, ChC	596	Blackmon,Charlie, Col	176
Granderson,Curtis, NYM	157	Granderson,Curtis, NYM	682	Kemp,Matt, SD	596	Phillips,Brandon, Cin	173
McCutchen,Andrew, Pit	157	Frazier,Todd, Cin	678	Polanco,Gregory, Pit	593	Harper,Bryce, Was	172
Pollock,A.J., Ari	157	Pollock,A.J., Ari	673	Phillips,Brandon, Cin	588	Votto,Joey, Cin	171

Singles		Doubles		Triples		Total Bases	
Gordon,Dee, Mia	169	Carpenter,Matt, StL	44	Peralta,David, Ari	10	Arenado,Nolan, Col	354
Phillips,Brandon, Cin	140	Arenado,Nolan, Col	43	Blackmon,Charlie, Col	9	Harper,Bryce, Was	338
Markakis,Nick, Atl	139	Frazier,Todd, Cin	43	Fowler,Dexter, ChC	8	Goldschmidt,Paul, Ari	323
LeMahieu,DJ, Col	138	Pollock,A.J., Ari	39	Gordon,Dee, Mia	8	Frazier,Todd, Cin	308
Escobar,Yunel, Was	133	Goldschmidt,Paul, Ari	38	Ethier,Andre, LAD	7	Pollock,A.J., Ari	303
Posey,Buster, SF	130	Harper,Bryce, Was	38	Grichuk,Randal, StL	7	Rizzo,Anthony, ChC	300
Pollock,A.J., Ari	127	Markakis,Nick, Atl	38	Realmuto,J.T., Mia	7	Gonzalez,Carlos, Col	299
Duffy,Matt, SF	123	Murphy,Daniel, NYM	38	8 tied with	6	Votto,Joey, Cin	295
Galvis,Freddy, Phi	121	Rizzo,Anthony, ChC	38			Carpenter,Matt, StL	290
Inciarte,Ender, Ari	121	McCutchen,Andrew, Pit	36			2 tied with	276

Runs Scored		RBI		Walks		Strikeouts	
Harper,Bryce, Was	118	Arenado,Nolan, Col	130	Votto,Joey, Cin	143	Bryant,Kris, ChC	199
Pollock,A.J., Ari	111	Goldschmidt,Paul, Ari	110	Harper,Bryce, Was	124	Desmond,Ian, Was	187
Goldschmidt,Paul, Ari	103	Rizzo,Anthony, ChC	101	Goldschmidt,Paul, Ari	118	Pederson,Joc, LAD	170
Fowler,Dexter, ChC	102	Kemp,Matt, SD	100	McCutchen,Andrew, Pit	98	Upton,Justin, SD	159
Carpenter,Matt, StL	101	Bryant,Kris, ChC	99	Pederson,Joc, LAD	92	Taylor,Michael, Was	158
Granderson,Curtis, NYM	98	Harper,Bryce, Was	99	Granderson,Curtis, NYM	91	Fowler,Dexter, ChC	154
Arenado,Nolan, Col	97	Gonzalez,Carlos, Col	97	Fowler,Dexter, ChC	84	Carpenter,Matt, StL	151
Votto,Joey, Cin	95	McCutchen,Andrew, Pit	96	Carpenter,Matt, StL	81	Goldschmidt,Paul, Ari	151
Rizzo,Anthony, ChC	94	Posey,Buster, SF	95	Rizzo,Anthony, ChC	78	Granderson,Curtis, NYM	151
Blackmon,Charlie, Col	93	Gonzalez,Adrian, LAD	90	Bryant,Kris, ChC	77	Russell,Addison, ChC	149

2015 National League Batting Leaders

Intentional Walks

Goldschmidt,Paul, Ari	29
Harper,Bryce, Was	15
Votto,Joey, Cin	15
Arenado,Nolan, Col	13
McCutchen,Andrew, Pit	12
Lind,Adam, Mil	11
Markakis,Nick, Atl	11
Gonzalez,Adrian, LAD	10
Murphy,Daniel, NYM	10
Posey,Buster, SF	10

BA Bases Loaded
(minimum 10 PA)

Zimmerman,Ryan, Was	.667
Murphy,Daniel, NYM	.583
Peterson,Jace, Atl	.563
Hernandez,Cesar, Phi	.556
Pollock,A.J., Ari	.556
Duffy,Matt, SF	.500
Kendrick,Howie, LAD	.500
Rizzo,Anthony, ChC	.500
3 tied with	.462

Sacrifice Hits

Teheran,Julio, Atl	14
Koehler,Tom, Mia	12
Miller,Shelby, Atl	11
Gonzalez,Gio, Was	10
Haren,Dan, Mia-ChC	10
Latos,Mat, Mia-LAD	10
5 tied with	9

Sacrifice Flies

Arenado,Nolan, Col	11
Zimmerman,Ryan, Was	10
Bruce,Jay, Cin	9
McCutchen,Andrew, Pit	9
Molina,Yadier, StL	9
Pollock,A.J., Ari	9
6 tied with	8

BA Close & Late
(minimum 50 PA)

Revere,Ben, Phi	.381
Prado,Martin, Mia	.375
Gordon,Dee, Mia	.372
Pollock,A.J., Ari	.359
Pena,Brayan, Cin	.358
Upton Jr.,Melvin, SD	.340
Paulsen,Ben, Col	.339
Venable,Will, SD	.333
Coghlan,Chris, ChC	.329
Markakis,Nick, Atl	.327

Batting Average w/ RISP
(minimum 100 PA)

Freeman,Freddie, Atl	.376
Arenado,Nolan, Col	.373
Duffy,Matt, SF	.366
McCutchen,Andrew, Pit	.361
Kendrick,Howie, LAD	.360
Maybin,Cameron, Atl	.356
Braun,Ryan, Mil	.354
Posey,Buster, SF	.351
Goldschmidt,Paul, Ari	.340
Lind,Adam, Mil	.336

SLG vs. LHP
(minimum 125 PA)

Goldschmidt,Paul, Ari	.620
Frazier,Todd, Cin	.608
Harper,Bryce, Was	.552
Braun,Ryan, Mil	.550
Duda,Lucas, NYM	.545
Votto,Joey, Cin	.542
Pollock,A.J., Ari	.511
McCutchen,Andrew, Pit	.508
Posey,Buster, SF	.496
Byrd,Marlon, Cin-SF	.496

SLG vs. RHP
(minimum 377 PA)

Harper,Bryce, Was	.689
Gonzalez,Carlos, Col	.633
Arenado,Nolan, Col	.611
Goldschmidt,Paul, Ari	.556
Peralta,David, Ari	.552
Carpenter,Matt, StL	.541
Votto,Joey, Cin	.541
Rizzo,Anthony, ChC	.527
Ethier,Andre, LAD	.517
Granderson,Curtis, NYM	.504

Leadoff Hitters OBP
(minimum 150 PA)

Carpenter,Matt, StL	.389
Markakis,Nick, Atl	.379
Span,Denard, Was	.365
Granderson,Curtis, NYM	.360
Gordon,Dee, Mia	.360
Aoki,Nori, SF	.357
Pollock,A.J., Ari	.354
Blackmon,Charlie, Col	.352
Fowler,Dexter, ChC	.350
Myers,Wil, SD	.343

Cleanup Hitters SLG
(minimum 150 PA)

Harper,Bryce, Was	.740
Gonzalez,Carlos, Col	.610
Arenado,Nolan, Col	.598
Peralta,David, Ari	.561
Frazier,Todd, Cin	.537
Zimmerman,Ryan, Was	.514
Bruce,Jay, Cin	.511
Bour,Justin, Mia	.502
Rizzo,Anthony, ChC	.496
Gonzalez,Adrian, LAD	.495

BA vs. LHP
(minimum 125 PA)

Goldschmidt,Paul, Ari	.364
Gordon,Dee, Mia	.350
Votto,Joey, Cin	.331
McCutchen,Andrew, Pit	.328
Fowler,Dexter, ChC	.326
Pollock,A.J., Ari	.326
Prado,Martin, Mia	.325
Harper,Bryce, Was	.318
Pagan,Angel, SF	.318
Braun,Ryan, Mil	.317

BA vs. RHP
(minimum 377 PA)

Harper,Bryce, Was	.335
Inciarte,Ender, Ari	.331
Gordon,Dee, Mia	.327
Peralta,David, Ari	.325
Posey,Buster, SF	.319
Escobar,Yunel, Was	.314
Pollock,A.J., Ari	.312
Duffy,Matt, SF	.310
Goldschmidt,Paul, Ari	.309
Markakis,Nick, Atl	.306

Home BA
(minimum 251 PA)

Harper,Bryce, Was	.345
Goldschmidt,Paul, Ari	.341
Peralta,David, Ari	.336
Escobar,Yunel, Was	.336
Gordon,Dee, Mia	.333
Blackmon,Charlie, Col	.331
Inciarte,Ender, Ari	.330
Lind,Adam, Mil	.328
McCutchen,Andrew, Pit	.327
LeMahieu,DJ, Col	.321

Away BA
(minimum 251 PA)

Gordon,Dee, Mia	.333
Posey,Buster, SF	.330
Votto,Joey, Cin	.326
Phillips,Brandon, Cin	.320
Harper,Bryce, Was	.316
Markakis,Nick, Atl	.315
Braun,Ryan, Mil	.315
Pollock,A.J., Ari	.314
Murphy,Daniel, NYM	.310
Yelich,Christian, Mia	.309

OBP vs. LHP
(minimum 125 PA)

Votto,Joey, Cin	.467
Goldschmidt,Paul, Ari	.462
Harper,Bryce, Was	.434
McCutchen,Andrew, Pit	.410
Rizzo,Anthony, ChC	.409
Braun,Ryan, Mil	.407
Fowler,Dexter, ChC	.399
Prado,Martin, Mia	.391
LeMahieu,DJ, Col	.390
Hernandez,Cesar, Phi	.381

OBP vs. RHP
(minimum 377 PA)

Harper,Bryce, Was	.471
Votto,Joey, Cin	.456
Goldschmidt,Paul, Ari	.428
McCutchen,Andrew, Pit	.399
Markakis,Nick, Atl	.398
Granderson,Curtis, NYM	.388
Carpenter,Matt, StL	.385
Posey,Buster, SF	.385
Peralta,David, Ari	.384
Ethier,Andre, LAD	.383

2015 National League Batting Leaders

Stolen Bases		Caught Stealing		Highest SB Success Pct (minimum 20 SBA)		Lowest SB Success Pct (minimum 20 SBA)	
Gordon,Dee, Mia	58	Gordon,Dee, Mia	20	Heyward,Jason, StL	88.5	Peterson,Jace, Atl	54.5
Hamilton,Billy, Cin	57	Blackmon,Charlie, Col	13	LeMahieu,DJ, Col	88.5	Rollins,Jimmy, LAD	60.0
Blackmon,Charlie, Col	43	Inciarte,Ender, Ari	10	Phillips,Brandon, Cin	88.5	Frazier,Todd, Cin	61.9
Pollock,A.J., Ari	39	Marte,Starling, Pit	10	Hamilton,Billy, Cin	87.7	Wong,Kolten, StL	65.2
Marte,Starling, Pit	30	Peterson,Jace, Atl	10	Braun,Ryan, Mil	85.7	Herrera,Odubel, Phi	66.7
Polanco,Gregory, Pit	27	Polanco,Gregory, Pit	10	Pollock,A.J., Ari	84.8	Inciarte,Ender, Ari	67.7
Segura,Jean, Mil	25	7 tied with	8	Revere,Ben, Phi	82.8	Polanco,Gregory, Pit	73.0
Braun,Ryan, Mil	24			Goldschmidt,Paul, Ari	80.8	Rizzo,Anthony, ChC	73.9
Revere,Ben, Phi	24			Segura,Jean, Mil	80.6	Fowler,Dexter, ChC	74.1
4 tied with	23			Owings,Chris, Ari	80.0	Gordon,Dee, Mia	74.4

Steals of Third		Grounded Into DP		Grounded Into DP Pct (minimum 50 GIDP Ops)		Hit By Pitch	
Hamilton,Billy, Cin	16	Escobar,Yunel, Was	24	Puig,Yasiel, LAD	1.56	Rizzo,Anthony, ChC	30
Blackmon,Charlie, Col	9	Peralta,Jhonny, StL	23	Belt,Brandon, SF	2.80	Marte,Starling, Pit	19
Gordon,Dee, Mia	8	Ramirez,Aramis, Mil-Pit	23	Granderson,Curtis, NYM	3.49	Kang,Jung Ho, Pit	17
Phillips,Brandon, Cin	8	Duffy,Matt, SF	22	Bryant,Kris, ChC	4.76	Wong,Kolten, StL	15
Pollock,A.J., Ari	8	Gonzalez,Adrian, LAD	21	Blanco,Gregor, SF	5.00	Duda,Lucas, NYM	14
Braun,Ryan, Mil	6	Braun,Ryan, Mil	20	Asche,Cody, Phi	5.06	Blackmon,Charlie, Col	13
Inciarte,Ender, Ari	6	LeMahieu,DJ, Col	20	Carpenter,Matt, StL	5.26	Dietrich,Derek, Mia	13
Bruce,Jay, Cin	4	5 tied with	19	Norris,Derek, SD	5.26	Turner,Justin, LAD	13
LeMahieu,DJ, Col	4			Freeman,Freddie, Atl	5.56	McCutchen,Andrew, Pit	12
7 tied with	3			2 tied with	5.68	2 tied with	11

Pitches Seen		At Bats Per Home Run (minimum 502 PA)		Highest GB/FB Ratio (minimum 502 PA)		Lowest GB/FB Ratio (minimum 502 PA)	
Votto,Joey, Cin	3020	Harper,Bryce, Was	12.4	Yelich,Christian, Mia	4.16	Duda,Lucas, NYM	0.54
Granderson,Curtis, NYM	2981	Gonzalez,Carlos, Col	13.9	Gordon,Dee, Mia	3.19	Frazier,Todd, Cin	0.69
Goldschmidt,Paul, Ari	2917	Arenado,Nolan, Col	14.7	Maybin,Cameron, Atl	2.89	Carpenter,Matt, StL	0.71
Fowler,Dexter, ChC	2819	Goldschmidt,Paul, Ari	17.2	LeMahieu,DJ, Col	2.80	Granderson,Curtis, NYM	0.73
Carpenter,Matt, StL	2807	Duda,Lucas, NYM	17.4	Simmons,Andrelton, Atl	2.51	Bryant,Kris, ChC	0.76
McCutchen,Andrew, Pit	2780	Frazier,Todd, Cin	17.7	Heyward,Jason, StL	2.44	Arenado,Nolan, Col	0.78
Rizzo,Anthony, ChC	2751	Pederson,Joc, LAD	18.5	Segura,Jean, Mil	2.43	Rizzo,Anthony, ChC	0.79
Blackmon,Charlie, Col	2727	Votto,Joey, Cin	18.8	Marte,Starling, Pit	2.37	Bruce,Jay, Cin	0.84
Markakis,Nick, Atl	2711	Rizzo,Anthony, ChC	18.9	Escobar,Yunel, Was	2.35	Upton,Justin, SD	0.88
Harper,Bryce, Was	2682	Braun,Ryan, Mil	20.2	Ramos,Wilson, Was	2.23	Belt,Brandon, SF	0.88

Pitches Per Plate App (minimum 502 PA)		Pct Pitches Taken (minimum 1500 Pitches)		Best BPS on OutZ (minimum 502 PA)		Worst BPS on OutZ (minimum 502 PA)	
Granderson,Curtis, NYM	4.37	Votto,Joey, Cin	63.3	Votto,Joey, Cin	.629	Coghlan,Chris, ChC	.246
Votto,Joey, Cin	4.35	Rendon,Anthony, Was	62.5	Gordon,Dee, Mia	.607	Ramos,Wilson, Was	.257
Carpenter,Matt, StL	4.22	Granderson,Curtis, NYM	62.5	Goldschmidt,Paul, Ari	.606	Russell,Addison, ChC	.257
Pederson,Joc, LAD	4.21	Werth,Jayson, Was	62.1	Rizzo,Anthony, ChC	.594	Peterson,Jace, Atl	.272
Goldschmidt,Paul, Ari	4.20	Goldschmidt,Paul, Ari	61.9	Arenado,Nolan, Col	.577	Taylor,Michael, Was	.285
Belt,Brandon, SF	4.17	Carpenter,Matt, StL	61.1	Molina,Yadier, StL	.570	Norris,Derek, SD	.301
Russell,Addison, ChC	4.12	Grandal,Yasmani, LAD	60.9	Harper,Bryce, Was	.566	Lind,Adam, Mil	.315
Harper,Bryce, Was	4.10	Prado,Martin, Mia	60.5	Inciarte,Ender, Ari	.556	Owings,Chris, Ari	.317
Duda,Lucas, NYM	4.09	Utley,Chase, Phi-LAD	59.1	McCutchen,Andrew, Pit	.556	Rollins,Jimmy, LAD	.318
Fowler,Dexter, ChC	4.09	Heyward,Jason, StL	59.0	Peralta,David, Ari	.553	Fowler,Dexter, ChC	.329

2015 National League Batting Leaders

Best OPS vs Fastballs (minimum 251 PA)		Best OPS vs Curveballs (minimum 50 PA)		Best OPS vs Changeups (minimum 50 PA)		Best OPS vs Sliders (minimum 32 PA)	
Harper,Bryce, Was	1.145	Bryant,Kris, ChC	1.264	Gordon,Dee, Mia	1.212	Pence,Hunter, SF	1.218
Votto,Joey, Cin	1.010	Votto,Joey, Cin	1.260	Turner,Justin, LAD	1.068	Paulsen,Ben, Col	1.204
Arenado,Nolan, Col	.969	Harper,Bryce, Was	1.132	Posey,Buster, SF	1.024	Harper,Bryce, Was	1.173
Goldschmidt,Paul, Ari	.969	Marte,Starling, Pit	1.058	Carpenter,Matt, StL	.986	Hernandez,Cesar, Phi	1.027
Rizzo,Anthony, ChC	.961	Gonzalez,Carlos, Col	.999	Castro,Starlin, ChC	.984	Blackmon,Charlie, Col	1.025
Frazier,Todd, Cin	.947	Byrd,Marlon, Cin-SF	.969	Lind,Adam, Mil	.977	Braun,Ryan, Mil	1.019
Pollock,A.J., Ari	.920	Goldschmidt,Paul, Ari	.939	Duffy,Matt, SF	.968	Hundley,Nick, Col	.990
Duda,Lucas, NYM	.919	Polanco,Gregory, Pit	.913	LeMahieu,DJ, Col	.963	Murphy,Daniel, NYM	.944
Kang,Jung Ho, Pit	.911	Granderson,Curtis, NYM	.901	Norris,Derek, SD	.958	Guerrero,Alex, LAD	.937
Peralta,David, Ari	.908	Blackmon,Charlie, Col	.871	Ethier,Andre, LAD	.939	Tulowitzki,Troy, Col	.937

OPS (minimum 502 PA)		OPS First Half (minimum 260 PA)		OPS Second Half (minimum 201 PA)		OPS by Catchers (minimum 251 PA)	
Harper,Bryce, Was	1.109	Harper,Bryce, Was	1.168	Votto,Joey, Cin	1.152	d'Arnaud,Travis, NYM	.835
Goldschmidt,Paul, Ari	1.005	Goldschmidt,Paul, Ari	1.064	Harper,Bryce, Was	1.043	Posey,Buster, SF	.825
Votto,Joey, Cin	1.000	Rizzo,Anthony, ChC	.955	Peralta,David, Ari	.977	Hundley,Nick, Col	.807
Rizzo,Anthony, ChC	.899	Stanton,Giancarlo, Mia	.952	Gonzalez,Carlos, Col	.975	Castillo,Welington, ChC-Ari	.803
Arenado,Nolan, Col	.898	Arenado,Nolan, Col	.926	Carpenter,Matt, StL	.950	Grandal,Yasmani, LAD	.780
Peralta,David, Ari	.893	Frazier,Todd, Cin	.922	Cespedes,Yoenis, NYM	.942	Cervelli,Francisco, Pit	.778
McCutchen,Andrew, Pit	.889	McCutchen,Andrew, Pit	.892	Goldschmidt,Paul, Ari	.931	Montero,Miguel, ChC	.769
Carpenter,Matt, StL	.871	Freeman,Freddie, Atl	.887	Pollock,A.J., Ari	.926	Pierzynski,A.J., Atl	.765
Pollock,A.J., Ari	.865	Lind,Adam, Mil	.887	Kang,Jung Ho, Pit	.913	Lucroy,Jonathan, Mil	.719
Gonzalez,Carlos, Col	.864	Posey,Buster, SF	.880	Granderson,Curtis, NYM	.898	Realmuto,J.T., Mia	.702

OPS by First Basemen (minimum 251 PA)		OPS by Second Basemen (minimum 251 PA)		OPS by Third Basemen (minimum 251 PA)		OPS by Shortstops (minimum 251 PA)	
Goldschmidt,Paul, Ari	1.014	Murphy,Daniel, NYM	.842	Bryant,Kris, ChC	.902	Tulowitzki,Troy, Col	.816
Votto,Joey, Cin	1.000	Panik,Joe, SF	.825	Arenado,Nolan, Col	.896	Crawford,Brandon, SF	.790
Rizzo,Anthony, ChC	.899	Gordon,Dee, Mia	.778	Turner,Justin, LAD	.886	Suarez,Eugenio, Cin	.760
Belt,Brandon, SF	.868	Spangenberg,Cory, SD	.774	Carpenter,Matt, StL	.866	Peralta,Jhonny, StL	.752
Gonzalez,Adrian, LAD	.852	Espinosa,Danny, Was	.771	Franco,Maikel, Phi	.829	Tejada,Ruben, NYM	.700
Duda,Lucas, NYM	.842	Walker,Neil, Pit	.758	Frazier,Todd, Cin	.809	Hechavarria,Adeiny, Mia	.689
Freeman,Freddie, Atl	.833	Kendrick,Howie, LAD	.749	Solarte,Yangervis, SD	.805	Desmond,Ian, Was	.672
Bour,Justin, Mia	.803	LeMahieu,DJ, Col	.744	Escobar,Yunel, Was	.793	Flores,Wilmer, NYM	.668
Lind,Adam, Mil	.800	Phillips,Brandon, Cin	.727	Duffy,Matt, SF	.791	Simmons,Andrelton, Atl	.661
Alvarez,Pedro, Pit	.780	Wong,Kolten, StL	.706	Kang,Jung Ho, Pit	.789	Galvis,Freddy, Phi	.655

OPS by Left Fielders (minimum 251 PA)		OPS by Center Fielders (minimum 251 PA)		OPS by Right Fielders (minimum 251 PA)		OPS by Pitchers (minimum 50 PA)	
Peralta,David, Ari	.916	McCutchen,Andrew, Pit	.893	Harper,Bryce, Was	1.087	Bumgarner,Madison, SF	.709
Holliday,Matt, StL	.815	Pollock,A.J., Ari	.866	Stanton,Giancarlo, Mia	.946	Ross,Tyson, SD	.652
Davis,Khris, Mil	.812	Blackmon,Charlie, Col	.808	Gonzalez,Carlos, Col	.860	Greinke,Zack, LAD	.575
Coghlan,Chris, ChC	.811	Span,Denard, Was	.796	Braun,Ryan, Mil	.836	Syndergaard,Noah, NYM	.530
Upton,Justin, SD	.796	Pederson,Joc, LAD	.770	Inciarte,Ender, Ari	.835	Scherzer,Max, Was	.463
Yelich,Christian, Mia	.785	Fowler,Dexter, ChC	.762	Granderson,Curtis, NYM	.820	Niese,Jon, NYM	.438
Marte,Starling, Pit	.782	Herrera,Odubel, Phi	.756	Ethier,Andre, LAD	.820	Heston,Chris, SF	.431
Byrd,Marlon, Cin-SF	.749	Gomez,Carlos, Mil	.749	Heyward,Jason, StL	.794	Arrieta,Jake, ChC	.428
Aoki,Nori, SF	.733	Maybin,Cameron, Atl	.697	Puig,Yasiel, LAD	.771	Wood,Alex, Atl-LAD	.420
Cuddyer,Michael, NYM	.723	Ozuna,Marcell, Mia	.678	Kemp,Matt, SD	.748	deGrom,Jacob, NYM	.417

2015 National League Batting Leaders

OPS Batting Left vs. LHP
(minimum 125 PA)

Votto,Joey, Cin	1.009
Harper,Bryce, Was	.986
Rizzo,Anthony, ChC	.881
Duda,Lucas, NYM	.878
Gordon,Dee, Mia	.823
Belt,Brandon, SF	.802
Gonzalez,Adrian, LAD	.782
Carpenter,Matt, StL	.752
Herrera,Odubel, Phi	.720
Crawford,Brandon, SF	.716

OPS Batting Left vs. RHP
(minimum 377 PA)

Harper,Bryce, Was	1.160
Votto,Joey, Cin	.997
Gonzalez,Carlos, Col	.997
Peralta,David, Ari	.936
Carpenter,Matt, StL	.926
Rizzo,Anthony, ChC	.905
Ethier,Andre, LAD	.900
Granderson,Curtis, NYM	.892
Lind,Adam, Mil	.883
Gonzalez,Adrian, LAD	.850

OPS Batting Right vs. LHP
(minimum 125 PA)

Goldschmidt,Paul, Ari	1.073
Braun,Ryan, Mil	.957
McCutchen,Andrew, Pit	.918
Frazier,Todd, Cin	.908
Pollock,A.J., Ari	.881
Fowler,Dexter, ChC	.865
Prado,Martin, Mia	.856
Posey,Buster, SF	.854
Kemp,Matt, SD	.824
Byrd,Marlon, Cin-SF	.820

OPS Batting Right vs. RHP
(minimum 377 PA)

Goldschmidt,Paul, Ari	.986
Arenado,Nolan, Col	.931
McCutchen,Andrew, Pit	.881
Bryant,Kris, ChC	.875
Pollock,A.J., Ari	.860
Upton,Justin, SD	.848
Posey,Buster, SF	.847
Braun,Ryan, Mil	.821
Duffy,Matt, SF	.803
Escobar,Yunel, Was	.798

OPS vs. LHP
(minimum 125 PA)

Goldschmidt,Paul, Ari	1.081
Votto,Joey, Cin	1.009
Harper,Bryce, Was	.986
Braun,Ryan, Mil	.957
McCutchen,Andrew, Pit	.918
Frazier,Todd, Cin	.908
Pollock,A.J., Ari	.881
Rizzo,Anthony, ChC	.881
Duda,Lucas, NYM	.878
Fowler,Dexter, ChC	.865

OPS vs. RHP
(minimum 377 PA)

Harper,Bryce, Was	1.160
Gonzalez,Carlos, Col	.997
Votto,Joey, Cin	.997
Goldschmidt,Paul, Ari	.984
Peralta,David, Ari	.936
Arenado,Nolan, Col	.931
Carpenter,Matt, StL	.926
Rizzo,Anthony, ChC	.905
Ethier,Andre, LAD	.900
Granderson,Curtis, NYM	.892

RC Per 27 Outs vs. LHP
(minimum 125 PA)

Goldschmidt,Paul, Ari	11.7
Votto,Joey, Cin	9.8
Rizzo,Anthony, ChC	8.4
Harper,Bryce, Was	7.8
McCutchen,Andrew, Pit	7.7
Braun,Ryan, Mil	7.0
Kemp,Matt, SD	7.0
Arenado,Nolan, Col	6.8
Byrd,Marlon, Cin-SF	6.3
Lagares,Juan, NYM	6.3

RC Per 27 Outs vs. RHP
(minimum 377 PA)

Harper,Bryce, Was	10.9
Votto,Joey, Cin	9.0
Gonzalez,Carlos, Col	8.3
Goldschmidt,Paul, Ari	8.0
Lind,Adam, Mil	7.7
Carpenter,Matt, StL	7.6
Granderson,Curtis, NYM	7.6
McCutchen,Andrew, Pit	7.5
Peralta,David, Ari	7.1
Bryant,Kris, ChC	6.8

Highest RBI %
(minimum 502 PA)

Arenado,Nolan, Col	45.06
Harper,Bryce, Was	43.67
Goldschmidt,Paul, Ari	43.50
Braun,Ryan, Mil	41.79
McCutchen,Andrew, Pit	41.56
Bryant,Kris, ChC	41.08
Carpenter,Matt, StL	40.66
Gonzalez,Carlos, Col	40.42
Rizzo,Anthony, ChC	40.42
Votto,Joey, Cin	40.14

Lowest RBI %
(minimum 502 PA)

Pagan,Angel, SF	21.59
Rollins,Jimmy, LAD	21.59
Owings,Chris, Ari	21.78
Simmons,Andrelton, Atl	23.24
Desmond,Ian, Was	25.96
Herrera,Odubel, Phi	26.23
Coghlan,Chris, ChC	26.50
Fowler,Dexter, ChC	26.65
Galvis,Freddy, Phi	26.82
Segura,Jean, Mil	26.90

Highest Strikeout per PA
(minimum 502 PA)

Taylor,Michael, Was	.309
Bryant,Kris, ChC	.306
Desmond,Ian, Was	.292
Pederson,Joc, LAD	.291
Russell,Addison, ChC	.285
Howard,Ryan, Phi	.274
Byrd,Marlon, Cin-SF	.267
Belt,Brandon, SF	.264
Owings,Chris, Ari	.261
Upton,Justin, SD	.256

Lowest Strikeout per PA
(minimum 502 PA)

Murphy,Daniel, NYM	.071
Simmons,Andrelton, Atl	.082
Posey,Buster, SF	.083
Solarte,Yangervis, SD	.098
Inciarte,Ender, Ari	.103
Phillips,Brandon, Cin	.109
Molina,Yadier, StL	.111
Escobar,Yunel, Was	.118
Markakis,Nick, Atl	.121
Prado,Martin, Mia	.123

Home Runs At Home

Gonzalez,Carlos, Col	24
Harper,Bryce, Was	23
Bryant,Kris, ChC	21
Arenado,Nolan, Col	20
Duda,Lucas, NYM	19
Frazier,Todd, Cin	19
Gonzalez,Adrian, LAD	17
Davis,Khris, Mil	16
Upton,Justin, SD	15
3 tied with	14

Home Runs Away

Arenado,Nolan, Col	22
Goldschmidt,Paul, Ari	20
Rizzo,Anthony, ChC	20
Harper,Bryce, Was	19
Braun,Ryan, Mil	17
Frazier,Todd, Cin	16
Gonzalez,Carlos, Col	16
Carpenter,Matt, StL	15
Votto,Joey, Cin	15
2 tied with	14

2015 National League Batting Leaders

Under Age 26: AB Per HR
(minimum 502 PA)

Harper,Bryce, Was	12.4
Arenado,Nolan, Col	14.7
Pederson,Joc, LAD	18.5
Bryant,Kris, ChC	21.5
Flores,Wilmer, NYM	30.2
Taylor,Michael, Was	33.7
Russell,Addison, ChC	36.5
Duffy,Matt, SF	47.8
Castro,Starlin, ChC	49.7
Wong,Kolten, StL	50.6

Under Age 26: OPS
(minimum 502 PA)

Harper,Bryce, Was	1.109
Arenado,Nolan, Col	.898
Bryant,Kris, ChC	.858
Yelich,Christian, Mia	.782
Pederson,Joc, LAD	.763
Duffy,Matt, SF	.762
Herrera,Odubel, Phi	.762
Inciarte,Ender, Ari	.747
Wong,Kolten, StL	.707
Flores,Wilmer, NYM	.703

Under Age 26: RC/27 Outs
(minimum 502 PA)

Harper,Bryce, Was	9.9
Bryant,Kris, ChC	6.6
Arenado,Nolan, Col	6.6
Duffy,Matt, SF	5.2
Yelich,Christian, Mia	4.9
Herrera,Odubel, Phi	4.8
Inciarte,Ender, Ari	4.7
Taylor,Michael, Was	4.3
Polanco,Gregory, Pit	4.3
Pederson,Joc, LAD	4.2

Swing and Miss %
(minimum 1500 Pitches Seen)

Pederson,Joc, LAD	35.1
Bryant,Kris, ChC	34.9
Soler,Jorge, ChC	33.4
Davis,Khris, Mil	32.6
Taylor,Michael, Was	32.6
Howard,Ryan, Phi	31.2
Reynolds,Mark, StL	31.1
Upton,Justin, SD	31.0
Alvarez,Pedro, Pit	30.3
Russell,Addison, ChC	30.2

Highest First Swing %
(minimum 502 PA)

Byrd,Marlon, Cin-SF	48.9
Taylor,Michael, Was	40.9
Crawford,Brandon, SF	40.2
Ramos,Wilson, Was	39.8
Molina,Yadier, StL	39.6
Desmond,Ian, Was	39.2
Belt,Brandon, SF	39.1
Frazier,Todd, Cin	39.1
Marte,Starling, Pit	39.1
Escobar,Yunel, Was	38.9

Lowest First Swing %
(minimum 502 PA)

Blackmon,Charlie, Col	5.9
Granderson,Curtis, NYM	8.3
Prado,Martin, Mia	11.9
Carpenter,Matt, StL	14.4
Pagan,Angel, SF	17.5
Lind,Adam, Mil	17.9
Markakis,Nick, Atl	18.0
Heyward,Jason, StL	18.7
Yelich,Christian, Mia	20.2
Duda,Lucas, NYM	20.3

Home RC Per 27 Outs
(minimum 251 PA)

Harper,Bryce, Was	11.5
Goldschmidt,Paul, Ari	9.7
Votto,Joey, Cin	9.7
Bryant,Kris, ChC	8.8
McCutchen,Andrew, Pit	8.7
Lind,Adam, Mil	8.5
Arenado,Nolan, Col	7.6
Gonzalez,Carlos, Col	7.4
Blackmon,Charlie, Col	7.3
Peralta,David, Ari	7.2

Road RC Per 27 Outs
(minimum 251 PA)

Votto,Joey, Cin	8.8
Harper,Bryce, Was	8.4
Goldschmidt,Paul, Ari	8.0
Braun,Ryan, Mil	7.2
Pollock,A.J., Ari	7.2
Freeman,Freddie, Atl	6.9
Granderson,Curtis, NYM	6.9
Rizzo,Anthony, ChC	6.8
Carpenter,Matt, StL	6.8
McCutchen,Andrew, Pit	6.6

Lead Changing RBI

Bryant,Kris, ChC	42
Kemp,Matt, SD	42
Arenado,Nolan, Col	38
Frazier,Todd, Cin	37
Goldschmidt,Paul, Ari	37
Harper,Bryce, Was	37
Gonzalez,Carlos, Col	36
Carpenter,Matt, StL	34
Gonzalez,Adrian, LAD	33
Posey,Buster, SF	33

2015 American League Pitching Leaders

Earned Run Average (minimum 162 IP)		Winning Percentage (minimum 15 Decisions)		Opponent Batting Average (minimum 162 IP)		Baserunners Per 9 IP (minimum 162 IP)	
Price,David, Det-Tor	2.45	Eovaldi,Nathan, NYY	.824	Estrada,Marco, Tor	.203	Keuchel,Dallas, Hou	9.23
Keuchel,Dallas, Hou	2.48	Price,David, Det-Tor	.783	Keuchel,Dallas, Hou	.217	Estrada,Marco, Tor	9.65
Gray,Sonny, Oak	2.73	McHugh,Collin, Hou	.731	Gray,Sonny, Oak	.217	Price,David, Det-Tor	9.80
Kazmir,Scott, Oak-Hou	3.10	Hutchison,Drew, Tor	.722	Archer,Chris, TB	.220	Gray,Sonny, Oak	9.82
Estrada,Marco, Tor	3.13	Keuchel,Dallas, Hou	.714	Salazar,Danny, Cle	.226	Carrasco,Carlos, Cle	9.90
Archer,Chris, TB	3.23	Gray,Sonny, Oak	.667	Santiago,Hector, LAA	.227	Kluber,Corey, Cle	9.93
Chen,Wei-Yin, Bal	3.34	Hernandez,Felix, Sea	.667	Carrasco,Carlos, Cle	.228	Sale,Chris, CWS	10.35
Odorizzi,Jake, TB	3.35	Lewis,Colby, Tex	.654	Price,David, Det-Tor	.230	Archer,Chris, TB	10.36
Quintana,Jose, CWS	3.36	Buehrle,Mark, Tor	.652	Kluber,Corey, Cle	.231	Salazar,Danny, Cle	10.51
Sale,Chris, CWS	3.41	2 tied with	.647	Odorizzi,Jake, TB	.231	Odorizzi,Jake, TB	10.52

Games		Games Started		Complete Games		Shutouts	
Jepsen,Kevin, TB-Min	75	Archer,Chris, TB	34	Buehrle,Mark, Tor	4	Gray,Sonny, Oak	2
Betances,Dellin, NYY	74	Dickey,R.A., Tor	33	Kluber,Corey, Cle	4	Hernandez,Felix, Sea	2
Shaw,Bryan, Cle	74	Gallardo,Yovani, Tex	33	Carrasco,Carlos, Cle	3	Keuchel,Dallas, Hou	2
Wilson,Justin, NYY	74	Keuchel,Dallas, Hou	33	Gray,Sonny, Oak	3	Montgomery,Mike, Sea	2
Tolleson,Shawn, Tex	73	Lewis,Colby, Tex	33	Keuchel,Dallas, Hou	3	Samardzija,Jeff, CWS	2
Herrera,Kelvin, KC	72	Volquez,Edinson, KC	33	Price,David, Det-Tor	3	20 tied with	1
Salas,Fernando, LAA	72	11 tied with	32	8 tied with	2		
Duke,Zach, CWS	71						
5 tied with	70						

Wins		Losses		No Decisions		Wild Pitches	
Keuchel,Dallas, Hou	20	Kluber,Corey, Cle	16	Karns,Nate, TB	14	Richards,Garrett, LAA	17
McHugh,Collin, Hou	19	Chavez,Jesse, Oak	15	Santiago,Hector, LAA	14	Karns,Nate, TB	15
Hernandez,Felix, Sea	18	Danks,John, CWS	15	Kazmir,Scott, Oak-Hou	13	Simon,Alfredo, Det	14
Price,David, Det-Tor	18	Porcello,Rick, Bos	15	Pelfrey,Mike, Min	13	Archer,Chris, TB	13
Lewis,Colby, Tex	17	Archer,Chris, TB	13	Quintana,Jose, CWS	13	Gray,Sonny, Oak	13
Buehrle,Mark, Tor	15	Samardzija,Jeff, CWS	13	Sabathia,CC, NYY	13	Porcello,Rick, Bos	12
Richards,Garrett, LAA	15	6 tied with	12	Chen,Wei-Yin, Bal	12	Duffy,Danny, KC	11
4 tied with	14			Dickey,R.A., Tor	11	Wilson,C.J., LAA	11
				Volquez,Edinson, KC	11	5 tied with	10
				10 tied with	10		

Strikeouts		Walks Allowed		Intentional Walks Allowed		Hit Batters	
Sale,Chris, CWS	274	Bauer,Trevor, Cle	79	Olson,Tyler, Sea	7	Martinez,Nick, Tex	13
Archer,Chris, TB	252	Richards,Garrett, LAA	76	Feliz,Neftali, Tex-Det	6	Sale,Chris, CWS	13
Kluber,Corey, Cle	245	Volquez,Edinson, KC	72	Gibson,Kyle, Min	6	Pelfrey,Mike, Min	12
Price,David, Det-Tor	225	Rodon,Carlos, CWS	71	Jennings,Dan, CWS	6	Samardzija,Jeff, CWS	12
Carrasco,Carlos, Cle	216	Santiago,Hector, LAA	71	8 tied with	5	Weaver,Jered, LAA	12
Keuchel,Dallas, Hou	216	Gallardo,Yovani, Tex	68			Dickey,R.A., Tor	11
Salazar,Danny, Cle	195	Jimenez,Ubaldo, Bal	68			Hutchison,Drew, Tor	11
Hernandez,Felix, Sea	191	Simon,Alfredo, Det	68			Jimenez,Ubaldo, Bal	11
Quintana,Jose, CWS	177	Archer,Chris, TB	66			Kluber,Corey, Cle	11
Richards,Garrett, LAA	176	Gibson,Kyle, Min	65			Lewis,Colby, Tex	11

2015 American League Pitching Leaders

Runs Allowed			Hits Allowed			Doubles Allowed			Home Runs Allowed	
Samardzija,Jeff, CWS	122		Samardzija,Jeff, CWS	228		Miley,Wade, Bos	51		Guthrie,Jeremy, KC	29
Lewis,Colby, Tex	114		Quintana,Jose, CWS	218		Chen,Wei-Yin, Bal	50		Hughes,Phil, Min	29
Simon,Alfredo, Det	112		Buehrle,Mark, Tor	214		Danks,John, CWS	47		Samardzija,Jeff, CWS	29
Danks,John, CWS	104		Lewis,Colby, Tex	211		Quintana,Jose, CWS	47		Sanchez,Anibal, Det	29
Hutchison,Drew, Tor	103		McHugh,Collin, Hou	207		Simon,Alfredo, Det	47		Santiago,Hector, LAA	29
Porcello,Rick, Bos	103		Miley,Wade, Bos	201		Buehrle,Mark, Tor	46		Chen,Wei-Yin, Bal	28
Guthrie,Jeremy, KC	101		Simon,Alfredo, Det	201		Kluber,Corey, Cle	45		Sabathia,CC, NYY	28
Buehrle,Mark, Tor	100		Pelfrey,Mike, Min	198		Lewis,Colby, Tex	44		Lewis,Colby, Tex	26
Miley,Wade, Bos	98		Porcello,Rick, Bos	196		Tillman,Chris, Bal	42		4 tied with	25
2 tied with	97		2 tied with	195		Gibson,Kyle, Min	41			

Run Support Per Nine IP			% Pitches In Strike Zone			Pitches Per Start			Pitches Per Batter	
(minimum 162 IP)			(minimum 162 IP)			(minimum 30 GS)			(minimum 162 IP)	
Buehrle,Mark, Tor	6.89		Chen,Wei-Yin, Bal	48.2		Sale,Chris, CWS	107.2		Buehrle,Mark, Tor	3.42
Lewis,Colby, Tex	6.20		Price,David, Det-Tor	47.8		Price,David, Det-Tor	105.9		Ramirez,Erasmo, TB	3.62
Keuchel,Dallas, Hou	5.82		Porcello,Rick, Bos	47.0		Keuchel,Dallas, Hou	105.8		Samardzija,Jeff, CWS	3.67
McHugh,Collin, Hou	5.79		Salazar,Danny, Cle	46.6		Quintana,Jose, CWS	105.4		Hernandez,Felix, Sea	3.68
Price,David, Det-Tor	5.60		Samardzija,Jeff, CWS	46.4		Samardzija,Jeff, CWS	104.3		Dickey,R.A., Tor	3.69
Ventura,Yordano, KC	5.51		Ramirez,Erasmo, TB	46.3		Kluber,Corey, Cle	102.3		Lewis,Colby, Tex	3.69
Miley,Wade, Bos	5.48		Dickey,R.A., Tor	46.2		Salazar,Danny, Cle	101.6		Kluber,Corey, Cle	3.69
Santiago,Hector, LAA	5.28		Archer,Chris, TB	46.1		Richards,Garrett, LAA	101.6		Gray,Sonny, Oak	3.70
Walker,Taijuan, Sea	5.25		Santiago,Hector, LAA	45.6		Archer,Chris, TB	101.4		Sabathia,CC, NYY	3.72
Volquez,Edinson, KC	5.21		Walker,Taijuan, Sea	45.5		McHugh,Collin, Hou	101.3		Porcello,Rick, Bos	3.72

Quality Starts			Batters Faced			Innings Pitched			Most Pitches in a Game	
Keuchel,Dallas, Hou	27		Keuchel,Dallas, Hou	911		Keuchel,Dallas, Hou	232.0		Fiers,Mike, Hou	134
Quintana,Jose, CWS	25		Samardzija,Jeff, CWS	910		Kluber,Corey, Cle	222.0		Estrada,Marco, Tor	129
Price,David, Det-Tor	24		Price,David, Det-Tor	888		Price,David, Det-Tor	220.1		Sale,Chris, CWS	125
Richards,Garrett, LAA	24		Kluber,Corey, Cle	886		Dickey,R.A., Tor	214.1		Carrasco,Carlos, Cle	124
Sale,Chris, CWS	23		Dickey,R.A., Tor	884		Samardzija,Jeff, CWS	214.0		Santiago,Hector, LAA	124
Gray,Sonny, Oak	22		Archer,Chris, TB	868		Archer,Chris, TB	212.0		Archer,Chris, TB	122
McHugh,Collin, Hou	21		Richards,Garrett, LAA	865		Sale,Chris, CWS	208.2		Keuchel,Dallas, Hou	122
4 tied with	20		Quintana,Jose, CWS	862		Gray,Sonny, Oak	208.0		Richards,Garrett, LAA	122
			Lewis,Colby, Tex	861		Richards,Garrett, LAA	207.1		Rodriguez,Wandy, Tex	122
			McHugh,Collin, Hou	859		Quintana,Jose, CWS	206.1		7 tied with	121

Stolen Bases Allowed			Caught Stealing Off			Stolen Base Pct Allowed			Pickoffs	
						(minimum 162 IP)				
Jimenez,Ubaldo, Bal	22		Weaver,Jered, LAA	10		Buehrle,Mark, Tor	0.0		Beimel,Joe, Sea	6
Weaver,Jered, LAA	22		Carrasco,Carlos, Cle	9		Price,David, Det-Tor	0.0		Guthrie,Jeremy, KC	5
Porcello,Rick, Bos	18		Pineda,Michael, NYY	9		Miley,Wade, Bos	25.0		Miley,Wade, Bos	5
Volquez,Edinson, KC	18		Archer,Chris, TB	8		Salazar,Danny, Cle	33.3		Eovaldi,Nathan, NYY	4
Young,Chris, KC	18		Hutchison,Drew, Tor	8		Ventura,Yordano, KC	33.3		Quintana,Jose, CWS	4
Betances,Dellin, NYY	17		Santiago,Hector, LAA	8		Archer,Chris, TB	46.7		Santiago,Hector, LAA	4
Karns,Nate, TB	17		5 tied with	7		Walker,Taijuan, Sea	50.0		Smyly,Drew, TB	4
Santiago,Hector, LAA	17					Richards,Garrett, LAA	54.5		Walker,Taijuan, Sea	4
Simon,Alfredo, Det	17					Sale,Chris, CWS	55.6		Weaver,Jered, LAA	4
Kluber,Corey, Cle	16					Estrada,Marco, Tor	58.3		9 tied with	3

2015 American League Pitching Leaders

Strikeouts Per 9 IP (minimum 162 IP)		Opp On-Base Percentage (minimum 162 IP)		Opp Slugging Average (minimum 162 IP)		Opponent OPS (minimum 162 IP)	
Sale,Chris, CWS	11.82	Keuchel,Dallas, Hou	.262	Keuchel,Dallas, Hou	.314	Keuchel,Dallas, Hou	.575
Archer,Chris, TB	10.70	Estrada,Marco, Tor	.269	Gray,Sonny, Oak	.316	Gray,Sonny, Oak	.590
Carrasco,Carlos, Cle	10.58	Price,David, Det-Tor	.271	Archer,Chris, TB	.331	Archer,Chris, TB	.613
Kluber,Corey, Cle	9.93	Gray,Sonny, Oak	.273	Price,David, Det-Tor	.350	Price,David, Det-Tor	.621
Salazar,Danny, Cle	9.49	Carrasco,Carlos, Cle	.277	Richards,Garrett, LAA	.359	Estrada,Marco, Tor	.633
Price,David, Det-Tor	9.19	Kluber,Corey, Cle	.279	Ramirez,Erasmo, TB	.363	Carrasco,Carlos, Cle	.646
Bauer,Trevor, Cle	8.69	Sale,Chris, CWS	.282	Estrada,Marco, Tor	.364	Sale,Chris, CWS	.649
Ventura,Yordano, KC	8.60	Archer,Chris, TB	.282	Sale,Chris, CWS	.368	Kluber,Corey, Cle	.650
Hernandez,Felix, Sea	8.52	Odorizzi,Jake, TB	.284	Carrasco,Carlos, Cle	.369	Ramirez,Erasmo, TB	.655
Keuchel,Dallas, Hou	8.38	Salazar,Danny, Cle	.286	Kluber,Corey, Cle	.371	Richards,Garrett, LAA	.664

Home Runs Per Nine IP (minimum 162 IP)		Batting Average vs. LHB (minimum 125 BF)		Batting Average vs. RHB (minimum 225 BF)		Opp BA w/ RISP (minimum 125 BF)	
Pelfrey,Mike, Min	0.60	Harris,Will, Hou	.129	Young,Chris, KC	.159	Chen,Wei-Yin, Bal	.170
Keuchel,Dallas, Hou	0.66	Betances,Dellin, NYY	.135	Kluber,Corey, Cle	.197	McCullers,Lance, Hou	.176
Price,David, Det-Tor	0.69	Davis,Wade, KC	.146	Estrada,Marco, Tor	.204	Karns,Nate, TB	.193
Quintana,Jose, CWS	0.70	Herrera,Kelvin, KC	.151	Paxton,James, Sea	.212	Santiago,Hector, LAA	.197
Volquez,Edinson, KC	0.72	Allen,Cody, Cle	.176	Archer,Chris, TB	.218	Odorizzi,Jake, TB	.201
Gallardo,Yovani, Tex	0.73	Keuchel,Dallas, Hou	.177	Tanaka,Masahiro, NYY	.219	Volquez,Edinson, KC	.202
Gray,Sonny, Oak	0.74	Brach,Brad, Bal	.184	Price,David, Det-Tor	.219	Salazar,Danny, Cle	.204
Ventura,Yordano, KC	0.77	Sabathia,CC, NYY	.189	Iwakuma,Hisashi, Sea	.219	Gibson,Kyle, Min	.214
Miley,Wade, Bos	0.79	Ramirez,Erasmo, TB	.193	Salazar,Danny, Cle	.220	Gallardo,Yovani, Tex	.215
Archer,Chris, TB	0.81	Rodon,Carlos, CWS	.194	Kazmir,Scott, Oak-Hou	.225	Quintana,Jose, CWS	.216

OBP vs. Leadoff Hitter (minimum 150 BF)		Strikeouts / Walks Ratio (minimum 162 IP)		Highest GB/FB Ratio (minimum 162 IP)		Lowest GB/FB Ratio (minimum 162 IP)	
Archer,Chris, TB	.215	Sale,Chris, CWS	6.52	Keuchel,Dallas, Hou	3.14	Santiago,Hector, LAA	0.56
Odorizzi,Jake, TB	.246	Kluber,Corey, Cle	5.44	Hernandez,Felix, Sea	2.09	Estrada,Marco, Tor	0.62
Tanaka,Masahiro, NYY	.248	Carrasco,Carlos, Cle	5.02	Gibson,Kyle, Min	1.99	Lewis,Colby, Tex	0.76
Estrada,Marco, Tor	.251	Price,David, Det-Tor	4.79	Richards,Garrett, LAA	1.96	Odorizzi,Jake, TB	0.92
Ramirez,Erasmo, TB	.253	Keuchel,Dallas, Hou	4.24	Pelfrey,Mike, Min	1.93	Danks,John, CWS	0.94
Kluber,Corey, Cle	.253	Quintana,Jose, CWS	4.02	Ventura,Yordano, KC	1.92	Bauer,Trevor, Cle	0.96
Gray,Sonny, Oak	.254	Walker,Taijuan, Sea	3.92	Carrasco,Carlos, Cle	1.72	Samardzija,Jeff, CWS	0.98
Santiago,Hector, LAA	.259	Porcello,Rick, Bos	3.92	Gallardo,Yovani, Tex	1.72	Walker,Taijuan, Sea	0.99
Keuchel,Dallas, Hou	.267	Archer,Chris, TB	3.82	Gray,Sonny, Oak	1.72	Chen,Wei-Yin, Bal	1.03
Walker,Taijuan, Sea	.275	Chen,Wei-Yin, Bal	3.73	Jimenez,Ubaldo, Bal	1.70	Price,David, Det-Tor	1.11

Sacrifice Flies Allowed		Sacrifice Hits Allowed		GIDP Induced		GIDP Per Nine IP (minimum 162 IP)	
Dickey,R.A., Tor	11	Buehrle,Mark, Tor	10	Pelfrey,Mike, Min	29	Pelfrey,Mike, Min	1.59
Lewis,Colby, Tex	11	Simon,Alfredo, Det	9	Buehrle,Mark, Tor	28	Buehrle,Mark, Tor	1.27
Richards,Garrett, LAA	10	Danks,John, CWS	8	Gibson,Kyle, Min	27	Gibson,Kyle, Min	1.25
Buehrle,Mark, Tor	9	Kluber,Corey, Cle	7	Keuchel,Dallas, Hou	21	Porcello,Rick, Bos	1.10
Samardzija,Jeff, CWS	9	Gibson,Kyle, Min	6	Porcello,Rick, Bos	21	Sabathia,CC, NYY	1.08
Chen,Wei-Yin, Bal	8	Milone,Tommy, Min	6	Sabathia,CC, NYY	20	Volquez,Edinson, KC	0.90
Price,David, Det-Tor	8	Richards,Garrett, LAA	6	Volquez,Edinson, KC	20	Gallardo,Yovani, Tex	0.88
Tanaka,Masahiro, NYY	8	Rodon,Carlos, CWS	6	Gray,Sonny, Oak	19	Kazmir,Scott, Oak-Hou	0.84
Tillman,Chris, Bal	8	10 tied with	5	Richards,Garrett, LAA	19	Carrasco,Carlos, Cle	0.83
4 tied with	7			6 tied with	18	Tillman,Chris, Bal	0.83

2015 American League Pitching Leaders

<table>
<tr><td colspan="2">Saves</td><td colspan="2">Blown Saves</td><td colspan="2">Save Pct</td><td colspan="2">Save Opportunities</td></tr>
<tr><td colspan="2"></td><td colspan="2"></td><td colspan="2">(minimum 20 Save Ops)</td><td colspan="2"></td></tr>
<tr><td>Boxberger,Brad, TB</td><td>41</td><td>Feliz,Neftali, Tex-Det</td><td>7</td><td>Miller,Andrew, NYY</td><td>94.7</td><td>Boxberger,Brad, TB</td><td>47</td></tr>
<tr><td>Street,Huston, LAA</td><td>40</td><td>Herrera,Kelvin, KC</td><td>7</td><td>Tolleson,Shawn, Tex</td><td>94.6</td><td>Street,Huston, LAA</td><td>45</td></tr>
<tr><td>Britton,Zach, Bal</td><td>36</td><td>Robertson,David, CWS</td><td>7</td><td>Uehara,Koji, Bos</td><td>92.6</td><td>Robertson,David, CWS</td><td>41</td></tr>
<tr><td>Miller,Andrew, NYY</td><td>36</td><td>Tazawa,Junichi, Bos</td><td>7</td><td>Perkins,Glen, Min</td><td>91.4</td><td>Britton,Zach, Bal</td><td>40</td></tr>
<tr><td>Tolleson,Shawn, Tex</td><td>35</td><td>Boxberger,Brad, TB</td><td>6</td><td>Britton,Zach, Bal</td><td>90.0</td><td>Allen,Cody, Cle</td><td>38</td></tr>
<tr><td>Allen,Cody, Cle</td><td>34</td><td>Rodney,Fernando, Sea</td><td>6</td><td>Allen,Cody, Cle</td><td>89.5</td><td>Miller,Andrew, NYY</td><td>38</td></tr>
<tr><td>Robertson,David, CWS</td><td>34</td><td>7 tied with</td><td>5</td><td>Street,Huston, LAA</td><td>88.9</td><td>Holland,Greg, KC</td><td>37</td></tr>
<tr><td>Holland,Greg, KC</td><td>32</td><td></td><td></td><td>Soria,Joakim, Det</td><td>88.5</td><td>Tolleson,Shawn, Tex</td><td>37</td></tr>
<tr><td>Perkins,Glen, Min</td><td>32</td><td></td><td></td><td>Boxberger,Brad, TB</td><td>87.2</td><td>Gregerson,Luke, Hou</td><td>36</td></tr>
<tr><td>Gregerson,Luke, Hou</td><td>31</td><td></td><td></td><td>Osuna,Roberto, Tor</td><td>87.0</td><td>Perkins,Glen, Min</td><td>35</td></tr>
</table>

<table>
<tr><td colspan="2">Easy Saves</td><td colspan="2">Regular Saves</td><td colspan="2">Tough Saves</td><td colspan="2">Holds Adjusted Saves %</td></tr>
<tr><td colspan="2"></td><td colspan="2"></td><td colspan="2"></td><td colspan="2">(minimum 20 Save Ops + Holds)</td></tr>
<tr><td>Boxberger,Brad, TB</td><td>31</td><td>Miller,Andrew, NYY</td><td>15</td><td>Allen,Cody, Cle</td><td>7</td><td>Cedeno,Xavier, TB</td><td>100.0</td></tr>
<tr><td>Street,Huston, LAA</td><td>24</td><td>Britton,Zach, Bal</td><td>13</td><td>Betances,Dellin, NYY</td><td>3</td><td>Davis,Wade, KC</td><td>97.2</td></tr>
<tr><td>Tolleson,Shawn, Tex</td><td>24</td><td>Street,Huston, LAA</td><td>13</td><td>Britton,Zach, Bal</td><td>3</td><td>Tolleson,Shawn, Tex</td><td>95.3</td></tr>
<tr><td>Holland,Greg, KC</td><td>23</td><td>Robertson,David, CWS</td><td>11</td><td>Perkins,Glen, Min</td><td>3</td><td>Miller,Andrew, NYY</td><td>94.7</td></tr>
<tr><td>Robertson,David, CWS</td><td>22</td><td>Soria,Joakim, Det</td><td>11</td><td>Street,Huston, LAA</td><td>3</td><td>Wilson,Justin, NYY</td><td>93.5</td></tr>
<tr><td>Allen,Cody, Cle</td><td>21</td><td>Tolleson,Shawn, Tex</td><td>11</td><td>14 tied with</td><td>1</td><td>Duke,Zach, CWS</td><td>93.1</td></tr>
<tr><td>Gregerson,Luke, Hou</td><td>21</td><td>Boxberger,Brad, TB</td><td>10</td><td></td><td></td><td>Uehara,Koji, Bos</td><td>92.6</td></tr>
<tr><td>Perkins,Glen, Min</td><td>21</td><td>Gregerson,Luke, Hou</td><td>10</td><td></td><td></td><td>Perkins,Glen, Min</td><td>92.1</td></tr>
<tr><td>Britton,Zach, Bal</td><td>20</td><td>Holland,Greg, KC</td><td>9</td><td></td><td></td><td>Madson,Ryan, KC</td><td>92.0</td></tr>
<tr><td>Miller,Andrew, NYY</td><td>20</td><td>Uehara,Koji, Bos</td><td>9</td><td></td><td></td><td>2 tied with</td><td>90.9</td></tr>
</table>

<table>
<tr><td colspan="2">Relief Wins</td><td colspan="2">Relief Losses</td><td colspan="2">Relief Games</td><td colspan="2">Holds</td></tr>
<tr><td>Davis,Wade, KC</td><td>8</td><td>Boxberger,Brad, TB</td><td>10</td><td>Jepsen,Kevin, TB-Min</td><td>75</td><td>Smith,Joe, LAA</td><td>32</td></tr>
<tr><td>Gregerson,Luke, Hou</td><td>7</td><td>Farquhar,Danny, Sea</td><td>8</td><td>Betances,Dellin, NYY</td><td>74</td><td>Wilson,Justin, NYY</td><td>29</td></tr>
<tr><td>Kela,Keone, Tex</td><td>7</td><td>Tazawa,Junichi, Bos</td><td>7</td><td>Shaw,Bryan, Cle</td><td>74</td><td>Betances,Dellin, NYY</td><td>28</td></tr>
<tr><td>Betances,Dellin, NYY</td><td>6</td><td>8 tied with</td><td>6</td><td>Wilson,Justin, NYY</td><td>74</td><td>Neshek,Pat, Hou</td><td>28</td></tr>
<tr><td>O'Day,Darren, Bal</td><td>6</td><td></td><td></td><td>Tolleson,Shawn, Tex</td><td>73</td><td>Duke,Zach, CWS</td><td>26</td></tr>
<tr><td>Robertson,David, CWS</td><td>6</td><td></td><td></td><td>Herrera,Kelvin, KC</td><td>72</td><td>Jepsen,Kevin, TB-Min</td><td>24</td></tr>
<tr><td>Shreve,Chasen, NYY</td><td>6</td><td></td><td></td><td>Salas,Fernando, LAA</td><td>72</td><td>Shaw,Bryan, Cle</td><td>23</td></tr>
<tr><td>Tolleson,Shawn, Tex</td><td>6</td><td></td><td></td><td>Duke,Zach, CWS</td><td>71</td><td>Kela,Keone, Tex</td><td>22</td></tr>
<tr><td>10 tied with</td><td>5</td><td></td><td></td><td>4 tied with</td><td>70</td><td>Smith,Carson, Sea</td><td>22</td></tr>
<tr><td></td><td></td><td></td><td></td><td></td><td></td><td>Herrera,Kelvin, KC</td><td>21</td></tr>
</table>

<table>
<tr><td colspan="2">Relief Innings</td><td colspan="2">Inherited Runners Scrd %</td><td colspan="2">Relief Opp On Base Pct</td><td colspan="2">Relief Opp Slugging Avg</td></tr>
<tr><td colspan="2"></td><td colspan="2">(minimum 30 IR)</td><td colspan="2">(minimum 50 IP)</td><td colspan="2">(minimum 50 IP)</td></tr>
<tr><td>Betances,Dellin, NYY</td><td>84.0</td><td>Cedeno,Xavier, TB</td><td>13.3</td><td>Davis,Wade, KC</td><td>.211</td><td>Miller,Andrew, NYY</td><td>.239</td></tr>
<tr><td>Brach,Brad, Bal</td><td>79.1</td><td>Rodriguez,Fernando, Oak</td><td>13.3</td><td>Miller,Andrew, NYY</td><td>.237</td><td>Davis,Wade, KC</td><td>.240</td></tr>
<tr><td>Tolleson,Shawn, Tex</td><td>72.1</td><td>Wilson,Justin, NYY</td><td>15.9</td><td>Harris,Will, Hou</td><td>.237</td><td>Betances,Dellin, NYY</td><td>.244</td></tr>
<tr><td>Harris,Will, Hou</td><td>71.0</td><td>Petricka,Jake, CWS</td><td>16.1</td><td>Osuna,Roberto, Tor</td><td>.241</td><td>Smith,Carson, Sea</td><td>.262</td></tr>
<tr><td>Smith,Carson, Sea</td><td>70.0</td><td>Duke,Zach, CWS</td><td>18.9</td><td>Robertson,David, CWS</td><td>.241</td><td>Jepsen,Kevin, TB-Min</td><td>.282</td></tr>
<tr><td>Herrera,Kelvin, KC</td><td>69.2</td><td>Gomes,Brandon, TB</td><td>20.0</td><td>Gregerson,Luke, Hou</td><td>.253</td><td>O'Day,Darren, Bal</td><td>.283</td></tr>
<tr><td>Jepsen,Kevin, TB-Min</td><td>69.2</td><td>Layne,Tommy, Bos</td><td>20.0</td><td>Cecil,Brett, Tor</td><td>.254</td><td>Britton,Zach, Bal</td><td>.286</td></tr>
<tr><td>Osuna,Roberto, Tor</td><td>69.2</td><td>Rzepczynski,Marc, Cle</td><td>20.6</td><td>Madson,Ryan, KC</td><td>.254</td><td>Harris,Will, Hou</td><td>.288</td></tr>
<tr><td>Allen,Cody, Cle</td><td>69.1</td><td>Salas,Fernando, LAA</td><td>20.8</td><td>O'Day,Darren, Bal</td><td>.257</td><td>Herrera,Kelvin, KC</td><td>.298</td></tr>
<tr><td>Davis,Wade, KC</td><td>67.1</td><td>Ramos,Cesar, LAA</td><td>21.2</td><td>Britton,Zach, Bal</td><td>.261</td><td>Allen,Cody, Cle</td><td>.305</td></tr>
</table>

2015 American League Pitching Leaders

Relief Opp BA Vs LHB
(minimum 50 AB)

Clippard,Tyler, Oak	.100
Harris,Will, Hou	.129
Betances,Dellin, NYY	.135
Tepera,Ryan, Tor	.137
Britton,Zach, Bal	.145
Pomeranz,Drew, Oak	.145
Davis,Wade, KC	.146
Schultz,Bo, Tor	.148
Layne,Tommy, Bos	.148
Herrera,Kelvin, KC	.151

Relief Opp BA Vs RHB
(minimum 50 AB)

Manship,Jeff, Cle	.103
Young,Chris, KC	.118
Miller,Andrew, NYY	.131
Davis,Wade, KC	.141
Tonkin,Michael, Min	.154
Freeman,Sam, Tex	.167
Smith,Carson, Sea	.169
Jepsen,Kevin, TB-Min	.172
Givens,Mychal, Bal	.174
Osuna,Roberto, Tor	.174

Relief Opp Batting Average
(minimum 50 IP)

Davis,Wade, KC	.144
Miller,Andrew, NYY	.151
Betances,Dellin, NYY	.157
Harris,Will, Hou	.168
Osuna,Roberto, Tor	.191
Geltz,Steve, TB	.192
Smith,Carson, Sea	.194
Robertson,David, CWS	.196
Cecil,Brett, Tor	.197
O'Day,Darren, Bal	.198

Relief Earned Run Average
(minimum 50 IP)

Davis,Wade, KC	0.94
Betances,Dellin, NYY	1.50
O'Day,Darren, Bal	1.52
Harris,Will, Hou	1.90
Britton,Zach, Bal	1.92
Lowe,Mark, Sea-Tor	1.96
Sipp,Tony, Hou	1.99
Miller,Andrew, NYY	2.04
Madson,Ryan, KC	2.13
Wilson,Alex, Det	2.28

Rel OBP 1st Batter Faced
(minimum 40 BF)

Robertson,David, CWS	.100
Lowe,Mark, Sea-Tor	.175
Rodriguez,Fernando, Oak	.179
Duensing,Brian, Min	.182
Davis,Wade, KC	.188
Salas,Fernando, LAA	.200
Madson,Ryan, KC	.206
Cecil,Brett, Tor	.206
Uehara,Koji, Bos	.209
Morin,Mike, LAA	.217

Rel Opp BA w/ Runners On
(minimum 50 IP)

Davis,Wade, KC	.110
Betances,Dellin, NYY	.115
Miller,Andrew, NYY	.129
Harris,Will, Hou	.143
Tolleson,Shawn, Tex	.177
Osuna,Roberto, Tor	.179
Smith,Carson, Sea	.192
Madson,Ryan, KC	.194
Brach,Brad, Bal	.195
Sipp,Tony, Hou	.208

Relief Opp BA w/ RISP
(minimum 50 IP)

Harris,Will, Hou	.097
Duke,Zach, CWS	.107
Betances,Dellin, NYY	.115
Davis,Wade, KC	.118
Miller,Andrew, NYY	.125
Madson,Ryan, KC	.164
Petricka,Jake, CWS	.167
Lowe,Mark, Sea-Tor	.170
Cecil,Brett, Tor	.174
Smith,Carson, Sea	.176

Fastest Avg Fastball-Relief
(minimum 50 IP)

Herrera,Kelvin, KC	98.1
Betances,Dellin, NYY	97.0
Davis,Wade, KC	95.9
Britton,Zach, Bal	95.9
Kela,Keone, Tex	95.6
Osuna,Roberto, Tor	95.6
Lowe,Mark, Sea-Tor	95.5
McAllister,Zach, Cle	95.4
Wilson,Justin, NYY	95.1
Wilhelmsen,Tom, Sea	95.0

Fastest Average Fastball
(minimum 162 IP)

Ventura,Yordano, KC	96.3
Richards,Garrett, LAA	95.5
Archer,Chris, TB	95.2
Salazar,Danny, Cle	94.8
Carrasco,Carlos, Cle	94.5
Sale,Chris, CWS	94.5
Walker,Taijuan, Sea	94.3
Samardzija,Jeff, CWS	94.2
Price,David, Det-Tor	94.2
Volquez,Edinson, KC	93.7

Slowest Average Fastball
(minimum 162 IP)

Dickey,R.A., Tor	81.5
Buehrle,Mark, Tor	83.4
Lewis,Colby, Tex	88.0
Estrada,Marco, Tor	89.3
Danks,John, CWS	89.4
Keuchel,Dallas, Hou	89.6
Sabathia,CC, NYY	90.1
Santiago,Hector, LAA	90.3
Gallardo,Yovani, Tex	90.4
McHugh,Collin, Hou	90.4

Pitches 100+ Velocity

Herrera,Kelvin, KC	143
Eovaldi,Nathan, NYY	62
Rondon,Bruce, Det	50
Ventura,Yordano, KC	28
Betances,Dellin, NYY	10
Diekman,Jake, Tex	8
Gausman,Kevin, Bal	5
Montas,Frankie, CWS	5
Jones,Nate, CWS	3
Hunter,Tommy, Bal	2

Pitches 95+ Velocity

Richards,Garrett, LAA	1684
Price,David, Det-Tor	1606
Ventura,Yordano, KC	1314
Archer,Chris, TB	1311
Salazar,Danny, Cle	1260
Kelly,Joe, Bos	1161
Eovaldi,Nathan, NYY	1159
Sale,Chris, CWS	999
Gausman,Kevin, Bal	887
Herrera,Kelvin, KC	810

Pitches Less Than 80 MPH

Dickey,R.A., Tor	2679
Kazmir,Scott, Oak-Hou	1340
Weaver,Jered, LAA	1295
Wright,Steven, Bos	1055
Buehrle,Mark, Tor	985
Estrada,Marco, Tor	919
McHugh,Collin, Hou	760
Keuchel,Dallas, Hou	642
Boyd,Matt, Tor-Det	550
Rodriguez,Wandy, Tex	546

Lowest % Fastballs
(minimum 162 IP)

Dickey,R.A., Tor	11.1
McHugh,Collin, Hou	33.6
Samardzija,Jeff, CWS	39.7
Hernandez,Felix, Sea	43.8
Danks,John, CWS	44.1
Simon,Alfredo, Det	45.9
Lewis,Colby, Tex	50.2
Buehrle,Mark, Tor	50.6
Odorizzi,Jake, TB	50.9
Volquez,Edinson, KC	51.0

Highest % Fastballs
(minimum 162 IP)

Pelfrey,Mike, Min	73.2
Salazar,Danny, Cle	68.9
Porcello,Rick, Bos	66.0
Tillman,Chris, Bal	65.0
Walker,Taijuan, Sea	64.8
Chen,Wei-Yin, Bal	64.0
Jimenez,Ubaldo, Bal	61.1
Richards,Garrett, LAA	61.0
Santiago,Hector, LAA	60.6
Gray,Sonny, Oak	60.2

Highest % Curveballs
(minimum 162 IP)

Quintana,Jose, CWS	30.9
Ventura,Yordano, KC	24.1
Volquez,Edinson, KC	24.0
McHugh,Collin, Hou	23.5
Hernandez,Felix, Sea	22.3
Kluber,Corey, Cle	15.6
Tillman,Chris, Bal	14.2
Gray,Sonny, Oak	14.0
Porcello,Rick, Bos	14.0
Danks,John, CWS	12.4

2015 American League Pitching Leaders

Highest % Changeups
(minimum 162 IP)

Odorizzi,Jake, TB	30.0
Danks,John, CWS	28.9
Estrada,Marco, Tor	28.1
Hernandez,Felix, Sea	27.8
Sale,Chris, CWS	27.7
Buehrle,Mark, Tor	25.2
Volquez,Edinson, KC	25.0
Ramirez,Erasmo, TB	23.0
Price,David, Det-Tor	22.6
Salazar,Danny, Cle	20.5

Highest % Sliders
(minimum 162 IP)

Archer,Chris, TB	39.2
McHugh,Collin, Hou	38.7
Lewis,Colby, Tex	35.0
Richards,Garrett, LAA	33.3
Gallardo,Yovani, Tex	29.4
Samardzija,Jeff, CWS	24.5
Carrasco,Carlos, Cle	22.3
Sabathia,CC, NYY	22.2
Bauer,Trevor, Cle	20.8
Keuchel,Dallas, Hou	20.3

Balks

Alburquerque,Al, Det	4
Mujica,Edward, Bos-Oak	3
Sanchez,Anibal, Det	3
Santiago,Hector, LAA	3
7 tied with	2

Strikeout/Hit Ratio
(minimum 50 IP)

Miller,Andrew, NYY	3.03
Betances,Dellin, NYY	2.91
Davis,Wade, KC	2.36
Smith,Carson, Sea	1.88
Robertson,David, CWS	1.87
Cecil,Brett, Tor	1.79
Allen,Cody, Cle	1.77
O'Day,Darren, Bal	1.74
Fields,Josh, Hou	1.72
Harris,Will, Hou	1.62

Opp OPS vs Fastballs
(minimum 251 BF)

Keuchel,Dallas, Hou	.594
Hahn,Jesse, Oak	.596
Gray,Sonny, Oak	.599
Price,David, Det-Tor	.611
Sanchez,Aaron, Tor	.630
Archer,Chris, TB	.635
Odorizzi,Jake, TB	.636
Estrada,Marco, Tor	.646
Kazmir,Scott, Oak-Hou	.647
Richards,Garrett, LAA	.650

Opp OPS vs Curveballs
(minimum 100 BF)

Hernandez,Felix, Sea	.377
Gray,Sonny, Oak	.472
Kluber,Corey, Cle	.493
Quintana,Jose, CWS	.546
McCullers,Lance, Hou	.548
Karns,Nate, TB	.560
Ventura,Yordano, KC	.568
Volquez,Edinson, KC	.580
McHugh,Collin, Hou	.581
Pomeranz,Drew, Oak	.713

Opp OPS vs Changeups
(minimum 100 BF)

Ramirez,Erasmo, TB	.507
Carrasco,Carlos, Cle	.518
Eovaldi,Nathan, NYY	.544
Wilson,C.J., LAA	.544
Gibson,Kyle, Min	.545
Sale,Chris, CWS	.548
Rodriguez,Eduardo, Bos	.550
Salazar,Danny, Cle	.552
Volquez,Edinson, KC	.553
Estrada,Marco, Tor	.559

Opp OPS vs Sliders
(minimum 64 BF)

Miller,Andrew, NYY	.343
Cedeno,Xavier, TB	.396
Keuchel,Dallas, Hou	.431
Betances,Dellin, NYY	.438
Tanaka,Masahiro, NYY	.454
Alvarez,Jose, LAA	.465
Street,Huston, LAA	.491
Lowe,Mark, Sea-Tor	.509
Hendriks,Liam, Tor	.525
Bassitt,Chris, Oak	.527

Earned Runs

Samardzija,Jeff, CWS	118
Lewis,Colby, Tex	106
Simon,Alfredo, Det	105
Guthrie,Jeremy, KC	98
Miley,Wade, Bos	96
Tillman,Chris, Bal	96
Porcello,Rick, Bos	94
Danks,John, CWS	93
Dickey,R.A., Tor	93
Hutchison,Drew, Tor	93

Hits Per Nine Innings
(minimum 162 IP)

Estrada,Marco, Tor	6.66
Gray,Sonny, Oak	7.18
Keuchel,Dallas, Hou	7.18
Archer,Chris, TB	7.43
Carrasco,Carlos, Cle	7.55
Salazar,Danny, Cle	7.59
Kluber,Corey, Cle	7.66
Price,David, Det-Tor	7.76
Bauer,Trevor, Cle	7.77
Santiago,Hector, LAA	7.77

2015 National League Pitching Leaders

Earned Run Average (minimum 162 IP)		Winning Percentage (minimum 15 Decisions)		Opponent Batting Average (minimum 162 IP)		Baserunners Per 9 IP (minimum 162 IP)	
Greinke,Zack, LAD	1.66	Greinke,Zack, LAD	.864	Arrieta,Jake, ChC	.185	Greinke,Zack, LAD	7.80
Arrieta,Jake, ChC	1.77	Arrieta,Jake, ChC	.786	Greinke,Zack, LAD	.187	Arrieta,Jake, ChC	8.02
Kershaw,Clayton, LAD	2.13	Wacha,Michael, StL	.708	Kershaw,Clayton, LAD	.194	Kershaw,Clayton, LAD	8.12
deGrom,Jacob, NYM	2.54	Cole,Gerrit, Pit	.704	Scherzer,Max, Was	.208	Scherzer,Max, Was	8.46
Cole,Gerrit, Pit	2.60	Kershaw,Clayton, LAD	.696	deGrom,Jacob, NYM	.215	deGrom,Jacob, NYM	8.91
Harvey,Matt, NYM	2.71	Bumgarner,Madison, SF	.667	Harvey,Matt, NYM	.222	Bumgarner,Madison, SF	9.36
Lackey,John, StL	2.77	Martinez,Carlos, StL	.667	Bumgarner,Madison, SF	.222	Harvey,Matt, NYM	9.41
Scherzer,Max, Was	2.79	Shields,James, SD	.650	Liriano,Francisco, Pit	.223	Cole,Gerrit, Pit	10.25
Bumgarner,Madison, SF	2.93	deGrom,Jacob, NYM	.636	Wacha,Michael, StL	.236	Lester,Jon, ChC	10.40
Martinez,Carlos, StL	3.01	Liriano,Francisco, Pit	.632	Ross,Tyson, SD	.237	Haren,Dan, Mia-ChC	10.57

Games		Games Started		Complete Games		Shutouts	
Siegrist,Kevin, StL	81	Arrieta,Jake, ChC	33	Arrieta,Jake, ChC	4	Arrieta,Jake, ChC	3
Melancon,Mark, Pit	78	Kershaw,Clayton, LAD	33	Bumgarner,Madison, SF	4	Kershaw,Clayton, LAD	3
Lopez,Javier, SF	77	Lackey,John, StL	33	Kershaw,Clayton, LAD	4	Scherzer,Max, Was	3
Watson,Tony, Pit	77	Miller,Shelby, Atl	33	Scherzer,Max, Was	4	Bumgarner,Madison, SF	2
Familia,Jeurys, NYM	76	Ross,Tyson, SD	33	Heston,Chris, SF	2	Miller,Shelby, Atl	2
Hughes,Jared, Pit	76	Scherzer,Max, Was	33	Leake,Mike, Cin-SF	2	8 tied with	1
Maness,Seth, StL	76	Shields,James, SD	33	Miller,Shelby, Atl	2		
Smith,Will, Mil	76	Teheran,Julio, Atl	33	Rusin,Chris, Col	2		
Strop,Pedro, ChC	76	Zimmermann,Jordan, Was	33	14 tied with	1		
3 tied with	73	8 tied with	32				

Wins		Losses		No Decisions		Wild Pitches	
Arrieta,Jake, ChC	22	Miller,Shelby, Atl	17	Hendricks,Kyle, ChC	17	Ross,Tyson, SD	14
Cole,Gerrit, Pit	19	Cashner,Andrew, SD	16	Anderson,Chase, Ari	15	Hale,David, Col	11
Greinke,Zack, LAD	19	Harang,Aaron, Phi	15	Hammel,Jason, ChC	14	Nelson,Jimmy, Mil	11
Bumgarner,Madison, SF	18	Kennedy,Ian, SD	15	Teheran,Julio, Atl	14	Hammel,Jason, ChC	10
Wacha,Michael, StL	17	Garza,Matt, Mil	14	Shields,James, SD	13	Latos,Mat, Mia-LAD	10
Kershaw,Clayton, LAD	16	Koehler,Tom, Mia	14	Anderson,Brett, LAD	12	Liriano,Francisco, Pit	10
5 tied with	14	5 tied with	13	Gonzalez,Gio, Was	12	Scherzer,Max, Was	10
				Haren,Dan, Mia-ChC	12	Kershaw,Clayton, LAD	9
				Liriano,Francisco, Pit	12	5 tied with	8
				2 tied with	11		

Strikeouts		Walks Allowed		Intentional Walks Allowed		Hit Batters	
Kershaw,Clayton, LAD	301	Ross,Tyson, SD	84	Garcia,Luis, Phi	8	Heston,Chris, SF	13
Scherzer,Max, Was	276	Shields,James, SD	81	Miller,Shelby, Atl	8	Nelson,Jimmy, Mil	13
Arrieta,Jake, ChC	236	Koehler,Tom, Mia	77	Chafin,Andrew, Ari	6	Morton,Charlie, Pit	12
Bumgarner,Madison, SF	234	Miller,Shelby, Atl	73	Lorenzen,Michael, Cin	6	Burnett,A.J., Pit	11
Shields,James, SD	216	Teheran,Julio, Atl	73	Morton,Charlie, Pit	6	Cole,Gerrit, Pit	10
Ross,Tyson, SD	212	Liriano,Francisco, Pit	70	Nicasio,Juan, LAD	6	Despaigne,Odrisamer, SD	9
Lester,Jon, ChC	207	Gonzalez,Gio, Was	69	Reed,Addison, Ari-NYM	6	Niese,Jon, NYM	9
deGrom,Jacob, NYM	205	Lynn,Lance, StL	68	Strop,Pedro, ChC	6	Perez,Williams, Atl	9
Liriano,Francisco, Pit	205	Cashner,Andrew, SD	66	Torres,Carlos, NYM	6	Shields,James, SD	9
Cole,Gerrit, Pit	202	2 tied with	65	Treinen,Blake, Was	6	Teheran,Julio, Atl	9

2015 National League Pitching Leaders

Runs Allowed		Hits Allowed		Doubles Allowed		Home Runs Allowed	
Cashner,Andrew, SD	111	Colon,Bartolo, NYM	217	Haren,Dan, Mia-ChC	44	Kendrick,Kyle, Col	33
de la Rosa,Rubby, Ari	103	Lackey,John, StL	211	DeSclafani,Anthony, Cin	43	Shields,James, SD	33
Garza,Matt, Mil	102	Zimmermann,Jordan, Was	204	Shields,James, SD	43	de la Rosa,Rubby, Ari	32
Kendrick,Kyle, Col	102	Cashner,Andrew, SD	200	de la Rosa,Rubby, Ari	42	Haren,Dan, Mia-ChC	31
Harang,Aaron, Phi	100	Wood,Alex, Atl-LAD	198	Lester,Jon, ChC	42	Kennedy,Ian, SD	31
Lohse,Kyle, Mil	99	Anderson,Brett, LAD	194	Colon,Bartolo, NYM	41	Lohse,Kyle, Mil	29
Teheran,Julio, Atl	99	DeSclafani,Anthony, Cin	194	Miller,Shelby, Atl	41	Scherzer,Max, Was	27
Koehler,Tom, Mia	96	de la Rosa,Rubby, Ari	193	Cashner,Andrew, SD	40	Teheran,Julio, Atl	27
Kennedy,Ian, SD	95	Niese,Jon, NYM	192	Hellickson,Jeremy, Ari	40	Harang,Aaron, Phi	26
Locke,Jeff, Pit	95	3 tied with	189	Scherzer,Max, Was	40	Colon,Bartolo, NYM	25

Run Support Per Nine IP		% Pitches In Strike Zone		Pitches Per Start		Pitches Per Batter	
(minimum 162 IP)		(minimum 162 IP)		(minimum 30 GS)		(minimum 162 IP)	
Wacha,Michael, StL	5.96	Colon,Bartolo, NYM	50.1	Arrieta,Jake, ChC	104.2	Colon,Bartolo, NYM	3.32
Shields,James, SD	5.92	Scherzer,Max, Was	48.3	Bumgarner,Madison, SF	103.5	Lackey,John, StL	3.49
de la Rosa,Rubby, Ari	5.77	Zimmermann,Jordan, Was	48.0	Kershaw,Clayton, LAD	102.8	Niese,Jon, NYM	3.51
Gonzalez,Gio, Was	5.33	Lackey,John, StL	47.3	Scherzer,Max, Was	101.8	Leake,Mike, Cin-SF	3.54
Heston,Chris, SF	5.17	Kershaw,Clayton, LAD	47.3	Greinke,Zack, LAD	101.2	Burnett,A.J., Pit	3.58
Zimmermann,Jordan, Was	5.09	Wacha,Michael, StL	46.9	Cole,Gerrit, Pit	101.2	Anderson,Brett, LAD	3.62
Hammel,Jason, ChC	5.01	Miller,Shelby, Atl	46.7	Shields,James, SD	101.1	Wood,Alex, Atl-LAD	3.63
Niese,Jon, NYM	4.99	Harvey,Matt, NYM	46.6	Cashner,Andrew, SD	100.3	Harvey,Matt, NYM	3.71
Liriano,Francisco, Pit	4.97	DeSclafani,Anthony, Cin	45.7	Lester,Jon, ChC	99.5	DeSclafani,Anthony, Cin	3.71
Haren,Dan, Mia-ChC	4.90	Niese,Jon, NYM	45.2	Teheran,Julio, Atl	99.2	Nelson,Jimmy, Mil	3.71

Quality Starts		Batters Faced		Innings Pitched		Most Pitches in a Game	
Greinke,Zack, LAD	30	Scherzer,Max, Was	899	Kershaw,Clayton, LAD	232.2	Kershaw,Clayton, LAD	132
Arrieta,Jake, ChC	29	Lackey,John, StL	896	Arrieta,Jake, ChC	229.0	Hamels,Cole, Phi	129
Kershaw,Clayton, LAD	27	Kershaw,Clayton, LAD	890	Scherzer,Max, Was	228.2	Cueto,Johnny, Cin	125
Lackey,John, StL	26	Arrieta,Jake, ChC	870	Greinke,Zack, LAD	222.2	Arrieta,Jake, ChC	123
Cole,Gerrit, Pit	25	Bumgarner,Madison, SF	869	Bumgarner,Madison, SF	218.1	Cueto,Johnny, Cin	123
deGrom,Jacob, NYM	23	Miller,Shelby, Atl	860	Lackey,John, StL	218.0	Kershaw,Clayton, LAD	123
Scherzer,Max, Was	23	Shields,James, SD	860	Cole,Gerrit, Pit	208.0	O'Sullivan,Sean, Phi	123
Bumgarner,Madison, SF	22	Greinke,Zack, LAD	843	Miller,Shelby, Atl	205.1	5 tied with	122
Zimmermann,Jordan, Was	22	Teheran,Julio, Atl	843	Lester,Jon, ChC	205.0		
4 tied with	21	Cole,Gerrit, Pit	832	Shields,James, SD	202.1		

Stolen Bases Allowed		Caught Stealing Off		Stolen Base Pct Allowed		Pickoffs	
				(minimum 162 IP)			
Lester,Jon, ChC	44	Ross,Tyson, SD	13	Martinez,Carlos, StL	28.6	Kershaw,Clayton, LAD	10
Ross,Tyson, SD	37	Cashner,Andrew, SD	11	deGrom,Jacob, NYM	40.0	Anderson,Brett, LAD	6
Burnett,A.J., Pit	33	Lester,Jon, ChC	11	Kershaw,Clayton, LAD	43.8	Zimmermann,Jordan, Was	6
Arrieta,Jake, ChC	27	Anderson,Brett, LAD	10	Heston,Chris, SF	45.5	Rusin,Chris, Col	5
Cole,Gerrit, Pit	25	Cole,Gerrit, Pit	10	Anderson,Brett, LAD	50.0	Teheran,Julio, Atl	5
Nelson,Jimmy, Mil	24	Burnett,A.J., Pit	9	Harang,Aaron, Phi	50.0	Wood,Alex, Atl-LAD	5
Jungmann,Taylor, Mil	18	Kershaw,Clayton, LAD	9	Leake,Mike, Cin-SF	50.0	7 tied with	4
Miller,Shelby, Atl	18	Shields,James, SD	8	Teheran,Julio, Atl	50.0		
DeSclafani,Anthony, Cin	16	3 tied with	7	Zimmermann,Jordan, Was	50.0		
Hamels,Cole, Phi	16			Gonzalez,Gio, Was	53.3		

2015 National League Pitching Leaders

Strikeouts Per 9 IP
(minimum 162 IP)

Kershaw,Clayton, LAD	11.64
Scherzer,Max, Was	10.86
Liriano,Francisco, Pit	9.88
Ross,Tyson, SD	9.73
deGrom,Jacob, NYM	9.66
Bumgarner,Madison, SF	9.65
Shields,James, SD	9.61
Kennedy,Ian, SD	9.30
Arrieta,Jake, ChC	9.28
Martinez,Carlos, StL	9.22

Opp On-Base Percentage
(minimum 162 IP)

Greinke,Zack, LAD	.231
Arrieta,Jake, ChC	.236
Kershaw,Clayton, LAD	.237
Scherzer,Max, Was	.242
deGrom,Jacob, NYM	.255
Bumgarner,Madison, SF	.263
Harvey,Matt, NYM	.265
Cole,Gerrit, Pit	.287
Lester,Jon, ChC	.288
Hammel,Jason, ChC	.289

Opp Slugging Average
(minimum 162 IP)

Arrieta,Jake, ChC	.271
Greinke,Zack, LAD	.276
Kershaw,Clayton, LAD	.284
deGrom,Jacob, NYM	.318
Ross,Tyson, SD	.330
Liriano,Francisco, Pit	.332
Cole,Gerrit, Pit	.336
Harvey,Matt, NYM	.344
Bumgarner,Madison, SF	.349
Miller,Shelby, Atl	.355

Opponent OPS
(minimum 162 IP)

Arrieta,Jake, ChC	.507
Greinke,Zack, LAD	.507
Kershaw,Clayton, LAD	.521
deGrom,Jacob, NYM	.574
Scherzer,Max, Was	.600
Harvey,Matt, NYM	.609
Bumgarner,Madison, SF	.612
Cole,Gerrit, Pit	.623
Liriano,Francisco, Pit	.631
Ross,Tyson, SD	.652

Home Runs Per Nine IP
(minimum 162 IP)

Arrieta,Jake, ChC	0.39
Gonzalez,Gio, Was	0.41
Ross,Tyson, SD	0.41
Cole,Gerrit, Pit	0.48
Greinke,Zack, LAD	0.57
Miller,Shelby, Atl	0.57
Kershaw,Clayton, LAD	0.58
Burnett,A.J., Pit	0.60
Martinez,Carlos, StL	0.65
Lynn,Lance, StL	0.67

Batting Average vs. LHB
(minimum 125 BF)

Melancon,Mark, Pit	.138
Arrieta,Jake, ChC	.159
Benoit,Joaquin, SD	.172
Cueto,Johnny, Cin	.173
Chafin,Andrew, Ari	.182
Hudson,Daniel, Ari	.186
Greinke,Zack, LAD	.194
Rosenthal,Trevor, StL	.194
Ramos,A.J., Mia	.202
Strasburg,Stephen, Was	.202

Batting Average vs. RHB
(minimum 225 BF)

deGrom,Jacob, NYM	.181
Greinke,Zack, LAD	.182
Scherzer,Max, Was	.184
Kershaw,Clayton, LAD	.192
Nelson,Jimmy, Mil	.202
Teheran,Julio, Atl	.207
Arrieta,Jake, ChC	.207
Syndergaard,Noah, NYM	.212
de la Rosa,Rubby, Ari	.214
Miller,Shelby, Atl	.214

Opp BA w/ RISP
(minimum 125 BF)

Greinke,Zack, LAD	.157
Arrieta,Jake, ChC	.170
Martinez,Carlos, StL	.181
Shields,James, SD	.191
Hellickson,Jeremy, Ari	.203
Wacha,Michael, StL	.208
Burnett,A.J., Pit	.209
Haren,Dan, Mia-ChC	.210
Lackey,John, StL	.210
Scherzer,Max, Was	.217

OBP vs. Leadoff Hitter
(minimum 150 BF)

Greinke,Zack, LAD	.199
Arrieta,Jake, ChC	.203
deGrom,Jacob, NYM	.209
Scherzer,Max, Was	.210
Harvey,Matt, NYM	.228
Kershaw,Clayton, LAD	.249
Bumgarner,Madison, SF	.253
Hendricks,Kyle, ChC	.254
Harang,Aaron, Phi	.261
Syndergaard,Noah, NYM	.261

Strikeouts / Walks Ratio
(minimum 162 IP)

Scherzer,Max, Was	8.12
Kershaw,Clayton, LAD	7.17
Bumgarner,Madison, SF	6.00
Colon,Bartolo, NYM	5.67
deGrom,Jacob, NYM	5.39
Harvey,Matt, NYM	5.08
Greinke,Zack, LAD	5.00
Arrieta,Jake, ChC	4.92
Cole,Gerrit, Pit	4.59
Lester,Jon, ChC	4.40

Highest GB/FB Ratio
(minimum 162 IP)

Anderson,Brett, LAD	3.58
Ross,Tyson, SD	3.09
Arrieta,Jake, ChC	2.47
Burnett,A.J., Pit	2.21
Niese,Jon, NYM	2.21
Martinez,Carlos, StL	2.14
Locke,Jeff, Pit	2.05
Heston,Chris, SF	2.04
Gonzalez,Gio, Was	2.02
Liriano,Francisco, Pit	1.95

Lowest GB/FB Ratio
(minimum 162 IP)

Haren,Dan, Mia-ChC	0.62
Scherzer,Max, Was	0.79
Harang,Aaron, Phi	0.83
Kennedy,Ian, SD	0.99
Hammel,Jason, ChC	1.03
Teheran,Julio, Atl	1.10
Colon,Bartolo, NYM	1.15
Zimmermann,Jordan, Was	1.16
Bumgarner,Madison, SF	1.17
Harvey,Matt, NYM	1.27

Sacrifice Flies Allowed

Anderson,Chase, Ari	9
Gonzalez,Gio, Was	9
de la Rosa,Jorge, Col	8
Locke,Jeff, Pit	8
Colon,Bartolo, NYM	7
deGrom,Jacob, NYM	7
Nelson,Jimmy, Mil	7
11 tied with	6

Sacrifice Hits Allowed

Niese,Jon, NYM	16
Wood,Alex, Atl-LAD	15
Lackey,John, StL	11
Scherzer,Max, Was	11
deGrom,Jacob, NYM	10
DeSclafani,Anthony, Cin	10
Teheran,Julio, Atl	10
Colon,Bartolo, NYM	9
Lynn,Lance, StL	9
Martinez,Carlos, StL	9

GIDP Induced

Lackey,John, StL	29
Heston,Chris, SF	26
Wood,Alex, Atl-LAD	25
Koehler,Tom, Mia	24
Anderson,Brett, LAD	23
Cole,Gerrit, Pit	22
DeSclafani,Anthony, Cin	22
Leake,Mike, Cin-SF	22
Liriano,Francisco, Pit	22
2 tied with	21

GIDP Per Nine IP
(minimum 162 IP)

Heston,Chris, SF	1.32
Lackey,John, StL	1.20
Wood,Alex, Atl-LAD	1.19
Koehler,Tom, Mia	1.15
Anderson,Brett, LAD	1.15
DeSclafani,Anthony, Cin	1.07
Liriano,Francisco, Pit	1.06
Leake,Mike, Cin-SF	1.03
Burnett,A.J., Pit	0.99
Cole,Gerrit, Pit	0.95

2015 National League Pitching Leaders

Saves			Blown Saves			Save Pct			Save Opportunities		
						(minimum 20 Save Ops)					
Melancon,Mark, Pit	51		Johnson,Jim, Atl-LAD	7		Melancon,Mark, Pit	96.2		Melancon,Mark, Pit	53	
Rosenthal,Trevor, StL	48		Axford,John, Col	6		Rodriguez,Francisco, Mil	95.0		Rosenthal,Trevor, StL	51	
Familia,Jeurys, NYM	43		Casilla,Santiago, SF	6		Jansen,Kenley, LAD	94.7		Familia,Jeurys, NYM	48	
Kimbrel,Craig, SD	39		Hoover,J.J., Cin	6		Rosenthal,Trevor, StL	94.1		Casilla,Santiago, SF	44	
Casilla,Santiago, SF	38		Ramos,A.J., Mia	6		Ziegler,Brad, Ari	93.8		Kimbrel,Craig, SD	43	
Rodriguez,Francisco, Mil	38		6 tied with	5		Grilli,Jason, Atl	92.3		Rodriguez,Francisco, Mil	40	
Jansen,Kenley, LAD	36					Papelbon,Jonathan, Phi-Was	92.3		Jansen,Kenley, LAD	38	
Chapman,Aroldis, Cin	33					Chapman,Aroldis, Cin	91.7		Ramos,A.J., Mia	38	
Ramos,A.J., Mia	32					Kimbrel,Craig, SD	90.7		Chapman,Aroldis, Cin	36	
2 tied with	30					Familia,Jeurys, NYM	89.6		2 tied with	34	

Easy Saves			Regular Saves			Tough Saves			Holds Adjusted Saves %		
									(minimum 20 Save Ops + Holds)		
Melancon,Mark, Pit	32		Melancon,Mark, Pit	19		Rosenthal,Trevor, StL	4		Lopez,Javier, SF	100.0	
Rosenthal,Trevor, StL	30		Kimbrel,Craig, SD	15		Familia,Jeurys, NYM	3		Melancon,Mark, Pit	96.3	
Casilla,Santiago, SF	26		Familia,Jeurys, NYM	14		Ziegler,Brad, Ari	3		Watson,Tony, Pit	95.5	
Familia,Jeurys, NYM	26		Rondon,Hector, ChC	14		Giles,Ken, Phi	2		Rodriguez,Francisco, Mil	95.0	
Rodriguez,Francisco, Mil	26		Rosenthal,Trevor, StL	14		Kimbrel,Craig, SD	2		Jansen,Kenley, LAD	94.9	
Jansen,Kenley, LAD	25		Storen,Drew, Was	13		Ramos,A.J., Mia	2		Romo,Sergio, SF	94.7	
Kimbrel,Craig, SD	22		Chapman,Aroldis, Cin	12		12 tied with	1		Ziegler,Brad, Ari	94.4	
Chapman,Aroldis, Cin	20		Ramos,A.J., Mia	12					Rosenthal,Trevor, StL	94.1	
Papelbon,Jonathan, Phi-Was	19		Rodriguez,Francisco, Mil	12					Strop,Pedro, ChC	93.9	
Ramos,A.J., Mia	18		2 tied with	11					3 tied with	92.3	

Relief Wins			Relief Losses			Relief Games			Holds		
Delgado,Randall, Ari	8		Cishek,Steve, Mia-StL	6		Siegrist,Kevin, StL	81		Watson,Tony, Pit	41	
Hoover,J.J., Cin	8		Garcia,Luis, Phi	6		Melancon,Mark, Pit	78		Romo,Sergio, SF	34	
Motte,Jason, ChC	8		Johnson,Jim, Atl-LAD	6		Lopez,Javier, SF	77		Benoit,Joaquin, SD	28	
Maurer,Brandon, SD	7		Strop,Pedro, ChC	6		Watson,Tony, Pit	77		Siegrist,Kevin, StL	28	
Siegrist,Kevin, StL	7		Torres,Carlos, NYM	6		Familia,Jeurys, NYM	76		Strop,Pedro, ChC	28	
Smith,Will, Mil	7		12 tied with	5		Hughes,Jared, Pit	76		Johnson,Jim, Atl-LAD	25	
Benoit,Joaquin, SD	6					Maness,Seth, StL	76		Dunn,Mike, Mia	23	
Giles,Ken, Phi	6					Smith,Will, Mil	76		Jeffress,Jeremy, Mil	23	
Howell,J.P., LAD	6					Strop,Pedro, ChC	76		Logan,Boone, Col	23	
Rondon,Hector, ChC	6					3 tied with	73		Hughes,Jared, Pit	21	

Relief Innings			Inherited Runners Scrd %			Relief Opp On Base Pct			Relief Opp Slugging Avg		
			(minimum 30 IR)			(minimum 50 IP)			(minimum 50 IP)		
De Fratus,Justin, Phi	80.0		Strickland,Hunter, SF	12.9		Jansen,Kenley, LAD	.215		Chapman,Aroldis, Cin	.235	
Familia,Jeurys, NYM	78.0		Lopez,Javier, SF	13.6		Rodriguez,Francisco, Mil	.229		Watson,Tony, Pit	.265	
Melancon,Mark, Pit	76.2		Choate,Randy, StL	14.0		Strickland,Hunter, SF	.241		Strop,Pedro, ChC	.270	
Watson,Tony, Pit	75.1		Avilan,Luis, Atl-LAD	16.1		Garcia,Yimi, LAD	.242		Ziegler,Brad, Ari	.272	
Chafin,Andrew, Ari	75.0		Hughes,Jared, Pit	16.1		Benoit,Joaquin, SD	.242		Wood,Travis, ChC	.279	
Caminero,Arquimedes, Pit	74.2		Dunn,Mike, Mia	16.3		Kontos,George, SF	.244		Giles,Ken, Phi	.283	
Gomez,Jeanmar, Phi	74.2		Thornton,Matt, Was	18.2		Melancon,Mark, Pit	.250		Bastardo,Antonio, Pit	.284	
Siegrist,Kevin, StL	74.2		Romo,Sergio, SF	18.4		Ziegler,Brad, Ari	.253		Blazek,Michael, Mil	.290	
Kontos,George, SF	73.1		Affeldt,Jeremy, SF	20.0		Watson,Tony, Pit	.260		Melancon,Mark, Pit	.291	
Ramos,A.J., Mia	70.1		Oberg,Scott, Col	20.5		Familia,Jeurys, NYM	.261		Ramos,A.J., Mia	.294	

2015 National League Pitching Leaders

Relief Opp BA Vs LHB
(minimum 50 AB)

Lopez,Javier, SF	.112
Machi,Jean, SF	.120
Garcia,Yimi, LAD	.123
Melancon,Mark, Pit	.138
Bastardo,Antonio, Pit	.138
Grimm,Justin, ChC	.140
Chapman,Aroldis, Cin	.143
Maurer,Brandon, SD	.158
Capps,Carter, Mia	.160
Robles,Hansel, NYM	.167

Relief Opp BA Vs RHB
(minimum 50 AB)

Benoit,Joaquin, SD	.144
Storen,Drew, Was	.146
Jansen,Kenley, LAD	.151
Cunniff,Brandon, Atl	.151
Strop,Pedro, ChC	.156
Torres,Alex, NYM	.157
Blanton,Joe, Pit	.158
Siegrist,Kevin, StL	.164
Aardsma,David, Atl	.167
Ramos,A.J., Mia	.169

Relief Opp Batting Average
(minimum 50 IP)

Benoit,Joaquin, SD	.159
Strop,Pedro, ChC	.167
Jansen,Kenley, LAD	.176
Chapman,Aroldis, Cin	.181
Ramos,A.J., Mia	.184
Kimbrel,Craig, SD	.185
Bastardo,Antonio, Pit	.188
Rodriguez,Francisco, Mil	.189
Robles,Hansel, NYM	.190
Strickland,Hunter, SF	.190

Relief Earned Run Average
(minimum 50 IP)

Chapman,Aroldis, Cin	1.63
Rondon,Hector, ChC	1.67
Giles,Ken, Phi	1.80
Familia,Jeurys, NYM	1.85
Ziegler,Brad, Ari	1.85
Collmenter,Josh, Ari	1.89
Watson,Tony, Pit	1.91
Rosenthal,Trevor, StL	2.10
Papelbon,Jonathan, Phi-Was	2.13
Siegrist,Kevin, StL	2.17

Rel OBP 1st Batter Faced
(minimum 40 BF)

Romo,Sergio, SF	.159
Cotts,Neal, Mil	.160
Wood,Travis, ChC	.178
Lopez,Javier, SF	.182
Ziegler,Brad, Ari	.182
Garcia,Yimi, LAD	.190
Petit,Yusmeiro, SF	.195
Siegrist,Kevin, StL	.200
Strop,Pedro, ChC	.211
Kimbrel,Craig, SD	.213

Rel Opp BA w/ Runners On
(minimum 50 IP)

Siegrist,Kevin, StL	.130
Rodriguez,Francisco, Mil	.139
Hoover,J.J., Cin	.157
Bastardo,Antonio, Pit	.161
Jansen,Kenley, LAD	.162
Kontos,George, SF	.165
Papelbon,Jonathan, Phi-Was	.168
Ramos,A.J., Mia	.170
Rondon,Hector, ChC	.171
Familia,Jeurys, NYM	.172

Relief Opp BA w/ RISP
(minimum 50 IP)

Rodriguez,Francisco, Mil	.081
Hoover,J.J., Cin	.120
Knebel,Corey, Mil	.140
Siegrist,Kevin, StL	.140
Rondon,Hector, ChC	.143
Collmenter,Josh, Ari	.150
Bastardo,Antonio, Pit	.158
Familia,Jeurys, NYM	.159
Ramos,A.J., Mia	.159
Kontos,George, SF	.160

Fastest Avg Fastball-Relief
(minimum 50 IP)

Chapman,Aroldis, Cin	99.5
Caminero,Arquimedes, Pit	97.9
Rosenthal,Trevor, StL	97.6
Kimbrel,Craig, SD	97.3
Diaz,Jumbo, Cin	97.3
Familia,Jeurys, NYM	97.1
Baez,Pedro, LAD	97.1
Strickland,Hunter, SF	96.9
Giles,Ken, Phi	96.5
Rondon,Hector, ChC	96.4

Fastest Average Fastball
(minimum 162 IP)

Harvey,Matt, NYM	95.9
Cole,Gerrit, Pit	95.6
Martinez,Carlos, StL	95.3
deGrom,Jacob, NYM	95.0
Cashner,Andrew, SD	94.8
Arrieta,Jake, ChC	94.6
de la Rosa,Rubby, Ari	94.3
Wacha,Michael, StL	94.2
Scherzer,Max, Was	94.2
Miller,Shelby, Atl	94.0

Slowest Average Fastball
(minimum 162 IP)

Haren,Dan, Mia-ChC	86.1
Hendricks,Kyle, ChC	88.3
Colon,Bartolo, NYM	88.3
Heston,Chris, SF	89.0
Wood,Alex, Atl-LAD	89.1
Niese,Jon, NYM	89.1
Harang,Aaron, Phi	89.5
Anderson,Brett, LAD	90.7
Burnett,A.J., Pit	90.9
Leake,Mike, Cin-SF	90.9

Pitches 100+ Velocity

Chapman,Aroldis, Cin	452
Caminero,Arquimedes, Pit	94
Rosenthal,Trevor, StL	45
Capps,Carter, Mia	27
Familia,Jeurys, NYM	23
Diaz,Jumbo, Cin	17
Vizcaino,Arodys, Atl	16
Syndergaard,Noah, NYM	15
Baez,Pedro, LAD	14
Giles,Ken, Phi	14

Pitches 95+ Velocity

Cole,Gerrit, Pit	1721
Syndergaard,Noah, NYM	1442
Harvey,Matt, NYM	1429
Cashner,Andrew, SD	1283
deGrom,Jacob, NYM	1189
Martinez,Carlos, StL	1090
Strasburg,Stephen, Was	1013
Arrieta,Jake, ChC	999
Rosenthal,Trevor, StL	881
Scherzer,Max, Was	876

Pitches Less Than 80 MPH

Haren,Dan, Mia-ChC	824
Heston,Chris, SF	750
Collmenter,Josh, Ari	629
Kershaw,Clayton, LAD	614
Hellickson,Jeremy, Ari	581
Bumgarner,Madison, SF	536
Jungmann,Taylor, Mil	507
Bolsinger,Mike, LAD	500
Fiers,Mike, Mil	497
Lester,Jon, ChC	487

Lowest % Fastballs
(minimum 162 IP)

Haren,Dan, Mia-ChC	37.7
Shields,James, SD	41.8
Leake,Mike, Cin-SF	44.3
Liriano,Francisco, Pit	46.8
Niese,Jon, NYM	47.1
Bumgarner,Madison, SF	49.6
Greinke,Zack, LAD	50.7
Arrieta,Jake, ChC	50.7
Ross,Tyson, SD	51.9
Anderson,Brett, LAD	52.3

Highest % Fastballs
(minimum 162 IP)

Lynn,Lance, StL	85.4
Colon,Bartolo, NYM	83.8
Hendricks,Kyle, ChC	68.1
Lackey,John, StL	67.6
Cashner,Andrew, SD	67.3
Cole,Gerrit, Pit	67.1
Miller,Shelby, Atl	66.6
Gonzalez,Gio, Was	65.7
Burnett,A.J., Pit	64.0
Zimmermann,Jordan, Was	62.5

Highest % Curveballs
(minimum 162 IP)

Burnett,A.J., Pit	29.3
Koehler,Tom, Mia	22.7
Wood,Alex, Atl-LAD	21.8
Nelson,Jimmy, Mil	21.1
Shields,James, SD	18.7
Gonzalez,Gio, Was	18.2
Kershaw,Clayton, LAD	18.1
Bumgarner,Madison, SF	17.0
Locke,Jeff, Pit	15.9
Arrieta,Jake, ChC	15.4

2015 National League Pitching Leaders

Highest % Changeups
(minimum 162 IP)

Locke,Jeff, Pit	22.7
Shields,James, SD	21.0
Greinke,Zack, LAD	20.9
Liriano,Francisco, Pit	20.5
Hendricks,Kyle, ChC	20.0
de la Rosa,Rubby, Ari	19.3
Martinez,Carlos, StL	17.2
Wacha,Michael, StL	16.8
Gonzalez,Gio, Was	16.1
Wood,Alex, Atl-LAD	15.7

Highest % Sliders
(minimum 162 IP)

Ross,Tyson, SD	41.6
Hammel,Jason, ChC	35.9
Liriano,Francisco, Pit	32.7
Bumgarner,Madison, SF	31.4
Kershaw,Clayton, LAD	27.6
Anderson,Brett, LAD	25.8
Martinez,Carlos, StL	24.1
DeSclafani,Anthony, Cin	23.7
Teheran,Julio, Atl	22.8
Lackey,John, StL	22.5

Balks

Cueto,Johnny, Cin	4
Kershaw,Clayton, LAD	3
Lackey,John, StL	3
Wisler,Matt, Atl	3
10 tied with	2

Strikeout/Hit Ratio
(minimum 50 IP)

Chapman,Aroldis, Cin	2.70
Jansen,Kenley, LAD	2.42
Kimbrel,Craig, SD	2.18
Strop,Pedro, ChC	2.08
Ramos,A.J., Mia	1.93
Kershaw,Clayton, LAD	1.85
Benoit,Joaquin, SD	1.75
Smith,Will, Mil	1.75
Siegrist,Kevin, StL	1.70
Robles,Hansel, NYM	1.65

Opp OPS vs Fastballs
(minimum 251 BF)

Arrieta,Jake, ChC	.511
Greinke,Zack, LAD	.547
Kershaw,Clayton, LAD	.556
Garcia,Jaime, StL	.589
Cole,Gerrit, Pit	.606
deGrom,Jacob, NYM	.612
Bumgarner,Madison, SF	.629
Harvey,Matt, NYM	.638
Lester,Jon, ChC	.643
Lackey,John, StL	.644

Opp OPS vs Curveballs
(minimum 100 BF)

Kershaw,Clayton, LAD	.427
Arrieta,Jake, ChC	.481
Jungmann,Taylor, Mil	.556
Strasburg,Stephen, Was	.572
Syndergaard,Noah, NYM	.622
Nelson,Jimmy, Mil	.631
Wood,Alex, Atl-LAD	.640
Koehler,Tom, Mia	.656
Bumgarner,Madison, SF	.661
Zimmermann,Jordan, Was	.664

Opp OPS vs Changeups
(minimum 100 BF)

Rodriguez,Francisco, Mil	.322
deGrom,Jacob, NYM	.418
Greinke,Zack, LAD	.424
Hamels,Cole, Phi	.529
Martinez,Carlos, StL	.542
Scherzer,Max, Was	.582
Hendricks,Kyle, ChC	.596
Anderson,Chase, Ari	.631
de la Rosa,Jorge, Col	.663
Collmenter,Josh, Ari	.664

Opp OPS vs Sliders
(minimum 64 BF)

Strop,Pedro, ChC	.388
Harvey,Matt, NYM	.442
Greinke,Zack, LAD	.464
Rondon,Hector, ChC	.481
Scherzer,Max, Was	.483
Kershaw,Clayton, LAD	.497
Romo,Sergio, SF	.507
deGrom,Jacob, NYM	.510
Storen,Drew, Was	.520
Liriano,Francisco, Pit	.523

Earned Runs

Kendrick,Kyle, Col	100
Lohse,Kyle, Mil	99
de la Rosa,Rubby, Ari	98
Garza,Matt, Mil	93
Harang,Aaron, Phi	93
Colon,Bartolo, NYM	90
Teheran,Julio, Atl	90
Cashner,Andrew, SD	89
Shields,James, SD	88
Koehler,Tom, Mia	85

Hits Per Nine Innings
(minimum 162 IP)

Arrieta,Jake, ChC	5.90
Greinke,Zack, LAD	5.98
Kershaw,Clayton, LAD	6.31
Scherzer,Max, Was	6.93
deGrom,Jacob, NYM	7.02
Harvey,Matt, NYM	7.42
Bumgarner,Madison, SF	7.46
Liriano,Francisco, Pit	7.47
Ross,Tyson, SD	7.90
Cole,Gerrit, Pit	7.92

2015 American League Fielding Leaders

2B Pivot %	
(minimum 98 G)	
Sanchez,Carlos, CWS	0.721
Kinsler,Ian, Det	0.707
Drew,Stephen, NYY	0.667
Odor,Rougned, Tex	0.667
Forsythe,Logan, TB	0.652
Dozier,Brian, Min	0.651
Altuve,Jose, Hou	0.651
Cano,Robinson, Sea	0.633
Giavotella,Johnny, LAA	0.583
Infante,Omar, KC	0.563

SS Pivot %	
(minimum 98 G)	
Iglesias,Jose, Det	0.721
Gregorius,Didi, NYY	0.687
Ramirez,Alexei, CWS	0.667
Semien,Marcus, Oak	0.654
Hardy,J.J., Bal	0.653
Lindor,Francisco, Cle	0.652
Andrus,Elvis, Tex	0.626
Escobar,Alcides, KC	0.622
Aybar,Erick, LAA	0.535
Bogaerts,Xander, Bos	0.489

Highest Pct CS by Catchers	
(minimum 600 INN or 50 SBA)	
Martin,Russell, Tor	38.5
McCann,James, Det	36.9
Rivera,Rene, TB	36.5
McCann,Brian, NYY	34.2
Castro,Jason, Hou	32.3
Gomes,Yan, Cle	31.6
Perez,Carlos, LAA	30.5
Joseph,Caleb, Bal	28.8
Perez,Salvador, KC	26.7
Vogt,Stephen, Oak	25.9

Lowest Pct CS by Catchers	
(minimum 600 INN or 50 SBA)	
Suzuki,Kurt, Min	9.1
Flowers,Tyler, CWS	14.5
Iannetta,Chris, LAA	21.4
Zunino,Mike, Sea	22.2
Chirinos,Robinson, Tex	23.7
Swihart,Blake, Bos	24.1
Vogt,Stephen, Oak	25.9
Perez,Salvador, KC	26.7
Joseph,Caleb, Bal	28.8
Perez,Carlos, LAA	30.5

2B Double Play %	
(minimum 98 G)	
Sanchez,Carlos, CWS	0.642
Kinsler,Ian, Det	0.620
Odor,Rougned, Tex	0.594
Cano,Robinson, Sea	0.572
Dozier,Brian, Min	0.570
Infante,Omar, KC	0.522
Drew,Stephen, NYY	0.520
Altuve,Jose, Hou	0.517
Kipnis,Jason, Cle	0.504
Giavotella,Johnny, LAA	0.492

3B Double Play %	
(minimum 98 G)	
Longoria,Evan, TB	0.545
Valbuena,Luis, Hou	0.514
Castellanos,Nick, Det	0.490
Plouffe,Trevor, Min	0.483
Machado,Manny, Bal	0.466
Donaldson,Josh, Tor	0.453
Seager,Kyle, Sea	0.444
Beltre,Adrian, Tex	0.411
Sandoval,Pablo, Bos	0.362
Lawrie,Brett, Oak	0.350

SS Double Play %	
(minimum 98 G)	
Iglesias,Jose, Det	0.682
Lindor,Francisco, Cle	0.648
Ramirez,Alexei, CWS	0.646
Gregorius,Didi, NYY	0.632
Andrus,Elvis, Tex	0.606
Semien,Marcus, Oak	0.597
Hardy,J.J., Bal	0.584
Bogaerts,Xander, Bos	0.554
Escobar,Alcides, KC	0.547
Aybar,Erick, LAA	0.516

Errors	
Semien,Marcus, Oak	35
Lawrie,Brett, Oak	24
Headley,Chase, NYY	23
Andrus,Elvis, Tex	22
Machado,Manny, Bal	21
Donaldson,Josh, Tor	18
Aybar,Erick, LAA	17
Beltre,Adrian, Tex	17
Miller,Brad, Sea	17
Odor,Rougned, Tex	17

Fielding Errors	
Semien,Marcus, Oak	17
Andrus,Elvis, Tex	14
Lawrie,Brett, Oak	12
Seager,Kyle, Sea	12
Aybar,Erick, LAA	11
Headley,Chase, NYY	11
Gregorius,Didi, NYY	10
Kinsler,Ian, Det	10
Machado,Manny, Bal	10
Odor,Rougned, Tex	10

Throwing Errors	
Semien,Marcus, Oak	18
Donaldson,Josh, Tor	13
Headley,Chase, NYY	12
Lawrie,Brett, Oak	12
Machado,Manny, Bal	11
Ramirez,Alexei, CWS	10
Miller,Brad, Sea	9
Andrus,Elvis, Tex	8
Beltre,Adrian, Tex	8
Santana,Danny, Min	8

Range Factor for 2B	
(minimum 98 games)	
Odor,Rougned, Tex	4.98
Dozier,Brian, Min	4.95
Kinsler,Ian, Det	4.85
Cano,Robinson, Sea	4.72
Altuve,Jose, Hou	4.49
Sanchez,Carlos, CWS	4.49
Infante,Omar, KC	4.35
Giavotella,Johnny, LAA	4.30
Drew,Stephen, NYY	4.29
Kipnis,Jason, Cle	4.27

Range Factor for 3B	
(minimum 98 games)	
Machado,Manny, Bal	3.09
Donaldson,Josh, Tor	2.90
Seager,Kyle, Sea	2.82
Plouffe,Trevor, Min	2.79
Headley,Chase, NYY	2.73
Beltre,Adrian, Tex	2.71
Moustakas,Mike, KC	2.65
Castellanos,Nick, Det	2.61
Lawrie,Brett, Oak	2.57
Longoria,Evan, TB	2.56

Range Factor for SS	
(minimum 98 games)	
Andrus,Elvis, Tex	4.90
Ramirez,Alexei, CWS	4.45
Bogaerts,Xander, Bos	4.40
Escobar,Alcides, KC	4.37
Semien,Marcus, Oak	4.28
Iglesias,Jose, Det	4.21
Gregorius,Didi, NYY	4.11
Aybar,Erick, LAA	4.06
Hardy,J.J., Bal	4.00
Lindor,Francisco, Cle	3.94

2015 National League Fielding Leaders

2B Pivot %		SS Pivot %		Highest Pct CS by Catchers		Lowest Pct CS by Catchers	
(minimum 98 G)		(minimum 98 G)		(minimum 600 INN or 50 SBA)		(minimum 600 INN or 50 SBA)	
Gordon,Dee, Mia	0.743	Simmons,Andrelton, Atl	0.841	Maldonado,Martin, Mil	37.0	Ruiz,Carlos, Phi	11.5
LeMahieu,DJ, Col	0.705	Ahmed,Nick, Ari	0.733	Ramos,Wilson, Was	36.2	Pena,Brayan, Cin	14.7
Panik,Joe, SF	0.692	Crawford,Brandon, SF	0.703	Rupp,Cameron, Phi	35.3	Montero,Miguel, ChC	17.4
Walker,Neil, Pit	0.684	Hechavarria,Adeiny, Mia	0.657	Molina,Yadier, StL	33.9	Pierzynski,A.J., Atl	18.3
Gennett,Scooter, Mil	0.662	Desmond,Ian, Was	0.650	Norris,Derek, SD	31.1	Cervelli,Francisco, Pit	18.5
Wong,Kolten, StL	0.636	Peralta,Jhonny, StL	0.636	Posey,Buster, SF	30.4	Stewart,Chris, Pit	19.6
Owings,Chris, Ari	0.621	Galvis,Freddy, Phi	0.635	Hundley,Nick, Col	27.5	Castillo,Welington, ChC-Ari	23.1
Peterson,Jace, Atl	0.614	Flores,Wilmer, NYM	0.609	Barnhart,Tucker, Cin	27.5	Ross,David, ChC	23.4
Phillips,Brandon, Cin	0.610	Mercer,Jordy, Pit	0.584	Realmuto,J.T., Mia	25.9	Grandal,Yasmani, LAD	25.3
Kendrick,Howie, LAD	0.569	Segura,Jean, Mil	0.537	Plawecki,Kevin, NYM	25.6	Lucroy,Jonathan, Mil	25.5

2B Double Play %		3B Double Play %		SS Double Play %	
(minimum 98 G)		(minimum 98 G)		(minimum 98 G)	
Walker,Neil, Pit	0.582	Prado,Martin, Mia	0.600	Simmons,Andrelton, Atl	0.795
Panik,Joe, SF	0.565	Turner,Justin, LAD	0.474	Hechavarria,Adeiny, Mia	0.657
Gordon,Dee, Mia	0.562	Arenado,Nolan, Col	0.464	Ahmed,Nick, Ari	0.634
Owings,Chris, Ari	0.536	Carpenter,Matt, StL	0.407	Galvis,Freddy, Phi	0.600
Peterson,Jace, Atl	0.526	Ramirez,Aramis, Mil-Pit	0.405	Crawford,Brandon, SF	0.593
LeMahieu,DJ, Col	0.516	Duffy,Matt, SF	0.396	Peralta,Jhonny, StL	0.586
Wong,Kolten, StL	0.513	Bryant,Kris, ChC	0.352	Mercer,Jordy, Pit	0.585
Gennett,Scooter, Mil	0.504	Frazier,Todd, Cin	0.322	Desmond,Ian, Was	0.580
Phillips,Brandon, Cin	0.436	Escobar,Yunel, Was	0.277	Segura,Jean, Mil	0.561
Kendrick,Howie, LAD	0.420			Flores,Wilmer, NYM	0.538

Errors		Fielding Errors		Throwing Errors	
Desmond,Ian, Was	27	Alvarez,Pedro, Pit	19	Segura,Jean, Mil	15
Castro,Starlin, ChC	24	Desmond,Ian, Was	18	Flores,Wilmer, NYM	10
Alvarez,Pedro, Pit	23	Castro,Starlin, ChC	17	Montero,Miguel, ChC	10
Frazier,Todd, Cin	19	Bryant,Kris, ChC	13	Crawford,Brandon, SF	9
Segura,Jean, Mil	19	Suarez,Eugenio, Cin	13	Desmond,Ian, Was	9
Suarez,Eugenio, Cin	19	Wong,Kolten, StL	12	Arenado,Nolan, Col	8
Arenado,Nolan, Col	17	Frazier,Todd, Cin	11	Frazier,Todd, Cin	8
Bryant,Kris, ChC	17	Russell,Addison, ChC	11	Stewart,Chris, Pit	8
Galvis,Freddy, Phi	17	Galvis,Freddy, Phi	10	6 tied with	7
Wong,Kolten, StL	17	Harrison,Josh, Pit	10		

Range Factor for 2B		Range Factor for 3B		Range Factor for SS	
(minimum 98 games)		(minimum 98 games)		(minimum 98 games)	
LeMahieu,DJ, Col	5.27	Arenado,Nolan, Col	3.24	Ahmed,Nick, Ari	4.82
Gordon,Dee, Mia	5.15	Duffy,Matt, SF	2.57	Simmons,Andrelton, Atl	4.78
Wong,Kolten, StL	5.08	Prado,Martin, Mia	2.52	Crawford,Brandon, SF	4.63
Peterson,Jace, Atl	5.04	Turner,Justin, LAD	2.49	Mercer,Jordy, Pit	4.55
Gennett,Scooter, Mil	4.93	Frazier,Todd, Cin	2.47	Castro,Starlin, ChC	4.45
Panik,Joe, SF	4.90	Bryant,Kris, ChC	2.46	Segura,Jean, Mil	4.40
Walker,Neil, Pit	4.81	Ramirez,Aramis, Mil-Pit	2.46	Hechavarria,Adeiny, Mia	4.39
Phillips,Brandon, Cin	4.80	Carpenter,Matt, StL	2.25	Galvis,Freddy, Phi	4.30
Kendrick,Howie, LAD	4.45	Escobar,Yunel, Was	1.81	Desmond,Ian, Was	4.26
Owings,Chris, Ari	4.34			Flores,Wilmer, NYM	4.16

2015 Active Career Batting Leaders

Batting Average (minimum 1000 PA)		On Base Percentage (minimum 1000 PA)		Slugging Average (minimum 1000 PA)		Home Runs	
Cabrera,Miguel	.321	Votto,Joey	.423	Pujols,Albert	.581	Rodriguez,Alex	687
Suzuki,Ichiro	.314	Cabrera,Miguel	.399	Cabrera,Miguel	.562	Pujols,Albert	560
Mauer,Joe	.313	Trout,Mike	.397	Trout,Mike	.559	Ortiz,David	503
Pujols,Albert	.312	Pujols,Albert	.397	Rodriguez,Alex	.554	Beltre,Adrian	413
Votto,Joey	.311	Goldschmidt,Paul	.395	Ortiz,David	.547	Cabrera,Miguel	408
Posey,Buster	.310	Mauer,Joe	.394	Stanton,Giancarlo	.547	Teixeira,Mark	394
Cano,Robinson	.307	McCutchen,Andrew	.388	Braun,Ryan	.545	Beltran,Carlos	392
Holliday,Matt	.307	Fielder,Prince	.387	Abreu,Jose	.540	Ramirez,Aramis	386
Altuve,Jose	.305	Holliday,Matt	.386	Goldschmidt,Paul	.535	Howard,Ryan	357
Braun,Ryan	.304	Harper,Bryce	.384	Votto,Joey	.534	Hunter,Torii	353

Games		At Bats		Hits		Total Bases	
Rodriguez,Alex	2719	Rodriguez,Alex	10341	Rodriguez,Alex	3070	Rodriguez,Alex	5734
Beltre,Adrian	2567	Beltre,Adrian	9712	Suzuki,Ichiro	2935	Pujols,Albert	4961
Hunter,Torii	2372	Suzuki,Ichiro	9362	Beltre,Adrian	2767	Beltre,Adrian	4636
Suzuki,Ichiro	2357	Rollins,Jimmy	9145	Pujols,Albert	2666	Ortiz,David	4432
Beltran,Carlos	2306	Hunter,Torii	8857	Beltran,Carlos	2454	Beltran,Carlos	4289
Pujols,Albert	2274	Beltran,Carlos	8749	Hunter,Torii	2452	Hunter,Torii	4087
Ortiz,David	2257	Pujols,Albert	8545	Rollins,Jimmy	2422	Cabrera,Miguel	4079
Rollins,Jimmy	2234	Ramirez,Aramis	8136	Cabrera,Miguel	2331	Ramirez,Aramis	4004
Ramirez,Aramis	2194	Ortiz,David	8103	Ortiz,David	2303	Rollins,Jimmy	3840
Pierzynski,A.J.	1978	Cabrera,Miguel	7258	Ramirez,Aramis	2303	Suzuki,Ichiro	3797

Doubles		Triples		Runs Scored		RBI	
Ortiz,David	584	Crawford,Carl	122	Rodriguez,Alex	2002	Rodriguez,Alex	2055
Pujols,Albert	583	Reyes,Jose	117	Pujols,Albert	1599	Pujols,Albert	1698
Beltre,Adrian	560	Rollins,Jimmy	114	Beltran,Carlos	1449	Ortiz,David	1641
Rodriguez,Alex	541	Suzuki,Ichiro	91	Rollins,Jimmy	1396	Beltre,Adrian	1467
Beltran,Carlos	503	Granderson,Curtis	84	Suzuki,Ichiro	1348	Cabrera,Miguel	1445
Rollins,Jimmy	503	Beltran,Carlos	78	Ortiz,David	1340	Beltran,Carlos	1443
Hunter,Torii	498	Victorino,Shane	70	Beltre,Adrian	1339	Ramirez,Aramis	1417
Ramirez,Aramis	495	DeJesus,David	65	Hunter,Torii	1296	Hunter,Torii	1391
Cabrera,Miguel	492	Fowler,Dexter	65	Cabrera,Miguel	1229	Teixeira,Mark	1254
Cano,Robinson	446	2 tied with	63	Ramirez,Aramis	1098	Howard,Ryan	1135

Walks		Intentional Walks		Hit By Pitch		Strikeouts	
Rodriguez,Alex	1324	Pujols,Albert	296	Utley,Chase	179	Rodriguez,Alex	2220
Ortiz,David	1239	Cabrera,Miguel	205	Rodriguez,Alex	175	Hunter,Torii	1741
Pujols,Albert	1165	Ortiz,David	194	Johnson,Reed	134	Howard,Ryan	1729
Beltran,Carlos	1016	Suzuki,Ichiro	179	Ramirez,Aramis	127	Ortiz,David	1664
Cabrera,Miguel	936	Fielder,Prince	163	Weeks,Rickie	127	Beltran,Carlos	1592
Teixeira,Mark	871	Howard,Ryan	152	Pierzynski,A.J.	126	Reynolds,Mark	1519
Swisher,Nick	817	Gonzalez,Adrian	145	Fielder,Prince	117	Beltre,Adrian	1518
Fielder,Prince	815	Mauer,Joe	127	Holliday,Matt	113	Granderson,Curtis	1459
Rollins,Jimmy	797	Martinez,Victor	104	Teixeira,Mark	109	LaRoche,Adam	1407
Bautista,Jose	794	Beltre,Adrian	102	2 tied with	108	Upton Jr.,Melvin	1406

2015 Active Career Batting Leaders

Sacrifice Hits		Sacrifice Flies		Stolen Bases		Seasons Played	
Andrus,Elvis	95	Rodriguez,Alex	108	Suzuki,Ichiro	498	Hawkins,LaTroy	21
Arroyo,Bronson	82	Beltran,Carlos	100	Crawford,Carl	480	Rodriguez,Alex	21
Kershaw,Clayton	80	Pujols,Albert	93	Reyes,Jose	479	Hunter,Torii	19
Wolf,Randy	79	Ramirez,Aramis	87	Rollins,Jimmy	465	Ortiz,David	19
Crisp,Coco	76	Beltre,Adrian	86	Bourn,Michael	326	Beltran,Carlos	18
Lohse,Kyle	75	Ortiz,David	85	Rodriguez,Alex	326	Beltre,Adrian	18
Cain,Matt	70	Martinez,Victor	74	Davis,Rajai	322	Colon,Bartolo	18
Lincecum,Tim	70	Morneau,Justin	72	Beltran,Carlos	311	Pierzynski,A.J.	18
3 tied with	69	Hunter,Torii	71	Ellsbury,Jacoby	301	Ramirez,Aramis	18
		Cabrera,Miguel	70	Crisp,Coco	299	3 tied with	17

At Bats Per Home Run		Grounded Into DP		Highest SB Success Pct		Lowest SB Success Pct	
(minimum 1000 AB)				(minimum 100 SBA)		(minimum 100 SBA)	
Stanton,Giancarlo	14.2	Pujols,Albert	312	Utley,Chase	88.8	DeJesus,David	51.6
Rodriguez,Alex	15.1	Hunter,Torii	262	Werth,Jayson	86.6	Castro,Starlin	62.5
Howard,Ryan	15.1	Rodriguez,Alex	257	Dyson,Jarrod	86.4	Parra,Gerardo	64.5
Pujols,Albert	15.3	Cabrera,Miguel	253	Beltran,Carlos	86.4	Hunter,Torii	66.3
Davis,Chris	15.4	Beltre,Adrian	249	McLouth,Nate	84.7	De Aza,Alejandro	67.7
Carter,Chris	15.9	Ramirez,Aramis	233	Trout,Mike	84.3	Hill,Aaron	68.0
Ortiz,David	16.1	Pierzynski,A.J.	228	Victorino,Shane	83.4	Hart,Corey	68.0
Bautista,Jose	16.5	Cano,Robinson	216	Ellsbury,Jacoby	83.4	Fowler,Dexter	68.3
Teixeira,Mark	16.6	Ortiz,David	214	Cain,Lorenzo	82.9	Martin,Russell	68.3
Cruz,Nelson	17.0	Martinez,Victor	211	Escobar,Alcides	82.4	Pence,Hunter	68.4

Strikeouts / Walks Ratio		At Bats Per GIDP		OPS		Secondary Average	
(minimum 1000 AB)		(minimum 1000 AB)		(minimum 1000 PA)		(minimum 1000 PA)	
Pujols,Albert	.839	Stubbs,Drew	143.8	Pujols,Albert	.977	Trout,Mike	.449
Hanigan,Ryan	.988	Bourn,Michael	142.2	Cabrera,Miguel	.961	Votto,Joey	.429
Aoki,Nori	.988	Gregorius,Didi	130.2	Votto,Joey	.957	Stanton,Giancarlo	.427
Pedroia,Dustin	1.037	Granderson,Curtis	129.8	Trout,Mike	.956	Goldschmidt,Paul	.426
Mauer,Joe	1.039	Gordon,Dee	123.0	Rodriguez,Alex	.937	Bautista,Jose	.421
Callaspo,Alberto	1.043	Blackmon,Charlie	118.9	Goldschmidt,Paul	.930	Ortiz,David	.417
Martinez,Victor	1.126	Schafer,Jordan	117.5	Ortiz,David	.925	Rodriguez,Alex	.417
Johnson,Dan	1.140	Bonifacio,Emilio	115.2	Braun,Ryan	.911	Pujols,Albert	.417
Santana,Carlos	1.148	Eaton,Adam	110.1	Stanton,Giancarlo	.909	Harper,Bryce	.402
Jaso,John	1.162	Suzuki,Ichiro	108.9	2 tied with	.904	Santana,Carlos	.388

Highest Strikeout per PA		Lowest Strikeout per PA		Plate Appearances		At Bats Per RBI	
(minimum 1000 PA)		(minimum 1000 PA)				(minimum 1000 AB)	
Carter,Chris	.334	Aoki,Nori	.077	Rodriguez,Alex	11964	Howard,Ryan	4.7
Flowers,Tyler	.333	Callaspo,Alberto	.092	Beltre,Adrian	10620	Ortiz,David	4.9
Zunino,Mike	.321	Simmons,Andrelton	.092	Suzuki,Ichiro	10101	Cabrera,Miguel	5.0
Reynolds,Mark	.316	Molina,Yadier	.093	Rollins,Jimmy	10074	Rodriguez,Alex	5.0
Maxwell,Justin	.311	Frandsen,Kevin	.094	Beltran,Carlos	9929	Pujols,Albert	5.0
Davis,Chris	.310	Revere,Ben	.094	Pujols,Albert	9902	Teixeira,Mark	5.2
Stubbs,Drew	.303	Pedroia,Dustin	.095	Hunter,Torii	9692	Goldschmidt,Paul	5.4
Saltalamacchia,Jarrod	.300	Pujols,Albert	.099	Ortiz,David	9465	Stanton,Giancarlo	5.5
Wallace,Brett	.295	Suzuki,Ichiro	.099	Ramirez,Aramis	8986	Hamilton,Josh	5.6
Alvarez,Pedro	.291	Solarte,Yangervis	.103	Cabrera,Miguel	8322	Fielder,Prince	5.6

2015 Active Career Pitching Leaders

Earned Run Average (minimum 750 IP)		Winning Percentage (minimum 100 Decisions)		Opponent Batting Average (minimum 750 IP)		Baserunners Per 9 IP (minimum 750 IP)	
Kershaw,Clayton	2.43	Kershaw,Clayton	.671	Rodriguez,Francisco	.204	Kershaw,Clayton	9.45
Rodriguez,Francisco	2.69	Price,David	.650	Nathan,Joe	.206	Strasburg,Stephen	10.10
Nathan,Joe	2.89	Wainwright,Adam	.644	Kershaw,Clayton	.207	Sale,Chris	10.12
Sale,Chris	2.91	Weaver,Jered	.630	Benoit,Joaquin	.223	Bumgarner,Madison	10.28
Wainwright,Adam	2.98	Scherzer,Max	.629	Sale,Chris	.224	Nathan,Joe	10.29
Bumgarner,Madison	3.04	Hudson,Tim	.625	Young,Chris	.224	Price,David	10.41
Price,David	3.09	Sabathia,CC	.624	Arrieta,Jake	.226	Rodriguez,Francisco	10.43
Strasburg,Stephen	3.09	Verlander,Justin	.618	Strasburg,Stephen	.228	Hamels,Cole	10.57
Hernandez,Felix	3.11	Lester,Jon	.617	Cain,Matt	.230	Weaver,Jered	10.66
Cueto,Johnny	3.30	Lee,Cliff	.611	Price,David	.233	Wainwright,Adam	10.68

Games		Games Started		Complete Games		Shutouts	
Hawkins,LaTroy	1042	Buehrle,Mark	493	Sabathia,CC	38	Colon,Bartolo	13
Rodriguez,Francisco	859	Hudson,Tim	479	Colon,Bartolo	36	Hudson,Tim	13
Qualls,Chad	781	Colon,Bartolo	467	Buehrle,Mark	33	Kershaw,Clayton	12
Nathan,Joe	777	Sabathia,CC	452	Lee,Cliff	29	Lee,Cliff	12
Affeldt,Jeremy	774	Burnett,A.J.	430	Hudson,Tim	26	Sabathia,CC	12
Lopez,Javier	771	Zito,Barry	421	Hernandez,Felix	25	Hernandez,Felix	11
Thornton,Matt	730	Lohse,Kyle	416	Burnett,A.J.	24	Buehrle,Mark	10
Rodney,Fernando	700	Lackey,John	387	Shields,James	22	Burnett,A.J.	10
Betancourt,Rafael	680	Harang,Aaron	381	3 tied with	21	4 tied with	9
Frasor,Jason	679	Haren,Dan	380				

Wins		Losses		Innings Pitched		Batters Faced	
Hudson,Tim	222	Buehrle,Mark	160	Buehrle,Mark	3283.1	Buehrle,Mark	13705
Colon,Bartolo	218	Burnett,A.J.	157	Hudson,Tim	3126.2	Hudson,Tim	13005
Buehrle,Mark	214	Colon,Bartolo	154	Sabathia,CC	2988.2	Colon,Bartolo	12588
Sabathia,CC	214	Harang,Aaron	143	Colon,Bartolo	2980.2	Sabathia,CC	12465
Lackey,John	165	Zito,Barry	143	Burnett,A.J.	2731.1	Burnett,A.J.	11665
Zito,Barry	165	Lohse,Kyle	141	Zito,Barry	2576.2	Zito,Barry	11001
Burnett,A.J.	164	Hudson,Tim	133	Lohse,Kyle	2522.1	Lohse,Kyle	10792
Verlander,Justin	157	Arroyo,Bronson	131	Lackey,John	2481.1	Lackey,John	10551
Haren,Dan	153	Haren,Dan	131	Haren,Dan	2419.2	Haren,Dan	10022
2 tied with	147	Sabathia,CC	129	Arroyo,Bronson	2364.2	Arroyo,Bronson	10016

Strikeouts		Walks Allowed		Hit Batters		Wild Pitches	
Sabathia,CC	2574	Burnett,A.J.	1100	Burnett,A.J.	143	Burnett,A.J.	161
Burnett,A.J.	2513	Zito,Barry	1064	Hudson,Tim	124	Hernandez,Felix	126
Colon,Bartolo	2237	Hudson,Tim	917	Lackey,John	112	Lackey,John	110
Hernandez,Felix	2142	Sabathia,CC	894	Arroyo,Bronson	103	Lincecum,Tim	104
Peavy,Jake	2105	Colon,Bartolo	856	Wolf,Randy	103	Haren,Dan	98
Hudson,Tim	2080	Wolf,Randy	831	Zito,Barry	97	Jackson,Edwin	88
Haren,Dan	2013	Marquis,Jason	769	Sabathia,CC	95	Jimenez,Ubaldo	85
Lackey,John	1965	Buehrle,Mark	734	Masterson,Justin	93	Hudson,Tim	84
Verlander,Justin	1943	Jimenez,Ubaldo	718	3 tied with	88	de la Rosa,Jorge	82
Hamels,Cole	1922	Harang,Aaron	712			Shields,James	81

2015 Active Career Pitching Leaders

Saves			Save Pct			Home Runs Allowed			Strikeouts Per 9 IP		
			(minimum 50 Save Ops)						(minimum 750 IP)		
Rodriguez,Francisco	386		Kimbrel,Craig	90.7		Buehrle,Mark	361		Rodriguez,Francisco	10.76	
Nathan,Joe	377		Britton,Zach	90.1		Colon,Bartolo	355		Strasburg,Stephen	10.44	
Papelbon,Jonathan	349		Holland,Greg	90.1		Arroyo,Bronson	324		Sale,Chris	10.30	
Street,Huston	315		Nathan,Joe	89.3		Lohse,Kyle	312		Scherzer,Max	9.79	
Rodney,Fernando	236		Chapman,Aroldis	89.0		Haren,Dan	305		Kershaw,Clayton	9.75	
Kimbrel,Craig	225		Papelbon,Jonathan	88.4		Harang,Aaron	298		Nathan,Joe	9.49	
Soriano,Rafael	207		Jansen,Kenley	88.2		Wolf,Randy	296		Perez,Oliver	9.40	
Soria,Joakim	202		Soria,Joakim	87.8		Sabathia,CC	293		Lincecum,Tim	9.33	
Gregg,Kevin	177		Rosenthal,Trevor	87.3		Zito,Barry	282		Liriano,Francisco	9.26	
Chapman,Aroldis	146		Frieri,Ernesto	86.9		Burnett,A.J.	263		Morrow,Brandon	9.23	

Opp On-Base Percentage			Opp Slugging Average			Hits Per Nine Innings			Home Runs Per Nine IP		
(minimum 750 IP)			(minimum 750 IP)			(minimum 750 IP)			(minimum 750 IP)		
Kershaw,Clayton	.268		Kershaw,Clayton	.304		Rodriguez,Francisco	6.68		Kershaw,Clayton	0.54	
Sale,Chris	.280		Rodriguez,Francisco	.330		Kershaw,Clayton	6.69		Wainwright,Adam	0.60	
Strasburg,Stephen	.280		Nathan,Joe	.331		Nathan,Joe	6.72		Lynn,Lance	0.67	
Nathan,Joe	.282		Sale,Chris	.347		Benoit,Joaquin	7.45		Billingsley,Chad	0.68	
Bumgarner,Madison	.284		Strasburg,Stephen	.350		Sale,Chris	7.46		Gonzalez,Gio	0.70	
Rodriguez,Francisco	.285		Hernandez,Felix	.353		Young,Chris	7.47		Hudson,Tim	0.71	
Price,David	.285		Arrieta,Jake	.354		Arrieta,Jake	7.54		Morton,Charlie	0.72	
Weaver,Jered	.290		Wainwright,Adam	.356		Strasburg,Stephen	7.60		Pelfrey,Mike	0.72	
Hamels,Cole	.290		Gonzalez,Gio	.357		Cain,Matt	7.64		Masterson,Justin	0.73	
Wainwright,Adam	.293		Wilson,C.J.	.358		2 tied with	7.87		Hernandez,Felix	0.73	

Strikeouts / Walks Ratio			Stolen Base Pct Allowed			GIDP Induced			GIDP Per Nine IP		
(minimum 750 IP)			(minimum 750 IP)						(minimum 750 IP)		
Sale,Chris	4.70		Cueto,Johnny	39.7		Buehrle,Mark	362		Porcello,Rick	1.14	
Strasburg,Stephen	4.69		Miley,Wade	42.1		Hudson,Tim	334		Qualls,Chad	1.12	
Bumgarner,Madison	4.22		Buehrle,Mark	42.1		Colon,Bartolo	277		Morton,Charlie	1.11	
Zimmermann,Jordan	4.09		Tillman,Chris	45.2		Sabathia,CC	267		Duke,Zach	1.08	
Haren,Dan	4.03		Fister,Doug	47.2		Burnett,A.J.	241		Pelfrey,Mike	1.04	
Lee,Cliff	3.93		Kershaw,Clayton	51.3		Lackey,John	233		Hernandez,Roberto	1.03	
Scherzer,Max	3.78		Lynn,Lance	52.3		Zito,Barry	220		Masterson,Justin	1.03	
Kershaw,Clayton	3.75		Duke,Zach	54.3		Hernandez,Felix	219		Richard,Clayton	1.02	
Hamels,Cole	3.73		Greinke,Zack	54.3		Marquis,Jason	216		Wilson,C.J.	1.01	
Greinke,Zack	3.71		Colon,Bartolo	55.8		Wolf,Randy	198		Affeldt,Jeremy	1.00	

Complete Game %			Quality Start Pct			Walks Per 9 IP			Games Finished		
(minimum 100 GS)			(minimum 100 GS)			(minimum 750 IP)					
Wainwright,Adam	0.10		Sale,Chris	74.1		Fister,Doug	1.77		Rodriguez,Francisco	602	
Keuchel,Dallas	0.09		Kershaw,Clayton	72.3		Zimmermann,Jordan	1.82		Nathan,Joe	586	
Lee,Cliff	0.09		Wainwright,Adam	70.1		Haren,Dan	1.86		Papelbon,Jonathan	555	
Kershaw,Clayton	0.09		Price,David	69.0		Lee,Cliff	1.94		Street,Huston	502	
Sabathia,CC	0.08		Hernandez,Felix	68.0		Buehrle,Mark	2.01		Rodney,Fernando	440	
Colon,Bartolo	0.08		Hamels,Cole	66.7		Bumgarner,Madison	2.06		Gregg,Kevin	382	
Hernandez,Felix	0.07		Weaver,Jered	65.6		Baker,Scott	2.07		Hawkins,LaTroy	373	
Shields,James	0.07		Bumgarner,Madison	65.6		Nolasco,Ricky	2.14		Soriano,Rafael	343	
Sale,Chris	0.07		Zimmermann,Jordan	64.6		3 tied with	2.18		Soria,Joakim	325	
Kluber,Corey	0.07		Greinke,Zack	64.1					Kimbrel,Craig	294	

2015 American League Bill James Leaders

Top Game Scores

Pitcher	Date	Opp	IP	H	R	ER	BB	SO	GS
Carrasco,Carlos, Cle	9/25	KC	9.0	1	0	0	2	15	98
Kluber,Corey, Cle	5/13	StL	8.0	1	0	0	0	18	98
Archer,Chris, TB	8/20	Hou	9.0	1	0	0	1	11	95
Fiers,Mike, Hou	8/21	LAD	9.0	0	0	0	3	10	94
Hill,Rich, Bos	9/25	Bal	9.0	2	0	0	1	10	92
Holland,Derek, Tex	8/30	Bal	9.0	3	0	0	0	11	92
Sale,Chris, CWS	6/19	Tex	8.0	2	0	0	0	14	92
Verlander,Justin, Det	8/26	LAA	9.0	1	0	0	2	9	92
Carrasco,Carlos, Cle	8/4	LAA	9.0	1	0	0	1	7	91
Iwakuma,Hisashi, Sea	8/12	Bal	9.0	0	0	0	3	7	91
Samardzija,Jeff, CWS	9/21	Det	9.0	1	0	0	0	6	91
Walker,Taijuan, Sea	7/31	Min	9.0	1	1	1	1	11	91

Worst Game Scores

Pitcher	Date	Opp	IP	H	R	ER	BB	SO	GS
Guthrie,Jeremy, KC	5/25	NYY	1.0	9	11	11	3	1	-11
Hernandez,Felix, Sea	8/15	Bos	2.1	12	10	10	1	2	-6
Lewis,Colby, Tex	7/5	LAA	4.0	12	10	10	2	1	-3
Samardzija,Jeff, CWS	9/15	Oak	3.0	11	10	10	3	3	-3
Lewis,Colby, Tex	5/27	Cle	2.2	11	10	9	1	2	-1
Montgomery,Mike, Sea	8/14	Bos	2.1	10	9	9	1	1	1
Eovaldi,Nathan, NYY	6/16	Mia	0.2	9	8	8	0	0	2
Archer,Chris, TB	9/26	Tor	3.2	10	9	9	5	3	3
Deduno,Samuel, Hou	5/6	Tex	4.2	11	10	10	3	4	3
4 tied with									4

Runs Created

Donaldson,Josh, Tor	131
Trout,Mike, LAA	131
Davis,Chris, Bal	117
Bautista,Jose, Tor	113
Encarnacion,Edwin, Tor	110
Fielder,Prince, Tex	110
Cruz,Nelson, Sea	108
Machado,Manny, Bal	107
Abreu,Jose, CWS	105
2 tied with	100

Runs Created Per 27 Outs

Trout,Mike, LAA	8.2
Cabrera,Miguel, Det	8.1
Donaldson,Josh, Tor	7.6
Encarnacion,Edwin, Tor	7.2
Davis,Chris, Bal	7.2
Bautista,Jose, Tor	6.9
Cruz,Nelson, Sea	6.9
Brantley,Michael, Cle	6.5
Fielder,Prince, Tex	6.5
Choo,Shin-Soo, Tex	6.3

Offensive Winning %

Trout,Mike, LAA	.804
Cabrera,Miguel, Det	.791
Donaldson,Josh, Tor	.768
Encarnacion,Edwin, Tor	.752
Bautista,Jose, Tor	.737
Cruz,Nelson, Sea	.734
Davis,Chris, Bal	.708
Abreu,Jose, CWS	.702
Martinez,J.D., Det	.675
Eaton,Adam, CWS	.661

Secondary Average
(minimum 502 PA)

Bautista,Jose, Tor	.503
Trout,Mike, LAA	.470
Davis,Chris, Bal	.450
Encarnacion,Edwin, Tor	.432
Ortiz,David, Bos	.426
Rodriguez,Alex, NYY	.403
Donaldson,Josh, Tor	.398
Santana,Carlos, Cle	.380
Cabrera,Miguel, Det	.378
Cruz,Nelson, Sea	.369

Isolated Power
(minimum 502 PA)

Davis,Chris, Bal	.300
Trout,Mike, LAA	.290
Bautista,Jose, Tor	.285
Encarnacion,Edwin, Tor	.280
Ortiz,David, Bos	.280
Donaldson,Josh, Tor	.271
Cruz,Nelson, Sea	.264
Martinez,J.D., Det	.253
Pujols,Albert, LAA	.236
Rodriguez,Alex, NYY	.235

Power / Speed Number
(minimum 502 PA)

Machado,Manny, Bal	25.5
Altuve,Jose, Hou	21.5
Cain,Lorenzo, KC	20.4
Betts,Mookie, Bos	19.4
Gardner,Brett, NYY	17.8
Trout,Mike, LAA	17.3
Dozier,Brian, Min	16.8
Pillar,Kevin, Tor	16.2
Eaton,Adam, CWS	15.8
Brantley,Michael, Cle	15.0

Speed Scores

Davis,Rajai, Det	8.27
Kiermaier,Kevin, TB	8.11
Reyes,Jose, Tor	8.00
Martin,Leonys, Tex	7.93
Cain,Lorenzo, KC	7.76
Eaton,Adam, CWS	7.75
Ellsbury,Jacoby, NYY	7.66
Gardner,Brett, NYY	7.46
Trout,Mike, LAA	7.28
Escobar,Alcides, KC	7.24

Cheap Wins

Hughes,Phil, Min	6
Eovaldi,Nathan, NYY	5
Buehrle,Mark, Tor	4
Simon,Alfredo, Det	4
Ventura,Yordano, KC	4
9 tied with	3

Tough Losses

Chavez,Jesse, Oak	6
Kluber,Corey, Cle	6
Quintana,Jose, CWS	6
9 tied with	5

2015 National League Bill James Leaders

Top Game Scores

Pitcher	Date	Opp	IP	H	R	ER	BB	SO	GS
Scherzer,Max, Was	10/3	NYM	9.0	0	0	0	0	17	104
Scherzer,Max, Was	6/14	Mil	9.0	1	0	0	1	16	100
Arrieta,Jake, ChC	8/30	LAD	9.0	0	0	0	1	12	98
Hamels,Cole, Phi	7/25	ChC	9.0	0	0	0	2	13	98
Heston,Chris, SF	6/9	NYM	9.0	0	0	0	0	11	98
Kershaw,Clayton, LAD	9/29	SF	9.0	1	0	0	1	13	97
Scherzer,Max, Was	6/20	Pit	9.0	0	0	0	0	10	97
Bumgarner,Madison, SF	8/16	Was	9.0	3	0	0	1	14	94
Bumgarner,Madison, SF	9/12	SD	9.0	1	0	0	0	9	94
Cueto,Johnny, Cin	7/7	Was	9.0	2	0	0	1	11	93
Strasburg,Stephen, Was	9/15	Phi	8.0	1	0	0	1	14	93

Worst Game Scores

Pitcher	Date	Opp	IP	H	R	ER	BB	SO	GS
Buchanan,David, Phi	8/11	Ari	1.2	11	11	11	2	1	-12
Rusin,Chris, Col	8/22	NYM	2.0	12	11	11	2	3	-11
Frias,Carlos, LAD	5/24	SD	4.0	12	10	10	2	0	-4
Garza,Matt, Mil	5/16	NYM	3.1	10	10	10	3	2	-1
Morton,Charlie, Pit	6/21	Was	0.2	8	9	9	1	1	0
Collmenter,Josh, Ari	5/11	Was	1.1	8	9	9	1	0	1
Bettis,Chad, Col	7/7	LAA	2.1	8	10	10	1	2	2
Hamels,Cole, Phi	7/10	SF	3.1	12	9	9	2	4	2
Correia,Kevin, Phi	7/4	Atl	3.1	10	9	9	2	1	3
Roark,Tanner, Was	6/28	Phi	3.1	12	8	8	1	0	3

Runs Created

Harper,Bryce, Was	138
Goldschmidt,Paul, Ari	135
Votto,Joey, Cin	135
McCutchen,Andrew, Pit	120
Arenado,Nolan, Col	116
Rizzo,Anthony, ChC	115
Carpenter,Matt, StL	108
Pollock,A.J., Ari	106
Bryant,Kris, ChC	104
Granderson,Curtis, NYM	104

Runs Created Per 27 Outs

Harper,Bryce, Was	9.9
Votto,Joey, Cin	9.3
Goldschmidt,Paul, Ari	8.8
McCutchen,Andrew, Pit	7.6
Rizzo,Anthony, ChC	6.9
Carpenter,Matt, StL	6.7
Bryant,Kris, ChC	6.6
Peralta,David, Ari	6.6
Arenado,Nolan, Col	6.6
Lind,Adam, Mil	6.5

Offensive Winning %

Harper,Bryce, Was	.846
Votto,Joey, Cin	.826
Goldschmidt,Paul, Ari	.811
McCutchen,Andrew, Pit	.774
Carpenter,Matt, StL	.741
Rizzo,Anthony, ChC	.737
Posey,Buster, SF	.723
Bryant,Kris, ChC	.720
Granderson,Curtis, NYM	.718
Peralta,David, Ari	.710

Secondary Average
(minimum 502 PA)

Harper,Bryce, Was	.568
Votto,Joey, Cin	.510
Goldschmidt,Paul, Ari	.494
Pederson,Joc, LAD	.406
Rizzo,Anthony, ChC	.396
McCutchen,Andrew, Pit	.389
Duda,Lucas, NYM	.382
Carpenter,Matt, StL	.382
Granderson,Curtis, NYM	.374
Bryant,Kris, ChC	.374

Isolated Power
(minimum 502 PA)

Harper,Bryce, Was	.319
Arenado,Nolan, Col	.287
Gonzalez,Carlos, Col	.269
Goldschmidt,Paul, Ari	.249
Frazier,Todd, Cin	.242
Duda,Lucas, NYM	.242
Rizzo,Anthony, ChC	.234
Carpenter,Matt, StL	.233
Votto,Joey, Cin	.228
Howard,Ryan, Phi	.214

Power / Speed Number
(minimum 502 PA)

Pollock,A.J., Ari	26.4
Goldschmidt,Paul, Ari	25.7
Braun,Ryan, Mil	24.5
Blackmon,Charlie, Col	24.4
Marte,Starling, Pit	23.3
Rizzo,Anthony, ChC	22.0
Upton,Justin, SD	22.0
Frazier,Todd, Cin	19.0
Fowler,Dexter, ChC	18.4
Bryant,Kris, ChC	17.3

Speed Scores

Gordon,Dee, Mia	8.74
Hamilton,Billy, Cin	8.71
Revere,Ben, Phi	8.20
Pollock,A.J., Ari	8.09
Span,Denard, Was	7.92
Blackmon,Charlie, Col	7.92
Polanco,Gregory, Pit	7.70
Inciarte,Ender, Ari	7.51
Owings,Chris, Ari	7.26
Heyward,Jason, StL	7.11

Cheap Wins

Burnett,A.J., Pit	4
Conley,Adam, Mia	3
de la Rosa,Rubby, Ari	3
Garcia,Jaime, StL	3
Heston,Chris, SF	3
Kendrick,Kyle, Col	3
Lohse,Kyle, Mil	3
Shields,James, SD	3
Wacha,Michael, StL	3
Zimmermann,Jordan, Was	3

Tough Losses

Scherzer,Max, Was	7
Cashner,Andrew, SD	6
Kershaw,Clayton, LAD	6
Anderson,Brett, LAD	5
Bumgarner,Madison, SF	5
Harvey,Matt, NYM	5
Kennedy,Ian, SD	5
Miller,Shelby, Atl	5
Ross,Tyson, SD	5
12 tied with	4

Additional Bill James Leaders

AL Batters Win Shares

Trout,Mike, LAA	42
Donaldson,Josh, Tor	32
Abreu,Jose, CWS	27
Altuve,Jose, Hou	27
Cain,Lorenzo, KC	27
Davis,Chris, Bal	27
Machado,Manny, Bal	27
Cabrera,Miguel, Det	26
Cruz,Nelson, Sea	26
3 tied with	25

NL Batters Win Shares

Harper,Bryce, Was	38
Goldschmidt,Paul, Ari	35
McCutchen,Andrew, Pit	35
Votto,Joey, Cin	33
Rizzo,Anthony, ChC	32
Bryant,Kris, ChC	30
Carpenter,Matt, StL	30
Granderson,Curtis, NYM	29
Posey,Buster, SF	29
Pollock,A.J., Ari	27

AL Pitchers Win Shares

Keuchel,Dallas, Hou	22
Davis,Wade, KC	19
Price,David, Det-Tor	19
Gray,Sonny, Oak	16
Britton,Zach, Bal	15
Quintana,Jose, CWS	15
Sale,Chris, CWS	15
9 tied with	14

NL Pitchers Win Shares

Arrieta,Jake, ChC	27
Greinke,Zack, LAD	26
Kershaw,Clayton, LAD	21
Cole,Gerrit, Pit	18
Scherzer,Max, Was	18
Bumgarner,Madison, SF	17
Lackey,John, StL	17
Melancon,Mark, Pit	17
Rondon,Hector, ChC	16
2 tied with	15

Batters Win Shares

Rodriguez,Alex	490
Pujols,Albert	446
Cabrera,Miguel	356
Beltran,Carlos	347
Beltre,Adrian	320
Suzuki,Ichiro	309
Rollins,Jimmy	301
Ortiz,David	292
Hunter,Torii	277
Ramirez,Aramis	273

Pitchers Win Shares

Buehrle,Mark	220
Hudson,Tim	219
Sabathia,CC	207
Colon,Bartolo	185
Hernandez,Felix	175
Nathan,Joe	163
Greinke,Zack	158
Rodriguez,Francisco	157
Verlander,Justin	157
Lackey,John	152

AL Component ERA
(minimum 162 IP)

Player	ERA
Keuchel,Dallas, Hou	2.26
Gray,Sonny, Oak	2.53
Price,David, Det-Tor	2.54
Estrada,Marco, Tor	2.64
Carrasco,Carlos, Cle	2.72
Kluber,Corey, Cle	2.74
Archer,Chris, TB	2.79
Sale,Chris, CWS	3.00
Odorizzi,Jake, TB	3.02
Salazar,Danny, Cle	3.10

NL Component ERA
(minimum 162 IP)

Player	ERA
Arrieta,Jake, ChC	1.53
Greinke,Zack, LAD	1.56
Kershaw,Clayton, LAD	1.67
Scherzer,Max, Was	2.11
deGrom,Jacob, NYM	2.13
Bumgarner,Madison, SF	2.43
Harvey,Matt, NYM	2.44
Cole,Gerrit, Pit	2.66
Lester,Jon, ChC	2.88
Liriano,Francisco, Pit	3.04

AL Highest Avg Game Score
(minimum 30 GS)

Keuchel,Dallas, Hou	62.70
Price,David, Det-Tor	61.78
Sale,Chris, CWS	60.32
Kluber,Corey, Cle	59.75
Gray,Sonny, Oak	59.61
Archer,Chris, TB	58.76
Carrasco,Carlos, Cle	58.33
Hernandez,Felix, Sea	57.03
Salazar,Danny, Cle	56.70
2 tied with	54.94

AL Lowest Avg Game Score
(minimum 30 GS)

Simon,Alfredo, Det	46.45
Pelfrey,Mike, Min	46.83
Danks,John, CWS	47.50
Tillman,Chris, Bal	47.84
Samardzija,Jeff, CWS	49.50
Lewis,Colby, Tex	49.76
Miley,Wade, Bos	49.94
Buehrle,Mark, Tor	50.06
Gallardo,Yovani, Tex	50.61
Jimenez,Ubaldo, Bal	51.56

AL Lowest Offensive Win %

Player	%
Ramirez,Alexei, CWS	.331
Sandoval,Pablo, Bos	.332
Gose,Anthony, Det	.358
Escobar,Alcides, KC	.359
Andrus,Elvis, Tex	.394
Semien,Marcus, Oak	.409
Cabrera,Asdrubal, TB	.413
Aybar,Erick, LAA	.419
Perez,Salvador, KC	.427
Garcia,Avisail, CWS	.438

NL Highest Avg Game Score
(minimum 30 GS)

Kershaw,Clayton, LAD	67.97
Arrieta,Jake, ChC	67.24
Greinke,Zack, LAD	67.06
Scherzer,Max, Was	64.36
deGrom,Jacob, NYM	61.80
Bumgarner,Madison, SF	61.69
Cole,Gerrit, Pit	59.50
Lester,Jon, ChC	57.59
Lackey,John, StL	57.39
Liriano,Francisco, Pit	57.19

NL Lowest Avg Game Score
(minimum 30 GS)

Locke,Jeff, Pit	48.27
Cashner,Andrew, SD	48.87
de la Rosa,Rubby, Ari	49.59
Koehler,Tom, Mia	50.23
Anderson,Brett, LAD	50.55
Colon,Bartolo, NYM	50.61
DeSclafani,Anthony, Cin	50.84
Wood,Alex, Atl-LAD	51.22
Kennedy,Ian, SD	51.30
Heston,Chris, SF	51.61

NL Lowest Offensive Win %

Player	%
Rollins,Jimmy, LAD	.271
Owings,Chris, Ari	.276
Ramos,Wilson, Was	.285
Simmons,Andrelton, Atl	.373
Desmond,Ian, Was	.385
Segura,Jean, Mil	.396
Bruce,Jay, Cin	.397
Castro,Starlin, ChC	.399
Pagan,Angel, SF	.400
Molina,Yadier, StL	.416

Home Run Robberies

Ben Jedlovec

The 2015 season may have been the last for the most legendary home run thief of all time: Torii Hunter. Hunter has brought back 12 home runs in the last 12 seasons (0 since 2010), but he had already established himself as the premier home run snatcher in the league (most memorably by swiping Barry Bonds' deep fly at the 2002 All-Star Game) by the time we started tracking Home Run Robberies in 2004 as part of Bill James' Good Plays/Misplays data.

Carlos Gomez has equaled Torii Hunter in our "since 2004" world, and with Tal's Hill potentially coming down in the next few seasons in Gomez's home park in Houston, it's entirely possible that Hunter will be finally overtaken.

If Gomez doesn't hold the top spot for long, it will likely be because Mike Trout has returned to his larcenous ways. Trout stole the show in his rookie 2012 season on both sides of the ball, but nothing stood out more than his four highlight reel pilferages that season. After stealing just one over the next three seasons, Trout broke out of his "slump" with three more crimes in 2015. His career total of eight places him in a tie for fifth on our career list.

Chris Davis had six home runs embezzled in 2015. Actually, that's not quite true. Chris Davis was swindled five times, and Khris Davis once. In our database, no other hitter has had more than three home runs (running out of synonyms here)...purloined...in a single season. Other highlights from this year's section include George Springer's grand salami heist and acts of burglary from J.B., J.D., A.J., J.B.J., and two from Mookie.

2015 Home Run Robberies

Date	Matchup	Fielder	Pos	Pitcher	Batter	Inn.	Outs	Men On	Score
04/06/2015	Twins@Tigers	Yoenis Cespedes	7	David Price	Kurt Suzuki	3	1	___	0-3
04/06/2015	Angels@Mariners	Mike Trout	8	Fernando Salas	Logan Morrison	8	2	___	1-4
04/12/2015	Giants@Padres	Justin Maxwell	9	Jake Peavy	Yangervis Solarte	3	2	___	2-0
04/12/2015	Astros@Rangers	George Springer	9	Tony Sipp	Leonys Martin	10	2	123	4-4
04/13/2015	Nationals@Red Sox	Mookie Betts	8	Rick Porcello	Bryce Harper	1	1	1__	0-0
04/15/2015	Rays@Blue Jays	Kevin Pillar	7	Todd Redmond	Tim Beckham	7	0	___	3-11
05/03/2015	Nationals@Mets	Michael Cuddyer	7	Dillon Gee	Ryan Zimmerman	4	0	___	1-0
05/07/2015	Orioles@Yankees	Delmon Young	9	Chris Tillman	Alex Rodriguez	1	0	1_3	1-0
05/12/2015	Blue Jays@Orioles	Travis Snider	7	Chris Tillman	Jose Bautista	5	2	12_	1-2
05/13/2015	Rockies@Angels	Mike Trout	8	Fernando Salas	Troy Tulowitzki	10	1	___	1-1
05/19/2015	Mariners@Orioles	Seth Smith	7	Taijuan Walker	Adam Jones	1	1	1__	1-0
05/26/2015	Padres@Angels	Will Venable	8	Odrisamer Despaigne	Mike Trout	3	1	1__	0-0
05/29/2015	Rockies@Phillies	Brandon Barnes	8	Chad Bettis	Ryan Howard	5	0	___	2-0
06/02/2015	Twins@Red Sox	Rusney Castillo	9	Clay Buchholz	Aaron Hicks	8	0	___	0-1
06/09/2015	Cubs@Tigers	Rajai Davis	8	Anibal Sanchez	David Ross	2	2	1__	0-1
06/10/2015	Diamondbacks@Dodgers	Joc Pederson	8	Brett Anderson	Yasmany Tomas	3	0	12_	1-4
06/10/2015	Astros@White Sox	Melky Cabrera	7	Jose Quintana	Preston Tucker	7	1	1__	1-1
06/13/2015	Blue Jays@Red Sox	Jose Bautista	9	R.A. Dickey	Rusney Castillo	3	0	___	3-0
06/22/2015	Astros@Angels	Kole Calhoun	9	Hector Santiago	George Springer	3	1	1__	1-0
06/25/2015	Diamondbacks@Rockies	Ben Paulsen	7	Justin Miller	Chris Owings	8	2	___	2-1
06/27/2015	Reds@Mets	Juan Lagares	8	Hansel Robles	Jay Bruce	8	0	___	1-1
06/28/2015	Reds@Mets	Marlon Byrd	7	Josh Smith	Wilmer Flores	3	2	___	1-2
07/04/2015	Orioles@White Sox	Avisail Garcia	9	David Robertson	Chris Davis	9	1	___	2-3
07/05/2015	Orioles@White Sox	J.B. Shuck	7	Scott Carroll	Chris Davis	8	1	_3	8-1
07/07/2015	Padres@Pirates	Justin Upton	7	Marcos Mateo	Andrew McCutchen	5	0	1__	2-1
07/12/2015	Athletics@Indians	David Murphy	9	Corey Kluber	Stephen Vogt	1	1	___	0-0
07/17/2015	Orioles@Tigers	J.D. Martinez	9	Anibal Sanchez	Chris Davis	3	2	1__	1-3
07/17/2015	Rangers@Astros	Colby Rasmus	9	Collin McHugh	Josh Hamilton	6	0	1__	1-3
08/01/2015	Yankees@White Sox	Avisail Garcia	9	John Danks	Didi Gregorius	3	0	1_3	0-2
08/01/2015	Rockies@Cardinals	Randal Grichuk	8	Seth Maness	Michael McKenry	7	2	_2_	6-1
08/01/2015	Cubs@Brewers	Jorge Soler	9	Jason Motte	Khris Davis	9	0	_2_	4-1
08/07/2015	Mets@Rays	Grady Sizemore	7	Jake Odorizzi	Wilmer Flores	6	0	___	0-1
08/09/2015	Rockies@Nationals	Michael Taylor	8	Felipe Rivero	Charlie Blackmon	7	0	___	4-4
08/09/2015	Phillies@Padres	Cody Asche	7	Jerome Williams	Derek Norris	7	1	___	3-1
08/11/2015	Reds@Padres	Will Venable	8	Colin Rea	Brandon Phillips	3	2	___	0-8
08/14/2015	Rays@Rangers	Kevin Kiermaier	8	Xavier Cedeno	Prince Fielder	5	2	1__	3-2
08/14/2015	Mariners@Red Sox	Jackie Bradley Jr.	9	Craig Breslow	Kyle Seager	8	0	___	1-14
08/16/2015	Athletics@Orioles	Henry Urrutia	7	Brian Matusz	Danny Valencia	7	2	1__	2-17
08/17/2015	Athletics@Orioles	Billy Burns	8	Drew Pomeranz	Chris Davis	7	1	___	2-4
08/19/2015	Giants@Cardinals	Juan Perez	8	Matt Cain	Stephen Piscotty	1	1	___	0-0
08/22/2015	Giants@Pirates	Starling Marte	7	Gerrit Cole	Brandon Crawford	2	1	___	0-0
08/31/2015	Rays@Orioles	Kevin Kiermaier	8	Chris Archer	Manny Machado	1	0	___	0-0
09/02/2015	Rays@Orioles	Steve Pearce	7	Kevin Gausman	Brandon Guyer	1	1	___	0-0
09/11/2015	Padres@Giants	Angel Pagan	8	Jake Peavy	Matt Kemp	7	1	___	1-5
09/13/2015	Brewers@Pirates	Khris Davis	7	Taylor Jungmann	Francisco Cervelli	2	1	___	2-1
09/13/2015	Cardinals@Reds	Jason Heyward	9	Michael Wacha	Ivan De Jesus	5	2	___	2-2
09/18/2015	Diamondbacks@Giants	A.J. Pollock	8	Daniel Hudson	Jarrett Parker	8	0	___	2-0
09/25/2015	Orioles@Red Sox	Mookie Betts	9	Rich Hill	Chris Davis	9	2	_2_	0-7
09/26/2015	Mariners@Angels	Mike Trout	8	Andrew Heaney	Jesus Montero	4	0	12_	2-1
09/26/2015	Mets@Reds	Jason Bourgeois	8	Collin Balester	Daniel Murphy	5	0	___	7-2

Win Shares

Joe Rosales

Generally speaking, if a pitcher can reach 20 Win Shares, he's going to be in the discussion for winning a Cy Young. Some years, like in 2011 when Justin Verlander had 27 Win Shares, reaching the 20 Win Shares threshold won't get you much more than a pat on the back. That was the year Verlander won both the American League Cy Young and MVP Awards. But those years are obviously rare. In the three years that Clayton Kershaw won Cy Young Awards, he had 23, 22, and 22 Win Shares, respectively. And in 2012, the two Cy Young winners, David Price and R.A. Dickey, both had 19 Win Shares.

All of those pitchers that have been mentioned so far are starting pitchers. What about relief pitchers, though? It's more rare for them to reach the heights of 20 Win Shares, but there is usually one or two that come close every year. The last time a relief pitcher won a Cy Young Award was 2003 when Eric Gagne did it in the National League. He had 25 Win Shares that year, which was the most by any pitcher, starter or reliever. So, clearly, he deserved that award. But, again, that kind of performance is a rare occurrence. In 2012, Aroldis Chapman had 21 Win Shares, and in 2008, Mariano Rivera had 20 Win Shares. They finished eighth and fifth in the Cy Young voting, respectively, in those years, so they weren't entirely unappreciated. But we might say that they were *under*appreciated. In fact, the year that Chapman had 21 Win Shares is the same year that Dickey and Price both won Cy Young Awards with 19 Win Shares.

For the 2015 season, no such controversy exists. Jake Arrieta and Zack Greinke had dominant seasons as starters in the NL, with 27 and 26 Win Shares, respectively. And Dallas Keuchel led the AL with 22 Win Shares. The relief pitcher that shows up highest on the list is Wade Davis with 19. Davis is interesting because, after beginning his career as a starter in Tampa Bay, he actually had a very successful year as a reliever in his third full season in the big leagues. However, when he was traded to Kansas City, both he and the team wanted him to be a starter again. That move didn't really take, but to Davis' credit, he didn't let that derail his career. Two years back in the bullpen full-time, and he is the best in the game right now.

Bill James devised Win Shares as a way to relate a player's individual statistics to the number of wins he contributed to his team. As a single number, Win Shares allows us to easily compare accomplishments of each player to other players and to compare players across positions.

The following pages contain the sum of a player's Win Shares prior to 2006, followed by his individual season totals from 2006 through 2015. Career totals are also included for each player.

For a complete description of how Win Shares are calculated, as well as countless essays using Win Shares to analyze various facets of the game, check out Bill James' book, *Win Shares*.

WIN SHARES BY YEAR												
Player	<06	06	07	08	09	10	11	12	13	14	15	Career
Aardsma,David	0	4	1	1	16	8		0	1		1	32
Abreu,Jose										29	27	56
Ackley,Dustin							14	16	11	12	3	56
Adams,Matt								1	12	15	3	31
Affeldt,Jeremy	22	3	5	6	10	3	6	5	1	6	0	67
Ahmed,Nick										1	8	9
Albers,Matt		0	0	4	2	5	3	6	5	1	6	32
Allen,Cody								1	8	14	12	35
Alonso,Yonder						0	4	17	12	6	8	47
Altuve,Jose							2	17	11	30	27	87
Alvarez,Henderson							4	5	7	14	0	30
Alvarez,Pedro						14	3	22	18	11	10	78
Amarista,Alexi							1	6	10	13	6	36
Anderson,Brett					8	9	4	3	0	3	8	35
Anderson,Cody											8	8
Andrus,Elvis					17	20	18	23	15	13	21	127
Aoki,Nori								15	17	17	12	61
Archer,Chris								0	10	11	14	35
Arenado,Nolan									9	12	26	47
Arencibia,J.P.						1	14	12	3	3	4	37
Arrieta,Jake						5	5	0	3	12	27	52
Asche,Cody									4	10	10	24
Avila,Alex					3	7	27	15	6	14	6	78
Aviles,Mike			17	2	10	5	10	8	5	3		60
Axford,John					1	11	15	7	3	3	7	47
Aybar,Erick		1	2	15	20	9	20	16	14	20	13	130
Badenhop,Burke				0	5	4	3	4	3	7	3	29
Bailey,Andrew						17	11	6	0	3	0	37
Bailey,Homer			2	0	5	5	5	12	11	8	0	48
Baker,Jeff	1	3	1	7	7	4	3	3	6	6	0	41
Baker,Scott	4	0	8	13	12	8	11		1	1	0	58
Balfour,Grant	5	0	11	5	6	8	15	10	4	0		64
Barmes,Clint	13	6	0	12	13	10	10	10	2	1	4	81
Barney,Darwin						1	14	15	5	6	1	42
Bastardo,Antonio				0	1	10	3	6	3	6		29
Bauer,Trevor								0	0	5	8	13
Bautista,Jose	0	9	12	8	6	34	36	13	18	28	25	189
Beckham,Gordon					12	11	14	13	7	5	3	65
Belisle,Matt	4	3	5	0	1	11	7	8	5	3	3	50
Belt,Brandon							5	17	24	5	20	71
Beltran,Carlos	150	34	25	29	14	8	26	18	22	7	14	347
Beltre,Adrian	128	17	16	13	10	26	16	25	22	27	20	320
Benoit,Joaquin	18	4	10	2		9	8	7	14	12	9	93
Betances,Dellin								0		14	14	28
Betancourt,Rafael	16	5	16	3	8	8	10	11	4		1	82
Betts,Mookie										8	23	31
Billingsley,Chad			6	12	16	9	11	6	8	1	0	69
Bird,Gregory											8	8
Blackmon,Charlie							1	1	7	16	20	45
Blanco,Andres	4	2		2	4	1				2	9	24
Blanco,Gregor			11	0	6		12	13	15	10		67
Blanks,Kyle					5	2	3	0	10	2	3	25
Blanton,Joe	13	10	13	7	11	4	1	5	0		8	72
Blevins,Jerry			0	3	1	3	2	7	5	2	2	25
Bloomquist,Willie	12	5	2	5	7	3	8	9	5	5	1	62
Boesch,Brennan						11	12	6	2	0		31
Bogaerts,Xander									1	7	22	30
Bonifacio,Emilio			1	2	7	5	20	6	7	11	1	60
Bour,Justin										3	12	15
Bourjos,Peter						3	16	5	4	7	2	37
Bourn,Michael		0	4	7	23	18	22	28	14	11	7	134
Boxberger,Brad								2	1	8	8	19
Brach,Brad						0	3	1	5	9		18
Bradley Jr.,Jackie									1	5	10	16
Brantley,Michael					3	5	11	18	21	31	21	110
Braun,Ryan			22	23	36	25	37	28	9	17	20	217
Breslow,Craig	1	1		6	6	8	3	6	7	0	3	41
Britton,Zach							6	3	1	17	15	42
Brothers,Rex							4	7	13	1	1	26
Brown,Domonic						0	4	5	19	10	5	43
Broxton,Jonathan	0	9	10	10	16	6	0	11	1	9	4	76
Bruce,Jay				7	9	16	22	18	21	10	10	113
Bryant,Kris											30	30

WIN SHARES BY YEAR												
Player	<06	06	07	08	09	10	11	12	13	14	15	Career
Buchholz,Clay			3	0	6	18	6	9	12	2	8	64
Buehrle,Mark	91	9	17	16	16	12	15	12	10	13	9	220
Bumgarner,Madison					1	8	12	11	12	16	17	77
Burnett,A.J.	49	9	11	14	12	4	5	11	9	3	10	137
Burns,Billy										0	15	15
Butler,Billy			7	8	18	20	17	21	16	12	9	128
Byrd,Marlon	27	2	13	12	20	19	8	1	23	16	12	153
Cabrera,Asdrubal			7	12	18	9	25	19	12	15	11	128
Cabrera,Everth					14	3	0	11	19	8	1	56
Cabrera,Melky	0	13	12	5	14	8	19	25	7	19	16	138
Cabrera,Miguel	58	33	29	20	25	30	38	32	37	28	26	356
Cahill,Trevor					7	16	9	11	6	0	2	51
Cain,Lorenzo						6	0	7	12	19	27	71
Cain,Matt	5	11	12	14	20	15	15	16	5	1	0	114
Calhoun,Kole								0	8	20	21	49
Callaspo,Alberto		1	1	6	17	11	17	15	13	5	4	90
Canha,Mark											12	12
Cano,Robinson	12	17	21	12	18	34	30	34	35	34	21	268
Carpenter,Matt							0	9	35	27	30	101
Carrasco,Carlos						0	3	5	0	12	14	34
Carter,Chris						0	0	8	13	15	10	46
Cashner,Andrew						2	1	2	10	9	3	27
Casilla,Santiago	0	0	4	3	0	8	8	9	6	12	9	59
Castellanos,Nick									0	13	13	26
Castillo,Welington						1	0	4	10	12	10	37
Castro,Jason							4		8	18	10	7	47
Castro,Starlin						12	25	23	7	20	13	100
Cecil,Brett					3	10	4	1	6	6	6	36
Cervelli,Francisco				0	3	7	4	0	3	7	17	41
Cespedes,Yoenis								24	14	18	27	83
Chacin,Jhoulys					0	10	12	4	15	2	2	45
Chafin,Andrew										1	8	9
Chamberlain,Joba			5	11	6	5	3	1	2	5	0	38
Chapman,Aroldis						2	4	21	12	13	13	65
Chen,Bruce	35	0	0		1	9	9	6	10	0	0	70
Chen,Wei-Yin								12	7	12	14	45
Chisenhall,Lonnie							6	4	7	18	9	44
Choo,Shin-Soo	0	4	1	16	23	27	8	25	31	9	25	169
Cishek,Steve						1	6	10	14	10	3	44
Clippard,Tyler			1	1	5	9	13	11	10	10	9	69
Coghlan,Chris					21	8	4	1	5	15	16	70
Coke,Phil				3	5	6	4	3	0	4	0	25
Colabello,Chris									1	3	13	17
Cole,Gerrit									8	7	18	33
Collmenter,Josh							10	5	7	12	6	40
Colon,Bartolo	130	1	1	2	3		8	9	17	7	7	185
Conforto,Michael											8	8
Correa,Carlos											18	18
Correia,Kevin	5	6	8	0	8	1	4	5	9	3	0	49
Cozart,Zack							1	11	12	8	4	36
Craig,Allen						2	10	20	26	6	0	64
Crawford,Brandon							5	13	11	22	20	71
Crawford,Carl	61	21	20	11	19	32	8	3	13	12	4	204
Crisp,Coco	45	9	16	11	4	14	15	18	21	15	0	168
Cron,C.J.										8	9	17
Cruz,Nelson	0	3	4	7	16	19	16	17	16	22	26	146
Cuddyer,Michael	21	22	16	7	17	15	17	6	19	6	7	153
Cueto,Johnny				6	7	12	12	21	5	22	12	97
Danks,John			4	17	16	16	8	1	3	7	5	77
d'Arnaud,Travis									1	8	11	20
Davis,Chris				8	7	1	4	19	33	12	27	111
Davis,Ike						16	6	15	7	10	3	57
Davis,Khris									6	12	11	29
Davis,Rajai		0	5	5	13	14	6	11	6	14	6	80
Davis,Wade					2	8	6	7	2	15	19	59
De Aza,Alejandro				1	1	1	9	18	16	11	8	65
de la Rosa,Jorge	2	2	3	5	12	8	4	0	12	11	9	68
deGrom,Jacob										11	15	26
DeJesus,David	25	14	15	22	16	11	8	15	12	4	5	147
Denorfia,Chris	0	2		2	0	10	7	12	17	7	5	62
Descalso,Daniel						1	10	5	11	3	1	31
DeShields,Delino											16	16
Desmond,Ian					2	11	16	18	25	19	12	103

Player	<06	06	07	08	09	10	11	12	13	14	15	Career
Dickerson,Corey									4	15	8	27
Dickey,R.A.	11	0		3	3	15	11	19	11	11	10	94
Donaldson,Josh						0		8	32	27	32	99
Doolittle,Sean								5	8	11	2	26
Dozier,Brian								4	19	19	24	66
Drew,Stephen		6	16	21	16	20	10	6	17	4	7	123
Duda,Lucas						0	11	13	8	25	17	74
Duensing,Brian					6	13	4	2	5	4	3	37
Duffy,Danny							1	2	3	12	7	25
Duffy,Matt										2	22	24
Duke,Zach	10	10	2	3	12	1	4	2	2	7	5	58
Dyson,Jarrod						2	2	8	7	9	6	34
Dyson,Sam								0	0	4	9	13
Eaton,Adam								2	5	20	24	51
Ellis,A.J.				0	0	4	3	20	16	7	10	60
Ellsbury,Jacoby			6	16	21	1	34	6	22	22	9	137
Encarnacion,Edwin	4	14	16	14	6	8	11	31	22	19	24	169
Eovaldi,Nathan							2	3	5	4	9	23
Escobar,Alcides				0	4	12	8	14	10	20	15	83
Escobar,Eduardo							0	2	2	13	14	31
Escobar,Yunel			12	13	24	14	20	9	18	10	16	136
Espinosa,Danny						4	22	18	2	6	10	62
Estrada,Marco				0	0	0	4	8	7	5	12	36
Ethier,Andre			11	13	23	21	22	18	22	16	10	171
Familia,Jeurys								0	0	9	15	24
Feldman,Scott	1	3	1	4	14	2	2	4	10	9	5	55
Feliz,Neftali					6	15	12	4	1	6	1	45
Fernandez,Jose									16	4	6	26
Fielder,Prince	2	16	27	23	36	23	33	27	18	3	24	232
Fiers,Mike							0	8	0	7	9	24
Fister,Doug					4	7	18	11	14	14	4	72
Flores,Wilmer									2	7	16	25
Flowers,Tyler					0	0	3	3	10	7		26
Floyd,Gavin	2	0	2	15	13	12	11	10	0	3	1	69
Forsythe,Logan							3	8	3	4	16	34
Fowler,Dexter				0	15	13	16	15	13	16	22	110
Franco,Maikel										1	13	14
Francoeur,Jeff	12	15	20	5	9	8	17	6	1	0	5	98
Frasor,Jason	15	4	3	2	10	5	5	2	5	5	4	60
Frazier,Todd							3	13	15	20	13	64
Freeman,Freddie						0	19	18	35	28	22	122
Freese,David					1	8	13	19	9	12	15	77
Frieri,Ernesto					0	4	4	11	8	0	1	28
Fuld,Sam		0			4	1	9	3	2	12	3	34
Gallardo,Yovani			9	2	10	11	13	16	8	9	14	92
Galvis,Freddy								3	4	2	15	24
Garcia,Avisail								1	5	4	10	20
Garcia,Jaime				1		12	7	6	2	2	12	42
Gardner,Brett				3	9	17	16	2	22	19	19	107
Garza,Matt		1	4	12	12	10	10	5	10	8	0	72
Gattis,Evan									11	12	11	34
Gee,Dillon						3	5	4	10	5	0	27
Gennett,Scooter									9	14	7	30
Gentry,Craig					0	0	5	9	11	8	0	33
Giavotella,Johnny							2	1	1	0	15	19
Gibson,Kyle									0	8	12	20
Giles,Ken										7	11	18
Gillaspie,Conor				0			1	0	9	16	3	29
Goins,Ryan									2	2	12	16
Goldschmidt,Paul							6	17	36	20	35	114
Gomes,Jonny	14	6	8	2	10	18	6	13	12	7	4	100
Gomes,Yan								2	14	18	5	39
Gomez,Carlos			2	13	6	4	7	12	21	27	14	106
Gonzalez,Adrian	2	16	25	24	34	35	27	24	24	26	22	259
Gonzalez,Carlos				6	9	25	20	15	15	5	18	113
Gonzalez,Gio				0	2	15	15	17	11	8	9	77
Gonzalez,Marwin								2	2	6	8	18
Gonzalez,Miguel								10	10	10	5	35
Gordon,Alex			12	15	2	3	24	20	21	26	16	139
Gordon,Dee							6	3	2	22	26	59
Gorzelanny,Tom	0	3	11	0	2	7	4	6	4	3	0	40
Gose,Anthony								4	2	3	8	17
Grandal,Yasmani								11	4	12	15	42

Player	<06	06	07	08	09	10	11	12	13	14	15	Career
Granderson,Curtis	6	20	25	20	20	16	26	21	4	17	29	204
Gray,Sonny									5	13	16	34
Gregerson,Luke					5	9	4	9	7	8	11	53
Gregg,Kevin	10	4	10	11	7	9	4	2	8	0	0	65
Gregorius,Didi								0	10	9	17	36
Greinke,Zack	12	1	9	15	26	11	10	16	17	15	26	158
Grichuk,Randal										1	12	13
Grilli,Jason	2	4	4	7	2		4	6	9	2	6	46
Guthrie,Jeremy	1	0	12	13	7	15	8	7	12	9	0	84
Gutierrez,Franklin	0	1	6	5	21	14	4	5	3		7	66
Guyer,Brandon							0	0		8	11	19
Gyorko,Jedd									12	11	11	34
Hamels,Cole		8	15	18	10	16	17	18	13	15	12	142
Hamilton,Josh			11	26	11	30	15	26	12	12	4	147
Hammel,Jason		0	2	3	10	8	5	10	4	9	9	60
Hanigan,Ryan			1	4	8	13	11	18	5	8	4	72
Happ,J.A.			0	2	15	6	1	5	3	7	10	49
Harang,Aaron	23	18	17	6	7	1	8	8	1	10	3	102
Hardy,J.J.	11	3	19	20	6	10	22	20	16	17	5	149
Haren,Dan	16	14	17	19	20	14	18	6	4	5	11	144
Harper,Bryce								21	19	9	38	87
Harris,Will								0	5	1	9	15
Harrison,Josh							5	4	3	25	12	49
Harrison,Matt				3	1	3	15	18	0	1	0	41
Hart,Corey	0	5	21	16	9	18	21	17		2	1	110
Harvey,Matt								5	14		14	33
Hawkins,LaTroy	71	4	5	6	10	0	6	2	7	9	4	124
Headley,Chase			0	8	16	15	16	32	17	15	16	135
Heaney,Andrew										0	8	8
Hechavarria,Adeiny								3	5	13	13	34
Heisey,Chris						4	8	8	5	3	3	31
Hellickson,Jeremy						3	15	11	4	1	5	39
Hendricks,Kyle										7	8	15
Hernandez,Cesar									3	1	12	16
Hernandez,David					3	6	10	9	3		1	32
Hernandez,Felix	8	8	14	13	26	23	16	15	16	22	14	175
Hernandez,Kiké										5	9	14
Hernandez,Roberto		1	22	3	0	12	2	0	3	4	2	49
Herrera,Kelvin							0	10	5	10	8	33
Herrera,Odubel											16	16
Heyward,Jason						23	11	22	14	23	21	114
Hicks,Aaron									4	4	11	19
Hill,Aaron	9	14	20	5	25	12	13	25	12	10	5	150
Hochevar,Luke			1	3	1	4	7	1	10		3	30
Holland,Derek					2	3	14	8	13	4	2	46
Holland,Greg						0	9	11	18	15	7	60
Holliday,Matt	26	19	27	21	25	25	21	21	25	26	12	248
Holt,Brock								3	1	12	14	30
Hosmer,Eric							13	10	18	14	22	77
Howard,Ryan	11	29	26	24	26	20	21	7	9	15	11	199
Howell,J.P.	1	2	0	11	11		0	3	6	5	6	45
Hudson,Daniel					1	9	16	0		0	5	31
Hudson,Tim	120	7	17	10	4	20	14	12	6	6	3	219
Hughes,Phil			4	0	10	11	1	9	2	14	8	59
Hundley,Nick				3	10	10	12	2	10	6	7	60
Hunter,Tommy				0	8	10	3	4	10	8	4	47
Hunter,Torii	92	17	22	21	20	23	17	24	16	13	12	277
Iannetta,Chris		1	5	17	10	3	16	8	10	17	8	95
Iglesias,Jose							0	1	13		12	26
Inciarte,Ender										10	15	25
Infante,Omar	25	5	4	9	7	19	18	14	16	9	3	129
Ishikawa,Travis		1		4	9	4		5	0	3	1	27
Iwakuma,Hisashi								8	20	11	8	47
Jackson,Austin						18	14	22	15	11	14	94
Jackson,Edwin	2	1	2	10	17	9	12	9	1	0	4	67
Jansen,Kenley						6	6	15	16	11	12	66
Janssen,Casey		4	10		0	5	8	11	11	6	1	56
Jaso,John				0		16	5	21	9	9	6	66
Jay,Jon						8	13	15	17	16	3	72
Jennings,Desmond						0	11	13	20	13	2	59
Jepsen,Kevin				0	4	5	0	4	1	6	12	32
Jimenez,Ubaldo		0	4	11	19	22	6	3	13	3	11	92
Johnson,Chris					0	15	8	17	20	11	3	74

WIN SHARES BY YEAR												
Player	<06	06	07	08	09	10	11	12	13	14	15	Career
Johnson,Jim		0	0	8	7	3	11	17	11	0	7	64
Johnson,Kelly	9		19	19	6	21	16	14	12	7	10	133
Johnson,Reed	30	16	3	13	3	3	8	8	3	3	0	90
Jones,Adam		1	0	9	13	15	16	26	23	25	15	143
Jones,Garrett			0		10	13	12	23	8	9	2	77
Joseph,Caleb										7	12	19
Joyce,Matt				6	1	10	19	13	11	10	1	71
Kang,Jung-ho											17	17
Karns,Nate									0	0	9	9
Kazmir,Scott	11	13	13	12	6	0	0		8	10	11	84
Kela,Keone											8	8
Kelly,Joe								5	9	5	6	25
Kemp,Matt		3	10	19	26	15	37	21	6	20	18	175
Kendrick,Howie		6	9	15	15	19	18	16	13	27	18	156
Kendrick,Kyle			9	3	2	5	7	8	5	4	2	45
Kennedy,Ian			2	0	0	11	20	11	2	9	4	59
Kershaw,Clayton				5	12	15	23	19	22	22	21	139
Keuchel,Dallas								0	3	16	22	41
Kiermaier,Kevin									0	9	19	28
Kimbrel,Craig						4	17	18	17	16	11	83
Kinsler,Ian		12	17	24	24	13	22	15	20	24	21	192
Kipnis,Jason							6	24	27	10	22	89
Kluber,Corey							0	1	9	21	14	45
Lackey,John	40	16	21	13	12	11	1		10	11	17	152
Lagares,Juan									7	15	13	35
Laird,Gerald	5	5	10	9	14	6	3	5	6	2	0	65
Lamb,Jake										1	9	10
LaRoche,Adam	18	16	16	16	17	16	1	22	14	20	5	161
Latos,Mat					1	13	8	16	13	5	3	59
Lawrie,Brett							10	14	9	10	13	56
Leake,Mike						7	9	8	12	10	10	56
LeMahieu,DJ							0	6	8	9	14	37
Lester,Jon		5	4	18	17	17	14	8	12	18	13	126
Lewis,Colby	2	0	0			13	11	8		3	10	47
Lincecum,Tim			8	25	22	14	16	0	4	3	3	95
Lind,Adam		3	7	7	21	9	11	9	15	13	20	115
Lindor,Francisco											14	14
Liriano,Francisco	0	16		4	2	14	4	4	12	7	12	75
Lohse,Kyle	41	4	9	12	3	0	9	16	12	11	0	117
Loney,James		3	16	14	18	18	16	5	19	13	6	128
Longoria,Evan				19	24	28	25	14	24	21	18	173
Lopez,Javier	6	2	4	6	0	6	6	4	5	3	5	47
Lowrie,Jed				7	1	8	5	11	23	11	6	72
Lucroy,Jonathan						4	15	15	19	26	10	89
Lynn,Lance							2	11	7	16	12	48
Machado,Manny								7	20	12	27	66
Madson,Ryan	15	4	5	8	10	8	12				9	71
Marcum,Shaun	1	3	10	12		14	13	8	0		1	62
Marisnick,Jake									2	5	9	16
Markakis,Nick		12	20	23	16	22	19	16	11	20	20	179
Marquis,Jason	39	2	8	15	0	6	3	4			0	85
Marte,Ketel											9	9
Marte,Starling								5	20	17	20	62
Martin,Leonys							0	1	14	14	5	34
Martin,Russell		14	22	20	16	9	14	12	16	22	17	162
Martinez,Carlos									1	4	14	19
Martinez,J.D.							6	7	3	19	25	60
Martinez,Victor	46	18	29	7	21	17	24		11	30	4	207
Masset,Nick		1	0	4	10	7	4			1	1	28
Masterson,Justin				7	5	5	15	6	14	0	2	54
Mathis,Jeff	0	0	2	7	4	3	4	5	4	1	1	31
Matusz,Brian					3	10	0	4	5	3	4	29
Mauer,Joe	28	30	21	30	32	27	10	25	23	14	18	258
Maxwell,Justin			1			3	2	12	5	0	4	27
Mayberry,John					1	1	11	9	7	4	1	34
Maybin,Cameron			0	3	2	8	17	13	0	5	16	64
McCann,Brian	6	22	15	18	20	19	23	12	16	19	21	191
McCann,James										0	10	10
McCarthy,Brandon	5	5	3	1	5		11	7	3	8	0	48
McCullers,Lance												
McCutchen,Andrew					18	22	28	40	34	33	35	210
McGee,Jake						0	2	8	5	15	7	37
McGehee,Casey				0	17	23	9	5		17	1	72

WIN SHARES BY YEAR												
Player	<06	06	07	08	09	10	11	12	13	14	15	Career
McHugh,Collin								0	0	13	13	26
Medlen,Kris				3	7	0	18	13			3	44
Melancon,Mark					1	2	10	0	15	15	17	60
Mercer,Jordy								2	13	10	8	33
Mesoraco,Devin							1	3	8	26	0	38
Miley,Wade							2	14	10	7	9	42
Miller,Andrew		0	2	0	2	0	2	4	2	9	14	35
Miller,Brad									10	11	15	36
Miller,Shelby								2	10	10	11	33
Milone,Tommy							2	10	6	5	8	31
Molina,Yadier	19	9	12	15	20	17	18	29	29	19	16	203
Montero,Miguel		0	3	4	13	9	29	26	10	15	12	121
Morales,Kendrys	2	2	0	23	8			14	17	2	21	89
Moreland,Mitch						6	8	9	10	3	16	52
Morneau,Justin	17	26	18	28	18	17	4	10	14	16	5	173
Morrison,Logan						9	11	4	7	11	9	51
Morrow,Brandon			5	7	4	7	10	0	0		2	42
Morse,Michael	5	2	2	0	2	9	25	13	3	13	3	77
Moss,Brandon			1	5	5	0	0	13	20	17	7	68
Motte,Jason				2	2	6	9	14		1	6	40
Moustakas,Mike							4	14	5	9	21	53
Mujica,Edward		1	0	0	4	4	8	7	10	4	2	40
Murphy,Daniel				6	10		14	20	22	21	19	112
Murphy,David		0	5	11	11	15	9	20	5	14	8	98
Myers,Wil									14	6	9	29
Napoli,Mike		10	8	12	10	12	23	12	16	10	8	121
Nathan,Joe	55	20	16	16	16		5	12	17	6	0	163
Nava,Daniel						5			18	11	2	41
Navarro,Dioner	4	5	6	17	5	2	3	4	11	17	5	79
Nelson,Jimmy									1	0	8	9
Niese,Jon				0	1	6	4	13	6	8	5	43
Nolasco,Ricky		5	0	14	6	7	5	8	9	3	0	57
Norris,Bud					3	3	7	4	8	11	0	36
Norris,Derek								7	11	16	19	53
Nova,Ivan						2	11	5	13	0	2	33
Nunez,Eduardo						2	8	4	6	3	6	29
O'Day,Darren				2	9	9	0	10	8	10	12	60
Odor,Rougned										11	16	27
Odorizzi,Jake								0	1	7	11	19
O'Flaherty,Eric		0	4	0	4	5	12	8	3	2	0	38
Ogando,Alexi						6	13	7	8	0	4	38
Ortiz,David	105	27	27	15	11	18	18	15	22	19	15	292
Osuna,Roberto											11	11
Ozuna,Marcell									8	19	10	37
Pagan,Angel		3	5	3	12	23	15	27	11	14	9	122
Panik,Joe										10	17	27
Papelbon,Jonathan	4	19	15	15	15	10	12	14	11	14	10	139
Parnell,Bobby				0	2	2	4	8	9	0	0	25
Parra,Gerardo					9	6	19	9	15	6	14	78
Pearce,Steve			2	2	2	1	0	6	4	19	5	41
Peavy,Jake	41	12	21	13	6	6	5	17	7	9	6	143
Pederson,Joc										0	15	15
Pedroia,Dustin		2	18	26	24	12	27	17	25	17	12	180
Pelfrey,Mike		0	1	12	4	12	3	2	3	0	7	44
Pena,Brayan	0	1	0	0	2	4	5	3	2	8	8	33
Pence,Hunter			18	19	17	21	24	18	25	26	7	175
Pennington,Cliff				3	7	19	18	10	5	4	3	69
Peralta,David										7	20	27
Peralta,Jhonny	30	15	21	19	10	16	22	12	19	22	20	206
Peralta,Joel	2	5	6	0	0	5	8	6	7	3	2	44
Perez,Carlos										8		8
Perez,Salvador							7	10	23	17	18	75
Perkins,Glen		1	2	7	2	0	8	10	13	9	9	61
Peterson,Jace										1	14	15
Phegley,Josh									2	0	8	10
Phillips,Brandon	5	14	17	19	19	18	22	19	22	13	17	185
Pierzynski,A.J.	82	14	8	8	10	12	11	19	17	6	14	201
Pillar,Kevin									1	1	15	17
Pineda,Michael						10				8	7	25
Piscotty,Stephen											11	11
Plouffe,Trevor						0	6	8	8	17	18	57
Polanco,Gregory										8	17	25
Pollock,A.J.								2	14	10	27	53

533

	WIN SHARES BY YEAR										
Player	<06	06	07	08	09	10	11	12	13	14	15	Career
Porcello,Rick				13	5	8	7	9	13	5		60
Posey,Buster					0	20	9	38	24	30	29	150
Prado,Martin		2	1	9	12	22	12	23	15	15	17	128
Price,David			1	6	17	13	19	12	16	19		103
Puig,Yasiel									17	27	9	53
Pujols,Albert	173	37	32	34	39	32	26	25	10	19	18	445
Qualls,Chad	11	9	9	11	8	0	5	1	6	7	3	70
Quintana,Jose								9	13	12	15	49
Raburn,Ryan	0		4	3	9	11	10	1	13	0	6	57
Ramirez,Alexei			18	15	20	20	14	15	21	16		139
Ramirez,Aramis	95	21	21	25	15	13	25	22	10	15	10	272
Ramirez,Erasmo								2	2	0	10	14
Ramirez,Hanley	0	25	27	32	34	22	10	17	23	18	7	215
Ramos,A.J.							0	5	8	14		27
Ramos,Wilson					3	13	3	8	10	11		48
Rasmus,Colby				13	17	11	15	20	8	15		99
Realmuto,J.T.									1	10		11
Reddick,Josh				0	1	7	16	13	13	17		67
Reed,Addison					0	7	12	7	4			30
Reimold,Nolan				10	0	11	4	0	2	6		33
Rendon,Anthony								12	26	9		47
Revere,Ben					0	9	11	10	16	17		63
Reyes,Jose	32	28	24	28	5	19	26	23	15	19	13	232
Reynolds,Mark		14	17	20	16	16	12	11	7	7		120
Richard,Clayton		0	8	10	2	7	0			3		30
Richards,Garrett					0	1	6	13	14			34
Rios,Alex	16	18	22	20	11	18	4	22	15	9	4	159
Rizzo,Anthony					0	12	14	28	32			86
Roark,Tanner								7	15	4		26
Robertson,David			2	3	4	11	7	12	12	13		64
Robinson,Clint							0		1	10		11
Rodney,Fernando	7	8	3	4	10	6	1	19	11	10	4	83
Rodon,Carlos										9		9
Rodriguez,Alex	314	25	37	23	23	21	14	14	4		16	491
Rodriguez,Eduardo										8		8
Rodriguez,Francisco	41	17	15	16	10	11	10	5	7	13	12	157
Rodriguez,Sean				3	0	9	10	8	4	6	2	42
Rodriguez,Wandy	2	2	7	9	16	11	10	9	3	0	4	73
Rollins,Jimmy	101	25	28	24	19	14	25	21	20	19	5	301
Romo,Sergio				4	4	8	9	11	9	8	5	58
Rondon,Hector								2	11	16		29
Rosario,Eddie										12		12
Rosario,Wilin					1	9	13	3	2			28
Rosenthal,Trevor							2	7	11	14		34
Ross,Cody	1	6	10	16	16	14	14	13	8	2	0	100
Ross,David	10	13	7	5	6	6	7	6	2	2	1	65
Ross,Tyson					0	3	0	5	13	12		33
Ruggiano,Justin		0	1		4	11	8	8	5			37
Ruiz,Carlos	2	13	6	13	19	18	24	9	15	3		122
Russell,Addison										13		13
Ryan,Brendan		5	2	14	8	13	11	4	1	2		60
Sabathia,CC	61	15	24	23	18	20	19	14	8	0	5	207
Salazar,Danny							4	4	14			22
Sale,Chris					5	11	19	15	17	15		82
Saltalamacchia,J		5	6	6	0	7	8	15	5	5		57
Samardzija,Jeff			3	0	0	7	8	7	11	6		42
Sanchez,Anibal		10	1	0	5	11	10	10	17	8	5	77
Sandoval,Pablo			6	27	9	23	18	22	21	6		132
Sano,Miguel										16		16
Santana,Carlos					7	22	21	26	22	14		112
Santana,Ervin	6	12	3	19	6	14	14	2	14	9	7	106
Santiago,Hector						1	7	8	5	11		32
Saunders,Michael				1	6	2	17	10	10	0		46
Schafer,Jordan				2		8	5	8	3	1		27
Scherzer,Max				4	9	13	10	14	20	18	18	106
Schoop,Jonathan									0	6	9	15
Schumaker,Skip	0	0	7	16	18	14	11	7	8	4	3	88
Schwarber,Kyle											10	10
Seager,Kyle						3	24	23	28	17		95
Segura,Jean							4	21	13	12		50
Semien,Marcus								2	7	10		19
Shaw,Bryan						3	4	7	8	7		29
Shields,James		6	12	15	11	3	20	12	18	15	9	121

	WIN SHARES BY YEAR										
Player	<06	06	07	08	09	10	11	12	13	14	15	Career
Siegrist,Kevin									6	0	12	18
Simmons,Andrelton								8	19	13	14	54
Simon,Alfredo				0	0	4	3	6	7	11	5	36
Sipp,Tony				3	4	7	2	1	6	6		29
Sizemore,Grady	29	24	29	26	13	1	5			7	5	139
Smith,Carson										2	11	13
Smith,Joe			3	6	2	3	8	6	9	14	8	59
Smith,Seth		1	3	14	9	13	11	10	20	11		92
Smoak,Justin				7	10	9	12	4	10			52
Smyly,Drew						6	10	10	5			31
Snider,Travis			3	4	8	3	5	5	10	5		43
Sogard,Eric				0	1	1	10	7	8			27
Solano,Donovan						8	9	10	1			28
Solarte,Yangervis								16	18			34
Soler,Jorge								4	10			14
Soria,Joakim		13	17	12	15	7		2	6	10		82
Soriano,Rafael	9	7	9	2	12	14	4	13	11	10	0	91
Soto,Geovany	0	0	3	21	8	15	10	5	8	2	3	75
Span,Denard			16	21	20	6	15	19	26	12		135
Spangenberg,Cory									2	10		12
Springer,George									10	13		23
Stammen,Craig				3	3	2	9	7	4	1		29
Stanton,Giancarlo					13	19	19	15	31	14		111
Stauffer,Tim	0	1	0		3	9	7	0	3	4	0	27
Storen,Drew					5	15	5	3	12	9		49
Strasburg,Stephen					5	2	14	11	13	8		53
Street,Huston	16	14	10	10	15	9	7	9	8	14	12	124
Strop,Pedro					0	0	3	10	5	6	8	32
Stubbs,Drew			5	18	13	6	10	11	2			65
Suarez,Eugenio									9	10		19
Suzuki,Ichiro	134	24	33	19	28	23	15	11	10	8	4	309
Suzuki,Kurt		7	17	17	10	8	10	6	14	8		97
Swihart,Blake										8		8
Swisher,Nick	13	20	18	12	18	22	19	24	17	5	4	172
Syndergaard,Noah										9		9
Tabata,Jose					14	8	6	12	3	1		44
Tanaka,Masahiro										12	10	22
Taylor,Michael									1	14		15
Teheran,Julio					0	0	12	15	8			35
Teixeira,Mark	69	21	25	28	26	24	22	16	1	10	17	259
Tejada,Ruben			3	11	14	4	15	11				58
Thole,Josh			2	8	9	4	1	2	0			26
Thornton,Matt	3	7	4	10	12	12	5	7	3	4	5	72
Tillman,Chris			2	1	1	8	14	13	6			45
Tolleson,Shawn					2	0	6	13				21
Travis,Devon										11		11
Trout,Mike				3	38	40	40	42				163
Trumbo,Mark				0	14	19	14	8	10			65
Tulowitzki,Troy		1	24	9	24	25	25	5	21	16	14	164
Turner,Justin				0	0	15	4	3	18	18		58
Uehara,Koji			4	9	8	5	18	13	9			66
Uggla,Dan		23	16	24	18	24	21	23	10	1	2	162
Upton,Justin		1	8	19	14	26	16	21	21	21		147
Upton Jr.,Melvin	4	2	22	23	13	18	20	17	3	9	9	140
Uribe,Juan	61	11	13	11	13	16	2	2	15	14	10	168
Utley,Chase	38	27	28	30	32	25	18	13	22	24	5	262
Valbuena,Luis			1	6	4	0	5	9	17	9		51
Valencia,Danny				12	10	1	5	4	12			44
Vargas,Jason	4	1	0		3	10	8	11	7	10	3	57
Venable,Will			3	8	15	12	17	14	10	10		89
Ventura,Yordano								1	13	10		24
Verlander,Justin	0	15	16	8	21	17	27	23	14	8	8	157
Victorino,Shane	1	11	11	20	22	23	23	17	19	2	4	153
Villanueva,Carlos		4	8	6	2	2	7	6	6	2	5	48
Vogelsong,Ryan	4	0				14	10	0	5	2		35
Vogt,Stephen						0	4	8	18			30
Volquez,Edinson	0	0	2	16	2	3	0	6	0	11	13	53
Votto,Joey		3	19	24	33	33	27	30	8	33		210
Wacha,Michael								4	7	14		25
Wainwright,Adam	0	9	13	11	21	20		9	16	23	3	125
Walden,Jordan					2	11	3	4	5	2		27
Walker,Neil			0	16	20	21	20	21	22			120
Warren,Adam					0	6	8	9				23

534

Player	<06	06	07	08	09	10	11	12	13	14	15	Career
WIN SHARES BY YEAR												
Watson,Tony							3	5	8	11	12	39
Weaver,Jered		14	12	11	17	19	24	16	10	12	5	140
Webb,Ryan					1	4	4	4	5	3	4	25
Weeks,Rickie	9	10	14	16	7	29	18	14	4	9	0	130
Werth,Jayson	22		13	17	26	22	17	13	26	27	6	189
Wieters,Matt					9	12	23	23	19	5	7	98
Wilhelmsen,Tom							3	13	8	8	7	39
Wilson,Alex									1	3	8	12
Wilson,C.J.	0	3	9	2	11	15	20	9	13	5	8	95
Wolf,Randy	65	2	5	7	14	9	12	2		0	0	116
Wong,Kolten									1	10	18	29
Wood,Alex									4	13	8	25
Wood,Travis						6	3	5	15	3	6	38
Worley,Vance						2	11	5	0	7	3	28
Wright,David	35	30	34	27	20	25	14	30	26	15	7	263
Yelich,Christian									8	22	15	45
Young,Chris	12	12	12	5	1	3	3	3		9	11	71
Young,Chris		2	14	17	8	19	21	9	7	8	9	114
Young,Delmon		2	17	13	7	22	10	7	7	8	2	95
Young,Eric					0	2	4	5	11	6	1	29
Ziegler,Brad				12	7	5	6	8	13	7	12	70
Zimmerman,Ryan	2	24	20	9	21	23	15	22	23	8	10	177
Zimmermann,Jordan					3	1	11	15	15	16	11	72
Zito,Barry	92	17	8	5	10	7	0	6	0		0	145
Zobrist,Ben		2	1	8	27	21	28	27	26	18	17	175

Instant Replay

Ben Jedlovec

We're two years into expanded usage of replay in major league baseball, and it almost feels like it's been here forever. Some of the 2014 speed bumps, such as neighborhood play and catcher collision rule confusion, are largely non-issues now. Time-wasting manager tantrums are far less frequent. Umpires don't always get the calls right, but when they don't, we know that within three or four minutes, the remote replay crew will straighten things out. There had always been small, looming fear that, even if things go perfectly for your favorite team, the umpires still might screw it up, and a less deserving team might prevail. The same ominous sense still prevails with certain events in other sports, such as fouls called by NBA referees. MLB's expanded replay system has lifted much of that doubt and brought us closer to a hypothetical world where the team who performs the best in a given game actually ends up winning.

There are still flaws in the process, of course. Television crews seem to be able to provide their viewers with the best angles within 30 seconds or a minute, while it takes two or three times as long to get an answer from New York. There are still calls that are not eligible for review, most notably balls and strikes. And, sometimes, the New York crew arrives at a completely different conclusion than the broadcast crew, and no explanation is provided. But, the game moves on, and within an out or two, we've forgotten about it entirely.

Some teams have used instant replay to their great advantage. Joe Maddon's Cubs, for instance, challenged 49 calls and had 28 overturned in their favor, the most in MLB for the second straight year. That's 28 calls that would have gone against the Cubs without replay; to put it another way, that's 28 games when Cubs fans might have gone home feeling like the umpires took the game away from them. Cubs' opponents had 18 calls overturned in their favor, a net of +10 calls in the Cubs' direction, tied for the largest such difference in 2015.

Maddon's successor in Tampa, Kevin Cash, did not fare as well. No one challenged more plays than the Rays' 53, but no team had a lower success ratio either (32.1 percent). Given that there's not really a penalty for unsuccessfully challenging a call (other than losing your challenge for the rest of the game), that's not necessarily a bad thing. The Yankees, on the other hand, were successful in 22 of 30 challenges this year, the best ratio in baseball.

As a final note, for the second straight year, umpire-initiated reviews were far less likely to be overturned (27 percent) than manager challenges (52 percent). In other words, umpires should stick to their guns; if they're wrong, the managers will let them know!

2015 Instant Replay Summary

Replay Type	Total Replays	Overturned	Percent
Tag Play	588	259	44.0
Force Play	492	299	60.8
Boundary Call (Over Fence)	102	33	32.4
Hit By Pitch	65	32	49.2
Fair or Foul	43	15	34.9
Trap or Catch	28	11	39.3
Missed Base	10	1	10.0
Record Keeping	6	1	16.7

2015 Challenges

Team	Challenges	Overturned	Pct	Oppenent Challenges	Overturned	Pct	Net
Twins	42	26	61.9	30	16	53.3	10
Cubs	49	28	57.1	33	18	54.5	10
Yankees	30	22	73.3	26	13	50	9
Phillies	38	24	63.2	29	15	51.7	9
Braves	46	23	50.0	35	15	42.9	8
Mariners	38	27	71.1	40	20	50	7
Reds	33	20	60.6	32	14	43.8	6
Astros	47	23	48.9	41	18	43.9	5
Padres	45	20	44.4	34	15	44.1	5
Blue Jays	45	20	44.4	33	15	45.5	5
Rockies	46	24	52.2	41	20	48.8	4
Pirates	46	25	54.3	44	21	47.7	4
Orioles	30	17	56.7	34	13	38.2	4
Indians	28	15	53.6	23	11	47.8	4
Angels	41	24	58.5	38	21	55.3	3
Royals	34	21	61.8	46	20	43.5	1
Mets	35	19	54.3	35	20	57.1	-1
Diamondbacks	34	22	64.7	48	24	50.0	-2
Athletics	29	16	55.2	36	18	50.0	-2
Red Sox	52	21	40.4	47	23	48.9	-2
Rays	53	17	32.1	43	21	48.8	-4
Marlins	31	19	61.3	42	23	54.8	-4
Cardinals	31	16	51.6	44	21	47.7	-5
Giants	40	21	52.5	43	27	62.8	-6
White Sox	41	21	51.2	48	30	62.5	-9
Dodgers	41	17	41.5	42	27	64.3	-10
Rangers	49	16	32.7	44	26	59.1	-10
Brewers	30	16	53.3	47	28	59.6	-12
Nationals	30	13	43.3	34	26	76.5	-13
Tigers	27	11	40.7	49	25	51.0	-14
Totals	1161	604	52.0				

Hall of Fame Monitor

Bill James

If you think about it, you will realize that "consensus" and "predictability" are related concepts. A consensus cannot form around an idea which is out of the mainstream; that's an oxymoron. That which is within the mainstream of ideas is that which is predictable, expected, normal.

The Hall of Fame is a consensus-driven process, and this makes it a predictable process to a certain extent. Players who will eventually be elected to the Hall of Fame tend to meet certain markers. If a player drives in 100 runs in a season, that moves him one step closer to the Hall of Fame; if he drives in 90 runs, that doesn't. If a player wins an MVP Award, that moves him significantly forward in the Hall of Fame march. If a player wins a Gold Glove, that's not nearly as significant, but it's a little step.

To reach the Hall of Fame, you have to take about a hundred little steps, which means that if the ONLY thing a player does in a season is to win a Gold Glove, then that player is not moving forward fast enough to be a Hall of Fame player. We've developed a process to try to keep track of all of the little things that a player does which are steps toward the Hall of Fame. If a player reaches 100 on that scale, then we believe that that player is a clear and certain Hall of Famer, unless he is Pete Rose or a steroid user. If the player reaches 70 or more on this scale, then he's a viable candidate for the Hall of Fame; he may go in or he may not, depending on factors that are outside the record books.

The charts that follow track the Hall of Fame progress of active and recently retired players.

Leading Hall of Fame Candidates Born in 1992	
Player	**Points**
Bryce Harper	17
Manny Machado	9
Kris Bryant	5

Leading Hall of Fame Candidates Born in 1991	
Player	**Points**
Mike Trout	41
Nolan Arenado	11

Leading Hall of Fame Candidates Born in 1990	
Player	**Points**
Jose Altuve	27
Starlin Castro	20
Salvador Perez	13
Trevor Rosenthal	13

Leading Hall of Fame Candidates Born in 1989	
Player	**Points**
Freddie Freeman	19
Giancarlo Stanton	16
Madison Bumgarner	15
Chris Sale	15
Anthony Rizzo	14
Jason Heyward	12

Leading Hall of Fame Candidates Born in 1988	
Player	**Points**
Clayton Kershaw	45
Craig Kimbrel	40
Aroldis Chapman	29
Elvis Andrus	20
Dee Gordon	16
Neftali Feliz	15
Dallas Keuchel	10

Leading Hall of Fame Candidates Born in 1987	
Player	**Points**
Buster Posey	41
Paul Goldschmidt	27
Justin Upton	20
Kenley Jansen	19
Michael Brantley	18
Zach Britton	15
Jason Kipnis	14
Kyle Seager	12
Jay Bruce	12
Austin Jackson	11
Pedro Alvarez	10
Alex Avila	10
Brian Dozier	10

Leading Hall of Fame Candidates Born in 1986	
Player	**Points**
Felix Hernandez	38
Andrew McCutchen	38
Chris Davis	26
Pablo Sandoval	18
Matt Wieters	17
Billy Butler	16
Jonathan Lucroy	16
Johnny Cueto	14
Carlos Santana	12
Dexter Fowler	12
Jake Arrieta	11
Jordan Zimmermann	11

Leading Hall of Fame Candidates Born in 1985	
Player	**Points**
Evan Longoria	29
David Price	26
Matt Carpenter	23
Josh Donaldson	22
Adam Jones	20
Greg Holland	20
Carlos Gonzalez	20
Mark Melancon	16
Asdrubal Cabrera	16
Neil Walker	13
Daniel Murphy	12
Ian Desmond	12

Leading Hall of Fame Candidates Born in 1984	
Player	**Points**
Prince Fielder	53
Brian McCann	40
Troy Tulowitzki	36
Matt Kemp	33
Tim Lincecum	31
Joakim Soria	28
Ryan Zimmerman	24
Jon Lester	24
Max Scherzer	23
Melky Cabrera	23
Alex Gordon	19
Chase Headley	17

Leading Hall of Fame Candidates Born in **1983**	
Player	Points
Miguel Cabrera	127
Joe Mauer	79
Ryan Braun	60
Hanley Ramirez	50
Justin Verlander	50
Dustin Pedroia	49
Joey Votto	48
Jose Reyes	47
Huston Street	42
Zack Greinke	34
Nick Markakis	26
Russell Martin	25

Leading Hall of Fame Candidates Born in **1981**	
Player	Points
Curtis Granderson	38
Josh Hamilton	36
Justin Morneau	33
Carl Crawford	31
Adam Wainwright	29
Ben Zobrist	29
Brandon Phillips	28
Jake Peavy	21
Alex Rios	17
James Shields	17
Alexei Ramirez	15
Omar Infante	13

Leading Hall of Fame Candidates Born in **1979**	
Player	Points
Adrian Beltre	68
Ryan Howard	54
Adam Dunn	50
Mark Buehrle	31
Rafael Soriano	26
Jayson Werth	24
Carlos Ruiz	20
Michael Cuddyer	17
Coco Crisp	17
Adam LaRoche	17
Juan Uribe	16
David DeJesus	13

Leading Hall of Fame Candidates Born in **1982**	
Player	Points
Robinson Cano	79
Francisco Rodriguez	76
Adrian Gonzalez	59
David Wright	55
Yadier Molina	53
Ian Kinsler	38
Jhonny Peralta	28
Jered Weaver	26
Shin-Soo Choo	24
Grady Sizemore	23
Andre Ethier	21
Aaron Hill	19

Leading Hall of Fame Candidates Born in **1980**	
Player	Points
Albert Pujols	163
Mark Teixeira	65
Jonathan Papelbon	63
Matt Holliday	61
CC Sabathia	45
Jose Bautista	41
Dan Uggla	30
Shane Victorino	22
Nelson Cruz	22
Nick Swisher	19
Dan Haren	18
C.J. Wilson	14

Leading Hall of Fame Candidates Born in **1978**	
Player	Points
Jimmy Rollins	68
Chase Utley	63
Victor Martinez	56
Aramis Ramirez	56
Cliff Lee	37
Jose Valverde	35
Vernon Wells	33
Jason Bay	31
Barry Zito	23
John Lackey	19
Kevin Gregg	14
Chad Qualls	10

Leading Hall of Fame Candidates Born in
1977

Player	Points
Carlos Beltran	71
Roy Halladay	61
Juan Pierre	36
Rafael Furcal	34
Fernando Rodney	32
Roy Oswalt	31
Marlon Byrd	16
A.J. Burnett	13
Bronson Arroyo	12
Grant Balfour	10
Javier Lopez	6

Leading Hall of Fame Candidates Born in
1976

Player	Points
Lance Berkman	72
Michael Young	69
Alfonso Soriano	63
Paul Konerko	50
A.J. Pierzynski	39
Matt Thornton	8
Jason Grilli	7
Randy Wolf	7

Leading Hall of Fame Candidates Born in
1975

Player	Points
Alex Rodriguez	200
David Ortiz	74
Torii Hunter	40
Tim Hudson	36
Placido Polanco	34
Koji Uehara	11
Rafael Betancourt	6

Leading Hall of Fame Candidates Born in
1974

Player	Points
Derek Jeter	164
Miguel Tejada	83
Bobby Abreu	79
Joe Nathan	79
R.A. Dickey	11

Leading Hall of Fame Candidates Born in
1973

Player	Points
Ichiro Suzuki	106
Todd Helton	98
Bartolo Colon	32

Leading Hall of Fame Candidates Born in
1972

Player	Points
Andy Pettitte	56
Raul Ibanez	30
LaTroy Hawkins	27

Reviewing our Projections
From the 2015 Handbook

Bill James

The quotation that it is but a short step from the sublime to the ridiculous is attributed to Napoleon Bonaparte in 1812, fleeing his disaster in Russia in a humble disguise, although actually this quotation or extremely similar ones had a long history before Napoleon. Thomas Paine in 1795, for example, wrote that "One step above the sublime makes the ridiculous, and one step above the ridiculous makes the sublime again."

Joc Pederson, a rookie outfielder with the Los Angeles Dodgers, struck out 170 times in 2015 in just 480 at bats, but also hit 26 homers and drew 92 walks. In the sabermetric community we like players who hit homers and draw walks, even at the cost of many strikeouts, but occasionally there is a player who takes it too far. Jack Cust was the most recent example of this; in his major league career he struck out in almost 40% of his at bats, but walked more than a hundred times a year and hit homers more often than Matt Williams, Roger Maris, Chipper Jones or Adrian Gonzalez. Rob Deer was another example of this, for those of you who are a little bit older; from Gorman Thomas to Rob Deer was but a short step.

Babe Ruth represents the sublime in this category; Babe Ruth, Barry Bonds, Jim Thome, Mickey Mantle and Harmon Killebrew. Joc Pederson is just a short step away from them; he just strikes out a little bit *too much*, or at least did as a rookie. We had not expected this, based on his minor league records. We had projected, a year ago, that Pederson would hit 26 homers and strike out 170 times, but not that his in-play average would be so low:

Hitter	Label	Score	G	AB	R	H	D	T	HR	RBI	BB	SO	SB	Avg	Slg
Pederson,Joc	Actual	882	151	480	67	101	19	1	26	54	92	170	4	.210	.417
Pederson,Joc	Projected	882	152	546	84	147	23	2	26	71	73	174	29	.269	.462

That's not a good projection; on an A to F scale that would be about a C-. While we got his power and strikeouts about right and we did anticipate that he would draw some walks, we had expected that he would be able to steal some bases, which he was not able to do, and we missed his batting average by 59 points, which is a very wide margin. Pederson had 28 hits fewer than he would have needed to have to hit .269, which is the largest under-performance (compared to projections) of any major league player in 2015. Two players (Xander Bogaerts and Dee Gordon) had a greater over performance than Pederson in terms of hits, but no one had a greater under performance:

Hitter	Label	Score	G	AB	R	H	D	T	HR	RBI	BB	SO	SB	Avg	Slg
Bogaerts,Xander	Actual	894	156	613	84	196	35	3	7	81	32	101	10	.320	.421
Bogaerts.Xander	Projected	894	156	592	76	156	33	2	16	66	53	135	4	.264	.407

Hitter	Label	Score	G	AB	R	H	D	T	HR	RBI	BB	SO	SB	Avg	Slg
Gordon,Dee	Actual	887	145	615	88	205	24	8	4	46	25	91	58	.333	.418
Gordon,Dee	Projected	887	145	598	83	165	22	9	2	36	39	99	62	.276	.353

Those are all relatively poor projections, not terrible. But back to Pederson, early in the season everything that Pederson hit found a hole. As of May 1 he had struck out 23 times in 60 at bats, but was hitting .300 because his in-play average was almost .400. Then the rest of the year his in-play average was about .240, which is exceptionally low.

Ordinarily, if a player has an extremely low in-play batting average, that's just because he was hitting in bad luck. Ordinarily, that's an effect that goes away over time. But unusual players get unusual results, and Pederson is an unusual player; thus, we can't really be sure whether it's a fluke or not. I'm assuming that Pederson almost always hits the ball in the air. If a player almost always hits the ball in the air, he may have a very low in-play average, as a permanent feature. Pederson's on that line, between ridiculous and sublime, and we can't say for sure where he will fall. That's baseball.

Well, if Pederson, Bogaerts and Dee Gordon had relatively poor projections in this section of the book last year, who had better projections? Alex Gordon, Billy Butler and Yunel Escobar had projections that were just one step better than the first three:

Hitter	Label	Score	G	AB	R	H	D	T	HR	RBI	BB	SO	SB	Avg	Slg
Gordon,Alex	Actual	900	104	354	40	96	18	0	13	48	49	92	2	.271	.432
Gordon,Alex	Projected	900	155	583	87	159	38	2	19	74	65	134	11	.273	.443

Gordon had an injury that took him out for a couple of months, but otherwise played as expected.

Hitter	Label	Score	G	AB	R	H	D	T	HR	RBI	BB	SO	SB	Avg	Slg
Butler,Billy	Actual	903	151	538	63	135	28	1	15	65	52	101	0	.251	.390
Butler,Billy	Projected	903	159	596	67	173	38	0	17	86	62	102	0	.290	.440

Butler's average was off 40 points.

Hitter	Label	Score	G	AB	R	H	D	T	HR	RBI	BB	SO	SB	Avg	Slg
Escobar,Yunel	Actual	906	139	535	75	168	25	1	9	56	45	70	2	.314	.415
Escobar,Yunel	Projected	906	150	544	60	143	24	1	9	53	54	73	2	.263	.360

As Escobar and Butler were one step better than Bogaerts and Pederson (in terms of the accuracy of the projection), our projections for Torii Hunter, Chris Davis and Khris Davis were two steps better:

Hitter	Label	Score	G	AB	R	H	D	T	HR	RBI	BB	SO	SB	Avg	Slg
Hunter,Torii	Actual	921	139	521	67	125	22	0	22	81	35	105	2	.240	.409
Hunter,Torii	Projected	921	140	535	72	151	28	1	17	79	35	103	5	.282	.434

Hitter	Label	Score	G	AB	R	H	D	T	HR	RBI	BB	SO	SB	Avg	Slg
Davis,Chris	Actual	921	160	573	100	150	31	0	47	117	84	208	2	.262	.562
Davis,Chris	Projected	921	154	547	84	138	31	1	36	99	59	194	3	.252	.510

Hitter	Label	Score	G	AB	R	H	D	T	HR	RBI	BB	SO	SB	Avg	Slg
Davis,Khris	Actual	927	121	392	54	97	16	2	27	66	44	122	6	.247	.505
Davis,Khris	Projected	927	140	512	75	134	38	1	25	79	44	116	6	.262	.486

Chris Davis missed having his second 50-homer season because outfielders kept robbing him of home runs. We're up now to like a "B"; these are "B" projections. A B+ projection would be like the projection for Didi Gregorius, Rougned Odor, or Marcus Semien:

Hitter	Label	Score	G	AB	R	H	D	T	HR	RBI	BB	SO	SB	Avg	Slg
Gregorius,Didi	Actual	947	155	525	57	139	24	2	9	56	33	85	5	.265	.370
Gregorius,Didi	Projected	947	110	402	55	104	18	5	7	38	34	61	4	.259	.381

Hitter	Label	Score	G	AB	R	H	D	T	HR	RBI	BB	SO	SB	Avg	Slg
Odor,Rougned	Actual	946	120	426	54	111	21	9	16	61	23	79	6	.261	.465
Odor,Rougned	Projected	946	149	517	63	141	19	8	16	68	26	87	11	.273	.433

Hitter	Label	Score	G	AB	R	H	D	T	HR	RBI	BB	SO	SB	Avg	Slg
Semien,Marcus	Actual	943	155	556	65	143	23	7	15	45	42	132	11	.257	.405
Semien,Marcus	Projected	943	136	492	78	124	28	3	18	62	65	108	13	.252	.431

I always like to see whether there is some player whose batting average, home runs and RBI we projected exactly correctly, but unfortunately there almost never is. We came really close on the doubles, triples and homers for Robinson Chirinos, pretty close for Evan Longoria:

Hitter	Label	Score	G	AB	R	H	D	T	HR	RBI	BB	SO	SB	Avg	Slg
Chirinos,Robinson	Actual	955	78	233	33	54	16	1	10	34	28	62	0	.232	.438
Chirinos,Robinson	Projected	955	94	299	34	73	16	0	10	39	25	61	1	.244	.398

Hitter	Label	Score	G	AB	R	H	D	T	HR	RBI	BB	SO	SB	Avg	Slg
Longoria,Evan	Actual	950	160	604	74	163	35	1	21	73	51	132	3	.270	.435
Longoria,Evan	Projected	950	156	588	85	156	35	1	27	98	68	136	4	.265	.466

We had some "A-" and "A" projections as well, but I'll save those for the end of the article so we can end on an up note. We started with the not-so-hot projections for Dee Gordon, Xander Bogaerts and Joc Pederson. Worse than those were the projections we made for Jonathan Schoop, Billy Hamilton and Chris Carter:

Hitter	Label	Score	G	AB	R	H	D	T	HR	RBI	BB	SO	SB	Avg	Slg
Schoop,Jonathan	Actual	865	86	305	34	85	17	0	15	39	9	79	2	.279	.482
Schoop,Jonathan	Projected	865	144	478	55	114	21	0	17	51	23	110	3	.238	.389

Hitter	Label	Score	G	AB	R	H	D	T	HR	RBI	BB	SO	SB	Avg	Slg
Hamilton,Billy	Actual	863	114	412	56	93	8	3	4	28	28	75	57	.226	.289
Hamilton,Billy	Projected	863	153	559	83	147	24	6	6	48	44	108	62	.263	.360

Hitter	Label	Score	G	AB	R	H	D	T	HR	RBI	BB	SO	SB	Avg	Slg
Carter,Chris	Actual	862	129	391	50	78	17	0	24	64	57	151	1	.199	.427
Carter,Chris	Projected	862	146	509	75	123	26	1	33	90	64	167	5	.242	.491

Not good, not good. Worse still were the projections we offered for Chris Colabello, Randal Grichuk and MVP candidate Josh Donaldson:

Hitter	Label	Score	G	AB	R	H	D	T	HR	RBI	BB	SO	SB	Avg	Slg
Colabello,Chris	Actual	848	101	333	55	107	19	1	15	54	22	96	2	.321	.520
Colabello,Chris	Projected	848	71	188	22	50	12	0	8	33	17	49	0	.266	.457

Hitter	Label	Score	G	AB	R	H	D	T	HR	RBI	BB	SO	SB	Avg	Slg
Grichuk,Randal	Actual	848	103	323	49	89	23	7	17	47	22	110	4	.276	.548
Grichuk,Randal	Projected	848	145	545	83	133	30	5	25	72	29	122	9	.244	.455

Hitter	Label	Score	G	AB	R	H	D	T	HR	RBI	BB	SO	SB	Avg	Slg
Donaldson,Josh	Actual	844	158	620	122	184	41	2	41	123	73	133	6	.297	.568
Donaldson,Josh	Projected	844	151	575	85	154	33	1	25	93	67	111	7	.268	.459

Another step down the ladder were our absurdly inaccurate projections for Leonys Martin, Jayson Werth and Josh Hamilton:

Hitter	Label	Score	G	AB	R	H	D	T	HR	RBI	BB	SO	SB	Avg	Slg
Martin,Leonys	Actual	816	95	288	26	63	12	0	5	25	16	69	14	.219	.312
Martin,Leonys	Projected	816	150	494	70	137	22	6	8	49	37	96	28	.277	.395

Hitter	Label	Score	G	AB	R	H	D	T	HR	RBI	BB	SO	SB	Avg	Slg
Werth,Jayson	Actual	815	88	331	51	73	16	1	12	42	38	84	0	.221	.384
Werth,Jayson	Projected	815	143	533	82	150	31	1	19	78	77	126	9	.281	.450

Hitter	Label	Score	G	AB	R	H	D	T	HR	RBI	BB	SO	SB	Avg	Slg
Hamilton,Josh	Actual	811	50	170	22	43	8	0	8	25	10	52	0	.253	.441
Hamilton,Josh	Projected	811	149	569	79	151	35	2	25	91	52	163	5	.265	.466

And finally we reach the bottom of the ladder, the F stop, our projections for Yasiel Puig, Danny Santana and Javier Baez:

Hitter	Label	Score	G	AB	R	H	D	T	HR	RBI	BB	SO	SB	Avg	Slg
Puig,Yasiel	Actual	746	79	282	30	72	12	3	11	38	26	66	3	.255	.436
Puig,Yasiel	Projected	746	153	572	102	181	39	7	23	81	67	119	15	.316	.530

Hitter	Label	Score	G	AB	R	H	D	T	HR	RBI	BB	SO	SB	Avg	Slg
Santana,Danny	Actual	743	91	261	30	56	10	5	0	21	6	68	8	.215	.291
Santana,Danny	Projected	743	145	577	84	166	35	9	7	50	27	124	29	.288	.416

Hitter	Label	Score	G	AB	R	H	D	T	HR	RBI	BB	SO	SB	Avg	Slg
Baez,Javier	Actual	730	28	76	4	22	6	0	1	4	4	24	1	.289	.408
Baez,Javier	Projected	730	152	612	79	148	33	1	32	72	48	214	23	.242	.456

Just a word about philosophy. Our belief is that if there is a chance that a young player coming out of the minors MIGHT play, then we should project that he WILL play. Our job is to tell you, as best we know, what kind of player a young man will be if he gets a chance to play. Whether he will get a chance or will not...nobody knows that, at this time, and it is not profitable to try to guess. This leads us to overproject playing time for untested, unproven players, but that's alright.

We're not soothsayers or psychics; we're just taking what players have done in the past and projecting it into the future. Sometimes it works pretty well- as for example, with Jhonny Peralta, Derek Dietrich and Pedro Alvarez:

Hitter	Label	Score	G	AB	R	H	D	T	HR	RBI	BB	SO	SB	Avg	Slg
Peralta,Jhonny	Actual	966	155	579	64	159	26	1	17	71	50	111	1	.275	.411
Peralta,Jhonny	Projected	966	148	551	65	146	34	1	18	76	53	118	2	.265	.428

Hitter	Label	Score	G	AB	R	H	D	T	HR	RBI	BB	SO	SB	Avg	Slg
Dietrich,Derek	Actual	963	90	250	38	64	14	3	10	24	23	65	0	.256	.456
Dietrich,Derek	Projected	963	88	315	55	80	15	3	15	44	25	74	3	.254	.463

Hitter	Label	Score	G	AB	R	H	D	T	HR	RBI	BB	SO	SB	Avg	Slg
Alvarez,Pedro	Actual	961	150	437	60	106	18	0	27	77	48	131	2	.243	.469
Alvarez,Pedro	Projected	961	151	540	66	130	25	2	29	88	60	168	6	.241	.456

Those are A- projections. And these are straight A's:

Hitter	Label	Score	G	AB	R	H	D	T	HR	RBI	BB	SO	SB	Avg	Slg
Rizzo,Anthony	Actual	980	160	586	94	163	38	3	31	101	78	105	17	.278	.512
Rizzo,Anthony	Projected	980	158	598	91	164	39	1	34	99	74	120	6	.274	.513

Hitter	Label	Score	G	AB	R	H	D	T	HR	RBI	BB	SO	SB	Avg	Slg
Walker,Neil	Actual	979	151	543	69	146	32	3	16	71	44	110	4	.269	.427
Walker,Neil	Projected	979	145	545	73	146	33	2	19	78	50	101	4	.268	.440

Hitter	Label	Score	G	AB	R	H	D	T	HR	RBI	BB	SO	SB	Avg	Slg
Romine,Andrew	Actual	975	109	184	25	47	5	0	2	15	11	46	10	.255	.315
Romine,Andrew	Projected	975	79	182	22	45	5	1	1	13	14	36	8	.247	.302

I'll never forget the first time I saw Anthony Rizzo in uniform; this was in late February in Ft. Myers, must have been 2008 or 2009. At that time the Red Sox had a big left-handed hitting first baseman who was supposed to be a super prospect, Lars Anderson, but for some reason his power never came around at game time. There were three huge left-handed hitters in a spring training hitting group, just blasting the ball—Anderson, Rizzo, and David Ortiz. I was standing about ten feet away from them. Anderson would hit the ball about 380 feet, then Rizzo would step in and hit it about 400 feet, and then David would step in and hit it about 420. The ball would just hang in the air for an hour and sometimes it would bounce up and hit the side of the team bus that was parked out there at what was supposed to be a safe distance, and then finally Rizzo got hold of one perfect and actually hit it over the bus. I was thinking, "Oh, my God; who's this guy?" Rizzo looked like David, as a hitter, and that's saying something, because there aren't that many David Ortizes running around. He's the same hitter as David, anymore; just about the same. But you know what? Rizzo is really good and he might be a Hall of Famer—but David is 14 years older, and he is still just a little bit better:

Hitter	Year	Score	G	AB	R	H	D	T	HR	RBI	BB	SO	SB	Avg	Slg
Rizzo,Anthony	2015	980	160	586	94	163	38	3	31	101	78	105	17	.278	.512
Ortiz,David	2015	961	146	528	73	144	37	0	37	108	77	95	0	.273	.553

2016 Hitter Projections

Hitter	Team	Age	G	AB	H	2B	3B	HR	R	RBI	RC	RC27	BB	SO	SB	CS	SB%	Avg	OBP	Slg	OPS
Abreu,Jose	CWS	29	151	596	185	36	2	34	88	109	118	7.46	46	125	1	0	1.00	.310	.373	.549	.922
Ackley,Dustin	NYY	28	112	361	90	18	2	10	46	38	45	4.27	35	67	5	3	.62	.249	.317	.393	.711
Adams,Matt	StL	27	148	546	154	34	2	22	64	85	83	5.48	33	114	3	2	.60	.282	.324	.473	.797
Adrianza,Ehire	SF	26	66	138	33	7	1	1	14	10	14	3.40	14	27	4	2	.67	.239	.318	.326	.644
Ahmed,Nick	Ari	26	142	446	109	21	4	7	54	40	46	3.50	31	71	9	5	.64	.244	.295	.357	.651
Almonte,Abraham	Cle	27	148	549	139	29	5	11	74	55	68	4.23	53	118	22	8	.73	.253	.319	.384	.703
Alonso,Yonder	SD	29	90	297	84	18	1	6	35	35	43	5.20	32	44	3	2	.60	.283	.356	.411	.767
Altherr,Aaron	Phi	25	149	524	133	36	5	17	70	71	73	4.77	46	115	19	7	.73	.254	.318	.439	.757
Altuve,Jose	Hou	26	157	639	202	41	3	11	85	61	101	5.82	36	66	40	14	.74	.316	.358	.441	.800
Alvarez,Pedro	Pit	29	150	489	118	22	1	28	63	82	72	5.03	55	151	3	1	.75	.241	.321	.462	.783
Amarista,Alexi	SD	27	116	290	69	12	3	3	30	30	28	3.26	19	46	6	2	.75	.238	.287	.331	.618
Andrus,Elvis	Tex	27	159	614	165	30	3	5	83	58	72	4.07	53	88	29	11	.73	.269	.330	.352	.682
Aoki,Nori	SF	34	140	532	149	23	3	6	68	40	67	4.46	47	44	17	8	.68	.280	.348	.368	.716
Arenado,Nolan	Col	25	156	596	171	45	3	32	86	104	103	6.27	35	88	2	2	.50	.287	.330	.534	.863
Arencibia,J.P.	TB	30	67	182	40	9	0	9	21	28	19	3.48	8	53	0	0	.00	.220	.260	.418	.678
Asche,Cody	Phi	26	134	435	117	27	2	14	50	54	61	4.97	33	99	2	1	.67	.269	.323	.437	.760
Avila,Alex	Det	29	102	303	69	16	1	9	36	39	39	4.33	51	106	0	0	.00	.228	.341	.376	.717
Aviles,Mike	Cle	35	69	145	36	7	0	3	18	14	15	3.55	7	20	3	1	.75	.248	.288	.359	.646
Aybar,Erick	LAA	32	154	587	160	31	3	6	74	53	66	3.95	29	70	15	7	.68	.273	.312	.366	.679
Baez,Javier	ChC	23	140	561	152	32	1	27	79	96	86	5.35	40	172	26	9	.74	.271	.319	.476	.795
Barnes,Clint	SD	37	95	234	53	12	0	4	23	22	21	3.00	14	56	1	1	.50	.226	.285	.329	.614
Barnes,Brandon	Col	30	87	175	44	10	1	4	21	17	20	3.88	12	46	5	3	.62	.251	.307	.389	.695
Barnhart,Tucker	Cin	25	67	141	34	6	0	2	11	14	14	3.40	15	23	0	0	.00	.241	.318	.326	.645
Bautista,Jose	Tor	35	154	571	147	28	1	39	103	106	111	6.76	108	116	7	3	.70	.257	.380	.515	.895
Beckham,Gordon	CWS	29	86	210	49	12	0	5	26	22	22	3.53	16	39	1	1	.50	.233	.303	.362	.665
Beckham,Tim	TB	26	83	248	62	12	2	6	34	31	29	3.99	19	66	6	3	.67	.250	.306	.387	.693
Bell,Josh	Pit	23	151	545	162	26	7	7	70	76	83	5.56	64	71	11	5	.69	.297	.371	.409	.780
Belt,Brandon	SF	28	147	512	140	35	4	19	72	71	84	5.81	61	147	9	4	.69	.273	.354	.469	.823
Beltran,Carlos	NYY	39	132	463	122	27	1	18	59	65	68	5.17	47	88	2	1	.67	.263	.334	.443	.777
Beltre,Adrian	Tex	37	153	596	176	34	1	23	81	87	96	5.93	44	78	1	1	.50	.295	.348	.471	.819
Bethancourt,Christian	Atl	24	112	342	91	19	0	7	35	40	39	3.99	14	59	7	3	.70	.266	.295	.383	.678
Betts,Mookie	Bos	23	150	611	189	45	7	20	110	85	117	7.07	62	77	28	8	.78	.309	.375	.504	.879
Bird,Gregory	NYY	23	147	539	144	33	1	25	78	88	87	5.71	64	122	1	1	.50	.267	.346	.471	.817
Blackmon,Charlie	Col	29	151	569	163	32	4	15	83	62	83	5.16	38	91	31	12	.72	.286	.340	.436	.776
Blanco,Andres	Phi	32	69	134	34	8	0	3	15	13	16	4.12	11	22	1	1	.50	.254	.320	.381	.700
Blanco,Gregor	SF	32	124	370	96	16	3	4	52	31	45	4.18	47	76	14	6	.70	.259	.346	.351	.697
Bogaerts,Xander	Bos	23	152	604	180	35	3	12	81	76	89	5.41	43	108	9	4	.69	.298	.348	.425	.773
Bour,Justin	Mia	28	144	511	136	30	0	23	63	93	78	5.39	51	101	2	1	.67	.266	.334	.460	.794
Bourgeois,Jason	Cin	34	60	132	34	5	1	1	16	10	14	3.64	9	15	5	2	.71	.258	.305	.333	.638
Bourjos,Peter	StL	29	118	241	57	10	4	5	35	20	26	3.60	19	67	7	4	.64	.237	.306	.373	.679
Bourn,Michael	Atl	33	130	455	113	18	4	2	57	32	46	3.42	44	117	19	8	.70	.248	.317	.319	.636
Bradley Jr.,Jackie	Bos	26	145	517	131	34	4	14	79	62	70	4.67	55	120	8	4	.67	.253	.329	.416	.745
Brantley,Michael	Cle	29	150	564	169	37	2	13	78	74	92	5.98	56	58	17	5	.77	.300	.366	.441	.807
Braun,Ryan	Mil	32	140	534	153	32	3	26	83	89	95	6.37	53	119	18	7	.72	.287	.356	.504	.860
Brown,Domonic	Phi	28	84	224	57	11	1	7	26	31	28	4.28	19	40	6	3	.67	.254	.316	.406	.722
Bruce,Jay	Cin	29	152	578	141	33	3	29	83	91	84	4.94	61	155	9	5	.64	.244	.319	.462	.781
Bryant,Kris	ChC	24	157	581	176	36	4	37	112	120	131	8.31	87	188	17	5	.77	.303	.399	.570	.969
Burns,Billy	Oak	26	146	607	164	23	7	4	89	41	71	4.08	44	92	38	10	.79	.270	.323	.351	.674
Butler,Billy	Oak	30	151	542	151	33	0	15	61	74	79	5.25	55	97	0	0	.00	.279	.350	.423	.773
Butler,Joey	TB	30	84	245	69	14	1	7	34	31	37	5.40	25	67	3	2	.60	.282	.351	.433	.783
Buxton,Byron	Min	22	148	537	133	18	9	10	84	59	62	3.90	40	130	33	9	.79	.248	.301	.371	.672
Byrd,Marlon	SF	38	142	506	126	27	2	18	59	64	61	4.16	29	145	2	1	.67	.249	.298	.417	.715
Cabrera,Asdrubal	TB	30	150	566	146	35	2	16	75	68	73	4.48	46	117	8	4	.67	.258	.320	.412	.732
Cabrera,Melky	CWS	31	142	589	169	33	3	12	75	70	81	4.98	42	81	5	3	.62	.287	.336	.414	.751
Cabrera,Miguel	Det	33	147	559	180	38	0	29	91	109	124	8.48	81	106	1	1	.50	.322	.411	.546	.956
Cain,Lorenzo	KC	30	141	510	153	29	4	11	77	62	78	5.56	35	93	24	8	.75	.300	.352	.437	.789
Calhoun,Kole	LAA	28	136	530	144	27	3	21	69	72	78	5.23	43	115	5	2	.71	.272	.330	.453	.783
Callaspo,Alberto	LAD	33	86	206	51	9	0	3	21	20	22	3.69	22	26	0	0	.00	.248	.323	.335	.658
Campbell,Eric	NYM	29	74	178	47	11	0	3	24	21	24	4.66	24	35	6	3	.67	.264	.358	.376	.734
Canha,Mark	Oak	27	131	389	105	24	2	15	58	62	59	5.36	37	83	5	2	.71	.270	.340	.458	.797
Cano,Robinson	Sea	33	159	617	182	40	1	22	84	90	100	5.94	51	96	3	3	.50	.295	.355	.470	.825
Carpenter,Matt	StL	30	158	611	169	46	3	19	106	79	102	5.96	88	138	4	3	.57	.277	.373	.455	.828
Carrera,Ezequiel	Tor	29	71	125	34	5	1	1	18	11	15	4.19	11	23	7	2	.78	.272	.336	.352	.688
Carter,Chris	Hou	29	120	357	78	18	1	21	48	59	50	4.64	47	134	2	1	.67	.218	.316	.451	.767
Casali,Curt	TB	27	73	239	58	15	0	11	29	34	36	5.17	33	66	1	0	1.00	.243	.339	.444	.783
Castellanos,Nick	Det	24	151	540	142	33	4	15	54	69	71	4.63	40	128	1	1	.50	.263	.315	.422	.737
Castillo,Rusney	Bos	28	141	542	145	21	2	10	65	58	62	3.97	35	96	17	9	.65	.268	.313	.369	.682
Castillo,Welington	Ari	29	111	374	95	19	0	16	41	53	50	4.66	30	91	0	0	.00	.254	.318	.433	.751
Castro,Jason	Hou	29	114	374	86	22	1	12	43	41	44	3.97	38	118	0	0	.00	.230	.306	.390	.696
Castro,Starlin	ChC	26	146	543	152	29	4	11	61	60	70	4.60	29	91	8	5	.62	.280	.322	.409	.731
Cervelli,Francisco	Pit	30	128	440	125	19	3	7	55	48	60	4.94	44	86	2	1	.67	.284	.355	.389	.743
Cespedes,Yoenis	NYM	30	156	614	167	36	4	30	93	101	94	5.42	38	139	7	4	.64	.272	.320	.490	.810
Chirinos,Robinson	Tex	32	99	326	78	18	1	12	40	43	41	4.26	33	75	0	0	.00	.238	.313	.409	.722
Chisenhall,Lonnie	Cle	27	147	493	132	32	1	14	62	68	66	4.73	37	95	4	2	.67	.268	.321	.422	.743
Choo,Shin-Soo	Tex	33	143	508	134	29	2	17	79	63	78	5.37	73	138	7	4	.64	.264	.371	.429	.801
Clevenger,Steve	Bal	30	52	112	31	7	0	2	12	13	15	4.81	10	15	0	0	.00	.277	.336	.393	.729
Coghlan,Chris	ChC	31	136	417	107	27	3	10	56	40	57	4.70	49	87	10	5	.67	.257	.338	.408	.745
Colabello,Chris	Tor	32	120	396	113	23	0	17	52	68	64	5.86	34	103	1	1	.50	.285	.345	.472	.817
Collins,Tyler	Det	26	131	419	104	21	2	12	47	53	51	4.14	38	92	11	5	.69	.248	.312	.394	.706

2016 Hitter Projections

Hitter	Team	Age	G	AB	H	2B	3B	HR	R	RBI	RC	RC27	BB	SO	SB	CS	SB%	Avg	OBP	Slg	OPS
Colon,Christian	KC	27	81	275	73	11	1	4	31	26	32	4.04	23	29	10	4	.71	.265	.322	.356	.679
Conforto,Michael	NYM	23	140	478	134	34	3	20	70	71	83	6.26	55	97	1	1	.50	.280	.356	.490	.845
Conger,Hank	Hou	28	80	228	54	12	0	8	26	29	28	4.18	23	54	0	0	.00	.237	.312	.395	.707
Corporan,Carlos	Tex	32	56	132	29	6	0	4	12	15	12	3.03	8	35	0	0	.00	.220	.280	.356	.636
Correa,Carlos	Hou	21	156	612	180	44	3	33	93	112	122	7.23	65	112	34	7	.83	.294	.363	.538	.900
Cozart,Zack	Cin	30	141	515	127	28	2	12	66	51	56	3.72	31	88	6	3	.67	.247	.293	.379	.672
Crawford,Brandon	SF	29	153	504	124	27	4	14	59	63	62	4.21	47	118	5	3	.62	.246	.317	.399	.715
Crawford,Carl	LAD	34	108	346	96	18	3	7	49	38	45	4.57	20	65	16	6	.73	.277	.322	.408	.730
Crawford,J.P.	Phi	21	147	530	129	30	8	7	66	43	64	4.11	63	67	11	4	.73	.243	.324	.370	.694
Crisp,Coco	Oak	36	112	416	100	19	2	9	58	40	49	3.97	47	66	17	5	.77	.240	.317	.361	.678
Cron,C.J.	LAA	26	127	451	122	28	2	18	51	70	63	4.95	21	86	3	2	.60	.271	.307	.461	.769
Cruz,Nelson	Sea	35	153	593	159	30	1	36	81	99	98	5.83	55	161	5	3	.62	.268	.334	.504	.839
Cruz,Tony	StL	29	60	137	30	7	1	2	11	14	12	2.92	8	27	0	0	.00	.219	.262	.328	.591
Cuddyer,Michael	NYM	37	107	350	95	20	1	12	46	46	50	5.08	28	76	3	1	.75	.271	.331	.437	.768
d'Arnaud,Travis	NYM	27	101	366	99	25	2	16	50	54	58	5.65	33	65	1	0	1.00	.270	.334	.481	.815
Davis,Chris	Bal	30	160	576	146	33	1	40	91	108	99	5.96	68	207	2	2	.50	.253	.339	.523	.862
Davis,Ike	Oak	29	126	447	107	27	0	16	54	61	61	4.65	65	107	1	1	.50	.239	.336	.407	.743
Davis,Khris	Mil	28	145	506	130	31	2	30	75	82	83	5.69	51	130	6	3	.67	.257	.329	.504	.833
Davis,Rajai	Det	35	134	449	115	23	4	7	63	41	50	3.77	26	94	29	11	.73	.256	.303	.372	.675
De Aza,Alejandro	SF	32	123	390	102	22	3	8	54	38	49	4.33	35	97	11	6	.65	.262	.330	.395	.725
DeJesus,David	LAA	36	79	175	43	9	1	3	20	17	20	3.91	17	33	2	1	.67	.246	.333	.360	.693
den Dekker,Matt	Was	28	85	200	53	11	1	6	28	23	27	4.71	17	45	6	2	.75	.265	.323	.420	.743
Denorfia,Chris	ChC	35	94	219	55	10	1	3	25	18	23	3.60	17	49	3	2	.60	.251	.308	.347	.655
DeShields,Delino	Tex	23	156	603	154	30	9	7	110	62	79	4.44	78	139	45	14	.76	.255	.343	.370	.712
Desmond,Ian	Was	30	158	604	152	33	2	20	73	73	75	4.25	44	178	16	7	.70	.252	.307	.412	.719
Dickerson,Corey	Col	27	148	566	172	39	8	26	88	82	105	6.86	39	116	5	4	.56	.304	.349	.539	.888
Dietrich,Derek	Mia	26	94	286	73	16	3	12	45	37	41	5.00	24	67	1	0	1.00	.255	.334	.458	.792
Donaldson,Josh	Tor	30	160	614	172	41	1	33	99	106	112	6.56	71	133	6	2	.75	.280	.359	.511	.871
Dozier,Brian	Min	29	158	615	147	37	3	23	96	72	81	4.44	66	138	13	6	.68	.239	.319	.421	.740
Drew,Stephen	NYY	33	100	276	62	15	2	9	33	32	32	3.87	29	62	1	1	.50	.225	.301	.391	.692
Drury,Brandon	Ari	23	132	509	140	36	1	7	49	55	61	4.25	26	75	4	4	.50	.275	.312	.391	.703
Duda,Lucas	NYM	30	150	506	125	31	0	25	67	76	78	5.31	70	142	1	1	.50	.247	.349	.457	.805
Duffy,Matt	SF	25	149	569	177	31	5	11	79	85	90	5.91	38	91	15	4	.79	.311	.358	.441	.800
Dyson,Jarrod	KC	31	105	245	62	8	3	1	37	18	27	3.69	21	43	31	7	.82	.253	.317	.322	.640
Eaton,Adam	CWS	27	148	590	172	32	7	10	97	51	88	5.36	56	107	19	9	.68	.292	.361	.420	.781
Ellis,A.J.	LAD	35	96	294	71	13	0	7	31	35	36	4.20	46	55	0	0	.00	.241	.348	.357	.705
Ellsbury,Jacoby	NYY	32	131	529	144	26	3	11	76	52	69	4.55	42	92	27	9	.75	.272	.332	.395	.727
Encarnacion,Edwin	Tor	33	148	536	142	30	0	36	85	100	99	6.50	74	95	4	2	.67	.265	.360	.522	.883
Escobar,Alcides	KC	29	153	588	157	25	4	4	71	49	61	3.63	26	79	20	6	.77	.267	.305	.344	.648
Escobar,Eduardo	Min	27	136	435	115	28	3	9	54	48	55	4.44	29	85	4	2	.67	.264	.312	.405	.716
Escobar,Yunel	Was	33	138	463	126	21	1	7	54	45	57	4.38	44	63	2	1	.67	.272	.343	.367	.710
Espinosa,Danny	Was	29	107	308	71	16	1	10	40	31	35	3.81	25	96	6	2	.75	.231	.307	.386	.693
Ethier,Andre	LAD	34	139	412	113	25	2	12	51	55	62	5.37	46	85	2	1	.67	.274	.354	.432	.786
Fielder,Prince	Tex	32	160	575	168	31	0	26	79	99	105	6.71	80	96	0	0	.00	.292	.388	.482	.870
Flaherty,Ryan	Bal	29	98	284	64	12	1	10	35	36	31	3.66	25	69	1	0	1.00	.225	.297	.380	.677
Flores,Wilmer	NYM	24	133	470	128	27	1	16	58	66	62	4.71	22	62	0	0	.00	.272	.308	.436	.744
Flowers,Tyler	CWS	30	114	345	85	15	0	13	35	43	42	4.20	29	110	0	0	.00	.246	.314	.403	.717
Forsythe,Logan	TB	29	152	536	142	28	2	14	70	61	73	4.77	59	107	9	4	.69	.265	.346	.403	.749
Fowler,Dexter	ChC	30	147	553	146	30	7	13	91	49	82	5.13	81	143	17	9	.65	.264	.362	.414	.776
Franco,Maikel	Phi	23	145	553	154	37	3	21	71	85	83	5.38	35	86	3	2	.60	.278	.324	.470	.794
Francoeur,Jeff	Phi	32	72	161	39	8	1	5	16	19	18	3.80	8	37	1	1	.50	.242	.291	.398	.688
Franklin,Nick	TB	25	78	231	56	12	1	8	28	27	30	4.41	26	61	5	2	.71	.242	.319	.407	.726
Frazier,Todd	Cin	30	156	584	150	36	2	28	78	84	85	5.01	48	135	12	7	.63	.257	.320	.469	.789
Freeman,Freddie	Atl	26	147	554	159	37	2	23	86	92	99	6.48	73	128	3	2	.60	.287	.376	.486	.862
Freese,David	LAA	33	145	453	120	25	1	13	54	63	60	4.67	40	116	1	1	.50	.265	.335	.411	.746
Fuld,Sam	Oak	34	115	271	59	12	2	2	33	21	24	2.89	30	49	10	4	.71	.218	.298	.299	.597
Gallo,Joey	Tex	22	132	487	114	24	2	35	71	93	81	5.62	66	217	6	2	.75	.234	.325	.507	.833
Galvis,Freddy	Phi	26	151	505	126	22	4	8	56	47	52	3.54	28	88	8	3	.73	.250	.290	.356	.647
Garcia,Adonis	Atl	31	98	322	89	18	1	8	38	38	40	4.43	13	45	4	2	.67	.276	.304	.413	.718
Garcia,Avisail	CWS	25	138	514	144	18	2	15	67	64	67	4.65	32	119	8	5	.62	.280	.327	.411	.738
Gardner,Brett	NYY	32	149	561	144	25	5	13	91	56	75	4.60	67	134	21	7	.75	.257	.341	.389	.730
Gattis,Evan	Hou	29	142	525	135	25	5	28	62	85	76	5.07	31	107	0	0	.00	.257	.304	.484	.787
Gennett,Scooter	Mil	26	129	428	121	24	3	7	53	40	53	4.45	19	67	4	3	.57	.283	.316	.402	.718
Giavotella,Johnny	LAA	28	107	389	108	24	2	5	48	45	51	4.69	33	46	6	2	.75	.278	.337	.388	.725
Gillaspie,Conor	LAA	28	100	289	75	15	2	6	29	32	35	4.25	23	48	0	0	.00	.260	.316	.388	.704
Gillespie,Cole	Mia	32	42	112	31	6	1	2	14	13	16	5.07	12	18	3	1	.75	.277	.347	.402	.749
Gimenez,Chris	Tex	33	48	132	31	6	0	3	16	15	14	3.57	15	30	1	1	.50	.235	.313	.348	.661
Goins,Ryan	Tor	28	124	366	93	19	2	4	40	37	39	3.69	29	72	3	2	.60	.254	.309	.350	.659
Goldschmidt,Paul	Ari	28	158	572	173	42	2	32	103	110	130	8.35	106	151	16	6	.73	.302	.413	.551	.964
Gomes,Jonny	KC	35	93	207	46	9	0	7	26	29	23	3.69	26	71	1	1	.50	.222	.326	.367	.694
Gomes,Yan	Cle	28	116	403	108	26	1	16	49	59	56	4.94	22	98	1	0	1.00	.268	.314	.457	.771
Gomez,Carlos	Hou	30	142	538	143	30	4	18	82	69	74	4.75	38	132	26	10	.72	.266	.325	.437	.762
Gomez,Hector	Mil	28	68	151	36	9	1	3	16	14	14	3.11	6	33	2	1	.67	.232	.266	.364	.630
Gonzalez,Adrian	LAD	34	159	599	168	37	0	27	80	103	101	6.09	66	116	0	0	.00	.280	.356	.477	.833
Gonzalez,Carlos	Col	30	131	490	138	28	3	29	82	89	88	6.45	43	122	7	3	.70	.282	.342	.529	.871
Gonzalez,Marwin	Hou	27	102	259	68	15	1	6	29	24	31	4.18	14	46	3	2	.60	.263	.305	.398	.703
Gordon,Alex	KC	32	156	575	155	35	2	19	83	73	88	5.40	71	141	7	4	.64	.270	.359	.437	.795
Gordon,Dee	Mia	28	147	610	183	23	7	3	86	40	80	4.66	34	91	57	19	.75	.300	.339	.375	.714
Gose,Anthony	Det	25	140	504	127	22	6	7	77	39	59	3.93	48	141	32	13	.71	.252	.321	.361	.682
Gosselin,Phil	Ari	27	45	112	31	6	1	1	14	10	13	4.12	7	18	2	1	.67	.277	.325	.375	.700
Grandal,Yasmani	LAD	27	120	356	90	20	0	14	49	50	55	5.38	62	86	0	0	.00	.253	.367	.427	.794

2016 Hitter Projections

Hitter	Team	Age	G	AB	H	2B	3B	HR	R	RBI	RC	RC27	BB	SO	SB	CS	SB%	Avg	OBP	Slg	OPS
Granderson,Curtis	NYM	35	155	570	136	26	3	25	88	72	80	4.74	79	157	10	5	.67	.239	.336	.426	.763
Gregorius,Didi	NYY	26	150	504	133	23	5	9	65	51	61	4.24	38	75	5	3	.62	.264	.323	.383	.706
Grichuk,Randal	StL	24	155	486	124	30	6	24	76	67	70	4.97	29	128	7	4	.64	.255	.300	.490	.790
Guerrero,Alex	LAD	29	122	256	66	12	2	13	29	41	34	4.63	8	58	2	1	.67	.258	.283	.473	.756
Gutierrez,Franklin	Sea	33	98	285	69	16	0	11	35	35	35	4.19	22	80	3	1	.75	.242	.301	.414	.715
Guyer,Brandon	TB	30	132	348	97	24	2	8	57	37	49	4.98	26	60	11	5	.69	.279	.348	.428	.776
Gyorko,Jedd	SD	27	124	451	116	21	0	18	51	67	59	4.57	36	100	1	1	.50	.257	.318	.424	.741
Hamilton,Billy	Cin	25	138	503	128	17	5	5	76	41	58	3.84	40	90	72	18	.80	.254	.311	.338	.649
Hamilton,Josh	Tex	35	99	335	89	20	1	14	46	53	49	5.16	28	96	2	1	.67	.266	.328	.457	.785
Hanigan,Ryan	Bos	35	84	236	55	9	0	3	23	23	24	3.45	31	42	0	0	.00	.233	.332	.309	.641
Hardy,J.J.	Bal	33	144	540	130	24	1	15	60	58	57	3.61	33	105	0	0	.00	.241	.286	.372	.658
Harper,Bryce	Was	23	151	531	161	32	4	36	105	83	132	9.18	115	129	8	4	.67	.303	.430	.582	1.012
Harrison,Josh	Pit	28	138	501	145	34	4	8	69	47	67	4.80	24	71	14	7	.67	.289	.328	.421	.749
Headley,Chase	NYY	32	152	554	143	31	1	14	68	64	72	4.53	61	139	4	2	.67	.258	.339	.394	.733
Hechavarria,Adeiny	Mia	27	143	509	137	20	6	4	53	48	55	3.79	27	79	8	5	.62	.269	.307	.356	.663
Hedges,Austin	SD	23	69	192	42	8	0	3	17	21	15	2.58	12	38	1	1	.50	.219	.268	.307	.576
Hernandez,Cesar	Phi	26	136	446	125	20	5	2	60	38	55	4.33	40	86	20	9	.69	.280	.341	.361	.702
Hernandez,Kiké	LAD	24	145	522	136	28	3	14	61	53	65	4.34	35	88	4	3	.57	.261	.308	.406	.714
Herrera,Dilson	NYM	22	136	506	145	29	3	16	76	65	78	5.45	46	102	20	11	.65	.287	.347	.451	.798
Herrera,Elian	Mil	31	137	467	128	26	2	6	61	46	58	4.38	38	97	12	5	.71	.274	.329	.377	.706
Herrera,Odubel	Phi	24	152	510	149	27	4	7	63	48	67	4.71	30	111	17	9	.65	.292	.336	.402	.738
Herrmann,Chris	Min	28	59	133	31	7	1	2	17	13	14	3.53	14	31	2	1	.67	.233	.311	.346	.657
Heyward,Jason	StL	26	149	546	152	31	4	17	82	66	87	5.66	66	98	19	6	.76	.278	.360	.443	.804
Hicks,Aaron	Min	26	134	428	113	22	4	11	66	47	61	4.94	54	86	13	6	.68	.264	.348	.411	.759
Hill,Aaron	Ari	34	116	320	80	18	1	9	37	40	38	4.07	25	55	5	3	.62	.250	.312	.397	.709
Holliday,Matt	StL	36	132	487	138	32	1	17	73	77	82	6.07	65	97	4	2	.67	.283	.378	.458	.836
Holt,Brock	Bos	28	119	415	117	23	4	2	54	35	53	4.56	39	76	9	4	.69	.282	.346	.371	.718
Hosmer,Eric	KC	26	145	551	157	32	3	16	78	77	84	5.50	52	97	7	3	.70	.285	.349	.441	.790
Howard,Ryan	Phi	36	131	482	111	24	1	20	57	84	61	4.27	46	158	0	0	.00	.230	.304	.427	.731
Hundley,Nick	Col	32	110	349	88	18	2	10	35	41	42	4.15	24	85	3	2	.60	.252	.304	.401	.705
Hunter,Torii	Min	40	135	491	127	24	1	15	59	69	60	4.26	33	100	3	2	.60	.259	.313	.403	.716
Iannetta,Chris	LAA	33	86	262	57	13	0	9	32	36	32	4.06	45	80	1	0	1.00	.218	.341	.370	.711
Iglesias,Jose	Det	26	136	471	132	17	2	3	53	33	52	3.91	28	55	12	7	.63	.280	.327	.344	.671
Inciarte,Ender	Ari	25	132	520	153	25	4	7	75	40	70	4.84	31	56	24	9	.73	.294	.336	.398	.734
Infante,Omar	KC	34	108	340	87	16	2	4	33	34	34	3.47	15	49	3	2	.60	.256	.289	.350	.639
Jackson,Austin	ChC	29	147	544	146	28	5	9	77	50	69	4.43	47	140	16	7	.70	.268	.330	.388	.718
Jaso,John	TB	32	102	301	77	19	1	7	39	37	42	4.85	43	59	2	1	.67	.256	.354	.395	.750
Jay,Jon	StL	31	108	307	86	15	1	4	41	30	38	4.41	25	54	5	3	.62	.280	.356	.375	.730
Jennings,Desmond	TB	29	131	498	126	27	4	11	75	45	64	4.38	54	107	22	8	.73	.253	.330	.390	.719
Johnson,Chris	Cle	31	82	221	59	12	0	5	20	25	26	4.15	11	61	1	1	.50	.267	.308	.389	.697
Johnson,Kelly	NYM	34	104	272	64	13	1	10	34	33	33	4.09	28	75	3	2	.60	.235	.311	.401	.712
Johnson,Micah	CWS	25	36	123	34	6	1	2	14	10	16	4.47	10	25	9	4	.69	.276	.336	.390	.726
Jones,Adam	Bal	30	154	618	173	32	2	29	88	91	91	5.28	27	123	6	3	.67	.280	.321	.479	.800
Joseph,Caleb	Bal	30	95	290	70	15	1	9	31	39	34	4.02	23	59	1	0	1.00	.241	.302	.393	.695
Joyce,Matt	LAA	31	125	401	93	23	1	13	49	51	51	4.28	55	105	3	2	.60	.232	.330	.392	.722
Kang,Jung Ho	Pit	29	145	484	143	29	2	18	71	69	78	5.88	34	104	5	4	.56	.295	.363	.475	.838
Kemp,Matt	SD	31	152	567	163	32	2	25	86	96	94	5.96	49	148	13	6	.68	.287	.347	.483	.831
Kendrick,Howie	LAD	32	144	566	163	31	3	11	72	67	76	4.86	34	106	8	4	.67	.288	.333	.412	.744
Kiermaier,Kevin	TB	26	151	504	140	25	11	11	71	44	71	4.96	32	89	19	8	.70	.278	.323	.437	.760
Kinsler,Ian	Det	34	157	638	172	37	3	16	97	77	85	4.68	53	82	12	6	.67	.270	.331	.412	.744
Kipnis,Jason	Cle	29	140	546	150	33	4	11	80	62	79	5.11	61	111	16	6	.73	.275	.353	.410	.763
Kubitza,Kyle	LAA	25	147	554	146	36	6	8	74	53	75	4.72	67	159	13	5	.72	.264	.343	.394	.736
Lagares,Juan	NYM	27	145	449	123	23	4	6	50	45	52	4.08	21	84	10	5	.67	.274	.312	.383	.695
Lamb,Jake	Ari	25	145	506	147	32	6	14	66	71	84	6.05	57	128	4	2	.67	.291	.363	.460	.824
LaRoche,Adam	CWS	36	107	306	70	15	0	12	36	41	38	4.19	39	88	1	0	1.00	.229	.320	.395	.715
Lawrie,Brett	Oak	26	138	513	137	28	4	17	66	62	70	4.80	33	108	7	3	.70	.267	.318	.437	.754
LeMahieu,DJ	Col	27	147	552	157	25	4	5	70	52	69	4.46	41	101	18	7	.72	.284	.335	.371	.706
Lind,Adam	Mil	32	143	493	137	29	1	20	63	78	79	5.77	52	102	0	0	.00	.278	.348	.462	.810
Lindor,Francisco	Cle	22	155	609	176	30	7	14	80	72	90	5.26	54	102	24	12	.67	.289	.348	.430	.778
Lobaton,Jose	Was	31	68	172	40	8	0	4	18	19	19	3.74	19	43	0	0	.00	.233	.313	.349	.661
Loney,James	TB	32	114	359	101	19	0	6	34	44	46	4.62	27	44	2	1	.67	.281	.335	.384	.719
Longoria,Evan	TB	30	158	595	158	36	1	25	82	92	91	5.39	63	135	3	2	.60	.266	.342	.455	.797
Lough,David	Bal	30	76	134	35	5	1	3	17	13	15	3.86	7	23	4	2	.67	.261	.303	.381	.683
Lowrie,Jed	Hou	32	130	481	121	31	1	13	63	60	62	4.47	51	84	1	1	.50	.252	.327	.401	.728
Lucroy,Jonathan	Mil	30	134	503	141	30	2	12	62	67	72	5.14	49	78	3	2	.60	.280	.347	.419	.766
Machado,Manny	Bal	23	158	620	178	37	3	29	96	82	106	6.14	56	101	16	7	.70	.287	.349	.497	.846
Mahtook,Mikie	TB	26	126	347	89	22	3	8	39	45	43	4.27	24	87	12	4	.75	.256	.306	.406	.713
Maldonado,Martin	Mil	29	74	176	40	7	0	5	16	21	18	3.44	15	45	0	0	.00	.227	.295	.352	.648
Marisnick,Jake	Hou	25	95	240	59	11	2	6	31	26	26	3.61	12	61	17	6	.74	.246	.290	.383	.674
Markakis,Nick	Atl	32	151	572	162	32	1	9	72	58	79	5.00	62	79	2	1	.67	.283	.356	.390	.746
Marte,Ketel	Sea	22	143	546	157	32	5	5	70	47	73	4.75	38	82	33	11	.75	.288	.334	.392	.726
Marte,Starling	Pit	27	151	575	171	32	6	18	89	69	89	5.55	31	122	31	13	.70	.297	.350	.468	.818
Martin,Leonys	Tex	28	128	416	110	20	3	8	55	41	50	4.11	29	82	23	10	.70	.264	.317	.385	.702
Martin,Russell	Tor	33	132	449	108	21	0	18	61	65	60	4.53	61	104	5	3	.62	.241	.343	.408	.751
Martinez,J.D.	Det	28	156	584	161	35	2	31	78	98	97	5.93	48	166	3	2	.60	.276	.334	.502	.836
Martinez,Victor	Det	37	150	555	159	31	0	17	64	86	84	5.52	51	61	1	0	1.00	.286	.351	.434	.785
Mauer,Joe	Min	33	135	509	147	32	1	9	68	64	77	5.52	67	96	2	1	.67	.289	.373	.409	.781
Maxwell,Justin	SF	32	59	113	27	5	1	4	16	14	14	4.18	12	36	2	1	.67	.239	.323	.407	.730
Maybin,Cameron	Atl	29	134	480	124	20	4	9	64	47	58	4.15	45	103	19	7	.73	.258	.324	.373	.697
McCann,Brian	NYY	32	136	487	118	20	0	25	60	82	67	4.72	52	94	1	0	1.00	.242	.324	.437	.762
McCann,James	Det	26	114	413	109	25	2	7	39	45	47	4.01	20	83	2	1	.67	.264	.300	.385	.685

554

2016 Hitter Projections

Hitter	Team	Age	G	AB	H	2B	3B	HR	R	RBI	RC	RC27	BB	SO	SB	CS	SB%	Avg	OBP	Slg	OPS
McCutchen,Andrew	Pit	29	157	589	174	37	4	23	97	86	112	6.90	89	128	15	7	.68	.295	.396	.489	.885
McKenry,Michael	Col	31	58	143	36	9	0	5	18	18	20	4.81	17	35	1	1	.50	.252	.335	.420	.755
Mercer,Jordy	Pit	29	132	433	113	26	1	8	47	47	51	4.12	31	72	4	2	.67	.261	.313	.381	.694
Mesoraco,Devin	Cin	28	110	370	94	22	1	16	45	58	54	5.07	38	78	2	1	.67	.254	.328	.449	.777
Middlebrooks,Will	SD	27	56	127	31	5	0	5	14	19	14	3.75	7	30	1	1	.50	.244	.294	.402	.696
Miller,Brad	Sea	26	138	444	117	21	4	13	58	53	62	4.86	48	92	11	5	.69	.264	.338	.417	.755
Molina,Yadier	StL	33	132	483	137	28	0	9	45	61	64	4.78	35	59	3	2	.60	.284	.336	.398	.733
Montero,Jesus	Sea	26	38	122	34	6	1	5	14	19	19	5.61	8	25	1	0	1.00	.279	.323	.467	.790
Montero,Miguel	ChC	32	119	357	88	18	0	12	38	51	47	4.54	44	93	0	0	.00	.246	.339	.398	.737
Moore,Tyler	Was	29	56	147	38	10	0	7	18	25	22	5.25	13	36	0	0	.00	.259	.323	.469	.792
Morales,Kendrys	KC	33	148	554	150	34	1	21	65	86	82	5.28	48	106	0	0	.00	.271	.334	.449	.784
Moreland,Mitch	Tex	30	137	464	120	27	1	19	56	71	65	4.90	39	109	1	1	.50	.259	.321	.444	.765
Morneau,Justin	Col	35	117	423	120	27	1	13	50	64	64	5.49	38	69	0	0	.00	.284	.347	.444	.791
Morrison,Logan	Sea	28	134	420	104	21	3	15	52	55	57	4.65	49	75	6	3	.67	.248	.331	.419	.750
Morse,Michael	Pit	34	86	209	52	11	0	8	21	26	26	4.31	16	64	0	0	.00	.249	.317	.416	.734
Moss,Brandon	StL	32	145	470	111	26	1	22	60	71	64	4.62	52	148	1	1	.50	.236	.319	.436	.755
Moustakas,Mike	KC	27	145	542	139	34	1	20	63	74	72	4.63	41	84	1	1	.50	.256	.317	.434	.751
Murphy,Daniel	NYM	31	148	596	174	42	2	13	76	76	86	5.25	38	67	7	4	.64	.292	.336	.435	.771
Murphy,David	LAA	34	135	382	101	21	1	10	42	49	49	4.52	31	59	2	1	.67	.264	.321	.403	.724
Murphy,John Ryan	NYY	25	67	170	43	11	0	4	21	19	20	4.09	14	38	0	0	.00	.253	.310	.388	.698
Myers,Wil	SD	25	154	602	168	34	2	26	98	97	100	5.91	68	146	15	6	.71	.279	.353	.472	.825
Napoli,Mike	Tex	34	124	388	93	20	1	19	51	57	58	5.08	57	126	2	2	.50	.240	.344	.443	.788
Nava,Daniel	TB	33	79	200	53	12	0	4	27	25	27	4.74	25	43	2	1	.67	.265	.366	.385	.751
Navarro,Dioner	Tor	32	55	176	46	8	0	5	17	22	22	4.40	15	29	0	0	.00	.261	.323	.392	.715
Nimmo,Brandon	NYM	23	124	397	99	18	4	6	45	27	46	3.96	45	83	6	4	.60	.249	.326	.360	.686
Norris,Derek	SD	27	137	464	122	28	1	16	68	68	67	5.06	51	107	5	2	.71	.263	.340	.431	.771
Nunez,Eduardo	Min	29	71	192	52	10	1	3	24	20	23	4.18	11	27	9	3	.75	.271	.314	.380	.694
Odor,Rougned	Tex	22	151	542	150	29	10	21	75	79	81	5.26	32	86	10	8	.56	.277	.328	.483	.811
Olivera,Hector	Atl	31	142	504	137	25	4	12	45	61	65	4.60	31	68	0	0	.00	.272	.317	.409	.725
Orlando,Paulo	KC	30	56	116	30	5	1	2	13	12	13	3.84	6	21	5	2	.71	.259	.301	.371	.672
Ortiz,David	Bos	40	142	516	135	33	0	28	66	93	90	6.14	76	100	0	0	.00	.262	.358	.488	.846
Owings,Chris	Ari	24	142	498	127	26	5	6	60	46	52	3.59	23	116	16	6	.73	.255	.289	.363	.653
Ozuna,Marcell	Mia	25	139	532	150	34	3	18	68	69	80	5.42	38	119	3	2	.60	.282	.332	.459	.791
Pagan,Angel	SF	34	117	412	110	21	3	4	52	36	47	3.98	29	71	11	5	.69	.267	.317	.362	.678
Panik,Joe	SF	25	150	570	165	32	3	8	77	56	79	5.03	51	62	5	3	.62	.289	.351	.398	.749
Paredes,Jimmy	Bal	27	59	123	33	6	1	3	15	13	15	4.24	6	32	4	2	.67	.268	.302	.407	.709
Parker,Jarrett	SF	27	121	351	92	18	2	16	51	51	54	5.28	41	126	13	7	.65	.262	.339	.462	.801
Parra,Gerardo	Bal	29	153	533	148	31	4	11	72	50	71	4.72	37	94	12	6	.67	.278	.329	.413	.742
Paulsen,Ben	Col	28	84	207	54	12	1	7	25	27	28	4.73	16	55	1	1	.50	.261	.317	.430	.747
Pearce,Steve	Bal	33	99	322	83	20	1	16	43	47	49	5.29	33	66	2	2	.50	.258	.334	.475	.809
Pederson,Joc	LAD	24	151	485	121	21	2	29	84	63	86	6.03	92	154	14	7	.67	.249	.375	.480	.855
Pedroia,Dustin	Bos	32	136	546	157	35	1	13	77	64	83	5.49	58	71	8	4	.67	.288	.359	.427	.786
Pena,Brayan	Cin	34	81	251	65	13	0	2	17	21	26	3.61	17	29	1	1	.50	.259	.309	.335	.643
Pence,Hunter	SF	33	156	612	167	31	3	24	88	89	91	5.26	52	130	11	5	.69	.273	.332	.451	.783
Pennington,Cliff	Tor	32	92	212	50	9	1	2	25	18	21	3.33	23	46	5	2	.71	.236	.316	.316	.632
Peralta,David	Ari	28	151	472	142	27	8	16	64	76	83	6.46	41	89	8	4	.67	.301	.360	.494	.854
Peralta,Jhonny	StL	34	153	564	148	32	1	17	63	75	75	4.68	52	117	1	1	.50	.262	.329	.413	.742
Perez,Carlos	LAA	25	107	308	79	18	0	5	28	29	35	3.96	24	50	3	1	.75	.256	.310	.364	.674
Perez,Hernan	Mil	25	63	109	29	6	1	1	10	9	12	3.85	4	17	4	1	.80	.266	.292	.367	.659
Perez,Roberto	Cle	27	78	233	55	14	1	6	31	31	31	4.53	38	69	0	0	.00	.236	.346	.382	.728
Perez,Salvador	KC	26	144	548	150	29	1	20	59	78	72	4.70	19	78	1	0	1.00	.274	.302	.440	.742
Peterson,Jace	Atl	26	151	543	136	27	5	6	62	55	61	3.80	60	112	15	10	.60	.250	.327	.352	.679
Pham,Tommy	StL	28	82	234	68	13	3	7	36	31	39	6.00	25	54	9	3	.75	.291	.359	.462	.821
Phegley,Josh	Oak	28	74	230	57	14	1	8	26	31	28	4.21	13	44	0	0	.00	.248	.291	.422	.713
Phillips,Brandon	Cin	35	145	575	157	26	1	13	69	72	70	4.29	32	81	14	6	.70	.273	.318	.390	.708
Phillips,Brett	Mil	22	128	466	122	31	8	2	72	46	58	4.27	45	121	21	9	.70	.262	.327	.376	.702
Pierzynski,A.J.	Atl	39	120	416	113	20	1	10	39	48	50	4.29	17	50	0	0	.00	.272	.310	.397	.706
Pillar,Kevin	Tor	27	124	423	121	29	2	9	57	46	58	4.90	21	58	17	6	.74	.286	.324	.428	.752
Piscotty,Stephen	StL	25	131	482	130	34	3	12	62	63	68	4.95	45	84	8	5	.62	.270	.333	.427	.761
Plawecki,Kevin	NYM	25	74	249	61	13	0	5	24	28	26	3.60	16	46	0	0	.00	.245	.299	.357	.656
Plouffe,Trevor	Min	30	145	525	129	32	2	19	66	71	68	4.45	45	116	2	1	.67	.246	.310	.423	.733
Polanco,Gregory	Pit	24	155	602	161	34	4	12	95	71	81	4.64	61	110	30	13	.70	.267	.336	.397	.733
Pollock,A.J.	Ari	28	156	602	178	39	5	15	97	67	96	5.76	48	84	31	9	.77	.296	.350	.452	.802
Pompey,Dalton	Tor	23	143	517	150	21	7	10	95	50	79	5.41	57	92	33	13	.72	.290	.362	.416	.778
Posey,Buster	SF	29	147	549	174	32	1	21	73	92	104	7.19	59	63	2	1	.67	.317	.387	.494	.881
Prado,Martin	Mia	32	147	569	160	32	2	11	67	66	75	4.74	42	75	3	2	.60	.281	.335	.402	.737
Puig,Yasiel	LAD	25	136	503	151	31	6	22	81	72	95	6.88	55	106	10	7	.59	.300	.377	.517	.894
Pujols,Albert	LAA	36	141	547	147	31	0	31	80	93	91	5.89	55	68	5	2	.71	.269	.341	.495	.836
Raburn,Ryan	Cle	35	91	224	54	14	0	8	27	31	28	4.28	20	61	0	0	.00	.241	.312	.411	.722
Ramirez,Alexei	CWS	34	155	589	154	30	1	11	64	64	65	3.82	29	75	16	7	.70	.261	.300	.372	.671
Ramirez,Hanley	Bos	32	136	546	151	30	1	23	85	80	86	5.58	53	103	13	6	.68	.277	.346	.462	.808
Ramirez,Jose	Cle	23	97	323	83	16	3	4	48	27	38	4.00	29	32	19	7	.73	.257	.320	.362	.682
Ramos,Wilson	Was	28	110	378	96	16	0	14	38	55	45	4.15	21	66	0	0	.00	.254	.293	.407	.701
Rasmus,Colby	Hou	29	122	406	94	22	2	19	58	52	54	4.49	41	136	3	1	.75	.232	.305	.436	.741
Realmuto,J.T.	Mia	25	126	452	121	25	6	10	60	57	59	4.57	30	68	12	5	.71	.268	.315	.416	.731
Reddick,Josh	Oak	29	145	530	138	28	4	21	75	76	77	5.06	51	85	8	4	.67	.260	.326	.447	.774
Reimold,Nolan	Bal	32	70	179	46	9	0	6	23	22	25	4.85	22	43	1	1	.67	.257	.342	.408	.749
Rendon,Anthony	Was	26	140	561	157	37	3	16	88	65	88	5.62	65	102	6	3	.67	.280	.359	.442	.801
Revere,Ben	Tor	28	144	577	172	17	5	1	73	36	70	4.39	29	58	34	10	.77	.298	.334	.350	.684
Reyes,Jose	Col	33	138	565	161	30	4	9	79	52	77	4.86	41	69	25	8	.76	.285	.333	.400	.733
Reynolds,Mark	StL	32	102	248	54	11	0	12	31	36	31	4.13	33	86	2	1	.67	.218	.322	.407	.729

2016 Hitter Projections

Hitter	Team	Age	G	AB	H	2B	3B	HR	R	RBI	RC	RC27	BB	SO	SB	CS	SB%	Avg	OBP	Slg	OPS
Rios,Alex	KC	35	110	361	94	20	2	7	42	41	40	3.93	18	66	11	4	.73	.260	.301	.385	.686
Rivera,Rene	TB	32	87	210	48	11	0	5	17	24	20	3.21	13	50	0	0	.00	.229	.280	.352	.632
Rizzo,Anthony	ChC	26	152	554	151	37	2	31	85	94	101	6.42	71	110	11	6	.65	.273	.371	.514	.886
Robinson,Clint	Was	31	90	232	63	15	1	7	30	30	35	5.38	27	41	0	0	.00	.272	.352	.435	.788
Rodriguez,Alex	NYY	40	132	503	121	21	0	24	69	78	72	4.88	72	139	5	2	.71	.241	.343	.425	.768
Rodriguez,Sean	Pit	31	83	128	30	7	1	4	16	15	14	3.68	8	36	2	1	.67	.234	.310	.398	.708
Rogers,Jason	Mil	28	84	216	61	12	1	8	31	32	35	5.83	25	41	1	1	.50	.282	.360	.458	.818
Rojas,Miguel	Mia	27	70	145	36	6	1	2	15	12	15	3.55	10	17	2	1	.67	.248	.297	.345	.642
Rollins,Jimmy	LAD	37	146	532	124	26	2	13	69	47	58	3.64	51	89	15	6	.71	.233	.301	.363	.664
Romine,Andrew	Det	30	72	121	30	4	0	1	15	9	11	3.04	9	25	6	3	.67	.248	.305	.306	.611
Rosario,Eddie	Min	24	138	512	132	25	10	14	67	59	62	4.17	22	114	12	7	.63	.258	.288	.428	.716
Rosario,Wilin	Col	27	97	287	78	16	1	13	36	43	41	5.08	13	60	2	1	.67	.272	.306	.470	.776
Ross,David	ChC	39	58	114	22	6	0	3	9	11	10	2.83	14	45	0	0	.00	.193	.281	.325	.606
Ruf,Darin	Phi	29	74	159	42	9	0	7	21	24	24	5.33	15	39	1	0	1.00	.264	.343	.453	.796
Ruggiano,Justin	LAD	34	94	262	68	15	1	10	34	35	37	4.83	25	73	8	5	.62	.260	.329	.439	.768
Ruiz,Carlos	Phi	37	71	234	58	14	0	4	24	24	27	3.97	24	35	1	1	.50	.248	.336	.359	.695
Rupp,Cameron	Phi	27	116	387	87	17	1	13	36	43	41	3.55	33	106	0	0	.00	.225	.289	.375	.664
Russell,Addison	ChC	22	156	575	151	37	1	20	79	78	79	4.80	47	150	7	4	.64	.263	.321	.435	.755
Rutledge,Josh	Bos	27	94	323	86	19	3	6	44	32	39	4.24	18	73	4	2	.67	.266	.311	.399	.710
Saladino,Tyler	CWS	26	138	479	114	17	4	8	59	51	52	3.62	44	90	34	8	.81	.238	.303	.340	.644
Saltalamacchia,Jarrod	Ari	31	114	383	88	25	0	15	50	52	48	4.23	42	137	1	0	1.00	.230	.308	.413	.720
Sanchez,Carlos	CWS	24	115	391	100	22	1	4	41	33	40	3.53	20	76	9	4	.69	.256	.295	.348	.643
Sandoval,Pablo	Bos	29	147	545	150	32	2	15	61	72	75	4.94	39	82	0	0	.00	.275	.328	.424	.752
Sands,Jerry	Cle	28	71	199	50	10	1	9	27	32	30	5.23	25	47	1	0	1.00	.251	.335	.447	.782
Sano,Miguel	Min	23	152	577	153	39	3	37	102	113	114	6.94	94	194	7	3	.70	.265	.369	.536	.905
Santana,Carlos	Cle	30	153	542	132	33	1	22	75	84	86	5.40	106	121	7	4	.64	.244	.370	.430	.800
Santana,Danny	Min	25	76	186	53	10	3	2	26	16	23	4.36	7	39	8	4	.67	.285	.318	.403	.721
Santana,Domingo	Mil	23	141	445	122	24	1	20	65	72	72	5.72	52	148	7	4	.64	.274	.354	.467	.821
Sardinas,Luis	Mil	23	132	471	118	20	3	1	50	35	42	3.04	18	74	17	6	.74	.251	.280	.312	.592
Saunders,Michael	Tor	29	98	297	71	15	2	8	40	32	36	4.07	35	85	7	4	.64	.239	.319	.384	.703
Schafer,Logan	Mil	29	71	124	30	7	1	1	15	10	13	3.56	10	21	2	1	.67	.242	.304	.339	.642
Schoop,Jonathan	Bal	24	135	474	115	23	0	20	56	57	54	3.90	21	110	3	1	.75	.243	.281	.418	.698
Schumaker,Skip	Cin	36	70	115	29	6	0	1	13	10	12	3.59	10	22	1	1	.50	.252	.317	.330	.648
Seager,Corey	LAD	22	155	589	170	43	4	21	93	88	97	5.96	46	97	6	2	.75	.289	.341	.482	.823
Seager,Kyle	Sea	28	161	619	167	37	1	24	80	83	92	5.25	58	108	7	4	.64	.270	.338	.449	.787
Segura,Jean	Mil	26	146	566	154	18	6	8	68	49	64	3.94	24	80	29	10	.74	.272	.306	.367	.674
Semien,Marcus	Oak	25	155	577	150	30	5	19	82	61	82	4.92	61	125	14	6	.70	.260	.332	.428	.760
Shaffer,Richie	TB	25	128	322	75	20	1	18	46	48	48	5.03	40	100	3	1	.75	.233	.321	.469	.790
Shaw,Travis	Bos	26	145	540	136	28	2	20	68	70	74	4.74	58	113	2	2	.50	.252	.326	.422	.748
Simmons,Andrelton	Atl	26	149	542	141	24	3	8	59	50	60	3.86	40	47	5	3	.62	.260	.315	.360	.674
Singleton,Jon	Hou	24	138	511	116	27	1	23	76	82	74	4.65	79	154	4	2	.67	.227	.331	.419	.749
Sizemore,Grady	TB	33	70	146	35	8	1	3	16	16	17	3.95	14	33	2	1	.67	.240	.319	.370	.689
Smith,Seth	Sea	33	136	423	106	29	3	13	57	50	60	4.91	53	102	1	1	.50	.251	.340	.426	.765
Smoak,Justin	Tor	29	130	314	72	16	0	13	37	43	40	4.30	38	84	0	0	.00	.229	.316	.404	.721
Smolinski,Jake	Oak	27	78	199	51	13	1	7	29	26	29	5.03	24	36	3	2	.60	.256	.342	.437	.779
Snider,Travis	Pit	28	86	233	59	14	1	7	29	31	31	4.61	24	59	2	1	.67	.253	.326	.412	.738
Sogard,Eric	Oak	30	104	259	65	11	1	2	31	24	24	3.43	22	31	6	3	.67	.251	.314	.324	.639
Solarte,Yangervis	SD	28	153	552	153	33	2	14	67	63	76	4.94	41	57	1	1	.50	.277	.331	.420	.751
Soler,Jorge	ChC	24	142	525	149	35	2	22	68	92	89	6.12	54	150	4	2	.67	.284	.353	.484	.837
Soto,Geovany	CWS	33	76	190	42	11	0	8	21	24	23	4.04	22	60	0	0	.00	.221	.305	.405	.710
Souza,Steven	TB	27	125	437	119	26	2	22	75	66	77	6.14	58	134	19	8	.70	.272	.361	.492	.853
Span,Denard	Was	32	144	576	165	31	5	6	85	48	79	4.90	54	67	22	8	.73	.286	.350	.389	.739
Spangenberg,Cory	SD	25	154	541	163	27	8	9	74	45	81	5.40	41	115	25	12	.68	.301	.352	.431	.782
Springer,George	Hou	26	143	551	154	26	2	31	94	83	103	6.61	75	160	25	8	.76	.279	.372	.503	.875
Stanton,Giancarlo	Mia	26	142	526	142	32	2	43	88	107	112	7.52	78	171	7	3	.70	.270	.367	.584	.951
Stewart,Chris	Pit	34	56	147	37	6	0	1	12	13	14	3.31	12	23	1	0	1.00	.252	.317	.313	.630
Stubbs,Drew	Tex	31	75	147	34	6	1	4	22	14	17	3.84	15	53	7	2	.78	.231	.311	.367	.678
Suarez,Eugenio	Cin	24	97	348	92	19	2	11	45	42	47	4.70	28	77	5	4	.56	.264	.325	.425	.750
Susac,Andrew	SF	26	52	171	42	11	1	6	21	23	24	4.84	20	48	0	0	.00	.246	.328	.427	.755
Suzuki,Ichiro	Mia	42	140	357	91	11	2	2	37	21	34	3.27	21	49	11	4	.73	.255	.298	.314	.612
Suzuki,Kurt	Min	32	119	369	92	19	0	5	34	43	38	3.57	26	48	1	0	1.00	.249	.311	.341	.652
Swihart,Blake	Bos	24	123	421	121	26	2	9	58	53	59	5.06	29	92	6	3	.67	.287	.335	.423	.758
Swisher,Nick	Atl	35	85	306	71	16	0	11	37	40	39	4.31	43	84	0	0	.00	.232	.332	.392	.725
Taylor,Michael	Was	25	147	504	135	20	2	20	70	74	73	5.03	47	159	24	8	.75	.268	.332	.435	.766
Teixeira,Mark	NYY	36	120	431	103	22	0	26	62	77	67	5.29	60	99	2	1	.67	.239	.340	.471	.811
Tejada,Ruben	NYM	26	122	384	96	21	1	3	40	30	40	3.59	37	68	3	2	.60	.250	.324	.333	.657
Thompson,Trayce	CWS	25	146	530	129	30	5	17	72	57	67	4.27	47	126	17	7	.71	.243	.305	.415	.720
Tomas,Yasmany	Ari	25	140	490	137	24	3	13	51	62	64	4.67	22	120	6	3	.67	.280	.313	.420	.734
Tomlinson,Kelby	SF	26	54	188	55	7	2	1	27	18	25	4.71	17	33	11	5	.69	.293	.354	.367	.721
Travis,Devon	Tor	25	138	484	136	31	3	14	77	62	73	5.38	43	85	11	5	.69	.281	.341	.444	.785
Trout,Mike	LAA	24	160	605	187	37	8	39	125	102	145	8.89	95	158	20	6	.77	.309	.410	.590	1.001
Trumbo,Mark	Sea	30	143	522	133	26	2	25	65	83	73	4.87	39	140	2	1	.67	.255	.308	.456	.764
Tucker,Preston	Hou	25	72	187	48	11	0	9	24	27	27	5.01	15	39	1	1	.50	.257	.319	.460	.779
Tulowitzki,Troy	Tor	31	134	471	137	28	1	22	77	76	84	6.52	51	99	2	1	.67	.291	.366	.495	.861
Turner,Justin	LAD	31	132	409	116	28	1	11	54	52	61	5.36	36	74	5	3	.62	.284	.350	.438	.788
Turner,Trea	Was	23	146	562	166	30	6	12	83	62	88	5.62	46	119	38	11	.78	.295	.349	.434	.783
Upton Jr.,Melvin	SD	31	109	315	73	16	2	9	42	32	37	3.88	35	101	14	6	.70	.232	.311	.381	.691
Upton,Justin	SD	28	155	576	157	32	3	29	96	88	100	6.12	72	165	15	6	.71	.273	.359	.490	.849
Uribe,Juan	NYM	37	111	369	93	19	0	11	37	46	44	4.16	27	82	2	1	.67	.253	.308	.395	.703
Urshela,Giovanny	Cle	24	134	441	109	24	2	12	51	50	50	3.92	25	70	0	0	.00	.247	.289	.392	.681
Utley,Chase	LAD	37	129	442	110	23	2	12	57	54	55	4.28	45	74	6	2	.75	.249	.335	.391	.726

2016 Hitter Projections

PLAYER			BATTING												BASERUNNING			AVERAGES			
Hitter	Team	Age	G	AB	H	2B	3B	HR	R	RBI	RC	RC27	BB	SO	SB	CS	SB%	Avg	OBP	Slg	OPS
Valbuena,Luis	Hou	30	138	439	104	25	1	18	59	53	59	4.57	54	104	2	1	.67	.237	.325	.421	.746
Valencia,Danny	Oak	31	138	464	120	29	1	16	56	66	60	4.51	31	102	2	2	.50	.259	.306	.429	.735
Van Slyke,Scott	LAD	29	102	247	69	18	1	10	32	37	42	6.07	30	63	4	2	.67	.279	.362	.482	.844
Vargas,Kennys	Min	25	59	142	38	6	0	6	19	23	21	5.25	16	36	0	0	.00	.268	.346	.437	.783
Vazquez,Christian	Bos	25	141	447	115	26	0	4	52	46	50	3.89	47	76	3	2	.60	.257	.328	.342	.670
Venable,Will	Tex	33	140	390	93	16	3	10	47	39	44	3.79	36	107	14	5	.74	.238	.308	.372	.679
Victorino,Shane	LAA	35	52	121	31	6	1	2	16	11	14	4.00	9	20	4	1	.80	.256	.338	.372	.710
Villar,Jonathan	Hou	25	61	148	37	6	1	3	21	14	18	4.03	13	41	16	5	.76	.250	.311	.365	.675
Vogt,Stephen	Oak	31	131	429	114	23	2	15	53	63	62	5.12	42	75	1	0	1.00	.266	.333	.434	.766
Votto,Joey	Cin	32	156	539	162	37	1	25	89	81	119	8.12	122	132	7	4	.64	.301	.433	.512	.945
Walker,Neil	Pit	30	147	521	139	32	2	17	67	72	74	5.01	46	102	4	2	.67	.267	.336	.434	.769
Werth,Jayson	Was	37	115	380	100	21	1	14	56	51	58	5.35	51	94	5	2	.71	.263	.358	.434	.792
Wieters,Matt	Bal	30	100	373	96	20	1	14	42	52	52	4.88	35	82	1	0	1.00	.257	.323	.429	.752
Winker,Jesse	Cin	22	136	489	130	27	2	14	73	56	74	5.29	78	95	9	5	.64	.266	.367	.415	.782
Wong,Kolten	StL	25	150	543	146	26	4	12	76	58	69	4.44	37	83	19	7	.73	.269	.325	.398	.723
Wright,David	NYM	33	109	408	114	25	1	12	56	57	63	5.50	50	93	8	4	.67	.279	.361	.434	.795
Yelich,Christian	Mia	24	136	529	160	32	4	10	82	54	87	6.02	61	110	18	7	.72	.302	.377	.435	.811
Young,Chris	NYY	32	123	334	78	21	1	13	47	43	43	4.32	37	83	6	3	.67	.234	.316	.419	.735
Young,Delmon	Bal	30	81	221	61	11	0	6	24	29	28	4.55	9	43	1	0	1.00	.276	.313	.407	.721
Zimmerman,Ryan	Was	31	127	463	124	28	1	19	64	74	71	5.43	48	101	2	1	.67	.268	.338	.456	.794
Zobrist,Ben	KC	35	148	571	153	37	3	15	83	71	86	5.30	79	89	7	4	.64	.268	.359	.422	.781
Zunino,Mike	Sea	25	94	286	59	12	1	13	33	34	28	3.21	16	92	0	0	.00	.206	.265	.392	.657

Pitcher Projections

Bill James

Traditional pitching statistics—that is, pitching statistics as they existed in 1980—are completely different than traditional batting statistics. Traditional batting statistics documented discrete events, one by one. That player hit a one base hit; we will record that as a single. That player hit the ball in such a manner that a run crossed home plate; we will record that as an RBI. That player went to the plate and did not produce anything; we will record that as an at bat.

The primary pitching stats, on the other hand, were "result" statistics which represented not single-event outcomes but end products. The main pitching stats were Wins, Losses, and Earned Run Average. A "win" is a result of (usually) about 80 plate appearances, around 40 by each team. An "earned run average" is a calculation produced by long sequences of events.

The process of modern sabermetric analysis in pitching, then, has run in the opposite direction from the process of sabermetric analysis in batting. For hitters, what we have done (mostly) is to CONSTRUCT "end-result" conclusions from what we know about the discrete events. For hitters, we have moved on from the counting stats to questions like "How many runs did this player create?", and "How many wins was he responsible for?" WAR is a win-based stat; Win Shares is a win-based stat. We have taken the counting stats, and made from them estimates of the answers to the great questions.

For pitchers, what we have done is the exact opposite. For pitchers, we have mostly DECONSTRUCTED the end results, moving toward the elements. For hitters, we have marched toward broad conclusions. For pitchers, we have marched away from them. WHIP is a step AWAY from a general conclusion, back to a more elemental level. OPS is a step TOWARD a general conclusion about the hitter.

This difference has profound implications for the process of making projections. It was relatively easy to make projections for hitters, in a certain sense. Alcides Escobar hit 4 homers in 2010, 4 in 2011, 5 in 2012, 4 in 2013, 3 in 2014, and 3 in 2015. It's not really that hard to predict how many he will hit in 2016.

He's not going to hit 20. Probably; there's always the Bert Campaneris, 1970, type season that pops up once in a while.

Anyway, when we project hitter's production for 2016, it's a pretty simple process of following the elements. But when we started to project pitcher's production, I at first thought that this was impossible, because we didn't have the "elements" to work with. Maybe I didn't say that right. My intuition was to try to project END RESULTS based on previous years' end results; in other words, if a pitcher won 14 games last year, I would try to project that he would win 14 again next year, just as you might do with home runs.

But that doesn't work, because wins and losses are large-scale results, and consequently are subject to many different influences. A pitcher might go 19-8, not because he has pitched well but because his team has scored six runs a game for him. Also, pitchers get hurt a lot, and pitcher's careers take unexpected turns. Jake Arrieta in 2012 was 3-9 with a 6.20 ERA. Now, if he is not Cy Young, he is at least Walter Johnson.

That kind of thing doesn't happen OFTEN with pitchers, but it does happen. It has probably never happened in the history of baseball with a hitter. There is nobody who started out as a .185 hitter and wound up as Miguel Cabrera. Well...Mike Schmidt, but that's not really the same. It can happen, for a pitcher, because the events combine into the end-result record, and a relatively small change in the elements can lead to a seemingly much more dramatic change in the results.

It took us longer to learn to project pitchers, because we had to learn to back away from the end products, and project the pitcher forward based on the elements of his performance, rather than the summary of his performance. I don't know if that makes sense; I hope that it does.

But we've been projecting pitchers for 15 or 20 years now, I guess, and we're starting to get a little bit more comfortable with it. Next year, we boldly predict that Clayton Kershaw will be really, really good. We have projected that Trevor Bauer will go 7-12 with a 4.29 ERA, which, you know...it has as much chance of being right as any other answer. It is entirely possible that Trevor Bauer, who has a good deal of ability, will turn it around next year and go 17-7; these things happen every year to several pitchers. We have made our best guesses, and it is our privilege to share them with you.

2016 Pitcher Projections

Pitcher	Team	Age	G	GS	IP	H	HR	BB	SO	HB	W	L	Pct	Sv	BR/9	ERA
Aardsma,David	Atl	34	35	0	31	25	3	14	32	2	2	2	.500	0	11.9	3.48
Abad,Fernando	Oak	30	63	0	51	49	6	17	44	2	2	3	.400	0	12.0	3.88
Adams,Austin	Cle	29	64	0	66	66	5	28	65	1	3	4	.429	0	13.0	3.95
Albers,Matt	CWS	33	45	0	54	52	5	13	39	2	3	3	.500	0	11.2	3.17
Alburquerque,Al	Det	30	63	0	58	49	5	30	70	2	3	3	.500	0	12.6	3.57
Allen,Cody	Cle	27	68	0	69	54	5	25	88	1	4	4	.500	36	10.4	2.74
Alvarez,Henderson	Mia	26	27	27	167	173	14	35	93	7	10	9	.526	0	11.6	3.66
Alvarez,Jose	LAA	27	73	0	71	73	8	24	53	4	3	5	.375	0	12.8	4.31
Anderson,Brett	LAD	28	31	31	184	194	16	50	134	4	10	10	.500	0	12.1	3.86
Anderson,Chase	Ari	28	26	26	148	148	17	42	123	6	8	8	.500	0	11.9	3.83
Anderson,Cody	Cle	25	20	20	125	131	14	37	77	3	6	8	.429	0	12.3	4.03
Andriese,Matt	TB	26	31	5	62	65	6	16	50	2	3	4	.429	0	12.0	3.77
Archer,Chris	TB	27	34	34	212	187	18	70	211	8	13	11	.542	0	11.2	3.35
Arrieta,Jake	ChC	30	33	33	226	187	17	55	210	8	18	7	.720	0	10.0	2.91
Asher,Alec	Phi	24	27	27	135	145	23	40	102	3	5	10	.333	0	12.5	4.60
Avilan,Luis	LAD	26	69	0	50	46	4	19	37	2	3	3	.500	0	12.1	3.42
Axford,John	Col	33	65	0	64	59	6	37	74	1	3	4	.429	15	13.6	4.22
Badenhop,Burke	Cin	33	67	0	65	67	4	18	42	2	4	4	.500	0	12.0	3.46
Baez,Pedro	LAD	28	60	0	60	55	6	14	58	2	4	3	.571	0	10.6	3.15
Bailey,Homer	Cin	30	18	18	118	115	13	35	98	5	6	7	.462	0	11.8	3.81
Banuelos,Manny	Atl	25	27	27	146	145	14	76	125	10	5	11	.313	0	14.2	4.62
Barnes,Matt	Bos	26	31	4	52	55	6	23	50	2	2	4	.333	0	13.8	4.67
Barrett,Aaron	Was	28	52	0	50	42	2	16	60	2	4	2	.667	0	10.8	2.52
Bass,Anthony	Tex	28	26	0	50	55	5	15	36	1	2	3	.400	0	12.8	4.32
Bassitt,Chris	Oak	27	25	25	163	151	6	57	137	13	9	9	.500	0	12.2	3.42
Bastardo,Antonio	Pit	30	72	0	67	49	5	32	80	2	5	3	.625	0	11.1	2.82
Bauer,Trevor	Cle	25	31	31	182	168	22	81	177	10	9	12	.429	0	12.8	4.10
Bedrosian,Cam	LAA	24	60	0	59	49	3	29	75	3	4	3	.571	0	12.4	3.20
Beimel,Joe	Sea	39	55	0	45	47	6	15	26	1	2	3	.400	0	12.6	4.40
Belisle,Matt	StL	36	57	0	56	60	4	19	44	2	3	3	.500	0	13.0	4.02
Benoit,Joaquin	SD	38	63	0	64	45	6	21	70	1	5	2	.714	0	9.4	2.39
Bergman,Christian	Col	28	33	3	46	51	7	10	28	1	2	3	.400	0	12.1	4.30
Betances,Dellin	NYY	28	73	0	86	66	6	36	109	6	6	4	.600	5	11.3	2.93
Bettis,Chad	Col	27	29	29	167	179	18	59	143	6	8	10	.444	0	13.1	4.42
Blanton,Joe	Pit	35	48	2	64	72	10	15	52	2	3	4	.429	0	12.5	4.64
Blazek,Michael	Mil	27	58	0	63	58	7	25	58	2	3	4	.429	0	12.1	3.71
Bolsinger,Mike	LAD	28	28	28	145	144	12	56	133	4	8	8	.500	0	12.7	3.91
Boxberger,Brad	TB	28	68	0	64	48	7	28	88	2	4	3	.571	43	11.0	2.95
Boyd,Matt	Det	25	26	26	140	136	22	42	125	4	7	9	.438	0	11.7	3.99
Boyer,Blaine	Min	34	63	0	64	65	6	17	42	1	3	4	.429	0	11.7	3.66
Brach,Brad	Bal	30	61	0	76	65	7	33	83	1	4	4	.500	0	11.7	3.32
Breslow,Craig	Bos	35	64	0	63	63	7	25	47	2	3	4	.429	0	12.9	4.29
Britton,Zach	Bal	28	63	0	68	67	5	20	53	2	4	4	.500	37	11.8	3.31
Brooks,Aaron	Oak	26	22	17	104	121	13	21	75	3	4	7	.364	0	12.5	4.41
Brothers,Rex	Col	28	42	0	36	31	3	30	43	1	2	2	.500	0	15.5	4.75
Brown,Brooks	Col	31	35	0	31	35	3	11	22	1	1	2	.333	0	13.6	4.94
Broxton,Jonathan	StL	32	70	0	66	58	5	23	67	2	4	3	.571	0	11.3	3.14
Buchanan,David	Phi	27	27	27	136	160	14	49	84	8	4	11	.267	0	14.4	5.10
Buchholz,Clay	Bos	31	28	28	171	164	15	44	136	7	10	9	.526	0	11.3	3.47
Buehrle,Mark	Tor	37	32	32	201	218	21	39	111	5	11	11	.500	0	11.7	3.85
Bumgarner,Madison	SF	26	32	32	222	193	20	44	213	4	16	9	.640	0	9.9	3.00
Butler,Eddie	Col	25	28	28	146	166	16	63	84	5	6	10	.375	0	14.4	5.12
Cahill,Trevor	ChC	28	29	1	47	46	5	22	34	2	2	3	.400	0	13.4	4.21
Cain,Matt	SF	31	30	30	183	161	20	57	148	6	11	9	.550	0	11.0	3.44
Caminero,Arquimedes	Pit	29	73	0	74	65	8	31	80	6	4	4	.500	0	12.4	3.65
Capps,Carter	Mia	25	62	0	62	54	5	24	82	4	4	3	.571	0	11.7	3.29
Carrasco,Carlos	Cle	29	31	31	194	182	19	46	189	7	12	10	.545	0	10.9	3.39
Carroll,Scott	CWS	31	17	0	36	41	3	13	20	2	1	3	.250	0	14.0	4.75
Cashner,Andrew	SD	29	31	31	186	181	16	59	156	5	11	10	.524	0	11.9	3.68
Casilla,Santiago	SF	35	67	0	62	50	5	23	55	3	4	3	.571	44	11.0	2.90
Cecil,Brett	Tor	29	65	0	57	55	6	19	52	2	3	3	.500	0	12.0	3.63
Cedeno,Xavier	TB	29	62	0	48	44	4	15	46	2	3	2	.600	0	11.4	3.19
Chacin,Jhoulys	Ari	28	10	8	53	50	4	20	38	2	3	3	.500	0	12.2	3.57
Chafin,Andrew	Ari	26	68	0	70	70	5	28	51	2	4	4	.500	0	12.9	3.86
Chapman,Aroldis	Cin	28	66	0	67	42	4	33	110	4	4	3	.571	38	10.6	2.28
Chatwood,Tyler	Col	26	20	20	111	123	9	40	73	4	5	7	.417	0	13.5	4.54
Chavez,Jesse	Oak	32	26	24	142	144	16	45	125	4	7	9	.438	0	12.2	3.93
Chen,Wei-Yin	Bal	30	31	31	195	198	26	41	149	4	10	11	.476	0	11.2	3.78
Choate,Randy	StL	40	65	0	31	26	2	8	27	3	2	1	.667	0	10.7	2.90
Cingrani,Tony	Cin	26	54	0	54	44	7	31	62	2	3	3	.500	0	12.8	3.83
Cishek,Steve	StL	30	65	0	60	53	3	23	62	2	4	3	.571	3	11.7	3.00
Clippard,Tyler	NYM	31	71	0	70	48	7	28	74	2	5	3	.625	0	10.0	2.57
Cobb,Alex	TB	28	12	12	66	61	5	19	59	3	4	3	.571	0	11.3	3.41
Cole,Gerrit	Pit	25	33	33	218	196	14	52	202	11	15	9	.625	0	10.7	3.14
Collmenter,Josh	Ari	30	34	0	59	57	7	13	41	1	4	3	.571	0	10.8	3.20
Colome,Alex	TB	27	45	15	126	124	8	42	105	7	7	7	.500	0	12.4	3.64
Colon,Bartolo	NYM	43	31	31	195	208	22	26	133	3	11	11	.500	0	10.9	3.65
Conley,Adam	Mia	26	29	29	163	158	11	62	135	8	9	9	.500	0	12.6	3.75
Contreras,Carlos	Cin	25	25	0	36	32	3	28	35	1	1	3	.250	0	15.2	4.75

561

2016 Pitcher Projections

Pitcher	Team	Age	G	GS	IP	H	HR	BB	SO	HB	W	L	Pct	Sv	BR/9	ERA
			HOW MUCH			**WHAT HE WILL GIVE UP**					**THE RESULTS**					
Corbin,Patrick	Ari	26	28	28	182	181	17	42	158	8	11	9	.550	0	11.4	3.61
Cosart,Jarred	Mia	26	26	26	156	146	11	75	110	4	8	9	.471	0	13.0	3.81
Cotts,Neal	Min	36	71	0	65	57	7	22	69	2	4	3	.571	0	11.2	3.18
Cueto,Johnny	KC	30	33	33	219	189	20	52	182	11	14	10	.583	0	10.4	3.12
Danks,John	CWS	31	30	30	174	182	24	58	121	5	7	12	.368	0	12.7	4.34
Darvish,Yu	Tex	29	13	13	85	68	9	30	105	3	6	4	.600	0	10.7	3.18
Davies,Zachary	Mil	23	30	30	170	175	11	65	143	4	8	11	.421	0	12.9	3.92
Davis,Wade	KC	30	68	0	69	63	6	23	63	2	4	4	.500	44	11.5	3.26
De Fratus,Justin	Phi	28	53	0	76	76	6	28	71	5	3	5	.375	0	12.9	4.03
de la Rosa,Jorge	Col	35	30	30	169	160	18	68	140	6	10	9	.526	0	12.5	3.89
de la Rosa,Rubby	Ari	27	31	31	180	179	22	65	151	6	9	11	.450	0	12.5	4.10
deGrom,Jacob	NYM	28	30	30	191	171	13	45	183	3	13	8	.619	0	10.3	3.06
Delgado,Randall	Ari	26	64	0	68	65	9	29	61	2	3	4	.429	0	12.7	4.10
DeSclafani,Anthony	Cin	26	31	31	189	196	18	54	159	7	9	12	.429	0	12.2	3.90
Despaigne,Odrisamer	SD	29	27	20	124	136	13	37	83	8	6	8	.429	0	13.1	4.35
Detwiler,Ross	Atl	30	46	3	45	52	4	22	30	2	1	4	.200	0	15.2	5.20
Diaz,Jairo	Col	25	62	0	60	57	6	33	65	3	3	4	.429	0	14.0	4.50
Diaz,Jumbo	Cin	32	63	0	60	53	6	20	59	3	4	3	.571	1	11.4	3.30
Dickey,R.A.	Tor	41	33	33	213	196	25	65	152	10	13	11	.542	0	11.5	3.63
Diekman,Jake	Tex	29	69	0	59	52	3	30	73	3	3	3	.500	1	13.0	3.51
Doolittle,Sean	Oak	29	58	0	59	43	4	10	72	1	4	2	.667	32	8.2	1.83
Duensing,Brian	Min	33	56	0	58	63	6	23	37	2	2	4	.333	0	13.7	4.50
Duffey,Tyler	Min	25	26	26	151	148	11	39	127	4	9	8	.529	0	11.4	3.46
Duffy,Danny	KC	27	29	29	161	148	16	60	139	8	8	10	.444	5	12.1	3.75
Duke,Zach	CWS	33	72	0	60	66	7	26	42	1	2	4	.333	0	14.0	4.80
Dull,Ryan	Oak	26	25	0	34	28	3	10	37	1	2	2	.500	0	10.3	2.91
Dunn,Mike	Mia	31	74	0	58	49	5	28	67	2	3	3	.500	0	12.3	3.41
Dyson,Sam	Tex	28	68	0	68	66	2	22	48	5	4	4	.500	0	12.3	3.31
Eickhoff,Jerad	Phi	25	30	30	188	179	24	61	165	7	9	12	.429	0	11.8	3.83
Elias,Roenis	Sea	27	26	26	147	146	16	55	126	9	7	9	.438	0	12.9	4.16
Eovaldi,Nathan	NYY	26	29	29	170	180	11	48	127	4	9	10	.474	0	12.3	3.81
Erlin,Robbie	SD	25	26	26	148	171	19	41	125	4	6	10	.375	0	13.1	4.68
Estrada,Marco	Tor	32	31	31	185	161	26	55	155	4	12	9	.571	0	10.7	3.45
Familia,Jeurys	NYM	26	72	0	74	66	5	23	72	2	5	3	.625	46	11.1	3.04
Farquhar,Danny	Sea	29	47	0	56	51	5	17	60	2	4	3	.571	0	11.2	3.21
Feldman,Scott	Hou	33	24	24	140	143	15	39	87	5	7	8	.467	0	12.0	3.92
Feliz,Neftali	Det	28	55	0	56	48	6	20	51	2	3	3	.500	18	11.2	3.21
Fernandez,Jose	Mia	23	31	31	195	146	13	50	233	5	16	5	.762	0	9.3	2.58
Fields,Josh	Hou	30	54	0	50	40	4	20	58	2	3	2	.600	0	11.2	2.88
Fien,Casey	Min	32	66	0	62	58	8	9	53	0	4	3	.571	0	9.7	3.05
Fiers,Mike	Hou	31	30	30	184	158	22	57	187	6	12	9	.571	0	10.8	3.38
Fister,Doug	Was	32	26	26	163	169	15	32	111	9	10	9	.526	0	11.6	3.70
Flande,Yohan	Col	30	17	10	61	71	6	18	39	2	3	4	.429	0	13.4	4.72
Foltynewicz,Mike	Atl	24	27	27	151	155	21	68	144	8	5	11	.313	0	13.8	4.77
Frasor,Jason	Atl	38	48	0	42	37	3	21	41	1	2	3	.400	1	12.6	3.64
Freeman,Sam	Tex	29	52	0	40	35	3	22	37	2	2	2	.500	0	13.3	3.83
Frias,Carlos	LAD	26	13	8	51	57	4	14	33	2	3	3	.500	0	12.9	4.24
Friedrich,Christian	Col	28	66	0	51	59	7	22	42	2	2	4	.333	0	14.6	5.29
Furbush,Charlie	Sea	30	58	0	51	44	6	14	52	2	3	2	.600	0	10.8	3.18
Gallardo,Yovani	Tex	30	32	32	178	174	18	61	152	2	10	10	.500	0	12.0	3.79
Garces,Frank	SD	26	48	2	45	42	5	24	42	2	2	3	.400	0	13.6	4.40
Garcia,Jaime	StL	29	27	27	178	172	14	41	144	4	11	8	.579	0	11.0	3.34
Garcia,Luis	Phi	29	71	0	65	63	4	35	61	1	3	4	.429	6	13.7	4.02
Garcia,Yimi	LAD	25	64	0	61	48	8	14	71	3	5	2	.714	0	9.6	2.66
Garza,Matt	Mil	32	26	26	155	151	18	54	126	4	8	10	.444	0	12.1	3.89
Gausman,Kevin	Bal	25	29	29	164	163	20	50	149	3	8	10	.444	0	11.9	3.84
Gee,Dillon	NYM	30	23	23	147	152	17	38	108	7	7	9	.438	0	12.1	3.98
Geltz,Steve	TB	28	66	1	62	44	8	25	72	2	4	3	.571	0	10.3	2.76
Germen,Gonzalez	Col	28	49	0	53	54	6	28	46	1	2	3	.400	0	14.1	4.75
Gibson,Kyle	Min	28	33	33	203	207	17	67	146	5	10	13	.435	0	12.4	3.86
Giles,Ken	Phi	25	65	0	72	56	2	25	94	1	5	3	.625	30	10.2	2.25
Gilmartin,Sean	NYM	26	49	0	56	61	6	19	45	1	3	4	.429	0	13.0	4.34
Goeddel,Erik	NYM	27	52	0	50	49	4	20	47	2	3	3	.500	0	12.8	3.96
Goforth,David	Mil	27	48	0	60	58	3	29	45	1	3	4	.429	0	13.2	3.90
Gomes,Brandon	TB	31	66	0	65	58	8	18	68	3	4	3	.571	1	10.9	3.18
Gomez,Jeanmar	Phi	28	62	0	74	79	7	21	49	2	3	5	.375	0	12.4	4.01
Gonzalez,Chi Chi	Tex	24	25	25	151	153	10	63	97	7	7	9	.438	0	13.3	4.05
Gonzalez,Gio	Was	32	32	32	186	167	13	71	182	4	12	9	.571	0	11.7	3.44
Gonzalez,Miguel	Bal	32	27	27	159	153	23	53	117	7	8	10	.444	0	12.1	3.96
Gorzelanny,Tom	Det	33	49	0	43	42	5	24	39	2	2	3	.400	0	14.2	4.60
Gott,Trevor	LAA	23	65	0	69	65	1	30	56	3	4	4	.500	0	12.8	3.39
Graham,J.R.	Min	26	44	0	60	66	4	21	46	4	2	4	.333	0	13.6	4.35
Gray,Jonathan	Col	24	30	30	158	166	14	57	147	6	8	9	.471	0	13.0	4.16
Gray,Sonny	Oak	26	32	32	212	190	14	65	179	4	13	10	.565	0	11.0	3.18
Greene,Shane	Det	27	18	13	78	90	8	27	62	5	3	6	.333	0	14.1	4.85
Gregerson,Luke	Hou	32	64	0	63	51	5	12	59	2	4	3	.571	39	9.3	2.29
Greinke,Zack	LAD	32	33	33	226	195	18	44	212	5	17	8	.680	0	9.7	2.91
Grilli,Jason	Atl	39	57	0	54	46	4	18	67	2	3	3	.500	0	11.0	3.00
Grimm,Justin	ChC	27	71	0	59	57	5	27	55	2	3	3	.500	0	13.1	3.97
Guaipe,Mayckol	Sea	25	51	0	56	56	6	15	47	3	3	3	.500	0	11.9	3.70
Guthrie,Jeremy	KC	37	26	26	160	176	23	44	91	9	6	12	.333	0	12.9	4.61

562

2016 Pitcher Projections

PLAYER			HOW MUCH			WHAT HE WILL GIVE UP					THE RESULTS					
Pitcher	Team	Age	G	GS	IP	H	HR	BB	SO	HB	W	L	Pct	Sv	BR/9	ERA
Hagadone,Nick	Cle	30	40	0	32	28	4	14	35	0	2	2	.500	0	11.8	3.66
Hahn,Jesse	Oak	26	27	27	164	147	8	52	130	10	10	8	.556	0	11.5	3.24
Hale,David	Col	28	25	25	128	145	13	45	90	6	6	8	.429	0	13.8	4.78
Hamels,Cole	Tex	32	33	33	222	199	22	63	210	8	14	11	.560	0	10.9	3.36
Hammel,Jason	ChC	33	31	31	164	162	21	41	134	7	10	9	.526	0	11.5	3.79
Hand,Brad	Mia	26	34	19	118	115	13	44	90	2	6	7	.462	0	12.3	3.89
Happ,J.A.	Pit	33	31	31	181	181	21	54	157	3	10	10	.500	0	11.8	3.83
Harang,Aaron	Phi	38	30	30	178	191	22	56	132	4	7	13	.350	0	12.7	4.30
Hardy,Blaine	Det	29	67	0	62	58	5	23	53	1	4	3	.571	0	11.9	3.48
Harris,Will	Hou	31	71	0	72	58	6	24	76	3	5	3	.625	0	10.6	2.75
Harvey,Matt	NYM	27	31	31	202	166	15	39	209	6	16	7	.696	0	9.4	2.76
Hatcher,Chris	LAD	31	66	0	60	57	6	19	60	1	4	3	.571	2	11.6	3.45
Hawkins,LaTroy	Tor	43	43	0	41	42	3	8	29	0	3	2	.600	0	11.0	3.29
Heaney,Andrew	LAA	25	30	30	178	173	14	49	152	8	11	9	.550	0	11.6	3.54
Hellickson,Jeremy	Ari	29	30	30	177	180	23	52	142	6	9	11	.450	0	12.1	4.02
Hembree,Heath	Bos	27	62	0	64	59	7	23	62	2	4	3	.571	0	11.8	3.66
Hendricks,Kyle	ChC	26	33	33	186	173	12	43	155	7	13	7	.650	0	10.8	3.19
Hendriks,Liam	Tor	27	61	0	61	64	5	9	48	2	4	3	.571	0	11.1	3.39
Hernandez,David	Ari	31	66	0	66	55	8	24	70	4	4	3	.571	0	11.3	3.27
Hernandez,Felix	Sea	30	32	32	208	181	17	52	201	7	15	8	.652	0	10.4	3.07
Herrera,Kelvin	KC	26	72	0	71	56	5	26	70	3	5	3	.625	0	10.8	2.66
Heston,Chris	SF	28	31	31	180	175	16	63	140	11	10	10	.500	0	12.4	3.85
Hill,Rich	Bos	36	30	8	64	54	5	33	72	6	4	3	.571	0	13.1	3.66
Hochevar,Luke	KC	32	57	0	61	61	8	24	48	2	3	4	.429	0	12.8	4.28
Holland,Derek	Tex	29	27	27	170	169	22	52	143	4	9	10	.474	0	11.9	3.92
Hoover,J.J.	Cin	28	63	0	61	46	6	29	64	2	4	3	.571	1	11.4	3.10
House,T.J.	Cle	26	26	26	153	175	14	64	117	8	6	11	.353	0	14.5	5.00
Howell,J.P.	LAD	33	68	0	42	34	3	16	39	2	3	2	.600	0	11.1	3.00
Hudson,Daniel	Ari	29	69	0	69	67	7	25	62	2	4	4	.500	2	12.3	3.78
Hughes,Jared	Pit	30	71	0	64	64	4	19	43	5	4	3	.571	0	12.4	3.66
Hughes,Phil	Min	30	30	30	186	201	26	20	148	5	9	11	.450	0	10.9	3.77
Hunter,Tommy	ChC	29	56	0	54	56	7	11	35	1	3	3	.500	0	11.3	3.83
Hutchison,Drew	Tor	25	31	31	179	185	23	57	167	11	9	11	.450	0	12.7	4.32
Iwakuma,Hisashi	Sea	35	29	29	188	171	22	28	158	2	13	8	.619	0	9.6	3.11
Jackson,Edwin	Atl	32	57	0	65	69	7	26	51	1	3	5	.375	0	13.3	4.43
Jansen,Kenley	LAD	28	65	0	66	43	5	14	101	2	5	2	.714	47	8.0	1.64
Janssen,Casey	Was	34	58	0	46	42	4	9	38	2	3	2	.600	0	10.4	2.93
Jeffress,Jeremy	Mil	28	71	0	72	70	4	26	71	2	4	4	.500	0	12.2	3.50
Jennings,Dan	CWS	29	60	0	62	63	3	27	54	0	3	4	.429	0	13.1	3.77
Jepsen,Kevin	Min	31	72	0	67	60	5	25	64	1	4	4	.500	29	11.6	3.22
Jimenez,Cesar	Mil	31	55	0	62	60	3	23	54	0	4	3	.571	0	12.0	3.34
Jimenez,Ubaldo	Bal	32	33	33	198	186	19	85	182	8	10	12	.455	0	12.7	3.91
Johnson,Erik	CWS	26	27	27	163	163	14	68	135	6	7	11	.389	0	13.1	4.09
Johnson,Jim	LAD	33	68	0	61	64	4	23	43	4	3	4	.429	0	13.4	4.28
Jones,Nate	CWS	30	64	0	67	61	6	24	71	1	4	4	.500	0	11.6	3.36
Jungmann,Taylor	Mil	26	32	32	187	180	16	83	156	15	9	12	.429	0	13.4	4.14
Kahnle,Tommy	Col	26	51	0	64	53	6	39	68	1	4	3	.571	0	13.1	3.80
Karns,Nate	TB	28	23	21	122	116	17	50	124	5	6	8	.429	0	12.6	4.20
Kazmir,Scott	Hou	32	31	31	180	171	19	54	155	7	10	10	.500	0	11.6	3.65
Kela,Keone	Tex	23	65	0	60	47	3	24	73	1	4	2	.667	0	10.8	2.55
Kelley,Shawn	SD	32	55	0	48	42	5	16	55	1	3	2	.600	0	11.1	3.19
Kelly,Joe	Bos	28	25	25	144	149	13	56	104	7	7	9	.438	0	13.2	4.25
Kendrick,Kyle	Col	31	28	28	157	175	22	47	89	7	7	10	.412	0	13.1	4.76
Kennedy,Ian	SD	31	31	31	182	180	24	60	171	8	9	11	.450	0	12.3	4.05
Kensing,Logan	Sea	33	37	0	31	29	3	12	26	1	2	2	.500	0	12.2	3.48
Kershaw,Clayton	LAD	28	33	33	230	169	13	41	253	4	21	5	.808	0	8.4	2.31
Keuchel,Dallas	Hou	28	33	33	231	225	19	54	171	5	15	11	.577	0	11.1	3.43
Kimbrel,Craig	SD	28	67	0	66	40	4	25	103	2	5	2	.714	45	9.1	1.77
Kluber,Corey	Cle	30	32	32	220	211	20	46	225	9	13	11	.542	0	10.9	3.40
Knebel,Corey	Mil	24	58	0	60	48	6	24	77	2	4	3	.571	0	11.1	3.15
Koehler,Tom	Mia	30	32	32	199	192	21	79	152	7	10	12	.455	0	12.6	3.98
Kontos,George	SF	31	73	0	73	64	8	15	64	1	5	3	.625	0	9.9	2.71
Lackey,John	StL	37	33	33	212	216	24	51	167	7	12	12	.500	0	11.6	3.82
Lamb,John	Cin	25	26	26	145	144	16	59	136	8	7	10	.412	0	13.1	4.28
Latos,Mat	LAA	28	30	30	174	159	16	51	151	4	11	8	.579	0	11.1	3.36
Layne,Tommy	Bos	31	66	0	45	45	3	23	35	3	2	3	.400	0	14.2	4.20
Leake,Mike	SF	28	31	31	191	191	23	47	127	6	10	11	.476	0	11.5	3.77
LeCure,Sam	Cin	31	37	0	40	40	4	17	35	2	2	3	.400	0	13.3	4.23
Lester,Jon	ChC	32	31	31	211	195	18	49	198	7	15	9	.625	0	10.7	3.24
Lewis,Colby	Tex	36	33	33	211	222	30	49	166	10	10	13	.435	0	12.0	4.14
Liberatore,Adam	LAD	29	52	0	61	54	3	22	60	2	4	3	.571	0	11.5	2.95
Lincecum,Tim	SF	32	22	22	111	101	11	49	109	3	6	6	.500	0	12.4	3.81
Liriano,Francisco	Pit	32	31	31	184	161	15	74	188	5	11	9	.550	0	11.7	3.52
Lobstein,Kyle	Det	26	14	10	56	65	5	20	45	1	2	4	.333	0	13.8	4.66
Locke,Jeff	Pit	28	29	29	167	166	16	62	129	7	9	10	.474	0	12.7	3.93
Loewen,Adam	Phi	32	39	0	39	35	3	26	36	3	1	3	.250	0	14.8	4.38
Logan,Boone	Col	31	62	0	38	38	5	17	43	2	2	2	.500	0	13.5	4.74
Lohse,Kyle	Mil	37	30	30	190	195	24	48	125	5	9	12	.429	0	11.7	3.88
Lopez,Javier	SF	38	78	0	38	32	1	16	26	1	3	2	.600	0	11.6	2.84
Lorenzen,Michael	Cin	24	34	16	92	98	11	39	63	4	4	7	.364	0	13.8	4.79
Loup,Aaron	Tor	28	65	0	65	61	5	20	55	7	4	3	.571	0	12.2	3.60

2016 Pitcher Projections

PLAYER			HOW MUCH			WHAT HE WILL GIVE UP					THE RESULTS				
Pitcher	Team	Age	G	GS	IP	H	HR	BB	SO	HB	W	L	Pct	Sv	BR/9	ERA
Lowe,Mark	Tor	33	61	0	56	55	6	16	56	1	3	3	.500	0	11.6	3.54
Lyles,Jordan	Col	25	12	12	71	79	7	26	50	4	3	5	.375	0	13.8	4.82
Lynn,Lance	StL	29	32	32	176	168	13	66	163	7	10	10	.500	0	12.3	3.73
Lyons,Tyler	StL	28	24	7	77	79	9	16	71	2	4	4	.500	0	11.3	3.62
Machi,Jean	Bos	34	66	0	64	59	6	20	51	1	4	3	.571	0	11.2	3.23
Madson,Ryan	KC	35	66	0	63	52	4	14	61	2	5	2	.714	2	9.7	2.43
Maness,Seth	StL	27	71	0	65	70	6	12	43	2	4	4	.500	0	11.6	3.60
Manship,Jeff	Cle	31	62	0	64	68	6	25	46	1	3	4	.429	0	13.2	4.22
Marimon,Sugar	Atl	27	46	0	59	65	8	23	39	2	2	5	.286	0	13.7	4.88
Martinez,Carlos	StL	24	29	29	173	160	11	61	165	10	10	9	.526	0	12.0	3.54
Martinez,Nick	Tex	25	25	25	144	150	16	54	87	9	6	10	.375	0	13.3	4.38
Masterson,Justin	Bos	31	26	5	51	51	4	25	43	4	2	3	.400	0	14.1	4.41
Mateo,Marcos	SD	32	62	0	61	57	6	24	63	4	3	3	.500	0	12.5	3.69
Mattheus,Ryan	Cin	32	64	0	65	69	5	20	45	2	3	4	.429	0	12.6	3.88
Matusz,Brian	Bal	29	66	0	50	51	6	19	44	2	2	3	.400	0	13.0	4.32
Maurer,Brandon	SD	25	55	0	54	59	5	17	45	2	3	3	.500	0	13.0	4.33
May,Trevor	Min	26	59	9	95	97	10	31	92	4	4	6	.400	0	12.5	4.07
McAllister,Zach	Cle	28	63	0	66	69	6	21	55	2	3	4	.429	0	12.5	4.09
McFarland,T.J.	Bal	27	41	0	61	69	4	21	41	2	3	4	.429	0	13.6	4.28
McGee,Jake	TB	29	60	0	56	44	4	14	65	1	4	2	.667	6	9.5	2.25
McHugh,Collin	Hou	29	31	31	195	185	17	51	170	9	12	10	.545	0	11.3	3.46
Medlen,Kris	KC	30	26	26	146	137	15	37	119	6	8	8	.500	0	11.1	3.45
Mejia,Jenrry	NYM	26	21	0	30	30	2	11	26	1	2	2	.500	0	12.6	3.90
Melancon,Mark	Pit	31	72	0	72	61	4	12	67	3	5	3	.625	49	9.5	2.25
Miley,Wade	Bos	29	31	31	185	189	18	63	144	3	10	11	.476	0	12.4	3.94
Miller,Andrew	NYY	31	65	0	71	60	6	23	84	4	5	3	.625	39	11.0	2.92
Miller,Justin	Col	29	60	0	65	55	5	21	65	5	5	3	.625	0	11.2	3.05
Miller,Shelby	Atl	25	33	33	211	189	22	77	187	7	11	12	.478	0	11.6	3.58
Milone,Tommy	Min	29	24	24	135	140	17	35	108	2	6	9	.400	0	11.8	3.93
Mitchell,Bryan	NYY	25	30	4	45	47	3	24	38	1	2	3	.400	0	14.4	4.60
Montero,Rafael	NYM	25	25	25	132	115	8	49	126	0	9	6	.600	0	11.2	3.27
Montgomery,Michael	Sea	26	26	26	140	149	15	55	105	7	6	9	.400	0	13.6	4.56
Moore,Matt	TB	27	29	29	162	143	18	62	167	6	9	9	.500	0	11.7	3.61
Morales,Franklin	KC	30	66	0	59	58	8	21	47	3	3	4	.429	0	12.5	4.27
Morgan,Adam	Phi	26	29	29	162	191	23	51	95	7	5	13	.278	0	13.8	5.11
Morin,Mike	LAA	25	62	0	54	51	4	15	57	3	3	3	.500	0	11.5	3.33
Morris,Bryan	Mia	29	73	0	65	63	6	26	50	3	3	4	.429	0	12.7	3.88
Morton,Charlie	Pit	32	27	27	152	154	11	51	110	14	8	9	.471	0	13.0	3.97
Motte,Jason	ChC	34	62	0	57	49	6	14	55	2	4	2	.667	0	10.3	2.84
Mujica,Edward	Oak	32	54	0	51	51	7	9	39	1	3	3	.500	0	10.8	3.35
Narveson,Chris	Mia	34	29	4	61	63	8	21	51	1	3	4	.429	0	12.5	4.43
Nelson,Jimmy	Mil	27	31	31	189	171	13	67	172	14	11	10	.524	0	12.0	3.52
Neris,Hector	Phi	27	50	0	66	63	8	30	61	3	3	5	.375	0	13.1	4.36
Neshek,Pat	Hou	35	62	0	51	44	6	10	45	2	4	2	.667	0	9.9	2.82
Nicasio,Juan	LAD	29	53	0	52	55	6	23	44	1	2	3	.400	0	13.7	4.50
Nicolino,Justin	Mia	23	25	25	152	172	14	36	74	5	7	10	.412	0	12.6	4.20
Niese,Jon	NYM	29	28	28	171	180	17	50	129	6	8	11	.421	0	12.4	4.00
Nolasco,Ricky	Min	33	22	22	132	147	14	36	105	4	6	9	.400	0	12.8	4.36
Nolin,Sean	Oak	26	12	12	58	57	6	25	49	2	3	4	.429	0	13.0	4.03
Norris,Bud	SD	31	35	13	92	98	13	32	83	5	4	6	.400	0	13.2	4.50
Norris,Daniel	Det	23	28	28	160	160	18	73	152	4	7	11	.389	0	13.3	4.33
Nova,Ivan	NYY	29	24	24	136	147	15	45	101	8	6	10	.375	0	13.2	4.50
Nuno,Vidal	Sea	28	32	12	91	89	13	21	75	3	5	5	.500	0	11.2	3.76
Oberg,Scott	Col	26	65	0	59	63	7	27	47	5	2	4	.333	0	14.5	5.03
O'Day,Darren	Bal	33	72	0	71	54	7	17	72	6	5	3	.625	2	9.8	2.41
Odorizzi,Jake	TB	26	31	31	192	176	23	58	177	4	11	10	.524	0	11.2	3.56
O'Flaherty,Eric	NYM	31	34	0	31	30	2	14	24	2	2	2	.500	0	13.4	4.06
Ogando,Alexi	Bos	32	61	0	61	55	8	27	49	2	3	4	.429	0	12.4	3.84
Osich,Josh	SF	27	58	0	61	52	6	24	56	1	4	3	.571	0	11.4	3.10
Otero,Dan	Oak	31	39	0	45	47	2	7	30	1	3	2	.600	0	11.0	3.00
Ottavino,Adam	Col	30	45	0	45	46	4	12	42	2	3	2	.600	0	12.0	3.80
Owens,Henry	Bos	23	29	29	167	145	15	77	158	6	10	9	.526	0	12.3	3.66
Papelbon,Jonathan	Was	35	59	0	66	54	5	13	70	4	4	3	.571	46	9.7	2.45
Parra,Manny	Cin	33	54	0	42	44	4	13	40	1	2	3	.400	0	12.4	3.86
Patton,Spencer	Tex	28	62	0	61	47	7	25	75	5	4	3	.571	0	11.4	3.25
Paxton,James	Sea	27	27	27	149	148	12	63	134	2	8	9	.471	0	12.9	3.99
Peavy,Jake	SF	35	27	27	162	152	19	43	134	5	10	8	.556	0	11.1	3.56
Pelfrey,Mike	Min	32	30	30	164	191	13	51	91	8	6	12	.333	0	13.7	4.66
Pena,Ariel	Mil	27	37	12	85	77	10	43	82	3	4	6	.400	0	13.0	4.13
Peralta,Joel	LAD	40	68	0	64	52	8	17	65	1	5	2	.714	0	9.8	2.81
Peralta,Wily	Mil	27	28	28	160	167	17	53	124	7	7	10	.412	0	12.8	4.16
Perez,Martin	Tex	25	23	23	139	152	12	40	99	3	7	9	.438	0	12.6	4.08
Perez,Oliver	Hou	34	70	0	42	41	5	17	45	3	2	3	.400	0	13.1	4.07
Perez,Williams	Atl	25	29	29	164	171	11	62	112	12	7	11	.389	0	13.4	4.17
Perkins,Glen	Min	33	54	0	51	52	6	9	45	2	3	3	.500	10	11.1	3.53
Pestano,Vinnie	LAA	31	56	0	51	42	4	19	60	3	3	2	.600	0	11.3	3.00
Petit,Yusmeiro	SF	31	41	5	91	89	12	17	83	1	5	5	.500	0	10.6	3.36
Petricka,Jake	CWS	28	60	0	51	53	2	21	36	1	2	3	.400	0	13.2	3.88
Phelps,David	Mia	29	33	14	93	93	10	32	78	4	5	6	.455	0	12.5	3.97
Pinder,Branden	NYY	27	59	0	61	60	6	24	55	1	3	4	.429	0	12.5	3.98
Pineda,Michael	NYY	27	28	28	165	154	17	21	158	5	11	7	.611	0	9.8	3.11

2016 Pitcher Projections

Pitcher	Team	Age	G	GS	IP	H	HR	BB	SO	HB	W	L	Pct	Sv	BR/9	ERA
Pomeranz,Drew	Oak	27	22	17	110	100	11	42	106	3	6	6	.500	0	11.9	3.60
Porcello,Rick	Bos	27	31	31	192	214	21	41	131	7	10	12	.455	0	12.3	4.13
Pressly,Ryan	Min	27	40	0	46	45	2	19	37	0	2	3	.400	0	12.5	3.52
Price,David	Tor	30	32	32	223	199	20	42	214	5	17	8	.680	0	9.9	3.03
Putnam,Zach	CWS	28	44	0	47	46	4	20	46	1	2	3	.400	0	12.8	3.83
Quackenbush,Kevin	SD	27	67	0	68	58	3	23	73	1	5	3	.625	0	11.1	2.65
Qualls,Chad	Hou	37	64	0	52	53	5	9	40	1	3	3	.500	0	10.9	3.29
Quintana,Jose	CWS	27	32	32	205	207	16	48	168	5	11	11	.500	0	11.4	3.56
Ramirez,Erasmo	TB	26	31	31	181	182	20	49	139	10	9	11	.450	0	12.0	3.88
Ramirez,Neil	ChC	27	58	0	54	45	5	24	60	3	3	3	.500	0	12.0	3.50
Ramos,A.J.	Mia	29	71	0	72	49	4	34	84	2	5	3	.625	41	10.6	2.38
Ramos,Cesar	LAA	32	69	0	57	57	5	21	42	2	3	3	.500	0	12.6	3.95
Rasmus,Cory	LAA	28	29	2	40	31	4	16	43	1	3	2	.600	0	10.8	2.92
Ray,Robbie	Ari	24	29	29	174	181	13	77	163	8	8	11	.421	0	13.8	4.34
Reed,Addison	NYM	27	65	0	64	57	7	21	68	1	4	3	.571	0	11.1	3.23
Richard,Clayton	ChC	32	40	3	62	66	7	14	35	2	3	3	.500	0	11.9	3.92
Richards,Garrett	LAA	28	32	32	206	190	16	72	168	7	12	10	.545	0	11.8	3.54
Roark,Tanner	Was	29	30	30	188	186	17	39	138	7	12	9	.571	0	11.1	3.49
Robertson,David	CWS	31	64	0	66	50	6	17	88	1	4	3	.571	37	9.3	2.32
Robles,Hansel	NYM	25	62	0	64	56	7	22	65	3	4	3	.571	0	11.4	3.38
Rodney,Fernando	ChC	39	68	0	62	54	4	28	62	4	4	3	.571	0	12.5	3.48
Rodriguez,Eduardo	Bos	23	31	31	182	186	15	53	158	4	10	10	.500	0	12.0	3.76
Rodriguez,Fernando	Oak	32	62	0	71	65	6	28	70	3	4	4	.500	0	12.2	3.55
Rodriguez,Francisco	Mil	34	64	0	60	49	8	14	65	1	4	2	.667	38	9.6	2.70
Roe,Chaz	Bal	29	62	0	62	64	5	25	52	4	3	4	.429	0	13.5	4.21
Romero,Enny	TB	25	37	0	44	44	4	20	37	1	2	3	.400	0	13.3	4.30
Romo,Sergio	SF	33	73	0	66	52	6	12	74	2	5	2	.714	0	9.0	2.18
Rondon,Bruce	Det	25	44	0	42	37	3	23	48	2	2	2	.500	18	13.3	3.86
Rondon,Hector	ChC	28	70	0	70	64	6	17	65	2	5	3	.625	44	10.7	2.96
Rosenthal,Trevor	StL	26	65	0	66	54	3	28	79	3	4	3	.571	50	11.6	3.00
Ross,Robbie	Bos	27	62	0	61	65	6	21	48	4	3	4	.429	2	13.3	4.43
Ross,Tyson	SD	29	32	32	200	188	13	81	188	9	12	11	.522	0	12.5	3.69
Rusin,Chris	Col	29	12	8	49	56	6	15	30	2	2	3	.400	0	13.4	4.78
Russell,James	ChC	30	39	0	31	31	4	10	22	1	2	2	.500	0	12.2	3.77
Ryan,Kyle	Det	24	26	5	53	59	5	17	32	1	2	3	.400	0	13.1	4.25
Ryu,Hyun-Jin	LAD	29	27	27	158	154	10	33	134	2	11	7	.611	0	10.8	3.25
Rzepczynski,Marc	SD	30	74	0	40	41	3	16	37	2	2	2	.500	0	13.3	4.05
Sabathia,CC	NYY	35	27	27	159	162	20	46	141	6	8	10	.444	0	12.1	3.96
Salas,Fernando	LAA	31	74	0	68	59	7	14	70	2	5	3	.625	0	9.9	2.78
Salazar,Danny	Cle	26	30	30	191	171	21	59	215	5	11	10	.524	0	11.1	3.44
Sale,Chris	CWS	27	31	31	211	176	21	44	248	12	14	9	.609	0	9.9	2.99
Samardzija,Jeff	CWS	31	31	31	206	199	23	48	181	9	11	12	.478	0	11.2	3.58
Sanchez,Aaron	Tor	23	30	30	179	156	14	96	137	10	10	10	.500	0	13.2	3.87
Sanchez,Anibal	Det	32	29	29	184	173	17	54	167	3	11	10	.524	0	11.2	3.47
Santana,Ervin	Min	33	31	31	195	187	24	62	154	7	10	12	.455	0	11.8	3.83
Santiago,Hector	LAA	28	31	31	179	163	22	73	159	11	9	11	.450	0	12.4	3.97
Scheppers,Tanner	Tex	29	45	0	43	43	5	23	38	3	2	3	.400	0	14.4	4.81
Scherzer,Max	Was	31	33	33	222	189	23	44	245	6	17	8	.680	0	9.7	3.00
Schultz,Bo	Tor	30	44	0	61	63	6	21	39	2	3	4	.429	0	12.7	4.13
Scribner,Evan	Oak	30	55	0	62	54	8	7	67	1	4	3	.571	0	9.0	2.61
Shaw,Bryan	Cle	28	70	0	63	57	5	19	52	3	4	3	.571	0	11.3	3.14
Shields,James	SD	34	32	32	204	202	25	66	182	8	11	12	.478	0	12.2	3.97
Shoemaker,Matt	LAA	29	28	28	168	176	23	38	139	6	9	10	.474	0	11.8	3.96
Shreve,Chasen	NYY	25	62	0	56	52	5	25	59	1	3	3	.500	0	12.5	3.70
Siegrist,Kevin	StL	26	78	0	72	52	5	33	88	4	5	3	.625	3	11.1	2.75
Simon,Alfredo	Det	35	31	31	188	188	22	63	127	11	9	12	.429	0	12.5	4.07
Sipp,Tony	Hou	32	57	0	54	41	7	16	60	1	4	2	.667	0	9.7	2.67
Skaggs,Tyler	LAA	24	25	25	151	144	13	48	138	6	9	8	.529	0	11.8	3.64
Smith,Carson	Sea	26	71	0	71	56	2	23	88	5	5	3	.625	38	10.6	2.41
Smith,Joe	LAA	32	71	0	68	56	4	18	57	3	5	2	.714	2	10.2	2.51
Smith,Josh	Cin	28	13	9	47	50	4	17	38	3	2	3	.400	0	13.4	4.40
Smith,Will	Mil	26	76	0	69	72	7	27	68	2	3	5	.375	0	13.2	4.30
Smyly,Drew	TB	27	29	29	167	148	19	53	168	3	10	9	.526	0	11.0	3.40
Soria,Joakim	Pit	32	68	0	65	54	6	17	67	2	5	2	.714	0	10.1	2.63
Stammen,Craig	Was	32	45	0	64	67	6	17	50	1	4	3	.571	0	12.0	3.80
Storen,Drew	Was	28	66	0	60	53	4	16	58	3	4	2	.667	7	10.8	2.85
Strasburg,Stephen	Was	27	32	32	202	170	19	42	234	7	15	7	.682	0	9.8	2.94
Street,Huston	LAA	32	66	0	68	54	8	20	65	0	5	3	.625	44	9.8	2.65
Strickland,Hunter	SF	27	67	0	64	52	5	10	67	2	5	2	.714	0	9.0	2.25
Stroman,Marcus	Tor	25	31	31	184	172	14	49	177	5	12	8	.600	0	11.1	3.33
Strop,Pedro	ChC	31	74	0	67	51	4	28	73	4	5	2	.714	2	11.1	2.69
Syndergaard,Noah	NYM	23	32	32	200	178	22	48	224	5	13	9	.591	0	10.4	3.24
Tanaka,Masahiro	NYY	27	27	27	175	155	24	30	168	3	11	8	.579	0	9.7	3.19
Tazawa,Junichi	Bos	30	63	0	60	60	6	14	61	1	4	3	.571	0	11.1	3.39
Teheran,Julio	Atl	25	33	33	215	203	25	67	181	10	11	13	.458	0	11.7	3.73
Tepera,Ryan	Tor	28	52	0	54	51	5	20	46	4	3	3	.500	0	12.5	3.83
Thatcher,Joe	Hou	34	54	0	31	29	2	12	33	2	2	2	.500	0	12.5	3.48
Thayer,Dale	SD	35	51	0	48	46	5	15	41	1	3	3	.500	0	11.6	3.75
Thornburg,Tyler	Mil	27	50	0	59	60	7	25	51	2	2	4	.333	0	13.3	4.58
Thornton,Matt	Was	39	65	0	46	41	2	12	41	2	3	2	.600	0	10.8	2.93
Tillman,Chris	Bal	28	31	31	176	171	23	61	136	4	9	11	.450	0	12.1	3.94

565

2016 Pitcher Projections

Pitcher	Team	Age	G	GS	IP	H	HR	BB	SO	HB	W	L	Pct	Sv	BR/9	ERA
			HOW MUCH			**WHAT HE WILL GIVE UP**					**THE RESULTS**					
Tolleson,Shawn	Tex	28	76	0	77	66	9	22	82	2	5	4	.556	40	10.5	3.04
Tomlin,Josh	Cle	31	28	28	171	172	27	23	123	4	9	10	.474	0	10.5	3.63
Tonkin,Michael	Min	26	62	0	60	55	4	16	59	3	4	3	.571	0	11.1	3.00
Torres,Alex	NYM	28	54	0	53	47	3	33	56	2	3	3	.500	0	13.9	3.91
Torres,Carlos	NYM	33	52	0	53	50	5	17	47	1	3	3	.500	0	11.5	3.57
Treinen,Blake	Was	28	70	0	74	77	4	25	58	3	4	4	.500	0	12.8	3.77
Tropeano,Nicholas	LAA	25	27	27	147	142	14	50	142	4	8	8	.500	0	12.0	3.73
Uehara,Koji	Bos	41	62	0	62	45	7	11	72	0	5	1	.833	38	8.1	1.89
Urena,Jose	Mia	24	26	7	60	64	5	18	39	2	3	4	.429	0	12.6	4.05
Venditte,Pat	Oak	31	44	0	49	43	4	18	47	1	3	3	.500	0	11.4	3.12
Ventura,Yordano	KC	25	32	32	202	187	16	77	192	10	11	12	.478	0	12.2	3.65
VerHagen,Drew	Det	25	37	0	51	54	3	19	31	3	2	3	.400	0	13.4	4.06
Verlander,Justin	Det	33	32	32	204	186	17	57	190	5	13	10	.565	0	10.9	3.31
Verrett,Logan	NYM	26	35	0	36	36	4	9	29	1	2	2	.500	0	11.5	3.75
Villanueva,Carlos	StL	32	31	0	56	53	7	17	49	2	3	3	.500	0	11.6	3.70
Villarreal,Pedro	Cin	28	34	0	61	67	8	15	44	3	3	4	.429	0	12.5	4.43
Vincent,Nick	SD	29	62	0	54	48	4	17	59	2	4	2	.667	0	11.2	3.00
Vizcaino,Arodys	Atl	25	65	0	64	59	4	25	67	3	3	4	.429	35	12.2	3.38
Vogelsong,Ryan	SF	38	22	22	125	125	13	48	101	5	6	8	.429	0	12.8	4.10
Volquez,Edinson	KC	32	33	33	194	181	18	72	163	9	10	12	.455	0	12.2	3.71
Wacha,Michael	StL	24	29	29	175	152	16	55	157	5	12	8	.600	0	10.9	3.24
Wada,Tsuyoshi	ChC	35	26	26	142	148	16	42	119	3	8	8	.500	0	12.2	3.99
Wainwright,Adam	StL	34	30	30	210	187	12	40	180	5	16	8	.667	0	9.9	2.91
Walden,Jordan	StL	28	41	0	37	31	2	17	42	0	2	2	.500	0	11.7	3.16
Walker,Taijuan	Sea	23	30	30	182	171	23	53	177	12	10	10	.500	0	11.7	3.76
Warren,Adam	NYY	28	48	13	116	116	10	35	92	5	6	7	.462	0	12.1	3.72
Watson,Tony	Pit	31	74	0	71	57	5	15	63	4	6	2	.750	0	9.6	2.28
Weaver,Jered	LAA	33	29	29	173	155	21	43	134	6	11	8	.579	0	10.6	3.38
Webb,Daniel	CWS	26	29	0	30	29	2	19	27	1	1	2	.333	0	14.7	4.80
Webb,Ryan	Cle	30	55	0	61	60	3	15	43	2	4	3	.571	0	11.4	3.10
Wheeler,Zack	NYM	26	27	27	153	135	12	65	148	8	9	8	.529	0	12.2	3.59
Wilhelmsen,Tom	Sea	32	62	0	74	63	5	35	67	3	4	4	.500	13	12.3	3.41
Williams,Jerome	Phi	34	41	17	121	138	17	33	79	5	4	9	.308	0	13.1	4.76
Wilson,Alex	Det	29	57	0	66	66	5	17	52	2	4	4	.500	0	11.6	3.55
Wilson,C.J.	LAA	35	30	30	170	155	14	68	148	9	10	9	.526	0	12.3	3.71
Wilson,Justin	NYY	28	75	0	66	56	5	25	60	3	4	3	.571	0	11.5	3.14
Wisler,Matthew	Atl	23	28	28	161	166	19	49	132	5	7	11	.389	0	12.3	4.02
Withrow,Chris	Atl	27	60	0	62	54	5	44	63	2	3	4	.429	0	14.5	4.21
Wood,Alex	LAD	25	33	33	200	190	14	60	175	5	13	10	.565	0	11.5	3.46
Wood,Travis	ChC	29	54	7	89	84	10	35	75	3	5	5	.500	0	12.3	3.84
Worley,Vance	Pit	28	32	12	86	94	8	20	63	3	4	5	.444	0	12.2	3.98
Wright,Mike	Bal	26	25	25	138	150	13	48	104	8	6	9	.400	0	13.4	4.43
Wright,Steven	Bos	31	11	7	56	58	6	19	42	2	3	3	.500	0	12.7	4.18
Yates,Kirby	TB	29	52	0	52	42	7	22	66	3	3	3	.500	0	11.6	3.46
Young,Chris	KC	37	34	12	97	87	15	35	65	1	5	6	.455	0	11.4	3.62
Ziegler,Brad	Ari	36	62	0	68	59	3	20	44	2	5	3	.625	42	10.7	2.65
Zimmermann,Jordan	Was	30	33	33	210	200	19	37	172	8	14	9	.609	0	10.5	3.30
Zych,Tony	Sea	25	56	0	59	62	3	15	52	4	3	3	.500	0	12.4	3.66

Three Up and Three Down in 2016

Scott Spratt

Batted ball location and velocity data has provided the backbone of advanced defensive analytics like Defensive Runs Saved for more than a decade, but it has been something of an untapped resource for offensive analysis. In general, hitters produce consistent results on their batted balls season after season, but that does not mean that outliers must be written off entirely as random variance. Just as we know that the average batting average on balls in play (BABIP) of a line drive (.681) is not the same as the average BABIP of a flyball (.127), it stands to reason that a hard groundball hit right down the third baseline has a better chance to become a hit than a medium groundball hit right at a shortstop. That line of reason drove Baseball Info Solutions to develop Defense-Independent Batting Statistics (DIBS).

The goal of DIBS is to get away from results-based thinking in the offensive evaluation of hitters. Rather than call a specific ball in play either a hit or an out, we compare that ball in play to similar ones historically based on its characteristics like location and velocity and assign it a chance of becoming a hit based on the ratio of hits to outs of those similar batted balls. That means that that hard-hit groundball down the third baseline becomes an expected 0.9 hits, even if Nolan Arenado makes an exceptional backhanded play to rob the batter of the actual hit in that specific instance.

In addition to the properties of the batted ball, we also factor in the batter's speed and handedness, the batter's power, whether the defense deployed a shift, and the ballpark. With all of those factors included in the framework, we found that DIBS was a much more consistent measurement of offense than traditional statistics, which suggests that it does a better job of capturing batter skill.

DIBS is not only a better method of evaluating the offensive production of hitters; it is also a powerful tool to project future hitter performance. DIBS can identify the hitters who benefited or suffered the most because of the defensive plays made or not made against them, and it can also assign an appropriate value to whatever discrepancy exists based on run expectancy. In the previous example, Arenado's great diving play did not only rob the batter of 0.9 expected hits. It also cost the hitter 0.7 expected doubles and 0.1 expected triples. We assign each of those fractions of hits a run value based on linear weights, which we combine in a single number called Batting Runs Above Average (BRAA) that is a comprehensive evaluation of hitter performance.

In future years, we plan to incorporate what we have learned from DIBS into improved Bill James Hitter and Pitcher Projections. This year, we wanted to provide you with a taste of the type of analysis that can be done with DIBS. What follows are three hitters who underperformed their expectations in DIBS in 2015 and so should be expected to improve in 2016 and three hitters who overperformed their expectations and should be expected to decline.

Three Hitters Who Should Improve in 2016

Victor Martinez, 2015

	PA	Hits	Doubles	Triples	Home Runs	AVG	BABIP	BRAA
Actual	485	108	20	0	11	.245	.253	-16.0
DIBS	485	125	27	1	11	.283	.307	4.4
Difference	0	-17	-7	-1	0	-.038	-.055	-20.4

In 2014, Victor Martinez may have been the best hitter in baseball. His .335 batting average trailed only Jose Altuve's .341 mark among qualified batters. Meanwhile, Martinez hit 32 home runs. No one else in the top five in batting average hit more than 20. Because of his command of the strike zone and all-fields approach, the 36-year-old Martinez appeared to be the epitome of a player who should age gracefully. Instead, in 2015, his offensive numbers fell off a cliff. His batting average fell by 90 points and he barely reached double-digit home runs despite close to 500 plate appearances.

A knee injury was no doubt responsible for some of Martinez's precipitous decline in performance, but his trajectory-based hitting statistics suggest he was also the unluckiest batter in baseball. Martinez had 17 fewer batted balls drop in for hits than would be expected based on their locations and velocities. And while his home run total was no different than expected, he wound up with seven fewer doubles than he should have.

His season was the kind that can shake a team's confidence in a veteran player. However, while the aging Martinez will likely never again reach the peak he enjoyed in 2014, his trajectory-based statistics paint a much more optimistic picture of his 2015 performance that bodes well for a bounce-back season in 2016.

Jayson Werth, 2015

	PA	Hits	Doubles	Triples	Home Runs	AVG	BABIP	BRAA
Actual	378	73	16	1	12	.221	.253	-5.5
DIBS	378	88	21	1	13	.265	.322	8.9
Difference	0	-15	-5	0	-1	-.044	-.069	-14.4

Jonathan Papelbon's and Bryce Harper's dugout altercation will provide the lasting image of the Nationals' disappointing 2015 season, but the player who may best represent the team's underperformance is Jayson Werth. Like Martinez, Werth had turned 36 years old but had maintained his exceptional level of play in recent seasons. And then, like Martinez, Werth suffered a complete offensive collapse in 2015 with a contributing injury—in his case, a wrist fracture due to a hit by pitch. Still, Werth managed to play in 88 games and see 378 plate appearances, in which time he hit just .221.

Relative to expectations for his batted balls, Werth underachieved across the board. He saw 15 fewer hits than expected, including 5 fewer doubles and 1 less home run. Even luck would have transformed his season from one in which he cost the Nationals 5.5 runs relative to average to one in which he provided the Nationals with 8.9 runs. Like with Martinez, do not count out a return to form for Werth next season.

Jonathan Lucroy, 2015

	PA	Hits	Doubles	Triples	Home Runs	AVG	BABIP	BRAA
Actual	415	98	20	3	7	.264	.297	-5.5
DIBS	415	108	25	2	7	.291	.334	6.7
Difference	0	-10	-5	1	0	-.027	-.037	-12.3

Because of all of the demands of the position, it can be difficult for even the best hitting catchers to excel offensively each year. To that point, it would be easy to look at Jonathan Lucroy's traditional statistics and assume his 2014 production was an outlier. The only time he performed as well as his .301/.373/.465 triple slash in 2014 was in 2012, when he was limited to 346 plate appearances. Meanwhile, his .264/.326/.391 triple slash in 2015 was more in line with his production over the rest of his career.

It is easy, then, to call Lucroy's 2014 performance his career year similar to how Joe Mauer produced one outlier season in 2009. However, Lucroy's DIBS numbers show that his batted ball trajectories have been much more similar over the last three seasons than those surface numbers would indicate.

Jonathan Lucroy, 2013

	PA	Hits	Doubles	Triples	Home Runs	AVG	BABIP	BRAA
Actual	580	146	25	6	18	.280	.290	10.3
DIBS	580	158	29	6	20	.302	.323	22.4
Difference	0	-12	-4	0	-2	-.022	-.033	-12.1

In 2013, Lucroy dramatically underachieved his DIBS expectations. He had 12 hits fewer than expected, including 4 fewer doubles and 2 fewer home runs. In fact, Lucroy's expected numbers were nearly identical to the actual numbers he produced the following season, in 2014, when his results were much more in line with his expected production.

Jonathan Lucroy, 2014

	PA	Hits	Doubles	Triples	Home Runs	AVG	BABIP	BRAA
Actual	655	176	53	2	13	.301	.324	24.4
DIBS	655	172	47	3	15	.294	.319	21.9
Difference	0	4	6	-1	-2	.007	.005	2.6

Entering 2016, Lucroy is in the same spot that he was in entering 2014. His trajectory-based statistics show that bad fortune cost him 10 hits in 2015. Because his actual numbers underachieved his expected numbers in two of the last three seasons, Lucroy has looked much less consistent than he actually has performed, and that consistency points to continued production for Lucroy in 2016.

Three Hitters Who Should Decline in 2016

Nelson Cruz, 2015

	PA	Hits	Doubles	Triples	Home Runs	AVG	BABIP	BRAA
Actual	655	178	22	1	44	.302	.350	43.1
DIBS	655	160	26	1	32	.271	.335	20.2
Difference	0	18	-4	0	12	.031	.015	22.9

Nelson Cruz proved many of his doubters wrong when he followed up his break-out power season in 2014 with an even better power season in 2015. Prior to 2014, Cruz had only once exceeded 30 home runs in a season. In 2014, he hit 40, and then in 2015, he hit 44 despite playing his home games in pitcher-friendly Safeco Field. While Cruz's trajectory-based statistics support the idea that he is an exceptional hitter, they also suggest that Cruz enjoyed tremendous fortune with the locations of his home runs. In fact, DIBS would have expected Cruz's batted balls to produce just 32 home runs, 12 fewer than his actual total.

The source of that disconnect between Cruz's home park and his home run luck was fortunate timing. Cruz actually hit 27 of his home runs on the road compared to just 17 at home. Meanwhile, many of those road home runs barely cleared the fences in the parks in which he hit them such that they would not have been home runs in many different parks, not just in Safeco. As such, Cruz will likely see a precipitous drop in his home run total in 2016.

Logan Forsythe, 2015

	PA	Hits	Doubles	Triples	Home Runs	AVG	BABIP	BRAA
Actual	615	152	33	2	17	.281	.323	16.1
DIBS	615	134	27	2	15	.247	.289	-0.4
Difference	0	18	6	0	2	.034	.034	16.6

Logan Forsythe went from a career part-time player to one of the best second basemen in baseball in 2015. The Rays seem to have a knack for discovering this sort of unexpected talent, and while Forsythe's trajectory-based numbers back up that conclusion, they also indicate that he enjoyed some good fortune. Across the board, Forsythe overachieved his expectations on his batted balls in 2015. He had 18 more hits than expected, including 6 more doubles and 2 more home runs.

Based on his actual numbers, Forsythe was similarly productive to Jose Altuve, Dee Gordon, and Joe Panik—the elite hitters at the position. Based on his expected numbers, he was more in line with Chase Utley, Brandon Phillips, and Jace Peterson.

Francisco Lindor, 2015

	PA	Hits	Doubles	Triples	Home Runs	AVG	BABIP	BRAA
Actual	438	122	22	4	12	.313	.348	12.1
DIBS	438	103	20	3	8	.264	.291	-4.0
Difference	0	19	2	1	4	.049	.057	16.1

It did not surprise anyone that Francisco Lindor made an immediate impact on the Indians when he was called up in mid-June. However, it was something of a surprise that the slick-fielding Lindor was one of the two most productive offensive rookies in the American League along with elite hitting prospect Carlos Correa. Unlike Correa, who saw a more moderate total of 8 hits gained in a similar number of plate appearances, Lindor enjoyed 19 hits more than would be expected based on his distribution of batted balls. In particular, good fortune boosted Lindor's numbers in the power department, where his 12 actual home runs were 4 more than expected. At just 21 years old, Lindor has an exceptionally bright future ahead of him, but it is probably unfair to expect this level of offensive success to continue next season.

The Favorite Toy

Bill James

The Favorite Toy is the method that I use to estimate a player's chance to hit 500 home runs, or to get 3,000 hits, or to break the career record for RBI, or something like that. I invented this method in the 1970s and have used it ever since. Recently I did some studies designed to determine how accurate the method is, and, as a result of that, made some small changes to the method (and also established that the method is, in fact, generally accurate.) The article reporting on that research can be found at Bill James Online, and is the article published October 2, 2015, entitled "Tinkering with The Favorite Toy."

But enough about me; let's talk about Miguel Cabrera. Cabrera, although he won the American League batting championship again in 2015, appears to be in an aging/decline phase. Still, he is 32 years old at the moment, and he has 2,331 career hits. Cabrera has more career hits than David Ortiz, who (a) is a great hitter himself, and (b) is almost eight years older than Cabrera. It is more likely than not that Cabrera will get 3,000 career hits—as is also true for Pujols, Adrian Beltre and, I guess, Ichiro. Robinson Cano, Jose Altuve, Jimmie Rollins and Nick Markakis probably won't get 3,000 career hits, but we can't rule it out, either. It is a battle of momentum against time. Each player is moving forward at a certain speed, and he has a certain number of years left until Father Time catches up with him.

We don't know when exactly Father Time will catch up with Miguel Cabrera, but we know certain things. We know it will happen before he is 45. We know that, by the time he is 40, he won't be the hitter that he is now. We can guess that, at 37, 38, he might not be the hitter that he is now, but we can't be certain of that; some players age better than others. Anyway, the Favorite Toy is the process of comparing the time that is left for the player with the distance that must be travelled and the speed with which the player is advancing.

Albert Pujols was 35 years old last year, and hit 40 home runs. He is 202 home runs away from Barry Bonds' career record, 762 homers. At 40 homers a year, that's five years. It's very unlikely that a 35-year-old player can keep moving forward at the same pace for another five years, but it's not impossible. We estimate Pujols chance of breaking Bonds' home run record at 6%. Pujols has a younger teammate, Mike Trout. Trout hit 41 homers, but he is 623 home runs away from the record. That's 15 years. Again, it is very, very unlikely that the player (Trout) can keep moving forward at the same pace for another 15 years, but it's not impossible, and also, Trout probably hasn't had his best home run seasons; when he is 30 he may well be hitting 50 homers a year. Again, we estimate the chance that he can get to 763 career homers at 6%.

Miguel Cabrera will probably hit 500 home runs in his career, but he will probably not hit 600. Albert Pujols will probably hit 600, but he will probably not hit 700. Alex Rodriguez will probably hit 700, but is very unlikely to hit 762. These are the conclusions of the method—unless, of course, somebody comes up with a new PED which is undetectable and causes the numbers to go haywire again. Then all bets are off.

3,000 Hits	
% chance to reach milestone	
Rodriguez,Alex	done
Suzuki,Ichiro	90%
Beltre,Adrian	80%
Pujols,Albert	69%
Cabrera,Miguel	52%
Cano,Robinson	42%
Markakis,Nick	27%
Altuve,Jose	18%
Rollins,Jimmy	16%
Reyes,Jose	15%
McCutchen,Andrew	15%
Andrus,Elvis	15%
Jones,Adam	14%
Trout,Mike	12%
Castro,Starlin	12%
Hosmer,Eric	11%
Cabrera,Melky	11%
Gonzalez,Adrian	10%
Butler,Billy	9%
Upton,Justin	9%
Brantley,Michael	9%
Heyward,Jason	7%
Machado,Manny	7%
Longoria,Evan	6%
Revere,Ben	6%
Mauer,Joe	5%
Harper,Bryce	5%
Freeman,Freddie	5%
Bogaerts,Xander	5%
Kinsler,Ian	5%
Rizzo,Anthony	4%
Fielder,Prince	4%
Escobar,Alcides	3%
Arenado,Nolan	3%
Seager,Kyle	3%
Goldschmidt,Paul	2%
Kemp,Matt	2%
Parra,Gerardo	1%
Peralta,Jhonny	< 1%
Kendrick,Howie	< 1%
Gordon,Dee	< 1%
Pedroia,Dustin	< 1%

Career Targets

762 Home Runs
% chance to break record

Trout,Mike	6%
Pujols,Albert	6%

2,298 RBI
% chance to break record

Cabrera,Miguel	7%
Pujols,Albert	4%

2,296 Runs Scored
% chance to break record

Trout,Mike	7%

4,257 Hits
% chance to break record

Altuve,Jose	< 1%

900 Home Runs
% chance to reach milestone

2,000 RBI
% chance to reach milestone

Rodriguez,Alex	done
Pujols,Albert	58%
Cabrera,Miguel	38%
Trout,Mike	7%

6,857 Total Bases
% chance to break record

Trout,Mike	7%
Cabrera,Miguel	< 1%
Pujols,Albert	< 1%

4,000 Hits
% chance to reach milestone

Altuve,Jose	5%
Trout,Mike	1%
Cabrera,Miguel	< 1%

800 Home Runs
% chance to reach milestone

Trout,Mike	3%

600 Home Runs
% chance to reach milestone

Rodriguez,Alex	done
Pujols,Albert	82%
Davis,Chris	17%
Cabrera,Miguel	14%
Trout,Mike	13%
Stanton,Giancarlo	10%
Harper,Bryce	7%
Encarnacion,Edwin	5%
Ortiz,David	4%
Arenado,Nolan	3%

793 Doubles
% chance to break record

Cabrera,Miguel	9%
Altuve,Jose	5%
Cano,Robinson	2%
Trout,Mike	2%

Most Likely No-Hitter
% chance to reach milestone

Kershaw,Clayton	36%
Sale,Chris	31%
Archer,Chris	24%
Scherzer,Max	22%
Carrasco,Carlos	22%
Kluber,Corey	18%
Ross,Tyson	18%
Arrieta,Jake	17%
Strasburg,Stephen	17%
Bumgarner,Madison	17%

700 Home Runs
% chance to reach milestone

Rodriguez,Alex	92%
Pujols,Albert	30%
Trout,Mike	9%
Davis,Chris	4%
Harper,Bryce	2%

500 Home Runs
% chance to reach milestone

Rodriguez,Alex	done
Pujols,Albert	done
Ortiz,David	done
Cabrera,Miguel	55%
Davis,Chris	31%
Encarnacion,Edwin	29%
Teixeira,Mark	27%
Trout,Mike	20%
Beltre,Adrian	20%
Bautista,Jose	18%

1,000 Stolen Bases
% chance to reach milestone

The 300-Win Candidates

Bill James

Clayton Kershaw is 27 years old at the moment and has 114 career wins. That is more wins than Grover Cleveland Alexander had at the same age, or Warren Spahn, or Steve Carlton, or Eddie Plank, or Nolan Ryan, or Don Sutton, or Phil Niekro, or Gaylord Perry, or Old Hoss Radbourn, or Tom Glavine, or Randy Johnson, or Lefty Grove or Early Wynn, and all of those went on to win 300 games. On the other hand, it is less than Fernando Valenzuela had at the same age, or Kenny Holtzman, or Dave McNally or Dwight Gooden, and all of those pulled up short of 200 career wins, so go figure. If Kershaw were to win 20 games next year, then 19 the year after that, then 18, 17, 16 and so on, he would get his 300th career win in 2029, at the age of 41. If, on the other hand, he were to win 21 games next year, then 20, 19, 18, 17 and so on, then he would get to 300 career wins at the age of just 39.

The odds against Kershaw are about two to one; we estimate that he has a 31% chance to get 300 career wins, which is a better chance than anyone else has. The list attached to this article says that R. A. Dickey and A. J. Burnett have a 1% chance each to win 300 games, which, you know...I doubt it. Aaron Harang has less than a 1% chance to win 300 games? Yeah; way less. But the player who is underrated on the list is CC Sabathia, who has 214 career wins and is only 34 years old. Obviously Sabathia had a poor year, but many pitchers have had poor years and snapped back to form. Sabathia had a 2.22 ERA over his last four starts, and he struck out 137 batters in 187 innings on the season. Both of those things indicate to me that he still has some ability, if he can get past the personal issues that prevented him from being effective in 2015.

I had intended to change this feature this year from tracking chances at 300 wins to tracking chances at 250 wins; I don't know that it is really realistic to talk about pitchers winning 300 games, with five-man rotations and eight-man bullpens. But I forgot to implement the change, and maybe it is for the better that I did. This is about magic numbers, and I don't know that 250 wins is a magic number *yet*; I am merely anticipating that it might be in the future.

Pitchers on Course For 300 Wins

Name	2015 Age	R/L	W	L	EWL	Momentum	Chance
Kershaw, Clayton	27	L	114	56	17.5	.896	31%
Price, David	29	L	104	56	16.0	.857	15%
Hernandez, Felix	29	R	143	101	15.1	.833	15%
Shields, James	33	R	127	97	13.4	.862	15%
Scherzer, Max	30	R	105	62	16.0	.852	14%
Bumgarner, Madison	25	L	85	58	16.6	.855	13%
Greinke, Zack	31	R	142	93	16.2	.793	11%
Colon, Bartolo	42	R	218	154	12.3	.693	9%
Buehrle, Mark	36	L	214	160	11.5	.713	8%
Lester, Jon	31	L	127	79	12.4	.808	5%
Hamels, Cole	31	L	121	91	12.5	.804	4%
Lackey, John	36	R	165	127	11.7	.761	4%
Cueto, Johnny	29	R	96	70	12.3	.792	2%
Dickey, R.A.	40	R	100	93	10.9	.780	1%
Burnett, A.J.	38	R	164	157	9.2	.729	1%
Sabathia, CC	34	L	214	129	7.2	.676	1%
Hudson, Tim	39	R	222	133	7.2	.613	<1%
Haren, Dan	34	R	153	131	10.4	.680	<1%
Weaver, Jered	32	R	138	81	8.8	.655	<1%
Lohse, Kyle	36	R	147	141	7.4	.674	<1%
Harang, Aaron	37	R	128	143	7.2	.620	<1%

EWL: Established Win Level

Baseball Glossary

% Inherited Scored
The percentage of inherited baserunners a relief pitcher allows to score.

% Pitches Taken
The percentage of pitches that a batter does not swing at out of the total number of pitches thrown to him.

1st Batter Average
The Batting Average that a relief pitcher allows to the first batter he faces when he enters a game.

1st Batter OBP
The On-Base Percentage that a relief pitcher allows to the first batter he faces when he enters a game.

1st to 3rd (Baserunning)
"Moved" is the number of times a runner goes from 1st base to 3rd base on a SINGLE. "Chances" are the number of times a runner is on 1st base and a batter is credited with a SINGLE.

1st to Home (Baserunning)
"Moved" is the number of times a runner goes from 1st base to home on a DOUBLE. "Chances" are the number of times a runner is on 1st base and a batter is credited with a DOUBLE.

2nd to Home (Baserunning)
"Moved" is the number of times a runner goes from 2nd base to home on a SINGLE. "Chances" are the number of times a runner is on 2nd base and a batter is credited with a SINGLE.

Active Career Batting Leaders
A list of batting leaders among active (appearing in the most recent season) players. An active player is eligible when he meets the minimum requirements for the following categories:

> 1,000 At Bats—Batting Average, On-Base Percentage, Slugging Average, At
>   Bats Per HR, At Bats Per GDP, At Bats Per RBI, Strikeout to Walk Ratio
> 100 Stolen Base Attempts—Stolen Base Success Percentage

Active Career Pitching Leaders
A list of pitching leaders among active (appearing in the most recent season) players. An active player is eligible when he meets the minimum requirements for the following categories:

> 750 Innings Pitched—Earned Run Average, Opponent Batting Average, all "Per
>   9 Innings" categories, Strikeout to Walk Ratio
> 250 Games Started—Complete Game Frequency
> 100 Decisions—Win-Loss Percentage

AVG Allowed ScPos
The Batting Average allowed by a pitcher while pitching with runners in scoring position.

AVG Bases Loaded

The Batting Average of a hitter while batting with the bases loaded.

Base Taken

A player is credited with a Base Taken whenever he moves up a base on a Wild Pitch, Passed Ball, Balk, Sacrifice Fly, or Defensive Indifference.

Batting Average

Hits divided by at bats.

Blown Save

When a relief pitcher enters a game in a Save Situation (see definition for Save Situation) and allows the other team to score the tying or go-ahead run.

Bomb (Intentional Walk)

An Intentional Walk is counted as a "Bomb" if
1. The next batter, after the IBB, does not ground into a double play, and
2. Multiple runs are scored in the inning, after the intentional walk.

BR Gain (Baserunning)

BR Gain (or Loss if a negative number) is the total of all the types of extra baserunning advances minus the (triple) penalty for all the BR Outs compared with what would be expected based on the MLB averages.

BR Outs (Baserunning)

BR Outs include the sum of Outs Advancing, Doubled Offs, and when a runner is tagged out on the bases when another runner moves up on a Wild Pitch, Passed Ball, or scores on a Sacrifice Fly.

BS Win

A Blown Save Win is a "win" credited to a reliever who has blown a save opportunity.

Career Targets

This method, once called the Favorite Toy, is a way to estimate the probability that a player will achieve a specific career goal. In this example, 3,000 hits will be used. The four components of the formula are:

1. Needed Hits. This is the number of Hits (or any statistic) that a player needs to reach a desired goal.

2. Years Remaining. This is the estimated number of years remaining in the player's career. It is determined using the player's age (on June 30th of the previous year; use 2015 when making the calculation after the 2015 season is complete). The formula is (42 - age) divided by two. This means a player who is 20 years old will have 11 remaining seasons, a player who is 25 years old will have 8.5 remaining seasons and a player who is 35 years old will have 3.5 remaining seasons. If the player is a catcher, then multiply his remaining seasons by .7. The only stipulation is that years remaining must always be greater than or equal to 1.5.

3. Established Hit Level. The Established Hit Level is a weighted average of the player's hits over the past three seasons. To calculate the Established Hit Level after the 2015 season is complete, add 2013 Hits, (2014 Hits multiplied by two) and (2015 Hits multiplied by three), then divide by six. If the Established Hit

Level is less than 75% of the most recent performance (2015 Hits in this case), then the Established Hit Level is equal to .75 times the most recent performance.

4. Projected Remaining Hits. This is calculated by multiplying Years Remaining by the Established Hit Level.

The probability of achieving the specified goal is found by dividing Projected Remaining Hits by Needed Hits, then subtracting .5. The maximum that any player has of achieving a goal is .85 raised to the power of (Need Hits / Established Hit Level). This prevents the possibility of a player reaching a goal from being higher than 100 percent, which is impossible.

Catcher's ERA
The ERA for a catcher is equal to the ERA of pitchers pitching while the catcher is playing behind the plate. It is calculated exactly like ERA for pitchers. Take the number of earned runs allowed while the catcher is playing, multiply it by 9 and then divide it by the total number of defensive innings that the catcher was behind the plate.

Cheap Win
A starting pitcher who wins the game with a game score under 50 gets credit for a cheap win. See Game Score.

Clean Outing
A Clean Outing is a game in which the reliever is not charged with a run (earned or otherwise) AND does not allow an inherited runner to score.

Cleanup Slugging Average
The Slugging Average of a batter when he bats in the cleanup spot, or fourth, in the batting order.

Close and Late
A situation in a game that is very similar to a Save Situation. The following requirements are necessary for a Close and Late game:
1. The game is in the seventh inning or later AND
2. The batting team is either leading by one run or tied OR
3. The tying run is on base, at bat, or on deck.

Component ERA (ERC)
A statistic that estimates what a pitcher's ERA should have been, based on his pitching performance. The ERC formula is calculated as follows:

1. Subtract the pitcher's Home Runs Allowed from his Hits Allowed.
2. Multiply Step 1 by 1.255.
3. Multiply his Home Runs Allowed by four.
4. Add Steps 2 and 3 together.
5. Multiply Step 4 by .89.
6. Add his Walks and Hit Batsmen.
7. Multiply Step 6 by .475.
8. Add Steps 5 and 7 together.

This yields the pitcher's total base estimate (PTB), which is:

$$PTB = 0.89 \times (1.255 \times (H - HR) + 4 \times HR) + 0.475 \times (BB + HB)$$

For those pitchers for whom there is intentional walk data, use this formula instead:

$$PTB = 0.89 \times (1.255 \times (H - HR) + 4 \times HR) + 0.56 \times (BB + HB - IBB)$$

9. Add Hits and Walks and Hit Batsmen.
10. Multiply Step 9 by PTB.
11. Divide Step 10 by Batters Facing Pitcher. If BFP data is unavailable, approximate it by multiplying Innings Pitched by 2.9, then adding Step 9.
12. Multiply Step 11 by 9.
13. Divide Step 12 by Innings Pitched.
14. Subtract .56 from Step 13.

This is the pitcher's ERC, which is:

$$\frac{(H + BB + HB) \times PTB}{BFP \times IP} \times 9 - 0.56$$

If the result after Step 13 is less than 2.24, adjust the formula as follows:

$$\frac{(H + BB + HB) \times PTB}{BFP \times IP} \times 9 \times 0.75$$

Consecutive Days
A count of how many times the pitcher was used after having pitched on the previous day or (in a few cases) in an earlier game on the same day.

Defensive Runs Saved
Defensive Runs Saved (Runs Saved, for short) is the innovative metric introduced by John Dewan in *The Fielding Bible—Volume II* and modified in *The Fielding Bible—Volume III* and *The Fielding Bible—Volume IV*. The Runs Saved value indicates how many runs a player saved or cost his team in the field compared to the average player at his position. A player of zero Runs Saved is about average; a positive number of runs saved indicates above-average defense, below-average fielders post negative Runs Saved totals. There are eight components of Runs Saved:

Range and Positioning Runs Saved (all positions except Catcher)
Adjusted Earned Runs Saved (Catchers)
Strike Zone Runs Saved (Catchers)
Stolen Base Runs Saved (Catchers, Pitchers)
Bunt Runs Saved (Corner Infielders, Pitchers, Catchers)
Double Play Runs Saved (Infielders)
Outfield Arm Runs Saved (Outfielders)
Good Play/Misplay Runs Saved (All Positions)

Double Play %
Successful Double Plays divided by the number of Double Play opportunities. This statistic includes both the fielder who started the play and the pivot man.

Double Play Opportunity
A fielder is considered to have a double play opportunity when a ground ball is hit with a runner on first base and less than 2 outs and that fielder is involved in the play. This is used to calculate Double Play % and Pivot %.

Doubled Off
A runner is Doubled Off when he is out for failing to get back to his base before he, or the base, is tagged after a ball hit in the air is caught.

Early Entry
A count of the number of times the reliever entered the game in the sixth inning or earlier.

Earned Run Average
The number of earned runs that a pitcher surrenders per nine innings that he pitches. It is calculated by multiplying the total earned runs allowed by nine and dividing by the total number of innings pitched.

Easy Save
This label is used to separate Saves by difficulty level (Easy or Tough). A Save is considered Easy if the relief pitcher enters the game, pitches one inning or less, and the first batter he faces does not at least represent the tying run.

Fielding Percentage
The percentage of plays a player makes in the field without making an error out of the total number of opportunities. It is calculated by adding (Putouts plus Assists) and dividing by (Putouts plus Assists plus Errors).

Games Finished
The relief pitcher who is in the game for each team when the game ends is credited with a Game Finished.

Game Score
To determine the starting pitcher's Game Score:
Start with 50.
Add 1 point for each out recorded by the starting pitcher.
Add 2 points for each inning the pitcher completes after the fourth inning.
Add 1 point for each strikeout.
Subtract 2 points for each hit allowed.
Subtract 4 points for each earned run allowed.
Subtract 2 points for an unearned run.
Subtract 1 point for each walk.

GDP
Grounded into Double Play.

GDP Opportunity

This is a situation where the batter has a chance to ground into a double play. It occurs with at least a runner on first base and less than two outs.

Ground / Fly Ratio (Grd/Fly, GB/FB)

Calculated for both batters and pitchers. For batters, it is the number of groundballs hit divided by the number of flyballs hit. For pitchers, it is exactly the same but uses the number of groundballs and flyballs allowed. Every fair batted ball is included except for bunts and line drives.

Hold

A relief pitcher is given a Hold anytime he enters the game in a Save Situation (see definition for Save Situation), records one out or more, and exits the game without giving up the lead. If the pitcher finishes the game, then he will only earn credit for a Save. He cannot receive credit for both a Hold and a Save.

Holds Adjusted Save Percentage (same as Save/Hold Percentage)

Holds plus Saves divided by Holds plus Saves Opportunities.

Inherited Runner

When a relief pitcher enters the game, any runner who was on base at the time is considered an Inherited Runner.

Isolated Power

Slugging Average minus Batting Average.

K/BB Ratio

Strikeouts divided by Walks.

Leadoff On-Base Percentage

The On-Base Percentage of a batter when he bats leadoff, or first, in the batting order.

Leverage Index

Leverage is the amount of swing in the possible change in win probability, compared to the average swing in all situations. The average swing value, by definition, is indexed to 1.00.

If the score of the game is 12-0 or 14-1 the possible changes in win probability will be very close to negligible. Whether the pitcher gives up a home run or gets a double play ball doesn't really change the outcome of the game. There won't be much swing in either direction for the probability of the win. But in the late innings of a close game, the change in win probability among the various events will have rather wild swings. With a runner on first, two outs, down by one, and in the bottom of the ninth, the game can hinge on one swing of the bat. A home run and an out will both end the game, but with different outcomes for the teams involved. The Leverage Index we use (LI) was developed at the website Tangotiger.net, and compiled at the website FanGraphs.com.

Long Outing

A Long Outing is one in which the starting pitcher throws more than 110 pitches. Prior to 2002, we used 120 pitches as the cutoff in the Manager's Record section.

Long Save
A Long Save is when the pitcher credited with a save pitches more than one inning.

Manufactured Runs
1. A run that scores without a hit, or a run on which the only hit(s) is/are infield hits, is always scored as a Manufactured Run.
2. A run which is driven in by a home run is never scored a Manufactured Run, under any circumstance.
3. A run which is driven in by a double or a triple is scored as a Manufactured Run only if *two* of the four bases result from advancing on one of these four acts: a sacrifice bunt, a stolen base, a hit and run, or a bunt single.
4. Otherwise, a run is considered to be a Manufactured Run if two of the four bases do not result from the runner being forced along by a walk, a hit batsman, or a safe hit reaching the outfield.
5. A forceout or fielder's choice which does not improve the position of the base runners should not be counted as contributing toward a Manufactured Run. Advancing on a forceout or a fielder's choice DOES count toward a manufactured run, if the play is one which improves the position of the baserunners.
6. A base "gained" on a double play does not count as a contribution to a Manufactured Run. A run scored on a double play is a Manufactured Run only if two of the OTHER bases are not attributable to forced advancement.

Not Good Outcome (Intentional Walk)
A Not Good Outcome (NG) for an Intentional Walk occurs when one run scored in the inning after the intentional walk (and the next batter after the intentional walk did not ground into a double play).

Offensive Winning Percentage (OWP)
A player's Offensive Winning Percentage is the winning percentage of a hypothetical team which has an offense consisting of nine of that player, and pitching and defense which is average for the player's league. It is calculated by taking the square of RC/27 (see the definition for Runs Created per 27 Outs), dividing it by the sum of the square of RC/27 and the square of the average runs scored per game in the league.

On-Base Percentage
(Hits plus Walks plus Hit by Pitcher) divided by (At Bats plus Walks plus Hit by Pitcher plus Sacrifice Flies).

$$\frac{H + BB + HBP}{AB + BB + HBP + SF}$$

Opponent Batting Average
Hits Allowed divided by (Batters Faced minus Walks minus Hit Batsmen minus Sacrifice Hits minus Sacrifice Flies minus Catcher's Interference).

$$\frac{H}{BFP - BB - HBP - SH - SF - CI}$$

Opposition OPS
The OPS of the hitters facing the pitcher.

Out Advancing

A runner is out advancing when he is tagged out attempting to score from 2nd base on a single or from 1st base on a double, or attempting to go from 1st base to 3rd base on a single.

PA*

Used in the denominator for the calculation of On-Base Percentage. It is calculated by subtracting (Sacrifice Hits plus Times Reached Base on Defensive Interference) from Plate Appearances (see definition for Plate Appearances).

Park Index

To calculate the park index for home runs in a given ballpark, we take the total home runs of both the home team and its opponents at the ballpark and compare it to the total home runs of the home team and its opponents in other games. We then divide each of those totals by the at-bats in the equivalent situations, so that if there are more at-bats in either situation the index is not skewed. The result is then multiplied by 100 to yield the familiar form.

The park indices for doubles, triples, walks, strikeouts and home runs by lefties and righties are determined like home runs above—relative to at-bats. Indices of at-bats, runs, hits, errors and infield fielding errors (E-Infield) are calculated relative to games. The three batting average indices are calculated as is, since these are already relative to at-bats.

PCS (Pitchers' Caught Stealing)

The number of runners officially scored as Caught Stealing where the pitcher initiated the play. The normal Caught Stealing is when a runner is out attempting to steal a base but the play was initiated by the catcher. PCS plays are often referred to as pickoffs, but differ when the runner breaks towards the next base as opposed to returning to the base he was currently on. Pickoffs occur when the pitcher throws to a base that a runner is leading from, and the runner is out attempting to return to that base. Pickoffs are not an official statistic.

Pitches per PA

The total number of pitches a hitter sees divided by his total Plate Appearances.

Pivot %

Successful Double Plays turned by pivot man divided by the number of Double Play opportunities with that pivot man involved.

Plate Appearances

At Bats plus Total Walks plus Hit By Pitches plus Sacrifice Hits plus Sacrifice Flies plus Times Reached on Defensive Interference.

Platoon Advantage %

Platoon Advantage % is the percentage of players in the starting lineup who have the platoon advantage (i.e. bats right against a left-handed pitcher or bats left against a right-hander) against the starting pitcher; e.g. if the opposing starting pitcher is right handed and the batting team has six left-handed batters in its lineup, the platoon advantage for that game would be 67%.

Power/Speed Number

A single number that reflects a combination of power and speed. To calculate the Power/Speed Number, multiply Home Runs by Stolen Bases by two, and divide by the sum of Home Runs and Stolen Bases.

$$\frac{2 \times HR \times SB}{HR + SB}$$

PPO (Pitcher Pickoff)

The number of baserunners thrown out when a pitcher throws to a base with a leading baserunner, and the runner is tagged out attempting to return to the base. PPO is not an official statistic and does not count toward Caught Stealing totals.

Productive Out

An out made by the batter which moves at least one baserunner up at least one base. See also Unproductive Out.

Quality Start

A game where the starting pitcher pitches for at least six innings and allows no more than three earned runs.

Quality Start Percentage

Quality Starts divided by Games Started (see the definition for Quality Start).

Quick Hooks

Used in the Manager's Record. For Quick Hooks and Slow Hooks a score is calculated for each game that is the sum of the number of Pitches plus 10 times the number of Runs Allowed. The bottom 25% of scores in the league are considered to be Quick Hooks.

Range and Positioning System

Formerly called the Plus/Minus System, the Range and Positioning System is a method for evaluating defensive play on batted balls. It is made possible by a game scoring system in which each batted ball is rated for type (line drive, grounder, etc.), velocity within its type (based on hang time for flyballs and time to the infielder or through the infield on groundballs), and location on the field. A player gets credit (a "plus" number) if he makes a play that at least one other player at his position missed during the season and he loses credit (a "minus" number") if he misses a play that at least one player made. The size of the credits are proportional to the percentage of times all players make the play. All plays for each player at his position are summed to get his total Plays Saved for the season. A total of zero would be average and any other number would approximate how many plays more or less the player made than the average player at the position for the number of chances the player had to field batted balls.

Range Factor

The number of Successful Chances (Putouts plus Assists) times nine divided by the number of Defensive Innings Played.

RBI %

The percentage of all potential runs driven in by a certain hitter. Simply put, it's RBIs divided by RBI Opportunities. RBI Opportunities are a weighted total for baserunners available to be driven in by the batter. They are defined like so:

1.00 for each runner on third base with less than 2 outs, plus

.70 for each runner on third base with 2 outs, plus

.70 for each runner on second base, plus

.40 for each runner on first base, plus

.10 for each bases-empty plate appearance.

Regular Saves

Any save which does not meet the definition either of an Easy Save or a Tough Save is a "Regular" Save.

Run Support Per 9 IP

The total number of runs scored by a pitcher's team while he is in the game multiplied by nine and divided by total Innings Pitched.

Runs Created

"Runs Created" is an estimate of the number of a team's runs which are created by each individual hitter. The Cincinnati Reds scored 820 runs last year, let us say. How many of those were created by Joey Votto? How many by Brandon Phillips? How many by Jay Bruce?

There are many different formulas for estimating runs created. . .did you want the one that involves swinging a dead cat in the cemetery under a full moon? Yeah, I don't blame you. . .worm-eaten persimmons are so hard to find in the modern world.

This is the one we use now; it is complicated enough. First, there is an "A" Factor in the formula, a "B" Factor, and a "C" factor. The "A" Factor, which represents the number of times the hitter is on base, is Hits, Plus Walks, Plus Hit Batsmen, Minus Caught Stealing, Minus Grounded Into Double Play. The "B" Factor, which represents the hitter's ability to advance other runners, is 1.125 times the player's Singles, plus 1.69 times his Doubles, plus 3.02 times his Triples, plus 3.73 times his Home Runs, plus .29 times his Walks and Hit Batsmen, not counting intentional walks, plus .492 times Sacrifice Hits, Sacrifice Flies and Stolen Bases, minus .04 times Strikeouts. The "C" Factor, which represents opportunities, is At Bats, Plus Walks, Plus Hit By Pitch, Plus Sacrifice Hits, Plus Sacrifice Flies.

Having made these initial calculations of the A, B and C factors, we then change the "A" factor to "A plus 2.4 times C".

We change the "B" factor to "B plus 3 times C".

We change the "C" factor to "9 times C".

Multiply A times B, divide by the new C ("9 times C"), and subtract .90 times by the original C.

This is our first, temporary estimate of the player's runs created. What we have done here is to ask these questions:

1. How many runs would a team probably score that consisted of eight "ordinary" type of hitters, plus this particular hitter?
2. How many of those runs would be created by the eight ordinary type of hitters?
3. What is the difference and thus, how many runs did our player create?

To estimate this, we have placed our player in the context of eight hitters with a .300 on base percentage (2.4 divided by 8) and a .375 advancement percentage (3 divided by 8). For each trip through the batting order, the eight ordinary-type hitters would produce 9/10 of a run (2.4 times 3, divided by 8). The "9" in the denominator is eight ordinary hitters plus our man. The "-.9" being subtracted at the end is the runs created by the "ordinary" hitters. In essence, we have placed the hitter in a neutral solution, measured the neutral solution without our hitter, measured it with our hitter, and then estimated the contribution of this hitter as being the difference between the two.

We're not quite done. After that, we adjust the player's runs created estimate for his performance in two "run-sensitive" situations. Suppose that a player whose overall batting average is .250, has batted 100 times with runners in scoring position, and has gone 30-for-100. That's five hits better than expected, 30 hits where we would have expected 25. His team will score an extra five runs because he has done that, and so we increase the player's runs created estimate by five runs. If the player has hit poorly with runners in scoring position, we decrease it by the shortfall in the same way.

Suppose that a player has batted 250 times with runners on base, 250 times with the bases empty, and that he has hit 20 home runs overall. We would expect him to have hit 10 with men on base, 10 with the bases empty, right?

Suppose that he didn't. Suppose that he hit 12 with the bases empty, 8 with men on base. His team would score two runs less than expected because he did this, and we would thus penalize him two runs for the shortfall.

This is our second runs created estimate the player's runs created, adjusted for his batting performance in run sensitive situations.

Suppose, however, that we figure the runs created for all of the individuals on a team, and we add them up, and it doesn't match the runs actually scored by the team? What if the formulas say that the team should have scored 800 runs, but they actually scored 820?

Then obviously, the formulas missed. We're trying to measure the runs ACTUALLY created by each hitter as best we can, in the real world, not the theoretical impact of some combination of singles, doubles, triples and walks. If the actual number is different than the estimates, we have to adjust the estimates to fit the facts. In this case—820 runs scored with only 800 runs created— we would multiply each runs created estimate by 820/800, or 1.025. Then we round it off to an integer, and that's the player's estimated runs created.

Let go of that cat, Arthur. Heck, the moon isn't full for three weeks, anyway.

Runs Created per 27 Outs (RC/27)

This statistic estimates the number of runs per game that a team made up of nine of the same player would score. To calculate RC/27, multiply Runs Created by league outs per team game, divide the result by outs made by the player (the sum of at bats plus sacrifice hits plus sacrifice flies plus caught stealing plus grounded into double plays, minus hits). The formula written out is:

$$\frac{\frac{RC \times 3 \times LgIP}{2 \times LgG}}{AB - H + SH + SF + CS + GDP}$$

Runs Saved

See Defensive Runs Saved.

Save Opportunities

The sum of Saves and Blown Saves (see Save Situation).

Save/Hold Percentage (same as Holds Adjusted Saves Percentage)

The sum of Saves and Holds, divided by the sum of Saves, Holds, and Blown Saves.
For several years we figured "Save Percentage", which is simply Saves divided by Save Opportunities, and this stat had some currency in the game. But the Save Percentage severely discriminates against middle relievers, who have no real chance to be credited with the Save, since they will be taken out of the game and replaced by the Closer even if they throw 110 miles an hour and strike out everybody they see. Middle relievers typically have Save Percentages of zero, even if they pitch well. The Save/Hold Percentage is a much more realistic evaluation of a pitcher's success in Save situations.

Save Percentage

A pitcher's Saves divided by the total number of Save Situations he faces (see definition for Save Situation).

Save Situation

A relief pitcher is in a Save Situation when he enters the game with his team in the lead, has the opportunity to finish the game, is not the winning pitcher of record at the time, and meets any one of the three following conditions:

1.The pitcher's team is leading by no more than three runs and the pitcher has the chance to pitch for at least one inning,

OR

 2.The pitcher enters the game with the potential tying run on base, at bat, or on deck,

OR

3. The pitcher pitches three or more effective innings regardless of the lead. The determination of a save in this situation is made by the official scorer.

It is not possible to have more than one save credited to a single team in a game.

SB Gain (Baserunning)

Stolen Base attempts must be successful greater than about two thirds of the time to have a positive result on the number of runs scored. SB gain is therefore the number of bases stolen minus two times the number of caught stealing (SB Gain = SB - 2CS). For example, a runner steals 30 bases and is caught stealing 7 times. His SB Gain would be 30 - 2*7 = +16. Another runner steals 10 bases and is caught stealing 6 times. His SB Gain (actually a loss) would be 10 - 2*6 = -2.

SB Success Percentage

Stolen Bases divided by the number of Stolen Base attempts (Stolen Bases plus Caught Stealing).

$$\frac{SB}{SB + CS}$$

Secondary Average

A number meant to reflect everything else except for batting average. A player will have a high Secondary Average if he hits for power, takes walks and steals bases. It is calculated with the following formula:

$$\frac{TB - H + BB + SB}{AB}$$

Similarity Score

A number which reflects the similarity between two different statistical lines, either for a player or for a team. A score of 1,000 means that the statistical lines are identical.

Slow Hooks

Used in the Manager's Record. For Quick Hooks and Slow Hooks a score is calculated for each game that is the sum of the number of Pitches plus 10 times the number of Runs Allowed. The top 25% of scores in the league are considered to be Slow Hooks.

Slugging Average

Total Bases divided by At Bats.

$$\frac{TB}{AB}$$

Speed Score

Speed score is an estimate of a player's running speed, based on six indicators of running speed found in his batting and fielding records. Those six indicators are stolen base success rate, the frequency of stolen base attempts, triples, grounding into double plays, runs scored as a percentage of times on base, and defensive position and range.

The full process of estimating Speed Scores is long and complex, and can be found on Bill James Online or by contacting Baseball Info Solutions.

Total Bases

Hits plus Doubles plus (2 times Triples) plus (3 times Home Runs).

$$H + 2B + (2 \times 3B) + (3 \times HR)$$

Tough Loss

A starting pitcher who loses the game with a game score (see definition for Game Score) over 50 gets credit for a tough loss.

Tough Save

This label is used to separate Saves by difficulty level (Easy or Tough). A Save is considered Tough if the relief pitcher enters the game with the tying run on base.

Unproductive Out

An out made by the batter which is not the third out of an inning, but comes with runners on base which fails to advance any baserunner, or results in a weaker baserunner configuration than before the out. See also Productive Out.

Win Probability

The probability of a team winning the game determined at any time during the game based on the score, inning, outs and base situation.

Winning Percentage

Wins divided by (Wins plus Losses).

Minor League Abbreviation Key

Abbreviation	Team	Level	League	MLB Affiliate	First Year	Last Year
Abrdn	Aberdeen IronBirds	A-	New York-Penn League	Baltimore Orioles	2011	2015
Akron	Akron Aeros	AA	Eastern League	Cleveland Indians	2011	2013
Akron	Akron RubberDucks	AA	Eastern League	Cleveland Indians	2014	2015
Albq	Albuquerque Isotopes	AAA	Pacific Coast League	Los Angeles Dodgers	2011	2014
Albq	Albuquerque Isotopes	AAA	Pacific Coast League	Colorado Rockies	2015	2015
Altna	Altoona Curve	AA	Eastern League	Pittsburgh Pirates	2011	2015
Amarill	Amarillo Sox	IND	Independent League	Independent	2013	2013
Angels	AZL Angels	R	Arizona League	Los Angeles Angels	2011	2015
Ark	Arkansas Travelers	AA	Texas League	Los Angeles Angels	2011	2015
As	AZL Athletics	R	Arizona League	Oakland Athletics	2011	2015
Ashvll	Asheville Tourists	A	South Atlantic League	Colorado Rockies	2011	2015
Astros	GCL Astros	R	Gulf Coast League	Houston Astros	2011	2015
Auburn	Auburn Doubledays	A-	New York-Penn League	Washington Nationals	2011	2015
Augsta	Augusta GreenJackets	A	South Atlantic League	San Francisco Giants	2011	2015
B Jays	GCL Blue Jays	R	Gulf Coast League	Toronto Blue Jays	2011	2015
Batvia	Batavia Muckdogs	A-	New York-Penn League	St Louis Cardinals	2011	2012
Batvia	Batavia Muckdogs	A-	New York-Penn League	Miami Marlins	2013	2015
Beloit	Beloit Snappers	A	Midwest League	Minnesota Twins	2011	2012
Beloit	Beloit Snappers	A	Midwest League	Oakland Athletics	2013	2015
BG	Bowling Green Hot Rods	A	Midwest League	Tampa Bay Rays	2011	2015
Billings	Billings Mustangs	R+	Pioneer League	Cincinnati Reds	2011	2015
Biloxi	Biloxi Shuckers	AA	Southern League	Milwaukee Brewers	2015	2015
Bklyn	Brooklyn Cyclones	A-	New York-Penn League	New York Mets	2011	2015
Bkrsfld	Bakersfield Blaze	A+	California League	Cincinnati Reds	2011	2014
Bkrsfld	Bakersfield Blaze	A+	California League	Seattle Mariners	2015	2015
Bluefld	Bluefield Blue Jays	R+	Appalachian League	Toronto Blue Jays	2011	2015
Bnghtn	Binghamton Mets	AA	Eastern League	New York Mets	2011	2015
Boise	Boise Hawks	A-	Northwest League	Chicago Cubs	2011	2014
Boise	Boise Hawks	A-	Northwest League	Colorado Rockies	2015	2015
Bowie	Bowie Baysox	AA	Eastern League	Baltimore Orioles	2011	2015
Bradtn	Bradenton Marauders	A+	Florida State League	Pittsburgh Pirates	2011	2015
Braves	GCL Braves	R	Gulf Coast League	Atlanta Braves	2011	2015
Brewrs	AZL Brewers	R	Arizona League	Milwaukee Brewers	2011	2015
Brham	Birmingham Barons	AA	Southern League	Chicago White Sox	2011	2015
Brstol	Bristol White Sox	R+	Appalachian League	Chicago White Sox	2011	2013
Brstol	Bristol Pirates	R+	Appalachian League	Pittsburgh Pirates	2014	2015
BrvdCt	Brevard Co. Manatees	A+	Florida State League	Milwaukee Brewers	2011	2015
Buffalo	Buffalo Bisons	AAA	International League	New York Mets	2011	2012
Buffalo	Buffalo Bisons	AAA	International League	Toronto Blue Jays	2013	2015
Burlgtn	Burlington IA Bees	A	Midwest League	Oakland Athletics	2011	2012
Burlgtn	Burlington IA Bees	A	Midwest League	Los Angeles Angels	2013	2015
Burlgtn	Burlington NC Royals	R+	Appalachian League	Kansas City Royals	2011	2015
Cards	GCL Cardinals	R	Gulf Coast League	St Louis Cardinals	2011	2015
Carlina	Carolina Mudcats	AA	Southern League	Cincinnati Reds	2011	2011
Carlina	Carolina Mudcats	A+	Carolina League	Cleveland Indians	2012	2014
Carlina	Carolina Mudcats	A+	Carolina League	Atlanta Braves	2015	2015
Casper	Casper Ghosts	R+	Pioneer League	Colorado Rockies	2011	2011
Charllt	Charlotte NC Knights	AAA	International League	Chicago White Sox	2011	2015
Charltt	Charlotte FL Stone Crabs	A+	Florida State League	Tampa Bay Rays	2011	2015
Chatt	Chattanooga Lookouts	AA	Southern League	Los Angeles Dodgers	2011	2014
Chatt	Chattanooga Lookouts	AA	Southern League	Minnesota Twins	2015	2015
Clinton	Clinton LumberKings	A	Midwest League	Seattle Mariners	2011	2015
Clmbs	Columbus Clippers	AAA	International League	Cleveland Indians	2011	2015
Clrwtr	Clearwater Threshers	A+	Florida State League	Philadelphia Phillies	2011	2015
ColSpr	Colorado Spr. Sky Sox	AAA	Pacific Coast League	Colorado Rockies	2011	2014
ColSpr	Colorado Spr. Sky Sox	AAA	Pacific Coast League	Milwaukee Brewers	2015	2015
Conn	Connecticut Tigers	A-	New York-Penn League	Detroit Tigers	2011	2015
CpChr	Corpus Christi Hooks	AA	Texas League	Houston Astros	2011	2015
Crpds	Cedar Rapids Kernels	A	Midwest League	Los Angeles Angels	2011	2012
Crpds	Cedar Rapids Kernels	A	Midwest League	Minnesota Twins	2013	2015
CtnSC	Charleston RiverDogs	A	South Atlantic League	New York Yankees	2011	2015
Cubs	AZL Cubs	R	Arizona League	Chicago Cubs	2011	2015

Minor League Abbreviation Key

Abbreviation	Team	Level	League	MLB Affiliate	First Year	Last Year
Danvle	Danville Braves	R+	Appalachian League	Atlanta Braves	2011	2015
Dayton	Dayton Dragons	A	Midwest League	Cincinnati Reds	2011	2015
Dbcks	AZL D-backs	R	Arizona League	Arizona Diamondbacks	2011	2015
Ddgrs	AZL Dodgers	R	Arizona League	Los Angeles Dodgers	2011	2015
Dlmrva	Delmarva Shorebirds	A	South Atlantic League	Baltimore Orioles	2011	2015
Dnedin	Dunedin Blue Jays	A+	Florida State League	Toronto Blue Jays	2011	2015
Drham	Durham Bulls	AAA	International League	Tampa Bay Rays	2011	2015
Dytona	Daytona Cubs	A+	Florida State League	Chicago Cubs	2011	2014
Dytona	Daytona Tortugas	A+	Florida State League	Cincinnati Reds	2015	2015
Elizab	Elizabethton Twins	R+	Appalachian League	Minnesota Twins	2011	2015
ElPaso	El Paso Chihuahuas	AAA	Pacific Coast League	San Diego Padres	2014	2015
Erie	Erie SeaWolves	AA	Eastern League	Detroit Tigers	2011	2015
Eugene	Eugene Emeralds	A-	Northwest League	San Diego Padres	2011	2014
Eugene	Eugene Emeralds	A-	Northwest League	Chicago Cubs	2015	2015
Everett	Everett AquaSox	A-	Northwest League	Seattle Mariners	2011	2015
Frdrck	Frederick Keys	A+	Carolina League	Baltimore Orioles	2011	2015
Fresno	Fresno Grizzlies	AAA	Pacific Coast League	San Francisco Giants	2011	2014
Fresno	Fresno Grizzlies	AAA	Pacific Coast League	Houston Astros	2015	2015
Frisco	Frisco RoughRiders	AA	Texas League	Texas Rangers	2011	2015
FtMyrs	Fort Myers Miracle	A+	Florida State League	Minnesota Twins	2011	2015
FtWyn	Fort Wayne TinCaps	A	Midwest League	San Diego Padres	2011	2015
GdJunc	Grand Junction Rockies	R+	Pioneer League	Colorado Rockies	2012	2015
Giants	AZL Giants	R	Arizona League	San Francisco Giants	2011	2015
Gr Falls	Great Falls Voyagers	R+	Pioneer League	Chicago White Sox	2011	2015
Grnsbr	Greensboro Grasshoppers	A	South Atlantic League	Florida Marlins	2011	2011
Grnsbr	Greensboro Grasshoppers	A	South Atlantic League	Miami Marlins	2012	2015
Grnvlle	Greeneville Astros	R+	Appalachian League	Houston Astros	2011	2015
Grnvlle	Greenville Drive	A	South Atlantic League	Boston Red Sox	2011	2015
Gt Lks	Great Lakes Loons	A	Midwest League	Los Angeles Dodgers	2011	2015
Gwnntt	Gwinnett Braves	AAA	International League	Atlanta Braves	2011	2015
Helena	Helena Brewers	R+	Pioneer League	Milwaukee Brewers	2011	2015
Hgrstn	Hagerstown Suns	A	South Atlantic League	Washington Nationals	2011	2015
Hi Dsrt	High Desert Mavericks	A+	California League	Seattle Mariners	2011	2014
Hi Dsrt	High Desert Mavericks	A+	California League	Texas Rangers	2015	2015
HiroCrp	Hiroshima Carp	IND	Independent League	Independent	2008	2015
Hkry	Hickory Crawdads	A	South Atlantic League	Texas Rangers	2011	2015
Hlsbro	Hillsboro Hops	A-	Northwest League	Arizona Diamondbacks	2013	2015
Hntsvl	Huntsville Stars	AA	Southern League	Milwaukee Brewers	2011	2014
Hrsbrg	Harrisburg Senators	AA	Eastern League	Washington Nationals	2011	2015
HudVal	Hudson Valley Renegades	A-	New York-Penn League	Tampa Bay Rays	2011	2015
Idaho	Idaho Falls Chukars	R+	Pioneer League	Kansas City Royals	2011	2015
Indns	AZL Indians	R	Arizona League	Cleveland Indians	2011	2015
Indy	Indianapolis Indians	AAA	International League	Pittsburgh Pirates	2011	2015
InldEm	Inland Empire 66ers	A+	California League	Los Angeles Angels	2011	2015
Iowa	Iowa Cubs	AAA	Pacific Coast League	Chicago Cubs	2011	2015
Jacksn	Jackson Generals	AA	Southern League	Seattle Mariners	2011	2015
Jaxnvl	Jacksonville Suns	AA	Southern League	Florida Marlins	2011	2011
Jaxnvl	Jacksonville Suns	AA	Southern League	Miami Marlins	2012	2015
Jhscty	Johnson City Cardinals	R+	Appalachian League	St Louis Cardinals	2011	2015
Jmstwn	Jamestown Jammers	A-	New York-Penn League	Florida Marlins	2011	2011
Jmstwn	Jamestown Jammers	A-	New York-Penn League	Miami Marlins	2012	2012
Jmstwn	Jamestown Jammers	A-	New York-Penn League	Pittsburgh Pirates	2013	2014
Jupiter	Jupiter Hammerheads	A+	Florida State League	Florida Marlins	2011	2011
Jupiter	Jupiter Hammerheads	A+	Florida State League	Miami Marlins	2012	2015
Kane	Kane County Cougars	A	Midwest League	Kansas City Royals	2011	2012
Kane	Kane County Cougars	A	Midwest League	Chicago Cubs	2013	2014
Kane	Kane County Cougars	A	Midwest League	Arizona Diamondbacks	2015	2015
Knapol	Kannapolis Intimidators	A	South Atlantic League	Chicago White Sox	2011	2015
Kngspt	Kingsport Mets	R+	Appalachian League	New York Mets	2011	2015
Knstn	Kinston Indians	A+	Carolina League	Cleveland Indians	2011	2011
Lakwd	Lakewood BlueClaws	A	South Atlantic League	Philadelphia Phillies	2011	2015
Lancst	Lancaster JetHawks	A+	California League	Houston Astros	2011	2015
LG	LG Twins	IND	Independent League	Independent	2005	2011
Lk Cty	Lake County Captains	A	Midwest League	Cleveland Indians	2011	2015

Minor League Abbreviation Key

Abbreviation	Team	Level	League	MLB Affiliate	First Year	Last Year
Lk Els	Lake Elsinore Storm	A+	California League	San Diego Padres	2011	2015
Lkland	Lakeland Flying Tigers	A+	Florida State League	Detroit Tigers	2011	2015
Lnsng	Lansing Lugnuts	A	Midwest League	Toronto Blue Jays	2011	2015
Lowell	Lowell Spinners	A-	New York-Penn League	Boston Red Sox	2011	2015
LsVgs	Las Vegas 51s	AAA	Pacific Coast League	Toronto Blue Jays	2011	2012
LsVgs	Las Vegas 51s	AAA	Pacific Coast League	New York Mets	2013	2015
Lsvlle	Louisville Bats	AAA	International League	Cincinnati Reds	2011	2015
LV	Lehigh Valley IronPigs	AAA	International League	Philadelphia Phillies	2011	2015
Lxngtn	Lexington Legends	A	South Atlantic League	Houston Astros	2011	2012
Lxngtn	Lexington Legends	A	South Atlantic League	Kansas City Royals	2013	2015
Lynbrg	Lynchburg Hillcats	A+	Carolina League	Atlanta Braves	2011	2014
Lynbrg	Lynchburg Hillcats	A+	Carolina League	Cleveland Indians	2015	2015
Mdest	Modesto Nuts	A+	California League	Colorado Rockies	2011	2015
Mdlnd	Midland RockHounds	AA	Texas League	Oakland Athletics	2011	2015
Memp	Memphis Redbirds	AAA	Pacific Coast League	St Louis Cardinals	2011	2015
Mets	GCL Mets	R	Gulf Coast League	New York Mets	2011	2015
MhVlly	Mahoning Valley Scrappers	A-	New York-Penn League	Cleveland Indians	2011	2015
Missi	Mississippi Braves	AA	Southern League	Atlanta Braves	2011	2015
Mobile	Mobile BayBears	AA	Southern League	Arizona Diamondbacks	2011	2015
Mont	Montgomery Biscuits	AA	Southern League	Tampa Bay Rays	2011	2015
Mrlns	GCL Marlins	R	Gulf Coast League	Florida Marlins	2011	2011
Mrlns	GCL Marlins	R	Gulf Coast League	Miami Marlins	2012	2015
MrtlBh	Myrtle Beach Pelicans	A+	Carolina League	Texas Rangers	2011	2014
MrtlBh	Myrtle Beach Pelicans	A+	Carolina League	Chicago Cubs	2015	2015
Ms	AZL Mariners	R	Arizona League	Seattle Mariners	2011	2015
Msoula	Missoula Osprey	R+	Pioneer League	Arizona Diamondbacks	2011	2015
Nashv	Nashville Sounds	AAA	Pacific Coast League	Milwaukee Brewers	2011	2014
Nashv	Nashville Sounds	AAA	Pacific Coast League	Oakland Athletics	2015	2015
Nats	GCL Nationals	R	Gulf Coast League	Washington Nationals	2011	2015
NewOr	New Orleans Zephyrs	AAA	Pacific Coast League	Florida Marlins	2011	2011
NewOr	New Orleans Zephyrs	AAA	Pacific Coast League	Miami Marlins	2012	2015
Nexen	Nexen Heroes	IND	Independent League	Independent	2011	2015
Nham	New Hampshire Fisher Cats	AA	Eastern League	Toronto Blue Jays	2011	2015
Nippon	Hokkaido Nippon Ham Fighters	IND	Independent League	Independent	2013	2015
Norfolk	Norfolk Tides	AAA	International League	Baltimore Orioles	2011	2015
NWArk	NW Arkansas Naturals	AA	Texas League	Kansas City Royals	2011	2015
NwBrit	New Britain Rock Cats	AA	Eastern League	Minnesota Twins	2011	2014
NwBrit	New Britain Rock Cats	AA	Eastern League	Colorado Rockies	2015	2015
Ogden	Ogden Raptors	R+	Pioneer League	Los Angeles Dodgers	2011	2015
OkCity	Oklahoma City RedHawks	AAA	Pacific Coast League	Houston Astros	2011	2014
OkCity	Oklahoma City Dodgers	AAA	Pacific Coast League	Los Angeles Dodgers	2015	2015
Omha	Omaha Storm Chasers	AAA	Pacific Coast League	Kansas City Royals	2011	2015
Orem	Orem Owlz	R+	Pioneer League	Los Angeles Angels	2011	2015
Orioles	GCL Orioles	R	Gulf Coast League	Baltimore Orioles	2011	2015
Padres	AZL Padres	R	Arizona League	San Diego Padres	2011	2015
Peoria	Peoria Chiefs	A	Midwest League	Chicago Cubs	2011	2012
Peoria	Peoria Chiefs	A	Midwest League	St Louis Cardinals	2013	2015
Phillies	GCL Phillies	R	Gulf Coast League	Philadelphia Phillies	2011	2015
Pirates	GCL Pirates	R	Gulf Coast League	Pittsburgh Pirates	2011	2015
PlmBh	Palm Beach Cardinals	A+	Florida State League	St Louis Cardinals	2011	2015
Pnscla	Pensacola Blue Wahoos	AA	Southern League	Cincinnati Reds	2012	2015
Portlnd	Portland ME Sea Dogs	AA	Eastern League	Boston Red Sox	2011	2015
Prnctn	Princeton Rays	R+	Appalachian League	Tampa Bay Rays	2011	2015
Ptomc	Potomac Nationals	A+	Carolina League	Washington Nationals	2011	2015
Pulski	Pulaski Mariners	R+	Appalachian League	Seattle Mariners	2011	2014
Pulski	Pulaski Yankees	R+	Appalachian League	New York Yankees	2015	2015
Pwtckt	Pawtucket Red Sox	AAA	International League	Boston Red Sox	2011	2015
QuadC	Quad Cities River Bandits	A	Midwest League	St Louis Cardinals	2011	2012
QuadC	Quad Cities River Bandits	A	Midwest League	Houston Astros	2013	2015
Rays	GCL Rays	R	Gulf Coast League	Tampa Bay Rays	2011	2015
Rchmd	Richmond Flying Squirrels	AA	Eastern League	San Francisco Giants	2011	2015
Rcuca	Rancho Cucamonga Quakes	A+	California League	Los Angeles Dodgers	2011	2015
Rdng	Reading Phillies	AA	Eastern League	Philadelphia Phillies	2011	2012
Rdng	Reading Fightin Phils	AA	Eastern League	Philadelphia Phillies	2013	2015

Minor League Abbreviation Key

Abbreviation	Team	Level	League	MLB Affiliate	First Year	Last Year
RdRck	Round Rock Express	AAA	Pacific Coast League	Texas Rangers	2011	2015
Reds	AZL Reds	R	Arizona League	Cincinnati Reds	2011	2015
RedSx	GCL Red Sox	R	Gulf Coast League	Boston Red Sox	2011	2015
Reno	Reno Aces	AAA	Pacific Coast League	Arizona Diamondbacks	2011	2015
RioGrnd	Rio Grande Valley WhiteWings	IND	Independent League	Independent	2011	2011
Rngrs	AZL Rangers	R	Arizona League	Texas Rangers	2011	2015
Roch	Rochester Red Wings	AAA	International League	Minnesota Twins	2011	2015
Rome	Rome Braves	A	South Atlantic League	Atlanta Braves	2011	2015
Royals	AZL Royals	R	Arizona League	Kansas City Royals	2011	2015
Salem	Salem Red Sox	A+	Carolina League	Boston Red Sox	2011	2015
Salt Lk	Salt Lake City Bees	AAA	Pacific Coast League	Los Angeles Angels	2011	2015
Savann	Savannah Sand Gnats	A	South Atlantic League	New York Mets	2011	2015
Sbend	South Bend Silver Hawks	A	Midwest League	Arizona Diamondbacks	2011	2014
Sbend	South Bend Cubs	A	Midwest League	Chicago Cubs	2015	2015
Scrmto	Sacramento River Cats	AAA	Pacific Coast League	Oakland Athletics	2011	2014
Scrmto	Sacramento River Cats	AAA	Pacific Coast League	San Francisco Giants	2015	2015
SlKzr	Salem-Keizer Volcanoes	A-	Northwest League	San Francisco Giants	2011	2015
SnAnt	San Antonio Missions	AA	Texas League	San Diego Padres	2011	2015
SnJos	San Jose Giants	A+	California League	San Francisco Giants	2011	2015
Spkane	Spokane Indians	A-	Northwest League	Texas Rangers	2011	2015
Sprgfld	Springfield Cardinals	AA	Texas League	St Louis Cardinals	2011	2015
Stcktn	Stockton Ports	A+	California League	Oakland Athletics	2011	2015
StCol	State College Spikes	A-	New York-Penn League	Pittsburgh Pirates	2011	2012
StCol	State College Spikes	A-	New York-Penn League	St Louis Cardinals	2013	2015
Stluci	St. Lucie Mets	A+	Florida State League	New York Mets	2011	2015
Stnlld	Staten Island Yankees	A-	New York-Penn League	New York Yankees	2011	2015
S-WB	Scranton WB Yankees	AAA	International League	New York Yankees	2011	2012
S-WB	Scranton WB RailRiders	AAA	International League	New York Yankees	2013	2015
Syrcse	Syracuse Chiefs	AAA	International League	Washington Nationals	2011	2015
Tacom	Tacoma Rainiers	AAA	Pacific Coast League	Seattle Mariners	2011	2015
Tampa	Tampa Yankees	A+	Florida State League	New York Yankees	2011	2015
Tenn	Tennessee Smokies	AA	Southern League	Chicago Cubs	2011	2015
Tigers	GCL Tigers	R	Gulf Coast League	Detroit Tigers	2011	2015
Toledo	Toledo Mud Hens	AAA	International League	Detroit Tigers	2011	2015
TriCity	Tri-City WA Dust Devils	A-	Northwest League	Colorado Rockies	2011	2014
TriCity	Tri-City NY ValleyCats	A-	New York-Penn League	Houston Astros	2011	2015
TriCity	Tri-City WA Dust Devils	A-	Northwest League	San Diego Padres	2015	2015
Trntn	Trenton Thunder	AA	Eastern League	New York Yankees	2011	2015
Tucsn	Tucson Padres	AAA	Pacific Coast League	San Diego Padres	2011	2013
Tulsa	Tulsa Drillers	AA	Texas League	Colorado Rockies	2011	2014
Tulsa	Tulsa Drillers	AA	Texas League	Los Angeles Dodgers	2015	2015
Twins	GCL Twins	R	Gulf Coast League	Minnesota Twins	2011	2015
Vancvr	Vancouver Canadians	A-	Northwest League	Toronto Blue Jays	2011	2015
Visalia	Visalia Rawhide	A+	California League	Arizona Diamondbacks	2011	2015
Vrmnt	Vermont Lake Monsters	A-	New York-Penn League	Oakland Athletics	2011	2015
Wichita	Wichita Wingnuts	IND	Independent League	Independent	2012	2012
Wilmg	Wilmington Blue Rocks	A+	Carolina League	Kansas City Royals	2011	2015
WinSa	Winston-Salem Dash	A+	Carolina League	Chicago White Sox	2011	2015
Wisc	Wisconsin Timber Rattlers	A	Midwest League	Milwaukee Brewers	2011	2015
Wmich	West Michigan Whitecaps	A	Midwest League	Detroit Tigers	2011	2015
Wmspt	Williamsport Crosscutters	A-	New York-Penn League	Philadelphia Phillies	2011	2015
Wsox	AZL White Sox	R	Arizona League	Chicago White Sox	2013	2015
WV	West Virginia Black Bears	A-	New York-Penn League	Pittsburgh Pirates	2015	2015
WV	West Virginia Power	A	South Atlantic League	Pittsburgh Pirates	2011	2015
Yakima	Yakima Bears	A-	Northwest League	Arizona Diamondbacks	2011	2012
Yanks1	GCL Yankees	R	Gulf Coast League	New York Yankees	2011	2015
Yanks2	GCL Yankees2	R	Gulf Coast League	New York Yankees	2013	2015

Baseball Info Solutions

It has been more than a decade since Baseball Info Solutions opened shop, and while interest and technology have allowed baseball analytics to expand more quickly than we ever could have imagined, our objective has remained the same. Our mission is to provide the most accurate, in-depth, timely professional baseball data, including cutting-edge research and analysis, striving to educate major league teams and the public about baseball analytics. It is our pleasure to work with 22 of 30 MLB teams.

The foundation of our work is our data collection operation. We have a staff of operation analysts who work with and coordinate our dozens of highly trained video scouts. Together, they scout every major league baseball game—and many minor leagues ones—multiple times to collect data and ensure its accuracy. That data begins with the basics that you would find in a typical box score and then expands to include everything from batted ball locations and velocities, pitch types and locations, defensive shifts and specific infielder alignments, and much more. We collect data that you cannot find anywhere else, such as Good Fielding Plays and Defensive Misplays—discrete observations of good and bad fielding plays as originally outlined by Bill James—and pitch command data.

Many clients work with the raw data that we collect, but our research and development team attempts to take that data to the next level with research projects and analytics that demonstrate the value that data can have. The most famous of that work is Defensive Runs Saved, which estimates the amount of runs defensive players save or cost their teams because of their range, positioning, throwing, pitch-framing, and several other factors. Most recently, the team has developed Defense-Independent Batting and Pitching Statistics (DIBS and DIPS) that use our batted ball location and velocity data to measure hitter and pitcher success based on the trajectories of their batted balls rather than the actual results.

John Dewan began Baseball Info Solutions in 2002, but he had already been at the forefront of baseball analysis for many years beforehand. He first entered the field as the Executive Director of Project Scoresheet, which was a Bill James-led effort to comprehensively collect baseball data. Those efforts are the reason that many of the statistics that today seem basic are even available.

If you would like to contact Baseball Info Solutions for data inquiries, potential job openings, or additional information, you can reach us at:

Baseball Info Solutions
41 S. 2nd Street
Coplay, PA 18037
610-261-2370
www.baseballinfosolutions.com

Acknowledgments

The Bill James Handbook takes an incredible amount of effort from everyone involved in its production. From when the regular season ended on October 4 to when we delivered the book to the publisher on October 16, we all spent days, nights, and weekends to ensure that every page was proofread and stat-checked and up to the high standard we set for ourselves. Because of that great effort, we want to thank everyone who helped the book come together.

That list can only start with Bill James, who began what would eventually become the Handbook as you see it now in his original Baseball Abstract in 1977. Bill remains intimately involved in the production of the Handbook today. This year, he helped design and wrote the introductions for the two new data sections, Stolen Base Attempt Times and Painting the Corners, as well as wrote the introductions for six other sections. In addition, he provided input on projections for many different hitters and pitchers.

John Dewan and his wife Sue Dewan are the owners of Baseball Info Solutions. Despite the many demands on their time, they put in extra effort to ensure that the Handbook stayed on schedule. Of note, one of the Dewans' many projects is the charity Franciscan Works, which does mission work in Ebola-ravaged Liberia. If you are interested in learning more, please check out   FranciscanWorks.org and consider making a donation.

President Ben Jedlovec has now been a part of seven Handbooks dating back to his Research and Development days. Now, he manages the project top to bottom, contributing as needed to the content and organization.

Director of IT Rob Dougherty survived his first Handbook experience this year. Rob brings 15 years of experience in the industry to BIS. He has been instrumental in ensuring that our clients' needs have continued to get met during this busy time.

Patrick Coyle is our version of Madison Bumgarner. He is excellent all year in his role of Senior IT Analyst, but then he takes his game to a new level come the play-offs. This was the third consecutive year that Pat handled the production of the Handbook. In addition, Greg Thomas, Ben Stanczak, Will Creager, and IT intern Mason McIntyre have all done an incredible job balancing the many IT demands of the Handbook process with their other responsibilities, including our new football initiative.

With our expanded collection efforts in recent seasons, the Operations Department of Jon Vrecsics, Jim Swavely, Dan Casey, Todd Radcliffe, Kevin Morrissey, Tim Kwilos, Dan Foehrenbach, James Mehall, Nathan Phares, and newly hired Jason Paff has been exceptional in keeping up with their increased responsibilities without neglecting the data quality controls. More than anyone, they are responsible for the accuracy of the statistics in the Handbook. In particular, Jon has now worked on 10 different Handbooks and is instrumental in leading the stat-checking effort. Every number in this book has been repeatedly checked over, and any discrepancies between our numbers and other published sources have been tracked down such that we are confident that the Handbook has the correct numbers.

The Research and Development Department of Joe Rosales and Scott Spratt handles a variety of Handbook tasks from managing the Fielding Bible Award voting and Hitter and Pitcher Projections processes to writing section intros to tracking down data discrepancies. They with interns Marat Biyashev, Andrew Kyne, and Jordan Wallach demonstrate the utility of our collected data with research projects and analytics.

Director of Business Development Jim Capuano and Business Development Associate Ryan Allor together lead the effort to bring our data, research, and analysis to our clients and the public.

Office Administrator Carol Olsen makes everyone's life much better. She handles much of the day-to-day running of the business, from Human Resources to Accounting to Office Management.

As our collection efforts continue to expand, so too does our collection of video scouts. Their dedication and attention to detail provide the foundation of our business. They include Ted Baarda, Curt Baylor, Cole Bieser, Ryan Binas, Troy Bogenschutz, Andy Brookshire, Patrick Canfield, Sam Cassell, Mike Churchward, Jason Davila, Joey Denton, Ben Douglas, Danny Duran, Pete Febbraro, Adam Feeley, Joe Firestone, Anthony Flora, Devon Frey, Zack Greenfield, Kieran Hall, Brandon Haney, Josh Hofer, Kyle Hunter, Nick James, Brendan Jenner, Jeremy Kaufman, Max Kraust, Chris Kumar, Wes LaValley, Stefan Lechmanik, Matt Lemming, Derek Lescarbeau, Chris Licata, Josh Lipman, Kyle McLain, Noah Michel, Spencer Moody, Connor Morris, Jonas Nordman, Jason Paff, Tim Paragone, Anthony Rescan, Vince Rinaldi, Jeremy Rochford, Ryne Rogers, Joe Romen, Adam Schopick, J.H. Schroeder, David Shevlin, Justin Stine, Tim Sylvester, Travis Trial, Josh Tuchman, Zeke Turrentine, and Dan Wallie.

Our partners at ACTA Publications include President Greg Pierce, as well as Tom Wright, Kate Glasgow, Mary Eggert, Abby Pierce, Brian Tobin, Patricia Lynch, Mary Doyle, and Hugh Spector.

Thank you to our friends in the baseball industry who have helped us over the years. They include Greg Ambrosius, Andy Andres, David Appelman, Jim Callis, Dave Cameron, Sean Forman, Peter Gammons, Vince Genarro, Marshall Greenhut, Jason Grey, Eric Karabell, Brian Kenny, Peter Kreutzer, Michael Lehrer, Gene McCaffrey, Bob Meyerhoff, Mike Murphy, Noel Nash, Rob Neyer, Alex Patton, Mike Phillips, David Pinto, Joe Posnanski, Adam Richman, Hal Richman, Peter Schoenke, Ron Shandler, Joe Sheehan, John Sickels, Mark Simon, Dave Studenmund, Tom Tango, Mark Watson, Rick Wilton, and Don Zminda.

Thank you to Steve Ruskowski for your assistance in stat-checking.

It is impossible for us to thank everyone who made this book possible in the space we have, and so thank you to everyone who made this possible. Finally, thank you to our readers. We make it through these hectic weeks because we know that you share our love of baseball and our commitment to attempt to understand all of its wonderful quirks.